D1032950

Guide to the Presidency

Guide to the Presidency

SECOND EDITION • VOLUME II

MICHAEL NELSON, Editor

 CONGRESSIONAL QUARTERLY INC.
WASHINGTON, D.C.

NO LONGER the property of Whitaker Library

117699

Copyright © 1996 Congressional Quarterly Inc.
1414 22nd Street, N.W., Washington, D.C. 20037

All rights reserved. No part of this publication may be reproduced or transmitted in any form or by any means, electronic or mechanical, including photocopy, recording, or any information storage and retrieval system, without permission in writing from the publisher.

Book design and production by Kachergis Book Design,
Pittsboro, North Carolina

Printed and bound in the United States of America

The paper used in this publication meets the minimum requirements of the American National Standard for Information Science—Permanence of Paper for Printed Library Materials, ANSI Z 39.48-1984.

Copyrights and acknowledgments: Excerpt, p. 329: from "On the Pulse of the Morning" by Maya Angelou. Copyright © 1993 by Maya Angelou. Reprinted by permission of Random House, Inc. Box, p. 896: from *What Americans Really Think?* by Barry Sussman. Copyright © 1988 by Barry Sussman. Reprinted by permission of Pantheon Books, a division of Random House, Inc. Figures 27-1 and 27-2, pp. 1079 and 1081: Copyright © 1978 Stephen J. Wayne, *The Legislative Presidency*. New York: Harper & Row, 1978. Published with permission of the author. Figure 27-4, p. 1083: from Samuel Kernell and Samuel Popkin, *Chief of Staff: Twenty-Five Years of Managing the Presidency*, 202. Copyright © 1986 The Regents of the University of California.

Illustration credits and acknowledgments begin on page 1705, Volume II, which is to be considered an extension of the copyright page.

LIBRARY OF CONGRESS CATALOGING-IN-PUBLICATION DATA
Congressional Quarterly's guide to the presidency/Michael Nelson,
[editor].—2nd ed.
   p.   cm.
   Includes bibliographical references and index.
   ISBN: 1-56802-018-x (set: alk. paper)
   ISBN: 1-56802-232-8 (v.1: alk. paper)
   ISBN: 1-56802-233-6 (v.2: alk. paper)

1. Presidents—United States.   I. Nelson, Michael, 1949-
II. Congressional Quarterly, inc.
JK516.C57 1996
353.03′13—dc20   96-18543
                                                          CIP

Summary Table of Contents

Table of Contents

The White House and the Executive Branch

CHAPTER 22

Housing of the Executive Branch

BY MARGARET H. SEAWELL

T HE BEST-KNOWN executive branch structure is surely the White House, the official residence of the best-known U.S. government employee. But the executive branch employs five million other people as well. They work in fourteen cabinet-level departments and sixty-two independent agencies in a vast network of buildings around the world. U.S. military installations, embassies and consulates, Social Security offices, and post offices all house executive branch employees. Approximately five hundred executive branch buildings, including the headquarters of the departments and agencies, are in the Washington, D.C., area alone.

Managing these properties is largely the job of the General Services Administration (GSA). In particular, GSA's Public Buildings Service (PBS) operates as the owner, developer, and manager of properties for all three branches of the government. It provides space for government employees by constructing new buildings, buying existing ones, and leasing space in others. PBS manages 227 million square feet of work space in approximately seven thousand office buildings ranging in size from the Social Security office in Monticello, Arkansas, with 1,339 square feet, to the Pentagon, with 3.8 million square feet. Since 1982 PBS has allowed some thirty departments and agencies to operate and maintain their own headquarters in the Washington area.

The White House

Along the East Coast of the United States, guides at historic sites often claim that "George Washington slept here." Although there is much uncertainty about just where the nation's first president did lodge, historians are sure about one thing—Washington never spent a night in the White House. In fact, Washington is the only president who never lived in the building known around the world as the symbol of the U.S. presidency. *(See box, Where Did President Washington Live? p. 930.)*

EARLY HISTORY

Although he never lived there, the nation's first president was instrumental in determining the location and appearance of the White House. Under Washington's direction, French engineer and architect Pierre Charles L'Enfant mapped out the new capital city. Together, they selected the site for the presidential residence.

Washington appointed three commissioners to oversee development of the federal city and its buildings, and in 1792 they conducted a public contest to choose the design for the house. Thomas Jefferson, under the pseudonym "A.Z.," submitted a plan, as did many others. The winner was James Hoban, a self-taught, Irish-born master builder who, in addition to the honor of becoming the architect of the "President's House," as Washington called it, received a $500 gold medal and a plot of land for his personal use. *(See box, What's in a Name? p. 938.)* The commissioners subsequently hired Hoban as general supervisor of construction.

Hoban designed a simple, three-story, boxlike structure that incorporated the harmonious proportions of late eighteenth-century Georgian architecture. The plan called for balustrading, a hipped roof, and columns at the main entrance. Symmetrical, rectangular windows would provide the main exterior ornamentation: windows on the first floor would be tall, with alternating arched and triangular pediments.

Hoban's interior design included a large entrance hall with a spacious ceremonial room on the east end of the building (today's East Room) balanced by a formal dining room on the west end (the State Dining Room). Three smaller drawing rooms (the Green Room, the Blue Room, and the Red Room) would line the transverse corridor joining the East Room and the State Dining Room. Hoban's plan for these rooms on the first floor (also called the "state floor") has not been changed significantly since he designed them.

Master stonemason Collen Williamson laid the cornerstone of the President's House on October 13, 1792, eleven months before George Washington laid the cornerstone of the Capitol. The White House is thus the oldest federal building in the District of Columbia.

The building is made of white-painted sandstone from the Aquia Creek Quarry in Virginia. The quarry, on an island in the Potomac about forty miles south of Washington, supplied the stone for many public buildings in the new capital from 1791 to 1837.

Money was in short supply from the beginning, and Congress held the purse strings tightly. To cut costs, Washington instructed Hoban to eliminate the third floor. (This floor eventually was added in 1927.) Major construction took eight years and cost approximately $240,000; but much work remained to be done when President John Adams (1797–1801) and his wife, Abigail, became the first residents of the President's House in November 1800, shortly before the end of his term.[1] In fact, only six rooms in the house were usable. "Not a chamber is finished of

WHERE DID PRESIDENT WASHINGTON LIVE?

The only chief executive who never lived in the White House—or the "President's House," as it was originally called—was the nation's first president, George Washington.

When he was sworn into office on April 30, 1789, New York was the temporary capital of the United States. The president and Martha Washington lived first in a residence on Cherry Street and later in a house on Broadway. An official residence for the president was under construction in New York when the government moved in 1790 to Philadelphia, named as the temporary capital until the new federal city could be finished.

In Philadelphia, President and Mrs. Washington lived at 190 High Street in a house owned by financier Robert Morris. Washington described the house as "the best *single* House in the City. . . . There are good Stables . . . and a Coach House which will hold all my Carriages."[1] Philadelphia, too, planned an official residence, but it was not finished in time for Washington to live there.

When his term ended in March 1797, Washington left Philadelphia to return to his home at Mount Vernon, Virginia. On the way he stopped in the city of Washington for a banquet in his honor and a visit to the White House, still under construction. Expecting the general, a crowd had gathered at the residence and cheered wildly for the first president. James Hoban directed the Washington Artillery Company in a sixteen-gun salute. Washington never attended another White House ceremony, because he died on December 14, 1799, eleven months before President John Adams moved into the President's House.[2]

1. Kenneth W. Leish, *The White House* (New York: Newsweek, 1972), 15.
2. William Seale, *The President's House*, 2 vols. (Washington, D.C.: White House Historical Association, 1986), 1: 74–75.

south side and a "porte cochere," or carriage porch, for the north. The South Portico was not finished until 1824; the North Portico, 1830. Both included elements of Hoban's original design.

James Madison (1809–1817) and his wife, Dolley, a well-known hostess, followed Jefferson to the President's House. Congress appropriated $14,000 for household furnishings and $12,000 for repairs when Madison took office. Dolley Madison redecorated, under the direction of Latrobe, who designed Greek Revival furniture for the Oval Room. In 1813 Elbridge Gerry Jr., son of the vice president, described the finished room as "immense and magnificent."[2] But the splendor was not to last.

In 1814, during the War of 1812, the British invaded Washington and burned the Capitol, the departmental buildings, the Navy Yard, and the White House. Through a spyglass from the White House roof, Dolley Madison watched British troops approach. Just before leaving the house, she demanded that the Gilbert Stuart portrait of George Washington be saved. She wrote to her sister:

Our kind friend, Mr. Carroll, has come to hasten my departure and is in a very bad humor with me because I insist on waiting until the large picture of General Washington is secured: and it requires to be unscrewed from the wall. This process was found too tedious for these perilous moments; I have ordered the frame to be broken and the canvas taken out; it is done, and the precious portrait placed in the hands of two gentlemen of New York for safe keeping. . . .[3]

Fire gutted the interior. Only the sandstone exterior walls, blackened from smoke and flames, were left standing.

The Madisons finished out their term first in Octagon House, an elegant New York Avenue mansion owned by Col. John Tayloe, and later in a smaller house at the corner of Nineteenth Street and Pennsylvania Avenue.

RENOVATIONS AND REFURBISHINGS

The White House has been hollowed out and its interior rebuilt twice in its history—after the fire of 1814 and from 1949 to 1952 during the administration of Harry S. Truman, when the building was found to be structurally unsound. Major, but less encompassing, structural renovation took place during Theodore Roosevelt's administration in 1902 and during Calvin Coolidge's administration in 1927. Between 1817 and 1902, however, the White House underwent only minor changes in its structure, although every first family engaged in some degree of redecorating, depending on the generosity of Congress.

Hoban Returns

One could say that James Hoban built the White House twice. After supervising its initial construction, he returned to rebuild the mansion after the fire of 1814. Beginning in March 1815 with only a burned and roofless shell, Hoban hired workers and acquired the materials necessary for reconstruction. Carpenters and stonecutters worked long days, and the President's House, which had taken almost ten years to build originally, was

the whole," wrote Abigail Adams of her new home. There was little firewood to warm the large, drafty rooms and no indoor bathroom. Plaster was still wet, the main staircase was unfinished, and water had to be carried to the house from a park five blocks away.

Still, Mrs. Adams made the best of things in her four-month stay. She used the vast, unfinished East Room as a place to hang her laundry, and each week she and President Adams held large, formal receptions—then called "levees"—in the Oval Room (known today as the Blue Room).

Thomas Jefferson (1801–1809) introduced a different style of living when he succeeded Adams as president. Instead of large receptions, he held small dinner parties where he seated no one by precedence. Instead of bowing to his guests, as had his predecessors, the new president preferred the more democratic gesture of shaking hands.

Jefferson worked with his architect, Benjamin Henry Latrobe, to complete and add to the President's House. Latrobe replaced the leaking roof and built pavilions on the building's east and west ends. He also proposed a semicircular portico for the

In 1792 master builder James Hoban won the competition for architect of the White House with this design.

reconstructed in just under three at a cost of $247,000.[4] By September 1817 the house was ready for the new president, James Monroe (1817–1825), who had been inaugurated in March.

Congress appropriated $20,000 for refurbishing the mansion, and Monroe proved more than equal to the task of spending it. He purchased for the White House furniture of high quality from the French Empire period and sold to the government many of his personal furnishings collected while he was U.S. ambassador to France. Items from the Monroe administration—particularly pieces made by French cabinetmaker Pierre-Antoine Bellangé—form the core of the White House's historic collection. The only item of greater historic significance is the portrait of Washington, rescued by Dolley Madison in 1814, which has belonged to the White House since 1800.

In 1824, during Monroe's second term, Hoban built the semicircular South Portico with Ionic columns two stories tall. (One hundred twenty-four years later, President Truman would object to the height of these columns and build a balcony on the second floor.) In 1829 Hoban began work on the North Portico, finishing it the following year.

Modernization and Popular Taste

Andrew Jackson (1829–1837) fancied himself the "people's president," and hundreds of newly enfranchised voters came to the White House to celebrate his inauguration. In the process, the East Room suffered mightily as rowdy supporters destroyed furniture and broke dishes and glassware. Jackson finally escaped the crowd and spent his first night as president at Gadsby's Hotel. The new president made up for the damage by decorating the East Room lavishly; he spent one-fifth of his $50,000 furnishings allowance on that room alone.[5] He ordered from

Pittsburgh a shipment of glassware that included twelve dozen tumblers and eighteen dozen wine glasses for $1,452 and bought a French porcelain 440-piece dinner service and 412-piece dessert set for $2,500.[6]

In 1833, during Jackson's first term, iron pipes were installed, which brought running water into the White House for the first time. Shortly thereafter, lines for the first sewer were laid.

Martin Van Buren (1837–1841), Jackson's successor, installed a furnace in 1840 to augment the twelve fireplaces Hoban had added in 1817. Although he spent less than Jackson on White House furnishings, Van Buren's purchases took on unusual political significance. In April 1840 Rep. Charles Ogle, a Whig from Pennsylvania, delivered a three-day oration criticizing what he called the "princely lifestyle" of the Democratic president. He proclaimed that Van Buren was living in "a palace as splendid as that of the Caesars" while the rest of the nation was suffering from a financial panic and economic depression. The speech—itself excessive and inaccurate in many respects—was delivered seven months before the 1840 election with the intention of swaying public opinion in favor of Ogle's preference for president, the simple "hard cider man," Gen. William Henry Harrison. Certainly Ogle alone did not decide the president's fate; but after the election of 1840, it was Harrison, not Van Buren, who called the White House home.

Harrison died of pneumonia after one month in office, and his successor, John Tyler (1841–1845), had a difficult time securing funds from Congress to refurbish an increasingly shabby executive mansion.

James K. Polk (1845–1849) received an appropriation of $14,900 for redecorating the White House, which had seen little improvement since Jackson's administration.[7] Polk was the first president to enjoy central heating (installed in 1845–1846) and gas lighting (installed in 1848).[8] He also purchased an icebox in 1845 for $25.

In 1850 Millard Fillmore (1850–1853) improved the kitchen further by adding a stove. Previously, food had been prepared in open fireplaces. Fillmore's wife, Abigail, saw to it that Congress appropriated $5,000 for a small White House library. When the former schoolteacher moved into the executive mansion, she had been surprised to find no books—not even a Bible or a dictionary.[9]

Fillmore's successor, Franklin Pierce (1853–1857), was the first president to have a bathroom with hot and cold running water in the second-floor family quarters.[10]

President James Buchanan (1857–1861) replaced much of the White House furniture after auctioning off numerous old pieces (including some of the Monroe collection, which would later find its way back to the White House). He also built the first of several conservatories, which supplied plants and flowers for the White House until the administration of Theodore Roosevelt.

Abraham Lincoln (1861–1865), who presided over the White House during the Civil War, was scrupulous about expenditures, but his wife was not. Mary Todd Lincoln purchased rosewood furniture and expensive upholstery, exceeding a congressional appropriation by $6,700. The angry president responded: "It would stink in the nostrils of the American people to have it said that the President of the United States had approved a bill overrunning an appropriation of $20,000 for *flub dubs* for this damned old house, when the soldiers cannot have blankets."[11]

Lincoln said he would make up the difference out of his own pocket, but Congress approved funds to cover the first lady's expenses. The president opened his house to the army and at one point quartered Union soldiers in the East Room.

After Lincoln's assassination, his grief-stricken widow remained cloistered for six weeks in a bedroom overlooking the North Portico. Meanwhile, souvenir-seekers, who had free access to the house, looted the state rooms, cutting swatches from draperies and upholstery and carrying off the china and silver.

Although Congress impeached President Andrew Johnson (1865–1869), it did give him funds to begin redecorating the executive mansion, left in poor condition after the Civil War. But in 1873 it was Ulysses S. Grant (1869–1877) who oversaw the most extensive refurbishing in decades. Although ceilings had cracked and settled (one had even collapsed), President and Mrs. Grant focused not on structural improvements but on redecoration of the mansion in an ostentatious style typical of the Gilded Age. In the East Room, for example, they installed ornamental beams and pillars, massive cut-glass chandeliers, and floral wall-to-wall carpet. The first family said their decorating scheme followed "the Greek style," but their critics called it "steamboat Gothic."

Rutherford B. Hayes (1877–1881) and his wife, known as "Lemonade Lucy" for serving only nonalcoholic beverages at parties, led modest lives and made few changes during their

President Ulysses S. Grant and his wife made extensive changes to the White House. They referred to the new style of the East Room, above, as "Greek," but their critics called it "steamboat Gothic."

White House tenure. One notable improvement, however, was the installation of a telephone in 1879.

Chester A. Arthur (1881–1885), nicknamed "Elegant Arthur" for his sophisticated tastes, became president when James A. Garfield was assassinated soon after taking office. He refused to move into the White House until extensive renovations took place, which he began by auctioning off twenty-four wagonloads of furnishings he considered worn or outmoded. (Almost another quarter-century would pass before first families would value historic use or ownership over the current fashion in furnishing the White House.) Arthur expanded the conservatories, installed an elevator, and engaged New York artist Louis Comfort Tiffany to redecorate the state rooms. Expenses for Arthur's refurbishing ran to $110,000 ($80,000 more than budget), the most that had been spent on the building since its reconstruction after the fire of 1814.

Throughout the nineteenth century, the greater part of the White House had served for the official duties of the president. Job-seekers, politicians, lobbyists, and sightseers milled about in droves on the first and second floors, leaving the first family little privacy. A mere eight rooms were available as family living quarters during Grant's presidency, and Benjamin Harrison (1889–1893) had to accommodate his family of eleven in only five bedrooms.

Caroline Harrison, the president's wife, devised three proposals for expanding the White House. One of the plans would have moved the family quarters to a separate residence on Sixteenth Street; the others added large wings to the mansion. Congress refused to fund any of the plans, and Mrs. Harrison was able to improve the house only by having rotting floorboards replaced and the kitchen modernized. Her hobby of painting china led her to begin the White House China Collection, which today contains pieces from almost every administration. The landmark improvement of the Harrison administration was the installation of electricity in 1891.

Presidents Grover Cleveland (1885–1889, 1893–1897) and William McKinley (1897–1901) also had plans to expand the White House that were never carried out. Not until the next administration did a major renovation take place.

Restoration and a Sense of History

Although he had a very large family, President Theodore Roosevelt (1901–1909) had no intention of abandoning the White House for another residence. Instead, he chose to take the offices out of the White House and expand the living quarters on the second floor. He hired architects William R. Mead, Charles F. McKim, and Stanford White of New York, who were known for their work in the historic style called "colonial" (referring to the early days of the Republic). Roosevelt assigned them the following five goals: make the White House structurally sound; move the offices out of the main building; provide for smoother handling of guests at large, official receptions; enlarge the State Dining Room; and remove the conservatories (or, as the exuberant president ordered, "Smash the glass houses!").[12]

Roosevelt received congressional approval in June 1902 and demanded that the work in the new office be finished in October of that year. The first family moved to a house on Lafayette Square as work got under way. The floors were rebuilt, and modern plumbing, heating, and wiring were installed.

On schedule, Roosevelt moved his offices to the new, white brick West Wing, which also included work and meeting space for the cabinet and the press. A colonnade connecting the offices to the residence was built on the foundations of Jefferson's original west terrace, discovered when the greenhouses were removed.

To accommodate crowds, the architects built an East Wing containing cloakrooms, restrooms, a porte cochere that could shelter three carriages, and a portico that could hold five hundred guests.

Inside the White House, McKim redecorated the state floor, removing all the Victorian furnishings of Roosevelt's predecessors. Hoban's original grand staircase, which had led from the west end of the transverse corridor to the executive offices on the second floor, was removed to allow more space for an expanded State Dining Room.

By December, when the renovation was complete, costs had reached $65,000 for the West Wing and $475,000 for the rest of the house. Since 1902, presidents and first ladies who have redecorated the White House have followed Roosevelt's example and conscientiously furnished the state rooms in a style appropriate to the early days of the Republic.

No renovation matched in scope that of the 1902 work until the Truman reconstruction of 1949–1952. Still, intervening presidents continued to make changes. Ellen Axson Wilson, first wife of Woodrow Wilson (1913–1921), added guest rooms to the attic. During Calvin Coolidge's administration (1923–1929), a study by the Army Corps of Engineers revealed that the roof was in

Theodore Roosevelt restored the White House to its classical interior. This is the East Room largely as it appears today.

During the Truman renovation of 1949–1952, only the exterior walls of the White House were left intact. Here, beneath steel scaffolding, a bulldozer excavates a new basement.

danger of collapse because the beams were rotten. President Coolidge, known for his frugality, responded that "there were plenty others who would be willing to take the risk" of living under that roof. Nonetheless, in 1927 the Coolidges moved to a mansion on Dupont Circle owned by the Patterson family, and the roof was replaced.

At this time the third story—eliminated from Hoban's 1792 design—finally was added to the White House, giving the mansion an additional eighteen rooms for guests, servants, and storage. A sun room, which Grace Coolidge called the "sky parlor," was built on the South Portico roof. Hidden from view from the ground by the balustrade, it affords both privacy and splendid views of the Mall.

Grace Coolidge also took an interest in furnishing the White House with antique or historic furniture and urged Congress to pass legislation authorizing presidents to accept such donations from the American public. A joint resolution of Congress, passed in February 1925, marked the first legal recognition of the White House as a museum. A committee established to evaluate the gifts remained in operation through the Eisenhower administration.

Franklin D. Roosevelt (1933–1945) was the next president to make permanent changes in the White House, although his alterations were largely utilitarian. The president and first lady of a nation in the midst of the Great Depression and then World War II had no interest in decoration for its own sake. Instead, they wanted the White House to be a comfortable and practical home for their large family.

The West Wing, which had been damaged by a fire in 1929 and was proving short of office space for the New Deal president, was rebuilt in 1934 and given new underground work space. Also added were three stories of office space to the East Wing and an underground bomb shelter in the basement of the Treasury Department, connected by passageway to the White House. Eleanor Roosevelt had the servants' quarters and the kitchen improved and enlarged. In 1933 the Roosevelts added an indoor swimming pool—paid for by private funds, largely in small donations from the people of New York—so that the polio-stricken president could take regular exercise.[13]

Harry S. Truman (1945–1953) left his mark on both the outside and the inside of the White House. In 1948 he had a second-floor balcony built over the South Portico, which cost $10,000 and earned him much criticism. But Truman stuck by his conviction that the balcony was both an aesthetic improvement (to divide the two-story columns, which he thought looked awkward) and a practical one (to shade the Blue Room, because there was no air conditioning, and to provide a cool place for the first family to relax in summer).

Later in 1948 engineers' reports concluded that the rest of the White House was structurally unsound. Although the first floor had been reinforced with steel in 1902, as had the third floor in 1927, the remaining walls and beams were largely those of the 1814–1817 reconstruction. They had been cut into many times to accommodate plumbing, wiring, and heating ducts and consequently were standing "purely by habit," as the commissioner of public buildings put it.[14] There was also visible evidence of the structural weakness of the building. In 1948 a leg of Margaret Truman's grand piano punctured the floor of her bedroom, causing portions of the ceiling in the room below to collapse. And chandeliers in the East Room often swayed—for reasons only the building itself knew.

The president had three options. First, he could move to a new presidential residence and have the White House designated a museum. Second, the entire White House could be razed and a replica reconstructed. Third, the exterior walls could be left intact, and the interior torn out and rebuilt.[15] The third—and most expensive—option was chosen, and in 1949 Congress appropriated $5.4 million for the work.[16]

The Trumans moved across the street to Blair House in November 1948 as architects and engineers began planning the reconstruction. Starting in December 1949, workers took apart the interior, setting aside mantelpieces and fixtures, labeling decorative moldings, and tagging paneling—all to be carefully reinstalled. Pieces that could not be reused—the walls and floors themselves—were demolished, except for small quantities of wood, brick, and stone that were sold as "relic kits."[17] By mid-1950, apart from supportive scaffolding, the entire White House, basement to roof, was hollow.

In twenty-seven months of rebuilding, fifty subcontractors and hundreds of workers (all of whom had to have security clearances) gave the President's House new foundations, two newly excavated basements, a new steel frame, fireproofing, and air conditioning. Interior details were faithfully restored.

Shortly after his return to the White House on March 27, 1952, President Truman conducted a televised tour of the mansion with Walter Cronkite. His was the first such tour, but not the most famous. Ten years later, on February 14, 1962, Jacqueline Kennedy would conduct another tour of the White House to a television audience of forty-six million.

In 1961 Mrs. Kennedy (1961–1963) created the Fine Arts Committee for the White House and the Special Committee on Paintings. She planned to furnish the White House with authentic American antiques and paintings of the eighteenth and nineteenth centuries and to dispose of the reproduction pieces, many of which were mediocre in quality and irrelevant to U.S. history. No public funds were available, so all contributions came from private donors. Before President Kennedy's death, Jacqueline Kennedy's Fine Arts Committee restored the state rooms on the first floor and several historic rooms on the second floor.

In September 1961 Congress passed legislation stating that White House acquisitions of "historic or artistic interest" would become part of the permanent White House collection. When not in use, they would be stored at the Smithsonian Institution. No longer would it be possible simply to lose track of historic pieces, as had happened so often in the past, or for furnishings to be sold to the highest bidder, as President Arthur had done when he moved into the White House in 1881.

On March 7, 1964, Lyndon B. Johnson (1963–1969) signed Executive Order 11145 establishing the Committee for the Preservation of the White House and the permanent office of White House curator. Still operating today, the committee advises the first family on the selection and use of furnishings for the executive mansion.

Throughout Richard Nixon's tenure in the White House (1969–1974), Patricia Nixon oversaw renovation of the main rooms on the ground and state floors. Nearly a decade of heavy use since the Kennedy refurbishing had left much of the furniture nearly threadbare. Under the guidance of curator Clement E. Conger, the Nixons continued the program of antiques collection begun by Jacqueline Kennedy. The swimming pool in the West Wing was boarded over to make more room for the fifteen hundred reporters accredited to the White House.

Gerald R. Ford (1974–1977) and Jimmy Carter (1977–1981) collected paintings rather than furniture during their terms of office. Ford acquired twenty-six works, including a small wax portrait of James Hoban, the only known likeness of the architect.[18] Carter added thirty-four paintings to the White House collection.[19]

Ronald Reagan (1981–1989) raised more than $1 million in private funds to redecorate the second and third floors. Since the Truman renovation, efforts to furnish the White House had focused entirely on the historic rooms of the ground and first floors, leaving for the family quarters and other second-floor rooms whatever furniture presidents chose to bring with them or could find in White House warehouses. Many pieces of nineteenth-century American furniture were retrieved from storage, refurbished, and returned to use in the executive mansion.

Major improvements to the building itself took place during the administrations of Reagan and of George Bush (1989–1993). From 1980 to 1992 workers performed the painstaking work of chemically removing 175 years' buildup of whitewash and paint from the exterior walls and repairing the delicate sandstone carvings beneath. When cleaned, some sections, under as many as thirty-two layers of paint, revealed the black scorch marks from the burning of the mansion in the War of 1812. The project, which cost more than $5 million, was scheduled for completion in 1997.

During the administration of Bill Clinton (1993–), private donations again funded redecoration, primarily of the Lincoln Sitting Room, the Treaty Room, and the Oval Office.[20]

THE WHITE HOUSE TODAY

The White House contains 132 rooms, including 32 bathrooms. The residence, which is 170 feet long and 85 feet wide, consists of four floors (referred to as the ground, first, second, and third floors) and two basements; the West and East wings each have three floors. The ground floor, opening onto the South Portico, is visible only from the south side of the house. The five state rooms open for tours are on the first floor, which contains the North Portico entrance facing Pennsylvania Avenue. The second floor contains seven historic rooms and the principal living quarters. On the third floor are additional rooms for the first family, the solarium, guest bedrooms, and storage areas.

The Committee for the Preservation of the White House works closely with the White House Historical Association, a nonprofit organization, to acquire furniture, paintings, and decorative objects through private donations. At the beginning of each presidential term since 1925, Congress has appropriated $50,000 for the president to paint and decorate the family living quarters.

FIGURE 22-1   Plan of the White House

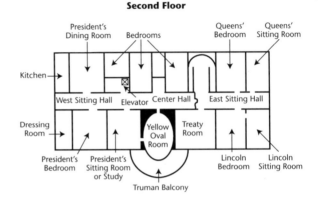

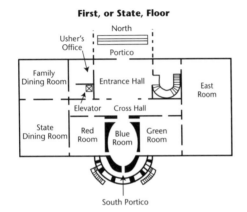

Note: Drawings are not to scale.

The East Wing and the Ground Floor

The public tour of the White House begins in the *East Wing Lobby*, a wood-paneled hall decorated with portraits of first ladies. The East Wing, built in 1902 during Theodore Roosevelt's administration, was rebuilt and enlarged in 1934 by Franklin Roosevelt. It contains the visitors' office and some offices of the first lady's staff, the president's military aides, some White House congressional liaison staff, and the Uniformed Division of the Secret Service. In 1942 Roosevelt added the East Wing Lobby and converted the cloakroom—known as the "Hat Box"—into a movie theater, still in use today. Adjacent to the lobby is the bright, informal *Garden Room,* which overlooks the Jacqueline Kennedy Garden. Visitors proceed through a glass-enclosed colonnade, built on the foundations of Thomas Jefferson's east pavilion, to the ground floor of the White House. Before the renovation of 1902, the *Ground Floor Corridor* (the only area open to the public on this floor) and adjacent rooms served as work and storage areas. The Truman renovation restored the clean lines of Hoban's groined arches and covered the walls and floors with marble. Portraits of first ladies hang in the hall.

The first room on the south side of the corridor is the *Vermeil Room* (also called the "Gold Room"), which contains a col-lection of gilded silver, given to the White House in 1956 by Margaret Thompson Biddle. Throughout the room are portraits of First Ladies Eleanor Roosevelt, Jacqueline Kennedy, Lady Bird Johnson, and Patricia Ryan Nixon. This display room also is used as a women's sitting room on formal occasions; powder rooms are adjacent.

The second room on the south side of the corridor is the *China Room,* so named in 1917 by Edith Bolling Wilson, Woodrow Wilson's second wife, to display the china collection begun by Caroline Harrison in 1889. Almost every presidential administration is represented. The white, red, and gold state china service commissioned by Nancy Reagan was donated to the White House in 1982. Howard Chandler Christy's 1924 por-trait of Grace Coolidge wearing a red dress determined the red and white color scheme of this room.

Portraits of the most recent first ladies usually hang in the Ground Floor corridor outside the *Diplomatic Reception Room.* Opening onto the South Portico, the Diplomatic Reception Room contains the south entrance to the White House, used by the first family and foreign dignitaries on informal occasions. (For state dinners, heads of state enter through the North Porti-co on the first floor; all other guests pass through security checks in the East Wing.) Franklin Roosevelt broadcast his fireside chats from this room in the 1930s and 1940s. In 1961 Jacqueline Kennedy redecorated the room with historic furnishings. "Scenic America," a wallpaper printed in 1834, forms a panorama of American scenes along the curved walls, one of Hoban's three oval rooms.

For President Roosevelt during World War II, the *Map Room,* next door to the Diplomatic Reception Room, served as a communications center where he tracked the movement of troops and ships. Today, the president and first lady use the room for private meetings and small receptions.

On the north side of the Ground Floor corridor is the *Library.* Used for storage in 1801, later as a laundry room, and in Theodore Roosevelt's day as a "Gentlemen's anteroom," the Library assumed its present use in 1937. Old timbers removed from the house during the Truman restoration were made into wood paneling for the room, now painted a soft gray after the fashion of "painted" rooms in the early 1800s. In 1961 a committee was formed to select books on American subjects for the Library. The collection for the Library and for the family living quarters continues to grow with presidential biographies and papers and with quadrennial gifts of 250 to 300 titles from the American Booksellers Association. Also on the ground floor are the main kitchen, the florist's workshop, and offices of the curator, the housekeeper, the president's physician, the auditor, and additional offices for the Secret Service.

The First Floor

The rooms on the first, or state, floor are those viewed by the public on morning tours and used by the president for official entertaining at other times. The five state rooms—the East Room, Green Room, Blue Room, Red Room, and State Dining Room—are the most historic and the most used parts of the White House. Consequently, these rooms undergo the most refurbishing.

The *North Entrance Hall,* opening onto the North Portico, and the *Cross Hall,* connecting the East Room and the State Dining Room, were part of Hoban's original design. The only major change since Hoban's time took place in 1902 when the main staircase at the west end of the Cross Hall was removed and a new one was installed across from the Green Room. During the Truman restoration, the staircase was repositioned so that it now descends into the Entrance Hall. Also between 1949 and 1952, marble was added to the floors and walls of the Cross Hall, where portraits of recent presidents hang.

The elegant but sparsely furnished *East Room* is probably the most famous room in the White House, for it is here that most White House press conferences are held. Decorated in the classical style of the late eighteenth century, the East Room appears today much as it did after the 1902 renovation by the architectural firm McKim, Mead, and White. It is eighty feet long by forty feet wide, with ceilings twenty-two feet in height. The walls are paneled in wood, intricately carved, and painted white. Three Bohemian cut-glass chandeliers hang above an oak floor

Just before fleeing the White House as British troops invaded Washington in August 1814, Dolley Madison removed this Gilbert Stuart portrait of George Washington so she could take it with her.

of Fontainebleu parquetry. The principal article of furniture is a Steinway grand piano with gilded legs in the shape of American eagles, which the Steinway Company donated to the White House in 1938. On the wall is the full-length Gilbert Stuart portrait of George Washington that Dolley Madison saved from the fire of 1814.

In addition to news conferences, the East Room is used for large gatherings on many sorts of occasions—bill signings, receptions, dances, concerts, after-dinner entertainment, weddings, and funerals. It was here that Abigail Adams hung her laundry in 1801; James Madison met with his cabinet in 1812; and Abraham Lincoln dreamed he saw his catafalque surrounded by mourners in 1865—which, but a few days later, it was. Seven presidents have lain in state in the East Room: William Henry Harrison in 1841, Taylor in 1850, Lincoln in 1865, McKinley in

1901, Warren G. Harding in 1923, Franklin Roosevelt in 1945, and Kennedy in 1963. Happier uses of the room include the wedding of President Grover Cleveland and Frances Folsom in 1886—the only White House wedding of a president.

Music at the White House has played an important role not only as entertainment but as a symbol of the first family's commitment to the cultural life of the country. In 1878 soprano Marie Selika performed for President and Mrs. Rutherford B. Hayes. Selika was probably the first black performer to give a concert at the White House. Jacqueline Kennedy established the White House as a cultural center with performances by premier artists such as cellist Pablo Casals in 1961. Jimmy and Rosalyn Carter began the practice of televised concerts from the East Room with a performance by pianist Vladimir Horowitz in 1978.[21]

On the tour, visitors enter the East Room from the Cross Hall and exit through a door to the *Green Room*. Hoban called this room the "Common Dining Room," but only Thomas Jefferson used it regularly for meals. For James Madison, it was a sitting room; for James Monroe, a card room. John Quincy Adams called it the "Green Drawing Room," establishing both its color and its function for future presidents. In the Green Room today small receptions and teas are held and occasionally a small formal dinner.

The room is furnished with Sheraton pieces from the Federal period (1800–1815), many from the New York workshop of cabinetmaker Duncan Phyfe. The walls are covered in green watered-silk, a fabric originally chosen by Jacqueline Kennedy in 1961 and matched and replaced by Patricia Nixon in 1971. The carpet in the Green Room, a large, multicolored Turkish Hereke, is unusual for its green field. On the walls are portraits of presidents and other paintings by well-known American artists.

Hoban designed three oval rooms for the White House, one on each floor at the midpoint of the south side of the house. The *Blue Room*, which Hoban called the "elliptic saloon," is the most historic of the three. Thomas Jefferson first decorated the room in blue, which for most of its history has been used for formal receptions. (The Blue Room is also the location of the official White House Christmas tree.) After the fire of 1814, President Monroe decorated the room with French Empire furnishings, largely with pieces made by Pierre Antoine Bellange, purchased in 1817. Items from Monroe's collection that were lost or sold at auction in the nineteenth century gradually have been located or reproduced in the twentieth. Refurbishings of 1902, 1962, 1972, and 1995 fully restored the French Empire style of the room. The 1995 work included installation of light gold wallpaper, blue satin draperies, and sapphire blue silk upholstery based on early nineteenth-century American and French designs.

The fourth state room open to the public, and the third of the three parlors on the first floor, is the *Red Room*. Decorated in the American Empire style (1810–1830) with red damask upholstery and wallpaper of red twill satin, the room has been used as a parlor since Jefferson's day. Earlier, it was John Adams's break-

---

WHAT'S IN A NAME?

French engineer and architect Pierre Charles L'Enfant, chosen by George Washington to plan the new capital city on the Potomac, insisted on calling the presidential residence the "President's Palace." But Washington preferred a less regal term and called the residence simply the "President's House." Others spoke of it as the "Executive Mansion."

Once the house was completed its appearance determined its name, for the painted white sandstone stood in sharp contrast to the brick and frame buildings surrounding it. In November 1810 a reporter for the *Baltimore Whig* first referred to the house in print as the "white house."[1] By the end of the Madison administration in 1817, the term had gained full currency.

Not until 1901, however, did the name become official. In that year Theodore Roosevelt issued an executive order changing the official name from the "Executive Mansion" to the "White House."[2] Today, the president's letterhead reads simply:

The White House
Washington

1. Amy La Follette Jensen, *The White House and Its Thirty-three Families* (New York: McGraw-Hill, 1962), 21.
2. William Seale, *The President's House*, 2 vols. (Washington, D.C.: White House Historical Association, 1986), 1088, 654.

---

fast room. Dolley Madison held her glittering Wednesday night receptions here, and Eleanor Roosevelt held press conferences in this room for women reporters, who were not allowed to attend her husband's meetings with the press. The Red Room gained political fame in 1877 as the place where Rutherford B. Hayes secretly was sworn into office during a party hosted by retiring president Grant. Because of a close race and a final decision challenged by Hayes's opponent, Grant was eager to ensure a smooth transition of government. (See *"The Compromise of 1876,"* p. 356, in Chapter 7.)

The last of the five state rooms on the public tour is the *State Dining Room*. First given this name by Andrew Jackson, the room earlier served as a drawing room, cabinet room, and office. The 1902 renovation enlarged the room by extending the north wall and removing the grand stairway at the end of the Cross Hall. The State Dining Room today can seat 140.

Similar to the spacious white and gold East Room, the State Dining Room has wood paneling painted in several shades of antique ivory to highlight the delicately carved Corinthian pilasters and neoclassical frieze. Golden silk damask draperies frame the floor-to-ceiling windows. The mantel over the fireplace is a 1962 reproduction of the bison-head mantel from Theodore Roosevelt's administration. In 1952 Truman replaced the Roosevelt mantel with a simpler molding and declared the original "surplus"; today the original mantel is in the Truman presidential library. The face of the mantel is inscribed with the following passage from a letter John Adams wrote to his wife on his second night in the White House:

I Pray to Heaven to Bestow
the Best of Blessings on
THIS HOUSE
and on All that shall hereafter
Inhabit it. May none but Honest
and Wise Men ever rule under this Roof.

Adjacent to the State Dining Room, in the northwest corner of the first floor, is the smaller *Family Dining Room.* Although President James Monroe gave his state dinners here and called it the "Public Dining Room," the room usually has served as the formal dining room for the president's family or for official entertaining of a small number of guests, most often at luncheons or breakfasts. During formal dinners in the State Dining Room, the White House staff drape the furniture and use this room as a pantry to lessen the inconvenience of having the kitchen and dining room on separate floors. The Family Dining Room appears today much as it did after the 1902 renovation, when its white vaulted ceiling and classical frieze were installed. The walls are painted a light yellow, and the furniture is from the Federal period.

The Second and Third Floors

The east half of the second floor contains historic areas—the Queens' Suite, the Lincoln Suite, the Treaty Room, and the Yellow Oval Room. The west half contains several rooms of the family living quarters. The third floor comprises additional family rooms as well as sitting rooms and bedrooms for guests. None of these rooms is open to the public, but it has not always been so.

The Historic Areas. "All sorts of people come upon all sorts of errands," wrote an assistant to Abraham Lincoln about the crowds milling about in the second-floor hall near the president's office. Throughout the nineteenth century, before offices were moved to the West Wing, the public was free to come and go—and wait—in what is now the *East Sitting Hall.* The room today is a small parlor, furnished largely with antiques from the White House collection. Filling the east wall of the hall, overlooking the East Wing and the Treasury Building, is Hoban's original double-arched window. To the north of the East Sitting Room is the *Queens' Suite,* comprising a small sitting room and a bedroom furnished in the American Federal style. The bed in the *Queens' Bedroom* is believed to have belonged to Andrew Jackson. The *Queens' Sitting Room* appears today much as it did during the Kennedy administration. Wall covering, draperies, and upholstery are made from a French fabric with ivory, neoclassical medallions on a blue field. The room is furnished with antiques from the American and French Empire periods held in the White House collection. Among the guests who have occupied the Queens' Suite are Queen Elizabeth, wife of Great Britain's King George VI, and her daughter Queen Elizabeth II; and Queen Wilhelmina of the Netherlands and Queen Juliana, her daughter.

On the south side of the East Sitting Hall is the *Lincoln Suite,* comprising the *Lincoln Bedroom* and the *Lincoln Sitting Room.* Used today as a guest room for friends of the president, the bedroom once was Lincoln's office and cabinet room. It was there that he signed the Emancipation Proclamation in 1863.

President Truman decorated the room with American Victo-

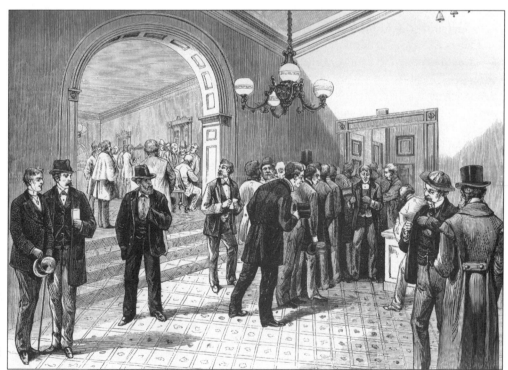

Nineteenth-century office seekers gather in the White House awaiting an interview with the president. Before Theodore Roosevelt built the West Wing offices, visitors milled about on the first and second floors of the White House, leaving the first family little privacy.

rian furnishings from the period 1850–1870. Notable pieces are a desk that Lincoln used and a rosewood bed—eight feet long and six feet wide—thought to have been purchased by Mary Todd Lincoln in 1861. Although Lincoln probably never used the bed, other presidents did, including Theodore Roosevelt and Woodrow Wilson. Lincoln was particularly fond of the portrait of Andrew Jackson that hangs in the room. Also in the Lincoln Bedroom is the only known copy of the Gettysburg Address titled, dated, and signed by President Lincoln.

The Lincoln Sitting Room is a small room with a fireplace on the southeast corner of the second floor. Throughout much of the nineteenth century it served as office space for presidential assistants, although English novelist Charles Dickens recorded on his visit to the White House during John Tyler's administration (1841–1845) that this room was the president's office. The Clintons decorated the room in high Victorian style. The red and gold patterned rug and draperies, late Empire chest, and four mahogany chairs purchased by Mrs. Lincoln complement the furnishings of the Lincoln Bedroom. A small mahogany desk in the room was built by White House architect James Hoban.

Also on the south side of the building, beside the Lincoln Bedroom, is the *Treaty Room*, so named during the Kennedy administration. The Treaty Room served as the cabinet room from 1865 to 1902 and as a sitting room from 1902 to 1961. Since 1961 presidents have signed several important documents here, including the instruments of ratification for the 1963 test ban treaty and the 1972 antiballistic missile treaty. In 1989 the Bushes redecorated the room and made it a private study for the president.

Clinton continued to use the Treaty Room as his personal study and redecorated it again. For his desk he chose a large Victorian walnut table, which President Grant purchased in 1869. On March 26, 1979, President Jimmy Carter had this table moved outdoors for the signing of the Egyptian-Israeli peace treaty.

Adjacent to the Treaty Room is the *Yellow Oval Room*, the third in the tier of Hoban's elliptical rooms. Today the room serves as a formal drawing room for the first family and as a reception room where the president greets foreign dignitaries before state luncheons and dinners. Throughout its history, the room has seen many other uses as well. President John Adams held the first White House reception here on January 1, 1801. It has been a bedroom, a family room, and an office, and Abigail Fillmore set up the first White House library here. Franklin Roosevelt and Harry Truman called the room their "oval study" and used it as a less formal working space than the Oval Office.

Dolley Madison decorated the room in yellow damask in 1809, and Jacqueline Kennedy chose a yellow color scheme again in 1961 when she added furnishings in the neoclassical style of Louis XVI. The Yellow Oval Room contains the works of several important American artists, including William Merritt Chase and Albert Bierstadt.

The Yellow Oval Room opens onto the Truman balcony, built in 1948, where first families occasionally dine, entertain guests, and on July 4 watch fireworks on the Mall.

The yellow and white *Center Hall* is today a large drawing room for the president's family and for foreign guests waiting to be received in the Yellow Oval Room. During the Truman administration, a cornice and bookshelves were installed. The hall is furnished with late eighteenth- and early nineteenth-century antiques from the White House collection and, like the Yellow Oval Room, is decorated with works of American artists.

The Family Living Quarters. With each first family, both the decor and the number of rooms used as the family living quarters change, for they become the Washington home of the person elected president. These rooms constitute a private home within a very public house; comfort and familiarity, not the historical record, govern their use and appearance.[22]

This part of the White House changes constantly, as President Truman discovered when he asked Chief Usher J. B. West whether his family's plan for the living quarters would be "tampering with history too much." West replied:

> The President may use the house any way he wishes. . . . It's always been so. Actually, the room that Mrs. Truman has chosen for her sitting room was probably where Lincoln slept. The Coolidges kept the Lincoln furniture there, and President and Mrs. Coolidge slept in the room together. The Hoovers slept in the same room, but they moved the Lincoln furniture across the hall. . . . You could just as easily move it down the hall over the East Room, because that was the Lincoln Cabinet Room.

To this convoluted history lesson Truman replied, "Now I know why they say Lincoln's ghost walks around up here all night. He's just looking for his bed!"[23]

The West Sitting Hall, opening off the Center Hall, is the first family's private living room, which, with each new administration, is decorated with personal items from the family's former home. Like the East Sitting Hall, one end of the room is dominated by Hoban's double-arched window, which overlooks the West Wing and the Old Executive Office Building. Before the 1902 renovation, this hall was little more than a stair landing. During the Truman renovation, the hall became a room when it was enclosed with solid partitions.

Jacqueline Kennedy disliked the Family Dining Room on the first floor and wanted a smaller, more intimate dining room for her family in their living quarters. So in 1961 she converted one of the Eisenhowers' sitting rooms on the north side of the West Sitting Hall into the President's Dining Room. Early in the century, this space had served as a bedroom, and Alice Roosevelt Longworth, daughter of Theodore Roosevelt, remembered having her appendix removed here.

The President's Dining Room is furnished largely with American Federal pieces donated to the White House in 1961 and 1962 through Jacqueline Kennedy's Fine Arts Committee. The mahogany sideboard was once owned by Daniel Webster; it still bears his initials. James Madison's portable walnut medicine chest on display here was taken from the house by a British soldier just before troops burned the mansion in 1814. A Canadian

WHITE HOUSE TOURS

A tour of the White House takes some planning, some patience, and, in the busy season, a ticket. The White House Visitor Center, in Baldrige Hall at the Department of Commerce, is the place for the public to get tickets for a visit. The White House is open for public tours Tuesday through Saturday, 10:00 a.m. to 12:00 p.m. The Visitor Center gives out free, same-day-only tickets on a first-come, first-served basis starting at 7:30 a.m. on the days the White House is open.

The Visitor's Center exhibit hall, showing a video and displays of White House history and everyday life, is open 7:30 a.m. to 4:00 p.m. every day.

The public, self-guided tours last about twenty minutes, as visitors are ushered through eight rooms of the White House (the Ground Floor Corridor, East Room, Green Room, Blue Room, Red Room, State Dining Room, Cross Hall, and Entrance Hall). Secret Service agents are stationed in each room and will answer questions about the room's furnishings and history.

The White House also offers free guided tours between 8:00 a.m. and 9:00 a.m., which include two additional rooms (usually the Library and Vermeil Room). Tickets for these tours must be obtained from one's senator or representative three to six months in advance. Availability is limited, as each member of Congress can give out only about ten tickets per week. These tours include about seventy people in each tour and last about thirty minutes.

In the spring and summer, as many as 5,000 people take the public tours of the White House each day, so tickets are required from mid-March through August 31. The Visitor Center recommends getting in line by 6:45 a.m. during cherry blossom season, by 7:30 a.m. during other days in April and May, and by 7:00 a.m. during the summer months. After August 31, tickets are not required for public tours, and visitors may line up outside the southeast entrance to the White House, between the White House and the Treasury Building.

In addition to spring and summer weekdays, the most popular visiting times are the third weekends in April and October, when both the house and South Lawn gardens are open to the public; Easter Monday for the annual children's Easter egg hunt (one must bring a child to get in); and the three Christmas candlelight tours, variously scheduled during the holiday season. The garden and Christmas tours draw roughly 11,000 visitors; the Easter egg hunt, about 30,000. Occasionally White House events (such as a visit by a head of state) necessitate closing the White House to public tours.

SOURCE: White House Visitor Center, Department of Commerce, 1450 Pennsylvania Avenue, N.W., 202-208-1631 or 202-456-7041 (recorded message with complete details and notice of any last-minute changes in tour availability).

descendant of the soldier donated the chest to the White House in 1939.[24] The wallpaper, called "The War of Independence," is a panorama of scenes from the American Revolution—some accurate in their details, some merely imagined by the artist.

The first family's private kitchen, built by the Kennedys in 1961 and renovated by the Clintons in 1993, is adjacent to the dining room on the northwest corner of the second floor. This was not, however, the first private kitchen in the family living quarters. Franklin Roosevelt did not like the food his wife's cook prepared, so in 1938 he had a kitchen built on the third floor and brought in his own cook from his Hyde Park home. Thereafter he took many of his meals with friends or staff in his second-floor study (now the Yellow Oval Room).

The room between the Yellow Oval Room and the president's bedroom on the south side of the house has been used as a bedroom, a study, and most recently as a sitting room. Presidents Ford, Carter, Bush, and Clinton used the room as a sitting room; President Reagan made it his study; and Presidents Franklin Roosevelt through Nixon chose this room as their bedroom. On the side of the mantelpiece is a small plaque that Jacqueline Kennedy had installed after her husband's assassination; it reads: "This room was occupied by John Fitzgerald Kennedy during the two years, ten months and two days he was President of the United States. January 20, 1961–November 22, 1963."

President and Mrs. Clinton share the bedroom adjacent to the sitting room, as did the Bushes, Reagans, Fords, and Carters. In earlier administrations, Mamie Eisenhower, Jacqueline Kennedy, Lady Bird Johnson, and Patricia Nixon made this room their bedroom. First families since the Eisenhowers have used the small adjoining room in the southwest corner of the second floor as a dressing room.

Family quarters extend to the third floor, although not all first families have used these rooms regularly. The Third Floor Center Sitting Hall, lined with bookshelves, follows the decorating style of the Central Hall on the second floor. Various parlors and guest bedrooms open onto the hall. The Solarium—or "sky parlor," as Grace Coolidge called it—has been a favorite retreat of first families since 1927. It served, for example, as a schoolroom for Caroline Kennedy, an entertaining room for Luci and Lynda Johnson (who had a soda fountain installed there), a family room for the Carters, and a playroom for the Bushes' grandchildren. Octagonal in shape with three walls of glass, the room overlooks the south lawn of the White House and the Mall.

The West Wing

The West Wing of the White House is where the chief executive conducts the official business of the presidency. In 1993 Hillary Rodham Clinton became the first first lady to establish her office in the West Wing rather than the East Wing of the White House.

Built during the Roosevelt renovation of 1902 as temporary offices, the West Wing has since become a permanent addition to the White House. It was doubled in size in 1909 and enlarged

The *Resolute* desk, a gift from Queen Victoria to President Rutherford B. Hayes in 1880, was made famous in this photograph of John F. Kennedy Jr. peeking out from behind the panel FDR had installed to conceal his leg braces. Presidents Reagan and Clinton also chose to use the desk.

again in 1927 and 1934. The structure was rebuilt in 1930 after a fire on Christmas Eve, 1929.

In 1969 President Nixon remodeled the West Wing. A north portico and driveway were added, and the swimming pool along the colonnade joining the West Wing and the mansion was boarded over to make more room for the press. The old press lobby, in use since 1902 on the north side of the wing, was converted to the *West Wing Reception Room* and is used today as an appointments lobby.

High-level staff meetings and conferences are held in the *Roosevelt Room*, which President Nixon named for both Theodore and Franklin Roosevelt, in honor of their contributions to the construction and expansion of the West Wing. Service flags from the army, navy, air force, Marine Corps, and Coast Guard stand at one end of the large conference table, which dominates the room. On the fireplace mantel is the medal presented to Theodore Roosevelt in 1906 when he won the Nobel Peace Prize for his role in settling the Russo-Japanese War—the only Nobel prize to be won by a U.S. president to date. Today the room is decorated with presidential portraits and American

landscape paintings, but during Franklin Roosevelt's administration it looked quite different. The New Deal president installed an aquarium and filled the room with mementos of his fishing trips, so the staff called it the "Fish Room." The tradition continued through the Kennedy administration when JFK mounted a sailfish on the wall.

In the *Cabinet Room*, added to the West Wing in 1909, the president meets with the cabinet, the National Security Council, and members of Congress and occasionally conducts award ceremonies. An oval, mahogany conference table seating twenty, purchased by President Nixon in 1970, fills the room. The back of the president's chair is two inches taller than the others. Each of the other chairs bears a small plaque with the cabinet member's name and title. (After his or her term, the cabinet member may purchase the chair as a keepsake.) Overlooking the Rose Garden, the Cabinet Room contains likenesses of former presidents and statesmen—the choice reflecting the preferences of the current chief executive.

The *Oval Office* is the president's formal office, where meetings with heads of government and chiefs of state are held. The first Oval Office was built in 1909 in the center of the West Wing. William Howard Taft was the first president to occupy the Oval Office. In 1934 the office was moved to its current location on the southeast corner of the wing, overlooking the Rose Garden. Each president has decorated the Oval Office to suit his tastes. The only features that remain constant are the presidential seal in the ceiling medallion and the two flags behind the president's desk—the U.S. flag and the president's flag.

In the Oval Office Presidents Clinton and Reagan used the desk Queen Victoria gave to President Hayes in 1880, made from timbers of the H.M.S. *Resolute*. In 1855 American whalers had rescued the ship trapped in Arctic ice, and the United States returned it to the British government. Later, when the *Resolute* was broken up, Queen Victoria had the desk made for the U.S. president in a gesture of appreciation. Truman used the desk, as did FDR, who installed a front panel to conceal his leg braces. Kennedy also used the *Resolute* desk, but it was John F. Kennedy Jr. who made the desk famous in a photograph of the boy peeking out from behind the central panel while his father worked above.

WHITE HOUSE GROUNDS

The eighteen acres surrounding the White House have changed a great deal since John and Abigail Adams's time. In November 1800 the grounds were muddy and littered with the shacks and supplies of workers still building the mansion.

Methods of groundskeeping have changed as well. The grass, for example, is no longer kept short by grazing sheep, as it was as recently as Woodrow Wilson's administration, or by William Howard Taft's cow, Pauline Wayne. Today, the National Park Service takes care of the house and grounds. Still, touches of the past remain.

Thomas Jefferson was an avid gardener and landscaped what he called the "President's Park." John Quincy Adams devoted much time to the gardens, and a massive American elm that he planted on the south lawn in 1825 stood until fall 1991 as a monument to his efforts. Growing tall beside the South Portico, the southern magnolias that Andrew Jackson planted in memory of his wife nearly conceal the windows of the president's bedroom on the second floor. Since the Wilson administration, every president has planted trees on the White House grounds. In December 1991 Barbara Bush planted a tree propagated from Adams's elm in the same location where the original had stood. In April 1995 Bill and Hillary Clinton planted a dogwood on the South Lawn in memory of those who died in that month's truck bombing in Oklahoma City.

Special Gardens

The *Rose Garden* is one of three special gardens on the grounds of the White House. Situated between the West Wing and the residence, the Rose Garden is planted in the style of a traditional eighteenth-century American garden. From early spring until the first frost, flowers and trees provide seasonal color within the rectangular frame of boxwood and osmanthus hedges.

Until 1902 conservatories and greenhouses covered the ground where the West Wing and Rose Garden now are. Theodore Roosevelt had them removed. Ellen Axson Wilson first planted roses here in 1913, and the garden remained largely unchanged until 1962 when President Kennedy asked Rachel Lambert Mellon to redesign it.[25]

The president receives special guests in the Rose Garden, such as foreign dignitaries, Medal of Honor winners, and U.S. astronauts. Occasionally, the president will host a state dinner in the garden. In June 1971 the first outdoor White House wedding took place there, when Tricia Nixon married Edward Cox.

The *Jacqueline Kennedy Garden,* located beside the East Wing of the White House is a setting for the first lady's informal receptions. Shaded by rows of lindens, the garden contains ornamental flowering trees, shrubs, and herbs around a rectangular lawn. In 1994 Hillary Clinton used it as an outdoor sculpture garden. Lady Bird Johnson named the garden for her predecessor in 1965, but Patricia Nixon called it "the east garden." Today, it again bears Mrs. Kennedy's name. On January 18, 1969, Lady Bird Johnson established a third special garden, this one in honor of the young children associated with the White House. The "Children's Garden" is decorated with plaques bearing the handprints and footprints of the Johnson, Carter, and Bush grandchildren.

Recreational Facilities

Presidents through the years have set up their own sports facilities on the White House grounds. Hayes played croquet, Harding played medicine ball, Hoover played golf (and trained his Airedale to retrieve the balls), and Truman played horseshoes. Ford installed the first outdoor swimming pool, and presidents since Theodore Roosevelt have enjoyed the tennis court on the south lawn. Bush added an artificial putting green and a

horseshoe pit. Clinton built a jogging track that encircles a portion of the South Lawn.

Children, too, have had their fun outdoors at the White House. Benjamin Harrison's grandson, Baby McKee, rode around the grounds in a cart pulled by His Whiskers—the boy's pet goat. Eleanor Roosevelt had a jungle gym and a sandbox built for her grandchildren and resisted the advice of groundskeepers against hanging an old-fashioned swing from a tree limb.[26] Theodore Roosevelt's son Quentin rode his pony Algonquin on the south lawn, and Caroline Kennedy riding her pony Macaroni was a favorite subject for photographers in the early 1960s.

An annual public treat for children begun in 1879 is the Easter Monday egg-rolling. Children are invited to bring their eggs to the party and compare their artistic and egg-rolling skills. In 1995, thirty-five thousand people attended the event.

SECURITY AND COMMUNICATIONS

The Secret Service is tight-lipped about White House security procedures, reasoning that the more that is known about its practices the better equipped a potential assassin could be.[27] Yet the Secret Service is keenly aware that the White House is a national monument and an important symbol to the American people. Consequently, the White House—even on a tour of its interior—appears remarkably accessible.

It is not. Round-the-clock protection of the president and the mansion is the duty of plainclothes Secret Service agents (the ones dressed in business suits with small white lapel pins) and of the White House Branch of the Uniformed Division of the Secret Service. *(See also "Protecting the President: The Secret Service," p. 1003, in Chapter 24.)* The agents, working in eight-hour shifts, are stationed throughout the residence and in the East and West wings. Officers of the Uniformed Division are positioned on the grounds of the residence, at the guardhouses, and at selected posts inside, such as the hallways and entrances to the Oval Office. Two main duties of the Uniformed Division are to police the grounds of the White House and to conduct and monitor visitors' tours.

The White House is surrounded by a black iron fence six and one-half feet tall. Sensors on the fence can detect intruders attempting to climb over. At each of the eight entrances to the grounds, at least two uniformed guards staff small white guardhouses, one standing outside and one watching over surveillance devices inside. The guardhouses are protected with bulletproof glass.

Electronic sensors and video equipment ensure thorough protection of the grounds. Buried seismic sensors can detect even the lightest footsteps. Television cameras disguised as lanterns or concealed in plantings provide visual surveillance. Uniformed guards regularly check the grounds from observation points on the roof of the White House and the Treasury Building next door, and sharpshooters watch from the roofs whenever the president is outdoors. Foot and vehicular patrols on small motorcycles cover the grounds and the streets around

In 1995 the segment of Pennsylvania Avenue directly in front of the White House was closed to vehicular traffic. This arrangement opened several blocks up to pedestrians, bicyclists, and skaters. In 1996 plans were under way for turning the closed segment of the street into a parklike area.

the White House. In October 1995 the Secret Service also started using bicycles on its patrols. A canine unit, trained in attacking and scouting, is used primarily to check the buildings and grounds for explosives.

In 1983 security of the house and grounds was stepped up significantly after bombings at the U.S. Capitol and of the U.S. Embassy and the Marine barracks in Lebanon. At a cost of $6.9 million, East Executive Avenue was closed and made into a park.[28] A wall of concrete barriers, installed in 1983, was replaced in 1988 by 274 barrel-shaped cement posts linked by heavy chains; they cost $670,000.[29] The posts, thirty-eight inches high and four feet apart, are placed so that only slow-moving vehicles can approach and enter the White House gate. The April 1995 bombing of the Alfred P. Murrah federal building in Oklahoma City led to strong recommendations that the block of Pennsylvania Avenue in front of the White House be closed to all but pedestrian traffic. It was closed in May 1995, as was State Place, adjacent to the White House. (See box, Public Access to the White House, right.)

The Secret Service also guards the airspace above the White House. A microwave Doppler radar system, installed in 1991, can detect someone attempting to parachute onto the grounds. Equipped with heat-seeking Stinger antiaircraft missiles, guards can shoot down airborne intruders. A communications link to the control tower at Washington's nearby National Airport allows air traffic controllers to alert the Secret Service to any planes flying off course and posing a threat.[30]

Several incidents occurred in 1994, however, that brought into question the effectiveness of these protective measures. Two were particularly alarming. In September 1994 a pilot crashed a Cessna 150 on the White House grounds, and the small plane crumpled up against the south wall of the White House—just outside the State Dining Room and just beneath the president's

PUBLIC ACCESS TO THE WHITE HOUSE

One hundred years ago anyone who wanted to meet with the president simply went to the second floor of the White House and waited outside his office. Dozens of people paid such calls every day. Gathered just outside the president's living quarters, the daily crowds eventually became unmanageable, and in 1902 Theodore Roosevelt built the West Wing suite of offices.

A little more than fifty years ago, visitors could stroll across the White House grounds, just as they might walk through any public park. But the bombing of Pearl Harbor on December 7, 1941, put a stop to that casual access, and President Franklin Roosevelt agreed to extend the perimeter of White House security to the iron fence at the property's edge.

By May 1995 the public's proximity to the White House had again become a security issue. After several security breaches on White House grounds and the car bombing of the federal building in Oklahoma City in April 1995, the block of Pennsylvania Avenue in front of the White House was closed to vehicular traffic. This enhanced security measure virtually eliminates the threat of a car bomb and makes it easier for police and White House security to monitor pedestrians.

In a democracy of such relatively short history, which has endured the assassinations of four presidents and numerous attempts, no one questions the need for adequate presidential security. Yet each distancing of the chief of state from the public, be it symbolic or real, forces the disturbing acknowledgment that the world—and, in particular, the "heart of the free world"—is an ever more dangerous place.

bedroom. (The president and first family were not in residence at the time.) Less than a month later, a man standing on the sidewalk outside the White House fence fired twenty-seven rounds from a semiautomatic rifle into the north wall of the mansion and a window in the press room. A mostly classified Treasury Department report issued in 1995 evaluated White House protection in light of these events.

The Uniformed Division also carefully monitors White House tours. Visitors enter through the East Wing and, as at airports, pass through a metal detector. Still more sensitive are the devices for detecting radioactive materials. In 1986 two women on a White House tour were questioned by the Secret Service when they set off these alarms. Several days before their White House visit, each had had a radioisotope scan for heart disease, and small amounts of radioactivity remained in their bodies.[31]

The uniformed guards inspect all handbags and packages and ask visitors to leave behind all newspapers, which conceivably could hide a weapon. Guards watch the tourists on closed-circuit television as they make their way through the five rooms and two hallways that are open to the public. Plainclothes Secret Service agents mingle with the visitors, watching and listening for signs of threatening behavior.

Careful security procedures extend well beyond the monitoring of tourists. Electronic sensing devices, embedded in the floors, ceilings, and walls, track all movement in the house. Secret Service agents know at all times exactly where the president and the first family are within the White House so that they can maintain a "protective ring" around them. All visitors and aides, even the president's closest advisers, must wear a visible security badge. Transparent bullet-proof shields cover the windows in the Oval Office, even though the office is not visible from the street. The president has the added security of a knee-high "panic button" located beneath the Oval Office desk. The president can push the button while appearing simply to shift position. Occasionally, the chief executive pushes the button by accident and is startled when a cadre of arms-wielding agents bursts into the office.

The Secret Service inspects all incoming packages and takes no chances with gifts of food—none ever reaches the president. The White House also is equipped with highly sensitive air and water filtration systems for detecting poisonous gas and bacteria. To ensure that no one tampers with the president's food, all food suppliers for the White House are cleared by the Secret Service. Even so, White House kitchen staff hand select many food items at random.

One of the most secure—and least discussed—areas of the White House is the Situation Room, the presidential communications nerve center. Located under the Oval Office in the basement of the West Wing, the Situation Room is run by a twenty-five person duty staff of communications experts from the U.S. Army Signal Corps. Twenty-four hours a day they operate the Signal Board, which links the White House with the Pentagon, the State Department, the Central Intelligence Agency, and other military and intelligence facilities. The Situation Room re-

Blair House, across Pennsylvania Avenue (now closed to vehicular traffic) from the White House, is used from time to time by the president and first family during White House renovations. The Trumans stayed here from 1949–1952. Visiting heads of state may also stay here at the invitation of the president. Presidents-elect also stay at Blair House before their inaugurations.

ceives thousands of messages daily.[32] Contrary to popular assumptions, the Washington-Moscow "hotline" is not in the White House; rather, it is part of the National Military Command Center at the Pentagon. (See "Department of Defense," p. 1174.)

With the Clinton administration, the White House entered the information superhighway. The Clinton White House was the first to use on-line services and to communicate with the public by electronic mail on the Internet. The White House also provides documents on-line such as speeches, briefings, and policy statements. In 1995 the White House's first World Wide Web site (http://www.whitehouse.gov) offered a virtual tour of the Executive Mansion, complete with sound effects from the first cat, Socks.

When presidents travel, they remain in constant, secure telephone contact not only with the Situation Room but with U.S.

military facilities throughout the world. The president's plane, *Air Force One*, is outfitted with a special switchboard that keeps the chief executive in touch while airborne. Always near the president is a military aide assigned to the White House Communications Agency (WHCA, pronounced "Whocka"). This staffer carries the "presidential emergency satchel," called the "football," containing the authentication codes and emergency declarations to be used in the event of war.[33]

Whether traveling by plane, car, or ship, walking at Camp David, attending a concert at the Kennedy Center, or visiting a foreign head of state, the president is said to be never more than thirty seconds away from the communications link to the White House command post.[34]

The Vice President's Residence

On the grounds of the Naval Observatory on Massachusetts Avenue, N.W., barely visible from the road, stands the official home of the vice president. Although the president has had an official Washington residence since 1800, not until July 1974 did Congress give the vice president a permanent home. The cost of securing and protecting the house of each new vice president had become greater than the cost of establishing and maintaining a single residence.

Formerly known as the Admiral's House, the residence served as the home of the superintendent of the Naval Observatory until 1928 and of the chief of naval operations until 1974. Adm. Elmo R. Zumwalt was the last military resident of the house.

Designed by Washington architect Leon E. Dessez and completed in 1893, the house is a Queen Anne-style, three-story, brick and wood-framed structure encompassing 12,000 square feet. The first floor consists of an entrance hall, dining room, living room, library, and administrative offices. Because the dining room can accommodate only thirty persons, vice presidents often have entertained large numbers of guests outdoors. The second and third floors contain four bedrooms plus a master bedroom suite, family room, kitchenette, and office. The main kitchen, laundry, and quarters for the staff and Secret Service are in the basement.

Outside, a pillared porte cochere forms the main entrance. A wide veranda extends from the right of the entrance along the front of the house and curves around the three-story Romanesque tower on the south, forming a porch on three sides. The steep roof of gray slate contains the three dormer windows of the third floor. The house is situated on twelve acres, landscaped in the style of an English park.

When Congress claimed the Admiral's House for the vice president in 1974, it appropriated $315,000 for renovation and installation of security devices. At that time the roof leaked, the floors sagged, the six fireplaces did not work, the wiring was unsafe, and the house was air-conditioned with twenty-two window units (since replaced with central air-conditioning). In 1995 the annual appropriation for operating the residence was

In 1974 Congress designated the home of the chief of naval operations at the Naval Observatory as the official residence of the vice president.

$415,000.[35] The navy, which still owns and maintains the house, also supplies staff for the vice president's residence, including six enlistees who serve as stewards.

Although the house has been available to six vice presidents, only four have lived there. Betty Ford began plans for decorating but had time to do little more than select china and crystal before her husband became president in August 1974. Vice President and Mrs. Nelson Rockefeller (1975–1977) continued to live in their home on Foxhall Road in Washington, but they supervised the renovation and contributed several pieces of their own artwork and furnishings to the house.

Vice President and Mrs. Walter F. Mondale (1977–1981) and their three children were the first full-time residents. Mrs. Mondale, an art historian, used the house as a showcase for works of contemporary American artists. The Mondales also established a household library of works by and about vice presidents.

Vice President and Mrs. George Bush (1981–1989) discovered the limitations of the initial $315,000 appropriation when the roof began to leak again, mortar between bricks began crumbling, and damp streaks appeared on the living room walls. As a result, the navy spent more than $260,000 for repairs. The Bushes began the practice of raising private, tax-deductible funds to redecorate the vice president's residence. They redecorated the house through approximately $200,000 in private donations and restored the interior by adding their personal furnishings and paintings borrowed from art museums in Washington and Houston.

Vice President and Mrs. Dan Quayle (1989–1993) added a bathroom and a wheelchair-accessible entrance and remodeled the attic to make more room for their family, at a cost of $340,000 in private funds. In 1989 they constructed a putting green, and in 1991, a swimming pool, hot tub, and poolhouse, again with private funds. Security enhancements in 1992 and 1993 cost an additional $4 million of government funds.[36]

A 1992 inspection revealed the need for major structural,

electrical, and mechanical renovations, which would take six months and require the house to be unoccupied. Vice President and Mrs. Albert Gore Jr. (1993–) agreed to remain in their nearby Virginia home until the overhaul could be completed. Within six months the wrap-around veranda was restored according to requirements of the National Historic Preservation Act; heating, air conditioning, plumbing, and ventilation systems were replaced; asbestos was removed; the electrical system was rewired; and the family quarters on the second floor were upgraded. Cost of the 1993 renovation was $1.6 million.[37]

Executive Office of the President

The Old Executive Office Building (OEOB), formerly the State, War, and Navy Building, may be the government's most maligned structure. Mark Twain called it "the ugliest building in America." Others have praised it for its "wedding-cake" grandeur. Herbert Hoover declared that it was "an architectural absurdity," and Harry Truman described it as "the greatest monstrosity in America." Excessive or engaging, the French Second Empire structure, now a historic landmark, remains a monument to the architectural enthusiasm of a victorious government after the Civil War.

Supervising Architect of the Treasury Alfred Bult Mullett designed the building, constructed from 1871 to 1888, for the State, War, and Navy departments. The State Department's south wing was completed in 1875; the Navy's east wing in 1879; and the War Department's north, west, and center wings in 1888. But these departments continued to grow, and by 1947 each had vacated the building for larger quarters. In 1939 the White House began moving some of its offices into the building, and in 1949 the State, War, and Navy Building was given over entirely to the Executive Office of the President (EOP). Today the building houses most of the White House Office, the National Security Council, the Office of Management and Budget, the Council of Economic Advisers, and the vice president's office.

The OEOB comprises 440,250 square feet—including 553 rooms, two miles of black-and-white-tiled corridors, and ten acres of floor space. When completed the OEOB was the largest office building in Washington and among the largest in the world. It is still one of the largest granite buildings, with four and one-half-foot exterior walls and many eighteen-foot ceilings. Construction costs totaled $10.1 million.

The French Second Empire styling makes the OEOB architecturally unique in Washington. It has seven floors and more than nine hundred columns. Its elaborate dormer windows, mansard roof of light green copper, and more than two dozen chimneys topped with oversize chimney pots make it a curious companion to the Georgian-style White House next door.

In 1934 and 1944 Congress approved plans to give the OEOB a Greek Revival façade to match its neighbor to the east of the White House, the Treasury Building. In 1957 a commission appointed by President Eisenhower recommended its demolition. But funds ran short after each proposal, and the OEOB re-

On the west side of the White House is the Old Executive Office Building (OEOB), formerly the State, War, and Navy Building, which today houses various offices of the Executive Office of the President and most of the vice president's staff.

mained untouched. Although Kennedy's Commission on Fine Arts recommended preservation of the building, full-scale restoration did not get under way until 1981, under President Reagan's Office of Administration.

When the carpeting, partitions, and dropped ceilings were removed, the three-story White House Law Library, formerly the War Department Library, revealed its colorful Minton tile floor and the delicate cast-iron tracery of its balcony railings. Also restored was the four-story State Department Library, which now serves as the White House Library and Research Center. Both libraries were constructed entirely of cast iron to reduce the danger of fire. The Indian Treaty Room, with its tile floor and coffered ceiling, is used for receptions, award ceremonies, and occasionally press conferences.

Five presidents worked in the OEOB before becoming chief executive, and more than one thousand treaties have been signed within its walls. It was in this building on December 7, 1941, that Secretary of State Cordell Hull confronted the two Japanese envoys who pretended to negotiate peace in the Pacific as Japanese warplanes bombed Pearl Harbor.

Less than twenty-five years after moving into the OEOB, the Executive Office of the President again needed more space. The solution became known as the New Executive Office Building (NEOB), a ten-story structure completed in 1968, one block across Pennsylvania Avenue from the OEOB at 17th and H Streets, N.W. Designed by John Carl Warnecke, the contemporary red-brick building contains 307,000 square feet of office space and houses approximately nine hundred EOP employees.

The Departmental Headquarters

When the federal government moved from Philadelphia to Washington, D.C., in 1800, the executive branch consisted of four departments—State, Treasury, War, and Navy. By 1820 each had its own brick building within short walking distance of the president's office in the White House. The entire executive branch was neatly contained within two city blocks. Today, there are fourteen departments and more than five hundred executive branch buildings in the Washington, D.C., area.

Only the Treasury Department is located on approximately its original site. Like its neighbors the White House and the Old Executive Office Building, it is a historic landmark, as designated by the interior secretary's National Park System Advisory Board.

Other departmental buildings are unusual for their history, their artwork (the Justice and Interior buildings contain exceptional examples of American art of the 1930s), or, simply, their size. Several were considered to be the largest office building in the world when completed. Today, it is said that the Pentagon holds that distinction.

DEPARTMENT OF AGRICULTURE

The Department of Agriculture headquarters on 14th Street, S.W., is contained in two structures—the Administration Building facing the Mall and the South Building facing Independence Avenue. The two are joined by two third-floor archways over Independence Avenue and an underground tunnel.

The neoclassical Administration Building, designed by Rankin, Kellogg, and Crane of Philadelphia, was built in three sections, largely of marble. The four-story, L-shaped east and west wings, constructed from 1904 to 1908, set the precedent for a four hundred-foot setback from the center line of the Mall. The five-story center section, with its imposing Corinthian colonnade, connects the east and west wings. It was built from 1928 to 1930. The Administration Building contains a gross floor area of 380,000 square feet, with 280,000 square feet of offices and other work areas. The secretary of agriculture's office is in this part of the departmental headquarters.

The seven-story South Building, with nearly six times as much office space as the Administration Building, was designed in the office of the Supervising Architect of the Treasury and constructed from 1930 to 1937. It contains seven miles of corridors and 1.5 million square feet of office space, divided into more than four thousand rooms. Its seven wings and six interior courtyards cover three city blocks. The exterior of the building is neoclassical, but less ornamented than the Administration Building. The 12th and 14th Street wings are finished in limestone; the rest of the exterior, in variegated tan brick and terracotta.

Approximately ten thousand people work in the headquarters building, which contains all but two bureaus of the Agriculture Department. Agriculture has field offices in every state and most major cities throughout the United States, including more than seventy Extension Service locations and approximately fifty offices of the Farmers Home Administration. With the passage of the Leahy/Lugar USDA reorganization bill in 1994, the Department of Agriculture will undertake major streamlining of the Washington staff and field offices.

DEPARTMENT OF COMMERCE

The Herbert Clark Hoover Building, named in 1982 for the former president (1929–1933) and commerce secretary (1921–1928), was the largest office building in the world when completed in 1932. The building encompasses 1.1 million square feet of work space, covers eight acres, contains 3,311 rooms, and houses approximately five thousand employees.

Construction of the seven-story building, designed by the New York architectural firm of York and Sawyer, began in 1927 on swampland the government purchased in 1910 for $2.5 million. The Commerce building sits atop Tiber Creek, and sections of the basement floor are three feet thick to withstand pressure from the water flowing underneath.

The building comprises three large rectangular sections joined by accordion-like expansion joints. Because these joints expand in the heat and contract in the cold, the Hoover Building may be three inches longer in July than it is in January. Filling three city blocks, Commerce is bounded by 14th and 15th Streets, N.W., on the east and west and by D Street and Constitution Avenue on the north and south. It cost $17.5 million to build.

Two unusual features of the building are on view to the public. A census "clock" digitally records births and deaths in the United States, showing an American born every eight seconds and dying every fourteen seconds (for a population growth rate of 0.9 percent). A basement aquarium displays more than one thousand fish from around the world.

DEPARTMENT OF DEFENSE

The Pentagon—headquarters of the Department of Defense (DOD)—is located in Arlington, Virginia, just across the Potomac River from Washington, D.C. Said to be the world's largest office building, it is the only departmental headquarters outside the District of Columbia.

Gen. Brehon B. Somervell's 1941 plan to house the nation's military establishment under one roof aroused controversy, but pressures of impending war hastened congressional approval of new headquarters for what later became the Defense Department. The government already owned more than half of the 583 acres needed for the proposed building, and it bought the rest—mostly swamps, dumps, and dilapidated buildings—for $2.2

Often called the world's largest office building, the Pentagon, headquarters of the Department of Defense, contains 3.7 million square feet of work space and seventeen and one-half miles of corridors.

million. Starting in August 1941, thirteen thousand laborers worked in shifts around the clock and completed construction in January 1943—a mere seventeen months later. The building itself cost $49.6 million; the total project, including outside facilities, $83.0 million.

With a gross floor area of 6.5 million square feet (3.7 million of which is work space), the Pentagon contains three times the floor space of the Empire State Building. Its other statistics also are impressive. The building covers twenty-nine acres and contains 150 stairways, nineteen escalators, thirteen elevators, 280 restrooms, 7,748 windows, and fifteen thousand light fixtures. The parking lot covers sixty-seven acres and has space for almost ten thousand cars. Twenty-six thousand military and civilian employees use the stores, restaurants, theaters, barbershop, post office, education centers, and libraries within the building. Each day, the Pentagon post office handles 130,000 pieces of mail, while the building's 22,500 telephones accommodate 225,000 calls.

Architects George E. Bergstrom and David J. Whitmer designed the five-sided steel and concrete structure to fit its site, which is bounded by five roads. The number five recurs throughout the building's design. Besides having five sides, the Pentagon contains five concentric rings; that is, the exterior ring surrounds four progressively smaller pentagons, each with five floors. A center courtyard with grass and trees covers five acres.

The total length of Pentagon hallways is seventeen and one-half miles, but because ten spoke-like corridors connect the five rings, it takes no more than seven minutes to walk from any one point to another.

A particularly well-known component of the Pentagon, one not on view to the public, is the Washington–Moscow Direct Communication Link, better known as the "hot line." It was set up in 1963 in response to the Cuban missile crisis and is located in the National Military Command Center. Today the hot line—actually an array of direct links rather than a single "line"—connects Washington not only with Russia but with other nuclear nations as well.

In 1990 Congress authorized $1.25 billion to renovate the Pentagon. Energy efficiency is a key goal of the project. Changes to the building will include the replacement of thousands of single-paned windows with tinted, double-paned glass; the use of nontoxic paints and natural-fiber carpets; the installation of elevators and ramps to provide access for the handicapped, insulation made of natural materials, automatic water-saving sensors in restrooms, energy-efficient computers; and the use of natural light where possible. Work began in early 1995 and is expected to take ten years to complete.[38]

Vast though the Pentagon is, less than 1 percent of the Defense Department's 3.2 million employees work there. Defense employs 1.1 million civilian and 2.1 million military personnel. Approximately 150,000 people work at more than twenty-five other Defense facilities in the Washington area—workplaces as diverse as the Walter Reed Army Medical Center, the Naval Observatory, and the National War College.

DEPARTMENT OF EDUCATION

The headquarters for the Department of Education, at 400 Maryland Avenue, S.W., is housed in Federal Office Building (FOB) No. 6, one of several modern, numbered office structures commissioned in the late 1950s in southwest Washington to accommodate the growing executive branch bureaucracy. FOB 6, designed by two Washington, D.C., firms—Faulkner, Kingsbury, and Stenhouse; and Chatelain, Gauger, and Holan—was built between 1959 and 1961 at a cost of $13.3 million. Its several hundred tall, narrow windows on the second through the sixth floors give an impression of greater height to the eight-story limestone building.

FOB 6 contains 401,544 square feet of office space and houses approximately nine hundred Education employees. Education staffers work in two other buildings in Washington and in ten regional offices throughout the country. In September 1994 the department relocated temporarily to FOB 10 at 600 Independence Avenue while FOB 6 was undergoing renovation. The project completion date for the work is fall 1997.

DEPARTMENT OF ENERGY

The Department of Energy moved into the James Forrestal Building at 1000 Independence Avenue, S.W., in 1977, the year the department was established. For its first seven years the building had housed employees of the Defense Department. In December 1963 Congress appropriated $33.7 million for the structure known as FOB No. 5 until it was named for former secretary of defense Forrestal. The contemporary-styled building of precast concrete was under construction from September 1965 to April 1970 and was designed by the architectural firms of Curtis and Davis, Fordyce and Hanby Associates, and Frank Grad and Sons.

The Forrestal Building is a sprawling, three-part structure with 1.1 million square feet of space in floors above and below ground. The South Building has eight floors above ground; the North Building has four; the West Building, two. Each building is constructed of architectural concrete with recessed window pockets one story tall. The three wings are connected by two floors of office space underground. The Forrestal Building houses forty-five hundred employees and all divisions of the Energy Department, except for the Federal Energy Regulatory Commission offices, which are on Capitol Hill.

DEPARTMENT OF HEALTH AND HUMAN SERVICES

The Hubert H. Humphrey Building, headquarters of the Department of Health and Human Services (HHS) at 200 Independence Avenue, S.W., is one of two departmental headquarters buildings designed by architect Marcel Breuer. Under construction from 1971 to 1975, the contemporary steel and concrete structure is heavily fenestrated with hundreds of convex trapezoidal windows cantilevered over the first floor. The walls of windows break off at each corner, leaving recesses for shafts, discreetly incorporated into the building's design, to vent exhaust fumes from the freeway tunnel that passes underneath.

The twelve-story building houses approximately 2,000 HHS staffers in 328,490 square feet of office space. The remaining 22,100 HHS employees in the Washington, D.C., area are scattered among fifty-nine other buildings, including the Parklawn Building in Rockville, Maryland, housing approximately 6,000 staffers. HHS employs more than 127,000 people throughout the United States in regional and field offices of the Social Security Administration, the Public Health Service, and other HHS agencies.

DEPARTMENT OF HOUSING AND URBAN DEVELOPMENT

The Housing and Urban Development (HUD) building, at 7th and D Streets, S.W., was the first of two departmental headquarters that the federal government commissioned from architect Marcel Breuer. Similar in design to Breuer's UNESCO headquarters in Paris, HUD is unique among Washington buildings for its curvilinear shape: from above, it looks like two Y's joined at their base. The American Institute of Architects awarded Breuer its 1968 gold medal for this design and other work.

Built between 1965 and 1968 at a cost of $22.5 million, HUD was the first federal structure made of precast concrete, a mark of the International style. The sculptural effects of precast concrete are apparent in the 1,585 recessed window units, each weighing ten tons, that form the curve of the walls. The building's ten stories rest on dozens of *pilotis,* or pillars, creating a 5.5-acre courtyard instead of a first floor at ground level.

Unlike the straight, seemingly endless hallways of the Pentagon (875 feet) and other government buildings, the longest corridor at HUD (180 feet) seems even shorter because the curving walls create an optical illusion that gives the building a more human scale. The building contains 543,000 square feet of office space for the thirty-five hundred employees working there. HUD has eighty-one regional and field offices throughout the United States. Its Washington bureaus are housed within the headquarters and three other buildings in the city.

DEPARTMENT OF THE INTERIOR

The Department of the Interior building, at 18th and C Streets, N.W., three blocks southwest of the White House, was the first project undertaken by the Public Works Administration (PWA) to provide work for the unemployed during the New Deal era. Constructed in only sixteen months, August 1935 to December 1936, the eight-story granite and limestone building contains sixteen acres of floor space and two miles of corridors, housing twenty-nine hundred employees.

President Franklin D. Roosevelt laid the cornerstone in 1936 with the same trowel George Washington had used to lay the Capitol cornerstone in 1793.

The building, designed by Waddy B. Wood, is utilitarian and plain on the outside but has an elaborately decorated interior containing more New Deal art than any other government structure. Bas-reliefs and murals by Heinz Warneke and Louis Bouché, among others, depict the themes and work of the department. Notable among Interior's murals is Henry Varnum Poor's nine-by-forty-two-foot work showing the origins of the conservation movement in the United States.

Harold Ickes Sr., interior secretary from 1933 to 1946 and head of PWA, took a keen interest not only in the building but in a state-of-the-art museum with exhibits of the department's programs. Today, one still can see the museum's original dioramas portraying each bureau's history as well as artifacts, documents, photographs, and crafts. An Indian arts and crafts shop and many areas of the building containing artwork are open to the public. Other Interior Department offices in the Washington area are the Bureau of Mines and the U.S. Geological Survey.

DEPARTMENT OF JUSTICE

The Department of Justice had numerous homes before Congress appropriated $12 million for its permanent headquarters in downtown Washington. Under construction from 1931 to 1935, the Justice building fills the block of Federal Triangle between 9th and 10th Streets, N.W., and Constitution and Pennsylvania Avenues.

The seven-story limestone structure contains a gross floor area of 1.2 million square feet, including 1,712 rooms, eighty-seven stairways, almost four miles of corridors, and underground parking for 150 cars. More than twenty-five hundred employees occupy the building.

Principal architects Clarence Zantzinger and Charles L. Borie Jr. made wide use of aluminum, an uncommon construction material for that period. The exterior doors (each twenty feet tall), frames for the 1,908 windows, all door trim, stair railings, and much ornamentation are aluminum. One observer remarked that the designers used enough aluminum to make "not only forks and spoons but pots and pans for a whole city."[39]

Although the exterior of the Justice headquarters, like many federal buildings, is classical revival in style, many of its decorative elements reflect the Art Deco influence of the 1920s and 1930s. Notable Art Deco features include the nine exterior doors and aluminum torchiers as well as John Joseph Earley's striking mosaic ceilings, the first made of American materials.

All sculptural work was designed by C. Paul Jennewein, who consulted philosophy professor Hartley B. Alexander in rendering a unified theme for the numerous exterior relief panels depicting the role of a justice department in a constitutional democracy. Still, his work aroused controversy. The president's Commission on Fine Arts objected to three nude male figures proposed for a six-by-fourteen-foot exterior relief panel and, in a letter to Jennewein, asked, "Do you think it would be possible to adopt the fig leaf for these figures?" Jennewein conceded and offered a second design. The commissioners again objected: "The fig leaves are not quite large enough," they wrote.[40] Today, the larger fig leaves may be seen in the pediment above the Constitution Avenue entrance.

Throughout the building, vast murals by noted New Deal artists Boardman Robinson, George Biddle, and John Steuart Curry depict themes of justice. The murals took six years to complete (1935–1941) and cost $68,000.

Other offices of the Justice Department include the Federal Bureau of Investigation and the Immigration and Naturalization Service in Washington and the U.S. Marshals Service in McLean, Virginia.

DEPARTMENT OF LABOR

The modern Department of Labor building, which occupies two city blocks at 200 Constitution Avenue, N.W., was dedicated by President Gerald R. Ford on its completion in 1974. Six years later President Jimmy Carter named the building for Franklin D. Roosevelt's labor secretary, Frances Perkins, on the centennial of her birth, April 10, 1980.

The six-story steel and limestone building, designed by two Texas architectural firms—Brooks, Barr, Graeber, and White of Austin, and Pitts, Mebane, Phelps, and White of Houston—comprises one million square feet of office space and two and one-half miles of corridors. It cost $95 million to build and houses approximately four thousand employees. Like Health and Human Services, the Labor headquarters was built above a freeway tunnel, so the architects had to incorporate exhaust shafts into the building's design.

To commemorate the country's bicentennial in 1976, the General Services Administration commissioned New York artist Jack Beal to paint four murals for the building. Called "The History of Labor in America," the work continues the tradition of Social Realist art exemplified by the New Deal artists in other government buildings in Washington.

The Labor Department also occupies twelve other buildings in Washington and numerous regional and field offices, including eight regional offices of the Bureau of Labor Statistics and ten of the Occupational Safety and Health Administration.

DEPARTMENT OF STATE

Until 1947 the State Department shared quarters with the War and Navy departments in the State, War, and Navy Building (now the OEOB) next-door to the White House. When the department needed more space, it moved to its current location at 21st and D Streets, N.W. The eight-story, neoclassical limestone building was designed by Gilbert S. Underwood and William Dewey Foster; Louis A. Simon served as supervising architect.

The department continued to grow, however, and by the mid-1950s—less than a decade after it moved—it occupied more than twenty-five annexes in addition to its main building. Congress approved funding for an extension, which was built from 1957 to 1961 under direction of the architectural firm of Graham, Anderson, Probst, and White.

The State Department building today covers 11.8 acres—the two blocks between 21st and 23rd Streets on the east and west and C and D Streets on the south and north. The building contains approximately 2.5 million square feet of gross floor space and houses the Agency for International Development (AID) and the Arms Control and Disarmament Agency in addition to State Department staff, approximately seven thousand employees altogether. Other AID and State employees staff approximately 250 U.S. embassies, consulates, and missions in 161 countries around the world.

At the C Street entrance of the contemporary-styled addition is the three-story Diplomatic Lobby. Television reporters covering the State Department often broadcast from this room, where the national flags of countries that have diplomatic relations with the United States form a colorful backdrop. At each end of the lobby is a plaque commemorating more than 150 State Department employees who have died "under heroic or tragic circumstances in foreign service." More than seventy-five names have been added since 1965. The Exhibition Hall on the first floor displays the Great Seal of the United States, in use since 1782 to seal instruments of ratification of treaties and the commissions of cabinet officers, ambassadors, and Foreign Service officers.

In 1961 the State Department's Fine Arts Committee began the Americana Project to remodel and redecorate—entirely through private funds—the sixteen diplomatic reception rooms on the eighth floor and the office of the secretary. The refurnished rooms, a showcase of the country's cultural heritage, contain museum-quality furniture, rugs, paintings, and silver from the classical period of American design, 1740–1825. Senior government officials, including the president and secretary of state, use the rooms for official functions.

DEPARTMENT OF TRANSPORTATION

The Nassif Building, which contains the principal offices of the Transportation Department, is the only departmental headquarters not built and owned by the federal government. The General Services Administration, the federal government's property manager, leases 1.7 million square feet of the building, bounded by D, E, 6th, and 7th Streets, S.W., for $29 million a year.

Edward Durell Stone, architect of the Kennedy Center and the National Geographic Society building in Washington, designed the modern ten-story structure for Boston real estate developer David Nassif. When completed in 1969 it was the largest private office building in Washington. The one-inch white marble exterior veneer comes from quarries in Carrara, Italy, as does the marble in the Kennedy Center.

The only major change or addition since Transportation first occupied the building in 1970 was the construction of a 22,873-square-foot computer room in 1983. Approximately fifty-five hundred of the department's more than eleven thousand employees work in the Nassif Building. Other Transportation offices in Washington include the headquarters of the Federal Aviation Administration and the Coast Guard.

DEPARTMENT OF THE TREASURY

The Treasury building is the oldest federal government departmental headquarters. The five-story granite structure in the Greek Revival style set a precedent for the design of many other government buildings in Washington. Constructed in stages from 1836 through 1869, it is Treasury's third home on this site. The first Treasury building was burned by the British in 1814; the second, by arsonists in 1833.

Treasury's five wings fill two city blocks at 15th Street and Pennsylvania Avenue, N.W., just east of the White House. Legend has it that President Andrew Jackson, annoyed at the protracted controversy over the exact location of the building, one day walked over from the White House, planted his cane in the ground, and declared, "Right here is where I want the cornerstone." Unfortunately, the building spoiled the clear view along Pennsylvania Avenue between the White House and Capitol. Treasury served as a barracks for Union soldiers during the Civil War and provided a temporary office for President Andrew Johnson while he waited six weeks for Mary Todd Lincoln to leave the White House after her husband's assassination.

Robert Mills, architect of the Washington Monument, designed the east and center wings (1836–1842). The most impressive feature of Mills's design is the east front colonnade—thirty Ionic columns, each thirty-six feet (three stories) tall, carved from a single block of granite. Thomas Ustick Walter, architect of the Capitol dome, did the preliminary design of the west and south wings (1855–1864). Ammi B. Young and Isaiah Rogers completed the plans, incorporating ornate details of late nineteenth-century tastes in their interior designs.

The architect of the north wing (1867–1869) was Alfred Bult Mullett, designer of the State, War, and Navy Building. *(See "Executive Office of the President," p. 947.)* In the north wing is the Cash Room, a two-story hall finished in nine varieties of marble. The seventy-two by thirty-two foot room was opened in 1869, in time to serve as the site of President Ulysses S. Grant's inaugural ball March 4 of that year.

At 450,000 square feet (290,000 of which is office space), Treasury was one of the largest office buildings in the world when it was finished. Today the headquarters houses only twelve hundred of the department's twenty thousand Washington-area employees. Others work in the Treasury Annex, connected to the main building by a tunnel under Pennsylvania Avenue, and in buildings housing the various bureaus of the department, including the Bureau of Printing and Engraving and the Internal Revenue Service. Treasury has field organizations in every state and offices in most major U.S. cities.

DEPARTMENT OF VETERANS AFFAIRS

The goal of consolidating under one roof all Washington employees handling veterans affairs has eluded the federal government throughout most of the twentieth century. In the early 1900s the department's predecessor, the Bureau of War Risk Insurance, operated out of seventeen different buildings. In late 1988, when the Veterans Administration gained cabinet-level status, the new Department of Veterans Affairs (DVA) occupied six buildings in the Washington metropolitan area. The main building, containing the office of the secretary, is at 810 Vermont Avenue, N.W.

The eleven-story structure in the classical revival style was designed by the architectural firm of Wyatt and Nolting to be a hotel. In 1918, however, the government bought the site and foundation for $1 million, redesigned the exterior, and modified the interior to accommodate offices rather than hotel rooms.

Construction of the War Risk Building, as it then was called, was completed in 1918 at a cost of $3.6 million. It comprises 442,000 square feet of office space. Today the building houses approximately 900 out of 3,500 DVA employees in the Washington area.

NOTES

1. The figure for the cost of construction was obtained from the White House Office of the Curator.

2. *The White House: An Historic Guide,* 18th ed. (Washington, D.C.: White House Historical Association, 1994), 114.

3. Joseph Nathan Kane, *Facts about the Presidents: A Compilation of Biographical and Historical Material* (New York: Wilson, 1981), 39.

4. According to White House historian William Seale, one reason the rebuilding proceeded so quickly was that Hoban substituted timber for brick in some of the interior partitions. Although he saved time, Hoban created a weaker structure than the original—one that would necessitate the interior reconstruction of 1949–1952 (William Seale, *The President's House,* [Washington, D.C.: White House Historical Association, 1986], 2 vols. 2: 142–143). The figure for the cost of reconstruction was obtained from the White House Office of the Curator.

5. Kenneth W. Leish, *The White House* (New York: Newsweek, 1972), 39.

6. Ibid., 119.

7. Seale, *The President's House,* 1: 265.

8. Ibid., 268.

9. Amy La Follette Jensen, *The White House and Its Thirty-three Families* (New York: McGraw-Hill, 1962), 72.

10. Seale, *The President's House,* 1: 316.

11. Leish, *The White House,* 128.

12. Ibid., 140.

13. Seale, *The President's House,* 2: 923.

14. Leish, *The White House,* 116.

15. Ibid.

16. Seale, *The President's House,* 2: 1028.

17. Ibid., 1035.

18. Ibid.

19. *The White House: An Historic Guide,* 16th ed. (Washington, D.C.: White House Historical Association, 1987), 153.

20. White House Office of the Curator.

21. Elise K. Kirk, "Music at the White House: Legacy of American Romanticism," in *The White House: The First Two Hundred Years,* ed. Frank Freidel and William Pencak (Boston: Northeastern University Press, 1994), 190, 196.

22. The number of rooms used by the first family in their living quarters changes with each family, depending on how many of the president's children live in the White House and how many guest rooms the family needs. The Clintons' redecorating of the family quarters and other rooms in the White House is described and illustrated in "A Visit to the White House," *House Beautiful,* March 1994, 108ff.

23. J. B. West, with Mary Lynn Kotz, *Upstairs at the White House: My Life with the First Ladies* (New York: Coward, McCann, and Geoghegan, 1973), 61–62.

24. Leish, *The White House,* 29.

25. Rachel Lambert Mellon, "President Kennedy's Rose Garden," *White House History* 1:1 (1983): 5–11.

26. Leish, *The White House,* 107.

27. Except where noted, details of Secret Service protection of the White House are from Philip H. Melanson, *The Politics of Protection: The U.S. Secret Service in the Terrorist Age* (New York: Praeger, 1984).

28. Judith Havemann, "Adding Up the Reagan Renovations," *Washington Post,* September 7, 1988, A1.

29. "White House Eyesore," *New York Times,* March 29, 1988, B6.

30. Melinda Liu and Douglas Waller, "Terror on the South Lawn," *Newsweek,* September 26, 1994, 42; Michael Duffy, "Flight of the Intruder," *Time,* September 26, 1994, 47.

31. Christine Russell, "Tourists' Telltale Hearts," *Washington Post,* September 25, 1986.

32. Bradley H. Patterson Jr., *The Ring of Power: The White House Staff and Its Expanding Role in Government* (New York: Basic Books, 1988), 49.

33. Ibid., 322.

34. Elmer Plischke, *Diplomat in Chief* (New York: Praeger, 1986), 56.

35. Public Affairs Office, Engineering Field Activity Chesapeake, Naval Facilities Engineering Command, Washington, D.C.

36. Patricia Dane Rogers, "Fixing the Gores' New House," *Washington Post,* May 13, 1993, Washington Home section, 14ff.

37. Kathleen Sampson, "EFA Chesapeake Restores Vice President's House," *Navy Civil Engineer,* Winter 1994, 26–27; Rebecca Rodgers, "The House on Observatory Hill," *Defense Housing,* March/April 1994, 11ff.

38. Keith Schneider, "What Has 5 Sides and Is Turning Green?" *New York Times,* February 22, 1995.

39. Lois Craig, "Hidden Treasures of a Walled City," *American Institute of Architects Journal* 67 (June 1978): 21.

40. Antonio Vasaio and the Justice Management Division, *The Fiftieth Anniversary of the U.S. Department of Justice Building, 1934–1984* (Washington, D.C.: Government Printing Office, 1984), 26.

SELECTED BIBLIOGRAPHY

Executive Office of the President, Office of Administration. *The Old Executive Office Building: A Victorian Masterpiece.* Washington, D.C.: Government Printing Office, 1984.

Freidel, Frank, and William Pencak. *The White House: The First Two Hundred Years.* Boston: Northeastern University Press, 1994.

Jensen, Amy La Follette. *The White House and Its Thirty-three Families.* New York: McGraw-Hill, 1962.

Leish, Kenneth W. *The White House.* New York: Newsweek, 1972.

The Living White House. 9th rev. ed. Washington, D.C.: White House Historical Association, 1991.

Look, David W., and Carole L. Perrault. *The Interior Building and Its Architecture and Its Art.* Washington, D.C.: Government Printing Office, 1986.

Oulahan, Richard. "Capital's Doughty Dowager Becomes a New Cinderella." *Smithsonian.* March 1986. 84–94.

Seale, William. *The President's House.* 2 vols. Washington, D.C.: White House Historical Association, 1986.

———. *The White House: The History of an American Idea.* Washington, D.C.: American Institute of Architects Press, 1992.

Vasaio, Antonio, and the Justice Management Division. *The Fiftieth Anniversary of the U.S. Department of Justice Building, 1934–1984.* Washington, D.C.: Government Printing Office, 1984.

West, J. B., with Mary Lynn Kotz. *Upstairs at the White House: My Life with the First Ladies.* New York: Coward, McCann, and Geoghegan, 1973.

The White House: An Historic Guide. 18th ed. Washington, D.C.: White House Historical Association, 1994.

CHAPTER 23

Executive Branch Pay and Perquisites

BY W. CRAIG BLEDSOE

T HE NATIONAL executive branch is staffed by approximately three million civilian employees. At the top of the federal hierarchy sits the president. The executive branch, however, has a quite diverse workforce. Executive branch employees include cabinet members, White House aides, national security advisers, Secret Service agents, Federal Bureau of Investigation agents, Foreign Service officers, policy analysts, computer programmers, engineers, physicians, forest rangers, and people from hundreds of other occupations.

An important feature of the executive branch is that most of its employees are hired under the requirements of civil service, ensuring that most executive branch jobs are filled on the basis of merit and that employees are not fired for political reasons. Along with this political protection, civil service employees are compensated according to a uniform federal salary scale.

Some executive branch positions remain political appointments, specifically those occupied by policy advisers to the president. Although most of the political positions do not pay as much as their occupants might make in similar positions in private business, they carry with them a number of perquisites that make them attractive to many potential appointees. The job of president itself has a modest salary (considering its importance), but over the years many perquisites of the office have evolved. Other executive branch positions, including the vice presidency, also carry with them a growing number of fringe benefits and extra courtesies that have become part of their official status. Because of its complexity and enormous number of positions, the executive branch uses a maze of compensation standards.

The President

The material rewards of the presidency are substantial. Although the president's annual salary of $200,000 is large by most standards, it pales in comparison to the value of the perquisites and other tangible benefits of the office. The value of all the privileges and fringe benefits that go with the job of president of the United States would amount to an annual income of millions of dollars, if the president were a private citizen.

Along with the special burdens and responsibilities of the office come the rewards. The president and the first family live in an environment of comfort and grandeur in the White House, a mansion provided by the government at public expense. At a combined cost of more than $8 million a year, utili-

ties and maintenance for the White House and a salaried staff of approximately one hundred are completely free to the president. In addition, the government maintains a vacation resort for the president at Camp David, Maryland. Several limousines, airplanes, and helicopters stand ready to transport the chief executive any time, anywhere. These amenities come with protection of the president, the vice president, and their families from more than two thousand Secret Service agents, which costs U.S. taxpayers about $356 million a year.[1]

Many of these perquisites are necessary to ensure the smooth functioning of a complex office. For example, the president's own plane can accommodate staff and some press, can avoid scheduling problems, and can ensure the president's security in ways commercial airlines cannot. Moreover, although many perquisites are intended to facilitate the president's many tasks, they also create and maintain an aura of majesty around the presidency. Most Americans want to look to the president (and the office of the president) with pride; the president represents the American people to others and to Americans themselves, embodying the idealism of American life. In this sense the salary and perquisites of the presidency are an object of interest and pride to Americans.

How much does all of this presidential pomp and circumstance cost U.S. taxpayers? Because many of these expenses are merged within the budgets of various departments, it is impossible to determine the exact cost. Undoubtedly, however, the cost is high. In the mid-1970s Dan Cordtz, writing on the excesses of the Nixon administration, estimated the cost to be more than $100 million a year. In the early 1990s, Christopher Georges estimated the cost to run approximately $150 million.[2] The costs for supporting the presidency far exceed what is actually appropriated by Congress for the White House. President Clinton requested $167.4 million in 1993 from Congress for the White House budget. But Ronald Kessler estimates this figure to be one-tenth the actual cost of running the White House. For example, Clinton's budget request did not include $90.6 million from the Defense Department for the White House Communications Agency, $185 million from Defense for White House travel, and $356 million from the Secret Service.[3]

PRESIDENTIAL SALARY

The president's salary is determined by Congress. Article II, section 1, of the Constitution makes the following provisions for the president's salary: "The President shall, at stated Times, receive for his Services, a Compensation, which shall neither be increased nor diminished during the period for which he shall have been elected, and he shall not receive within that Period any other Emolument from the United States, or any of them." On September 24, 1789, the First Congress set the salary for the president of the United States at $25,000 a year.

The issue of paying the president had caused some controversy at the Constitutional Convention. The delegates were concerned that their president not become their king, and there was some discussion about making the office of the president one with no or little pay. Benjamin Franklin suggested that the chief executive of the new nation not be paid any salary at all. Franklin argued that the love of money was the root of much political evil, and he proposed to allow the president to receive "no salary, stipend, fee or reward" above what was necessary to defray the expenses of office.[4]

Franklin's proposal was postponed and conveniently forgotten, but his goal of making the presidency largely an office of honor and not of profit was achieved when George Washington declined any share of personal compensation to which he was constitutionally entitled, proclaiming in his inaugural address: "I must decline as inapplicable to myself any share of the personal emoluments which may be indispensably included in a permanent provision for the executive department, and must accordingly pray that the pecuniary estimates for the station in which I am placed may during my continuance in it be limited to such actual expenditures as the public good may be thought to require."

With changing times and with the increased importance of the office of the presidency, the president's salary has gradually been adjusted upward. Not until after the Civil War, when Ulysses S. Grant became president, did Congress pass the first increase in the president's salary, however. From the beginning, the salaries of all public officials in the United States were low when compared with those of other nations. In 1873, in an effort to keep top public officials from having to draw on their own private resources, Congress voted to increase the salaries of some of the major federal government positions, including those of Congress, the president, and other executive branch officials. At this time the president's salary was doubled to $50,000 a year. (See Table 23-1.) Even though most of the country viewed these increases in pay as justifiable, much resentment was created when Congress decided to vote its own pay raises retroactive to 1871. This action aroused so much resentment among the public that it became known as "the salary grab." Eventually, Congress repealed the retroactive pay. Public indignation continued to be so great, however, that the members of Congress finally reduced their own salaries back to their former levels but left the president's raise untouched. Since Congress initially had approved the increase on March 3, 1873, a day before Grant's second term began, Grant served his first term at half of what he was paid for his second term.

As a result of political pressure against raising the salaries of public officials, subsequent presidential pay increases have not

TABLE 23–1 Presidential Compensation

September 24, 1789	$25,000 salary
March 3, 1873	$50,000 salary
March 4, 1909	$75,000 salary
January 19, 1949	$100,000 salary $50,000 expense account
January 20, 1969	$200,000 salary $50,000 expense account

NOTE: Under the 1949 legislation authorizing the president's expense account, the $50,000 allowance was not taxable to the president. An act of October 20, 1951, made the expense allowance taxable effective January 20, 1953. Since 1979, however, the annual appropriations bill has stipulated that the allowance is nontaxable but that any unspent funds must be returned to the Treasury.

come frequently. Congress voted for a second pay raise for the president in 1909, increasing the annual salary to $75,000. President William Howard Taft was the first to benefit from this increase in salary.

In 1949 Congress raised the salary of the president to $100,000 a year. It also decided that the president henceforth would be paid monthly rather than quarterly, as previous presidents had been paid. In addition, Congress for the first time recognized the need to assist the president in defraying the expenses of official presidential duties. President Harry S. Truman was the first president to receive the $100,000 yearly salary and a $50,000 yearly tax-free expense account. In the Revenue Act of 1951, however, Congress reversed itself and subjected the president's expense account, as well as the expense accounts of members of Congress, to income taxes.

The most recent presidential pay raise occurred on January 20, 1969. Acting upon a recommendation by President Lyndon B. Johnson, Congress voted to double the president's salary. Less than a week later Richard Nixon became the first president to receive a yearly salary of $200,000. Congress also voted to give the president a $100,000 travel allowance and a $12,000 entertainment allowance, both tax free. Although the 1989 Commission on Executive, Legislative, and Judicial Salaries recommended that the president's salary be raised to $350,000, neither the president nor Congress has taken any action that would raise the presidential salary.

Some presidents have been wealthy in their own right. Of the recent presidents, John F. Kennedy, Johnson, Nixon, Jimmy Carter, Ronald Reagan, and George Bush were all millionaires. But only one president besides Washington ever indicated that he would be willing to take a cut in salary: President Kennedy returned his entire salary to the U.S. Treasury.[5]

Presidential pay does not tell the whole story, however. In addition to the $200,000 annual salary and expense, travel, and entertainment accounts, presidents receive many more tangible benefits from being in office. It would be impossible to put a price tag on some of the presidential perquisites. Cordtz has remarked that some of the best rewards of the office, such as the top consideration in air traffic given *Air Force One* or the priori-

THE INCREDIBLE SHRINKING PRESIDENTIAL SALARY

Although many Americans might think their chief executive's salary is too high, the real dollar value of the president's salary has been steadily declining. From 1984 to 1994 the value of the U.S. president's $200,000 annual salary decreased 25 percent. According to economists Michael J. Ahearn and Paul E. Greenberg, William Howard Taft received the highest real pay of any president. Taft earned $100,000 in 1909 dollars, worth $1,533,000 in 1994 dollars. The decline in real dollar values for presidential salaries has occurred as America's private sector CEOs saw their average cash compensation climb 44 percent, to $1.5 million, over the last ten years.

SOURCE: Jacqueline M. Graves, "An Underpaid President?" *Fortune*, May 30, 1994, 20.

ty the president's car takes over other traffic, are invaluable. Perquisites make the job worth a great deal more than the annual salary of the officeholder.

PERQUISITES OF OFFICE

Concerned about the prospects for a burgeoning monarchy in the new American nation, Patrick Henry warned, "Your president may easily become king."[6] *The Federalist Papers,* written to ease the concerns of citizens in New York about the coming constitution, tried to allay the fears that the presidency would become too powerful and would resemble the British monarchy. Alexander Hamilton in defending the constitutional provisions for the presidency argued that no similarities existed between the new American presidency and the British monarchy. He derided those who saw the president with "imperial purple flowing in his train . . . seated on a throne surrounded with minions and mistresses, giving audience to the envoys of foreign potentates in all the supercilious pomp and majesty . . . decorated with attributes superior in dignity and splendor to those of the king of Great Britain."[7]

The presidency has not become a monarchy in the sense of the eighteenth-century British monarchy. Yet, over the years the presidency has developed not only a regal style but a lavish splendor. Much of the pomp and circumstance that Hamilton refused to believe would accompany the growth of the presidency now exists. In fact, the perquisites of the presidency led President Nixon to remark candidly about his life in the White House, "We're roughing it pretty nicely."[8]

Early Perquisites

When George Washington became president, he attempted to establish a protocol of behavior for future presidents to follow. As an aristocrat he believed that the presidency should be honored and esteemed above the other branches of the federal government. In 1789, when Washington traveled from Mount Vernon, in Virginia, to New York City for his inauguration, his journey was punctuated by tolling bells, booming cannons, and cheering citizens. Once in office Washington presented a demeanor of grandeur. When he traveled among the citizenry, he did so in a stately cream-and-gilt coach drawn by six matched horses, the best in the United States. When he went out on horseback, he rode a white stallion covered with a leopard-skin blanket; the horse's hooves were painstakingly blackened, and its teeth were cleaned. Given to much formality, Washington refused to accept private invitations but dispensed his own social invitations to political leaders and prominent individuals to attend elegant receptions and ceremonial affairs. Receiving his guests with a bow rather than a handshake, Washington gave the appearance of a strong and dignified leader. When Thomas Jefferson, the nation's third president, took the oath of office in 1801, he shunned the ornate horse-drawn coaches of Washington and John Adams and simply walked from his boardinghouse to the Capitol to give his inaugural address to members of Congress. He then walked back to his lodgings for dinner. The story is told that upon arriving at the common dinner table the new president found all of the chairs occupied. At first Jefferson was ignored. But eventually one woman recognized him and offered him her seat. Jefferson refused, however, and waited until others had finished their meal before taking his seat at the table.

Jefferson's presidential style reflected his approach to American democracy. He spurned the brilliant display of the two previous Federalist administrations and tried to create an atmosphere of egalitarianism. Most presidents after Jefferson tended to follow his example. It was considered far more important to have been born in a log cabin than to exhibit aristocratic tendencies in office. Consequently, for political as well as financial reasons, most early presidents lived a much more Spartan existence than had Washington.

Washington, Jefferson, and the other early presidents did not enjoy the large expense accounts of modern presidents. Until the presidency of Calvin Coolidge, presidents had to pay for all the food consumed in the White House, including food at state dinners. During his eight years in office, Jefferson recorded that he spent $10,855.90 on wine alone. With these types of expenses, and a salary of only $25,000 a year, Jefferson left office $20,000 in debt. Presidents still pay for all the food they and their families consume privately at the White House, but in the 1920s U.S. taxpayers began paying for most of the expenses of state dinners.

Some of the nation's first presidents actually endured physical hardships while in office. John Adams, the first president to live in the White House, found life there not very comfortable. Mrs. Adams said that the unfinished mansion did not offer many of the "luxuries" of her old home. She dried her washing in the partially finished audience hall (now the East Room) and suffered the indignity of an outdoor privy. On the night Franklin Pierce moved into the White House in 1853, the mansion had little furniture and no lights. Pierce could find only a single candle to illuminate his way to a mattress on the floor of his bedroom. Congress subsequently allocated $25,000, however, for Pierce to refurbish the White House—at that time the largest sum ever set aside for improvements to the president's home. Pierce installed the White House's first furnace and had the presidential residence painted inside and out. Yet, Congress balked at providing funding for someone to tend the new furnace.

Some presidents brought their own furniture to the White House and took it with them when they left. Others, such as James Monroe, left their furniture for future occupants.

Transportation was usually furnished by private individuals or companies to the presidents and their families. Occasionally, someone gave the president a horse or carriage to use, and the railroads allowed the president and the first family to travel free on their lines. But until the presidency of Taft, no funds were available for official travel expenses.

Retirement from office brought little in the way of financial rewards to the first chief executives. Most found themselves without pensions and with few benefits. Thomas Jefferson retired to Monticello at the age of sixty-five. Even though he was a prolific writer, a creative inventor, and an expert architect, musician, and lawyer, he found himself in almost immediate financial crisis. Heavily in debt from his days in the presidency, Jefferson had to accept a gift of $16,500 to save himself from bankruptcy. When James Monroe left office at sixty-six, he was forced to sell one of his two Virginia estates, Ash Lawn, to help pay his debts. He later sold his Oak Hill estate and moved to New York City. At his death, seven years after his retirement, he left an estate drained of funds. In 1880, after Ulysses S. Grant tried unsuccessfully for a third term in the White House, he set up an investment firm in New York that eventually went bankrupt. Things got so bad for Grant that even his swords and presidential souvenirs were eventually sold. Before his death of throat cancer, however, he published a two-volume personal memoir that earned his family nearly $500,000. (*See Chapter 32, Former Presidents.*)

Modern-day Perquisites

Presidential lifestyles gradually became easier and more enjoyable. The White House switched from animal transportation to the automobile during Theodore Roosevelt's administration, and Congress established a travel allowance for the president; Taft was the first to receive it. Woodrow Wilson was the first to travel in a yacht; Franklin Roosevelt was the first to use airplanes; and Dwight D. Eisenhower added the first helicopter squadron to the president's means of transportation. In the 1920s Congress allocated an entertainment allowance for the president's official functions, and during President Truman's administration it put meals for servants under the federal budget.

From these rather modest beginnings presidential living evolved impressively to the point of the "imperial" presidential lifestyle of Richard Nixon, whom many Americans believed abused the perquisites available to a president by spending al-

President Nixon is noted for the regal touches he added to the White House lifestyle. Among the changes he introduced were new ceremonial uniforms for White House guards.

most $10 million in government funds to upgrade his two private homes. Nixon is noted for making the royal style of life part of the American presidency. Bill Gulley, who served in the White House under Presidents Johnson, Nixon, Ford, and Carter as director of the Military Office, has written: "The buzz word around the Nixon White House for projecting the proper image was 'Presidential.' If a thing or place wasn't dignified enough . . . then it wasn't 'Presidential.' And that meant money had to be spent on it."[9]

To a large extent the perquisites a president enjoys have been the result of the president's style. Thus, the rewards of office vary from time to time and from administration to administration. In an effort to back away from the image of the imperial presidency of Nixon, President Carter took many symbolic measures to deflate the image of excessive White House perquisites. Within a few weeks of his inauguration, Carter sold off two presidential yachts and reduced the motor pool by 40 percent. In addition, he removed three hundred television sets and two hundred AM-FM radios from the White House and the Executive Office Building. Even with these reductions in presidential perquisites, few would argue that the quality of life was bad at the White House during the Carter years.

President Reagan restored many of the ceremonial touches that Carter had removed. Carter had ended the practice of a marine band playing "Ruffles and Flourishes" and "Hail to the Chief" at major social events. Reagan reinstated both and stationed a marine in full dress uniform at the entrance of the West

Lobby of the White House just to salute and open the door. Military aides escorted each member of the official guest party at state dinners, and a color guard preceded the Reagans and their guests of honor. Fringe benefits for the presidential staff also improved under Reagan. Among other things, Reagan expanded the White House motor pool to allow senior staff members to use limousines for their business around town.

President Bush attempted to curtail the expansion of White House fringe benefits by assigning to the deputy assistant to the president for White House operations, Rose Zamaria, the job of controlling fringe benefits within the White House. One of Zamaria's jobs was to ration the cuff links, tie clips, and other trinkets that the president and aides might distribute to White House visitors. Bush would hand out cuff links and tie clips with the presidential insignia worth about $35 to visitors. Aides could dispense a less valuable $5 version of these. Although the cost of these trinkets was covered by the Republican National Committee, Zamaria tried to restrict their distribution in an effort to make them more valuable to those who did receive them. In addition, she held a tight rein on the use of other presidential fringe benefits, such as staff use of presidential boxes at the Kennedy Center for the Performing Arts and invitations to personal parties thrown by the president. Despite the Bush administration's relative restraint in the use of some presidential benefits, like presidents before him Bush enjoyed the luxurious accommodations of the White House and the other trappings of the presidency.

The trappings of the presidency can be very seductive for a president and his staff. Early in his administration, President Clinton, who like some presidents before him had promised to avoid the arrogance of presidential perquisites, found himself in one of the worst blunders of his administration. Before takeoff from Los Angeles International Airport, Clinton summoned Cristophe Schatteman, a Beverly Hills hair stylist, to the privacy of *Air Force One* for a haircut. Although Clinton paid for the $200 haircut himself, the act closed two runways and diverted air traffic for at least an hour. When reporters got hold of the story, many Americans took Clinton to task for falling prey to what was perceived to be the luxury and arrogance of the presidency.

Just how many rewards of office do Americans want their chief executive to enjoy? The question is difficult to answer. Presidential scholar James David Barber has noted that Americans seem ambivalent on the issue: "We want our President to be plain and fancy at the same time, up there with all the other monarchs and yet be Abraham Lincoln, too."[10] Perhaps there is a need for some Americans to see a little regality in their president. But no matter how Americans may feel about the perquisites of the presidency, whether because of necessity or personal style, they are considerable.

Residences. One of the luxuries that presidents and their families enjoy is the rent-free White House mansion. *(See "The White House Today," p. 935, in Chapter 22.)* The full-time staff of about one hundred includes butlers, cooks, stewards, gardeners, plumbers, electricians, maids, and other assistants. Almost every imaginable convenience is available to the president within the White House complex and the adjoining Executive Office Building, including a theater, a swimming pool, a gymnasium, tennis courts, a bowling alley, a putting green, a jogging track, and a library regularly supplied by the publishing industry. With all these amenities at the personal disposal of the president, the operating cost of the White House has risen considerably. The annual cost of $13,800 to run and maintain the mansion a century ago seems meager compared with today's costs of more than $8 million a year. Within the West Wing the president enjoys the advantages of the Oval Office, one of the best equipped office complexes in the world. Total operating expenses for the White House Office exceed $39 million a year. Almost every new chief executive wants to refurbish the White House. Some of the presidents' remodeling has been at public expense. President Kennedy, however, concerned about the public's perception of his wealthy background, refused to use public money to pay for redecorating. When Kennedy's father commissioned a mural to brighten up the White House swimming pool area, an overzealous aide ordered the General Services Administration to install better lighting to highlight the mural. When the president found out about it, he insisted that he be billed for the $56,000 expense. Jacqueline Kennedy began the practice of making souvenir books available for purchase by White House tourists to help offset the costs of remodeling. Recently, presidents mostly have used donated funds to cover refurbishing expenses. When Gerald Ford became president, the government made plans to build a $500,000 pool and fitness center to replace the pool that Nixon had covered over to make a press room. Later, however, these plans were modified, and privately donated funds were used to build a $55,000 outdoor pool. President Carter did very little redecorating, but President Reagan raised more than $1 million in private donations to refurbish the family living quarters of the mansion. President Clinton refurbished both the private living quarters and the Oval Office area, including the Treaty Room, attempting to restore them to the style of the Lincoln era. Privately raised funds paid for the total cost of $337,000.[11]

Camp David, hidden away on Maryland's Catoctin Mountain, serves as the president's second official residence, or weekend retreat. Franklin Roosevelt built this 180-acre estate and called it *Shangri-La.* Renamed *Camp David* by Eisenhower in honor of his grandson, the estate has become a posh recreational park. Presidents and their guests can enjoy a number of recreational facilities, including a heated pool, a bowling alley, archery and skeet ranges, tennis courts, a small golf course, a movie theater, and many miles of nature trails. As commander in chief of the armed forces, the president also has access to the best accommodations available on any one of the nation's widespread military bases. Since some of these bases are located in exotic places, they have provided presidents some very good

CAMP DAVID

About fifty miles northwest of the nation's capital, nestled in nearly 6,000 rolling acres of Catoctin Mountain National Park, lies one of the most popular presidential perquisites, Camp David. Since 1942 presidents have used this 180-acre retreat for solitude, relaxation, and important diplomatic negotiations. For most recent presidents, Camp David has served as a place where they could "escape" the burdens and the day-to-day demands of the office. For most Americans, however, it has remained something of a mystery.

In the spring of 1942 the federal government, at the request of Franklin Roosevelt, set up the beginnings of the Camp David compound on the highest land in Catoctin Mountain Park. President Roosevelt wanted a secluded retreat that was closer to Washington than his home in Hyde Park, New York. Roosevelt's doctor wanted him to be able to get away to a place that was cool and at least 2,000 feet above sea level. The camp, located in a hardwood forest of oaks, hickories, hemlocks, tulip trees, and sugar maples, met his doctor's criteria. Roosevelt named the camp Shangri-La. Originally, the compound was rugged, composed of a large cottage made by moving together three log cabins built by the Civilian Conservation Corps during the 1930s. It contained a kitchen, a butler's pantry, a combined living and dining room, four bedrooms, and two bathrooms. Over the years Camp David matured. During the Reagan administration the retreat consisted of ten cabins, plus a dining lodge. The president has a separate cabin with a valley view, a stone patio, and a swimming pool. There are also tennis and basketball courts, a bowling alley, and a trampoline.

Because the retreat received little publicity, Roosevelt could slip away to the mountains and escape the hectic pace of Washington. He could relax at Shangri-La, where he worked on his stamp collection and played poker with his secretary, Grace Tully, and other friends. He entertained a variety of guests there, including Prime Minister Winston Churchill. Most Americans did not know until after Roosevelt's death that Shangri-La existed.

The retreat experienced a decline in importance during the Truman years. Preferring the sea, the Trumans found Shangri-La rather dull. Eisenhower, however, enjoyed the Maryland retreat at least as much as Roosevelt had. He spent almost every other weekend there, and after suffering a heart attack, he convalesced there for several months. Eisenhower eventually renamed the compound *Camp David* after his grandson.

President Kennedy preferred Cape Cod to Camp David, but he made the compound available to his staff. President Johnson and his family used the camp regularly, frequently inviting guests for the weekend. President Nixon liked Camp David so much that he spent almost every other weekend there in 1972 and regularly made it available to his staff. President Ford used Camp David as a family retreat and took advantage of the pool and tennis courts to keep in shape. President Carter enjoyed some of the best trout fishing in Maryland in sparkling Big Hunting Creek. And the Reagans regularly helicoptered to Camp David with many of their aides. President Reagan enjoyed horseback riding, swimming, and hiking the many trails throughout the camp.

The Bushes frequently visited Camp David on the weekends. President Bush often invited his children and grandchildren, administration officials, and sometimes foreign leaders such as Soviet leader Mikhail Gorbachev. The weekend after the Gulf War began, the Bushes hosted House Speaker Tom Foley and his wife.

In the first three years of his administration President Clinton rarely used Camp David, however. The official White House explanation for Clinton's lack of interest in the retreat was that there was little to do there except read. Some observers believed the main reason for Clinton's infrequent use of Camp David was that the environment there aggravated his allergies.

Over the years Camp David has proven to be more than a recreational retreat. It often has served as a secluded getaway where presidents have conducted sensitive negotiations with foreign dignitaries. In 1959 Eisenhower invited Soviet premier Nikita Khrushchev to Camp David for informal discussions of foreign affairs. Out of this meeting the media coined the phrase "the spirit of Camp David," meaning a spirit of serious negotiation and compromise. Probably the most notable diplomatic negotiations at Camp David occurred in September 1978 when Carter met with President Anwar Sadat of Egypt and Prime Minister Menachem Begin of Israel. This meeting, embodying the spirit of Camp David, produced the Camp David peace accords.

---

lodgings. The president may choose either the VIP quarters, which are usually staffed and well maintained, or the quarters of the commanding officer. The cost to the taxpayer is small since military bases usually provide good security and communications facilities and would require less expense than private residences or hotels to bring them up to security standards. Truman occasionally took vacations in the sun at the naval base in Key West, Florida, and Eisenhower from time to time visited the base at Newport, Rhode Island. Most recent presidents, however, have not taken advantage of this fringe benefit.

Finally, many presidents prefer to have their own "private" residences, which serve as hideaways from the hustle and bustle of Washington life. Johnson frequently withdrew to his 400-acre LBJ Ranch in Texas; Nixon regularly visited his two homes, in Key Biscayne, Florida, and San Clemente, California; Carter often returned to his farm in Plains, Georgia; Reagan frequently flew home to his ranch in California; and Bush would return to his family home in Kennebunkport, Maine. Although Clinton did not own a country house or private home, he occasionally vacationed in resort areas such as Martha's Vineyard, Massachusetts, or Jackson Hole, Wyoming. When presidents have chosen to return to their private residences for vacations, public money often had to be spent on them to ensure the president's safety. An estimated $10 million of public funds was spent on renovat-

President Reagan and his wife, Nancy, often spent weekends at Camp David. Reagan, wearing riding boots in this photo, particularly enjoyed horseback riding at the secluded compound.

ing and bringing up to security standards Nixon's private homes.

Transportation. Perhaps the most misleading presidential expense account is the $100,000 annual travel allowance. This sum does not begin to cover even the annual salary of the crew of *Air Force One*, a cost actually borne by the Department of Defense and not charged against the president's travel allowance. In 1992 Congress considered a bill that would have raised the president's travel budget to $185 million, which was an estimate of what is actually spent on White House travel. The bill would have required the White House to reimburse from that sum all federal agencies that pay for any transportation costs incurred by the president, vice president, and White House staffers. Although the bill did not pass Congress, its consideration brought to light the total costs of transporting the president and the president's family and staff.

Presidents' use of automobiles has increased tremendously since President Taft used the first official limousine provided at public expense. Today, the presidential motor pool consists of thirty-five automobiles. A dozen limousines are available for the president's use, including a $500,000, armor-plated Lincoln. The Secret Service provides drivers for the presidents' automobiles and additional automobiles for others in the presidential party. No one would dispute the need for presidents to have their own carefully protected cars. Yet, over the years, various presidents have been accused of abusing their limousine privileges. President Nixon was criticized for giving his Irish setter, King Timahoe, a solitary ride to Camp David in an official automobile.

NIXON'S SECOND HOMES

President Richard Nixon maintained two controversial private residences in addition to his official White House address. Both houses, one in Key Biscayne, Florida, and the other in San Clemente, California, required extensive repairs and renovations to make them sufficiently secure and comfortable for a president. Nixon purchased both of the residences with his own money, but various agencies of the federal government—including the Secret Service, General Services Administration, and Defense Department—paid for most of the renovations on the estates because the improvements were necessary to protect the president and maintain the properties.

Among the improvements necessary to make the Key Biscayne and San Clemente properties suitable for a president were helicopter pads to transport the president to *Air Force One* and office complexes for himself and his staff. In addition, both homes were inherently hard to protect. The Key Biscayne property, for example, fronted on busy Biscayne Bay. To screen it off, neighboring houses had to be leased, and the Coast Guard had to patrol the waters continuously near the house. Nonrecurring construction and equipment expenses came to more than $1.3 million just for Key Biscayne. At San Clemente, bullet-proof glass was installed in all windows and in a screen that shielded the swimming pool from

seaborne attackers and cold Pacific breezes. Some renovations, however, involved more than security and the normal overhead of maintaining the residence.

In 1973 the congressional Joint Committee on Internal Revenue Taxation, an investigatory and policy recommending committee, came to the conclusion that a number of repairs to Nixon's Key Biscayne and San Clemente homes served more to enrich the value of the estates than to provide increased security. Questionable expenditures on the Nixon homes included: $18,494 for a forced-air heating system, $621.50 for an ice-cube-making machine, $1,600 for four picture windows facing the ocean, $388.78 for an exhaust fan for a fireplace, $4,981.50 for a gazebo, and $2,329 for a flagpole. The committee found that many of these improvements had little to do with protecting the president or maintaining him in a reasonable manner.

Nixon defended the expenditures by announcing that he and Mrs. Nixon would donate their San Clemente estate to the public after their deaths. Instead, Nixon sold the San Clemente estate in 1979 and demanded that the Secret Service bear the cost of removing any improvements made for the sake of security. Nixon did write the government a check for $2,329 to cover the cost of the flagpole.

AIR FORCE ONE

When presidents first became airborne, the Army Air Corps (later to become the Air Force) became air chauffeur to the commander in chief and has been in charge of selecting and piloting presidential planes ever since. The first official plane used by a president was a U.S. Army Air Corps Douglas C-54 Skymaster, dubbed the *Sacred Cow* by the press. Shortly before his death in 1945, Franklin D. Roosevelt used the plane on one trip. Harry S. Truman, who enjoyed flying, used the *Sacred Cow* often for presidential trips. In the summer of 1947 the official presidential plane was upgraded to a state-of-the-art Douglas Aircraft DC-6. Named the *Independence* after Truman's hometown in Missouri, the plane was equipped with weather radar, long-range capability, and a teletype system that allowed the president to stay in touch with Washington even when he was three thousand miles away. The *Independence* served him throughout his administration.

Dwight D. Eisenhower enjoyed flying even more than Truman. Although he did not pilot the planes himself, he did possess a pilot's license. President Eisenhower's first official plane was a Lockheed Constellation 749. Named *Columbine II*, after the military craft he used during World War II and the official flower of his wife's home state of Colorado, the model was a personal favorite of his. Because of rapidly advancing aviation technology, the plane was replaced in 1954 by *Columbine III*, a Lockheed 1049C Super-Constellation, which remained the official plane for the remainder of Eisenhower's administration. On a whirlwind, eighteen-day tour of eleven countries in Europe, Africa, and Asia in 1959, Eisenhower chose not to use the propeller-driven *Columbine III* and became the first president to travel by jet.

The distinction of being the first president to travel regularly by jet, however, belonged to John F. Kennedy. Assigned a propeller-driven Douglas VC-118A by the Air Force, Kennedy preferred the much faster Boeing jets. In fact, he used his assigned plane only for travel to airports at which the runways were not long enough for the jets to land. In 1962, as a result of the increased demands for faster presidential travel, a Boeing 707 was delivered to Kennedy and became officially known as *26000* and designated *Air Force One*, as is any plane in which the president might be riding. Previous planes had been military in appearance, but designer Raymond Loewy, along with Jacqueline Kennedy, created a new exterior that would become widely recognized around the world. Among the changes, "United States Air Force" was replaced with "United States of America" on the body of the craft. And Mrs. Kennedy added a number of amenities for which the plane became famous.

President Kennedy was not able to enjoy *Air Force One* for very long, however. On the day of his assassination, November 22, 1963, Kennedy's body was flown from Dallas to Washington in the plane he had used for just over thirteen months. Nine years later, the plane Kennedy had first used became the backup to a newer version of the Boeing 707. These two planes remained the president's planes for more than twenty-five years. By the 1980s, however, the 707s were obsolete: their range, space, and amenities were limited; factory parts were hard to obtain; and their engines were too loud to meet many local airport noise rules.

George Bush was the first president to fly on the most recent version of *Air Force One*. Two identical Boeing 747-200Bs, at a cost of approximately $400 million, were supposed to have been ready during the Reagan administration but were not delivered until September 1990. The new *Air Force One* has a top speed of 640 miles per hour and can fly at least twice as far without refueling—more than 7,140 miles—than the older 707s could. With ninety-three seats and the capability of serving a hundred meals at a time, the plane can accommodate seventy passengers and twenty-three crew members.

Equipped with every amenity imaginable, the plane provides the president with an excellent work environment. The Boeing 747 has a conference room, a staff room, several work stations with computers, a guest area, space for members of the media and their telex equipment, a facsimile machine, eighty-five telephones, and medical facilities, including an operating room for emergency surgery by the personal doctor who always travels with the president. Communications equipment and the crew are upstairs. The president's bedroom suite, including a dressing room and lavatory with a shower-tub, is in the nose of the aircraft. Other special touches include fresh flowers and memo pads, napkins, playing cards, boxes of M&Ms, and matches embossed with the presidential seal and the words "Aboard Air Force One."

Perhaps the most historic flight of the new *Air Force One* occurred in November 1995 when former presidents Carter and Bush joined President Clinton in attending the funeral of Prime Minister Yitzhak Rabin of Israel. Others aboard the flight to Israel included Senate Majority Leader Bob Dole, House Speaker Newt Gingrich, House Minority Leader Richard Gephardt, Senate Minority Leader Tom Daschle, Secretary of State Warren Christopher, Secretary of Defense William Perry, and former secretaries of state Cyrus Vance and George Shultz.

Only recently have presidents begun to make many long-distance trips. In fact, before World War II, only two presidents traveled outside the country while in office. Theodore Roosevelt made a quick boat trip to Panama, and Wilson ventured to Europe at the end of World War I to attend the Paris Peace Conference. By the next world war, however, long-distance presidential travel had become more of a necessity. In January 1943 Franklin Roosevelt became the first president to fly overseas when he went to Casablanca, Morocco, to meet with British prime minister Winston Churchill and Allied commanders to plan the D-Day invasion. (Only after the trip did the rest of the world learn of the historic flight.) Roosevelt made the trip in a commercial airplane that had been pressed into wartime service. Compared with the amenities of contemporary presidential air travel, Roosevelt's trip was arduous.

Today, the best and certainly the most expensive travel bene-

Air Force One, the president's personal aircraft, is probably the most visible symbol of the presidency. The latest model, a converted Boeing 747, went into service in 1990.

fit for the president is the air fleet maintained by the military for the president's official use. At the president's disposal are a half-dozen Air Force jets, each outfitted with a bedroom and an office, and several sound-proofed Marine Corps helicopters for short trips. The president also has access to several Lockheed Jet Stars stationed at Andrews Air Force Base, which serve as courier planes to transport mail and staff when the president is out of Washington. Although the presidential air fleet was created primarily for the use of the president and the vice president, presidents have recently made the jets available to members of their immediate families for personal trips. They have felt justified in doing so for security reasons, since threats of violence against presidents and their families have multiplied.

The centerpiece of the presidential air fleet is *Air Force One.* (Technically, the designation *Air Force One* is reserved for whatever plane the president is flying on at the time.) Equipped with the latest technology, *Air Force One* is a quick and comfortable means of transportation that allows the president to keep in constant contact with Washington and the rest of the world through an extensive communications center. The Secret Service tries to keep secret most of the communications facilities aboard *Air Force One,* but President Reagan once boasted that he could place a telephone call to anywhere in the world and speak freely on a "secure" line (a telephone line supposedly safe from being tapped).[12]

Designers wanted to produce a plane that would provide not only luxury and communications but also the greatest possible security. In addition to a gourmet kitchen, numerous televisions and VCRs, a stereo system, and movie facilities, the plane has several important security features; for example, it has been hardened against the electromagnetic pulses that would be created by a nuclear explosion. Also, the president has extra securi-ty personnel who can watch welcoming crowds on television screens as the plane taxis up the runway.

On any presidential trip at least two large jets—a back-up plane and a communications plane—accompany *Air Force One.* And sometimes a large cargo plane carrying the chief executive's bullet-proof limousine will precede the presidential entourage. Also, somewhere aboard *Air Force One* is a compartment for the "black box," which contains the secret codes for the president in case of a nuclear crisis.

Entertainment. Like many of the other perquisites of the presidential office, the amount of money and staff resources expended on entertainment depends significantly on the person holding the office. Even though protocol requires all presidents to do some entertaining of foreign heads of state and foreign and U.S. government notables, the social pace at the White House largely depends on the inclination of the president. The Trumans, for example, seldom entertained, but other presidents and their families have taken advantage of the many entertainment opportunities the White House affords. The Kennedys, Johnsons, Fords, Nixons, and Bushes all enjoyed busy social calendars. The Carters cut back on White House social events, but the Reagans stepped up the presidential social pace, delighting in state dinners, congressional breakfasts, political teas, luncheons, barbecues, receptions, and various command performances. In 1984 *U.S. News and World Report* found that President Reagan had entertained 222,758 persons during his first three years in office.[13] After President Clinton's first year in office, one Washington columnist complained that the Clintons had entertained so many politicians, dignitaries, and Hollywood stars as overnight guests at the White House that they were devaluing the trappings of the presidency by overusing them. Fred Barnes noted that the practice had become so excessive that he

The pace and style of entertaining at the White House are determined largely by the president's tastes. Pablo Casals, world-renowned cellist, was among President Kennedy's invited performers.

expected to see bumper stickers that said: "Honk, if you haven't slept at the White House."[14]

Even though the president receives an annual entertainment allowance of $12,000, most entertainment expenses are not paid out of the White House budget. The State Department pays for all state banquets and functions. *(See box, An Evening at the Clinton White House, p. 995.)* Periodically, various entertainers are asked to come to the White House and perform for the president and White House guests. The distinction of performing at a White House function is so great that celebrities do so without charge. In fact, many will even cancel previously scheduled appearances to accommodate the president. At most White House affairs, the army, navy, air force, or marine bands continuously play for the pleasure of the president and White House guests. Smaller groups, such as the Army Chorus, the Air Force Strolling Strings, and the Navy Sea Chanters, may also perform. Since these are military groups, the Defense Department bears the costs of their performances. Also, a number of White House functions are paid for by the organizations that benefit from them. During the Reagan and Bush administrations, the Republican National Committee picked up the tab for several fetes for Republicans.

In addition to entertaining at the White House, from time to time presidents will entertain dignitaries while abroad. Several presidents have gone to extremes to carry the pageantry and glamour of a White House dinner to other countries. It was not uncommon for Johnson and Nixon to take with them White House china and crystal for entertaining government officials in the countries they visited. In 1981 President and Mrs. Reagan hosted six hundred Chinese and American guests in the banquet facilities of Beijing's Great Wall Hotel—one of the largest state dinners ever held outside the United States. The Reagans

treated their guests to a "typical American meal" of turkey and dressing. To accommodate the large crowd with the best possible meal, forty frozen turkeys were flown in from California, and a professor from the Beijing Agricultural College was asked to oversee the selection of vegetables to make sure they were garden fresh. Some of the vegetables came from the hotel's own greenhouse. Canned cranberries were flown in from Hong Kong. The amount of food required for the dinner was massive: 176 pounds of beef for consommé; 440 pounds of prawns, scallops, Mandarin fish, and turbot for the seafood mousse appetizer; 132 pounds of hearts of palm for the salad; and twenty-two pounds of almonds, 600 eggs, thirty-six quarts of cream, and three bottles of Grand Marnier for the praline ice cream dessert. The Reagans selected three types of California wine for the event. Seventy-six chefs and 120 staffers were required to assist in the preparation. Special arrangements were made with the hotel to provide place settings of German chinaware, Irish linen, and French crystal, candelabra, and silverware. A twelve-piece Chinese orchestra played music chosen by the Reagans, including works by Irving Berlin, George Gershwin, and Rodgers and Hammerstein.[15]

For four decades presidents had the use of a 105-foot yacht, the *Sequoia,* for entertaining friends and dignitaries. In 1976, however, President Carter sold it for $286,000, a symbolic sacrifice in the interest of cutting back on presidential pomp. At the urging of several friends and advisers—among them former House Speaker Thomas P. "Tip" O'Neill—the Reagan administration tried to replace the yacht. Many felt it had served a useful purpose in the past by providing the president a more intimate environment for official entertaining and lobbying. The cost of replacing it proved prohibitive, however.

Protection. Most presidents have viewed the Secret Service as a mixed blessing. Probably the most necessary and important presidential perquisite, it is also the most annoying. Since the assassination of President Kennedy and the failed, but close, attempts on presidents Ford and Reagan, the growing need for greater security has dictated an increase in Secret Service protection and a decrease in the personal freedoms of the chief executives. During the Clinton administration, several attempts were made to breach White House security measures. In fact, during a one-week period in May 1995, two intruders climbed over the White House fence. Both were intercepted by White House guards and posed no real threat to the president. A few months earlier, in late October 1994, the White House had been sprayed with bullets by a disgruntled Colorado Springs upholsterer. These breaches of security resulted in even tighter security around the executive mansion. Every month almost six thousand new pieces of information concerning possible threats to the president pour into Secret Service headquarters. Sometimes the information may be just a report of a malicious statement, such as someone in a bar saying, "That jerk in the White House ought to be shot." Or a person might report that a next-door neighbor blames the president for losing their job. Even though all tips are taken seriously, some are viewed with the utmost urgency. In November 1981 intelligence sources warned that Libya's Col. Muammar Qaddafi had sent assassination teams to murder top-ranking government officials, including President Reagan. Even though nothing came of the threat, the Secret Service put the tightest possible security measures in place. In 1991, during the Persian Gulf War, the Secret Service quietly intensified its security measures around the White House as a result of information about a possible terrorist attack on the White House. As of 1995, the Secret Service had computerized files on some 50,000 individuals who had threatened the president or other government officials at some time, or who had done something to make the Secret Service suspicious and concerned. The Secret Service divides these potential threats into three categories. Only about one hundred people are listed as Category 3, the most serious.[16]

Abraham Lincoln was the first president to have bodyguards, paid for by the state of Ohio during the Civil War. After the assassination of William McKinley in 1901, the Treasury Department's Secret Service, which had primarily investigated counterfeiting, was charged with the protection of the president. Florence Harding was the first first lady to appropriate the services of her own Secret Service agent, and during Calvin Coolidge's administration, Secret Service protection was extended to the president's immediate family. Even though the Secret Service undertakes other activities, such as detecting and arresting counterfeiters and offering and paying rewards for information contributing to the arrest of criminals, the majority of its budget goes to protecting the president of the United States. At the time of the Kennedy assassination, the Secret Service had 389 agents and a budget of $8 million. In the mid-1990s the Secret Service employed about 4,600 people worldwide, including

more that 2,000 agents, and had a budget of more than $475 million. (See "Protecting the President: The Secret Service," p. 1003, in Chapter 24.)

No longer can a president take a casual stroll through the streets of Washington, as Truman frequently did. Nor can they elude their Secret Service agents, as Kennedy did to visit friends in Georgetown. They cannot even take a walk around the grounds of the White House without Secret Service protection, a pleasure that Johnson enjoyed. But those days are long gone. Reagan became a virtual prisoner of the White House after he was wounded in an assassination attempt in 1981. Before the shooting, the Reagans occasionally went to church. After the attempt on the president's life, however, the Reagans decided to quit attending services altogether because members of any church they visited would have been subjected to checks by metal detectors and other security-related annoyances. Because of Secret Service protection, Nancy Reagan could not even go shopping without disrupting a store's normal business. Instead, she ordered from catalogs and asked her secretary to shop for her.[17]

Both the Bushes and Clintons enjoyed getting out of the White House and going to Washington restaurants. When they did so, however, the Secret Service had to take elaborate security measures. Agents visited and searched the restaurants before the presidential party arrived and subjected restaurant guests to metal-detectors and explosives-sniffing dogs. Although President Clinton had a jogging track built around the White House in order to avoid disrupting early morning traffic, he continued to jog outside the gates of the executive mansion to avoid what he called the "splendid prison" of the White House. Doing so required that a dozen Secret Service vehicles follow him through downtown traffic.[18]

Even in the White House itself the president and the first family are restricted in their activities by security requirements. They live on the second and third floors in approximately thirteen of the 132 rooms of the White House. The rest of the rooms are used for offices or for the president's official duties. The Secret Service makes sure that the White House is one of the most secure places on earth. At every exit and throughout the White House, security guards and the Secret Service stand a careful watch. When the president entertains, guests must be approved in advance by the Secret Service before they can even enter the White House. Any presents given to the president or to family members must be opened by someone else. And as a routine security measure, the Secret Service confiscates all food that arrives at the White House by mail. The agents constantly monitor, using hidden television cameras and electronic sensors, the almost nineteen acres of White House grounds and routinely test the air for poisonous gases and bacteria. As groups tour the mansion, Secret Service agents discreetly mingle with the crowd.

Occasionally, threats against presidents and their families will force the Secret Service to take extraordinary measures of protection. After the attempted assassination of Reagan, the 1983 bombings of the U.S. Marine barracks in Beirut and of a corridor in the U.S. Capitol, and several specific threats against Reagan's life, Secret Service agents decided to blockade the entrances to the White House. Protected by police vans and dirt-filled dump trucks, the White House came to resemble an outpost in a battle zone. These steps were in addition to the steel gates and sensors already in place at the entrances and on the grounds of the White House. Eventually, the Secret Service replaced these vehicles with more attractive, permanent concrete barriers standing three feet high.

In 1995 Pennsylvania Avenue in front of the White House was closed to automobile traffic and converted into a pedestrian mall. The White House had suffered assault three times in the few months preceding the closure: a deranged gunman fired shots that struck the White House, a small plane crashed just short of the president's bedroom, and an unknown assailant fired shots at the White House grounds. Although closing Pennsylvania Avenue would have done little to prevent the attacks, a panel of security experts appointed to review White House security after the assaults recommended the action to protect the White House from a potential car bomb attack, similar to the one that destroyed a federal building in Oklahoma City on April 19, 1995. Closing Pennsylvania Avenue to car traffic rerouted the estimated 26,000 cars that drove between 15th and 17th Streets every day.

Safety precautions are not confined to possible ground assaults. In 1994 the White House was subjected to an air strike of sorts. An amateur pilot flying a small Cessna airplane was able to breach White House security, crashing on the South Lawn just outside the president's private quarters. At the time the Cessna crashed, President Clinton and his family were spending the night across the street at Blair House. Secret Service agents indicated that had the president been in the White House, they would have responded differently, rather than just letting the plane attempt to land on the White House lawn. But the fact that someone with limited flying skill could almost crash into the president's bedroom raised tremendous concerns about White House security against trained assassins.

Airborne attacks appear to be the greatest weakness for White House security. In the Old Executive Office Building, next-door to the White House, a command and control center closely monitors all aircraft using National Airport, a mere three miles from the White House. There have been rumors for years that ground-to-air missiles are hidden near the White House, but those rumors have never been substantiated. And even if they are true, security experts believe that planes are impossible for the White House to defend against because a pilot approaching National Airport could easily veer off course and be on the White House lawn in less than twenty seconds. Even if the Secret Service were able to track an errant aircraft, there is some speculation about whether or not agents would actually attempt to shoot it down, possibly risking innocent lives on the airplane itself and the lives of other people in downtown Washington.

When the president makes a public appearance, the Secret Service takes special precautions. Wherever the president is scheduled to speak, the Secret Service works with local law enforcement officials to make sure any risk is minimal. Security officers carefully check the motorcade route to the president's destination for any places where an assassin would have an open shot. They look for possible sniper posts and inspect utility holes and bridges for bombs. In case of an emergency, the Secret Service selects alternate routes and designates certain hospitals to have a ready supply of the president's blood type. Moreover, in every city or town where a public appearance is scheduled, agents search local files to see if there are people in the area who could pose a threat to the president. Anyone considered suspicious is interrogated and put under constant surveillance.

When *Air Force One* arrives at an airport, the Secret Service quickly escorts the chief executive from the airplane into the armored presidential limousine, fitted with bullet-proof tires and windows. An agent drives the limousine, and a second agent rides in the back with the president. Twenty or so agents jog alongside the car or follow in cars equipped with submachine guns, tear gas, emergency tools, and medical supplies. As the motorcade passes through the streets, sharpshooters with high-powered binoculars and rifles watch warily from the rooftops. Other agents with pistols watch the motorcade from strategic locations along the way. Some agents closely observe onlookers for anything suspicious. At the destination, the president will often speak in a "secured" room, that is, one that has been thoroughly checked by Secret Service agents. Before sealing off the room, agents use specially trained dogs to sniff out bombs. And as people enter the room, they pass through metal detectors and have their bags or purses inspected. Although the Secret Service prefers that the president speak in a secure auditorium, the president will sometimes address an audience outdoors. Since the Secret Service cannot screen everyone in the crowd, these venues place an extra burden on them. They must station agents on the rooftops of nearby buildings and place extra agents in the crowd.

Protecting presidents when they travel or go on vacation often entails elaborate measures. When President Eisenhower took golfing vacations, he usually was followed around the golf course by an athletic-looking twosome with high-powered rifles in their golf bags. When President Ford vacationed in Vail, Secret Service agents would ski alongside him. And when President Reagan visited his ranch, agents adept at horseback riding would accompany him on trail rides. Both Bush and Clinton were shadowed by Secret Service agents wherever they would go jogging, either around Washington or on vacation.

Sometimes, especially when a president visits other countries, the Secret Service takes what may seem to be ludicrous precautions. When President Reagan visited Costa Rica in December 1982, he arrived with a C-5 cargo plane carrying three bullet-proof Lincoln Continentals and an entourage of three hundred Secret Service agents. Costa Ricans were amused at these protective measures in their peaceful, democratic country, for the Costa Rican president can walk about in public without security guards.[19] But, understandably, the Secret Service would rather err on the side of caution.

Retirement. Few executive officers of major corporations enjoy the generous retirement benefits that former presidents of the United States have today. Yet, until 1958, when the first annual pension of $25,000 was given to Truman, neither presidents nor their families received any pension or benefits after retirement from the highest public office in the country. Calvin Coolidge moved from the White House into a $36-a-month rented duplex. When the Trumans left the White House and went back to Missouri, they paid their own train fares.

During his retirement years, Truman refused to accept any job that might take advantage of his former occupation as presi-

dent. Because he was not independently wealthy and spent much of his time answering large quantities of mail, he faced real financial hardship just a few short years after retiring. To help Truman and to rectify past negligence, Congress passed the Former Presidents Act of 1958, which gave Truman his pension and provided him with an additional $50,000 a year for office and staff.

Since January 1989 every ex-president has received an annual pension equal to the salary of a cabinet secretary ($148,400 when George Bush retired in 1993). A president's widow receives $20,000 a year. In addition, the retired president also receives $150,000 annually for a staff for the first thirty months out of office and a $96,000 annual allowance thereafter. But there are other retirement benefits as well. The government provides each ex-president with unlimited postage for nonpolitical correspondence and a furnished office. Ex-presidents receive these benefits in addition to $1.5 million budgeted by the Presidential

---

PRESIDENTIAL LIBRARIES

Recent presidents have established libraries to house their presidential papers and memorabilia, as well as films, tapes, and clippings relating to their administrations. These libraries were built with private funds but are maintained by the federal government. Richard Nixon's presidential papers, however, are not housed in the privately maintained Richard Nixon Library and Birthplace in Yorba Linda, California. Everything pertaining to Nixon's presidential years, including the Nixon White House tapes, was taken by the

federal government as a result of the Watergate affair and eventually placed in the Nixon Presidential Materials Project, a section of the National Archives and Records Administration. The Richard Nixon Library and Birthplace houses many of Nixon's prepresidential papers, including items from his congressional and vice presidential years, and much of his postpresidential materials.

The following is a list of these libraries, their locations, and the date each was dedicated.

The Herbert Hoover Presidential Library
Parkside Drive
West Branch, Iowa 52358
Phone: (319) 643-5301
Dedicated: August 10, 1972

The Franklin D. Roosevelt Library
Albany Post Road
Hyde Park, New York 12538
Phone: (914) 229-8114
Dedicated: July 4, 1940

The Harry S. Truman Library
U.S. Highway 24 and Delaware Street
Independence, Missouri 64050
Phone: (816) 833-1400
Dedicated: July 6, 1957

The Dwight D. Eisenhower Library
Southeast Fourth Street
Abilene, Kansas 67410
Phone: (913) 263-4571
Dedicated: May 1, 1972

The John F. Kennedy Library
Morrissey Boulevard
Boston, Massachusetts 02125
Phone: (617) 929-4500
Dedicated: October 20, 1979

The Lyndon B. Johnson Library
2313 Red River Street
Austin, Texas 78705
Phone: (512) 482-5137
Dedicated: May 22, 1971

The Richard Nixon Library and Birthplace
18001 Yorba Linda Boulevard
Yorba Linda, California 92686
Phone: (714) 993-5075
Dedicated: July 19, 1990

The Nixon Presidential Materials Project
National Archives at College Park
8601 Adelphi Road
College Park, Maryland 20740
Telephone: (301) 713-6950

The Gerald R. Ford Library
1000 Beal Avenue
Ann Arbor, Michigan 48109
Phone: (313) 668-2218
Dedicated: April 27, 1981

The Jimmy Carter Library
One Copenhill Avenue
Atlanta, Georgia 30307
Phone: (404) 331-3942
Dedicated: October 1, 1986

The Ronald Reagan Presidential Library
40 Presidential Drive
Simi Valley, California 93065
Phone: (805) 522-2977
Dedicated: November 4, 1991

The George Bush Presidential Library
Texas A&M University
College Station, Texas
To be opened in 1997

Transitions Effectiveness Act of 1988 to ease the transition from president to former president and help the president and vice president wind up their official affairs.

The most expensive presidential retirement perquisite for the federal government is the operational budget for the increasing number of presidential libraries. American taxpayers paid more than $20 million to operate presidential libraries in 1993. Seven deceased presidents (Herbert Hoover, Roosevelt, Truman, Eisenhower, Kennedy, Johnson, and Nixon) and three living presidents (Ford, Carter, and Reagan) have libraries that house their presidential papers and related memorabilia. The George Bush Presidential Library and Museum was due to open at Texas A & M University in College Station, Texas, in 1997. Construction of these facilities was paid for by funds raised through private donations, but since 1955 the federal government has picked up the expense of maintaining them. Although the libraries were built mainly for research, the National Archives, which maintains them, estimates that the number of researchers looking at presidential documents is a tiny fraction of the total number of visitors. Most visitors to the libraries are more interested in the presidential museums, which are usually housed in the same buildings, than in presidential papers. In recent years many members of Congress have felt that these libraries serve more as monuments than research centers and have proposed limits on the size of new presidential libraries.[20]

The cost of Secret Service protection for ex-presidents ranks close behind the cost of maintaining presidential libraries. In 1962, shortly before President Kennedy was assassinated, Congress ordered the Secret Service to begin protecting ex-presidents and to continue to do so for a "reasonable time." Then, in 1965, Congress approved lifetime protection for all retired chief executives, their spouses, and their children under the age of sixteen. Lawmakers also granted a president's widow Secret Service protection as long as she did not remarry. When Amy Carter turned sixteen, she lost her Secret Service protection, as did Jacqueline Kennedy when she remarried. Occasionally, a president will decline some allowable protection. In 1984 Nixon dropped Secret Service protection for himself and his wife, Pat, who had suffered a stroke and thereafter rarely traveled.

The General Services Administration (GSA) controls presidential retirement funds and keeps an eye on how former presidents make use of public money. The GSA approves most requests for funds for office allowances and other items. Some of the items that ex-presidents have requested and received include: Nixon's subscriptions to a variety of newspapers and magazines, including the *Wall Street Journal,* the *New York Times,* the *Washington Post, Foreign Affairs, Fortune, Facts on File, Time,* and *U.S. News and World Report;* Ford's cable television service; and Carter's computer equipment complete with service contract. The GSA rejects items it feels breach the bounds of propriety. Shortly after leaving the presidency, Carter began to set up his new office in Atlanta. Initially, he asked GSA for an allowance of $15,000 for a wool rug for his office and

$3,500 for two chandeliers. The GSA refused, and Carter had to "settle" for buying a rug costing $12,600 and for installing chandeliers that cost only $1,850. The GSA also rejected Carter's request for funds to pay for photographs of Amy Carter to be sent to children writing her and asking for pictures.

Much controversy surrounds the upkeep of former presidents. Under heavy pressure to slash the federal budget, members of Congress in the 1980s introduced several bills to curtail the steady increase in the amount of money allocated to former presidents. Sen. Lawton Chiles (D-Fla.) introduced bills in 1980 and 1981 that would have limited the size of presidential libraries that the government would pay to maintain. The bills also would have limited Secret Service protection to eight years. The secretary of the Treasury could have extended the service two more years, if it was deemed necessary. And Secret Service protection for widows would have been cut off six months after their husbands' deaths. Another provision of the bills would have cut back on the practice of using federally funded staffs to help prepare presidential memoirs. Although Chiles's bills never became law, they served to reflect the reservation many Americans had about spending large sums of tax money to support ex-presidents.

Today, ex-presidents typically are millionaires. Former presidents remain in the public spotlight, and they take advantage of the lingering interest in their tenure at the White House. As a result, they become marketable and coveted commodities. Through speaking engagements, serving as consultants, serving on corporate boards, and writing books, former chief executives can profit handsomely. After his retirement, for example, Bush was able to command up to $100,000 for speeches. The Republican National Committee (RNC) supplements Reagan's and Bush's retirement. Since his 1989 retirement, Reagan has been paid $12,500 by the RNC toward maintenance of his Los Angeles office. Bush received $50,000 to cover his first four months back in private life.[21] On the one hand, critics contend that the public should not be asked to subsidize this wealth any more than is absolutely necessary. On the other hand, defenders contend that ex-presidents still have public responsibilities and should be financially supported in their activities.

The Vice President

The trappings of political office have always been important to vice presidents. Yet, they have never shared in the pomp and grandeur of the office of president. Neither the pay nor the perquisites of the vice presidency have been as substantial as those of the presidency. In fact, until relatively recently the vice presidency was an insignificant office, not only in terms of its power and functions but also in terms of the privileges and honor of the position. Because most presidents did not give meaning to the vice president's role, the job failed to win meaningful fringe benefits. Since the mid-1970s, however, vice presidents have enjoyed a wider range of benefits, and they certainly

Marine Corps helicopters afford the president, vice president, and their aides convenient transportation in and out of Washington, D.C. *Marine One,* as the president's helicopter is called, awaits President Bill Clinton and Vice President Al Gore on the South Lawn of the White House.

have lived in a style that many Americans would envy. Nonetheless, the splendor of their perquisites still does not approach that of the president's.

VICE-PRESIDENTIAL SALARY

On September 24, 1789, when Congress first fixed the president's salary at $25,000 a year, it placed the annual salary of the vice president at $5,000. When Congress doubled the president's salary in 1873, it also doubled the vice president's. No more consideration was given to the vice president's salary until 1906, when Congress raised it from $10,000 to $12,000 annually. This amount was well below the $50,000 a year that the president was given, and it reflected the relative unimportance of the job to most Americans.

However, since the late 1940s the vice president's salary has increased substantially. The Legislative Reorganization Act of 1946 contained a measure that provided for a $20,000 salary for the vice president. In 1949 Congress raised the vice-presidential salary from $20,000 to $30,000 a year and added an annual tax-free expense account of $10,000. Twelve years later Congress voted the vice president a $5,000 raise. The Federal Employee Act of 1964 again raised the compensation, from $35,000 to $43,000 a year; and in 1969, when Congress increased the president's salary to $200,000, it raised the vice president's salary to $62,500. The vice president received several raises thereafter, and in 1994 earned $171,500 in salary (over 83 percent of the president's salary of $200,000) and was given an expense account of $10,000 a year, all of which was taxable.

VICE-PRESIDENTIAL PERQUISITES

In the George Gershwin musical comedy *Of Thee I Sing,* Alexander Throttlebottom felt so neglected as vice president

that he complained that he had to take the public tour even to get into the White House. Many vice presidents have felt that they were excluded not only from administration policy making but also from White House perquisites. Although Gershwin's characterization of vice-presidential prestige was extreme, it does represent the historical lack of fringe benefits for vice presidents.

Although most vice presidents have enjoyed a certain amount of fringe benefits of the job itself, the actual importance of a specific vice president's job and the benefits that follow depend largely upon the president. If a president recognizes the importance of the vice presidency and uses the vice president for things other than receiving visiting delegations of Boy Scouts, then the vice president will likely share in many of the trappings of the presidential office.

Franklin Roosevelt had little use for the vice presidency, prompting his first vice president, John N. "Cactus Jack" Garner, to tell Lyndon Johnson that the office "ain't worth a cup of warm spit." Until the Ford administration, most presidents seemed to ignore their vice presidents, giving them few responsibilities or privileges and little recognition. Of recent vice presidents, Johnson, Humphrey, and Agnew seemed almost to disappear in office. Their presidents seldom recognized their importance or sought their advice.[22] A former Humphrey assistant noted the reality of vice-presidential privileges: "It used to take an act of Congress to get us into the White House. We had to get cleared in by somebody because we didn't have White House passes. . . . We were treated like little children, allowed to look but not to touch. . . . We didn't have any symbols of power and that was currency in the White House."[23] In contrast, more recent vice presidents, such as Walter Mondale, George Bush, Dan Quayle, and Albert Gore Jr., found that their counsel was consistently sought and their positions recognized through the granting of White House fringe benefits.

Although the relation between perquisites and power is uncertain, the advancement of vice-presidential perquisites does seem to reflect the rise in the vice president's position. Instead of having their main office in the Old Executive Office Building, across the street from the White House, recent vice presidents, including Mondale, Bush, Quayle, and Gore, were allowed an office in the West Wing of the White House and greater access to the president than their predecessors had. In addition, their staffs were expanded and granted greater access to the White House and given more privileges than earlier vice-presidential staffs.[24] Simply having White House mess privileges meant that the vice president's staff rubbed elbows with the president's staff, allowing greater contact and accessibility.

The location of the vice president's office is one of the most important perquisites for the second in command. The formal office of the vice president, in the Old Executive Office Building, contains all the amenities befitting a vice president. A Mondale aide once described it in glowing terms: "That EOB office is nothing less than magnificent. Royal blue carpeting. Two entrances, both protected by huge mahogany doors. Great view of the White House and monuments. Good location. Balcony. High ceilings."[25] But for all the splendor of that office, the real perquisite is to be located in the West Wing of the White House. The West Wing vice-presidential office is small and not nearly as grand, but it provides the vice president with greater access to the president. As another former Mondale aide remarked: "The West Wing Office is really quite grubby. It is cramped and closed in. There's a lot of traffic and the view isn't so hot out the back window. It's got lots of advantages if you want to be a player, but it isn't that great if you're into offices."[26] Today the vice-presidential office in the Old Executive Office Building is used mostly for ceremonial functions. The vice president also maintains an office on Capitol Hill to serve the constitutional function as the presiding officer of the Senate.

During the past thirty years the vice president's staff has grown tremendously, indicating the increased importance of the position. In 1959, when Nixon was vice president, the staff of the vice president was fewer than twenty. By the time Bush served in the office, it had increased to more than seventy. In fact, the vice president's office staff today is almost a replica of the president's staff. The vice president has a national security adviser, a press secretary, an issues staff, a counsel's office, a chief of staff, a scheduling team, an appointments secretary, and an advance team. An enlarged staff not only increased the ability of vice presidents to stay abreast of the issues, it gave them the appearance of importance and the intangible perquisite of clout.

Recent years have seen an increase in other tangible vice-presidential fringe benefits, such as improved airplanes, more limousines, and an official residence. Until the Carter administration, vice-presidential air travel paled in comparison to the president's *Air Force One.* Humphrey had to travel in a small jet

with enough room for only ten or twelve persons, which prevented the media from going along. Agnew moved up a bit to an Air Force transport without windows. Often called "Air Force Thirteen" by Agnew's staff, it resembled a flying coffin. Vice President Ford's air travel accommodations were hardly much better. He traveled in *Air Force Two,* an aging turboprop Convair that "creaked and groaned its way through the skies."[27] By the time Mondale assumed the office, vice-presidential air travel had improved markedly. He always had one plane on standby and two or three others at his disposal. During the 1980 presidential campaign, his aircraft was equipped to carry representatives from the media. As one of his longtime aides gratefully remarked, "We had two or three planes that could not be moved without our permission. And they were decent airplanes. Windows, engines, wheels, the whole package."[28]

Only recently have vice presidents been given an official residence. *(See "Vice President's Residence," p. 946, in Chapter 22.)* On April 9, 1966, Congress authorized the planning, design, construction, furnishing, and maintenance of an official vice-presidential residence to be built on the site of the United States Naval Observatory in Washington, D.C. However, it never appropriated any money for the project. Finally, on July 12, 1974, Congress selected the Admiral's House—a building almost a century old on a twelve-acre section of the seventy-two-acre observatory property—as the official residence of the vice president. This time, Congress also authorized expenditures for its repair. On January 20, 1977, Mondale became the first vice president to occupy the renovated building. In the late 1980s private donations provided for further renovations to the vice-presidential residence to accommodate Vice President Quayle's young family. In 1993 the residence underwent a $1.6 million renovation to rid the mansion of asbestos and other dangerous materials. The renovations were paid for by the not-for-profit Vice President's Residence Foundation.

White House Staff and Executive Agencies

When President Washington established his cabinet, salaries were based on the perceived difficulty of the position. The first three cabinet officers Washington selected were Secretary of State John Jay, Secretary of War Henry Knox, and Secretary of the Treasury Alexander Hamilton. The annual salary for the secretary of war was $3,000; for the two other cabinet secretaries, $3,500 each. Later, the attorney general and the postmaster general became members of Washington's cabinet at $1,500 a year. Finally, the secretary of the navy was added as a sixth cabinet member at an annual salary of $3,000. Compared with Washington's $25,000 annual salary, cabinet officers' salaries were quite low.

Establishing salaries for members of the top echelon of presidential aides and the executive branch has always posed special problems for lawmakers. On the one hand, there is the belief

TABLE 23–2 Executive Branch Salaries and Quadrennial Commission Recommendations

Position	1987 compensation	Quadrennial Commission recommendation	1988 actual	1996 actual
Executive Level I	$88,000	$155,000	$99,500	$148,400
Executive Level II	77,400	135,000	89,500	133,600
Executive Level III	75,800	125,000	82,500	123,100
Executive Level IV	74,500	120,000	80,700	115,700
Executive Level V	70,800	115,000	75,500	108,200

SOURCES: Quadrennial Commission on Executive, Legislative, and Judicial Salaries; Karen Riley, "Large Salary Increases Are Urged for Congress, Judges, Cabinet Officers," *Washington Times*, December 16, 1986; Barbara Vobejda, "Citizens Celebrate as Raise Collapses," *Washington Post*, February 8, 1989; Office of Personnel Management.

NOTE: Executive Level I comprises cabinet secretaries; Executive Level II, deputy secretaries and heads of offices and agencies; Executive Level III, under secretaries and chairs of regulatory commissions; Executive Level IV, assistant secretaries and members of regulatory commissions; Executive Level V, directors of major bureaus within the cabinet departments.

that top members of the executive branch should be the brightest and the best people available and that salaries for executive positions should be high enough to attract such people. On the other hand, many Americans are uneasy when their public servants earn more than they do. This is complicated by the fact that the issue of federal executive compensation often becomes a political football. As John W. Macy, Bruce Adams, and J. Jackson Walter observed in their study on appointing presidential aides, "Much as they may desire to set government salaries high enough to attract talented people into the public service, members of Congress are profoundly sensitive to the electoral backlash that federal pay policies can inspire."[29] As a consequence, the salaries of top-level executive branch staff are lower than the salaries of their private-sector counterparts; most key presidential aides could earn much more in private life. There are, however, other incentives for staying in public service.

STAFF AND AGENCY SALARIES

Congress, recognizing the political difficulties involved in raising federal pay to levels that would permit recruitment and retention of top-quality people, attempted to insulate salary increases from political pressures by passing the Postal Revenue and Federal Salary Act of 1967. The act created a nine-member Commission on Executive, Legislative, and Judicial Salaries. The president appointed three members of the commission, and the president pro tempore of the Senate (the presiding officer of the Senate in the absence of the vice president), the Speaker of the House, and the chief justice each appointed two members. Known as the Quadrennial Commission because it was to convene every fourth fiscal year, the commission reviewed the salaries of members of Congress, federal judges, and top officers of the executive branch covered under the Executive Schedule and made recommendations to the president. Under the provisions of the act, the president was free to revise the recommendations or submit them unchanged in the annual budget message to Congress. The president's recommendations became law automatically within thirty days unless both houses of Congress disapproved them or Congress submitted its own salary structure. In 1975 Congress enacted the Executive Salary Cost-of-Living Adjustment Act, which supplemented the Quadrennial Commission's work by providing cost-of-living adjustments during the interim period.

This system was not very successful, however, in keeping executive branch salaries competitive with private-sector salaries. Regardless of the recommendations of the Quadrennial Commission and cost-of-living adjustments, Congress was reluctant to increase federal executive pay. Much of the problem resulted from the practice begun in 1969 of linking salaries of executive officials to those of members of Congress. Macy, Adams, and Walter wrote,

Members of Congress always find it difficult to raise their own salaries, especially if an election is approaching. Nothing more clearly reflects this difficulty than the fact that congressional pay has been increased less than a dozen times in this century. As long as the linkage of executive and congressional salaries remains in effect, there appears little likelihood of establishing an executive compensation system that is objective and consistent.[30]

Federal executives received only a 5 percent raise from 1969 to 1976, and that came in 1975. Upon the recommendation of President Carter, Congress froze executive pay for 1978.

Even though White House aides and cabinet officers received small increases in pay after 1978, their salaries did not keep up with the cost of living. In December 1986 the Quadrennial Commission reported that the cost of living for the average citizen had risen more than 225 percent since 1969, resulting in a 40 percent decline in real earnings for senior government officials, whose salaries had not kept pace with inflation.[31] The commission recommended that top employees in all three branches of the federal government receive raises of as much as 60 to 80 percent. *(See Table 23-2.)* It argued that these increases were necessary to offset the prolonged erosion of top executives' earning power. President Reagan recommended to Congress that it raise salaries for his staff and other top officials in his administration, as well as for federal legislators and judges, from 2 to 16 percent. Even though some members of Congress attempted to kill the raises, they became law after the required thirty-day period had elapsed. Salaries of cabinet secretaries increased from $88,800 to $99,500; those of deputy cabinet secretaries and heads of government agencies increased from $81,100 to $89,500; and those of other top-level executives increased at comparable rates.

These raises met stiff opposition not only from Congress but from some consumer groups as well. In response to the raises, consumer advocate Ralph Nader wrote President Reagan and urged him to reconsider: "Nothing is more absurd in this perennial debate than the assertion by legislators, judges, and other government officials that they can't get by at salary plus benefit levels five times greater than what the average American worker receives."[32] In fact, the Office of Management and Budget estimated that each 10 percent increase in top officials' pay in all three branches of government would cost American taxpayers $100 million annually, when increased life insurance, pensions, Social Security, and the costs of severance pay were considered.

Before leaving office in January 1989 President Reagan accepted the Quadrennial Commission's recommendations that executive, legislative, and judicial salaries be raised by 51 percent to make up for the cost of inflation since 1969. The increase was voted down in the eleventh hour by both houses of Congress. Nader led citizens from around the country in protesting the recommendations of the commission. Rep. Jim Slattery (D-Kan.) argued that relying on the commission was an "abdication by Congress" of the responsibility for setting executive, legislative, and judicial salaries.[33]

Congress's failure to deal effectively with increasing executive, legislative, and judicial salaries led to the passage of the Ethics Reform Act of 1989 (103 Stat. 1716). The legislation contained pay raises of 7.9 to 9.9 percent for executive, legislative, and judicial officials in 1990 and raises of 25 percent in 1991. In addition, the act included provisions reforming the system by which federal salaries were to be determined. Under the new guidelines, the nine-member Quadrennial Commission that met every four years to recommend salary hikes for top federal officials was replaced by an eleven-member Citizens' Commission on Public Service on Compensation. (During its tenure, the Quadrennial Commission made recommendations for pay raises six times in twenty years, with increases going into effect three times.) The new Citizens Commission includes five people chosen by lot from voter registration lists from various regions of the country, two by the president, two by congressional leaders, and two by the judiciary.

The Citizens' Commission is to meet every four years and report its recommendations to the president by December 15. Presidents then must make their recommendations to Congress within the following thirty days. Congress must either approve or disapprove these recommendations. However, under the terms of the Ethics Reform Act of 1989 there must be an election of the House of Representatives before any approved increase in executive, legislative, and judicial salaries can go into effect. In addition, the act provided for automatic, annual cost-of-living adjustments (COLAs) for members of Congress and top executive officials of 0.5 percentage points less than the previous year's Economic Cost Index, which measures inflation of private industry salaries. A ceiling of 5 percent was set on annual COLAs.

Despite the increases implemented in 1990 and 1991, wages for most federal employees remained below those of private employees. In a 1991 wage study, the General Accounting Office found that federal white-collar jobs paid 6 to 39 percent less than the same jobs within the private sector, depending on the job and the area of the country where the government employee lived.[34] As of 1994, executive branch salaries had still not reached levels recommended by the 1986 Quadrennial Commission.

STAFF AND AGENCY PERQUISITES

Most White House aides and top executive branch officials could make more money in private business, but the prestige and fringe benefits of working in the White House are considerable. Senior White House aides not only share indirectly in the president's perquisites by accompanying him aboard *Air Force One,* they also have at their disposal a fleet of official aircraft and limousines. In addition, many aides eat in the White House mess and carry beepers that allow the White House switchboard to get in touch with them at all times. Most carry business cards with "The White House" inscribed on them.

The distribution of perquisites to White House aides and top executive officials is uneven. That is, which White House officials get what perquisites is left up to the president and, therefore, varies from administration to administration. At the discretion of the president, the Military Office at the White House controls access to perquisites such as *Air Force One,* the Marine

---

THE WHITE HOUSE MESS

One of the most valued of all perks enjoyed by the White House staff is the privilege of eating in the White House mess. Only a few of the president's top advisers, including cabinet secretaries and assistants and deputy assistants to the president, are accorded the prestige of the White House mess. (It is known by the naval term because it is run by the navy.) Although the basement room is well appointed—with seven tables, wood paneled walls adorned with pictures of navy carriers, and upholstered seats—the ultimate perk is coveted not for the room or the food but for the prestige.

When presidential aides arrive for lunch they are greeted at the door by a navy steward who knows their names and the tables where they like to sit. The president often eats lunch in the mess with his top aides. The meals are not lavish, but they are quite good. The menu changes daily. Thursday is Tex-Mex day; Friday is crabcake day. Both days are very popular. There is always fresh fish on the menu. The food is about 25 percent cheaper than what an aide would pay in a comparable restaurant in the Washington area. The mess keeps a monthly tab for its patrons.

SOURCE: Christopher Georges, "Executive Sweet," *Washington Monthly,* January–February 1993, 1.

Corps Helicopter Squadron, Camp David, the White House motor pool, the White House stewards, and the White House mess. Although these fringe benefits were meant for the comfort and convenience of the president, many staffers also have enjoyed these perquisites. Bill Gulley, former director of the Military Office, wrote,

The Military Office holds the White House perks, the status symbols, and staff members, high and low, devote more time and ingenuity to trying to get access to them than they do to high affairs of state. Literally. They impress the hell out of themselves and each other by getting the use of a White House car or a ride on *Air Force One.*[35]

The demand for White House perquisites always has been high, and often abused. For example, not only did Nixon White House and executive branch officials enjoy the comfort and convenience of *Air Force One* on trips to San Clemente and Key Biscayne, but many Nixon staffers were able to arrange for their wives and children also to have access to *Air Force One* on these trips. Senior White House aides on official business also may use the other military planes that are part of the presidential air fleet. The practice was rare until 1987, however, when Secretary of State George Shultz could not reach either national security adviser Frank Carlucci or chief of staff Howard Baker because they were on commercial flights. After that incident, President Reagan authorized the chief of staff and the national security adviser to make use of the air fleet. The practice was curtailed significantly in 1990, however, when Bush chief of staff John Sununu abused the privilege by taking seventy-seven flights. Under present guidelines, the White House Counsel must decide if a military plane is appropriate for any trip by a White House aide.

Access to official White House limousine service is another perquisite that has been widened by some administrations and curtailed by others, in response to the political climate and specific instances of abuse. Cordtz has reported that Nixon's press secretary, Ron Ziegler, while in Key Biscayne, Florida, would take his tennis partners to the courts in a Continental Mark IV rented by the government. During the Ford administration, Sheila Weidenfeld, press secretary for the first lady, continually badgered the Military Office for some of the same perquisites, including a chauffeur-driven limousine, that the president's press secretary, Ron Nessen, enjoyed.

President Carter objected to some staff members' using limousines to commute from home to work, so he cut back on the number of limousines available to staffers. Since 1986 only cabinet secretaries, deputy cabinet secretaries, the budget director, and up to six White House aides of the president's choosing have been permitted to use the presidential motor pool to take them home, known as portal-to-portal service. Bush limited portal-to-portal service to only four White House aides: chief of staff Sununu, chairman of the Council of Economic Advisers Michael Boskin, national security adviser Brent Scowcroft, and deputy national security adviser Robert Gates. Other presidential assistants and deputy assistants can continue to take advantage of the White House motor pool, however, to take them on trips for either official business or to social events such as lunches or dinner parties.

Although most staffers seek them, presidents differ in their generosity in allocating White House perquisites. In the Nixon White House, Chief of Staff H. R. Haldeman controlled the awarding of the most important perquisites, generally reserving them for those aides closest to the president. President Johnson enjoyed keeping a tight reign on White House perquisites. His administration kept track of staff violations of the use of presidential planes, automobiles, Camp David, the yacht, the White House mess, and special telephones and radios. President Carter also was dedicated to not allowing his staff to take advantage of government-funded perquisites of office. When Carter's secretary of state, Cyrus Vance, was working abroad on peace negotiations between Israel and Egypt, he wanted to fly back to the United States for his son's college graduation. When it was suggested that it would be easier and quicker to fly Vance back by military aircraft, Carter said no and made him fly back by commercial airline. Once, Secretary of Health, Education, and Welfare Joseph Califano had his driver drop his wife at the beauty shop. He was promptly called in and threatened with loss of his car privilege. Still, there is some evidence Carter allowed a double standard to exist in his administration. According to Gulley, "Family, or those close to it, were allowed advantages others weren't. During the transition, before Carter was even inaugurated, his son Chip and wife Caron, and their dog, lived in a government owned house in Lafayette Square, across from the White House."[36]

Early in his administration, President Bill Clinton faced a similar embarrassment over the abuse of White House perquisites. In May 1994, a Frederick, Maryland, newspaper ran a photograph of W. David Watkins, assistant to the president for administration and management, and two other aides dressed in casual clothes and carrying golf clubs, climbing into a presidential helicopter. Further embarrassing the administration, the photograph showed a marine in full dress uniform saluting the aides as they entered the helicopter. Clinton immediately asked for Watkins's resignation and requested that he pay for the cost of the trip—$13,129.66. When Watkins initially refused, other White House aides volunteered to chip in and cover the expenses. Watkins, however, eventually agreed to pay for the trip.[37]

Even though presidential perquisites have sometimes been abused by staff and family members, many of them are legitimate and serve the best interests of the country. For example, presidents must carry certain aides on cross-country trips and, as a matter of expediency, these staff members get to enjoy the luxury and comfort of *Air Force One.*

The most important perquisite that comes from working with the president has yet to be mentioned. Not only are White House aides and executive-level staffers provided with the perquisites that go along with the presidency, but by their association with the president they also have the biggest psychological fringe benefit of all—clout.

The Federal Civil Service System

The way presidents fill positions in the federal government has been a volatile issue throughout much of U.S. history. In the nineteenth century, most federal jobs were filled through patronage; that is, presidents awarded jobs to their supporters. Patronage, however, was a power shared with Congress. Although it had no constitutional mandate, Congress by the end of the nineteenth century was able to exert tremendous influence on presidential appointments. Under the patronage system, widespread turnover in jobs occurred after almost every presidential election. Employees who were qualified for specific jobs but were not of the president's political party had trouble finding positions with the government. Today, however, only a small percentage of federal employees—usually top-ranking policy makers—are replaced with each new administration. Most jobs in the federal government are filled through the competitive civil service and are awarded according to the competence of the applicant.

By any standard, the federal government has grown extremely large and complex since its early days. As the United States matured and expanded, the executive branch in general—and the presidency in particular—also grew. As the presidency itself expanded, the president's role in dispensing federal jobs for political loyalty became increasingly controversial. The civil service evolved to place executive branch employees under a merit system of appointment, making the federal government less susceptible to political manipulation.

The number of federal employees remained low and relatively stable until the early part of the twentieth century. The population of the United States at the time of George Washington's presidency was about three and a half million, just a little more than the number of civilian federal employees in the mid-1990s. At the beginning of Washington's administration, there were only nine employees in the State Department, fewer than 100 in the War Department, and only about 350 throughout the entire federal government. The largest department was the Post Office, with seventy-five offices throughout the nation. By the beginning of the nineteenth century, the number of executive branch employees had increased to about 2,100. At the time of the Civil War the federal government employed approximately 37,000 people, or about two-tenths of one percent of the population of 31 million. By 1900 the federal civil service comprised only 208,000 employees, or less than 0.3 percent of the population.

During and after World War I, however, the number of employees on the executive branch payroll began to expand more rapidly, reaching 570,000 by 1923. The years of the New Deal immediately following the depression saw a tremendous amount of growth in the number of federal employees, from 620,000 in 1933 to 1.3 million in 1939. Federal workers constituted 0.7 percent of the population of 130 million in 1939. By the end of World War II the number of employees in the federal civil service reached an all-time high of 3.8 million. Even after the massive war effort ended and federal employment declined, the number of federal workers remained high. In fact, political scientist Bruce D. Porter has argued that it is precisely because of American involvement in World Wars I and II and in the Korean and Vietnam Wars that the bureaucracy has expanded:

The principal cause of the expansion of the United States government has been the nation's involvement in four foreign wars in the twentieth century. This is true for the entire executive branch, not just for the defense-related sectors of the bureaucracy. Modern warfare requires national economic mobilization, and the non-defense bureaucracy must be enlarged to accomplish this task.... Following the wartime expansion of the bureaucracy, a "ratchet" effect comes into play and the bureaucracy retains much of its growth despite postwar layoffs. This ratchet effect occurs because Congress lacks the political will to force deep cutbacks.... Wartime gains in federal employment that are not trimmed within five years will generally become permanent.[38]

In 1994 the federal government comprised approximately 3 million civilian employees, most working under some type of merit protection. *(See Table 23-3.)*

Under the present civil service system most jobs are awarded according to the abilities of the applicants. Throughout much of U.S. history, however, the president (with the influence of Congress) had wide latitude in deciding which job seeker received which job. Many positions were awarded through patronage, the decisions based on the "spoils system" (from the maxim "To the victor belong the spoils"). In other words, until relatively recently, most presidents were able to offer federal government jobs as a reward for loyalty. From the beginning, however, Congress increasingly has exerted its influence in the appointment process. It was impossible for presidential administrations to know all office seekers. Consequently, as early as John Adams's administration it was accepted practice to consult with Congress on federal appointments.

In his book *Democracy and the Public Service,* Frederick C. Mosher divides the history of the growth of the merit system into six distinct stages. Each of these stages reflects the values held by both the public and the president during the evolution of the federal civil service.[39]

GOVERNMENT BY GENTLEMEN, 1789–1829

When George Washington became president in 1789, he had the opportunity to build an entirely new executive structure. The federal government under the Articles of Confederation had been small, and many government employees returned to private life when the new government was established. Washington was unique among U.S. presidents in that he had the chance to appoint a fresh slate of civil servants. Not surprisingly, many people attempted to influence his selection of employees. From the beginning of the nation's history, therefore, people seeking office for themselves or their friends tried to force their interests on the president.

In setting an early standard, Washington sought to nominate individuals to office on grounds of "fitness of character." He refused appointment even to many veterans of the Revolutionary War, arguing that past service did not outweigh the need for ex-

TABLE 23-3 Civilian Employees, Executive Branch, 1818–1994

Year	Number of employees	Year	Number of employees
1818	4,837	1962	2,514,197
1821	6,914	1963	2,527,960
1831	11,491	1964	2,500,503
1841	18,038	1965	2,527,915
1851	26,274	1966	2,759,019
1861	36,672	1967	3,002,461
1871	51,020	1968	3,055,212
1881	100,020	1969	3,076,414
1891	157,442	1970	2,981,574
1901	239,476	1971	2,883,000
1911	395,905	1972	2,823,000
1921	561,142	1973	2,775,000
1931	609,746	1974	2,847,000
1941	1,437,682	1975	2,848,000
1942	2,296,384	1976	2,832,000
1943	3,299,414	1977	2,789,000
1944	3,332,356	1978	2,820,000
1945	3,816,310	1979	2,823,000
1946	2,696,529	1980	2,821,000
1947	2,111,011	1981	2,806,000
1948	2,071,009	1982	2,768,000
1949	2,102,109	1983	2,819,000
1950	1,960,708	1984	2,854,000
1951	2,482,666	1985	2,964,000
1952	2,600,612	1986	2,967,000
1953	2,558,416	1987	3,030,000
1954	2,407,676	1988	3,054,000
1955	2,397,309	1989	3,064,000
1956	2,398,736	1990	3,067,000
1957	2,417,565	1991	3,048,000
1958	2,382,491	1992	3,020,000
1959	2,382,804	1993	2,946,000
1960	2,398,704	1994	2,908,000
1961	2,435,804		

SOURCES: Data 1818–1970 from *Historical Statistics, Colonial Times to 1970* (Washington, D.C.: Census Bureau, 1976); data 1971–1994 from Office of Management and Budget, *Budget of the United States, Fiscal Year 1996: Historical Tables* (Washington, D.C.: U.S. Government Printing Office, 1995), 245.

cellence in the job. He also did not allow kinship to be a reason for appointment.

Washington's idea of competence was not necessarily job related, however; that is, he did not always look for a person who possessed specific qualifications for a certain job. Instead, he was interested in the honesty and integrity of his appointees and in the loyalty of the individual to the new federal government. Technical expertise mattered much less than reputation. (Moreover, during this period of civil service history, few jobs required technical or specialized knowledge.) In creating this early form of merit, Washington also strove for equitable representation; that is, he made sure his principal appointments came from all regions of the country. Nonetheless, Washington appointed those who strongly supported the new federal form of government, creating a civil service that came from the elite of society—the well educated, well to do, and well respected.

As the first political parties began to develop in the 1790s, Washington began to make more partisan appointments. Early in his administration he had offered government positions to

some Anti-Federalists (members of the opposition party); but as the parties grew stronger, he came under increasing pressure to appoint members of his own political party, the Federalists. Nonetheless, historians generally agree that Washington took great effort to appoint a federal executive workforce that exhibited a high degree of competence.

Adams's administration moved further toward partisanship in the use of presidential appointments. Although Adams's conscience and personal honesty prevented him from using his patronage powers fully, his Federalist administration began increasingly to manipulate political appointments to maintain its partisan advantage. Civil service historian Paul P. Van Riper has written, "Adams normally tried to be above partisanship, but caught in the dilemma of conflict policies, his actions did not always match his ideals. . . . The trend was fairly clear. Appointments were more factional than under Washington."[40] When Thomas Jefferson came into office, many expected him to expand the base of political appointments because Jefferson, as a Democratic-Republican, had a sincere commitment to broadening the democratic foundation of government. Upon assuming office he found that Federalists held nearly every government position. In a letter to a friend Jefferson complained: "If a due participation of office is a matter of right, how are vacancies to be obtained? Those by death are few; by resignation none. Can any other mode than that of removal be proposed?"[41] Believing that his presidential election victory in 1800 was a mandate for change, Jefferson set out to achieve what political scientist Herbert Kaufman describes as a "balance between Republicans and Federalists in the civil service corresponding to their proportionate shares in the general population, which, once achieved, would allow him to make appointments purely on the basis of honesty, ability, and loyalty to the constitution."[42]

Jefferson used prudence in replacing employees. Although he did turn out some of the early Federalist appointees, he retained many more than he fired. During the course of his administration, however, Jefferson took the opportunity to fill many positions with Democratic-Republicans by either removing existing Federalist appointees or through attrition. By the end of his administration he had replaced almost half of the Senate-approved Federalist appointees. Significantly, he continued to fill vacancies in his administration from the elite of society.

During the twenty years after Jefferson's presidency the pattern of executive personnel appointments changed very little. Because presidents James Madison and James Monroe came from the same political party as Jefferson (the Democratic-Republican Party), they found little reason to replace existing employees. And as a matter of integrity and conscience, the sixth president, John Quincy Adams, did not significantly alter the civil service. As a result, from 1803 to 1828 the makeup of the civil service changed little.

In this forty-year period from 1789 to 1829 most government employees hired were from the elite. They were generally white, male, and from the upper class. This system of political appointment was initiated by Washington and practiced by both his Federalist and Democratic-Republican successors. It became the standard for this period—a pattern of filling positions on the basis of both character and competence.

GOVERNMENT BY THE COMMON MAN, 1829–1883

Andrew Jackson's inauguration as president in 1829 pushed the civil service into a new era. Although many people attribute the spoils system and its bleak consequences to Jackson, it is probably more accurate to say that Jackson's actions reflected his desire to democratize the American public service rather than a lack of commitment to merit. Whatever his intentions, he nonetheless was one of the most outspoken early American defenders of the spoils system.

In running for the presidency in 1828, Jackson appealed to many propertyless voters who recently had won the vote when property ownership was abolished as a voting requirement. Jackson promised civil service "reform" and stated that he would appoint "men whose diligence and talents will insure in their respective stations able and faithful cooperation."[43] And in his inaugural address, Jackson defended the practice of rotating federal employees in government jobs because, he said, the duties of public offices did not require any special abilities. Furthermore, he argued that no one had any intrinsic right to an official position.

Because Jackson had campaigned on a theme of reform, he felt the American people had voted for change when they elected him, and he did not intend to disappoint them. He instituted a large-scale system of spoils. Those who came from his own political party were awarded jobs. In this respect, Jackson's concern for competence was not as strong as his concern for loyalty.

Jackson is identified with the spoils system more because of what he said than what he did. The term *spoils system* did get its name during Jackson's administration, but not from Jackson. Sen. William L. Marcy of New York popularized the term in 1832 when he remarked that politicians "see nothing wrong in the rule, that to the victor belong the spoils of the enemy." Yet Jackson, under his method of dispensing spoils, removed only a few more persons from office than his predecessors had. He replaced 90 percent of the previous administration's top executive officers; Jefferson had replaced 80 percent. During his full eight years in office Jackson removed from the entire federal workforce only about one employee in five.

Just as Washington's initial system of hiring the competent elite had set a pattern for other administrations to follow, so did Jackson's egalitarian philosophy. Jackson's public advocacy of the spoils system made it easier for subsequent presidents to manipulate patronage to strengthen their political parties and gain congressional support for their programs. By appointing the friends and patrons of various members of Congress, presidents were able to trade patronage for congressional votes. Even though the opposition Whigs were extremely critical of the way Jackson and his successor, Martin Van Buren, used the appoint-

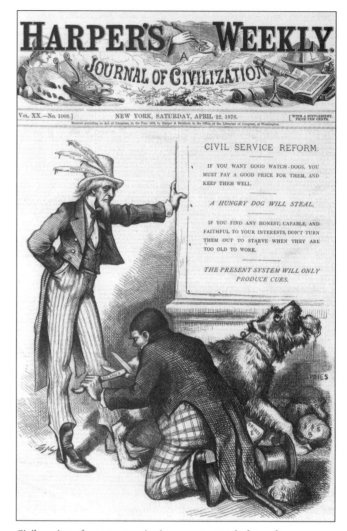

Civil service reform was a major issue many years before reform was enacted in 1883. In this 1876 cartoon, Uncle Sam criticizes the "Statesman" for not recognizing that low salaries and the spoils system are responsible for corruption among government employees.

ment power, they nonetheless employed the same tactics—although not to the same degree. Whig Party workers wanted political jobs just as much as the Jacksonian Democrats had. When William Henry Harrison, a Whig, assumed office in 1841, he faced the demands of an estimated thirty to forty thousand office seekers.

The pattern of removal and appointment of federal employees continued under succeeding presidents. As Kaufman has noted, up to the mid-1850s "every four years, with the regularity of tides, the civil service was swept nearly bare and restaffed."[44] The spoils system reached its peak during Abraham Lincoln's presidency. In 1861, in an effort to consolidate the federal government behind his program and the war effort, Lincoln made a more thorough house cleaning of federal employees than any president before him. In the higher levels of his administration, he replaced the employees in nearly every position with members of his party. Lincoln's use of patronage was not without purpose, however, for through it he skillfully won cooperation and concessions from a predominantly Republican Congress in managing the Civil War.

Although Jackson's open support of the spoils system had drawn widespread public attention, the subsequent problems and misbehavior of patronage appointees in the administrations of Andrew Johnson and Ulysses S. Grant attracted even more attention to the procedure. No real evidence exists that corruption in the civil service increased during and following Jackson's presidency, but the press had certainly begun to pay more attention to corruption and to the problems of the spoils system by the late 1860s. Van Riper has suggested that reform of the patronage system became part of a larger reform movement:

Not until the late eighteen sixties did reform become more than a dream. Then the powerful energies and ideals of the Anti-Slavery Society and similar organizations of the forties and fifties took up the cudgels. As the sixties moved into the seventies, civil service reform and its new generation of champions, along with other reform movements involving such things as money and the tariff, slowly but surely came to occupy a prominent place among the current political issues.[45]

Consequently, civil service reform became a popular concern among legislators and critics. By the time Ulysses S. Grant became president in 1869, a great deal of public disapproval surrounded the spoils system. In fact, the corrupt Grant administration did much to contribute to this public dissatisfaction. During Grant's presidency several top officials were found to be involved in various scandals, including kickbacks, land speculation, fraud, embezzlement, and tax evasion. Reformers argued that all of these problems could be traced directly to the spoils system. True or not, this argument gave conviction and determination to the reform movement beginning to take shape.

Ironically, one of the first attempts at reforming the spoils system occurred during the Grant administration. In 1871 President Grant sought relief from continuing and increasing pressure to appoint more of his supporters and successfully pushed Congress to pass a "rider" (a nongermane amendment) to an appropriations bill that would establish a system to promote efficiency and determine the fitness of candidates for public service. Under the authority of this law, Grant appointed the first U.S. Civil Service Commission, consisting of seven members, three of whom were full-time federal employees. In 1872 the Civil Service Commission conducted the first competitive examinations for entry into the federal workforce. In the following year, however, because President Grant continued to give in to the pressure of patronage and ignored the work of his own creation, Congress refused to continue funding the commission, and this first effort at reform was aborted in 1875.

Calls for civil service reform continued to be heard in Washington. President Rutherford B. Hayes, who succeeded Grant in 1877 and had campaigned on a reform-in-government Republican Party platform, also tried to promote a system of merit appointment. But because of opposition from the more conservative elements in his own party he, too, was unsuccessful. Hayes, like Grant, continued to use civil service appointments as a means of rewarding those who had helped him reach the presi-

dency. In the late 1870s, several civil service reform associations sprang up throughout the country. The first of these was the New York Civil Service Reform Association, founded in 1877. By 1881 the thirteen existing state reform associations merged to form the National Civil Service Reform League. Carefully judging the climate of opinion as not favorable to massive changes, the league pushed for very modest goals. The reformers were interested primarily in instituting minimal examinations for entry into some federal clerical jobs, limiting the president's ability to remove officeholders for political reasons, and prohibiting the custom of assessing party contributions on officeholders. Reformers remained unsuccessful in reaching any of these goals until Congress and the public were convinced that they were needed.

One small triumph for the reformers resulted from an initiative by President Hayes. Hayes requested that Dorman P. Eaton, an early reformer, prepare at his own expense two reports on the effects of two separate reform movements. One of the reports was on the British civil service, which in 1870 had created a system of competitive examinations covering most civil service positions. The second report concerned Hayes's efforts to institute competitive examinations in the New York City customhouse in 1879. Both reports showed that improvements had been achieved, which provided reformers with new ammunition.

The Garfield Assassination

Significant civil service reform did not occur, however, until after the assassination of President James A. Garfield. As a member of the House of Representatives, Garfield had supported civil service reform, so when he became president in 1881, reformers had high expectations that he would quickly institute meaningful changes in the system. But Garfield did not initiate reform immediately; the new president instead spent much of his time trying to satisfy literally thousands of demands for federal jobs by party workers who had helped him in the election. It is estimated that for every appointment Garfield was able to make, twenty office seekers were turned down.

Among those who did not receive an appointment was Charles J. Guiteau, who on July 2, 1881, shot Garfield in a Washington railroad station. After suffering for eleven weeks, Garfield died on September 19, 1881. Many saw the spoils system as the cause of his death. In 1880 Guiteau, a member of the Stalwart faction of the Republican Party, had supported the nomination of Grant to a third presidential term. When the nomination went instead to Garfield, the Republicans nominated Arthur, a Stalwart, for the vice presidency. Guiteau switched allegiances, worked for Garfield's election, and after the election moved to Washington expecting a position in Garfield's administration. Looking for an appointment as consul to Paris, Guiteau waited around the halls of the State Department and the White House and sent numerous letters to Garfield. Finally, in May 1881, he was met in the hall of the White House by Secretary of State James G. Blaine, who told Guiteau never to bother him again about the Paris consulship. Depressed and unemployed, Gui-

The assassination of President Garfield by a disgruntled office-seeker in 1881 spurred Congress to institute civil service reform.

teau decided to remove Garfield from the presidency and make way for Vice President Arthur to become president. When seized after shooting Garfield, Guiteau shouted, "I am a Stalwart; now Arthur is president!" The implication was that, with a member of his faction of the party in the White House, he would now get a federal job. At his trial Guiteau requested that all who had benefited politically from Garfield's assassination contribute to his defense fund.

Garfield's death provided the final impetus for civil service reform. Newspapers ran numerous editorials deploring Guiteau's actions and the spoils system in general. President Arthur himself began to support reform measures. Ironically, Garfield's greatest achievement as president may have been the result of his death. His assassination shocked the nation into taking action to eliminate abuses in the federal hiring system. As political scientist Robert S. Lorch has observed, "The bullet that killed Garfield also killed the federal spoils system."[46]

Civil Service Act of 1883

Meaningful civil service reform finally came on January 16, 1883, when President Arthur signed into law the Civil Service Act of 1883 (the Pendleton Act). *(See box, Civil Service Reforms, p. 979).* This act had been introduced in Congress by Sen. George H. Pendleton (D-Ohio) in 1880, but it was not until after Garfield's death that it finally gained enough momentum to become law. Inspired by the British civil service system, the reformers believed that power to make federal appointments had to be transferred from the president to a nonpolitical, neutral agency. Entitled "An Act to Regulate and Improve the Civil Service of the United States," the Pendleton Act created a bipartisan commission of three members to help the president make rules for filling government positions. The act required that govern-

ment employees be chosen "from among those graded highest" in competitive examinations. In addition, it prohibited assessments of federal employees for money to help party candidates.

Even though the Civil Service Act created a new system of appointing federal officeholders based on an equal chance for all to compete in job-related skills, the act did not immediately end the massive turnover of personnel at the end of each presidential administration. In fact, the act initially affected only about fourteen thousand positions, or 10.5 percent of federal employees. Under the provisions of the act, however, the president could issue executive orders extending the coverage to other appointees. As succeeding presidents exercised their option to extend merit coverage, almost all federal employees eventually came under a merit system.

GOVERNMENT BY THE GOOD, 1883–1906

Passage of the Civil Service Act in 1883 brought about a new era in the administration of civil service jobs. It did not effect a complete change in the way that presidential appointments were made, but it did signal the beginning of a change in direction. The Civil Service Act actually built upon the tradition of egalitarianism and equal opportunity that prevailed during the earlier period of public employment. In other words, the authors of the act did not abandon the Jacksonian belief in widespread access to jobs in the federal administrative structure. Instead, they provided for "practical" entrance tests that would ensure that the applicants would be able to do their jobs. The framers of the act had no intention of filling federal positions with an "administrative class" specially educated to administer the government permanently.

The Civil Service Act placed the Civil Service Commission

CIVIL SERVICE REFORMS

With the passage of the Civil Service Act of 1883 (Pendleton Act), the executive branch experienced its most dramatic restructuring since George Washington first set up the federal bureaucracy. Known as the Magna Carta of civil service reform, the act:

• Created a bipartisan Civil Service Commission of three members appointed by the president with the consent of the Senate; members were subject to removal by the president at any time

• Gave the Civil Service Commission a mandate to prepare rules for the management of the competitive civil service, consisting of those federal employees who were under the rules and regulations of the commission

• Allowed the president to issue executive orders bringing positions into the competitive service that had previously been outside. It also allowed the president to remove any positions at any time from the competitive service

• Based entrance into the merit system on competitive examination

• Provided that examinations should test the practical skills required to do the job

• Allowed applicants, regardless of age, to enter into the competitive civil service at any rank or grade for which they were qualified

• Provided that competitive civil service employees could not be removed for refusing to contribute money or services to a political party

In 1978 Congress passed the Civil Service Reform Act. This act represented the major civil service reform effort of the twentieth century. The act became effective January 1, 1979, and incorporated a wide variety of provisions. The reform act:

• Created the Office of Personnel Management and the Merit Systems Protection Board, replacing the Civil Service Commission

• Delegated personnel management authority to agencies themselves

• Streamlined the process used to dismiss employees

• Strengthened procedures to protect whistle-blowers

• Established a comprehensive statutory framework for conducting labor-management relations

• Authorized a merit pay system for midlevel supervisors, based on performance rather than longevity

• Established a Senior Executive Service (SES) for top-level career decision-makers

• Required that objective and job-related performance standards be developed for members of the SES

• Enacted both a set of explicit merit principles and a statement of prohibited personnel practices

SOURCE: Adapted from George J. Gordon, *Public Administration in America* (New York: St. Martin's, 1992), 284.

within the executive branch. Specifically, the act allowed the president to use the commission to make rules and regulations governing the selection of personnel to fill executive positions. The president, with the advice and consent of the Senate, appointed the three-member commission. No more than two members of the commission could be from the same political party. The effect of the act, Kaufman maintains, was "to substitute the Commission for Congressional and party officials in providing appointment advice to the President and his department heads."[47] The act did not eliminate presidential influence on appointments covered by the Civil Service Act altogether. Presidents had influence on the commission itself just by their power to appoint and remove commission members. It was hoped, though, that the members of the commission would raise a loud enough public cry to embarrass any president who tried to bypass their efforts.

Although the framers of the act were sincere in their desire to provide an effective mechanism for civil service reform, they initially failed to provide sufficient funding for the commission. They gave very little consideration to funding a staff for the three commissioners apart from the secretary, stenographer, messenger, and chief examiner provided for in the act. By omitting provisions for any further staffing, the act implied that employees of other federal agencies would perform many of the duties of the commission. Through the years this dependency on other agencies threatened to compromise the commission's neutrality. By 1890, the commission, dissatisfied with its lack of personnel, began to submit requests for an expanded staff.

The merit system under the new Civil Service Commission experienced slow but steady growth. Although they faced a real challenge in increasing the number of employees in the competitive system, the reformers were generally successful. In an effort to reduce the remaining effects of patronage, reformers put pressure on presidents and Congress to bring as many federal employees as possible under the jurisdiction of the commission. A major obstacle was persuading presidents to increase equitably the number of employees in the "classified civil service," that is, federal jobs that can be entered only by competitive examinations. The Pendleton Act originally placed only clerical and technical employees under the protection of the civil service. As subsequent presidents increased the number of positions to be classified as civil service positions, they tended not only to increase the number of clerical positions under civil service but also to place more and more policy-making positions under civil service shortly before they left office. Since only new appointees had to take examinations, these presidents were able to "blanket in" their supporters.

When Grover Cleveland became president in 1885 he attempted to change the balance of federal workers to favor Democrats by firing Republicans, but made no effort to jeopardize the 10 percent of federal positions that were already classified. Only upon leaving office did he extend classification to positions that had not been competitive previously. This extension not only broadened the merit system but also blanketed in

Cleveland's political appointments, ensuring that whole agencies would be staffed with Democrats for some time to come. Cleveland's appointees were political; that is, they had not been required to take competitive examinations. Their successors, however, would have to take examinations.

When Benjamin Harrison assumed the presidency in 1889, he followed Cleveland's pattern by firing many opposition party federal workers, hiring members of his own party, and blanketing in many of his party before leaving office. He dismissed more than thirty-five thousand employees in the first year of his administration alone, appointing replacements from the Republican Party.

In 1893, when Cleveland became president for the second time, he once again appointed mostly partisans to fill executive offices. In 1896, at the end of his administration, he again blanketed in a large number of his appointees by increasing the classified civil service, this time by a full one-third. This extension brought to 85,000 the total number of competitive positions out of 205,000 in the entire civil service. Cleveland and Harrison had established a pattern of increasing the classified civil service, but at the same time protecting their own political employees. Patronage and merit had merged.

Even though many political employees were protected in their jobs through classification, the number of positions under the merit system increased through this process. By 1897 the newly inaugurated president, William McKinley, had the smallest percentage of patronage jobs to offer of any previous president. Some Republicans suggested that positions placed under the merit system by Cleveland be made political appointments again. But that became unnecessary when many new, unclassified jobs became available as the federal civil service expanded to conduct the Spanish-American War. This increase allowed McKinley to make many political appointments without taking many positions out of the classified category. McKinley's complaint that too many jobs had been classified during Cleveland's tenure led the Senate to conduct an investigation, after which it recommended that a substantial number of jobs be unclassified. Consequently, in 1899 McKinley removed more than nine thousand positions from the competitive service.

Several important civil service advances occurred during McKinley's presidency. McKinley strengthened the position of the competitive services by weakening the potential for political removals. He ordered that classified employees not be removed from office unless they had been given sufficient written notice of the charges against them and a chance to respond in writing to the accusations. In addition, McKinley, bowing to partisan Republican pressures for jobs, increased the number of competitive employees by blanketing in more than nineteen thousand positions. This increase brought the total number of federal employees covered by civil service to 41 percent. McKinley also extended the merit system to the newly acquired territories. "In the contest between spoils and merit," Kaufman has stated, "merit pushed steadily ahead."[48]

Theodore Roosevelt played a significant role in the growth of the merit system. President Harrison's appointment of Roosevelt as chairman of the Civil Service Commission in 1889 began a period of innovation and expansion for the merit service during which Roosevelt made major changes. He introduced a promotion system based on the efficiency records of the individual employee, instituted a program that systematized the hiring of workers in the navy yards, and successfully classified the Indian service, which had suffered through many patronage-related scandals.

After he became president in 1901, Roosevelt continued to be a friend to the merit system. He blanketed in to the classified services an additional thirty-five thousand jobs while he was president, making almost 64 percent of federal jobs merit positions. And because he was a Republican who succeeded a Republican, he felt no need to remove vast numbers of federal employees from office because of their political affiliations. Roosevelt therefore was able to effect many civil service improvements without the pressure and demands of patronage. In addition, he made procedural reforms that further strengthened the Civil Service Commission and its overall position within the federal system. Specifically, he defined the principles of removal by specifying the reasons for which an employee might be fired.

The main emphasis during the Government by the Good period was neutrality. The framers of the Civil Service Act and civil service reformers believed that the proper administration of government lay outside the sphere of politics. They felt that the administration of public duties should be apolitical; that is, it should not be manipulated by the partisan politics of either the White House or Congress. Consequently, reformers wanted the Civil Service Commission to be politically independent of both. At first, the commission did little more than screen applicants. Later, especially under the presidency of Roosevelt and with the advantage of greater funding, it began to play an increasingly important role in a broader range of personnel policy decisions. The main concern of the commission was to end corruption in the hiring practices of federal agencies. The power of political appointment—previously a common practice among presidents—came to be equated with corruption.

At all levels of government, morality became an increasingly important consideration in appointments for public service, and state and local governments came to regard the Civil Service Commission as a model of political neutrality for the management of personnel. The commission provided the buffer between the politics of the White House and of Congress and the appointment of federal employees. One way it did so was through its use of the "rule of three." Originally established under the Pendleton Act, the rule required that the commission provide a list of the three best-qualified candidates for a job and that the executive branch appoint one of these three. Because the commission could not make the actual choices but only offer advice in the form of a list of candidates, the rule ensured the commission's neutrality. The rule of three was passed on to state and local civil service organizations and became accepted practice to ensure the independence of their commissions as well.

GOVERNMENT BY THE EFFICIENT, 1906–1937

The principle of the separation of politics from personnel administration continued to be of primary importance during the fourth period of personnel administration, but a desire on the part of reformers to make government as efficient as possible exerted increasing influence. This desire stemmed mainly from developments in business administration, dominated during this period by the scientific management school. The main value of scientific management was efficiency, or doing the job with the least resources. According to political scientist Nicholas Henry, during this period efficiency became sufficiently integrated with the concept of neutrality to produce "a somewhat inconsistent but soothing amalgam of beliefs . . . that packed goodness, merit, morality, neutrality, and science into one conceptual lump."[49]

Specifically, during this stage in the development of the federal merit system the Civil Service Commission concentrated on classifying jobs that had a logical relationship to one another and on developing job descriptions for each position. In 1923 Congress passed the Classification Act, which guaranteed the principle of equal pay for equal work. This act allowed jobs to be defined by the responsibilities and qualifications necessary to carry them out. Also, the classification of positions made it possible for examinations to measure objectively the qualifications for a particular position. Merit was no longer based on the qualifications of honesty and general education but on an applicant's ability to perform a set of tasks well.

The overall effect of scientific management theory during this period was to depersonalize the civil service. Examinations were more objective, as were several other aspects of the federal personnel system. Training personnel in the specific knowledge and skills of a set of job classifications became an important function of the civil service. Also, efficiency ratings came into use as a better way to supervise and promote workers objectively. Central to all of these advances was the new system of classifying jobs according to content and requirements, which made it possible to be more objective about examining, training, and rating the performance of employees. This method of classification significantly reduced the president's direct influence in naming specific persons to federal jobs. And as succeeding presidents placed more and more jobs under the protection of civil service, partisan patronage continued to diminish.

Generally, presidents during this period treated the classified civil service favorably. Republican presidents had controlled the office for twelve years by the time another Republican, William Howard Taft, succeeded Theodore Roosevelt in 1909. Taft therefore was not inclined to effect large-scale turnover in the positions that had not yet been classified. He added thirty-nine thousand positions to the classified service and vetoed a bill to limit the amount of time one could spend in the civil service to seven years. This bill would have reduced the overall level of experience in the civil service.

When Democratic president Woodrow Wilson took office in 1913 after sixteen years of Republican control, he faced tremendous pressure to clean house. The Democratic Party pushed for opportunities for patronage, and Wilson's supporters descended on Washington much as other job seekers had in previous years. Wilson acceded to some of the demands and exempted eight thousand internal revenue deputy collectorships from the classified service. But he opposed other attempts to increase patronage and actually contributed to the growth of the merit system. Before his election Wilson had been an enthusiastic supporter of civil service reform, serving as vice president of the National Civil Service Reform Association. As president he introduced several reform measures to make the civil service more impartial. Perhaps his greatest contribution was withstanding pressure from his party to take partisan advantage of World War I. As the war began to occupy more of the federal government's resources and energy, new agencies developed, and the number of federal employees increased. Resisting pressure to make these patronage positions, Wilson placed most of the new positions in the competitive service.

In 1921 Warren G. Harding, a Republican, confronted many of the same pressures Wilson had faced in succeeding a president of the opposing party. The Republicans were as hungry for patronage after eight years of Democratic Party control of the White House as the Democrats had been after the Republicans' sixteen years. Harding, however, was in a much more difficult position than Wilson. As the war machinery demobilized and there was no longer the need for as large a federal civil service, it became extremely difficult to satisfy Republican Party office seekers. As a result, Harding reversed some of the earlier reforms, exercising a small measure of patronage by dismissing some employees for rather peculiar reasons. In early 1922, for example, President Harding by executive order dismissed thirty-one employees in the Bureau of Printing and Engraving for reasons "of the service" and even abolished the positions themselves, later creating new positions and filling them with his own appointees.[50] Kaufman concluded that "the merit system did well to hold its own ground in this period."[51] Presidents Calvin Coolidge and Herbert Hoover treated the merit system more favorably. Together they classified about thirteen thousand positions during their tenures in office. More significantly, they were both committed to the concept of a competent and efficiently run government and thus did not allow the reduction of the federal workforce caused by the end of World War I to be accompanied by a corresponding reduction of the classified civil service. As a result, the percentage of classified jobs in relation to the entire number of federal jobs amounted to about 80 percent by 1924. Even though the civil service began to grow again by the end of the 1920s, enough of the new positions had been classified that by the end of Hoover's administration the percentage of merit employees remained approximately the same.

When Franklin D. Roosevelt became president in 1933, he faced some of the same demands for patronage as earlier presidents had. Once again Democrats were eager for patronage jobs after twelve years of Republican control of the White House. This time the Depression compounded the pressure for political appointments. With the unusual lack of private sector jobs, the prospect of public employment was especially appealing to Democratic Party loyalists. The security of jobs in the merit system, and what were regarded as outstanding benefits, such as sick leave, retirement pensions, and paid vacations, made it especially attractive to those seeking employment of any kind. In the face of this challenge, the future of the merit system seemed uncertain. But as before when under pressure, the merit system survived the demands placed upon it. Confronted with the economic disasters of the depression, Roosevelt inaugurated the most extensive peacetime program of public employment the country has ever known. Countless agencies, all needing staff, were created to handle the problems of the depression. Through these agencies Roosevelt undertook programs he judged indispensable for the well-being of the nation. At the same time, by not placing these new jobs under the authority of the Civil Service Commission, he was able to provide patronage positions to Democratic Party workers, an opportunity he would not have had otherwise. Without removing positions from the classified service, Roosevelt satisfied the pressure from his party for patronage. Because the federal government expanded dramatically, the percentage of jobs in the classified civil service was reduced temporarily to less than 61 percent in 1936. But this expansion laid the foundation for further growth in the merit system during the later years of the Roosevelt administration, when many of these new positions were eventually classified under civil service.

GOVERNMENT BY ADMINISTRATORS, 1937–1955

By 1937 the civil service had noticeably shifted its emphasis from efficiency to what Mosher labels "administration." This shift resulted from the depression and from Roosevelt's attempts to solve the ensuing problems of society and the economy. As the government grew larger in its efforts to solve these problems, there was more need for a strong and active administration. And as government assumed a more active role, public administrators (that is, civil servants) found themselves more involved in establishing policy.

Proper management of federal programs became a political objective in that many felt that the purposes of the programs were political. No longer was efficiency the primary consideration. Many now viewed politics as an essential element of the administration of the New Deal programs. Mosher has written, "More important than efficiency in carrying out given tasks were initiative, imagination, and energy in the pursuit of public purposes." Furthermore, those purposes were viewed as political, and "administrators charged with responsibility for them . . . had to be politically sensitive and knowledgeable."[52]

Two major reports prepared for two different presidents mark the beginning and end of this period. The first was the Brownlow Report, named after Louis Brownlow, chairman of President Roosevelt's Committee on Administrative Management. Roosevelt had formed the committee late in his first term to study reforms and reorganizations that would improve presidential management of the executive branch. The second report was prepared for President Dwight D. Eisenhower.

In January 1937 the Brownlow Committee issued its report, calling on the president to accept greater responsibility and authority in conducting the affairs of the executive branch. The committee interpreted executive power to include administrative power, which meant that the president should be involved in both the discharging of existing policies and the creating of new policies. Specifically, the commission called for the extension of the merit system "upward, outward, and downward." And it was critical of the Civil Service Commission's policy of encouraging a narrow, specialized federal workforce; it called instead for the hiring of administrators with broad, general skills. Overall, the aim of the Brownlow Report was to centralize the powers and responsibilities of the president, blurring the distinction between politics and administration that had previously been established by reformers most concerned with efficiency and the elimination of patronage.

President Roosevelt responded to the Brownlow Report in several ways. He began to take a more active role in the day-to-day administration of the federal bureaucracy, personally attending to such matters as directing the bureaucracy and defining more precisely the lines of authority. The effect of these reforms was to show that the administration of executive personnel was a function of the president's responsibility as chief administrator. Ultimately, the president's personal involvement in running the government served to blend politics with administration of the bureaucracy.

The classified service continued to grow from 1937 to 1945. After President Roosevelt's initial problems of providing patronage to his Democratic supporters, the number of classified positions in the merit system soared to new heights. It became apparent to Roosevelt's administration that the complete success of New Deal programs depended upon their efficient administration. As the public began to rely more and more on relief programs, it also became concerned with their administration. As a result, interest in civil service reform increased. During World War II the whole federal government had to mobilize, so figures from this period are distorted; but by 1948, 83.7 percent of all civil service employees were in classified positions.

Roosevelt's extension of merit had a twofold purpose, however. Not only did he attempt to increase the efficiency of New Deal programs by putting a large number of positions in the protected category, he also intentionally blanketed in thousands of Democrats who had been placed in their jobs through patronage. Roosevelt's moves caused Republicans a great deal of concern. If they opposed him, they would open themselves to the charge of opposing the merit system itself. Their only option was to wait for a new Republican administration and face the problem then.

As more FDR Democrats were blanketed in, many reformers

HATCH ACT RESTRICTIONS ON FEDERAL EMPLOYEES

The Act to Prevent Pernicious Political Activities (the Hatch Act) was enacted in 1939 to protect the political neutrality of the federal civil service. The act placed limits on the partisan political activities of federal employees and empowered the Civil Service Commission to enforce the act. At the same time, the act protected federal employees by making it illegal for their superiors to demand partisan political actions—such as donations to political campaigns—on the part of subordinates.

Critics of the act have charged that the limitations it imposes on political activity infringe the First Amendment rights of federal employees, but the Supreme Court has upheld the act more than once. In *United Public Workers v. Mitchell* (1947) and *United States Civil Service Commission v. National Association of Letter Carriers* (1973), the Court ruled that Congress had a compelling reason to pass the act despite the infringement of employees' rights.

Critics also objected that it was vaguely worded, often leaving federal workers to guess whether a particular action was legal, and unnecessarily stringent. Many contended that restrictions on political activity by federal employees could be relaxed without undermining the spirit or intent of the act.

Congress, in response, amended the Hatch Act with the Federal Employees Political Activities Act of 1993. This act spelled out in greater detail which activities were legal and which were not. Overall, it tightened on-the-job restrictions and eased off-duty limits on political activity. Employees, for example, cannot wear campaign buttons at work, a form of political expression permitted under the original Hatch Act. While not at work, however, they can hold office in a political party, participate in political campaigns and rallies, and endorse candidates. Running for partisan elective offices or soliciting contributions from the general public continue to be banned under the new law. Specifically, federal employees may:

• Register and vote as they choose
• Be candidates for public office in nonpartisan elections
• Assist in voter registration drives
• Express opinions about candidates and issues
• Contribute money to political organizations and attend fundraising functions
• Be an active member of a political party or club
• Hold office in a political party or club
• Campaign for or against candidates in partisan elections
• Campaign for or against referendum questions, constitutional amendments, or municipal ordinances
• Attend and be active at political rallies
• Distribute campaign literature in partisan elections
• Make campaign speeches for candidates in partisan elections

Employees may not:
• Use their official authority or influence to interfere with an election
• Solicit political contributions unless both individuals are members of the same federal labor organization or employee organization and the one solicited is not a subordinate employee
• Engage in political activity while on duty
• Knowingly solicit or discourage the political activity of anyone with business before the employee's agency
• Engage in political activity while wearing an official uniform
• Engage in political activity while using a government vehicle
• Solicit political contributions from the general public
• Be candidates for public office in partisan elections
• Wear a political campaign button while on the job

SOURCE: Adapted from "Hatch Act Provisions," *1993 CQ Almanac* (Washington, D.C.: Congressional Quarterly, 1994), 203–204.

---

became concerned that the principle of political neutrality would be violated. Since the majority of those who worked in federal agencies owed their jobs to FDR and the Democratic Party, it seemed normal for them to campaign for the Democratic Party. In the election of 1938, however, a coalition of Republicans and conservative Democrats won control of Congress and passed the Act to Prevent Pernicious Political Activities of 1939, known as the Hatch Act. The original Hatch Act prohibited federal workers from taking an active role in the political management of campaigns.[53] Federal workers could vote, attend political rallies, and talk privately about politics. But they were prohibited from participating in partisan voter registration drives, endorsing candidates, or working for or against a candidate in any way. In addition, the Hatch Act made illegal the use of rank to force federal employees to support certain candidates or to make political contributions.

When Truman became president in 1945 he faced very little demand for patronage jobs; the Democrats had been in control

of the executive branch since 1933. Between 1946 and 1951 Truman blanketed in another thirty-five thousand jobs, bringing the percentage of executive branch jobs in the classified service to 87 percent. Even though the percentage went down during the Korean War as emergency agencies were created to handle the pressures of the war, it once again climbed to the prewar figure as more wartime-related jobs were classified.

Not surprisingly, Republican president Dwight D. Eisenhower faced patronage problems when he took office in 1953, for the presidency had been controlled by Democrats since 1933. No president since McKinley had as few patronage positions to distribute as he did, and never before had so many workers from the opposition party been locked into their jobs. Many Republicans wanted government jobs, yet very few jobs were available. Eisenhower ultimately resorted to a technique used many times by presidents before him. He unclassified a large number of jobs that had originally been filled on a noncompetitive basis and then been put under merit protection. Because previous Democratic administrations had blanketed in so many positions that only about 15,000 employees were immediately open to removal for political purposes, the Eisenhower administration felt justified in unclassifying some positions. On March 31, 1953, Eisenhower canceled civil service removal protection for 134,000 full-time positions. Half of this number, however, retained removal protection through the Veteran's Preference Act of 1944, and 68,000 were positions overseas not usually subject to patronage. Van Riper estimated that all in all only about 30,000 positions were affected.[54] Although he did not engage in a wholesale housecleaning, Eisenhower's unclassifications were a setback for the merit system and caused debate among reformers.

The second major report of this period was prepared by President Eisenhower's Commission on Organization of the Executive Branch of Government, chaired by former president Hoover and known as the Hoover Commission. This commission was to look at administrative problems unique to the transition of presidential power from Truman to Eisenhower. The federal government had grown tremendously between 1933—when Hoover, the last Republican president, left office—and 1953, the year Eisenhower was inaugurated. After twenty years of Democratic domination, few Republicans had experience in federal government.

Further confusing matters for Republicans was that Democrats held many of the important policy positions, and they were protected from dismissal by civil service regulations on neutrality. Thus, Eisenhower's transition to power was complicated by the problem of making a largely Democratic federal bureaucracy responsive to the policies of a new Republican administration. Conflicts existed between political appointees and career employees, or those whose activities the new political appointees would oversee. Many newcomers doubted that career officers would change their goals for the new administration. Mosher writes, "Some feared, and may have even experienced, sabotage in the carrying out of the changed policies." The Eisenhower administration recognized that "some protected civil servants were in positions which could influence effective public policy."[55]

In an early attempt to ensure that the bureaucracy's goals were the same as those of his administration, Eisenhower created a section of the federal service called "Schedule C" by executive order on March 31, 1953. Schedule C was composed of fifteen hundred confidential or policy-determining positions, which for political reasons Eisenhower and the Civil Service Commission felt should be exempt from merit testing and qualifications and made subject to direct appointment by the president. (Every four years, just after a presidential election, either the House or Senate committee of jurisdiction publishes a list of federal positions that may be subject to noncompetitive appointment, including Schedule C appointments; formally titled *United States Government Policy and Supporting Positions,* the list is known among Washingtonians as the "plum book.") Although the move was controversial because it involved Eisenhower's attempt to gain control of the federal bureaucracy by staffing it with his own appointees, it nonetheless was considered a reasonable effort to define the relationship between an administration's chief policy makers and career bureaucrats.

In 1955, after two years of deliberation, the Hoover Commission delivered its report, which included a sweeping analysis of the relations between political appointees and career administrators. One of the specific recommendations for smoothing relations between these two groups was the creation of a "Senior Civil Service." The Senior Civil Service would comprise politically neutral employees with particular skills and competencies who could be transferred to similar jobs in different agencies. The creation of a Senior Civil Service would place more importance on managerial ability than on the specific requirements of a position. Although this recommendation was not incorporated into the civil service, the Hoover Commission did spawn the modern idea that high-level civil service employees should be capable of being transferred from one agency to another. In addition, the commission's suggestion of a Senior Civil Service generally endorsed the distinction between career bureaucrats and political employees made by the Eisenhower administration's creation of Schedule C.

Schedule C epitomized this period. It answered the complaints of the Eisenhower administration about executive control of the bureaucracy. As the Brownlow Report and the Hoover Report both pointed out, the need existed for presidents to exert more control over the bureaucracy. Consequently, administration became a more important part of the chief executive's duties. Thus, centralization of power in the president and the emergence of a new genre of civil servants were trademarks of this period. Both innovations allowed the president to take a more active role in managing the federal bureaucracy.

GOVERNMENT BY PROFESSIONALS, 1955 TO THE PRESENT

In 1955 the civil service started requiring applicants to take the Federal Service Entrance Exam (FSEE). This exam had several important objectives. First, it served as a single point of entry to the civil service system. Applicants could take a standard examination that could be used as a core of information for personnel decisions. Second, the common entrance examination made it easier to move employees from one agency to another. When each agency had its own entrance qualifications and examinations, it was difficult to foster an environment in which broad, general skills were encouraged. Third, the FSEE made recruiting more efficient. Recruiters from the Civil Service Commission could visit college and university campuses and offer potential applicants a standardized examination that required no special skills to take.

By placing a premium on professional skills, the FSEE marked another change in emphasis in the federal civil service. Professionalism became a major concern among reformers who desired that the civil service be run as effectively as possible. As professionalism increased in the business community, so too did it grow in the federal government. Consequently, since 1955 the federal government has hired more professionally trained personnel than ever before—military officers who have entered the civil service, those who have trained to become Foreign Service officers, civil engineers, physicians, educators, lawyers, foresters, and scientists from almost all disciplines. In addition, several new professions centered on government service have developed during this period, including penologists, recreation specialists, environmental specialists, public health professionals, and employment security officers.

Professionalism has had broad implications for the civil service. According to political scientist George J. Gordon, it has caused the civil service to shift its emphasis from the job itself to the people filling the job. Previously, reformers had expended much effort to classify administrative positions by functions and responsibilities and to develop the mechanisms—such as competitive examinations—necessary to fill those jobs through merit (that is, through job competence). Since 1955, professionalism, and its emphasis on the career needs of people filling government positions, has challenged the egalitarian tradition of the merit system.[56]

Professionalism nurtures a career-oriented system that tends to be somewhat elitist since it places a greater emphasis on the person than on the position. Henry has drawn a distinction between the civil service system and the "career system." He writes, "where what one does in a job is of paramount importance in the civil service system, how one does it is of major significance in the career system." Furthermore, "where neutral and autonomous control of the entire public personnel system is valued by the civil service system, planned and autonomous control of the individual professional is the concern of the career system."[57] This means that in the most recent period of federal government employment, professional methods and standards of behavior have been emphasized over merit and autonomy. In other words, the trend among federal employees is to look not at the civil service job but at the specific profession of the employee. For example, since the 1960s federal agencies have increasingly relied on graduates of government-focused higher education programs, such as criminal justice and public administration, to fill such jobs as police officers, assessors, penologists, and purchasing experts.

Since the mid-1970s, in a reflection of the demand for professionally trained employees, the Civil Service Commission and Office of Personnel Management (OPM) have exempted more than ninety professions from their oversight and have established separate salary schedules in designated personnel grades for certain professionals. The creation in 1974 of the Professional and Administrative Career Examination (PACE) to replace the FSEE also reflected the growth of professionalism in the civil service. Rather than measuring only the general education and background of applicants, PACE was designed to assess the professional training of prospective employees. Accessible to college graduates who majored in almost any field, PACE examined applicants for federal government careers rather than for specific jobs. In 1981 OPM dropped PACE for administrative

'Go through this door, take a left, then a right, then a left, a right, a left, another left, a right . . .'

generalists because minority group advocates argued that it tended to institutionalize racism by stressing education that only middle-class whites would possess.

During the 1980s OPM shifted the focus of entry-level hiring away from a single entry point by developing several new agency-level examinations to replace more than half of the old PACE positions. Addressing concerns that such agency-specific hiring processes detracted from the idea of a professional core of highly skilled merit workers, OPM finally introduced a replacement evaluation process for PACE in 1990, called Administrative Careers with America (ACWA). ACWA attempted to avoid the problems of PACE, which was accused of too narrowly measuring educational skills. Using methods to test both job specific skills and a potential employee's academic and work accomplishments, ACWA is based on what OPM calls the "whole person approach."

Merit and Responsiveness to Presidential Direction

In addition to the growth of professionalism, the history of the civil service since the 1960s reflects a desire on the part of presidents and reformers both to make the civil service responsive to presidential direction and to continue it as a true merit system.

During this period opportunities for patronage continued to decline. In 1969 President Nixon issued an executive order that placed about 70,000 postmasters and rural letter carriers under the protection of the federal merit system. These positions had been considered the "last great pool of patronage." Since Nixon's action, presidents have had comparatively little patronage to dispense. In 1970 the Postal Reorganization Act removed more than 700,000 employees from the auspices of the Civil Service Commission and placed them under their own civil service system administered by the new United States Postal Service. As was true under the federal Civil Service Commission, political influence in appointments to the postal civil service is prohibited. Today, presidents still have approximately three thousand high-level policy positions, such as cabinet and subcabinet jobs, agency heads, and Executive Office of the President appointments, that they can fill through patronage, but they do not have the large number of low-level patronage posts earlier presidents had.

As patronage has declined, presidents of both parties have tried to make the civil service more responsive to the goals of their administrations. President Kennedy, for example, tried to become involved in the day-to-day direction and control of his administration by communicating his objectives to his top-level administrators. Frustrated by a continued lack of responsiveness among career bureaucrats, Kennedy finally complained that dealing with bureaucracies was like trying to nail jelly to the wall.

Nixon attempted to make his administration more responsive by devising ways of circumventing the merit system. Through the White House Personnel Office, Nixon directed that each department set up a special assistant to the secretary who would write a job description for job openings within the department. In order to circumvent civil service requirements, these job descriptions were written to fit particular persons the Nixon administration wanted in the position. In the *Federal Political Personnel Manual,* or the Malek Report, produced as an unofficial political "textbook" for departmental personnel offices, Nixon loyalists were told how to fake job descriptions and manipulate selection procedures to gain positions or promotions.

Although other presidents from time to time had been guilty of some of the same intrigues, no other president violated civil service regulations so boldly and on such a wide scale. This scheme initially gave Nixon some control over the civil service, but the Watergate scandal eventually loosened his grip. After Nixon resigned, the Civil Service Commission gave documented information to the House Committee on Post Office and Civil Service, which led to a House investigation of Nixon's civil service practices. The commission eventually pressured Nixon's successor, Gerald Ford, to strengthen merit procedures.

Civil Service Reform Act of 1978

The schizophrenic function of the Civil Service Commission, as both manager and watchdog of civil servants, led many reformers to demand that the functions of the commission be split into two separate agencies. Chief among the reformers was Sen. Joseph Clark (D-Pa.) who introduced a bill in the early 1960s to transfer most of the commission's staff and functions to an office of personnel management in the Executive Office of the President. This would have left the Civil Service Commission to function only as a watchdog of the merit system. Even though it received widespread support from political scientists and public administrators, Congress refused to pass the Clark bill.

By the late 1970s the political atmosphere was more conducive to the reforms Clark had called for more than a decade earlier. President Jimmy Carter oversaw the most sweeping reform of the civil service since 1883. The Civil Service Reform Act of 1978 (CSRA), primarily the work of Alan K. Campbell, head of the Civil Service Commission during the Carter administration, abolished the ninety-five-year-old commission. In its place the act set up the Office of Personnel Management and the Merit Systems Protection Board. Similar to Senator Clark's earlier bill, the CSRA recognized the conflict between the dual functions of personnel management and protection of employees against merit violations by setting up new administrative machinery to carry out these functions. One of the main goals of the CSRA was to increase presidential control of the bureaucracy by increasing the political responsiveness of top career civil servants. Civil service restructuring became effective on January 1, 1979.

Office of Personnel Management

The Office of Personnel Management was created as an independent executive agency and was made accountable for approximately 2.1 million out of 2.8 million federal civil service employees. The director of OPM is appointed by the president and confirmed by the Senate. OPM advises the president and agency managers on personnel policies and is generally responsible for providing guidelines for classifying positions, recruiting and examining applicants, and determining levels of compensation. Each of these functions plays a vital role in the civil service system today.

Classification. Each federal agency is responsible for classifying its own positions, but it follows specific OPM guidelines to maintain consistency in classifications from one agency to another. Many positions in different agencies entail similar duties and responsibilities, so these jobs are grouped into the same classification. This standardization allows the federal civil service to maintain a coherent personnel system for most of the executive branch and to follow uniform procedures for recruitment, examination, and pay.

OPM ensures this uniformity by classifying positions for most of the civil service within the General Schedule (GS). Positions are ranked according to their difficulty and are assigned a specific GS grade. Generally, GS-1 through GS-6 comprise lower-grade positions; GS-7 through GS-12, middle grade; GS-13 through GS-18, higher grade. Although many federal agencies have set up their own classification systems, they usually have based them on OPM's General Schedule. OPM also administers the Wage Grade for blue-collar positions. These standardized systems allow applicants to be sent to an agency that requires a job with skills that fit the applicants and salaries to be awarded by the standard of "equal pay for equal work."

Recruitment. OPM acts as a recruiting agency for the federal bureaucracy. Its primary tools for recruitment are the Federal Job Information Centers (FJICs) located throughout the country. The sole purpose of the FJICs is to provide information and application forms to anyone seeking federal employment. The

FEDERAL JOB INFORMATION AVAILABLE ONLINE

Federal job seekers have a new tool in their quest for employment: Internet sites and bulletin board systems (BBSs) that offer free federal job information. *(See also box, How to Get a Government Job; p. 1415.)*

Although several Internet sites and BBSs provide federal job information, the Federal Job Opportunity Board (FJOB) is the most important site. FJOB, which is operated by the Office of Personnel Management Staffing Service Center in Macon, Georgia, offers lists of federal job openings across the United States and overseas, information about how to apply for a federal job, the optional application form for federal employment, a list of Federal Job Information Centers, details about student work programs, and much more.

The lists of federal jobs are updated daily, Tuesday through Saturday, at 5:30 a.m. EST. Users can download the job files, which are divided by region and state, or search all of the job files online. The job files can be searched by series number or job title, and users can narrow their searches by specifying a state to search or a grade level.

For some jobs, the full text of the vacancy announcement is available on the board. For others, users can leave a message on the BBS requesting that the application materials be mailed to them.

The Federal Job Opportunity Board can be accessed through Telnet, FTP, or Dial-in:

To access Telnet: *fjob.mail.opm.gov*
To access FTP: *ftp.fjob.mail.opm.gov*
   Login: anonymous
   Password: your e-mail address
To access Dial-in: 912-757-3100
Voice: 912-757-3090

FJOB is available twenty-four hours a day except Monday from 2 a.m. to 4 a.m. EST and Tuesday through Saturday from 4:30 a.m. to 6 a.m. EST.

SOURCES: Bruce Maxwell, *How to Access the Government's Electronic Bulletin Boards: Washington Online*, 2d ed. (Washington, D.C.: Congressional Quarterly, 1995); Bruce Maxwell, *How to Access the Federal Government on the Internet: Washington Online*, 2d ed. (Washington, D.C.: Congressional Quarterly, 1996).

centers also send out information about federal jobs to college and university placement offices to recruit students for federal employment. When a job opens up in a federal agency, OPM applies the "rule of three" and refers a list of three eligible candidates to the agency. The agency has to hire someone from this list.

Examination. Almost 62 percent of all appointed federal officials are part of the competitive service. In other words, they have been appointed after they have satisfied the requirements of a written exam administered by OPM or have met certain selection criteria formulated by the hiring agency and approved by OPM. Most examinations are written and are designed to measure both aptitude and competence. Occasionally, consideration is given to education and experience, which sometimes substitute for taking an exam. For example, entry into the mid-level grades of the federal service (GS-9 through GS-12) is usually based upon the applicant's background and qualifications. An applicant's acceptance, however, into the civil service most often is based upon a combination of written and oral examinations and education and experience. OPM also uses a system of veteran's preference in which disabled veterans and certain members of their families may receive up to ten extra points on their examination scores; honorably discharged veterans receive five additional points. These additional points make it possible for a veteran to score as high as 110 on an exam.

The remaining 38 percent of the federal workforce constitute the excepted service, or those who do not come under the authority of OPM or under qualifications designed or approved by OPM. They have been excepted either by order of OPM or by federal statute. They include Post Office employees, agents of the Federal Bureau of Investigation, Foreign Service officers in the State Department, and Secret Service agents. Most of these positions are nonpartisan and are filled through merit systems independent of OPM. There are basically no differences between the excepted service and the competitive service in terms of salaries and personnel regulations. Less than 3 percent of the excepted employees are appointed on a basis other than, or in addition to, merit. These include presidential appointments (such as cabinet officers, judges, and ambassadors), Schedule C positions (policy-making positions), and noncareer executive assignments (high-ranking members of the civil service who are involved in high-level policy making, such as subcabinet positions). These three groups constitute the president's remaining patronage.

An additional part of the examination process is a personal investigation conducted by OPM of the reputation, character, and loyalty to the United States of those who apply for appointment to government positions. These investigations help OPM to enforce civil service regulations and, by evaluating qualifications, help to determine the suitability of applicants for positions that affect national security or entail professional skills. (If the job is a highly sensitive national security position, such as one on the National Security Council staff, the FBI may conduct the investigation.) In addition, new civil service employees must swear or affirm their allegiance to the Constitution of the United States and swear not to participate in a strike against the federal government or any agency of the government.

Compensation. About half of all federal workers are under the General Schedule for white-collar positions. These include administrative, technical, and clerical employees. Within this schedule, there are fifteen grades, or levels, and ten steps within each grade. *(See Table 23-4.)* Former grades sixteen to eighteen now make up the Senior Executive Service and are compensated by a different system. Each October the president may change the pay rate, corresponding to rate changes in the private sector for comparable jobs. Most federal employees not under the General Schedule fall under the Wage Grade schedule. These workers are paid the prevailing wage in their geographical location for the type of work they are doing. Most of these positions are skilled labor positions such as electricians, machinists, toolmakers, masons, welders, and painters. OPM periodically surveys standard rates for typical work in each geographic region.

Federal government employees at the GS-13, GS-14, or GS-15 level may be rewarded for meritorious service under the Merit Pay System. The amount of the salary increases for these grades depends entirely on performance appraisals. Unlike employees at lower grades, those at the GS-13 level and above do not advance through the grades on the basis of length of service and continued adequate performance. If performance appraisals are high enough, employees may receive raises that exceed those on the regular GS scale.

The compensation system for federal workers got its first real overhaul in twenty years when Congress passed the Federal Employees Pay Comparability Act of 1990. The act was intended to resolve gradually over a period of years the pay gap between federal white-collar workers and those who hold similar jobs with private employers. In a review conducted between June 1989 and February 1991, the General Accounting Office compared federal and private sector salaries of professional, administrative, technical, and clerical workers in twenty-two metropolitan areas. The pay deficit ranged from 6 percent in San Antonio, Texas, to 39 percent in San Francisco.[58] At the heart of the Federal Employees Pay Comparability Act is "locality pay," intended to bring salaries for federal jobs closer to those for comparable private-sector jobs in the same geographic area by providing raises which vary from locality to locality. The act established a formula by which federal workers would receive locality pay increases over a nine-year period beginning in 1994 until their salaries were within five percent of their private-sector counterparts.

Merit Systems Protection Board

Separate from OPM under the 1978 reform is the Merit Systems Protection Board (MSPB). This independent, quasi-judicial agency is really the successor agency to the Civil Service Commission. It has three members, serving nonrenewable, three-year terms. As with the old Civil Service Commission, no more than two of its members may be from the same political party. They are appointed by the president and confirmed by the Senate. MSPB has responsibility for hearing and adjudicating appeals of personnel actions taken by OPM. These cases may include removals, suspensions, demotions, denials of periodic pay raises, and merit system violations. In addition, MSPB has the authority to review rules and regulations issued by OPM to determine if they meet merit system standards.

MSPB was given authority to protect employee rights and to enforce provisions of the act that forbade certain personnel practices, including reprisals against "whistleblowers" (civil servants who expose possible wrongdoing). Under provisions of

TABLE 23–4 GS Ratings and Their Respective Minimum and Maximum Salaries, 1996

Ratings	Minimum salary in grade	Maximum salary in grade
GS-1	$12,384	$15,489
GS-2	13,923	17,519
GS-3	15,193	19,747
GS-4	17,055	22,176
GS-5	19,081	24,805
GS-6	21,269	27,650
GS-7	23,634	30,726
GS-8	26,175	34,032
GS-9	28,912	37,588
GS-10	31,839	41,388
GS-11	34,981	45,475
GS-12	41,926	54,508
GS-13	49,856	64,814
GS-14	58,915	76,591
GS-15	69,300	90,090

SOURCE: *Federal Register* (Washington, D.C.: U.S. Government Printing Office, January 3, 1996), 239, 246.

NOTE: There are ten "steps" within each pay grade. The minimum and maximum pay rates given above are, respectively, step 1 and step 10 in each grade. In January 1994 most general schedule employees began receiving "locality pay" as a salary supplement. Intended to reduce the discrepancy between federal and nonfederal rates of pay in designated geographical areas, locality pay is calculated as a percentage of salary, ranging from a low of 4.13 percent to a high of 9.4 percent. The figures above are the baseline salaries before locality pay is added.

the Civil Service Reform Act of 1978, the Office of Special Counsel (OSC) was set up within the MSPB to receive and investigate allegations of prohibited personnel practices and to recommend corrective action if there was evidence of a violation. These provisions put new force into the concept of a federal merit system and, simultaneously, eliminated the conflict that had existed within the old Civil Service Commission between its dual roles.

The Whistleblower Protection Act of 1989 separated the Office of Special Counsel from the MSPB but still allowed the OSC to bring violations before the board. The act was intended to insure the independence of the OSC and to reinvigorate the mandate of the OSC to protect whistleblowers.

Senior Executive Service

In addition to dividing the functions of the Civil Service Commission, the Civil Service Reform Act of 1978 included another important reform: it classified about eight thousand positions as the Senior Executive Service (SES). The second Hoover Commission had proposed this reform with the hope of creating a large pool of professionally mobile, all-purpose senior executives, ideally to serve three functions. First, these executives could be transferred with no loss of rank to agencies requiring their managerial skills. Second, top political executives who wanted to assemble their own management teams would have a pool of talent from which to choose. Third, this group of talented executives, ready to go anywhere on behalf of the president, would improve the quality of presidential management through collective responsiveness.[59]

SES was designed in part after the British civil service system, which traditionally has stressed general training and mobility over technical specialization. Senior executives who choose to join SES have less job security and are liable to being transferred from one organization to another. As a reward, however, they are eligible for substantial cash bonuses for superior service instead of automatic pay raises awarded for length of service. Theoretically, the federal administrators constituting SES will be more responsive and responsible to the president because the president will have more discretion in rewarding or removing them. Of those eligible to join SES (mostly administrators at the GS-16 through GS-18 levels), well over 90 percent have joined. Apparently, the enticement of financial rewards for merit performance has outweighed job security.

Bonuses for SES merit performance take several forms. Originally, as many as 50 percent of SES executives were eligible to earn performance bonuses of up to 20 percent of their base pay in the regular bonus system. Congress reduced that number to 25 percent of SES members, but the bonus system remains in effect today. In addition, SES members are eligible for two "presidential ranks": up to 1 percent of SES executives may earn the rank of Distinguished Executive, providing a $20,000 bonus; up to 5 percent may be awarded the rank of Meritorious Executive, which carries a $10,000 award.

The "Thickening" of the Federal Government

The reform effort during the "Government by Professionals" period was intended to make the bureaucracy not only more professional but more responsive to the president as well. Political scientist Paul C. Light argues that just the opposite occurred, however. Government actually became less responsive to presidential will during this period because it became more bloated. Light notes that between 1960 and 1992 the number of senior executives and political appointees in the executive branch increased from 451 to 2,393, up nearly 430 percent. In the Department of Agriculture alone, the number of high level positions shot up from 81 to 242. While the number of department secretaries increased from ten to only fourteen, deputy secretaries, under secretaries, deputy under secretaries, assistant secretaries, and deputy assistant secretaries flourished. This increase in the number of high level executives resulted in a proliferation of layers of executives at the top of the federal government. In 1960 there were seventeen layers of management in any given agency; in 1992, there were thirty-two.[60] Light calls this proliferation of management layers the "thickening" of government.

Thickening occurred in large part because of presidential attempts to professionalize the bureaucracy. Both the Brownlow Committee and Hoover Commission had backed increased presidential staff support to enhance the president's control of government. Political scientist Richard P. Nathan observes that in heeding the Brownlow and Hoover reports, presidents have created an "administrative presidency" by adding a multitude of handpicked, loyal aides throughout the upper levels of govern-

ment.[61] Although the goal was responsiveness, this proliferation of staff helped thicken the federal government.

Light found that Republican presidents tended to increase layers of government at the top, while Democrats tended to increase layers at the lower levels of the upper hierarchy, "where most policy gets delivered." Most Republican presidents have distrusted career bureaucrats, believing that civil servants could thwart their policy-making efforts. President Eisenhower, for example, followed Hoover Commission recommendations and increased levels of hierarchy in an effort to coordinate and control the executive branch, assuming that "more leaders equal more leadership." Given their view of the civil service as an ally, Democratic presidents have distributed most of the layers further down in the civil service system.[62]

One of the main culprits of thickening has been the Senior Executive Service. From 1988 to 1992, the number of SES appointees increased to just over 8,100, up 22 percent. The reason Congress created the SES was to provide a cadre of flexible generalists, ready to go anywhere in the bureaucracy on behalf of the president. According to Light, mobility has rarely characterized the SES. Members of the SES reach their positions through well-established career ladders in a single agency. Contrary to the intentions of the Civil Service Reform Act of 1978, the SES has become a haven for "home grown" specialists rather than professional generalists ready to move to a new agency at a moment's notice. Only one percent of the SES move from one agency to another in any given year. Light writes, "With the numbers and specialization rising, the career SES may have become a powerful force for thickening. If one becomes a member only through increasing experience, which is measured by progression through a series of specific job titles, the SES creates momentum for creation of those jobs."[63] Professionalism and responsiveness have given way to thickening.

Creating new positions is not especially expensive by federal budget standards. Once new positions are created, however, they almost always remain. Thickening makes it difficult for government to do its job by threatening organizational capability and accountability, distorting information reaching leaders, and making it more difficult to recruit and keep capable officials. Presidents are thwarted in their search for bureaucratic responsiveness and accountability. Light argues that thickening undermines the executive will. Presidents "must win with a secretary, who must win with a chief of staff, who must win with two deputy secretaries, who must win with four under deputy under secretaries. . . . Since in each game there is the potential for defeat, the risk of flawed implementation increases with each player added."[64]

NOTES

1. Ronald Kessler, *Inside the White House* (New York: Pocket Books, 1995), 8.

2. Dan Cordtz, "The Imperial Lifestyle of the U.S. President," *Fortune*, October 1973, 144; Christopher Georges, "Executive Sweet (White House Perks)," *Washington Monthly*, January–February 1993, 35.

3. Kessler, *Inside the White House*, 8.

4. Quoted in Joseph E. Kallenbach, *The American Chief Executive: The Presidency and the Governorship* (New York: Harper and Row, 1966), 196.

5. Robert Sherrill, *Why They Call It Politics*, 4th ed. (New York: Harcourt Brace Jovanovich, 1984), 14.

6. Quoted in Norine Dickson, *Patrick Henry: Patriot and Statesman* (Old Greenwich, Conn.: Devin-Adair, 1969), 345.

7. Alexander Hamilton, *Federalist* No. 67, in *The Federalist*, introduction by Edward Gaylord Bourne (New York: Tudor, 1937), ii, 30.

8. Quoted in Sherrill, *Why They Call It Politics*, 13.

9. Bill Gulley, with Mary Ellen Reese, *Breaking Cover* (New York: Simon and Schuster, 1980), 147.

10. Quoted in Tom Morganthau and Eleanor Clift, "Hail, Hail to the Chief," *Newsweek*, May 25, 1981, 44.

11. Kessler, *Inside the White House*, 197.

12. Jack Messmer and Ellen Messmer, "All the President's Planes," *Popular Mechanics*, February 1986, 164.

13. Patricia A. Avery, "Reagan White House Steps Up Social Pace," *U.S. News and World Report*, January 23, 1984, 54.

14. Fred Barnes, "How Special," *The New Republic*, March 21, 1994, 42.

15. J. Frank Diggs and Patricia A. Avery, "Reagan White House—Glitter and Grace," *U.S. News and World Report*, June 1, 1981, 43.

16. Kessler, *Inside the White House*, 52.

17. Sara Fritz and Patricia A. Avery, "Why They Call the White House a 'Gilded Cage,'" *U.S. News and World Report*, February 15, 1982, 50.

18. Kessler, *Inside the White House*, 76, 232.

19. Sherrill, *Why They Call It Politics*, 16–17.

20. "When Uncle Sam Turns Librarian," *U.S. News and World Report*, May 2, 1983, 24.

21. *Business Week*, June 28, 1993, 43.

22. Unlike his predecessors, President Ford showed a willingness to listen to Vice President Nelson Rockefeller. This elevated Rockefeller to a position of importance that other vice presidents had not enjoyed up to that time. Political scientist Paul C. Light has written, "Much of Ford's willingness came from circumstances surrounding Watergate. Rockefeller had a considerable store of political and policy resources, but he also brought legitimacy to an administration already weakened by the Nixon pardon" (Paul C. Light, *Vice-Presidential Power: Advice and Influence in the White House* [Baltimore: Johns Hopkins University Press, 1984], 162).

23. Ibid., 74–75.

24. Ibid., 123, 162–164.

25. Ibid., 122.

26. Ibid.

27. Gerald Ford, "On the Threshold of the White House," *Atlantic Monthly*, July 1974, 63.

28. Light, *Vice-Presidential Power*, 74.

29. John W. Macy, Bruce Adams, and J. Jackson Walter, *America's Unelected Government: Appointing the President's Team* (Cambridge, Mass.: Ballinger, 1983), 76.

30. Ibid., 80.

31. Bill Whalen, "Congress Figures a Pay Raise's Cost," *Insight/Washington Times*, February 2, 1987.

32. Quoted in Judith Havemann, "Top Salary of $135,000 Proposed," *Washington Post*, December 14, 1986.

33. Tom Kenworthy, "Pay Raise Debacle Poses Challenges for Congress," *Washington Post*, February 9, 1989, A21.

34. Doug McDaniel, "Uncle Sam's Workers Earn 6%–39% Less," *Indianapolis Star*, B2.

35. Gulley, *Breaking Cover*, 159.

36. Ibid., 276.

37. Kessler, *Inside the White House*, 184.

38. Bruce D. Porter, "Parkinson's Law Revisited: War and Growth of American Government," *Public Trust* (summer 1980): 44.

39. Frederick C. Mosher, *Democracy and the Public Service*, 2d ed. (New York: Oxford University Press, 1982), chaps. 3, 4.

40. Paul P. Van Riper, *History of the United States Civil Service* (Evanston, Ill.: Row, Peterson, 1958), 21.

41. Letter in Saul K. Padover, *The Complete Jefferson* (New York: Tudor, 1943), 518.

42. Herbert Kaufman, "The Growth of the Federal Personnel System," in *The Federal Government Service: Character, Prestige, and Problems* (New York: Columbia University, 1954), 23.

43. Quoted in James D. Richardson, *Messages and Papers of the Presidents*, vol. 2 (Washington, D.C.: Bureau of National Literature and Art, 1903), 438.

44. Kaufman, "Growth of the Federal Personnel System," 27.

45. Van Riper, *History of the Civil Service*, 63.

46. Robert S. Lorch, *Public Administration* (St. Paul, Minn.: West, 1978), 94.

47. Kaufman, "Growth of the Federal Personnel System," 35–37.

48. Ibid., 38.

49. Nicholas Henry, *Public Administration and Public Affairs* (Englewood Cliffs, N.J.: Prentice-Hall, 1975), 191.

50. Van Riper, *History of the Civil Service*, 207.

51. Kaufman, "Growth of the Federal Personnel System," 38.

52. Mosher, *Democracy and the Public Service*, 79–80.

53. A second Hatch Act, passed in 1940, extended the same restrictions to state and local employees whose salaries were funded at least in part by the federal government. The 1939 act is therefore sometimes referred to as the "first" or "original" Hatch Act.

54. Van Riper, *History of the Civil Service*, 497.

55. Mosher, *Democracy and the Public Service*, 85–86.

56. George J. Gordon, *Public Administration in America*, 2d ed. (New York: St. Martin's, 1982), 307.

57. Henry, *Public Administration and Public Affairs*, 197.

58. McDaniel, "Uncle Sam's Workers Earn 6%–39% Less."

59. G. Calvin Mackenzie, "The Paradox of Presidential Personnel Management," in Hugh Heclo and Lester M. Salamon, eds. *The Illusion of Presidential Government* (Boulder, Colo.: Westview, 1981), 130.

60. Paul C. Light, *Thickening Government: Federal Hierarchy and the Diffusion of Accountability* (Washington, D.C.: Brookings, 1995), 7.

61. Richard P. Nathan, *The Plot That Failed: Nixon and the Administrative Presidency* (New York: Wiley, 1975).

62. Light, *Thickening Government*, 30, 118.

63. Ibid., 55.

64. Ibid., 64.

SELECTED BIBLIOGRAPHY

Albertazzie, Ralph, and Jerald F. terHorst. *The Flying White House: The Story of Air Force One*. New York: Coward, McCann, and Geoghegan, 1979.

Avery, Patricia A. "Reagan White House Steps Up Social Pace." *U.S. News and World Report*. January 23, 1984.

Barnes, Fred. "All the President's Perks." *New Republic*. September 2, 1991.

———. "How Special." *New Republic*. March 21, 1994.

Collins, Herbert R. *Presidents on Wheels: The Complete Collection of Carriages and Automobiles Used by Our American Presidents*. Washington, D.C.: Acropolis Books, 1971.

Cordtz, Dan. "The Imperial Lifestyle of the U.S. President." *Fortune*. October 1973.

Dickson, Norine. *Patrick Henry: Patriot and Statesman*. Old Greenwich, Conn.: Devin-Adair, 1969.

Diggs, J. Frank, and Patricia A. Avery. "Reagan White House—Glitter and Grace." *U.S. News and World Report*. June 1, 1981.

Ford, Gerald. "On the Threshold of the White House." *Atlantic Monthly*. July 1974.

Fritz, Sara, and Patricia A. Avery. "Why They Call the White House a 'Gilded Cage.'" *U.S. News and World Report*. February 15, 1982.

Gordon, George J. *Public Administration in America*. 2d ed. New York: St. Martin's Press, 1982.

Gulley, Bill, with Mary Ellen Reese. *Breaking Cover.* New York: Simon and Schuster, 1980.

Hamilton, Alexander, John Jay, and James Madison. *The Federalist.* Introduction by Edward Gaylord Bourne. New York: Tudor, 1937.

Harvey, Donald R. *The Civil Service Commission.* New York: Praeger, 1970.

Havemann, Judith. "Top Salary of $135,000 Proposed." *Washington Post.* December 14, 1986.

Henry, Nicholas. *Public Administration and Public Affairs.* Englewood Cliffs, N.J.: Prentice-Hall, 1975.

"House Guards." *Time.* December 21, 1983.

Kaiser, Frederick M. *Presidential Protection: Assassinations, Assaults, and Secret Service Protective Procedures.* Washington, D.C.: Congressional Research Service, 1981.

Kallenbach, Joseph E. *The American Chief Executive: The Presidency and the Governorship.* New York: Harper and Row, 1966.

Kaufman, Herbert. "The Growth of the Federal Personnel System." In *The Federal Government Service: Character, Prestige, and Problems.* New York: Columbia University, 1954.

Kessler, Ronald. *Inside the White House.* New York: Pocket Books, 1995.

Kilian, Michael, and Arnold Sawislak. *Who Runs Washington?* New York: St. Martin's Press, 1982.

Lawford, Valentine. "The Presidential Yacht U.S.S. Sequoia." *Architectural Digest.* January 1983.

Light, Paul C. *Thickening Government: Federal Hierarchy and the Diffusion of Accountability.* Washington, D.C.: Brookings, 1995.

——. *Vice-Presidential Power: Advice and Influence in the White House.* Baltimore: Johns Hopkins University Press, 1984.

Lorch, Robert S. *Public Administration.* St. Paul, Minn.: West, 1978.

Macy, John W., Bruce Adams, and J. Jackson Walter. *America's Unelected Government: Appointing the President's Team.* Cambridge, Mass.: Ballinger, 1983.

Messmer, Jack, and Ellen Messmer. "All the President's Planes." *Popular Mechanics.* February 1986.

Morganthau, Tom, and Eleanor Clift. "Hail, Hail to the Chief." *Newsweek.* May 25, 1981.

Mosher, Frederick C. *Democracy and the Public Service.* 2d ed. New York: Oxford University Press, 1982.

Nathan, Richard P. *The Plot That Failed: Nixon and the Administrative Presidency.* New York: Wiley, 1975.

Parker, Nancy W. *The President's Car.* New York: Crowell, 1981.

Richardson, James D. *Messages and Papers of the Presidents.* 2 vols. Washington, D.C.: Bureau of National Literature and Art, 1903.

Rowan, Carl T., and David M. Mazie. "Shield against Assassins: The Secret Service." *Reader's Digest.* April 1982.

Shafritz, Jay M., Norma M. Riccucci, David H. Rosenbloom, and Albert C. Hyde. *Public Personnel in Government: Politics and Process.* 4th ed. New York: Marcel Delcher, 1991.

Sherrill, Robert. *Why They Call It Politics.* 4th ed. New York: Harcourt Brace Jovanovich, 1984.

Sidey, Hugh. "The Loftiest Chariot." *Time.* July 21, 1986.

Vivian, James F. *The President's Salary: A Study in Constitutional Declension, 1781–1990.* New York: Garland, 1993.

Whalen, Bill. "Congress Figures a Pay Raise's Cost." *Insight/Washington Times.* February 2, 1987.

"When Uncle Sam Turns Librarian." *U.S. News and World Report.* May 2, 1983.

CHAPTER 24

Daily Life of the President

BY STEPHEN L. ROBERTSON

ALTHOUGH IN THEORY just another citizen, the president does not live like one. The first family occupies the White House, a fully staffed, 132-room structure that combines personal living quarters and an office complex. Located at 1600 Pennsylvania Avenue in Washington, D.C., the Executive Mansion sits on an immaculate eighteen-acre estate, which is maintained by the National Park Service. Within its walls are thousands of beautiful items of furniture, art, china, and antiques, many of which are invaluable. Should the president or first lady not like the paintings on the walls, the National Gallery of Art will provide new ones.

White House Life

Newly elected presidents receive $50,000 to spend over the course of their presidency on redecorating the White House, which is repainted every four years at no extra charge. Because the redecorating allowance does not go very far, some presidents and first ladies, most recently Ronald and Nancy Reagan, have conducted campaigns to raise private funds and material donations, such as furniture, for the mansion. In addition to offices and the first family's living quarters, the Executive Mansion houses exercise rooms and recreational facilities for the president, who may invite guests or staff to use them as well. On the ground floor are an office for the president's physician and a small clinic with a staff of thirteen that is adequate for routine medical care. (Major or specialized treatment is available at one of Washington's hospitals.) There are also a dental clinic, a barbershop, a tailor's shop, a cafeteria, laundry rooms, a carpenter's shop, a machine shop, a painter's shop, and a bomb shelter. If the president needs a few moments with nature to meditate or clear his mind, just outside the mansion are grounds that hold the Rose Garden and the Jacqueline Kennedy Garden, where the chefs sometimes gather herbs to season the first family's meals.

PRESIDENTIAL PERQUISITES
AND EXPENSES

Since 1969 the president has drawn annually a salary of $200,000, a taxable expense account of $50,000, and a travel allowance of $100,000. In reality, because the president travels almost exclusively on government transportation, the cost of which is covered by government agencies such as the Department of Defense, most of the president's travel allowance is available for other uses. The president has access to more than a dozen limousines and cars—including an armor-plated limousine with a detachable roof—which are leased by the manufacturer to the government at a small fee. Family members and designated staff on official business may also use the cars, and up to six presidential assistants may be named to "portal to portal" privileges: being chauffeured from their home to the White House door. The president also may use a Marine Corps helicopter for short trips such as to Camp David, the presidential retreat in Maryland. (See also Chapter 23, Executive Branch Pay and Perquisites.)

For longer journeys, a small fleet of airplanes is available, including Air Force One, the primary jet, which was replaced during the administration of George Bush at a cost of $400 million. The new Air Force One is a modified Boeing 747 that can carry seventy passengers and has a special crew of twenty-three. It has comfortable compartments with desks, sofas, and beds, a presidential office, a conference room, a computer center, food service facilities, medical facilities (including an operating room for an emergency), and communications equipment, including eighty-five telephones and one fax machine, for constant access to the rest of the world. The president's family and invited guests also may fly on these official aircraft; however, unless they are on official business, they must pay their own way. By custom of the White House Military Office, which operates the aircraft, the fare is calculated at the commercial airlines' first-class rate plus one dollar. The cost of maintaining the plane is about $40,000 per hour.[1]

A flight with the president is an enormous status symbol, and one that is eagerly sought by almost everyone in the administration and in Congress. The new Air Force One was originally designed to hold up to 140 passengers, but it was scaled back because the Reagan administration (which ordered the jet) feared that a larger plane would enormously multiply the demands to hitch a ride with the president. Naturally, for a ride on Air Force One to be a status symbol, there needs to be proof of it:

Those who get a ride have a tangible way of letting folks know. They can swipe special M&Ms with the presidential seal and "Air Force One" on the box, then leave the candy in plain view at home or office. . . . In 1988 the White House contacted M&M—Mars Company and asked it to design a presidential candy box in time for Reagan's trip to the Moscow summit.[2]

Security and communications considerations dictate that the president use government transportation almost exclusively. The president's guardians, the Secret Service, have discouraged

Roving musicians entertain guests at a state dinner during the Bush administration.

the use of private transportation by the president since the Truman administration. When President Harry S. Truman's mother-in-law died, Truman, seeking privacy, wanted to return to his Missouri home on a commercial train, but the service refused to allow it.

The expenses incurred in operating the White House itself are paid by the government. For example, the electric bills, which can total more than $180,000 per year, are paid by the federal Treasury. Similarly, the White House telephone service, which operates through an in-house switchboard and is among the best in the world, is provided at no charge to the president. In 1994 operating expenses for the White House totaled $553,000.

Despite the lavish accommodations and generous perks that presidents receive, the many items that the government does not pay for can be a serious drain on the president's personal resources. As a general rule, personal items—toiletries, clothing, gifts, and so on—must be purchased by the president. The president also must absorb the cost of the food served to the first family and their personal guests, as well as the maintenance of personal items such as appliances and furniture that the first family brought to the White House.

A similar distinction exists in White House entertainment. The government will pay for official entertaining. The tab for a state dinner, for example, will be picked up by the State Department. For any strictly political functions the president's political party may help defray expenses. The cost of any other entertaining, however, such as receptions, dinners, recitals, or parties that are not directly connected to business on behalf of the U.S. government, is covered by the president. For example, a White House reception honoring a Nobel laureate or a party for thirty

members of Congress would be a private expense. Although a military band is always available, and many entertainers and performers gladly donate their time to the White House, the expense of entertaining easily can become quite high. During the administration of Lyndon B. Johnson, for example, entertainment bills were sometimes as much as $10,000 a month.[3] (See box, An Evening at the Clinton White House, p. 995.)

Despite the size of the president's salary and benefits, living in the White House is far from inexpensive, as first families learn to their dismay. Rosalynn Carter wrote of her shock when the food bill for her first ten days in the White House in 1977 came to $600.[4] Other first ladies have expressed similar feelings. Thus, they look for ways to economize: Bess Truman scrutinized every line of the budget, and Mamie Eisenhower searched newspaper advertisements for bargains. Lady Bird Johnson's cook sometimes made the round of supermarkets looking for specials. When Mrs. Johnson's daughter Luci once asked for a second dress to wear to a festival, the first lady, citing the budget, refused to buy it. Although most were fairly wealthy, each first lady has echoed Jacqueline Kennedy's orders to her staff: "I want you to run this place just like you'd run it for the chintziest president who ever lived."[5]

Some presidents take their desire to save money even further. For example, to symbolize his concern for economy in government, Lyndon Johnson constantly harassed staff and family alike to turn off the lights in the White House when they were not needed. The harassment continued until finally Johnson came home one night to a blacked-out White House; the only light in the entire mansion was a single candle on the table where his brother, Sam Houston Johnson, was writing. Other presidents have taken steps to save resources, if not actually

AN EVENING AT THE CLINTON WHITE HOUSE

An invitation to a White House state dinner—a black tie affair hosted by president and first lady for visiting heads of state—is one of the most prized in the capital. The invitees, who generally bring a spouse or guest, usually are a mix of top White House officials, senators and representatives (from both parties), prominent individuals with dealings with the invited nation, friends of the president, business leaders, and other celebrated Americans. For the February 1996 state dinner the Clintons hosted for French president Jacques Chirac and his wife, along with a handful of French ministers and dignitaries, top U.S. administration officials included the vice president, secretary of state, secretary of the Treasury, national security adviser, White House chief of staff, U.S. ambassador to the UN, and U.S. ambassador to France. There were also business and labor heads, such as Michael Eisner of the Disney Corporation, Randolph A. Hearst of Hearst Publications, and John Sweeney of the AFL-CIO. Celebrity guests included actress Candice Bergen, designer Oscar de la Renta, actor Michael Douglas, author John Grisham, cyclist Greg LeMond, actor Gregory Peck, architect I. M. Pei, and composer Stephen Sondheim.

When Bill and Hillary Clinton moved into the White House, they brought their own style of entertaining with them. Abandoning the heavier French style of cooking previous White House occupants preferred, the Clintons hired a new White House chef, Walter Scheb III, who sought a "healthier" American cuisine. Some food was baked rather than fried and some steamed rather than sautéed. Scheb explained, "If there is a way to get the fat out without making the taste or texture suffer, we do it."[1] At the 1996 state dinner for the French president, the White House served the following menu:

Lemon thyme lobster with roasted eggplant soup
Rack of lamb with winter fruit and pecans
Sweet potato puree, root vegetables
Tarragon huckleberry sauce
Layered artichoke, leek and herbed cheese with greens and endive balsamic dressing
Apple and cherry sherbert pyramid
Apple brandy sauce
Peanut butter truffles
White almond bark chocolate fudge

Three wines from California were served with dinner. The tables in the State Dining Room were set with the gold Eisenhower base plates with the Roosevelt china and Morgantown crystal used for service. For flatware, the Clintons were fond of using the White House's collection of vermeil, gilded pieces of solid silver that had not been used at state dinners since the Johnson administration. Following the dinner, opera singer Thomas Hampson entertained the guests with songs by Aaron Copeland, Stephen Collins Foster, and Richard Rodgers and Oscar Hammerstein.[2]

1. Marian Burros, "At Dinner: Hot Lights, Light Food," *New York Times,* September 28, 1994, A6.
2. The White House.

money. President Jimmy Carter tried to save energy by ordering all the White House thermostats turned down in the winter, and President Bill Clinton started recycling the family trash.

Purchases for the White House, including many of the president's personal wants, are made by the staff. For example, the first family's food is bought wholesale from selected stores (limited in number partly due to security). After the White House menu is fixed, government trucks visit the stores, where White House staff members and carefully screened store employees collect the food. Such purchases are paid with the president's personal check. Other types of purchases are made in a similar way.

It is rarely if ever possible for the president or the first lady to go on public shopping trips. As late as the 1920s Grace Coolidge shopped virtually unnoticed. On one such trip she even encountered another customer who told her that she resembled the first lady. Such informality rapidly disappeared, however. In 1945, Bess Truman drove herself around Washington, but she soon began to cause traffic jams and had to stop. More recently, in 1977, Rosalynn Carter tried to fly quietly on a commercial airliner to New York City to buy some clothes, only to find a mob of journalists waiting for her when she left the store. In December 1993 President Clinton created pandemonium at a nearby Washington, D.C., mall when he shopped for Christmas presents for his wife and daughter.

The Executive Mansion is fully staffed. The White House domestic staff has nearly one hundred permanent, full-time employees who remain from president to president and whose primary loyalty is to the presidency itself. Although this staff is not protected by civil service status, staffers are fired infrequently. Moreover, because jobs within the White House have a certain prestige, turnover is low. Accounts indicate that the staff takes great pride in serving the president. For example, when Lady Bird Johnson, aware of her husband's erratic working hours, encouraged the White House butlers to go home early, they refused to hear of it.

The most important member of the White House domestic staff is the chief usher. Responsible for the general operation of the White House, the chief usher manages the mansion's budget; hires, directs, and dismisses personnel; and oversees the various White House activities under way. Should the president or the first family want something done around the White House, they seek out the chief usher. Chief ushers have been charged with coordinating the mansion's redecoration, organizing a president's last-minute reception for hundreds of people, supervising a president's funeral, and even acquiring animals for the president's children. (See box, *Chief Usher of the White House, p. 996.*)

Below the chief usher is the large permanent White House workforce, including butlers, maids, cooks, operating engineers, electricians, carpenters, plumbers, painters, floral designers, and a seamstress. In the mid-1990s, staff salaries totaled $3.9 million. The staff is sufficiently diversified to handle most problems internally. On occasion in the past other government employees

CHIEF USHER OF THE WHITE HOUSE

The chief usher of the White House has one of the most varied jobs anywhere in the government, as seen in the following job description taken from the U.S. Civil Service Commission's position description form:

Subject only to the general direction of the President of the United States, serves as "Chief Usher" of the White House. As such is the general manager of the Executive Mansion, and is delegated full responsibility for directing the administrative, fiscal, and personnel functions involved in the management and operation of the Executive Mansion and grounds, including construction, maintenance, and remodeling of the Executive Mansion.

Is responsible for the preparation and justification of budget estimates covering administrative and operating expenses, and for the construction and maintenance projects of the Executive Mansion . . . , as well as for the allotment, control, and proper expenditure of funds appropriated for these purposes.

Is responsible for the direction and supervision of the activities of approximately one hundred employees of the President's household including their selection, appointment, placement, promotion, separation, disciplinary action, etc. In addition, exercises responsibility over the mechanical and maintenance forces in connection with the maintenance and repair of buildings and grounds.

Serves as the receptionist at the White House, and as such is responsible for receiving and caring for all personal and official guests calling on the President or the First Lady. These guests include, among others, members of the Congress and their families, members of the Judicial Branch, governors, foreign dignitaries, and heads of state. Is responsible for arranging for accommodations for house guests, their comfort, their acquaintance with customs of the household, etc. Is responsible and arranges for all personal and official entertainments, receptions, dinners, etc., in the Executive Mansion, which frequently include the heads of the sovereign states, and several hundred persons. Is responsible for the procurement of all food consumed by the President's family and their guests. Makes personal appointments for the President and other members of his official family.

Is responsible for answering a large volume of correspondence regarding the Executive Mansion, its history and furnishings, historical subjects, sightseeing, Congressional requests with regard to the Mansion and Grounds, State function, etc.

Is completely responsible for the efficient operation, cleanliness, and maintenance of the 132 rooms of the Executive Mansion containing 1,600,000 cubic feet. . . .[1]

1. J. B. West, *Upstairs at the White House: My Life with the First Ladies* (New York: Coward, McCann, and Geohegan, 1973), 10–11.

have been drafted to supplement the domestic staff. For example, when President Johnson, at the end of the period of mourning for John F. Kennedy, decided suddenly to invite the entire Congress to the White House for a Christmas party, additional government personnel had to be brought in to assist with the preparations. Such short-term borrowing is rare, however.

The first family is permitted to place a small number of personal servants on the government payroll. These employees, although paid temporarily by the government, are in fact distinct from the rest of the domestic staff. They are employed by the president and first lady and leave with them. Their pay is generally on a par with that of the permanent staff; some, however, may live in the White House itself and therefore draw a smaller salary. Included among such employees would be the president's valet(s), personal cook, and barber, and the first lady's personal secretary and maids.

THE PRESIDENT'S WORKDAY

The workload of the president has changed a great deal during the twentieth century. Although it is probably true, as George Reedy, Lyndon Johnson's press secretary, has said, that no president has ever died from overwork, the load certainly seems to have been much heavier after 1930 than before.

Before 1930 most presidents had a fairly light workload. Congress dominated American government, and the president was expected to do little. Indeed, the federal government as a whole was not expected to do much, for most government activities took place at the state and local levels. In general, people expected the federal government to take a hands-off attitude to most problems. Consequently, presidents did not have to work very long or hard.

In the 1800s a schedule such as Benjamin Harrison's was typical: arrive at the office around nine in the morning, work for two or three hours, and take the rest of the day off. Later, in 1905, Theodore Roosevelt disposed of government in the morning and devoted his afternoons to exercise and his evenings to reading. Calvin Coolidge spent fairly little time in his office from 1923 to 1929 because he felt the government should do little. There were exceptions—James K. Polk (1845–1849) worked so long and hard that he ruined his health and died three months after leaving the presidency at age fifty-three, thereby perhaps disproving Reedy's dictum. However, most presidents in the nineteenth and early twentieth century did not find the job terribly taxing. Fighting off the would-be officeholders was more demanding.

The presidential workload began to increase in the 1930s when problems arose that were beyond the capacities of the states. The Great Depression, followed by World War II, led to new expectations of the federal government, which increased its role in society and the economy with each passing year. Concurrently, people began to look to the president more than to Congress for direction and solutions. Just as the federal government was expected to solve the nation's problems, so the president was expected to lead the government. Longer presidential workdays were therefore inevitable. Herbert Hoover (1929–1933) spent many more hours in the Oval Office than most of his predecessors, and his successor, Franklin D. Roosevelt (1933–1945), spent all day at work, with brainstorming sessions often held over meals. Harry Truman (1945–1953) arose at five-thirty in the morning, exercised, had breakfast by eight o'clock, and went straight to work. Although he did not labor under the same pressures as Roosevelt, he worked a full day.

By 1952 the public viewed the presidency as a full-time job. Many Americans therefore found Dwight D. Eisenhower's approach to the job somewhat disconcerting. Relying on his extensive staff, Eisenhower (1953–1961) tried to return to the old work patterns. He concentrated his work into the mornings and tried to take afternoons off as much as possible. Unlike Roosevelt and Truman, Eisenhower avoided working on weekends. He argued that a rested president made better decisions than an overworked one, but not everyone agreed. He was criticized for the amount of time he spent playing golf, and a bumper sticker appeared, which read: "Ben Hogan for President. If We're Going to Have a Golfer, Let's Have a Good One."

For the most part John F. Kennedy (1961–1963) did not work long hours either. As a senator he had had a reputation as a four-day legislator; as president he consistently took weekends off. Kennedy worked through the morning, paused in the afternoon for a swim, lunch, and a nap, and then returned to the office for a time in the late afternoon.

Life under Lyndon Johnson (1963–1969) was not so relaxed.

A driven man who possessed almost superhuman energy, Johnson wanted to accomplish more than any other president and drove himself, and everyone else, accordingly. He arose early and held bedroom meetings with selected staff members; he then spent the morning in his office. After lunch he took a nap, on doctor's orders, from two to four. Thus refreshed, he started the day all over again, frequently working late into the night. It was not at all unusual for LBJ to hold staff meetings at nine or ten in the evening and to work until after midnight. He drove his staff as hard as himself, demanding that they be available at all times of the night and day.

Although Richard Nixon (1969–1974) was not as frantic as Johnson, he too worked long hours. He generally arose at seventhirty in the morning and was at his office by eight-thirty. Meetings began at nine and lasted throughout the morning. After a brief lunch, Nixon would resume work until early evening. A workday of ten to eleven hours, with perhaps an hour for lunch, was common. At times, Nixon would return to his office around nine in the evening to read and work another hour or two. He generally went to bed between midnight and one in the morning.

The habit of presidents working long days continued with

A PRESIDENT'S WORK SCHEDULE

The president of the United States is a very busy person, who may work from the dawn's early light to the twilight's last gleaming, and well beyond. The schedule that follows is a day (April 4, 1995) in the life of President Bill Clinton, who quickly earned a reputation as one of the most energetic and workaholic presidents. On the day chronicled here, Clinton began the morning jogging at the residence of his mother-in-law in Little Rock, Arkansas, where he had been making a brief weekend visit, before flying back to Washington, meeting with the visiting British prime minister, putting in office hours, attending an evening fund-raiser, and ending the night with the British prime minister at a Georgetown restaurant.

6:00 a.m. The president takes an early morning run in Little Rock, Arkansas.

7:00 a.m. The presidential motorcade departs Dorothy Rodham's residence en route to Adams Field near Little Rock.

7:30 a.m. The presidential party departs Adams Field via *Air Force One* en route Andrews Air Force Base, Maryland.

10:30 a.m. *Air Force One* lands at Andrews Air Force Base.

10:45 a.m. The president departs Andrews Air Force Base via the *Marine One* helicopter en route to the White House.

11:00 a.m. The president arrives at the White House.

11:10 a.m. In the Oval Office Clinton meets with Leon Panetta, White House chief of staff.

11:25 a.m. Clinton meets with Anthony Lake, national security adviser.

12:00 p.m. The president greets visiting British prime minister John Major.

12:05 p.m. The president and prime minister have a short private meeting.

12:30 p.m. The president and prime minister have lunch in the Old Family Dining Room.

1:30 p.m. The president and prime minister have an extended meeting with advisers in the Cabinet Room.

2:30 p.m. In the East Room the president and prime minister deliver prepared statements and answer press questions.

3:00 p.m. The president escorts the prime minister to the Blue Room before the prime minister departs the White House.

3:15 p.m. The president meets with Laura D'Andrea Tyson, chairwoman of the Council of Economic Advisers.

3:30 p.m. Clinton meets with presidential aide Billy Webster, director of scheduling.

3:40 p.m. The president meets with White House council, Abner Mikva.

4:00 p.m. Clinton meets with head speechwriter, Donald Baer, to go over the speech he is to give that night.

4:30 p.m. The president spends two more hours in the Oval Office, going over paperwork, making phone calls, and signing documents and letters.

7:00 p.m. The presidential motorcade departs the White House in twenty-minute drive to Sen. Edward Kennedy's home in northern Virginia for a fund-raiser.

8:30 p.m. The presidents dines and gives his speech.

10:00 p.m. On the drive back to Washington, the president makes an unannounced stop at a local restaurant to have dessert with Prime Minister Major and British ambassador Robin Renwick.

11:00 p.m. Clinton returns to the White House.

Gerald R. Ford (1974–1977) and Jimmy Carter (1977–1981), both of whom put in full days and not a few nights. By then it was believed that the president had to work twelve-hour days because the burdens of government were so great. One of Carter's commercials during his 1980 reelection campaign illustrated and played on that belief; it pictured a dark White House late at night, with a solitary light where Carter worked alone.

The workday of Ronald Reagan (1981–1989), in contrast, was usually over by four in the afternoon. He also generally took Wednesday and Friday afternoons off and took frequent vacations. Like Eisenhower, he did not care to immerse himself in details and thought he made better decisions with less work. However, by the 1980s the public had become accustomed to more workaholic presidents, and there was criticism from many quarters about Reagan's "banker's hours" approach to the presidency. It is worth noting, however, that even though Reagan had a shorter workday than his immediate predecessors, he labored longer than most presidents before 1930.

Reagan's successors, both more hands-on presidents, worked longer hours. For Bush, the workday began at about seven in the morning and lasted until six or six-thirty in the evening. He tried to take weekends off, generally preferring to leave Washington altogether. Clinton worked even more. A man who needed only about five hours sleep a night and who, in one associate's words, "works whenever he's awake," Clinton started his workday at seven in the morning after his jog and continued up to sometime between seven and ten at night. At times, he returned to the Oval Office even later to catch up on more work. He rarely took weekends off. Thus Saturday and Sunday became regular workdays at his White House. (*See box, A President's Work Schedule, p. 997.*)

Such workdays put enormous stress on the president's staff, who must work at least as long and hard as the president does. Bush's staff averaged between a fifty- and an eighty-hour workweek, frequently working from six in the morning until eight at night. Bush domestic policy adviser Roger B. Porter at one point was sleeping in his office during the week. For the Clinton staff, it was worse. Because the boss worked weekends, so did the staff, and so twelve to fifteen hours per day, seven days a week, was not an uncommon schedule. In addition, the president had an ambitious agenda, yet, to fulfill a campaign promise, had cut the size of his staff. Thus the demands became enormous. Of course, the Oval Office is only a one-minute walk from the Executive Mansion, and so the president can always retreat there to snatch a few minutes' respite during the busy day. White House staffers, most of whom average a forty-five-minute to an hour commute to the White House, have no such luxury.[6]

THE PRESIDENT'S RECREATION

With its long hours and psychological burden, the modern presidency is a stressful job. Consequently, rest and relaxation are important to the well-being of the president.

Among the recreational facilities available at the White House is a heated outdoor swimming pool, built with private funds by President Ford. The original White House swimming pool was built in 1933 with publicly donated funds for Franklin Roosevelt, who used it frequently, at least during his early years in office. Truman, Kennedy, and Johnson also used the pool often, but Eisenhower did not. Nixon later eliminated the pool to make space for a press room.

The White House also contains a small gymnasium, a tennis court that was built originally for Theodore Roosevelt, and a one-lane bowling alley that was particularly popular with Nixon. There is a movie theater where the first family and their guests can watch their favorite movies. Presidential requests for movies that are in current release are filled quickly by the film studios.

The White House library regularly receives new books from publishing houses, which send titles that match each president's interests. For example, when the Eisenhowers moved in the White House the library was flooded with western and romance titles, which were the favorites of the president and first lady, respectively.

Presidents have managed to relax in a variety of ways. Benjamin Harrison took walks or used the billiard table in the basement of the White House. In fact, the entire Harrison family played the game, despite the terrible condition of the basement in the 1890s. Harrison's successor (and predecessor), Grover Cleveland (1885–1889; 1893–1897), also relaxed at the billiard table, and he enjoyed taking carriage rides through the city as well. Although Cleveland spent more time at his desk than many previous presidents, he still got away for hunting and fishing.

Because of the time he spent caring for his frail, epileptic wife, William McKinley (1897–1901) was unable to indulge in many recreational activities. He took walks and, like Cleveland, enjoyed an occasional carriage ride. He also enjoyed visits from his friends and an infrequent game of cards. His greatest pleasure, however, was the cigar that was his constant companion. It was perhaps the one indulgence he permitted himself.

A "man's man," Theodore Roosevelt walked and hiked regularly, jogged often, excelled at horsemanship, hunted, swam in the Potomac, and played tennis on the White House courts with invited guests. Roosevelt's tennis guests were members of Congress, diplomats, cabinet members, and other political figures. An invitation to play tennis with Roosevelt was a privilege, and only those who played well were invited back. Roosevelt also enjoyed fencing, boxing, and wrestling, and he often devoted entire afternoons to any one of them. He even practiced the martial arts and once set up a contest between American wrestling and Japanese jujitsu to see which was superior. Yet he also loved to read and frequently devoted his evenings to a book or the latest magazines. The entire Roosevelt household read with him.

William Howard Taft (1909–1913), not being a fan of the strenuous life, preferred less demanding recreation. Taft took walks and occasional automobile rides, and he enjoyed reading

Among his many athletic pursuits, Theodore Roosevelt was an excellent horseman.

the newspapers and having massages. A baseball fan, Taft was the first president to open a season by tossing out the first pitch. He also played golf often.

For Woodrow Wilson (1913–1921) golf was never more than an amusement; he never tried to be good at it. Rides in his car, billiards, solitaire, particularly Canfield, and the theater were among his other favorite pastimes. Warren G. Harding (1921–1923) played golf and walked a little for exercise, but he preferred spending his spare time playing cards—poker and bridge—with old cronies from Ohio.

Calvin Coolidge relaxed by taking walks and working jigsaw puzzles. One of his Secret Service agents taught him to fish and he became an avid angler, although all he did was hold the rod. His agents baited the hook and removed the fish for him. One day, when he noticed someone catching fish from the stream in front of his South Dakota vacation house, he sent the Secret Service to confiscate them and tell the trespassers, "They are my fish." His favorite relaxation, however, was sleeping. Coolidge

slept at least eleven hours a day, getting nine hours a night and taking two- to four-hour naps each afternoon.

Herbert Hoover, who spent his 1929–1933 term grappling unsuccessfully with the Great Depression, seems to have relaxed very little in the White House. Irwin Hood "Ike" Hoover (no relation to the president), then chief usher at the White House, noted that the president "labored practically all his waking hours and never spent any time with his family."[7] Hoover worked out with a medicine ball in the mornings, however, and read often. It was his complaint about being unable to find adequate reading material in the White House that led to publishers' donations. And the Hoovers apparently enjoyed dinner companions; in fact they rarely ate alone.

Franklin Roosevelt's inability to walk because of polio limited the forms of recreation he could enjoy. At first, Roosevelt swam frequently in the White House swimming pool, but as the cares of his office mounted, he used the pool less and less; he had largely abandoned it by 1945. In the way of hobbies Roosevelt was a skilled bird-watcher, and he liked to collect stamps, books, and models of sailing ships. His White House study in fact was filled with these things, much to the dismay of the housekeeping staff.[8] Roosevelt also relaxed by taking weekend trips to his mountain hideaway, Shangri-La (now Camp David), in the Maryland countryside. He also frequently enjoyed the quiet and privacy of long automobile rides in the country, and he liked to fish from the presidential yacht. Roosevelt's yacht was one of several vessels that had been maintained by the navy and made available to presidents since the Theodore Roosevelt administration. President Carter sold the last of these boats during his administration, and now there is no presidential yacht. President Truman maintained an exercise regime while in the White House. He began the day with an hour's brisk walk at six, followed by a swim in the pool, a workout on the rowing and exercise machines, some calisthenics, and another dip in the pool. From 1949 to 1950 part of the well-publicized daily walks were devoted to viewing the renovation of the White House, which had to be almost totally rebuilt due to accumulated structural problems. (During the renovation, the Trumans lived at Blair House, which is situated across Pennsylvania Avenue from the White House.) The walks stopped after an aborted assassination attempt on Truman in 1950. Truman also relaxed by playing the piano during quiet evenings with his family.

Believing that proper rest was vital to effective work, Eisenhower carefully guarded his leisure time while president. An avid golfer, he made a putting green out of the lawn outside the Oval Office—he threatened to shoot the squirrels that kept burying nuts there—and practiced his swing on the South Lawn. He played golf often at the Burning Tree Country Club in Bethesda, Maryland. The president also enjoyed painting and set up a studio in the White House. He liked to watch movies, particularly westerns; preferred to read westerns, mysteries, and cookbooks; and was the first president to spend much time watching television.

Eisenhower plays golf at a club in Newport, Rhode Island, while onlookers watch and take pictures.

President Kennedy relaxed by leaving Washington. Almost every weekend he was off to his family's property in Massachusetts or Florida, a friend's home in rural Virginia, or Camp David. Many of these holidays were taken without his wife, who often vacationed separately. While at the White House itself, Kennedy used the White House pool. He would take a nude swim in the afternoon, return to his room for a nap, go back to work, and then return to the pool afterward. J. B. West, chief usher at the White House from 1957 to 1969, wrote that Kennedy followed this routine every day that he was at the mansion.[9] Because the president had a chronically bad back that hampered his physical activity, he exercised regularly to strengthen it, and he kept a rocking chair in the Oval Office for relief from his back pain. But despite his ailment, Kennedy enjoyed sailing and was a good golfer.

Lyndon Johnson was a human dynamo who never seemed to need rest. For Johnson, a man always on the move, work itself seemed to be a form of relaxation. When he sought some other form of activity, he swam in the pool, played an occasional game

of dominoes, and sometimes watched a movie. The president also enjoyed dancing; at parties he took turns dancing with different partners and often danced with his daughters, Luci and Lynda. Because Johnson liked a good massage, when he left the White House he arranged to have his masseur, a navy officer, transferred to Bergstrom Air Force Base near his Texas ranch.

The more sedate Richard Nixon rarely swam and had the pool filled in. Nixon, however, watched an occasional movie, sometimes played golf, and used the White House bowling alley. Moreover, he went out frequently on the White House yacht. Nixon also often read for relaxation and seemed to find comfort in the White House fireplaces, which were used even in the summer; the air-conditioning was turned up to compensate. In the way of spectator sports, Nixon liked baseball and greatly enjoyed football. In fact, he was an avid fan of the Washington Redskins and followed the team closely when he could. He even suggested plays to the Redskins' coaching staff. According to Dennis McCarthy, a member of Nixon's Secret Service detail, one evening after a game Nixon came outside and sat on the porch with him "just like two guys getting together over a couple of beers to discuss the game, except there was no beer."[10]

Gerald Ford was a former football player who enjoyed watching the game, but he also liked more active recreation. An outdoor swimming pool was built during Ford's term, and the president lifted weights, rode an exercise bicycle, and skied in the winter. Ford's greatest pleasure, however, was golf. He played whenever he could and unfortunately developed a reputation as a rather erratic player after hitting a spectator or two with his golf shots.

Like many of his predecessors, Jimmy Carter relaxed with a swim. He jogged on the White House grounds, bowled in the bowling alley, and played tennis on the mansion's courts. The Carter family particularly enjoyed the movie theater, which by Rosalynn Carter's account became one of their favorite places to escape. The family frequently retreated there with popcorn or an entire meal to watch movies, including to-be-released titles with the director or an actor as a guest. Carter enjoyed classical and some pop music, and, as a speed reader who could read two thousand words per minute with 95 percent retention, he could read three or four books a week.

After the attempt on his life, Ronald Reagan regularly followed an exercise routine that actually increased his muscular strength while he was president. Evenings with friends were a favorite pastime; he was an excellent storyteller who loved a good joke. Reagan also enjoyed the outdoors, particularly riding horses and working at his California ranch in the Santa Yaez Mountains.

George Bush seemed to attack his recreation time. Perhaps because he had been the captain of the baseball team at Yale, he developed a preference for active relaxation and pursued it with zest. He spent time playing golf, often speeding around the course, and had an artificial putting green installed on the mansion's grounds. He jogged regularly, swam, played some softball, and made frequent use of the White House tennis court. He en-

President Bill Clinton jogs past cherry trees in bloom along the tidal basin in Washington.

joyed hunting and fishing and sometimes raced his powerboat off the Maine coast. Having developed a passion for horseshoes, he had a horseshoe pit built at the White House and played often.

On the other hand, workaholic Bill Clinton sometimes seemed never to relax at all. However, he did have a morning jog each day, sometimes on a special track built on the South Lawn. He was an avid reader, particularly of mysteries and novels, and a sports fan, especially of the University of Arkansas basketball team. He also played golf and occasionally hunted and went biking or boating.

ALTERNATIVES TO THE WHITE HOUSE

When the pressures of the presidency become too great, it may not be enough to retreat to the movie theater or the swimming pool. Presidents often feel the need to leave the White House altogether to put their problems behind them. For that purpose the government maintains a presidential retreat in the mountains of Maryland, known as Camp David. Originally

named Shangri-La, Camp David was built for Franklin Roosevelt, who traveled there frequently. Eisenhower renamed it Camp David in honor of his grandson, Dwight David Eisenhower II, and made it his weekend home for the early part of his administration.

Subsequent presidents, particularly since Johnson, have found Camp David an invaluable source of solitude for self-renewal. It also has been a place where presidents can retreat to meditate on problems, design programs, and write speeches. For example, it was at Camp David that FDR plotted much of the strategy for the Normandy invasion of World War II. The retreat even has been used for international diplomacy. In 1978 Carter hosted an important summit meeting there between Egyptian president Anwar Sadat and Israeli prime minister Menachem Begin, which led to the signing of the Camp David peace accords.

When first used in 1942, the buildings at Camp David looked unfinished and were filled with furniture from the White House attic. The modern Camp David complex, which is far from rustic, is designed to let the president relax in comfort. It has a four-bedroom, air-conditioned lodge and additional guest cabins. Conference rooms are also provided. Like the White House, Camp David has a swimming pool, bowling alley, and tennis court. For presidents who like to fish, there is a stream stocked with trout; for shooting, there is an archery and skeet-shooting range; and for playing golf, there is a par-three hole. Jacqueline Kennedy, a skilled rider, particularly appreciated the camp's riding stables.

Most important, Camp David is private. It is thirty minutes by helicopter from the White House, but it contains adequate communications equipment to keep in touch with the rest of the world. The grounds are surrounded by a chain link fence topped with barbed wire and are patrolled by Marine guards. No one enters without an invitation from the first family; even the omnipresent White House press corps is left outside the compound. As President Reagan has noted, Camp David is one of the few places where a president can just step outside and go for a walk. The cost of maintaining this retreat has been estimated at more than $1.6 million a year.[11]

Even with the availability of Camp David, most presidents like the alternative of a private home for rest and relaxation. Such homes, popularly known, for example, as the western (Nixon) or Georgia White House (Carter), are equipped with communications and security facilities at public expense. Whereas Camp David is used frequently for weekend escapes, a president generally will use the alternate White House for extended vacations.

Almost every recent president has had at least one such retreat. FDR withdrew to his family estate in Hyde Park, New York, or to Warm Springs, Georgia, where he could undergo physical therapy. Truman went home to Independence, Missouri, or traveled to the Key West, Florida, naval base when he took a vacation. Eisenhower sometimes vacationed in Denver, Colorado, near his wife's family. He was there when he suffered a heart attack in 1955. Eisenhower had a Gettysburg farmhouse that he had purchased and remodeled, and before he left office it had become his weekend and vacation retreat.

Kennedy used several retreats. Originally avoiding Camp David because he was sure he would not like it if the Eisenhowers had, he vacationed instead at his family's compound at Cape Cod, Massachusetts, his father's house in Palm Beach, Florida, or at a friend's house, leased for his use, at Glen Ora, Virginia. After leaving the Glen Ora house the Kennedys decided to build their own retreat near Glen Ora, and it was virtually finished when they decided they liked Camp David after all. Kennedy and his wife made news with their separate vacations. Mrs. Kennedy traveled without the president to India, Italy, and the Mediterranean.

Johnson retreated to the LBJ Ranch on the Pedernales River in the Texas hill country. He loved to oversee the operation of his spread, speeding around it in his car and showing it off to visitors. The president also enjoyed hosting barbecues, sometimes on the spur of the moment. He challenged his Secret Service detail to speedboat races on the ranch's lake. The service always let him win the races so that they could secretly keep the fastest boat.

President Nixon had two retreats: a home in Key Biscayne, Florida, and one in San Clemente, California. The Nixon homes became involved in the Watergate controversy, when it was charged that funds were used improperly in their purchase. Other critics claimed that the remodeling of the Nixon homes, done in the name of security, in fact increased their resale value at the taxpayers' expense.

President Ford maintained only one retreat, a home in California, and President Carter went back to his longtime home in Plains, Georgia, for a break from Washington. Ronald Reagan enjoyed his California ranch while president and vacationed there frequently. In fact, Reagan enjoyed his ranch so much that he was criticized for taking too many vacations; he spent some 200 days there in his first term.

President Bush escaped White House pressures by retreating to Houston, Texas, where he stayed in a house he rented from friends. The Bushes' retirement home in Houston was not ready for occupancy until after he left the presidency. Much of his vacation time was spent in Kennebunkport, Maine, where he had a summer home on land his family had owned since 1902. Bush's Kennebunkport retreat had a large house, two smaller ones, a swimming pool, and a tennis court.

Thinking that he would not like the atmosphere of the retreat with its military guards, President Clinton rarely used Camp David early in his term, although he went there more as time passed. Unlike many of his predecessors, Clinton had no private estate to use for vacations. Instead, staying in borrowed lodgings, the Clintons vacationed in the summers of 1993 and 1994 at Martha's Vineyard, Massachusetts, and spent their vacation in 1995 at Jackson Hole, Wyoming. *(See box, A President's Vacation, right.)*

A PRESIDENT'S VACATION

All presidents face the problem of how to get away from it all and escape the pressures of the office. To some extent, it is impossible to escape, for some presidential matters cannot be delayed "until next week." Also, presidents cannot simply "take off" like an average American; since they are recognized everywhere they go and everyone wants to see them, they cannot easily find solitude.

This is a particular problem for a president such as Bill Clinton, who did not own a private retreat. Lyndon Johnson and Ronald Reagan had ranches where they could relax; Richard Nixon had a vacation home in California, George Bush went to Maine, and John Kennedy went to the family retreat in Massachusetts. The Clintons had none of these, and so they had to look for vacation spots.

In 1993 and 1994, the Clintons vacationed in Martha's Vineyard, off the coast of Massachusetts. The island was chosen because of its relative seclusion and because the inhabitants are so used to the rich and famous—Art Buchwald, Walter Cronkite, Katherine Graham, Vernon Jordan, Robert McNamara, Jacqueline Onassis, Beverly Sills, Carly Simon, and James Taylor among others vacationed there—that a president would hardly seem worthy of notice. During his time on the island, Clinton was able to unwind by walking the beach, playing golf, being with his family, and sleeping late. However, predictions that the glitterati would ignore the president's presence were wrong; Clinton was wined and dined by local residents and spent a lot of his time at parties and dinners. Although some locals grumbled beforehand about the inconvenience of it all, when the president arrived he became the center of attention.

In 1995 the Clintons decided to vacation in a more remote location, Jackson Hole, just south of the Grand Teton National Park, in Wyoming. Apparently they wanted more solitude than Martha's Vineyard could provide. Moving into a home owned by Sen. John D. Rockefeller IV (D-W.Va.), the Clintons hiked and rode horseback, went whitewater rafting down the Snake River, and toured Grand Teton and Yellowstone.

Jackson Hole is remote, but not remote enough to escape the trappings and burdens of the presidency. There were still neighbors who wanted the president to dine with them; there were still the aides, the media, and the Secret Service surrounding him; there were still the telephone and the briefings; and there were still national problems to deal with, such as the wildfires on Long Island and the accidental deaths of three American diplomats in Bosnia. (Clinton sent federal aid to help extinguish the fires and interrupted his vacation to return to Washington for the funerals of the diplomats.)

The Clinton experience indicates that presidents cannot truly escape from the pressures of their office; they can, at most, briefly put them in the background. An incident on Clinton's Jackson Hole vacation illustrates this well: President Clinton traveled to Old Faithful in Yellowstone—by helicopter—and was met there not by the local four-wheel drive vehicles, but by two black limousines.

Protecting the President: The Secret Service

One of the major benefits provided presidents is the full-time personal protection for them and their families. While the bulk of the president's security is provided by the U.S. Secret Service, other government agencies also contribute to the effort to protect the president.[12] The Federal Bureau of Investigation (FBI) points out to the Secret Service those people within the United States who might pose a threat to the president, and the Central Intelligence Agency (CIA) provides information on potential assassins in other countries, a source of increasing concern to the service.

Because the number of Secret Service personnel is insufficient to fill all the human resource demands of protecting the president, local and foreign police may be used, depending on where the president travels. The air force provides a fighter escort for *Air Force One;* the navy furnishes backup in case an emergency develops while the president flies over the ocean; the army provides communication equipment; and the Marine Corps posts a detachment to guard Camp David. Finally, the General Services Administration (GSA) arranges for any renovations needed to improve security at a presidential residence.

Although all these agencies contribute to the president's safety, the central body is the Secret Service, which coordinates their activities. Any measures taken by GSA, for example, are at the request of the service, and it is the service that provides the human shield needed to protect the president.

ORIGINS OF THE SECRET SERVICE

What is now known as the Secret Service was created in July 1865 to reduce the wholesale counterfeiting of U.S. currency. By the end of the Civil War, counterfeiting had reached such proportions that as many as one-third of all bills in circulation may have been bogus. In one of the last official acts of his life, President Abraham Lincoln agreed to the creation of a unit within the Treasury Department that would have the permanent task of catching forgers and counterfeiters. The Secret Service Division proved quite successful at this task. During its first few years it captured more than two hundred counterfeiters a year.

Because at that time the service was the only federal government agency that acted as a general law enforcement body, it found that its role expanded rapidly. By 1874 it was investigating fraud, peonage, and slavery cases, as well as the Ku Klux Klan. The service also began to acquire the form and structure of a bureaucratic institution and, unfortunately, a reputation for unsavory tactics; agents freely made searches and arrests without warrants and even spied on Andrew Johnson while he was still in the White House. In 1874 a distrustful Congress stripped it of all but its original functions.

The Secret Service languished until 1898 and the Spanish-American War, when President McKinley, needing an intelligence agency to gather information about the Spanish, asked for its help. During the war the service operated as both a military espionage body and a domestic counterintelligence body, and by the end of the war it had established itself as one of the best such units in the world. After the war the intelligence role was de-emphasized, but it was restored during World War I. Although the Secret Service worked well with the State Department during the conflict, it found itself out of the spy game by World War II. The growth of the FBI and military intelligence rendered the service's activities in that area superfluous.

The service's quite active anticounterfeiting operations remained intact throughout this period, however. In 1917 alone it obtained more than one thousand arrests and convictions and seized nearly $300,000 in fraudulent money. It also conducted investigations into official misconduct and played a major part in uncovering the Teapot Dome scandal during the Harding administration.

Protection of the president was not part of the service's original function. For many years presidents who wanted bodyguards had to hire them themselves, and most did without. Confronted with a would-be assassin in 1835, President Andrew Jackson himself attacked his assailant and drove him off. On the night he was killed, President Lincoln was guarded by a single District of Columbia policeman; the guard had wandered off when assailant John Wilkes Booth arrived. Secret Service agents were nearby when Presidents James A. Garfield and McKinley were shot, but none of them were responsible for protecting the president. In McKinley's case there were three agents next to him, but their only job was crowd control. Indeed, early efforts by the service to protect the president were rebuffed by Congress, and it was not until 1906 that the first presidential detail was authorized.

The coverage given by the service gradually expanded through the years, and with the decline in its intelligence role, protection became its second major function. In 1940 the service survived a threat to that function from the FBI, which had taken on the job of protecting the vice president from 1929 to 1932, when a proposed relocation of the service into the Justice Department failed. In fact, the Secret Service was only permanently granted the job of presidential protection in 1951; until that time its authorization had to be renewed annually.

ORGANIZATION AND PERSONNEL

In keeping with its original anticounterfeiting role, the Secret Service is an arm of the Treasury Department, which administers the service with a very light touch. The director of the Secret Service is not a political appointee; he or she is selected by the secretary of the Treasury from the ranks of the experienced agents. There are approximately 36,000 employees in the agency, of whom about 1,800 are special agents, the elite who handle personal protection or counterfeiting cases. The remaining employees consist of the Uniformed Division and the support staff. A very small but growing number of female special agents have been assigned to every aspect of the service's work, including the presidential detail.

The annual budget of the service is about $180 million, but

budgeting can be difficult because it is hard to know in advance exactly how much protection may be needed. The total varies with the changing number of protectees and the activities in which they engage.

Structurally, the service has five divisions (or offices) under the director and deputy director. The most important of these are the Office of Investigations, the Office of Protective Research, and the Office of Protective Operations.

The Office of Investigations is responsible for forgery and counterfeiting cases. Its experts investigate, analyze documents, and provide evidence in forgery cases. The office also conducts background checks on government employees and investigates threats against service protectees—but not actual assassination attempts, which are the responsibility of the FBI. Finally, it maintains control of the Treasury Security Force, which protects the Treasury building itself. Because the agency's regional offices normally deal with forgery and counterfeiting cases, those offices are supervised by the Office of Investigations.

The Office of Protective Research compiles data on individuals who, for whatever reason, have come to the service's attention as potential threats to its protectees. Its files contain more than forty thousand people, about 1 percent of whom are on a "watch list" as serious threats. Others are singled out depending on the president's travel plans. In addition to identifying dangerous persons to be monitored, the Office of Protective Research also conducts searches to ensure that any environment the president will occupy is safe and secure, without dangerous objects such as explosives or surveillance devices.

The agents who actually protect the president are in the Office of Protective Operations. Each of its divisions is responsible for a particular protectee. The division for the president contains the White House detail. Other divisions are responsible for the vice president, each of the living former presidents, and any widowed first ladies. Thus, for example, Jimmy Carter and Lady Bird Johnson have their own divisions within the Secret Service's Protective Operations Office. Should a protectee die or decline coverage, his or her division is disbanded. The service is also responsible for protecting announced presidential candidates and foreign heads of state, but the Candidate/Nominee Protective Division and the Dignitary Protective Division are basically skeletal and only staffed as needed.

Also within Protective Operations is the Uniformed Division, which originally was part of the District of Columbia Police Department. President Harding, who wanted better control over it, removed it from the department in 1922. In 1930, after a stranger walked unchallenged into President Hoover's dining room one evening, the Secret Service was given authority over the division. The Uniformed Division is responsible for the White House security guards, and since 1970 it has also provided protection for foreign embassies in Washington. When the service provides protection for an embassy, it protects only that; guards do not leave the grounds, and they take action only if someone trespasses onto the property.

Most Secret Service employees have demanding jobs, and the training for special agents is particularly arduous. To be a special agent an applicant must be between twenty-one and thirty-five years of age and able to pass a physical exam, the Treasury Enforcement Agent Exam, an extensive interview, and a security check. Candidates who pass the initial screening undergo an intensive training program to prepare them for both parts of the service's mission. They are first sent to the Federal Law Enforcement Facility in Brunswick, Georgia, to learn to deal with forgery and counterfeiting. Then they move on to the service's 420-acre school in Beltsville, Maryland, to learn the details of investigation and protection. A superb training ground, the Beltsville facility has classrooms and laboratories in which sophisticated methods for detecting forgeries are taught.

To prepare for their protective role, prospective agents are taught emergency medical principles, abnormal psychology, hand-to-hand combat, investigative techniques, and evasive driving tactics. They also become firearms experts. They study movies of previous assassination attempts and engage in simulations in which their own responses are videotaped and studied. Using full-size mock-ups of the White House and of a city street, new agents can refine their skills.

Secret Service agents are civil service employees and are paid according to the federal government's General Schedule (GS). Depending on experience and education, agents usually begin at the GS5, 6, or 7 levels, which pays between $17,000 and $27,000 per year. (The upper range is more common). Advancement to GS12 or 13 is usually fairly rapid; within six to eight years, an agent may earn better than $50,000 annually.

Agents start in a field office, move to a protective detail after a few years if they are good enough, and after a few more years go back to a field office and eventually an administrative job. For people on protective details, particularly the president's, the stress can be extreme; thus agents tend to be rotated regularly. Moreover, the hours can be long and irregular; agents may find themselves on duty for sixteen hours and more. Because an agent can be called on duty on short notice and sent anywhere around the world, a normal family and personal life is often unachievable. Indications of this are found in the fact that the average age of an agent is only thirty-five, and that the service teaches its agents the warning signs of psychological disorders and alcoholism.[13]

THE ROLES OF THE SECRET SERVICE

With its roles of defender of the nation's currency and protector of the president, the Secret Service is in a sense two agencies in one: a criminal investigation unit and a bodyguard service. Unfortunately, the two roles do not always fit together very well, and some agents are not equally comfortable in both. The skills required to crack a counterfeiting ring are not the same as those needed to foil an assassination attempt. The service thinks the juxtaposition is useful, but not everyone agrees.

Because relatively few agents regularly participate in the protective role, the major task for most agents is the prevention of counterfeiting and forgery. In 1994 the service closed more than

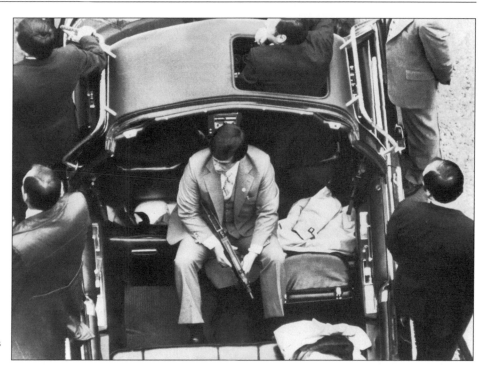

Secret Service agents equipped with machine guns ride in the car following President Ronald Reagan's limousine during his 1981 inauguration parade.

37,765 counterfeiting cases, arresting 9,166 people and confiscating more than $45.7 million in counterfeit currency. It obtained convictions in 98 percent of the cases it prosecuted. The service attempts to break counterfeiting rings before the bogus bills go into service, targeting the big distributors. It also investigates cases of forged checks and documents and has recently investigated food stamp fraud. Of particular interest are cases involving stolen government checks and bonds. The service tries to combine public awareness with the latest technology to control these crimes.

The better-known part of the service's mission is protection of the president. That role has expanded considerably since its inception. The first White House detail, assigned to Theodore Roosevelt in 1901, had only two agents. The detail expanded to ten by 1918 and to thirty-seven by 1940. In 1989 it numbered seventy. The protection has broadened as well. Originally, it included just the president, but in 1908 it was extended to the president-elect. In 1962 the vice president came under the agency's full-time protection. (Previously, protection of the vice president was on a request-only basis.) Further additions to the service's workload were made in 1965, when retired presidents, widows of presidents, and their children under age sixteen were protected. Coverage was extended to presidential candidates in 1968, to foreign heads of state in 1971, and to candidates' wives (on a limited basis) in 1976. In addition, the president in 1971 was granted the right to request protection for anyone thought to need it, as Jimmy Carter did for Edward Kennedy in 1980 before the senator became an official presidential candidate. Any of these people can refuse Secret Service protection, but few do; one of those few was Richard Nixon, who terminated his protection in 1985.

Because of these extensions of coverage and increased travel and activity by public figures, the demand for protection results in a considerable load for the service, particularly in election years, when it may be forced to borrow from elsewhere in the Treasury Department to meet its obligations. This is true even though the service normally protects only those candidates who can raise enough campaign funds to warrant matching funds from the federal Treasury.

Occasionally, the service finds itself with other tasks. During World War II, for example, it was responsible for protecting the original Constitution and the Declaration of Independence on display at the National Archives in Washington, D.C. Similarly, when Leonardo da Vinci's painting *Mona Lisa* toured the United States in 1962, it was guarded by the service.

PROTECTING THE PRESIDENT: TACTICS AND PROBLEMS

All of the training undertaken by agents in the Secret Service's operations divisions is aimed at keeping the president alive and unharmed. The service has adopted numerous tactics to ensure the president's continued safety in a world filled with dangers.

The service prefers, of course, that the president remain in the White House, where there are numerous safeguards and a controlled environment. Although the service does not reveal any details, it is clear that White House security arrangements are elaborate. Anyone entering the mansion on business is checked; anyone working there, including presidential aides, must wear a photo badge. All incoming packages and visitors are also carefully monitored; bomb-sniffing dogs are available to check suspicious packages or vehicles. Armed guards and plain-

clothes agents keep watch around the premises, and sharpshooters are posted on the roof. The grounds are protected by reinforced fences, guardhouses, television cameras, and electronic
sensors. There is a Doppler radar system that looks directly up
to detect any parachute assault, antiaircraft weapons (reportedly
heat-seeking, shoulder-fired Stinger missiles), and a bomb shelter. Finally, should the president need help, there is a "panic button" under the desk in the Oval Office that can unobtrusively
summon agents at any time. (See "Security and Communications," p. 943, in Chapter 22.)

Despite the trained agents and all of the equipment, the system sometimes fails. In 1977 an intruder was able to walk up to
the windows outside the Oval Office and speak directly to President Carter. In 1981 a man with a history of mental illness
gained access to the White House grounds and was there unchallenged for ten minutes; he made it to the mansion itself before he was stopped.[14] In the early morning on September 12,
1994, a man flying a small airplane eluded radar detection and
crash-landed on the White House grounds. The pilot was killed
as the plane crumpled up against the mansion itself, directly under the president's bedroom. The first family was not in the
White House at the time and it was not certain whether the incident was an attack on President Clinton or a failed stunt.
Nonetheless, security measures were carefully reevaluated. In
1995, in an effort to protect against vehicular attack, part of
Pennsylvania Avenue in front of the White House was closed to
traffic and converted into a pedestrian mall.

When the president travels, the challenges for the service are
greater because the variables that can be easily controlled are
fewer. The White House detail and the field offices in the areas
where the president plans to travel must make extensive security
arrangements. Working with the local police, they secure the
airport where the president will arrive and depart. They carefully plan and survey the routes to be traveled, secure the buildings
in which the president will appear, and arrange that rooftops
and other overlooks be patrolled. Sharpshooters may be posted
on roofs. Procedures for screening onlookers are introduced.
The service's files are checked for any people known to be a possible threat to the president; some of them may be watched during the visit. Preparations extend to identifying a hospital to use
in case of emergency and ensuring that it has adequate supplies
of the president's blood type.

In recent years security arrangements have not permitted
publicity about the president's travel plans. Formerly, in an
effort by political supporters to ensure the largest crowds possible, it was customary to publicize the president's travel route.
For example, President Kennedy's exact route through Dallas on
November 22, 1963, was available to anyone who picked up a
Dallas newspaper. This is no longer true. When the president
travels today, the arrival and departure times and the itinerary
are not public knowledge.

The most visible part of the presidential protection effort is
the cordon of agents that surrounds the president. These agents
are with the president at almost all times, even in the White
House, except the family quarters. They stand guard both inside
and outside of every room occupied by the president. When the
president leaves the White House, the agents form (as best they
can) a human shield around the chief executive. The service
tries to maintain what it calls a "safe zone" or clear space around
the president, so that the agents have a better chance to spot a
potential assailant. Their efforts to keep a safe zone have sometimes led to criticism of their tactics.

Because these agents represent the last line of defense for the
president, they are under enormous pressure. Beyond watching
for any known dangerous people who may be around, agents
scan the crowds in search of unusual or threatening behavior: a
man wearing an overcoat on a warm day, a person carrying a
newspaper in a strange way, a woman too eager to get close to
the president, or even a face that keeps reappearing in different
places. Because the goal of the service is prevention, not retribution, agents must develop a sixth sense to anticipate trouble. An
instinct for danger and quick reactions are critical to keeping
the president safe.

Should an attack occur, agents shield the president first, then
subdue the assailant, and finally, once the president is safely removed, secure the area and assist any injured bystanders. Agents
are trained to become a human shield for the president. As he
watched agents stand to practice with firearms, President Reagan commented that they made a very large target that way; he
was told that that was the point. In Dallas in 1963 agent Rufus W.
Youngblood covered Vice President Lyndon Johnson with his
own body when the presidential motorcade came under attack.
Videotapes of the 1981 assassination attempt on President Reagan show agent Timothy J. McCarthy, with arms and legs spread
wide, walking directly toward the assailant, John W. Hinckley Jr.,
thus blocking his view of the president. (McCarthy was shot, but
he recovered.)

The service has encountered several serious difficulties in its
efforts to protect the president, and several of these have had to
do with presidents themselves. Some presidents have been quite
cooperative with the service, but others have balked at its requests, generally for two reasons.

One reason is strictly political. Most presidents like crowds,
and even if they do not, it is simply good politics for them to be
seen mingling with their adoring supporters. Thus, while the
service probably would prefer that presidents spent their days in
one room in the White House, political realities dictate that
presidents get out and "press the flesh." The more they do that,
the harder it is for the service. President Johnson, for example,
loved to dive into crowds, much to his bodyguards' dismay. On
that fateful day in Dallas in 1963, Kennedy had the protective
cover removed from his limousine so that the crowds could see
him better.

Even a president like Nixon, who was something of a loner
and thus easier to protect, was a problem for political reasons.
Nixon's staff constantly wanted to show how much Nixon was

loved by the people and looked for close public contacts to prove it. Thus, the staff consistently fought the service over security arrangements, which it regarded as too restrictive for its aims. One argument over where the crowd restraining line was to be was so bitter that the chief of Nixon's protective detail threatened to arrest Chief of Staff H. R. Haldeman for his interference.

The second reason for the lack of cooperation with the service is the presidents' desire for privacy. Agents are a constant intrusive presence in the president's life, which may lead to presidential resentment and resistance. President Johnson complained that the service would not hesitate to occupy his bedroom, and when he was at his ranch, he would often try to lose his detail by jumping in the car and ordering his driver to drive as fast as possible. When at Kennebunkport, President Bush would sometimes zoom off in his powerboat, leaving his guardians behind.

The Secret Service, however, has ways to get around presidents and first ladies, who may find their protection particularly burdensome. Eleanor Roosevelt, for example, flatly refused to accept her protective detail. Finally, the service worked out a deal: if she would carry and learn to fire a handgun, the service would stop tailing her. In fact the gun stayed in her dresser drawer, and the service put undercover agents at her every stop. Early in his term Harry Truman liked to walk to the bank, but the service did not like the fact that he waited on street corners for the lights to change, so agents fixed all the traffic lights on his route to turn red in all directions at once—thus Truman would never have to wait on a corner again. He soon caught on, however, and ordered the service to stop.[15] Pat Nixon tried to keep the number of agents with her on trips around Washington smaller than the service wanted, but her wishes were ignored. When one day she noticed the second car of agents that was accompanying her, she was reassured that it was only there in case her car had engine trouble.[16]

Presidents also tend to be fatalistic, further complicating the service's job. Many presidents, in fact, begin to feel that personal risk is part of the job. The feeling expressed by Lyndon Johnson that "all a man needs is a willingness to trade his life for mine" seems common to most presidents. This sense that "no amount of protection is enough" in the face of a determined assassin makes the service's job more difficult, for it leads presidents to be less cautious than their guardians would like. Not all presidents are fatalistic to the same degree, but those who are prove quite difficult for the service. Indeed, one of the most fatalistic of presidents, John Kennedy, was also one of the hardest to protect.

Another problem the service faces is trying to identify a potential assassin, a critical step in preventing an attack on the president. The master files maintained by the service of anyone who may pose a risk to the president—for example, people who have made threats, mentally disturbed and violent people, or members of political extremist groups—are updated constantly and sorted by degree of threat. Before the president moves from the White House, a watch list is put together of anyone in the files who resides where the president is going, and the agents in charge account for everyone they can and keep special watch for the rest.

In practice, however, this system has several flaws. First, the service has to rely on the FBI for much of the information that goes into its files, and communication between the two agencies sometimes fails. The service also must rely on local police for information about individuals, and the quality of the data obtained may vary.

Second, the service, which is a rather small agency, lacks the human resources to evaluate reports as carefully as it would like. Thus, the watch list is limited to about four hundred people, primarily because the agents cannot handle many more. After the attempt on President Reagan in 1981, some critics argued that John Hinckley's arrest for trying to carry a gun onto an airplane in 1980 should have put him on the watch list. Unfortunately, the agency lacked the people necessary to investigate that case and evaluate the risk.

The major problem, however, is that there is no consistent way to identify an assassin, either in the files or among the public at large. Despite its best efforts, the service has never managed to develop any statistical or psychological techniques that would allow it to distinguish unerringly a real assassin from all the false alarms in its own files, nor does it have any sure way to spot one in a crowd. In fact,

despite the impressive progress in the fields of computer technology and psychiatry, the service has few clues as to how to look for potential assassins. Without a reliable set of profiles or indices that can be used to identify those who are actually dangerous, as opposed to potentially dangerous, neither the agents nor their computers can derive much benefit from increased quantities of intelligence data.[17]

Such profiles simply do not exist. Thus, compilation of a watch list becomes a matter of subjective judgment by the agents in charge, as does the determination of which reports warrant inclusion in the master files.

With no foolproof guide to help evaluate information, truly dangerous people can be and are overlooked. In fact, none of the people who have shot at service protectees since 1960—Lee Harvey Oswald (President Kennedy, 1963), Sirhan Sirhan (Robert Kennedy, 1968), Arthur Bremer (Gov. George Wallace, 1972), Lynette Alice Fromme (President Ford, 1975), Sara Jane Moore (President Ford, 1975), and John Hinckley (President Reagan, 1981)—were in the agency's files before the attack.

Complicating the service's mission further is the increased threat of foreign terrorist activity against the president. Although such a threat may be mostly hypothetical, the service cannot take chances and must treat it seriously. Thus, in late 1981 it spent two months in a state of constant alert because of reports that Libya's Muammar Qaddafi had sent a "hit team" to kill President Reagan. Rumors flew about the nature and location of the team. In the end, however, nothing happened, and the hit squad may never have existed. This case indicates the additional burden thrown upon the service in an era of international terrorism. Given the agency's limited resources, such a threat spreads the service thin and makes its job even more difficult.

Today, presidents frequently travel abroad, which also increases the problems for the Secret Service. The service must then coordinate its activities with those of a foreign country's security agencies; the difficulty of anticipating and spotting potential assassins are multiplied by the unfamiliar environment. That there are risks is shown in the attempt on former president Bush's life in April 1993. While on a visit to Kuwait, Bush was the target of a car bomb that was planted by the Iraqi intelligence service, in retribution for his role in leading Desert Storm. The plot failed and the bomb was never detonated, but the attempt indicates the potential danger and the difficulties of the service's job in protecting presidents and their families.

NOTES

1. Christopher Georges, "Executive Suite," *The Washington Monthly,* January/February 1993, 36.

2. Fred Barnes, "All the President's Perks," *The New Republic,* September 2, 1991, 25.

3. J. B. West, *Upstairs at the White House: My Life with the First Ladies* (New York: Coward, McCann, and Geohegan, 1973), 342.

4. Rosalynn Carter, *First Lady from Plains* (Boston: Houghton Mifflin, 1984), 144.

5. Quoted in West, *Upstairs at the White House,* 209.

6. Some description of the life of the staff can be found in two pieces by Burt Solomon: "The Work's Hard, the Hours Long, But the Rewards Are Worthwhile" (*National Journal,* February 17, 1990, 406–407) deals with the Bush staff, and "When the Next H-Hour Strikes, Will Clinton's Aides Be Awake?" (*National Journal,* June 11, 1994, 1362–1363) deals with Clinton's.

7. Irwin Hood Hoover, *Forty-Two Years in the White House* (Boston: Houghton Mifflin, 1934), 267.

8. West, *Upstairs at the White House,* 20.

9. Ibid., 204–205.

10. Dennis V. McCarthy, *Protecting the President: The Inside Story of a Secret Service Agent* (New York: Morrow, 1985), 195.

11. W. Dale Nelson, *The President Is at Camp David* (Syracuse, N.Y.: Syracuse University Press, 1995), 143.

12. The discussion of the Secret Service that follows relies heavily on Philip H. Melanson's *The Politics of Protection: The U.S. Secret Service in the Terrorist Age* (New York: Praeger, 1984), an excellent study of the origins and operations of the service.

13. For a firsthand account of the stress of a service job, see McCarthy, *Protecting the President,* especially chap. 5.

14. Melanson, *The Politics of Protection,* 92.

15. Ibid., 128.

16. McCarthy, *Protecting the President,* 172.

17. Melanson, *The Politics of Protection,* 115.

SELECTED BIBLIOGRAPHY

Caroli, Betty Boyd. *First Ladies.* Exp. ed. New York: Oxford University Press, 1995.

Carter, Rosalynn. *First Lady from Plains.* Boston: Houghton Mifflin, 1984.

Freidel, Frank, and William Pencak, eds. *The White House: The First Two Hundred Years.* Boston: Northeastern University Press, 1993.

Furman, Bess. *White House Profile: A Social History of the White House, Its Occupants and Its Festivities.* Indianapolis: Bobbs-Merrill, 1954.

Hoover, Irwin Hood. *Forty-Two Years in the White House.* Boston: Houghton Mifflin, 1934.

Johnson, Lady Bird. *A White House Diary.* New York: Holt, Rinehart, and Winston, 1970.

Kessler, Ronald. *Inside the White House.* New York: Pocket Books, 1995.

McCarthy, Dennis V. *Protecting the President: The Inside Story of a Secret Service Agent.* New York: Morrow, 1985.

Melanson, Philip H. *The Politics of Protection: The U.S. Secret Service in the Terrorist Age.* New York: Praeger, 1984.

Nelson, W. Dale. *The President Is at Camp David.* Syracuse: Syracuse University Press, 1995.

"Safeguarding the President's Life: Where the Money Goes." *U.S. News and World Report,* August 13, 1973, 24–26.

Thomas, Helen. *Dateline: White House.* New York: Macmillan, 1975.

West, J. B. *Upstairs at the White House: My Life with the First Ladies.* New York: Coward, McCann, and Geohegan, 1973.

"Why It Will Be Hard to Stay 'Just Plain Folks.'" *U.S. News and World Report,* January 24, 1977, 23–26.

Youngblood, Rufus W. *Twenty Years in the Secret Service: My Life with Five Presidents.* New York: Simon and Schuster, 1973.

CHAPTER 25

The First Lady, the First Family, and the President's Friends

BY STEPHEN L. ROBERTSON

T HE PRESIDENCY has been described as the loneliest job in the world, and in terms of the heavy responsibilities of the office, it no doubt is. No president, however, comes into office truly alone. Almost every president has been accompanied to the White House by a wife, and all have had family and friends who, along with the first lady, form a network of support for the president. Family members and friends of the president do not remain in the background long, however. As time passes in the media age, they become more prominent in the public eye, and, through association, they may assist or harm the administration as the president attempts to carve a place in history.

The First Lady

As the president's wife, the first lady is one of the most prominent women in the country. Many first ladies have had little to distinguish them except the position they have held by marriage, but others have achieved distinction on their own. Particularly since 1900 the first lady has been increasingly active politically and visible to the public. She is now among the best-known figures in American politics, better known in fact than members of Congress and cabinet secretaries, and often even the vice president. (See "Biographies of the First Ladies," p. 1019.)

The term *first lady* was not applied to the president's wife until after the Civil War. In its early days, the Republic, uncertain of how much respect was due its leader's wife, tried several titles without success. Among them were Lady Washington, Mrs. President, presidentress, and republican or democratic queen. Sometimes no title was used at all. Julia Grant was the first presidential spouse to be called the "first lady," in 1870, but the title did not gain wide acceptance until Lucy Hayes held the position from 1877 to 1881.[1]

The modern first lady has a varied, demanding role. She acts as the manager of the White House as well as the gracious hostess at receptions, parties, and formal dinners. She also is expected to play a political role and participate in social causes on behalf of her husband's administration—all while continuing to fulfill her responsibilities as wife and mother. Yet the first lady holds no official position—the Constitution does not mention her—and earns no salary. Instead, her modern importance stems from history and changing customs.

THE FIRST LADY AS HOSTESS

Since the first presidential administration in the late eighteenth century, the public has held that the primary responsibility of the first lady is to organize and to act as hostess at White House social events. Presidents, too, are concerned with such events; they view the social calendar as a political tool. George Washington used the first social season to serve his political aims just as, more than a century and a half later, Lyndon B. Johnson used White House functions as occasions to persuade people to adopt his point of view.

Although the first lady has both a personal and the White House domestic staff to assist her, the basic responsibility for arranging any teas, receptions, banquets, coffees, and state dinners that the president may have is still hers, even on those occasions when she does not have to act as hostess. Most first ladies have carefully selected the menus, entertainment, decorations, and even chairs for social events. For example, Mamie Eisenhower (1953–1961) replaced all the banquet chairs in the mansion after she decided the old ones were too small. But not all first ladies have been willing to accept the social role generally expected of them. Some, such as Dolley Madison (1809–1817) and Julia Tyler (1844–1845), seemed to relish company and loved to entertain at the White House. For others, such as Helen Taft (1909–1913) and Eleanor Roosevelt (1933–1945), entertaining was largely a necessary formality. Still others avoided it altogether; for example, Letitia Tyler (1841–1842), Margaret Taylor (1849–1850), and Abigail Fillmore (1850–1853) made few, if any, social appearances, leaving relatives to act as hostess. (See box, White House Hostesses: Surrogate First Ladies, p. 1052.)

In her social role, the first lady frequently can use parties and other social events to soothe ruffled feathers and charm the uncommitted, thereby helping the president. Perhaps the best first lady at this was Dolley Madison, famous for her glorious parties. Mrs. Madison's charm and ability to put people at ease won numerous friends for her aloof husband, James Madison, who once was described by American writer Washington Irving as a "withered little applejohn."[2]

THE FIRST LADY AS MANAGER

Besides organizing parties, the first lady is expected to be the traditional homemaker. But when one's home is the White

House, that may be a rather tall order. The first lady acts as the general supervisor of the White House, much like the mistress of a large estate. She oversees food selection, decorations, furnishings, cleaning, and other household duties. Again, some first ladies have been much more concerned with these duties than others. Eleanor Roosevelt had little or no interest in how well the White House was kept up. One visitor to the White House, after soiling her gloves on the banisters, wrote that Mrs. Roosevelt should spend less time traveling and more time cleaning the house.[3]

In contrast, her successor, Bess Truman (1945–1953), was quite concerned with the cleanliness of the mansion and had a running battle with the housekeepers to improve their cleaning in general and their dusting in particular. Mamie Eisenhower, who succeeded Mrs. Truman and who too was a demanding mistress, was particularly fussy about the carpets, insisting that they be vacuumed several times each day so as not to show footprints. Mrs. Eisenhower was used to running a tight ship; one of her first demands was that she alone approve all menus.

Despite the best managerial efforts of the first lady, however, the White House staff is not always readily responsive. As with any organization, the large permanent staff has a natural inertia, which leads it to resist the first lady even as it tries to serve her. Thus a new first lady who suddenly wants neglected corners made spotless may find the housekeepers slow to respond to her demands. For the first lady and the staff, there is a process of mutual accommodation, in which she adjusts to their established ways as they adjust to her desires.

THE FIRST LADY AS PUBLIC FIGURE

The first lady always has had a social role to play; receptions and dinners have long been part of Washington life. Similarly, the duties of household manager are not new. The letters of First Lady Abigail Adams, wife of President John Adams (1797–1801), reveal her continual concern with her budget and her home, and first ladies since have had the same worries in managing the White House.

But as far as politics, the early first ladies were not expected to play any role at all. Being the gracious hostess at social functions was the norm, and any activities beyond that were frowned on. The established model for women was that of passive purity. Placed on a pedestal, they were thought to be both above and unsuited for the dirty world of politics. A woman had her place, and the first lady, like any other woman, was expected to remain there.

Unlike her predecessors, however, the modern first lady undertakes a wide range of public activities. Indeed, rarely have first ladies been as visible as they are today, and the public expectations of the first lady are higher than ever before. It is no longer enough for the first lady to be a good hostess and to manage the White House well. Now she also must be publicly engaged in some social cause (or causes) that benefits the nation. If she is not so engaged, she is open to serious criticism.

Thus the burdens of the position of first lady have increased along with the public role.

At the same time, there are still limits to the public's expectations of the first lady's proper role. Certain areas remain off-limits; if she ventures into them, she is criticized for exercising too much power or behaving inappropriately. In general, "social" issues are the proper sphere for a first lady; "political" ones are not. Thus first ladies are expected to be prominently involved in efforts to combat drug abuse or reduce illiteracy, whereas efforts to represent the president to foreign leaders or to spearhead major policy reform are open to criticism.

EVOLUTION OF THE FIRST LADY'S ROLE

Early first ladies were apolitical and often relegated to the background. For most of these first ladies, life in the White House was very restricting, for it was imperative that the president's wife display only "proper" behavior. Martha Washington (1789–1797) declared herself to be a virtual prisoner as first lady. Elizabeth Monroe (1817–1825) avoided Washington life altogether, and Louisa Adams (1825–1829) played the part of social lady but never assumed any other public role. Dolley Madison, however, was much more prominent and became the grande dame of Washington, but her fame was limited strictly to her social role; she espoused no political views.

The limits on first ladies were most clearly evident during the tenure of the nation's second first lady, Abigail Adams. A very intelligent woman with excellent judgment, she took a keen interest in politics and political figures. Her husband, John Adams, frequently sought her advice on issues of the day and privately acknowledged her importance as an adviser. Yet all of her political activity was strictly behind the scenes; when she displayed her political leanings in public, she was roundly criticized for inappropriate and unladylike behavior. Her strong political views and clear influence on John Adams were offensive to many.

During the first half of the nineteenth century, the White House was occupied by a series of first ladies who, in keeping with the accepted image of the day which depicted upper-class women as fragile, often sickly creatures, maintained almost no public profile. Several first ladies thus avoided a public role on the grounds of ill health—Letitia Tyler (1841–1842), Margaret Taylor (1849–1850), Abigail Fillmore (1850–1853), and Eliza Johnson (1865–1869)—or personal tragedy—Jane Pierce (1853–1857). But there were exceptions to this trend. John Tyler's young second wife, Julia (1844–1845), relished attention; as first lady she hired a press agent and received guests while seated on a raised platform. Mary Lincoln (1861–1865) was very prominent in Washington, to her detriment; crushed by the Civil War and personal tragedy, she became compulsive and neurotic, and her mental instability and erratic behavior drew widespread public attention and negative publicity. Yet none of these first ladies was politically active.

Throughout the nineteenth century, the ideal of a demure,

polite, proper first lady persisted, and many first ladies remained obscure. The second half of the century, however, saw public interest in first ladies grow. As a result of two developments in particular—higher literacy rates, especially among women, and the development of mass communication, spurred by the invention of the linotype press in 1885—these latter first ladies were much better known than their predecessors. A related development—the spread of mass-circulation newspapers and magazines—helped to stimulate curiosity about the president's family and increased coverage of its activities. Historian Betty Boyd Caroli has pointed out several reasons for the growing media interest in first ladies:

> The absence of any clearly defined role for presidential wives, the possibility that they exercised some private influence on their husbands, and their place as symbols of how women ought to behave made them the object of the same kind of media attention that surrounded actresses, sports figures, and society women.[4]

The first lady emerged in the mass media with the publicity that surrounded the wedding of Frances Folsom and Grover Cleveland on June 2, 1886. After the wedding, which was the first presidential wedding to take place in the White House (President Tyler's wedding was held in New York), the newspapers continually tried to invade the couple's privacy, leading the president to bitterly assail "those ghouls of the press." The intense media scrutiny of the first lady that began with Frances Cleveland has never abated. Today, the first lady is the target of an unrelenting media barrage; dozens, if not hundreds, of publications, ranging from scholarly journals to supermarket tabloids, run articles or photographs featuring her.

The traditional view of women as passive, delicate creatures began to fade in the 1870s as pressure grew for greater equality for women. Much of this trend was symbolized in the drive for women's suffrage. Only after fifty years, however, would this trend directly affect the role of first lady.

Edith Roosevelt (1901–1909), the twentieth century's first first lady and the second wife of Theodore Roosevelt, took advantage of the changing public outlook toward women. Realizing the growing importance of the news media and recognizing the public interest in her boisterous family of six children, Mrs. Roosevelt carefully managed the news coming from the White House in order to protect their privacy. Although she was not active politically, it was well known that her husband sought and listened to her advice; unlike Abigail Adams, she was not criticized for offering it. During Edith Roosevelt's stay in the White House, the first lady attained new importance as the leader of Washington society. Mrs. Roosevelt's meetings with the cabinet wives and her regular evening musicales helped to ensure new prestige for the first lady.

Edith Roosevelt also began the process of institutionalizing the office of the first lady. She hired a social secretary to assist with her growing load of mail and to deal with press releases and reporters' questions. This marked the beginning of a permanent staff for the first lady, independent from that of the president, to handle the first lady's business. As such, it was a major step in the evolution of the modern first lady.

The first ladies who followed Edith Roosevelt contributed in different ways to the institution's development. Helen Taft (1909–1913), for example, began to alter the notion that first ladies were to be politically seen but not heard. It was widely known that William Howard Taft never would have become president had it not been for the driving ambitions of his wife. It also was known that Mrs. Taft was interested in political issues and sought to advise her husband; only a stroke kept her from being an important if unofficial player in the Taft administration.

Woodrow Wilson's first wife, Ellen (1913–1914), was the first first lady to support publicly social legislation (a housing bill) pending before Congress. After Wilson suffered a major stroke in 1919, his second wife, Edith (1915–1921), controlled the information and paper flow to and from the president. In fact, she was widely perceived to be running the country (debate continues to this day over her precise role during Wilson's illness). Neither Grace Coolidge (1923–1929) nor Lou Hoover (1929–1933) were involved in politics, but both were very visible and had an interest in social causes.

The increasing attention of the media to the first lady, the changing attitudes toward women's roles, and the development of the first lady's office came together with Eleanor Roosevelt, who from 1933 to 1945 redefined the role of the first lady. She expanded the initiatives of her predecessors, reaching into areas previously untouched by a first lady. She gave the office her unique stamp and changed its place in American politics.

Mrs. Roosevelt realized the potential of her position for publicity, and she exploited it to the hilt. She regularly granted interviews and routinely held her own press conferences, which were open to women journalists only. In 1933 journalistic coverage of the president was almost exclusively a man's job; Mrs. Roosevelt hoped her press conferences would stimulate opportunities for women in journalism. She quickly mastered the art of posing publicly for staged photographs with children or working people, thereby anticipating the later development of the "photo op." She was in the newspapers and newsreels almost daily.

Of course, to be in the news Mrs. Roosevelt had to do something, and here she again broke new ground. Her level of activity was incredible and unprecedented for a first lady. She always was in motion; projects followed one another in rapid succession. She visited the rural poor, miners, prisoners, soldiers in their foxholes, hospitals, and "New Deal" programs. She seemed everywhere. Sometimes she traveled for the president, other times for herself. Her frequent outings were the subject of jokes and cartoons as well as of admiration.

Mrs. Roosevelt also was politically active to an unprecedented degree. She took up social causes publicly; for example, she pushed openly for an end to racial segregation. She drew attention to the plight of the poor in the slums, the unemployed, and the war veterans who had lost pensions. She advocated equality

From 1933 to 1945 Eleanor Roosevelt redefined the role of the first lady, constantly plunging into political activities and humanitarian projects. Here she holds a press conference for women journalists.

for women. During World War II, she served as deputy director of the Office of Civilian Defense. She scrutinized various New Deal programs, offering suggestions when possible, and kept close watch over her favorites. In an effort to push her programs, she frequently pressured President Roosevelt, sometimes to the point that he would have to leave the room. If FDR avoided someone his wife thought he should see, she might invite that person to dinner. Her political clout was thought to be extensive, and she became a kind of liaison for the general public.

She also answered thousands of letters herself, gave speeches and lectures, broadcast her own radio program, and wrote a syndicated newspaper column, "My Day," and numerous magazine articles. She even wrote a best-selling autobiography, *This Is My Story*. Although most of the money from her writing was given to charity, she enjoyed the satisfaction of having her own source of income.

When Eleanor Roosevelt left the White House in 1945, the role of first lady had been changed drastically and permanently. She had established it as something separate from the presidency, and with her outspokenness, activity, and visibility had made it independent from, although linked to, the Oval Office. She also changed forever the public's expectations of the first lady. After her, the public would begin to look for an active woman in the White House; the passive, retiring first lady was gone for good.

Still, Mrs. Roosevelt's immediate successors, Bess Truman and Mamie Eisenhower, were more retiring than she. Mrs. Truman regarded the White House as the "Great White Jail" and, noting that "we are not any of us happy to be where we are," said that she "most definitely" would not have become first lady of her own choice.[5] Although she shrank from publicity and re-

fused to grant interviews, it was well known that Bess Truman was very influential with her husband and gave him considerable, if general, political advice. She also helped to keep his famous temper under control, no doubt saving him much political embarrassment. Truman himself acknowledged her help and claimed that she was frequently objective about things when he was not.

Despite her weak heart and chronic inner ear problems, Mrs. Eisenhower was more visible than Mrs. Truman. Her political involvement was negligible, but she was widely admired, and her bangs, her clothes, her favorite pastels of pink and green, and even her cooking recipes were copied by thousands of women across the country. Although Mrs. Truman and Mrs. Eisenhower did not take center stage as first ladies, neither did they retreat to the extent of earlier first lady Jane Pierce who, burdened by the death of her son, simply withdrew from public view.

A startling contrast to her predecessors, Jacqueline Kennedy (1961–1963) elevated the position of first lady to a glamorous high. Young, attractive, cosmopolitan, fluent in French, Mrs. Kennedy became a media star and largely gave the Kennedy White House its "Camelot" image. Little interested in politics, the popular first lady focused instead on art and culture. She worked to bring historical antiques to the White House, and entertainment under Mrs. Kennedy featured some of the finest talent from the opera and the classical concert stage. Although in many ways the most private of people, Jacqueline Kennedy succeeded in transforming the first lady's office into a grand public stage. Her cultured charm and poise, seen best in her televised tour of the White House in 1962, left her successors with a high-profile position to fill.

Lady Bird Johnson plants flowers as part of her national beautification program, which was designed by her to improve the quality of life in urban and rural areas.

Lady Bird Johnson (1963–1969) may have lacked some of Mrs. Kennedy's style, but she resurrected the political possibilities of the first lady. She used her position as a means of helping to achieve policy goals and as a platform to speak to the public and push for action. Believing that improved surroundings meant a better quality of life, Mrs. Johnson traveled thousands of miles across the country to support her beautification program and lobbied Congress in behalf of the Highway Beautification Act of 1965. Her repeated emphasis of the nation's natural beauty helped to fuel the environmental movement. And, among other things, she worked to improve conditions in Washington's slums. In an unprecedented move, Mrs. Johnson also campaigned independently for her husband, touring the South by herself to gather support for his reelection bid in 1964. In essence, she became a presidential aide, and in doing so she raised the level of the first lady's political involvement.

Pat Nixon (1969–1974) was not as publicly prominent as her immediate predecessors or successors. She disliked politics and had little or no input into her husband's political decisions. By nature reserved in public, she dutifully made the necessary appearances, but the fixed smile and stiff demeanor she protectively adopted led to the unfair nickname of "Plastic Pat." Because she also tried to avoid publicity whenever possible, many people did not know that she was one of the most widely traveled first ladies, that she visited a hospital at the front lines in Vietnam, and that she was the first first lady to represent the president abroad in peacetime. The president's staff, which initially seemed to want to hide her, came to realize that she was the "human" face on the administration. Soon after, however, the Watergate scandal broke, and she withdrew more and more from public view.

Mrs. Nixon's major contribution was historical: she worked hard to collect authentic pieces of furniture and artwork (as opposed to replicas and copies) for refurnishing the White House, and to make the mansion more accessible to visitors. Typically, she insisted on downplaying her achievements for fear of diminishing the earlier efforts of Jacqueline Kennedy.[6]

Unlike Pat Nixon, Betty Ford (1974–1977) was active in a variety of social causes, and she encouraged the fine arts whenever possible (she had been trained in dance). She worked in behalf of the poor, the elderly, and the handicapped, and became perhaps the nation's most visible spokesperson for women's rights in general and the Equal Rights Amendment (ERA) in particular. She even personally called Illinois legislators to try to win support for the ERA. Her "pillow talks" with her husband about issues became common knowledge. She also proved to be one of the most candid of first ladies; she was willing to discuss almost everything, including controversial issues, such as abortion and premarital sex, and personal difficulties, such as her own breast cancer. Mrs. Ford thus increased the social concerns and the visibility of the first lady, but she also made the first lady a sort of Everywoman, to whom everyone could relate.

Rosalynn Carter (1977–1981) pushed her office to its limits during her four years in the White House. She testified before Congress in support of legislation promoting mental health, one of her major interests; advocated improved programs for the elderly; and supported the ERA. What distinguished Rosalynn Carter was the extent of her political involvement, which went far beyond that of any predecessor. She was in some ways a partner in her husband's presidency. Mrs. Carter sat in on cabinet meetings; she traveled abroad and met heads of state as her husband's representative; and she held weekly working lun-

Hillary Rodham Clinton speaks to the press after a meeting with congressional leaders on health care reform. Her open, powerful role in the Clinton administration brought both admiration and criticism.

cheons with the president. She effectively functioned as a presidential adviser, and her influence with President Carter was extensive and openly acknowledged by both. In fact, she seemed to be involved in almost everything, which led to widespread criticism; the public was perhaps unprepared for so much activism in a first lady.

Nancy Reagan (1981–1989) pulled back from the extreme exposure of Mrs. Carter. Her public political activity was slight; she exercised her influence behind the scenes. After a Carter administration that had been viewed as "austere," she was interested in restoring "elegance" to the White House. When she moved into the White House in 1981, Mrs. Reagan announced that she was not interested in social work; her husband was her project, she said. The public no longer accepted such a limited role for the first lady, however, and Mrs. Reagan's public image suffered. She did not begin to gain wide public favor until she began to travel widely and host conferences aimed at reducing drug abuse among young people in the United States. She also promoted the Foster Grandparents Program.

Barbara Bush (1989–1993) focused her public activity as first lady on eliminating illiteracy. In keeping with her husband's "Thousand Points of Light" theme, she also encouraged voluntarism and community service. She was not publicly prominent in political affairs, and in her memoirs Mrs. Bush described her own political judgment as poor and denied any influence on policy matters. Yet some observers felt that she had extensive influence with President Bush. They exchanged ideas over breakfast each day, and she brought news articles to his attention. Indeed, Mrs. Bush was not hesitant to give her opinion; one reporter noted that the first lady "weighs in on everything from policy to personnel" and the reporter "quoted a close aide as

saying that the president 'clears his mind' by first discussing issues and speeches with her."[7] Bush publicly acknowledged that he respected and valued her opinions.

Hillary Rodham Clinton, who became first lady in 1993, was possibly the most powerful of all first ladies. A successful lawyer before becoming first lady, she became a powerful figure in the White House and was known as the president's "most important advisor."[8] Mrs. Clinton, the first first lady to have an office in the West Wing of the White House, led the commission in 1993 that formulated the president's health care reform plan and spearheaded the administration's failed efforts to pass it. In doing so, she appeared publicly before five different congressional committees, thus becoming only the third first lady—after Eleanor Roosevelt and Rosalynn Carter—to appear before Congress. *(See box, First and Second Ladies on the Hill, p. 1015.)* Besides health care, Mrs. Clinton was particularly concerned with children's issues. Overall, she was to an unprecedented degree an equal to the president. She had free access to all meetings, input into any decision she chose, and a staff that considered itself equal in rank to the president's. Inside the White House, aides watched her as closely as they watched the president. Hillary Clinton pushed her office's power to the limits of the time; outsiders also recognized her power and frequently criticized her for it. Her high political profile also drew criticism and made her the major focus of investigations into the Clintons' Whitewater real-estate venture dating from the late 1970s and her role in the 1993 firings in the White House Travel Office.

The modern first lady, then, is part of her husband's team. In one sense, this always has been true. Every first lady has had at least a social role to play; the success with which she has filled it has been important to the success of her husband's administra-

FIRST AND SECOND LADIES ON THE HILL

Formal appearances by first ladies on Capitol Hill have been rare. Before 1940, no first lady had testified before any congressional committee. But since then, three first ladies and three second ladies have appeared before Congress. Of these appearances, the most important has been that of Hillary Rodham Clinton, who spent a week testifying extensively about a proposed major social reform.

December 10, 1940: Eleanor Roosevelt testifies before the House Select Committee to Investigate the Interstate Migration of Destitute Citizens about people forced by the Great Depression to wander the nation looking for work.

January 14, 1942: Mrs. Roosevelt appears before the House Select Committee Investigating National Defense Migration about the problems caused by people moving to industrial centers to find defense work.

February 7, 1979: Rosalynn Carter testifies before the Senate Labor and Human Resources Committee in support of more federal funding for mental health programs.

April 30, 1979: Mrs. Carter appears before an oversight hearing by the House Science and Technology Committee.

June 26, 1979: Joan Mondale, wife of Vice President Walter F. Mondale, testifies before the Senate Labor and Human Resources Committee on the Arts, Humanities and Museum Services Act of 1979.

September 25, 1979: Mrs. Mondale testifies before the Senate Governmental Affairs Committee on the subjects of art and architecture.

February 7, 1980: Mrs. Mondale appears before the House Select Committee on Aging to discuss senior citizens and art.

March 3, 1980: Mrs. Mondale testifies before the House Education and Labor Committee during hearings on the reauthorization of both the 1965 National Foundation for the Arts and the Humanities Act and the 1976 Museum Services Act.

April 23, 1990: Marilyn Quayle, wife of Vice President Dan Quayle, appears before the House Committee on Energy and Commerce to discuss women's health issues.

May 16, 1990: Mrs. Quayle testifies before the House Select Committee on Aging on breast cancer.

May 13, 1993: Tipper Gore, wife of Vice President Al Gore, appears before the Senate Labor and Human Resources Committee to discuss mental health care.

September 27–31, 1993: Hillary Rodham Clinton appears before five different committees—House Ways and Means Committee, House Education and Labor Committee, House Energy and Commerce Committee, Senate Finance and Labor Committee, and Senate Human Resources Committee—to explain and defend the president's health care reform proposal.

SOURCE: Thomas H. Moore, "First Ladies on the Hill," *Congressional Quarterly Weekly Report*, October 2, 1993, 2641.

tion. Yet over the years the position has expanded beyond simply "hostess" as first ladies have enlarged their roles. Today, the first lady takes positions, works for causes, makes public appearances and speeches, and often is an important figure in her own right. First ladies now may take a much more active role in electoral politics as well. At one time, the idea of a woman campaigning was inconceivable, and even the otherwise irrepressible Eleanor Roosevelt did not campaign separately for her husband. This, however, has changed. Lady Bird Johnson led the way by campaigning alone in the South for her husband's re-election in 1964.

At the same time, public expectations of the first lady have changed; she no longer is expected to be a shrinking violet. The legacy of Eleanor Roosevelt and her activist successors is that Americans now anticipate that the first lady will take up some social problem as her own and work for its solution. When Betty Ford became first lady, one of the first questions she was asked was "What is your program going to be?" And as Nancy Reagan discovered, the consequences of having no program can be serious.

Over the years, the first lady's office has evolved in response to changing social attitudes and the efforts of a succession of women. The modern first lady has her own staff and set of offices in the East Wing of the White House. *(See "The First Lady's Staff," p. 1017.)* She remains responsible for the social functions and management of the mansion, but she also is a political activist with her own special issues, a distinct political figure in her own right, and an integral part of the president's administration. The wife of the president can largely shape the role of the first lady to her needs and desires, yet it is clear that a set of imprecise yet definite expectations about her role has emerged. The first lady must satisfy them if she is to be a success and an asset to the president.

Hillary Clinton has been described as "a transitional first lady, taking on a new, bolder role as woman, mother, and policy maker."[9] The difference between Mrs. Clinton and previous first ladies is not that she exercised power, but that she did it so openly. As the first career woman to be elevated to the position of first lady, she may be the vanguard of an important change in the institution. It seems likely that future first ladies, fresh from careers in business or professions, may be more prominent and more visibly political than their predecessors. Mrs. Clinton may be the first of a new generation that will expand the possibilities of the office of the first lady. And, of course, the day will surely come when a woman occupies the Oval Office and her husband will define anew the role of the "first spouse" in American politics.

THE FIRST LADY AS ASSET AND LIABILITY

First ladies have proven to be either assets or liabilities to the political standing and support of their husbands. Some first ladies, such as Dolley Madison, were assets to their husbands through their social roles—indeed, her entertaining made her the star of Washington. Although he was a brilliant and privately charming man, James Madison was cool and aloof in public. Mrs. Madison's grace, compassion, and sunny disposition, however, more than offset her husband's weaknesses. By her admission, she was primarily interested in people, and she had a great ability to make them relax and feel at ease. When a young guest spilled his drink at one of her receptions and became flustered and embarrassed, she reassured him with the smiling remark that in such great crowds accidents were unavoidable. She also had a remarkable memory for names and faces and seemed to have a genuine concern for everyone.

Mrs. Madison's courage and composure were renowned as well. When the British burned the White House during the War of 1812, it was Dolley Madison who stayed behind until the last possible minute to rescue papers and the Gilbert Stuart portrait of George Washington. In fact, she was so popular that James G. Blaine, who tried for the presidency himself in the 1870s and 1880s, wrote that "she saved the administration of her husband. . . . But for her, DeWitt Clinton would have been chosen president in 1812."[10]

Seventy years after Dolley Madison left the White House, another woman arrived who proved to be a similar asset to her husband. Frances Cleveland married into the White House on June 2, 1886, and her youth, beauty, and grace made her instantly and immensely popular—quite in contrast to dour, grumpy Grover Cleveland, who sometimes ignored visitors altogether. She stood in reception lines shaking hands for so long that her arms required a massage afterward. The president's new wife also became a trendsetter in fashion; if Mrs. Cleveland wore it, so did everyone else. Merchants even began using her unauthorized likeness in their advertisements. She was so popular that one Republican official lamented, "It will be so much harder for us to win against both Mr. and Mrs. Cleveland."[11] In the election of 1888, which Cleveland lost to Benjamin Harrison, Mrs. Cleveland was a focal point of the campaign. The Democrats put her picture above the president's on their campaign posters, while the Republicans circulated unfounded rumors that Cleveland beat his wife.

The first lady who in many ways was the biggest asset to her husband was Eleanor Roosevelt. Mrs. Roosevelt's assistance to her husband went beyond a transfer of popularity, for although she was widely admired and respected, she also was disliked intensely by many. Her real importance to the president lay elsewhere. Crippled by polio, the president relied on his wife to be his eyes and ears, to go to places where he could not and report back to him. She became his link to the public, keeping him informed on what the people wanted, how New Deal programs were working, and what kinds of new projects were needed.

Her well-publicized independence from the president proved a tremendous asset as well. Eleanor Roosevelt frequently took positions on issues such as racial desegregation and women's rights that went well beyond those of FDR himself. When she did so, the praise she won went in part to him by association as

her husband, and thus he was able to broaden his base of support through her. To those whom she offended he could say, "That's my wife" and "I can't do a thing with her." Her separate identity let him have it both ways. Eleanor's daily newspaper column, "My Day," which began as a public diary but soon was discussing issues of the day, also helped the president; he sometimes used it to send up trial balloons, and politicians read it in an effort to anticipate the president's intentions.[12]

Two recent first ladies whose popularity rubbed off on their husbands were Jacqueline Kennedy and Betty Ford. Beautiful and stylish, Mrs. Kennedy emerged as the star of the Kennedy administration. She became immensely popular, and her hairstyle and clothing were widely copied—everyone wanted the "Jackie look." She also was the subject of constant media attention and drew big crowds when she made public appearances. When she traveled with President Kennedy, the crowds preferred her to him. Realizing what an asset she was, the president took advantage of it, sometimes introducing himself (as he did on a trip to France) as "the man who accompanied Jacqueline Kennedy."

Similarly, Mrs. Ford was more popular than her husband, Gerald, who jokingly wished that "I could just get my ratings up to hers." Mrs. Ford's courage and candor won her thousands of admirers, and she became one of the world's most popular women. She publicly discussed her bout with breast cancer. Her support for the ERA and her remarks about the possibilities of drug use or premarital affairs by her children angered some people but won great support from others. By 1976 she was so popular that buttons began to appear saying "Betty's Husband for President" and "Keep Betty in the White House." She continued to gain admirers after leaving the White House by speaking openly of her successful struggle to overcome an addiction to alcohol and prescription painkillers, and in 1982 she founded the Betty Ford Center for Drug and Alcohol Rehabilitation to assist those recovering from chemical dependency.

Other first ladies have been helpful to their husbands in different ways. Mrs. Coolidge's cheerful personality proved a welcome contrast to "Silent Cal," and Mrs. Truman advised her husband and kept his famous temper under control. Mrs. Johnson's campaigning won votes for Lyndon. Mrs. Carter was a "partner" in Jimmy's presidency, discussing numerous issues with him and giving advice.

But not every first lady has been an asset to the president, especially during the 1800s. For example, Elizabeth Monroe, aristocratic and reserved, refused to participate in the expected social round; the sharp contrast with her predecessor, Dolley Madison, brought much ill will toward James Monroe. Likewise, Jane Pierce contributed little to her husband, Franklin. She was in poor health, was frequently depressed, and acutely disliked her husband's political career. She was burdened as well by the death of her son. Thus the White House, far from being a cheerful place to win friends for the president, was shrouded in gloom for four years.

Betty Ford was one of the most popular first ladies. By the time of the 1976 campaign, buttons began to appear saying, "Betty's Husband for President" and "Keep Betty in the White House."

Mary Lincoln, the first lady who was perhaps the biggest liability to her husband, was emotionally unstable. She meddled in appointments, bought clothes compulsively, and was prone to irrational jealousy and emotional outbursts. Mrs. Lincoln was the target of vicious criticism from all sides, with charges ranging from poor taste to treason. In the presidential campaign of 1864 she became a major issue, and newspapers attacked her as much as or more than the president himself. As the pressure increased, her behavior deteriorated. Far from helping, the first lady was a political and personal millstone to a husband trying to deal with the Civil War.

The modern first lady can find it difficult to be an asset to her husband's administration largely because of the conflicting expectations Americans have of her. On the one hand, the public believes that the first lady should be the perfect housewife, her husband's loyal helpmate, and a devoted mother—all while holding down an outside job, which, in this case, is promoting some social issue. On the other hand, only certain issues are acceptable, and too much involvement in politics will bring public censure. For example, Rosalynn Carter's open assistance to her husband was so great that it aroused animosity in many citizens, who felt an unelected first lady had no business doing as much as she did.[13]

The dilemma of conflicting public expectations is perhaps best illustrated by Nancy Reagan's case. At first, Mrs. Reagan indicated that she had no social causes and that her only interests were returning elegance to the White House and taking care of her husband. This led to widespread criticism of the first lady as selfish and insensitive; in fact, so unpopular was she that Reagan's aides worried she would harm his 1984 reelection campaign. When she then became publicly involved in an antidrug campaign (a long-standing interest), her popularity improved dramatically. During Reagan's second term, however, she was the object of more criticism. This time, her backstage maneuverings led to the perception that she was deeply involved in political dealings and was actually dominating her husband. The revelation that she regularly consulted an astrologer before making decisions further damaged her public standing—and by extension, the president's.

This is the dilemma for a first lady: if she does too little, she is a liability, and if she does too much, or does the wrong sort of thing, she is still a liability.[14] Critics assailed Hillary Clinton for her extensive involvement in health care reform and politics in general. The unelected and unaccountable first lady, critics charged, was intruding into inappropriate areas. No doubt in part because of such criticism, Mrs. Clinton seemed to downplay politics and emphasize the more traditional role of the first lady as the Clinton administration progressed. Her predecessor, however, had had no such problem. In fact, perhaps no first lady has achieved the proper balance better than Barbara Bush. She had an acceptable social cause—literacy—which she combined with a grandmotherly image that pleased most Americans. To the very end of her stay at the White House, her popularity remained high.

THE FIRST LADY'S STAFF

The permanent staff that assists the first lady in her duties is completely separate from the White House domestic staff that she also oversees. On a flow chart the domestic staff appears under the chief usher's office.

Barbara Bush, talking here to children about reading, campaigned for programs to increase literacy.

Before 1900, the first lady had no staff, and few first ladies had any reason to need one. First ladies did little except to entertain in season, and most remained quietly within the White House, with the occasional exception such as Julia Tyler, who had a press agent. At a time when the president needed little or no staff, there certainly was no reason for the first lady to have any.

In 1901 the first step toward establishing an East Wing staff was taken by Edith Roosevelt. The growth of literacy and of the media had created a greater interest in the White House and therefore an increase in letters to and press coverage of the first family. Aware of the need to satisfy public curiosity, yet wanting to protect her family's privacy, Mrs. Roosevelt hired Belle Hagner as her secretary. Hagner became an all-purpose aide to the first lady; she released photographs and news stories about the Roosevelts and helped to answer the mail and supervise the operation of the White House. With that, the secretary's position was permanently established, to be passed down to the first ladies who followed.

For about fifty years, the permanent staff for the first lady remained quite small: one or two people, as well as an occasional person on loan from some government agency. Even Eleanor Roosevelt, who received some 300,000 letters in 1933 alone, had only one full-time person working under her; she had to borrow help from the president's staff. The first lady's staff began to grow during the Eisenhower administration to help the popular Mamie Eisenhower with her correspondence. By the Kennedy administration, Letitia Baldridge, Mrs. Kennedy's social secretary, claimed to have as many as forty people working for the first lady.

The size of the staff has varied slightly with each first lady. In recent years the permanent staff has numbered between twenty-one and twenty-six, with some allowance made for borrowing from other sources when needed. Even so, the first lady often is pressed for help. Rosalynn Carter, for example, pleaded repeatedly with her husband for more staff, but she never got it. He also refused to let her borrow staff from other agencies.[15]

The staff was diversified and restructured by Lady Bird Johnson, who formally separated the press and social functions of her staff. Bess Abell, her social secretary, was responsible for arranging parties, banquets, and receptions, and Elizabeth S. "Liz" Carpenter was press secretary and overall staff supervisor.

The organization and duties of the staff have varied with each first lady. Like the president, the first lady uses staffers as she sees fit, and in fact her smaller staff gives her more flexibility that way. Most staffs, however, are now divided into social, press, and policy sections. The press secretary handles media inquiries; the social office plans events and compiles invitation lists; and policy advisers address policy questions that interest the first lady. In addition, a scheduling director ensures that the first lady's travels are properly coordinated, and a correspondence office deals with her mail. There also is a calligrapher's office to take care of any engraving, such as invitations, needed. (The calligrapher's office also holds the presidential seal and grants permission for its use.) The organization of Lady Bird Johnson's staff was typical: six people handled media relations, four organized social functions, four answered correspondence, and two dealt with the "beautification" issue.[16] The numbers change, but the basic divisions remain.

Biographies of the First Ladies

The women who have served as first lady have acted as hostesses, political activists, and presidential advisers. They represent a range of personalities: some have been quiet and withdrawn, figures in the shadows; others have been colorful, visible, and even controversial. The stories of some are ones of success; of others, tragedy. But all contributed to the success of the presidency and to the development of the office of the first lady.[17]

Martha Washington

BORN: June 21, 1731;[18] New Kent County, Virginia
PARENTS: Col. John and Frances Jones Dandridge
SPOUSES: Col. Daniel Parke Custis; June 1749; New Kent County
George Washington; January 6, 1759; New Kent County
CHILDREN: By Daniel Parke Custis: John Parke (1754–1781); Martha "Patsy" Parke (1756–1773)
DIED: May 22, 1802; Mount Vernon, Virginia

The early years of Martha Dandridge Custis Washington are not well documented. Her father was a small plantation owner, who, although not well-to-do, was part of the Virginia aristocracy. Martha was well trained in the social graces but apparently had little schooling, as her erratic spelling attests.

In 1749 Martha met and married Col. Daniel Parke Custis, son of a wealthy Virginia plantation owner. Custis, by whom Martha had four children (two died in infancy), was twice her age. Daniel's father left his son his considerable estate when he died in November 1749. Thus when Daniel himself died of heart failure on July 8, 1757, the estate passed on to Martha, making her a very wealthy widow at the age of twenty-six.

George Washington probably had met Martha before her husband's death, and shortly afterward he came to pay his respects to the widow. Courtship followed, and although many historians have argued that Martha was not Washington's first love, the pair married in 1759. The addition of Martha's estate to George's plantation, Mount Vernon, where the Washingtons lived, made the couple wealthy, and the years until 1775 were spent tending to the plantation. But this period was punctuated by two sorrows: the Washingtons' failure to have more children and the 1773 death of Martha's daughter, Patsy, from an epileptic seizure.

With the onset of the American Revolution in 1775, George left Mount Vernon to lead the American army. Martha spent the summers of the war at Mount Vernon, but each winter, when the armies paused in their struggle, she joined her husband in camp, endeavoring to cheer him and his troops. When the war drew to a successful conclusion in 1781, Martha looked forward to a quiet retirement with George, but instead he became the nation's first president on April 30, 1789.

Martha did not join George in New York, the temporary capital of the new nation, until May 1789. She found being first lady

Martha Washington

(although not called such then) to be somewhat restrictive: "I live a very dull life here. . . . I am more like a state prisoner than anything else." Martha may not have been well read, but she was a pleasant and engaging hostess who generally enjoyed entertaining; her Mount Vernon home rarely had been empty. As the nation's first first lady, she established practices that were followed by her successors, such as the regular Friday afternoon parties for ladies and the custom of opening the White House to all visitors on New Year's Day. The latter custom remained in effect until 1931, when it was discontinued by the Hoovers.

George and Martha retired to Mount Vernon in 1797. The time left was not easy; financial worries nagged them, for the plantation had not been very profitable in recent years, and Martha's health had begun to deteriorate. "Lady Washington" lived quietly at her home until her death in 1802. She was buried on the plantation grounds next to George, who had died two years earlier.

Abigail Adams

BORN: November 11, 1744; Weymouth, Massachusetts
PARENTS: Rev. William and Elizabeth Quincy Smith
SPOUSE: John Adams; October 25, 1764; Weymouth
CHILDREN: Abigail Amelia (1765–1813); John Quincy (1767–1848); Susanna (1768–1770); Charles (1770–1800); Thomas Boylston (1772–1832)
DIED: October 28, 1818; Quincy, Massachusetts

Abigail Adams

Outspoken Abigail Smith Adams was the second of four children born to a New England minister and his wife. Abigail was sickly as a child, and she had no formal schooling, yet she acquired a considerable education in the private library of her family. Her intelligence, sharp wit, and willingness to speak out impressed those people who knew her.

One such person was John Adams, who made his first reference to Abigail in his diary when she was only fourteen. After overcoming the objections of her parents, who did not consider him to be in her social class, John and Abigail married in 1764. Abigail quickly proved to be an adept manager of their household. She ran their family farm efficiently, prosperously, and largely on her own while John was pursuing his legal and political careers and serving as an American diplomat abroad. She also helped to educate their children, teaching them Latin after first teaching herself.

In 1784, after a six-year separation, she sailed to London and rejoined John, who was then the first American minister to England. She spent four years in London and Paris, not entirely approving of the customs there, before returning to the United States in 1789 when John became vice president. Abigail became first lady when John was elected president in 1796. In many ways the four years that she spent as first lady were difficult for her. The expense of entertaining was a strain on the president's $25,000 salary, and the demands on her left her with almost no time of her own. Although she managed to save some money and find some private time, she complained bitterly (but pri-

vately) about both problems. Moreover, John was not a popular president and was subjected to constant vilification in the press, which angered Abigail greatly.

In 1800 Abigail supervised the move from Philadelphia, the temporary capital, to the new presidential mansion in Washington. Unfortunately, the mansion was far from finished when she arrived; only a few rooms were habitable and many facilities were lacking. But as a practical New Englander, she hung her laundry in the East Room. The nation's new capital was in no better condition, with mud roads and half-built buildings, and Abigail was privately unhappy at having left Philadelphia for it. Nevertheless, she spent her time there laying the foundations of a proper social life for the new capital.

Abigail was a prolific letter writer (more than two thousand of her letters still exist) and from them it is clear that, unlike most other first ladies for years to come, she took an active interest in politics and did not hesitate to express her views on the issues and personalities of the day. For example, in 1775 Abigail had urged John to support American independence and later to back more education for women and the abolition of slavery. As a pioneering feminist, Abigail repeatedly urged her husband to "remember the ladies" in forming the new government. She attacked his political enemies such as Alexander Hamilton, who opposed Adams's nomination for a second term and whom she called "the very devil." Her husband had a very high regard for her judgment and intelligence, and her influence and political involvement were clear to her contemporaries. Many of them, however, took exception to both as unbecoming a woman. The extent of her political activism, while perhaps not as great as that of some modern first ladies, would be unmatched for years to come.

Roundly disliked by Federalists for refusing to go to war with France and by the Republicans for being a "monarchist," John Adams served only one term as president before retiring to Massachusetts. Abigail lived there for seventeen years, her health gradually deteriorating but her mind remaining alert, before she died of typhoid fever at the age of seventy-four. She was buried in Quincy. John, who outlived her by six years, was buried next to her. Shortly before his death, John wrote of the love and admiration that he always had had for his wife and spoke of his gratitude for her "never-failing support" during his political career.

Dolley Madison

BORN: May 20, 1768; New Garden, North Carolina

PARENTS: John and Mary Coles Payne

SPOUSES: John Todd; January 7, 1790; Philadelphia, Pennsylvania

James Madison; September 15, 1794; Harewood, Jefferson County, Virginia

CHILDREN: By John Todd: John Payne (1792–1852); William Temple (1793)

DIED: July 12, 1849; Washington, D.C.

Dolley Madison

calls, knowing that to do so would help her husband. So popular was Dolley that even her habit of taking snuff, which was considered very unladylike, was overlooked. Although Dolley greatly loved social life and company, she was not one-dimensional. As a Quaker, she was a well-educated woman for her time, and her managerial skills were good as well. But she downplayed her intelligence and strong will to help her husband.

During the War of 1812 when the British threatened Washington, she displayed her courage by staying behind in the White House to supervise the removal of documents. When she finally was forced to leave the mansion, she took with her the portrait of George Washington by American portraitist Gilbert Stuart. (Contrary to popular legend, the painting was not cut out of its frame. Dolley had its frame broken, and it was rolled up.)

When Madison's second term expired in 1817, he and Dolley retired to their Virginia estate, Montpelier. Life was not easy in retirement; Dolley still entertained, but financial woes plagued them, aggravated by the wastefulness of her son, John Payne. After Madison died in 1836, Dolley was reduced to near poverty and had to sell first James's papers on the Constitutional Convention and then Montpelier itself to pay her debts. Finally, she returned to Washington and spent the rest of her life there.

Even as she grew older, she remained the center of Washington society, admired by every president through James K. Polk. She was even granted a lifetime seat on the floor of the House of Representatives. In 1849 her funeral was attended by every dignitary in the capital. She was buried in Washington but later was removed to rest beside Madison at Montpelier.

Perhaps the most popular of the early first ladies, the elegant Dorothea "Dolley" Payne Todd Madison was born into a Quaker family of nine children.[19] Her family lived on a Virginia plantation until she was five, when her father freed their slaves and moved his family to Philadelphia. There, in 1789, Dolley met a young Quaker lawyer, John Todd, whom she married a year later. They had been married for three years when a yellow fever epidemic struck Philadelphia and claimed Dolley's husband and younger son.

Shortly after Todd's death, Dolley met James Madison and within a year married him. For the indiscretion of marrying outside her faith (James was Episcopalian), she was expelled from the Friends, but this only seemed to allow her true self to shine through. She discarded her plain gray Quaker garments for bright clothing and elegant turbans. Moreover, she found that she loved entertaining and delighted in giving large, formal dinner parties. In fact, she was greatly admired as a hostess, particularly because of her memory for names and her remarkable ability to put everyone at ease. In this, she was an asset to Madison's political career, for he was generally withdrawn and cool around crowds.

With Dolley as first lady the White House became a festive place. Although she occasionally had served as hostess for the widowed Thomas Jefferson, Dolley came into her own when Madison was elected president in 1808. Her weekly receptions always were lively and gay. And she paid all the expected social

Elizabeth Monroe

BORN: July 30, 1768; New York City
PARENTS: Capt. Lawrence and Hannah Aspinwall Kortright
SPOUSE: James Monroe; February 16, 1786; New York City
CHILDREN: Eliza Kortright (1786–1835); James Spence (1799–1801); Maria Hester (1803–1850)
DIED: September 23, 1830; Oak Hill, Virginia

Elizabeth Kortright Monroe, who brought a new touch of aristocracy to the White House, was born into one of New York's premier families. Not much is known of her younger years. She met James Monroe in 1785, and although her family and friends disapproved of both his politics and his social status, she married him the next year.

The Monroes moved from New York to Virginia in 1789. James was elected to the U.S. Senate in 1790, and from 1794 to 1796 he served as ambassador to France. While in France, Elizabeth, on learning that the wife of the Marquis de Lafayette (America's friend in the Revolutionary War) was facing execution, boldly drove to the prison to speak with her publicly. The gesture earned Madame Lafayette's release. James later served on other diplomatic missions to Europe (1803–1807), and Elizabeth spent much of that time in Paris, where she found the environment convivial.

Elizabeth Monroe

Louisa Adams

While in Europe, the Monroes adopted European formality, believing that it helped them to deal with Europeans. That formality was carried into the White House when James became president in 1817, for the Monroes believed it to be appropriate to the presidential office. The contrast between the haughty Elizabeth Monroe and her predecessor, the warm, friendly Dolley Madison, was dramatic and, so far as social Washington was concerned, very unfavorable for Elizabeth. Quiet and somewhat aloof, she refused to follow the accepted Washington custom of paying social calls. Her many critics decried her as too aristocratic and French, and for a time they boycotted her receptions. Her elder daughter, Eliza, angered many with her arrogant behavior, and Elizabeth angered them further when she refused to extend mass invitations to younger daughter Maria's wedding, the first in the White House.

Bothered by chronically weak health and disliking much of her role as first lady, Elizabeth nonetheless continued her entertaining until she left the White House in 1825. Her last years were spent at the Monroe mansion, Oak Hill, in Virginia, but they were clouded by financial difficulties. She died in 1830 and was buried at Oak Hill. Monroe died in New York a year later and was buried next to her.

Louisa Adams

BORN: February 12, 1775; London, England
PARENTS: Joshua and Catherine Nuth Johnson
SPOUSE: John Quincy Adams; July 26, 1797; London

CHILDREN: George Washington (1801–1829); John (1803–1834); Charles Francis (1807–1886); Louisa Catherine (1811–1812)
DIED: May 15, 1852; Washington, D.C.

Louisa Catherine Johnson Adams did not see the United States until she was twenty-six. She was born in 1775 in England, where her father represented an American tobacco firm, but her family moved shortly to France and lived there until 1790. In 1790 they returned to England. There, in 1795, she met John Quincy Adams, who was on a diplomatic mission for the United States. Two years later they married. The early years of their marriage were somewhat strained because their personalities were quite different in many ways—she was outgoing, sensitive, and forgiving; he was stern, dogmatic, and demanding. They grew much closer in later years, however.

Louisa's time abroad has led some to call her "the most traveled woman of her time." From England she went to Berlin, where John Quincy was the American minister to Prussia during the administration of his father, John Adams (1797–1801). When Jefferson became president in 1801, John Quincy was recalled, bringing Louisa to the United States for the first time. There she finally met her in-laws, who received her with reservations. (Abigail Adams, in particular, questioned Louisa's foreign childhood, her associations with British royalty, and whether the younger woman was good enough for Abigail's favorite son.) From 1803 to 1808, Louisa lived in Massachusetts while John Quincy served in the U.S. Senate.

In 1809 President James Madison appointed him minister to

Russia. Concerned about the expenses of living abroad, John Quincy forced Louisa to leave her two oldest sons—George, eight, and John, six—behind with their grandmother. The time in Russia was difficult for Louisa. The harsh weather adversely affected her health, and her only daughter died after living less than a year. Moreover, Louisa was frequently lonely, particularly after John Quincy left for Belgium in 1814 to negotiate the treaty ending the War of 1812. Early in 1815 he sent word to her that his mission in Russia was finished and that she should join him in France. After packing their goods and disposing of their property in St. Petersburg, she set out with her young son in the dead of the Russian winter for Paris; only her courage and resourcefulness got them through the perilous two thousand-mile journey.

An intelligent and talented woman, Louisa spoke French fluently and enjoyed sketching and playing the harp and piano. Yet she seems to have had virtually no effect on John Quincy's political career. By her own admission, "no woman certainly had interfered less in [politics] than I have." For his part, John Quincy deliberately shared none of his professional life with her.

President James Monroe appointed John Quincy secretary of state in 1817, and in 1825 he became president. Louisa's time as first lady was not a pleasant one, however. The regular receptions that she held were a strain on her and, although well attended, were not thought exciting. She suffered from poor health in the form of recurrent migraine headaches and fainting spells, and she was hurt by the vicious criticism that was aimed at her husband, particularly after his controversial victory over Andrew Jackson in 1824. No doubt she was pleased to return to Massachusetts in 1829 when his term expired.

Louisa came back to Washington when John Quincy was elected to the House of Representatives in 1830. There she lived quietly the rest of her life, generally apart from Washington society. In 1848 John Quincy suffered a stroke on the floor of the House and died without regaining consciousness. Despite the strains their marriage had endured in earlier times, Louisa's letters indicate her anguish at losing her husband of fifty years so abruptly. She died four years later and was buried next to him in Quincy, Massachusetts.

Anna Harrison

BORN: July 25, 1775; Walpack Township, New Jersey
PARENTS: John and Anna Tuthill Symmes
SPOUSE: William Henry Harrison; November 25, 1795; North Bend, Ohio
CHILDREN: Elizabeth Bassett (1796–1846); John Cleves Symmes (1798–1830); Lucy Singleton (1800–1826); William Henry Jr. (1802–1838); John Scott (1804–1878); Benjamin (1806–1840); Mary Symmes (1809–1842); Carter Bassett (1811–1839); Anna Tuthill (1813–1845); James Findlay (1814–1817)
DIED: February 25, 1864; North Bend

Almost a footnote in White House history, Anna Symmes Harrison never saw the executive mansion that she was supposed to run. Anna's father was a New Jersey farmer and an

Anna Harrison

army officer. She was educated at some of the better schools for girls in the young nation and is the first first lady for whom there is a definite record of her schooling. In 1795 Anna's father took her to the new Ohio settlement of North Bend, where she met William Henry Harrison, a military officer who was stationed there. The two eloped the same year over the objections of Anna's father, who did not believe that an army man could adequately support his daughter. The life Anna adopted was that of an army officer's wife. She traveled with her husband until her family became too large. The couple lived primarily in a substantial log cabin in North Bend during their marriage, but they did spend a few years in Vincennes when Harrison was governor of the Indiana Territory. There Anna managed to care for her large family, frequently without any help from her absent husband.

Anna was intelligent and much better educated than most frontier women, and she was a devout Presbyterian. The years on the frontier were hard on her health, however. Moreover, the Harrisons rarely had any excess money, particularly after they were forced to assume the debts of their eldest son, who owed the government $12,000 when he died.

When the country went wild over the "Tippecanoe and Tyler Too" campaign in 1840 ("Tippecanoe" was Harrison's nickname), Anna was far less enthusiastic. Her husband had been content in retirement, and she thought he should stay there. She was concerned about her ability to be a satisfactory hostess—although she had proved able to entertain capably when necessary—and about her reception in Washington. When William Henry left for the capital in February 1841, Anna was too ill to accompany him; she decided to wait for spring before going herself. But Harrison died after only a month in office, and Anna never left Ohio.

Anna Harrison lived for nearly twenty-three more years in North Bend. In fact, she outlived all but one of her children. After her home burned down, she spent her final years in the home of her last surviving son, John, and there she died in 1864. Despite being the wife of one president and the grandmother of another (Benjamin Harrison), Anna never saw Washington. She was buried next to her husband and her father in North Bend.

Letitia Tyler

BORN: November 12, 1790; Cedar Grove, New Kent County, Virginia

PARENTS: Col. Robert and Mary Brown Christian

SPOUSE: John Tyler; March 29, 1813; Cedar Grove

CHILDREN: Mary (1815–1848); Robert (1816–1877); John Jr. (1819–1896); Letitia (1821–1907); Elizabeth (1823–1850); Anne Contesse (1825); Alice (1827–1854); Tazewell (1830–1874)

DIED: September 10, 1842; Washington, D.C.

Letitia Christian Tyler was born into a wealthy Virginia plantation family; her father was a friend of President George Washington. Although Letitia apparently had no formal education, she learned at home the skills needed to be the mistress of a southern plantation. Modest and reserved, she had many friends.

Letitia met John Tyler in 1808, and after a five-year courtship in part imposed by her parents, they married. Letitia's skills as a manager were needed quickly, for John's law practice and budding political career—he had been elected to the Virginia House of Delegates in 1811—kept him away from home frequently. Apparently, Letitia was an excellent manager and ran the growing Tyler plantation very effectively. She refused to go to Washington when John was elected senator from Virginia in 1826, both because she was needed on the plantation and because she disliked the unpleasant conditions then found in the capital. She also was a quiet woman who was devoted to her family and preferred to remain in her husband's shadow.

By the time John became president upon William Henry Harrison's death in 1841, Letitia's health had deteriorated dramatically. She had suffered a serious stroke in 1839 and had only partially recovered. Although she could still oversee the plantation, she was largely homebound. Letitia finally came to the White House, but she took no part in the mansion's public life. During her time as first lady, her daughter Letitia managed the White House, and her daughter-in-law Priscilla served as hostess. Her only public appearance was at daughter Elizabeth's White House wedding in January 1842. Otherwise, she remained out of sight, a semi-invalid, content to read her Bible and prayer book.

Letitia Tyler

On September 9, 1842, Letitia suffered another stroke. She died one day later, becoming the first president's wife to die in the White House. The depressed president ordered the White House hung in black for an extended period of mourning. Letitia was buried in Virginia on her father's estate, Cedar Grove.

Julia Tyler

BORN: May 4, 1820; Gardiners Island, New York

PARENTS: David and Juliana McLachlan Gardiner

SPOUSE: John Tyler; June 26, 1844; New York City

CHILDREN: David Gardiner (1846–1927); John Alexander (1848–1883); Julia Gardiner (1849–1871); Lachlan (1851–1902); Lyon Gardiner (1853–1935); Robert Fitzwalter (1856–1927); Pearl (1860–1947)

DIED: July 10, 1889; Richmond, Virginia

Vivacious Julia Gardiner Tyler, who brought cheer back to the Tyler White House, was a dark-haired beauty from a wealthy New York family. She was educated at an elite New York finishing school, and she was very popular in New York society. Somewhat impetuous and daring, at age nineteen Julia scandalized her family by posing for a department store advertisement, which polite ladies did not do in 1839. Her family promptly took her to Europe to avoid more embarrassments.

Julia first met President Tyler at a reception in 1842 while her family was visiting Washington, but he did not take much notice

Julia Tyler

of her until after the death of his wife, Letitia. Julia refused his first marriage proposal in early February 1843, but she changed her mind after her father was killed in an accident on board a U.S. Navy frigate a year later. In June 1844 the couple was wed in a secret ceremony in New York. The wedding was so secret in fact that even Tyler's children were not told in advance. As a result, relations between several of them and Julia were strained for years. Julia produced seven additional Tyler offspring during her marriage, the youngest when John was seventy.

The energetic Julia's time in the White House was brief, but she enjoyed it enormously. She established her own "court," despite the ridicule of the press, and entertained lavishly. She was the first first lady to have her own press agent (although she hardly needed one), and she initiated the custom of playing "Hail to the Chief" for the president. The Tylers left the White House in 1845 for their Virginia plantation. Conservative and defensive of her husband's politics, Julia became increasingly prosouthern, and by the time of the Civil War, both she and John wholeheartedly supported the Confederacy.

The years after John's death in 1862 were very difficult for her. The Civil War and Reconstruction destroyed most of the Tyler estate, and Julia had very little money. Moreover, she was plagued by legal battles over her property and her share of her mother's estate, contested by estranged members of her family. When she petitioned Congress for a pension, the pleas of the widow of the traitor Tyler were not favorably received for some

years. Much of what she did have was lost in an economic panic in the early 1870s. Not until the late 1870s was Julia able to begin rebuilding her estate.

In 1882 Congress included her in a pension it extended to widowed ex-first ladies, enabling her to be more comfortable in her last years. In July 1889 Julia Tyler died of a stroke in the same Richmond hotel in which John had died twenty-seven years earlier. She was buried next to him in Richmond.

Sarah Polk

BORN: September 4, 1803; Murfreesboro, Tennessee
PARENTS: Capt. Joel and Elizabeth Whitsitt Childress
SPOUSE: James K. Polk; January 1, 1824; Murfreesboro
CHILDREN: None
DIED: August 14, 1891; Nashville, Tennessee

One of the most politically minded of the first ladies, Sarah Childress Polk was born on her father's plantation in Rutherford County, Tennessee. She was educated at a private school in Nashville and spent one year at the Moravian Female Academy in North Carolina, one of the best schools of its kind in the South, before her father's death forced her to return home. In 1819 she began a courtship with James K. Polk, who was a clerk in the Tennessee Senate. They married in 1824.

Intelligent and strong-willed, Sarah began to play an important role in her husband's career. Far from being a reluctant

Sarah Polk

partner, she shared and actively encouraged his political ambitions, and, unlike other politicians' wives in those days, she routinely assisted her husband in his political activities. For example, she served as his personal secretary, marking papers important for him to read, and kept him informed about political matters when he was absent and provided advice on questions of the day. Her high profile led many observers to conclude that Polk was under her thumb, but she insisted that she was helping because of his delicate health.

During the presidential campaign of 1844, Sarah let it be known that she had no intention of churning butter and keeping house if she became first lady, and she kept her word. Impatient with social functions, she preferred to spend time with her husband on political matters and often did so until late at night. The Polks worked together without a vacation for four years. While she dutifully carried out her social responsibilities as first lady, Sarah, a devout Presbyterian, dismayed Washington society by banning drinking and dancing at the White House.

Worn out by his exertions in the White House, James died a few months after his term ended in 1849, and for the rest of her life Sarah always wore a bit of black. Showing great business skill, she operated profitably the Mississippi plantation that James had acquired while president until—perhaps anticipating the changes coming to the South—she sold it in 1860. She continued to live alone at Polk Place in Nashville—from which she had run the plantation—until her death in 1891. The southern woman who said that she belonged to the entire nation remained respected and admired by all, even during the turmoil of the Civil War. She and James are buried on the grounds of the Tennessee capital building in Nashville.

Margaret Taylor*

BORN: September 21, 1788; Calvert County, Maryland
PARENTS: Walter and Ann Mackall Smith
SPOUSE: Zachary Taylor: June 21, 1810; Jefferson County, Kentucky
CHILDREN: Ann Mackall (1811–1875); Sarah Knox (1814–1835); Octavia Pannel (1816–1820); Margaret Smith (1819–1820); Mary Elizabeth "Betty" (1824–1909); Richard (1826–1879)
DIED: August 18, 1852; Pascagoula, Mississippi

One of the most obscure of first ladies, Margaret Mackall Smith Taylor was born into a prosperous Maryland family, but very little record of her early years has survived. It is known, however, that she attended a New York finishing school and that she met Zachary Taylor in 1809 while visiting her sister in Kentucky. She and Taylor married a year later.

For the better part of the next thirty years, Margaret led the life of a military wife, following her husband to various posts from Wisconsin and Minnesota to Louisiana and throughout the South. She was unable to make a truly permanent home un-

*No portrait known

til 1840, when Zachary became southwestern commander and was assigned to Baton Rouge, Louisiana. Even then, he had to leave her to fight in the Mexican War. The constant moving took a toll on Margaret's health and that of her family. A malaria outbreak in Louisiana in 1820 claimed two of her daughters and almost killed her.

By 1848 Margaret Taylor was a semi-invalid who wanted only to live peacefully with her husband. She was appalled at Zachary's nomination and election to the presidency in that year, regarding it as a plot to deprive her of his company. Thus she came to Washington very reluctantly, and once there she completely abdicated her duties as first lady in favor of her youngest daughter, Betty. Because her time in the White House was spent upstairs as a semirecluse, wild rumors soon spread through Washington that she was a pipe-smoking simpleton. But in fact she was quite articulate with the few old friends she saw, and tobacco smoke made her acutely ill. So withdrawn was she that many people did not know until Zachary died that there even was a Mrs. Taylor.

Devastated by President Taylor's sudden death in July 1850, Margaret left the White House and went to live with family in Mississippi. Two years later she died there without ever referring to her days as first lady. No portrait or photograph of her remains, and her obituary in the New York Times failed to give her Christian name. She was buried next to Zachary near Louisville, Kentucky.

Abigail Fillmore

BORN: March 13, 1798; Stillwater, New York
PARENTS: Rev. Lemuel and Abigail Newland Powers
SPOUSE: Millard Fillmore; February 5, 1826; Moravia, New York
CHILDREN: Millard Powers (1828–1889); Mary Abigail (1832–1854)
DIED: March 30, 1853; Washington, D.C.

Growing up on the frontier, Abigail Powers Fillmore had little formal education. Yet she was able to educate herself well from the large library left by her father, who died when she was two. By sixteen, Abigail was a teacher in New Hope, New York, where she met Millard Fillmore, who was one of her students, although only two years younger than she. After a seven-year romance, the couple overcame the objections of her family, who found him beneath her socially, and married.

For the first two years of their marriage Abigail continued to teach, which was unusual at a time when married women rarely worked. She did not cease working until Millard's election to the New York State legislature in 1828. She continued to educate herself, however, learning to speak French and to play the piano.

Intelligent and well informed, Abigail took an active interest in her husband's political career, and she was able to join in political discussions with friends. Her political sense was keen, and she advised Millard frequently throughout his career. He ac-

Abigail Fillmore

SPOUSE: Franklin Pierce; November 19, 1834; Amherst, Massachusetts

CHILDREN: Franklin (1836); Frank Robert (1839–1843); Benjamin (1841–1853)

DIED: December 2, 1863; Andover, Massachusetts

Jane Means Appleton Pierce was born in 1806 to a Congregationalist minister and his wife, who hailed from a wealthy New England family. Jane's father, the excessively hard-working president of Bowdoin College in Brunswick, Maine, died in 1819. Under her parents' strict Calvinist influence, Jane became a very religious yet almost morbid young woman, possessed of delicate health and a fragile beauty that she hid in her simple dress. Although she had little formal schooling, it is likely that she gained a reasonable education from her father and various tutors.

Jane met Franklin Pierce, a graduate of Bowdoin, at her widowed mother's house in Amherst around 1826. Because of resistance from Jane's family, who looked unfavorably on Franklin's political ambitions, they did not marry until 1834. After their marriage they moved to Washington, D.C., as Franklin was then a member of Congress from New Hampshire. Jane, however, passionately hated both Washington and politics. Thus she stayed away from the capital as much as possible and tried to convince Franklin to leave politics for his law practice. In 1842 he surrendered to her pleas and resigned his seat in the U.S. Senate.

But the quiet, happy life that Jane wanted in New Hampshire was not to be. Her first child lived only three days; her second died of typhoid fever at the age of four. These tragedies accentuated her tendency toward depression and nervous tension so

knowledged that he consulted her on any important matter. Yet despite her private importance in Millard's life, she felt a public role for herself was inappropriate and refused public speaking opportunities.

Abigail remained in New York when Millard became vice president in 1849 and did not arrive in Washington until October 1850, after he had become president upon the death of Zachary Taylor. As first lady, Abigail turned much of the formal entertaining over to her daughter, Mary, generally limiting herself to more casual evening receptions and musicales. In part this was due to an old ankle injury which made prolonged standing difficult for her, but she also had little interest in Washington social life. She preferred a quiet evening with a book to a party and thought that social Washington would find her dull. Appalled at finding few books in the White House, Abigail sought and received a congressional appropriation to start the mansion's first library.

In March 1853 Abigail insisted on attending the outdoor inauguration of Millard's successor, Franklin Pierce, despite her poor health and the bad weather. A chill turned into pneumonia, and Abigail Fillmore died less than a month later in Washington. She and Millard, who died twenty-one years later, were buried in Buffalo.

Jane Pierce

BORN: March 12, 1806; Hampton, New Hampshire

PARENTS: Rev. Jesse and Elizabeth Means Appleton

Jane Pierce

much that Franklin had to refuse an appointment as U.S. attorney general. He did, however, volunteer for the Mexican War. He also maneuvered himself into the Democratic presidential nomination in 1852, despite assuring Jane he would not do so. When Jane discovered his deception, her trust in him was shattered. She prayed for his defeat in the presidential election of 1852 and was greatly depressed when he was elected.

In January 1853 the Pierce family was involved in a train wreck in Massachusetts. Franklin and Jane were unhurt, but their remaining son, Bennie, was killed before his mother's eyes. Jane never recovered from this disaster. She believed Bennie's death to be some sort of divine judgment of Franklin's election. She did not come to Washington until after the inauguration of her husband, and when she did arrive, she stayed upstairs in the White House and wrote letters to her dead son. She did not make an appearance as first lady until New Year's Day 1855. Her sense of duty led her to carry out her social responsibilities for the rest of Franklin's term, but she had no enthusiasm for them. Throughout her stay in Washington she was considered an invalid, and the White House was regarded as a gloomy place.

An admittedly sick woman by 1857, Jane left the White House to travel abroad—the West Indies and Europe—for her health. The cure was ineffective, however, and she returned to Massachusetts, depressed and ill. She died of tuberculosis in 1863 and was buried beside her children (and eventually her husband) in Concord, New Hampshire.

Mary Lincoln

BORN: December 13, 1818; Lexington, Kentucky
PARENTS: Robert and Elizabeth Parker Todd
SPOUSE: Abraham Lincoln; November 4, 1842; Springfield, Illinois
CHILDREN: Robert Todd (1843–1926); Edward Baker (1846–1850); William Wallace (1850–1862); Thomas "Tad" (1853–1871)
DIED: July 16, 1882; Springfield

Perhaps the most controversial of the first ladies, Mary Todd Lincoln was one of fifteen children born to a prominent Lexington, Kentucky, businessman and his wife. Her parents provided her with a good education; Mary spoke French and studied dance and music. By age twenty-one she had gone to live with a sister in Springfield, Illinois. Mary was attractive, intelligent, and witty, but she was troubled by severe insecurity and a mercurial temperament that worsened as she grew older.

While in Springfield, she met Abraham Lincoln, whom she married when she was twenty-four. The motive for her decision to marry Lincoln, as with so many of Mary's actions, is not clear. Some scholars believe that she claimed to see a future president in the man she chose above other suitors, but the early years of their marriage were hardly presidential. They lived in near poverty for the first year, and, although circumstances improved as Abraham served in Congress and then was a Springfield lawyer, Mary still lacked the luxury she had known as a girl.

Mary's belief in her husband was justified when he was elect-

Mary Lincoln

ed president in 1860, but her dream of being first lady was to become a nightmare. The difficulties of her young married life, including the death of her son Edward at age four, had combined with her moody temperament to leave her emotionally unstable. Abraham called her his "child wife," and often he had to treat her as one. By the time she became first lady, she was extremely nervous and prone to blinding headaches. Her moods swung erratically and violently, making her extremely impetuous and unpredictable. Her insecurity often showed as well, frequently in displays of irrational jealousy. Her instability made her a burden on a president trying to deal with war.

During Mary's stay at the White House, she was the target of unceasing criticism. With the Civil War on, she fought with Congress for more money to renovate the White House. Her family's ties to the Confederacy led many to call her a traitor, and she was even investigated by a congressional committee. When she held White House receptions, she was criticized for her inappropriate frivolity during a national crisis. If she chose not to host social functions, she was attacked for "adding to the gloom" of the day. When her son Willie died of typhoid in 1862, her unrestrained grief was condemned as excessive in a time of national tragedy. Indeed, her grief at Willie's death was "uncontrolled"; Abraham had to treat her like a "sick child." She refused ever again to enter the rooms where the boy died and was embalmed. She also banned flowers and music from the White

House (for which she was criticized as well) and conducted séances with his spirit.

The constant pressure and criticism intensified Mary's emotional problems, and her behavior became even more extreme. For example, driven by her insecurity and the pressures of living in the White House, Mary compulsively bought clothes without Abraham's knowledge, and her clothing bills soon exceeded his yearly salary. She fearfully awaited the returns of the 1864 elections, knowing that a loss would force her to face creditors she could not pay. When Abraham won, she bought more clothes.

Mary was forty-seven when her husband was assassinated in 1865. She did not attend his funeral and stayed in mourning in the White House for five weeks. Her behavior after leaving the White House became increasingly erratic. Among other things, she developed an obsession that she was impoverished—although Abraham's estate left her $35,000 after settling debts. Mary petitioned Congress for a pension, but she was so clumsy in her appeals that she alienated most members of Congress as well as the public.

To escape the criticism, she went with her favorite son, Tad, to Europe and did not return until Congress gave her a small pension in 1870. When Tad died of typhoid in 1871 she developed symptoms of paranoia and kept her money and securities sewed into her coat. Her behavior became so erratic that in May 1875 her remaining son, Robert, had her committed to a mental hospital. After one of her sisters arranged her release from the sanitarium a few months later, Mary moved to France and lived there alone until she fell and badly injured her back in 1879.

Sick and unhappy, estranged from her only remaining son, and largely forgotten, Mary went back to Springfield and died there of a stroke in 1882. She was buried next to her husband and children in Springfield.

Eliza Johnson

BORN: October 4, 1810; Leesburg, Tennessee

PARENTS: John and Sarah Phillips McCardle

SPOUSE: Andrew Johnson; May 17, 1827; Greeneville, Tennessee

CHILDREN: Martha (1828–1901); Charles (1830–1863); Mary (1832–1883); Robert (1834–1869); Andrew Jr. (1852–1879)

DIED: January 15, 1876; Greeneville

Eliza McCardle Johnson was born a few miles from Greeneville in east Tennessee. Her father was a shoemaker who died when she was still very young, but her mother was able to support herself and her daughter by weaving, and Eliza managed to acquire a basic education. She met Andrew Johnson, a tailor newly arrived in Greeneville, in 1826. Within a year they married. While the Johnsons lived frugally on Andrew's income as a tailor, Eliza taught him to read and write and otherwise improved his education.

In 1828, two years after arriving in Greeneville, Andrew's political career began when he was elected town alderman. That career would take him to the U.S. House of Representatives, the

Eliza Johnson

Tennessee governorship, the U.S. Senate, and the vice presidency. Throughout his career, however, Eliza shunned the attendant social life, preferring instead to focus on the efficient operation of her home.

With Andrew's work and Eliza's management, the family prospered, but Eliza's health did not. She suffered from a form of tuberculosis, and by 1853 the disease already had progressed so far that she felt unable to move to Nashville when Andrew became governor. During the Civil War, Eliza was forced from her east Tennessee home by the Confederate army, but she returned when the troops left and stayed there even when Andrew was elected vice president in 1864. Lincoln's assassination in April 1865, which elevated Andrew to the presidency, changed her plans, and she arrived in Washington in August of that year.

Although Eliza lived in the White House during her husband's turbulent administration, she took very little part in it. By then largely an invalid, she usually stayed in an upstairs room overlooking the front lawn, making only two public appearances during her time as first lady. Her daughter Martha served as White House hostess and supervised the renovation of the mansion after the Civil War. Although Eliza had no influence on Andrew's politics, her support for him never wavered. When told of his acquittal on impeachment charges, she said that she had known he would be vindicated.

With the expiration of Johnson's term in March 1869, Eliza

returned to east Tennessee, where she lived for the next seven years. She died at the age of sixty-five, six months after her husband's death, and was buried next to him in Greeneville.

Julia Grant

BORN: January 26, 1826; St. Louis, Missouri

PARENTS: Col. Frederick and Ellen Wrenshall Dent

SPOUSE: Ulysses S. Grant; August 22, 1848; St. Louis

CHILDREN: Frederick Dent (1850–1912); Ulysses Simpson Jr. (1852–1929); Ellen "Nellie" Wrenshall (1855–1922); Jesse Root (1858–1934)

DIED: December 14, 1902; Washington, D.C.

Julia Boggs Dent Grant was born at White Haven, her father's large farm about five miles west of St. Louis, Missouri. From ages ten to seventeen she attended a private school in St. Louis. In 1843 she met Ulysses S. Grant, an army officer stationed in St. Louis, who had been a classmate of her brother at the U.S. Military Academy. The pair soon decided to marry, but opposition from Julia's father and the outbreak of the Mexican War delayed them for five years.

The first twelve years of their marriage were not always easy ones for Julia. Ulysses's army career led to several moves and then a long separation when he was transferred to the Pacific coast. In 1854 he left the army and returned to civilian life, but his attempts at farming and business were failures. Julia, who

had been brought up in a slave-owning family, struggled to raise four children and manage her household largely on her own and with very little income. She also had to deal with Ulysses's tendency to drink excessively. The Civil War gave Ulysses the chance to escape oblivion. By its end, his battlefield success had made him the most popular man in the United States, except perhaps for President Lincoln, and he was easily elected president in 1868.

As first lady, the engaging Julia was a striking contrast to her immediate predecessors. At great expense she refurbished the White House, and she entertained lavishly—formal banquets had as many as twenty-nine courses. The country loved her style and her lively family. Politics was of no interest to her, but no one expected it to be; her society was sufficient. She was so prominent that, according to one historian, she was the first first lady to become a truly "national" figure.

After eight years in the White House, the Grants toured the world and then settled in New York City. Another bad business deal left them penniless, but Grant's memoirs, written while he was dying of cancer, brought Julia an adequate income. She lived for seventeen years after his death in 1885 and wrote her own autobiography—the first president's wife to do so. It remained unpublished, however, until 1975. The woman who was the first to be called the "first lady of the land" died in Washington, D.C., and was buried next to her husband in New York City.

Lucy Hayes

BORN: August 28, 1831; Chillicothe, Ohio

PARENTS: Dr. James and Maria Cook Webb

SPOUSE: Rutherford B. Hayes; December 30, 1852; Cincinnati, Ohio

CHILDREN: Birchard Austin (1853–1926); James Webb Cook (1856–1934); Rutherford Platt (1858–1927); Joseph Thompson (1861–1863); George Crook (1864–1866); Fanny (1867–1950); Scott Russell (1871–1923); Manning Force (1873–1874)

DIED: June 25, 1889; Fremont, Ohio

Lucy Ware Webb Hayes was the daughter of an Ohio doctor, who died in 1833 while on a trip to Kentucky to free his family's slaves. From her parents Lucy acquired a strong opposition to slavery. She was educated in private schools in Chillicothe and graduated from Wesleyan Women's College in Cincinnati in 1850, the first first lady to have a college degree.

Lucy met Rutherford B. Hayes in 1847, before entering college. He later set up a law practice in Cincinnati and eventually proposed to her, in 1851. Lucy was a serious, intelligent woman, who took an active interest in her husband's military and political careers. During his service in the Civil War, she traveled regularly to the camps where he stayed, and once brought him to Ohio to recuperate after being wounded. She was very interested in politics and kept abreast of the issues of the day. It was Lucy's persuasion that helped to turn Rutherford against slavery, and at least in her early days she displayed feminist leanings.

Julia Grant

Lucy Hayes

SPOUSE: James A. Garfield; November 11, 1858; Hiram

CHILDREN: Elizabeth Arabella (1860–1863); Harry Augustus (1863–1942); James Rudolph (1865–1950); Mary "Molly" (1867–1947); Irvin McDowell (1870–1951); Abram (1872–1958); Edward (1874–1876)

DIED: March 14, 1918; South Pasadena, California

Lucretia Rudolph Garfield was born to parents who strongly believed in education. Her father was one of the founders of what became known as Hiram College in Hiram, Ohio. With the encouragement of her parents, Lucretia grew into a studious, thoughtful young woman, who attended the school her father had founded. There her intelligence impressed many.

While at Hiram, Lucretia came to know James A. Garfield, who was both a student and a teacher at the school. Although James admired Lucretia's intellect, he initially found her "dull." The romance that developed between them was an off-and-on affair that lasted nine years before their marriage, in part because Lucretia was reluctant to surrender her independence and in part because James mistrusted what he saw as her feminist leanings. Initially, their marriage was a strained one, aggravated by frequent separations during its first four years. A close bond did not begin to develop between them until after the death of their first child in 1863. By then, James was on his way to Congress.

As the wife of a member of Congress, Lucretia had little impact on Washington society. She preferred to spend time at the

Her compassion for people showed in her kindness toward wounded soldiers and her concern for orphans and the poor while Rutherford was governor of Ohio.

Lucy became first lady in 1877. Her simplicity and frugality marked a dramatic change from the extravagance characteristic of the Grant administration. Devoutly religious and a teetotaler, Lucy instituted daily morning worship in the White House and banned alcohol from White House functions. The latter act, which earned her the derisive nickname of "Lemonade Lucy," was in fact as much a political as a moral gesture, for temperance was a burning issue of the day. Beyond this issue, however, she displayed no political leanings while first lady. She was a popular national figure who received letters from women throughout the country asking for help and advice. She initiated the custom of the children's Easter egg roll on the White House lawn.

After one term as president, Hayes retired to Fremont, Ohio, in 1881. Lucy spent the next few years busy with her family and various charitable activities. On June 21, 1889, she suffered a severe stroke and died four days later. She was buried in Fremont, where Rutherford was laid to rest in 1893.

Lucretia Garfield

BORN: April 19, 1832; Hiram, Ohio

PARENTS: Zebulon and Arabella Mason Rudolph

Lucretia Garfield

Library of Congress, which was near her home, and joined the Washington Literary Society. She also took a hand in her children's education in the classics and advised her husband when asked. She had become a political wife.

James became president in 1881, but Lucretia's time as first lady was very brief. She was making plans to redecorate the White House in a historical manner and undertaking research for accuracy when she was stricken with malaria in May 1881. She then left Washington to recuperate. James was on his way to visit her when he was shot in July; he died on September 19. Lucretia's stoic courage through his ordeal won her the admiration of the country. Unlike any previous first lady, she both organized his funeral and appeared publicly at it.

Lucretia Garfield lived for thirty-six more years, avoiding publicity while living briefly in Europe and then in Ohio. She died at her winter home in California and was buried next to James in Cleveland, Ohio.

Frances Cleveland

BORN: July 21, 1864; Buffalo, New York
PARENTS: Oscar and Emma Harmon Folsom
SPOUSES: Grover Cleveland; June 2, 1886; Washington, D.C.
Thomas J. Preston Jr.; February 10, 1913; Princeton, New Jersey
CHILDREN: Ruth (1891–1904); Esther (1893–1980); Marion (1895–1977); Richard Folsom (1897–1974); Francis Grover (1903)
DIED: October 29, 1947; Baltimore, Maryland

Frances Cleveland

Frances Folsom Cleveland, the daughter of a Buffalo, New York, attorney, was born in 1864. One of the first people to see the infant Frances was her father's close friend Grover Cleveland, who became her de facto guardian after her father, Oscar Folsom, was killed in an accident in 1875. Frances was educated in public schools in Buffalo and attended Wells College in Aurora, New York. She grew into a lively and attractive young woman, who maintained close ties with her friend Grover Cleveland.

In 1884 Cleveland became the first bachelor elected to the presidency since James Buchanan. For two years rumors about potential romances surrounded him—including one linking him with Frances's mother—until the White House announced his engagement to Frances in May 1886. Their wedding, the first of a president to be held in the White House, was small and yet a public sensation.

Frances Cleveland was admired widely. Her hairstyle and clothing became national fads, and her picture was used without her permission in various advertisements. Numerous causes solicited her endorsement without success. She held public receptions at the White House on evenings and Saturdays so that working women could come, and thousands did so. At one such reception nine thousand people came through her receiving line, and Frances's arms had to be massaged afterward. Her formal parties were just as popular. Frances's charm and beauty served as a valuable contrast to Grover, who could be rude and

boorish. In fact, the public curiosity about her was so great that the Clevelands rented a second residence in Washington to use as living quarters, and Grover commuted to the White House.

Frances's six years as first lady were interrupted by the term of Benjamin Harrison (1889–1893). During the campaign of 1888, she became a campaign issue as the Republicans accused the president of beating his wife; Frances had to refute the charges publicly. Her picture eventually appeared on Democratic campaign posters, the first time a politician's wife had been used in that way. When Frances returned to the White House in 1893, she reduced her social schedule to accommodate her growing family. Her second daughter, Esther, was the first child to be born in the White House.

In 1897 the Clevelands retired to Princeton, New Jersey. Eleven years later Grover died. Frances remained in Princeton and eventually married Thomas J. Preston Jr., an archaeology professor who later taught at Princeton University. She remained active in social and charity work and was a key figure in distributing clothes to the poor during the depression. On October 29, 1947, Frances died suddenly while visiting her son Richard in Baltimore. She was buried in Princeton next to Grover.

Caroline Harrison

BORN: October 1, 1832; Oxford, Ohio
PARENTS: Rev. John and Mary Neal Scott
SPOUSE: Benjamin Harrison; October 20, 1853; Oxford
CHILDREN: Russell Benjamin (1854–1936); Mary Scott
(1858–1930)
DIED: October 25, 1892; Washington, D.C.

Caroline Lavinia Scott Harrison was the second of three children born to one of the "most illustrious educators of the early West." Because her parents believed in education for women, Caroline was well taught; she displayed outstanding artistic and musical talents as well.

Caroline first met Benjamin Harrison in 1848 while he was a student at Farmer's College in Cincinnati, Ohio, where the Reverend Scott was teaching. In 1849 the Reverend Scott took his family back to Oxford, Ohio, Caroline's birthplace, to establish the Oxford Female Institute, and in 1850 Benjamin transferred to Miami University in Oxford. Both Benjamin and Caroline were serious and intelligent and soon were attracted to one another; in 1853 they married. Within a year they settled in Indianapolis, Indiana, where they made their home until 1881.

Benjamin became a successful lawyer, and in 1881 he was elected by the Indiana legislature to the U.S. Senate. For her part, Caroline never completely developed her artistic abilities. Spurred perhaps by the needs of her husband's career, she concentrated on civic work and was active in her church. In con-

trast to her aloof husband, Caroline was a lively, cheerful person who made guests welcome and spent much time teaching art, music, and needlepoint.

Benjamin was elected president in 1888. Caroline came to the White House with the hope of not just refurbishing the mansion but also structurally changing or rebuilding it. She had three different plans for major changes drawn up. Congress refused to approve any of them, however, and she was left with a more modest remodeling that included repairing the furniture, redoing the floors and plumbing, repainting, exterminating the mice and insects, and adding bathrooms (an important consideration since the Harrisons had several relatives staying with them). Electricity also was installed in the White House while Caroline was first lady, but she was so fearful of it that she would never touch the switches. Caroline designed her own china pattern and started the White House china collection by gathering pieces from previous administrations. Outside the White House she played an important role in making the new Johns Hopkins medical school coeducational.

Caroline's health became a problem as her term as first lady wore on. She had been seriously ill in 1883 and in 1886, but she had recovered. By 1892, however, she was so sick with tuberculosis that Benjamin refused to appear publicly in his reelection bid (his opponent, Grover Cleveland, also refrained from campaigning). Caroline continued to deteriorate through the summer and died two weeks before the election that turned her husband out of the White House. She was buried in Indianapolis, where Benjamin was buried as well nine years later.

Ida McKinley

BORN: June 8, 1847; Canton, Ohio
PARENTS: James and Catherine Dewalt Saxton
SPOUSE: William McKinley; January 25, 1871; Canton
CHILDREN: Katherine (1871–1875); Ida (1873)
DIED: May 26, 1907; Canton

Ida Saxton McKinley was one of three children born to a wealthy Canton, Ohio, banker from a prominent family. Active and headstrong as a young woman, she attended Brook Hall Seminary in Media, Pennsylvania, and worked in her father's bank for the pleasure of it, something rare for a woman in the 1860s. While working, she met William McKinley, a Civil War veteran and Canton lawyer, whom she married within a year.

For a brief time things went well for Ida. The family lived comfortably in Canton, and their first child was born within a year of their marriage. Then in early 1873 Ida's mother died. Shortly thereafter her second daughter was born, but the sickly infant lived only a few months. Less than two years later the McKinleys' other child, Katy, also died. Ida never recovered physically or emotionally from these successive shocks. She developed a form of epilepsy and was subject to frequent seizures. She also suffered from severe headaches and phlebitis and was frequently depressed and irritable. For the rest of her life Ida re-

Ida McKinley

Edith Roosevelt

BORN: August 6, 1861; Norwich, Connecticut

PARENTS: Charles and Gertrude Tyler Carow

SPOUSE: Theodore Roosevelt; December 2, 1886; London, England

CHILDREN: Theodore Jr. (1887–1944); Kermit (1889–1943); Ethel Carow (1891–1977); Archibald Bulloch (1894–1979); Quentin (1897–1918)

DIED: September 30, 1948; Oyster Bay, New York

mained an invalid who made extreme demands on the time and patience of her husband. Yet William remained devoted to her, tending carefully to her needs despite his flourishing political career, which led him to the presidency in 1896. Ida returned his devotion with a love that was almost worship.

Unlike previous first ladies who had been ill, Ida refused to remain in the background. She insisted on playing her role as White House hostess, and on attending all the social functions, despite the difficulties caused by her health. Special arrangements had to be made for every event to deal with the possibility of her becoming acutely ill. The president even changed the seating at formal dinners to place Ida next to him. If a minor seizure struck in the presence of guests, he would calmly cover her face with his handkerchief until it had passed and she could rejoin the conversation. Quick exits followed a major seizure. She also insisted on traveling with him, even though she was often too weak to do more than just be seen. William developed a reputation as a saint for his care of his wife, and his foremost concern upon being shot in 1901 was for her. Ida, however, displayed surprising strength during his decline, death, and funeral, despite the anguish recorded in her diary.

She returned to Canton to live, sick and lonely, for six more years. At first, she prayed daily to die, but later she decided that she wanted to live until completion of the McKinley mausoleum. She died four days before its dedication and was buried in Canton next to William and her two long-dead daughters.

Edith Kermit Carow Roosevelt was a childhood acquaintance of her future husband. They grew up in the same neighborhood, where she was a close friend of Theodore's younger sister. Although Edith did not attend college, she was a voracious reader and was considered well educated. Edith was not Theodore's first love; his first wife had died in 1884 after a four-year marriage. A year later Theodore renewed his long association with Edith, and in 1886 they married.

Edith was intelligent and serious, and she possessed a detached serenity that served her well in managing the boisterous Roosevelt household. She had five children of her own, a stepdaughter, Alice, from Theodore's first marriage, and Theodore himself, whom she often seemed to regard as another child. Because she also was politically astute, Theodore, who respected her intelligence, frequently looked to her for advice. Her stepdaughter, Alice, noted that the afternoon walks that Edith and Theodore took regularly seemed to have a "calming" effect on him.

Edith's organizational skills were valuable to her as first lady. To eliminate friction and control expenses, she held weekly meetings of cabinet wives to coordinate entertainment. And in running the White House, she used caterers for formal entertaining and a personal secretary to help handle correspondence. Edith introduced other innovations as well. She began carrying bouquets of flowers to avoid having to shake hundreds of hands during receptions, and she initiated a portrait gallery so that there would be a permanent memorial to each first lady. A music lover, Edith replaced the customary White House socials with musicales. Edith also worked to ensure that her family had some measure of privacy in the fishbowl of the White House. Realizing that public curiosity about the president's family would have to be satisfied, she released posed photographs and managed stories to produce more, instead of less, privacy. To the same end, when the White House was remodeled in 1902, she arranged to have the first family's living quarters separated from the White House offices and placed off-limits. She also controlled the publicity surrounding Alice's elaborate White House wedding in 1906.

Public opinion was very favorable about Edith when she left the White House in 1909 to retire with Theodore to Oyster Bay. After his death in 1919, Edith traveled widely throughout the world, engaged in charity work, and continued her ties with the Republican Party—she actively opposed Franklin Roosevelt's presidential bid in 1932. Her last years were spent quietly at Oyster Bay, and, after her death in 1948, she was buried there next to Theodore.

Helen Taft

Helen Taft

BORN: June 2, 1861; Cincinnati, Ohio
PARENTS: John and Harriet Collins Herron
SPOUSE: William Howard Taft; June 19, 1886; Cincinnati
CHILDREN: Robert Alphonso (1889–1953); Helen Herron (1891–1987); Charles Phelps (1897–1983)
DIED: May 22, 1943; Washington, D.C.

Helen Herron Taft was the eldest daughter of the eleven children born to a Cincinnati judge and his wife. During a quiet childhood, she attended private schools and became a skilled pianist. Later she taught school for a few years and was part of a group of the city's young people who met frequently to discuss ideas. Although the Herrons knew the Tafts well, Helen did not meet William Howard until she was eighteen. Over the next seven years a romance gradually developed between the two, and they married in 1886.

Ambitious and discontented with a quiet life in Ohio, Helen prodded her less-driven husband in his career, which he had begun as a lawyer. She had visited the White House in 1888 and greatly wanted to return to it as its mistress. Although Taft was content with a place on the federal bench in Ohio, Helen pushed him to accept nationally important positions, first as U.S. solicitor general, then as governor of the Philippines (1901–1904), and finally as Theodore Roosevelt's secretary of war. Her objections

twice led him to refuse a possible appointment to the U.S. Supreme Court during the Roosevelt administration. In 1908, despite his reluctance, Helen encouraged him to run for the presidency. It was widely known that without her push, he never would have made the effort.

In the inaugural parade of 1909, Helen broke precedent by riding next to her husband. The symbolism was appropriate, for she was intimately involved in his political decisions and frequently assisted and advised him on political matters. Her influence over him was obvious. She had little patience for social events and tried to downplay them as much as possible to remain where important things happened. She even complained that when traveling with the president, she was often shunted to some idle social frivolity while he was engaged in important meetings.

But Helen's drive for William's success strained her health. During her stay in the Philippines, she had been forced to go to Europe for treatment for nervous exhaustion. After two months as first lady she suffered a severe stroke that temporarily impaired her speech and took her out of the public eye for more than eighteen months. Typically, she found the forced absence from the political councils far more aggravating than missed social duties.

Taft served only one term as president, and Helen left the White House bitter toward Roosevelt, whom she believed had ruined her husband's chance at reelection. The Tafts then moved to New Haven, Connecticut, where William taught at Yale Law School. In 1921 they returned to Washington when he was appointed chief justice of the Supreme Court. No longer politically active, Helen remained in Washington after William's death in 1930, until her own death in 1943. She was the first first lady to be buried in Arlington National Cemetery. Helen Taft left at least one enduring legacy: Washington's famed cherry trees were planted at her request.

Ellen Wilson

BORN: May 15, 1860; Savannah, Georgia
PARENTS: Rev. Samuel and Margaret Hoyt Axson
SPOUSE: Woodrow Wilson; June 24, 1885; Savannah
CHILDREN: Margaret Woodrow (1886–1944); Jessie Woodrow (1887–1933); Eleanor Randolph (1889–1967)
DIED: August 6, 1914; Washington, D.C.

Ellen Louise Axson Wilson was born into a family of Presbyterian ministers. She was an intelligent woman who, according to her father, was "entirely too much inclined" to make her own decisions. She attended Rome Female College in Georgia, and, as a talented artist, she spent a year taking art classes in New York City. Ellen continued to paint throughout her life and maintained a studio on the third floor of the White House while she was first lady. She was a member of what is now the National Association of Women Artists, and her work was publicly displayed at a one-woman exhibition in 1913.

In 1883, while still at home in Georgia, she met Woodrow Wilson, who was visiting Rome on legal business. He was immediately attracted to her and proposed within five months. Ellen returned his affection, but their marriage had to wait for two years; because her mother was dead and her father was emotionally unstable, Ellen felt that she had to remain at home to care for her younger siblings. Her father's sudden death in 1884 provided her with the freedom and money to pursue her interest in art and then to marry Woodrow.

Woodrow's academic career took the Wilsons to Bryn Mawr College in Pennsylvania, Wesleyan University in Connecticut, and Princeton University in New Jersey, where he became the university's president. Ellen was an immense asset to him. By tending to the daily household details he disliked, Ellen freed Woodrow for his work. More facile in language than he, she learned German to help translate materials he needed. Her calm disposition provided stability for her intense husband. When Woodrow left Princeton to become governor of New Jersey in 1910, Ellen again proved invaluable; her incisive intellect and her intuitive understanding of people and politics made her one of his most trusted advisers.

Throughout their years together the Wilsons maintained a special relationship. Although there is no evidence that Woodrow ever had an affair, he did prefer the company of attractive women, yet Ellen never displayed any jealousy. Because the Wil-

Ellen Wilson

sons were frequently apart for various reasons, they maintained a constant correspondence that eventually totaled about fourteen hundred letters. In those letters their devotion to each other is obvious.

As first lady, Ellen maintained a hectic schedule of entertainment and social concerns. Perhaps because of her three career-oriented daughters, two of whom had White House weddings, Ellen became interested in women's suffrage. She supported the vote for women long before Woodrow did but never advocated it publicly. Instead, she took an interest in charitable work; for example, the revenue from her 1913 art exhibition went to a school for the underprivileged. After the problem of substandard housing in Washington came to her attention, she toured the capital's ghettos and then openly pushed for legislation to improve the decrepit African American neighborhoods. When a housing bill eventually passed in 1914, it was popularly known as "Ellen Wilson's bill." (The Supreme Court later declared the law unconstitutional, however.)

But Ellen Wilson did not live to enjoy her legislative success. She was terminally ill with Bright's disease, a kidney ailment, and her health began failing rapidly in late 1913. In fact, she was on her deathbed when her legislation was passed. Ellen, who died a few days before World War I began in Europe, was buried in Rome, Georgia, next to her parents.

Edith Wilson

BORN: October 15, 1872; Wytheville, Virginia
PARENTS: William and Sallie White Bolling
SPOUSES: Norman Galt; 1896; Washington, D.C.
Woodrow Wilson; December 18, 1915; Washington, D.C.
CHILDREN: None
DIED: December 28, 1961; Washington, D.C.

Born into a family of eleven children, Edith Bolling Galt Wilson received most of her education at home and had only a few years of formal schooling. At age twenty-four she married Norman Galt, an older man who was a Washington, D.C., jeweler. But in 1908 Galt died suddenly and left his store to his wife. Edith continued to manage the business, and she lived well, dressing fashionably and often making trips to Europe.

In March 1915 Edith was introduced to Woodrow Wilson by Wilson's cousin, Helen Bones, who was helping him to manage the White House after Ellen Wilson's death. Edith and Woodrow were immediately attracted to one another, and a romance developed rapidly. After hesitating briefly because of the possible political consequences of Woodrow marrying too soon after Ellen's death, they wed quietly at Edith's home. Despite the fears of his aides, Wilson suffered no political fallout, and he was re-elected president in 1916.

Self-assured and decisive, the new Mrs. Wilson brought life and entertainment back to the White House. She also proved to be an important assistant to the president, working as his personal secretary and helping with his papers. Her primary interest was her husband; she was not particularly interested in politics and denounced the women's suffrage movement as "unladylike." When the United States entered World War I, Edith tried to set an example for the country by observing the various meatless and gasless days, sewing items for the Red Cross, curtailing entertainment, and using sheep to keep the White House lawn trimmed (she donated their wool to the war effort).

While battling the Senate for ratification of the Treaty of Versailles after the war, Wilson's health broke down. By October 1919 a stroke had largely paralyzed him. Edith immediately stepped in to protect and shield her husband. She screened all papers, business, and visitors, keeping as much as possible away from him while he recovered. For a time, almost no one saw Wilson except his wife. Exactly how much power she wielded and how long she held it have never been determined conclusively. Critics then and now have argued that she was actually the acting president and essentially ran the country for the balance of Wilson's term. Edith herself claimed that her "regency" lasted but a few weeks and that Woodrow always made the important political decisions.

Sick and disillusioned, Woodrow Wilson lived only three years after leaving the White House. Edith survived him by almost thirty-eight years. During that time she traveled widely, participated in Democratic politics, wrote her memoirs, and served as a director of the Woodrow Wilson Foundation. She died of heart disease in 1961 and was buried with Woodrow in the nave of Washington's National Cathedral. Their house on S Street in Washington is now a museum.

Florence Harding

BORN: August 15, 1860; Marion, Ohio
PARENTS: Amos and Louisa Bouton Kling
SPOUSES: Henry A. DeWolfe; 1880; Marion
Warren G. Harding; July 8, 1891; Marion
CHILDREN: By Henry DeWolfe: Eugene Marshall (1880–1915)
DIED: November 21, 1924; Marion

Florence Kling DeWolfe Harding was born into one of the wealthiest families in Marion, Ohio. She was educated at the local schools and then attended the Cincinnati Conservatory of Music. Willful and tenacious, Florence fought repeatedly with her domineering father. In 1880 she eloped with Henry De-Wolfe, the son of a local coal dealer, and six months later had her only child. A man who liked to drink and hated to work, De-Wolfe proved unreliable and abandoned Florence in 1882; she divorced him in 1886. She then allowed her parents to adopt her son, and she eked out a living giving piano lessons.

In 1890 she met Warren G. Harding, then a Marion newspaperman, and married him a year later over the violent objec-

Florence Harding

tions of her father. Strong and demanding where Warren was weak and pliable, Florence quickly became the dominant force in the Harding household. She took charge of his newspaper, the *Marion Star,* and made it into an effective business, thereby freeing him for politics. She also pushed his political career, helping him into the U.S. Senate in 1914 and into the presidency in 1920. A believer in astrology, Florence at first hesitated to urge Warren to seek the presidency because a fortune-teller had predicted that although Warren would win the office, he also would die there.

Florence's personal life was not so successful. Health problems deprived her of the limited beauty she had enjoyed, and she knew that Warren, who was quite handsome, was having affairs. Her shrill voice and domineering manner led to further difficulties between them. Unflatteringly, Warren once had nicknamed her "Duchess." Their relationship continued to be strained during his presidency.

As first lady, Florence showed no interest in running the White House; she preferred to meet people. She entertained constantly, if not lavishly, opened the White House to the public, and shook hands for hours. She frequently visited wounded war veterans. She also tried to control the news coming from the White House, partly to conceal the continued indiscretions of Warren and their unhappy marriage, and partly to downplay his unsteady health. Her own health was poor; the one kidney she had (the other had been lost in 1905) was frequently infected. In fact, she almost died in 1922. Nevertheless, assertive and de-

manding, Florence continued to influence strongly her husband, but she later destroyed most of the papers that could have indicated her exact role.

As scandals began to break over the Harding administration in 1923, the president traveled to the West Coast, where he died suddenly on August 2. His death was so unexpected—the true state of his weak health had been well hidden—that rumors circulated that Florence had poisoned him. She coldly ignored them. The night before his state funeral she sat for hours with his body, speaking to it as a mother would speak to a child.

Florence then returned to Marion, where Warren was buried. Based again on astrological forecasts, she believed that she had only a short time left to live. In fact, her diseased kidney continued to weaken, and she died fifteen months after leaving the White House. Ironically, one of the songs sung at her funeral was "The End of a Perfect Day." She was buried next to her husband.

Grace Coolidge

BORN: January 3, 1879; Burlington, Vermont
PARENTS: Andrew and Lemira Barrett Goodhue
SPOUSE: Calvin Coolidge; October 4, 1905; Burlington
CHILDREN: John (1906–   ); Calvin Jr. (1908–1924)
DIED: July 8, 1957; Northampton, Vermont

An only child, Grace Anna Goodhue Coolidge was born to parents from old New England families. She attended public

Grace Coolidge

high school and graduated from the University of Vermont in 1902, making her the first president's wife to have attended a co-educational university. After graduation from college, she spent three years teaching at the Clarke Institute for the Deaf in Northampton, Vermont. She remained interested in the hearing impaired throughout her life.

In 1903, while teaching at Clarke, Grace met Calvin Coolidge. Looking up from her gardening one morning, she noticed a man standing by the window shaving while wearing only a felt hat and his underwear. The sight struck her as ludicrous, and she burst out laughing. The man was Coolidge, who heard her laughter and arranged to meet her. A romance developed between the two (which many friends, then and later, found hard to understand because Grace and Calvin seemed so different), and they married two years later.

Calvin's political career led him to the White House upon Warren G. Harding's death in 1923; he was elected to the presidency in his own right in 1924. Along the way Grace was a great asset to her husband. She was never involved politically (Calvin refused to allow it nor would he permit her to be interviewed), and there is no indication she ever gave him any political advice; she learned that he was not running for reelection in 1928 from reporters. But her outgoing personality and her remarkable memory for names and faces were a great contrast to tight-lipped Calvin's dour disposition, and she often won friends for him.

As first lady, Grace's good-natured cheerfulness made her extremely popular. Many thought that her cheerful vitality epitomized the 1920s. She was charming, friendly, and colorful, and was seen frequently with children or her pet animals. Her passion for baseball made her popular with men. Moreover, she loved music and the theater and brought notables in both fields to entertain at the White House. When the White House was renovated in 1927, Grace campaigned to have authentic period furniture donated to the mansion, but few people gave. Grace's stay at the White House was marred by one tragedy: the death of her younger son in 1924 from blood poisoning contracted from a blister on his toe.

Calvin Coolidge died four years after leaving the White House, but Grace lived and remained active for twenty-four more years. As first lady, she had helped to raise $2 million for the Clarke School, and she spent much of her retirement trying to help meet the needs of the hearing impaired. During World War II, she worked with the Red Cross and civil defense programs. In her last years her health slowly failed, and she died in 1957. Grace was buried next to her husband and younger son in Plymouth Notch, Vermont.

Lou Hoover

BORN: March 29, 1874; Waterloo, Iowa
PARENTS: Charles and Florence Weed Henry
SPOUSE: Herbert Hoover; February 10, 1899; Monterey, California

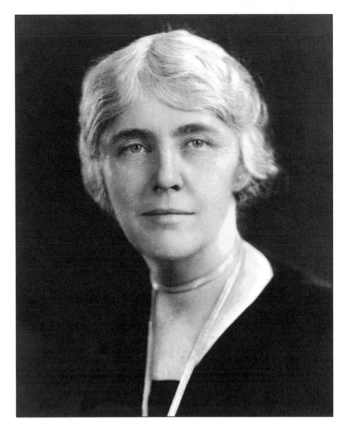

Lou Hoover

CHILDREN: Herbert Clark Jr. (1903–1969); Allan Henry (1907–1993)
DIED: January 7, 1944; New York City

One of the best educated of the first ladies, Lou Henry Hoover was born in 1874 about one hundred miles from the birthplace of Herbert Hoover, West Branch, Iowa. She lived in Waterloo, Iowa, attending public schools, until 1884, when, because of Mrs. Henry's poor health, her family moved to California. A public lecture on geology that she heard in Pacific Grove, California, led her to enroll at Stanford University in 1894; she was the first woman to major in geology there. Lou was an intelligent woman who learned to speak five languages (she later would converse with her husband in Mandarin when they wanted to speak privately in public). She also translated a sixteenth-century mining treatise from Latin into English.

In 1894 Lou met Herbert Hoover, also a Stanford geology student; four years later, she graduated from Stanford and accepted a marriage proposal from Herbert, who wired it from his job site in Australia. In 1899 he returned to California to marry her, and a week later they set out for China, where he had accepted a position with a mining firm. Thus began a global odyssey that would make Lou Hoover the most-traveled first lady in a century.

In China the Hoovers found themselves in the middle of the Boxer Rebellion, and Lou tried to assist people wounded in the conflict. From China they went to Great Britain and were there when World War I began in 1914. Lou helped Herbert's relief efforts, working with the needy in England and traveling in the United States and abroad in search of donations of food, clothes, and money to aid war victims. For her work Belgium's King Leopold awarded her the Cross of Chevalier, one of the country's highest honors.

In 1929 Lou Hoover became first lady. As first lady, Lou preferred a more active public role than earlier cabinet wives and recent first ladies. She supported social causes, advocated better social status for women, and was national president of the Girl Scouts of America. She made radio broadcasts from the White House. When Lou became mistress of the White House, she found it drab and spent some of her private funds to refurbish it. Also at her own expense, she had a photographic record made of the mansion's furnishings.

The Hoover administration was barely eight months old when the collapse of the stock market triggered the Great Depression. Touched by the suffering of the needy, Lou donated generously to charity and publicly urged others to do the same. She put the White House on a tight budget, using her own money to supplement the public funds. Almost all of her generosity, however, was kept from public view. This, combined with the Hoovers' formal and reserved manner and Herbert's inability to resolve the crisis, led to the perception that the Hoovers were cold and uncaring. Even the White House staff, which was kept at arm's length (staff members were instructed to stay out of sight when the president or first lady passed), shared this feeling. The staff also was bothered by the frequent and often impulsive entertainment carried out in the Hoover White House.

Overwhelmed by the depression, Herbert Hoover was defeated for reelection in 1932. Lou remained active in social causes after leaving the White House, particularly the Girl Scouts. With the outbreak of World War II, she began organizing efforts to provide necessities for war refugees. She was still at work when she suffered a heart attack and died in her New York apartment in 1944. So carefully had she guarded her privacy that even her husband did not realize how many people she had helped until he examined her papers after her death. In her desk drawer was a stack of uncashed checks from people who had tried to repay her generosity; she had kept them as souvenirs.

Lou Hoover was buried in Palo Alto, California; her body was later moved to West Branch, Iowa, and placed next to Herbert's.

Eleanor Roosevelt

BORN: October 11, 1884; New York City

PARENTS: Elliott and Anna Hall Roosevelt

SPOUSE: Franklin D. Roosevelt; March 17, 1905; New York City

CHILDREN: Anna Eleanor (1906–1975); James (1907–1991); Franklin (1909); Elliott (1910–1990); Franklin Delano Jr. (1914–1988); John Aspinwall (1916–1981)

DIED: November 7, 1962; New York City

Eleanor Roosevelt

Anna Eleanor Roosevelt Roosevelt, perhaps the most dynamic of all the first ladies, was born into a distinguished New York family. Her mother died of diphtheria when she was eight; her father, of whom she was very fond, was an alcoholic who died when she was ten. An unhappy girl, Eleanor was raised by a strict great aunt and taught by tutors. Her formal education consisted of three years at Allenwood School in London between ages fifteen and eighteen. In 1902 Eleanor met Franklin Delano Roosevelt, a distant cousin, and married him two years later. Their wedding date was set for the convenience of Eleanor's uncle, President Theodore Roosevelt, who gave the bride away.

Ironically, Eleanor, who became one of the most prominent first ladies, was very shy and insecure as a youngster. She was a plain girl, in contrast to her beautiful mother, and she felt the difference keenly. So serious was her disposition that her own mother nicknamed her "Granny." Things only grew worse when she married. Franklin's witty and urbane friends made her feel inadequate, and her mother-in-law, Sara Delano Roosevelt, was a domineering personality who largely ran Eleanor's household. Eleanor was even intimidated by the nursemaids who looked after her children.

Not until she was in her thirties did she begin to emerge

from her shell. A series of events—including a move away from Sara to Washington, exposure to the capital's politics, the discovery of her husband's affair with her social secretary, Lucy Page Mercer, and finally Franklin's polio attack in 1921—combined to bring her into public life. Knowing that Franklin's political career depended on having an active wife, she learned to make public appearances and to participate in New York politics even before he assumed the governorship in 1928. Her new energy spilled over into other aspects of her life. She began teaching history, English, and drama at Todhunter, a private school for girls; she wrote and lectured; and she even opened a furniture factory with two other women.

Her whirlwind of activity continued when she became first lady in 1933. Although she had to give up her teaching job, she made it clear that she did not intend to surrender any of her other activities. She continued to earn her own income from her writing, primarily for the satisfaction of doing so, but she donated most of her money to various charities. As President Roosevelt's eyes and ears, she was everywhere. She traveled throughout the country, visiting coal mines and impoverished Appalachian farms. During World War II, she regularly traveled abroad to cheer American troops. She was the first first lady to fly and advocated air travel when most Americans were afraid of it.

Refusing to be a quiet helpmate as first lady, Eleanor adopted a variety of causes and fought openly for them all. She called for programs to assist the young and the rural poor. An advocate of women's rights (although not of an equal rights amendment), she was influential in the selection of the first female cabinet member, Secretary of Labor Frances Perkins, and helped to expand government employment opportunities for women. She was an outspoken critic of racial discrimination, symbolized in her public resignation from the Daughters of the American Revolution because of the group's racist policies, and she pushed for better job opportunities for African Americans. Her activism made many criticize her harshly, but only her concern with Franklin's reelection kept her from being more vocal than she was. Although she publicly denied influencing the president, privately she regularly, and often passionately, discussed her views on policy and legislation with him and clearly was an important factor in many decisions.

No first lady has been more visible than Eleanor Roosevelt. She was active in the National Youth Administration and acted as deputy director of the Office of Civilian Defense. In addition to her travels and political activism, she, like Franklin, held regular news conferences, but she invited only women reporters since only men attended his. She made frequent radio broadcasts, continued writing magazine articles and giving public lectures, and began her own daily newspaper column. She also kept up a steady correspondence, personally answering most of the thousands of letters she received, and she did it all with only a tiny staff to help her. Her tremendous energy allowed her to work eighteen-hour days regularly.

Eleanor's time as first lady ended abruptly when Franklin Roosevelt died on April 12, 1945, but she did not fade away. Named as a delegate to the infant United Nations in 1946, she was instrumental in writing the Universal Declaration of Human Rights. She actively supported Adlai E. Stevenson's presidential bids in 1952 and 1956 and continued to speak and write in favor of more equality in American society. Her last public appointment came at the age of seventy-seven when in 1961 she was selected by John F. Kennedy to chair the President's Commission on the Status of Women.

Seriously ill with bone marrow tuberculosis, Eleanor Roosevelt failed rapidly during the summer and autumn of 1962. The woman who was called "first lady of the world" died in November 1962 at her New York home. She was buried next to her husband on their Hyde Park estate.

Bess Truman

BORN: February 13, 1885; Independence, Missouri
PARENTS: David and Madge Gates Wallace
SPOUSE: Harry S. Truman; June 28, 1919; Independence
CHILDREN: Mary Margaret (1924–   )
DIED: October 18, 1982; Independence

Elizabeth Virginia "Bess" Wallace Truman was one of four children born into a prominent family in Independence, Missouri. Besides attending school, Bess was something of a

Bess Truman

tomboy, who enjoyed baseball, basketball, tennis, and fencing, as well as throwing the shot put. Her father committed suicide when she was eighteen, leaving her to help her mother with her younger siblings. The trauma of this event, according to her daughter, Margaret, largely led to her later insistence on privacy for her own family.

Her relationship with Harry S. Truman, whom she had known since childhood, developed slowly for some eighteen years before they were married in 1919 after he returned from World War I. As her husband went into the very public career of politics, Bess, who argued that publicity was unbecoming to a lady, carefully remained in the background. She was far from insignificant in Harry's career, however. A calm and practical woman, she exerted an enormous influence over Harry. She was essentially his partner, reviewing his speeches, working on his correspondence and papers, and moderating his hot temper. She was so important to Harry that he put her on his Senate staff, arguing that "I need her there. . . . I never make a report or deliver a speech without her editing it."

The same pattern held when Bess became first lady in 1945, for she was determined not to be changed by the White House and actually became annoyed if old acquaintances treated her differently than before. Harry consulted her on every problem, including major ones such as the Marshall Plan and the Korean intervention, claiming that "her judgment [is] always good." She continued to restrain Harry's impulsive anger, and her admonishing "you didn't have to say that" was legendary among the White House staff. She insisted on remaining private, generally refusing to take stands on issues or make public statements, except for appeals for charities or on the question of repairing the White House (which by then badly needed it). Unlike Eleanor Roosevelt, Bess did not hold regular press conferences; in fact she spoke with the press very reluctantly. So successful was she at remaining in the background that, despite her importance in Harry's decisions, she was a virtual unknown. In 1949 the news media dubbed her a "riddle," and many of the "facts" reported about her were wrong. Throughout, however, the Trumans remained one of the closest families ever to occupy the White House.

Harry and Bess retired to Independence in 1953. Although he had been unpopular when he left Washington, Harry gradually acquired a reputation as a sort of folk hero, while Bess was considered one of the grand ladies of America. She went on living as quietly as ever, however, until her death from heart failure at the age of ninety-seven. She was buried next to Harry, who had died a decade earlier, in Independence.

Mamie Eisenhower

BORN: November 14, 1896; Boone, Iowa
PARENTS: John and Elivera Carlson Doud
SPOUSE: Dwight D. Eisenhower; July 1, 1916; Denver, Colorado

Mamie Eisenhower

CHILDREN: Doud Dwight (1917–1921); John Sheldon Doud (1922–   )
DIED: November 1, 1979; Washington, D.C.

Marie "Mamie" Geneva Doud Eisenhower, the last first lady born in the nineteenth century, was raised in Iowa by well-to-do Scandinavian parents. When Mamie was seven her mother's poor health prompted the family to move to Colorado, where Mamie attended high school and finishing school. The Douds later bought a winter home in San Antonio, Texas. There, in 1915, Mamie met Dwight D. Eisenhower, an army officer assigned to a nearby base. They married less than a year later.

For the next thirty-five years Mamie moved constantly as Dwight went from one military assignment to another. They moved in fact twenty-eight times, and they did not have a permanent home until they bought a farm in Gettysburg, Pennsylvania, in 1950. The longest time spent in one place before retirement was the Eisenhowers' eight-year occupancy of the White House.

Throughout these years, Mamie suffered from poor health, becoming critically ill in 1937. She was bothered by a weak heart, which apparently was a hereditary problem that had killed her sister as a young woman. She also suffered from Ménière's disease, a chronic inner ear condition that interfered with her balance and often caused her to stumble and bump into things. This condition led to groundless rumors that she was an alcoholic. Because of another illness she was unable to care for her first son when he contracted scarlet fever in 1921; his death from the disease was a devastating blow to the Eisenhowers and led to a temporary but serious strain on their marriage.

As first lady, Mamie brought frills and lace to the White House and became the nation's model for femininity. Although more visible than her predecessor Bess Truman, she took no interest at all in politics, preferring to concentrate on her managerial and social duties. She claimed to enjoy entertaining, and she worked diligently at being a good hostess. Mamie became very popular all over the country. Women copied her clothes, her bangs (a hairstyle she adopted to please her husband), and even her recipe for fudge. Her health continued to be a problem, however, and many of her friends feared she would not survive a second Eisenhower term. Yet despite her apparent delicacy, she was a strong and demanding woman who ran the White House with a firm hand, often conducting white-glove inspections.

The Eisenhowers left the White House and retired to Gettysburg in 1961. When Dwight suffered a series of heart attacks in 1968–1969, he spent almost eleven months in the hospital with Mamie at his side. She lived quietly after his death in 1969, until she had a stroke in September 1979. She never recovered and died two months later; she was buried in Abilene, Kansas. Her birthplace in Iowa is now a national museum. Abigail Adams is the only other first lady so honored.

Jacqueline Kennedy

BORN: July 28, 1929; Southampton, New York
PARENTS: John and Janet Lee Bouvier III
SPOUSES: John F. Kennedy; September 12, 1953; Newport, Rhode Island
Aristotle Onassis; October 20, 1968; Skorpios, Greece
CHILDREN: Caroline Bouvier (1957–); John Fitzgerald Jr. (1960–); Patrick Bouvier (1963)
DIED: May 19, 1994; New York City

The embodiment of "Camelot" and one of the most glamorous of the first ladies, Jacqueline Lee Bouvier Kennedy was the daughter of a New York stockbroker. Her parents divorced in 1940, however, and her mother later married the very wealthy Hugh Auchincloss.

Intelligent and strikingly attractive, Jacqueline grew up in high social circles. In fact, she was noted in the society columns at age two. She attended private schools and then Vassar, the Sorbonne (Paris), and George Washington University, graduating in 1951 with a degree in art. She worked as a writer for a time on the *Washington Times-Herald* and became its "Inquiring Camera Girl" and columnist.

Jacqueline met Massachusetts senator John F. Kennedy at a dinner party in 1951 and, after an off-and-on romance, married him two years later. But she found being a political wife sometimes trying, for she had little interest in politics and had to learn to temper her wit for public consumption. With her beauty, intelligence, and youth—she was thirty-one when John be-

Jacqueline Kennedy

came president in 1961—Jacqueline cut a much higher profile as first lady than her immediate predecessors. She made the White House a center for promoting culture and the arts, and she worked to obtain authentic antiques to furnish the mansion. As part of these efforts, she led a televised tour of the White House in February 1962, which enhanced her popularity. Women throughout the country found "Jackie" glamorous and began copying her fashions (particularly her fondness for pillbox hats) and hairstyle, much as they had done with Mamie Eisenhower. Citing the needs of her small children, she stubbornly insisted on a restricted social schedule. Her independence streak also showed when she took vacations separately from the president.

Despite its fairy tale appearance, life was not always easy for Jacqueline. Childbirth proved traumatic: her first child was stillborn, the next two were difficult Caesarean births, and her last child, Patrick, died after only two days. Moreover, shadowing her marriage were the extramarital affairs of her husband, which were hushed up at the time. Finally, in 1963, on one of the infrequent political trips that she took with John, he was assassinated as she rode next to him through the streets of Dallas, Texas. En route to Washington later the same day, she witnessed the swearing-in of Vice President Lyndon B. Johnson while still wearing a pink suit stained with her husband's blood. Back in Washington, she largely planned her husband's funeral.

After leaving the White House Jacqueline tried to maintain a more private life, despite constant pressure by inquisitive outsiders. In 1968 she married Aristotle Onassis, a wealthy Greek shipping tycoon, but his death in 1975 left her a widow for a second time. Her interest in the arts then led her to pursue a career in publishing beginning in 1975, and she accepted a position as a senior editor for Viking Press and then Doubleday. She also became involved in historical preservation.

In February 1994 the former first lady revealed that she was suffering from non-Hodgkin lymphatic cancer. The disease quickly spread to her brain and liver and proved untreatable. After contracting pneumonia, she abruptly worsened and died on May 19 in her New York apartment. She was buried next to President Kennedy in Arlington National Cemetery.

Lady Bird Johnson

BORN: December 22, 1912; Karnack, Texas
PARENTS: Thomas and Minnie Pattillo Taylor
SPOUSE: Lyndon B. Johnson; November 17, 1934; San Antonio, Texas
CHILDREN: Lynda Bird (1944–); Luci (originally Lucy) Baines (1947–)

Lady Bird Johnson

Her given name was Claudia Alta Taylor, but a nursemaid nicknamed her "Lady Bird" while she was still an infant. Her father was a successful farmer and merchant, but her mother, who suffered from health problems, died from a fall when Lady Bird was five. Thus the young Texan was raised mostly by a maternal aunt.

Lady Bird graduated from high school in Marshall County, Texas, at age fifteen, and spent two years at St. Mary's School for Girls in Dallas. From there she attended the University of Texas, where she finished in the top ten of her class with degrees in liberal arts and journalism. She earned a teaching certificate as well.

In 1934 she met Lyndon B. Johnson, then a secretary to a member of Congress, and married him after a courtship of only two months. A skillful and frugal homemaker, Lady Bird handled all of the family's financial and domestic matters. She also proved to be an astute businesswoman. In 1942 she borrowed from her inheritance to purchase a nearly bankrupt Austin radio station. Under her supervision, the station expanded into a multimillion-dollar broadcasting empire known as the Texas Broadcasting Corporation. Although the extent of her active management of the corporation varied over the years, she always maintained some involvement in its operation.

Lady Bird had virtually no experience in politics, but she quickly became a capable political wife. She learned to entertain numerous guests on short notice and became adept at remembering names, faces, and places. She borrowed from her inheritance to provide money for Lyndon's first race for Congress in 1937, and when he volunteered for active duty at the beginning of World War II, she ran his congressional office by herself for a few months. She was so capable that, according to some observers, she could have won elected office herself, although she never showed any interest in doing so. During her time as the vice president's wife (1961–1963), she substituted for the first lady at several formal events when Jacqueline Kennedy, who zealously guarded her time, refused to appear.

Lady Bird became first lady when President John F. Kennedy was assassinated in 1963. When her husband sought election to the presidency in 1964, he faced serious opposition in the South because of his support for civil rights legislation. To shore up his support among southerners, the likable Lady Bird hit the campaign trail, where she made forty-seven speeches and gained votes from people who would have refused to listen to the president himself.

With Lyndon elected, she turned her attention to her national "beautification" project, which she saw as symbolic for improving the quality of life in both urban and rural areas. She and her staff rallied public and private support for her program. Lady Bird also traveled 200,000 miles to make speeches in its behalf and personally lobbied Congress for passage of the Highway Beautification Act of 1965. She took an interest in education policy as well. In all, despite her attempt to avoid controversial policy issues such as the Vietnam War, she was the most active first lady since Eleanor Roosevelt. She also was an excellent manager. Observers have claimed that she ran her wing of the White House much better than the president ran his.

President Johnson's decision not to run for reelection in 1968—which was as much of a surprise to Lady Bird as everyone else—led to their retirement to their Texas ranch. After Lyndon's death in 1973 Lady Bird largely withdrew from public life. She continued to manage her business interests successfully and pursue her interests in natural resources, including publishing the book *Wildflowers Across America* in 1988.

Pat Nixon

BORN: March 16, 1912; Ely, Nevada
PARENTS: William and Katharine Bender Ryan
SPOUSE: Richard Nixon; June 21, 1940; Riverside, California
CHILDREN: Patricia (1946–); Julie (1948–)
DIED: June 22, 1993; San Clemente, California

Thelma Catherine Ryan Nixon was the daughter of an Irish miner, who nicknamed her "Pat" because her birthday was so close to St. Patrick's Day. Her father took up farming in Artesia, California, when she was two. In 1925 her mother died, leaving Pat to take care of the house. When her father died four years later after a lengthy illness, she went to New York to work.

In 1932 Pat returned to California and entered the University of Southern California. After graduating cum laude she took a teaching job in Whittier and there met Richard Nixon at a local theater production in which both were playing. He proposed to her on the night of their first meeting. Startled, Pat at first refused, but she eventually changed her mind and they married two years later. Richard became successful as a small-town lawyer, but he sought more and entered politics after World War II.

For Pat, the decision proved to be a trying one, one that—as she once acknowledged—she never would have made herself. She did not relish the constant public exposure, and as Richard sought higher offices and the campaigns became more intense and vicious, she came to dislike politics. In September 1952 rumors about financial misconduct forced Richard to make his famed Checkers speech in a successful effort to save his vice-presidential candidacy. Although for him it was a great triumph, for Pat it was a public humiliation as the family finances became common knowledge.

As early as 1950 she extracted a pledge from Richard not to seek office again, but he broke it repeatedly. Dutifully, Pat learned to be a proper political wife, but her lively personality was replaced, at least in public, by the stiff, formal, almost "doll-like" demeanor that earned her the unkind nickname of "Plastic Pat." The years between 1960 and 1968 were spent in private life, much to Pat's satisfaction, but Richard Nixon became president in 1969.

As first lady, Pat gathered more than five hundred authentic antiques and original paintings to refurnish the White House, more than any other first lady. She also tried to make the mansion more accessible to the public: she initiated Christmas candlelight tours and seasonal garden tours, introduced multilingual guidebooks, and made the mansion more accessible to the disabled. The most traveled of first ladies, Pat visited eighty-three countries. Because she knew that public expectations of first ladies had changed and required more social activism, Pat attempted to embrace various social projects, promoting educa-

Pat Nixon

tion and voluntarism, but her efforts were largely ineffective. Of the modern first ladies, she was one of the least active. This stemmed in part from her own difficulties in dealing with the public and in part from the White House staff's insistence that she maintain a low profile. She seemed to have little influence on her husband's political business and was left out of many important decisions, including his decision to run for president in 1968. As the Watergate scandal broke over Richard Nixon in 1973, Pat urged him to destroy the White House tapes, arguing that they were a private diary and not public fare. Her husband chose to ignore her warning, however. He resigned from the presidency in 1974.

Freed at last from the burden of politics, Pat withdrew from all but family and close friends. In 1976, while at home in California, she suffered a stroke and had to undergo several months of physical therapy; she had a second but milder stroke in 1983. Battling emphysema and chronic lung infections, her health deteriorated steadily over her last years. She died of lung cancer in 1993, on the day after her fifty-third wedding anniversary.

Betty Ford

BORN: April 8, 1918; Chicago, Illinois
PARENTS: William and Hortense Neahr Bloomer
SPOUSES: William C. Warren; 1942; Grand Rapids, Michigan

Gerald R. Ford; October 15, 1948; Grand Rapids
CHILDREN: Michael Gerald (1950–); John Gardner (1952–); Steven Meigs (1956–); Susan Elizabeth (1957–)

Betty Ford

Elizabeth "Betty" Bloomer Warren Ford was the daughter of a Chicago salesman who moved to Grand Rapids, Michigan, when she was three. As a young girl, Betty decided to become a dancer. Thus in 1935 she graduated from the Calla Travis Dance Studio and then spent time at the Bennington School of Dance in Bennington, Vermont. From 1939 to 1941 she worked in New York City as a dancer and model. After returning to Grand Rapids, she married William C. Warren, a local salesman, in 1942, but their marriage ended after five years.

Betty met Gerald R. Ford in 1947 and married him the next year. Three weeks after their wedding Gerald was elected to Congress for the first time, and Betty took on the role of political wife. She joined the organizations expected of the wife of a rising member of Congress, and, because her husband frequently was away on speaking trips or campaigning for fellow House Republicans, she took a major role in raising their four children. But the demands on her were great, and the strain finally forced her to seek psychiatric counseling in 1970. In 1973, just as she was learning stress management and had fixed a date with Gerald for his retirement from politics, he was named Richard Nixon's vice president, replacing Spiro T. Agnew who had resigned.

When Nixon resigned from the presidency on August 9, 1974, Betty Ford found herself first lady. Her outspoken honesty quickly brought her considerable attention. She strongly endorsed the Equal Rights Amendment, which was faltering in its

drive for ratification, and personally lobbied state legislators for its passage. Although the ratification effort eventually failed, she worked to increase the number of women in high government positions and pushed unsuccessfully for a woman on the Supreme Court. She also supported more assistance for the arts, the handicapped, and the mentally retarded.

Some of her statements proved to be controversial, however. Her endorsement of the Supreme Court's abortion decision, discussion of a hypothetical affair by her daughter, and comments on her children's experimentation with drugs all created a storm of protest. The courage and openness she displayed in her bout with breast cancer, which ended in a radical mastectomy, won her admirers and helped to focus public attention on that health problem. Her influence on President Ford was considerable. He acknowledged the value he placed on her opinions, while she referred to the importance of the "pillow talk" she had with him over issues.

Betty Ford left the White House in 1977 and retired with Gerald to Palm Springs, California. By the time she left she had become one of the most outspoken, and one of the more popular and respected, of the first ladies. She was praised when she acknowledged publicly her dependency on drugs and alcohol (caused by pain from an inoperable pinched nerve and arthritis together with the emotional stress of being a political wife) and told of her struggle to overcome it. She received awards for her work in behalf of women's rights and against cancer, and she helped establish the Betty Ford Center for Drug and Alcohol Rehabilitation in Rancho Mirage, California.

Rosalynn Carter

BORN: August 18, 1927; Plains, Georgia
PARENTS: Wilburn and Frances "Allie" Murray Smith
SPOUSE: Jimmy Carter; July 7, 1946; Plains
CHILDREN: John William (1947–); James Earl "Chip" III (1950–); Donnel Jeffrey (1952–); Amy Lynn (1967–)

Rosalynn Smith Carter was born and grew up about three miles from the Plains, Georgia, home of her future husband, Jimmy Carter. Her father died of leukemia when she was thirteen, leaving her to help her mother with the family. After serving as valedictorian of her high school class, Rosalynn attended Georgia Southwestern Junior College in Americus so that she could remain near home. She had known Jimmy for some time, but her first date with him was not until she was seventeen; she married him a year later.

Jimmy was a naval officer at the time of their marriage, and for the first time Rosalynn moved away from Plains, spending time in California, Pennsylvania, Hawaii, Virginia, and Connecticut. She enjoyed her new independence and the opportunities it offered. When her father-in-law died in 1953 and Jimmy decided to resign his commission to run the family peanut business, Rosalynn reluctantly returned to Plains.

Despite her initial resistance, she soon began to like her life

Rosalynn Carter

in Plains. She helped with the business and became active in local organizations. Rosalynn overcame an acute fear of public speaking so that she could help Jimmy when he entered politics; she traveled the state when he ran unsuccessfully for governor of Georgia in 1966, and again in 1974, when he was elected. When he decided to run for the presidency in 1976, Rosalynn again set off alone to campaign for him, traveling thousands of miles to give speeches in his behalf.

Few first ladies have achieved the prominence that Rosalynn Carter attained between 1977 and 1981. She frequently was compared to Eleanor Roosevelt, even by her husband—she was always on the go. It has been noted that "in her first two years as first lady, she made 248 speeches or public comments, gave 154 press interviews, attended 641 briefings, and visited 36 foreign countries." She fought for better treatment of the mentally ill and appeared before congressional subcommittees to support her views. Problems of the aged and equality for women were causes she supported. Rosalynn also traveled abroad on the president's behalf, most notably to Latin America in 1977. She frequently sat in on cabinet meetings and even participated in President Carter's Camp David negotiations between Egyptian president Anwar Sadat and Israeli prime minister Menachem Begin. Rosalynn was thus Jimmy's alter ego; she discussed policy matters and appointments with him daily. Their partnership in policy making was so openly equal that Rosalynn Carter has

been called one of the most influential of all the first ladies. In fact, in a poll of historians she was rated much more effective as first lady than her husband was as president.

Burdened by an economic downturn and his failure to obtain the release of American diplomats being held hostage in Iran, Jimmy Carter was defeated in his bid for reelection in 1980. He and Rosalynn retired to Plains where they wrote separate accounts of their years in the White House. She also worked with Jimmy to establish the Carter Center, a foundation in Atlanta devoted to promoting human rights and peace around the world, and she was active in Habitat for Humanity and other charitable organizations. In 1987 she and Jimmy coauthored *Everything to Gain: Making the Most of the Rest of Your Life,* which described their activities and lifestyle since leaving the White House.

Nancy Reagan

BORN: July 6, 1923;[20] New York City

PARENTS: Kenneth and Edith Luckett Robbins

SPOUSE: Ronald Reagan; March 4, 1952; Riverside, California

CHILDREN: Patricia Ann (1952–); Ronald Prescott (1958–)

Nancy Reagan was the daughter of an auto salesman and a stage actress. Her father left the family shortly after she was born, and her mother, determined to pursue a stage career, left young Nancy with relatives. Born Anne Frances Robbins, Nancy, as she was nicknamed, lived until age six with an aunt in Washington, D.C. In 1929 her mother married a Chicago physician, and Nancy went to live with them. She was legally adopted at age fourteen and became Nancy Davis. Later, Nancy attended a private high school in Chicago and Smith College in Massachusetts. While attending Smith, she had a brief romance with a Princeton student, who was accidentally struck by a train and killed.

Like her mother, Nancy decided to pursue an acting career. She had been in theatrical productions in high school and had majored in drama at Smith. In 1943 Nancy began her stage career, and in 1949 she moved to Hollywood to break into movies. There she met Ronald Reagan, then president of the Screen Actors Guild, who cleared her of a baseless charge of communist associations. After the couple married in 1952, Nancy largely abandoned her acting career to be a homemaker, returning to the screen only for very brief intervals when financially necessary. She made her last movie in 1954.

She returned to the public eye, however, when Ronald entered politics and became governor of California in 1966 and president in 1980. Initially as first lady, Nancy argued that her only concern was taking care of her husband. She thus attempted to remain out of sight. Her first two years in the White House were stormy ones, however. She was criticized sharply for her fashionable wardrobe, her rich friends, and the general image of

Nancy Reagan

Barbara Bush

luxury that she projected while the president cut spending on programs for the poor. Particularly attacked were her $900,000 remodeling of the White House and the $200,000 china set she ordered (although most of the money used for both was from private donations).

By 1982 Nancy was making determined efforts to improve her public image and to establish better relations with the news media. Among other things, she became active in drug abuse programs, a longtime concern, and supported antidrug efforts, both domestically and internationally. By 1985 Nancy had gone from being one of the most disliked first ladies to being more popular than the president. Beyond these efforts, she also was a great influence on the president himself. Moreover, she displayed an iron will in protecting the interests of the more easygoing Ronald. Nancy kept abreast of current events, but she was more interested in personalities. Even the president acknowledged that she was very perceptive in personnel matters. Her behind-the-scenes influence, particularly on personnel, was strong. Several White House insiders even attested to her power to remove people she thought a liability to her husband.

In 1989, after two terms in the White House, the Reagans retired to Los Angeles, California. Nancy, the only first lady to publish an autobiography before entering the White House, later wrote a memoir of her years there, *My Turn: The Memoirs of Nancy Reagan.*

BORN: June 8, 1925; Rye, New York
PARENTS: Marvin and Pauline Robinson Pierce
SPOUSE: George Bush; January 6, 1945; Rye
CHILDREN: George Walker (1946–); Pauline Robinson "Robin" (1949–1953); John Ellis (1953–); Neil Mellon (1954–); Marvin Pierce (1956–); Dorothy Walker (1959–)

Barbara Pierce Bush was born in Rye, New York, a suburb of New York City. Her father was the publisher of *McCall's* magazine; her mother was the daughter of an Ohio Supreme Court justice. Her family was well-to-do, and she attended school at prestigious Ashley Hall in South Carolina.

She met George Bush at a Christmas dance in 1942 and became engaged to him a year later. Their marriage was delayed, however, while George served in the U.S. Navy. In 1945 Barbara dropped out of school after two years at Smith College to marry him. After George graduated from Yale University in 1948, the Bushes moved to Odessa, Texas, where George entered the oil business. That was the beginning of an odyssey that included twenty-eight homes in seventeen cities.

After succeeding in oil, George became active in politics, serving as a member of Congress from Texas, U.S. ambassador to the United Nations, chair of the Republican National Committee, U.S. representative to China, director of the Central Intelligence Agency, and finally vice president and president. In the midst of traveling around the country and the world, Barbara had six children, the second of which, Robin, died of leukemia just before her fourth birthday.

A strong believer in voluntarism, Barbara Bush donated much of her time before becoming first lady to helping the less fortunate. She was honorary chair of the Leukemia Society of America and won the Distinguished American Woman Award in 1987. Her primary concern was illiteracy in the United States, and she was actively involved in programs to improve literacy.

These concerns continued for Barbara when she became first lady. She started the Barbara Bush Foundation for Family Literacy and donated the entire proceeds from her best-selling book, *Millie's Book,* to it. (Revenues from her earlier book, *C. Fred's Story,* also had been given to literacy groups.) Remembering her deceased daughter, she often visited chronically ill children in the hospital; a widely circulated photograph of her holding an AIDS-infected baby helped to reduce prejudice against victims of the disease. And she spoke out in behalf of the homeless and of poor and single parents.

Barbara also traveled widely as first lady, visiting sixty-eight countries, and she was very active in her social duties, hosting almost twelve hundred events while attending over eleven hundred others in her four years. These efforts, with her grandmotherly appearance and self-deprecating wit, made her immensely popular, so much so, in fact, that *Good Housekeeping* named her to its list of most admired Americans for four straight years, and another poll declared her to be the world's most popular woman.

Finally, she was a close if informal adviser to President Bush, reviewing papers and discussing policy with him. Although she downplayed her own political instincts, others regarded her as a "key element" in the Bush presidency.

After George lost his reelection bid in 1992, the Bushes retired to Houston, Texas. Barbara continued to travel and to enjoy reading, needlepoint, gardening, and spending time with her family, which included eleven grandchildren. Her autobiography, *Barbara Bush: A Memoir,* was published in 1994.

Hillary Rodham Clinton

BORN: October 26, 1947; Chicago, Illinois
PARENTS: Hugh and Dorothy Rodham
SPOUSE: Bill Clinton; October 11, 1975; Fayetteville, Arkansas
CHILDREN: Chelsea Victoria (1980–)

Hillary Rodham Clinton was raised in the Chicago suburb of Park Ridge by parents whose strong support for education and self-reliance were important factors in her growth and development. She attended public high school in Chicago and then went to Wellesley College, where her intelligence and skills as a mediator won praise, and her political views became more liberal. She delivered her class commencement address, punctuating it with an attack on the day's guest speaker, Massachusetts senator Edward Brooke, as a representative of establishment politics. The verbal fireworks earned her national publicity in *Life* magazine.

Hillary Rodham Clinton

After graduating from Wellesley, Hillary attended Yale Law School. There she became interested in children's rights issues, joined the Yale Child Study Center, and assisted in the preparation of two books on child development. She also met and began dating Bill Clinton, a fellow law student.

After her graduation from Yale in 1973, Hillary worked at the Children's Defense Fund for a brief time and then, in January 1974, joined the U.S. House of Representatives Judiciary Committee's Impeachment Inquiry staff, which was grappling with legal questions surrounding the possible impeachment of President Richard Nixon. Her work with the committee led to several prestigious job offers after Nixon's resignation, but she decided to join Bill in Arkansas. She taught law at the University of Arkansas in Fayetteville and married Bill in a house he had purchased there for them.

In 1976 Bill was elected attorney general of Arkansas, and the Clintons moved to Little Rock where Hillary joined a prominent law firm, working in family law, commercial litigation, and criminal law. She quickly established herself as one of the city's best lawyers. Two years later, Bill became governor. During this time, Hillary founded the Arkansas Advocates for Children and Families, was appointed by President Carter to chair the Legal Services Corporation, and served on the board of the Children's Defense Fund. But as first lady of Arkansas, Hillary's high profile, outspokenness, and "liberal" ideas—such as continuing to use her maiden name—made her a lightning rod for criticism and contributed to Bill's reelection defeat in 1980.

In 1982 Bill Clinton rebounded to be reelected governor of Arkansas; he held the office for the next decade. Finally adjusting to Arkansas realities, Hillary changed her image while remaining prominent and became one of the state's more popular first ladies. In the meantime, she spearheaded education reform by serving as the chair of the Arkansas Education Standards Committee. And, not least, she served as an adviser to her husband, evincing political skills good enough to earn her mention as a gubernatorial candidate in her own right. Her law practice and her reputation also grew, and by 1989 the *National Law Journal* had cited her as one of the nation's "100 Most Powerful Lawyers."

In the 1992 presidential campaign, her intelligence and proven abilities, which sometimes led the campaign to claim the public would be getting "two for the price of one" in a Clinton presidency, proved to be a double-edged sword. It won many supporters, some of whom thought her better qualified than her husband to be president, but it also left her open to attacks from political opponents, particularly the Republican right, who claimed that she had too much influence with her husband and that her views were "antifamily." Similar charges plagued her as first lady.

Once the Clintons were in the White House, Hillary was appointed by the president to head the commission established to create a health care reform program. When after eight months the commission produced a plan, Hillary became its foremost advocate, lobbying behind the scenes and appearing publicly before five different congressional committees to explain and defend it. She also served as one of her husband's most important informal advisers on almost every topic; "Ask Hillary" was the watchword in the White House. By 1996 she stood as one of the most active and powerful of the first ladies. As one commentator noted, she was unique because she had a "strong separate source of power inside the administration with a mandate of authority from the president and an operational base from which to carry it out."

While first lady, Hillary continued to address issues involving women and children, and she attended the United Nations conference on women in Beijing, China, in 1995. She also wrote a weekly newspaper column and published a book, *It Takes a Village.*

As in Arkansas, the first lady's prominence led to controversy. Legal and ethical questions persisted about her role in the 1993 firing of the White House Travel Office staff and in the handling of the Clintons' Whitewater real-estate venture. In the latter case, she responded to questions from a Senate investigation committee and, in February 1996, became the first sitting first lady to be subpoenaed by, and to testify before, a grand jury.

Family and Friends of the President

Family and the presidency have gone hand in hand; only two bachelors, James Buchanan and Grover Cleveland, have ever been elected president, and Cleveland married during his term. Most presidents have been family men, with wives, children, and other family members.

Given the burdens of the office, one might suppose that an unmarried person, unencumbered by family worries, would be better suited for the job. But, in fact, those burdens may increase the importance of a family for the president. The first family provides the president with a support system, a refuge where the problems of the nation can be put aside. For many people, the president's family life is an important indicator of whether the president is a stable, healthy, and mature individual, capable of handling the responsibilities of adulthood and the presidency. Politically, the family symbolizes traditional American values and therefore becomes invaluable to the man or woman who would be president.[21]

Presidential families have come in considerable variety. They have been large and small, close-knit and distant. Some family members have been quiet; others have been colorful. Some have proven to be real assets to a president; others have been liabilities. Whatever the case, the increasing attention paid to the White House in recent years has elevated the president's family to a new prominence.

CHILDREN IN THE WHITE HOUSE

Several presidents have had older children who already had left home when they entered office, but others have brought their children, some young, into the White House. Two of Abraham Lincoln's three sons were young when he was president, and Ulysses S. Grant brought a ten-year-old son to the White House. Benjamin Harrison brought such a large extended family to the White House that the mansion was not really large enough to accommodate it.

Perhaps the most famous White House family was that of Theodore Roosevelt. Roosevelt arrived in Washington in 1901 with six children, ages four to fourteen. Like their father, they were boisterous and active and often made their presence known, even at official activities. When Roosevelt was governor of New York, they had kept a small zoo of their own in the basement of the governor's mansion, and at least one official dinner had been cut short when the aroma of their animals had drifted through the open windows.

Having established a reputation in New York, the Roosevelt children quickly became the delight of Washington. They came to the White House just as press coverage of—and interest in—the president's family was beginning to grow, and although their mother carefully controlled the news about them, their exploits were soon the talk of the entire country. The White House was a "bully" playhouse for Roosevelt's brood. They crawled into the spaces between the ceilings and floors, explored out-of-the-way corners of the attic and the basement, and poked into all sorts of

Archie Roosevelt, one of Theodore's sons, rides his Shetland pony on the South Lawn in front of the West Wing.

other places where people had not been for years. They slid down the banisters, rode bicycles and roller-skated on the hardwood floors, walked on stilts in every room, climbed the trees, swam in the fountains, and used the furniture for leapfrog games. They kept pets everywhere and produced them for visitors at the slightest encouragement; their pony got rides on the White House elevator. Once, son Quentin Roosevelt used mirrors to flash light into government offices, thus disrupting work there.

Far from restricting his children, the president seemed to encourage their activities and often took part in their games. To a visitor who suggested that he do something about his irrepressible daughter Alice, who interrupted a meeting by repeatedly rushing into the Oval Office, he replied, "I can do one of two things. I can be president of the United States or I can control Alice. I cannot possibly do both." He also once said that no one had had more fun in the White House than he, and an observer noted that "you must remember that the president is about six."[22] Edith Roosevelt herself frequently seemed to treat him like a big child. When he cut his chin with a hatchet, she complained that he was spoiling the rugs by bleeding all over the house. Roosevelt's boisterous family proved to be a great asset for him. Their antics drew attention to the president and "reinforced the image of a vibrant, energetic man in the White House."[23]

More than half a century later another family with young children came into the White House. When John Kennedy moved into the mansion in 1961, his daughter, Caroline, was three years old and his son, John, was only an infant. Like

TABLE 25-1 Historians' Rankings of First Ladies

In 1982 Thomas Kelly and Douglas Lonnstrom of the Siena Research Institute, Loudonville, New York, conducted a poll of history professors to rank the first ladies. The poll included White House hostesses but did not include presidents' wives who did not live in the White House. Because the poll was taken early in the Reagan administration, it may not reflect accurately Nancy Reagan's later rating.

Ranking		Score
1	Eleanor Roosevelt	93.3
2	Abigail Adams	84.6
3	Lady Bird Johnson	77.5
4	Dolley Madison	75.4
5	Rosalynn Carter	73.8
6	Betty Ford	73.4
7	Edith Wilson	71.8
8	Jacqueline Kennedy	69.5
9	Martha Washington	67.5
10	Edith Roosevelt	65.4
11	Lou Hoover	63.5
12	Lucy Hayes	63.1
13	Frances Cleveland	62.3
14	Louisa Adams	62.0
15	Bess Truman	61.7
16	Ellen Wilson	61.5
17	Grace Coolidge	61.3
18	Martha Jefferson Randolph (daughter of Thomas Jefferson)	61.0
19	Helen Taft	61.0
20	Julia Grant	60.7
21	Eliza Johnson	60.7
22	Sarah Polk	60.5
23	Anna Harrison	60.1
24	Elizabeth Monroe	60.1
25	Mary Arthur McElroy (sister of Chester A. Arthur)	60.1
26	Emily Donelson (niece of Andrew Jackson)	60.0
27	Julia Tyler	59.9
28	Abigail Fillmore	59.8
29	Harriet Lane (niece of James Buchanan)	59.8
30	Lucretia Garfield	59.8
31	Mamie Eisenhower	59.7
32	Martha Patterson (daughter of Andrew Johnson)	59.6
33	Margaret Taylor	59.4
34	Caroline Harrison	59.4
35	Letitia Tyler	59.3
36	Angelica Van Buren (daughter-in-law of Martin Van Buren)	59.3
37	Pat Nixon	58.5
38	Jane Pierce	57.6
39	Nancy Reagan	57.4
40	Ida McKinley	57.0
41	Florence Harding	55.8
42	Mary Lincoln	52.9

SOURCE: Betty Boyd Caroli, *First Ladies*, exp. ed. (New York: Oxford University Press, 1995), 417–418.

Over the course of the American presidency, particularly between 1828 and 1868, several presidents' wives have refused or have been unable, usually for health reasons, to fulfill the social duties of first lady. Other presidents had no wife. When these situations have arisen, surrogates have carried out the social responsibilities of the first lady.

HOSTESSES SERVING WIDOWER OR BACHELOR PRESIDENTS

Six presidents had no wife to act as first lady during part or all of their tenure in office: four presidents (Jefferson, Jackson, Van Buren, and Arthur) entered the White House as widowers, and two others (Buchanan and Cleveland) were bachelors; Cleveland married while in office.

Martha Jefferson Randolph.

The need for a surrogate first lady first occurred during the term of Thomas Jefferson, who had been a widower for eighteen years when he became president in 1801. Although Jefferson did less formal entertaining than his predecessor John Adams, the Jefferson White House was still the center of much social activity. Dolley Madison, wife of Secretary of State James Madison, and Jefferson's daughter, Martha Jefferson Randolph, frequently filled the role of first lady for Jefferson.

Martha Randolph was the eldest of Jefferson's six children and one of only two to live to maturity. She was born in 1772 at Monticello, her family's home in Virginia. After her mother died in 1782, Martha went to a boarding school in Philadelphia. In 1784, when Jefferson became U.S. minister to France, Martha went with him. She attended an elite convent school in Paris for five years, until her decision to become a nun prompted her father to remove her from the school and hire tutors instead. Martha's girlhood letters indicate a great interest in her studies and her personal habits and appearance.

After returning to the United States in 1789, Martha married her cousin, Thomas Mann Randolph, in 1790 and had the first of her five children in 1791. The demands of her family prevented her from acting regularly as White House hostess. Her only extended stays at the mansion were during the winters of 1802–1803 and 1805–1806. An intelligent and very practical woman, Martha skillfully managed the White House and later Monticello. After the deaths of her father in 1826 and her husband in 1828, Martha was forced to sell the Virginia estate to settle debts. Her last appearance in Washington society was during Andrew Jackson's administration when Secretary of State Martin Van Buren, needing a hostess for a state dinner, turned to Martha. She died of apoplexy in 1836.

Emily Donelson.

Andrew Jackson came to the presidency in 1829 newly widowed; his wife, Rachel, died in the interval between his election and the inauguration. For much of his time in office the role of first lady was played by his niece, Emily Donelson, who was born in 1808 in Davidson County, Tennessee. Emily was educated at the Old Academy in Nashville and at age sixteen married a cousin who served as Jackson's secretary. She had four children.

After the election and before her death, Rachel Jackson, who was uncomfortable in Washington society, had asked Emily to handle many of the social functions of the White House. Despite her relative lack of sophistication and education, Emily was charming, gracious, and very popular in Washington society. She remained a hostess there until shortly before her death in 1836 from tuberculosis.

Angelica Singleton Van Buren.

Martin Van Buren's wife, Hannah, died nineteen years before he reached the White House in 1837. His daughter-in-law, Angelica Singleton Van Buren, served as the mansion's hostess during his administration. The daughter of a wealthy South Carolina planter, Angelica was related to several powerful southern families and was a distant relative of Dolley Madison. She met President Van Buren's eldest son, Abraham, at a state dinner in March 1838 and married him eight months later. President Van Buren, who until that time had had no White House hostess and had done little entertaining, asked Angelica to take charge of the mansion's social life. Her first social function was the New Year's reception of 1839. For the remainder of Van Buren's term in office, Angelica enlivened the White House.

Harriet Lane.

Because James Buchanan never married, his niece, Harriet Lane, served as hostess during his administration (1857–1861). Born in 1831, Harriet was orphaned at age nine, and her guardianship passed to Buchanan. He found homes with relatives for her siblings but chose to raise Harriet as his own daughter. She was sent to the best schools, concluding with two years at an elite Georgetown convent school. In 1853, when Buchanan became minister to England, he took Harriet with him.

Few women have come to the White House as well prepared for their social duties as the lively and attractive Harriet Lane. In fact, Buchanan's term was judged by many contemporaries to be the "gayest administration" because of her skill as a hostess. As with other immensely popular first ladies, fashions changed in response to her preferences, and the lower necklines she favored suddenly became the rage. Yet Harriet was more than just a capable hostess. Having been exposed for years to political discussions at Buchanan's table, she was well informed, and it is likely that the president listened to her opinions on many questions. She also was seen as an intermediary by those with problems and therefore received many appeals for help from the general public.

Buchanan served just one term. In 1866 Harriet married Henry Johnston and had two sons, neither of whom lived beyond age fourteen. When Buchanan died in 1869, he left his Pennsylvania estate to Harriet, and she lived there until her husband died in 1884. Harriet's remaining years were spent in Washington and abroad. Her extensive art collection formed the basis of the collection of the National Gallery of Art, which was opened to the public in 1941. She died in 1903.

Rose Cleveland.

Grover Cleveland (1885–1889) was the second bachelor president to reside in the White House. He eventually married while president, but until then his sister Rose served as White House hostess. The youngest child in the family, Rose Cleveland was born in Fayetteville, New York, in 1846. Rose was an intelligent and well-educated woman; she taught at Houghton Seminary and gained a favorable reputation as a college lecturer. She knew several languages and published scholarly studies on literature. Although a sparkling conversationalist and a gracious hostess, she sometimes intimidated visitors with her intellect. At times, she was bored with her social duties. Finding receiving lines dull, Rose would occupy herself by silently conjugating Greek verbs. After Cleveland married Frances Folsom in 1886, Rose returned to her scholarly work and lived in Europe until her death in 1918.

OTHER SURROGATE FIRST LADIES

From 1828 to 1868, several presidents whose wives were living prevailed on other family members to act as first lady, usually because they were in poor health.

Jane Irwin Harrison.

The first of these presidents was William Henry Harrison, whose widowed daughter-in-law, Jane Irwin Harrison, agreed to assist as White House hostess. Harrison's term lasted only a month after his inauguration in 1841, however, and thus Jane was left as a footnote in White House history.

Priscilla Cooper Tyler.

When John Tyler succeeded Harrison in 1841, his first wife, Letitia, who had suffered a stroke, was a semi-invalid. She died in 1842. His daughter-in-law, Priscilla Cooper Tyler, acted as his hostess. Born in 1816, Priscilla was one of the nine children of actor Robert Cooper. She performed on stage herself for a time as a young woman, but she lived in severe financial straits. In 1837 she met Tyler's son Robert after he saw her perform as Desdemona in Shakespeare's *Othello.* They were married in September 1839. Priscilla served as hostess until Tyler's marriage to Julia Gardiner in 1844. Her letters convey both her devotion to the president and her wonder at being acting first lady. She died in 1889 in Montgomery, Alabama.

Mary Elizabeth Taylor.

When Zachary Taylor came to the White House in 1849, his wife, Margaret, lacked the health or the desire to act as first lady. That role was played by her youngest daughter, Mary Elizabeth "Betty." Betty Taylor was born in 1824 in Jefferson County, Kentucky. Although her father had little formal education, he was concerned with that of his children, and Betty was sent to boarding school in Philadelphia. She married Maj. William Bliss, her father's adjutant, in 1848. After his death, she married Philip Pendleton Dandridge in 1858. Contemporaries have noted that she was charm-ing, gracious, and lovely, and a popular hostess while in the White House, particularly in contrast to the more austere Sarah Polk, her predecessor. Betty died in 1909 in Winchester, Virginia.

Mary Abigail Fillmore.

Abigail Fillmore, who followed Margaret Taylor into the White House, also lacked the interest or health to be hostess and so let her daughter take her place. Mary Abigail Fillmore was born in 1832 in Buffalo, New York, and was educated in schools in Massachusetts and New York. She taught school for a time before coming to Washington in 1850 when her father became president. A talented young woman, Mary spoke five languages and played the guitar, piano, and harp. At age twenty-two, less than two years after Millard Fillmore left the presidency, she contracted cholera and died in Aurora, New York.

Abby Kent Means.

For the first two years of Franklin Pierce's presidency (1853–1857) his wife, Jane, crushed by the tragic death of her only remaining child, refused to participate in White House society. Mrs. Abby Kent Means, a longtime friend of Jane Pierce and the second wife of Jane's uncle, thus filled in as first lady. With the help of Varina Davis, wife of Secretary of War Jefferson Davis, Abby attempted to maintain pleasantness in a melancholy White House and held receptions twice a week. But despite her efforts, the White House was a gloomy place, even after Jane Pierce assumed her duties.

Martha Johnson Patterson.

Andrew Johnson's wife, Eliza, suffered from tuberculosis when she became first lady, and her daughter, Martha Johnson Patterson, became hostess instead. Martha was born in Greeneville, Tennessee, in 1828 and married David Patterson in 1855. When her father became president in 1865, she was both White House hostess and wife of a U.S. senator. Proclaiming herself to be "plain folks from Tennessee," Martha put cows on the White House lawn to provide milk and butter. Her simplicity and calm dignity earned her respect and admiration during the turbulent Johnson years. She died in Greeneville in 1901.

Mary Arthur McElroy.

When Chester A. Arthur succeeded James A. Garfield as president in 1881, his wife, Ellen, had been dead for about eighteen months. Although Arthur personally took a great interest in White House entertainment, the official hostess in his administration was his younger sister, Mary Arthur McElroy. Mary was born in Greenwich, New York, in 1842 and was educated in private schools, concluding with Mrs. Willard's Female Seminary in Troy, New York. She married John McElroy in 1861. While White House hostess, Mary continued to live in Albany, New York, traveling to Washington for the social season each year. Although Mary was popular as a hostess, she also was careful to protect the privacy of both the president and her family. She died in 1917.

Theodore Roosevelt's children, Caroline and "John-John" were the subject of much curiosity, and they were constantly photographed and written about. Strongly wanting them to have a "normal" childhood, Jacqueline Kennedy carefully protected them and managed the publicity about them. She even went so far as to have holly trees and rhododendrons planted to block the view of the White House from the street. A playground with a tree house, slide, tunnel, sunken trampoline, and swing was built outside the president's office for the children, and there they frequently played within sight of Kennedy as he worked. There also was a small zoo with rabbits, guinea pigs, dogs, lambs, ducks, and ponies. (The ducks eventually were removed—they ate the flowers, and the dogs ate them.) There was an effort as well to get Irish deer and peacocks for the children, but none ever came to the South Lawn.

Mrs. Kennedy insisted on keeping her afternoons free for her children and skipped several social functions to do so; she and the children took regular walks around the White House driveway.

On the third floor of the White House a nursery school was built for Caroline and was equipped with books, a sandbox, goldfish, toys, and plants. Mother and daughter slipped in at night to play in the sand. Nine other children shared the school with her. After Kennedy's assassination in 1963, the school remained for the rest of that semester before being dismantled, and little Caroline was driven to the White House every day for school.[24]

The Kennedy children were not as publicly rambunctious as the Roosevelt clan, yet they remain the most photographed of any White House family. Images of the pair are part of American lore: running to meet their father, walking with their mother, dancing in the Oval Office, Caroline holding her mother's hand at her father's funeral as John-John salutes his coffin. The public attention continued to follow them as adults; Caroline

had to give up a job as a photojournalist because she became the focus of attention wherever she went.

The charm of younger children has proven an asset to presidents. Jimmy Carter came to the White House with a nine-year-old daughter, still young enough to be a symbolic help to him. Amy Carter showed up as a Typical Girl: strawberry blonde with freckles and glasses, a good student, lonely when her parents were out campaigning, and not at all eager to leave her friends in Plains, Georgia. As such, she became someone everyone could identify with, and she was a popular public figure well before Carter was elected president in 1976. Her parents too wanted her to have a normal childhood while living in the White House. Amy caused a sensation by attending public school in Washington; on her first day of class, members of the news media turned out in droves to cover the event. She had parties for her friends in the White House movie theater and in the tree house her father built on the South Lawn. She also learned to play the violin, studied astronomy from the mansion's roof, and received as presents an elephant from Sri Lanka and reindeer from Finland (they were given to the National Zoo). Although Amy knew little of Washington behavior when she arrived—she showed up for her first state dinner with a book in her hand—she soon learned, and she appeared at several public receptions, such as that held for the Energy Department's youth conservation program.

It is possible to escape the limelight and live a largely normal childhood in the White House. The Clintons made great efforts to minimize the public attention to Chelsea, who was almost thirteen when her father became president. Few stories appeared in the media about her, and little official information was provided. The stories that did appear showed a teenager much like any other: attending school and church, studying dance, going out with friends, and having slumber parties.

For younger children, living in the White House is not a

Bill and Hillary Clinton went to great lengths to protect the privacy of their daughter, Chelsea, pictured here in front of her parents at the 1992 Democratic national convention

Often overlooked in discussions of first ladies are the four women who died before their husbands reached the White House: Martha Jefferson, Rachel Jackson, Hannah Van Buren, and Ellen Arthur.

Martha Jefferson.

Martha Wayles Skelton Jefferson was born October 19, 1748, in Charles City County, Virginia. Her parents were John and Martha Eppes Wayles. When she was seventeen, Martha married Bathhurst Skelton, a lawyer and landowner, by whom she had one son. Skelton died in 1768, and four years later, on January 1, 1772, she married Thomas Jefferson. She and Jefferson had six more children, but only two—daughters Martha "Patsy" Washington (1772–1836) and Mary "Polly" (1778–1804)—lived more than two years.

Relatively little is known of Martha Jefferson. Few references to her remain, and none of her correspondence still exists. Although there are no portraits of her, she was apparently a very attractive woman who had considerable talent on the piano and harpsichord, as well as the practical ability to keep accounts for the Jeffersons' Virginia plantation, Monticello. Moreover, her inheritance made her fairly wealthy. Never very strong, Martha's health was weakened by the repeated burdens of childbearing and a flight through the snow and freezing weather from British troops in 1780. The birth of her last child, in May 1782, proved too much for her, and she died on September 6, 1782, at Monticello. Jefferson was so distraught at her death that he refused to leave his room for three weeks. He never remarried.

Rachel Jackson.

Rachel Donelson Robards Jackson hailed from a pioneering family. Her parents, John and Rachel Stockley Donelson, were among the first settlers of Nashville, Tennessee. Rachel was born on June 15, 1767, in Halifax County, Virginia; she moved with her family to Tennessee in 1780. She had little formal education.

In 1784 Rachel married Lewis Robards, a Kentucky landowner, and moved to Kentucky with him. Robards, however, proved to be insanely jealous and abusive. Fearing physical harm, Rachel fled back to Nashville. She returned once to Robards, but shortly afterward left again in the company of Andrew Jackson, who had been sent to her aid by her family. To protect her from Robards, Jackson took her on to Natchez, Mississippi.

In 1791, on receiving word that Robards had been granted a divorce, Andrew and Rachel married. But the information was wrong: Robards only had been given permission to seek the divorce in Kentucky, and the actual divorce did not occur until 1793. When the Jacksons were informed, they immediately remarried on January 17, 1794, but the damage was done. The fact that Rachel was technically an adulteress would haunt her for the rest of her life, and Andrew fought several duels to protect her honor.

Rachel stayed at the Hermitage, the Jackson estate in Nashville, for much of her married life. She wanted only to remain quietly at home with her husband, but his ambition frequently took him away for long intervals. Although she moved to Washington after he became a senator, she was generally reclusive. Short, stout, and interested only in friends, family, and church, she favorably impressed some visitors with her unassuming ways, but others thought her to be detrimental to Jackson's career. Rachel accepted Jackson's election to the presidency in 1828 with great reluctance, saying that she "would rather be a doorkeeper in the house of God than live in that palace in Washington." She feared that she was unsuited to be first lady.

During the 1828 campaign, Jackson's opponents had viciously resurrected the story of Rachel's "adultery." The details, however, were kept from her until, in Nashville to be fitted for an inaugural gown, she overheard some women discussing them disparagingly. Friends found her weeping hysterically. Rachel suffered a heart attack a few days later and died on December 22, 1828, at the Hermitage. She was buried there in the gown that had been made for the inaugural ball. Jackson never remarried.

Hannah Van Buren.

The first president's wife to be born an American citizen, Hannah Hoes Van Buren entered the world on March 8, 1783, at Kinderhook, New York. Her parents, Johannes and Maria Quackenboss Hoes, were Dutch, and Hannah grew up speaking that language. She knew Martin Van Buren as a child, and by age eighteen the couple was engaged. Because Martin wanted to study law and gain admittance to the bar before they wed, the wedding did not take place until February 21, 1807, in Catskill, New York.

Shortly after their marriage, Martin began his political career. He was a New York state senator from 1812 to 1820 and state attorney general from 1816 to 1819. From 1808 to 1817, Hannah spent much of her time in their home in Hudson, New York, raising their new family. They had four children: Abraham (1807–1873), John (1810–1866), Martin (1812–1855), and Smith (1817–1876). In 1817 she moved the family to Albany, where the weather proved bad for her health. She contracted tuberculosis and gradually declined. She never left her home after September 1818 and died on February 5, 1819, at the age of thirty-five.

Very little is written about Hannah Van Buren. She left no correspondence or writing of her own, and her husband's autobiography, so descriptive of public matters, says virtually nothing about his wife of twelve years. Apparently she was an attractive although shy woman who was religious and very concerned with the poor and the needy. Originally buried in Albany, Martin later had her reburied in Kinderhook.

Ellen Arthur.

Ellen Lewis Herndon Arthur, the daughter of William and Frances Hansbrough Herndon, was born on August 30, 1837, at Fredericksburg, Virginia. After her father, a naval officer, died at sea in 1857, she and her mother moved to New York City. There she met Chester A. Arthur, a young lawyer, in 1858, and they married on October 25, 1859. Chester's law practice proved very successful, and he entered New York State politics. The Arthurs continued to live in New York City, where Ellen cared for their three children: Billy (1860–1863), Chester Jr. (1864–1937), and Ellen (1871–1915). A gifted singer, Ellen was active in the Mendelssohn Glee Club and performed publicly several times. She also was active in charity work. Her musical and charitable work helped Chester's developing political career. In early January 1880, Ellen became ill after waiting outside in the cold for a carriage. Her illness was not considered serious at first, but she worsened abruptly and died of pneumonia on January 12. She was buried in Albany. Chester never remarried; he placed flowers before her portrait every day and kept her room in their home as she had left it.

problem. Since most of their families are well-to-do, the large house is normal. A greater adjustment is required of older children, who may find the mansion a restriction as much as a pleasure. One major problem is the glare of publicity that surrounds the president and the first family. The children's faces become almost as well known as the president's own, which makes going out a difficult prospect. It is now rare that a president's child can pass unnoticed in public. Incidents such as the one in which Lyndon Johnson's daughter Lynda was approached by an unwitting fellow student at the University of Texas and told that "the president's daughter was a student on campus somewhere" are infrequent.

More likely, every move the child of a president makes is subject to public scrutiny and public opinion. Thus the public learned all about Susan Ford's eighteenth birthday, her senior prom, how much she charged for baby-sitting (a dollar an hour), and the rides she rode at Disney World. Chelsea Clinton was at the center of a controversy when her parents decided to send her to an elite Washington private school instead of a public one. Some children may enjoy such publicity, but it is hard on others. Quiet Tricia Nixon shrank from all the attention and remained so reclusive that her sister once referred to her as "the Howard Hughes of the White House."

Another problem is that it is not easy for a teenager to have much of a social or romantic life in the White House. The constant public watchfulness makes it as difficult to have a quiet date as to go out for pizza with friends. Then too the omnipresent Secret Service agents who accompany every president's child impede the development of intimate relationships. Although agents maintain as discreet a distance as circumstances permit, knowledge of their presence may be inhibiting. The president's children therefore often wish to lose their protective detail and occasionally have tried. Early in her White House days, Luci Johnson would jump in her car and drive away before the agents were ready to go; they eventually stopped her by confiscating her car keys.

Older presidential offspring are much more aware of the political fallout from the actions of the president. They may suffer from guilt by association, or they may be the target of criticism. Like it or not, they frequently are in the center of the storm. Julie Nixon, for example, often encountered hostility while a student at Smith College during the Vietnam War. Her husband, David Eisenhower, skipped his commencement exercises at Amherst College because of antiwar tensions on the campus.

Despite the drawbacks, most children of presidents have seemed to enjoy life at the White House. Perhaps one cannot go out as much, but there are many opportunities for entertaining, as well as resources that cannot be had elsewhere.

PRESIDENTIAL RELATIVES AS ASSETS

The president's relatives have become much more prominent in recent years. As media coverage of the first family has increased, attention has expanded from just the president to the first lady and then to the children and the extended family. Be-

fore World War II, it was very unusual to hear much about the president's extended family. Occasionally some relative would be newsworthy, but most remained in the background.

The visibility and importance of the president's relatives began to change after 1945. Public curiosity about the president spread to his family until today anyone remotely connected to the president gets at least some attention. Some relatives naturally have proven more interesting and important than others. Many, in fact, have been quite valuable to the president.

Several family members have served as advisers to the president, either formally or informally. Milton Eisenhower, the younger brother of President Eisenhower, never held any official position in the Eisenhower administration, but he was a close confidant of the president. Because Milton had made his career in government, he had an understanding of its workings and nuances that his brother, a career military officer, lacked. More important was the relationship that existed between the brothers; they were close enough that the president was able to try out ideas on his brother and get honest advice in return. As Milton Eisenhower put it:

President Eisenhower found it helpful to reveal his innermost thoughts and plans to one who was not subservient to him, was not an advocate of special interests, had no selfish purpose to serve, and would raise questions and facts solely to help the president think through his problems without pressing for a particular decision.[25]

Milton Eisenhower's role was so important that some observers considered him to be the most helpful person, official or unofficial, around President Eisenhower.

There is little doubt that the most important adviser to John Kennedy was his brother Robert. Unlike Milton Eisenhower, however, Robert F. Kennedy had an official position in his brother's administration. Risking charges of nepotism, the president named his brother attorney general, despite his extremely limited experience in the legal profession. (A congressional act passed in 1967 banned future presidents from appointing relatives to cabinet positions.) In fact, Robert Kennedy's title meant little, for although he did spearhead an assault on organized crime, his real importance lay in his ties to his brother. Robert Kennedy was almost an alter ego to the president. He ran John Kennedy's Senate campaign in 1952 and his presidential race in 1960 and gradually developed a strong bond with him. The two brothers complemented each other well. Passionate where John was detached, a stern and demanding taskmaster where John was easygoing, Robert provided a driving force and both accomplished things and took the heat for his brother. The two even began to think alike, so much so that they could communicate without talking. Robert Kennedy's closeness and unquestionable loyalty to his brother allowed him to make suggestions and criticisms that no one else could.

The best illustration of Robert's importance was the 1962 Cuban Missile Crisis. Although by his formal position he should not have been involved at all, the attorney general not only sat in on the deliberations of the Executive Committee that was convened to advise the president on the American response to the crisis, but also was a central actor. When President Kennedy removed himself from the ExCom's deliberations to promote freer debate, it was Robert Kennedy who took charge, aggressively probing and questioning the other members of the committee to obtain the best decision possible.

Other presidents may have sought advice from relatives, but Milton Eisenhower and Robert Kennedy are the most prominent examples of presidential relatives who served as advisers. In other administrations, relatives have been assets to the president without being advisers. For example, Mary McElroy, sister of widowed Chester A. Arthur, and Rose Cleveland, sister of Grover Cleveland, both won favor for their respective brothers with their work as White House hostesses.

A president's family also can prove an asset in times of trouble. Strong support by family members may not make the problem disappear, but it can be both politically and personally advantageous to the president. For example, Richard Nixon's younger daughter, Julie Eisenhower, rallied to his defense during the Watergate affair. In 1973–1974, as the Watergate scandal consumed Nixon's presidency, both Pat Nixon and older daughter Tricia Cox gradually faded into the background; sunny and outgoing Julie stepped forward in her father's defense. She made numerous public appearances, granted interviews, and met the press in her father's behalf. The most famous of her public appearances was a televised Saturday morning press conference with her husband, David (President Eisenhower's grandson), in May 1974 in which she vigorously defended her father. She also became one of her father's closest confidantes. Her courage and her spirited, dogged defense of Nixon won the respect of many observers, and, although she could not save Nixon's presidency, her constant support may have been critical to his emotional survival.[26]

A different sort of asset was President Carter's mother, Lillian, who gave new meaning to the term *first mother*. Other presidents' mothers who have survived to see their sons take office have had such low profiles as to be almost invisible. Lillian Carter, however, was a star in her own right. She was lively and intelligent, outspoken, and down to earth. She courageously welcomed African Americans into her south Georgia home long before it was acceptable for southern whites to do so. In 1966, at age sixty-eight, she joined the Peace Corps and went to India. When Jimmy Carter became president in 1977, she became his goodwill ambassador. She toured drought-stricken East Africa, represented the president at state funerals in India and Israel, and made other trips on his behalf. She also traveled around the country to gather support for Carter among Democrats. In 1977 the Synagogue Council of America gave "Miss Lillian" the Covenant of Peace award for aiding "international justice, understanding, and peace." Her style and substance drew public support to an otherwise beleaguered president.

The efforts of the president's extended family also can prove useful in campaigning. The Kennedy clan pioneered in this area; before them, presidential family members rarely participated publicly in campaigns, but Kennedy's race in 1960 was a family affair. His brother Robert served as campaign manager, and his brother Edward had responsibility for producing votes in the western states. Joseph P. Kennedy, JFK's father, was a driving force as well, especially in his son's early congressional campaigns. The elder Kennedy, who had pushed his son John into politics, dominated his campaigns so much that only Robert proved able to cope with him. Joseph Kennedy also provided abundant funds and contacts for his son. JFK himself would joke about charges that his father was "buying elections" for him. Referring to the West Virginia primary in 1960, he remarked, "I got a wire from my father: Dear Jack. Don't buy one more vote than is necessary. I'll be damned if I'll pay for a landslide." His mother, Rose Kennedy (who died in January 1995), and his sisters Eunice Shriver, Pat Lawford, and Jean Smith rang doorbells and attended receptions and banquets on a carefully orchestrated schedule aimed at maximizing family exposure. In particular, Rose Kennedy proved a natural politician, plugging her son to everyone she met and turning every situation to his advantage. Even Kennedy's brother-in-law Stephen Smith played an important administrative role in the campaign. The family effort was very important to JFK's run for the White House; he might not have been nominated and elected without it.[27]

PRESIDENTIAL RELATIVES AS LIABILITIES

Many relatives of presidents have been perceived as liabilities. Some presidential relatives have come under direct public criticism; others, because the president believed that they would in some way foster negative publicity in a media-dominated era, have been kept out of sight. For example, JFK's sister, Rosemary, who was mentally disabled and eventually had to be institutionalized, was carefully excluded from public view. Later, Sam Houston Johnson, Lyndon Johnson's younger brother, was seen as a liability by LBJ, although the reasons are not entirely clear. Once referred to as his primary political adviser by Lyndon Johnson himself, Sam Houston was relegated to obscurity when his brother reached the White House. He seemed to be dominated by the president and totally dependent on him both before and during LBJ's term; he had no home of his own and no steady job. Moreover, Sam Houston was in poor health and was struggling with alcoholism. Apprehensive about the image his brother projected, the president put him under virtual house arrest; during LBJ's term, Sam Houston lived on the third floor of the White House, unable to do anything without the president's prior approval. The primary job of the Secret Service agent assigned to Sam Houston was to keep track of everywhere he went and everyone he spoke with. His contact with the outside world was restricted to the White House domestic staff, and he was mentioned in the press only four times in the five years of the Johnson administration.[28]

One of Richard Nixon's younger brothers, Donald, who was struggling to make a business venture succeed in the 1950s, borrowed money from Howard Hughes, a major manufacturer of defense equipment. The loan, however, was never repaid, and it became an issue (influence buying) in the 1960 presidential campaign and again in the 1962 California gubernatorial campaign. Nixon thus became seriously concerned that this and other of his brother's financial dealings (none of which were illegal) might be embarrassing to him as president. After Richard Nixon became president, Donald Nixon was kept under wraps; his telephone was tapped, he was placed under physical surveillance, and a report on his activities was prepared for Nixon's aides.

A more public problem was caused by Jimmy Carter's younger brother, Billy. In the early days of the Carter administration, Billy was actually an asset to the president; his folksy, down-home, beer-drinking, country boy image made austere Jimmy seem a bit more accessible. Billy Carter became an instant celebrity. He appeared on television talk shows, made paid public appearances, and had his own beer marketed. The press loved him and even commented on his shrewd business sense.

Unfortunately, by 1979 most of the good feeling toward Billy had been replaced by public criticism and ridicule. Some of his escapades and comments received extremely unfavorable publicity: once he urinated outdoors at an Atlanta airport, and another time he made remarks that were widely interpreted as being antisemitic. Allegations of financial irregularities, including the diversion of a business loan to his brother's campaign, were made but never proven. Billy also was criticized for a reception he cohosted for Libyan officials and a free trip he took to that country. In 1980 it was learned that Billy had accepted more than $200,000 in "loans" from Libya and also was apparently in technical violation of a law requiring him to register as a Libyan agent. These disclosures led to a Senate investigation later that year of Billy Carter's affairs. The president's brother argued that the Libyan money had been needed for living expenses; so much of the family business had been put into a blind trust during President Carter's term that Billy had been forced to sell his own share and had been left without income.

Although the congressional hearings into "Billygate" produced no evidence of anything beyond poor judgment, Billy Carter remained a liability to his brother. Republicans seized on the lingering claims of his financial improprieties to challenge President Carter's integrity in the 1980 elections. Moreover, people believed that the president should somehow muzzle his brother, who was seen as a national embarrassment. When the president would not or could not keep Billy Carter "under control," it reinforced the public perception of a weak president. Certainly, the poor image Billy Carter had acquired damaged the president's hopes for reelection in 1980.

Relatives sometimes can pose difficulties for the president even if they are not alcoholics or in financial hot water. Just as the American public expects the first lady to be the epitome of womanhood, so it expects the first family to be the essence of harmonious family life, with the implication that something is wrong if it is not. Such expectations can bedevil presidents who have tensions within their families. Ronald Reagan, for one, had

to deal with such problems. At the outset of his first term, relations were strained between his older children, Maureen and Michael, and their stepmother, Nancy. When Maureen ran for the U.S. Senate in 1981 the Reagans gave her no help, and Michael complained publicly in 1985 that the president had never seen his two-year-old granddaughter because of Nancy Reagan's "jealousy." Daughter Patti Davis sharply criticized her parents in her autobiography. The rifts later were patched over successfully, but such familial stresses can be damaging to presidents with less popular appeal than Reagan.

The hint of impropriety in the family also can harm the president. In 1990 President Bush's son Neil came under suspicion for his actions as a director of the Silverado Savings and Loan in Denver, Colorado. The S&L failed, leading to a $1 billion federal bailout, and the younger Bush was accused by investigators of conflict of interest, negligence, and unsafe and unsound business practices, although no criminal charges were ever brought (a civil suit was filed, however). Neil Bush consistently denied any wrong-doing, and the suit eventually was settled with only very minor penalties. Democrats, nevertheless, attacked President Bush for his son's "misconduct" and the "lax" punishment. In addition, the picture that emerged in the media of the wealthy Neil Bush seemingly getting special treatment was damaging to a president who already was seen as out of touch with the average American.

Sometimes merely being unconventional can reflect poorly on the president. President Clinton's standing was not aided by his half-brother, Roger. Younger and "wilder" than the president, Roger made news by being an aspiring rock-and-roll singer, shouting at a photographer in a department store, getting into an altercation with a heckler at a New York Knicks basketball game, and marrying his girlfriend less than two months before their first child was born.

PRESIDENTIAL FRIENDS

Over the years, several friends and close associates of the president have been important, if informal, players on the political scene. The reason for this is simple: because presidents are surrounded every day by people who expect something from them or who have a cause to endorse or a personal interest to protect, they naturally look for those who ask for nothing. As Franklin Roosevelt noted, the president needs someone "who asks for nothing except to serve [the president]." Such people are usually found among old friends.

Herein lies the origin of the so-called kitchen cabinet. Many members of the president's official cabinet are appointed for reasons other than friendship or compatibility; they may have expertise in the subject area of the cabinet department, or the appointment may be based on political necessities. Once named, cabinet appointees frequently develop a loyalty to the department in which they serve that overrides their loyalty to the president. In the words of Nixon aide John Ehrlichman, "They go off and marry the natives and we never see them again."[29] Presidents thus look to old friends to provide the unbiased advice and a fresh perspective that the cabinet may not give. Such old friends usually are not caught up in Washington politics; they look at politics from the outside in. Most presidents have had one or two, and sometimes several, such advisers.

The kitchen cabinet was created by President Andrew Jackson (1829–1837). Jackson's first official cabinet was a relatively weak body; several of its members had been appointed to satisfy factions within the Democratic Party, most notably the one led by Vice President John C. Calhoun. As a result, Jackson tended to rely on his unofficial advisers much more than his official ones. Most members of the kitchen cabinet had been important in Jackson's 1828 presidential campaign. Some were old Tennessee associates, such as Maj. John H. Eaton and Andrew J. Donelson; others, such as Amos Kendall, Issac Hill, and Francis P. Blair, were important newspapermen. Finally, there were political figures such as Roger B. Taney and Martin Van Buren. Several of these men remained in the background, but others occupied important places in the government: Eaton was secretary of war (1829–1831), Taney became attorney general (1831–1836) and then chief justice of the Supreme Court (1836–1864), and Van Buren was first secretary of state (1829–1831) and then vice president (1833–1837). The kitchen cabinet never dominated Jackson, but it was a significant source of advice, particularly between 1829 and 1831.

Not every kitchen cabinet had so many members. From 1913 to 1920, Woodrow Wilson had a one-man advisory board, Col. Edward M. House. A wealthy man who entered politics for the excitement of it, Colonel House met Wilson in 1911 and became his closest confidant throughout much of his presidency. Ike Hoover, chief usher at the White House in the Wilson years, noted that Wilson was in constant contact with House and "there was nothing too big, too important, too secret, or too sacred to discuss with Colonel House."[30] Wilson sought House's advice on various aspects of public policy, and even on personal matters such as the details of his wedding to Edith Galt. The colonel also became the president's emissary, representing him in Europe in efforts to mediate World War I. Later, House helped to lay the foundations of the Versailles peace conference that ended the war. He was recognized as being so close to Wilson that people came to him to get their ideas before the president. Although House and Wilson eventually had a falling out and never spoke after 1919, their relationship has become the symbol of closeness between president and adviser.

Another president who had a particularly close relationship with his unofficial advisers was Franklin Roosevelt. Although he had some appointees of notable ability in his cabinet, Roosevelt also drew on many sources outside the cabinet for information. One of the most important in the early days of the New Deal was the "brain trust," a group of academicians led by Rexford G. Tugwell, Raymond Moley, and Adolph A. Berle Jr. Each held minor posts in government but were instrumental in stimulating ideas on dealing with the depression.

Of greater importance was the influence of two longtime associates, Louis McHenry Howe and Harry Hopkins. Howe, once

On matters both personal and political, Col. Edward M. House was Woodrow Wilson's closest confidant throughout much of his presidency.

described as a "wizened gnome," was a newspaperman who had recognized Roosevelt's potential while FDR was still in the New York state legislature. He was Roosevelt's closest political adviser throughout the early years of the New Deal, and he strongly encouraged Eleanor Roosevelt to become involved in politics. Perhaps the most intimate of Roosevelt's advisers and one who was blessed with acute political instincts, Howe, who died in 1935, was particularly important in pointing out errors to the president and was the only man who could speak bluntly to him and get away with it. Harry Hopkins, who lived at the White House, had been part of FDR's New York state administration. He was a major adviser during World War II and served as an important figure in Roosevelt's operation of the war effort.

Whereas presidential friends and cronies often have been valuable sources of advice to the president, some friends of presidents have embarrassed and injured them by dishonesty and corruption. For example, Ulysses S. Grant came to the White House in 1869 as a career army officer with no experience in politics. To fill the various offices in his administration, Grant turned to his old friends and appointed so many of them that Massachusetts senator Charles Sumner declared it to be a case of "dropsical nepotism swollen to elephantitis."[31]

Unfortunately, many of Grant's old friends and associates were dishonest, but Grant, although honest himself, was reluctant to crack down on them. The result was one of the most scandal-plagued administrations in history. In 1875 it was learned that Grant's personal secretary, Gen. Orville E. Babcock, was involved first in a questionable scheme to annex Santo Domingo and later in the Whiskey Ring, which defrauded the government of millions of dollars in taxes. In 1876 Secretary of War William W. Belknap was impeached by the House of Representatives for selling licenses for the sale of goods to the Indians; he avoided conviction in the Senate because he resigned first. Grant was slow to respond to these and other scandals—not until the very end of his second term did he begin to acknowledge them—and they have severely damaged his historical reputation.

In 1920 Warren G. Harding was elected president, a position for which he was unsuited in many ways. Although Harding was a personable and attractive man, he was of but moderate intelligence, and he knew it. A trusting person, he seemed unable to recognize misconduct by his close associates. A contemporary joke was that George Washington could not tell a lie, but Harding could not tell a liar. He was very weak and pliable as well. His father once noted that if his son had been a girl, he would "have always been in a family way" because he could not refuse anyone.

Harding was simply one of the boys, and he brought his cronies to Washington with him. Upstairs in the White House, Harding and his friends such as Interior Secretary Albert B. Fall and Attorney General Harry H. Daugherty would play cards and drink from the president's private bar, even though Prohibition was then in force. Soon, however, scandals began breaking around Harding. The head of the Veterans' Bureau, Charles R. Forbes, was indicted for taking kickbacks in connection with the building of veterans' hospitals, and soon after, the Teapot Dome scandal, involving the illegal sale of oil leases in the western states, erupted. Fall eventually went to prison for his part in the Teapot Dome scandal; Daugherty was implicated in several crimes, but he was never convicted due to lack of evidence. The emerging accounts of corruption were devastating to Harding, who complained bitterly about his "goddamned friends." Already in uncertain health, he was put under great stress by the misdeeds of his cronies, which contributed to his sudden death from pneumonia and coronary thrombosis in 1923.

Other presidents have suffered as well from the misdealings of their associates, although few to the extent of Grant and Harding. In 1945 President Truman brought to Washington a number of his old Missouri cronies, some of whom turned out to be associated with an influence-peddling scandal. This error in judgment undercut Truman's chances to run in 1952. The allegations of financial wrongdoing that surrounded President Carter's old friend and budget director Bert Lance also helped to undercut the Carter administration in its early days.

In the modern presidency, with its emphasis on image, activities far less serious than legal misconduct can cause the president problems. When Bill Clinton arrived in Washington, he was accompanied by old friends and television producers Harry Thomason and Linda Bloodworth-Thomason. They helped to produce a mammoth, five-day inaugural gala for Clinton (including $500,000 worth of bunting for Pennsylvania Avenue), which was well attended by Hollywood figures. Bloodworth-Thomason also had the costume designer for a popular sitcom redo Clinton's wardrobe. Unfortunately, the infusion of the "Hollywood set" contrasted unfavorably with the image Clinton had used to get elected—that of identity with the average American. Within a few months, under a barrage of criticism, the "Friends of Bill" had withdrawn, and Bloodworth-Thomason had returned to Hollywood to make a sitcom satirizing Washington life.

NOTES

1. Betty Boyd Caroli, *First Ladies*, exp. ed. (New York: Oxford University Press, 1995), xv.

2. Quoted in ibid., 14.

3. Quoted in Paul F. Boller Jr., *Presidential Wives: An Anecdotal History* (New York: Oxford University Press, 1988), 296.

4. Quoted in Lewis L. Gould, "First Ladies," *American Scholar* (autumn 1986): 528–535.

5. Quoted in Boller, *Presidential Wives*, 319–320.

6. Margaret Truman, *First Ladies* (New York: Random House, 1995), 198.

7. Quoted in Carl Sferrazza Anthony, *First Ladies: The Saga of the Presidents' Wives and Their Power*, vol. 2 (New York: Morrow, 1991), 426.

8. Bob Woodward, *The Agenda: Inside the Clinton White House* (New York: Simon and Schuster, 1994), 103. Woodward's account of the inner operation of the Clinton administration indicates that Mrs. Clinton possessed extensive power.

9. Ibid., 332.

10. Boller, *Presidential Wives*, 46.

11. Quoted in ibid., 169.

12. Ibid., 296.

13. Gould, "First Ladies," 534.

14. For a discussion of this dilemma, especially in Mrs. Reagan's case, see James G. Benze Jr., "Nancy Reagan: China Doll or Dragon Lady?" *Presidential Studies Quarterly* (fall 1990): 777–789.

15. Rosalynn Carter, *First Lady from Plains* (Boston: Houghton Mifflin, 1984), 158–159.

16. Caroli, *First Ladies*, 241–242.

17. A number of sources were used to prepare the biographies of the first ladies. The major ones were: Anthony, *First Ladies*, vols. 1 and 2; Caroli, *First Ladies*; Sol Barzman, *The First Ladies* (New York: Cowles, 1970); William A. De Gregorio, *The Complete Book of the Presidents* (New York: Dembner Books, 1984); Joseph Nathan Kane, *Facts about the Presidents* (New York: Wilson, 1985); and Tim Taylor, *The Book of Presidents* (New York: Arno Press, 1972).

18. Scholars disagree about Martha Washington's actual birth date. June 21, 1731, is the date most commonly used, but several others also have been mentioned.

19. Dolley Madison's given name is not clear. Some scholars have declared that "Dorothea" was her given name and "Dolley" a nickname. Others have insisted that Dolley was her real name.

20. The birth records for Nancy Reagan have been lost, but school records indicate that she was born in 1921. Mrs. Reagan claims that she was born in 1923.

21. Barbara Kellerman, *All the President's Kin* (New York: Free Press, 1981), 26.

22. Quoted in Paul F. Boller Jr., *Presidential Anecdotes* (New York: Oxford University Press, 1981), 206.

23. Caroli, *First Ladies,* 120.

24. See J. B. West, *Upstairs at the White House: My Life with the First Ladies* (New York: Coward, McCann, and Geohegan, 1973), 216–220.

25. Quoted in Kellerman, *All the President's Kin,* 4.

26. Ibid., chap. 6.

27. Ibid., 8–10.

28. Ibid., 215–219.

29. Quoted in Stephen J. Wayne, *The Legislative Presidency* (New York: Harper and Row, 1978), 49.

30. Irwin Hood Hoover, *Forty-Two Years in the White House* (Boston: Houghton Mifflin, 1934), 87.

31. Quoted in Boller, *Presidential Anecdotes,* 157.

SELECTED BIBLIOGRAPHY

Akers, Charles W. *Abigail Adams: An American Woman.* Boston: Little, Brown, 1980.

Anderson, Alice E., and Hadley V. Baxendale. *Behind Every Successful President: The Hidden Power and Influence of America's First Ladies.* New York: S.P.I. Books, 1992.

Anthony, Carl Sferrazza. *First Ladies: The Saga of the Presidents' Wives and Their Power.* 2 vols. New York: Morrow, 1991.

Baker, Jean H. *Mary Todd Lincoln: A Biography.* New York: Norton, 1987.

Barzman, Sol. *The First Ladies.* New York: Cowles, 1970.

Boller, Paul F., Jr. *Presidential Wives: An Anecdotal History.* New York: Oxford University Press, 1988.

Bush, Barbara. *Barbara Bush: A Memoir.* New York: Simon and Schuster, 1994.

Caroli, Betty Boyd. *First Ladies.* Exp. ed. New York: Oxford University Press, 1995.

Carter, Rosalynn. *First Lady from Plains.* Boston: Houghton Mifflin, 1984.

Furman, Bess. *White House Profile: A Social History of the White House, Its Occupants and Its Festivities.* Indianapolis: Bobbs-Merrill, 1954.

Gould, Lewis L. "First Ladies." *American Scholar* (autumn 1986): 528–535.

Gutin, Myra G. *The President's Partner: The First Lady in the Twentieth Century.* New York: Greenwood Press, 1989.

Hofstadtler, Beatrice K. "How to Be First Lady." *American Heritage* 34 (August–September 1983): 98–100.

Johnson, Lady Bird. *A White House Diary.* New York: Holt, Rinehart, and Winston, 1970.

Kellerman, Barbara. *All the President's Kin.* New York: Free Press, 1981.

Levin, Phyllis Lee. *Abigail Adams: A Biography.* New York: St. Martin's Press, 1987.

Reagan, Nancy, with William Novak. *My Turn: The Memoirs of Nancy Reagan.* New York: Random House, 1989.

Thomas, Helen. *Dateline: White House.* New York: Macmillan, 1975.

Truman, Margaret. *First Ladies.* New York: Random House, 1995.

Whitton, Mary Ormsbee. *First First Ladies, 1789–1865.* New York: Hastings House, 1948.

Woodward, Bob. *The Agenda: Inside the Clinton White House.* New York: Simon and Schuster, 1994.

Youngs, William T. *Eleanor Roosevelt: A Personal and Public Life.* Boston: Little, Brown, 1984.

CHAPTER 26

Office of the Vice President

BY MICHAEL NELSON

T HE CONSTITUTIONAL and statutory responsibilities of the vice presidency are few and unimportant—legally, it is a weak office. The additional roles and resources that the vice president enjoys are delegated—and can be revoked—at the discretion of the president. "The president can bestow assignments and authority and can remove that authority and power at will," wrote Hubert H. Humphrey, who served as vice president with President Lyndon B. Johnson. "I used to call this Humphrey's Law—'He who giveth can taketh away and often does.'"[1] Accordingly, the activities and influence of individual vice presidents vary considerably from administration to administration.

During the twentieth century, however, the office of the vice president has been enhanced in several ways, especially since the end of World War II, when a cluster of events took place that aroused public concern about the vice presidency. In April 1945, after President Franklin D. Roosevelt died, Vice President Harry S. Truman succeeded to the presidency in virtual ignorance of both the administration's plans for the postwar period and the existence of the atomic bomb. Within a few years, the United States had entered into an ongoing "cold war" with the Soviet Union, a conflict that was heightened by both nations' possession of nuclear weapons that could be launched with intercontinental ballistic missiles. The possiblity that a virtually instantaneous war of unprecedented destruction could take place led many Americans to insist that vice presidents be sufficiently competent and informed so that, if the need for a presidential succession should arise, no lapse in national leadership would occur.

In response to this concern, most modern nominees for president, wishing to satisfy the voters, have examined the talents and abilities of the candidates they have considered as vice-presidential running mates before making a choice and, once in office, have kept the vice president informed and in the public eye. Some of the tasks with which presidents have entrusted their vice presidents, such as foreign travel and the right to give political and policy advice in weekly private meetings, have involved real responsibility; what is more, precedents have been created that subsequent vice presidents have been able to follow. To help carry out these new responsibilities, vice presidents have won additional resources for their office—perhaps most important, a larger and more professional staff. As a result, the vice presidency has become institutionalized, both in the narrow sense that it is organizationally larger and more complex than it

used to be and in the broader sense that certain kinds of vice-presidential activities now are taken for granted.

Evolving Roles

The myriad roles that modern vice presidents perform can be grouped into four categories: constitutional, statutory, advisory, and representative. The resources that vice presidents now have available to fulfill these roles are discussed in the next section.

CONSTITUTIONAL ROLES

The original Constitution assigned two roles to the vice president: to serve as the president of the Senate, voting only to break ties, and to succeed to the presidency in the event of a presidential death, resignation, removal, or disability. In 1967, the Twenty-fifth Amendment clarified the vice president's responsibilities as presidential successor and as acting president during periods of presidential disability. The amendment also made the vice president the central figure in determining whether a president is disabled.

President of the Senate

In the early years of the Republic, when the Senate was small and relatively informal, the vice president's role as president of the Senate allowed vice presidents to influence the Senate's agenda, steer debate, name the members of its committees, and cast relatively frequent tie-breaking votes. Vice Presidents John Adams and John C. Calhoun, for example, decided twenty-nine and twenty-eight tie votes, respectively. (See Chapter 3, History of the Vice Presidency, Vol. I.)

In contrast, modern vice presidents spend little time performing their constitutional role in the Senate. Because the Senate has become more institutionalized, the powers of the presiding officer are circumscribed and largely ceremonial—the vice president is expected to follow the advice of the Senate's parliamentarian, not to lead independently. Because the Senate is much larger today than it was when Adams and Calhoun presided, tie votes are highly infrequent. Vice President Lyndon Johnson cast no tie-breaking votes; Vice President Spiro T. Agnew, two; Vice President Walter F. Mondale, one; Vice President George Bush, eight; and Vice President Dan Quayle, none. Uniquely among recent vice presidents, Al Gore broke ties on two crucial budget measures during his first year in office.

The successor role of the vice president has been the most important throughout the history. Here Vice President Nelson A. Rockefeller meets in the Oval Office with President Gerald R. Ford, who himself as vice president succeeded to the presidency.

Equally important, the vice presidency has recently come to be associated much more closely with the presidency than with Congress. Vice President Richard Nixon estimated that he spent 90 percent of his time on executive tasks and only 10 percent fulfilling his Senate responsibilities.[2] Vice President Mondale presided over the Senate on only nineteen occasions one year, for a total of eighteen hours.

Successor

The language of the original Constitution was unclear about the vice president's responsibilities as presidential successor. If the president died, resigned, was impeached and removed, or was disabled, was the vice president to assume the office of president or merely its powers and duties? Was the succession to last until the end of the departed president's four-year term or only until a special election could be called? When President William Henry Harrison died in 1841, Vice President John Tyler set the pattern for future successions by claiming the office for the balance of Harrison's unexpired term. In 1967, the Twenty-fifth Amendment codified this precedent by declaring that "in case of the removal of the President from office or of his death or resignation, the Vice President shall become President." Nine vice presidents—Tyler, Millard Fillmore, Andrew Johnson, Chester A. Arthur, Theodore Roosevelt, Calvin Coolidge, Truman, Lyndon Johnson, and Gerald R. Ford—have become president by succession. *(See Chapter 8, Selection by Succession, Vol. I.)*

In one sense, the vice president's role as presidential successor resembles what physicists call "potential" energy: it is dormant unless triggered by a vacancy in the presidency. But, as noted above, since World War II, concern about the vice president's successor role has prompted presidents to entrust the vice presidency with other responsibilities in order to assure the nation that the vice president will be prepared, literally at a moment's notice, to step into the presidency if needed.

Codeterminer of Presidential Disability

The original Constitution listed presidential disability as one of the situations that would prompt a vice-presidential succession but created no procedure for determining when such a disability existed. Since 1967, the Twenty-fifth Amendment has empowered presidents to declare themselves disabled. It also has provided for situations in which a disabled president is unable or unwilling to make such a declaration. In these situations, the amendment requires that both the vice president and a majority of the heads of the departments (commonly referred to as the "cabinet") agree that the president is unable to fulfill the powers and duties of the office. Clearly, however, the vice president is, constitutionally, the most important figure in this decision: although the amendment authorizes Congress to replace the cabinet with some other body in disability determinations, it cannot replace the vice president. Further, the vice president is the only individual whose vote for a declaration of presidential disability is required.

The one occasion when a vice president nearly exercised the new power, however, suggests that it may be more a burden than a blessing. In 1981, shortly after President Ronald Reagan was shot and taken into surgery, White House counsel Fred Fielding prepared documents that would guide the vice president and cabinet in deciding whether to declare the president disabled and to transfer temporarily the powers and duties of the presidency to Vice President Bush. Other presidential aides, especially Richard Darman, the deputy assistant to the president, headed Fielding off for fear of confusing the nation and making the president look weak. Vice President Bush, anxious that the White House staff not regard him as an interloper, remained silent.[3]

Acting President

The Twenty-fifth Amendment also provides that while a president is disabled, whether by self-declaration or by determination of the vice president and the cabinet, "the Vice President shall immediately assume the powers and duties of the office as Acting President" and shall wield them until the president is once again able to resume office or until the term expires, whichever comes first. This, too, clarifies an ambiguity in the original Constitution, which seemed to imply that a vice-presidential succession in response to a presidential disability had the same legal status and was to be handled in the same way as a succession after a president's death, resignation, or impeachment and removal.

As with the vice president's role in determining whether a president is disabled, however, this new power may be at best a mixed blessing for the vice presidency. In 1985, in anticipation of extensive cancer surgery, President Reagan reluctantly signed over the powers and duties of the presidency to Vice President Bush, reclaiming them soon afterward. Eager not to offend the president or his aides with even the slightest hint of official activity, Bush played tennis and chatted with friends at the vice-presidential residence during his eight hours as acting president. Even this self-effacing behavior did not satisfy White House chief of staff Donald Regan, who would have preferred that Bush stayed at his vacation home in Maine.

Statutory Roles

In contrast to the presidency, to which numerous responsibilities have been assigned by law, the vice presidency has only two statutory roles: member of the National Security Council (NSC) and member of the Board of Regents of the Smithsonian Institution. The latter role is inconsequential—an aide to Vice President Mondale described it as "a dinosaur that will be with the vice presidency forever."[4] Membership on the NSC seems important, but it is less so than meets the eye.

The vice president was added to the NSC by Congress in 1949, partly at the behest of President Truman. As the only council member whom the president cannot remove from office, the vice president is entitled to attend all NSC meetings for the entire term. It is a prestigious post and, for Vice President Nixon—the one vice president whose president, Dwight D. Eisenhower, relied heavily on the formal advisory structures of the executive branch—NSC membership really did provide an important channel of influence.

But few presidents have wanted to feel obligated to involve the vice president in important foreign policy deliberations. As a result, most either have called a limited number of NSC meetings or used the meetings as forums to announce, rather than make, policy. During the Cuban missile crisis, for example, President John F. Kennedy ignored the NSC, creating instead an ad hoc Executive Committee of the National Security Council to deal with the crisis. The "Excom" included not only all the NSC members except Vice President Johnson, but also others, such as the attorney general and some White House aides. (For discussion of NSC and NSC staff, see *The National Security Council* p. 1119, in Chapter 28.)

ADVISORY ROLES

Vice presidents perform two sets of roles that are informal—that is, not grounded in the law or the Constitution. These informal roles originated and have evolved during the twentieth century. They were created by presidents for their vice presidents, reflecting the vice presidency's ever closer identification with the executive rather than the legislative branch. One set of roles, discussed in the next section, involves representing the president and the administration to foreign, intragovernmental, and public audiences. The other set of roles is advisory to the president—as cabinet member, commission chair, and senior adviser.

Cabinet Member

Every vice president since John Nance Garner has attended cabinet meetings at the invitation of the president. Vice President Garner was invited to meet regularly with the cabinet by President Franklin Roosevelt, who, as a candidate for vice president in 1920, had written an article urging that vice presidents be included.[5] (So had cousin Theodore Roosevelt in an 1896 article, but, as president, he did not practice what he preached with his own vice president, Charles W. Fairbanks.)[6]

Garner was not the first vice president to sit with the cabinet. A few earlier presidents had issued invitations to their vice presidents to attend cabinet meetings, notably President George Washington to Vice President John Adams and President Woodrow Wilson to Vice President Thomas R. Marshall, but only in exceptional cases. Nor was Franklin Roosevelt the first president who wanted to establish the practice of vice-presidential membership in the cabinet. In 1921, President Warren G. Harding tried to set a precedent by inviting Vice President Coolidge "to arrange to be present on all such meetings," on the grounds "that the second official of the Republic could add materially to the fullness of his service in this way." Coolidge accepted, writing later that the vice president "should be in the Cabinet because he might become President and ought to be informed on the policies of the Administration." As president, however, Coolidge was turned down even before he could offer cabinet membership to his own vice president, Charles G. Dawes. Dawes declared after his and Coolidge's election in 1924 that he did not want to bind future presidents with a precedent that would force them to include vice presidents they did not want at cabinet meetings.[7] Coolidge's successor as president, Herbert Hoover, did not invite Vice President Charles Curtis to join the cabinet. (*See Chapter 3, History of the Vice Presidency, Vol. I.*)

For all its symbolic value, cabinet membership seldom has been a position of real influence for the vice president. (The exceptions were Vice Presidents Garner and, especially, Nixon, who presided over nineteen cabinet meetings during President Eisenhower's various illnesses.) One reason is that cabinet meetings themselves have become less important in recent years. (*See Chapter 29, Cabinet and Executive Departments.*) In addition,

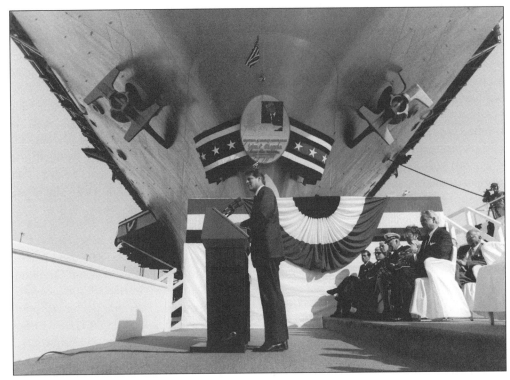

Vice President Albert Gore Jr. delivers a ship's christening address at Newport News Shipbuilding in 1993. Although the importance of the vice presidency has increased in recent decades, ceremonial roles still consume much of the vice president's time.

most vice presidents have felt bound to sit in near silence at such meetings, listening to the discussions of presidents, department heads, and others who are responsible for administering the executive branch.

Commission Chair

Eisenhower was the first president to appoint a vice president to chair a presidential commission, a practice that most of his successors have followed. For a long time, being chair of a commission was more a burden than a blessing for the vice president. But Vice Presidents Quayle and Gore have reversed this pattern, at least temporarily.

Nixon to Bush. Vice President Nixon was charged to monitor and end racial discrimination in federal contracting as head of the newly created government contracts commission in 1953; later he chaired the Cabinet Committee on Price Stability for Economic Growth. President Kennedy named Vice President Johnson as chair of both the President's Committee on Equal Employment Opportunity, a more powerful successor to Nixon's government contracts commission, and the National Aeronautics and Space Council. As president, Johnson assigned numerous commissions to Vice President Humphrey, such as youth opportunity, Native American opportunity, recreation and natural beauty, and tourism. But when civil rights became a major part of the administration's agenda, Johnson stripped Humphrey of responsibility for the equal employment opportunity commission and assigned it to members of the presidential staff.

For ideological reasons, President Nixon abolished most of the commissions Vice President Humphrey had headed, but

made his own vice president, Spiro Agnew, chair of a new commission on intergovernmental relations. Agnew's successor, Gerald Ford, headed only a commission on privacy during his brief vice presidency. After succeeding to the presidency, however, Ford appointed Vice President Nelson A. Rockefeller to chair several commissions, including the National Commission on Productivity and Work Quality, the President's Panel on Federal Compensation, the National Commission on Water Quality, and a commission to investigate abuses by the Central Intelligence Agency (CIA).

Most of these commission assignments were burdensome for the vice president. Typically, presidents created commissions to symbolize their concern for an issue or constituency; they named their vice presidents as chairs because the vice presidency is a visible and prestigious office and because they wanted to convince the public that the vice president was actively involved in the business of government. Seldom, however, did presidents entrust vice-presidential commissions with substantial powers and responsibilities. Rockefeller said of his assignments, "If it hadn't been that I had a lifetime of organizing and studying commissions, I could have been kissed goodbye and lost in the morass."[8] *(See Chapter 31, Presidential Commissions.)*

After Mondale's election as vice president in 1976, he asked President Jimmy Carter to spare him commission duties so that he could be free to serve the president as general adviser and troubleshooter. In doing so, Mondale was following the advice of Humphrey and Rockefeller, the two vice presidents who, to their regret, had been most active as commission chairs. Mondale argued that commissions inevitably rouse the ire of the agencies of the bureaucracy whose activities they study, that neither commissions nor the vice president have any authority to enact any goals, that commission assignments demean the vice presidency by wasting the vice president's time, and that the vice president lacks the staff to do an effective job as commission chair. Carter granted Mondale's request.

No vice president in the period 1953–1989 enjoyed chairing commissions (Vice President Nixon does not even mention his assignments in his memoirs), and all regarded the task as a distraction from other, potentially more useful, roles. Still, every vice president except Mondale felt compelled to chair one or more commissions in order to establish credibility within their administrations. During his first year in office, for example, Vice President Bush was still too much the outsider in the Reagan White House to pass up any opportunity to demonstrate his loyalty. In one case, to head off a major struggle that was developing among the president's top foreign policy advisers about responsibilty in times of international crisis, Bush was asked to head a newly formed Special Situations Group for crisis management. He agreed, which pleased the president and his aides, but shrewdly downplayed the assignment, placating the secretary of state, the head of the CIA, and the president's national security adviser. Later, Bush chaired the President's Task Force on Regulatory Relief.

Quayle and Gore. Initially, the commission role seemed likely to be as much of a nuisance for Vice President Quayle as for his predecessors. But Quayle was able to turn his first assignment from President Bush, as chief of the National Space Council, into a substantial position—so much so that when he spearheaded a major reorganization of the space program, including the replacement of Richard Truly as head of the National Aeronautics and Space Administration (NASA), Sen. Al Gore (D-Tenn.) complained that Quayle was trying to run NASA from the vice president's office.

Quayle's real power came later in his term when he chaired the White House Council on Competitiveness. "Initially a nominal assignment," writes political scientist Joseph Pika, "the council became the administration's principal weapon against regulations that were regarded as antibusiness and anti-free market." Business groups often received a favorable and definitive ruling when they appealed regulations (usually concerning the environment) that had been issued by federal agencies to Quayle's council, and President Bush supported his vice president. As Pika found, "the unwritten White House rule was for 'no appeals' of council decisions to the president."[9]

Quayle was succeeded as vice president by Gore. Having seen, as an outside critic, how valuable a commission role with clout could be for a vice president, Gore jumped at the chance to chair the National Performance Review Commission for President Bill Clinton in 1993. The commission was an effort to "reinvent government" by consolidating functions, changing personnel processes, and applying new technologies to government work. Gore's report, which was publicized widely when he unveiled it in September 1993, included a proposed reduction of 252,000 government jobs, eight hundred suggestions about how to improve efficiency, and a proposal for the federal government to change to a two-year budget cycle.[10]

Senior Adviser

Throughout history, some vice presidents have been sought out by the president, at least occasionally, for advice and counsel. But, until recently, these vice presidents were very much the exception. Before President Franklin Roosevelt won for presidential candidates the right to name their own running mates, party leaders invariably used the vice-presidential nomination as a means to unite the party, usually by pairing the nominee for president with a vice-presidential nominee from an opposing faction. Thus, presidents typically took office with little trust in their vice presidents, much less a willingness to rely on them for political or policy advice.

Since 1940, the year of President Roosevelt's convention coup, presidential candidates have been able to name political leaders they trust as running mates. And since 1945, the year President Roosevelt died, leaving Truman to serve out the term during wartime, they have had every political incentive to choose vice-presidential candidates who are talented and accomplished in their own right. Not surprisingly, then, most recent presidents have turned to their vice presidents after the inauguration for advice on matters about which they are knowledgeable or experienced. President Eisenhower respected Vice President Nixon's judgments about Congress and the Republican Party. President Ford valued the expertise of his vice president, former New York governor Rockefeller, on domestic policy. President Reagan made good use in foreign policy of Vice President Bush's experience as director of the CIA, ambassador to the United Nations, and chief U.S. diplomat in China. President Bush respected Vice President Quayle's understanding of Congress. President Clinton relied on Vice President Gore's demonstrated expertise in environmental and technological issues.

Vice President Mondale extended the vice president's role as presidential adviser beyond all previous limits. He had an unusually strong relationship with President Carter, who had selected him with great care and who, as a former governor, valued his experience as a Washington politician. After the 1976 election, Mondale wrote a memorandum to Carter arguing that the vice presidency is, by design, a nationally elected office unburdened by specific constitutional responsibilities and that these qualities suit it best for the role of senior adviser to the president. Mondale further urged that to perform this role, he would need full access to all the information that the president received, the right to require other administration officals to meet his requests for facts and assistance, a staff of his own, a close relationship with the White House staff, the right to participate in all of the administration's important policy groups, access to the president whenever necessary, and freedom from specific ongoing assignments. Carter approved Mondale's recommendations and added to them an office for the vice president in the West Wing of the White House.[11]

Mondale's proposed arrangement worked well in practice for the entire length of Carter's term because the vice president gave the president consistently sound advice and gave it discreetly. As Mondale later counseled his successor, Vice President Bush,

Advise the president confidentially. The only reason to state publicly what you have told the president is to take credit for his success and to try to escape blame for failure. Either way there is no quicker way to undermine your relationship with the president and lose your effectiveness. . . . Don't wear a president down. . . . Give your advice once and give it well. You have a right to be heard, not obeyed. . . . The vice president should remember the importance of personal compatability. He should complement the president's skills. . . .[12]

Bush took Mondale's advice and eventually was able to attain a similar wide-ranging role as trusted adviser in the Reagan White House. (It took a while because some hard feelings lingered from Bush's aggressive challenge to Reagan for the Republican presidential nomination in 1980.) Bush in turn brought Quayle, a much younger man whom he treated as a developing protégé, into an expanding range of advisory roles. Clinton leaned as heavily (or more) on Gore as Carter had on Mondale; close observers of the Clinton White House discovered that Gore was one of three or four people (including Hillary Rodham Clinton) whose advice Clinton sought on virtually every important matter that crossed his desk.[13]

REPRESENTATIVE ROLES

In recent years, presidents have called on vice presidents to represent their administrations to a variety of constituencies. Within the government, the modern vice president serves as a liaison from the president to Congress. Vice presidents also are used as envoys to foreign governments. Finally, the vice president publicly defends the president to a variety of domestic audiences.

Legislative Liaison

Even as the Senate responsiblities of the vice presidency have declined in importance and its affiliation with the executive branch has grown, vice presidents have developed a new role on Capitol Hill as legislative liaison. Since 1933, eleven of fourteen vice presidents—Garner, Truman, Alben W. Barkley, Nixon, Johnson, Humphrey, Ford, Mondale, Bush, Quayle, and Gore—have been former members of Congress. (Henry A. Wallace, Agnew, and Rockefeller are the only modern vice presidents who have not.) Six of them—Vice Presidents Garner, Truman, Nixon, Mondale, Bush, and Gore—served presidents who lacked legislative experience themselves, and the vice presidents often did so with great skill. Not surprisingly, then, vice presidents are frequently used to pass information and advice back and forth between representatives and senators on one end of Pennsylvania Avenue and the president on the other, working in conjunction with the White House staff's team of legislative lobbyists. The vice president's suite in the Capitol building, which was assigned many years ago in recognition of the office's constitutional role as Senate president, provides a convenient setting for such discussions, as well as for "head counts" on pending legislation.

Not all vice presidents are skillful legislative liaisons, and blunders born of inexperience can backfire on both the vice president and the president. When Vice President Agnew wandered onto the Senate floor in 1969 to ask Sen. Len Jordan, a fellow Republican, if the administration could count on his vote for a tax bill, Jordan barked, "You had it until now," then vowed to henceforth oppose any bill that Agnew asked him to support.[14] Rockefeller also blundered, ruling in what was regarded as a biased way in favor of liberal senators who wanted to dilute the Senate rule that protected filibusters.[15] Even Lyndon Johnson, arguably the most effective Senate leader in history before his election as vice president in 1960, was rebuffed by Senate Democrats when he asked to be allowed to continue presiding over meetings of the Senate Democratic conference at the start of his term in 1961. As Sen. Clinton Anderson, who had been one of Johnson's closest political allies, protested, Johnson no longer was a member of the legislative branch.[16]

Special Envoy

Garner was the first vice president to make an official trip abroad. After attending, as a representative of the Senate, the installation of the first president of the Philippines, Garner undertook a goodwill mission to Mexico at the behest of President Franklin Roosevelt. Vice President Nixon established the precedent of extensive vice-presidential travel as a special presidential envoy, making seven trips to fifty-four countries during his eight years in office. Two of these missions were especially memorable—the trip to the Soviet Union in which Nixon conducted an impromptu "kitchen debate" with the Soviet leader, Nikita Khrushchev, and the trip to South America in which he was attacked and spat on by leftist rioters. Johnson took ten trips as vice president, Humphrey twelve, Agnew seven, Ford one, Rockefeller six, and Mondale fourteen. Bush set the record with forty-one foreign trips during his two terms as vice president, and as president he sent out Vice President Quayle at a similar pace during his four years in office.[17] Gore traveled abroad less frequently than his recent predecessors, but for a reason that spoke well of him: President Clinton valued his advice on foreign policy so highly that he was reluctant to have him leave the White House for any extended period of time. Early accounts of Clinton administration foreign policy making noted Gore's active presence at almost every crucial Oval Office meeting.[18]

Many, perhaps most, special envoy assignments have been almost entirely symbolic in nature—the president simply wished to demonstrate the goodwill of the United States toward the visited country without having to undertake a trip personally. "I go to funerals," lamented Vice President Rockefeller. "I go to earthquakes."[19] But often the vice president has carried an important message to a foreign government, affirmed U.S. support for a beleaguered regime, or negotiated on a small diplomatic matter. And even relatively inconsequential trips are of political value to vice presidents, who gain greater-than-usual press coverage

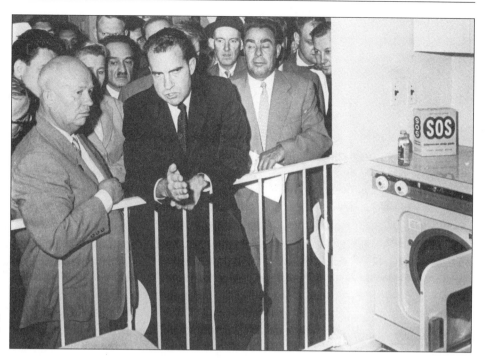

Vice President Richard Nixon conducts an impromptu "kitchen debate" with Soviet leader Nikita Khrushchev, left, during their tour of an American exhibition in Moscow in 1959.

while they are abroad and reinforce their image among the voters as knowledgeable world leaders.

Administration Defender

Modern vice presidents are most frequently seen in their role as defender of the president's leadership, policies, and party to a variety of public audiences, including interest groups, the news media, state and local party organizations, and the general public. The role of administration defender is one that the vice president must perform vigorously, enthusiastically, and with unquestioned loyalty, lest the wrath of the president's supporters—both inside the administration and in the nation at large—be aroused. Journalists, White House staffers, and politicians are constantly on the watch for any sign of disagreement between the president and the vice president.

The role of administration defender offers significant political benefits to the vice president who performs it well. It builds trust for the vice president with the president and the White House staff, endears the vice president to the party faithful, and increases the vice president's political visibility. Taken together, these benefits usually give the vice president the inside track for a subsequent presidential nomination. Vice Presidents Nixon (1960), Humphrey (1968), Mondale (1976), and Bush (1988) stepped directly from the vice presidency into their party's nomination for president, and even Vice President Agnew was an early favorite for the 1976 Republican presidential nomination.

But the administration defender role can be dangerous to the vice president as well. Despite their success in winning presidential nominations, no incumbent vice president was elected president from 1836 until 1988, when Bush accomplished the feat. Vice presidents may appear to be narrow, divisive figures, espe-

cially when defending the administration involves attacking its critics, as Vice Presidents Nixon, Agnew, and Quayle did with great fervor. Slashing partisan rhetoric may alienate the general electorate even as it gratifies the party faithful. In addition, vice presidents may come to seem weak and parrot-like, always defending the ideas of another while submerging their own thoughts and expertise. Vice President Bush, for example, was excoriated as a "wimp" and "lap dog" by political columnists and cartoonists. Finally, vice presidents may feel compelled to defend administration policies with which they profoundly disagree, as Vice President Nixon frequently did.[20]

Institutional Resources

Historically, the institutional resources of the vice presidency have been meager, consisting for many years of a suite of offices in the Capitol building and a small staff paid for by Congress's own budget. In recent years, the development of new vice-presidential roles has been a wellspring of added resources, as has the vice presidency's closer affiliation with the executive branch. The enhanced resources of the vice presidency have enabled it, in turn, both to assume new roles and to fulfill its traditional roles more effectively.

GROWING RESOURCES

The 1960s and 1970s were marked by substantial gains in the resources of the vice presidency that the 1980s and 1990s have not undone. In 1961, Vice President Lyndon Johnson won for the office an impressive suite in the Executive Office Building, adjacent to the White House. At the beginning of Vice President Agnew's term in 1969, he requested and received a line item in the budget of the executive branch to supplement the traditional

The old vice-presidential seal, left, created in 1948, seemed to many people to portray the low esteem in which the office was held. In 1975 Vice President Rockefeller ordered the design of a more imposing seal, right, still in use.

congressional appropriation. Taken together, these two developments freed vice presidents from their earlier dependence on Congress for office space and operating funds. In 1972, the vice presidency was listed for the first time as a part of the Executive Office of the President in the *United States Government Organization Manual.*

Even more substantial institutional advances were registered by Vice Presidents Ford and Rockefeller during the mid-1970s. Ford received President Nixon's consent both to name his own staff members, rather than rely on White House-approved appointees, and to increase the size of the vice president's staff. (By 1993, the vice president oversaw a staff of sixty-six with an annual budget of $3.1 million.) Ford and his successor, Vice President Rockefeller, then reorganized the staff to make it resemble more closely the White House staff, including a press secretary, counsel, and national security adviser. This additional staff freed the vice president's political and policy specialists from administrative and other distractions and fostered better communications and working relationships between members of the presidential and vice-presidential staffs. From 1974 to 1977, the vice president and high-ranking staff members also received certain perquisites that enhanced the prestige of the office within the status-conscious Washington community. The new symbols of vice-presidential status included an official residence (the Admiral's House at the Naval Observatory on Washington's Massachusetts Avenue), a better airplane for *Air Force Two,* and an impressive new seal of office, showing a star-shrouded, arrow-clutching eagle at full wingspread. New privileges for the vice president's staff included use of the White House mess and official automobiles. *(See "The Vice President's Residence," p. 946, in Chapter 22.)*

One reason that Vice Presidents Ford and Rockefeller were able to secure these resources for their office is that the presidents who invited them to become vice president very much needed their help. Both were appointed vice president, the first to be selected under the Twenty-fifth Amendment. After Vice

President Agnew resigned in 1973, President Nixon, who was embroiled in the Watergate affair, chose Ford because, as the minority leader of the House of Representatives, he was well liked and certain to be confirmed by Congress. When Ford became president after Nixon's 1974 resignation, he urgently wanted Rockefeller to become vice president because of the stature the former New York governor and presidential candidate could bring to the administration. As part of his agreement to serve, Rockefeller won the right to a weekly private meeting with the president.

Vice President Mondale, whom President Carter had selected out of respect for his talents, experience, and loyalty, consolidated the institutional gains his predecessors had made and added more, notably an office in the West Wing of the White House near the president's Oval Office, full access to the White House paper flow, a weekly private lunch with the president, and the right to attend all presidential meetings. Although neither Bush nor Quayle was an administration insider at the start of his term as vice president, they, too, were able to reap the gains their predecessors had made. Gore did so as well, with two additions: he was able to place several longtime aides on the president's staff and to reserve a spot in most White House staff meetings for one of his representatives.

RELATION OF ROLES AND RESOURCES

The roles and institutional resources of the modern vice presidency are linked in a synergistic way. Resources help to shape traditional roles. The vice president's office in the Capitol has made participation in legislative liaison sensible; the president's own liaison staff often uses the office as a headquarters while involving the vice president in the ongoing business of congressional relations. Similarly, the availability of free time has left vice presidents free to tour the country as administration defenders.

New resources also have paved the way for new roles for the vice presidency. The vice president's ability to serve usefully as a senior adviser is greater than it used to be because the creation in 1969 of a vice-presidential line item in the executive budget allowed vice presidents to hire talented staff. In 1977 the granting of a West Wing office put the vice president literally in the middle of the informal policy flow that surrounds the Oval Office.

Finally, new roles have generated new institutional resources. Almost all of the gains Vice President Mondale was able to make for the vice presidency flowed from his success in convincing President Carter that his main role in the administration should be that of general adviser. Mondale argued successfully that he could not fulfill this role unless he had full access to the president, the White House staff, and the documents that flowed back and forth between them.

To be sure, the major roles of the vice presidency, and virtually all of its resources, exist at the sufferance of the president. "If the next president does not want an active vice president and does not want to spend time in conference with his running mate," writes political scientist Paul Light, "there is no law or constitutional provision that can compel him to do so." [21] But practice, if repeated long and often enough, eventually becomes precedent that can be broken only at some political cost. As Pika points out, "to violate any of the expectations [about new vice-presidential roles and resources] would run the risk of embarrassing both the vice president and the administration." [22]

NOTES

1. Hubert H. Humphrey, "Changes in the Vice Presidency," *Current History* 67, no. 396 (August 1974): 59.

2. "Nixon's Own Story of 7 Years in the Vice Presidency," *U.S. News & World Report,* May 16, 1960, 98.

3. Lawrence I. Barrett, *Gambling with History: Ronald Reagan in the White House* (Garden City, N.Y.: Doubleday, 1983), chap. 7.

4. Quoted in Paul C. Light, *Vice-Presidential Power: Advice and Influence in the White House* (Baltimore: Johns Hopkins University Press, 1984), 34.

5. Franklin D. Roosevelt, "Can the Vice Presidency Be Useful?" *Saturday Evening Post,* October 16, 1920, 8.

6. Theodore Roosevelt, "The Three Vice-Presidential Candidates and What They Represent," *Review of Reviews,* September 1896, 289.

7. Irving G. Williams, *The Rise of the Vice Presidency* (Washington, D.C.: Public Affairs Press, 1956), 122–123, 134–135.

8. Michael Nelson, "Nelson A. Rockefeller and the American Vice Presidency," in *Gerald R. Ford and the Politics of Post-Watergate America,* eds. Bernard J. Firestone and Alexej Ugrinsky (Westport, Conn.: Greenwood Press, 1993), 139–159.

9. Joseph A. Pika, "The Vice Presidency: New Opportunities, Old Constraints," in *The Presidency and the Political System,* 4th ed., ed. Michael Nelson (Washington, D.C.: CQ Press, 1995), 516. See also David S. Broder and Bob Woodward, *The Man Who Would Be President: Dan Quayle* (New York: Simon and Schuster, 1992).

10. *Congressional Quarterly Weekly Report,* September 11, 1993, 2381–2389.

11. Light, *Vice-Presidential Power,* 201–202.

12. Quoted in Thomas E. Cronin, "Rethinking the Vice Presidency," in *Rethinking the Presidency,* ed. Thomas E. Cronin (Boston: Little, Brown, 1982), 339–340.

13. Bob Woodward, *The Agenda: Inside the Clinton White House* (New York: Simon and Schuster, 1994).

14. Quoted in Light, *Vice-Presidential Power,* 43–44.

15. Gerald Benjamin, "Nelson Rockefeller and the Emergence of the Appointive Vice Presidency," in *Gerald R. Ford and the Politics of Post-Watergate America,* 170.

16. Rowland Evans and Robert Novak, *Lyndon B. Johnson: The Exercise of Power* (New York: New American Library, 1966), 305–307.

17. Joseph Pika, "Bush, Quayle, and the New Vice Presidency" in *The Presidency and the Political System,* 3rd ed., ed. Michael Nelson (Washington, D.C.: CQ Press, 1990), 501–528.

18. See, for example, Elizabeth Drew, *On the Edge: The Clinton Presidency* (New York: Simon and Schuster, 1994).

19. Quoted in Joseph E. Persico, *The Imperial Rockefeller* (New York: Simon and Schuster, 1982), 262.

20. Stephen E. Ambrose, *Nixon: The Education of a Politician, 1913–1962* (New York: Simon and Schuster, 1987), chaps. 15–27.

21. Light, *Vice-Presidential Power,* 248–249.

22. Pika, "Vice Presidency: New Opportunities, Old Constraints," 514.

SELECTED BIBLIOGRAPHY

Cronin, Thomas E. "Rethinking the Vice Presidency." In *Rethinking the Presidency,* ed. Thomas Cronin. Boston: Little, Brown, 1982.

Light, Paul C. *Vice-Presidential Power: Advice and Influence in the White House.* Baltimore: Johns Hopkins University Press, 1984.

Milkis, Sidney M., and Michael Nelson. *The American Presidency: Origins and Development, 1776–1993.* Washington, D.C.: CQ Press, 1994.

Nelson, Michael. *A Heartbeat Away.* New York: Unwin Hyman, 1988.

——. "Nelson A. Rockefeller and the American Vice Presidency." In *Gerald R. Ford and the Politics of Post-Watergate America,* ed. Bernard J. Firestone and Alexej Ugrinksy. Westport, Conn.: Greenwood Press, 1993.

Pika, Joseph A. "Bush, Quayle, and the New Vice Presidency?" In *The Presidency and the Political System,* ed. Michael Nelson. 3d ed. Washington, D.C.: CQ Press, 1990.

——. "The Vice Presidency: New Opportunities, Old Constraints." In *The Presidency and the Political System,* ed. Michael Nelson. 4th ed. Washington, D.C.: CQ Press, 1995.

Quayle, Dan. *Standing Firm.* New York: HarperCollins, 1994.

Williams, Irving G. *The Rise of the Vice Presidency.* Washington, D.C.: Public Affairs Press, 1956.

CHAPTER 27

Executive Office of the President: White House Office

BY STEPHEN L. ROBERTSON

IN CONTRAST to the early days of the presidency, when presidents had little or no staff to help them, the modern presidential establishment is a bureaucracy with thousands of employees, all of whom work for the president. The Executive Office of the President (EOP) is the president's tool for coping with Congress and the far-flung executive branch.

In no real sense is the EOP an "office"; rather, it is a collection of agencies whose only tie is their direct responsibility to the president. The components of the EOP have changed many times over the years as the needs of the presidency have changed. Today some of the major elements of the EOP are the National Security Council, Office of Management and Budget, Council of Economic Advisers, Office of Science and Technology Policy, Office of the U.S. Trade Representative, and White House Office. Of these, perhaps the most important and surely the closest to the president is the White House Office.

Although all of the EOP does the president's business, the White House Office consists of the president's most intimate and trusted advisers. Of the entire presidential establishment, the White House Office is the most loyal to the president and has his or her particular interests most at heart. It can be a tremendous asset, advancing the administration's programs to fruition and avoiding the potential pitfalls that undermine a president's credibility. Indeed, much of the president's success depends on the ability of the White House staff, while many of the president's failures result from the staff's failures.

Examples of the importance of the White House staff abound. On the one hand, the vision and skill of President John F. Kennedy's staff were very important to his legislative success. The same was true in the early days of Lyndon B. Johnson's administration; the ability of Johnson's staff to deal with Congress was crucial in passing the "Great Society" programs. The disorganization and inexperience of President Jimmy Carter's staff, on the other hand, undermined his chances of achieving much in Congress. It was the staff's failure to anticipate problems adequately and protect the president's interests that led to Watergate, which destroyed the presidency of Richard Nixon, and to the Iran-contra affair, which haunted and weakened Ronald Reagan's second term.

Although the White House staff is important to the president, there is no set pattern for its selection or organization. In fact, the office itself has been in existence only since 1939.

The problem of how to count the White House Office staff is a factor in any discussion of its growth. No universally accepted figures exist on the precise size of the White House staff, and published estimates vary considerably depending on who is counting and how. There are several reasons for this discrepancy: short-term fluctuations in staff size, placement of White House people elsewhere in government, use of detailees (personnel borrowed from other executive departments), and hiring of staff out of the discretionary funds (such as the Special Projects account) that are available to the president. Consequently, the figures that follow should be treated with caution; they are indicators of trends but are not necessarily exact.[1]

Origins and Development of the White House Office

Early presidents had little or no staff to assist them, and what staff did exist was strictly clerical. There were no specialized or resident policy advisers, speechwriters, or liaison personnel. Believing that presidents should take care of their own business, Congress did not specifically appropriate funds for staff until 1857, when it provided an allowance for a presidential secretary. Presidents who wanted more help were forced to hire it themselves and to pay for it out of their own pockets. George Washington hired his nephew to assist him in 1792 and paid him $300 a year from his own salary.

Several later presidents followed Washington's lead and retained relatives or cronies in the White House. For most of those employed, the pay remained low and the jobs menial. Staff duties consisted almost exclusively of clerical work and scheduling the president's appointments. Over the years the common practices of nepotism and cronyism resulted in the appointment of several advisers and presidential secretaries who proved hopelessly inadequate. For example, President Andrew Johnson appointed his son Robert as his secretary even though Robert was a womanizer and an alcoholic. Ulysses S. Grant's secretary, Gen. Orville E. Babcock, was a corrupt power grabber who was involved in the Whiskey Ring, a group of liquor producers who were illegally avoiding federal liquor taxes. Babcock eventually was indicted for fraud. Rutherford B. Hayes chose as his secretary William K. Rogers, an old classmate who had failed in three careers. Rogers proved inept at that job, too.

Given the limitations of presidents' personal financial resources, as well as the small size of the government as a whole, the White House staff remained small throughout the nineteenth century. Presidents rarely could afford much staff, and they generally made more use of their cabinet as advisers than presidents do today. Benjamin Harrison was able to house his entire staff next to his living quarters on the second floor of the White House. Herbert Hoover doubled the number of his administrative assistants from two to four (which caused a minor sensation). Besides them, Hoover had only military and naval attachés and about forty clerks and typists.

To some extent the small size of these staffs is misleading. Historically, presidents have resorted to "detailing," or borrowing, personnel from the executive departments to carry out various tasks. Thus, a president who needs assistance might requisition an aide or two from the Defense or State Department. Presidents also have placed trusted advisers in positions within the executive branch to keep them readily available. Andrew Jackson named his close friend Amos Kendall as fourth auditor of the Treasury Department, but Kendall did little work there; instead he spent his time assisting Jackson. To keep his "brain trust" around him, Franklin D. Roosevelt appointed them not to his staff (which was still the size of Hoover's) but to posts in other departments: Raymond Moley became an assistant secretary of state, Rexford G. Tugwell was named assistant secretary of agriculture, and Adolph A. Berle Jr. was appointed as counsel to the Reconstruction Finance Commission. They did almost no work for their departments; instead, they assisted Roosevelt.

Although the use of detailees was a great asset to presidents, the growing demands of the office meant that presidents needed more in-house advisers who were not encumbered by even minimal jobs elsewhere. As the nation and its government grew in the early twentieth century, the need for a larger presidential staff increased, and the work of some of the presidential secretaries showed the potential value of a larger staff. Daniel G. Rollings, who was secretary to Chester A. Arthur, assisted the president in writing speeches and legislative proposals for Congress. Daniel Lamont was an able administrator, campaign manager, and adviser for Grover Cleveland. Joseph P. Tumulty, secretary to Woodrow Wilson, was an all-purpose aide who "functioned as an appointments secretary, political adviser, administrative manager, and public relations aide" as well as a White House doorkeeper.[2] Calvin Coolidge's secretary, C. Bascom Slemp, was an important liaison between the president and Congress, as well as between the president and his own party. And Louis McHenry Howe was a highly important influence on Franklin Roosevelt until Howe's death in 1935.

Even more significant was the work of aides George B. Cortelyou and William Loeb Jr. Cortelyou, who later became the first secretary of the Department of Commerce and Labor, was presidential secretary under William McKinley and Theodore Roosevelt. As secretary, particularly to McKinley, he drafted speeches and messages, scheduled appointments, organized trips, ran the White House clerical staff, and tended to First Lady Ida McKinley, who suffered from poor health. He helped to defeat a possible move against Roosevelt as the vice-presidential nominee in the Republican national convention of 1900. In the immediate aftermath of McKinley's assassination, Cortelyou operated as the de facto president, greatly easing the transition for the vice president.

Loeb followed Cortelyou as Roosevelt's presidential secretary and was just as valuable in keeping the White House and its occupants running smoothly. Loeb also served as the president's sounding board and had no small influence on Roosevelt and his policies. As a political operative, he was instrumental in pulling together support for William Howard Taft in the Republican national convention of 1908.

In the hands of aides such as Cortelyou and Loeb, the position of secretary to the president was the crucial one on the presidential staff; indeed, to a large extent it *was* the staff. The presidential secretary was a jack-of-all-trades: legislative drafter, congressional liaison, press and public relations coordinator, appointments and junkets scheduler, political manipulator, and White House manager.

By the 1930s, however, the responsibilities of the position had outstripped the abilities of any one person to fill them. When Franklin Roosevelt appointed Howe as his secretary in 1933, he also appointed Stephen T. Early as press secretary and Marvin H. McIntyre as appointments secretary. But when Howe died, the position died with him. Roosevelt never filled it, and its responsibilities were eventually distributed throughout a growing White House bureaucracy.

FDR: CREATING THE PRESENT STAFF SYSTEM

The present staff system began during the administration of Franklin Roosevelt (1933–1945). The White House staff had been growing slowly for several years, but it still remained quite small. Like his predecessors, Roosevelt regularly borrowed help from elsewhere in the executive branch, using at least a hundred detailees in each year from 1934 to 1945. Unlike his predecessors, however, he concluded that such arrangements were hopelessly inadequate, and, as an activist president faced with an unprecedented economic crisis, he decided to change them. In his mind, dealing with the nation's problems required a larger permanent staff that worked solely for him. He was not alone in his belief; at least nine proposals for reorganizing the executive branch appeared between 1918 and 1937, and all recognized the need for more executive efficiency and planning capability.[3]

Roosevelt found the justification for his larger staff in the work of the Committee on Administrative Management, more popularly known as the Brownlow Committee. Created on March 20, 1936, the committee—consisting of Louis Brownlow, chairman, and members Charles Merriam and Luther Gulick—was directed to study the staffing needs of the presidency. Declaring that "the American Executive must be regarded as one of the very greatest contributions by our Nation to the development of modern democracy," the committee concluded that

Although FDR's staff remained small, unstructured, and free of specific titles, Harry Hopkins, left, a special assistant to the president, was a forerunner of today's White House chief of staff.

"the President needs help . . . in dealing with managerial agencies and administrative departments of the Government" and recommended the creation of additional staff to assist him. The committee also recommended that

these assistants . . . not be interposed between the president and the heads of his departments. They would not be assistant presidents in any sense. Their function would be . . . to assist [the president] in obtaining quickly and without delay all pertinent information possessed by any of the executive departments so as to guide him in making his responsible decisions; and then when decisions have been made, to assist him in seeing to it that every administrative department and agency affected is properly informed. . . . They would remain in the background, issue no orders, make no decisions, emit no public statements. . . . They should be men in whom the president has personal confidence and whose attitude and character are such that they would not attempt to exercise power on their own account. They should be possessed of high competence, great vigor, and a passion of anonymity. They should be installed in the White House itself, directly accessible to the president.[4]

The Brownlow Committee report was submitted to the president in January 1937. Immediately endorsing its findings, with which he completely agreed and over which he had had significant influence, Roosevelt quickly forwarded the report to Congress for authorization to implement the committee's recommendations. However, Congress was angry over Roosevelt's ill-fated attempt to pack the Supreme Court, and it refused to act upon the report. Not until April 1939 did Congress agree to most of the Brownlow proposals. *(See Chapter 28, Executive Office of the President: Supporting Organizations.)*

Under the congressional authorization the president was allowed to hire six new administrative assistants, although Roosevelt initially hired only three. Congress also permitted the president to undertake a partial reorganization of the executive branch. On September 8, 1939, Roosevelt issued Executive Order 8248, creating the Executive Office of the President and transferring the Bureau of the Budget (renamed the Office of Management and Budget in 1970) into it from the Treasury Department. The president intended the EOP to be a permanent and professional support staff—the institutionalized infrastructure of the presidency—while the White House staff were seen as the president's personal assistants.

Executive Order 8248 represents the birth of the modern presidency, including the modern White House Office staff. Roosevelt did not greatly increase the size of the staff, however. He preferred and was able to manage with a staff small enough to allow him to interact with all of his aides equally. Thus, the number of presidential aides never exceeded twelve, and the total number of full-time White House employees was less than sixty-five.[5] The latter figure stayed relatively low despite a huge increase in mail to the White House, which required the hiring of more clerical staff to handle it.

Roosevelt's staff remained not only small but also rather unstructured. Disliking flow charts and rigid hierarchies, the president preferred to work on an ad hoc basis, distributing assignments to whoever was available at the time. Few of his aides had specific titles. Aside from Press Secretary Early and Appointments Secretary McIntyre, only Harry L. Hopkins, who bore the title of special assistant to the president, and Samuel I. Rosenman, who was the counsel to the president, had special designations.

Nevertheless, the first steps toward the differentiated structures maintained by later presidents were taken under Roosevelt. Hopkins, who had extensive influence in foreign affairs during the war years, was another forerunner of the chief of staff who would appear in later administrations. Rosenman's position was created just for him on the grounds that the president required an in-house legal adviser. Thus, by the end of the Roosevelt administration, the need for a larger staff had been recognized, and its expansion and differentiation had begun. The increasing role of the national government, both domestically and internationally, would fuel further staff growth over the next decades.

TRUMAN: INSTITUTIONALIZED GROWTH

Roosevelt's White House staff had swelled to meet the demands of the war years. Distrusting the larger staff and fearing that it would impede his interaction with his cabinet and the rest of the government, President Harry S. Truman (1945–1953) initially planned to return the White House staff to its prewar size. He quickly found that this was impossible. With Europe in ruins, the United States was the leader in the international community. At home the difficulties of restoring the economy to a peacetime status and repairing the dislocations caused by war created economic and political tensions for the federal government. The result was increasing pressure on the Truman White House for action, which inevitably led to a staff size that exceeded that of the Roosevelt years. Furthermore, whereas Roosevelt had maintained a fairly small permanent staff and used a large number of detailees, by 1947 Truman had reversed that trend, employing an in-house staff of two hundred or more while detailing only a handful of other aides. The earlier practice of storing advisers in various government posts also came to an end. After Truman, presidents simply brought whatever advisers they wished into the White House, creating new positions for them if necessary.

The staff evolved in structure as well as size during the Truman years. When he became president, Truman inherited Roosevelt's relatively unstructured staffing system, which provided everyone with access to the president and allowed Roosevelt to play off his advisers against one another. Truman valued the accessibility the open system allowed, but he found the intrastaff competition it fostered too chaotic and soon called for more order. To this end, Truman created the position of assistant to the president in 1946 and named John Roy Steelman to fill it. One of Steelman's duties was to serve as a link with the domestic agencies and to resolve many of their problems and disputes. As such, he too was a direct forerunner of the chief of staff who would emerge in later administrations. Unfortunately, Steelman was not very successful at keeping problems from the president; he was reluctant to bruise feelings, and Truman was unable to

distance himself from the everyday problems of his administration.

Besides Steelman, Truman's staff consisted of a press secretary, an appointments secretary, a personnel director, a special counsel, a legislative drafter, a military aide and a naval aide, a special assistant, a minority liaison, a few speechwriters (who also doubled as general assistants), and the more institutionalized position of budget director. Clerical and subordinate aides made up the remaining staff.

During the Truman years Congress created two new bodies within EOP to assist the president. The National Security Act of 1947 established the National Security Council (NSC) to help the president deal with foreign policy problems. The NSC membership (after an amendment of the act in 1949) consisted of the president, the vice president, the secretaries of state and defense, and anyone else the president wished to invite. The NSC was designed to ensure coordination among the foreign policy agencies so that the president would be given the necessary facts and options about a problem quickly and efficiently. Skeptical of a body that had been thrust upon him, Truman made little use of the NSC before the Korean War; the decision to intervene in Korea was made without formally consulting the NSC at all. During the war Truman found ways to use the NSC to his advantage and met with it more frequently, but the importance of the NSC as a personal staff remained minor.

The second body created by Congress to assist Truman was the three-member Council of Economic Advisers (CEA), intended to be the president's primary source of economic information and advice. As with the NSC, Truman rarely used the CEA at first, in part because under chairman Edwin G. Nourse it provided theoretical advice devoid of any political considerations. It was only when Leon Keyserling replaced Nourse as chairman in 1949 that the CEA emerged as an important body. *(See Chapter 28, Executive Office of the President: Supporting Organizations.)*

The Truman administration also saw the emergence of staffers as policy advocates. Truman's special counsel, Clark M. Clifford, was a key figure in advocating liberal positions before the president. Such a role defied the original vision of the Brownlow Committee, which had proposed that aides be neutral facilitators of policy decisions; policy advocacy was to be left to the cabinet. Clifford's role of policy advocate represented a potentially major change in the role of the White House staff, but the extent of this change would not be realized until later.

Thus, under Truman the White House staff increased in size and took on a more formal structure. Differentiation increased as particular staff members were assigned specific areas of responsibility, and White House assistants began to acquire small staffs of their own. In addition, Congress added two new bodies to the White House to assist the president. Finally, policy advocacy began to move into the White House and out of the cabinet where it theoretically belonged. Despite these important developments, however, the Truman White House staff did not wield much power overall. With the exception of Clifford and W. Averell Harriman, who was in the administration only briefly, no major names or dominant personalities stood out on Truman's staff. Moreover, Truman preferred to use his cabinet as policy advisers; his staff was not allowed to gain much influence. The makings of a powerful staff were there but were not realized until later administrations.

EISENHOWER: THE FORMALIZED STAFF

Under Dwight D. Eisenhower (1953–1961) the staff grew in both size and complexity. As a former general and a career military officer, Eisenhower recognized the benefits of a properly structured staff. A well-organized staff could handle the simple problems and minor tactical details at the lower levels, allowing the commander to concentrate on the major problems and questions. Reacting to what he saw as confusion within the Roosevelt and Truman administrations, Eisenhower preached that organization could provide a more efficient, high-quality government. His message resulted in the most highly structured and diversified White House staff seen up to that time.

Eisenhower's staff included many of the elements found in the Truman White House. His press secretary, James C. Hagerty, won a considerable reputation for his skillful handling of the position. Other staff members were an appointments secretary, a special counsel, and, of course, the much-needed clerks, typists, and messengers.

Several new positions were created as well. The Congressional Relations Office was established to facilitate interaction between the White House and Congress. The liaison aide was responsible for conveying the president's wishes to Congress, lobbying there for the president's programs, and relaying congressional feedback. This was not a completely new position; Matthew Connelly had fulfilled the same functions without the title under Truman, while others had acted in the same capacity for Roosevelt. Still, Eisenhower was the first to operate openly a congressional liaison office and to give it a formal place in the White House.

To improve the flow of paperwork through the channels of the administration, Eisenhower created the positions of staff secretary and secretary to the cabinet. The cabinet secretary's job was to improve the cabinet's ability to advise the president by coordinating meetings and facilitating communications between the two. Eisenhower also used the position of special adviser to the president to bring in his own experts as needed. For example, he responded to the Soviet launching of *Sputnik* in 1957 by naming a science adviser. Many of these special advisers made a significant contribution to the Eisenhower administration. The president's Open Skies proposal of 1955, which called for surveillance flights to allow each superpower to monitor the other's military installations, was devised by Nelson A. Rockefeller, who was then serving as a special adviser.

All these additions, made in the name of efficiency, naturally swelled the White House staff. The number of professionals appointed by the president in the White House increased from thirty-two in 1953 to fifty by 1960.[6] Overall, the size of the permanent staff increased by some ninety people, to 355, during the same period. Eisenhower also made important changes in the way some existing personnel were used. One major change concerned the National Security Council. Truman rarely met with the NSC before the outbreak of the Korean War in 1950 and never gave it much structure. To Eisenhower, however, the NSC appeared much more useful. He created an extensive apparatus that could examine problems and produce analyses and options for him. Under Eisenhower the NSC became an important element in the foreign policy process, although certainly not the dominant one. The lead in U.S. foreign policy remained with Secretary of State John Foster Dulles and the State Department.

The president also created the post of national security adviser. This new adviser served as the administrative head of the NSC and as the president's personal aide in foreign policy matters. For Eisenhower, the national security adviser had the important job of coordinating America's foreign policy apparatus and providing him with timely information.

In one other major staff change Eisenhower elevated the role of the assistant to the president, which under Truman had not been very important. Believing in hierarchy and not wanting to be bothered with unnecessary details, Eisenhower sought an aide to manage the White House, much as his chief of staff had managed his headquarters staff in the army. In creating this post, Eisenhower's assistant, Sherman Adams, became the gatekeeper to the president during Eisenhower's first six years in office.

As presidential chief of staff, Adams was perceived as possessing enormous power; anyone wishing to do business with the president had to pass through Adams first. It seemed certain that Adams was making a great many decisions, given Eisenhower's distaste for routine matters. Commentators described Adams as an "assistant president," particularly in domestic affairs, in which Eisenhower had less interest. Indeed, some saw Adams as running domestic policy during his stint as assistant to the president. One contemporary observer noted that

Adams has handled a considerable amount of the work that in past administrations has been done by the president himself. . . . While it has not been an inflexible rule, it has been the general practice that almost everything of importance in the White House bearing on domestic and political policy clears through Adams. . . . He is the channel through which many of the most important projects in domestic affairs reach the president . . . [and] by the time [they] have reached the president they have already been shaped in part by Adams himself. Time and again when a caller or official springs an idea on Eisenhower, the president will tell him, "Take it up with Sherman."[7]

In reality, Adams probably did not have that much power. Witnesses within the administration have recalled that while Adams had great influence over administrative matters in the White House, he rarely was involved in policy discussions. Others remember considerable interaction among staff members, despite the staff hierarchy. In any case it is certain that Adams, in his role of official presidential choke point, possessed a degree of influence that was unprecedented for a White House staffer. It would pave the way for powerful staffs in the future.

Eisenhower thus introduced many changes in the White House staff; he increased its numbers, formalized its structure, and built a fairly strict operational hierarchy. With the exception of Adams, however, his staff remained largely anonymous and relatively uninfluential. Eisenhower believed that his staff should be subordinate to the cabinet and remain in the background, and he tried to operate his administration along those lines. To him, the staff was supposed to move information and help policy makers, not make policy itself.

KENNEDY AND JOHNSON: THE BIRTH OF THE ACTIVIST STAFF

John F. Kennedy (1961–1963) came to the presidency determined to eliminate the elaborate mechanisms that Eisenhower had created in the White House. Convinced that Eisenhower's staff structure was too restrictive and left the president too removed from his administration, Kennedy deliberately attempted a return to a staff more akin to that of Franklin Roosevelt. He replaced the committees and secretariats that had supported the cabinet and the NSC under Eisenhower with a few senior aides who had distinct yet overlapping responsibilities. The overlap occurred because the staff structure was fluid, and because Kennedy tended to hand out assignments as they arose to whoever was available rather than channeling them to a predesignated individual.

Kennedy's staff included several of the now-established White House positions: press secretary, special counsel, appointments secretary, congressional liaison, and national security adviser. He had no formal chief of staff. Appointments secretary Kenneth P. O'Donnell doubled as White House administrator, while Kennedy himself controlled the paper flow, personally receiving reports from subordinates. He also had no designated speechwriters; as with Roosevelt, speech-writing duties were spread among his aides, most notably to his special counsel, Theodore C. Sorensen.

In spite of the dismantling of Eisenhower's staff system, the Kennedy White House did not decrease in size. Under Kennedy the regular White House employees numbered between 300 and 350, which was less than during Eisenhower's second term (but not his first). Kennedy used far more detailees than Eisenhower, however. His White House employed between 429 and 476 full-time personnel—figures unmatched by any previous administration. The continual growth of the White House staff reflected the increasing tendency of the public to look to Washington, and particularly the White House, for solutions to the nation's problems. This tendency was only accelerated by events such as the building of the Berlin Wall and the Cuban Missile Crisis. As one scholar noted:

The White House was allowed to keep growing because there was no resistance to growth. Indeed, creating another White House office was

often the easiest way to solve a personnel or constituent problem, a conferring of high status with little effort. The White House was the only place in government where the president could totally control expenditures and was free to move personnel and establish units at will.[8]

The ease with which the White House staff could be expanded made such expansion irresistible.

The most significant development in the staff during the Kennedy years was not the increase in its size but the increase in its responsibilities and influence. As a group, Kennedy's senior aides had far more influence than those in any previous administration. They meshed well with one another and with the boss. Because they thought along the same lines as Kennedy and often could anticipate him, they were readily able to speak for the president. This gave them a good deal of clout in Washington.

Beyond this, the influence of Kennedy's staff was increased by the governing style of the president himself. Kennedy was an activist president who wanted to fulfill his campaign promise to get the country moving again. He sought actions and results. Inevitably, perhaps, he became frustrated with the permanent government, which was filled with elaborate standing routines and career bureaucrats who shared neither his goals nor his sense of urgency. He quickly came to regard the bureaucracy as "an institutional resistance movement . . . a force against innovation with an inexhaustible capacity to dilute, delay, and obstruct presidential purpose."[9] To prod and even avoid the bureaucracy, he turned to his staff, and they, being activists also, were eager to respond. *(See Chapter 35, The President and the Bureaucracy.)* Like other presidents, Kennedy came into office intending to rely on his cabinet for policy innovations and advice. He quickly discovered, however, that cabinet meetings were dull and unproductive (he soon discontinued them) and that the loyalty of many of his department heads to him (rather than their departments) was open to question. He thus turned to other resources.

As a result, Kennedy's staff became involved in policy making to an unprecedented degree. Previous presidents had, with exceptions, prevented the White House staff from crossing the line that separated facilitating decisions from making decisions. The staff aided but rarely advised. Kennedy's senior staff became advisers and advocates more than aides. They were involved directly in many policy decisions, and as their importance swelled accordingly, they began acquiring larger staffs to assist them.

Kennedy was in fact beginning to pull policy making, and thus power, out of the executive departments and concentrate it within the White House. Kennedy's "New Frontier" was devised and advocated by his staff, largely under Sorensen's direction, not by the bureaucracy. Many other programs were handled similarly. Perhaps the staff's greatest influence lay in foreign policy. Having destroyed Eisenhower's elaborate NSC apparatus, and highly frustrated by the State Department, Kennedy turned to his national security adviser, McGeorge Bundy, and gave him a central role in the formulation and conduct of his foreign policy.

Kennedy's staff lacked the "passion for anonymity" that the

Brownlow Committee had advocated. As the "president's men," they clearly stood apart from the rest of the government and were more visible than previous staffs. And while it was probably not anyone's conscious intent—for in theory the staff was still just a link between the president and the bureaucracy—the White House staff began to take on the characteristics of a shadow government, parallel to the bureaucracy.

When he became president on November 22, 1963, Lyndon B. Johnson inherited Kennedy's staff and its organization, which for various reasons he found acceptable and so left intact. Like Kennedy, he intended to follow the example of Franklin Roosevelt, and the fluid nature of Kennedy's staff suited him. The White House staff continued to grow in influence during the Johnson administration (1963–1969). Johnson too was an activist president who wanted rapid access to the information and ideas needed to help him formulate new policies. He also wanted his staff to have sufficient authority to supervise policy implementation. LBJ found the cabinet departments to be too slow and ponderous to be truly useful, but he continued to hold cabinet meetings merely to obtain endorsement of his plans. This concentration of power in the White House was reinforced by Johnson's dominant personality, which led him to extend his control as much as possible. Later, the public outcry against his conduct of the Vietnam War caused him to withdraw into the sanctuary of the White House, relying on his staff even more.

Initially, Johnson kept Kennedy's people and staff arrangements, but as they gradually left he began clarifying the areas of responsibility within his staff. He maintained the usual press secretary, appointments secretary, special counsel (and deputy counsels), and congressional liaison offices. The latter received particular attention under Johnson, who had an extensive background in Congress. Speechwriters generally were drawn from other positions. Johnson also used his aides as links to groups outside the White House such as business, labor, and various religious and ethnic organizations. He was in fact operating a public liaison staff, although no formal structure or title was ever devised.

The major structural development of the Johnson administration was the creation of a domestic policy staff within the White House. The notion of a domestic policy adviser was not new; although he had had the title special counsel, Theodore Sorensen had performed a similar function for Kennedy. Johnson established the role as a separate position with a small staff of assistants and placed it in the hands of Joseph A. Califano Jr. Califano was responsible for isolating domestic problems, producing proposals for possible solutions, and assisting with the formulation of Johnson's legislative programs.

Although the president's activism and desire for control caused more authority to be vested in the White House staff, the staff's visibility decreased somewhat. Johnson preferred the public limelight for himself, particularly during the early days of his administration, and he downplayed his staff. Overall, the White House staff increased in size and authority during the Johnson administration. Because the president used many de-

tailees, his White House staff always numbered more than four hundred, and in 1967 there were almost five hundred. The demands of his office and his own personality caused Johnson to concentrate more power within the White House than any previous president. Thus, the White House staff that Johnson passed on to Nixon was both the largest and the most influential up to that time.

NIXON: THE IMPERIAL WHITE HOUSE

By 1969 two major trends characterized the development of the White House staff. The first was a continuing trend toward increased size and complexity; the second was a tendency for presidents to consolidate resources and hence power within the White House. Eisenhower had demonstrated the virtues of a large and structured staff, while Kennedy and Johnson had developed the staff to promote policy. These trends came together in the Nixon administration (1969–1974).

The White House Office of Richard Nixon had by far the most elaborate structure seen up to that time. As vice president during the Eisenhower administration, Nixon had observed firsthand the benefits of Eisenhower's staff hierarchy. Like Eisenhower, Nixon believed that he as president should deal with broad policies, not trivial details. He was also a private man who valued his solitude and preferred to make decisions alone, working from briefing papers. The staff he installed was designed to operate smoothly and to protect him from the outside distractions he disliked.

As originally constructed, Nixon's White House Office had four areas of operations: foreign policy, domestic affairs, congressional relations, and White House operations. (See Figure 27-1.) Each was headed by an administrative assistant responsible for its coordination and operation, assisted by a large number of specialists in various policy areas. The system was designed to channel expertise to the president and to facilitate the

FIGURE 27-1 Organization of the Nixon White House, 1972

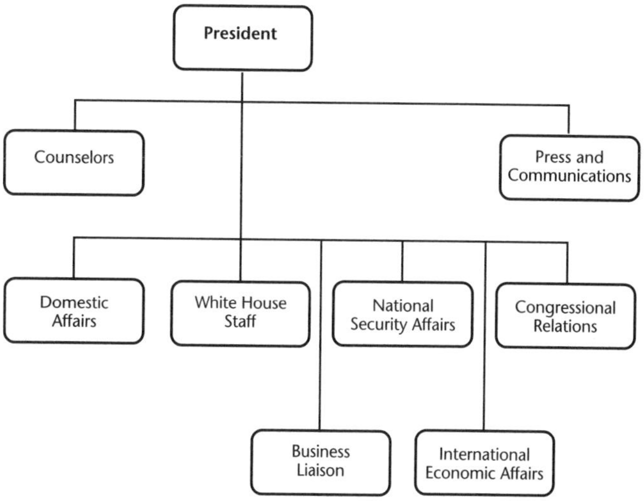

SOURCE: Stephen J. Wayne, *The Legislative Presidency* (New York: Harper and Row, 1978), 48.

implementation of his decisions. Nixon maintained the traditional offices of press secretary, appointments secretary, and special counsel, as well as a personnel office for staff selection and a small political operations staff. He also gathered a stable of designated speechwriters, something Kennedy and Johnson had abandoned.

Specialization was important on the Nixon White House staff. For example, Nixon had three primary speechwriters: Patrick J. Buchanan, William Safire, and Raymond Price, who represented, respectively, the right, center, and left of the Republican Party. Nixon never combined the talents of these men; rather, he used them selectively, depending on the nature of the speech he wanted to deliver. It was a highly specialized arrangement.[10]

The cornerstone of the structure was the chief of staff, a position Nixon resurrected and gave to H. R. Haldeman. Haldeman's task was to shield the president from unwanted paperwork, problems, or visitors, and to see that the business of the White House was carried out efficiently. He proved to be ruthlessly effective in his job. As the president's gatekeeper, he had as much or more authority than any staffer had ever possessed.

Staff innovations during the Nixon administration included a formalized Domestic Council. Unlike Kennedy and Johnson, who had maintained an untitled domestic adviser on their staffs (Sorensen and Califano, respectively), Nixon originally had two domestic advisory staffs, one under Daniel Patrick Moynihan and the other under Arthur F. Burns. Because the liberal Moynihan and the conservative Burns generally took opposing sides on policy questions, Nixon found himself being an arbitrator, a role he acutely disliked, and he began using his special counsel, John D. Ehrlichman, as an intermediary. Eventually, Ehrlichman replaced both Burns and Moynihan, and in November 1969 he was officially named as assistant to the president for domestic affairs.

Eight months later Nixon established the Domestic Council, a counterpart to the NSC, and Ehrlichman became its director. The Domestic Council was supposed to coordinate the domestic policy-making apparatus, isolating and analyzing problems and providing possible solutions to the president. Several presidents had attempted to improve the domestic policy machinery, but the council was the most formal attempt to do so.

Nixon also originated the White House Communications Office, which essentially was a public relations arm of the White House. Other presidents such as Kennedy had been concerned with public relations, but they had left it to the press secretary's office, which rarely had much time for it. To Nixon, public relations was far more important; as much as one-fifth of his entire staff dealt with press and public relations.[11] The Communications Office became a separate operation, a sister to the press secretary's office, and it continued to operate separately even after Nixon's press secretary, Ronald Ziegler, also became communications director.

This specialized structure naturally demanded still more personnel within the White House. In fact, Nixon had the largest White House staff in history. The number of detailees dropped dramatically after 1970, but the decrease was matched by an increase in permanent staff. In all, the Nixon White House never employed fewer than five hundred people, and in 1970 the number of staffers exceeded six hundred.

During the Nixon administration the White House Office became a small bureaucracy. The patterns of growth and formalization that had been developing for years culminated under Nixon in a largely depersonalized staff that was out of contact with the president it served. Franklin Roosevelt had worked closely with all his aides; in the Nixon White House there were assistants to the president who rarely, if ever, saw him. Nixon could not hope to supervise his staff personally; the staff had to control itself.

At the same time Nixon's staff acquired power to such an extent that the White House largely superseded the rest of the executive branch, relegating much of the regular government to a role of secondary importance. Problems were identified, options evaluated, and decisions made and implemented with minimal, if any, help from the traditional bureaucratic agencies. An increasing number of decisions and details formerly left to the executive departments were taken over by the White House staff. The White House bureaucracy mirrored and then overshadowed the permanent bureaucracy. Those who had problems learned to go not to the executive departments and agencies but to the appropriate official in the White House, where the real power was. Interest groups, members of Congress, and even executive department officials had to take their business to the White House if they hoped to get decisions and actions. Sen. Ernest F. Hollings (D-S.C.) complained:

It used to be that if I had a problem with food stamps, I went to see the secretary of agriculture, whose department had jurisdiction over that problem. Not anymore. Now, if I want to learn the policy, I must go to the White House to consult with John Price. If I want the latest in textiles, I won't get it from the secretary of commerce, who has the authority and responsibility. No, I am forced to go to the White House and see Mr. Peter Flanigan. I shouldn't feel too badly. Secretary [of Commerce Maurice] Stans has to do the same thing.[12]

To an unprecedented degree the White House staff was actually running the government's agencies. The extent of the staff's power was seen most clearly in the role of the National Security Council under Henry A. Kissinger. The NSC structure resembled that of the State Department, with "desks" for the various world regions. Important foreign policy decisions originated in the NSC, which also played a key role in implementing them, and not the State Department. For example, Nixon's China initiative was conducted without the knowledge of the State Department. Similarly, overtures toward the Soviet Union and Vietnam, among others, were largely devised and executed by the White House. The State Department generally was bypassed and the secretary of state reduced to a figurehead. So dominant was the NSC that at one point Secretary of State William P. Rogers had to publicly insist that he really did participate in the administration's foreign policy process.

Although all the power amassed in the Nixon White House and the EOP allowed the presidency to operate the government almost autonomously, this organization, having been designed to serve the president, was unable to distinguish between his best interests and those of the country. The staff's power, its zeal in serving Nixon, and its lack of outside supervision contributed to the political and legal excesses known collectively as Watergate. Watergate would cost many staffers, including Haldeman and Ehrlichman, their positions and eventually would drive Nixon from the White House. It also arrested, or at least slowed, the steady trend toward a larger and more powerful White House staff.

FORD AND CARTER: ATTEMPTS AT OPENNESS

The perceived power of Nixon's staff, with its tight shielding of the president and the abuses stemming from its blind loyalty, led to protests about the increasing authority gathered within the White House. Partly in response, both Gerald R. Ford (1974–1977) and Jimmy Carter (1977–1981) tried to create staff structures that avoided the excesses of the Nixon White House.

On paper, Ford's staff was structured much like the Nixon staff he had inherited, with its characteristic hierarchy and specialization. *(See Figure 27-2.)* Ford wanted more openness, however, and so he increased the number of advisers who had ready access to him. Whereas hardly anyone beyond Haldeman, Ehrlichman, and Kissinger had had easy access to Nixon, all of

Ford's senior aides could see him at any time. In fact, Ford soon discovered that he had become too available and began to restrict access so that he could use his time better.

Carter attempted a return to the Roosevelt-Kennedy models of White House staffing. Ford had tried to downplay the role of the chief of staff; Carter tried to eliminate it altogether. He wanted an informal structure in which a number of aides would have ready access to him, and he would be staff coordinator. The Nixon hierarchy was abandoned. Like Ford, Carter found this arrangement unworkable. By 1977 the White House had become so large and complex that some hierarchical structure was essential. *(See Figure 27-3, p. 1082.)*

Both Ford and Carter became bogged down in details and problems that swallowed up the time they needed for more important matters. They also found themselves settling turf disputes among their aides. Eventually, both turned to a chief of staff and reimposed hierarchy upon the White House. Neither president was able to reduce the staff's influence as much as he wanted. Both sang the praises of cabinet government, but both found it confusing and ineffective.

In what had become a very large and diversified White House, both Ford and Carter maintained the basic offices of press secretary, special counsel, appointments secretary, speechwriters, congressional liaison, cabinet secretary, staff secretary, public liaison, and domestic and national security advisers. Many of these offices had become rather large. For example, under Ford's press secretary, Ron Nessen, there were two deputy

FIGURE 27-2 Organization of the Ford White House, 1976

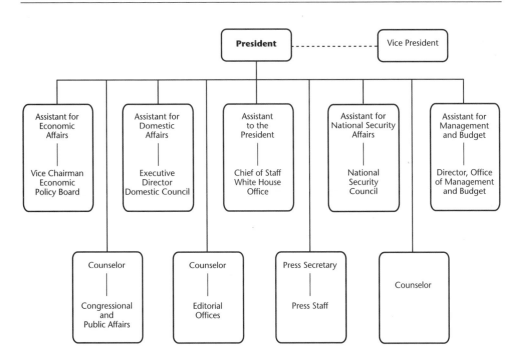

SOURCE: Stephen J. Wayne, *The Legislative Presidency* (New York: Harper and Row, 1978), 53.

FIGURE 27-3 Organization of the Carter White House, 1980

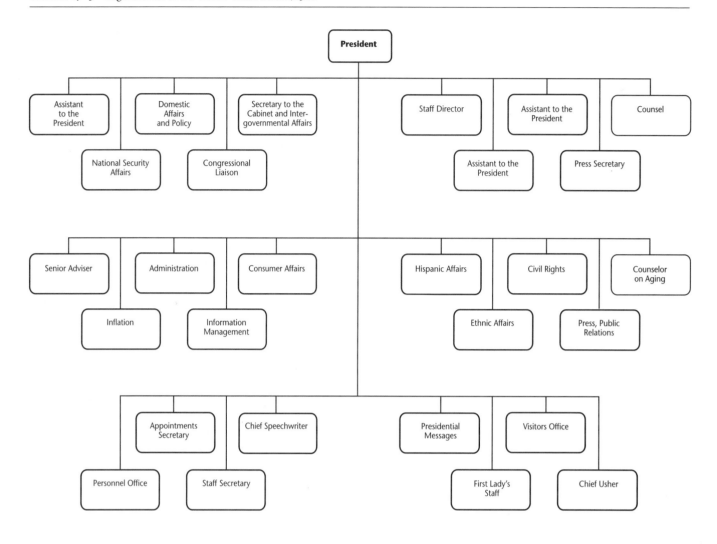

SOURCE: Hugh Heclo and Lester M. Salamon, eds., *The Illusion of Presidential Government* (Boulder, Colo.: Westview Press, 1981), 314.

press secretaries, eight assistant secretaries (including ones for domestic affairs, foreign affairs, and administration), a personal photographer to the president, and clerical workers.

White House growth also reflected the rise of special-interest groups in American politics. Between 1975 and 1979 White House liaison offices were established for business and trade associations, minorities, Hispanic Americans, civil rights, consumer affairs, youth, women, and senior citizens. There was also an assistant for human resources and a director of White House conferences.

Such specialization meant that the staff remained large, despite the efforts of Ford and Carter to reduce it. Ford's total staff remained at between 500 and 550, but Carter was able to reduce his staff to about 460 by 1978. By the end of his administration, however, it had returned to about 500. By 1980 the White House had developed to such a size and complexity that major staff reductions had become difficult, if not impossible, to make. It also

was impossible to operate the staff without a chief of staff and clear lines of authority. To structure the staff in the Rooseveltian manner would mean too great a loss of efficiency and control.

REAGAN: SPECIALIZED HIERARCHICAL STAFF

Just as Ford and Carter organized their staffs in partial reaction to the Nixon experience, Ronald Reagan (1981–1989) built a staff with one eye on the problems faced by his immediate predecessors. Moreover, Reagan saw no reason to tie himself up with technical details, preferring to concentrate instead on general strategies and broad policies as well as political leadership. In response to Carter's perceived obsession with details, President Reagan removed himself from the minutiae of governing perhaps more than any president in the modern era.

The Reagan staff was designed to help the president avoid unnecessary details. It was carefully structured to work out the

FIGURE 27-4   Organization of the Reagan White House, 1981

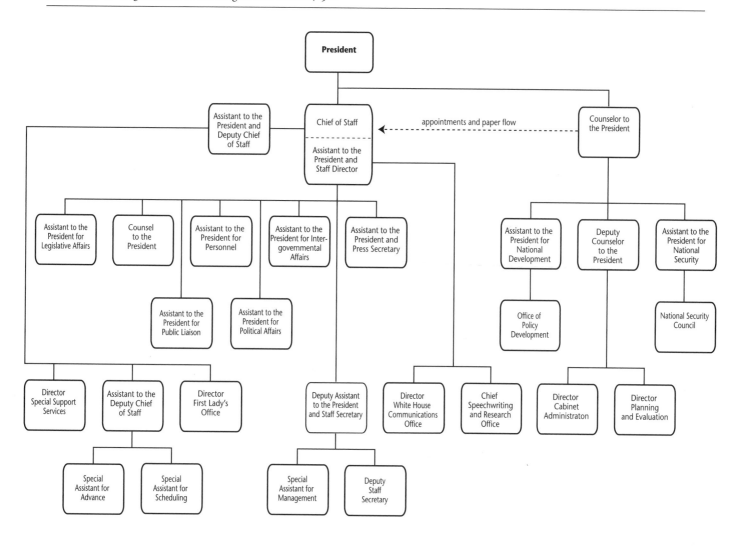

SOURCE: Samuel Kernell and Samuel L. Popkin, eds., *Chief of Staff: Twenty-five Years of Managing the Presidency* (Berkeley: University of California Press, 1986), 202.

specifics of policy issues at lower levels; only the most important questions and broad outlines of policy were taken to the president. The staff was sufficiently specialized and hierarchical to ensure that Reagan could focus on his role as the "Great Communicator." He retained most of the offices that had become an institutionalized part of the White House, including a chief of staff and a special counsel, and created a new position, counselor to the president, for his close adviser Edwin Meese III. (*See Figure 27-4.*)

One innovation in the Reagan White House was the Office of Planning and Evaluation (OPE), which coordinated the development of Reagan's policies with the public mood. The OPE conducted public opinion surveys to gauge public receptiveness to Reagan's programs and made long-range plans for their form and nature accordingly. This office represented the most sophisticated use of pollsters to date by the White House. Although all presidents since FDR had used polling data, only Carter had a

pollster on his staff even on an informal basis, and none had institutionalized public opinion studies like the Reagan White House.[13]

Other innovations in the Reagan White House included the creation of a cabinet secretariat to coordinate interaction between the White House and the cabinet departments and an office of political affairs to work with political elements outside the White House such as the Republican Party.

The Reagan staff was also original in its initial structure. As first created, the staff was subdivided to separate policy formulation from political action. Specialized units were charged with formulating administration policy and implementing it. A third section of the staff handled administrative details for the White House. The White House staff had for many years been engaged in both policy development and policy advocacy, but an institutionalized division between the two functions was unique in the evolution of the White House Office.

The Reagan White House remained large and specialized. President Reagan entered office declaring his love of cabinet government, but like Ford and Carter, he found that goal unattainable. His staff did decline in size—he began with about 450 permanent employees, with a budget of $21 million, and managed to reduce the staff to 357 by 1988[14]—but the shrinkage, at least in part, was an illusion. Presidential scholar Thomas E. Cronin has argued that the staff reduction was achieved on paper by moving the Office of Administration and the Office of Policy Development from the White House Office into the EOP, where they performed the same duties as before.[15]

Within the staff there was a shift as the roles of its most influential members—the national security and domestic advisers—were de-emphasized and the role of budget director was upgraded, reflecting Reagan's predominant concern with the domestic economy. Reagan had originally intended to return to cabinet government, but, like other presidents, found it unworkable. Instead, his administration created a set of cabinet councils. The councils were committees—originally seven, which later collapsed to two—of cabinet members who worked in shared policy areas; from their meetings would come policy suggestions. In Reagan's first term, the entire structure was organized and supervised by Edwin Meese, and so it remained under the tight control of the White House; during Reagan's second term, the councils were rarely used. Thus, the White House staff remained an influential force in the federal government.

BUSH AND CLINTON: HANDS-ON PRESIDENCY

The administration of George Bush (1989–1993) initially saw a brief decline in the staff's power. By being a far more "hands-on" president than his predecessor, Bush reduced the staff's ability to act autonomously. He also named several political friends to head the executive departments rather than appointing them to the White House staff, as other presidents tended to do, thereby creating something of an independent power base for those departments. Thus, although he rarely referred to "cabinet government," Bush probably came closer to it, at least early in his term, than any president since Eisenhower.

Even so, as his term wore on, authority slipped back into the White House at the expense of the executive departments. There were several reasons for this. First, devolving authority to the cabinet resulted in some positive initiatives but also some embarrassing slip-ups; for instance, "in late 1990, Bush's commitment to civil rights suffered . . . following an Education Department ruling, which the White House later rescinded, that college scholarships designated exclusively for minority students were not permissible."[16] Such embarrassments outweighed the value of cabinet initiatives, and the autonomy of the Education Department was curtailed. The missteps, coupled with the rise to prominence of chief of staff John Sununu as a policy adviser and the convenience of centralization, led Bush to reconsolidate power in the White House as other presidents had done.

The Bush White House carried over most of the structure of the Reagan administration. *(See Table 27-1, p. 1085.)* One change was the addition in 1989 of the Office of National Drug Control Policy (ONDCP). The ONDCP was created in reaction to public demand for presidential action on drug abuse and drug trafficking; in response, President Bush created an agency within the White House to coordinate government policy on the problem. The ONDCP was organized with divisions to tackle the supply and demand sides of the drug problem. Critics contended that it was bloated and filled with politicos.[17]

The Clinton administration pulled power further into the White House. Clinton was an activist president who compared himself to Kennedy, and like Kennedy, he seemed to have little patience with the established bureaucracy. Moreover, Clinton, who was once described as "a wonk's wonk," liked to immerse himself in the details of problems and solutions. The result was "an extremely president-centered White House";[18] Clinton tried to consolidate policy making in the White House, using ad hoc task forces to cope with issues as they emerged, and so maintain a direct hand in shaping policies. Perhaps the best example of this was his proposed health care reform, which was devised by a special commission led by First Lady Hillary Rodham Clinton; this far-reaching policy proposal was formulated almost entirely within the White House, with little input from the permanent bureaucracy. *(See Table 27-2, p. 1085.)*

Clinton's consolidation of power was accomplished with a reduced presidential bureaucracy. During the 1992 election campaign, candidate Clinton promised to reduce the size of the federal government; in 1993 President Clinton began cutting the EOP staff by 25 percent from its high point under his predecessor. Some areas were particularly hard hit. The ONDCP, for example, was cut by 83 percent.

The Modern White House Staff

By 1994 the White House staff had evolved into an institutionalized bureaucracy that existed solely to assist the president. In fiscal year 1994, after President Clinton's cuts in the presidential bureaucracy, the White House Office had 389 full-time employees and expenses of $38.8 million. (As noted before, the actual number of White House staff can vary depending on how one counts; some critics argued that some of Clinton's reductions were cosmetic.) Its influence remains formidable; even under Carter and Reagan, who sought to de-emphasize their staffs, the White House dominated the policy apparatus and monitored the bureaucracy. And it still had the ability to conduct operations on its own, as the Iran-contra affair—devised and run by the NSC—indicated. It remains "the directing force of the presidential branch."[19]

Successive presidents have sought with little success to reduce the power and size of the White House, but today the White House bureaucracy has become a permanent fixture of American politics. Presidential scholars have noted several reasons for this. Perhaps the major reason is the public's tendency, in an era of ongoing crises, to expect the president to solve every

TABLE 27-1 Makeup of the Bush White House, 1991

EXECUTIVE OFFICE OF THE PRESIDENT

Office of the Chief of Staff
Office of the Staff Secretary
    Scheduling
    Executive Clerk
    Records Management
    Correspondence
Office of Communications
    Speechwriting
    Research
    Media Relations
    Public Affairs
    Public Liaison
Office of Press Secretary
    News Summary
Office of Management and Administration
Office of Intergovernmental Affairs
Office of the Cabinet Secretary
Office of the Counsel
Office of National Security Affairs
White House Military Office
Office of Legislative Affairs
Office of Economic and Domestic Policy
Office of Special Activities and Initiatives
    Advance Office
Office of Political Affairs
Office of Presidential Personnel
Office of the First Lady

OFFICE OF THE VICE PRESIDENT

Chief of Staff
Office of Domestic Policy and Council on
    Competitiveness
National Security Affairs
Legislative Affairs

AGENCIES OF THE EXECUTIVE OFFICE OF THE PRESIDENT

Office of Administration
Council of Economic Advisers
Council on Environmental Quality
Domestic Policy Council
Economic Policy Council
National Critical Materials Council
National Security Council
Central Intelligence Agency
National Space Council
Office of Management and Budget
Office of National Drug Control Policy
Office of National Service
Office of Policy Development
Office of Policy Planning
Regulatory Information Service Center
Office of Science and Technology Policy
Office of U.S. Trade Representative

SOURCE: Ann L. Brownson, ed., *1991 Federal Staff Directory/1* (Mount Vernon, Va.: Staff Directories, 1991), 3–36.

TABLE 27-2 Makeup of the Clinton White House, 1995

OFFICE OF THE PRESIDENT OF THE UNITED STATES

Office of the Chief of Staff
    Policy
    Strategic Planning
    Speechwriting
Office of the Staff Secretary
    Correspondence
    Executive Clerk
    Records Management
Office of Press Secretary
    Media Affairs and News Analysis
Office of Public Liaison
Office of Intergovernmental Affairs
Office of Management and Administration
    White House Military Office
Office of the General Counsel
Office of Legislative Affairs
    House Liaison
    Senate Liaison
    Correspondence
Office of Political Affairs
National AIDS Policy
Office of Presidential Personnel
Office of Scheduling and Advance
Office of Cabinet Affairs
Office of the First Lady
White House Fellowships

OFFICE OF THE VICE PRESIDENT

Chief of Staff
National Security Adviser
Legislative Affairs
Domestic Policy

AGENCIES OF THE EXECUTIVE OFFICE OF THE PRESIDENT

Office of Administration
Office of Policy Development
Domestic Policy Council
Council on Environmental Quality
National Economic Council
Council of Economic Advisers
National Security Council
Central Intelligence Agency
Office of Management and Budget
Office of National Drug Control Policy
Office of Science and Technology Policy
Office of U.S. Trade Representative

SOURCE: Ann L. Brownson, ed., *1995 Federal Staff Directory/1* (Mount Vernon, Va.: Staff Directories, 1995), 3–37.

problem from national defense and economic recession to terrorism and AIDS. The president then responds by appointing more staff to deal with all these expectations. The creation of the ONDCP by President Bush is a perfect example of this dynamic in action.

More presidential staff are also needed to coordinate policy within the executive branch. Problems and the policies to deal with them now often spill across neat departmental divisions; farm policy, for example, may be the province not only of the Department of Agriculture but also of the Departments of Treasury, Commerce, Labor, and even State. Coordination of all these agencies requires some direction from the top—and therefore more staff.

A correlation between the level of presidential skepticism about the performance of the permanent bureaucracy and the size of the White House staff is also evident. Either because they become impatient with the snail's pace maintained by the executive departments (Kennedy, Johnson, or Clinton), or because they see a bureaucracy filled with personnel left over from previous administrations and perhaps unsympathetic to their programs (Nixon), presidents often try to control within the White House as much of the development and implementation of their programs as possible. The most activist presidents have the largest staffs. *(See Chapter 35, The President and the Bureaucracy.)*

The growth of the White House staff also parallels the growth of the congressional staff. In an effort to offset the capabilities of the executive departments, Congress has increased the size of both its personal and committee staffs over the last forty years. In 1957 the total congressional staff (personal and committee staff) was 4,489. By 1993 the number of total staff had swollen to 14,679, and either chamber had more staff than the entire Congress of 1955: the Senate staff numbered 5,132, while the staff of the House of Representatives numbered 9,547.[20] Since most of the contact between the president and Congress takes place at the staff level, an increase in congressional staff almost inevitably leads to a corresponding increase in presidential staff.

White House staff growth also has been prompted by the inclusion of special-interest representation within the White House. Since the Truman administration, presidential aides have been designated, at first unofficially but then more formally, as liaisons to certain groups in society such as labor or religious groups. The trickle of recognition has gradually grown into a torrent as literally dozens of groups have gained a voice within the White House. Cronin has noted that

a partial listing of staff specializations that have been grafted onto the White House in recent years . . . [forms] a veritable index of American society: budget and management, national security, economics, congressional matters, science and technology, drug abuse prevention, telecommunications, consumers, national goals, intergovernmental relations, environment, domestic policy, international economics, military affairs, civil rights, disarmament, labor relations, District of Columbia, cultural affairs, education, foreign trade and tariffs, the aged, health and nutrition, physical fitness, volunteerism, intellectuals,

Blacks, youth, women, Wall Street, governors, mayors, "ethnics," regulatory agencies and related industry, state party chairmen.[21]

The multitude of interests with ties to the White House and the larger staff needed to deal with them helps explain the growth not only of the White House Office but also of the entire EOP.

A final factor in the growth of the White House staff is its increased concern with the president's public image. Every president has wanted to put forward the best image possible, but the emphasis has been increasing and the techniques have grown more sophisticated, beginning with the Nixon administration. The modern White House maintains considerable staff to manage the news and to handle public relations in an effort to "sell" the president and presidential programs to the people. Even pollsters have become part of the presidential staff.

Structure of the White House Staff

As the president's personal staff, members of the White House organization provide the president with the advice and information needed to make decisions and try to ensure that presidential decisions are carried out. Their loyalty is to the president, whose best interests they always keep in mind. Within the government the White House Office is the president's only exclusive domain.

Unlike other parts of the Executive Office of the President, the White House staff is not institutionalized and can change in size and form to suit a president's managerial style. Congress has been careful not to impose any structure on it. Members of the White House staff are appointed solely by the president and are not subject to congressional confirmation. Staffers have no government status and no tenure in their position; they serve at the president's discretion and can be dismissed at any time for any reason. Staffers are also expected to put in long hours. That a president may work long hours is well known; the image of the lights burning late into the night in the Oval Office is familiar to us all. Often forgotten is that the president's staff works just as long and hard (or harder) as the president.

Although staffers may have enormous influence, that influence depends entirely on their relationship with the president. With no independent power base, staff members may find that their influence will wax and wane according to their intimacy with the boss. Staffers with offices near the Oval Office, or those who have ready access to the president, are likely to be very powerful. Those who are stuck in the Old Executive Office Building and see the president only by appointment are much less influential. Within the White House staff, proximity is everything. Thus, allotment of offices and the right to be the first or last to see the president each day become vital matters.

The following description of units within the White House Office must be prefaced with a caveat. Very simply, there is nothing fixed about these units. Presidents can create, abolish, or reorganize its offices as they choose. *(Compare Tables 27-1 and 27-2, p. 1085)*. Indeed, presidents are free to eliminate the entire staff if they wish. Similarly, the functions assigned to a given office may vary from one administration to another, and sometimes even within an administration. Presidents are free to change the job description of any office at any time, whether it is an office passed down from a previous administration or one of their own invention. Titles do not always accurately indicate who does what in the White House, nor do they always reveal whom the president consults on important matters. Presidents tend to seek advice from those assistants with whom they feel most comfortable, regardless of the staffer's position or the subject matter.

CHIEF OF STAFF

The most important position in the present-day White House is chief of staff. This senior aide is responsible for the smooth operation of the White House, which is no small task. Materials must be made available to the president in a timely manner, and the president's requests and directives must be acted upon and implemented quickly. The swift and accurate flow of business is a primary goal. The chief also acts as head gatekeeper to the president, and by reviewing all papers and visitors, he or she channels as many as possible around the president. Sherman Adams in the Eisenhower administration and H. R. Haldeman in the Nixon administration were very effective in this role. The gatekeeping function provides the chiefs of staff with a great deal of influence, since anyone wishing to bring an issue before the president must obtain their approval.

Although most chiefs of staff have denied playing a role in policy making, the position has acquired a policy function as well. Because most chiefs have a close working relationship with presidents, it is only natural for presidents to seek and heed their opinions. Hamilton Jordan, who served as Carter's chief of staff, was an important voice in the administration, and James A. Baker III was an adviser as well as a political operative under Reagan and Bush. Bush acknowledged even before taking office that his first chief of staff, John H. Sununu, would be an administrator and a policy adviser, and indeed Sununu was, notably in domestic affairs. (See Table 27-3.)

Another important function of the chief is presidential hatchet wielder. All presidents have had jobs that they wanted to avoid, confrontations that they wished to dodge. Haldeman once noted that "every president needs his son-of-a-bitch" to do the dirty work.[22] The chief of staff is that person. Adams reprimanded or dismissed people to save Eisenhower the unpleasantness of doing it himself. Haldeman did the same for Nixon. After the 1972 election, Nixon called a staff meeting and thanked everyone for their efforts in his behalf. Then, just before leaving, he turned the meeting over to Haldeman, who without preface immediately demanded everyone's resignation. The demand was really Nixon's and everyone knew it, but Haldeman had the task of carrying it out. Failure to be tough enough can lead to a staff that is ineffective and in disarray. Clinton's first chief, Thomas F. "Mack" McLarty III, was seen as too easygoing (he

TABLE 27-3   Chiefs of Staff, 1932–1996

President	Chief of Staff	Years
Roosevelt	—	—
Truman	John R. Steelman[a]	1946–1952
Eisenhower	Sherman Adams[a]	1953–1958
	Wilton Persons[a]	1958–1961
Kennedy	—	—
Johnson	—	—
Nixon	H. R. Haldeman	1969–1973
	Alexander M. Haig Jr.	1973–1974
Ford	Donald Rumsfeld	1974–1975
	Richard B. Cheney	1975–1977
Carter	Hamilton Jordan	1979–1980
	Jack H. Watson Jr.	1980–1981
Reagan	James A. Baker III	1981–1985
	Donald T. Regan	1985–1987
	Howard H. Baker Jr.	1987–1988
	Kenneth Duberstein	1988–1989
Bush	John H. Sununu	1989–1991
	Samuel Skinner	1991–1992
	James A. Baker III	1992–1993
Clinton	Thomas F. "Mack" McLarty III	1993–1994
	Leon Panetta	1994–

SOURCES: Presidential libraries and the White House.
NOTES: The Roosevelt, Kennedy, and Johnson presidential libraries each reported that there was no chief of staff or even a presidential assistant who served in that role.   a. These aides carried the title of "assistant" rather than "chief of staff."

was nicknamed "Mack the Nice") and was blamed for much of the perceived confusion in the staff. He eventually was replaced with budget director Leon Panetta.

Finally, the chief often shoulders the blame for the president. Performing unpleasant jobs such as dismissals, which may have political significance, and taking responsibility for misstatements or other errors in fact made by the president are two ways in which the chief may act as presidential shield. Or the chief may act as a lightning rod to draw criticism away from the president. This function will not be found in any job description, but the possibility of being a scapegoat for the president is part of the job, and most chiefs know it. Sununu's failure to play this role adequately for Bush was one of the major factors in his ouster as chief of staff.

SPECIAL COUNSEL

The position of special counsel has varied in importance over the years. In creating the position, Franklin Roosevelt argued that the White House needed its own lawyer because the attorney general, the nation's chief law officer and the government's first lawyer, was too busy to give the White House the necessary time. In reality, Roosevelt envisioned a larger role for his counsel.

The special counsel is the president's private lawyer. (He is not, however, the president's personal lawyer; the counsel was not responsible for President Clinton's defense in the Whitewater affair.) The special counsel provides legal advice on an assortment of topics, reviews legislation before it is sent to Con-

President Bill Clinton meets with his national security advisers in the Oval Office in 1994. From left to right, National Security Adviser Anthony Lake, Secretary of Defense William Perry, Clinton, Chairman of the Armed Forces Joint Chiefs of Staff John Shalikashvili, and Deputy National Security Adviser Samuel R. Berger.

gress, and may even check potential treaties for legal problems. The president also may seek the counsel's advice on the legality of certain actions. The counsel's office is concerned as well with "overseeing security clearances for presidential appointees, supervising the selection of new federal judges, maintaining liaison with the Justice Department and the legal counsels in the other federal departments, and monitoring internal conflict-of-interest guidelines for employees" of the EOP.[23] Since Watergate, the special counsel's office also has been responsible for ensuring the proper behavior of the presidential staff.

Beyond these duties the office has often served presidents as a place to put valuable aides. Franklin Roosevelt named a special counsel primarily to create a place for Samuel Rosenman, who served him as an adviser and a speechwriter. Clark Clifford performed similar functions while occupying the same post under Truman. Kennedy named Theodore Sorensen special counsel and used him as a speechwriter and domestic policy adviser. Under Carter, the office was used in two different ways: Robert J. Lipshutz confined himself to legal matters, but his successor, Lloyd Cutler, advised the president on a wide range of issues, both foreign and domestic.

NATIONAL SECURITY AND DOMESTIC ADVISERS

The national security adviser is one of the president's primary advisers on foreign policy. Created originally as a largely administrative post, the national security adviser was responsible for overseeing the functioning of the National Security Council and coordinating the various elements of the foreign policy establishment, such as the State Department, Defense Department, and Central Intelligence Agency. Over the years the position has retained these administrative functions, and the Reagan

administration, at least in its initial days, tried to reemphasize them. (See Table 27-4 and Chapter 28, Executive Office of the President: Supporting Organizations.)

Given the central location of the national security adviser in the policy process, it was natural that presidents began turning to them for advice as well as coordination. National security advisers became important policy-making figures; men such as Bundy, Kissinger, and Zbigniew Brzezinski (under Carter) were major players, if not the crucial figures, in the development of their administrations' foreign policy. Under these advisers the role of foreign policy designer began to overshadow that of administrator.

The prominence of the national security adviser has led to an

TABLE 27-4 National Security Advisers, 1961–1996

President	National security adviser	Years
Kennedy	McGeorge Bundy	1961–1963
Johnson	McGeorge Bundy	1963–1966
	Walt W. Rostow	1966–1969
Nixon	Henry A. Kissinger	1969–1974
Ford	Henry A. Kissinger	1974–1975
	Brent Scowcroft	1975–1977
Carter	Zbigniew Brzezinski	1977–1981
Reagan	Richard Allen	1981–1982
	William P. Clark	1982–1983
	Robert C. McFarlane	1983–1986
	John M. Poindexter	1986
	Frank C. Carlucci	1986–1987
	Colin Powell	1987–1989
Bush	Brent Scowcroft	1989–1993
Clinton	Anthony Lake	1993–

SOURCES: *Congressional Quarterly Weekly Report*, various issues.

occasional controversy about the position. The possibility that a national security adviser could dominate the execution of U.S. foreign policy has led to calls for congressional confirmation of appointees to the post. Demands for congressional approval have been particularly strident when evidence has surfaced of uncontrolled or excessive NSC activity, such as that during the Iran-contra affair.

The domestic policy adviser has existed under different names in several administrations. Some scholars have contended that Adams was a de facto domestic adviser under Eisenhower. Sorensen served as one under Kennedy. The role was given to Califano in the Johnson administration, and the Domestic Council was formalized under Ehrlichman in the Nixon years. Carter rechristened it the Domestic Policy Staff, and Reagan renamed it yet again, designating it the Office of Policy Development. In the Clinton administration, the Office of Policy Development was subordinated to the Domestic Policy Council, but Clinton made little use of it. *(See Chapter 28, Executive Office of the President: Supporting Organizations.)*

By whatever name, the office of the domestic policy adviser has responsibilities that parallel those of the office of the national security adviser. The domestic adviser coordinates domestic policy making and acts as a policy adviser. The adviser's office settles disputes between domestic agencies and uses input from them to formulate legislative proposals. The president may also turn to the domestic adviser for advice on domestic problems. The domestic adviser has not been as influential or as effective a coordinator as the national security adviser. This stems from the larger number of agencies and constituencies in the domestic adviser's domain, many of which are powerful and active. Thus, the domestic adviser cannot exercise the same degree of control as his or her foreign counterpart.

WHITE HOUSE LIAISON OFFICES

Several offices in the modern White House are concerned with its links with the world outside its gates. The oldest of these is the office of the press secretary. The press secretary manages the administration's relations with the news media. News summaries and daily briefings issued by the secretary for journalists provide information on the president's activities and decisions. The press secretary is regarded as the spokesperson for the administration, and his or her words are taken to be the president's position. Because of their proximity to the president, press secretaries may also become policy advisers. James Hagerty functioned in that dual capacity for Eisenhower, as did the Nixon administration's Ronald Ziegler, who eventually was named as an assistant to the president as well.

A key role of the press secretary is to maintain good relations between the president and the media and thereby perhaps improve the coverage given to the president. A skillful press secretary can release information selectively and help push the stories the president wants; a personable one can reduce antagonism between the White House and the media and so help the president "get a break" in the coverage. An example of this was

Dee Dee Myers, serving under President Clinton from 1993 to 1994, was the first woman to be White House press secretary.

in the Clinton administration. Under Communications Director George Stephanopoulos and Press Secretary Dee Dee Myers (who was the first woman White House press secretary), a level of hostility with the media existed and the president's press coverage was very negative. This was partly due to the communication structure of the Clinton White House. Myers was never a part of the information loop of the White House's top advisers, a mistake that had often hampered press secretaries in previous administrations. The press felt Myers was amiable enough but uninformed. Michael McCurry, who replaced Myers in 1994, was not only given access to the top information denied Myers, he knew how to manipulate flow of information to maximize stories favorable to the president. He also created a more relaxed and open relationship between the administration and the press. The result was that favorable media coverage of President Clinton increased dramatically.

Closely related to the press secretary is the Communications Office. The two offices were actually one through the Johnson administration, with the press secretary handling all press relations, but the increasing workload caused by the government's growth and the electronic era necessitated a division of labor. The Communications Office was separated from the press secretary's office by President Nixon in 1969, and it has remained a separate entity since.

Like the press secretary's office, the Communications Office is concerned with the news media, but it is more involved in managing the news. The communications director responds to reporters' inquiries, provides information and briefings, and arranges interviews. The director also tries to get the administration's point of view across, using press releases, interviews, mailings, and other techniques to promote the president's side of a story. In short, the Communications Office functions as an advertising department and the public relations agency for the White House. During the Nixon presidency, for example, the office sent out summaries of administration accomplishments to some five thousand journalists and commentators. During Watergate, it acted as a liaison between the White House and various groups opposing a possible Nixon impeachment.[24]

The White House also maintains offices to facilitate communication with important groups. One of the most important of these is the congressional liaison office, which has been called the Office of Legislative Affairs since the Reagan administration. Used to control the interaction between the president and Congress, this office was formally established during the Eisenhower administration, although previous presidents had unofficial liaison personnel. Subsequently, it has grown as Congress has grown.

The congressional liaison staff, with its components for the House and the Senate, tries to maintain a two-way flow of information between the White House and Congress. Staff members present the president's positions to Congress and sell presidential programs there. They also nurture good relationships with individual members of Congress who might support the administration on various bills. Information and materials are provided as well to help the administration's congressional friends persuade others in Congress and defend themselves back home.

In facilitating communications from Congress to the White House, the liaison staff relays and tries to resolve problems that members of Congress may be having with the administration. It is a channel through which members of Congress can talk to the president. The liaison staff also keeps the president informed on the mood in Congress and the chances of success there. For specific bills the liaison staff must work with the president's congressional supporters to help determine when a bill should be introduced, how it should be worded, how it should be promoted and modified, and when it should be brought to a vote. Staff members also must keep accurate counts of the number of votes available to the president for a bill. They then know exactly who is wavering, and either can be won over or must be reinforced, and what incentives are needed to gain a member's vote. The staff also must know when and to what degree direct presidential involvement is needed to save a bill. Any slip-up may mean losing a salvageable bill or wasting valuable presidential resources.

The public liaison office was established during the Ford administration, and it has remained a White House fixture. Its goal is to build support for the administration's policies among the general public. Liaison staffers contact constituency groups and try to educate them about the administration's goals and actions. One of President Carter's assistants for public liaison, Anne Wexler, invited influential groups to the White House to hear administration officials, including the president, explain the administration's positions on particular issues. Her goal was to increase public support for the president. Other White House liaison offices maintain ties with various specific constituency groups.

The White House also has a staff of presidential speechwriters. On earlier staffs, speechwriters were not specifically designated as such. The first "speechwriting specialist" was Emmet Hughes, a former journalist who wrote for Eisenhower. The Eisenhower practice was discarded by Kennedy but resumed by Johnson and has continued ever since. In 1996 the Clinton administration had at least five aides who were designated as "Special Assistant to the President for Speechwriting."

Presidential speechwriters are the administration's wordsmiths: they compose the addresses, statements, and messages that the president delivers to Congress and the general public, both at home and abroad. Much of President Kennedy's famed inaugural address, for example, was written by Theodore Sorensen, Kennedy's special counsel. Many phrases that have defined an administration were created by speechwriters, not by the president who spoke them. For example, the "kinder, gentler" Bush administration, with its "thousand points of light," was a creation of speechwriter Peggy Noonan. Because words define policy, speechwriters also may have a role in policy making. Indeed, in the Roosevelt, Truman, and Kennedy administrations, speechwriters were policy advisers as well.

PERSONNEL OFFICE

During every administration numerous vacancies occur in the executive branch, and all presidents' staffs maintain a personnel office to find people to fill them. This office locates potential officeholders, checks on qualifications and conducts interviews, and along with the special counsel's office arranges for background checks, often by the Federal Bureau of Investigation. If all is in order, the office presents the nominee to the president for approval and submission to the Senate, if necessary. It also might brief the appointee on the questions he or she may face from that body. The rigor with which the personnel office does its business varies from administration to administration, methods range from using computer data banks to making informal queries.[25]

The Personnel Office can be a very important tool for presidents to use in staffing their administration. A large office with clear guidelines can carefully screen potential appointees to ensure that they are ideologically compatible with, and will be loyal to, the president. Controlling as many appointments as possible from the White House, as opposed to selecting department heads and letting them choose their own subordinates (as Carter did), can reduce the difficulties the president encounters in managing his administration.

Recruiting the White House Staff

Because the success or failure of an administration may depend largely on the abilities of the White House staff, the problem of how to find good people is of major concern to presidents. Certainly, there is no lack of applicants: during the Bush transition, which was from one Republican administration to another and therefore had less turnover than many, more than 45,000 applications and recommendations were received (*after* the deletion of duplicates; the original number was close to 70,000).[26] How can presidents select the most suitable people from such a mass? Unfortunately, few studies have examined critically how presidents choose their staffs and what factors determine how and why staffers are selected.

Recent presidents have had both an inner and an outer staff. In a bureaucracy that includes hundreds if not thousands of people (depending on whether one includes the EOP), not everyone can have the ear of the president. The term "inner staff" refers to those senior aides who are close to the president and can reasonably expect admission to the Oval Office when they need it. The "outer staff" refers to the other members of the presidential establishment, who perform specialized functions in the lower echelons of the White House but see the president rarely, if ever. The distinction between the two staffs is of some importance, for presidents may choose personnel for each in different ways.

Historically, the senior inner staff is chosen from among the president's close friends and political allies. To fill these staff positions, presidents usually look to the people with whom they have worked closely in the past, tending to select campaign workers or old friends to take the top staff positions. In 1968, for example, President Nixon chose his campaign manager as his White House chief of staff. President Clinton named Mack McLarty, a close friend since childhood, as his first chief of staff. Technical qualifications thus may not matter as much as a good relationship with the president.

Presidents often bring their inner staff to Washington with them. Truman appointed a number of old political friends from Missouri to various staff positions. Kennedy had his "Irish Mafia," staffed by men from Harvard and the Northeast; Carter's "Georgia Mafia" was drawn from his native state; Clinton filled his staff with associates from Arkansas politics. Johnson brought old Texas associates such as Jack Valenti and Bill Moyers, while Reagan brought William P. Clark, Edwin Meese III, and Michael K. Deaver from California to serve in his administration. Virtually all of Bush's first- and second-level aides were long-term associates of the president and of one another.

Presidents tend to choose their inner staff from the ranks of close friends and associates for good reasons. In the first place, these people are nearby when a new president starts forming the White House team. In the crush of a presidential transition period, the new president has a multitude of details to worry about, and an extended search to fill staff appointments is often

not possible. Indeed, a new president needs help immediately after the election; the only way to get that help is to call on friends and associates to fill staff positions.

More important, the president usually chooses the inner staff from among close associates because these are the people the president feels he can trust when seeking political or personal advice. The need for trustworthy confidants is particularly keen for a president. When FDR's Republican opponent in the 1940 election, Wendell L. Willkie, asked Roosevelt why he continued to keep assistant Harry Hopkins, he replied,

I can understand that you wonder why I need that half man around me. But someday you may be sitting here where I am now as president of the United States. And when you are, you'll be looking through that door over there and knowing that practically everybody who walks through it wants something out of you. You'll learn what a lonely job this is, and you'll discover the need for somebody like Harry Hopkins who asks for nothing except to serve you.[27]

Although most members of the inner staff are chosen from the president's friends and former aides, presidents sometimes choose senior aides primarily on the basis of reputation, and close working relationships may follow. For example, President Nixon selected Henry Kissinger as his national security adviser after just one meeting with him. The selection was based on Kissinger's writings on foreign policy and international politics. Only later did Kissinger develop a good working relationship with Nixon. Similarly, James Baker was far from a close confidant of President Reagan when he was selected to fill the position of chief of staff. Thus, although special knowledge or qualifications may become important in filling high-profile senior posts such as budget director or national security adviser, new presidents continue to select most senior aides on the basis of old ties.

Lower-level White House personnel, who fill more specialized roles, may be appointed on the basis of either connections or merit. Depending on the desires of the president, such staffers are selected in a systematic screening process similar to that used for other executive branch personnel. Potential staff who meet the criteria of loyalty to the president, agreement with the president's program, and competence may be subjected to background checks (to prevent something embarrassing to the administration from surfacing later) before taking their positions. White House staff appointments do not require congressional confirmation.

Every recent administration has had a White House personnel office responsible for finding and screening potential appointees. The care with which such searches are undertaken, however, varies from one administration to another. Under Lyndon Johnson, a computerized file was set up to keep records on possible appointees; whenever a position became available, Johnson's personnel staff could scan the computer banks and find people qualified for the job. Other presidents have employed less advanced methods. After President Nixon's election in 1968 his staff tried to find personnel by soliciting recommendations from everyone in *Who's Who in America* (which included such political notables as Casey Stengel and Elvis Presley; a letter also was sent to Nixon himself).[28]

What seems to be more common than computers and systematic searches is the BOGSAT method of appointing personnel: "a bunch of guys sitting around a table" saying, "Whom do you know?" Frequently, White House staff selection appears to be based on connections; it is a matter of knowing a person who knows a person who knows the president. As one Bush transition team member put it, "There are lots of ways people get jobs in the White House, but one of them isn't by sending in a resume. . . . [T]he process doesn't get people jobs, people get people jobs."[29]

Like Franklin Roosevelt, many presidents have chosen a large part of their staff by drawing on friends, colleagues, campaign workers, the "old boys' network," and party operatives to fill posts both in the White House and in the administration at large. Although most administrations worked this way, the Johnson, Carter, and Reagan administrations, which were more systematic than most in their selection of executive personnel, avoided the BOGSAT method to some degree.

Profiles of White House aides over the years are strikingly consistent—no doubt partly because of the way in which they are chosen. From 1948 through 1974 the staff was almost exclusively white men: 98 percent were white and 98 percent were male. Eighty-six percent had college educations. Of these, 57 percent had undertaken some advanced graduate work, particularly in law. Sixty-nine percent of the staffers were between the ages of thirty and fifty, and the average age has tended to decline over the years. The private sector has produced 60 percent of the White House staffers; the predominant fields have been law (16 percent), business (15 percent), journalism (13 percent), and education (11 percent); nonelected government positions produced 29 percent of the staff; 4 percent were former elected officials; and 6 percent were former military men.[30] While more women and minorities have been included on recent staffs, especially in Democratic administrations, this basic pattern still seems to hold. The Bush staff, for example, was "mainly affable white men in their 30s and 40s who [were] experienced in Washington's ways."[31] The Clinton senior staff, while somewhat younger than most, still had only two African Americans, one Hispanic, and five women (out of nineteen)—and three of the women were also the ethnic minorities.

Styles of Presidential Management and Organization

No formal rules govern the way presidents shape their staffs; the only variables are their preferences and work habits. At the same time, certain patterns of organization have recurred over the years. Scholars have discerned two types of patterns: pyramidal and circular.

As the name suggests, pyramidal staffs are structured as a hierarchy with the president occupying the top position. Immediately under the president there is usually a chief of staff who has a few key assistants who are close to the president; some may have direct access to the Oval Office. Arranged in order of importance below these close aides are the other assistants, whose numbers increase as their relative importance decreases. This structure is designed to ensure a clear chain of command and provide precise channels of communication for information going up and directives coming down. It permits specialization at the lower levels and control at the top. In theory, aides higher up in the system are able to provide the president with more accurate information in a timely manner, filtering out and eliminating unnecessary information. President Eisenhower argued that "a president who doesn't know how to decentralize will be weighted down with details and won't have time to deal with the big issues."[32]

Critics of the pyramidal staff have contended that the structure may distort information and problems. Highly complex problems may resist compression into the one-page memoranda preferred by Presidents Eisenhower and Reagan; information and policy alternatives that the president should have may be lost or discarded at the lower staff levels. A staff pyramid also may malfunction and isolate the president. In acting as a screen, the staff may not only keep unnecessary information from the president; it may also filter out necessary but unpleasant information. What staff member wants to be the bearer of bad news? Critics charge that pyramidal staffs can cause the president to lose contact with reality. Indeed, it may happen that the staff is controlling the president more than the president is controlling the staff.

In the circular or "spokes of the wheel" method of organizing the White House, the president acts as chief of staff. Surrounded by a number of trusted advisers, all of whom have approximately equal access to the Oval Office, the president makes assignments, receives reports, and largely determines how presidential time is allotted among staffers. Essentially, the president sits in the middle of a ring of advisers who funnel information to and are in equal contact with the Oval Office, much like the hub of a wheel.

The circular approach to staff organization permits the president to obtain information from a variety of sources. Properly pursued, this approach reduces the possibility that dissenting voices getting lost in the shuffle and never reaching the president. Because not all details are worked out at the lower staff levels, the president can have more control of the specifics of the administration's policies, thereby ensuring that an important idea is not lost in the evolution of a brief policy memo. As some scholars have noted, activist presidents who want an exchange of ideas at the highest levels have tended to prefer this approach.

The circular staff arrangement may permit too much access to the president, however. Given the size of the modern White House staff, a president who does not have someone else to control the flow of people and paper to the Oval Office is at serious risk of being inundated and swept away. There is simply not enough of the president to go around. H. R. Haldeman once observed that "if everyone who wanted to see [the president] got in, nobody would get in because there wouldn't be room."[33] And as President Ford noted,

[B]ecause power in Washington is measured by how much access a person has to the president, almost everyone wanted more access than I had access to give. I wanted to have an "open" door, but it was very difficult; my working day grew longer and longer, and the demands on my time were hindering my effectiveness. Someone . . . had to be responsible for scheduling appointments, coordinating the paper flow, following up on decisions I had made. . . .[34]

Circular staffing arrangements also have been criticized as stimulating unhealthy friction between staffers, who may find themselves competing for the president's attention. Most (but not all) presidents have found such jealousies disruptive to peak staff performance. The opposite of internal bickering could also occur: a circular staff could easily become excessively collegial and lose its critical perspective, thus developing what is referred to as "groupthink."[35]

ROOSEVELT AND THE COMPETITIVE STAFF

Some presidential scholars have drawn a distinction between the circular model employed by Franklin Roosevelt and those of other presidents. The Rooseveltian model has been characterized as a "competitive" one in which members of the president's staff are given conflicting assignments. Out of the competition between staffers to win the president's favor, the president can get a better array of options and data, more forcefully argued. Other presidents with circular staffs have used a "collegial" approach, intended to facilitate staff cooperation and to promote harmony and efficiency.

Roosevelt surrounded himself with a small staff of about a half-dozen administrative assistants, most of whom were simply "special assistants," or generalists, able to handle whatever problems emerged. Formal staff meetings were rare because the president preferred informal gatherings with any assistant who needed to see him. There were no experts on particular policy areas, no special-interest liaisons, and no rigid lines of authority; aides moved across policy areas as the president saw fit. The president served as his own chief of staff and handed out assignments himself on a seemingly random basis, often selecting the aide most readily available. He could be so flexible in his assignments because he had created a staff that could move readily from one problem to another. Roosevelt expected his aides to take on whatever assignment that he might give them, resulting in a very fluid staff structure. Roosevelt also received all of the staff's reports personally.

In his constant search for more information about problems and issues, Roosevelt tapped numerous sources, both within and outside of his immediate staff, for facts and advice. For Roosevelt, a separate chief of staff to sort out incoming information would have been an unwelcome obstruction. A master politician and manipulator, he wanted all the facts to come directly to him so that he personally could evaluate and use them.

Roosevelt's staff, which in most ways was a prototypical circular arrangement, was unique in the extent to which he turned it upon itself. Most presidents have disliked internal staff competition and infighting, but Roosevelt seemed to thrive on it. Instead of trying to discourage intrastaff competition, he promoted it. Instead of worrying about stress and struggles within his staff, he encouraged them. In fact, Roosevelt often gave the same assignment to more than one assistant, thus setting them potentially in conflict. Yet he always maintained control of the competition; unlike most presidents he did not even feel the need to maintain a facade of internal staff harmony.

For Roosevelt, operating a staff by the principle of competition had several distinct advantages. The president reasoned that putting aides in competition would stimulate them to work faster, dig harder for needed information and critical insights, and devise more creative solutions to national problems. This was something Roosevelt was constantly seeking, particularly in his early years. He also was better able to evaluate his personnel and their ideas. And the conflict itself apparently appealed to Roosevelt; as Kennedy adviser Richard E. Neustadt has noted, he encouraged his staff to jostle and "evidently got a kick out of bruised egos."[36]

To an outsider, Roosevelt's staff operation seemed chaotic, strife-ridden, and often wasteful of time and resources. It appeared that too many people were duplicating efforts and that there was no organization or planning. However, the open staff system provided what Roosevelt wanted: a flow of ideas. For that, the lack of order was a fair trade-off. Roosevelt was able to retain sufficient control over the operation due to his manipulative skills and the small size of the staff. His staff arrangement remains unique; no other president has been willing or able to operate with the somewhat acrimonious confusion in which Roosevelt thrived.

President Truman certainly was not willing to adopt the Rooseveltian style and set out to alter it soon after becoming president. Although he maintained a basically open and circular staff system, he took steps to provide more order and reduce the intrastaff competition that had been so dear to his predecessor. Assignments were more functional; overlap was reduced. Still, Truman preferred to remain at the center of the wheel.

KENNEDY, JOHNSON, AND THE COLLEGIAL STAFF

Two later Democratic presidents also operated circular staffs. Indeed, President Kennedy's staff is often cited as a prototype of the collegial staff system. When he organized his White House staff, Kennedy made a conscious decision to return to the informal staffing arrangements once employed by Roosevelt. In this decision, which was encouraged by advisers such as Richard Neustadt, he was reacting to the outgoing Eisenhower administration. Kennedy believed that Eisenhower's staff structure was too rigid and that it stifled creativity and debate. His staff system was designed to avoid this rigidity. Like Roosevelt, Kennedy created an open, circular staff structure in which he was accessible to all of his advisers equally. Because the president made assignments and received papers personally, the business of his government moved through him. There was no chief of staff to censor the flow of papers and advisers.

As an activist president, Kennedy thought that his circular staff would be more creative in dealing with problems and devising policy. The bureaucracies were too slow in their operation and too traditional in their thinking to suit him; he wanted more originality and faster action, and he set up an interactive staff to produce it. The president's tendency toward an informal staff structure was no doubt reinforced by the number of crises that arose during his administration, particularly, in foreign affairs. Kennedy had to deal with the Bay of Pigs fiasco, the Berlin crisis, and the Cuban Missile Crisis. Crisis management is necessarily improvised, and the frequency of the crises confronting Kennedy's administration strengthened the president's belief in fluid staff patterns.[37]

The Kennedy staff was very fluid in structure. On paper there was more organization than had existed under Roosevelt, but in practice the dividing lines were not often observed. Like Roosevelt, Kennedy wanted a staff of generalists; he wanted every aide to be able to assume whatever duties were called for at a given moment. The staff was composed of equals, all of whom were free to interact with the president or one another.

The Kennedy staff was notable for its harmony. Most presidents have encountered jealousies among staffers, sometimes to the extent of disrupting staff performance, but an unusual degree of collegial spirit existed in the Kennedy White House, perhaps because the president's staff perceived itself to be on the cutting edge of the New Frontier, distinct from the rest of the Washington establishment. This camaraderie helped Kennedy's circular staff structure function effectively.

In the aftermath of Kennedy's assassination on November 22, 1963, Johnson tried to keep most of his predecessor's advisers around him, believing that he needed the expertise and the legitimacy that their presence would provide. At the same time, he began to bring in his own people gradually, often without dislodging the Kennedy staff. Thus, Johnson ran a dual staff for a time, overlapping former Kennedy staffers with his own personnel.

The circular staffing structure that Kennedy had employed appealed to the new president. A great admirer of Franklin Roosevelt, Johnson was a very active president, eager to create a Great Society through social programs to help the nation's poor and disadvantaged. In doing this, he wanted to emulate Roosevelt and overshadow Kennedy. He was eager for new ideas and programs and sought any pertinent facts aggressively, particularly in the early days of his administration before the Vietnam quagmire engulfed him. Thus, the Johnson White House was idiosyncratic and loosely structured to fit the whims of an energetic and mercurial president. It was so loosely structured, in fact, that anyone who asked for its organization chart was told that there was no such thing. Aides declared that drawing one up would simply be a waste of time, because no one would follow it anyway.

The collegiality that had marked the Kennedy staff was much less evident under Johnson. Unlike the Kennedy staff, Johnson's aides were in constant competition for the president's ear. Preferring informal arrangements and one-on-one encounters, Johnson avoided large staff meetings. He particularly liked to meet with selected staffers in his bedroom, either first thing in the morning or last thing at night, and aides who were admitted to such meetings were viewed as very influential.

Although the structure of Johnson's staff was similar to Kennedy's, the atmosphere was quite different. A man of incredible energy, Johnson drove his staff mercilessly. He would work from seven o'clock in the morning until two in the afternoon, when he would stop for lunch, a short nap (on his doctor's orders; he already had had a heart attack), a shower, and a change of clothes. Then, from four until nine o'clock or later, he would resume working as furiously as ever. Aides were supposed to be available at any time, night or day; no excuses were acceptable. (When Joseph Califano failed one day to answer a presidential phone call because he was in the bathroom, Johnson ordered him to put an extension in there.) The pace and pressure of White House staff work under Johnson wore his staff down.

EISENHOWER, NIXON, AND THE STAFF PYRAMID

Eisenhower made the first attempt at creating a more formal, hierarchical staff structure. An orderly person, Eisenhower was repelled by the chaos of the Roosevelt staff, even after it had been refined somewhat by Truman. His military experience had taught him the benefits of organization, and the result was a degree of differentiation and specialization previously unseen in the White House. Eisenhower's staff was the traditional pyramid, with none of the fluid and shifting assignments that Roosevelt had used. Everyone had specific areas of responsibility and knew what they were. Eisenhower was more interested in good management than spontaneity; specialization was the name of the game. This arrangement allowed the president to know exactly where to go for information or action.

The demarcation of specific areas of responsibility among the staff naturally led to a bigger staff, which, for better organization, was divided into subunits. One example of this was the National Security Council staff. The first president to give much organization to the NSC, Eisenhower created a rather elaborate system of working groups to analyze particular problems and to produce studies and recommendations. The NSC operation was criticized by opponents as a useless paper mill, but it typified the organization and specialization that Eisenhower wanted in his staff.

Unlike Roosevelt, Eisenhower did not want to be involved in every detail of operation or policy; he believed that presidents were supposed to make big decisions and leave little ones to subordinates. His attitude is captured in his remarks to Defense

Unlike FDR and Truman, Eisenhower ran a structured and diversified staff. Sherman Adams became the gatekeeper to the president during Ike's first six years in office.

Secretary Charles E. Wilson, who repeatedly came to him with minor problems early in the administration: "Charlie, you have to run Defense. We can't both run it. And I won't run it."[38] To ensure that problems found their appropriate level, Eisenhower created a chain of command to control the paper flow through the staff. Problems and papers came up from the lower levels until they reached a point of decision (which in most cases was below the president), and then orders went back down. Eisenhower was thus relieved of the need to bother with most problems at all, while ensuring that they were being dealt with systematically.

At the top of the pyramid was the president, but because Eisenhower preferred to distance himself from everyday business, the most important operations figure was the chief of staff. From 1953 to 1958 that person was Sherman Adams. He was followed by Maj. Gen. Wilton B. (Jerry) Persons. The chief of staff managed the operation of the staff, making sure that it ran smoothly and efficiently, and kept unimportant matters and people away from the president. Adams in particular acted as gatekeeper and arbiter for Eisenhower, restricting access to the Oval Office and forcing decisions, whenever possible, to be made somewhere else. "We must not bother the president with this" was his refrain.[39] Adams's authority over the president's business and Eisenhower's distance from daily events, particularly in domestic affairs, led to the perception that the chief of staff, with his extensive power, was a sort of "assistant president." Adams was seen as being so influential that a joke began to make the rounds: "Wouldn't it be awful if Eisenhower died and Nixon became president? Yes, but what if Adams died and Eisenhower became president?" In fact, if Adams had so much authority as presidential gatekeeper, it was because the president wanted it that way.

Beneath Adams the Eisenhower staff was the prototypical hierarchy. At least at the top, however, it was not completely rigid in its organization. There were lines of command, but they were not irrevocable; Eisenhower's staff structure was meant to control staff interaction, not eliminate it. Senior staff had access to the president and participated in policy discussions whenever appropriate.

The hierarchical staff, abandoned after Eisenhower, was resurrected by Nixon in 1969. Having served as Eisenhower's vice president, Nixon knew the organizational merits of a more formal staff structure. It also served his personal needs well. An intensely private man who preferred to work alone, making decisions in solitude on the basis of the many briefing papers he received, Nixon used his staff to insulate himself from the rest of the world. In the Nixon White House with its pyramidal structure, information and options were passed up the chain of command from specialists at the lower staff levels, and decisions and requests were returned down the ladder from the top. Much more information made its way to the top, however, than during the Eisenhower years. Unlike Eisenhower, who wanted one-page policy summaries and oral briefings, Nixon wanted details and read extensively.

Nixon used the staff as a buffer even more than Eisenhower did. Senior staff members contended that no unreasonable restrictions were placed on the flow of traffic through the Oval Office, but complaints from outsiders about the difficulties encountered in attempting to meet with the president were numerous. Transportation Secretary John Volpe, frustrated over lack of access to the president, once pulled a list of problems out of his pocket while greeting Nixon in a church reception line.

At its peak, the Nixon staff was a model of efficiency. Everyone knew their roles; everyone knew the chain of command. As one staffer noted, "The place had a structure, had a way of doing things, had a flow and a follow-up system that was beyond belief. Things happened." There was relentless pressure from the top to get work done quickly and thoroughly. The staffer who was late or sloppy in his assignments was immediately brought into line. Nixon aide John W. Dean remembered that

I spent too much time preparing my answers to a few action memoranda, let the due dates slide by, and discovered the consequences. First a secretary in the staff secretary's office called my secretary, asking where the answer was, and when the explanation was found unsatisfactory, a very bitchy Larry Higby called to say, "What's the matter, Dean, can't you meet a deadline? Do you think you're somebody special?" When I explained I was working on the response, Higby snapped, "Work a little faster." Higby was chewed out by Haldeman when the paper did not flow as the chief of staff wanted, so he leaned on others.[40]

The man who ran this machine with a firm hand was chief of staff H. R. Haldeman. Haldeman performed many of the same functions that Sherman Adams had performed for Eisenhower, and in fact once acknowledged himself that he was more like Adams than any other past staffer. But where Eisenhower had placed Adams alone at the top of the pyramid, Nixon included more specialists at the lower levels and broadened the top, making his chief of staff first among equals instead of a majordomo. In reality, although Haldeman remained the major figure on the staff, two other members also had ready access to the president: John Ehrlichman, who was first counsel to the president and later domestic adviser, and Henry Kissinger, the national security adviser. Increasingly, Haldeman, Ehrlichman, and Kissinger became the filter through which the outside world, including cabinet secretaries, had to pass to see the president. Because Nixon's distrust of the permanent bureaucracy led him to concentrate more authority within the White House, the influence wielded by the "Big Three" became formidable indeed.

In order to improve the organization and efficiency of the White House staff and to concentrate authority over the government within the White House, Nixon devised a new plan for structuring his staff. In July 1973 he unveiled a supercabinet proposal, in which the various executive departments were grouped into three blocks, each of which was to report to a presidential counselor who doubled as a department head. The counselors in turn would report to Ehrlichman, who was to oversee the entire operation. How well this plan might have worked will never be known. No sooner had it been introduced than the Watergate controversy began to overwhelm the Nixon administration. After the resignations of Haldeman and Ehrlichman in early 1974, the system was dismantled.

Because staff arrangements are a reflection of the president and the president's needs, the Nixon White House did not change greatly in structure with the replacement of Haldeman by Gen. Alexander M. Haig Jr. Like Haldeman, Haig sat atop the White House bureaucracy, controlling the flow of business to the president. Although he tried to coordinate the administration's domestic programs, the increasing disarray of the staff

and the growing congressional hostility made his task difficult. His efforts to expand the circle of White House advisers went for naught; the embattled Nixon increasingly withdrew into himself as the Watergate affair destroyed his presidency. By the end of his administration, Nixon was seeing few people besides Haig, Kissinger, and Press Secretary Ziegler.

FORD, CARTER, AND VARIATIONS ON THE PYRAMID

The pattern of staff organization used in the White House has reflected not only each president's personality, but also his desire to avoid the errors of his predecessors. Thus, Kennedy adopted a circular staff in part because he saw Eisenhower's staff as overcentralized, and Nixon returned to a centralized staff because of the disarray he perceived in Johnson's staff. Similarly, Gerald Ford and Jimmy Carter tried to incorporate more openness into their staffs in response to what they saw as the excessive authority of the "Prussian guards" under Nixon. Neither was completely successful.

President Ford inherited his staff from the departing Nixon. Desiring continuity, Ford kept many of the Nixon staffers for a time, particularly those at the lower and middle levels of the White House bureaucracy; most higher-level staffers were replaced early in the Ford administration. Ford set out quickly, however, to modify Nixon's staff structure.

Ford's desire to open the Nixon structure stemmed in part from the apparent excesses of the Watergate period and in part from his long congressional experience, which led him to prefer personal interaction. Ford therefore changed the Nixon pyramid into a rectangle. Each of nine senior aides was given a specific area of responsibility, a small staff, and equal access (at least in theory) to the president. The chief of staff position was abolished. Donald Rumsfeld was put in charge of White House operations, the traditional chief of staff duty, but Ford insisted carefully that there was no real chief. Ford did not entirely abandon hierarchy, however. His staff design was supposed to delineate staff responsibilities clearly and thus maintain more order than a circular staff while providing more accessibility and more channels of communication than the traditional pyramid.

In practice, the staff rectangle failed to operate as Ford had hoped. Despite his preference for receiving information orally and having personal contact, the president found that his staff arrangements permitted too many people to have access to him and make too many demands on his time. Eventually, Ford was forced to have someone control the flow of traffic to his office. He thus appointed Richard B. Cheney chief of staff, in fact if not in title. The rectangle had become a pyramid again.

President Carter came into office seeking to re-create the circular staff system used by his Democratic predecessors Roosevelt, Kennedy, and Johnson. Carter wanted to serve as his own chief of staff, sitting in the middle of a circle of advisers who would keep him in touch with the events of his administration. Like the presidents he was emulating, Carter wanted innovation and valued new ideas, and he thought that a circular staff system would encourage them.

No doubt Carter thought that he could manage a circular staff, even a large one, because of his ability to handle facts and details. Like Ford, however, he soon found that there was not enough of him to go around. With no gatekeeper, too many people brought too many problems to his attention, and Carter was soon handling such trivial matters as the allocation of parking spaces in the White House garage. It was no wonder that he was quickly overwhelmed by the volume of demands on his time. Overall policy and long-range goals were lost as he tried to cope with the mass of visitors and papers that descended upon him.

In the end, Carter was forced to capitulate to the reality of the modern White House. In 1979, attempting to shake off the "great malaise," he reorganized his staff into a more pyramidal form. He appointed a chief of staff (originally Hamilton Jordan, who was Carter's closest aide, and later Jack H. Watson Jr.) to control the president's business. Formal staff meetings replaced small informal gatherings. Although his staff never became as structured as Nixon's or Eisenhower's, Carter necessarily adopted a more systematic approach to his staff as his term wore on.

REAGAN AND THE TRIUMVIRATE STAFF

The most unusual staff arrangement of any president was that employed by President Reagan during his first term in office. Although it resembled the traditional pyramid structure in the concentration of power at the top, Reagan did not use a single chief of staff to guard the door to the Oval Office. Instead, the president divided his staff into separate units, each headed by a senior staff member who had direct access to him. The senior staff linked the president to the lower staff. One can visualize the staff as a set of columns supporting the president. Initially, the Reagan staff comprised three divisions. One addressed policy development; another dealt with the political problems of promoting the president's programs; and the third ran the operation of the White House. A fourth division was added later when William P. Clark arrived as national security adviser. This division of the staff by function was unique in the history of the White House staff.

Policy development was handled by a staff supervised by presidential counsel Edwin Meese. Staff units under Meese included the Office of Policy Development, the Office of Planning and Evaluation, and initially the National Security Council. This portion of the White House staff was supposed to formulate policy options and proposals for the president to consider.

The task of organizing political support for President Reagan's programs and pushing them through Congress and into action was given to a staff unit headed by chief of staff James A. Baker III. Baker supervised the White House liaison units—including liaison to Congress, the public, other government agencies, and political organizations—as well as the press secretary's office, the Communications Office, and the speechwriters.

Operation of the White House was supervised by the deputy chief of staff, Michael Deaver. Deaver's staff handled the support services, travel arrangements, and scheduling for the president. Deaver's influence was much greater than his title or nominal duties might indicate, however. An old confidant of the president, he was closely involved in many presidential decisions and was important to the smooth operation of the staff. Indeed, another staff member referred to Deaver as "the glue that holds this [staff] together."[41]

A few months into the Reagan administration, the triumvirate of Meese, Baker, and Deaver was joined by William Clark, who replaced Richard Allen as national security adviser. Although Clark knew little about foreign affairs, he was an old friend of the president and so was included immediately in the inner circle. Clark envisioned himself as the honest broker in the foreign policy process and supported the consensus view of the foreign policy establishment.

The foursome of Baker, Clark, Deaver, and Meese was the cornerstone of the Reagan staff. They operated as equal partners, working together to ensure coordination and to facilitate the transmission of information from below and direction from above. The president met with them regularly, and they in turn worked with their sections of the White House staff. Responsibilities were assigned by mutual decision among them.

That the four-pillar staff functioned at all is perhaps remarkable. As Deaver once noted, the staff arrangement worked "in spite of the fact that it probably shouldn't have worked. . . . You see, you are supposed to have a chief of staff, but in fact what you have are three or four different systems that are all working here."[42] Yet despite some tension, and despite the potential for discord and infighting that is always present in the White House bureaucracy, the Reagan staff managed to operate relatively harmoniously and effectively. The impressive string of political successes rung up by President Reagan during his first term testifies to the efforts of his senior staff to make his unique staffing arrangement work.

Unique and effective as it seemed to be, the original Reagan staff plan did not survive into his second term. Each of the four key staffers who made it function had left the White House by early 1985. Meese moved from his position as counsel to the president to that of attorney general. Clark first became secretary of the interior and then went home to California. Deaver resigned his position to go into private business. And Baker, in a rather unusual move, swapped jobs with Donald T. Regan: he became secretary of the Treasury, while Regan took over as White House chief of staff. By the beginning of Reagan's second term the pillar-and-platform structure that had characterized his White House staff had collapsed into the traditional pyramid. In effect, new chief of staff Regan was replacing four top staffers.

A successful business executive and powerful chief executive officer with little political experience, Regan preferred to operate the White House like a business. Seeing himself as the White

House CEO, he tried to draw all the staff's business through him and to have a hand in all aspects of the White House operations. The staff Regan created was perhaps the most centralized of any ever found in the White House, equaling or exceeding the level of centralization in the staff under Sherman Adams or H. R. Haldeman. He also was among the most visible of White House chiefs; in the aftermath of the 1985 Reykjavik summit, Regan gave fifty-three media interviews. A man who was used to being prominent, he did not shrink from public view, or from asserting the extent of his authority.

Unfortunately for Regan, his highly centralized staff failed to equal the successes of Reagan's first term (although some of the reasons for that were beyond his control), and his high profile made him a natural target when the Iran-contra controversy erupted in late 1986. Having claimed to have control over all aspects of the White House, Regan became the focus of criticism when the staff went awry. He resigned under pressure in February 1987 after the Tower Commission's report blamed him for failing to control his subordinates and to protect the president's interests.

The basic staff structure remained the same under Regan's successors, former U.S. senator Howard H. Baker Jr. (R-Tenn.) and Kenneth Duberstein. The new chiefs were not as aloof and domineering as Regan, but the basic organization was left in place. This structure and process were very important in producing policy options for a president who did not care to concern himself with the details of policy.

BUSH, CLINTON, AND THE TREND TOWARD FLEXIBILITY

Under George Bush, the White House staff system continued to be hierarchical, but somewhat more flexible. The staff pyramid continued, and the paper and people still flowed through the chief of staff, but Bush combined hierarchy with informality. Under Bush, although there were specific lines of authority, staffers often crossed them to pursue particular areas of interest. A staff member who took an interest in a policy area often could contribute to the formation of policy, even if it was not within the usual scope of his or her office. Thus, C. Boyden Gray, the White House counsel, became involved in questions concerning the National Endowment for the Arts, alcohol fuels, the environment, and the disabled—none of which were normally within the counsel's province.

The Bush White House retained the system of cabinet councils that had been introduced under Reagan. Different councils coordinated policy in domestic, economic, and national security areas. The councils met once a week or so to formulate policy options for the president. The president would sit in on many of the meetings; he liked to hear the verbal exchanges because they helped to sharpen his thinking. Often, after the formal meeting, Bush would talk to other knowledgeable people in order to gain more information.

The policy groups were important very early in the Bush ad-

In 1994 President Bill Clinton named Leon E. Panetta, a well-respected representative from California with sixteen years of congressional experience, to be his chief of staff. Panetta brought order and efficiency to the White House staff.

ministration, but they soon lost influence as power became more centralized due to the rise in influence of Chief of Staff John H. Sununu. Sununu, who controlled the legislative liaison office, became the administration's key domestic policy adviser as well. Far more than a paper pusher, Sununu was a policy advocate, particularly in domestic affairs, although he also became involved in foreign issues when Bush's prestige might be at risk. On many issues of personal interest, Sununu micromanaged; for example, he handled every detail of the administration's conference on global warming in 1989.[43]

If "flexible organization" characterized Bush's staff, at least initially, "organizational facade" characterized Clinton's. The Clinton White House had an organization chart, and on paper looked much like the White House of its recent predecessors, with a designated chief of staff. Within that structure, however, Clinton tended to revert to the old Democratic tendency to be the center of the wheel. At least at first, Clinton was essentially his own chief of staff as well as his own top domestic and economic adviser (although other people had those titles). As many as eight to ten advisers had walk-in privileges to the Oval Office. Policy tended to be made by task forces assembled to deal with specific issues: "war rooms" was the term used in the White

House for these groups. One commentator characterized this arrangement as government by "adhocracy."[44]

The consequences of Clinton's organizational style were twofold. On the one hand, the White House staff had great flexibility in dealing with any issue that might arise; it could quickly bring alternatives to the president and could readily meet any change in circumstances or new problems. On the other hand, it tended toward disorganization and frequently gave the impression of being in disarray and out of control. Clinton was forced to rework his staff system several times in his first two years in an effort to improve efficiency. The first staff changes occurred only 107 days after his inauguration.

In the Clinton staff, flow charts meant nothing and theoretical lines of authority were flexible at best. The staff's operation reflected both the president's enormous energy and his tendency, for better or for worse, to flit restlessly from problem to problem. The Clinton administration provided another reminder that the White House inevitably reflects the president who operates it.

Criticism of the White House Staff

The steady growth of the White House Office over the past fifty years has given presidents more resources to handle problems and more personnel to deal with the increasing demands on their time and energy. Given the size of the federal government and the active role it plays in American society, the president could not hope to keep up with either the sprawling executive branch or a growing and diverse Congress without the assistance of a large White House staff, which has become a permanent fixture of the presidential establishment.

Despite this, or perhaps because of it, a number of scholars have subjected the enlarged White House staff to serious criticisms, all related to its increased size and prominence. Some of these criticisms have been echoed by White House insiders. For one, critics have pointed out that the White House staff has grown too large to be supervised and managed adequately. Instead of an efficient personal staff, the White House Office is a small bureaucracy that is often unwieldy and inefficient. Complaints about the excessive size of the staff are not limited to scholars; recent White House chiefs of staff have agreed that the staff has grown too much and should be reduced as much as possible.[45] Despite this, none have had significant success at reducing the staff while they were in office.

The larger the staff, the greater the possibility that needed information may be distorted or lost as it passes through different hands on its way to the president. This problem inevitably stems from the pyramidal organization needed to manage a large staff. It is complicated by staffers who try to shield the president from what they see as unnecessary or unpleasant information. Delays in implementing presidential directives as the directives work their way back down the chain of command are also a problem.[46] Moreover, members of an oversized staff who are under-

employed and undersupervised may look for their own (generally unauthorized) projects to pursue and may wind up embarrassing the president. The Iran-contra affair was largely such a project and indicates the managerial problems that large staffs pose for the president.

Critics also have contended that the size of the White House staff has passed the point of diminishing returns for the president. The overly large staff can provide more information than a president with a limited supply of time and attention to devote to solving problems can hope to use. In this view, much of the staff is superfluous, if not actually counterproductive. Political scientist Aaron B. Wildavsky has argued that "after a while, the addition of new staff just multiplies [the president's] managerial problems without giving him valuable service in return. Forcing a president to 'count hands' all the time, by making him consider endless strings of alternatives, is a good way of rendering him useless."[47]

A second major criticism leveled at the modern White House is that the president's staff has entirely too much influence on policy. Presidential assistants have always had a political role, but their input into the policy-making process is a recent development. The Brownlow Committee report issued during Franklin Roosevelt's administration envisioned a staff of neutral aides who would efficiently provide the president with objective information and options; policy advocacy or formation was not part of the staff's role.

For reasons put forth elsewhere in this chapter, that ideal has been lost over the years. No longer does the White House staff practice "neutral competence." Instead, a better way to describe the staff would be "responsive competence"—how quickly and effectively the staff can respond to the president's desire for action. Responsive competence is a combination of centralization of power and politicization of attitude. It is far removed from paper pushing and impartial presentations of options. Modern White House staffs engage in responsive competence; it is what presidents want.[48] Of the recent staffs, only the Bush staff in its early days even approached the Brownlow's Committee's ideal.

According to the critics, the modern White House staff now operates as a policy-making organism, often in unequal competition with the federal bureaucracy. Indeed, the staff frequently relegates a secondary role in policy making to the established departments. Although the staff rarely dominates the bureaucracy to the extent it did in the Nixon administration, it still tends to be the primary actor in the policy-making process. *(See Chapter 35, The President and the Bureaucracy.)*

Critics argue that there are problems with this increased power of the White House staff. First, the staff has too narrow a focus: it tends to see everything through the limited perspective of the president's needs. Unlike the bureaucracy, the staff has no institutional memory and may easily overlook the problems of implementing a policy. The result may be policy that is idiosyncratic and lacks long-term perspectives on what is feasible and effective.[49] Second, there is something disturbing about major policy decisions in a constitutional democracy being made by the presidential staff, whose members are unelected and are responsible to no one except the president.

A third major criticism of the enlarged presidential staff is that the presence of so many special interests pleading for the president's attention is not in the president's best interests. Over the years liaison aides for many different social groups have been added to the White House. Although a few were dropped by the Reagan administration, the majority remain.

Finally, as the staff grows, it increasingly isolates the president from the rest of the government. As a consequence, depending on the personality of the president, the large and influential staff may only reinforce the natural doubts that the president may have about the bureaucracy's loyalty and efficiency. In any event, the president is at serious risk of becoming a prisoner of the staff, dependent on it alone for information and options and able to be no more effective and to make no better decisions than the staff's abilities will allow.

NOTES

1. A good discussion of this problem is found in John Hart, *The Presidential Branch* (New York: Pergamon Press, 1987), 96–109. Unless noted otherwise, the figures on staff size used in this chapter are from Stephen J. Wayne, *The Legislative Presidency* (New York: Harper and Row, 1978), 220–221.

2. George Edwards and Stephen J. Wayne, *Presidential Leadership: Politics and Policy Making* (New York: St. Martin's Press, 1985), 181.

3. Edward H. Hobbs, "An Historical Review of Plans for Presidential Staffing," *Law and Contemporary Problems* 21 (August 1956): 666–675.

4. The President's Committee on Administrative Management, *Report of the Committee* (Washington, D.C.: Government Printing Office, 1937), 5.

5. The figures cited are taken from U.S. Congress, House, *Congressional Record*, daily ed., 92d Cong., 2d sess., June 20, 1972, H21512; and from Wayne, *The Legislative Presidency*, 220.

6. Stephen Hess, *Organizing the Presidency*, rev. ed. (Washington, D.C.: Brookings, 1988), 70.

7. Quoted in Patrick Anderson, *The President's Men: White House Assistants of Franklin D. Roosevelt, Harry S Truman, Dwight D. Eisenhower, John F. Kennedy, and Lyndon B. Johnson* (Garden City, N.Y.: Doubleday, 1968), 152–153.

8. Hess, *Organizing the Presidency*, 84.

9. Ibid., 83.

10. Ibid., 112.

11. Dom Bonafede, "Dual Capacity Brings Power to Ronald Ziegler," *National Journal*, March 2, 1974, 325.

12. Quoted by Thomas E. Cronin in "The Swelling of the Presidency," *Saturday Review of the Society* 1 (August 1973): 33.

13. Dom Bonafede, "As Pollster to the President, Wirthlin Is Where the Action Is," *National Journal*, December 12, 1981, 2184–2188.

14. Dick Kirschten, "The White House Office: Where the Power Resides," *National Journal*, April 25, 1981, 678; the 1988 data is from Harold W. Stanley and Richard G. Niemi, *Vital Statistics on American Politics*, 5th ed. (Washington, D.C.: CQ Press, 1995), 249.

15. Thomas E. Cronin, "The Swelling of the Presidency: Can Anyone Reverse the Tide?" in *American Government: Readings and Cases,* 9th ed., ed. Peter Woll (Boston: Little, Brown, 1987), 336.

16. John P. Burke, *The Institutional Presidency,* (Baltimore: Johns Hopkins University Press, 1992), 164.

17. W. John Moore, "Status Up, Spending Down," *National Journal,* June 19, 1993, 1495.

18. Fred I Greenstein; quoted in Burt Solomon, "A One-Man Band," *National Journal,* April 24, 1994, 970.

19. Hart, *The Presidential Branch,* 94.

20. Congressional staff figures are taken from *Guide to Congress,* 4th ed. (Washington, D.C.: Congressional Quarterly, 1991), 483; and Norman J. Ornstein, Thomas E. Mann, and Michael J. Malbin, *Vital Statistics on Congress 1995–1996* (Washington, D.C.: Congressional Quarterly, 1995), 131–132.

21. Cronin, "The Swelling of the Presidency," in Woll, *American Government,* 346–347.

22. Quoted in Dan Rather and Gary Paul Gates, *The Palace Guard* (New York: Harper and Row, 1974), 240.

23. Dom Bonafede, "There's More to the Counsel's Job than Just Giving Legal Advice," *National Journal,* December 22, 1979, 2139.

24. Dom Bonafede, "President Still Seeks to Restore Staff Efficiency, Morale," *National Journal,* January 5, 1974, 1–6.

25. For more on the selection process for the executive branch, see John W. Macy, Bruce Adams, and J. Jackson Walter, *America's Unelected Government: Appointing the President's Team* (Cambridge, Mass.: Ballinger, 1983).

26. James P. Pfiffner, "Establishing the Bush Presidency," *Public Administration Review* (January/February 1990): 68.

27. Quoted in Anderson, *The President's Men,* 7.

28. More details of presidential appointment practices can be found in Matthew B. Coffey, "A Death at the White House: The Short Life of the New Patronage," *Public Administration Review* 34 (September 1974): 440–444; and in Macy, Adams, and Walter, *America's Unelected Government,* especially chaps. 2 and 3.

29. Ed Rogers, "Transition Admission," *Washington Monthly,* January/February 1993, 39.

30. Figures are from Patricia S. Florestano, "The Characteristics of White House Staff Appointees from Truman to Nixon," *Presidential Studies Quarterly* 7 (Fall 1977): 186.

31. Quoted in Anderson, *The President's Men,* 135.

32. Quoted in Burt Solomon, "In Bush's Image," *National Journal,* July 7, 1990, 1644.

33. Quoted in Rather and Gates, *The Palace Guard,* 239.

34. Quoted in Edwards and Wayne, *Presidential Leadership,* 203.

35. Ibid., 188.

36. Quoted in Wayne, *The Legislative Presidency,* 32.

37. Hess, *Organizing the Presidency,* 84.

38. Quoted in Richard T. Johnson, *Managing the White House: An Intimate Study of the Presidency* (New York: Harper and Row, 1974), 84.

39. Quoted in Anderson, *The President's Men,* 152.

40. Both quotations in this paragraph are from Wayne, *The Legislative Presidency,* 47.

41. Quoted in John H. Kessel, "The Structures of the Reagan White House," *American Journal of Political Science* 28 (May 1984): 253.

42. Ibid., 251.

43. A good analysis of the Bush staff organization can be found in Burke, *The Institutional Presidency,* chap. 7, from which this discussion is largely borrowed.

44. Richard N. Haass, "Bill Clinton's Adhocracy," *New York Times Magazine,* May 29, 1994, 40–41.

45. Samuel Kernell and Samuel L. Popkin, eds., *Chief of Staff: Twenty-five Years of Managing the Presidency* (Berkeley: University of California Press, 1986), 199.

46. Hess, *Organizing the Presidency,* 5.

47. Aaron B. Wildavsky, "Salvation by Staff: Reform of the Presidential Office," in *The Presidency,* ed. Aaron B. Wildavsky (Boston: Little, Brown, 1969), 697.

48. Burke, *The Institutional Presidency,* 181–185.

49. Hess, *Organizing the Presidency,* 5.

SELECTED BIBLIOGRAPHY

Anderson, Patrick. *The President's Men: White House Assistants of Franklin D. Roosevelt, Harry S. Truman, Dwight D. Eisenhower, John F. Kennedy, and Lyndon B. Johnson.* Garden City, N.Y.: Doubleday, 1968.

Burke, John P. *The Institutional Presidency.* Baltimore: Johns Hopkins University Press, 1992.

Cronin, Thomas E. "The Swelling of the Presidency: Can Anyone Reverse the Tide." In *American Government: Readings and Cases,* ed. Peter Woll. 9th ed. Boston: Little, Brown, 1987.

Cronin, Thomas E., and Sanford D. Greenberg. *The Presidential Advisory System.* New York: Harper and Row, 1969.

Hart, John. *The Presidential Branch: From Washington to Clinton.* 2d ed. Chatham, N.J.: Chatham House, 1995.

Hess, Stephen. *Organizing the Presidency.* Rev. ed. Washington, D.C.: Brookings, 1988.

Johnson, Richard T. *Managing the White House: An Intimate Study of the Presidency.* New York: Harper and Row, 1974.

Kernell, Samuel, and Samuel L. Popkin, eds. *Chief of Staff: Twenty-five Years of Managing the Presidency.* Berkeley: University of California Press, 1986.

Koenig, Louis W. *The Invisible Presidency.* New York: Holt, Rinehart, and Winston, 1960.

Macy, John W., Bruce Adams, and J. Jackson Walter. *America's Unelected Government: Appointing the President's Team.* Cambridge, Mass.: Ballinger, 1983.

Patterson, Bradley H., Jr. *The Ring of Power: The White House Staff and Its Expanding Role in Government.* New York: Basic Books, 1988.

Redford, Emmette S., and Richard T. McCulley. *White House Operations: The Johnson Presidency.* Austin: University of Texas Press, 1986.

Walcott, Charles E., and Karen M. Hult. *Governing the White House: From Hoover Through LBJ.* Lawrence: University Press of Kansas, 1995.

Wayne, Stephen J. *The Legislative Presidency.* New York: Harper and Row, 1978.

Weko, Thomas J. *The Politicizing Presidency: The White House Personnel Office, 1948–1994.* Lawrence: University Press of Kansas, 1995.

Wildavsky, Aaron B. "Salvation by Staff: Reform of the Presidential Office." In *The Presidency,* ed. Aaron B. Wildavsky. Boston: Little, Brown, 1969.

CHAPTER 28

Executive Office of the President: Supporting Organizations

BY W. CRAIG BLEDSOE AND LESLIE RIGBY

BEYOND THE PRESIDENT'S inner circle of White House Office aides lies an outer circle of presidential advisers who head the supporting organizations of the presidency. These organizations, together with the White House Office, form the Executive Office of the President (EOP). Most of these offices are housed adjacent to the White House in the new and old Executive Office buildings.

While EOP organizations perform services directly for the president, their staff members may or may not have daily access to the Oval Office. The heads of EOP organizations, like the president's closest White House advisers, are appointed by the president. Unlike the president's personal staff, however, the top positions in the EOP are subject to Senate approval.

Only recent presidents have enjoyed the increased management and control that the EOP provides. Based on the recommendations of the Brownlow Committee on Administrative Management, and with congressional authorization, President Franklin D. Roosevelt established the Executive Office of the President in 1939 to help him manage the burgeoning bureaucracy resulting from his "New Deal" programs. At that time the EOP consisted of five units, the most important of which were the Bureau of the Budget (now the Office of Management and Budget) and the White House Office. As federal programs proliferated and the ensuing bureaucracy grew even larger, the EOP became the more specialized and complex organization needed to coordinate federal activities.

Since 1939, fifty-five different boards, offices, and councils have been established within the EOP. *(See Table 28-1, p. 1104.)* Congress created some of these, but many others were created by executive order. President Clinton's initial EOP consisted of the White House Office *(see Chapter 27, Executive Office of the President: White House Office; Table 27-2, p. 1085)*, Office of Management and Budget, National Security Council, Council of Economic Advisers, Office of the U.S. Trade Representative, Office of Science and Technology Policy, Office of Policy Development (under which falls the National Economic Council and the Domestic Policy Council), Council on Environmental Quality, Office of Administration, Office of National Drug Control Policy, and Office of the Vice President *(see Chapter 26, Office of the Vice President)*. Some of these organizations are so large that they may be considered small bureaucracies themselves. Even though the components of the EOP have changed from one ad-

ministration to the next, the functions of the EOP have continued to fall into several general categories. According to presidential scholar Richard M. Pious, four functions traditionally have been carried out by EOP organizations. First, organizations such as the Office of Economic Opportunity (1964–1975), though they gained autonomous "presidential status," really performed departmental functions. Second, offices such as those for consumer affairs (1971–1973), science and technology (1962–1973), and drug abuse policy (1976–1978) represented the interests of various constituencies. Third, EOP units such as the National Security Council (1947 to present) and the Council of Economic Advisers (1946 to present) develop policy. And finally, offices such as the Office of Management and Budget (1970 to present) perform management functions.[1]

The organization and structure of EOP have changed considerably over the years, but this change has not occurred systematically. Most presidents have altered the composition of EOP based on their needs and problems, resulting in its rather piecemeal development. Recent presidents have attempted, nevertheless, to centralize and streamline the operations of EOP to make it more responsive to their programs and objectives.

The Appointment Process

While most federal jobs are filled by appointment procedures designed to ensure that selections are made on the basis of qualifications and without political influence, the president is responsible for appointing staff to certain federal positions. The legal authority for making such appointments is derived from two sources: the Constitution and the various statutes that created the federal agencies requiring presidential appointments. Article II of the Constitution empowers the president to make many federal appointments with "the advice and consent of the Senate." While there occasionally has been some dispute over which executive officers require confirmation by the Senate, it generally is recognized that the very top positions in the organizations of the EOP are subject to such review. In fact, Congress has absolute power to make any officer of the EOP subject to Senate confirmation.

No consistent legal principle clearly defines, however, which middle-level jobs in the EOP are appointed by the president and confirmed by the Senate and which jobs are appointed by an

TABLE 28-1 Units in the Executive Office of the President, 1939–1996

Unit	President	Duration
White House Office	Roosevelt	1939–
Council on Personnel Administration	Roosevelt	1939–1940
Office of Government Reports	Roosevelt	1939–1942
Liaison Office for Personnel Management	Roosevelt	1939–1943
National Resources Planning Board	Roosevelt	1939–1943
Bureau of the Budget[a]	Roosevelt	1939–1970
Office of Emergency Management	Roosevelt	1940–1954
Committee for Congested Production Areas	Roosevelt	1943–1944
War Refugee Board	Roosevelt	1944–1945
Council of Economic Advisers	Truman	1946–
National Security Council	Truman	1947–
National Security Resources Board	Truman	1947–1953
Telecommunications Adviser to the President	Truman	1951–1953
Office of Director of Mutual Security	Truman	1951–1954
Office of Defense Mobilization	Truman	1952–1959
Permanent Advisory Committee on Government Organizations	Eisenhower	1953–1961
Operations Coordinating Board	Eisenhower	1953–1961
President's Board of Consultants on Foreign Intelligence Activities	Eisenhower	1956–1961
Office of Civil and Defense Mobilization	Eisenhower	1958–1962
National Aeronautics and Space Council	Eisenhower	1958–1973
President's Foreign Intelligence Advisory Board[b]	Kennedy	1961–1977, 1981–
Office of Emergency Planning	Kennedy	1962–1969
Office of Science and Technology	Kennedy	1962–1973
Office of Special Representative for Trade Negotiations	Kennedy	1963–
Office of Economic Opportunity	Johnson	1964–1975
Office of Emergency Preparedness	Johnson	1965–1973
National Council on Marine Resources and Engineering Development	Johnson	1966–1971
Council on Environmental Quality	Nixon	1969–
Council for Urban Affairs	Nixon	1969–1970
Office of Intergovernmental Relations	Nixon	1969–1973
Domestic Policy Council/Domestic Policy Staff[c]	Nixon	1970–1978
Office of Management and Budget	Nixon	1970–
Office of Telecommunications Policy	Nixon	1970–1977
Council on International Economic Policy	Nixon	1971–1977
Office of Consumer Affairs	Nixon	1971–1973
Special Action Office for Drug Abuse Prevention	Nixon	1971–1975
Federal Property Council	Nixon	1973–1977
Council on Economic Policy	Nixon	1973–1974
Energy Policy Office	Nixon	1973–1974
Council on Wage and Price Stability	Nixon	1974–1981
Energy Resource Council	Nixon	1974–1977
Office of Science and Technology Policy	Ford	1976–
Intelligence Oversight Board	Ford	1976–1993
Office of Administration	Carter	1977–
Office of Drug Abuse Policy	Carter	1977–1978
Office of Policy Development	Carter	1978–
Office of Private Sector Initiatives	Reagan	1981–1989
National Critical Materials Council	Reagan	1984–1993
Office of National Drug Control Policy	Bush	1989–
Office of National Service	Bush	1989–1994
National Space Council	Bush	1990–1993
Points of Light Foundation	Bush	1990–1993
National Economic Council	Clinton	1993–

SOURCE: Adapted from Lyn Ragsdale, *Vital Statistics on the Presidency: Washington to Clinton* (Washington, D.C.: Congressional Quarterly, 1996), 272–273.

NOTES: This list does not include short-term advisory commissions, study councils, and cabinet-level coordinating committees. a. Unit currently in operation as Office of Management and Budget. b. Unit abolished by President Carter and recommissioned by President Reagan. c. Unit currently in operation as Office of Policy Development.

office head. Some scholars have suggested that the rules of appointment stem from whatever presidential-legislative relations exist at the time a particular component of the EOP is created.[2] Thus, while the president is responsible for appointing staff to the top-level positions in the EOP, a presidential subordinate, such as the chief of staff or the special assistant to the president for management and administration, may appoint staff to many other positions, including high-level ones.

A president-elect must fill vacancies in the EOP during the period of transition (about seventy-five days) from the old to the new administration. Unfortunately, it is during this period that the new president is least prepared to make the best choices. According to presidential scholar Stephen Hess, just three weeks after his election John F. Kennedy reacted to the difficulty he had in finding qualified people by saying, "People, people, people! I don't know any people. I only know voters."[3]

Public relations considerations further complicate the EOP staffing procedure. A president's first appointments indicate the tone and style of the new administration. The kind of individuals the president has chosen to fill EOP positions and the policy direction the new administration appears to be taking will be of keen interest to both the media and the public. Political party activists and other supporters will wonder whether the initial presidential appointments to EOP will reflect the president's campaign goals.

The president also has the political problem of appointing people who agree with the administration's policy positions and who will be loyal to the administration and its objectives. According to the authors of *America's Unelected Government:*

[The president] will want to build teams that can work together when they share jurisdiction over critical issues like the economy or national security. He will want to pick appointees who can command the respect of the career civil servants and of foreign governments. And, of course, he will want people whose ability to do their jobs effectively is beyond doubt.[4]

The president is not always successful in appointing people of his own choosing, however. Pressures from congressional supporters will influence some appointments; in fact, the number of congressional recommendations for executive office vacancies is quite large. Frederic V. Malek, President Richard Nixon's personnel director, claimed that during his tenure the White House received five hundred letters each month from Congress requesting positions in the executive branch, including some in the EOP. Frank Moore, head of President Jimmy Carter's congressional liaison office, estimated that during Carter's first month in office the administration received over a thousand requests for jobs from legislators.

The demands of political party patronage will influence appointments as well. Shortly after Dwight D. Eisenhower's election to the presidency, Sen. Robert A. Taft of Ohio, the Republican leader in the Senate, led a delegation of Republicans to the president-elect's headquarters. They complained that Eisenhower and his staff were ignoring traditional patronage considerations and trying to depoliticize the executive recruitment process. Eisenhower acquiesced to political party pressure and instructed his staff to make more staffing decisions on the basis of patronage.

Although the president may pay off political debts by filling some positions with appointees who may or may not be competent to fill them, other positions will be filled by people with whom the president has had little or no personal contact but who are eminently qualified to work in the EOP. As a result, some EOP officeholders feel a strong sense of loyalty to the president's programs, while others do not and may be at odds with them.

Staffing of the EOP does not end with the close of the presidential transition period. The turnover that occurs during any presidential administration requires presidents to continue to make major personnel decisions throughout their tenure in office. Often the factors and conditions that govern these in-term decisions are different from those that prevail during the transition period. Since most electoral debts have been paid off, presidential attention turns to finding people who will best help accomplish administration goals. Presidential appointments scholar G. Calvin Mackenzie found that in-term appointment decisions usually are based on two very practical questions: Will the quality and character of the executive appointee have a strong impact on the president's ability to control and direct the government? And will the appointee improve the president's relation with Congress?[5] In-term appointments therefore usually reflect presidential concerns in dealing with the bureaucracy and Congress, and they thus become a central part of an administration's political and administrative strategy.

Some presidents have struggled to remedy the initial and ongoing helter-skelter EOP staffing process, and make it more responsive to the administration's needs, by use of a transition appointments staff. But throughout their administrations presidents face a flood of personnel decisions that would benefit from some kind of centralized personnel management. Recent presidents have attempted to handle ongoing staffing problems by incorporating full-time personnel managers into their administrations.

Presidents, with their different needs and policy objectives, have used a variety of styles and methods for filling positions in the Executive Office of the President. Although presidents generally have relied on the traditional methods of presidential appointments—such as appointing friends and colleagues—the growth of the modern EOP is making such methods increasingly impractical. Indeed, presidents have had to make innovations in the appointment process, including establishment of a staffing agency in the White House to locate talented administrators who also exhibit loyalty to the president's programs.

THE EARLY YEARS

As the EOP began to expand in the early 1940s, President Franklin Roosevelt recognized the need for greater presidential control over the appointment process. When initially staffing the EOP Roosevelt relied on old friends and colleagues: those who had served in his New York gubernatorial administration, some of his 1932 campaign workers, people from the "old boys' network," and Democratic Party activists. His method of appointment lacked coordination and control. As one presidential scholar noted: "Roosevelt's staffing practices were primarily a haphazard blend of fortuity, friendship, obligation, and pressure, as were those of presidents who followed him. He was luckier than most and his network of acquaintances was larger than most."[6]

In 1939 Roosevelt designated a personnel manager to coordinate his EOP staffing procedure. Partisan politics played a significant role, however, in even this attempt at appointment coordination. As Roosevelt's administration evolved, it became obvious that the primary responsibility of the president's personnel manager was to serve as the presidential liaison to the Democratic National Committee and to certify potential appointees' Democratic credentials.

Presidents Harry S. Truman and Dwight Eisenhower viewed the appointment of their White House staffs and the top positions in the supporting organizations of the EOP as an important way to control their presidencies, but they usually left mid- and lower-level appointments to the office heads. Truman took a more active role than Eisenhower, however, because he enjoyed dealing with people directly by calling them to the White House for personal interviews. Because Truman assumed office upon the death of Roosevelt, he faced an EOP made up of Roosevelt loyalists. He was determined, however, that his appointees would be loyal to him and his administration's goals, and he wasted little time in actively replacing carryover officials who could not give their allegiance to him. Not sharing in Truman's enthusiasm for the day-to-day routine of dealing with possible appointees, Eisenhower decentralized the appointment process by allowing many heads of offices to make the initial recommendations for staff selection. The president, however, always reserved the right to make the final decision.

Eisenhower had little choice in delegating most of his appointment authority. The size of the ever-expanding EOP—which grew from 1,183 to 2,779 employees between 1953 and 1960—made his personal involvement in every personnel decision increasingly difficult. Thus, early in his first term Eisenhower created the position of special assistant for executive appointments. Although the special assistant, Charles F. Willis Jr., was responsible for managing the appointment process for the administration's executive offices, he did not choose the president's appointees. Instead, he managed the paperwork and served as the president's liaison with the Republican National Committee and members of Congress who solicited appointments for their political allies. The special assistant and his staff then weeded through the various lists of nominees presented to the president and identified the strongest candidates with the fewest political drawbacks.

Eisenhower had two major criteria for selecting personnel to fill executive posts: loyalty and demonstrated success. Presiding over the first Republican administration in twenty years, he wanted a federal government bureaucracy that was responsive to his programs. In addition, according to Hess, "Eisenhower believed that a successful person, someone who had already proven that he could run something big, would be best able to tame a government department."[7]

THE KENNEDY ADMINISTRATION

Shortly after his election in 1960, President-elect Kennedy set up a loosely organized staff, known as "Talent Hunt," to sift through the possible appointees to his administration. Composed of some of his best campaign aides, Talent Hunt was designed to reward people who had helped Kennedy win the presidency by giving them jobs in his administration and to identify the most important jobs in the administration and the best-qualified persons to fill them. After the transition a more permanent staffing operation was established in the White House. Headed by Dan Fenn Jr., this operation reached out beyond the traditional political channels and established a "contact network" as a source of potential appointees. By drawing on contacts at the Brookings Institution and other "think tanks," Fenn was able to make a list of several hundred national leaders in industry, labor, state government, academia, and other sectors. These "contacts" then either suggested potential appointees or served as references for appointees suggested by others.

The Kennedy administration used this list of contacts to circumvent normal political channels. Kennedy did not intend to depoliticize the appointment process, however. Rather, he wanted a personnel operation that would allow him to triumph in the political conflict among his administration, his political party, and Congress over executive office positions. According to presidential scholars John W. Macy, Bruce Adams, and J. Jackson Walter, "With an independent recruiting capability the president could often find better qualified candidates than those recommended to him by his party, by members of Congress, and by the leaders of interest groups."[8] Kennedy could also expect a higher degree of loyalty and responsiveness from his own nominees than from patronage appointees.

Kennedy's appointments to EOP generally reflected what presidential historian William Manchester has called his "generational chauvinism." Kennedy felt more comfortable with people with whom he had something in common. Among the factors he considered in his appointments to the EOP were age, military service, quality of education, and participation in his campaign for the presidency. As a result, the three original members of the Council of Economic Advisers were relatively young at forty-five, forty-four, and forty-two, very close to Kennedy's age of forty-three. Moreover, the educational backgrounds of Kennedy's appointees were impressive; fifteen Rhodes scholars served in the EOP during his administration. And many of his top EOP appointees had been members of his campaign team since 1956.[9]

THE JOHNSON ADMINISTRATION

When Lyndon B. Johnson suddenly became president in 1963 after Kennedy's assassination he moved very slowly in replacing Kennedy appointees with his own. To Johnson, the nation's need for stability was greater than his need for loyal appointees. After six months, however, President Johnson found himself filling many EOP positions and taking a strong personal interest in appointment decisions. Johnson was even more concerned than Kennedy about outside influence on these decisions; to him, loyalty was essential. Political scientists Emmette S. Redford and Richard T. McCulley have noted that in making new appointments "Johnson was extremely cautious in selecting people to meet his qualifications for executive performance and especially careful to assure their loyalty to his objectives and to him personally. Even when responding to political influence in appointments, he normally sought assurance of loyalty."[10]

Like Kennedy, Johnson set up a systematized personnel office in the White House for help in making appointments, but unlike Kennedy, he relied on it extensively. Johnson eventually appointed John W. Macy as head of his personnel selection operation. Although the selection of Macy was unusual, since he also served as chairman of the Civil Service Commission, it helped Johnson distance his appointments from political pressures. In fact, Johnson often used Macy's civil service position to dissuade potential job seekers and their patrons on the grounds that Macy insisted that all appointments be based on merit and that Macy had a well-qualified candidate of his own. This relieved President Johnson from having to rely excessively on appointments that fulfilled some political obligation.

Macy introduced a systematic approach to the presidential appointment process. The computer system he designed, known as the White House Executive Biographic Index, provided the president with quick and accurate information about a pool of potential appointees. By the end of the Johnson administration, almost thirty thousand names were in the index. When a position opened up, Macy sent Johnson names from the talent bank for his consideration. Johnson then chose the nominee and sent the name back to Macy, who had the nominee's background checked by the Federal Bureau of Investigation.

Curiously, Johnson's appointees to second-echelon slots in the EOP tended to come up through the civil service, because he found it difficult to attract qualified outsiders to his administration. During President Johnson's first eighteen months in office, career civil servants filled almost half of the major appointments, and the political turmoil characterizing the last part of his administration prolonged the president's difficulty in attracting quality people from outside government. Even though Johnson looked for loyalty in his appointees, his inability to find many staffers beyond the confines of the civil service limited his staff's devotion to his programs. Former Kennedy staffer and presidential scholar Theodore C. Sorensen reported, "Lyndon Johnson complained privately that too many of his policy positions went by default to career civil servants who were willing, available, and technically competent but had no 'fire in their bellies.'"[11] They lacked the drive and devotion to administration programs that Johnson desired.

THE NIXON ADMINISTRATION

Early in his administration, President Richard Nixon asserted that ability, not loyalty, would be the standard for appointment. Beyond his top White House aides and cabinet members, however, Nixon expressed little interest in personally choosing members of the EOP, and most of the time he delegated responsibility for making appointments to members of his White House staff. When he did express an interest, it was usually to approve or reject a candidate recommended by his staff.

In the transition period and early stages of the Nixon administration the appointment process was slow and awkward; no systematic appointment procedure was in place. Macy, Adams, and Walter noted that because of this lack of control over the appointment process and Nixon's early lack of interest in staffing, "the management needs of the president were often a low-level consideration in appointment decisions, and far too many appointees were people who did not agree with the president on important substantive matters."[12] Nixon eventually recognized the need to tie personnel to his management needs, however, and his administration developed a more sophisticated staffing system.

By 1971 Nixon and his senior White House staff members had recognized the important relationship between loyalty and talent in selecting people to fill executive positions. Consequently, Nixon hired Frederic Malek to take over the personnel staffing operation. Based on his experience as a student of scientific management and a former manager in the Department of Health, Education, and Welfare, Malek implemented a personnel system that aggressively pursued Nixon's policies by appointing loyal and skilled executives. Under the direction of Malek the practice of achieving White House policy objectives by appointing officials who were loyal to the president soon became official White House procedure.

In the process of linking personnel to policy objectives, Malek created the White House Personnel Operation (WHPO) to bring professional executive practices to the EOP appointee search procedure. WHPO was composed largely of private sector "headhunters." Following models established by the Kennedy and Johnson administrations, WHPO rated potential appointees and recommended those who expressed loyalty to Nixon's objectives. Primarily, Nixon wanted to exert control over almost all noncareer appointments in the federal government.

By developing the largest and most systematic evaluation system ever found in the executive branch, the Nixon administration effectively tied its management objectives to its appointments. Following Malek's departure in 1972 to direct the Office of Management and Budget, however, the Nixon personnel operation took on a life of its own. WHPO tried to push its influence beyond the scope of its original conception, and some of its members attempted to influence the appointment of civil service assignments, generating a damaging controversy in the press and in Congress.

Loyalty continued to be the most important consideration in choosing personnel for the EOP throughout Nixon's tenure in office. During his first term the White House produced the *Federal Personnel Manual*, which advised the appointment of only those persons who held the same partisan beliefs as the administration. As a guideline for appointments the manual argued that policy control depended on political control of appointees:

The record is quite replete with instances of the failures of the program, policy, and management goals because of sabotage by employees of the Executive Branch who engage in frustration of those efforts because of their political persuasion and their loyalty to the majority party of Congress rather than the Executive that supervises them.[13]

Moreover, according to G. Calvin Mackenzie,

Eventually, perhaps inevitably, the territorial aggressiveness of the postelection WHPO began to get out of control. Political criteria were applied to appointments to competitive positions in the civil service. A variety of ingenious ways to circumvent the merit system were developed and employed. . . . Subsequent investigations by congressional committees, journalists, and grand juries uncovered abundant evidence of agency, departmental, and White House efforts to subvert civil service merit hiring procedures for political purposes.[14]

THE FORD ADMINISTRATION

Because of the political situation that triggered his rise to the presidency, Gerald R. Ford moved into the White House with little planning for staffing his Executive Office. From the beginning, however, Ford played an active role in the appointment process. He initially appointed a four-member transition team composed of some of his closest friends and colleagues: Donald Rumsfeld, Rogers C. B. Morton, William W. Scranton, and John O. Marsh Jr. In the aftermath of Watergate, and faced with a possibly brief tenure in the White House, the administration and its transition team had to go to extra lengths to attract talented and loyal personnel from outside government. Ford's participation in the appointment process, however, facilitated the recruitment of appointees.

Although Ford tried to follow the recommendations of his transition team by replacing all Nixon appointees, he did not succeed as quickly as he would have liked. Early in his administration the EOP was made up of both Nixon and Ford appointees. This resulted in a dilution of staff loyalty to Ford's programs and objectives, and Ford thus began appointing those with whom he felt comfortable; his early appointments reflected his reliance on old friends and colleagues.

According to presidential scholar Edward D. Feigenbaum, the EOP appointments made by Ford during his administration originated from four groups: the "old boys' network," including colleagues from the House of Representatives and some of Ford's congressional aides; the Grand Rapids crowd, or those from his Michigan past; the New York set, or colleagues of Vice President Nelson A. Rockefeller, a former New York governor (they were appointed primarily to the Domestic Council); and the "New Wave" group, who were primarily young and energetic and were appointed to highly responsible positions.[15]

THE CARTER ADMINISTRATION

When Jimmy Carter became president in 1976, he already had a personnel selection system in place. In the summer before the national election and a possible transition to the presidency, he had set up a small staff in Atlanta, known as the Policy Planning Office (PPO). Under the direction of Jack H. Watson Jr., this group identified important positions in the new administration and people qualified to fill them. After the election the PPO became known as Talent Inventory Program (TIP) and was firmly established in the White House. Like similar programs before it, TIP provided a comprehensive inventory of potential candidates for the EOP and other positions.

The good intentions of TIP were upset, however, by political infighting within the Carter administration. While Watson intended to make personnel selection a nonpolitical undertaking, the Georgia politicians who had managed Carter's campaign wanted some political control of the process. Macy, Adams, and Walter reported that as a result, "no central coordinating mechanism emerged to manage the appointment process, and much of the work done by TIP was simply disregarded." Even though a personnel organization eventually emerged in the White House, "its ability to control the appointment process was undermined by a confused mandate."[16]

The confusion surrounding appointments arose from two conflicting concerns. Like most presidents, Carter wanted a responsive administration, staffed by appointees who were not only qualified but also loyal and free of conflicts of interest. At the same time, however, Carter came into office committed to a cabinet administration in which departments would run their own show, including selection of their personnel. While these concerns little affected the selection of EOP members, they fostered in the Carter administration a conflict and ensuing paralysis that frustrated the filling of many EOP appointments. Many of the positions in Carter's executive branch went unfilled until the spring of his first year in office.

At first, Carter took an active interest in the appointment process. As time went on, however, he lost his enthusiasm for filling executive positions, and the task of filling most of the major vacancies became one of the primary responsibilities of Hamilton Jordan. One of Carter's top assistants from his home state of Georgia, Jordan was fiercely loyal to Carter. And in seeking similar loyalty in Carter appointees, Jordan made the appointment process a decidedly political affair. This set up a power struggle between Jordan and Watson over the control of appointments, which Jordan eventually won because of his close relationship to President Carter.

Carter's appointment process throughout his administration largely reflected the conflicting styles of Watson and Jordan. Major appointments were made either by department and agency heads or by Carter's staff through the "old boys' net-

work." Consequently, there was little consistency in their quality and character.

One of Carter's most important EOP appointments indicates the problems the Carter administration faced in staffing. In nominating Bert Lance, a Carter supporter from Georgia, for director of the Office of Management and Budget, Carter's staff either failed to identify or ignored important information. Carter demanded a rather rigorous security and conflict-of-interest check on each appointee, but the system broke down in the case of Lance. Facing political pressures for appointment, the administration overlooked evidence that Lance may have been involved in questionable banking practices and campaign conduct. After several press revelations to this effect, Lance was forced to resign in September 1977.

THE REAGAN ADMINISTRATION

Ronald Reagan, like Carter, set up a presidential staffing organization during the 1980 presidential campaign that was carried over into the new administration. Headed by E. Pendleton James, a professional headhunter who had worked in the Nixon administration, this organization attempted to increase the president's control over his administration by tying policy objectives to executive appointments. Appointees not only had to have the qualifications and talent necessary to carry through on policies, but they also had to agree with Reagan's objectives. Reagan's chief advisers believed that only then could the administration be confident that the president's programs would be implemented.

Unlike the Carter administration, the Reagan administration showed consistency in its appointments, and the appointment procedure worked well under James. While there was much internal debate over various nominees, almost always agreement was reached on the criteria for appointment and the objectives to be sought in potential appointees. The Reagan administration's stated criteria for appointment to the EOP were fairly straightforward: "Support for Reagan's objectives, integrity, competence, teamwork, toughness, and a commitment to change."[17]

During the transition period and the first year of his administration, Reagan consistently displayed an active interest in the appointment process. Reportedly, he made all the important staffing decisions. This helped reduce congressional influence on administration appointments because congressional leaders did not attempt to exert as much influence on Reagan, to whom their access was limited, as they might have exerted on his staff if his staff were making the final decisions.

Political party influence over the appointment process also declined during the Reagan administration. In the past, political parties had served as clearinghouses for patronage requests and had put pressure on the White House to make certain appointments for political reasons. During the Reagan administration, however, potential appointees went directly to the president and his staff to apply for EOP jobs. This situation relieved some of the pressure on the president to appoint candidates who may not have been his choice, but it also created something of a logistical problem. It placed a tremendous burden on Reagan's personnel staff at a time when the staff was not in the best position to handle it, during the transition and the early stages of the new administration.

Further complicating the selection procedure for Reagan (and future presidents) were the increasingly rigorous ethical and conflict-of-interest considerations mandated by Congress after the Watergate scandals. This increased scrutiny not only delayed the appointment process by requiring much more complicated investigation and disclosure procedures, but it also made recruiting much more difficult by raising the stakes for public employment. Potential EOP officeholders had to endure a thorough background check. And in many cases they had to give up control of their financial holdings by putting them into some form of financial trust to avoid potential conflicts of interest. Such measures caused many to think more than once about leaving a lucrative private endeavor to serve the federal government.

THE BUSH ADMINISTRATION

Almost a year before his election, George Bush asked Charles Untermeyer to begin working on plans for staffing a new administration. Untermeyer, a Bush loyalist who had interned in the future president's congressional office in the mid-1960s, was eventually put in charge of the Office of White House Personnel after the successful presidential bid. Bush's choice of Untermeyer and his desire to begin the initial stages of the appointment process as soon as he did indicated the significance Bush placed on the staffing of EOP.

The main criteria for appointment to Bush's EOP were loyalty and professional competence. Bush's definition of loyalty differed drastically from Reagan's, however. Whereas Reagan placed great importance on ideological loyalty, Bush wanted a team in EOP (and the rest of his administration) that exhibited personal loyalty to him. John Podhoretz, a Bush staffer, described the process of weeding out candidates as one of finding someone who was "either directly beholden to Bush or someone to whom Bush was directly beholden."[18] In other words, Bush wanted people who had worked for or had given money to his campaign.

Although Bush emphasized personal loyalty in staffing EOP, he paid little personal attention to most EOP appointments. Bush filled some of the top positions himself but left most EOP appointments under the ultimate control of his chief of staff, John Sununu. This detachment from much of the appointment process reflected the president's interests and priorities. Bush saw himself above the political process and wanted to concentrate his efforts on foreign policy. It was no coincidence that some of Bush's best appointments were those he made himself, and those were in the foreign policy sections of EOP. National security adviser Brent Scowcroft, for example, reflected the type of EOP appointee that Bush sought. Scowcroft was a competent professional who had extensive experience in foreign affairs and shared a long personal friendship with Bush.

As was the case with Scowcroft, the criterion of "personal loyalty" came to mean past service with Bush. The early transition team reviewed potential nominees to ensure that preference was given to those who had a proven record of working with Bush.

In selecting mid- and low-level staff for the White House Office, chief of staff John Sununu's aides, Andy Card and Ed Rogers, often found themselves making decisions based on the recommendations of campaign advisers such as Lee Atwater, the chairman of the Republican National Committee. Rogers explained the process:

How did people get in? Lee Atwater, for example, might stop by our office, pull up a chair, hand me four resumes and say, "I want these people to get jobs. Call me back later today and let me know where they will be working." They were usually people who had been in the Republican community or had played a role in the campaign. Remember the process doesn't get people jobs, people get people jobs.[19]

Unless Bush himself or some other highly placed Bush loyalist, such as Sununu or campaign manager James Baker, gave a nominee a personal recommendation, potential staffers had to provide proof that they were in fact personally loyal to Bush. EOP office seekers had to fill out forms asking them to specify their "Bush experience."[20]

Beyond personal loyalty, Bush sought competence over ideology. Although most of his appointees were conservative, the Bush administration, unlike its predecessor, fought no ideological battles over EOP staff. With the exception of Sununu, who was an outspoken conservative, few ideological crusaders were recruited into the Bush EOP. Presidential scholar James P. Pfiffner found appointees to the Bush EOP to be competent and "marked by professionalism and a low-visibility approach to White House service."[21] In addition, Bush tried to "stay the course" of the Reagan administration while replacing Reagan staffers. Bush believed he was elected to build on the Reagan legacy. At the same time, however, he also believed that he had to put his imprint on the presidency. Bush gave Untermeyer a direct order to clean house. In most cases, this meant merely taking the old Reagan organizational chart, erasing the names of Reagan appointees, and replacing them with Bush loyalists.

THE CLINTON ADMINISTRATION

Following the precedent of the previous three administrations, Bill Clinton established a formal transition and staffing organization for his possible administration during the presidential election campaign in 1992. The Clinton-Gore Presidential Transition Planning Foundation, located in Little Rock, Arkansas, and directed by Mickey Kantor, Clinton's campaign chairman, was responsible for ensuring a smooth and quick staffing procedure. After the election, Kantor asked to be named chairman of the transition and White House chief of staff. But a

Since its creation by Franklin D. Roosevelt in 1939, the Executive Office of the President (EOP) has been a constantly changing entity. The strength and composition of the EOP under a particular president in the final analysis have depended on the president. Some chief executives have preferred a formal organization; others have opted for informality. Some have relied on a small inner circle of advisers; others have drawn on a larger pool of talent. The distinction between a White House office or advisory body and an EOP office often has been blurred. Moreover, some offices were created first in the EOP and then transferred to the White House, or vice versa.

As presidential scholar Stephen Hess has noted, EOP offices frequently experience conflicting pulls between their mandate to serve the institution of the presidency as "objective" advisers and their loyalty toward a particular president and administration policies. At times Congress has tried to impose its view on the kind of advice a president needs by creating offices that an administration does not want. (Presidents, however, always can ignore such statutory advisers.)

President Franklin Roosevelt relied on an informal coterie of close White House advisers, as well as a larger group of perhaps a hundred outside advisory bodies. At the same time, he established many new offices within the executive branch (primarily interdepartmental), the proliferation of which led to chaos. To address this problem the Brownlow Committee on Administrative Management, which was convened in 1937, recommended changes in the White House staff and the creation of the Executive Office of the President. When the office finally came into being in 1939, the Bureau of the Budget (the predecessor of the Office of Management and Budget) and the National Resources Committee (renamed the National Resources Planning Board or NRPB) were added to it. The NRPB consisted of three part-time advisers who were responsible for planning long-range public works, assisting state and local governments, and informing the president of economic trends. The board was not very effective, however, and Congress abolished it in 1943. Another agency transferred to EOP in 1939 was the Office of Government Reports (a public information clearinghouse that became part of the Office of War Information in 1942). Roosevelt also established the Office of War Mobilization in 1939 as part of the Executive Office. The Committee for Congested Production Areas (1943–1944) and the War Refugee Board (1944–1945) were added later.[1]

During the presidency of Harry S. Truman the Council of Economic Advisers (CEA), the National Security Council, and the Office of Defense Mobilization, among others, were added to EOP. The mission of the latter was to direct and coordinate federal agency activities during the Korean War. "Possibly no other legal act of either the Congress or the President ever came so close to the actual creation of an Assistant President," wrote John R. Steelman and H. Dewayne Kreager of the office's wide-ranging powers.[2] In 1951 the Office of Director for Mutual Security was established to provide military, economic, and technical aid to other nations. In 1953 its functions were transferred to the Foreign Operations Administration.

Eisenhower's EOP staff, like his cabinet, was composed primarily of business leaders, not politicians, and pragmatic "doers," rather than strictly conservative theoreticians. In contrast to Roosevelt's informal and somewhat haphazard methods of seeking advice, Eisenhower—drawing on his military background—established an ordered chain of command and was not averse to delegating authority. He relied heavily on the National Security Council and CEA and was the first president to appoint a special assistant for national security affairs. During Eisenhower's tenure the directors of the Bureau of the Budget and Defense Mobilization, as well as the mutual security administrator, regularly attended the weekly cabinet meetings.

The White House EOP complex expanded considerably under President John F. Kennedy, who established the Office of the Special Representative for Trade Negotiations, the Office of the Food for Peace Program, and others. Lyndon B. Johnson's "Great Society" programs resulted in a further expansion of EOP, including addition of the Office of Consumer Affairs and the Office of Economic Opportunity.

Richard Nixon also established a number of EOP offices during his presidency. Among them were the cabinet-level Council for Urban Affairs (precursor of the Domestic Council), the Office of Intergovernmental Relations, the Council on Environmental Quality, the Council for Rural Affairs, the Council on International Economic Policy, the Special Action Office for Drug Abuse Prevention, and the Office of Telecommunications Policy, which dealt with highly technical questions. At the same time, Nixon abolished a number of offices, including the Space Council and Office of Economic Opportunity. He shifted the advisory functions of the Office of Science and Technology to the National Science Foundation and transferred the duties of the Office of Emergency Preparedness to other agencies.

During his brief tenure in the White House, President Gerald R. Ford did little restructuring in the EOP except to replace Nixon's Special Action Office for Drug Abuse Prevention with the Office of Drug Abuse Policy. Most of Ford's organizational changes took place within the White House Office, which he reorganized to insure an open administration and accessibility to the president.

President Jimmy Carter reduced the White House office staff by 28 percent and the EOP staff by 15 percent. His Reorganization Plan 1, which was implemented in April 1978, eliminated seven of the seventeen units in the Executive Office: the Office of Drug Abuse Policy, the Office of Telecommunications Policy, the Council on International Economic Policy, the Federal Property Council, the Energy Resources Council, the Economic Opportunity Council, and the Domestic Council (the latter, however, was reorganized). Congressional criticism of the plan focused primarily on the elimination of the Office of Drug Abuse Policy. Critics complained that the office had been created by Congress less than a year before and had not been given time to prove itself.

Although Presidents Ronald Reagan and George Bush sought to streamline further the Executive Office, it swelled to more than 1,500 employees and to a budget of over $150 million in 1992. In addition to filling the offices in both the New and Old Executive Office Buildings, staff members also occupied several other smaller building surrounding the White House.[3]

Like all presidents, President Bill Clinton reorganized the EOP to reflect his priorities and the changing concerns of the day. He centralized economic policy making within a new National Economic Council, and he abolished several Bush-era organizations, including the National Space Council, the National Critical Materials Council, and the Competitiveness Council. In addition, he "cut" the number of White House and EOP employees by 25 percent, but he achieved the reduction in part by "borrowing" personnel from other executive branch departments. For example, staff members cut from the National Security Council were replaced by staffers from the State Department, whose salaries continued to be paid by the State Department.

1. Stephen Hess, *Organizing the Presidency* (Washington, D.C.: Brookings, 1976), 38.

2. John R. Steelman and H. Dewayne Kreager, "The Executive Office as Administrative Coordinator," *Law and Contemporary Problems* 21 (autumn 1956): 704.

3. John P. Burke, *The Institutional Presidency* (Baltimore: Johns Hopkins University Press, 1993), 13.

dispute arose among Kantor and other Clinton campaign advisers—especially political strategist James Carville, campaign communications chief George Stephanopoulos, media strategist Mandy Grunwald, and pollster Stanley Greenberg, collectively known as the Gang of Four—and Kantor was pushed aside.

The transition organization that Kantor had set up was left headless. As a result, the plans for a smooth and fast transition and for naming appointees immediately after the election were in jeopardy. Clinton, who had run as an outsider, turned to two veteran lawyers with strong Washington ties. Vernon Jordan, former president of the National Urban League, and Warren Christopher, Jimmy Carter's deputy secretary of state, were brought on as chairman and director of the transition, respectively. Christopher had gained considerable clout with the president-elect by successfully conducting Clinton's search for a vice-presidential running mate. Unlike Bush, Clinton took an active interest in the appointment process, trying to guarantee his imprint on the new administration. Journalist Bob Woodward reports that, in the end, most of the important appointments were made by Clinton, Christopher, Hillary Rodham Clinton, Vice-president-elect Albert Gore Jr., and former law partner and loyalist Bruce Lindsey.[22] Although controversial, Hillary Clinton's role in this inner circle of advisers was significant because never before had a first lady played such a public and important role in advising a president on potential staffers. Sidney Blumenthal

described her as "Bill's Bobby Kennedy, his James Baker."[23] No one else had her access to the president-elect.

This new inner circle of advisers worked diligently to appoint Clinton loyalists to major EOP positions. Known as "Friends of Bill" (FOBs), most of these appointees were long-time Arkansas acquaintances and included Thomas (Mack) McLarty, one of Clinton's closest friends, as White House chief of staff. The purpose of appointing as many FOBs as possible in the EOP was twofold. First, loyalists throughout the administration would provide the president with a constant flow of inside information on the government. Second, the Clinton administration was attempting to avoid the mistakes of the Carter administration. A transition memo, "Transition Workplan for Reviewing the Staffing and Organization of the White House and Executive Office of the President," drafted by Harrison Wellford, a Carter budget official, argued that a "political perspective" had to be taken on the White House and EOP. The memo argued that Carter had failed to connect policy making with politics by relying too heavily on his cabinet to make policy. Clinton believed that Reagan, on the other hand, had understood the need to bring policy making under the control of the president by appointing political loyalists throughout the administration. Clinton's appointment of FOBs reflected his desire to centralize policy making.

Clinton's appointments to EOP also reflected his administration's priorities. Just as Bush had concentrated on foreign policy appointments, Clinton concentrated on domestic and economic policy appointments. In the area of domestic policy, Clinton had campaigned on a moderate "New Democrat" theme with the promise of change in Washington, and he initially wanted appointees to share his New Democrat ideology. The New Democrat ideology consisted of a middle-of-the-road approach to such issues as race and social spending and a commitment to free trade and international competitiveness. Few critical appointments to EOP met this criterion, however, due in part to an ideological debate that emerged in the transition stage of the new presidency. In an effort to secure the ideological perspective he sought in his administration, Clinton placed Al From, president of the Democratic Leadership Council (DLC) and a personal friend, in charge of domestic policy for the transition staff. The DLC, which Clinton had chaired, sought to move the Democratic Party away from some of its more liberal positions. Among moderates, From's appointment was generally seen as a decisive move by Clinton to assure a new momentum of change in Washington. But Clinton undermined From's influence by appointing Robert Reich, a professor at Harvard's Kennedy School of Government, to direct economic policy during the transition. Reich, also a close Clinton friend, took a much more activist view of government than From. Clinton gave Reich tremendous power during the transition by asking him to develop several policy options for the new administration. As the transition progressed, Reich was named labor secretary, and From and his moderate influence on administration appointments returned home.

Office of Management and Budget

The history of the Office of Management and Budget (OMB), previously known as the Bureau of the Budget (BOB), is inextricably linked to the development of the president's Executive Office, which was established in 1939. The budget office, created in 1921, was one of several offices to be reconstituted in the EOP, where it later was joined by the National Security Council and Domestic Policy Council and became one of the three primary Executive Office advisory organizations. Indeed, the budget office has considered itself "first among equals" in the Executive Office, according to many observers.

The Office of Management and Budget, as it has been known since 1970, has far-reaching influence over not only how much the federal government spends but also how it spends and how the states disburse what they are allocated. The office is the final arbiter of the budgets that the cabinet departments and other agencies propose to send to the president and Congress for authorization and appropriation. It is a principal broker in distributing the taxpayers' dollars.

As OMB has described its own role:

The actions of OMB touch the lives of all Americans. Nowhere are those actions more directly and broadly felt in society than in OMB's preparation of the budget. . . . The budget is essentially a resource allocation plan for the vast amount of federal funds and staff involved in activities that range from agriculture to zoology and cover locations that range from a lone fire lookout tower in Idaho to a housing project in the heart of New York City, from research in the Antarctic to a Peace Corps office in Ecuador, from salaries for all government employees to school lunch subsidies, and from the operating budget of the Supreme Court to funds for the launch of a spacecraft.[24]

Throughout its existence the president's budget office has been a steadfast accountant of federal expenditures. It also has played a major role in fashioning government policy by virtue of its recommendations, its director's access to the president, and periodic self-reappraisals of its functional efficacy and organization.

Shifts in the office's influence on presidential—and subsequent congressional—decisions have been caused largely by each director's relations with the president and Congress, each director's perception of the role of the budget office, and, more indirectly, changes in overall relations between the executive branch and Capitol Hill. But OMB is the president's right-hand adviser on what federal spending and revenue should be. The president, in close consultation with the budget office, approves or modifies the proposals made by OMB. The president's budget is then sent to Congress, which modifies the spending and revenue program as it sees fit.

Projections of the vast spending of the federal government (amounting to $1.61 trillion in 1996, or about 20 percent of the nation's gross national product) are contained in several volumes produced by a rather small budget office staff (numbering about 550 in 1995). These volumes are compiled from submissions by federal agencies on a timetable that allows little latitude for further extensive revision by those agencies.

What the administration proposes to spend in the forthcoming fiscal year, beginning October 1, is presented by the president to Congress in a January message. This document is supplemented by a thick appendix that details the administration's plans (and gives a sharp insight into its overall goals), by a less technical hundred-page "Budget in Brief," and by other analytical documents on special topics. Congress then decides item by item, through the relevant authorization and appropriation committees and subcommittees and finally on the floor, which parts of the president's program it will accept, modify, or reject. The budget office plays a central role throughout the process.

Since 1974 the president's budget office has had something of an analytical counterpoint on Capitol Hill. In enacting the Congressional Budget and Impoundment Control Act (PL 93-344), Congress established a Congressional Budget Office to oversee deadlines on clearing appropriations bills and to make recommendations on government spending. Another check on the federal government's expenditures is provided by the General Accounting Office (GAO), which was established in 1921 by the same act that created the Bureau of the Budget. While GAO's initial mandate and activities have grown (initially it was intended as a congressional arm for overseeing and auditing federal spending but has since become more involved in policy analysis), so too the executive branch budget office has expanded its role, increasingly injecting itself into areas that some critics have viewed as being beyond the bounds of its initial mandate of providing objective accounting and analysis. The history of the budget office is one of the push and pull between a nonpartisan "factual" adviser and a premier executive office with an obligation to promote the office of the presidency, if not always the policies of a particular president.

ORIGINS AND DEVELOPMENT OF THE BUDGET OFFICE

Before 1921 no system existed in the executive branch for unified consideration or control of fiscal policy. The secretary of the Treasury usually did no more than compile the estimates of the various departments before forwarding them to Congress for approval. No coordination, analysis, or recommendation was attempted, and it became increasingly apparent that the procedure was inadequate.

In 1911 President William Howard Taft appointed a Commission on Economy and Efficiency to review the budget process. The panel recommended creation of a central office, but this measure was not enacted for several years, largely owing to the preoccupation of Taft's successor, Woodrow Wilson, with World War I and its aftermath. The next president, Warren G. Harding, refocused attention on the idea, however, and in 1921 Congress enacted the Budget and Accounting Act, thereby ending the right of federal departments and agencies to decide for themselves what appropriations levels to seek. The act established the Bureau of the Budget to serve as a central clearinghouse for the president's budget requests; the office, however, initially was placed in the Department of the Treasury. The bill authorized

BOB "to assemble, correlate, revise, reduce or increase the requests for appropriations of the several departments or establishments." The bureau also was authorized to develop "plans for the organization, coordination and management of the Executive Branch of the Government with a view to efficient and economical services." The act further required the new office, at the request of any congressional committee having jurisdiction over revenue or appropriations, to provide that panel with the assistance or information it requested.

Budget Circular 49, approved by President Harding on December 19, 1921, called for all agency proposals for appropriations to be submitted to the president before they were sent to Congress. The proposals were to be reviewed for their relationship to "the president's financial program" and were to be forwarded to Capitol Hill only if the president approved them.

Early Directors of BOB

Much depended on the personality and capabilities of the first budget director, as well as his relationship with the president. Gen. Charles G. Dawes, a former chief of supply procurement for the U.S. Army in France and later vice president (1925–1929) under Calvin Coolidge, was selected by President Harding for the post. Hard working and enthusiastic, Dawes established a close working relationship with the president, who allowed him frequent access to cabinet officials. Although Dawes set out to develop long-range tasks, his major emphasis was on efficiency and economy in government agency programs, including his own bureau's operations.

Dawes believed that Treasury was not the place for BOB because it should be independent of any agency influence and answerable solely to the president. He was a strict constructionist, however, concerning his organization's role as policy maker, firmly believing that BOB should be impartial and nonpolitical. According to the 1945 budget bureau *Staff Orientation Manual,* "Dawes had not prepared the bureau for the assumption of functions more typical of a general administrative staff agency. The broader aspects of administrative management, outside the province of economical conduct of business transactions, had not received the attention they deserved."[25]

The three succeeding bureau directors, including Franklin D. Roosevelt's first appointment, Lewis W. Douglas, had similar views about BOB's role. As a result, the agency's staff remained relatively small given its broad statutory mandate, and its effectiveness was curtailed. Douglas disagreed with Roosevelt's burgeoning New Deal projects and their hefty expenditures, and he resigned in 1934. He was succeeded by a Treasury Department staffer, Daniel W. Bell, who served as acting BOB director for the next five years. Although relations between Bell and the president were not close, a number of changes effected during the period enhanced the bureau's standing.

An Expanded Role and New Home

In 1935 President Roosevelt broadened the budget office's clearinghouse function to include other legislation than just appropriations requests, saying that he had been "quite horrified—not once but a dozen times—by reading in the paper that some department or agency was after this, that or the other without my knowledge."[26] According to political scientist Richard E. Neustadt, Roosevelt's actions were not merely designed to extend the budget process. "On the contrary . . . this was Roosevelt's creation, intended to protect not just his budget, but his prerogatives, his freedom of action, and his choice of policies in an era of fast-growing government and of determined presidential leadership."[27]

In 1939 Roosevelt heeded the recommendations of his Committee on Administrative Management—chaired by Louis Brownlow and appointed to study the organization of the executive branch—by issuing the first reorganization plan in the nation's history. Approved by Congress, it created the Executive Office of the President, of which BOB was a major part. A second reorganization plan established divisions of the Executive Office and gave more power to BOB to improve and coordinate statistical services. (See box, *Presidential Reorganization Authority, p. 1161.)*

The budget office expanded considerably under the direction of Harold Smith, who served as its director from 1939 to 1946, the longest tenure of any budget director. Growing from a staff of forty to more than six hundred in 1944, BOB retained its position as the central budget review agency and increased its powers in the areas of legislative clearance and administrative management. Whereas before it had been empowered to send departmental legislative requests to the president—and, with presidential approval, to Congress—only if they had fiscal implications, during Smith's tenure BOB was given oversight authority for all proposed legislation, executive orders and proclamations, and recommendations for reorganization plans. According to presidential scholar Stephen Hess, under Smith BOB attracted competent young professionals who recommended far-reaching management changes in federal departments.[28]

During World War II the budget office played a central role in managing the war effort. According to Roger Jones, a former BOB official, "There was rapid acceleration of attention to the Budget Bureau's role as an organization and management planner for the President and as a sorter out of fiscal priorities and possibilities."[29]

Smith was succeeded by James E. Webb, a little-known bureaucrat from Texas who proved to be an effective manager. "While Harold Smith was responsible for creating the modern BOB, James Webb was instrumental in redirecting bureau staff work into the program development process," wrote Larry Berman in his history of OMB. "Many observers viewed the Webb period as the golden age of the Bureau of the Budget."[30] Under Webb's direction the bureau assumed responsibility for drafting complex legislation such as the 1946 Employment Act (which created the Council of Economic Advisers) and the Taft-Hartley Labor-Management Relations Act of 1947. BOB's relations with Congress also expanded; congressional committees increasingly requested the bureau's opinion on pending legislation.

Hiatus and Reorganization

Because of BOB's added responsibilities it soon became apparent that a restructuring was needed to bring more efficiency and coordination to the budget office's operations. Although postponed by Webb's resignation in 1948, a major overhaul of BOB was carried out in 1952. Budgetary analysis, fiscal analysis, and administrative management were divided along functional lines, and five operating divisions were established to work directly with government agencies on program, budgetary, economic, and management issues.

Although streamlined, the bureau became less central to policy making during Dwight D. Eisenhower's two-term presidency. Two of Ike's BOB directors were bankers, and two were accountants; none had experience in public administration. The president, wrote Berman, viewed the budget office primarily as "his agent for obtaining control of spending trends."[31] Yet Eisenhower's initial appointment as budget director, Joseph M. Dodge (who served from January 1953 to April 1954), was the first to hold cabinet rank. Later, in 1958, when the president named deputy director Maurice Stans to head the office, a senior budget official said it was "like opening up all the curtains in the building and letting the sun shine in. There was confidence, there was leadership, everything turned around. . . ."[32]

Despite that assessment, others expressed the view that BOB had lost some initiative, flexibility, and creativity. Outside pressure for reform was growing as well. In 1957 the President's Advisory Committee on Government Organization, chaired by Nelson A. Rockefeller, proposed an overhaul of BOB that would reconfigure it as an Office of Administration reporting directly to the president. The recommendation was opposed by Stans, who suggested instead reorganizing and upgrading the bureau into an Office of Executive Management. In 1959, while these proposals were pending, the budget office initiated its own internal review of operations.

In 1960 President-elect John F. Kennedy asked the Brookings Institution (a prestigious Washington think tank) to study the role of the Bureau of the Budget. The Brookings report recommended that the BOB director possess "sensitivity to political and administrative as well as financial and organizational matters."[33] In fact, the political emphasis dominated during Kennedy's three years in office. BOB directors David E. Bell and Kermit Gordon were program oriented and served as close personal advisers to the president. But in doing so, oversight of the day-to-day management of the office fell by the wayside, and the bureau's operations suffered.

The Great Society and the Bureau

Questions about BOB's role, organization, purpose, and efficiency deepened during the presidency of Lyndon B. Johnson with the advent of his complex and financially burdensome "Great Society" programs. The numerous task forces established by Johnson advocated new welfare and other programs with little attention to their cost or how they would work together. As a result, the focus of the budget office shifted from its primary in-stitutional mandate as budget overseer to that of coordinator of interagency activities.

The problem BOB confronted by the end of the Johnson presidency in 1969 is reflected in the figures. In 1949 the bureau employed 534 people to oversee federal expenditures of $40 billion. By 1969, 503 staffers had to contend with a budget of $193 billion, involving scores of innovative programs, conflicting agency priorities, and uncoordinated activities.

Dissatisfaction with the bureau's performance was apparent both within and outside the office. A task force established in 1965 by Budget Director Charles L. Schultze concluded that BOB needed to "develop a clear definition of its role and of its organization and staff requirements under the pressure of new federal programs and responsibilities."[34] According to an internal staff survey, the bureau's prestige was at an all-time low because of too much attention to detail, personnel problems, lack of internal management (the director spent too much time advising the president and too little time attending to the agency's organization), a rapidly growing workload, lack of feedback on what was wanted, and inadequate skills for dealing with current problems. A number of outside studies also were highly critical of BOB's management of the Great Society programs.

From BOB to OMB

Like Kennedy, President-elect Richard Nixon established a task force to study government organization. The panel gave top priority to revising the structure of the Executive Office and White House staff and to renewing the president's expired authority to make organizational changes. Congress granted the authority in March 1969, and in April Nixon established an advisory council, headed by industrialist Roy L. Ash, to study the issues confronting the establishment of more effective executive branch operations. The Ash panel recommended creation of an Office of Executive Management and a Domestic Policy Council. The primary responsibility of the Office of Executive Management (which would include a substantially revised budget bureau) was to manage programs, while the Domestic Policy Council would make forecasts, analyze alternative policies, and suggest program revisions. (See "Office of Policy Development," p. 1122.)

After renaming the proposed Office of Executive Management the Office of Management and Budget (and dropping "Policy" from the Domestic Policy Council), Nixon sent Reorganization Plan 2 to Congress on March 12, 1970. It was accompanied by a message:

The Domestic Council will be primarily concerned with what we do; the Office of Management and Budget will be primarily concerned with how we do it, and how well we do it. . . . The creation of the Office of Management and Budget represents far more than a mere change of name for the Bureau of the Budget. It represents a basic change in concept and emphasis, reflecting the broader management needs of the Office of the President.[35]

The House Subcommittee on Executive and Legislative Reorganization approved a resolution of disapproval. Some top staffers at BOB also opposed the reorganization, but the House of Representatives approved the measure on May 13, 1970 (after strenuous lobbying by the Ash committee), and the Senate followed suit on May 16. On July 1, 1970, by means of Executive Order 11541, the Bureau of the Budget was officially redesignated the Office of Management and Budget.

This redesignation did not downgrade the budgeting function of the office; rather, it amplified it. The budget office's existing responsibilities were expanded, and greater emphasis was placed on organization and management systems, development of executive talent and a broader career staff, better dissemination of information, and appropriate use of modern techniques and equipment. All of these changes were intended to enhance the capability of the executive branch to coordinate, evaluate, and improve the efficiency of government programs. Thus in one new role, OMB was to help implement major legislation, such as bills to preserve the environment, under which several agencies would share responsibility for action.

Another important new task assigned to OMB was coordination of the complex system of federal grants. This often involved more than one federal agency as well as agencies and government entities at the state and local levels. Finally, OMB was asked to evaluate the cost-effectiveness of particular programs and the relative priority of the needs they were designed to meet.

Some observers have speculated that OMB was established to strengthen the budget planners' hand in questioning the expenditure requests of the Department of Defense. This task had become difficult as Pentagon budgets skyrocketed and became almost uncontrollable.

George P. Shultz, OMB director from 1970 to 1972, established himself as a principal adviser in domestic affairs. Under his leadership, career officers were replaced by noncareer officers who served as assistant directors and dealt with policy decisions. The career officers retained responsibility for day-to-day OMB operations.

During the Watergate crisis, when the president was under siege and his domestic policy adviser, John D. Ehrlichman, and several others on the White House staff were under investigation, OMB assumed de facto responsibility for much of the day-to-day management of the government. Yet according to observers, OMB, even with its expanded role, did not fare well under the Nixon presidency. "The Office of Management and Budget was a major casualty of the Nixon presidency, in part for what it did, but also for what it appeared to be doing," wrote Berman. "By responding to the partisan needs of the president, OMB depleted valuable credibility with its other clients—leading many observers to maintain that OMB could not serve the long-range needs of the presidency."[36]

Controversies over the Role and Directors of OMB

Partly in reaction to what was perceived as OMB's partisan role, Congress enacted legislation in 1973 that required Senate approval of the office's director and deputy director. James Lynn, who served under Nixon's successor, Gerald R. Ford, was the first head of OMB to be subject to confirmation. He did much to repair the agency's "overly politicized" image.

Bert Lance was appointed OMB director by President Jimmy Carter, who succeeded Ford in 1977. Lance followed Lynn's philosophy of reestablishing the agency's image as an objective assistant to the presidency, rather than a partisan political adviser. He was one of Carter's closest confidants, however. Lance resigned after less than a year in office when faced with accusations of unethical banking practices during his years as a Georgia bank president. He was succeeded by James T. McIntyre Jr., who had been serving as deputy director of OMB.

During President Ronald Reagan's first term in office (1981–1985), OMB found itself the center of political attention with Reagan's appointment of David A. Stockman, a two-term Republican representative from Michigan, to the director's post. Reagan selected Stockman to lead his revolutionary campaign to cut both government spending and taxes after Stockman caught the presidential candidate's eye in 1980 while playing the role of independent candidate John B. Anderson in a practice debate. Stockman began his career in Washington in 1970 as a legislative assistant to Anderson.

Reagan was particularly impressed with Stockman's knowledge of economics. And Stockman's November 1980 "manifesto" on how the new Republican administration could avoid an "economic Dunkirk" seemed to seal his fate as Reagan's chief economic adviser. In fact, Stockman was credited with being the main architect of the massive 1981 tax and budget cuts that he and others in the administration said would lower inflation, spur economic growth, and eventually eliminate the deficit.

Instead, the economy began to sour, and in the December 1981 issue of the *Atlantic Monthly* Stockman conceded that the tax cutting had gone too far and defense spending should have been restrained. He revealed other doubts as well about the administration's economic policy, saying, "None of us really understands what's going on with all these numbers."

Publication of the article, it was thought, would mean the end of Stockman's time in office. He offered his resignation, but instead of accepting it, Reagan took Stockman to the "woodshed" for a verbal beating. Afterward, Stockman's influence was primarily in behind-the-scenes negotiations on the budget. During the following three years he was credited with using his knowledge of the minutiae of the federal budget to help steer through Congress several deficit-reduction measures that cut spending and raised taxes.

Nonetheless, during his latter days in office Stockman's growing exclusion from the inner circle in the administration cost him influence on Capitol Hill, according to members of Congress. Frustrated by his inability to bring down the deficit, Stockman resigned in July 1985. "He was an extraordinarily talented and capable person," said House Budget Committee Democrat Thomas J. Downey (N.Y.), who often disagreed with Stockman on policy. "He had a tenacity and ability to frame the issues politically. Those qualities will be missed."[37]

OMB Director Richard G. Darman holds a copy of the fiscal year 1991 budget that successfully curbed the rising federal deficit. The budget, however, ended up being a major political liability for his boss, President George Bush.

Stockman was succeeded by James C. Miller III, then chairman of the Federal Trade Commission and former administrator of OMB's Office of Information and Regulatory Affairs.

OMB in the Bush and Clinton Administrations

During President George Bush's term the OMB regained the visibility that it had enjoyed in the early 1980s under Stockman as the principal agency for shaping the president's economic objectives. In addition, Bush's OMB director, former Reagan Treasury official Richard G. Darman, played a dominant role within the president's inner circle in shaping domestic policy. With Bush devoting much of his attention to national security issues, Darman and White House chief of staff John Sununu became the point men and chief negotiators for the administration's domestic legislative agenda. They concentrated their efforts on consolidating Reagan's legacy of deregulation and scaling back of federal programs, most notably in the areas of environment and energy, and frequently overruled cabinet secretaries in the development of policy.

Darman and Sununu were the two top White House negotiators on the 1990 budget pact in which Bush abandoned his trademark 1988 campaign slogan, "Read my lips: No new taxes." In January 1990 Bush had released a $1.2 trillion budget plan for fiscal year 1991, projecting a deficit of $126.9 billion. In its annual reestimate of the president's budget, the Congressional Budget Office (CBO) projected a deficit nearly $70 billion higher, with most of the difference explained by less optimistic economic assumptions and additional funds for the savings and loan bailout.

Concerned about the worsening economy and rising deficit projections, Bush and top congressional leaders appointed twenty negotiators to begin a series of closed-door sessions. Although they agreed on a deficit-reduction goal—cutting $50 billion in the first year and $500 billion over five years—negotiators were deadlocked until June when Bush, under pressure from congressional leaders and his own team, released a statement that "tax revenue increases" would have to be part of any deficit-reduction plan. The following month, Darman released a revised deficit projection of $231.4 billion for fiscal year 1991 and warned that unless immediate steps were taken, mandatory across-the-board cuts would be necessary under the Gramm-Rudman antideficit law, which set a deficit target of $64 billion for fiscal year 1991.

The budget summit continued through the summer, with conservative Republicans refusing to fall in line with the administration's concession on higher taxes. The Omnibus Budget Reconciliation Act of 1990 was finally approved on October 27, after an initial deal was defeated in the House, with Republicans angrily divided on the measure. The bill was saved largely through Darman's negotiations with senior Democrats, at the expense of alienating many rank-and-file Republicans.

Although the bill was the most ambitious effort ever to turn the tide on federal spending, many Republicans faulted Darman and Sununu for persuading Bush to renege on his campaign pledge, and Bush himself claimed shortly afterward that he regretted the tax-increase agreement. Party members also complained that Darman's overly confident forecasts had been partially responsible for the prolonged wrangling over the budget package and had weakened the administration's control over spending and tax issues. The final agreement cut discretionary spending, including defense, by $182.4 billion and raised taxes by $146.3 billion over five years. An additional $99 billion was to be cut from entitlement programs, such as Medicare and farm-price supports, for an overall reduction in the deficit of almost $500 billion over five years. The 1990 bill was a success for Darman, but a costly political risk for Bush, leaving him exposed to criticism from within his party. Furthermore, the 1990 agreement ultimately did not reduce the deficit, which grew to $290.4 billion by Bush's last year in office.

Bill Clinton's first budget director, Democratic representative Leon E. Panetta of California, was a sharp contrast to his hard-charging predecessor. Unlike Bush, Clinton took a hands-on approach to domestic policy, and under Panetta the OMB focused more on budgetary matters. Although trained as a lawyer, many thought that Panetta had been preparing for the budget post since coming to Congress in 1977. A converted Republican, Panetta had been forced to resign as director of President Nixon's Office of Civil Rights because the White House thought he was doing his job too aggressively. He was elected to Congress as a Democrat in 1976 and soon made the budget his area of expertise, serving as chairman of the House Budget Committee from 1989 until his appointment to the Clinton administration. He was an acknowledged expert on the technical details of budgeting, which enabled him to play a leading role in the 1990 budget-summit negotiations. He was also known as a dogged enforcer of the budget rules and a true believer in the importance of deficit reduction.

During his confirmation hearing, Panetta proposed a new long-term goal of reducing the ratio of the deficit to the gross domestic product (GDP) from 4.9 percent to 1 percent, a level that had not been reached since 1974. By linking the deficit to the GDP, Panetta set a goal that could be met by reducing the size of the deficit, enlarging the economy, or some combination of the two. Despite his reputation as a "deficit hawk," Panetta acknowledged that there would always be a deficit of some size.

Clinton's fiscal year 1993 deficit-reduction proposal came on the heels of the Senate defeat of his first piece of fiscal legislation, the 1993 economic stimulus package. Panetta had been an active lobbyist for the stimulus bill, which would have provided $16.3 billion in supplemental appropriations for fiscal 1993 through a blend of job-creation and economic-development measures, social programs for the poor, and high-technology purchases for the government. Several Democratic senators joined Republicans in refusing to accept an increase in the deficit in exchange for several thousand new temporary jobs. Panetta had more success in persuading nervous Democrats to accept the budget-reconciliation package, which relied heavily on tax increases to reduce the deficit by an estimated $500 billion over five years. The bill also made substantial cuts in entitlement spending and changed budget laws to freeze discretionary spending for five years. Panetta's hawkish fiscal reputation gave the president's plan much needed credibility within his party, although some Republicans claimed that Panetta had not been as responsive to them. And even though Panetta's 1993 budget was credited with being more honest than previous proposals, critics still questioned the validity of OMB's estimates. By 1995 the Clinton administration had proven its critics wrong as the deficit had been cut nearly in half to $163.5.

In mid-1994 Clinton selected Panetta to be White House chief of staff and appointed his deputy, Alice M. Rivlin, as OMB director. Rivlin had been the first director of CBO when that agency was formed in 1975, and before joining the administration had been a senior research fellow in economics at the Brookings Institution. Like Panetta, Rivlin was a fierce and consistent "deficit hawk." During White House strategy sessions on the 1993 budget-reconciliation plan, Rivlin had argued for a lower deficit and criticized several of the president's reduction measures. Her role in producing the president's 1996 and 1997 budgets became quickly overshadowed by the new Republican majority in Congress, which battled President Clinton over control of the budget process. *(See "Clinton Administration," p. 721, in Chapter 16, Vol. I.)*

ORGANIZATION AND FUNCTIONS OF OMB

The organization and functions of the president's budget agency have changed often through the years. The scope of its purview has reflected the growth of the economy and federal budget, each president's political inclinations and perception of what the office should do, changing relations within the executive branch and with Congress, and the office's perception of its mission. Internal organizational realignments usually have accompanied such changes.

Organization of OMB

OMB is headed by a director who is assisted by a deputy director. Both are appointed by the president and confirmed by the Senate.

The office, which had 550 employees in 1995, is broken down into budget and management divisions, as well as an administrative and support staff. The budget staff is grouped into program areas: national security and international affairs; human resources; health; economics and government; and natural resources, energy, and science. Staff members are responsible for preparing agency funding requests, supervising spending authorized by Congress, and formulating economic and financial analyses and forecasts. Special study groups within the division conduct detailed reviews of selected programs. The work of the budget analysts is compiled by the Budget Review and Concepts and the Budget Analysis and Systems divisions, which look at the programs in light of overall federal spending. These divisions also are responsible for developing better management techniques for formulating and presenting the budget.

The Office of Federal Procurement Policy provides overall direction to governmentwide procurement policies, regulations, procedures, and forms. Its authority extends over procurement by executive agencies; recipients of federal grants or assistance; services, including research and development; and construction, alteration, repair, or maintenance of real property.

Functions of OMB

In 1970 OMB was designated "the president's principal arm for the exercise of his managerial functions." This responsibility grew in 1974 with enactment of the Congressional Budget and Impoundment Control Act; the act added responsibility for meeting congressional budget reporting deadlines to the office's workload, among other tasks. The same year, Congress established a forty-person Office of Federal Procurement within OMB to handle procurement and contracting policy development. In 1980 the Office of Information and Regulatory Affairs

(OIRA) was created in OMB to coordinate the administration's efforts to cut down on federal regulations and paperwork. By 1995 OMB's responsibilities included:

• Preparing the budget and formulating the government's fiscal program

• Supervising execution of the executive branch budget

• Reviewing the organizational structures and management procedures of the executive branch

• Evaluating the performance of federal programs

• Encouraging interagency and intergovernmental cooperation and coordination

• Coordinating and clearing with the president departmental recommendations for proposed legislation to be sent to Congress and for presidential action on bills passed by Congress

• Assisting the relevant departments and the White House in the consideration, clearance, and preparation of executive orders and proclamations

• Keeping the president advised of activities proposed, actually initiated, and completed by federal agencies

• Coordinating interagency activities to ensure that funds appropriated by Congress were spent with the least possible overlap[38]

By far the most important of OMB's functions is its central role in the federal budget process. The administration's budget proposes specific levels of new spending authority for appropriations, as well as outlays (amounts to be spent for the fiscal year) for all government agencies and functions. The budget presents as well a detailed account of the administration's program. *(See Table 11-1, Budget Timetable in the Executive Branch and Congress, p. 498, Vol. I.)*

Controversial New Role: OIRA and Regulation

President Reagan entered office in 1981 determined to cut down on the number of federal regulations and the amount of paperwork that the private sector must contend with in doing business. The 1980 Paperwork Reduction Act (PL 96-511) established the Office of Information and Regulatory Affairs as a principal unit of OMB. Its task is to oversee and review the actions of all major regulatory agencies to determine whether they meet administrative guidelines for studying the costs and benefits of proposed and existing regulations.

All of Reagan's top economic advisers favored regulatory reform and deregulation wherever possible, and plans for the attack were developed before Reagan was inaugurated. Incoming OMB director Stockman called for an "orchestrated series of unilateral administrative actions to defer, revise, or rescind existing and pending regulations where clear legal authority exists."[39]

On February 17, 1981, less than one month after taking office, Reagan issued Executive Order 12291, which required executive branch agencies to prepare a regulatory impact analysis for all new and existing major regulations. OMB's regulatory office was authorized to issue criteria for deciding when a regulation was needed and to order an agency to perform a regulatory impact analysis that would assess the potential benefits, costs, and net benefits of a regulation.

A second executive order (12498), issued in January 1985, required agencies to give OMB their agendas for each year, including activities such as studies that might lead to regulation. The order gave OMB authority to determine whether agency plans met administration objectives and guidelines.

The zeal with which OIRA assumed its role, however, came under criticism from outside experts, regulators, and Congress. Congressional critics of the expanded OMB function argued that the office had become a regulatory czar and that department and other federal agency personnel—not the budget office staff—should have final authority over rules needed to implement laws passed by Congress. According to a May 1986 report by the Senate Environment and Public Works Committee, "OMB's ability to . . . substantively influence agency regulations and to delay their promulgation is inappropriate encroachment upon congressional legislative authority and upon agency independence and expertise. . . ."[40]

In February 1986 that position was upheld by a federal district court in Washington, D.C. The court ruled (in *Environmental Defense Fund v. Thomas*) that OMB's ability to delay or force changes in agency regulations was "incompatible with the will of Congress and cannot be sustained as a valid exercise of the president's Article II powers" (Article II of the Constitution delineates the president's powers).[41]

The result of congressional ire over OMB's new regulatory authority was a 1986 attempt to eliminate funding for OIRA. Although that effort failed and a compromise measure authorized the office through 1989, the authorizing bill required that future administrators of OIRA be presidential appointees, subject to Senate confirmation. The bill also restricted OMB's regulatory oversight functions to reviewing requests for information contained in proposed rules or regulations.

In addition to OMB's regulatory authority, which was a source of contention during the Reagan administration, Congress scrutinized the entire structure of the federal government's budgetary procedures. In June 1986 the Senate Governmental Affairs Committee approved a sweeping bill that would create within OMB an Office of Financial Management, two deputy director positions, and an executive deputy director position. Although the bill died, its introduction and testimony on the legislation indicated dissatisfaction on Capitol Hill with the office. As stated by Governmental Affairs chairman William V. Roth Jr. (R-Del.), "We're dissatisfied with the 'M' [in OMB]."[42]

In 1993 President Clinton issued Executive Order 12866, which revoked both of Reagan's executive orders. In place of broad OMB oversight of regulatory agencies, Clinton's order reemphasized the responsibilities of the agencies, the vice president, and other policy advisers in the regulatory process. Although restricting the role of the OMB in reviewing regulations, Clinton's executive order still gave the OMB the authority to identify duplication, overlap, and conflict in rules, which agencies were then required to rectify; to develop procedures for cost-benefit analysis; to recommend changes in laws authorizing regulatory activity; to monitor compliance with the executive order; and to schedule existing rules for agency review.

Indeed, throughout its long history the president's budget office has assumed functions and responsibilities so vast that it has not been difficult to find some critics of aspects of its work. Yet the overall consensus appears to be that OMB is dedicated to performing its functions well and that, although some internal restructuring might be needed, the agency has a secure place in the Executive Office structure.

National Security Council

In the decades following World War II the Executive Office of the President assumed an increasingly important role in all aspects of the management of foreign and defense policy. A key vehicle used by most presidents to expand their authority in these areas has been the National Security Council (NSC).

Formally, the NSC is composed of the president, the vice president, and the secretaries of state and defense, with the director of central intelligence and the chairman of the Joint Chiefs of Staff serving as advisers. It is the highest-level advisory body to the president on military and diplomatic issues.

The National Security Council was established in 1947 to help the president coordinate the actions of government agencies into a single cohesive policy for dealing with other nations. Many members of Congress saw the new panel also as another institutional check on President Harry S. Truman's power in the areas of foreign affairs and defense. The council has acted as a true decision-making body on only a few important occasions. In 1956, for example, members of the NSC helped formulate President Dwight D. Eisenhower's response to the Soviet invasion of Hungary.

Instead, the prime significance of the NSC has stemmed from its development into an apparatus used by presidents to implement their personal visions of U.S. foreign policy. The NSC staff comprises policy experts who analyze foreign policy issues and make recommendations to the president. They are distinct from the formal members of the council. Presidents have turned to the NSC because it is subject to little effective control from Congress and is without the independent institutional loyalties frequently evident in the State, Defense, and other departments.

The role of the NSC has varied greatly over the years, usually depending on the personal influence of the president's national security adviser, who heads the NSC staff. When the national security adviser has been a relatively weak figure within the government, the NSC staff has been merely a bureaucratic shell with little power. At other times, however, it has been the dominant institutional force in setting foreign policy; this was the case under President Richard Nixon's national security adviser, Henry A. Kissinger.

During the Reagan administration, NSC staffers, including

Marine Lt. Col. Oliver North, played key roles in carrying out secret plans to sell arms to Iran and to divert the proceeds to guerrillas fighting the leftist government of Nicaragua. The so-called Iran-contra affair was a major political embarrassment for President Reagan during his second term.

Since Kissinger's term as national security adviser, a debate has raged about how much independent authority the NSC staff should exercise. Many experts in the area of foreign policy argue that the NSC staff should be limited to managing the flow of information and policy options from the departments to the president. But some former national security advisers argue that the NSC and its staff should have considerable authority to help the president define overall policy and to control the departments to ensure that this policy is carried out.

ORIGINS AND DEVELOPMENT OF NSC

Formation of the NSC represented the first institutional attempt in U.S. history to foster coordination and cooperation among the organizations contributing to U.S. national security policy. Before its formation, the president was essentially the only person able to impose harmony on the often opposing positions and actions of the State and War Departments and other agencies.

The conflicts and lack of coordination among the military services and civilian agencies during World War II convinced many government officials that a fundamental reorganization of the national security structure was needed. This realization led in 1947 to passage of the National Security Act, landmark legislation that created the Defense Department out of the old War and Navy Departments. The act also established the Central Intelligence Agency (CIA).

Passage of the National Security Act was marked by bitter debate in Congress and in the services about the creation of a single military command system. But the law's provisions establishing the NSC as a permanent agency for policy coordination enjoyed broad support. According to the act, the purpose of the NSC was to "advise the president with respect to the integration of domestic, foreign, and military policies relating to the national security. . . ."[43]

The role played by the NSC in the decades that followed was generally determined by the attitudes of succeeding presidents toward it. As a 1978 Congressional Research Service study of the NSC observed, "The NSC was a malleable organization, to be used as each President saw fit. Thus, its use, internal substructure and ultimate effect would be directly dependent on the style and wishes of the President."[44]

In its early years under President Truman, the NSC was not a major factor in the formulation of foreign and defense policy. Truman viewed the council as only an advisory body and rarely attended its meetings. President Eisenhower, by contrast, carried out a major expansion and institutionalization of the NSC. Perhaps most important, he appointed an assistant to the president for national security affairs—a position not mentioned in the 1947 act—to head the council staff. He frequently attended NSC meetings, moreover, and relied on its advice during times of international crisis.

Eisenhower's heavy reliance on the NSC led to complaints from the Senate Government Operations Committee and others that the council had become "overinstitutionalized." President John F. Kennedy came into office determined to rely more on a small group of personal advisers than on the NSC bureaucracy. Although Kennedy worked closely with his national security adviser, McGeorge Bundy, he ordered a substantial reduction in the staff and responsibilities of the NSC. President Lyndon B. Johnson followed a pattern similar to Kennedy's. Although the NSC system as a whole was not a major factor in determining policy, Walt W. Rostow, who became national security adviser in 1966, played an important role in encouraging Johnson to order a major escalation of the Vietnam War.

The role of the NSC underwent a radical change under Nixon and his national security adviser, Kissinger. The NSC staff tripled in size, to about fifty high-level professional experts, and it wielded unprecedented power within the Washington bureaucracy. Kissinger himself became the coarchitect of Nixon's key foreign policy moves, including the negotiated end to the Vietnam War, the opening to Communist China, and the onset of détente with the Soviet Union.

Kissinger enlarged the power of his office in two major ways. One was by shifting from the strictly advisory role played by his predecessors to an active involvement in diplomatic negotiations. Beginning in 1969, for example, he engaged in secret diplomacy with the North Vietnamese, holding private talks with enemy leaders in Paris that eventually led to a peace settlement. Even more dramatic was his secret trip to China in 1971. At that point, Nixon and Kissinger were ready to end the decades-old hostility of the United States toward the Communist Chinese regime, but they were unwilling to reveal their intentions to the world. On a trip to Pakistan, Kissinger eluded the press and observers and flew unnoticed to Peking, where he met with Communist leaders. After Kissinger returned to the West, Nixon made an announcement that shook world power diplomacy: the potential alliance of the United States and China against the Soviet Union.

Kissinger also succeeded in completely overshadowing Nixon's secretary of state, William P. Rogers. He worked to exclude Rogers from key information and negotiations, resulting in a strong personal and institutional antagonism that continued to affect relations between subsequent national security advisers and secretaries of state. In his memoirs, Kissinger revealed the bitter strains between the two men. Rogers was an "insensitive neophyte," Kissinger wrote, while acknowledging that Rogers viewed him as an "egotistical nitpicker."[45]

The conflict between the national security adviser and the secretary of state ended in 1973 when Kissinger assumed the latter post while retaining the former. Tensions resumed at a relatively low level under the administration of Gerald R. Ford, who became president following Nixon's resignation in 1974. In November 1975 Kissinger relinquished his position as Ford's national security adviser to Lt. Gen. Brent Scowcroft. Scowcroft viewed his responsibilities primarily in terms of coordinating and overseeing foreign policy actions; he did not attempt to challenge Kissinger's primacy in determining foreign policy.

President Jimmy Carter came into office proclaiming his intention to place more responsibility in the departments and agencies while reducing the policy-making role of the NSC. Almost from the start, however, sharp conflicts arose between National Security Adviser Zbigniew Brzezinski and Secretary of State Cyrus R. Vance. Not content with being a mere facilitator of the policy views of others, Brzezinski was determined to assert his views, which centered on a policy of hard-line confrontation with the Soviet Union. Carter did not indicate whether he agreed with Brzezinski or with Vance, who stressed mutual cooperation and arms control agreements with the Soviets. As a result, the American public and foreign governments frequently were left in confusion about which man truly reflected U.S. foreign policy. Finally, however, Vance resigned in protest against the unsuccessful 1980 attempt to conduct a military rescue of American hostages held in Iran, leaving Brzezinski with more influence over foreign policy during the last year of Carter's presidency.

Ronald Reagan assumed the presidency affirming cabinet government as his model. Although Reagan was somewhat more willing than his immediate predecessors to hold formal NSC meetings with the vice president and secretaries of state and defense, he de-emphasized the role of the NSC staff and dismantled much of the elaborate system of NSC staff committees that analyzed and formulated policy. He did not move to establish a formal NSC structure until 1982. At the same time, he designated the secretary of state as his principal foreign policy adviser.

During his first six years in office, Reagan had four national security advisers, who were viewed in Washington as relatively weak figures, lacking either strong foreign policy experience or close ties to the president. The four—Richard V. Allen, William P. Clark, Robert C. McFarlane, and John M. Poindexter—were virtually unknown to the public. Behind the scenes, however, two of the advisers and their staffs were directing operations of pivotal importance to Reagan's presidency. Investigations of the Iran-contra affair revealed that McFarlane and Poindexter had masterminded the secret plan to sell arms to Iran in exchange for the release of American hostages held in Lebanon. Moreover, NSC staffer Lt. Col. Oliver L. North, with Poindexter's approval, arranged for the allegedly illegal transfer of proceeds from the sales to Iran to the "contra" guerrillas in Nicaragua. In carrying out these activities, McFarlane, Poindexter, and North became involved in the operational side of foreign policy at a level far beyond that achieved by Kissinger even at his most active. In the wake of disclosures in late 1986 about the secret transactions, Reagan replaced Poindexter with Frank C. Carlucci, who moved to scale back the power of the NSC staff.

President George Bush's choice for national security adviser, Brent Scowcroft, reflected the characteristics common to all of

Bush's foreign policy appointees, whom one writer termed a "mix of professionals and buddies."[46] Scowcroft, a retired lieutenant general, had served as Ford's national security adviser following Kissinger's resignation and had chaired the Scowcroft Commission on arms control in the early 1980s. He was also a trusted associate of the president, dating back to the Ford administration, when Bush served first as U.S. liaison to China and then as director of the CIA. Furthermore, Scowcroft had served as a member of the 1987 Tower Commission on the Iran-contra affair, which had strongly criticized staff members of the NSC for circumventing the law to divert funds to the contras and Reagan himself for delegating too much authority to the NSC staff. Poindexter and North were both convicted of felony charges, but the convictions eventually were overturned on the grounds that they had been influenced by testimony given under congressional immunity.

Unlike Reagan, Bush was actively involved in the formulation and management of national security policy, and he had a collegial and trusting relationship with Scowcroft throughout his term. Scowcroft, like Secretary of State James Baker III and Secretary of Defense Richard Cheney, was a powerful player both behind-the-scenes and publicly in an administration whose greatest accomplishments were in foreign policy, particularly in the mobilization of a multinational coalition against Iraq during the 1991 Gulf War. Although Scowcroft restored an image of purpose and accountability to the NSC, major national security decisions, such as the invasion of Panama, continued to be made behind closed doors by Bush's collective foreign policy team. Formal NSC meetings were infrequent.

In December 1989 Scowcroft led a surprise trip to China, ostensibly to brief the Chinese government on the recently concluded Malta summit talks between the United States and the Soviet Union. Shortly thereafter it was disclosed that Scowcroft had been on an earlier mission, in July of that year, only a month after the Chinese government's violent suppression of the student-led democracy uprising in Tiananmen Square. Although the administration described the earlier trip as an attempt to underscore U.S. concern over the crackdown, both trips were widely criticized as attempts to placate the Chinese government in the wake of U.S. sanctions and the possible revocation of China's most-favored-nation trading status because of human-rights violations.

President Bill Clinton's national security adviser, Anthony Lake, had been a special assistant to Kissinger in the Nixon White House, resigning in 1970 to protest the secret U.S. invasion of Cambodia. During the Carter administration Lake was the director of policy planning at the State Department, and later he became one of Clinton's foreign policy advisers during the 1992 campaign. A professor of international relations, Lake was viewed as bringing intellectual depth to the administration's national security strategy, which had taken up little space on candidate Clinton's platform. Immediately after taking office Clinton's foreign policy team was faced with challenges throughout the world, especially the Balkans, Somalia, Haiti, Korea, and

Iraq. Almost from the outset, the Clinton administration was criticized by the press and members of both parties in Congress for its inconsistent stance on such crises as the escalating violence in Bosnia and the precarious role of U.S. forces in UN peacekeeping operations in Somalia. In contrast to the implementation of foreign policy under Bush, the Clinton team presented a fractured front. Lake had entered the NSC pledging to serve the president as an "honest broker," and although he was respected as a behind-the-scenes policy coordinator, the administration's early foreign policy performance was widely seen as uneven.

Early in Clinton's term the NSC deliberative system was restructured to stress the primacy of the economic dimensions of Clinton's post–cold-war national security policy and to formalize the interagency decision-making process. The secretary of the Treasury and the director of the new National Economic Council (NEC) met with NSC members on high-priority issues before the issues were brought up in formal NSC meetings. Less immediate concerns were covered in meetings of a "deputies committee," headed by the deputy assistant for national security and attended by the deputy chiefs of staff for key agencies. And "working groups" convened over medium-term matters.

ORGANIZATION AND FUNCTIONS OF NSC

The organizational structure of the NSC over the years has been as fluid as the roles to which different presidents have assigned it. Other than the presence, since Eisenhower's presidency, of a national security adviser as head of the NSC staff, there has been little consistency in either the organization of the NSC staff hierarchy or in the large number of interagency working groups and oversight committees established within the NSC. Nor has the number of NSC employees remained constant. Reaching a high of around three hundred under Kissinger, the number of employees at all levels within the NSC fell to perhaps a quarter of that under Brzezinski and rose again to 180 by the end of Reagan's first term. It remained at that level during the Bush administration and was reduced to 151 by the end of Clinton's first year in office.

One theme has been consistent over time, however: the high degree of independence of the NSC from outside control. Like other parts of the Executive Office of the President, the NSC is institutionally responsible only to the chief executive. Thus over the years, presidents have relied increasingly on the council's staff because of their confidence in the staff's accountability. Presidents frequently have questioned the loyalty of staff members of the State and Defense Departments, the CIA, and other agencies, who may have long-term institutional commitments that are at odds with the president's personal agenda. That concern usually does not apply to NSC staffers, however, as they are dependent on the president alone.

Presidents also have acted to strengthen the loyalty of NSC staffers to themselves. Originally, the staff was thought to be a nonpolitical group of experts, who, like many of the fiscal experts at the Office of Management and Budget, might hold their positions over the course of several administrations. Beginning with President Kennedy, however, new presidents have purged the ranks of the NSC upon taking office, substituting their own supporters for those of the outgoing president.

The president selects a national security adviser without fear of congressional questioning or rejection. The position is not subject to Senate confirmation, which, according to a long-standing Washington tradition, means that the officeholder cannot be compelled to testify before Congress. It was not until 1980 that a national security adviser made his first formal appearance before a congressional committee, and subsequent appearances have been rare.

Another factor that increases the autonomy of the NSC is the relative lack of congressional controls over its budget. Although Congress sets the NSC's budget, council officials are able to exceed that limit by having staffers detailed, or lent, by other agencies. At the end of 1994 about two-thirds of the 151 NSC staff members were detailed from other agencies.

As the history of the council and its staff shows, views about how the NSC should function have changed many times over the years. Many foreign policy scholars argue that the NSC staff should not be a strong, independent force in decision making. According to this viewpoint, national security advisers and their staffs should be facilitators rather than policy makers, "honest brokers" who present the views of different departments to the president without prejudice and monitor the departments' actions to make sure presidential policies are being followed. National security advisers should not contest the secretary of state's role as chief foreign policy spokesperson for the administration, nor should they assume a direct role in international negotiations and the management of covert operations.[47]

Surprisingly, this view came to be held even by Kissinger, the foremost practitioner of NSC power. "Though I did not think so at the time, I have become convinced that a President should make the secretary of state his principal adviser and use the national security adviser primarily as a senior administrator and coordinator to make certain that each significant point of view is heard," wrote Kissinger in his memoirs. "If the security adviser becomes active in the development and articulation of policy he must inevitably diminish the Secretary of State and reduce his effectiveness."[48]

Other experts argue, however, that the NSC needs the authority to strive for unity and cohesiveness among the competing forces in an administration. Even some of those who were most critical of the NSC staff's moves into covert action in the Reagan administration complained that the council as an institution did not have the strength to insure agreement within the administration on key issues. Critics frequently found foreign policy disarray within the administration—for example, the continuing differences between the State and Defense Departments over arms control negotiations with the Soviet Union—and some attributed this disarray to the weakness of the NSC.

Past national security adviser Brzezinski thought that the system would work best if

the practical coordination and definition of the strategic direction would originate from [the president's assistant for national security affairs], who would then tightly coordinate and control the secretary of state, the secretary of defense, the chairman of the joint chiefs, and the director of central intelligence as a team, with them knowing that he was doing so on the president's behalf.[49]

Office of Policy Development

Established in 1977 as the Domestic Policy Staff, the Office of Policy Development (OPD, redesignated as such in 1981) coordinates and implements policy for the White House Domestic and Economic Policy Councils. It is unique among Executive Office agencies in that *all* staff members (including nonprofessionals) are political appointees. Its history is therefore closely tied to that of the White House staff (its head serves as a special assistant to the president), and it has one client: the president.

ORIGINS AND DEVELOPMENT OF OPD

In 1970 President Richard Nixon established the first formal office for domestic policy; his predecessors had relied on ad hoc arrangements for advice on domestic policy making. For example, with the growth of the presidency as an institution under Franklin D. Roosevelt, domestic planning was centralized in the White House. There was no organized staff structure, however. Instead, Roosevelt—to ensure his control over policy making—established a web of overlapping responsibilities for his advisers.

President Harry S. Truman depended on a small core of advisers headed by his special counsel, Clark M. Clifford. During the Truman presidency, however, as George Washington University political scientist Stephen J. Wayne observed, "policy initiative clearly rested with the individual department secretaries."[50]

The same kind of informal system was used by Dwight D. Eisenhower, whose chief of staff, Sherman Adams, coordinated domestic policy. Under John F. Kennedy, policy planning was further centralized in the White House. Kennedy's top domestic aide, special counsel Theodore C. Sorensen, assumed an active role in forging the "New Frontier" legislation.

The seeds of an institutional domestic policy staff were planted during the presidency of Lyndon B. Johnson. His chief of staff, Joseph A. Califano Jr., formed a cadre of aides who played a key role in drafting Johnson's Great Society programs. The idea of establishing a formal domestic policy council to strengthen the president's capacities for formulating policy arose as early as 1964, when White House staffer Richard Goodwin wrote Johnson: "I suggest the establishment of a Domestic Policy Planning [Council]. There is such a staff on foreign policy . . . yet the need is far more obvious in the field of domestic policy. . . . This would be a full-time council of experienced people—scholars, government people, etc. Its director would be on your staff. It could be attached to the Bureau of the Budget or operate independently and report directly to you."[51]

Nixon's Reorganization

It was not until Richard Nixon entered the White House that Goodwin's idea caught hold. Granted formal authority by Congress to make organizational changes, Nixon in April 1969 set up an advisory panel, headed by industrialist Roy L. Ash, to propose ways to streamline and formalize policy-making procedures. The Ash panel recommended redesigning the Bureau of the Budget to form an Office of Management and Budget (OMB) and creating a Domestic Council. Acting on the panel's advice, Nixon sent Congress Reorganization Plan 2 in March 1970, proposing these changes. While OMB's function was conceived as primarily budgetary and managerial oversight, the Domestic Council was to serve in a broader policy-making capacity. (*See "Office of Management and Budget," p. 1112.*)

Under the reorganization plan, the new Domestic Council would be composed of the president (who would act as chair), the vice president, the attorney general, and the secretaries of the Treasury; interior; agriculture; commerce; labor; health, education, and welfare; housing and urban development; and transportation. The president could designate others to serve on the council as relevant issues arose. The staff of the council, located in the Executive Office, would be headed by an executive director who would act as an assistant to the president.

"The staff of the Domestic Council formalized the development over the last decade of a substantial policy group in the White House," observed political scientist Peri E. Arnold. "The Domestic Council staff would greatly increase the president's support system for developing policy proposals at the same time that it removed that system from the White House, thus appearing to fulfill the Nixon pledge for a lean White House."[52]

According to the president, the creation of a council had two assets. First, it placed those responsible for domestic policy making in the forefront of the effort. A second, more important asset was suggested by Nixon in his message transmitting the reorganization plan to Congress:

The Council will be supported by a staff. . . . Like the National Security Council staff, this staff will work in close coordination with the President's personal staff but will have its own institutional identity. By being established on a permanent, institutional basis, it will be designed to develop and employ the "institutional memory" so essential if continuity is to be maintained, and if experience is to play its proper role in the policy-making process.[53]

Some members of Congress were troubled by Nixon's concept of the proposed staff. During hearings on the reorganization plan—at which Ash and Dwight A. Ink Jr., assistant director of management for the budget bureau, appeared—Rep. Chester E. Holifield (D-Calif.) queried the meaning of "institutional memory," noting that the staff would be "a political organization headed by a political appointee, none of whom have civil service tenure, and the director, of course, not being confirmed by the Senate." Ink admitted that would be the case, but he said the staff would be heterogeneous: "It is not expected that they have tenure," he declared. He then added that "institutional memory" should not be "interpreted as necessarily going from

administration to administration," to which Holifield responded that it must be "a four-year institutional memory."[54]

The problem of relations with OMB also threatened congressional acceptance of the reorganization plan. The Domestic Council was charged with developing domestic policy; yet the budget director was not a statutory member. Moreover, the council was to have a large, expert staff, implying that the new OMB was in fact being demoted. The administration denied that was the case; budget director Robert P. Mayo testified, "The Budget Bureau makes policy recommendations to the President. . . . This will continue as far as I know. . . ."[55] Another troubling point for skeptical members of Congress was the first section of the reorganization plan. It stated: "There are hereby transferred to the President . . . all functions vested by law . . . in the Bureau of the Budget or the Director of the Budget." This implied that the statutory functions of the bureau could be placed anywhere at the president's discretion.

Despite these misgivings and the fact that the head of the Domestic Council staff, like the new OMB director, was not subject to Senate confirmation (and therefore was not required to testify on Capitol Hill), Congress approved the plan.

Like OMB, the Domestic Council "never quite fulfilled the expectations of the Ash Council," wrote Arnold. "Far from becoming a mechanism for policy formulation, the Domestic Council became a large staff for presidential errands, admittedly increasing presidential reach, but providing little analytic or formulative capacity over policy."[56] During Nixon's tenure the cabinet-level council and its subcommittees met infrequently. Despite the apparent ineffectiveness of the council staff, however, its head wielded great power in the Nixon White House.

President Nixon had described the Domestic Council as "a domestic counterpart to the National Security Council" (NSC), which was established in 1947.[57] Although the two agencies had been conceived as cabinet-level advisory groups, during the Nixon years the staffs of both were overshadowed and marginalized by their heads—Henry A. Kissinger of the NSC and John D. Ehrlichman of the Domestic Council—who were among the president's closest advisers. Ehrlichman and OMB director George P. Shultz (the latter gained influence with Nixon as Watergate consumed the presidency and led to Ehrlichman's downfall) were the "czars" of domestic policy and agency budgets. "Traditionally, Cabinet officers . . . had the right of appeal to the President when negotiating their budgets; now this right was to be denied them," wrote presidential scholar Stephen Hess. "Shultz and Ehrlichman became the final arbiters."[58] Although the stated function of the council was coordination of domestic policy making, under Ehrlichman its major activity was to overrule departmental agencies, who complained that they in fact had less access to the president than before. The staff under Ehrlichman was viewed as "high handed"; during the Watergate crisis, however, Ehrlichman (and by extension, the council) ceased to play much of a role in domestic policy making, while the role of Schultz (and OMB) grew.[59]

Despite the concentration of power and influence in the person of Ehrlichman, during Nixon's tenure the Domestic Council staff became highly professional, according to political scientist John H. Kessel.[60] Of its twenty-one professional members, twelve had law degrees, seven had Ph.D. degrees, and two had degrees in business administration. Each of the six assistant directors covered a policy field (transportation and crime; energy, environment, and agriculture; and so forth). In addition, ad hoc working groups were formed to address specific policy areas. Such a group might consist of representatives of the Domestic Council and OMB staffs and assistant secretaries from each of the concerned departments.

Changes under Ford and Carter

President Gerald R. Ford gave his vice president, Nelson A. Rockefeller, control of the Domestic Council. Rockefeller then installed a longtime colleague, James M. Cannon, as associate director. The staff did not jell, however, largely because of its members' varied allegiances (some were holdovers from the Nixon presidency). Moreover, the austerity-minded president gave the council and its staff little to do.

In February 1977 President Jimmy Carter, in an effort to streamline White House operations, sought—and subsequently was granted—legislation to restore presidential reorganization authority, which had expired in 1973. He then submitted Reorganization Plan 1, which abolished the Domestic Council and reorganized it into the Domestic Policy Staff. Georgia lawyer Stuart E. Eizenstat, who headed the redesignated office, soon was described as "one of the most powerful men in Washington."[61] Under his purview the Domestic Policy Staff launched a host of varied and important legislative initiatives, among them a tax on oil windfall profits, hospital cost-control proposals, criminal code revisions, and a Social Security overhaul. The staff steadily gained influence as well, overseeing the framing of legislation and resolving interagency conflicts. "Often, it has the last word on the shape of an administration bill before it is sent to Capitol Hill," wrote reporter Larry Light in 1979.[62] Eizenstat did point out, however, that the staff did not initiate legislation. "Rather, we coordinate it," he said.[63]

Eizenstat also served as a principal adviser to the president. "I give personal advice to the president himself, telling him what I think he should do," noted Eizenstat.[64] Carter's domestic adviser was a member, moreover, of the Economic Policy Group, composed of government officials concerned with fiscal policy. And during Eizenstat's tenure a close working relationship with OMB was developed.

The Domestic Policy Staff included twenty-seven professionals, generally young and highly educated, who won high praise from Congress. The total staff numbered eighty, even though President Carter sought a leaner White House and Executive Office. Under the director there were ten associate directors, each responsible for an "issues cluster" such as economics or government reorganization; the remainder of the staff worked in one of those clusters.

The staff played a central role in formulating the domestic legislative agenda and maintained close ties with White House lobbyists on Capitol Hill. Although the Domestic Policy Staff itself did not lobby, it briefed members of Congress on legislative issues. Much of its stature resulted from Eizenstat's personal influence with the president and Congress.

ORGANIZATION AND FUNCTIONS OF OPD IN THE 1980S AND 1990S

Soon after entering office in 1981 Ronald Reagan restructured the Domestic Policy Staff, renaming it the Office of Policy Development. At first, the House of Representatives refused to fund the office because the administration declined to send anyone to testify on its behalf. To explain that decision, White House counsel Fred F. Fielding wrote Rep. Edward R. Roybal (D-Calif.), chairman of the House Appropriations Subcommittee on the Treasury-Postal Service: "The President is not subject to questioning as to the manner in which he formulates executive policy." And, according to Fielding, the principle applied equally to senior members of the president's staff.[65] The Senate, however, restored the $3 million requested for the office, and the funds cleared Congress.

Reagan's Office of Policy Development proved to be a leaner version of its predecessor. Its staff was reduced (numbering forty-one in 1981), as were professional titles (under Carter, almost all professional staff members were associate or assistant directors). Reagan's first appointment as domestic policy adviser (assistant to the president for policy development) was Martin C. Anderson, an economist who had made his name as a critic of welfare and urban renewal. During Anderson's tenure, the policy development staff was organized around seven cabinet councils (commerce and trade, economic affairs, food and agriculture, human resources, legal policy, management and administration, and natural resources and the environment). A senior member of the policy development staff served as executive secretary to each, while a second member of the staff served as OPD's representative on the "staff secretariat."

The cabinet council system collapsed under its own weight, however, and on April 11, 1985, Reagan announced the consolidation of the seven councils into a Domestic Policy Council and an Economic Policy Council. The former was composed of the attorney general (who served as chairman pro tempore); the secretaries of the interior, health and human services, housing and urban development, transportation, energy, and education; and the director of OMB. The heads of nonmember departments were invited to participate in the council's deliberations whenever matters affecting their organizations were on the agenda. The vice president and chief of staff served as ex officio members of both councils.[66] "Under Reagan, the White House domestic staff concept has come nearly full circle to the idea originally put forth by the Ash council: a White House support mechanism designed to facilitate discussion and decision making by the Cabinet itself," wrote reporter Dick Kirchten at the time.[67]

By 1987 there had been four assistants to the president for

policy development in the Reagan administration. Among the staff the turnover rate was high. The organization of the office (always extremely fluid) consisted then of a director, three assistant directors, and several special assistants. They served both the Domestic and Economic Policy councils. Total staff numbered thirty-nine—all political appointees.

The major functions of the OPD were threefold: (1) to provide the president with an early warning of important domestic issues likely to arise, (2) to produce an independent evaluation of policies, and (3) to oversee implementation and follow-up of initiatives in domestic legislation. Two major areas of OPD activity in 1986–1987 concerned drug abuse programs and welfare reform.[68]

Perhaps because of its political nature, the domestic policy staff—whatever its name—had not by 1987 evolved into a lasting, "institutional" center of power and influence. One reason might be that, as Kirchten observed, no administration had been willing to commit itself to a "permanent" staff with an "institutional memory."[69] In any event, the domestic policy staff continued to be overshadowed by the firmly entrenched budget office.

This was especially true during George Bush's term in office, as both OMB director Richard Darman and White House chief of staff John Sununu regularly intervened in both major and low-level domestic policy issues. Roger Porter, a former professor at Harvard's Kennedy School of Government, served as assistant to the president for economic and domestic affairs and as director of the OPD. Bush retained both the Domestic Policy Council and the Economic Policy Council, which were provided staff support by the OPD and the White House Office of Cabinet Affairs. The two councils were composed of cabinet officials and charged with developing policy strategies for the president's review. On economic affairs in particular, however, Darman and Sununu were the dominant players, and Porter's Economic Policy Council met rarely and did not establish a formal procedure for preparing issues for presidential decision.[70]

This system continued until early 1992, when Bush replaced the two councils with a Policy Coordinating Group, in which the Economic Policy Council would continue as a working group. The intention was to create a domestic equivalent to the National Security Council, but like earlier offices, the coordinating group did not become an institutionalized body and it was abolished by President Bill Clinton in 1993.

Clinton reorganized the OPD into two distinct clusters: the National Economic Council (NEC) and the Domestic Policy Council. Each was headed by an assistant to the president responsible for coordinating the development and implementation of policy among the relevant cabinet agencies. Early in his administration Clinton had sought to eliminate the existing White House Council on Environmental Quality (CEQ) and fold its responsibilities into a new Office of Environmental Policy, to be organized under an assistant to the president similar to the NEC and DPC. Legislation to abolish the CEQ died in Congress, however.

President Clinton continued the tradition of appointing individuals with academic backgrounds to the Council of Economic Advisers. His first CEA chair, Laura D'Andrea Tyson, had been an economics professor at the University of California at Berkeley.

The assistant to the president for domestic policy, Carol Rasco, chaired the Domestic Policy Council, which was composed of the vice president, cabinet heads, and other EOP officers. The council functioned through committees, task forces, and interagency working groups on such issues as welfare reform, crime, and immigration. However, the major domestic initiative of the first two years of the administration, health care reform, was led not by the council but by First Lady Hillary Rodham Clinton and presidential adviser Ira Magaziner.

The NEC was intended, not unlike Bush's Policy Coordinating Group, to be the economic equivalent of the National Security Council. The council included the heads of cabinet departments and other executive offices, with the chair coordinating the discussions and preparing policy initiatives for the president's decision. Although it was still unclear whether the council would evolve into a permanent executive office, its first chairman, Robert E. Rubin, wielded greater influence than most of his predecessors. Before joining the Clinton administration, Rubin had worked for twenty-six years at the Wall Street investment bank Goldman, Sachs & Co., eventually becoming cochairman of the firm and a major fund-raiser for Democratic campaigns.

In his role of assistant to the president for economic policy, Rubin gained a reputation as an "honest broker" to the president similar to that envisioned by several past national security advisers.[71] During White House strategy sessions on the 1993 budget, which combined tax hikes and spending cuts to close the deficit by an estimated $500 billion over five years, the NEC was the primary forum for interagency negotiations. Although some critics charged that the NEC would gain influence at the expense of other appointed positions, such as the budget director and trade representative, Rubin himself was highly regarded as an effective coordinator of the often competing priorities of the different agencies.

Following Lloyd Bentsen's resignation in late 1994, Rubin was nominated to be Treasury secretary and was unanimously confirmed by the Senate in January 1995. He was replaced at the NEC by Laura D'Andrea Tyson, the chair of Clinton's Council of Economic Advisers (CEA). Tyson, a professor of economics at the University of California at Berkeley, had been supported for the post by Rubin. As head of Clinton's CEA, Tyson had been outspoken on a number of domestic issues, including advocating an increase in the minimum wage and questioning the economics of the administration's health care reform plan. Before entering the Clinton White House, Tyson was seen as a protectionist on trade issues, but as head of the CEA she had pushed for the implementation of the North American Free Trade Agreement over the objections of Democratic opponents.

Council of Economic Advisers

Twenty-five years after Congress established the Bureau of the Budget (renamed the Office of Management and Budget—OMB—in 1970), another organization was authorized to help the president handle the economy. The Council of Economic Advisers (CEA) was a central part of the 1946 Employment Act, which created a three-member committee to advise the president on wide-ranging issues confronting the nation's economic future. In the CEA the president had a means of documenting problems and their solutions.

The position of the CEA in the Executive Office of the President (EOP) is unique. Unlike other presidential offices of its stature, the council acts independently, advising the president instead of rigidly adhering to administration policy pronouncements. Throughout its existence the CEA has viewed its mission as professional—that of an adviser to the president to point out trends in the economy. Yet there is an unstated conflict in its role as an "objective observer" for the president: the council naturally wants to point out measures the president should take to adjust economic policies in light of its own analyses. Because the president appoints—and the Senate confirms—all three members of the council, the CEA has become an important presidential policy-making tool.

According to professor of public administration Edward S. Flash Jr., in an opinion shared by many observers, "The Council of Economic Advisers, originally characterized as a source of objective and politically neutral expertise, has instead emerged as an active and frequently influential font of knowledge and ideas, which often provides a foundation for the President's economic policy."[72]

This relationship has continued to characterize the status of the CEA within the Executive Office structure. Its small staff, supplemented by a large number of consultants, works closely with the White House, OMB, and congressional committees to advocate the administration's view of economic trends and policies, to identify the trouble spots and opportunities that lie ahead, and to suggest what the federal government might do to avoid or promote them.

Although slight fluctuations in staff size and some reorganization have occurred over the years, CEA's functions and character "have remained remarkably consistent," noted Roger Porter in his 1983 study of the CEA.[73] Its members and staff have come primarily from academe, usually "on loan" for two to three years. Political party affiliation is of little importance in selection of staff, and institutional loyalty to the council is not strong. The CEA, noted Porter, is primarily an analyst, not a policy broker. "It has no 'constituency'; rather, it has a 'client,' the president."[74]

ORIGINS AND DEVELOPMENT OF THE CEA

According to political scientist David Naveh, "The creation of the President's Council of Economic Advisers was a landmark in transforming the science of economics into a policymaking tool."[75] The CEA was an integral part of the 1946 Employment Act—post–World War II legislation that was born of the recognition that a laissez-faire economic policy would be inadequate for dealing with the transition from a wartime, high-production environment to a civilian economy. Transition aids and new economic goals were needed.[76] In general, the 1946 legislation was intended to provide employment opportunities for those returning to a civilian economy who were willing and able to work and to promote maximum employment, production, and purchasing power for the nation as a whole. At the same time the act emphasized the government's continued commitment to a free enterprise system.

To assist the administration in carrying out the mandate of the act, Congress, in a bipartisan effort, established the CEA. It was a unique undertaking: never before had an independent, professional council (instead of a single adviser) been established to provide the president with an objective overview of where the economy was headed. Moreover, the bill's requirement that the three members of the CEA be confirmed by the Senate also was unique at the time. The Capitol Hill initiative was viewed by many observers as an attempt to reassert congressional control over economic policy making, which had been conducted rather haphazardly during Franklin D. Roosevelt's presidency. Congress also established the Joint Committee on the Economic Report (later renamed the Joint Economic Committee), composed of House and Senate members, to prepare its own annual analysis of the economy and to critique the CEA findings.

Section 4 (a) of the Employment Act set out the qualifications for the three members of the CEA panel, "each of whom shall be a person who, as a result of his training, experience and attainment, is exceptionally qualified to analyze and interpret economic developments, to appraise programs and activities of the Government . . . and to recommend national economic policy to promote employment, production and purchasing power under free competitive enterprise." Each council member was to receive a salary of $15,000, and the total council budget was not to exceed $345,000.

The CEA's initial mandate—which has changed little over the years—was fivefold:

1. To assist and advise the president in preparing the president's annual economic report to Congress in January and to submit an annual report to the president during the previous December.

2. To gather, analyze, and interpret information on economic developments and trends.

3. To assess federal government programs in light of how well they are satisfying the president's goals and those of the Employment Act.

4. To provide ongoing studies and advice to the president on the state of the economy.

5. To provide additional studies and reports to the president as requested or on its own initiative.

Early Years of the CEA

Like other EOP offices, from the beginning the CEA and its stature have been highly dependent upon the chairman's (and the president's) perception of its mission. The relationship of the council members—particularly the chairman—to the president, as well as to Congress, also has been important. Perhaps the most decisive factor in the status of the council has been whether the CEA chairman has viewed his role as primarily that of an economic analyst or that of a major voice in economic policy making.[77]

President Harry S. Truman did not propose creation of the CEA. It was first proposed by the House Committee on Executive Expenditures. Congress overwhelmingly passed the measure, and in signing the bill on February 20, 1946, the president hailed it as "a commitment to take any and all measures necessary for a healthy economy."[78] The act did not specify whether the "exceptionally qualified" members of the CEA should come from academe. The president therefore received hundreds of applications from people of varied backgrounds. Even congressional supporters of the legislation were divided about whether the council's members should have solid academic credentials or practical experience in either government or business. The former attribute prevailed.

Truman nominated Edwin G. Nourse to serve as the first chairman of the CEA. Vice president of the Brookings Institution, Nourse was a highly regarded moderate conservative with a background in academics and agricultural policy. According to Erwin C. Hargrove and Samuel A. Morley in their oral history of the CEA, this appointment was seen as an "indication of [Truman's] desire to appoint a person of professional standing rather than partisan loyalty."[79] Truman named as vice chairman, however, an experienced government professional, Leon Keyser-

ling, who was a firm advocate of Roosevelt's New Deal policies and a principal drafter of the 1946 Employment Act. The third CEA member, John D. Clark, also was a liberal.

Differences soon emerged in the members' interpretations of the CEA's mission. Nourse, for example, did not wholeheartedly embrace the administration's economic policies, and he was firmly convinced that the economic advisers should assume a "scientifically objective" view without injecting themselves into policy making. Perhaps because he hailed from academe, Nourse found it difficult to adapt to the quick decision making and policy formulation that were facts of life for anyone seeking influence in Washington (although several succeeding "academic" CEA chairs adjusted to the atmosphere quite well). In any event, relations between Nourse and Truman were not close. Looking back on the situation some years later, Gerhard Colm, a CEA staff member during Nourse's term, observed that the president might have felt uncomfortable in dealing with the CEA chairman because Truman "did not feel equal to discussing economics with a man whom he respected as a great scholar and authority."[80] Nourse himself recognized the difficulties in his relations with the president:

After the lapse of a little more than a year, it can be said that there has been no single case when he [Truman] has called upon us in any specific situation for counsel in his study of any matter of national economic policy. While he has accepted the material which we have presented to him for use in the Economic Report and passed it on without material change . . . there is no clear evidence that at any juncture we had any tangible influence on the formation of policy. . . .[81]

In an article written in 1948, Nourse emphasized that the council's function was to assist the president in a strictly advisory manner.[82] But the chairman soon found himself outvoted on a controversial issue—whether CEA members should testify on Capitol Hill before the Joint Committee on the Economic Report. Nourse refused to appear on the grounds that doing so would jeopardize the CEA's relationship of confidentiality with the president and that the council's economic policy role was to advise, not advocate. (The Employment Act did not require CEA congressional testimony, nor did it mandate council accountability to the joint committee.)

Nourse thus viewed the CEA's role as somewhat like that of a top administrator in a large corporation—primarily advisory, with policy decisions and implementation left in the hands of professional executives.[83] During his tenure the CEA expanded its research capabilities, drawing on a coterie of outside specialists for consultation. Professionalism, not politics, was the trademark of Nourse's council.

With the 1948 presidential elections approaching, Keyserling and Clark expressed their wish to be helpful by testifying in behalf of the administration's economic programs. Truman encouraged such activity, and the two CEA members complied, thereby fueling dissension within the council's ranks. In 1948 a midyear CEA economic review contained a minority statement written by Chairman Nourse. A few months earlier the Hoover Commission on the Organization of the Executive Branch had recommended ending the ambiguity in relations between the CEA chairman and members by forming an Office of Economic Adviser with a single head. Although a version of this recommendation was to take effect later, no action was taken at the time.

Nourse resigned in November 1949 and was succeeded by Keyserling, who almost immediately set about redefining the CEA's philosophy and position. Although he played a more active role as chairman than Nourse, Keyserling tolerated statements of disagreement by his colleagues. He was more interested than his predecessor in organization of the staff, and he encouraged outside contacts and informality. Keyserling also established a number of interagency committees chaired by council staff, thereby affording a greater role for the CEA in developing government programs. He continued, however, like Nourse, to hire staff analysts who were familiar with government bureaucracy and legislative procedures.

"Unlike Nourse, Keyserling perceived the CEA as trustee for the president's economic programs in Congress," wrote Hargrove and Morley. "He rejected Nourse's claims to objectivity and nonpartisanship, claiming instead that the Council was part of the administration and should act accordingly."[84] The result was a closer relationship with the president and White House staff. Keyserling contributed to drafts of presidential speeches, used the media to publicize the CEA's work, and was made a de facto member of the cabinet and National Security Council. Indeed, he viewed the CEA's role as equivalent to that of a cabinet office, which included appearances before Congress to explain and defend presidential economic proposals. Keyserling himself became increasingly active in Democratic Party politics. Partly for this reason, he clashed with the Republican-controlled Joint Committee on the Economic Report, which issued a critique of the CEA's Economic Report as overly political and paving a path to a controlled economy.

Nonetheless, according to presidential scholar Stephen Hess, the CEA under Keyserling

became a serious contending force in the formulation of administration policy.... Freed of operating responsibility (with the exception of preparing the Economic Report) and located in close proximity to the President, the CEA had ample opportunity to develop and to expound its judgments within the higher reaches of the administration....

Congress was wrong in its belief that it could direct the president to accept economic advice; the experience under Nourse graphically proved otherwise. But it was right in believing that the quantity and quality of economic advice might be force-fed. The presence of a group of professional economists in the White House resulted in additional sources of information and analysis, which the President absorbed, often through his personal staff, sometimes by osmosis.[85]

Changes under Eisenhower

By the time Dwight D. Eisenhower entered office, the CEA's existence was in jeopardy. The Republicans in Congress had taken issue with the council's role and activities under Keyserling. Thus, in considering a bill providing continuing appropriations for the council, Congress was uncertain whether to grant sup-

plemental funding to continue the existing CEA or to pass new legislation restructuring it. Congress finally decided to provide monies for the rest of the fiscal year, but for only one economic adviser. Shortly after his inauguration, however, Eisenhower decided to continue the CEA, but in its previous form as a strictly professional, nonpolitical body whose primary mission was to provide factual advice. He asked his White House staff to seek out "the best man in the country on the ups and downs of business."[86] On the advice of Gabriel Hauge, Eisenhower's assistant on economic matters, the president selected Arthur F. Burns, a highly respected economist, to assume the post. Burns, a "Democrat for Eisenhower," had impressive academic credentials as a professor of economics at Columbia University and the director of the National Bureau of Economic Research. He also was well known for his study of business cycles. "The CEA survived its crucial transition in administrations because of the increased stake of the President in the behavior of the economy, because the council members and their staff were congenial to the President, and because they provided the President with information that he considered immediately useful," concluded Hess.[87]

In August 1953, shortly after assuming office, Eisenhower issued Reorganization Plan 9, which effected far-reaching changes in the CEA's structure. Much of the rearrangement had been suggested by Burns. The major change of the brief reorganization order was to make the chairman—not the three-person council—the linchpin of CEA contacts with the president. The post of CEA vice chairman was eliminated. In a letter accompanying the reorganization plan, Eisenhower declared that its purpose was "to take the appropriate actions to reinvigorate and make more effective the operations of the CEA."

Burns, a newcomer to the Washington scene, soon made his mark on the CEA. Not only was he the preeminent member of the council as its spokesman to the president, but as CEA chairman he also had the sole authority for employing staff, specialists, and consultants. Only three members of the staff had remained on board from the Keyserling era, and Burns set about filling the vacancies with a substantial number of academic economists. He felt more comfortable working with colleagues from academe, and he viewed their presence as "a means to depoliticize the CEA and establish its professional credibility."[88]

Like Nourse, Burns viewed his role as independent, but he was less objective. Hargrove and Morley observed that "if the Burns Council was determined to stay out of the political spotlight, it nevertheless took an active role in policy formation that extended beyond the scientific expertise and neutral competency that Edwin Nourse had sought during his tenure."[89] Adhering to the policies of the first CEA chairman, Burns refused to appear before the Joint Economic Committee in public hearings (a decision that severely strained his relations with Congress), yet he made numerous public appearances to defend the president's programs. "While Keyserling had encouraged policy considerations by the staff, Burns felt the staff's role was simply to advise him, providing him with whatever information he needed to make the necessary policy decisions," wrote Hargrove and

Morley. "He wanted a completely objective support staff."[90] Burns controlled all staff contacts with administration agencies (the staff totaled thirty full-time and part-time professionals as well as consultants).

During his tenure as council chairman, Burns developed close contact with the president, and he regularly advised the cabinet. In 1953 he was designated chairman of the new Advisory Board on Economic Growth and Stability, an economic sub-cabinet. Task forces and interagency groups abounded under Burns.

Burns resigned in December 1956 and was replaced by CEA member Raymond J. Saulnier, who, like his predecessor, viewed the council's mission as that of an objective adviser. Saulnier, however, was more inclined to delegate responsibility to his colleagues on the council. Although his relationship with the president was not as close as that enjoyed by Burns, the CEA chairman continued to attend all cabinet meetings, and he helped draft speeches and legislation. The council was in fact an active participant in policy making.

That role was spurred in part by Treasury Secretary Robert B. Anderson, who in 1957 suggested that he, Saulnier, Federal Reserve chairman William McChesney Martin Jr., and presidential economic adviser Hauge consult regularly on economic issues and trends. The group, known as the "little four" or "financial committee," was a consultative, not a policy-making, body. It was the precursor of President John F. Kennedy's Troika and Quadriad.

The CEA in the 1960s

The tendency to appoint academics to CEA positions intensified during President Kennedy's three years in office, beginning in 1961. Kennedy nominated Walter W. Heller, a well-respected economics professor from the University of Minnesota, to chair the council, and he selected professors James Tobin of Yale University and Kermit Gordon of Williams College as the remaining members. When the president approached Tobin with the offer of the position, the professor hesitated, remarking, "I'm afraid I am only an ivory tower economist." Kennedy responded, "That is the best kind. I am only an ivory tower president."[91] All three council members, however, had extensive Washington experience.

As before, staff vacancies were filled primarily by academicians. Most were young and lacking government experience, but they were eager to apply their knowledge to the many challenges of the New Frontier.[92] "They were, in short, 'action intellectuals,'" wrote Hess. "They knew the proper way to lecture the President, and a CEA memorandum reached Kennedy's desk on the average of once every third day. Before long, CEA members were taking on the sort of programmatic assignments that had been unknown to prior councils, such as developing legislative proposals regarding poverty and transportation."[93]

One of the president's close personal advisers, Heller was an active chairman, concerned more with policy than economic theory. According to Hargrove and Morley, "He saw nothing wrong with the CEA publicly advocating the policies it felt to be economically wise and educating the public in the 'New Economics' espoused by himself and his colleagues."[94] President Kennedy was a bit more conservative than his CEA, but he encouraged Heller and his colleagues to expound their views in public congressional testimony, speeches, and articles.

As chairman of the CEA, Heller established the Quadriad—composed of the heads of the CEA, Federal Reserve Board, BOB, and Treasury—which met regularly. (The Troika was composed of the heads of the CEA, BOB, and Treasury.) The CEA assumed an active role in wage-price stabilization policy in 1961 and began work on poverty programs. This role continued under President Lyndon B. Johnson (1963–1968), who wholeheartedly embraced the War on Poverty and continued the wage-price guideposts.

Heller resigned in November 1964 and was succeeded by Gardner Ackley, a professor of economics at the University of Michigan, who had served as a CEA member since 1962. Ackley made few policy changes. The council's staff remained small (sixteen professional economists), but the chairman retained full access to the president. Ackley was succeeded for a brief period by Arthur M. Okun (1968–1969), the youngest chairman in the council's history (he was thirty-nine), who had been responsible for the CEA's economic forecasts. Under both Ackley and Okun the CEA gained influence as the Vietnam War impinged on the economy and the president became increasingly preoccupied with the conflict, leaving much of domestic policy making to others.

The Nixon and Carter Eras

Shortly after his victory in 1968, Republican president-elect Richard Nixon announced that Paul W. McCracken, a member of the CEA under Eisenhower, would become its new chairman. Characterized as a "centrist," the new CEA chairman believed that fiscal policies (which determine the amount of taxing and spending) and monetary policies (which determine the amount of currency and credit in the country) were equally important in establishing the nation's long-term economic goals.

Although Nixon retained the Troika and Quadriad, the Troika worked more closely with the White House staff than with the president, while the Quadriad assumed a larger role in macroeconomic policy making. The CEA also participated in the cabinet's Council on Economic Policy as well as White House working groups on economic matters convened by John D. Ehrlichman, the president's domestic policy adviser. Although the council was represented in daily White House staff meetings, Nixon's establishment of the Domestic Council under Ehrlichman and reorganization of the Bureau of the Budget into the Office of Management and Budget cut into the CEA's influence on economic policy.

The major economic problem confronting the administration during Nixon's first term was inflation. McCracken was a principal force in the president's decision to impose wage and price controls in 1971. He served as chairman of the Executive

Policy Committee of the Cost of Living Council (CLC), which was established to monitor the freeze. The policy committee was responsible for interpreting existing policies and recommending new ones to the CLC.

In January 1972 Herbert Stein, a council member and senior fellow at the Brookings Institution, became chairman of the CEA, serving until September 1974. Although Stein was "perhaps the most ardent free-marketer and opponent of economic controls within the Nixon administration,"[95] by the time he assumed the CEA leadership he had come to believe in the necessity of wage and price controls. During his tenure the CEA continued to be represented on the CLC, the Council on Economic Policy, the Domestic Council, and the Council on International Economic Policy, but its influence diminished as that of the Treasury secretary grew under John B. Connally and his successor, George P. Shultz.

That situation was reversed with the accession of Nixon's vice president, Gerald R. Ford, to the presidency following Nixon's resignation in 1974. The new CEA chairman, Alan Greenspan, had already been recruited by Nixon. Unlike previous heads of the CEA, Greenspan came from the business community, where he was a consultant. He was a critic of government intervention in the economy and an advocate of reduced government spending to achieve a balanced budget. Greenspan's "sound reputation as a forecaster and his plans for restoring the CEA to an advisory role easily won him the support of the profession," wrote Hargrove and Morley. "Although he was perhaps the most conservative chairman in the council's history, even the more liberal past chairmen affirmed their respect for his abilities as an economist. He announced intentions to 'depoliticize' the CEA and avoid a public role."[96] According to Greenspan, he did this by assuming a low profile as CEA chairman, making few speeches, reducing congressional contacts, and canceling monthly press briefings. And during his tenure the Troika and Quadriad all but faded from view.

President Jimmy Carter entered the White House in 1977 as unemployment was running at 6–7 percent, the budget deficit was rising, and inflation was pegged at 5–6 percent. Carter's new CEA chairman, Charles L. Schultze, came from the Brookings Institution; he also had served in the CEA and OMB. Much of Schultze's preinaugural package of programs to stimulate the economy (with the goal of returning to full employment without inflation) was adopted by the Carter administration. "It is difficult to imagine a selection for the CEA chairmanship who could have won more respect or have been more in the mainstream of pragmatic, liberal approaches to economic policy," wrote Hargrove and Morley.[97] Schultze has been described as a liberal Democrat and a Keynesian economist who believed that government could actively influence the economy through fiscal policy to insure healthy expansion. But he also was known as a hard-headed skeptic when it came to assessing the value of government spending programs.

Congress adopted Schultze's plan to stimulate the economy

quickly through tax refunds that would generate business and consumer confidence. Testifying before the House Budget Committee in January 1977, the CEA chairman noted, "This package has been designed to tread prudently between the twin risks of over- and under-stimulation."[98]

Regulatory reform was another concern of the president and his economic adviser. As chairman of both the CEA and the Regulatory Analysis Review Group, Schultze focused attention on the inflationary consequences of many proposed regulations and favored in some cases the use of taxation, rather than specific standard setting, as a cost-effective approach to compliance. Regulatory reform became even more of a major issue during Ronald Reagan's presidency, but primary responsibility for it was lodged in OMB. (See "Office of Management and Budget," p. 1112.)

The CEA under Reagan

Reagan's first appointment to the CEA leadership, Murray Weidenbaum, reflected the president's view that one of the major tasks of his administration was to cut down on federal regulations. Weidenbaum, a former assistant secretary of the Treasury and head of the Center for the Study of American Business at Washington University in St. Louis, was a conservative who advocated a cost-benefit analysis approach to weeding out unnecessary government rules.

It became apparent soon after his appointment to the CEA, however, that Weidenbaum's talents would be better used in a position in which he had a decisive role in pruning federal regulations—and that position had been created in the OMB's new Office of Information and Regulatory Affairs. Weidenbaum also had come under attack for his 1981 congressional testimony that played down the importance of deficits, appearing to contradict years of Republican rhetoric. Even though White House spokespersons later denied that Weidenbaum's remarks reflected administration policy, stunned Senate Republicans denounced the CEA chairman's comments as "incredible," "disheartening," and "foolish."[99]

Weidenbaum was succeeded by Martin S. Feldstein, a professor at Harvard University and president of the National Bureau of Economic Research. Feldstein served as CEA chairman for almost two years (from October 1982 to July 1984), but, ironically, his outspoken calls for deficit reduction above all other issues—including the need to increase defense spending—angered other administration officials.

Feldstein's replacement was an undersecretary of the Treasury, Beryl W. Sprinkel, who was confirmed by the Senate in April 1985. Sprinkel, a former Chicago bank executive and economics professor, had close personal ties to Donald T. Regan, the president's chief of staff. Although Sprinkel had direct contacts with the president, Treasury Secretary James A. Baker III was the Reagan administration's chief economic spokesperson. Sprinkel's first economic forecast, envisioning strong economic growth, was attacked as excessively rosy by members of Congress when it was presented to them in February 1986. Other economists appearing before the Joint Economic Committee were equally skeptical about the CEA's projected economic growth rate.

The controversy continued in 1987. In presenting the annual Economic Report to Congress, Sprinkel observed that "the U.S. economy demonstrates continued strength as it moves into the fifth year of the current economic expansion, but . . . important sectoral and structural problems remain." Those problems, discussed in the report, included the large and persistent budget and trade deficits.[100]

Under George Bush's appointee as CEA chair, Stanford economist Michael Boskin, the role of the CEA shifted toward greater involvement in deficit-reduction issues. Boskin, a noted monetarist, was part of the powerful "economic subpresidency" within the Bush White House, and although he did not wield the influence shared by budget director Richard Darman and chief of staff John Sununu, he frequently acted as spokesperson for the administration.[101]

In his first annual economic report, released in March 1990, Boskin gave overall praise to the earlier Reagan economic policies and endorsed a continuation of the Gramm-Rudman Act beyond 1993. That act, passed in 1985 and modified in 1987, specified annual deficit targets and an automatic spending-cut process. The original Gramm-Rudman (named after its congressional authors) bill set a goal of a balanced budget by 1992, later pushed back to 1993. In his report, Boskin forecast the elimination of the federal budget deficit by 1996, and was immediately criticized for relying on overly optimistic economic projections and disproportionate cuts in domestic spending. His second annual report, released at the height of the 1991 Persian Gulf War, contained a less rosy forecast, reflecting the expenses of the massive Operation Desert Storm, higher than expected costs to bail out the savings and loan industry, and slower economic growth due to the recession. Nonetheless, Boskin anticipated a speedy recovery from the recession.

Boskin was also a member of Vice President Dan Quayle's controversial Council on Competitiveness, which had been established to review the costs and benefits of regulation, particularly concerning the environment, and to revise or suspend those that were seen as unnecessarily burdensome to industry. The council met in closed session, and in the second half of the Bush administration it successfully pressured the EPA and other agencies to hold up numerous environmental rules and regulations. The council's secret operations drew protests that it was acting illegally by violating established administrative and regulatory procedures. Boskin was also among the conservative White House officials who urged the president to reject the 1991 Department of Energy (DOE) comprehensive national energy strategy, objecting to the larger governmental role and strengthened conservation measures called for by the original DOE plan. Together with Darman and Sununu, Boskin created the final administration plan, which emphasized energy production initiatives and eliminated proposed increases in energy taxes.

Like most of his predecessors, President Bill Clinton appointed a member of the academic community to the CEA post. A professor of economics at the University of California at Berkeley, Laura D'Andrea Tyson had concentrated on trade and competitiveness issues and was seen by some as too much of a protectionist on trade issues. During her confirmation hearings, however, Tyson emphasized her commitment to free-market principles and called for the government to become more involved in opening foreign markets, expanding civilian research, and training workers to help U.S. industry compete against subsidized and protected foreign competitors. During her first year at the CEA, Tyson helped Clinton defend the North American Free Trade Agreement (NAFTA) against its critics in the Democratic Congress. In 1994 the council was also optimistic about the benefits of the new General Agreement on Tariffs and Trade (GATT), estimating that the opening of new export markets would increase U.S. national income by $100 billion ten years after GATT went into effect in 1995.

Although the council remained a primary advisory body to the president on economic issues, some of its stature was absorbed by the new National Economic Council (NEC), which coordinated policy between several agencies and served as a gatekeeper to the president on major economic decisions, such as the administration's deficit reduction proposals. Nonetheless, Tyson won praise for her pragmatism and analytical skills; the CEA correctly forecast the 1993 growth rate and slightly underestimated improvements in inflation, unemployment, and interest rates, in contrast to previous administrations' overly optimistic forecasts. In February 1995 Tyson became chair of NEC, replacing Robert E. Rubin, who left to become secretary of Treasury. In her place, Clinton appointed Joseph E. Stiglitz, a Stanford University professor who had been a member of the CEA since 1993.

ORGANIZATION AND FUNCTIONS OF THE CEA

The activities of the president's Council of Economic Advisers include:

• Briefing the president on overall economic policy objectives and programs that need to be implemented

• Preparing an annual economic report to the president and an Economic Report of the President for submission to Congress in January

• Informing the president on a continuing basis of major policy issues, including international economic issues

• Chairing an interagency forecasting group that includes the Treasury and OMB for developing economic projections

• Participating in the cabinet-level National Economic Council to discuss the economic effects of tax reform, trade and balance-of-payments issues, international policy coordination, and budget reform

The CEA participates as well in the cabinet-level Domestic Policy Council and has dealt with such issues as agricultural problems, regulatory and antitrust reforms, catastrophic health insurance, welfare reform, energy policy, transportation and communications regulation, and tax policy.

The CEA chair also heads the economic policy committee of the twenty-four-nation Organization for Economic Cooperation and Development (OECD) and other OECD committees as well. In 1995 the professional staff of the three-member council consisted of a special assistant and thirty-five full-time employees, evenly divided between economists and support staff.

Most CEA heads and staff members have been outspoken in their belief that the council's staff should remain small and transitory (most have tenured positions elsewhere). Indeed, the small size of the staff and its transitory nature have been considered advantages. The party affiliations of staff members remain of little importance.

The CEA has continued to avoid operational responsibility for programs, serving instead as an adviser to the president to forecast economic trends and provide analyses of issues. The CEA's influence on administration economic policy making has always depended on three factors: the quality of its advice, the chair's perception of CEA's role, and the relation between the president and the council (particularly the chair). But these factors have their nuances. "The CEA was created by Congress in 1946 to force presidents to accept economic advice in a particular form. Yet they have chosen to use or not use the CEA largely on the basis of whether they preferred working with an individual council chairman to receiving economic advice from other sources," wrote Hess.[102] According to former CEA chair Arthur Okun,

When the President's economists decide to go on public record, they cannot serve two masters. They cannot speak for both the President and for the [economics] profession. And they cannot speak for the Profession publicly and still maintain confidence and rapport internally with the President. The choice should be clear. It is far more important for society and for the Profession to have economists who maintain rapport with the President and thus have the greatest influence on the inside.[103]

Office of the U.S. Trade Representative

The Office of the Special Representative for Trade Negotiations was established in 1963 and redesignated the Office of the U.S. Trade Representative (USTR) in 1980. The original office was created in response to a perception that a presidential spokesperson was needed to deal with the increasingly complex issues facing the nation in its economic contacts with foreign nations. In 1962 the government's trade philosophy—both in Congress and within the Kennedy administration—advocated opening the doors to international transactions and promoting free trade.

ORIGINS AND DEVELOPMENT OF THE TRADE OFFICE

The removal of barriers to the free flow of international trade was a principal goal of American foreign policy for more than two decades following World War II.[104] With little variation, presidents Harry S. Truman, Dwight D. Eisenhower, John F. Kennedy, and Lyndon B. Johnson held that a liberal trade policy, no less than foreign aid, was an essential means of establishing a more secure and prosperous world. Each was forced to do battle, however, with an array of protectionist interests whose pressures on Congress complemented a historic legislative view that tariffs were a domestic matter, not to be subordinated to foreign policy objectives.

By 1962 there were new and compelling reasons for the United States to champion the free flow of trade. Although exports and imports remained small in relation to a gross national product of more than $500 billion, they occupied an increasingly important role in an economy beset by a slow rate of growth. Moreover, despite its substantial and continuing surplus of exports over imports, the United States was experiencing severe deficits in its total international accounts because of heavy expenditures abroad for military and other purposes. Of the several alternatives for bringing the payments deficit under control, rapid expansion of exports was in many ways the most desirable.

Creation of the Trade Office

The expansion of exports depended, however, upon reversal of a new trend toward protectionism abroad, as evidenced in the common tariff wall constructed by the six-member European Community (EC or Common Market) in 1957. In 1962 the large economic stake of the United States in the freest possible access to world markets, as well as the overriding political interest of the United States in building a strong and interdependent free world, led Congress to authorize President Kennedy to take a new initiative in behalf of trade liberalization. Even though some U.S. industries were unable or unwilling to compete with the products of other nations, the Trade Expansion Act of 1962 reflected the majority view that freer trade was no longer a choice but a necessity for the United States.

In a special message sent to Capitol Hill on January 25, 1962, Kennedy asked Congress for unprecedented authority to negotiate with the Common Market for reciprocal tariff concessions. With the help of strong bipartisan support in the business community and concessions to potentially obstructive interests, Kennedy finally got substantially all that he wanted in the Trade Expansion Act of 1962 (PL 88-794). The act granted the president far-reaching tariff-cutting authority and provided safeguards against damage to American industry and agriculture. The act also authorized the formation of a cabinet-level Interagency Trade Organization and the establishment of the post of special representative for trade negotiations, to act as the chief U.S. spokesperson in trade talks. On January 15, 1963, Kennedy appointed Christian A. Herter, secretary of state under Eisenhower, to the new post. According to a former trade negotiator, Herter "had supported the purposes of the bill from the outset and had the courage to resist any efforts of special interest groups to divert him from achieving them."[105] Herter was the chief U.S. negotiator for the "Kennedy round" of tariff-cutting talks (1963–1967), held under the auspices of the General Agreement on Tariffs and Trade (GATT, formed in 1947, had a membership of about 124 nations in 1995).

1974 Trade Act

By the late 1960s and early 1970s competition for world markets was growing, the U.S. share of world trade was in persistent decline, and protectionist sentiment was on the rise. Like his predecessors, however, President Richard Nixon remained committed to free trade, although conflicts with the EC and Japan, in particular, over trade reciprocity and quotas were occurring more frequently. In late 1969 the president sent Congress legislation that would have permitted him to retain his tariff-cutting authority while increasing assistance to U.S. businesses harmed by imports. But the protectionist mood on Capitol Hill was strong, and by the end of 1970 the administration's bill had been altered severely by the House of Representatives. The measure never reached the president's desk.

In 1973 Nixon resubmitted proposals for new trade-negotiating authority, largely in response to growing trade deficits and as the major industrial nations were preparing for another series of trade negotiations (known as the Tokyo round). In December 1974, after a year's delay, Congress passed the 1974 Trade Act (PL 93-618), which authorized U.S. participation in the tariff negotiations and established a cabinet-level special trade representative's office within the Executive Office of the President. The office was given the powers and responsibilities needed to coordinate trade policy.

Carter Reorganization

The Tokyo round of negotiations on reducing nontariff barriers to trade was completed in 1979. The bill (PL 96-39) implementing the agreement, submitted by President Jimmy Carter that same year and quickly approved by Congress, consolidated and coordinated U.S. trade policy making.[106] Carter effected the consolidation and coordination by Executive Order 12188 in January 1980. Under this act, the U.S. trade representative was designated as the nation's chief trade negotiator and U.S. representative in the major international trade organizations. The act also transferred domestic oversight of most trade programs from the Treasury to the Department of Commerce, including responsibility for determining whether countervailing tariffs or antidumping duties should be imposed for what were considered unfair trade practices or excessive foreign imports. Carter's final trade reorganization plan was close to House proposals but fell short of demands made by the Senate for a separate trade department.

Reagan's Trade Representative

President Ronald Reagan continued his predecessors' commitment to free trade despite the deepening trade deficit, mounting concern about the competitiveness of U.S. products abroad, and growing criticism about the restrictiveness of other

nations' markets. All three concerns applied primarily to Japan. Reagan's first trade representative, William E. Brock III, remained an advocate of free trade. As he noted in January 1983: "In recent years four out of five of the new U.S. jobs in manufacturing have been created by international trade. One out of every three acres planted by American farmers is producing crops for export internationally and the potential for growth is unlimited."[107] But Brock also summarized the ironies and difficult choices in the protectionism versus free-trade debates. "Everyone is against protectionism in the abstract," he said in 1983. "That is easy. It is another matter to make the hard, courageous choices when it is your industry or your business that appears to be hurt by foreign competition."[108]

Brock was succeeded in June 1985 by Clayton Yeutter, who was head of the Chicago Mercantile Exchange when nominated. Yeutter had served as deputy special trade representative during the administration of Gerald R. Ford and as assistant secretary of agriculture under Nixon. In his confirmation hearings Yeutter said he was prepared to take a more aggressive approach to dealing with trade pressures. He pledged to step up enforcement of existing statutes, including provisions that protected U.S. business from foreign products sold in the United States at unfairly low prices. And he emphasized the need for international trade talks, identifying the biggest problem as that of convincing other nations to lower nontariff barriers, such as foreign government purchasing programs, that discriminated against U.S. exports. To set the agenda for trade talks, Yeutter planned to consult actively with Congress and the business community. He also indicated that he was prepared to take a pragmatic approach to trade.[109]

Trade in the 1990s

By the end of the 1980s the U.S. trade balance had fallen deeply into deficit as imports outpaced exports by tens of billions of dollars each year. Under President George Bush the activities of the USTR received increasing public and media attention as the administration negotiated two major trade agreements, the Uruguay round of the GATT and the North American Free Trade Agreement (NAFTA), which would join the United States, Canada, and Mexico into a free-trade zone. Bush appointed Carla A. Hills, a Washington, D.C., lawyer and former secretary of housing and urban development under President Ford.

The Uruguay round, which began in 1986, was the seventh GATT renegotiation and was considered the most ambitious since GATT was established after World War II. In general, the Uruguay round was aimed at reducing worldwide tariffs by more than one-third and reducing agricultural subsidies. When the talks opened, Reagan's trade secretary, Yeutter, had set out to eliminate agricultural subsidies by the year 2000, but Hills pulled back from that goal and instead sought deep cuts in subsidies in coming years. The Uruguay round had been scheduled to end in 1990, but late that year the talks broke down because of disagreements between the United States, Japan, and the twelve-

Trade was a major issue from the outset of the Clinton administration. U.S. Trade Representative Mickey Kantor, despite a limited background in international trade issues, played a pivotal role in wrapping up negotiations on the North American Free Trade Agreement and the revised General Agreement on Tariffs and Trade. Above, Kantor testifies during his January 19, 1993, Senate confirmation hearing.

member European Community (EC) over farm subsidies. Before the talks resumed in early 1991, Ambassador Hills put the likelihood of reaching an agreement at 25 percent.

The White House lobbied Congress intensively for a renewal of "fast-track" procedures governing approval of trade agreements. Fast-track authority required Congress to approve or disapprove a trade agreement within sixty days of its introduction, and also required an up or down vote without amendments. The measure covered both the stalled GATT talks and the recently opened NAFTA talks. It was intended to pressure negotiators to complete the Uruguay round and to give NAFTA negotiators confidence that the terms they reached would not be dismantled or rejected by congressional opponents. Hills met personally with about 150 members of Congress, including two-thirds of the Senate. The deputy trade representative and chief GATT negotiator, Rufus Yerxa, was brought back from his post in Geneva to lobby members of the House Ways and Means Committee, where he had once been a top committee aide. In winning approval of fast-track procedures, the administration made some concessions on its NAFTA plans, including promises to reject any weakening of U.S. environmental laws, to provide adjustment assistance to displaced workers, and to provide long transition periods for some U.S. industries threatened by the pact.

Shortly before he left office, President Bush signed NAFTA, which would eliminate tariffs, duties, and other trade barriers among the three countries over fifteen years. The challenge of getting the pact through Congress was left to his successor, Bill Clinton.

Clinton's trade representative, Mickey Kantor, was a close friend who had been active in high-level Democratic politics for more than twenty years and had served as Clinton's campaign manager in 1992. A Los Angeles lawyer and experienced lobbyist, Kantor did not have any previous international trade experience, but he had a reputation as a skilled negotiator.

Kantor persuaded Clinton to reopen NAFTA talks to negotiate side agreements with Mexico ensuring enforcement of labor and environmental laws. Although these measures were intended to win over the trade pact's staunchest congressional opponents, the debate about the implementing legislation, considered under fast-track procedures with the side agreements, remained explosive, particularly in the House of Representatives. Final congressional approval of NAFTA in late 1993 ranked as one of Clinton's most important victories.

Likewise, the Uruguay round of GATT talks continued into the Clinton administration and were finally completed in December 1993, with final signing by more than 117 member nations in April 1994. Kantor was credited with gaining the long-sought cuts in agricultural subsidies that had plagued earlier U.S. negotiators and with orchestrating an agreement on lowering industrial tariffs, known as the Market Access Agreement. Although not as bitter as the fight over NAFTA, the GATT-enacting legislation faced similar debate in Congress. It was approved in late 1994 in a rare lame-duck session, after both houses postponed the GATT vote until after the midterm election. *(See also International Trade Negotiations, p. 738, in Chapter 16, Vol. I.)*

ORGANIZATION AND FUNCTIONS OF THE TRADE OFFICE

The trade office is headed by the U.S. trade representative (USTR), a cabinet-level official with the rank of ambassador who is directly responsible to the president and Congress.[110] The representative is confirmed by the Senate and thus testifies before congressional committees. Of the three deputy representatives, who also have ambassadorial rank, two are located in Washington, D.C., and one is in Geneva, Switzerland (GATT headquarters).

The USTR is the president's chief adviser on international trade policy and is responsible for developing this policy and coordinating its implementation. The holder of this position also acts as the nation's chief negotiator for international trade agreements. The USTR serves as an ex officio member of the boards of directors of the Export-Import Bank and the Overseas Private Investment Corporation and sits on the National Advisory Council for International Monetary and Financial Policy.

With the advice of the cabinet-level National Economic Council, of which it is a member, the USTR office provides policy guidance on issues related to international trade, including the expansion of U.S. exports; matters concerning GATT; overall U.S. trade policy on unfair trade practices; international trade issues involving energy; and direct investment matters, to the extent they are trade related.

As the principal trade negotiator for the United States, the U.S. trade representative is the chief U.S. representative at international negotiations. These include all activities of GATT; discussions, meetings, and negotiations within the Organization for Economic Cooperation and Development (OECD) on matters affecting trade and commodity issues; meetings of the United Nations Conference on Trade and Development (UNCTAD) and other multilateral institutions dealing with trade and commodity issues; and other bilateral and multilateral negotiations at which trade, including East-West trade or commodities, is the primary issue.

The deputy USTR in Geneva is the U.S. representative to GATT and also is responsible for negotiations on commerce and trade under UNCTAD. One of the deputy trade representatives located in Washington, D.C., oversees trade policy coordination and bilateral and multilateral negotiations outside GATT and UNCTAD. This official is also responsible for USTR's offices for trade policy and analysis, trade policy coordination, and bilateral trade negotiations. The second deputy located in Washington is responsible for sectoral and external affairs and management, including industry and services, agriculture and commodities, congressional affairs, public affairs and private sector liaison, management, and computer operations. The chief textile negotiator, who also has ambassadorial rank, has primary responsibility for negotiating textile agreements and representing the government in matters related to textile trade.

The office has assistant trade representatives for the different region-specific offices: Canada and Mexico; Japan and China; Latin America, Caribbean, and Africa; Asia and the Pacific; and Europe and the Mediterranean. There also are assistant U.S. trade representatives responsible for special issues such as dispute resolution, trade policy coordination, industry, intellectual property and the environment, agriculture, and services, investment, and science and technology. Finally, the USTR office includes a counselor to the trade representative who provides advice on trade policy and represents the United States on the OECD trade committee.

In 1995 the staff of the office of the U.S. Trade Representative numbered 168.

Office of Science and Technology Policy

Although it was formally established in 1976, the president's Office of Science and Technology Policy (OSTP) has had a long history that began during World War II, when the government recognized that science and technology were vital to the nation's military capabilities.

According to the National Science and Technology Policy, Organizations, and Priorities Act of 1976 (PL 94-282), OSTP was to provide "a source of scientific and technological analysis and judgment for the president with respect to major policies, plans and programs of the federal government." Its mission became even more central to the government during the late 1970s and 1980s as scientific and technological breakthroughs in other parts of the world challenged America's leadership. The urgency of the situation was addressed in stark terms by the OSTP in its 1983–1984 biennial report:

A quarter century ago, U.S. industry had few worries about competition. The United States dominated essentially all industrial technologies and had always been able to develop and introduce them at its own pace. Today we must use our technological resources much more aggressively.

In the decades after World War II, the United States built the world's largest research and development capability, primarily through investment of Federal money. . . . Industry was strongly stimulated by and benefited from this Federal role. But the commercial market for technology has expanded tremendously in the past decade. . . . Non-Federal spending for research and development reached that of the Federal Government in 1978 and has been rising ever since.

Today, Federal research and development [R & D] spending is about 46 percent of the national total. It is industry, not Government, that is pushing hardest at technological frontiers in many areas.[111]

Although OSTP has tried to encourage the government to participate in a wide range of R & D efforts, the science counselors in the Executive Office of the President (EOP), like the academicians who generally compose the Council of Economic Advisers, have often found it difficult to make their voices heard in the highly political and bureaucratic environment of the nation's capital.

ORIGINS AND DEVELOPMENT OF OSTP

During World War II a number of White House advisory panels were created, primarily to serve the war effort. In 1950 President Harry S. Truman signed a bill establishing the National Science Foundation (NSF); a year later he appointed a Science Advisory Committee in the Office of Defense Mobilization. That panel was a forerunner of President Dwight D. Eisenhower's Presidential Science Advisory Committee (PSAC). According to Lee A. Dubridge, President Richard Nixon's science adviser, "PSAC and the science adviser were regarded as the capstone of the government's scientific advisory structure. . . ." The president, said Dubridge, "found it very helpful to have an unbiased, broadly-based and distinguished scientific group helping him to unravel the many technical problems which he faced in defense, space, and various civilian enterprises." Under Eisenhower, concluded Dubridge, "PSAC developed some extraordinarily penetrating and far-reaching recommendations."[112]

The need to upgrade U.S. scientific efforts was perceived as even more urgent after the Soviet Union launched the *Sputnik I* satellite in 1957. Americans, who had considered their country in the forefront of scientific and technological know-how, were shocked that their major adversary appeared to be taking the lead in space efforts. In light of that concern, PSAC recommended creation of the National Aeronautics and Space Administration (NASA).

According to James R. Killian Jr., science adviser to Eisenhower and chairman of PSAC (after *Sputnik I,* he was given the title of special assistant to the president for science and technology), PSAC worked very closely with the president, the National

Security Council, and the budget bureau. Most PSAC members were nonpartisan, with no political ambitions (sometimes they were criticized for being too conservative and unimaginative). "They were motivated primarily by a feeling of obligation to make their specialized learning and skills available to the government in time of need," said Killian.[113]

After John F. Kennedy's election to the presidency in 1960, the position of science adviser was further upgraded. Jerome B. Wiesner, Kennedy's science adviser and chairman of PSAC, found the president extremely receptive to science advice. Indeed, according to Wiesner's successor, Donald F. Hornig, the science adviser "became the White House contact point for the entire governmental science apparatus."[114]

Reorganization Plan 2, implemented in 1962, institutionalized the Office of Science and Technology (OST) in the Executive Office of the President, with its own budget and staff. Its director also served as an official special science adviser to the president, which gave the office more statutory responsibility. Wiesner and PSAC members were apprehensive that the move from the White House Office to EOP might downgrade their access to and influence with the president. Yet, under Kennedy OST took on greater responsibility for energy, environment, and natural resource policies, as well as other civilian technology concerns. At the same time the science office continued to be involved in arms control, defense, and space issues.

Wiesner's apprehensions were perhaps well founded, not so much because of the reorganization, but because President Lyndon B. Johnson, unlike Kennedy, was not particularly comfortable with scientists and academicians. Although OST grew during Johnson's presidency (the staff numbered about twenty professionals, and the office employed between two hundred and three hundred consultants), federal sponsorship of research and development was drastically reduced. Hornig, who served as director during that period, noted that his relationship to the president could be described as "friendly but arms-length." According to Hornig, Johnson "used the talents of PSAC, the OST staff, and the Science Adviser and was happy to hear from them, but one never had the feeling that he depended on them to shape his views."[115] The president's growing preoccupation with the Vietnam War made him even less accessible to his domestic advisers. OST had more contact with members of Congress—and in fact was required to appear before its committees—but it spent less time advising the president.

The science adviser's influence in the White House was further eroded with the accession of Richard Nixon to the presidency in 1969. Under Nixon, White House staff members placed themselves between the science adviser and the president; at the same time, PSAC began to criticize openly the president's policies. The result was Nixon's decision to abolish OST, PSAC, and the position of science adviser. According to one observer, Nixon's science adviser, Dubridge, was unable to develop a close personal rapport with the president. His opposition to presidential policies, including the development of the supersonic transport (SST) aircraft, also distanced him from the White House.[116]

President Gerald R. Ford was more comfortable with and interested in science policy. In June 1975 he introduced legislation that established the Office of Science and Technology Policy (OSTP) within the Executive Office; it was enacted in 1976. The director was chief policy adviser to the president on science and technology for major national policies, programs, and issues. OSTP was authorized to examine the adequacy of federal programs, the use of new ideas and discoveries, and the coordination of government scientific activities. Ford was "receptive and interested" in science advice, commented the OSTP's first director, H. Guyford Stever.[117] Vice President Nelson A. Rockefeller further promoted the science advisory role; under the Ford administration, the government's R & D budget began to grow, and initiatives were undertaken in basic research.

The 1976 act had assigned OSTP the responsibility for producing a five-year outlook and annual reports to the president and Congress. But in 1977 these reporting responsibilities were transferred to the National Science Foundation (they were later assumed by the National Academy of Sciences), because of a general feeling that OSTP was overly taxed with reports to Congress and that its prime function was to serve as adviser to the president. Subsequently, OSTP was asked to submit a biennial report.

The position of OSTP under President Jimmy Carter was somewhat ambiguous. Frank Press (who served as presidential science adviser from 1977 until 1981 and who later became president of the National Academy of Sciences) maintained a low profile. He was well respected, however, by the president, the scientific community, government departments, and the Office of Management and Budget (OMB), which was important because OSTP had to work closely with OMB. Under the Carter presidency more emphasis was placed on the role of the science office in encouraging R & D, but according to presidential scholar James Everett Katz, OSTP's role under Carter was nevertheless "greatly diminished."[118] The staff was proscribed from taking policy initiatives, particularly in the areas of defense, natural resources, and energy. "The vision of a vigorous, politically significant science policy office was snuffed out, largely because the President's top advisers recognized that many areas of science and technology were politically sensitive and hence should be handled at the political level," wrote Katz.[119] Press reduced the office's already small staff by 30 percent.

Press was succeeded by G. A. Keyworth II, who served as President Ronald Reagan's first appointee to the post (Benjamin Huberman was acting science adviser from January to August 1981). On January 1, 1986, John P. McTague, the deputy director, became acting science adviser and acting OSTP director until May of that year. Between May and October, Richard G. Johnson served as acting OSTP director, until William R. Graham was appointed science adviser and OSTP director.

The OSTP maintained its low profile under President George Bush's science adviser, D. Allan Bromley. Bromley was an advocate of greater spending for basic R & D, one of the few areas that received increases higher than inflation in the 1992 budget.

He also supported federal funding for the development of supercomputers and a high-speed network to link them, and was assigned to set goals for and coordinate the efforts of the nine federal agencies involved in supercomputer R & D. However, on more controversial matters relating to such issues as energy policy and climate, White House chief of staff John Sununu was the key player, and frequently circumvented or overrode the suggestions of EOP deliberative bodies such as the Domestic Policy Council.

When Bill Clinton took office the OSTP was expected to play a more active role in coordinating policy. Vice President Al Gore had major responsibilities in the formulation of both environmental and technology initiatives, but Clinton's science adviser, physicist John Gibbons, retained the primary advisory role and was an influential participant in EOP decision making. In 1995 the OSTP had forty full-time staff members and a budget of almost $5 million.

ORGANIZATION AND FUNCTIONS OF OSTP

The director of OSTP, who is appointed by the president and confirmed by the Senate, also serves as the president's science adviser. In this capacity the director advises the president on how science and technology will affect, for example, the nation's economy, national security, foreign relations, health, energy, environment, and resources. The OSTP head also assists the president in coordinating the government's R & D programs and evaluates existing government science and technology efforts as a basis for recommending appropriate action. Finally, the director advises the president on science and technology considerations in the federal budget and works with OMB on the review and analysis of research and development items in the budgets of all federal agencies.[120]

The National Security Council seeks advice from the director on matters related to science and technology. Moreover, the director works closely with the Council of Economic Advisers, the National Economic Council, and the Council on Environmental Quality, as well as with other government agencies.

Four associate directors are nominated by the president as well, subject to Senate confirmation, and are responsible for technology, national security and international affairs, science, and environment. An assistant director assists in national security issues, and a small group of policy analysts deal with specialized policy fields. Finally, an executive secretary is responsible for the Federal Council for Science, Engineering and Technology, which receives support from OSTP.

Most of OSTP's coordination tasks are carried out through special committees. In the 1980s and 1990s these committees addressed such topics as national aeronautics policy, agricultural research, Arctic research, health issues surrounding the defoliant Agent Orange used during the Vietnam War, biotechnology, basic research in defense and space policy, the nation's scientific and technological competitiveness in national security matters, emergency preparedness planning, energy policy issues, and international scientific cooperation.

OVERALL POSITION OF OSTP

"The most effective science advisers were those with clear understanding of the government, and how to make it work," observed David Z. Robinson, who served on the science adviser's staff in the 1960s.

Technical skill is available outside the government, and a science adviser can find technical help. The help needed to accomplish goals is harder to find. Successful advisers had long experience with government agencies. They knew how far to push things. . . . They knew how to form alliances, both with the agencies and with key parts of the Executive Office. . . . In summary, they were first-rate politicians.[121]

William G. Wells Jr., former staff director of the House Subcommittee on Science, Resources, and Technology, agreed:

There should be at least a general political rapport between a president and his science adviser. This is not to argue that the post of science adviser should be strictly a political appointment. . . . Yet, there is no escaping the reality that the White House is a political place, that the problems of the public sector are primarily political, and that a science advisory apparatus—especially the president's science adviser—must be able to function in an intensely political environment.[122]

Katz has noted the problems inherent in OSTP's umbrella function.[123] On many issues it serves as the lead agency, assembling and chairing interagency panels, often tapping outside organizations for human resources, money, and administrative support. Yet the office's regular outreach program to draw in private sector experts entails a potential conflict by relying on private organizations to contribute to public policy work. Furthermore, OSTP has been spread thin by the demands of a growing "user" group—state and local governments—as well as by coordination problems with other executive agencies. "The massive workloads combined with this high rate of dispersal of the tasks to various agencies and organizations have led to problems of coordination for the OSTP," wrote Katz. "It is difficult for the director and the second-rung assistant directors to know what is going on in each division and the information problem is magnified for those lower down in the hierarchy. In the past the lack of communication has led to inefficiency and overlapping responsibilities within OSTP."[124]

"The need for balance and diplomacy means that there is no simple recipe for a science adviser's effectiveness," concluded Katz. "Each science adviser must carve out his own niche within the flow of the dynamic and powerful forces surrounding the central position in the U.S. political system, or be swept away by them."[125]

Council on Environmental Quality

Like the Office of Science and Technology Policy (OSTP), in which the director acts in a dual capacity as OSTP head and science adviser to the president, the chair of the Council on Environmental Quality (CEQ) also serves as director of the Office of Environmental Quality (OEQ), whose staff provides support for the council. The council was established by the National Environmental Policy Act of 1969 (PL 91-190). The three members of the council are appointed by the president, subject to Senate confirmation, and the president designates one member as chair. Although the chair interacts with the cabinet, cabinet rank does not accompany the position.

The 1970 Environmental Quality Improvement Act (PL 91-224) established the OEQ in the Executive Office of the President "to provide the professional and administrative staff for the Council." Although the council received permanent authorization, periodic reauthorization is required for the OEQ.[126]

Because the oversight responsibility of the council and the office is extremely broad, they have been selective in choosing areas of study. These areas have depended on the priorities of their varied constituents, which include their own members and staff, Congress, the president, the American public, and the international community. Their relations with federal agencies, state and local governments, and private interests have made it even more difficult for the council and office to preside over the formulation of a unified national environmental policy.

ORIGINS AND DEVELOPMENT OF CEQ AND OEQ

Both CEQ and OEQ were created in response to the nation's increasing concern about declining air and water quality and a general deterioration of the environment. The dramatic blowout of an oil well in the channel off the coast of Santa Barbara, California, in late January 1969, focused public attention on the seriousness of environmental problems. Miles of beaches were covered with oil, and thousands of fish and wildfowl were killed.

On June 3, 1969, four months after the Santa Barbara incident, President Richard Nixon established by executive order the cabinet-level Environmental Quality Council. Congress was not satisfied, however, calling the formation of the council a patchwork approach to environmental problems. In December 1969 Congress passed the National Environmental Policy Act (NEPA), which made environmental protection a matter of national policy. The act required federal agencies to submit environmental impact statements for all proposed actions and created the Council on Environmental Quality to replace the Environmental Quality Council. NEPA was denounced by many industry groups, but conservation organizations such as the Sierra Club hailed it as "an environmental Magna Carta."[127]

During its early days the Nixon administration was criticized widely for not displaying a strong commitment to environmental protection. In 1970, as the pressure for corrective action mounted, the president submitted to Congress a plan to consolidate the federal government's widespread environmental efforts into a single Environmental Protection Agency (EPA). There was little congressional opposition, and on December 2, 1970, the EPA was created by executive order as an independent agency within the executive branch. The Council on Environmental Quality continued to exist as an advisory and policymaking body. While EPA was charged with setting and enforcing pollution control standards, CEQ focused on broad envi-

ronmental policies and coordination of the federal government's activities in that area.

ORGANIZATION AND FUNCTIONS OF CEQ AND OEQ

Environmental policy analysis and development are the primary responsibilities of the CEQ chair and the two council members, who provide the president with expert opinion and policy advice on environmental issues. The council chair participates in discussions of the Domestic Policy Council when matters concerning the environment arise, and the other members of the CEQ serve on two White House subcabinet working groups on environmental policy.

A primary function of the council is preparation of a lengthy annual Environmental Quality Report, which details how activities of the federal, state, and local governments, as well as private enterprise, are affecting the environment. This report is based on CEQ's own research, work with other federal agencies, the findings of the OEQ staff, and contract studies. The council also publishes reports on specific topics.

The second major responsibility of CEQ and OEQ—interagency coordination of environmental quality programs—includes overseeing the implementation and monitoring of regulations related to the National Environmental Policy Act, coordination of federal environmental programs, and participation in the review process conducted by the Office of Management and Budget (OMB) for proposed legislation related to environmental quality. CEQ members also regularly testify before Congress on the administration's environmental policies.

The role of CEQ and OEQ in the acquisition and assessment of environmental data has been directed toward coordinating an interagency effort to update information about environmental data sources. For example, the council's chair joined the EPA administrator in heading an Interagency Toxic Substances Data Committee. A management fund established in 1985 supports OEQ participation in interagency environmental policy studies by allowing it to enlist outside expertise.

Another of CEQ's major functions has been monitoring federal compliance with provisions of the NEPA. This act required CEQ to prepare detailed statements (environmental impact statements) on proposed legislation and other major federal actions that would significantly affect the quality of the human environment. But the process became increasingly burdensome as litigation over environmentally sensitive development escalated. As CEQ chairman and OEQ director A. Alan Hill testified on April 9, 1987, "By the mid-1970s significant problems had become associated with the NEPA process. As the number of court cases increased, so too, the number of pages in [environmental impact statements] doubled and tripled, and complaints about the paperwork and delay associated with the process were frequently heard."[128] In 1977, in response to this problem, President Jimmy Carter issued Executive Order 11991, which provided CEQ with the legal authority to issue regulations to federal agencies for implementing the procedural provisions of the

NEPA. The order also established a referral process to CEQ for any conflicts among agencies about NEPA implementation. The executive order directed that the regulations "be designed to make the environmental impact statement more useful to decision makers and the public," thereby reducing the paperwork involved and turning the attention to the "real environmental issues and alternatives." After soliciting reviews and comments, CEQ issued the NEPA regulations in November 1978; they became effective for all federal agencies in 1979.

With the accession of Ronald Reagan to the presidency in 1981 the NEPA regulations were reviewed and approved by his newly created Task Force on Regulatory Reform, chaired by Vice President George Bush. CEQ later amended the regulations, however, to deal with cases of incomplete or inadequate information on environmental impact. The new rules, which went into effect in May 1986, required federal agencies to point out in the statements that accompanied and documented their material any inadequacy in or lack of information.

The CEQ is also active in international environmental conferences and in the resolution of issues that go beyond national boundaries. For example, in 1981 the CEQ chair headed the Global Issues Working Group, which was established at President Reagan's request. Composed of senior policy representatives from eighteen federal agencies, the group was convened to coordinate the administration's policies on international issues dealing with environmental protection, population, and the use and protection of natural resources. In 1986 and 1987 the council participated in the World Commission on Environment and Development, an independent group which had its origins in a United Nations General Assembly resolution calling for preparation of an "environmental perspective to the year 2000 and beyond." The commission examined a wide range of topics, including air, water, and ocean pollution; hazardous and nuclear waste; deforestation and soil erosion; human shelter; land tenure; and industrial and environmental controls.

Other CEQ and OEQ projects undertaken during the Reagan administration included studies of depletion of the ozone layer and related issues of climatic change stemming from the "greenhouse effect"; participation in an international conference on the assessment processes for environmental impacts held in Nairobi, Kenya, in June 1987; and participation in bilateral environmental agreements with the Soviet Union and Japan.[129]

Considering its broad responsibilities, the Office of Environmental Quality had a small staff of ten in 1987, a few of whom were detailed temporarily to the OEQ from various federal agencies. Between 1975 and 1985, CEQ's budget dropped by more than 80 percent (in constant dollars) and its ability to oversee and implement environmental policy also declined. For most of the 1980s the office had difficulty producing its mandated report on environmental quality, which frequently ran several years behind schedule. President George Bush increased the staff and budget of the council, but by 1993 its budget was still significantly less than it had been during the 1970s, and its future was uncertain.

On entering office, President Bill Clinton proposed abolishing the CEQ as part of a larger plan to elevate the Environmental Protection Agency to a cabinet-level department. Some of CEQ's functions would have been transferred to the new Department of Environment, and its advisory role would have been assumed by a new Office of Environmental Policy, which Clinton proposed in 1993 to coordinate the federal government's response to environmental problems. Clinton reversed his position on abolishing the CEQ after intense lobbying by environmental groups and key lawmakers, who argued that it played a vital role in mediating interagency disputes and that abolishing it would weaken the power of the executive branch to enforce environmental laws.

Legislation to create a new Department of Environment stalled in 1995 in the Republican-dominated 104th Congress, and Clinton nominated Kathleen McGinty to the council's chair, which had been vacant for the first two years of his term. His proposed budget for the CEQ in 1996 was $2.2 million, and staff at the newly expanded CEQ numbered twenty full-time employees.

Office of Administration

As the scope and activities of the Executive Office of the President (EOP) expanded following its establishment in 1939, it became apparent that the support functions of all EOP offices needed to be centralized in a single agency. Reorganization Plan 1 of 1977 (implemented by Executive Order 12028, issued on December 12, 1977) established the Office of Administration within EOP. The director of the office, who is appointed by and directly responsible to the president, has the task of "ensuring that the Office of Administration provides units within the Executive Office of the President common administrative support and services" (Section 2, Executive Order 12028).

The office provides administrative support services to all EOP offices in the White House. These services include personnel management; financial management; data processing; library services, record-keeping, and information services; and office services and operations, including mail handling (except for presidential mail), messenger service, printing and duplication, graphics, word processing, procurement, and supply.

In 1995 the Office of Administration was divided into five sections: personnel management; financial management; library and research services; information systems and technology; and general services. The two printing plants of the office prepare the Budget Message and other documents for distribution. (For large print quantities, the Government Printing Office either prints and binds the publication itself or seeks an outside printer and binder.) For all EOP offices the Administration Office maintains accounts, recruits employees (with the exception of the Office of Policy Development and White House staff, all of whose employees are political appointees), and maintains official records, including those of the White House. In 1994 the Office of Administration received almost $30 million to provide services to White House agencies, with approximately half of those funds paying for computer systems for the Executive Office. Three libraries (not open to the general public) come under its oversight as well: a general reference library located in the New Executive Office Building and reference and law libraries in the Old Executive Office Building.

Office of National Drug Control Policy

The Office of National Drug Control Policy was established by the National Narcotics Leadership Act of 1988 and began operating in January 1989. The director of national drug control policy, or "drug czar," is responsible for coordinating all federal antidrug programs and developing an annual drug control strategy for the president to submit to Congress. Most of the programs are financed outside of the drug czar's office; interdiction and enforcement programs are financed by the Departments of Treasury, Defense, Justice, and Transportation, and drug prevention and treatment programs are financed by the Departments of Education, Labor, and Health and Human Services.

ORIGINS AND DEVELOPMENT

The National Narcotics Leadership Act of 1988 grew out of public fear of the rapid spread of illegal drugs, particularly crack cocaine, and the increase in drug-related and gang violence. Antidrug proposals, such as for stiffer penalties for drug traffickers and mandatory drug testing for certain workers, were a staple of political campaigns throughout the 1980s. Congress routinely cleared major antidrug legislation in each election year, and the funds for all federal antidrug programs rose from $1 billion in 1981 to just under $4 billion in 1988.

The office of drug czar had first been proposed in 1982 legislation, but President Ronald Reagan vetoed the measure on the grounds that it was unnecessary and likely to produce turf battles. The office was finally authorized in the 1988 bill, which also allowed the federal death penalty for major drug traffickers, stiffened penalties for drug dealers, directed more funds toward drug interdiction efforts, and raised the authorization level for drug-treatment programs.

President George Bush declined to make the first drug policy director, William J. Bennett, a member of his cabinet. Although some observers claimed that Bush's decision diminished from the start the clout of the position, Bennett did not shy from using the office as a bully pulpit to pressure Congress and state and local governments to use stronger measures to stop the use of illegal drugs. Bennett had been a controversial secretary of education under Reagan, whose administration had antagonized Education's constituents by calling for the elimination of the department itself.

As drug czar, Bennett remained confrontational and often sparred with lawmakers in his efforts to push the president's first drug strategy through Congress. Bush's first plan called for assistance to Colombia, Peru, and Bolivia and required schools to implement programs aimed at preventing illegal substance abuse by students and employees. Bush's second strategic plan, released in January 1990, largely reiterated the first but included provisions to widen federal death-penalty laws to cover drug felons even in those cases that did not involve murder. This and other controversial measures, such as mandatory drug testing by the states for all arrestees, prisoners, and parolees, eventually were dropped from the final appropriations bills. Although Bennett was frequently criticized for emphasizing military and interdiction approaches over prevention and treatment, federal spending for drug treatment programs nearly doubled, to $1.5 billion, in the first two years of the Bush administration.

Bennett resigned in late 1990 and was replaced by recently defeated Florida Republican governor Bob Martinez. Like Bennett, Martinez as governor had also been faulted for short-changing drug education and treatment at the expense of enforcement. During his four-year tenure as governor, Martinez had been a strong proponent of increased U.S. military involvement in fighting international drug trafficking and had stiffened penalties for drug dealers in Florida. Many viewed Martinez's role in the office as that of caretaker, following Bennett's stormy tenure. The office remained a target of criticism, however, and Democratic lawmakers successfully pushed through a measure to prohibit the drug czar's involvement in partisan politics, such as public appearances for political campaigns.

During the Bush administration, the office also had come under attack for being a repository for political appointees. When Bill Clinton assumed the presidency, the staff and budget of the office were reduced sharply. From a fiscal year 1992 budget of $101 million and staff of 112, the office was reduced to a budget of $5.8 million and a staff of 25 in fiscal year 1993. Although Clinton made his drug czar, Lee P. Brown, a member of the National Security Council, Brown maintained a low profile in the Clinton administration, as health care and welfare reform supplanted the "war on drugs" as the burning domestic policy initiatives of the new administration.

During Brown's tenure, even more of the government's antidrug efforts were shifted to agencies outside the office. In 1993 congressional appropriators created a new "Federal Drug Control Programs" account that was financed by the Justice, Treasury, and Health and Human Services (HHS) Departments. This account financed programs directing money to law enforcement agencies operating in high-intensity drug-trafficking areas, block grants for the HHS Substance Abuse and Mental Health Services Administration, and antigang programs and enforcement research.

Brown's national drug control strategy of 1995 called for a record $14.6 billion in antidrug spending, an increase of almost 10 percent over the previous year. The administration's proposal contained $5.3 billion in spending on treatment and prevention and greater spending on U.S. efforts at enforcement in drug-producing countries. The 1995 strategic plan faced hurdles in Congress, however, as the new Republican Congress sought through anticrime legislation to reduce funds for the new law enforcement officers in drug courts and prevention programs that would be instrumental to the Clinton proposal.

In fact, the Office of National Drug Control Policy narrowly escaped being abolished altogether in 1995. In July, the Senate Appropriations Committee voted to cut all funding to the office in fiscal year 1996. Aggressive lobbying by the Clinton administration and congressional supporters saved the office, which secured $23.5 million in funding for 1996. To underscore the revitalization of the office, President Clinton announced during his 1996 State of the Union address that he was nominating Gen. Barry McCaffrey, formerly commander in chief of the U.S. military's Southern Command, to replace Lee Brown as head of the office.

ORGANIZATION

The office is headed by a director, who is appointed by the president and confirmed by the Senate. The director is assisted by deputy directors for demand reduction and for supply reduction. The associate director for national drug control policy oversees the Bureau of State and Local Affairs, a separate division within the Office of National Drug Control Policy. Additional offices include that of the chief of staff; Office of Planning, Budget, and Administration; general counsel; the Commission on Model State Drug Laws; the President's Drug Advisory Council; and the Counter-Drug Technology Assessment Center.

The office designates recipients of funding from the federal High Intensity Drug Trafficking Areas Program, established in 1990 to provide funds to federal, state, and local law enforcement agencies in areas most adversely affected by drug trafficking. The Special Forfeiture Funds, established in 1988, is also administered by the director. Forfeited funds from the Treasury and Justice departments are transferred to drug control agencies in accordance with the director's annual drug control strategy.

NOTES

1. Richard M. Pious, *The American Presidency* (New York: Basic Books, 1979), 253.

2. John W. Macy, Bruce Adams, and J. Jackson Walter, *America's Unelected Government: Appointing the President's Team* (Cambridge, Mass.: Ballinger, 1983), 4.

3. Stephen Hess, *Organizing the Presidency* (Washington, D.C.: Brookings, 1976), 14.

4. Macy, Adams, and Walter, *America's Unelected Government*, 7.

5. G. Calvin Mackenzie, *The Politics of Presidential Appointments* (New York: Free Press, 1981), 8–9.

6. Hess, *Organizing the Presidency*, 29.

7. Ibid., 62.

8. Macy, Adams, and Walter, *America's Unelected Government*, 30.

9. Hess, *Organizing the Presidency*, 79–80.

10. Emmette S. Redford and Richard T. McCulley, *White House Operations: The Johnson Presidency* (Austin: University of Texas Press, 1986), 137.

11. Theodore C. Sorensen, *Watchmen in the Night* (Cambridge, Mass.: MIT Press, 1973), 36.

12. Macy, Adams, and Walter, *America's Unelected Government*, 33.

13. Quoted in Stephen J. Wayne, *The Legislative Presidency* (New York: Harper and Row, 1978), 187.

14. Mackenzie, *The Politics of Presidential Appointments*, 54–55.

15. Edward D. Feigenbaum, "Staffing, Organization, and Decision-making in the Ford and Carter White Houses," *Presidential Studies Quarterly* 10 (summer 1980): 366–367.

16. Macy, Adams, and Walter, *America's Unelected Government*, 37.

17. Ibid., 49.

18. John Podhoretz, *Hell of a Ride: Backstage at the White House Follies, 1989–1993* (New York: Simon and Schuster, 1993), 89.

19. Ed Rogers, "Transition Admission," *Washington Monthly* 25 (January–February 1993): 38.

20. Podhoretz, *Hell of a Ride*, 89.

21. James P. Pfiffner, *The Modern Presidency* (New York: St. Martin's, 1994), 80.

22. Bob Woodward, *The Agenda: Inside the Clinton White House* (New York: Simon and Schuster, 1994), 59.

23. Sidney Blumenthal, "Waiting for the Call: The Rush for Positions in the Clinton Administration," *The New Yorker* 68 (January 25, 1993): 50.

24. Office of Management and Budget, "The Work of the Office of Management and Budget," mimeographed (Washington, D.C.: OMB, 1987).

25. Bureau of the Budget, *Staff Orientation Manual* (Washington, D.C.: Government Printing Office, 1945), 38.

26. Quoted in *Congress and the Nation, 1969–1972* (Washington, D.C.: Congressional Quarterly, 1973), 3:73.

27. Richard E. Neustadt, "Presidency and Legislation: The Growth of Central Clearance," *American Political Science Review* 48 (September 1954): 641–671.

28. For a discussion of this period, see the chapter on Franklin D. Roosevelt in Hess, *Organizing the Presidency*.

29. Quoted in Larry Berman, *The Office of Management and Budget and the Presidency, 1921–1979* (Princeton, N.J.: Princeton University Press, 1979), 28.

30. Ibid., 42.

31. Ibid., 52.

32. Ibid., 55.

33. Brookings Institution, *Study of the 1960–61 Presidential Transition: The White House and the Executive Office of the President* (Washington, D.C.: Brookings, 1960), 33.

34. "Task Force Report on Intergovernmental Program Coordination: The Bureau of the Budget During the Administration of Lyndon Baines Johnson," mimeographed (Washington, D.C.: U.S. Executive Office of the President, Bureau of the Budget, November 14, 1968).

35. *Presidential Documents*, March 16, 1970 (Washington, D.C.: Government Printing Office, 1970), 355–357.

36. Berman, *The Office of Management and Budget and the Presidency*, 125.

37. *Congressional Quarterly Weekly Report*, July 13, 1985, 1356.

38. Office of Management and Budget, "The Work of the Office of Management and Budget," 5.

39. *Federal Regulatory Directory, 1983–84* (Washington, D.C.: Congressional Quarterly, 1983), 66.

40. Quoted in Julie Rovner, "OMB's Activities Draw Fire in Congress, Courts," *Congressional Quarterly Weekly Report*, June 14, 1986, 1341.

41. See *Congressional Quarterly Weekly Report*, June 14, 1986, 1340.

42. Quoted in Dave Kaplan, "Senate Committee Approves OMB Overhaul," *Congressional Quarterly Weekly Report*, June 28, 1986, 1488.

43. From Title I, "Coordination for National Security," of the National Security Act, PL 80-253. See *Congress and the Nation, 1945–1964* (Washington, D.C.: Congressional Quarterly, 1965), 1:247.

44. Mark M. Lowenthal, "The National Security Council: Organizational History," Congressional Research Service, Washington, D.C., June 27, 1978.

45. Henry A. Kissinger, *White House Years* (Boston: Little, Brown, 1979), 31.

46. Larry Berman and Bruce W. Jentleson, "Bush and the Post–Cold-War World," in *The Bush Presidency: First Appraisals*, ed. Colin Campbell

and Bert A. Rockman (Chatham, N.J.: Chatham House, 1991): 99–102.

47. For a description of this "conventional wisdom" on the NSC, see I. M. Destler, "National Security Management: What Presidents Have Wrought," *Political Science Quarterly* 95 (winter 1980): 81.

48. Kissinger, *White House Years*, 30.

49. Quoted in Allen Weinstein and Michael R. Beschloss, "The Best National Security System: An Interview with Zbigniew Brzezinski," *Washington Quarterly* (winter 1982): 74.

50. Quoted in Larry Light, "White House Domestic Policy Staff Plays an Important Role in Formulating Legislation," *Congressional Quarterly Weekly Report*, October 6, 1979, 2202.

51. Quoted in Peri E. Arnold, *Making the Managerial Presidency: Comprehensive Reorganization Planning 1905–1980* (Princeton, N.J.: Princeton University Press, 1986), 285.

52. Ibid., 284–285.

53. Public Papers of the Presidents of the United States, Richard Nixon, 1970 (Washington, D.C.: Government Printing Office, 1971), 257.

54. House Committee on Government Organization, *Hearings, Reorganization Plan No. 2 of 1970*, 91st Cong., 2d Sess., 1970, 55–56.

55. Ibid., 23.

56. Arnold, *Making the Managerial Presidency*, 298.

57. Quoted in Hess, *Organizing the Presidency*, 131.

58. Ibid., 132.

59. Dick Kirchten, "Policy Development Office: A Scaled-down Operation," *National Journal*, April 25, 1981, 684.

60. John H. Kessel, *The Domestic Presidency: Decision-Making in the White House* (Boston, Mass.: Duxbury Press, 1975), 29.

61. Light, "White House Domestic Policy Staff," 2199.

62. Ibid., 2199.

63. Ibid., 2200.

64. Ibid.

65. Quoted in *Congressional Quarterly Almanac: 1981* (Washington, D.C.: Congressional Quarterly, 1982), 356. The letter was dated July 8, 1981.

66. Text of announcement in *Congressional Quarterly Weekly Report*, April 20, 1985, 757.

67. Kirchten, "Policy Development Office," 684.

68. The organization and functions of the OPD were provided by special assistant Michael Driggs in a May 19, 1987, interview.

69. Kirchten, "Policy Development Office," 684.

70. Norman C. Thomas and Joseph A. Pika. *The Politics of the Presidency*, 4th ed. (Washington, D.C.: Congressional Quarterly, 1994): 345–358.

71. Bob Woodward, *The Agenda: Inside the Clinton White House* (New York: St. Martin's, 1994), 156.

72. Edward S. Flash Jr., "The Broadening Scope of the President's Economic Advisers," *The George Washington Law Review* 35, no. 2 (December 1966): 286.

73. Roger Porter, "Economic Advice to the President from Eisenhower to Reagan," *Political Science Quarterly* (fall 1983): 404.

74. Ibid., 405.

75. David Naveh, "The Political Role of Academic Advisers: The Case of the U.S. President's Council of Economic Advisers, 1946–76," *Presidential Studies Quarterly* 11 (fall 1981): 492.

76. The origins and politics of the act have been well documented by Stephen K. Bailey in *Congress Makes a Law* (New York: Columbia University Press, 1950).

77. For a good discussion of this issue, see E. Ray Canterbury, *The President's Council of Economic Advisers* (New York: Exposition Press, 1961).

78. Quoted in Edwin G. Nourse and Bertram M. Gross, "The Role of the Council of Economic Advisers," *American Political Science Review* (April 1948).

79. Erwin C. Hargrove and Samuel A. Morley, eds., *The President and the Council of Economic Advisers: Interviews with CEA Chairmen* (Boulder, Colo.: Westview, 1984), 47.

80. Gerhard Colm, "The Executive Office and Fiscal and Economic Policy," *Law and Contemporary Problems* 21 (autumn 1956): 716.

81. Edwin G. Nourse, *Economics in the Public Service* (New York: Harcourt Brace, 1953), 380.

82. Nourse and Gross, "The Role of the Council of Economic Advisers."

83. Edwin G. Nourse, "The Employment Act and the Economic Future," *Vital Speeches XII* (January 1, 1946).

84. Hargrove and Morley, *The President and the Council of Economic Advisers*, 50.

85. Hess, *Organizing the Presidency*, 55.

86. Quoted in Hugh S. Norton, *The Council of Economic Advisers: Three Periods of Influence* (Columbia, S.C.: Bureau of Business and Economic Research, 1973), 23.

87. Hess, *Organizing the Presidency*, 75.

88. Naveh, "The Political Role of Academic Advisers," 497.

89. Hargrove and Morley, *The President and the Council of Economic Advisers*, 91.

90. Ibid., 90.

91. Quoted in Arthur M. Schlesinger Jr., *A Thousand Days: John F. Kennedy in the White House* (Boston: Houghton Mifflin, 1965), 137.

92. Edward S. Flash Jr., *Economic Advice and Presidential Leadership* (New York: Columbia University Press, 1965), 209.

93. Hess, *Organizing the Presidency*, 90.

94. Hargrove and Morley, *The President and the Council of Economic Advisers*, 163.

95. Ibid., 359.

96. Ibid., 409.

97. Ibid., 459.

98. *Congress and the Nation, 1977–1980* (Washington, D.C.: Congressional Quarterly, 1981), 5: 233.

99. *Congressional Quarterly Almanac: 1981* (Washington, D.C.: Congressional Quarterly, 1982), 270.

100. Council of Economic Advisers, *Economic Report of the President* (Washington, D.C.: Government Printing Office, January 1987).

101. Thomas and Pika, *The Politics of the Presidency*, 385.

102. Hess, *Organizing the Presidency*, 167.

103. Quoted in Naveh, "The Political Role of Academic Advisers," 501.

104. For a general history of U.S. trade policy, see *Trade: U.S. Policy Since 1945* (Washington, D.C.: Congressional Quarterly, 1984).

105. John W. Evans, *The Kennedy Round in American Trade Policy: The Twilight of the GATT?* (Cambridge, Mass.: Harvard University Press, 1971), 156.

106. See, among other sources, *Congress and the Nation, 1977–1980* 5:273.

107. *Trade*, 2.

108. Quoted in Clyde M. Farnsworth, "William Brock: Our Man for Trade," *New York Times Magazine*, November 13, 1983.

109. *Congressional Quarterly Weekly Report*, June 29, 1985, 1303.

110. Information on the organization and functions of the USTR was supplied by interviews with staff members and a mimeographed article produced by the office.

111. Office of Science and Technology Policy (in cooperation with the National Science Foundation), *Biennial Science and Technology Report to the Congress: 1983–1984* (Washington, D.C.: Government Printing Office, 1985), 4. This report summarizes OSTP's wide-ranging activities.

112. Lee A. Dubridge, "Science Advice to the President: Important and Difficult," in *Science Advice to the President*, ed. George Bugliarello and A. George Schillinger, a special issue of *Technology and Society* (New York: Pergamon Press, 1980), 2:11. These volumes provide invaluable articles by former presidential science advisers, observers, and legislative experts on the evolution of the science advisory role.

113. James R. Killian Jr., "The Origins and Uses of a Scientific Presence in the White House," in *Science Advice*, 31.

114. Donald F. Hornig, "The President's Need for Science Advice: Past and Future," in *Science Advice*, 42.

115. Ibid., 47.

116. William G. Wells Jr., "Science Advice and the Presidency," in *Science Advice,* 214. Wells served as staff director of the House Subcommittee on Science, Resources, and Technology at the time.

117. H. Guyford Stever, "Science Advice—Out of and Back to the White House," in *Science Advice,* 74.

118. James Everett Katz, "Organizational Structure and Advisory Effectiveness," in *Science Advice,* 230.

119. Ibid.

120. For greater detail, see Office of Science and Technology Policy, *Biennial Science and Technology Report.*

121. David Z. Robinson, "Politics in the Science Advising Process," in *Science Advice,* 163.

122. Wells, "Science Advice and the Presidency," 214.

123. Katz, "Organizational Structure." Katz himself noted, "Conventional wisdom dictates that the science advisor's usefulness is predicated entirely on his personal rapport with the president" (p. 243).

124. Ibid., 233.

125. Ibid., 243.

126. To learn the full relevant statutory authority at the time, see Executive Office of the President, Council on Environmental Quality, *Regulations for Implementing the Procedural Provisions of the National Environmental Policy Act* (Washington, D.C.: Government Printing Office, November 1978), reprint 43FR 55978–56007.

127. For background, see *Federal Regulatory Directory, 1983–84,* 113.

128. Ibid., 8.

129. For summaries of CEQ and OEQ activities, see the annual reports of the Council on Environmental Quality, particularly the eleventh and fifteenth reports (Washington, D.C.: Government Printing Office, 1981). Other reports of particular interest are: *Report of an Expert Meeting on Research Needs and Opportunities at Federally-supervised Hazardous Waste Site Clean-ups* (Washington, D.C.: Executive Office of the President, Council on Environmental Quality, October 20, 1986); and *Report on Long-term Environmental Research and Development* (Washington, D.C.: Executive Office of the President, Council on Environmental Quality, Office of Environmental Quality, March 1985).

SELECTED BIBLIOGRAPHY

Arnold, Peri E. *Making the Managerial Presidency: Comprehensive Reorganization Planning 1905–1980.* Princeton, N.J.: Princeton University Press, 1986.

Bailey, Stephen. *Congress Makes a Law.* New York: Columbia University Press, 1950.

Berman, Larry. *The Office of Management and Budget and the Presidency, 1921–1979.* Princeton, N.J.: Princeton University Press, 1979.

Blumenthal, Sidney. "Waiting for the Call: The Rush for Positions in the Clinton Administration." *The New Yorker* 68 (January 25, 1993): 48–53.

Bugliarello, George, and A. George Schillinger, eds. *Science Advice to the President,* a special issue of *Technology in Society.* Vol. 2, nos. 1 and 2. New York: Pergamon Press, 1980.

Campbell, Colin, and Bert A. Rockman, eds. *The Bush Presidency: First Appraisals.* Chatham, N.J.: Chatham House, 1991.

Feigenbaum, Edward D. "Staffing, Organization, and Decision-making in the Ford and Carter White Houses." *Presidential Studies Quarterly* 10 (summer 1980): 364–377.

Hargrove, Erwin C., and Samuel A. Morley, eds. *The President and the Council of Economic Advisers: Interviews with CEA Chairmen.* Boulder, Colo.: Westview, 1984.

Hess, Stephen. *Organizing the Presidency.* Rev. ed. Washington, D.C.: Brookings, 1988.

King, Anthony. *Both Ends of the Avenue: The Presidency, the Executive Branch, and Congress in the 1980s.* Washington, D.C.: American Enterprise Institute, 1983.

Light, Larry. "White House Domestic Policy Staff Plays an Important Role in Formulating Legislation." *Congressional Quarterly Weekly Report,* October 6, 1979, 2199–2204.

Macy, John W., Bruce Adams, and J. Jackson Walter. *America's Unelected Government: Appointing the President's Team.* Cambridge, Mass.: Ballinger, 1983.

Mosher, Frederick C. *A Tale of Two Agencies: A Comparative Analysis of the General Accounting Office and the Office of Management and Budget.* Baton Rouge: Louisiana State University Press, 1984.

Naveh, David. "The Political Role of Academic Advisers: The Case of the U.S. President's Council of Economic Advisers, 1946–76." *Presidential Studies Quarterly* 11 (fall 1981).

Pfiffner, James P. *The Modern Presidency.* New York: St. Martin's Press, 1994.

Pious, Richard M. *The American Presidency.* New York: Basic Books, 1979.

Podhoretz, John. *Hell of a Ride: Backstage at the White House Follies, 1989–1993.* New York: Simon and Schuster, 1993.

Redford, Emmette S., and Richard T. McCulley. *White House Operations: The Johnson Presidency.* Austin: University of Texas Press, 1986.

Rogers, Ed. "Transition Admission," *Washington Monthly* 25 (January–February 1993): 38–41.

Sorensen, Theodore C. *Watchmen in the Night.* Cambridge, Mass.: MIT Press, 1973.

Thomas, Norman C., and Joseph A. Pika. *The Politics of the Presidency.* 4th ed. Washington, D.C.: Congressional Quarterly, 1996.

Trade: U.S. Policy Since 1945. Washington, D.C.: Congressional Quarterly, 1984.

Vig, Norman J., and Michael E. Kraft, eds. *Environmental Policy in the 1990s.* 2d ed. Washington, D.C.: Congressional Quarterly, 1994.

Wayne, Stephen. *The Legislative Presidency.* New York: Harper and Row, 1978.

Woodward, Bob. *The Agenda: Inside the Clinton White House.* New York: Simon and Schuster, 1994.

CHAPTER 29

The Cabinet and Executive Departments

BY W. CRAIG BLEDSOE AND LESLIE RIGBY

T HE CABINET is one of the most unusual institutions of the presidency. Although not specifically mentioned in the Constitution or provided for in statutory law, the cabinet has become an institutionalized part of the presidency. The secretaries of the executive departments make up the majority of the cabinet. Executive departments are the largest units of the federal executive branch. Each department covers broad areas of responsibility. As of 1996, there were fourteen cabinet departments: Agriculture, Commerce, Defense, Education, Energy, Health and Human Services, Housing and Urban Development, Interior, Justice, Labor, State, Transportation, Treasury, and Veterans Affairs.

The country's first president, George Washington, initiated the practice of meeting with the secretaries of state, Treasury, and war as well as his attorney general, to seek their advice on domestic and foreign policy. The modern presidential cabinet consists of the president, vice president, heads of the fourteen executive departments, and any other officials the president might wish to invite, such as the head of the Office of Management and Budget and the ambassador to the United Nations. Although some presidents have used their cabinets regularly, recognizing that a presidency that effectively uses its cabinet is still considered ideal, presidential cabinets have for the most part been a sidelight of the presidency. In fact, because cabinet members usually become advocates of their departments, they contribute little to presidential decision making unless the decisions involve matters that concern their respective bailiwicks.

Origin and Development of the Cabinet

The idea of some kind of advisory council for the president was discussed at the Constitutional Convention. Gouverneur Morris and Charles Cotesworth Pinckney, the first delegates to use the term "cabinet" at the convention, proposed creation of a council of state, composed of the executive department heads, to advise the president. This proposal failed to win adoption, but advocates of a cabinet kept the idea alive throughout most of the convention. Indeed, less than two weeks before finalization of the Constitution, Benjamin Franklin continued to insist that a council of state "would not only be a check on a bad president but be a relief to a good one."[1]

The cabinet concept ultimately failed to win majority support among the convention's delegates, however. Most of the Founders apparently feared that the presidency might become too overburdened with unnecessary advisory councils. Alexander Hamilton explained the Founders' concerns in *Federalist No. 70*: "A council to a magistrate, who is himself responsible for what he does, are generally nothing better than a clog upon his good intentions; are often the instruments and accomplices of his bad, and are almost always a cloak to his faults."[2] Consequently, when the Committee on Style finished drafting the Constitution, all that remained of the idea was the authorization that the president "require the Opinion, in writing, of the principal Officer in each of the executive Departments, upon any Subject relating to the duties of their respective Offices" (Article II, section 2).

Having no constitutional or statutory mandate for the institution of a cabinet, presidents have relied on the constitutional mandate that allows them to require the advice of their principal executive branch officers. Under the Articles of Confederation, several executive departments already existed. Thus, in reality Washington's first cabinet merely evolved out of an already established executive pattern that began in the early 1780s. President Washington understood that the constitutional language about the responsibility of the departments was ambiguous. His biographer, James Thomas Flexner, has written: "Whether what was defined as 'the heads of the great departments' were to be under the jurisdiction of the president was not stated: the president was merely empowered to require their opinions relating to their duties."[3] When Washington was inaugurated in 1789, he consulted with Hamilton, James Madison, and others about the powers and duties of the presidency and permanently settled the matter by instituting the modern cabinet. Early in his administration, Washington took the view that department heads should be assistants to the president and not to Congress.

Seeking both administrative and advisory help in his new administration, Washington asked Congress to create three executive departments to oversee, respectively, foreign affairs, military affairs, and fiscal concerns. During the months before the executive branch was firmly in place, Washington relied on the services of those who had served in the same positions under the Articles of Confederation. John Jay continued temporarily as secretary of foreign affairs, Henry Knox remained at the secretary of war post, and the old Treasury Board continued to manage fiscal concerns.

For more than two months Congress debated the proper establishment of these three executive departments. Primarily concerned with the relationship of each department to Congress and believing that not all departments should be alike in this relationship, most members of Congress preferred that the departments concerned with foreign affairs and war be primarily under the control of the executive. The Treasury, however, had some legislative purposes and thus should fall more under the control of Congress. The statutes setting up the departments reflected these preferences. On July 27, 1789, Congress established the Department of Foreign Affairs. The secretary of foreign affairs was given the responsibility of performing duties assigned by the president. (Two months later Congress changed the name to the Department of State.) Similarly, the statutory language setting up the War Department placed it squarely under the control of the president. But the Treasury Department was not designated by Congress as an "executive department." Instead, the secretary of the Treasury was directed to report fiscal matters to Congress. Part of the rationale for this special status was the constitutional requirement that revenue bills originate in the House of Representatives.

Hamilton did much to increase the prestige and independence of the cabinet. Early in his administration Washington asked Hamilton to head the Treasury, and there is some evidence that the secretary contributed greatly to the drafting of the Treasury Act. Hamilton, who had served as Washington's chief adviser during the organization of the new government, virtually assumed the role of prime minister after his confirmation as secretary of the Treasury on September 11, 1789. In addition to his abilities and his special relationship with Washington, Hamilton's ascension to a position of such prominence was assisted by the relative statutory importance of the Treasury Department. He assumed an office that Congress had intended as an extension of its own authority and made it a stronghold of executive power. According to presidential scholar R. Gordon Hoxie, "With his admiration of the British model and his high regard for Washington, Hamilton conceived of executive power as generated through a cabinet of department heads, administered by a judicious executive head. In such a system, by the sheer vent of his energies and genius, Hamilton came to be Washington's dominant adviser."[4]

Washington's use of the cabinet soon resulted in the institution that the Framers of the Constitution had declined to include. The president eventually appointed Knox as secretary of war (September 12, 1789) and Thomas Jefferson, who had been serving as minister to France, as secretary of state (March 22, 1790). In addition, Edmund Randolph was named attorney general, although there was no Department of Justice until 1870.

Washington initially believed that the Senate would fill the role of an advisory council, but that hope faded in August 1790 when Washington, accompanied by Knox, went to the Senate floor seeking advice on an Indian treaty. The senators made it clear that they were uncomfortable meeting with the president and that they would not serve in the capacity of an advisory council. As a result, Washington gradually began to rely on the advice of his department heads, the attorney general, Vice President John Adams, and Chief Justice John Jay.

Although the Treasury secretary was not part of the original cabinet, Alexander Hamilton made the department a stronghold of executive power and became Washington's dominant adviser.

At first Washington consulted with each individually, both in person and in writing. Later, in 1791, when he was preparing to leave the capital for a few days, he authorized his vice president, the chief justice, and the secretaries of Treasury, state, and war to meet and discuss government matters during his absence. In the following year the president conferred frequently with his department heads and attorney general, omitting the vice president and the chief justice. These meetings occurred even more often during the undeclared naval war with France. By 1793 Madison was applying the term "cabinet" to these conferences. The name stuck, and the cabinet became a permanent addition to the executive branch.

Like many presidents after him, Washington had hoped that his advisers would consult with one another and work together harmoniously. Early cabinet meetings, however, were marred by a growing rift between Jefferson and Hamilton, who differed on a number of important policy positions. Although Washington tried to get them to work together, they quarreled continuously. Jefferson finally resigned in the summer of 1793. Less than two years later Hamilton retired from government service to return to his lucrative law practice, yet Washington continued to write him for advice during his remaining two years in office. In fact, the president apparently abandoned his hopes of the cabinet serving as an advisory board.

When Washington replaced Jefferson and Hamilton in his cabinet, he chose men of cooler heads but lesser talents, and evidently he did not value their advice as much as that from his first cabinet. Flexner wrote: "Unlike their predecessors they were not consulted concerning executive decisions; they were limited to the routines of their departments."[5] This disillusionment and uncertainty surrounding the proper role of the cabinet has afflicted almost every administration since Washington's.

President John Adams, who retained all of Washington's cabinet members, was even more disillusioned with his cabinet than his predecessor. Early in his administration important differences of opinion developed between Adams and his department heads. Indeed, his cabinet members were more loyal to Hamilton than to him. And because the president was often away from the capital, cabinet members began to advise each other and to seek Hamilton's advice. In the final year of his administration Adams removed two cabinet members. Yet during his administration the formal cabinet remained the president's principal official advisory unit. The role of the cabinet under Washington and Adams thus entailed ambiguity that has endured throughout the history of the presidency. According to Hoxie,

The twelve Federalist years had established the joint consultation between the president and the department heads as a body, but it was clear that the president was bound neither to consult nor to accept the advice received. Nor was the cabinet an administrative body. The business of government was carried out throughout the executive departments.[6]

NINETEENTH-CENTURY CABINETS

The first part of the nineteenth century witnessed a gradual decline in the importance of the cabinet. Few cabinets got along all that well, and few presidents relied on their cabinets as advisory groups. Because the selection of cabinet members became more and more dictated by political and geographic considerations, presidents increasingly appointed cabinet members whom they did not know personally or necessarily trust. Indeed, many times presidents had to struggle to maintain control over their cabinets. If because of a lack of interest in using the cabinet a president declined to prepare an agenda for a cabinet meeting, the secretaries would take the initiative.

Appointments to earlier cabinets were based primarily on the appointees' abilities. Beginning with President James Madison's administration (1809–1817), however, political and geographic factors often took precedence over ability or loyalty. For example, the Senate strongly opposed Madison's selection of Albert Gallatin, Jefferson's secretary of the Treasury, to succeed Madison as secretary of state. Rather than provoke a battle with the Senate over Gallatin, the president reluctantly appointed Robert Smith, the brother of an influential senator, to the position. For the first time the president was not in complete control of the cabinet selection process.

Because of these pressures, as well as his own personality, Andrew Jackson (1829–1837) was the first president largely to ignore his collective cabinet. During his first two years in office, he did not even meet with the cabinet, and he convened it only sixteen times during his eight years as president. Jackson preferred the intimacy of his "kitchen cabinet," a group of close personal advisers (many of whom were newspapermen who kept him in touch with public opinion), to the formality of his official cabinet. Throughout his administration, he steadfastly refused to use his formal cabinet to help him make decisions. As he explained: "I have accustomed myself to receive with respect the opinions of others, but always take the responsibility for deciding for myself."[7]

Abraham Lincoln (1861–1865) appointed strong political leaders, many of them his political antagonists, to his cabinet. In fact, some of his cabinet members believed themselves superior to Lincoln. This resulted in some rather bitter relationships between cabinet members and the president. Cabinet officers during the Lincoln administration were known for their intrigues. Secretary of State William H. Seward, for example, considered himself Lincoln's prime minister. Salmon P. Chase, secretary of the Treasury, schemed with a few members of the Senate to remove Seward and increase his own influence. Lincoln's strong leadership, however, allowed him to retain control of his cabinet and use it for his own ends. Indeed, as the story goes, when seeking advice on one critical decision, Lincoln polled his entire cabinet, only to be overwhelmingly outvoted. He then proclaimed: "Seven nays and one aye, the ayes have it." The critical decisions, such as issuing the Emancipation Proclamation, were his alone, although he usually sought cabinet endorsement. Hoxie wrote: "Just as he was the strongest nineteenth-century president, he had the strongest cabinet members, who worked strenuously in their respective departments, although as a body they were subordinated to him."[8]

During the latter part of the nineteenth century an attempt was made to transfer responsibility for the cabinet from the White House to Congress, thereby giving Congress considerable access to information from the executive branch. Chief among the members of Congress introducing legislation to accomplish this goal was George Hunt Pendleton (D-Ohio), who in 1864 proposed a bill that would allow secretaries of executive departments to occupy seats on the House floor. Supported strongly by others in Congress (including future president James A. Garfield), the bill came up for debate in 1865 and several times thereafter. It was never voted into law.

TWENTIETH-CENTURY CABINETS

Early in the twentieth century the cabinet grew in size but continued to play only a modest role as an advisory body. As the federal government became more complex and the power of the presidency began to expand, the size of the cabinet expanded as well. In 1913, at the start of Woodrow Wilson's administration (1913–1921), the cabinet swelled to ten members. President Wilson, however, rarely met with his cabinet. Even during World

Truman called for a strong, active cabinet, yet not once did he convene his cabinet to discuss the North Korean invasion of South Korea.

War I Wilson did not consult with his cabinet about the 1915 sinking of the *Lusitania* or his 1917 call for Congress to declare war. Instead, he relied for advice on his Council of National Defense, which was created in 1916 and consisted of the secretaries of war, navy, interior, agriculture, commerce, and labor. As one department secretary complained, "Nothing talked of at Cabinet that would interest a nation, a family, or a child. No talk of the war."[9]

Under Franklin D. Roosevelt (1933–1945) cabinet meetings continued to be more a forum for discussion than for decision making. During cabinet meetings Roosevelt customarily went around the table and asked each cabinet member what was on his or her mind. His secretary of the interior, Harold L. Ickes, summarized Roosevelt's attitude: "The cold fact is that on important matters we are seldom called upon for advice. We never discuss exhaustively any policy of government or question of political strategy. . . . Our cabinet meetings are pleasant affairs, but we only skim the surface of routine affairs."[10] In addition, Roosevelt often interceded in the activities of his cabinet members. According to Hoxie,

Roosevelt constantly interposed in the executive departments both in domestic and foreign policy. He became, in essence, his own secretary of state, war, and navy. Secretary of State Cordell Hull and Secretary of War [Henry L.] Stimson both voiced their unhappiness. So did Roosevelt's new vice-president, Harry S Truman, who was neither consulted nor informed of what was going on.[11]

President Truman (1945–1953) boasted that he had "revived the cabinet system," believing that the cabinet should be similar to a board of directors. Indeed, Truman called for a strong, active cabinet: "The cabinet is not merely a collection of executives administering different governmental functions. It is a body whose combined judgment the president uses to formulate the fundamental policies of the administration."[12] Unlike Roosevelt, Truman actually asked his cabinet to vote on some major issues. Toward the end of his administration, however, he backed away

from the board of directors approach. For example, when North Korea attacked South Korea in 1950 Truman never convened his cabinet to discuss the matter. He relied instead on an informal group—consisting of the secretaries of defense and state, the Joint Chiefs of Staff, and some of his closest aides—to advise him on the entry of the United States into the war. Throughout his administration Truman reserved the most difficult decisions for himself. Presidential scholar Stephen Hess has written: "Over the years he [Truman] drew back from the board of directors concept; powers delegated could be powers lost, and Truman, while modest about himself as president, was zealous in protecting those prerogatives that he felt were inherent in the presidency."[13]

Dwight D. Eisenhower (1953–1961) took his cabinet more seriously than any other twentieth-century president. He established a cabinet secretariat (one of the cabinet secretaries set the agenda and served as liaison with the president), and he charged his cabinet to advise him on major issues and to see that every decision was carried out.

Eisenhower expanded cabinet meetings to include not only department secretaries but also important aides such as the U.S. ambassador to the United Nations, the budget director, the White House chief of staff, the national security affairs assistant, and other top White House advisers. *(See box, Cabinet Status, p. 1149.)* Vice presidents have served on cabinets since Franklin Roosevelt's first administration, but Eisenhower was the first president to use his vice president effectively in the cabinet. He made the vice president chair of several cabinet committees and acting chair of the cabinet if he was unable to attend a meeting. Eisenhower's cabinet, which usually numbered around twenty or more, held regularly scheduled, weekly meetings which often lasted three or more hours.

Although Eisenhower accepted responsibility for final decisions, he attempted to make the cabinet more than just a body of advisers by including wide-ranging, important issues on the

CABINET STATUS

Membership in the president's cabinet is not limited to the secretaries of the executive departments. Since the cabinet as an institution lacks foundation in the Constitution or statutory law, presidents are free to promote any government official they please to cabinet-rank status. The practice of inviting top officials to join the cabinet dates to the presidency of George Washington. Washington set a precedent when he asked his first attorney general, Edmund Randolph, as well as his two subsequent attorneys general, to join the cabinet even though they did not head a department. (Justice was not elevated to an executive department until 1870.)

Presidents ask top officials other than department secretaries to join their cabinets for a variety of reasons. One is to solicit the advice of knowledgable specialists. In the post–World War II period, dominated by the cold war, arms race, and international threats to U.S. security, it became common to invite the director of the Central Intelligence Agency to join the cabinet. More recently, the U.S. trade representative has sat in the cabinet, reflecting the greater importance and complexity of international trade. Although these individuals are full-fledged members of the cabinet, by virtue of the executive order that promotes them, they often attend only those cabinet meetings or portions of cabinet meetings in which their respective areas of expertise are discussed.

A second reason to expand the cabinet beyond the executive departments is to call attention to an issue or agency. Presidents can exhibit concern for a particular issue, such as environmental protection or foreign trade, by promoting the top administrators of the relevant organizations to cabinet status. Also, on rare occasions, cabinet status has been accorded to reward an agency or agency

head for a job well done. This was the explanation offered by President Bill Clinton for promoting James Lee Witt, head of the Federal Emergency Management Agency (FEMA), to cabinet rank in February 1996. FEMA, a much-maligned agency in previous administrations, had received public approbation for its effective response to several major natural disasters, including floods in the Midwest in July–August 1993 and California in March 1995 and the Northridge, California, earthquake in January 1994.

Cabinet rank affords no additional benefits apart from status, enhanced visibility, and perhaps greater access to the president. If the president seldom convenes the cabinet or relies on it for advice, then a seat at the cabinet table may not enhance access to the president very much. These cabinet members continue to receive their normal pay rates, which are below those of department secretaries. The attorney general, for example, even though a member of the cabinet since Washington's administration, did not reach parity in pay with the department secretaries until Justice became a department, in 1870.

Elevation to cabinet rank is at the president's discretion, and presidents have used the power to varying degrees. President Bush elevated only two to cabinet rank: the director of the Office of Management and Budget and the U.S. trade representative. By early 1996 President Clinton, in contrast, had elevated seven: the chief of staff to the president, the chairman of the Council of Economic Advisers, the administrator of the Environmental Protection Agency, the director of the Office of Management and Budget, the U.S. representative to the United Nations, the U.S. trade representative, and the FEMA director.

---

cabinet agenda. According to noted presidential scholar Thomas E. Cronin,

[Eisenhower] did, within certain limits, encourage his cabinet members to take an independent line of their own and argue it out within the cabinet session. Eisenhower fully appreciated the limits of a cabinet system but seemed motivated to use the cabinet sessions both as a means to keep himself informed and as a way to prevent the personality conflicts, throat-cutting, and end-running that had characterized the history of past administrations.[14]

In his relationship with his cabinet, John F. Kennedy (1961–1963) did not follow the example set by President Eisenhower. Although he spent time with his department heads individually, President Kennedy held cabinet meetings as seldom as possible. Historian Arthur M. Schlesinger Jr. has quoted Kennedy as saying, "Cabinet meetings are simply useless. Why should the Postmaster General sit here and listen to a discussion of the problems of Laos?"[15] Because he believed that few subjects warranted discussion by the entire cabinet, Kennedy preferred to spend his time with the aides and secretaries most concerned with a specific issue. Eisenhower was highly tolerant of meetings because of his long military experience, but Kennedy

wanted to avoid them. Hess wrote: "Kennedy was too restless to sit for long periods, too impatient with long-winded speakers, and too mentally agile to accept repetitious, circuitous Cabinet-NSC discussions as a tolerable method for receiving information."[16]

Although Lyndon B. Johnson (1963–1969) used his cabinet much more than Kennedy, cabinet meetings were mostly for show and contained little in the way of substantive discussion. Johnson, in fact, used cabinet meetings to create the impression of consensus within his administration. According to Johnson's press secretary, George Reedy, "Cabinet meetings were held with considerable regularity, with fully predetermined agendas and fully prewritten statements. In general, they consisted of briefings by cabinet members followed by a later release of the statements to the press. It was regarded by all participants except the president as a painful experience."[17] Johnson thus gave little credit to the cabinet as a consultative body, keeping many of his cabinet officers at a distance. His use of the cabinet to dispense information and to promote the appearance that a substantive debate was taking place led one of his cabinet officers to complain: "Cabinet meetings under L.B.J. were really perfunctory.

They served two purposes: to let Dean Rusk brief us on the state of foreign affairs and let the president give us some occasional new political or personnel marching orders."[18]

Prior to his election in 1968 Richard Nixon (1969–1974) seemed to call for a powerful cabinet in his administration: "I don't want a government of yes-men. . . . [I want] a cabinet made up of the ablest men in America, leaders in their own right and not merely by virtue of appointment . . . men who will command the public's respect and the president's attention by the power of their intellect and the force of their ideas."[19] After his election Nixon took the unprecedented step of introducing his soon-to-be appointed cabinet on national television.

Despite his announced intention to use a cabinet system, President Nixon held few cabinet meetings and relegated the cabinet to a position of lesser importance than that of his White House staff. At one point Secretary of the Interior Walter J. Hickel, complaining that he had had only two or three private meetings with the president, advised Nixon: "Permit me to suggest that you consider meeting, on an individual and conversational basis, with members of your cabinet. Perhaps through such conversations we can gain greater insight into the problems confronting us all, into solutions of these problems."[20] Because of his disdain for his original cabinet, Nixon had a totally new one in place five years later.

Both Gerald R. Ford (1974–1977) and Jimmy Carter (1977–1981) pledged to use their cabinets as decision-making bodies. Although both held regular cabinet meetings at the beginning of their administrations, only Ford came close to making his cabinet a meaningful advisory group. Convinced that Watergate had resulted from Nixon's carelessness in allowing his personal aides to gain too much power at the expense of the cabinet, Ford restored the cabinet secretariat established by Eisenhower but abandoned by subsequent presidents. Like Eisenhower, he asked a cabinet secretary to draw up formal agendas for cabinet meetings, which often were used to gauge the views of his department heads on different issues. Hoxie noted: "More than any other president in the period from 1916 to 1981, he [Ford] restored the cabinet as a deliberative, meaningful advisory and administrative body."[21]

Jimmy Carter, in contrast, failed to achieve his goal of revitalizing the cabinet. Early in his administration Carter made this promise: "There will never be an instance while I am in office where the members of the White House staff dominate or act in a superior position to the members of the cabinet."[22] Early on, however, the Carter White House became embroiled in a controversy over the cabinet's status. Aide Jack Watson advocated a strong cabinet, but close Carter adviser Hamilton Jordan preferred that major decisions be made by high-level White House staffers. Jordan finally won, and Carter's cabinet lost any hope of achieving much prominence in presidential decision making. In fact, fewer and fewer cabinet meetings were held as the administration progressed. Carter met with his cabinet weekly during the first year of his administration; biweekly during the second

year; monthly during the third year; and only sporadically during his last year in office.[23]

Similarly, Ronald Reagan (1981–1989) met less frequently with his cabinet as his term in office progressed. Coming into office, Reagan intended to meet with his cabinet appointees weekly to discuss the major problems facing the government. Determined to avoid the friction between the cabinet and the White House staff that Nixon and Carter faced, Reagan quickly consolidated power over administration policy, personnel decisions, and budget priorities within the White House staff. His administration was more successful, however, in using the cabinet as an advisory group. Early in his first term Reagan divided the cabinet into seven councils, each of which addressed a specific substantive area: economic affairs, commerce and trade, food and agriculture, human resources, national resources and environment, legal policy, and management and administration. Under this system, cabinet members could concentrate on matters germane only to them and not to the government as a whole. Indeed, in some respects this system restored the advisory function that the cabinet enjoyed during the Eisenhower administration. By Reagan's second term, however, seven councils proved to be cumbersome, and the number of councils was reduced to just two—economic policy and domestic policy.

Although George Bush (1989–1993) did not indicate he would implement cabinet government in his presidential campaign, he made more use of his cabinet than most of his predecessors. Bush retained the cabinet council system of the Reagan years with three councils—economic policy, domestic policy, and national security policy. As Bush's strong chief of staff, John Sununu, exerted more influence and control over policy making within the White House, the frequency of formal cabinet meetings followed the typical pattern of decline. Yet Bush's use of the cabinet was more informal than formal. He created an atmosphere of organizational informality that kept cabinet officers in the policy-making process. Analyzing the cabinet structure of the Bush presidency, political scientist John P. Burke wrote, "Bush . . . generously delegated responsibility to his cabinet officers, permitting them to establish whatever patterns of contact with the White House they [were] most comfortable with."[24] As a result of these informal cabinet relationships, secretaries were often given the opportunity to offer advice and counsel to the president.

Like Bush, Bill Clinton offered no promise of cabinet government in his presidential campaign, and early in his administration none was evident. Soon after his election to the presidency, Clinton decided to centralize as much power within the White House as possible. By controlling subcabinet appointments, the White House hoped to avoid the chaos that characterized the Carter cabinet. The fact that Clinton sought great demographic diversity in his cabinet appointments made cabinet government difficult. Clinton's tendency to micromanage policy (his desire to attend all meetings and hear all arguments on a policy issue) contributed to the decision to centralize policy making as well

Early in the Clinton administration, Treasury Secretary Lloyd Bentsen, right, and the chairman of the National Economic Council, Robert Rubin, left, were instrumental in formulating economic policy. Rubin later replaced Bentsen at Treasury.

as personnel matters within the White House. Early in the Clinton administration, cabinet members complained that Clinton was not delegating policy decisions to the cabinet, that cabinet members were often informed too late of policy decisions, and that their objections to policy matters were often disregarded. Clinton, however, successfully used small councils made up of both cabinet and noncabinet members to provide policy advice. For example, the National Economic Council, headed by White House adviser Robert Rubin and including Secretary of Treasury Lloyd Bentsen (later replaced in that post by Rubin), Secretary of Labor Robert Reich, and Secretary of Commerce Ron Brown, helped Clinton set economic policy in the first part of his administration.

Role and Function of the Cabinet

Most presidents have come to expect little from their cabinets except the opportunity to exchange information. At best, the cabinet may serve as a source of advice for the president, but this use of the cabinet has been rare. Even when presidents, such as Nixon and Carter, emphasized the importance of their cabinets early in their administrations, their commitment to a strong cabinet soon diminished. As administrations mature, daily administrative matters and domestic and international crises often take more and more of a president's time. Moreover, presidential programs and goals become fixed, and cabinet secretaries, as heads of their departments, may find themselves competing for scarce resources. Cabinet meetings thus become less frequent, less enthusiastic, and less cordial, as well as a burden for both the department secretary and the president. Indeed, some department secretaries see cabinet meetings as nothing more than opportunities for their peers to take pot-shots at their departments' programs. Seeking to protect their administrative turf and hoping to avoid excessive and detrimen-

tal departmental sniping, many secretaries intentionally exercise restraint in cabinet meetings. Jesse H. Jones, Franklin Roosevelt's secretary of commerce, declared: "My principal reason for not having a great deal to say at cabinet meetings was that there was no one at the table who could be of help to me except the president, and when I needed to consult him, I did not choose a cabinet meeting to do so."[25]

CABINETS AS ADVISERS

Although many presidents have intentionally avoided placing their cabinets in an advisory role, some still consider such a role the ideal one for the presidential cabinet. In 1940 the leading British scholar on the presidency, Harold J. Laski, offered this description of what a good cabinet should do for an American president:

A good cabinet ought to be a place where the large outlines of policy can be hammered out in common, where the essential strategy is decided upon, where the president knows that he will hear, both in affirmation and in doubt, even in negation, most of what can be said about the direction he proposes to follow.[26]

No American presidential cabinet has lived up to Laski's model, however, and some presidents—Jackson, Wilson, and Kennedy, for example—have even gone to great lengths to avoid taking advice from their cabinets. Only Eisenhower came close to the model suggested by Laski, and even his cabinet procedures came up lacking.

Historically, cabinets have served presidents as an advisory group in one of three ways. First, in the cabinet meetings of some presidents, department heads discussed issues and problems informally, primarily to exchange information. This custom was generally followed by Franklin Roosevelt, Truman, Kennedy, Johnson, and Nixon. Second, the Eisenhower cabinet regularly considered specific issues, using papers authored by cabinet members and circulated prior to meetings. Both the president and the cabinet were aided by agendas, concise records, and a small secretariat. Third, under both Eisenhower and Truman, the National Security Council provided summaries of issue papers that earlier had been subjected to a thorough interdepartmental review, with dissenters identified and alternative language proposed.[27]

Why do most presidents avoid using their cabinets as advisory groups? Primarily, presidents are rarely willing to delegate the decision-making power needed to make the cabinet an effective advisory board. Many presidents feel that doing so might challenge their power. Moreover, a strong, institutionalized cabinet with its own staff might put the president at a disadvantage in the control of federal resources and information. According to presidential scholar Richard M. Pious, "A collective cabinet with its own staff could become a competitor for 'The Executive Power' and come to function as a 'council of state'—the system rejected at the Constitutional Convention."[28] Consequently, presidents have tended to downgrade the importance of their cabinets.

The presidential reluctance to use cabinets as advisory groups also stems from situations in which presidents are forced to choose cabinet appointees who may be weak or who may not represent the goals of their administrations. Schlesinger has contended that "genuinely strong presidents are not afraid to surround themselves with genuinely strong men [in the cabinet]."[29] Presidents, however, have rarely had more than one or two notable departmental secretaries at one time. Most of the time cabinet selections are influenced heavily by political considerations. Hess has written:

Historically, presidents have selected their cabinets on the basis of traditions, trade-offs, and obligations. . . . Once the obligations were fitted into the appropriate slots, balances had to be made. . . . The end result was often that a new president found himself surrounded with some people of less than inspiring ability, personalities that were incompatible, and even some cabinet members of questionable loyalty.[30]

Because presidents seldom have been closely associated with their cabinet officers, they have tended to rely on their White House staffs for advice. Since the establishment of the Executive Office of the President and the White House staff in 1939, the White House staff has acted as a threat to the cabinet's role as a policy-making institution. With their closer proximity to the Oval Office, White House staffers have more access to the president than the cabinet. Moreover, these staffers often are long-time personal assistants of the president, and they exhibit loyalty not necessarily found among members of the cabinet. Presidents Nixon and Carter reduced the influence of their cabinets in favor of the personal loyalties of certain members of their staffs. Indeed, both presidents asked their cabinets to resign en masse to allow them to appoint new "loyal" cabinet members. Specifically, cabinet advice gave way to Nixon's reliance on his trusted aides John Ehrlichman and Henry Kissinger and Carter's close connections with aide Hamilton Jordan and press secretary Jody Powell. Writing about this tendency for presidents to rely on advice from their staffs rather than their cabinets, British author Godfrey Hodgson noted:

The cabinet has been losing ground to the White House staff for a long time now. . . . Where successive presidents . . . have all come to rely more and more on their own staff and less and less on their cabinet members, where, moreover, two such different presidents as Richard Nixon and Jimmy Carter have both turned to their staff for help after an initial, apparently sincere effort to reverse the trend and give more authority to cabinet members, it is tempting to come to the conclusion that the decline of the cabinet is inevitable.[31]

The result is that the stronger and more assertive presidents attempt to be, the less likely they are to use their cabinets as vital advisory bodies. Thus, to protect their powers and to guard against a vigorous cabinet system that they may regard as more of a threat than a help, presidents may use cabinet meetings as devices for generating enthusiasm or displaying cabinet unity rather than as devices for a thorough discussion of problems facing the nation. Most presidents want advice when they ask for it, but they also want to reserve the right to either disregard it or not even seek it. A strong cabinet system that imposes advice upon them is then something to be resisted.

The Inner Cabinet

Although presidents may shun their cabinets as sources of information for decision-making purposes, individual cabinet members may serve as important sources of experience and advice. According to political scientist Frank Kessler, "Seasoned political veterans in the cabinet can provide a president one thing that the most dedicated and informed White House staffer often cannot, and that is a sense of perspective gained from years of experience and political savvy."[32] Certain cabinet members, by virtue of either their close relationship with the president or the department they head, may find themselves with greater access to the president and often the opportunity to influence the administration's policy. In fact, every cabinet usually has one or two members who have dominant personalities and who form close relationships with the president. In the Truman administration, for example, Secretary of State Dean Acheson and George C. Marshall, who served at different times as secretary of state and secretary of defense, overshadowed the rest of the cabinet. With his strong and outspoken foreign policy positions, Secretary of State John Foster Dulles dominated the Eisenhower cabinet. As defense secretary during the Vietnam War, Robert S. McNamara enjoyed close ties with both Presidents Kennedy and Johnson. Most of these cabinet members also had a significant influence on presidential decision making based on their personal friendships with the president. Acheson's friendship with Truman, for example, allowed him to influence the president greatly. However, influence wielded on the basis of intimate friendship and confidences was never transferred to colleagues or successors.

Access to the president is often influenced by the importance that the president places on a particular department. Because the departments of defense and state receive much attention from presidents, their secretaries usually have a more cordial relationship with their presidents based on the frequency of their contacts. On occasion some departments, and thus their secretaries, increase in importance in the eyes of the president. For example, the Department of Health, Education and Welfare (HEW) took on more significance as the number and size of social programs increased during the 1960s. John W. Gardner, secretary of HEW, gained status within the cabinet as he began the significant task of managing the Johnson administration's major education and health programs. And in the early months of the Clinton administration, Secretary of Treasury Lloyd Bentsen had more influence than any other cabinet member as Clinton developed a plan for deficit reduction. Usually, however, presidents devote most of their time and attention to national security and foreign policy. Consequently, some staff members, particularly the national security adviser, may have more access to the president than most cabinet members.

Composition of the Inner Cabinet

Cronin has suggested that contemporary presidential cabinets can be divided into inner and outer cabinets.[33] Based on extensive interviews with White House aides and cabinet officers about their views of the departments and their access to the president, Cronin found that the inner cabinet generally includes the secretaries of state, defense, and Treasury and the attorney general (a body analogous to President Washington's first cabinet). Because of the importance of their departments to the making of public policy, these cabinet members have been the most successful in influencing presidential decisions in a broad range of policy areas. The departments that deal almost exclusively with domestic policy and commerce form the outer cabinet. Their secretaries usually are more concerned with advocacy for their departments' constituent groups than with advising the president on policy issues.

Because presidents usually are very selective in filling inner cabinet positions, the views of these cabinet members are likely to mirror those of the chief executive. In addition, these appointees are often Washington veterans such as John Foster Dulles, Cyrus R. Vance (Carter's secretary of state), George P. Shultz (Reagan's secretary of state), or James Baker (Bush's secretary of state). Although President Clinton chose Washington outsiders for most of his cabinet positions, he turned to two well-known and well-respected insiders, Warren Christopher (secretary of state) and Lloyd Bentsen (secretary of Treasury), for his inner cabinet. Significant responsibility and visibility accompany these cabinet positions, and the officials holding them are usually in contact with the president on a daily basis. In addition to the top four cabinet positions, the inner cabinet frequently includes White House aides who have a close consultative relationship with the president.

The inner cabinet is generally divided into two subgroups, the first of which Cronin labeled the national security cabinet. This group is composed of the two cabinet members responsible for national security policy, the secretaries of state and de-

fense. Recent presidents have met at least weekly with their national security cabinets and have maintained telephone contact with them daily. One Johnson aide believed that President Johnson trusted just two of his cabinet members, Secretary of State Dean Rusk and Secretary of Defense Robert McNamara. Likewise, Secretary of State Cyrus Vance and Secretary of Defense Harold Brown were probably Carter's closest cabinet counselors.[34] And James Baker and Richard Cheney had close relationships with Bush.

In addition to the national security part of the inner cabinet, presidents rely heavily on the legal and economic counsel that they receive from their attorneys general and secretaries of the Treasury—the second inner cabinet subgroup. In recent years the Justice Department has been headed by close friends or relatives of the president. John Kennedy, for example, appointed his brother Robert, and Richard Nixon appointed his law partner and trusted friend John Mitchell. Jimmy Carter named his close friend Griffin Bell, and Ronald Reagan, during his second term in office, appointed one of his longtime California advisers and friends, Edwin Meese III.

The secretary of the Treasury has been an important presidential adviser since Alexander Hamilton advised George Washington. Although the formal responsibility of the Treasury Department may have been somewhat diminished with its loss of the Bureau of the Budget and the creation of the Council of Economic Advisers as an independent presidential advisory board, the secretary of the Treasury continues to play a significant role in domestic monetary and fiscal matters as well as in international commerce and currency. The latter area brings the Treasury secretary into the inner cabinet of foreign policy counselors. Cronin has suggested that the importance of the Treasury secretary as a member of the inner cabinet is to some degree a function of the intelligence and personality of the secretary. President Eisenhower said of his Treasury secretary George M. Humphrey: "In cabinet meetings, I always wait for George Humphrey to speak. I sit back and listen to the others talk while he doesn't say anything. But I know that when he speaks, he will say just what I was thinking."[35]

One curious feature of the inner cabinet is that its members tend to be more noticeably interchangeable than the members of the outer cabinet. Henry L. Stimson, for example, served as William Howard Taft's secretary of war, Herbert C. Hoover's secretary of state, and Franklin Roosevelt's secretary of war. Dean Acheson was undersecretary of the Treasury under Roosevelt and secretary of state under Truman. Eisenhower's attorney general, William P. Rogers, later became Nixon's first secretary of state. Elliot L. Richardson served as undersecretary of state, secretary of health, education and welfare, defense secretary, and attorney general. George Shultz, another versatile cabinet member, served as Nixon's secretary of the Treasury and later as Reagan's secretary of state. James Baker, one of Bush's closest friends and advisers, served as both secretary of Treasury in the Reagan administration and secretary of state under Bush. Warren Christopher served as deputy U.S. attorney general in the final two years of the Johnson administration and as deputy secretary of state for the duration of the Carter administration before becoming Clinton's secretary of state. When Kennedy was trying to attract Robert McNamara to the cabinet, he reportedly offered him his choice of either the defense post or the Treasury post. There has been some movement between the inner and outer cabinets, but most shifts in position have remained in the inner cabinet.

Although outsiders are brought into the inner cabinet by all presidents, why is there so much reliance on people who have served within that cabinet? Cronin has suggested simply that presidents look for appointees with whom they feel comfortable for these positions.

This interchangeability may result from the broad-ranging interests of the inner-cabinet positions, from the counseling style and relationships that develop in the course of an inner-cabinet secretary's tenure, or from the already close personal friendship that has often existed with the president. It may be easier for inner-cabinet than for outer-cabinet secretaries to maintain the presidential perspective; presidents certainly try to choose men they know and respect for these intimate positions.[36]

CABINETS AS ADVOCATES: THE OUTER CABINET

The outer cabinet deals with more highly organized and specialized clientele than the inner cabinet. While inner cabinet members are selected more on the basis of personal friendships and loyalty, outer cabinet members are selected more on the basis of geographical, ethnic, or political representation. And because they have fewer loyalties to the president, they often adopt an advocacy position for their departments.

The secretaries of interior, agriculture, commerce, labor, health and human services, housing and urban development, transportation, energy, education, and veterans affairs form the outer cabinet. Because their interests are so specialized, these secretaries are under extreme pressure from their clientele groups and political parties to serve specific interests. According to Cronin, "Whereas three of the four inner cabinet departments preside over policies that usually, though often imprudently, are perceived to be largely nonpartisan or bipartisan—national security, foreign policy, and the economy—the domestic departments almost always are subject to intense crossfire between partisan and domestic interest groups."[37]

Department secretaries are torn between loyalty to their presidents and loyalty to the departments they represent. Almost all secretaries go through what political scientist Richard P. Nathan has called "the ritualistic courting and mating process with the bureaucracy."[38] Because most outer cabinet members have only limited contact with the president, they usually are "captured" by the permanent bureaucracies. In fact, it is often in the best interest of secretaries to adopt the concerns of the departments they administer, thereby gaining the confidence of the career bureaucrats who work daily to further the pursuits of the department. Political scientist Hugh Heclo wrote: "Fighting your counterparts in other departments creates confidence and support beneath you. . . . Less politically effective executives may be personally admired by civil servants but have little to offer in return for bureaucratic support."[39] Not surprisingly, the tendency of cabinet secretaries to assume an advocacy role for their respective departments increases over the term of an administration. As they see their influence with the president diminishing, department secretaries try to build their political base of support within their own bureaucracies by forging goodwill with their bureaucrats.

Cabinet members who adopt an advocacy position contrary to the president's may find life in Washington difficult. The history of the presidency is full of examples of department secretaries who were "fired" by their presidents for not publicly supporting the president's programs. Truman fired Henry Wallace, his secretary of commerce, for criticizing his foreign policy, and Eisenhower fired Secretary of Labor Martin P. Durkin. In appointing Durkin, former head of the Plumbers and Pipe Fitters Union, Eisenhower was seeking to broaden the perspective of his cabinet. Durkin proved to be more of a spokesperson for labor than Eisenhower had expected. Later, Nixon fired Secretary of the Interior Walter J. Hickel, who, it turned out, was an outspoken opponent of some of the Nixon administration's programs. In fact, few cabinet members stay the length of a president's administration. Since World War II, the average tenure of a cabinet member has been less than thirty-five months, although turnover varies greatly from administration to administration. (See Table 29-1.) In the five years of his administration Nixon replaced his entire cabinet and made a total of thirty appointments, making the average tenure of a cabinet member in the Nixon administration about eighteen months. Over a period

TABLE 29-1 Tenure of Cabinet Secretaries Appointed 1945–1995, by Department

Department	Number of secretaries	Average months of service
IN EXISTENCE THROUGHOUT THE PERIOD		
State	16	38
Treasury	18	34
Justice	20	31
Interior	16	38
Agriculture	14	44
Commerce	22	28
Labor	18	34
CREATED IN THE PERIOD		
Defense (1947)	19	31
HEW/HHS (1953/1980)	18	29
HUD (1965)	10	37
Transportation (1966)	12	30
Energy (1977)	7	33
Education (1980)	6	32
Veterans Affairs (1989)	2	42

SOURCE: Adapted from Charles O. Jones, *The Presidency in a Separated System* (Washington, D.C.: Brookings, 1994), 65.

of a year and a half Nixon had five attorneys general.[40] In comparison, Eisenhower made only twenty appointments during the eight years he was in office. Cabinet turnover also varies greatly among cabinet departments. Although the Department of Justice has had frequent turnover since 1945, the Departments of Agriculture, State, and Interior have had long-serving secretaries.[41]

Relations between presidents and their cabinet members—sometimes even members of the inner cabinet—deteriorate rapidly after the inauguration. For example, scarcely eighteen months after being sworn into office, Secretary of State Alexander M. Haig Jr. left the Reagan administration when he failed to gain the confidence of the president and his aides. More often than not, however, friction develops between presidents and cabinet members because cabinet secretaries adopt the view of the departments and constituencies they represent.

As a cabinet secretary assumes a larger advocacy role, the relationship between president and cabinet member becomes more strained. Cabinet meetings become increasingly confrontational, and the cabinet becomes less useful to the president as an effective advisory body. If cabinet secretaries carefully build their bases of support, they can frustrate a president's policy-making initiatives. Franklin Roosevelt often complained about the difficulty he had in dealing with the bureaucracies:

The Treasury is so large and so far-flung and ingrained in its practices that I find it almost impossible to get the action and results that I want even with Henry [Morgenthau] there. But, Treasury is nothing compared with the State Department. You should go through the experience of trying to get any changes in thinking, policy, and action of the career diplomats and then you'd know what a real problem was.[42]

Close presidential advisers usually view outer cabinet members as more of a burden than a help to presidential decision making. Over the years, many high-level White House staffers have performed cabinet-level roles for the president. Some actually found themselves attending cabinet meetings. Eisenhower, for example, designated aide Sherman Adams to serve as an ex officio member of his cabinet. Other presidents have simply trusted and confided in their close aides more than their cabinets. For his important decisions, Kennedy preferred the advice of aides Theodore C. Sorensen and McGeorge Bundy to that of his cabinet members. Such White House advisers believe that they have the president's best interests in mind. In their view, most outer cabinet members neglect the president's interests for those of their own clientele. One close Carter aide explained: "Nobody expects Ray Marshall at Labor to be a spokesman for anything other than big labor. You just have to live with this. . . ."[43] The White House does not view advocacy as anything positive.

Advocacy alienates outer cabinet members from the president even more than they already are. For example, in response to pressure from western Republicans, President Nixon appointed Walter Hickel, a former governor of Alaska, to head the Department of the Interior, instead of his first choice, Rogers C. B. Morton from Maryland. At first feared by environmentalists,

Nixon fired Interior Secretary Walter J. Hickel, who, it turned out, was an outspoken opponent of some of the Nixon administration's programs.

Hickel turned out to be an opponent of big oil's plans to route the Alaskan pipeline through some northern wilderness lands. Hickel's opposition to the Nixon administration's programs and his tendency to be outspoken quickly got him into hot water with the president, who then considered Hickel an adversary. Hickel explained:

Initially I considered it a compliment because, to me, an adversary in an organization is a valuable asset. It was only after the president had used the term many times and with a disapproving inflection that I realized he considered an adversary an enemy. I could not understand why he would consider me an enemy.

As I sensed that the conversation was about to end, I asked, "Mr. President, do you want me to leave the administration?" He jumped from his chair, very hurried and agitated. He said, "That's one option we hadn't considered." He called in Ehrlichman and said: "John, I want you to handle this. Wally asked whether he should leave. That's one option we hadn't considered."[44]

A week later Hickel was fired. Although extreme, Hickel's case is typical of what most outer cabinet members face when they consider their relationships with their presidents.

In reality, presidents rarely fire cabinet members; cabinet members usually anticipate presidential dissatisfaction and resign. Sometimes cabinet members become so disenchanted with presidential programs and policies that they decide to leave on their own accord. For example, after becoming increasingly concerned about the direction of U.S. foreign policy during the late 1970s, Secretary of State Cyrus Vance finally decided to part company with the Carter administration over the attempted Iranian hostage rescue mission. Although he disagreed privately with many of Carter's foreign policy decisions during his tenure, Vance did not make his concerns public until three weeks after his resignation.

CABINET ALTERNATIVES

Has the presidential cabinet outlived its usefulness? Presidents continue to seek the advice of their inner cabinets, but rarely in the history of the presidency have collective cabinet meetings been meaningful. Many scholars believe that as long as presidents are subject to political pressures to appoint certain cabinet members who are not personally loyal to them and as long as cabinet secretaries are captured by their departments, the collective cabinet will remain useless as an advisory group.

Presidents and presidential scholars have explored alternatives to the present cabinet system. Most presidents have used task forces composed of several cabinet or subcabinet members and White House aides to help them study specific problems. President Kennedy, for example, used many such task forces—often chaired by his brother, Attorney General Robert F. Kennedy—to study national security problems. Kennedy required these study groups to produce both majority and minority reports.

Although task forces have produced some meaningful and innovative policy analysis, they have had some problems. Typical of the Kennedy task forces was the executive committee he created to advise him during the Cuban Missile Crisis in 1962. It was composed of the president, Vice President Lyndon Johnson, Secretary of State Dean Rusk, Secretary of Defense Robert McNamara, Secretary of Treasury C. Douglas Dillon, Attorney General Robert Kennedy, Special Foreign Affairs Assistant McGeorge Bundy, Chairman of the Joint Chiefs of Staff Gen. Maxwell Taylor, White House aide Theodore Sorensen, CIA director John McCone, and three people from outside the executive branch: Paul Nitze, George W. Ball, and Llewellyn Thompson. Kennedy ordered the task force to put any other duties they might have aside. The system worked well for the missile crisis, but would it have worked if there had been anything else pressing the administration for attention? According to Kessler, "Presidential task forces and White House staff–created options provided a certain creative chaos to the Kennedy system for gathering foreign policy ideas. The arrangements proved useful in moving from crisis to crisis but left much to be desired in heading off crises before they reached the flash point. Long-range policy making suffered. . . ."[45]

Some scholars such as Stephen Hess have maintained that the cabinet should be strengthened and made more collegial. Hess has argued for a presidency in which responsibility is shared by the president and the cabinet:

Effective presidential leadership in the immediate future is likely to result only from creating more nearly collegial administrations in which presidents rely on the cabinet officers as the principal sources of advice and hold them personally accountable—in the British sense of "the doctrine of ministerial responsibility"—for the operations of the different segments of government.[46]

Benjamin V. Cohen, one of Franklin Roosevelt's chief advisers during the 1930s, suggested a similar idea in a 1974 lecture at the University of California. Cohen called for the creation of an executive council composed of five to eight distinguished citizens appointed by the president. The council would have staff, access to information, and the power to monitor and coordinate government activities. The president would be obliged to consult with this group before making critical decisions.[47]

President Nixon considered introducing a "supercabinet" in his second term. In his 1971 State of the Union address he proposed merging the eight existing domestic departments into four new superagencies: natural resources, human resources, economic affairs, and community development. Although Congress refused to approve his plan, Nixon proceeded to name four cabinet members (the secretaries of Treasury, agriculture, HEW, and HUD) as presidential counselors. As White House aides as well as cabinet members, they assumed functional responsibility over the areas served by the proposed superagencies. Nixon's efforts in this area were soon sidetracked, however, as he became engulfed in the Watergate scandal.

Several recent presidents have formed cabinet councils in an attempt to integrate the advice of department secretaries and White House advisers on important policy matters. Organized on the basis of broad policy areas, the councils functioned much like Eisenhower's full cabinet: they deliberated policy recommendations, developed administration positions, and coordinated presidential decisions. The president, nominally in charge of each council, usually designated one of the department heads as chair. Because the White House provided staff support, the councils were able to act fairly independently of the departments.

Presidents Ford, Reagan, and Bush, who tended to delegate much of their authority, used cabinet councils. Roger Porter, an aide to all three presidents, pioneered the idea in the Ford administration. Porter favored a system of "multiple advocacy," in which the president received advice on policy issues from several different sources and perspectives, and cabinet councils helped centralize decision making by integrating opposing advice.[48]

Reagan established five cabinet councils in 1981—Economic Affairs, Commerce and Trade, Human Resources, Natural Resources and Environment, and Food and Agriculture—and two in 1982—Legal Policy and Management and Administration. Each council had between six and eleven members. Reagan usually designated one of his cabinet members or White House aides to chair a council in its initial stages of discussion. During the final sessions the president presided. Interested cabinet

TABLE 29-2 Appointments, Personnel, and Budget Authority, by Department

Department	Year established	Presidential appointments		Personnel (thousands)		Budget authority ($ billions)	
		Schedule C appointments[a]	Total appointments[b]	1994 actual	1995 estimate	1994 actual	1995 estimate
Agriculture	1889	131	197	109.8	108.9	$65.6	$61.9
Commerce	1913	152	237	36.0	36.0	3.8	4.1
Defense[c]	1947	103	202	868.3	834.1	251.4	252.6
Education	1980	116	156	4.8	5.1	27.0	33.5
Energy	1977	107	170	19.8	20.5	17.2	15.5
Health and Human Services[d]	1980	89	176	63.4	62.8	307.7	302.7
Housing and Urban Development	1965	83	123	13.1	12.9	26.3	25.8
Interior	1849	54	111	76.3	76.3	7.5	7.5
Justice	1870	64	170	95.3	102.0	10.2	12.8
Labor	1913	91	124	17.5	17.6	38.2	33.8
State	1789	97	194	25.2	25.0	5.8	6.0
Transportation	1966	57	113	66.4	65.2	42.3	40.4
Treasury	1789	75	129	157.3	161.4	309.3	353.1
Veterans Affairs	1989	13	32	233.1	229.9	36.8	38.2
TOTALS		1,232	2,134	1,786.3	1,757.7	$1,149.1	$1,187.9

SOURCES: Budget authority and personnel figures are from Executive Office of the President, *Budget of the United States Government, Fiscal Year 1996* (Washington, D.C.: Government Printing Office, 1995), 215, 222. Presidential appointment figures are from the Office of Personnel Management.

NOTES: Civilian employment as measured by full-time equivalents. a. Schedule C appointees are top-level presidential aides and are exempted from the testing and qualification requirements of the civil service merit system. b. Figures include noncareer employees in the Senior Executive Service and public law positions, such as State Department Foreign Service officers. c. Personnel figures include only civilian employees. Budget authority figures exclude civil defense. d. The Social Security Administration (SSA) became independent of HHS effective March 1995; to provide consistent numbers across the period 1994–1995, SSA employment and budget authority have been subtracted from the 1994 HHS figures. e. Figure does not include U.S. marshals or U.S. attorneys. f. Figure does not include U.S. ambassadors unless members of the Foreign Service.

members not on a specific council were often invited to attend a council's meetings.

Patterned after the National Security Council, Reagan's cabinet councils were designed to make cabinet members part of the presidential decision-making process by centralizing policy discussions. The council system initially worked well. During the first eighteen months of the Reagan administration the councils considered approximately two hundred issues. Reporting directly to White House presidential advisers, the councils allowed Reagan to delegate issues in the early stages of discussion. During his second term, Reagan replaced much of his cabinet and White House staff, and the council system became unwieldy and collapsed.

The Bush administration implemented its own council system, with three councils—Economic Policy, chaired by Treasury secretary Nicholas Brady, Domestic Policy, chaired by Attorney General Richard Thornburgh, and National Security, chaired by the national security adviser, Brent Scowcroft. Councils met regularly but not for significant amounts of time. The domestic and economic councils met for one hour every other week. The national security council met more frequently because of the emphasis Bush placed on foreign policy.

Although the council system worked well during the early stages of presidential administrations, it generally fell into disuse as administrations matured. The councils, designed to increase the influence of cabinet members in the policy-making process, may have done just the opposite. Critics have argued that cabinet councils unduly centralize decision making in the

White House or in an even smaller group similar to the inner cabinet. Also, by creating additional policy-making layers, the council system may actually slow down decision making and make it more cumbersome.

Styles and Methods of Appointment

Selection of the department secretaries is crucial because the cabinet is the most prominent feature of the president's team. Although the number of appointments each president makes is small when compared with the size of the departments themselves, appointments to the cabinet and subcabinet (the more than one thousand deputy secretaries, undersecretaries, assistant secretaries, and deputy assistant secretaries who manage the departments) indicate both the policy direction and credibility of a new administration. *(See Table 29-2.)* Consequently, most new presidents face intense public scrutiny of their cabinet appointments. In fact, after the 1980 election the public interest was so great that in the two and a half months between the election and Ronald Reagan's inauguration the *New York Times* printed one hundred articles and editorials on the incoming administration's cabinet appointments. Twenty-one of these articles appeared on the front page.[49] Beyond their symbolic importance, however, cabinet appointments provide presidents with their best early opportunity to show their leadership. Moreover, the first step toward a successful administration is in all likelihood the wise and prudent selection of a new cabinet.

The cabinet secretary's job is by any standard a difficult one.

The relationships that secretaries maintain with the president and their individual departments have an important bearing on the success of an administration. Presidential scholar Richard M. Pious has pointed out that department secretaries "must manage their departments and set priorities; represent constituencies to the president and the president to constituencies; help make administration policy and propose new policy initiatives; offer advice to the president."[50]

Ideally, some argue, cabinet appointees should be able to demonstrate that they are uniquely qualified to head one of the major departments of the federal government, and presidents should make appointments to cabinet positions based upon the administrative qualifications of the nominee. In practice, however, presidents rarely make appointments based solely on administrative ability. Instead, they consider such factors as personal loyalty, political party, ideological compatibility, acceptability to Congress, geographic representation, constituent group representation, reputation, expertise, and prior government experience.

Different presidents use different strategies for filling cabinet positions. Although no president has ever adhered to a single appointment strategy, political scientist Nelson W. Polsby found that most recent presidents have used at least one of three major approaches.[51] First, some presidents base appointments primarily on constituent concerns. They find appointees who already have strong connections or political associations with groups served by the department. Although such an arrangement may serve the department and certain constituent groups well in some respects, it also may prove to be divisive because very few departmental secretaries will be acceptable to all clientele groups. For example, conservationists might welcome a particular secretary of the interior, while miners might find the appointee to be completely unsympathetic to their concerns. In addition, some appointees chosen on the basis of constituency concerns may not be completely representative of constituents. In assembling his cabinet in late 1992, President Clinton set out to appoint a cabinet that "looks like America" in an effort make his cabinet a model of ethnic, racial, and gender diversity. In making his appointments, Clinton apparently ignored financial diversity. *Time* reported that as many as ten of Clinton's initial thirteen cabinet appointees were millionaires. (This compared with the Reagan administration, which had seven, and the Bush administration, with six.)[52]

Second, for some presidents expertise in the policy area served by the department is the primary criterion for appointment. For example, nominees for secretaries of defense and state tend to have substantial backgrounds in foreign affairs. However, secretaries appointed on the basis of their technical mastery of the substantive concerns of the departments are often oblivious to the political goals of the president's administration.

A third approach used by presidents is the appointment of generalists to cabinet positions. Such secretaries are not connected to the constituent groups served by the department, nor do they have expertise in the substantive interests of the department. They are sought instead for their loyalty to the president. Thus in theory, appointees are able to focus on implementing the president's programs and not on a narrow set of policies advocated by constituents or the department. Polsby contends, however, that the generalist's loyalty to the president can become pathological. Departmental officers not obligated by the charter of the department or ties to clientele groups would be much more likely to oblige a president who asks them to do things that are illegal or immoral to further the president's political cause. For example, Attorney General John Mitchell's loyalty to President Nixon superseded his obligation to serve as the nation's chief legal officer and allowed him to engage in questionable and illegal activities in an effort to protect Nixon during the 1972 election.

After electoral debts have been paid off with the initial cabinet selections and the media attention has begun to fade, presidents often turn to appointees who will help them accomplish their objectives. Competence and loyalty become the most important criteria for selection. Presidents need competent and loyal cabinet officers to help them deal with the federal bureaucracy and with Congress. According to presidential appointments scholar G. Calvin Mackenzie, "It is characteristic of interm selection decisions to reflect the president's concerns in dealing with the executive establishment and with Congress. . . . In-term personnel selections . . . often become a central part of an administration's political and administrative strategies for accomplishing its policy objectives."[53] Although the criteria that presidents use in filling cabinet positions often call for certain selections, the appointment process itself can impose additional restrictions on their ability to choose the best possible cabinet. Unlike some presidential appointments, cabinet nominations must be submitted to the Senate for majority confirmation. Some nominees are unwilling to submit to the scrutiny that accompanies the Senate confirmation process, which can be long and demanding. After a particularly exhausting confirmation hearing in the summer of 1975, Gov. Stanley K. Hathaway of Wyoming, President Gerald R. Ford's appointee for secretary of the interior, suffered a nervous breakdown. Although this type of confirmation hearing is hardly the rule, it indicates the potential hazards of a tough Senate confirmation procedure.

Other nominees may not be willing to make the financial sacrifice necessary to enter public service. In their study of the presidential appointment process, John W. Macy, Bruce Adams, and J. Jackson Walter found that almost all executives in the private sector are better paid than those holding positions at similar levels of responsibility in the public sector.[54] Consequently, presidential appointees recruited from the private sector usually take a cut in salary to work for the federal government. It is not unusual that a cabinet appointee give up a $500,000 annual salary for a cabinet post that pays $148,400 a year. Similarly, the rigors of financial disclosure are a disincentive to some nominees. Some conflict-of-interest regulations, such as those imposed on President Jimmy Carter's appointees, contain very precise demands. From his nominees Carter required full financial disclosure of their net worth, a promise not to return to Washington to lobby for pay for at least one year after leaving federal employment, and a commitment to shed all financial holdings that might be affected by a later official decision.

Those who decide to accept the challenges of the confirmation process and the terms of presidential appointment now face higher standards for appointment to public office, as well as the increased expectations of the American public. Thus, cabinet officers must have the management skills necessary to administer a large public bureaucracy, as well as some knowledge of what their departments do. The personal lives of appointees are subject to higher standards as well. Former Texas senator John Tower, President George Bush's nominee for secretary of defense in 1989, saw his nomination defeated on the Senate floor following allegations of drunkenness and sexual improprieties. President Bill Clinton's first nominee to head the Justice Department, Zoë Baird, withdrew from the Senate confirmation process after it was revealed that she had hired an illegal immigrant as a nanny and had not paid Social Security taxes on the nanny's salary. The failure of the Tower and Baird nominations has caused many to look on the confirmation process with some degree of cynicism. Yale law professor Stephen L. Carter has described the modern confirmation process as one that allows disqualifications to overshadow questions of ability and policy. He writes, "We presume the nominees to be entitled to confirmation absent smoking guns, and then we look for smoke in order to disqualify them."[55]

How well do cabinet officers meet these public demands? A 1967 Brookings Institution study analyzed the background, tenure, and later occupations of those in high executive positions, including cabinet posts, from 1933 through April 1965. It found that most high federal officeholders had high levels of education and substantial federal administrative experience; generally they were well prepared for their positions. But the study also suggested that with their short tenure, top executives rarely had enough time to learn the issues and personalities of the job.[56]

A comparable study conducted by the National Academy of Public Administration (NAPA) in 1987 found that political executives for the period 1964–1984 were very similar to those in the Brookings Institution study. Using data on federal political executives, , the NAPA study reported very little difference in these appointees and those holding office fifty years earlier. Executive-level appointees remained predominantly white, middle-aged males with degrees from prestigious universities. Although the number of women and members of racial minorities in cabinet positions had increased, their proportions did not reflect their representation in the general population.[57]

The NAPA survey also pointed out a few significant changes in the characteristics of executive appointees. For example, career public servants increasingly were filling executive-level ap-

pointments. As a result, fewer people were being recruited from business, professional, and academic careers, and more appointees were coming from public service "professions" such as state and local governments, congressional staffs, and other noncareer and career federal positions.[58]

In general, presidents replace cabinet members frequently, leading critics to argue that cabinet members are not in their positions long enough to learn all the important aspects of their jobs. How long does a typical cabinet member stay in office? The 1967 Brookings study found that cabinet secretaries remained in office a median period of 3.3 years, while the more recent NAPA study found that the length of tenure of cabinet secretaries had dropped significantly, to a median of 1.9 years. The authors of the Brookings study argued, however, that length of tenure in a particular office is not as important as length of tenure in the federal government. The NAPA survey discovered that cabinet secretaries have a median of four years of experience in the federal government, indicating that many have come from public service with several years of experience.

Nominees to cabinet or subcabinet positions often view their appointment as a ticket to a later position in private business. In the NAPA twenty-year survey almost 93 percent of those questioned decided to leave public service for the private sector. The Department of Defense suffered the most from this public service drain. Two-thirds of its top political appointees later found their way into business positions.

Some presidents have come into office determined to control the staffing of the more than one thousand high-level department positions directly below those of the department secretaries. In seeking to accomplish their programs and goals, presidents want these high-ranking department executives to be loyal. The Reagan and Clinton administrations, for example, sought to keep the appointment of subcabinet officials squarely within the control of the White House, allowing little counsel from the department secretaries. Richard Nixon and Jimmy Carter, in contrast, initially invited their department secretaries to make their own senior departmental appointments. Both presidents wanted their cabinets to be independent of the White House. Later, however, Nixon and Carter spent a great deal of energy trying to bring decision-making power under their control to maintain some degree of loyalty to administration objectives.

RECENT PRESIDENTIAL APPOINTMENTS

No president is ever really free from political concerns in making cabinet or subcabinet appointments. Political parties, special-interest groups, members of Congress, and constituent concerns all play a role in the selection process. The role of these political concerns is not constant, however; sometimes one factor has been more important than others, and at other times presidents have ignored some or all of these factors. A look at cabinet selection decisions may better illustrate how presidents select cabinet appointees.

Franklin D. Roosevelt

In staffing his administration Roosevelt usually relied on five sources: friends and colleagues from his younger years, participants in his New York gubernatorial administration, his 1932 presidential campaigners, the "old boys' network" (or people-who-knew-people-who-knew-Roosevelt), and the rank and file of the Democratic Party.[59] As a result, his selection of nominees for cabinet positions outwardly showed no underlying purpose or consistency. For example, Frances Perkins, the first female cabinet member, was appointed secretary of labor because Roosevelt wanted a woman in his cabinet. He appointed Harold L. Ickes, a nominal Republican, as secretary of the interior, Henry A. Wallace, a noted agricultural economist and also a nominal Republican, as secretary of agriculture, and Daniel C. Roper, an old friend who was not well known in public life, as secretary of commerce.

Presidential scholar Stephen Hess contends that in reality Roosevelt had two principles that dictated his cabinet appointment strategy. First, early in his administration Roosevelt sought to appoint only cabinet members who would not overshadow him or threaten him politically. The only appointee of any real national prominence was Secretary of State Cordell Hull. As World War II approached, however, Roosevelt appointed cabinet members, such as Henry L. Stimson, Hoover's former secretary of state, and Frank Knox, the 1936 Republican candidate for vice president, who had more national stature. This early strategy of appointing relative unknowns to the cabinet was designed to make sure that the public perceived the administration to be distinctively Rooseveltian. Second, Roosevelt embarked on a deliberate strategy of appointing opposites to his cabinet; he reveled in the give and take of opposing opinions. For example, by appointing both fiscal conservatives, such as Secretary of the Treasury William H. Woodin, and fiscal liberals, such as Secretary of Commerce Harry L. Hopkins, to the cabinet, Roosevelt was able to play each side against the other and hear both sides of an issue. He once told Frances Perkins, "A little rivalry is stimulating. . . . It keeps everybody going to prove he is a better fellow than the next man. It keeps them honest, too."[60]

Similarly, Roosevelt insisted on being involved in the appointments to lower-level cabinet positions, and he succeeded in appointing exceptional subcabinet members. These young intellectuals and academics, who had little experience in politics but shared Roosevelt's ideological beliefs, included such undersecretaries and subcabinet members as Dean G. Acheson, Jerome Frank, and James Landis. Although Roosevelt's cabinet secretaries may not have approved of this selection process, they nevertheless yielded to the president's selections.

Harry S. Truman

Upon Roosevelt's death in 1945, Harry Truman at first encouraged his inherited cabinet to remain in the new administration. Within three months, however, he had replaced six of Roosevelt's ten department heads, as he found that he did not enjoy the conflicting policy advice offered by Roosevelt's diverse cabinet. Truman replaced Roosevelt's appointees with personal acquaintances and others whom he felt were qualified as well as loyal to him.

Because he wanted to have his own team in place by late 1945, the president gladly accepted the resignations of Roosevelt loyalists. Their replacement by appointees loyal to Truman's programs and goals became a major task of his administration. To show his keen interest in the selection of his new cabinet, Truman invited nominees to the White House to inform them personally of their nomination. For Truman, loyalty to him and experience in government were the two major criteria for appointment to his cabinet. Thus, in an attempt to justify the nomination of Lewis B. Schwellenbach (a former senator from Washington) as secretary of labor, Truman argued that he and Schwellenbach "saw right down the same alley on policy."[61] As for the criterion of experience in government, four of Truman's first six cabinet appointments were former members of Congress. He also chose more members of his administration from

Frances E. Perkins, whom New York governor Franklin D. Roosevelt had named administrative head of the state labor department, became the first woman named to the cabinet when President Roosevelt appointed her secretary of labor in 1933. She was instrumental in framing the social security system and remained in the cabinet until June 1945.

PRESIDENTIAL REORGANIZATION AUTHORITY

The power to reorganize the executive branch of government—to shift duties from one department to another, to shift responsibilities from one agency within a department to another, and to create new departments and agencies—lies with Congress. Prior to World War I, executive branch reorganizations were affected through the normal legislative process, whereby Congress acts on bills submitted by the president. To cope with the exigencies of the war, however, Congress passed the Overman Act of 1918, which for the first time delegated to the president broad authority to coordinate and consolidate government agencies to make them more efficient. The authority lasted only through the end of the war.

In 1932 Congress granted President Herbert Hoover's request for authority to reorganize the executive branch. The Economy Act of 1932 granting Hoover's request contained a novel mechanism, the legislative veto, that allowed Congress to retain some control over the reorganization process. If either house of Congress passed a resolution disapproving a reorganization within sixty days, the reorganization was voided. In the Economy Act of 1933 Congress again delegated its reorganization authority to the president but modified the legislative veto such that both houses of Congress would have to concur in a bill opposing the reorganization, but the president would then have the opportunity to veto that bill.

The authority granted to the president by the Economy Act of 1933 expired in 1935 and was not renewed until 1939. At that time, the legislative veto provisions were once again modified. Like the 1933 act, the 1939 legislation stipulated that to kill a reorganization, both houses of Congress would have to pass a resolution opposing it. But the 1939 act did not give the president the opportunity to veto the congressional resolution. President Franklin D. Roosevelt submitted five reorganization plans to Congress before the 1939 act expired on January 20, 1941, one of which created the Executive Of-

fice of the President. None were blocked by Congress. The First War Powers Act of 1941 extended the president's authority to reorganize the government for the duration of the national emergency.

In the postwar period, Congress routinely granted extensions of the president's reorganization authority, tinkering with provisions of the legislative veto each time. Some presidents made wide use of the power. President Truman, acting on the recommendations of a bipartisan Commission on Organization of the Executive Branch of the Government, known as the Hoover Commission after its chairman, former president Herbert Hoover, sent forty-one reorganization plans to Congress. President Dwight D. Eisenhower submitted a dozen plans in 1953, one of which created the Department of Health, Education, and Welfare.

Under two presidents—John F. Kennedy and Richard M. Nixon—Congress intentionally allowed the authority to lapse. Kennedy angered Congress in 1962 by trying to create a department of urban affairs and housing, which Congress had specifically rejected a year earlier. And when a 1971 grant of authority lapsed on April 1, 1973, while Nixon was in office, Congress declined to renew it. President Carter requested and received a new grant of authority in 1977.

In 1983 the long-standing reorganization procedures were dealt a blow by the Supreme Court. In *Immigration and Naturalization Service v. Chadha*, the Court declared that legislative vetoes such as the one used by Congress to pass judgment on presidential reorganization plans were unconstitutional. Congress, unwilling to delegate authority to the president without some means of control, refused to renew the president's 1977 grant of authority, which had expired in 1981. Consequently, reorganizations of the government can now be achieved only through laws passed by both houses of Congress and signed by the president.

the ranks of the federal government than did any of his successors. Truman believed that success in government could be transferred to the political arena of the presidential cabinet. He wrote:

I consider political experience absolutely necessary, because a man who understands politics understands free government. Our government is by the consent of the people, and you have to convince a majority of the people that what you are trying to do is right and in their interest. If you are not a politician, you cannot do it.[62]

For the most part Truman chose highly qualified, experienced cabinet appointees, especially in areas dealing with foreign affairs. His most celebrated cabinet appointments included Secretaries of State George C. Marshall and Dean Acheson, Secretaries of Defense James V. Forrestal and Robert A. Lovett, and Secretary of War Robert P. Patterson. Although some Truman appointees were members of America's governing elite, who went to the most prestigious schools and belonged to the Amer-

ican upper class, the president generally appointed those with whom he had the most in common and knew the best—government employees.

Dwight D. Eisenhower

As the first Republican president in twenty years, Dwight Eisenhower had to look beyond the Democratic-controlled federal government for cabinet appointees. Unlike Truman, he was not involved personally in most of these decisions. Even though Republican leaders were extremely interested in the new administration's choices for these positions, Eisenhower did not seek their advice in selecting his cabinet. The job of filling new government positions, including those of the cabinet, went to two friends, Herbert Brownell Jr., a New York attorney, and Gen. Lucius Clay, chairman of the board of Continental Can Company. Although Brownell and Clay made the initial selections for the cabinet, the choice of a subcabinet was left to the cabinet secretaries themselves.

Eisenhower strongly disliked the role that patronage played in the appointment process. Expressing the "profound hope" that he would not have to become too involved in the distribution of federal patronage, Eisenhower wrote in his diary: "Having been fairly successful in late years learning to keep a rigid check on my temper, I do not want to encounter complete defeat at this late date."[63]

With his distaste for patronage and a desire to delegate as much administrative responsibility as possible, Eisenhower found himself with a cabinet made up almost entirely of strangers and Republican Party members who were not nationally well-known. Only two of Eisenhower's ten initial choices, Attorney General Brownell and Postmaster General Arthur E. Summerfield, had played a major role in his presidential campaign.

The lack of conservative Republican Party notables particularly offended party leaders. Although Eisenhower had appointed primarily Republicans to his cabinet, most were from the moderate faction of the party. When Sen. Robert A. Taft (R-Ohio), the Republican leader in the Senate, took exception to being excluded from the cabinet selection process, Eisenhower agreed to allow members of Congress to advise the departments in their selection of subcabinet appointees. This compromise did not entirely please congressional leaders. It succeeded in making Eisenhower aware, however, of the importance of political considerations in making cabinet selections.

The *New Republic* described Eisenhower's first cabinet as "eight millionaires and one plumber." The millionaires not only had money, but they also were leaders in their professions. According to Stephen Hess, "Eisenhower believed that a successful person, someone who had already proven that he could run something big, would be best able to tame a government department."[64] Only three members of his cabinet did not have backgrounds in management. Two of them, Secretary of State John Foster Dulles and Brownell, were attorneys. Secretary of Labor Martin P. Durkin was the most notable exception. The nomination of Durkin, head of the Plumbers and Pipe Fitters Union and an Adlai Stevenson supporter, surprised many observers. Apparently, Eisenhower wanted to appease the unions and broaden the perspective of the cabinet. Out of harmony with the rest of the Eisenhower administration, Durkin resigned within the first year.

John F. Kennedy

John Kennedy was elected president in 1960 by one of the narrowest margins in history. This factor, probably more than any other, dictated the selection of the Kennedy cabinet. Although Kennedy expressed a desire to choose men of superior quality, he was restricted by a number of political factors. Kennedy viewed the appointment of department secretaries primarily as an opportunity to consolidate various political factions and to enlarge his popular base of support. Consequently, he appointed representatives of both political parties, all sections of the country, a variety of religious backgrounds, and a wide range of professions as his first ten cabinet members. They included a corporation president, Robert S. McNamara, as secretary of defense, and a Republican who had contributed heavily to Richard Nixon's campaign, C. Douglas Dillon, as secretary of the Treasury.

Like his predecessors, President Kennedy wanted to make the federal government responsive to his programs and direction. He therefore sought cabinet members who would support his agenda and carry out his directives. After eight years of Republican control of the bureaucracy, Kennedy expressed the fear that the departments had developed a life of their own. As G. Calvin Mackenzie noted, Kennedy did not want his department heads to be "simply the instruments or mouthpieces of the organizations they were appointed to lead."[65] He wanted a cabinet on which he could rely to pursue his goals vigorously in the departments; otherwise, his task as president would be much more difficult. From this perspective it was not surprising that Kennedy appointed his younger brother, Robert, as his attorney general. While Robert F. Kennedy had no judicial experience, he was personally close to the president and could be counted on to carry out the president's program in the Department of Justice. Some of Kennedy's other appointments, however, were surprising. Both McNamara and Secretary of State Dean Rusk were unknown to Kennedy. They were the products of an informal network of talent hunters that produced much of Kennedy's cabinet and White House staff. To screen candidates for his cabinet, Kennedy called upon friends and acquaintances across the country to help him assess the qualifications or abilities of potential appointees. He then interviewed candidates himself, and he made the final decisions on appointments. This informal network and Kennedy's personal interest helped him recruit individuals who had proven themselves in business, professional, and university communities.

Robert McNamara, president of Ford Motor Company and a nonpolitical Republican, impressed Kennedy from the beginning. McNamara's management abilities meant that Kennedy would not have to worry about the day-to-day business of the Defense Department. Dean Rusk, an assistant secretary of state during the Truman administration, understood the folkways of the State Department. Kennedy expected this to be helpful in accomplishing his goal of moving the primary responsibility for foreign policy decision making from the National Security Council to the State Department. Rusk proved not to be assertive enough, however, in pushing for Kennedy's goals of diplomacy. Hess wrote: "In constructing a national security triumvirate of Rusk-McNamara-Bundy [McGeorge Bundy was Kennedy's national security adviser], the President put the most diffident [person] in the post that required the most assertive."[66]

Early in his administration Kennedy also focused his attention on appointments to secondary cabinet positions, primarily in the State Department. Some of Kennedy's lower-level appointments in the State Department, many of whom were named before he nominated the secretary, were more qualified than Rusk to be head of the department. They included Adlai E.

Stevenson, W. Averell Harriman, and Chester Bowles. Although Kennedy apparently was attempting to spread talent and diversity throughout the State Department, he soon found the task of naming subcabinet appointees wearisome. Thus, he eventually gave McNamara an almost free hand in naming his top subordinates in the Pentagon. As a result, most of McNamara's appointees remained in the Defense Department for the duration of his tenure. In contrast, top-level State Department personnel left the department on average after about fourteen months.

Lyndon B. Johnson

Feeling the need to maintain stability in the government, Lyndon Johnson made no changes in the Kennedy cabinet until September 1964—ten months after President Kennedy's assassination—when Robert Kennedy resigned as attorney general. After the 1964 election, however, Johnson decided to put his own stamp on the administration. Thus, during his term in office, he selected fifteen of the twenty-five men who served in his cabinet; the others he inherited from Kennedy.

Even though Johnson relied heavily on a personnel staff to help him make his cabinet decisions, he participated in almost every step of the selection process. In fact, probably no other recent president has maintained the continuing interest that Johnson exhibited in the selection of all of his executive personnel. Although he usually followed his personnel staff's recommendations, he always reserved the final decision for himself.

Johnson applied very explicit criteria to his cabinet selections, which included not only intelligence and ability but also some important political considerations. For example, because he wished to increase the number of minorities in the federal government, in 1966 Johnson appointed Robert C. Weaver, the first black cabinet member, as secretary of housing and urban development (HUD).

At first Johnson appeared to pay little attention to political party affiliation. He boasted, for example, that he was unaware that John W. Gardner was a Republican until shortly before he announced Gardner's nomination as secretary of health, education and welfare (HEW). Loyalty to his programs, however, was very important. As Johnson's presidency matured and friction developed between some of his advisers and the remaining Kennedy staffers, it became increasingly clear that he needed to have his own team in place in the cabinet. According to journalist David Halberstam, Johnson, when discussing loyalty among his cabinet members, said: "If you ask those boys in the cabinet to run through a buzz saw for their president, Bob McNamara would be the first to go through it. And I don't have to worry about Rusk either. Rusk's all right. I never have to worry about those two fellows quitting on me."[67]

Nevertheless, Johnson soon began to confuse loyalty with blind allegiance to his Vietnam policies. G. Calvin Mackenzie observed that this made it increasingly difficult for Johnson to find people for all of his executive positions. "The more criticism the war engendered, the more concerned Johnson became that his appointees support his war policies. The effect of his

President Lyndon B. Johnson appointed Robert C. Weaver, the first African American cabinet member, as secretary of housing and urban development.

concern was to narrow the range of people from which executive selections were made."[68] Johnson thus began to turn increasingly to people who already held major positions in his administration, and his cabinet was a good example of Johnson's preference for appointing those who already had experience in government. Of the fifteen cabinet members he appointed, only four came from outside the federal government. The others were internal promotions, such as Wilbur J. Cohen's appointment as Johnson's last HEW secretary; Cohen had spent most of his career at the Social Security Administration. The Johnson cabinet thus tended to represent well the clientele of the agencies, but it also did not have much political independence from the president.

Richard Nixon

Soon after his election in 1968 Nixon turned over direction of the effort to select a cabinet to his law partner John Mitchell and a Wall Street banker named Peter Flanigan. On December 11, 1968, after a "crash program" of selection lasting five weeks, Nixon went before a national television audience in prime time to introduce twelve men of "extra dimension" who were to form his first cabinet.

In choosing a cabinet that proved more diverse than Eisenhower's, Nixon relied on some traditional sources of recruitment: personal friends (John Mitchell as attorney general, Robert H. Finch as secretary of HEW, and William P. Rogers as secretary of state); Republican governors (Walter J. Hickel as secretary of the interior, George W. Romney as secretary of housing and urban development, and John A. Volpe as secretary of transportation); academics (Clifford M. Hardin as secretary of agriculture and George P. Shultz as secretary of labor); members of Congress (Melvin R. Laird [R-Wis.] as secretary of defense); and business people (Winton M. Blount as postmaster general, David M. Kennedy as secretary of the Treasury, and Maurice H. Stans as secretary of commerce). He also followed the traditional patterns of constituency representation: he chose a westerner for Interior, a banker for Treasury, and a midwesterner with an agricultural background for Agriculture. Even though Nixon appointed a number of millionaires, they were generally self-made men who rose from meager beginnings.

In other ways Nixon chose a nontraditional cabinet. For example, traditionally presidents have appointed at least one member of the defeated party; there were no Democrats on Nixon's cabinet. Nixon ignored other prominent groups as well by not including any labor union members, African American, Jews, or women. And because Republicans had gained little top-level federal experience during the last eight years, Nixon's cabinet was somewhat short on Washington executive experience. According to Mackenzie, "The selection process [for Nixon's cabinet] seems to have been guided by little more than the desire to follow convention, to pay off some personal and electoral debts, and to surround the new President with people who seemed to share his political outlook."[69] Historian Arthur M. Schlesinger Jr. publicly criticized Nixon's cabinet appointments for a lack of independence, asking, "Who in President Nixon's cabinet will talk back to him?"[70]

Early in 1969 President Nixon told his cabinet that they would have the primary responsibility for filling subcabinet positions. Specifying that the selection process should be based on ability first and loyalty second, Nixon thus delegated to his cabinet the authority for determining the responsiveness of the federal government to his programs. Mackenzie wrote: "Nixon recognized almost immediately that in granting this discretion he had made an error in judgment. As he left the cabinet room after the meeting, he is reported to have said to an aide, 'I just made a big mistake.'"[71]

After Nixon delegated subcabinet appointment power to his department heads, the White House personnel staff found it difficult to exert much control over these appointments. The White House staff spent a great deal of time trying to reconfirm its right to approve nominations made by department heads.

By 1970 Nixon realized that he needed to install in the White House a selection process that would ensure that high-level departmental appointees were loyal enough and bold enough to carry out his programs. As a result, Frederic V. Malek, deputy undersecretary of HEW, was put in charge of studying the White House personnel operation. When Malek recommended that all personnel decisions be centralized in a new White House Personnel Operation (WHPO), Nixon agreed and asked him to run the operation.

By centralizing the appointment procedure in the WHPO, the Nixon White House hoped to protect the president's nominations from outside influences, thereby making it easier to limit appointments to those well in line with Nixon's policies. For all its good intentions, however, the WHPO was not entirely successful. Nixon continued to remain aloof from the nominating process. Often he even refrained from meeting his subcabinet nominees when they joined the administration. This lack of interest made it difficult for the Nixon administration to instill loyalty to Nixon's policies and goals in its cabinet and subcabinet officers.

Gerald R. Ford

After Nixon's resignation Gerald Ford came into office facing many of the same problems that Truman and Johnson confronted after the deaths of presidents Roosevelt and Kennedy. Primarily, Ford faced the need to place his own mark on the federal government. He entered the presidency with Nixon's cabinet and not much preparation for his new job. Thus, several months passed before his administration began to take shape. When he finally found himself in a position to make changes, he encountered many potential nominees who were hesitant to take executive positions in his administration because of the possibility that Ford would not win reelection in his bid for the presidency and the nominee would face a very short tenure in office.

Ford sought geographical balance and group representation in all of his appointments by nominating women, minorities, and young people to his administration. Because of the Watergate scandal, which had forced Nixon's resignation, Ford asked his personnel staff to be particularly sensitive to political considerations; he sought nominees who shared his political beliefs and reflected his administration's goals. He was, however, less strenuous about political compatibility than many of his predecessors, and he thus appointed several cabinet members who were not responsive to Republican Party demands: Secretary of Transportation William T. Coleman Jr.; Secretary of Housing and Urban Development Carla A. Hills; Secretary of Labor John T. Dunlop; Secretary of Health, Education and Welfare F. David Mathews; and Attorney General Edward H. Levi. Most were not Republicans, and many represented minorities.

Jimmy Carter

Even though Jimmy Carter won the 1976 election by a slim margin, his cabinet selections did not reflect any obligations that he may have had to the groups that helped put him over the top. He came into office believing that he owed little to anyone, except African Americans, and promising that his administration would appoint new leaders to key posts based on merit and well-balanced geographical representation. In an oft-quoted comment, Carter's closest adviser, Hamilton Jordan, stated during the transition period: "If, after the inauguration, you find a Cy Vance as Secretary of State and Zbigniew Brzezinski as head of national security, then I would say we failed. And I'd quit. But that's not going to happen. You're going to see new faces, new ideas. The government is going to be run by people you have never heard of."[72]

Promises of this kind set up many unfulfilled expectations. Carter nominated Vance as secretary of state and Brzezinski as national security adviser. Other initial cabinet and executive position selections did little to satisfy either traditional Democratic Party supporters or those hoping for new leadership. Democratic legislators expressed dismay when their suggestions were not heeded. Minority groups and women, who felt they had contributed significantly to Carter's election, were disappointed in his selections; only two women, Patricia Roberts Harris (secretary of housing and urban development) and Juanita M. Kreps (secretary of commerce), and two African Americans, Harris and Andrew Young (as ambassador to the United Nations) were appointed to the cabinet. In an unprecedented move the Democratic National Committee adopted a resolution criticizing the Carter administration for failing to confer with Democratic state officials in making federal appointments.

Carter in fact was attempting to take firm control of the nomination process, and in doing so he sacrificed many traditional Democratic ties. Mackenzie wrote: "By failing to recognize some legitimate political claims and by promising a good deal more than it could deliver, the Carter administration failed to capitalize fully on the political opportunities the selection process provides, especially in the initial stages of a new administration."[73]

No president had started as early as Carter in finding personnel for his administration. In the summer of 1976, even before the election, Carter established a Policy Planning Office (PPO). Headed by Jack H. Watson Jr., the PPO was charged with finding qualified nominees and giving the new administration a head start on the selection process during the transition. The early start in appointing executives to the new administration did little to speed up the cabinet selection process, however. Carter took longer to select his cabinet than had any of his postwar predecessors. Although all cabinet members were sworn in within a week of the inauguration, many subcabinet positions remained unfilled for several months.

In addition to the deliberateness of Carter's selection process, new strict ethics and conflict of interest guidelines also contributed to the uncommon slowness of the appointment process. During his transition Carter initiated some of the toughest standards ever required of executive branch appointees. Although these guidelines were not enacted into law by Congress until 1978, the president-elect imposed them on nominees for his staff and cabinet. These ethics requirements covered three

Although President Carter's goal for his cabinet was to choose new faces, he ended up with Washington insiders. Cyrus Vance, top, held the post of secretary of state; Zbigniew Brzezinski, bottom, headed the National Security Council.

main areas: public disclosure of financial assets, divestiture of assets that could involve appointees in conflicts of interest, and restrictions on the employment of policy makers after they left the government. The rigorousness of the new standards could be seen in the difficulty Office of Management and Budget (OMB) Director Bert Lance had in complying with the requirement that policy-making officials divest themselves of any investments that could prove to be conflicts of interests. Although appointed to head OMB, Lance had to resign his post after a congressional investigation in 1977.

Carter insisted on participating directly in the selection of his department heads, and he preferred to pick all appointees in a specific department before moving on to another. Because he was concerned about compatibility among his top advisers, Carter tried to ascertain the quality and compatibility of potential nominees by holding joint meetings with candidates in the same policy area. So many candidates were involved in these meetings that it was difficult to keep them out of the public eye. This process had the advantage, however, of giving Carter feedback from observers who might have an interest in the nomination. Carter compiled a list of potential cabinet nominees by soliciting suggestions countrywide from experts in foreign policy, domestic affairs, defense, economics, education, and other areas covered by cabinet appointments. He then turned his list of names over to Hamilton Jordan, who undertook a thorough analysis of each candidate. Before making his final decision, Carter talked to the individuals being considered.

Carter's firm control of nominations occurred only at the department head level, however. Initially, Carter invited his department secretaries to make their own senior departmental appointments, as he wanted to establish an independent cabinet. But this freedom of selection set up a power struggle between Jordan, who retained overall responsibility for personnel selection, and the department heads. According to presidential scholar R. Gordon Hoxie, "During the first year a warfare erupted between departmental personnel and White House staff over control of the turf and the action. The staff rationale was that *their* coordination, their orchestration, was required in all matters."[74] Eventually, because of his closeness to the president, Jordan and the White House staff won, and the process of selecting subcabinet personnel became concentrated in the White House.

Ronald Reagan

Following Carter's example, Ronald Reagan started the process of selecting cabinet members and other executive personnel during the election campaign. E. Pendleton James, a professional executive recruiter, headed the overall personnel selection process. James believed it important that the president exercise his appointment power in a manner that would insure his control of his administration. Thus, the president had to appoint not only people who were loyal to him and shared his objectives, but also those who were competent and committed to implementing them.

Unlike the Carter administration, however, the Reagan administration initially succeeded in keeping the appointment process firmly within the White House under the control of James. Reagan supported the process and actively participated in it. During the transition, Reagan made the final decisions on all important appointments, especially cabinet selections. This made it difficult for the departments and agencies—and even for members of Congress—to exert much influence on the selection process.

Like Carter, Reagan required an excessive amount of time to get his administration fully in place. As in the Carter administration, post–Watergate-mandated security checks and conflict-

Environmental conservation organizations opposed President Reagan's nomination of James G. Watt as secretary of the interior, and his tenure as secretary was stormy. He resigned before the end of Reagan's first term.

of-interest disclosures contributed to the delay in the Reagan appointments. The diminished role that political parties played in Reagan's appointment process slowed the process as well. By the Reagan presidency, political parties no longer served as clearinghouses for political appointments. Instead, applications went directly to the White House, generating an administrative logjam. Appointment experts Macy, Adams, and Walter noted that "this creates an enormous and politically delicate logistical problem at a time when a new administration is unlikely to be well equipped to handle it."[75]

Another problem facing the Reagan administration was the growing conflict between differing ideologies and political philosophies in the White House and Congress. Senate confirmation hearings thus became even more difficult. For example, Reagan appointee Warren Richardson, nominated as assistant secretary of health and human services, withdrew his name from consideration when members of the Senate Labor and Human Resources Committee objected to his ultra-conservative political views. Although Richardson denied it, he was charged with holding both racist and anti-Semitic views. In another incident, Sen. Jesse Helms (R-N.C.) and other conservative senators effectively delayed the nomination of twenty-nine State Department appointees before receiving assurances from Secretary of State George P. Shultz that six conservative employees of the

State Department would not be fired. Faced with this kind of ideological tightrope, Reagan had difficulty finding acceptable cabinet appointees.

Reagan's initial cabinet nevertheless reflected many traditional political considerations. It was a combination of political cronies and strangers, well-known politicians, and obscure state officials. Political scientist Ross K. Baker divided members of Reagan's cabinet into "mailmen" (management-oriented moderates) and "Grail seekers" (conservative advocates). The mailmen in Reagan's first cabinet were Treasury Secretary Donald T. Regan, Secretary of Housing and Urban Development Samuel R. Pierce Jr., Secretary of Commerce Malcolm Baldrige, Secretary of Labor Raymond J. Donovan, and Secretary of Transportation Drew Lewis. His grail seekers included Secretary of the Interior James G. Watt, Secretary of Energy James B. Edwards, and Secretary of Agriculture John R. Block.[76] More than anything else, Reagan's cabinet represented his electoral constituencies. Groups that did not support Reagan (liberals, environmentalists, and labor unions) were not represented in his cabinet, while groups that helped give him his electoral majority (farmers, developers, and big business) were well represented.

George Bush

As the first sitting vice president since 1836 to succeed in his bid to become president, George Bush faced the difficult task of creating an administration that built upon the legacy of the previous administration but firmly established its own identity. Bush believed he had no mandate to change the course set by the Reagan administration. Yet he wanted an administration filled with people loyal to him—an administration that clearly bore the imprint of George Bush.

Bush considered the task of staffing the executive branch so important that he placed Charles Untermeyer, a former Reagan administration official but a Bush loyalist, in charge of finding people to fill most executive branch positions through the Office of Presidential Personnel. Actually given his directive a year before the presidential election, Untermeyer's orders were to clean house in the executive branch and find loyal Bush appointees. Loyalty and competence became the main criteria for selection. Unlike Reagan, Bush did not seek ideologues. Instead, he sought individuals who could be considered pragmatic and experienced. For example, Bush appointed James Baker III as secretary of state and Richard Cheney as secretary of defense. Typical of Bush's cabinet nominations, both were pragmatists and longtime friends of Bush. Journalist Burt Solomon writes:

Bush put into place a cabinet and a White House staff that foretell a style of governance—a conscientious, relentlessly mainstream Republican administration filled with pragmatists who prize public niceness. Bush promised fresh faces but hired old friends.[77]

Bush, along with Baker and chief of staff John Sununu, made the final selections for the heads of the executive departments. Unlike Reagan, however, Bush left most of the staffing for subcabinet positions to the discretion of department secretaries.

CABINET HOLDOVERS

When President-elect Herbert C. Hoover sent his list of cabinet nominations to the Senate for approval in 1929, he failed to mention that his predecessor's controversial Treasury secretary, Andrew W. Mellon, would be staying on the job. "He wanted to minimize the fight" by shielding Mellon from a confirmation battle, said Senate historian Richard A. Baker. Mellon had already been confirmed once when President Warren G. Harding tapped him for the Treasury post in 1921. And he had held the job throughout Calvin Coolidge's 1923–1929 presidency as well. Hoover's decision to keep Mellon on drew howls of protest from liberal and progressive lawmakers who opposed Mellon's economic policies. But the president-elect had ample precedent for his move. From the time of John Adams's presidency, cabinet members appointed by one administration had been passed to the next without having to wait for Senate approval. In fact, holdovers were quite common. John Adams retained five members of George Washington's cabinet. Between then and 1929, 110 cabinet appointees served in consecutive administrations. The majority of those, however, were retained between terms of the same president. From Washington's time to the present, only forty-two appointees have been held over from one administration to the next when there was a clear change of power.

In 1989 George Bush followed in Hoover's footsteps. Three of his cabinet appointments—Treasury Secretary Nicholas F. Brady, Education Secretary Lauro F. Cavazos, and Attorney General Dick Thornburgh—were holdovers from the Reagan administration. None had to be reconfirmed.

In the years between Hoover and Clinton, many presidents retained their closest advisers from one term to the next. When a president died in office, his successor often kept the cabinet team intact. In fact, when Lyndon B. Johnson was elected in his own right in 1964, he held on to eight cabinet members originally appointed by John F. Kennedy. The Bush cabinet, however, marked the first time since Hoover took over from Coolidge that a completely new administration retained department heads named by a former president. In part, that is because it was the first time since 1929 that there had been a "friendly takeover" at the White House, with the incoming president belonging to the same party as his predecessor. Bush was on firm legal ground when he asserted that his holdovers did not need to be reconfirmed. "Nowhere in the Constitution is there a specific termination date" for cabinet secretaries, a Senate legal adviser explained. "They are appointed for an indefinite period of time, and unless they are dismissed by the president [or resign], they are not subject to reconfirmation." Cavazos and Thornburgh submitted letters of resignation in compliance with President Reagan's efforts to clear the way for Bush. But Reagan did not accept those letters once Bush made his choices public. Brady was writing his letter when Bush asked him to stay on the job November 15. He never finished it.

SOURCE: Adapted from Macon Morehouse, "Cabinet Holdovers Need No Senate Approval," *Congressional Quarterly Weekly Report*, November 26, 1988, 3390.

Since Bush made no attempt to centralize the subcabinet appointments within the White House, cabinet secretaries chose, in consultation with Untermeyer's Office of Presidential Personnel, their own subcabinet appointments. As a result, the Bush administration moved slowly in filling subcabinet positions. Finding Bush loyalists to fill these positions helped slow the staffing process, just as finding ideological loyalists helped slow the process for Reagan. Although Bush granted more discretion than Reagan to his cabinet secretaries, he insisted that the appointment process follow traditional patronage requirements. A "Special Schedule C Project" was set up in the Office of Presidential Personnel, under the direction of Scott Bush, the president's nephew, to insure that campaign workers and friends were appointed to top positions within the departments. Although Schedule C appointments are legally the responsibility of department secretaries, lists of potential appointees were sent to the secretaries with strong recommendations from the Office of Presidential Personnel. Presidential scholar James P. Pfiffner writes, "This placement of campaign personnel caused some administrative problems when departments had to absorb lists of people before subcabinet appointments had been made."[78] Feeling no great urgency to replace Republicans with other Republicans and facing a slow and sometimes hostile Democratic Senate confirmation process, the Bush personnel system operated at a surprisingly slow pace.

Bill Clinton

After twelve years of Republican control of the White House, Bill Clinton faced the difficult task of putting together a government staffed by Democrats who had relatively little experience in top policy positions in the federal government. In addition, during the presidential election Clinton promised to set a new agenda and change the course of the federal government. Finding talented people who were committed to his agenda proved to be difficult, given the smaller pool of experienced Democrats.

In addition, Clinton made a specific promise to appoint a cabinet that "looks like America," a cabinet that mirrored the diversity of America. The staffing mechanism he put in place produced the most demographically diverse cabinet and subcabinet of any previous administration. Clinton appointed three women, one an African American, to head the Justice, Energy, and Health and Human Services Departments. In addition, he appointed African Americans to head the Commerce, Agriculture, and Veterans Affairs Departments and Hispanics to head the Housing and Urban Development and the Transportation Departments. Since these appointments, although fulfilling a commitment to ethnic, racial, and gender diversity, also produced a cabinet of millionaires and lawyers, the Clinton administration was still criticized for its failure to represent America completely.

During the transition period, control of the appointment power shifted from campaign chair Mickey Kantor, who had originally been put in charge of the Clinton-Gore Presidential Transition Planning Foundation, to former deputy secretary of state Warren Christopher, whom Clinton brought on board to give the transition effort more stature. Cabinet decisions ultimately were made by Clinton, Christopher, Vice President-elect Albert Gore, Clinton loyalist Bruce Lindsey, and Hillary Rodham Clinton. One primary goal of the cabinet selection team was to centralize subcabinet selections within the White House. In this respect the Clinton team was reacting to what it perceived as a weakness of the Carter administration's commitment to an independent cabinet. Whereas Carter had turned control over subcabinet positions to his department secretaries, Clinton insisted that all subcabinet appointments had to be negotiated with the White House.

President Bill Clinton introduces four of his appointees to the media: from left, Chairwoman of the Council of Economic Advisors Laura D'Andrea Tyson, EPA Administrator Carol M. Browner, Secretary of Health and Human Services Donna Shalala, and Secretary of Labor Robert Reich. Diversity was the hallmark of Clinton's appointments.

Although the transition team sought to build and solidify traditional Democratic Party loyalties, most of the emphasis was placed on gender and ethnicity. In the end, Clinton's commitment to diversity caused him to neglect some traditional patterns of political patronage. For all the effort devoted to balance within the new administration, Clinton's cabinet contained no one from the industrial heartland of Illinois, Michigan, Ohio, or Pennsylvania—important political states with large numbers of electoral votes that had gone to Clinton. Also, with the exception of Mike Espy, who was named secretary of agriculture, the cabinet contained no prominent campaign supporters. Those who had supported Clinton during the primaries and had been important to his overall success in the election felt neglected and betrayed.

Even with the Clinton transition's commitment to finding cabinet and subcabinet appointees who reflected America's diversity, his appointment process still fell prey to the extraordinarily strong demands of Democratic Party constituencies. When women's groups criticized Clinton for not appointing enough women to top positions, he at first lashed out at what he called "bean counters," who were more concerned with numbers of representatives of ethnic and gender groups than the quality and substance of the appointees themselves. Several days later, however, in what most analysts saw as partial capitulation to interest group pressure, the transition team announced the next attorney general would be a woman.

Ironically, the presidents who started the earliest to select executive appointees (Carter, Reagan, Bush, and Clinton) took the longest to staff their administrations. Part of the delay in the nomination and confirmation process can be attributed to the amount of effort the Clinton administration put into its quest for diversity. Elevating gender and ethnicity as primary selection criteria put more demands on an already strained and cumbersome selection process. Fairly tough ethics standards that were put in place early in the transition process also contributed to the delay. Finding qualified people willing to submit themselves to stringent clearances and ethics commitments proved difficult. Clinton's desire to control the subcabinet appointment process from within the White House also contributed to a slow and tedious staffing procedure. When coupled with Clinton's micromanaging style, the administration's efforts to insure political control over the subcabinet produced long delays in many appointments. The slowness of the staffing process drew criticism from presidential scholar Stephen Hess, who claimed that it had resulted in the "least successful transition I've seen since 1960."[79]

Department of Agriculture

The U.S. Department of Agriculture (USDA) was established in 1862 and elevated to cabinet status in 1889. In 1995 it employed almost one hundred ten thousand people, with about ten thousand of them in Washington, D.C.

USDA assists the nation's farmers through a variety of pro-grams, among them, subsidies, credit, and rural development (through loans for improved water systems, recreation areas, electrification, telephone service, and housing). USDA also oversees the nation's food quality through inspections of processing plants, and it establishes quality standards for every major agricultural commodity. It provides nutrition education programs as well. USDA's research facilities investigate animal production, plant and animal diseases, pest controls, crop production, marketing and use of agricultural products, food safety, and forestry. Moreover, the department supports environmental protection through its energy, soil, water, and forest resource conservation programs. Other responsibilities of the department include administering school lunch, food stamp, food-for-the-needy, and overseas distribution programs; managing the nation's 191 million acres of national forests and grasslands; and helping developing nations improve food production.

Despite the importance of USDA, in 1971 President Richard Nixon proposed abolishing the department, and in 1977 President Jimmy Carter suggested transferring a number of USDA's functions to other agencies. Neither happened. But the Clinton administration proposed and in 1994 Congress passed a major overhaul of USDA that would eliminate 7,500 staff positions over five years and reorganize the USDA bureaucracy.

FROM SMALL BEGINNINGS

The idea of establishing an agricultural agency in the federal government first surfaced in 1776, when farmers made up nearly 90 percent of the nation's population and virtually all exports were farm products. President George Washington recommended creating such an agency in 1796, but it was not until 1839 that Congress appropriated $1,000 for collecting agricultural statistics, conducting agricultural investigations, and distributing seeds. These functions were assigned at first to the Patent Office because Henry L. Ellsworth, commissioner of patents, had initiated the seed distribution idea.

The pressure to establish a federal agricultural agency mounted, led by the U.S. Agricultural Society, which was organized in 1852. The society found an ally in the Republican Party, which pledged in 1860 to enact agrarian reforms. The law authorizing the department in 1862 instructed it "to acquire and to diffuse . . . useful information on subjects connected with agriculture in the most general and comprehensive sense of the word." In carrying out this mandate, the commissioner of agriculture was to conduct experiments, collect statistics, and "procure, propagate, and distribute among the people new and valuable seeds and plants."

The first commissioner of the department was Isaac Newton, a Pennsylvania dairy farmer and personal friend of President Abraham Lincoln. He had a staff of four clerks and a gardener as well as an annual budget of about $50,000. In his 1862 annual report the commissioner proposed a research and information program that was to become the basis of the department's activities during the next several years. The agency published statistical and research reports and dispatched scientists overseas to study other nations' agricultural practices.

Newton's successor, Norman J. Coleman, became the first secretary of agriculture in 1889, although he served in that capacity for only three weeks. A lawyer and lieutenant governor of Missouri, Coleman was active in state, regional, and national agricultural organizations. He played a key role in the passage of the 1887 Hatch Agricultural Experiment Stations Act, which authorized the establishment of such stations, under the direction of the land-grant colleges, in each state and territory.

Coleman's successor, Jeremiah M. Rusk, who was appointed by President Benjamin Harrison, reorganized the department and inaugurated publication of farmers' bulletins. He created USDA's first assistant secretary post—to oversee the department's scientific work—and he named Edwin Williams to head the office.

EXPANSION OF FUNCTIONS

A new era for the department began in 1897 with the appointment of James ("Tama Jim") Wilson as secretary. Wilson, who served sixteen years—twice as long as any secretary before or since—had been director of the Iowa state agricultural experiment station and had served three terms in the House of Representatives. During his tenure the department became known as one of the great agricultural research institutions of the world. Wilson established new bureaus which operated autonomously under the leadership of well-known scientists. The Forest Service was established in 1905, as oversight of the national forests was transferred from the Department of the Interior to USDA. USDA was given additional regulatory authority as well, including responsibility for administering the 1906 Meat Inspection and Food and Drugs Acts (the latter was transferred to the Food and Drug Administration in 1940). By 1912 the number of employees (13,858) and the department's budget were nearly seven times what they had been in 1897.

Under the leadership of David F. Houston (1913–1920), the department focused its efforts increasingly on the farmers' social and economic plight. Houston also made significant organizational changes, centralizing the department and establishing the Office of Markets and the Office of Information. Passage of the Smith-Lever Agricultural Extension Act in 1914 allowed the department and land-grant colleges, under formal cooperative agreements, to carry the fruits of research directly to farmers. This arrangement resulted in creation of the Cooperative Extension Service, which served as a model for similar programs abroad.

In 1916 the department became active in establishing standards and grades for grain and cotton. Subsequently, standards were established for other products. The 1921 Packers and Stockyards Act barred unfair, deceptive, discriminatory, and monopolistic practices in livestock, poultry, and meat marketing.

The World War I years were accompanied by a surge in farm production and speculation. At the same time, farmers confronted declining prices for their products and high mortgage indebtedness. In the 1920s agriculture's economic decline preceded the Great Depression. To help farmers meet market needs, the Bureau of Agricultural Economics was established in 1922 to foster statistical and economic research. During the depression Congress responded to the farmers' plight by passing a number of significant laws, among them the 1933 Agricultural Adjustment Act (AAA), which provided for production adjustment to be achieved principally through direct USDA payments to farmers. The Farm Credit Act, passed the same year, consolidated all farm credit programs under the Farm Credit Administration. The Soil Conservation Service was established in 1935, as were the Resettlement Administration (which later became the Farm Security Administration and Farmers Home Administration) and the Rural Electrification Administration. In 1936 the Supreme Court declared the AAA unconstitutional; Congress responded by passing the Soil Conservation and Domestic Allotment Act.

In addition to assisting farmers during the depression, USDA joined the welfare agencies in aiding the poor in rural and urban areas through programs designed to distribute surpluses to the needy.

POSTWAR FARM POLICY

Responding to overseas food needs following World War II, USDA urged U.S. farmers to expand their productive capacity. By the time the Korean War ended in 1953, however, the policy of emphasizing maximum production had resulted in surpluses and falling farm prices. Faced with that problem, President Dwight D. Eisenhower's secretary of agriculture, Ezra Taft Benson, chose to institute programs to expand markets rather than establish high price supports. A Soil Bank Program was put into place nevertheless, whereby farmers were paid to take farmland out of cultivation. The Rural Development Program was inaugurated in 1955 to help low-income farmers. That program was greatly expanded under Benson's successor, Orville L. Freeman (1961–1969). Passage of the Food Stamp Program, and expansion of the school lunch, school milk, and other food donation programs during this period, not only provided food aid to low-income families but also reduced farm surpluses to more manageable levels. At the same time, "Food for Peace" activities were increased. More than 100 million people in 115 countries received U.S. food surpluses.

Clifford M. Hardin took over as USDA secretary in 1969 and was succeeded by Earl L. Butz in 1971. Butz, a controversial appointee, was forced to resign in 1976.

Fifty years after the federal government first paid farmers to plow under crops and slaughter surplus livestock, the Reagan administration launched a drive to end many depression-era farm programs and eliminate the assumption that the federal government is directly responsible for farmers' well-being. Reagan's first USDA secretary, John R. Block (an Illinois farmer), and others—including portions of the farm community—argued that earlier programs had in fact destabilized American agriculture and had to be changed radically.

During his tenure Block was alternately praised and criticized as a well-intentioned but often ineffectual advocate of the president's free-market philosophy for agriculture. Block came into office hoping to free farmers from relying so heavily on government programs, yet the crisis in agriculture—high interest rates and declining agricultural exports caused by the strength of the dollar—only deepened each year he was in office, despite unprecedented tax expenditures for price supports and income subsidies. Although Block lasted longer than all but three of Reagan's original cabinet officials, his influence on Capitol Hill waned considerably; he resigned in February 1986.

To replace Block, Reagan chose longtime associate Richard E. Lyng, an agriculture consultant and lobbyist and a former California seed company executive with wide experience in government. He was known to be Reagan's original choice for the cabinet post following the 1980 election, but congressional pressure had led Reagan to pick Block because he was a "working farmer" from the midwestern state of Illinois. Lyng instead took the number-two job in the department. He remained in that position through Reagan's first term, overseeing day-to-day operations and often acting as lightning rod on Capitol Hill for the administration's more controversial farm policies.

George Bush's first secretary of agriculture, Clayton Yeutter, had served as U.S. trade representative under Reagan and had staked his reputation in that job on negotiations to end "trade distorting" agricultural subsidies throughout the world, particularly in Japan and the European Community. Arriving at the USDA when the farm economy was gradually improving, Yeutter called for continued reductions in farm payments but did not propose the politically risky cutbacks for the sake of free-market principles that had shaped agricultural debates during the Reagan era. His pragmatic style gave the administration more leverage in debates over the 1990 farm bill, which froze subsidy levels at existing rates and achieved some of the administration's goal to give farmers more flexibility to participate in federal farm programs, allowing them to plant crops with high market prices. Yeutter was criticized by farm-state lawmakers for his vagueness on subsidy reductions, however, and he was unable to win the concessions from U.S. agricultural interests that the administration was concurrently demanding from its foreign partners at the General Agreement on Tariffs and Trade talks.

In 1991 Yeutter resigned to become chairman of the Republican National Committee and was replaced by Rep. Edward Madigan, a Republican from Illinois who had lobbied aggressively for the position. As the ranking member of the House Agriculture Committee, Madigan had been a key negotiator in the 1985 and 1990 farm bill conferences and was regarded as a knowledgeable and open-minded legislator by members of both parties. In early 1993 just before Bush's term expired, Madigan announced plans to revamp the USDA field office structure, which according to a 1991 GAO report maintained offices in 85 percent of the nation's counties, only 16 percent of which were considered farming communities.

The Agriculture Department, founded in 1862 and elevated to cabinet rank in 1889, expanded greatly during the Great Depression. Today its mandate extends to food and nutrition programs, consumer education, rural housing, and environmental protection, in addition to its core agricultural and forestry responsibilities.

President Bill Clinton's nominee, Mike Espy, promised during his confirmation hearings to make restructuring the entire USDA a priority. Espy, the nation's first African American agriculture secretary, had served three terms as a Democratic representative from Mississippi and was one of Clinton's earliest congressional supporters during the 1992 campaign. As a member of the House Agriculture Committee Espy had been an active backroom negotiator on farm legislation, and as chairman of a domestic task force on hunger he was familiar with the often unwieldy nutrition programs, such as food stamps and the school lunch program, under USDA jurisdiction. He received high praise from agricultural interests for his understanding of complex U.S. farm programs and his sympathy for farmers' needs, particularly following his successful coordination of federal relief to farmers affected by the 1993 floods in the Midwest. As secretary he elevated the assistant secretary for food and consumer services to the rank of undersecretary and also established an office of consumer affairs, gaining public support for his promise to strengthen the government's meat inspection programs following a food-poisoning outbreak from tainted meat in early 1993.

Espy made USDA a model for Clinton and Vice President Al Gore's plans to "reinvent government" by reducing bureaucracy. Building on the plan drafted under Madigan, Espy proposed to close 1,200 field offices, eliminate 7,500 jobs, reduce the number of USDA agencies from 43 to fewer than 30, and overhaul the federal crop insurance program. For Espy, enactment of the overhaul legislation was overshadowed by his resignation in October 1994 in response to allegations that he had accepted gifts from businesses regulated by the department, including Tyson Foods, an Arkansas poultry conglomerate owned by a prominent Clinton supporter. In December Clinton nominated Democratic representative Dan Glickman of Kansas, who had lost his seat in the 1994 election. Glickman had been an early critic of USDA bureaucracy and as chairman of the House Subcommittee on Wheat, Soybeans and Feed Grains had played a pivotal role in the 1990 debate on price-support programs. Glickman's confirmation was delayed until March 30, 1995, by questions of whether he had adequately reimbursed the House of Representatives and his congressional campaign for personal expenses charged on credit cards in the 1980s.

ORGANIZATION

USDA has been reorganized a number of times in response to different problems and the gradual addition of functions. The greatest expansion of the department took place during the 1930s in response to the Great Depression. Between the depression and 1994, the only major organizational change was a 1953 move to increase the number of assistant secretaries from one to five.

In 1994 USDA underwent a major reorganization as part of President Clinton's reinventing government initiative. USDA is headed by a secretary, who is assisted by a deputy secretary, six undersecretaries (farm and foreign agriculture services; food, nutrition and consumer services; food safety; natural resources and environment; research, education and economics; and rural economic and community development) and three assistant secretaries (administration, congressional relations, and marketing and regulatory programs). The offices of budget and program analysis, the general counsel, the judicial officer, and the inspector general report directly to the secretary.

Department of Commerce

Between 1850 and 1900 the nation's rapid economic growth fueled demands for business representation at the highest levels of government. The Panic of 1893 and the ensuing depression led the newly formed National Association of Manufacturers to lobby strenuously for formation of a department of commerce and industry that would include the Department of Labor (which had been established as a noncabinet-rank department

in 1888). Congress responded by authorizing a U.S. industrial commission to study commercial problems.

In 1901, in his first State of the Union address, President Theodore Roosevelt proposed a combined department of commerce and labor. Labor representatives argued that workers needed a separate department, but business interests were willing to accept Roosevelt's compromise. In the end the latter prevailed, and the Department of Commerce and Labor came into being in 1903. The new department was one of the largest and most complicated in the federal government; within five months its employees numbered 10,125. Its responsibilities included foreign and domestic commerce; mining, manufacturing, shipping, and fishery industries; labor interests; and transportation.

As the nation's manufactured exports continued to expand and workers moved from farms to industry, pressures built up on both sides to separate labor and commerce into independent departments. As a result a March 4, 1913, law gave labor cabinet status and the Department of Commerce was born.

EXPANSION OF THE DEPARTMENT

President William Howard Taft signed the bill on his last day in office. In 1913, his Democratic successor, Woodrow Wilson, appointed the first commerce secretary, William C. Redfield, a manufacturing executive and politician. Despite the constraints of a $60,000 budget and elimination of funding for collecting domestic statistics, Redfield established a cadre of bilingual commercial attachés with business experience, opened branch offices in eight cities, and sent specialists overseas to study foreign markets.

Commerce came into the limelight during Herbert Hoover's tenure as secretary (1921–1928). Hoover was determined to make Commerce the most powerful department in the government. His primary interest was to expand trade, and, indeed, by 1925 U.S. exports had increased by one-third over the figure recorded in 1913. During Hoover's stewardship, Commerce acquired a Building and Housing Division (1922), the Bureau of Mines and the Patent Office (both were transferred from Interior in 1925), an Aeronautics Division (1926; it was the forerunner of the Federal Aviation Administration), and a Radio Division (1927; it later became part of the Federal Communications Commission).

Keenly interested in revitalizing the department's statistical functions, Hoover instituted in 1921 a program of balance-of-payments reporting, publishing the data in the first *Survey of Current Business*. The department also developed safety codes for industry and transportation (including assistance in developing traffic signals and air and road safety standards, as well as expansion of its previous responsibility for safe ocean travel). In tandem with its increased responsibilities was the growth in the department's budget, from $860,000 in 1920 to more than $38 million in 1928.

Hoover left Commerce in 1928 to become president. His first year in office saw the beginning of the Great Depression. The national income declined drastically, and U.S. exports fell below their 1913 levels. Franklin D. Roosevelt, who defeated Hoover in the 1932 election, slashed Commerce's budget and reduced its activities. There was even some thought of abolishing the department.

World War II and the years that followed ushered in a new role for Commerce. The National Bureau of Standards gained importance through its efforts to insure interchangeability of weapons parts, while the Civil Aeronautics Administration significantly expanded its pilot training programs. The Bureau of Public Roads and the Maritime Administration were moved to Commerce in 1949 and 1950, respectively. Until the Department of Transportation was established in 1967, Commerce was the principal overseer of national transportation programs.

Although Commerce has remained an important source of economic information, it now shares responsibilities in international economics with special presidential advisers, the Treasury, and the Office of the U.S. Trade Representative.

ORGANIZATION AND FUNCTIONS

In the Department of Commerce the general counsel, inspector general, Office of Business Liaison, Office of Policy Planning and Coordination, and Office of Public Affairs report directly to the secretary and the deputy secretary. Six undersecretaries are responsible for oceans and atmosphere, international trade, export administration, economic affairs, technology, and travel and tourism. The department has assistant secretaries for legislative and intergovernmental affairs, administration, patents and trademarks, communications and information, and economic development. A number of key offices are administered by directors. Commerce has offices in more than seventy-five major U.S. cities and more than seventy posts overseas. The department is organized according to the following functions.

Trade

The International Trade Administration (ITA) is the agency most closely associated with the department's mandate "to foster, promote and develop the commerce and industry of the United States." Congress authorized establishment of ITA in 1980 to help deal with soaring U.S. merchandise trade deficits. ITA helps formulate foreign trade and economic policies, works with the U.S. Trade Representative and other agencies, and administers legislation to counter unfair foreign trade practices.

The Bureau of Export Administration, established in 1987, formulates U.S. policy for the control of high-technology exports and monitors such exports. This program is designed to prevent the loss of commodities and technologies that would harm the nation's security and advance the military capabilities of adversaries. ITA originally had jurisdiction over this function.

The National Tourism Policy Act of 1981 replaced the U.S. Travel Service, established in 1961 to address a $1.2 billion balance-of-payments deficit in tourism, with the U.S. Travel and Tourism Administration (USTTA).

Economics

Created by President John F. Kennedy in 1961 to help coordinate the formulation of economic policy, the Office of Economic Affairs provides foreign and domestic economic data, analyses, and forecasts, based on information provided by its two bureaus, Economic Analysis and Census. The Constitution stipulates that censuses are to be taken, but it was not until 1902 that Congress enacted legislation making the Census Bureau a permanent organization.

Science and Technology

In 1970 Congress authorized establishment of the National Oceanic and Atmospheric Administration (NOAA) in response to the presidentially commissioned report "Our Nation and the Sea," which called for bringing several existing agencies into a unified program. NOAA, one of the largest agencies in Commerce, monitors and predicts the weather, charts the seas and the skies, protects ocean resources, and collects data on the oceans, atmosphere, space, and sun.

The Office of Technology Administration, established by Congress in 1988, helps U.S. businesses to become more competitive abroad by fostering government and private partnerships to stimulate the spread of innovative technologies. OTA oversees the National Institute of Standards and Technology (NIST) and the National Technical Information Service (NTIS). The latter serves as a clearinghouse for scientific, technical, and engineering information and analysis. It is self-supporting through its sales of information products and services.

The National Institute of Standards and Technology was created in 1901 as the National Bureau of Standards, when the United States was the only major commercial nation without a standards laboratory. The earlier bureau—first located in Treasury and transferred to Commerce and Labor in 1903—was charged with custody, comparison, and, when needed, establishment of standards. It was renamed NIST under the Omnibus Trade and Competitiveness Act of 1988, which formalized the agency's growing role in the development of advanced technology, through in-house research and joint development ventures for other federal agencies and private businesses.

In 1978 an executive order merged the Office of Telecommunications in the Executive Office of the President with the Office of Telecommunications in Commerce. The product of this merger was the National Telecommunications and Information Administration. Its mandate is to develop policies on the advancement and use of new technologies in common carrier, telephone, broadcast, and satellite communications systems.

The Patent Office, one of the oldest federal agencies, was authorized by Article I, section 8, of the Constitution. In 1802 a full-time Patent Office was established in the State Department; the office was transferred to Commerce in 1925. The Patent Office began registering trademarks in 1870. In 1975, one year after the one millionth trademark was registered, the office's name was changed officially to the Patent and Trademark Office.

Development

Created in 1965, the Economic Development Administration (EDA) works to generate and preserve private sector jobs in economically depressed areas by using public works funds, business loans, loan guarantees, technical assistance, long-range economic planning, and economic research.

The Minority Business Development Agency was created in 1979 to promote minority businesses by generating private capital—and, later, by providing federal contracts and grants.

The Office of Business Liaison (1981) is a central source of information for people interested in doing business overseas or with the federal government.

Department of Defense

"The role of a Defense Secretary is to rein in the disparate interests in the defense establishment and shape a military program to suit the overall goals of himself and his administration," wrote Richard A. Stubbing, a defense analyst at the Office of Management and Budget for twenty years. "Given his limited time and political resources, the task is enormous, in some ways impossible, but the performance of the Defense Secretary is vitally important to the overall effectiveness and efficiency of the defense program."[80]

The Department of Defense (DOD) officially became part of the cabinet only in 1949. In terms of human resources it is the largest of the fourteen departments that make up the cabinet. Providing the umbrella for the army, navy, marine corps, and air force, DOD is composed of about 1.5 million men and women on active duty. They are backed, in case of emergency, by the one million members of the reserve components. In addition, more than 900,000 civilian employees work for DOD. The defense appropriations bill for fiscal year 1996 totaled $243 billion.

CREATION OF THE NATIONAL MILITARY ESTABLISHMENT

Before the twentieth century there was little need for a centralized defense establishment; the army fought on land and the navy fought at sea. The acquisition of overseas territories and the growing U.S. role in international affairs, however, led many observers to conclude that a more coordinated national security system was needed—an observation that proved to be all the more true with the advent of air power in the period between World Wars I and II. The Air Corps, as the air force was then called, lobbied for equality with the other branches; although it was nominally a part of the army, it in fact operated independently.

Between 1921 and 1945 at least fifty bills aimed at unifying the armed forces were introduced in Congress. But the major argument for unification also acted as the stumbling block to an interservice agreement. The Army Air Corps' desire for separate status—was practicable only within a framework that provided some degree of unified direction at the top. To the navy, however, the logic of separate services for land, sea, and air represented the potential loss of naval aviation to the air force and the marine corps to the army.

Despite the navy's opposition, Congress passed the National Security Act of 1947 (PL 80-253) on July 25. This act provided "a comprehensive program for the future security of the United States" and gave the three services "authoritative coordination and unified direction under civilian control" without merging them. The law thus created a national military establishment, to be headed by the secretary of defense and to consist of the Departments of the Army, Navy, and Air Force. The secretary was designated "the principal assistant to the President in all matters relating to the national security." At the same time, however, the

Richard B. Cheney, upon becoming secretary of defense, reviews an honor guard at the Pentagon with President George Bush, March 21, 1989.

three service departments were to be "administered as individual executive departments by their respective Secretaries," who retained the right to present "to the President or to the Director of the Budget . . . any report or recommendations relating to his department which he may deem necessary." The secretary of defense was not allowed to establish a military staff and was restricted to three civilian assistants. The Joint Chiefs of Staff (JCS), including a chief of staff, were given statutory authority as "the principal military advisers to the President and the Secretary of Defense," with authority to prepare strategic plans, "establish unified commands," and "review major material and personnel requirements of the military forces."

President Harry S. Truman signed the law on July 26, 1947, and immediately named Navy Secretary James V. Forrestal as the first secretary of defense.

1949 AMENDMENTS

Concern about the high cost of national defense—not its adequacy—was the major factor that persuaded Congress to amend the National Security Act in 1949. The report of the Hoover Commission on Organization of the Executive Branch had recommended (1) giving the secretary of defense complete statutory authority over the three services, (2) eliminating the three military departments and demoting the service secretaries to undersecretaries of defense, and (3) appointing a chairman of the JCS responsible to the secretary. Truman essentially adopted the proposals and sent them to Congress.

As enacted, the National Security Act amendments of 1949 converted the national military establishment into an executive cabinet-level Department of Defense. The amended act incorporated the military departments of the three services and stipulated that each was to be "separately administered" by a secretary under the "direction, authority, and control" of the secretary of defense. The secretary was barred, however, from acting to transfer, abolish, or consolidate any of the services' combatant functions. Moreover, nothing was to "prevent a Secretary of a military department or a member of the Joint Chiefs of Staff from presenting to the Congress, on his own initiative, . . . any recommendations relating to the Department of Defense that he may deem proper."

The law also provided for a deputy secretary of defense, three assistant secretaries, and a nonvoting chairman of the Joint Chiefs of Staff (to replace the chief of staff to the president), who was to rank first but hold no command. Finally, provision was made for adding comptrollers to the Defense Department and the three military departments and for instituting uniform accounting and budgetary procedures.

Dwight D. Eisenhower assumed the presidency committed to the same general foreign policy and security objectives as his predecessor, yet he pledged to bring about a sharp reduction in defense spending and a reorganization of DOD. For civilian leadership in the Pentagon, Eisenhower turned to the business world, selecting Charles E. Wilson, president of General Motors Corporation, as defense secretary. The deputy secretary and secretaries of the army, navy, and air force also came from the business community.

Like World War II, the Korean War revealed the organizational shortcomings of the military complex. President Eisenhower thus asked a group of prominent citizens to propose changes in the Defense Department, and their recommendations were embodied in a reorganization plan that the president submitted to Congress. Although there were some objections from legislators, the plan was adopted, providing for six additional assistant secretary positions and giving the secretary the power to select the director of the joint staff of the Joint Chiefs of Staff.

Between 1953 and 1957 Eisenhower and Wilson were largely successful in holding down attempts to increase defense spending to levels unacceptable to them. But in the aftermath of the 1957 Soviet launch of the first unmanned satellite, *Sputnik I,* the administration found itself under attack from Republicans as well as Democrats, who called for major changes in the defense program. These changes included a reorganization of the Defense Department to speed decision making in the development of new weapons systems and to curtail waste and duplication of effort by the three services.

The administration reluctantly agreed to go along with some of the proposed changes. The Department of Defense Reorganization Act of 1958 authorized the secretary to consolidate common supply and service functions and to assign responsibility for the development and operation of new weapons systems. It also authorized the secretary to transfer, reassign, abolish, or consolidate existing combat functions of the three services, subject to congressional veto. The act established the position of director of defense research and engineering as the principal adviser to the secretary for all scientific and technological matters. An administration proposal to appropriate all defense funds to the secretary—rather than to the military departments—to "remove all doubts" about the secretary's authority was dropped because of strong Republican as well as Democratic criticism.

SECRETARIES MCNAMARA, LAIRD, AND BROWN

Within six months of taking office, President John F. Kennedy had added almost $6 billion to Eisenhower's defense request of $41.8 billion for fiscal year 1962, initiating a sharp acceleration of strategic programs and a major expansion of conventional forces. In moving to a higher level of defense spending, however, the president and Defense Secretary Robert S. McNamara did not abandon all considerations of cost. On the contrary, McNamara continued and strengthened the policy of cutting back, terminating, or postponing programs of marginal or dubious effectiveness.

McNamara, president of the Ford Motor Company when Kennedy nominated him as secretary, quickly gained a reputation as a highly intelligent and forceful "boss" of the Pentagon. The new secretary asserted the full authority of his office under the 1958 reorganization act, achieving a greater degree of centralization and control over the services than had ever existed. In the field of management, he introduced a planning-programming-budgeting process that attempted to tie together, in terms of national objectives, the requirements and projected activities of all elements of the military establishment.

Richard Nixon's choice of Melvin R. Laird as secretary of defense was widely considered to be an astute one. Laird, an eighth-term Republican representative from Wisconsin (1953–1969), was the first member of Congress to serve as DOD secretary. A professional politician who had served on committees dealing with defense, Laird had a reputation as a "mover and shaker" in Congress. He recognized his relative lack of managerial experience, however, and he chose David Packard, a highly successful industrialist, as his deputy to run the day-to-day business of the department. The two established a close working relationship.

Laird believed strongly in the power of appointments for both civilian and military posts; he personally selected the three service secretaries and met separately with them each week. He also held weekly meetings with his assistant secretaries. Despite major budget and force cutbacks and an end to the draft, Laird was popular among military personnel, and he developed a close rapport with Gen. Earle G. Wheeler, chairman of the Joint Chiefs of Staff.

Laird left Defense in 1973 to assume the position of presidential assistant for domestic affairs, which had been vacated by John D. Ehrlichman in the wake of the Watergate scandal. He was replaced in January 1973 by Elliot L. Richardson, who was reassigned the following May to Justice as attorney general. Richardson's tenure as defense secretary was the briefest in the twenty-six-year history of the office.

Nixon's third selection as DOD secretary was James R. Schlesinger, who had just been named director of the Central Intelligence Agency in January. Although Schlesinger was viewed as an intellectual, his approach to defense issues was pragmatic, and, unlike McNamara, whose emphasis on cost-effectiveness Schlesinger had criticized, he was willing to negotiate. Nonetheless, management suffered during Schlesinger's tenure; he did not get along well with President Gerald R. Ford, who fired the secretary in 1975 over policy disagreements. In his place Ford appointed Donald Rumsfeld, who held the post until the end of the administration.

In contrast to the musical chairs of the Nixon and Ford administrations, Harold Brown's tenure as defense secretary lasted throughout the administration of Jimmy Carter. A physicist and former McNamara protege, Brown was secretary of the air force from 1965 to 1969 before becoming president of the California Institute of Technology. Brown brought with him a thorough knowledge of defense programs and a sterling reputation. He was, above all, a scientist and administrator, not a politician. As secretary he used a more centralized management style than that favored by Laird or Schlesinger, and he took a more active role in making budget and program decisions.

During his first year in office Brown ordered a comprehensive review of DOD's organization. As a result, fewer people reported directly to the secretary, and a number of headquarters activities were consolidated. A General Accounting Office report concluded that no substantial economies had been effected, however. "Defense recently completed a Harold Brown ordered economy movement that resulted in almost no economy and even less movement," commented the *Washington Post* on October 7, 1978.[81]

One of Brown's major difficulties in asserting his role as secretary was Carter's personal involvement in defense issues, even small ones. Brown was unwilling to challenge the president and generally was overshadowed by him.

BUILDUP UNDER REAGAN

Caspar W. Weinberger was Ronald Reagan's choice as secretary of defense when the Republican entered office in 1981. A longtime friend of the president, Weinberger had a distinguished career in public service and private business. When he was nominated to be DOD secretary, however, opponents criticized Weinberger's lack of background in defense policy and feared that he would manage the Pentagon's budget too tightly. But he quickly established himself as a relentless advocate of a rapid military buildup.

After Reagan's first few years in office, Congress became less willing to back the defense buildup at the pace sought by the president and Weinberger. There was a growing sense that Pentagon funds were used poorly. Weinberger was hesitant to override the budget requests of the services and gave them a relatively free hand in setting military priorities and making program decisions. The secretary's "hands-off" approach and his inattention to management resulted in strained relations with Congress, which were not helped by the increasingly perfunctory character of the secretary's dealings with Capitol Hill. Defense committees asked him for advice on where to find budget cuts, but Weinberger insisted that his requests were the minimum required for the nation's safety. Hardliners applauded his tenacity, but many congressional defense specialists contended that by refusing to bargain, he dealt himself out of the process.

Citing personal reasons, Weinberger resigned in November 1987. He was replaced by his longtime associate Frank C. Carlucci, who had established a reputation as a shrewd operator of the machinery of government.

DEFENSE UNDER BUSH AND CLINTON

George Bush's nomination of former senator John Tower of Texas sparked one of the most divisive confirmation battles in Senate history. While Republican chair of the Senate Armed Services Committee in the early 1980's, Tower's hawkish views and partisan style had antagonized Democratic colleagues. During his 1989 confirmation hearings, the Democratic majority claimed that Tower's personal life, especially accusations of drunken behavior and womanizing, made him unfit for the sensitive post. Tower's supporters accused Democrats of waging a vindictive political campaign against Bush through his nominee. Although Bush refused to abandon the nomination, it failed on the Senate floor; it was the first time that a newly elected president's cabinet choice was not confirmed.

Within weeks of the Tower fiasco Bush had nominated and the Senate had confirmed Rep. Richard Cheney of Wyoming. Cheney had been President Ford's chief of staff and while in the House had served on the Intelligence Committee and as ranking member of the congressional committee investigating the Iran-contra affair. As part of Bush's close-knit foreign policy team, Cheney was one of the president's closest advisers and oversaw the deployment of U.S. troops in the multinational coalition against Saddam Hussein in Iraq. Reputed differences arose between Cheney and Secretary of State James Baker III over the diminished Soviet threat in view of Soviet president Mikhail Gorbachev's reforms and the collapse of the Warsaw Pact, with Cheney stressing the political instability of Gorbachev and urging a cautious approach in conventional and strategic arms negotiations. The dramatic changes in East-West relations, however, had strengthened demands for a "peace dividend" and Cheney began a retrenchment of the DOD budget, initiating a defense management review that streamlined the Pentagon's weapons procurement, maintenance, and supply systems. His military base closure proposal drew fire from Democrats, who accused the secretary of drawing up a political "hit list" that targeted bases and jobs in their districts. In 1991 an independent commission was charged with reviewing the list, and after protracted deliberation and opposition from Congress the vast majority of Cheney's recommendations were approved and thirty-four military installations were scheduled to be closed between 1992 and 1997.

In 1993 President Bill Clinton selected the chair of the House Armed Services Committee, Les Aspin of Wisconsin, for the defense portfolio. Aspin had been regarded as a centrist on military issues and, although not a longtime Clinton associate, shared the president's style of political wrangling and compromise to solve complex policy problems. Aspin came to the Pentagon promising a major "bottom-up" review of U.S. military needs in the post–cold war world. His early proposed troop and materiel cuts were criticized as dangerously excessive by top military officials, including Joint Chiefs of Staff Chairman Gen. Colin Powell Jr. Aspin further alienated the military establishment, already chilly to Clinton because of his draft deferment and opposition to the Vietnam War, by suggesting that U.S. military force could be used for limited objectives with uncertain outcomes as an instrument of foreign policy.

Early in his term Aspin was bogged down by inherited problems and was criticized for a lack of administrative skills. Aspin was noncommittal on Clinton's campaign pledge to end the ban on gays in the military and relinquished authority to Gen. Powell and Senate Armed Services Committee chairman Sam Nunn, both critics of Clinton's proposal. Aspin received the brunt of public and congressional anger over the Clinton administration's ambivalent policy on the mission of American troops in Somalia and became a lightning rod for dissatisfaction with Clinton's foreign policy overall. After a disastrous raid in Soma-

lia in October 1993 in which eighteen U.S. soldiers were killed, it was revealed that Aspin had denied requests to reinforce the troops with heavy armor. Aspin resigned in January 1994.

Clinton nominated retired admiral Bobby Ray Inman, a former director of navy intelligence and deputy director of the CIA, as Aspin's successor. Although the nomination was well received across the political spectrum, Inman abruptly withdrew from consideration, claiming he had been unfairly criticized by newspaper columnists. Clinton soon named Aspin's deputy, William J. Perry, to the post. Unlike Aspin, Perry had a record of managerial expertise in both corporate and government service. Trained as a mathematician, he had been the president of a military electronics company before joining the Carter administration as DOD supervisor of defense research and development. As Aspin's deputy he had concentrated on developing high-tech weaponry and managing weapons acquisition.

ORGANIZATION AND FUNCTIONS

DOD is structured around four principal elements: the office of the secretary, the military departments, the Joint Chiefs of Staff, and the unified commands. The secretary's line of command is direct to both the staff and fighting forces. Nonetheless, "the responsibilities of the job [of DOD secretary] are not matched by corresponding powers," wrote John G. Kester, former special assistant to Defense Secretary Harold Brown. "The Secretary is an official whose position is impinged upon from many directions, and who often must feel that he is sitting on top of a centrifuge. Without a lot of pulling at the center, the Defense Department tends to fly off in all directions."[82]

The secretary of defense is assisted by a deputy secretary, three undersecretaries (acquisition and technology; policy; and personnel and readiness), and ten assistant secretaries (command, control, communications, and intelligence; health affairs; legislative affairs; regional security; reserve affairs; economic security; international security policy; special operations and low-intensity conflict; strategy and requirements; and policy and plans). The comptroller, general counsel, inspector general, director of the National Security Agency, and directors of operational test and evaluation and administration and management report directly to the secretary.

Reporting to the office of the secretary via defense assistant secretaries and undersecretaries are the following agencies: mapping, legal services, contract audit, security assistance, investigative service, logistics, advanced research projects, nuclear, on-site inspection, information systems, finance and accounting, commissary, central imagery, and intelligence. In January 1984, in response to Reagan's directive, the Strategic Defense Initiative Organization (later renamed the Ballistic Missile Defense Organization) was established as a Defense agency reporting directly to the secretary of defense.

The Joint Chiefs of Staff—consisting of the chairman; vice chairman; chief of staff, U.S. Army; chief of naval operations; chief of staff, U.S. Air Force; and commandant of the marine corps—constitutes the immediate military staff of the defense secretary. The members of the JCS are the senior military officers of their respective services. The chairman of the JCS is the senior military adviser to the president, the National Security Council (NSC), and the secretary of defense. The JCS is served by the joint staff, which is composed of not more than four hundred officers selected in approximately equal numbers from the army, navy (including the marine corps), and air force.

Each military department is organized separately under its own secretary, who is responsible to the secretary of defense. In addition, there are a number of unified commands. A "unified command" is a force under a single commander that is engaged in a broad, continuing mission, assisted by assigned personnel from two or more services. The unified commands are the European, Atlantic, Central, Pacific, Southern, Transportation, Special Operations, Strategic, and Space.

Department of Education

President Jimmy Carter entered office in 1977 with one much-publicized legislative priority in the area of education. During the 1976 presidential election campaign, he had vowed to establish a cabinet-level department to oversee education. In return, he received the endorsement of the 1.7 million-member National Education Association, the first campaign endorsement given in the organization's history. Congress passed legislation creating the Department of Education in 1979.

PREDECESSORS OF THE DEPARTMENT

Unlike many other countries, for which a centralized educational system was a vital component of nation building, the United States traditionally has avoided a strong federal role in education. It was not until 1867 that President Andrew Johnson called for the creation of an education department "for the purpose of collecting such statistics and facts as shall show the condition and progress of education in the several States and Territories, and of diffusing such information respecting the organization and management of schools and school systems, and methods of teaching. . . ." The new department had a staff of four: Commissioner of Education Henry Barnard and three clerks. Their combined annual salary was $7,800.

The first Department of Education was downgraded quickly to the status of a bureau in the Interior Department. For the next seventy years it limped along as a small recordkeeping office, collecting information on the modest federal education efforts. Proposals for a separate department surfaced periodically, but they went nowhere. In 1939 the renamed Office of Education was transferred to the Federal Security Agency, which became the Department of Health, Education and Welfare (HEW) in 1953.

With the tremendous expansion of federal education programs in the postwar period, arguments for a separate department grew more persuasive. During the 1960s several studies recommended establishment of a separate department, as did related reorganization proposals. In 1972 Congress established

within HEW an Education Division, headed by an assistant secretary for education. It included the existing Office of Education.

CONTROVERSY OVER ITS CREATION

One of the main arguments for a separate education department was the confusing and contradictory structure of the existing federal educational administration. In 1978 the hundreds of federal educational programs were located in more than forty different agencies.

Grouping all these programs in one department, however, proved to be very difficult politically. For every program going into the department, some other department would have to lose power and money. Agencies and interest groups fought against giving up long, established relationships for an uncertain future in the Education Department. The bill creating the new department also was opposed by a coalition of labor and civil rights groups, which feared that their influence would be reduced in a department dominated by professional educators. The strongest supporters of the new department were those in elementary and secondary education. Higher education organizations were basically neutral on the question.

At first it appeared that the bill would clear Congress easily despite some bitter struggles among administration officials, interest groups, and members of Congress over exactly what should be in the new department. But, faced with dilatory tactics, House leaders decided to shelve the bill in 1978. Opposition was vigorous when the legislation came before Congress again in 1979, but effective lobbying by the proposal's supporters—including President Carter—provided the margin needed to create the department. Congress completed action on the bill on September 27, and Carter signed it on October 17. Some 152 federal education-related programs were consolidated in the new agency, which at its creation became the fifth largest department handling the eighth largest budget.

Shirley M. Hufstedler, the first secretary of education, took office on December 6, 1979. A member of the U.S. Court of Appeals for the Ninth Circuit since 1969, Hufstedler brought no professional education credentials to her new job other than her experience as a member of the boards of trustees of three California institutions of higher education. That lack of experience caused some concern in the education community. Defenders of Carter's appointment argued, however, that Hufstedler's lack of experience and close connection with one or another of the sectors of the education community was a virtue. They said she would bring a fresh perspective to the deep-seated problems of the nation's public education system.

The new department formally opened its doors on May 7, 1980. By 1995 its budget totaled $23.2 billion. The department is constrained in its authority, however, by the long-standing tradition in the United States that education is primarily a state and local function. Congress restated the commitment to decentralized control when it declared in the act that created the department that "the establishment of the Department of Education shall not . . . diminish the responsibility for education which is reserved to the states and the local school systems and other instrumentalities of the state." It is they who make policies on such matters as the length of the school day and year, textbook selection, teacher certification, high school graduation requirements, grading scales, and other instructional and administrative policies.

The Department of Education distributes most of its program funds directly to the states as formula grants. The amounts are based on the number of students in various special categories, and the states then distribute the money to local districts under Education-approved plans.

The existence of the department was precarious during its first years. Ronald Reagan, riding a wave of voter dissatisfaction with what was seen as widespread federal intervention into local affairs, promised during the 1980 election campaign to dismantle the young agency and reduce Washington's role in education programs. His selection of Terrel H. Bell as secretary of education was viewed, however, as an indication that the president would abandon, or at least scale back, his campaign pledge to abolish the department. Bell had been U.S. commissioner of education from 1974 to 1976 and Utah commissioner of higher education since 1976. Education groups were pleased by the selection of a fellow educator with long experience. Bell had supported creating the department, and he stated during his confirmation hearings that he did not want to see a return to the days when education was a low-status unit of the massive Department of Health, Education and Welfare.

After 1981 Reagan made little progress in his efforts to reduce spending and restructure federal involvement in education. Although in 1982 he proposed abolishing Education, Congress ignored the suggestion, and the proposal gradually faded from view.

Bell fought within the administration to moderate proposals to curb education spending, and as a result, he was criticized frequently by conservatives. He resigned as secretary at the end of 1984 and was succeeded in February 1985 by William J. Bennett, former chairman of the National Endowment for the Humanities. When Bennett resigned in 1988, Reagan named Lauro F. Cavazos to the post, making him the nation's first Hispanic cabinet member. When George Bush became president in 1989, he retained Cavazos as secretary.

Bush had campaigned on a pledge to be the "education president," but by the midpoint of his term he had not offered any major legislation that outlined his goals to improve the country's education system. Cavazos, the former president of Texas Tech University, was seen as ineffective by members of Congress, the education community, and other administration officials. Although he had been credited with opening up lines of communication with Congress that had been shut by Bennett, Cavazos was asked to resign in December 1990, after Senate Republicans blocked Bush's modest "Educational Excellence Act" at the end of the 101st Congress.

Cavazos was succeeded by Lamar Alexander, the president of the University of Tennessee and a former Republican governor of that state. As governor, Alexander had gained national attention for pushing a major education reform package through a Democratic-controlled legislature. Despite concerns about lucrative investments he had made with little of his own money, Alexander was confirmed easily and his appointment gave credibility to Bush's stated intention to make education his domestic policy priority.

One of Alexander's first duties was to dampen the controversy surrounding the administration's confusing stance on minority scholarships. The administration initially proposed a ban on race-based scholarships from schools receiving federal aid and then backed down to allow the awards if they were privately funded. Alexander eventually announced that he would allow the scholarships as long as race was not the only factor considered.

Alexander formulated Bush's "America 2000" proposal, a plan to overhaul the nation's education system using limited federal funds to promote change through model schools and financial incentives, such as federally subsidized vouchers to allow parents to send their children to private schools. Opposition to the "school-choice" initiative and proposed national examinations to monitor students' progress plagued the progress of "America 2000" through Congress, and Bush's proposals died in the Senate. Alexander was unable to persuade Bush to veto a 1992 higher education bill that included provisions for direct loans to students, which the secretary argued would create new federal debt by erasing the role of banks. In that election year, Republicans convinced the president that he could not afford to be seen as blocking the bill's major provisions, which expanded middle-class eligibility for college loans.

President Bill Clinton's appointment of former South Carolina governor Richard W. Riley as secretary drew high praise from the education community. Like Clinton, Riley was seen as at the vanguard of the education reform movement at the state level, where he had successfully implemented a school improvement plan by slightly raising sales taxes. His South Carolina reform plan had included initiatives to emphasize preschools, improve teacher training and workplace conditions, and improve testing and student performance, all parts of Clinton's agenda.

As secretary, Riley was sometimes criticized for failing to develop national proposals that lived up to the reform zeal of the Clinton campaign. In 1994 Congress passed a Clinton school improvement package, "Goals 2000," closely patterned on Bush's earlier proposal. Riley's effort to revise the formula for distributing federal money to schools, the Title I grants program, in order to direct it to states with a high percentage of poor students had limited success. But he received bipartisan support for his cooperation with Labor Secretary Robert B. Reich to develop another Clinton initiative, a federal school-to-work program to provide career training for students who do not attend college.

ORGANIZATION AND FUNCTIONS

The Department of Education is headed by a secretary who serves as the president's chief adviser on education and supervises the department's staff. The secretary also performs certain functions related to five federally aided corporations: American Printing House for the Blind in Lexington, Kentucky; Gallaudet University (for assisting the deaf) in Washington, D.C.; Howard University in Washington, D.C.; National Institute for Literacy in Washington, D.C.; and National Technical Institute for the Deaf (part of Rochester Institute of Technology) in New York State. The secretary is assisted by a deputy secretary, undersecretary, general counsel, inspector general, and nine assistant secretaries who serve in the following offices.

The Management Office coordinates the day-to-day activities of the department and provides administrative guidance to the secretary. The Office of Intergovernmental and Interagency Affairs serves as the liaison between the department and its ten regional offices, state and local governments, and other federal agencies. The Office of Legislation and Congressional Affairs is the principal advisory body to the secretary on legislative matters and congressional relations.

The Office of Elementary and Secondary Education provides state and local education agencies with the financial assistance needed to help improve preschool, elementary, and secondary education—both public and private. Its largest program, authorized under Title I of the 1965 Elementary and Secondary Education Act, is aimed at disadvantaged children. The office also administers funds provided by the Indian Education Act. It oversees voluntary and court-ordered school desegregation programs, provides assistance to school districts affected by federal activities that overburden local tax sources (impact aid), and helps districts struck by natural disasters.

The Office of Special Education and Rehabilitative Services assists in the education of handicapped children and in the rehabilitation of disabled adults.

The Office of Postsecondary Education supports financially needy young people who want to go to college or a vocational training school after high school. The office also supports programs for institutional development, student services, housing and facilities, veterans' affairs, cooperative education, international education, graduate education, historically black colleges, foreign language and area studies, innovative teaching methods and practices, and other subjects related to the improvement of postsecondary education.

The Office of Vocational and Adult Education helps states and communities provide specialized vocational education so that young people and adults can acquire marketable skills, or so that they can obtain a high school diploma or its equivalent.

Research and demonstration projects designed to improve education at all grade levels—preschool through graduate school—are funded by the Office of Educational Research and Improvement. The office also deals with libraries, museums, and educational programming by the media.

The Office for Civil Rights is responsible for seeing that educational institutions comply with federal statutes that prohibit discrimination in programs and activities receiving federal financial assistance from the department.

Department of Energy

The 1973–1974 Arab oil embargo brought with it dramatic evidence that the U.S. government needed to formulate a more coherent and comprehensive energy policy and centralize its energy-related programs, which then were scattered among various federal agencies. The initial federal response to this need was creation in 1974 of the Energy Research and Development Administration (ERDA) and the Federal Energy Administration (FEA) to administer federal policy for energy planning and regulation. It soon was recognized, however, that additional steps were needed. Thus, on August 4, 1977, President Jimmy Carter signed into law a bill (PL 95-91) that created a cabinet-level Department of Energy (DOE). The new department came into existence on October 1, 1977.

The first new cabinet department since the Department of Transportation was created in 1966, DOE assumed the powers and functions of FEA, ERDA, the Federal Power Commission (FPC), and the four regional power commissions. DOE also absorbed energy-related programs formerly administered by the Departments of the Interior, Defense, Commerce, and Housing and Urban Development and the Interstate Commerce Commission. The department assumed as well the role of consultant to the Department of Transportation and the Rural Electrification Administration on energy-related matters.

The first secretary of energy was James R. Schlesinger, President Carter's chief energy adviser during the early months of the administration. Although Schlesinger had a long record of government service, he drew vigorous criticism for his lack of administrative skill in putting the new department into working order; he resigned in mid-1979. Carter replaced him with Charles W. Duncan Jr., deputy secretary of defense since 1977, who won high marks for his management of the new department.

DOE initially employed almost twenty thousand people—virtually all of them transferees from the existing energy programs in other departments and agencies. Its fiscal year 1978 budget was $10.6 billion.

RESPONSE TO THE ENERGY CRISIS

President Richard Nixon was the first president to suggest that the federal agencies dealing with energy be reorganized and consolidated. In 1971 he proposed creation of a Department of Natural Resources, based on the Department of the Interior, but including such energy-related programs as those run by the Atomic Energy Commission. Congress greeted Nixon's proposal with yawns, and it progressed no further than the hearing stage. In 1973 Nixon resubmitted his proposal. Once again, it went nowhere on Capitol Hill. As the energy crisis became a fact of life, however, Congress responded in 1974 to Nixon administration requests to create FEA and ERDA.

One of President Gerald R. Ford's last official actions was to submit a plan to Congress for reorganizing the energy bureaucracy into a Department of Energy. Congress had requested such a plan when it passed legislation in 1976 extending the life of the FEA. Ford's plan was in many respects similar to that proposed by Carter a few months later. "Nowhere is the need for reorganization and consolidation greater than in energy policy," Carter said in a March 1, 1977, message to Congress unveiling his reorganization plan. "All but two of the executive branch's Cabinet departments now have some responsibility for energy policy, but no agency . . . has the broad authority needed to deal with our energy problems in a comprehensive way."

The bill that finally reached Carter's desk for his signature differed in only one major respect from his original proposal. Carter and Congress disagreed over who in the new energy structure should have the power to set prices for natural gas, oil, and electricity. Carter would have given this power to the secretary, but the majority in both chambers of Congress was opposed on the ground that it was unwise to give such power to a single person who served at the pleasure of the president. To shield such sensitive and far-reaching economic decisions from political pressure, Congress included in the DOE legislation language that created an independent Federal Energy Regulatory Commission (FERC) that would set energy prices. If the president found that a national emergency required quick action on such matters, however, the secretary could circumvent the commission on the question of oil prices.

DECLINING INTEREST IN ENERGY

During Ronald Reagan's administration, Congress all but forgot the national energy problems that it had spent the previous decade trying to solve. Indeed, by 1985 the stormy political debates over energy policy that had marked the 1970s had lost their thunder. With no crisis to raise an alarm, members of Congress who were still concerned about the adequacy of the nation's long-term fuel supplies could generate little political momentum for challenging Reagan's determination to scale back federal control over U.S. energy markets.

During the 1980 presidential campaign, Reagan had contended that federal actions had caused, rather than alleviated, the nation's energy problems. Declaring that "America must get to work producing more energy," he pledged to keep the government from interfering with marketplace supply-and-demand incentives that would encourage domestic fuel development. Reagan also vowed to abolish DOE; conservatives viewed the department as an unneeded instrument for federal meddling in energy matters. Congress refused to comply, but Reagan's first-term energy secretaries—former South Carolina governor James B. Edwards (an oral surgeon) and Donald P. Hodel (former deputy secretary of the interior)—de-emphasized the department's programs to promote conservation, encourage solar and other alternative technologies, and develop new ways to burn fossil fuels.

Edwards had little experience in dealing with energy issues.

As South Carolina's governor, however, he had been an unabashed advocate of developing nuclear power. Environmental groups were dismayed by his strong backing of the commercial reprocessing of spent nuclear fuel into fresh fuel, plutonium, and liquid wastes. As energy secretary, Edwards continued to back nuclear research and development as offering the best long-term solution to U.S. energy needs.

In selecting Hodel to replace Edwards, the administration ignored environmental groups' criticism of Hodel's close ties to Interior Secretary James G. Watt and his record of supporting nuclear power. Hodel was able, however, to improve the morale of DOE employees by playing down talk of abolishing the department. He also won praise from some members of Congress, even Democrats who opposed his policies. While Edwards and Hodel gave DOE a low profile, Watt, as chairman of Reagan's cabinet council on Natural Resources and the Environment, took the lead in shaping the administration's agenda for easing federal regulatory restraints on the U.S. energy industry.

In January 1985 Reagan nominated John S. Herrington, then an assistant to the president for personnel, to replace Hodel, who was nominated to be secretary of the interior after the controversial Watt was forced to resign. The announcement came amid new rumors that Reagan would seek to abolish DOE and merge its functions into the Interior Department. But Herrington played down this possibility in an appearance before the Senate Energy and Natural Resources Committee, saying, "The president has nominated me to be a full-time secretary of energy, not a caretaker." The Senate confirmed both nominations in February. The idea of a merger faded.

In 1989 President George Bush appointed as secretary James D. Watkins, a former nuclear submarine skipper and chief of naval operations. He hoped that Watkins's expertise in nuclear energy would lead to solutions for the nation's problem-plagued weapons reactor complex.

The 1989 DOE estimate for cleanup of its principal plants and laboratories, on EPA's "superfund" list of the nation's worst toxic dumps, was $200 billion spread over thirty years. Acknowledging that long-term neglect of environmental and safety standards had generated these costs, Watkins pledged an emphasis on safety and environmental concerns, reflecting both the nation's changing defense needs and the importance of restoring public confidence in the program. His proposed restructuring of the weapons complex included a smaller nuclear stockpile and a transfer of more of the department's nonnuclear work to the private sector. Watkins had more difficulty in his efforts to open DOE nuclear waste-storage facilities. The sites, facing opposition from lawmakers over safety issues, opposition from the states in which they were to be placed, and defeats in federal court trials to withdraw the land for storage use, were eventually cleared to be opened with provisions for environmental oversight by the EPA.

The issue of energy consumption, which had faded from view during the Reagan administration, surfaced again in the early days of the Persian Gulf War. Concern about higher prices and U.S. reliance on oil imports (which were now threatened) shaped the development of Watkins's comprehensive energy plan. Following nationwide public meetings and extensive department review, Watkins proposed modifications to federally mandate fuel efficiency standards for passenger vehicles and other energy conservation measures. The plan was watered down, however, by conservative antiregulatory forces within the White House, principally Chief of Staff John Sununu and budget director Richard Darman. The administration plan submitted to Congress favored increased domestic production over incentives to reduce consumption. In the lengthy debate about the energy bill, Bush's White House team, rather than the DOE, acted as the administration's primary negotiators. The final bill, signed by Bush in October 1992, contained some significant policy advances, such as a restructured and more competitive electric utility industry, streamlined licensing requirements for nuclear power plants, and greater promotion of alternative fuels. But it did not live up to the possibility of a major rewrite of energy policy that many felt the Gulf War had opened up, reflecting Watkins's lack of influence in Bush's conservative and election-oriented inner circle.

Clinton's choice for secretary of energy, Hazel O'Leary, was a relative unknown in Washington policy circles. A Minnesota utilities executive, she had worked for Ford and Carter in the Department of Energy and its predecessor, the Federal Energy Administration, as a regulator of petroleum, natural gas and electric industries, and energy conservation programs. On entering office in 1993 she pledged to shift the emphasis of energy policy from production and fossil fuels to conservation, energy efficiency, and renewable fuels.

An early goal of the Clinton administration was to speed up the pace of environmental cleanup at DOE facilities and to dismantle the U.S. nuclear arsenal in compliance with international treaties. In 1993 DOE was not producing nuclear weapons or material, but the costs of cleanup remained high and action on waste disposal remained at an impasse. O'Leary began a two-year review, incorporating public comment, of the department's regulatory structure, and in early 1995 released a preliminary proposal for the downsizing and reorganization of the nation's nuclear-weapons complex. Although cleanup remained the focus of the program, the proposal included plans to begin restoring the department's weapons-building activities with a new facility to produce tritium, a radioactive form of hydrogen used in nuclear weapons.

ORGANIZATION AND FUNCTIONS

The Department of Energy is organized around four broad groups of activities. The largest includes energy research, development, and demonstration. The next largest encompasses nuclear weapons development, cleanup, production, waste management, and surveillance. The remaining two major functions are oversight of the interstate transmission of natural gas, oil, and electricity, performed by the Federal Energy Regulatory Commission; and the collection and analysis of energy data, undertaken by the Energy Information Administration.

The secretary is responsible for the overall planning, direction, and control of DOE activities. The deputy secretary has the primary oversight responsibility for the department's policies on energy efficiency and renewable energy technology, fossil energy, nuclear energy, energy information, civilian radioactive waste management, and the power marketing administrations.

The undersecretary for energy has primary responsibility for defense programs, environmental safety and health, waste management, intelligence and national security programs, energy research, science education and technical information programs, and laboratory management.

The assistant secretary for defense programs manages and directs DOE's programs for nuclear weapons research, development, testing, production, and surveillance.

The assistant secretary for environmental management is responsible for the cleanup of inactive sites, the continuation of effective waste management operations, and research and development of long-term solutions to storing radioactive waste. The assistant secretary for environment, safety, and health is responsible for ensuring that all active DOE facilities comply with applicable environmental laws and regulations and for protecting the safety and health of DOE employees and the public.

The assistant secretary for energy efficiency and renewable energy oversees development of departmental programs to increase production and use of renewable energy, such as solar, biomass, wind, geothermal, and alcohol fuels. The assistant secretary for fossil energy is responsible for research and development of fossil fuels.

The assistant secretary for congressional and intergovernmental affairs develops policies and procedures for the conduct of relations with Congress and state, local, Native American, and territorial governments.

The assistant secretary for policy directs international energy policy and coordinates cooperative international energy projects with foreign governments and international organizations, such as the International Energy Agency and the International Atomic Energy Agency.

The Office of Nuclear Energy administers the department's fission power generation and fuel technology programs. The office also conducts analyses and provides advice concerning nonproliferation. Nonproliferation and arms control policy is developed by the Office of Nonproliferation and National Security, which also provides the intelligence community with technical and analytical expertise on foreign nuclear and energy issues and manages the department's Emergency Management System.

The Nuclear Waste Policy Act of 1982 established within DOE an Office of Civilian Radioactive Waste Management to focus on research and development leading to the siting, construction, and operation of geologic repositories for the disposal of civilian and defense high-level radioactive wastes and spent nuclear fuel.

The director of energy research advises the secretary on DOE physical research programs, the department's overall energy research and development programs, and university-based education and training activities.

The Energy Information Administration collects, processes, and publishes data on all energy reserves, the financial status of energy-producing companies, production, demand, consumption, and other areas. The administration also analyzes short- and long-term energy trends.

The Energy Department oversees the operations of the Southeastern, Southwestern, Western Area, and Alaska Power Administrations. These administrations market electric power generated by federally owned hydropower projects.

Other offices in DOE are: Human Resources and Administration; General Counsel; Inspector General; Hearings and Appeals; Economic Impact and Diversity; and Public and Consumer Affairs. Finally, DOE has an extensive network of field organizations.

Department of Health and Human Services

The Department of Health and Human Services (HHS) was established in 1979 as the successor to the Department of Health, Education and Welfare (HEW). It is one of the largest of the federal departments, with fiscal year 1995 budget authority estimated at $302.7 billion.

PRODUCT OF REORGANIZATION

HEW evolved in a series of presidential reorganization plans and laws that became effective between 1939 and 1953. In 1939 President Franklin D. Roosevelt sent Congress his first presidential reorganization plan, creating a new federal office, the Federal Security Agency (FSA). The plan transferred a number of existing agencies to FSA, among them the Public Health Service (PHS) from Treasury, the Social Security Board (established in 1935 as an independent agency), and the Office of Education from Interior. A 1940 reorganization plan transferred additional units to FSA; among them, the most important was the Food and Drug Administration (FDA) from Agriculture. The 1943 Barden-LaFolette Act authorized an expanded federal-state vocational rehabilitation program, which led to the creation of a separate office of vocational rehabilitation in FSA.

A 1946 reorganization plan transferred the Children's Bureau to FSA (from Labor) and the Office of Vital Statistics to PHS (from the Census Bureau in Commerce). The Social Security Board was abolished and its functions handed over to the FSA administrator, who subsequently created a Social Security Administration (SSA) to oversee the program. In 1948 management of the Federal Credit Union Act of 1934 was shifted from the Federal Deposit Insurance Corporation to FSA, where a bureau of federal credit unions was established. One year later the Bureau of Employment Security (responsible for unemployment compensation) was transferred from Labor to FSA.

On March 12, 1953, President Dwight D. Eisenhower submitted to Congress a reorganization plan that transformed FSA into a cabinet-level Department of Health, Education and Welfare. There was little opposition in either party to the substance of the plan, which took effect April 11. Republicans and many southern Democrats, who had opposed similar efforts by President Harry S. Truman in 1949–1950, supported Eisenhower's initiative, as did the American Medical Association, which also had criticized the Truman proposals. Objections to the earlier plans had stemmed largely from fears that creation of a new department would enhance the power of Oscar R. Ewing, then FSA administrator and a staunch advocate of compulsory national health insurance. Ewing was expected to be the president's choice as secretary, and in that capacity he was expected to help the Truman administration advance its national health insurance proposals. Republicans had resisted the earlier plans also on the grounds that they would submerge education and health matters in a welfare-oriented agency and subject decisions on health matters to "nonprofessional" bureaucratic control.

Later in 1953 those fears were obviated by several factors. First, Oveta Culp Hobby, a strong opponent of national health insurance, was nominated to be the new secretary rather than Ewing. Second, the 1953 plan did not vest all departmental powers directly in the new secretary; it left the functions of the PHS and Office of Education as the responsibility of those two agencies, which were to be subordinate units of the new department operating under the secretary's general supervision. (This was the existing setup under FSA.) Finally, the plan provided for the creation of a new post of special assistant to the secretary for health and medical affairs. The special assistant, to be appointed by the president, was to be a person of wide nongovernmental experience in that field, but not necessarily a physician. The plan also gave the new secretary the power to administer Social Security and welfare programs (as it had been vested in the FSA administrator since 1946), but it provided for the presidential appointment of a commissioner of Social Security, subject to Senate confirmation, to carry out whatever duties in connection with those programs might be assigned by the secretary.

EXPANSION OF RESPONSIBILITIES

During the next few years the responsibilities of HEW increased significantly. In 1954 far-reaching changes were made in the Old Age and Survivors Insurance (OASI) program, greatly extending coverage. In 1956 OASI was changed to OASDI to include disability insurance. Also that year, Congress authorized the PHS to create a National Library of Medicine (its initial stock consisted of the existing Armed Forces Medical Library), which subsequently became one of the world's largest specialized libraries.

The department's purview continued to expand under Presidents John F. Kennedy and Lyndon B. Johnson. One of the most enduring legacies of the Johnson administration was the wide range of innovative social programs initiated under the banner of the "Great Society." Certainly the most dramatic development was enactment of the Medicare program in 1965 to provide hospital insurance for the elderly, financed through the Social Security system. Also in 1965 a Medicaid program of aid to the poor for medical expenses was enacted. Existing programs were broadened, including community mental health and retardation as well as aid to education for doctors, nurses, and other health specialists. Social Security was revised, with retirement benefits raised and eligibility requirements eased.

Despite Richard Nixon's desire to shift power and funding from the federal government to the states and localities, entitlement programs—among them, Social Security—continued to grow.

President Jimmy Carter's first HEW secretary, Joseph A. Califano Jr., wasted little time in pushing forward internal reorganization at HEW in an attempt to manage more effectively one of the government's largest bureaucracies, a task that had stymied many before him. Califano made changes in both the policies and procedures of his department. In March 1977 he announced a restructuring of the bureaucracy that he said was expected to save $2 billion a year in the long run. He consolidated administration of the Medicare and Medicaid programs in a new Health Care Financing Administration (HCFA). In July he announced a reorganization of the department's regional offices, and in September he pledged a thorough review of the department's voluminous regulations—six thousand pages in thirteen volumes. The overhaul was labeled "Operation Common Sense."

A much more dramatic reorganization occurred in 1979 when Congress voted to consolidate the education functions of HEW and several other cabinet departments in a separate Department of Education, with the remaining HEW responsibilities vested in the renamed Department of Health and Human Services.

Throughout the 1980s efforts to separate the Social Security Administration (SSA) from HHS were cleared by the House of Representatives. Presidents Reagan and Bush objected to the legislation and the measures died in the Senate. Proponents had maintained that SSA independence would raise the agency's visibility and distance it from the White House. In 1994 both houses of Congress passed and President Bill Clinton signed legislation making the SSA independent by March 31, 1995. The SSA would be administered by a commissioner and deputy commissioner appointed by the president to six-year terms, subject to Senate confirmation. They would be advised by a seven-member board, to which the president would appoint three members and Congress would appoint four.

ORGANIZATION AND FUNCTIONS

HHS has nine offices: Inspector General, General Counsel, Civil Rights, Consumer Affairs, Management and Budget, Legislation, Personnel Administration, Public Affairs, and Planning and Evaluation. The last five are headed by assistant secretaries. The Office of Consumer Affairs is located within HHS but re-

ports directly to the president. The department has four operating divisions.

Administration on Aging

The Administration on Aging is the principal office for carrying out the provisions of the 1965 Older Americans Act. It advises the secretary and other federal departments on the characteristics and needs of older people and develops programs designed to promote their welfare. The Administration on Aging operates the largest of the department's social service programs not aimed at those with low incomes. These provide funds to help run six thousand senior citizens centers, hot-meal programs both in seniors' homes and in group settings, legal assistance, and homemaker, home-health, and other services needed by older people to continue living at home. The agency also administers formula grants to states to develop state and community-based programs, and a program of grants to establish programs for older Native Americans.

Public Health Service

The Public Health Service (PHS) had its origin in a July 16, 1798, act which authorized a Marine Hospital Service for the care of American merchant sailors. Subsequent legislation vastly broadened the scope of its activities, and it was renamed the Public Health Service in 1912. The Public Health Service Act of July 1944 consolidated and revised substantially all existing legislation related to PHS. The service's basic responsibilities have been expanded many times since then.

PHS now administers grants to states for health services, financial assistance to educational institutions for the health professions, and national health surveys; grants to state and local agencies for comprehensive health planning; health services for American Indians and native Alaskans; and funds for research in improving the delivery of health services.

The Agency for Health Care Policy and Research, formerly the PHS National Center for Health Services Research and Health Care Technology Assessment, develops and administers a program of health services research, evaluation, research training, and related grant- and contract-supported research on the financing, organization, quality, and use of health services.

Established by the HEW secretary in 1973, the Centers for Disease Control and Prevention (CDC), based in Atlanta, Georgia, administers national programs for the prevention and control of communicable and vector-borne diseases and other preventable conditions. CDC is a leading federal agency in efforts to combat AIDS, using its funds to track cases of AIDS and HIV, finance blood testing programs, and provide counseling, education, and prevention services. The CDC oversees the activities of the National Center for Health Statistics, which collects, analyzes, and disseminates health statistics and conducts basic and applied research on health data systems and statistical methodology.

The activities of the Agency for Toxic Substances and Disease

Registry, established in 1983, are designed to protect both public health and worker safety and health from exposure to and the adverse effects of hazardous waste sites and hazardous substances released in fires, explosions, or transportation accidents.

The Food and Drug Administration was first established in the Agriculture Department in 1931, although similar law enforcement functions had been in existence under different organizational titles since 1907, when the 1906 Food and Drug Act became effective. The activities of FDA are directed toward protecting the health of the nation from impure and unsafe foods, drugs, and cosmetics as well as other potential hazards. Within FDA are centers for drug evaluation and research, biologics, food safety and applied nutrition, veterinary medicine, devices and radiological health, and toxicological research.

The Health Resources and Service Administration develops health care and maintenance systems in response to the public's needs. It is composed of bureaus of primary health care, health professions, resource development, and maternal and child health.

The Indian Health Service provides a comprehensive health services delivery system for American Indians and Alaska natives and serves as their principal federal advocate in the health field. It operates hospitals, health centers, and clinics, primarily on reservations, for Native Americans and assists tribes in obtaining and using health resources through federal, state, and local programs. The service also provides health management training, technical assistance, and human resource development to help develop Native American health programs.

The mission of the National Institutes of Health (NIH) is to improve the health of the American people by conducting and supporting biomedical research into the causes, prevention, and cure of diseases; supporting research training and the development of research resources; and communicating biomedical information.

In 1992 the Alcohol, Drug Abuse, and Mental Health Administration was dismantled and its research functions were transferred to NIH, which took over the direction of the National Institute for Mental Health, the National Institute on Drug Abuse, and the National Institute on Alcohol Abuse and Alcoholism. The administration's health care delivery operations were incorporated into a new division of the Public Health Service, the Substance Abuse and Mental Health Services Administration. The agency consists of three centers: the Center for Mental Health Services, the Center for Substance Abuse Treatment, and the Center for Substance Abuse Prevention. The agency provides block grants and technical assistance to states to help operate prevention, treatment, and rehabilitation programs and supports training for substance abuse practitioners and other health professionals.

The surgeon general advises the public on health issues such as smoking, AIDS, immunization, diet, nutrition, and disease prevention. The surgeon general oversees the activities of all members of the Public Health Service Commissioned Corps.

Health Care Financing Administration

The HCFA was established by an internal HEW reorganization in 1977, which placed under one administration oversight of the Medicare and Medicaid programs and related federal medical care quality control staffs.

Administration for Children and Families

The Administration for Children and Families (ACF), formerly the Family Support Administration (FSA), is responsible for federal programs that promote the economic and social well-being of families, children, individuals, and communities. It recommends actions and strategies designed to improve coordination of family support programs among HHS, other federal agencies, state and local governments, and private sector organizations. Among its administrative and regulatory responsibilities are the Aid to Families with Dependent Children program, which provides temporary financial assistance to needy families with dependent children; Head Start services to preschool children from low-income families; child support enforcement; programs for children with developmental disabilities and their families; refugee resettlement; foster care and adoption assistance programs; and Native American social and economic self-sufficiency programs. ACF distributes block grants to local communities for programs that promote self-sufficiency among low-income individuals, including the elderly, and carries out the Low-Income Home Energy Assistance Program to help low-income families meet the costs of home energy.

Department of Housing and Urban Development

After four years of lobbying by Presidents John F. Kennedy and Lyndon B. Johnson, Congress elevated the federal government's role in housing to cabinet-level importance in 1965 by establishing the Department of Housing and Urban Development (HUD). This move was viewed as a response to the urgent problems arising from urbanization; more than 70 percent of the U.S. population lived in the cities and suburbs—a percentage that was growing rapidly. Programs to deal with the problems of urban and suburban living—housing shortages, pollution, lack of mass transit, urban renewal, inadequate roads—were in disarray, scattered among federal, state, and local governments. The disarray often led to illogical government action: a new public housing project or hospital might be located far from public transportation, while slums might be replaced by parking lots or new high-rent dwellings.

HUD is principally responsible for federal housing and urban development programs affecting the development and preservation of communities and the provision of equal housing opportunities. These responsibilities include administering Federal Housing Administration (FHA) mortgage insurance programs that help families become homeowners and facilitate the construction and rehabilitation of rental units; rental assis-

The Department of Housing and Urban Development, formed in 1965 as one of Lyndon Johnson's Great Society initiatives, traces its roots to the U.S. Housing Corporation, which was formed during World War I to build housing for war workers.

tance programs for lower-income families who otherwise are unable to afford decent housing; the Government National Mortgage Association (GNMA, or Ginnie Mae) mortgage-backed securities that help insure an adequate supply of mortgage credit; programs to combat housing discrimination and promote fair housing; assistance to promote community and neighborhood development and preservation; programs that protect the home buyer in the marketplace; and programs to provide temporary and transitional housing for homeless people.

HUD was established by one of two major housing bills that became law in 1965. The first bill, which passed Congress on August 10, authorized rent supplements for poor persons unable to pay for decent housing from their own incomes. The bill establishing HUD soon followed and was signed into law on September 9. Accompanying legislation, passed between 1965 and 1968, gave the department additional, and controversial, responsibilities: administering rent supplements to help the poor who could not afford decent housing, a model cities program intended to pump extra federal funds into needy cities, and a program to promote home ownership by the poor.

CREATION OF HUD

The idea of establishing a department of housing was controversial from the time of its initial proposal by Kennedy in 1961. He promised to make House and Home Finance Agency (HHFA) Director Robert C. Weaver, an African American, secretary of the new department. In the Senate, however, a leadership head count found almost solid southern Democratic and Republican opposition, ensuring defeat. Using his reorganization authority, Kennedy submitted a plan to create a housing

and urban development department, but the House disapproved the resolution to put the plan into effect.

On March 2, 1965, in his "Message on the Cities," Lyndon Johnson called for a department of housing and urban development "to give greater force and effectiveness to our effort in the cities." The president's proposal had rough sledding, however: on Senate and House roll calls, a majority of Republicans and southern Democrats voted against the bill, which nonetheless passed the House on June 16 by a 217–184 vote. The Senate concurred on August 11, with much less contention.

As signed by the president on September 9, 1965, the HUD bill basically upgraded the existing HHFA to cabinet-level status. The HHFA then consisted of the Office of the Administrator and five operating units: the Federal Housing Administration, the Public Housing Administration, and the Federal National Mortgage Association—all three of which had specific authorization in law—as well as the Community Facilities Administration and the Urban Renewal Administration—both of which were created administratively within the HHFA.

The new department was not given authority to administer all federal programs related to cities and urban problems. One section of the bill, however, required a study of the functions of other agencies to determine if any should be transferred to HUD. The bill did not attempt to define an urban area or to limit the size of communities that could benefit from a HUD program. Small towns and villages as well as large cities were thus within the department's scope.

HUD became the eleventh cabinet-level department at midnight on November 8, 1965, under provisions of the bill ordering it created no later than sixty days after the president approved the legislation. Johnson, however, postponed HUD's actual establishment until a special study group completed a report on the government's role in solving urban problems. On January 13, 1966, he appointed HHFA director Weaver as HUD secretary.

DEVELOPMENT OF HUD'S PROGRAMS

The young department was thrust immediately into the fray of administering several major controversial and extremely complex housing laws. Rent supplements and the model cities program, as well as a program to promote home ownership by the poor, immediately came under HUD's purview. By the time Johnson left office in 1969, these programs were reasonably well established and were expected to survive. Even after precariously close votes on enactment of the basic authorization, however, Congress threatened several times to deny implementing funds.

By the late 1970s the federal government was providing a wide range of housing assistance, including direct mortgage and rent subsidies and government-insured mortgages, loans, secondary market programs, and programs designed to help special-risk homeowners and renters. In addition to HUD, the Veterans Administration and the Department of Agriculture's Farmers Home Administration participated in these programs.

During the presidency of Jimmy Carter, attention turned to revising community development programs intended to improve the nation's cities and counties. In 1977 the administration introduced a new urban development program—Urban Development Action Grants (UDAG)—which was an immediate success among the nation's cities. Aimed at urban areas with the most severe problems, UDAG used federal funds to spur private investment. But a year later, Congress took away some of HUD's authority to regulate community development projects. HUD Secretary Patricia Harris had wanted to require cities to spend 75 percent of federal community development funds for projects benefiting low- and moderate-income persons. After strenuous objection from House Banking Committee members, however, HUD retreated from the proposal and required instead that at least 51 percent of the block grant funds (federal money given to state and local governments to fund a group— or "block"—of programs) be set aside for low- and middle-income projects. In addition, the final legislation allowed the House and Senate banking committees to review all proposed regulations and delay their effective date for ninety days.

By 1980 the fights over allocating community development funds had subsided. The Reagan administration, however, proposed a fundamental shift in federal housing and urban policies in the early 1980s. Blight, housing shortages, and economic decline, Reagan said, represented the failure of past federal social programs. He sought to reduce the federal role in solving urban problems, while increasing incentives for a larger role by the private sector. Although the president persuaded Congress to accept substantial reductions in federal housing programs, lawmakers resisted his attempts to eliminate or sharply curtail community development and other projects.

Reagan continued his effort to cut the housing budget in 1988, proposing a 26 percent reduction—to $13.8 billion—in HUD's outlays for housing credit, commerce, and community development programs, which would have killed urban development action grants, rental development grants, economic development assistance grants, and loans for redevelopment and rehabilitation assistance. Early in the year the administration was the subject of congressional criticism when it came to light that HUD Secretary Samuel R. Pierce Jr. had not testified before any of the agency's three oversight committees for almost three years.

Early in George Bush's presidency a detailed picture began to emerge of massive fraud and mismanagement at HUD during the Reagan administration. Beginning in April 1989, after the release of a critical report by HUD's inspector general, a congressional subcommittee investigated allegations of influence-peddling by Pierce and other HUD officials. Months of hearings uncovered numerous instances of political favoritism in the awarding of housing and community development projects, some in the form of consulting fees to former officials in the Reagan administration, including Reagan's first secretary of interior, James G. Watt. The ongoing probe prompted the passage in November 1989 of legislation that subjected HUD's management to more scrutiny, limited its discretionary powers, threatened violators with huge penalties, and curtailed the ability of private firms to make large profits through HUD contracts.

Bush attorney general Dick Thornburgh ordered the appointment of an independent counsel in February 1990 to investigate charges of criminal conduct by Pierce, his top assistant, Deborah Gore Dean, and others associated with the housing scandal. By early 1995 the independent counsel had obtained sixteen convictions by trial or guilty plea, and Dean had been sentenced to twenty-one months in prison on perjury, conspiracy, and other charges. In February of that year a federal grand jury indicted former interior secretary Watt on twenty-five felony charges, including fraud, perjury, and obstruction of justice. Pierce had earlier admitted without being charged that his mismanagement of HUD had fostered an atmosphere in which corruption flourished.

Inheriting the scandal-ridden agency in February 1989 was Bush's nominee for secretary, Jack Kemp, a former Republican representative from New York. Kemp had sought the Republican presidential nomination in the 1988 campaign but dropped out of the race following a weak showing in the early primaries. As chair of President Bush's task force on "economic empowerment," Kemp took over at HUD pledging to redefine the war on poverty and seeking to make his mark on housing policy by getting the federal government out of the business of subsidized housing. Although he was regarded as one of the more ideological members of the Bush team and frequently clashed with lawmakers, in his first two years Kemp managed to win congressional passage of legislation enabling him to take steps to prevent the types of fraud and abuse that had occurred under his predecessor. Kemp was one of the few Bush secretaries to take a leading domestic policy role, which other cabinet members frequently ceded to White House Chief of Staff John H. Sununu and budget director Richard Darman.

In November 1990 Bush signed the first major overhaul of housing programs since 1974. The legislation authorized Kemp's hallmark empowerment program, HOPE, an acronym for Homeownership and Opportunity for People Everywhere. The program was designed to give public housing tenants and other poor people a stake in their communities by helping them to buy their homes, including public housing projects, through HUD grants. However, by the end of the Bush administration, no agreement had been reached with Congress on appropriating funds for HOPE, as lawmakers remained concerned that the money would be diverted from existing housing programs.

Following the 1991 riots in Los Angeles, Kemp tried to revive the president's earlier support of enterprise zones—blighted inner-city areas in which businesses would be given tax breaks. He had little success overcoming the objections of the White House inner circle and Republican lawmakers, and Bush vetoed a 1992 urban aid bill because it contained other tax-raising provisions. Although a keystone of Kemp's urban development agenda, the first enterprise zone legislation was not enacted until President Bill Clinton signed it as part of a 1993 budget-reconciliation package.

Clinton's choice of former San Antonio mayor Henry G. Cisneros as HUD secretary received bipartisan praise, including from outgoing secretary Kemp, who spoke on the nominee's behalf during Senate confirmation hearings. As a mayor in the 1980s, Cisneros had emphasized economic development through innovative government-industry partnerships to revitalize urban areas. He was mentioned frequently as a potential senator or governor and had been seriously considered as Walter Mondale's vice-presidential running mate in 1984. His reputation was later tainted, however, by a highly publicized extramarital affair with a campaign supporter, and Cisneros chose not to run for reelection in 1989. Before his appointment to the cabinet, he remained active in San Antonio civic affairs and was instrumental in focusing the 1992 Clinton campaign on Hispanic voters.

Among the urgent matters facing Cisneros was HUD's inability to dispose of buildings it inherited when private developers defaulted on FHA-insured mortgages. Legislation passed in 1987 required HUD to provide long-term rental subsidies on foreclosed apartment buildings as a condition of sale. The legislation had been intended to prevent the Reagan administration from disposing of public housing without providing plans for replacing it. In addition to these restrictions, HUD did not have the money for the subsidies or to maintain the housing projects in the interim. In 1993 HUD owned 190 such projects, with 31,225 housing units, and held the mortgages on an additional 2,446 properties. The cost to subsidize and sell the buildings under existing law was projected to be $5.4 billion.

In April 1994 Cisneros gained the flexibility he had sought to dispose of the properties. But by the end of that year he faced the possibility that HUD funding would be drastically reduced, or the department even eliminated, by Vice President Al Gore's National Performance Review. Cisneros had been an early advocate of the administration's attempt to "reinvent government," but the threat from within the White House and, after the 1994 elections, from the new Republican Congress prompted him to craft a more aggressive restructuring of the agency to ensure its survival. In early 1995 he submitted a five-year "reinvention blueprint" that would shift HUD's programs to local agencies, combine the agency's sixty major programs into three "performance block grants," and turn the FHA into a government-owned corporation. Some of the reforms were certain to be enacted; some, including creation of two block grants, were incorporated into HUD's fiscal 1996 appropriations bill, which President Clinton vetoed.

Two years into his term at HUD, Cisneros was confronted with controversies surrounding his earlier extramarital affair. In March 1995 Attorney General Janet Reno appointed an independent counsel to investigate charges that Cisneros had made false statements during FBI background checks leading up to his confirmation as secretary. The charges revolved around payments that Cisneros had made to his former girlfriend, which court papers stated were considerably larger than Cisneros had told the FBI. Cisneros offered to resign in mid-March, but the president rejected the offer.

ORGANIZATION AND FUNCTIONS

The HUD secretary is assisted by a deputy secretary; both are advised by two assistants, one for field management and the other for labor relations. The office of the secretary also contains four staff offices with departmentwide responsibility in specialized functional areas: Indian and Alaskan native programs, small and disadvantaged business utilization, administrative and judicial proceedings, and contract appeals. ·

In addition to the general counsel and inspector general offices, there are eight assistant secretaries, who are responsible for public affairs, congressional and intergovernmental relations, administration, community planning and development, fair housing and equal opportunity, federal housing, public and Indian housing, and policy development and research.

Other offices include Federal Housing Enterprise Oversight, established in 1992 to oversee the financial safety and soundness of the Federal National Mortgage Association (Fannie Mae) and the Federal Home Loan Mortgage Corporation (Freddie Mac), and the Office of Lead-Based Paint Abatement and Poisoning Prevention, which provides overall direction to HUD's lead-based paint activities. In addition, two external organizations complement the department's responsibilities. The Interagency Council on the Homeless, which receives administrative support from HUD, is responsible for reviewing and coordinating the programs and activities of seventeen federal agencies designed to help the homeless. The Federal Housing Finance Board, established as an independent agency within the executive branch in 1992, oversees the Federal Home Loan Banks.

The GNMA, or Ginnie Mae, a government corporation

within the department, administers support programs for government-sponsored mortgages through its mortgage-backed securities programs. The latter are designed to increase liquidity in the secondary mortgage market and attract new sources of financing for residential loans.

Department of the Interior

As the nation's principal conservation agency, the U.S. Department of the Interior is responsible for almost 600 million acres of public lands, or about 30 percent of the total U.S. land area. The Department of Agriculture oversees the nation's forests.

During the nation's early years, functions that would be carried out by an "interior," "home," or "internal affairs" department were apportioned by Congress among other agencies. To streamline these activities, proposals to establish a home office were made as early as 1789, but to no avail.

Shortly before the War of 1812 a House committee appointed to study the operations and organization of the Patent Office revived the idea of setting up a separate home department. And in 1816, after the war, a cabinet report recommended that a new home department be established to supervise territorial governments, construction of federal highways and canals, and the Post Office, Patent Office, and Indian Office. President James Madison endorsed the report, and a bill was introduced in the Senate in 1817, but again no action was taken.

Interest in creating a home department lagged during the next decade. Various efforts to establish one were made beginning in 1827, but none proved successful until 1848 and the administration of James K. Polk. In December of that year Secretary of the Treasury Robert J. Walker sent Congress a proposal to create a Department of the Interior. Before becoming Treasury secretary, Walker had served in the Senate (D-Miss.) and chaired its Committee on Public Lands. During the 1830s he had advocated selling public lands only to settlers to discourage land speculation. That proposal served as the basis of his plan to establish a new executive department.

By the late 1840s the Treasury Department had become burdened by increasing fiscal duties, and Walker did not wish to become involved in managing the vast domain acquired from the Louisiana Purchase of 1803, the Mexican War of 1846–1848, and the 1848 treaty with Great Britain by which the United States acquired the Oregon Territory. The nation's expansion, he argued, had made the responsibilities of the Treasury greater than it could handle.

CONGRESSIONAL STRUGGLE OVER INTERIOR

On February 12, 1849, the House Ways and Means Committee reported out a bill to establish a Department of the Interior. Samuel F. Vinton, an Ohio Whig and chairman of the committee, was a key figure in securing enactment of the legislation. The House passed the bill three days later with only minimal de-

bate. The Senate Finance Committee reported out the bill on March 3, the last day of the Thirtieth Congress. That night, in a dramatic session, the full Senate chamber approved the measure by a margin of only six votes, 31–25.

"The bill to establish the Home Department has become law, having passed the Senate after a long, arduous and rather stormy debate; and a new and valuable Department has thus been added to the Government," noted the Washington, D.C., *Daily National Intelligencer* on March 5, 1849. Almost one hundred years later, Harold L. Ickes, a longtime secretary of the interior (1933–1946) and one of the most famous of its chiefs, speculated that the long delay in establishing the department resulted primarily from "states' rights and the ever occurring problem of expenditures in government."

Congress transferred to the new Interior Department the General Land Office from the Treasury Department, the Patent Office from the State Department, and the Bureau of Indian Affairs and Pension Office from the War Department. Other responsibilities assigned to the department included supervising the commissioner of public buildings, the Board of Inspectors, the Warden of the Penitentiary of the District of Columbia, and the Census of the United States, as well as the accounts of marshals and other officers of the U.S. courts and of lead and other kinds of mines in the United States.

EVOLUTION OF THE DEPARTMENT'S POLICY

For a long time Interior's policy mirrored the more general public sentiment that natural resources were the limitless foundation on which a powerful nation could be built. As a result, public policy on their exploitation was extremely permissive.

Gradually, however, Americans realized that their natural resources were not inexhaustible. The environmental movement of the 1960s and 1970s resulted in the establishment of the Council on Environmental Quality and the Environmental Protection Agency, which share responsibility for overseeing natural resources with Interior. The Energy Department, created in 1977 in response to growing awareness of the need to conserve fuel resources, also plays a role in establishing environmental policy.

Throughout most of the 1960s environmentalists found an ally in Interior Secretary Stewart L. Udall, a former representative (D-Ariz.) who was appointed to the position by President John F. Kennedy. Udall had been a well-known supporter of conservation, reclamation, and national park improvement during his tenure in the House. As interior secretary he added significantly to the department's role in water planning, outdoor recreation, and national parks programs.

The federal government's philosophy underwent an abrupt turnaround with Richard Nixon's selection of Walter J. Hickel to succeed Udall. Hickel's nomination became controversial after conservation groups questioned his dedication to natural preservation and others criticized his ties with oil companies. At a December 1968 news conference he stated that he was opposed to "conservation for conservation's sake" and that the high national standards for clean water "might even hinder industrial development."

Hickel was criticized for his opposition, as governor of Alaska, to plans to create a foreign trade subzone for oil at Machiasport, Maine, which would result in cheaper fuel for New England. Another complaint concerned his opposition, as governor, to an Interior Department freeze on the status of Alaskan public lands until Congress settled pending claims to the land by native Alaskans.

Despite the controversy the Senate confirmed Hickel's nomination. The Alaskan claims, giving natives 40 million acres of land and $962.5 million, were cleared in 1971, but Hickel's ideology and outspokenness led to his downfall; the president fired him in November 1970.

The environmental movement waned during the early 1970s, but President Jimmy Carter's appointment of conservationist Idaho governor Cecil D. Andrus as interior secretary brought praise from environmentalists and criticism from mining, logging, and other development interests. While Interior was headed by Andrus (1977–1981), major legislation was enacted to control strip mining, protect millions of acres of wilderness in Alaska, and clean up chemical contamination.

Although conservationists generally found an ally in whoever was the interior secretary, President Ronald Reagan's first appointee to the post, James G. Watt, aroused considerable controversy when he attempted to make broad changes in the department's programs and personnel. Although he was generally considered an able administrator, Watt's rhetoric was occasionally abrasive. Moreover, his philosophy of emphasizing private use of resources in the public domain and of returning to the states more control over government lands did not sit well with environmentalists.

Initially, Reagan stood by his secretary, but Watt was forced to resign in October 1983. He was succeeded by William P. Clark, who took over temporarily and was followed in 1985 by Donald P. Hodel, who had been secretary of energy and previously had served as undersecretary of interior under Watt.

During the 1988 presidential campaign George Bush pledged that if elected he would be an "environmental president," thus hoping to distance himself from Reagan's controversial record on natural-resource and land-use policy. Once in office, however, Bush appointed as secretary Manuel Lujan Jr., a retired Republican representative from New Mexico who had scant support among environmentalists.

In 1990 the reauthorization of the 1973 Endangered Species Act, one of the most popular and well-known laws ever passed by Congress, became bogged down in a protracted "jobs-versus-environment" debate. The most contentious arguments were about the management of old-growth forests in the Northwest, where timber-industry interests opposed efforts to protect the habitat of the threatened northern spotted owl. In 1992 Lujan convened the high-level Endangered Species Committee, known as the "God Squad," which was authorized to grant exemptions to Endangered Species Act provisions after considering their effects on jobs and businesses. The committee voted to allow logging on some of the disputed old-growth timber tracts, but court injunctions prevented even this compromise from taking effect. Lujan was criticized by both sides and by lawmakers seeking to mediate the dispute, all of whom claimed that the panel's decision had further polarized the logging debate and stymied reauthorization of the act. Similar battles slowed down congressional efforts to overhaul the rules governing mining and grazing on public lands, with Lujan generally siding with western business interests and echoing the antiregulatory stance adopted by the Bush White House.

Environmentalists applauded President Bill Clinton's 1993 appointment of Bruce Babbitt, a former Arizona governor and 1988 Democratic presidential contender. Regarded as one of the country's foremost conservationists, Babbitt had served as president of the League of Conservation Voters, the self-described political arm of the environmental movement. As governor, however, he had successfully balanced conservation and development interests on such issues as groundwater management, and early in the Clinton administration Babbitt continued to win praise for his willingness to listen to all sides. Babbit oversaw major wilderness protection advances in the California desert and the Florida Everglades, but these were overshadowed by the early failures of more ambitious plans to reshape federal land-use policy through mining and grazing reform. Babbitt's attempt to impose higher grazing fees on ranchers using federal lands was blocked by the Senate in 1993. In early 1995 the department announced a modified public-range management strategy that provoked further criticism from environmentalists that the changes gave local and state governments too much control in the development of land-management policy. Similar plans to update the 1872 Mining Law by imposing higher royalties and environmental standards died in the Senate in 1994.

In early 1995 Secretary Babbitt faced renewed and potentially explosive battles over the stalled reauthorization of the Endangered Species Act, which had expired in 1992 with its enforcement kept alive only by annual appropriations. In addition, the new Republican majority in the 104th Congress targeted the department for budget cuts, including a reduction in the number of national parks and elimination of the U.S. Geological Survey and National Biological Survey, a new agency established in 1993 to inventory all plant and animal species in the country. Babbitt had promoted the latter as a means to anticipate and prevent disputes about endangered species, but it was criticized by conservatives as forcing regulatory decisions that would restrict the rights of private property owners.

ORGANIZATION AND FUNCTIONS

The Interior Department consists of some thirty major bureaus and offices. The secretary is responsible for meshing departmental activities, with the assistance of an undersecretary and five assistant secretaries (fish and wildlife and parks, Indian affairs, land and minerals management, territorial and international affairs, and water and science). An assistant secretary for policy, budget, and administration serves as principal policy adviser to the secretary. The department is divided into functional offices, which are responsible for a wide variety of managerial, regulatory, promotional, planning, and research activities.

The U.S. Geological Survey (USGS) was established in 1879 to provide a permanent federal agency to conduct the systematic and scientific "classification of the public lands, and examination of the geological structure, mineral resources, and products of the national domain." USGS is the federal government's largest earth science research agency, the nation's largest civilian mapmaking agency, the primary source of data on the nation's surface water and groundwater, and the employer of the largest number of professional earth scientists.

The Bureau of Indian Affairs (BIA) is the federal agency with primary responsibility for working with tribal governments to provide services for approximately 1 million American Indians and Alaska natives from 321 federally recognized tribes and 223 native villages in Alaska. Other federal agencies may deal with American Indians or native Alaskans as members of an ethnic group or simply as individuals, but the BIA is distinctive in that it deals with them in a government-to-government relationship. One of BIA's principal programs administers and manages some 56 million acres of land held in trust by the United States for American Indians.

The mandate of the U.S. Fish and Wildlife Service is to conserve, protect, and enhance fish, wildlife, and their habitats. Its primary focus is on migratory birds, endangered species, freshwater and anadromous fisheries, and certain marine mammals. Headquartered in Washington, D.C., the service has seven regional offices and numerous field units, including national wildlife refuges, national fish hatcheries, research laboratories, and a nationwide network of law enforcement agents.

Established in 1946, the Bureau of Land Management oversees about 270 million acres of public lands, located primarily in the West and in Alaska and comprising about one-eighth of the total U.S. land area. Day-to-day management of these lands and related resources is decentralized into twelve state offices. The bureau is also responsible for development of mineral resources on an additional 582 million acres administered by other federal agencies and certain private lands on which the United States reserves the mineral rights.

The 1977 Surface Mining Control and Reclamation Act established the Office of Surface Mining Reclamation and Enforcement to collect funds from coal companies and disburse funds for reclamation of coal lands mined before August 1977. The office also establishes and enforces standards and regulations ensuring that current and future mining will be environmentally sound.

The Bureau of Reclamation was chartered in 1902 to reclaim the arid lands of the western United States for farming by providing a secure, year-round supply of water for irrigation. Among its most notable projects were the Grand Coulee Dam on the Columbia River and Hoover Dam on the Colorado River.

In addition to irrigation, the bureau's responsibilities include hydroelectric power generation, municipal and industrial water supplies, river regulation and flood control, outdoor recreation, enhancement of fish and wildlife habitats, and research.

The Minerals Management Service, created in 1982, is responsible for collecting revenues generated from mineral leases offshore (including the outer continental shelf) and on federal and Indian lands. It is also charged with the orderly development of offshore energy and mineral resources while safeguarding the environment. These revenues from these leases, the largest federal source of revenue outside the Treasury Department, are distributed to Indian tribes and the appropriate states, the Land and Water Conservation Fund, the Historic Preservation Fund, and the U.S. Treasury.

The National Park Service, established in 1916, administers the National Park System, which comprises 367 parks, monuments, historic sites, battlefields, seashores and lakeshores, and recreation areas. The service also directs programs that assist states, other federal agencies, local governments, and individuals in the protection of historical, natural, architectural, engineering, and archeological resources that lie outside the National Park System. It maintains the National Register of Historic Places and a registry of natural sites.

The National Biological Survey was created in 1993 to conduct a comprehensive inventory of the nation's plants and animals. A nonregulatory agency, the survey consolidated biological research activities within Interior and related agencies under a director to be appointed by the president and confirmed by the Senate.

The office of the assistant secretary for territorial and international affairs is responsible for coordinating federal policy in the territories of American Samoa, Guam, the Virgin Islands, the Commonwealth of the Northern Mariana Islands and the freely associated states: Federated States of Micronesia, Republic of the Marshall Islands, and Republic of Palau. The office also oversees and coordinates various international activities of the Interior Department.

Department of Justice

The U.S. attorney general was one of the first positions to be established, with cabinet rank, in the federal government. The Judiciary Act of September 24, 1789, made the attorney general the chief legal officer of the federal government. At the time, the nation's top law officer was assisted by one clerk. The Department of Justice itself was established in 1870, with the attorney general as its head. Through its thousands of lawyers, investigators, and agents, the department investigates violations of federal law (ranging from income tax evasion to criminal syndicates), supervises the custody of those accused or convicted of federal crimes, oversees legal and illegal aliens, and directs U.S. domestic security against threats of foreign or internal subversion. Moreover, Justice polices narcotics trafficking; helps state and local governments expand and improve police departments, courts, and correctional institutions (through federal aid); advises the president and other government agencies on legal matters; and drafts legislation. The Justice Department also conducts all suits in the Supreme Court to which the U.S. government is a party. The attorney general supervises and directs these activities, as well as those of the U.S. attorneys and U.S. marshals in the nation's various judicial districts.

Justice is one of the smallest cabinet departments in number of employees. Writer Richard Harris has noted that "the federal government has only a small fraction of the manpower that is required to combat crime nationally," largely because the Constitution gives the policing power to the states. Nonetheless, Harris observed, "Limited as the federal role is . . . it can be critically significant. . . . [I]t provides a model for every lesser jurisdiction, and the federal government's overall approach . . . will probably determine whether or not the nation's traditional freedoms are preserved."[83]

EVOLUTION OF THE DEPARTMENT IN THE 1960S

Before the 1960s the department's mission was perceived as primarily one of prosecuting violations of the Internal Revenue Code, instituting some antitrust suits, and keeping watch over "subversives" and "public enemies." In the 1960s, however, Justice became intimately involved with major domestic issues—racial violence, mass demonstrations, riots, draft resistance to the Vietnam War, and rising crime rates, among others. To cope with its increased responsibilities the department created a number of new divisions, and by 1970 Justice had 208 units.

Crime as a national political issue became the most emotionally charged, and perhaps the most crucial, of all domestic concerns in the 1968 elections. President Lyndon B. Johnson's attorney general, Ramsey Clark, was keenly interested in civil rights, but it was his approach to crime that brought him the greatest criticism and made him an issue in the 1968 presidential campaign. An uncompromising opponent of efforts to maintain order at the expense of due process, Clark became a natural target of those who advocated a "get tough" policy on crime. "If we are going to restore order and respect for law in this country, there's one place we're going to begin; we're going to have a new attorney general of the United States of America," stated Richard Nixon on accepting the Republican presidential nomination.

NIXON'S "WAR ON CRIME" AND WATERGATE

Crime was increasing at a frightening pace when Nixon, elected on a tough "law and order" platform, was sworn in for his first term in 1969. But five years and billions of dollars later, with stringent new federal anticrime laws in place, the crime rate was still climbing. Late in 1974, plainspoken attorney general William B. Saxbe declared the war on crime a "dismal failure." But even before Nixon left office in 1974, national opinion polls showed that the public's attention had shifted away from concern with street crime to economic problems, the energy crisis, and Watergate.

Climbing even more swiftly than the crime rate during the Nixon and Ford years was the amount of federal dollars spent on law enforcement. In fiscal year 1971 the Justice Department had its first billion-dollar budget. In fiscal year 1975 its budget hit $2 billion. Justice spending leveled off just above the $2 billion mark in fiscal year 1976.

In a peculiar twist on the Nixon administration's "law and order" theme, the crimes that drew national attention in its last years were those committed by or charged against some of its highest officials, including the president himself. Among the Nixon administration officials indicted for crimes during this period was Attorney General John N. Mitchell. Mitchell was convicted in early 1975 of conspiracy and obstruction of justice for his participation in the effort to cover up White House involvement in the Watergate break-in at Democratic National Headquarters in June 1972. The attorney general, who was also Nixon's campaign manager, was aloof, blunt, and a product of Wall Street. Unlike Clark, Mitchell stated that he believed Justice "was an institution for law enforcement, not social improvement."[84]

In 1972 Mitchell was replaced by Richard G. Kleindienst, who pleaded guilty in May 1974 to charges that he did not testify fully before the Senate Judiciary Committee when it was investigating charges that political pressure had figured in the settlement of the government's case against International Telephone and Telegraph Corporation. After Kleindienst was forced to leave office in 1973, Secretary of Defense Elliot L. Richardson took over. He resigned on October 10, 1973, however, rather than obey the president's order to fire special Watergate prosecutor Archibald Cox. Nixon then selected William Saxbe as attorney general.

JUSTICE UNDER FORD, CARTER, AND REAGAN

With the accession of Gerald R. Ford to the presidency, the tone of the federal anticrime effort changed markedly. Emphasizing that law enforcement should focus more upon the needs of the victims of crime than upon the criminal, Ford asked Congress to authorize financial aid for the victims of crime, to approve a revised criminal code, to provide mandatory minimum sentencing for certain crimes, to provide for more consistency in sentences, and to enact a mild control on gun ownership.

Crime was not a top priority in the White House or on Capitol Hill from 1977 to 1980. Access to justice, rather than a war on crime, was the theme of the Carter administration's law enforcement program. That emphasis was explicable in light of the fact that the top two law enforcement officials in the administration—Attorney General Griffin B. Bell and Federal Bureau of Investigation Director William Webster—had served a total of more than twenty years on the federal bench before moving to the executive branch. In the Justice Department, Bell set up a new entity, the Office for Improvements in the Administration of Justice. Out of that office came proposals to expand the powers of federal magistrates—a measure that was passed in 1979.

Crime was mentioned little during Ronald Reagan's first years in office, even though the nation appeared more concerned about this issue than it had been during Carter's administration. The Federal Bureau of Investigation (FBI) nevertheless became a billion-dollar operation for the first time in fiscal year 1984, spending more than the entire federal court system, whose funding rose from $631 million in fiscal year 1981 to $977.9 million in fiscal year 1985.

William French Smith, once Reagan's personal lawyer, served as the administration's first attorney general. Professing a desire to return to private life, Smith announced his resignation January 23, 1984, pending confirmation of his successor. On the same day, Reagan nominated White House counselor Edwin Meese III, one of his closest advisers, to succeed Smith. Questions about Meese's personal finances, however, led to a prolonged investigation that delayed Senate confirmation until February 23, 1985. As attorney general, Meese was criticized for his failure to conduct a thorough investigation of the Iran arms sales and contra aid scandal when it became public in November 1986. He also was probed for connections with individuals tied to a New York defense contractor, the Bronx-based Wedtech Corporation, which was the subject of federal investigations of fraud and bribery of public officials. In 1987 independent counsel James C. McKay was appointed to investigate Meese's personal finances, his involvement with Wedtech, and several other instances of alleged wrongdoing. After a fourteen-month investigation, McKay concluded in an 814-page report made public July 18, 1988, that although he would not indict Meese for criminal wrongdoing, the attorney general had "probably violated" the law. Before the report's release, Meese had announced on July 5 that he intended to resign in August. He left Justice on August 12, and Reagan appointed Dick Thornburgh to replace him.

JUSTICE UNDER BUSH AND CLINTON

When President George Bush took office, Thornburgh remained as attorney general and was initially credited with setting higher ethical standards and restoring morale at the department. The possibility of improved departmental relations with lawmakers, however, grew dimmer as the Bush administration entered into ideological battles with the Democratic-controlled Congress over civil-rights and worker-protection legislation. At Thornburgh's urging, Bush vetoed the Civil Rights Act of 1990, the first rejection of a major civil-rights bill in twenty-five years. Throughout the yearlong negotiations, Thornburgh had made known his opposition to the package, which he charged would force businesses to adopt quotas in hiring and promotion. Last-minute changes to the bill to ease the burden of proof on employers and cap punitive damages attracted the support of moderate Republicans, who were eager to see their party associated with civil-rights legislation. But the quota issue eclipsed debate on all other provisions and the Senate failed by one vote to override the president's veto.

Thornburgh came under fire for the Justice Department's mild treatment of the Bank of Credit and Commerce International (BCCI), a worldwide banking empire accused of fraud and money laundering. In 1990 BCCI agreed to plead guilty and paid a relatively low fine for laundering money in the United States through its Florida branches. Under Thornburgh the department also went through several personnel crises, including the conviction of one of his aides on drug charges. In another incident, Thornburgh had ordered an investigation to find out who had leaked news of an FBI inquiry of Rep. William H. Gray III (D-Pa.), who was running for Democratic whip at the time. Gray had actually not been the target of the probe, and months later when Thornburgh closed the investigation without determining the leaker, it was revealed that one of his top aides had played a role in the original story about the representative.

Thornburgh resigned in August 1991 to run for the Senate in Pennsylvania. Acting attorney general William P. Barr was confirmed in November, again amid hopes that the appointment would lead to more cooperative relations between the Justice Department and Congress. Barr had been at the department for three years and previously had worked in the CIA and on the White House domestic policy staff. During his confirmation hearings, Barr broke precedent with previous judicial nominees' reticence and announced his opposition to legalized abortion.

In 1992 Barr refused to appoint an independent counsel to investigate possible crimes surrounding U.S. assistance to Iraq before its invasion of Kuwait. Revelations of unauthorized loans to Saddam Hussein and documents concerning arms sales in the 1980s cast a shadow over the U.S.-led military triumph in the Persian Gulf War. Although Barr proceeded with a preliminary investigation of the charges, this was not made public until after the November elections, prompting allegations that he was dragging his feet to prevent the release of embarrassing or incriminating material. His refusal to appoint a panel came in the midst of congressional efforts to reauthorize the Watergate-era law that provided for the appointment of an independent counsel, separate from the Justice Department, to investigate federal officials accused of wrongdoing. Barr opposed the law, which was due to expire at the end of 1992, on the grounds that it usurped the attorney general's prosecutorial authority, and the law was not revived until 1993, the first year of Bill Clinton's presidency.

Clinton's attempts to fill the attorney general position resulted in a series of blunders and cast doubt on the judgment and political skills of his transition team. His first choice, corporate attorney Zoë Baird, had to withdraw her nomination amid widespread public anger over her hiring of an illegal immigrant as a nanny and failure to pay required Social Security taxes for her. The "nanny" controversy also clouded the planned nomination of Clinton's second choice, district court judge Kimba M. Wood of New York, even though she had employed an undocumented worker as a nanny when it was not illegal to do so and had paid the applicable taxes.

In February 1993 Clinton's third nominee, Miami prosecutor Janet Reno, was unanimously confirmed by the Senate and became the first woman to serve as attorney general. Reno had served as the chief prosecutor in Dade County for fifteen years, having been reelected five times. She had received national attention for innovations in the criminal justice field, including a special court to deter young drug offenders, and for her aggressive prosecution of sexual and child abuse cases.

Reno brought to the department a reputation for evenhandedness and she became one of the administration's most visible and popular officials. Early on, however, she had to contend with a number of crises, including the investigation of the terrorist bombing of the World Trade Center in New York City, allegations of ethical misconduct by FBI Director William S. Sessions, and a tense standoff between federal law enforcement agents and the Branch Davidians, a religious sect near Waco, Texas. A February raid on the sect's compound by the Bureau of Alcohol, Tobacco and Firearms (BATF) had resulted in the deaths of four BATF agents and led to a two-month, nationally televised siege of the compound. In April Reno authorized the FBI to use nonlethal tear gas in an effort to drive out the Branch Davidians, but fire erupted throughout the compound, killing eighty-five people, including at least twenty-five children. A subsequent internal Justice Department report faulted Reno for failing to involve herself in the details of the standoff and also contradicted several of the explanations she had given for authorizing the attack. Reno took full responsibility for the decision and this ultimately added to her reputation for being candid and fair.

In some cases, Reno's visibility reflected her willingness to stand apart from the administration. She continued to support the controversial nomination of Lani Guinier to head the department's Civil Rights Division even when it became clear that Clinton would bow to conservative pressure to abandon the nominee because of her academic writings and perceived radical stance on voting-rights issues. During the debate on the 1994 crime bill Reno continued to emphasize crime prevention rather than the tough enforcement measures that the White House trumpeted to sell its package, and she successfully prevented the merger of the Drug Enforcement Administration and FBI in Vice President Al Gore's reinventing government proposal.

ORGANIZATION AND FUNCTIONS

The attorney general provides overall policy and program direction for the offices, divisions, bureaus, and boards of the department and represents the United States in legal matters generally; the attorney general also makes recommendations to the president about appointments to federal judicial positions. The attorney general is assisted by a deputy attorney general and associate attorney general, who are the principal agents for managing the department.

The office of the solicitor general supervises and conducts government litigation in the Supreme Court. Such litigation comprises about two-thirds of all cases decided by the Court each year. The solicitor general, often called the "tenth justice" of the Court, determines which cases the government will seek to have the Supreme Court review as well as the position the government will take on each case. Another function of the office is to decide which cases, of those lost before the lower courts, the United States should appeal.

In addition to its divisions and bureaus, the department consists of various offices, some headed by an assistant attorney general. The assistant attorney general in charge of the Office of Legal Counsel assists the attorney general as legal adviser to the president and all the executive branch agencies. The office drafts the formal opinions of the attorney general and provides written opinions and informal advice in response to requests. The staff frequently prepares and delivers testimony to Congress on a variety of legal issues, particularly constitutional matters such as legislative vetoes, executive privilege, and the power of the president to enter into executive agreements.

The assistant attorney general in charge of the Office of Legislative Affairs is responsible for liaison between the department and Congress. Under the direction of the assistant attorney general for administration, the Justice Management Division assists senior management officials with matters related to basic department policy for selected management operations and provides direct administrative services to offices, boards, and divisions of the department.

The Office of the Pardon Attorney receives and reviews all petitions for executive clemency, initiates the necessary investigations, and recommends to the president which form of executive clemency—including pardon, commutation of sentence, remission of fine, and reprieve—it finds appropriate in certain cases.

The Community Relations Service (CRS), created by Title X of the Civil Rights Act of 1964, falls under the general authority of the attorney general and is headed by a director, who is appointed by the president with the advice and consent of the Senate. The CRS helps resolve disputes through its field staff of mediators and conciliators, who work out of ten regional and three field offices. It also is charged with continuing integration, processing, resettlement, and care of Cubans and Haitians who have entered the country since 1980 without documentation or imminent prospects of returning to their homelands and have subsequently been detained by the Immigration and Naturalization Service.

The Office of Professional Responsibility, which reports directly to the attorney general, investigates allegations of criminal or ethical misconduct by employees of the department.

The Office of Policy and Communications (OPC) is responsible for developing and coordinating department policy and communicating with the media, the law enforcement community, and the public. Within OPC, the Office of Liaison Services represents the attorney general in dealings with external interest groups, justice- and law-enforcement-related constituencies, and all legislatures and other governmental and nongovernmental entities—both foreign and domestic—except Congress. OPC consists of an Office of Policy Development and Office of Public Affairs.

Under the supervision of the deputy attorney general, the Executive Office for United States Attorneys provides the U.S. attorneys with general executive assistance and nonlitigative oversight. It also publishes the *United States Attorneys' Manual* and the *United States Attorneys' Bulletin.*

The Office of Intelligence Policy and Review is responsible for advising the attorney general on all matters relating to the national security activities of the United States. The office prepares and files all applications for surveillance under the Foreign Intelligence Surveillance Act of 1978, represents the department on a variety of interagency committees, and serves as adviser to other agencies, including the Central Intelligence Agency and the Departments of State and Defense, on matters relating to oversight of and guidelines for domestic and overseas intelligence operations.

U.S. trustees insure compliance with the federal bankruptcy laws and supervise the administration of cases and trustees in cases filed under various provisions of the 1978 Bankruptcy Code. Initially established as a pilot program with limited jurisdiction, the U.S. trustee program—under the Bankruptcy Judges, United States Trustees, and Family Farmer Bankruptcy Act of 1986—became a permanent, nationwide system for the administration of bankruptcy cases.

The Inspector General's office enforces fraud, waste, abuse, and integrity laws and regulations within the department.

The Office of Special Counsel for Immigration Related Unfair Employment Practices was established in 1986 to investigate and prosecute charges of discrimination based on national origin and citizenship status. Its jurisdiction over charges is limited to those not covered by the Equal Employment Opportunity Commission.

Divisions

As a law enforcement agency, the Antitrust Division prosecutes criminal and civil antitrust cases, primarily under the Sherman and Clayton Antitrust Acts. Two major areas of enforcement are investigation, detection, and criminal prosecution of price fixing, and investigation and civil litigation to prevent anticompetitive mergers and bid rigging. The division serves as the administration's principal authority on competition policy in regulated industries and advises governmental agencies on the competitive implications of their policies. The division also appears as a competition advocate before congressional committees and federal regulatory agencies.

The Civil Division is known as the "government's lawyer." This is sometimes a complicated role, because in every case there are two clients: the agency concerned and the people of the United States. The division's clients include more than a hundred federal agencies and commissions, individual federal employees acting in their official capacities, and, in some instances, members of Congress and the federal judiciary. The di-

vision's litigation is organized into seven major groups: commercial, federal program, tort, appellate staff, immigration, consumer, and management program.

Established in 1957, the Civil Rights Division enforces the nation's laws and executive orders relating to civil rights, including statutes under the Civil Rights Act of 1964, Voting Rights Act of 1965, Fair Housing Act of 1968, Equal Educational Opportunities Act of 1974, and Americans with Disabilities Act of 1990. The division works primarily on litigation and connected matters. The division prosecutes criminal cases, which are tried before a jury, as well as suits filed in equity (based on principles of fairness rather than strictly applied statutes); which are usually tried before a single judge and seek injunctive relief.

The assistant attorney general in charge of the Criminal Division formulates criminal law enforcement policies and enforces and generally supervises all federal criminal laws except those specifically assigned to the other divisions. This division—by far the most active of the principal Justice divisions—also supervises certain civil litigation related to federal law enforcement activities (such as federal liquor, narcotics, counterfeiting, gambling, firearms, customs, agriculture, and immigration laws). It supervises as well litigation resulting from petitions for writs of habeas corpus by members of the armed forces, actions brought by or on behalf of federal prisoners, alleged investigative misconduct, and legal actions related to national security issues.

The Environment and Natural Resources Division represents the United States in all litigation concerning the protection, use, and development of public lands and natural resources, environmental quality, Native American lands and claims, wildlife resources, and the acquisition of federal property. The fastest growing area of its responsibility involves civil and criminal enforcement of environmental statutes. The division works closely with Federal Bureau of Investigation and Environmental Protection Agency criminal investigators to prosecute violators of such statutes as the Clean Air Act, Superfund, and the Resource Conservation and Recovery Act (RCRA). It also tries both civil and criminal cases concerning the protection of wildlife and marine resources, including the illegal hunting, smuggling, and black-market dealing of protected species.

In all courts except the U.S. Tax Court, the Tax Division represents the United States and its officers in civil and criminal litigation involving federal, state, and local taxes. The Internal Revenue Service (IRS) is the division's principal client. The division collects federal revenues by instituting many types of actions at the request of IRS and defends tax refund and other suits brought by taxpayers.

Bureaus

Established in 1908, the Federal Bureau of Investigation is the principal investigative arm of the department. It is charged with gathering and reporting facts, locating witnesses, and compiling evidence in cases involving federal jurisdiction.

The Federal Bureau of Prisons is responsible for the care and custody of persons convicted of federal crimes and sentenced by the courts to incarceration in a federal penal institution. The bureau operates a nationwide system of maximum-, medium-, and minimum-security prisons and community program offices.

The U.S. Marshals Service is the nation's oldest federal law enforcement agency, having served as a link between the executive and judicial branches since 1789. Approximately 3,500 presidentially appointed marshals and additional administrative personnel operate from 427 office locations in each of the ninety-four federal judicial districts in all fifty states, Guam, Puerto Rico, and the Virgin Islands. They are responsible for providing support and protection for federal courts, apprehending most federal fugitives, operating the Federal Witness Security program, executing court orders and arrest warrants, and responding to emergency circumstances. The director of the service is appointed by the president and provides overall supervision.

The United States National Central Bureau (USNCB) represents the United States in the International Criminal Police Organization (INTERPOL). INTERPOL was created to promote mutual assistance between all law enforcement authorities in the prevention and suppression of international crime. Established in 1923 and reorganized in 1946, it has grown from an organization composed of a few European countries to a worldwide consortium of 142 member countries. In 1977 Justice and Treasury officials were given dual authority to administer USNCB, which represents federal, state, and local law enforcement agencies.

The Immigration and Naturalization Service (INS), established in 1891, has four major areas of responsibility: (1) aliens entering the United States (controlling entry into the country, facilitating the entry of qualified persons, and denying admission to illegal aliens); (2) aliens within the United States (providing immigration benefits, maintaining information on alien status, and deporting illegal aliens); (3) naturalization and citizenship; and (4) aliens who enter illegally or whose authorized stay in the United States has expired (apprehending and removing such individuals).

The Drug Enforcement Administration (DEA) is the lead federal agency in enforcing the laws and regulations governing narcotics and controlled substances. Created in 1973, DEA concentrates on high-level narcotics smuggling and distribution organizations in the United States and abroad, working closely with such agencies as the Customs Service, the Internal Revenue Service, and the Coast Guard.

The Justice Assistance Act of 1984 restructured the criminal justice research and statistics units of the department and established a program of financial and technical assistance to state and local governments. The act also established the Office of Justice Programs, headed by an assistant attorney general, to coordinate the activities of some existing offices (including statistics and juvenile justice and delinquency prevention) and to oversee a new program designed to locate and recover missing

children. The office oversees the National Institute of Justice, the research and development arm of the Justice Department.

Boards

Seven boards are associated with the Justice Department. They are the Executive Office for Immigration Review, Board of Immigration Appeals, Office of the Chief Immigration Judge, Office of the Immigration Judge, Office of the Chief Administrative Hearing Officer, United States Parole Commission, and Foreign Claims Settlement Commission of the United States. The U.S. Parole Commission has been abolished effective 1997, ten years after the implementation of the U.S. Sentencing Guidelines, which instituted mandatory sentencing for all offenders whose crimes were committed after November 1, 1987.

Department of Labor

On March 4, 1913, President William Howard Taft signed a bill that established a cabinet-level department "to foster, promote, and develop the welfare of the wage earners of the United States, to improve their working conditions, and to advance their opportunities for profitable employment." Although the beginnings of the Department of Labor were rather small and somewhat inauspicious, the department was enforcing hundreds of laws by the 1990s. They deal with wide-ranging and significant areas of workers' well-being, including unemployment insurance and workers' compensation, minimum wages and overtime pay, occupational health and safety, antidiscrimination in employment, protection of pension rights, job training, and strengthening free collective bargaining. The department compiles statistics on prices, employment, and other appropriate subjects and strives to improve the employment opportunities of minorities, youth, older workers, women, and people with disabilities.

ADVOCACY FOR A LABOR DEPARTMENT

As labor unions grew in strength, pressures increased after the Civil War to create a federal office that represented workers. This effort was led by William Sylvis, a well-known labor leader who argued that existing federal departments were closely tied to wealthy businesses and that no federal agency had as its "sole object the care and protection of labor." Sylvis and others lobbied President Andrew Johnson to support a secretary of labor, with cabinet status, to be selected from labor's ranks. According to labor historian Jonathan Grossman, more than one hundred bills and resolutions to create a labor department were introduced in Congress between 1864 and 1900.[85]

In 1884 Congress passed and President Chester A. Arthur signed a bill that established a Bureau of Labor in the Interior Department. The bureau was to gather information pertaining to workers and devise a "means of promoting their material, social, intellectual, and moral prosperity."

It took some time for Arthur to name the first commissioner of labor. The unions had expected that he would appoint Terence Powderly, leader of the Knights of Labor union, but the president found Powderly too radical. Instead, he appointed Carroll D. Wright of the Massachusetts Bureau of Labor Statistics. Under Wright's leadership the new bureau flourished.

Arthur's successor, Grover Cleveland, pressed for enlarging the bureau and empowering it to investigate and arbitrate labor disputes. The Knights of Labor lobbied for creation of a cabinet-level department and succeeded in having a bill introduced in 1888. The legislation was watered down, however; the bill that emerged, with little debate, established an independent Department of Labor, without cabinet status. Cleveland signed the legislation on March 21 and chose Wright to head the new agency.

During the next few years the department gained in stature as the most important federal statistics-gathering agency and as author of significant reports on such subjects as labor legislation, compulsory insurance, housing, railroad labor, and the status of women in the workforce. In 1895 it began publishing the *Bulletin of Labor* (today called the *Monthly Labor Review*).

MERGER, THEN INDEPENDENCE

On becoming president after William McKinley's assassination, Theodore Roosevelt suggested appointing a secretary of commerce and industries, with cabinet status. "It should be his province to deal with commerce in its broadest sense, including among many other things whatever concerns labor and all matters affecting the great business corporations. . . ." Legislation reflecting this view was introduced in the Fifty-seventh Congress. It was opposed vigorously by Democrats, who argued that mutual distrust between business and labor would paralyze the department and that the powers of the existing independent Department of Labor would in fact be weakened. But Republicans, who were in the majority, responded that the two groups had mutual interests and that a new department would be more efficient in obtaining and synthesizing economic information scattered through existing departments. Their position predominated; legislation creating the new department, its name changed to the Department of Commerce and Labor, was signed into law in February 1903.

Democrats won control of the House in 1910, and fifteen union members were elected to Congress. Rep. William Sulzer (D-N.Y.) introduced a bill for a separate Department of Labor in 1912; it cleared both chambers and was signed into law on March 4, 1913. Although President Taft opposed the bill, a veto was fruitless: President-elect Woodrow Wilson had already selected William B. Wilson, a trade unionist and member of the House (D-Pa.), to be his secretary of labor.

During its early years the fledgling department faced rough going: businesses distrusted it, and conservative members of Congress slashed at its funds and functions. For many years Labor was the smallest and least influential cabinet department. But under President Franklin D. Roosevelt's labor secretary, Frances Perkins (the first woman named to the cabinet), the department's authority and stature grew considerably. Thereafter, other functions and responsibilities were added to the depart-

Formed in 1913, the Department of Labor seeks to improve the working conditions and well-being of workers. Of its many undertakings, the department arbitrates labor disputes, fights discrimination in hiring practices, regulates occupational health and safety standards, and provides job training.

ment's purview with the passage of significant labor relations legislation and Supreme Court decisions upholding these acts and workers' rights in general.

From the viewpoint of organized labor, the administration of Lyndon B. Johnson produced one of the most fruitful legislative periods in American history with the enactment of Johnson's "Great Society" programs. Congress also cleared an administration measure for a far-reaching extension of minimum wage size and coverage. Business interests and their allies emerged victorious, however, over both the labor unions and the administration when Congress refused to enact laws expanding unemployment compensation and lifting restrictions on construction site picketing by striking unions. Overseeing labor's interests during these years was secretary W. Willard Wirtz, who had served in the administration of John F. Kennedy and remained through the Johnson presidency.

Labor interests did not fare so well under Richard Nixon's presidency, when the administration was bent on cutting back domestic social programs. Jimmy Carter's administration began optimistically enough—labor interests had hoped to take advantage of a labor-supported president and Congress—but those hopes quickly faded. Although Congress enacted traditional labor legislation such as an increase in the minimum wage, it rejected or qualified a number of items on labor's agenda, including legislation broadening picketing rights at construction sites, legislation mandating cargo handling preferences, and legislation making it easier for unions to organize. This happened despite the efforts of Carter's labor secretary, F. Ray Marshall, whose nomination had broad appeal to key elements of Carter's coalition: unions, civil rights groups, and the South. Marshall brought with him a distinguished career in economics—his work focused on employment problems of African Americans and rural human resource and poverty issues.

LABOR SECRETARIES IN THE 1980S AND 1990S

The influence of organized labor declined during the Reagan presidency. Moreover, the voice of labor's representative in the cabinet was weakened when Reagan's first labor secretary, Raymond J. Donovan, resigned his post March 15, 1985. Donovan was the last member of Reagan's original cabinet to win Senate approval because his confirmation was held up by the Senate Labor and Human Resources Committee. The committee was investigating charges, made by a Federal Bureau of Investigation informer, that Donovan and Schiavone Construction Company, a New Jersey firm Donovan had worked for since 1958, had provided illegal payoffs to corrupt union officials to maintain "labor peace." Other informants said the company had close ties with organized crime. Although the Senate confirmed the appointment, with only Democrats dissenting, a special prosecutor was appointed in December 1981 to investigate the charges, and in October 1984 a grand jury named Donovan in a 137-count indictment. Donovan pleaded not guilty, but he asked for a leave of absence. He resigned after a New York Supreme Court judge refused to dismiss larceny and fraud charges against him. On May 25, 1987, he was acquitted.

Reagan's choice of U.S. Trade Representative William E. Brock III to succeed Donovan drew praise from organized labor. "While we have not always agreed [with Brock], he has earned our respect," said AFL-CIO President Lane Kirkland.[86] Throughout Donovan's tenure, Labor's budget cuts and allegedly lax enforcement of labor laws came under steady criticism from union officials, most of whom opposed Reagan's reelection in 1984.

Brock resigned in November 1987, and Reagan named Ann Dore McLaughlin to succeed him. McLaughlin, whose specialty was public affairs, had not worked in the Labor Department but had held ranking posts in Treasury and Interior. She was handily confirmed by the Senate on December 11, 1987. McLaughlin had three goals: (1) ensure enforcement of the existing labor statutes; (2) use changes in the workforce—largely the growing proportion of women—as an opportunity to galvanize labor and management to solve problems such as child care; and (3)

along with the Education and Commerce Departments, move quickly to develop retraining and education programs for workers in the fast-changing economy.

Under President George Bush's first secretary of labor, former Reagan transportation official Elizabeth H. Dole, the department saw a warming in its relations with organized labor. During her two years at the labor post, Dole was credited with negotiating an increase in the minimum-wage, strengthening enforcement of job-safety and child-labor laws, encouraging companies receiving government contracts to move more women and minorities into managerial positions, and placing more women and minorities in policy positions at the Labor Department itself. She was also praised for helping to resolve an intractable coal-field dispute, but resisted pressure from organized labor and federal mediators to intervene in the 1989 pilots' strike at Eastern Airlines, which later declared bankruptcy.

The Occupational Safety and Health Administration (OSHA) had seen its budget severely reduced under Reagan, whose labor administrators were unsympathetic to OSHA's primary mission of promoting worker safety and health. On entering office, Dole pledged to make worker safety a priority and under Bush the agency saw its first budget increase in more than a decade. Dole still had to contend with opposition to revived OSHA mandates from key White House domestic policy players, particularly budget director Richard Darman, who regarded the worker-safety laws as unduly costly to employers. When Dole resigned in 1989 to head the American Red Cross, her supporters charged that her effectiveness and political initiative had been thwarted by antilabor forces within the Bush administration.

Dole was the first member of Bush's cabinet to resign. Her successor, Lynn Martin, was a former Republican representative from Illinois who had recently lost a bid for a Senate seat. Martin was a moderate with long-standing ties to Bush, having supported his first presidential bid in 1980 and served as national cochair of his 1988 campaign. On labor issues, however, she had remained independent from the president, supporting parental leave and employment-rights legislation vetoed by Bush and in 1989 voting to override a presidential veto of a minimum-wage bill. On appointment to the labor post, Martin echoed Dole's priorities of strengthening child-labor and worker-safety laws, ending discrimination in the workplace, and improving job training.

Organized labor had supported Bill Clinton's presidential campaign and it also backed his nominee for the labor post, Robert B. Reich. Reich, a lecturer at Harvard University's Kennedy School of Government, had been director of policy planning at the Federal Trade Commission under President Carter and an assistant solicitor general in the Ford administration Justice Department. He had been a close friend of Clinton's since their days as Rhodes scholars at Oxford and, though he was not an economist, he headed the economic policy-planning group during the Clinton transition.

Reich took a leading role in trying to sell Clinton's 1993 economic stimulus plan, which was designed to spur the economy by creating temporary jobs through a blend of public works projects, employment programs for youths and unskilled laborers, and social programs for the poor. Although Senate Democrats were forced to strip all the administration's proposals from the package save a $4 billion unemployment-benefit extension, Reich continued to press for the liberal policy initiatives that had been part of Clinton's campaign. Long an advocate of higher wages and better benefits for workers, Reich successfully urged Clinton to seek an increase in the minimum wage, which Clinton proposed in early 1995 despite strong opposition from business interests and the newly elected Republican Congress. Reich also implemented a "school-to-work" transition program, which would provide grants to state and business partnerships for vocational job training for students who did not attend college.

Despite organized labor's overwhelming opposition to the North American Free Trade Agreement (NAFTA), Reich was a loyal spokesperson for the administration's difficult campaign for NAFTA's passage. The Clinton administration negotiated side agreements with Canada and Mexico to ensure compliance with U.S. environmental and labor laws, and a retraining program for workers who lost their jobs due to NAFTA was incorporated in the pact's enacting legislation, which cleared Congress in late 1993. Despite these efforts, relations between the White House and labor groups became acrimonious during the push for the NAFTA vote and remained lukewarm afterward.

In early 1995 labor organizations geared up to resist changes to the federal job-training system. Leading Republicans called for ending most federal job-training programs and turning the remaining programs over to the states. In a preemptive response to the Republican plan, Reich proposed streamlining the system by consolidating up to seventy education and training programs and replacing others with a voucher system for displaced workers.

ORGANIZATION AND FUNCTIONS

The secretary of labor is the principal adviser to the president on the development and execution of policies and the administration and enforcement of laws relating to wage earners, their working conditions, and their employment opportunities. The secretary is assisted by a deputy secretary and a deputy undersecretary for international labor affairs. The department has four assistant secretaries in charge of congressional and intergovernmental affairs, public affairs, administration and management, and policy. The secretary's office includes the Women's Bureau, an inspector general, a solicitor, the Benefits Review Board, the Employees' Compensation Appeals Board, the Office of Administrative Law Judges, the Office of Small Business and Minority Affairs, the Department of Labor Academy, and the Wage Appeals Board.

In addition to the commissioner of labor statistics, there are seven assistant secretaries responsible for the following areas: occupational safety and health, employment and training, mine safety and health, pension and welfare benefit programs, veter-

ans' employment and training services, employment standards, and an Office of the American Workplace.

The department's functions that most affect American workers are those administered by the Employment and Training Administration (ETA), which is responsible for employment services, work experience, work training, and unemployment insurance. ETA operates the Job Training Partnership Program and a program to assist dislocated workers (primarily those affected by plant closings) as well as oversees an employment and training program for Native Americans. The Job Corps provides a wide range of training, educational, and support services for disadvantaged youths aged sixteen to twenty-one. The Senior Community Service Employment Program helps older Americans obtain employment. The NAFTA Transitional Adjustment Assistance Program (NTAA) assists workers who are laid off or forced into part-time work as a result of the North American Free Trade Agreement (NAFTA). This includes help for family farmers and farm workers who do not qualify for unemployment compensation. ETA offers on-site services to workers threatened by layoffs, including job placement, income support, employment counseling, and job search and relocation allowances. ETA also administers apprenticeship programs and unemployment benefits.

The Employment Standards Administration (ESA) regulates minimum wage and overtime standards through its wage and hour division and attempts to achieve nondiscrimination in employment by federal contractors through the Office of Federal Contract Compliance Programs. ESA also administers three major disability programs through its Office of Workers' Compensation Programs.

Worker safety and health are the responsibility of the Occupational Safety and Health Administration, which formulates safety and health standards for the workplace, and the Mine Safety and Health Administration, which operates in all types of mines. The Veterans' Employment and Training Service ensures that national employment and training programs for veterans are carried out by local employment services and the private sector. It has a nationwide field staff and also cooperates with the Department of Veterans Affairs to provide other services and benefits to veterans.

The Pension and Welfare Benefits Administration is responsible for administering the Title I provisions of the Employee Retirement Income Security Act of 1974 (ERISA). The agency monitors and investigates administration of employee benefit and pension plan funds and has the authority to enforce ERISA by bringing civil action in federal courts.

The Office of the American Workplace was established in 1993 to work with government, business, and labor to encourage the adoption of high-performance work practices and cooperative labor-management relations. It took over some of the functions of the former Labor-Management Office, including assistance to collective bargaining negotiators and oversight of labor organizations under the Labor Management Reporting and Disclosure Act.

The Bureau of Labor Statistics is the principal fact-finding agency for data on labor requirements, labor force, employment, unemployment, hours of work, wages and employee compensation, productivity, technological developments, and general economic trends. It publishes the *Monthly Labor Review, Consumer Price Index, Employment and Earnings, Compensation and Working Conditions, Producer Prices and Price Indexes,* and *Occupational Outlook Quarterly,* among numerous other publications.

Department of State

Although it has far-flung responsibilities, the State Department—the senior executive department of the U.S. government—has remained one of the smallest departments in the cabinet. About one-third of its approximately twenty-six thousand employees serve domestically; of the two-thirds serving abroad, slightly more than one-third are American citizens, and the rest are foreign nationals. The department's fiscal year 1995 budget totaled roughly $6.0 billion (excluding U.S. contributions to more than fifty major multinational organizations and their affiliates). Americans employed by the department are members of either the Civil Service or the Foreign Service. Those in the Civil Service generally do not serve abroad, while Foreign Service personnel spend approximately 60 percent of their years of service in foreign countries.

HISTORY OF THE DEPARTMENT

The present-day Department of State had its beginnings in 1781, when Congress established a Department of Foreign Affairs, redesignated as the Department of State in September 1789. During Secretary Thomas Jefferson's tenure (1789–1793), the department consisted of five clerks, two messengers, and a part-time translator of French. It maintained legations in London and Paris, a diplomatic agency in The Hague, and two consular missions. Only ten persons were added to the staff in the ensuing thirty years.

The department was reorganized by Secretary Louis McLane (1833–1834) into bureaus dealing with diplomatic, consular, internal, and servicing functions. That arrangement continued until 1870, when Secretary Hamilton Fish (1869–1877) split the diplomatic and consular bureaus into two geographically oriented units. In the early 1900s Secretaries Elihu Root (1905–1909) and Philander C. Knox (1909–1913) reorganized the department into regional divisions, which is the basis of the contemporary structure. The 1924 Rogers Act combined the diplomatic and consular services in a single Foreign Service.

Throughout the 1920s and 1930s most of the State Department's work was carried out by its geographical divisions, which formulated policy and drafted instructions. Because of the small size of the divisions, it was relatively easy to conduct the nation's foreign policy. World War II, however, thrust the United States into the unambiguous position of world leader. Responding to the expansion of State's activities, Secretary Cordell Hull (1933–1944) regrouped related functions under individual assistant secretaries and established eleven coordinating offices.

According to author Martin Mayer, "The modern State Department is essentially the creation of George C. Marshall [1947–1949], who . . . immediately saw what was wrong. No staff . . . no planning: no real sense of who the other actors were, domestically."[87] Marshall put the undersecretary (who was Dean G. Acheson at the time) in charge of the daily operations of the department; staff wishing access to the secretary had to be cleared by him first. Marshall also established a Policy Planning Staff, with George F. Kennan (later U.S. ambassador to the Soviet Union) in charge. Marshall's reorganization and the strength of the Policy Planning Staff (subsequently renamed the Policy Planning Council) gave the State Department preeminence in foreign policy making.

After the Hoover Commission on government reorganization recommended a thorough overhaul of the department in 1949, Secretary Acheson (1949–1953) rearranged the existing eighteen offices into five bureaus (four geographic and a Bureau of United Nations Affairs), as well as units dealing with economic, intelligence, public, and press affairs. The budgetary, personnel, and operating facilities were assigned to a deputy undersecretary. Eventually, there were six substantive and eight functional agencies.

During Dwight D. Eisenhower's first term the information service and foreign aid programs were taken away from State, and Congress reinstated the Foreign Agricultural Service in the Department of Agriculture. By 1953–1954, Sen. Joseph R. McCarthy's (R-Wis.) virulent accusations of communist penetration of the State Department had severely weakened its stature; recruitment into the Foreign Service came to a halt. In response, Secretary of State John Foster Dulles appointed a commission to examine the department's organization and personnel procedures. The commission recommended a sizable expansion of the Foreign Service, achieved primarily by giving Foreign Service officer status to the department's Civil Service employees.

Another major reorganization occurred in 1970, following a period of intensive internal review by several task forces. Secretary William P. Rogers (1969–1973) phased in a number of managerial changes that strengthened the policy formulation process and assigned decision-making and managerial responsibilities to the secretary and assistant secretaries. Nonetheless, complaints continued to abound about what were considered an excessive number of meetings and the huge quantity of paperwork (including more than two million words of cable traffic a day) generated by the department.

In 1995 the new Republican Congress prepared to make sweeping cuts in foreign aid programs, focusing on U.S. contributions to UN peacekeeping missions and support for the World Bank and other international financial institutions. In an effort to preempt these deep budget cuts and fulfill the administration's "reinventing government" strategy to reduce federal bureaucracy, Secretary Warren Christopher offered a foreign policy reorganization plan. Under his proposal, the State Department would absorb several independent agencies—the Agency for International Development, the Arms Control and Disarmament Agency, and the United States Information Agency—to eliminate their duplicative functions. The proposal was widely criticized by the heads of these agencies as a "power grab" by senior State officials and a heated and high-level public relations campaign prevented the proposed merger. The State Department made plans to cut its programs by closing fifteen overseas missions and eliminating one bureau at Washington headquarters, but it still faced steep budget cuts and legislative proposals to limit its operations.

SECRETARY'S POSITION

The secretary of state, along with the secretaries of defense, Treasury, and justice, is generally considered a member of the president's inner cabinet, although the influence of the department has varied according to personalities and circumstances. President Harry S. Truman, for example, relied heavily on the advice of Secretary Marshall in the postwar reconstruction of Europe. In the following years of mounting international tension, presidents continued to look to their secretaries for principal foreign policy leadership: Acheson under Truman, Dulles under Eisenhower, Dean Rusk (1961–1969) under presidents John F. Kennedy and Lyndon B. Johnson, and Henry A. Kissinger (but not his predecessor, William Rogers) under Richard Nixon.

Before 1968, according to Mayer, "Presidents usually spent considerable time with their Secretaries of State—Dean Rusk estimated that he saw Kennedy more than two thousand times in the thousand days. Recently, and unfortunately, both President and Secretary have become too busy, and too tightly cosseted by their staffs."[88]

Recent secretaries have had their ups and downs in relations with the president. Jimmy Carter's first secretary of state, Cyrus R. Vance (1977–1980), brought to the administration broad experience in foreign policy and crisis management. He offered to foreign governments the reassurance of a well-known and widely respected figure in charge of U.S. diplomacy. It was primarily President Carter himself, however, who assumed the foreign policy initiative in reaching the major foreign policy achievement of his administration: the 1979 Camp David Peace Accords between Israel and Egypt.

Ronald Reagan's first secretary of state was Alexander M. Haig Jr., a former army general and NATO commander known for his loyal service as President Nixon's White House chief of staff during the Watergate period. Haig remained controversial during his year and a half in office, declaring himself Reagan's foreign policy "vicar" and engaging in jealous turf fights over policy formulation with other administration figures. He resigned suddenly in June 1982, later saying that his departure was not entirely voluntary.

George P. Shultz—a former economics professor, corporate executive, and Nixon cabinet officer—succeeded Haig. Shultz changed both the style and substance of U.S. foreign policy, using a less aggressive posture and more quiet diplomacy.

George Bush's secretary of state, James A. Baker III, was the central figure in the president's foreign policy team and was seen as a skilled negotiator and pragmatist as well as a Bush loyalist. Baker was a close friend of Bush, having served as campaign manager for his fellow Texan's 1980 and 1988 presidential campaigns, and had been chief of staff and then secretary of the Treasury in the Reagan White House. Baker was a leading player in creating the president's post–cold war policy and was credited with easing diplomatic tensions between the United States and the Soviet Union. Like Bush, Baker's style of diplomacy was nonconfrontational and personal. Frequent meetings and an ongoing rapport with their Soviet counterparts fostered a number of major developments in East-West relations, including the Strategic Arms Reduction Treaty (START), close cooperation on German reunification, an agreement to reduce conventional forces in Europe, and Soviet support for the U.S.-led multinational force against Iraq during the Persian Gulf War. Baker resigned toward the end of Bush's term to manage the president's reelection campaign and was replaced by Deputy Secretary Lawrence S. Eagleburger.

Bill Clinton selected his campaign adviser and transition-team manager, attorney Warren M. Christopher, as secretary of state. Christopher had served as deputy secretary in the Carter State Department, and his tenure had earned him a reputation as a competent and cautious diplomat, which was later enhanced by his leadership of a commission investigating the Los Angeles police following the riots of 1992. Early in his term critics charged that, like Clinton, Christopher lacked the international stature and vision to formulate the broad geopolitical philosophy necessary in the post–cold war world. Christopher often took the brunt of ongoing complaints that Clinton's response to crises in Somalia, Bosnia, Haiti, and the former Soviet Union were inconsistent and ineffective.

ORGANIZATION AND FUNCTIONS

The secretary of state is responsible for the overall direction, coordination, and supervision of U.S. foreign relations and for the interdepartmental activities of the U.S. government overseas. The secretary is the first-ranking member of the cabinet and a member of the National Security Council.

The secretary is assisted by a deputy secretary and five undersecretaries: arms control and international security affairs; global affairs; political affairs; economic, business, and agricultural affairs; and management. Also attached to the secretary's office are the U.S. ambassador to the United Nations, several ambassadors-at-large, who undertake special missions, the chief of protocol, and the Policy Planning Staff.

Regional Bureaus

Primary substantive responsibility in the department rests with the six regional bureaus (European and Canadian Affairs,

African Affairs, East Asian and Pacific Affairs, Inter-American Affairs, Near Eastern Affairs, and South Asian Affairs), which are headed by assistant secretaries. These bureaus advise the secretary on the formulation of U.S. policies toward countries within their regional jurisdiction and guide the operations of the U.S. diplomatic establishments in those countries.

The Bureau of International Organization Affairs manages U.S. participation in the United Nations and its system of programs and agencies. The bureau also deals with international problems such as food production, air traffic safety, communications, health, human rights, education, and the environment. In addition, the bureau is responsible for U.S. participation in international conferences, some hosted by the United States.

Functional Bureaus

The remaining bureaus are organized by function. The Bureau of Economic and Business Affairs deals with international energy policy, international monetary developments, trade policy, aviation, shipping, patents, trademarks, commodity matters, and other international economic concerns.

The Political-Military Affairs Bureau originates and develops policy and provides general direction within the department on issues that affect U.S. security policies, military assistance, nuclear nonproliferation and conventional arms transfer policy, and arms control matters.

The Bureau of Democracy, Human Rights, and Labor implements U.S. policies relating to human rights. It prepares an annual review of human rights worldwide and provides the Immigration and Naturalization Service with advisory opinions regarding asylum petitions.

The Bureau of International Narcotics and Law Enforcement Affairs is responsible for coordinating the federal government's international drug control activities, including policy development, diplomatic initiatives, bilateral and multilateral assistance programs in producer and transit nations, technical assistance and training for foreign personnel. The bureau represents the United States at international meetings and conferences on drugs, narcotics, and psychotropic substances.

Established by Congress in 1974, the Bureau of Oceans and International Environmental and Scientific Affairs ensures that scientific, technological, and environmental developments are taken into account in the formulation and execution of U.S. foreign policy.

The Bureau of Population, Refugees, and Migration develops and implements programs and policies on international refugee matters, including repatriation and resettlement programs. It funds and monitors overseas relief, assistance, and repatriation programs and manages refugee admission to the United States.

The Bureau of Administration provides supply, procurement, and administrative services for the department and for U.S. government-owned real estate in 265 cities abroad.

The Bureau of Consular Affairs, under the direction of an assistant secretary, assists Americans who travel or live abroad. Its Passport Services Office issues more than four million passports

a year. Through 265 U.S. diplomatic and consular posts abroad, the Overseas Citizens Services Office assists Americans in a number of ways, including distribution of federal benefits checks to help when sudden illness or death strikes. U.S. consular officers in the Visa Services Office interview foreign nationals applying to come to the United States to settle, work, study, or visit.

The Bureau of Diplomatic Security, established in 1986, provides a secure environment for conducting American diplomacy and promoting American interests abroad. Its security officers guard the department, protect visiting foreign dignitaries, and supervise security—provided by marine security guards (numbering about 1,500) and about 150 State Department security agents—at U.S. embassies and consulates.

The Bureau of Finance and Management Policy is directed by a chief financial officer, who serves as the department's budget officer and assists in managing the department and its posts.

The Office of Foreign Missions regulates the benefits, privileges, and immunities granted to foreign missions and their personnel in the United States on the basis of the treatment accorded U.S. missions abroad and considerations of national security, public safety, and welfare. The office is authorized to control the numbers, locations, and travel privileges of foreign diplomats and diplomatic staff in the United States.

The legal adviser is the principal adviser to the secretary, and through the secretary to the president, on all matters of international law arising in the conduct of U.S. foreign policy.

The Bureau of Intelligence and Research has three principal functions. First, it prepares current and long-range intelligence analyses for the department, overseas missions, and other government agencies. Second, it serves as the department's coordinator with other members of the U.S. intelligence community to assure conformity of their programs with U.S. foreign policy. And, third, the bureau manages the department's external research, which provides foreign policy expertise from outside the government.

The Bureau of Public Affairs, headed by an assistant secretary, advises other bureaus in State on public opinion and arranges continuing contacts between department officials and the public through conferences, briefings, and speaking and media engagements. The spokesperson of the department and the bureau's press office conduct daily press briefings. The bureau also produces and distributes publications (including the encyclopedic series, *The Foreign Relations of the United States*), films, and other information and educational materials on U.S. foreign policy.

The Bureau of Legislative Affairs supervises and coordinates all departmental legislative activities (other than administrative matters) with Congress and other executive agencies.

The Bureau of International Communications and Information Policy is the principal adviser to the secretary on international telecommunications policy issues affecting U.S. foreign policy and national security.

Some of these programs are carried out in cooperation with

other federal agencies, including the Agency for International Development, the Immigration and Naturalization Service in the Department of Justice, and the Office of Refugee Resettlement in the Department of Health and Human Services.

Foreign Service

The United States has diplomatic relations with 160 countries. In some smaller countries where the United States does not maintain a mission, official contacts are channeled through embassies in neighboring countries or the United Nations. Ambassadors are the personal representatives of the president as well as representatives of the Department of State and all other federal agencies. They have full responsibility for the implementation of U.S. foreign policy by all U.S. government personnel within their country of assignment, except those under military commands.

As chiefs of mission, each ambassador heads a "country team" which typically includes a deputy chief of mission; heads of political, economic, consular, and administrative sections; defense, agricultural, and foreign commercial service attachés; a public affairs officer; the director of the Agency for International Development (AID) mission; and, as needed, representatives of other agencies of the U.S. government.

Department of Transportation

Development of a coordinated national transportation policy—long a goal of Congress and the executive branch—eluded lawmakers in the early 1960s. Instead, Congress was, for the most part, content to extend existing programs, which President John F. Kennedy had described as "a chaotic patchwork of inconsistent and often obsolete legislation [evolving] from a history of specific actions addressed to specific problems of specific industries at specific times."

The search for integrated programs that would lead to a diversified transportation system was complicated by the fact that each mode of transportation had a vested interest in existing policies, regulations, and legislation—and each had its own spokespersons in the administration and Congress. They tended to oppose any changes that would alter these advantages, while often advocating changes designed to improve their own situations.

Kennedy's successor, Lyndon B. Johnson, nonetheless pursued the idea of establishing a transportation department, and Congress acceded to his wishes in 1966. As the president requested, Congress excluded from the new Department of Transportation (DOT) all economic regulatory and rate-setting activities conducted by existing federal agencies. The urban mass transportation programs administered by the Department of Housing and Urban Development (HUD) also were excluded pending further study of their logical place in the executive branch (they later were transferred to DOT). The final legislation substantially weakened the powers proposed for the secretary of transportation, effectively denying the secretary inde-

Under the Department of Transportation Enabling Act, signed by President Johnson on October 15, 1966, ninety thousand government employees and thirty-eight agencies or functions were transferred to the new department. One the department's major responsibilities is maintaining the nation's 45,280-mile interstate highway system.

pendent authority to coordinate or revise existing federal transportation policies and programs. This stemmed partly from the desire of Congress to retain direct influence over transportation activities and partly from the desire of various private transportation groups to preserve their relationships, built up over many years, with existing federal agencies.

The bill creating DOT established a National Transportation Safety Board—independent of the secretary and other units—to oversee major accident investigations, determine the cause of such accidents, and review appeals of licenses and certificates issued by the Department of Transportation. The existing separation of aviation safety functions was continued by transferring the Federal Aviation Agency's safety duties to the new federal aviation administrator, whose decisions would be administratively final. The Civil Aeronautics Board's responsibilities, which included accident investigations, probable cause determination, and review of appeals, were given to the safety board. On other safety matters, the secretary was directed to enforce the 1966 auto and highway safety laws; the federal railroad and federal highway administrators (not the secretary) were given statutory authority over the safety functions transferred to them from the Interstate Commerce Commission; and the U.S. Coast Guard was to continue to enforce maritime safety.

Johnson named Alan S. Boyd, undersecretary of commerce for transportation, as the first DOT secretary. Earlier, Boyd had been a member of the Civil Aeronautics Board, serving as chairman from 1961 to 1965. The Senate confirmed his appointment on January 12, 1967, and the department officially began operation on April 1.

THE FIRST TWO DECADES

With its inception, DOT assumed responsibility for administering the High Speed Ground Transportation Program transferred from the Department of Commerce. In July 1967 the Urban Mass Transportation Administration was shifted from HUD to DOT. During 1967 DOT issued the first thirteen national highway safety standards under the Highway Safety Act, and the first set of federal motor vehicle standards became effective that year.

In 1970 DOT and the Department of Defense announced their cooperation in a project called Military Assistance for Safety in Traffic. The 1970 Airport and Airways Development Act provided for a long-term airport/airway development project under the auspices of DOT but strictly supervised by Congress.

During the administration of Jimmy Carter, Congress enacted legislation to deregulate the airline, railroad, and trucking industries. The new laws, for which DOT was the major overseer, pared away years of federal regulations that threatened the health of the industries and, in many cases, resulted in higher consumer costs. As for other major actions, in 1978 Congress provided nearly $54 million in aid for highway and mass transit programs administered by DOT. The controversial Chrysler Corporation Loan Guarantee Act of 1979 directed the secretary of transportation to prepare an assessment of the long-term viability of the corporation. Another hotly debated measure was the department's promulgation of final rules requiring recipients of DOT financial aid to make their facilities accessible to the handicapped. That was followed in 1979 by a ruling that all buses purchased after September 1, 1979, had to be accessible to the elderly and handicapped.

Other transportation highlights included passage of the 1980 Aviation Safety and Noise Abatement Act; passage in 1980 of the Staggers Rail Act, giving railroads more freedom in rate making and service options; authorization in 1981 of the Northeast Corridor Rail Improvement Project under the Federal Railroad Administration, and establishment in 1984 of the Office of Commercial Space Transportation.

Deregulation continued under Ronald Reagan with the sale of Conrail (the freight rail system). The president proposed cutting federal subsidies for Amtrak passenger service, phasing out mass transit subsidies, and returning responsibility for most roads, including the interstate system, to state and local governments. By the mid-1980s, however, DOT, parent organization of the Coast Guard, was focusing on combating terrorism and drug trafficking.

TRANSPORTATION UNDER BUSH AND CLINTON

Samuel K. Skinner, secretary of transportation under George Bush, had more success shaping a new transportation strategy by giving states greater flexibility but fewer federal funds for aviation, highway, and mass transit programs. In 1991 he shepherded a $151 billion, six-year highway, safety, and mass transit bill through Congress. The new law retained the federal role in maintaining the nation's highways in a newly designated National Highway System composed of the interstate network and primary arterial roads. Much of the rest of transportation policy was shifted to the states, and key funding programs were consolidated into one Surface Transportation Program, from which states were free to spend funds on nearly any transportation project. State transit officers were also given more flexibility to spend funds on mass transit programs, which were slated to receive $31.5 billion over six years, the largest funding increase since the federal government began supporting mass transit in 1964. The bill also mandated air bags for all passenger cars made after September 1, 1995, and provided grants to states to improve safety on highways.

By 1991 the turbulence caused by deregulation of the nation's airlines had resulted in an industrywide shakeout, with strong carriers buying up international routes and weakened carriers filing for bankruptcy. Higher fuel prices during the Persian Gulf War and the recession caused a record industry loss of $2 billion in the first quarter of 1991. The growing list of carrier casualties continued even after the end of the war, and key lawmakers began a reregulatory effort to deal with concerns about airline prices and the trend toward consolidation.

Secretary Skinner resisted pressure to intervene through regulation and concentrated instead on steering the debate toward the global market. He granted British carriers new access to U.S. cities and won access to the London routes of troubled and defunct carriers for the healthiest U.S. companies. He also began talks with Canada on an open-skies treaty, and relaxed rules allowing foreign investors to own up to 49 percent of an airline's equity.

Reviving the troubled airline industry was also high on the agenda of Federico F. Penā, a former Denver mayor, who served as secretary under President Bill Clinton. He supported the work of a commission established in 1992 to study the financial condition of the airline industry, but, like Skinner, rejected reregulation in favor of paring unnecessary regulations that drove up costs and sought more landing rights for U.S. airlines in foreign countries. The Clinton administration supported a commission recommendation that the government quickly modernize the air-traffic control system, but calls for a government-run air-traffic corporation and measures to make the FAA independent stalled in political disputes and interrupted the flow of federal funds to airports. The Clinton administration rejected the commission's recommendation to cut taxes for the industry, and the final 1994 FAA reauthorization addressed few of the commission's suggestions, making only minor changes in aviation policy.

Similar efforts by Peña to bolster the maritime industry by extending subsidy contracts to shipping lines and shipyards were also frustrated by both congressional and White House opposition. Direct federal subsidies to shipyards had been ended in 1981, and most of the contracts were due to expire in 1997, which the U.S. shippers claimed would kill an industry already disadvantaged by heavily subsidized yards in other countries and higher building costs and taxes in this country. Clinton continued to oppose direct subsidies, including a Peña proposal for a ten-year subsidy program for U.S.-flag operators, which the secretary argued was essential to preventing companies from shifting their vessels to foreign registries.

In early 1995, Peña announced a Transportation reorganization plan that would consolidate the department into three agencies based on transportation over land, sea, and air. A new Aviation Administration would control all FAA functions except air-traffic control, which would be under a separate government corporation. The Intermodal Transportation Administration would incorporate highway, mass transit, railroad, maritime and other agencies, and the U.S. Coast Guard would remain intact.

ORGANIZATION AND FUNCTIONS

The secretary of transportation, assisted by a deputy secretary, oversees the nine operating administrations that compose the department, eight of which are concerned with a specific form of transportation. The secretary's office also develops and updates national transportation policy, prepares transportation legislation, issues licenses for commercial expendable space launch vehicle operations, and helps negotiate international transportation agreements. Reporting to the secretary are the Office of Civil Rights, the Board of Contract Appeals, the Office of Small and Disadvantaged Business Utilization, the Office of Commercial Space Transportation, the general counsel, the Executive Secretariat, the Office of Intelligence and Security, the Office of Intermodalism, the inspector general, and the Bureau of Transportation Statistics. Five assistant secretaries are assigned, respectively, to aviation and international affairs, budget and programs, governmental affairs, administration, and transportation policy.

Created by Secretary of the Treasury Alexander Hamilton in 1790 to combat smugglers, the U.S. Coast Guard has seen its role and mission expand tremendously over the years. Coast Guard personnel go out on some seventy thousand search and rescue missions each year. They investigate and clean up oil spills, regulate operation of the U.S. merchant fleet, enforce U.S. maritime laws, operate the nation's only fleet of icebreakers, and help in the search for drug smugglers and illegal aliens. The Coast Guard maintains more than 45,000 navigational aids, which include buoys, lighthouses, and offshore towers. As one of the nation's five military services, the Coast Guard protects U.S. ports from sabotage, and it has participated in U.S. military conflicts abroad.

The principal mission of the Federal Aviation Administration (FAA) is to promote aviation safety while insuring efficient use of the nation's airspace. The administration is responsible for issuing and enforcing safety rules and regulations; certifying aircraft, aircraft components, air agencies, and airports; conducting aviation safety-related research and development; and managing and operating the national airspace system. FAA oversees approximately 710,000 licensed pilots, 274,000 mechanics, 18,000 air traffic controllers, and 43,000 flight engineers. It operates and maintains 24 air route traffic control centers, 400 airport traffic control towers, 316 flight service stations, 4 international flight service stations, 109 air route surveillance radars, 200 airport surveillance radars, and 851 instrument landing systems. Following the 1988 bombing of a Pan Am flight over Lockerbie, Scotland, the FAA implemented stronger airport security measures, including the establishment of federal security managers to serve as the FAA liaison with airport managers and law enforcement agencies, and provisions for notifying passengers of terrorist threats to flights.

The Federal Highway Administration (FHWA) is responsible for administering the federal aid program for highways, which subsidizes the maintenance of more than 276,000 bridges, the 45,280-mile interstate highway system, and over 800,000 miles of other roads, making up a network that carries about two-thirds of the nation's motor vehicle traffic. The FHWA also regulates and enforces federal requirements on the safety of trucks and buses engaged in interstate or foreign commerce, as well as the transport of hazardous cargoes.

The principal duties of the Federal Railroad Administration (FRA) are to issue standards and regulations designed to improve passenger and freight rail safety. FRA inspectors at eight regional offices monitor safety equipment and procedures. The FRA also provides policy guidance on legislative matters affecting rail transportation—such as the transportation of hazardous materials and financial assistance to the National Railroad Passenger Corporation (Amtrak)—and oversees the development of the northeast high-speed rail corridor between Washington, D.C., and Boston.

Created by Congress in 1966, the National Highway Traffic Safety Administration (NHTSA) is authorized to issue motor vehicle safety standards and to investigate possible safety defects. In recent years the agency has waged a campaign against drunk drivers and for use of safety belts. The NHTSA also supervises a program of state grants for motor vehicle, driver, and pedestrian safety programs and has authority to prescribe fuel-use economy standards for motor vehicles.

The Federal Transit Administration (formerly the Urban Mass Transportation Administration) provides financial and planning assistance to the nation's public transit systems, including buses, subways, trolleys, commuter trains, and ferry boats. Although the federal government's involvement in mass transportation began in 1961, the existing transit program started with passage of the 1964 Urban Mass Transportation Act. About half of transit administration funds come from the mass-transit account of the Highway Trust Fund, which in 1994 received 1.5 cents of the 18.4-cents-per-gallon federal gasoline tax.

Created by legislation in 1954, the St. Lawrence Seaway Development Corporation constructed the U.S. facilities of the St. Lawrence Seaway navigation project, operated jointly by the United States and Canada. The corporation continues to operate and maintain that part of the seaway between Montreal and Lake Erie, within the territorial limits of the United States, and it is responsible for developing the full seaway system from the western tip of Lake Superior to the Atlantic Ocean—a distance of twenty-three hundred miles.

The Maritime Administration (MARAD), which initially was excluded from DOT's purview, became part of the department in 1981. Like its predecessor agencies dating back to the creation of the United States Shipping Board in 1916, MARAD is responsible for developing and maintaining a merchant marine capable of meeting the nation's requirements for both commercial trade and national defense. The agency administers financial and technical programs, develops promotional and marketing programs, trains ships' officers at the U.S. Merchant Marine Academy at Kings Point, New York, negotiates bilateral maritime agreements, and maintains the National Defense Reserve Fleet.

In contrast to DOT's eight other administrations which focus on a single transportation sector, the purview of the Research and Special Programs Administration (RSPA) extends to all transportation modes. Established in 1977 by combining the functions of other offices, RSPA consists of the Office of Hazardous Materials Safety; Management and Administration; the Office of Pipeline Safety; the Office of Research, Technology, and Analysis; and the Volpe National Transportation Systems Center in Cambridge, Mass., which plans, develops, and manages programs in all fields of transportation research and development. RSPA is also responsible for ensuring that the nation's civil transportation system will continue to operate effectively during an emergency.

Department of the Treasury

Management of the monetary resources of the United States is the primary function of the Department of the Treasury. Among other responsibilities, it regulates national banks, assesses and collects income taxes and customs duties, manufactures coins and bills, advises the president on international economic policy, reports the federal government's financial transactions, conducts international and domestic economic research, enforces tax and tariff laws, directs anticounterfeiting operations, and provides executive protection.

One of the oldest cabinet departments, Treasury was established by the first session of Congress on September 2, 1789. Yet many of its functions were carried out even before the signing of the Declaration of Independence; the Continental Congress issued paper money to finance the revolutionary war and appointed treasurers to oversee the effort.

The new republic's finances, however, remained in disarray until September 1789 when President George Washington appointed Alexander Hamilton to be the first secretary of the Treasury. Hamilton's shrewd financial policies resulted in renewed confidence in the Bank of the United States, which issued money in the government's name. As Treasury's first secretary, Hamilton established a precedent for the position's power in advising the president, as well as the controversy surrounding many of its holders. The department is not only intrinsically influential; its secretaries also have numbered among the presidents' closest advisers.

More than 150 years after Hamilton advised Washington, President Dwight D. Eisenhower was quoted as saying of his Treasury secretary: "In Cabinet meetings, I always wait for George Humphrey to speak. I sit back and listen to the others talk while he doesn't say anything. But I know that when he speaks, he will say just what I was thinking."

EVOLUTION OF THE DEPARTMENT

Treasury's authority expanded considerably during the Civil War. The loss of customs revenues from the seceded southern states necessitated the establishment of the Bureau of Internal Revenue, as well as the printing of paper currency and the institution of a national banking system. The growth of international trade following World Wars I and II resulted in a central role for Treasury in the 1944 Bretton Woods Conference, which established the International Monetary Fund and the postwar monetary system.

Many federal functions that originally resided in Treasury have been transferred over the years to other departments. For example, Treasury administered the Postal Service until 1829. The General Land Office, which was the core of the Interior Department, was part of Treasury from 1812 to 1849. Business activities were under Treasury's purview until the Department of Commerce and Labor was established in 1903. The functions of the Office of the Supervising Architect of the Treasury were transferred to the General Services Administration in 1949. The Coast Guard, the oldest seagoing armed service in the United States, was part of Treasury until its transfer to the Department of Transportation in 1967. Other marine interests initially administered by Treasury were passed on to other departments. The Bureau of the Budget was transferred from Treasury to the Executive Office in 1939.

ORGANIZATION AND FUNCTIONS

Treasury is divided into two major components: the office of the secretary and the operating bureaus. The secretary, who is officially the second-ranking cabinet officer, has primary responsibility for formulating and recommending domestic and international financial, economic, and tax policy; participating in the preparation of broad fiscal policies that have general sig-

The Treasury Department has been responsible for issuing currency since its founding in 1789. Here department employees trim currency in 1907.

nificance for the economy; and managing the public debt. As chief financial officer of the government, the secretary serves as chair pro tempore of the Economic Policy Council and as U.S. governor of the International Monetary Fund, International Bank for Reconstruction and Development, Inter-American Development Bank, Asian Development Bank, and African Development Bank. The Treasury secretary is required by law to submit periodic reports to Congress on the government's fiscal operations, including an annual report.

The secretary is assisted by a deputy secretary, two undersecretaries for domestic finance and international affairs, a general counsel, and an inspector general. Nine assistant secretaries are responsible for the following areas: economic policy, international affairs, fiscal affairs (including the Financial Management Service and the Bureau of the Public Debt), financial institutions, legislative affairs, management, tax policy, public affairs and public liaison, and enforcement (which includes enforcement activities of the U.S. Customs Service, U.S. Secret Service, Bureau of Alcohol, Tobacco and Firearms, Federal Law Enforcement Training Center, and Office of Foreign Assets Control).

The Office of the Treasurer of the United States was established on September 6, 1777. Initially, the treasurer was responsible for the receipt and custody of government funds. Over the years, however, these duties have been dispersed throughout various Treasury bureaus. In 1981 the treasurer was assigned oversight of the Bureau of Engraving and Printing and the United States Mint.

The Office of the Comptroller of the Currency, created February 25, 1863, is an integral part of the national banking system. The comptroller oversees the execution of laws related to nationally chartered banks (including trust activities and overseas operations) and promulgates rules and regulations governing their operations.

The Bureau of Alcohol, Tobacco and Firearms (ATF) was established on July 1, 1972, as successor to the Alcohol Tax Unit of the Bureau of Internal Revenue. ATF enforces federal laws that require excise taxes on alcoholic substances, control of firearms and explosives, and regulation of the tobacco industry.

In 1927 the Bureau of Customs was established as a separate agency within the Treasury Department; in August 1973 it was redesignated the U.S. Customs Service. The Customs Service collects revenue from imports and enforces customs and related laws. Customs also administers the 1930 Tariff Act. As the principal border enforcement agency, the service's mission has been extended over the years to cover the administration and enforcement of a wide range of safety standards on behalf of more than forty federal agencies. Customs monitors three hundred ports of entry into the United States in the fifty states, Virgin Islands, and Puerto Rico.

The Bureau of Engraving and Printing began operations in July 1862, when the government started printing "greenback" currency to finance the Civil War. It designs and prints a large variety of security products, including all paper currency; U.S. postage, customs, and revenue stamps; Treasury bills, notes, and bonds; permits; and certificates of award. The bureau produces about 8 billion bills per year and more than 31 billion stamps. It is the largest printer of security documents in the world, issuing more than 40 billion annually.

Responsibility for the government's cash management, credit management, debt collection programs, and central reporting and accounting systems originally rested with the Register of the Treasury. In 1920 those functions were transferred to the newly created Office of the Commissioner of Accounts and Deposits, which was renamed the Bureau of Government Financial Operations in 1974 and became the Financial Management Service (FMS) in 1984. FMS issues approximately 440 million Treasury checks and close to 350 million electronic fund transfer payments annually for federal salaries and wages, payments to suppliers of goods and services to the government, income tax refunds, and payments under major government programs such as Social Security and veterans' benefits.

The Bureau of Internal Revenue came into existence on July 4, 1862, to collect new income taxes—money that was used to pay for the Civil War. The Supreme Court declared the national income tax unconstitutional in 1894, but it was reinstated by the 16th Amendment to the Constitution in 1913. Reorganized in 1953, the bureau was renamed the Internal Revenue Service (IRS). The largest of Treasury bureaus, IRS employs more than 120,000 people in its Washington headquarters, seven regional offices, and sixty-two districts.

Congress created the Mint of the United States on April 2, 1792, and placed it in the State Department. In 1799 the Mint was made an independent agency, and in 1873 it became part of Treasury as the Bureau of the Mint. It was placed under the supervision of the treasurer of the United States in 1981, and its name was changed to the United States Mint in 1984. The Mint's principal function is to produce coins and medals; it also has custody over Treasury gold and silver bullion.

Management of the national debt was consolidated from several departments into the Public Debt Service in 1920; it became a bureau in 1940. A commissioner oversees the primary responsibilities of the Bureau of the Public Debt including the management of the public debt, issuing U.S. securities, and managing receipts and expenditures. The department's Savings Bond Division was authorized in 1945 as successor to a number of World War II agencies. The division promotes and directs the sale and holding of U.S. savings bonds and notes.

The U.S. Secret Service was created in 1865 to halt counterfeiting operations. It continues to pursue this goal, but its more well-known function is executive protection, which it assumed after the assassination of President William McKinley in 1901. *(See "Protecting the President: The Secret Service," p. 1003 in Chapter 24.)*

Established in March 1970, the Federal Law Enforcement Training Center, located in Georgia, is an interagency training facility serving more than seventy federal law enforcement organizations, including the Secret Service, Customs, and Bureau of Alcohol, Tobacco and Firearms, as well as the Federal Bureau of Investigation and other non-Treasury agencies.

The Office of Thrift Supervision was created in 1989 as part of the Financial Institutions Reform, Recovery, and Enforcement Act, popularly known as the thrift bailout law. The office is responsible for supervising all of the approximately 2,000 state- and federally chartered savings and loans. The office is funded through fees and assessments on the thrift institutions it regulates.

Department of Veterans Affairs

Following the English precedent, the American colonies as early as 1636 enacted laws providing that returning disabled soldiers should be "maintained competently" by the colonies for the rest of their lives.[89] The Continental Congress, in an effort to encourage enlistment during the American Revolution, continued that policy, and, in fact, benefits were paid to veterans of the Revolutionary War and their dependents until 1911.

In the meantime, Congress in 1789 passed a pension law that initially was administered by Congress and was subsequently transferred in 1818 to the secretary of war. In 1849 the Office of Pensions was moved from the War Department to the newly created Interior Department. During the Civil War, Congress authorized benefits for federal volunteers on the same basis as those already provided for the regular army. In his second inaugural address in March 1865, President Abraham Lincoln called on Congress and the American people "to care for him who shall have borne the battle and for his widow, and his orphan." (The phrase subsequently became the VA's motto.)

Early veterans legislation emphasized pensions, with direct medical and hospital care provided by states and localities. It was not until 1811 that Congress authorized the first medical facility for veterans, the U.S. Naval Home in Philadelphia, as a "permanent asylum for disabled and decrepit Navy officers, seamen and Marines." During the nineteenth century, other homes were established—among them the U.S. Soldiers Home—to provide care for the indigent and disabled veterans of the Civil War, Indian wars, Spanish-American War, and Mexican War, and the discharged regular members of the armed forces. An honorable discharge from military service was one of the requirements for admission.

Congress greatly expanded veterans benefits after the United States entered World War I in 1917, establishing disability compensation, insurance for service personnel and veterans, a family allotment program for service personnel, and vocational rehabilitation for the disabled. With the exception of the last of these programs, all were administered by the Bureau of War Risk Insurance, which had been created in 1914. At the same time, another agency, the Public Health Service, also provided medical and hospital care.

CONSOLIDATION OF VETERANS' PROGRAMS

The division of responsibilities for veterans among various departments and agencies proved unwieldy. Responding to the recommendations of a presidential study commission to consolidate functions in a single agency, Congress in 1921 established the United States Veterans' Bureau. Nonetheless, two other agencies also continued to administer veterans benefits: the Bureau of Pensions in the Interior Department and the National Homes for Disabled Volunteer Soldiers.

In 1930 Congress authorized the president further to "consolidate and coordinate government activities affecting war veterans." The three existing agencies became bureaus within the new Veterans Administration (VA). Brig. Gen. Frank T. Hines, then head of the Veterans' Bureau, was named the first administrator of veterans affairs, a post he held until 1945.[90] Given its wide-ranging responsibilities, the new agency had a relatively small staff of 31,600.

The VA served about 4.7 million veterans during its first year; by the end of World War II, their numbers had swelled to almost 19 million. To deal with this challenge, VA facilities were substantially enlarged, and significant new programs, such as those created by the GI bill (signed into law June 22, 1944), were established. Other new programs and legislation included vocational rehabilitation legislation (1943, expanded in 1980), establishment of a VA Department of Medicine and Surgery (1946), the Korean Conflict GI Bill (1952), creation of the Department of Veterans Benefits (1953), a new GI bill for veterans with service between 1955 and 1977 (1966), and a Veterans Educational Assistance Program for post–Vietnam-era veterans.

ESTABLISHING THE DEPARTMENT

Bills to elevate the Veterans Administration to cabinet-level status had been introduced in at least seventeen successive Congresses without success. Nonetheless, only a week after President Reagan announced his support for a cabinet-level VA, the House of Representatives on November 17, 1987, overwhelmingly passed its version of implementing legislation, and the Senate followed suit in July 1988. The action came despite a nonpartisan, congressionally mandated report that found "little evidence" such a move would improve government services for veterans. The report, by the National Academy of Public Administration (NAPA), concluded that "there is no compelling reason why the VA . . . should be elevated to cabinet status." The report said the creation of a cabinet-level department would not "significantly improve access to the president, affect the adequacy of necessary resources or improve the organization, management and delivery of high-quality services and benefits." Furthermore, the report pointed out that an enlarged cabinet tended to "reduce its value to the president" and added that VA elevation could strengthen the argument for upgrading other federal agencies, such as the Social Security Administration. But NAPA stopped short of recommending against a Department of Veterans Affairs.

Proponents of placing the VA in the cabinet pointed out that the work of the agency reached far beyond the 27.4 million U.S. veterans. The VA also served millions of dependents and survivors of veterans. Altogether, they amounted to about one-third of the nation's population. Giving the agency a seat at the cabinet table would enhance its access to the president and improve its ability to defend itself during budget decisions, supporters maintained. They argued that giving the VA cabinet status would also allow better coordination of policy with other departments. Opponents of the legislation pointed out, however, that Reagan could have had his VA chiefs attend cabinet sessions

through executive order and without legislative action, as had his Democratic predecessor, Jimmy Carter.

Legislation establishing the VA as the Department of Veterans Affairs (it retained the acronym VA) was signed into law by President Reagan on October 25, 1988. Perhaps somewhat ironically, Reagan had stated as a presidential candidate that he would view his election "as a mandate to reduce the size of government. . . ."[91] He also had advocated abolishing the Departments of Education and Energy, both of which were still in place at the end of his tenure.

The VA Department came into being on March 15, 1989, making it the fourteenth executive department and the fifth to be created since 1953. President George Bush named Edward J. Derwinski, a twelve-term member of the House of Representatives, to the post of secretary.

DEPARTMENT'S EARLY YEARS

Under Derwinski, funding for veterans' health care rose $1 billion each year through 1992, despite the threat of budget cuts. Derwinski, a former Republican representative from Illinois, was also successful in implementing a program to compensate Vietnam War veterans suffering from illnesses resulting from their exposure to the chemical defoliant Agent Orange. His support for the compensation program was well received by veterans groups, whose claims of the link between Agent Orange and certain forms of cancer had been dismissed by the Reagan administration, other federal agencies, and some members of Congress.

Overall, however, Derwinski's tenure was marked by a series of run-ins with various veterans organizations, including one over his agreement to a request from administration POW-MIA negotiators to give Vietnam $250,000 in obsolete VA medical equipment to encourage cooperation in resolving the lingering issue of missing U.S. servicemen in that country. In 1991 Derwinski and HHS secretary Louis W. Sullivan proposed that VA hospitals in some poor rural communities accept nonveteran patients who had no other access to local health care. The proposal was part of Derwinski's plan to expand funding sources for VA health care by bringing in Medicare dollars. Veterans opposed the plan, arguing that empty beds in VA hospitals were a result of restrictive eligibility requirements for veterans, and Derwinski later dropped the plan.

Later that year he further angered veterans when he announced that VA hospitals would no longer sell tobacco products and issued a directive requiring VA health facilities to be smoke-free by the end of 1993. Members of Congress joined veterans in opposing Derwinski, and the smoking ban was reversed by a provision inserted in an omnibus veterans health bill in 1992. Derwinski's controversial decisions were seen as threatening veteran support for the Bush reelection campaign, and he resigned in September 1992. Deputy VA Secretary Anthony J. Principi served as acting secretary for the remainder of Bush's term.

President Bill Clinton's choice for secretary, Jesse Brown, was warmly received by veterans advocacy groups. Brown, a Vietnam War veteran who had received the Purple Heart, had worked for twenty-five years at the 1.3 million member nonprofit group, Disabled American Veterans, where he had last served as executive director. Departmental affairs did not loom large in the Clinton agenda, but Brown carefully guarded VA interests in the administration's evolving health care reform package. Although the reform effort eventually failed, Brown had ensured that veterans would have expanded access to VA hospitals if those hospitals were opened up to nonveterans.

In other departmental matters, Brown, arguing that current law prohibited him from compensating veterans disabled by an undiagnosed condition, gained special authorization to pay benefits to veterans suffering from "Persian Gulf syndrome," a catchall for a variety of conditions with no known cause affecting personnel who served in the Gulf War. Brown had more difficulty initiating a program to expand health care for women veterans, who numbered 1.2 million in 1993. Opponents of a 1994 measure that would have provided comprehensive care for female veterans argued that authorizing pregnancy-related and pre- and postnatal services could be interpreted to allow the VA to perform abortions. After repeated attempts at compromise failed, most of the women's health provisions were abandoned.

ORGANIZATION AND FUNCTIONS

The secretary of veterans affairs is assisted by a deputy secretary. Reporting directly to the secretary are the inspector general, general counsel, veterans service organization liaison, office of small and disadvantaged business utilization, and the boards of veterans' and contract appeals. Six assistant secretaries provide policy guidance and managerial support in the following areas: finance and information resources management, policy and planning, human resources and administration, public and intergovernmental affairs, acquisitions and facilities, and congressional affairs.

Before the establishment of the cabinet-level department, the VA's programs were administered by three separate departments—Medicine and Surgery, Veterans Benefits, and Memorial Affairs—which varied greatly in number of employees and budget. These departments were continued essentially unchanged under the new VA.

The Veterans Health Administration, formerly the Department of Medicine and Surgery, is the nation's largest government-funded health care system. The undersecretary for health is responsible for the operation of VA facilities nationwide and also administers programs to support treatment of veterans and their dependents by non–VA institutions and physicians. Although most of the agency's resources go to the health care delivery system, some funding is channeled to related activities, such as medical and prosthetic research.

The undersecretary for benefits administers the Department of Veterans Benefits (formerly the Veterans Benefits Administration), which covers all nonmedical benefits to veterans and their

families. Most of its funding is allocated for pension and compensation benefits, including monthly payments for surviving spouses and dependents of military personnel who died as a result of injuries connected to active duty service. Permanently disabled veterans and those older than sixty-five also qualify for pensions, which may go to their families after they die. The department also administers the VA education, vocational rehabilitation, home-loan guaranty, and insurance programs.

The Veterans Assistance Service provides assistance and advice to veterans and their families concerning benefits legislated by Congress for veterans of active duty army, naval, air services, the Public Health Service, the National Oceanic and Atmospheric Administration, and the World War II Merchant Marine. It also cooperates with state and local agencies to develop veteran employment opportunities and referral systems for resolving veterans' socioeconomic, housing, and other problems. And it provides field investigative services for other VA components.

The National Cemetery System (NCS) replaced the Department of Memorial Affairs. It is headed by a director who oversees the operations of 147 national cemeteries. Qualified military personnel, veterans, their spouses, and certain children are eligible for burial and a headstone in any national cemetery where space is available. Next of kin also can receive burial, plot, and marker allowances for internment of a veteran in a private cemetery. NCS, which is supported by three area offices, also administers the State Cemetery Grants Program, which provides financial assistance to states for establishing and improving state veterans cemeteries.

NOTES

1. See Richard F. Fenno Jr., *The President's Cabinet* (New York: Vintage, 1959), 12.

2. Alexander Hamilton, John Jay, and James Madison, *The Federalist*, intro. by Edward Gaylord Bourne (New York: Tudor, 1937), ii, 57.

3. James Thomas Flexner, *Washington: The Indispensable Man* (Boston: Little, Brown, 1974), 220.

4. R. Gordon Hoxie, "Cabinet," in *Encyclopedia of American Political History: Studies of the Principal Movements and Ideas*, 3 vols., ed. Jack P. Greene (New York: Scribner's, 1984), 1:149.

5. Flexner, *Washington: The Indispensable Man*, 326.

6. Hoxie, "Cabinet," 152.

7. Quoted in Emmet John Hughes, *The Living Presidency: The Resources and Dilemmas of the American Presidential Office* (Baltimore: Penguin, 1973), 147.

8. Hoxie, "Cabinet," 156.

9. Quoted in Fenno, *The President's Cabinet*, 123.

10. Quoted in ibid., 125.

11. Hoxie, "Cabinet," 158–159.

12. Quoted in Thomas E. Cronin, *The State of the Presidency*, 2d ed. (Boston: Little, Brown, 1980), 263.

13. Stephen Hess, *Organizing the Presidency* (Washington, D.C.: Brookings, 1976), 46.

14. Cronin, *The State of the Presidency*, 271.

15. Arthur M. Schlesinger Jr., *A Thousand Days* (New York: Fawcett, 1967), 632.

16. Hess, *Organizing the Presidency*, 84.

17. George Reedy, *The Twilight of the Presidency* (New York: New American Library, 1970), 74.

18. Quoted in Cronin, *The State of the Presidency*, 266.

19. Excerpted from a radio address of September 19, 1968, in Robert Hirschfield, ed., *Power of the Modern Presidency*, 2d ed. (Chicago: Aldine, 1973), 165–166.

20. *New York Times*, May 7, 1970, C18.

21. Hoxie, "Cabinet," 161.

22. Quoted in Edward D. Feigenbaum, "Staffing, Organization, and Decision-Making in the Ford and Carter White Houses," *Presidential Studies Quarterly* 10 (summer 1980): 371.

23. George C. Edwards III and Stephen J. Wayne, *Presidential Leadership* (New York: St. Martin's Press, 1985), 173.

24. John P. Burke, *The Institutional Presidency* (Baltimore: Johns Hopkins Press, 1992), 164.

25. Quoted in Robert J. Sickels, *Presidential Transactions* (Englewood Cliffs, N.J.: Prentice-Hall, 1974), 31.

26. Harold J. Laski, *The American Presidency: An Interpretation* (New York: Harper, 1940), 257–258.

27. Bradley H. Patterson Jr., *The President's Cabinet: Issues and Questions* (Washington, D.C.: American Society for Public Administration, 1976), 113.

28. Richard M. Pious, *The American Presidency* (New York: Basic Books, 1979), 241.

29. Arthur M. Schlesinger Jr., "Presidential War," *New York Times Magazine*, January 7, 1973, 28.

30. Hess, *Organizing the Presidency*, 180.

31. Godfrey Hodgson, *All Things to All Men: The False Promise of the Modern American Presidency* (New York: Simon and Schuster, 1980), 109–112.

32. Frank Kessler, *The Dilemmas of Presidential Leadership: Of Caretakers and Kings* (Englewood Cliffs, N.J.: Prentice-Hall, 1982), 92.

33. Cronin, *The State of the Presidency*, 276–293.

34. Ibid., 278.

35. Quoted in ibid., 280.

36. Ibid., 282.

37. Ibid., 283.

38. Richard P. Nathan, *The Plot That Failed* (New York: Wiley, 1975), 40.

39. Hugh Heclo, *A Government of Strangers* (Washington, D.C.: Brookings, 1977), 196.

40. Pious, *The American Presidency*, 238.

41. Charles O. Jones, *The Presidency in a Separated System* (Washington, D.C.: Brookings, 1994), 63.

42. Quoted in Kessler, *The Dilemmas of Presidential Leadership*, 93.

43. Quoted in Cronin, *The State of the Presidency*, 283.

44. Walter J. Hickel, *Who Owns America?* (Englewood Cliffs, N.J.: Prentice-Hall, 1971), 259.

45. Kessler, *The Dilemmas of Presidential Leadership*, 106.

46. Hess, *Organizing the Presidency*, 154.

47. Benjamin V. Cohen, "Presidential Responsibility and American Democracy," Royer Lecture, University of California, Berkeley, May 23, 1974; quoted in Cronin, *The State of the Presidency*, 361–362.

48. Roger Porter, *Presidential Decision Making* (Cambridge, England: Cambridge University Press, 1980).

49. James D. King and James W. Riddlesperger Jr., "Presidential Cabinet Appointments: The Partisan Factor," *Presidential Studies Quarterly* 14 (spring 1984): 231.

50. Pious, *The American Presidency*, 936.

51. Nelson W. Polsby, "Presidential Cabinet Making: Lessons for the Political System," *Political Science Quarterly* 93 (spring 1978): 19–20.

52. "The Club," *Time*, February 8, 1993, 18.

53. G. Calvin Mackenzie, *The Politics of Presidential Appointments* (New York: Free Press, 1981), 9.

54. John W. Macy, Bruce Adams, and J. Jackson Walter, *America's Unelected Government: Appointing the President's Team* (Cambridge, Mass.: Ballinger, 1983), 76–82.

55. Stephen L. Carter, *The Confirmation Mess: Cleaning Up the Federal Appointments Process* (New York: Basic Books, 1994), 7.

56. David T. Stanley, Dean E. Mann, and Jameson W. Doig, *Men Who Govern: A Biographical Profile of Federal Executives* (Washington, D.C.: Brookings, 1967).

57. Linda Fisher, "Fifty Years of Presidential Appointments," in *The In-and-Outers: Presidential Appointees and Transient Government in Washington*, ed. G. Calvin Mackenzie (Baltimore: Johns Hopkins University Press, 1987), 28.

58. Ibid.

59. Hess, *Organizing the Presidency*, 28.

60. Ibid., 30.

61. Mackenzie, *The Politics of Presidential Appointments*, 12.

62. Harry S. Truman, *1945, Year of Decisions* (New York: Signet, 1955), 364.

63. Dwight D. Eisenhower, *Mandate for Change* (New York: Signet, 1963), 137.

64. Hess, *Organizing the Presidency*, 62.

65. Mackenzie, *The Politics of Presidential Appointments*, 22.

66. Hess, *Organizing the Presidency*, 82.

67. David Halberstam, *The Best and the Brightest* (New York: Random House, 1972), 434.

68. Mackenzie, *The Politics of Presidential Appointments*, 39.

69. Ibid., 41.

70. Schlesinger, "Presidential War," 28.

71. Mackenzie, *The Politics of Presidential Appointments*, 45.

72. Quoted in Dom Bonafede, "Cabinet Comment," *National Journal*, vol. 8 (December 11, 1976), 1784.

73. Mackenzie, *The Politics of Presidential Appointments*, 64.

74. R. Gordon Hoxie, "Staffing the Ford and Carter Presidencies," *Presidential Studies Quarterly* 10 (spring 1984): 393.

75. Macy, Adams, and Walter, *America's Unelected Government*, 40.

76. Ross K. Baker, "Outlook for the Reagan Administration," in *The Election of 1980: Reports and Interpretations*, ed. Gerald Pomper (Chatham, N.J.: Chatham House, 1981), 164.

77. Burt Solomon, "Bush Promised Fresh Faces . . . But He's Hiring Old Friends," *National Journal*, January 21, 1989, 142.

78. James P. Pfiffner, "Establishing the Bush Presidency," *Public Administration Review*, January/February 1990, 69.

79. Quoted in Jeffrey H. Birnbaum and Michael K. Frisby, "Clinton's Slow Start Picking a Team and Policies Dooms His Hope of Hitting the Ground Running," *The Wall Street Journal*, January 13, 1993, A16.

80. Richard A. Stubbing, with Richard A. Mendel, *The Defense Game* (New York: Harper and Row, 1986), 259–260.

81. *Washington Post*, October 7, 1978.

82. John G. Kester, "Thoughtless JCS Change Is Worse Than None," *Armed Forces Journal International* (November 1984): 113.

83. Richard Harris, *Justice: The Crisis of Law, Order, and Freedom in America* (New York: Dutton, 1970), 33–34.

84. Ibid., 161.

85. Jonathan Grossman, "The Origin of the Department of Labor," *Monthly Labor Review*, March 1973.

86. Quoted in Janet Hook, "Brock Selected to Replace Donovan at Labor," *Congressional Quarterly Weekly Report*, March 23, 1985, 549.

87. Martin Mayer, *The Diplomats* (New York: Doubleday, 1983), 211.

88. Ibid., 240.

89. From *VA History in Brief* (Washington, D.C.: Government Printing Office, 1986).

90. Like the earlier Veterans' Bureau, the Veterans Administration originally used the apostrophe (Veterans' Administration), but the apostrophe eventually was dropped from the name.

91. Quoted in *Congressional Quarterly Weekly Report*, October 19, 1988, A-21.

SELECTED BIBLIOGRAPHY

Baker, Ross K. "Outlook for the Reagan Administration." In *The Election of 1980: Reports and Interpretations,* ed. Gerald Pomper. Chatham, N.J.: Chatham House, 1981.

Bonafede, Dom. "Cabinet Comment." *National Journal* 8 (December 11, 1976), 1784.

Burke, John P. *The Institutional Presidency.* Baltimore: Johns Hopkins University Press, 1992.

Campbell, Colin, and Bert A. Rockman, eds. *The Bush Presidency: First Appraisals.* Chatham, N.J.: Chatham House, 1991.

Carter, Stephen L. *The Confirmation Mess: Cleaning Up the Federal Appointments Process.* New York, N.Y.: Basic Books, 1994.

Congressional Quarterly Almanac. Washington, D.C.: Congressional Quarterly, annual.

Cronin, Thomas E. *The State of the Presidency.* 2d ed. Boston: Little, Brown, 1980.

Edwards, George C., III, and Stephen J. Wayne. *Presidential Leadership.* 3d ed. New York: St. Martin's, 1994.

Eisenhower, Dwight D. *Mandate for Change.* New York: Signet, 1963.

Federal Regulatory Directory. 7th ed. Washington, D.C.: Congressional Quarterly, 1994.

Feigenbaum, Edward D. "Staffing, Organization, and Decision-Making in the Ford and Carter White Houses." *Presidential Studies Quarterly* 10 (summer 1980): 364–377.

Fenno, Richard F., Jr. *The President's Cabinet.* New York: Vintage, 1959.

Fisher, Linda. "Fifty Years of Presidential Appointments." In *The In-and-Outers: Presidential Appointees and Transient Government in Washington,* ed. G. Calvin Mackenzie. Baltimore: Johns Hopkins University Press, 1987.

Flexner, James Thomas. *Washington: The Indispensable Man.* Boston: Little, Brown, 1974.

Halberstam, David. *The Best and the Brightest.* New York: Random House, 1972.

Hamilton, Alexander, John Jay, and James Madison. *The Federalist.* Intro. by Edward Gaylord Bourne. New York: Tudor, 1937.

Heclo, Hugh. *A Government of Strangers.* Washington, D.C.: Brookings, 1977.

Hess, Stephen. *Organizing the Presidency.* Rev. ed. Washington, D.C.: Brookings, 1988.

Hickel, Walter J. *Who Owns America?* Englewood Cliffs, N.J.: Prentice-Hall, 1971.

Hirschfield, Robert, ed. *Power of the Presidency.* 3d ed. Chicago: Aldine, 1982.

Hodgson, Godfrey. *All Things to All Men: The False Promise of the Modern American Presidency.* Rev. ed. New York: Penguin, 1984.

Hoxie, R. Gordon. "Cabinet." In *Encyclopedia of American Political History: Studies of the Principal Movements and Ideas,* Vol. 1, ed. Jack P. Greene. New York: Scribner's, 1984.

———. "Staffing the Ford and Carter Presidencies." *Presidential Studies Quarterly* 10 (spring 1980): 378–401.

Hughes, Emmet John. *The Living Presidency: The Resources and Dilemmas of the American Presidential Office.* Baltimore: Penguin, 1973.

Jones, Charles O. *The Presidency in a Separated System.* Washington, D.C.: Brookings, 1994.

Kessler, Frank. *The Dilemmas of Presidential Leadership: Of Caretakers and Kings.* Englewood Cliffs, N.J.: Prentice-Hall, 1982.

King, James D., and James W. Riddlesperger Jr. "Presidential Cabinet Appointments: The Partisan Factor." *Presidential Studies Quarterly* 14 (spring 1984): 231–237.

Laski, Harold J. *The American Presidency: An Interpretation.* New York: Harper, 1940.

Mackenzie, G. Calvin. *The Politics of Presidential Appointments.* New York: The Free Press, 1981.

Macy, John W., Bruce Adams, and J. Jackson Walter. *America's Unelected Government: Appointing the President's Team.* Cambridge, Mass.: Ballinger, 1983.

Nathan, Richard P. *The Plot That Failed.* New York: Wiley, 1975.

Patterson, Bradley H., Jr. *The President's Cabinet: Issues and Questions.* Washington, D.C.: American Society for Public Administration, 1976.

Pfiffner, James P. "Establishing the Bush Presidency." *Public Administration Review,* January/February 1990: 64–73.

Pious, Richard M. *The American Presidency.* New York: Basic Books, 1979.

Polsby, Nelson W. "Presidential Cabinet Making: Lessons for the Political System." *Political Science Quarterly* 93 (spring 1978): 16–24.

Porter, Roger. *Presidential Decision Making.* Cambridge, England: Cambridge University Press, 1980.

Reedy, George. *The Twilight of the Presidency.* Rev. ed. New York: New American Library, 1987.

Rovner, Julie. "On Policy Front, Home Is Not Where Bush's Heart Is," *Congressional Quarterly Weekly Report,* Feb. 2, 1992, 292.

Schlesinger, Arthur M., Jr. *A Thousand Days.* New York: Fawcett, 1971.

———. "Presidential War." *New York Times Magazine.* January 7, 1973, 28.

Sickels, Robert J. *Presidential Transactions.* Englewood Cliffs, N.J.: Prentice-Hall, 1974.

Stanley, David T., Dean E. Mann, and Jameson W. Doig. *Men Who Govern: A Biographical Profile of Federal Executives.* Washington, D.C.: Brookings, 1967.

Thomas, Norman C., and Joseph A. Pika, eds. *The Politics of the Presidency.* 4th ed. Washington, D.C.: CQ Press, 1996.

Truman, Harry S. *1945, Year of Decisions.* New York: Signet, 1955.

Vig, Norman J., and Michael E. Kraft, eds. *Environmental Policy in the 1990s.* 2d ed. Washington, D.C.: CQ Press, 1994.

CHAPTER 30

Government Agencies and Corporations

BY W. CRAIG BLEDSOE AND LESLIE RIGBY

I N ADDITION to the fourteen cabinet departments, the executive branch includes several other kinds of agencies. Some of these agencies are independent of any cabinet department, whereas others are part of the cabinet hierarchy but have the power to operate largely as separate entities. No matter what kind of organizational relationship these agencies have to the rest of the executive branch, however, the president has direct legal responsibility for them and often exerts considerable control over them.

These independent and semi-independent agencies have different objectives, powers, methods of determining their members, and organizations. Any similarity is derived from their existence largely outside the traditional lines of authority of the executive departments. Their independent or semi-independent status results from either the desire of Congress to remove their operations from the control of the cabinet hierarchy or presidential attempts to show concern for specific problems that could best be solved in an environment lacking political pressure. These agencies can be divided into three general categories: regulatory agencies, independent executive agencies, and government corporations.

Regulatory Agencies

Regulatory agencies and commissions regulate various aspects of the economy and, more recently, consumer affairs. The commerce clause of the Constitution (Article I, section 8) gives the federal government the legal authority "to regulate Commerce with foreign Nations, and among the several States. . . ." Although there is no universally accepted definition, in 1977 the Senate Government Operations Committee (subsequently renamed the Governmental Affairs Committee) defined a federal regulatory agency as "one which (1) has decision-making authority, (2) establishes standards or guidelines conferring benefits and imposing restrictions on business conduct, (3) operates principally in the sphere of domestic business activity, (4) has its head and/or members appointed by the president . . . and (5) has its legal procedures generally governed by the Administrative Procedure Act."[1]

Regulatory agencies are organizationally either independent of the cabinet hierarchy or part of an existing executive department. Independent regulatory agencies are governed by bipartisan commissions of five or more members. These commissioners usually serve lengthy, fixed terms, and they cannot be re-

moved by the president. Among the major independent regulatory agencies are the Federal Reserve Board (FRB), National Labor Relations Board (NLRB), Federal Communications Commission (FCC), Federal Trade Commission (FTC), and Securities and Exchange Commission (SEC).

Semi-independent regulatory agencies—agencies within an executive branch department—serve under the authority of the department in which they are located. The individuals who head these agencies are subject not only to presidential appointment but also to presidential dismissal. Presidents may appoint and dismiss these agency heads either personally or through their department secretaries. Regulatory agencies within executive branch departments include the Food and Drug Administration (FDA), located in the Department of Health and Human Services, and the Occupational Safety and Health Administration (OSHA), located in the Department of Labor.

Although independent regulatory agencies oversee a wide variety of activities, they share certain jurisdictional and organizational characteristics. Sometimes called quasi-agencies because they are legally empowered to perform quasi-legislative, quasi-executive, and quasi-judicial functions, they can issue rules that govern certain sectors of the economy, oversee implementation of those rules, and adjudicate disputes over interpretation of the rules.

In creating these organizations Congress has attempted to protect their independence. For example, commissioners, who are appointed by the president and confirmed by the Senate, serve overlapping fixed terms, usually of four-to-seven years. Even though they are political appointees, presidents cannot simply fire them. In a further attempt to ensure political independence from the president, Congress made these commissions bipartisan and placed limits on the number of appointees from any single political party. Generally, neither political party may have a majority of more than one. This organizational design makes these agencies and commissions independent of other executive organizations and places responsibility for the execution of their policies with the commissioners rather than the president.

Presidents, however, have at times attempted to bring various regulatory agencies under their authority by removing commissioners who have proven uncooperative. The courts have generally upheld the independence of commissioners from executive control. In 1935 the Supreme Court ruled that President Franklin D. Roosevelt had acted unconstitutionally when he fired a member of the FTC. In that case, *Humphrey's Executor v. United States,* the Court held that presidents cannot remove regulatory commission members for ruling in ways that might displease the president or members of Congress.

Presumably, appointees to regulatory commissions should be not only experts in the policy area they have been chosen to oversee but also objective parties who would not unfairly favor one side over another in a policy dispute. In practice, however, regulatory agencies tend to develop reciprocal relationships with the interests they are supposed to regulate. Political scientist Samuel Huntington has suggested that regulatory agencies inevitably are "captured" by the interest groups they are supposed to be regulating.[2] Thus, the FDA would look out for the interests of drug manufacturers, and the Nuclear Regulatory Commission (NRC) for the interests of the nuclear industry.

Some regulatory agencies seem to go through a life cycle. Regulatory agency scholar Marver H. Bernstein has argued that agencies are most aggressive when they are new. Over the years, however, they gradually lose their stamina and become captives of the interests they are supposed to regulate, or they become dormant. As public attention moves from the initial problem that prompted the regulation, the regulatory agency, out of public scrutiny, might become free to operate as it wishes.[3] Even if a regulatory life cycle exists, however, some agencies have been spurred on to new action by the public. In the 1950s and 1960s, for example, the FDA became much more aggressive about drug testing after the public expressed concern about unsafe drugs.

Whereas the original regulatory activity of the federal government was primarily economic regulation, modern agencies undertake regulation that goes beyond the traditional economic spheres, moving more and more into the area of social concerns. Although these social concerns usually are related to economic activities, their scope is different in that they touch upon issues that are of importance to individual consumers. For this reason regulatory activity can be divided into economic regulation and social regulation.

ECONOMIC REGULATION

In 1887 the federal government undertook its first major regulation of a private sector of the economy when Congress, exercising its constitutional right to regulate interstate commerce, created the Interstate Commerce Commission. According to political scientist Robert E. Cushman, "The Interstate Commerce Commission was an innovation not because it was endowed with a new type of power, but because it represented a new location of power in the federal system."[4]

Ironically, Congress initially did not intend to make the Interstate Commerce Commission independent of the control of the president. During congressional debate on creation of the ICC, matters of independence and presidential control were never considered. Congress first placed the ICC in the Interior Department, which subjected its budget, staff, and internal management to control by an executive department. Two years later, Congress gave the ICC control over its own affairs.

It was several years after achieving independence from Interior that the ICC gained any real measure of power. Initially, the ICC lacked the power to do anything more than issue cease-and-desist orders to stop railroads from violating provisions of the Interstate Commerce Act of 1887. It had neither the authority to set or adjust railroad shipping rates nor any coercive power to enforce its rulings. Moreover, in the early years the courts closely reviewed ICC orders, often substituting their own judgments favoring the railroads for those of the commission. The railroads quickly learned that they could circumvent the ICC by appealing judgments to the courts.

Gradually the ICC became powerful. In 1906 Congress passed the Hepburn Act, which gave the commission the authority to adjust rates that the ICC deemed unreasonable or unfair. And in 1910, with passage of the Mann-Elkins Act, Congress strengthened the commission's enforcement ability by authorizing it to suspend and investigate new rate proposals and to set original rates.

Abandoning the idea that the ICC might be able to handle the regulation of all commerce, Congress created a network of new regulatory agencies patterned after the ICC. In 1913 the Federal Reserve System began to regulate banking and the supply of money. The following year saw creation of the Federal Trade Commission to regulate business practices and control monopolistic behavior. Between 1915 and 1933, the beginning of Franklin Roosevelt's administration, Congress set up seven other regulatory agencies, including the Tariff Commission (1916), Commodities Exchange Authority (1922), Customs Service (1927), and Federal Power Commission (1930).

After the onset of the Great Depression and beginning with Roosevelt's "New Deal," an extraordinary flood of regulatory programs passed Congress. Between 1932 and 1938 eight major regulatory agencies were set up to handle problems created by the economic crisis of the depression. These included several agencies that have become mainstays in the American way of life. For example, the Federal Deposit Insurance Corporation (FDIC), created by the Banking Act of 1933, continues six decades later to regulate state-chartered, insured banks that are not members of the Federal Reserve System and to provide federally guaranteed insurance for bank deposits. The Securities and Exchange Commission, founded in 1934 to protect the public against fraud and deception in securities and financial markets, carries out the same mandate today. Finally, the Wagner Act of 1935 created the National Labor Relations Board, which continues to prevent "unfair labor practices" and to protect the right of collective bargaining.

SOCIAL REGULATION

The New Deal was the true beginning of large-scale federal regulation of the economy, but it also provided the foundation for the many social regulatory agencies that arose in the 1960s and 1970s. As New Deal programs expanded the scope of the federal government, the American people came to accept the federal government's role in solving the nation's economic and social problems. By the mid-1960s the federal government was providing medical care, educational aid, nutritional help, urban renewal, and job training, among other services. And by the mid-1970s social activism had grown to such an extent that many consumer and environmental groups were calling for a new wave of regulation intended to achieve certain social goals such as clean air and consumer protection. These social regulatory agencies can be thought of as divided into four areas of concern: consumer protection, environmental protection, workplace safety, and energy regulation.[5]

By the early 1970s the consumer movement had begun to have a significant impact on American life. Consumers were vocal in demanding protection against false advertising and faulty products. Organized groups pressed for safer and better products and lower prices for food, fuel, and medical care. Earlier, in 1965, Ralph Nader had almost single-handedly launched consumerism as a political movement with the publication of his book *Unsafe at Any Speed*, which attacked the automobile industry's poor safety record. Through Nader's efforts and those of other consumer advocates interested in automobile safety, the National Highway Traffic Safety Administration (NHTSA) was created within the Department of Transportation in 1970. With its authority to set automobile safety and fuel efficiency standards, the agency represents one of the early efforts at consumer legislation. In contrast to the semi-independent NHTSA, the Consumer Product Safety Commission (CPSC) was created as a wholly independent consumer protection agency. With passage of the Consumer Product Safety Act in 1972, Congress gave the commission the task of protecting consumers against unreasonable risks of injury from hazardous products.

Advocates of a cleaner environment were also part of the consumer movement; the creation of the Environmental Protection Agency (EPA) in 1970 stemmed directly from their efforts. Set up as an independent executive agency, EPA was charged with supervising and protecting the nation's environment, including its air, water, and land, and with reducing noise pollution. EPA has become one of the most controversial of all federal agencies, largely because of its wide-ranging responsibilities and the costs of the programs that it implements to clean up the environment.

Workplace safety was another concern of the consumer movement. Consumers wanted to minimize hazards in the workplace by establishing guidelines for improving safety and health on the job. The Occupational Safety and Health Administration, established as an agency within the Labor Department in 1970, was charged with promulgating and enforcing worker safety and health standards. It is authorized to conduct unannounced on-site inspections and to require employers to keep detailed records on worker injuries and illnesses. OSHA thus has considerable regulatory power that it can wield in carrying out its quasi-legislative, quasi-executive, and quasi-judicial functions.

In the 1970s the United States was confronted with the dual problems of a dwindling energy supply and rising costs of energy. In an attempt to insulate consumers from growing energy problems, Congress created a number of agencies. In 1973 it established the Federal Energy Administration (FEA) to alleviate short-term fuel shortages, and in 1974 it created the Energy Research and Development Administration (ERDA) to develop nuclear power and new energy sources. Also in 1974 Congress created the Nuclear Regulatory Commission to regulate nuclear safety. All of these agencies, except the NRC, were abolished in 1977 when their functions were moved to the newly created Department of Energy.

METHODS OF REGULATION

Regulatory agencies use a variety of techniques to carry out their mandates. The range of methods that each agency uses may be limited by the legislation that created the agency in the first place. For example, Congress may find an issue of such importance that it tells the agency exactly how to regulate the area of concern. For issues of lesser importance, Congress may give the agency a free hand to use whatever regulatory methods it believes appropriate.

One of the most common methods of regulation is to require disclosure of information. For example, the Food and Drug Administration requires manufacturers of a variety of food products to list their products' ingredients and nutritional value. The agency often requires manufacturers to place labels on their products warning consumers of the risks attached to product use. Health warnings on cigarette packages is one of the best-known examples.

The most extreme form of regulation is mandatory licensing—that is, certain professionals and businesses must obtain licenses to practice their trade, to take certain actions, or own certain goods. In most cases, failure to obtain the license results in civil or criminal action. Licenses usually are required when the consumer is unable to determine the qualifications of the individuals offering their services. Various federal agencies and commissions license such diverse businesses as radio and television stations (by the Federal Communications Commission) and nuclear power plants (by the Nuclear Regulatory Commission). Licensing requires a massive amount of paperwork and intrusive oversight, but for successful applicants it provides some economic benefit in that it allows them to practice their trade or provide their service while protecting their interests by keeping the unqualified out.

When information about certain products cannot be provided conveniently to consumers, or when the potential harm of a product is very high, agencies often will set standards with which companies must comply. Failure to maintain the standards could result in legal penalties. Agencies can impose two kinds of standards. Performance standards require simply that minimum goals be met, but no guidelines are given on the method or methods to be used. Thus, EPA could require a specific city to meet minimum air pollution standards without reference to how that city achieves those standards. Specification standards, in contrast, spell out exactly how certain requirements are to be met. EPA would tell a city exactly what kind of equipment to use to reduce pollution.

Standards are only as effective as the agency's ability to enforce them. One method of enforcing regulatory rules or standards is taxation—historically a tool of regulation. Higher taxes often are imposed on companies or persons who refuse to comply with voluntary rules. The tariffs placed on imported goods to protect American manufacturers were early examples of a regulatory tax.

Some agencies have the power to recall consumer products that could harm their users. *Consumer Reports* estimates that between 1973 and 1980 the Consumer Product Safety Commission recalled more than 120 million items in more than twenty-six hundred separate actions—about eighty recalls a week. From the time automobile recalls began in 1966 to 1980 more than 86 million automobiles, trucks, vans, and other vehicles were recalled. Recalls do not always result, however, in effective regulation. Whether the product is corrected is usually left up to the consumer.

Independent Executive Agencies

Independent executive agencies are similar to independent regulatory agencies in that they are not part of a cabinet department. But they are normally considered to be part of the presidential hierarchy and report to the president. The most important of these agencies are the National Aeronautics and Space Administration (NASA) and the General Services Administration (GSA).

Many of these agencies were created in an effort to overcome bureaucratic inertia, which often resulted in the failure of existing departments to accomplish their objectives. In 1964, for example, the Johnson administration created the Office of Economic Opportunity (OEO) to help implement its "Great Society" programs. By locating OEO in the Executive Office of the President and not in a specific department, the White House was able to exert more control over its operation and ensure that the administration's antipoverty objectives were carried out. Similarly, NASA was located outside the control of a specific department to help expedite its formation and operation, free from the traditional demands of departmental control. In addition, it was set up apart from the Defense Department to ensure that the U.S. space program would be controlled by civilians rather than the military.

Often agencies are made independent in response to vested interests. Members of Congress and interest groups want to guarantee that these agencies are responsive to their wishes. In addition, presidents and Congress often want these agencies free from the traditional constraints and methods of old-line departments. For example, in an effort to challenge directly actions detrimental to the environment, Congress made the EPA independent of old-line departments that might have had traditional environmental interests.

Since they have some degree of autonomy from hierarchical executive control, independent executive agencies can maneuver more openly than departmental agencies in ways that will maximize their objectives. This kind of freedom, however, often means that independent agencies will have few allies in the executive branch, possibly diminishing their overall influence on the formulation of executive policy. Some agencies—the Civil Rights Commission (CRC), for example—have been successful at developing coalitions with groups not traditionally represented by executive departments. The CRC, established in 1957 as a bipartisan, six-member independent agency, used its autonomous organizational status to become a constructive critic of federal civil rights policies. Between 1959 and 1970, by forging coalitions outside the executive branch, the commission was able to get more than two-thirds of its recommendations either enacted into law or included in executive orders.

Executive independence can result, however, in overlapping jurisdictions and conflicts between the independent agencies and other executive organizations. Until it was replaced by the Office of Personnel Management in 1978, the Civil Service Commission's independence made it an easy target for groups seeking to influence particular aspects of federal personnel policy. An interviewee cited in a Brookings Institution report noted the divided loyalties of the commission: "Well, we think it [the CSC] works first for its congressional committees, second for the status of employees, third for the American Legion in support of veterans' preference laws, fourth for the civil service employees' unions, and possibly fifth for the President."[6] The attempt to remove politics from the federal personnel selection process resulted in just the opposite; politics became a primary factor in determining federal job selection.

Government Corporations

A third type of agency, which operates either independently or semi-independently of the regular departmental structure, is the government corporation. Even though investors in them cannot buy stock and collect dividends, these organizations operate much like a private corporation that sells a service. Government corporations usually provide a service that the private sector has found too expensive or unprofitable to offer.

Three of the best-known government corporations are the Tennessee Valley Authority (TVA), created in 1933 to develop electric power and navigation in the Tennessee Valley region; the National Railroad Passenger Corporation, or Amtrak, the nation's passenger train service; and the U.S. Postal Service. Several successful government corporations have been based on the TVA model, including Comsat, which sells time-sharing on NASA satellites.

The Postal Service became a government corporation only in 1970. Originally created in 1775 by the Continental Congress with Benjamin Franklin as its postmaster general, this longtime cabinet department assumed its corporate status during the administration of Richard Nixon. In urging reorganization of the Postal Service, Nixon argued that it would operate more effi-

In 1780, three years after its founding, the postal service had thirty-two employees. In 1994 the United States Postal Service employed 692,000 and handled 171 billion pieces of mail.

ciently if freed from the direct control of the president and Congress and the resulting bipartisan pressure.

By incorporating these organizations Congress has given them greater latitude in their day-to-day operations than that given to other agencies. As corporations, federal agencies can acquire, develop, and sell real estate and other kinds of property, acting in the name of the corporation rather than the federal government. They have the power as well to bring lawsuits on behalf of the corporation, and they can be sued. Also like private corporations, these agencies are headed by a board of directors or board of commissioners. Some corporations such as the Postal Service have a single head who is assisted by a board. Corporation heads and members are appointed by the president and confirmed by the Senate. They serve long, staggered terms to prevent any one president from controlling the corporation.

Government corporations are not dependent on annual appropriations, as are the other executive departments and agencies. Their earnings may be retained by the corporation and deposited back into their operations. Consequently, they are less subject to financial control by the president or Congress, and they are free of the annual process of defending their estimates for the fiscal year before the Office of Management and Budget (OMB), the president, and Congress. Even so, their operations are reviewed annually by all three, using a review process that tends to be less demanding than that applied to the departments and other agencies, since they are not requesting appropriations. Because some government corporations have difficulty operating in the black, Congress is committed to providing long-term appropriations for their operations.

Government corporations also are free to raise some of their own financing. The Postal Service not only uses revenues that it generates from its own activities, but it is also empowered to borrow money by issuing bonds.

Compared to their modern counterparts, the original government corporations, such as the Federal Savings and Loan Insurance Corporation, founded in 1934, had more independence, as well as much more fiscal freedom, to realize their goals. Almost unheard of until the New Deal, government corporations became particularly important during World War II as a means of accomplishing specific tasks such as developing raw materials. The Rubber Development Corporation, Petroleum Reserves Corporation, and other war-era government corporations operated almost identically to private corporations. Initially, Congress gave them start-up funding, which they sustained through their revenues.

In 1945, however, Congress passed the Government Corporation Control Act, which sought to make these agencies more accountable to the president and Congress. While preserving some of the previous independence of government corporations, the act set limits on their autonomy. The act provided that Congress must first authorize the corporate form of organization, specifying what the corporation may and may not do; that Congress may modify the authority or responsibilities of the corporation, or even dissolve it; and that Congress, if it chooses, may withhold working capital.

Sometimes the federal government takes over an ailing corporation in an effort to insure its survival. Amtrak, the nation's railway service, is a prime example. Although Amtrak is a losing proposition in terms of its multibillion-dollar federal subsidy, Congress decided that the survival of passenger train service in the United States is in the public interest.

Styles and Methods of Appointment

The heads and commissioners of almost all independent and semi-independent agencies are selected according to Article II, section 2, of the Constitution, which states that the president "shall nominate, and by and with the advice and consent of the Senate, shall appoint Ambassadors, other public Ministers and Consuls, Judges of the Supreme Court and all other Officers of the United States. . . ." The Founders decided, however, to permit the president or heads of the departments to appoint such "inferior officers" as they thought proper. Once the Senate has confirmed a nominee, it may not reconsider the nomination.

The president has the power to remove for any reason the heads of agencies within the executive branch, but independent agency heads and commissioners usually may be removed only for inefficiency, neglect of duty, or misconduct. Even though removal is rare, it occasionally occurs. In 1975 President Nixon set about to remove the chairman of the Civil Aeronautics Board, Robert D. Trimm, for "incompetence." Trimm resigned out of respect for the office of the president. If he had chosen to fight his removal, however, the Nixon administration would have had to submit proof of Trimm's incompetence.

Although the Constitution does not specify qualifications for agency heads and commissioners, Congress has required statutorily that appointees to certain agencies meet certain criteria. For example, the act creating the Federal Reserve Board requires its members to be a fair representation of financial, agricultural, industrial, commercial, and geographical interests. Similarly, appointees to the Federal Aviation Administration must be not only qualified administrators but also civilians with aviation experience.

One of the requirements for most agencies, especially regulatory, is that neither political party have more than a one-person majority of commissioners. Ironically, then, administrations pay more attention to nominees from the opposition party than from their own. According to executive branch scholar William E. Brigman, "By careful scrutiny every administration has managed to find members of the opposition party, or registered independents, who are supportive of administration goals."[7] By choosing members of the opposition party who agree with their views, presidents are able to bypass the intent of bipartisanship. Richard Nixon, for example, once attempted to nominate the Tennessee leader of "Democrats for Nixon" to a Democratic slot on a commission. When the Democratic-controlled Senate refused to confirm the nominee, Nixon successfully appointed him as an independent. Although bipartisan representation may exist in terms of numbers, rarely does a true minority party view exist in an agency or commission.

Because presidents are authorized to name the heads of most agencies and commissions, they usually take this opportunity to appoint someone from their own party. If they name one of the sitting commissioners as the new commission head, the retiring chair does not have to leave the commission until his or her term of appointment has expired. Many, however, decide to leave anyway. The terms of most heads of agencies and commissions are fixed. For example, the chair of the Federal Reserve Board serves a four-year term.

SELECTION AND NOMINATION

Appointees to independent agencies and regulatory commissions represent a significant percentage of all major executive appointments made by the president. Thus, selecting these personnel is one of the president's most important jobs.[8]

As for most presidential appointments, the president relies heavily on others—such as advisers or a formal personnel office—to help search for, screen, and recommend potential appointees. Presidents are presented then with several choices, and they often make the final decision themselves; however, this may mean simply affirming the selection of their advisers.

Few presidents have played active roles in the process of selecting and nominating appointees to independent agencies and regulatory commissions, but President Gerald R. Ford paid attention to almost every such appointment. Yet even Ford did not meet with the nominees. That privilege was reserved for individuals he was nominating as chairs.

Even though presidents invest very little time in the appointment of commissioners, their selection is one of the most important sources of influence that presidents have over independent agencies and regulatory commissions. Despite the organizational independence of these agencies, every administration has sought some measure of influence over them. Wielding influence appears to be a simple matter of appointing ideologically compatible partisans, but factors other than political philosophy must be considered. Moreover, measuring partisan purity and loyalty in potential nominees is difficult.

Traditionally, most presidents have viewed agency seats as important political rewards and have instructed their advisers to use them as such. Agency vacancies thus have become an important way to pay political debts as well as to influence policy.

Few people are nominated who are not politically acceptable to the White House. Although a potential appointee's educational background, geographical origin, and party loyalty are all important, political connections may be the most important presidential consideration. Congressional sponsorship has also been particularly useful to appointees. In a study of thirty-eight appointments to four regulatory agencies over a fifteen-year period, the Senate Governmental Affairs Committee found that congressional sponsorship most often determined selection of the nominee.[9] And very few administrations do not first consult with members of Congress and special-interest groups to obtain some type of informal clearance for the nominee.

Whether regulatory commissioners should come from the industries that they are supposed to regulate is one of the more controversial questions confronting the appointment process. The most logical place to turn for experts on the industry to be controlled is that industry itself. But appointing someone who has such an association leaves the commissioner open to a conflict-of-interest charge. Most presidents, however, at least check with representatives of the industry to be regulated.

Yet there are often pressures in the other direction as well. Because presidents want to avoid confirmation fights, they usually have their aides consult with key public-interest groups. According to presidential appointments scholar G. Calvin Mackenzie,

The appointment of regulatory commissioners . . . rarely aroused much interest or controversy before 1970. But the growing political prominence of a number of self-declared public interest groups sharply increased the conflict engendered by these appointments in the decade that followed. . . . The likely effect . . . is that the president's freedom of choice will be circumscribed.[10]

PRESIDENTIAL USE OF APPOINTMENTS

Recent presidents have looked upon the appointment of a strong and loyal agency or commission chair as the most effective method for influencing agency policies. Consequently, presidents pay close attention to the selection of commission chairs. With the exception of the Federal Communications Commission, which has resisted attempts at consolidating power within its chair, there are very few collegial decisions within the agencies and commissions. Chairs have power over budgets and personnel, and they have more information than the other commissioners. They therefore wield substantial powers in the direction and control of their agencies. Brigman wrote:

Realizing that a strong chairman can accomplish the administration's goals without explicit intervention, thereby preserving the fiction of regulatory independence, the White House pays much more attention to the selection of chairmen than it does to ordinary commissioners.[11]

The desire of presidents to control a regulatory commission often stems from their philosophy of both regulation and the role of government in general. By appointing agency heads and commissioners who share their philosophical views, presidents are best able to leave their imprint on the government. Regulation itself represents the expanding role of government in an individual's life. The differing philosophies toward regulation of Presidents Jimmy Carter, Ronald Reagan, George Bush, and Bill Clinton were reflected in their appointments to the regulatory commissions and agencies.

Even though President Carter indicated an interest in reducing regulation through several of his appointments to executive branch and regulatory posts, he still appointed a significant number of "activists" to head agencies concerned with consumer protection and health and safety standards. For example, he appointed Michael Pertschuk, who had been instrumental in developing the Consumer Product Safety Commission, as chairman of the Federal Trade Commission. Pertschuk pushed the FTC into an activist position on the issues of television advertising directed at children and automobile advertisements that promoted more driving during periods of gas shortages. Carter also named Joan Claybrook, former director of Ralph Nader's public-interest group Congress Watch, as director of the National Highway Traffic Safety Administration. During her tenure, NHTSA proposed the mandatory installation of airbags in automobiles. In addition, Carter appointed to CPSC some of its most activist commissioners.

President Reagan, in contrast, made extensive use of the appointment process to promote his policy of reducing the role of the federal government. Many of Reagan's appointees to regulatory agencies and independent agencies and commissions shared his hostility to most governmental regulations and con-

trols. By appointing Thorne Auchter to head the Occupational Safety and Health Administration, Reagan instilled in OSHA a philosophy sympathetic to businesses that complained of high regulatory costs. Reagan's appointment of Raymond Peck as NHTSA's administrator created in that agency a philosophy favorable to looser regulation of the automobile industry, reversing the support for mandatory airbags NHTSA expressed during the Carter administration. And his appointment of S. R. Shad, a vice president of E. F. Hutton and Company, to head the Securities and Exchange Commission narrowed the SEC's view of its role in regulating the marketing of new securities. The SEC's independent and aggressive staff traditionally had sought tough enforcement of disclosure requirements and antifraud provisions.

Bush administration appointments sent mixed signals about the role of regulation. In his campaign rhetoric Bush promised to maintain the antiregulatory policies of his predecessor. As president, however, Bush showed no predisposition to appoint ideologues who would pursue confrontational politics in the regulatory process. Presidential scholar Bert A. Rockman characterized Bush's appointees as "firefighters rather than flamethrowers."[12] In fact in the first three years, the Bush administration pursued more active regulatory policies than the Reagan administration had. For example, Bush appointed William Reilly, a career conservationist, as head of the EPA. Although Reilly frequently found himself in conflict with Bush's chief of staff, John Sununu, an antienvironmentalist, he was able to persuade the president to support the Clean Air Act of 1990, which imposed stricter regulations on power plant emissions and chemical plants.

Later in his administration, as the economy grew weaker, Bush moved away from his earlier support of regulatory policies and gave free rein to the Competitiveness Council, a group of cabinet level officials headed by Vice President Dan Quayle and dedicated to deregulation. The Competitiveness Council attacked regulatory programs on the basis of the costs they imposed on businesses. Proactive regulators, such as Reilly, often found themselves in conflict with the goals and policies of the Competitiveness Council.

President Clinton, on the other hand, pursued an overtly activist regulatory policy through his appointment of proactive regulatory commissioners. At the EPA, Clinton appointed Carol Browner, an environmental activist and the former director of the Florida Department of Environmental Regulation. Early in the administration, Browner moved to expedite the cleanup of toxic waste sites through expansion of the government's Superfund program. Clinton also appointed Antoinette Cook to head the FCC. As senior staff counsel to the Senate Commerce Committee before her appointment to the FCC, Cook was largely responsible for writing the tough legislation that reregulated cable television rates and passed Congress in 1992 over President Bush's veto. Cook's appointment brought a decidedly activist view to the regulatory policy of the FCC.

Administrative Conference of the United States

The Administrative Conference of the United States is a permanent, independent federal agency that recommends improvements in the administration of regulatory, benefit, and other government programs. Established by the Administrative Conference Act of 1964, the Administrative Conference is headed by a chair who is appointed to a five-year term by the president, with Senate confirmation. A council, which acts as an executive board, consists of the chair and ten other members appointed by the president for three-year terms. In addition to the council, the membership of the conference is composed of fifty-five federal government officials and forty-five private lawyers, university faculty members, and other experts in administrative law and government who serve two-year terms. Members representing the private sector are appointed by the chair, with council approval.

The Administrative Conference provides a forum for agency officials, private lawyers, university professors, and other experts to study procedural problems and to develop improvements. The entire membership meets at least once each year. Membership is divided into six standing committees: adjudication, administration, governmental processes, judicial review, regulation, and rule making. The committees study subjects selected by either the chair, the council, or the assembly. The assembly has authority to approve, reject, or amend any recommendations presented by the committees. Although the final recommendations of the Administrative Conference are nonbinding, the chair is authorized to encourage departments and agencies to adopt the proposed changes.

African Development Foundation

The African Development Foundation (ADF) is an independent public corporation created by Congress to provide development assistance to indigenous nongovernmental African groups and individuals. Congress authorized ADF in 1980 as a complement to U.S. foreign aid programs; its aim is to deliver economic assistance directly to African communities and grassroots organizations. Aid is awarded primarily for farming, education, husbandry, manufacturing, and water management projects. In the legislation that created ADF, Congress required that the corporation's beneficiaries design and implement their own projects. In 1994 grants ranged in size from under $10,000 to $250,000 and were awarded to 112 development and research projects in 31 African countries. The foundation is governed by a seven-member board of directors appointed by the president with Senate confirmation. Board members serve staggered terms ranging from two to six years. By law five members are chosen from the private sector and two from the government.

The goal of ADF is to make local communities responsible for their own development through programs appropriate for their needs and to give priority to objectives established by the community. ADF also seeks to demonstrate the value of local or traditional methods, so as to avoid social and economic disruption caused by the introduction of new equipment or production systems.

Because its purpose is to provide grassroots assistance, ADF requires that a basic level of community organization be in place at the time a request is made. In addition, a proposed project must involve the community at large, and the community must understand and accept the responsibilities of implementing the project and paying its recurring costs. Communities requesting ADF aid also must demonstrate the skill and capacity to manage project funds effectively.

In addition to funding grassroots development activities, ADF supports applied research conceived and executed by Africans. ADF's field staff includes African regional liaison officers (RLOs) who serve as liaisons between ADF and applicants in each of ADF's five African regions. RLOs provide technical support, assist ADF in monitoring projects, and provide information about funding procedures. Country resource facilitators provide the same support in those countries in which they are resident.

American Battle Monuments Commission

The American Battle Monuments Commission (ABMC) is responsible for commemorating the services of American armed forces where they have served since the United States entered into World War I on April 6, 1917. A small independent agency, ABMC oversees the design, construction, operation, and maintenance of permanent U.S. military burial grounds in foreign countries. ABMC also controls the design and construction of U.S. military monuments and markers in foreign countries by U.S. citizens and organizations both public and private.

Created by Congress in 1923, ABMC administers, operates, and maintains twenty-four permanent U.S. military burial grounds, twenty-one separate monuments, and three markers in twelve countries worldwide. The policy-making body of the commission comprises eleven members who are appointed by the president for an indefinite term and serve without pay. The board members, who elect a chair and vice chair from among their number, serve at the pleasure of the president. New appointments can immediately be made by an incoming president. A professional staff of full-time civilian employees consists of U.S. citizens and foreign nationals from countries where ABMC installations are located. Field offices in Paris, Rome, and Tunisia supervise operations in Europe, North Africa, and the Mediterranean. The superintendents of the cemeteries in Mexico City, Corozal, Panama, and Manila report directly to the Washington office.

The commission provides assistance in locating grave and memorial sites and general information on travel and accommodations for visitors. For immediate family traveling overseas specifically to visit a grave or memorial site, the commission provides letters authorizing "nonfee" passports and other services at the grave site.

Appalachian Regional Commission

The Appalachian Regional Commission (ARC) administers a comprehensive program for the economic development of the Appalachian region. Created by the Appalachian Regional Development Act of 1965, the commission consists of fourteen members, including the thirteen sitting governors of states within the Appalachian region and a federal chair, appointed by the president and subject to Senate confirmation. A cochair also is appointed. The federal cochair serves at the pleasure of the president. Members' terms run concurrently with their terms as governor.

The Appalachian region, as defined by the Appalachian Regional Development Act as amended, includes all of West Virginia and parts of New York, Pennsylvania, Maryland, Virginia, Ohio, Kentucky, Tennessee, North Carolina, South Carolina, Georgia, Alabama, and Mississippi. It incorporates 397 counties, covers 195,000 square miles, and has a population of more than twenty million. In fiscal year 1995 Congress appropriated $282 million for commissions programs and administrative costs.

Federal efforts to revitalize the economy of the Appalachian region had been considered as early as 1902. The region had been poor and underdeveloped even though it is rich in resources. By 1964 per capita income in many areas of the region was less than half the national average, and education levels in the region were far below the national average.

Central Intelligence Agency

The Central Intelligence Agency (CIA) is an independent agency established by the National Security Act of 1947 to coordinate the nation's intelligence activities and to correlate, evaluate, and disseminate intelligence that affects national security. The CIA is responsible for the production of political, military, economic, biographical, sociological, and scientific and technical intelligence to meet the needs of national policy makers.

The CIA is headed by a director and a deputy director who are appointed to an indefinite term by the president with Senate confirmation and serve at the discretion of the president. The director of central intelligence (DCI), in addition to heading the CIA, heads the intelligence community and is the primary adviser to the president and the National Security Council on national foreign intelligence matters. The director of the CIA is not a cabinet-level position, but presidents by executive order may elevate to cabinet status anyone they wish. William Casey, who was appointed CIA director by President Ronald Reagan, was designated as a cabinet officer.

In addition to the DCI's office staff, the intelligence community consists of the CIA, the National Security Agency, the Defense Intelligence Agency, the offices within the Department of Defense responsible for collection of specialized national for-

The Central Intelligence Agency was founded in 1947 to collect and analyze foreign intelligence. The agency has no police, subpoena, or law enforcement powers or internal security functions.

eign intelligence, the Bureau of Intelligence and Research of the Department of State, and the intelligence elements of the military services, the Federal Bureau of Investigation, and the Departments of Treasury and Energy.

In 1949 the National Security Act of 1947 was amended by the Central Intelligence Agency Act. The legislation permits the CIA to use confidential fiscal and administrative procedures, and it exempts the agency from certain limitations on expenditure of federal funds. The act allows CIA funds to be included in the budgets of other agencies and then transferred to the CIA without regard to the restrictions placed on the initial appropriation. The amount of CIA funds held by other agencies is classified. The 1949 act also exempted the CIA from having to disclose its organization, functions, number of personnel, and the names, titles, and salaries of its employees.

The CIA conducts covert activities abroad in support of U.S. foreign policy objectives. These actions are executed so that the role of the U.S. government is not apparent or acknowledged publicly. Only the president can authorize covert actions, upon the recommendation of the National Security Council. When initiating a covert action, the DCI must notify the intelligence oversight committees of Congress.

The agency has no law enforcement or security functions either at home or abroad. The CIA is expressly prohibited by executive order from routinely engaging in the domestic use of electronic, mail, or physical surveillance, monitoring devices, or physical searches. These restrictions can be lifted only under the most extraordinary conditions of concern for the national security and only with the approval of the U.S. attorney general.

Oversight of the CIA is conducted by the Intelligence Oversight Board. The board consists of three members appointed by the president from the public sector. Board members serve indefinite terms at the discretion of the president. The chair of the board is also a member of the president's Foreign Intelligence Advisory Board. In 1995 President Bill Clinton signed a classified executive order establishing a committee of senior White House, Defense, and State Department officials to coordinate and review intelligence operations. The move was seen as an effort to ensure that the users of intelligence information had a role in deciding what type of information would be gathered and also to limit the CIA's freedom to set its priorities and measure its own performance without interagency coordination.

Commission of Fine Arts

The Commission of Fine Arts was established by Congress in 1910 to advise the government on matters pertaining to the arts and the architectural development of Washington, D.C. The commission, comprising seven members including a director who are appointed by the president to four-year terms, initially was authorized to advise on statues, fountains, and monuments within the District of Columbia. Subsequent executive orders and acts of Congress greatly expanded the commission's duties to include the preservation of places of national interest and approval of architectural designs of government buildings.

The commission also reviews plans for private structures within the District and advises on building height limits and architectural standards in the Old Georgetown and Shipstead-Luce areas. Land to be acquired as parkland in the District of Columbia, Maryland, and Virginia also falls under commission responsibility.

The commission's members advise on matters of art and architectural development when requested to do so by the president or by a member of Congress. Contracting officers of the federal and district governments also are directed to call for the commission's advice on such matters. Among the more significant areas, monuments, and buildings reviewed by the commission have been the Mall, the Lincoln Memorial, the Federal Triangle, the National Gallery of Art, and the Vietnam Veterans Memorial. The commission is not required by law to be bipartisan, and members serve at the pleasure of the president.

Commission on Civil Rights

Established by the Civil Rights Act of 1957, the Commission on Civil Rights is an independent fact-finding agency that monitors developments in civil rights under the Constitution. The Civil Rights Act of 1983 increased the commission's membership from six to eight commissioners, four of whom are appointed by the president and four by Congress. Not more than four members may be of the same party. With the approval of a majority of the commission, the president designates a chair and a vice chair from among its members. An incoming president can appoint a new chair.

Commissioners serve either six- or three-year terms and can be removed by the president only for neglect of duty or malfeasance in office. A full-time staff director oversees the day-to-day activities of the commission.

The commission assesses the laws and policies of the federal government to determine the nature and extent of denial of equal protection under the law on the basis of race, color, religion, sex, national origin, age, or disability, and it submits reports to the president and to Congress. Areas of study include employment, voting rights, education, and housing.

In its fact-finding capacity, the commission may hold hearings and issue subpoenas for the production of documents and the attendance of witnesses at such hearings. Subpoenas may be issued in the state in which the hearing is being held and within a fifty-mile radius of the site. The commission maintains advisory committees and consults with representatives of federal, state, and local governments and private organizations. The commission lacks direct enforcement powers but refers complaints to appropriate government agencies for action.

Advisory committees are located in each state and in the District of Columbia. Each committee comprises citizens familiar with local and state civil rights issues. The members serve without compensation and assist the commission with its fact-finding, investigative, and information dissemination functions. Six regional offices coordinate the commission's regional operations and assist the state advisory committees in their activities. Each office is staffed by a director, equal opportunity specialists, researchers, attorneys, and other administrative personnel.

The commission maintains a library that serves as a national clearinghouse for civil rights information and conducts studies of discrimination against certain groups, including women, African Americans, Hispanics, eastern and southern Europeans, and Asian and Pacific island Americans. The commission also issues public service announcements to discourage discrimination and denial of equal protection under the law.

Commodity Futures Trading Commission

The Commodity Futures Trading Commission (CFTC) is an independent regulatory agency established in 1975 to administer the Commodity Exchange Act of 1936. Congressional legislation established the CFTC in 1974 for four years. This mandate was renewed in 1978, 1982, 1986, and 1992.

The purpose of the commission is to ensure that futures markets function smoothly. Oversight regulation is needed to guard against manipulation, abusive trade practices, and fraud. Specific responsibilities of the commission include regulating commodities exchanges, approving futures contracts, registering commodities traders, protecting customers, and monitoring information. The commission has three major operating units: the Divisions of Economic Analysis, Enforcement, and Trading and Markets. The CFTC disseminates information about commodities markets. It publishes weekly commodity reports, *Monthly Commitments of Traders,* and relevant books and pamphlets. It also provides training courses to people in the field. The commission maintains large regional offices in Chicago and New York and smaller offices in Kansas City and Los Angeles.

The CFTC is headed by five commissioners who are appointed by the president with the consent of the Senate. They serve staggered five-year terms, and no more than three commissioners can be of the same political party. The president designates one commissioner as chair. A majority vote by the commissioners is required for major policy decisions and committee actions.

In 1981 the CFTC registered the National Futures Association (NFA) as an industrywide self-regulatory organization. The NFA safeguards the interests of public and commercial users of futures markets by establishing codes of conduct and offering advice. If a dispute arises between customers and sellers, the NFA can provide arbitration. In 1982 Congress passed a law requiring the NFA and the CFTC to share regulatory responsibilities.

Consumer Product Safety Commission

The Consumer Product Safety Commission (CPSC) is an independent regulatory agency established by Congress to protect consumers from unreasonable risks of injury associated with consumer products. Created by the 1972 Consumer Product Safety Act (CPSA), which was passed in response to the consumer movement, the CPSC comprises five commissioners, not more than three of whom may be members of the same political party. Commissioners are appointed to seven-year terms by the president, with Senate confirmation. The president also designates one of the commissioners to serve as chair. The chair and commissioners can be removed by the president for neglect of duty or malfeasance but for no other reason. A newly elected president, however, can appoint a new chair.

In addition to the Consumer Product Safety Act, the CPSC administers the Flammable Fabrics Act, the Federal Hazardous Substances Act, the Poison Prevention Packaging Act of 1970, the Refrigerator Safety Act, the Lead Contamination Act of 1988, and the Child Safety Protection Act. The commission's statutory mandate provides a broad range of regulatory authority over consumer products. In addition to banning unsafe products, CPSC responsibilities include developing uniform safety standards, safety test methods and testing devices, and consumer and industry education programs. Consumer products not regulated by the CPSA include boats, cars, planes, food, drugs, cosmetics, pesticides, medical devices, alcohol, tobacco, and firearms. Standards set by the CPSC preempt any state or local law that establishes lower safety standards; however, states and localities may set stricter standards that produce a greater degree of consumer protection as long as they do not place undue burden on interstate commerce.

Responsibility for correcting potentially hazardous products belongs primarily with manufacturers, who are required to certify that the consumer products they produce meet all applicable safety standards issued under the Consumer Product Safety Act. They must allow the CPSC to test their products for compliance and inspect and investigate their factories. If a manufacturer fails to comply with a standard or certification require-

ment, charges may be brought against the company by the Justice Department in U.S. district court.

Corporation for National Service

The Corporation for National Service is an independent corporation created in 1993 to administer federally sponsored domestic volunteer programs. Two existing agencies, the Commission on National and Community Service and ACTION, were incorporated into the new agency, which was charged with funding and administering all previously authorized programs. The mission of the corporation is to provide disadvantaged people with services, foster civic responsibility, and provide educational opportunities for those who make a substantial commitment to service. Participants of all ages and backgrounds engage in community-based service programs that address the nation's educational, health, public safety, and environmental needs.

A fourteen-member board of directors is appointed by the president and confirmed by the Senate, as is the chief executive officer, who serves as an ex officio member of the board and as the assistant to the president for national service. The president also appoints, subject to Senate confirmation, the director of external affairs, the chief management officer, and the directors of the AmeriCorps/Vista and National Civilian Corps programs.

The centerpiece of the reorganized national service agency is AmeriCorps, a community service program in which participants receive education awards. In 1996 more than 25,000 AmeriCorps members served full- or part-time in more than 400 programs nationwide. Participants in the program work as nurse's aides in hospitals, tutors and mentors for youth, assistants in police departments and conflict resolution efforts, in housing construction, as relief workers in areas hit by natural disasters, and in conservation jobs in parks. They must be seventeen years of age or older and have received a high school or general equivalency diploma. They receive education awards of up to $4,725 each year for no more than two years of full-time or three years of part-time service. Participants must use these awards for higher education or vocational training within five years of completing a term of service. One thousand AmeriCorps members serve in the National Civilian Community Corps, a residential program in which participants are housed in downsized military bases and are dispatched in teams to provide emergency relief services.

Two-thirds of AmeriCorps funds go directly to state commissions on national service. Each state is required to establish a commission on national service in order to receive a federal grant. State commissions are composed of fifteen to twenty-five members appointed by the governor on a bipartisan basis. State commissions also are required to develop national service plans and prepare applications to the corporation for funding. The commissions themselves cannot operate programs, but they can fund state and local agencies that do. Eligible organizations include those run by nonprofit organizations, higher education institutions, school and police districts, local, state, and federal governments, and Native American tribes.

The corporation also oversees several former ACTION programs. The National Senior Service Corps is a network of programs that help senior citizens find service opportunities in their home communities. In the Foster Grandparents Program, low-income volunteers sixty years old and over provide companionship and guidance to mentally, physically, or emotionally disabled children and to those in the juvenile justice system. The Retired and Senior Volunteer Program (RSVP) is the largest program, with 500,000 volunteers serving through more than 65,000 public and nonprofit community agencies. RSVP places retirees age sixty and over with nonprofit organizations and public agencies in need of volunteer services. The Senior Companion Program was established in 1974 under the Domestic Volunteer Service Act. Under the program, low-income persons age sixty or over provide care and companionship to other adults, particularly the homebound elderly.

The goal of Volunteers in Service to America (VISTA) is to alleviate poverty in the United States. Volunteers serve on a full-time basis and work through locally sponsored community projects. VISTA volunteers receive a basic subsistence allowance for housing, food, and incidentals. More than half of VISTA's programs are designed to serve young people.

The corporation also supports service-learning initiatives for K-12 schools and institutions of higher education in its Learn and Serve America program. Grants are awarded to programs that are designed to make service an integral part of the educational experience of students.

Defense Nuclear Facilities Safety Board

The Defense Nuclear Facilities Safety Board is an independent agency established in 1988 to oversee the standards relating to the design, construction, and operation of the nuclear defense facilities of the Department of Energy (DOE). In 1990 the board's jurisdiction was expanded to include facilities and activities involved with the assembly, disassembly, and testing of nuclear weapons. The board is also responsible for investigating any health and safety issues at the facilities. The agency makes recommendations to the secretary of energy but is not under his or her direction. If any aspect of operations, practices, or occurrences at the facilities is determined to present an imminent or severe threat to public health and safety, the board makes its recommendations directly to the president.

The board is composed of five members who are appointed by the president and confirmed by the Senate. Board members are selected from among U.S. citizens who are experts in the field of nuclear safety. The board is supported by a general counsel, general manager, technical manager, and investigative and support staff.

The board has jurisdiction over nine DOE weapons facilities and six DOE material processing and waste management facilities. Since the late 1980s the DOE's nuclear weapons program has been beset by safety, environmental, and management problems, and nearly half of the department's defense program budget goes to clean up nuclear weapons facilities and develop waste management technologies. Since the breakup of the Soviet Union, the DOE has halted the construction of nuclear warheads and, at least temporarily, the periodic testing of nuclear weapons in the United States. Research activities continue at several DOE installations, including the Lawrence Livermore National Laboratory in California, the Los Alamos National Laboratory in New Mexico, the Sandia national laboratories in New Mexico and California, and the Nevada test site. The Mound plant in Ohio, the Kansas City plant, and the Pinellas plant in Florida all manufacture nonnuclear components for nuclear weaponry. Although no nuclear materials are currently being produced, the board also has responsibility for standards at the Oak Ridge Plant in Tennessee, which handles uranium from dismantled nuclear warheads and provides long-term storage of nuclear warheads; the Savannah River site in South Carolina, which acts as a reserve for the possible future production of tritium; and the Pantex plant in Texas, which disassembles warheads. Three other former facilities—at Hanford, Washington, Rocky Flats, Colorado, and the Idaho National Engineering Laboratory—are currently undergoing extensive environmental restoration.

Environmental Protection Agency

The Environmental Protection Agency (EPA) is an independent regulatory agency responsible for implementing the federal laws designed to protect the environment. EPA was created in 1970 through an executive reorganization plan that consolidated components of five executive departments and independent agencies into a single regulatory agency.

The agency is directed by an administrator and a deputy administrator appointed by the president with Senate confirmation. Nine assistant administrators manage specific environmental programs or direct other EPA functions. The agency's general counsel and its inspector general also are named by the president with Senate confirmation. The agency has ten regional administrators across the country. All governing members of EPA are appointed to no fixed term and serve at the pleasure of the president.

EPA administers nine comprehensive environmental protection laws that authorize the agency to protect the public health and welfare from harmful effects of pollutants and toxic substances. The Clean Water Act authorizes EPA to restore and maintain the "chemical, physical, and biological integrity of the Nation's waters." Under the Safe Drinking Water Act of 1974, EPA establishes national standards for drinking water from both surface and ground water sources. The fundamental objective of the Clean Air Act is to protect the public health and welfare from harmful effects of air pollution. Regulation of current and future waste management and disposal practices was authorized by the Resource Conservation and Recovery Act. In 1980 Congress passed the Comprehensive Environmental Response, Compensation, and Liability Act, also called the "Superfund." The Superfund program provides EPA with a trust fund, collected mainly through taxes, and in 1995 allocated about $1.5 billion to clean up hazardous and toxic materials and for emergency response to chemical accidents.

EPA's Office of Pesticide Programs administers two statutes regulating pesticides. The Federal Insecticide, Fungicide, and Rodenticide Act governs the licensing or registration of pesticide residue levels in food or feed crops. The Toxic Substances Control Act authorizes EPA to identify and control chemicals that pose an unreasonable risk to human health or the environment. In addition, EPA administers the Marine Protection, Research, and Sanctuaries Act and the Uranium Mill Tailings Radiation Control Act.

The agency maintains a research office that provides data in six major research areas: engineering and technology; environmental processes and effects; modeling, monitoring systems and quality assurance; health research; health and environmental assessment; and exploratory research. For technical advice and review, EPA relies on its Science Advisory Board, consisting of eminent non-EPA scientists. Congress created the board to advise the agency on scientific issues and to review the quality of EPA scientific research.

Enforcement of EPA regulations is supported by state agencies and the agency's National Enforcement Investigation Center in Denver, Colorado. The agency also maintains a criminal investigation unit with specialized training in criminal law enforcement techniques. The agency enforces its regulations through compliance promotion, administrative monetary penalties, negotiated compliance schedules, and judicial enforcement entailing criminal proceedings.

Efforts to elevate the EPA to cabinet rank began under President George Bush and were continued by President Bill Clinton. Clinton gave his EPA administrator, Carol M. Browner, a seat at the cabinet table by executive order, but congressional debate over EPA's authority and other environmental initiatives continued to stall legislative proposals for the new department through 1995.

Equal Employment Opportunity Commission

The Equal Employment Opportunity Commission (EEOC) is an independent agency established in 1965 to eliminate employment discrimination based on race, color, religion, sex, or national origin. EEOC is composed of five commissioners, not more than three of whom may be of the same political party. The commissioners are appointed by the president and confirmed by the Senate for staggered five-year terms. The president designates one member to serve as chair and another to serve as vice chair. The general counsel also is nominated by the president and confirmed by the Senate for a four-year term. The

Early in the tenure of Carol M. Browner, EPA administrator in the Clinton administration, tensions ran high between environmentalists and proponents of private property rights.

chair is responsible for the administration of the commission. The five-member commission decides equal employment opportunity policy and approves all litigation undertaken by the commission. The general counsel is responsible for conducting all commission litigation. All appointees to the EEOC serve at the pleasure of the president.

The commission was created by Title VII of the Civil Rights Act of 1964. The Equal Employment Opportunity Act of 1972 extended the commission's jurisdiction to include state and local governments, public and private educational institutions, public and private employment agencies, and private businesses that ship or receive goods across state lines and employ fifteen or more persons. EEOC jurisdiction also covers labor unions with fifteen or more members and joint labor-management committees for apprenticeships and training.

The commission has authority to investigate, conciliate, and litigate charges of discrimination in employment. It also has the authority to issue guidelines, rules, and regulations and to require employers, unions, and others covered by Title VII to report regularly the race, ethnic origin, and sex of their employees and members. In cases where a charge of discrimination cannot be conciliated, EEOC has the authority to file a lawsuit in federal district court to force compliance with Title VII.

In addition to administering Title VII, EEOC enforces the Equal Pay Act of 1963, which requires equal pay for equal work, and the Age Discrimination in Employment Act of 1967. In 1978, the Pregnancy Discrimination Act amended the Civil Rights Act of 1964 to prohibit discrimination on the basis of pregnancy, childbirth, or related medical conditions. The 1964 Act was further amended by the Americans with Disabilities Act of 1990, extending the rights under Title VII to disabled Americans, including those with AIDS, and by the Civil Rights Act of 1991, which provided for compensatory and punitive damages for intentional discrimination.

EEOC also administers Executive Order 12067, which requires oversight and coordination of all federal equal employment opportunity regulations, practices, and policies. Executive Order 11478 protects people with disabilities and aged workers from discrimination in federal employment. Responsibility regarding discrimination against the disabled in federal employment was transferred to the commission from the former Civil Service Commission. In 1995 legislation extended Title VII nondiscrimination laws to congressional employees, but the provisions were to be enforced by a legislative office of compliance rather than the EEOC.

Export-Import Bank of the United States

The Export-Import Bank (Eximbank) is an independent, corporate agency that stimulates foreign trade by supporting export financing of U.S. goods and services. Founded in 1934, Eximbank was intended to increase foreign trade during the Great Depression. The agency's first loan, in 1935, financed the Cuban government's purchase of silver from U.S. mines. Eximbank also financed construction of the Burma Road in the late 1930s and the Pan American Highway through Latin America in the 1940s. After World War II, Eximbank helped U.S. companies participate in the reconstruction of Europe and Asia. Eximbank supports U.S. exports by neutralizing the effect of export credit subsidies from other governments and absorbing risks the private sector will not accept.

Eximbank's board of directors consists of five full-time members appointed for four-year terms by the president with Senate confirmation. One member is appointed by the president to serve as chair. All members of the board serve at the discretion of the president. In addition, the secretary of commerce and the U.S. trade representative serve as ex officio, nonvoting members. The board is responsible for Eximbank's activities and policies and approves support for individual transactions.

Eximbank's loans provide competitive fixed-interest-rate financing for U.S. exports facing foreign competition that is backed with subsidized official financing. Evidence of foreign competition is not required for exports produced by small businesses where the loan amount is $2.5 million or less. Eximbank extends direct loans to foreign buyers of U.S. exports and intermediary loans to fund parties that lend to foreign buyers.

The Insurance Group is responsible for Eximbank's export credit insurance programs. The agency's Foreign Credit Insur-

ance Association provides credit insurance policies for nonpayment on export credit transactions that cover political and commercial risks. Political risks include war, cancellation of an existing export or import license, expropriation, confiscation of or intervention in the buyer's business, and transfer risk (failure of foreign government authorities to transfer the foreign currency deposit into dollars). Commercial risks cover nonpayment for reasons other than specified political risks.

Eximbank's policies are coordinated with overall U.S. government foreign and economic policies and are designed not to compete with private financing but to supplement it when adequate funds are not available in the private sector. The bank is authorized to have outstanding dollar loans, guarantees, and insurance in aggregate amounts not to exceed $75 billion at any one time. Eximbank also is authorized to have a capital stock of $1 billion and to borrow up to $6 billion from the Treasury at any one time.

Farm Credit Administration

The Farm Credit Administration (FCA) is an independent financial regulatory agency established in 1933 to oversee the Farm Credit System. FCA was created in response to the need for increased lending to rural farmers unable to obtain credit from bankers headquartered in large U.S. cities.

FCA is administered by a three-member board appointed by the president with Senate confirmation. Members serve six-year terms and are not eligible for reappointment. The president selects one member to serve as chair and chief executive officer. Board members can be removed for neglect of duty or malfeasance but for no other reason. New appointments including the chair can be made immediately by an incoming president. As head of FCA, the board provides for the examination and regulation of and reporting by institutions within the Farm Credit System, a nationwide network of agricultural lending institutions and their service organizations.

The Farm Credit System comprises two types of banks: the farm credit banks and banks for cooperatives. The farm credit banks were created in 1988 through a merger of the earlier federal land banks and the federal intermediate credit banks. In 1916 Congress passed the Federal Farm Loan Act, which divided the country into twelve farm credit districts and created and funded a federal land bank in each of them. The land banks made long-term farm mortgage loans through local federal land bank associations. In 1923 Congress passed the Agricultural Credits Act, establishing and funding twelve federal intermediate credit banks. The banks provided short- and intermediate-term loan funds to production credit associations and other financing institutions serving agricultural producers.

The Farm Credit Act of 1971 established thirteen banks for cooperatives to provide financing for agricultural cooperatives. The banks participate with the district banks on loans that exceed their individual lending capacities. They also participate in international lending activities that benefit U.S. cooperatives. In an effort to improve the financial condition of the FCA following the farm crisis of the 1980s, the Farm Credit Act amendments of 1985 and the Agricultural Credit Act of 1987 restructured the Farm Credit System and authorized voluntary and mandated mergers between its institutions. The reorganized Farm Credit System is composed of eleven farm credit banks and three banks for cooperatives. These banks provide credit to local associations, which extend credit to agricultural producers. The number of lending associations with the system had dropped from 800 in 1984 to 238 in 1994. This drop is attributable in part to the federally mandated merger of many federal land bank associations and production credit associations (PCAs) into agricultural credit associations (ACAs) and the creation of federal land credit associations (FLCAs). Long-term loans are made through ACAs and FLCAs, which have direct lending authority, and FLCAs also provide long-term real estate loans to farmers and ranchers. Short- and intermediate-term loans are made through PCAs and ACAs and also through other financial institutions serving farmers, ranchers, rural homeowners, commercial fishermen, and certain farm-related businesses for production purchases such as fertilizer, seed, and chemicals.

The Farm Credit System raises its loan funds through the Federal Farm Credit Banks Funding Corporation, which sells debt securities on the New York bond market to private investors. The bonds are not government guaranteed, although they are exempt from state and local taxes. In 1987 the Farm Credit System Insurance Corporation Assistance Board was established as an independent government-controlled corporation. Its purpose is to ensure timely payment of principal and interest on insured notes, bonds, and other obligations issued on behalf of Farm Credit System banks. The Federal Agricultural Mortgage Corporation (Farmer Mac), also established in 1987, aids in the development of a secondary market for agricultural real estate mortgages.

In its regulatory capacity, the FCA has a broad range of authority, including the power to issue cease-and-desist orders, levy civil monetary penalties, and remove officers and directors of system institutions. The FCA also is responsible for direct examination of the corporations within the Federal Credit System.

Federal Communications Commission

The Federal Communications Commission (FCC) is an independent regulatory agency charged with regulating interstate and international communications by radio, television, wire, satellite, and cable. Established by the Communications Act of 1934, the FCC assumed regulatory authority previously exercised by the Federal Radio Commission (which was abolished), the secretary of commerce, and the Interstate Commerce Commission. FCC jurisdiction covers the fifty states, the District of Columbia, and the possessions of the United States.

The FCC is composed of five commissioners, not more than three of whom may be members of the same political party. The commissioners are nominated by the president and confirmed by the Senate for staggered five-year terms. The terms are arranged so that no two expire in the same year. The president designates one of the members to serve as chair. The chair can be removed for neglect of duty or malfeasance but for no other reason unless replaced by an incoming president.

The commissioners supervise all FCC activities, delegating responsibilities to staff units, bureaus, and committees. The FCC allocates frequency bands to nongovernment communications services and assigns frequencies to individual stations. The commission also licenses and regulates stations and operators. It regulates the technical aspects and equal employment practices of cable systems and monitors competition in the cable industry.

The FCC does not regulate the broadcast networks or programming practices of individual stations, but it does have rules governing obscenity, slander, and political broadcasts. The FCC has no authority over government communication or other communications media, including movies, newspapers, and books.

Six bureaus, each headed by a chief, conduct FCC regulatory activities. The Mass Media Bureau regulates AM, FM, and television broadcast stations and related facilities. The Cable Services Bureau administers and enforces cable television rules and licenses private microwave radio facilities used by cable systems. The Common Carrier Bureau regulates common carriers of wire and radio communications including telephone, telegraph, and satellite companies. The Wireless Communications Bureau regulates private radio services, primarily two-way communication, such as use of radio by police, fire, and public safety officials, state and local governments, marine and aviation operations, land transportation companies, and amateur (ham) radio operators. It also is responsible for licensing emerging wireless technologies, such as cellular communications. The Compliance and Information Bureau detects violations of radio regulations, monitors transmissions, inspects stations, investigates complaints of radio interference, and issues violation notices. This bureau maintains special enforcement facilities to enforce rules of the Citizens Radio Service (CB) and through its district offices administers examinations for commercial and amateur radio operator licenses. In 1994 a new International Bureau was created out of the Office of International Communications to handle the expansion of international telecommunications. The bureau ensures the coordination of commission international policy activities and represents the commission in international organizations.

The FCC is supported by a general counsel, who advises the commission on legal issues, coordinates its legislative program, and represents the commission in court. A chief of engineering and technology advises the commission on the radio frequency spectrum and the types of equipment using the spectrum and is responsible for research into spectrum propagation and innovation. The chief of plans and policy develops and evaluates long-range plans and policy recommendations and serves as account manager for contract research studies funded by the FCC.

Federal Deposit Insurance Corporation

The Federal Deposit Insurance Corporation (FDIC) is an independent agency that provides insurance to bank depositors and serves as the federal regulator and supervisor of insured state banks that are not members of the Federal Reserve System. The FDIC was established by the Banking Act of 1933 to provide protection against mounting bank failures that followed the stock market crash of October 1929. The corporation insures funds of bank depositors up to $100,000. Separate $100,000 coverage is provided to holders of Keogh Plan Retirement Accounts and Individual Retirement Accounts.

Management of the corporation is carried out by a five-member board of directors, three of whom are appointed by the president with Senate confirmation for six-year terms. One of these appointed directors is designated by the president to be chair. Board members can be removed for neglect of duty or malfeasance but for no other reason, although the president may appoint another director as chair at any time. The comptroller of the currency and the director of the Office of Thrift Supervision also serve on the board of directors. No more than three members of the board may be of the same political party.

Many states require state-chartered banks that are not members of the Federal Reserve System to apply to the FDIC for federal insurance coverage. The FDIC examines banks to determine the adequacy of their capital structure, prospects for future earnings, the general character of each bank's management, and the needs of the community in which each bank is located. National banks and state banks that are members of the Federal Reserve System receive FDIC insurance with their charters and do not require investigation by the corporation.

Since 1990 the FDIC has averaged about five thousand bank examinations and investigations each year. Each examination includes a report that outlines any unacceptable banking practices or violations of law and suggests corrective steps. Usually, the FDIC then attempts to work with the bank management informally by obtaining its approval of a corrective agreement or by privately issuing a proposed notice of charges and a proposed cease-and-desist order. If, after a meeting with the bank and the appropriate state supervisory authority, the bank does not consent to comply with the proposed order, the FDIC will initiate formal proceedings by publicly issuing the notice of charges and holding a hearing before an administrative law judge.

The FDIC also can terminate a bank's insurance if it finds the bank has been conducting its affairs in an unsound and unsafe manner. When insurance is terminated, existing deposits, less subsequent withdrawals, continue to be insured by the FDIC for two years. If a bank becomes insolvent, the FDIC attempts to arrange a deposit assumption, in which another bank takes over many of the assets of the failed bank and assumes both insured and uninsured deposits. If such a transaction cannot be arranged, the FDIC pays off all depositors to the insured maximum limit.

The FDIC receives no annual appropriations from Congress. Funding is raised from assessments on deposits held by insured banks and from interest on the required investment of its surplus funds in government securities. The FDIC can withdraw up to $30 billion from the Treasury to augment its Deposit Insurance Fund, but this option never has been exercised. From 1934 through 1993 a total of 2,056 banks failed, of which 2,038 required disbursements by the FDIC to pay off insured depositors at a cost of $211 billion. Almost all of the depositors in failed FDIC-insured banks have recovered their total deposits.

In January 1996 the FDIC assumed from the defunct Resolution Trust Corporation (RTC) responsibility for managing failed savings and loan associations. The RTC had been established by Congress in 1989 to act as the government conservator or receiver of thrift institutions that had become insolvent.

Federal Election Commission

The Federal Election Commission (FEC) is an independent regulatory agency created in 1975 to administer and enforce the provisions of the Federal Election Campaign Act of 1971 as amended. The commission comprises six members appointed by the president and confirmed by the Senate. The commissioners serve staggered six-year terms, and no more than three commissioners may be members of the same political party. The chair and vice chair must be members of different political parties and are elected annually by their fellow commissioners. The chair can be removed only by impeachment and cannot be replaced by the president until the chair's term expires. From 1975 to 1993 the clerk of the House of Representatives and the secretary of the Senate served as nonvoting members of the commission. In 1993 a federal appeals court ruled that the presence of two congressional employees violated the constitutional separation of the legislative and executive branches. The Supreme Court let stand the appeals court judgment without ruling directly on the separation of powers issue.

The Federal Election Campaign Act of 1971, as amended, requires the disclosure of sources and uses of funds in campaigns for any federal office, limits the size of individual contributions, and provides for partial public financing of presidential elections. The act was amended in 1974, 1976, and 1979 to establish public financing of presidential primary elections, limits on campaign contributions, an independent body (the FEC) to oversee the campaign finance law, and simplified reporting requirements that would apply to all political committees and candidates.

Any candidate for federal office and any political group or committee formed to support a candidate must register with the FEC and file periodic reports on campaign financing. Individuals and committees making expenditures in behalf of a candidate must also file reports.

Contributions from national banks, corporations, labor organizations, government contractors, and nonresident foreign nationals are prohibited. Also prohibited are contributions of cash in excess of $100, contributions from one person given in the name of another, and contributions exceeding legal limits.

FEC staff members review the reports for omissions, and, if any are found, they request additional information from the candidate or committee. If the missing information is not supplied, the FEC has the authority to seek a conciliation agreement, to impose a fine, or to sue for the information in U.S. district court. These procedures also apply to cases in which the FEC discovers a violation of campaign finance law. If any matter involves willful violations, the commission may refer the case to the Justice Department.

The commission also administers provisions of the law covering the public financing of presidential primaries and general elections.

Federal Emergency Management Agency

The Federal Emergency Management Agency (FEMA) is an independent agency responsible for the federal government's civil emergency preparedness, mitigation, and response activities in both peace and war. The director of FEMA is appointed by the president with consent of the Senate and serves at the pleasure of the president.

In 1979 a presidential directive consolidated five federal agencies to form FEMA and transferred closely allied functions from other departments to the new agency. The former federal agencies that make up FEMA are: the Defense Civil Preparedness Agency, the Federal Disaster Assistance Administration, the Federal Preparedness Agency, the Federal Insurance Administration, and the United States Fire Administration. Other programs transferred to FEMA include weather emergency preparedness, Earthquake Hazard Reduction, dam safety coordination, and oversight of the Federal Emergency Broadcast System. In addition, two new functions were added to the agency's responsibilities—coordination of emergency warnings and federal response to consequences of terrorist incidents.

FEMA's Response and Recovery Directorate develops and coordinates federal programs to ensure that government at all levels is able to respond to and recover from national emergencies. Its responsibilities include arrangements for succession to office and emergency organization of federal departments and agencies. The directorate assesses national mobilization capabilities and develops programs for resource management during national and civil emergencies.

The Preparedness, Training, and Exercises Directorate provides funding, technical assistance, supplies, equipment, and training for state and local emergency programs.

The agency administers the President's Disaster Relief Program, which provides supplemental federal assistance when the president declares an emergency or major disaster. Requests for assistance under this program are made by the governor of the affected state and are directed to the president before being sent to the FEMA regional director. FEMA then evaluates the damage and assistance requirements and makes recommendations to the president. Direct disaster assistance can be extended to state and local governments and to individual victims and their families.

FEMA's National Flood Insurance Program provides insurance coverage to participating communities and works with local government officials to reduce future flood damage through floodplain management. FEMA also administers the Federal Crime Insurance Program, which offers protection to home and business owners against financial loss from robbery or burglary, and the National Earthquake Hazards Reduction Program, which develops seismic resistance design codes and construction methods.

The United States Fire Administration seeks through education and research programs to reduce the loss of life and property because of fire. FEMA maintains the National Emergency Training Center in Emmitsburg, Maryland, which conducts education programs for federal, state, and local officials, volunteer groups, and providers of emergency services in hazard mitigation, emergency preparedness, fire prevention and control, disaster response, and long-term disaster recovery. There are ten FEMA regional offices nationwide. Each office is headed by a regional director who reports to the FEMA director and is responsible for all FEMA programs in the region.

Federal Housing Finance Board

The Federal Housing Finance Board (FHFB) is an independent agency that supervises the Federal Home Loan Bank System. FHFB was created in August 1989 by the Financial Institutions Reform, Recovery, and Enforcement Act and assumed some of the responsibilities of the Federal Home Loan Bank Board. The FHFB is governed by a five-member board of directors, four of whom are appointed by the president and confirmed by the Senate. The secretary of housing and urban development serves *ex officio* as the fifth member.

The bank system originated with the Federal Home Loan Bank Act of 1932. The act was a response to the Great Depression, which had undermined the nation's banking system and created a need for a reserve credit system to ensure the availability of funds for home financing. The Federal Home Loan Bank System consists of twelve district banks and is similar to the Federal Reserve System. System banks are mixed-ownership government corporations managed by a board of directors appointed by the FHFB. These banks borrow funds in the capital markets to lend to their members. Members must be primarily home financing institutions that reinvest the funds as home mortgages. Members of the system include commercial banks, insured savings and loans associations, mutual savings banks, credit unions, and insurance companies.

The twelve federal home loan district banks are also required to contribute funds to the Affordable Housing Program, which lends money to banks below market cost to finance purchase and renovation of housing for families with incomes at 80 percent below the median for their community.

The board supervises all activities of the system banks, implements the affordable-housing and other community-oriented mortgage lending advance programs, prescribes rules and conditions upon which a bank will be authorized to borrow, acts on applications for bank membership, and issues consolidated bonds, loans, or debentures, which are the joint and several obligations of all the federal home loan banks.

The FHFB carries out board policy in regulating, monitoring, and supervising the bank system. The agency is self-supporting, and its operating costs are paid from a U.S. Treasury account funded by assessments on the twelve district banks.

Federal Labor Relations Authority

The Federal Labor Relations Authority (FLRA) is an independent agency established to administer Title VII of the Civil Service Reform Act of 1978. The FLRA is chartered to serve as a neutral third party in the resolution of labor-management disputes arising among unions, employees, and federal agencies. The FLRA also is charged with resolution of labor-management disputes among all employees, both U.S. citizens and foreign nationals, of the Panama Canal area.

The chairman of the authority is appointed by the president and serves as the chief executive and administrative officer. The general counsel has direct responsibility for the investigation of alleged unfair labor practices and the filing and prosecuting of complaints. The office of the general counsel also provides training on rights and responsibilities under the Federal Service Labor Relations Statute and facilitates partnership programs between federal agencies and labor organizations.

The Federal Service Impasses Panel is an entity within the FLRA whose function is to assist in resolving negotiation impasses between agencies and unions. If the parties are unable to reach a settlement after assistance from the panel, the panel may hold hearings and take whatever action it deems necessary to resolve the impasse. The panel consists of a chairman and six other members appointed by the president. The panel is not bipartisan by law, and members serve five-year terms. The Foreign Service Labor Relations Board and the Foreign Service Impasse Disputes Panel oversee the labor-management relations statutes for employees of the Foreign Service.

Specifically, the FLRA is empowered to determine the appropriateness of organizations representing federal employees. The authority supervises or conducts elections of labor organizations by employees and sets criteria for representation of national federal labor organizations. The authority also conducts hearings to resolve complaints of unfair labor practices and exceptions to awards granted by federal arbitrators.

Federal Maritime Commission

The Federal Maritime Commission (FMC) is an independent regulatory agency established by executive order in 1961 when the responsibilities of the Federal Maritime Board were divided. FMC assumed jurisdiction as regulator of the ocean commerce of the United States, and responsibility for promoting the nation's merchant marine devolved to the Transportation Department's Maritime Administration.

The FMC has five members who are appointed by the president with Senate confirmation. No more than three of the commissioners may be members of the same political party. The president designates one of the commissioners to serve as chair at the president's discretion. Members serve five-year terms.

The FMC consists of six offices directly responsible to the chair: the offices of the managing director, the secretary, the inspector general, equal employment opportunity, the general counsel, and administrative law judges. Five bureaus report to the director of programs and are responsible for trade monitoring and analysis; tariffs, certification, and licensing; hearings counsel; investigations; and administration.

As required by the Shipping Acts of 1916 and 1984, the commission regulates the rates charged for shipping in domestic commerce, monitors the rates in foreign commerce, and licenses ocean freight forwarders. The commission also regulates the formation by shipping companies of rate-setting cartels (conferences) that would otherwise be in violation of antitrust statutes (the ocean carrier conferences were exempted from antitrust laws by both acts).

Other responsibilities of the FMC include review of rates filed by common carriers and investigation of charges of discriminatory practices in ocean commerce. The commission does not have the authority to approve or disapprove general rate increases or individual commodity rates in U.S. foreign commerce except for certain foreign government-owned carriers. Charges of discriminatory treatment are investigated and resolved by administrative proceedings conducted by FMC staff.

Federal Mediation and Conciliation Service

The Federal Mediation and Conciliation Service (FMCS) is an independent federal agency created to prevent and to minimize labor-management disputes having a significant effect on interstate commerce or national defense. Created by the Labor-Management Relations Act of 1947 (also known as the Taft-Hartley Act), FMCS is headed by a director who is appointed by the president with Senate confirmation. The director serves an indefinite term at the discretion of the president. An incoming president can appoint a new director at any time.

The FMCS's objective is to prevent or minimize work stoppages by providing free mediation of labor-management disputes in both the public and private sectors of the economy. Collective bargaining, mediation, and voluntary arbitration are the processes encouraged by FMCS for settling labor-management issues. FMCS does not mediate labor-management disputes in the railroad and airline industries, which fall under the jurisdiction of the National Mediation Board.

The Labor-Management Relations Act requires parties to notify FMCS thirty days before a contract termination or modification date so that mediation services may be proffered. If, in the opinion of the president, a threatened or actual strike may imperil the national health or safety, a board of inquiry, appointed from an agency list of arbitrators, may be appointed to submit a report on the dispute. After receiving the report, the president can seek to enjoin the strike for not more than eighty days.

FMCS offers various types of technical assistance programs: arbitration, labor management committees, training, preventive mediation, alternative dispute resolution, and conferences and seminars. Labor-management committees are cooperative efforts by disputing parties directed at improving specific work site problems, including safety and health, organization of work quality, productivity, and absenteeism. The committees also address common issues such as worker training and retraining and introduction of new technology. To encourage cooperation among disputing parties FMCS regulations provide that information obtained by mediators in the course of their duties shall not be subsequently revealed in judicial, arbitration, or administrative hearings. The Labor-Management Cooperation Act of 1978 empowered FMCS to provide financial assistance to eligible applicants for the establishment and operation of labor-management committees.

Parties having disputes under collective bargaining agreements fall under the responsibility of the FMCS Division of Arbitration Services. FMCS maintains a roster of qualified private citizens experienced in the collective bargaining process. Upon request, FMCS will furnish a panel of these arbitrators from which the parties select the one most mutually acceptable to hear and provide a final decision on their particular dispute. In most cases a panel of arbitrators is provided only on joint request of the disputing parties. Alternative dispute resolution projects are undertaken to assist other federal agencies by providing mediation and technical assistance to reduce litigation costs and speed federal processes. These projects are funded through interagency agreements.

Federal Mine Safety and Health Review Commission

The Federal Mine Safety and Health Review Commission is an independent, quasi-judicial agency established by the Federal Mine Safety and Health Act of 1977. The commission reviews and decides on contested enforcement actions by the secretary of labor and also adjudicates claims by miners and their representatives concerning their rights under the Mine Safety and Health Act of 1977.

The commission is composed of five members who are appointed by the president and confirmed by the Senate. The chairman is selected by the commission and serves at the pleasure of the president. Other members serve staggered six-year terms.

The Labor Department's Mine Safety and Health Administration sets standards for and conducts inspections of the nation's surface and underground coal, metal, and nonmetal mines. *(See "Department of Labor," p. 1196.)* The Mine Safety and Health Administration has enforcement authority, which includes citation, mine closure orders, and proposals for civil penalties for violations of mandatory health and safety standards. Cases that are contested by mine operators or miners are brought before the commission. The commission also has jurisdiction over allegations of discrimination filed by miners or their representatives in connection with their health and safety rights and over complaints for compensation filed on behalf of miners made jobless through the enforcement of mine closure orders issued by the Mine Safety and Health Administration.

Cases are assigned to the Office of Administrative Law Judges, and hearings are conducted, as far as practicable, at locations convenient to the affected mines. The administrative law judge's decision becomes final (but not precedential) forty days after issuance unless the commission decides to review the case in response to a petition or on its own motion. When a review is conducted, the decision of the commission is final after thirty days unless a party adversely affected seeks review in the U.S. Circuit Court of Appeals in Washington, D.C., or in the circuit in which the mine subject to litigation is located. In 1994 the commission's administrative law judges heard more than 12,000 cases and decided more than 4,000; commission reviews totaled more than 150, of which almost 100 were decided.

Federal Reserve System

The Federal Reserve System (the "Fed") is an independent regulatory and monetary policy-making agency established by the Federal Reserve Act in 1913. The Fed is the nation's central bank and is charged with making and administering policy for the nation's credit and monetary affairs. It also has supervisory and regulatory power over banking in general and over state-chartered banks that are members of the system.

By buying and selling government securities, the Fed influences the supply of credit and the level of interest rates, in turn strongly affecting the pace of economic activity. The Fed also regulates credit activities, collects economic data, and oversees the activities of bank holding companies.

The Fed consists of five major parts: the board of governors, the Federal Open Market Committee, the twelve Federal Reserve banks, the Federal Advisory Council, and the member banks of the system. The Fed is administered by a board of seven governors who are nominated by the president and confirmed by the Senate. Governors are appointed to a single fourteen-year term. One governor is designated by the president to serve as chair for a four-year term and can be reappointed. All appointees serve at the pleasure of the president.

The board's primary function is the formulation of monetary policy. It has authority to change the discount rate, which is the rate the twelve Federal Reserve Banks charge for loans to member banks; to change the amount of reserves that banks in the Federal Reserve System must keep on hand; to set margin requirements for financing of securities traded on national security exchanges; and to set maximum interest rates on time deposits (such as certificates of deposit) and savings deposits of its member banks.

The Federal Open Market Committee is composed of the seven members of the board of governors and five reserve bank presidents, one of whom is the president of the New York reserve bank. The other bank presidents serve on a rotating basis. The committee establishes the extent to which the Fed buys and sells government and other securities. Purchases and sales of securities in the open market are undertaken to supply the credit and money needed for long-term economic growth, to offset cyclical economic swings, and to accommodate seasonal demands of businesses and consumers for money and credit. The committee also oversees the system's operations in foreign exchange markets.

The operations of the Fed are conducted through a nationwide network of twelve Federal Reserve banks and twenty-five branches. Each reserve bank is an incorporated institution with its own board of directors. Under supervision of the board of governors, they determine interest rates the bank may charge on short-term collateral loans to member banks and on any loans extended to nonmember institutions.

The Federal Advisory Council consists of one member from each of the Federal Reserve districts. The council meets in Washington, D.C., at least four times a year. It confers with the board of governors on economic and banking matters and makes recommendations regarding the affairs of the system.

The Fed receives no funding from Congress. Interest paid on government securities purchased by the Fed constitutes about 90 percent of the Fed's earnings. In addition, the Fed earns money from the fees it charges for its services, from interest on its discount window loans, and from its foreign currency operations.

Federal Retirement Thrift Investment Board

The Federal Retirement Thrift Investment Board is an independent agency responsible for establishing policies for the investments, management, and administration of the Thrift Savings Plan (TSP) for federal employees. Created by the Federal Employees' Retirement System Act of 1986, the board consists of five part-time members who are appointed by the president with consent of the Senate. The president designates one member as chair. A sixth member is appointed by the board as executive director, responsible for the management of the agency and TSP.

The board operates TSP solely for the benefit of the partici-pants and their beneficiaries. Investments in the plan and earnings on those investments cannot be used for any other purpose. The tax-deferred retirement savings and investment plan is chartered by Congress to provide federal employees with the same savings and tax benefits that many private corporations offer their employees. Because TSP is a defined contribution plan, the maximum amount employees and their agencies may contribute to an account is established by law. Plan benefits are determined by the amount contributed and the earnings on the contributions. TSP is one of the three parts of the Federal Employees' Retirement System (FERS). FERS participants may invest up to 10 percent of their salary and are eligible for up to 5 percent in employer matching contributions.

The plan began operation on April 1, 1987, with $148 million invested in retirement savings accounts for 563,000 federal and postal employees. As of 1995 thrift savings fund investments totaled $25 billion by 2.1 million participants.

Federal Trade Commission

The Federal Trade Commission (FTC) is an independent agency created to regulate interstate commerce in the United States. The FTC is headed by five commissioners who are nominated by the president and confirmed by the Senate for seven-year terms. One commissioner is designated chair by the president, and no more than three of the commissioners may be members of the same political party. Commissioners are removable only for cause. The chair serves at the discretion of the president but remains a commissioner if removed as head of the commission.

Established in 1914 by the Federal Trade Commission Act, the FTC was created to be the federal government's chief trust-buster. That same year, Congress passed the Clayton Antitrust Act, giving the FTC broad powers to define and prohibit unfair methods of competition and specific business activities tending to lessen competition or create monopolies. Consumer protection was added to the FTC's responsibilities in 1938 through passage of the Wheeler-Lea amendment to the original FTC act.

In 1974 the Magnuson-Moss Warranty/Federal Trade Commission Improvement Act empowered the FTC to issue trade regulation rules (TRR). TRRs have the force of law and can apply to an entire industry or only to companies in a specific geographical region. The Bureau of Competition handles investigations and actions related to anticompetitive behavior. The Bureau of Consumer Protection handles consumer issues and problems.

Once the FTC determines that a company has engaged in illegal activities, it either negotiates an agreement with the company to stop the practice voluntarily, or it initiates adjudicative proceedings to order the practice stopped. The FTC also can order violators to make restitution to consumers harmed by their actions.

At the request of a business or an individual, the FTC may issue an advisory opinion on whether a practice violates FTC restrictions. The opinions define the limits of the law as they relate to that particular business practice. Advisory opinions may be overturned by the commission, which then must give the individual or business originally affected by the opinion a reasonable amount of time to alter practices to conform to the new ruling.

In complaints alleging anticompetitive or anticonsumer practices, the FTC initiates adjudicative proceedings. Before beginning a proceeding, the FTC conducts an investigation to determine whether charges of illegal behavior should be brought. The party charged is notified and given thirty days to respond to the complaint. If the respondent decides not to dispute the charge, the illegal practice must be stopped. The respondent also may dispute the charge in a hearing before an administrative law judge. If a respondent fails to comply with an FTC cease-and-desist order or TRR, the commission can obtain a court order imposing a penalty of $10,000 a day for each rule or order the respondent ignores. Further failure to comply can result in contempt-of-court charges.

The FTC operates an outreach program to apprise businesses of laws and regulations. The commission also publishes pamphlets and other materials for consumers to warn them of fraudulent practices and to inform them of their rights under the law.

General Services Administration

The General Services Administration (GSA) is an independent agency responsible for federal procurement, property, and telecommunications services. Established in 1949, GSA, with more than twenty thousand employees nationwide, services congressional, judicial, and executive agencies and many of their international facilities. GSA's principal components are the Federal Supply Service (FSS), the Public Buildings Service (PBS), the Office of Information Technology Service (OITS), and the Office of Federal Telecommunications System 2000 (FTS2000).The administrator and deputy administrator of GSA are appointed by and serve at the pleasure of the president.

The Federal Supply Service purchases and distributes goods and services for government use. Goods include office furniture and supplies, industrial items, and scientific and medical equipment. Services supplied by GSA include use of prenegotiated contracts for freight and household moves and for maintenance and repair of government items. FSS controls a fleet management system consisting of eleven centralized, computerized maintenance and repair control centers across the country. The system oversees GSA's motor pool of 140,000 vehicles and manages the federal government's travel program.

Federal workspace is controlled by the Public Buildings Service, which functions as owner, developer, and property manager of federal work sites, including office buildings, laboratories, and warehouses. PBS provides space by constructing new buildings, purchasing existing buildings, or leasing workspace. PBS also sells surplus government land, buildings, and other materials or distributes those items between federal agencies. Unneeded real property can be donated to state and local governments or can be made available for homeless assistance purposes when deemed suitable.

The Office of Information Technology Service provides federal agencies with products and services relating to telecommunications, data processing, office automation, and information management. It also develops policies and procedures for GSA's Local Service Program and manages the Federal Secure Telephone Service and the National Security Emergency Preparedness Telecommunications Program.

The GSA-run Federal Telecommunications Service 2000 provides long-distance telecommunications services to the federal government. FTS2000 manages two multibillion-dollar, ten-year contracts that were awarded in 1988 to Sprint and American Telephone & Telegraph.

GSA also assists other federal agencies in developing acquisition policies. In conjunction with the Department of Defense and the National Aeronautics and Space Administration, GSA developed the Federal Acquisition Regulation, the primary regulation used by all executive agencies for procuring supplies and services.

GSA also issues the Federal Information Resources Management Regulations governing telecommunications, automated data processing, and records management. GSA operates Business Services Centers in ten major cities across the country to provide information to anyone interested in doing business with the federal government. Public inquiries are handled by GSA Federal Information Centers. Federal publications are promoted and distributed to the public by GSA's Consumer Information Center in Pueblo, Colorado.

Inter-American Foundation

The Inter-American Foundation (IAF) is an independent government corporation established to promote assistance programs in Latin America and the Caribbean. Created in 1969, the IAF was granted authority to conduct its affairs independently of other U.S. foreign policy agencies. The IAF is based in Rosslyn, Virginia, and is governed by a nine-member board of directors appointed by the president and confirmed by the Senate. Six members of the board are drawn from the private sector and three from the government. The president appoints one member as chair. Members of the board can be removed for neglect of duty or malfeasance but for no other reason.

The IAF supports local and private development efforts through grants and educational programs. The majority of IAF grants go to grassroots organizations such as agricultural cooperatives, community associations, and small urban enterprises. Other grants are awarded to large organizations that work with local groups, providing credit, technical assistance, training, and marketing services. Funding comes from congressional appropriations and the Social Progress Trust Fund administered by the Inter-American Development Bank.

The IAF awards fellowships to doctoral and masters degree candidates at U.S. universities to conduct field work on grassroots development issues. Fellowships also are awarded to scholars from Latin America and the Caribbean wishing to study development issues at U.S. universities. In 1986 the IAF inaugurated an Office of Learning and Dissemination to document and evaluate projects conducted through IAF grants. The office's findings are made available through seminars and conferences. In addition, the IAF publishes a quarterly journal in three languages, which reports on projects and issues affecting IAF countries.

Legal Services Corporation

The Legal Services Corporation (LSC) is a nonprofit, independent organization established by Congress to provide financial support for legal assistance in noncriminal matters to persons unable to afford such assistance. Established by the Legal Services Corporation Act of 1974, the LSC assumed responsibility for the nation's legal services program from the Office of Economic Opportunity. The creation of the LSC was an attempt by Congress to depoliticize the provision of legal services. LSC was chartered as a private corporation with a bipartisan board and with restrictions on lobbying and political advocacy. Funding for LSC is provided by Congress and by outside sources, such as interest earned on participating lawyers' trust accounts.

In keeping with its independent status, LSC officers and employees are not considered officers and employees of the federal government. LSC financial statements are audited by an independent firm of certified public accountants and included in the corporation's annual report, which is submitted to Congress. The LSC is governed by an eleven-member board of directors appointed by the president with Senate confirmation. Six of the board members serve three-year terms, and five serve two-year terms. By law no more that six members may be of the same political party. The board selects a chair from among its members by a vote of seven or more directors.

The board is authorized to provide financial assistance to qualified programs furnishing legal assistance to eligible clients. The maximum income level prescribed by the corporation for eligible clients is 125 percent of the official poverty threshold. Each program's board of directors, taking local living costs into account, sets its own financial eligibility standards for clients and cannot go beyond the corporation level without LSC approval. Eligibility is determined primarily by family income, fixed debts and obligations, medical bills, child care expenses, liquid and nonliquid assets, and seasonal income variations.

The corporation is responsible for ensuring that recipient programs provide services efficiently and effectively and that all recipients comply with the Legal Services Corporation Act, the terms of appropriations bills, and all rules and regulations issued by the corporation. Oversight of recipient programs is provided by advisory councils established in each state. Each state's advisory council consists of nine members appointed by the

governor from among the attorneys admitted to practice in the state. The advisory council is charged with notifying the LSC of any apparent violation of the provisions of the LSC act.

Merit Systems Protection Board

The Merit Systems Protection Board (MSPB) is an independent quasi-judicial agency created to safeguard against partisan politics in federal merit systems and to protect employees against unlawful abuses by agency management. The board was established in 1979 by the Civil Service Reform Act of 1978. The act abolished the Civil Service Commission and divided its responsibilities among the MSPB, the Office of Personnel Management (OPM), and the Federal Labor Relations Authority. In addition to its Washington, D.C., headquarters, the board maintains regional offices in eleven major cities around the country.

Operating under bipartisan leadership, the board consists of a chair, a vice chair, and one other member. No more than two of its three members may be from the same political party. Board members are appointed by the president with Senate confirmation and serve overlapping, nonrenewable, seven-year terms. The chair can be removed by the president without cause but remains a board member unless cause for dismissal is shown. The Office of Special Counsel, an independent agency created in 1979, investigates allegations of prohibited personnel practices and prosecutes cases before the MSPB. Under the Whistleblower Protection Act of 1989, the MSPB and Office of Special Counsel were given a mandate to protect federal workers who report wrongdoing within their agencies from reprisals.

The reform act of 1978 established merit system principles for federal employment that include the selection and promotion of employees based on merit through fair, open competition and equal pay for work of equal value in the private sector. In addition, the principles guarantee employees' constitutional rights, protection for whistleblowers, and rights of privacy. The reform act also outlines a number of prohibited personnel practices, including discrimination and coercion of an employee to participate in political activities.

The board hears and decides appeals brought by employees concerning agency actions and reviews cases of discrimination. The board also reviews employment regulations established by OPM to determine if they conflict with established personnel principles and cases brought by the special counsel, who investigates prohibited personnel practices such as reprisals against whistleblowers and violations of the Freedom of Information Act. Discrimination complaints that do not involve adverse actions, such as removal, demotion, or suspension of more than fourteen days, go to the Equal Employment Opportunity Commission. Cases involving examination ratings and classification decisions are reviewed by the Office of Personnel Management.

The board conducts special studies of particular merit systems to measure compliance with established principles. If the board finds an agency in violation of the reform act, the agency has fifteen days to show evidence of compliance, a schedule for full compliance, and a statement of actions completed, in progress, or remaining.

National Aeronautics and Space Administration

After the Soviet Union launched *Sputnik I*, the world's first artificial satellite, on October 4, 1957, Congress and the administration of President Dwight D. Eisenhower agreed to combine the government's existing space efforts into one agency, which would manage the national space program. The National Aeronautics and Space Act of 1958 created the National Aeronautics and Space Administration (NASA), a civilian agency chartered to exercise control over U.S. aeronautical and space activities.

NASA is headed by an administrator who is charged with responsibility for all functions and authorities assigned to the agency. The administrator is appointed by the president with Senate confirmation to an indefinite term and serves at the pleasure of the president. The NASA Advisory Council advises the NASA administrator on the agency's aeronautics and space plans, programs, and issues. Council members are chosen by the administrator from the scientific community to serve at the pleasure of the administrator.

The problem of launch vehicles occupied much attention in NASA's first years, and on January 31, 1958, the first American satellite, *Explorer 1,* went into orbit. On April 12, 1961, however, the Soviet Union achieved the first successful manned space mission. NASA responded on May 5, 1961, with the *Freedom 7* Mercury spacecraft. On May 25, 1961, President John F. Kennedy addressed a joint session of Congress and called for a national goal of "landing a man on the moon and returning him safely to Earth" within a decade. The U.S. manned space program continued with the Gemini series in 1965–1966, and on July 20, 1969, *Apollo 11* landed the first man on the moon.

In addition to space flight, NASA is responsible for many other scientific research programs, including studies in the fields of space science, aeronautics, solar system and planetary science, astrophysics, life science, and earth science. NASA employs more than twenty-two thousand people in eight space flight centers and six research centers and other installations throughout the United States.

The agency's Washington, D.C., headquarters determines programs and projects, establishes management policies, procedures, and performance criteria, evaluates progress, and reviews and analyzes the agency's aerospace program.

Following the explosion of the space shuttle *Challenger* in 1986, a presidential committee organized to study the accident issued a report recommending nine changes in the agency's organization and operations. The recommendations included creating an office of Safety and Mission Assurance, which reports directly to the administrator. Three separate committees of the National Research Council were organized to provide oversight

NASA is a civilian agency created in 1958 to manage U.S. aeronautical and space activities. NASA placed the first American in orbit in 1961 and landed the first astronauts on the moon eight years later.

of space shuttle redesign efforts, including redesign and testing of the shuttle's booster rocket O-rings, whose failure was determined to be the cause of the *Challenger* explosion.

National Archives and Records Administration

The National Archives and Records Administration (NARA) is responsible for identifying, preserving, and making available to the federal government and to the people of the United States all forms of government records not restricted by law that have been determined to have sufficient historical, informational, or evidential value to warrant being preserved.

The National Archives was created as an independent agency in 1934. In 1949 the archives was incorporated into the newly established General Services Administration and renamed the National Archives and Records Service. In 1984 Congress once again established the archives as an independent agency, renaming it the National Archives and Records Administration.

The archives is headed by the archivist of the United States, who is appointed by the president with Senate confirmation to no fixed term. The archivist can be removed only for cause. NARA's major organizational elements are the offices of Management and Administration, National Archives, Public Programs, Records Administration, Federal Register, Presidential Libraries, Federal Records Centers, and Special and Regional Archives.

Daily operations of NARA are managed by the office of Management and Administration. The office's responsibilities include the agency's budget, property, personnel, and security and safety management.

The office of the National Archives oversees the reference and maintenance of permanently valuable records in the National Archives in Washington, D.C., and twelve field branches throughout the country.

The Public Programs office oversees public outreach programs that include distribution of audiovisual materials, workshops, lectures, exhibitions, volunteers, ceremonial events, and publications such as *Prologue,* the quarterly journal of the National Archives.

The office of Records Administration determines the appropriate disposition of all federal records including those produced by federal agencies. These records include microforms, maps, charts, drawings, photographs, motion pictures, sound recordings, and electronic and paper records. The office reviews the retention periods proposed by each agency for its documents and determines how documents will be handled once they are no longer held by the agencies. The Records Administration office also identifies records of continuing value to be preserved in the National Archives. These records may document the organization, policies, and activities of the federal government or contain information of high research value.

The office of the Federal Register publishes the official text of laws, administrative regulations, and presidential documents. It publishes the daily *Federal Register,* the *Code of Federal Regulations,* the *United States Government Manual,* the *Weekly Compilation of Presidential Documents,* the *Public Papers of the Presidents,* and the *Codification of the Presidential Proclamations and Executive Orders.* The office also is responsible for publication of slip laws (early and separate prints of statutes), the *United States Statutes at Large,* and the *Privacy Act Compilation,* and it ensures the accuracy of the official count of electoral college votes for president and vice president.

As of 1994, the Office of Presidential Libraries maintained eleven presidential libraries dedicated to preserving and displaying records of presidents Herbert C. Hoover, Franklin D. Roosevelt, Harry S. Truman, Dwight D. Eisenhower, John F. Kennedy, Lyndon B. Johnson, Richard Nixon, Gerald R. Ford, Jimmy Carter, Ronald Reagan, and George Bush. The office also maintained the Gerald R. Ford Museum in Ann Arbor, Michigan.

The 1993 estimate of the holdings in the National Archives was 1.7 million cubic feet of records, not including records held by the presidential libraries. Archive records include over 3 billion paper documents, 2.2 million maps and charts, 200,000 video and sound recordings, 123,000 motion pictures, 9.2 million aerial photographs, and 7,000 reels of computer tape.

National Capital Planning Commission

The National Capital Planning Commission (NCPC) is the central development planning agency for the federal government in the Washington area. Established in 1924 as a park planning agency, NCPC's role was expanded under the National Capital Planning Act of 1952 to include central planning for the federal and District of Columbia governments. In 1973 the National Capital Planning Act was amended by the D.C. Home Rule Act, which made the mayor of the District of Columbia the chief planner for the District.

NCPC prepares the federal components of the Comprehensive Plan for the National Capital (the District of Columbia and federal property within the region), which is a statement of goals, policies, and guidelines for the future development of the national capital. In addition to work facilities for federal employees, historic preservation, and parks within the region, NCPC is responsible for reviewing plans for all new federal buildings in the area. NCPC also prepares and submits annually to the Office of Management and Budget a five-year Federal Capital Improvements Program that contains land acquisitions and development proposals from all federal agencies. NCPC planning activities cover the national capital region, which includes the District of Columbia and Prince George's and Montgomery counties in Maryland, and Arlington, Fairfax, Prince William, and Loudoun counties in Virginia.

The commission consists of five appointed and seven ex officio members. Three citizen members are appointed by the president and two by the mayor of the District of Columbia. Presidential appointees include one resident each from Maryland and Virginia and one from anywhere in the United States. The two mayoral appointees must be District residents. Ex officio members include the secretaries of defense and interior, administrator of the General Services Administration, the D.C. mayor, chair of the D.C. city council, chair of the Senate Committee on Governmental Affairs, and chair of the House Government Reform and Oversight subcommittee on the District of Columbia. The president designates a chair from among the twelve members.

National Credit Union Administration

The National Credit Union Administration (NCUA) is an independent agency created to regulate the nation's federal credit unions. NCUA approves or disapproves applications for federal credit union charters and examines federal credit unions to determine their financial condition. NCUA issues charters to credit unions whose applications are approved and supervises credit union activities.

Established by a 1970 amendment to the Federal Credit Union Act of 1934, NCUA is based in Washington, D.C., and maintains six regional offices nationwide. Before 1970, administration of the original Federal Credit Union Act was shifted among several federal agencies. The Financial Institutions Regulatory and Interest Rate Control Act of 1978 reorganized NCUA and replaced the agency's single administrator with a three-member governing board. Board members are appointed by the president with Senate confirmation to six-year terms. The president designates one member to serve as chair, and not more than two members may be of the same political party. Board members can be removed only for cause. An incoming president may, however, appoint another member as chair.

A credit union is a cooperative association designed to promote thrift among its members. Membership in a credit union is limited to persons having a common bond of occupation or association and to groups within a well-defined neighborhood, community, or rural district. The credit union accumulates a fund from savings to make loans to members for useful purposes at reasonable interest rates. Credit unions are managed by a board of directors and committees made up of members of the credit union. After expenses and legal reserve requirements are met, most of the earnings of a credit union are returned to the members in the form of dividends on share holdings. There are two types of credit unions: federal credit unions, chartered by NCUA, and state credit unions, chartered by state agencies. In 1994 the federal credit union system consisted of 7,572 credit unions with total assets of $180 billion.

Federal credit unions pay an annual operating fee to NCUA and provide the agency with financial reports at least annually. NCUA also regulates the operations of the Central Liquidity Facility (the central bank for loans) and administers the National Credit Union Share Insurance Fund (NCUSIF). All federally chartered credit unions are insured by NCUSIF, which was authorized in 1970. Insurance coverage for member accounts was increased from $40,000 to $100,000 in 1980. The fund also insures member accounts in 90 percent of state-chartered credit unions.

National Foundation on the Arts and Humanities

The National Foundation on the Arts and the Humanities is an independent agency established by Congress in 1965 to promote progress and scholarship in the humanities and the arts in the United States. The foundation consists of the National Endowment for the Arts, the National Endowment for the Humanities, the Institute of Museum Services, and the Federal Council on the Arts and the Humanities.

Each endowment is itself an independent agency and is governed by its own council comprising a chair and twenty-six members who are appointed to four-year terms by the president with Senate confirmation. Council members, chosen for their expertise in the arts or humanities, advise the chair on policies and procedures and review applications for financial support. Members can be removed only for cause.

The National Endowment for the Arts (NEA) was created to support American arts and artists. The endowment awards matching grants to nonprofit, tax-exempt arts organizations of outstanding quality and both matching and nonmatching fellowships to artists of exceptional talent. By law, the agency also provides a minimum of 20 percent of its program funds in matching grants to state arts agencies and to regional arts organizations. Programs receiving endowment funds include dance, design arts, folk arts, literature, media arts, music, opera-musical theater, theater, and visual arts. Funding of endowment programs is guided by advisory panels of private citizens who are artists or recognized experts in their particular field. The council reviews the panel decisions and makes final recommendations on grants and policy to the chair.

The National Endowment for the Humanities (NEH) was created to support research, education, and public programs in the humanities. According to the legislation that created the endowment, the term *humanities* includes, but is not limited to, the study of history, philosophy, languages, linguistics, literature, archaeology, jurisprudence, comparative religion, ethics, the social sciences that employ historical or philosophical methods, and the history, criticism, and theory of arts. The endowment provides grants through six operating divisions—Education Programs, Fellowships and Seminars, Public Programs, Research Programs, Preservation and Access, and State Programs—and one office, the Office of Challenge Grants.

The Institute of Museum Services is an independent agency established by Congress in 1976 to assist museums in maintaining, increasing, and improving their services to the public. The institute makes grants to museums subject to policy directives and priorities set by the National Museum Services Board. The board comprises fifteen nonvoting members appointed by the president with Senate confirmation to indefinite terms, and four ex officio, nonvoting members. Members serve at the discretion of the president.

The Federal Council on the Arts and Humanities consists of twenty members, including the NEA and NEH chairs and the director of the Institute of Museum Services. Membership is made up of heads of federal agencies whose service with the council is determined by their agency position. The council is designed to coordinate the activities of the two endowments and related programs of other federal agencies.

National Labor Relations Board

The National Labor Relations Board (NLRB) is an independent federal agency created in 1935 to administer the National Labor Relations Act (the Wagner Act), the nation's principal labor relations law. NLRB has five board members (including a chair) who are appointed by the president, with Senate confirmation, to staggered five-year terms. The board also has a general counsel who is appointed to a four-year term. By law the board is bipartisan, and the president can reappoint or remove members for neglect of duty or malfeasance in office but for no other cause.

As chief administrator of the National Labor Relations Act, NLRB seeks to reduce interruptions in commerce caused by industrial strife. In its statutory assignment, NLRB determines and implements, through secret-ballot elections, the choice of employees whether or not to be represented by a union and, if so, by which one. The act also is intended to prevent unfair labor practices by either employers or unions. It outlaws practices such as interference with employees' freedom to organize and bargain collectively, domination of unions, antiunion discrimination, and refusal to bargain. In 1947 the Taft-Hartley Act added prohibitions against various union practices such as intimidation of employees and restraint or coercion of neutral employers. In 1959 the act was again amended, and steps were taken to eliminate gaps between federal and state jurisdiction in labor relations disputes.

The five-member board acts primarily as a quasi-judicial body in deciding cases brought before it by one of its thirty-three regional offices or sixteen field offices throughout the country. The general counsel is responsible for the investigations and prosecution of charges of violations of the act. NLRB does not bring action on its own but responds to charges or petitions filed by employees or employers.

Charges are initially investigated by regional or field office staff who then determine whether formal proceedings are warranted. If so, the parties involved are encouraged to reach a voluntary settlement. If the case cannot be settled, a formal complaint is issued and the case is heard before an NLRB administrative law judge. The administrative law judge's decision may be appealed to the board; if left unchallenged, it becomes the order of the board. In cases of representation disputes, the thirty-three regional directors are authorized to process all petitions, rule on contested issues, and direct elections or dismiss the request. Actions of the regional directors are subject to review by the board on limited grounds.

National Mediation Board

The National Mediation Board (NMB) is an independent agency that governs collective bargaining and representation disputes in the airlines and railroads as prescribed by the Railway Labor Act of 1926. Established in 1934, the NMB comprises three members appointed by the president with Senate confirmation. Members serve staggered three-year terms, and not more than two members may be of the same political party. The position of chair, which is decided by the board, rotates annually among the three members. Board members serve at the pleasure of the president.

The NMB administers the Railway Labor Act, the oldest labor relations statute in the United States. The act is intended to maintain a free flow of commerce and to ensure the right of employees to organize and bargain collectively through representatives of their own choosing. Originally enacted to cover only the railroad industry, the act was extended in 1936 to include the nation's airlines.

The NMB is the only federal labor relations agency authorized to handle both mediation and representation disputes. Between 1935 and 1993 the board resolved more than sixty-two hundred representation issues and approximately thirteen thousand rail and air mediation cases. The board mediates contract disputes between employees and the carriers over wages, rules, and working conditions. These are known as "major disputes." When negotiations reach a stalemate, either party may request mediation by the board, or the board may intervene in negotiations at its own initiative.

Once the NMB becomes involved in a dispute, the status quo must be maintained until the board decides to release the parties from negotiations. If the NMB is unsuccessful in its mediation efforts, the disputing parties are urged to submit to voluntary arbitration for final and binding settlement. If arbitration is rejected by either party, a thirty-day "cooling-off" period begins during which the parties must continue to maintain the status quo and refrain from self help. If the dispute continues and threatens to interrupt interstate commerce and deprive sections of the country of essential transportation services, the NMB may notify the president who may then appoint an emergency board. The president's board has thirty days to investigate the dispute and report its findings, which are nonbinding. If either side rejects the findings, neither party may act, except to reach an agreement, for thirty more days. If after that time an agreement still has not been reached, the parties are then legally free to act.

Representation disputes involving labor organizations and railroad or airline employees also fall under NMB jurisdiction. The board is authorized to determine the appropriate crafts or classes of rail or airline employees and to designate an employee representative through secret ballot of the employees or through other appropriate methods.

The National Railroad Adjustment Board in Chicago is authorized by the NMB to mediate "minor disputes," which are disagreements over the interpretation and applications of existing contracts between individual carriers and employees.

National Railroad Passenger Corporation (Amtrak)

The National Railroad Passenger Corporation (Amtrak) is an operating railroad corporation whose capital assets are owned by the U.S. government through the Department of Transportation. Created in 1970 by the Rail Passenger Service Act, Amtrak began operation on May 1, 1971, with a $40 million appropriation from Congress.

By 1970 railroads carried less than 7 percent of the intercity passenger traffic in the United States and there were fewer than

450 trains in operation. But the nation's highway and air transportation systems were beginning to be overwhelmed by the growing need for transportation between the major population centers. Revitalization of the railways, which already had thousands of miles of existing tracks and rights-of-way into major cities, was viewed by some as more economical than constructing new highways and airports.

The new corporation inherited, however, antiquated locomotives, passenger cars, and other railroad assets. The Amtrak fleet consisted of twenty- to thirty-year-old steam-heated cars, and the average age of Amtrak's locomotives was seventeen years. For the first two years of operation, Amtrak was almost totally dependent on private railroads from which it leased equipment and facilities. When created, Amtrak assumed responsibility for managing intercity passenger train service over twenty-three thousand route miles connecting twenty-one major population centers. In 1973 Amtrak received its first new equipment, and in 1976 the corporation acquired a major portion of the busy 455-mile Northeast Corridor between Washington, D.C., and Boston. Also in 1976, Congress passed the Railroad Revitalization and Regulatory Reform Act, which authorized spending $2.5 billion to rebuild the Northwest Corridor. The corporation continued to upgrade its facilities, and by 1982 all fifteen hundred of Amtrak's cars were new or rebuilt.

Management of Amtrak was assigned to a board comprising nine members. They include the president of Amtrak, who is appointed by the board, and the secretary of transportation. Three members are appointed by the president of the United States with Senate confirmation: one of the three is selected from a list recommended by the Railway Labor Executives Association; one is selected from among the governors of the states with an interest in rail transportation; and one is selected as a representative of business connected with rail transportation. Two additional members are selected by the president from a list recommended by commuter agencies that provide service over the Amtrak-owned Northeast Corridor; and two members are selected annually by the Department of Transportation, which is the preferred stockholder of the corporation. Board members serve staggered one- to two-year terms and can be removed only for cause. The board of directors meets ten times each year at Amtrak's Washington, D.C., headquarters. Meetings consist of a closed session for the discussion of personnel and proprietary matters and a session open to the media and interested persons.

National Science Foundation

The National Science Foundation (NSF) is an independent federal agency established to promote and advance scientific progress in the United States. Created by the National Science Foundation Act of 1950, the NSF was an outgrowth of the important contributions made by science and technology during World War II. Since its inception the NSF has provided financial and other support for research, education, and related activities in science, mathematics, and engineering. The NSF is headed by

a director, deputy director, and a twenty-four-member governing board; members are appointed by the president and confirmed by the Senate and serve six-year terms, except for the deputy director, who serves an unspecified term. Board members include scientists, engineers, educators, physicians, and industry officials.

Each year the NSF receives thousands of proposals for research and graduate fellowships from academic institutions, private research firms, industrial laboratories, and major research facilities and centers. The NSF staff is divided into grant-making divisions covering various disciplines and fields of science and engineering. Outside advisers from the scientific community serve on formal committees or as ad hoc reviewers of the proposals. Applicants receive verbatim, unsigned copies of reviews of their proposals and can appeal decisions, which are made by NSF staff members. Awardees are wholly responsible for doing their research and preparing the results for publication. The NSF does not assume responsibility for research findings or their interpretation.

Specific fields of research funded by the NSF are the mathematical and physical sciences, all fields of engineering, biological and environmental sciences, the social sciences and economics, behavioral and neural sciences, computer and information science, atmospheric, earth, and ocean sciences, and engineering education. The NSF does not support projects in clinical medicine, the arts and humanities, commerce, or social work.

The NSF does not conduct research itself but funds large-scale cooperative facilities for scientists and engineers. National and regional facilities supported by the NSF include research centers for physics, astronomy and atmospheric sciences, supercomputer centers, oceanographic vessels, and Materials Research Laboratories. In addition, the NSF manages a long-term U.S. scientific research program in Antarctica.

Other NSF programs provide funding for cooperative research efforts between industry, government, and academia and outreach programs with state government and private organizations. The NSF also monitors resources for science and engineering and publishes analyses and statistical studies on the supply and demand for personnel and funding in those fields.

National Transportation Safety Board

The National Transportation Safety Board (NTSB) is an independent agency authorized to investigate transportation accidents and to formulate safety recommendations. Established by the Department of Transportation Act of 1966, the NTSB was made entirely independent of the Department of Transportation by the Independent Safety Board Act of 1974.

The safety board is composed of five members appointed by the president with Senate confirmation. Members serve five-year terms, and the president designates two members to serve as chair and vice chair for two-year terms. No more than three members can be of the same political party, and all serve at the pleasure of the president.

The board is authorized to investigate and determine the probable cause of air, rail, highway, and marine accidents. The board also investigates pipeline accidents involving a fatality or substantial property damage. The NTSB assembles investigative teams that are dispatched to accident scenes to gather data and interview witnesses. The teams consist of NTSB staff personnel skilled in various types of accident investigation. For accident investigations requiring off-site engineering studies or laboratory tests, the board operates its own technical laboratory. The laboratory has the capability to read out "black boxes" containing aircraft cockpit voice recorders and flight data recorders. The laboratory's metallurgists can determine whether failures resulted from a design flaw, from overloading, or from deterioration in static strength through fatigue or corrosion.

Following an accident, the board may hold a public hearing to collect additional information. A board member presides over the hearings, and witnesses testify under oath. Upon completion of the fact-finding phase, the data are reviewed at NTSB headquarters where the "probable cause" of the accident is determined. The final accident report is then presented to the full five-member board for discussion and approval at a public meeting in Washington.

To increase safety, the board makes a safety recommendation as soon as a problem is identified, without necessarily waiting until an investigation is completed and the probable cause of an accident determined. Each recommendation designates the person or party expected to take action, describes the action the board expects, and clearly states the safety need to be satisfied. The Department of Transportation is required to respond to each board recommendation within ninety days. The board also is empowered to conduct special studies that go beyond examination of a single accident to broader transportation and safety problems. In 1994 the NTSB completed twenty-two major accident investigation reports, 2,300 other accident investigation reports, and two special investigations. It issued 345 safety recommendations.

Nuclear Regulatory Commission

The Nuclear Regulatory Commission (NRC) was established by the Energy Reorganization Act of 1974 to regulate the civilian uses of nuclear materials in the United States. When President Gerald R. Ford signed the legislation creating the NRC in 1975 the commission formally took over the nuclear regulatory and licensing functions of the Atomic Energy Commission (AEC), which was abolished.

The NRC is headed by five commissioners appointed by the president and confirmed by the Senate. No more than three commissioners may be of the same political party. Commissioners serve five-year terms with one commissioner appointed by the president to serve as chair. The chair directs the day-to-day operations of the agency and is responsible for the commission's response to nuclear emergencies. Commission members can be removed only for cause.

The NRC's Office of Nuclear Reactor Regulation licenses nuclear reactors used for testing, research, and power generation. A construction permit must be granted before construction can begin on a nuclear facility, and an operating license must be issued before fuel can be loaded and the reactor started. The office reviews license applications to determine what effect the proposed facility will have on the environment and whether it can be built and operated without undue risk to public safety and health. Applicants are investigated to determine whether they are properly insured against accidents. No application to construct a new nuclear plant has been filed since 1979.

Public hearings on applications for construction permits are mandatory. Hearings are conducted by the Atomic Safety and Licensing Board in communities near proposed nuclear facilities. Notices of these hearings are published in the *Federal Register* and the local newspaper and are posted in the nearest public document room. Interested parties can petition for the right to participate in the public hearings.

The Office of Nuclear Material Safety and Safeguards ensures that public health and safety, national security, and environmental factors are considered in the licensing and regulation of nuclear facilities. Safeguards also are reviewed and assessed against possible threats, thefts, and sabotage. The Office of Nuclear Regulatory Research administers the commission's research program, develops nuclear safety standards for the construction of nuclear power plants, and establishes standards for the preparation of environmental impact statements. The Office of Nuclear Reactor Regulation inspects nuclear facilities to determine whether they are constructed and operated in compliance with license provisions and NRC regulations. Analysis of operating data, enforcement of NRC regulations, and special projects are controlled by separate offices within the agency.

After the accident at Pennsylvania's Three Mile Island nuclear power plant on March 28, 1979, President Jimmy Carter appointed a commission to study government and industry safety practices in nuclear energy. The conclusions of the commission led to a reorganization of the NRC in 1980, in which greater responsibility for directing the commission's response to nuclear emergencies was transferred to the office of the chair. The new plan also provided that the NRC's executive director for operations report directly to the chair. Formerly, supervision of the operating staff was left to the collective commission.

Occupational Safety and Health Review Commission

The Occupational Safety and Health Review Commission (OSHRC) is an independent, quasi-judicial agency created to review contests of citations or penalties prescribed by the Occupational Safety and Health Administration (OSHA). Established in 1971 by the Occupational Safety and Health Act of 1970, the review commission is based in Washington, D.C., and is independent of OSHA and the Department of Labor. The commission comprises three members who are appointed by the president, with Senate confirmation, and their administrative staff. Members are appointed for staggered six-year terms.

After the issuance of citations or penalties by OSHA, an employer has fifteen days to contest the assessment. If the employer does not contest the citations or penalties, they become the final order of the commission. If a citation is contested, the review commission usually holds a hearing before an OSHRC administrative law judge. The judge's decision becomes final thirty days after the commission receives it, unless a petition for discretionary review is filed. Decisions also can be reviewed at the discretion of one or more commission members. Penalties imposed by the commission range from $1,000 fines for "other than serious violations" to $10,000 fines and imprisonment for up to six months for willful violations resulting in the death of an employee.

In fiscal year 1994 the review commission received 3,697 new cases, of which 3,414 were resolved without a hearing. In addition to the Washington, D.C., office, review commission judges are stationed in four regional offices.

Office of Government Ethics

The Office of Government Ethics, previously part of the Office of Personnel Management (OPM), was established in 1978 by the Ethics in Government Act of 1978 and became a separate executive agency in 1989. It was created to help prevent conflicts of interest in the executive branch and to promote public confidence in federal officials. The office develops, in consultation with the attorney general and the director of OPM, rules and regulations on conflicts of interests, standards of conduct, restrictions on postemployment activities, and public and confidential financial disclosure. It also provides guidance to officials to help them comply with ethics rules, determines whether violations have occurred, and recommends corrective action. Violations of law are referred to the Justice Department.

The office also has the authority to set limits on the gifts that federal employees may receive from anyone with an interest in the activities of the employee's agency. Generally, only gifts worth less than $25 are allowed and then only if the source does not give more than $100 in gifts per year. The legislation establishing the agency also imposed a governmentwide honoraria ban, prohibiting all federal employees from accepting speaking or writing fees, even if the topic was unrelated to the employee's work. Criticism that the sweeping ban would restrict rank-and-file civil servants from pursuing hobbies—such as fiction writing, genealogical studies, and theater performances—prompted the office to modify the ban in 1990. Exempted activities include writing fiction or poetry, teaching a course, and performing comedy routines in dinner theaters. Accepting payment for nonfiction articles remained prohibited, as did receiving payment for any outside speech or appearance.

The director of the office is appointed by the president and confirmed by the Senate for a five-year term. He or she is supported by a deputy director and general counsel. The agency's operations are carried out by three associate directors for administration, education, and program assistance and review. In addition to its monitoring role, the office provides ethics program assistance and information to the executive branch, recommends appropriate new legislation or amendments, and evaluates the effectiveness of the Ethics Act, conflict of interest laws, and other related statutes.

Office of Personnel Management

The Office of Personnel Management (OPM) is an independent agency that sets and carries out personnel policies for the federal workforce. OPM was created by the Civil Service Reform Act of 1978, replacing the U.S. Civil Service Commission, which had been established in 1883 by the Pendleton Act. The 1978 act also established the Office of Government Ethics within OPM to direct executive branch policies toward preventing conflicts of interest by executive branch personnel; in 1989 the Office of Government Ethics was made a separate executive agency.

Headquartered in Washington, D.C., OPM has approximately 3,200 permanent employees and maintains five regional offices nationwide. In 1995 OPM personnel policies covered a workforce of more than two million nonpostal federal employees. The director of OPM is appointed by the president with Senate confirmation and serves as chief adviser on personnel policies governing civilian employment in executive branch agencies and some legislative and judicial agencies. The director is appointed to a four-year term and can be removed only for cause. An incoming president can appoint a new director at any time.

As the U.S. government's central personnel agency, OPM is responsible for recruiting and examining federal employees, providing development and training programs, classifying jobs, investigating personnel to support its selection and appointment processes, evaluating agency personnel programs, and overseeing pay administration. Positions covered by OPM include the federal civil service from General Schedule grades one through fifteen and Wage Grade (blue-collar) positions. The agency also administers the Qualifications Review Board examining process for career Senior Executive Service appointments.

OPM oversees federal employee retirement and insurance programs and enforces government policies on labor relations and affirmative action. In 1994 OPM provided approximately $40 billion in health, life insurance, and retirement benefits to 1.7 million retirees and more than 600,000 survivors. OPM is chartered to administer federal employment under a merit system based on knowledge and skills through the Merit Systems Protection Board.

OPM's Incentive Awards program gives cash and honors to employees who provide suggestions that improve government operations and whose performance is judged superior. OPM also administers the Presidential Rank Awards program for recognition of sustained high-quality accomplishment by career members of the Senior Executive Service.

Office of Special Counsel

The Office of Special Council (OSC) was established in 1979 to protect federal employees, former employees, and applicants for employment from prohibited personnel practices. It investigates allegations of prohibited personnel practices and other activities and when appropriate prosecutes these cases before the Merit Systems Protection Board. If warranted, OSC also initiates corrective or disciplinary action. Under the Whistleblower Protection Act of 1989 the office was charged with providing federal employees with a protected confidential means to disclose wrongdoing within federal agencies. OSC is also responsible for enforcing the Hatch Act, which restricts the political activities of federal employees. When the agency was reauthorized in 1994 all of its protections were extended to medical employees of the Department of Veterans Affairs and whistleblower protections to 82,000 employees of government corporations.

The office is headed by the special counsel, who is appointed by the president and confirmed by the Senate. He or she is assisted by a deputy special counsel and associate special counsels for prosecution, management, and planning and advice. There are also directors for management and for the legislative and public affairs office.

The primary role of OSC is to protect workers from reprisal for whistleblowing. Whistleblower protection covers federal employees who report violations of law or regulation, gross mismanagement, gross waste of funds, abuse of authority, or substantial danger to public health or safety. OSC may transmit whistleblower allegations to the head of the agency concerned and to Congress and the president when appropriate. In 1994 the office received 653 allegations of whistleblowing reprisals, 3,073 of other personnel violations, and 140 of Hatch Act violations. In that year OSC also filed twenty-three enforcement actions before the Merit Systems Protection Board.

Panama Canal Commission

The Panama Canal Commission manages, operates, and maintains the Panama Canal under the Panama Canal Treaty of 1977. The treaty abolished the former canal organization—the Panama Canal Company and the Canal Zone Government. Two years later Congress passed the Panama Canal Act of 1979, which established the commission as the managing agency of the Panama Canal until the year 2000, when the treaty expires. At that time the entire facility will be turned over to the government of Panama, which is committed to keeping the canal open to international marine traffic.

The commission is supervised by a nine-member board. Five members are U.S. nationals appointed by the president with Senate confirmation. Four members are Panamanian nationals proposed by their government for appointment by the U.S. president. The commission administrator is a Panamanian citizen, and the deputy administrator is a U.S. citizen. The deputy administrator serves at the pleasure of the president.

The canal is approximately fifty-one miles long and runs across the Isthmus of Panama connecting the Pacific and Atlantic oceans. A canal on the Isthmus of Panama was first proposed by King Charles I of Spain in 1534. In 1880 the French under Count Ferdinand de Lesseps, the builder of the Suez Canal, began work on the Panama Canal; but disease and financial problems ended the French effort almost twenty years later. In 1903, shortly after Panama's independence from Colombia, Panama and the United States signed a treaty by which the United States, under President Theodore Roosevelt's administration, undertook to construct the canal. The project was completed eleven years later at a cost of $387 million. In 1994, 12,478 oceangoing vessels transited the canal.

Peace Corps

The Peace Corps is an independent agency created by executive order in 1961 to help developing countries meet their basic needs for health care, food, shelter, and education. The corps trains volunteers to participate in its programs in Latin America, Africa, the Near East, Asia, central and eastern Europe, and the Pacific. Peace Corps volunteers offer skills in education, health, nutrition, agriculture, small business development, urban development, and the environment. The goals of the Peace Corps as set by Congress are: to help developing countries to meet their needs for trained workers, to help promote a better understanding of Americans on the part of the peoples served, and to help promote a better understanding of other peoples on the part of Americans.

The corps is headed by a director who is appointed by the president with Senate confirmation. There is no fixed term, and the director serves at the discretion of the president.

The Peace Corps's overseas operations are administered through four regions comprising thirty-three countries in sub-Saharan Africa; eighteen in Asia and the Pacific; twenty in North Africa, eastern and central Europe, and the former Soviet Union; and twenty-three in the Inter-American region. In 1995 the Peace Corps had more than seven thousand volunteers worldwide and was planning to expand its programs in the republics of the former Soviet Union, Africa, and Latin America.

The idea of the Peace Corps originated in 1960 when Sen. Hubert H. Humphrey (D-Minn.) introduced a bill calling for establishment of a "Peace Corps." Although Congress defeated the bill, less than four months later, in a campaign speech at the University of Michigan, presidential candidate John F. Kennedy questioned his audience whether they would be willing to volunteer their services overseas as representatives of the United States. The idea became a presidential directive soon after Kennedy's election and was funded out of the White House. In 1961 Congress approved funds and legislation formally establishing the Peace Corps with the mandate to "promote world peace and friendship."

In 1971 President Nixon created ACTION to incorporate various federal voluntary organizations, including the Peace Corps, under one umbrella agency. After complaints from the corps' leadership that the corps had lost its identity, President Carter in 1979 signed legislation granting the Peace Corps special independence within ACTION. The International Security and Development Cooperation Act of 1981 made the Peace Corps a fully independent agency.

Volunteers must be U.S. citizens, at least eighteen years old, and medically qualified. There is no upper age limit. If married, an applicant must serve with his or her spouse. Although they participate in a U.S. agency program, Peace Corps volunteers are not officials of the U.S. government and have no diplomatic privileges. All volunteers receive intensive, short-term technical and language training. They also are offered studies of the history, customs, and social and political systems of the host country. The normal tour of duty is twenty-four months following three months of training. Volunteers receive a monthly allowance for rent, food, travel, and medical needs.

Pennsylvania Avenue Development Corporation

The Pennsylvania Avenue Development Corporation (PADC) was established by Congress in 1972 to plan the development and use of the area adjacent to Pennsylvania Avenue between the U.S. Capitol and the White House. The legislation that created the PADC charged the corporation to create a plan for developing and administering the area in a manner "suitable to its ceremonial, physical and historic relationship to the legislative and executive branches of the federal government." The corporation's Pennsylvania Avenue Plan includes oversight responsibilities of the government buildings, monuments, memorials, and parks in and around the area.

A board of directors comprising fifteen voting members and eight nonvoting members heads the PADC. Eight of the voting members are appointed by the president to serve six-year terms. Seven other voting members representing specific public interests include heads of federal agencies, the mayor of the District of Columbia, and the city council chair (or designees of the mayor and council chair). All voting members can be removed only for cause. The seven nonvoting members are advisory officials expert in or responsible for cultural, historic, or planning activities in the District. The chair of the corporation is appointed by the president.

The PADC maintains four operating committees: Design and Planning, Finance and Administration, Development Operations, and Public Improvements. The legislation that created the PADC provides for various powers, including review and approval authority over public and private development. The corporation also has authority to construct and to rehabilitate buildings, to manage property, and to establish restrictions, standards, and other requirements that ensure conformance to the plan.

Pension Benefit Guaranty Corporation

The Pension Benefit Guaranty Corporation (PBGC) was created by Title IV of the Employee Retirement Income Security Act of 1974. PBGC ensures that participants in the pension plans it insures will receive their benefits in the event the plans become insolvent. PBGC also may force a plan to terminate if the agency determines that the pension fund is in danger of default. In 1994 more than 41 million workers participated in more than 67,000 covered plans.

PBGC is a nonprofit corporation wholly owned by the federal government. It is financed by premiums levied against covered pension plans, the assets of plans it places into trusteeship, and investment income. The corporation is administered by a board of directors and an executive director. The board comprises the secretaries of labor, commerce, and the Treasury; the labor secretary serves as chair. A seven-member advisory committee made up of two labor representatives, two business representatives, and three public members advises the corporation.

PBGC coverage is mandatory for single-employer, private sector defined-benefit pension plans—plans whose benefits are determined by using a formula including factors such as age, length of service, and salary. The agency also protects the pension benefits of participants in multiemployer pension plans. Multiemployer plans are based on collective bargaining agreements involving a union and two or more employers.

Postal Rate Commission

The Postal Rate Commission (PRC) is an independent regulatory agency established to consider proposed changes in postal rates, fees, and mail classifications and to make recommendations on these matters to the governors of the Postal Service. The PRC was created by the Postal Reorganization Act of 1970, which also changed the old Post Office Department into the U.S. Postal Service.

The commission consists of five members appointed by the president and confirmed by the Senate, who can be removed only for cause. Members serve six-year terms, and no more than three may be members of the same political party. The president designates one of the commissioners as chair. An incoming president can appoint a new chair.

In addition to reviewing proposed changes in rates and classifications, the PRC considers changes in the availability of postal services and customers' appeals of Postal Service decisions to close or consolidate post offices. The PRC also investigates complaints concerning postal rates, fees, and mail classifications or services.

After receiving a rate proposal and supporting testimony from the Postal Service, the PRC issues public notice of the filing and appoints an officer of the commission, who is a staff member of the PRC's Office of the Consumer Advocate, to represent the interest of the general public before the commission.

After a discovery period and public hearings, during which the commission receives oral and written testimony, the PRC issues a written recommendation, which is then forwarded to the Postal Service board of governors. The governors may either accept the decision, in which case the proposed rate is implemented, or reject the decision and return it for reconsideration by the commission. The governors also may allow the commission's recommendation to stand, but under protest. In this case the rate proposal will be implemented under protest, while the decision either undergoes judicial review by the Postal Service or is returned to the PRC for reconsideration. Decisions on mail classifications (which are official definitions of the different services available from the Postal Service) and proposed changes in postal services undergo similar reviews by both the PRC and the Postal Service governors.

Railroad Retirement Board

The Railroad Retirement Board (RRB) is an independent agency created to administer retirement and unemployment programs for the nation's railroad employees. The board, which is based in Chicago, is made up of three members who are appointed by the president with Senate confirmation. Members serve staggered five-year terms. By law, one member is appointed upon recommendations made by railroad labor organizations, one upon recommendations of railroad employers, and the third member, the chair, is in effect independent of the employees and employers and represents the public interest. The president also appoints an inspector general for the board who reports directly to the chair. Board members serve five-year terms and can be removed only for cause.

The function of the board is to determine and pay benefits under the retirement-survivor and unemployment-sickness programs. The board maintains lifetime earnings records for covered employees, a network of field offices to handle claims, and examiners to adjudicate the claims.

The railroad retirement system is based on three federal laws: the Railroad Retirement Act of 1934, as amended, the Railroad Unemployment Insurance Act, and the Railroad Retirement Tax Act. The original Railroad Retirement Act of 1934 set up the first retirement system for nongovernment workers to be administered by the federal government. But the act was declared unconstitutional. A federal district court held that neither employees nor their employers could be compelled to pay railroad retirement taxes. Congress responded by passing the Railroad Retirement Carriers' Taxing Acts of 1935, and the RRB began awarding annuities in 1936. The act was amended in 1937 to establish the railroad retirement system. In 1946 and 1951 the act was again amended to coordinate in certain areas with the Social Security system. In 1974 Congress adopted a two-tier system of benefits that would provide amounts equal to Social Security benefits and other industrial pension systems. The system was designed to phase out dual railroad retirement/Social Security benefits being collected by railroad employees. With several modifications the two-tier system remains intact today.

From 1936, when the board first began issuing benefits, through September 1994 benefits under the railroad retirement system have been awarded to 1.7 million retired employees, and 2.2 million spouses and survivors. In 1994, $8.1 billion in benefits was paid to roughly 912,000 retirees and survivors.

Securities and Exchange Commission

The Securities and Exchange Commission (SEC) is an independent, quasi-judicial regulatory agency created in 1934 to administer federal securities laws. The commission is composed of five members, not more than three of whom may be of the same political party. The commissioners are nominated by the president and confirmed by the Senate for staggered five-year terms and serve at the discretion of the president. The president designates one of the members to serve as chair. A general counsel serves as the chief legal officer for the commission.

The origins of the SEC may be traced to the stock market crash of October 29, 1929. The crash and the ensuing economic depression focused public attention on stock manipulations and unscrupulous trading during the 1920s. A Senate investigation of securities trading eventually prompted the passage of the Securities Act of 1933, also known as the "truth-in-securities" bill. The act required anyone offering securities for sale in interstate commerce or through the mails to file information with the Federal Trade Commission (FTC) on the financial condition of the issuing company. The following year Congress passed the Securities Exchange Act of 1934, which created the SEC and transferred to it the functions that had been assigned to the FTC under the 1933 law. The 1934 act required companies whose securities were traded on national exchanges to file periodic financial reports. The measure also required that exchanges and over-the-counter dealers and brokers conduct business in line with principles of fair and equitable trade.

The SEC maintains four divisions with specific areas of responsibility for various segments of the federal securities laws. The Division of Corporation Finance has the overall responsibility of ensuring that disclosure requirements are met by publicly held companies registered with the commission.

The Securities Exchange Act requires the registration of "national securities exchanges" (those having a substantial trading volume) and of brokers and dealers who conduct an over-the-counter securities business in interstate commerce. Exchanges establish their own self-regulatory rules, although the commission, through its Division of Market Regulation, may alter or supplement them if it finds that the rules fail to protect investors. The division also examines applications from brokers and dealers to determine if they conform to business practices and standards prescribed by the commission.

Since 1934 Congress has passed three additional securities measures, including the Public Utility Holding Company Act of

1935, the Investment Company Act of 1940, and the Investment Advisers Act of 1940. Administration of these acts is the primary responsibility of the commission's Division of Investment Management.

Investigation and enforcement of securities laws is the primary responsibility of the commission's Division of Enforcement. Although most investigations are conducted through informal inquiry, the commission has the authority to issue subpoenas requiring sworn testimony and the production of books, records, and other documents pertinent to the subject under investigation. If the investigations show possible fraud or other violation, the securities laws provide several courses of action or remedies. The commission may apply for a civil injunction enjoining those acts or practices alleged to violate the law or commission rules. If fraud or other willful violation is indicated, the commission may refer the facts to the Department of Justice with a recommendation for criminal prosecution. The commission also may, after a hearing, issue orders that suspend or expel members from exchanges, censure firms or individuals, or bar individuals from employment with a registered firm.

Selective Service System

The Selective Service System is an independent agency that provides personnel to the armed forces in emergencies and administers the alternative service program for conscientious objectors. The legislation under which the agency operates is the Military Selective Service Act. The Selective Service was originally mandated by the Selective Service Act of 1948, which ordered that men be selected for the draft on a fair and equitable basis consistent with the maintenance of an effective national economy. The act replaced the expired Selective Training and Service Act of 1940, which established the first peacetime draft in U.S. history.

The last draft calls issued under the 1948 legislation were made in 1972, and the president's authority to conscript men into the armed forces expired on July 1, 1973. Mandatory registration continued until 1975, at which time it was suspended; it was reinstated in the summer of 1980 by the Military Selective Service Act. The act states that male U.S. citizens and male aliens residing in the United States who are between the ages of eighteen and a half and twenty-six are required to register with Selective Service. Failure to register or otherwise comply with the act is, upon conviction, punishable by a fine or imprisonment, or both. According to the act, a person who knowingly counsels, aids, or abets another to violate the act is subject to the same penalties.

The director of the Selective Service is appointed by the president and confirmed by the Senate. The director is appointed to an indefinite term and serves at the discretion of the president. The staff of 205 full-time employees is composed of civilians and active duty military officers.

The Selective Service System headquarters is in Washington, D.C. The agency maintains six regional offices throughout the country in addition to offices in each state. The Selective Service also trains Reserve and National Guard officers to operate the registration and draft systems in case their mobilization is required.

Local boards are allocated to counties or corresponding political subdivisions. The local boards make judgments about registrant claims for deferment or exemption from military service if a draft is resumed. Conscientious objectors who are found to be opposed to any service in the armed forces are required to perform civilian work in lieu of induction into the armed forces. Registrants who have been deferred remain liable for training and service in the armed forces until age thirty-five. The local board members are the only officials permitted to make initial decisions about claims of conscientious objections, hardship, or religious ministry. The local board also can review claims denied by the area office for other classifications or student postponements if a registrant requests a review.

District appeal boards are maintained in areas corresponding to federal judicial districts. The boards review and affirm or change any decision appealed to them from local boards in their areas. Members of both the local boards and the district appeal boards are civilians appointed by the president who serve without pay. If a claim for classification is denied by the district appeal board by less than a unanimous vote, the registrant can appeal to the president through the National Selective Service Appeal Board. Decisions of the National Appeal Board are final.

Small Business Administration

The Small Business Administration (SBA) is an independent federal agency that provides both new and established small businesses with financial assistance, management counseling, and training. Created by the Small Business Act of 1953, the authority of SBA was expanded by the Small Business Investment Act of 1958. The act authorized SBA to aid, counsel, and assist the interests of small businesses in order to promote free, competitive enterprise. The agency's Office of Advocacy works to ensure that a fair proportion of the total purchases and contracts for supplies and services for the government be placed with small business enterprises.

SBA is headed by an administrator and a deputy administrator. The administrator, the agency's chief counsel for advocacy, and its inspector general are appointed by the president with Senate confirmation. The deputy administrator is appointed by the administrator. The appointees serve at the discretion of the president with no fixed term.

Most SBA aid is in the form of guarantees of loans made by banks. In particular, loans are provided to assist small businesses that have sustained substantial economic injury from sources such as: major natural disasters; urban renewal or highway construction programs; construction programs conducted with federal, state, or local funds; and the closing or reduction in op-

The "Castle" was the Smithsonian Institution's first museum building. It was designed by James Renwick Jr. and completed in 1855.

eration of major federal military installations. SBA also makes loans to businesses to assist them in meeting requirements imposed by federal laws and by federal air and water pollution standards. In addition, loans are provided to homeowners who have suffered economic injury as a result of natural disasters. Special programs expand and promote ownership of businesses by women and minorities.

SBA licenses, regulates, and lends to small business investment companies (SBICs). These companies provide venture capital to small businesses in the form of equity financing, long-term loans, and management services. SBA determines SBIC loan requirements, approves SBIC charters and articles of incorporation, reviews specific terms of financing and interest rates to be charged, and enforces regulations and penalties regarding investments.

Through its Office of Business Initiative, the SBA sponsors conferences, prepares informational booklets, and encourages small business research. The Office of Small Business Development provides assistance and training to businesses through fifty-three small business development centers. The Office of Private Sector Initiatives coordinates agency programs involving partnerships with the private sector and proposes legislation supporting private-sector involvement in small business assistance and other agency programs. Assistance to small business owners new to exporting is provided through the Office of International Trade. The office also develops programs in coordination with the Department of Commerce to foster small-business involvement in overseas export development activities.

Two pieces of legislation affecting SBA were signed into law

in 1980. Both acts were intended to aid small businesses that cannot absorb the costs of regulation compliance. The Regulatory Flexibility Act requires the federal government to anticipate and reduce the effects of federal regulations on small business. The Small Business Investment Incentive Act exempts certain small- and medium-sized businesses from the registration requirements of securities laws.

Smithsonian Institution

The Smithsonian Institution, which encompasses the world's largest museum complex, is an independent trust devoted to public education, research, and national service in the arts, sciences, and history. The Smithsonian complex comprises the National Zoological Park and fourteen museums and galleries—thirteen in Washington, D.C., and one in New York City. Nine of the museums are on the National Mall between the U.S. Capitol and the Washington Monument. The institution also maintains research facilities in nine states and the Republic of Panama.

The institution is governed by a board of regents, which is composed of the vice president of the United States, the chief justice of the United States, three members of the Senate, three members of the House of Representatives, and nine citizen members, nominated by the board and approved by Congress in a joint resolution signed by the president. The chief justice traditionally has served as chancellor of the institution, and the chief executive officer is the secretary, who is appointed by the board.

In 1829 James Smithson, a British scientist, drew up his will naming his nephew, Henry James Hungerford, as beneficiary. The will stipulated that should Hungerford die without heirs (as he did in 1835), the estate would go to the United States "to found at Washington, under the name of the Smithsonian Institution, an establishment for the increase and diffusion of knowledge among men." Smithson's fortune—105 bags containing approximately 100,000 gold sovereigns worth more than $500,000—was brought to the United States in 1838. Eight years later, on August 10, 1846, an act of Congress signed by President James K. Polk established the Smithsonian Institution. James Smithson never visited the United States. He died in 1829 in Genoa, Italy, where he was buried in a small English cemetery. In 1904, when the burial ground was to be displaced by the enlargement of a quarry, his remains were exhumed, escorted to the United States by Alexander Graham Bell, and reinterred in the original Smithsonian building.

The original building, commonly known as "the Castle," was completed in 1855 and today houses the institution's administrative offices and the Visitor Information and Associates Reception Center. The Castle also serves as headquarters for the affiliated Woodrow Wilson International Center for Scholars. Other Smithsonian facilities include the Arts and Industries Building, which serves as a showplace for items from the institution's collections in the fields of history and technology; the Arthur M. Sackler Gallery, which is the museum of Near Eastern and Asian art; the Freer Gallery of Art; the Hirshhorn Museum and Sculpture Garden, which is devoted to the exhibition, interpretation, and study of modern and contemporary art; the National Air and Space Museum; the National Museum of African Art; the National Museum of American History; the National Museum of Natural History; and the Cooper-Hewitt Museum in New York City, which is the only museum in the United States devoted exclusively to the study and exhibition of historical and contemporary design.

Smithsonian research facilities include the Archives of American Art, the Center for Folklife Programs and Cultural Studies, the Smithsonian Astrophysical Observatory, the Environmental Research Center, and the Tropical Research Institute. In addition to the Smithsonian trust funds, which include endowments, donations, and other revenues, the institution receives an annual appropriation from Congress.

Social Security Administration

The Social Security Administration (SSA) was established during the Truman administration, on July 16, 1946. Its predecessor, the Social Security Board, had been created by Franklin D. Roosevelt in 1935 as part of his New Deal efforts to provide a safety net during the Great Depression. In 1953 SSA was transferred from the Federal Security Agency to the Department of Health, Education, and Welfare, which in 1980 evolved into the Department of Health and Human Services. Effective March 31, 1995, SSA became an independent executive agency.

The Social Security Administration (SSA) administers the national program of contributory social insurance whereby employees, employers, and the self-employed pay contributions that are pooled in trust funds. Part of the contributions go into a hospital insurance trust fund for Medicare. When earnings stop or are reduced because a worker retires, dies, or becomes disabled, monthly cash benefits are paid to replace partially the earnings the worker has lost. SSA also administers part of the black lung benefits program, established by the 1969 Coal Mine Health and Safety Act.

The principal SSA programs are Old Age and Survivors Disability Insurance (OASDI) and Supplemental Security Income (SSI) for the aged, blind, and disabled. (Funds for SSI come out of general revenues rather than a trust fund). Within SSA are ten regional offices, six program service centers, and more than thirteen hundred local offices.

SSA is administered by a commissioner and deputy commissioner who are appointed to six-year terms by the president with Senate confirmation. The commissioner and deputy commissioner are advised by a bipartisan board appointed by the president and Congress.

State Justice Institute

The State Justice Institute is a private, nonprofit corporation created to further the development and improvement of the administration of justice in the state courts. Established by the State Justice Institute Act of 1984, the institute is based in Alexandria, Virginia. It is administered by a board of directors consisting of eleven members appointed by the president, with consent of the Senate, to three-year terms. By law the board membership comprises six judges, a state court administrator, and four members of the public, of whom no more than two may be of the same political party. The board may remove its own members only for cause.

The board of directors selects a chair from among its members to act as governor of the institute's quarterly meetings. The board also selects an executive director, who serves as an ex officio board member and manages the daily business of the institute.

The institute's statute contains fourteen broad areas of interest including education for judges and support personnel of state court systems, access to a fair and effective judicial system, and coordination and cooperation of the state courts with the federal judiciary. The institute provides grants and funds cooperative agreements with individuals or organizations interested in carrying out innovative programs. All funding for the institute and its programs is appropriated by Congress. Interested parties submit concept papers to the institute for review. Those chosen by the board of directors may receive grants from the institute of up to $300,000, although grants of more than $200,000 are unusual. In 1995 the institute awarded $13 million in grants.

Tennessee Valley Authority

The Tennessee Valley Authority (TVA) is an independent corporate agency of the federal government, charged with responsibility for developing the resources of the Tennessee Valley region. Established by Congress in 1933, TVA serves ninety-one thousand square miles in the southeast United States comprising parts of seven states—Tennessee, Alabama, Mississippi, Kentucky, Virginia, North Carolina, and Georgia. TVA is responsible for flood control and improving navigation on the Tennessee River, producing electric power, and promoting agricultural, economic, and industrial development.

TVA is headed by a three-member board of directors appointed by the president with Senate confirmation. Directors serve staggered, nine-year terms, and one director is designated as chair by the president. Daily affairs are managed by an executive vice president and vice presidents for water management, land management, and governmental relations.

The three major administrative offices of TVA are in Muscle Shoals, Alabama, and Knoxville and Chattanooga, Tennessee. A small liaison staff is in Washington, D.C., and seven district offices are located throughout the Tennessee Valley region. Day-to-day operations of TVA are conducted by three divisions: Power and Engineering, Natural Resources and Economic Development, and Agricultural and Chemical Development.

The Office of Power and Engineering is responsible for the overall electrical supply program in the TVA area. The office oversees the design, construction, and daily operation and maintenance of the TVA power system, the nation's largest. The TVA electric power system serves more than seven million consumers through 160 municipal and cooperative power distributors. The power system is self-supporting from revenues from power sales. Other TVA programs, such as fertilizer development and flood control, are funded by Congress.

The Office of Natural Resources and Economic Development manages programs designed to use and protect the natural resources of the Tennessee Valley area. Programs include reservoir land use, aquatic plant control, and water conservation, development, and management.

Through TVA facilities, the Office of Agricultural and Chemical Development researches and develops new fertilizers and fertilizer manufacturing processes. The office is chartered to improve and preserve agricultural resources and to encourage soil conservation in the Tennessee Valley area.

Trade and Development Agency

The Trade and Development Agency (TDA) was established in 1980 as the Trade and Development Program of the International Development Cooperation Agency. In 1992 it was made an independent agency to fund services that help U.S. firms involved in overseas development projects. The agency supports projects that foster U.S. export potential and enhance the use of U.S. technology, goods, and services. Grants go to major development projects in the developing world, including projects in the former Soviet Union.

TDA is headed by a director and deputy director, both of whom are appointed by the president and confirmed by the Senate. Regional directors and country managers oversee the Divisions of Africa and the Middle East; Central, Eastern, and Southern Europe; Newly Independent States, South Asia, and Mongolia; South Asia and Pacific Islands; Latin America and Caribbean; and Special Projects. Additional staff include the general counsel, economist/evaluation officer, financial officer, contracting officer, and administrative officer. TDA frequently employs outside consultants.

The agency funds feasibility studies and other project-planning services for major development projects, such as those that are funded by the World Bank or other international financial institutions, or by the host country's government. Grants fund only services performed by U.S. firms. The agency also has the authority to serve as a coordinating and authorizing agency to provide government-to-government technical assistance on a fully reimbursable basis. TDA provided $54 million in grants, subsidies, and contributions in 1994.

United States Arms Control and Disarmament Agency

The United States Arms Control and Disarmament Agency (ACDA) is an independent government agency mandated by Congress to formulate, implement, and support arms control and disarmament policies. The agency has four main tasks: to prepare for and manage U.S. participation in negotiations on disarmament and arms control, to conduct research, to participate in verifying compliance with existing agreements, and to disseminate information on arms control and disarmament to the public.

ACDA is headed by a director and deputy director who are appointed by the president with Senate confirmation. The appointees serve an unspecified term at the discretion of the president. The director and deputy director advise the president, the National Security Council, the secretary of state, and other senior government officials on arms control and disarmament matters. The director of the agency is supported by a General Advisory Committee, which is composed of up to fifteen members who are also appointed by the president and approved by the Senate.

Before ACDA was created, disarmament negotiations usually were handled by the State Department's Office of United Nations Affairs. While campaigning for president, John F. Kennedy proposed the establishment of the U.S. Arms Control Research Institute. The new agency, which was renamed as a result of a compromise between the Kennedy administration, the Senate, and the House, was signed into law in 1961.

ACDA maintains four bureaus and four offices. The Bureau of Strategic and Eurasian Affairs develops, for presidential approval, arms control policy, strategy, tactics, and language for ongoing arms limitation talks with the republics of the former Soviet Union. The bureau also provides agency representatives and advisers for U.S. delegations to international negotiations.

The Multilateral Affairs Bureau develops arms control policy, strategy, tactics, and language for ongoing multilateral arms limitations negotiations and provides organizational support, delegation staffing, and advice for multilateral negotiations.

The Bureau of Intelligence, Verification, and Information Support is responsible for policies and studies dealing with the verifiability of provisions of current and projected arms control agreements. The bureau also provides operations analysis, intelligence, and computer support for all ACDA's activities.

The Bureau of Nonproliferation and Regional Arms Control performs ACDA work on nuclear nonproliferation issues, chemical weapons, arms and technology transfers, arms control impact studies, defense economics and economics of arms control, military expenditure recording and analysis, and weapons analyses.

The Office of General Counsel is responsible for all matters of domestic and international law relevant to ACDA's work and provides advice and assistance in drafting and negotiating arms control treaties and agreements. The Office of Administration has responsibility for the daily operation of the agency and its negotiating staffs in Geneva, Stockholm, and Vienna.

United States Information Agency

The United States Information Agency (USIA) is an independent agency responsible for the U.S. government's overseas information, educational exchange, and cultural programs. Its director reports to the president and receives policy guidance from the secretary of state. The director, deputy director, and four associate directors are appointed by the president with Senate confirmation and serve at the discretion of the president.

USIA originated as the Voice of America (VOA) in 1942 during World War II. The Smith-Mundt Act established the information program as a long-term, integral part of U.S. foreign policy in 1948, and in 1953 Congress created USIA. The State Department retained control over educational and cultural affairs until 1978.

In 1994 USIA had more than 200 posts in 147 countries. Overseas posts are maintained at U.S. diplomatic missions and are grouped in five geographical areas: Africa; Europe; East Asia and the Pacific; the American Republics; and North Africa, the Near East, and South Asia. Each post reports to an area office in the agency's Washington, D.C., headquarters. USIA officers overseas engage in political advocacy of American foreign policy objectives. In addition to its radio service, the Voice of America, the agency uses personal contacts with foreign leaders and films, videotapes, magazines, and direct satellite to carry out its mission. USIA also maintains a library open to the public in many of its overseas posts.

The chief of the agency's program in any country usually has the diplomatic designation of counselor of the embassy for public affairs. These public affairs officers advise U.S. ambassadors on the articulation of U.S. policies.

Overall program direction and administration are handled by the agency's Washington office. U.S.-based personnel conduct the broadcasting operations of the Voice of America and the Television and Film Service and produce agency publications, films, exhibits, and other support materials for field posts. USIA's Washington office is also responsible for advising the president and others in the foreign affairs community on the implications of foreign opinion for the United States. USIA provides analyses of world opinion on international issues as well as daily summaries of foreign media treatment of U.S. actions and policies.

The Voice of America is the global radio network of USIA. It produces and broadcasts in English and forty-seven foreign languages to more than two thousand affiliate stations overseas. USIA's Worldnet is an interactive international television service that provides direct communication on international issues between U.S. spokespersons and foreign leaders and journalists. USIA also sponsors educational exchange programs including the Fulbright Scholars Program, which operates all over the world and awards more than 4,700 scholarships each year.

The International Broadcasting Act of 1994 provided for the transfer of Radio Free Europe/Radio Liberty (RFE/RL) to USIA by the end of 1995. Formerly under the Board for International Broadcasting, which was abolished, RFE/RL broadcasts to central and eastern Europe and the republics of the former Soviet Union. The act also consolidated all nonmilitary international broadcasting under a Broadcasting Board of Governors within USIA. The board administers the Voice of America, the Worldnet Television and Film Service, radio and television broadcasting to Cuba, Radio Free Asia, and RFE/RL.

United States Institute of Peace

The United States Institute of Peace is an independent, federal, nonprofit corporation created to develop and disseminate knowledge about the peaceful resolution of international conflict. Established in 1984, the institute is governed by a bipartisan fifteen-member board of directors. Board members are appointed by the president with Senate confirmation and serve at the discretion of the president. Members of the board include the deputy director of the U.S. Arms Control and Disarmament Agency, the assistant secretary of state for intelligence and research, the president of the National Defense University, and the undersecretary of defense for policy. The president of the board is the only nonvoting member.

The institute awards grants to nonprofit organizations and to public institutions and individuals researching the nature and processes of peace, war, and international conflict management. The institute also administers an internal research and studies program and a fellowship program for scholars and practitioners of conflict management. Other activities include an education and public information program and a research library program. The institute produces a biennial report to Congress and the president and the *United States Institute of Peace Journal.* All funding for the institute and its activities is appropriated by Congress.

United States International Development Cooperation Agency

The United States International Development Cooperation Agency (IDCA) was established by Congress in 1979 to plan and coordinate U.S. policy on economic issues affecting developing countries. The director of IDCA serves as the principal international development adviser to the president and to the secretary of state.

IDCA incorporates the Agency for International Development and the Overseas Private Investment Corporation. In 1992, a third IDCA component, the Trade and Development Program, was made an independent agency and renamed the Trade and Development Agency *(See "Trade and Development Agency," p. 1248.)* Responsibility for U.S. participation in multilateral development banks is shared by the director of IDCA and the secretary of the Treasury. The director of IDCA also shares policy responsibility for the Food for Peace Program with the Department of Agriculture. The agency guides U.S. participation in certain programs of the United Nations (UN) and the Organization of American States (OAS), including the UN Development Program, the UN Children's Fund, the World Food Program, and the OAS Technical Assistance Funds.

As head of the primary policy-making agency for U.S. assistance programs, the director of IDCA is a member of the Trade Policy Committee and chairs the Development Coordination Committee, a broad interagency body that coordinates development and development-related policies and programs.

United States International Trade Commission

The United States International Trade Commission is an independent, quasi-judicial agency that investigates the effect of U.S. foreign trade on domestic production, employment, and consumption. Created by Congress in 1916 as the United States Tariff Commission, the agency acquired its present title under the Trade Act of 1974.

The commission comprises six members appointed by the president with Senate confirmation for terms of nine years, unless appointed to fill an unexpired term. A commissioner who has served for more than five years is not eligible for reappointment. No more than three commissioners may be of the same political party. The chair and vice chair are designated by the president and serve two-year terms. No chair may be of the same political party as the preceding chair.

As a fact-finding agency, the commission has broad powers to study and investigate all aspects of U.S. foreign trade, the competitiveness of U.S. products, and foreign and domestic customs laws. It does not set policy, although its technical advice forms a basis for economic policy decisions on U.S. international trade.

The commission examines whether increasing imports cause serious injury to U.S. industry and whether importers are infringing on U.S. patents, copyrights, or trademarks. The commission may initiate an investigation or arrange one after receiving a complaint.

After receiving a petition from an industry representative or from the Commerce Department, the commission investigates whether there are reasonable indications that U.S. industries are threatened or materially injured by imports that are subsidized or sold in the United States at prices lower than foreigners would charge in their home market (a practice known as "dumping"). At the same time, the Commerce Department examines whether those subsidies or pricing practices are unfair. If the outcome of both preliminary investigations warrants further action, the commission conducts a final investigation to determine whether a U.S. industry is being materially injured or threatened by unfairly priced imports. If the commission finds that such harm is occurring, the Commerce Department must order that a duty be placed on the imports equal to the amount of the unfair subsidy or price. That duty cannot be lifted by the president.

United States Postal Service

The United States Postal Service (USPS) is the second oldest department or agency of the U.S. government. Its forebear, the Post Office Department, was established on July 26, 1775, by the Continental Congress meeting in Philadelphia. By 1780 the Post Office Department consisted only of a postmaster general, a secretary/comptroller, three surveyors, one inspector of dead letters, and twenty-six post riders. When the seat of government and postal headquarters were moved to Washington, D.C., in 1800, officials were able to carry all postal records, furniture, and supplies in two wagons. In 1994 the U.S. Postal Service employed approximately 692,000 people and handled 171 billion pieces of mail in approximately 40,000 post offices, branches, and stations throughout the United States.

The growth of the USPS during its long history reflects the rapid expansion of the nation and has been marked by both great successes and great difficulties. Benjamin Franklin was appointed the first postmaster general, and the methods and organization of mail delivery that he created remained intact for almost two hundred years. By 1966, however, years of financial neglect and lack of centralized control had left the Post Office Department unable to deal efficiently with the increasing demands of the modern era.

The problems led Winton M. Blount, postmaster general under President Richard Nixon, to propose in 1969 a reorganization of the Post Office Department. Reforms passed by Congress less than a year later failed to rectify the situation, however, and on March 16, 1970, approximately 152,000 postal employees in 671 locations began a work stoppage. The department and leaders of the seven unions representing the postal employees worked out a plan for reorganization. That plan was submitted to Congress, and on August 12, 1970, President Nixon signed into law the most comprehensive postal legislation since the founding of the country.

The new organization, renamed the United States Postal Service, began operating on July 1, 1971, under the vested authority of a board of governors. The board comprises eleven members, nine of whom are appointed by the president on a bipartisan basis with the advice and consent of the Senate. The nine members in turn appoint a tenth member of the board, the postmaster general, who serves as the chief executive officer of the Postal Service. The nine members and the postmaster general appoint the deputy postmaster general, who serves as the eleventh member of the board. The 1970 legislation also established an independent Postal Rate Commission of five members, appointed by the president, to recommend postal rates and classifications for adoption by the board of governors. *(See "Postal Rate Commission," p. 1243.)*

NOTES

1. Quoted in *Federal Regulatory Directory, 1983–84* (Washington, D.C.: Congressional Quarterly, 1983), 3.

2. Samuel Huntington, "The Marasmus of the ICC," *Yale Law Journal* 61 (April 1952): 467–509.

3. Marver H. Bernstein, *Regulating Business by Independent Commission* (Princeton, N.J.: Princeton University Press, 1955).

4. Robert E. Cushman, *The Independent Regulatory Commissions* (New York: Oxford University Press, 1941), 19.

5. *Federal Regulatory Directory,* 7th ed. (Washington, D.C.: Congressional Quarterly, 1994), 89.

6. Marver H. Bernstein, *The Job of the Federal Executive* (Washington, D.C.: Brookings, 1958), 172.

7. William E. Brigman, "The Executive Branch and the Independent Regulatory Agencies," *Presidential Studies Quarterly* 11 (spring 1981): 251.

8. Linda Fisher, "Fifty Years of Presidential Appointments," in *The In-and-Outers: Presidential Appointees and Transient Government in Washington,* ed. G. Calvin Mackenzie (Baltimore: Johns Hopkins University Press, 1987), 4.

9. Cited in *Federal Regulatory Directory, 1983–84,* 37.

10. G. Calvin Mackenzie, *The Politics of Presidential Appointments* (New York: Free Press, 1981), 82–83.

11. Brigman, "The Executive Branch," 249.

12. Bert A. Rockman, "The Leadership Style of George Bush," in *The Bush Presidency: First Appraisals,* ed. Colin Campbell and S. J. and Bert A. Rockman (Chatham, N.J.: Chatham House, 1991), 11.

SELECTED BIBLIOGRAPHY

Bernstein, Marver H. *Regulating Business by Independent Commission.* Princeton, N.J.: Princeton University Press, 1955.

——. *The Job of the Federal Executive.* Washington, D.C.: Brookings, 1958.

Brigman, William E. "The Executive Branch and the Independent Regulatory Agencies." *Presidential Studies Quarterly* 11 (spring 1981): 244–261.

Congressional Quarterly Almanac, vol. 49. Washington, D.C.: Congressional Quarterly, 1993.

Cushman, Robert E. *The Independent Regulatory Commissions.* New York: Oxford University Press, 1941.

Federal Regulatory Directory, 1983–84. Washington, D.C.: Congressional Quarterly, 1983.

Federal Regulatory Directory. 7th ed. Washington, D.C.: Congressional Quarterly, 1994.

Fisher, Linda. "Fifty Years of Presidential Appointments." In *The In-and-Outers: Presidential Appointees and Transient Government in Washington,* ed. G. Calvin Mackenzie. Baltimore: Johns Hopkins University Press, 1987.

Huntington, Samuel. "The Marasmus of the ICC." *Yale Law Journal* 61 (April 1952): 467–509.

Kohlmeier, Louis, Jr. *The Regulators: Watchdog Agencies and the Public Interest.* New York: Harper and Row, 1969.

Mackenzie, G. Calvin. *The Politics of Presidential Appointments.* New York: Free Press, 1981.

CHAPTER 31

Presidential Commissions

BY W. CRAIG BLEDSOE

SINCE THE BIRTH of this nation, presidents have been appointing commissions to probe subjects that normally are beyond the daily scope of presidential advisory organizations. Twentieth-century presidents have relied on commissions to gather information and to focus public attention on specific problems.

Although commissions can be created either by the president or by Congress, they are usually placed within the executive office. Carl Marcy, an early scholar of presidential commissions, has noted that commissions "grow out of the inadequacies in the executive departments or in Congress, or, in some instances, they develop because of the unusual nature of the problem to be met."[1] In recent years the number and variety of presidential commissions have increased tremendously. Often they have been ridiculed by presidential scholars and the press for their seemingly meaningless objectives and empty conclusions. In truth, not all presidential commissions have worked well; some, however, have proven valuable and important.

Presidents have no specific constitutional grant of authority to appoint commissions. They usually justify such a step, however, by pointing to the general grant of authority in the Constitution to "take care that the laws be faithfully executed" and "from time to time give to the Congress information on the State of the Union, and recommend to their consideration such measures as he shall judge necessary and expedient" (Article II, section 3). President John Tyler (1841–1845), in naming a presidential commission to investigate corruption in the New York City customhouse, was the first president to cite his constitutional authority to do so. Tyler asserted that the information collected by the commission was for his use as president, but that it probably would find its way to Congress in the form of proposed legislation. He argued: "The expediency, if not the necessity, of inquiries into the transactions of our customs houses, especially in cases where abuses and malpractices are alleged, must be obvious to Congress."[2] His constitutional justification of presidential commissions has stood up over the years.

Although it is generally recognized that presidents have the power to establish commissions, they often seek congressional approval anyway. One reason for requesting congressional authorization to form a commission is that the funds required to operate and staff the commission would then be specifically appropriated by Congress. Some presidential commissions, however, are created by an executive order of the president and are financed by emergency, executive, or special projects funds,

Although presidential commissions are largely a twentieth-century phenomenon, they date back to George Washington's administration, when he appointed a commission to investigate the Whiskey Rebellion.

which are appropriated by Congress to be spent at the president's discretion. President Herbert C. Hoover (1929–1933), who significantly expanded the use of presidential commissions by appointing sixty-two during his first sixteen months in office, reportedly raised at least $2 million in private funds to finance them.

Presidential commissions date back to the administration of George Washington (1789–1797), who appointed a commission to investigate the Whiskey Rebellion. In this incident a group of liquor distillers in western Pennsylvania threatened civil disorder over the federal liquor tax. Washington, perplexed over a situation potentially divisive to the young nation, took the problem to a group of distinguished citizens; he clearly had confidence in their findings. In his sixth annual address to Congress, Washington flatly stated: "The report of the commissioners marks their firmness and abilities, and must unite all virtuous men."[3]

Most nineteenth-century presidents used commissions to meet the specific needs of their administrations. President Martin Van Buren (1837–1841), for example, appointed a commission to examine the European postal systems. Strong presidents have used commissions freely. Andrew Jackson (1829–1837) appointed two commissions just to check up on the actions of the navy. The use of presidential commissions is nevertheless primarily a twentieth-century phenomenon. The first serious study of commissions found that some one hundred had been appointed up to 1940.[4] A 1970 study found that another forty-four had been appointed since 1945.[5] In the mid-1990s the General Service Administration (GSA) listed forty-six commissions or committees directly advising the president.[6]

Not all executive branch commissions are "presidential" commissions, however. Presidential commissions are a part of a larger number of federal advisory bodies that provide advice on a broad range of topics to various departments and agencies of the executive branch. Of the 1195 executive branch committees or commissions in operation during fiscal year 1994, only 46 (or 3.4 percent) were classified by the GSA as "presidential advisory committees" that directly advised the president.[7] Presidential commissions or committees are as varied as the President's Council on Physical Fitness and Sports, the President's Committee on the Arts and Humanities, the Presidential HIV/AIDS Advisory Council, and the recently created Advisory Committee on Personal Motor Vehicle Greenhouse Gas Reductions.

Over the years presidential commissions have played significant roles in many policy areas. Recent commissions have investigated business regulation, tariffs, government waste, defense spending, the space program, Social Security, the Iran-contra affair, government reorganization, and health care. Theodore Roosevelt (1901–1909) introduced the use of commissions for substantive policy advice to the president. Inspired by the royal commissions used extensively in Great Britain to investigate policy questions, Roosevelt appointed a number of commissions during his administration, including the Aldrich Commission, whose recommendations led to establishment of the Federal Reserve System. Herbert Hoover, after his retirement from the presidency, headed two important commissions on government reorganization appointed by Presidents Harry S. Truman and Dwight D. Eisenhower, respectively. Presidential commissions also have been sent overseas to supervise national elections and investigate the stability of foreign governments. In 1917, for example, after the overthrow of Czar Nicholas II, President Woodrow Wilson sent a special commission to Russia to find out how democratic the regime of Aleksandr Fyodorovich Kerensky would be.

Although the objectives of presidential commissions have varied, most have been important to presidential decision making, and many have contributed significantly to the development of government policy. For example, Franklin D. Roosevelt's most notable commission, the President's Committee on

Administrative Management (known as the Brownlow Committee), developed the blueprint for the Executive Office of the President. *(See Chapter 27, Executive Office of the President: White House Office.)*

Types of Presidential Commissions

Presidential commissions fall into three broad categories: permanent advisory organizations, ad hoc or blue-ribbon commissions, and White House conferences.

PERMANENT ADVISORY ORGANIZATIONS

When presidents want advice from sources outside the White House staff and the cabinet, they often establish a permanent advisory organization—committee, commission, council, board, or task force—within the executive branch. These organizations formulate and coordinate recommendations for the president on specific policy issues over an indefinite period of time. A permanent advisory organization is placed either in an agency in the Executive Office of the President (EOP) or in the department to which it is most germane. *(See Table 31-1.)* For example, both the National Critical Technologies Panel and the President's Council of Advisors on Science and Technology are located in the Office of Science and Technology Policy, an agency in the EOP. The National Partnership Council, the President's Cancer Panel, and the Presidential HIV/AIDS Advisory Council are located in Health and Human Services.

Permanent advisory organizations usually have the right to review and question presidential initiatives and programs. Congress may give these organizations broad grants of authority, and it usually specifies membership qualifications and the terms of office for members. Because permanent advisory organizations often are set up in response to interest group pressure, their composition frequently to reflects the respective interests. Normally, qualifications for advisory organization membership are couched in statutory language open to broad interpretation, but statutory provisions usually make interest group representation mandatory. The Federal Council on the Aging, for example, must have members representative of older Americans and national organizations that have an interest in the aging.

Although permanent advisory organizations are designed to facilitate presidential decision making, presidents sometimes view them as an uninvited burden. The National Council on Marine Resources and Engineering Development (1966–1971), established to develop a comprehensive program of marine science exploration, was forced upon Lyndon B. Johnson's administration by interest groups trying to protect their industry. Both Presidents Johnson and Richard Nixon often clashed with the council. Thus, Nixon dismantled the group, moving its functions into existing departments. Presidential scholar Richard M. Pious has described the effects of these organizations: "The president has little time to consider their proposals and may wall himself off from officials who run them. He may become

TABLE 31-1 Presidential Advisory Organizations, 1995

Organization	Location	Organization	Location
Advisory Board for Cuba Broadcasting	USIA	National Commission on Alcoholism and Other	
Advisory Committee for Trade Policy and Negotiations	USTR	Alcohol-Related Problems	HHS
Advisory Committee on Human Radiation Experiments	DOE	National Critical Technologies Panel	OSTP
Advisory Committee on Personal Motor Vehicle Greenhouse		National Education Goals Panel	ED
Gas Reductions	EPA	National Partnership Council	HHS
Advisory Council on Unemployment Compensation	DOL	National Women's Business Council	NWBC
Bipartisan Commission on Entitlement Reform	HHS	President's Advisory Commission on Educational Excellence	
Board of Visitors, U.S. Air Force Academy	DOD	for Hispanic Americans	ED
Board of Visitors, U.S. Military Academy	DOD	President's Board of Advisors on Historically Black Colleges	
Board of Visitors, U.S. Naval Academy	DOD	and Universities	ED
Committee for the Preservation of the White House	DOI	President's Cancer Panel	HHS
Competitiveness Policy Council	CPC	President's Commission on White House Fellowships	OPM
Cultural Property Advisory Committee	USIA	President's Committee on Mental Retardation	HHS
Defense Base Closure and Realignment Commission	DOD	President's Committee on the Arts and the Humanities	NEA
Federal Council on the Aging	HHS	President's Committee on the International Labor Organization	DOL
Federal Fleet Conversion Task Force	DOE	President's Committee on the National Medal of Science	NSF
General Advisory Committee on Arms Control and Disarmament	ACDA	President's Council of Advisors on Science and Technology	OSTP
Glass Ceiling Commission	DOL	President's Council on Physical Fitness and Sports	HHS
Martin Luther King Jr. Federal Holiday Commission	KFHC	President's Council on Sustainable Development	DOI
Motor Vehicle Titling, Registration and Salvage Advisory		President's Export Council	DOC
Committee	DOT	Subcommittee on Export Administration	DOC
National Advisory Council on Educational Research		President's National Security Telecommunications	
and Improvement	ED	Advisory Committee	DOD
National Advisory Council on Maternal, Infant and		Presidential HIV/AIDS Advisory Council	HHS
Fetal Nutrition	USDA	Risk Assessment and Management Commission	EPA
National Agricultural Research and Extension Users		Technical Advisory Committee on Verification of Fissile Material	
Advisory Board	USDA	and Nuclear Warhead Controls	DOE
National Commission for Employment Policy	DOL	United States Advisory Commission on Public Diplomacy	USIA

SOURCE: *Twenty-Third Annual Report of the President on Federal Advisory Committees, Fiscal Year 1994*, July 10, 1995, 53.

NOTES: ACDA–Arms Control and Disarmament Agency; CPC–Competitive Policy Council; DOC–Department of Commerce; DOD–Department of Defense; DOE–Department of Energy; DOI–Department of Interior; DOL–Department of Labor; ED–Department of Education; EPA–Environmental Protection Agency; HHS–Department of Health and Human Services; KFHC–Martin Luther King Jr. Federal Holiday Commission; NWBC–National Women's Business Council; OPM–Office of Personnel Management; NEA–National Endowment for the Arts; NSF–National Science Foundation; OSTP–Office of Science and Technology Policy, Executive Office of the President; USDA–Department of Agriculture; USIA–United States Information Agency; USTR–Office of the United States Trade Representative, Executive Office of the President.

impatient with long-range planning and irritated at lack of consideration for his political problems."[8]

AD HOC COMMISSIONS

Ad hoc commissions investigate particular issues or related policy questions. They consist of three or more members who are appointed directly by the president for a specified period of time. A commission is considered ad hoc when it has a termination and reporting date not more than three years after its creation. Created either by executive order, by congressional legislation, or by a combination of legislation and executive order, ad hoc commissions (like all presidential commissions) are purely advisory, with no power to implement their findings or recommendations, which are published and made available to the public. At least one member of an ad hoc commission must be from outside the executive branch. Members, however, may be from Congress, the federal judiciary, or state or local governments, or they may be private citizens. Many ad hoc commissions have been composed entirely of private citizens.[9]

Ad hoc commissions are sometimes called blue-ribbon commissions when their members have distinguished records in the public or private sector. In this way, national leaders in business, agriculture, science, technology, and other important fields, who otherwise might not accept permanent positions in the federal government or might not make suitable permanent advisers, are able to serve in a temporary but official advisory capacity to the president. A 1979 study of the effect of ad hoc commissions on presidential policy making found that of the thirteen hundred commissioners studied "over 60 percent were prestigious members of some national elite at the time of their appointment."[10]

Ad hoc commissions usually are asked to examine a particular problem and to offer advice on how to deal with that problem. According to political scientist David Flitner Jr., such commissions are either procedure oriented, situation oriented, or crisis oriented.[11] Procedure-oriented commissions examine the operating procedures of existing agencies before recommending improvements to increase their efficiency or making judgments about their overall utility. These commissions have examined, among other things, postal procedures, criminal code reform, and general government operations. For example, the 1980 Grace Commission on More Effective Government examined the efficiency of virtually all federal government operations in the United States.

Situation-oriented commissions investigate broad areas of vital concern to large sectors of the population. Such commissions have included the Commission on Law Enforcement and the Administration of Justice (Katzenbach Commission), the Commission on Obscenity and Pornography (Lockhart Commission), the Commission on Population Growth and the American Future (Rockefeller Commission), and the National Commission on Marijuana and Drug Abuse (Shafer Commission).

As their name implies, crisis-oriented commissions arise from a particular event or crisis. Such a commission may or may not investigate the more fundamental cause underlying the crisis. Examples of crisis-oriented commissions have included the President's Commission on the Assassination of President Kennedy (Warren Commission), the National Advisory Commission on Civil Disorders (Kerner Commission), the National Commission on the Causes and Prevention of Violence (Eisenhower Commission), the President's Commission on Campus Unrest (Scranton Commission), the President's Commission on the Space Shuttle *Challenger* Accident (Rogers Commission), and the HIV/AIDS Advisory Council.

WHITE HOUSE CONFERENCES

The White House conference is another means of going beyond the traditional executive branch advisory bodies. Invitees to such a conference (often as many as several hundred attend) usually meet for several days to discuss a specific topic. Like ad hoc commissions, White House conferences are temporary and must report back to the president on the subject of their investigation.

Customarily, organizational meetings are convened in advance to prepare an agenda for the conference itself. The 1995 White House Conference on Small Business, for example, followed the recommendations submitted by thirteen small panels of experts from fields ranging from family business to venture capital.

Most conferences meet only once or in a series of panels or committees that make recommendations to the entire conference.[12] Another small committee usually writes the report of the conference.[12] The White House Conference on International Cooperation, held in late 1965, was typical of this kind of conference. Called in recognition of the International Year of Cooperation, designated by the United Nations, the conference was designed to promote a dialogue between private citizens and government officials on international problems and prospects for world peace. A National Citizen's Commission on International Cooperation, composed of 230 members working in thirty separate committees, was convened to lay the groundwork for the conference. Additional government and private experts were added as the committees went about their deliberations. All together, more than a thousand people from various areas of expertise took part in the discussions before the conference was held in December 1965. Although all the committees did not come together until the final conference, they put in many hours in their separate meetings; some committees even subdi-

As president, Herbert Hoover significantly expanded the use of presidential commissions, appointing sixty-two during his first sixteen months in office. As a former president, he chaired two presidential commissions examining the organization of the executive branch.

vided further. For example, the Committee on Culture and Intellectual Exchange divided itself into twelve subcommittees and held six meetings of the full committee, and the Arms Control and Disarmament Committee held four full committee meetings, with many of its members meeting regularly in smaller groups. The final conference produced a report entitled "Blueprint for Peace," which contained more than four hundred recommendations.[13]

The Commissioners

Although White House conferences tend to be large affairs, most presidential commissions are relatively small, with between fifteen and twenty-five members. The size of a commission usually depends on its scope and possible political impact. One of the smallest recent ad hoc commissions was the three-member President's Special Review Board, or Tower Commission, which in 1987 investigated the White House's involvement in the Iran-contra affair. One of the largest was the twenty-four-member ad hoc Commission on Population Growth and the American Future, established during the early 1970s to study the effects of population growth on the United States. The more narrowly defined the commission's topic, the more likely it is that the commission will be small. The 1970 President's Commission on Campus Unrest, founded to study disorder and violence on college and university campuses, had only nine members. The larger commissions usually are given more time to conduct their studies.

The appointment of commissioners is related to how the commission was established. If a president establishes a commission by executive order, the president is responsible for appointing all members of the commission. If Congress at the request of the president or through its own initiative establishes a commission through statutory law within the executive branch, appointment power is divided among several sources, with the president having the majority of appointments. The two Hoover-chaired Commissions on the Organization of the Executive Branch of Government of 1949 and 1955 are good examples of presidential commissions established by statutory law with appointment power divided among different sources. Both commissions were set up by unanimous votes of Congress. Each commission had twelve members—four appointed by the president, four by the vice president, and four by the Speaker of the House. Of these, at least two members had to come from the private sector and two from the public sector. Moreover, appointments had to be based on proportional partisan representation. The first Hoover Commission comprised six Democrats and six Republicans; the second, five Democrats and seven Republicans. The Commission on Population Growth and the American Future had a congressionally mandated membership composed as follows:

(1) two members of the Senate who shall be members of different political parties and who shall be appointed by the President of the Senate; (2) two members of the House of Representatives who shall be members of different political parties and shall be appointed by the Speaker of the House of Representatives; and (3) not to exceed twenty members appointed by the President.[14]

Most commissions attempt to represent a number of constituencies. According to Frank Popper, a scholar of presidential commissions, "A commission generally includes at least one businessman, labor leader, lawyer, educator, editor, farmer, woman, Negro, Protestant, Catholic, Jew, Easterner, Midwesterner, Southerner, Westerner, federal government official, congressman, member of a previous administration, enlightened amateur, and friend of the president."[15] Even though many of these constituencies may be represented by one person, most major sectors of American society will be represented on a single commission. Presidents customarily attempt to maintain bipartisanship on commissions; to do otherwise would completely discredit the results of the commission's investigation.

Commission appointments usually are not considered political plums, but most commissioners tend to be well known, with outstanding records in either public or private service. Representatives of the private sector are primarily attorneys, college professors, and other professionals. Some scholars see the elite nature of commissions as a positive characteristic that allows them to forge a consensus among various elite interests. Daniel Bell, a member of the National Commission on Technology, Automation, and Economic Progress (1964–1965), has written: "The distinctive virtue of the government commission arrange-

ment is that there is a specific effort to involve the full range of elite or organized opinion in order to see if a real consensus can be achieved."[16] Popper has noted that most commissioners are more like each other than like their constituents.

[Commission members] know, or know of, each other. They are primarily administrators, and they are used to working in committees. They have already succeeded in their careers, and their commission service is an honor rather than a steppingstone. They do not really need the nominal payment they get for their commission service. Some have national power, and all share what may be called the conservatism of personal success.[17]

Others complain, however, that despite efforts to recruit representatives from a broad range of constituencies, most commissioners come from a group of individuals who tend to shift continuously between the private and public sectors. Journalist Jason de Parle sarcastically characterizes the job description for a commissioner:

[T]hose ideally suited for the job include university presidents, former ambassadors, former ambassadors who are now university presidents, governors, former governors who are now university presidents, Wall Street bankers, and other kindred spirits—like Theodore Hesburgh, John Gardner, Milton Eisenhower, Tom Watson, John J. McCloy, any Rockefeller.[18]

Although elites are represented on commissions, leaders of some interest groups are not. And because of the elite nature of representation, representatives of most minority groups are seldom on the rosters of commissions.[19] Any group that is out of the mainstream of American politics is not represented at all. Political scientists Thomas E. Cronin and Sanford E. Greenberg noted that during the Eisenhower, Kennedy, and Johnson administrations, presidential commissions were "extraordinarily skewed in composition in favor of the best educated and the professionally well established."[20]

Elite participation on commissions is so complete that often the same names appear on commission rosters again and again. In seeking bipartisanship, both Democratic and Republican presidents often appoint the same people. And ad hoc commissions have been especially popular ways for former government officials to return to the policy-making process. From 1950 to 1970 seven individuals served on three commissions each, and twenty-five served on two commissions each.[21] Milton Eisenhower, President Eisenhower's brother, served on some twenty commissions. Among those who served on more than one commission during the Reagan administration (1981–1989) were former senator John G. Tower (R-Texas) and former secretary of state Edmund S. Muskie (National Commission on the Public Service and the President's Special Review Board), retired Air Force lieutenant general Brent Scowcroft (Commission on Defense Management and President's Special Review Board), former astronaut Neil Armstrong (*Challenger* Commission and National Commission on Space), former Virginia governor Charles S. Robb (National Commission on the Public Service and National Bipartisan Commission on Central America), and business executive J. Peter Grace (President's Private Sector Survey on Cost Control, Peace Corps Advisory Council, and Presidential Commission on World Hunger). The tendency to appoint former government officials to commissions has created an "established class of commissioners who are tapped repeatedly for service."[22] A Johnson aide explained:

There is a problem that the same damn names turn up time after time. It is as hard as the devil to find new people. There was a lot of talk about finding that bright young man in Iowa in the Kennedy Administration. They didn't find him. There is really a sort of a liberal house establishment. The same people keep turning up on the same problems. You have a deuce of a time trying to reach out to get outside of the major cities.[23]

This situation results in what presidential commission critic Thomas R. Wolanin has described as a "ho-hum-those-guys-again" attitude from the public, which reduces the effectiveness and persuasiveness of a commission's work.[24]

SELECTION PROCESS FOR COMMISSION MEMBERS

Shortly after the decision has been made to establish a commission, a presidential aide usually is put in charge of developing a list of potential nominees. Political considerations almost always are part of the deliberations that go into formulating a list of members. One Johnson aide described the process:

After we had a topic, we'd make up a list of the general skills and areas we wanted represented, but no names. The lists were a lot alike. We'd check with the appropriate departments, the Budget Bureau, and the Civil Service Commission. They'd suggest specific names which would go to the president. He would add, subtract, or substitute names or categories. He'd add the people we wanted for general wisdom-at-large delegates. When he didn't like a list, he'd say things like "That guy's been on everything lately," or "Everyone's from New York and Texas. See if you can spread it out a little."[25]

Most administrations have maintained lists of people who were recommended for appointment to various federal positions, or who came to the attention of the White House because of their distinguished accomplishments. In addition to consulting these files, presidential aides consult various constituent groups. Sometimes people in these groups themselves volunteer, or groups submit names for consideration. Certain groups will be asked to submit names, especially if their support is crucial to the success of the commission. The Kennedy administration, for example, wanted the support of both political parties for an investigation into the increasing costs of campaigning. It thus asked the Republican National Committee to submit a list of names for the President's Commission on Campaign Costs (1961–1962).

In addition nominees often are chosen from lists of people who have served on previous commissions, who held positions in past administrations, or who testified at congressional hearings in the relevant area.[26] Once the list of potential appointees has been narrowed, it is given to the president for final approval. As in most presidential appointments, the amount of interest that individual presidents show in the final selection varies. President Johnson, for example, paid meticulous attention to his commission appointments. Other presidents have given little attention to final decisions on commission personnel, especially if the commission is of minor importance. If the commission is politically important, however, presidents may intervene just before the final selection is made by deleting or adding names for personal or political reasons. For example, at the last minute President John F. Kennedy added one of his personal friends to the list of nominees for the President's Commission on Campaign Costs. One of Kennedy's assistants explained, "He was conservative as hell but the president respected him. Kennedy had served in the House with him and may have served on the same committee with him."[27]

SELECTION PROCESS FOR COMMISSION CHAIRS

Because the chairs of commissions serve as the public symbols of their groups (their names may even be used as a shorthand way of referring to a commission), selection of the chair is an important presidential decision. The most famous example of this is probably the President's Commission on the Assassination of President Kennedy, which became known as the Warren Commission after its chairman, Chief Justice Earl Warren. Similarly, the Kerner Commission (named after former Illinois governor Otto Kerner) and the Grace Commission (named after industrialist Peter Grace) both became better known by the names of their chairs. The heads of commissions assume most of the responsibility for the operation of their groups. They publicize their commission's work by testifying before congressional committees, giving speeches, making television appearances, and writing articles about the commission's investigation. Presidents also may ask chairs to play a role in the selection of other commission members.

Most important, however, commission heads are responsible for leading their commissions to a consensus and producing a report with specific recommendations at the conclusion of their investigations. The chair sets the tone for the commission and is responsible for its success or failure. Because chairs preside at meetings, they are in a position to provide the commission with leadership. Indeed, as Wolanin has noted, they can exercise social leadership and facilitate the process of producing the commission's report: "The role of the chairman is most often primarily political, producing agreement, and administrative, producing a report, rather than substantive."[28] Lloyd M. Cutler, executive director of the 1968–1969 National Commission on the Causes and Prevention of Violence (also known as the Eisenhower Commission on Violence), has described the importance of an effective chair:

Our chairman was Dr. Milton Eisenhower, an able and devoted man who . . . was the key to the success of the entire commission. Dr. Eisenhower was a man with whom all of the commissioners were ready to agree even though they might disagree a great deal with one another. It was his presence and his continuing force on the commission that I think led to the largely unanimous reports that were filed. He is also

The 1987 three-member Tower Commission investigated the White House's involvement in the Iran-contra affair. From left: Sen. John Tower, President Ronald Reagan, Edmund Muskie, and Gen. Brent Scowcroft.

quite a draftsman in his own right and . . . every word in this report was at least reviewed and edited by Dr. Eisenhower and a very large number of those words were written in the first instance by him.[29]

Commission chairs should have multidimensional qualities. According to Flitner, "The chairman must, ideally, exhibit the integrity and fairness of a judge, the administrative skills of an executive, and the intellectual abilities of a scholar."[30] President Johnson had to make a very thoughtful decision about his selection of a chair for the Commission on the Assassination of President Kennedy. In his memoirs Johnson commented on the politically sensitive appointment and his choice for the post:

The Commission had to be bipartisan, and I felt that we needed a Republican chairman whose judicial ability and fairness were unquestioned. I don't believe that I ever considered anyone but Chief Justice Earl Warren for chairman. I was not an intimate of the Chief Justice. We had never spent ten minutes alone together, but to me he was the personification of justice and fairness in this country. . . . We had to bring the nation through that bloody tragedy, and Warren's personal integrity was a key element in assuring that all the facts would be unearthed and that the conclusions would be credible.[31]

The most important characteristics sought in a commission chair are national prominence and a reputation for fairness.

Although few potential nominees refuse in the end to chair a commission, presidents occasionally have to use some persuasion. When Johnson asked Milton Eisenhower to chair the Commission on Violence, for example, Eisenhower proved somewhat reluctant. Johnson persuaded him by pointing out that a press conference already was scheduled for that day to announce the appointments to the commission. Most potential appointees end up agreeing to serve as chair because, as one commission member put it, "You just don't say no to the President of the United States."[32]

Commission Staff

One of the first and most important responsibilities of a commission chair is selection of the commission's staff. The staff provides the support services necessary to carry out the commission's mandate and does most of the commission's work. This includes collecting data, preparing briefings, coordinating meetings, and working out differences of opinion among commission members. Staffers usually are younger and not as well known as commissioners. They tend to be lawyers or academics, and they often come from federal agencies working in the commission's area of interest. Staffers not recruited from federal agencies most often come from universities, private industry, research firms, and private law practices.

Generally, a commission's staff comprises an executive director, subordinate staff, consultants, and a general counsel.

EXECUTIVE DIRECTOR

Although presidents may designate a commission's executive director, most often this task is left to the newly appointed commission chair, who may confer with the president or with other commission members. Most executive directors are known by someone in the White House or the federal agency that advocated creation of the commission. The executive director, perhaps with the assistance of the commission chair, is generally responsible for recruiting other staff members. If the staff is large, the higher-level staff members may recruit their own staff. In almost all cases, however, recruitment of staff members occupies a major portion of the executive director's initial time and efforts. Recruitment is especially difficult for executive directors of short-lived ad hoc commissions. Few potential staffers are willing to leave their permanent jobs for positions that will last no longer than a few months. Lloyd Cutler, executive director of the

Eisenhower Commission on Violence, reportedly spent ten weeks of the eighteen-month commission lining up thirty-one staff members.[33]

In addition to hiring staff the executive director serves as mediator between the staff and the commission. According to political commentator Elizabeth Drew, the relationship between the commission and the staff is usually one of mutual contempt.

The staff is often composed of young, less experienced people who still think that the world can and should be changed; the commissioners know better. . . . [In addition] the commissioners, being important people, are not very interested in chewing things over with a lot of young staff members. . . . So the policy alternatives go up from the staff, and the policy directives come down from the commission, and seldom do the twain meet, except in the person of the exhausted, whipsawed executive director.[34]

Executive directors thus serve not only as administrators but also as diplomats who must motivate and fashion the work of the commission. Popper observed that executive directors

must prevent commissioners from taking the commission in contradictory or irrelevant directions. He has the nearly impossible task of making commissioners and staff members regard the commission as a cohesive group, and not as a fragmented and temporary collection of individuals. But above all, he must infuse the commissioners and staff with a sense of urgency.[35]

Executive directors are responsible as well for overseeing and coordinating the entire operation of their commissions. They are, above all, administrators, and they devote much of their time to activities that have little to do with the substance of the commission's work. The rest of the staff researches and writes the report. Drew noted that much of the job of an executive director is

begging for money from executive agencies, which have their own problems, . . . cutting through civil service regulations so that the staff can be hired before the commission expires; arguing with the General Services Administration over office space and typewriters and with the Government Printing Office over how long it will take to print the report.[36]

SUBORDINATE STAFF

Past commission staffs have ranged in size from just a few staffers to well over a hundred. To some extent the size of the staff depends on the scope of the investigation—the narrower the scope, the smaller the staff. The Warren Commission, which conducted a very narrow investigation using the resources of the Federal Bureau of Investigation, had a relatively small staff of only 27. The Kerner Commission on Civil Disorders had a much broader scope and a staff of 115. No hard and fast rule can be applied to staff size, however. The most important determinant of the size of a commission's staff is the commission's budget, and that frequently is a political consideration. Popper has written:

The fact that some technical commissions have a small staff often means that the president does not really want much substantive advice from them; he is doing little more than showing concern for a special-

ized group. If he had wanted more from them, he would have given them more money to hire larger staffs. Such funds are given to the small, highly publicized commissions from which he expects broad political impact.[37]

Not all commissions have the same positions. Staff titles may include: deputy or associate director, administrative officer, editorial officer, public affairs officer, and director of research.[38] Staff members usually are chosen for their competence in the areas relevant to the work of the commission. The staff director also tries not to rely too heavily on any one source of staff, thereby promoting the objectivity and independence of the staff in the eyes of the public. Finally, to establish political credibility, staff appointees often have ties to important constituencies with which the commission must deal.[39]

CONSULTANTS

Commissions often use outside consultants and researchers—individuals, consulting firms, or "think tanks"—to supplement the work of the permanent staff. The 1967 President's Commission on Postal Organization relied on Arthur D. Little, Inc., a consulting firm in Cambridge, Massachusetts, for most of its research, and the Eisenhower Commission on Violence (1968–1969) hired the Louis Harris organization to take several polls. Consultants write most of the technical supplements that accompany a commission's final report, and they are free to disagree with the overall findings of the commission.[40] At least two ad hoc commissions used consulting organizations exclusively: the National Advisory Commission on Libraries (1969–1970) used nine private firms, and the President's Commission on an All-Volunteer Armed Force (1969–1970), three outside firms.[41]

Although consultants provide commissions with a variety of talents, commissioners and staffers often question their work. But, in fact, faced with time constraints, many consultants feel rushed and uncomfortable with their own efforts. Nevertheless, their work is an important part of a commission's effort.

According to Popper, "The consultant's work, regardless of its quality and its pertinence to the report, is fundamentally valuable to a commission, not for its intellectual merits or policy proposals, but because it involves the appropriate academic, professional, and technical communities in the work of the commission."[42]

GENERAL COUNSEL

The complexity of the legal issues encountered by most commissions requires the services of legal counsel. Commissions having a large number of attorneys on staff may not appoint a general counsel, but this is the exception rather than the rule. Depending on the nature of a commission's investigation, its legal counsel may consist of only one attorney or an entire legal staff. The Warren Commission, for example, had in addition to its regular staff of twenty-seven a fourteen-member legal team to investigate the assassination of President Kennedy. The general counsel is usually consulted on any legal questions that arise during the commission's investigation.

How Commissions Operate

Permanent commissions operate much like any federal agency; they carry out their investigations and business on an ongoing basis, funded by annual congressional appropriations. Ad hoc commissions, in contrast, operate under quite different circumstances because of the money and time constraints arising from their temporary status.

Ad hoc commissions must work toward a deadline. President Johnson called on the Kerner Commission, for example, to produce a preliminary report in March 1968, just seven months after the commission was established. Thus, as sociologist Amitai Etzioni has observed, "More than anything else, commissions are part of government by fire-brigade."[43] After forming, commissions spend much of their time hiring staff. They then organize to distribute the workload, investigate their area of concern, and report their findings, and they disband without any means of implementing their findings or recommendations. Whether good or bad, temporary ad hoc commissions are a stopgap method of solving problems. James F. Campbell, general counsel to the Eisenhower Commission on Violence, viewed the fast pace of ad hoc commissions in a positive light.

It's a very hectic pace . . . but at least one is thinking, deliberating, researching, and so on. You have the same kind of pace in the executive branch to "put out fires," and to meet budget deadlines, and to get something up to the Hill. The pace is just as fast there and there's no time for thinking or deliberating or writing or researching. . . . At least with commissions one is "hectically thinking."[44]

Commissions have varied in how often they meet. The Kerner Commission, for example, had a reputation for hard work and met a total of forty-four days over its lifetime of seven months. The mid-1960s President's Commission on Law Enforcement and the Administration of Justice had a more typical pace of only nineteen days of meetings over seventeen months. Meetings usually are held on weekends for the convenience of the participants and rarely take place more than once a month. Attendance also varies from commission to commission. Small, highly publicized commissions might have a normal attendance as high as 80 percent. Some commissions, however, rarely have more than 50 percent of their commissioners at a given meeting.[45] Wolanin found that most commissioners and staff members did not find poor attendance to be a problem; in fact, they found attendance at commission meetings adequate for exercising commission responsibilities. Although attendance at subcommittee meetings and hearings also tends to vary from commission to commission, it generally is considered good.[46]

Some passive members may attend commission meetings but not participate actively in commission proceedings. Most commissioners who attend meetings, however, participate in the debates and deliberations of the commission. Popper has reported that the commissioners who make the most useful contributions have the greatest sense of urgency about the commission's topic.[47] For most commissioners, their acceptance of a commission appointment indicates their high interest and involvement in the subject of the commission and therefore the commission's work. The extent of their involvement is reflected in the writing of the report. According to one staff member of the National Commission on Technology, Automation, and Economic Progress, "The report went through fourteen bloody drafts, and I mean bloody. You couldn't recognize the relation between the first two drafts and the final report. This indicates the impact that the commissioners had."[48]

Wolanin has divided the approaches that commissioners take to their work into two categories: the commissioner as statesman or stateswoman and the commissioner as constituency representative. Commissioners with the first perspective view the problem under investigation in terms of the public interest; those representing constituencies view their work primarily in terms of its impact on their clientele. As one labor leader explained, "When I serve [on a commission], I do so as an individual citizen, but always with the thought of labor's viewpoint, of course. . . . I just sit as a member and discuss the report, in particular how it affects the workers."[49]

Most commissioners are statesmen or stateswomen because of their initial objectivity, which usually figures in their selection for the commission, or because of their growth during the commission's investigation. Commissioners apparently undergo a period of learning which leads to their advocacy of positions that they ordinarily might oppose. Flitner called this phenomenon "collegial intellectual growth among commissioners," reflecting an exposure to facts that dispel the commissioner's preconceptions. He quoted Milton Eisenhower, whose Commission on Violence made eighty-one nearly unanimous recommendations: "It was a revelation to me. . . . We freed our minds of all preconceptions. When we started we couldn't agree on anything."[50]

Commissions carry out their investigations differently. Some commissions divide themselves into study groups or task forces that investigate specific areas within the broader scope of the commission. The 1967 Commission on Pornography, for example, had four study groups: (1) legal, (2) traffic and distribution, (3) effects, and (4) positive approaches. Each area was assigned commissioners, staff, consultants, and advisers. Some commissions do not use task forces at all, whereas others allow the staff to form task forces. The Eisenhower Commission on Violence, for example, did not assign its commissioners to task forces. Instead, it allowed its staff the freedom to work on task force problems, and the commission then reviewed the staff's work.[51]

In addition to their private meetings and deliberations, commissions often hold public hearings. With the exception of the final report, hearings are the most visible activity of a commission, and they allow commissioners to become better acquainted with their subject. Hearings may be open or closed. Closed hearings are primarily for informational purposes. The Warren Commission heard direct testimony from ninety-four witnesses in closed testimony. Its legal staff heard testimony from 395 others and received sixty-one sworn affidavits. These witnesses provided commissioners and staffers with a wealth of information from a variety of perspectives otherwise unavailable. Hearings generally allow a commission to be more thorough and impartial. According to Popper, "There is a general agreement, even among commissioners, that hearings inform commissioners so that, by the time the report is being written, their knowledge of the commission's subject is often comparable to the staff's."[52] Public hearings also allow commissions to establish legitimacy and to generate publicity. Political scientist Martha Derthick found that members of the President's Commission on Campus Unrest "knew that by making hearings public, whatever value they might have as sources of information would be lost." The commission held public hearings anyway, however, "to demonstrate that it would listen to diverse opinions."[53] Howard Shuman, executive director of the National Commission on Urban Problems (1967–1968), has pointed out the dramatic effect of its public hearings:

Among the best things the Commission did was to hold hearings in the ghettos of the major cities of the country. . . . The best testimony received was from the ordinary citizens. It had a fire and a spirit which was unmatched by the experts we heard. . . . The hearings and inspections provided a common experience for the members of our commission and united them as no other action could have done.[54]

Most presidential commission hearings receive more publicity than their congressional counterparts. For example, in investigating the ghetto racial riots of the summer of 1967, the Senate Permanent Subcommittee on Investigations, chaired by Democratic senator John L. McClellan of Arkansas, found the possible causes of the riots to be conspiracies, the involvement of antipoverty workers, and the moral degeneracy of the rioters. Public hearings conducted by the National Advisory Commission on Civil Disorders, an ad hoc presidential commission created to investigate the same problem, found no evidence of conspiracy, no misconduct on the part of antipoverty workers, and no evidence of the moral degeneracy of the rioters. Although the two investigations came to different conclusions, the Commission on Civil Disorders received greater publicity than McClellan's Senate investigation and its report became more widely accepted.[55]

Depending on their budget and the perceived importance of their mission, some presidential commissions may release preliminary technical and staff reports. The 1970 Commission on Obscenity and Pornography, for example, had enough funding to commission and publish technical reports by independent social scientists on the effects of viewing erotic material. In contrast, the 1986 Attorney General's Commission on Pornography (Meese Commission), generally considered underfunded, commissioned no new research and produced only its final report.[56] Most commissions are not funded well enough to sponsor new research. Consequently, commissions often face criticism for contributing little new information on a particular subject. Annette Strauss, cochair of the 1992 President's Commission on Urban Families and former mayor of Dallas, defended her commission's reliance on previous studies and the work of other commissions by stating, "We're not going to reinvent the wheel. A lot of good work has been done."[57]

For any commission, all of the staff work, investigations, public and private hearings, subcommittee meetings, and full commission deliberations are conducted with the goal of the final report in sight. Reports have varied in length from the three-page letter to the president produced by the President's Commission on the World's Fair (1959) to the six-volume report produced by the National Commission on Higher Education (1946–1947) or the nineteen-hundred-page Meese Commission report. Reports often include appendices of technical reports, subcommittee studies, and hearing transcripts.

Wolanin found that commissions generally use one of three methods in producing a report.[58] In the most common approach, subcommittees of commissioners review the data, and the staff for each group then produces position papers. After reviewing these papers, the subcommittees make recommendations to the full committee. The full commission then reviews the subcommittees' reports and recommendations, making revisions and producing a mutually acceptable final report. The second method frequently used by commissions is similar to the first, except that the subcommittees do not make detailed reports and recommendations to the full commission. Instead, all the subcommittees meet together acting as a committee of the whole, which undertakes all revisions itself. This method is generally used by smaller commissions with narrowly defined mandates. In the third and least used method, the commission makes policy decisions and then directs the writing of the report to conform to its decisions.

As the writing of the final report looms ever larger on the commission's agenda, tensions rise among the staff and the commissioners. Reports often go through draft after draft with certain commissioners seemingly impossible to satisfy. Some chapters of the final report of the Warren Commission reportedly went through twenty drafts. Staffers often spend day and night working on the final report and endure endless criticism from all sides. In describing this growing tension among the staff and commissioners, Popper recalled the words of a journalist who worked with several commissions:

All the strands of activity and hostility always come together in the writing. The first few commission meetings haven't done anything more than introduce the commissioners to each other. They size up each other. Then in the next few meetings, attendance drops off and the staff begins to show its strength. Then the staff trots out its early drafts, and all of a sudden the swing members, the ones with open minds and without ideological preconceptions, assert themselves. They make worthwhile, influential suggestions about the drafts. Apparently vulnerable people like women and clergymen can pull a lot of weight here. Finally, in the last few meetings, the staff produces drafts all over the place, the homework swamps the commissioners, and the staff sneaks in everything they think they can get away with. They get away with a lot, because by this time the commissioners have fourteen chapters to read in two days, and it's too late to change anything anyway.[59]

THE FEDERAL ADVISORY COMMITTEE ACT

Presidential advisory committees fall under the authority of the Federal Advisory Committee Act (FACA). Passed in 1972, FACA established guidelines for the operation of most federal government advisory committees. Congress enacted FACA in response to criticism that federal advisory committees were often nonrepresentative of the population and to a desire to open committee proceedings and reports to the public. Congress also addressed concerns about the large number of advisory committees and the pervasiveness of their influence.

FACA regulates a committee's charter and duration and requires an advisory committee to open its meetings and records to the public if at least one member of the committee is not a full-time federal officer or employee. The act also requires Congress and OMB to inventory and review annually existing advisory committees and recommend reorganization or abolition of committees deemed superfluous. In addition, FACA requires a presidential response to a committee's final recommendations. Some one thousand federal advisory committees fall under the authority of FACA. In 1994, forty-six of these committees advised the president directly.

Even though some scholars believe FACA represents a congressional challenge to executive power, presidents have chosen not to challenge the act in the courts. Through FACA Congress did exert some control over executive branch advisory committees by regulating their activities, which may be seen as a violation of the separation of powers between the presidency and Congress.[1] Recent presidents, however, rather than chafe at the restrictions, have accepted FACA as a way of reducing federal spending by eliminating unnecessary committees. For example, under provisions of FACA, President Clinton in February 1993 issued an executive order directing OMB to eliminate at least one-third of all federal advisory committees not required by Congress. As a result, the Clinton administration reported a net reduction of 42 percent in advisory committees by the middle of 1995.

FACA, however, was also a source of consternation for the Clinton administration. During the 1992 presidential campaign, candidate Clinton had promised national health-care reform. Shortly after his inauguration, the president appointed a presidential advisory committee, the Task Force on National Health Care Reform, to fashion a health care reform system that would guarantee health care to all Americans and reduce the rising rate of health care spending. Clinton appointed both cabinet members and White House staffers to the task force. In an unusual move, the president appointed his wife, Hillary Rodham Clinton, to chair the committee. As part of the task force, the administration set up fifteen working groups on different health care topics. Members included more than a hundred congressional staffers who dealt with health care policy, and health care policy experts from both the public and private sector.

Within a month of its formation, the task force came under attack for violating FACA regulations. The Association of American Physicians and Surgeons filed suit seeking to make the group's meetings and records public. Arguing that Hillary Clinton was neither a public official nor a federal employee, they charged that the task force came under the jurisdiction of FACA and should not be allowed to close its meetings to the media and the public.

The district court issued a ruling that confirmed the application of FACA to the task force. The court made a distinction between the cabinet members and White House staff, who made recommendations to the president, and the working groups, which were investigating and formulating alternative policies. Although the court enjoined the working groups from meeting in private, cabinet members and White House staffers were permitted to continue meeting privately to formulate and give recommendations to the president. The Clinton administration appealed the decision to the United States Court of Appeals for the D.C. Circuit.

The court of appeals overturned the district court's ruling that the task force fell under the jurisdiction of FACA because of Hillary Clinton's involvement. Ruling that the first lady was a full-time federal employee, the appeals court affirmed that the task force was free to make its recommendations to the president in private. The court ruled, however, that it had insufficient information to determine the status of the fifteen working groups and remanded the case to the district court for discovery about the membership and tasks of the groups. The district court ordered the Clinton administration to make public the membership and procedural documents of the working groups. The White House responded by releasing the list of people who served on the working groups and documents of meetings, travel reimbursements, and financial disclosure forms. By the time court proceedings were over and the documents were released, the task force had finished it work.

1. See Jay S. Bybee, "Advising the President: Separation of Powers and the Federal Advisory Committee Act," *Yale Law Journal*, October 1994, 51–128.

In their final reports, however, commissioners seek accommodation and compromise. Efforts also are made to ensure that relations among commissioners and staffers do not fragment beyond repair. A strong, competent chair is likely to intervene and call for more temperate rhetoric from commissioners.

Commissions often seek unanimity in their reports because they believe that it instills more legitimacy in their work. According to Martha Derthick, this goal leads to inaccuracies in reports. "Commissions frequently decide that it would be best not to confuse the nation with divided counsel. Since the commissioners usually are divided on important issues, this guarantees that a large number of these issues will be fudged."[60]

Although dissenting footnotes could be added to the final report, they usually are not. Instead, commissioners seek consensus, and "consensus can nearly always be made to cover up differences."[61] For example, the Warren Commission was divided on whether President Kennedy and Texas governor John B. Connally were hit by the same bullet. Three commissioners believed that both men had been hit by the same bullet, while three others believed that the men were hit by different bullets. In seeking a unanimous report, the commission entered into a debate over adjectives. One commissioner wanted the report to state that there was "compelling" evidence that the same bullet had hit both Kennedy and Connally. The commission finally compromised on the adjective "persuasive." The issue was never really settled by the commission.

Functions of Commissions

Although used ostensibly to supplement standard presidential advisory procedures, presidential commissions serve a variety of functions. Some scholars, however, have argued that commissions serve no useful purposes and should not be a part of the presidential advisory system. Others have argued, somewhat skeptically, that presidents use commissions for their own purposes—that is, either to generate support for existing policies or to postpone effective action by passing the problem off on a presidential commission. Elizabeth Drew has listed eight rather cynical reasons for appointing a commission:

1. To obtain the blessing of distinguished men for something you want to do anyway.

2. To postpone action, yet be justified in insisting that you are working on the problem.

3. To act as a lightning rod, drawing political heat away from the White House.

4. To conduct an extensive study of something you do need to know more about before you act, in case you do.

5. To investigate, lay to rest rumors, and convince the public of the validity of one particular set of facts.

6. To educate the commissioners, or get them aboard on something you want to do.

7. Because you can't think of anything else to do.

8. To change the hearts and minds of men.[62]

Another factor further complicates trust in the efficacy of commission work: once a commission's report is written, presidents can choose either to follow or to ignore the report's recommendations. They sometimes choose to ignore them, fueling the fires of the critics. Sen. Edward M. Kennedy (D-Mass.) has characterized commissions as "so many Jiminy Crickets chirping in the ears of deaf presidents, deaf officials, deaf congressmen, and perhaps a deaf public."[63]

What functions do commissions actually serve? The conventional wisdom is that presidents appoint commissions to avoid confronting an issue, to delay action, or to divert public attention. Yet research indicates that most presidents heed and act favorably on the reports they receive from their commissions.[64] Commissions serve a variety of other purposes, however, besides merely providing presidents with advice. Political scientist George T. Sulzner has classified these ulterior functions into two general categories. Functions in the first category generally re-

late to solving problems. They include investigating, defining, and recommending action on specific problems and generating public demands for such action. Functions in the second category relate to presidential management of conflict. They include consensus building and pacifying political groups.[65] Each presidential commission may go beyond the purely advisory function for which the commission was nominally created. Presidents may, and often do, use commissions to manage conflict during their administrations.

The first and most obvious function of commissions is to provide presidents with the information needed to make informed decisions. Although some scholars have impugned this motive, most presidents have appointed commissions to facilitate the fact-finding activities of the executive branch. According to Wolanin, "Most commissions are formed because the president wants to act but is not sure how, or is not sure that important segments of public opinion, congressional leadership, or executive branch agencies are ready to support him."[66] In fact, commission recommendations are usually accepted and often implemented. For example, President Truman's response to the growing demand for action against the lynchings of African Americans in the fall of 1946 was appointment of the President's Committee on Civil Rights in late 1946 to look into civil rights violations across the nation. In his memoirs, Truman explained that he took this action "because of repeated anti-minority incidents immediately after the war in which homes were invaded, property was destroyed, and a number of innocent lives were taken. I wanted to get the facts behind these incidents of disregard for individual and group rights which were reported in the news with alarming regularity. . . ."[67] The moral weight of the final report of the commission forced congressional consideration and implementation of its various proposals.

Presidents often turn to commissions to obtain information about a problem that regular presidential advisory mechanisms are unable to handle. Flitner has reported that a primary function of commissions is "surmounting the pathologies of organizational complexity: for avoiding duplication of effort and circumventing bureaucratic obstacles."[68] Both the Warren Commission and the President's Commission on the Space Shuttle *Challenger* Accident serve as examples of commissions formed to investigate expeditiously incidents that traditional presidential advisory mechanisms found difficult to handle. Some presidential commissions are able to bring together resources, skills, and information in a way that is unachievable by other advisory agencies of the executive branch. For example, the President's Private Sector Survey on Cost Control (1982–1983), or the Grace Commission, was composed entirely of private sector appointees, who were charged with recommending where the government could spend its money more efficiently. The 170 members of the Grace Commission issued a report that proposed 2,478 cost-cutting measures, which in theory would have saved the government $425 billion. Judging from the bureaucratic and congressional debate that ensued over the proposals, it is doubtful that any other executive branch advisory mechanism could have produced such a report. Four years after the report was is-sued, only about thirteen hundred of its recommendations were in place, reportedly saving the government almost $39 billion.

In addition to their advisory function, presidential commis-sions allow presidents to manage conflict by building a consen-sus for their programs. As many critics have charged, presidents use commissions to sell their programs to the country. Political commentator Harlan Cleveland has observed that "Commis-sions can . . . help the president build support for what he has already decided to do."[69] And according to Daniel Bell, the abili-ty of presidents to use commissions to build consensus has be-come so pronounced that there is a danger that presidents may use commissions primarily to manipulate public opinion.[70] Other observers believe, however, that presidents can use com-missions to focus the nation's attention on problems that other-wise would not gain legitimacy.

The very presence of "blue-ribbon" commissioners, who rep-resent a variety of interests, lends credibility to a commission's work. As an example, Etzioni pointed to the composition of the National Commission on the Causes and Prevention of Vio-lence, which refocused the national dialogue on the causes and prevention of violent behavior: "If ten wise men drawn from such a cross-section of the nation support a set of conclusions, the country is more likely to go along with them than if these conclusions are advocated by ten experts."[71] Similarly, the Na-tional Bipartisan Commission on Central America (1984) gave the Reagan administration a report that essentially upheld the administration policy of increased military assistance to El Sal-vador and continued aid to the Nicaraguan rebels. Because of its distinguished commissioners, headed by former secretary of state Henry Kissinger, and its bipartisan character, including former Democratic National Committee chairman Robert Strauss, criticism of the final report was muted.

Increasingly, however, the blue-ribbon nature of some com-missions has been questioned, leaving some final commission reports suspect. For example, the composition of the 1988 Presi-dential Commission on the Human Immunodeficiency Virus Epidemic (AIDS Commission) offended both ends of the politi-cal spectrum. The Reagan administration had nominated indi-viduals representing various interests in the AIDS crisis. Liber-als, however, were offended by the participation of such conser-vatives as state representative Penny Pullen of Illinois, who au-thored a mandatory AIDS testing bill, and conservatives were outraged by the inclusion of an avowed homosexual, New York geneticist Dr. Frank Lily. The medical community complained, as well, noting that not enough medical personnel were repre-sented. As a result, the commission's final report did not receive the widespread support enjoyed by most other commission re-ports.

The symbolic functions of commissions can be the most use-ful to presidents in managing conflict. The very creation of a commission sends signals to various groups and individuals that the administration is concerned about a specific problem. According to Flitner,

By their existence, commissions symbolize the highest cognizance and concern over a situation. Commissions communicate that the presi-dent is aware of a situation and will begin a process of directing atten-tion to it. This implies a search for facts and answers and willingness to give the disaffected members of society a "fair hearing." . . . In short, commissions represent the fact that the president is at least doing something.[72]

In many respects the creation of the 1988 AIDS Commission was a symbolic response of the Reagan administration to the grow-ing AIDS crisis. Similarly, in both 1994 and 1995, amid public calls for renewing civic values in education, President Clinton convened the White House Conferences on Character Building for a Democratic, Civil Society. The roughly two-hundred at-tendees included individuals from both ends of the political spectrum. Civic leaders such as former vice president Dan Quayle and First Lady Hillary Clinton meet for four days each year to deliberate the merits of "various character-education proposals."[73]

Some critics charge that the symbolic function of commis-sions undermines effective policy making by allowing presi-dents to delay action. Cleveland has contended: "On the whole, presidential commissions are probably better adapted to smoth-ering problems with well-publicized inaction than to paving the way for novel action."[74] This assessment may have been true in some cases, but overall it does not seem to be the motivation be-hind most presidential commissions,

Delay does occur, however. Sulzner has suggested that the de-lay that results from the appointment of commissions is an inte-gral part of the policy-making process by which government adapts to emerging social problems. It promotes political pacifi-cation through a cooling-off period. "Frequently, commissions hold public hearings where they solicit representative testimony from diverse sources, and these hearings can serve as outlets for the airing of grievances. Moreover, the opportunity for expres-sion may have cathartic effects for the interests involved that may be as rewarding to them as the provision of concrete reme-dies."[75]

Over the years some commissions have been abused or ig-nored in their efforts. Commission recommendations often do not become policy; sometimes they do. The final report of the Commission on Law Enforcement and the Administration of Justice is generally credited with having prompted the passage of the Safe Streets Act of 1968, for example. But more than just making policy recommendations, commissions have served other important, although often symbolic, functions. According to Flitner,

They have affected the attitudinal atmosphere of society. They have helped demythologize subjects such as the conspiracy theory or riot origins and the assumption that increasing population growth is nec-essarily advantageous. Commissions have helped lower the emotional content of certain issues, such as marijuana use. . . . Commissions have altered the terms in which issues are discussed and, although they have by no means either reached or convinced everyone of their findings, they have spread awareness to all levels of society, a not undesirable function in a democracy.[76]

NOTES

1. Carl Marcy, *Presidential Commissions* (New York: King's Crown Press, 1945), 97.

2. Quoted in ibid., 8.

3. Quoted in Elizabeth B. Drew, "On Giving Oneself a Hotfoot: Government by Commission," *Atlantic Monthly*, May 1968, 45.

4. Marcy, *Presidential Commissions*, 8.

5. Frank Popper, *The President's Commissions* (New York: Twentieth Century Fund, 1970), 66–67.

6. *Twenty-Third Annual Report of the President on Federal Advisory Committees, Fiscal 1994*, General Services Administration, July 10, 1995, 4.

7. Ibid.

8. Richard M. Pious, *The American Presidency* (New York: Basic Books, 1979), 164.

9. Alan L. Dean, "Ad Hoc Commissions for Policy Formulation," in *The Presidential Advisory System*, ed. Thomas E. Cronin and Sanford E. Greenberg (New York: Harper and Row, 1969), 101–102.

10. Terrence R. Tutchings, *Rhetoric and Reality: Presidential Commissions and the Making of Public Policy* (Boulder, Colo.: Westview, 1979), 12.

11. David Flitner Jr., *The Politics of Presidential Commissions* (Dobbs Ferry, N.Y.: Transnational Publishers, 1986), 28–29.

12. Thomas R. Wolanin, *Presidential Advisory Commissions: Truman to Nixon* (Madison: University of Wisconsin Press, 1975), 10.

13. Henry Fairlie, "Government by White House Conference: Two Views," in Cronin and Greenberg, *The Presidential Advisory System*, 144–149.

14. Flitner, *The Politics of Presidential Commissions*, 45.

15. Frank Popper, *The President's Commissions* (New York: Twentieth Century Fund, 1970), 15.

16. Daniel Bell, "Government by Commission," in Cronin and Greenberg, *The Presidential Advisory System*, 121.

17. Popper, *The President's Commissions*, 18.

18. Jason DeParle, "Advise and Forget," *Washington Monthly*, May 1983, 43.

19. Flitner, *The Politics of Presidential Commissions*, 46.

20. Cronin and Greenberg, *The Presidential Advisory Commission*, xix.

21. Popper, *The President's Commissions*, 17.

22. "The Commission: How to Create a Blue Chip Consensus," *Time*, January 19, 1970, 20.

23. Quoted in Wolanin, *Presidential Advisory Commissions*, 85.

24. Ibid.

25. Quoted in Popper, *The President's Commissions*, 20.

26. Wolanin, *Presidential Advisory Commissions*, 82–83.

27. Quoted in ibid., 83.

28. Ibid., 123.

29. Quoted in Flitner, *The Politics of Presidential Commissions*, 50–51.

30. Ibid., 50.

31. Lyndon Baines Johnson, *The Vantage Point—Perspectives on the Presidency, 1963–1969* (New York: Popular Library, 1971), 26.

32. Wolanin, *Presidential Advisory Commissions*, 84.

33. Popper, *The President's Commissions*, 22.

34. Drew, "On Giving Oneself a Hotfoot," 48.

35. Popper, *The President's Commissions*, 24.

36. Drew, "On Giving Oneself a Hotfoot," 48.

37. Popper, *The President's Commissions*, 22.

38. Flitner, *The Politics of Presidential Commissions*, 59.

39. Wolanin, *Presidential Advisory Commissions*, 108.

40. Popper, *The President's Commissions*, 24.

41. Tutchings, *Rhetoric and Reality*, 27.

42. Popper, *The President's Commissions*, 26.

43. Amitai Etzioni, "Why Task Force Studies Go Wrong," *Wall Street Journal*, July 9, 1968, 18.

44. Quoted in Flitner, *The Politics of Presidential Commissions*, 63.

45. Popper, *The President's Commissions*, 27.

46. Wolanin, *Presidential Advisory Commissions*, 112.

47. Popper, *The President's Commissions*, 28.

48. Quoted in Wolanin, *Presidential Advisory Commissions*, 113.

49. Ibid., 121.

50. Flitner, *The Politics of Presidential Commissions*, 79–80.

51. Ibid., 65–66.

52. Popper, *The President's Commissions*, 37.

53. Martha Derthick, "On Commissionship—Presidential Variety," Brookings Reprint No. 245 (Washington, D.C.: Brookings, 1972), 627, 636.

54. Quoted in Flitner, *The Politics of Presidential Commissions*, 77.

55. Popper, *The President's Commissions*, 36–37.

56. Nicholas F. S. Burnett, "Considering Commissions Critically," in *Government Commission Communication*, ed. Christine M. Miller and Bruce C. McKinney (Westport, Conn.: Praeger, 1991), 19.

57. Quoted in W. David Snowball, "Rhetorical Constraints on Government Commissioning," in *Government Commission Communication*, 38.

58. Wolanin, *Presidential Advisory Commissions*, 110–111.

59. Popper, *The President's Commissions*, 31–32.

60. Derthick, "On Commissionship," 629.

61. Popper, *The President's Commissions*, 33.

62. Drew, "On Giving Oneself a Hotfoot," 45–47.

63. Quoted in Flitner, *The Politics of Presidential Commissions*, 2.

64. Thomas E. Cronin, "On the Separation of Brain and State: Implications for the Presidency," in *Modern Presidents and the Presidency*, ed. Marc Landy (Lexington, Mass.: Lexington Books, 1985), 60–61.

65. George T. Sulzner, "The Policy Process and the Uses of National Governmental Study Commissions," in *Perspectives on the Presidency: A Collection*, ed. Stanley Bach and George T. Sulzner (Lexington, Mass.: D. C. Heath, 1974), 207.

66. Wolanin, *Presidential Advisory Commissions*, 193.

67. Harry S Truman, *Memoirs* (Garden City, N.J.: Doubleday, 1955–1956), 2: 180.

68. Flitner, *The Politics of Presidential Commissions*, 180.

69. Harlan Cleveland, "Inquiry into Presidential Inquirers," in *The Dynamics of the American Presidency*, ed. Donald B. Johnson and Jack L. Walker (New York: Wiley, 1964), 292.

70. Bell, "Government by Commission," 121.

71. Etzioni, "Why Task Force Studies Go Wrong," 18.

72. Flitner, *The Politics of Presidential Commissions*, 180.

73. Benjamin DeMott, "Morality Plays," *Harper's Magazine*, December 1994, 67.

74. Cleveland, "Inquiry into Presidential Inquirers," 292.

75. Sulzner, "The Policy Process," 216.

76. Flitner, *The Politics of Presidential Commissions*, 180–181.

SELECTED BIBLIOGRAPHY

Bach, Stanley, and George T. Sulzner, eds. *Perspectives on the Presidency: A Collection.* Lexington, Mass.: D.C. Heath, 1974.

Bell, Daniel. "Government by Commission." In *The Presidential Advisory System*, ed. Thomas E. Cronin and Sanford E. Greenberg. New York: Harper and Row, 1969.

Burnett, Nicholas F. S. "Considering Commissions Critically." In *Government Commission Communication*, ed. Christine M. Miller and Bruce C. McKinney. Westport, Conn.: Praeger, 1991.

Bybee, Jay S. "Advising the President: Separation of Powers and the Federal Advisory Committee Act." *Yale Law Journal*, October 1994, 51–128.

Cleveland, Harlan. "Inquiry into Presidential Inquirers." In *The Dynamics of the American Presidency*, ed. Donald B. Johnson and Jack L. Walker. New York: Wiley, 1964.

Cronin, Thomas E. "On the Separation of Brain and State: Implications for the Presidency." In *Modern Presidents and the Presidency*, ed. Marc Landy. Lexington, Mass.: Lexington Books, 1985.

Cronin, Thomas E., and Sanford E. Greenberg, eds. *The Presidential Advisory Commission.* New York: Harper and Row, 1969.

Dean, Alan L. "Ad Hoc Commissions for Policy Formulation." In *The Presidential Advisory System,* ed. Thomas E. Cronin and Sanford E. Greenberg. New York: Harper and Row, 1969.

DeMott, Benjamin. "Morality Plays." *Harper's Magazine,* December 1994, 67–77.

DeParle, Jason. "Advise and Forget." *Washington Monthly,* May 1983, 41–46.

Derthick, Martha. "On Commissionship—Presidential Variety." Brookings Reprint No. 245. Washington, D.C.: Brookings, 1972.

Drew, Elizabeth B. "On Giving Oneself a Hotfoot: Government by Commission." *Atlantic Monthly,* May 1968, 45–49.

Etzioni, Amitai. "Why Task Force Studies Go Wrong." *Wall Street Journal,* July 9, 1968, 18.

Fairlie, Henry. "Government by White House Conference: Two Views." In *The Presidential Advisory System,* ed. Thomas E. Cronin and Sanford E. Greenberg. New York: Harper and Row, 1969.

Flitner, David, Jr., *The Politics of Presidential Commissions.* Dobbs Ferry, N.Y.: Transnational Publishers, 1986.

Johnson, Donald B., and Jack L. Walker, eds. *The Dynamics of the American Presidency.* New York: Wiley, 1964.

Landy, Marc, ed. *Modern Presidents and the Presidency.* Lexington, Mass.: Lexington Books, 1985.

Marcy, Carl. *Presidential Commissions.* New York: King's Crown Press, 1945.

Miller, Christine M. and Bruce C. McKinney, eds. *Government Commission Communication.* Westport, Conn.: Praeger, 1991.

Popper, Frank. *The President's Commissions.* New York: Twentieth Century Fund, 1970.

Snowball, W. David. "Rhetorical Constraints on Government Commissions," In *Government Commission Communication,* ed. Christine M. Miller and Bruce C. McKinney. Westport, Conn.: Praeger, 1991.

Sulzner, George T. "The Policy Process and the Uses of National Government Study Commissions." In *Perspectives on the Presidency: A Collection,* ed. Stanley Bach and George T. Sulzner. Lexington, Mass.: D.C. Heath, 1974.

"The Commission: How to Create a Blue Chip Consensus." *Time,* January 19, 1970, 20.

Tutchings, Terrence R. *Rhetoric and Reality: Presidential Commissions and the Making of Public Policy.* Boulder, Colo.: Westview, 1979.

Twenty-Third Annual Report of the President on Federal Advisory Committees, Fiscal Year 1994. Washington, D.C.: General Services Administration, July 10, 1995.

Wolanin, Thomas R. *Presidential Advisory Commissions: Truman to Nixon.* Madison, Wis.: University of Wisconsin Press, 1975.

CHAPTER 32

Former Presidents

BY MICHAEL NELSON

W HEN THE FRAMERS of the Constitution reject-ed a proposal by Alexander Hamilton that the president be elected to a lifetime term, they unwit-tingly created an unofficial office: the ex-presidency. At noon on January 20, 1993, George Bush became the nation's thirty-sec-ond former president. (Eight presidents died while still in office.) Collectively, Bush's thirty-one predecessors had lived more than three hundred years after leaving the White House, including four—Richard Nixon, Gerald R. Ford, Jimmy Carter, and Ronald Reagan—who were former presidents during the entire Bush presidency. (See Table 32-1.) Bush's addition to their ranks meant that from January 20, 1993, until Nixon's death on April 22, 1994, there were five living former presidents. Only once before had that many former presidents been alive at the same time: Martin Van Buren, John Tyler, Franklin Pierce, Mil-lard Fillmore, and James Buchanan all lived between March 4, 1861, when Buchanan left office, and January 18, 1862, when Tyler died.

On four other occasions—each of them in the early- or mid-nineteenth century—the nation had four living ex-presidents: March 4, 1825–July 4, 1826 (John Adams, Thomas Jefferson, James Madison, and James Monroe); March 1, 1845–June 8, 1845 (John Quincy Adams, Andrew Jackson, Van Buren, and Tyler); March 4, 1857–March 4, 1861 (Van Buren, Tyler, Fillmore, and Pierce); and January 18, 1862–July 24, 1862 (Van Buren, Fillmore, Pierce, and Buchanan). In contrast, on five occasions there have been no living former presidents at all: for one year after George Washington died (1799–1801), for two years after Andrew John-son died (1875–1877), for one year after Grover Cleveland died (1908–1909), and from January 22, 1973, when Lyndon B. John-son died, until August 9, 1974, when Nixon resigned.

According to the historian Daniel J. Boorstin, "The number of living former presidents is likely to increase, with the decline in smoking and the increasing longevity of the American popu-lation and especially since the passage of the Twenty-second Amendment to the Constitution, which prevents a president from serving more than two terms."[1] To this list one might add the rapid turnover of presidents that has characterized recent American politics: from John F. Kennedy to Bill Clinton, eight presidents, only one of whom (Reagan) managed to serve two full terms, have occupied the office.

"[F]ormer presidents," observed the political scientist Alan Evan Schenker, "are a mixed bag, older and younger, Democrat and Republican, willing and unwilling retirees, healthy and ill,

TABLE 32–1 Former Presidents: Length of Life after Leaving Office

President	Date left office	Date of death	Length of life after leaving office
1. Washington	March 4, 1797	Dec. 14, 1799	2 years, 285 days
2. J. Adams	March 4, 1801	July 4, 1826	25 years, 122 days
3. Jefferson	March 4, 1809	July 4, 1826	17 years, 122 days
4. Madison	March 4, 1817	June 28, 1836	19 years, 116 days
5. Monroe	March 4, 1825	July 4, 1831	6 years, 122 days
6. J. Q. Adams	March 4, 1829	Feb. 23, 1848	18 years, 356 days
7. Jackson	March 4, 1837	June 8, 1845	8 years, 96 days
8. Van Buren	March 4, 1841	July 24, 1862	21 years, 142 days
9. Tyler	March 4, 1845	Jan. 18, 1862	16 years, 320 days
10. Polk	March 4, 1849	June 15, 1849	103 days
11. Fillmore	March 4, 1853	March 8, 1874	21 years, 4 days
12. Pierce	March 4, 1857	Oct. 8, 1869	12 years, 218 days
13. Buchanan	March 4, 1861	June 1, 1868	7 years, 89 days
14. A. Johnson	March 4, 1869	July 31, 1875	6 years, 149 days
15. Grant	March 4, 1877	July 23, 1885	8 years, 141 days
16. Hayes	March 4, 1881	Jan. 17, 1893	11 years, 319 days
17. Arthur	March 4, 1885	Nov. 18, 1886	1 year, 260 days
18. Cleveland[a]	March 4, 1889	June 24, 1908	15 years, 112 days
19. B. Harrison	March 4, 1893	March 13, 1901	8 years, 9 days
20. T. Roosevelt	March 4, 1909	Jan. 6, 1919	9 years, 309 days
21. Taft	March 4, 1913	March 8, 1930	17 years, 4 days
22. Wilson	March 4, 1921	Feb. 3, 1924	2 years, 337 days
23. Coolidge	March 4, 1929	Jan. 5, 1933	3 years, 308 days
24. Hoover	March 4, 1933	Oct. 20, 1964	31 years, 231 days
25. Truman	Jan. 20, 1953	Dec. 26, 1972	19 years, 340 days
26. Eisenhower	Jan. 20, 1961	Mar. 28, 1969	8 years, 67 days
27. L. Johnson	Jan. 20, 1969	Jan. 22, 1973	4 years, 2 days
28. Nixon	August 9, 1974	April 22, 1994	19 years, 256 days
29. Ford	Jan. 20, 1977	—	—
30. Carter	Jan. 20, 1981	—	—
31. Reagan	Jan. 20, 1989	—	—
32. Bush	Jan. 20, 1993	—	—

SOURCE: Congressional Research Service.

NOTE: a. Even though Grover Cleveland was elected to the presidency two different times (not in succession—he was also president from March 4, 1893, to March 4, 1897), he is counted only once as a former president.

rich and poor, loved and hated."[2] Some former presidents were young when they left office: Theodore Roosevelt was fifty (the youngest to date), and Pierce, Fillmore, and James K. Polk were all in their early fifties. Indeed, Schenker has noted, the majority of postpresidential years have been lived by men in their fifties and sixties. Other former presidents were old at the time of their retirement: Dwight D. Eisenhower was seventy, Buchanan and Jackson were sixty-nine, and Harry S. Truman was sixty-eight. Reagan, the oldest person ever to be elected to the presidency, was also the oldest ever to leave it: he turned seventy-eight on February 6, 1989.

Former presidents have left office under a variety of circumstances. Some were retired against their will: Pierce, Truman, and Lyndon Johnson were among those who, in effect, were denied renomination by their parties to run for another term; Cleveland, William Howard Taft, Hoover, Ford, Carter, and Bush were renominated but were defeated in the general election; Nixon resigned from the presidency to avoid impeachment; and Eisenhower and Reagan were denied the opportunity to run for a third term by the Twenty-second Amendment (1951).

Washington, in contrast, yearned for "the shade of retirement" (a phrase he used in his Farewell Address) and stepped down willingly at the end of his second term. Jefferson, Madison, and Monroe followed suit. Several former presidents actively sought another term—Van Buren as the candidate of the Free Soil Party in 1848, Fillmore as the nominee of the American Party in 1856, Cleveland as the Democratic nominee in 1892, and Theodore Roosevelt, who ran as the Progressive (or Bull Moose) nominee in 1912 after failing to win the Republican nomination. Hoover conducted a barely concealed campaign for the Republican nomination in 1940. Only Cleveland was successful: in 1892 he defeated the candidate who had defeated him in 1888, Benjamin Harrison.

Some former presidents lived long after exiting the White House, including Hoover (almost thirty-two years), John Adams (twenty-five years), Fillmore (twenty-one years), and Nixon (twenty years). Polk and Chester A. Arthur, both of them young, lived only three months and two years, respectively, after their terms expired.

Almost from the beginning, former presidents have been uncertain about what they should and should not do after leaving office. Taft suggested that the former president should be given "a dose of chloroform or . . . the fruit of the lotus tree" in order to "fix his place in history and enable the public to pass on to new measures and new men."[3] Some have remained in politics, including not just the five who sought a return to the presidency, but also three who were elected to Congress (John Quincy Adams, Andrew Johnson, and, in the Confederate congress, Tyler), and one (Taft) who became chief justice of the United States. Others have left the political arena almost entirely; still others (notably Hoover) have served the federal government in one or more special assignments. Whether politically active or not, however, "nearly every president has been critical of his successor," according to the author James Clark. "Even George Washington criticized John Adams for spending too much time away from his office."[4]

Some former presidents, such as Ulysses S. Grant and Ford, have traded on their status in an effort to become wealthy. Grant was disastrously unsuccessful; Ford, as ex-president, became a multimillionaire for the first time in his life. Others (including Jefferson, Madison, Monroe, and several other nineteenth-century presidents) have ended their lives heavily in debt. Until recently, no pension or expense money was provided to former presidents or their widows, a situation that was remedied by the passage of the Former Presidents Act of 1958 and later legislation. Since the 1970s, some critics have argued that presidents now are provided for too generously after they leave the White House.

The longer the time that passes after a former president leaves office, the more appreciative historians usually become. Hoover ranked twentieth of twenty-nine presidents in a 1948 survey of historians by Arthur M. Schlesinger Sr.; in a 1981 survey by Robert K. Murray and Tim H. Blessing, he ranked twenty-first of thirty-six. Franklin D. Roosevelt rose from third in 1948 to second in 1981. Truman, in a 1962 Schlesinger survey of historians, scored ninth of thirty-one presidents; by 1981 he was eighth of thirty-six. Eisenhower registered the most impressive gain of all, from twenty-second (in the bottom third) in 1962 to eleventh (the top third) in 1981. Of the more recent former presidents, the reputations of Nixon (ranked thirty-fourth in 1981) and Carter (ranked twenty-fifth) already seem to be on the rise. Kennedy, however, was so admired by historians after he was assassinated in 1963 that his standing seems likely to fall.[5] (See Chapter 4, Rating the Presidents, Vol. I.)

Just as former presidents are to some extent uncertain about what is expected of them, Americans seem ambivalent about the ex-presidency as an institution. The titles of recent articles on the subject mirror the range of feelings Americans have: from respect ("Presidents Emeritus") to resentment ("Caring for Ex-Presidents Can Cost a Bundle") to bewilderment ("What Shall We Do with Our Ex-Presidents?").[6]

Evolution of the Ex-Presidency

Former presidents were not thought of as a group—nor was the ex-presidency regarded as even an unofficial office—until recently. "The evolution of the ex-presidency has been rather haphazard," observed the historian John Whiteclay Chambers II in 1979. "For most of its history the nation has left the former presidents to fend for themselves and to work out their own post-executive careers. But in the last thirty years, the quasi-public 'Office of the Ex-President' has emerged with quite well-defined perquisites, and some of the trappings of power."[7]

The evolution of the ex-presidency may be divided into three main periods. The first period began with the first former president, George Washington, and ended during the postpresidential career of Grant. Although Washington established some precedents for later ex-presidents to follow, great uncertainty prevailed for many years about what the proper role of a former chief executive should be. The 1870s until the mid-1950s (Rutherford B. Hayes to Truman) constitute a second era in the evolution of the ex-presidency, one in which widespread concern was expressed about what activities were appropriate for former presidents and how they should be supported. The third period has witnessed the development of what Chambers called the "Office of Ex-President," with a panoply of quasi-institutional roles and resources.

GEORGE WASHINGTON TO ULYSSES S. GRANT

Washington is most admired by historians for the precedents he set for future presidents. Less remarked on are the precedents he set for future former presidents. First—and, perhaps, foremost—Washington eschewed the opportunity to remain in office (probably, for life, if he had chosen to stand for reelection every four years) and voluntarily became a former president at the end of his second term on March 4, 1797. Equally important, in deciding to return to his plantation in Virginia, Washington departed from the seat of government instead of remaining behind as an active or potential rival to his successor. Finally, as former president, Washington responded to a call of duty that later was issued. When the nation faced war with France in 1798, Washington accepted President John Adams's request to serve as commanding officer of the army. Fortunately, war was avoided.

Adams was the first president to be defeated for reelection. He also was one of the longest lived former presidents, surviving for twenty-five years after leaving office at age sixty-five. Initially, Adams was bitter at his defeat and avoided politics. Eventually, however, he entered into one of the most fabled and friendly correspondences in U.S. history with Thomas Jefferson, his erstwhile political rival and the candidate who had beaten him in the election of 1800.[8] In 1820, at the age of eighty-five, Adams was a delegate to the Massachusetts constitutional convention. (He also served his home town of Quincy, Mass., as a surveyor of roads, a selectman, and an assessor.) Four years later, in 1824, Adams became the only former president to witness the election of his son (John Quincy Adams) as president. On July 4, 1826, the fiftieth anniversary of the signing of the Declaration of Independence, Adams and Jefferson both died.

Jefferson was the first president to leave office after two terms as a matter of principle. *(See "Twenty-second Amendment," p. 49, in Chapter 1, Vol. I.)* Sixty-six at the time, Jefferson's final years were financially disastrous, partly because he was untalented as a farmer, but also because he "was one of America's major attractions, and it appeared that every visitor to America made a point of breaking his journey at Jefferson's lovely home" Monticello near Charlottesville, Virginia.[9] Jefferson died with more than $100,000 in debts.

Several of Jefferson's successors as former president also suffered the consecutive burdens of neglecting their own financial affairs while serving in the White House (at an annual salary of $25,000), then bearing the responsibilities of entertainment, correspondence, and the other obligations of fame when out of office. Former presidents received no pension or expense money; nor did their widows. Three of the four presidents who followed Jefferson—Madison, Monroe, and Jackson—endured considerable financial distress in retirement. Monroe actually had to leave his home state of Virginia to live with a daughter

After his presidency, John Quincy Adams served eighteen years in the House of Representatives. Adams is the earliest president of whom there is a photograph; this daguerrotype was made shortly before his death in 1848.

and son-in-law in New York, where he died. In 1841 Congress did vote to give $25,000 (equal to one year's presidential salary) to the widow of William Henry Harrison, who was the first president to die in office. More grudgingly, Congress in 1870 approved a small annual pension for the unpopular Mary Todd Lincoln, whose husband Abraham Lincoln was assassinated in 1865.

In contrast, the postpresidential career of John Quincy Adams, who was chosen as president in the disputed election of 1824 and roundly defeated by Jackson four years later, was happier than his presidency ("the four most miserable years of my life," Adams later said).[10] In 1830 Adams was asked by voters in Quincy, Massachusetts, if he would consider election to the U.S. House of Representatives to be degrading. "No person could be degraded by serving the people as a representative," Adams replied. "Nor, in my opinion, would an ex-president be degraded by serving as a selectman of his town, if elected thereto by the people."[11] Adams served eighteen years in Congress until his death at age eighty. His most famous legislative victory came in 1844, when he secured the repeal of the House's 1836 "gag resolution," under which antislavery petitions were automatically tabled without consideration.

For a time, most of Adams's successors as former president followed his precedent of active involvement in politics. Van Buren unsuccessfully sought the Democratic presidential nomination in 1844 and accepted the nomination of the Free Soil Party in 1848. (He received 10 percent of the popular vote but no electoral votes.) Fillmore was nominated for president by the American, or Know Nothing Party in 1856: he won 21.5 percent of the popular vote and eight electoral votes. In 1861 the Virginian Tyler presided over the Peace Conference, which sought vainly to avert civil war, then was elected to the lower house of the congress of the Confederate States of America. (He died before taking his seat.) After being impeached, almost convicted, and denied renomination to run for president in 1868, Andrew Johnson won a vindication of sorts when the Tennessee legislature narrowly elected him to the U.S. Senate in 1874.

Few of the early former presidents did much writing of consequence after leaving office. One exception was James Buchanan, who wrote a labored defense of his generally unsuccessful presidency called *Mr. Buchanan's Administration on the Eve of the Rebellion*. Buchanan waited until 1866 to publish his book so that it would not be regarded as an effort to embarrass President Lincoln. It sold only five thousand copies. Grant was much more successful as an author. His two-volume *Memoirs* of his service as general during the Civil War earned $440,000 for his estate. Grant died of cancer three days after completing the work. His memoirs said nothing about his presidency.

Unfortunately, Grant also traded on his status as a former president to engage in some tarnished business dealings. He and his son joined with an unscrupulous speculator to form a Wall Street investment house called Grant and Ward. The firm went bankrupt in 1884, destroying the savings of thousands of investors who, in many cases, had been attracted to the firm by Grant's reputation.

Grant's business affairs seemed especially notorious because in 1873, at the start of his second term as president, Congress had voted to double the president's salary to $50,000. The reason for doing so, explained the House Judiciary Committee in the report that recommended the legislation, was that although no law prevented "an ex-president of the United States from engaging in the business pursuits of life for the purpose of acquiring property, . . . custom and public sentiment" were "decided against such a course." The committee felt that a former president "ought to have a sufficient provision while in office to enable him when he leaves it to retire from all active, or at least all money making, pursuits."[12]

After the bankruptcy of his investment house in 1884, Ulysses S. Grant wrote his memoirs to make ends meet. This photograph was taken at Grant's New York cottage in 1885, the year of his death.

RUTHERFORD B. HAYES TO HARRY S. TRUMAN

Grant's financial indiscretions notwithstanding, the belief grew over the years that business was an unsuitable activity for former presidents—not because private enterprise was regarded as inherently bad, but because a company's motive in hiring a former president presumably would be to trade on the prestige of the office. Calvin Coolidge expressed the attitude of many of his colleagues in rejecting an offer that would have paid him much more than he ever had been paid as president. "These people are trying to hire not Calvin Coolidge, but a former president of the United States," he argued. "I can't do anything that might take away from the presidency any of its dignity, or any of the faith the people have in it." Truman later echoed this sentiment: "I could never lend myself to any transaction, however respectable, that would commercialize on the prestige and dignity of the presidency."[13]

Congress periodically raised the president's salary—to $75,000 in 1909 and $100,000 in 1949—in order that presidents would be able to save for their retirement and so not need to pursue commercial careers.[14] The industrialist Andrew Carnegie's 1912 offer—evidently benign in origin—to fund personally an annual pension of $25,000 a year to ex-presidents was rejected by former presidents Taft, Theodore Roosevelt, and Coolidge as unnecessary and was disapproved of as unseemly by many members of Congress.

A quiet retirement was one choice available to former presidents, assuming they had accumulated sufficient savings before or during their tenure in the White House to be able to afford to retire. At age fifty-seven, Coolidge and his wife returned to Northampton, Massachusetts, and rented (at $32 per month) a duplex at 21 Massasoit Street. Tourists annoyed them so much that they eventually moved to a larger home on the outskirts of town. Truman bought train tickets for himself and his wife and rode from Washington to their modest family home at 219 North Delaware Street in Independence, Missouri. "I tried never to forget who I was, where I came from, and where I would go back to," he later said.[15]

Most former presidents (including Truman) pursued one or more active roles in retirement that were widely regarded as appropriate to their status. Among these were: law, writing, service in temporary public assignments, testimony before congressional committees, and, in ways more restricted than for the early presidents, politics.

Law

For a time, beginning in the late-nineteenth century, several former presidents (notably Cleveland, Benjamin Harrison, and Taft) resumed legal careers of one sort or another. Fillmore had rejected such a career for himself as improper for a former president, but Harrison actually argued cases before Supreme Court justices whom he had appointed. Cleveland declined to appear in court but wrote legal briefs for clients. Taft, shortly after leaving the presidency in 1909, became the Kent professor of law at Yale University.

Writing

Grant established writing as a normal activity for former presidents. Among his predecessors, John Quincy Adams (the sole president to become a published poet until Jimmy Carter published a book of poems in 1994), Van Buren, and Buchanan had been the only presidents to write extensively after leaving office. But Grant wrote a series of articles (at a rate of $500 each) for *Century Magazine* about his Civil War experiences and later expanded them into his critically and commercially successful *Memoirs*. Cleveland wrote numerous magazine articles and books on subjects as diverse as the presidency *(Presidential Problems)* and hunting and fishing *(Fishing and Hunting Sketches)*. Theodore Roosevelt averaged one book per year in the decade after his tenure as president ended, along with hundreds of magazine articles and newspaper editorials. Taft also wrote frequently for newspapers and magazines such as the *Saturday Evening Post* and the *Ladies Home Journal,* as did Coolidge. Taft's 1916 book, *Our Chief Magistrate: His Office and Powers,* is still widely quoted for its defense of the presidency as an office of

limited powers. Hoover compiled collections of his speeches for publication in a series of books called *Addresses Along the American Road* and wrote other books as well, including his *Memoirs* and *The Ordeal of Woodrow Wilson.* (Theodore Roosevelt and Coolidge each published a book called *Autobiography.*) Truman's two-volume *Memoirs* and a later book about his retirement *(Mr. Citizen)* sold very well and provided his main source of income.

Temporary Service in Government

Although Rutherford B. Hayes served in no official capacity after leaving the presidency, he stated the simple creed that has guided most ex-presidents ever since: "Let him, like every good American citizen, be willing and prompt to bear his part in every useful work that will promote the welfare and happiness of his family, his town, his state, and his country."[16]

Most former presidents have accepted temporary assignments of one sort or another from the federal government. For example:

• Grant served as U.S. commissioner to Mexico in 1882 to negotiate a commercial treaty.

• Benjamin Harrison accepted an appointment to the Permanent Court of Arbitration.

• At the request of President Theodore Roosevelt, Cleveland headed a study commission during the coal strike of 1902.

• Theodore Roosevelt was the U.S. delegate to the funeral of Great Britain's King Edward VII in 1910.

• During World War I, Taft was cochair of the National War Labor Board and served as a member of several war commissions.

No president has taken on more temporary assignments than Hoover, especially during the Truman administration. (Franklin Roosevelt was uninterested in Hoover's services: told after World War II broke out that Hoover was willing to serve in government, Roosevelt snapped, "Well, I'm not Jesus Christ, and I'm not raising him from the dead.")[17] In 1946 Hoover headed the Truman-appointed Famine Emergency Committee, which helped to save millions of lives by documenting the need for food relief after the end of World War II. In anticipation of the Marshall Plan for postwar economic aid to Europe, Hoover led the President's Economic Mission to Germany and Austria in 1947. In 1947 and 1953 he directed the first and second "Hoover commissions" (Commission on Organization of the Executive Branch of the Government) and recommended numerous reorganization plans for the federal bureaucracy, several of which were adopted.

Testimony before Congress

John Tyler was the first and only former president in the nineteenth century to appear before a congressional committee.[18] Tyler was subpoenaed in 1846 to shed light on accusations—groundless, as it turned out—that had been made against former secretary of state Daniel Webster. Of the twentieth-century former presidents, Theodore Roosevelt, Taft, Hoover, Truman, Ford, and Carter testified to Congress on several occasions. In some cases, their testimony bore on decisions that had been made while they were president. Roosevelt, for example, was called on to defend both an antitrust decision and his 1904 campaign fund-raising practices. At other times, the testimony of the former president related to policy issues (Taft on budgeting, Truman on repeal of the two-term limit on presidents, Carter on mediating the Bosnia conflict) about which he had a particular concern. A former president's service in a temporary assignment often was the occasion of congressional testimony. Hoover's record-setting twenty appearances before Congress mainly concerned his work on famine relief and the first and second Hoover commissions.

All of the twentieth-century appearances of former presidents before congressional committees have been voluntary, none by subpoena. Indeed, when the House Committee on Un-American Activities sent a subpoena to Truman in 1953 to testify about the promotion of alleged communists in his administration, he refused it by claiming the same immunity, on grounds of separation of powers and executive privilege, that the incumbent president traditionally had enjoyed.[19]

Politics

In contrast to several of their predecessors, former presidents since Grant have not pursued or accepted other offices after leaving the White House. Some, however, have tried to return to the presidency, and one, Cleveland, succeeded. Among those who were less successful was Theodore Roosevelt, who, after failing to wrest the Republican nomination from President Taft in 1912, ran for president on the Progressive (Bull Moose) Party ticket. (He finished second—ahead of Taft—with 27.4 percent of the popular vote and eighty-eight electoral votes.) Despite the scandals that tainted the Grant administration, the physical disability that crippled Woodrow Wilson, and the devastating electoral defeat that drove Hoover from office, each seems to have hoped that he would be drafted by his party to run for another presidential term. Hoover also hoped (forlornly) that he would be appointed to fill Hiram Johnson's Senate seat when the California senator died in 1945.

Taft was perhaps history's happiest former president. He always would have preferred to have been chief justice of the United States rather than president. When Chief Justice Edward D. White died in 1921, Taft was elevated to that position by President Warren G. Harding. "Next to my wife and children, the Court is the nearest thing to my heart in life," Taft declared on one occasion. In 1925 he wrote blissfully: "The truth is that in my present life I don't remember that I ever was president."[20]

The "Office of the Ex-President"

Since the 1950s, the "ex-presidency" has taken on many of the trappings of a government institution—"a form of public of-

Having yearned to head the Supreme Court, even over the presidency, William Howard Taft finally got his wish. He was appointed chief justice by President Warren Harding in 1921.

fice," in the words of the historian John Whiteclay Chambers. "This has not been the result of any coherent, deliberate policy; developments have often been fortuitously related to other events. Nevertheless, more codification has taken place [since 1950] than in the first 150 years of the Republic."[21] Indeed, the ex-presidency to some degree has become institutionalized in both senses of the word—its size and complexity are greater than in the past, and new expectations exist of its incumbents.

Chronologically, the ex-presidency has developed in four main stages:

• The generally successful assertion by former president Truman of a right for former presidents to make constitutional claims of executive privilege (see "Testimony before Congress," p. 1273.)

• The passage of the Presidential Libraries Act of 1955, which funded the maintenance of libraries and museums for each recent former president

• The passage of the Former Presidents Act of 1958 and later legislation, which provided each former president with a pension, protection by the Secret Service, and money for office, staff, and other expenses

• The granting to former presidents of the right to address the Senate.

Since the mid-1970s, these developments have triggered a re-action against what critics sometimes call the "imperial ex-presidency."[22] The ex-presidency has become an expensive office (see Table 32-2)—taken together, the cost to the Treasury of presidential libraries, pensions, and other expenses rose from nothing in 1954 to $147,000 in 1958 to $28 million in 1987, with roughly two-thirds of that amount going to maintain presidential libraries.[23] Former presidents also are largely unaccountable. As Chambers has noted, "despite the growth of the office and of the sums of public funds spent on its maintenance, a former chief executive is under virtually no obligation to do, or not to do, anything at all."[24]

PRESIDENTIAL LIBRARIES

Among the precedents George Washington established as a former president was the right to claim private ownership of his presidential papers. During the nineteenth century, several groups of presidential papers were purchased from former presidents or their estates by the federal government and stored at the State Department. In 1903 the Library of Congress began taking possession of the papers that the government had purchased: its manuscript division now has most of the papers of every president from Washington to Coolidge. Still, significant collections of the papers of the first twenty-nine presidents remain scattered about the country. Some former presidents gave away parts of their papers as souvenirs; others burned their papers or mutilated them.

During his second term, President Franklin Roosevelt conceived the idea of creating a Roosevelt presidential library, and he organized a private committee to fund and construct one in his home town, Hyde Park, New York. Roosevelt asked Congress to authorize the National Archives to receive the library and his papers as a gift, agreeing in turn to see to it that the library's operation and maintenance were publicly financed. In 1939 Congress consented to do so. The Franklin D. Roosevelt Library opened to researchers in 1946.

Encouraged to make similar arrangements by committees that were planning libraries for former president Truman and President Eisenhower, Congress passed the Presidential Libraries Act in 1955. The Harry S. Truman Library opened in Independence, Missouri, in 1957; the Dwight D. Eisenhower Library in Abilene, Kansas, in 1962; the Herbert Hoover Library in West Branch, Iowa, in 1962; the Lyndon Baines Johnson Library in Austin, Texas, in 1971; the John F. Kennedy Library in Boston, Massachusetts, in 1979; the Gerald R. Ford Library in Ann Arbor, Michigan, in 1980; the Jimmy Carter Library in Atlanta, Georgia, in 1986; the Richard Nixon Library in Yorba Linda, California, in 1990; and the Ronald Reagan Library in Simi Valley, California, in 1991. A George Bush Library in College Station, Texas, is scheduled to open by the spring of 1997.

The Carter library is unique among the presidential libraries because it includes the Carter Center, which is devoted to the study and melioration of public policy problems, most of them international. With an annual budget (most of it raised by Carter) of more than $20 million and a staff of more than one hundred, the center includes programs such as Global 2000, which conducts health and agricultural projects in Africa and Asia, the Council of Freely-Elected Heads of Government, which was established to assist emerging democracies in the Western Hemisphere, and the International Negotiating Network (INN), which was designed to help resolve civil wars. (Although the vast majority of wars are civil wars, international bodies such as the UN are restricted to dealing with conflicts between nations.) As chair of the heads of government council, Carter has been invited to monitor the fairness of elections in Panama, Nicaragua, and Haiti; as head of the INN, Carter has tried to mediate conflicts like the one between the government of Ethiopia and the Eritrean People's Liberation Front.

Nine of the presidential libraries (all but the privately run Nixon library) are part of the presidential library system that was created by the 1955 act. They are administered by the Office of Presidential Libraries, a division of the National Archives and Records Administration. Funding policies, as well as the traditional policy of individual presidential control over the papers of their administrations, have been modified by laws passed in 1974, 1978, and 1986. (See "Official Reactions," p. 1280.)

SUPPORT AND PROTECTION

Until 1958, former presidents were virtually the only officials or employees of the federal government who were not covered by some sort of retirement plan. Congress briefly included former presidents in a 1942 pension act that was mainly intended to cover its own members, but public outcry against congressional avarice during wartime prompted the act's quick repeal. After World War II ended, Congress enacted another pension program but did not include former presidents in its coverage.

In 1955, however, the financial plight of former president Truman led members of both houses of Congress to introduce

TABLE 32-2 Allowances for Former Presidents, Fiscal Year 1994

Allowance	Nixon[a]	Ford	Carter	Reagan	Bush
Pension	$148,400	$148,400	$148,400	$148,400	$148,400
Staff salaries	96,000	93,252	96,000	96,000	150,000
Staff benefits	25,200	18,000	5,000	28,800	45,750
Travel	18,700	45,200	2,100	46,200	46,000
Motor pool	0	0	2,400	0	0
Rental payments	150,688	92,542	83,496	361,466	135,990
Telephone	22,600	12,500	39,900	32,200	24,120
Postage	4,800	10,400	14,000	10,400	8,576
Printing	4,400	4,400	28,700	23,200	16,584
Supplies and materials	7,000	13,600	16,200	15,200	19,356
Equipment	4,300	9,700	20,300	2,700	1,960
Transportation of things	300	300	0	2,300	1,680
Other services	614	17,270	12,510	14,942	12,584
TOTAL	$483,002	$465,564	$469,006	$781,808	$611,000

SOURCE: General Services Administration, June 24, 1993.
NOTE: a. Died on April 22, 1994.

At the funeral for Richard Nixon in California on April 27, 1994, President Bill Clinton stands with his wife Hillary along with all the living ex-presidents and their wives: George and Barbara Bush, Ronald and Nancy Reagan, Jimmy and Rosalynn Carter, and Gerald and Betty Ford.

legislation to provide office and staff assistance to ex-presidents and pensions for both them and their widows. Truman had complained to Speaker of the House Sam Rayburn that it cost him $30,000 a year just to answer mail and fulfill requests for speeches and public appearances. He had turned down numerous business offers because he thought they were improper activities for a former president. But, Truman added, if federal assistance was not provided, he would be forced to "go ahead with some contracts to keep ahead of the hounds."[25] Herbert Hoover, the only other living ex-president in 1955, indicated formally to Congress that he did not want a pension.[26]

Debate on the proposed legislation extended over three years. House Majority Leader John W. McCormack urged passage on grounds that "a former president is considered a dedicated statesman, available, if desired, for service to our country; his responsibility does not end when his term of office has ended; and a former president is not expected to engage in any business or occupation which would demean the office he once held." Republicans on the House Committee on Post Office and Civil Service argued publicly that the law would create in effect a new office: a "separate entity" for former presidents, with "an aura of official standing yet a wholly undefined relationship to the constitutional functions of the federal government." Privately, Republicans grumbled that they were being asked to subsidize Truman's attacks on their party.[27]

The Former Presidents Act was passed in 1958. It provided all presidents who left office, unless by impeachment and conviction, with a pension of $25,000 per year (roughly comparable to the salary then paid to members of Congress), a generous allowance to hire a staff, office space and furnishings in a federal building of their choice, franking (that is, free mailing) privileges for nonpolitical mail, and a pension of $10,000 per year for their widows. Hoover and Truman were the first beneficiaries of the new presidential pension; Eleanor Roosevelt and Edith Wilson were the first to receive the widows' pension.

Several additional benefits were added to the ex-presidency during the 1960s. In 1962 Congress extended Secret Service protection to former presidents for a period of six months after they left office. The following year, after President Kennedy was assassinated, such protection was granted to his widow and children. In 1965, after a Treasury Department official testified that former presidents and their families are subject to "annoyance by the idly curious" and remain possible targets of the "mentally deranged," Congress passed a law to grant lifetime Secret Service protection to presidents and their spouses, as well as to the widows of former presidents until they remarry and to their children until they reach the age of sixteen.[28]

With one exception, every former president and his family have accepted the protection of the Secret Service: Patricia Nixon (in 1984) and Richard Nixon (in 1985) decided to rely instead on private security guards. The attitude of former president Carter is more typical: he said that the Secret Service is "very necessary because wherever a former president goes, crowds gather and it's comforting to know they are around."[29] In some cases, however, Secret Service agents have acted more as servants and staff than as guardians. After the death of President Eisenhower, for example, Mamie Eisenhower relied on her Secret Service agents mainly to take her to church and to run errands. William Bell, a former agent assigned to Lady Bird Johnson, complained that Secret Service protection "becomes a glorified valet service. There were times when I felt it was a waste of taxpayer money. I absolutely refused to carry any shopping bags into the house. Other agents did that to ingratiate themselves."[30] The excesses of former first ladies were satirized in the 1994 movie, *Guarding Tess.*

The Presidential Transition Act of 1963 provided outgoing presidents with $300,000 to cover the costs of leaving the White House, mainly office rental and staff assistance during their first six months out of office. During this period, the office and staff provisions of the Former Presidents Act do not apply. In 1976 Congress raised the amount of the transition subsidy for the outgoing president to $1 million. The incoming administration receives $2 million under the act.

In 1969 a historic Victorian townhouse in Washington was designated as the Former Presidents' Residence and made available for the use of former presidents when they are visiting the capital. The approximately two-thousand-square-foot house, at 716 Jackson Place, N.W. (about one block from the White House), was first used in 1977 by former president Ford and has been used an average of six times per year since 1980, mostly by Ford.

Congress attached an escalator to the presidential pension in 1970, setting it as equal to the annual salary of department heads. Bush retired with a pension of $143,800 per year, plus his pensions from other government jobs. Congress also raised the widow's pension to $20,000 a year.

SENATE PRIVILEGES

Over the years, the most frequently offered suggestion to involve former presidents formally in the activities of the federal government has been to make them nonvoting members of the Senate. President Rutherford B. Hayes opposed the idea as "inconsistent with the principles of popular government" when it was debated in Congress in 1879, as did President Taft three decades later. Truman, however, with the endorsement of former president Hoover, sought to persuade Congress to revive the nonvoting senator proposal after he left office. In 1963 the Senate relented in part by modifying its rules to read: "Former presidents of the United States shall be entitled to address the Senate upon appropriate notice to the presiding officer who shall thereupon make the necessary arrangements." Truman made some bantering remarks on the occasion of his eightieth birthday in 1964, but no former president has used the Senate as a forum to make a formal address.

EXECUTIVE PRIVILEGE

Several former presidents have testified voluntarily before congressional committees *(see "Testimony before Congress," p. 1273.)*, but, until 1953, only Tyler was ordered to do so under a subpoena. (He complied.) In 1953 former president Truman rejected a subpoena from the House Committee on Un-American Activities to provide information about the promotion to a higher government position of an alleged Communist during his administration. Truman asserted the same rights of executive privilege that presidents historically had claimed while in office. *(See "Presidential Immunities," p. 1389, in Chapter 34.)*

Constitutional scholars disagreed over the legitimacy of Truman's assertion, but the committee backed down. Citing this precedent, former president Nixon refused in 1977 to testify before a House subcommittee that was investigating his administration's negotiations with North Vietnam. "If the doctrine of separation of powers and the independence of the presidency is to have any validity at all," Nixon argued, "it must be equally applicable to a president after his term of office has expired when he is sought to be examined with respect to any act occurring while he is president." Although Nixon agreed to speak informally on the telephone with a few subcommittee members, Congress's acquiescence to his initial refusal seemed to affirm the acceptability of Truman's assertion.

AUTHORS AND ADVISERS

For all the newfound privileges of their position, former presidents in the modern era are not completely unlike their predecessors. All have spent the major portion of their first years out of office writing memoirs, usually after negotiating a large advance payment from a book publisher (Reagan received a record $6 million advance) and always with the help of research assistants. Eisenhower wrote two books about his presidency—*Mandate for Change: The White House Years, 1953–1956* (1963), which covered his first term as president, and *Waging Peace: The White House Years, 1956–1961* (1965), which treated his second term. Johnson wrote *The Vantage Point: Perspectives on the Presidency, 1963–1969* (1971). Nixon, who resigned from office in disgrace and desperately needed the income a publisher could offer, was obliged to write a somewhat franker and, regarding Watergate at least, more confessional memoir, *RN, The Memoirs of a President* (1978). (He later wrote *In the Arena: A Memoir of Victory, Defeat, and Renewal* [1990], which was more assertive in tone.) Most presidential memoirs, however, are extended defenses of their authors' actions in office, a pattern that was restored with Ford's *A Time To Heal: The Autobiography of Gerald R. Ford* (1979) and preserved with Carter's *Keeping Faith: Memoirs of a President* (1982) and Reagan's *An American Life* (1990). (Carter subsequently published a memoir of his first political race, *Turning Point: A Candidate, a State, and a Nation Come of Age* [1992].) Bush began the task of writing memoirs of his administration's foreign policy shortly after leaving office in 1993.

GERALD R. FORD

Gerald Ford was appointed to the vice presidency after Vice President Spiro T. Agnew resigned in October 1973; he then became president in August 1974 when Nixon resigned. Defeated just twenty-seven months later in his bid for a full term as president, Ford met in the White House with Hollywood agent Norman Brokaw to plan his future. Ford, who had never been wealthy, wanted to make money without foreclosing a possible political comeback. He initially resisted business offers in favor of a Brokaw-negotiated, million-dollar publishing contract for himself and his wife, Betty Ford, along with public consulting roles with the American Enterprise Institute and the NBC television network.

In 1978 Ford campaigned actively for Republican congressional candidates. While eschewing an active presidential bid in 1980, he made known his availability for a draft. None was forthcoming, and on March 15, 1980, Ford announced his withdrawal from presidential politics. Ronald Reagan, who was nominated by the Republican party in 1980, made an effort to woo Ford onto the ticket as his vice-presidential running mate. After trying unsuccessfully to negotiate an arrangement that would enable him, as vice president, to exercise some of the president's powers in office, Ford declined Reagan's offer.

Freed from any concern about the political effects of bad publicity, Ford (who had never worked in business) accepted numerous lucrative offers to serve on corporate boards of directors and as a business consultant. Corporations like Santa Fe International, whose board Ford joined twelve days after withdrawing from the presidential race in 1980, G. K. Technologies, which he joined six weeks later as board member and consultant, and Shearson Loeb Rhoades, which he joined eight days after that (again as board member and consultant), appreciated the prestige and publicity that the presence of a former president on the board brought. According to an article in the February 15, 1987, issue of the *Los Angeles Times Magazine,* in 1986 Ford earned at least $541,300 from companies he was affiliated with, along with more than a quarter million dollars from lecture fees, a substantial stipend from the American Enterprise Institute, and more than $150,000 in congressional and presidential pensions.

Ford was severely criticized in 1978 when he endorsed a commercially produced series of presidential medals. The *New York Times* lamented in an editorial, "We wish he could earn his way without dragging the presidency into it." An investment company Ford formed with Leonard Firestone (called Fordstone) became controversial when environmental groups opposed a real estate development project it was financing in California.

No former president since Ulysses S. Grant has been involved in business to the extent that Ford has. In recent years, having turned 80 in 1993, Ford has retired from business and political life.

JIMMY CARTER

Jimmy Carter, like Herbert Hoover, was a politically unsuccessful president who conducted himself as former president in ways that brought almost universal applause. In contrast to Nixon (a Californian who settled in New York City, then moved to its New Jersey suburbs) and Ford (a lifelong resident of Michigan who moved to California after leaving the White House), Carter returned to his modest home in Plains, Georgia, along with his wife, Rosalynn Carter. Like most recent former presidents, Carter worked to raise money to construct a presidential library, in his case on the campus of Emory University in Atlanta. But in designing the library, Carter emphasized the importance of attaching a center (the Carter Center) that could be used to address important topics of public policy.

Carter eschewed business endeavors and abandoned any political ambitions in order to pursue activities he considered more interesting and worthwhile. He wrote his critically and publicly well-received memoirs (*Keeping Faith: Memoirs of a President*) and followed it with books on the Middle East, retirement, and hunting and fishing. Carter lent his talents as a carpenter to the Christian organization Habitat for Humanity, which builds and repairs houses for poor people in the United States and abroad. He continued to teach Sunday School at his Baptist church in Plains.

The Carter Center has been Carter's base for numerous activities, some of which have dominated the world's headlines. For example, since 1987 he has monitored the fairness of several Latin American and African elections. In 1994 Carter brokered an agreement in Haiti that restored to office the exiled elected president, Jean-Bertrand Aristide, and averted a U.S. invasion. Other activities have been more controversial. Although Carter has said that he worked more closely with the Bush administration than with any other administration, in 1991 he privately sent letters to the heads of United Nations Security Council member states urging them to vote against a resolution authorizing armed intervention in the Persian Gulf.

Carter has risen steadily in scholarly and public esteem since he left office. A June 24, 1988, article in the *Wall Street Journal* found strong evidence of "Carter revisionism" among political scientists and historians, who now concede that he handled the unusually difficult problems of his time courageously. In 1994 Carter ranked second in Gallup's annual "most admired man" poll, the highest that any former president has ever ranked. The Gallup poll also has found consistently that Americans approve more highly of Carter's conduct as a former president than any other former president.

RONALD REAGAN

In contrast to Carter, Ronald Reagan was a popular president whose public standing fell after he left office. In 1989, shortly after his return to private life in his home state of California, Reagan was heavily criticized for accepting $2 million to give a few speeches in Japan. Later that year, attorneys for Oliver North, a National Security Council staff member in the Reagan administration, forced the government to release a document that showed Reagan to have been far more involved in the Iran-contra affair than he had ever admitted. North, who continued to profess himself a Reagan loyalist, repeated the charge that "Reagan knew everything" about the Iran-contra affair in his 1991 autobiography, *Under Fire.*

Reagan blasted North when the latter sought the Republican nomination for U.S. senator from Virginia in 1994. Violating his own "11th commandment" (thou shalt not speak ill of another Republican), Reagan declared, "I am getting pretty steamed about statements coming from Oliver North . . . I certainly did not know anything about the Iran-contra diversion." As for the frequent private meetings that North claimed to have had with Reagan, they "just didn't happen." North won the nomination but lost the election.

Reagan's fall in public esteem (except among conservative Republicans) was widespread. His memoirs, *An American Life,* sold poorly in 1990, a year that also saw him plead memory loss around 150 times during two days of testimony in the trial of his former national security adviser, John Poindexter. A June 1992 Gallup poll found that only 50 percent of Americans approved of the way he had handled his job as president, and only 52 percent approved of his performance as a former president. In contrast, 70 percent approved of Carter's postpresidency performance and 61 percent approved of Ford's.

In November 1994 much of the public's dormant affection for Reagan was revived when he announced in a handwritten open letter that he had Alzheimer's disease, an illness that destroys brain cells, gradually causing memory loss, confusion, and personality changes. Reagan made the news public in the hope of drawing public attention to Alzheimer' s, much as Franklin D. Roosevelt had in starting the March of Dimes to combat polio and first ladies Betty Ford and Nancy Reagan had in making their breast cancer known. "I now begin the journey that will lead me into the sunset of my life," Reagan wrote. "I know that for America there will always be a bright dawn ahead."

GEORGE BUSH

"Don't need any new suits for the rest of my life," George Bush told Hugh Sidey of *Time* magazine in March 1994, little more than a year after leaving office. Noting to the author George Plimpton that his passport listed his occupation as "retired," Bush declared that he was "trying hard to be a non-imperial ex-president."

After his term as president ended in January 1993, Bush and his wife Barbara retired to their home town of Houston, Texas, where they built a house on what to many reporters seemed a surprisingly small lot. Bush eschewed interviews for a year and withheld comment on his successor, Bill Clinton. He also worked on a book with his former national security adviser, Brent Scowcroft. Bush described the book as being not the usual memoir, but rather a work focused on "how decisions were made on German reunification, NAFTA, China, and Desert Storm."

Even in retirement, Bush has stepped into the public eye on a few occasions. In 1993 he made a triumphal visit to Kuwait, which he had liberated in the 1991 Gulf War. (After Bush returned to the United States, President Clinton bombed Iraq in response to a report that Iraqi agents had planned to kill Bush during his visit.) In 1994 Bush did some low-profile campaigning for Republican candidates. Two of Bush's sons, George W. Bush and Jeb Bush, ran for governor of Texas and Florida, respectively, in that year's elections. George won but Jeb lost. In 1995 Bush publicly quit the National Rifle Association, which had sent out an inflammatory fund-raising letter around the time of the April 19 car bombing of the federal office building in Oklahoma City.

Several recent former presidents, like some of their predecessors, also have written books on subjects other than themselves. Nixon wrote extensively on international affairs, including *The Real War* (1980), *Leaders* (1982), *No More Vietnams* (1985), *Real Peace* (1985), *1999* (1988), *Seize the Moment: America's Challenge in a One-Superpower World* (1992), and *Beyond Peace* (1994). Carter has written books on topics as varied as the Middle East (*The Blood of Abraham,* 1985), retirement (*Everything to Gain: Making the Most of the Rest of Your Life,* 1987, written with his wife, Rosalynn Carter), and camping and fishing (*An Outdoor Journal,* 1988). A book of his poems, called *Always a Reckoning* was published in 1994.

Each of the four most recent first ladies also has written one or more books. Betty Ford, with Chris Chase as coauthor, wrote *The Times of My Life* (1978); she and Chase later recounted her struggles with drugs and alcohol in *Betty: A Glad Awakening* (1987). Critics found Rosalynn Carter's *First Lady from Plains* (1984), a memoir of her years in the White House, to be more insightful in some ways than Jimmy Carter's book. Nancy Reagan answered her critics in *My Turn: The Memoirs of Nancy Reagan* in 1989, and Barbara Bush revealed her disagreement with her husband on the abortion issue in *Barbara Bush: A Memoir* (1994).

In addition to writing books, recent former presidents have emulated their predecessors' willingness to provide confidential advice to and accept temporary assignments from the president. In 1981, for example, Reagan dispatched all three living former presidents—Nixon, Ford, and Carter—to represent the United States at the funeral of assassinated Egyptian leader Anwar Sadat. Each also has commented on public policy issues and, except for Nixon, participated in political campaigns.

Critics

During the 1970s and 1980s, the "office of ex-president" came under severe criticism from some quarters. A 1979 *Washington Monthly* article that assailed "The Imperial Ex-Presidency" was typical of many such writings.[31] Bills were introduced in Congress to reduce the privileges, benefits, and, consequently, the cost of supporting former presidents. A bill sponsored by Rep. Andrew Jacobs Jr. (D-Ind.) was called the "Former Presidents Enough Is Enough and Taxpayers' Relief Act." The historian Arthur Schlesinger Jr., in a 1981 article, reflected the tone of much of the recent criticism: "Ex-Presidents, like other old folk, tend to live in the past, preoccupied with the issues, remedies, and self-justifications of another time. . . . We recognize all this in the private sector. When presidents retire from corporations or from universities, no one wants them offering advice." Schlesinger cautioned against succumbing to what he called "the patriarchal illusion. If our three living ex-presidents Nixon, Ford, and Carter are really all that wise, they would surely have been better presidents."[32]

To some degree, the backlash against the ex-presidency resulted from the changed roster of former presidents. In the late 1960s and early 1970s, Truman, Eisenhower, and Hoover died and were replaced by Johnson and Nixon, each of whom had been forced to withdraw from office, then Ford and Carter, both of whom were defeated in their bids for reelection as president. Criticism also was born of the growing cost to the Treasury of supporting former presidents with pensions, offices, staff, Secret Service protection, and maintenance of their libraries. "They can make a million dollars or so a year going around and being ornaments and making dull speeches," charged Representative Jacobs. "Let them pay their own office rent and let them pay for their own secretaries."[33] Jacobs, Democratic senator Lawton M. Chiles Jr., of Florida, and other critics seemed particularly offended by the money-making activities of former president Ford, who earned hundreds of thousands of dollars annually from serving on corporate boards, consulting for corporations, and giving speeches to business groups. (See box, Four Living Former Presidents: Ford, Carter, Reagan, and Bush, p. 1278.)

OFFICIAL REACTIONS

Critics of the ex-presidency won several victories for their cause, some legislative, some legal, and some administrative.

In response to the various Watergate investigations that were going on at the time, Congress passed the Presidential Recordings and Materials Preservation Act of 1974, which deprived Nixon of control over his papers and tape recordings. (Nixon's secret tape recordings of White House conversations provided vital evidence of administration wrongdoing.) Under the act, the administrator of the General Services Administration (GSA) was enjoined to obtain "complete possession of all papers, documents, memorandums, transcripts, and other objects and materials which constitute the presidential historical materials of Richard M. Nixon." Nixon and, later, his estate launched a legal war against efforts to release these materials, however, and their disposition still is not settled.

Four years later, the Presidential Records Act of 1978 broadened the requirements of the 1974 act by granting the government complete ownership and control of all presidential records, beginning with the next president. (Ronald Reagan, who was elected in 1980, was the first to be covered.) Former presidents were permitted, however, to restrict access to some of their papers for as many as twelve years.

In 1986 Congress passed a law to reduce the government's responsibility for future presidential libraries. Previously, such libraries had been constructed with privately raised funds but maintained at the expense of the National Archives. The new law required that endowments be created by the organizations that built the libraries to help pay for their maintenance. President Reagan's request for an exemption from this requirement was granted, but future presidential libraries, including Bush's, will be covered.

A federal court ruled in 1976 that a former president could be held accountable for personal misconduct in office. The judge

---

ELECTION MYTH

One generally overlooked aspect of the Reagan legacy is that the former president has laid to rest the myth of "Tecumseh's Curse."

According to the curse, each president who is elected in a year ending in a zero is destined to die in office. It supposedly originated with the great Shawnee chief Tecumseh, who was defeated in a battle during the War of 1812 by Gen. William Henry Harrison. However implausible the story (what would have prompted an enraged Tecumseh to utter such an oddly detailed curse?), Harrison, who was elected president in 1840, died in office. So did the presidents who subsequently were elected in 1860 (Abraham Lincoln), 1880 (James A. Garfield), 1900 (William McKinley), 1920 (Warren G. Harding), 1940 (Franklin D. Roosevelt), and 1960 (John F. Kennedy).

Adherents of Tecumseh's Curse must have felt especially confident when Ronald Reagan was elected in 1980. Reagan supplanted Harrison (by one year) as the oldest person ever to be elected president: he turned sixty-nine on February 6, 1980. Two weeks after leaving office, hale and hearty, Reagan turned seventy-eight, eight years older than any other former president. And he took the curse with him.

---

found former president Nixon personally liable for damages to Morton Halperin, a former Nixon aide, because of an illegal wiretap that Nixon had authorized to be placed on Halperin's telephone. The principle was more important than the damages, however, which were set at one dollar.

The GSA, which is charged to administer the benefits former presidents receive, became harsher in its discretionary judgments. The law on office space and furnishings, for example, is vague, requiring only that the GSA administrator should provide "suitable office space appropriately equipped with furniture, furnishings, office machines and equipment, and office supplies, as determined by the administrator." Nixon was enjoined to accept an office in New York in a federal building rather than (at triple the expense) in the Chrysler Building. Carter was told to buy a less expensive Persian rug than the one he had in mind for his office.

ADDITIONAL PROPOSALS

Critics of the modern ex-presidency still object to many aspects of the largely informal institution. Some would restrict further the cost of the benefits provided to former presidents, notably Secret Service protection, and office and staff expenses. Others fret that the laws governing benefits for former presidents are too vague—someone who served as president for even one day would be fully eligible, for example.

Legislation was introduced in Congress in 1985 (but not passed) to limit Secret Service protection for a former president to five years, to the widow of a former president for six months, and to the former president's children only when they are with the former president. (These limits could be extended at the discretion of the secretary of the Treasury.) Proponents argued that the danger to former presidents and their families does not justify the expense—with the exception of Theodore Roosevelt, who was running for president in 1912, no assassination attempt has ever been made against a former president or any member of a former president's family. Yet each former president requires twenty-four agents, eight per eight-hour shift. Extensions of Secret Service protection to family members raised the annual cost of such protection from $50,000 in 1968 to nearly $15 million in 1993, even though the number of living former presidents was small in each year. In the face of a wave of international terrorism, however, Congress was reluctant to reduce security of any kind.

The General Services Administration has urged Congress to establish specific guidelines for former presidents' office furniture, travel expenses, and office size and location. In 1985 the House of Representatives (but not the Senate) passed a bill that would have placed ceilings on the amount of government funds former presidents could spend for office and staff. These ceilings would decrease every year the president was out of office.

Critics of presidential libraries have charged that their dispersed geographical locations make them difficult for researchers to use. Indeed, all but a few visitors to presidential libraries are tourists visiting the adjoining museums.[34] One proposed remedy is to create a central depository for the papers of all former presidents.

NOTES

1. Daniel J. Boorstin, "Saving a National Resource: An Address on the Role of Former Presidents in American Public Life," in *Farewell to the Chief: Former Presidents in American Public Life,* ed. Richard Norton Smith and Timothy Walch (Worland, Wyo.: High Plains, 1990), 140.

2. Alan Evan Schenker, "Former Presidents: Suggestions for the Study of an Often Neglected Resource," *Presidential Studies Quarterly* 12 (fall 1982): 545.

3. John Whiteclay Chambers II, "Presidents Emeritus," *American Heritage* 30 (June 1979): 16. When the question of "What shall we do with our former presidents?" was broached in a Chicago meeting at which Grover Cleveland spoke, Cleveland said he opposed a newspaper editor's suggestion that they be taken out in "a five acre field and shot." He explained: "In the first place, a five acre lot seems needlessly large, and in the second place, an ex-president has already suffered enough." (Lowell H. Harrison, "Presidents in Retirement," *American History Illustrated* 8 [December 1973]: 41).

4. James C. Clark, *Faded Glory: Presidents Out of Power* (New York: Praeger, 1985), v.

5. Arthur M. Schlesinger Sr., "The U.S. Presidents," *Life,* November 1, 1948, 67–74; Schlesinger, "Our Presidents: A Rating by 75 Historians," *New York Times Magazine,* July 29, 1962, 12–13, 40–43; Robert K. Murray and Tim H. Blessing, *Greatness in the White House: Rating the Presidents, Washington Through Carter* (University Park: Pennsylvania State University Press, 1988).

6. Chambers, "Presidents Emeritus"; Dom Bonafede, "Life after the White House: Caring for Ex-Presidents Can Cost a Bundle," *National Journal,* August 31, 1985, 1943–1947; Milton S. Mayer, "What Shall We Do with Our Ex-Presidents?" *Forum* 89 (March 1933): 185–189.

7. Chambers, "Presidents Emeritus," 17.

8. *The Adams-Jefferson Letters,* ed. Lester J. Cappon (Chapel Hill: University of North Carolina Press, 1959).

9. Harrison, "Presidents in Retirement," 37.

10. Ibid., 34.

11. Ibid., 35.

12. Quoted in Stephanie Smith, *Federal Benefits to Former Presidents and Their Widows,* CRS Report 85–173 GOV (Washington, D.C.: Library of Congress, Congressional Research Service, August 19, 1985), 12–13.

13. Chambers, "Presidents Emeritus," 18; Harrison, "Presidents in Retirement," 37. In his memoirs, Truman described a number of lucrative offers he received after leaving office. (He rejected all the offers):

A chain of clothing stores wanted me to be its vice president at an annual salary in six figures. A sewing machine company wanted me to be its chairman of the board, also at a salary in six figures but with no work to do except appear in public ceremonies for the company. The chief executive of a motion picture company called on me to try and interest me in a merger of several producing companies, saying that the deal could be consummated only if I agreed to join and head it up. He offered a fabulous salary and added that I could name my own terms. Several oil companies thought I would be a good man to have around. One proposal of an eight-year contract, requiring only an hour's "work," guaranteed over a half million dollars.

14. In 1913 Taft told President-elect Woodrow Wilson that he had saved nearly $100,000 from his salary as president. "Congress is very generous to the president," he told Wilson. The only expenses a president has are "those of furnishing food to a large boarding house of servants and to your family, and your own personal expenses of clothing, etc." (Smith, "Federal Benefits to Former Presidents," 12).

15. Quoted in David McCullough, "The Man of Independence: Harry S. Truman in Retirement," in *Farewell to the Chief,* 47.

16. Harrison, "Presidents in Retirement," 37. Hayes was no hypocrite: He worked hard in the service of a number of private charities and causes.

17. Quoted in Richard Norton Smith, "Outliving the Bastards: Herbert Hoover as a Former President," in *Farewell to the Chief,* 30.

18. This section is based on Stephen W. Stathis, "Former Presidents as Congressional Witnesses," *Presidential Studies Quarterly* 13 (summer 1983): 458–481.

19. Unaware of his predecessors' many appearances before congressional committees, Truman told reporters after voluntarily testifying to the Senate Foreign Relations Committee in 1955: "I think I made history yesterday in being the first president to allow himself to be questioned by a legislative committee." Ibid., 458.

20. Harrison, "Presidents in Retirement," 35.

21. Chambers, "Presidents Emeritus," 21.

22. Teresa Riordan, "The Imperial Ex-Presidency," *The Washington Monthly,* April 1983, 24–28.

23. Stephanie Smith, "Federal Expenditures for Former Presidents," CRS Issue Brief (Washington, D.C.: Library of Congress, Congressional Research Service, January 12, 1988), 1.

24. Chambers, "Presidents Emeritus," 17.

25. Marie B. Hecht, *Beyond the Presidency* (New York: Macmillan, 1976), 187.

26. Nonetheless, Hoover accepted the pension and other benefits that subsequently were offered to former presidents by law.

27. Smith, "Federal Benefits to Former Presidents," 15.

28. Ibid., 33.

29. Ibid., 34.

30. Ronald Kessler, *Inside the White House: The Hidden Lives of the Modern Presidents and the Secrets of the World's Most Powerful Institution* (New York: Pocket Books, 1995), 75.

31. Riordan, "The Imperial Ex-Presidency."

32. Arthur M. Schlesinger Jr., *Parade,* June 21, 1981.

33. Bonafede, "Life after the Oval Office," 1946.

34. The Ford library is on the campus of the University of Michigan in Ann Arbor. The university required that the museum be elsewhere, however, and it was built in Grand Rapids, Michigan.

SELECTED BIBLIOGRAPHY

Chambers, John Whiteclay, II. "President Emeritus." *American Heritage* 30 (June 1979).

Clark, James C. *Faded Glory: Presidents Out of Power.* New York: Praeger, 1985.

Harrison, Lowell H. "Presidents in Retirement." *American History Illustrated* 8 (December 1973): 41.

Hecht, Marie B. *Beyond the Presidency.* New York: Macmillan, 1976.

Schenker, Alan Evan. "Former Presidents: Suggestions for the Study of an Often Neglected Resource." *Presidential Studies Quarterly* 12 (fall 1982).

Smith, Richard Norton, and Timothy Walch, eds. *Farewell to the Chief: Former Presidents in American Public Life.* Worland, Wyo.: High Plains, 1990.

Smith, Stephanie. *Federal Benefits to Former Presidents and Their Widows.* CRS Report 85–173 GOV. Washington, D.C.: Library of Congress, Congressional Research Service. August 19, 1985.

———. "Federal Expenditures for Former Presidents." Washington, D.C.: Library of Congress, Congressional Research Service. January 12, 1988.

Stathis, Stephen W. "Former Presidents as Congressional Witnessess." *Presidential Studies Quarterly* 13 (summer 1983).

PART VI

Chief Executive and Federal Government

CHAPTER 33

The President and Congress

BY ROBERT J. SPITZER

In framing a government which is to be administered by men over men, the great difficulty lies in this: you must first enable the government to control the governed; and in the next place oblige it to control itself.

—James Madison
Federalist No. 51

The constitutional convention of 1787 is supposed to have created a government of "separated powers." It did nothing of the sort. Rather, it created a government of separated institutions sharing *powers.*

—Richard E. Neustadt
Presidential Power

I have been told I was on the road to Hell, but I had no idea that it was just a mile down the road with a dome on it.

—Abraham Lincoln

The Framers of the Constitution who convened in Philadelphia in the summer of 1787 disagreed about much when it came to the size, nature, and functions of the national government. They were in substantial agreement, however, that the American government should consist of three branches—legislative, executive, and judicial. This agreement stemmed from both the colonial experience and the failure of the Articles of Confederation. Each colony had established some version of a three-branch governing system. When the first national government set up under the Articles deviated from this pattern by establishing a legislature-centered system, its failings were attributed in part to the absence of separate, coequal branches. In particular, the absence of a strong executive was felt keenly, as many believed that an executive was essential to provide some measure of leadership and to serve as well as a check on legislative excesses.

The arrangement implemented by the Founders—separation of powers—was designed to ensure that each of the three branches of government would perform different governing functions. At the same time, however, the Founders introduced checks and balances, whereby each branch needed the cooperation of the others to perform most important aspects of governing. Political scientist Richard E. Neustadt, who is quoted at the beginning of this chapter, summarized this complex relationship as a system of "separated institutions *sharing* powers." To understand this relationship, characterized by patterns of conflict and cooperation, is to understand much about the relationship between the president and Congress.

"Separated Institutions"

Most Americans take for granted the division in the Constitution of governing responsibilities into three separate, if interrelated, categories. Yet for the Framers, this decision represented a major change from the pattern of government followed at the time by most other nations.

CONSTITUTIONAL PROVISIONS

The Constitution treats the legislative and executive branches for the most part separately. Article I describes in considerable detail the powers and responsibilities assigned to Congress, and states that, in concept, Congress has the sole power to legislate. According to Article I, "All legislative Powers herein granted shall be vested in a Congress of the United States. . . ." The power to enforce the law, and exercise other executive-type powers, is reserved to the president, as specified in Article II: "The executive Power shall be vested in a President of the United States of America."

The distinction between the branches is seen partly in the separate selection of the members of each branch. Members of the House of Representatives are elected for two-year terms from districts within each state. Senators serve staggered six-year terms, with two elected from each state. Under the original Constitution, state legislatures elected their U.S. senators; the Seventeenth Amendment, ratified in 1913, changed this to provide for direct election of senators. The president, in contrast, is elected every four years by the electoral college, which in turn is selected by the outcome of the popular vote for president in each state.[1]

This election cycle has an important effect on the president's political relations with Congress. Since the entire membership of the House and one-third of the Senate is up for reelection every two years, most members of Congress face reelection during midterm elections when the presidency is not up for grabs. During presidential election years the victorious presidential candidate may succeed in helping to elect members of his or her political party seeking election for congressional or other offices (called the "coattail effect"). But during midterm elections the president's political party usually loses seats in Congress, resulting in a weakening of the president's influence over legislators. By incorporating an electoral cycle of midterm elections, the Founders were helping to ensure that coordination between the two branches of government would not be too close.[2] *(See Party*

After many initial disagreements over the size and function of the national government, on September 17, 1787, the Framers signed the Constitution, providing for three separate by equal branches and a strong executive.

Affiliations in Congress and the Presidency, 1789–1995, p. 1681, in Reference Materials.)

The Constitution also stipulates in Article I, section 6, that individuals may not serve in more than one branch at the same time (such as a member of Congress serving simultaneously in the president's cabinet); such dual service is the norm in parliamentary cabinet government systems such as that found in Great Britain. As James Madison noted in the *Federalist* No. 51, this division was constructed carefully "to render [the branches of government], by different modes of election and different principles of action, as little connected with each other as the nature of their common functions and their common dependence on the society will admit." The president is further protected from improper congressional influence by the provision in Article II, section 1, that the president's salary, which is approved by Congress, "shall neither be increased nor diminished during the Period for which he shall have been elected. . . ." Thus, the two branches are separated by structure and selection procedures.

REFORM?

Although this separation has been an integral component of the relationship between the legislative and executive branches, some critics have proposed that the terms for members of the House be extended to four years, coterminous with the president's election, and that senatorial terms be lengthened similarly to eight years. This presumably would lead to a greater likelihood that the same political party would control both branches at the same time, thus minimizing the oft-heard complaint that modern governing is typified by paralysis and gridlock rather than decisive leadership.

The prevalence of divided party control was evident in the forty-four-year period from 1952 to 1996; during that time, the presidency and both houses of Congress were controlled by the same political party for only sixteen years (a little over a third of the time). In the twenty-eight-year period from 1968 to 1996, same-party control existed for only six years (less than a quarter of the time). As a 1950 report critical of the current system noted, "If the elections for these offices always coincide, recurrent emphasis upon national issues would promote legislative-executive party solidarity."[3]

The idea of a four-year term for members of the House was not considered at the Constitutional Convention of 1787; at that time, representatives in state legislatures served one-year terms.[4] At one point, however, the convention approved a three-year term for House members. The question of how long legislators should serve has been the subject of long-standing contention. In fact, a proposal to change term lengths was advanced with renewed vigor during the 1987 bicentennial celebration of the Constitution. As one critic observed, "The midterm election cannot result in a clearly defined change in governmental direction. . . . All it can do is deadlock the government. . . ."[5] The coterminous term proposal was advanced in other important writings during the bicentennial as well.[6]

CUSTOM AND TRADITION

The ambiguity of constitutional wording has meant that the actual separation between the legislative and executive branches has varied according to historical circumstance and the predilections of the leaders of both branches. For example, writing in the 1830s, Supreme Court Justice Joseph Story observed that the president was "compelled to resort to secret and unseen influences, to private interviews, and private arrangements, to accomplish his own appropriate purposes instead of proposing and sustaining his own duties and measures by a bold and manly appeal to the nation in the face of its representatives."[7] Story was reflecting the dominant view of the time that presidents ought to respect scrupulously the preeminence of Congress over lawmaking. Yet by modern standards such appeals by the president to Congress and the nation are considered integral to the president's involvement in the legislative process.

This concern for the proper boundary between executive and legislative powers was evident in the early 1800s in debates over the propriety and constitutionality of public threats by presidents to use the veto power. Although presidential veto power over legislation was clearly stated in the Constitution, there was a strong sense that a publicly issued threat to use the veto represented an improper and even unconstitutional presidential intrusion into the legislative process. (See "Veto Power," p. 1310.)

President James Monroe provoked considerable dissent in Congress when he announced his intention to veto internal transport improvement legislation in 1817. Although Monroe used the veto only once in his eight years as president, this statement prompted the House to set up a special committee to review his views. The committee concluded that if the president's threat had any influence on congressional deliberations, it would amount to stripping Congress of its duly authorized preeminence over lawmaking. President Andrew Jackson relied more heavily on veto threats, provoking anguished howls from congressional critics that he was intruding unconstitutionally into the legislative sphere. By the middle of the nineteenth century, however, such intrusions had become an accepted norm. This change occurred because presidents set precedent by using the veto aggressively (and successfully), and because Congress found it useful to glean the president's preferences on major legislation, which in turn invited greater presidential involvement in legislative affairs. This greater involvement included freer use of the veto.[8] Today, no one would question the constitutionality of a presidential veto threat.

EXECUTIVE PRIVILEGE

The separation between the branches has been cloudy as well in the area of executive privilege. Under this privilege the president and other executive officials have the right to withhold sensitive documents and information from Congress or the courts. Presidents have argued that executive privilege is necessary to safeguard certain information in the public interest, including secret negotiations, without fear of interrupting the flow of legitimate government business. In short, presidents have argued that executive privilege is an important component of executive power.

In rebuttal, Congress has argued that it has an equally legitimate "right to know" about executive business, especially as it relates to congressional oversight of administrative matters. In the overwhelming majority of cases, congressional requests for sensitive executive documents have been granted eventually.

Uncertainty over the extent and nature of this privilege dates back to President George Washington, who refused to give information to the House of Representatives about the Jay Treaty. Most presidents have had similar confrontations with Congress (although the term *executive privilege* was not coined until the Eisenhower administration), but differences generally have been resolved through accommodation and compromise. Even so, presidents generally are free to define what communications are and are not covered, especially in the area of national security.

Arguments about executive privilege came to a head during the administration of Richard M. Nixon. The special prosecutor appointed to investigate the Watergate crimes subpoenaed tape recordings of conversations between the president and his aides as part of the evidence being compiled in a criminal prosecution. Nixon refused to turn the tapes over, however, arguing that the communications were protected by executive privilege. The case was taken to the Supreme Court, which ruled unanimously in 1974 that Nixon had to comply with the subpoena. Although the Court ruled against Nixon in *United States v. Nixon,* it recognized the concept of executive privilege for the first time.[9] Speaking for the Court, Chief Justice Warren E. Burger recognized the need for such privilege as it applied to the president's "need for complete candor and objectivity from advisers" and "to protect military, diplomatic, or sensitive national security secrets." As with many Court rulings the question of executive privilege was not resolved in 1974, and the nature, legitimacy, and limitations of the concept continue to be debated hotly.[10]

AMBIGUOUS ROLE OF THE VICE PRESIDENT

The United States is almost the only nation in the Western world to have formally created a "standby" executive. Most other nations fill chief executive vacancies with a caretaker or through a special election until a new executive is selected. This anomaly is compounded by the fact that the vice president is granted only two significant powers in the Constitution—one executive and the other legislative. (See Chapter 26, Office of the Vice President.)

According to Article II, section 1, the vice president becomes the chief executive in case of the death, resignation, or disability of the president. The vice president also serves as president of the Senate—clearly a legislative function. Both of these powers reflect the long-standing truism that the vice presidency is a position of little real power or importance during the normal course of events.

The vice president's position as president of the Senate takes on real significance only when a tie vote occurs on the floor of the Senate. The vice president may then cast the tie-breaking vote, an occurrence that arises on average only once every couple of years. In 1993, for example, Vice President Albert Gore Jr. cast the tie-breaking vote to win passage of President Bill Clinton's Omnibus Budget Reconciliation Act.

The position of president of the Senate is, and has always been, considered primarily ceremonial, even when the vice president came from the Senate. For example, Lyndon B. Johnson had served as Senate majority leader for eight years before his selection as John F. Kennedy's running mate in 1960. After the presidential election, Johnson proposed that he be allowed to serve as presiding officer over the Senate Democrats, but Senate leaders sharply rebuffed this proposal. In arguing against such an idea an otherwise sympathetic senator said that to grant Johnson such a position "would violate the spirit of separation of powers."[11]

The ambiguity of the vice presidency stems from several concerns of the Framers of the Constitution when creating that office. First, some of the Founders believed it important that the presiding officer of the Senate be selected from outside the body, so that no Senator would have to lose his vote by serving in this position. (Originally the Senate was composed of only twenty-six members. The same problem did not exist for the larger House of Representatives.)

Second, the Founders followed many of the provisions of the New York State constitution, which provided for a lieutenant governor. Thus, the principle of vice-presidential succession is based on a similar provision in that constitution.

Third, the Founders were looking for a means of facilitating the election and enhancing the legitimacy of the president. By specifying that the president and the vice president "shall not be an Inhabitant of the same State"—thereby ensuring that at least two states would be represented on the national ticket—the Constitution's Framers were hoping to minimize the state rivalries that might prevail in presidential elections. A situation in which candidates hailed from the same state was especially likely to occur under the original system in which the vice presidency went to the presidential candidate who received the second-highest number of electoral votes. In changing this system, the Twelfth Amendment provided for a ticket composed of a presidential and a separately designated vice-presidential candidate.[12] With the rise of national political parties and improved communications and transportation, the presidential race became "nationalized."

The lack of a lengthier and more detailed constitutional charge for the vice president, combined with a vice president's political dependence on the president for meaningful work and a political identity, has resulted in an institution that has remained mostly in the shadows. Yet in recent years the growth of the institutional presidency has helped prod the growth of an institutional vice presidency. Recent vice presidents—notably Walter F. Mondale, George Bush, Dan Quayle, and Al Gore—have assumed active advisory and policy-shaping roles. If this trend continues, the vice president's dilemma of sharing both executive and legislative functions may be resolved through the expanded involvement of the vice president in the affairs of the executive branch.[13]

"Sharing Powers"

Just as the constitutional system consists of three separate branches, it is equally true that, under most circumstances, no one branch can operate without the other two. This reality especially applies to the relationship between the president and Congress. The familiar list of constitutionally granted powers makes it clear that most powers cannot be carried out without some degree of cooperation between the two branches.

CONSTITUTIONALLY SHARED POWERS

Congress passes laws, but they cannot be enacted until they cross the president's desk for a signature or veto. If vetoed, they are returned to the congressional house of origin for a possible override vote. A bill is enacted over a veto if two-thirds majorities are mustered in both houses. When the president wishes to veto a bill after "Congress by their Adjournment prevent its [the bill's] Return," (from Article I, section 7, of the Constitution), the president may exercise a "pocket veto," meaning that the bill dies if the president withholds his signature. (See "Veto Power," p. 1310.)

As for other constitutionally shared powers in Article II, section 3, the president is charged with giving Congress "Information of the State of the Union" and recommending for its consideration "such Measures as he shall judge necessary and expedient." The president also can call special sessions of Congress. Presidential nominations to important administrative and judicial positions must be approved by the Senate, and treaties with other nations negotiated by the president must be ratified by a two-thirds Senate vote. The president holds commander-in-chief powers over the military, but Congress declares war and finances and regulates the armed forces.

In the case of misconduct ("high crimes and misdemeanors"), the president is subject to impeachment and removal from office by Congress. In such an eventuality articles of impeachment are voted by the House, and an impeachment trial is held in the Senate. In 1868 President Andrew Johnson was impeached by the House (that is, charges were brought); in the Senate trial Johnson avoided conviction by a single vote. In 1974 the House Judiciary Committee voted three articles of impeachment against President Richard Nixon. In the face of mounting political opposition and a likely Senate trial and conviction, Nixon resigned.

Even in the case of a presidential election Congress may play a role. If no presidential candidate receives an absolute majority of electoral college votes, the presidential election is thrown into the House of Representatives, which then ballots with each state casting one vote until one candidate receives a majority of state votes. The vice president is selected separately by the Senate if no vice-presidential candidate wins a majority of electoral votes. Although this procedure has been used only once since 1824 (when the Senate selected a vice president in 1836), it illustrates one additional way the branches may interact.

Congress and the president must work together to enact laws. Here President Bill Clinton visits Capitol Hill in May 1993 to discuss his economic program with congressional leaders. From left are Vice President Al Gore, Senate Majority Leader George Mitchell, Clinton, and House Speaker Thomas Foley.

SHARING POWERS BY LEGAL DELEGATION

One of the key sources of presidential authority has arisen from concerted efforts by Congress to delegate some of its authority by statute to the president and other executive officials. (In a challenge to the Judiciary Act of 1789, Chief Justice John Marshall observed that Congress could in fact delegate certain powers to either of the other two branches.) This delegation of congressional powers is based on several considerations. First, until this century Congress typically was in session for only a few months of the year. Thus, Congress found it necessary to delegate certain powers to the executive branch to ensure the smooth functioning of government programs while it was not in session.

Second, the need for flexibility in the timing of legislative policy often has resulted in delegation. In 1799, for example, Congress voted to renew commercial restrictions against France, but it allowed the president the option of ending them "if he shall deem it expedient and consistent with the interest of the United States."[14]

Third, delegation of power to the president is based on the long-practiced tradition that presidents act as channels for communication with foreign nations. For example, an 1822 law barred British West Indies ports from shipping to America unless the president received satisfactory information that American ships could enter the British ports.

Fourth, the president has long been considered the one representative of the American people. Thus, Congress has delegat-

ed many powers to the executive to avoid the political fragmentation and controversy that often attend congressional decision making. This was seen, for example, in attempts to delegate tariff powers to the executive in the early twentieth century.

A fifth consideration underlying delegation of powers is the president's responsibility for fact-finding and coordination. This is especially true when intervention in the economy is necessary; measures designed to stimulate or otherwise direct the economy depend directly on the quality and timeliness of information. Because the executive branch gathers and generates much of this information, it often has proven to be the logical source of timely action. The Federal Pay Comparability Act of 1970 was enacted to ensure that federal pay levels remained roughly comparable with those for similar jobs in the private sector. Such assessments depend on data supplied by several federal bureaus. Based on these data the president makes recommendations to Congress.

Finally, national emergencies have been a reason for delegating power to the president. During times of war and economic crisis, the desire for speed and flexibility, and respect for presidential expertise, contribute to congressional willingness to give broad powers to the president.[15]

The delegation of congressional powers to the executive is a practice that extends back to the beginning of the country. Over the last two centuries Congress has delegated authority in hundreds, perhaps even thousands, of instances. An excellent example of the nature and effect of congressional delegation of authority to the president is illustrated by the evolution of budgetary authority.

Federal Budgetary Authority

Before 1921 Congress was vested with the sole budget-making authority. Many presidents and Treasury secretaries played important roles in formulating national spending priorities, but Congress bore principal responsibility for the budget, and it had relatively little difficulty in formulating annual spending priorities up to the time of the Civil War. The magnitude of wartime spending placed a great strain on the legislative committee structure, however, and Congress responded by dispersing budgetary authority among several committees, including the newly created Appropriations Committee, and separating authority over the appropriation and revenue components of budget making.

In the latter part of the nineteenth century the increasing fragmentation of budget authority among more congressional committees encouraged railroad interests, land speculators, other business interests, and many individuals seeking government pensions to obtain lucrative concessions in the budget. The fiscal consequence was extravagant use of public funds. The only public figure to stand up consistently against this abuse was the president. President Grover Cleveland in particular gained a reputation as "protector of the purse" by his prolific use of the veto. In his first term alone he vetoed 304 bills—almost three times as many as all of his predecessors combined. Of those vetoes, 241 were aimed at private and general pension bills. (Private bills are ones that affect named individuals or other very specific matters, such as bills that grant citizenship status or pensions to particular individuals.)

From the early 1900s on, the swell of reformers' cries (including many in Congress) called for giving greater budgetary authority to the president. In 1921 Congress enacted the Budget and Accounting Act, which provided for an executive Bureau of the Budget (BOB) and allowed the presidential appointment of a budget director. For the first time BOB would formulate and submit to Congress a comprehensive budget document. In 1933 Congress passed the Economy Act, which centralized and reorganized various budgetary authorities within the executive. And in 1939 President Franklin D. Roosevelt used the reorganization authority granted by Congress to bring BOB into the newly created Executive Office of the President.

In 1970 President Nixon issued an executive order based on reorganization authority granted by Congress that broadened the mandate of BOB from simply preparing the budget to assessing and evaluating existing programs. Nixon changed the name of the bureau to the Office of Management and Budget to reflect its enhanced authority. In 1974, however, in reaction to the excesses of the Nixon administration, including expanded use of impoundment power (refusing to spend funds duly appropriated by Congress), Congress passed the Budget and Impoundment Control Act. This act reasserted some congressional control over the budget and ended the practice of presidential impoundment of funds.[16]

This case illustrates how congressional authority over the budget was delegated to the president, resulting in a significant increase in presidential authority. The progressively greater scope of that authority was challenged only when the institutions concerned came into sharp political dispute over claims that the executive had abused its authority. The increase in the president's budget power could not have occurred without congressional willingness to delegate its authority to the executive.

Challenges to Delegation

Legal challenges to congressional delegation of power to the executive have arisen periodically. The thrust of court decisions addressing the question generally has included an assertion that Congress cannot delegate its power (or can do so only within certain limits). At the same time, however, the courts have ruled in favor of the delegations raised in particular cases. This pattern has appeared in several Supreme Court cases, including *Wayman v. Southart*,[17] *Field v. Clark*,[18] and *S. W. Hampton, Jr. & Co. v. United States*.[19] The Court has recognized nonetheless that limits on congressional delegation to the president are greater in the area of foreign policy than in domestic policy. This position was laid out clearly in *United States v. Curtiss-Wright Export Corporation*.[20] *(See* "United States v. Curtiss-Wright Export Corporation," *p. 1597, in the Reference Materials.)*

In another important case, *Schechter Poultry Corp. v. United States*,[21] the Court invalidated a provision of the National Industrial Recovery Act on the grounds that the delegation of legislative power to the president was too broad. As Justice Benjamin N. Cardozo observed, "This is delegation run riot."[22] Although *Schechter* has not been overturned, it has been neglected as precedent. Some observers have argued that the *Schechter* principle should be reexamined as a means of limiting the extent to which Congress can delegate its authority.[23]

THE POLITICS OF SHARED POWERS

Louis Fisher, a keen observer of relations between the executive and legislative branches, has noted that separation of powers and a system of checks and balances are by no means contradictory, even though the first calls for separation and the second for intermixing. "Far from being contradictory, they complement and support one another. An institution cannot check unless it has some measure of independence; it cannot retain that independence without the power to check."[24] Without a doubt, powers are shared, yet each branch retains sole domain over certain actions. Both Congress and the president can claim ties to popular sovereignty, as the members of each branch are elected popularly. Yet differing bases of representation may result in the two branches holding very different views of what the American people want their government to do. These differences are visible in several areas where the branches interact.

Foreign Affairs

The relationship between Congress and the presidency in the area of foreign affairs is marked in general by the historic dominance of the president over Congress. The president's ascendance in foreign affairs is such that one political scientist has concluded that there are actually "two presidencies"—one for domestic policy and the other for foreign policy. Despite variations according to historical era and area, presidents generally have realized more of their objectives in foreign affairs than in domestic politics.[25]

Despite presidential ascendance, the Constitution is by no means one-sided in favoring one branch over the other. In Article II, section 2, the president is empowered to serve as "Commander in Chief of the Army and Navy of the United States, and of the Militia of the several States, when called into the actual Service of the United States. . . ." The president also has the power to "make Treaties," with two-thirds concurrence of the Senate, and to nominate "Ambassadors, other public Ministers and Consuls" subject to Senate approval. Other presidential responsibilities are receiving ambassadors and ensuring that the laws are "faithfully executed." Some presidential scholars believe that presidential influence over foreign affairs also stems from Article II, section 1, which vests "executive power" in the president. Finally, the presidential oath of office requires that the executive "preserve, protect and defend the Constitution of the United States."

Congress is charged with several responsibilities in Article I, section 8. Among these are providing for "the common Defence and general Welfare of the United States" and regulating commerce with other nations. Congress punishes crimes on the high seas and settles "Offenses against the Law of Nations." It also has the power to "declare War, grant Letters of Marque and Reprisal, and make Rules concerning Captures on Land and Water." Other congressional responsibilities are raising and supporting an army, providing for a navy, making the rules that govern both, calling up and regulating the militia, and making all laws considered "necessary and proper" to carry out its other responsibilities.

Despite what appears to be a rough balance in powers and responsibilities between the executive and legislative branches, from the beginning many presidents have sought to extend their influence in foreign affairs. The first three presidents all provided forceful leadership in this area. In 1793, for example, President George Washington issued a Proclamation of Neutrality in the war between France and Britain. Pro-French Americans, led by Thomas Jefferson, publicly criticized the proclamation, however, arguing that Washington was usurping congressional authority. Alexander Hamilton then defended Washington's action, saying that the conduct of foreign relations was an executive function. This dispute was aired in a series of articles published in a Philadelphia newspaper and written by Hamilton and James Madison, who defended the Jeffersonian position. Hamilton wrote under the name "Pacificus" and Madison under the name "Helvidius."

Other factors have contributed as well to presidential ascendance in foreign policy. First, Congress by its nature is more likely to be drawn to concerns that are close, substantively and geographically, to the hearts of its constituents. Thus, service by members of Congress on the Agriculture or Public Works committees, for example, is likely to be of greater interest to con-

stituents for the immediate impact those committees may have on representatives' home districts than service on the House Foreign Affairs or Senate Foreign Relations committees. Similarly, as the only political leader elected at the national level, the president often is viewed as a purely national leader, who is more likely to receive political credit for, and thus benefit from, foreign policy initiatives.

Second, the president benefits from the unitary nature of the position. Although the modern presidency incorporates a large administrative apparatus, the president can act authoritatively as a single individual. Especially in times of emergency and crisis, the president can move with decisiveness, secrecy, and dispatch. Even presidential critics acknowledge the necessity that a government speak with a single voice to the rest of the world. The president is the obvious leader to fulfill such a role.

Third, presidents are always on hand. Because until the end of the 1930s Congress held session for only part of the year, many responsibilities fell on presidential shoulders out of simple necessity, including many pertaining to foreign affairs.

Fourth, strong presidents set precedent. Although the history of presidential-congressional relations is marked by periods in which each has held some degree of ascendance, the cumulative effect of unilateral presidential actions in areas that include war making, diplomacy, and intelligence has buttressed arguments that presidential assertiveness in these areas is appropriate, if not obviously constitutional. (Particular examples are considered in succeeding sections.)[26]

Finally, court decisions generally have supported an expansive interpretation of the presidential prerogative in foreign affairs. The courts largely have avoided constitutional challenges to presidential initiatives abroad (often arguing that such questions are "political" and thus not justiciable). In a few cases, however, the courts have spoken to presidential power. Perhaps the strongest statement favoring presidential authority in foreign affairs came in the Supreme Court case of *United States v. Curtiss-Wright Export Corp.* Speaking for the majority, Justice George Sutherland referred to "the very delicate, plenary and exclusive power of the President as the sole organ of the federal government in the field of international relations. . . ."[27]

Two reasons can be offered for the courts' apparent deference and infrequency of ruling in such cases. First, the wording of Article II of the Constitution is less specific than that of Article I. Thus, presidents possess more leeway to interpret the wording so that it fits their political goals. For example, the first sentence of Article I says that Congress is given "All legislative Powers herein granted." Many specific powers are then enumerated in the rest of the article. Article II, on the other hand, says that "The executive Power shall be vested in a President." Constitutional scholars and others have debated for two centuries whether this sentence is merely a definition of the presidential office, or whether the sentence confers executive-type powers (the latter interpretation would mean a more powerful president).

Second, and related to the first reason, an aura of nearly

monarchical dimensions has surrounded the office of the president for most of the country's history. Phrases such as "Sun King complex," "textbook presidency," "cult of the presidency," and "American monarchy" refer to enduring popular images of the president as moral leader, problem solver, and benevolent, omniscient parent figure. The enduring popular support emanating from these images has been a vital basis for the growth of presidential power.[28] The fundamental recognition of popular support for presidential actions that might be otherwise subject to constitutional challenge has contributed to the discouragement of such challenges, or the recognition that the political consensus behind presidential actions may be more potent than seemingly narrow constitutional interpretation.

War Powers and Use of Military Force

Although ambiguity surrounds many of the Founders' deliberations, little uncertainty exists about the construction of war powers. The power to initiate war was vested in Congress. In a draft of the Constitution circulated to the convention members on August 6, 1787, the legislature was to have the power "to make war." In subsequent debate this phrase was changed to "declare war." As Madison's notes revealed, he and Elbridge Gerry "moved to insert '*declare*,' striking out '*make*' war; leaving to the Executive the power to repel sudden attacks."[29] Thus, the purpose of the change was not to enhance the president's power; rather, it was to permit the president to take actions "to repel sudden attacks." Only one delegate to the convention, Pierce Butler, proposed giving the president war-making powers, but his proposal found no support. Both Madison and James Wilson assured the convention that the power of war and peace was a legislative, not an executive function, and that world history had shown that executives were most prone to war making.[30]

In addition to repelling sudden attacks on the United States, it also was understood that the president would direct and lead the armed forces and put them to any use specified by Congress, as the president was dependent on, and responsible to, final legislative authority. Jefferson summarized the thinking of many when he wrote to Madison in 1789: "We have already given in example one effectual check to the Dog of war by transferring the power of letting him loose from the Executive to the Legislative body, from those who are to spend to those who are to pay."[31]

As with many shared powers the practice of war making and deployment of troops was shaped by necessity, ambition, and enterprise. During the nineteenth century, presidents used American armed forces on their own authority to suppress piracy and the slave trade, to pursue criminals across frontiers, and to protect American lives and property in primitive or undeveloped areas. Some presidents, such as James K. Polk, Ulysses S. Grant, and William McKinley, interpreted the commander-in-chief powers broadly, while others, such as George Washington, Thomas Jefferson, James Buchanan, and Grover Cleveland, were more deferential to the war powers of Congress. Regardless of these differences, however, the dominant view of the time was

that the president could deploy the military outside of U.S. borders so long as the military was not used to commit an "act of war" (using military force against a sovereign nation without that nation having declared war on or used force against the United States).[32]

This pattern changed in the twentieth century. Presidents from Theodore Roosevelt on began to use the military against sovereign nations without congressional authorization. Roosevelt, for example, directed the U.S. Navy against Colombia to prevent Colombia from suppressing the Panamanian insurrection. Presidents William Howard Taft and Woodrow Wilson both used American troops freely in Central America and the Caribbean without congressional authorization. And President Franklin Roosevelt exercised even greater discretion over the use of American troops abroad prior to the start of World War II.[33] (*See box, Major U.S. Military Interventions, 1946–1995, p. 1293.*)

After the war America emerged for the first time from its predominantly isolationist posture in world affairs, assuming instead an assertive internationalist and interventionist role. This trend opened the door to a more active military role, with military initiatives arising from presidential initiative and congressional acquiescence.

President Harry S. Truman committed American troops to Korea in 1950 without congressional authorization. Truman himself offered no explanation for declining to seek congressional assent (although he did consult with congressional leaders after the initial commitment of troops), but a State Department bulletin asserted that "the President, as Commander in Chief of the Armed Forces of the United States, has full control over the use thereof."[34] The following year Secretary of State Dean Acheson defended Truman's actions before a congressional hearing by asserting that the president had acted properly by carrying out American foreign policy and that Congress could not interfere.

President Dwight D. Eisenhower, in contrast, took care to seek congressional authorization in the case of the Formosa Resolution of 1954, which empowered the president to employ American forces to defend the island of Formosa, off the coast of China. But in subsequent resolutions, including the Middle East Resolution of 1957, the Cuba Resolution of 1962 (under President John F. Kennedy), and the Gulf of Tonkin Resolution of 1964 (under President Lyndon B. Johnson), the concept of seeking congressional authorization was dropped. Rather, the terminology used implied acceptance of the idea that the president already had the power to use the armed forces in the ways mentioned in the resolutions.

Presidents from Eisenhower through Nixon all asserted unrestricted executive authority to commit American forces without prior congressional consent. With some minor exceptions Congress acquiesced in this arrangement until 1973.

The War Powers Resolution

The 1960s and 1970s saw American engagement in the longest war in U.S. history. Although the scale of American in-

MAJOR U.S. MILITARY INTERVENTIONS, 1946–1995

The following are major instances of U.S. military intervention since World War II (not including participation in multinational peacekeeping forces, such as those deployed in Lebanon in the 1980s and Somalia and Bosnia in the 1990s):

July–August 1946. President Harry S. Truman sends U.S. naval units to Trieste, near the Italian-Yugoslav border, anticipating an attack from Yugoslav-Soviet forces. After U.S. Army transport planes are shot down, reinforcements arrive in Italy.

August 1946. To counter Soviet threat to Turkish control of Bosporus Straits, President Truman dispatches powerful carrier force as a display of resolve.

September 1946. One U.S. carrier is stationed off Greece during attempted communist takeover.

January 1948. Marine reinforcements sent to the Mediterranean are seen as a warning to Yugoslavia to stay away from the five thousand U.S. Army troops in Trieste.

July 1948. During the Arab-Israeli War a consular guard is detached from the U.S.S. *Kearsarge* and sent to Jerusalem to protect the U.S. consul general. Two marines are later wounded.

April 1948–November 1949. Marines are sent to Nanking and Shanghai to protect the U.S. embassy and to aid evacuation of American nationals in wake of communist takeover of China.

June 1950–July 1953. Korean War.

July 1954–February 1955. Five U.S. carriers arrive at the Tachen Islands north of Taiwan to evacuate American and Taiwanese civilians and military personnel threatened by Chinese communist bombing.

November 1956. During the Suez crisis one marine battalion evacuates fifteen hundred people, most of them Americans, from Alexandria, Egypt.

February 1957. Marines stationed 550 miles northeast of Sumatra are poised to intervene for protection of Americans during revolt in Indonesia.

July 1957. Four U.S. carriers are sent to defend Taiwan during Chinese communist shelling of Kinmen Island (Quemoy).

January 1958. When mob violence breaks out in Caracas, Venezuela, the U.S.S. *Des Moines*, with one company of U.S. marines on board, is stationed nearby.

March 1958. A marine company, attack squadron, and helicopter squadron are deployed with the Seventh Fleet off Indonesia to protect U.S. citizens.

July–October 1958. Following civil unrest in Beirut, President Dwight D. Eisenhower sends five thousand marines to Lebanon to "protect American lives" and to "assist Lebanon in preserving its political independence." Eventually, fourteen thousand U.S. soldiers and marines occupy areas in Lebanon. The last U.S. forces withdraw in late October.

July 1959–April 1975. Vietnam era. Sent as troop trainers, the first U.S. military are killed in South Vietnam in July 1959. In October 1961 President John F. Kennedy decides to send Green Beret "military advisers." In August 1964 Congress passes Gulf of Tonkin

Resolution. In March 1973 last U.S. troops withdraw. At the end of April 1975 last Americans are evacuated from Saigon.

November 1959–February 1960. A Marine Ground Task Force is deployed to protect U.S. nationals in Cuba during the revolution.

November 1961. Navy ships and planes arrive off the Dominican Republic as show of force to discourage members of Trujillo family from attempting to retake the government they lost when dictator Rafael Trujillo was assassinated the previous May.

May–July 1962. A marine expeditionary unit of five thousand lands in Thailand to support the government against threat of outside communist pressure. Marines depart nine weeks later.

October–December 1962. Challenging a Soviet introduction of missiles into Cuba, President Kennedy orders 180 U.S. Navy ships and a B-52 bomber force carrying A-bombs into the Caribbean to effect a quarantine. Troop carrier squadrons of the U.S. Air Force Reserve are being recalled to active duty when Soviet premier Nikita Khrushchev agrees to withdraw the missiles.

May 1963. A U.S. Marine battalion is positioned off the coast of Haiti in the wake of domestic protest against the Duvalier regime and a threat of intervention by the neighboring Dominican Republic.

November 1964. U.S. transport aircraft in the Congo carry Belgian paratroopers in an operation to rescue civilians, among them sixty Americans held hostage by antigovernment rebels near Stanleyville.

May 1964–January 1973. Beginning as retaliation for the downing of American reconnaissance planes flying over Laos, U.S. Navy jets attack Pathet Lao communist strongholds. Air attacks on Laos continue into the 1970s.

April 1965. Following a communist-leaning revolt in the Dominican Republic, President Lyndon B. Johnson dispatches 21,500 U.S. troops to protect Americans and to offer supplies and military assistance to locals. By fall, constitutional government is restored.

June 1967. During the Arab-Israeli War, President Johnson sends the U.S. Sixth Fleet within fifty miles of the Syrian coast as a warning to the Soviet Union against entering the conflict.

July–December 1967. Responding to an appeal from Congolese president Joseph-Désiré Mobutu, President Johnson sends three C-130 transport planes with crews to aid government forces battling white mercenaries and Katangese rebels.

April–June 1970. U.S. ground troops attack communist sanctuaries in Cambodia.

May 1975. President Gerald R. Ford sends combined force of navy, marine, and air force to rescue thirty-nine crew members of the U.S. merchant ship *Mayaguez*, which had been captured by Cambodian communists.

April 1980. Ninety-man U.S. commando team in Iran aborts effort to rescue American hostages held in the U.S. embassy in Tehran. Eight die in collision between transport plane and helicopter.

October 1983. U.S. Marines and troops from neighboring eastern Caribbean nations invade the island of Grenada.

(Continued on page 1294)

April 1986. President Ronald Reagan orders air strikes from the Gulf of Sidra against Libyan military installations in response to terrorist attacks.

1986–1988. American ships patrol the Persian Gulf during Iran-Iraq war. Thirty-seven American sailors killed in attack on U.S. vessel in 1987.

December 1989. After fatal attack on an American serviceman in Panama, President George Bush sends 27,000 American troops into Panama, overthrowing dictator Manuel Noriega.

January–February 1991. After Iraq invades and occupies Kuwait in August 1990, Bush begins massive American military buildup in the Mideast (eventually about 500,000 U.S. soldiers). In January 1991 Congress invokes War Powers Resolution for the second time and authorizes use of military force. From January 16 to February 23, United States and its allies fly almost 100,000 air missions against Iraqi positions. After brief pause, a land invasion is launched. Iraqi troops are routed in 100 hours of fighting; seventy-two U.S. soldiers are killed.

December 1994. President Bill Clinton sends troops to Haiti to restore peacefully the regime of Bertrand Aristide.

SOURCE: *Congressional Quarterly Weekly Report*, October 29, 1983, 2222, and various issues.

volvement in the Vietnam War was less than that of World War II, for example, the length of the war and the growing doubts about its justification and its progressively greater human and material costs fanned the flames of discontent nationwide. Congressional leaders pressed for means to curtail the president's relatively free hand, which in turn sparked renewed interest in reinvigorating congressional influence over war making. This pressure culminated in the passage of the War Powers Resolution in 1973. Although vetoed by President Richard Nixon, Congress enacted the bill over the veto.

The resolution incorporates three key provisions. First, the president must consult with Congress "in every possible instance" before introducing U.S. forces into hostilities. The resolution fails to identify with whom the president should consult, but the assumption of the resolution's drafters and presidents has been that consultation should include the party leaders in each chamber, and the heads and ranking minority members of key committees involved with foreign policy and defense matters. Second, the president must submit a written report to Congress (specifically to the Speaker of the House and president pro tempore of the Senate) within forty-eight hours of the introduction of American forces into hostilities. And third, the president must withdraw forces within sixty days (or up to ninety days, if the president certifies to Congress the necessity for a prolonged engagement) unless Congress provides appropriate authorization. Congress may direct the president to withdraw forces at any time by passage of a concurrent resolution (a con-

current resolution does not normally cross the president's desk, but in the two instances in which the War Powers Resolution has been invoked—the Lebanon resolution of 1983 and the Persian Gulf resolution of 1991—Congress used the regular legislative process). The sixty-to-ninety-day period does not begin, however, until the president submits a written report. *(See box, War Powers Provisions, p. 644, Vol. I.)*

Despite what initially was considered a successful attempt to involve Congress more meaningfully in war making, the War Powers Resolution has been the subject of much criticism and debate. Some critics have argued that it attempts improperly to tie the president's hands, while others view it as an invitation for the president to conduct war freely for sixty days.[35] In any case, presidents from Ford to Clinton have avoided full compliance, and all except Clinton have questioned the act's constitutionality, mostly on the grounds that the act improperly infringes on the president's constitutional prerogatives. This has raised the added objection that the act lacks any mechanism to force the president to comply with it (aside from the concurrent resolution provision), as it provides no means of impelling the president to submit an initial report or even to consult with Congress. While President Clinton has not specifically argued that the War Powers Resolution is unconstitutional, he has asserted presidential war powers claims similar to those of his immediate predecessors in the case of the 1994 Haiti incursion and the deployment of U.S. troops to Bosnia in 1995.

In 1975 the War Powers Resolution was invoked on four occasions. The first three occurred in April and involved the evacuation of refugees and U.S. citizens from Vietnam and Cambodia in the waning days of the Vietnam War. In these cases, "consultation" with Congress occurred, but the rescue attempts were concluded quickly.

The fourth instance occurred in May, when a Cambodian gunboat captured an American vessel, the *Mayaguez*. President Ford then ordered air strikes against Cambodia and called up the marines, who launched a costly invasion of Koh Tang Island in the erroneous belief that the *Mayaguez* crew was being held there. Despite problems with the military operation, the crew was returned two days later (although apparently not as a result of the military assaults), and Ford's actions prompted euphoria at a time when the country was still feeling the sting of Vietnam. In this instance Ford did not consult with Congress, but he did inform some members of Congress as the military carried out the operation.

When President Jimmy Carter launched an unsuccessful military effort in April 1980 to rescue American hostages being held in Iran, he did not consult with Congress, citing the need for secrecy. He submitted a brief report to Congress, but he argued that the War Powers Resolution did not apply as the mission was a humanitarian effort.

Lebanon. The presidency of Ronald Reagan saw several clashes between the executive and legislative branches over the deployment of American troops abroad. In August 1982 Reagan sent marines to Lebanon to serve as part of an international force, which included French and Italian (and later British) troops deployed to help bring peace to that war-torn nation. Despite agreement that a state of hostilities existed, Reagan submitted a report to Congress that was consistent with the War Powers Resolution rather than under its terms. That is, Reagan technically ducked the provision of the resolution requiring reporting under its terms by using the phrase "consistent with." Thus, he did not set in motion the sixty-to-ninety-day limit the resolution imposes (although the resolution gives Congress the power to start the clock regardless of whether the president reports).

The continued presence of American troops in Lebanon in what was considered an untenable military situation raised doubts about the mission.[36] Such doubts were aggravated when marines were killed in several bombing incidents. The worst attack occurred on October 23, 1983, when a Moslem fundamentalist drove a truck full of explosives into marine headquarters, killing 241 marines.

In the absence of the automatic triggering of the War Powers clock, Congress moved to direct the president to withdraw the troops. Protracted negotiations between the administration and congressional leaders ensued, spanning many months. Congress passed and President Reagan signed a bill in the fall of 1983 giving him authority to keep troops in Lebanon for eighteen months. Despite uneasiness over the length of this period, many in Congress felt it politically prudent to see that this period extended past the 1984 elections so that Congress would not suffer adverse political effects if the congressionally set deadline proved to be a political or military embarrassment. They also believed that Reagan would acknowledge the legitimacy of the War Powers framework. Instead, the president made it clear that he did not consider himself bound by the act, and that he would consider keeping troops in Lebanon past the eighteen-month deadline.[37]

By early 1984 the military situation was deteriorating steadily. On February 7, 1984, Reagan ordered the marines withdrawn to American ships.

Grenada. On October 25, 1983, President Reagan launched an invasion of the tiny Caribbean island of Grenada (population, about 110,000). The operation employed more than nineteen hundred soldiers from all service branches.

In 1979 the ruling government of Prime Minister Eric Gairy was overthrown in a coup led by Maurice Bishop. In October 1983 Bishop was overthrown. The Reagan administration had viewed the Bishop regime with suspicion because of its leftist leanings, and it feared that a new regime would be even more sympathetic to Cuba. Moreover, approximately one thousand Americans were living on the island at the time, six hundred of whom were medical students.

Reagan briefed congressional leaders the night before the invasion and submitted a report on the day of the invasion. Despite their overwhelming military superiority, U.S. forces took

Despite congressional opposition, President Ronald Reagan sent marines into Lebanon as part of a multinational peacekeeping force in August 1982. After the deaths of 241 marines in the bombing of their barracks, U.S. forces left Lebanon in February 1984.

about a week to win control of the island. Nineteen U.S. soldiers were killed and 116 were wounded; twenty-four Cubans were killed, as were forty-five Grenadians (twenty-seven were killed accidentally when U.S. forces bombed a mental hospital). By the end of October both houses of Congress had taken steps to begin the sixty-day War Powers clock, but by December only about three hundred American personnel were still on the island.

Critics of the invasion questioned whether the Americans on Grenada were in fact in danger, and, if so, whether an armed invasion was the appropriate response. They also criticized the U.S. military's decision in not allowing news reporters to accompany the invading U.S. troops, as had been the practice in previous wars. The Defense Department claimed that reporters were excluded for their own safety, but after the invasion the department announced that it would allow a few reporters to cover future similar military actions.[38]

Gulf of Sidra. On April 14, 1986, President Reagan ordered air strikes against port and military installations in Libya, in response to Libya's widely reputed support of terrorism. The air strike was prompted by two particular incidents: the terrorist bombing of a nightclub in West Germany frequented by U.S. soldiers and U.S. naval maneuvers in the Gulf of Sidra. Libya claimed all of the gulf as its territorial waters, but the Reagan administration ordered maneuvers to be conducted there anyway.

President Reagan summoned congressional leaders to the White House for a late afternoon briefing after American F-111 bombers had already left their bases in Great Britain (they were joined in the raid by carrier-based aircraft). After the mission the Reagan administration admitted that the naval maneuvers held inside the gulf were designed to provoke Libya's leader, Muammar Quaddafi, into military action to provide a basis for a U.S. response. The air strikes also were an attempt to assassinate Quaddafi, who narrowly escaped death when planes bombed his residence.

Persian Gulf. When the Iran-Iraq war of the 1980s spilled over into the Persian Gulf, a central shipping lane for oil, oil tankers became targets of raids by both countries. Although American ships already had been patrolling the gulf and the Indian Ocean, patrols were stepped up in 1986 in response to requests by Kuwait that its oil tankers be "reflagged" under U.S. registry to provide a basis for armed U.S. protection. American ships and personnel were involved in several skirmishes. In one instance an Iraqi Exocet missile hit the frigate U.S.S. *Stark,* killing thirty-seven crew members and injuring twenty-one. Although the attack was a mistake and Iraq immediately apologized, it underscored the vulnerability of American vessels to harm from missiles, mines, and small attack speedboats.

As with the situation in Lebanon, many in Congress and the country were concerned that the American purpose and mission were ill-defined. Although the Persian Gulf was considered "the most dangerous body of water in the world for shipping," and U.S. soldiers there were given "imminent danger" pay, the Reagan administration argued that the War Powers Resolution did not apply.[39] In response, 112 members of Congress filed suit in federal court to force the president to comply.[40] In early 1988 the Reagan administration announced that it was cutting back on the American presence in the gulf. With the subsequent end of the Iran-Iraq war, the threat to shipping subsided.

Panama. Throughout the 1980s Panama was ruled by General Manuel Noriega. Although Noriega was backed by the United States, his connections with drug trafficking and his anti-American statements escalated tensions between his regime and U.S. leaders. In October 1989 America expressed sympathy for an unsuccessful attempt to overthrow him. The Bush administration was criticized for failing to intervene militarily.

After the killing of an unarmed American soldier on December 17, Bush authorized a massive assault on Panama, carried out on December 20. The invasion involved 27,000 American soldiers, including 13,000 already stationed in the American-controlled Panama Canal Zone. Despite encountering unexpectedly tough fighting from some of Noriega's troops, U.S. forces were successful in subduing resistance within a few days. Noriega himself eluded capture and took refuge at the Vatican Embassy on December 24. After two weeks of negotiations, he surrendered to American forces. According to the Department of Defense, twenty-three U.S. soldiers and three American civilians were killed, and 324 American soldiers were wounded. Between 300 and 700 Panamanians were killed, and about 1,500 were wounded.

The Bush administration kept congressional leaders apprised of developments before the invasion and informed them by phone of the impending attack a few hours before it began. After the start of the operation, the administration sent formal notice to Congress, which also included an assertion that the War Powers Act was unconstitutional. These steps, plus general support for the action against Noriega, muted what little criticism was heard.[41]

The Gulf War. America's reluctant support for Iraq, and its ruthless leader Saddam Hussein, during the Iran-Iraq war soured when Iraq turned its attention to its vulnerable, oil-rich neighbor, Kuwait. After protracted negotiations over border lands to which both nations lay claim, Iraq invaded Kuwait on August 2, 1990, quickly overrunning Kuwait's small army. Fearing an assault on Saudi Arabia and an interruption of oil supplies, President Bush began a massive American military buildup, dubbed Operation Desert Shield. Bush and a small circle of top White House advisers made this decision. Only one member of Congress, Sen. Sam Nunn (D-Ga.), was informed of the decision beforehand. Within two weeks, the United States had deployed nearly 100,000 troops in and around Saudi Arabia.

Bush labored to build international support for military intervention, including support from other Middle East nations. As the military buildup continued, criticism at home began to escalate from both liberals and conservatives. At first, Bush claimed that no congressional approval was necessary for the military buildup. Yet congressional alarm rose when on November 8 (two days after the midterm congressional elections) Bush announced a doubling of U.S. troop strength, presaging a shift from a militarily defensive to an offensive posture. By the end of 1990, U.S. troop strength had reached 400,000.

After the November elections, Congress conducted a series of hearings on the intervention, and a consensus began to emerge that Congress needed to debate formally and come to a decision about American involvement. On January 10, 1991, Congress began consideration of two resolutions. One, sponsored by the Democratic leadership, called for continued use of economic sanctions. It was defeated on January 12 in the Senate by a vote of 53–46, and in the House by a vote of 250–183. That same day, Congress approved an administration-backed resolution authorizing the president to use force, subject to notification of congressional leaders. It passed on January 12 by votes of 52–47 in the Senate and 250–183 in the House. The measure also included a specific invocation of the War Powers Resolution. (*See box,*

INTELLIGENCE COMMUNITY

The agencies and bureaus that collect and analyze information on foreign affairs for the executive branch are collectively known as the *intelligence community*. As specified in Executive Order 12333, issued by President Ronald Reagan on December 4, 1981, the intelligence community consists of the Central Intelligence Agency; the National Security Agency; the Bureau of Intelligence and Research in the Department of State; the Defense Intelligence Agency and the intelligence offices of the army, navy, air force, and marine corps in the Department of Defense; the Federal Bureau of Investigation; intelligence offices in the Department of Energy and the Department of the Treasury; and staff elements of the director of central intelligence.

Intelligence is only a minor part of the overall activities of some of these agencies. Nevertheless, the intelligence collected is important in terms of national security and the total flow of information to the U.S. government.

SOURCE: Cecil V. Crabb Jr. and Pat M. Holt, *Invitation to Struggle: Congress, the President and Foreign Policy*, 4th ed. (Washington, D.C.: CQ Press, 1992), 25–26.

Congressional Resolution on the Gulf Crisis of 1991, p. 1305.) Congress won high praise for the quality of debate, and willingness to assume its constitutional role over war making, even though Bush's actions up to that time served to force Congress's hand. Even so, congressional leaders made it clear that the president would be legally bound by the will of Congress, whatever the outcome.

Eighteen hours after the January 15 deadline for the withdrawal of Iraqi troops, Operation Desert Storm began. Between then and February 23, the United States and its allies flew about 100,000 air missions against Iraqi targets. On February 23, a massive ground assault was launched. In the span of 100 hours, Iraqi troops were routed, and the allies suffered far fewer casualties than had been expected. In all, seventy-two Americans were killed and two hundred were wounded. More than 100,000 Iraqi soldiers surrendered, and tens of thousands were killed. Yet despite this stunning victory, allied forces stopped short of deposing Saddam, and he remained in control of his country, continuing to rebuild his shattered forces.[42]

PRESIDENTIAL WAR MAKING

Despite the attempt by Congress to reinsert itself in the war-making process, it is evident that presidents who wish to project U.S. military strength still have considerable ability to do so. Several reasons help explain this persisting trend.

First, even when taken at face value the War Powers Resolution contains a number of loopholes for presidents with predilections to military action. The resolution states, for example, that "Nothing in this joint resolution . . . is intended to alter the constitutional authority of the . . . president. . . ." Other loopholes and ambiguities, such as concern that the sixty-to-ninety-day period provides the president with an open invitation to make war for that period, are highlighted by the cases summarized above. Presidents also have argued that parts of the act are simply impractical. In discussing the *Mayaguez* incident, President Ford noted later that many key legislators were out of town, making consultation difficult. He also observed that legislators have other concerns that minimize the attention they can give to a single problem, that the need to gain a congressional consensus may inhibit speed of action, and that information may leak from Congress.[43]

Second, the historical record indicates that presidents usually benefit politically when they engage in foreign military operations. Most foreign policy crises and operations, especially when brief, boost a president's popularity ratings.[44] More to the point, Congress is less likely to challenge the president if it perceives that the public supports the president's actions.

Third, the political reality is that an apparently successful military action invariably outweighs seemingly mundane constitutional and legal questions. The military necessity of both the *Mayaguez* and Grenada incidents was questioned, for example; yet such questions were far outshadowed by national feelings of euphoria. Moreover, although members of Congress recognized in the *Mayaguez* incident that President Ford had not followed the law, they muted their criticism because of the positive reaction to the president's actions.[45]

Fourth, Congress has by no means been unified in opposing presidential military initiatives. Many in Congress support presidential actions for ideological or partisan reasons, and many believe that the president indeed has the constitutional power, in effect, to wage war. Some would just as soon let the president take the lead, given the political risks of military adventures that fail. And once a military operation has begun, members of Congress invariably are reluctant to interfere in a way that might be interpreted later as having contributed to the defeat of, or harm to, U.S. soldiers. This was a key consideration in the reluctance of Congress to force Reagan's hand in Lebanon.

Admittedly, then, congressional attempts to limit unilateral presidential actions, or to involve members of Congress more meaningfully, have met with limited success. Still, the War Powers Resolution has served as a focal point for the debate on war making.

Treaty Making and Executive Agreements

Treaty making is treated succinctly in Article II, section 2, of the Constitution, which gives the president the power "to make Treaties, provided that two-thirds of the Senators present concur. . . ." The House of Representatives clearly is excluded from the treaty process, yet it becomes involved when appropriations or enabling legislation is required to put a treaty into effect. *(See also "The Treaty Power," p. 601, and "Executive Agreements," p. 606, in Chapter 13, Vol. I.)*

Treaty-making power was discussed frequently at the Constitutional Convention. Initially, the Founders proposed that power over treaties remain solely in the hands of the legislature, as had been the case under the Articles of Confederation. But late in the convention the Founders yielded to the argument that the president should "make treaties." The exclusion of the House was defended by Alexander Hamilton and John Jay in *The Federalist Papers* Nos. 64, 69, and 75, where they argued that the Senate's smaller size and institutional continuity (attributable to senators' longer terms of office and staggered election cycle) would facilitate secrecy and dispatch in the treaty process.

The Founders envisioned that the president actually would consult with the Senate while treaty formulation was under way. But when President Washington attempted such a process with an Indian treaty in 1789, it proved entirely unsatisfactory. Washington went personally to the Senate, expecting the body to approve the treaty on the spot. Feeling rushed, the Senate was unwilling to do this, asking for more time and information. Washington became angry and left without treaty approval, although the Senate approved the treaty shortly thereafter. Washington abandoned in-person consultation. From that time to the present the Senate has played more of a "consent" role than an "advice" role.[46] In fact, the Senate (and Congress as a whole) has been more active in peace-related matters than war-related matters. According to one study an inverse relationship exists between the active involvement of Congress and the presence of military hostilities in a situation. Stated another way, the greater the specter of armed conflict, the less likely it is that Congress will play a key role.[47]

Although the Senate as an institution typically enters the treaty-making process when the president presents a treaty to it, individual senators often have participated in negotiations with other countries. As early as 1814, for example, President Madison appointed two members of Congress to negotiate a peace treaty with Great Britain. More recently, in 1945, Senators Arthur H. Vandenberg (R-Mich.) and Thomas T. Connally (D-Texas) were key participants in drawing up the United Nations Charter. And President Kennedy's negotiations with the Soviet Union over the nuclear test ban treaty of 1963 occurred with Senate members present. Many observers argue that the absence of senators during Wilson administration negotiations on the League of Nations agreement at the end of World War I contributed to the treaty's defeat by the Senate in 1919. After Woodrow Wilson's experience, senators were often appointed to important international conferences, especially by Presidents Warren G. Harding, Herbert C. Hoover, Franklin Roosevelt, and Harry Truman.[48]

The relationship between the Senate and the president in the treaty process often is viewed as one of conflict, characterized by presidential defeat, especially considering the two-thirds approval requirement. Examples that seem to support this proposition are the defeat of the League of Nations treaty by the Senate in 1919, the withdrawal of the SALT II Treaty by President Carter in 1980 in the face of vocal Senate opposition, and Carter's protracted battle to win ratification of the Panama Canal Treaty in 1978. President Clinton faced a fierce, though successful, struggle to win ratification of the North American Free Trade Agreement (NAFTA) in 1993. Yet from 1789 to 1994 only twenty-two major treaties (about 1 percent) were voted down by the Senate. About 15 percent were accepted by the Senate after alteration. (*See Table 13-1, Major Treaties Killed by the Senate, 1789–1994, p. 605, Vol. I.*)

The very nature of treaty making has provided the president with an immediate advantage in dealing with the Senate. Since the process of negotiating treaties falls clearly (although not necessarily exclusively) to the president, the White House staff and the State Department in particular are associated closely with the construction of the treaty document. (The president may invite members of Congress to participate or may permit key legislators to have a say in the selection of the negotiating team.) Thus, the administration is likely to have control over, if not a monopoly on, information about the content and political process leading up to finalization of an agreement. The proposed treaty is presented to the Senate as the president's document, carrying the weight and prestige of the chief executive. Since the president also is recognized as the nation's chief international spokesperson, the political initiative rests with the president in a way that it does not with routine legislation, especially since Senate involvement in the negotiation process is likely to occur only at the invitation of the president.[49]

The treaty-making process incorporates three stages. First, the president's representatives, usually including the secretary of state, engage in negotiations with a foreign government, the result of which is a treaty. As was the case with the Panama Canal Treaty, such negotiations often span decades and several administrations. Congress may offer advice and opinions about negotiations, but legally they carry no special weight. Second, the document is transmitted to the Senate, which has several options. It can approve the treaty, reject it, amend it (in which case it may have to go back to the foreign country for reapproval), or attach reservations and understandings designed to clarify treaty provisions and language. Third, at the conclusion of the Senate's deliberations, the treaty must be "proclaimed," or accepted, by the president.[50] As this sequence reveals, the president retains the political initiative throughout, but Senate involvement at every stage is by no means precluded. At any stage other than ratification, however, such involvement must be at the president's request.

Although the treaty process favors the president's political predilections, the chief executive cannot take Senate support for granted. Presidents must lay the political groundwork carefully to improve the chances of ratification, even when substantial support for proposed treaties already exists.

ENDING TREATIES

The Constitution is silent on the question of treaty termination. Scholar Louis Fisher has noted that Article V of the Constitution vests federal statutes and treaties with the same status, yielding the conclusion that Congress possesses the power to end a treaty by the normal legislative process.[51] Other scholars have argued that, since the Senate must ratify treaties, it follows that Senate consent is necessary to terminate a treaty. At the same time several presidents have claimed for themselves the power to end treaties. President Franklin D. Roosevelt, for example, ended a commerce and friendship treaty with Japan two years before the United States entered World War II.

More recently a political and legal challenge was raised against President Carter's termination of treaties with the Republic of China (Taiwan) as a prelude to full recognition of the People's Republic of China (mainland China). Contention centered on the Mutual Defense Treaty of 1954, which allowed either party to end the treaty on a year's notice. Carter announced the termination of the treaty in December 1978, while Congress was out of session. Sen. Barry M. Goldwater (R-Ariz.) then filed suit in federal court to block Carter's action. Although a federal district court sided with Goldwater, the federal court of appeals ruled that the president possessed the power to terminate the treaty. In the case of *Goldwater v. Carter,* a divided Supreme Court upheld the lower court ruling.[52]

The ruling in the *Goldwater* case also clarified an important point about recognition of foreign governments. Termination of the treaty with Taiwan was a necessary step to the full recognition of the Beijing government, which was the goal of Carter's actions. Supreme Court Justice William J. Brennan Jr. noted in his opinion: "Our cases firmly establish that the Constitution commits to the President alone the power to recognize, and withdraw recognition from, foreign regimes."

TREATY-MAKING SUCCESS: PANAMA CANAL TREATIES

Since the American-inspired Panamanian revolution in 1903, the United States has controlled a ten-mile-wide strip of land running through the middle of Panama. This arrangement allowed the United States to construct the Panama Canal and maintain complete control over its operation. The terms of the agreement granting American control "in perpetuity" were so favorable to the United States that, despite treaty renegotiations in 1936 and 1955, Panamanians grew increasingly resentful of continued U.S. domination. In contrast, most U.S. leaders felt little need to alter significantly the terms of the relationship, as it had been very advantageous to this country.

In the early 1960s riots broke out in Panama and the U.S.-controlled Canal Zone. Although the immediate cause of the riots was whether the Panamanian flag would be flown along with the American flag in the zone, the riots were symptomatic of growing resentment in Panama over continued U.S. domination.

In the spring of 1964 treaty negotiations began again; they did not conclude until 1977. During the long negotiations, some in Congress—especially the House Merchant Marine and Fisheries Committee and its subcommittee on the Panama Canal—kept a watchful eye on their development. Both the full committee and its subcommittee were sources of opposition to changes

The battleship U.S.S. *New Jersey* sails through the Panama Canal. Although U.S. control of the canal will be turned over to Panama in the year 2000, U.S. warships will still retain the right of expeditious transit through the canal.

that might arise from a new treaty, and in 1975 the House passed an amendment that barred any use of federal funds in relinquishing U.S. rights to the Canal Zone. This measure failed in the Senate, but it was reintroduced in the House in 1976 and 1977.

Treaty negotiations ended during the summer of 1977, and two treaties were transmitted to the Senate on September 16. The first, the Panama Canal Treaty, superseded the 1903 treaty and abolished the Canal Zone. The United States maintained the right to manage, maintain, and operate the canal through a new administrative apparatus (that would include Panamanians) until the end of 1999, when complete control of the canal would pass to Panama. At that time the United States would relinquish some of its control over administration of the canal and would increase payments to Panama for continued favored treatment of the United States. The other treaty, the Neutrality Treaty, asserted that the canal would operate under a permanent state of neutrality, and that Panama alone would operate the canal after 1999. As a special concession to the United States, U.S. warships were to be allowed expeditious transit through the canal.

From the beginning, treaty ratification was an open question. There were a large number of undecided senators. Many citizens and government officials simply had assumed that the canal properly belonged to the United States. Indeed, public opinion surveys revealed majority opposition to treaty ratification, although those citizens better informed about the treaties were more likely to support them.[53] Part of the suspicion surrounding the treaties arose from concern that relinquishment of legal control would result in a compromise of U.S. security.[54]

Thus, when President Carter tackled the task of winning treaty ratification in the Senate, he faced several political obstacles. He began to lay the political groundwork in the spring of 1977 by apprising key members of the Senate of treaty developments and soliciting their views. Besides rallying public opinion, Carter had to satisfy members of his own administration and a Congress that had maintained a long-term interest in the affairs of the Panama Canal. According to scholar William L. Furlong, "Few foreign policy issues in the history of the United States have involved the Congress more than negotiations and relations regarding the Panama Canal."[55] Although this involvement is not typical of congressional interest in foreign affairs, the Panama case reveals much about how the president and Congress interact during the formulation and ratification of treaties.

House ratification is not needed for treaties, but the House had made its political weight felt in previous attempts to influence funding affecting the canal. During the ratification process for the two canal treaties, the House served as an important forum for generating both support for and opposition to the treaties. In particular, three House committees held hearings on the canal and the treaties: Merchant Marine and Fisheries, International Relations, and Armed Services.

In the Senate, the Judiciary, Armed Services, and Foreign Relations committees conducted the hearings. Those of the Foreign Relations Committee were the lengthiest and the most detailed. In addition, forty-two of the Senate's one hundred members traveled to Panama, as did many members of the House. On the floor of the Senate the debate continued for thirty-eight days and was the second longest treaty debate in the Senate's history—only the Treaty of Versailles debate was longer. No fewer than eighty-eight changes were proposed and voted on. Of these, more than twenty reservations, understandings, and conditions were added.

Most of the senators who visited Panama did so to gather information, but some actually negotiated directly with the Panamanian leadership. Such negotiations, after finalization of the terms of the treaty by the heads of government, were highly unusual and represented a degree of Senate involvement not seen since consideration of the Treaty of Versailles in 1919. President Carter responded to the specific concerns of undecided senators. In one key incident a first-term senator—Dennis W. DeConcini (D-Ariz.)—succeeded in attaching an amendment to the treaty (with Carter's consent) that allowed the United States to use military force if necessary to keep the canal open after the year 2000. The addition infuriated the Panamanians,

and some last-minute bargaining was necessary to satisfy both the Senate, including DeConcini, and Panama. Carter's concession on the DeConcini amendment was obviously a move to win his support, yet it nearly collapsed the treaty process.

DeConcini's pivotal influence illustrates a larger point about ratification. Senators who remained undecided found themselves in the best political position to influence the terms of the treaty, and also to extract concessions (often unrelated to the treaty issue) from the president in exchange for their support. Indeed, some senators who initially had committed themselves to the treaty backed off in an attempt to gain some leverage with the White House.[56]

After months of intense investigation, bargaining, and debate, the Senate approved the Neutrality Treaty on March 16, 1978, and the Panama Canal Treaty on April 18. Both passed by the same 68 to 32 margin—one vote more than the necessary two-thirds.

TREATY-MAKING FAILURE: SALT II TREATY

Since 1968, the United States has engaged in systematic talks with the Soviet Union and, after 1991, with Russia and the independent states, designed to control aspects of the nuclear arms race. For the Nixon, Ford, and Carter administrations these talks were known by the acronym SALT (Strategic Arms Limitation Talks). The two most important treaties emerging from this process were SALT I, completed and ratified in 1972, and SALT II, completed in 1979 but withdrawn from the Senate shortly after completion because it was clear that it could not achieve the necessary two-thirds affirmative vote.[57]

SALT II negotiations had begun in November 1972 and had stretched on for seven years, spanning three presidential administrations. The treaty dealt with a variety of complex issues, but in general it set limits on how many of the vehicles (including missiles and bombers) used to deliver nuclear warheads each side could have. It also included a three-year "protocol" that addressed the controversial issues dividing the two nations and a statement that addressed President Carter's "deep cuts" proposal, which called for significant reductions in weapons numbers set out in prior agreements. The negotiations process stretched on during Carter's first two years in office because of disagreements about how to deal with particular weapons systems, such as the cruise missile and the Soviet Backfire bomber.

As with the Panama Canal treaties the president had to deal domestically not only with the Senate, but also with the House, his own administration, and public opinion. In Congress, key members had been vocal about the negotiations process since the early 1970s. Certain House members had been influential in shaping the SALT debate nationally, and various attempts had been made to influence the nature and direction of the treaty through control of funding. (Members of Congress were excluded from actual negotiations of SALT I.)

In fact, Carter made good on his campaign promise to involve key legislators by appointing a group of thirty senators and fourteen House members as advisers to, and participants in, the SALT II negotiations. The Carter administration sought the views of some Senate hardliners as well as a means of ultimately winning their support. These efforts prompted Senate Minority Leader Howard H. Baker Jr. (R-Tenn.) to praise Carter for his bipartisan approach. In addition, prevailing congressional sentiment often was used as a bargaining chip with the Soviets, as the U.S. negotiators would sometimes argue for or against a certain proposed provision based on predictions about what the Senate would or would not accept.

Despite all these careful steps, SALT II encountered a series of roadblocks. Many in Congress, for example, sought to link the SALT agreement to other issues not related to the nuclear balance in an attempt to alter Soviet policy in these areas. Others were concerned that some of Carter's negotiators, such as Arms Control and Disarmament Agency head Paul Warnke, would not be sufficiently tough. And still others believed that the treaty gave away too much, or that some provisions would be difficult to verify. These and related criticisms were presented forcefully at a time when Congress was moving to assert itself generally in policy making, and the presidency was still suffering from the aftermath of Vietnam and Watergate.

The final provisions of the treaty were worked out in May 1979, and the agreement was signed on June 14. By the time the treaty was sent to the Senate the public SALT debate had been going on for several years. Thus, the major issues were well known to the principals. The Senate Foreign Relations Committee held four months of both open and closed hearings on the treaty. The Armed Services Committee undertook consideration of the military consequences of the treaty.

After narrowly averting several attempts to kill the treaty, the Senate Foreign Relations Committee agreed to send the treaty to the full Senate by a lukewarm vote of 9–6. In addition, it attached twenty-three conditions to the ratification resolution. It thus became clear that the treaty would not be approved without changes, and yet Carter was unwilling to renegotiate the treaty. Also in 1979 congressional critics were noting with alarm the presence of Cuban troops in Africa and the taking of American hostages in Iran in November. Shortly thereafter, a group of nineteen senators urged Carter to put off a vote on the treaty. Finally, Carter asked the Senate to postpone consideration of the treaty in the aftermath of the Soviet invasion of Afghanistan in December. The treaty was never brought back to the Senate, although its terms were followed generally by both sides throughout the 1980s.

The withdrawal of SALT II was facilitated by external events, but also by persistent divisions within the government over the goals and purposes of the SALT process. Some observers have suggested that the substantial involvement of Congress was instrumental to SALT's demise. Yet it was the exclusion of key legislators from the negotiations for SALT I that did much to energize congressional opposition to the SALT process that followed.

TREATIES, THE PRESIDENT, AND CONGRESS

The Panama Canal treaties and the SALT II Treaty were both high-visibility treaty efforts involving a single presidency—that of Jimmy Carter. They nevertheless reveal much about the politics of treaty making. First, the rise of congressional assertiveness in the 1970s reinvigorated the role of Congress. Thus, the president now must take greater care when laying the political groundwork for approval of major or controversial treaties.

Second, the president cannot ignore the House. Through the appropriations process, committee investigations, and the ability to gain public attention, the House (especially through key committees) can have a profound effect on the treaty process.

Third, the door is clearly open for greater direct involvement by members of Congress in the actual process of formulating treaties, despite the possible pitfall of involving too many hands in the negotiations process. In many respects this is consistent with the intent of the Framers of the Constitution. Moreover, political circumstances make such involvement desirable.

Fourth, political bargaining occurs over treaty support just as it does over more mundane domestic political issues. The two-thirds requirement means that thirty-four senators can veto a treaty. This extraordinary majority requirement therefore gives a relatively small number of legislators a disproportionately great influence. Most treaties are relatively noncontroversial and deal with minor matters, but those treaties that are likely to raise questions invite senators to use the two-thirds threshold as a lever to extract concessions (whether related or unrelated to the treaty issue at hand) from the president. While one might question the trading of a favorable vote on an important treaty for funding of an unrelated pet project in a senator's home state, such processes are part of the currency of presidential-congressional relations.

Fifth, organizationally the modern Congress is more decentralized than it used to be. Party and chamber leaders possess less control over the behavior of members, and committees and committee chairs are extremely influential. Thus, a president needing to win two-thirds support in the Senate must be sensitive to the concerns of a variety of influential senators, including party leaders, committee leaders, ideological leaders, and regional leaders.

Finally, treaties belong, in a political sense, primarily to the president. It is the job of the chief executive to build coalition support by any available means. Given the historical record, it is clear that presidents have carried this burden with considerable success. Yet in recent years presidents increasingly have avoided the treaty route altogether in favor of a means of reaching international agreements without involving Senate ratification.

EXECUTIVE AGREEMENTS

Agreements with other countries are achieved not only by treaties, but also by executive agreements. An executive agreement is an understanding reached between heads of state or their designees. It can be oral or written and may require either prior congressional authorization or later congressional approval. An executive agreement, however, does not go to the Senate for ratification. It nevertheless has the force of law and, compared with a treaty, possesses "a similar dignity."[58]

Many executive agreements involve routine matters, from fishing rights to postal agreements. Yet some important international agreements have been concluded through the executive agreement route, including the 1940 exchange of fifty American destroyers for some British military bases undertaken by President Franklin Roosevelt and British prime minister Winston Churchill, and a series of agreements in the 1950s and 1960s between the White House and South Vietnamese leaders promising military and other assistance.

Executive agreements date back to the founding of the country. In 1792, for example, the postmaster general initiated an agreement on international postal arrangements. Presidents have frequently used executive agreements since then, but since World War II the number of executive agreements has skyrocketed. About 95 percent of all international understandings since the war have taken the form of executive agreements.

This rise in executive agreements is attributable partly to the greater role of the United States in international military, political, and economic affairs since World War II. But it also represents presidential efforts to make foreign policy commitments without having to go through the laborious treaty process. This trend is based in part on the president's increased political influence, congressional willingness to allow the president wide latitude in this area, and the fundamental legal ambiguity in deciding when an understanding should be treated as a treaty and when it can be handled as an executive agreement.

As a result, an international understanding is likely to be handled as an executive agreement, unless it deals with a politically important subject and Congress expresses sufficient objections to avoidance of the treaty route. Presidents often test the political waters by suggesting that an understanding might be treated as an executive agreement. President Carter did exactly this with both the Panama Canal treaties and the SALT II agreement. In both cases, however, congressional objections were sufficiently strenuous that he decided to deal with them as treaties.

Congressional dissatisfaction with the president's more frequent use of executive agreements—including some agreements arrived at secretly without the knowledge of Congress—culminated in the passage of the Case Act of 1972. Congress was not informed, for example, of important executive agreements reached between the president and Ethiopia in 1960, Laos in 1963, Thailand in 1964 and 1967, and Korea in 1966.[59] The Case Act directs the president to transmit all executive agreements to Congress within sixty days of their completion, including secret agreements (although access within Congress to information about secret agreements is restricted).

Some critics have found the Case Act too weak. Because the act does not define executive agreements, presidents have ap-

plied their own definitions, which have excluded understandings that many in Congress believed were agreements. President Nixon, for example, promised South Vietnamese president Nguyen Van Thieu that the United States would "respond with full force" if North Vietnam violated the Paris Peace Agreement, but he did not inform Congress of this promise. The pledge proved to be an embarrassment in 1975 when the North Vietnamese overran South Vietnam, and Congress declined to provide assistance. One member of Congress estimated in 1975 that from 1972 (when the Case Act was enacted) until then, presidents had entered into four hundred to six hundred understandings with other governments that had not been reported to Congress.[60]

Other Aspects of Foreign Affairs

For about the first twenty years after World War II, U.S. foreign policy was characterized by relatively strong bipartisanship. Republicans and Democrats alike in Congress and the White House shared a deep antipathy toward communism and the Soviet Union. During this cold war era, arms sales, foreign aid programs, and direct military efforts usually focused on some aspect of anticommunism. The president provided the principal leadership, and both houses of Congress generally followed closely in step.

During the mid-1960s, however, dissent began to rise in Congress and throughout the country over the president's conduct of the Vietnam War. Although conduct of the war was in many respects consistent with past policies, many onlookers began to question the monolithic view of communism that had been the basis of U.S. policy up to that time. This questioning then manifested itself in the growing division between the executive and legislative branches of government. American involvement in the Vietnam War began with the approval and support of Congress, but it soon became identified with the two presidents most heavily committed to waging the war—Johnson and Nixon. As the institutional rift between the branches widened, so too did presidential-congressional differences over other aspects of foreign policy.

The immediate evidence of this rift was repeated congressional efforts to end or otherwise limit American involvement in Vietnam. But evidence surfaced in other areas as well, such as the handling of arms sales.

In 1974, for example, an amendment passed by Congress required the president to report arms sales of more than $5,000 to Congress (although multiple sales under that amount did not have to be reported), and it provided a mechanism whereby Congress could move to block some arms sales. This act helped prod Congress to challenge proposed presidential arms sales. In 1978 members of Congress fought unsuccessfully to block the sale of fighter jets to Egypt and Saudi Arabia. Congress succeeded, however, in stalling or forcing the withdrawal of proposed arms sales to Turkey, Chile, Argentina, Libya, Iraq, and other nations.[61]

SAUDI ARMS DEAL

The Reagan administration tried to expand arms sales and trade, but Reagan too met opposition to proposed major arms sales. In 1985, for example, Reagan had planned to propose the sale of a billion-dollar arms package to Saudi Arabia, including F-15 jet fighters, M-1 tanks, helicopter gunships, and other equipment. This plan was scratched before it was formally proposed, however, because of informal but overwhelming Senate opposition that would have ensured defeat of the package. This sentiment stemmed partly from an experience with Iran in 1979, when billions of dollars in recent-vintage American military and other hardware sold to the Shah of Iran fell into the hands of the unfriendly Khomeini regime during that country's revolution.[62]

In the spring of 1986 the Reagan administration proposed a scaled-down $354 million missile package for Saudi Arabia that included air-to-sea Harpoon missiles, air-to-air Sidewinder missiles, and ground-to-air, shoulder-held Stinger missiles. Congressional resistance to even this modified package was stiff because of Saudi support for Syria and the Palestine Liberation Organization (PLO), Saudi refusal to support Egypt and Jordan in the peace process, and the continued belligerence of Saudi Arabia toward Israel.

Congress had fifty days in which to block the sale, and both the Republican-controlled Senate and the Democratic-controlled House did so. President Reagan then vetoed the disapproval on May 21. The relatively rapid and lopsided vote against the arms sale was partly a function of the administration's decision to avoid lobbying Congress to block the initial vote against the sale. Rather, the administration decided to veto the bill if it passed, and then lobby to uphold the veto, a simpler political task because the administration only had to marshal one-third plus one vote in a single house to sustain a veto.

Congressional critics decried the use of arms sales as a primary means of diplomacy and lamented in particular the inclusion of Stinger missiles in the package. One persistent concern was that given the volatility of the Middle East, such weapons might find their way into the hands of terrorists (the Stinger was referred to as a "terrorist's delight").

The White House argued that Saudi Arabia had remained a friend of the United States, was a key source of oil, and was a moderate voice in the Arab world. It also argued that the package was needed to counter Soviet and Iranian influence in the region. Then in a significant concession the president eliminated the Stingers from the package. White House pressure to uphold the Reagan veto was facilitated by a recurring argument—namely, the president's ability to conduct foreign policy could be impaired if his wishes were denied by Congress. At least one senator changed his vote in favor of the president in response to this argument. Then after last-minute pressure from the White House, the Senate upheld the veto by the exact margin required, 66–34 (67 votes were needed to override).

FOREIGN AID

Presidential-congressional relations with respect to foreign aid have followed a similar path in recent years. In the 1970s Congress began to press the president to tie foreign assistance to progress on human rights. And in 1973 Congress enacted the Foreign Assistance Act, in which it inserted two provisions expressing the opinion or "sense" of Congress that the president should deny foreign aid to any country that practiced incarceration of its citizens for political purposes. One provision stated this as a general principle; the other provision specifically addressed the government of Chile, which recently had undergone a coup (with the covert assistance of the U.S. Central Intelligence Agency) that deposed its elected president, Salvador Allende, and replaced him with a harsh military regime. The human rights abuses of Chile's new Pinochet regime provoked Congress into tying U.S. aid to human rights practices. Similar human rights-related restrictions were tied to aid packages for Argentina, Cambodia, El Salvador, Guatemala, Haiti, Mexico, Nicaragua, South Africa, South Korea, and Uganda.

Two members of Congress, Rep. Charles A. Vanik (D-Ohio) and Sen. Henry M. Jackson (D-Wash.), spearheaded an effort to link U.S. trade relations with the Soviet Union to Soviet human rights practices by making U.S. approval of trade agreements contingent on evidence that improvement in human rights practices was occurring. They were especially eager to encourage more liberal emigration policies for Soviet dissidents, Jews, and others. Despite resistance by the White House, which felt that quiet diplomacy could accomplish more, the policy was enacted. Some critics of this policy have argued that it actually resulted in a constriction of emigration from the Soviet Union.[63]

From 1976 to 1980 Congress strengthened the legal language tying foreign aid to human rights practices. This effort was facilitated by the Carter administration, which elevated concern for human rights to a leading policy goal, applying not just to foreign aid but also to the overall conduct of foreign policy (including policy toward the Soviet Union). Congress worked progressively to apply rigorous standards for human rights in security assistance and multilateral aid programs, but it was less rigorous in programs aimed at development assistance and food aid, since the latter programs were targeted at more fundamental human needs.

The struggle between Congress and the White House intensified during the Reagan administration, which sought a more conciliatory policy toward nations with records of human rights abuses such as South Africa, El Salvador, Chile, and the Philippines under President Ferdinand Marcos. The thinking of the Reagan administration, as articulated, for example, by United Nations Representative Jeane Kirkpatrick, was that the United States should continue to aid its allies even if human rights problems existed, because such nations supported the United States, did not violate human rights to the same degree as other nations, and would likely improve their human rights practices.[64] Others in Congress and elsewhere argued that the United States was in the best position to influence the human rights practices of these nations.[65]

During the Bush administration, Congress urged the president to support a lifting of some Jackson-Vanik restrictions to reward the Soviet Union for its loosening of emigration restrictions. Bush resisted these efforts because of the Soviet Union's failure to meet the goal of an open emigration policy as written in Soviet law. Similar issues arose with regard to China. Bush resisted pressure from Congress to eliminate China's most-favored-nation (MFN) trading status in the aftermath of its ruthless suppression of the democracy movement during the summer of 1989. Twice in 1992, Bush vetoed bills to revoke China's MFN status. President Clinton faced a similar dilemma, in that China continued to operate large forced labor camps for political prisoners and other dissidents. Despite its mixed human rights record, Clinton renewed China's MFN status in 1994.

The political pattern of presidential-congressional relations for foreign aid generally follows closely that noted for war making and other foreign policy areas. The president continues to be the dominant actor, even when Congress attempts to reassert its role in various foreign policy areas. Political initiative typically belongs to the president, but Congress can meaningfully affect the course of policy when it wishes.

"INTERMESTIC" ISSUES

Cheap and plentiful gas and oil supplies were taken for granted in the United States until 1973, when the Arab nations imposed an oil embargo on the nations that supported Israel during the Arab-Israeli War of that year. For the first time Americans recognized their interdependence with Mideast nations, and the relationship between gasoline prices in the United States and events across the globe. This is an example of an "intermestic" issue (one with both international and domestic effects), and it is an area in which the political pattern of presidential-congressional relations resembles that of conventional domestic politics.

One long-standing intermestic policy has been the use of food. Since 1954 the Food for Peace program (also known as PL 480) has provided food for humanitarian, diplomatic, and political purposes abroad and has been a means of disposing of domestic agricultural surpluses. The program has expanded in high-surplus years and contracted when surpluses were small. In high-surplus years the program has provided American farmers with a major subsidy.

The Food for Peace program has grown steadily over the years, largely because of domestic political pressure and support from the Foreign Agricultural Service of the U.S. Department of Agriculture, the relevant congressional subcommittees, farmers' groups, and shipping interests. Although the program has served an important foreign policy objective, its political impetus lies in conventional interest group politics.

In the 1970s an executive-legislative dispute arose over administrations' increasing tendency to use the Food for Peace program abroad to reward political allies and coax other nations into greater cooperation with the United States. Many members of Congress opposed this use of the program, arguing that its purpose should be fundamentally humanitarian. Even though this debate persisted—strategic considerations continued to influence the distribution of food abroad—the program continued to thrive throughout the 1980s (despite budget cutbacks in other foreign aid programs) largely because of its solid domestic support.[66]

Domestic political forces also play an important role in trade and tariff policies. American steel and auto manufacturers, and the unions representing workers in these areas, take a keen interest in policies that affect the import of foreign-made steel and cars. With American jobs apparently at stake, these groups lobby Congress and the president to see that they are not driven out of business by foreign competition. In this way vital domestic concerns expressed through conventional domestic political means may shape foreign policy.

A high-profile example of such an issue involved Clinton's advocacy of the North American Free Trade Agreement (NAFTA) in 1993. The agreement sought to end trade barriers between the United States and its North American neighbors, Canada and Mexico. Organized labor, otherwise a traditional Democratic ally, feared that the agreement would accelerate the flight of American companies to Mexico, where labor costs are far lower than in the United States. Clinton in turn argued that the expanded trade resulting from the agreement would, in the long run, result in more jobs and greater prosperity for American workers. Most business leaders strongly supported NAFTA. In Congress, House Democratic Majority Leader Dick Gephardt (Mo.) and Majority Whip David Bonior (Mich.) broke ranks with the president to oppose NAFTA. Also lining up against NAFTA was an array of environmental groups that feared adverse environmental consequences if companies sought to avoid tougher American pollution standards by going elsewhere, and some farm groups that feared accelerated import of cheaper produce from abroad. With the support of most Republicans, House Speaker Tom Foley (D-Wash.), and most Senate leaders, NAFTA passed in November 1993 by a vote of 234 to 200 in the House, and by a more comfortable margin of 61 to 38 in the Senate.

Not all intermestic issues involve jobs and the economy. Jewish organizations take a strong interest in U.S. policy toward Israel. Pressure from African American groups helped push the United States toward taking a harder line against the apartheid regime that controlled South Africa in the 1980s. Greek Americans and Turkish Americans are represented by groups who work to influence U.S. policy toward those traditionally antagonistic nations. Opponents of abortion have pressed Congress and the president to cut family planning aid to Third World nations that use abortion as a means of limiting population. In all of these intermestic issues domestic political forces substantially affect foreign policy as it is shaped by the president and Congress.

CONTROL OVER INTELLIGENCE AGENCIES

Control over sensitive information pertaining to national security and intelligence matters is a key source of presidential ascendancy. Virtually all intelligence gathering is conducted through executive agencies. In 1981 Executive Order 12333 (issued by President Reagan) listed thirteen agencies as composing the intelligence community. Six of these were affiliated with the Department of Defense and the rest with the Executive Office of the President or a cabinet agency. In theory Congress plays the same role in relation to intelligence agencies that it plays with other government agencies: it provides the legal basis for such agencies and oversees agency actions. In reality, however, Congress had little control of government intelligence efforts until the 1970s. *(See box, Intelligence Community, p. 1297.)*

The need for intelligence has always existed, but the executive appetite for information accelerated with America's expanded role in international affairs after World War II. In 1947 Congress passed the National Security Act, which created the Central Intelligence Agency (CIA); its forerunner was the Office

---

CONGRESSIONAL RESOLUTION ON THE GULF CRISIS OF 1991

PL 102-1

To authorize the use of United States Armed Forces pursuant to United Nations Security Council Resolution 678.

Whereas the Government of Iraq without provocation invaded and occupied the territory of Kuwait on August 2, 1990; and

Whereas both the House of Representatives (in H.J. Res. 658 of the 101st Congress) and the Senate (in S. Con. Res. 147 of the 101st Congress) have condemned Iraq's invasion of Kuwait and declared their support for international action to reverse Iraq's aggression; and

Whereas, Iraq's conventional, chemical, biological, and nuclear weapons and ballistic missile programs and its demonstrated willingness to use weapons of mass destruction pose a grave threat to world peace; and

Whereas the international community has demanded that Iraq withdraw unconditionally and immediately from Kuwait and that Kuwait's independence and legitimate government be restored; and

Whereas the U.N. Security Council repeatedly affirmed the inherent right of individual or collective self-defense in response to the armed attack by Iraq against Kuwait in accordance with Article 51 of the U.N. Charter; and

Whereas, in the absence of full compliance by Iraq with its resolutions, the U.N. Security Council in Resolution 678 has authorized member states of the United Nations to use all necessary means, after January 15, 1991, to uphold and implement all relevant Security Council resolutions and to restore international peace and security in the area; and

Whereas Iraq has persisted in its illegal occupation of, and brutal aggression against Kuwait; Now, therefore, be it

Resolved by the Senate and House of Representatives of the United States of America in Congress assembled,

SECTION 1.

SHORT TITLE

This joint resolution may be cited as the "Authorization for Use of Military Force Against Iraq Resolution."

SECTION 2.

AUTHORIZATION FOR USE OF U.S. ARMED FORCES

(a) AUTHORIZATION.—The President is authorized, subject to subsection (b), to use United States Armed Forces pursuant to United Nations Security Council Resolution 678 (1990) in order to achieve implementation of Security Council Resolutions 660, 661, 662, 664, 665, 666, 667, 669, 670, 674, and 677.

(b) REQUIREMENT FOR DETERMINATION THAT USE OF MILITARY FORCE IS NECESSARY.—Before exercising the authority granted in subsection (a), the President shall make available to the Speaker of the House of Representatives and the President pro tempore of the Senate his determination that—

(1) the United States has used all appropriate diplomatic and other peaceful means to obtain compliance by Iraq with the United Nations Security Council resolutions cited in subsection (a); and (2) that those efforts have not been and would not be successful in obtaining such compliance.

(c) WAR POWERS RESOLUTION REQUIREMENTS.—

(1) SPECIFIC STATUTORY AUTHORIZATION.—Consistent with section 8(a) of the War Powers Resolution, the Congress declares that this section is intended to constitute specific statutory authorization within the meaning of section 5(b) of the War Powers Resolution.

(2) APPLICABILITY OF OTHER REQUIREMENTS.—Nothing in this resolution supersedes any requirement of the War Powers Resolution.

SECTION 3.

REPORTS TO CONGRESS

At least once every 60 days, the President shall submit to the Congress a summary on the status of efforts to obtain compliance by Iraq with the resolutions adopted by the United Nations Security Council in response to Iraq's aggression.

of Strategic Services, formed to gather intelligence during the war. Yet Congress paid little attention to the agency or its activities. Other intelligence agencies such as the Defense Intelligence Agency and the National Security Agency were created by executive order. Because funds for these agencies were included in lump sum appropriations, members of Congress were unaware of the specific purposes of the funds and the actual amounts budgeted. Congressional interest in intelligence was aroused only when embarrassing problems arose, such as when an American U-2 spy plane was caught flying over the Soviet Union in 1960, and when the Bay of Pigs invasion (a CIA-sponsored invasion of Cuba by anti-Castro Cuban exiles) failed in 1961. The few members of Congress informed of intelligence activities rarely questioned executive priorities. As the chair of one "watchdog" committee, Sen. John C. Stennis (D-Miss.), said, "You have to make up your mind that you are going to have an intelligence agency and protect it as such and shut your eyes and take what is coming."[67]

Congress was finally emboldened to involve itself more actively in intelligence-related matters when it was revealed that both the CIA and the Federal Bureau of Investigation had been involved in illegal surveillance and investigation of Americans (mostly anti–Vietnam War protesters) in the late 1960s and early 1970s at the behest of the Nixon administration, and that the CIA had played an active role in the violent overthrow of the popularly elected regime of President Salvador Allende in Chile. Several important congressional investigations helped bring these activities to light, especially the investigation headed by Sen. Frank F. Church (D-Idaho) in 1975 and 1976. Executive branch authorization of such activities at home and abroad raised fundamental questions about control over and misuse of the American intelligence establishment.

In 1974 Congress passed the Hughes-Ryan Amendment, which required that covert actions of the CIA (that is, operations designed to do more than gather information) be reported to the appropriate congressional committees. The act did not have dramatic consequences, as the executive was to report "in a timely fashion," and the CIA and the president interpreted this to mean after the conclusion of an operation.

In 1975 President Ford created a special commission to examine CIA activities. Based on the commission's findings, Ford directed the CIA to refrain from engaging in further assassination plots. This action followed revelations that the CIA had plotted to assassinate Cuban dictator Fidel Castro and other heads of government deemed unfriendly.

As a result of these revelations each house of Congress created a permanent Select Committee on Intelligence. Although the jurisdiction of each committee is slightly different, both are designed to provide some meaningful oversight. Each committee has a substantial staff and the power to compel testimony, demand information, and review reports. In addition, these committees control budgetary authorizations (that is, they grant legal permission to spend appropriated money) for intelligence agencies. For the sake of secrecy neither committee operates

with the openness characteristic of other congressional committees. And despite fears that Congress cannot keep secrets, both committees have favorable records of not disclosing national security information.

To help ensure that the committees would engage in meaningful oversight and would not be co-opted by the intelligence agencies, as had happened in the past, a limit was put on the number of terms a member could serve on the committees, and their leadership is rotated.

In 1980 Congress passed the Accountability for Intelligence Activities Act. This act stipulated that the two intelligence committees would be the sole funnels for information about covert activities, and it required the committees to be fully informed of all intelligence activities. It also terminated the Hughes-Ryan Amendment. Finally, despite wording designed to strengthen and clarify the role of Congress, the act granted the president wide discretion and freedom of action in covert operations.[68]

Although Congress assumed a more active role in intelligence activities, controversial covert operations continued. Beginning in 1981, for example, the Reagan administration engaged in a large-scale covert program to aid rebels (called contras) fighting against the Sandinista regime in Nicaragua. In December the administration informed the intelligence committees of its support for the contras.

In 1982 Congress enacted for the first time an amendment aimed at curtailing Reagan's support for the contras. Successively stronger amendments were enacted in 1983, 1984, and 1985, and were attached to authorization and appropriations bills. These amendments were known collectively as the Boland Amendment, named after Rep. Edward P. Boland (D-Mass.), their prime sponsor. The strongest measure, enacted in 1984, barred all military and covert assistance (direct and indirect) to the contras during fiscal year 1985.

In 1985 and 1986 the administration succeeded in gaining congressional permission to expand support for the contras. Yet in 1986, Reagan's national security advisers and other members of the administration were implicated in an "off the books" operation to fund the contras covertly by selling arms to Iran and using the profits to purchase weapons for the contras. This operation was designed to maintain funding for the contras despite the congressional ban. Throughout the summer of 1987 a joint Senate-House committee chaired by Sen. Daniel P. Inouye (D-Hawaii), a former Senate Intelligence Committee chair, conducted hearings to investigate the Iran-contra affair.

The committee's majority report concluded that members of the National Security Council (NSC) and others (including private businesspeople) had consciously attempted to circumvent the law through private means. The political embarrassment accompanying these revelations was heightened by the scheme to sell arms to Iran, an avowed enemy of the United States. Iran was in the market for weapons to help in its protracted war with Iraq.

The Iran-contra affair dramatized how difficult it is for Congress to influence the conduct of covert operations and an intelligence process that is structured to serve the president. Despite renewed congressional efforts in the 1970s and 1980s, Congress continues to be handicapped because of its lack of involvement with, and influence over, the National Security Council staff and adviser, who have acquired substantial control over the formulation and coordination of national security matters, although under Presidents Bush and Clinton the secretary of state has reasserted the position's traditional role as leader of administration foreign policy. Some political scientists have suggested that nominees for the national security adviser position be subject to congressional ratification.[69] *(See Chapter 27, Executive Office of the President: White House Office.)*

Appointment Power

Article II, section 2, of the Constitution says that the president shall have the power to nominate,

with the Advice and Consent of the Senate . . . Ambassadors, other public Ministers and Consuls, Judges of the supreme Court, and all other Officers of the United States, whose Appointments are not herein otherwise provided for, and which shall be established by law; but the Congress may by Law vest the Appointment of such inferior Officers . . . in the President alone, in the Courts . . . or in the Heads of Departments.

The Constitution (Article I, section 6) also forbids members of Congress to serve simultaneously in an executive position, such as a cabinet post, or to serve in any position created by Congress if the position in question was created during the term of a member, or if the salary for the position in question was raised during the member's term. *(See also "The Appointment Power," p. 487, in Chapter 11, Vol. I.)*

The Founders clearly paid close attention to many aspects of the appointment power. The appointment process itself involves close interaction between the executive and legislative branches. Its importance is underscored by the roughly sixty thousand appointments (most of them military) that arise each year.[70]

Presidential appointments fall into four broad categories: federal judges, executive branch officials, ambassadors, and heads of regulatory agencies. The power to nominate belongs, in principle, solely to the president. Alexander Hamilton stated in the *Federalist* No. 66 that the Senate would not choose nominees: "They may defeat one choice of the Executive, and oblige him to make another; but they cannot themselves *choose*—they can only ratify or reject the choice of the President." In fact, many political forces intervene before a name is sent to the Senate.

Senators from the same political party as the president may suggest potential nominees from their home states for judicial, federal marshal, and federal attorney positions. But if presidents are dissatisfied with senatorial suggestions, they may bargain to find a mutually acceptable nominee. Possible nominees also may be suggested by party leaders, judges, and other executive officials.

Private interest groups may take a hand as well. The American Bar Association, for example, has screened judicial nominees since 1946. Presidents also may consult sympathetic private groups when searching for nominees for agencies and departments related to a group's concerns. Labor unions, for example, take a keen interest in appointments to the position of secretary of labor. The influence of such outside groups is directly related to the extent to which presidents are sympathetic to their concerns. Interest groups play an even more active role after nominees are forwarded to the Senate.

The appointment process is vital to the functioning of an administration. Presidents who pay inadequate attention to the process may wind up with administrative and judicial appointees who are incompetent, unqualified, corrupt, or at odds with the president's philosophy. President Kennedy summarized the problem facing presidents at the beginning of their terms when he said, "For the last four years I spent so much time getting to know people who could help me get elected President that I didn't have time to get to know people who could help me, after I was elected, to be a good president."[71] Richard Nixon faced difficulties filling positions at the beginning of his administration, and both he and Jimmy Carter later reevaluated their appointments, as many positions filled hurriedly at the outset of their administrations were occupied by individuals either inadequately in tune with the goals of the president or simply not well qualified. Ronald Reagan delayed filling many positions during his first year in office to ensure that his nominees conformed with his political philosophy. President Clinton sought to construct a cabinet and administration that "looked like America," appointing more women, African Americans, and Hispanics to top positions.

Another important factor influencing the course of nominations is "senatorial courtesy," a long-standing informal practice in which presidents and senators defer to (that is, show great respect for) the evaluations offered by their fellow senators who represent nominees from (or who are appointed to positions within) their home states. The relative influence of a senator is considerably greater if he or she is in the same political party as the president. Although senatorial courtesy is occasionally violated, senators usually respect the wishes of their colleagues because they want other senators to do the same when individuals are nominated from their own states. Presidents usually respect this courtesy as well to maintain good relations with the Senate, at least when it comes to "advice and consent."

COURT NOMINATIONS

Presidents make nominations to all federal courts, but Supreme Court nominations attract the most political attention. The Constitution gives the president the power to select nominees, and it gives the Senate the right to confirm or reject them. Historically, the Senate has rejected about one of every five nominees to the Supreme Court. Some critics of this system have suggested erroneously that senatorial rejection of a nominee for political reasons is unconstitutional.[72] The 80 percent confirmation average for Supreme Court nominees, however, indicates that, other things being equal, presidents are entitled to have their nominees confirmed. (The rejection rate was one out of three in the nineteenth century.) And even more to the point, of the nine hundred nominees submitted to the Senate from 1945 to 1974 to fill positions on the federal courts of appeal, federal district courts, and other federal courts, only four were not confirmed.[73]

Three key struggles over rejected Supreme Court nominees in recent years illustrate the interdependence of the two branches when the Senate does not simply accept the president's nomination. The first occurred during President Richard Nixon's term. In May 1969 a vacancy on the Supreme Court was created by the resignation of Justice Abe Fortas. Nixon's nominee to the position was Clement Haynsworth, a competent if undistinguished conservative southern judge who fulfilled Nixon's ideological and regional preferences. During his confirmation hearings, however, Haynsworth demonstrated indifference to the discovery of financial and other improprieties, which the Senate could not overlook especially because Fortas had resigned when charges of similar improprieties surfaced. These and other concerns about Haynsworth's civil rights and civil liberties record led the Senate to reject his nomination by a vote of 55–45.[74]

The Senate's rejection of Haynsworth infuriated Nixon, who believed the rejection to be based on Haynsworth's southern conservatism. He followed up the rejection by nominating G. Harrold Carswell, a Florida judge with at best marginal credentials. This appointment was considered "an act of vengeance" by Nixon.[75] As with the Haynsworth nomination, the Senate was disposed initially to ratify Carswell. Investigations revealed, however, that he had at one time firmly supported racial segregation, that he had participated in an effort to keep a Florida golf course segregated, and that he had one of the highest reversal rates of any sitting judge. After several months Carswell too was rejected by the Senate.

After this second stinging rejection Nixon criticized the Senate for robbing him of his right to have his nominations confirmed (although no such right exists). In the spring of 1970 Nixon nominated to the Court a Minnesota judge, Harry A. Blackmun, who was readily confirmed.[76]

A similar scenario occurred in 1987 when President Ronald Reagan moved to fill a Court vacancy left by the June retirement of Lewis Powell, a Nixon appointee. Reagan's nominee was Robert H. Bork, a well-known conservative legal scholar and federal judge. But unlike most Court nominees, Bork had been outspoken over the years about both his judicial philosophy and his opposition to dozens of Supreme Court decisions that expanded civil rights and liberties. His opinions and writings revealed what critics considered extreme conservatism and a rejection of some well-established Court doctrines, such as the right to privacy. Civil rights, women's rights, and civil liberties groups complained bitterly that Bork's views placed him beyond the bounds of even traditional conservatism. According to them, his attitudes toward the rights of African Americans,

women, and others made him unfit to serve on the nation's highest court.[77]

The Bork hearings received unprecedented media attention and were broadcast on network television. As the hearings progressed, public opposition grew, and private groups on both sides mounted intense campaigns to either oppose or support Bork. After months of hearings and debates the Senate rejected Bork's nomination in October 1987 by the widest margin ever cast against a Supreme Court nominee, 58–42.

Following the Bork rejection Reagan nominated Douglas H. Ginsburg, a California law professor with brief judicial experience. Although Ginsburg was considered to be almost as conservative as Bork, his nomination was not expected to engender as much controversy as that of Bork, given Ginsburg's briefer and less public career. Investigations revealed, however, that Ginsburg had experimented with marijuana, not only as a student, but also while a law professor. This revelation was particularly embarrassing to the White House as the Reagan administration and First Lady Nancy Reagan were engaged in a vigorous antidrug campaign. Thus, the administration pressured Ginsburg to withdraw his name. Had the marijuana question not arisen, Ginsburg's ratification by the Senate would have been difficult nonetheless because of his conservatism, lack of judicial experience, and hints of conflict-of-interest problems.

Reagan's third nominee was Anthony M. Kennedy, a respected California judge considered to be more moderate than Bork and Ginsburg. The Senate confirmed Kennedy by a unanimous vote, and he took his seat on the Court in February 1988.

An even more intense controversy arose in 1991 when President Bush sought to replace retiring Justice Thurgood Marshall, the Court's first African American member, with another black, Clarence Thomas. Thomas's conservative views, including his opposition to affirmative action, prompted bitter criticism from the congressional black caucus and other liberal groups. Despite such opposition, and Thomas's unwillingness to discuss his views on such matters as abortion, his confirmation seemed assured. The day before the Senate Judiciary Committee was scheduled to vote, however, word leaked out that Anita Hill, a law professor from the University of Oklahoma who had worked for Thomas at the Equal Employment Opportunity Commission (EEOC), claimed to have been sexually harassed by him. This allegation forced the committee to hold two more days of emotionally charged hearings that were nationally televised. Hill leveled a series of detailed charges against Thomas, who in turn categorically denied them. No firm conclusion was reached concerning the validity of the charges, and the Senate confirmed Thomas by a vote of 52 to 48. The key votes on behalf of Thomas came from several southern Democrats who believed that their black constituents favored the nominee.

Several important observations stem from these admittedly unusual cases. First, initially the Senate is not inclined to resist a presidential nominee, even when senators have personal reservations about a nominee's qualifications or politics. Senate rejection of a judicial nominee invariably engenders resentment and anger in the White House, because each president exerts significant political resources to see a nomination through to a successful conclusion.

Second, politics plays a part. All the rejected nominees described in the preceding account were rejected in part because of their politics. In particular, their stands on civil rights and civil liberties were scrutinized by senators and private interests. Although such scrutiny is by no means limited to conservative judicial nominees (as seen, for example, in Justice Fortas's forced withdrawal as Johnson's nominee to the position of chief justice in 1968), senators take political considerations into account. In the case of Reagan's nominees, liberal senators made it clear that they were not out to oppose all conservative nominees; they cautioned, however, that nominees to the highest court should not be too far to the ideological extreme. Another Reagan appointee to the Court, Antonin Scalia, was ratified by the Senate unanimously in 1986, his well-known conservatism notwithstanding.

Third, timing plays a role. Had Haynsworth been nominated after Carswell instead of before, he might well have been confirmed. Had Bork been nominated for the 1981 Court vacancy (a position that was filled by Sandra Day O'Connor), Reagan might have been able to exert sufficient pressure to obtain Bork's confirmation. Reagan's political strength was greatest in his first year, when the Republicans controlled the Senate. (Party control of the Senate changed after the 1986 elections.) Had Hill's allegations come out earlier, the Thomas nomination might have been derailed, since public support for Hill increased as events unfolded.

Fourth, partisanship is also important. The president is likely to face a more difficult confirmation process when the opposition party controls the Senate, as was the case for the rejections just described.

Fifth, the Senate does not like confrontation over judicial and other appointments. Carswell, for example, was rejected because it was clear that he was less qualified than Haynsworth. The Judiciary Committee was at first reluctant to delay its vote on Thomas, despite Hill's charges, but it was forced to hold additional hearings in response to mounting public pressure. The Senate's inclination is to go along with and not challenge presidential appointees.

Presidents select judicial and other nominees hoping that they will act according to the president's ideological leanings. But the record of how Supreme Court justices have voted after joining the Court indicates that it is difficult to predict how an appointee will act after joining the Court. Although presidents have been personally acquainted with about three-fifths of their Supreme Court nominees, one scholar has concluded that one Supreme Court appointee in four has turned out to be quite different from what the appointing president wanted.[78]

President Truman once noted that trying to pack the Supreme Court with loyal appointees "just doesn't work. . . . Whenever you put a man on the Court, he ceases to be your friend."[79] Eisenhower's appointment of Earl Warren to be chief justice of the Supreme Court provided the Court with a leader who proved to be far more activist and liberal than Eisenhower anticipated. A former Republican governor of California, Warren became one of the Court's great champions of civil rights, civil liberties, rights of the accused, and a generally more activist Court. Another Eisenhower appointee, William Brennan, also proved to be far more liberal than the president who appointed him. This independence demonstrated by Court appointees is explainable by the life terms that they serve and (unlike most other appointees) their location in a separate branch of government.

OTHER APPOINTEES

The Senate has shown greater deference to presidential appointees to cabinet, ambassadorial, and agency positions than to appointees to judicial positions. From 1945 to 1974 the Senate rejected less than 1 percent of more than 3,300 nonjudicial appointees.[80] From 1959 to 1994, the Senate rejected only two cabinet secretary nominees—Lewis L. Strauss, Eisenhower's nominee for commerce secretary in 1959, and John Tower, George Bush's nominee for defense secretary in 1989. These statistics do not, however, take into account prospective nominees whose names were not forwarded to the Senate because of informal opposition or pressure exerted before the actual nomination. (See Table 33-1.)

TABLE 33-1 Nominations Submitted to and Confirmed by the U.S. Senate, 1961–1994

Congress		Number submitted	Confirmed	With-drawn	Rejected[a]	Uncon-firmed
87th	(1961–1962)	102,849	100,741	1,279	0	829
88th	(1963–1964)	122,190	120,201	36	0	1,953
89th	(1965–1966)	123,019	120,865	173	0	1,981
90th	(1967–1968)	120,231	118,231	34	0	1,966
91st	(1969–1971)	134,464	133,797	487	2	178
92d	(1971–1972)	117,053	114,909	11	0	2,133
93d	(1973–1974)[b]	134,384	131,254	15	0	3,069
94th	(1975–1976)	132,151	131,378	6	0	3,801
95th	(1977–1978)	137,504	124,730	66	0	12,713
96th	(1979–1980)	154,797	154,665	18	0	1,458
97th	(1981–1982)	186,264	184,844	55	7	1,346
98th	(1983–1984)	97,893	97,262	4	0	610
99th	(1985–1986)	99,614	95,811	16	0	3,787
100th	(1987–1988)	89,193	88,721	23	1	5,922
101st	(1989–1990)	93,368	88,078	48	1	7,951
102d	(1991–1992)	76,446	75,349	24	0	756
103d	(1993–1994)	77,384	76,122	1,080	0	2,741

SOURCE: Harold W. Stanley and Richard G. Niemi, *Vital Statistics on American Politics*, 5th ed. (Washington, D.C.: CQ Press, 1995), 259.

NOTES: a. Includes only those nominations rejected outright by a vote of the Senate. Most nominations that fail to win approval of the Senate are unfavorably reported by committees and never reach the Senate floor, having been withdrawn. In some cases, the full Senate may vote to recommit a nomination to committee, in effect killing it. b. Forty-six nominations were returned to the president during the October–November 1974 recess in accordance with Senate Rule 38, which states: "[I]f the Senate shall adjourn or take a recess for more than thirty days, all nominations pending and not finally acted upon at the time of taking such adjournment or recess shall be returned by the Secretary to the President, and shall not again be considered unless they shall again be made to the Senate by the President."

In 1993, for example, President Clinton announced that he planned to nominate a law school professor, Lani Guinier, to serve as head of the civil rights division of the Department of Justice. Guinier's views on how to rectify racial discrimination in state legislative districts, among other issues, were sharply criticized, and Clinton ultimately asked her to withdraw her name before Senate review began.

Questions of competence are sometimes raised, but they rarely have a decisive effect. The nominations of James T. Lynn to serve as secretary of the Department of Housing and Urban Development in 1973 and of Carla A. Hills to the same position two years later (after Lynn's resignation) raised questions about their lack of experience for the job, yet both were confirmed. In 1981 President Reagan nominated California judge and close associate William Clark to serve as an assistant secretary of state for African affairs. During the confirmation hearings Clark exhibited a lack of elementary knowledge of African politics and geography that startled and enraged some senators, yet he was ratified by the Senate.

Both the president and the Senate have been accused of not paying enough attention to the quality of appointments to regulatory agencies. Unlike those in many other appointed positions, the appointed heads of agencies often need substantial knowledge about the object of regulation. Of even greater concern, however, is the tendency to appoint individuals from the industries or sectors being regulated to top agency positions. Such appointments call into question the independence and veracity of subsequent agency actions.[81] *(See Chapter 30, Government Agencies and Corporations.)*

REMOVAL POWER

An ongoing debate has accompanied the question of who has the power to remove appointed officials. While the Constitution clearly states that the president and federal judges may be removed by impeachment, it provides little clarity on the matter of removing other appointed officials.

Some scholars and officials have suggested that other executive officers must be impeached to be removed. Most, however, argue that removal rests with either the president as head of the executive branch, or Congress, which creates the offices filled by appointment, allowing it as well to attach conditions and limitations to service in such offices.

The question of removal has been a major concern of several presidents, especially Andrew Johnson. When Johnson tried to suspend and then remove Secretary of War Edwin M. Stanton in violation of the Tenure of Office Act of 1867, he was subjected to a vote of impeachment in the House and a trial in the Senate. (Enacted over Johnson's veto, the act provided for Senate involvement in the removal of executive officials.) After a presidential-congressional clash over the Senate's involvement in removal during the Cleveland administration, the Tenure of Office Act was repealed in 1886. The power of the president to remove cabinet secretaries and other cabinet officials the president appoints is now well recognized.

Since repeal of the Tenure of Office Act, the Supreme Court has recognized that Congress may establish grounds for the removal of other appointed officials. Moreover, Congress may remove an official by abolishing the office in which he or she serves. Congress also can establish the terms of office. On occasion Congress has enacted nonbinding resolutions expressing its sense that the president should remove an official. It can apply informal political pressure as well to force the resignation of an appointee. In fact, one study concluded that pressure from Congress resulted in more firings and personnel reassignments than pressure from the president.[82]

At the other extreme, Congress may act to protect an appointee whose job is threatened for inappropriate reasons. In 1968, for example, a procurement specialist, Ernest Fitzgerald, admitted before a Senate committee that the C-5A cargo plane had incurred $2 billion in cost overruns. Because of his admission Fitzgerald was stripped of his civil service protection, demoted, investigated by the air force, and eventually fired. After years of litigation and congressional outcry, Fitzgerald was given back his job, with a promotion, in 1982. Congress has continued to help protect federal officials who reveal agency misdeeds and mistakes from arbitrary suspension, removal, demotion, or reassignment.[83]

Veto Power

The presidential veto is one of the cornerstone powers in the Constitution, tying the president to the legislative process. Veto power was included as a presidential power from the beginning of the Constitutional Convention—it was included in the Virginia Plan—even though use of the veto by British monarchs and colonial governors had been a key source of irritation for the colonists. Despite the opinions of Alexander Hamilton and James Wilson at the convention that the president's veto should be absolute (that is, no provision for an override vote by both houses of Congress), as was that of the British monarch, the veto remained qualified. At one point, the Founders agreed to a three-fourths override vote for vetoes, but they eventually settled on a two-thirds override. *(See also "The Veto," p. 551, in Chapter 12, Vol. I.)*

The first six presidents used the veto sparingly—only ten times. George Washington was the first president to exercise the power when he vetoed a congressional reapportionment bill on April 5, 1792. President Andrew Jackson drew heavy political fire for using the veto twelve times in eight years for plainly political reasons. President John Tyler used the veto ten times in his single term of office, and he was even subject to a vote of impeachment in the House for one of his vetoes. The loud congressional outcry that followed these early vetoes—especially those of Jackson and Tyler—was founded partly in political opposition, but also in the belief that the veto should only be used against bills of questionable constitutionality. (Although the Constitution places no restrictions on veto use, this was the principal charge used against Tyler.) Also, many felt that frequent use of

TABLE 33-2 Fate of Veto-threatened Bills, 1961–1989

President	Total threatened bills	Average per year	Congress backs down; bill dies	Compromise	President backs down; bill enacted	Bill passed as is and vetoed	Veto overridden
Kennedy	0	0	0	0	0	0	0
Johnson	0	0	0	0	0	0	0
Nixon	5	1	0	0	0	5	1
Ford	10	4	2	0	0	8	1
Carter	12	3	3	5	2	2	1
Reagan	48	6	9	19	4	16	5

SOURCE: Robert J. Spitzer, *The Presidential Veto* (Albany: State University of New York Press, 1988), 103; and updated by author.

NOTE: The numbers of veto threats listed above are not considered definitive. Threats may have been delivered by Presidents Kennedy and Johnson, for example, but not reported in the newspapers. There is no doubt, however, that presidents with larger numbers of threats used these more, as the potency of threats depends largely on the extent to which they are widely known.

the veto was simply inappropriate and reminiscent of the abuses of British monarchs. By the mid-nineteenth century, however, these objections had subsided. *(See Table 33-2.)*

After the Civil War, presidents used the veto more frequently, with the significant increase attributable to greater presidential involvement in legislative affairs and to a flood of private pension bills (many of them of questionable justification) stemming from war-related claims. The veto allowed presidents to exert greater influence over the legislative process in the nineteenth century, first through the veto itself, then through the presidential threat to use the veto, and finally through anticipation of the president's legislative preferences as a means of avoiding the veto.

The veto continues to be an important weapon in the president's dealings with Congress; about 93 percent of all vetoes subject to override have been sustained. When broken down by public and private bills, presidential vetoes of public bills have been upheld about 81 percent of the time; vetoes of private bills have been upheld more than 99 percent of the time. A public bill affects the people as a whole and relates to individuals only by classification or category. In contrast, a private bill names the individual or entity who will receive some form of relief—such as payment of a claim or pension—from the federal government.

Several factors help to explain why presidents veto, or are more likely to veto, legislation. When the presidency and Congress are controlled by different political parties, presidential vetoes occur more often. Presidents also are more likely to veto when they have little or no prior service in Congress (stemming from a presumed lack of sensitivity to congressional nuance), when they are in their second and fourth years of their term (resulting from greater congressional independence in an election year), when the role of government expands, and when public support for the president sags. Congress is more likely to override a veto when party control is split between the branches, when the president's political standing is low, and in times of economic crisis.[84]

The veto poses a paradox for presidents who contemplate its use. With the exception of vetoes of private bills in the twentieth

century, frequent use of the veto by presidents invariably tends to erode their reservoir of political resources. This occurs because Congress becomes more resentful and confrontational when its measures are vetoed too frequently. Moreover, even though the Founders viewed the veto as a creative, positive tool (it was often called the "revisionary power") that could be used to mold better legislation in concert with Congress, today the veto is predominantly viewed as a negative power used by presidents to frustrate and block. A president who uses the veto in the latter fashion in the twentieth century faces a significant political obstacle in dealing with Congress.

Indeed, more frequent use of the veto usually means that presidents have not succeeded in establishing a pattern of positive leadership based on the president's legislative program. Presidents who establish such leadership usually are able to avoid numerous vetoes either by winning passage of their important programs or by obtaining a favorable compromise with congressional leaders. Thus, presidents who most need the veto are those who lack other sources of power to compensate, while presidents needing the veto least exert greater influence over Congress and have more sources of power, such as a high standing in the eyes of the public.[85]

President Franklin Roosevelt was the most prolific veto user of all the presidents (although his per year veto average was second to that of President Grover Cleveland). Unlike most frequent veto users, however, Roosevelt faced a sympathetic Congress during his twelve years in office. His frequent use of the veto indicated his willingness to use all the tools at his disposal in dealing with Congress, as indicated by his well-known "send me a bill I can veto" attitude. That is, Roosevelt found it useful to exercise the veto periodically simply as a way of letting Congress know that he was willing to be tough on Congress. More to the point, however, the vast majority of Roosevelt's vetoes were of private bills or other matters that garnered little attention and less interest. Although Roosevelt believed that the veto was a key presidential power, it received relatively little attention during a time when more attention was focused on the depression, the "New Deal," and World War II.

Roosevelt's successor also valued the veto as a presidential tool. Facing a more hostile Congress, Harry Truman and his vetoes attracted more attention. Best known was his veto of the Taft-Hartley Labor-Management Relations Act of 1947, which Congress enacted into law over his veto. Truman took pride in the claim that he gave his veto messages careful personal attention, and he used them to set forth administration policy. Of the veto, he said that it was "one of the most important instruments of his authority."[86]

Dwight Eisenhower faced a Congress controlled by the opposition party for six of his eight years in office, and thus the veto was an important tool. Eisenhower did not use the veto lightly, but he did rely on it more heavily later on in his second term, especially as a device to "subdue" the overwhelmingly Democratic Congress of 1959–1960.

During the presidencies of Democrats John Kennedy and Lyndon Johnson, the Democratic Party controlled the executive and legislative branches. Both presidents were relatively influential over congressional actions (Johnson more so), and neither needed to rely on the veto as a major weapon. Nevertheless, occasional vetoes were viewed as useful, even therapeutic, for interbranch relations. As an aide to Johnson later noted, "It is inevitable that the President will use the veto at some point. It's the best method to show the Congress he means business."[87] When Kennedy and Johnson did use the veto, they were careful to avoid a successful override, and none of their vetoes were overridden.

Appreciating the negative consequences of frequent veto use, Richard Nixon used the veto rarely in his first three years in office. This pattern changed, however, when he vetoed seventeen bills during a six-month period in 1972 after concluding that a broad attack on congressional spending was needed. Nixon's aides also recognized that minimal effort can be devoted to upholding a veto, since all that is needed is the support of one-third plus one of the membership of one house of Congress. It was understood, nevertheless, that use of the veto represented a failure to alter or block undesired bills before they reached the president's desk.

The veto power was a vital tool for the brief administration of Gerald Ford. Ford's political position was weak from the start because of how he became president (appointed vice president by a president who himself later resigned). Moreover, he had little opportunity to formulate his own legislative program after becoming president. This left Republican Ford few options beyond reacting to the initiatives of the Democratic-controlled Congress. As the first post-Watergate president, he faced a strong anti-Republican, anti-"imperial presidency" backlash. Ford hoped to gain initiative by winning the 1976 election, but instead he was defeated by Jimmy Carter. During his two and one-half years in office, Ford vetoed sixty-six bills; of these, fifty-four were sustained. Insofar as the veto was a cornerstone of his legislative relations, his presidency was the only one in this century to adopt a true veto strategy. Ford's aides recognized the

adverse effects of the numerous vetoes, but they believed that they had few other options.

Jimmy Carter's administration saw a return to sparing use of the veto on a par with that of the Kennedy and Johnson years. Despite Democrat Carter's reputed difficulties with the Democratic-controlled Congress, he found relatively little need to resort to the veto. Unlike Ford, Carter established a substantial legislative agenda from the start of his presidency, which impelled Congress to react to him rather than the opposite. Most of Carter's thirty-one vetoes aroused little interest in Congress.

The presidential veto played an important role in the administration of Republican Ronald Reagan, but not in the way that it had for Ford. During Reagan's two terms in office, he averaged less than ten vetoes per year, most of which concerned relatively noncontroversial measures. This is explained partly by his legislative successes (despite Democratic Party control of the House throughout and Republican control of the Senate for only six years). Yet, veto rhetoric played a large role in his administration. He often challenged Congress to send him bills that exceeded his spending guidelines, even using a well-known line from a Clint Eastwood movie in daring Congress to "make my day." He persistently advocated that he be granted item veto powers and he issued numerous veto threats. Despite these public statements, many conservatives continued to urge Reagan to use the veto more often as a brake on federal spending.[88]

George Bush relied even more heavily on the veto, averaging more than eleven vetoes per year. More significantly, the veto proved to be a primary focal point of relations between Bush and Congress. He vetoed such major pieces of legislation as minimum wage, family and medical leave, civil rights, unemployment insurance, campaign finance reform, and voter registration reform. Of his forty-five vetoes, only one bill—a measure to regulate cable television—was overridden and enacted into law. The Bush administration took great pride in its record of upholding vetoes, but this belied the larger fact that, at least in domestic policy, Bush's record was similar to that of Ford, in that he failed to develop a comprehensive domestic agenda. This placed Bush on the defensive with Congress, which took the initiative in many policy areas.

In addition, Bush was a prolific user of veto threats, and he also advocated a presidential line-item veto. In an unusual twist, he even claimed for a time that the Constitution already provided for a line-item veto for the president, based on the view of a few conservative scholars that the Founders defined bills as being limited to single subjects. Thus, according to the argument, today's multisubject bills could be separated into separate "bills" by the president and vetoed selectively. Other scholars noted that the Constitution does not define "bill," and that the Founders, as well as early Congresses, routinely enacted multisubject bills. Despite promises that he would attempt to use such a power and let Congress take him to court if it object-

On December 6, 1995, President Bill Clinton, using the pen that Lyndon Johnson used to sign Medicare into law in 1965, vetoes legislation that he argued would have drastically cut Medicare spending.

ed, Bush never followed through on the threat, and eventually renounced the theory behind the idea.[89]

The election of Bill Clinton in 1992 returned the executive and legislative branches to one-party control for the first time since 1980. This fact, coupled with Clinton's willingness to pursue a broad menu of executive-inspired initiatives, resulted in no vetoes during his first two years in office. The veto question arose only once during that time, when Clinton promised in his 1994 State of the Union address to veto any health care bill that did not provide for universal coverage.

Veto patterns shifted dramatically in the second half of Clinton's term. When Republicans won control of both houses of Congress in the 1994 midterm elections, Clinton found himself using the veto to beat back several Republican initiatives, including several key budget measures to which Republicans had attached provisions objectionable to Clinton. In 1995 Clinton used the veto eleven times (the same veto average per year as George Bush). Clinton's heavy veto use reflected the scope of conflict between Congress and the president. Congress overrode one of those vetoes.

THE VETO THREAT

For as long as the veto power has existed, so too has the veto threat. Writing in the *Federalist* No. 73, Alexander Hamilton noted that the veto often would have "a silent and unperceived, though forcible, operation" that might give pause to those seeking to challenge the president. President Washington, for example, voiced his displeasure about a tonnage bill (imposing duties on imports based on weight) that Congress passed just four months into his first term. Because it was too late for Congress to take back or alter the original bill, Congress passed another bill that was more to Washington's liking.

The veto threat can be used as a tool to shape, alter, or deter legislation before it reaches the president's desk. Like the veto itself, however, a threat applied too often loses its potency, and a threat not considered credible is not a threat at all.

Veto threats have been important tools for modern presidents. For example, a legislative coordinator during the Nixon-Ford years estimated that the veto threat resulted in legislative alterations favorable to the president in twenty to thirty cases.[90] President Carter's threat to veto any bill containing tuition tax credits prompted Congress to remove such a program from its 1978 education bill.

Four possible actions can occur in the aftermath of a veto threat: (1) Congress may back down; (2) a compromise bill may be constructed, leading to passage of a modified bill; (3) the president may reconsider; or (4) neither side may back down, and the bill may be passed and vetoed. As Table 33-2 shows, Kennedy and Johnson did not use the public veto threat. Although threats were used by Carter, the three Republican presidents (Nixon, Ford, and Reagan), all of whom contended with a Congress controlled partially or entirely by the opposition party, faced the greatest number of confrontations over the threat.

The frequent use of veto threats by presidents who face a Congress controlled by the opposing party was illustrated by both Presidents Bush and Clinton. Bush was a prolific user of veto threats; in the first eighteen months of his term alone, Bush issued over 120 veto threats. Bush's threats retained a high degree of credibility because Congress failed to override any of his vetoes until his final year in office, when Bush's veto of a bill regulating cable television was successfully overridden.

In his first two years as president, Clinton issued only one veto threat, when he warned Congress in his 1994 State of the Union address that he would veto any health care reform bill that did not meet his specifications. After the Republicans took control of Congress in 1995, Clinton issued numerous veto threats in an effort to stave off Republican attempts to curtail federal programs dramatically in such areas as welfare, Medicaid, and environmental regulations.

PRIVATE BILL VETOES

About 63 percent of all vetoes have involved private bills. The historically large volume of private bill vetoes is attributable to a rush of war-related pension and other claims. Most of these vetoes were applied by Presidents Cleveland (for Civil War claims), Franklin Roosevelt (for World War I claims), and Truman and Eisenhower (for World War II claims).

Vetoes of private bills are much more likely to be sustained because of the extremely narrow focus of such bills. Given congressional workloads and interests, it is unlikely that the veto of a legislator's pet private bill will spark sufficient interest to cause a serious override effort. Moreover, after passage private bills are subject to a relatively nonpartisan assessment by the appropriate executive departments and agencies. When the recommendation to veto emerges and is carried out, it is perceived in many ways as a nonpolitical judgment, unlike vetoes of public bills.

POCKET VETO

Although the Founders rejected an absolute veto for the president, they nevertheless gave the president a pocket veto, which is in effect an absolute veto. According to Article I, section 7, of the Constitution, "If any bill shall not be returned by the President within ten days (Sundays excepted) after it shall have been presented to him, the same shall be a law, in like manner as if he had signed it, unless the Congress by their adjournment prevent its return, in which case it shall not be a law."

A bill thus automatically becomes law if the president takes no action within ten days, leaving the president unable to block legislation simply by withholding a signature. This provision is modified, however, by the phrase referring to adjournment. This phrase was inserted to prevent Congress from passing a law objectionable to the president and then quickly adjourning to prevent the president from vetoing the bill. (According to the regular veto procedure a bill must be returned to Congress, but this cannot be done if Congress adjourns to avoid receiving a vetoed bill.) If a bill is pocket-vetoed, it dies, and Congress must begin the law-making process again during its next session if it wishes to attempt passage of the bill again.

Roughly 40 percent of all vetoes have been pocket vetoes. The use of the pocket veto did not become common until after the Civil War, simply because the volume of end-of-session legislation was small until this time, and because the veto itself was rarely used. Although the pocket veto has been used frequently, a continuing controversy exists over the question of what constitutes an adjournment by Congress. If the president is able to return a vetoed bill, the pocket veto is not permissible.

The question of the relation between the pocket veto and adjournment has arisen in several court cases. In 1929 the Supreme Court ruled in the *Pocket Veto Case* that the key question concerning when the pocket veto was appropriate was not whether adjournment was final (as in the end of a Congress) or interim (as with a holiday recess), but whether presidents were prevented from returning a vetoed bill to Congress. That is, a bill might still be returnable to Congress if Congress designated agents to receive vetoed bills, a procedure analogous to Congress's legal presentation of passed bills to the president's representatives even when the president is out of the country.[91] If the president was indeed prevented from returning a bill, then the pocket veto was appropriate. In the *Pocket Veto Case* the Court ruled in favor of the pocket veto in question.

In 1938 the Court ruled in *Wright v. United States* that Congress could designate agents to receive veto messages when it was not in session, just as the executive designated agents to serve as legal representatives to receive messages and the like.[92] As a result of these rulings, use of the regular (also called the return) veto was favored over the absolute pocket veto, as long as Congress designated an agent to receive vetoes. The only time

Congress is unable to do this is at the end of its two-year sessions; by the World War II era, Congress began to meet year-round.

Two more recent court challenges have questioned a liberal use of the pocket veto. When President Nixon pocket-vetoed a bill during a six-day Christmas recess in 1970, Sen. Edward M. Kennedy (D-Mass.) filed suit, claiming that the pocket veto was unjustified. Kennedy contended that there had been no adjournment and that the bill could have been return-vetoed. Both the federal district court and federal court of appeals ruled the veto unconstitutional, emphasizing that the pocket veto was unjustified as long as duly designated agents were on hand to receive possible veto messages.[93] The Nixon administration declined to appeal the case to the Supreme Court.

During the 1970s both Presidents Ford and Carter avoided pocket vetoes during intra- and intersession adjournments and cooperated with efforts by Congress to formalize procedures for receiving presidential messages during adjournments. This arrangement changed during the Reagan administration, which used the pocket veto twice when the vetoed bill could have been returned. The second incident prompted a court challenge by thirty-three members of Congress. On March 9, 1984, a federal district court judge ruled in favor of the pocket veto of a bill tying aid to El Salvador with that nation's progress on human rights.[94] The judge ruled that the *Pocket Veto Case* had set precedent. A three-judge court of appeals panel then reversed the lower court ruling in a 2–1 decision. The majority ruled that as long as Congress made arrangements to receive veto messages during recesses and adjournments, the return veto was preferred.[95] On appeal, the Supreme Court ruled 6–2 that the case was moot, because the provisions of the bill had ended by the time of the court ruling. The case was therefore dismissed without a judgment as to its merits.[96]

President Bush continued to argue in behalf of a broader interpretation of pocket veto powers, prompting Congress to consider a bill in 1989 and 1990 to define the pocket veto as appropriate only at the end of a two-year congress. In one instance, Bush claimed he was exercising a pocket veto of a bill providing for appropriations for the District of Columbia, yet returned the bill to Congress as if it were a regular veto. The action was treated like a regular veto, but Congress failed to override. In two other instances, Bush claimed to exercise a pocket veto because the bills reached his desk during congressional recesses, and he did not return the bills to Congress. The two bills, dealing with the enrollment of HR 1278, and with a national environmental scholarship program, were nevertheless enacted into law and entered as part of the U.S. Code because Bush failed to sign them.

The political ambiguity about proper use of the pocket veto thus has played itself out in a series of court and political disputes. Resolution of the dispute depends on the willingness of the president to seek an accommodative relationship with Congress.

LINE-ITEM VETO

Since the last quarter of the nineteenth century, presidents and others have argued that the presidential veto should be expanded to incorporate the power to veto parts or items of a bill. The call for a *line-item veto* (or *item veto*) was predicated partly on the bluntness of the existing veto power, in that presidents may be compelled to veto a bill that includes provisions they favor or to sign a bill that includes provisions they oppose. Congress has long attached "riders" (amendments not related to the bills to which they are attached) to legislation as a means of circumventing a veto. The line-item veto also has been viewed as a way in which the president can trim excess from spending measures and eliminate special-interest projects.

The item veto first appeared in the constitution of the Confederacy in 1861. Although Confederate president Jefferson Davis used the regular veto powers thirty-eight times, he never exercised the item veto. After the Civil War, the item veto was included in Georgia's constitution of 1865 and that of Texas in 1866. It was included in most other state constitutions by about 1915.[97]

In 1873 President Ulysses Grant became the first president to call for the power at the federal level. During the next one hundred years more than 150 proposals for the presidential line-item veto were offered in Congress, but only one proposal reached the floor of Congress, in 1884. Presidents who have called for the power have included Rutherford B. Hayes, Chester A. Arthur, Grover Cleveland, Woodrow Wilson, Franklin Roosevelt, Harry Truman, Dwight Eisenhower, and Gerald Ford. Presidential opponents of the line-item veto have included Benjamin Harrison, William Howard Taft, and Jimmy Carter. More recently, President Reagan called for line-item veto powers for the president in his State of the Union addresses from 1984 to 1988.[98]

In the late 1980s and early 1990s, some commentators advanced the argument that the Constitution already allowed for a presidential line-item veto, based on the idea that the Founders' definition of a bill was limited to a single subject or single appropriation, as compared to modern bills, which often incorporate multiple unrelated subjects and omnibus appropriations. President Bush supported such an interpretation for a time, but then reversed his position. Yet such an argument finds little support, since early legislation did include omnibus measures, as well as multiple subjects. In any case, congressional authority over lawmaking incorporates the power to define and construct legislation as it chooses.[99] President Clinton supported an effort in Congress in 1993 to grant the president a limited line-item veto over appropriations bills, called modified budgetary rescission authority. The effort failed in a Senate floor vote.

In 1995, however, both houses of Congress passed slightly different versions of limited item veto power as part of the Republicans' "Contract with America." A joint Senate-House conference report passed in the Senate 69 to 31 on March 27, 1996, and the House passed it 232 to 177 the following day. The historic measure, which goes into effect on January 1, 1997, gives the president the power to eliminate selected discretionary spending items in appropriations bills. The president also will have limited authority to cancel targeted tax benefits, as well as new or increased entitlement programs. Congress retains the power to override any items "canceled" by the president by a two-thirds vote.

Opponents of the line-item veto have argued that it would serve principally to enhance the president's already considerable power over the legislative process. During the last one hundred years the predominant trend in relations between the executive and legislative branches has been a steady rise in presidential influence over virtually every phase of the legislative process. The addition of the line-item veto would, according to critics, only exacerbate the existing imbalance between the branches.

Accordingly, the claim that presidents would use the power impartially to cut excess spending and special-interest programs overlooks the political and special interests of each president. Nothing could prevent a president from using a line-item veto to serve political ends by, for example, threatening to line-item-veto favored programs of presidential opponents, while sparing those of allies. Moreover, a line-item veto would be effective against only a small proportion of the federal budget, as most of the federal budget is composed of spending resulting from contractual, legal, or other obligations and commitments.[100]

Critics also have argued that the existing veto power gives the president an ample, if imperfect, means of dealing with riders and excess spending. The veto threat alone is often incentive enough for Congress to alter legislation. And when that is not effective, presidents have used the veto successfully to force the hand of Congress. This is evident in the frequency of vetoes, their high rates of success, and the fact that Congress stands to suffer as much from legislative bottlenecks as the president.

As of April 1996, forty-three state governors had line-item veto powers. The experiences of the states have provided no ready model for the presidency, critics have argued, because state governing systems are centered more heavily around the executive, with legislatures that meet for only part of the year (meaning that governors need greater powers to govern when the legislatures are not in session). Moreover, state governors use their line-item vetoes for political purposes in ways that critics fear presidents might adopt under similar circumstances.[101]

A practical problem arises from the difficulty in defining and identifying particular items in legislation. So-called pork barrel projects typically are not itemized in legislation but are incorporated into lump sum amounts. The spending for such projects is stipulated in committee reports, not the law itself. This practice is the product of mutual consent between Congress and federal agencies, because it allows agencies some discretion in adapting spending to changing circumstances. In any case, members of Congress seeking to avoid a line-item veto could find many ways to circumvent the identification of particular items.[102]

In addition to the uncertainty of whether presidents would use the line-item veto as a way to cut excess spending or as a powerful club to bully Congress, the passage of the statutory version of the line-item veto in 1996 raised constitutional questions. Many believed that such a surrender of congressional authority to the executive branch could only be done through a constitutional amendment. It was widely anticipated that the Supreme Court would rule on the constitutionality of the measure.

LEGISLATIVE VETO

The legislative veto, which came into being in the 1930s, is an action taken by Congress to prevent something from happening in the executive branch. It can be invoked by a vote of both houses of Congress (usually through a concurrent resolution), by a vote of one house (through a simple resolution), or even through the actions of a congressional committee. In 1952, for example, Congress authorized the chair of the House Appropriations Committee to veto proposals made by the director of the budget to amend a budget circular.

A legislative veto, unlike regular legislative action, does not cross the president's desk, although the authority creating each legislative veto must be enacted in prior legislation that does cross the president's desk. In this way, Congress reserves the right to review and disapprove present and future actions of the executive branch.

The legislative veto was first employed during the presidency of Herbert Hoover. In 1930 Hoover asked Congress to enact legislation for reorganization of the executive branch. When Congress failed to do so, he asked for the authority to do it himself, subject to congressional "power of revision." Congress delayed responding until June 1932, when the then-Democratic-controlled Congress was reluctant to grant such power to a Republican president. Congress realized, however, that the president was in the best position to oversee such a reorganization, and out of this quandary emerged the legislative veto. Congress reversed the usual legislative procedure by letting the president reorganize, subject to congressional veto, with no authority in the executive to override. Thus, Hoover was allowed to reorganize by executive order, but each order had to be transmitted to Congress and would be undone if disapproved within sixty days by either house.

Since then, the legislative veto has become a standard provision in reorganization legislation and has appeared in many other types of legislation as well. Up to 1983 about two hundred legislative veto provisions had been inserted into legislation. One well-known legislative veto is found in the War Powers Resolution of 1973. According to the provision, Congress may enact a concurrent resolution to force the president to withdraw military forces from hostilities in other nations. A provision of the Budget and Impoundment Control Act of 1974 stipulates that either house can vote to disapprove presidential impoundment of funds and thus compel expenditures. A similar provision is found in the International Security Assistance and Arms Control Act of 1976, which allows Congress to override a decision by the president to sell military hardware to other nations.[103]

Presidents have objected to the idea of the legislative veto by arguing that it represents an improper invasion of executive power. Yet despite this, they have set aside their objections and accepted the validity of reorganization authority.

Critics argue that the legislative veto infringes on the executive's constitutional duty to carry out the laws, because of the way Congress uses the veto to direct administrative action. Some also argue that it violates the presentment clause of Article I, section 7, of the Constitution, which says that binding actions emanating from the legislature must be presented to the president for a signature or veto. Finally, the legislative veto is said to reverse the normal relationship between the two branches, since the president or an agency can take an action unless Congress "vetoes" the action.

In arguing for the legislative veto, proponents first point out that Congress legally delegates rule-making authority to executive branch agencies and the president with regularity. Thus Congress may circumscribe or limit that delegated power by making it subject to legislative veto. Second, although the legislative veto is not subject to presidential assent, it is based on prior statutory authority, which must cross the president's desk. Third, in 1976 Supreme Court Justice Byron R. White noted in the case of *Buckley v. Valeo* that the legislative veto "no more invades the President's powers than does a regulation not required to be laid before Congress."[104] Fourth, the legislative veto has been a key political tool for Congress at a time when it has needed such tools to make its oversight more effective.

The legal arguments for and against the legislative veto came to a head in the 1983 Court case of *Immigration and Naturalization Service v. Chadha*.[105] Speaking for the seven-member majority, Chief Justice Warren Burger said that the legislative veto violated the presentment clause and the principle of bicameralism. (The *Chadha* case involved a one-house veto.) The following month the Court upheld two lower court rulings striking down one- and two-house legislative vetoes.

Despite the sweeping nature of the *Chadha* case the legislative veto is still employed. For example, from 1983 to 1986, 102 legislative veto provisions were implemented through "ingenious and novel methods" developed jointly by Congress and federal agencies. These methods included informal agreements between congressional committees and federal agencies, reliance on bill language that was sufficiently vague or arcane so that only the affected parties were familiar with the language's consequences, and use of internal congressional rules. From 1987 to 1990 an additional 100 such provisions were enacted. Despite President Reagan's stated opposition to the legislative veto, he vetoed none of the bills containing these provisions. One critic of the *Chadha* case has asserted that it has resulted in "a record of non-compliance, subtle evasion, and a system of lawmaking that is now more convoluted, cumbersome, and covert than before."[106] The use of these provisions is nevertheless an example of a vital political accommodation between the branches that was not impeded even by a sweeping Court ruling.

The President as Chief Legislator

The Constitution explicitly involves the president in the legislative process, but the president's present-day extensive role in legislative affairs extends far beyond the initial bounds set by the Constitution. *(See also "The President's Program," p. 561, in Chapter 12, Vol. I.)*

According to Article II, section 3, the president shall give Congress information about the state of the Union, recommend to Congress measures judged "necessary and expedient," and convene "on extraordinary occasions" one or both houses of Congress. The president also makes treaties with the Senate's advice and consent and vetoes bills. Thus, within the ordinary routine of enacting legislation the Constitution allows the president to make proposals to Congress and to veto when legislation emerges. Yet when added together, these powers do not explain how the president has acquired the title of "chief legislator."[107]

Early presidents took great care to avoid trespassing on legislative prerogatives. During his eight years in office, George Washington proposed only three specific measures to Congress and used the veto only twice. Some of Washington's cabinet members, such as Alexander Hamilton, played a more active role by testifying before committees, requesting appropriations, and mobilizing support. Washington's successor, John Adams, faced a more contentious and partisan Congress, and relations deteriorated.

Thomas Jefferson's presidency saw an upturn in relations, aided by close partisan ties between the president and his Democratic-Republican Party allies who controlled Congress. Jefferson's own superb political skills helped as well. Members of Jefferson's cabinet considered and actually formulated legislation. Jefferson's degree of influence over the shape and direction of legislation stood as a high-water mark for nineteenth-century presidents; not until the twentieth century would presidents again wield so much influence over the course of legislation.

The next three presidents—James Madison, James Monroe, and John Quincy Adams—could not match Jefferson's skills, nor were they able to maintain ascendance over their party. They continued to work with congressional leaders and cabinet members, but the predominant pattern was deference to the legislature in all things legislative.[108] This is evident in a House committee report issued in December 1817 in response to a comment in President Monroe's 1817 message to Congress. In the message, Monroe questioned the constitutional right of Congress to establish and finance internal improvements, and he implicitly threatened to veto any bill along these lines. In response the House report stated that the president's expression of opinion should have no influence whatsoever over congressional actions. Furthermore, should a presidential statement announcing a possible veto be made and deter Congress from enacting a measure it might otherwise have passed, "the Presidential veto would acquire a force unknown to the Constitution, and the legislative body would be shorn of its powers from a

want of confidence in its strength."[109] Despite these concerns, Monroe only vetoed one bill during his eight years in office.

Legislative reactions to perceived presidential incursions intensified during subsequent administrations. Andrew Jackson was unable to sway congressional leaders and thus appealed directly to the people, using patronage and the veto with considerable effectiveness. (He vetoed twelve bills, more than all of his predecessors combined.) His vetoes, and veto threats, infuriated his opponents in Congress, who accused him of improperly trying to tamper with the legislative process. Critics rejected Jackson's suggestion that congressional leaders should have consulted the president first to avoid a veto and produce better legislation. To these critics the constitutional pronouncement in Article I—"All legislative powers herein granted shall be vested in Congress"—meant plainly that the president was not to intrude until a bill was presented for a presidential signature or veto. This rift over guiding the course of legislation contributed directly to Senate passage in 1834 of a nonbinding motion to censure Jackson (although the motion was later repealed).

The ascendance of the Whig Party in the 1830s and 1840s helped to legitimize the "Whiggish" view of the presidency, which emphasized that legislating should be left to the legislature. The country's first Whig president, William Henry Harrison, said in his inaugural address: "I cannot conceive that by a fair construction any or either of its [the Constitution's] provisions would be found to constitute the President a part of the legislative power."

President Abraham Lincoln moved effectively during his first term in office to gain more influence over the flow of legislation. Aided by a wartime crisis and a truncated Congress (the Southern states withdrew their representatives at the start of the Civil War), Lincoln proposed legislation and worked for its passage, and he even engaged in some bill drafting. With the ascension of the Radical Republicans after the 1864 elections, presidential influence waned, and Lincoln's successors fared poorly with a postwar Congress that held the political initiative for most of the rest of the century.

Presidents William McKinley and Theodore Roosevelt worked closely with party leaders in Congress. Roosevelt in particular relied on House Speaker Joseph G. Cannon (R-Ill.) to rally support for presidential proposals. Support from the House Speaker was especially crucial during this period because congressional power was at its most hierarchical. From about 1910 on, power in Congress became more and more decentralized, affecting not only the way Congress conducted its business, but also the way Congress interacted with the president.

An important revitalization of presidential influence over legislation occurred during the presidency of Woodrow Wilson. Wilson viewed his role as similar to that of the British prime minister. (He was a close observer and great admirer of the parliamentary system.) To that end he formulated a coordinated series of proposals addressing important national problems, helped draft legislation, used cabinet members to influence

Congress, and established his own direct ties to key congressional leaders. Wilson, in fact, became the first president since John Adams personally to deliver his State of the Union address before Congress. The upshot of these efforts was that Wilson obtained passage of a number of pieces of landmark legislation, including the Clayton Antitrust Act, and the Federal Reserve Act, and creation of the Federal Trade Commission. The end of Wilson's second term saw a decline in his political fortunes, however, capped by the Senate's defeat of the Treaty of Versailles in 1919.

Wilson's three Republican successors, Warren Harding, Calvin Coolidge, and Herbert Hoover, all adopted a more modest attitude toward influencing the legislative process. Like the nineteenth-century Whigs, their conservatism extended to their relations with Congress.

The economic crisis of the 1930s precipitated not only the election of Franklin Roosevelt in 1932, but also his unprecedented domination of the legislative agenda. The relationship between the two branches would never be the same again. From the beginning of his first term Roosevelt sought legislative initiative to deal with the depression; in fact, the day after Roosevelt took office, he called a special session of Congress. During the one-hundred-day session, Congress enacted an enormous volume of major New Deal legislation aimed at the country's economic woes. Roosevelt and his aides designed and guided this legislation through Congress. A second great wave of legislative activity (called the second New Deal) occurred from 1935 to 1936, again based on White House initiative.

Roosevelt used all the resources at his command to influence every aspect of the legislative process. He used aides, advisers, and cabinet secretaries both to formulate legislation and to shepherd it through Congress. He expanded the role of the Bureau of the Budget to control more firmly the requests of the burgeoning federal bureaucracy. And he employed patronage and used the veto more often than any other president.[110]

In sum, Roosevelt's actions had two important consequences. First, for future presidents his actions set a precedent that placed a high premium on decisive, positive, vigorous legislative leadership. It was a precedent accepted not only by presidents, but also by most members of Congress. Second, Roosevelt presided over the creation of the Executive Office of the President (EOP), which then included, among other offices, the Bureau of the Budget. *(See Chapter 27, Executive Office of the President: White House Office.)* The EOP established the administrative framework that enabled future presidents to exercise legislative leadership. The expectations of such leadership were thus firmly established, as were the mechanisms for that leadership.

Harry Truman worked to establish a comprehensive legislative program for Congress. This effort was hampered, however, by the difficulties in adjusting to peacetime, the strains in foreign alliances, and the many problems associated with building a new White House structure after the unexpected death of Roosevelt. Truman's 1948 messages to Congress presented for the first time in his presidency the kind of detailed and comprehensive programs that had been associated with his predecessor. His subsequent proposals were even more comprehensive.

When Dwight Eisenhower took office in 1953 he was criticized widely for not proposing a detailed, defined program to Congress. In 1954 "Eisenhower espoused a sweeping concept of the President's initiative in legislation and an elaborate mechanism for its public expression."[111] From this point on, every president would submit a detailed, comprehensive legislative program that would serve as the basis for congressional action in the coming year.

Besides Franklin Roosevelt, Lyndon Johnson probably had more success in dealing with Congress than any other president. With the assistance of an overwhelmingly Democratic Congress (the famous Eighty-ninth Congress of 1965–1966), he succeeded in enacting an enormous volume of legislation known as his "Great Society" program. These achievements were curtailed first when the Republican Party made electoral inroads in the midterm elections of 1966, and later when the country became more deeply enmeshed in the Vietnam War. As Johnson escalated U.S. involvement in the war, more resources had to be drawn from domestic programs. Johnson's critics then grew in both number and intensity over his conduct of the war. An antiwar challenge from within his own party resulted in his decision not to seek reelection in 1968.

The political troubles that accompanied the Vietnam War not only interrupted Johnson's Great Society, but also ushered in a period of deadlock between the branches of government. This resulted from, among other things, efforts by Congress to reassert itself in the face of presidential dominance, mostly divided party control of the executive and legislative branches, national economic stagnation, and spreading dissatisfaction with the government's ability to solve national problems. Despite all these difficulties, the president remained at the center of the legislative process.

Ronald Reagan swept into office in 1981 after defeating incumbent Jimmy Carter by 10 percent of the vote. Bringing with him a Republican-controlled Senate, and with the assistance of conservative Democrats in the House (where Democrats still held a majority), Reagan won passage of a 25 percent tax cut, dramatic increases in defense spending, and cutbacks in domestic social programs. After these and other achievements in his first two years, however, Democrats succeeded in stopping other Reagan objectives, and his success rate in Congress fell off. When Reagan's vice president, George Bush, won election to the presidency in 1988, he pledged to continue the Reagan agenda. But Bush's primary interest lay in foreign affairs, where he devoted much of his effort. This, plus the fact that he faced a Congress firmly lodged in Democratic hands, resulted in little domestic legislative action with Congress.

Bill Clinton succeeded in winning passage of a large volume of legislation in his first two years in office. Even though the passage of important legislation, such as his first-year budget act, the NAFTA agreement, and the first crime bill passed by Congress in six years, were all enacted by narrow margins, his overall support scores in Congress were among the highest in decades. Yet Clinton suffered a stunning reversal of fortunes in 1995, when the Republican Congress handed him the lowest support score rate of any president since 1953 (although his support score in the Senate was significantly higher than in the House, where Republicans led by Speaker Newt Gingrich more aggressively fought Clinton and his initiatives). *(See Presidential Support in Congress, 1953–1995, p. 1704, in Reference Materials.)*

EXTENT OF THE CHIEF LEGISLATOR'S ROLE

The president's involvement in the legislative domain originates not only in custom and precedent, but also in law. According to the Budget and Accounting Act of 1921, for example, the president must present Congress with an annual budget message. The Employment Act of 1946 calls for presidential submission of an annual economic report as well. In addition, hundreds of other presidential messages, reports, communications, and suggestions are sent to Congress to meet legal requirements.[112]

These legal requirements, enacted by Congress over the years, underscore how much Congress relies on the president's annual legislative program. In fact, Congress is critical of presidents when such programs are not forthcoming. In 1953 an important House committee chair reportedly told an Eisenhower administration official, "Don't expect us to start from scratch on what you people want. That's not the way we do things here— *you* draft the bills and *we* work them over."[113] The difference between this attitude and that of Congress in the nineteenth century illustrates how far the president's participation in legislative affairs has evolved.

Liaison

Presidents always have maintained informal relations with congressional leaders. Woodrow Wilson was the first president in this century to lobby personally on Capitol Hill. Franklin Roosevelt sent his top aides directly to the Capitol to push for his proposals, but President Truman was the first to establish a White House office to maintain ties between the president and Congress. Eisenhower enlarged and reorganized the office, and it grew to maturity under the guidance of Lawrence O'Brien, special assistant to Presidents Kennedy and Johnson for congressional affairs. O'Brien's office acted as a focal point for the liaison activities of the executive agencies and departments, and he and his staff also spent much time roaming the halls of Congress. The liaison office prepared weekly reports for the president and made projections about the week to come. President Johnson also played an active role in building support in Congress for his programs and proposals.[114]

President Nixon constructed a strong liaison staff, but its judgments and operations were preempted by Nixon's top assistants, including H. R. Haldeman and John Ehrlichman. After two frustrating years, Nixon's liaison head, Bryce Harlow, re-

signed. Harlow's successors were similarly frustrated by broadside administration attacks against Congress. By 1973 the liaison office had lost its effectiveness, and liaison efforts were left to a few top Nixon aides.

President Carter took office with high expectations for legislative policy achievement in such areas as energy, welfare, and health care, but they were dashed soon by his mishandling of legislative liaison. Frank Moore, Carter's choice to head the liaison office, had been his liaison with the state legislature when Carter was governor of Georgia; but Moore had no Washington experience. He and his staff neglected the early construction of solid relations with an initially receptive Democratic Congress. Moreover, the liaison office was organized by issue categories (such as agriculture, labor, health, welfare, etc.) rather than by regional blocs (that is, lobby efforts targeted to representatives from particular regions of the country). These failures combined with the flood of initial legislation forwarded to Congress to produce poor and relatively unproductive relations between the branches. (In contrast, Johnson sent important bills to Congress one at a time.)

President Reagan's initial liaison efforts were successful, despite Republican control of only one house of Congress (the Senate). Early in the Reagan administration, White House staff members conducted a study of the first three months of each past administration, beginning with that of Franklin Roosevelt. They concluded that their best chance of success lay in working early and hard on a few key proposals. Reagan selected an experienced Washington hand, Max Friedersdorf, to head liaison efforts, and he was also careful to extend personal favors and courtesies to the key congressional leaders of both parties. As a result of these efforts Reagan achieved many early successes, including enactment of his tax cut package.[115]

George Bush sought to emulate the successes of his predecessor. Bush's choice for liaison head was Frederick D. McClure, a former senatorial staff member. Bush won early praise for taking a pragmatic and personal approach to Congress. Yet the White House came under increasing criticism for bypassing the liaison office, and relying instead on Chief of Staff John Sununu, Budget Director Richard Darman, and White House Counsel C. Boyden Gray to lobby Congress. Bush's preoccupation with foreign policy and relative neglect of domestic matters placed the administration in an increasingly defensive posture with Congress.

Bill Clinton's style was also one of greater personal involvement. Unlike Bush, however, Clinton placed primary emphasis on domestic policy. Clinton's first legislative liaison head was Howard Paster, who served for about one year. He was succeeded by Patrick Griffin, a former top aide to Sen. Robert C. Byrd (D-W.Va.). While Clinton's liaison office actively cultivated strong ties with members of Congress (a fact reflected in Paster's resignation when he cited burnout as one reason for leaving), Clinton relied on a multipronged approach with Congress, enlisting top aides and advisers, as well as cabinet secretaries, Vice President Al Gore, and First Lady Hillary Rodham Clinton.

Central Clearance

Concomitant with the expansion of the president's legislative role, the growth of the federal bureaucracy, and the need for greater fiscal economy, budgetary authority was delegated to the president in 1921 with enactment of the Budget and Accounting Act. This act stated that any agency or department planning to request legislation for the expenditure of funds must first have approval from the newly created Bureau of the Budget (BOB). In the 1930s this "central clearance" process was extended to all executive branch requests for legislation. BOB then determined whether the requests were consistent with the president's legislative priorities. *(See Chapter 28, Executive Office of the President: Supporting Organizations.)*

At the other end of the legislative process BOB also assessed all enrolled bills (those passed by Congress but not yet signed by the president). These were forwarded to the agencies affected, which in turn informed BOB whether the bill should be signed or vetoed by the president. BOB then sent its final recommendation to the president. Communication between the president and the bureau was made easier in 1939 when the office was moved from the Treasury Department to the newly created Executive Office of the President. According to one expert, the clearance and enrolled bill processes "lie at the core of the legislative presidency."[116]

From the Franklin Roosevelt period to about 1965 the Bureau of the Budget tried to avoid overt political considerations in its recommendations, concerning itself more directly with budgetary limitations and the objective merits of bills. Primary responsibility for these activities fell to the Legislative Reference Division within BOB. Because of the volume of legislation, BOB recommendations carried considerable weight, as did those of the career civil servants within the bureau who assumed the brunt of the work. Toward the end of his term, however, President Johnson created a high-level, politically appointed (as opposed to civil service) position at the bureau with the aim of giving the president an added political voice within the agency. This appointment marked the beginning of a greater general politicization within BOB.

The Johnson White House also began to take a more active role in determining the bureau's political and policy priorities and their relationship to the president's broader agenda. Legislative items of special interest to the president were given higher priority and often were handled by White House aides. This greater White House interest in BOB was accompanied by an expansion of Johnson's domestic policy staff.

When BOB was reconstituted as the Office of Management and Budget (OMB) under Nixon in 1970, it was given greater managerial responsibilities, and four new politically appointed associate directors assumed key duties. As a consequence, central clearance and assessment of enrolled bills came under the purview of political appointees rather than civil servants. Moreover, OMB was less receptive to the suggestions and recommendations of civil servants and federal agencies, and it increasingly served as an instrument for extending White House policy preferences into these agencies. This process of politicizing OMB accelerated under the Reagan administration, as OMB increasingly served as a political force for the president. Using its control over the budget process, OMB became a primary tool for the president to ensure that other federal agencies were operating according to the president's policy preferences. This pattern continued under Bush and Clinton.[117]

WINNING SUPPORT IN CONGRESS

Presidents and their staffs rely on personal persuasion to gain congressional approval of presidential initiatives. Although Congress seeks a presidential agenda, it has few inhibitions about changing presidential proposals once consideration begins. Presidents use other informal methods as well to realize their legislative objectives.

Party Leadership

Presidents whose political party controls both houses of Congress begin with an immediate political advantage. Those who have had the greatest success with Congress—such as Thomas Jefferson, Theodore Roosevelt, Woodrow Wilson, Franklin Roosevelt, and Lyndon Johnson—have used party ties to chamber and committee leaders to cement support for important programs. Sometimes, however, presidents have run up against their congressional party leaders. President Kennedy, for example, found that conservative southern Democrats who held influential positions in Congress blocked many of his programs because of ideological differences. President Carter also encountered difficulties with members of his party in Congress because of his lack of experience and that of his staff. President Clinton met with a similar, if less severe, problem with unsympathetic conservative southern Democrats during his first two years in office. In particular, Sen. Richard Shelby (D-Ala.) often sided with Republicans on key, close votes. (Shelby switched to the Republican Party in November 1994.)

Even presidents who find the opposition party in control of Congress discover ways of dealing with partisan differences. President Reagan amassed a series of major successes during his first year in office by relying on the Republican majority in the Senate and a working House majority composed of minority Republicans and "Boll Weevil" Democrats (conservative southern Democrats who were sympathetic to many of Reagan's objectives). The centerpiece of Reagan's efforts was a controversial three-year tax cut plan, enacted only a few months after its introduction. Reagan also won passage in 1981 of major shifts in budget priorities, including significant cuts in domestic social programs and a major increase in defense spending.

Patronage

Presidents readily rely on patronage as a means of winning support. Although civil service limits the extent to which federal jobs may be filled by presidential appointment, presidents nevertheless have the authority to fill thousands of federal positions, including judgeships, federal marshal and attorney positions, customs collector posts, and slots on selective service boards. Such appointments can be used to curry favor among members of Congress.

Presidents also can wield substantial personal patronage, such as making campaign trips to the home district of a member of Congress to boost fund-raising efforts, extending special White House invitations to legislators, and even providing tickets to the president's box at the John F. Kennedy Center for the Performing Arts. Such favors can have an effect on those of either party whose support is sought by the president.

Presidents have great influence as well over the kind of patronage found in distributive (often called pork barrel) policies. Presidents may reward friends and punish enemies by throwing their support to or withholding support from certain distributive policies such as public works projects, construction projects, defense contracts, rivers and harbors work, and agricultural subsidies. President Carter incurred the ire of many in Congress when he attempted to eliminate nineteen water resource projects in 1978; Congress ultimately defeated his efforts. In contrast to Carter, Reagan encouraged water development. Similarly, he overrode the recommendations of his budget director, David Stockman, and continued to back price supports for tobacco growers during the major effort in 1981 to reduce elements of the federal budget. In the case of the water projects, Reagan was lending his support to programs that benefited the western states, which had provided him with vital support during his election. Tobacco supports were of great importance to key southern states, including North Carolina and Virginia.

In 1993 President Clinton used patronage agreements extensively to swing support in the House of Representatives on behalf of the North American Free Trade Agreement (NAFTA). He made deals with more than fifty members of the House to win their votes. Some of the deals included special protections for sugar growers, citrus farmers, and vegetable producers; the awarding of special air routes and defense contracts; tariff reductions for certain appliances; cuts in grazing fees for federal lands; and cuts in helium subsidies. Each of these agreements provided special benefits for constituents in the congressional districts of the representative whose NAFTA vote Clinton obtained. One estimate said that the sum total of such deals could cost as much as $50 billion during a five-year period.[118]

Another aspect of the president's support for pork barrel projects is illustrated by a study of presidential proposals sent to Congress from 1954 to 1974. It found that presidents propose more distributive policies to Congress during presidential election years than at any other time in the four-year term cycle.[119]

Public Support

One of the president's most important bases of political strength is public support. Abraham Lincoln once noted, "Public sentiment is everything. With public sentiment nothing can fail, without it nothing can succeed."[120] In the early days of his presidency, Lyndon Johnson often quoted poll results to demonstrate the extent of public support for his programs. Later in his presidency, as public support faded, so too did his success with Congress. Likewise, the Watergate revelations eroded Richard Nixon's popular support after his landslide reelection in 1972, thereby sapping his political strength and support for his policy initiatives in Congress.

A remarkable jump in the polls early in Ronald Reagan's first term had an important effect on the passage of his economic program. After the first three months of Reagan's presidency, his public standing according to the polls was about two to one in his favor. Then on March 30, 1981, John Hinckley Jr. attempted to assassinate the president. Reagan was hit with a single bullet, but he recovered. According to White House assistant Richard Beal, this incident helped endear the president to the public. "His personal attributes might never have come across without the assassination attempt."[121] Because people admired Reagan's courage, calmness, and humor, his standing in the polls rose to a three-to-one favorable rating after the assassination attempt. When Reagan's aides then met to decide how best to capitalize on this new reservoir of good feeling, they concluded that enactment of Reagan's economic program should receive priority. Thus, the president's first public speech after the assassination attempt dealt with that subject. (See Presidential Approval Ratings, Gallup Poll, 1945–1995, p. 1698, in Reference Materials.)

In the aftermath of the 1991 Persian Gulf War, President Bush's popularity stood at 89 percent, the highest rating ever recorded for a president since such polling began in the 1930s. Bush supporters urged him to use the opportunity to push priority bills in Congress; yet the relatively little attention Bush had given to domestic concerns left him flat-footed. He pushed no major agenda items, and failed to take advantage of the opportunity.

A president's standing in the eyes of the public is at its greatest immediately after the presidential election. As a result, presidential resources and opportunities are most plentiful then. Unfortunately, administrations often lack the experience and skills necessary to take full advantage of this so-called honeymoon period. Later in the term, when the requisite skills and experience are on hand, the president invariably stands lower in the polls and thus possesses less of a mandate to act. Presidents thus are best off trying early in the term to enact important programs if they are to realize any benefit from their popularity.[122]

WHO FORMULATES LEGISLATION?

Many scholars have studied the question of who bears the primary responsibility for the formulation and initiation of legislation, and many have argued that Congress has not received the credit that it deserves. Although Congress waits on the president's annual legislative program, a large number of the ideas and suggestions found in the president's program may come from Congress or elsewhere, such as private interest groups.

In the first important study of legislative initiative, Lawrence Chamberlain examined ninety major pieces of legislation passed by Congress from 1870 to 1940. According to his results, published in 1946, presidential influence predominated in nineteen cases; congressional influence in thirty-five cases; joint influence in twenty-nine cases; and pressure group influence in seven cases. The study's principal conclusion was that it is "not that the president is less important than generally supposed, but that Congress is more important."[123]

A follow-up study by William Goldsmith applied similar methods to sixty-three major pieces of legislation enacted into law from 1945 to 1964. This study concluded that "the President has indeed become a major partner in the legislative process, and . . . very little significant legislation is now passed that either does not emanate from the Executive branch, or is not significantly influenced by executive action at some stage of its legislative history."[124] Another presidential scholar, writing at the height of the Johnson era, concluded: "The President now determines the legislative agenda of Congress almost as thoroughly as the British Cabinet sets the legislative agenda of Parliament."[125]

Several political scientists, arguing that the role of Congress has been undervalued, have challenged the conclusion that the president has come to play the primary role. For example, one study of the period 1940–1967 revealed many areas in which Congress played a decisive role, including the economy, transportation, agriculture, urban policy, and technology. It concluded that "Congress continues to be an active innovator and very much in the legislative business."[126] Other studies have explored as well what many observers view as Congress's undervalued role in legislative initiation and enactment.[127]

Still other analyses emphasize that the president's influence over Congress is indeed marginal. Political scientist George C. Edwards III asserts that presidents operate "at the margins" of the presidential-congressional relationship, in that they operate as facilitating Congress, rather than leading it. Edwards finds political party and public opinion to be the most important factors in explaining what motivates Congress, concluding that presidents ". . . are essentially limited to exploiting rather than creating opportunities for leadership. . . ."[128] Similarly, political scientists Jon R. Bond and Richard Fleisher assert that presidential success in Congress is determined more by Congress-cen-

tered factors (party and ideology) than by president-centered factors (public support and leadership skills). They find the president to be ". . .a relatively weak legislative actor. . . ."[129] Political scientist Mark A. Peterson finds a more balanced relationship between the two branches, arguing that the constitutional relationship between the two branches has yielded a relationship of the two institutions operating in tandem, with each branch needing the cooperation of the other.[130]

These apparent contradictions can be resolved by recognizing several facts. First, it is often impossible to identify the original source of legislation. And even if it is possible, credit is frequently shared. For example, many of the Great Society initiatives enacted during Lyndon Johnson's presidency were adapted from proposals formulated in the 1950s by Democratic members of Congress (with those ideas in turn often coming from policy experts, interest groups, or others), who deserve recognition for their initial work. Likewise, President Johnson deserves credit for putting the weight of the presidency behind these proposals and seeing them through to enactment. President Kennedy received credit for enacting the Area Redevelopment Act of 1961, even though several Democratic senators advanced the idea in the late 1950s, when it was successfully blocked by President Eisenhower.

Second, some scholarly studies are shaped by contemporary politics. The Roosevelt and Johnson eras, for example, were periods of relative presidential dominance. But Congress played a more assertive role during the Eisenhower presidency and even more so during the 1970s. Studies with the mid-1960s as their endpoint would almost certainly come to a different conclusion about presidential-congressional relations than studies completed during the mid-1970s, for example.

Third, a rearrangement of data from different studies often uncovers greater consistencies. For example, when the data from the Chamberlain and Goldsmith studies are rearranged chronologically, they illustrate that, over time, the president's influence has increased progressively, while that of Congress has declined progressively; joint responsibility is also on the rise. (See Table 33-3.)

Fourth, recent more empirical studies of presidential-congressional relations are limited in their scope and applicability.

TABLE 33-3 Responsibility for Passage of Major Legislative Proposals

	President		Congress		Joint		Pressure group		Total	
1870–1910	17%	(5)	53%	(16)	20%	(6)	10%	(3)	100%	(30)
1911–1930	12	(4)	48	(16)	27	(9)	12	(4)	99	(33)
1931–1940	37	(10)	11	(3)	52	(14)	0	—	100	(27)
1945–1954	33	(12)	17	(6)	44	(16)	6	(2)	100	(36)
1955–1964	56	(15)	4	(1)	41	(11)	0	—	100	(27)

SOURCE: Robert J. Spitzer, *The Presidency and Public Policy* (University: University of Alabama Press, 1983), 92. Reprinted by permission of the publisher.

NOTE: Variations from 100 percent are due to rounding error. Data taken and readjusted from Lawrence Chamberlain, "The President, Congress, and Legislation," in *The President: Roles and Powers*, ed. David Haight and Larry Johnson (Chicago: Rand McNally, 1965), 301–303; and William Goldsmith, *The Growth of Presidential Power* (New York: Chelsea House, 1974), 3: 1398–1399. Goldsmith claimed to use the same evaluation standards and techniques as Chamberlain. Data from 1870 to 1940 are from the Chamberlain study. Data from 1945 to 1964 are from the Goldsmith study.

These studies measure presidential success by roll call votes, which is limited only to the last few decades, and precludes the many decision points where president and Congress interact before and after roll call votes are taken. Most of the ways and means the president uses to influence Congress as discussed in this chapter fall outside of the narrow bounds of what can be measured in roll call votes.

MEASURES OF AND FACTORS IN PRESIDENTIAL SUCCESS

Factors related to the president's success in dealing with Congress include political party, the kind of policy (for example, domestic or foreign) being addressed by legislation, and term cycle, referring to whether the president is at the start, middle, or end of a term in office. Personal leadership skills play a role in all of these factors.

Several scores have been used to measure the president's track record in Congress. One such measure is the presidential Boxscore, or success score. From 1954 to 1975 Congressional Quarterly kept track of proposals that composed the president's annual legislative program (excluding both proposals emanating from the executive branch but not specifically endorsed by the president, and those endorsed by the president but not specifically included in the White House program). While the Boxscore provided a ready means for comparing numbers of proposals and their rates of success, it also had its limitations. For example, it did not take into account the relative importance of bills. It included a large number of foreign policy proposals, in which the president was more likely to gain congressional approval. It did not indicate which were measures favored by the president but were not included in the formal proposal list because of overwhelming congressional opposition. And it did not take into account measures included solely because the president anticipated that they would be enacted anyway.[131]

Despite these limitations the Boxscore has provided a source of information for those interested in comparing the track records of presidents, variations in their success rates, and the kinds of proposals that presidents have selected for inclusion in their legislative menus. Problems with use of the data arise when the summary percentages are used as the sole indicators of a president's success.

Another measure kept by Congressional Quarterly is presidential support scores. Collected annually since 1953, this measure summarizes all public statements and messages of the president to determine the president's position on pending roll call votes in the House and Senate. These votes may or may not involve presidential proposals. Although support scores indicate how often Congress supports the president's position, this measure has its limitations. It disregards the reasons for the president's positions on legislation, and it does not indicate which measures are more important to the president. Support scores provide a basis for comparison between presidents, however. *(See Presidential Support in Congress, 1953–1995, p. 1704, in Reference Materials.)*

Presidential support scores are higher than their respective Boxscores, because support scores merely indicate what bills the president favors, and all presidents have an interest in supporting legislation that is more likely to pass. Support scores also are usually highest at the start of a presidential term, especially during the honeymoon period.

A third measure used by Congressional Quarterly is key votes, pivotal issues of great importance to Congress and the president. To be judged a key vote, a roll call vote must involve a major controversy or constitute an important test of political power or a decision that will have a great impact on the country. Such criteria weed out less important legislative efforts and reveal the priorities and interests of both branches when the political stakes are high.

One important study of key votes found that presidents fared well on key votes from 1957 to 1972, but not as well from 1973 to 1978. Dividing support on key votes by party, the study reported that support from the president's party in Congress remained about the same from 1957 to 1973. After 1973, however, a major drop in support occurred among opposition party members, especially in foreign policy matters.[132]

Key votes do not focus solely on issues of concern to the president, but, not surprisingly, the president takes a position on most such votes. The usefulness of this measure is limited by the relatively small number of bills that are included in the key votes score each year. In 1957, for example, only five House and five Senate roll call votes (for which individual member votes are recorded) were included, while in 1965, during the height of the Johnson administration, eighteen roll call votes from each chamber were included.

Finally, the number of presidential vetoes and the record for sustaining vetoes sometimes are used as a measure of presidential success. Although veto scores are readily available, by themselves these scores say little about presidential rates of success. The veto is an indisputably important power, but as an aggregate measure it reveals little because it applies only to bills that the president seeks to block at the very end of the legislative process, and because of its relatively rare use by most presidents.

The measures of presidential success just described support the proposition that presidents do better when their political party maintains control of Congress. Thus, virtually all presidents and presidential candidates have devoted political efforts and resources to this end. Like Ronald Reagan, however, some presidents have logged important successes in Congress despite their lack of political party control.

George C. Edwards III has concluded that members of the president's party in Congress find that their political future usually is related to that of the president. Thus, when the president's public standing and popularity are high, legislators from the same party face a better chance at reelection and also stand to benefit from presidential favors. Moreover, members of the president's political party often feel a sense of personal loyalty to the president, which often transcends ideological or other differences.[133]

TABLE 33-4 Losses by President's Party in Midterm
Elections, 1862–1994

Year	Party holding presidency	President's party: gain/loss of seats in House	President's party: gain/loss of seats in Senate
1862	R	−3	8
1866	R	−2	0
1870	R	−31	−4
1874	R	−96	−8
1878	R	−9	−6
1882	R	−33	3
1886	D	−12	3
1890	R	−85	0
1894	D	−116	−5
1898	R	−21	7
1902	R	9[a]	2
1906	R	−28	3
1910	R	−57	−10
1914	D	−59	5
1918	D	−19	−6
1922	R	−75	−8
1926	R	−10	−6
1930	R	−49	−8
1934	D	9	10
1938	D	−71	−6
1942	D	−55	−9
1946	D	−55	−12
1950	D	−29	−6
1954	R	−18	−1
1958	R	−48	−13
1962	D	−4	3
1966	D	−47	−4
1970	R	−12	2
1974	R	−48	−5
1978	D	−15	−3
1982	R	−26	1
1986	R	−5	−8
1990	R	−8	−1
1994	D	−53	−8

SOURCE: Norman J. Ornstein, Thomas E. Mann, and Michael J. Malbin, *Vital Statistics on Congress, 1995–1996* (Washington, D.C.: Congressional Quarterly, 1996), 55.

NOTES: Each entry is the difference between the number of seats won by the president's party in that midterm election and the number of seats won by that party in the preceding general election. Because of changes in the overall number of seats in the Senate and House, in the number of seats won by third parties, and in the number of vacancies, a Republican loss is not always matched precisely by a Democratic gain, or vice versa.   a. Although the Republicans gained nine seats in the 1902 elections, they actually lost ground to the Democrats, who gained twenty-five seats after the increase in the overall number of representatives after the 1900 census.

Another important factor related to the president's success in dealing with Congress is the kind of policy being addressed by legislation. Studies have demonstrated that presidents have greater success in obtaining passage of foreign policy proposals, for example, than domestic policy proposals, although this trend has varied over time. (For example, Congress challenged presidential foreign policy initiatives more in the 1970s than it had in the past.)

Different kinds of domestic policies also yield various political configurations and thus various political outcomes. Political

scientist Steven A. Shull has noted that "variations in the content of policies . . . produce variations in the roles and behavior of actors."[134] Several studies have concluded that different policies—such as those dealing with social benefits, civil rights, government management, and agriculture—have different political patterns.[135] In other words, some policies by their nature are more or less controversial, are more or less likely to involve interest group pressure, are more or less likely to be dominated by the president, and so on.

A leading student of policy making, Theodore J. Lowi, has proposed reversing the usual analysis of policy making in Congress and elsewhere. Most examinations of policy making focus on how political relationships affect policies produced by the political system. Lowi proposed instead examining how different kinds of policies affect politics.[136] He then described four kinds of policies—constituent, redistributive, distributive, and regulatory—each of which produces its own political pattern.

A study by Robert Spitzer applied these four policy types to the presidency, arguing that the kind of policy that presidents proposed to Congress determined the political configuration that ensued, resulting in "four presidencies." The "administrative president" prevails when the president proposes constituent policies related to the running of the government, including those pertaining to government reorganization, election laws, and budgeting. Congress's struggle to enact campaign finance reform in 1994 is a specific example of constituent policy. As chief executive the president is perceived as having great authority over such administrative matters. Thus, the president has the greatest success in dealing with Congress when advancing constituent policy legislation. For the president, this area is less politically rewarding than other policy areas, however, because constituent policies usually attract little attention or interest in the country.

The "public-interest president" results from presidential concern with redistributive policies, which are broad in scope, affecting large groups of people. Examples include Social Security, welfare, and the progressive income tax. A specific example is Congress's 1993 extension of unemployment benefits. Given the nationwide scope of redistributive policies, Congress looks for presidential leadership in this area. The resulting politics may be contentious, but presidents usually have success in this area. As opposed to constituent policies, redistributive policies, which are wider in scope and of greater interest to Congress and the country, present presidents with more obstacles. Yet presidents continue to take a strong interest in redistributive policies, which often represent a litmus test of presidential leadership.

The "special-interest president" emerges when the president proposes distributive policies. These policies, which are narrow in scope and purpose, are often labeled patronage or pork barrel policies. Although presidents can exert political influence when proposing these policies to Congress, they must pay careful attention to congressional preferences. Distributive policies—such as construction projects and rivers and harbors legislation—directly affect the economies of the localities where they

FIGURE 33-1 Arenas of Power Applied to Presidential Policy Making

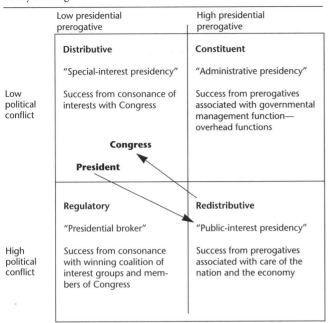

	Low presidential prerogative	High presidential prerogative
Low political conflict	**Distributive** "Special-interest presidency" Success from consonance of interests with Congress	**Constituent** "Administrative presidency" Success from prerogatives associated with governmental management function—overhead functions
High political conflict	**Regulatory** "Presidential broker" Success from consonance with winning coalition of interest groups and members of Congress	**Redistributive** "Public-interest presidency" Success from prerogatives associated with care of the nation and the economy

Source: Robert J. Spitzer, *The Presidency and Public Policy* (University: University of Alabama Press, 1983), 152. Reprinted by permission of the publisher.

are targeted, and members of Congress are keenly interested in such projects when they are associated with their districts. Thus, presidents challenging congressional preferences in this area are likely to face a fierce struggle. A specific example is Congress's enactment of a bill in 1973 to construct the Alaska oil pipeline.

Presidents assume a "presidential broker" role when dealing with regulatory policies. These policies affect the formation and enforcement of laws that manipulate economic and social conduct, usually through use of sanctions and penalties. Common examples include regulations on unfair competition, elimination of substandard goods, gun control, and antitrust legislation. Although presidents frequently try to take the lead in this area, they often are frustrated and unsuccessful. By their nature, regulatory policies arouse deep passions in those doing the regulating and those being regulated. Thus, even presidents at the peak of their power (such as Lyndon Johnson after his election in 1964) often find that enactment of such proposals in Congress is extremely difficult. *(See Figure 33-1.)* A specific example is the crime bill enacted by Congress in 1994. While President Clinton favored the crime bill, interest group lobbying was extremely intense, and the measure was subject to protracted debate and angry rhetoric. Various provisions were added, and compromises struck, to win sufficient votes to realize passage.

Spitzer's study of presidential policy making in Congress concluded that presidents have faced comparable political problems in dealing with Congress, according to the kind of policy being proposed. This pattern has held true despite differences in the president's party affiliation, reputed leadership skills, or party support in Congress.[137]

Another factor related to a president's success with Congress is the presidential term cycle. Political scientist Richard E. Neustadt has observed a rhythmic cycle in the presidential term. The first eighteen months usually are devoted to learning the job, establishing routines, and setting patterns with Congress, while the fourth year is a "period of pause," dominated by concern with reelection. By the seventh year national attention is beginning to focus on the president's successor. According to Neustadt, the most important years for presidents seeking to achieve their objectives are the third, fifth, and sixth.[138]

A study of presidencies of the 1960s and 1970s concluded that presidential success hinged on two conflicting cycles—one of decreasing influence and one of increasing effectiveness. Presidential resources—and thus influence—are greatest immediately after election or reelection (although the second term holds less potential than the first), when presidents and their staffs possess the least experience and skill. They are therefore in a poor position to exploit their maximal influence. As the term progresses, the administration acquires more experience and skill but loses resources. The capacity for effectiveness then increases, but diminished resources mean that success is less likely. Not surprisingly, this paradoxical pattern has been labeled the "No-Win Presidency." According to White House aides, minimizing the no-win problem and maximizing the president's success hinge on a large electoral margin, a high rate of public approval, and presidential party control of Congress.[139]

Forces Promoting Conflict and Cooperation

Structural factors do much to explain the interrelationship between the president and Congress. The effect of these factors is tempered, however, by informal political habits and traditions.

ORGANIZATION OF CONGRESS

The structure and hierarchy of the authority of Congress are related directly to the president's association with the nation's lawmakers. When in the past congressional authority has been concentrated in the hands of a few strong leaders, presidents usually have won congressional support by earning the support of those leaders. Theodore Roosevelt, for example, chalked up important legislative successes because of his close ties to House Speaker Joseph G. Cannon (R-Ill.). Cannon's tenure as Speaker represented an apex of strong congressional leadership.

Since the early 1900s, however, power in Congress has become much more decentralized, although House Speaker Newt Gingrich has sought to centralize power to a greater extent than has been seen in decades. Still, congressional power continues to be dispersed. Presidents seeking congressional support must now curry favor not only with party leaders, but also with committee and subcommittee chairs, regional leaders, and spokespersons for particular interests. When President Carter proposed his comprehensive energy program in 1977, no fewer than

Speaker of the House Newt Gingrich (R-Ga.) consolidated power in the speakership in 1995 and sought to return to an era of congressional government by wresting control of the national agenda from the executive branch.

thirty congressional committees and subcommittees claimed jurisdiction over some portion of the program. In addition, House Speaker Thomas P. "Tip" O'Neill Jr. (D-Mass.) set up a special ad hoc committee to oversee and coordinate the many facets of the energy legislation.

In short, presidents must be prepared to work within existing channels of congressional authority if they are to be successful. And they must be sensitive to the importance of seniority, the committee and subcommittee system, the role of party leaders, and other factors that affect the distribution of power in the legislative branch.

Seniority

Although it is only a custom, seniority has been the principal means of selecting leaders of standing committees and resolving other power-related matters in both houses of Congress. In the seniority system, length of continuous service is rewarded with enhanced power and perquisites within the institution. Consecutive length of service in Congress is congressional seniority; length of service on a committee is committee seniority.

Before the twentieth century seniority was only one of several criteria used to determine committee leadership positions. But in the latter part of the nineteenth century, as legislation became more complex and the average length of congressional careers increased, reliance on the principle of seniority increased as well (although it came to the House more slowly than to the Senate, where terms were longer and experience was more venerated). In this century the norm of seniority has been violated only occasionally, and then under extraordinary circumstances.[140] In 1975 dissatisfaction with three elder House com-

mittee chairs caused them to lose their seats. In 1985 eighty-year-old Melvin Price (D-Ill.) lost his chairmanship of the House Armed Services Committee to seventh-ranked member Les Aspin (D-Wis.). In 1991 two committee chairs were ousted. In 1995 three senior Republicans were passed over for committee chair positions in favor of less senior Republicans who maintained greater personal loyalty to, and ideological compatibility with, House Speaker Gingrich. In almost every instance, the ousted chairs were faulted for their poor committee leadership and failure to respond to the needs and preferences of committee members. Although competence claims were made for the three Republicans passed over in 1995, greater weight was placed on the issue of loyalty to the Speaker.

Seniority is the basis for determining influence on congressional committees. The committee chair is typically the most senior member of the majority party, which holds numerical majorities on all committees. The most senior member of the minority party on each committee, known as the ranking minority member, is also accorded some deference for continuous years of committee service. In addition to access to and influence on committees, seniority affects the assignment of office space, access to congressional patronage, and the respect of colleagues.

Party leaders in both houses are not selected according to seniority, but lengthy service in Congress is generally a necessary prerequisite for service as chamber leader. For example, one of the most respected House leaders of the twentieth century was Sam Rayburn. A Democrat from Texas, Rayburn served in the House for twenty-four years before becoming majority leader in 1937. He became Speaker of the House in 1940 and served in that position until his death in 1961. Democrat Tip O'Neill of Massachusetts was elected House majority leader in 1973 after twenty years of service, and he served as Speaker from 1977 until his retirement in 1986. Jim Wright (D-Texas) became Speaker in 1987 after thirty-two years of service. Tom Foley (D-Wash.) became Speaker in 1989 after twenty-five years of service. Newt Gingrich (R-Ga.) assumed the position of Speaker in 1995 after sixteen years of service. Yet Gingrich's relatively rapid succession only occurred because Republican House leader Robert Michel (Ill.) decided to retire in 1994 after thirty-eight years in the House and fourteen years as minority leader (Michel expressed regret over missing the opportunity to serve as Speaker).

Because the principle of seniority rewards length of continuous service, it has tended to empower representatives elected from "safe" constituencies—that is, districts or states that reelect their representatives by consistently high percentages. Most often, these have been more conservative, one-party regions. For example, the South was almost entirely Democratic for many years, and southern conservative Democrats controlled many important committee leadership positions from the 1950s to the 1970s. *(See Table 33-5.)* Rural areas in the Midwest and Far West have been Republican strongholds for many years, as have large urban areas for the Democrats. Several of these urban districts have become strongholds for African American representatives, who have in turn acquired committee leadership positions. In

One of the most respected twentieth-century House Speakers, Sam Rayburn (D-Texas), served in the post for seventeen years.

TABLE 33-5 Southern Democratic Membership and Committee Leadership, House of Representatives, 1967–1979

Year and Congress	Southern members (% of all House Democrats)		Southern leaders (% of all chairs)	
	Number of all Democrats	% Southern	Number of all chairs	% Southern
1967 (90th)	(248)	33	(20)	45
1969 (91st)	(243)	33	(21)	38
1971 (92d)	(255)	31	(21)	38
1973 (93d)	(248)	30	(21)	38
1975 (94th)[a]	(291)	28	(20)	50[b]
1977 (95th)	(292)	27	(21)	24
1979 (96th)	(276)	28	(21)	24

SOURCE: Barbara Hinckley, *Stability and Change in Congress* (New York: Harper and Row, 1988), 130.

NOTES: a. Excludes standing committees newly created for the Ninety-fourth Congress: Budget and Small Business. b. According to the strict operation of seniority. After the challenges the figure is 35 percent.

the 103d Congress (1993–1995), Ron Dellums (D-Calif.), for example, represented the cities of Oakland and Berkeley and chaired the Armed Services Committee; and John Conyers (D-Mich.) chaired the Government Operations Committee and represented the city of Detroit.[141] Both of these Democrats had to give up their chairs when the Republicans took control of Congress after the 1994 election.

Committee System

Congressional committees constitute the heart of Congress. In committees, policy is formulated, reputations are made, and power is wielded. Woodrow Wilson wrote in 1886 that "Congress in session in its committee-rooms is Congress at work."[142]

The importance of committees is seen partly in their workload. Virtually all bills introduced in Congress are referred to one or more committees. During the 103d Congress (1993–1995), 9,824 measures were introduced in Congress. Of these, 473 bills were enacted into law; most of the rest died in committee. In the 104th Congress, the House maintained nineteen regular standing committees (after eliminating three) and ninety-eight subcommittees (after eliminating twenty-five), while the Senate had seventeen standing committees and eighty-six subcommittees. According to Democratic Party caucus rules, in the House no member can chair more than one subcommittee. The Senate also imposes restrictions on chairing multiple committees. As a result, most majority party members of Congress, including very junior members, have the opportunity to wield added power as a chair. Various special, select, and joint committees are engaged in important work as well. *(See Table 33-6.)*

The average senator sits on ten committees or subcommittees, while the average House member serves on seven. In 1987 Senate committees employed about one thousand staff members, while House committees had a staff of two thousand. In 1995 the Republican House leaders slashed congressional staffs by one-third. Smaller cuts were also made in Senate staff size.

Committees are also recognized for their members' expertise. Deference by the rest of Congress to committee recommendations reflects the respect accorded committee actions by the full House and Senate.

A committee's work begins by examining its assigned legislation. According to House procedural guidelines, committees "are not infallible, but they have had long familiarity with the subject under discussion, and have made an intimate study of the particular bill before the House and after mature deliberation have made formal recommendations and, other considerations being equal, are entitled to support on the floor."[143]

After committees receive a bill they may hold hearings to solicit the opinions of government leaders and private interests on the merits of the legislation. This can be done in either the committee or an appropriate subcommittee, or in both. With a positive committee recommendation, the bill is sent to the full chamber for consideration and vote. Expertise, specialization, and experience, then, are the hallmarks of committee work and the foundation for deference to committee and subcommittee

TABLE 33-6 Standing Committees of the House and Senate, 104th Congress, 1996

Committee	Size	Party ratio	Number of sub-committees
HOUSE			
Agriculture	49	(R27/D22)	5
Appropriations	58	(R33/D25)	13
Banking and Financial Services	51	(R28/D23)	5
Budget	42	(R24/D18)	—
Commerce	49	(R27/D22)	5
Economic and Educational Opportunities	43	(R24/D19)	5
Government Reform and Oversight	51	(R28/D23)	7
House Oversight	12	(R7/D5)	—
International Relations	44	(R24/D20)	5
Judiciary	35	(R20/D15)	5
National Security	55	(R30/D25)	5
Resources	49	(R27/D22)	5
Rules	13	(R9/D4)	2
Science	50	(R27/D23)	4
Select Intelligence	16	(R9/D7)	2
Small Business	43	(R23/D20)	4
Standards of Official Conduct	10	(R5/D5)	—
Transportation and Infrastructure	61	(R33/D28)	6
Veterans' Affairs	33	(R18/D15)	3
Ways and Means	39	(R23/D16)	5
SENATE			
Agriculture, Nutrition and Forestry	18	(R10/D8)	4
Appropriations	28	(R15/D13)	13
Armed Services	21	(R11/D10)	6
Banking, Housing and Urban Affairs	16	(R9/D7)	5
Budget	22	(R12/D10)	—
Commerce, Science and Transportation	19	(R10/D9)	6
Energy and Natural Resources	20	(R11/D9)	5
Environment and Public Works	16	(R9/D7)	4
Finance	20	(R11/D9)	6
Foreign Relations	18	(R10/D8)	7
Governmental Affairs	15	(R8/D7)	3
Indian Affairs	16	(R9/D7)	—
Judiciary	18	(R10/D8)	6
Labor and Human Resources	16	(R9/D7)	4
Rules and Administration	16	(R9/D7)	—
Select Ethics	6	(R3/D3)	—
Select Intelligence	17	(R9/D8)	—
Small Business	19	(R10/D9)	—
Special Aging	19	(R10/D9)	—
Veterans' Affairs	12	(R7/D5)	—

SOURCE: *Players, Politics and Turf of the 104th Congress,* Committee Guide (Washington, D.C.: Congressional Quarterly, 1996).

actions. Members of Congress who attempt to circumvent the judgment of a committee may find their own pet legislation subject to challenge by others.[144]

All this being said, deference to committees has undergone some change since the 1970s. Committee actions are more likely to be challenged on the floor as members develop expertise on selected issues, as the norm of deference declines, and as greater decentralization takes hold. This move away from traditional committee ascendance is seen partly in challenges to committee leadership.

In the 1970s an influx of new members of Congress prompted a move to grant junior members more influence. In addition, the autonomy of subcommittees was increased, which had the effect of limiting the power of the committee chair.[145] Previously, committee chairs had had the power to name subcommittee chairs, create or abolish subcommittees, call committee meetings, and hire staff. Some committee chairs abused their power, however, by refusing to convene a committee meeting as a means of blocking legislation favored by other committee members, for example. Most were more circumspect in the use of their powers and paid careful attention to building a coalition within their committees. Still, the clamor for reform grew. This movement peaked in 1975, when three sitting House Democratic committee chairmen were deposed by the Democratic Caucus—Wright Patman (Texas) from the Banking and Currency Committee, W. R. Poage (Texas) from the Agriculture Committee, and F. Edward Hebert (La.) from the Armed Services Committee. Although seniority was violated in these three cases, it was observed in seventeen others.[146]

After 1975 seniority was observed in every instance until 1985, when the sitting chair of the Armed Services Committee, C. Melvin Price (D-Ill.), was deposed by seventh-ranked Democrat Les Aspin (Wis.). Price was eighty years old at the time, and he had not provided the committee with strong leadership.[147] Although Aspin had begun his career as a maverick liberal on the Armed Services Committee, he had earned the respect of both liberals and conservatives, and he moved quickly to soothe relations among committee members after his election.

In 1991 two House committee chairs were deposed. Glenn Anderson (D-Calif.) and Frank Annunzio (D-Ill.) lost their positions as heads of Public Works and Transportation and House Administration, respectively. Both were criticized by colleagues for their lack of leadership and effectiveness. Seniority was by no means irrelevant, however, as Anderson was succeeded by the committee's second-ranking Democrat, and Annunzio by his committee's third-ranking Democrat.

Subcommittees

Many committees, such as the House Agriculture and Appropriations committees, have long relied on subcommittees to handle most of the important work. Subcommittees hold the initial hearings and make the first recommendations on bills. Congress relies on the specialization and division of labor represented by subcommittees in dealing with the overwhelming amount of work that it faces annually.

Subcommittees in the House gained a greater role in the 1970s with the adoption of the so-called subcommittee bill of rights. Approved in 1973, this agreement ensured that subcommittees would have clearly defined jurisdictions, could meet with or without the approval of the committee chair, and would have their own budgets and staff. Moreover, committee members could choose at least one subcommittee assignment.

Seniority is also the principal basis for determining subcommittee leadership positions, although it is violated more frequently than for committee leadership selection. From 1959 to 1981 about 5 percent of all subcommittee chairs owed their positions to violations of seniority. This percentage remained constant both before and after the changes of the 1970s.[148]

The number of subcommittees has grown, and their workload has increased as well. In the 1950s subcommittees held about 30 percent of all hearings. By the late 1970s this figure had increased to more than 90 percent. Even though the number of subcommittees in Congress was reduced by Democratic leaders in 1993 and by Republican leaders in 1995, their impact was and is felt in committee work, as well as on the chamber floor, where the extension of specialization and decentralization is reflected in the key influence often exerted by subcommittee chairs acting as legislative shepherds. The greater role of subcommittees also has meant that they have generated even more business—such as hearings and press conferences—in Congress.[149]

Leaders

Since the post–Civil War period, when the modern two-party system was established in Congress, congressional leadership has been based on partisan divisions. Although members of Congress are elected as representatives of small geographic regions, they also are elected as Republicans or Democrats. The party that holds the numerical majority in each house uses that majority to select chamber leaders.

In the House the chief chamber leader is the Speaker, who also serves as the leader of the majority party. *(See Table 33-7.)* Each party then has its majority and minority floor leaders (depending on which party holds a numerical majority) and majority and minority assistant floor leaders, called whips.

The Senate has no position comparable to that of the House Speaker. As specified in the Constitution, the U.S. vice president serves as president of the Senate, but this position is ceremonial, and the vice president participates only to cast a tie-breaking vote. The next highest officer is the president pro tempore, also a ceremonial position, which is awarded to the most senior member of the majority party of the Senate. The most important Senate leaders are the majority and minority floor leaders, followed by the majority and minority whips.

While the committee system is a source of decentralization in Congress, congressional leaders work to provide centralization, coherence, and a measure of party discipline to their chambers. The principal job of the leaders is to rally support for, or opposition to, partisan programs. To do this, they negotiate with committee leaders, resolve jurisdictional disputes between committees, schedule floor action for bills, use rules and procedures to best advantage, and gather support for important votes.

Leadership in the modern Congress is problematic compared with leadership patterns of the past. In the Senate of the 1950s, for example, Majority Leader Lyndon Johnson held more personal authority than his successors from the 1970s to the present. A few senior, mostly southern leaders prevailed in the Senate during Johnson's tenure; thus, he could advance his goals by dealing with a smaller number of individuals. Decision making itself was more centralized, since fewer committees existed. Staff

TABLE 33-7 Speakers of the House, 1899–1995

Speaker	Dates of service as Speaker	Years of service	Years in House before election as Speaker
David B. Henderson (R-Iowa)	1899–1903	4	16
Joseph G. Cannon (R-Ill.)	1903–1911	8	28
Champ Clark (D-Mo.)	1911–1919	8	16
Frederick H. Gillett (R-Mass.)	1919–1925	6	26
Nicholas Longworth (R-Ohio)	1925–1931	6	20
John N. Garner (D-Texas)	1931–1933	2	28
Henry T. Rainey (D-Ill.)	1933–1934	1	28
Joseph W. Byrns (D-Tenn.)	1935–1936	1	26
William B. Bankhead (D.-Ala.)	1936–1940	4	19
Sam Rayburn (D-Texas)	1940–1947, 1949–1953, 1955–1961	17	27
Joseph W. Martin Jr. (R-Mass.)	1947–1949, 1953–1955	4	22
John W. McCormack (D-Mass.)	1962–1971	9	34
Carl Albert (D-Okla.)	1971–1977	6	24
Thomas P. O'Neill Jr. (D-Mass.)	1977–1987	10	24
James C. Wright Jr. (D-Texas)	1987–1989	2	32
Thomas S. Foley (D-Wash.)	1989–1995	6	25
Newt Gingrich (R-Ga.)	1995–	—	16
AVERAGE[a]		5.9	24.7

SOURCES: Roger H. Davidson and Walter J. Oleszek, *Congress and Its Members* (Washington, D.C.: CQ Press, 1985), 175; *Congressional Quarterly Weekly Report*, various issues.

NOTES: The House was technically without a Speaker for short periods following the deaths of Rainey and Rayburn. Congress had adjourned, and their successors were not elected until the next Congress convened. a. Excluding Gingrich.

resources were controlled by a few senior members, the Senate workload was smaller than in later years, its junior members were far less independent-minded than contemporary junior senators, and the institution employed more closed, secretive decision making.[150]

Modern congressional leaders have limited resources at their disposal. Nevertheless, they can employ persuasion, use bill scheduling authority to reward or punish, influence committee assignments, appoint special committees, direct campaign contributions toward or away from members, and use White House contacts to exert pressure.

Informal Caucuses

In addition to the fragmenting effects of the committee system, leaders must contend with a vast array of informal caucuses, groups, alliances, cliques, and coalitions that serve to unify like-minded congressional groups. Each party in each chamber has its own party caucus, incorporating a number of particular policy- and issue-related concerns. The House Democratic Party caucus also was used to institute many of the reforms of the 1970s. The Boll Weevils, an important party caucus of the 1950s and 1960s composed of conservative southern Democrats, were energized during the 1980s, when they provided President Reagan with key support for his conservative agenda.

Of the other unofficial congressional groups (technically called "legislative service organizations") formed in recent years, some are active and influential, although others are paper organizations that exist mostly to attract favorable public attention. Some state caucuses, composed of representatives from the larger states, have been influential in promoting state and regional concerns.

Various private interests also have encouraged the establishment of congressional caucuses. The American Mushroom Institute, for example, inspired the creation of the Mushroom Caucus in 1977 to protect mushroom producers from foreign competition. And a variety of ethnic groups have promoted ethnic caucuses in Congress. Among the best known and most influential are the black, women's, and Hispanic caucuses.

Regional and economic interests have prompted the formation of caucuses as well. Representatives of the northeastern states, for example, formed a "Frost Belt" coalition to stem what they believed to be a flow of resources from the Northeast to the Sunbelt states. The Steel Caucus was formed to promote steel-related economic interests.

Assessments of the political power of these groups are divided. Without question, some caucuses have been influential in the passage of important legislation. Some observers view the groups as a positive basis around which like-minded legislators can organize to promote legitimate interests. Critics complain that these caucuses simply add to the list of parochial interests that must be satisfied to transact important business. As House Speaker Tip O'Neill observed, the "House has over-caucused itself."[151]

Consequences

The sum total of these organizational characteristics points to an institution where centrifugal forces predominate, despite the best efforts of chamber leaders. This situation invites presidential leadership in the legislative sphere. As Randall Ripley, an expert on Congress, has observed, "The principal centralizing factor in the legislative equation remains outside Congress in the form of the president and the institutional presidency."[152]

Presidents seeking to establish a positive working relationship with Congress turn first to their party leaders in Congress. This helps strengthen the hand of the president, since it demonstrates respect for the opinions of chamber leaders. Likewise, it helps party leaders, as it allows them to represent themselves to the rest of the chamber as a presidential conduit. In addition, presidents must show sensitivity toward other important congressional leaders, including committee chairs, caucus leaders, and influential private interests. President Reagan, for example, launched a multipronged effort in 1981 to win congressional approval of his controversial economic program. He persuaded several governors to hold meetings with undecided legislators; he contacted Boll Weevil (that is, southern conservative) Democrats to line up their support; he sent aides into key congressional districts to rally public pressure on behalf of the program; and he made a nationwide television appeal to bolster support. The result was enactment of the program.[153]

In 1994 President Clinton won enactment of a $30 billion crime package after a fierce struggle with Republicans, but also with key elements within his party. In particular, many rural conservative Democrats opposed the bill because it included a ban on the sale and possession of nineteen types of assault weapons. Many members of the congressional Black Caucus opposed the bill for a different reason: it included a provision barring the use of statistics to demonstrate racial bias in criminal cases involving the death penalty, and it expanded the number of federal death penalty crimes. On an initial House vote in August, the president's bill was defeated, thanks to the defection of fifty-eight Democrats (mostly rural conservatives and eleven African American representatives). After considerable White House pressure, the bill was brought back for a second vote ten days later. This time, the bill passed, thanks to the Clinton administration's ability to win over the votes of four black representatives and several moderate Republicans.

Presidential success turns on the president's recognition that Congress incorporates numerous decision points. A lack of support at any point can mean the end of a presidential initiative.

PARTISAN BALANCE

According to an oft-stated aphorism, the most important single factor accounting for congressional voting patterns is political party affiliation. It is evident, however, that other factors also affect congressional voting, including those tied to region, ideology, and peer influence. Students of Congress typically examine roll call votes when studying the influence of political party and other factors, as most important votes are conducted by roll call. Such studies have found that political party voting—those votes in which a majority of one party opposes a majority of the other party—has declined during the twentieth century. Early in the century about two-thirds of all roll call votes were party votes; that is, for these two-thirds of roll call votes, a majority of Democrats voted one way, and a majority of Republicans voted the other way. By the post–World War II period, however, that proportion had fallen to about 50 percent, and then to 40 percent during the 1970s. Despite this trend, from the 1960s to the 1980s Republicans and Democrats from both houses still supported their parties about 70 percent of the time. And during the first three years of the Clinton presidency, party voting in Congress increased to record levels over the previous several years. Admittedly, these apparently strong partisan trends may mask other factors such as region, ideology, or leadership pressure.[154] (See Table 33-8.)

The presence of party voting also is evident in the interest group ratings of congressional voting records undertaken to observe support for liberal, conservative, and labor-related concerns, for example. Such ratings show that Democrats generally receive high scores from labor and liberal groups, whereas Republicans receive high scores from conservative groups.[155]

To the extent that party voting occurs in Congress, it is beneficial to the president who belongs to the majority party. If this is not the case, the president must endeavor to split the majority party coalition and woo support for the minority party. But the president wins no guarantees of loyalty simply by belonging to the party controlling Congress. In 1978, for example, Democratic House Speaker Tip O'Neill and Majority Leader Robert Byrd both deserted President Carter by voting to override his veto of a major public works bill. Although the veto was upheld, many Democrats defended the public works program for the benefits it provided to local constituencies.

In 1993 Democratic Majority Leader Richard Gephardt (Mo.) and Majority Whip David Bonior (Mich.) deserted Democratic President Bill Clinton over approval of the NAFTA agreement. The free trade agreement was strongly opposed by labor unions, a traditionally strong force within the Democratic Party. Bonior in particular was strongly pressured to oppose NAFTA because of the strength of the automobile unions in his home state of Michigan.

The limitations of party ties are illustrated even more clearly by the Johnson presidency. During the Eighty-ninth Congress (1965–1966), Johnson enjoyed a Democratic Party advantage in the House of 295 Democrats to 140 Republicans (more than two to one). The legislative accomplishments of that Congress were prolific and well known, including major bills dealing with civil rights, education, and many other social programs. After the 1966 elections the Democrats lost forty-seven seats in the House, so that the partisan split was then 248 to 187. Although this was still a sizable favorable margin for Johnson and the Democrats, the president found it necessary to draw on liberal Republicans for support. On issues such as rent supplements, open housing, and poverty programs, Johnson lost his working majority, despite having a sixty-one-vote cushion within his party.[156] Presidents Eisenhower and Reagan were able to achieve important successes despite the absence of majority support in one or both houses of Congress.

PRESIDENTIAL LOBBYISTS

Although the president and the executive branch are now an institutionalized part of the lawmaking process, representatives of the executive branch engage in congressional lobbying, as do private interests.

Executive lobbying begins, but does not end, with the White House. Its legislative liaison office is relatively small. Under the

TABLE 33–8 Congressional Voting in Support of the President's Position, 1954–1994 (percent)

President and year	House			Senate		
	All Democrats	Southern Democrats	Republicans	All Democrats	Southern Democrats	Republicans
Eisenhower (R)						
1954	54	n.a.	n.a.	45	n.a.	82
1955	58	n.a.	67	65	n.a.	85
1956	58	n.a.	79	44	n.a.	80
1957	54	n.a.	60	60	n.a.	80
1958	63	n.a.	65	51	n.a.	77
1959	44	n.a.	76	44	n.a.	80
1960	49	n.a.	63	52	n.a.	76
Kennedy (D)						
1961	81	n.a.	41	73	n.a.	42
1962	83	71	47	76	63	48
1963	84	71	36	77	65	52
Johnson (D)						
1964	84	70	42	73	63	52
1965	83	65	46	75	60	55
1966	81	64	45	71	59	53
1967	80	65	51	73	69	63
1968	77	63	59	64	50	57
Nixon (R)						
1969	56	55	65	55	56	74
1970	64	64	79	56	62	74
1971	53	69	79	48	59	76
1972	56	59	74	52	71	77
1973	39	49	67	42	55	70
1974	52	64	71	44	60	65
Ford (R)						
1974	48	52	59	45	55	67
1975	40	48	67	53	67	76
1976	36	52	70	47	61	73
Carter (D)						
1977	69	58	46	77	71	58
1978	67	54	40	74	61	47
1979	70	58	37	75	66	51
1980	71	63	44	71	69	50
Reagan (R)						
1981	46	60	72	52	63	84
1982	43	55	70	46	57	77
1983	30	45	74	45	46	77
1984	37	47	64	45	58	81
1985	31	43	69	36	46	80
1986	26	37	69	39	56	90
1987	26	36	64	38	42	67
1988	27	34	61	51	58	73
Bush (R)						
1989	38	49	72	56	66	84
1990	26	35	65	39	49	72
1991	35	43	74	42	53	83
1992	27	38	75	33	41	75
Clinton (D)						
1993	80	81	39	87	84	30
1994	78	68	49	88	88	44

SOURCE: Norman J. Ornstein, Thomas E. Mann, and Michael J. Malbin, *Vital Statistics on Congress, 1995–1996* (Washington, D.C.: Congressional Quarterly, 1996), 206–207.

NOTES: Percentages indicate number of congressional votes supporting the president divided by the total number of votes on which the president had taken a position. The percentages are normalized to eliminate the effects of absences, as follows: support = (support)/(support + opposition). Figures are not available (n.a.) for Southern Democrats for 1954–1961, and for House Republicans in 1954.

Reagan administration, for example, it consisted of ten staff members—five who covered the House, four who covered the Senate, and liaison head Max Friedersdorf (Ken Duberstein also served in this position for a time). The office was about the same size under Clinton and his first liaison head, Howard Paster. The Office of Management and Budget, particularly its Office of Legislative Reference, conducts extensive liaison work. The latter keeps track of all bills of interest to the executive, whether substantial or minor. In addition, each executive department devotes staff to legislative matters, since these agencies have a direct stake in policy and appropriation actions taken in Congress. The Department of Defense alone has more than two hundred staff assigned to liaison work. According to one estimate, the entire executive branch has as many as fifteen hundred employees assigned to liaison efforts. Both the White House and the OMB staff coordinate departmental liaison activities.[157]

Much executive lobbying consists of routine information gathering. This task is important because it dovetails with the two-pronged nature of lobbying. Lobbyists, whether executive or otherwise, use information to press their case for or against legislation. But members of Congress also rely on lobbyists for information when they are still formulating their own views. Although lobbying by definition involves presenting a one-sided argument rather than a balanced view, lobbyists are experts whose opinions often are valued by sympathetic legislators (although White House lobbyists are not necessarily subject-matter experts in the way lobbyists for other groups are). Executive lobbyists possess not only expertise, but also the added legitimacy of being part of the government.

Liaison officials must be sensitive to the preferences and leanings of key legislators. The Carter administration, for example, resisted the creation of tax credits designed to aid private and parochial schools. Yet when it encountered an influential legislator, such as a committee chair, who strongly favored such a program, the liaison staff labored to find some compromise or alternate program that might satisfy the chair.

The Carter administration also employed a procedure known as the troublesome bills process. Early in the legislative session OMB compiled a list of bills that were likely to face difficulty in Congress. The list then was reviewed regularly by OMB, the domestic policy staff, and liaison personnel to determine what positive steps might be taken to advance these bills. The maintenance of such a list also minimized the likelihood of unwelcome surprises.

Much of the executive lobbying effort is devoted to projecting the preferences of legislators on administration-favored bills. Both the Carter and Reagan liaison staffs categorized legislators into those supporting the administration on given bills, those opposed, and those undecided. Executive lobbyists then concentrated on the undecided and those whose commitments were less than firm. The chief executive is often brought in at key moments to apply presidential prestige and personal skills to sway wavering legislators. In June 1981, for example, President Reagan contacted undecided legislators to marshal the support necessary to ensure enactment of his budget package. Even so early in Reagan's term, the liaison staff had little difficulty in identifying the key legislators.

Similar tactics were applied by Clinton in his successful effort to win passage of NAFTA. Yet Clinton's liaison chief, Howard Paster, quit after the passage of NAFTA in November 1993 because of his frustration over the administration's scatter-shot approach. That is, liaison activities were not coordinated among the liaison office, the White House, and outside experts brought in by the administration.

Liaison staff do more than just lobby; they also engage in policy making. When involved in face-to-face bargaining, liaison staff often must make promises and commitments that constitute policy agreements. For example, in a 1961 meeting with congressional leaders President Kennedy's liaison head, Lawrence O'Brien, found himself agreeing to a level and amount of coverage for the proposed new minimum wage without consulting the White House. Because such situations can arise, the liaison staff must be well informed and have the trust of the president.

Frequently, liaison staff are incorporated into other White House policy groups. Reagan's liaison chief, Max Friedersdorf, for example, participated in morning senior White House staff meetings, cabinet council meetings, weekly luncheon meetings with the president, and meetings of the Legislative Strategy Group.

Liaison is often most effective when it does not directly involve the liaison staff. If liaison staff can succeed, for example, in getting key decision makers together, a favorable and expeditious resolution may be more likely. Similarly, if a key member of Congress adopts and is willing to promote aggressively the president's position, the result is more likely to be favorable to the president. Acting as an institutional insider, a committee chair, for example, can deal effectively with his or her fellow chamber members. The Reagan administration found that House Minority Leader Robert H. Michel (R-Ill.) and Minority Whip C. Trent Lott (R-Miss.) were effective in gathering congressional support for key administration initiatives.

Personal presidential persuasion is a decisive lobbying force as well. President Carter disliked such personal lobbying, but he applied it well in a few instances, while Reagan's personal efforts often provided a needed nudge. In one instance, a bill dealing with standby petroleum allocations, championed by conservative Republican senator James A. McClure (Idaho) and opposed by the Reagan administration, passed both houses. The administration considered a veto, but it promised McClure that he could present his case for the bill to the president before the veto decision was made. After McClure did so, Reagan vetoed the bill on March 20, 1982. Both the Senate Republican leader and McClure were contacted after the veto by Reagan, who justified his action. On March 24 the Senate sustained the veto. Despite the defeat of a bill important to McClure, hard feelings were minimized by regular communication and presidential involvement.[158]

President Bush also relied frequently on personal persuasion.

Late in 1989 Bush vetoed a bill that would have protected Chinese students studying in the United States from deportation to China after the expiration of their visas. This move was taken in the aftermath of the student-led democracy movement in China. Although supportive of the measure, Bush vetoed it, saying that he preferred to implement the measure administratively. He also argued that the congressional action was an infringement of executive authority. Congressional leaders were outraged by the action, and a successful override was considered likely. On January 24, 1990, the House overrode the veto 390–25. The next day, however, Bush's veto was sustained in the Senate by a vote of 62–37, five votes short of the necessary two-thirds. The surprising result was attributed to Bush's forceful personal intervention, including phone calls and personal notes. Bush argued strongly that an override would harm the president's prestige abroad, and that the Chinese students would be protected.

In 1994 President Clinton managed to revive his $30 billion crime bill after the House had initially voted to kill it. Usually, a negative floor vote on a bill spells the bill's end for the balance of the congressional session. Clinton refused to accept defeat, however, and he launched a strenuous personal campaign that included speeches around the country, high-profile meetings with law enforcement organizations, and personal lobbying of swing members of Congress. Junior moderate House Republicans found themselves in the unusual circumstance of bargaining with a president of the opposing party. Ten days after the crime bill's initial defeat, a second House vote was held, and the bill was passed and signed into law in September.

THE PRESIDENT AND THE PEOPLE

Abraham Lincoln once observed, "Public sentiment is everything. With public sentiment nothing can fail, without it nothing can succeed." History has confirmed this observation: presidents with a high popular standing are more successful in dealing with Congress than presidents with a low public standing.

Political scientist George C. Edwards III has proposed two explanations for the close connection between a president's popular standing and the willingness of Congress to support the president's program. One posits that legislators believe it is their job to reflect public opinion. When the president's public standing is high, members of Congress are inclined to follow public dictates by supporting the president because such support is in accordance with popular preferences. When the president's standing falls, Congress moves to reflect changing popular sentiments.

The second explanation ties congressional responses to legislators' own electoral fortunes. According to this view, members of Congress believe that their constituents will respond to congressional support for, or opposition to, presidential initiatives. They thus see a link between their electoral fortunes and the president's popular standing. Members of Congress who oppose a popular president may risk losing support in their home districts. Similarly, opposition to an unpopular president may improve their standing back home.[159] The close electoral tie between the president and Congress is reflected in the congressional seats gained by the president's party in every presidential election year from 1904 to 1992 except six (1908, 1916, 1956, 1960, 1988, 1992). Conversely, from 1880 to 1994, the president's party lost seats in every midterm election, with one exception (1934).

These two explanations correspond to those offered by an earlier study, which found that popular perceptions of the president overshadowed popular opinions of Congress, leading to a situation in which Congress was evaluated more positively when the president was regarded more positively, even when Congress was controlled by the opposition party. In short, "a large portion of the general public evaluates Congress by first assessing the President."[160] This finding is supported by the fact that citizens are better informed about, and more interested in, the presidency than in Congress.

Regardless of the explanation for the connection between congressional support for the president and the president's public standing, the connection itself is well accepted. For the years 1953 to 1976, Edwards examined the connection between the president's popular standing (as measured in Gallup polls) and congressional support for presidential programs (as measured in roll call votes). He found a high correlation between the two, but he noted that members of the House, who face the voters every two years, were more likely to respond to fluctuations in the president's popularity than senators. This relationship also was found to be closely related to partisanship.[161]

Presidential Coattails

A successful presidential candidate who is sufficiently popular may aid other party members running for lower offices. When voters decide to vote for members of Congress partly because of the popularity of the presidential candidate at the top of the ticket, the presidential candidate is said to possess coattails. Thus the popularity of a president or presidential candidate can have a direct, measurable effect on members of Congress.

The coattail phenomenon is often discussed, but it is also often misunderstood. Many people assume, for example, that the wider the margin of victory for a presidential candidate, the greater the candidate's pulling power. Many also assume that the coattail effect is present in every presidential election. Neither assumption is necessarily true. In 1972, for example, Richard Nixon was reelected president by one of the largest margins in the century—more than 60 percent. Yet the Republican Party picked up only twelve seats in the House and actually lost two seats in the Senate. Indeed, the Republicans might have done even worse had Nixon not done as well, but he demonstrated little in the way of coattails, especially when 1972 is compared with other presidential elections. In fact, in a tight presidential race, an incumbent president may benefit from a reverse coattail effect—that is, the president may be helped by support for party candidates lower on the ballot.

In 1964, by way of contrast, President Johnson too was elected by a margin of more than 60 percent. Yet the Democrats gained thirty-seven seats in the House and one in the Senate, enhancing the already sizable Democratic majority in Congress.

A related question is the size of the parties' majorities in Congress before the election. If one party holds a large congressional majority before an election and gains only modestly after the election, a greater victory may have occurred than if the party holds a slim lead in Congress but makes the same modest numerical gain.

The coattail effect is important because presidential candidates like to bring as many party allies as possible into Congress to ensure greater legislative success there. Members of Congress elected because of the popularity of the president also may feel a sense of gratitude, identity, and even obligation to the chief executive. A member of Congress who shares party affiliation with the president but feels no similar sense of attachment is more likely to behave independently of the president.

Adequate understanding of the coattail effect depends on understanding the motivations of voters as well as the information derived from vote statistics. The first of these is difficult to study, in part because it is extremely difficult to determine whether voters base their votes for lower offices on their choice for president. Although one cannot determine voter motivations from election results, this source of information can help explain the nature and effect of coattails.

One study examined the coattail effect on House races coinciding with presidential elections from 1952 to 1980. It concluded that seventy-six coattail victories occurred during the period (an average of 9.5 per election), ranging from a high of seventeen in Johnson's 1964 race to a low of four in Carter's 1976 election. Of the seventy-six victories, seventy-five involved races in which there was no incumbent. Clearly, a congressional candidate's best chance to benefit from the coattail effect occurs for open seats in which the incumbent has either retired, been defeated in a primary, or died. (*See Table 33-9.*)

Also according to this study, a president who wins more votes in a district than a House candidate of the same party is not necessarily demonstrating coattails. Such a difference in votes actually may indicate weak presidential coattails, because the presi-

TABLE 33-10 Ticket Splitting between Presidential and House Candidates, 1900–1992

Year	Districts[a]	Districts with split results[b] Number	Districts with split results[b] Percentage
1900	295	10	3.4
1904	310	5	1.6
1908	314	21	6.7
1912	333	84	25.2
1916	333	35	10.5
1920	344	11	3.2
1924	356	42	11.8
1928	359	68	18.9
1932	355	50	14.1
1936	361	51	14.1
1940	362	53	14.6
1944	367	41	11.2
1948	422	90	21.3
1952	435	84	19.3
1956	435	130	29.9
1960	437	114	26.1
1964	435	145	33.3
1968	435	139	32.0
1972	435	192	44.1
1976	435	124	28.5
1980	435	143	32.8
1984	435	190	43.7
1988	435	148	34.0
1992	435	100	23.0

SOURCE: Norman J. Ornstein, Thomas E. Mann, and Michael J. Malbin, *Vital Statistics on Congress, 1995–1996* (Washington, D.C.: Congressional Quarterly, 1996), 70.

NOTES: a. Before 1952 complete data are not available on every congressional district.   b. Congressional districts carried by a presidential candidate of one party and a House candidate of another party.

dent is unable to extend presidential popularity to the congressional candidate. In close elections such as those in 1960, 1968, and 1976, the president often ran behind or on a par with congressional candidates who nevertheless benefited from coattails.[162]

Many observers believe that the coattail effect is on the decline. This decline has been attributed to the decline of straight-ticket voting among voters and the decline of political parties as vital forces in national elections, reflected in the tendency for candidates to rely more on their own resources (or those of nonparty organizations such as political action committees) to finance election campaigns. This does not imply, however, that the coattail effect is related solely to party ties.

The decline of the coattail effect is illustrated by the rise in the number of congressional districts with split results—that is, House districts where the president won a majority of the vote, but the district elected a legislator from the opposition party. (*See Table 33-10.*) The number of districts with split ticket results has increased dramatically since 1920, with a high point reached in 1972. (One would expect a 50 percent result if there were no relationship at all between presidential and congressional elections.

Despite the best efforts of presidential candidates and party

TABLE 33-9 Coattail Victories, House Elections

Year	President	Number of coattails	President tied or ran behind
1952	Eisenhower	13	0
1956	Eisenhower	8	0
1960	Kennedy	7	6
1964	Johnson	17	2
1968	Nixon	10	9
1972	Nixon	12	1
1976	Carter	4	3
1980	Reagan	5	1
TOTAL		76	22

SOURCE: George C. Edwards III, *The Public Presidency: The Pursuit of Popular Support* (New York: St. Martin's Press, 1983), 26. Copyright © 1983 by St. Martin's Press. Reprinted by permission of the publisher.

organizations, neither may be able to exert much direct influence over the likelihood of coattails. A downturn in the economy during an election year, for example, may spell the end of coattail possibilities for the incumbent president, while an economic upturn may have the opposite effect. Nevertheless, even though the coattail effect lessened during the 1970s and 1980s, it continues to have an effect on congressional and other elections.

Midterm Elections

A similar electoral intersection between the president and Congress is observable during elections held in the middle of presidential terms. The election of all 435 members of the House and one-third of the Senate invites presidential attempts to fortify the executive's party strength in Congress. Yet the overwhelming trend has been the reverse. In every midterm election in this century, except that in 1934, the president's party has lost seats in the House. (With only a third of the Senate elected every two years, its results are a less accurate gauge of the mood of the country.) *(See Table 33-4, p. 1324.)*

This midterm dip has been labeled the "surge and decline" phenomenon. It is predicated on the assumption that the president's party usually does better during presidential years than the national partisan balance would otherwise indicate because of the strength of the winning presidential candidate. Thus, the system corrects itself in years when the president is not running, with a more nearly normal partisan balance taking hold.

The problem with this explanation is that the correlation between the presidential and congressional vote has declined during the last several decades, and congressional incumbency has become a much more important factor in explaining congressional outcomes. Two other factors also given greater weight in explaining midterm swings are the condition of the economy and the president's popularity.[163] Midterm elections are largely perceived as referenda on presidential performance during the previous two years, and the number of seats lost by the president's party—the dominant trend—is related to the state of the economy and the president's popular standing. When such indicators turn down, it is more difficult for the president's party to raise money and field strong candidates for office. If congressional members of the opposition party are not challenged by motivated, well-financed members of the president's party in the congressional races, the likelihood that the president's party will suffer is greater.

An example of this phenomenon was the 1974 midterm elections. The incumbent president until August 1974, Republican Richard Nixon, had suffered precipitously in public standing after his 1972 reelection because of the damaging revelations of the Watergate investigation. Thus, the Republicans—who also were coping with an economic downturn—found it extremely difficult to raise money and select strong candidates for office. Moreover, an unusually large number of legislators (mostly Republican) decided to retire in 1974, thereby enhancing the Democratic challengers' chances. Finally, Democratic antipathy toward Nixon (and his appointed successor, Gerald Ford, who in turn pardoned Nixon) and the Republicans was fanned by revelation of Watergate misdeeds throughout much of 1974, in part because these offenses were directed against Democratic Party leaders. As a result, Democrats at all levels were motivated to run for office, give more money, and otherwise work to defeat the party of Watergate. The net result in Congress was a gain of forty-nine Democratic seats in the House and four in the Senate. Some of the Democratic House gains occurred in districts that had been Republican strongholds.

Evaluation of the president is not the only basis for voter decisions during midterm elections. Despite the long-term erosion of partisanship, political party ties continue to play an important role. A study of midterm elections in the 1970s noted that party identification, incumbency, and personal attributes of candidates were strong predictors of voter choices.[164]

Still, the inexorable erosion of support for the president's party at midterm elections emphasizes the large shadow that the president casts over congressional elections. As the only nationally elected leader the president is a natural referent for voter choices. Moreover, some observers argue that the electorate is more likely to vote against policies or candidates than for them. Given that the president's standing is almost invariably highest at the start of the term, followed by a decline (although this decline may be mitigated by short-term factors), it is likely that at midterm a president, and his or her political party, will be hurt by critics more than helped by supporters.

It has been suggested that midterm elections may provide a source of affirmation for, or rejection of, the president's positions on the issues, but there is little reason to believe that this is true. First, experts agree that the public knows little about the positions of congressional candidates on the issues, even the controversial ones. Moreover, voters' awareness of issues during midterm elections is even lower than during presidential elections. Second, many congressional races are not competitive. In 1988, for example, of 410 House members seeking reelection, seventy-nine ran unopposed. In 1990, of 406 incumbents seeking reelection, seventy-four ran unopposed. Third, congressional candidates are likely to de-emphasize specific issues in their campaigns, focusing instead on broader abstractions such as government efficiency and invocations of political symbols. Fourth, turnout in midterm elections is low. In 1982, for example, only 38 percent of the national electorate voted. Even in the contentious 1994 midterm election, the national turnout rate was 38 percent. This level of turnout is not a measure of public opinion, and those who do vote are not representative of the population as a whole. Finally, issues that are raised in congressional campaigns are bound to vary from district to district, in part because they spring from local concerns.[165]

In 1994 Republican House candidates banded together and signed on to a set of Republican policy objectives called the "Contract with America." The signees pledged to carry out this ten-point program if elected. A Republican sweep at election time gave the new congressional Republican majority the opportunity to follow through on this promise. Many pointed to the fifty-four-seat House Republican gain as proof that the nation had rejected President Clinton's governing approach. Yet even in this election, the actual effect of national forces was far less than many supposed. For example, a national survey conducted by the *Los Angeles Times* at election time showed that fewer than 20 percent of Americans had even heard of the Contract with America; of those, more than half called it "unrealistic." Another survey, conducted by Republican pollster Richard Wirthlin, found that only 4 percent of voters had heard of and approved of the contract. In addition, the incumbency reelection rate in the House was still very high—90 percent.

High and Low Presidential Standing

Presidents who stand tall in the eyes of the public hold the political high ground in their dealings with Congress. Presidents who lack high standing face a politically problematic situation in which Congress actually might gain politically from jousting with the president. Presidents have long appreciated the political clout accompanying popular approval, especially when it comes to dealing with Congress.

In the aftermath of his overwhelming victory in 1964, President Johnson moved ahead quickly to enact major legislation, particularly the highly controversial Voting Rights Act of 1965. Despite warnings that the bill was too explosive and that he ought to bide his time more carefully, Johnson knew from his years of Senate experience that presidents had to act when their popularity stood high.

Many presidents before and since have seen the wisdom in capitalizing on public standing to promote important programs in Congress. When presidents are reelected to a second term, their annual programs are infused with new proposals as part of the postelection mandate. By the end of their terms, however, a far larger proportion are recycled proposals from earlier in the administration. This trend reflects realization that the president no longer possesses the popular mandate necessary to mount successful drives in Congress for major new legislation. The progressive erosion of the president's public standing results in a more assertive Congress and a less influential president.

PRESIDENTIAL LEADERSHIP SKILLS

Shortly before leaving office, Harry Truman observed that his successor, former general Dwight Eisenhower, would be in for a rude awakening when he assumed the presidency. Truman predicted: "He'll sit here . . . and say, 'Do this! Do that!' *And nothing will happen.* Poor Ike—it won't be a bit like the Army. He'll find it very frustrating."[166]

Political scientist Richard Neustadt made a vital point about the modern American presidency when he quoted President Truman, his former boss. In observing that presidential power to command was both overrated and overstated, he was arguing that presidential power was primarily the power to persuade. Reliance on persuasion and bargaining has become a hallmark of the presidency, Neustadt observed, because the responsibilities, demands, and expectations now inherent in the presidential office have outstripped the powers of the office. As a consequence, presidents must rely on informal bargaining skills to accomplish their goals.

Concern for the appropriate level of presidential leadership skills was articulated by two early twentieth-century presidents. Theodore Roosevelt advocated an aggressive stewardship role for the president. He argued that the president was entitled, even obliged, to act as necessary to promote the needs, goals, and interests of the people, unless such action was explicitly unconstitutional. Roosevelt's successor, William Howard Taft, called instead for a restrained or Whiggish view of the presidency, proposing instead that presidents could and should exercise only those powers explicitly granted in the Constitution.[167] Both these approaches require some level of presidential leadership skills, but they vary widely as to the scope and limitation of these skills.

While the philosophical debate over the relative merits of the stewardship and Whiggish views of presidential leadership persists, no modern president can ignore the fundamentals of effective executive leadership. To win enactment of important (and therefore usually controversial) legislation, the president cannot simply submit legislation and sit back to wait for the finished product. Specialized coalitions often must be built in Congress, even across party lines. Lyndon Johnson, for example, admitted that he could not have gained passage of key civil rights legislation without the support of moderate Republicans, even though his party held substantial majorities in both houses.

Often considered one of the most adept legislative strategists ever to occupy the White House, Johnson knew more than most about the key leadership role of the president. Johnson summarized his philosophy when he said: "There is only one way for a President to deal with the Congress, and that is continuously, incessantly, and without interruption."

Although many factors other than the president's leadership skills play a vital role in shaping presidential-congressional relations, presidents are nevertheless the personifications of their administrations. They take personal credit for successes and personal blame for failures (although seldom willingly). More to the point, presidents are personal, readily available reservoirs of influence. They are an administration's handiest political balm.

Some presidents such as Lyndon Johnson bring with them intimate knowledge of Congress, while others acquire such knowledge on the job. As president, Johnson paid close attention to even small legislative details, and he always made himself available to members of Congress who wanted to see him.

Presidents also learn that the timing of legislative maneuvers often contributes to a successful outcome. For example, successful passage of Reagan's economic program owed much to the rise in Reagan's popularity following the 1981 attempt on his life. Lyndon Johnson similarly found that sending bills to Congress at the right time was important to a favorable outcome.

Consultation also plays a vital role in executive-legislative relations. Presidents who do not bother to consult with key mem-

A president's influence over Congress varies with each president's personality. Lyndon Johnson, aggressive as Senate majority leader, was just as comfortable employing embarrassment and bullying to get his way as president, in this case with Democratic senator Theodore Francis Green of Rhode Island.

bers of Congress often find that they have made opponents out of potential allies. President Nixon, for example, probably lost the support of Republican senator Margaret Chase Smith for the Carswell nomination to the Supreme Court when his administration informed members of the Senate that she was going to support Carswell; the truth was she had not made up her mind. Smith eventually voted against Carswell.

Frequently, presidents have found their cabinets to be an important source of expertise and political pressure. Johnson devoted much cabinet meeting time to pending legislation, and he also directed his cabinet secretaries to apply their departments to legislative ends. Clinton used his cabinet secretaries often to press key measures through Congress, even when the bill in question did not relate directly to the departments represented by the secretaries. To win passage of the Brady bill in 1993 (imposing a five-day waiting period and background checks on handgun purchases) and a major crime bill in 1994, Clinton pressed several cabinet secretaries into service, including Robert Reich, secretary of labor; Donna Shalala, secretary of health and human services; and Henry Cisneros, secretary of housing and urban development. Aside from lobbying efforts, cabinet secretaries and lower department officials often testify before congressional committees, and the president can shape that testimony to advantage.

One of the president's most important legislative resources is a personal appeal. Whether over the phone or face to face, such an appeal is usually an effective (although by no means unfailing) means of winning support. Some presidents—such as Johnson, Ford, Reagan, and Clinton—were frequent and effective users of personal appeals. Others—such as Eisenhower and Carter—were less comfortable with the personal approach. Richard Nixon actively avoided substantive personal contact with members of Congress. Phone calls from members to the

president were screened carefully, with most not even getting through to the president himself. His view of himself as more of an administrator than a power broker, as well as his apparent aloofness and detachment, did little to endear Nixon to members of Congress. Admittedly, direct access to the president is normally limited, even for members of Congress. But some presidents, such as Reagan, Bush, and Clinton, placed greater emphasis on such direct links.

As with any resource, the effect of direct involvement by the president may decline if employed too frequently. Presidents usually reserve personal pressure for close votes on important bills and for instances when the president's prestige is on the line. A good example of both of these cases is presidential attempts to defeat a veto override vote. In 1986, for example, Reagan tried to win support for his veto of a congressional effort to block an arms sale to Saudi Arabia by personally contacting twelve senators. One senator who changed his vote to support Reagan's veto was John P. East (R-N.C.). He was persuaded that "the president should be allowed to make foreign policy without being managed at every turn by Congress." In this instance Reagan's veto was upheld by the precise minimum of thirty-four votes.

Although there is no consensus on the extent and effectiveness of bargaining, it is indisputably an integral presidential resource. President Kennedy, for example, struck a bargain with Sen. Robert S. Kerr (D-Okla.) over an Arkansas River project. (The Arkansas River runs through Kerr's home state of Oklahoma.) When Kennedy asked Kerr for help in getting an investment tax credit bill out of the Senate Finance Committee, Kerr responded by raising the Arkansas River bill, insisting on a trade. Kennedy replied, "You know, Bob, I never really understood that Arkansas River bill before today." Kerr's project was supported and enacted; in exchange, Kerr backed the Kennedy bill.

Sometimes, presidents fail to engage in enough bargaining and consultation with Congress. Among Clinton's first priorities when he assumed office in 1993 was passage of an economic stimulus package. Originally offered as a $20 billion package, Sen. Robert Byrd (D-W. Va.) assured Clinton that the bill would sail through Congress. Yet Clinton did not consult more carefully with other key congressional leaders, and the bill was eventually stripped down to $1 billion before it was sent to the president.

Every president engages in some degree of bargaining, but the technique has its limitations. First, bargaining resources are limited. The president cannot afford to use bargaining or favor trading as a principal means of obtaining action. If bargains are made frequently and explicitly, everyone in Congress will likely want to make such deals. Like personal contact, bargains are most effective when used prudently and implicitly. Moreover, members of Congress may not be swayed by the bargaining option, especially if they are motivated by such factors as constituent pressure, ideology, or party ties. Although presidents use bargaining to pursue their policy objectives, most of the pressure for bargains emanates from Congress.

Sometimes, presidential influence extends to applying coercion. Strictly speaking, the president can do little to twist arms. Some presidents, such as Eisenhower, found strong-arm tactics distasteful. Even after repeated attacks against him and his administration by Sen. Joseph R. McCarthy (R-Wis.), Eisenhower declined to respond aggressively. Johnson, on the other hand, was not reluctant to employ embarrassment, bullying, and threats to promote his ends.

The Nixon administration also employed arm-twisting tactics, although Nixon himself avoided personal involvement. These tactics came into play in 1969 over such controversial issues as the antiballistic missile system and the Haynsworth and Carswell nominations to the Supreme Court. In addition, the Nixon administration threatened rebellious representatives with reelection trouble. A well-known example is the administration's support of James L. Buckley, who was running for the Senate from New York in 1970. Because the Republican incumbent, Charles E. Goodell, had become a strong administration critic, the administration threw its support informally behind Buckley, the nominee of the New York Conservative Party. The weight of the Nixon administration helped Buckley defeat Goodell and the Democratic nominee, Richard Ottinger. Despite this and other periodic successes for the arm-twisting technique, it frequently does not work, and it often serves to fan and fortify opposition.

Presidents can provide a variety of services to members of Congress. These include presidential visits to home districts, fund raising, assistance with favored pork barrel and other projects, patronage appointments, constituent service assistance (such as giving out presidential memorabilia and signed photographs, arranging special White House tours, interceding with federal agencies), access to privileged or other inside information, campaign assistance, and personal favors and amenities for members of Congress (from cuff links to choice theater tickets). The use of amenities and social courtesies builds positive personal relations. Early in his term President Lyndon Johnson was careful to apportion credit for important legislation, but as Vietnam-related criticism mounted, he began to refer to programs as his own, which further eroded his relations with Congress. As with other tactical devices, services and amenities are limited in effectiveness.

Besides these direct means of influence, presidents can marshal outside pressure, including that exerted by constituents. Thus, presidents may appeal directly to geographic or other constituencies to urge that pressure be placed on representatives. President Kennedy's legislative chief, Lawrence O'Brien, frequently contacted state governors to urge them to pressure state representatives. Federal agencies also may be called on to mobilize support for presidential policies. Farmers, unions, business groups, and regional or other interests may be persuaded to side with the administration in attempting to swing congressional support. President Johnson forged a coalition of the major religious denominations and educational groups in support of the Elementary and Secondary Education Act of 1965 even before the bill was introduced. In fact, Johnson deliberately held the bill until both the National Education Association and the National Catholic Welfare Conference agreed on the bill's basics.[168]

The sheer length of this list of leadership tools available to the president may seem to provide convincing evidence that presidential persuasion is irresistible when applied firmly and consistently. Yet the actual presidential record suggests almost the opposite. Many examples of all of these factors in operation can be cited, but in fact the persuasive tools and abilities of presidents constitute only one category of factors that influence the legislative process. One penetrating analysis has concluded that the use of presidential skills in influencing Congress has been overstated, partly because of the tendency of such activities to attract headlines. According to this study, "Presidential legislative skills do not seem to affect support for presidential policies, despite what conventional wisdom leads us to expect."[169]

The Public Presidency

Presidents often use their rhetorical skills to bypass Congress and sway public opinion. The potency of aroused public sentiment already has been summarized. It is not surprising, then, that presidents often seek public favor to build support for major legislation or to head off possible opposition.

One of the best-known examples of presidents seeking public support to sway Congress occurred before the era of television. In 1919 Woodrow Wilson stumped the country to rally support for the beleaguered League of Nations treaty that was then before the Senate. Although he gave forty speeches in twenty-two days, Wilson's efforts fell short. He suffered exhaustion, then a stroke, and the Senate defeated the treaty by a fifteen-vote margin.

President Johnson also found a public appeal desirable, and

even necessary, to impel congressional action. When Johnson's tax surcharge bill stalled in the House Ways and Means Committee, he appealed to the people through several public forums, including his 1968 State of the Union address. The impasse was eventually overcome, despite some congressional resentment over the public approach.

Early in his administration President Carter used a series of television addresses to rally public support for his proposed energy legislation. To symbolize his commitment to energy conservation, Carter wore a cardigan sweater instead of the traditional suit jacket. Despite his appeal to the public, Carter's energy program faced difficult sailing in Congress.

To cite a more recent example, Ronald Reagan met increasing opposition from both Congress and the country to his efforts to cut back on education aid programs in 1983. (Polls indicated popular disapproval of Reagan's cutbacks by a two-to-one ratio.) In response, the White House launched a communications offensive, emphasizing the themes of excellence in education, merit pay for teachers, and greater classroom discipline, and Reagan made more than twenty-five personal appearances to repeat these themes. Later polls indicated that the public supported Reagan's education program by a two-to-one ratio, even though no programmatic changes had occurred. By altering public perceptions, Reagan also helped to alleviate pressure from Congress.

The Bush administration recognized from the start of the crisis with Iraq in the fall of 1990 the importance of rallying public support in behalf of military intervention. Throughout the fall, Bush sought to impress on the American people what he thought was a dire threat from Iraq. He likened Iraq's leader, Saddam Hussein, to Hitler; he spoke of the importance of Middle East oil; he argued repeatedly that Iraq's human rights abuses were intolerable actions that the United States and the rest of the world community could not ignore. The effort to rally public support for military action was buttressed by the Kuwaiti government, which hired the Washington public relations firm of Hill and Knowlton to launch a vigorous media campaign to rally American sympathy and support.

Presidents also try to take advantage of changing public sentiments. Immediately after the 1968 assassination of Martin Luther King Jr., President Johnson pressed congressional leaders to act on his Fair Housing Act, which had been stalled in committee for more than two years. Within seven days of King's death the bill was signed into law. One day after Robert F. Kennedy's assassination in 1968, Congress enacted the Omnibus Crime Control and Safe Streets Act, even though the bill had been tied up in Congress for more than a year. In both instances, dramatic swings in public sentiment resulting from unforeseen events provided the impetus needed to push a White House-favored proposal through Congress.

The presidential public appeal is nothing new, but many political scientists have noted that modern communications technology, along with political changes, have encouraged presidents to use the public forum to pressure Congress. Presidents can command network television time almost at will, and no modern president would think of launching a major political effort involving Congress without incorporating public communications channels. Indeed, presidents have progressively expanded their prime time exposure. President Clinton expanded his media exposure opportunities by making appearances on television and radio talk shows. Using a technique popularized in the 1992 election, Clinton periodically made himself available to such talk-show hosts as Don Imus (a New York City radio personality) in order to answer critics or emphasize issues of importance.

Political scientist Samuel Kernell has argued that modern

FIGURE 33-2 Presidential Addresses, 1929–1990 (Yearly Averages for First Three Years of First Term)

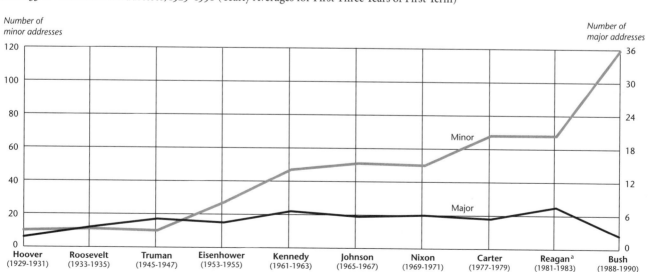

Source: Samuel Kernell, *Going Public: New Strategies of Presidential Leadership* (Washington, D.C.: CQ Press, 1993), 92.
Notes: To eliminate public activities inspired by concerns of reelection rather than governing, only the first three years have been tabulated. For this reason, Gerald Ford's record of public activities during his two and one-half years in office have been ignored.   a. The Reagan entry only includes television addresses. With radio included, Reagan averaged twenty-four addresses a year.

presidents "go public" more than their predecessors; they attempt to place themselves, and their proposals, directly before the people in order to improve their political fortunes in Washington. These efforts may target particular groups or segments of the population, but since virtually any presidential action is news, national coverage usually results.

The consequence of this trend is that presidents, their allies, and their foes have all become much more concerned with public relations as a political tactic. Both allies and critics agree that, among modern presidents, "No president has enlisted public strategies to better advantage than did Ronald Reagan."[170] Reagan's acting background dovetailed with a growing understanding of the influence of presidential images to produce a presidency that cultivated Reagan's national image as a means of promoting his congressional agenda.

The idea that modern presidents can obtain powerful political capital from public support is taken further by Theodore J. Lowi.[171] He argues that because the country has entered an era in which the government is centered around the presidency, presidential appeals have taken on a plebiscitary nature—that is, presidents seek popular support or even adoration, as did the autocrats of ancient Rome and the more recent French empires. And, according to Lowi, the forceful ascendance of the personal presidency has come at the expense of the separation of powers (especially in a denigration of the role of Congress) and the two-party system. The cult of presidential personality has been accompanied by expansion of the formal and informal powers of the presidency, although these heightened powers cannot match public expectations. Under these conditions the president may operate outside the traditional presidential-congressional relations to impel Congress to act according to the president's wishes.

Thus, the powers and skills most important to presidents seeking an effective presidency have changed since the 1950s. Communications skills have always been important, but past presidents known for their communications skills—such as Theodore Roosevelt, Woodrow Wilson, and Franklin Roosevelt—did not rely solely or even primarily on speech making and public oration to gain political results in Congress. Modern presidents have found public appeals to be an increasingly important supplement to the traditional bargaining with Congress. With the erosion of strong party ties, the traditional institutional and partisan links between the president and Congress have been further weakened.[172]

Presidents as Leaders

Each president has left a mark on the presidency. Historians, journalists, political scientists, and others pay close attention to the strengths and weaknesses of each president, and they often rank presidents according to their relative "greatness."[173] These rankings have been criticized for their unstated assumptions (such as the assumption that activism equals greatness), their reliance on subjective and reputational considerations, and the lack of agreement about what constitutes greatness. Yet the varying leadership styles of recent presidents reveal much about their dealings with Congress.[174] *(See also Chapter 4, Rating the Presidents, Vol. I.)*

Roosevelt. Franklin Roosevelt oversaw the expansion of the modern presidency, in particular the legislative realm. Early in his four-term presidency he shepherded through Congress the enormous volume of legislation that composed his New Deal program. And because he served as president during World War II, he benefited from the wartime deference to presidential authority. In both instances, severe national crises afforded Roosevelt singular opportunities to shape and direct legislative affairs, and even to redefine the president's role. His singular leadership skills were important as well.

As Richard Neustadt has noted, "No president in this century has had a sharper sense of personal power. . . . No modern president has been more nearly master in the White House. . . . He wanted power for its own sake; he also wanted what it could achieve."[175]

Besides the personal enjoyment he derived from the use of power, much of Roosevelt's legacy is his continued influence on the institution of the presidency. He created the Executive Office of the President and brought the Bureau of the Budget into it from the Treasury Department. He increased staff and other executive resources, and he focused these expanded resources on Congress to provide the necessary presidential leadership and to ensure the enforcement of presidential preferences.

Roosevelt also knew how to use the media and other external forces to bring pressure to bear on Congress. His celebrated fireside chats highlighted his ability to use the still new electronic medium of radio as a means of rallying public support for his political agenda. Later, during the war years, Roosevelt used the radio to instill confidence and fan patriotic fervor.

For all of Roosevelt's skill, however, he made his share of blunders and suffered his share of defeats. During his second term he miscalculated congressional (and national) sentiments when he proposed increasing the number of seats on the Supreme Court so that he could appoint additional justices more receptive to his agenda. Congress balked at Roosevelt's attempt at "court packing," and the president suffered no little political humiliation. In the 1938 primaries, Roosevelt ran pro-Roosevelt Democrats against Democratic legislators who had not been adequately receptive to many of his initiatives in Congress. With one exception, every effort failed, and southern Democrats in particular harbored resentment for years.

Truman. Harry Truman sought to extend the legislative work of his predecessor. His "Fair Deal," which emphasized economic security for Americans, was a continuation of Roosevelt's New Deal. Truman set forth a twenty-one-point program, which included proposals related to the minimum wage, urban development, national health insurance, Social Security, and full employment. Unlike his predecessor, however, Truman met vociferous opposition. In the midterm elections of 1946 the Republicans gained control of both houses of Congress for the first time since 1928, and Truman's programs were savaged, as was he in the press. Nonetheless, he challenged the Republicans head on, and in one of the great upsets in modern presidential elections, he defeated his Republican rival, Thomas E. Dewey, in 1948 and carried into office Democratic congressional majorities.

Truman could not match Roosevelt's reputation or adroit leadership, but he was not without experience and skill. Truman had served in the Senate for ten years before becoming vice president in 1945, and he both knew and respected the congressional decision-making process. But Roosevelt's death took everyone by surprise, and Truman had little knowledge of White House decision making. He spent his first two years establishing a coherent White House structure to deal with legislative matters. While contributing to the institutionalization process begun by Roosevelt, Truman also took personal interest in and control over legislative matters. The well-known sign he kept on his desk, proclaiming, "The buck stops here," embodied his personal involvement.

Another indication of Truman's attitude was his frequent use of the veto—250 times in eight years. He used his well-known veto of the Taft-Hartley Act in 1947 to enforce his image as defender of the average worker. Truman took special care with his veto messages and worked on them personally. He became enmeshed in the unpopular Korean War during his final two years in office and suffered a precipitous decline in public standing that was matched only by Nixon's decline during Watergate.

Eisenhower. The election of former general Dwight Eisenhower represented the ascension of a relatively apolitical public figure inexperienced in the ways of civilian governing. Initial assessments of Eisenhower's presidential leadership, such as that of Richard Neustadt, portrayed him as a man who served more out of a sense of duty than a love of power, and as a president who saw his role as that of referee rather than politician in chief.

Yet many presidential observers have argued that Eisenhower's leadership skills have been underrated. Despite facing a Congress controlled by the opposition party for six out of eight years, Eisenhower saw many of his important programs enacted, presided over an era of peace and economic good times, and was elected twice by large margins. Philosophically, he did not share the aggressive activism of his two predecessors. In his first year in office he sent no coordinated legislative program to Congress, but after stern criticism from Congress, he followed through with annual programs for the remainder of his term. His personal role was one of relative detachment compared to his predecessors. He relied more on his staff and organizational hierarchies, and he generally disdained the backslapping, armtwisting style favored by some politicians.

One revised assessment of Eisenhower's leadership style has argued that it was a "hidden hand" style; that is, Ike was in fact "politically astute and informed, engaged in putting his personal stamp on public policy, a president who applied a carefully thought-out conception of leadership to the conduct of his presidency."[176] In addition to the hidden hand, Eisenhower's political strategies included his careful use of language, analysis of the personalities of those with whom he was dealing in assessing options, refusal to engage in personality conflicts, and selective delegation of authority to others. Eisenhower's leadership style with Congress and the country was relatively low key and detached. He benefited from and relied on persistent public support. Given the strong opposition congressional leadership of Democratic House Speaker Sam Rayburn and Senate Majority Leader Lyndon Johnson, Eisenhower probably deserves more credit for having leadership skills suited to the circumstances of the time than critics initially conceded.

Kennedy. Although his presidency conveyed a certain mystique, John F. Kennedy entered the White House on a razor-thin margin that left him little in the way of a political base. Congress was in the hands of the Democrats, but southern conservatives held tight reins, and many of Kennedy's most important "New Frontier" initiatives (including Medicare, aid to education, creation of an urban affairs department, establishment of a youth conservation corps, and civil rights) remained bottled up.

Kennedy had served in the Senate for eight years, but he had taken little interest in Senate affairs and in the traditional paths of congressional power. When he became president, his desire to exert leadership was to some extent frustrated by Republicans and conservative Democrats in Congress, and his inexperience. In the area of civil rights, for example, Kennedy had pledged important advances, but, having lost twenty Democratic seats in the House in the 1960 elections, he failed to win passage of any important civil rights legislation. In response to political pressure, Kennedy did issue a series of executive orders directed at improving civil rights, and he appointed more African Americans to judicial and other positions than any of his predecessors. Kennedy achieved some notable legislative successes, including a minimum wage bill, aid to depressed areas, and a housing bill. As leadership specialist Barbara Kellerman has noted, Kennedy might have realized greater successes in areas such as civil rights had he been willing to apply more of the rewards and sanctions available to him. Kennedy lacked "an appreciation of the *politics* of leadership. He failed to exert sufficient influence on those political actors whose support he needed to win."[177]

With staffing, Kennedy shed Eisenhower's formalistic, hierarchical arrangements, preferring instead a flexible arrangement that fed information more directly to him. Kennedy's top aides also had considerable discretion to act on his behalf. Although these mechanisms could have maximized Kennedy's personal ability to have an effect on the legislative process, his fear of outpacing his mandate did much to slow his efforts.

Johnson. In many respects, Lyndon Johnson was the political opposite of Kennedy. He knew Congress like few other politicians, having served there since 1937 and risen through the ranks to become majority leader during the Eisenhower administration. As a southerner, he knew how to play to southern Democratic conservatives and Republican leaders in Congress. He also appreciated the subtleties of promoting controversial legislation. In 1964, for example, he succeeded where Kennedy had failed in enacting a major civil rights bill. After the 1964 elections, when the Democrats rolled up large congressional majorities, he stepped up the legislative pace.

Johnson's Great Society followed in the tradition of the legislative agendas of Democratic presidents back to Roosevelt. His successes were considerable during 1965–1966; of eighty-three major Johnson proposals, eighty were enacted. Many of his proposals dated back to the Roosevelt era. Johnson's prodigious record of achievement was the product of both an overwhelming electoral mandate in the 1964 election and his well-known personal leadership skills. To be the object of the "Johnson treatment" was to be stroked, prodded, flattered, bullied, encouraged, and cajoled into supporting the president. Johnson was "the very model of a political president."[178]

Johnson's highly personal, hands-on style was reflected in his staff organization. Johnson actively participated in political and policy matters, reserving most important decisions for himself. Members of his White House staff, of course, were heavily involved in such matters as well. When Johnson's energy was directed at Congress, it produced numerous achievements, but his pattern of close personal involvement served him poorly when his attention turned to Vietnam. As Johnson's public support lessened and the country became more committed to the Vietnam War, Johnson brooked little dissent and less disagreement. He continued to log some legislative successes during the last two years of his administration, but his unwavering commitment to the Vietnam War inexorably sapped resources, political capital, and goodwill from his legislative agenda. Johnson's considerable leadership skills could not extract him from his own unyielding commitment to fight an increasingly unpopular war.

Nixon. The 1968 elections inaugurated a period of divided government—that is, one political party controlled the presidency (Nixon was a Republican), and the other party (the Democrats) held majorities in the two houses of Congress. Although he had served in both houses of Congress and as Eisenhower's vice president for eight years, Richard Nixon failed to carry with him either house of Congress. He was the first president to face this difficulty since Zachary Taylor in 1848.

At the outset of his administration Nixon forwarded more than forty legislative proposals to Congress, including election law reform, tax reform, crime-related proposals, welfare reform, and drug control. But despite these early efforts, Nixon encountered problems with Congress almost from the beginning, notably over the Haynsworth and Carswell nominations to the Supreme Court. Nixon's initial organizational approach to Congress differed from that of his immediate predecessors. He sought to emulate Eisenhower's strong cabinet model, emphasizing organizational hierarchy and more limited personal involvement by the president in day-to-day decisions. As his term progressed, however, the strong cabinet model was overthrown in favor of an administrative approach, where power was concentrated in the hands of key political aides. During Nixon's first

term, he sought to achieve policy successes through legislative remedy. By the second term, however, he had turned increasingly to an administrative strategy that emphasized circumventing congressional channels to the extent possible. This approach suited Nixon's personal leadership style, which emphasized detachment, hierarchy, and managerial values.[179]

Nixon's principal leadership efforts concerned foreign policy. He began to scale down U.S. involvement in Vietnam by reducing the number of American troops there (although he actually escalated the war by expanding the fighting into Cambodia, provoking much criticism from Congress and the nation), opened ties to China, and completed the first Strategic Arms Limitation Treaty with the Soviet Union. The Vietnam War was a persistent source of friction between Congress and the White House, with struggles over efforts to end funding for the war and constitutional questions about the extent of Nixon's discretion over the use of U.S. forces. Congress scored several important legislative victories, including passage of the War Powers Resolution.

Nixon's administrative approach conformed to his disdain for congressional critics, and he began to treat his political opponents as enemies. This we-versus-they mentality did much to foster the Watergate scandal, which was marked by efforts to turn the apparatus of government against Nixon's political opponents. Nixon's reelection campaign also diverted resources to political sabotage, dirty tricks, and other illegal activities. As public exposure of Nixon campaign and administration misdeeds surfaced, a siege mentality gripped Nixon and his White House more tightly. Despite the personal mandate Nixon could claim accompanying his landslide 1972 reelection, White House efforts focused increasingly on political damage control. Relations with Congress continued to deteriorate; moreover, congressional investigations were responsible for Nixon's resignation.

Ford. The presidency of Gerald Ford was the product of historical accident. Had Vice President Spiro T. Agnew not resigned over financial improprieties committed during his tenure as governor of Maryland, Ford never would have become president. Without the benefit of a national campaign, Ford had no opportunity to construct and promote his own political and policy agenda. This simple fact explains much of the difficulty Ford faced with Congress.

Ford's elevation to the presidency was welcomed by a country eager to put the troubled Nixon presidency behind it. Ford's simple, direct, unassuming style provided a refreshing contrast to the cold and distant Nixon. Congress too welcomed Ford. As House Republican minority leader, he was known as a partisan, but also likable, honest leader. The Ford honeymoon was cut short, however, when he pardoned Richard Nixon. The pardon provoked a sharp drop in Ford's popularity and did little to improve Ford's standing in the Democratic-controlled Congress.

Because the circumstances under which he became president precluded proposal of a full-blown legislative agenda at the beginning of his term, Ford had to rely primarily on a veto strategy in his dealings with a Congress whose Democratic majority had been enhanced significantly in the 1974 midterm elections. The inherent negativity of this approach fanned congressional resentment, and it engendered a public image of Ford as a naysayer. (Ford vetoed sixty-six bills in his two and one-half years in office.) Ford's aides were keenly aware of these problems, but they felt that they had little room to maneuver until Ford won his own mandate in the 1976 elections.

Ford attempted a major legislative initiative in 1975 when he sent an energy plan to Congress, but Congress challenged and revised the Ford proposal. Ford's overall support rate in Congress was among the lowest of any president since such records were kept. His administrative apparatus was far more open and flexible than that of Nixon, but it operated less decisively and authoritatively.

It is unclear whether another individual with more adroit leadership skills could have exceeded Ford's performance given the circumstances. Nevertheless, Ford's presidential leadership style was similar to his style as minority leader—that of a good person with limited vision who held the reins of power loosely.

Carter. Former Georgia governor Jimmy Carter entered the White House as a Washington outsider. Because in his four years as president he failed to shed the outsider status, his legislative record was pockmarked with unfulfilled expectations and outright failures.

Carter's campaign promises filled more than one hundred pages, and he meant to carry all of them out. Although Congress was controlled by the president's party, Democrats mistrusted Carter, and Carter did little to assuage the mistrust. He underestimated the importance of building careful relations with key congressional leaders, and he overwhelmed Congress from the start by sending to Capitol Hill numerous important bills all at once. This contrasted with Johnson's practice of sending over one major bill at a time. Carter's experiences testified to Johnson's wisdom.

Carter's top aides, including his legislative liaison chief, Frank Moore, were non-Washingtonians, who were inexperienced in Washington politics and did little to cultivate deep-seated support for the president. The Carter staff was known for not returning phone calls, not informing key legislators of important decisions, and ignoring personal courtesies such as making photo sessions available for those interested in being photographed with the president.

The post-Watergate Congress was not disposed to accept proposals simply because they came from the White House. The composition of Congress also militated against docility and pliability. Of the 289 Democratic House members elected in 1976, 118 had served no more than two terms. The large proportion of junior members was interested in a share of congressional power, and Carter was less disposed than most recent presidents to court members of Congress.

Carter achieved some legislative successes, but most observers saw him as incapable of getting an important program through a Congress controlled by his party. For example, his 1977 energy package—really an amalgam of different bills—encountered difficulties. Carter tried to rally public support for the program as a means of overcoming congressional hurdles, but he found such support broad and diffuse and insufficient for overcoming conventional congressional obstacles.

With foreign affairs he had more success, most notably the Camp David accords that helped establish bonds between Israel and Egypt. Carter also concluded negotiations for the Panama Canal Treaty, although Senate ratification proved difficult.

Carter's leadership incorporated two divergent tendencies. First, he was a technocrat who immersed himself in the details of complex programs. Second, he was a born-again Christian who espoused high moral standards. What he lacked was a mid-level concern for conventional political relationships.

Reagan. Like Carter, Ronald Reagan ran for president against the Washington establishment. Unlike Carter, Reagan's administration labored to gain political insider status, partly by learning from Carter's mistakes. Bringing with him a Republican-controlled Senate (the Democrats retained control of the House) and an electoral mandate based on carrying forty-four states, Reagan worked to lay careful political groundwork from the start.

After conducting a study of the first three months of past presidencies, Reagan's aides concluded that they should push a few selected initiatives and work to restore the informal social courtesies and connections that Carter had neglected. The outsider image successful in the campaign was sublimated after the election in the interest of building better relations with Capitol Hill. Reagan selected Max Friedersdorf, a Washington insider with experience in two previous Republican administrations, as his legislative liaison chief.

Like Carter, Reagan sought to rally public support for high-priority programs, but the Reagan administration paid greater attention to image-building, and Reagan excelled as the "Great Communicator." No president since Eisenhower has demonstrated such enduring personal popularity.

The primary issue thrust for the Reagan administration in 1981 was an economic package, incorporating large increases in defense spending, cuts in social welfare programs, and a major tax cut predicated on supply-side economics. Reagan's political strategies and wide public support resulted in a major policy victory that has been compared to Roosevelt's early successes during the New Deal's first one hundred days. Reagan's political support in Congress stemmed from the Republican Senate majority, the Republican minority in the House, and conservative southern Democrats.

By 1985 Reagan's support level in Congress had dropped to levels comparable to Nixon's low point. In his second term Reagan faced increasingly stiff opposition to several proposals, including his expensive Strategic Defense Initiative, his advocacy of continued aid to the Nicaraguan contras, his continued efforts to cut social programs, and his efforts to restrict abortion. In 1986 the Republicans lost control of the Senate. The following

President Ronald Reagan confers with Republican congressional leaders at a White House meeting in June 1984.

year Reagan lost a bitter fight to have Supreme Court nominee Robert H. Bork confirmed by the Senate. In 1987 Congress launched an investigation of the Iran-contra affair, which involved administration efforts to trade U.S. arms for hostages being held in the Middle East and to use profits from the arms sales to fund the Nicaraguan contras. In 1988 those top White House aides who participated in the affair were indicted.

Despite these pitfalls, Reagan continued to maintain a high level of personal popularity. The enduring appeal of Reagan's personal qualities provided a constant to an otherwise roller-coaster presidency, and earned him the nickname "the Teflon president" ("nothing bad ever stuck to him").

Bush. After serving in Reagan's shadow as vice president for eight years, George Bush won election in his own right in 1988. Unlike Reagan, however, his victory was much more narrow, and the Democrats retained solid majorities in both houses of Congress. In fact, the Republicans lost seats in both houses.

At the outset of his administration, Bush sought to establish good relations with Congress, emphasizing his active personal involvement. Among the most pressing policy imperatives was a budget deal that would curtail the spiraling federal deficit inherited from Reagan. Such efforts were hampered by Bush's flamboyant campaign pledge of "read my lips, no new taxes." In the summer of 1990, Bush reneged on his no-tax pledge by agreeing to an income tax increase as part of a major deficit-reduction package with Democratic leaders, a decision that was politically embarrassing, but necessary for any meaningful deficit reduction. Yet Bush also relied increasingly on vetoes and veto threats as a primary tool for influencing Congress. In his four years in office, Bush vetoed forty-five bills, with only one congressional override. Moreover, he was a prolific user of veto threats. In his first year and a half alone, he issued 120 veto threats.

One problem with this veto strategy was that it angered and

alienated many in Congress (as had happened in the Ford administration). A second problem was that it underscored Bush's failure to promote a systematic domestic policy agenda in Congress. Thus, popular measures widely supported in Congress and in the country, such as civil rights, minimum wage, and family medical leave, were blocked by the Bush veto. Bush was increasingly criticized for his weak and ineffectual approach to domestic policy and his failure to promote viable policy alternatives.[180]

Political scientist Charles Tiefer put a somewhat different spin on Bush's policy approach, arguing that Bush "generally disdained moving a legislative program." At the same time, Tiefer argues, Bush pursued a strategy of circumventing Congress by seeking to operate through administrative means, some of which were of dubious legality.[181]

In foreign policy, Bush operated more aggressively and actively. The clearest example arose from the Iraqi crisis of 1990–1991. Bush labored unceasingly to rally international and domestic support for armed intervention against Iraq in the aftermath of that nation's conquest of Kuwait in August 1990. In the late summer and fall of 1990, most members of Congress supported Bush's military actions to counterbalance Saddam Hussein's aggression. Yet as Bush continued the buildup, a rising chorus in Congress insisted that Congress be involved more actively. Bush stated repeatedly that congressional approval was not necessary for the commitment of American troops and that he possessed the necessary authority. Rejecting this, Congress held hearings, debated, and provided statutory approval for armed intervention in January 1991, specifically invoking the terms of the War Powers Resolution.[182]

By the conclusion of the fighting, Bush's public approval rating stood at 89 percent, the highest approval rating ever recorded for a president. Bush's path to reelection seemed assured. Yet a declining economy and Bush's continued intransigence with Congress made him vulnerable to defeat in 1992.

Clinton. Bill Clinton sought to set himself up as the antidote to the problems of the Bush years. Clinton promised an end to gridlock with Congress by providing same-party control of the two branches of government for the first time since 1980 (the Republicans won control of one house of Congress, the Senate, in 1980), assuming that the Democrats would retain control of both houses of Congress in the 1992 election, which they did. He promised to "focus like a laser beam" on the economy and to pursue aggressively a comprehensive domestic agenda at a time when Americans were less concerned with foreign policy than at any time in the previous fifty years. Clinton was elected with only 43 percent of the popular vote, the remainder was split between Bush and third party contender Ross Perot.

Expectations and hopes were high when Clinton took office, and he set to work immediately on a broad front. Displaying youthful energy and enthusiasm, Clinton logged an impressive series of policy achievements in his first two years. He won congressional approval of his budget package, instituted the longest period of sustained deficit reduction since the Truman administration, and won passage of such bills as family medical leave, motor voter registration, a five-day waiting period on handgun purchases, the North American Free Trade Agreement (NAFTA), regulation of mining on public lands, a $30 billion crime bill (including an assault weapons ban), and highway transportation improvement. A major disappointment was the failure of the 103d Congress to enact health care reform. Nevertheless, according to Congressional Quarterly's presidential support score for 1993, Congress supported Clinton's position almost 87 percent of the time, a score not matched since the early days of the Johnson administration.[183]

Despite these significant achievements, the Clinton administration was dogged by a series of decisions and actions that gave fuel to Clinton's critics. For example, Clinton had promised to end the ban on gays in the military, yet ultimately he had to settle for a modest change in military policy, largely because of congressional criticism. Several of his prospective nominees for executive branch positions came under criticism, causing Clinton to back down and suffer political embarrassment. Despite the country's greater interest in domestic matters, such foreign policy trouble spots as Somalia, the former Yugoslavia, Haiti, and North Korea all posed continuing problems, in that Clinton seemed to have no consistent policy for dealing with these crises. In 1995 Clinton overrode congressional objections and sent over 20,000 American troops to Bosnia as part of a multinational peacekeeping force. This action, plus the maintenance of stability in other parts of the world, helped to quiet critics.

Clinton exhibited a consistent interest in and willingness to work with Congress on major issues. In particular, passage of NAFTA was considered a major political achievement. Yet Clinton's style, and that of his staff, reflected a youthful, inexperienced, but zealous approach. The White House was often caught unprepared for many of the political conflicts that pockmarked the administration. It would then scramble frantically to mend fences and repair damage, often succeeding in grabbing a victory out of the jaws of defeat. By one account, the Clinton White House was nothing less than chaotic, with little firm organizational direction coming from the top, and with Clinton himself seeking to be involved in every important decision.[184] Concerned about the possibility of losing a Democratic majority in the Senate (and possibly even the House) in the 1994 midterm elections, the Clinton White House sought to get as much through Congress as possible before the election, despite the fear of overwhelming Congress.

The Republican takeover of Congress in the 1994 midterm elections caught President Clinton by surprise. In the first several months of the 104th Congress (1995–1997), Clinton was eclipsed by the flurry of activity surrounding the GOP's efforts to enact portions of their "Contract with America." Against Clinton's preferences, Congress attempted to reduce welfare spending by $70 billion over seven years; impose cuts of $270 billion in Medicare and $170 billion in Medicaid, and turn the remaining money over to the states in the form of block grants, a move that would give the states much greater control over this spending; enact constitutional amendments for term limits and a balanced budget; cut government subsidies to agriculture; repeal the assault weapons ban and the five-day waiting period for handgun purchases; end federal direct student loan programs; roll back environmental regulations; and repeal abortion rights. Many of these measures bogged down in the Senate, or as the result of presidential intervention or veto. Yet Congress succeeded in dictating and redirecting the national policy agenda. It failed to reach any accommodation with the president, however, and that produced a prolonged stalemate over enactment of the 1996 fiscal year federal budget. As the stalemate dragged on, public sentiment turned against Congress, which more people believed bore the main responsibility for the impasse.

Seizing the initiative, Clinton sought to take the high road and regain some political initiative. He emphasized the willingness of the White House to bargain and compromise with congressional Republicans, while defending, among other things, Medicare, federally directed social service programs, education programs, and environmental protection. As the 1996 presidential election neared, Republicans feared that the continuing stalemate would harm their party more than the Democrats. The president and Congress finally reached a budget agreement at the end of April 1996—seven months into the fiscal year. Although the final appropriations bill cut $22 billion in domestic spending, it fell short of the ambitious cuts the Republicans originally sought. Clinton was successful in protecting his priorities in education, job training, and environmental protection.

NOTES

1. For more on the electoral college, see Judith V. Best, *The Case against Direct Election of the President* (Ithaca, N.Y.: Cornell University Press, 1975); Lawrence D. Longley and Alan G. Braun, *The Politics of Electoral College Reform* (New Haven, Conn.: Yale University Press, 1975); and Neil R. Peirce,

The People's President: The Electoral College in American History and the Direct Vote Alternative (New York: Simon and Schuster, 1968).

2. Many have proposed that the electoral cycle be changed so that there is greater connection between congressional and presidential races. See, for example, Donald L. Robinson, ed., *Reforming American Government* (Boulder, Colo.: Westview, 1985); Donald L. Robinson, *"To the Best of My Ability"* (New York: Norton, 1987); James L. Sundquist, *Constitutional Reform and Effective Government* (Washington, D.C.: Brookings, 1986).

3. Committee on Responsible Parties, American Political Science Association, *Toward a More Responsible Two-Party System* (New York: Rinehart, 1950), 75. See also President's Commission for a National Agenda for the Eighties, *The Electoral and Democratic Process in the Eighties*, Paul G. Rogers, chairperson (Englewood Cliffs, N.J.: Prentice-Hall, 1981), 35–36.

4. See Max Farrand, *The Records of the Federal Convention of 1787*, 4 vols. (New Haven, Conn.: Yale University Press, 1966), 1:214–215.

5. Sundquist, *Constitutional Reform*, 115.

6. See Robinson, *"To the Best of My Ability,"* 270–271; and Committee on the Constitutional System, *A Bicentennial Analysis of the American Political Structure* (January 1987), 10–11.

7. Quoted in George B. Galloway, *History of the House of Representatives* (New York: Crowell, 1961), 236–237.

8. See Robert J. Spitzer, *The Presidential Veto* (Albany: State University of New York Press, 1988), chap. 2.

9. *United States v. Nixon*, 418 U.S. 683 (1974).

10. For example, see Raoul Berger, *Executive Privilege: A Constitutional Myth* (New York: Bantam Books, 1984); Robert G. Dixon Jr., "Congress, Shared Administration, and Executive Privilege," in *Congress against the President*, ed. Harvey C. Mansfield Sr. (New York: Praeger, 1975), 125–140; Mark J. Rozell, *Executive Privilege* (Baltimore: Johns Hopkins University Press, 1994); and Gary J. Schmitt, "Executive Privilege: Presidential Power to Withhold Information from Congress," in *The Presidency in the Constitutional Order*, ed. Joseph M. Bessette and Jeffrey Tulis (Baton Rouge: Louisiana State University Press, 1981), 154–194.

11. Quoted in Thomas E. Cronin, "Rethinking the Vice-Presidency," in *Rethinking the Presidency*, ed. Thomas E. Cronin (Boston: Little, Brown, 1982), 328.

12. James W. Davis, *The American Presidency: A New Perspective* (New York: Harper and Row, 1987), 396–397; Joel K. Goldstein, *The Modern American Vice Presidency: The Transformation of a Political Institution* (Princeton, N.J.: Princeton University Press, 1981), 4–6.

13. See Michael Dorman, *The Second Man* (New York: Dell, 1970); Paul C. Light, *Vice-Presidential Power: Advice and Influence in the White House* (Baltimore: Johns Hopkins University Press, 1984); and Irving G. Williams, *The American Vice-Presidency: A New Look* (Garden City, N.Y.: Doubleday, 1954).

14. Quoted in Louis Fisher, *President and Congress* (New York: Free Press, 1972), 60.

15. An excellent discussion of delegation of power is found in ibid., chap. 3. See also Richard M. Pious, *The American Presidency* (New York: Basic Books, 1979), 213–217.

16. This account is taken from Louis Fisher, *Presidential Spending Power* (Princeton, N.J.: Princeton University Press, 1975), chaps. 1 and 2. For more on budgeting, see Daniel P. Franklin, *Making Ends Meet* (Washington, D.C.: CQ Press, 1993); Dennis Ippolito, *Congressional Spending* (Ithaca, N.Y.: Cornell University Press, 1981); Lance T. LeLoup, *Budgetary Politics* (Brunswick, Ohio: King's Court Communications, 1986); Howard E. Shuman, *Politics and the Budget* (Englewood Cliffs, N.J.: Prentice-Hall, 1988); and Aaron Wildavsky, *The New Politics of the Budgetary Process* (Glenview, Ill.: Scott, Foresman, 1988).

17. *Wayman v. Southart*, 10 Wheat. 1 (1825).

18. *Field v. Clark*, 143 U.S. 649 (1891).

19. *S. W. Hampton, Jr. & Co. v. United States*, 276 U.S. 394 (1928).

20. *United States v. Curtiss-Wright Export Corp.*, 299 U.S. 304 (1936).

21. *Schechter Poultry Corp. v. United States*, 295 U.S. 495 (1935).

22. Quoted in Gerald Gunther, *Constitutional Law* (Mineola, N.Y.: Foundation Press, 1975), 424.

23. See, for example, Theodore J. Lowi, *The End of Liberalism* (New York: Norton, 1979).

24. Louis Fisher, *The Politics of Shared Power: Congress and the Executive*, 3d ed. (Washington, D.C.: CQ Press, 1993), 4.

25. See Aaron Wildavsky, "The Two Presidencies," in *Perspectives on the Presidency*, ed. Aaron Wildavsky (Boston: Little, Brown, 1975), 448–461. Wildavsky noted: "In the realm of foreign policy there has not been a single major issue on which Presidents, when they were serious and determined, have failed" (p. 449). Although Vietnam and subsequent events altered the truth of this statement, an ever-expanding role for the president in foreign policy continues to prevail. For more on the "two presidencies" thesis, see Steven A. Shull, ed., *The Two Presidencies* (Chicago: Nelson-Hall, 1991).

26. Robert J. Spitzer, *President and Congress: Executive Hegemony at the Crossroads of American Government* (New York: McGraw-Hill and Temple University Press, 1993), chaps. 5 and 6.

27. Quoted in Gunther, *Constitutional Law*, 422.

28. See Louis Koenig, *The Chief Executive*, 4th ed. (New York: Harcourt Brace Jovanovich, 1981), 7–8; Thomas E. Cronin, *The State of the Presidency* (Boston: Little, Brown, 1980), chap. 3; and George Reedy, *The Twilight of the Presidency* (New York: New American Library, 1970), chap. 1.

29. Farrand, *The Records of the Federal Convention*, 2:318. As early as 1552 the verb "declare" was synonymous with the verb "commence," as in *to begin* or *initiate*. See David Gray Adler, "The President's War-Making Power," in *Inventing the American Presidency*, ed. Thomas E. Cronin (Lawrence: University Press of Kansas, 1989), 123.

30. Spitzer, *President and Congress*, 150.

31. Quoted in Gunther, *Constitutional Law*, 436; also see Gunther's discussion of war powers. Alexander Hamilton summarized the president's responsibility to Congress in war making in the *Federalist* No. 69. A useful historical accounting of the evolution of war powers is found in Richard J. Barnet, *The Rockets' Red Glare: War, Politics and the American Presidency* (New York: Simon and Schuster, 1990); Demetrios Caraley, ed., *The President's War Powers: From the Federalists to Reagan* (New York: Academy of Political Science, 1984); and Francis D. Wormuth and Edwin B. Firmage, *To Chain the Dog of War* (Urbana: University of Illinois Press, 1989).

32. See Gunther, *Constitutional Law*, 437–439.

33. For more on this, see Louis Fisher, *Constitutional Conflicts Between Congress and the President* (Princeton, N.J.: Princeton University Press, 1985), chap. 9.

34. Quoted in Gunther, *Constitutional Law*, 439. See also Louis Fisher, "The Power of Commander in Chief," in *The Presidency and the Persian Gulf War*, ed., Marcia Lynn Whicker, James P. Pfiffner, and Raymond A. Moore (Westport, Conn.: Praeger, 1993), 53–57.

35. For more on this debate, see Stephen Carter, "The Constitutionality of the War Powers Resolution," *Virginia Law Review* 70 (1984); Kenneth M. Holland, "The War Powers Resolution: An Infringement on the President's Constitutional and Prerogative Powers," in *The Presidency and National Security Policy*, ed. R. Gordon Hoxie (New York: Center for the Study of the Presidency, 1984); Robert Scigliano, "The War Powers Resolution and the War Powers," in Bessette and Tulis, *The Presidency in the Constitutional Order*, 115–153; William Spong Jr., "The War Powers Resolution Revisited: Historical Accomplishment or Surrender?" *William and Mary Law Review* 16 (1975).

36. The Joint Chiefs of Staff, it was later revealed, had unanimously opposed sending the marines to Lebanon. See Cecil V. Crabb Jr. and Pat M. Holt, *Invitation to Struggle: Congress, the President, and Foreign Policy*, 4th ed. (Washington, D.C.: CQ Press, 1992), 147. In all, 264 marines were killed and 134 were wounded.

37. Fisher, *Constitutional Conflicts*, 317.

38. See Michael Rubner, "The Reagan Administration, the 1973 War Powers Resolution, and the Invasion of Grenada," *Political Science Quarterly* 100 (winter 1985–1986): 627–647.

39. See John H. Cushman Jr., "Iraqi Missile Hits U.S. Navy Frigate in Persian Gulf," *New York Times*, May 18, 1987, A12.

40. *Lowry et al. v. Reagan* (87-2196).

41. Spitzer, *President and Congress*, 179–181.

42. Robert J. Spitzer, "The Conflict Between Congress and the President Over War," in *The Presidency and the Persian Gulf War,* 25–44.

43. John Spanier and Eric M. Uslander, *American Foreign Policy Making and the Democratic Dilemmas* (New York: Holt, Rinehart, and Winston, 1985), 73–74.

44. See, for example, Theodore J. Lowi, *Incomplete Conquest: Governing America* (New York: Holt, Rinehart, and Winston, 1981), 313–315; and Theodore J. Lowi, *The Personal President* (Ithaca, N.Y.: Cornell University Press, 1985), chap. 1. This trend has broken down in a few instances—such as during the Vietnam War and the Iranian hostage crisis—when the involvement stretched on without the prospect of a "winning" outcome.

45. Davis, *The American Presidency,* 196.

46. Larry Berman, *The New American Presidency* (Boston: Little, Brown, 1987), 36–37.

47. See James A. Robinson, *Congress and Foreign Policy-Making* (Homewood, Ill.: Dorsey Press, 1967), 67–69.

48. Koenig, *The Chief Executive,* 215; *Guide to Congress,* 4th ed.(Washington, D.C.: Congressional Quarterly, 1991), 174.

49. The Supreme Court case of *United States v. Curtiss-Wright Export Corp.* stated: "The President alone has the power to speak or listen as the chief representative of the nation."

50. Crabb and Holt, *Invitation to Struggle,* 14.

51. Fisher, *Constitutional Conflicts,* 269.

52. *Goldwater v. Carter,* 444 U.S. 996 (1979). For more on treaty termination, see David Gray Adler, *The Constitution and the Termination of Treaties* (New York: Garland, 1986).

53. Bernard Roshco, "The Polls: Polling on Panama—Si, Don't Know; Hell No!" *Public Opinion Quarterly* 42 (1978): 551–562.

54. These and other basic facts are drawn from Cecil V. Crabb Jr. and Pat M. Holt, *Invitation to Struggle: Congress, the President, and Foreign Policy,* 2d ed. (Washington, D.C.: CQ Press, 1984), chap. 3. See also George D. Moffett III, *The Limits of Victory: The Ratification of the Panama Canal Treaties* (Ithaca, N.Y.: Cornell University Press, 1985).

55. William L. Furlong, "Negotiations and Ratifications of the Panama Canal Treaties," in *Congress, the Presidency and American Foreign Policy,* ed. John Spanier and Joseph Nogee (New York: Pergamon Press, 1981), 78.

56. Crabb and Holt, *Invitation to Struggle,* 2d ed., 91.

57. This account is drawn from Stephen J. Flanagan, "The Domestic Politics of SALT II: Implications for the Foreign Policy Process," in *Congress, the Presidency,* chap. 3. See also Spanier and Uslander, *American Foreign Policy Making,* 204–217.

58. This was stated in *United States v. Pink,* 315 U.S. 203 (1942). Although executive agreement power is not stipulated in the Constitution, it generally is recognized as coming from four sources: the presidential responsibility to represent the country in foreign affairs, the presidential authority to receive ambassadors, the president's role as commander in chief of the military, and the president's obligation to "take care that the laws be faithfully executed." See Fisher, *Constitutional Conflicts,* 272–283.

59. See Benjamin I. Page and Mark P. Petracca, *The American Presidency* (New York: McGraw-Hill, 1983), 269–270. The greater presidential reliance on executive agreements is discussed in Loch Johnson and James M. McCormick, "Foreign Policy by Executive Fiat," *Foreign Policy* 28 (fall 1977).

60. Robert E. DiClerico, *The American President* (Englewood Cliffs, N.J.: Prentice-Hall, 1983), 51.

61. Spanier and Uslander, *American Foreign Policy Making,* 12, 47, 88.

62. This account is taken from Spitzer, *The Presidential Veto,* chap. 3.

63. See Dan Caldwell, "The Jackson-Vanik Amendment," in *Congress, the Presidency,* chap. 1.

64. Jeane Kirkpatrick, "Human Rights and American Foreign Policy: A Symposium," *Commentary* 72 (November 1981): 42–45.

65. For example, Alan Tonelson, "Human Rights: The Bias We Need," *Foreign Policy* 49 (winter 1982–1983): 52–74.

66. Randall B. Ripley and Grace A. Franklin, *Congress, the Bureaucracy, and Public Policy* (Homewood, Ill.: Dorsey Press, 1987), 190–191.

67. Quoted in Frank Kessler, *The Dilemmas of Presidential Leadership* (Englewood Cliffs, N.J.: Prentice-Hall, 1982), 110.

68. See Crabb and Holt, *Invitation to Struggle,* 4th ed., chap. 6.

69. DiClerico, *The American President,* 51–54. See also Harold Hongju Koh, *The National Security Constitution* (New Haven, Conn.: Yale University Press, 1990).

70. Erwin C. Hargrove and Michael Nelson, *Presidents, Politics and Policy* (Baltimore: Johns Hopkins University Press, 1984), 210.

71. Quoted in George C. Edwards III and Stephen J. Wayne, *Presidential Leadership* (New York: St. Martin's Press, 1985), 370.

72. Fisher, *Constitutional Conflicts,* 40.

73. George C. Edwards III, *Presidential Influence in Congress* (San Francisco: Freeman, 1980), 26.

74. Henry J. Abraham, *Justices and Presidents* (New York: Oxford University Press, 1985), 15.

75. Ibid., 16.

76. Ibid., chap. 2.

77. Everett C. Ladd, "The Political Battle for the Federal Courts," *Ladd Report,* no. 7 (New York: Norton, 1988), 10–21.

78. See Robert Scigliano, *The Supreme Court and the Presidency* (New York: Free Press, 1971), 96–99, 146–158.

79. Quoted in Kessler, *The Dilemmas of Presidential Leadership,* 215.

80. Edwards, *Presidential Influence in Congress,* 26.

81. This and other aspects of the appointment process are discussed in Fisher, *Constitutional Conflicts,* chap. 2.

82. Harold Seidman, *Politics, Position, and Power* (New York: Oxford University Press, 1980), 54.

83. Fisher, *The Politics of Shared Power,* 131–132. See also Fisher, *Constitutional Conflicts,* chap. 3.

84. See Jong Lee, "Presidential Vetoes from Washington to Nixon," *Journal of Politics* 37 (May 1975): 522–545; Gary Copeland, "When Congress and the President Collide: Why Presidents Veto Legislation," *Journal of Politics* 45 (August 1983): 696–710; and David Rohde and Dennis M. Simon, "Presidential Vetoes and Congressional Response: A Study of Institutional Conflict," *American Journal of Political Science* 29 (August 1985): 397–427.

85. See Spitzer, *The Presidential Veto,* chaps. 2 and 3.

86. Quoted in Herman Finer, *The Presidency* (Chicago: University of Chicago Press, 1960), 75.

87. See Paul Light, *The President's Agenda* (Baltimore: Johns Hopkins University Press, 1982), 111.

88. Robert J. Spitzer, "The Disingenuous Presidency: Reagan's Veto and the 'Make-My-Day' President," *Congress and the Presidency* 21 (spring 1994): 1–10.

89. Robert J. Spitzer, "Presidential Prerogative Power: The Case of the Bush Administration and Legislative Powers," *PS: Political Science and Politics* 24 (March 1991): 38–42; Charles Tiefer, *The Semi-Sovereign Presidency* (Boulder, Colo.: Westview, 1994).

90. Stephen J. Wayne, *The Legislative Presidency* (New York: Harper and Row, 1978), 159.

91. *The Pocket Veto Case,* 279 U.S. 644 (1929).

92. *Wright v. United States,* 302 U.S. 583 (1938).

93. See *Kennedy v. Sampson,* 364 F. Supp. 1075 (D.D.C. 1973); and *Kennedy v. Sampson,* 511 F. 2d 430 (D.C.C. 1974).

94. *Barnes v. Carmen,* 582 F. Supp. 163 (1984).

95. *Barnes v. Kline,* 759 F. 2d 21 (1985).

96. *Burke v. Barnes,* 491 U.S. 361 (1987). See also U.S. Congress, House of Representatives, Committee on Rules, Subcommittee on the Legislative Process, *Hearing on a Bill to Clarify the Law Surrounding the President's Use of the Pocket Veto, July 26, 1989* (Washington, D.C.: Government Printing Office, 1989).

97. For more on the item veto controversy, see Spitzer, *The Presidential Veto,* chap. 5.

98. For more on arguments for the line-item veto, see Judith A. Best, "The Item Veto: Would the Founders Approve?" *Presidential Studies Quarterly* 14 (spring 1984): 183–188; Russell M. Ross and Fred Schwengel, "An Item Veto for the President?" *Presidential Studies Quarterly* 12 (winter 1982): 66–79; and Andrew Taylor, "Congress Hands President a Budgetary Scalpel," *Congressional Quarterly Weekly Report,* March 30, 1996, 864–867.

99. Anthony Haswell, "Partial Veto Power—Does the President Have It Now?" *Federal Bar News and Journal* 36 (March/April 1989): 142–146; Michael B. Rappaport, "The President's Veto and the Constitution," *Northwestern University Law Review* 87 (spring 1993): 735–786.

100. House Committee on the Budget, "The Line-Item Veto: An Appraisal," 98th Cong., 2d sess., February 1984 (Washington, D.C.: Government Printing Office, 1984).

101. See Louis Fisher and Neal Devins, "How Successfully Can the States' Item Veto Be Transferred to the President?" *Georgetown Law Journal* 75 (October 1986): 159–197.

102. The item veto proposals are criticized in Thomas E. Cronin and Jeffrey J. Weill, "An Item Veto for the President?" *Congress and the Presidency* 12 (autumn 1985): 127–151; Fisher, *Constitutional Conflicts,* 159–162; and Robert J. Spitzer, "The Item Veto Reconsidered," *Presidential Studies Quarterly* 15 (summer 1985): 611–617.

103. For more on the legislative veto, see Fisher, *Constitutional Conflicts,* 162–183; Murray Dry, "The Congressional Veto and the Constitutional Separation of Powers," in *The Presidency in the Constitutional Order,* 195–233; Congressional Research Service, "Studies on the Legislative Veto," prepared for the Subcommittee on Rules of the House Committee on Rules, U.S. House of Representatives (Washington, D.C.: Government Printing Office, 1980); and Spitzer, *President and Congress,* 118–126.

104. *Buckley v. Valeo,* 424 U.S. 1 (1976).

105. *Immigration and Naturalization Service v. Chadha,* 462 U.S. 919 (1983).

106. Louis Fisher, "Judicial Misjudgments about the Lawmaking Process: The Legislative Veto Case," *Public Administration Review* 45 (November 1985): 711; and communication with Louis Fisher.

107. The title of "chief legislator" was popularized by Clinton Rossiter's book *The American Presidency* (New York: New American Library, 1960). Rossiter asserted, "The President alone is in a political, constitutional, and practical position to provide such leadership, and he is therefore expected, within the limits of constitutional and political propriety, to guide Congress in much of its lawmaking activity" (p. 26).

108. Wayne, *The Legislative Presidency,* 8–10.

109. *Annals of Congress* (December 15, 1817), 452.

110. Wayne, *The Legislative Presidency,* 12–18.

111. Richard E. Neustadt, "Presidency and Legislation: Planning the President's Program," in *The Presidency,* 559.

112. Fisher, *The Politics of Shared Power,* 19.

113. Quoted in Neustadt, "Presidency and Legislation," 594.

114. Davis, *The American Presidency,* 159.

115. Harold M. Barger, *The Impossible Presidency* (Glenview, Ill.: Scott, Foresman, 1984), 128–129. For more on legislative liaison, see Abraham Holtzman, *Legislative Liaison* (Chicago: Rand McNally, 1970).

116. Wayne, *The Legislative Presidency,* 72.

117. Ibid., chap. 3; Stephen J. Wayne and James F. C. Hyde Jr., "Presidential Decision-Making on Enrolled Bills," *Presidential Studies Quarterly* 8 (summer 1978): 284–296.

118. Sarah Anderson and Ken Silverstein, "Oink Oink," *The Nation,* December 20, 1993, 752–753.

119. See Robert J. Spitzer, *The Presidency and Public Policy* (University: University of Alabama Press, 1983), 98–100.

120. Quoted in Davis, *The American Presidency,* 163.

121. Sidney Blumenthal, "Marketing the President," *New York Times Magazine,* September 13, 1981, 112.

122. For more on the importance of popularity or "public prestige," see Richard E. Neustadt, *Presidential Power* (New York: Wiley, 1980), chap. 5; and Edwards, *Presidential Influence in Congress,* chap. 4.

123. See Lawrence Chamberlain, *The President, Congress, and Legislation* (New York: Columbia University Press, 1946); and Lawrence Chamberlain, "The President, Congress, and Legislation," in *The President: Roles and Powers,* ed. David Haight and Larry Johnson (Chicago: Rand McNally, 1965), 304.

124. William Goldsmith, *The Growth of Presidential Power* (New York: Chelsea House, 1974), 3: 1400.

125. Samuel Huntington, "Congressional Responses to the Twentieth Century," in *The Congress and America's Future,* ed. David Truman (Englewood Cliffs, N.J.: Prentice-Hall, 1965), 23. Huntington goes on to propose that law making be left to the president and that Congress devote its energies to constituent work and bureaucratic oversight.

126. Ronald C. Moe and Steven C. Teel, "Congress as Policy-Maker: A Necessary Reappraisal," *Political Science Quarterly* 85 (September 1970): 468. See also Hugh Gallagher, "Presidents, Congress, and the Legislative Functions," in *The Presidency Reappraised,* ed. Rexford Tugwell and Thomas E. Cronin (New York: Praeger, 1974), 232–233.

127. See, for example, John R. Johannes, "The President Proposes and Congress Disposes—But Not Always: Legislative Initiative on Capitol Hill," *The Review of Politics* 36 (July 1974): 356–370.

128. George C. Edwards III, *At the Margins: Presidential Leadership of Congress* (New Haven, Conn.: Yale University Press, 1989), 212.

129. Jon R. Bond and Richard Fleisher, *The President in the Legislative Arena* (Chicago: University of Chicago Press, 1990), x.

130. Mark A. Peterson, *Legislating Together* (Cambridge, Mass.: Harvard University Press, 1990), 7–9.

131. The presidential Boxscore is discussed critically in Wayne, *The Legislative Presidency,* 168–171; Cronin, *The State of the Presidency,* 169–173; and Spitzer, *The Presidency and Public Policy,* 93–94.

132. Lee Sigelman, "A Reassessment of the Two Presidencies Thesis," *Journal of Politics* 41 (November 1979): 1195–1205.

133. Edwards, *Presidential Influence in Congress,* 66.

134. Steven A. Shull, *Domestic Policy Formation* (Westport, Conn.: Greenwood Press, 1983), 10.

135. See Aage R. Clausen, *How Congressmen Decide* (New York: St. Martin's Press, 1973); John W. Kingdon, *Congressmen's Voting Decisions* (New York: Harper and Row, 1973); and Peterson, *Legislating Together,* 175–181.

136. Lowi proposed this scheme in "American Business, Public Policy, Case Studies, and Political Theory," *World Politics* 16 (July 1964): 677–715. See also Theodore J. Lowi, "Four Systems of Policy, Politics, and Choice," *Public Administration Review* 32 (July–August 1972): 298–310.

137. Spitzer, *The Presidency and Public Policy,* chap. 7. Shull also applies three of Lowi's four categories to presidential-congressional relations in *Domestic Policy Formation.*

138. Neustadt, *Presidential Power,* 149.

139. Light, *The President's Agenda,* 32, 202–206.

140. The evolution of the seniority system is chronicled in Nelson W. Polsby, Miriam Gallaher, and Barry Rundquist, "The Growth of the Seniority System in the U.S. House of Representatives," *American Political Science Review* 63 (September 1969): 787–807.

141. For more on seniority, see Barbara Hinckley, *The Seniority System in Congress* (Bloomington: Indiana University Press, 1971); and *How Congress Works,* 2d ed. (Washington, D.C.: Congressional Quarterly, 1991), 78–79, 84–85.

142. Woodrow Wilson, *Congressional Government* (Boston: Houghton Mifflin, 1886), 69.

143. Clarence Cannon, *Cannon's Procedure in the House of Representatives* (Washington, D.C.: Government Printing Office, 1963), 221.

144. For more on the rules and procedures followed by committees and Congress as a whole, see Lewis A. Froman, *The Congressional Process* (Boston: Little, Brown, 1967); and Walter J. Oleszek, *Congressional Procedures and the Policy Process,* 4th ed. (Washington, D.C.: CQ Press, 1996).

145. See Norman J. Ornstein and David W. Rohde, "Political Parties and Congressional Reform," in *Parties and Elections in an Anti-Party Age,* ed. Jeff Fishel (Bloomington: Indiana University Press, 1978), 280–294.

146. Barbara Hinckley, *Stability and Change in Congress* (New York: Harper and Row, 1988), 123, 138–140.

147. Ibid., 132.

148. Randall Ripley, *Congress: Process and Policy* (New York: Norton, 1983), 66.

149. Hinckley, *Stability and Change in Congress,* 158–163. For more on the committee and subcommittee system, see Richard F. Fenno, *Congressmen in Committees* (Boston: Little, Brown, 1973); Steven S. Smith and

Christopher J. Deering, *Committees in Congress* (Washington, D.C.: CQ Press, 1990); *How Congress Works*, 73–99.

150. Roger H. Davidson and Walter J. Oleszek, *Congress and Its Members* (Washington, D.C.: CQ Press, 1996), chap. 6; John J. Kornacki, ed., *Leading Congress* (Washington, D.C.: Congressional Quarterly, 1990); Barbara Sinclair, *Majority Leadership in the U.S. House* (Baltimore: Johns Hopkins University Press, 1983).

151. Quoted in ibid., 352; see also 46, 190, 352–355.

152. Ripley, *Congress: Process and Policy*, 160.

153. Davidson and Oleszek, *Congress and Its Members*, 308.

154. Hinckley, *Stability and Change in Congress*, 204.

155. Alan R. Gitelson, M. Margaret Conway, and Frank B. Feigert, *American Political Parties* (Boston: Houghton Mifflin, 1984), 270–275.

156. Fred I. Greenstein and Frank B. Feigert, *The American Party System and the American People* (Englewood Cliffs, N.J.: Prentice-Hall, 1985), 133–135.

157. John H. Kessel, *Presidential Parties* (Homewood, Ill.: Dorsey Press, 1984), 138.

158. Ibid., 137–144. See also Wayne, *The Legislative Presidency*, chap. 5; and Holtzman, *Legislative Liaison*.

159. Edwards, *Presidential Influence in Congress*, 88–90.

160. Roger H. Davidson, David M. Kovenock, and Michael K. O'Leary, *Congress in Crisis* (Belmont, Calif.: Wadsworth, 1966), 64.

161. Edwards, *Presidential Influence in Congress*, 90–100.

162. George C. Edwards III, *The Public Presidency* (New York: St. Martin's Press, 1983), 1–4, 83–88. See also Gary C. Jacobson, *The Politics of Congressional Elections* (Boston: Little, Brown, 1983), 131–137; and Barbara Hinckley, *Congressional Elections* (Washington, D.C.: CQ Press, 1981), chap. 7.

163. For more on the relationship between elections and the economy, see Edward R. Tufte, *Political Control of the Economy* (Princeton, N.J.: Princeton University Press, 1978). See also James E. Campbell, *The Presidential Pulse of Congressional Elections* (Lexington: University Press of Kentucky, 1993).

164. Hinckley, *Congressional Elections*, 114–131.

165. Edwards, *The Public Presidency*, 25–30.

166. Neustadt, *Presidential Power*, 9.

167. See Theodore Roosevelt, *The Autobiography of Theodore Roosevelt* (New York: Scribner's, 1958), 197–200; and William Howard Taft, *The President and His Powers* (New York: Columbia University Press, 1916), 138–145.

168. See Edwards, *Presidential Influence in Congress*, chaps. 5 and 6. See also Light, *The President's Agenda*, esp. intro. and chap. 1.

169. Edwards, *Presidential Influence in Congress*, 202.

170. Samuel Kernell, *Going Public: New Strategies of Presidential Leadership*, 2d ed.(Washington, D.C.: CQ Press, 1993), 4.

171. Lowi, *The Personal President*.

172. Mary E. Stuckey, *The President as Interpreter-in-Chief* (Chatham, N.J.: Chatham House, 1991); Jeffrey K. Tulis, *The Rhetorical Presidency* (Princeton, N.J.: Princeton University Press, 1987).

173. These measures are summarized in Steven A. Shull, *Presidential Policy Making* (Brunswick, Ohio: King's Court, 1979), 326–330; and Spitzer, *President and Congress*, 88–93.

174. The following assessments of individual presidents are drawn partly from Berman, *The New American Presidency*, chaps. 6–8; and Wayne, *The Legislative Presidency*, 32–59, unless otherwise noted.

175. Neustadt, *Presidential Power*, 118–119.

176. Fred I. Greenstein, *The Hidden-Hand Presidency* (New York: Basic Books, 1982), 57.

177. Barbara Kellerman, *The Political Presidency* (New York: Oxford University Press, 1984), 87.

178. Ibid., 155.

179. See Richard P. Nathan, *The Administrative Presidency* (New York: Wiley, 1983).

180. Barbara Sinclair, "Governing Unheroically (and Sometimes Unappetizingly): Bush and the 101st Congress," in *The Bush Presidency*, ed. Colin Campbell and Bert A. Rockman (Chatham, N.J.: Chatham House, 1991), 168–176; Michael Duffy and Dan Goodgame, *Marching in Place: The Status Quo Presidency of George Bush* (New York: Simon and Schuster, 1992).

181. Tiefer, *The Semi-Sovereign Presidency*, x. See also Walter Williams, "George Bush and Executive Branch Policymaking Competence," *Policy Studies Journal* 21 (winter 1993): 700–717.

182. Spitzer, "The Conflict Between Congress and the President over War."

183. Phil Duncan and Steve Langdon, "When Congress Had to Choose, It Voted to Back Clinton," *Congressional Quarterly Weekly Report*, December 18, 1993, 3427–3431.

184. Bob Woodward, *The Agenda: Inside the Clinton White House* (New York: Simon and Schuster, 1994). See also Fred I. Greenstein, "The Presidential Leadership Style of Bill Clinton: An Early Appraisal," *Political Science Quarterly* 108 (winter 1993–94): 589–602.

SELECTED BIBLIOGRAPHY

Binkley, Wilfred E. *President and Congress*. New York: Vintage, 1962.

Crabb, Cecil V., Jr., and Pat M. Holt, eds. *Invitation to Struggle: Congress, the President and Foreign Policy*. 4th ed. Washington, D.C.: CQ Press, 1992.

Edwards, George C. III. *At the Margins: Presidential Leadership of Congress*. New Haven, Conn.: Yale University Press, 1989.

Fisher, Louis. *Constitutional Conflicts Between Congress and the President*. Lawrence: University Press of Kansas, 1991.

——. *The Politics of Shared Power: Congress and the Executive*. 3d ed. Washington, D.C.: CQ Press, 1993.

——. *President and Congress*. New York: Free Press, 1972.

Gimpel, James G. *Fulfilling the Contract: The First 100 Days*. Boston: Allyn and Bacon, 1996.

LeLoup, Lance T., and Steven Shull. *Congress and the President: The Policy Connection*. Belmont, Calif.: Wadsworth, 1993.

Light, Paul C. *The President's Agenda*. Rev. ed. Baltimore: Johns Hopkins University Press, 1991.

Mezey, Michael L. *Congress, the President, and Public Policy*. Boulder, Colo.: Westview, 1989.

Peterson, Mark A. *Legislating Together: The White House and Capitol Hill from Eisenhower to Reagan*. Cambridge, Mass.: Harvard University Press, 1990.

Spitzer, Robert J. *The Presidency and Public Policy*. University: University of Alabama Press, 1983.

——. *President and Congress: Executive Hegemony at the Crossroads of American Government*. New York: McGraw-Hill and Temple University Press, 1993.

——. *The Presidential Veto*. Albany: State University of New York Press, 1988.

Sundquist, James L. *The Decline and Resurgence of Congress*. Washington, D.C.: Brookings, 1985.

Thurber, James A., ed. *Divided Democracy: Cooperation and Conflict Between the President and Congress*. Washington, D.C.: CQ Press, 1991.

Wayne, Stephen J. *The Legislative Presidency*. New York: Harper and Row, 1978.

CHAPTER 34

The President and the Supreme Court

BY JOHN R. VILE

IN 1776 the American Declaration of Independence proclaimed that legitimate government rested on "the consent of the governed." Eleven years later, the writers of the U.S. Constitution began their preamble with the words "We the People." The Framers of the Constitution grounded it on popular consent, but they favored a representative, or indirect, rather than a direct, or pure, democracy.[1] Accordingly, they designed institutional structures and constitutional guarantees that would temper majority rule with protections for minority rights and respect for the rule of law.

The Framers' scheme of checks and balances divided government powers both vertically and horizontally. The Framers devised a federal system in which the new national government shared powers with existing state governments. Within the national government, the Framers separated powers and responsibilities among the legislative, executive, and judicial branches.

The Framers also delineated the general lines of authority between the national government and the states and among the three branches of the national government. Still, they realized that the government they created was a unique hybrid and that allocations of power were sometimes unclear and overlapping. If the Constitution was to succeed in its objective of balancing power, it would need an arbiter. It would also require an institution that could enforce constitutional limits. In part by the Framers' design and in part by historical practice and historical necessity, the judicial branch of the government has assumed these roles. Both functions bring the judiciary in contact with the executive branch.

The Judicial System: Origins and Development

The American judicial system is more than two hundred years old, but many of its most important features can best be understood by examining its constitutional foundations and early history. Although the Framers envisioned the judiciary as one of three branches of the new national government, the position of the early judiciary as an unelected branch of government within a republican system was precarious. Its initial exercises of power were tentative and controversial. To a remarkable degree, Chief Justice John Marshall, who served on the Court from 1801 to 1835, helped define the role of the judicial branch of government and set it on the course familiar to Americans today.

CONSTITUTIONAL FOUNDATIONS

In 1787 fifty-five delegates assembled in Philadelphia to amend the Articles of Confederation, which had provided for a weak national government. It soon became apparent that the wiser course was to scrap the Articles and write a new document, the U.S. Constitution.

Under the Articles, Congress was the only independent branch of government. From the introduction of the Virginia Plan at the beginning of the Constitutional Convention and through most of the convention's subsequent discussions, delegates agreed to balance the legislative branch with an executive and a judicial branch. The delegates devoted most of their deliberations to the two elected branches. They began their constitutional outline by describing the legislative branch and entrusted to this body a broad array of powers including some, like the regulation of interstate commerce, that it had not exercised under the Articles of Confederation. Congress was to be responsive to the people. The Framers specified that voters would directly select members of the lower house, the House of Representatives, who would serve two-year terms. Members of the upper house, the Senate, would serve six-year terms and be more indirectly responsible to the voters. State legislatures chose senators under the original Constitution. In 1913 the states ratified the Seventeenth Amendment, which ushered in direct election of senators.

Because the people, directly or indirectly, elected members of Congress, the Framers expected that it would be the most powerful and important of the three branches. They therefore concluded that it was also the branch most in need of constraint and control. As he surveyed the existing state legislatures, James Madison observed, "The legislative department is everywhere extending the sphere of its activity, and drawing all power into its impetuous vortex."[2] The Framers' decision to divide Congress into two houses, the principle of bicameralism, was one indication of their desire to temper and slow its deliberations.

The creation of a powerful unitary executive and an independent judiciary further demonstrated the Framers' desire to balance the authority of the legislative branch.[3] They rejected, however, a proposal providing for a "council of revision" consisting of the president and members of the judiciary with power to veto laws. Still, the Framers constructed these branches so that they can unite in opposition to legislative authority.

Article II of the Constitution specifies that a single individual serving a four-year term is to head the executive branch. The

Constitution entrusted the president with relatively broad authority, including the powers to veto laws, make appointments, execute laws, issue pardons and reprieves, and serve as commander in chief of the armed forces. Even though the president is not elected directly by the voters, but by electors from each state, the power of the president and vice president is enhanced by the fact that they are the only two American officials elected by the nation as a whole. *(See "Role of the Electoral College and the Selection of Electors," p. 187, in Chapter 5, Vol. I.)*

The foundations of judicial power are far more complex than the foundations of legislative or executive power. They rest in part on constitutional moorings, in part on historical practice, and in part on the power of symbolism and on respect for the rule of law. Article III of the Constitution, the last and briefest of the three "distributing" articles, outlines the judicial power of the United States. Section I mentions the Supreme Court, but does not specify how many members it will have. Because the delegates to the Constitutional Convention wished to delay a controversial decision, Article III entrusts the establishment of other, "inferior" courts to Congress at its discretion.

Article II, section 2, specifies that the president shall appoint justices of the U.S. Supreme Court subject to the "Advice and Consent of the Senate." This provision also includes other judges of any inferior court established under Article III. Convention records indicate that the process of appointment and confirmation represents a compromise between delegates who wanted the president to appoint judges and those who wanted Congress to exercise this power.

Section 1 of Article III stipulates that judges will serve "during good Behaviour," meaning that judges serve until they resign, retire, die, or are impeached, convicted, and removed from office in accordance with procedures outlined in the Constitution. The Framers also hoped to guarantee judicial independence without subjecting judges to the long-term eroding effects of inflation during lives of extended service. Accordingly, section 1 allows Congress to raise, but not lower, judges' pay.

JUDICIAL JURISDICTION

Section 2 of Article III deals with jurisdiction, the kinds of cases the Supreme Court and the other courts established by Congress would handle. The Framers intended to strengthen the new national government while preserving state powers. A federal system necessarily calls for arbitrationamong the various levels of government. A system that relied solely on state courts might find the maintenance of central powers problematic. Accordingly, the Founders assigned to the federal courts all matters that would have a bearing on the distribution of powers under the new system.

Under Article III federal courts are granted jurisdiction over some cases based on the subject matter of the case and others based on the nature of the parties to the suit. In the first category, the Constitution extends the judicial power of the United States to "all Cases, in Law and Equity [law and equity refer to two distinct branches of English law, which were then adjudicated by separate courts but combined by this constitutional provision in the same U.S. courts], arising under this Constitution, the laws of the United States, and Treaties made, or which shall be made under their Authority." With a view to the limits of state borders and the need to govern interstate and foreign commerce, the Constitution extends federal jurisdiction "to all Cases of admiralty and maritime Jurisdiction."

In the second category, the nature of the parties to the suit, the Constitution entrusts to federal courts cases involving diplomatic personnel. Just as with controversies between U.S. states or citizens and foreign states and their citizens, to which the Constitution also extends U.S. jurisdiction, cases involving diplomats could have an impact on American foreign policy. Article III extends the judicial power of the United States to cases in which the U.S. government is a party, to disputes involving different states or citizens from different states, and to controversies in which citizens of a state claim land under grants made by other states. And, anticipating a provision that would be included in the Bill of Rights, Article III guarantees jury trials in all criminal cases other than impeachment. This provision helps ensure that the people ultimately temper the power of federal judges.

The Constitution left the division of power among national courts largely to future congressional judgments. It did specify, however, that the Supreme Court would have original jurisdiction, acting as a trial court, in two classes of cases, those "affecting Ambassadors, other public Ministers and Consuls" and "those in which a State shall be Party." Congress has subsequently granted concurrent original jurisdiction in most such cases to lower federal courts, leaving the Supreme Court with relatively few exclusive cases of original jurisdiction; what remains mostly involves disputes between states. Even in these cases, the Court often appoints special masters to recommend action for its consideration.

As the capstone of a much larger federal judicial hierarchy, the Supreme Court is primarily an appellate court. The Constitution vests the Court with appellate jurisdiction in all cases other than the two specified. With a view toward political checks and balances, Article III specifies that the Court shall exercise appellate jurisdiction "with such Exceptions, and under such Regulations as the Congress shall make." This provision raises the possibility that Congress could impose limits on jurisdiction that could undermine judicial independence. *(See "Congressional Regulation of Judicial Jurisdiction," p. 1302.)*

In retrospect, the most striking feature of the grants of judicial power in Article III is the failure to specify what the courts were to do when judges concluded that state or federal laws or executive actions conflicted with the fundamental law of the Constitution. There are hints in the document, especially when it mentions possible instances of state law conflicting with the federal Constitution. For example, Article VI contains the famous supremacy clause:

This Constitution, and the Laws of the United States which shall be made in Pursuance thereof; and all Treaties made, or which shall be made, under the Authority of the United States, shall be the supreme Law of the Land; and the Judges in every State shall be bound thereby, any Thing in the Constitution or Laws of any State to the contrary notwithstanding.

As important as this clause is, it addresses itself primarily to state rather than to federal judges. Only with difficulty (perhaps by focusing on laws "made in Pursuance thereof") can it be read as a mandate to the courts to examine the constitutionality of federal laws. The power of courts to invalidate laws—the power that brings the judiciary into conflict with the other two branches and which scholars today call judicial review—rests less on the specific words of the constitutional text than on other sources. These sources include the implications to be drawn from (1) a written Constitution unchangeable by ordinary legislative means; (2) a system dividing power between the national government and the states; and (3) a plan that divides power among three branches, each with distinct, if somewhat limited and overlapping, functions.

FEDERALIST AND ANTI-FEDERALIST VIEWS

Once the Constitution was written, the document went for ratification to the states, where Federalists and Anti-Federalists debated its merits and the future of the nation. Because the members of the judiciary were to be appointed rather than elected, Anti-Federalist opponents of the new Constitution were especially concerned about this branch of the new government. They saw what Herbert Storing described as "the tracks of a consolidating aristocracy."[4] Robert Yates, an Anti-Federalist who wrote under the name Brutus, anticipated the power of judicial review with disfavor. He argued, "If . . . the legislature pass any laws, inconsistent with the sense the judges put upon the constitution, they will declare it void; and therefore in this respect their power is superior to that of the legislature." Noting that judges would be "independent of the people, of the legislature, and of every power under heaven," Brutus observed, "Men placed in this situation will generally soon feel themselves independent of heaven itself."[5]

The most important defense of the Constitution that emerged from the Federalist/Anti-Federalist debates was a series of eighty-five articles that appeared in New York newspapers during that state's debate over ratification and was subsequently published as *The Federalist Papers*. Alexander Hamilton, James Madison, and John Jay wrote as "Publius," a name they took from a prominent Roman statesman. Hamilton, mindful of Anti-Federalist criticisms of the judiciary, devoted most of the *Federalist* essays from No. 78 to the end to defending it. All the essays concerning the judiciary shed light, but No. 78 is the most famous and instructive. In it Hamilton portrayed the judicial branch of the new government as "the least dangerous to the political rights of the Constitution." He argued that

while the president would dispose the "honors" and bear the "sword" of the community, and Congress would control the "purse" and prescribe the "rules," the judiciary would "have neither FORCE nor WILL but merely judgment." Moreover, Hamilton argued that in exercising its powers the judiciary "must depend ultimately upon the aid of the executive arm even for the efficacy of its judgments." Hamilton used this argument about judicial weakness to justify judicial "permanency in office," and he argued that judicial independence was essential "in a limited Constitution."[6]

Hamilton also tackled the issue of judicial review. Rather than contradicting Brutus's assertion that courts would exercise such power, Hamilton appeared to take it for granted. Instead of agreeing that such power would elevate the judicial branch over the legislative branch, Hamilton argued that the power to void unconstitutional legislation would enforce the Constitution that the people had adopted. Opposing those who thought that the legislative branch should judge its own constitutional powers, subject to electoral controls, Hamilton wrote:

> It is far more rational to suppose that the courts were designed to be an intermediate body between the people and the legislature in order, among other things, to keep the latter within the limits assigned to their authority. The interpretation of the laws is the proper and peculiar province of the courts. A constitution is, in fact, and must be regarded by the judges as, a fundamental law.[7]

Although Hamilton argued in subsequent essays that a bill of rights was not necessary, in a sense he helped lay the groundwork for modern conceptions of these guarantees. In arguments later echoed by Thomas Jefferson and James Madison,[8] Hamilton argued that the independence of judges would allow them to serve as guardians of the

> rights of individuals from the effects of those ill humors which the arts of designing men . . . sometimes disseminate among the people themselves . . . and which . . . have a tendency . . . to occasion dangerous innovations in the government, and serious oppressions of the minor party in the community.[9]

Having portrayed judges as defenders of individual rights, Hamilton returned to the benefits that would flow from judicial permanence and independence. He argued that the permanence of judicial offices would attract individuals who combined "the requisite integrity with the requisite knowledge." Hamilton further argued that tenure would enable judges to master the "strict rules and precedents which serve to define and point out their duty in every particular case that comes before them."[10]

THE JUDICIARY ACT OF 1789

Although the delegates to the Constitutional Convention were relatively clear about how Congress and the presidency would be organized, they deferred a number of matters involving the judicial branch, especially its relation to the existing state courts. Given this ambiguity, the action of the First Congress in adopting the Judiciary Act of 1789 proved to be especially significant. Oliver Ellsworth, a Connecticut delegate to the conven-

THE CONSTITUTIONAL CONVENTION AND JUDICIAL SELECTION

The convention that wrote the U.S. Constitution met in Philadelphia in the summer of 1787 and included fifty-five delegates from all of the existing thirteen states except Rhode Island. The delegates spent far more time discussing the legislative and executive branches than the judiciary, but this branch of government also raised some crucial issues. Among the most important was judicial selection. Some delegates wanted the president to appoint judges, while others thought the Senate should have this power.

James Wilson of Pennsylvania generally favored a strong presidency, so it is not surprising that he also supported presidential appointment of judges. He contrasted appointment by a "single responsible person" with appointment by a more numerous legislative body where "intrigue, partiality, and concealment" might prevail.[1]

Arguing for the other side, Maryland's Luther Martin said that, as a body composed of members from all the states, the Senate "would be best informed of characters and most capable of making a fit choice."[2] Connecticut's Roger Sherman reaffirmed that, as a body with more members, the Senate would also have "more wisdom" than a single executive.[3]

James Madison of Virginia twice suggested a provision that appears quite close to the modern legislative veto mechanism. He proposed "that the judges should be nominated by the executive, and such nominations become appointments, unless disagreed to by two-thirds of the second branch of the legislature."[4]

Pennsylvania's Benjamin Franklin (also known for proposing that the new president serve without pay) made the most novel suggestion regarding judicial appointments, but he may not have been completely serious. He cited the alleged Scottish practice of entrusting the power of appointing judges to lawyers. Franklin noted that, with such a system, the lawyers "always selected the ablest of the profession in order to get rid of him and share his practice among themselves."[5]

Ultimately, the delegates at the Constitutional Convention chose the current arrangement, first proposed by Alexander Hamilton. It provides that all federal judges are selected by the president with the "advice and consent" of the Senate. High-profile confirmation battles, including the unsuccessful nomination of Judge Robert Bork in 1987 and the ultimately successful nomination of Associate Justice Clarence Thomas in 1991, have brought new scrutiny to this process.

1. Saul K. Padover, *To Secure These Blessings: The Great Debates of the Constitutional Convention of 1787, Arranged According to Topics* (New York: Washington Square Press, 1962), 400. Debate from June 5, 1787.
    2. Ibid., 401. Debate from July 18, 1787.
    3. Ibid., 402. Debate from July 18, 1787.
    4. Ibid., 405. Debate from July 21, 1787.
    5. Ibid., 399–400. Debate from June 5, 1787.

tion, who would become chief justice in 1796, was largely responsible for drafting this law. The beauty of the Judiciary Act, some of which is still in effect, is that it "upheld the principle of federal supremacy," while bringing about compromise between "states' rights and centralization."[11] The law also created a tripartite system of federal courts, the central outlines of which are recognizable today.

Section 1 of the Judiciary Act provided that the Supreme Court would consist of the chief justice and five associates who would meet semiannually, with four justices required for a quorum. The act created thirteen district courts, one for each of the eleven states then in the Union, and one each for Kentucky and Maine, which were not yet states. The law further specified that a single judge residing within the district would preside over each district court. The Judiciary Act specified that intermediate circuit courts (today generally referred to as courts of appeal) would consist of two Supreme Court justices riding circuit and one district judge, with a minimum of two judges required to conduct business. The law barred district judges from hearing appeals from their own decisions.[12]

The most significant part of the Judiciary Act is section 25. Consistent with Hamilton's understanding in *Federalist* No. 82, section 25 provided for national supremacy and uniformity by permitting appeals, or writs of error, from the highest court within each state to the Supreme Court in three broad categories of cases. These were (1) cases in which state courts had questioned the validity of a U.S. treaty or statute; (2) cases in which state courts had upheld a state statute against claims that it conflicted with the U.S. Constitution, treaties, or laws; and (3) cases in which parties were denied rights on the basis of claims made under the federal "Constitution, treaty, statute or commission."[13]

Section 9 of the act outlined the jurisdiction of the district and circuit courts. Significantly, the law entrusted to federal courts "exclusively of the courts of the several States, cognizance of all crimes and offences that shall be cognizable under the authority of the United States, committed within their respective district, or upon the high seas."[14] The lower federal courts shared concurrent jurisdiction with the states over other civil matters.

Today's circuit courts are primarily appellate courts. Under the Judiciary Act of 1789, however, in addition to hearing appeals from the district courts, the circuit courts served primarily as courts of first resort for civil cases of more than $500 involving the United States, individual states, or aliens. Federal courts exercised this power concurrently with existing state courts.

One other provision of the Judiciary Act, section 13, proved to be especially important. This section attempted to designate those cases in which the U.S. Supreme Court exercised original and appellate jurisdiction. The law specified that in some cases the Court's original jurisdiction would be exclusive, but in others it would be concurrent. This article also provided for the Supreme Court to issue writs of mandamus, or written orders, to officials of the federal government.

THE EARLY COURT

In contrast to the dramatic developments that occurred in the early history of Congress and the presidency, the first decade of the Supreme Court was relatively inauspicious. Indeed, the justices had no cases to hear in their first two sessions. They had to devote far more of their time and energies to the unappealing duties of riding their designated circuits, at a time when transportation and accommodations were primitive, than to their work on the high court. This circuit-riding duty, however, had the advantage of bringing the people into contact with some federal authority.

President George Washington selected John Jay of New York as the first chief justice. Washington sought nationalist sentiment and geographical balance in choosing the other five initial nominees. They were John Rutledge of South Carolina, William Cushing of Massachusetts, James Wilson of Pennsylvania, John Blair of Virginia, and James Iredell of North Carolina. Jay resigned in 1795 to become governor of New York, a position he considered more important. Oliver Ellsworth succeeded Jay after the Senate refused to approve Washington's recess appointment of John Rutledge. Ellsworth also accepted a diplomatic assignment, which limited his participation on the Court, and he resigned in 1800 citing poor health.

While riding circuit in 1792, Chief Justice Jay and other justices struck a blow for judicial independence and for the doctrine of separation of powers in a decision known as *Hayburn's Case*.[15] They refused to examine the claims of disabled veterans under the Pension Act of 1792. They based their decision on the fact that this was not a judicial duty and that other government officials had the power to review these claims. Moreover, in 1793 Jay set an important precedent that has lasted to this day. He refused to render an advisory opinion to President Washington regarding his Neutrality Proclamation of 1793. In a letter to Washington, Jay noted the separation of powers among the three branches and commented:

These being in certain respects checks upon each other, and our being judges of a court in the last resort, are considerations which afford strong arguments against the propriety of our extrajudicially deciding the questions alluded to, especially as the power given by the Constitution to the President, of calling on the heads of departments seems to have been *purposely* as well as expressly united to the *executive* departments.[16]

Despite the scarcity of cases, the Supreme Court rendered several significant opinions in its early years. These included *Ware v. Hylton* (1796), in which the Court asserted the supremacy of federal treaties over conflicting laws; *Hylton v. United States* (1796), in which the Court upheld a federal carriage tax as an excise that did not need to be apportioned according to population; and *Calder v. Bull*, a 1793 decision limiting the definition of ex post facto laws to retrospective criminal (and not civil) laws.[17]

In *Chisholm v. Georgia* (1793) the Court ruled, contrary to assurances that Hamilton and other Federalists had made, that

John Jay, the first chief justice of the United States, served until June 29, 1795. During his tenure on the Court, Jay negotiated a treaty with Great Britain, which had been impressing Americans into the British navy. Such a diplomatic mission would be unthinkable for any member of today's Supreme Court.

citizens from other states could sue a state.[18] The Eleventh Amendment, ratified in 1798, overturned this decision. Significantly, the state of Georgia felt so strongly about its sovereignty in this case that it refused even to send a representative to the Supreme Court to argue its case. The state subsequently threatened to hang anyone who enforced the Court's judgment.[19] This setback undoubtedly contributed to the common perception that the Court was unlikely to become a fully equal coordinate branch of the federal government.

A TIME OF TRANSITION

The waning days of President John Adams's Federalist administration (1797–1801) proved critical for the future history of the Supreme Court and for the development of relations between the Court and the presidency. After Jay refused Adams's offer to nominate him for a second time as chief justice, Adams nominated John Marshall of Virginia. While many presidents have been disappointed in their judicial selections, Adams would later say, "My gift of John Marshall to the people of the United States was the proudest act of my life."[20] In his thirty-four years on the Court, Marshall established its power and elevated its position in a way few people, familiar only with the earlier Court, could have imagined.

Marshall's tenure had an inauspicious beginning. He was an ardent Federalist, and members of President Thomas Jefferson's incoming Democratic-Republican administration deeply resented his appointment. Federalist passage in 1798 of the Alien and Sedition Acts, directed to restricting immigration and limiting partisan criticism of those in power, had stung leaders of the new administration. The outgoing Federalist Congress now confronted the incoming administration with the passage of the Judiciary Act of 1801. This law, which mixed needed reforms with partisan politics, added six new federal circuit courts with sixteen additional judges. It eliminated the irksome need for Supreme Court justices to ride circuit. The act also reduced the size of the Supreme Court by one justice effective with the next vacancy and added forty-two new justices of the peace and a new district court for the District of Columbia.[21] On his final night as president, Adams sat signing the commissions of new justices of the peace. He filled these positions with Federalist supporters who could be expected to work against the incoming administration.

Early in 1802 the incoming Democratic-Republicans repealed the Judiciary Act. Vigorously, and somewhat hypocritically, leading Federalists argued that Republican actions were motivated by partisanship. They also argued that the law unconstitutionally violated provisions in Article III assuring judicial tenure. The Supreme Court prudently rejected this argument in *Stuart v. Laird* (1803).[22]

Fortunately, partisanship did not blind the Democratic-Republicans to the very real need for some structural changes in the courts. They partially met this need when they adopted the 1802 Amendatory Act increasing the number of circuits from three to six. The new law did not, like the 1801 law, eliminate the circuit-riding duties of the justices. Instead, it assigned only one justice to each circuit, rather than the two assigned under the Judiciary Act of 1789.[23] Another provision of the 1802 law reduced the Supreme Court sessions from two to one per year, which had the not unwelcome side effect of postponing the Court's next session until 1803.

MARBURY V. MADISON AND THE POWER OF JUDICIAL REVIEW

The 1803 session was historic. The Court issued its opinion, written by Chief Justice John Marshall, in *Marbury v. Madison*. This case is important because it marked the first time the Supreme Court struck down an act of federal legislation. However implicit the exercise of judicial review might have been in the system of checks and balances established by the Constitution, the power was not explicitly stated there. Prior to *Marbury*, the Court had predicated a number of its decisions on its possession of this power, but the Court had neither exercised nor defended it. Marshall's defense of judicial review in *Marbury* continues to be the classic exposition of the subject.

The case arose from the midnight appointments that had preceded Jefferson's inauguration and included actions by two U.S. presidents and their advisers. President Adams signed a

John Marshall became chief justice in 1801 and served for thirty-four years. He delivered 519 of the 1,215 opinions of the Supreme Court during his tenure, among them some of the best known in the Court's history: *Marbury v. Madison, McCulloch v. Maryland, Dartmouth College v. Woodward,* and *Gibbons v. Ogden.*

commission designed to make William Marbury a justice of the peace in the District of Columbia. Although Adams signed and sealed Marbury's commission, the outgoing secretary of state, who just happened to be John Marshall himself, did not deliver it. Jefferson subsequently directed James Madison, his secretary of state, to withhold Marbury's commission. Marbury, in turn, proceeded under the authority of section 13 of the Judiciary Act of 1789 to ask the Supreme Court for a writ of mandamus, an order to compel an executive official—in this case, Madison—to carry out a particular act or duty.

Marshall undoubtedly recognized that the Democratic-Republican administration might well refuse to heed an order vindicating Marbury's rights, but he was intent on establishing the Court's power to restrain both legislative and executive abuses. In his opinion, Marshall declared that the Court could offer Marbury no remedy because provisions of the Judiciary Act of 1789 that appeared to give the Court authority to issue writs of mandamus in a case of original jurisdiction not specified in Article III were unconstitutional. While that reasoning denied Marbury the remedy he sought, it did not stop Marshall from using his opinion as a platform to lecture Jefferson on his responsibility.

Marshall's opinion took the form of three questions: (1) Did Marbury have a right to his commission? (2) Did the laws offer him a legal remedy? and (3) Was this remedy a writ of mandamus from the Supreme Court? Marshall answered the first question in the affirmative. He argued that Marbury's commission was complete when signed and sealed. The secretary of state's duty to deliver it was therefore an obligatory ministerial act rather than a discretionary political act. Here Marshall chided the Jefferson administration for failing to carry out its duty.

In answering the second question, Marshall further argued that, if the government was to be "a government of laws, and not of men," then courts should be able to issue writs to executive officers who failed to honor individual rights.[24] Marshall expanded on this idea when, examining the third question, he addressed the nature of the writ of mandamus. He noted that, while the Judiciary Act of 1789 appeared to allow the Supreme Court power to issue the writ in this case, Congress had no authority to expand the original jurisdiction of the Court beyond that delineated in Article III. *(See "Judicial Jurisdiction," p. 1284.)*

Here Marshall, using arguments similar to those Hamilton had advanced in *The Federalist Papers,* established the foundation for judicial review. He concluded that, although Marbury had been unjustly treated, the Supreme Court could offer him no judicial remedy. Marshall based his central argument on the existence of a written constitution designed as "a superior paramount law, unchangeable by ordinary means." By ignoring the words of the Constitution when applying the laws, the courts would effectively "overthrow in fact what was established in theory." However, Marshall argued, "It is emphatically the province and duty of the judicial department to say what the law is." In cases of apparent conflict, the Court should apply the paramount law of the Constitution over an act of Congress. Any other alternative would give "the legislature a practical and real omnipotence with the same breath which professes to restrict their power within narrow limits."[25]

Marshall supplemented this central point with a number of arguments and examples. Because Article III gave the Court the responsibility of hearing cases "arising under the Constitution," Marshall argued that it would be absurd for the courts not to examine this Constitution. He cited various constitutional provisions, some addressed specifically to the judiciary, that could become nullities if the Court concurred in blatant congressional attempts to subvert them. Marshall further stated that the judicial oath obliged judges to apply the Constitution they were sworn to uphold. Finally, he argued that the supremacy clause of Article VI did not declare all laws to be the supreme law of the land but "those only which shall be made in pursuance of the constitution." Concluding that "a law repugnant to the constitution is void," Marshall said that Marbury could obtain no relief.[26] No matter how much Jefferson despised the Court's claim of authority in this case, he could do nothing about it because Marshall did not order him to do anything that he might have refused to do.

The Modern Court System

The power of the president may vary significantly with the individual who occupies the office, but power is more stable and evenly distributed in the judicial system. The structure established in the Judiciary Act of 1789 provides the essential outlines of today's system.[27] It continues to be federal, with an overlapping network of state and national courts. The federal judicial system is also hierarchically arranged into three main tiers with the Supreme Court at the pinnacle. Although the Supreme Court exercises increased discretion over which cases it accepts on appeal, a number of internal and external restraints still limit its power. The most important of these restraints is the way justices are appointed: they are nominated by the president and confirmed by the Senate.

The Constitution did not abolish existing state court systems; rather, it added another layer of courts beside and, to some extent, over them. State courts continue to hear the majority of cases argued in the United States each year. Since the Constitution was adopted, individual state court systems have evolved unique features and nomenclatures, but most of these systems resemble the hierarchical features of the federal system. Six states now have a single set of trial courts. The others divide the work among specialized courts of limited jurisdiction (juvenile courts, traffic courts, domestic relations courts, and others) that handle less serious civil and criminal matters and courts of general jurisdiction that deal with more serious civil and criminal cases. Many states have consolidated and more clearly defined the jurisdictions of these state trial courts and added a layer of intermediate appellate courts. Typically, parties to a suit may appeal decisions of these appeals courts to a state supreme court.[28]

Influenced by notions of Jeffersonian and Jacksonian democracy, some states elect their judges or combine methods of appointment and election. State judges often serve for limited terms and/or have mandatory retirement ages. State courts may exercise concurrent jurisdiction over some federal questions. Consistent with the scheme established in the Judiciary Act of 1789, losing litigants may also take appeals from state supreme courts to the U.S. Supreme Court in cases involving a substantial federal question.

LOWER FEDERAL COURTS

The federal system is neatly arranged into three tiers, with the Supreme Court at the top. Lower U.S. district and U.S. courts of appeal are generally the first to hear cases that eventually find their way to the Supreme Court.

Ninety-four U.S. district courts form the base of the federal system of constitutional courts. These courts exercise powers originally shared by district and circuit courts established by the

Judiciary Act of 1789. About 650 judges and about half as many U.S. magistrates work in U.S. district courts. U.S. district courts are courts of original jurisdiction. They deal with the following six categories of cases: (1) cases involving crimes against the United States; (2) civil actions in excess of $50,000 that fall under the U.S. Constitution or laws and treaties; (3) cases of more than $50,000 involving aliens or citizens of different states; (4) admiralty and maritime cases; (5) cases involving the review or enforcement of federal administrative agencies; and (6) other matters prescribed by congressional law.[29] Although the U.S. Supreme Court has discretion over its docket, lower courts do not. Individuals falling within the jurisdiction of the U.S. district courts appear there as a matter of right.

Consistent with the federal scheme, district courts follow state or territorial boundaries except for Wyoming's, which covers parts of Yellowstone Park within neighboring states. Each state has at least one district court, and the most populous have four. Typically, a single judge presides over a district court, although occasionally three-judge courts are used. A district court judge may hear a case alone or in conjunction with a jury, which renders the verdict.

The Judiciary Act of 1789 created two different types of federal trial courts. The Judiciary Act of 1891 refined the system by creating circuit courts of appeal (since 1948 usually referred to as courts of appeal), of which there are currently thirteen. Of these, eleven are numbered circuits that hear appeals from states according to geographical groupings of three or more states; in 1995 Congress began to consider splitting up the Ninth Circuit, currently the largest. There is an additional circuit court for the District of Columbia and another specialized court that hears appeals in cases once heard by the Court of Claims and the Court of Customs and Patent Appeals. Circuit courts were once composed of district judges and circuit-riding Supreme Court justices. Congress periodically trimmed, but did not end, this duty until 1891.

Today, more than 175 judges preside over U.S. circuit courts. While judges within a circuit occasionally sit as a group (*en banc*), they usually hear cases in panels of three. Most cases come to the courts of appeal via the U.S. district courts from which individuals may appeal as a matter of right. Courts of appeal also take cases from a variety of other specialized courts—for example, the U.S. Claims Court, various territorial courts, and the U.S. Court of International Trade—as well as from federal administrative departments and agencies.[30] The caseload of the courts of appeal has increased significantly in recent years, and, because the U.S. Supreme Court can hear only a limited number of appeals, most appeals court decisions are final. Because U.S. district courts and courts of appeal are federal constitutional courts created under the authority of Article III, the president appoints all their judges, with the advice and consent of the Senate, and judges serve "during good Behaviour." The U.S. Court of Military Appeals, the U.S. Tax Court, the U.S. Court of Veterans Appeals, and several territorial courts are cre-

ated under Article I. As legislative courts, they do not have the same protections as constitutional courts.

In the 1970s Harvard's Paul A. Freund headed a commission that issued a call, supported by Chief Justice Warren E. Burger, for a national court of appeals to stand midway between the U.S. courts of appeal and the Supreme Court. Advocates believe that a court at this level would help ease the Supreme Court's workload. In recent years, however, the Supreme Court has decreased its workload by accepting fewer cases. Moreover, fears that a new appellate court might become a kind of second Supreme Court and weaken the existing institution have dampened support for a new court and prevented it from being established.[31]

THE U.S. SUPREME COURT

Despite its importance in the federal scheme, the U.S. Supreme Court has always been the least well-known branch. Unlike their counterparts in Congress and the White House, its members usually avoid the limelight. They make few public appearances, and most confine their speaking engagements to gatherings of lawyers and judges. Until 1935 the Supreme Court did not even have its own building in Washington, D.C.; rather, it met in the U.S. Capitol, occupying several different spaces over the years. Since October 1935 and thanks to the efforts of Chief Justice William Howard Taft, the Court has been housed in an impressive marble building across the street from the Capitol. Today, the Court is clearly recognized as the pinnacle of a coordinate branch of the federal government, and its decisions receive substantial news coverage.

The Constitution gives Congress the power to decide the number of justices, which has varied from five to ten. Congress set the number at nine in 1869 and has not subsequently changed it.

Article III of the Constitution spells out the original jurisdiction of the Supreme Court, some of which it exercises concurrently with other courts. These cases, however, constitute only a small percentage of its overall caseload. The Supreme Court's appellate jurisdiction still includes cases involving substantial federal questions that make it to the highest courts within each state. It also hears appeals from federal constitutional courts and most federal legislative courts.

The Supreme Court accepts appellate cases by way of three writs, or petitions. The writs are the instruments individuals and their attorneys use to bring the Court's attention to the legal issues at stake in a case. Writs of appeal are technically compulsory, but the Supreme Court may dismiss them in cases where it does not find a substantial federal issue. The writ of certification is an appeal by which lower courts ask the Supreme Court to answer disputed questions of law.

The most frequently used route to the Court is the writ of certiorari, accounting for about 90 percent of its cases. The Court can choose which of these appeals to accept and which to reject. Rule 17 of the Supreme Court states, "A review on writ of

COURTS AND PUBLICITY

Of the three branches of the federal government, the judiciary is the least known to the public. A survey conducted by the *Washington Post* in December 1995 showed that only 6 percent of respondents knew that William Rehnquist was the chief justice of the United States.[1]

In part this ignorance may stem from the fact that, apart from a few well-publicized confirmation hearings, justices are usually able to stay out of the limelight. Unlike presidents, who are photographed nearly everywhere they go, and members of Congress, who are televised during sessions, federal judges enjoy a greater degree of anonymity. At present, cameras are not allowed in federal courts, including the U.S. Supreme Court.

Until recently, some forty-five state and federal courts had permitted such coverage.[2] However, in September 1994 the United States Judicial Conference, headed by Chief Justice Rehnquist, ended a three-year experiment that allowed cameras in some civil and criminal federal trials. It decided to discontinue this practice for fear of distracting witnesses.

Cameras have never been permitted to cover sessions of the U.S. Supreme Court. Justices apparently fear that the presence of cameras might cause disruptions. They also have indicated that cameras might cause a tendency to make justices behave in uncharacteristic ways.

Someone making a first visit to the Court might be surprised by the way justices vigorously question the attorneys appearing before them. The justices sometimes exchange comments with one another and often divert the attorneys from their prepared texts. Justices might feel less free to engage in such repartee in front of cameras.

Ultimately, however, the decision to keep cameras out may be personal, reflecting the uniqueness of a branch of government whose members do not run for office. Justices may simply wish to preserve their privacy. As Tony Mauro, a reporter for *USA Today* noted, "They very much covet their privacy and their anonymity. They're very loath to lose that."[3]

The justices' experience with televised confirmation hearings may be an additional factor leading them to oppose television coverage. After the notorious Robert Bork hearings, Justice Thurgood Marshall, who had originally favored televised coverage of the Court, said, "No one's going to stick a camera up my nose."[4]

In 1955 Chief Justice Earl Warren initiated the practice of making tape recordings of arguments before the Court. These tapes have been deposited in the National Archives and have been available primarily to scholars. In 1993 political scientist Peter Irons published a set of tapes and transcripts from twenty-three of these cases, including *United States v. Nixon* (1974), which concerned President Nixon's attempt to keep private recordings made in the Oval Office.[5] Chief Justice Rehnquist sharply criticized Irons for unauthorized use of the recordings. Questions also have been raised about Irons's editing and rearrangement of some of the tapes.[6] Whatever the ultimate scholarly judgment, the recordings afford some insight into the exciting process of oral argument before the Supreme Court.

1. Richard Morin, "Who's in Control? Many Don't Know or Care," *Washington Post* January 29, 1996, A6.
2. Cited by Richard Davis, *Decisions and Images: The Supreme Court and the Press* (Englewood Cliffs, N.J.: Prentice-Hall, 1994), 150.
3. Ibid., 152.
4. Ibid., 154.
5. Peter Irons and Stephanie Guitton, *May It Please the Court* (New York: New Press, 1993).
6. Edward Lasarus, "Electronic Hash," *Atlantic Monthly*, October 1994, 36–41.

certiorari is not a matter of right, but of judicial discretion, and will be granted only when there are special and important reasons therefor."[32] After the justices and their clerks—typically recent graduates of prestigious law schools—review the petitions for certiorari, the justices vote on which to review and which to refuse. The Court operates by the "rule of four," meaning that four justices must vote to hear a case before an appeal is accepted, although the votes are rarely this close. When the Court refuses to accept a case, the decision of the lower court stands. Leaving the decision in place does not necessarily mean that the Court would agree with it on review. It may merely indicate that the justices do not think the issue raised in the case is significant or yet "ripe" for review.

Of the thousands of petitions that come to the Court annually, about half are *in forma pauperis* petitions filed by individuals who are too poor to afford attorneys. One such petitioner was the plaintiff in *Gideon v. Wainwright* (1963), the historic case in which the Court decided to extend the right to state-appointed counsel to indigent defendants in nonfelony cases.[33] In the past, the Court typically agreed to hear about 200 cases each year, rendering full verdicts in about 150 of them and dealing with the rest by issuing *per curiam* (unsigned) opinions or short memorandum orders.[34] Recently, the Court has begun to accept about one hundred cases a year. In part by cutting back on the number of *in forma pauperis* petitions that it hears, the Court issued eighty-two signed and six *per curiam* opinions in the 1994–1995 term.[35] Although this number is the lowest since 1955, observers cannot be certain whether the Court's restriction of its caseload is a trend or an aberration.

When the Supreme Court accepts a case, both sides file full written briefs. Other interested parties and special-interest groups often ask permission to file amicus curiae (friend of the court) briefs in support of those submitted by the parties to the suit. Attorneys subsequently present their cases orally before the Supreme Court. The solicitor general, a Justice Department official appointed by the president to represent the government before the Court, argues cases in which the U.S. government is involved. After oral arguments, the justices meet in conference behind closed doors, discuss and vote on each case, and accept writing assignments. *(See "The Chief Justice—Primus Inter Pares," p. 1294.)* The justices who write opinions then circulate them among their colleagues for comments. Final decisions represent collective judgments: justices have the right to suggest modifications and to switch their votes before the opinions are printed and made public. On "opinion days" the justices announce their verdicts from the bench, sometimes reading parts aloud. The official *U.S. Reports* and other unofficial compilations then publish the decisions. In addition, several on-line computer services provide the text of Supreme Court opinions.

Typically, a majority or, in some cases, a plurality, of the justices issues an opinion for the Court. In sensitive cases, the Court may give weight to its decision by issuing a unanimous opinion. Chief Justice Earl Warren worked for months to get a unanimous opinion in *Brown v. Board of Education* (1954), which ended the long-standing policy of racial segregation in public education.[36] Four years later, in a follow-up opinion designed to assert judicial power to order desegregation at Central High School in Little Rock, Arkansas, the justices took the extraordinary step of listing their names at the beginning of the opinion.[37] When President Richard Nixon, in connection with the Watergate investigation, threatened to defy an order to produce tapes for the special prosecutor, all eight members of the Court who voted joined in a single opinion.[38]

In more routine cases, justices individually or collectively may file concurring opinions. Justices write concurrences when they agree with the majority decision but not with its reasoning. Justices may also write dissenting opinions in which they outline reasons for voting against the majority decision. An evenly split decision, which can occur when the seat of one of the nine justices is vacant, leaves the lower court decision in place.

APPOINTMENT AND CONFIRMATION

The president and members of Congress achieve their legitimacy from their election by, and their accountability to, the voters. In contrast, the links between the people and their judges are indirect. The president nominates and the Senate confirms judicial nominees, but once they reach the bench, the pale threat of impeachment and conviction is the only legal sanction for individual judges. The Constitution specifies minimal age requirements for members of the two elected branches; it makes no such specifications for the judiciary, perhaps in the belief that legal training and the process of presidential appointment and senatorial confirmation will ensure a modicum of competence.

From time to time, individuals call for "merit" selection of judges. President Jimmy Carter chose to make merit nominations to lower federal courts from suggestions submitted by special committees. In most cases, however, the process of becoming a federal judge or Supreme Court justice is a "supremely political" process.[39] Part of the problem is that merit is an elusive concept, and no one can know whether prior judicial experience will lead to judicial greatness. Moreover, as liberal justice Hugo

Only two women have been appointed to serve on the Supreme Court since its establishment in 1789. President Ronald Reagan nominated Sandra Day O'Connor, right, of Arizona in 1981 and President Bill Clinton named Ruth Bader Ginsburg, left, of New York in 1993.

Black's past membership in the Ku Klux Klan demonstrated, there is no certainty that past behavior and affiliations are a guide to future conduct. More important, as the role of the courts has expanded in American society, presidents want to appoint individuals most likely to reflect their ideological perspectives. Although senators recognize that presidents do their best to get like-minded individuals onto the bench, senators may also try to block appointments that they find personally distasteful or far out of line with their own thinking.

A tradition of "senatorial courtesy" has developed in regard to federal judges in U.S. district courts. In effect, this custom allows individual senators from the president's party to blackball candidates from their state whom they oppose. Presidents therefore have a strong incentive to consult with senators before making such appointments.

Individual senators do not have as much power over nominees to the U.S. circuit courts of appeal or the Supreme Court, but collectively senators often exercise their prerogative to block presidential nominations. Although the Senate in 1981 confirmed President Ronald Reagan's nomination of Sandra Day

O'Connor as the first woman to serve as an associate justice by a 99–0 vote, and later confirmed his 1986 and 1988 nominations of Antonin Scalia and Anthony Kennedy by 98–0 and 97–0, respectively, it confirmed William Rehnquist's promotion to chief justice in 1986 by a closer 65–33. In 1987 the Senate defeated, 42–58, the nomination of conservative standard-bearer Robert Bork, and, by reflecting the public firestorm that erupted after it was revealed that nominee Douglas Ginsburg had smoked marijuana as a law professor, persuaded Ginsburg to withdraw from consideration.

The Senate confirmed President George Bush's nomination of David Souter in 1990 by a 90–9 vote, but came close to rejecting Clarence Thomas. Thomas was perceived as ideologically much more conservative than Souter, and he was accused of sexual harassment by law professor and former employee Anita Hill in televised congressional hearings in 1991 before the Senate Judiciary Committee. President Bill Clinton's 1993 and 1994 nominations of Ruth Bader Ginsburg and Stephen Breyer proved relatively uncontroversial. However, conservative opponents, many of whom were still bitter over the Bork defeat, had threatened an all-out fight if Clinton nominated a liberal standard-bearer such as Laurence Tribe, a Harvard law professor and noted attorney.

In addition to ideology, personal friendship and considerations of political expediency or popularity may influence presi-

---

THE ORDEAL OF CLARENCE THOMAS

Of all the confirmation hearings for Supreme Court justices, probably none have been more dramatic than those of nominee Clarence Thomas in 1991. President George Bush selected Thomas to fill the seat vacated by the retirement of Justice Thurgood Marshall. Marshall, the first African American to sit on the Court, previously had served as legal counsel for the NAACP, where he headed the Legal Defense and Education Fund that successfully argued *Brown v. Board of Education* (1954). President John F. Kennedy appointed Marshall to the U.S. court of appeals, and Lyndon Johnson selected him first as solicitor general and then in 1967 as an associate justice. In his almost twenty-five years on the Court, Marshall established himself as a liberal who championed government action designed to protect racial minorities and the poor.

In contrast, Thomas was a conservative who stressed individual achievement and responsibility and was wary of centralized government. A graduate of Yale Law School with an extensive record of service in the Reagan and Bush administrations, Thomas had been appointed to the Circuit Court for the District of Columbia just one year before President Bush nominated him to the Supreme Court.

In 1987 President Reagan's nomination of another appeals court judge, Robert Bork, had been defeated largely because of questions concerning his conservative views. Thomas's publicly stated views were close enough Bork's to make him appear vulnerable. In his favor, Thomas had been born in humble circumstances in Pin Point, Georgia, and his career in government was impressive.

The Senate Judiciary Committee questioned Thomas and was evenly divided on whether he should be confirmed, but a date was set for a vote by the full Senate, which appeared to be leaning in his direction. His chances were helped by the strong support of Sen. John Danforth, a Missouri Republican for whom Thomas had worked early in his career.

Before the full Senate could vote, however, reports began to surface in the media that law professor Anita Hill had accused Thomas of sexual harassment. Hill was an African American and a fellow Yale Law School graduate. She had worked for Thomas at the Equal Employment Opportunity Commission and the Department of Education.

Once the allegations of sexual harassment became public, some senators were unwilling to support Thomas without a hearing. With the nation watching, the Judiciary Committee reconvened and listened to dramatic public testimony in which Hill described in detail numerous incidents of alleged sexual harassment. Probing questions from Sen. Arlen Specter left the viewing audience divided about Hill's credibility.

Thomas adamantly denied all charges and refused even to watch the televised hearings. Senator Danforth has stated that Thomas went through tremendous personal agony and described Thomas's ordeal as similar to a death. In his response to the Senate Judiciary Committee after Hill's testimony, Thomas came out swinging against what he perceived as the unfairness of this very public process:

This is a circus. It is a national disgrace. And from my standpoint, as a black American, as far as I am concerned, it is a high-tech lynching for uppity blacks who in any way deign to think for themselves, to do for themselves, to have different ideas, and it is a message that, unless you kow-tow to an old order, this is what will happen to you, you will be lynched, destroyed, caricatured by a committee of the U.S. Senate, rather than hung from a tree.[1]

Thomas denied all of Hill's allegations, and she decided not to reappear before the committee for further questioning.

President Bush continued his public support for Thomas, but many, especially feminists, were convinced that Hill had told the truth. The committee was left with a he said/she said story and a confused public that at first believed Hill but then found Thomas's testimony persuasive.

Unable to confirm or refute the charges against Thomas, the Senate Judiciary Committee took no further vote. The full Senate confirmed him, 52–48, the closest such vote in the twentieth century. For many, the Thomas hearings stand as a vivid example of the perils of the modern confirmation process.

1. Quoted by John C. Danforth in *Resurrection: The Confirmation of Clarence Thomas* (New York: Viking, 1994), 148.

dential selection of judges. Presidents almost always nominate members of their own party, but occasionally a president reaches across party lines. For example, President Franklin D. Roosevelt, a Democrat, promoted to the post of chief justice a Republican, Harlan Fiske Stone, who had been appointed to the Court by Calvin Coolidge. As war approached, Roosevelt may have been trying to forge national unity.

Certain traditions have played a role in appointments. Presidents have aimed for regional balance on the Court as a way of making it appear to be representative of the nation and increasing judicial legitimacy. In similar fashion, since President Andrew Jackson nominated Roger B. Taney, a Roman Catholic, to be chief justice in 1835, the Court has seen some religious diversity in its members. For many years, there have been both a "Jewish" seat—first held by Justice Louis Brandeis but vacant for some time after the retirement of Justice Abe Fortas—and a "Catholic" seat on the Court. Race appears to have been a significant factor in President Lyndon Johnson's appointment of Thurgood Marshall in 1967 and Bush's appointment of Clarence Thomas to replace Marshall when he retired in 1991. Ronald Reagan undoubtedly viewed Antonin Scalia's Italian ethnicity as a plus at a time when many anticipated that New York governor Mario Cuomo, also of Italian descent, might be the Democratic nominee in the next presidential election.

Fulfilling a campaign promise, President Reagan appointed the first woman to the Court in 1981. President Carter also had promised to appoint a woman to the Court, but no vacancy occurred during his term. President Clinton undoubtedly gained some political advantage by giving his first Supreme Court appointment to Ruth Bader Ginsburg, the second woman and first Jewish woman to serve on the Court. Justice Harry Blackmun's retirement in 1994 prompted renewed but unsuccessful pressures on the president to appoint the first Hispanic nominee to the Court. Clinton turned instead to Stephen G. Breyer, an appeals court judge and former Harvard law professor. The media devoted little attention to the fact that Breyer was Jewish.

Of the 144 individuals nominated to the Supreme Court, the Senate either rejected or did not act on twenty-eight. Henry Abraham has identified eight factors that seem to have been prominent in Senate decision making, although he notes that usually more than one issue has been at work. The factors, a blend of political and substantive reasons, are as follows:

(1) opposition to the nominating president, not necessarily the nominee; (2) the nominee's involvement with one or more contentious issues of public policy . . . ; (3) opposition to the record of the incumbent Court . . . ; (4) senatorial courtesy (closely linked to the consultative nominating process); (5) a nominee's perceived political unreliability on the part of the party in power; (6) the evident lack of qualification or limited ability of the nominee; (7) concerted, sustained opposition by interest or pressure groups; and (8) fear that the nominee would dramatically alter the Court's jurisprudential lineup.[40]

A great irony of the appointment and confirmation process is that, no matter how hard presidents try, they can never be certain of getting their ideological soul mates on the Court. Two

years after his appointment of Oliver Wendell Holmes Jr., President Theodore Roosevelt reacted to one of Holmes's antitrust decisions by noting that he "could carve out of a banana a Judge with more backbone than that!"[41] On one occasion, President Harry Truman referred to Justice Tom C. Clark as his "biggest mistake" and said, "He hasn't made one right decision that I can think of."[42] President Dwight D. Eisenhower came to regret his appointments of Chief Justice Earl Warren and Associate Justice William Brennan, both of whom became known as judicial activists with a liberal bent.

The Senate rejected two of President Nixon's nominations to the Supreme Court (Clement Haynsworth and G. Harrold Carswell) after acrimonious controversy. Still, Nixon generally succeeded in using his four appointments to the Supreme Court to stem if not reverse the liberal judicial tide created by the Warren Court in criminal justice and school busing. However, one of Nixon's appointees, Justice Harry Blackmun, was the author of the Court's controversial decision legalizing abortion in *Roe v. Wade* (1973).[43]

In his early years on the Court, Blackmun's jurisprudence so often reflected that of his conservative friend and fellow Minnesotan, Warren Burger, that commentators sometimes referred to them as the "Minnesota twins." By the time Blackmun retired in 1994, he was generally identified as the most liberal member of the Court. In what must have been a bitter disappointment for President Nixon, three of his appointees—Chief Justice Burger and Justices Blackmun and Lewis Powell—voted against his claim of executive privilege in the controversial tapes case of 1974. The verdict was 8–0; Nixon's fourth appointee, William Rehnquist, a former Justice Department employee, recused himself.

Judicial tenure helps insulate federal judges from day-to-day political pressures. Judges often serve over long time periods during which the Court's focus changes, the justices' own views may alter, and issues that their appointing presidents never contemplated come to the fore. Nominating presidents and confirming senators can influence the ideological disposition of the judiciary, but their influence ultimately is limited.

SPECIAL JUDICIAL PERSONNEL

Although all justices have an equal vote, the chief justice has special responsibilities that make this position worthy of separate treatment. The solicitor general and the attorney general—neither of whom is purely a judicial officer—also play roles that are especially important in linking the judicial and executive branches of government.

The Chief Justice—Primus Inter Pares

The only mention of the chief justice in the Constitution is its description of the chief's responsibility for presiding over trials of presidential impeachment in the U.S. Senate. Early in the history of the Court, John Marshall demonstrated that a chief justice can have a substantial impact on the Court and the nation. Scholars typically, albeit not altogether accurately, refer to a Court by the name of the chief justice who led it. On the Court, the chief justice is *primus inter pares,* first among equals. As with other justices, the president appoints the chief with the advice and consent of the Senate. A president may choose to elevate a sitting justice, but most chief justices have come from outside the Court. Once confirmed, the chief justice retains that position.

The chief justice presides over Court sessions, both public and private. Some chiefs are more adept than others at guiding discussions, achieving judicial consensus, and promoting personal harmony among their fellow justices. While scholars sometimes classify chiefs according to whether they exercise effective task leadership or social leadership or both,[44] the chief's colleagues make their own more personal assessments. Speaking of Chief Justice Taft (1921–1930), whom scholars generally regard as a good social leader (his friend Van Devanter was the Court's task leader), Justice Holmes noted, "He is good-humored, laughs readily, not quite rapid enough, but keeps things moving pleasantly."[45] In contrast, when Justice Stone was elevated to chief, a position he held from 1941 to 1946, Judge Learned Hand's observation that Stone had a "certain inability to express himself orally and maintain a position in a discussion" proved accurate.[46] Scholars generally do not regard him as either a good task or social leader. By almost any measure, chiefs like John Marshall (1801–1835) and Earl Warren (1953–1969) were adept leaders, while others were not as successful.

In addition to their work with colleagues, some chiefs—Taft and Burger are notable examples—paid particular attention to judicial administration and/or to legislation directly affecting the judiciary, and some—again Taft—attempted to influence the president's choice of new justices. The chief justice also heads the Judicial Conference of the United States, a group of twenty-eight lower court judges that meets twice a year to draw up rules designed to promote efficient judicial administration.

Whatever role the chief justice plays in representing the Court to the outside world, this individual also participates in judicial decision making. The chief has the same vote when it comes to deciding cases as do the other justices. The chief's power is enhanced, however, by a long-standing practice of the Court. When voting with the majority, the chief is responsible for either writing the opinion of the Court or choosing a justice to write it. In especially important cases, the chief may write the decision; in other cases, the chief may assign the opinion to a justice who, in the chief's thinking, will write the most acceptable opinion or garner the most support within the Court and with the public. When the chief votes in the minority, the power to write or assign the opinion goes to the justice in the majority with the longest tenure on the Court.

The Solicitor General: The Tenth Justice

Of all the links between the executive and judicial branches, perhaps none is as important as the solicitor general, who is appointed by the president with the advice and consent of the Senate. This office was created in 1870 to provide the attorney general with someone to represent the government in cases before the Supreme Court. Because of this vital role, commentators often call the solicitor general the "tenth justice." In addition to an office at the Justice Department, the solicitor general has an office at the Supreme Court, and attorneys general usually allow solicitors to exercise considerable discretion. One of the solicitor's main duties is to decide which of the government's cases should be appealed. Because the solicitor screens out so many appeals, the Court is far more likely to accept those he makes than others. The Court generally grants the solicitor permission to file amicus curiae briefs in cases affecting the government, and the solicitor sometimes argues before the Court as an amicus.

The solicitor general has certain privileges, including "lodging," the practice whereby the solicitor brings to the Court's attention outside information not evident in the formal legal briefs. The solicitor general can also "confess error" and ask the Court to reconsider a decision that was decided in the government's favor. Historically, scholars have viewed the solicitor as both an advocate for the executive and the keeper of the government's conscience. In 1980 President Reagan launched an aggressive campaign contending that many Supreme Court precedents were based on mistaken interpretations of the Constitution. At the same time, he envisioned a more partisan role for the solicitor, who would challenge decisions on abortion and other social policies with which the administration disagreed. Reagan's policies highlight the difficult balance between law and politics that solicitors must maintain.

Some solicitors have become Supreme Court justices. These include William Howard Taft (1890–1892), Robert Jackson (1938–1940), who also served as attorney general, Stanley Reed (1935–1938), and Thurgood Marshall (1965–1967). Other well-known solicitors are John Davis (1913–1918), the 1924 Democratic presidential nominee, Archibald Cox (1961–1965), the first special prosecutor in the Watergate case, and Robert Bork (1973–1977), later a U.S. appellate judge and unsuccessful Supreme Court nominee.[47] It was Bork who carried out President Nixon's order to fire Special Prosecutor Archibald Cox after Attorney General Elliot Richardson and his top assistant, William Ruckelshaus, resigned rather than comply with the president's command.

The Attorney General: Between Law and Politics

Like the solicitor general, the attorney general of the United States serves both the executive and the judicial branches. The office was originally created not when laws were made for the executive branch but as part of the Judiciary Act of 1789. This may have been a way of recognizing that the attorney general would be "a quasi-judicial officer of the court."[48] The Department of Justice, which the attorney general heads, was not established until 1870.

The attorney general often must straddle the fine line between law and politics. The attorney general serves both as a legal adviser (although presidents also have personal lawyers on the White House staff) and as a member of the cabinet and political adviser to the president. As a legal adviser, the attorney general frequently gives an opinion on the constitutionality of a given law or practice, sometimes with significant implications for the scope of presidential powers. From the time in 1791 that President Washington rejected Edmund Randolph's view that the creation of a national bank was unconstitutional, however, the president has not always heeded the attorney general's advice. In cases where no judicial decisions subsequently confirm the constitutionality of rulings by attorneys general, the legal force of such opinions is likely to be disputed.

A thorough study of the attorney general's office has identified two models of attorneys general. One type serves as a partisan advocate for presidential policies. Such individuals may even have been active in the president's election. Robert Kennedy, who served under his brother, and John Mitchell, who served in the Nixon administration, are good examples. The other type projects a more detached image of neutrality in the service of the law. Gerald Ford's attorney general, Edward Levi, is a good example. Scholars frequently call for attorneys general to emulate the latter model, but ideological affinity with a president's programs and close personal friendship with the president as an individual may enhance the attorney general's powers. Moreover, some of the nation's most effective attorneys general—Kennedy, for example—have shown that an attorney general can successfully devote attention to both law and politics.[49]

Although the president carries out some law enforcement responsibilities through the Treasury Department and other cabinet-level departments, a strong Justice Department is essential to the forceful execution of the laws, whether they deal with civil rights, antitrust actions, taxes, national security, immigration and naturalization, or federal criminal law. Attorneys general are likely to be careful to distance themselves from any matters that might involve presidential criminal culpability, leaving such investigations to modern-day special prosecutors. Still, attorneys general often must make decisions about overall departmental priorities—for example, how vigorously to pursue antitrust matters, white collar crime, or mob activities—that can significantly affect federal law enforcement authority.

Statutory Interpretation and Judicial Review

In *Federalist* No. 78 Hamilton responded to Anti-Federalist critics of the new government by arguing that the judiciary would be the weakest of the three branches of the government. He contended that the judiciary would exercise neither the power of the purse nor the sword but merely the power of "judgment."[50] Hamilton may have correctly assessed the relative weight of judicial power when compared with that of the two elected branches. To contemporary ears, however, his analysis underestimates the authority of what has arguably become the most powerful judicial system in the world.

The power of American courts derives from two practices.

The first is statutory interpretation. This power was implicit in John Marshall's assertion in *Marbury v. Madison* that courts have the responsibility "to say what the law is" in cases arising before them.[51] This responsibility often requires a court to ascertain whether a president is properly interpreting or enforcing the law. *Rust v. Sullivan* (1991) is a good example. The question in *Rust* was whether President Reagan's policy (followed by President Bush, but subsequently discontinued by President Clinton) of cutting off funds to family planning agencies that offered abortion counseling was constitutional.[52] The Supreme Court's decision to accept the Republican administrations' interpretation significantly affected Bush's policies.

The second practice is judicial review, which is the examination of state and federal laws and executive actions to determine if they are in conflict with the U.S. Constitution and therefore void. A president may take a forceful action, such as President Truman's seizing of the steel mills in 1952 to avoid a threatened strike during the Korean War, only to find that the Court does not support him.[53] As powerful as this judicial instrument is, it is nowhere specifically stated in the Constitution. Rather, it follows from its consistency with constitutional themes like the rule of law and the importance of a written constitution unchangeable by ordinary legislative means.

THE REACTIVE NATURE OF THE AMERICAN JUDICIARY

Citizens often expect the president, as the nation's chief elected official, to exercise leadership by taking bold initiatives. Courts are more passive. Indeed, one of the aspects of statutory interpretation and judicial review that makes them palatable to democratic theory is that American courts do not exercise a general right to examine the meaning of laws or to question their constitutionality. Instead, courts perform these functions only when they adjudicate concrete cases and controversies involving two parties contending over a live issue. Courts often devote considerable attention to the doctrines of "standing" and "justiciability." These doctrines are designed to guarantee that those who bring cases before them have genuine grievances that the judiciary can resolve.

In *Valley Forge Christian College v. Americans United for Separation of Church and State* (1982) the Court rejected a religious watchdog group's challenge to a transfer of government property to a parochial college. The group had no direct interest in the controversy, but had heard about the transfer in the news.[54] In *Allen v. Wright* (1984) the Court denied standing to parties in a class action suit. They were challenging IRS designations of tax-exempt status to certain private schools alleged to be practicing discriminatory conduct.[55] The Court ruled that these individuals, whose children attended public schools, had not demonstrated a clear connection between the alleged acts of segregation and any direct harm to themselves.

The Court has other doctrines by which it can limit the cases it hears. For example, the Court may dismiss cases that it thinks are not "ripe" for review. In 1947 it refused to hear a suit by a

The Supreme Court did not have a home of its own in the nation's capital until this marble building, designed by architect Cass Gilbert, was completed in 1935. Previously, the Court had met in the Capitol on the Senate side. The Capitol, however, provided no office space for the justices or their assistants.

group of public workers who sought to forbid enforcement of the Hatch Act, which limited their participation in politics, because the workers were not engaged in any political activities.[56] The Court may also dismiss cases that it believes have become moot. In *DeFunis v. Odegaard* (1974) the Court refused to accept a challenge to an affirmative action program for minorities by a white law school student who had been admitted by order of the lower courts and was about to graduate.[57]

Even in cases where the Court has jurisdiction, it may decide that, although harm has occurred, the government is not at fault. In *DeShaney v. Winnebago Social Services* (1989) the Court declared that the state was not responsible under the due process clause of the Fourteenth Amendment for serious injury that a father inflicted on his child after the state returned the child to his custody. Acknowledging that the facts of the case were "undeniably tragic," Chief Justice Rehnquist said that the due process clause did not protect individual rights "against invasion by private actors." Rehnquist elaborated on the clause:

It forbids the State itself to deprive individuals of life, liberty, or property without "due process of law," but its language cannot fairly be extended to impose an affirmative obligation on the State to ensure that these interests do not come to harm through other means.[58]

While there are a few exceptions, federal courts generally do not accept so-called taxpayer suits in which litigants try to get standing simply because of their status as taxpayers. In *United States v. Richardson* (1974) the Court refused to accept a taxpayer challenge to the CIA's failure to publish its budget as Article I, section 9, of the Constitution seems to require all government agencies to do.[59] Suits involving complaints about the effects of the defoliant Agent Orange on Vietnam War veterans or the safety of the Dalkon Shield intrauterine device or breast implants demonstrate that the courts sometimes accept class action suits where the interests of multiple litigants who are simi-

larly situated are presented in a single case. Individuals and interest groups also commonly initiate test cases specifically designed to challenge the constitutionality of a law or other government action.

OTHER CHARACTERISTICS OF JUDICIAL DECISION MAKING

Americans value their rights, and the judicial role in upholding them undoubtedly contributes positively to the Court's public standing. There is a classic American distinction that, although blurry around the edges, is no less important on that account. This distinction is between law and politics. Especially when they adhere to precedents and to the constitutional text, judges can claim not to be enforcing their political will but their studied legal judgments on the meaning of the Constitution. Whether the courts should have a monopoly on constitutional interpretation is a legitimate question, but at least the courts are insulated from day-to-day public opinion in a number of ways designed to give them independence. Judges are appointed rather than elected; they serve for life rather than for fixed terms; and their salaries are protected against pay cuts. These protections are designed to ensure that judicial decisions on constitutional matters will be based on respect for the rule of law rather than on political considerations.

The emphasis on law is evident by the fact that it is considered inappropriate for individuals to "lobby" courts the way they might try to influence members of Congress or the president. Furthermore, judges typically seek to justify their opinions through legal reasoning rather than appeals to public opinion. Alone among public officials, judges emerge from their chambers in black robes that emphasize their authority and continuity with legal tradition. Typically, judges hold sessions on raised platforms and in settings designed to convey solemnity and deliberation. Moreover, judges sometimes deprecate their powers by describing themselves as apolitical actors. Felix Frankfurter once said, "When a priest enters a monastery, he must leave—or ought to leave—all sorts of worldly desires behind him. And this Court has no excuse for being unless it's a monastery."[60]

Although Justice Frankfurter's words conflicted with some of his actions, judges realize that they wield little direct power. Ultimately, their authority, that is, their power to issue binding decisions, rests upon the support of the other two branches and the states. The public perception that courts have exercised legitimate authority also contributes to judicial power.

THE INESCAPABLE BURDEN OF INTERPRETATION

However much judges seek to justify or cloak their power behind appeals to the law, those who disagree with the courts periodically argue that they have assumed too much power in an otherwise democratic society. Advocates of judicial restraint, who believe that the courts have become too "activist" or that their interpretations of the Constitution have strayed from the intent of the Framers and the words of the Constitution, may find ammunition in dissenting opinions of the Court. Sometimes the attacks come from the president or members of the administration.

Intense arguments have erupted over the methods of constitutional interpretation that judges should employ. Those who believe courts should stick close to the Framers' intent or to the constitutional text generally call themselves originalists. Nonoriginalists are more willing for courts to make judgments on the basis of legal principles, on behalf of broad conceptions of human rights, or on the developing nature of the Constitution. Critics have accused the Court of attempting to make the law or rewrite the Constitution rather than interpret it, citing cases such as *Miranda v. Arizona* (1966),[61] the Court's expansive decision on the rights of criminal defendants, or *Roe v. Wade* (1973), the case that initially legalized a fairly broad right to abortion.

Part of the problem is that many of the clauses that judges must interpret (phrases like the Fourteenth Amendment's "equal protection of the laws" and the Eighth Amendment's prohibition of "cruel and unusual punishment") are rife with interpretive ambiguity. Writing in *Youngstown Sheet & Tube Co. v. Sawyer,* also known as the *Steel Seizure Case,* in 1952, Justice Robert Jackson noted:

A judge, like an executive advisor, may be surprised at the poverty of really useful and unambiguous authority applicable to concrete problems of executive power as they actually present themselves. Just what our forefathers did envision, or would have envisioned had they foreseen modern conditions, must be derived from materials almost as enigmatic as the dreams Joseph was called upon to interpret for Pharaoh.[62]

Whatever the technical divisions between the legislative and judicial branches, judges necessarily engage in some law making. The line between what is appropriate and inappropriate may well depend not only on the language of the Constitution but also on the nature of the case before the Court and the temper of the times.

Restraints on Judicial Power

Both internal and external restraints limit the Supreme Court. Observed over time, these restraints have kept the Court from extreme interpretations that lean in either an overly activist or an overly deferential direction. Such restraints also may enable the Court to avoid direct conflict with the presidency.

INTERNAL RESTRAINTS

The judiciary is unique among the three branches of government. While its members frequently wield great powers, their legal training typically gives them great respect for legal precedents. Their education may further impress judges with the importance of deferring where possible to decisions made by members of the elected branches of government. Judges are the first to acknowledge that they have achieved their positions not by popular mandate but by presidential nomination and senatorial confirmation. In a democratic republican form of government like that in the United States, the method of judicial selection necessarily means that judges and justices are once, if not twice, removed from majority will. Moreover, while members of the judiciary may largely have been selected because of their ideology, their oath obliges them to uphold the U.S. Constitution rather than their own policy preferences.

Judges are not the sole decision makers in their courtrooms. U.S. district judges frequently preside over trials in which juries decide the outcome. Moreover, two higher tiers of courts review district court decisions, limiting the potential for individual mischief. Stephen Carter notes that "Harold Cox, appointed to the federal district court in Mississippi by President John Kennedy, issued half-crazy, generally racist rulings but was regularly slapped down by the appellate court."[63] Other federal judges sit on panels where they undoubtedly strive for the respect of their colleagues and members of their profession. Often they must compromise to arrive at consensus.

The Restraining Influence of Precedents

In *Federalist* No. 78 Hamilton noted that judges "would be bound down by strict rules and precedents which serve to define and point out their duty in every particular case that comes before them."[64] He exaggerated. Judges are not mere machines, and precedents do not cover "every particular case" that comes before them. Especially when it comes to constitutional matters, justices of the Supreme Court sometimes take the position that it is better to get an issue "right" than simply to follow precedents. Some of the most important decisions of the twentieth century, including the Court's desegregation decision in *Brown v. Board of Education* (1954), overturned earlier precedents.[65] Moreover, courts sometimes distinguish between the *ratio decidendi,* the core legal principles announced in earlier cases, and mere *obiter dicta,* the extraneous judicial comments. Still, judges and justices frequently express their support for the principle of *stare decisis,* adherence to existing precedents. Rarely do judges start from scratch when making decisions, especially in important constitutional or statutory matters.

An interesting example of *stare decisis* occurred in the 1992 decision in *Planned Parenthood of Southeastern Pennsylvania v. Casey.* Justices O'Connor, Kennedy, and Souter, all Reagan and Bush appointees, wrote this opinion. While accepting somewhat greater restrictions on abortion, they decided not to overturn the Court's holding in *Roe v. Wade,* which recognized a woman's right to procure an abortion. In deciding *Casey,* the three justices consciously weighed the need for "continuity over time" against the possibility that *Roe* was so clearly in error that "its enforcement was for that very reason doomed." Here the justices took four considerations into account:

whether *Roe*'s central rule has been found unworkable; whether the rule's limitations on state power could be removed without serious inequity to those who have relied upon it or significant damage to the stability of the society governed by the rule in question; whether the law's growth in the intervening years has left *Roe*'s central rule a doctrinal anachronism discounted by society; and whether *Roe*'s premises of fact have so far changed in the ensuing two decades as to render its central holding somehow irrelevant or unjustifiable in dealing with the issue it addressed.[66]

The justices answered each question negatively and decided to preserve the *Roe* precedent. Precedents rarely dictate a decision, but they certainly exercise a restraining force on most judges and justices.

Restraints Imposed by Interpretive Principles

Constitutional interpretation is a difficult enterprise. The vigor of judicial dissents testifies to the wide range of possible interpretations of constitutional language. Court observers frequently classify judges as conservative or liberal or as advocates of judicial restraint or judicial activism, but such labels tend to obscure the complexity of the matter. Whatever their persuasions, most judges feel constrained by the constitutional text, historical understandings, precedents, and their view of the judicial role and its place in a tripartite federal system. Consistent with these understandings, judges and justices often proclaim their adherence to principles of judicial restraint or deference to the elected branches, or what Alexander Bickel called "the passive virtues."[67] While judges do not always exercise these "virtues" in individual cases, many certainly pay them more than mere lip service. Political scientist Ronald Kahn notes, "The polity and rights principles held by various justices prevent them, at important times in Court deliberations, from supporting policy outcomes that they personally favor."[68]

A Note on the Political Questions Doctrine

Among the doctrines of judicial restraint that have special importance to relations between the judiciary and the elected branches, probably none is at once more elusive and revealing than the political questions doctrine. The doctrine's very name demonstrates the often elusive distinction between law and politics.

The roots of the political questions doctrine go deep into judicial history. In *Marbury v. Madison* John Marshall said, "The province of the court is, solely, to decide on the rights of individuals. . . . Questions by their nature political, or which are, by the constitution and laws, submitted to the executive, can never be made in this court."[69] The Court used similar reasoning in deciding that the president had the authority under the Enforcement Act of 1795 to call out state militias during the War of 1812. In *Martin v. Mott* (1827) Justice Joseph Story wrote for a unanimous Court, "We are all of opinion that the authority to decide whether the exigency has arisen, belongs exclusively to the President, and that his decision is conclusive upon all other persons."[70]

The political questions doctrine blossomed in the Supreme Court's 1849 decision in *Luther v. Borden.* During the Dorr Rebellion in Rhode Island, President John Tyler decided to recognize the long-standing charter government rather than the newly formed Dorr government. A litigant subsequently asked the Court in a trespass action against an agent of the charter government to recognize the rival Dorr government. His claim centered on the clause in Article IV of the Constitution known as the guarantee clause because it guarantees to each state "a republican form of government."

Identifying the issue as a political question, Chief Justice Taney said that determining which state government to recognize was a matter for Congress to decide. It typically did so when it determined which delegation to seat in the legislature. In the shorter term, Congress had passed legislation vesting in the president the responsibility for deciding which state government to recognize. The president's position in the public eye would be likely to protect against abuse of power. Taney concluded that, while the Court should be ready to accept those responsibilities which the Constitution delegated, "it is equally its duty not to pass beyond its appropriate sphere of action, and to take care not to involve itself in discussions which properly belong to other forums."[71]

The Court took a similar position in two Reconstruction cases, both of which petitioned the Court to enjoin President Andrew Johnson or his subordinates from carrying out Reconstruction laws. The first case was *Mississippi v. Johnson* (1867). There the Court distinguished between duties that were ministerial, meaning that the president or his subordinates might be commanded by the courts to act, and those that were political, meaning that judicial intervention could lead to stalemate or confrontation. It concluded that the case before it involved the latter situation. If the Court issued an order that the president refused to obey, it had no way to compel him to do so. If the president complied, he might find (as he eventually did) that he would be impeached and subject to a Senate trial.[72] In *Georgia v. Stanton* (1868) the Court argued that it had no jurisdiction. It decided that the matters at issue required "the judgment of the court upon political questions, and upon rights, not of persons or property, but of a political character."[73]

The Supreme Court also applied the political questions doctrine to other areas. In *Coleman v. Miller* (1939) it decided, contrary to a number of earlier precedents, that the Constitution vested resolution of questions of amending procedure in Congress.[74] In *Colegrove v. Green* (1946) a Court plurality rejected a challenge to the Illinois system of legislative apportionment under the guarantee clause. It decided that such matters were political questions because they were inappropriate for, and perhaps incapable of, adequate judicial resolution.[75]

The Court significantly transformed the political questions doctrine in *Baker v. Carr* (1962). Here the majority decided, over vigorous dissents, that it now viewed issues of state legislative apportionment as justiciable under the equal protection clause of the Fourteenth Amendment. Justice William Brennan wrote the Court's decision. He identified six areas—none of which he believed to be involved in this particular case—in which the political questions doctrine was still applicable:

Prominent on the surface of any case held to involve a political question is found a textually demonstrable constitutional commitment of the issue to a coordinate political department; or a lack of judicially discoverable and manageable standards for resolving it; or the impossibility of deciding without an initial policy determination of a kind clearly for nonjudicial discretion; or the impossibility of a court's undertaking independent resolution without expressing lack of the respect due coordinate branches of government; or an unusual need for unquestioning adherence to a political decision already made; or the potentiality of embarrassment from multifarious pronouncements by various departments on one question.[76]

In *Powell v. McCormack* (1969) the Supreme Court examined the congressional decision to exclude Adam Clayton Powell from the House of Representatives. Powell was a flamboyant, controversial African American, duly elected by his Harlem district, and he met the constitutionally specified age and residency requirements. The Court reversed the congressional action, deciding, as in *Baker v. Carr,* that no political question was involved.[77] In *Goldwater v. Carter* (1979) the Court rejected as not "ripe" for consideration a plea by members of Congress who challenged President Carter's unilateral termination of a treaty with Taiwan. However, only four justices—Rehnquist, Burger, Potter Stewart, and John Paul Stevens—took the position that this sensitive matter of foreign affairs was a nonjusticiable political question.[78]

Whatever its precise contours, the political questions doctrine still has some force, especially in foreign relations, an area in which courts traditionally defer to actions by the two elected branches, especially the president. Lower federal courts avoided ruling on the constitutionality of the Vietnam War. Subsequently, the Supreme Court (over a vigorous dissent by Justice William O. Douglas) followed their example by refusing to accept a suit in *Massachusetts v. Laird* (1970).[79] In *Crockett v. Reagan* (1982) a U.S. district judge dismissed a suit that members of Congress brought under the War Powers Resolution of 1973.

Rep. Adam Clayton Powell, a Democrat of New York, speaking to the press. During an investigation into his activities, the House of Representatives attempted to exclude him despite the fact that he had been duly elected. In 1969 the Supreme Court said Powell met the constitutional standards for membership and the House could not refuse to seat him.

This suit questioned the legality of President Reagan's military aid to El Salvador.[80] Judge Joyce Green decided that her court was not in as good a position as Congress to ascertain whether American forces had been introduced into a hostile situation or to decide when or whether the sixty-day period specified in the War Powers Resolution had been triggered. The exact status of the political questions doctrine is difficult to ascertain, but it still appears "to have some life left in it." The doctrine serves in judges' minds as a continuing "subjective caution against inappropriate judicial participation in certain kinds of policy issues."[81]

EXTERNAL RESTRAINTS ON JUDICIAL POWER

In addition to internal norms, a variety of structural features constrain courts, or can be brought to bear on them. Chief among the restraints on judicial power is the process for nominating and confirming judges. Presidents are usually anxious to appoint justices they think reflect their views, and recent presidents are no exception. Especially when dominated by members of the opposing party, the Senate may subject nominees to extensive hearings. Generally, nominees refuse to answer direct questions about cases they think will come before them if they are confirmed. Their silence on specific issues does not keep senators either from asking questions or from trying to assure themselves that nominees are in the judicial mainstream. Each nomination raises the issue as to whether the president or Senate should be applying a "litmus test" to nominees, for example, support of or opposition to abortion rulings. Clearly, if a president and a Senate from opposite parties were to apply too many tests, the system would ultimately break down. Moreover, scrutiny of a candidate that seems grossly disproportionate or unfair may backfire on the party that makes it.

Congress has a more direct way to exercise control over the Court. Because the Framers of the Constitution did not specify how many Supreme Court justices there should be, Congress determines the number and could some day adjust it, as has sometimes been done in the past, to partisan advantage. A lame duck session of the Federalist Congress decreased the number of justices just prior to the inauguration of the Democratic-Republican administration. During the Civil War, Republicans increased the number of justices from nine to ten—an action the Judiciary Act of 1869 reversed—to give President Lincoln another appointment. Franklin Roosevelt's notorious court-packing plan, which he offered just after his second election to the presidency, was the last serious attempt to alter the number of Supreme Court justices. Critics argued that Roosevelt's plan threatened checks and balances, and, even though the Democrats controlled Congress, that body rebuffed his plan. The experience makes future alterations in the number of justices unlikely. *(See "Franklin D. Roosevelt and the Court-packing Plan," p. 1307.)*

Perhaps the most serious check on power is the threat of impeachment and removal from office. The Senate has never voted by the necessary majority to remove a Supreme Court justice or a U.S. president whom the House of Representatives had impeached. The Democratic-Republicans' unsuccessful attempts to remove Justice Samuel Chase during the Jefferson administration is a powerful, and arguably salutary, example of the limits of this approach. A provision in Article II, section 4, of the Constitution serves as a critical barrier to widespread use of this mechanism. The language describes impeachable offenses As "Treason, Bribery, or other high Crimes and Misdemeanors." Although these words are somewhat ambiguous, the general scholarly consensus is that the phrase limits the grounds for removing individuals from office to serious breaches of public trust and not to mere political differences.[82]

Practice, however, has not always followed such clear-cut understandings. In 1803 the Democratic-Republican-dominated Congress removed district judge John Pickering, the first federal judge to be impeached and convicted, not because he was guilty of a crime but because he was alcoholic and probably insane. The Constitution makes no explicit provisions for such circumstances.

In more recent times, partisan considerations appear to have motivated threats of impeachment against Chief Justice Earl Warren and Justice William Douglas, both of whom were fairly liberal justices. Moreover, Rep. Gerald R. Ford stated that "an impeachable offense is whatever a majority of the House of Representatives considers it to be at a given moment in history."[83] Threats of impeachment against Justice Abe Fortas are more difficult to assess but appear to have stemmed from a blend of partisan motives and genuine ethical concerns. Just as

the threat of impeachment and conviction later influenced President Nixon's decision to step down, such possibilities probably also figured in Fortas's decision to resign.

In a 1993 case, Walter Nixon, a U.S. district court judge, unsuccessfully challenged the legality of his impeachment and conviction. Nixon had challenged the trial as illegal, complaining that the Senate had entrusted the central proceedings to a committee rather than devoting its full attention to his trial. The Court decided that Nixon's claim was nonjusticiable. Speaking for the Court, Chief Justice Rehnquist focused on the language of Article I, section 3. This provision states that the Senate should have the "sole" power to try impeachments. Rehnquist also observed:

Judicial involvement in impeachment proceedings, even if only for purposes of judicial review, is counterintuitive because it would eviscerate the "important constitutional check" placed on the Judiciary by the Framers.

Rehnquist noted that, if the Court accepted jurisdiction over Senate impeachment proceedings, it "would place final reviewing authority with respect to impeachments in the hands of the same body that the impeachment process is meant to regulate."[84]

Constitutional Amendments

The ability to amend the Constitution provides another external restraint on the power of the courts. When the Supreme Court exercises statutory interpretation and issues a pronouncement on the meaning of a law or regulation that is contrary to what Congress says it intended, there is no need for an amendment. Congress can simply clarify its will by passing a new statute. For example, in 1986 the Court upheld a military regulation that prohibited a member of the air force from wearing a yarmulke while on duty, so Congress amended a military authorization bill and reversed this judgment.[85] An earlier example involved the Court's declaration that employee health plans that excluded pregnancy coverage did not violate existing civil rights laws. In response, Congress adopted the Pregnancy Discrimination Act of 1978 and overturned the Court's decision.[86] Likewise, in 1993 Congress passed the Religious Freedom Restoration Act largely as a means of reversing the Supreme Court's 1990 ruling in *Employment Division v. Smith.*[87] In that case, the Court appeared to back away from its earlier use of the compelling state interest test when dealing with matters involving the free exercise of religion. Congress feared that the Court's new standard would not adequately protect religious freedom.

Supreme Court decisions based on the U.S. Constitution, rather than statutes, are more difficult to reverse. There are, however, times when the Court reverses itself. Some reversals are prompted by passage of another law in which Congress reasserts its understanding of the situation and gives the Court a second chance to examine the issue. For example, after the Supreme Court issued a 5–4 decision in *Texas v. Johnson* (1989) declaring that a Texas statute making it a crime to desecrate an American flag was in conflict with the First Amendment to the

Constitution, Congress adopted the Flag Protection Act with a similar purpose. In this case, however, the Court reasserted its position and overruled the new law in another 5–4 vote the following year in *United States v. Eichman*.[88] If Congress remains determined, the formal amending process is the only way to overturn a decision.

Article V of the Constitution outlines the formal process of constitutional amendment. It states that two-thirds majorities in both houses of Congress must approve a proposed amendment, which then must be ratified by three-fourths of the state legislatures—or, as in the case of the Twenty-first Amendment, which repealed Prohibition, by special conventions held in the states. Another mechanism exists but has yet to be used. Article V provides that two-thirds of the states may petition for a constitutional convention to propose amendments. The difficulty of the process is demonstrated by the fact that although nearly eleven thousand amending proposals—most of which have been redundant—have been introduced in Congress, the legislature has passed only thirty-three amendments by the necessary two-thirds majority. Of these, only twenty-seven have survived the state ratification gauntlet. And controversy remains about whether the Twenty-seventh Amendment, which forbids Congress from raising its pay without an intervening election, is valid. It was proposed in 1789 but not ratified until 1992.

Constitutional amendments have overturned a number of major Supreme Court decisions. The Eleventh Amendment, ratified in 1798, reversed the Supreme Court's 1793 decision dealing with judicial jurisdiction in *Chisholm v. Georgia*. By prohibiting involuntary servitude and guaranteeing citizenship rights on the basis of birth, the Thirteenth and Fourteenth Amendments (ratified in 1865 and 1868) had the effect of overturning the notorious *Scott v. Sandford* decision (1857) in which the Court declared that African Americans, even if emancipated, could not be citizens of the United States and questioned the power of the government to exclude slavery from the territories.[89] In *Pollock v. Farmers' Loan & Trust Company* (1895) the Supreme Court declared that the national income tax was unconstitutional, but the Sixteenth Amendment, which was ratified in 1913, reversed the decision.[90] The Nineteenth Amendment, ratified in 1920, extended voting rights to women long after the Court ruled in *Minor v. Happersett* that the Fourteenth Amendment and other constitutional provisions did not grant this right.[91] The Twenty-sixth Amendment, ratified in 1971, extended the right to vote to eighteen-year-olds after the Supreme Court declared in a 1970 decision, *Oregon v. Mitchell,* that the federal government could set such policies for national, but not state elections.[92]

Members of Congress have introduced amendments to overturn other decisions in areas such as abortion, busing, prayer in public schools, and legislative term limits, none of which has succeeded. Senate Minority Leader Everett Dirksen of Illinois led a vigorous effort in the 1960s to call a special constitutional convention to address the Supreme Court's reapportionment decisions. His efforts fell a single state short of the three-fourths majority needed.

Congressional Regulation of Judicial Jurisdiction

The provision within Article III that grants the Court appellate jurisdiction "with such Exceptions, and under such Regulations as the Congress shall make" raises a fascinating possibility for limiting the power of the Supreme Court. Periodically, Congress has attempted to use this mechanism to withdraw certain topics from the Court's appellate purview. The Jenner bill sought unsuccessfully in the 1950s to limit judicial jurisdiction over internal security matters. Subsequent proposals calling for limited judicial jurisdiction over subjects such as abortion or prayer in public schools also have failed.

In a Reconstruction case, *Ex parte McCardle* (1869), the Court, weakened by its disastrous decision in *Scott v. Sandford*, acquiesced in a congressional law that withdrew its jurisdiction in a pending case. In *McCardle*, Chief Justice Salmon Chase noted:

Without jurisdiction the court cannot proceed at all in any cause. Jurisdiction is power to declare the law, and when it ceases to exist, the only function remaining to the court is that of announcing the fact and dismissing the cause.[93]

In 1872, however, the Court ruled in *United States v. Klein* that Congress could not restrict its jurisdiction in cases where individuals had relied on a presidential pardon.[94] Although members of Congress periodically threaten to restrict the Court's appellate jurisdiction, such action might result in the perpetuation of discordant decisions at the lower court level and could ultimately threaten individual rights. Should the situation arise, the Court might declare, as in *Klein*, that Congress had exceeded constitutional limitations. The extent of this congressional power therefore remains unresolved.

Nonenforcement or Noncompliance

One of the most important internal restraints on judges may simply be that they live and work in the society for which they help to render judgments. Judges often act courageously to enforce the law. A classic study has chronicled the immense pressures on U.S. district court judges who were called upon to enforce desegregation in the wake of the Supreme Court's desegregation decision.[95] In addition to the reactions they elicit from the public, judicial decisions are regularly analyzed and critiqued in law reviews and other scholarly forums. The fact that judges and justices frequently cite scholarly works in their decisions is an indication of their possible influence.

In *The Federalist Papers*, Hamilton noted that the judiciary would be unable to enforce its own judgments, but would depend for help on the other branches, particularly the presidency. Despite a few important historical examples, the days of outright congressional or presidential defiance of court orders appear to be past. However, if the president only halfheartedly enforces, or if Congress or a state legislature only halfheartedly

EXTRAJUDICIAL ACTIVITIES OF THE JUSTICES

Article I, section 6, of the Constitution specifically prohibits members of Congress from holding other civil offices, but the Constitution imposes no such limit on Supreme Court justices. By law the chief justice serves in a number of other administrative capacities (chancellor of the Smithsonian Institution, for example), and the Constitution entrusts the chief with the responsibility of presiding over the Senate in cases of presidential impeachment. In the past, presidents have asked justices to take on nonjudicial assignments, some of which may have breached the separation of powers. The criticisms to which past justices were often subjected suggests that future justices are unlikely to participate in such activities.

The first chief justice, John Jay, spent part of his term in office, along with fellow justice Oliver Ellsworth, serving on a diplomatic mission for George Washington. Justice Joseph Bradley served on the controversial commission that eventually tipped the disputed 1876 election to fellow Republican Rutherford Hayes and consequently brought criticism to the Court. Justice Owen Roberts investigated the Pearl Harbor attack, and Justice Robert H. Jackson accepted the role of chief American prosecutor at the Nuremberg war trials of former Nazi officials. Chief Justice Warren accepted President Lyndon Johnson's request to head the commission that investigated the assassination of President John F. Kennedy.

When justices accept such assignments and the results prove unpopular or controversial, the prestige of the Court may suffer. Colleagues on the Court who must carry heavier workloads may also prove resentful—Justices Jackson and Hugo Black engaged in an ongoing public feud exacerbated by Jackson's assignment in Nuremberg. This may be one reason that Chief Justice Warren Burger resigned from the Court before accepting, in June 1986, the responsibility of chairing the commission celebrating the bicentennial of the U.S. Constitution.

Similar considerations will probably limit future informal contacts between members of the judiciary and members of the two elected branches whose actions the justices may later be called upon to judge. Posthumous revelations that Justices Louis Brandeis and Felix Frankfurter played active roles advising legislators and presidents long after they were appointed to the bench stirred considerable academic controversy. Moreover, although there were other ideological and ethical concerns, much of the opposition to President Lyndon Johnson's unsuccessful attempt to promote his friend Abe Fortas, then an associate justice, to replace Earl Warren as chief justice stemmed from revelations that Fortas had actively advised the president on day-to-day public policy matters involving both domestic and foreign affairs. The chief justice will likely continue participating in ceremonial functions such as swearing in a new president and attending the annual State of the Union address, as well as supporting legislation directly related to matters that concern the judiciary. Considerations of prudence make it unlikely that justices will accept many other substantive nonjudicial assignments or advisory functions that bring them into direct contact with members of the elected branches.

Justices are also sensitive to perceived conflicts of interest and are likely in such cases to recuse themselves, or abstain from participating in the decision. The situation in *Marbury v. Madison*, wherein Chief Justice John Marshall examined the legitimacy of a commission he himself had failed to deliver when he was secretary of state, would be extremely unlikely to occur today.

---

funds a court judgment, its chances for success may be significantly affected. President Eisenhower generally gave only the most grudging and tepid support to the Court's desegregation decisions, and members of Congress have openly opposed busing, affirmative action, and other subsequent remedies. Public support or lack of it may also limit judicial exertions of power. While state powers are not as strong as they once were, state resistance may also impede judicial judgments.

Studies carried out in the 1960s demonstrated significant variations in compliance with judicial rulings related to *Miranda* warnings, and with court mandates on juvenile justice, obscenity, and prayer and Bible reading in public schools.[96] Moreover, during this time, a substantial number of scholars began to criticize the judicial activism of the Warren Court and the increasingly active policies of lower court judges who sometimes responded to complaints by in effect taking over the administration of state prisons, hospitals, and school systems. Donald L. Horowitz has argued that the judiciary was not well equipped to handle most matters of public policy. Such matters often required continued attention that courts, largely dependent on the individual initiative of claimants, find it difficult to sustain.[97] Horowitz also focused on how judicial decisions often resulted in unintended consequences. In a more recent work focusing on judicial decision making in the areas of civil rights, food and drug regulation, and occupational health standards, Jeremy Rabkin has also argued that excessive attention to legal issues often distorts public policy.[98]

Political scientist Gerald Rosenberg has written one of the most striking reexaminations of the impact of judicial decisions. Rosenberg focused on areas long thought to demonstrate the positive impact of judicial decisions—namely, civil rights, abortion and women's rights, and issues related to the environment, reapportionment, and criminal law. He concluded that, although courts often ride the waves of change that are already present, many have had far less independent influence in these areas than is generally thought. Rosenberg argues that judicial influence more frequently resembles "the cutting of the ribbon on a new project than its construction."[99] According to Rosenberg, some resources diverted into judicial contests might have been better invested elsewhere.

Rosenberg focuses on three limitations on judicial powers. These are the "limited nature of constitutional rights," the "lack of judicial independence," and the "judiciary's lack of powers of implementation."[100] In attempting to explain those cases in which judicial decisions have proved successful, Rosenberg identifies four circumstances where they have a greater likelihood of success. These include cases where other members of government offer rewards to those who comply with judicial judgments; cases where such officials offer punishments; cases where the free market system provides positive incentives for compliance; or cases where the decisions provide "a shield, cover, or excuse" for people already disposed to act in the manner the Court has directed.[101] Rosenberg's focus on the dependence of the courts on other actors is especially relevant to the relation between the judiciary and the presidency.

The President and the Courts: A Natural Alliance?

On the surface, there are substantial differences between the executive and the judicial branches of the federal government. A single individual heads the executive branch and is responsible for its operations. In contrast, power is diffused throughout the judicial branch, with its highest court consisting of nine individuals with relatively equal powers. The president is elected and limited by the Twenty-second Amendment to serving two full terms. Judges are nominated by the president and confirmed by the Senate, and they serve during good behavior. Although the president exercises a great many discretionary powers, Article II invests a number of specific powers in this office. In the judicial branch, almost all powers have developed through custom and constitutional interpretation. The executive demonstrates energy, while the judiciary is passive; it has to wait for cases to come to it.

Despite these differences, there may be greater affinity between the executive and judicial branches than first meets the eye.[102] John Locke and the Baron de Montesquieu significantly influenced the American Founders. Both clearly distinguished between the legislative and executive functions, but neither described the executive and judicial branches separately. When Locke described the three parts of government, he referred to the legislative, the executive, and the federative (dealing with foreign policy making) rather than the legislative, executive, and judicial powers.[103] Although Montesquieu at one point suggested that juries needed to be separated from legislative and executive influence, he divided the powers of government into "the legislative; the executive in respect to things dependent on the law of nations; and the executive in regard to matters that depend on the civil law."[104]

Robert Scigliano has noted that many of the American Founders appeared to anticipate that judges "were to engage in

the execution of the laws." As evidence, he notes both that the Constitution did not exclude members of the judiciary—as it did members of Congress—from serving in the executive branch and that many early justices accepted executive assignments. Scigliano further distinguishes between the more active "tough executive" functions that American presidents, who are expected to act energetically and with force, carry out, and the more passive "soft executive" functions that members of the judiciary perform when they simply wait for controversies to come before them. Pointing to the important role that the solicitor general plays in representing the interests of the government before the Supreme Court, Scigliano notes that the Court typically accepts "between two-thirds and three-fourths of the government's appeals and 90 percent of the appeals supported by the government as *amicus curiae*."[105]

Although there have been obvious points of tension between the two branches, Scigliano believes that the Framers, ever fearful of the expanding nature of legislative powers, intended that "the president and judges would usually share a common outlook on matters that came to them," and that they typically "would form a limited defensive alliance against an encroaching Congress."[106] Significantly, *The Federalist Papers* moves directly from its discussion of the presidency (Nos. 66–77) to the judicial branch (Nos. 78–85).

Hamilton wrote, "Energy in the executive is a leading character in the definition of good government," but many of the Framers appeared to have underestimated how presidential and judicial powers would expand.[107] Not surprisingly, while the judiciary has often sided with the executive against Congress, it has also frequently opposed executive initiatives and sought to curb executive discretion.

PRESIDENTIAL POWERS: CONSTITUTIONAL FOUNDATIONS

The U.S. president is a powerful figure. A brief look at Article II of the Constitution will explain why. It entrusts the president with the "executive Power" of the United States. Article II, section 2, designates the president as "Commander in Chief" of the United States armed forces. It gives the president the power to issue "reprieves and pardons," to make treaties, and, with the advice and consent of the Senate, to appoint "Ambassadors, other public Ministers and Consuls, Judges of the supreme Court, and all other Officers of the United States." Article II grants the president power to fill vacancies when Congress is not in session and entrusts the president with power to inform Congress of the state of the Union and to make recommendations to that body. The president may convene and, in some cases, adjourn Congress. Article I, section 7, gives the president a qualified veto of congressional legislation. The president receives ambassadors, executes the laws, and commissions U.S. officers.

Writing in defense of this powerful institution, Hamilton carefully stressed that the president's "due dependence on the people" and his "due responsibility" to them would provide "safety," but he appeared to devote far more attention to the need for sufficient "energy" in this office.[108] Hamilton argued that a number of constitutional provisions strengthened such energy. They included provisions for a unitary executive, the president's "duration in office" (now somewhat modified by the Twenty-second Amendment), "adequate provision" for support, and "competent powers."

In describing presidential powers, Hamilton might also have mentioned another factor that strengthens the office. In many nations, the chief executive, usually called a prime minister or chancellor, is head of the government, and another person, typically a monarch, serves as the national symbol or head of state. The U.S. Constitution in effect combines these roles in the presidency. The dual role magnifies the American president's constitutional powers and gives this officeholder an extraordinary place among world leaders. More than one observer has likened the American president to an elected king.[109]

Historically, a major aspect of executive power is its exercise of discretionary, or prerogative, powers. In part, these powers derive from the power to issue reprieves and pardons. Quite beyond this specific power, however, is the notion that the chief executive may sometimes need to act outside or even against the law. In his classic formulation of executive power, Locke described prerogative powers as the power "to act according to discretion, for the publick [sic] good, without the prescription of the Law, and sometimes even against it."[110]

Even Thomas Jefferson, who was theoretically opposed to presidential prerogative powers, sometimes exercised them, as in his purchase of the Louisiana Territory. Others—Abraham Lincoln and the two Roosevelts—showed less compunction about the exercise of such power. However essential this power may sometimes be, it can lead to potential abuse and disputes in a nation historically dedicated to the rule of law. Despite long periods of cooperation and judicial acquiescence to expanded executive powers, American history has witnessed a number of extraordinary conflicts between the executive and the courts.

CASES OF CONFLICT AND COOPERATION

Judicial decisions usually uphold executive power, just as presidents usually enforce judicial decisions. When conflicts between the president and the judiciary occur, however, they can be dramatic. As a consequence, accounts of conflicts often dominate discussions of the president and the Court.

Thomas Jefferson's Conflicts with the Court

Presidents Washington and Adams had the opportunity to appoint members of the judiciary who were compatible with their judicial philosophies. When Jefferson arrived in office, however, he faced a judiciary that had been stacked against him by the Federalists, who consistently opposed many of his political ideas. Jefferson favored states' rights, but the Marshall Court was attempting to consolidate national powers. Jefferson em-phasized that freedom of speech should be exempt from federal coercion, but the lower federal courts had enforced the notorious Sedition Act of 1798.

Jefferson's and Marshall's views of the role of the Supreme Court also conflicted. Marshall believed the Court was the final arbiter of interbranch disputes, but Jefferson advocated a form of what scholar Susan Burgess calls "departmentalism." Jefferson articulated this view when he pardoned those who had been convicted under the Sedition Act of 1798:

The Judges, believing the Sedition Law constitutional, had a right to pass a sentence of fine and imprisonment; because that power was placed in their hands by the Constitution. But the Executive, believing the law to be unconstitutional, was bound to remit the execution of it because the power had been confided to him by the Constitution. The instrument meant that its co-ordinate branches should be checks on each other. But the opinion which gives to the Judges the right to decide what laws are constitutional, and what are not, not only for themselves in their own sphere of action, but for the Legislative and Executive also in their spheres, would make the Judiciary a despotic branch.[111]

Conflict between Jefferson and the courts developed in at least three areas. The act that resulted in the Supreme Court decision in *Marbury v. Madison* was Jefferson's order to his secretary of state to withhold a commission from Marbury. The outgoing administration had appointed Marbury as a justice of the peace, but the commission was not delivered, and Marbury sued. Marshall used his opinion to lecture Jefferson and assert the authority of the judiciary to void acts of legislation that the Court believed to be in conflict with the Constitution. However, Marshall's decision declaring that a writ of mandamus could not issue from his Court meant that he made no command that Jefferson might refuse to obey. *(See* "Marbury v. Madison *and the Power of Judicial Review," p. 1288.)*

The impeachment of Justice Samuel Chase was the second occasion for conflict. Heartened by the successful removal of John Pickering, a New Hampshire federal district judge who had gone insane, the Democratic-Republicans moved against Justice Chase in 1803. While riding circuit, Chase had made partisan and injudicious remarks criticizing the Democratic-Republicans and their philosophy. As president, Jefferson directed the attention of members of Congress to Chase's behavior. He asked one of them, "Ought this seditious and official attack on the principles of our Constitution and on the proceedings of a State, go unpunished?" Jefferson personally stayed out of the fray, however, proclaiming, "For myself, it is better that I should not interfere."[112]

However justified the Democratic-Republicans must have felt, their action threatened to convert a constitutional protection designed to punish gross malfeasance into a tool to punish officeholders for mere expressions of opinion. When members of Congress took up Jefferson's challenge, the resulting threat to judicial independence caused even John Marshall to waver. He weakly testified in Chase's Senate trial and suggested in one letter that Congress should be able to review judicial decisions.[113]

Ultimately, Maryland's Luther Martin and other Chase defenders who stood firmly on the Constitution's narrow grounds for impeachable offenses prevailed over Virginia's John Randolph and others who argued for impeachment on broader political grounds. Chase's opponents could muster only nineteen of the twenty-three votes needed for a two-thirds majority, and he was acquitted. Had the trial turned out differently, the Democratic-Republicans might have gone after other justices, perhaps even Marshall. This would have seriously threatened the independence of the judiciary as a coequal branch of government.

Two years after the Chase trial, Jefferson battled once again with Marshall. As part of his circuit-riding duties, Marshall presided at the trial in Richmond of Aaron Burr, who Jefferson hoped would be convicted. Burr was charged with treason in connection with a trip down the Mississippi River that he may have made for the purpose of separating the Southwest from the rest of the country. The evidence against him was sketchy, however, and Marshall insisted on a strict interpretation of the constitutional provision on treason. This insistence resulted in Burr's acquittal. Scholars justly credit Marshall's actions with putting "the American law of treason beyond the easy grasp of political expediency."[114] Most fascinating is the fact that the circuit court Marshall presided over twice subpoenaed Jefferson for documents. While he denied the court's power on both occasions, Jefferson apparently yielded each time and submitted the documents.[115]

Andrew Jackson and Constitutional Interpretation

Like Jefferson, Andrew Jackson was a strong president who made a permanent imprint on the executive branch. Jackson made his most important contribution to the ongoing debate between the presidency and the Court in his message vetoing the renewal of the national bank. John Marshall had clearly affirmed the constitutionality of the bank in *McCulloch v. Maryland* (1819), one of his most nationalistic opinions, which not only upheld the constitutionality of the bank but also struck down state powers to tax it. Arguing that the national government "though limited in its powers, is supreme within its sphere of action," Marshall had advanced the theory of broad constitutional construction that Alexander Hamilton had used to convince President Washington that the bank was proper. In Marshall's words:

Let the end be legitimate, let it be within the scope of the constitution, and all means which are appropriate, which are plainly adapted to that end, which are not prohibited, but consist with the letter and spirit of the constitution, are constitutional.[116]

However, Jackson and his attorney general, Roger Taney, a future chief justice, negatively associated the bank with Eastern monied interests. In one of his most notable public papers, Jackson denied that judicial precedent settled the matter. Like Jefferson, Jackson asserted that each branch of government was independently responsible for interpreting the Constitution:

If the opinion of the Supreme Court covered the whole ground of this act, it ought not to control the coordinate authorities of this Government. The Congress, the Executive, and the Court must each for itself be guided by its own opinion of the Constitution. Each public officer who takes an oath to support the Constitution swears that he will support it as he understands it, and not as it is understood by others. It is as much the duty of the House of Representatives, of the Senate, and of the President to decide upon the constitutionality of any bill or resolution which may be presented to them for passage or approval as it is of the supreme judges when it may be brought before them for judicial decision.[117]

Jackson's message did not require that he disobey any court order, but it clearly set the stage for future conflicts in cases where executive and judicial views of the Constitution differed.

Abraham Lincoln and Constitutional Interpretation

The Supreme Court generally supported President Lincoln's wartime endeavors, but he had a number of run-ins with judges and justices, including the chief justice. Taney questioned Lincoln's power to suspend the writ of *habeas corpus,* which is used to determine if a person is being legally held in custody, and to try civilians in military courts. Lincoln in turn reaffirmed and refined Jefferson's and Jackson's views that Supreme Court decisions were not necessarily the final word on the constitutionality of a law.

One of the defining issues in the presidential contest of 1860 was the legitimacy of Taney's 1857 decision in *Scott v. Sandford.* Dred Scott was a slave whose master, an army surgeon, took him to a free territory and then back to a slave state. Scott subsequently sued for his freedom. Taney denied that Scott's previous residence in a free territory had made him free. Instead, Taney declared that, because blacks were not and could not be U.S. citizens, Scott could not bring suit in federal court. He further declared that Congress could not exclude slavery, as the Missouri Compromise had sought to do, from the territories.

In the famous debates with Lincoln for a Senate seat from Illinois in 1858, Stephen Douglas argued that this case settled the constitutional issue. Lincoln did not deny that the case settled the matter for Scott, but Lincoln was concerned about slavery spreading to the territories. Accordingly, both in the debates and in his first inaugural address, Lincoln denied that the Court's word was necessarily final. He went on to say that:

if the policy of the Government upon vital questions affecting the whole people is to be irrevocably fixed by decisions of the Supreme Court, the instant they are made in ordinary litigation between parties in personal actions the people will have ceased to be their own rulers, having to that extent practically resigned their Government into the hands of that eminent tribunal.[118]

On a number of occasions, Lincoln asserted his own views of constitutional interpretation over those of the courts. Ultimately, the Thirteenth and Fourteenth Amendments overturned the position that Taney espoused in *Scott.*

Chief Justice Roger Brooke Taney served from 1836 until his death in 1864. Although his reputation with the public rests almost completely on his disastrous decision in *Scott v. Sandford*, (1857), professors of law, history, and political science rank Taney as one of the great justices.

Franklin D. Roosevelt and the Court-packing Plan

Of all the conflicts between the president and the judiciary, probably none is more controversial or pivotal than that involving President Franklin Roosevelt's attempt to "pack" the Court.[119] Elected to office in the throes of the Great Depression, Roosevelt in his first one hundred days in office demonstrated the power implicit in the president's ability to formulate legislation. The New Deal Roosevelt launched stands as the most ambitious legislative program in American history. Many New Deal programs called for expansive readings of constitutional powers under the commerce clause and other grants of power to Congress. To promote economic recovery, Congress passed laws that were in tension with fairly conservative Court decisions such as *Lochner v. New York* (1905).[120] In *Lochner* and similar rulings, the Court had interpreted the due process clauses of the Fifth and Fourteenth Amendments to guarantee "liberty of contract" and other tenets of laissez-faire economics against attempts at government regulation. In a number of other cases, the Court had also struck down federal legislation as an invasion of state police powers protected by the Tenth Amendment.

At the beginning of his presidency, Roosevelt confronted a Court divided into three ideological blocs. The first was the so-called "Four Horsemen"—Justices Pierce Butler, James McReynolds, George Sutherland, and Willis Van Devanter—a solid conservative bloc that was generally critical of economic regulation by government. Justices Benjamin Cardozo, Louis Brandeis, and Harlan Fiske Stone composed the second bloc. They were liberals who usually upheld expansive government programs. The third bloc, Justice Owen Roberts and Chief Justice Charles Evans Hughes, held the swing votes, at least one of which (usually Roberts) almost always favored the conservatives.

At first, the justices appeared to back a number of Roosevelt's initiatives. In three cases known as the *Gold Clause Cases*, the Court in 1935 upheld a controversial law that Congress had adopted providing for the payment of contracts in currency rather than in gold.[121] In *Home Building and Loan Association v. Blaisdell* (1934) the Court upheld a Minnesota law that extended the payment time for mortgages. Although *Blaisdell* dealt specifically with state powers, the Court's comments must have been comforting to the president. Noting that "Emergency does not create power," Chief Justice Hughes went on to say that it "may furnish the occasion for the exercise of power." Referring to a power that was not immediately at issue, the Court said:

the war power of the Federal Government is not created by the emergency of war, but it is a power given to meet that emergency. It is a power to wage war successfully, and thus it permits the harnessing of the entire energies of the people in a supreme cooperative effort to preserve the nation.[122]

In what seemed to be a good omen for the New Deal, Hughes appeared to accept an expansive view of constitutional powers:

It is no answer to say that this public need was not apprehended a century ago, or to insist that what the provision of the Constitution meant to the vision of that day it must mean to the vision of our time. If by the statement that what the Constitution meant at the time of its adoption it means today, it is intended to say that the great clauses of the Constitution must be confined to the interpretation which the framers with the conditions and outlooks of their time, would have placed upon them, the statement carries its own refutation. It was to guard against such a narrow conception that Chief Justice Marshall uttered the memorable warning: "We must never forget, that it is a *constitution* we are expounding."[123]

Despite these initial causes for hope, on May 27, 1935, a day often referred to as Black Monday, the Court issued three unanimous decisions that threatened the future of Roosevelt's New Deal. In *Louisville Bank v. Radford,* the Court struck down mortgage relief provisions of the Frazier-Lemke Act. In *Humphrey's Executor v. United States,* it limited the president's power to remove members of independent regulatory agencies. In *Schechter Poultry Corp. v. United States,* it struck down powers delegated to the president by Congress to establish industry codes of fair competition under the National Industrial Recovery Act.[124] Although the margins were closer, with the chief justice siding with the Court's liberals, the next year the Court proceeded to void other important pieces of New Deal and progressive state legislation. These included the Agricultural Adjustment Act, which the Court invalidated in *United States v. Butler:* the Bituminous Coal Conservation Act of 1935, which it ruled against in

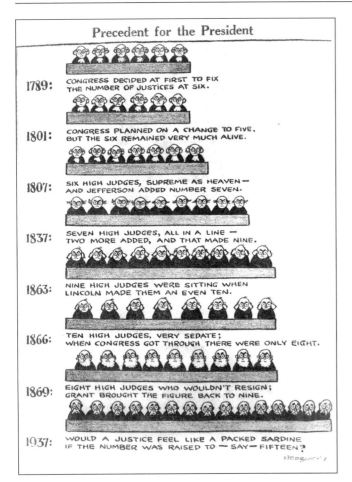

Precedent for the President

1789: CONGRESS DECIDED AT FIRST TO FIX THE NUMBER OF JUSTICES AT SIX.

1801: CONGRESS PLANNED ON A CHANGE TO FIVE, BUT THE SIX REMAINED VERY MUCH ALIVE.

1807: SIX HIGH JUDGES, SUPREME AS HEAVEN — AND JEFFERSON ADDED NUMBER SEVEN.

1837: SEVEN HIGH JUDGES, ALL IN A LINE — TWO MORE ADDED, AND THAT MADE NINE.

1863: NINE HIGH JUDGES WERE SITTING WHEN LINCOLN MADE THEM AN EVEN TEN.

1866: TEN HIGH JUDGES, VERY SEDATE; WHEN CONGRESS GOT THROUGH THERE WERE ONLY EIGHT.

1869: EIGHT HIGH JUDGES WHO WOULDN'T RESIGN; GRANT BROUGHT THE FIGURE BACK TO NINE.

1937: WOULD A JUSTICE FEEL LIKE A PACKED SARDINE IF THE NUMBER WAS RAISED TO — SAY — FIFTEEN?

Congress has the power to decide how many justices sit on the Supreme Court. In 1937 President Franklin Roosevelt, frustrated by the Court's reversals of his economic recovery legislation, offered Congress a plan to expand the Court's membership by as many as six.

Carter v. Carter Coal Co.; and a New York minimum wage law, which it declared unconstitutional in *Morehead v. New York ex rel. Tipaldo.*[125]

Biding his time until after his second election, Roosevelt surprised the nation when, in February 1937, he proposed that Congress reorganize the judiciary. The heart of this plan called for adding one Supreme Court justice (up to a total of fifteen) for every justice over age seventy who did not resign. Roosevelt justified this bill as a response to the Court's workload and to the age of the justices, who were often referred to as the "nine old men." By March 1937 Roosevelt was more forthright about his intentions. In a "fireside chat," Roosevelt likened the three branches of the federal government to three horses, one of which was pulling in the wrong direction.[126]

While the proposed law was within the constitutional powers of Congress, conservatives and many liberals alike viewed Roosevelt's plan as a blatant attempt to exert direct political influence on the Court and undermine judicial independence. The Senate Judiciary Committee issued a report that said:

We recommend the rejection of this bill as a needless, futile, and utterly dangerous abandonment of constitutional principle. . . .

It is a proposal without precedent and without justification.

It would subjugate the courts to the will of Congress and the President and thereby destroy the independence of the judiciary, the only certain shield of individual rights. . . .

It points the way to the evasion of the Constitution and establishes the method whereby the people may be deprived of their right to pass upon all amendments of the fundamental law.[127]

Moreover, the unexpected death of Joe Robinson, Roosevelt's floor leader in the Senate, probably doomed the president's plan.

Although he lost the battle, Roosevelt won the war. The Court issued its opinion in *West Coast Hotel Co. v. Parrish* just two months after the court-packing plan was proposed. Chief Justice Hughes wrote the 5–4 decision in which the Court upheld a minimum wage law for women and children in the state of Washington, overturning a 1923 precedent.[128] Referring to earlier decisions in which the Court had affirmed the sanctity of liberty of contract, Hughes now noted that such liberty was not absolute.

About two weeks later, the Court issued another 5–4 decision in *National Labor Relations Board v. Jones & Laughlin Steel Corporation,* which Hughes also wrote. Here the Court upheld the congressional ban on unfair labor practices. Earlier decisions had limited federal powers under the Tenth Amendment, which reserves powers to the states. These decisions also had distinguished between the unwarranted regulation of production and the permissible regulation of subsequent commerce as well as between activities that had an indirect rather than a direct effect on commerce. Here, in contrast, the Court read federal commerce powers generously:

When industries organize themselves on a national scale, making their relation to interstate commerce the dominant factor in their activities, how can it be maintained that their industrial labor relations constitute a forbidden field in which Congress may not enter when it is necessary to protect interstate commerce from the paralyzing consequences of industrial war?[129]

In both cases, Justice Roberts, who had often sided with the Four Horsemen, provided the swing vote. Court observers began to refer to "the switch in time that saved nine," because the Court's new stance relieved what pressure remained to adopt the court-packing plan.

Supreme Court retirements further ensured that the Court would be more sympathetic to Roosevelt's legislative objectives. The first to retire was Justice Van Devanter, who was replaced in 1937 by Alabama senator Hugo Black, a supporter of the court-packing plan. Still, Roosevelt's failure to get congressional authorization to increase the number of justices suggests that this mechanism is unlikely to work, at least in the foreseeable political future.

Harry S. Truman and the Steel Seizure Case

Like his predecessor, Harry Truman found himself on the losing side of an important Supreme Court decision involving one of the most controversial actions of his administration. During America's military involvement in Korea, technically described as a "police action," Truman faced the imminent threat of strike in the U.S. steel industry. Truman feared that a strike would interfere with production of materials needed for the conflict. When neither labor nor management would budge, Truman ordered his secretary of commerce, Charles Sawyer, to seize the steel mills until the crisis was over. The president's seizure triggered an immediate appeal and a great deal of criticism.

In *Youngstown Sheet & Tube Co. v. Sawyer* (1952), also known as the *Steel Seizure Case*, the Supreme Court ruled against Truman, 6–3. It decided that Truman's actions could not be justified either by his inherent powers or by any congressional legislation. The president had weakened his claim by failing to invoke the cooling-off period provided in the Taft-Hartley law. Although Truman was surprised by the decision and believed that it represented a mistaken constitutional judgment, he quickly complied with it and averted a constitutional crisis.[130] *(See "Other Domestic Powers Related to National Security," p. 1325.)*

Dwight D. Eisenhower and Little Rock

Few presidents could have desired a constitutional crisis any less than Truman's successor in office. Although President Eisenhower faced major changes in judicial decisions regarding civil rights, he never welcomed them and supported them only tepidly. In Little Rock, Arkansas, however, a governor's opposition to federal power ultimately prompted Eisenhower to take strong executive action.[131]

Responding to the Supreme Court's historic desegregation decision in *Brown v. Board of Education* (1954), the Little Rock school board drew up a plan to begin desegregating Central High School in September 1957. Gov. Orval Faubus, an ardent segregationist, called out the Arkansas National Guard to prevent black students from entering the school. He later responded to a U.S. district court order by withdrawing the guard and permitting chaos and mob violence to ensue. Faced with defiance of federal authority, Eisenhower federalized the Arkansas National Guard and sent in units of the U.S. Army's 101st Airborne Division to restore order and to escort black students to their classes. Rarely has a president acted more reluctantly. Against the advice of those who understood the situation, Eisenhower had met with Faubus and thought the two had struck a satisfactory deal. Moreover, Eisenhower was fearful that the use of troops would encourage violence, so after deploying them, he insisted that they were there *"not to enforce integration but to prevent opposition by violence to orders of a court."*[132]

In an unusual opinion signed by each justice, the Supreme Court refused in *Cooper v. Aaron* (1958) to permit further delay in the implementation of desegregation in Little Rock. The Court's assertion of its power was as forceful a statement of the doctrine of judicial supremacy as it has ever made. The Court said that *Marbury v. Madison* had established

the basic principle that the federal judiciary is supreme in the exposition of the law of the Constitution, and that principle has ever since

In 1957 President Dwight D. Eisenhower federalized the Arkansas National Guard to prevent violence from stopping a court order to integrate Central High School in Little Rock. The following year the Supreme Court ruled unanimously that the state could not delay or obstruct integration.

been respected by this Court and the Country as a permanent and indispensable feature of our constitutional system. It follows that the interpretation of the Fourteenth Amendment enunciated by this Court in the *Brown* Case is the supreme law of the land, and Art. VI of the Constitution makes it of binding effect on the States "any Thing in the Constitution or Laws of any State to the Contrary notwithstanding."[133]

While the Court's words were forceful, scholars have questioned whether the Court could have taken this "'high constitutional ground' if Eisenhower . . . had decided not to send the troops to Little Rock." From this perspective, *Cooper v. Aaron* may be "more a testament to judicial dependency on the executive than an assertion of judicial power."[134]

Richard Nixon and Executive Privilege

Richard Nixon entered office in 1969 determined to use the power of appointment to reverse liberal trends in judicial decision making. He became better known for testing the limits in areas such as impoundment of congressional funds, injunctions against pending publications, unauthorized wiretapping, and presidential war making. His most controversial claim, raised in connection with the Watergate incident, concerned executive privilege. Nixon's defeat on this issue ultimately led to his resignation.

Nixon's difficulty began with a series of illegal acts committed by his subordinates. The most notorious of these was the

CONGRESSIONAL INVESTIGATIONS

One of the ways Congress can keep the executive in check is through a power that is not explicitly stated in the Constitution—the power to call witnesses and conduct investigations. Supreme Court decisions have consistently recognized this power as implicit in the so-called elastic clause in the last sentence of Article I, section 8, which grants to Congress the power "To make all Laws which shall be necessary and proper for carrying into Execution the foregoing Powers, and all other Powers vested by this Constitution in the Government of the United States." For example, in *McGrain v. Daugherty,* a case centering on a congressional investigation of the conduct of the Justice Department during the Harding administration, Justice Willis Van Devanter concluded that "the power of inquiry—with process to enforce it—is an essential and appropriate auxiliary to the legislative function."[1]

Congressional investigations have ranged far and wide—sometimes too wide. During the McCarthy era, congressional investigations were used to create suspicion and ruin reputations rather than to provide information for legislation. The Supreme Court provided some relief. In *Watkins v. United States* (1957), a 6–1 decision written by Chief Justice Earl Warren, the Court threw out a contempt conviction of a labor leader who testified before the House Un-American Activities Committee (HUAC) about his associations with the Communist Party but refused to provide information about individuals he believed were no longer party members. Agreeing that the power of investigation was broad, Warren also said it was not unlimited. As he explained, "There is no general authority to expose the private affairs of individuals without justification in terms of the functions of the Congress." Moreover, Congress is not "a law enforcement or trial agency"; these functions belong to "the executive and judicial departments of government."[2]

Subject to intense criticism for its opinion, the Court limited somewhat the immediate effect of the *Watkins* decision in *Barenblatt v. United States* (1959). Even though the Court rejected a broad First Amendment claim of a college professor who refused to testify before HUAC about his past associations, the central holding in

Watkins still stands.[3] However broad congressional powers may be, individuals do not shed their constitutional rights when they appear before congressional committees—including the Fifth Amendment right to refuse to testify on the grounds that they might incriminate themselves.[4]

Investigations by congressional committees often focus on allegations of executive wrongdoing and are therefore a vital component of the system of checks and balances among the three branches of government.[5] Investigations were critical in exposing the Watergate abuses that eventually led to President Richard Nixon's resignation. Ironically, Nixon's own investigations of Alger Hiss in the 1950s had been one reason for his political rise. Investigations pried into the Reagan administration's running of the Environmental Protection Agency and into the Iran-contra scandal, which involved the transfer of monies from sales of weapons to Iran to finance Latin American anticommunist forces after Congress had limited direct government appropriations for that purpose. Investigations often center on proposed constitutional amendments, some of which are designed to overturn Supreme Court opinions.

Congressional committees also investigate individuals slated for high government posts. In the past, nominees to the Supreme Court were likely to appear before the Senate Judiciary Committee only when their nominations appeared to be in jeopardy. Since John Marshall Harlan testified before this committee in 1955, such appearances have been routine. The televised confirmation hearings involving Robert Bork and Clarence Thomas became public spectacles with millions of viewers, leading some scholars to call for consideration of a less public means of scrutiny.

1. *McGrain v. Daugherty,* 237 U.S. 135, 174 (1927).
2. *Watkins v. United States,* 254 U.S. 178, 187 (1957).
3. *Barenblatt v. United States,* 360 U.S. 109 (1959).
4. Congress, however, may extend immunity from prosecution for testimony given before it, which subjects a recalcitrant witness to charges of contempt.
5. See James Hamilton, *The Power to Probe: A Study of Congressional Investigations* (New York: Random House, 1976).

botched break-in during the 1972 presidential campaign at Democratic National Headquarters, then housed in the Watergate complex in Washington, D.C. His attempts to cover up executive branch participation in this illegal action led him into deeper trouble. Eventually, televised hearings by the Senate Select Committee on Presidential Campaign Activities, chaired by Sam Ervin (D-N.C.), revealed in 1973 that the president had recorded all conversations made in the Oval Office.

In the meantime, public pressure had led Nixon to appoint a special prosecutor, Archibald Cox, to look into executive wrongdoing. In the "Saturday Night Massacre," so-called because it resulted in the firing of so many officials, Nixon ordered Robert Bork to dismiss Cox, who had attempted to get documents from the president. The action generated a considerable public outcry. Nixon next appointed Leon Jaworski as the new special

prosecutor, and Jaworski continued the quest for tapes of White House conversations. He believed they were necessary for determining the president's role in the Watergate affair (Nixon had been named by a Washington, D.C., grand jury as an "unindicted co-conspirator") and for the prosecution of important presidential subordinates such as advisers John Ehrlichman and Bob Haldeman and Attorney General John Mitchell. Nixon, in turn, asserted that the separation of powers doctrine prevented the special prosecutor from seeking this information and that "executive privilege" permitted him to withhold it. Perhaps more important, the president purposely kept the nation in the dark as to whether he would obey the decision.

The Court ruled against Nixon, 8–0. Three of the four justices Nixon had appointed voted against him, and William Rehnquist, a former Justice Department employee in the president's administration, recused himself. Rejecting the separation of powers argument, the Court pointed to the unique situation that had prompted the appointment of a special prosecutor. Quoting from *Marbury v. Madison*, the Court also reasserted its authority "'to say what the law is' with respect to the claim of privilege presented in this case."[135] Although the Court recognized a legitimate need for presidential privacy and confidentiality, especially in foreign affairs, it decided that, in this case, the need for grand juries to have access to the best evidence outweighed the president's generalized claim of executive privilege.

Nixon reluctantly complied with the Court's order. Release of the tapes provided evidence of Nixon's active participation in the Watergate cover-up and led to his resignation on August 9, 1974. Still, Nixon's earlier refusal to commit himself to releasing the tapes if the Court went against him left open the chance that he might well have disobeyed a more ambiguous ruling from a divided Court. Such a threat may have served as a catalyst for the Supreme Court's unanimous ruling.

Ronald Reagan and Constitutional Interpretation

Like Nixon, Ronald Reagan assumed office intending to appoint justices who would reverse a number of Supreme Court decisions and bring the judicial branch closer to his conservative leanings. Reagan favored constitutional amendments designed to restore the voluntary recitation of prayers in public schools and to reverse the Supreme Court's permissive stance toward abortion. He opposed affirmative action policies that the courts had sanctioned, and he advocated the death penalty, which Justice Brennan's and Justice Marshall's expansive readings of the Eighth and Fourteenth Amendments threatened. More generally, Reagan favored greater state control over matters such as criminal justice and the regulation of pornography. Over the years, the Court had undermined state control by its "incorporation" of most of the guarantees of the Bill of Rights—which had initially applied only to the national government—into the due process clause of the Fourteenth Amendment, where they now applied to states as well. Other conservative presidents had been largely content to work around the edges of constitutional interpretation. Reagan decided to challenge the precedents directly. Accordingly, he chose a highly political attorney general, Edwin Meese III, who was also a close friend and adviser, and further politicized the solicitor general's office.

The administration's most direct clash with the judicial branch came not in court but in a July 1985 speech by Meese to the American Bar Association in which he declared his support for "a jurisprudence of original intention." In retrospect, the attorney general's speech, while hardly presenting the final word on constitutional interpretation, was not all that extraordinary. Arguing that the justification for judicial review centered on an interpretable written constitution, Meese said:

Where the language of the Constitution is specific, it must be obeyed. Where there is a demonstrable consensus among the framers and ratifiers as to a principle stated or implied by the Constitution, it should

be followed as well. Where there is ambiguity as to the precise meaning or reach of a constitutional provision, it should be interpreted and applied in a manner so as to at least not contradict the text of the Constitution itself.[136]

Meese contended that this standard of review was more consistent with democratic theory than a standard based on appeals to the "spirit" of the Constitution or to broad concepts like "human dignity."[137] Citing a brief the Reagan administration had filed before the Court, Meese noted:

The further afield interpretation travels from its point of departure in the text, the greater the danger that constitutional interpretation will be like a picnic to which the framers bring the words and the judges the meaning.[138]

Meese further argued that a jurisprudence of original intention would help to "depoliticize the law" by leaving "to the more political branches the matter of adapting and vivifying its principles in each generation." Such a jurisprudence would also give to "the people of the states" what Meese called "those responsibilities and rights not committed to federal care."[139]

If commentators had viewed Meese's words as a scholar's commentary on constitutional interpretation, the speech probably would not have provoked much response. Because of his position in the administration, however, many, including some members of the Supreme Court, viewed Meese's words as an attack on the liberal jurisprudence that the Warren Court had initiated. Three months later, Justice William Brennan—who, along with Justice Thurgood Marshall, was considered one of the most liberal members of the Court—delivered a sharp counterattack in a symposium at Georgetown University. Arguing that the Constitution "embodies the aspiration to social justice, brotherhood and human dignity," Brennan referred to the "amended Constitution" as "the lodestar for our aspirations." Brennan declared, "The phrasing is broad and the limitations of its provisions are clearly marked. Its majestic generalities and ennobling pronouncements are both luminous and obscure."[140] Lest there be any doubt as to Brennan's target, he specifically contrasted his view to a somewhat simplified version of the view Meese had advanced.

There are those who find legitimacy in fidelity to what they call "the intentions of the Framers." In its most doctrinaire incarnation, this view demands that Justices discern exactly what the Framers thought about the question under consideration and simply follow that intention in resolving the case before them. It is a view that feigns self-effacing deference to the specific judgments of those who forged our original social compact. But in truth it is little more than arrogance cloaked as humility.[141]

The scholarly debate that followed may have been more productive than Brennan's speech in establishing the strengths and weaknesses of Meese's interpretative stance. Brennan's choice of a nonjudicial forum in which to respond to a speech by a U.S. attorney general remains unusual.

More important, Brennan's speech may have been one of the factors that led many opponents of Robert Bork, whose views on constitutional interpretation were similar to Meese's, to per-ceive that he was vulnerable when Reagan nominated him to the Supreme Court in 1987. The resulting controversy was so bitter that a new word was coined to describe it—to "Bork," meaning to sink, a particular nominee. Bork was a former Yale University Law School professor and a federal appeals judge who was a prolific writer and a strong defender of original intent. The Senate eventually rejected his nomination by a 58–42 vote after extensive hearings and unprecedented lobbying by outside interest groups. Noting the tie to the earlier debates over the doctrine of original intent, one scholar says that the Bork hearings "came closer than any before to a national debate; in [Sen. Joseph] Biden's words, 'a referendum on the past progress of the Supreme Court and a referendum on the future.'"[142]

Bork's rejection created intense partisan rancor that bubbled up again in 1991 when George Bush's nominee, Clarence Thomas, appeared before the Senate Judiciary Committee. Neither of Bill Clinton's nominees, Ruth Bader Ginsburg and Stephen Breyer, proved to be as controversial. Both had fairly extensive tenures on federal appeals courts, and both were perceived as judicial moderates.

Presidential Powers in Domestic Affairs

Aaron Wildavsky has cogently argued that there are in effect two presidencies, one for domestic affairs and the other for defense and foreign policy.[143] Not all scholars agree that the line of division is this clear-cut, but Wildavsky's dichotomy is a useful starting point for outlining presidential powers as the courts have interpreted them. Presidents have broad powers in both areas, but courts generally have accorded them greater powers and more deference in foreign policy making than in domestic affairs.

APPOINTMENT AND REMOVAL POWERS

The power to appoint diplomatic officials, judges, and other officers is one of the most important powers that the Constitution confers on the president. In a compromise with those at the Constitutional Convention who thought the power of appointment should be vested in Congress, the Framers made the presidential power of appointment contingent on senatorial confirmation. The Senate is not averse to exercising its veto power over a president's nominees, especially when it is controlled by the opposite party. Generally, however, the Senate accords far more deference to the president's selection of cabinet members who will work directly for the administration than to judicial choices.[144] Typically, it also gives less scrutiny to nominees to lower federal courts than to the Supreme Court. Certainly, shrewd presidents keep likely senatorial reactions in mind when they make their judicial selections. From 1789 to 1995, only twenty-nine nominations to the Supreme Court have failed. (See Table 34-1.)

Of all the lacunae in the Constitution, few are as puzzling as the document's failure to specify how appointed officials, who

TABLE 34-1 Supreme Court Nominations That Failed

Nominee	Year of nomination	President	Action
William Paterson	1793	Washington	withdrawn
John Rutledge	1795	Washington	rejected, 10–14
Alexander Wolcott	1811	Madison	rejected, 9–24
John Crittenden	1828	J. Q. Adams	postponed
Roger B. Taney	1835	Jackson	postponed
John Spencer	1844	Tyler	rejected, 21–26
R. Walworth	1844	Tyler	withdrawn
Edward King	1844	Tyler	postponed
Edward King	1844	Tyler	withdrawn
John Read	1845	Tyler	not acted on
G. Woodward	1845	Polk	rejected, 20–29
Edward Bradford	1852	Fillmore	not acted on
George Badger	1853	Fillmore	postponed
William Micou	1853	Fillmore	not acted on
Jeremiah Black	1861	Buchanan	rejected, 25–26
Henry Stanbery	1866	A. Johnson	not acted on
Ebenezer Hoar	1869	Grant	rejected, 24–33
George Williams	1873	Grant	withdrawn
Caleb Cushing	1874	Grant	withdrawn
Stanley Matthews	1881	Hayes	not acted on
W. B. Hornblower	1893	Cleveland	rejected, 24–30
Wheeler H. Peckham	1894	Cleveland	rejected, 32–41
John J. Parker	1930	Hoover	rejected, 39–41
Abe Fortas[a]	1968	L. Johnson	withdrawn
Homer Thornberry	1968	L. Johnson	not acted on
C. Haynsworth	1969	Nixon	rejected, 45–55
G. H. Carswell	1970	Nixon	rejected, 45–51
Robert Bork	1987	Reagan	rejected, 42–58
Douglas Ginsburg[b]	1987	Reagan	not submitted

SOURCE: Harold W. Stanley and Richard G. Niemi, *Vital Statistics on American Politics*, 5th ed. (Washington, D.C.: CQ Press, 1995), 271.

NOTES: a. In 1968, Fortas, an associate justice, was nominated for chief justice. b. Publicly announced but withdrawn before the president formally submitted the nomination to the Senate.

do not—like judges—serve during good behavior, are to be removed. Did the Framers expect that the president, who is responsible for making nominations, would exercise this removal power alone, or did they anticipate that the president would share this power with the Senate, the body responsible for confirming nominations? A number of important cases have addressed this issue and have established fairly clear parameters.

Myers v. United States (1926) is the leading case in this area. It arose when President Woodrow Wilson fired a first class postmaster, who then filed an appeal. Although the law required the Senate to confirm the postmaster's appointment and to consent to his removal prior to the end of his four-year term, Wilson dismissed him without approval. Chief Justice Taft (the only person in American history to serve as president and chief justice) wrote the 5–3 majority decision expansively interpreting the president's removal powers. Taft based his decision partly on his view of the Framers' intentions as shown in debates held in the first session of Congress and partly on the nature of the presidential office and its responsibility for enforcing the laws. Taft argued that, as the nation's chief administrator, the president would have a better knowledge of and more responsibility

Chief Justice William Howard Taft (third from left) and the associate justices examine the architect's model for a new Supreme Court building in 1929. Taft persuaded Congress to fund the building and oversaw its planning and initial construction. He died five years before its completion.

WILLIAM HOWARD TAFT

Only one individual has ever served as the chief executive and the chief justice of the United States. That individual was the portly Republican, William Howard Taft (1857–1930). Taft also served as a judge of an Ohio superior court, as solicitor general in the administration of Benjamin Harrison, as a federal judge of the U.S. sixth circuit, as civil governor of the Philippines under William McKinley, and as secretary of war under Theodore Roosevelt.[1]

More at home as a judge than as a politician, Taft was nudged into the presidency both by his wife and by Roosevelt's decision not to seek reelection in 1908. As president from 1909 to 1913, Taft made six appointments to the Supreme Court, a record for a one-term president. Taft's decision to elevate a Democrat, Associate Justice Edward White, to the position of chief justice when Melville Fuller died in 1910 appears to have been motivated by Taft's hope that he might himself become chief when the more elderly White retired.

Chief Justice White died in 1921, and President Warren G. Harding fulfilled Taft's dream by appointing him to the vacancy. Taft's reputation was such that the Senate confirmed him the same day, skipping the committee hearings and debates that have become so common, and occasionally contentious, in modern times. When Taft retired in 1930, he was replaced by Charles Evans Hughes, whom Taft had appointed an associate justice in 1910. Hughes had resigned his seat to run against Woodrow Wilson for president.

As chief justice, Taft worked hard, although not always with success, to achieve unanimity. Beginning in 1925, when Harlan Fiske Stone was appointed to the Court, it was common for Oliver Wendell Holmes Jr. and Louis D. Brandeis to join Stone in dissent.[2]

Taft was generally regarded as a conservative, especially on matters of economic regulation, but he could be flexible in his opinions.

For example, he voted in dissent to uphold a minimum wage for women in *Adkins v. Children's Hospital*.[3]

Taft thought presidential powers were strictly limited by the Constitution. In *Myers v. United States*, however, Taft wrote an opinion for the Court strongly affirming the president's power to remove a first class postmaster without congressional consent.[4] Taft's opinion still stands in regard to individuals like cabinet members and diplomatic representatives who are serving in executive capacities. In subsequent cases, the Court modified Taft's reasoning so that it does not apply to attempted presidential removals of individuals serving in quasi-legislative and quasi-judicial capacities.

Because of his role in promoting judicial reform, Taft is sometimes regarded as the first "modern" chief justice. He helped to create the Judicial Conference of the United States, which coordinated activities among federal courts, and to win passage of the Judiciary Act of 1925, which gave the Court increased control over the cases it would hear. Taft also successfully lobbied for a separate building for the Supreme Court. Although Taft helped to oversee the design and early construction of the large marble building across from the Capitol, he did not see it completed. The Court moved in 1935, five years after his death.[5] The building serves as a visible symbol of the Court's coequal status with the two elected branches of government.

1. See Jonathan Lurie, "Taft, William Howard," in *The Oxford Companion to the Supreme Court of the United States*, ed. Kermit L. Hall (New York: Oxford, 1992), 854–856.

2. Alpheus T. Mason, *The Supreme Court from Taft to Burger*, 3d ed. (Baton Rouge: Louisiana State University Press, 1979), 61.

3. *Adkins v. Children's Hospital*, 261 U.S. 525 (1923).

4. *Myers v. United States*, 272 U.S. 52 (1926).

5. *The Supreme Court Justices: Illustrated Biographies, 1789–1995*, 2d ed., ed. Clare Cushman (Washington, D.C.: Congressional Quarterly, 1995), 345–346.

for any flaws in the performance of subordinates than would the Senate. He concluded, "The power to remove inferior executive officers, like that to remove superior officers, is an incident of the power to appoint them, and is in its nature an executive power."[145]

Taft's reasoning undoubtedly applied to members of the cabinet and other top executive officers. It is not so clear that it applied to functionaries at the level involved in *Myers*. Moreover, Taft proceeded to expand his argument quite beyond the facts of the case. He conceded that a president could not interfere directly with the duties of executive officers engaged in activities of a "quasi-judicial character" involving individual claims. Even in these cases, however, he said that the president "may consider the decision after its rendition as a reason for removing the officer, on the ground that the discretion regularly entrusted to that officer by statute has not been on the whole intelligently or wisely exercised."[146]

Justices McReynolds and Holmes dissented. They argued that because Congress had created the office of first class postmaster and could have vested the appointment elsewhere, Congress should be involved in removals. Justice Brandeis contended that Senate concurrence in such removals was the natural development of the idea of the civil service, whose members are not subject to presidential removal. He argued that Taft's decision did not provide adequate checks and balances.

Two subsequent cases have qualified Taft's *obiter dicta*, which, by definition, were not essential to deciding the case. One was *Humphrey's Executor v. United States* (1935), a case that led to Roosevelt's court-packing plan. In this case, Justice Sutherland wrote the opinion for a unanimous Court. He ruled that the president did not have the power to remove a member of the Federal Trade Commission except for cause. Sutherland characterized the commission as

an administrative body created by Congress to carry into effect legislative policies embodied in the statute in accordance with the legislative standard therein prescribed, and to perform other specified duties as a legislative or as a judicial aid.

Accordingly, Sutherland did not believe that the commission could "in any proper sense be characterized as an arm or an eye of the executive."[147] Moreover, Sutherland feared that judicial recognition of presidential removal powers over this agency would apply to other independent regulatory commissions that functioned as "quasi-legislative and quasi-judicial bodies," and undermine their effectiveness.[148]

In *Wiener v. United States* (1958) Justice Frankfurter wrote an opinion for a unanimous Court in which he denied President Eisenhower's authority to remove without cause a member of the War Claims Commission whom President Truman had appointed for the commission's duration. Like Sutherland, Frankfurter based his opinion on the belief that this position was not executive but quasi-judicial in nature. As such it required independence:

If, as one must take for granted, the War Claims Act precluded the President from influencing the Commission in passing on a particular

claim, *a fortiori* must it be inferred that Congress did not wish to have hang over the Commission the Damocles' sword of removal by the President for no reason other than that he preferred to have on that Commission men of his own choosing.[149]

Humphrey's Executor and *Wiener* appear to sanction the delegation of legislative powers to independent regulatory commissions. Beginning with the Interstate Commerce Commission (1887), these bodies have assumed an increasingly important role in national affairs. But agencies such as the Federal Trade Commission, the Federal Communications Commission, the Securities and Exchange Commission, and the Federal Reserve Board fit awkwardly in a system of separated powers. Sometimes they exercise legislative powers without being subject to the president's veto. At other times they perform executive functions without their members, who are appointed by the president for specific terms, being subject to executive removal. As unusual as these agencies appear, it may be that the Framers, who recognized that the division of authority among branches would sometimes be ambiguous, would have been willing to tolerate the inconsistencies.[150]

Significantly, the modern Court often reviews decisions by executive agencies to ascertain whether they have exceeded their powers or have adhered to guidelines to assure procedural due process. For example, in *Bob Jones University v. United States* (1983) the Supreme Court reviewed and ultimately upheld a decision by the Internal Revenue Service to withhold tax-exempt status from religious colleges that practice racial discrimination.[151] The Reagan administration had opposed the IRS policy. In *Dalton v. Specter* (1994) the Supreme Court rejected a suit brought by Sen. Arlen Specter of Pennsylvania. The Court decided that Congress, in passing the 1990 Base Closure Act, did not intend for the Court to review actions taken by a commission established to recommend the closure of military bases. Chief Justice Rehnquist noted that the president, not the commission, made the ultimate decision on base closures. Rehnquist concluded, "How the President chooses to exercise the discretion Congress has granted him is not a matter for our review."[152]

A number of cases since *Humphrey's Executor* and *Wiener* have further addressed appointment and removal powers. Some have applied fairly formalistic separation of powers reasoning. In *Buckley v. Valeo* (1976) the Court ruled a provision of the 1974 amendments to the Federal Election Campaign Act unconstitutional because it vested appointment of members of the Federal Election Commission in Congress rather than in the executive.[153] In *Bowsher v. Synar* (1986) the Court decided that the comptroller general was not an executive officer. The Court based the decision on the facts that the comptroller was appointed by the president from a list of names submitted by Congress and was removable by and therefore accountable to Congress. The Court decided that the comptroller could not be entrusted with executive functions, and that, accordingly, this official had no authority to recommend budget cuts to the president under the Balanced Budget and Emergency Deficit Control Act, better known as the Gramm-Rudman-Hollings law.[154]

In *Metropolitan Washington Airports Authority v. Citizens for the Abatement of Aircraft Noise* (1991) the Court ruled that Congress could not give a nine-member board, consisting of members of Congress, power over the Metropolitan Washington Airports Authority. Here the Court appeared to put Congress on the horns of a dilemma:

If the power [exercised by the board] is executive, the Constitution does not permit an agent of Congress to exercise it. If the power is legislative, Congress must exercise it in conformity with the bicameralism and presentment requirements of Art. I, 7.[155]

The Court took a more flexible view in *Morrison v. Olson* (1988). There it addressed the constitutionality of Title VI of the Ethics in Government Act, as applied to an investigation of an attorney in the Environmental Protection Agency alleged to have lied to Congress.[156] The Watergate scandal had prompted this law, which provided, on the application of the attorney general, for the appointment by a special court of a special prosecutor to examine alleged executive branch wrongdoing. The prosecutor would be subject to supervision by the attorney general, but could be removed only for cause.

Chief Justice Rehnquist wrote the 7–1 majority decision. He acknowledged that the constitutional line between inferior and principal officers was not "exact." Still, he decided that the special prosecutor was an "inferior officer" whose appointment could, under provisions of Article II, section 1, be vested in the courts.[157] Rehnquist also upheld the restrictions on presidential removal as consistent with the nature of the position:

we simply do not see how the President's need to control the exercise of that discretion is so central to the functioning of the Executive Branch as to require as a matter of constitutional law that the counsel be terminable at will by the President.[158]

Rehnquist further asserted that the special prosecutor did not violate the doctrine of separation of powers. While the law reduced presidential control of the office, Rehnquist argued that the act permitted through the attorney general's office "sufficient control over the independent counsel to ensure that the President is able to perform his constitutionally assigned duties."[159] In dissent, Justice Antonin Scalia argued that the provisions did not ensure adequate political accountability over the office and therefore posed a potential threat to executive powers.

Like *Morrison v. Olson, Mistretta v. United States* represents a fairly flexible view of departmental powers. In *Mistretta* the Court upheld the constitutionality of the U.S. Sentencing Commission. The commission consisted of seven voting members, at least three of whom were judges, approved by the president from a list submitted to him by the Judicial Conference of the United States. The Senate approved members of the commission, whom the president could remove only for cause. The commission's function was to establish binding sentencing guidelines. Acknowledging that the Sentencing Commission was "a peculiar institution within the framework of our Government," Justice Blackmun denied either that it represented an excessive delegation of legislative powers or that it "upset the

constitutionally mandated balance of powers among the coordinate Branches." As in *Morrison,* Justice Scalia dissented. He likened the commission to "a sort of 'junior-varsity Congress'" that was not, like Congress, accountable to the people and that did not therefore accord with constitutional requirements.[160]

ENFORCEMENT OF THE LAWS

Article II, section 3, of the Constitution specifies that the president shall "take Care that the Laws be faithfully executed." The classical description of a system of separated powers depicts Congress as making the laws, the president as enforcing them, and the courts as interpreting them. Here, as elsewhere in government, reality is considerably more complex.

The language of Article II, section 3, does not say that the president will directly execute the laws; instead, it says that the president will "take Care" that they be "faithfully executed," presumably by subordinates. Moreover, by its very nature, executive power is ambiguous. Harvey C. Mansfield Jr. notes that, while the dictionary may refer to an executive as one who "carries out" policy, an executive is more likely to envision and refer to the role as the more active one of "law enforcement."[161] In truth, the president's duties may involve both kinds of functions.

John Marshall recognized this duality in his classic decision in *Marbury v. Madison.* Marshall divided the president's duties into two categories: discretionary and ministerial. When it comes to discretionary political acts, "he [the president] is to use his own discretion, and is accountable to his country in his political character and to his conscience." Placing the power to name executive officials in the discretionary category, Marshall further noted, "In such cases, their acts are his acts; and whatever opinion may be entertained of the manner in which executive discretion may be used, still there exists, and can exist, no power to control their discretion."[162] In the ministerial category, there are occasions "when the legislature proceeds to impose on that officer other duties; when he is directed peremptorily to perform certain acts; when the rights of individuals are dependent on the performance of those acts." In these instances, Marshall argued that the president and his subordinates are "amenable to the laws . . . and cannot . . . sport away the vested rights of others."[163]

It is much easier to recognize that a distinction exists between discretionary and ministerial duties than to define their boundaries. The development of independent regulatory commissions that mix legislative and executive duties has made this task even more complicated.

One commentator has observed that scholars have attempted to explain the president's power to execute the laws by using both an active and a passive theory, neither of which is adequate. The active view, similar to Chief Justice Taft's opinion in *Myers v. United States,* portrays the president as the direct enforcer of the laws. Under this theory, "no act of execution could be accomplished except under the direction and control of the President."[164] The passive view, "while preserving for the President a limited role in oversight of the executive branch, permits Congress to effect independent execution of the laws through independent agencies or by formally independent executive officers."[165] It can be argued that the active view would augment presidential powers unduly. Descriptively, it probably overestimates the degree of control that the dismissal power and existing law give to modern presidents. The passive view, however, would leave the presidency as a "shell" and tempt Congress to assume too much power.[166] How a balance between the active and passive views should be found may not be clear, but such ambiguity may be implicit in the variety of functions that a modern president oversees.

In addition to *Marbury v. Madison* and the cases involving the president's removal powers, a number of other cases speak to the president's powers over law enforcement. In *Kendall v. United States ex rel. Stokes* (1838) the Court directed the postmaster general to follow a congressional law and honor a contract negotiated by his predecessor.[167] In the case of *In re Neagle* (1890) the Court upheld the president's inherent power to assign law enforcement officers to guard a Supreme Court justice.[168] In 1895 the Court sustained the attorney general's decision to seek an injunction and a subsequent contempt sentence against Eugene Debs, president of the American Railway Union, which was conducting a strike against railroads using Pullman cars. The case was *In re Debs*. The government, the Court proclaimed, had broad powers under the Sherman Antitrust Law to protect the mail and interstate commerce:

The entire strength of the nation may be used to enforce in any part of the land the full and free exercise of all national powers and the security of all rights entrusted by the Constitution to its care. The strong arm of the national government may be put forth to brush away all obstructions to the freedom of interstate commerce or the transportation of the mails. If the emergency arises, the army of the nation, and all its militia, are at the service of the nation to compel obedience to its laws.[169]

The Court clearly believed that President Cleveland had also been justified in sending in federal troops to break the strike.

Rarely will presidential actions executing the laws be so dramatic. The president's influence is usually more subtle. He may use the presidential platform to give a certain "tone" to the administration. He decides which areas of the law to emphasize and makes appointments and sets priorities that affect government decision making.

PARDON AND CLEMENCY POWERS

Article II, section 2, of the Constitution grants to the president "Power to grant Reprieves and Pardons for Offenses against the United States, except in Cases of Impeachment." Throughout American history, courts have interpreted this power broadly. Because the clause refers to "Offenses against the United States," it does not reach to offenses against individual states or intervention in civil suits.[170] In *Ex parte Grossman* (1925), however, the Supreme Court declared that the power to pardon can extend to criminal contempts of federal courts.[171] Moreover, presidents have sometimes issued pardons for contempts of Congress.[172]

In *The Federalist Papers*, Alexander Hamilton argued that the pardon power was more than a method of mitigating the effects of the law in cases involving an injustice. He also defended the pardon power—and the fact that it could be extended even in cases of treason—as a means of restoring domestic peace. He wrote that

in seasons of insurrection or rebellion, there are often critical moments when a well-timed offer of pardon to the insurgents or rebels may restore the tranquillity of the commonwealth; and which, if suffered to pass unimproved, it may never be possible afterwards to recall.[173]

Consistent with this intention, courts have included general amnesties within the pardon power. Presidents Washington, Adams, Madison, Lincoln, Andrew Johnson, and Carter have all granted such amnesties. Carter's amnesty, which extended to Vietnam-era draft evaders, some of whom had fled to Canada, was constitutionally sound, but politically controversial. As with Gerald Ford's earlier pardon of Richard Nixon, Carter's act met with criticism from some quarters, showing that public opinion remains a check on the exercise of the pardon and clemency powers.

Early in U.S. history, the Court advanced the theory that pardons were not valid unless the parties to whom they were offered accepted them. In *United States v. Wilson* (1833), for example, Chief Justice Marshall accepted an individual's refusal of a presidential pardon for robbing the U.S. mail and putting a driver's life in jeopardy. By refusing the pardon, the individual was able to shield himself under the constitutional prohibition against double jeopardy from further prosecution. Marshall said:

A pardon is a deed, to the validity of which delivery is essential, and delivery is not complete without acceptance. It may then be rejected by the person to whom it is tendered; and if it be rejected, we have discovered no power in a court to force it on him.[174]

In *Biddle v. Perovich* (1927), however, the Court reversed course in a case involving a presidential commutation of a death sentence to life imprisonment. Speaking for the Court, Justice Holmes noted that a pardon was "not a private act of grace from an individual happening to possess power," but rather "a part of the Constitutional scheme." Therefore, he said, "Just as the original punishment would be imposed without regard to the prisoner's consent and in the teeth of his will, whether he liked it or not, the public welfare, not his consent, determines what shall be done."[175]

In a leading pardon case, *Ex parte Garland* (1867), the Supreme Court upheld President Andrew Johnson's pardon of a former Confederate sympathizer against the Test Act of 1865, which was intended to prohibit from practicing law anyone who had sided with the rebellion. The Court decided that a pardon had the effect of restoring its recipient to his status prior to an offense. The Court upheld broad presidential powers, indicating that an executive pardon "extends to every offense known to the law, and may be exercised at any time after its commission, either before legal proceedings are taken, or during their penden-

A DISTRICT COURT MAKES A DIAGNOSIS: THE PRESIDENT AS REBEL

It is rare for judges to lambaste a president or former president, but Richard Nixon could certainly take little comfort from a U.S. district court decision, even though it validated the pardon he had received from President Gerald Ford. Chief Justice Noel Fox of the U.S. District Court for the Western District of Michigan issued the decision.

Fox was hearing an unusual case. An attorney, George Murphy, had brought an action against President Ford seeking a judicial declaration that Ford's pardon of Nixon was unconstitutional. Ford had issued his unconditional pardon shortly after taking over the duties of the former president.

In examining Alexander Hamilton's discussion of the pardon power in *Federalist* No. 74, Judge Fox noted that Hamilton had praised the pardon as an instrument that might be employed "in seasons of insurrection or rebellion" for "insurgents or rebels."[1] Following this lead, Judge Fox argued, "Few would today deny that the period from the break-in at the Watergate in June 1972, until the resignation of President Nixon in 1974 was a 'season of insurrection or rebellion' by many actually in government." Judge Fox said, "Evidence now available suggests a strong probability that the Nixon Administration was conducting a covert assault on American liberty and an insurrection and rebellion against constitutional government itself."[2]

Despite the judge's pointed analysis of Nixon's conduct, he concluded that Ford's pardon was valid. He cited Ford's concern about ending the divisiveness caused by Watergate and the need to address pressing social and economic problems. He concluded that Ford's action was "thus within the letter and the spirit of the Presidential Pardoning Power granted by the Constitution. It was a prudent public policy judgment."[3] Judge Fox cited a previous Supreme Court decision, *Ex parte Garland,* as authority, as well as a contemporary Florida case.

As if to reiterate his opinion of Nixon's guilt, however, Judge Fox highlighted a section of the latter case: "it [the pardon] does not obliterate the fact of the commission of the crime and the conviction thereof; it does not wash out the moral stain; as has been tersely said, 'it involves forgiveness and not forgetfulness.'"[4]

1. *Murphy v. Ford,* 390 F. Supp. 1372 (1975). Cited at 1373.
2. Ibid.
3. Ibid.
4. Ibid., 1375.

The most controversial pardon in this century, if not in American history, was the "full, free, and absolute pardon . . . for all offenses against the United States which he had committed or may have committed or taken part in" that President Ford gave to former president Nixon.[178] Ford said he wanted to focus his energies on more important matters and was concerned about the former president's ability to receive a fair trial.[179] Ford drew considerable criticism for his action, which may even have cost him the presidential election in 1976. A U.S. district court upheld the pardon, which most commentators believe to have been a legitimate exercise of power.[180] Sen. Walter Mondale proposed an amendment that would have allowed both houses of Congress to disapprove such a pardon by a two-thirds vote, but Congress rejected it.[181]

During his presidency, Ronald Reagan demonstrated his concern with crime by attempting to tighten up on pardons. Generally, he did not issue them until several years after criminals had served their sentences.[182] Despite speculation that he might do so, Reagan did not pardon Oliver North and others involved in the sale of arms to Iran (a deal designed to encourage the Iranians to pressure those holding American hostages in Lebanon to release them). Profits from the arms sale were funneled to the contra rebels in Nicaragua in violation of a congressional ban. The courts eventually overturned North's conviction because of the possibility that testimony he gave under a congressional grant of immunity in the publicly televised Iran-contra hearings had tainted his conviction.[183] In December 1992 President Bush pardoned former secretary of defense Caspar Weinberger, former national security adviser Robert McFarlane, and four other Reagan officials who had been convicted of offenses in connection with the Iran-contra affair. Bush argued that their convictions had represented the "criminalization of policy differences."[184]

PRESIDENTIAL LEGISLATIVE POWERS

Congress is the branch of government responsible for passing legislation, but the president's veto power is a clear indication that the Framers expected the chief executive to play a role in this process. Article II, section 3, provides that the president shall give Congress information on the state of the Union and "recommend to their Consideration such Measures as he shall judge necessary and expedient." The presidential role has significantly expanded as, in a development unanticipated by many of the Founders, the president also has become a party leader.

The Presidential Veto Power

The "presentment clause" in Article I, section 7, sets forth the power of presidential veto. The provision applies to all congressional actions except for actions of a single house or concurrent resolutions applying only to routine housekeeping matters or constitutional amendments. The Constitution already requires Congress to propose amendments by a two-thirds vote of both houses of Congress, the same congressional majority needed to override a veto.

cy, or after conviction and judgment."[176] In *Schick v. Reed* (1974) the Court upheld the constitutionality of a conditional pardon that President Eisenhower had extended to a member of the military. The Court said that the purpose of the constitutional pardon provision was "to allow plenary authority in the President to 'forgive' the convicted person in part or entirely, to reduce a penalty in terms of a specified number of years, or to alter it with conditions which are in themselves constitutionally unobjectionable."[177]

By the presentment clause, a president in essence has three options: (1) to sign a bill into law; (2) to return a bill with objections to it spelled out and veto it, subject to a two-thirds override by both houses of Congress (a regular veto); or (3) to do nothing. Normally, a bill becomes law in ten days—excluding Sundays—without the president's signature. If the president receives a bill during the last ten days of a congressional session, however, a failure to sign results in a so-called pocket veto. Designed in large part as an instrument for protecting the president's constitutional prerogatives, the veto has also been a highly effective political tool. Congress has overridden only 103 of 1,426 regular vetoes exercised from 1789 to 1991, and, while the president's success in having a veto stand is more likely in cases of private bills affecting single individuals (for example, in the area of pensions) than of public bills, there is a greater than 80 percent presidential success rate for the latter.[185] Because of this success, even a threat of a veto may prompt members of Congress to seek effective compromise.

The pocket veto prevents Congress from presenting the president with a bill likely to be vetoed and then adjourning before that takes place. In the *Pocket Veto Case* of 1929 the Supreme Court ruled that such a congressional adjournment need not be at the end of its two-year session. Writing for a unanimous Court and relying in part on a memorandum prepared by the attorney general's office, Justice Edward Sanford said:

We think that under the constitutional provision the determinative question in reference to an "adjournment" is not whether it is a final adjournment of Congress or an interim adjournment, but whether it is one that "prevents" the President from returning the bill to the House in which it originated within the time allowed.[186]

Less than a decade later, however, the Supreme Court issued a decision in *Wright v. United States* (1938) that called into question whether a recess by a single branch of Congress could trigger a pocket veto if that house had designated a secretary to receive veto messages.[187] A number of appeals court decisions have subsequently invalidated pocket vetoes in cases where Congress has recessed but designated officials to receive veto messages.[188] In a case that might have resolved the question, the Supreme Court sidestepped the issue by declaring that the bill in question, a military aid bill to El Salvador, had expired before the Court reviewed it, and the question was therefore moot.[189]

In some states, governors exercise a line-item veto, which gives them the ability to strike individual items of an appropriations bill. In March 1996 Congress passed a type of line-item veto through legislation that allows the president to rescind individual budget items subject to congressional disapproval. Some people believe that such a measure can be adopted only through consitutional amendment, and the constitutionality of this law is likely to be challenged. The effects of a federal line-item veto are as yet unknown; some observers believe such a measure will help trim existing federal budget deficits, but others fear that it may tilt the balance between the two elected branches toward the president.

Delegated Legislative Powers

As government grew more complex, Congress found it advantageous to adopt laws that vest in the president discretion in implementing them in accordance with changing circumstances. The Court has been especially open to the delegation of power in foreign affairs, where the president already shares broad authority with Congress. *J. W. Hampton, Jr. & Co. v. United States* (1928) was an important case that recognized the power of the president, under authority of a tariff law, to raise or lower duties on imported goods. In that decision, the Court ruled:

If Congress shall lay down by legislative act an intelligible principle to which the person or body authorized to fix such rates is directed to conform, such legislative action is not a forbidden delegation of legislative power.[190]

In domestic affairs, however, critics fear that the delegation of legislative powers may intrude upon the principle of separation of powers by in effect granting the president or an independent regulatory commission powers that Congress should be exercising. In three cases from the New Deal period, the Court struck down laws for vesting undue legislative discretion in the president.

The first was *Panama Refining Company v. A. D. Ryan* (1935). It dealt with powers delegated to the president in the National Industrial Recovery Act of 1934 (NIRA), which Congress adopted to deal with the effects of the Great Depression. The provision tested in this case regulated "hot oil," or oil produced in excess of quotas established by the states. Declaring that "Congress manifestly is not permitted to abdicate, or to transfer to others, the essential legislative functions with which it is thus vested," Chief Justice Hughes issued the 8–1 majority opinion voiding the act, finding that "Congress left the matter to the President without standard or rule, to be dealt with as he pleased."[191]

In *Schechter Poultry Corp. v. United States* (1935), known as the "sick chicken case," the Court examined another NIRA provision. This provision permitted the president to enforce elaborate codes of fair competition that were drawn up, not by Congress, but by industry representatives. Again, the Court struck down the law. Hughes wrote:

In view of the scope of that broad declaration, and of the nature of the few restrictions that are imposed, the discretion of the President in approving or prescribing codes, and thus enacting laws for the government of trade and industry throughout the country is virtually unfettered.[192]

Justice Benjamin Cardozo approved the delegation of power at issue in *Panama*. In *Schechter*, however, he had to agree with the majority. "The delegated power of legislation which has found expression in this code is not canalized within banks, that keep it from overflowing. It is unconfined and vagrant," he wrote.[193]

In striking down the Bituminous Coal Conservation Act of 1935 in *Carter v. Carter Coal Co.* (1936), the Court focused again on the improper delegation of legislative powers. Noting that the law delegated power to fix hours and wages to producers and miners, Justice Sutherland said:

This is legislative delegation in its most obnoxious form; for it is not even delegation to an official or an official body, presumptively disinterested, but to private persons whose interests may be and often are adverse to the interests of others in the same business.[194]

The judicial "switch in time" in 1937 left the validity of these precedents clouded. In *Yakus v. United States* (1944) the Court upheld a delegation of power to a price administrator whom the president had appointed under the Emergency Price Control Act of 1942. Congress had granted the administrator the power to fix prices at a "fair and equitable" level to combat wartime inflation. In upholding the administrator's authority, Chief Justice Stone wrote:

The Constitution as a continuously operative charter of government does not demand the impossible or the impracticable. It does not require that Congress find for itself every fact upon which it desires to base legislation or that it make for itself detailed determinations which it has declared to be prerequisite to the application of the legislative policy to particular facts and circumstances impossible for Congress itself properly to investigate.

Stone further stated:

Only if we could say that there is an absence of standards for the guidance of the Administrator's action, so that it would be impossible in a proper proceeding to ascertain whether the will of Congress has been obeyed, would we be justified in overriding its choice of means for effecting its declared purpose of preventing inflation.[195]

The Court has never repudiated its warnings against broad delegations of legislative power to the president. Since the 1930s, however, it has not invalidated a single act of congressional legislation on this ground. Both commentators and dissenting justices continue to raise this issue, which might one day serve again as the basis for a Supreme Court decision.

Meanwhile, in a number of decisions, the Court has been fairly permissive in this area. In *Arizona v. California* (1963), for example, the Court upheld broad delegations of power to the secretary of the interior in allocating Colorado River waters among the states.[196] And in *Bowsher v. Synar* (1986), while deciding that the comptroller general could not specify budget cuts under the Gramm-Rudman-Hollings act, the Court did not rule that such authority was an unconstitutional delegation of legislative powers.

A Special Case—The Legislative Veto

Of all the twentieth century constitutional innovations that have affected the potential relationship between the president and Congress, none was probably more significant than the legislative veto. Originally developed in response to President Hoover's attempt to reorganize the executive branch, the legislative veto gave the president authority to make certain administrative changes subject to disapproval by one or both houses of Congress. And, beginning with Hoover, presidents consistently expressed their objections to this device, often while signing a bill containing it. In a sense, however, presidents also gained from the arrangement because Congress was generally willing to entrust more decision making to the executive branch subject to

such a check than it would have been willing to grant without it.

In *Immigration and Naturalization Service v. Chadha* (1983) the Supreme Court ruled that the legislative veto was unconstitutional.[197] The case involved an East Indian from Kenya with a British passport. The Immigration and Naturalization Service (INS) granted his petition for permanent resident status under authority that Congress had delegated to the attorney general. The House of Representatives subsequently vetoed the INS approval. When Chadha challenged the constitutionality of the legislative veto, the INS, former president Jimmy Carter, and President Ronald Reagan all agreed with him. Members of Congress filed amicus briefs in behalf of the mechanism, leaving the Court to resolve the dispute.

Writing for a 7–2 majority, Chief Justice Burger ruled that the legislative veto was unconstitutional even though it was part of more than two hundred existing laws. Burger followed strict separation of powers logic and the language of the Constitution. As he viewed the legislative veto, it ran afoul of both the presentment provisions and the bicameralism requirements. As to the first, a legislative veto became effective without the president's signature or a veto override, which, in Burger's view, was inconsistent with the Framers' wish to guard against "oppressive, improvident, or ill-considered measures" that Congress might on its own adopt.[198] Moreover, the fact that only the House of Representatives had adopted the veto in the case at hand meant that the second constitutional requirement, the principle of bicameralism, had also been violated. Burger acknowledged that many commentators viewed the legislative veto as a "convenient shortcut" and an "appealing compromise." He also noted that "the Framers ranked other values higher than efficiency" and decided that the veto was therefore unconstitutional.[199] Justice Lewis Powell agreed with the decision in this case but preferred a narrower ruling. He focused on the fact that Congress appeared in this instance to be violating the doctrine of separation of powers by exercising a judicial function.

Justice Byron White wrote a vigorous dissent. White praised the legislative veto as "an important if not indispensable political invention that allows the president and Congress to resolve major constitutional and policy differences, assures the accountability of independent regulatory agencies, and preserves Congress' control over lawmaking." White further argued that the majority had presented Congress with a Hobson's choice:

either to refrain from delegating the necessary authority, leaving itself with a hopeless task of writing laws with the requisite specificity to cover endless special circumstances across the entire policy landscape, or in the alternative, to abdicate its lawmaking function to the executive branch and independent agencies.[200]

Although the Supreme Court continues to uphold its decision, critics still question its efficacy.[201] Congress removed a number of vetoes from existing bills, sometimes providing that presidential initiatives would now require positive legislative approval, rather than be subject to a veto. However, from the *Chadha* decision through October 1992, Congress also had enacted more than two hundred new legislative vetoes.[202] Moreover, rather than providing statutory mandates, Congress has worked out informal nonstatutory agreements with many executive agencies, which depend on Congress for funding. Under the agreements, these agencies continue to seek committee authorization for decisions over which they desire more than the usual degree of discretion. Louis Fisher has argued that the *Chadha* decision "simply drives underground a set of legislative and committee vetoes that formerly operated in plain sight."[203] In this respect, *Chadha* may be another indication of the limits of judicial decision making.

Another Special Case—Presidential Impoundment

If the legislative veto appeared to encroach on presidential powers, the presidential exercise of impoundment seemed to threaten congressional prerogatives. The practice of impoundment goes back to Jefferson's day. Jefferson decided not to spend congressionally appropriated funds for gunboats he believed were no longer needed in light of changed circumstances. President Nixon significantly escalated the use of impoundments, refusing to spend money even on projects that Congress had adopted over his veto.

The Court partly rebuffed Nixon's actions, albeit in a case that dealt chiefly with statutory construction rather than with the underlying constitutional issue.[204] Congress also responded by passing the Budget and Impoundment Control Act of 1974. This law distinguished between presidential impoundments that attempt to delay or defer spending and those that attempt to terminate programs or cut authorized spending. Under provisions of this law, Congress could disapprove attempts to delay spending, thereby forcing the release of funds—a form of legislative veto later declared unconstitutional in the *Chadha* case—while attempts to rescind spending altogether required bicameral support within forty-five days.[205] In 1986 Reagan upset an earlier informal understanding with Congress and attempted to use the deferral powers under this law. A district judge, whose decision was affirmed in an appeals court decision, subsequently ruled that, because the legislative veto provision of the law was unconstitutional, the law was no longer in effect.[206] In 1987 Congress subsequently limited such deferrals to what Louis Fisher has described as "routine managerial actions."[207]

EXECUTIVE ORDERS

The doctrine of separation of powers suggests that Congress alone makes laws, but that is not strictly true. A kind of executive equivalent to statutes, known as the executive order, has developed. Executive orders have been assigned numbers since 1907, and more than fifteen thousand have been recorded during this time period.[208]

President Clinton demonstrated the power—and possible limits—of the executive order shortly after assuming office. He successfully used the device to lift the bans that Presidents Reagan and Bush had imposed on fetal tissue research and on abortion counseling at federally funded facilities. But Congress rebuffed Clinton when he attempted to order an end to the ban on immigrants with the HIV virus, and he was forced to compromise over his plan to permit homosexuals to serve in the military.[209]

Statutes provide authority for most executive orders. A study of 1,769 orders signed from 1945 through 1965 found that 1,474, or 83 percent, fell into this category.[210] General grants of power within the Constitution provide the basis for others. Virtually indistinguishable from presidential proclamations, executive orders are particularly prominent in military affairs. During the Civil War, President Lincoln issued several, the most important of which was the Emancipation Proclamation. Justified as a war measure, the proclamation extended freedom to slaves behind enemy lines. Franklin Roosevelt issued orders providing for curfews and for the removal of Japanese Americans to detention camps during World War II. President Truman's order to seize the steel mills to avert a strike during the Korean conflict also took the form of an executive order.

Executive orders have also been significant in civil rights. For example, Truman used Executive Order 9981 to desegregate the military in 1948. After Congress refused to include minority hiring requirements for government contractors in the Civil Rights Act of 1964, President Lyndon Johnson issued an executive order to get it done.

On occasion justices express reservations about executive orders. In a concurring opinion in *Peters v. Hobby* (1955), a decision on the actions of loyalty boards created by the president, Justice Black observed, "These orders look more like legislation to me than properly authorized regulations to carry out a clear and explicit command of Congress." Black further noted that "the Constitution does not confer lawmaking power on the President."[211] In *Jenkins v. Collard* (1891), however, the Supreme Court said that executive orders carry "the force of public law."[212] Glendon A. Schubert Jr.'s 1957 list of cases in which the validity of executive orders has been recognized includes twenty examples, many from lower federal courts.[213] Judging the constitutionality of a given order can, however, be fairly complex:

While a statute may be held unconstitutional only if it contravenes some provision of the Constitution, an Executive order is held invalid if it conflicts with provisions either of the Constitution or of a statute, or even with the implied intent of Congress. The invalidation of an order found to conflict with a statute has occurred even in an area where the President has a special constitutional status, such as Commander in Chief.

On the other hand, Congress may "ratify" by statute a prior Executive order either by making direct reference to it or by implication.[214]

DOMESTIC PREROGATIVE OR INHERENT POWERS

The U.S. Constitution is a constitution of enumerated, or granted, powers. The description of the legislative branch in Article I, section 1, begins with a reference to "All legislative Powers herein granted." Article I, section 8, proceeds to list the specific powers entrusted to Congress. Scholars often refer to the last provision of this section as the elastic or sweeping clause. It specifies that Congress shall have the power "[t]o make all Laws which shall be necessary and proper for carrying into Execution the foregoing Powers, and all other Powers vested by this Constitution in the Government of the United States, or in any Department or Officer thereof." Chief Justice Marshall used this provision as the textual basis for the doctrine of implied powers in *McCulloch v. Maryland.* Giving a broad rather than a narrow definition of the words "necessary and proper," Marshall argued that Congress had a wide choice of means in furthering constitutionally granted powers or ends, means that here extended to creating a banking corporation.

Article I of the Constitution vests all "legislative Powers *herein granted*" in Congress. Article II states more simply, "The executive Power shall be vested in a President of the United States." Going back at least as far as Alexander Hamilton, some commentators have argued that the difference between the wording of these two grants of power indicates that executive powers, often tied in political theory to the doctrine of prerogative, might be more expansive than legislative powers.[215] This doctrine has been more important in foreign affairs, where the United States is assumed to have equal standing among and equal prerogatives to other nations, than in domestic affairs. Still, courts have recognized certain domestic executive prerogatives.

The Supreme Court decision that most clearly establishes executive prerogative or inherent powers in domestic affairs is *In re Neagle* (1890). Because of a threat on Justice Stephen Field's life, the U.S. attorney general had appointed a U.S. marshal, David Neagle, to protect Field as he rode circuit in California. The threat came from a former colleague on the California Supreme Court. Neagle subsequently killed this man while defending Field. California authorities arrested Neagle, and he sought release through a writ of *habeas corpus.* Even though no statute specifically authorized the protection that Neagle had provided to Field, the Court ordered Neagle's release. The Court noted that Article II, section 3, of the Constitution authorized the president to see that laws were faithfully executed. It decided that this grant included the right not merely to enforce congressional acts in "their express terms" but also the duty to enforce "the rights, duties and obligations growing out of the constitution itself." The Court concluded that the president's duty to protect the "peace of the United States" included the power to assign a federal marshal to protect a Supreme Court justice.[216]

Presidential Immunities

American presidents are highly visible public figures who exercise broad powers over numerous areas of policy at a time when society appears to be growing more litigious. Presidents exposed to the risk of personal lawsuits for routine public policy decisions could be hampered in carrying out their duties. It is not surprising, therefore, that the Supreme Court has carved out an area of presidential immunity here.

Presidential immunity is not exclusive. The Court has recognized some type of immunity from civil actions for members of all three branches of the federal government as well as for a variety of state officials. State executive officials, judges, state prosecutors, and aides to members of Congress all have such immunity, although, in some cases, courts have qualified it. *Butz v. Economou* (1978), dealing with cabinet officers, is an example.[217]

IMMUNITY FROM LAWSUITS

The central case involving presidential immunity from lawsuits is *Nixon v. Fitzgerald* (1982). This case involved a suit brought against President Nixon by a former civilian air force employee. The employee had embarrassed the administration by blowing the whistle on his department's cost overruns. The president subsequently concurred in the employee's dismissal from his job after his department was reorganized. Writing for a 5–4 majority, Justice Lewis Powell decided that the president should have absolute immunity against civil suits resulting from his official acts. Powell described this immunity as "a functionally mandated incident of the President's unique office rooted in the constitutional tradition of the separation of powers and supported by our history." Powell argued that the threat of impeachment and conviction and the president's desire both for reelection and continuing prestige were adequate safeguards against abuse. Immunity from civil suits would not place the president above the law. The dissenters argued that the Court had gone too far, that this interpretation of presidential immunity not only elevated the president above the law but also left aggrieved private parties without adequate redress.[218]

Ruling 8–1 in a companion case, *Harlow v. Fitzgerald* (1982), however, the Court decided that presidential aides were entitled to only a qualified good faith immunity. Using this standard, courts would be able to dismiss frivolous lawsuits through summary judgments.[219]

Presidents have been called upon to provide information to, and testify before, congressional committees and criminal trials involving others. Especially where the information sought concerns diplomatic and military affairs or matters entrusted exclusively to the White House, the president may refuse to comply on the grounds of executive privilege. In addition, courts rarely treat presidents and ex-presidents as they would ordinary private parties. Instead, courts are likely to summon them only in cases where their testimony is directly relevant, and courts may permit them to submit taped depositions or otherwise accommodate their schedules. In 1989 U.S. District Judge Gerhard A. Gesell indicated his belief that "the Court has power to enforce its compulsory process," but he did not require that President Reagan testify in the Oliver North trial because he did not believe that North had demonstrated adequate need for the testimony.[220]

Like judges and justices, presidents may be impeached by the House of Representatives and tried in the Senate. The House Judiciary Committee had voted impeachment charges against Richard Nixon when he decided to resign from office, but to date Andrew Johnson remains the only president that the House has impeached. In his case, the Senate fell one vote shy of the necessary two-thirds the Constitution requires for conviction.

Although the Supreme Court has not spoken directly to the matter, some scholars believe that, while members of the legislative and judicial branches may be indicted while in office, criminal charges against the president can be initiated only by the constitutional impeachment process.[221] Special Prosecutor Leon Jaworski insisted that the grand jury investigating the Watergate affair name President Nixon as an *unindicted* coconspirator.

In 1994 an Arkansas woman, Paula Jones, filed a civil suit against President Clinton alleging that, when he was governor of Arkansas, he had denied her a promotion after she refused his sexual advances. This case raised a new question: Is the president immune from prosecution for actions taken prior to assuming office? Clinton claimed executive immunity. Judge Susan Webber Wright of a U.S. district court ruled in December 1994 that he could be questioned about this matter while he was president, but that any trial would have to wait until his term in office was over. Pleased with the postponement, Clinton's lawyers indicated that they would appeal the decision permitting pretrial discovery during his tenure in office. However, a federal court of appeals ruled in January 1996 that this compromise was unacceptable and that the trial did not have to wait until Clinton left office.[222] The resulting appeals seemed likely to postpone resolution of this issue until after the 1996 presidential election.

IMMUNITIES RELATIVE TO PRIVACY AND CONFIDENTIALITY

From time to time throughout American history, presidents have claimed the right to withhold information from congressional investigating committees. Presidents have been especially concerned about protecting sensitive matters of foreign policy that might embarrass the nation. President Nixon widened this claim and refined it into the claim of executive privilege that the Court addressed in *United States v. Nixon* (1974).

At issue was a subpoena *duces tecem* (requiring production of documents) that Leon Jaworski secured against Nixon. Jaworski was leading the investigation of a number of top presidential advisers, and he wanted the tapes of specific conversations between the president and his aides that had been made in the Oval Office. Jaworski thought (correctly) that these tapes had bearing on possible criminal wrongdoing. Judge John Sirica of the U.S. district court ordered Nixon to produce these tapes for an *in camera* (in chambers) inspection to determine their relevance. Nixon asserted his right to refuse on separation of powers grounds. He alleged that the controversy was an intrabranch executive dispute between the president and the special prosecutor. He also asserted executive privilege.

The Supreme Court dismissed the first argument by pointing to the special prosecutor's unique legal mandate and by noting the Court's historic duty "to say what the law is."[223] As to the broad claim of executive privilege, or the need for confidentiali-

This subpoena *duces tecum* (a writ to produce documents or other evidence) was issued by the first special prosecutor July 23, 1973. It ordered President Richard Nixon or his subordinates to appear before the grand jury and to bring tapes relevant to the Watergate investigation.

ty, the Court noted that although the privilege was not specifically stated in the Constitution, "to the extent this intent relates to the effective discharge of a President's powers, it is constitutionally based."[224] In addition to the ordinary privacy needs of everyday citizens, the president had an additional interest in seeing that his aides did not temper their advice because of fears of future disclosures. Claims of privilege might be especially important in regard to sensitive matters of foreign relations. Here, however, no such matters were at issue. Moreover, presidents and their advisers would have few occasions to fear that their conversations would be subpoenaed for use in ongoing criminal prosecutions. Consequently, the Court decided that the special prosecutor's more particular and important interest in upholding the rule of law outweighed the president's generalized claim of privilege.

The Supreme Court accepted a similar limitation on executive privilege in 1977 when, in *Nixon v. Administrator of General Services*, it voted 7–2, with Chief Justice Burger and Justice Rehnquist dissenting, to uphold the Presidential Recordings and Preservation Act of 1974. This law abrogated an agreement between Nixon and the administrator of the General Services Administration limiting access to Nixon's presidential papers. Tape recordings made in the Oval Office, including those that had led to evidence of Nixon's complicity in the Watergate affair, would have been destroyed in time. The law required that the administrator return private materials to Nixon, but preserve others for relevant judicial proceedings and eventual public access, and that President Nixon be compensated for them.

The law was unique. First, it applied directly only to Nixon. Second, in the past presidential papers had been regarded as the president's personal property. In this case, however, the Court cited several reasons why the public interests outweighed Nixon's desire for privacy. The Court noted "[t]he limited intrusion of the screening process, . . . appellant's status as a public figure, . . . his lack of expectation of privacy in the overwhelming majority of the materials, . . . the important public interest in preservation of the materials, and . . . the virtual impossibility of segregating the small quantity of private materials without comprehensive screening."[225] With this public interest in view, the Court majority also denied that the law constituted an illegal bill of attainder, or legislative punishment without benefit of a trial, intended to penalize the former president rather than provide for the public good.

In 1995 renewed attention was focused on the issue of executive privilege when, for a time, President Clinton instructed White House counsel William Kennedy to refuse to turn over notes he had made of a meeting between Clinton and his attorneys and aides shortly after the suicide of Vincent Foster, deputy counsel to the president. A Senate committee investigating the Whitewater matter, a land deal in Arkansas that involved a failed savings and loan institution with which Bill and Hillary Clinton had contacts, voted to subpoena the notes. The Senate upheld the vote. Before releasing the notes to Special Prosecutor Kenneth Starr, Clinton received assurances that by releasing them, he was not waiving his broader attorney-client privileges.

As the controversy continued, Starr made history in January 1996 when he issued the first subpoena ever to a sitting first lady. Hillary Clinton was required to appear under oath before a grand jury—her earlier depositions had been taken at the White House. The grand jury was inquiring into the sudden appearance at the White House of documents that the prosecutor had subpoenaed two years earlier. The documents in question were her billing records at the Rose law firm in Little Rock, where she had worked prior to Clinton's presidency. The billing records were needed to determine the extent of her representation of parties involved in the Whitewater land deal.

Presidential Powers in Defending the Nation

The conduct of a nation's foreign affairs is critical; unless a nation is relatively secure, it cannot pursue other goals. The Constitution grants the president wide powers in foreign affairs, but they are not exclusive. Instead, the Constitution divides these powers between the president and Congress. For example, the president negotiates treaties, but a two-thirds majority of the Senate ratifies them. The Constitution grants Congress the power to "declare" war, but it designates the president as commander in chief of the armed forces, giving the president the power to "wage" it. Debates over the appropriate balance of power between the president and Congress date back to the Pacificus (Hamilton)/Helvidius (Madison) debate over the constitutionality of President Washington's 1793 Proclamation of Neutrality in the war between Britain and France. In this debate Hamilton argued for strong executive powers in foreign affairs,

and Madison, goaded on by Jefferson, argued for legislative control.

Compared with other areas, judicial powers are fairly restricted when it comes to foreign affairs. For all practical purposes, the national government exclusively exercises foreign-policy-making powers rather than sharing them with the states. Consequently, the Supreme Court has never voided a treaty or executive agreement because of alleged conflict with state powers.[226] Moreover, although the Court occasionally draws boundary lines between exercises of power by the other two branches of the national government, broad disputes over policies are often more prominent in the area of foreign policy making than the vindication of personal rights.[227] Courts therefore usually defer to initiatives by the two elected branches and often avoid or delay resolving conflicts between them.

PRESIDENTIAL POWERS DIRECTED INWARD

No matter how presidential powers over domestic and foreign affairs are divided, at times they overlap. Cases involving presidential exercises of power on the domestic front during wartime and rebellion, and especially exercises of martial law, are clear examples.

Domestic Trials by Military Authorities

Article I, section 8, of the U.S. Constitution grants Congress power "to make Rules for the Government and Regulation of the land and naval Forces." On the basis of this clause, Congress has created a system of justice for individuals serving in the nation's armed forces. Trials under this system are known as courts-martial and are chiefly governed by the Uniform Code of Military Justice (1950). The U.S. Military Appeals Court and, ultimately, the U.S. Supreme Court may review these trials. On this point, in January 1994 the Supreme Court upheld a conviction in *Eric J. Weiss and Ernesto Hernandez v. United States*.[228] The defendants had questioned the current method of appointing military judges as well as their lack of fixed terms of office.

There would be obvious potential for conflict if military courts could try civilians, but such incidents have been rare in American history. Two cases arose during the Civil War in areas where military districts overlapped with existing civilian court boundaries. One involved Clement Vallandigham, a former Ohio representative. A military commission convicted him for expressing support for the rebels and sentenced him to prison.[229] President Lincoln commuted this sentence to banishment to the South. Because he was no longer behind bars, Vallandigham could not apply to the Supreme Court for a writ of *habeas corpus*. He then appealed directly to the Court for a writ of certiorari, but the Court avoided a decision on the merits of Vallandigham's trial. It unanimously declared in 1864 that it lacked jurisdiction under Article III to hear an appeal from a military court.[230]

The Court was considerably more sympathetic to civilians in

Ex parte Milligan (1866). Because the Court decision came after the war was over, however, Clinton Rossiter has argued that the opinion's vivid language had "practically no value whatsoever."[231]

Milligan was a Confederate sympathizer who lived in Indiana. A military commission established by President Lincoln tried and convicted him for conspiracy to seize federal weapons and liberate Confederate prisoners. Speaking through Justice David Davis, a Lincoln friend and appointee, a Court majority granted Milligan the writ of *habeas corpus* for which he petitioned. Davis observed:

The Constitution of the United States is a law for rulers and people, equally in war and in peace, and covers with the shield of its protection all classes of men, at all times, and under all circumstances. No doctrine involving more pernicious consequences, was ever invented by the wit of man than that any of its provisions can be suspended during any of the great exigencies of government.[232]

Noting that Congress had not created the commission that tried Milligan, the Court observed that the president had no power to do so. Instead, the president "is controlled by law, and has his appropriate sphere of duty, which is to execute, not to make, the laws."[233] The Court further recognized that Milligan was a civilian, that he resided in a loyal state that had not been invaded, that the civilian courts were open at the time of his trial, and that the military had conducted the trial without the constitutionally guaranteed right to a jury. Justice Davis questioned whether even Congress would have power to empower a military commission to hear cases involving civilians in such circumstances.

Chief Justice Chase, joined by three colleagues, wrote a fascinating concurring opinion. While Chase agreed that Congress had not sanctioned the military commission in this case, he believed that Congress did have power to create such a court when necessity so required. As Chase saw it,

We cannot doubt that, in such a time of public danger, Congress had power, under the Constitution, to provide for the organization of a military commission, and for trial by that commission of persons engaged in this conspiracy. The fact that the Federal courts were open was regarded by Congress as a sufficient reason for not exercising that power; but the fact could not deprive Congress of the right to exercise it. Those courts might be open and undisturbed in the execution of their functions, and yet wholly incompetent to avert threatened danger, or to punish, with adequate promptitude and certainty, the guilty conspirators.[234]

Many years later, the Court confirmed this concurring opinion in *Milligan* in *Ex parte Quirin* (1942). In this case, on the basis of the joint authority of the president and Congress, the Court upheld the conviction by a military commission of eight German saboteurs. They had violated the laws of war by landing in the United States dressed in civilian clothes. Although most of these individuals, six of whom were executed shortly afterwards, were not American citizens, the Court rested its decision on their status as enemy belligerents, not whether they were citizens.[235] In 1946 the Court upheld the conviction of a Japanese

general whom a military commission had sentenced to death for war crimes. The case was *In re Yamashita*.[236] In *Duncan v. Kahanamoku*, decided the same year, the Court ruled that the Organic Act of 1900, under which Hawaii had been placed under martial law and the civilian courts had been suspended after the attack on Pearl Harbor, did not contain adequate authorization for the latter action.[237]

In *Reid v. Covert* (1957) the Supreme Court confronted another case involving military trials of civilians.[238] Here the Court voided an executive agreement between the United States and Great Britain that permitted military courts to try spouses of armed forces personnel serving overseas. Significantly, by voiding Clarice Covert's conviction for killing her husband, this case also helped ease fears stirred by *Missouri v. Holland* (1920). In that case the Court had used a treaty regulating migratory birds as authority to override a state game law that lower courts had previously upheld as an exercise of state police power over a federal law.[239] (See "*The Power to Make and Terminate Treaties*," p. 1328.) Some observers had interpreted *Holland* to mean that treaties might be able to override constitutional guarantees. In *Reid v. Covert*, however, Justice Black said:

It would be manifestly contrary to the objectives of those who created the Constitution, as well as those who were responsible for the Bill of Rights—let alone alien to our entire constitutional history and tradition—to construe Article VI as permitting the United States to exercise power under an international agreement without observing constitutional prohibitions.[240]

In a related matter, in *Solorio v. United States* (1987) the Court overturned an earlier precedent and declared that the jurisdiction of courts-martial was based on the status of defendants as members of the armed services, whether or not their alleged offenses were service-connected.[241]

Curfew and Exclusion Orders

Few incidents in American judicial history have occasioned more criticism than the treatment meted out to Americans of Japanese ancestry during World War II.[242] After the sudden and unexpected attack on Pearl Harbor, some Americans became suspicious of the approximately 112,000 Japanese Americans living in the United States. Many lived in communities near the West Coast and maintained ties with their homeland. Their connections to Japan fueled concerns that they constituted a potential "fifth column" and a danger to the United States if the enemy invaded the mainland. In retrospect, it is clear that long-standing racial prejudice served as the foundation for these fears. But at the time, official reports that had the authority of military commanders, including Gen. John L. DeWitt, behind them, appeared to substantiate public anxiety. President Franklin Roosevelt subsequently signed executive orders that Congress unanimously implemented. The orders provided for curfews, exclusion zones, and relocation centers.

In *Hirabayashi v. United States* (1943) the Court upheld the curfew orders. The Court granted that "distinctions between citizens solely because of their ancestry are by their very nature odious to a free people whose institutions are founded upon the doctrine of equality." Still, it unanimously decided that there were cases where such a background "may in fact place citizens of one ancestry in a different category from others."[243]

The Court extended this decision in its 6–3 ruling in *Korematsu v. United States* (1944). Following the judgment of military authorities as confirmed by the president and Congress, the Court upheld the exclusion of Japanese Americans from the Pacific coast. Although this exclusion was tied to requirements that Japanese Americans report to an assembly center for relocation, the Court sidestepped the constitutionality of that more intrusive order.[244]

Writing for the Court, Justice Black accepted the military's claim that the exclusions were not based on racism, but on military necessity and the inability to separate loyal Japanese Americans from the disloyal. Black further asserted that "hardships are part of war, and war is an aggregation of hardships."[245] In the long run, Black may have advanced the fight against racial discrimination in nonmilitary cases by declaring that racial classifications were "immediately suspect."[246] This judgment provided the basis for the Court to give more exacting scrutiny to such classifications in future cases.

There was considerable truth in the view that Justice Robert Jackson expressed in dissent. He argued that "a judicial construction of the due process clause that will sustain this order is a far more subtle blow to liberty than the promulgation of the order itself," and he voiced his fear that the Court's decision would be like "a loaded weapon ready for the hand of any authority that can bring forward a plausible claim to urgent need."[247] In 1944 the Court permitted a Japanese American judged to be loyal to secure release on a writ of *habeas corpus* in *Ex parte Endo,* but it never struck down the military's use of relocation camps.[248]

In the 1980s federal courts held some unusual rehearings under ancient and little used *coram nobis* petitions. A claimant may file this petition when there is evidence that an original conviction was based on government misconduct. In 1987 U.S. district and circuit courts decided that the Japanese exclusion orders had been unconstitutional.[249] In 1988 Congress adopted legislation providing monetary reparations for Japanese Americans who had been interred. When President Reagan signed the bill, which acknowledged that a "grave injustice" had been committed, he said, "It's not for us today to pass judgment upon those who may have made mistakes while engaged in this great struggle. Yet we must recognize that the internment of Japanese Americans was just that, a mistake."[250]

Suspension of the Writ of Habeas Corpus

The writ of *habeas corpus* contains one of the great protections for civil liberties. Literally an order to "produce a body," this writ permits those who are detained by the government to ascertain the charges against them. Article I, section 9, of the U.S. Constitution protects this right; without it individuals would have no way to challenge false imprisonments. Section 9 also provides for the writ's suspension when "in Cases of Rebellion or Invasion the public Safety may require it." Although the Framers placed this phrase under the article that deals with congressional powers, the language does not conclusively indicate who has power to suspend *habeas corpus.*

This constitutional ambiguity led to one of the most striking legal skirmishes of the Civil War. Faced with strong rebel sentiments in a number of border states, President Lincoln had suspended the writ of *habeas corpus* in these areas. As a result, authorities arrested John Merryman, a rebel sympathizer in Maryland, and detained him in Fort McHenry. Chief Justice Taney, holding circuit court in Baltimore in 1861, granted Merryman a writ of *habeas corpus.* Taney directed Gen. George Cadwalader, who was holding Merryman in custody, to produce him. Cadwalader sent an aide to refuse the order. When a guard at Fort McHenry refused to allow a U.S. marshal to serve an attachment of contempt against the general, all Taney could do was pronounce the president's conduct illegal.[251]

Other Domestic Powers Related to National Security

A number of other wartime assertions of executive power have had important domestic policy repercussions. *Youngstown Sheet & Tube Co. v. Sawyer* (1952), called the *Steel Seizure Case,* was among the most important. The case arose when President Truman bypassed the Taft-Hartley Act dealing with labor relations and ordered his reluctant secretary of commerce to seize the steel mills. Truman was hoping to avert a threatened strike that he thought would weaken the American war effort in Korea. The steel companies obtained expedited review of the case, and a 6–3 Court majority declared the seizure to be unconstitutional.

Ignoring the idea of inherent powers, Justice Hugo Black wrote the majority opinion asserting that presidential exercises of power "must stem either from an act of Congress or from the Constitution itself." Here Congress had given the president no authority to seize industries. Moreover, the president's executive powers did not extend to law making, and his powers as commander in chief were restricted to the theater of war.[252]

Justice Jackson reiterated this point in his justly famous concurring opinion. He noted:

I should indulge the widest latitude of interpretation to sustain his [the president's] exclusive function to command the instruments of national force, at least when turned against the outside world for the security of our society. But, when it is turned inward, not because of rebellion but because of a lawful economic struggle between industry and labor, it should have no such indulgence.[253]

In another carefully crafted distinction, Jackson argued that presidential exercise of power fell into three categories: (1) actions pursuant to congressional authority; (2) actions in the absence of congressional authority; and (3) actions contrary to such authority. Presidential powers were strongest in the first category. The second category constituted "a zone of twilight in which he and Congress may have concurrent authority, or in which its distribution is uncertain." Presidential powers were at their weakest in the third area.[254] Because Congress had specifically denied entrusting the president with seizure powers when it adopted the Taft-Hartley Act, Jackson thought that Truman's actions in this case fell within the third category and could not be sanctioned by the Court.

New York Times Co. v. United States (1971), the so-called *Pentagon Papers Case,* is another that involves the attempted exercise of presidential powers relative to foreign affairs in the domestic arena. The case arose from President Nixon's request for the first injunction ever sought by the national government against a publication in American history. Nixon wanted to prevent the *Times* and other newspapers from publishing a classified Defense Department study that was critical of U.S. entry into and participation in the Vietnam War. Nixon believed that disclosure of these papers would undermine American security, but his claim was not linked to a specifically verifiable harm. Pointing to the strong presumption against any prior restraint of publication that the Court had always found in the First Amendment, a 6–3 majority rejected Nixon's plea in a short *per curiam,* or unsigned, opinion, followed by individual opinions by each justice. The Court stopped short of declaring freedom of the press to be absolute. Even Justice Brennan, known for his liberal decisions on the First Amendment, indicated that the government might have the right to "prevent actual obstruction to its recruiting service or the publication of the sailing dates of transports or the number and location of troops."[255] Still, the Court certainly erected a high bar to exercises of presidential authority in this area.[256]

The president is not the only party who has invoked national security to curtail individual rights. The national government and states from time to time have sought to limit speech for fear that it would pose a threat to national security. The contemporary Court is more sympathetic to First Amendment rights and less sympathetic to counterclaims of national security than were earlier Courts. However, some important cases illustrate the Court's acceptance of the national security rationale.

One of these is *Schenck v. United States* (1919). In upholding the conviction under the Espionage Act of 1917 of individuals who had mailed leaflets to potential World War I draftees urging them to resist the draft, Justice Holmes formulated the "clear and present danger test." Under this test, Congress might curtail speech that the First Amendment would normally protect if the speech presented a clear and present danger that Congress had a right to prevent.[257]

The Court took an even more deferential posture toward a state criminal anarchy law in *Gitlow v. New York* (1925). In upholding the conviction of a member of the Socialist Party who had distributed leaflets advocating the forceful overthrow of the government, Justice Sanford applied the dangerous tendency test. It was designed, in his words, to "suppress the threatened danger in its incipiency."[258]

In *Dennis v. United States* (1951) the Court upheld the conviction of several leading members of the American Communist Party under the Smith Act of 1940. This law made it a federal crime to advocate or organize a group for the purpose of overthrowing the government. Writing for the Court, Chief Justice Vinson noted that protection of the government against forceful overthrow was "the ultimate value of any society, for if a society cannot protect its very structure from armed internal attack, it must follow that no subordinate value can be protected."[259]

Prior to American entry into World War II, the Court dealt with the constitutionality of regulations of symbolic speech. Local school boards required students to salute the American flag each day or be expelled from school. This requirement fell with particular force on Jehovah's Witnesses, who believed that saluting the flag was a sinful display of idolatry. In 1940 the Court deferred to the school board's judgment about the need to promote national loyalty,[260] but it reversed itself just three years later in *West Virginia State Board of Education v. Barnette* (1943). In a ringing decision, Justice Robert Jackson decided that the compulsory flag salute violated the First Amendment. Jackson declared:

If there is any fixed star in our constitutional constellation, it is that no official, high or petty, can prescribe what shall be orthodox in politics, nationalism, religion, or other matters of opinion or force citizens to confess by word or act their faith therein.[261]

The Court's later decisions protecting flag-burning as a form of symbolic protest were directed against state and congressional actions.[262] President Bush had strongly supported such laws.

National security claims may pose a threat to rights other than those in the First Amendment. The Nixon administration used the national security claim in 1972 to justify warrantless wiretaps of individuals it believed were engaged in domestic subversion. In *United States v. United States District Court* (1972) the Court unanimously rejected this contention.[263] It decided that here, as elsewhere, the provisions of the Fourth Amendment required that the president obtain prior judicial approval before engaging in electronic surveillance.[264]

National security considerations have sometimes been used to justify restrictions on travel. In *Kent v. Dulles* (1958), however, the Supreme Court said that the secretary of state could not withhold a passport from an individual who refused to indicate whether he was or ever had been a communist.[265] In *Aptheker v. Secretary of State* (1964) the Court overturned a law denying passports to communists on the basis that the law was "supported only by a tenuous relationship between the bare fact of organizational membership and the activity Congress sought to proscribe."[266] In *Zemel v. Rusk* (1965) the Court upheld travel restrictions imposed against a particular country, in this case Cuba, rather than a person.[267] After the Supreme Court later ruled in *United States v. Laub* (1967) that individuals traveling to Cuba in violation of such restrictions could not subsequently be prosecuted, Congress adopted a law to rectify the situation.[268] In *Haig v. Agee* (1981) the Supreme Court sanctioned the revocation of the passport of a former CIA agent who made it his mission to travel abroad exposing American intelligence operations.[269] The unique facts of this case appear to have shaped the Court's decision.

Occasionally, Congress has attempted to punish individuals who have fled the draft, deserted, or voted in foreign elections by depriving them of their citizenship.[270] With a few exceptions that have since been overruled, the Court has taken the position, exemplified in *Afroyim v. Rusk* (1967), that an individual has "a constitutional right to remain a citizen in a free country unless he voluntarily relinquishes that citizenship."[271]

The Court, however, has validated other exercises of political power in connection with war making and national security.[272] To cite two examples, in *Hamilton v. Kentucky Distilleries Co.* (1919) the Court upheld the War-Time Prohibition Act, which had been signed into law after the armistice with Germany and was to remain in effect until the president proclaimed that the period of war and demobilization were complete. Justice Brandeis noted that the United States had not yet signed a peace treaty, the national government was still exercising control over the railroads, other war-related activities had not been terminated, and the nation had not yet demobilized its armed forces and returned "to a peace footing." He therefore could not find a basis for declaring the continuing application of the law to be invalid.[273] In *Woods v. Miller* (1948) the Court reasoned that "the war power includes the power 'to remedy the evils which have arisen from its rise and progress' [quoted from *Hamilton v. Kentucky Distilleries*] and continues for the duration of that emergency" and upheld the Housing and Rent Act of 1947.[274] This law limited rents in so-called defense-rental areas.

Statutes frequently have provided for enhanced presidential powers in times of emergency. A 1973 Senate report identified more than 470 such provisions. It found that, from a legal standpoint, the nation had been in a state of emergency from the day that Franklin Roosevelt declared it in 1933. Concerned with the implications of long-standing authorizations, Congress in 1976 adopted the National Emergency Act. It provided for the termination of all existing states of emergency within two years and for congressional review of future delegations.[275]

PRESIDENTIAL POWERS DIRECTED ABROAD

The Constitution designates the president as commander in chief of the armed forces. The president serves both as symbolic head of state and as the principal elected official within the government. The U.S. president therefore combines roles that parliamentary systems divide between a monarch and a prime minister. The president's powers in foreign affairs can be particularly awesome. Although the courts have sometimes patrolled the edges of this power, they have far more consistently either avoided constitutional issues by citing the political questions doctrine or affirmed broad presidential powers that make the president the equal of other world leaders.

United States v. Curtiss-Wright: *The President as Sole Organ*

The case that dominates discussion of presidential powers in foreign affairs is the Court's 1936 decision in *United States v.*

Curtiss-Wright Export Corp. The central issue was the delegation of legislative powers to the president, an area where the Court had already proved quite generous in foreign affairs. For example, in *The Brig Aurora* (1813) the Court had accepted a law investing the president with the power to declare an embargo. In *Field v. Clark* (1892) it had upheld presidential power to impose tariffs. In *J. W. Hampton & Co. v. United States* (1928) it had permitted the president both to impose and to alter tariff rates.[276]

Justice Sutherland wrote the *Curtiss-Wright* decision. Although he was one of the conservative "Four Horsemen" who opposed New Deal domestic programs, Sutherland was also a strong nationalist. He predicated his opinion on an expansive view of presidential powers. This view has been at the base of many subsequent assertions of executive power in foreign affairs.

At issue in *Curtiss-Wright* was the constitutionality of a proclamation that President Franklin Roosevelt issued under the authority of a joint congressional resolution. Congress had specified that, if he judged that the situation so warranted, Roosevelt could proclaim an embargo of military equipment to the Chaco region of South America. The Court issued its decision at a time when it had been stringent about legislative delegations of power in the domestic sphere.[277] Perhaps as a way to distinguish *Curtiss-Wright* from these precedents, Sutherland emphasized the differences between government powers over internal affairs and those over external affairs.

The internal powers of the national government were limited to those enumerated or implied in the Constitution, Sutherland argued, but external powers were not. Rather than being delegated to the nation by the individual states, Sutherland argued that sovereignty over external affairs passed directly from the British Crown to the colonies in their collective capacity. Therefore, he wrote,

the investment of the federal government with the powers of external sovereignty did not depend upon the affirmative grants of the Constitution. The powers to declare and wage war, to conclude peace, to make treaties, to maintain diplomatic relations with other sovereignties, if they had never been mentioned in the Constitution, would have vested in the federal government as necessary concomitants of nationality.[278]

After explaining the foundations of federal power over foreign affairs, Sutherland proceeded to elevate presidential powers within this area. He cited a similar statement that John Marshall had made in his capacity as secretary of state, saying, "The President is the sole organ of the nation in its external relations, and its sole representative with foreign nations."[279] Sutherland concluded that in external affairs "the President alone has the power to speak or listen as a representative of the nation."[280] Roosevelt's proclamation, therefore, carried with it not only any powers that Congress had delegated but also "the very delicate, plenary and exclusive power of the President as the sole organ of the federal government in the field of international relations." Such powers require that the Court grant to the president "a degree of discretion and freedom from statutory restriction which would not be admissible were domestic affairs alone involved."[281] Sutherland pointed to the president's "confidential sources of information," the frequent need for secrecy in foreign affairs, and historical precedent. He focused special attention on the fact that Congress *directs* the president to furnish information about other departments of government, but, when dealing with the State Department, it *requests* such materials.[282] Sutherland opposed the congressional imposition of narrow standards in the field of foreign affairs and upheld Roosevelt's embargo proclamation.

Perhaps more important, however, Sutherland gave a distinctive executive tilt toward foreign policy making. The Court's frequent resort to the political questions doctrine in the area of foreign affairs and the broad stewardship theory of the presidency that Theodore Roosevelt and others had advanced have further accented this tilt. Roosevelt wrote:

> I declined to adopt the view that what was imperatively necessary for the Nation could not be done by the President unless he could find some specific authorization to do it. My belief was that it was not only his [the president's] right but his duty to do anything that the needs of the Nation demanded unless such action was forbidden by the Constitution or by the laws.[283]

Presidents have been especially likely to espouse such a view in foreign affairs where the survival of the nation may be at stake.

The Power to Make and Terminate Treaties

The Constitution outlines treaty-making responsibilities in its delineation of presidential powers. Accordingly, some individuals have followed Sutherland's reasoning in *Curtiss-Wright* and have portrayed this power as almost exclusively executive. However, the treaty-making power in Article II, section 2, of the Constitution is worded and qualified so that some degree of cooperation with Congress is assured: "He [the president] shall have Power, by and with the Advice and Consent of the Senate, to make Treaties, provided two thirds of the Senators present concur." Moreover, a president like Woodrow Wilson who excludes the Senate from the treaty-making process may find, as Wilson did in regard to the Treaty of Versailles, that the Senate is unwilling to approve the treaty.[284]

It has been noted that the Senate has four options when it confronts a treaty: (1) consenting to it unconditionally, (2) rejecting it, (3) requesting amendments to it, or (4) attaching reservations.[285] These possibilities are complicated, however, by the development of the executive agreement. The president does not have to submit these written agreements with foreign governments to the Senate for approval. The apparently clear-cut nature of the treaty-making process can be further complicated if the House of Representatives wants to exert pressure by refusing or threatening to refuse to appropriate money to implement treaties. In addition, presidents may sometimes accomplish through joint congressional resolutions what a two-thirds majority of the Senate is reluctant to authorize by treaty.[286] Examples include the 1954 agreement with Canada over the St. Lawrence Seaway and the controversial 1994 North American Free Trade Agreement, which President Clinton signed with Canada and Mexico.

The supremacy clause of Article VI of the Constitution declares that "all Treaties made, or which shall be made, under the Authority of the United States, shall be the supreme Law of the Land." States have sometimes been reluctant to accept the fact that federal authority negates conflicting state laws. The Court has reiterated this point a number of times in its history.

Among the most important decisions establishing the sovereignty of federal treaties over conflicting state laws is a 1920 case, *Missouri v. Holland*. The Court ruled that a treaty signed by the United States and Great Britain concerning birds that migrate between the United States and Canada superseded state hunting regulations. What makes the case remarkable is that the Supreme Court had earlier ruled that congressional legislation passed without the authorization of a treaty invaded state police powers under the Tenth Amendment. In upholding legislation passed under authority of a treaty, Justice Holmes argued, "There may be matters of the sharpest exigency for the national well-being that an act of Congress could not deal with but that a treaty followed by such an act could." While a state normally controlled "the great body of private relations," Holmes noted that "a treaty may override its power."[287]

Pointing to the language of the supremacy clause, Holmes suggested that the distinction in terminology might be deliberate and instructive: "Acts of Congress are the supreme law of the land only when made in pursuance of the Constitution, while treaties are declared to be so when made under the authority of the United States."[288] A more likely reason for this difference in language, however, stems from the Framers' desire to maintain the legitimacy of treaties that the nation had made prior to the writing of the Constitution.[289] In any case, in *Missouri v. Holland*, Holmes noted that the treaty the United States had signed did not "contravene any prohibitory words to be found in the Constitution."[290] Subsequent cases have established that specific constitutional prohibitions apply to treaties just as they do to other laws. The Court continues to face situations where it has to decide whether state laws relative to inheritance by foreign citizens and other matters impinge negatively on foreign affairs or whether they conflict with agreements already covered by federal treaties.[291]

Judicial decisions have established that laws and treaties are on the same legal level. A law or treaty has the effect of voiding prior laws or treaties with which it may conflict. As the Court has observed:

> By the Constitution a treaty is placed on the same footing, and made of like obligation, with an act of legislation. Both are declared by that instrument to be the supreme law of the land, and no supreme efficacy is given to either over the other. When the two relate to the same subject, the courts will always endeavor to construe them so as to give effect to both, if that can be done without violating the language of either; but if the two are inconsistent, the last one in date will control the other, providing always the stipulation of the treaty on the subject is self-executing.[292]

Louis Henkin has described the principle at issue as that of *"leges posteriores priores contrarias abrogant* (the last expression of the sovereign always controls)."

As with laws, the meaning of treaties is not always self-evident. Presidential interpretations of treaties that differ from the Senate's may spark conflict. For example, President Reagan, in pursuing his Star Wars defense program, read the 1972 Antiballistic Missile Treaty with the Soviet Union more permissively than did most senators. The Supreme Court never adjudicated this controversy.

Especially in those cases where the two elected branches do not appear to be in conflict, the Court is likely to defer to presidential interpretations. In *United States v. Alvarez-Machain* (1992) the Court accepted President Bush's view that the presence of an extradition treaty with Mexico did not prevent the United States from trying a medical doctor who had been forcibly kidnapped in Mexico and brought to the United States.[293] American law enforcement authorities alleged that the doctor had participated in the kidnapping and murder of a Drug Enforcement Administration agent in Mexico. A U.S. district court subsequently dismissed this unusual case against Alvarez-Machain for lack of evidence.[294]

The Constitution does not specify who shall terminate treaties, although Congress clearly can do so by adopting a conflicting law or treaty. In 1978, as part of U.S. recognition of the People's Republic of China, President Carter terminated a defense treaty with Taiwan. Practically, this decision stood, but legally, the issue of unilateral presidential actions has not been resolved. Four justices sidestepped a suit brought by Sen. Barry Goldwater and twenty other members of Congress, who challenged this action, by declaring that the issue was a "political question" for the two elected branches to resolve. The other justices either argued that the issue was not yet "ripe" for review or wanted to uphold the president's actions. Justice Brennan articulated the latter view:

Abrogation of the defense treaty with Taiwan was a necessary incident to Executive recognition of the Peking Government, because the defense treaty was predicated upon the now-abandoned view that the Taiwan Government was the only legitimate authority in China. Our cases firmly establish that the Constitution commits to the President alone the power to recognize, and withdraw recognition from, foreign regimes.[295]

Executive Agreements

In one form or another, executive agreements date back to the Washington administration. On occasion, as in Franklin Roosevelt's 1940 destroyers-for-bases deal with Great Britain, executive agreements have been vitally important to the conduct of American foreign policy. These agreements often have some statutory or treaty authority behind them and, unlike the Roosevelt arrangement with Britain, deal with fairly routine matters. Presidents have based some executive agreements on their power to extend diplomatic recognition to foreign governments.[296] Far more problematic are secret agreements. In 1954 a constitutional amendment that, among other things, would

have limited executive agreements (the so-called Bricker Amendment) fell but a single vote short of the necessary two-thirds majority in the Senate.[297] In 1972 Congress required the president to report all executive agreements to Congress, but presidents use other mechanisms to bypass this requirement.[298]

In *United States v. Belmont* (1937) the Supreme Court reiterated its position that state laws were subservient to international agreements. The Court upheld an action by the U.S. government, which had claimed assets that had been deposited in a New York bank. The Soviets had confiscated these assets from a Russian corporation and transferred them to the United States.[299] What makes this case particularly noteworthy is that the agreement the Court upheld was not a formal treaty that had been confirmed by a two-thirds vote of the Senate. Instead, it was an executive agreement (the Litvinov Agreement) that President Franklin Roosevelt had made when he extended diplomatic recognition to the communist government of the Soviet Union.

As in *United States v. Curtiss-Wright Export Corp.*, Justice Sutherland argued, "Governmental power over external affairs is not distributed, but is vested exclusively in the national government." As in *Curtiss-Wright*, Sutherland also asserted that the president was the "sole organ" of the national government. Just as important, however, in pointing to compacts such as *protocols, modus vivendis,* and *postal conventions,* Sutherland ruled that "an international compact, as this was, is not always a treaty which requires the participation of the Senate."[300] The Supreme Court reiterated its stance on the validity of executive agreements and their supremacy over any conflicting state policies in *United States v. Pink* (1942), another case dealing with Russian assets.[301]

Dames & Moore v. Regan (1981) dealt with the validity of a presidential action that impinged on a private business. Dames & Moore had a claim against Iran for work done in connection with the Atomic Energy Organization of that country. After mobs seized the U.S. embassy in Tehran and took Americans hostage in November 1979, President Carter ordered that Iranian assets in the United States be frozen. The hostages were held until January 19, 1981, Carter's last full day in office. On that day Carter issued executive orders transferring the Iranian assets to the Federal Reserve Bank of New York, where they were to be held until returned to Iran. A month after he was inaugurated, President Reagan issued executive orders that in effect "ratified" Carter's orders. As part of the agreement, Iran set aside one billion dollars in a special account from which the Iran–United States Claims Tribunal would settle claims. The executive agreement temporarily blocked the judgment that Dames & Moore had secured against Iran in U.S. courts.

This case is fascinating because neither the International Emergency Economic Powers Act (IEEPA), as revised in 1977, nor an earlier hostage act provided "specific authorization of the President's action suspending claims." Still, writing for a unanimous Court, Justice Rehnquist argued that both acts taken in context were "highly relevant in the looser sense of indicating congressional acceptance of a broad scope for executive action in circumstances such as those presented in this case." Noting that presidents had used executive agreements in the past for similar purposes, Rehnquist said:

where, as here, the settlement of claims has been determined to be a necessary incident to the resolution of a major foreign policy dispute between our country and another, and where, as here, we conclude that Congress acquiesced in the President's action; we are not prepared to say that the President lacks the power to settle such claims.[302]

In *Weinberger v. Rossi* (1982) the Supreme Court ruled that, when the law prevented discrimination against U.S. citizens on overseas military bases, unless permitted by "treaty," the term "treaty" was intended to embrace executive agreements as well. In this case the Court upheld a preference for Philippine nationals accepted by executive agreement.[303]

War-making Powers

Many of the major constitutional issues that surround U.S. foreign policy making center on the appropriate balance between legislative and executive power. While this debate is important, it must be kept in perspective. No matter which institution has the balance of power at any given moment, both are elected branches of government dominated by civilians. The principle of civilian control of the military sets the United States apart from many other nations where military authorities control civilian politics. There are sometimes differences of opinion between elected officials and the military top brass—as in Lincoln's persistent criticism of his generals or the well-known Truman-MacArthur conflict over military policies in Korea, which resulted in Gen. Douglas MacArthur's dismissal. In such controversies, the weight of the Constitution is clearly on the side of civilian control.

When working on the Constitution, delegates in Philadelphia initially gave Congress the power "to make war" but subsequently changed the language so that it would have the power "to declare war."[304] The power to "make" or "wage" war, while obviously subject to congressional powers of the purse, is generally considered to be a power connected to the president's role as commander in chief of the armed forces. Two factors have complicated the situation. First, as commander in chief the president can put American troops in a situation in which war is almost inevitable. President James K. Polk provoked a war with Mexico by ordering American troops to occupy disputed territory. Second, although the United States has been engaged in scores of conflicts, Congress has declared war only five times—the War of 1812, the Mexican War, the Spanish-American War, and World Wars I and II. Many of the other conflicts have been minor, but some—like the so-called "police action" in Korea, the struggle in Vietnam, and the Persian Gulf War—have been major national commitments. Presidential actions waged in the absence of an official congressional declaration can raise sensitive legal issues. The Court has avoided most of these by invoking the political questions doctrine.

A challenge to presidential war-making powers arose during the Civil War. The Union viewed the conflict as an insurrection,

COTTON IN THE STOCKS.

M. Mercier :—"HOW MUCH LONGER IS THIS TO LAST? OR ARE YOU WAITING UNTIL WE INTERFERE?"

The Union blockade against Southern ports during the Civil War held up cotton exports and caused a slump in European textile production. In this cartoon, Henri Mercier, the French minister to Washington, threatens the United States with intervention if the blockade is not lifted. The legality of the blockade in the period before Congress officially authorized the war was decided by the *Prize Cases* in 1863.

or rebellion, rather than a conflict between two sovereign nations, or War Between the States, as the Confederacy claimed. Therefore, the Union never officially declared war. Moreover, the conflict, which erupted in 1861, began during a congressional recess, leaving Lincoln free to act on his own executive authority. His actions included the declaration of martial law and the suspension of the writ of *habeas corpus*.

One of Lincoln's most forceful actions was the blockading of Southern ports, which Congress approved several months after the fact. In the *Prize Cases* (1863) the Court examined the legitimacy of this blockade. The fate of a number of captured ships rested on the Court's decision. In upholding their seizures, albeit by a 5–4 vote, the Court, speaking through Justice Robert Grier, recognized a de facto state of civil war. Grier wrote, "By the Constitution, Congress alone has the power to declare a national or foreign war." However, according to Grier, as chief executive and as commander in chief of the armed forces and of the militia, the president

is authorized to call out the militia and use the military and naval forces of the United States in case of invasion by foreign nations, and to suppress insurrection against the government of a State or of the United States.[305]

On the basis of this authority, Grier concluded:

Whether the President in fulfilling his duties, as Commander-in-Chief, in suppressing an insurrection, has met with such armed hostile resistance, and a civil war of such alarming proportions as will compel him to accord to them the character of belligerents, is a question to be decided *by him*, and this Court must be governed by the decisions and acts of the political department of the Government to which this power was intrusted. "He must determine what degree of force the crisis demands."[306]

In a forceful dissenting opinion, Justice Samuel Nelson argued that only Congress could declare war, and that, unless a de jure war was officially declared, the president's blockade was illegal.

The war in Vietnam was among the most troubling in American history. As U.S. participation in this distant and protracted conflict escalated, President Lyndon Johnson sought congressional approval for his actions. Rather than requesting an official declaration of war, however, Johnson relied on the Gulf of Tonkin Resolution, which Congress overwhelmingly passed in 1964 in response to an alleged attack against American ships. The resolution authorized the president "to take all necessary measures to repel any armed attack against the forces of the United States and to prevent further aggression." It also authorized taking "all necessary steps, including the use of armed force, to assist any member or protocol state of the Southeast Asia Collective Defense Treaty requesting assistance in defense of its freedom."[307] Congress repealed this resolution in 1971, after the United States got bogged down in the war, casualties mounted, and domestic protests increased. John Hart Ely, however, has noted that "Congress threw so many anchors to windward, leeward, and every other whichward that by the time it got through it was difficult to determine what, if any, course it intended to chart."[308]

The War Powers Resolution of 1973

Partly because of confusion over the Gulf of Tonkin Resolution, and partly because of the congressional conviction that presidential powers over war making had grown excessive, Congress adopted the controversial War Powers Resolution of 1973 over President Nixon's veto. Congress justified this law as a means of fulfilling the intent of the Framers to "insure that the collective judgment of both the Congress and the President will apply to the introduction of United States Armed Forces into hostilities." The law also sought to limit the president's introduction of troops into hostile situations to cases "pursuant to (1) a declaration of war, (2) specific statutory authorization, or (3) a national emergency created by an attack upon the United States, its territories or possessions, or its armed forces."[309]

To this end, the law sets forth a number of requirements. In one of its vaguest sections (section 3), the law requires the president to consult with Congress when troops are introduced into hostile situations. The law further provides that when the president sends troops without a declaration of war, this action must be reported to Congress within forty-eight hours and at least every six months thereafter. The report is supposed to explain the circumstances under which the president acted, "the constitutional and legislative authority under which such introduction [of troops] took place," and an estimate of the anticipated "scope of duration of the hostilities or involvement." The most controversial part of the law requires that after sixty days (with the possibility of a thirty-day extension mandated by "unavoidable military necessity respecting the safety of the United States Armed Forces"), the president shall terminate American involvement in conflicts

unless the Congress (1) has declared war or has enacted a specific authorization for such use of United States Armed Forces, (2) has extended by law such sixty-day period, or (3) is physically unable to meet as a result of an armed attack upon the United States.[310]

Alternatively, Congress may at any time direct that troops be withdrawn.

Factors such as "presidential defiance, congressional irresolution, and judicial abstention" have complicated discussions of the status of the War Powers Resolution.[311] The law also contains a legislative veto provision like the one the Court invalidated in the *Chadha* case. *(See "A Special Case—The Legislative Veto," p. 1319.)* The consultation provisions of the law are extremely ambiguous, and presidents have successfully bypassed its central provision by refusing to make reports that would officially trigger the sixty-day troop limit.[312] Neither the president nor Congress has been anxious to test the law in court. If the law is tested, the Supreme Court might well declare that the matter is a political question for the two elected branches to resolve.

Some presidents have ignored the law, especially in cases of short-term troop commitments. Still, the existence of the War Powers Resolution probably has made presidents more aware of the need to seek congressional support for their foreign policy initiatives. In America's largest troop commitment since the passage of the resolution—its participation in the Persian Gulf War—President Bush sought and obtained congressional approval for offensive operations.[313] Significantly, Congress granted its approval after a federal judge imitated the kind of evasive action that courts have often followed in other cases involving foreign affairs. In *Dellums v. Bush* (1990) Judge Harold Greene agreed that an injunction against the president's use of force against Iraq was technically possible. He decided, however, that the case—brought by just over fifty members of Congress (far short of a majority) at a time when Bush's intentions with regard to the use of U.S. troops were not yet clear—was not "ripe" for judicial resolution. Judge Greene wrote, "The principle that the courts shall be prudent in the exercise of their authority is never more compelling than when they are called upon to adjudicate on such sensitive issues as those trenching upon military and foreign affairs."[314]

The War Powers Resolution continues on the books. On October 7, 1993, President Clinton set March 31, 1994, as the date American troops would be withdrawn from Somalia. President

Bush had sent them there in December 1992 on a humanitarian mission that had become increasingly dangerous. Observers viewed Clinton's actions as a response to nonbinding congressional resolutions of the previous month asking for an outline of U.S. objectives by October 15 and asking the president to seek congressional approval for further troop involvement.[315] Clinton's subsequent military intervention in Haiti in September 1994, which was designed to restore democracy to that nation, also prompted Congress to adopt nonbinding congressional resolutions setting a specific date for American troop withdrawal. When Clinton decided in December 1995 to send twenty thousand American troops to Bosnia as part of a larger peacekeeping force, Congress responded with a resolution of support for the troops rather than for Clinton's decision to send them. Clinton, in turn, promised to end the mission in one year.

Conclusion

Edward S. Corwin has described the U.S. Constitution as "an invitation to struggle."[316] The establishment of the three branches of the federal government has perpetuated this struggle. In domestic affairs, it may result in clashes among any of the three branches, and conflicts between the president and the Supreme Court are not uncommon. In foreign affairs, the two elected branches are most likely to battle, with judicial intervention improbable. Even on basic matters such as the authoritative interpretation of the Constitution, controversy continues, and it is unlikely that it will be resolved as long as the present form of limited government endures. Perhaps in part because of its deference to the political branches on sensitive matters involving foreign affairs, however, the judicial branch has earned a right to be heard and is usually heeded on those occasions when it decides to proclaim "what the law is."

NOTES

1. See *The Federalist Papers,* with an introduction by Clinton Rossiter (New York: New American Library, 1961), No. 10, 77–84.

2. Ibid., No. 48, 309.

3. These matters are discussed in greater length by John R. Vile, in *A Companion to the United States Constitution and Its Amendments* (Westport, Conn.: Praeger, 1993).

4. Herbert J. Storing, *What the Anti-Federalists Were For* (Chicago: University of Chicago Press, 1981), 50.

5. *Federalist* No. 15, cited in *Free Government in the Making,* by Alpheus T. Mason and Gordon E. Baker (New York: Oxford University Press, 1985), 250.

6. *The Federalist Papers,* 465–466.

7. Ibid., 467.

8. Mason and Baker, *Free Government in the Making,* 276–298.

9. *The Federalist Papers,* 469.

10. Ibid., 471.

11. See Alfred H. Kelly, Winifred A. Harbison, and Herman Belz, *The American Constitution: Its Origins and Development,* 2 vols., 7th ed. (New York: Norton, 1991), 1:158.

12. The central provisions of the Judiciary Act may be found in *From Settlement Through Reconstruction,* vol. 1 of *Documents of American Constitutional and Legal History,* by Melvin I. Urofsky (New York: Knopf, 1989), 129–132.

13. Ibid., 131.

14. Ibid., 130.

15. *Hayburn's Case,* 2 Dall. 409 (1792).

16. Letter of August 8, 1793, as printed in Jean E. Smith, *The Constitution and American Foreign Policy* (St. Paul: West, 1989), 49.

17. *Ware v. Hylton,* 3 Dall. 199 (1796); *Hylton v. United States,* 3 Dall. 171 (1796); *Calder v. Bull,* 3 Dall. 386 (1793).

18. *Chisholm v. Georgia,* 2 Dall. 419 (1793).

19. Melvin I. Urofsky, *A March of Liberty* (New York: Knopf, 1988), 144.

20. Quoted in ibid., 177.

21. Ibid., 175–176.

22. *Stuart v. Laird,* 1 Cranch 299 (1803).

23. Urofsky, *A March of Liberty,* 181.

24. *Marbury v. Madison,* 1 Cranch (5 U.S.) 137, 163 (1803).

25. Ibid., 177–178.

26. Ibid., 180.

27. Revisions of the Judiciary Act were passed in 1801, 1802, 1837, 1866, 1869, 1891, and 1925, with the 1891 law establishing the hierarchy in place today. See entries under individual judiciary acts in *The Oxford Companion to the Supreme Court of the United States,* ed. Kermit L. Hall (New York: Oxford University Press, 1992), 472–476.

28. G. Alan Tarr, *Judicial Process and Judicial Policymaking* (St. Paul: West, 1994), 46–51.

29. Henry J. Abraham, *The Judicial Process,* 6th ed. (New York: Oxford University Press, 1993), 156.

30. Ibid.

31. Ibid., 183.

32. Cited by Walter F. Murphy and C. Herman Pritchett, in *Courts, Judges, and Politics: An Introduction to the Judicial Process,* 4th ed. (New York: Random House, 1986), 111.

33. *Gideon v. Wainwright,* 372 U.S. 335 (1963). For a vivid account of this case that gives good insight into the workings of the federal court system, see Anthony Lewis, *Gideon's Trumpet* (New York: Vintage, 1964).

34. Abraham, *The Judicial Process,* 179.

35. Kenneth Jost, *The Supreme Court Yearbook, 1994–1995* (Washington, D.C.: Congressional Quarterly, 1995), 64, 66.

36. *Brown v. Board of Education,* 347 U.S. 483 (1954). For an account of Warren's efforts, see Richard Kluger, *Simple Justice,* 2 vols. (New York: Knopf, 1975), 2:830–883.

37. *Cooper v. Aaron,* 358 U.S. 1 (1958).

38. *United States v. Nixon,* 418 U.S. 683 (1974).

39. John Massaro, *Supremely Political: The Role of Ideology and Presidential Management in Unsuccessful Supreme Court Nominations* (Albany: State University of New York Press, 1990).

40. Henry J. Abraham, *Justices and Presidents: A Political History of Appointments to the Supreme Court,* 3d ed. (New York: Oxford University Press, 1992), 39.

41. Quoted by David M. O'Brien in *Storm Center: The Supreme Court in American Politics,* 3d ed. (New York: Norton, 1993), 123.

42. Abraham, *Justices and Presidents,* 248.

43. *Roe v. Wade,* 410 U.S. 113 (1973).

44. See David J. Danelski, "The Influence of the Chief Justice in the Decisional Process," in Murphy and Pritchett, *Courts, Judges, and Politics,* 568–577.

45. Ibid., 570.

46. Ibid., 571.

47. See Lincoln Caplan, *The Tenth Justice: The Solicitor General and the Rule of Law* (New York: Vintage, 1987). For a more succinct summary, see Caplan's essay on the solicitor general in *Oxford Companion,* 803–804.

48. Nancy V. Baker, *Conflicting Loyalties: Law and Politics in the Attorney General's Office, 1789–1990* (Lawrence: University Press of Kansas, 1992), 46.

49. Ibid., 166–179.

50. *The Federalist Papers,* 465.

51. *Marbury v. Madison,* 177.

52. *Rust v. Sullivan,* 500 U.S. 173 (1991).

53. *Youngstown Sheet & Tube Co. v. Sawyer,* 343 U.S. 579 (1952).

54. *Valley Forge Christian College v. Americans United for Separation of Church and State,* 454 U.S. 464 (1982).

55. *Allen v. Wright,* 468 U.S. 737 (1984).

56. *United Public Workers v. Mitchell,* 330 U.S. 75 (1947).

57. *DeFunis v. Odegaard,* 416 U.S. 312 (1974).

58. *DeShaney v. Winnebago Social Services,* 489 U.S. 189 (1989). For a defense of this controversial decision, see Eugene W. Hickok and Gary L. Mc-Dowell, *Justice vs. Law: Courts and Politics in American Society* (New York: Free Press, 1993).

59. *United States v. Richardson,* 418 U.S. 166 (1974).

60. Quoted by David M. O'Brien, "Supreme Court Justices' Personal Relations with Presidents," *Encyclopedia of the American Presidency,* 4 vols., ed. Leonard W. Levy and Louis Fisher (New York: Simon and Schuster, 1994), 4:1421.

61. *Miranda v. Arizona,* 384 U.S. 436 (1966).

62. *Youngstown Sheet & Tube Co. v. Sawyer,* 634.

63. Stephen L. Carter, *The Confirmation Mess: Cleaning Up the Federal Appointments Process* (New York: Basic Books, 1994), 123–124.

64. *The Federalist Papers,* 471.

65. *Brown v. Board of Education* overturned the Court's earlier decision upholding separate but equal accommodations in *Plessy v. Ferguson,* 163 U.S. 537 (1896).

66. *Planned Parenthood of Southeastern Pennsylvania v. Casey,* 112 S. Ct. 2791, 2808–09 (1992).

67. Alexander M. Bickel, *The Least Dangerous Branch: The Supreme Court at the Bar of Politics* (New Haven, Conn.: Yale University Press, 1986).

68. Ronald Kahn, *The Supreme Court and Constitutional Theory* (Lawrence: University Press of Kansas, 1994), 59.

69. *Marbury v. Madison,* 168.

70. *Martin v. Mott,* 12 Wheat. (25 U.S.) 19, 30 (1827).

71. *Luther v. Borden,* 48 U.S. 1, 47 (1849).

72. *Mississippi v. Johnson,* 71 U.S. 475, 500–501 (1867).

73. *Georgia v. Stanton,* 73 U.S. 50, 77 (1868).

74. *Coleman v. Miller,* 397 U.S. 433 (1939). This case and subsequent cases dealing with the amending process are discussed at greater length in *Contemporary Questions Surrounding the Constitutional Amending Process,* by John R. Vile (Westport, Conn.: Praeger, 1993), 24–38.

75. *Colegrove v. Green,* 328 U.S. 549 (1946).

76. *Baker v. Carr,* 369 U.S. 186, 217 (1962).

77. *Powell v. McCormack,* 395 U.S. 486 (1969).

78. *Goldwater v. Carter,* 444 U.S. 996 (1979).

79. *Massachusetts v. Laird,* 400 U.S. 886 (1970).

80. *Crockett v. Reagan,* 558 F. Supp. 893 (D.D.C. 1982).

81. The judgment is that of Joel B. Grossman, in "Political Question," *Oxford Companion,* 653.

82. The Committee on Federal Legislation of the Bar Association of the City of New York, *The Law of Presidential Impeachment* (New York: Harrow Books, 1974), 17–19. Also see Raoul Berger, *Impeachment: The Constitutional Problems* (Cambridge, Mass.: Harvard University Press, 1973).

83. Quoted in Berger, *Impeachment,* 53.

84. *Nixon v. United States,* 113 S. Ct. 732 (1993).

85. *Goldman v. Weinberger,* 475 U.S. 503 (1986). See Louis Fisher, "One of the Guardians Some of the Time," in *Is the Supreme Court the Guardian of the Constitution?* ed. Robert A. Licht (Washington, D.C.: American Enterprise Institute, 1993), 96.

86. *Gedulig v. Aiello,* 417 U.S. 484 (1974); and *General Electric v. Gilbert,* 429 U.S. 125 (1976).

87. *Employment Division v. Smith,* 494 U.S. 872 (1990).

88. *Texas v. Johnson,* 491 U.S. 397 (1989); and *United States v. Eichman,* 496 U.S. 310 (1990).

89. *Scott v. Sandford,* 19 How. (60 U.S.) 393 (1857).

90. *Pollock v. Farmers' Loan & Trust Company,* 158 U.S. 601 (1895).

91. *Minor v. Happersett,* 21 Wall. (88 U.S.) 162 (1875).

92. *Oregon v. Mitchell,* 400 U.S. 112 (1970).

93. *Ex parte McCardle,* 74 U.S. 506, 514 (1869).

94. *United States v. Klein,* 80 U.S. 128 (1872).

95. Jack W. Peltason, *Fifty-Eight Lonely Men: Southern Federal Judges and School Desegregation* (Urbana: University of Illinois Press, 1971).

96. The best collection of compliance studies is no doubt *The Impact of Supreme Court Decisions,* 2d ed., ed. Theodore L. Becker and Malcolm M. Feeley (New York: Oxford University Press, 1973). In this collection, Stephen L. Wasby advanced forty-one factors that appeared to affect compliance in individual cases (pp. 214–217). For a more recent study, see Christopher E. Smith, *Courts and Public Policy* (Chicago: Nelson-Hall, 1993).

97. Donald L. Horowitz, *The Courts and Social Policy* (Washington, D.C.: Brookings, 1977).

98. Jeremy Rabkin, *Judicial Compulsions: How Public Law Distorts Public Policy* (New York: Basic Books, 1989).

99. Gerald N. Rosenberg, *The Hollow Hope: Can Courts Bring About Social Change?* (Chicago: University of Chicago Press, 1991), 338.

100. Ibid., 35.

101. Ibid., 33–35.

102. This argument has been ably made by Robert Scigliano, "The Two Executives: The President and the Supreme Court," in *The American Experiment: Essays on the Theory and Practice of Liberty,* ed. Peter A. Lawler and Robert M. Schaefer (Lanham, Md.: Rowman and Littlefield, 1994), 277–293.

103. John Locke, *Two Treatises of Government,* ed. Peter Laslett (New York: New American Library, 1965), 409–411, or para. 143–146 of the second treatise.

104. Baron de Montesquieu, *The Spirit of the Laws,* 2 vols., trans. Thomas Nugent (New York: Hafner Press, 1949), 1:151–152.

105. Scigliano, "The Two Executives," 278–283.

106. Ibid., 285–286.

107. *The Federalist Papers,* No. 70, 423.

108. Ibid., 423–424.

109. See Michael Novak, *Choosing Our King: Powerful Symbols in Presidential Politics* (New York: Macmillan, 1974); and George E. Reedy, *The Twilight of the Presidency* (New York: New American Library, 1970), 17–28.

110. Locke, *Two Treatises of Government, Second Treatise,* 422.

111. See Susan R. Burgess, *Contest for Constitutional Authority: The Abortion and War Powers Debates* (Lawrence: University Press of Kansas, 1992), 3–4.

112. Albert J. Beveridge, *The Life of John Marshall,* 4 vols. (Boston: Houghton Mifflin, 1919), 3:170, citing a letter of Jefferson to Joseph Nicholson dated May 13, 1803.

113. Ibid., 177.

114. R. Kent Newmyer, *The Supreme Court under Marshall and Taney* (New York: Crowell, 1968), 34.

115. Robert Scigliano, *The Supreme Court and the Presidency* (New York: Free Press, 1971), 32.

116. *McCulloch v. Maryland,* 4 Wheat (17 U.S.) 316, 421 (1819).

117. *A Compilation of the Messages and Papers of the Presidents, 1789–1908,* 11 vols., ed. James E. Richardson (Washington: Bureau of National Literature and Art, 1908), 2:582.

118. Ibid., 6:9.

119. The best account of this crisis is still Robert H. Jackson, *The Struggle for Judicial Supremacy: A Study of a Crisis in American Power Politics* (New York: Vintage, 1941).

120. *Lochner v. New York,* 198 U.S. 45 (1905). In *Lochner,* the Court had struck down a New York law regulating the hours of bakers on the basis that it interfered with "due process" protections (chiefly, what the Court identified as "liberty of contract") in the Fourteenth Amendment.

121. *Norman v. Baltimore & Ohio Railroad Co.,* 294 U.S. 240; *Nortz v. United States,* 294 U.S. 317; *Perry v. United States,* 294 U.S. 330 (1935).

122. *Home Building and Loan Association v. Blaisdell,* 290 U.S. 398, 425–426 (1934).

123. Ibid., 442–443. Hughes quoted from *McCulloch v. Maryland.*

124. *Louisville Bank v. Radford*, 295 U.S. 555 (1935); *Humphrey's Executor v. United States*, 295 U.S. 602 (1935); and *Schechter Poultry Corp. v. United States*, 295 U.S. 495 (1935).

125. *United States v. Butler*, 297 U.S. 1 (1936); *Carter v. Carter Coal Co.*, 298 U.S. 238 (1936); and *Morehead v. New York ex rel. Tipaldo*, 298 U.S. 587 (1936).

126. See Jackson, *The Struggle for Judicial Supremacy*, 328–337 and 340–351 for Roosevelt's messages.

127. Cited in Mason and Baker, *Free Government in the Making*, 686.

128. *West Coast Hotel Co. v. Parrish*, 300 U.S. 379 (1937); the overturned decision was *Adkins v. Children's Hospital*, 261 U.S. 525 (1923).

129. *National Labor Relations Board v. Jones & Laughlin Steel Corporation*, 301 U.S. 1, 41 (1937).

130. Maeva Marcus, *Truman and the Steel Seizure Case: The Limits of Presidential Power* (New York: Columbia University Press, 1977), 215.

131. See Tony Freyer, *The Little Rock Crisis: A Constitutional Interpretation* (Westport, Conn.: Greenwood Press, 1984).

132. Quoted in *The President*, vol. 2 of *Eisenhower*, by Stephen E. Ambrose (New York: Simon and Schuster, 1984), 420.

133. *Cooper v. Aaron*, 18.

134. Otis H. Stephens Jr. and John M. Scheb II, *American Constitutional Law* (St. Paul: West, 1993), 96.

135. *United States v. Nixon*, 705.

136. See Meese's speech titled, "Interpreting the Constitution," in *Interpreting the Constitution: The Debate over Original Intent*, ed. Jack N. Rakove (Boston: Northeastern University Press, 1990), 17.

137. Ibid.

138. Ibid., 19.

139. Ibid.

140. See Brennan's remarks, "The Constitution of the United States: Contemporary Ratification," in *Interpreting the Constitution*, 23.

141. Ibid., 25.

142. David M. O'Brien, "The Reagan Judges: His Most Enduring Legacy?" in *The Reagan Legacy: Promise and Performance*, ed. Charles O. Jones (Chatham, N.J.: Chatham House, 1988), 93. O'Brien describes the Bork controversy on pages 90–95.

143. Aaron Wildavsky, "The Two Presidencies," in *The Two Presidencies: A Quarter Century Assessment*, ed. Steven A. Shull (Chicago: Nelson-Hall, 1991), 11.

144. Stephen Carter notes that "only 7 of our 250 cabinet-level nominees have been defeated or withdrawn since World War II." *The Confirmation Mess*, 32.

145. *Myers v. United States*, 272 U.S. 52, 161 (1926).

146. Ibid., 135.

147. *Humphrey's Executor v. United States*, 628.

148. Ibid., 629–639.

149. *Wiener v. United States*, 357 U.S. 349, 356 (1958).

150. See Lawrence Lessig and Cass R. Sunstein, "The President and the Administration," *Columbia Law Review* 94 (January 1994): 1–123.

151. *Bob Jones University v. United States*, 461 U.S. 574 (1983).

152. *Dalton v. Specter*, 114 S. Ct. 1719 (1994). The decision is described by Holly Idelson and Pat Towell in "House and Supreme Court Take Hands-Off Stance," *Congressional Quarterly Weekly Report*, May 28, 1994, 1404.

153. *Buckley v. Valeo*, 424 U.S. 1 (1976).

154. *Bowsher v. Synar*, 478 U.S. 714 (1986).

155. *Metropolitan Washington Airports Authority v. Citizens for the Abatement of Aircraft Noise*, 501 U.S. 252 (1991).

156. *Morrison v. Olson*, 487 U.S. 654 (1988). This case and other issues surrounding the special prosecutor are analyzed by Katy J. Harriger in *Independent Justice: The Federal Special Prosecutor in American Politics* (Lawrence: University Press of Kansas, 1992), especially 95–116.

157. *Morrison v. Olson*, 671–673.

158. Ibid., 691–692.

159. Ibid., 696.

160. *Mistretta v. United States*, 488 U.S. 361, 384, 412, 427 (1989).

161. Harvey C. Mansfield Jr., "The Ambivalence of Executive Power," in *The Presidency in the Constitutional Order*, ed. Joseph M. Bessette and Jeffrey Tulis (Baton Rouge: Louisiana State University Press, 1981), 314–333, especially 314–316.

162. *Marbury v. Madison*, 166.

163. Ibid.

164. Bruce Ledewitz, "The Uncertain Power of the President to Execute the Laws," *Tennessee Law Review* 46 (1979): 760.

165. Ibid.

166. Ibid., 805.

167. *Kendall v. United States ex rel. Stokes*, 12 Pet. (37 U.S.) 524 (1838).

168. *In re Neagle*, 135 U.S. 1 (1890).

169. *In re Debs*, 158 U.S. 564, 582 (1895).

170. See William F. Duker, "The President's Power to Pardon: A Constitutional History," *William and Mary Law Review* 18 (spring 1977): 475–538.

171. *Ex parte Grossman*, 267 U.S. 87 (1925).

172. Duker, "The President's Power to Pardon," 529.

173. *The Federalist Papers*, No. 74, 449.

174. *United States v. Wilson*, 7 Pet. (32 U.S.) 150, 161 (1833).

175. *Biddle v. Perovich*, 274 U.S. 480, 486 (1927).

176. *Ex parte Garland*, 71 U.S. 333, 380 (1867).

177. *Schick v. Reed*, 419 U.S. 256, 266 (1974).

178. Quoted by Forrest McDonald, "Pardon Power," *Oxford Companion*, 620.

179. Gerald R. Ford, *A Time to Heal: The Autobiography of Gerald R. Ford* (New York: Harper and Row, 1979), 159–178.

180. *Murphy v. Ford*, 390 F. Supp. 1372 (1975). See Mark J. Rozell, "President Ford's Pardon of Richard M. Nixon: Constitutional and Political Considerations," *Presidential Studies Quarterly* 24 (winter 1994): 121–137.

181. Duker, "The President's Power to Pardon," 537.

182. McDonald, "Pardon Power," 620.

183. See *United States v. North*, 910 F. 2d 843 (D.C. Cir. 1990); *United States v. North*, 920 F. 2d 940 (D.C. Cir. 1990); *United States v. North*, 111 S. Ct. 223 (1991).

184. Holly Idelson, "Bush Leaves Partisan Mark With Surprise Pardons," *Congressional Quarterly Weekly Report*, January 2, 1993, 31.

185. Robert J. Spitzer, "Veto, Regular," *Encyclopedia of the American Presidency*, 4:1553. See also Robert J. Spitzer, *The Presidential Veto: Touchstone of the American Presidency* (Albany: State University of New York Press, 1988).

186. *Okanogan Indians v. United States (Pocket Veto Case)*, 279 U.S. 655, 680–681 (1929).

187. *Wright v. United States*, 302 U.S. 538 (1938).

188. Congressional Quarterly, *Guide to the U.S. Supreme Court*, 2d ed., ed. Elder Witt (Washington, D.C.: Congressional Quarterly, 1990), 221.

189. *Burke v. Barnes*, 479 U.S. 361 (1987).

190. *J. W. Hampton, Jr. & Co. v. United States*, 276 U.S. 394 (1928). For an earlier case, see *Field v. Clark*, 143 U.S. 649 (1892).

191. *Panama Refining Company v. A. D. Ryan*, 293 U.S. 388, 421, 418 (1935).

192. *Schechter Poultry Corp. v. United States*, 541–542 (1935).

193. Ibid., 551.

194. *Carter v. Carter Coal Co.*, 311.

195. *Yakus v. United States*, 321 U.S. 414, 424, 426 (1944).

196. *Arizona v. California*, 373 U.S. 546 (1963).

197. *Immigration and Naturalization Service v. Chadha*, 462 U.S. 919 (1983). For an analysis, see Barbara H. Craig, *Chadha: The Story of an Epic Constitutional Struggle* (New York: Oxford University Press, 1988).

198. *Immigration and Naturalization Service v. Chadha*, 947–948.

199. Ibid., 958.

200. Ibid., 959.

201. See, for example, *Metropolitan Washington Airports Authority v. Citizens for the Abatement of Aircraft Noise*.

202. Louis Fisher, "The Legislative Veto: Invalidated, It Survives," *Law and Contemporary Problems* 56 (autumn 1993): 273–292.

203. Ibid., 288–291, 292.

204. See *Train v. City of New York*, 420 U.S. 35 (1975).

205. Louis Fisher, *The Politics of Shared Power: Congress and the Executive*, 3d ed. (Washington, D.C.: CQ Press, 1993), 67.

206. See *New Haven v. United States*, 634 F. Supp. 1449 (D.D.C. 1986); and *New Haven v. United States*, 809 F.2d 900 (D.C. Cir. 1987).

207. Fisher, *The Politics of Shared Power*, 68.

208. Jethro R. Lieberman, *The Evolving Constitution* (New York: Random House, 1992), 192.

209. John R. Vile, *Constitutional Change in the United States: A Comparative Study of the Role of Constitutional Amendments, Judicial Interpretations, and Legislative and Executive Actions* (Westport, Conn.: Praeger, 1994), 57–60.

210. Ruth P. Morgan, *The President and Civil Rights: Policy Making by Executive Order* (New York: St. Martin's Press, 1970), 4.

211. *Peters v. Hobby*, 349 U.S. 331 (1955).

212. *Jenkins v. Collard*, 145 U.S. 546, 560–561 (1891).

213. Glendon A. Schubert Jr., *The Presidency in the Courts* (Minneapolis: University of Minnesota Press, 1957), 314n. 38.

214. Morgan, *The President and Civil Rights*, 7.

215. See Hamilton's first Pacificus essay of 1793 in *Documents of American Constitutional and Legal History*, 145.

216. *In re Neagle*, 64, 69.

217. *Butz v. Economou*, 438 U.S. 789 (1978).

218. *Nixon v. Fitzgerald*, 457 U.S. 731, 749, 797 (1982).

219. *Harlow v. Fitzgerald*, 457 U.S. 800 (1982).

220. See Harold H. Koh, *The National Security Constitution: Sharing Power After the Iran-Contra Affair* (New Haven, Conn.: Yale University Press, 1990), 33.

221. See, however, Raoul Berger, "The President, Congress, and the Courts," *The Yale Law Journal* 83 (May 1974): 1123–1136.

222. Neil A. Lewis, "Court Rejects Move to Delay Clinton Case," *New York Times*, January 10, 1996.

223. *United States v. Nixon*, 703, 705. Quoted from *Marbury v. Madison*.

224. Ibid., 711.

225. *Nixon v. Administrator of General Services*, 433 U.S. 425, 465 (1977).

226. J. Woodford Howard Jr., "Foreign Affairs and Foreign Policy," *Oxford Companion*, 307.

227. Michael M. Uhlmann, "Reflections on the Role of the Judiciary in Foreign Policy," in *Foreign Policy and the Constitution*, ed. Robert A. Goldwin and Robert A. Licht (Washington, D.C.: American Enterprise Institute, 1990), 42.

228. *Eric J. Weiss and Ernesto Hernandez v. United States*, 114 S. Ct. 752 (1994).

229. *Ex parte Vallandigham*, 1 Wall. (68 U.S.) 243 (1864).

230. Herman Belz, "Civil War," *Oxford Companion*, 153.

231. Clinton Rossiter, *The Supreme Court and the Commander in Chief*, introductory note and additional text by Richard P. Longaker (Ithaca, N.Y.: Cornell University Press, 1976), 34.

232. *Ex parte Milligan*, 4 Wall. (71 U.S.) 2, 120–121 (1866).

233. Ibid., 121.

234. Ibid., 140–141.

235. *Ex parte Quirin*, 317 U.S. 1, 37 (1942).

236. *In re Yamashita*, 327 U.S. 1 (1946).

237. *Duncan v. Kahanamoku*, 327 U.S. 304 (1946).

238. *Reid v. Covert*, 354 U.S. 1 (1957).

239. *Missouri v. Holland*, 252 U.S. 416 (1920).

240. *Reid v. Covert*, 17.

241. *Solorio v. United States*, 483 U.S. 435 (1987). The earlier precedent was *O'Callahan v. Parker*, 395 U.S. 258 (1969).

242. These cases are treated by Jacobus tenBroek, Edward N. Barnhart, and Floyd W. Matson in *Prejudice, War and the Constitution* (Berkeley: University of California Press, 1968); and by Peter Irons in *Justice at War: The Story of the Japanese American Internment Cases* (New York: Oxford University Press, 1983).

243. *Hirabayashi v. United States*, 320 U.S. 81, 100 (1943). A companion case also sustaining the curfew was *Yasui v. United States*, 320 U.S. 115 (1943).

244. *Korematsu v. United States*, 323 U.S. 214, 221–222 (1944).

245. Ibid., 219.

246. Ibid., 216.

247. Ibid., 345–346.

248. *Ex parte Endo*, 323 U.S. 283 (1944).

249. For the circuit court opinion, see *Hirabayashi v. United States*, 828 F. 2d 591 (9th Cir. 1987). Documents relevant to this extraordinary decision may be found in *Justice Delayed: The Record of the Japanese American Internment Cases*, ed. Peter Irons (Middletown, Conn.: Wesleyan University Press, 1989).

250. "War Internee Measure Enacted," *Facts on File Yearbook 1988* (New York: Facts on File, 1989), 594.

251. This incident is described by Rossiter in *The Supreme Court and the Commander in Chief*, 18–26. For the case, see *Ex parte Merryman*, F. Cas. 9487 (1861).

252. *Youngstown Sheet & Tube Co. v. Sawyer*, 585, 587.

253. Ibid., 645.

254. Ibid., 635–638. Quotation is from 637.

255. *New York Times Co. v. United States*, 403 U.S. 713, 726 (1971). Sanford J. Ungar discusses this case in *The Papers and the Papers* (New York: E. P. Dutton, 1972).

256. For a related development, in which the national government sought an injunction to prevent publication of an article on making hydrogen bombs, see *United States v. The Progressive, Inc.*, 467 F. Supp. 990 (1979).

257. *Schenck v. United States*, 249 U.S. 47, 52 (1919).

258. *Gitlow v. New York*, 268 U.S. 652, 669 (1925).

259. *Dennis v. United States*, 341 U.S. 494, 509 (1951).

260. *Minersville School District v. Gobitis*, 310 U.S. 586 (1940).

261. *West Virginia State Board of Education v. Barnette*, 319 U.S. 624, 642 (1943).

262. *Texas v. Johnson and United States v. Eichman*. In *United States v. O'Brien*, 391 U.S. 367 (1968), the Court upheld the conviction of an individual who had burned his draft card in protest of the Vietnam War. The Court decided that the national interest in the selective service system was both weighty and independent of any attempt to suppress the protester's free speech rights.

263. *United States v. United States District Court*, 407 U.S. 297 (1972).

264. In *Katz v. United States*, 389 U.S. 342 (1967), the Court had decided that such prior judicial authorization was needed in ordinary matters of law enforcement. *Katz* had overturned *Olmstead v. United States*, 277 U.S. 438 (1928).

265. *Kent v. Dulles*, 357 U.S. 116 (1958). For analysis, see Smith, *The Constitution and American Foreign Policy*, 275–277.

266. *Aptheker v. Secretary of State*, 378 U.S. 500, 514 (1964).

267. *Zemel v. Rusk*, 381 U.S. 1 (1965).

268. *United States v. Laub*, 385 U.S. 475 (1967). See Smith, *The Constitution and American Foreign Policy*, 276.

269. *Haig v. Agee*, 453 U.S. 280 (1981).

270. See Smith, *The Constitution and American Foreign Policy*, 274–275.

271. *Afroyim v. Rusk*, 387 U.S. 253, 268 (1967).

272. For an excellent review of such cases, see Christopher N. May, *In the Name of War: Judicial Review and the War Powers Since 1918* (Cambridge, Mass.: Harvard University Press, 1989).

273. *Hamilton v. Kentucky Distilleries Co.*, 251 U.S. 146, 163 (1919).

274. *Woods v. Miller*, 333 U.S. 138, at 141 (1948).

275. Donald L. Robinson, "Presidential Emergency Powers," *Oxford Companion*, 665–666.

276. *The Brig Aurora*, 7 Cr. (11 U.S.) 382 (1813); *Field v. Clark*, 143 U.S. 649 (1892); *J. W. Hampton & Co. v. United States*, 276 U.S. 394 (1928). For

discussion of all these cases, see Stephens and Scheb, *American Constitutional Law*, 327–328.

277. See *Panama Refining Co. v. Ryan, Schechter Poultry Corp. v. United States*, and *Carter v. Carter Coal Co.*

278. *United States v. Curtiss-Wright Export Corp.*, 299 U.S. 304, 318 (1936). For a good analysis of this case, which is critical of Sutherland's historical interpretations, see Charles A. Lofgren, "United States v. Curtiss-Wright Export Corporation: An Historical Reassessment," *The Yale Law Journal* 83 (November 1973): 1–32. For a view more sympathetic to Sutherland, see Hadley Arkes, *The Return of George Sutherland: Restoring a Jurisprudence of Natural Rights* (Princeton, N.J.: Princeton University Press, 1994), 198–241.

279. *United States v. Curtiss-Wright Export Corp.*, 319. Lofgren, "United States v. Curtiss-Wright Export Corporation," 25, denies that this statement in context was intended as "an endorsement of unlimited executive discretion in foreign policy-making."

280. *United States v. Curtiss-Wright Export Corp.*, 319.

281. Ibid., 320.

282. Ibid., 321.

283. Quoted by Louis Henkin in *Foreign Affairs and the Constitution* (New York: Norton, 1972), 39–40.

284. In *The Politics of Shared Power*, 151, Fisher notes that the Treaty of Versailles was "the most conspicuous casualty of a presidential determination to negotiate unilaterally." Fisher cites the North Atlantic Treaty as a good example of executive/legislative cooperation in making a treaty. He further notes that Congress has developed a "fast-track" procedure for ratifying trade treaties that it has helped negotiate.

285. Smith, *The Constitution and American Foreign Policy*, 108.

286. Fisher, *The Politics of Shared Power*, 152–153.

287. *Missouri v. Holland*, 433, 434.

288. Ibid., 433.

289. Henkin, *Foreign Affairs and the Constitution*, 138.

290. *Missouri v. Holland*, 433.

291. See, for example, *Zschernig v. Miller*, 504 U.S. 655 (1968).

292. *Whitney v. Robertson*, 124 U.S. 190, 194 (1888).

293. *United States v. Alvarez-Machain*, 112 S. Ct. 2188 (1992).

294. David M. O'Brien, *Supreme Court Watch—1993* (New York: Norton, 1993), 38.

295. *Goldwater v. Carter*, 1007.

296. Fisher, *The Politics of Shared Power*, 156.

297. See Duane Tananbaum, *The Bricker Amendment Controversy: A Test of Eisenhower's Political Leadership* (Ithaca, N.Y.: Cornell University Press, 1988), 180–181.

298. Fisher, *The Politics of Shared Power*, 157.

299. *United States v. Belmont*, 301 U.S. 324 (1937).

300. Ibid., 330.

301. *United States v. Pink*, 315 U.S. 203 (1942).

302. *Dames & Moore v. Regan*, 453 U.S. 654, 677, 688 (1981).

303. *Weinberger v. Rossi*, 456 U.S. 25 (1982).

304. David M. O'Brien, *Struggles for Power and Governmental Accountability*, vol. 1 of *Constitutional Law and Politics* (New York: Norton, 1991), 216.

305. *The Prize Cases*, 2 Black (67 U.S.) 635, 668 (1863).

306. Ibid., 670.

307. Quoted by John H. Ely in *War and Responsibility: Constitutional Lessons of Vietnam and Its Aftermath* (Princeton, N.J.: Princeton University Press, 1993), 16.

308. Ibid., 32.

309. Quoted in ibid., 132.

310. Ibid., 133–135.

311. Ibid., 49.

312. Ibid., 53.

313. Fisher, *The Politics of Shared Power*, 167.

314. *Dellums v. Bush*, 752 F. Supp. 1141 (D.C.C. 1990), 1149.

315. "U.S. Sets Somalia Pullout Deadline," *Facts on File*, October 7, 1993, 53:743–746.

316. Edward S. Corwin, *The President: Office and Powers, 1787–1984*, 5th rev. ed., ed. Randall W. Bland, Theodore T. Hindson, and Jack W. Peltason (New York: New York University Press, 1984), 201.

SELECTED BIBLIOGRAPHY

Abraham, Henry J. *The Judicial Process*. 6th ed. New York: Oxford University Press, 1993.

——. *Justices and Presidents: A Political History of Appointments to the Supreme Court*. 3d ed. New York: Oxford University Press, 1992.

Biskupic, Joan, and Elder Witt. *Guide to the U.S. Supreme Court*, ed. Elder Witt. 3d ed. Washington, D.C.: Congressional Quarterly, 1997.

Burgess, Susan R. *Contest for Constitutional Authority: The Abortion and War Powers Debates*. Lawrence: University Press of Kansas, 1992.

Corwin, Edward S. *The President: Office and Powers, 1787–1984*, ed. Randall W. Bland, Theodore T. Hindson, and Jack W. Peltason. 5th rev. ed. New York: New York University Press, 1984.

Ely, John H. *War and Responsibility: Constitutional Lessons of Vietnam and Its Aftermath*. Princeton, N.J.: Princeton University Press, 1993.

Fisher, Louis. *The Politics of Shared Power: Congress and the Executive*. 3d ed. Washington, D.C.: CQ Press, 1993.

Goldman, Sheldon, and Thomas P. Jahnige. *The Federal Courts as a Political System*. 3d ed. New York: McGraw-Hill, 1985.

Henkin, Louis. *Foreign Affairs and the Constitution*. New York: Norton, 1972.

Jackson, Robert H. *The Struggle for Judicial Supremacy: A Study of a Crisis in American Power Politics*. New York: Vintage, 1941.

Kelly, Alfred H., Winfred A. Harbison, and Herman Belz. *The American Constitution: Its Origins and Development*. 2 vols. 7th ed. New York: Norton, 1991.

Koh, Harold H. *The National Security Constitution: Sharing Power After the Iran-Contra Affair*. New Haven, Conn.: Yale University Press, 1990.

May, Christopher N. *In the Name of War: Judicial Review and the War Powers Since 1918*. Cambridge, Mass.: Harvard University Press, 1989.

Murphy, Walter F., and C. Herman Pritchett. *Courts, Judges, and Politics: An Introduction to the Judicial Process*. 4th ed. New York: Random House, 1986.

O'Brien, David M. *Storm Center: The Supreme Court in American Politics*. 3d ed. New York: Norton, 1993.

The Oxford Companion to the Supreme Court of the United States, ed. Kermit L. Hall. New York: Oxford University Press, 1992.

Rehnquist, William H. *The Supreme Court: How It Was, How It Is*. New York: Morrow, 1987.

Rossiter, Clinton. *The Supreme Court and the Commander in Chief*. Introduction by Richard P. Longaker. Ithaca, N.Y.: Cornell University Press, 1976.

Rozell, Mark J. *Executive Privilege: The Dilemma of Secrecy and Democratic Accountability*. Baltimore: Johns Hopkins University Press, 1994.

Schwartz, Bernard. *A History of the Supreme Court*. New York: Oxford University Press, 1993.

Scigliano, Robert. *The Supreme Court and the Presidency*. New York: Free Press, 1971.

Smith, Jean E. *The Constitution and American Foreign Policy*. St. Paul: West, 1989.

Spitzer, Robert J. *The Presidential Veto: Touchstone of the American Presidency*. Albany: State University of New York Press, 1988.

Supreme Court Historical Society. *The Supreme Court Justices: Illustrated Biographies, 1789–1995*, ed. Clare Cushman. 2d ed. Washington, D.C.: Congressional Quarterly, 1995.

Tarr, G. Alan. *Judicial Process and Judicial Policymaking*. St. Paul: West, 1994.

Urofsky, Melvin I. *A March of Liberty*. New York: Knopf, 1988.

Vile, John R. *A Companion to the United States Constitution and Its Amendments*. Westport, Conn.: Praeger, 1993.

CHAPTER 35

The President and the Bureaucracy

BY MARK E. BYRNES

The Treasury is so large and far-flung and ingrained in its practices that I find it almost impossible to get the action and results I want. . . . But the Treasury is not to be compared with the State Department. You should go through the experience of trying to get any changes in the thinking, policy, and action of the career diplomats. . . . But the Treasury and the State Department put together are nothing compared with the Navy. . . . To change anything in the Navy is like punching a feather bed. You punch it with your right and you punch it with your left until you are finally exhausted, and then you find the damn bed just as it was before you started punching.

—Franklin D. Roosevelt

He'll sit here and he'll say, "Do this! Do that!" And nothing will happen. Poor Ike—it won't be a bit like the Army. He'll find it very frustrating.

—Harry S. Truman

Before I became president, I realized and was warned that dealing with the federal bureaucracy would be one of the worst problems I would have to face. It has been worse than I had anticipated.

—Jimmy Carter

The term *bureaucracy* does not appear in the U.S. Constitution, yet the bureaucracy has become one of the most powerful elements of modern American government. In fact, it often is called the "fourth branch" of government because of its prominence in contemporary politics. From their vantage point in the White House, presidents quickly discover that they can accomplish little without help from the bureaucracy. Thus their relationship with it is one of the most important aspects of any administration.

For many people, the term *bureaucracy* conjures up images of red tape, impersonality, and rigidity, and applies wherever those images are found—from government to universities to large corporations. In this chapter the term is used without any negative connotations; *bureaucracy* simply refers to the units of the executive branch of the U.S. national government—staffed mainly by unelected public officials—which carry out public policy. Except where noted, the term does not encompass the uniformed services of the military.

The bureaucracy comprises many agencies. In this chapter *agency* may refer to one of the cabinet departments, a part of a department, or an executive branch entity independent of the departments. *Bureau* is used interchangeably with agency. *Department* refers solely to one of the fourteen cabinet departments. Finally, although commonly used as a slur, here the label *bureaucrat* simply refers to someone who works in the bureaucracy.

Evolution of the Federal Bureaucracy

The Founders probably would be startled by the scope and complexity of today's federal bureaucracy. It did not, however, take its present shape suddenly; the bureaucracy has been evolving for more than two hundred years.

CONSTITUTIONAL FOUNDATIONS

Although the Constitution barely mentions the executive branch and says nothing at all about a bureaucracy, the document is nevertheless crucial to the bureaucracy. The evolution of the bureaucracy has been shaped by what the Founders thought about the executive branch and by what the Constitution says—and does not say—about it. Subsequent constitutional interpretations also have played a role.

The Founders issued relatively explicit guidelines for the presidency, the Congress, and, to a lesser extent, the judicial system, but they said little about how the government's decisions were to be executed or about how the executive branch should be organized. Some delegates to the Constitutional Convention suggested, to no avail, that the details of the executive branch be fleshed out. The clauses that were inserted into the Constitution, though brief, did at least set the boundaries for the development of the modern bureaucracy.

The position of the executive branch in the Constitution's overall scheme of government is ambiguous. Article II, section 1, states that "the executive Power shall be vested in a President of the United States of America," but it does not spell out exactly what that power includes. The next section provides only some help by specifying two powers. First, the president "may require the Opinion, in writing, of the principal Officer in each of the executive Departments, upon any Subject relating to Duties of their respective Offices." And, second, the president "shall nominate, and by and with the Advice and Consent of the Senate, shall appoint Ambassadors, other public Ministers and Consuls, Judges of the Supreme Court, and all other Officers of the United States, whose Appointments are not herein otherwise provided for, and which shall be established by Law." The second power comes with a condition, however: "The Congress may by Law vest the Appointment of such inferior Officers, as they think proper, in the President alone, in the Courts of Law, or in the

Heads of Departments." These few provisions are all that the Constitution says specifically about the executive branch.

Organization of Executive Power

The Founders' relative lack of attention to executive power does not mean that they thought it was unimportant. To the contrary, the short yet turbulent history of the American colonies clearly indicated the critical role of administration. The colonists had suffered "a long train of abuses" at the hands of British administrators and thus had developed an intense distrust of, but a grudging respect for, strong executive power.

America's own attempts at administration also had taught some lessons. The Continental Congress, intent on avoiding the dangers of executive power, had tackled the immense executive task of running the Revolutionary War without outside administrative help. Instead, committees composed of members of Congress had been formed to deal with even the most minor executive issues. Congress quickly discovered that this system was unwieldy and ineffective, but administration by committees of amateurs serving part time continued throughout the war and under the government established by the Articles of Confederation.

When they met to construct a new form of government, the Founders were determined to correct the executive situation. Aware of the problems created by administrative committees, they agreed that executive functions should be grouped in a limited number of executive departments, each with a single head. Although the Constitution does not mandate this specific structure, references to "the principal Officer in each of the executive Departments" and "Heads of Departments" support this interpretation. The major disagreement at the Constitutional Convention concerned how heads of departments would be selected and to whom they would be responsible. The delegates decided that the president, with the advice and consent of the Senate, would choose department heads, but they left the question of responsibility unanswered.

Another question left unanswered was the removal of officials appointed by the president with Senate approval: Did the president alone have the power to dismiss such officials? The First Congress (1789–1791) debated this issue at length before narrowly deciding that presidents can remove appointees from office on their own authority. Although that decision makes executive branch officials technically subordinate to the president, Congress still holds tremendous influence.

One major source of influence is the considerable freedom that the Constitution gives Congress in deciding how to organize the executive branch. Congress has the right to create and abolish departments and agencies, to arrange them as it sees fit, and to decide how many employees they have and how those employees are selected. Congress also exerts control over the bureaucracy by appropriating money and conducting investigations.

The Constitution grants the president "executive power" to "take Care that the Laws be faithfully executed," but it is am-

biguous about what that power and responsibility entail. Congress settled one issue by deciding that the president has the authority to remove appointed officials from office, but much of the relationship between the president and the executive branch hinges on the attitudes and strategies of individual presidents. In this context, the words "executive power," applied to the president by Article II, have been called a "term of uncertain content," the meaning of which can be supplied only by a particular president.[1]

Results of the Constitutional Framework

The Founders' handling of the executive branch—and their use of checks and balances to ensure that no one part of the U.S. government can subjugate the other parts or the public—demonstrates their fear of centralized government power. Neither the president nor Congress can dominate the executive branch; each checks the other. The president is granted executive power and the right to appoint officials, but that presidential power is countered by the requirement for Senate approval of appointees and by congressional control of the organization of the executive branch. This arrangement vividly illustrates the separation of powers doctrine inherent in the U.S. Constitution.

The constitutional foundations of the executive branch have had some significant ramifications for the development of the bureaucracy and for the U.S. government in general. First, although these foundations have helped to prevent excessive concentrations of power, they also have increased the fragmentation of government, making the formulation of coherent public policy difficult. Second, the Constitution's ambiguity and lack of restrictions on the executive branch have allowed the federal bureaucracy to grow to proportions unimagined by the Founders. Finally, the system of dual control of the executive branch by the president and Congress has resulted in a system of limited control.[2] Executive departments and agencies quickly learned to play one branch against the other and to develop an independent power base, thus setting the stage for the historical process that has made the federal bureaucracy one of the most powerful forces in American society.

GROWTH OF THE BUREAUCRACY

The U.S. bureaucracy has grown dramatically over the years. Although various people and events throughout American history have fueled bureaucratic growth, some periods are particularly noteworthy, including the nation's earliest years, the Jacksonian era, the Civil War and its aftermath, the Progressive era, and the administration of Franklin D. Roosevelt and beyond.

Historical Development

The modern federal bureaucracy had humble beginnings. George Washington's administration began with only three executive departments—State, Treasury, and War—and very few federal workers. The first State Department, for example, had only nine employees.[3] Creation of the U.S. Post Office in 1792 caused a small surge in federal employment, but the entire government workforce still numbered only about three thousand in 1801.[4] Although the early bureaucracy was small and informal, competition for jobs was intense. Washington looked for "men of character," whom he knew personally if possible and could trust to exercise good judgment and to perform competently.

This personalized system of recruitment continued largely unchanged until the presidency of Andrew Jackson (1829–1837), when the country found itself outgrowing its highly informal system of administration. Jackson appointed his friend Amos Kendall to head the Post Office, where lack of structure and established procedures were especially harmful. Kendall made changes—such as setting up clear lines of authority, specifying job descriptions, and establishing strict accounting practices—that replaced informality with routinization. Thus the bureaucracy began to take on the more formal character that it has today.

In making appointments to the bureaucracy, Jackson applied the "spoils system"—a practice in which presidential election winners rewarded their supporters with federal government jobs. Although Jackson was not the first president to give public jobs to friends and allies, his openness and unapologetic attitude were new. His behavior was not entirely cynical, however, because he based this practice on his support of "rotation in office." Jackson believed that a regular change of public officials made the government more democratic by giving more people the chance to participate, thereby preventing the rise of a bureaucratic elite unrepresentative of the general public. The president was convinced that any reasonably intelligent person could perform the duties of public office.

In 1849 President James K. Polk signed into law a bill adding another cabinet department, the Department of the Interior. The new department was created to administer the millions of acres of new territory acquired by the country after the Mexican War and to supervise the Native Americans who lived there.

The Civil War (1861–1865) sparked tremendous growth in the size of the bureaucracy. New agencies were created, including the predecessor of the Department of Agriculture, and thousands of new employees were hired as the Union prepared for and conducted the war. After the war, another new agency was established to respond to the needs of Northern veterans.

The Civil War also revealed some of the bureaucracy's weaknesses, most notably the existence of fairly widespread corruption and inefficiency. The problems undoubtedly existed before the war, but they were exacerbated by wartime pressures. Proposals for reform of the bureaucracy soon surfaced and then intensified as scandals over government employment practices appeared after the war. Rapid industrial growth and expansion of government activities placed additional strains on the bureaucracy. In response, Congress created new executive agencies and departments, such as the Department of Justice and the Interstate Commerce Commission, to help meet the increasing demands for government service.

Presidents of the era recognized the need to reform the bureaucracy. Rutherford B. Hayes (1877–1881) wanted to dismantle the spoils system, but Congress did not pass his proposed legislation. Hayes's successor, James A. Garfield, denounced the spoils system both as a candidate and as president. Once in office, he was particularly vexed by the amount of time he had to spend dealing with political appointments and the people who wanted them. Garfield wrote in his diary: "My day is frittered away with the personal seeking of people when it ought to be given to the great problems which concern the whole country."[5]

The reform movement got its biggest push in a roundabout and tragic way. One man who tried but failed to get a government job, Charles J. Guiteau, vented his frustration by assassinating Garfield just a few months after the president's 1881 inauguration. *(See Chapter 9, Removal of the President, Vol. I.)* Public outrage at the killing focused attention on the problems of the spoils system and spurred Congress into action. The Pendleton Act, passed in 1883, mandated that federal jobs be granted to the most qualified applicants rather than those with the best political connections. It also provided those employees with job security, thus ending the mass rotation in office that had occurred with every new president.

The first few decades of the twentieth century also brought sizable increases in the bureaucracy. The Progressive movement of that time blossomed in reaction to abuses of workers and consumers by unregulated businesses. Progressive leaders advocated more government regulation of the economy and the creation of new agencies—such as the Department of Labor, Federal Trade Commission, Food and Drug Administration, and Forest Service—to do the regulating. Similarly, America's entry into World War I generated more government activity and therefore more bureaucracy.

Franklin Roosevelt won election to the White House in 1932 on a platform that promised vigorous government action—a "New Deal"—to combat the depression that had plagued the country for three years. Roosevelt kept his promise by persuading Congress to enact a variety of programs. During his first term (1933–1937), Congress passed laws designed by Roosevelt to provide relief to those hardest hit by the depression, to help the economy recover, and to reform the economy to prevent future depressions. Among the more than sixty new agencies created during the New Deal were the Social Security Administration (SSA), Federal Deposit Insurance Corporation (FDIC), Securities and Exchange Commission (SEC), and Tennessee Valley Authority (TVA).

The New Deal not only established many new bureaucratic agencies but also signified a fundamental shift in the role of government in American society.[6] The federal government was now expected to take an active role in fighting the nation's problems—a role that required adding to the bureaucracy. By 1937, even the U.S. Supreme Court, which for years had restricted the amount of regulation undertaken by the bureaucracy, had accepted the government's new role.

America's tremendous commitment to World War II also led to a burgeoning bureaucracy, most noticeably in the military

Franklin D. Roosevelt greatly expanded the size and reach of the federal bureaucracy in his efforts to cope with the Great Depression. Critics of government bureaucracy, both at the time and for years afterward, complained that the "alphabet soup" of new programs and agencies changed the character and purpose of the federal government.

but also domestically. Another important consequence of the war was the dramatic increase in the amount of money raised and spent by the federal government. From 1940 to 1945, total federal revenues skyrocketed from under $7 billion to over $45 billion, again enlarging the influence of bureaucracy.[7] Even after Germany and Japan fell, U.S. taxes did not; resources were directed to continued military readiness and domestic social programs. By the early 1950s, the number of federal civilian employees had reached about 2.6 million.[8]

Another spurt of bureaucratic growth occurred in response to the Soviet Union's launching of *Sputnik,* the world's first satellite, in 1957. Americans were alarmed by the Soviet achievement and demanded action from their government. The next year, Congress created the National Aeronautics and Space Administration (NASA) to manage the U.S. space effort. Because *Sputnik* had suddenly made the American education system, especially science education, seem inadequate, the federal government also became deeply involved in education at all levels.[9]

In the 1960s, the federal government greatly enlarged its efforts to solve many social problems and, in the process, created new government programs and agencies. President Lyndon B. Johnson pursued his vision of a "Great Society" in part by persuading Congress to establish new organizations—such as the Department of Housing and Urban Development, Department of Transportation, Organization for Economic Opportunity (OEO), and Equal Employment Opportunity Commission (EEOC)—and major new government programs—such as Medicare and Medicaid.

Growing concern about the environment in the 1970s

sparked the creation of the Environmental Protection Agency (EPA) and the Department of Energy. The Departments of Education and Health and Human Services also were born during that decade. The elevation of the Veterans Administration to cabinet status in 1989 (becoming the Department of Veterans Affairs) boosted the number of cabinet departments to fourteen.

Explaining Bureaucratic Growth

Why has this remarkable growth occurred in the size and scope of the federal bureaucracy? As the history of the federal government suggests, the fundamental reason is that a larger bureaucracy is needed to carry out new demands placed on government. Public demands for additional services have led Congress and the president to create new government programs, which have required new agencies and employees to run them. Thus the bureaucracy has grown because Americans have increasingly expected the government to solve society's problems.

Scholars often cite four more specific explanations for bureaucratic growth.[10] One explanation maintains that government must have more employees with specialized knowledge to keep up with the rapid technological changes taking place throughout society. According to the second explanation, increasing government regulation of the economy and the attendant need for more federal agencies are the primary forces behind expansion of the bureaucracy. The third explanation concerns how the government responds to crises. When a crisis such as a war, an economic depression, or a natural disaster occurs, the federal government usually takes measures—frequently requiring new government agencies and additional employees—to end the crisis or limit its effects. Once the crisis has passed, however, the additional bureaucracy is rarely dismantled. The fourth explanation for bureaucratic growth is the political pressure exerted by various segments of society, who demand services from the government and then support the agencies established to fulfill their demands.

THE MODERN FEDERAL BUREAUCRACY

The federal bureaucracy's growth and its policy-making functions have made it one of the most important political forces in this country. Yet it also is one of the least-understood political institutions.

Dimensions of the Federal Bureaucracy

Many Americans believe that the federal bureaucracy is growing at an alarming, almost uncontrollable, rate. Part of this perception is based on the pervasive influence of the bureaucracy on American life. The federal bureaucracy generates rules and regulations that govern the lives of Americans literally from womb to tomb, as well as what goes on in between. The air they breathe, the food they eat, the cars they drive, the television programs they watch, and virtually all other aspects of American life are affected by bureaucracy. It is no wonder that the federal bureaucracy seems to be continually expanding.

ONLINE GATEWAYS TO FEDERAL INFORMATION

The federal government offers a vast wealth of information for free through computer bulletin board systems (BBSs) and Internet sites. The online systems offer transcripts of presidential speeches, the full text of bills introduced in Congress, extensive health information, consumer publications about everything from buying a home to helping children learn to read, and lots more.

To access a bulletin board, a user needs a computer, a modem, communications software, and a telephone line. To access an Internet site, a user also needs an Internet account.

More than 1,000 BBSs and Internet sites offer access to federal government information. Although most of these systems are operated by federal agencies, departments, and courts, colleges and universities run some of the best sites and private individuals run a few others. The five sites described below are major gateways to federal BBSs or Internet sites. Using a gateway, one can seamlessly connect to hundreds of other federal computer systems.

WELCOME TO THE WHITE HOUSE: AN INTERACTIVE CITIZENS' HANDBOOK

This site offers presidential documents such as speeches, transcripts of press briefings, and the full text of the proposed federal budget. It also has the National Performance Review report, the National Information Infrastructure report, the North American Free Trade Agreement (NAFTA), and the General Agreement on Tariffs and Trade (GATT).

Welcome to the White House also offers interior and exterior pictures of the White House and links to dozens of Internet sites operated by federal agencies and departments.

To access World Wide Web: *http://www.whitehouse.gov*
E-mail: *feedback@whitehouse.gov*

THE VILLANOVA CENTER FOR INFORMATION LAW AND POLICY

This site provides access to the Federal Web Locator, which has links to hundreds of World Wide Web sites operated by federal agencies, departments, and courts.

Using Villanova as a starting point, users can connect to Internet sites operated by the House of Representatives, the Federal Judicial Center, the Department of Commerce, the Department of Labor, the Department of State, the Central Intelligence Agency, the Defense Nuclear Facilities Safety Board, the Federal Emergency Management Agency, the National Aeronautics and Space Administration, the National Archives and Records Administration, the Securities and Exchange Commission, the Small Business Administration, the Social Security Administration, and many other agencies.

To access World Wide Web: *http://www.law.vill.edu/fed-agency/ fedwebloc.html*
E-mail: *feedback@mail.law.vill.edu*

LC MARVEL

Operated by the Library of Congress, LC MARVEL offers links to hundreds of Gophers, FTP sites, and Telnet sites that provide federal information. It also has links to state and local government sites arranged by state, and foreign government sites arranged by country.

In addition to the links, LC MARVEL has extensive information about the Library of Congress and its collections, details about how to access the library's online card catalog, documents about copyright, congressional directories, and links to hundreds of Internet sites around the world, arranged by subject.

To access Gopher: *marvel.loc.gov*
To access Telnet: *telnet marvel.loc.gov*
Login: marvel

FEDWORLD

This site offers a huge collection of federal information, although its most popular feature is a gateway to more than 100 federal BBSs. If one accesses FedWorld through the World Wide Web, FedWorld also provides a gateway to dozens of federal government Internet sites. The Internet sites are arranged by subject.

Besides the gateways, FedWorld offers hundreds of IRS tax forms and publications, White House documents, cancer information from the National Cancer Institute, publications for investors from the Securities and Exchange Commission, lists of federal job openings, documents about problems at nuclear power plants from the Nuclear Regulatory Commission, images from weather satellites, and much more.

To access World Wide Web: *http://www.fedworld.gov*
To access Telnet *telnet fedworld.gov*
Login: new (then register)
To access FTP: *ftp.fedworld.gov*
Login: anonymous
Password: your e-mail address
To access Dial-in: 703-321-3339
Login: new (then register)
E-mail: *helpdesk@fedworld.gov*
Helpful files: FEDUSER.DOC (uncompressed) or FEDUSER.ZIP (compressed), ALLFILES (uncompressed) or ALLFILES.ZIP (compressed)

UNIVERSITY OF MICHIGAN DOCUMENTS CENTER, "FEDERAL GOVERNMENT RESOURCES ON THE WEB."

The Documents Center of the University of Michigan offers twenty-three broad categories of federal government resources and, within them, numerous links to national and international internet sites. The budget category, for example, provides both the current and next year's federal budgets, access to the related congressional legislation, and media coverage of the budget debate. In addition to the standard categories on various aspects of the three branches of government, related information on political science and statistics is available from wide-ranging sources and sites.

To access World Wide Web:
http://www.lib.umich.edu/libhome/Documents.center/federal.html

Sources: Bruce Maxwell, *How to Access the Government's Electronic Bulletin Boards: Washington Online,* 2d ed. (Washington, D.C.: Congressional Quarterly, 1995); Bruce Maxwell, *How to Access the Federal Government on the Internet: Washington Online,* 2d ed. (Washington, D.C.: Congressional Quarterly, 1996).

In truth, however, the number of federal government employees is not swelling. About three million civilians work for the federal government, a number that has not changed significantly in the last twenty-five years. In fact, there are fewer federal employees today than there were at the end of World War II, when the government employed over 3.8 million.[11] The size of the bureaucracy varies somewhat over time, increasing during periods of national crisis and then stabilizing or even decreasing somewhat as normal conditions return. (See Table 35-1 and Table 35-2.)

Most federal bureaucrats do not work in Washington, D.C.; only about 11 percent of federal civilian employees are located in the nation's capital.[12] This percentage, as well as the tremendous number of state and local government employees nationwide, illustrates how decentralized government is in the United States. Employment at the state and local levels of government has grown dramatically in recent decades: as of 1992 about 4.6 million people worked for state governments, while local governments employed a staggering 11.1 million people.[13]

But the power of the federal bureaucracy cannot be judged by the number of its employees alone. Although it is true that the number of federal employees has not risen since World War II, the size of the federal budget has increased sharply. In 1947, for example, federal spending was $34.5 billion—a huge figure but one that seems minuscule when compared with the government's 1996 budget of about $1.6 trillion (inflation accounts for part of that increase, however).[14]

The federal government accommodates these vastly larger budgets without hiring more employees to help administer them through a system of proxy, or indirect, administration. Many programs are funded by the federal government and car-

TABLE 35-2 Size of Independent Federal Agencies for 1980 and 1992

Agency	Paid civilian employees	
	1980	1992
ACTION	1,837	421
American Battle Monuments Commission	386	401
Board of Governors, Federal Reserve System	1,498	1,594
Commission on Civil Rights	304	89
Environmental Protection Agency	14,715	18,360
Equal Opportunity Employment Commission	3,515	2,873
Export-Import Bank	385	368
Farm Credit Administration	271	486
Federal Communications Commission	2,244	1,872
Federal Deposit Insurance Corporation	3,520	22,775
Federal Emergency Management Agency	3,427	3,730
Federal Labor Relations Authority	349	252
Federal Mediation and Conciliation Service	503	322
Federal Trade Commission	1,846	993
General Services Administration	37,654	21,094
International Trade Commission	424	495
Interstate Commerce Commission	1,998	627
National Aeronautics and Space Administration	23,714	26,011
National Endowment for the Arts	362	279
National Labor Relations Board	2,936	2,199
National Science Foundation	1,394	1,352
National Transportation Safety Board	384	367
Nuclear Regulatory Commission	3,283	3,564
Office of Personnel Management	8,280	6,984
Panama Canal Commission	8,700	8,519
Railroad Retirement Board	1,795	1,812
Securities and Exchange Commission	2,056	2,610
Selective Service System	97	254
Small Business Administration	5,804	5,182
Smithsonian Institution	4,403	5,621
Tennessee Valley Authority	51,714	19,479
U.S. Postal Service	660,014	791,986
All others	20,062	24,394
TOTAL	1,100,363	977,365

SOURCE: Lyn Ragsdale, *Vital Statistics on the Presidency: Washington to Clinton* (Washington, D.C.: Congressional Quarterly, 1996), 280.

TABLE 35-1 Size of Executive Departments for Selected Years

Executive department	Year established	Paid civilian employees	
		1980	1992
Agriculture	1889	126,139	133,049
Commerce[a]	1913	45,563	38,356
Defense[b]	1947	960,116	1,001,322
Education	1980	7,364	5,117
Energy	1977	21,557	21,351
Health and Human Services[c]	1980	155,662	134,321
Housing and Urban Development	1965	16,964	13,862
Interior	1849	77,357	84,617
Justice	1870	56,327	97,941
Labor	1913	23,400	18,111
State	1789	23,497	25,986
Transportation	1966	72,361	70,745
Treasury	1789	124,663	164,658
Veterans Affairs[d]	1989	228,285	259,406
TOTAL		1,942,255	2,068,842

SOURCE: Lyn Ragsdale, *Vital Statistics on the Presidency: Washington to Clinton* (Washington, D.C.: Congressional Quarterly, 1996), 279.
NOTES: a. Originally the Department of Commerce and Labor, established in 1903 and split in 1913.   b. Originally the Department of War, established in 1789.   c. Originally the Department of Health, Educations and Welfare, established in 1953.   d. Originally Veterans Administration.

ried out by private organizations or state and local governments—a practice that increased under the Republican-controlled 104th Congress (1995–1997) that favored devolving power to the states. For example, the federal government pays for the food stamp program, but state governments administer it. The practice of proxy administration masks the number of people who actually rely on the federal bureaucracy for their livelihood. According to one estimate, for every person who works directly for the federal government, as many as four people may work for it indirectly.[15]

Public Attitudes Toward the Bureaucracy

Bureaucracy has a bad reputation. Deserved or not, criticism is heaped on the bureaucracy by Americans from all walks of life. Much of the public harbors an image of small-minded bureaucrats entrenched in minor offices making life miserable for everyone else by issuing petty regulations and generating miles of frustrating red tape. Although the U.S. bureaucracy certainly is not perfect, many of the accusations against it are unjustified.

The media relish stories of bureaucratic foul-ups and wastefulness. Some of the incidents revealed in the press are disturbing; others are ruefully amusing. No taxpayer enjoys reading that the Defense Department purchased some $659 ashtrays and $7,000 coffee makers,[16] and few citizens can be comfortable with the knowledge that the Department of Energy included among millions of declassified documents directions on how to build a hydrogen bomb.[17] On the lighter side, it is hard not to smile on learning that the Department of Health and Human Services sent fifteen chimpanzees to a laboratory to start a chimp breeding program—and that all those chimps were males.[18]

During the last forty years, academics have joined in the chorus of abuse. They tend to castigate the bureaucracy on more general grounds than the media, pointing to organizational problems, policy failures, and excessive political power. One of the first and foremost students of the bureaucracy, German sociologist Max Weber, warned that bureaucracy is "a power instrument of the first order" which can be a threat to democracy.[19]

Politicians also have frequently engaged in bureaucracy bashing. For example, Democratic senator William Proxmire of Wisconsin used his "Golden Fleece Awards" to highlight examples of bureaucratic waste, and Gerald R. Ford and Jimmy Carter included attacks on the bureaucracy in their campaigns for the presidency. In 1993 Vice President Albert Gore Jr. charged that the federal government was "failing the American people."[20] Gore frequently criticized the bureaucracy while promoting the administration's plan to "reinvent government." But no one has surpassed President Ronald Reagan in condemning the federal bureaucracy. His calls to curb the size and spending of the civilian bureaucracy were central to his hallmark pledge to get government "off the backs of the people."

Considering the frequency of assaults on the bureaucracy from these sources, it is hardly surprising that the general public often views the bureaucracy negatively. One observer has called the public fear and dislike of bureaucracy "a raging pandemic."[21] Many citizens view the bureaucracy as inefficient, unresponsive, and out of control, and complaining about the bureaucracy has almost become a national pastime.

One public opinion survey conducted in the early 1970s by Robert L. Kahn et al. showed that the majority of Americans thought government agencies did not treat most people fairly or handle their problems efficiently.[22] Americans also tend to think that federal bureaucrats waste tax money. Sixty-three percent of respondents to a 1992 survey thought bureaucrats wasted "a lot" of money; 33 percent said "some" money was wasted; only 4 percent believed "not very much" money was squandered.[23] In general, many Americans apparently believe that the bureaucracy is not doing its job.

Dislike of the bureaucracy is not universal, however, and some observers have come to its defense. They argue that the U.S. bureaucracy, especially when compared with those of other countries, actually performs pretty well.[24] Mistakes occur, of course, but no organization is totally error-free. Moreover, charges of bureaucratic inefficiency often are based on isolated cases. There also is the question of whether efficiency should be the primary goal of government agencies. For example, the Department of Veterans Affairs could operate more efficiently if it cut some of its programs, but then the services it provides to veterans would not be the same.

In a different vein, the defenders of the bureaucracy contend it has become a scapegoat for many of the problems of modern society. It is a convenient target of criticism because it is big, powerful, hard to change, and relatively anonymous. When people become frustrated with government or feel powerless over their lives, they channel their discontent toward the bureaucracy and thus help to perpetuate the myth that the bureaucracy is the source of problems, not solutions.

The survey conducted by Kahn et al. supports this theory. Although respondents were unhappy with the bureaucracy generally, the overwhelming majority had had satisfactory personal encounters with bureaucratic agencies. These results indicate that people cling to bureaucratic stereotypes despite personal experiences to the contrary. Kahn et al. attribute this to a larger pattern of political attitudes in which Americans are patriotic and happy with their own contacts with government but are generally distrustful of politicians and government agencies.[25] Charles T. Goodsell's analysis of more recent survey results also reveals that most citizens are satisfied with their own experiences with the bureaucracy.[26]

Structure of the Federal Bureaucracy

The federal bureaucracy is extremely complicated. Understanding its place in American life and its relation to the president requires some grasp of its complex structure.

CHARACTERISTICS OF ALL BUREAUCRACIES

All bureaucracies share certain characteristics.[27] Although many people call any large organization a *bureaucracy,* the term properly refers only to entities exhibiting the characteristics described below.

Hierarchy. Each member of a bureaucracy is part of a chain of command, accepting authority from above and exercising authority downward. This hierarchy of authority is vital in performing the large-scale, complex functions usually assigned to bureaucracies. Because each bureaucrat can complete only a small part of the agency's tasks, centralized control is vital in coordinating the work of employees. In general, instruction flows down the hierarchy, and information flows both up and down the chain of command.

Specialization. Bureaucracies have clear divisions of labor. Like a worker on a factory assembly line, each bureaucrat specializes in a limited set of duties and ordinarily becomes an expert in that narrow area. Specific responsibilities usually are developed carefully; in fact, each of the roughly three million employees of the federal bureaucracy has a written job description.[28] This kind of job specialization allows bureaucracies to shoulder greater loads of more complicated work and do it better and more quickly.

Record Keeping. Bureaucracies are designed to function consistently regardless of changes in personnel. Organized files of records (particularly memoranda and details of decisions made and actions taken) help to make this possible. Employees consult agency records to review what has been done in the past, and supervisors use agency records to monitor the work of subordinates. *(See box, Bureaucratic Lingo, right.)*

Rules. Rules serve some of the same purposes as records. They tell each employee what to do and what not to do in certain situations, thereby facilitating bureaucratic consistency and coordination. Because most employees are highly specialized and supervisors are not always available to advise them, they often need to consult rules to know how best to handle situations outside their area of specialization. Unfortunately, because some rules may be unclear or burdensome to follow, they may seem more like annoying red tape than helpful guides.

Impersonal Operation. Bureaucrats strive to handle each business matter objectively, on its merits, rather than emotionally. Such an approach makes the bureaucracy more efficient by keeping employees from becoming mired in the unhappy consequences that sometimes result from bureaucratic decisions, and it ensures a more uniform application of the rules. Thus impersonality increases fairness. A negative effect is the impression of indifference or coldness that impersonality often leaves with members of the public who come into contact with the bureaucracy, especially those who believe the uniqueness of their situations has been ignored.

Personnel Practices. Bureaucratic personnel systems generally are based on two factors: merit (ability to do the job well) and seniority (length of employment). Merit is usually the main requirement for employment by the bureaucracy, with qualifications often measured by competitive examinations. Both merit and seniority play a role in promotions.

Size of Operation. Bureaucracies usually are large. According to scholar Anthony Downs, an organization is large when its highest-ranking leaders know fewer than half its staff members personally.[29] Bureaucracies must be big enough to handle the extensive chores they are given, but their immense size leads to many of the coordination and control problems described in this section. For example, the Defense Department has the gigantic job of providing for U.S. security. Thus as a huge agency—with more than one million civilian employees—it enjoys benefits and suffers problems because of its size.

Types of Functions. Bureaucracies generally perform functions that are not carried out elsewhere in society. The economic free market of private organizations acting primarily in their own interests simply does not provide everything society needs. According to Downs, in democratic societies with free-market economies governments must tackle large societal problems such as pollution; furnish services such as national defense that benefit the entire society; undertake any major redistribution of

BUREAUCRATIC LINGO

Bureaucrats often seem to speak a language of their own. The major characteristic of bureaucratic lingo is its lack of clarity and directness. Many bureaucrats apparently adopt "Smith's Principle" when communicating: "If it can be understood, it's not finished yet."[1] For example, in the wake of the explosion of the space shuttle *Challenger,* which killed seven astronauts, the National Aeronautics and Space Administration (NASA) called the incident an "anomaly."[2] A National Park Service official engaged in some bureaucratic lingo when he termed the service's plan to kill burros in the Grand Canyon (they were eating the vegetation and causing erosion) a "direct reduction."[3] The Central Intelligence Agency (CIA) referred to an extermination of a different kind—assassination—as "termination with extreme prejudice" and termed the less violent activity of illegal break-ins as "uncontested physical searches."[4]

Why do bureaucrats engage in such tortuous use of the language? The principal reason is probably to protect themselves and their agencies by burying unpleasant facts under mounds of barely comprehensible verbiage or disguising them with euphemisms. "Acheson's Rule of the Bureaucracy" (elucidated by Dean Acheson, secretary of state under Truman) says that "a memorandum is written not to inform the reader, but to protect the writer."[5] In the *Challenger* case, NASA's use of euphemisms may have eased slightly the emotional situation for everyone concerned, but it also was probably aimed at protecting whatever remnants of the agency's good public image remained after the accident. Similarly, both the CIA and the Park Service officials gained some small degree of protection from negative public reaction through their use of euphemistic terminology.

The following guidelines for speaking and writing in "bureaucratese" are helpful in deciphering bureaucratic lingo:

1. Use nouns as if they were verbs.

Don't say, *"We gave the department this task";* say instead, *"We tasked the department."*

2. Use adjectives as if they were verbs.

Don't say, *"We put the report in final form";* say instead, *"We finalized the report."*

3. Use several words where one word would do.

Don't say, *"at this point";* say instead, *"at this point in time."*

4. Never use ordinary words where unusual ones can be found.

Don't say you *"made a choice";* say you *"selected an option."*

5. No matter what subject you are discussing, employ the language of sports and war.

Never say *"progress";* say *"breakthrough."* Never speak of a *"compromise";* instead, consider *"adopting a fallback position."*

6. Avoid active verbs.

Never say, *"Study the problem";* say instead, *"It is felt that the problem should be subjected to further study."*[6]

1. Paul Dickson, *The Official Rules* (New York: Delacorte Press, 1978), 170.

2. "Doublespeak at NASA," *Space World,* February 1987, 7.

3. William Safire, *On Language* (New York: Times Books, 1980).

4. Ibid.

5. Quoted in Dickson, *Official Rules,* 1.

6. James Q. Wilson, *American Government: Institutions and Policies,* 2d ed. (Lexington, Mass.: D.C. Heath, 1983), 362.

income, including welfare programs; regulate the economy; protect consumers; provide law and order; and maintain the government itself.[30]

ORGANIZATION OF THE FEDERAL BUREAUCRACY

The day-to-day activities of the U.S. federal bureaucracy, which consists of more than two thousand separate units, receive little public attention. Much of the population, then, does not understand how the bureaucracy is organized.

Types of Agencies

Bureaucratic agencies can be sorted into five categories: departments, independent agencies, government corporations, agencies attached to Congress and the president, and other agencies.

Departments. The fourteen executive, or cabinet, departments compose the first layer of bureaucracy under the president. The heads of these departments (also known as secretaries except in the case of the Justice Department, which is headed by the attorney general) are members of the president's cabinet. Department secretaries and their immediate subordinates are appointed by the president with the approval of the Senate. The departments conduct some of the bureaucracy's most important business and employ about 65 percent of all federal workers.[31] The fourteen executive departments are: Agriculture, Commerce, Defense, Education, Energy, Health and Human Services, Housing and Urban Development, Interior, Justice, Labor, State, Transportation, Treasury, and Veterans Affairs.

Congress determines the number and jurisdictions of cabinet-level departments, but the president can request changes.

FIGURE 35–1 The Government of the United States, 1996

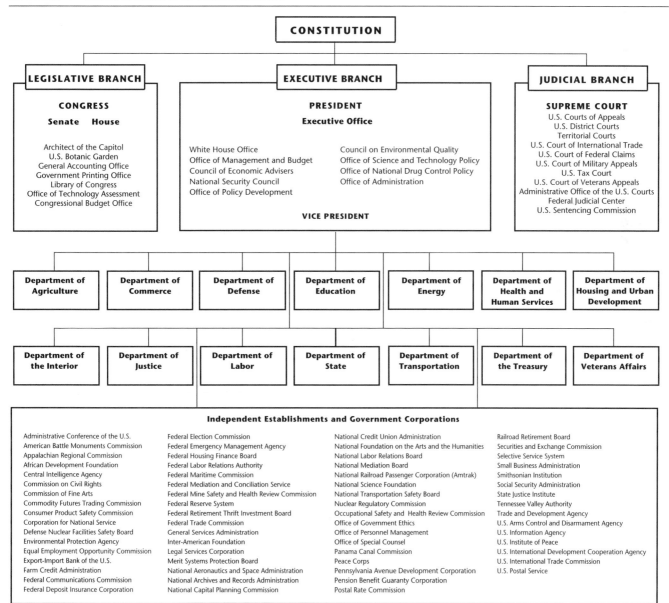

The Departments of State, Treasury, and War were established in 1789 to meet immediate national needs; other departments were created as the nation developed and new needs arose. Some departments—such as Justice and Interior—serve the general needs of the entire country. Others—such as Commerce, Labor, Agriculture, and Veterans Affairs—serve particular segments of society.

Each of the fourteen executive departments is broken down into smaller units—offices, administrations, services, and bureaus—which administer the department's programs. The specific functions of these units vary from department to department. Among these department subunits are the Food Safety and Inspection Service and the Agricultural Marketing Service in the Department of Agriculture, the National Highway Traffic Safety Administration and the Federal Railroad Administration in the Department of Transportation, and the Bureau of African Affairs and the Bureau of International Narcotics Matters in the Department of State. *(See Chapter 29, Cabinet and Executive Departments.)*

Independent Agencies. The approximately sixty independent agencies within the federal bureaucracy, which are roughly equivalent to the department subunits in size and influence, are either independent executive agencies or independent regulatory agencies.[32] Both types exist outside of and independent from the cabinet departments. Agencies are made independent for several reasons. First, such agencies are less tied to the traditional ways of doing things and thus can be more innovative than the executive departments. Second, with their independent status, these agencies are theoretically less susceptible to outside political pressures. And, third, some agencies, such as the National Aeronautics and Space Administration, are independent simply because their missions do not fall naturally within any of the departments.[33]

Independent executive agencies, usually headed by one person who serves at the president's pleasure, perform a single function and report directly to the president. Presidents wield significant influence over independent executive agencies. Such agencies include the Central Intelligence Agency, General Services Administration, and Environmental Protection Agency.

Independent regulatory agencies regulate parts of the private economic sector to protect the public interest. These agencies are usually headed by a bipartisan group—often called a commission or a board—rather than an individual. Commission members, who serve terms of fixed length, are appointed by the president and approved by the Senate, but they report directly to neither. Independent regulatory agencies—including the Federal Communications Commission, Federal Trade Commission, and Securities and Exchange Commission—are designed to operate independently from all three branches of government. *(See Chapter 30, Government Agencies and Corporations.)*

Government Corporations. When confronted with tasks similar to those carried out by private business, the federal government can form a government corporation to take advantage of the rights enjoyed by private corporations. Government corpo-

ABBREVIATIONS FOR BUREAUCRATIC AGENCIES AND CABINET DEPARTMENTS

ACDA	Arms Control and Disarmament Agency
ACIR	Advisory Commission on Intergovernmental Relations
AMTRAK	National Railroad Passenger Corporation
BIA	Bureau of Indian Affairs
CEA	Council of Economic Advisers
CIA	Central Intelligence Agency
CPSC	Consumer Product Safety Commission
DEA	Drug Enforcement Agency
DIA	Defense Intelligence Agency
DOD	Department of Defense
DOE	Department of Energy
DOT	Department of Transportation
EEOC	Equal Employment Opportunity Commission
EOP	Executive Office of the President
EPA	Environmental Protection Agency
FAA	Federal Aviation Administration
FBI	Federal Bureau of Investigation
FCC	Federal Communications Commission
FDA	Food and Drug Administration
FDIC	Federal Deposit Insurance Corporation
FEC	Federal Election Commission
FEMA	Federal Emergency Management Agency
FLRA	Federal Labor Relations Authority
FRB	Federal Reserve Board
FTC	Federal Trade Commission
GAO	General Accounting Office
GSA	General Services Administration
HHS	Department of Health and Human Services
HUD	Department of Housing and Urban Development
INS	Immigration and Naturalization Service
IRS	Internal Revenue Service
NASA	National Aeronautics and Space Administration
NHTSA	National Highway Traffic Safety Administration
NIH	National Institutes of Health
NLRB	National Labor Relations Board
NRC	Nuclear Regulatory Commission
NSC	National Security Council
NSF	National Science Foundation
NTSB	National Transportation Safety Board
OMB	Office of Management and Budget
OPM	Office of Personnel Management
OSHA	Occupational Safety and Health Administration
SBA	Small Business Administration
SEC	Securities and Exchange Commission
SSA	Social Security Administration
TVA	Tennessee Valley Authority
USDA	U.S. Department of Agriculture
USPS	U.S. Postal Service
WHO	White House Office

rations have greater freedom of operation than most other government agencies. They can buy and sell property, borrow money, bring legal suits in their own names (and be sued), earn a profit, and even sell stock. Congress finds this structure appealing because it allows transfer of responsibility to a supposedly nonpartisan body and because the costs of such corporations do not appear in the federal budget.

Like private corporations, government corporations are run by boards of directors. Board members come from both political parties and usually serve long, fixed terms. Some of the best-known government corporations are the U.S. Postal Service, Tennessee Valley Authority, Federal Deposit Insurance Corporation, and Amtrak. *(See Chapter 30, Government Agencies and Corporations.)*

Presidential and Congressional Agencies. The staffs of both the president and Congress have grown so drastically in recent decades that each now has its own supporting bureaucracy. Not surprisingly, these two bureaucracies frequently clash with other parts of the federal bureaucracy. The White House Office within the Executive Office of the President (EOP) is composed of the president's special assistants, legislative liaisons, and press secretaries. The other supporting organizations within the EOP assist the president primarily with policy issues. One of the most notable agencies is the Office of Management and Budget, which constructs the federal budget and assesses the fiscal side of legislation. Other EOP agencies include the National Security Council and Council of Economic Advisers. *(See Chapter 28, Executive Office of the President: Supporting Organizations.)*

Congress employs about eighteen thousand people, who serve on the members' personal staffs, on committee staffs, and in research agencies such as the Library of Congress and the Congressional Budget Office.[34] The General Accounting Office acts as congressional watchdog over federal programs. Other congressional agencies, such as the Government Printing Office, fulfill responsibilities not directly related to policy making.

Other Agencies. Hundreds of advisory committees and other minor boards operate within the federal government. Presidential advisory committees, which can be either temporary or permanent, give expert advice on a particular subject. Presidents like such committees because their creation demonstrates to the public that the administration cares about the problems being examined and because they provide an opportunity to pay political debts with committee appointments. Examples of the many presidential advisory committees include the President's Council on Physical Fitness and Sports, the President's Science Advisory Committee, and the President's Foreign Intelligence Advisory Board.

Many of the other minor boards and commissions sponsored by the federal government have no permanent staff and can only make recommendations. Examples of these organizations, which generally are established for a single purpose, include the Warren Commission, which investigated the 1963 assassination of President John F. Kennedy, the Grace Commission, which in 1984 made recommendations on how to cut the size of the federal government, and the Rogers Commission, which studied and reported on the explosion of the space shuttle *Challenger* in 1986. *(See Chapter 31, Presidential Commissions.)*

Functions of the Bureaucracy

Bureaucratic functions fall into four categories: regulatory, clientele, regional, and housekeeping.

Regulatory. Congress establishes regulatory agencies to oversee and regulate parts of the private economic sector. Regulatory agencies do not provide services as such; instead, they formulate and enforce rules and regulations. Many independent agencies are regulatory. Examples of regulatory agencies are the Federal Trade Commission and the National Labor Relations Board. *(See Chapter 30, Government Agencies and Corporations.)*

Clientele. Clientele agencies address the problems and concerns of a specific segment of society. Although such agencies generally are quite responsive to their target groups, the groups do not always approve of what the agencies do. On the contrary, clientele groups can be some of the agencies' harshest critics. Clientele agencies include the Departments of Agriculture, Labor, Veterans Affairs, and Commerce, as well as the Bureau of Indian Affairs and some independent agencies.

Regional. Some agencies concentrate on specific parts of the country. For example, the Department of Housing and Urban Development devotes most of its attention to the problems of the inner cities, and the Tennessee Valley Authority encourages economic development of the Tennessee Valley region. Other regional agencies are the Mississippi River Commission and the Appalachian Regional Commission.

Housekeeping. Housekeeping agencies serve other government agencies. For example, the General Services Administration supervises most government buildings and oversees contracts for equipment. Another housekeeping agency, the Office of Personnel Management, helps to run the federal personnel system.

FEDERAL PERSONNEL SYSTEM

Employees of the federal civilian bureaucracy are hired either through a merit-based system or by presidential appointment. The debate over merit systems versus patronage (political appointments) is an old one. Advocates of merit systems emphasize the goals of recruiting competent employees, maintaining a fairly stable public workforce, and striving for "neutral competence" in administration. Supporters of patronage, or what used to be called the "spoils system," believe that government works better when elected political leaders appoint bureaucrats who can be counted on for their loyalty and enthusiasm. Although both kinds of systems are used, in practice some elements of each appear in the other.

Merit Systems

Merit-based employment began in 1883 with the passage of the Pendleton Act. This act served as the basis for the merit system until it was modified by the Civil Service Reform Act of 1978. Over 90 percent of all federal bureaucrats work under one of four merit systems: the civil service, the senior executive service, separate merit systems, and the excepted service.

Civil Service. The career civil service system, managed by the Office of Personnel Management (OPM), is the largest merit system, covering three-fifths of federal employees.[35] OPM strives to ensure that employees are hired on the basis of qualifications, promoted on the basis of good performance, and provided with job security. The civil service system revolves around the General Schedule (GS), which classifies positions and sets the pay scale for clerical, administrative, and professional personnel. *(See box, How to Get a Government Job, right.)*

The General Schedule lists fifteen grades, from GS-1 to GS-15. Job type and an employee's qualifications determine at what grade the schedule is entered. Clerical employees are placed in the first four grades, while college graduates usually enter at GS-5, and those with advanced degrees at GS-9 or higher.[36] Steps within each grade are decided by seniority, job performance, and type of skill.

Senior Executive Service. In an effort to make the upper stratum of federal employees more productive and more responsive to the president's policy goals, Congress passed the Civil Service Reform Act of 1978, which moved more than seven thousand civil service employees from the top three GS grades (GS-16 through GS-18) into the Senior Executive Service (SES). Incentives for SES employees include higher pay and eligibility for financial bonuses, but they have less job security than other federal employees and can be transferred fairly easily. The SES has increased the president's influence over the bureaucracy, but some SES members have become discouraged because their salaries have not kept pace with those for similar jobs in the private sector and because of the continued "bureaucrat bashing" by politicians and the media.[37] Today, the SES numbers about eight thousand employees.

Separate Merit Systems. Some federal agencies have their own merit personnel systems, independent of OPM control. About 30 percent of federal bureaucrats work under these systems.[38] Although the specific procedures of the separate systems vary from agency to agency, they are created for some of the same reasons: to make recruitment of professionals easier, to give the agency more freedom in hiring and firing than allowed under the civil service system, and to enable closer screening and supervision of applicants and employees.[39]

Separate systems also add credibility to the notion that employment in these agencies is a career rather than simply a job. Agencies that operate their own personnel systems include the U.S. Postal Service (which has the largest system by far), Department of State (for foreign service officers), Federal Bureau of Investigation, Tennessee Valley Authority, Department of Veterans Affairs, and U.S. Public Health Service.

Excepted Service. Two categories of federal jobs, Schedule A and Schedule B, are excepted from competitive hiring and other merit-based procedures, but very few of the jobs go to political

HOW TO GET A GOVERNMENT JOB

Although there probably are few children who dream of growing up to become federal bureaucrats, some adults find the prospect appealing. Federal employment usually offers job security, good benefits, and, depending on the type of job, reasonably good pay. The vast majority of federal employees fall under merit employment systems, which base hiring, promotion, and firing decisions on qualifications and performance rather than on political connections. *(See "Federal Personnel System," p. 1415, and box, Federal Job Information Available Online, p. 987.)*

The Office of Personnel Management (OPM) oversees the federal government's hiring practices, but it gives some departments and agencies considerable discretion over hiring. Running the government's personnel system is a huge task, even in an era in which the total number of federal jobs is being cut. *(See box, "Reinventing Government," p. 1437.)* Retirements, resignations, firings, and new programs requiring new employees continually create openings in the bureaucratic workforce. In the early 1990s, between fifty thousand and seventy thousand "new hires" of white-collar employees were made annually.[1]

Procedures for getting a federal government job were streamlined somewhat as a result of the Clinton administration's National Performance Review (NPR), but the process is still not simple. Interested persons must first determine what government jobs are open. That information is available to the public twenty-four hours a day, seven days a week through an automated telephone system, an electronic bulletin board accessible by computer modem, and the Internet. In some cities, potential applicants can visit Federal Employment Information Centers in person.

Each job announcement specifies how to apply for that particular job. Procedures vary somewhat from job to job and from agency to agency. The government no longer requires a standard application form for most jobs, but applicants must provide certain information including personal data, educational background, work experience, and other job-related qualifications.[2]

Persons seeking lower-level government jobs usually take written exams that determine their ranking on a roster of applicants (veterans of the U.S. military generally receive bonus points that move them up the list). Applicants for higher-level jobs are typically judged on their resumes. In either case, the OPM usually certifies the top three applicants as qualified for the position. The hiring agency then selects one of those three for the job or asks the OPM to certify someone else.[3]

U.S. citizenship is required to be eligible for most federal jobs. In addition, males over age eighteen who were born after December 31, 1959, must be registered with the Selective Service System or have an exemption to be considered. Federal law also prohibits government employees from appointing, promoting, or recommending their relatives.

1. James W. Fesler and Donald F. Kettl, *The Politics of the Administrative Process* (Chatham, N.J.: Chatham House, 1991), 115.
2. U.S. Office of Personnel Management, *Applying for a Federal Job*, OF 510, September 1994.
3. Fesler and Kettl, *Politics of the Administrative Process*, 115.

appointees. Schedules A and B apply to nonpolicy-making positions that cannot be filled practically using normal civil service system methods. The difference between the two schedules is that applicants for Schedule B jobs must take a noncompetitive exam, and those for Schedule A jobs need not. Many Schedule A employees are lawyers. Treasury Department bank examiners, among others, fall under Schedule B.

Characteristics of Civil Servants. All kinds of people work for the federal bureaucracy. Employees of the merit systems are "ordinary people" in that, in terms of education, sex, race, social background, income, region of origin, and occupation, they reflect the diversity of the American population.[40] (The same cannot be said for presidents, members of Congress, or federal judges, who are overwhelmingly well-educated white males from middle- or upper-class backgrounds.) Furthermore, on most political issues government employees hold views similar to those of the general public.[41] (*See box, The "Typical" Federal Employee, right.*)

The ordinariness of bureaucrats begins to disappear, however, higher up in the civil service ranks. White males hold a disproportionate share of the jobs in the top few grades of the General Schedule.[42] Political partisanship is another difference between bureaucrats and the general public. Civil servants of all ranks generally favor the Democratic over the Republican Party, which is not surprising given Republican attacks on "big government." Whatever the demographic characteristics of bureaucrats, however, there is little evidence to suggest that these characteristics exert much influence on how public employees do their jobs.[43]

Presidential Appointments

The president appoints only a small fraction of the government's employees, but those appointees hold some of the most important jobs in the bureaucracy.

Number and Types of Appointments. Few of the nation's bureaucrats get their jobs through presidential appointment: the president has the authority to appoint only about three thousand of the approximately three million civilian federal workers.[44] Presidential appointments, however, include the high-level policy-making positions. Thus although the number of appointments is relatively small, they provide the president with significant leverage over the bureaucracy.

Presidential appointments fall into three major categories: those authorized by statute, Schedule C jobs, and noncareer senior executives. By law, the president has the power to appoint the secretary of each cabinet department and the secretary's immediate subordinates; federal judges, marshals, and attorneys; ambassadors; and members of certain boards and commissions. In addition, the president appoints the White House staff, fills about ten positions in each major independent agency, and names the heads of some minor agencies. Schedule C lists about sixteen hundred jobs at GS-15 and below in the bureaucracy that the president can use for patronage purposes. And about eight hundred noncareer senior executives act as ad-

---

THE "TYPICAL" FEDERAL EMPLOYEE

What is the typical federal employee really like? According to political scientist Stephen J. Wayne and colleagues, there is no typical civil servant. They were able, however, to pull together a composite portrait from data about federal civilian, full-time, permanent, nonpostal employees:

AGE: 43.2 years
LENGTH OF GOVERNMENT EMPLOYMENT: 14.2 years
EDUCATION: bachelor's degree or more, 36.5 percent
GENDER: male, 56 percent; female, 44 percent
RACE AND NATIONAL ORIGIN: 28.1 percent belong to minorities (16.8 percent African American; 5.6 percent Hispanic; 3.8 percent Asian/Pacific Islander; 1.9 percent Native American)
HANDICAPPED: 7 percent
ANNUAL BASE SALARY: $37,718
AVERAGE GS GRADE: 9.0

Source: Stephen J. Wayne et al., *The Politics of American Government* (New York: St. Martin's Press, 1995), 516.

---

vocates for presidential programs at the upper levels of the bureaucracy.

Selection Process. Although the figure of three thousand presidential appointees seems insignificant when compared with the total number of federal jobs, this number appears much higher when a president faces the task of filling each of these positions. Presidents have long found personnel selection an onerous task. Jimmy Carter articulated his frustration shortly after entering office:

I have learned in my first two and a half weeks why Abraham Lincoln and some of the older Presidents almost went home when they first got to the White House. The handling of personnel appointments, trying to get the right person in the right position at the right time is a very, very difficult question.[45]

Several factors help account for the trouble that presidents often have in deciding on appointees for government posts.[46] Lack of time is a big constraint. Presidents-elect have less than three months between the election and the inauguration not only to search for and recruit people to join the new administration, but also to do all the other things necessary to prepare to take office. To make matters worse, presidents-elect and their staffs often are exhausted during this transition period from the just-concluded electoral campaigns.

The selection process also is hindered by the president's usual compulsion to consider demographic characteristics such as race, sex, geography, religion, and whatever other traits the president believes must be represented among appointees. This constraint persists throughout the president's term in office. Whenever a vacancy occurs, the best-qualified person may be passed over if he or she does not possess the desired demographic characteristics.

Finally, politics influences presidential appointments. The president-elect finds that many of the political IOUs passed out during the campaign are called in during the personnel selection process. Many supporters want either to obtain jobs themselves or to recommend others for positions. Interest groups, members of Congress, and other party loyalists also want a say in the composition of the new administration. The situation becomes even more complicated when the White House and the newly appointed department secretaries do not agree on appointments. The secretaries frequently want control over appointments in their departments, but this hampers presidential efforts to place people in the bureaucracy who will remain loyal to the White House. *(See "Styles and Methods of Appointment," p. 1157, in Chapter 29.)*

Active presidential involvement in the selection process is crucial to its success.[47] Presidents may be tempted to leave this chore mainly to others, but that can lead to long-term trouble. Richard Nixon, for example, ran into personnel difficulties partly because he was not attentive enough to appointments at the beginning of his administration. Like Nixon, Jimmy Carter allowed his cabinet secretaries to choose their immediate subordinates even though they were technically presidential appointees.[48]

In contrast, President Ronald Reagan and his staff devoted much energy to controlling the selection process, placing special emphasis on recruiting officials who agreed with Reagan's political philosophy. As a result, Reagan was able to exercise more control over the bureaucracy than any other modern president.[49] George Bush was concerned more with finding appointees who were professionally competent and loyal to him than with demanding ideological purity.[50]

After his election, Bill Clinton pledged to create a government that "looked like America," and his initial cabinet was quite demographically diverse (although there was a disproportionate number of lawyers).[51] Like Reagan, Clinton had potential appointees carefully scrutinized by the White House staff before offering them jobs, which helps to explain why appointed positions were filled so slowly in the Clinton administration. Clinton's push for diversity as well as his (and the first lady's) personal involvement in the selection process also slowed things down.[52] The Clinton experience continued the trend evident in the last few decades of presidents taking more time to make appointments. The average time from inauguration day taken by a president to fill a position rose from 2.1 months for John Kennedy to 8.1 months for George Bush.[53]

Another factor that can slow the selection process is the requirement that most presidential nominees receive Senate approval before taking office. The Senate usually confirms the president's nominations, but there are exceptions. In 1989 the Senate rejected John G. Tower, Bush's nominee for secretary of defense, over allegations of misconduct in his personal life and conflicts of interest in his professional life. In 1993 Bill Clinton had to drop two potential choices for attorney general, first corporate lawyer Zoë Baird and then federal judge Kimba Wood, when questions arose over their use of illegal immigrants as domestic workers.

"Government of Strangers." Political scientist Hugh Heclo has asserted that the system for making presidential appointments to the executive branch creates a "government of strangers."[54] Appointees are strangers in several respects. The president usually does not know them personally before they are selected, and, other than cabinet members and a few other top administrators, the president does not get to know them well even after their appointment. Political appointees also generally do not know many, if any, of the other appointees who are asked to serve the president.

One reason presidents do not know many of their appointees is that they have been so busy running for office. After his election John Kennedy remarked to an assistant, "For the last four years I spent so much time getting to know people who could help me get elected president that I didn't have time to get to know people who could help me, after I was elected, to be a good president."[55]

Many presidential appointees also are strangers to working in the federal government. Because even those with government experience rarely understand all aspects of their new jobs, virtually all newly appointed political executives spend much of their time learning the ropes. This learning process generally takes from twelve to eighteen months—a long time considering that the average upper-level presidential appointee keeps the job only about two years.[56] Such a rapid turnover prevents the appointees from ever being totally settled and ensures that the federal bureaucracy remains, at least partially, a government of strangers.

Characteristics of Presidential Appointees. Most presidential appointees have economically and socially elite backgrounds.[57] They usually are white, male, middle-aged, affluent urbanites, who are graduates of prestigious schools and members of high-status occupations. Most appointees to the cabinet or subcabinet (deputy secretaries and assistant secretaries in the cabinet departments) have had some experience working for the federal government.[58] Thus, although many presidential appointees have no government experience, those placed in the most senior positions usually do. The executive branch, then, is run mainly by people knowledgeable about the government.

Presidential appointees are drawn from many different sources. Some, as noted, are former politicians or government officials; others hail from business, universities, think tanks, law firms, or labor unions. More recent presidents have tended to look for expertise or administrative experience rather than political prominence in their appointees. For the most part, once appointees finish their stint in government, they go back to private life and do not return to government service.[59] This contradicts the commonly held belief that the government is largely controlled by men and women who rotate in and out of public office.

Bureaucratic Policy Making

For many years the study of public administration in America was dominated by the notion, espoused by Woodrow Wilson and other political scientists, that politics—the process of deciding what public policy should be—and administration—the process of carrying out those policy decisions—were clearly separable. Within this scenario, the bureaucracy existed solely to implement the policies made by elected officials. Although such a description may have been fairly accurate a hundred years ago, the modern American bureaucracy helps to form public policy and to execute it. One reason for this change is the large role played by the federal government in contemporary American life and the tremendous government workload this role generates. Today the president and Congress cannot possibly make all policy decisions alone.

The organization of the federal government also promotes bureaucratic policy making. Because of their profound fears of concentrated power, the Framers of the Constitution deliberately created a highly fragmented system of government. Not only do the three branches of the federal government check each other, but the state governments also check the federal government. The political party system that has developed in the United States does little to counter this constitutionally induced fragmentation. U.S. political parties—loose coalitions unable to impose much discipline on their members—generally are more concerned with winning elections than with generating specific policy proposals. The fragmentation of the American political system thus means that there is no central control of public policy and that numerous political players—including the federal bureaucracy—can shape policy.[60]

BUREAUCRATIC TASKS

The kinds of tasks assigned to the federal bureaucracy also strengthen its influence on policy making. Most government programs tackle extremely complex problems, and large organizations usually are needed to run the programs. For example, preservation of the environment requires grappling with many difficult and often complex issues; thus the Environmental Protection Agency must be large enough to do so. Program size alone can present formidable challenges; the Social Security Administration, for example, processes about 39 million checks each month.[61] Public programs also demand expert knowledge, and the federal bureaucracy employs a wide array of specialists to supply this knowledge.

Despite the popular belief that the bureaucracy moves at a snail's pace, it can respond rapidly when the need for a new policy arises. For example, the U.S. Department of Agriculture quickly issued new guidelines for cooking meat in response to the many cases of food poisoning in 1993 reportedly linked to the tainted beef served by a popular restaurant chain. And whenever an airliner crashes, the National Transportation Safety Board (NTSB) immediately launches an investigation. The bureaucracy, then, is designed to meet such requirements of public policy making and implementation, and it can exert great influence in doing so.

The federal bureaucracy may participate in all stages of setting and implementing public policy, but its main job continues to be that of implementing policy. The bureaucracy is able to exercise considerable discretion in the implementation of most policies because the laws passed by Congress are often quite vague. In general, such laws express the goals of Congress and leave it up to the bureaucracy to find the best means of achiev-

Investigators from the National Transportation Safety Board (NTSB) promptly investigate every aircraft accident. Here, NTSB officials inspect the wreckage of a test aircraft in February 1995 to determine why it crashed.

ing them. The less explicit the law, the greater is the bureaucratic influence on the policy.

Bureaucratic agencies write specific rules and regulations to implement laws passed by Congress. For example, Congress passed the Clean Air Act in 1990 but gave the Environmental Protection Agency the responsibility to write and enforce the specific air quality standards. About two thousand federal agencies have rule-making powers.[62] Congress first established the process for bureaucratic rule making in the Administrative Procedures Act of 1946. Today the process includes announcing proposed new regulations in the *Federal Register,* soliciting public comments and holding hearings on the proposed regulations, researching the likely effects of the regulations, and consulting with other government officials and agencies. After the new regulations are adopted, they are published in the *Federal Register.*[63] Agency rules carry the force of law unless overturned by Congress or the courts.

Lack of time is a major reason that most of the laws passed by Congress are vague. Congress considers hundreds of bills each year, and it simply does not have time, even with the help of staff, to write laws specific enough to fit every potential situation. Congress also lacks the expert knowledge required to construct highly technical programs. Even if Congress could produce more specific legislation, the outcome might be little improved; the bureaucratic discretion accompanying vague legislation probably leads to better policy. The bureaucracy can respond to societal changes affecting policy, and make the appropriate programmatic alterations, more quickly and more easily than Congress.

SELF-INTEREST AT WORK

According to political scientist Morris P. Fiorina, the growth of bureaucratic policy-making power is based on self-interest. Fiorina has contended that the present political system owes its evolution to members of Congress, bureaucrats, and voters, who have, over the years, pursued their self-interests. Members of Congress gear their behavior toward achieving reelection, which is their foremost goal. Typical bureaucrats want to see the size and power of their agency increase, which in turn enhances their own status and power. Finally, voters want to get as many benefits as possible from government for the least possible cost.[64]

Congress engages in three basic kinds of activities: (1) developing and considering legislation and law making; (2) securing government benefits for members' home districts (so-called pork-barrel projects); and (3) helping constituents who have problems with the federal government or who request some other kind of assistance (casework). Fiorina has argued that because so many members of Congress are interested primarily in getting reelected, they tend to devote more time and energy to pork barrel and casework activities—from which they reap greater political benefits—at the expense of law making.

Law making is less appealing to the reelection-minded member for two reasons. First, legislation is often controversial, and

any stand on divisive issues can upset voters and thus cost the member support in the election. Second, even if the legislation is popular, it is hard to take personal credit for it when hundreds of other people also were involved in its passage. Pork barrel and casework efforts, however, present neither difficulty. These tasks are rarely controversial, and the people who benefit not only know who provided the help but also usually express their gratitude at the polls. Such gratitude may even withstand a severe political crisis. For example, Democratic representatives Gerry E. Studds and Barney Frank of Massachusetts have been reelected despite highly publicized scandals involving sex. And in 1994 three of the four members of Congress running for reelection while under indictment won their races.

The ambiguity of many laws passed by Congress also serves the interests of individual members of Congress. Lawmakers can claim credit for having passed a law to solve a problem, but they also can blame the bureaucracy if constituents are unhappy with the way the law is executed. Ironically, such an arrangement gives legislators more opportunities to do casework for constituents as complaints arise about the law's implementation.

The bureaucracy is a willing partner in this arrangement because it satisfies bureaucrats' drive for more power. Vague laws enable federal agencies to decide the specifics of programs and therefore to exercise tremendous power in policy making. Moreover, the bureaucracy expands as Congress, in its zeal to gain political benefits, continues to enact imprecise laws that must be carried out by the bureaucracy. The outcome, observed Fiorina, is that "more and more bureaucrats promulgate more and more regulations and dispense more and more money."[65]

Most voters are pleased with the system because they benefit from it, and even those concerned about government spending seldom hold individual members of Congress responsible for the overall pattern of federal government expenditures. In general, then, the system may serve the immediate self-interests of legislators, bureaucrats, and the voting public, but "the long-term welfare of the United States is no more than an incidental by-product."[66]

Not all scholars subscribe to Fiorina's view. Political scientist Arthur Maass, for example, has found Congress to be a responsible and responsive political institution, which works for the common good of the American people. He has argued, moreover, that Congress provides a valuable forum for the discussion of different points of view, including those of interest groups, and the generation of new political proposals.[67]

Bureaucratic Power

The federal bureaucracy wields considerable power and can be, depending on the situation, one of the president's primary allies or chief rivals in government and politics. Not all parts of the bureaucracy enjoy the same clout, however. For example, the Selective Service System does not have nearly as much influence as the Department of Defense. Understanding the sources and limits of bureaucratic power is crucial to understanding why the bureaucracy in general is powerful and why certain federal agencies are more powerful than others. Bureaucratic power is one of the key variables in the relationship between the bureaucracy and the president.

SOURCES OF BUREAUCRATIC POWER

Bureaucratic power springs from two kinds of sources: internal and external. Because no two agencies are exactly alike, no two will draw the same amount of power from the same sources. An agency's specific characteristics largely determine the extent of its power, but it can take certain actions to expand its power.

Internal Sources

Sources of power inside a bureaucratic agency itself include the agency's expertise, control of information, size and complexity, inertia, leadership, cohesion, and popular appeal.

Expertise. Many of today's political issues are so technically complex that only experts can fully understand them. For example, the intricacies of defense issues such as the quality of advanced weapons systems and of environmental concerns such as the depletion of the ozone layer are beyond the comprehension of most people. Thus citizens, and in turn their political leaders, look to bureaucracy for such expertise.

The federal government employs tens of thousands of professionals—including engineers, architects, physicians, scientists, and lawyers—thereby bringing tremendous expertise to the bureaucracy.[68] Because Americans generally hold professionals in high regard, professionals heighten an agency's prestige. Bureaucratic agencies employ specialists in the technical areas within their purview. The Department of Agriculture, for example, employs agronomists, soil scientists, and economists, among other experts. Similarly, the State Department is home to experts on countries and issues vital to U.S. foreign policy. Unlike members of Congress, who are confronted with dozens of issues at the same time, the experts working for the bureaucracy can devote their complete attention to a single project.

Because the agency experts usually are able to generate effective public policy, or at least policy more effective than that devised by nonexperts, political leaders seek their advice when making policy decisions. Experienced politicians realize that they can be saved from embarrassing policy and political errors by consulting with the agency experts.

The respect accorded bureaucrats by politicians enhances the credibility, prestige, and power of their agencies. Despite the frequent antibureaucracy rhetoric by members of Congress and other politicians, they like and fund bureaucratic agencies that produce good results. Indeed, a kind of cycle is formed: bureaucratic experts study the issues and reach sound conclusions; politicians seek bureaucratic advice and recognize its expertise; agencies parlay their increased credibility into more power, which they use to maintain and develop their expertise; and the role of the agency experts in government decision making expands. To take one example, experts in the Environmental Pro-

tection Agency advise Congress on the technical aspects of legislation for pollution control and other complex environmental issues. Each time Congress accepts EPA's advice, the agency's credibility and influence are enhanced, which in turn generally leads to increased political support for the agency. EPA takes advantage of that support to expand its expertise—and thus its role in environmental policy making.

Control of Information. Information is the raw material of politics, central to the decision-making process. Thus control of information can greatly influence policy. Largely because of their technical expertise, bureaucratic agencies are asked regularly to advise political leaders on policy issues. The information and recommendations passed along by the agencies shape what comes out of the political decision-making process by shaping much of what goes into it.

From an agency's standpoint, the ideal situation is one in which the agency has a monopoly on the information about a particular subject, making that agency an indispensable participant in policy making in its area of interest. That situation rarely occurs, however, since information on most issues is widely available from other bureaucratic agencies, universities, interest groups, and congressional staff, among others. Generally, the less available the outside information, the greater is the influence of the agency. The Central Intelligence Agency, for example, often enjoys considerable influence because it frequently has information not available from other sources.

The large number of professionals working in the bureaucracy makes the information it provides both more credible and easier to control. The credibility of such information stems from its stamp of professional approval, especially from highly trusted professionals such as physicians and scientists (lawyers and economists, among others, are somewhat less revered). Its control is facilitated by its extremely technical nature or its cryptic jargon, making it unintelligible to the lay public. Bureaucratic professionals can then control the flow of information simply by deciding how much (or how little) of their work to explain to the public.

Natural scientists have enjoyed remarkable bureaucratic success because the sensational scientific achievements of the last few decades—from discovering a vaccine for polio to sending a man to the moon—seem all the more impressive to a public that does not understand how these feats were accomplished. Political scientist Francis E. Rourke has argued that agencies prosper most when they produce benefits that the public understands and appreciates via methods that it cannot fathom.[69] The National Science Foundation and NASA (at times) have fit this description.

When decision makers have preexisting notions about a policy issue, bureaucrats can appear to be influential by supplying the decision makers with information and advice that match those preconceptions. In fact, politicians ordinarily choose advisers with attitudes similar to their own. This dangerous practice can encourage narrow-mindedness, and presidents are well advised to seek information from as many different sources as possible. President Franklin Roosevelt, for example, went to great lengths to get many separate opinions. Bill Clinton also was known for seeking many different opinions before making decisions. Whatever advice experts provide, the public usually accepts presidential policy decisions more readily when the policy is perceived to be based on the information and recommendations of experts.

Size and Complexity. The size and complexity of the federal bureaucracy increase its power and autonomy by making it difficult for the president, Congress, and the courts to exert control over it. About three million federal civilian employees work in hundreds of separate departments, agencies, offices, corporations, and commissions. They spend billions of taxpayer dollars and produce thousands of pages of rules and regulations each year. The federal bureaucracy pervades American society.

In addition to its sheer enormity, the bureaucracy is very complicated. Its functions are highly complex, and its overall organization and overlapping jurisdictions can be perplexing, making it hard to determine which agency is responsible for which matters. For example, the State Department, Defense Department, and National Security Council all participate in foreign policy decisions, as do other agencies, depending on the specific issue. When Jimmy Carter set out to create a separate Department of Education, he discovered that the responsibility for education was distributed throughout the bureaucracy; the Defense Department, for example, handled the education of military dependents stationed overseas.

Another characteristic complicating the bureaucracy is the interdependence of its many constituent parts—the goals and actions of one agency affect other agencies. For example, attempts to reduce America's reliance on imported oil led to the encouragement of practices such as the increased burning of wood and coal, which is contrary to the environmental goals of fighting air and water pollution.

The dispersion of the bureaucracy also hampers outside control. Although the political actors interested in managing the bureaucracy are concentrated in the Washington, D.C., area, federal offices are scattered all over the country. Bureaucrats must go where their services are needed, and their presence around the country gives them some protection from outside intervention.

Inertia. Bureaucratic inertia is an internal source of power for the same reason that large size and complexity are internal sources of power—inertia makes outside management of the bureaucracy extremely difficult. It is hard to spur bureaucracies to take new action and equally challenging to stop bureaucratic routines once they have begun. Rourke has expressed this phenomenon in what he calls the "celebrated law" of bureaucratic inertia: "Bureaucracies at rest tend to stay at rest, and bureaucracies in motion tend to stay in motion."[70] Inertia results from several bureaucratic characteristics, including reliance on traditional policies and methods, employees' desire for security, and the potential clash between new policies and the interests of individual bureaucrats and their agencies.

Bureaucratic inertia frustrates presidents, who have a limited time in office and generally want to act quickly and dramatically. Presidents seldom have the patience to wait for the desired changes to pass through the exasperatingly slow and incremental bureaucratic process. The deliberate movement of the bureaucracy sometimes can benefit the president, however, by providing time to reconsider possibly rash decisions. For example, while the military bureaucracy slowly prepared to execute President Nixon's 1969 orders for an air strike against North Korea in retaliation for its destruction of an American plane, Nixon changed his mind.

Momentum—the tendency for bureaucratic agencies to continue established programs—also restricts presidential control. Agencies want to maintain their programs, even if they no longer are productive, to protect their employees and budgets. In fact, much bureaucratic activity is mandated by law and cannot be easily changed by the president. In recent years, 75 percent or more of the federal budget has gone to relatively "uncontrollable" expenditures—including entitlement programs, interest on the national debt, national defense, and contractual obligations—that the government is virtually required to fund. The president has little room for maneuvering with so much of the bureaucracy's time and resources already committed.

In contrast to the annoying effects that it has on presidents, bureaucratic inertia does not bother permanent civil servants; they can afford to be patient in the pursuit of their goals. Bureaucrats also benefit from the small but steady growth characteristic of bureaucratic momentum, which eventually will increase their agency's size significantly.

Momentum can lead to bad public policy, however. Some scholars have argued that America's deep involvement in the Vietnam War resulted partly from the incremental steps taken by the bureaucratic agencies assigned to oversee America's efforts in Southeast Asia.

Leadership. Another determinant of a bureaucratic agency's power is the quality of its leadership. More than any other individual, an agency's leader affects that agency's power. Whether an appointee or a career civil servant, the leader must exercise a variety of political skills if the agency is to thrive. No one exemplifies the importance of an agency leader better than J. Edgar Hoover, who molded the Federal Bureau of Investigation (FBI) into a potent political force during his nearly fifty-year reign as FBI director.

Leaders of government agencies have responsibilities both inside and outside their agencies. Duties inside their agencies include building up internal sources of bureaucratic power such as expertise, control of information, and cohesion. Leaders also must supervise the daily operations of their agencies, which includes overseeing the management of programs and settling disputes. One of the most vital functions of a leader is to create and maintain enthusiasm and commitment to common goals among agency employees. One reason Anne Gorsuch Burford failed dismally as head of the Environmental Protection Agency early in the Reagan administration was her disastrous effect on employees' morale. EPA careerists became dispirited largely because they perceived Burford as hostile to the agency's mission—a perception based on her probusiness record on environmental issues and her voluntary acceptance of cuts in EPA's budget and personnel while she was head of the agency.

The primary outside goal of agency leaders is to generate political support for their agencies, especially from the president and Congress. A leader's own reputation plays a crucial role in this effort. An agency head who is widely respected and trusted finds the job of gaining support much easier than an unpopular chief. For example, David Stockman's reputation for expertise and candor as the head of the Office of Management and Budget in the Reagan administration helped that agency take a prominent place in the federal budgeting process.

Relations between agency leaders and the president become tricky when the president's policy desires clash with the best interests of the agency. Much to the dismay of the president, agency heads generally place their interests and those of their agencies first. Since the president can be a powerful ally (or foe), effective agency leaders try to emphasize how their agency is helping to fulfill presidential goals and work to minimize the frequency and severity of clashes with the occupant of the Oval Office.

In dealing with Congress, leaders of federal agencies must be sensitive to the electoral needs of its members. This entails avoiding actions that could embarrass legislators in their districts and providing quick assistance when they intercede in the bureaucracy in behalf of a constituent with a problem. Agency leaders gain influence over members of Congress by mobilizing political support for their agencies in members' districts. This task calls for effective communication and public relations skills. Hoover's legendary success at the FBI was partly attributable to his genius at publicity and his ability to generate public support for his agency. Thus few elected officials were willing to criticize him.

Much of a leader's external success also depends on the image he or she projects. Although the nature of the particular agency has much to do with the leader's image—the director of the Peace Corps, for example, starts out with an inherently better public image than the commissioner of the Internal Revenue Service—the individual's personality and leadership skills make a difference.

Finally, agency leaders must carefully balance their inside and outside functions. Sometimes the things done in one sphere can be detrimental in the other.

Cohesion. Cohesion is the commitment felt by bureaucrats to their agency and its goals. Employees who strongly believe in the mission of their agency will generally work harder at their jobs. This sense of cohesion with the agency means not only that employees will accept longer working hours when necessary, but also that they will apply greater dedication and imagination to their jobs. Harder working employees improve an agency's effectiveness, which in turn enhances the agency's political position and power.

Agencies promote cohesion by carefully recruiting employees who have values or interests similar to those of the agency. Job applicants themselves assist this process by seeking employment in agencies with values that appeal to them. For example, an ecology-minded applicant might well be attracted to the Environmental Protection Agency, while a job seeker interested in consumer rights might gravitate toward the Federal Trade Commission. Agencies also strive to increase their cohesion by conducting orientation programs for new employees as well as by informal socialization into the ways of the organization.

Cohesion comes more easily to some agencies than to others. Agencies that perform clearly identifiable, emotionally attractive functions such as EPA, FBI, the Marine Corps, and the Peace Corps have a natural advantage in cultivating cohesion. Other agencies are not so fortunate. As one scholar has wryly commented, slogans such as "the General Accounting Office is looking for a few good accountants" or "the few, the proud, the letter carriers" are less than inspirational.[71]

Popular Appeal. An agency's popular appeal is an internal source of power that affects its political clout and its recruitment of prospective employees. Such appeal helps agencies to garner public support—which translates into political clout—and it allows them to develop cohesion.

The functions of some agencies make them inherently more appealing than others. NASA is an excellent example of an agency that traditionally has profited from popular appeal. The glamorous and exciting business of space exploration captures the attention and imagination of the public in a way that few other bureaucratic activities can. For years, NASA benefited from hefty budgets partly because of its popular support. The president and Congress, ever sensitive to the preferences of voters, provided those budgets more willingly because of the agency's popularity. NASA's case also illustrates, however, that appeal can be short-lived. The comparative lack of public interest in the space shuttle, NASA's major program during most of the 1970s and 1980s, coupled with the explosion of the *Challenger* in 1986 and other problems, tarnished the space agency's appeal and weakened its political power.

External Sources

External sources of bureaucratic power are outside the agency itself but they are within the political arena in which the agency operates. External sources of power include the president, other bureaucratic agencies, Congress, interest groups, public opinion, and legal protection.

The President. Although the president and the bureaucracy clash frequently, the president may at times actively support bureaucratic agencies and their goals. Presidential support is one of the most valuable sources of bureaucratic power. Agencies and individuals blessed with presidential favor enjoy a distinct advantage over those without such status. The Central Intelligence Agency (CIA), having been on both sides of that fence, can attest to the importance of presidential support. In 1961 the

CIA lost a great deal of standing and political power when, because of its role in the Bay of Pigs fiasco, it lost the support of President Kennedy.

Presidential support of an agency comes in two forms: diffuse and specific. A president provides diffuse support by approving and backing the general functions and goals of an agency. For example, through his vigorous promotion of the "War on Poverty" Lyndon Johnson gave strong diffuse support to the agencies that helped the needy. And Ronald Reagan's ardent commitment to building up America's national defense lent crucial diffuse support to the Department of Defense.

Presidential advocacy of an agency's particular proposal or program is specific support. Although this kind of support is less common than diffuse support, it tends to be quite potent. Presidents seldom give specific support to bureaucratic agencies because they simply do not have the time to become deeply involved in the bureaucracy's business. Intervention is usually reserved for matters of particular personal interest. For example, President Reagan's dogged support of the Strategic Defense Initiative (dubbed "Star Wars") represented a deep personal commitment to that program.

Agencies that work closely with the president and the White House staff, such as the State Department, have the best chance of gaining presidential support, either diffuse or specific, simply because of regular contact. By giving special emphasis to programs that forward the president's policy objectives or by administering programs in ways favored by the president, other agencies can try, however, to win the president's backing. For example, several agencies tried to gain favor with President Carter by stressing managerial efficiency, one of Carter's goals. Agencies seeking presidential support also try to avoid public conflict with the president.

Other Bureaucratic Agencies. Agencies with common interests and goals often find it mutually advantageous to join forces in pursuing their shared objectives—the larger and more influential the coalition, the greater the chance for political success. For example, several agencies—among them, the Department of the Interior, Department of Agriculture, and Department of Defense—joined NASA in pushing for approval and support of the space shuttle program because they all wanted the regular and inexpensive means of putting satellites into orbit that the program promised.

Some agencies make stronger allies than others. For agencies located within a larger department, it is always useful to have the backing of agencies higher up the departmental chain of command. This is especially true in departments where authority is centralized in the upper echelons of management. One agency that can be a powerful ally for any other agency is the Office of Management and Budget (OMB), which has considerable influence. OMB constructs the president's annual budget request and holds internal hearings to determine budget levels for federal agencies. Because Congress rarely appropriates funds in excess of OMB's recommendations, OMB plays a large part in deciding how much money an agency gets every year. And, not least, all agency requests for additional authority that require congressional approval must be cleared first by OMB.

Other agencies also can be quite helpful. Agencies with strong ties to either the president, such as the Treasury and Justice Departments, or to Congress, such as the Department of Veterans Affairs and the Army Corps of Engineers, make especially good allies. Agencies that provide services to other bureaucratic agencies also can be useful friends. The Office of Personnel Management, for example, oversees the federal merit employment system and thus can affect an agency's recruitment and retention of employees. The General Services Administration, which supervises government buildings and grounds, also provides services essential to the comfort and efficiency of agencies.

Despite the possible benefits of interagency alliances, agencies tend to enter them cautiously since each organization generally views others as potential rivals. Ironically, agencies that share the most interests also are the ones most likely to fight over jurisdictions and money. Thus alliances usually are of brief duration. For example, the army, navy, and air force all profit from higher defense spending and work together to help support such spending, but among themselves they maintain an intense and long-standing rivalry.

Congress. Congress is an important external source of bureaucratic power because it controls two of an agency's most vital resources: authority and money. By passing the laws that create, reorganize, or destroy agencies and that stipulate what their functions and authority will be, Congress has the power to shape the bureaucracy at the most basic level. Congressional command over the budget also exerts tremendous influence. Although all agencies must have some congressional support, those without much backing from other external sources are particularly dependent on it.

Agencies want not only support from Congress as a whole, but also the assistance of individual members of Congress. A member of Congress is one of the best friends an agency can have because legislators more readily accept advice from colleagues than from outsiders. Agencies are especially fortunate when some members of Congress also belong to their organization. For example, the armed services usually have a few lawmakers in their reserve units, and these lawmaker/reservists are especially sensitive to the needs of their respective services. Agencies that exert a great deal of influence in particular legislative districts often succeed in gaining the support of the congressional representatives of those districts. The Department of Agriculture, for example, can rely on help from rural legislators.

The congressional committee structure makes some members more important to agencies than others. Because much of the work of Congress is handled by committees and subcommittees that have jurisdiction over certain policy areas, bureaucrats most need the support of members who serve on the committees that oversee their agency. For the most part, committee members enthusiastically support the agencies under their jurisdiction. Exceptions to this rule are the House and Senate Appropriations Committees, which tend to be concerned with controlling spending and are therefore more skeptical of agency requests.

Agencies ordinarily receive support from congressional committees with ease because, among other reasons, members of Congress are assigned to committees on the basis of their backgrounds and the nature of their constituencies. For example, a member who worked as a banker before entering politics might be appointed to the banking committee, and a member representing a district with areas of great natural beauty or particular natural resources might serve on a committee dealing with the environment. In either case, the member probably will be predisposed toward favoring the proposals of agencies working in those areas because the areas interest the member.

Agencies ensure good relations with Congress by responding quickly to requests made by legislators for information or for help on any problems that legislators' constituents may have with the agency. Agencies also emphasize programs known to interest particular legislators. They may even try to anticipate the political needs and policy preferences of members of Congress and then act accordingly. In general, agencies try to do whatever they can to maintain and increase their congressional support.

Interest Groups. An agency also may receive political support from private interest groups concerned with issues falling within the agency's mandate. For example, the Environmental Protection Agency may receive support from the National Wildlife Federation, the Sierra Club, and manufacturers of pollution control equipment.

Because bureaucratic agencies and interest groups each command power and resources valuable to the other, their relationship revolves around mutually beneficial trade-offs. On the one hand, an agency's biggest strength is its control over government programs that affect the goals of interest groups. On the other hand, interest groups have political resources that agencies need to build and keep power. Thus a general pattern of cooperation is formed: the agency, by listening to the interest group's opinions and providing it with access to the agency's decision makers, allows the interest group to participate in the government's decision-making process, and in return the interest group gives the agency political support. Specific deals usually are not made; instead, the process is one of long-term, implicit bargaining. This kind of relationship between agencies and interest groups is exemplified by the stable, mutually beneficial relations maintained between the Nuclear Regulatory Commission (NRC) and nuclear plant operators. The NRC consults the operators on regulation of the nuclear plants, particularly on an issue of vital concern to plant operators—when plants must be shut down. In return for this access to the agency's decision-making process, operators give the NRC valuable political support.

Interest groups provide agencies with many political services. These include acting as political cheerleaders, heralding the agency's accomplishments, and defending it against attackers; providing the agency with both technical data and news of the political situation; and pressuring other political actors, including the president and Congress, to support the agency.

Some interest groups pack more political punch than others. Groups whose members are dispersed geographically, such as the American Association of Retired Persons (AARP), have influence in more congressional districts and therefore enjoy more political clout than groups whose members are concentrated in a single area. Groups with highly cohesive memberships dedicated to the group's goals and willing to work to achieve them—the National Rifle Association (NRA) is one example—also have an advantage. Prestige is another factor. Groups whose members are generally respected, such as doctors or scientists, fare better than others. Finally, groups that are organized efficiently and understand how the political system works tend to succeed more easily. The National Education Association (NEA), which represents teachers nationwide, is such a group. Well organized, from the national entity to the many state and local affiliates, with a great deal of political savvy and with a committed membership, the NEA was in the forefront of the successful political battles to establish a separate Department of Education in 1979 and to block President Reagan's attempt to abolish that department a few years later.

Public Opinion. Public opinion constitutes the greatest external bureaucratic power because it underlies virtually all sources of political power in a democratic society. Politicians and the government respond when the American general public evinces an opinion strongly enough. A bureaucratic agency that enjoys strong public support can take primary control of its actions, at least as long as the support lasts.

Unfortunately for the agencies, however, the public rarely becomes enthused about bureaucratic issues. The vast majority of Americans are too busy leading their own lives and worrying about their own problems to be concerned about the bureaucracy. Even when a particular bureaucratic activity is publicized, many people do not understand it. For example, one survey of the public found that only 30 percent claimed to understand the functions of the Securities and Exchange Commission.[72] (The survey did not say, however, how many actually did.) Other agencies were more familiar, but the point is clear.

Even the lesser-known agencies occasionally receive temporary bursts of publicity and public attention. For example, the Nuclear Regulatory Commission was fairly obscure to the general public until the 1979 nuclear accident at Three Mile Island in Pennsylvania, as was the Bureau of Alcohol, Tobacco, and Firearms before its 1993 raid on the Branch Davidian cult compound in Waco, Texas. Similarly, as the problem of illegal drugs has climbed higher on the national agenda, the Drug Enforcement Administration has achieved greater public recognition. These episodes of public attention can be quite brief, however, and most recognized agencies sink back into relative obscurity after the crisis that precipitated the publicity has passed.

When the public has no definite opinion about a specific agency, its attitude toward the agency's overall mandate becomes especially important. For example, during the peak of the environmental protection movement the budget of the Environmental Protection Agency grew dramatically. Likewise, during the late 1970s and early 1980s growing public approval of defense spending led to significantly larger military budgets. Because the public tends to support certain bureaucratic functions over others, agencies performing the favored functions are more likely to generate public support. Opinion polls indicate that the public backs spending on education, health care, crime control, treatment for drug addiction, environmental protection, and Social Security much more strongly than spending on foreign aid, space exploration, and welfare.[73]

Agencies may try to mobilize public opinion in their behalf by tying the agency and its programs to the kinds of government activities that the public usually supports; the FBI succeeded in doing just that by capturing the public interest through a pattern of dramatic action, and the U.S. Postal Service used a public relations campaign to spread its message in the mid-1990s. Moreover, many agencies have created home pages on the World Wide Web to spread information about themselves to the public. Whatever an agency's efforts, however, often the only members of the public paying close attention to it are those directly affected by its actions. Even agencies that manage to win public support should not rely on it too heavily as it is apt to change; the recent decline in support for space exploration and NASA illustrates this phenomenon.

Legal Protection. An agency's legal position, the final source of bureaucratic power, usually protects it from many kinds of political attacks. Laws passed by Congress establishing an agency's functions, authority, and place within the government cannot be changed without additional congressional action. The president and other political elites may try to control the bureaucracy through a variety of methods, but they must act within these legal constraints.

Some agencies have more secure legal positions than others. For example, the president can exert greater influence over agencies within the Executive Office of the President than over most independent agencies. To prevent sudden and potentially disruptive shifts in policy, independent agencies that regulate parts of the economy—such as the Federal Reserve Board and the Securities and Exchange Commission—are granted substantial legal protection.

The bureaucracy's various merit employment systems provide a great deal of legal protection. *(See "Federal Personnel System," p. 1415.)* In addition to its other functions, the merit system is designed to give bureaucrats job security. Employees under any one of the federal merit systems—more than 90 percent of all civilian employees—are protected from being fired for solely partisan political reasons. The days of the spoils system are over, and the result is a more professional, independent bureaucracy.

Under J. Edgar Hoover, the FBI made effective use of legal protection as a source of bureaucratic power. Although the FBI is part of the Justice Department, Hoover ensured that the statutes governing his agency allowed it considerable autonomy

J. Edgar Hoover, director of the Federal Bureau of Investigation from 1924 to 1972, built the agency's power and influence to unprecedented heights. Hoover often abused his power, however, by collecting intelligence information, often through wiretaps and surveillance, for political as opposed to law enforcement purposes.

within the department. He also ensured that the laws setting out the FBI's functions gave it tasks that would fatten its record of solved crimes, such as recovering stolen cars and catching bank robbers, but not messier jobs such as drug enforcement and fighting organized crime. These and other laws governing the FBI, including the one that enabled the agency to establish its own personnel system, have given the agency tremendous legal protection and therefore have made it more powerful.

LIMITS TO BUREAUCRATIC POWER

Just as bureaucratic agencies draw power from many diverse internal and external sources, they must act within the limits imposed by numerous internal and external political forces. Several sources of bureaucratic power also can act as limits to that power.

Internal Limits

In a sense, the most basic internal constraint facing agencies springs from their internal dynamics, which shape bureaucratic goals and behavior. Agencies are unlikely to take steps that clash with firmly held agency goals, even if those steps could increase the agency's power. For example, the Environmental Protection Agency probably would gain the political support of wealthy, powerful developers and industrialists if the agency issued regulations making it much easier for their businesses to reap profits at the expense of the environment. Most likely this would not happen, however, since such regulations would contradict EPA's mission of protecting the environment.

The power of the bureaucracy also is limited by the personal ethics of bureaucrats. When an agency's goals are morally objectionable to some of its own employees, they may try to defeat the agency, or at least they will not support it. Although bureaucrats develop their personal codes of ethics in much the same way that nonbureaucrats do, bureaucrats are exposed to additional standards specifically applicable to government employees. The American Society for Public Administration has formally adopted a list of such standards, including admonitions for bureaucrats to be honest, respectful, responsive, and fair.[74]

As limits to bureaucratic power, ethics have advantages and disadvantages. On the positive side, once bureaucrats have accepted ethics, they always are in effect; no outsider must be there to apply them. Moreover, bureaucrats may be less likely to evade ethical restraints since the punishment for doing so comes from their own conscience.

One drawback to relying on ethics is that in many situations the right ethical choice is unclear. For example, in weighing an effort to help stop the spread of acquired immune deficiency syndrome (AIDS), which would be the more ethical decision: allowing the government or private organizations to provide intravenous drug users with clean needles, or prohibiting such action on the grounds that it might increase drug addiction? Another difficulty is that many ethical concepts are ambiguous; determination of the right thing to do is not always easy. Finally, every individual's code of ethics will differ according to his or her background, training, and values.

For years the American federal bureaucracy has tried deliberately to hire employees who represent a cross section of the country's population. Such a practice ensures not only equal opportunity for government employment, but also nondiscriminatory bureaucratic procedures and policy decisions. The idea is that representatives of any affected groups working in the bureaucracy would recognize discrimination and see that it is eliminated.

When bureaucrats spot instances of waste or wrongdoing within their own agencies, they may become "whistle-blowers" and make the information public. During the Nixon administration, a Pentagon employee testified before Congress about large cost overruns on the C-5A troop transport plane (so incensing President Nixon that he ordered the Defense Department to "get rid of that _____"). Whistle-blowing can be an effective internal limit on bureaucratic agencies, but many employees are reluctant to blow the whistle. Although federal law now protects whistle-blowers from retaliation and even pro-

vides for financial rewards in some cases, they often are treated as outcasts by their colleagues.

External Limits

Restraints on agency power also originate from sources outside the agency itself, including the president, other bureaucratic agencies, Congress, the courts, interest groups, public opinion, and the media.

The President. Presidents need control over the bureaucracy to fulfill their constitutional obligations to exercise "executive power" and to see that the laws are faithfully executed. Presidents also need the bureaucracy's cooperation in pursuing presidential policy objectives. Conflict between the president and the bureaucracy is almost guaranteed, however, because the bureaucracy tends to place its own goals above those of the president. *(See "President's View of the Bureaucracy," p. 1430.)*

Other Bureaucratic Agencies. Bureaucratic agencies work in close proximity to one another, and because their organizational interests differ, they come into conflict and thus limit each other's power. The causes and effects of these conflicts depend on the agencies involved. For example, just as the Office of Management and Budget, the Office of Personnel Management, and other agencies with authority over the bureaucracy can be valuable allies, they also can be formidable opponents. Without the support or at least the neutrality of such offices, the power of other bureaucratic agencies is severely limited. The relationship, however, is a two-way street. If an agency's primary function is to deal with other parts of the bureaucracy, it needs the support of other agencies because it has no clientele outside the bureaucracy. The General Services Administration (GSA), for example, would be in a perilous situation if it antagonized the agencies it serves because interest groups do not have much incentive to work in the GSA's behalf.

Agencies clash because they are pursuing goals that are either fundamentally opposite or basically the same.[75] The cause of conflict in the first case is obvious; to the extent that one of the agencies succeeds, the other fails. For example, the Department of Agriculture, concerned mainly with the interests of farmers, has differed with the State Department on the issue of grain embargoes. The State Department considers such embargoes useful tools of foreign policy, while the Department of Agriculture sees them as threats to farmers' prosperity.

Agencies working toward the same goals often clash because they feel threatened by one another. Like some animals, bureaucratic agencies stake out their own territories and become defensive when rivals try to invade. For a bureau, its territory is its jurisdiction over certain policy areas; thus other agencies working in the same areas frequently are perceived as invaders. This fear is not merely paranoia; one law of bureaucratic behavior is that agencies should try to expand their jurisdictions—and therefore their political power.[76] A classic territorial battle is that between the State Department and the president's National Security Council staff over foreign policy making. This kind of competition can limit the power of agencies in two ways: first, by the potential loss of territory to a rival agency; and, second, by the necessity to invest precious time and resources in the struggle against other agencies.

Congress. Congress has the power to exert more influence over the bureaucracy than any other external group or institution.[77] Although Congress by no means dominates the bureaucracy, it can guide the bureaucracy in a variety of ways using its legal authority. In practice, however, Congress seldom chooses to use its powers to control the bureaucracy.

The two congressional powers over the bureaucracy—legislation and budgeting—can be potent means of control. By passing legislation, Congress can change or restrict the authority of agencies, or it can take the even more drastic and unusual step of abolishing agencies altogether. Legislation is used frequently and effectively to shape administrative policy. If an agency upsets Congress, it may find its funding cut, or at least its funding threatened. Under such circumstances, bureaucrats usually are much more agreeable to the wishes of Congress.

Another method of congressional control is the legislative veto. Until 1983, when the Supreme Court declared some of its uses unconstitutional, the legislative veto allowed one or both houses of Congress to "veto" bureaucratic decisions. Congress passed laws giving agencies the power to take certain actions—enabling the Department of Defense to close military bases, for example—but with the provision that Congress could overturn any decisions it found objectionable.

Congress also influences the bureaucracy through its oversight authority, which entails gathering information on bureaucratic activity. Congress collects this information by holding committee or subcommittee public hearings, conducting staff investigations, and commissioning audits by the General Accounting Office. Oversight can be the first step in the legislative or budgeting process, or it can be an end in itself.[78] Public hearings are an especially effective vehicle for members of Congress to make their views known. The 1987 hearings into the Iran-contra affair, in which Congress delved into the actions of the National Security Council and other agencies, were a vivid example of congressional oversight. One scholar estimates that 25 percent of congressional hearings deal with oversight.[79]

Bureaucratic power also is limited by congressional influence over who receives top federal jobs. According to the Constitution, the president must obtain the "advice and consent" of the Senate in making upper-level appointments to the executive branch, and senators are not shy about giving such advice. Even House members feel free to comment on the president's choices despite their lack of formal authority. Although the Senate consents to the vast majority of presidential nominations, an occasional one is rejected, thereby ensuring continued congressional influence over the leadership of the bureaucracy.

Finally, Congress influences the bureaucracy through its informal contacts with bureaucrats and their agencies, usually in response to a constituent's request for help in dealing with a federal agency. One estimate has placed the total number of

Although the organization and activities of the bureaucracy are shaped largely by the president and the executive branch, Congress and the Supreme Court also influence the bureaucracy. The bureaucracy is sometimes referred to as "the fourth branch of government."

constituent requests at 200,000 annually.[80] Legislators also talk informally to bureaucrats about policy matters. The cumulative effects of these contacts on agencies can be substantial; repeated contacts from Congress may indicate to agencies that some changes are needed.

The Courts. Citizens unhappy with bureaucratic decisions can challenge them in court. If the court has jurisdiction over the matter and sees fit to do so, it can overrule the action of a federal agency. The judicial system has become immersed in a wide array of administrative issues affecting groups of people, including the drawing of school district boundaries, the running of prison systems, and the oversight of agency employment practices. In addition, the courts hear complaints from individuals dissatisfied with agency decisions as they affect those individuals personally (people denied benefits from government programs, for example).

Judicial involvement in administrative matters has increased as the amount and scope of bureaucratic activity have grown. Since the end of World War II, the federal bureaucracy has expanded in many areas, including regulatory activity and the administration of federal government benefit programs. More bureaucratic activity in these areas inevitably has meant more people unhappy with agency decisions, which in turn has resulted in more litigation and thus more opportunities for the courts to intervene in the bureaucracy.

The courts generally base their reviews of administrative action on two basic standards: procedural and statutory.[81] The procedural standard is applied when determining whether agencies followed the proper procedures in reaching the decision in question. Agencies must have complied with their own organizational procedures, any procedures mandated by Congress, and the general procedures of due process of law. Thus agencies are not allowed to ignore the rules even if those rules become inconvenient. Agencies also are required to obey the laws, or statutes, that are on the books. This includes staying within the bounds of legislative intent; taking action beyond what Congress intended is prohibited. The courts are mainly interested in whether these two standards are met, not in the effectiveness or fairness of the agency's policy.

Going to court is an effective strategy for some people dissatisfied with bureaucratic decisions, including environmentalists, who have, by filing lawsuits, succeeded in delaying hundreds of construction projects they oppose. This often is not a feasible alternative, however. Litigation is slow, risky, and very expensive. Even if a citizen wins the case, there is no guarantee that the agency will provide the desired response; it just may start its decision-making process over again.

Interest groups. Interest groups may be dangerous enemies of agencies for many of the same reasons that make them valuable friends. The political resources that groups mobilize to help agencies they like also can be used against agencies they do not like. Unfortunately for federal agencies, it is nearly impossible to take any action without upsetting at least one interest group.

Ironically, often the groups most infuriated by agency decisions are those that normally support the bureau. This is especially likely when the same segment of society is represented by two or more interest groups. Because these groups frequently disagree on issues, the agency has a dilemma; whatever it decides, some portion of its supporters will be unhappy. For example, American farmers are represented by the National Farmers' Union (NFU) and the American Farm Bureau Federation (AFBF), which traditionally have differed on the issue of government subsidies for agriculture. Thus the secretary of agriculture is in a no-win situation. By advocating high subsidies, the secretary pleases the NFU but not the AFBF, whereas by promoting lower subsidies, the reverse is true.[82]

Some agencies and interest groups are natural enemies because their goals are incompatible. For example, groups representing developers of natural resources often are frustrated by the Environmental Protection Agency, and businesses frequently bristle at safety regulations imposed by the Occupational Safety and Health Administration. Agencies in this kind of situation must strive not to alienate their friends since they already have permanent opponents.

Similar inherent enmity is widespread between different interest groups. The National Rifle Association and Handgun Control Inc., for example, are archenemies. When an agency must act on an issue contested by rival groups, it is guaranteed to draw the ire of at least one group. The Federal Aviation Administration (FAA), for example, prohibited smoking on many plane flights, leaving antismoking groups overjoyed and representatives of smokers wrathful.

Public opinion. Public opinion is another political force that can be both a source of and a limit to bureaucratic power. Although the general public seldom pays close attention to the bureaucracy, Americans nevertheless tend to have great expectations about its performance. The bureaucracy is expected to execute its functions effectively and creatively, to be loyal and responsive to citizens, and to be honest and fair.[83] When a bureaucrat or an agency fails to live up to these general expectations or adopts an unpopular policy, negative public reaction can result in political punishment for the offender.

The sporadic episodes of intense public attention that agencies often receive when current events (together with media coverage) highlight their existence and functions—as when a plane crash spotlights the FAA—can be a threat to agencies as well as an opportunity to generate public support.[84] In many cases, the agency is making the news because of some dramatic failure or oversight on its part, which often results in calls for changes in the agency—usually an unwelcome prospect. In the 1960s the Food and Drug Administration captured national attention when use of the drug thalidomide by pregnant women resulted in a high incidence of birth defects. Similarly, interest in the Nuclear Regulatory Commission mushroomed in 1979 in the wake of the accident at the Three Mile Island nuclear plant. At other times, the cause of attention is less sensational. For example, every time the U.S. Postal Service increases postage rates, it is accused of gross inefficiency and its privatization is suggested.

When the public becomes incensed enough about the bureaucracy to want change, it can pressure its elected officials, especially the president and members of Congress, to exert some control over the bureaucracy and make the changes, or it can vote for candidates who promise to take the desired actions. In his 1980 campaign for president, Ronald Reagan pledged to scale back the size and power of the bureaucracy, and at least in some areas he fulfilled that promise after entering office.

The public also influences the bureaucracy through informal contacts—personal conversations, phone calls, and letters. Agencies, ever concerned about public support, will likely give serious attention to matters raised frequently through these means. In addition, agencies stay abreast of public opinion by monitoring newspaper editorials and opinion polls. Citizens can make their views known more formally during public hearings that agencies occasionally conduct on controversial issues. Finally, a few agencies regularly consult members of the public throughout the process of policy design and implementation.

The Media. The news media, another limit to bureaucratic power, are related to public opinion—and help to shape it.[85] Television, radio, newspapers, and magazines play a crucial role in informing the public about the bureaucracy. The media are a blessing for agencies looking for a conduit to provide information or to sell an image to the public, but they also can create problems by reporting agency failures or exposing bureaucratic secrets. The *National Journal* and *Washington Monthly* devote much attention to the activities of the federal bureaucracy.

Traditionally, American reporters have enjoyed ferreting out juicy government scandals, especially since the lionization of the two *Washington Post* reporters, Bob Woodward and Carl Bernstein, who were largely responsible for uncovering the Watergate scandal in the Nixon administration. This tradition has produced investigative reporters hungry for a scoop and skeptical of the official government line.

But reporters' incessant needs for news can leave them vulnerable to manipulation by the agencies, which often feed reporters information designed primarily to make the agencies look good. Other inducements used by agencies to capture reporters include special access to sources and advance notice of stories. Although relatively few reporters are captured by agencies, those who are become little more than tools for spreading the agency point of view.

Many parts of the bureaucracy are covered closely by specialized trade journals, which concentrate on a particular agency or group of agencies working in the same field. For example, *Broadcasting Magazine* intensely covers the Federal Communications Commission. Although these kinds of publications effectively reach citizens interested in a particular area of policy, the general public usually responds to bureaucratic activity only when the mass media, such as the weekly news magazines or the nightly network newscasts, report on an issue.

President's View of the Bureaucracy

Traditionally, presidents have viewed the federal bureaucracy as one of their biggest political headaches. Rather than a system of compliant agencies faithfully executing the president's will, the bureaucracy is more often—especially from the perspective of the Oval Office—the source of many difficult problems. Presidents may feel a variety of emotions toward the bureaucracy—frustration, anger, disappointment, disdain, boredom, distrust, or despair—but rarely complete satisfaction.

Unlike most presidents, Franklin Roosevelt seemed to enjoy his involvement with the bureaucracy. This is illustrated in a tongue-in-cheek memo written by FDR in response to a minor bureaucratic jurisdictional dispute:

I agree with the Secretary of the Interior. Please have it carried out so that fur-bearing animals remain in the Department of the Interior.

You might find out if any Alaska bears are still supervised by (a) War Department (b) Department of Agriculture (c) Department of Commerce. They have all had jurisdiction over Alaska bears in the past and many embarrassing situations have been created by the mating of a bear belonging to one Department with a bear belonging to another Department.

F.D.R.

P.S. I don't think the Navy is involved but it may be. Check the Coast Guard. You never can tell![86]

In sharp contrast to FDR, Richard Nixon profoundly distrusted the bureaucracy and had an almost paranoid fear that many bureaucrats were out to get him:

When a bureaucrat deliberately thumbs his nose, we're going to get him. . . . The little boys over in State particularly, that are against us, will do it: Defense, HEW—those three areas particularly. . . . Now, goddamnit, those are the bad guys—the guys down in the woodwork.[87]

Jimmy Carter, another frequent critic of the bureaucracy, expressed his anger toward several bureaucrats who displeased him by telling them, "You are the cause of the problem."[88]

Ronald Reagan's diatribes against the bureaucracy were heard often. Much of his first successful campaign for the White House revolved around his promises to tame the wild bureaucracy and to get the federal government off the backs of the people. As president, such comments continued. In his inaugural address Reagan declared that "government is not the solution to our problem; government is the problem."[89]

Early in the Reagan administration, appointees in the Department of Agriculture made the surprising announcement that ketchup was an acceptable substitute for a vegetable in school lunches. Responding to the ensuing criticism, Reagan explained that "somebody got overambitious in the bureaucracy."[90] Reagan made an even more remarkable statement during his 1988 summit conference with Soviet leader Mikhail Gorbachev in Moscow. Reagan exempted Gorbachev and the communist system from any blame for Soviet violations of human rights by saying, incredibly, "I'm blaming [the Soviet] bureaucracy."[91] For Reagan, bureaucracy was apparently responsible not only for creating problems at home, but also for putting the evil into the "evil empire."

George Bush entered office with a dramatically different attitude toward the federal bureaucracy. He promised cooperation rather than conflict with the bureaucracy and heaped praise on government workers. Bush described government service as "a noble calling" and said that bureaucrats deserved "to be recognized, rewarded, and appreciated."[92] His kind words and other probureaucracy actions, including support of a pay increase for senior bureaucrats, paved the way for a smoother relationship between the bureaucracy and the White House.

But even Bush could not resist bashing the bureaucracy when he came under pressure from his Democratic opponent during his 1992 reelection campaign. Bill Clinton promised he would slash the federal payroll if elected. In response, Bush advocated reducing the salaries of the highest-paid federal workers—a stance that made bureaucrats feel betrayed.[93] Bush also imposed a moratorium on new federal regulations.

Although Clinton refrained from castigating bureaucrats the way Reagan had, some criticism was certainly implicit in his espousal of the pressing need to "reinvent government." Bureaucrats also were given cause to worry by some provisions of Clinton's 1993 National Performance Review, including the plan to cut 252,000 federal jobs over a period of years. According to one observer, Clinton's move to "reinvent government" made blaming the bureaucracy fashionable once again.[94]

CONFLICTING GOALS

Bureaucratic goals frequently conflict with presidential goals. Bureaucrats and presidents play vastly different roles in the political system. Most bureaucratic agencies serve a relatively small segment of the population; the president is responsible to the entire nation. Although bureaucrats usually keep their jobs for years, the president is in office only a short time. The president thus wants quick, dramatic government action—the kind often hated by bureaucrats—in order to formulate policy on a large scale and tackle the problems and crises of the day. Overall, the starkly different roles and interests of the bureaucracy and the president almost inevitably lead to conflict.

When the goals of the president and the bureaucracy clash, the bureaucracy often resists the president's plan. This resistance usually is not declared explicitly and often takes the form of passive opposition, but it is real nonetheless. Even presidents who believe that their election to office was a clear mandate from the people cannot escape bureaucratic resistance to change. Arthur M. Schlesinger Jr., an aide to President Kennedy, wrote: "Getting the bureaucracy to accept new ideas is like carrying a double mattress up a very narrow and winding stairway. It is a terrible job, and you exhaust yourself when you try it. But once you get the mattress up it is awfully hard for anyone else to get it down."[95]

Resistance from the bureaucracy makes the jobs of the president and the White House staff that much harder. Presidents expend a great deal of time and effort developing policy even before it reaches the hands of the bureaucracy: problems must be identified and evaluated, possible solutions weighed, decisions made, political support built, and members of Congress convinced. Then the bureaucracy must be faced. As another Kennedy assistant said, "Everybody believes in democracy until he gets to the White House and then you begin to believe in dictatorship, because it's so hard to get things done. Every time you turn around, people resist you and even resist their own job."[96]

When President Reagan encountered bureaucratic resistance to the deep budget cuts he proposed early in his term, he responded by saying, perhaps with some justification, that the resisters were "more worried about losing their position than . . . about the people they represent."[97] Resistance is not always based on selfish motives, however. During the Nixon administration, the FBI, CIA, and Internal Revenue Service all opposed the president's attempts to use their power illegally against his political enemies. Other cases of resistance have been more mundane. In 1977 Jimmy Carter instructed seventy-five federal agencies to draft regulations discouraging federally insured construction projects in low-lying areas where flooding was possible. Two years later only fifteen of those agencies had acted on Carter's order.[98]

PRESIDENTIAL INCENTIVES AND THE BUREAUCRACY

The overriding goal of most first-term presidents is reelection, while second-term presidents want to leave their mark on history.[99] Neither objective is easily achieved through close supervision and leadership of the bureaucracy—an activity that fails to inspire the masses. Instead, presidents usually concentrate on proposing and passing bold new programs, which, regardless of their effectiveness, attract the public's attention. Presidents have little incentive to worry about how well programs are implemented—the bureaucracy's job—because the public generally does not hold the president accountable for the actual functioning of programs, nor does it give the president credit when those programs run well.

Presidents also tend to concentrate on the broad issues of foreign affairs because in this area they enjoy greater freedom of action from the constraints posed by Congress and the bureaucracy. Moreover, crises that demand immediate presidential attention arise more frequently in foreign affairs than in the domestic realm, and this kind of dramatic action best complements presidential goals.

Supervision of the bureaucracy is therefore usually low on the president's list of priorities, well below taking valiant action, developing new policies, conducting foreign affairs, and performing the symbolic (but politically valuable) duties of head of state. Even though it is the president's constitutional duty to see that the laws are faithfully executed, lack of presidential attention to administrative detail commonly means that orders are not obeyed and programs do not operate as intended, leading to big problems. David Gergen, a top adviser to both President Reagan and President Clinton, has remarked: "It's unfortunately true that the management of the bureaucracy becomes one of the lowest priorities of almost every administration that comes to this city. Every administration pays a heavy price before it's over."[100]

Presidents do want to control the bureaucracy on certain occasions, however.[101] When they have a particular interest in a program, they want to ensure that the bureaucracy handles it properly. Richard Nixon, for example, was vitally concerned with the issue of busing students for purposes of racial desegregation, and after he prescribed specific guidelines for the Departments of Justice and Health, Education and Welfare to follow, he carefully monitored their performance. Years later, George Bush found that he needed the cooperation of numerous agencies in his efforts to interdict the flow of illegal drugs into the country. Presidents also watch the bureaucracy when they want to control government expenditures. Many presidents have embarked on budget-cutting plans that started with the bureaucracy.

Partisan politics also plays a role in how much attention the president gives the bureaucracy. The thousands of presidential appointees to jobs in federal agencies stand a better chance of success when they enter an environment receptive to the president's views. Moreover, appointees welcomed by their prospective agencies ordinarily receive Senate approval more easily. Presidents with some influence over the bureaucracy can act to improve that bureaucratic reception.

DIFFICULTY OF PRESIDENTIAL CONTROL

Harry S. Truman described with characteristic bluntness his efforts to control the bureaucracy: "I thought I was the president, but when it comes to these bureaucracies I can't make 'em do a damn thing."[102] His successor in the White House did not learn that harsh lesson so well. Six years into Dwight D. Eisenhower's term, one of his aides said, "The President still feels that when he's decided something, that ought to be the end of it . . . and when it bounces back undone or done wrong, he tends to react with shocked surprise."[103] By now the lesson should be clear: all presidents must battle the bureaucratic dragon.

According to a much-quoted maxim, first proposed by an assistant to Franklin Roosevelt, to get anything done, a president must ask for it three times. Bureaucrats feel that only one request from the president means that the matter can be safely ignored. Upon the second request, the president can be told that the matter is being investigated. The third time the president asks, the deed should be done. Presidents, however, rarely ask for anything three times.[104] John Kennedy discovered this maxim's validity when he tried to have a sign that gave directions to the CIA's Langley, Virginia, headquarters taken down. After issuing two directives through proper channels that yielded no results, Kennedy finally telephoned the person in charge of signs in the area and ordered the offending marker removed. "I now understand," he declared, "that for a president to get something done in this country, he's got to say it three times."[105]

Jimmy Carter became exasperated with the bureaucracy over the unlikely issue of a dead and increasingly smelly mouse inside a wall of the Oval Office. The General Services Administration (GSA), which maintains federal buildings, denied responsibility for the mouse's removal because it had recently exterminated all the mice in the White House. That meant the decaying rodent must have been an "outside mouse," which made the Department of the Interior, the agency in charge of the White House grounds, responsible for the problem. But Interior officials declined to act since the creature was no longer actually outside and their department only handled outside problems. Carter eventually summoned officials from both agencies to his office and angrily exclaimed, "I can't even get a damn mouse out of my office!" Finally a special task force was formed to remove the malodorous mouse corpse.[106]

Unfortunately, not all cases of bureaucratic resistance are as harmless as the sign that annoyed John Kennedy or the mouse that irritated Jimmy Carter. Soon after entering office, Kennedy twice ordered the State Department to remove some obsolete American missiles that were installed in Turkey. The State Department encountered some opposition to the idea from the Turks, and so it simply failed to execute the order, hoping that Kennedy would not press the issue—and he did not. But later, Kennedy was furious and dismayed when he learned, during the October 1962 Cuban Missile Crisis, that the missiles had not been dismantled. If the United States had bombed the Soviet missiles in Cuba, the American missiles in Turkey would have provided the Soviet Union with a legitimate target for a retaliatory strike—a potential step up the ladder toward all-out nuclear war.[107] Here, bureaucratic resistance made an already perilous situation even more dangerous.

Another case of potentially deadly bureaucratic obstruction occurred under Richard Nixon. In 1970 Nixon ordered the CIA to destroy its supply of biological weapons. The directive moved down the CIA chain of command to reach the appropriate mid-level official, who ignored it. Five years later, the illegal toxins were discovered during a routine inventory.

Like Kennedy's hard-fought victory over the sign to the CIA, Nixon also relished a minor win over the bureaucracy. He struggled for over a year to have two old government buildings near the White House demolished. After the structures were eventually destroyed, Nixon summoned his aides and told them with pride and relief, "We have finally gotten something done."[108] But apparently that was small comfort for Nixon. According to his close aide H. R. Haldeman, by his third year in office Nixon "realized that he was virtually powerless to deal with the bureaucracy in every department of government. It was no contest."

Is the situation really as bad for the president as these anecdotes suggest? Probably not. Even though management of the bureaucracy is no easy task, presidents can improve their performance of that task. One lesson is apparent: the need for follow-up on presidential orders and programs. Had Kennedy or his personal staff checked on compliance with his instructions to remove the missiles from Turkey and had Nixon followed up on his directive to destroy the CIA weapons, their orders might have been fulfilled satisfactorily.

Presidential Power over the Bureaucracy

Although presidents often find it difficult to control the federal agencies, they are far from powerless in the relationship. Presidents have certain advantages, according to one scholar, that allow them to slowly but surely increase their influence over the bureaucracy.[109]

SOURCES OF PRESIDENTIAL POWER

The Constitution and subsequent statutes grant presidents many powers over federal agencies. Although these powers are legally available to all presidents, they cannot be used successfully in every situation; political considerations and personal attributes constrain presidential actions.

Appointment and Removal Powers

Although the approximately three thousand presidential appointees to federal agencies are but a small fraction of the total three million federal workers, it is an important fraction because it includes most of the higher-level officials—cabinet members, subcabinet members, and agency heads—who make policy. Presidents can exercise power over the bureaucracy by appointing to key positions people who share their political philosophies and thus are more likely to support their political goals. This is sometimes known as "politicizing" the bureaucracy.

The removal power complements the appointment power. Although not specifically granted by the Constitution, removal power has been bestowed on the president by tradition, statute, and a string of Supreme Court decisions. Presidents can remove from office appointed officials who fail to perform their duties satisfactorily or who clash with the president on policy matters. In practice, however, presidents rarely fire officials outright; it usually is possible to ease them out of office. Presidents often ask for the resignations of officeholders they want ousted or have them informed indirectly that they are no longer welcome. If these methods do not work, presidents always can revert to direct dismissal.

In an effort to avoid some of the personnel problems suffered by its predecessors, the Reagan administration devoted an unusually large amount of time and attention to the appointment process. Reagan and his close aides painstakingly sought appointees, even for the lower levels of the bureaucracy, who were compatible ideologically with the president. By waiting to fill many top posts, Reagan had fewer bureaucrats around to oppose his proposed budget cuts. Reagan also reshaped the bureaucracy by using provisions of the Civil Service Reform Act of 1978 to reassign or terminate hundreds of influential Senior Executive Service (SES) members. Bill Clinton and his staff also spent much time and effort on evaluating potential appointees.

Use of the appointment and removal power to exercise some control over the bureaucracy has its limitations, however. First, a relatively small number of employees are under the president's direct supervision; the vast majority of federal workers enjoy the protection of merit employment systems and thus are insulated from presidential intervention. Presidential appointees frequently have policy-making power, but they still find guiding the bureaucracy difficult because only a few appointees reside in any particular agency. At least in terms of numbers, career civil servants overwhelmingly dominate the bureaucracy. *(See box, Firing Bureaucrats, p. 1434.)*

Second, even if presidential appointees are dedicated to the president's goals, they may not know enough about working in the executive branch or in their particular agency to be much help in achieving them. Moreover, they may find themselves unable to buck the deeply ingrained bureaucratic system. In the end, many appointees are ready to leave government service by the time they have learned the ropes.

Third, the president cannot even rely on the undivided loyalty of appointees who are knowledgeable about the bureaucracy because they have personal goals of their own. In addition, appointees wishing to execute a presidential directive almost always need the cooperation of career civil servants, whose own objectives may differ from those of the president.

Finally, Congress has much to say about who gets appointed to the bureaucracy. High-ranking appointed officials such as cabinet members must be confirmed by the Senate. Congress also decides which lower-level positions can be filled through presidential appointment and, if it desires, can establish qualifications that must be met by presidential appointees to specific offices. Congress cannot appoint executive officials itself, however, or force the president to fill vacant positions.

Leadership Skills

A president's leadership skills are an important factor in dealing with the bureaucracy because even the most potent power loses effectiveness if used improperly. Political scientists Erwin C. Hargrove and Michael Nelson identified four skills central to presidential leadership: strategic sense, communication skills, tactical skills, and management of authority.[110] Each of these skills can help the president to battle the bureaucracy. The historical circumstances and the president's own talents and preferences influence which type of skill is relied on most.

A good strategic sense enables the president to understand what kind of general political action the American people want at any particular time, and communication skills help the president to capture and hold the public's attention. Franklin Roosevelt's famous "fireside chats" on the radio, in which he allayed the public's fear of the depression and instilled hope for the future, exemplify effective presidential communication. Tactical skills such as timing and persuasion are used in making and carrying out political choices designed to help fulfill goals. Persuasion is one of the most important presidential tactics. In fact, presidential scholar Richard E. Neustadt has argued that "presidential power is the power to persuade."[111] Neustadt supported his assertion with a quote from Harry Truman: "I sit here all day trying to persuade people to do the things they ought to have sense enough to do without my persuading them. . . . That's all the powers of the president amount to."[112]

Yet another presidential leadership skill—and the one most directly relevant to leadership of the bureaucracy—is the management of authority, which includes supervising the president's staff and organizing the overall government.[113] Presidents need respect, loyalty, honesty, and candor from their personal staffs. Without these attributes, the staff will be of little help to the president. Presidents also need the assistance of the rest of the government—especially the bureaucracy—and such help will most likely be forthcoming if the government is organized efficiently and managed wisely. John Kennedy engendered tremendous personal loyalty from his staff, and he worked hard, and fairly successfully, to obtain the best effort from both his staff and the bureaucracy. As one staffer fondly recalled, "You always had the feeling that the most competent ideas would win out."[114]

Effective management of authority helps the president to lead the bureaucracy in two important kinds of activities: policy formation and policy implementation. Presidents rely on their staffs and on bureaucrats in the executive departments to construct specific policy proposals that mesh with presidential intentions. Thus the better managed these workers are, the greater is the likelihood that presidents will receive satisfactory results from them.

Implementation—the carrying out of presidential policies—is by no means automatic. There are so many obstacles to smooth implementation that policies made by the president can be delayed, distorted, or even ignored by the people who are supposed to implement them. Although effective management

FIRING BUREAUCRATS

We have no discipline in this bureaucracy. We never fire anybody. We never reprimand anybody. We never demote anybody. We always promote the sons-of-bitches that kick us in the ass.

—Richard Nixon

President Nixon clearly was not happy about the tremendous job security enjoyed by most bureaucrats. In fact, virtually all presidents have become frustrated with the difficulty encountered when firing bureaucrats. It is enough to make presidents yearn for the good old days of the spoils system, when presidents had much greater control over who held government jobs at all levels.

Ironically, it was widespread dissatisfaction with the spoils system that led to the present situation which so vexes modern presidents. Responding to concerns that the spoils system bred government inefficiency and corruption, Congress passed the Civil Service Act in 1883. This law and a series of others like it placed most government jobs under merit employment systems, which establish and enforce standards for the hiring and firing of employees. People are hired on the basis of their qualifications and fired only when they misbehave in office or fail to perform their duties—not for strictly political reasons.

The merit plans succeeded in crushing the spoils system. In the process of protecting employees from politically motivated dismissal, however, these merit systems have made it hard to fire workers for any reason, including misbehavior and incompetence. To fire a protected bureaucrat is now a time-consuming and convoluted undertaking, requiring much effort and reams of paperwork.

Passage of the Civil Service Reform Act of 1978 was an attempt to streamline the process. The law outlines the following procedure for firing or demoting civil servants. The employee must receive written thirty-days notice of the proposed action and a reasonable amount of time to prepare a response to the charges. The agency must provide a written decision explaining the reasons for the action. The employee can appeal the agency's decision to the Merit Systems Protection Board (created by the 1978 law specifically for this purpose), which reviews the case. Decisions on cases involving alleged discrimination also are reviewed by the Equal Employment Opportunity Commission. As a final step, the employee may take the case to the U.S. Court of Appeals for the Federal District.[1]

The result of this process, according to Jimmy Carter aide Jody Powell, is that "it is damn near impossible to fire someone from this government for failure to do their job." Statistics back up Powell's assessment: of the approximately three million bureaucratic employees, only between twelve thousand and thirty thousand are fired each year.[2]

Because it is so difficult to fire bureaucrats, presidents (and bosses throughout the bureaucracy) often resort to other ways of handling unwanted subordinates. One of the most common methods is to transfer the person in question to another position within the bureaucracy. As Jimmy Carter remarked, it is "easier to promote and transfer incompetent employees than to get rid of them."[3] Richard Nixon described the tactic more bluntly and colorfully:

There are many unpleasant places where Civil Service people can be sent. . . . We got to get in these departments. . . . Well, maybe he is in the regional office. Fine. Demote him, or send him to the Guam regional office. There's a way. Get him the hell out. . . . Let people know that when they don't produce in this administration, somebody's ass is kicked out.[4]

Other methods of banishing bureaucrats include encouraging early retirement and the more radical move of reorganizing the agency to eliminate the target's job.

One notable exception to the rule that few bureaucrats are fired occurred in 1981, when Ronald Reagan dismissed 11,400 federal air traffic controllers. As members of the Professional Air Traffic Controllers Organization, the controllers were on strike despite a statute prohibiting strikes by federal employees.[5] Not only was Reagan's action upheld by the U.S. Court of Appeals, but a poll indicated that the general public approved of it by a two-to-one margin.[6]

1. Ellen M. Bussey, *Federal Civil Service Law and Procedures: A Basic Guide* (Washington, D.C.: Bureau of National Affairs, 1984), 7–8, 69–71.

2. David V. Edwards, *The American Political Experience: An Introduction to Government*, 4th ed. (Englewood Cliffs, N.J.: Prentice-Hall, 1988), 280.

3. Quoted in George C. Edwards III and Stephen J. Wayne, *Presidential Leadership: Politics and Policy Making*, 3d ed. (New York: St. Martin's Press, 1994), 280.

4. "Transcript of an April 19, 1971, Meeting Attended by Nixon, Ehrlichman, and Shultz," *New York Times*, July 20, 1974, 14.

5. Norman C. Thomas and Joseph A. Pika, *The Politics of the Presidency*, 4th ed. (Washington, D.C.: CQ Press, 1996), 264.

6. Landon Butler, "Reagan Botched the Strike," *Newsweek*, August 31, 1981, 9.

of authority cannot eliminate all problems, it can increase the chances of successful implementation. After it became apparent that many parts of his Great Society program were not being implemented properly, Lyndon Johnson learned the importance of attention to implementation.

President's Staff

As Dwight Eisenhower once observed,

The government of the United States has become too big, too complex, and too pervasive in its influence on all our lives for one individual to pretend to direct the details of its important and critical programming. Competent assistants are mandatory.[115]

For that reason, the president's staff plays a big role in virtually all of the president's activities, including management of the bureaucracy.

In 1937 the Committee on Administrative Management, chaired by Louis Brownlow, studied the modern presidency and then issued a report that declared: "The president needs help."[116] The Brownlow Committee recognized that more staff assistance was needed to help the president meet the growing duties and responsibilities of the office. President Franklin Roosevelt and Congress agreed with the committee's recommendations, which spurred a dramatic growth in the size and influence of the president's staff. Since the late 1930s, the White House staff has expanded from a few dozen to several hundred employees. The Executive Office of the President (EOP), created in 1939, has likewise evolved into an assortment of powerful offices.

The White House Office is staffed by the special assistants to the president, including the press secretary, appointments secretary, legal counsel, and various policy and political advisers. Presidents enjoy considerable freedom in staffing and using the White House Office, and they often put their closest and most trusted advisers there. Over the years, White House staffers have been drawn from diverse backgrounds, including the law, the military, journalism, academics, business, and, of course, politics. *(See Chapter 27, Executive Office of the President: White House Office.)*

The Executive Office of the President is designed to help presidents meet their awesome managerial and policy responsibilities. EOP boasts about seventeen hundred full-time workers, although the precise number of EOP employees is difficult to determine because federal workers often are assigned there temporarily. The EOP staff has somewhat greater independence than the White House staff, but it remains primarily a servant of the president, playing a crucial role in the president's efforts to control the bureaucracy. Agencies within EOP include the Office of Management and Budget, the National Security Council, the Council of Economic Advisers, and the Office of Policy Development. *(See Chapter 28, Executive Office of the President: Supporting Organizations.)*

The president tends to rely heavily on assistants from the White House and executive offices, many of whom the president knows and trusts, unlike appointees to the other executive departments. Often these officials, particularly those working in the White House, are longtime friends or employees of the president; many probably worked on the president's electoral campaign. For example, Jimmy Carter brought fellow Georgians Hamilton Jordan, Bert Lance, and Jody Powell to Washington; Ronald Reagan appointed old friends such as Michael K. Deaver and Edwin Meese III to important posts; and Bill Clinton employed Thomas F. "Mac" McLarty III and numerous other "Friends of Bill" in his administration.

Presidents give their staff authority over federal programs in an effort to control the bureaucracy. The underlying logic is that because the staff is primarily loyal to the president and is thus much less susceptible to influence from outside constituent and interest groups than are bureaucrats in the departments, programs overseen by the staff will be run more in accordance with presidential desires. In general, the more suspicious the president is of the bureaucracy, the more likely this strategy will be used. Presidents favorably inclined toward the bureaucracy usually emphasize the appointment of loyalists to the departments. Both presidents Eisenhower and Nixon tried to centralize power over the bureaucracy in the hands of their staffs, while Reagan used this tactic in conjunction with carefully chosen appointments to the departments.

Another way presidents use their staffs to control the bureau-

cracy is by requiring that OMB or other entities that serve the president clear agency decisions. Presidents since Truman have employed this method to examine the legislative requests of agencies, but recent presidents have expanded the practice to include other kinds of agency decisions. Under the Reagan administration, central clearance was directed especially at controlling the rules and regulations issued by bureaucratic agencies. In fact, Reagan used this tactic so much that it generated opposition from some interest groups and congressional leaders, who attacked it as violating numerous federal statutes and perhaps even the constitutional separation of powers.

Taking a different tack, the Bush administration created a special board, the Council on Competitiveness, to review government regulation of business. Its goal was to prevent the bureaucracy from issuing regulations that might reduce the competitiveness of American companies. The council, headed by Vice President Dan Quayle, provided business with a way to go over the heads of regulatory agencies with their complaints about regulation. From the administration's perspective, it was a way both to keep business happy and to oversee the bureaucracy.

By giving control of bureaucratic programs to the White House Office and EOP staffs, the president is able to exert more influence over the bureaucracy, but problems can arise. For one thing, the president's staff can bog down quickly when trying to control the bureaucracy. Decisions are inevitably drawn upward, and presidential assistants, distrustful of the department heads, begin handling issues more properly settled in the departments, while department heads, mindful of White House scrutiny, decide questions that could be handled at lower levels. Thus presidential aides—and sometimes presidents themselves—soon become immersed in the details of bureaucratic programs rather than concentrating on the broader policy issues.

Attempts to harness the bureaucracy using the president's staff typically result in hefty increases in the staff's size. As the staff becomes more involved in the minutiae of bureaucratic decision making, more staff members are needed to deal with specialized matters. And as the staff grows, it takes on many bureaucratic characteristics such as hierarchy, interoffice rivalries, communication problems, overspecialization, and inadequate coordination.[117] Ironically, presidential efforts to control the bureaucracy by using staff actually can transform the president's staff itself into a bureaucracy.

Presidential distrust and efforts to bypass the executive departments weaken and demoralize the people who work there. Cabinet members and other high-level appointees feel usurped by assistants to the president. Many of their functions are taken over by the president's assistants, who also tend to monopolize the president's time and attention. Civil servants working in the bureaucracy become frustrated when their recommendations are viewed automatically as suspect by the president's staff and when the staff interferes in the normal operation of their departments.

Finally, the president's assistants can become dangerously

powerful. Because presidential assistants act in the name of the president, they usually get what they want. In addition, their often over-zealous attempts to protect the president may even seal the president off from the rest of the world. Now-famous examples of such assistants were Nixon aides H. R. Haldeman and John Ehrlichman, who jealously guarded President Nixon but isolated him in the process.

The tremendous power of presidential staffs raises two problems, one theoretical and one practical. In terms of democratic theory, this power is troubling; the men and women who serve on the president's staff are not elected, and Congress has no role in their selection as it has in most other presidential appointments. In practical terms, the actions taken by the staff, especially those initiated without outside consultation, can be disastrous. Ronald Reagan's powerful National Security Council staff undertook the ill-advised and probably illegal action that became known as the Iran-contra affair. This action had serious consequences for both American foreign policy and Reagan's political standing.

Reorganization

Presidential reorganization, and therefore control, of the bureaucracy can take several forms: creating new bureaucratic agencies or abolishing existing ones, merging agencies, or moving agencies within departments or to other departments. Presidents and scholars of organizational theory have long placed great faith in the benefits of reorganization. As Harold Seidman and Robert Gilmour, prominent observers of the federal government's structure, have remarked, "Reorganization has become almost a religion in Washington."[118] (See box, "Reinventing Government," p. 1437.)

Traditionally, reorganization has been hailed by presidents and others as a means of making government more efficient and economical. In fact, reorganization does not appear to work that way.[119] Despite the rhetoric about efficiency, reorganization is primarily a method for pursuing policy and political objectives. Franklin Roosevelt, a keen political analyst, understood the point: "We have to get over the notion that the purpose of reorganization is economy. . . . The reason for reorganization is good management."[120] Indeed, presidents can increase their control over the bureaucracy in a number of ways through successful reorganization.

An agency's position within the government greatly influences its power, prestige, and political support. Thus changes, or threatened changes, in the position of an agency can alter radically its situation and act as leverage for presidents attempting to guide the bureaucracy. For example, President Nixon granted the National Cancer Institute independent and favorable status both to help the agency and to signify his own commitment to fighting the disease. Conversely, Ronald Reagan demonstrated his belief in a limited role for the federal government by proposing to abolish the Departments of Education and Energy. Several candidates for the 1996 Republican presidential nomination also advocated abolishing one or more departments.

In addition to directly influencing the bureaucracy, presidents can reap other political benefits from reorganization. This device gives them the appearance of taking action, provides a method for rewarding political friends and punishing enemies, and assists efforts to centralize executive power in their hands and in the hands of their staff. (See box, Presidential Reorganization Authority, p. 1161.)

In a series of reorganization acts passed since 1939, Congress has given the president the power to reorganize the executive branch, subject to congressional approval. For their part, presidents are fond of declaring that reorganization is needed. Jimmy Carter's statement is typical: "We must give top priority to a drastic and thorough reorganization of the federal bureaucracy."[121] Yet even though Congress usually approves presidential reorganization requests, presidents do not make them often.[122] As with most presidential powers, reorganization has its drawbacks.

Despite its high percentage of approvals of presidential reorganization schemes, Congress sometimes opposes such plans, particularly when interest groups express strong objections. Richard Nixon's ambitious proposals—including one to merge seven cabinet departments into four "superdepartments"—ran into fatal difficulties in Congress. The Clinton administration's plan to merge the Drug Enforcement Agency (DEA) into the Federal Bureau of Investigation also had to be dropped in the face of opposition.

Congress frequently places restrictions on the reorganization power it grants the president. Its authorizations, for example, can impose time limits, exempt certain agencies, or prohibit the president from creating or destroying departments.

With its arsenal of potent political weapons, the bureaucracy itself can be a formidable opponent to reorganization plans. (See "Bureaucratic Power," p. 1420.) Agencies threatened by reorganization proposals fight them with all their considerable might, and many presidents who attempt reorganization do not develop comprehensive political strategies to help them achieve their goals.

Reorganization does offer presidents enhanced control over the bureaucracy but not without significant costs. Presidents attempting to reorganize the bureaucracy ordinarily must invest substantial time, effort, and political resources, all of which are precious commodities. Most presidents are understandably reluctant to expend large amounts of those resources in the mundane realm of bureaucratic reorganization.

Budgetary Powers

As a means of controlling the bureaucracy, the president can influence how much money agencies receive, particularly during the budget process. Although Congress actually appropriates the money that government spends, the president wields power at both the beginning and end of the budget process.

With the help of the Office of Management and Budget, an EOP agency, the president prepares a budget for each year's government spending and presents it to Congress for review. OMB

During his 1992 campaign for the presidency, Bill Clinton bemoaned the inefficiency he saw plaguing the federal bureaucracy and promised to "reinvent government" if elected. "It is time," he wrote in his campaign manifesto, *Putting People First,* "to radically change the way government operates."[1] Once in office, Clinton charged Vice President Al Gore with developing a plan to keep that promise. As part of that planning process, Clinton declared, "We'll challenge the basic assumptions of every program, asking does it work, does it provide quality service, does it encourage innovation and reward hard work?"[2]

Gore and his staff spent six months in 1993 scrutinizing the federal bureaucracy and reviewing previous reorganization schemes. They also interviewed many of the bureaucrats working in the federal government, asking for information and suggestions. Gore's efforts culminated in a plan, known officially as the National Performance Review (NPR) and informally as the "reinventing government" initiative. Clinton and Gore unveiled the plan in September 1993 on the White House lawn; behind them were forklifts loaded with hundreds of manuals filled with government regulations. Implementing the NPR, the president asserted, would lead to a government that "works better and costs less."

The fundamental goal of the NPR was to make the bureaucracy more "entrepreneurial"—that is, to improve governmental efficiency by injecting market forces into it. This was to be done by, among other things, cutting red tape, reducing spending, decentralizing authority and empowering employees, using incentives, and assessing outcomes. Many of the principles underlying the NPR can be traced back to writers David Osborne and Ted Gaebler, whose 1992 book on the "entrepreneurial spirit" intrigued candidate Clinton.[3]

The NPR called for a variety of actions, which, if enacted, would save the government $108 billion over five years (although some critics questioned whether the savings would be that high). About $40 billion of the savings would accrue from cutting 252,000 federal jobs. Other savings would result from making specific changes in the various departments and agencies, revising the federal government's procurement system, computerizing government activities more effectively, and changing the administration of federal grants to state and local governments.[4] In all, the report made about eight hundred specific recommendations.

Clinton and Gore promoted the plan enthusiastically, with Gore even appearing on David Letterman's *Late Show* to discuss it. Public and congressional support for the NPR was strong, even though some critics initially saw it simply as another in a long list of forgettable plans to reform the government. (Since 1905, eleven major efforts to reorganize the executive branch have been made.)

A year after it was proposed, political scientist Donald F. Kettl called the NPR "one of the Clinton Administration's few clear victories."[5] Indeed, many of the NPR's recommendations have been carried out. Numerous bureaucratic rules and procedures have been simplified, the procurement process has been reformed, management practices have been improved, innovation by federal managers has been encouraged, and even the culture of government has started to change.[6]

One especially notable victory was the radical pruning of the ten thousand-page *Federal Personnel Manual,* which instructed government personnel managers on everything from how to label file folders to how to register federal employees after a thermonuclear war.[7] Also well received was the NPR's plan to reduce the federal workforce; Congress liked the idea so much that it voted to trim federal employment even further.

Despite the early successes of the NPR, a year into the program Kettl saw two major problems.[8] One was a preoccupation with short-term savings over improved government performance, evidenced by the rapid downsizing of the federal workforce to produce quick savings rather than a slow reduction after careful planning. This alienated many government workers who already were being asked to change radically the way they did their jobs.

The second problem was the lack of a clear strategy for dealing with Congress. NPR officials initially thought that most of the reforms they sought could be achieved without pursuing congressional approval. The experience of the first year, however, taught them that few significant changes were possible without some degree of congressional support and that members of Congress were apt to balk at individual parts of the plan they did not like. Overall, Kettl argued, the NPR was off to a promising start but keeping it going would "require hard work that has only just begun."[9]

1. Bill Clinton and Al Gore, *Putting People First* (New York: Times Books, 1992), 23–24.

2. Quoted in Jon Meacham, "What Al Gore Might Learn the Hard Way," *Washington Monthly,* September 1993, 17.

3. David Osborne and Ted Gaebler, *Reinventing Government: How the Entrepreneurial Spirit Is Transforming the Public Sector from Schoolhouse to State House, City Hall to Pentagon* (Reading, Mass.: Addison-Wesley, 1992).

4. *From Red Tape to Results: Creating a Government That Works Better and Costs Less, Report of the National Performance Review* (Washington, D.C.: Government Printing Office, 1993), iii–iv.

5. Donald F. Kettl, "Did Gore Reinvent Government? A Progress Report," *New York Times,* September 6, 1994, A17.

6. Donald F. Kettl, *Reinventing Government? Appraising the National Performance Review* (Washington, D.C.: Brookings, 1994), 1–2.

7. Stephen Barr, "OPM Turns Over 10,000 New Leaves," *Washington Post,* January 28, 1994, A21.

8. Kettl, *Reinventing Government?* v–vii; and Kettl, "Did Gore Reinvent Government?" A17.

9. Kettl, "Did Gore Reinvent Government?" A17.

evaluates each federal agency's request for funds and recommends to the president what amount should be placed in the budget. (See "Office of Management and Budget," p. 1112, in Chapter 28.)

The president makes the final decisions on the proposed budget based on the advice from OMB and from other sources such as the Council of Economic Advisers. The amount fixed in the budget by the president and OMB is tremendously important to the agencies. Although Congress is not obligated to accept the president's recommendations, in practice the amounts appropriated by Congress generally follow those recommendations closely.[123]

A president who is unhappy with congressional budget decisions may impound—refuse to spend—funds appropriated by Congress. Presidents have long used this method to control government spending. In the modern era, controlling spending also has meant controlling the federal bureaucracy. Controversy over impoundment arose in the early 1970s because President Richard Nixon used the practice prodigiously, prompting Congress to pass legislation stipulating that it can overturn impoundments. Although presidential impoundment of funds is still possible, deferral—delaying expenditures for up to one year, which is harder for Congress to prevent—also is an option. The most spectacular use of these powers came in 1981, when President Reagan successfully deferred $7 billion and impounded another $14 billion appropriated by Congress.[124]

Yet another means of controlling agency funding is legislative clearance. Under this system, all agency requests for legislation, even those not requiring additional funding, must be cleared with OMB before going to Congress. Legislative clearance gives the president an opportunity to study the proposals. The president also has certain discretionary powers, informally granted by congressional appropriations committees, which allow the president to transfer funds from one program to another.[125] Moreover, the chief executive can spend large amounts of money on a confidential basis, including expenditures for intelligence activities.

There are limits, however, to the effectiveness of the president's budgetary powers in controlling the bureaucracy. First, the federal budget is immense, complicated, and—unless the head of OMB is exceptionally sharp (as was Reagan's first OMB chief, David Stockman)—not easy to manipulate. Because the budget process is so complex, it is constructed incrementally—that is, an agency's funding for any one year is based largely on the amount received the previous year. Thus any changes in an agency's budget will likely be small since any radical variation from one year to the next rarely occurs. Such stability provides the bureaucracy with a measure of protection from presidential interference.

Second, the federal budget is highly inflexible. A large proportion of it—75 percent or more—is very difficult to control. Items such as interest on the national debt, pensions for retired federal employees, payments for contracts already made, and funding for Social Security and other entitlement programs such as Medicare and Supplemental Security Income must be included in the budget. These spending requirements significantly reduce the president's ability to direct funds to personal priorities.

Finally, Congress can foil the best-laid presidential plans. Congress takes the budget process very seriously and exercises considerable influence over it. The president's budgetary powers are less effective in cases where Congress disagrees with the president's objective.

Control of Information

The old saying that knowledge is power seems especially applicable to the relationship between the president and the bureaucracy.[126] Expert knowledge is one of the primary sources of bureaucratic power, particularly when the information is not easily available elsewhere. Presidents who become totally dependent on agencies for information are at a disadvantage, whereas those who use their powers wisely not only avoid that problem but also control information so that they are better able to influence the bureaucracy.

Presidents by themselves, however, cannot gather and assess all the information they need to cope with the expanded role of the federal government in the twentieth century and the increasing technological complexity of its tasks. Recent presidents have gotten much of the assistance they need from the Executive Office of the President, which is an important alternative and a thoroughly loyal source of information available to the president for use in making choices and countering the bureaucracy.

In recent years, the size and information capabilities of EOP have grown, as have its authority and responsibility. Assistants to the president and EOP staffers frequently act in the president's name, which enhances the president's ability to acquire and disseminate information through subordinates.

Presidents also have other sources of information. Sources outside the government include newspapers, magazines, television, interest groups, the private sector, and academia. Sources within the government include supporters in Congress and the federal agencies. When agency jurisdictions overlap, the ensuing duplication of information sources provides a way to collect and verify information. Presidents also may cultivate informal channels of communication to back up formal ones or bypass uncooperative layers of the bureaucracy and extract information from lower-level bureaucrats. This was a favorite tactic of President Kennedy.

Franklin Roosevelt was a master at controlling information. Even though he had comparatively few personal staff assistants, he managed to keep a constant flow of ideas, opinions, and information coming into the Oval Office. He encouraged his staff to brainstorm for new ideas, fostered competition among his staffers, and sought information from a wide array of sources both within and outside the government. All these strategies helped Roosevelt to command the bureaucracy. He depended on no single source for information, and thus no one knew exactly what information he had or what his thinking was. He controlled the information he needed to make knowledgeable political and policy choices.

The acquisition of accurate information can be difficult. Aside from the possibility of factual errors, presidents face other problems. For example, because subordinates tend to filter the information they pass along to superiors, that information can be quite distorted by the time it gets to the top. Subordinates do not necessarily lie, but they often emphasize information that makes them look good and de-emphasize or omit information that is not flattering to them or is unlikely to appeal to their superiors. Information that travels through several layers of hierarchy is therefore often of questionable quality.[127]

Whatever the president's efforts at generating alternate sources of information, inevitably some information—facts on agency performance, for example—must come from bureaucratic agencies themselves. This raises the possibility that agencies will provide information biased in their own favor. Moreover, bureaucratic agencies usually operate on the assumption that the president is informed about agency activities only when something out of the ordinary occurs. This tendency further restricts the president's ability to squeeze accurate information from the bureaucracy.

Agenda Setting

The public expects the president to put forth ideas, actions, and proposals—an agenda—designed to solve problems and make the country a better place to live. The president's agenda is then subject to national political consideration and debate. If the president proceeds carefully and effectively, the national agenda can be a powerful political tool used to influence the bureaucracy.

Presidents can use agenda setting to control the bureaucracy by determining what issues agencies must handle. Whether or not agencies support an item placed on the agenda by the president, they must devote time and attention to it. When an agency likes a proposal, it will work for its adoption, and when it does not like a proposal it may try to stop it. In either case, the president, not the bureaucracy, has decided what the issue will be. When President Reagan proposed massive budget cuts for most federal agencies in 1981, he quickly captured the attention of the agencies to be affected. Bill Clinton's proposed overhaul of the nation's health care system, even though it was rejected in 1994, received plenty of notice in the bureaucracy and elsewhere.

This being said, presidents need to limit carefully the number of items on their agendas.[128] As evidenced by the gigantic federal deficits, there is not enough money to meet all the public's demands or all the president's desires. By limiting their agenda, presidents can concentrate on a few goals and keep public attention focused on them. Jimmy Carter's agenda suffered when he overloaded it with proposals. Presidents also must try to establish and move items quickly, particularly early in their terms when they can take advantage of the traditional "honeymoon" period with Congress and the public.

And, not least, presidents should try to keep a national per-spective and a long-range view when formulating an agenda and not get too bogged down in details. Carter, for example, devoted too much time to trivia.[129] Some sources claim that early in his term Carter diligently checked the arithmetic in budget tables and even personally reviewed the scheduling of the White House tennis court!

Because presidents want to give the best possible presentation of their views, their statements on potential agenda issues usually are carefully staged. Using speeches and television appearances, the president can reach millions of citizens at a time. Presidential addresses to the nation and press conferences are televised regularly, and the network news programs feature stories on the president almost nightly. (In fact, the White House encourages network coverage by staging media events and photo opportunities specifically designed to attract the media's attention.) Television is a more effective tool for some presidents than others. Kennedy and especially Reagan were natural performers and communicators; Nixon, Carter, and Bush were less comfortable in front of the camera. *(See Chapter 19, The President and the News Media, Vol. I.)*

Planning

According to scholars Norman C. Thomas and Joseph A. Pika, planning—"anticipating problems and developing solutions to them"—traditionally has been done more successfully by private corporations than by the federal government.[130] Recent presidents have used different types of planning to make the bureaucracy and its processes more amenable to presidential direction. These attempts at planning for the bureaucracy have yielded only mixed results, however.

One of the first large-scale efforts at government planning was the program planning budgeting system (PPBS) instituted throughout the federal government in 1965 by President Johnson. PPBS sought to improve planning before budget decisions were made, make programs rather than agencies the focus of the budget process, relate budget decisions to long-range national goals, and analyze programs on a cost-benefit basis.[131] The overall aim was to promote rational budgetary decision making. PPBS had worked fairly well in the Department of Defense during the Kennedy administration, and hopes were high for its effectiveness on a broader scale. Those hopes were soon dashed, however, as agencies rebelled against the extensive paperwork required by the system and Congress saw it as a threat to its role in the budgetary process.

A technique similar to PPBS, management-by-objective (MBO), was introduced by Richard Nixon to try to increase presidential direction of the bureaucracy. This technique called for agencies to compile lists of their objectives, ranked in order of priority. Once approved by OMB, these lists were sent to the president for his consent. The objectives then became the standard for evaluating agency performance. MBO offered certain benefits: it quickly uncovered conflicting objectives, facilitated White House oversight of agency actions, and highlighted areas of dispute between the agencies and OMB or the president. But

President Bill Clinton and Vice President Al Gore announce their plan to make government leaner and more customer-oriented amid forklifts piled with federal regulations. The administration hoped that public disgust with government red tape would help to overcome bureaucratic and congressional inertia.

MBO failed to help agencies formulate their objectives or state them unambiguously, and these failings were of greatest concern to the president.[132]

Jimmy Carter's principal contribution to planning was zero-base budgeting (ZBB). In theory, agencies would justify each year not only their proposed funding increases but also their entire budget—that is, they would assume a zero base. They then would estimate their output at various levels of funding (for example, at 80, 90, 100, and 110 percent of current funding), so that the estimates could be analyzed to determine the influence of the different levels of funding on long-term agency production and objectives.[133] Finally, the analysis would be used to make rational budget decisions. In practice, however, ZBB did not operate much differently from the traditional incremental budgeting process.

The National Performance Review issued in 1993 by the Clinton administration called for many changes in government planning. "Reinvention laboratories" were established throughout the bureaucracy to generate fresh ideas from all interested employees, employee training was revamped, and more widespread computerization of government activities took place. Also recommended, but not implemented, was a major change in planning: the institution of biennial budgets and appropriations.

Attempts to apply rationality to the uncertain and occasionally irrational world of politics face significant obstacles. The formulation of clear, widely acceptable objectives is rarely easy in a democratic political system. Planners cannot mandate ob-

jectives; specific goals are formed, if at all, through the bargaining and compromise inherent in politics—a process that does not guarantee rational decisions. Thus, although presidents can achieve some control over the bureaucracy through planning, that planning inevitably becomes dominated by politics, thereby losing much of its worth.[134]

Executive Orders

Executive orders are presidential proclamations that carry the force of law. The president's power to issue executive orders is essentially a legislative power since the orders may require agencies or individuals to perform acts not mandated by Congress. Executive orders may be used to enforce the Constitution or treaties with foreign countries, implement legislative statutes, or direct bureaucratic agencies.[135] Thus the executive order is a powerful presidential weapon which can be used against the bureaucracy.

Although the Constitution does not grant the power of executive orders explicitly, it does require the president to "take care that the laws be faithfully executed." When presidents occasionally must act quickly and decisively to fulfill this directive, the executive order is one way of doing so. Modern presidents have maintained that Article II of the Constitution grants them inherent power to take whatever actions they judge to be in the nation's best interests so long as those actions are not prohibited by the Constitution or law.[136] Presidents therefore view executive orders as perfectly acceptable exercises of presidential power, and the Supreme Court generally has upheld this interpretation.

Presidents have used executive orders in such areas as the economy, civil rights, and national security, as well as to direct the bureaucracy. During World War II, Franklin Roosevelt created two powerful agencies—the Office of Price Administration and the Office of Economic Stabilization—through executive orders. Richard Nixon tried, and sometimes succeeded, in using the power to abolish bureaucratic programs and agencies established by Congress. He also took advantage of executive orders to strengthen particular agencies, notably the CIA and the FBI. Ronald Reagan used executive orders to curb the bureaucracy's role in promulgating regulations for the private sector. George Bush issued an executive order to create a commission on ethics for public servants, and Bill Clinton issued executive orders to implement parts of the National Performance Review.

One problem with executive orders arises from the ambiguous nature of the president's authority to issue them. Although the practice itself is clearly accepted, the limits of its use are somewhat vague. This leaves some orders open to questions of validity. For example, Nixon's 1971 use of executive orders to freeze wages and prices, even though explicitly allowed by Congress, was challenged in federal court. That particular use of executive orders was upheld, but as Harry Truman had discovered earlier, there is no guarantee of such success in court. His seizure, through executive order, of the steel industry during the Korean War was struck down by the Supreme Court.[137]

Commander-in-chief Powers

The Constitution names the president commander in chief of the nation's armed forces. The position also gives the president a great deal of influence over the civilian bureaucracy, where presidential decisions on military questions can affect the funding, status, and support of several bureaucratic agencies. One obvious example is the Department of Defense, which prospered as a result of military decisions made by the Reagan administration.

Despite the authority that accompanies the role of commander in chief, the president rarely can issue instructions to the bureaucracy and have them obeyed immediately. As former secretary of state Henry A. Kissinger commented, "The outsider believes a presidential order is consistently followed out. Nonsense."[138] One official in the Nixon administration asserted that frustration over the difficulty in having commands carried out explains certain presidential behavior: "That's why [presidents] all love to play Commander in Chief; at least the military *pretends* to obey."[139]

In some instances, however, presidential orders are carried out expeditiously. Political scientist Richard Neustadt studied three cases in which presidents issued commands and had them obeyed readily: Truman's dismissal of Gen. Douglas MacArthur, Truman's seizure of the American steel industry during the Korean War, and Eisenhower's use of federal troops to force the desegregation of Little Rock, Arkansas, schools. After examining the circumstances that promoted such obedience, Neustadt concluded that presidential orders are obeyed swiftly only when

five conditions are met. First, subordinates must know that the order comes directly from the president, not merely from a presidential staffer. Presidents can ensure that their personal involvement is known by controlling how the announcement of the decision is made. Second, the president's order must be clear and unambiguous; it should state precisely what action the president wants taken. Third, the order must be widely publicized so that any official who disobeys the order draws the attention of the media and the White House. Fourth, whoever receives the order must be able to act on it. There is little reason to expect success if the order cannot possibly be fulfilled. Fifth, recipients of presidential orders must believe that the president has the legitimate authority to issue that particular order; subordinates are more likely to disobey an order that appears to be illegitimate. Yet, as Neustadt acknowledged, rarely are all five conditions met simultaneously, making it seldom likely that presidential orders will be obeyed rapidly. Thus the primary power of the president is the power to persuade.[140] *(See "Leadership Skills," p. 1433.)*

Neustadt's analysis clearly reveals that the president's powers as commander in chief are limited. But even if relatively few presidential directives are obeyed immediately and without question, the power to give those orders is still an important one. Presidential follow-up or cajoling may be needed to get the desired results, but the president's role as commander in chief is a benefit in dealing with the bureaucracy.

Crisis Leadership

During times of crisis the public expects the president to take charge of the situation, and it ordinarily approves of whatever action the president takes. National crises may include wars, riots, other acts of violence, economic upheavals, and natural disasters such as floods, droughts, blizzards, hurricanes, and earthquakes. The sense of urgency engendered by crises usually means that during crises presidents find that accomplishments come more easily, including control of the bureaucracy.

During a war, the severest kind of crisis, presidents have the greatest freedom of action. They can freeze prices, create new agencies, allocate jobs, and even censor the press.[141] In the past, presidential actions have even restricted fundamental civil liberties—for example, Abraham Lincoln suspended *habeas corpus* during the Civil War, and Franklin Roosevelt interned Japanese Americans during World War II. In the midst of a crisis, presidents find that they can do almost anything in the name of national security.

During the Great Depression of the 1930s, FDR got virtually everything he wanted from Congress during his first one hundred days in office, and he used that influence to create much of the modern federal bureaucracy. In 1970 Richard Nixon saw the potential for inflation as a crisis and imposed wage and price controls in an effort to forestall it.

Because presidents find the public support of their actions that appears in crises (sometimes called the "rally round the flag" effect) so appealing, they may try to make a genuine problem look like an immediate crisis in an effort to create public support and increase congressional backing. For example, Lyndon Johnson declared "an unconditional war on poverty" in 1964, and Carter described the energy shortage as the "moral equivalent of war" in 1977.[142] Johnson made more progress in his War on Poverty than Carter made in the energy crisis for two reasons. First, unlike Carter, Johnson worked long and hard to build congressional support for his programs. Second, LBJ was able to capitalize on emotions dredged up by the assassination of John Kennedy. Jimmy Carter's experience demonstrates one potential danger of crisis leadership: failure to handle crises effectively can lead to loss of political standing. Carter's mismanagement of the energy crisis seriously wounded his image, but a subsequent crisis that he did not manufacture caused even greater damage. In November 1979 a mob of fanatical Iranians overran the U.S. embassy in Tehran and captured about fifty Americans. Initially, public support was behind the president, but it steadily decreased as Carter's year-long attempts to free the hostages failed dismally. By most accounts, Carter's ineffectual management of the Iranian crisis contributed to his defeat in the 1980 election.

Crisis leadership is thus a double-edged sword for presidents. On the one hand, it allows considerable freedom of action, which can be a welcome change from the normal constraints on presidential behavior. The public support for the president characteristic of crises, particularly in their early stages, offers the president additional power. On the other hand, that supply of support is not inexhaustible, and presidents who bungle crises can suffer major political damage.

LIMITS TO PRESIDENTIAL POWER

Although presidents can use a variety of powers in their efforts to control the bureaucracy, each power has particular disadvantages that limit its usefulness. Unfortunately for presidents, however, those are not the only limits they must confront. The other factors hampering presidential attempts to harness the bureaucracy are time constraints, lack of information, "iron triangles," "issue networks," and bureaucratic preferences.

Time Constraints

Time works against presidential endeavors to oversee the bureaucracy in several ways. First, the president and the bureaucracy have wholly different perspectives on time. Longevity is one of the bureaucracy's strongest weapons; many problems facing it diminish after enough time passes. If the president is hostile to a particular agency, for example, the best defense for that agency is often just to wait for the arrival of a new president. Similarly, if conditions do not favor action by an agency, those conditions probably will change eventually.

Presidents do not have the luxury of being able to wait indefinitely. Their relatively short terms in office, as well as their desires to be reelected and then to make a mark on history, demand quick, dramatic action. Thus, with the bureaucracy's seemingly infinite capacity to delay filling presidential requests,

the passage of time generally works to the advantage of the bureaucracy and to the disadvantage of the president.

Second, presidents are faced with tremendous daily demands on their time. Even if presidents had more time to devote to controlling the bureaucracy, it is so vast and performs so many functions that becoming fully familiar with it, much less controlling it, would be an impossible task.

Third, the president's staff faces the same kinds of time limitations. They too have many different tasks, and, like the president, they are continually confronted with unanticipated problems. In the fall of 1978, for example, President Carter and his assistants were dealing with the beginnings of the Iranian revolution, the aftermath of the Camp David meetings, negotiations with the Soviets over the SALT II agreement, secret talks with the Chinese, and trouble with Nicaragua.[143] That is undoubtedly plenty to do, even without considering domestic issues and the bureaucracy.

Finally, even if presidents have abundant time, they are not likely to delve into areas—including many activities of the bureaucracy—that they find uninteresting or unimportant. In fact, a lack of presidential concern with the daily operations of many of the bureaucratic agencies is entirely understandable. Lyndon Johnson's response to a reporter's question about something the president considered a "minor administrative matter" clearly makes the point. Johnson roared at the reporter: "Why do you . . . ask me, the leader of the Western World, a chickenshit question like that?"[144]

Lack of Information and Experience

Even with a White House staff numbering in the hundreds the president cannot match the bureaucracy's information on all the activities of the federal bureaucracy and its three million employees. The expertise and specialization of the bureaucracy, perhaps largely because of its size, give it the advantage in information-gathering.

Time constraints also limit the information available to the president and the White House staff. In most cases, they have access to the raw information they need, but they do not have time to process and evaluate it. David Stockman, Reagan's first head of OMB, commented on his role in constructing the federal budget:

I just wish that there were more hours in the day or that we didn't have to do this so fast. I have these stacks of briefing books and I've got to make decisions about specific options. . . . I don't have time, trying to put this whole package together in three weeks, so you just start making snap judgments.[145]

If the president's staff does not even have enough time to consider the budget carefully, it certainly does not have time to generate and assess information about the routine functions of many bureaucratic agencies.

Lack of information can be a particular problem in presidential efforts to oversee the bureaucracy's implementation of programs and directives. Limited time and staff frequently force the president to rely on data provided by the implementing agencies themselves, which naturally raises questions about the information's accuracy and objectivity. This happens in several policy areas, including health care and protection of the environment.

Few chief executives enter the White House with experience in managing the federal bureaucracy, and some have little background in managing any kind of large organization. Any expectations that they can effectively control the mammoth U.S. bureaucracy are therefore unreasonable.

Five of the ten post–World War II presidents—Truman, Kennedy, Johnson, Nixon, and Ford—spent most of their political careers before assuming the presidency in Congress. Presidential candidates frequently claim that service in Congress is excellent preparation for the White House, but apparently that is not the case for handling the bureaucracy. Congressional contact with the bureaucracy is more cooperative than hierarchical; legislators ask for favors and the agencies are more than happy to respond.[146] This arrangement hardly prepares a president for the less congenial reception the bureaucracy often gives the occupant of the Oval Office.

Moreover, the skills learned in Congress are not especially helpful when managing the bureaucracy as president. Congress revolves around tactics and deal making and, for the most part, it leaves an issue behind once legislation is passed. But according to Seidman and Gilmour, "Unlike a legislator, a president should view the passage of a law as a beginning, not an end."[147] The president is, after all, the chief executive. Training in Congress rarely produces chief executives interested in or skilled at implementing programs.

George Bush's varied career—including, among other positions, a stint as head of a bureaucratic agency, the CIA—prepared him well to deal with the bureaucracy. Other recent presidents—Jimmy Carter, Ronald Reagan, and Bill Clinton—underwent their political preliminaries as state governors. They perhaps had an advantage over former members of Congress who occupied the Oval Office because they assumed the presidency with experience in managing their state bureaucracies. As the former governors quickly discovered, however, the huge and complex federal bureaucracy is in an entirely different league than the relatively small state bureaucracies. Franklin Roosevelt was perhaps the president best prepared to tackle the bureaucracy.[148] He not only had experience with the bureaucracy of a large state as governor of New York, but he also had been exposed to the federal bureaucracy when serving as assistant secretary of the navy.

"Iron Triangles"

As the name implies, an "iron triangle" is a strong three-sided alliance among groups of political participants—federal agencies, interest groups, and congressional committees or subcommittees—with stakes in a particular policy area. Each member of the alliance, or each point of the triangle, has a mutually beneficial relationship with the other two members, and all members work together to pursue common goals. Iron triangles sometimes are called "subgovernments" because they exert so much influence on government decisions in their policy areas. Hundreds of such alliances have sprung up in Washington.

Iron triangles tend to work behind the scenes. Representatives of the groups involved—agency careerists, interest group lobbyists, and members of Congress and their staffers—discuss policy issues and then agree on preferred outcomes. Likely topics of discussion are proposed legislation, budgetary matters, reorganization plans, personnel concerns, and potential regulations.[149] The interests of the allies do not always coincide completely, but the close personal relationships that frequently form between participants help to smooth the differences. Bureaucrats, lobbyists, and members of Congress often hold the same jobs for two decades or more, and thus they have plenty of opportunity to become friends with their allies.

Each side helps the others and receives help in return. From Congress, bureaucrats want generous funding as well as legislation granting them maximum authority and discretion. In return, members of Congress want preferential treatment for their constituencies, technical assistance for their staffs, and often help in drafting legislation. Legislators also look to interest groups for information and assistance in formulating proposals, as well as financial and political help in their campaigns and sometimes paid speaking engagements. Interest groups in turn want members of Congress to ensure their access to bureaucratic agencies and to pass and fund programs that benefit the groups. Interest groups also rely on Congress for help in having group members appointed to and confirmed for key government jobs.

The third side of the triangle connects the interest groups and bureaucratic agencies. Interest groups want to have a strong say in agency decisions, including the writing of regulations, ideally through a formal advisory system that would give the interest group either formal or informal veto power over such decisions. The agencies in turn want the political support of interest groups, including positive congressional testimony and lobbying for additional funds for the agency.

Examples of iron triangles are plentiful. The members of one iron triangle—the Department of the Interior; interest groups representing farmers, ranchers, and forestry and mining companies; and various congressional committees (including the Senate Environment Committee and the House Interior Committee, among others)—work together to form land- and water-use policies, which are particularly important in the western states. On the issue of highways, the driver's seat is shared by the Department of Transportation; interest groups representing the auto, tire, and oil industries; and members of the congressional transportation committees. One of the more infamous iron triangles is the so-called "military-industrial complex" that dominates the defense system. Its members include the Department of Defense, weapons contractors and related firms, and assorted congressional committees, particularly the armed services committees.

By bringing together the most interested parties on issues and having them work toward common goals, iron triangles greatly influence policy formulation. One effect is continuity in policy, arising from the expertise, longevity, and political clout of iron triangles. Although such an effect may benefit the public when presidents are concerned with other matters, it also can work against the public when citizens are anxious for a change. Moreover, the cozy relationships within iron triangles can result in lax government regulation of the private sector, can stifle free competition by giving some groups preferential treatment, and can penalize the poor or unorganized.[150]

The power of iron triangles limits presidential control of the bureaucracy because agencies within iron triangles always can turn to their congressional and interest group allies for help against the president. An assistant to Jimmy Carter assessed presidential control of the bureaucracy this way: "There isn't any government down there to manage. There is a series of sub-governments pursuing single interests of one kind or another."[151]

Congress is an especially valuable friend of federal agencies, and presidents find that those agencies with strong ties to Congress are the hardest to influence. One career bureaucrat put it bluntly: "I don't care who sits in the Oval Office. I depend on Congress for my livelihood."[152] The Army Corps of Engineers, which spreads pork barrel projects across the country, is renowned for its favored status with Congress and for its attendant invulnerability to presidential intervention.

The president can still exercise some influence over agencies, of course, particularly when their iron triangles are weakened. For example, iron triangles may clash with other subgovernments, receive negative publicity, or suffer from internal dissension. The weapons procurement iron triangle was weakened in 1988 when some of its members were shown to have participated in bribery and fraud. Some observers believed this scandal provided an opportunity for the president to clamp down on wasteful defense spending. And the interests of iron triangles and presidents occasionally do coincide. When Ronald Reagan pushed for increased defense spending in the early 1980s, for example, the weapons procurement iron triangle was eager to help. Thus the relationships are not always adversarial.

"Issue Networks"

Other forces that can impede presidential control of the bureaucracy are what scholar Hugh Heclo has called "issue networks."[153] Like iron triangles, issue networks are coalitions of individuals and groups who want to influence particular areas of executive policy. Issue networks, however, differ from iron triangles in several important respects. Issue networks are larger and more complex than iron triangles, as well as more open and fluid. Participants in such networks have varied backgrounds and may include journalists, academics, foundation officers, lobbyists, White House and congressional staff members, and bureaucrats.[154]

Because issue networks are less structured than iron triangles, people move in and out of them freely, and the networks themselves change as public issues change. Moreover, the goals of issue networks are likely to be different from those of iron triangles. Members of iron triangles are interested mainly in pursuing personal benefits—career security for bureaucrats, reelection for members of Congress, and economic gain for most interest groups—whereas those active in issue networks want to influence public policy, perhaps by encouraging rationality and innovation in decision making, promoting greater government efficiency, or pushing specific proposals. Activists in issue networks are generally professionals who enjoy exercising influence over public policy for the prestige, power, and personal satisfaction that such influence offers.

The making of agriculture policy is a good example of an issue network. The Department of Agriculture, farmers' organizations, and the congressional agriculture committees are joined by representatives of other backgrounds and professions in shaping agriculture policy. Nutrition experts, health care professionals, activists concerned with world hunger, and foreign policy analysts (American agricultural products are exported throughout the world) voice their opinions, as do members of "think tanks" and local community groups. Environmentalists concerned with the effects of pesticide use on farms, bankers holding farm mortgages, and energy experts looking at farmers' dependence on imported oil products also take part in the issue network, further illustrating its complexity and openness.

Issue networks sometimes clash with iron triangles. This is not surprising given their conflicting goals: self-interest for iron triangles versus good policy for issue networks (at least their participants' ideas of good policy). For example, analysts within the defense issue network but outside the weapons procurement iron triangle criticize the system of purchasing weapons as woefully wasteful. Similarly, environmentalists upset over acid rain battle the iron triangles that protect the "smokestack" industries contributing to the problem.[155]

Issue networks form and operate differently than iron triangles. Networks come into being when concerned citizens realize that they share similar points of view about a particular issue and often disintegrate when that issue is settled. Thus networks appear, disappear, and fluctuate over time, whereas iron triangles are much more stable. Members of networks want to convince the president and Congress that the network's position is the right one. They also want to have some network members appointed to government posts and to advise the president and Congress regularly of their views.[156] Unlike iron triangles, issue networks seek publicity and use the media to produce and shape public attention. Many members of issue networks are former high government officials, eager for the chance to regain influence over policy making.

Issue networks frustrate presidential control of the bureaucracy in several ways. In general, even though issue networks do not act with the unanimity of iron triangles, they do increase the fragmentation of public policy formulation and therefore the difficulty of presidential control over it.[157] Issue networks draw more people, most of them independent of the president and holding diverse opinions, into the policy-making process.

The federal bureaucracy—composed of hundreds of agencies and millions of workers—is immense and complex. Presidents have found managing the bureaucracy one of the most difficult aspects of their office.

The networks further reduce presidential power by supplying Congress and the bureaucracy with information and political backing that they can use to pursue their own objectives and to thwart presidential intervention.

The conflict that frequently erupts within issue networks can be an advantage to the president, however. Because issue networks are open and contain many diverse participants, disagreements within networks are common. For example, members of the agricultural issue network split sharply on the question of whether embargoes on exports of U.S. agricultural products should be used as tools of foreign policy. Conflicts such as this tend to produce different policy proposals from members of the same issue network. When a variety of proposals are put before the public, the president has an opportunity to weigh the alternatives and assess public opinion before acting. The information generated in such debates is quite useful to the president in making policy decisions. The conflict also may establish the president as the final arbiter of the dispute. Finally, issue networks may lead to better public policy and to enhanced political stature for the president by increasing the number of experts involved and improving the quality of the debate on policy.

Bureaucratic Preferences

Probably the most important restraint on presidential control of the bureaucracy stems from bureaucratic preferences. Presidents usually find it difficult to get the bureaucracy to do what it does not want to do. One reason for this difficulty is that the bureaucracy does not speak with a single voice. Although it is frequently thought to be a single entity, the federal bureaucracy is composed of hundreds of agencies and millions of employees with various interests and policy preferences. Bureaucratic preferences fall into three basic categories, however: those of

agencies, those of civil servants, and those of political appointees.

Federal agencies generally want to survive and, if possible, expand. Thus any presidential proposals that go counter to those goals are almost certain to draw opposition from the bureaus affected. For example, not surprisingly President Reagan's efforts to abolish the Departments of Education and Energy drew vigorous resistance from the agencies.

Agencies also may oppose the president on matters that do not threaten them directly. For example, an agency occasionally resists the president in behalf of other agencies that are allies. Or an agency may simply disagree with the president's decision and prefer another alternative when it believes a presidential decision is ill advised or unworkable. Disagreement also may spring from ideological differences. When given the chance, agency employees tend to act according to their own beliefs.[158] Welfare administrators, for example, opposed the Nixon administration's plan to require able-bodied welfare recipients to work in exchange for their payments, and the proposal eventually was discarded.[159] Similarly, some welfare workers reacted coolly to Clinton's welfare reform plan.

The goals of civil servants working within bureaucratic agencies also hamper presidential control of the bureaucracy. Permanent civil servants are committed to their careers and to their agencies and programs.[160] Thus their preferences, which emphasize their goals of stability and regularity, inevitably clash with those of the president, who usually wants rapid, bold action from the bureaucracy to help fulfill the presidential goals of reelection and historical significance. The security and longevity of civil servants make them formidable opponents of presidential actions they dislike. *(See "Conflicting Goals," p. 1430.)*

Even though they are selected by the president, political appointees also have goals that often conflict with the president's. Because most appointees serve in government only a short time, they want to establish their reputations quickly. This could require taking actions that do not toe the presidential line. Conflicting goals also result when political appointees adopt the positions and attitudes of their agencies and become more representatives of their agencies to the president than the other way around.

Outcomes of a Complex Relationship

The relationship between the president and the bureaucracy is clearly a complex one, and several important questions about this relationship have not yet been addressed. First, who wins, and why, when the president and the bureaucracy clash? Second, what effects does bureaucratic power have on democratic government? And, third, can the president actually control the bureaucracy?

EXPLAINING OUTCOMES

Who wins, and why, when the president and the bureaucracy clash? Unfortunately, there is no precise answer to this question. Each case differs, and the reasons for outcomes vary according to the specifics of the case. Much of the answer, however, lies in the powers and restraints applicable to the president and the bureaucracy in a particular case. In 1981 Ronald Reagan triumphed over the striking air traffic controllers in part because the strike was clearly illegal, making it easier for Reagan to fire the strikers. Additional factors, including the kind of policy and presidential goal in question, also come into play and must be considered in explaining outcomes.

Types of Policies

The extent and success of presidential efforts to control bureaucratic agencies depend in part on the type of policy involved. Policies can be separated into two categories: domestic and foreign. Domestic policies can be further divided into distributive, regulatory, and redistributive policies.

Distributive Policies. Implemented nationwide, distributive policies (sometimes called "pork barrel" policies) work toward general goals and provide benefits directly to the populace.[161] Distributive policies are manifested, for example, in the national park system, the interstate highway system, grants to state and local governments, and federal insurance of bank deposits. The bureaucratic agencies running distributive programs usually are fairly small, but they often participate in powerful iron triangles or issue networks because many distributive programs profit relatively narrow but influential segments of the population. For example, the interstate highway system benefits road contractors and oil companies, among others.

Agencies that implement distributive policies are among the most powerful within the bureaucracy, and thus they are not readily amenable to presidential control. Their strength stems from the backing of interest groups benefiting from their poli-

cies, as well as from the enthusiastic support of Congress, which likes distributive policies because of their widespread applicability, political attractiveness, and low political risk. Some distributive agencies are the Army Corps of Engineers, the Department of Education, and the National Park Service.

The functions of agencies handling distributive policies also help to shield them from presidential intervention. Because legislation creating the programs is generally loosely drafted, the implementing agencies have plenty of latitude in their operations and thus can implement programs as they see fit.[162] Designed to take action and combat problems, distributive agencies possess ample quantities of expertise, leadership, and cohesion—as well as popular support. In addition, because of their public and congressional support these agencies usually enjoy comfortable budgets. Presidents, who after all are politicians too, rarely want to attack popular programs that provide benefits to people all across the country.

Regulatory Policies. Regulatory policies establish government-specified rules of behavior for individuals and institutions—and penalties for violation of the rules.[163] The federal government regulates many aspects of society—including business and industry, public health and safety, and natural resources—and enforces federal criminal laws. Because the scope of government regulation is very broad, many bureaucratic agencies participate in its formulation and enforcement. Regulatory agencies include the Federal Communications Commission, Food and Drug Administration, and Environmental Protection Agency.

Support for regulatory policies is mixed. Activist groups often strongly support the government's regulatory efforts; for example, the Sierra Club and other ecology-minded groups encourage vigorous and stringent regulation of the environment by the EPA. As far as it is aware of governmental regulation, the public also is inclined to support it. Opposition often comes from the regulated, however, who may assail regulations as unwarranted government intervention. Congress tends to support the principle of government regulation, but in practice it is concerned about the possibility of upsetting constituents and political allies.[164] Overall, the support received by regulatory agencies is significantly less than that for distributive agencies, which is understandable considering that distributive agencies provide benefits, not rules and regulations.

Regulatory agencies also seldom enjoy the other advantages of distributive agencies. For example, most regulatory agencies do not have the large research staffs and expertise that constitute a source of agency power. Strong leadership also may be a problem because many regulatory agencies are governed not by a single individual but by a board of directors—an arrangement that ordinarily requires greater compromise. Another problem: agency cohesion may be difficult to generate because the functions of regulatory agencies, including the formulation and application of sometimes tedious rules, are relatively less appealing. The Environmental Protection Agency and the Federal Trade Commission are noteworthy exceptions; their employees are frequently zealous and dedicated. Most regulatory agencies are thus not very powerful, leaving them more open to presidential control than other types of agencies. Ironically, the more effective agencies contribute to their own weakness by skillfully making and enforcing rules that engender more active opposition from the regulated.[165]

Presidents exert some influence over regulatory agencies in their appointments of agency heads and manipulation of agencies' proposed budgets, and they can try to persuade agencies to interpret regulations in ways acceptable to the administration. Presidents also control regulatory agencies and policy through the judicial and legislative branches by having the Justice Department file friend-of-the-court briefs in regulatory test cases and by attempting to change regulations through the passage of new legislation. Finally, presidents can choose which regulations the administration will emphasize. By initially appointing EPA administrators who were hostile to the agency's mission, President Reagan clearly signaled that his administration intended to de-emphasize regulation of the environment.[166]

Although presidents are able to exercise significant control over regulatory agencies, they often choose not to do so. The political price can be high for intervention in the regulatory arena, as Reagan discovered in his relations with EPA. His moves upset Congress and the public so much that he was forced to back away from his position and to appoint an environmentalist to lead the agency.[167]

Redistributive Policies. Redistributive policies use the taxes taken from one group of people to provide benefits to another group of people.[168] These policies, which are among the most controversial in the country, include Medicaid, housing programs, and a variety of welfare programs.[169] Public support for redistributive programs varies, largely according to how many and what kind of people benefit from particular programs. Some redistributive programs lean toward being distributive—that is, they spread benefits widely through society for purposes that are widely approved. The Social Security program, for example, which makes payments to a large segment of the population, is a redistributive program with distributive characteristics. As a general rule, the greater the distributive element in a redistributive program, the greater is the political support it receives.[170] Not only do such programs have more political backing because they serve more people, but they also are not as likely to be dubbed "welfare," a term that still rankles many Americans.

The most important task—and thus power—of redistributive agencies is the distribution of funds. Redistributive agencies make and influence funding decisions at several levels. At the highest levels, they advise the president and Congress on legislation dealing with redistributive policies and related matters. Frequently, agencies even initiate policies themselves. At the agency level, daily decisions that affect how money is spent are made in conjunction with oversight of program operations and determination of which individuals are eligible to receive program benefits. Despite the influence of these agencies over spending practices, however, Congress has the final say and usually structures redistributive programs carefully, thereby limiting agency discretion.[171] Examples of redistributive agencies are the Social Security Administration, Farmers Home Administration, and Federal Housing Administration.

Because redistributive programs are so large, expertise is an important source of power for the agencies running them. Leadership and cohesion may become sources of power for redistributive agencies, but not easily because many of these programs are actually administered at the state and local levels. That method of administration also means that there are relatively few redistributive bureaucrats—even though redistributive agencies spend more than half the federal budget, only 7 percent of federal employees work in these agencies.[172] Overall, redistributive agencies enjoy more political clout than regulatory agencies but less than distributive ones.

Ideology influences the relationship between presidents and the agencies implementing redistributive policies. Conservative presidents are less supportive of redistributive policies and the agencies executing them than liberal presidents. This is especially true of welfare programs that serve only a narrow, and politically inactive, segment of society. But it is unlikely that any president will attack redistributive programs that benefit large numbers of relatively affluent and politically active citizens—as the inviolability of the Social Security system illustrates.

Presidential control of redistributive agencies also is affected by two other major issues. First, in an era of budgetary austerity, presidents must face the problem of increasingly scarce resources—and redistributive programs are expensive. Second, presidents quickly notice how difficult enforcement of the rules of redistributive programs can be, particularly because the points of service delivery are scattered all over the country.[173] Redistributive agencies also can be difficult to control because the programs often have strong public support and receive considerable attention from Congress.

Foreign Policy. Presidents devote more time to foreign policy than to domestic issues because they tend to be more interested in it, and because they often believe they can exert greater control over foreign policy than over domestic policy. Even presidents like Bill Clinton, who promised to emphasize domestic policy, often are forced by international events to focus on foreign policy. Presidents also view foreign policy achievements as an effective way to increase their popularity, improve their chances for reelection, and make their place in history.[174]

As commander in chief of the armed forces, presidents have significant authority over foreign policy questions, particularly issues requiring rapid action. Their power to make treaties with foreign nations and their position as head of state also enhance their role in foreign affairs. Despite these advantages, however, presidents continue to encounter problems with the bureaucratic agencies that deal most with foreign policy, the Departments of State and Defense.

The State Department, with its deep-seated attitudes and routines, has frustrated presidents for many years. Its foreign service officers, who represent the United States worldwide, are attuned primarily to the goals and procedures of the department, not the president. Presidents who try to use the State Department to provide bold new ideas or to carry out risky plans frequently are disappointed.[175] Therefore presidents sometimes circumvent the department, as when Clinton sent former president Jimmy Carter to negotiate a solution to the 1994 crisis in Haiti.

One challenging aspect of any president's job is controlling the military and dealing with the rivalry that exists among its branches. Presidents also must supervise the enormously complicated business of weapons procurement.[176] The Reagan administration's failure to do the latter helps to explain the 1988 weapons scandal, in which fraud and bribery were uncovered in Pentagon procurement practices.

Problems with the foreign policy bureaucracy have led recent presidents to rely increasingly on their White House national security staff and to make their national security adviser a key player in international relations. Henry Kissinger fulfilled this role during Nixon's first term. Although such tactics have certain advantages for presidents—including more information, greater discretion, and rapid responses to foreign policy issues—they also have some dangers, as shown by the Iran-contra scandal in the Reagan administration. Heavy reliance on the White House national security staff increases the tension between the White House and the executive agencies, decreases continuity between administrations, and encourages a narrow view of foreign relations.[177]

Presidents who try to control the foreign policy bureaucracy often have two problems.[178] First, agencies sometimes resist fulfilling presidential orders. Because presidents tend to believe that they can shape foreign policy and deal with foreign leaders better on their own than through the bureaucracy, they may make foreign policy decisions without consulting the bureaucracy or against its advice. And when the bureaucracy disagrees with presidential orders, it often resists those orders in the hope that the president will either forget about the matter or have a change of heart. The second problem is that presidential directives sometimes are misunderstood by agencies and thus are not implemented in the way the president intended.

These problems are similar to those that plague presidents in domestic politics. The major difference is that presidents can use their relatively greater authority in foreign policy to counter the problems presented by federal agencies. Also, there is rarely a need to involve state and local bureaucracies in foreign policy.

Presidential Goals

Although virtually all presidential goals require the cooperation if not the assistance of the bureaucracy, some goals are more easily achieved than others. Thus the nature of those goals is an important variable in the relationship between the president and the bureaucracy.

Presidential scholars Erwin C. Hargrove and Michael Nelson have proposed a cycle theory that categorizes presidents according to their goals.[179] What the public wants at any particular point in time also affects the cycle because skillful presidents adjust their goals to fit the public mood. According to this theory, three types of presidents appear in a cycle: a president of consolidation, who follows a president of achievement; a president of preparation, who follows a president of consolidation; and a president of achievement, who follows a president of preparation. Each type of president responds to different cues from the public and generates different goals. Presidents of achievement enter office with a mandate for change from the public, and they proceed to propose and get enacted broad and dramatic legislative programs that alter the role of the federal government in American life. Woodrow Wilson, Franklin Roosevelt, Lyndon Johnson, and Ronald Reagan were presidents of achievement.

Presidents of consolidation concentrate on refining, legitimizing, and rationalizing the changes brought about by their predecessors. They generally pursue no major new programs. Calvin Coolidge, Dwight Eisenhower, Richard Nixon, and George Bush exemplified this type of president.

Finally, presidents of preparation identify public problems, formulate possible solutions, and lay the political groundwork for the following president of achievement. Theodore Roosevelt, John Kennedy, Jimmy Carter, and Bill Clinton fall into this category.

Each of the three types of presidents relates differently to the bureaucracy because their goals differ. Presidents of achievement enter office with overwhelming public support for change. That support is short-lived, however; thus these presidents must act quickly in formulating and passing programs to take advantage of the existing support. One important consequence is that programs often are hastily devised, with little thought given to how they will be implemented—and the implementation stage is where the bureaucracy is particularly powerful. Presidents of achievement usually succeed in fulfilling their goals—resulting perhaps in big changes for the bureaucracy (FDR's "New Deal" expansion and Reagan's cutbacks on some types of federal spending are examples)—but they often have trouble getting the bureaucracy to implement their programs.

Presidents of consolidation try to solve the implementation problems left by presidents of achievement. They work with the bureaucracy to see that programs run as smoothly and effectively as possible. For example, rather than trying to repeal the Great Society programs passed by Lyndon Johnson, the Nixon administration attempted to make those policies run more efficiently. Good relations with the bureaucracy are therefore especially important for presidents of consolidation, and they are probably maintained more easily because the relationship is basically a cooperative one.

One of the most crucial tasks of presidents of preparation is generating new ideas, a process that usually is carried out by the White House staff, not the bureaucracy. This is not surprising since the bureaucracy is renowned for its love of routine and its aversion to proposals that conceivably might harm its standing. The bureaucracy plays a useful role in the process, however, by acting as the devil's advocate and stressing realism and practicality. Because clashes between the president and the bureaucracy can erupt when the president favors an idea unpopular with bureaucrats, presidents of preparation sometimes have stormy relations with the bureaucracy. For example, Jimmy Carter encountered opposition from the Department of Labor when he tried to develop a welfare reform proposal, and he faced resistance from several departments over his proposed urban policies.

Other Influences

Other influences also affect the outcome of clashes between the president and the bureaucracy, including the type of bureaucracy engaged in the conflict. Some agencies outside those in the Executive Office of the President are inherently more receptive to presidential control than others. Sometimes called presidential agencies, these entities ordinarily do not distribute tangible benefits to large areas of the country, nor do they exert direct influence within congressional districts. Presidential agencies include the Justice Department, Central Intelligence Agency, Treasury Department, and the Arms Control and Disarmament Agency.[180]

Other agencies, whose actions affect congressional constituents or districts directly, are more oriented toward Congress. Because such agencies can be valuable politically, Congress tends to take a strong interest in them, while presidential control over them is more tenuous. Congressional agencies include the Departments of Agriculture, Interior, and Veterans Affairs, and the Army Corps of Engineers.

Some agencies do not fit neatly into either category. The president has greater influence over these agencies than over congressional agencies, but not as much as over presidential agencies.

Another consideration in explaining the outcome of presidential-bureaucratic clashes is whether the agency is doing something the president does not like or whether the agency is not doing something the president wants it to do. The president is much more likely to succeed in halting agency action than in instigating agency action.[181] As is true throughout most of the American political system, it is much easier to stop initiatives than to complete them. The president can use, or threaten to use, several powers—including appointment and removal, budgetary measures, and reorganization—to halt whatever the agency is doing. Scholar Dennis D. Riley has put the odds of a president being able to stop an agency's actions at about fifty-fifty.[182]

Unfortunately for the president, the odds of being able to get agencies to do something new are much worse. Bureaucratic inertia works against the president, and in some instances the agencies do not have the authority to do what the president wants (here the president's chances are especially slim because Congress must first be convinced to grant the agency the authority to perform the action in mind). Even when agencies already have the necessary authority, the president must grapple with the reasons why the agency chose not to exercise that authority.[183]

Another factor to be considered in explaining outcomes of the clashes between the president and the bureaucracy is the question of where and how bureaucratic programs are implemented. As difficult as presidents find it to control the federal bureaucracy, that task seems simple compared to the presidential effort required to control the state and local organizations that carry out many federal programs.[184]

A final factor is the president's current political standing. The better it is, the easier will be control of the bureaucracy and most other political chores.[185] Also, presidents late in their second terms are weakened politically by their lame duck status and therefore find it harder to control the bureaucracy.

BUREAUCRATIC ACCOUNTABILITY

The tremendous power of the federal bureaucracy raises some important questions about America's democratic government. First, because the bureaucrats who exercise that power are not elected by the public, does the bureaucracy really respond to the public's desires—that is, is the bureaucracy accountable for its actions, and if it is, how? Second, how much accountability is necessary to ensure bureaucratic responsiveness? And third, should the president be responsible for holding the bureaucracy accountable?

Is the Bureaucracy Accountable?

Some scholars, pointing to the difficulty in holding the bureaucracy accountable, believe that little bureaucratic accountability is exercised in the modern political system. One problem is interpreting the public will. That task is difficult enough on major political issues, but divining the public's desires on the less visible matters ordinarily handled by the bureaucracy is an even more daunting prospect.

Furthermore, the huge size and complexity of the bureaucracy make it hard to keep track of what the bureaucracy is doing, much less to assess its actions and compare them to the public will. It also is unclear exactly who will do the accounting because the bureaucracy is technically subordinate to the president, Congress, and the courts, none of whom usually has much incentive to watch the bureaucracy closely.

Despite these obstacles, some observers claim that the federal bureaucracy is reasonably accountable to the public.[186] Scholars Peter Woll and Rochelle Jones even go so far as to assert that "the bureaucracy is at least as accountable and controlled as the three original branches [of the federal government]."[187] This line of argument admits that there is no clear single authority that governs the bureaucracy. Rather, the multiplicity of forces that influences the bureaucracy ensures an adequate degree of accountability. Thus the will of the public, at least as it manifests itself in interest groups and elected officials, who let the bureaucracy know their feelings, influences bureaucratic behavior.

How Much Accountability Is Necessary?

Almost everyone agrees that some accountability and control over the bureaucracy are needed to see that laws are implemented more or less in accordance with legislative intent and that the bureaucracy is responsive to the needs of the public. But how much accountability is in the public's best interests? Some observers believe that the greater that control, the better, whereas many others note the benefits of having a bureaucracy with a certain degree of autonomy.

One benefit usually reaped from a bureaucracy with some discretion is better policy. Because bureaucratic agencies have specific functions and use employees with specialized skills to carry them out, bureaucratic discretion is a good thing, the argument goes, as the bureaucrats themselves are best suited to make administrative decisions. Rigid control of the bureaucracy by outsiders may well reduce bureaucratic efficiency, not only because the interference causes inconvenience, but also because outsiders frequently do not know enough about the bureaucracy's functions to exercise control intelligently.[188] As German sociologist Max Weber observed, bureaucratic expertise and specialization often mean that "the 'political master' finds himself in the position of the 'dilettante'" when trying to control the bureaucracy.[189]

The notion that the bureaucracy must be placed under strict control assumes, probably unfairly, that bureaucrats will somehow misbehave if left to their own devices. But in fact many observers argue that most bureaucrats strive to serve the public interest—perhaps more diligently than some elected officials.[190]

A relatively autonomous bureaucracy can provide other benefits by acting as an additional check on the other three branches of government and by making many decisions on its own, without having to consult with those providing oversight. The latter benefit allows the bureaucracy to implement the laws more efficiently and also gives the overseers—whether the president, Congress, or the courts—more time to attend to their own business.

Thus how much control of the bureaucracy is needed? The answer seems to be some but not too much. As scholar Kenneth J. Meier has written, "Controls should be strong enough to guarantee the responsiveness of bureaucratic policymaking to the policy directives of the people yet not be so strong as to stifle bureaucratic initiative."[191] Although that answer may be frustratingly vague, it also may be the only answer available.

Should the President Do the Accounting?

Many observers of the bureaucracy believe that presidents must take the lead in controlling it.[192] After all, the president is elected nationally and thus presumably reflects the will of the public. Moreover, the Constitution charges the president with seeing that the laws are executed faithfully, which certainly requires some oversight of the bureaucracy. Most proponents of presidential control of the bureaucracy agree that such control is no easy task, but they disagree over whether the president possesses the necessary tools for the job. Some scholars contend

that the president does have all the powers needed to control the bureaucracy and that it is the skillful use of existing powers, rather than the addition of new ones, that is required.[193] Others argue that the president should be granted additional resources and authority to be used in battles against the bureaucracy.[194]

Some doubts about the president's potential role as overseer of the bureaucracy also have been raised. One reservation is that although presidents are elected on a national basis, those elections offer at best only rather vague mandates. Few specific issues are discussed in presidential campaigns; thus presidential direction of the bureaucracy based on the president's electoral mandate may be stretching things somewhat. Members of Congress also are elected officials; should not they have some say over bureaucratic actions? The courts and interest groups too can claim the right to exercise influence.

The extent of the president's role in supervising the bureaucracy is yet another question that cannot be settled completely. It is widely agreed that the president must take some responsibility for the bureaucracy, but exactly how much is unclear. As a result, it is largely up to presidents themselves to decide how much attention they wish to give to the bureaucracy.

CAN PRESIDENTS CONTROL THE BUREAUCRACY?

Is presidential control of the bureaucracy even possible? According to traditional wisdom, the federal bureaucracy is so intransigent that presidents are incapable of exercising much control over it.[195] The history of several recent presidencies and more contemporary scholarship, however, paint a slightly different picture. Thus the best answer to the question seems to be that although presidents cannot control everything the bureaucracy does, they can indeed exert significant influence over it.

Although presidents can influence the bureaucracy, it is by no means an easy job. Influencing the bureaucracy is a skill, and presidents who develop and use that skill effectively will enjoy more success with the bureaucracy than those who do not. Presidential scholars Hargrove and Nelson have called this skill "institutional leadership," and they have defined it as the ability of presidents to get the bureaucracy to adopt and work toward presidential goals.[196] Presidents employing this kind of institutional leadership must call on many of the powers of their office.

The experiences of several modern presidents demonstrate how the nation's chief executive can in fact influence the bureaucracy. John Kennedy took primary control of foreign policy making by relying on White House assistants instead of the executive departments, and Lyndon Johnson used his budgetary powers to sway the military bureaucracy. Richard Nixon took advantage of reorganization and other management techniques to achieve some control over the welfare system.[197] Jimmy Carter appointed like-minded people to help pursue his objective of deregulating numerous private sector industries.[198]

But no modern president has been more successful at controlling the bureaucracy than Ronald Reagan, and his presidency did the most to contradict the notion that presidents are helpless in the face of the massive federal bureaucracy.[199] Reagan was especially careful to appoint bureaucrats who shared his political ideology; in fact, political compatibility was the principal criterion for landing a political job in the Reagan administration. Reagan also used his staff and budget powers effectively. As a result, the federal bureaucracy began working for policies—items on Reagan's conservative agenda—that were radically different from those put forth by previous presidents, proving that presidents can exert some control over the bureaucracy. Reagan accomplished this feat using constitutional and statutory powers that have been available to presidents for decades.[200]

Some scholars have pointed to several trends that seem to be weakening the bureaucracy's ability to resist the president and enhancing presidential control of the bureaucracy.[201] One of these trends is the decline in the public's belief that experts can solve the nation's most difficult problems, including drug abuse, inner-city decay, and international crises. Because expertise is one of the primary sources of bureaucratic power, the bureaucracy loses strength when its expertise is tarnished. Another trend, arising from the growing number of government programs, is the expanding overlap of agency jurisdictions. The resulting struggles for power among agencies divert their attention from other issues and create stalemates that frequently must be resolved by the White House, giving the president more power. Finally, more and more interest groups are taking part in the policy process and consequently competing. Agencies thus can no longer count on having stable relations with interest groups.

Presidential control of the bureaucracy is not easy and probably never will be. The Framers of the Constitution virtually guaranteed that by giving the president and Congress joint custody of the bureaucracy, an arrangement that thwarts presidential command.[202] Forced by the Constitution to work within its separation of powers and faced with all the other obstacles to presidential control of the bureaucracy, the chief of the executive branch has a daunting job indeed.

NOTES

1. Richard P. Nathan, *The Administrative Presidency* (New York: Wiley, 1983), 2.

2. Michael Nelson, "The Irony of American Bureaucracy," in *Bureaucratic Power in National Policy Making*, 4th ed., ed. Francis E. Rourke (Boston: Little, Brown, 1986), 169.

3. Karen O'Connor and Larry J. Sabato, *American Government: Roots and Reform*, brief ed. (New York: Macmillan, 1994), 265.

4. Benjamin I. Page and Mark P. Petracca, *The American Presidency* (New York: McGraw-Hill, 1983), 198.

5. Quoted in O'Connor and Sabato, *American Government*, 267.

6. Page and Petracca, *American Presidency*, 201.

7. *Budget of the United States Government, Fiscal Year 1995, Historical Tables* (Washington, D.C.: Government Printing Office, 1994), 13.

8. Harold W. Stanley and Richard G. Niemi, *Vital Statistics on American Politics*, 5th ed. (Washington, D.C.: CQ Press, 1995), 291.

9. Carl E. Lutrin and Allen K. Settle, *American Public Administration: Concepts and Cases*, 4th ed. (St. Paul: West, 1992), 28.

10. George J. Gordon, *Public Administration in America*, 4th ed. (New York: St. Martin's Press, 1992), 18–19.

11. Stanley and Niemi, *Vital Statistics on American Politics*, 291–292.

12. Kenneth J. Meier, *Politics and the Bureaucracy: Policymaking in the Fourth Branch of Government*, 3d ed. (Pacific Grove, Calif.: Brooks/Cole, 1993), 31.

13. Stanley and Niemi, *Vital Statistics on American Politics*, 291–292.

14. *Budget of the United States Government, Fiscal Year 1995, Historical Tables*.

15. James Q. Wilson, *American Government: Institutions and Policies*, 2d ed. (Lexington, Mass.: D.C. Heath, 1983), 353.

16. Meier, *Politics and the Bureaucracy*, 3.

17. Charles T. Goodsell, *The Case for Bureaucracy*, 2d ed. (Chatham, N.J.: Chatham House, 1985), 3.

18. Ibid.

19. Quoted in Ibid., 7–8.

20. Quoted in Charles T. Goodsell, *The Case for Bureaucracy*, 3d ed. (Chatham, N.J.: Chatham House, 1994), 179.

21. Herbert Kaufman, "Fear of Bureaucracy: A Raging Pandemic," *Public Administration Review* (January/February 1981): 1.

22. Robert L. Kahn et al., "Americans Love Their Bureaucrats," in Rourke, *Bureaucratic Power*.

23. Thomas R. Dye, *Politics in America* (Englewood Cliffs, N.J.: Prentice-Hall, 1994), 476.

24. Kaufman, "Fear of Bureaucracy"; Goodsell, *Case for Bureaucracy*, 3d ed.; Meier, *Politics and the Bureaucracy*, 4–7.

25. Kahn et al., "Americans Love Their Bureaucrats," 290–292.

26. Goodsell, *Case for Bureaucracy*, 3d ed., 25–39.

27. See Anthony Downs, *Inside Bureaucracy* (Boston: Little, Brown, 1967); David Nachmias and David H. Rosenbloom, *Bureaucratic Government USA* (New York: St. Martin's Press, 1980); and Peter K. Eisinger et al., *American Politics: The People and the Policy* (Boston: Little, Brown, 1978).

28. Nachmias and Rosenbloom, *Bureaucratic Government USA*, 12.

29. Downs, *Inside Bureaucracy*, 24–25.

30. Ibid., 33–35.

31. Meier, *Politics and the Bureaucracy*, 18.

32. Ibid., 24.

33. Ibid., 25.

34. Ibid., 29.

35. Ibid., 33.

36. Ibid., 34.

37. James W. Fesler and Donald F. Kettl, *The Politics of the Administrative Process*, (Chatham, N.J.: Chatham House, 1991), 166–167.

38. Meier, *Politics and the Bureaucracy*, 36.

39. Ibid.

40. Goodsell, *Case for Bureaucracy*, 3d ed., 105; Dye, *Politics in America*, 467.

41. Gregory B. Lewis, "In Search of the Machiavellian Milquetoasts: Comparing Attitudes of Bureaucrats and Ordinary People," *Public Administration Review* (May/June 1990): 220–227.

42. Dye, *Politics in America*, 467–468.

43. Wilson, *American Government*, 359.

44. James P. Pfiffner, *The Modern Presidency* (New York: St. Martin's Press, 1994), 122.

45. Hugh Heclo, *A Government of Strangers* (Washington, D.C.: Brookings, 1977), 94.

46. George C. Edwards III and Stephen J. Wayne, *Presidential Leadership: Politics and Policy Making*, 3d ed. (New York: St. Martin's Press, 1994), 275–279.

47. Norman C. Thomas and Joseph A. Pika, *The Politics of the Presidency*, 4th ed. (Washington, D.C.: CQ Press, 1996), 250.

48. Pfiffner, *Modern Presidency*, 126.

49. Thomas and Pika, *Politics of the Presidency*, 250.

50. Pfiffner, *Modern Presidency*, 127.

51. Norman C. Thomas, Joseph A. Pika, and Richard A. Watson, *The*

Politics of the Presidency, rev. 3d ed. (Washington, D.C.: CQ Press, 1994), 464–465.

52. Ibid., 463, 466.

53. Pfiffner, *Modern Presidency,* 128.

54. Heclo, *Government of Strangers.*

55. Edwards and Wayne, *Presidential Leadership,* 276.

56. Thomas and Pika, *Politics of the Presidency,* 251.

57. Heclo, *Government of Strangers,* 100.

58. Wilson, *American Government,* 320.

59. Heclo, *Government of Strangers,* 102–103.

60. Meier, *Politics and the Bureaucracy,* 51–52.

61. Ibid., 53–54.

62. Dye, *Politics in America,* 453.

63. Ibid., 453–454.

64. Morris P. Fiorina, "Congress and Bureaucracy: A Profitable Partnership," in Rourke, *Bureaucratic Power.*

65. Ibid., 230.

66. Ibid.

67. Arthur Maass, *Congress and the Common Good* (New York: Basic Books, 1983).

68. Meier, *Politics and the Bureaucracy,* 69.

69. Francis E. Rourke, *Bureaucracy, Politics, and Public Policy,* 3d ed. (Boston: Little, Brown, 1984), 94.

70. Ibid., 32.

71. Meier, *Politics and the Bureaucracy,* 75.

72. Ibid., 58.

73. Ibid., 60.

74. Ibid., 194–195.

75. Rourke, *Bureaucracy, Politics, and Public Policy,* 77.

76. Downs, *Inside Bureaucracy,* 263–264.

77. Dennis D. Riley, *Controlling the Federal Bureaucracy* (Philadelphia: Temple University Press, 1987), 96; Richard M. Pious, *Essentials of American Politics and Government* (New York: McGraw-Hill, 1987), 459.

78. Meier, *Politics and the Bureaucracy,* 157.

79. Joel D. Aberbach, *Keeping Watchful Eye: The Politics of Congressional Oversight* (Washington, D.C.: Brookings, 1990), 35.

80. Meier, *Politics and the Bureaucracy,* 160.

81. Ibid., 162–163; Pious, *Essentials of American Politics and Government,* 468–469.

82. Wilson, *American Government,* 367.

83. Meier, *Politics and the Bureaucracy,* 121.

84. Rourke, *Bureaucracy, Politics, and Public Policy,* 51.

85. Ibid., 196–199.

86. Quoted in Harold Seidman and Robert Gilmour, *Politics, Position, and Power: From the Positive to the Regulatory State,* 4th ed. (New York: Oxford University Press, 1986), 89.

87. Quoted in Robert Sherrill, *Why They Call It Politics: A Guide to America's Government,* 4th ed. (San Diego: Harcourt Brace Jovanovich, 1984), 260.

88. Quoted in Thomas E. Cronin, *The State of the Presidency,* 2d ed. (Boston: Little, Brown, 1980), 241.

89. Quoted in Lyn Ragsdale, *Presidential Politics* (Boston: Houghton Mifflin, 1993), 403.

90. Quoted in David L. Barnett, "A War Reagan's Winning: Taming the Bureaucracy," *U.S. News & World Report,* April 5, 1982, 27.

91. Quoted in George J. Church, "Good Chemistry," *Time,* June 13, 1988, 14, 21.

92. Quoted in Robert B. Denhardt, *Public Administration: An Action Orientation* (Pacific Grove, Calif.: Brooks/Cole, 1991), 15.

93. Goodsell, *Case for Bureaucracy,* 3d ed., 177.

94. Ibid., 179.

95. Quoted in Sherrill, *Why They Call It Politics,* 251.

96. Quoted in Cronin, *State of the Presidency,* 223.

97. Quoted in Page and Petracca, *American Presidency,* 217.

98. Ibid.

99. Erwin C. Hargrove, *The Missing Link: The Study of the Implementation of Social Policy* (Washington, D.C.: Urban Institute, 1975), 111.

100. Quoted in Edwards and Wayne, *Presidential Leadership,* 261.

101. Robert J. Sickels, *The Presidency: An Introduction* (Englewood Cliffs, N.J.: Prentice-Hall, 1980), 194–198.

102. Quoted in David V. Edwards, *The American Political Experience: An Introduction to Government,* 4th ed. (Englewood Cliffs, N.J.: Prentice-Hall, 1988), 289.

103. Quoted in Richard E. Neustadt, *Presidential Power: The Politics of Leadership from FDR to Carter* (New York: Wiley, 1980), 9.

104. Graham T. Allison, *Essence of Decision: Explaining the Cuban Missile Crisis* (Boston: Little, Brown, 1971).

105. Quoted in Peter Goldman, "The Bureaucratic Man," *Newsweek,* January 26, 1981, 41.

106. Ragsdale, *Presidential Politics,* 402.

107. Allison, *Essence of Decision,* 101–102.

108. Quoted in Edwards and Wayne, *Presidential Leadership,* 287.

109. Terry M. Moe, "The Presidency and the Bureaucracy: The Presidential Advantage," in *The Presidency and the Political System,* 4th ed., ed. Michael Nelson (Washington, D.C.: CQ Press, 1994), 409.

110. Erwin C. Hargrove and Michael Nelson, *Presidents, Politics, and Policy* (New York: Knopf, 1984), 87–90.

111. Neustadt, *Presidential Power,* 25.

112. Quoted in ibid., 9.

113. Hargrove and Nelson, *Presidents, Politics, and Policy,* 89.

114. Ibid., 104.

115. Quoted in Gordon, *Public Administration in America,* 221.

116. Quoted in Sickels, *The Presidency,* 173.

117. Cronin, *State of the Presidency,* 244.

118. Seidman and Gilmour, *Politics, Position, and Power,* 3.

119. Rourke, *Bureaucracy, Politics, and Public Policy,* 169.

120. Quoted in Seidman and Gilmour, *Politics, Position, and Power,* 13.

121. Quoted in Riley, *Controlling the Federal Bureaucracy,* 42.

122. Ibid.; Page and Petracca, *American Presidency,* 214.

123. Gordon, *Public Administration in America,* 107.

124. Meier, *Politics and the Bureaucracy,* 175.

125. Thomas and Pika, *Politics of the Presidency,* 270.

126. See Gordon, *Public Administration in America,* 226–230.

127. Downs, *Inside Bureaucracy,* 116–118.

128. Edwards and Wayne, *Presidential Leadership,* 261–266.

129. Frank Kessler, *The Dilemmas of Presidential Leadership* (Englewood Cliffs, N.J.: Prentice-Hall, 1982), 68.

130. Thomas and Pika, *Politics of the Presidency,* 276.

131. Ibid., 277–278; Gordon, *Public Administration in America,* 351–352.

132. Thomas and Pika, *Politics of the Presidency,* 278; Gordon, *Public Administration in America,* 409–410.

133. Gordon, *Public Administration in America,* 353–354.

134. Thomas and Pika, *Politics of the Presidency,* 277.

135. Steffen W. Schmidt, Mack C. Shelley II, and Barbara A. Bardes, *American Government and Politics Today,* 2d ed. (St. Paul: West, 1987), 392.

136. Thomas and Pika, *Politics of the Presidency,* 264–265.

137. Ibid., 266.

138. Quoted in Page and Petracca, *American Presidency,* 342.

139. Quoted in Goldman, "The Bureaucratic Man," 42.

140. Neustadt, *Presidential Power,* 16–21.

141. Sherrill, *Why They Call It Politics,* 32.

142. Ibid., 33.

143. Edwards and Wayne, *Presidential Leadership,* 200.

144. Quoted in Riley, *Controlling the Federal Bureaucracy,* 18.

145. Quoted in Edwards and Wayne, *Presidential Leadership,* 200–201.

146. Meier, *Politics and the Bureaucracy,* 168.

147. Seidman and Gilmour, *Politics, Position, and Power,* 70.

148. Sickels, *The Presidency,* 198.

149. Pious, *Essentials of American Politics and Government,* 469.

150. Ibid., 470.

151. Goldman, "The Bureaucratic Man," 42.

152. Ibid.

153. Hugh Heclo, "Issue Networks and the Executive Establishment," in *The New American Political System,* ed. Anthony King (Washington, D.C.: American Enterprise Institute, 1978), 87–124.

154. Pious, *Essentials of American Politics and Government,* 471.

155. Ibid.

156. Ibid., 472.

157. Gordon, *Public Administration in America,* 65; Thomas et al., *Politics of the Presidency,* 249–250.

158. Meier, *Politics and the Bureaucracy,* 180.

159. Edwards and Wayne, *Presidential Leadership,* 273.

160. Hargrove, *Missing Link,* 114.

161. Hargrove and Nelson, *Presidents, Politics, and Policy,* 238–239.

162. Meier, *Politics and the Bureaucracy,* 104–106.

163. Hargrove and Nelson, *Presidents, Politics, and Policy,* 239.

164. Ibid.

165. Meier, *Politics and the Bureaucracy,* 94.

166. Hargrove and Nelson, *Presidents, Politics, and Policy,* 240–241.

167. Ibid.

168. Meier, *Politics and the Bureaucracy,* 94.

169. Ibid., 96.

170. Hargrove and Nelson, *Presidents, Politics, and Policy,* 241.

171. Meier, *Politics and the Bureaucracy,* 100.

172. Ibid., 96.

173. Hargrove and Nelson, *Presidents, Politics, and Policy,* 242.

174. Edwards and Wayne, *Presidential Leadership,* 433.

175. Hargrove and Nelson, *Presidents, Politics, and Policy,* 243–244.

176. Ibid., 244–245.

177. Edwards and Wayne, *Presidential Leadership,* 441–444.

178. Hargrove and Nelson, *Presidents, Politics, and Policy,* 248.

179. Ibid., chap. 3.

180. Wilson, *American Government,* 365.

181. Riley, *Controlling the Federal Bureaucracy,* 53–54.

182. Ibid.

183. Ibid.

184. Hargrove and Nelson, *Presidents, Politics, and Policy,* 234.

185. Riley, *Controlling the Federal Bureaucracy,* 55.

186. Peter Woll, *American Bureaucracy,* 2d ed. (New York: Norton, 1977), 246; Gordon, *Public Administration in America,* 66–70.

187. Peter Woll and Rochelle Jones, "The Bureaucracy as a Check on the President," *Bureaucrat* 3 (April 1974): 19.

188. Riley, *Controlling the Federal Bureaucracy,* 169–170.

189. Max Weber, "Essay on Bureaucracy," in Rourke, *Bureaucratic Power,* 70.

190. Gordon, *Public Administration in America,* 70–71.

191. Meier, *Politics and the Bureaucracy,* 226.

192. Ibid., 168; Cronin, *State of the Presidency,* 225.

193. Meier, *Politics and the Bureaucracy,* 232.

194. Cronin, *State of the Presidency,* 225–226.

195. Francis E. Rourke, "Grappling with the Bureaucracy," in *Politics and the Oval Office: Towards Presidential Governance,* ed. Arnold J. Meltsner (San Francisco: Institute for Contemporary Studies, 1981), 135.

196. Hargrove and Nelson, *Presidents, Politics, and Policy,* 238.

197. Rourke, "Grappling with the Bureaucracy," 138.

198. Meier, *Politics and the Bureaucracy,* 232–233.

199. Elizabeth Sanders, "The Presidency and the Bureaucratic State," in *The Presidency and the Political System,* 3d ed., ed. Michael Nelson (Washington, D.C.: CQ Press, 1990), 410.

200. Sanders, "The Presidency," 410.

201. Rourke, "Grappling with the Bureaucracy," 139–140.

202. Moe, "The Presidency and the Bureaucracy," 408–439.

SELECTED BIBLIOGRAPHY

Downs, Anthony. *Inside Bureaucracy.* Boston: Little, Brown, 1967.

Edwards, George C. III, and Stephen J. Wayne. *Presidential Leadership: Politics and Policy Making.* 3d ed. New York: St. Martin's Press, 1994.

Fesler, James W., and Donald F. Kettl. *The Politics of the Administrative Process.* Chatham, N.J.: Chatham House, 1991.

Goodsell, Charles T. *The Case for Bureaucracy: A Public Administration Polemic.* 3d ed. Chatham, N.J.: Chatham House, 1994.

Gordon, George J. *Public Administration in America.* 4th ed. New York: St. Martin's Press. 1992.

Hargrove, Erwin C., and Michael Nelson. *Presidents, Politics, and Policy.* New York: Knopf, 1984.

Heclo, Hugh. *A Government of Strangers: Executive Politics in Washington.* Washington, D.C.: Brookings, 1977.

Meier, Kenneth J. *Politics and the Bureaucracy: Policymaking in the Fourth Branch of Government.* 3d ed. Pacific Grove, Calif.: Brooks/Cole, 1993.

Neustadt, Richard E. *Presidential Power: The Politics of Leadership from FDR to Carter.* New York: Wiley, 1980.

Page, Benjamin I., and Mark P. Petracca. *The American Presidency.* New York: McGraw-Hill, 1983.

Pfiffner, James P. *The Managerial Presidency.* Pacific Grove, Calif.: Brooks/Cole, 1991.

———. *The Modern Presidency.* New York: St. Martin's Press, 1994.

Pious, Richard M. *Essentials of American Politics and Government.* New York: McGraw-Hill, 1987.

Riley, Dennis D. *Controlling the Federal Bureaucracy.* Philadelphia: Temple University Press, 1987.

Rourke, Francis E. *Bureaucracy, Politics, and Public Policy.* 3d ed. Boston: Little, Brown, 1984.

———, ed. *Bureaucratic Power in National Policy Making.* 4th ed. Boston: Little, Brown, 1986.

Seidman, Harold, and Robert Gilmour. *Politics, Position, and Power: From the Positive to the Regulatory State.* 4th ed. New York: Oxford University Press, 1986.

Thomas, Norman C., and Joseph A. Pika. *The Politics of the Presidency.* 4th ed. Washington, D.C.: CQ Press, 1996.

Wilson, James Q. *Bureaucracy: What Government Agencies Do and Why They Do It.* New York: Basic Books, 1989.

PART VII

Biographies of the Presidents and Vice Presidents

CHAPTER 36

Biographies of the Presidents

BY DANIEL C. DILLER

THE CONSTITUTION requires only that a president be at least thirty-five years of age, a natural born citizen or a citizen at the time of the adoption of the Constitution, and a resident within the United States for fourteen years. Although these constitutional requirements disqualify few Americans, the forty-one persons who have become president have come from a relatively narrow slice of American society.

All presidents have shared several important characteristics. First, all have been men. Through the 1992 election, no woman had been nominated for president by a major political party.

Second, each of the forty-one presidents descended from northern European ancestors. Moreover, of the forty-one, only five trace their roots to continental Europe. The ancestors of Martin Van Buren, Theodore Roosevelt, and Franklin D. Roosevelt were Dutch; Herbert C. Hoover's were Swiss; and Dwight D. Eisenhower's were German. The forebears of the thirty-six other presidents came to America primarily from the British Isles.

Third, no president has reached the presidency without significant experience as a public servant. Most presidents have served in at least one elective office at the national or state level. Twenty-four presidents have been members of Congress; sixteen have been governors of a state; and fourteen have been vice presidents. Presidents have also served as cabinet members, diplomats, state legislators, mayors, judges, sheriffs, and prosecutors on their way to higher office. Because George Washington was the first president, he did not have the opportunity to run for Congress, but he served the nation as a general and a delegate to the Continental Congress. Three presidents, Zachary Taylor, Ulysses S. Grant, and Eisenhower, were career generals without civilian political experience. Two others, William Howard Taft and Hoover, never had been elected to a national political office or a governorship but had served the nation as cabinet officers. Taft was Theodore Roosevelt's secretary of war; Hoover was secretary of commerce under Warren G. Harding and Calvin Coolidge.

Beyond these three characteristics common to each of the first forty-one presidents, two characteristics have been shared by all but one of them: marriage and Protestantism. James Buchanan was the only president who never married. Five others entered the presidency without a wife: Grover Cleveland did not marry until after he became president, and Thomas Jefferson, Van Buren, Andrew Jackson, and Chester A. Arthur took office as widowers. Not until the election of Ronald Reagan in

1980, however, did the American people elect a president who had been divorced.

Until John F. Kennedy became the first Catholic president in 1961, all chief executives had come from Protestant backgrounds with the Episcopalian, Presbyterian, and Unitarian denominations predominating. Although all presidents have professed their belief in God, they have varied widely in their religious convictions and practices. Jefferson's political opponents accused him of being an atheist—a charge he denied. Although Abraham Lincoln frequently quoted the Bible in his speeches, he belonged to no specific denomination and felt compelled early in his political career to make a statement declaring his belief in God. A few presidents have been outwardly religious men. James Garfield was a lay preacher for the Disciples of Christ before beginning his congressional career. Jimmy Carter described himself as a born-again Christian during the 1976 presidential campaign.

If one considers all these characteristics together, a distinct profile of the American president emerges. Presidents typically have been American-born, married men who were at least forty-two years old (Theodore Roosevelt being the youngest to hold office), descended from northern European, Protestant ancestors, and have had some type of public service career at the state or national level.

From this well-defined societal group, however, presidents have come into office from a variety of personal backgrounds.

Some presidents descended from the American aristocracy, including Jefferson, James Madison, John Quincy Adams, John Tyler, William Henry Harrison and his grandson Benjamin Harrison, the Roosevelts, Taft, Kennedy, and George Bush. These presidents had the advantages of wealth and family connections when building their political careers. Other presidents, including Jackson, Lincoln, Andrew Johnson, and Garfield, were self-made men from poor, sometimes destitute circumstances. Several presidents, such as Hoover, Richard Nixon, Reagan, and Bill Clinton, did not grow up in poverty but received little financial support from their parents as they started their careers.

The educational background of presidents ranges from that of Woodrow Wilson, who earned a Ph.D. from Johns Hopkins University, to Andrew Johnson, who never attended a school of any type. Other presidents, such as Washington and Lincoln, received only rudimentary formal education. Thirty-two presidents attended college, including every twentieth-century president except Harry S. Truman.

Presidents also have worked in all types of professions before starting their careers in public service. The most common profession for presidents has been law; twenty-five were admitted to the bar. Only two, however, of the last ten presidents, Gerald Ford and Nixon, have practiced law. Over half the presidents had some experience in agriculture, either as a plantation owner, dirt farmer, rancher, field worker, or son of a farming family. Seven presidents were teachers. Several others were professional soldiers, merchants, surveyors, or journalists.

Presidents have made progress toward the presidency at different times in their lives. Jackson and Nixon, for example, began their political careers with election to the U.S. House of Representatives at the ages of twenty-nine and thirty-three, respectively, and Clinton was elected attorney general of Arkansas at age thirty. In contrast, Wilson and Reagan were not elected to their first political offices—governor of New Jersey and governor of California, respectively—until they were in their mid-fifties. No one could have foreseen in 1922 that Truman, then the owner of a failing haberdashery who had never gone to college or run for public office, would be president in twenty-three years. In contrast, twenty-three years before John Quincy Adams became president, he had graduated Phi Beta Kappa from Harvard, served as minister to Holland and Prussia, been elected to the Massachusetts State Senate, and narrowly lost election to the U.S. House of Representatives.

Thus, despite their similarities, every president has come to office at a different pace, under different circumstances, and with different experiences that affect their leadership.

Just as the prepresidential experiences of the chief executives have varied, so have their postpresidential experiences. While many chief executives have retired from public life after leaving the presidency, a few have continued their political careers, and several have run again for president. Cleveland was the only president to be reelected president after leaving office. Van Buren, Millard Fillmore, and Theodore Roosevelt ran unsuccessfully for reelection after leaving office. Former president Ulysses S. Grant came close to receiving the Republican nomination in 1880, but the Republican National Convention chose dark-horse candidate Garfield instead.

Two former presidents were elected to Congress after retiring from the presidency. John Quincy Adams was elected to the U.S. House of Representatives in 1830 and served there until 1848; he died in the Capitol after suffering a stroke. Andrew Johnson was elected to the Senate in 1875 and served briefly before his death that year. Tyler was elected to the Confederate Congress in 1861 but died before taking his seat. Taft fulfilled his highest personal ambition when Harding appointed him chief justice of the United States in 1921. Taft served on the Court until he retired in 1930.

Most former presidents have served as unofficial advisers to their party or to the incumbent president. Several, including Taft and Hoover, have served on advisory commissions or administrative boards appointed by the incumbent president. One former president, Carter, has taken on numerous diplomatic

missions as a personal envoy of the incumbent president. And since Coolidge, every president who has survived his term has written an autobiography or memoirs about his time in office.

George Washington

BORN: February 22, 1732; Westmoreland County, Virginia
PARTY: Federalist
TERM: April 30, 1789–March 4, 1797
VICE PRESIDENT: John Adams
DIED: December 14, 1799; Mount Vernon, Virginia
BURIED: Mount Vernon

George Washington was born into a moderately wealthy family, who owned several plantations in northern Virginia. His father, Augustine, had ten children, six with Mary Ball, of which George was the eldest, and four by a previous marriage. When the eleven-year-old George's father died, he was left in the custody of his eldest half brother, Lawrence, whom he loved and admired.

George's early education was adequate, though far from exceptional. He was tutored and attended school on an irregular basis from ages seven to fifteen, but had no formal education beyond grammar school. George's exposure to the well-mannered intellectual atmosphere created by Lawrence compensated for the youngster's limited book learning. He also received an education in the outdoor occupations of Virginia. In his early teens he was already a skilled woodsman, tobacco planter, and surveyor. When George was sixteen, he joined the first of several survey expeditions that he would make to the Virginia frontier.

In 1751 George took the only overseas trip of his life, to Barbados with Lawrence, who was suffering from tuberculosis and thus hoping that the Caribbean climate would relieve his condition. There George contracted a mild case of smallpox, which left him scarred. Lawrence died in July 1752, after he and George returned to the colonies.

The following November, Washington began his frontier military career as a major in the Virginia militia. His first assignment was to inform the French commander at Fort Le Boeuf in Pennsylvania that unless the French evacuated the Ohio Valley they risked war. The French refused to budge, ensuring hostilities with the British.

After returning from the mission Washington was promoted to lieutenant colonel with the help of influential friends. In early 1754 he marched west with 160 recruits to reinforce British troops at the fork of the Ohio and Monongahela rivers. During this journey his men fired what many historians regard as the first shots of the French and Indian War. The nervous recruits ambushed a detachment of thirty French soldiers, killing ten, including their commander, Coulon de Jumonville. The attack gained Washington a measure of infamy because Jumonville was on a diplomatic mission to the British. Six weeks later Washington's force was besieged and defeated at Fort Necessity. Before allowing his men to return to Virginia, the French forced Washington to sign a statement written in French, which he did not understand. In it he admitted to being an assassin. Washington's reputation was damaged by the episode, especially among British military officers. Upon returning to Virginia, Washington resigned his commission.

In December 1754 Lawrence's last living child died, and Washington inherited the right to rent Lawrence's estate at Mount Vernon from his late half brother's remarried widow, Ann Lee. In 1761, when Mrs. Lee died, he inherited Mount Vernon outright.

Washington returned to military service in the spring of 1755 when he was appointed aide-de-camp to Maj. Gen. Edward Braddock. After several years of service in the French and Indian War, in which he achieved the rank of colonel, Washington resigned in 1758 to run for the Virginia House of Burgesses. He served there for nine years. He was not known as a dynamic or creative legislator, but he gained the admiration of his colleagues and firsthand knowledge of representative government.

REVOLUTIONARY WAR

As tensions mounted between the British and the colonies, Washington became increasingly involved in the patriot cause.

In 1769 he helped lead a movement to establish restrictions on the importation of British goods throughout the colonies. And in 1774 he attended the First Continental Convention in Philadelphia as a delegate from Virginia. Afterward, he returned to Virginia and began training militia forces using his own money. On June 16, 1775, Washington accepted a commission from the Second Continental Convention as the commanding general of the Continental army. Patriot leaders hoped the choice of a military leader from a southern state would unite the colonies behind the rebellion that already had begun in New England.

As a general, Washington's inspirational and administrative abilities were more exceptional than his military knowledge. He made several tactical blunders during the war, including the ill-considered deployment of part of his army in an exposed position on Long Island in 1776, which resulted in the loss of five thousand troops and the British occupation of New York City. Yet despite his lack of experience in commanding large forces, Washington did show flashes of strategic brilliance. The celebrated triumphs of his army at Boston, Trenton, Princeton, and Yorktown demonstrated his superior generalship. Nevertheless, Washington's skill at maintaining morale, inspiring loyalty, and holding his army together, as exemplified during the harsh winter of 1777–1778 at Valley Forge, Pennsylvania, was more crucial to the success of the Revolution than his tactical abilities.

After the decisive defeat of the British at Yorktown in 1781, discontent within the Continental army became the primary threat to the young nation. Many soldiers believed that Congress had not compensated them adequately or recognized their service to the nation. In May 1782 Washington angrily rejected an idea proposed by one of his officers that he allow himself to be crowned king. In March 1783 a more serious threat to Republican government emerged. Many officers were considering using the army to depose Congress and set up their own government. Washington addressed an assembly of his officers on March 15 in Newburgh, New York, where he persuaded them to give up their plan and support Congress.

With the war officially ended by the Treaty of Paris, signed on September 3, 1783, Washington retired to Mount Vernon. He managed his plantation until 1787, when he agreed to accept an appointment as one of Virginia's delegates to the Constitutional Convention in Philadelphia. His presence lent legitimacy to the convention, and its delegates unanimously elected him presiding officer. After a long summer of debate during which Washington said little, the convention agreed on a new constitution. Washington and his fellow delegates signed the document on September 17, 1787.

PRESIDENCY

Washington was the inevitable choice of his nation to be the first president under the new Constitution. He alone had the nonpartisan reputation needed to transcend sectional and ideological conflicts, so that the United States would have time to establish effective government institutions and gain the trust of the people. In early 1789 presidential electors unanimously elected Washington president. After a triumphant overland journey from Mount Vernon to New York City, during which he was met by cheering crowds at every stop, Washington took the oath of office in New York on April 30, 1789.

During Washington's first term Congress passed the Bill of Rights, and the states that had not yet ratified the Constitution did so. In an attempt to inspire confidence in the federal government and to establish a spirit of national unity Washington toured the northern states in late 1789 and the southern states in the spring of 1791. Mindful of the problems caused by the weakness of the federal government under the Articles of Confederation, Washington was careful throughout his presidency to assert the primacy of the federal government over the states.

Washington was usually deferential toward Congress; he believed that the president should veto a bill only if it were unconstitutional. He often made decisions after listening to his two most important and eloquent advisers, Secretary of State Thomas Jefferson and Secretary of the Treasury Alexander Hamilton, debate an issue. Secretary of War Henry Knox, Attorney General Edmund Randolph, and Postmaster General Samuel Osgood completed the cabinet. Although Washington endeavored to avoid any partisanship, he usually agreed with Hamilton on important issues. In particular, he backed Hamilton's plans to have the federal government assume the wartime debts of the states and to establish a national bank. After much debate Congress passed both measures, and Washington signed the debt assumption bill in 1790 and the bank bill in 1791.

Washington's primary goal in foreign policy was maintaining the neutrality of the United States in the war between France and Great Britain. Washington believed that the young nation had to avoid alliance entanglements if it were to survive and remain united during its early years. Secretary of State Thomas Jefferson urged that the United States aid France, which had helped the colonies defeat the British in the Revolutionary War, but Washington rejected Jefferson's counsel. The president issued a neutrality proclamation on April 22, 1793, which declared that the United States would be "friendly and impartial" toward the belligerents. Jefferson's disputes with Washington's policies led him to resign at the end of 1793. The following year Congress passed the Neutrality Act of 1794, which endorsed Washington's policy of neutrality. In 1795 Washington signed the Jay Treaty with Great Britain. The agreement, which had been negotiated in London by Chief Justice John Jay, increased commerce between the two nations and settled several disputes. The treaty was highly unpopular, however, with pro-French Democratic-Republicans who attacked Washington for concluding what they perceived as a pro-British agreement.

In 1794 Washington faced a domestic crisis when a rebellion broke out in western Pennsylvania over the federal tax on whiskey. Washington believed that he had to put down the rebellion quickly to avoid the impression that the federal government was weak. Thus, he ordered the governors of Pennsylvania, Maryland, New Jersey, and Virginia to supply the federal government with fifteen thousand militia and rode to Pennsylvania to oversee their preparations personally. The show of force was sufficient to quell the Whiskey Rebellion, and Washington never had to lead the militia into battle.

During his presidency Washington strove to avoid partisan politics; he believed that political factions could destroy the unity of the young nation. Thus, in his famous Farewell Address published on September 17, 1796, he cautioned against excessive partisanship as well as foreign influence and permanent alliances. But despite his efforts to prevent the development of parties, before his presidency had ended two factions had already emerged in American politics: the Federalists, with whom Washington most closely identified, led by Alexander Hamilton and Vice President John Adams, and the Democratic-Republicans, led by Thomas Jefferson and House member James Madison.

RETIREMENT

In 1796 Washington refused to consider running for a third term. He had been wounded during his second term by criticism from the Democratic-Republican press over the Jay Treaty and other issues and was anxious to return to the quiet life of a gentleman farmer at Mount Vernon. He spent the last years of his life managing his estate and entertaining friends. In 1799, when war seemed imminent with France, President John Adams asked Washington to accept an appointment as lieutenant general and commander in chief of the army. Washington accepted on the condition that he would not have to take active command of the forces except in an emergency. War with France was averted, and Washington's retirement was not disturbed. On December 12, 1799, after riding about his estate on a cold day, he suddenly fell ill, probably with pneumonia. His condition deteriorated rapidly, and he died on December 14 at Mount Vernon.

Washington married Martha Dandridge Custis on January 6, 1759. Martha was a wealthy widow, who added fifteen thousand acres to Washington's estate. The couple had no children, but they raised Martha's two surviving children from her previous marriage. Martha's daughter, Patsy, died in 1773 as a teenager, and when her son John died in 1781, George and Martha assumed custody of his two children.

Thomas Jefferson, looking back on Washington's life in 1814, wrote:

His mind was great and powerful without being of the very first order; his penetration strong, though not so acute as that of a Newton, Bacon, or Locke; and as far as he saw, no judgement was ever sounder. It was slow in operation, being little aided by invention or imagination, but sure in conclusion. . . .

Perhaps the strongest feature in his character was prudence, never acting until every circumstance, every consideration, was maturely weighed. . . . His integrity was most pure, his justice the most inflexible I have ever known.

John Adams

John Adams

BORN: October 30, 1735; Braintree (now Quincy), Massachusetts

PARTY: Federalist

TERM: March 4, 1797–March 3, 1801

VICE PRESIDENT: Thomas Jefferson

DIED: July 4, 1826; Quincy, Massachusetts

BURIED: Quincy

John Adams was born into a well-established family of farmers whose descendants had immigrated to Massachusetts from England a century before his birth. He was the oldest of three sons born to John and Susanna Adams. Young John received a grammar school education designed to prepare him for college. He enrolled in Harvard University in 1751 intending to become a Congregational minister. However, before he graduated in 1755 he had decided against a career in the ministry in favor of either law or medicine. After briefly teaching school in Worcester,

Adams began studying law. By 1758 he had been admitted to the Massachusetts bar and was practicing law in Braintree.

Adams soon became recognized throughout Massachusetts as an outspoken advocate of colonial causes. He authored Braintree's protest against the British Stamp Act of 1765, which was used as a model for similar protests by many other Massachusetts towns. Adams also published a series of anonymous letters in the *Boston Gazette* in which he theorized that the rights of English citizens were derived solely from God, not from the British monarchy or parliament. In 1770 Adams demonstrated his commitment to due process of the law when he defended the British soldiers on trial for the murder of colonial citizens at the Boston Massacre. His reputation withstood the unpopularity of his action, and the following year he was elected by an overwhelming margin to the Massachusetts state legislature.

In 1774 Adams became a delegate to the First Continental Congress. He was an early and influential advocate of separation from Britain and was appointed to the committee assigned to draft a declaration of independence. Adams retired from Congress in November 1777, intending to return to Massachusetts and his law practice. Within a month, however, Congress appointed him to the American commission in France. He set sail to join Benjamin Franklin and Arthur Lee in Paris on February 13, 1778, but a treaty of alliance had already been concluded by the time he arrived. Adams spent a year in Europe before returning to America in the summer of 1779. Upon his arrival he was elected as a delegate to the Massachusetts constitutional convention. He almost single-handedly wrote the first draft of the new state constitution, which the convention adopted with only minor changes. He returned to Europe in 1780 where he would spend the next eight years in various diplomatic posts, including minister to Holland and minister to Great Britain. He signed the armistice ending war with the British in 1783 and negotiated several loans and commercial treaties with the European powers.

Adams was serving as envoy to Great Britain when the Constitutional Convention was held, but his *Defense of the Constitutions of Government of the United States,* written while he was in Europe and published in 1787, contained insights into constitutional theory that were cited by delegates to the convention. When Adams received a copy of the Constitution in Great Britain, he immediately gave it his support. By this time he had grown tired of the unwillingness of the British government to improve relations with the United States. He resigned his post and returned to the United States.

When he arrived in Boston on June 17, 1789, he had already been elected to Congress under the new Constitution. He never served in this capacity, because he would also be elected vice president by virtue of his second place finish to George Washington in the balloting for president. Adams was dismayed at winning the vice presidency with only thirty-four votes. The disparity between his total and the unanimous sixty-nine received by Washington was caused by the machinations of

Alexander Hamilton, who persuaded many delegates to scatter their second vote to dilute Adams's influence.

Adams dutifully fulfilled his constitutional function of presiding over the Senate. Since the original Senate had only twenty-two members, the vice president was often in a position to break tie votes as prescribed by the Constitution. During Adams's two terms he had twenty-nine opportunities to decide issues with his tie-breaking vote, more than any subsequent vice president. However, he was seldom consulted by Washington on important issues and complained that the vice presidency was an insignificant and mechanical job—a lament of many of the men who would follow Adams in office. Nevertheless, Adams's relationship with Washington remained cordial.

After eight years as vice president, Adams was Washington's heir apparent. Fellow Federalist Alexander Hamilton, however, attempted to arrange the election of a candidate more agreeable to him than Adams. He persuaded a number of Federalist delegates to vote for intended vice-presidential candidate Thomas Pinckney, but not for presidential candidate John Adams. Hamilton hoped that Adams would lose the presidency to Pinckney, who Hamilton believed would be more receptive to his influence. But the maneuver backfired when many of Adams's supporters withheld their second votes from Pinckney to ensure Adams's victory, thereby allowing Democratic-Republican candidate Thomas Jefferson to finish second and win the vice presidency.

The most important and contentious issue of Adams's presidency was an impending war with France. French vessels had been preying on American shipping since 1795, and, just before Adams's inauguration, Paris issued a decree legitimizing the seizure of virtually any American ship. Adams faced intense political pressure from pro-British Hamiltonians who believed that the United States should join Britain in fighting to prevent French domination of Europe and to preserve American dignity. Jefferson's Democratic-Republicans opposed a war with France, but they did not have the votes in Congress to stop a declaration of war if Adams had wanted one. Adams chose to strengthen the nation's military, particularly the navy, while continuing negotiations with the French. He dispatched John Marshall, Charles C. Pinckney, and Elbridge Gerry to Paris in the summer of 1797 to seek an agreement that would avoid war and end French attacks on American shipping. But the diplomatic mission failed when the American representatives were greeted with demands for a bribe for French foreign minister Talleyrand, a loan to France, and an official apology for Adams's criticisms.

In April 1798 Adams's release of documents relating to the incident (which came to be known as the XYZ affair) aroused American opinion against France and rallied public support behind Adams. By this time an undeclared naval war between the two nations had already begun, and Congress granted Adams's request for further defense measures, including the establishment of the Navy Department. But he resisted calls for a full-scale declared war against France, even though he could have

bolstered his own political fortunes by yielding to the militant sentiment of the American public.

While Adams was enthusiastic about building a strong navy, he grudgingly agreed to the enlargement of the army. He asked George Washington to come out of retirement to command it. Washington accepted on the conditions that he would not have to take the field until there was fighting and that Alexander Hamilton would be his second in command in charge of building and training the army. Adams feared giving the powerful and ambitious Hamilton control of the army, but he believed if war did occur Washington's presence was indispensable to the unity of the country, so he assented to Washington's conditions.

In early 1799 France began sending conciliatory signals, which prompted Adams to send another peace commission before the year was over. Hamilton had tried to rally Federalist support for war with France and had proposed a joint British-American venture against Spanish holdings in North America. But increased taxes to support war preparations had diminished public enthusiasm for military adventurism. Adams stood by his policy of avoiding a declared war unless it was forced upon him by the French. The following May, when the immediate danger of a land war with France had passed, Adams ordered a drastic reduction in the army. In November word reached the United States that the American delegation had successfully concluded a treaty of peace and commerce with France.

By this time the Democratic-Republicans had taken control of the state legislatures of several key states, thus setting the stage for Adams's defeat in the 1800 presidential election. One of the reasons for the growing disaffection with the Federalist Party was its support of the Alien and Sedition Acts. In 1798 the Federalist majority in Congress attempted to put an end to the vituperative attacks on Federalist members of Congress and cabinet members in the Democratic-Republican press. The Sedition Act provided for imprisonment and fines for individuals who wrote, published, or uttered anything false or malicious about federal government officials. The Sedition Act together with the Alien Act of the same year, which gave the president broad authority to deport aliens suspected of subversive activity, constituted the greatest legislated suppression of freedom of expression in the history of the United States. Adams signed these bills into law but was not active in enforcing them. Despite the disunity of the Federalist Party and the unpopularity of the Alien and Sedition Acts, the 1800 election was close. Adams received sixty-five electoral votes, eight fewer than Jefferson and Aaron Burr.

Before leaving office Adams pushed for judicial reforms and appointed more than two hundred new judges, attorneys, clerks, and marshals. Some of these "midnight appointments" were removed by Jefferson, but many retained their offices. Adams also appointed John Marshall chief justice of the United States, a selection Adams was especially proud of in his later years.

When Adams's term ended, he returned to his farm in Massachusetts without attending Jefferson's inauguration. Adams spent much of his retirement writing his autobiography and corresponding with former colleagues about politics, philosophy, and religion. He wrote a letter of reconciliation to Thomas Jefferson at the insistence of their mutual friend Dr. Benjamin Rush in December 1811. Jefferson replied immediately, and they established a lasting correspondence. Adams died on July 4, 1826, the fiftieth anniversary of the Declaration of Independence. His last words reportedly were "Thomas Jefferson still lives." Adams had no way of knowing that Jefferson had died only a few hours before.

Adams married Abigail Smith in 1764. Her correspondence with her husband, family, and friends provides a valuable historical record of her husband's activities and the period in which they lived. They had five children: Abigail, John Quincy, Susanna, Charles, and Thomas. Susanna died while she was an infant. John Quincy became a prominent diplomat, congressman, and the sixth president of the United States. Adams's parents were Susanna Boyleston Adams and John Adams, a respected farmer and shoemaker who was active in local politics. The famous New England radical patriot Sam Adams was John's distant cousin.

Thomas Jefferson

BORN: April 13, 1743; Goochland (now Albemarle) County, Virginia

PARTY: Democratic-Republican

TERM: March 4, 1801–March 4, 1809

VICE PRESIDENTS: Aaron Burr; George Clinton

DIED: July 4, 1826; Charlottesville, Virginia

BURIED: Charlottesville

Thomas Jefferson was the eldest son and third of the ten children of Peter and Jane Jefferson. Peter Jefferson was a wealthy plantation owner, and Jane was a member of the prominent Randolph family, which was descended from British royalty.

As a boy, Thomas received instruction in Latin, Greek, French, mathematics, and philosophy from local scholars. When Peter Jefferson died in 1757, Thomas inherited Shadwell, the thousand-acre Virginia estate on which he was born. In 1760, at the age of seventeen, Thomas entered the College of William and Mary in Williamsburg, Virginia. There he studied vigorously for two years under the tutelage of Dr. William Small, a professor of mathematics, history, and philosophy. He left the college in the spring of 1762, however, without taking a degree.

Jefferson then studied law in Williamsburg for five years under the well-respected lawyer George Wythe. During Jefferson's stay in Williamsburg, Wythe and Small introduced him to many members of Virginia's government, including Francis Fauquier, the royal governor of the colony. In 1767 Jefferson was admitted to the Virginia bar and began a successful legal practice. Two years later he took a seat in Virginia's House of Burgesses. During his six years in that body, Jefferson distinguished himself as a powerful literary stylist. His colleagues often called upon him to draft proclamations and legislative documents.

Jefferson brought his reputation as a gifted writer to the Continental Congress in 1775. The following year, at the age of thirty-three, he was appointed by Congress to the committee charged with writing the Declaration of Independence. His fellow committee members—John Adams, Benjamin Franklin, Robert Livingston, and Roger Sherman—chose him to draft the document. Although the committee made minor changes in Jefferson's original draft and the entire Congress asked that several passages be deleted or modified, the Declaration of Independence was largely Jefferson's work.

Jefferson returned to Virginia in 1776 to a seat in the state legislature. In 1779 he became governor of his home state. His first experience as a chief executive was not impressive. In 1781 he was forced to abandon the Virginia capital of Richmond when British troops advanced upon the city. Some Virginians accused him of cowardice, but after a long debate the Virginia legislature passed a resolution stating that Jefferson's retreat was justified. He declined renomination for governor in 1781.

DIPLOMAT AND SECRETARY OF STATE

In 1784 Congress sent Jefferson to Paris as its minister to France. During his five years at this post, Jefferson witnessed the many events of the French Revolution. He applauded the revolution's stated democratic goals and had many friends among its leaders. Jefferson, like John Adams, missed the drafting of the Constitution because of his diplomatic service in Europe.

In 1789 Jefferson returned to the United States to become the country's first secretary of state. In this capacity Jefferson was more than just the nation's leading diplomat. Like the other members of George Washington's cabinet, Jefferson served as an adviser to Washington on matters outside the area of policy traditionally associated with his position. Washington often preferred to have his cabinet debate issues while he listened dispassionately to their reasoning. In these debates Jefferson was usually pitted against Treasury Secretary Alexander Hamilton. Hamilton, who was closer ideologically to Washington than Jefferson, was undoubtedly the most influential member of the cabinet. On July 31, 1794, Jefferson announced that he would resign at the end of the year because of his disagreements with administration policies. In particular, he objected to Hamilton's creation of a national bank and Washington's strict neutrality between Britain and France despite the 1778 treaty of alliance with France, which Jefferson believed should have been honored.

By 1796 the Democratic-Republican Party, which opposed the Federalists, had begun to emerge with Jefferson as its leader. That year he lost the presidential election to John Adams by three electoral votes, and, according to the original election rules of the Constitution, his second-place finish earned him the vice presidency. In this office he actively opposed the policies of Adams and the Federalists.

PRESIDENCY

After the election of 1800 the Twelfth Amendment introduced new election rules, which called for the president and vice president to run as a team, thereby eliminating the possibility of a candidate intended for the vice presidency receiving more votes than the presidential candidate. In the 1800 election, however, Jefferson was paired on the Democratic-Republican ticket with Aaron Burr. When the ambitious Burr received as many electoral votes as Jefferson, he refused to concede to his running mate. The tie gave the House of Representatives, where the Federalists and Alexander Hamilton were still in the majority, the responsibility of electing the president. To Hamilton's credit, he worked for the election of Jefferson, his political archenemy, whom he thought less dangerous and more reasonable than

Burr. The tie-breaking process took thirty-six ballots, but Jefferson was elected eventually.

Despite the acrimony between the Democratic-Republicans and the Federalists (outgoing president John Adams did not even attend Jefferson's inauguration), Jefferson entered office preaching reconciliation. He transformed the atmosphere surrounding the presidency from the stiff, regal style of Washington and Adams to his own democratic informality. Jefferson immediately freed all persons who had been jailed under the Alien and Sedition Acts enacted during the Adams administration. The Alien Act gave the president the authority to jail or deport aliens in peacetime, and the Sedition Act gave federal authorities broad power to prosecute persons who criticized the government. He also worked with Congress, which had come under the control of his party after the 1800 election, to cut the government budget and federal taxes.

In foreign policy Jefferson acted decisively to meet the threat to American shipping in the Mediterranean from pirates operating from the Barbary Coast of North Africa. American and European nations had been paying tribute to the governments of Morocco, Algiers, Tunis, and Tripoli to protect their ships from harassment. Jefferson, however, refused demands for increased tribute payments and sent a squadron of warships to the Mediterranean to protect U.S. shipping. After U.S. forces defeated Tripoli in a naval war, a treaty was concluded in 1805 that ended tribute payments to that state. The United States continued tribute payments to other North African states, however, until 1816.

Jefferson's most important act during his first term as president was the Louisiana Purchase. In 1803 the French owned the port of New Orleans as well as a vast area that stretched from New Orleans to present-day Montana, known as the Louisiana Territory. Jefferson, fearing that the French could block U.S. navigation of the Mississippi and threaten American settlements in the West, sent ambassadors to France in the hope of purchasing the port of New Orleans. The French instead offered to sell the entire Louisiana Territory. The American representatives, James Monroe and Robert Livingston, saw the opportunity to create an American empire and improve the security of the western frontier. Thus, they struck a deal with French emperor Napoleon to buy all of the Louisiana Territory for $15 million.

Jefferson recognized that to support the agreement he would have to ignore his own principles of strict constructionism, since the Constitution did not specifically authorize the president to acquire territory and Congress had not appropriated money for the purchase. He believed that the purchase would greatly benefit the nation and that the offer from Napoleon might be withdrawn if he hesitated. Therefore, Jefferson approved the deal and urged Congress to ratify it and appropriate funds for the purchase. In the fall of 1803 Congress bowed to his wishes and appropriated the $15 million. With the addition of the 828,000 square miles of the Louisiana Territory, the area of the United States nearly doubled.

In 1804, Jefferson, who was at the height of his popularity, easily won reelection. He lost only two states and defeated Charles C. Pinckney in the electoral college by a vote of 162–14.

Jefferson's second term was troubled by war between Britain and France. In 1806 both powers were blockading each other's ports and seizing American sailors and cargo. Jefferson was determined, however, not to become involved in the war. Thus, he persuaded Congress to pass the Embargo Act of 1807, which prohibited the shipping of U.S. products to other nations. Jefferson hoped that by cutting off all foreign trade he would prevent provocations on the seas that could lead to war.

The Embargo Act was a total failure. It severely hurt American businesses and farmers by denying them export markets. As the U.S. economy stagnated, Federalists and some Democratic-Republicans argued that the federal government's authority to regulate foreign commerce did not give it the power to stop foreign commerce altogether. Many merchants defied the embargo, causing Jefferson to order harsh enforcement measures that led to abuses of civil rights. On March 1, 1809, three days before the end of his term, Jefferson signed the Non-Intercourse Act, which ended the embargo against nations other than Britain and France and made provisions to lift the embargo against those two nations if they stopped violating U.S. neutrality. Despite the unpopularity of the Embargo Act, Jefferson's chosen heir and secretary of state, James Madison, won the 1808 presidential election.

RETIREMENT

When his second term expired Jefferson retired to Monticello, his home outside of Charlottesville, Virginia, which he had designed himself. He devoted his time to managing his estate, entertaining visitors, corresponding with former colleagues, and reveling in his many intellectual pursuits. Jefferson, who suffered from financial troubles caused by his generous entertaining and the defaults by several friends on loans he had cosigned, sold his 6,500-volume library to Congress in 1815. Congress's original collection of books had been burned by the British during the War of 1812. Jefferson's books formed the nucleus of the collection that would become the modern Library of Congress.

In 1819 the University of Virginia was chartered under Jefferson's supervision. He planned the curriculum, chose the faculty, drew up the plans for its buildings, and served as its rector until his death. Jefferson died at Monticello on July 4, 1826, the same day as John Adams and the fiftieth anniversary of the Declaration of Independence. Jefferson is buried at Monticello beneath a gravestone that he willed should read: "Here was buried Thomas Jefferson, Author of the Declaration of American Independence, of the Statute of Virginia for Religious Freedom, and the father of the University of Virginia."

Jefferson married Martha Wayles Skelton, a wealthy twenty-three-year-old widow, on January 1, 1772. The couple had six children, but only two, Martha and Maria, reached maturity. Martha Jefferson's father, John Wayles, died in 1773, leaving a forty-thousand-acre estate to the Jeffersons that doubled their landholdings. Wayles was heavily in debt, however, and Jefferson struggled for many years to pay off the balance. On September 6, 1782, Martha Jefferson died at the age of thirty-three. Little is known about Martha, and there is no authentic portrait of her in existence. Jefferson never remarried.

James Madison

BORN: March 16, 1751; Port Conway, Virginia
PARTY: Democratic-Republican
TERM: March 4, 1809–March 4, 1817
VICE PRESIDENTS: George Clinton; Elbridge Gerry
DIED: June 28, 1836; Orange County, Virginia
BURIED: Orange County

James Madison, oldest of the ten children of James and Eleanor Madison, was raised at Montpelier, the family plantation in Virginia. Young James Madison was an excellent scholar. He graduated from the College of New Jersey (now Princeton University) in 1771 and spent an extra six months studying theology under John Witherspoon, president of the college. In 1772 James returned to Virginia to continue his study of law and religion. Like John Adams, he considered entering the ministry after college, but the lure of a political career and the urgency of the patriot cause led him away from the ministry and into public service.

In 1775 he assumed his first government office, a slot on the committee of public safety of his native Orange County. By the spring of 1776 he had earned sufficient notice and respect to be elected as a delegate to Virginia's constitutional convention. There he served on the committee that drafted a declaration of rights and was primarily responsible for the constitutional article on religious freedom. As a member of the state constitutional convention, Madison automatically became a state legislator in the new Virginia government. There he met Thomas Jefferson, who became his close friend and political mentor. In 1777 Madison was defeated in his attempt to be elected to the state legislature, but the same year he was elected to the governor's council, an advisory body in which he served governors Patrick Henry and Thomas Jefferson.

FATHER OF THE CONSTITUTION

In 1780 Madison's political focus was broadened when he was chosen to serve in the Continental Congress, where he worked to bring greater organization to the federal government under the new Articles of Confederation. During this period, however, Madison began to believe that the articles had to be strengthened if the government was going to survive. Congress had no means of implementing its decisions and was completely dependent on the goodwill of the states. For example, in June 1783 Madison had witnessed a band of Revolutionary War veterans surround the Philadelphia statehouse where Congress was meeting and demand that the legislators vote them back pay. When Congress asked Pennsylvania for militia to disperse the band, the state government refused. Such humiliations convinced Madison that the federal government had to be restructured.

At the end of 1783 Madison returned to Virginia where he was reelected to the state legislature. He served there until 1786. During this period Madison studied the history of government and began to form ideas about how to strengthen the national government. In September 1786 he attended the Annapolis Convention, a national meeting called to consider trade. Only five states were represented at the convention, but the delegates in Annapolis issued a call for a second national convention to be held in Philadelphia the following year.

Madison led a group of nationalists who wanted to establish a broad mandate for the Philadelphia convention. They urged all thirteen states to send delegates, obtained a congressional endorsement of the convention, and enhanced the prestige of the convention by convincing George Washington to attend. At the Constitutional Convention in Philadelphia in 1787, Madison's extensive study and contemplation of political theory paid off for his nation. More than any other individual, he was responsible for the content of the Constitution produced by the conven-

tion. The "Virginia Plan," which served as the basis of the Constitution, was submitted to the convention by Edmund Randolph, but it was largely Madison's work.

Following the convention Madison wrote a series of essays, known as the *Federalist Papers,* with Alexander Hamilton and John Jay. These essays explained and defended the new Constitution, which had to be ratified by the states before it could become law. He also led the successful fight for ratification at Virginia's ratifying convention in 1788. That year Madison was prevented from being elected to the new U.S. Senate by powerful state legislator and former Virginia governor Patrick Henry, who had opposed the Constitution. Madison won election to the U.S. House of Representatives, however. There he proposed nine amendments to the Constitution, which became the basis for the Bill of Rights.

Madison legislated according to a strict interpretation of the Constitution; he opposed the government's exercise of powers not specifically granted in the document. He fought unsuccessfully against Treasury Secretary Alexander Hamilton's plans to establish a national bank and have the federal government assume the war debts of the states. He also wrote a series of articles, under the name "Helvidius," that argued against the expansion of presidential power and attacked Washington's proclamation of neutrality toward warring Britain and France in 1793 as unconstitutional.

From his position in Congress, Madison assumed a leading role, second only to Thomas Jefferson, in the formation of the Democratic-Republican Party. In 1797, after four terms, he retired from Congress.

In 1801, newly elected president Thomas Jefferson appointed Madison secretary of state. He served in this post for all eight years of Jefferson's presidency, and he supported all the president's major diplomatic initiatives, including the Louisiana Purchase.

With Jefferson's support, Madison was nominated for president by the Democratic-Republicans in 1808. Although he lost five northern states, Madison received 122 electoral votes to Federalist Charles C. Pinckney's 47.

PRESIDENCY

Madison's presidency focused on issues related to the war under way in Europe between Britain and France. British warships were boarding American commercial ships, seizing cargo, and impressing any sailor they suspected of being British. Members of Congress known as the War Hawks, a group that included Henry Clay and John Calhoun, urged Madison to declare war on the British. The War Hawks, most of whom were from the South and the West, also wanted to launch military adventures into Canada and to halt Indian attacks in the West, which they believed were encouraged by the British. By 1812 Madison saw no alternative to war, and on June 1 he asked Congress for a declaration of war. The declaration passed on June 18, 19–13 in the Senate and 79–49 in the House. That fall, Madison ran for reelection against DeWitt Clinton of New York, the nominee of an anti-Madison faction of the Democratic-Republican Party. The Federalists, who did not nominate a candidate, threw their support to Clinton. Madison defeated Clinton 128–89 in the electoral college.

The United States was not prepared for war. Its navy was small compared to the British fleet, and throughout the war the army had great difficulty fulfilling its recruitment goals. Moreover, the nation was not united behind the war effort. The war was opposed by many citizens in the Northeast, who favored the British in their fight with France. In addition, the merchants of that region preferred the occasional seizure of their neutral vessels by the British to a war that could end trade completely. Indeed, some New England Federalists openly discussed secession during the war.

The United States prevailed in several sea battles, and frontier generals William Henry Harrison and Andrew Jackson won decisive victories over Britain's Indian allies, but overall the war went badly for the United States. The worst humiliation occurred in August 1814 when the British occupied Washington, D.C., and burned government buildings, including the Executive Mansion and Capitol. On December 24, 1814, Britain and the United States signed the Treaty of Ghent, which ended the war without resolving the issues for which it had been fought. The British gave no guarantees that it would allow U.S. ships safe passage in the future.

In spite of the many defeats suffered by the United States, the end of the war brought a resurgence of nationalism. The Treaty of Ghent and Andrew Jackson's overwhelming victory over the British at the Battle of New Orleans on January 8, 1815, two weeks after the peace treaty had been signed, convinced many Americans that the war had been won. Federalist opposition to the war crippled that party, leaving Madison's Democratic-Republicans in a commanding position.

Madison's last two years in office were successful ones. Congress backed the president's proposal to appropriate funds to strengthen the armed forces. Madison also supported the establishment of the Second Bank of the United States and increased tariffs to protect U.S. industries.

RETIREMENT

After leaving office Madison returned to Montpelier, his estate in Virginia. He remained a close friend of Thomas Jefferson, who lived thirty miles away. When Jefferson died in 1826 Madison assumed his job as rector of the University of Virginia. In 1829 he cochaired a Virginia convention aimed at revising the state constitution. During his retirement Madison also edited the secret daily record he had kept at the Constitutional Convention, which has been invaluable to historians when reconstructing its events. His wife sold Madison's *Notes on the Federal Convention* to Congress in 1837. The year before Madison had died peacefully at Montpelier at the age of eighty-five.

On September 15, 1794, at the age of forty-three, Madison married widow Dorothea Payne Todd, who was called "Dolley." The couple had no children, but they raised Dolley's one surviving child from her previous marriage. Dolley was an outgoing woman who loved entertaining. As first lady her social charms compensated for her husband's reserved nature. After her husband's death Dolley participated in many Washington social functions until her death in 1849.

James Monroe

BORN: April 28, 1758; Westmoreland County, Virginia
PARTY: Democratic-Republican
TERM: March 4, 1817–March 4, 1825
VICE PRESIDENT: Daniel D. Tompkins
DIED: July 4, 1831; New York City
BURIED: Richmond, Virginia

James Monroe was the eldest of the five children of Elizabeth and Spence Monroe, a well-established Virginia planter of modest means. James entered the College of William and Mary in Williamsburg, Virginia, when he was sixteen but left two years later to join the Continental army. As a lieutenant he fought in numerous battles, including Trenton, Brandywine, Germantown, and Monmouth. At Trenton he was wounded in the shoulder and promoted to captain for his bravery by Gen. George Washington. In 1778 he was promoted again, to lieutenant colonel, but he was not able to recruit enough Virginia volunteers to form a new regiment that he could command.

Monroe left the army in 1780 to study law under Thomas Jefferson, then governor of Virginia. Monroe quickly developed a close personal and professional relationship with his mentor that lead to a career in politics and public service. In 1782 he was elected to the Virginia legislature and, a year later, he was chosen along with Jefferson to represent Virginia at the Continental Congress in New York City. While in Congress Monroe became an expert on frontier issues after making two fact-finding journeys into the Ohio Valley. When Monroe's third term expired in 1786, he moved to Fredericksburg, Virginia, where he established a law practice. That year Monroe was again elected to the Virginia legislature.

Although Monroe attended the national convention in Annapolis, Maryland, which created momentum for the writing of the Constitution, he was not a delegate to the Constitutional Convention of 1787. His belief that the Constitution gave the president and Senate too much power led him to oppose the document vigorously at Virginia's ratifying convention in 1788. Nevertheless, after ratification by Virginia, he ran for the U.S. House of Representatives but lost to James Madison.

Monroe soon adopted a national political perspective, and when Virginian William Grayson, an anti-Federalist, died in 1790, Monroe was appointed to his Senate seat. In the Senate Monroe worked against Treasury Secretary Alexander Hamilton's fiscal policies. Monroe helped Jefferson and Madison establish the foundations of the Democratic-Republican Party that would challenge the Federalists after George Washington's retirement.

In 1794 Washington appointed Monroe ambassador to France. In Paris, however, his outspoken support of the French conflicted with Washington's careful policy of neutrality in the Franco-British war. After the president recalled him in 1796, Monroe published A View of the Conduct of the Executive, in which he attacked the administration's policies toward France. In 1799 Monroe was elected governor of Virginia and served effectively for three years.

Thomas Jefferson was elected president in 1800, ushering in a period of Democratic-Republican dominance over national affairs. In January 1803, after Monroe's third term as governor of Virginia had expired, Jefferson asked him to travel to France to negotiate the purchase of New Orleans. When Napoleon offered to sell not just New Orleans but the entire Louisiana Territory, Monroe and Ambassador Robert Livingston seized the opportunity to double the size of the United States. Acting without authority, they closed the deal for $15 million. The purchase added 828,000 square miles to the United States. Monroe continued to function as a special ambassador in Europe for four more years. He tried unsuccessfully to purchase the Floridas from the Spanish and to conclude a treaty with the British ending that country's capture of American vessels.

Monroe returned to Virginia in 1807 and practiced law until he was again elected governor in 1811. When newly elected president James Madison offered Monroe the post of secretary of state, however, he resigned the governorship to return to nation-al service. Monroe helped write Madison's request for a declaration of war against the British in 1811. The United States was ill-prepared, however, for the War of 1812. The first two years of fighting brought several humiliating defeats, including the capture and burning of Washington, D.C., by the British in August 1814. In September of that year Madison appointed Monroe secretary of war in addition to his duties as secretary of state. Monroe then worked tirelessly to reorganize the nation's defenses and to end the confusion that had prevailed in the War Department. In March 1815, three months after the war ended, an exhausted Monroe resigned as secretary of war and went to his home in Virginia for a rest. He returned to Washington six months later and resumed his duties as secretary of state.

With Madison's backing, Monroe was nominated as the Democratic-Republican presidential candidate in 1816. He easily defeated the Federalist candidate, Sen. Rufus King of New York, 183–34 in the electoral college. Less than three months after taking office, Monroe followed George Washington's example and toured the Middle Atlantic and New England states. Reacting to the enthusiastic reception of the president in the North, a Boston newspaper declared the time to be a political "era of good feelings." These good feelings extended to the 1820 presidential election. Monroe ran unopposed and received all but one electoral vote that was cast for John Quincy Adams by an elector who wished to preserve George Washington's distinction as the only president ever to be elected unanimously.

Monroe's presidency, however, was not without its problems. When Missouri sought admission to the United States as a slave state, sectional tensions over the slavery issue erupted. Monroe was a slaveholder who believed that the institution should eventually be abolished. He also believed, however, that new states entering the Union had the constitutional right to determine for themselves if they would permit slavery. In 1820, after a lengthy debate, Congress passed the Missouri Compromise. The plan allowed Missouri to enter the Union as a slave state simultaneously with the admission of Maine as a free state. The compromise also prohibited slavery north of latitude 36° 30 minute symbol in the territory acquired in the Louisiana Purchase. Monroe doubted the constitutionality of the plan, but he approved it because he considered it the best way to avoid sectional conflict and possibly the secession of southern states.

In foreign policy Monroe's administration had several notable successes. The Rush-Bagot Agreement signed with Great Britain in 1817 limited the number of warships each country could deploy on the Great Lakes and led to the demilitarization of the Canadian frontier. In 1819 Secretary of State John Quincy Adams concluded a treaty in which Spain transferred control of the Floridas to the United States and agreed to a border dividing the United States and Spanish territory in western North America.

Monroe's administration is best known, however, for the foreign policy doctrine that bears his name and continues to influence U.S. policy toward Latin America. In October 1823 Great Britain suggested that the United States join it in resisting European intervention in Latin America, where several revolutions had succeeded in overthrowing Spanish colonial rule. Although former presidents Jefferson and Madison advised Monroe to accept the British proposal, Monroe was swayed by the arguments of Secretary of State Adams, who advocated an independent U.S. declaration against European intrusions into the Western Hemisphere. In his annual message to Congress in 1823 Monroe announced that the United States intended to stay out of European conflicts and would not interfere in the existing Latin American colonies of the European powers. Monroe warned the Europeans, however, that any attempt to establish new colonies in the Western Hemisphere or interfere in the affairs of independent American nations would be regarded by the United States as an "unfriendly" act. At the time the Monroe Doctrine was issued it had little force because the United States did not possess the military strength to defend Latin America. As the nation developed, however, the Monroe Doctrine became a cornerstone of U.S. foreign policy.

While serving in the Continental Congress in New York in 1785 Monroe met his wife-to-be, Elizabeth Kortright; they married in 1786. The Monroes raised two daughters and had one son who died at the age of two. Monroe experienced financial difficulties after he retired from the presidency and was forced to sell Ash Lawn, one of his two Virginia homes in 1825. After his wife died in 1830, he sold his other Virginia estate, Oak Hill, and moved to New York City to live with his daughter and her husband. On July 4, 1831, Monroe became the third president, along with John Adams and Thomas Jefferson, to die on Independence Day.

John Quincy Adams

BORN: July 11, 1767; Braintree (now Quincy), Massachusetts
PARTY: Democratic-Republican
TERM: March 4, 1825–March 4, 1829
VICE PRESIDENT: John C. Calhoun
DIED: February 23, 1848; Washington, D.C.
BURIED: Quincy

John Quincy Adams was the oldest son and second of the children of John and Abigail Adams. He was the only son of a president ever to become president. As a boy in Massachusetts, John Quincy lived through the early stages of the Revolutionary War and was an eyewitness to the battle of Bunker Hill. He lived in Europe from 1778 to 1785 while his father served as a diplomat. He was educated at schools in France and the Netherlands and learned to speak several languages. In 1781, when he was just fourteen, he left his family for two years to serve as secretary and translator for Francis Dana, the first U.S. ambassador to Russia.

When Adams returned to America in 1785 he enrolled in Harvard University and graduated two years later. After passing the bar in 1790, he established a law practice in Boston. His distinguished diplomatic career began in 1794 when George Washington appointed him ambassador to the Netherlands. In 1796 he was about to move to Portugal to become ambassador when

his father was elected president. President Adams reassigned his son to the post of minister to Prussia, which he held throughout his father's term.

When Thomas Jefferson defeated John Adams in his try for reelection in 1800, John Quincy returned to the United States where he embarked on a legislative career as a Federalist. In 1802 he was elected to the Massachusetts Senate, which sent him to the U.S. Senate the following year. Adams, however, angered his fellow Federalists by insisting on considering each issue independently, rather than voting with the party. When he supported President Jefferson's Embargo Act in 1807, the Massachusetts legislature elected his successor six months before his term expired. Adams thus resigned in protest and returned to Massachusetts to practice law and teach at Harvard University.

Despite Adams's Federalist background, Democratic-Republican President James Madison appointed him minister to Russia in 1809. While in St. Petersburg, Adams witnessed Napoleon's disastrous invasion of Russia and declined an appointment to the U.S. Supreme Court. In 1814 Adams was sent to Ghent to head the U.S. delegation to the negotiations seeking an end to the War of 1812. The treaty negotiated by Adams and his delegation and signed on December 24, 1814, extricated the United States from the embarrassing war without having to make significant concessions. Adams was then sent to London where he served as minister to Great Britain until 1817.

President James Monroe called Adams home from London in 1817 to become secretary of state. Adams distinguished himself in this post by conducting successful negotiations with Spain on the cession of the Floridas. The Adams-Onis Treaty with Spain, concluded on February 22, 1819, provided for the transfer of East and West Florida to the United States and the establishment of a border between Spanish and U.S. territory running from the Gulf of Mexico to the Rocky Mountains and along the forty-second parallel to the Pacific Ocean. Historians regard the treaty as a brilliant act of diplomacy, and Adams himself called its conclusion "the most important event of my life." Adams also was the mind behind the Monroe Doctrine, which warned that the United States would oppose any European interference in the internal affairs of an American nation or further European colonization of territory in the Western Hemisphere.

The 1824 presidential election was one of the most confused in U.S. history. The remnants of the Federalist Party had faded away during Monroe's presidency, leaving the Democratic-Republican Party the only significant party in existence. The Democratic-Republican congressional caucus nominated W. H. Crawford of Georgia as the party's candidate, but several state caucuses refused to be guided by the judgment of this group. Consequently, John Quincy Adams, Andrew Jackson, and Henry Clay were nominated as regional candidates. The four-candidate race split the electoral vote, and no one received the majority required to be elected. Jackson led Adams 99 to 84 votes, with Crawford and Clay receiving 41 and 37 votes, respectively. This stalemate threw the election into the House of Representatives. There Henry Clay, a powerful member of the House, gave his support to Adams, who emerged victorious despite having received less than one-third of the popular vote. Jackson's supporters were furious that their candidate had been denied the presidency. When Adams selected Clay to be his secretary of state, the new president's opponents charged that he had made a "corrupt bargain."

Despite the absence of an electoral mandate and the disadvantage of a Congress poised to oppose him, Adams attempted to implement a program of public improvements. To stimulate the economy he advocated construction of a federally funded system of roads and canals and the implementation of high protective tariffs. He also called for federal funding of a national university, a national observatory, and scientific expeditions. The president's proposals failed, however, to attract significant support. Adams gained respect from certain groups for his anti-slavery and Indian rights stands, but he was out of step politically with the majority of the American public, especially in the South and West. By his own admission he was not a popular president. When he ran for reelection in 1828 against Andrew Jackson, he did well in his native New England but lost the South and West, and therefore the election, by a landslide.

In 1830 the Twelfth District of Massachusetts elected the former president to the U.S. House of Representatives. Adams welcomed the chance to get back into national politics, free of the burdens and constraints of the presidency. He wrote, "No election or appointment conferred upon me ever gave me so much pleasure." Although not a radical abolitionist, Adams won respect for his conscientious opposition to slavery. He also was a leading congressional critic of the annexation of Texas and the Mexican War. Adams's life of public service ended in February 1848 when he became ill at his desk in the House chamber, fell into a coma, and died two days later in the Capitol.

While serving as a diplomat in Europe in 1797 Adams married Louisa Catherine Johnson, the daughter of Joshua Johnson, a merchant who was also the American consul-general in London. They had four children. Their youngest son, Charles Francis Adams, had a distinguished diplomatic career, serving as minister to Great Britain during the American Civil War.

Andrew Jackson

BORN: March 15, 1767; Waxhaw, South Carolina
PARTY: Democratic
TERM: March 4, 1829–March 4, 1837
VICE PRESIDENTS: John C. Calhoun; Martin Van Buren
DIED: June 8, 1845; Nashville, Tennessee
BURIED: Nashville

Andrew Jackson was the youngest of the three sons of Andrew and Elizabeth Jackson, who had emigrated from Ireland. The couple were poor farmers in the Waxhaw region of South Carolina near the North Carolina border. The boy's father died a few days before Andrew was born from internal injuries sustained while lifting a heavy log. Andrew was raised by his mother, with the help of his uncle and older brother.

By the time he was five Andrew had learned to read at a country school, but he received only a rudimentary education. When he was just thirteen Andrew and his older brother Robert joined the militia. Their oldest brother Hugh had already been killed in the Revolutionary War, and Andrew and Robert were wounded and captured by the British in 1781. While a prisoner, Andrew was scarred on the hand by a British officer who struck him with a saber for refusing to clean the officer's boots. Because the boys contracted smallpox while in a British prison in South Carolina, they were allowed to return to their mother. Andrew's experiences during the war caused him to develop a hatred toward the British that he would feel for the rest of his life.

Andrew's brother Robert died two days after being released by the British, and his mother died later that year. Andrew was then left in the care of his mother's relatives. When he was sixteen he received an inheritance worth several hundred pounds from his paternal grandfather in Ireland. By this time, however, Andrew had adopted a wild lifestyle, and he gambled much of the money away.

In 1784 Jackson moved to Salisbury, North Carolina, where he began studying law in the office of Spruce Macay. He was admitted to the bar and began practicing law in 1787. In 1788 he

Andrew Jackson

brief term ended, within months he was elected to fill a vacant Senate seat. He served in the Senate from November 1797 to April 1798, when he again resigned. He then returned to Tennessee because of financial difficulties and his dislike of being separated from his family. In November of that year he was appointed to a seat on the Tennessee Superior Court. He served there until 1804, when he resigned to manage his estate.

Although Jackson had become a prominent citizen, he still possessed the temper of his youth. During his years in Tennessee he was involved in several duels and fights. Some of these incidents came to nothing, including a duel in 1803 with Tennessee governor John Sevier in which no shots were fired. In 1806, however, Jackson fought a duel with Charles Dickenson, who had questioned the propriety of Jackson's marriage. Dickenson fired first, wounding Jackson in the chest. The athletic Jackson shrugged off his wound, straightened himself, and mortally wounded Dickenson with his volley. Because Dickenson's bullet was lodged near Jackson's heart, it could not be removed, and caused Jackson periodic pain for the rest of his life. In 1813 Jackson got into a fight with Thomas Hart and Jesse Benton in Nashville. He emerged from the brawl with two bullet wounds, one that almost forced the amputation of his arm.

MILITARY CAREER

Since 1802 Jackson had held the rank of major general of the Tennessee militia. When the United States declared war on Great Britain in 1812, Jackson offered the services of his militia against the British. The government was slow to accept his offer but eventually sent Jackson to fight the Creek Indians, who were allied with the British. Jackson, whose troops had earlier nicknamed him "Old Hickory" in tribute to his toughness, engineered a five-month campaign that culminated in the decisive defeat of the Creeks at the Battle of Horseshoe Bend, Alabama, on March 27, 1814. Soon after, he was commissioned as a brigadier and then major general in the U.S. Army.

Following a brief campaign in which Jackson's forces captured Pensacola, Florida, from the British, the general was ordered west to defend New Orleans. After a large British force landed near the city, Jackson launched a surprise attack on December 23, 1814, which slowed the British advance. He then ordered his forces to retire to earthen fortifications blocking the route to New Orleans. When the British attacked on January 8, 1815, Jackson's motley army of U.S. regulars, Tennessee backwoodsmen, free blacks, friendly Indians, and pirate Jean Lafitte's crew laid down a deadly fire that left the canefield where the battle was fought littered with British dead. In about a half hour over two thousand British troops were killed or wounded. Only about forty of Jackson's men were killed, wounded, or missing. The decisive victory at New Orleans raised the morale of the nation, which had suffered many embarrassing military defeats during the war, and made Jackson a folk hero.

After the war Jackson remained military commander of the Southern District of the United States. In late 1817, acting on vague orders to defend the frontier near Spanish Florida from

moved to the new settlement of Nashville, where he became the prosecuting attorney of the Western District of North Carolina, which would become the state of Tennessee.

In 1796 Jackson became a member of the convention that drafted Tennessee's constitution, and that same year he was elected without opposition as Tennessee's first representative to the U.S. House of Representatives. Because Tennessee had become a state shortly before regular congressional elections were to be held, Jackson's term lasted only from December 1796 until March 1797. During his brief tenure in the House he was one of a handful of members to vote against a farewell tribute to George Washington. Jackson was critical of Washington's support for the Jay Treaty, which he believed allowed the British to continue preying on American shipping. Although Jackson declined to run for reelection and returned to Tennessee when his

Indian attacks, Jackson launched an invasion of Florida that led to the capture of several Spanish posts. When Spain protested, the general was in danger of being reprimanded for exceeding his orders and infringing upon the right of Congress to declare war. Secretary of State John Quincy Adams, however, defended Jackson's actions, which he recognized increased pressure on the Spanish to cede the territory to the United States. President James Monroe stated his qualified support of Jackson's campaign, and in 1819 Adams concluded a treaty in which Spain renounced its claims to the Floridas.

PRESIDENCY

Although Jackson denied any interest in seeking the presidency, his supporters in Tennessee maneuvered to make him a candidate. In 1823 Jackson was elected to the U.S. Senate by the Tennessee legislature, sending him back to Washington as an obvious contender for the presidency.

The 1824 election was a confusing affair in which all the candidates were Democratic-Republicans and no one received a majority of electoral votes. One hundred and thirty-three electoral votes were needed for election, but Jackson, the leading vote-getter, received only 99 votes. John Quincy Adams finished second with 84, and William Crawford and Henry Clay received 41 and 37 votes, respectively. The election was thus thrown into the House of Representatives. Jackson lost the election when the House elected Adams after Clay threw his support to the second-place finisher.

The 1828 presidential election, in which Jackson defeated incumbent Adams, was a watershed in American politics. Jackson was not only the first person from the West to be elected president, but also he was the first to have been elected with the overwhelming support of the masses of common farmers and citizens who recently had been enfranchised in most states. Tens of thousands of voters descended on Washington for Jackson's inauguration. After his swearing-in Jackson opened the White House to his supporters, whose rowdy behavior confirmed the perceptions of many members of the conservative eastern political establishment that the country had succumbed to mob rule. The jubilant throngs at the White House broke furniture and china, muddied carpets, and forced Jackson to evacuate the premises for his own safety.

Jackson, like many presidents of his era, faced sectional tensions. In 1832 Congress had passed a high tariff despite the opposition of many southern states. Southerners objected to high tariffs because they protected the manufacturing interests in the North, while trade reprisals from Europe denied the South markets for its agricultural products. In response to the tariff law, the South Carolina legislature declared that the federal tariff was null in that state. Jackson met the challenge to the Constitution by denouncing nullification and requesting authority from Congress to send troops to South Carolina if needed to enforce the tariff. Congress granted this authority, which helped convince South Carolina to accept a compromise tariff bill backed by Jackson. The episode led to the estrangement of Jackson from his vice president, John C. Calhoun, who had supported South Carolina's nullification of the tariff.

Although Jackson was a strong defender of the primacy of the federal government, he did not support all its activities. In 1832 Jackson vetoed the bill that would have rechartered the Second Bank of the United States on the grounds that the bank was unconstitutional and a monopoly that benefited the rich. Jackson's political opponents hoped to turn the issue against him in the 1832 election, but the popular president easily defeated Whig Henry Clay. Unfortunately, the lack of a central bank weakened controls over state and local banks and contributed to the inflation and overspeculation that were partially responsible for the severe depression that began in 1837 after Jackson left office.

On January 30, 1835, Jackson became the first president to be the target of an assassination attempt. As Jackson was emerging from the Capitol, Richard Lawrence fired two pistols at him at point-blank range. Miraculously, both misfired. Jackson went at his assailant with his walking stick as onlookers seized Lawrence. The deluded young man, who claimed Jackson was preventing him from assuming the British throne, later was committed to an insane asylum.

When Jackson's second term expired, he retired to the Hermitage, his estate near Nashville. Although he never again sought public office and suffered from several ailments that left him weak, he retained his avid interest in politics. His support was important to the presidential victories of Martin Van Buren in 1836 and James K. Polk in 1844. Jackson died in 1845 at the Hermitage.

When Jackson met Rachel Donelson Robards in Nashville in 1788, she was separated from but still married to Lewis Robards. But when Jackson married her in 1791, they believed she had been granted a divorce. In late 1793, however, they learned that Rachel's divorce had not become legal until a few months before. Thus, to avoid any legal difficulties Andrew and Rachel repeated their wedding ceremony in January 1794.

Although the couple had no children, in 1810 they adopted Rachel's nephew, whom they renamed Andrew Jackson Jr. During the 1828 presidential campaign, Jackson's political opponents dredged up old accusations that Jackson's marriage was improper. Rachel was upset by the scrutiny of her past and longed for a quiet life in Tennessee with her husband. The charges may have affected Rachel's health, for it grew progressively worse, and she eventually died of a heart attack on December 22, 1828, after Jackson had been elected president but before his inauguration.

Martin Van Buren

BORN: December 5, 1782; Kinderhook, New York
PARTY: Democratic
TERM: March 4, 1837–March 4, 1841
VICE PRESIDENT: Richard M. Johnson
DIED: July 24, 1862; Kinderhook
BURIED: Kinderhook

Martin Van Buren was the third child of Abraham and Maria Van Buren. Martin's father was a farmer and tavern keeper who had fought in the Revolution. His mother, who had been widowed before marrying Abraham, had two sons and a daughter by her previous marriage.

Van Buren, the first president not of British descent, was raised in the Dutch community of Kinderhook, New York. Despite having received only a rudimentary education as a child, he began studying law when he was only fourteen under Francis Silvester. He moved to New York in 1801 and continued his law studies. After being admitted to the bar in 1803 he returned to Kinderhook and opened a law practice.

In 1808 Van Buren moved to Hudson, New York, where he was appointed surrogate of Columbia County. He began his rapid rise to power in New York politics in 1812 when he was elected to the state senate. He was appointed state attorney general in 1815 and retained his Senate seat while serving in that post. By 1820 Van Buren had become one of the most powerful politicians in New York. Before pursuing a national political career, Van Buren organized the "Albany Regency," a political machine that controlled New York politics through patronage, party newspapers, and a tightly controlled Democratic caucus in the state legislature.

In 1821 the New York State legislature elected Van Buren to the U.S. Senate as a member of the Democratic-Republican Party. He was reelected in 1827. While serving in the Senate, Van Buren was one of the most vocal critics of President John Quincy Adams.

Van Buren's rise to the presidency was aided by his association with Andrew Jackson. Although Van Buren and Jackson had little in common but political skill, they became close allies. By 1827 Van Buren had become Jackson's most powerful supporter from the northeastern states. In 1828 Van Buren resigned from the Senate to help Jackson's presidential campaign in New York by running for governor. Jackson was elected president and Van Buren won the governorship, but Van Buren resigned after only three months to become Jackson's secretary of state.

As secretary of state, Van Buren was the most influential member of Jackson's cabinet. He not only became a successful diplomat respected by foreign governments for his discretion and negotiating ability, but he also continued to be Jackson's principal political adviser. In 1831 Van Buren further endeared himself to Jackson, when he concurred with Jackson's defense of Peggy Eaton, Secretary of War John Eaton's wife, who had been rejected by Washington society for her alleged past promiscuity. Soon after the Eaton affair Van Buren resigned from his office to allow Jackson to reconstruct his cabinet free of supporters of Van Buren's political rival, Vice President John C. Calhoun. Jackson then appointed Van Buren ambassador to Great Britain, but when the Senate confirmation vote resulted in a tie, Calhoun voted against confirming Van Buren, who had already arrived in London. In 1832 Van Buren replaced Calhoun as Jackson's vice-presidential running mate. The Jackson-Van Buren team was elected easily, and Van Buren continued to exercise influence over Jackson's policies.

In 1836, with President Jackson's backing, Van Buren received the Democratic presidential nomination. The Whig Party, believing that no single candidate had a good chance to beat Van Buren, nominated several regional candidates, hoping to divide the electoral vote and force the election into the House of Representatives. Van Buren, however, won a majority of the popular and the electoral vote. He needed 148 electoral votes to win the election outright, and he received 170 votes with William Henry Harrison, his closest Whig opponent, receiving 73 votes.

Van Buren pledged at his inauguration to continue the policies of Jackson, and he reappointed Jackson's cabinet. The former president's economic policies, however, contributed to the depression that dominated Van Buren's presidency and did not subside until he had been defeated for reelection. In 1832 Jackson had vetoed the bill to recharter the National Bank. Without the central control provided by the National Bank, many state and local banks engaged in wild speculation that led to financial disaster.

In 1837 overspeculation and a natural downturn in the business cycle caused many banks and businesses to fail. While unemployment soared, Van Buren followed the conventional economic wisdom of the period by cutting government expenditures. But these restrictive fiscal policies only deepened the depression. Like his mentor, Van Buren also opposed a national bank, but he believed the federal government should handle its own funds rather than placing them in state banks as Jackson had done. He therefore proposed an independent federal treasury system. After several years of political maneuvering and debate Congress passed the Independent Treasury Act in July 1840. It established subtreasuries in seven U.S. cities.

On the issue of slavery Van Buren promoted the moderate course of allowing slavery to continue where it existed but blocking its extension. His opposition to the annexation of Texas, which would have added another slave state to the Union, avoided conflict with Mexico but cost him support in the South and West and damaged his relationship with Andrew Jackson.

Van Buren also had to deal with conflict on the U.S. border with Canada. He refused to support a movement by some U.S. citizens to aid a Canadian attempt to overthrow British rule in Canada. He defused the crisis by issuing a neutrality proclamation and sending Gen. Winfield Scott to Buffalo to enforce the peace. In 1839 a dispute developed over the uncertain legal boundary between Maine and Canada. Maine's governor, John Fairfield, called up a force of Maine militia and was preparing to fight with the Canadians over the issue when Van Buren intervened by negotiating an agreement with the British ambassador to the United States and sending Gen. Scott to Maine to block any military adventure by Fairfield.

In 1840 Van Buren was renominated unanimously by the Democratic Party, but Whig William Henry Harrison was a formidable opponent. Not only was Harrison a national hero for his Indian fighting exploits before and during the War of 1812, but also he was portrayed as the candidate of the common man who was truer to Jacksonian principles than Van Buren. Although Van Buren won 47 percent of the popular vote, Harrison trounced him in the electoral college 234–60. Van Buren even failed to win his home state of New York.

Despite his defeat in 1840 Van Buren did not retire from presidential politics. He attempted to run again for his party's nomination in 1844 but was defeated by dark horse candidate James K. Polk, who outflanked Van Buren by openly advocating the annexation of Texas. In 1848 Van Buren ran for president as the candidate of the new antislavery Free Soil Party. His long-shot candidacy split the Democratic vote in New York, helping Whig Zachary Taylor win the state and defeat Democrat Lewis Cass by 163–127 electoral votes. In 1850 Van Buren returned to the Democratic Party, and he supported Franklin Pierce's presidential candidacy in 1852.

Van Buren was the first former president to tour Europe. From 1853 to 1855 he visited Britain, France, Italy, Belgium, Holland, and Switzerland. During his retirement he wrote *Inquiry into the Origin and Course of Political Parties in the United States.*

The manuscript was unfinished when he died in 1862 after suffering severe asthma attacks, but it was edited by his sons and published in 1867.

Van Buren married his childhood sweetheart and distant cousin Hannah Hoes on February 21, 1807. They had four sons and a fifth child who died soon after birth. Hannah died in 1819 before her husband attained national prominence. Van Buren never remarried, and the role of White House hostess was performed by Angelica Singleton Van Buren, the wife of his oldest son and White House secretary, Abraham.

William Henry Harrison

BORN: February 9, 1773; Berkeley, Virginia
PARTY: Whig
TERM: March 4, 1841–April 4, 1841
VICE PRESIDENT: John Tyler
DIED: April 4, 1841; Washington, D.C.
BURIED: North Bend, Ohio

William Henry Harrison was the youngest of the seven children of Benjamin and Elizabeth Harrison. William's father, a prosperous Virginia planter who served as a member of the Continental Congress and governor of Virginia, also signed the

Declaration of Independence. When William was fourteen his parents sent him to Hampden-Sydney College in his home state. Before graduating, however, he left for Philadelphia to study medicine under Dr. Benjamin Rush, a prominent physician and signer of the Declaration of Independence.

When his father died in 1791, Harrison quit medicine to join the army. He was commissioned as a lieutenant and assigned as an aide to Gen. Anthony Wayne at Fort Washington near Cincinnati. In 1794 Harrison fought in the Battle of Fallen Timbers where General Wayne's forces defeated eight hundred Indians. Harrison was promoted to captain in March 1795 and was given command of Fort Washington late that year.

In 1798 President John Adams appointed Harrison secretary of the Northwest Territory. The following year Harrison traveled to Washington, D.C., as the delegate of the Northwest Territory to Congress. There he worked successfully for legislation that separated the Indiana Territory from the Northwest Territory. In 1800 Adams appointed Harrison governor of the Indiana Territory, a post that he held until 1812. In November 1811 Harrison led the Indiana territorial militia in a battle fought near Tippecanoe Creek against a confederation of Indians under the Shawnee chief Tecumseh. The battle was inconclusive, but it made Harrison a nationally famous Indian fighter. During the War of 1812 Harrison was appointed brigadier general in command of the U.S. Army in the Northwest. Two years after the Battle of Tippecanoe Harrison again met Tecumseh, who had formed an alliance with the British. At the battle of Thames River in Ontario, Harrison's troops decisively defeated the Indians. Tecumseh was killed, and the federation of Indians was broken. The importance of the Thames River battle was overshadowed, however, by Harrison's earlier fight against the Indians, which had earned him the catchy nickname "Tippecanoe."

After the war Harrison was elected first to the U.S. House of Representatives, then to the Ohio Senate, and finally to the U.S. Senate. In 1828 Andrew Jackson appointed him ambassador to Colombia, but Harrison served there only eight months before returning to North Bend, Ohio, to manage his farm. In 1834 he accepted an appointment as clerk of his county's court of common pleas to help pay his heavy debts. While serving in this relatively insignificant post, he began campaigning actively for the 1836 presidential nomination of the Whig Party.

After witnessing the ease with which popular Democrat Andrew Jackson won two presidential elections, leaders of the Whig Party decided that they too needed a candidate who was a war hero from the West. The Whigs thus ran several regional candidates, including Harrison, against Jackson's chosen successor, Martin Van Buren. Van Buren won the election, but Harrison demonstrated his appeal by winning seven states.

Harrison's strong showing in the 1836 presidential election made him the logical Whig candidate in 1840. Even with Andrew Jackson's endorsement, Van Buren's hold on the presidency was vulnerable because of an economic depression that had started in 1837. The Whig's campaign of 1840 was a study in political manipulation of the electorate. Party leaders promoted "Tippecanoe" as a champion of the common man and war hero who was raised in a log cabin and preferred to drink hard cider. Meanwhile, they portrayed Van Buren as the rich person's candidate who lived like a king in the White House. The Whigs buried political issues under a mountain of slogans, songs, picnics, stump speeches, and parades. And the strategy worked, with Harrison receiving 230 electoral votes to Van Buren's 60.

Harrison's inaugural address, delivered on March 4, 1841, while hardly the most memorable in presidential history, was probably the most fateful. A driving rainstorm soaked Harrison as he rode to the Capitol on a white horse and it continued throughout his address, which was the longest inaugural speech ever delivered. It contained over eight thousand words and lasted an hour and forty-five minutes. Ironically, in his speech, he advocated a constitutional amendment limiting presidents to one term in office and pledged to serve only one himself. Harrison caught a severe cold from his long exposure to the elements. On March 27 his condition deteriorated, and he was confined to his bed with what doctors diagnosed as pneumonia. He died on April 4, exactly one month after his inauguration.

Harrison married Anna Symmes on November 25, 1795, while he was an army lieutenant stationed in Ohio. They had six daughters and four sons. One of their sons, John Scott, was the father of Benjamin Harrison, who became the twenty-third president.

John Tyler

BORN: March 29, 1790; Charles City County, Virginia
PARTY: Whig
TERM: April 6, 1841–March 4, 1845
VICE PRESIDENT: None
DIED: January 18, 1862; Richmond, Virginia
BURIED: Richmond

John Tyler had much in common with his 1840 presidential running mate, William Henry Harrison. Both men were born in Charles City County, Virginia, and both were sons of prominent Virginia planters who had served as governor of that state.

John was the sixth of the eight children born to John and Mary Tyler. His mother died when he was just seven years old. Throughout his early life John set high goals for himself and attempted to follow his father's example of an active life of public service. He attended William and Mary College in Williamsburg, Virginia, graduating in 1807 when he was just seventeen. He then studied law under his father and was admitted to the bar two years later.

In 1811 Tyler was elected to the Virginia House of Delegates as a Jeffersonian Democratic-Republican. He was reelected five times and remained in office until 1815. During the War of 1812 he served briefly as captain of a Virginia militia company, but he saw no action. In November 1816 he was elected to the U.S. House of Representatives, but he retired from Congress in 1821,

John Tyler

citing poor health. During his early political career Tyler was noted for his support of slavery and states' rights.

In 1823 Tyler was again elected to the Virginia House of Delegates, where he served until he was elected governor in 1825. After he resigned the governorship in 1827 he won a seat in the U.S. Senate which he held until 1836.

As a senator, Tyler promoted the compromise tariffs that eased the nullification crises in South Carolina in 1832. Although he doubted that the states could legally nullify federal laws, he vigorously opposed Jackson's threats to use force against South Carolina. In 1836 Tyler resigned his Senate seat after refusing to follow the instructions of the Virginia legislature that he vote for the deletion of a 1833 censure of Andrew Jackson from the Senate *Journal*. The Senate had censured Jackson for his removal of public funds from the Second Bank of the United States without proper congressional approval.

Tyler's unhappiness with Jackson and the Democratic Party led him to join the Whig Party, despite the antislavery and nationalistic positions of many of its leaders. As one of several regional Whig vice-presidential candidates in 1836, Tyler received forty-seven electoral votes. Democrats Martin Van Buren and

Richard Johnson won the presidency and vice presidency, respectively.

Considering their similar beginnings, it is ironic that Tyler was chosen as Harrison's running mate to balance the ticket. Harrison was promoted by the Whigs as "Old Tippecanoe," a tough Indian fighter who, like Andrew Jackson, was a champion of the common people. Tyler added southern gentility and a proslavery background that the Whigs hoped would appeal to the South. The Whig campaign of 1840 avoided policy issues and promoted its candidates through parties, parades, songs, and catchy slogans such as "Tippecanoe and Tyler too." The Whig ticket easily defeated President Martin Van Buren, whose popularity had been damaged by an economic depression that had lasted throughout his term.

Tyler appeared destined to have a small role in the Harrison administration. Daniel Webster, Henry Clay, and other Whig leaders had planned to exercise considerable influence over the aging Harrison, and there would be little place for Tyler, whose views were outside the Whig mainstream. Tyler, however, was thrust into the presidency when Harrison died only one month after taking office. The Constitution did not specify whether a vice president was to become president upon the death of an incumbent or merely assume the powers and duties of the office. Since Tyler was neither a Democrat nor a true Whig, leaders of both parties sought to limit his power. Many members of Congress and other national leaders contended that Tyler should be recognized only as acting president. But Tyler ignored his critics and assumed not only the duties of the presidency but also its title and all of its power.

Unlike the aging William Henry Harrison, who would likely have been dominated by Whig Party leaders, Tyler adopted policies that were entirely his own. His strict constructionist principles led him to oppose the major goals of the Whig leadership, including the National Bank, high tariffs, and federally funded internal improvements. As a result, he was excommunicated from the Whig Party while still president.

Although Tyler had little influence in Congress, he wished to make Texas, which had declared its independence from Mexico in 1836, a part of the United States. He thus oversaw the negotiation of a treaty of annexation with Texas in early 1844. On April 22 of that year he submitted the treaty to the Senate for approval. The Senate, however, rejected the treaty on June 8.

Tyler wished to run for reelection in 1844, but neither of the major political parties wanted to nominate him. He therefore organized a new Democratic-Republican Party dedicated to states' rights and the annexation of Texas. He gave up his candidacy, however, when the Democrats nominated James K. Polk, who had the support of Andrew Jackson and also advocated annexing Texas.

On December 4, Tyler, now a lame-duck president, sent his last State of the Union message to Congress. In it he proposed that the Texas annexation treaty be approved by a simple majority of both houses. The proposal was controversial not only because annexation of Texas would have implications for the slavery issue, but also because such a method of granting congressional consent would ignore the constitutional provision requiring a two-thirds vote by the Senate for approval of treaties. The House passed the joint resolution by a vote of 120–98 on January 25, 1845, and the Senate followed suit by a vote of 27–25 on February 27, 1845. Tyler's strategy had worked, and an important legislative precedent was set. Tyler signed the bill into law on March 1, three days before leaving office.

When his term expired, Tyler retired to Sherwood Forest, his Virginia estate. As a private citizen, he remained an outspoken advocate of southern interests. He believed that states had a constitutional right to secede, but he worked to preserve the Union. In early 1861 he presided over the Washington Peace Conference, an eleventh-hour attempt to resolve sectional differences and avoid civil war. When Virginia seceded, however, he pledged his loyalty to the South. In November 1861 Tyler was elected to the new Confederate Congress in Richmond, Virginia. He died there in a hotel room on January 18, 1862, before he could take his seat.

Tyler married Letitia Christian in 1813 on his twenty-third birthday. They had eight children. Mrs. Tyler died in the White House in 1842 after an extended illness. Several months after his first wife's death, Tyler became infatuated with Julia Gardiner, a young socialite from New York. After a year of courtship they were married in New York on June 26, 1844. Tyler had seven children by his second wife giving him a total of fifteen, the most of any president. Tyler's second marriage caused a minor scandal in the capital because his bride was only twenty-four years old. Their wedding came in the wake of a tragic accident on the Potomac River in which Julia's father, David Gardiner, and several members of Tyler's cabinet were killed. In fact, many members of Washington society, including Julia and the president, were also on board at the time of the accident, when a cannon that was being demonstrated on board the navy frigate *Princeton* exploded.

James K. Polk

BORN: November 2, 1795; Mecklenburg County, North Carolina

PARTY: Democratic

TERM: March 4, 1845–March 4, 1849

VICE PRESIDENT: George M. Dallas

DIED: June 15, 1849; Nashville, Tennessee

BURIED: Nashville

James Knox Polk was the eldest of the ten children born to Samuel and Jane Polk. Samuel Polk was a prosperous North Carolina farmer who was interested in politics. When James was ten his family moved to Duck River, Tennessee, a settlement without a school on the edge of the frontier. There his parents taught him mathematics and reading. As a boy, Polk was frail and often ill. When he was seventeen he survived an operation

to remove gallstones without the benefit of anesthesia. His health improved dramatically after the surgery.

In 1818 Polk graduated from the University of North Carolina with honors. He then moved to Nashville, Tennessee, where he studied law for two years in the office of Felix Grundy before being admitted to the bar.

Polk began his political career in the Tennessee legislature in 1823 at the age of twenty-seven. Two years later he was elected to the U.S. House of Representatives from Andrew Jackson's former district. Polk rose quickly to positions of power in the House, becoming chairman of the Ways and Means Committee, majority leader, and finally Speaker in 1835. During his years in the House he earned the nickname "Young Hickory" because of his unswerving support for Andrew Jackson. In 1839 he left the House when the Democratic Party in Tennessee drafted him as its candidate for governor. He won that election and served a two-year term. He ran for reelection in 1841 and 1843 but was defeated both times by the Whig candidate.

At the 1844 Democratic National Convention in Baltimore Polk's political career was resurrected dramatically from those gubernatorial defeats. Martin Van Buren was favored to receive the Democratic presidential nomination, but neither he nor his chief rival, Lewis Cass, could muster the two-thirds vote required to secure the nomination. With the balloting hopelessly deadlocked, the convention turned unanimously to Polk as a compromise candidate on the ninth ballot. He thus became the first dark-horse presidential candidate of a major party.

Polk campaigned on an expansionist platform that advocated annexation of Texas and a settlement with Britain that would fix the northern boundary of Oregon at 54° 40'. He also received the invaluable endorsement of Andrew Jackson. Polk defeated his better-known Whig opponent, Henry Clay, 170–105 in the electoral college. The election, however, was closer than the electoral vote indicates. Polk received only forty thousand votes more than Clay, and he won New York's thirty-six electoral votes—which would have given Clay a 141–134 victory—by just five thousand votes.

The most important issue confronting the new president was westward expansion. Polk and most of the nation wished to resolve the Oregon boundary question with Great Britain, acquire California and other lands in the Southwest from Mexico, and annex Texas. An agreement signed in 1818 provided for joint U.S.-British ownership of the Oregon Territory, which extended from California to above the fifty-fourth parallel. Although Polk had campaigned on the slogan "54° 40' or fight," the battle cry of those who wanted all of the Oregon Territory, he offered to divide Oregon with the British at the forty-ninth parallel. When the British refused, Congress, at his request, terminated the joint ownership agreement on April 23, 1846. Realizing that lack of a settlement could mean war, the British accepted Polk's original offer.

Three days before Polk's inauguration, President Tyler had signed a joint resolution annexing Texas, as Polk had advocated during his campaign. The southern border of Texas, however, remained in dispute, and tensions with Mexico over Texas and other territories in the Southwest threatened to lead to war. In 1846 Polk sent U.S. troops under Gen. Zachary Taylor into the territory between the Nueces River and the Rio Grande. The action was provocative, since the area was claimed by both Mexico and Texas but occupied by Mexicans. Polk had already decided to ask Congress for a declaration of war when news reached Washington that Mexican forces had attacked the American contingent. The president then claimed that Mexico was the aggressor and asked Congress to declare war, which it did, despite opposition from some northern lawmakers. American forces under Gen. Zachary Taylor and Gen. Winfield Scott won major victories over the Mexican army and eventually occupied Mexico City. In 1848 Mexico agreed to the treaty of Guadalupe Hidalgo, which ceded California and New Mexico to the United States in return for $15 million and recognized the Rio Grande as the boundary of Texas.

In domestic policy Polk also achieved his major goals. With his backing, Congress narrowly passed the Walker Tariff Act in 1846, which greatly reduced tariffs. Although the bill was opposed in the North, it stimulated trade and the U.S. economy. Polk also persuaded Congress to pass an independent treasury bill in 1846, which reestablished a system of subtreasuries first set up under Van Buren to handle government funds. Before Polk reestablished the subtreasuries, these funds had been deposited in state banks.

At the beginning of his term, Polk reputedly had told a friend that his four main goals as president were resolution of the territorial dispute over Oregon, acquisition of California and New Mexico, a lowered tariff, and reestablishment of a subtreasury system. He successfully achieved all four goals, and historians generally believe that he provided the strongest presidential leadership between the terms of Presidents Jackson and Abraham Lincoln.

Upon entering office, Polk had declared that he would not run for a second term. He kept his promise in 1848 by not seeking the Democratic presidential nomination. After attending Zachary Taylor's inauguration, the former president left Washington and toured the South on his way to his recently purchased home in Nashville. Polk, who worked long hours and almost never took a day off during his presidency, was not to enjoy a long retirement. The stress of the presidency and his work schedule may have weakened his health. He died in Nashville at the age of fifty-three, only three and a half months after leaving office.

Polk married Sarah Childress on January 1, 1824. She served not only as White House hostess but also as the president's personal secretary. The Polks had no children. After her husband's death Sarah retired in Nashville, Tennessee, where she lived as a widow until her death in 1891.

Zachary Taylor

BORN: November 24, 1784; Orange County, Virginia
PARTY: Whig
TERM: March 4, 1849–July 9, 1850
VICE PRESIDENT: Millard Fillmore
DIED: July 9, 1850; Washington, D.C.
BURIED: Louisville, Kentucky

Zachary Taylor was born into a prominent family of Virginia planters related to both James Madison and Robert E. Lee. His father, Richard Taylor, had served as an officer in the Revolutionary War. When Zachary's mother, Sarah, was pregnant with him, the Taylors left Virginia to establish a farm near Louisville, Kentucky. Zachary, the third of nine children, was born at a friend's home along the way. Because the Kentucky frontier lacked schools, Zachary was given a rudimentary education by occasional tutors and his well-educated parents.

In 1808 at the age of twenty-three Taylor was commissioned as a lieutenant in the army. He participated in William Henry Harrison's Indian campaigns in the Indiana Territory and fought in the Ohio Valley during the War of 1812. After the war he resigned from the army over a dispute about his rank but returned a year later when he was recommissioned as a major. He then served in a series of garrison posts on the frontier. In 1832 Taylor was promoted to colonel during the Black Hawk War and was among the officers who accepted Chief Black Hawk's surrender. He was reassigned in 1837 to Florida where the army was fighting the Seminole Indians. On Christmas Day of that year his troops defeated the Seminoles in a major battle that earned him a promotion to brigadier general, and on May 15, 1838, he assumed command of all forces in Florida. In 1841 Taylor was given command of the southern division of the army and reassigned to Baton Rouge, Louisiana, where he bought a large plantation.

When the United States annexed Texas in 1845, President James K. Polk ordered Taylor to defend it against a Mexican invasion. In January 1846 Polk instructed the general to take the provocative step of deploying his forces on territory claimed by Mexico between the Nueces River and the Rio Grande. When Mexico declared war and launched an attack against Taylor's army, the general invaded Mexico and won a series of quick victories at Palo Alto, Resaca de la Palma, and Monterrey.

Taylor's victories earned him a promotion to major general and popularity among the American public. President Polk, however, recognized that Taylor's heroics made him an attractive Whig presidential candidate and maneuvered to prevent further boosts to the general's reputation. The president ordered Taylor to command a small force of five thousand troops in northern Mexico, while Gen. Winfield Scott was given most of the troops who had served under Taylor and the more glamorous duty of leading an expedition to capture Mexico City. Taylor, however, turned this assignment to his advantage when his soldiers routed twenty thousand Mexicans at Buena Vista in February 1847. The victory made Taylor a hero in the United States, and, as Polk had feared, the Whig Party sought to capitalize on "Old Rough and Ready's" popularity by offering him its nomination for president.

Taylor declared that he disliked partisan politics and preferred to run without party affiliation. Eventually, however, he accepted the Whig Party's nomination but announced that he thought of himself as a national candidate rather than a Whig candidate. Taylor's reputation as a war hero was enough to earn him a close 163–127 electoral vote victory over Democratic candidate Lewis Cass. Martin Van Buren's third party candidacy contributed to Taylor's victory by splitting New York's Democratic vote, thereby allowing Taylor to capture the state's thirty-six electoral votes that would have given Cass a majority.

Taylor's primary weakness as a chief executive was his lack of political experience. At Taylor's inauguration James Polk found the general to be "exceedingly ignorant of public affairs." Despite this handicap Taylor refused to be just a Whig figurehead. Among his proposals were greater government aid for agriculture and the development of a transcontinental railroad.

The major issue confronting Taylor was whether slavery would be allowed to exist in the West where territories soon

would be applying for statehood. Southerners feared that new states entering the Union, particularly California, would outlaw slavery and upset the equilibrium between slave and free states in Congress. Congressional leaders, led by Henry Clay of Kentucky, attempted to legislate a compromise that would satisfy both the North and the South. Taylor, however, supported the right of states to decide for themselves whether they would permit slavery. He also hoped that the bestowal of statehood on California would bring order to that territory, where local government had been unable to cope with the thousands of settlers who came after the discovery of gold there. He thus encouraged New Mexico and California to apply for statehood and declared that he would oppose the compromise plan being developed by Congress.

Although Taylor was a slave-owning southerner, he believed the Union must be preserved at all costs. He warned southern leaders that if their states rebelled against federal authority because of California statehood or any other issue, he would use the army to enforce the law and preserve the Union. Taylor never had to veto a congressional compromise plan or confront the secession of southern states, however. After sitting through ceremonies at the Washington Monument on a hot July Fourth he fell ill and died in the White House five days later at the age of sixty-five. His vice president, Millard Fillmore, succeeded to the presidency and threw executive support behind the Compromise of 1850, which held the Union together temporarily by making concessions to the South in return for California's entrance into the Union as a free state.

In 1810, while a young army officer, Taylor married Margaret Mackall Smith. They had six children, two of whom died as infants. Their only son, Richard, served as a general in the Confederate army. One of their daughters, Sarah Knox, married Jefferson Davis, who would become president of the Confederacy. She died of malaria only three months after the wedding.

Millard Fillmore

BORN: January 7, 1800; Cayuga County, New York
PARTY: Whig
TERM: July 10, 1850–March 4, 1853
VICE PRESIDENT: None
DIED: March 8, 1874; Buffalo, New York
BURIED: Buffalo

Millard Fillmore was the second oldest of the nine children of Nathaniel and Phoebe Fillmore, a poor New York farm couple. When Millard was fourteen he was apprenticed to a cloth-maker, but he bought his freedom from apprenticeship for thirty dollars and took a job teaching school. While teaching, he studied law with a local county judge and was admitted to the bar in 1823.

Fillmore began his political career as a member of New York's Anti-Masonic Party, which opposed secret societies in the United States. In 1828 he was elected to the New York State Assembly with the support of Anti-Masonic Party boss Thurlow Weed. While in the legislature, Fillmore drafted a bill that abolished imprisonment for debtors; it eventually became law. After being reelected twice he left the legislature to establish a lucrative law practice in Buffalo with his future postmaster general, Nathan K. Hall. From 1833 to 1835 and 1837 to 1843 Fillmore served in the U.S. House of Representatives. In 1834 he followed Weed into the Whig Party and soon became a prominent member of its northern wing. While in the House, Fillmore was an ally of Sen. Henry Clay (Whig-Ky.). In 1843 Fillmore returned to New York to practice law and enter state politics. He was defeated narrowly for the governorship in 1844 by Democrat Silas Wright but won election as New York's comptroller three years later.

In 1848 the Whigs nominated Mexican War hero Zachary Taylor as their presidential candidate. The party's search for a vice-presidential candidate to balance the ticket with the slave-owning Taylor led to Fillmore, who had impressed many party leaders with his good looks and political skills. The Taylor-Fillmore ticket then narrowly defeated Democrats Lewis Cass and William Butler.

As vice president, Fillmore was excluded from policy making

in the Taylor administration, but he dutifully presided over the Senate as that body struggled with the slavery issue. Fillmore was a staunch opponent of slavery, but he believed a moderate course was necessary to preserve the Union. He therefore supported the Compromise of 1850 devised by Sen. Henry Clay. The plan sought to relieve sectional tensions by making concessions to both the North and the South. President Taylor, however, opposed the compromise and was prepared to veto it and use force to put down any rebellions in the South that might result. Fillmore foresaw a close vote in the Senate and informed the president that if a tie vote should occur his conscience obligated him to vote for the compromise despite Taylor's opposition. Before the Senate could vote on the plan, Taylor died suddenly on July 9, 1850.

Because Fillmore believed Taylor's cabinet was against the compromise, he accepted the resignations of all seven men and appointed a new cabinet that supported it. With Taylor dead, the threat of a presidential veto of Clay's plan was removed and work on the compromise moved forward. In September 1850 Fillmore signed a series of bills that made up the Compromise of 1850. Under the compromise, California was admitted to the Union as a free state, the territories of Utah and New Mexico were established without mention of slavery, and Texas was paid

$10 million for surrendering its claim to New Mexico. Other provisions made federal officials responsible for capturing and returning runaway slaves and outlawed the slave trade in the District of Columbia while affirming the right to own slaves there. Many southerners objected to the compromise because it set a precedent: it allowed the federal government to pass legislation on slavery rather than leaving the issue to the states. Abolitionists, however, thought the compromise favored the South. They especially detested the Fugitive Slave Law, which Fillmore felt obligated to enforce despite his recognition that in doing so he was committing political suicide. The president believed the compromise would work only if the federal government upheld all of its provisions with equal force.

No one was entirely satisfied with the Compromise of 1850, which did nothing to resolve the slavery issue. It resulted, however, in a few years of relative calm. During this period Fillmore oversaw the modernization of the White House, worked to secure federal funds for railroad construction, and opposed the efforts of private U.S. citizens to overthrow Spanish rule in Cuba. Before Fillmore left office in 1853 he sent Commodore Matthew Perry on a cruise across the Pacific to open up Japan to American trade.

Fillmore attempted to secure the Whig presidential nomination in 1852, but the convention chose Gen. Winfield Scott, a Mexican War hero, on the fifty-third ballot. Scott then lost to the Democrat Franklin Pierce in a landslide. Fillmore's wife, Abigail, became ill after attending Pierce's inauguration on a cold March day. She died three weeks later, on March 30, 1853.

In 1853 Fillmore lost not only his wife but also his party. After the election of 1852 the Whig Party disintegrated. Their most visible leaders, Daniel Webster and Henry Clay, had died in 1852, and Fillmore's enforcement of the Fugitive Slave Act had disaffected many northern Whigs who helped form the new Republican Party in 1854. Fillmore declined to join the Republicans and instead accepted the 1856 presidential nomination of the ultraconservative American or "Know-Nothing" Party. The Know-Nothings were named for their practice of responding "I know nothing" to questions about their rituals. The party was based on an opposition to immigrants and Catholics. The Know-Nothings believed these groups threatened the United States by plotting against the government and promoting radical ideologies. In the election Fillmore received over 800,000 popular votes but just eight electoral votes. He thus finished a distant third behind Democrat James Buchanan and Republican John Fremont.

After this embarrassment Fillmore retired from politics. In 1858 he married Caroline McIntosh, a wealthy forty-four-year-old widow, and settled in Buffalo. He died of a stroke on March 8, 1874. Fillmore had one son and one daughter by his first wife, Abigail Powers.

Franklin Pierce

BORN: November 23, 1804; Hillsboro, New Hampshire
PARTY: Democratic
TERM: March 4, 1853–March 4, 1857
VICE PRESIDENT: William R. King
DIED: October 8, 1869; Concord, New Hampshire
BURIED: Concord

Franklin Pierce was the sixth of the eight children born to Anna and Benjamin Pierce. His father, who would become governor of New Hampshire, married Anna after the death of his first wife. Pierce's parents sent him to private schools as a child, and at the age of fifteen he enrolled at Bowdoin College in Brunswick, Maine. Pierce did well at Bowdoin, graduating third in his class in 1824. After college he studied law and was admitted to the bar in 1827. In 1829 he was elected to the New Hampshire legislature while his father was governor.

When he was elected to the U.S. House of Representatives in 1833, Pierce left the New Hampshire legislature, where he had become Speaker of the House. Although Pierce's loyal support of the Jackson administration earned him a second term, he served only a few months because the New Hampshire legislature elected him to the U.S. Senate in 1836. In 1842, however, he retired from the Senate at the urging of his wife and returned to New Hampshire to practice law. In 1844 President James K. Polk appointed Pierce U.S. district attorney for New Hampshire.

As district attorney and chairman of the Democratic Party in New Hampshire, Pierce remained a powerful political figure, but he refused a series of important political appointments, partly because his wife did not want to move back to Washington, D.C. When the president appointed Sen. Levi Woodbury (D-N.H.) to the Supreme Court in 1845, Pierce declined to replace Woodbury in the Senate. The same year he turned down the New Hampshire Democratic gubernatorial nomination. In 1846 Polk offered him the U.S. attorney generalship, but Pierce again refused so he could remain in New Hampshire with his family. After the United States declared war on Mexico, however, Pierce accepted a commission as a colonel and began recruiting a New England regiment. Before he sailed for Mexico in May 1847, he was promoted to brigadier general. Pierce saw little action during his five and one-half months in Mexico because of an intestinal ailment and an injury sustained when his horse fell. Nevertheless, in January 1848 he returned to a hero's welcome in Concord where he resumed his law practice. That same year he again refused the Democratic nomination for governor.

Pierce's rise to the presidency was sudden and unexpected. The 1852 Democratic nominating convention produced a stalemate between James Buchanan, Lewis Cass, William Marcy, and Stephen A. Douglas. Because none of these candidates was able to garner a majority of the votes, the convention began searching for a fifth candidate. On the forty-ninth ballot the Democrats nominated Franklin Pierce, who several months before had announced he would not turn down such a nomination. As a northerner with southern sympathies and a spotless record, Pierce was an acceptable compromise candidate, although he had not served in an elective office since 1842. His Whig opponent was Gen. Winfield Scott, a hero of the Mexican War. Scott's campaign, however, was crippled by the defection of many northern Whigs to the Free Soil Party. Pierce remained in New Hampshire during the months before the election, letting his fellow Democrats, who had united behind his candidacy, campaign for him. The uncontroversial Democratic platform of strict observance of the Compromise of 1850 gained Pierce a 254–42 victory in the electoral college.

Pierce took office advocating tranquillity and prosperity at home and the extension of U.S. territories and commercial interests abroad. Most of his domestic policies favored the South. In his inaugural address he had declared his belief that slavery was constitutional and that "states where it exists are entitled to efficient remedies" to enforce it. The Compromise of 1850 enacted under Millard Fillmore had calmed temporarily tensions over the slavery issue, but that calm did not last through Pierce's presidency. In 1854 Pierce signed the Kansas-Nebraska Act into law. It repealed the 1820 Missouri Compromise that had outlawed slavery north of 36° 30', thereby enabling Kansas to declare itself a slave state if its citizens favored that course. Pierce,

who believed that each state should decide for itself whether to permit slavery, strongly supported the act, which had been sponsored by Illinois senator Stephen A. Douglas. The act, however, turned Kansas into a war zone. Proslavery southerners and abolitionist northerners raced into Kansas hoping to seize control of the territory's government for their side. Many atrocities were committed by both groups, causing the territory to be dubbed "Bleeding Kansas."

In international affairs Pierce supported Millard Fillmore's initiative of sending Commodore Matthew Perry to Japan to open that country's ports to Western trade. Perry negotiated a treaty that gave U.S. ships access to two ports and guaranteed humane treatment of U.S. sailors shipwrecked off Japan's coasts.

After leaving the presidency in 1857 Pierce never again sought public office. He and his wife, Jane Means Appleton Pierce, traveled in Europe from 1857 to 1859 and then retired to their Concord, New Hampshire, home. They had three sons, two of whom died in infancy. Their third son, eleven-year-old Benjamin, was killed when a train on which he and his parents were passengers wrecked near Andover, Massachusetts, a few weeks before Pierce's inauguration. The tragedy deeply affected Pierce's wife, who remained in a state of mourning during the first two years of Pierce's presidency. Pierce was a close college friend of American author Nathaniel Hawthorne, who wrote Pierce's campaign biography. Pierce was at Hawthorne's bedside when the writer died in 1864.

James Buchanan

BORN: April 23, 1791; Stony Batter, Pennsylvania
PARTY: Democratic
TERM: March 4, 1857–March 4, 1861
VICE PRESIDENT: John C. Breckinridge
DIED: June 1, 1868; Lancaster, Pennsylvania
BURIED: Lancaster

James Buchanan was the second oldest child and oldest son of the eleven children born to James and Elizabeth Buchanan. Young James grew up working in the family's thriving frontier trading post in Mercersburg, Pennsylvania.

James received an elementary education at common schools and attended a secondary school in Mercersburg before entering Dickinson College in Carlisle, Pennsylvania, in 1807. A year later he was expelled for disorderly conduct, but he was reinstated with the help of the president of the board of trustees of the college. James graduated with honors in 1809 and returned to Lancaster to study law. In 1812 he was admitted to the bar, and the following year he was appointed assistant prosecutor for Lebanon County, Pennsylvania.

In August 1814, after the British burned Washington, D.C., Buchanan joined a company of men from Lancaster that marched to Baltimore to fight the British. The British withdrew from Baltimore soon after the company arrived. The unit was disbanded, and Buchanan returned to Pennsylvania where he

was elected to the state assembly. He served two terms before leaving politics to establish a successful law practice.

Buchanan began his national political career in 1820 with his election to the U.S. House of Representatives as a Federalist. He served in the House for ten years. He was a staunch opponent of John Quincy Adams and in 1828 gave his allegiance to Andrew Jackson and the Democratic Party. Jackson appointed Buchanan minister to Russia in 1831. While in St. Petersburg, Buchanan negotiated a treaty of commerce favorable to the United States. He returned home in 1833 and was elected to the U.S. Senate by the Pennsylvania legislature the following year. He quickly became a leading conservative Democrat and chairman of the Foreign Relations Committee. Buchanan chose to stay in the Senate despite President Martin Van Buren's offer of the attorney generalship and President John Tyler's offer of a seat on the Supreme Court. When President James K. Polk, for whom Buchanan had campaigned, offered Buchanan the post of secretary of state, however, he accepted. As secretary of state, Buchanan took a leading role in the negotiations with Britain that produced a compromise on fixing the boundary of the Oregon Territory.

After losing the 1848 Democratic presidential nomination to Lewis Cass, Buchanan retired to Lancaster. In 1853, however, he accepted an appointment from President Franklin Pierce as minister to Great Britain. While in Britain, Buchanan collabo-

rated with the U.S. ambassadors to Spain and France in writing the Ostend Manifesto of 1854. This diplomatic report advocated the acquisition of Cuba from Spain by force if Spain refused to sell it. Its intent was to prevent the possibility of a slave uprising on the island that might spread by example to the United States. The document, which was not acted upon, was denounced in the North but increased Buchanan's popularity in the South.

After returning from Britain in 1856, Buchanan was nominated for president by the Democrats. His absence from the country during the bloody fighting in Kansas precipitated by the Kansas-Nebraska Act made him more acceptable than either President Pierce or Sen. Stephen Douglas, both of whom had supported the act. Buchanan faced John Fremont of the newly formed Republican Party and former president Millard Fillmore of the right-wing American (Know-Nothing) Party. Buchanan received only 47 percent of the popular vote but won every southern state in defeating Fremont 174–114 in the electoral college.

Buchanan's presidency was dominated by the tensions between North and South over the slavery issue. Although Buchanan considered slavery to be unjust, he believed people in the southern states had the constitutional right to own slaves. He was a committed Unionist who tried to steer a middle course between the forces for and against slavery, but most of his policies appeared to northerners to favor the South. He enforced the Fugitive Slave Act, tried to quell northern antislavery agitation, and supported the Supreme Court's Dred Scott decision. The latter denied the citizenship of slaves, recognized the right of slaveowners to take their slaves wherever they chose, declared the Missouri Compromise restricting slavery to below 36° 30' to be unconstitutional, and implied that neither Congress nor the territorial governments created by Congress had the authority to exclude slavery from the territories. Buchanan not only supported the 7–2 decision, but also lobbied Associate Justice Robert Grier to support it.

The Dred Scott case did not resolve the slavery question as Buchanan had hoped. In 1858 Buchanan split his party when he sent a proslavery constitution written by the minority southern faction in Kansas to Congress and recommended that Kansas be admitted as a slave state. Many Democratic leaders, including Stephen Douglas, denounced the constitution and distanced themselves from Buchanan. The Senate approved the plan to admit Kansas under the proslavery constitution, but the House rejected it. Kansas remained a territory until 1861 and continued to inspire conflict between North and South.

The 1860 election produced the secession crisis that Buchanan had hoped to prevent. When Abraham Lincoln of the antislavery Republican Party was elected, southerners began to debate secession. Buchanan supported compromise solutions proposed by members of Congress and other leaders. He backed a proposal to reestablish the Missouri Compromise line and a constitutional amendment that would guarantee the right to own slaves in states that wanted it, but none of the plans was acceptable.

After Lincoln's election secessionists seized most federal forts in the South without much resistance. Buchanan considered secession to be unconstitutional, but he believed that the right to rebel against unjust rule was a basic right of all people and was even embodied in the Declaration of Independence. He also believed that the federal government could not wage war against a state or group of states. Therefore, he refrained from responding with force to the acts of rebellion. He did request, however, the power to call out the militia and increase the size of the armed forces, but Congress refused. By the time Buchanan's term ended, seven states had seceded, and the nation was headed toward civil war.

After Lincoln's inauguration Buchanan retired to Wheatland, his home in Lancaster, Pennsylvania. He corresponded with friends and political associates but was not active in public affairs. During his retirement the northern press criticized him for failing to prevent the Civil War and accused him of allowing federal forts to remain vulnerable and participating in plots to arm the South before the war. In an attempt to justify his actions and the policies of his administration, he published his memoirs, *Mr. Buchanan's Administration on the Eve of the Rebellion*, in 1866. Buchanan believed that he vindicated himself through his book, which placed primary blame for the war on northern radicals. Buchanan died at Wheatland in 1868.

Buchanan was the only president never to marry. His close relationship with William R. King, who became vice president under Franklin Pierce, has led some historians to speculate that Buchanan was homosexual. His niece, Harriet Lane, served as White House hostess during his administration. In 1819, while practicing law, he became engaged to Ann Coleman, who was from a wealthy Lancaster family. But after a quarrel with Buchanan she broke the engagement and left for Philadelphia to visit her sister. She died mysteriously a few days later on December 9, 1819, amid rumors that she committed suicide. Her family did not allow Buchanan to attend her funeral.

Abraham Lincoln

BORN: February 12, 1809; near Hodgenville, Kentucky
PARTY: Republican
TERM: March 4, 1861–April 15, 1865
VICE PRESIDENTS: Hannibal Hamlin; Andrew Johnson
DIED: April 15, 1865; Washington, D.C.
BURIED: Springfield, Illinois

Abraham Lincoln was born in a one-room log cabin on a backwoods farm in Kentucky. He was the second of the three children of Nancy and Thomas Lincoln, a poor farmer who also did carpentry work. Abe's younger brother died in infancy, and his mother died when he was nine. In 1819, Thomas Lincoln married Sarah Bush Johnston, who was a loving stepmother to Abe. She brought her three children by her previous marriage into the family.

During Abe's childhood the Lincolns lived on farms in Ken-

Abraham Lincoln

tucky and Indiana. Abe attended country schools sporadically, learning to read, write, and do elementary math. He possessed a quick, inquisitive intellect, however, and spent much free time reading the family Bible and whatever books he could borrow. Abe worked at numerous odd jobs while in his teens, including farmhand, grocery store clerk, and ferry boat rower. In 1828 and 1831 he took trips down the Mississippi River to New Orleans as a flatboat deck hand. While in New Orleans during the second trip he reputedly developed his hatred of slavery after witnessing the maltreatment of slaves.

Abe had moved with his family to a farm near Decatur, Illinois, in 1830, but after returning from New Orleans in 1831, he settled in New Salem, Illinois. There he worked in a store and became known for his prowess as a storyteller and wrestler. In 1832, Lincoln volunteered to fight Sauk Indians led by Chief Black Hawk. After serving several months in the army, he was discharged without participating in any combat. He returned to New Salem from his military service and made an unprepared attempt to win a seat as a Whig in the Illinois state legislature, but he was defeated.

Later in 1832 Lincoln bought half interest in a general store. When the store failed the following year, Lincoln was left with debts that he would not be able to pay off completely for seventeen years. After his failed business venture, Lincoln was appointed postmaster of New Salem and also worked as a surveyor.

EARLY POLITICAL CAREER

In 1834 Lincoln ran again for the state legislature and this time won a seat. He began studying law by reading borrowed law books. Shortly after being reelected to a second term in 1836, Lincoln was licensed to practice law. In 1837 he moved to Springfield, Illinois, and began practicing law when the legislature was not in session. He was reelected to the legislature in 1838 and 1840, serving for a time as Whig floor leader.

In 1846 Lincoln was elected to the U.S. House of Representatives. Despite the popularity of the Mexican War in his district, he joined fellow Whigs in denouncing the war as unjust. Lincoln also opposed the extension of slavery into the territories but did not advocate abolishing slavery where it already existed. Lincoln had promised Illinois Whig Party leaders that he would serve only one term, so when his term expired he returned to Springfield. He spent the next several years reading and developing his successful law practice.

In 1854 Lincoln ran for the Senate but backed out of the race when his candidacy threatened to split the antislavery vote. Two years later, Lincoln joined the new Republican Party, which had formed in 1854. He campaigned for its 1856 presidential candidate, John C. Fremont, who lost to Democrat James Buchanan.

The Illinois Republican Party nominated Lincoln for senator in 1858. He faced incumbent Democrat Stephen A. Douglas, author of the Kansas-Nebraska Act of 1854, which was favored by many proslavery Democrats. The act gave the people in the territories of Kansas and Nebraska the option to permit slavery.

Lincoln challenged Douglas to a series of seven debates focusing on slavery that were attended by huge crowds. In the debates Lincoln questioned the morality of slavery and firmly argued against its expansion into territories where it did not exist already. The state legislature elected Douglas over Lincoln 54–46, but the debates made Lincoln famous throughout the country and a credible candidate for the Republican presidential nomination in 1860. During the next two years he made several highly publicized speaking tours, including one to the East in early 1860. His name was placed in nomination at the Republican National Convention in Chicago in 1860, but he trailed New York senator William Seward on the first and second ballots. On the third ballot, however, Lincoln secured the nomination.

The Democratic Party, meanwhile, split into two factions. Stephen Douglas was nominated by northern Democrats, and Vice President John C. Breckinridge of Kentucky was nominated by southern Democrats. The remnants of the Whig and Know-Nothing Parties further complicated the election by joining to nominate John Bell as the candidate of their new Constitutional Union Party. Lincoln won the four-candidate race with less than 40 percent of the popular vote. He captured eighteen northern states with 180 out of the total 303 electoral votes. Breckinridge and Bell followed with 72 and 39, respectively.

Douglas, who finished second to Lincoln in the popular vote, won only Missouri's 12 electoral votes.

PRESIDENCY

Lincoln's election precipitated the secession crisis that the nation had feared for several decades. In December 1860, South Carolina left the Union, followed by six more states early in 1861. The rebelling states formed a confederacy and elected Jefferson Davis as their president.

Lincoln tried to ease southern fears that he intended to abolish slavery. He declared in his first inaugural address that he had no intention or authority to "interfere with the institution of slavery where it already exists." But he warned the Southern states that he did not recognize their secession and would enforce federal law and defend the Union. He declared, "In your hands, my dissatisfied fellow-countrymen, and not in mine, is the momentous issue of civil war." War came when rebels attacked and captured Fort Sumter in Charleston harbor in April 1861. The attack on the federal fort signaled the South's unwillingness to return to the Union. On April 15, Lincoln called for seventy-five thousand volunteers to put down the rebellion. Soon after, four more Southern states seceded, raising the number of states in the Confederacy to eleven.

During the next three months Lincoln refused to call Congress into session, while he took extraordinary actions to prepare for war, many of which violated the Constitution. He blockaded the South, doubled the size of the armed forces, suspended the writ of *habeas corpus* in some areas, and spent Treasury funds, all without congressional approval. Finally, on July 4, he convened Congress, which ratified most of his war measures.

Lincoln and the North hoped that the rebellion could be put down quickly, but the war turned into a protracted and bloody conflict. The Union won victories in the West under Gen. Ulysses S. Grant; but in the East, Union generals were repeatedly outmaneuvered by Robert E. Lee and other Confederate generals. On January 1, 1863, Lincoln issued the Emancipation Proclamation, which declared that the slaves in the rebellious states were free. *(See "Emancipation Proclamation," p. 1589, in Reference Materials.)* So that the proclamation would have greater credibility, he had waited to make this move until after the Union won a victory, which came at the battle of Antietam in September 1862. In July 1863 the Union victory at the Battle of Gettysburg in Pennsylvania put the Confederacy on the defensive. Lincoln traveled to Gettysburg on November 19 where he delivered his famous Gettysburg Address during a ceremony to dedicate the battlefield's cemetery. *(See "Gettysburg Address," p. 1589, in Reference Materials.)*

In 1864 Lincoln took an important step toward winning the war when he ordered Grant east to take command of all Union armies. That year Lincoln ran for reelection against Democratic candidate George B. McClellan, one of his former generals. Lincoln had relieved McClellan of his command of the Union army in 1862 because the general was overcautious and ineffective.

During the spring of 1864 Lincoln's reelection had been in doubt as Grant's army fought a series of indecisive and costly battles in Virginia at the Wilderness, Spotsylvania, and Cold Harbor. But by September, Union general William T. Sherman had captured Atlanta, and Grant had besieged Petersburg, Virginia. Voters sensed that the Union was close to victory and reelected the president. Lincoln won all but three states and defeated McClellan 212–21 in the electoral college.

During the final year of the war, Grant fought a battle of attrition against Lee's forces in Virginia, while Sherman's army drove though Georgia and North and South Carolina destroying Southern crops and industries. Finally, on April 9, 1865, Lee surrendered to Grant at Appomattox Court House in Virginia, ending the war.

In his second inaugural address, delivered on March 4, 1865, Lincoln had proposed a magnanimous peace, saying "with malice toward none, with charity for all, with firmness in the right as God gives us to see the right, let us strive on to finish the work we are in, to bind up the nation's wounds." *(See "Lincoln's Second Inaugural Address," p. 1590, in Reference Materials.)*

Lincoln, however, did not have the opportunity to implement his generous reconstruction plans. On April 14, 1865, while watching a production of the play *Our American Cousin* at Ford's Theater in Washington, D.C., he was shot in the back of the head at close range by actor John Wilkes Booth. After shooting Lincoln, Booth jumped from the presidential box to the stage, fled the theater, and rode south. On April 26 federal troops surrounded and killed him at a farm in Virginia. Booth, who had sympathized with the Confederacy, was part of a conspiracy to kill several government officials, including Vice President Andrew Johnson. With the exception of Secretary of State William Seward, who received a nonfatal stab wound at his home, the other targets of assassination escaped harm.

Lincoln was treated by a doctor at the theater, then carried across the street to a house where he died the next morning, April 15, without regaining consciousness. Vice President Johnson took the oath of office later that day. Lincoln's body lay in state in the Capitol and White House before being carried back to Illinois on a train viewed by millions of mourners.

Lincoln married Mary Todd on November 4, 1842. Of their four sons, only Robert, their eldest, reached adulthood. He served as secretary of war under Presidents James A. Garfield and Chester A. Arthur and minister to Great Britain under Benjamin Harrison. Their second son, Edward, died at the age of three; their third son, William, died of typhoid fever in the White House in 1862 at the age of eleven. Their youngest son, Thomas (Tad), survived his father but died at the age of eighteen in 1871.

Lincoln originally had been engaged to marry Mary Todd on January 1, 1841, but their wedding did not take place for reasons that are unclear. Afterwards, Lincoln suffered an emotional and physical breakdown and lived in Kentucky for a period while he recovered. In 1842 Lincoln resumed his relationship with Mary, and they married that year. Their marriage was a stormy one

that was complicated by the deaths of their children and Mary's lavish spending, superstitions, and bouts with depression.

Andrew Johnson

BORN: December 29, 1808; Raleigh, North Carolina
PARTY: Democratic
TERM: April 15, 1865–March 4, 1869
VICE PRESIDENT: None
DIED: July 31, 1875; Carter's Station, Tennessee
BURIED: Greeneville, Tennessee

Andrew Johnson was the younger of the two sons born to Jacob and Mary Johnson. Andrew's father, who died when he was three, was a laborer, and his mother was a seamstress. Neither parent could read or write, and Johnson received no formal education.

When Andrew was thirteen he was apprenticed to a tailor in Raleigh, North Carolina, his birthplace. Andrew's fellow workers taught him to read, although he did not learn to write until several years later. In 1824, after two years as an apprentice, Andrew ran away from his master, James Selby, and worked as a journeyman tailor in Laurens, South Carolina. Although Selby was still offering a reward for his return, Johnson came back to Raleigh in 1826 and convinced his mother and stepfather to move west with him. They settled in Greeneville, Tennessee, where Johnson opened a tailor shop.

In 1828 the people of Greeneville elected the young tailor alderman. After two years on the city council, Johnson was chosen mayor at the age of twenty-one. In 1835 he made the step up to state politics when he was elected as a Democrat to the Tennessee legislature. He espoused the ideals of Andrew Jackson, became an advocate of the common farmer and small business owner, and earned a reputation as a powerful orator. In 1837 he was defeated for a second term in the Tennessee legislature, but he won reelection in 1839. Two years later he was elected to the state senate, and in 1843 his congressional district sent him to the U.S. House of Representatives.

In Washington, Johnson supported the Mexican War and the Compromise of 1850. He served four terms in the House, but an 1853 Whig redistricting plan made his reelection impossible. Consequently, Johnson ran for governor of Tennessee and won two terms before the Tennessee legislature sent him to the U.S. Senate in 1857.

In 1860 Johnson was proposed as a presidential candidate, but he withdrew his name from nomination and supported John Breckinridge. When Abraham Lincoln was elected, Johnson surprised many of his fellow southerners by declaring his loyalty to the Union. He campaigned against the secession of Tennessee, and when his state did secede in June 1861, he was the only southern senator to remain in the Senate. In 1862, after Union forces had captured most of Tennessee, Lincoln appointed Johnson military governor of his state. With Johnson's urging, Tennessee became the only seceding state to outlaw slavery before the 1863 Emancipation Proclamation.

Johnson's loyalty to the Union was rewarded with a vice-presidential nomination in 1864. Lincoln's first-term vice president, Hannibal Hamlin, wanted to be renominated, but Lincoln refused to back his candidacy. Delegates to the National Union convention in Baltimore (the Republican nominating convention expanded to include Democrats loyal to the Union) hoped that having a southern Democrat on the ticket would attract support from northern Democrats and voters in border areas.

Lincoln and Johnson defeated Democrats George McClellan and George Pendleton by 212–21 electoral votes. Some Johnson supporters, however, changed their minds about him when he showed up drunk for the inauguration on March 4, 1865. Lincoln shrugged off the incident and expressed confidence in his vice president.

Johnson served as vice president only six weeks before President Lincoln died on April 15 from a gunshot wound inflicted by assassin John Wilkes Booth. The new president thus faced the immense problem of reconstructing a broken South, which had surrendered six days before. Johnson tried to implement the lenient Reconstruction program envisioned by Lincoln, but he was blocked by radical Republicans in Congress who were intent upon punishing the region and limiting the influence of white Southerners in national politics. Johnson successfully vetoed several harsh Reconstruction bills early in his presidency, but in the 1866 congressional elections the radical Republicans gained overwhelming control of Congress and were in a position to override the president's vetoes.

On March 2, 1867, Congress passed the first Reconstruction Act over Johnson's veto. It established martial law in the South, granted universal suffrage to blacks, and limited the voting rights of Southern whites. The same day Congress overrode Johnson's veto of the Tenure of Office Act, which prohibited the president from removing without Senate approval any appointee who had been confirmed by the Senate. Johnson's defiance of this act forced a showdown between the president and Congress. On August 12, 1867, while Congress was in recess, Johnson replaced Secretary of War Edwin Stanton with Gen. Ulysses S. Grant without the Senate's approval. On January 13, 1868, the Senate declared the president's action illegal and reinstated Stanton. Gen. Grant complied with the Senate's order, but Johnson again dismissed Stanton and ordered Maj. Gen. Lorenzo Thomas to take Stanton's place. Three days later, on February 24, 1868, the House voted 126–47 to impeach the president. Radical Republicans had been searching for an excuse to impeach Johnson since early 1867.

The president's fate was then in the hands of the Senate, which could remove him from office with a two-thirds vote. On March 13 Johnson's trial began in the Senate chambers with Chief Justice Salmon P. Chase presiding. The Senate voted 35–19 for the impeachment articles, one vote short of the necessary two-thirds needed for conviction. Although Johnson's radical Republican opponents controlled the Senate, seven believed that the charges against Johnson did not warrant his removal and voted against conviction despite the consequences for their political careers. The decisive vote belonged to freshman Sen. Edmund G. Ross (R-Kan.), whose "not guilty" acquitted Johnson.

Although Johnson's presidency was dominated by Reconstruction and his battles with Congress, he and his secretary of state, William H. Seward, achieved a notable foreign policy success in 1867 when they negotiated the purchase of Alaska from Russia for only $7.2 million.

When Johnson's term expired in 1869 he returned to Tennessee, where he ran for the U.S. Senate. He lost that year and was defeated for a seat in the House in 1872. Finally, in 1874 the Tennessee legislature elected him to the Senate. He returned to Washington, where he resumed his fight for more lenient Reconstruction policies. Johnson only served five months of his Senate term before he died of a stroke in 1875 while visiting his daughter at Carter's Station, Tennessee.

Johnson married sixteen-year-old Eliza McCardle on May 17, 1827, in Greeneville, Tennessee, where he had opened a tailor shop. She had received some primary education and was able to teach Johnson, who could already read, to write and do elementary mathematics. The couple had three sons and two daughters. Eliza died in Tennessee less than six months after her husband.

Ulysses S. Grant

BORN: April 27, 1822; Point Pleasant, Ohio
PARTY: Republican
TERM: March 4, 1869–March 4, 1877
VICE PRESIDENTS: Schuyler Colfax; Henry Wilson
DIED: July 23, 1885; Mount McGregor, New York
BURIED: New York City

Ulysses S. Grant was the eldest of the six children born to Jesse and Hanna Grant. Jesse Grant was a tanner, but his son disliked the business and preferred doing chores on the family farm. Grant attended a series of schools as a child, and received an appointment to the United States Military Academy at West Point, New York, in 1839 through the efforts of his father. Although Grant had no interest in a military career, he accepted the appointment.

Grant's name at birth was Hiram Ulysses, but when he enrolled at West Point he reversed the order of these two names. The school, however, officially recorded his name as Ulysses S.

Grant. Rather than correct the mistake, Grant adopted West Point's version of his name without expanding his new middle initial. In 1843 Grant graduated twenty-first in his class of thirty-nine at West Point. He did well in mathematics and hoped one day to be a math teacher. He also was recognized for his outstanding handling of horses, a skill he had developed as a boy on his father's farm. His class rank, however, was not high enough to earn him an appointment to the cavalry.

Grant's first assignment was as a second lieutenant in an infantry regiment stationed near St. Louis. In 1844 his unit was transferred to Louisiana, and from there to Texas in 1845. He was among the troops under Gen. Zachary Taylor ordered by President James Polk to occupy the disputed area north of the Rio Grande. When Mexican forces attacked Taylor's forces, Polk persuaded Congress to declare war. Although Grant had deep reservations about the Mexican War's morality, he fought in most of its major battles including Palo Alto, Resaca de la Palma, Monterrey, Vera Cruz, Cerro Gordo, and Chapultepec. He was recognized for his bravery and promoted to first lieutenant after the capture of Mexico City in September 1847.

In July 1848, Grant returned to the United States and was stationed at several posts around the country. In 1852 he reluctantly left his wife and children behind in St. Louis when he was transferred to California. Grant hated being separated from his family and drank heavily to ease his loneliness. Finally, in 1854 after a drinking episode, his commanding officer forced him to resign his commission.

The next few years were humbling ones for Grant. He returned to his family in Missouri where he failed as a farmer and as a real estate broker. In 1860 his younger brother offered him a job as a clerk in their father's hardware and leather store in Galena, Illinois. With no better options, Grant accepted the salary of $800 per year and moved his family to Galena.

CIVIL WAR

In April 1861 Grant had worked in the store only eleven months when President Abraham Lincoln called for volunteers to put down the insurrection in the South. Because of his military experience, Grant was appointed colonel of an Illinois regiment in June. He impressed his superiors and in August was promoted to brigadier general. Grant obtained permission from Gen. Henry Halleck in January 1862 to launch a military campaign into the South. On February 6, Grant's troops defeated Confederate forces at Fort Henry, Tennessee. Ten days later he won the first major Union victory of the war, when his forces captured Fort Donelson on the Cumberland River in Tennessee. The battle netted Grant fifteen thousand Confederate prisoners, a promotion to major general, and a national reputation. Grant's demand that the Confederates surrender unconditionally earned him the nickname "Unconditional Surrender" Grant.

Grant moved his troops deeper into Tennessee where on August 6 and 7, 1862, they repelled a furious Confederate surprise attack at Shiloh Church near Pittsburg Landing. Heavy Union casualties at Shiloh prompted some of Lincoln's advisers to urge the president to relieve Grant of his command. Lincoln dismissed their advice, saying, "I can't spare this man. He fights." In July 1862, Grant had gained command of all Union forces in the West when Halleck was promoted to general in chief and transferred to Washington, D.C. During the next twelve months, Grant slowly maneuvered to capture the imposing Confederate fortifications at Vicksburg, Mississippi. On July 4, 1863, the Confederate commander at Vicksburg and twenty thousand troops surrendered to Grant. The victory gave the Union control of the Mississippi River and split the South in two.

In March 1864 President Lincoln promoted Grant to lieutenant general and appointed him general in chief of the army. Grant used his army's numerical superiority to fight a battle of attrition in Virginia against the main body of the Confederate army under Gen. Robert E. Lee. After a year of heavy fighting in which tens of thousands of troops on both sides were killed or wounded, Lee surrendered to Grant at Appomattox Court House in Virginia on April 9, 1865.

After the war Grant toured the South and issued a report advocating a lenient Reconstruction policy. In 1866 he was promoted to the newly established rank of general of the armies of the United States. The following year Grant, who throughout his military career had tried to remain aloof from politics, became involved in a political controversy. President Andrew Johnson had fired Secretary of War Edwin M. Stanton in violation of the Tenure of Office Act, which required the approval of Congress for dismissal of a cabinet member. In August Johnson appointed Grant to take Stanton's place, but the general resigned when Congress reinstated Stanton. Johnson felt betrayed by Grant, whom he hoped would stay in office to force a court battle over the Tenure of Office Act. The split with the Democratic president moved Grant closer to the Republicans. In 1868 they nominated him as their candidate for president. Grant, whose Civil War record had made him the most idolized person in America, received 52.7 percent of the popular vote and defeated Democrat Horatio Seymour 214–80 in the electoral college.

PRESIDENCY

When Grant took office, Reconstruction of the South was the primary issue confronting his administration. Grant supported the Reconstruction laws enacted during Andrew Johnson's administration and the ratification of the Fifteenth Amendment giving African Americans the right to vote. The amendment was ratified on March 30, 1870. Although Grant opposed blanketing the South with troops to guarantee the rights of blacks and to oversee other aspects of Reconstruction, he did respond to violations of the law with force. As Grant's term progressed, however, many northerners came to believe that federal attempts to keep southern whites from controlling state governments could not go on forever and were causing southern whites to use intimidation and terror to achieve their ends. Grant, therefore, was less willing and able to rally support for an activist Reconstruction policy.

Grant also pursued a conservative financial course. In March 1869, he signed the Public Credit Act, which pledged the government to redeem its debts in gold rather than paper money issued during the Civil War. Grant also advocated a gradual reduction of the public debt left over from the war.

In foreign affairs, Grant and Hamilton Fish, his capable secretary of state, successfully negotiated the Treaty of Washington with Great Britain. The treaty, signed in May 1871, provided for the settlement of U.S. claims against Great Britain for destruction caused during the Civil War by the *Alabama* and other ships built in Britain for the Confederacy. Grant was unsuccessful, however, in his attempts to annex Santo Domingo. His personal secretary, Orville Babcock, negotiated a treaty of annexation, but it was rejected by the Senate.

Grant retained his popularity during his first term and in 1872 won an overwhelming victory over Horace Greeley, editor of the *New York Tribune.* Greeley had been nominated by the Democratic Party and the Liberal Republican Party, a faction of former Republicans pledged to fight corruption and implement a conciliatory policy toward the South. Grant defeated Greeley, 286 electoral votes to 66. Greeley died less than a month after the election.

Like his former commander, Zachary Taylor, Grant had no political experience before becoming president. Although Grant himself was honest, many of his appointees and associates were not; and Grant's administration, particularly his second term, is remembered for its scandals. Before Grant's second inauguration, the Crédit Mobilier scandal was revealed. Grant's outgoing vice president, Schuyler Colfax, and incoming vice president, Henry Wilson, both were implicated in the bribery scheme, which involved skimming profits made from the construction of the transcontinental railroad. In 1875 a Treasury Department investigation revealed that several prominent Republicans, including Orville Babcock, were involved in the Whiskey Ring, a group that had used bribery to avoid taxes on liquor. In 1876 Grant's secretary of war, William Belknap, resigned just before being impeached by the House of Representatives for accepting bribes. In his last annual message to Congress in 1876, Grant acknowledged that he had made mistakes during his presidency but assured its members that "failures have been errors of judgement, not of intent."

RETIREMENT

Upon leaving office Grant embarked with his wife on a round-the-world tour. He traveled in Europe, Africa, and Asia for two and a half years. He received a hero's welcome in foreign capitals and was entertained like royalty by many heads of state. The trip repaired Grant's popularity in the United States, and he was the preconvention favorite for the 1880 Republican presidential nomination. On the first ballot at the Republican convention in Chicago, Grant received 304 of the 378 votes necessary for nomination. Despite the support of Sen. Roscoe Conkling and his New York political machine, the anti-Grant factions had enough strength to prevent the former president's nomination on subsequent ballots. The convention remained deadlocked until the thirty-fifth ballot, when compromise candidate James A. Garfield was nominated.

After the convention, Grant retired from politics and moved to New York City. In May 1884 a brokerage firm in which he was a silent partner failed, and he was forced to sell much of his property to pay his debts. In August of that year he was diagnosed as having cancer. He began writing his memoirs in an attempt to give his family financial security before his death. Although suffering extreme pain, Grant lived longer than his doctors had predicted and finished his memoirs on July 19, 1885, four days before his death. The two-volume *Personal Memoirs of U.S. Grant* sold 300,000 copies and earned Grant's widow nearly a half million dollars in royalties.

Grant married Julia Boggs Dent on August 22, 1848, in St. Louis after he returned from the Mexican War. She was the sister of his West Point roommate. They had three sons and one daughter. Their eldest son rose to the rank of major general in the U.S. Army and served as minister to Austria-Hungary during Benjamin Harrison's administration.

Rutherford B. Hayes

BORN: October 4, 1822; Delaware, Ohio
PARTY: Republican
TERM: March 4, 1877–March 4, 1881
VICE PRESIDENT: William A. Wheeler
DIED: January 17, 1893; Fremont, Ohio
BURIED: Fremont

Rutherford Birchard Hayes was the youngest of the five children of Rutherford Hayes, a merchant who died two months before his son's birth. His father's estate was substantial, and his mother, Sophia, was able to send her children to private schools. Hayes enrolled at Kenyon College in Gambier, Ohio, when he was sixteen and graduated four years later, in 1842, as the valedictorian of his class. He studied law for a year at a law firm in Columbus, Ohio, before enrolling in Harvard Law School. In 1845 he graduated and was admitted to the Ohio bar.

In 1846 Hayes practiced law in Lower Sandusky (now Fremont), Ohio, but moved in 1850 to Cincinnati, where he established a thriving law office whose clients included several fugitive slaves. Hayes joined the Republican Party when it was formed in the mid-1850s. In 1858 the city council of Cincinnati appointed Hayes to an unexpired term as city solicitor, his first public office. He won reelection to the post in 1859 but was defeated in 1861.

When the Civil War began Hayes was commissioned as a major and given command of a regiment of the Twenty-third Ohio Volunteers, which he had helped organize. He was promoted to lieutenant colonel in October 1861 and colonel in September 1862 after he led a charge at the Battle of South Mountain, Maryland, despite being shot in the arm. In August 1864 he was nominated for the U.S. House of Representatives. When Ohio Republican leaders suggested that he take a furlough to cam-

paign, Hayes replied, "An officer fit for duty, who at this crisis would abandon his post to electioneer for a seat in Congress, ought to be scalped." Hayes's devotion to duty and his bravery in battle, where on several occasions he joined with his troops in hand-to-hand combat against the enemy, impressed voters more than any campaign speech he could have made. After being elected, however, he still refused to leave the army until the war was over. In October 1864, after the battle of Cedar Creek, Virginia, where he was wounded for the fourth time, he was promoted to brigadier general. On June 8, 1865, two months after Robert E. Lee had surrendered at Appomattox, Hayes finally resigned from the army to take his seat in Congress.

Hayes served two terms in the House before being elected governor of Ohio in 1867 in a close race. He was reelected two years later but declined to run for a third term. In 1872 he was defeated in his try for a House seat and turned down an offer from President Ulysses S. Grant of the post of assistant Treasury secretary. He retired to Fremont in 1873 and a year later inherited a large estate from his uncle, Sardis Birchard. Although Hayes did not seek the 1875 Republican nomination for a third term as governor of Ohio, he accepted his party's draft and was elected.

In March 1876 Hayes was put forward as a favorite son presidential candidate by the Ohio delegation at the Republican convention. James G. Blaine of Maine, the preconvention favorite, received the most votes on the first ballot but fell short of the number required for nomination. Blaine's opponents recognized they had to coalesce behind a single candidate and chose Hayes primarily because he was uncontroversial and free of scandal. Despite trailing four other candidates on the first ballot, Hayes was nominated on the seventh.

Hayes's chances for election were weakened by the scandals of the Grant administration, poor economic conditions, and the infrequency of his own campaign appearances. When the votes had been counted, Tilden had beaten Hayes by about 260,000 votes in the popular election and 203–166 in the electoral college. Republican leaders, however, were determined to retain the presidency and challenged the results in Florida, Louisiana, and South Carolina on the grounds that blacks had been intimidated from going to the polls. If the electoral votes of these three states were given to Hayes he would triumph 185–184. Southern Republican election officials from the three disputed states disqualified votes from Democratic precincts and declared Hayes the winner. Democratic leaders from these states accused the Republicans of corruption and sent rival sets of electoral votes to Congress, which was left to deal with the mess. With no way to determine who really deserved the electoral votes, members of Congress struck a deal. Democratic members agreed to the formation of an election commission that favored the Republicans in return for secret assurances that federal troops would be withdrawn from the South. The commission voted 8–7 for Hayes, who was officially declared president on March 4, 1877, just two days before his inauguration.

When Hayes became president he honored the agreement made with the Democrats to withdraw federal troops from the South. This move ended the Reconstruction era and enabled white Democrats to reestablish their political control over the southern states.

Hayes was a well-intentioned president, but the stigma of the deal that had made him president, his quarrels with conservatives in his party, and Democratic control of the House from 1877 to 1879 and the Senate from 1879 to 1881 limited his ability to push legislation through Congress. When Congress tried to stimulate the economy by coining overvalued silver coins, Hayes, an advocate of sound money, vetoed the inflationary measure. Congress, however, passed the bill over Hayes's veto. The president's calls for civil service reform also had little effect, as Congress refused to act on his proposals. In 1877, however, Hayes demonstrated his ability to take decisive action when he dispatched federal troops to stop riots that had broken out in several cities as a result of a nationwide railroad strike.

When his term expired, Hayes retired to Fremont, Ohio, where he managed several farms he had bought. He also promoted humanitarian causes, including prison reform and education opportunities for southern black youth. While returning to Fremont from a business trip, Hayes had a heart attack aboard a train on January 14, 1893. He died three days later.

Hayes married Lucy Ware Webb December 30, 1852, in Cincinnati, Ohio. They had seven sons and one daughter; three of their sons died in infancy. Lucy Hayes was deeply religious and lived according to strict moral principles. Her refusal to allow alcoholic beverages to be served at White House functions made her a symbol of the Women's Christian Temperance Union and earned her the nickname "Lemonade Lucy." She was the first college-educated first lady, having graduated from Wesleyan Female College in Cincinnati.

James A. Garfield

BORN: November 19, 1831; Orange, Ohio
PARTY: Republican
TERM: March 4, 1881–September 19, 1881
VICE PRESIDENT: Chester A. Arthur
DIED: September 19, 1881; Elberon, New Jersey
BURIED: Cleveland, Ohio

James Abram Garfield was born in a log cabin on an Ohio farm. When he was one year old, his father, Abram, died, leaving his mother, Eliza, to raise James and his three older siblings. After she sold fifty acres of the farm to pay family debts, the Garfields survived by farming just thirty acres. James worked on the farm during the summer months and attended elementary schools in the winter. When he was seventeen he spent a year driving horse and mule teams that pulled barges on the Ohio and Erie Canal.

In 1849 Garfield entered Geauga Seminary in Chester, Ohio, a local denominational secondary school. He paid for his tuition by working as a carpenter. Two years later he enrolled in the Western Reserve Eclectic Institute (later Hiram College). After a semester the school hired him as an English teacher. He taught and studied there until September 1854, when he had saved enough money to enroll at Williams College in Williamstown, Massachusetts. He graduated with honors in 1856 and returned to Hiram, Ohio, where he became president of Western Reserve Eclectic Institute with its five-member faculty. While presiding over the school, Garfield studied law and became known as an eloquent public speaker and preacher. He was elected to the Ohio Senate as a Republican in 1859 and was admitted to the bar in 1860.

When the Civil War began in 1861 Garfield received a commission as a lieutenant colonel and command of a regiment of Ohio volunteers. After being promoted to colonel, he led a brigade to a dramatic victory over a superior number of Confederate troops at the battle of Middle Creek, Kentucky, on January 10, 1862. Garfield's success brought him a promotion to brigadier general. He participated in the Battle of Shiloh on April 7, 1862, before falling ill and returning to Ohio in July.

In September 1862, Garfield was elected to the U.S. House of Representatives, but he declined to retire from military service. After the Battle of Chickamauga in September 1863, he was promoted to major general for his bravery, although he had endorsed the battle plan of Gen. William S. Rosecrans that led to the Union defeat.

Garfield resigned his commission in December to take his seat in the House. There his oratory and leadership on important committees made him a prominent Republican member of Congress. Garfield dramatically demonstrated his rhetorical skills on April 15, 1865, the day after President Lincoln was assassinated. When a New York mob threatened to avenge Lincoln's death by destroying the headquarters of the *New York World*, a newspaper that had been a severe critic of Lincoln, Garfield quieted the crowd with a short speech given from the balcony of the New York Stock Exchange. It concluded: "Fellow citizens, God reigns and the government of Washington still lives."

Garfield served in the House until 1880. During this time he supported the harsh Reconstruction policies of the radical wing of his party. In 1877 he served on the election commission formed to decide the disputed outcome of the Hayes-Tilden presidential election of 1876. In fact he helped craft the backroom political deal that made Hayes president. While the Democrats controlled the House during the Hayes presidency, Garfield held the post of Republican minority leader.

At the 1880 Republican National Convention the party was sharply divided over whom to nominate for president. President Hayes had declined to run for reelection and could not have

won the nomination had he tried. The radical Stalwart faction of the Republican Party, headed by New York senator Roscoe Conkling, a powerful political boss, supported former president Ulysses S. Grant, while the less radical Half-Breed faction backed Sen. James G. Blaine (R-Maine). Garfield, who had been elected to the Senate earlier in the year but had not yet taken his seat, had promoted the compromise candidacy of John Sherman of Ohio. The convention, however, nominated Garfield himself on the thirty-sixth ballot. In a gesture to the Stalwarts the convention nominated Chester A. Arthur, a Conkling associate, for vice president.

Garfield faced Democrat Winfield Scott Hancock of Pennsylvania, a hero of the battle of Gettysburg, in the general election. During the campaign the Democrats tried to capitalize on Garfield's role in the Crédit Mobilier bribery scandal that occurred during the Grant administration. Garfield had received a $329 dividend check in 1868 from the Crédit Mobilier holding company but had not actually bought stock in it. The scandal had ruined several other politicians, including Grant's first vice president, Schuyler Colfax, but Garfield's relatively minor role had not crippled his career. Despite the corruption charges and his unpopularity in the South, where he lost every state, Garfield won in the electoral college, 214–155. In the popular vote, however, Garfield received just ten thousand more votes than Hancock.

As president, Garfield's broad-based appointments and support for anticorruption measures angered Stalwarts. On March 23 he appointed Conkling's political rival, William Robertson, to the coveted post of collector of the port of New York. Although Garfield had appointed many Conkling supporters to patronage positions, the powerful senator was determined to block Robertson's confirmation. When Robertson was about to be confirmed, Conkling resigned his seat in protest. The move backfired, however, when the New York State legislature refused to reelect Conkling to the Senate as he had expected.

On July 2, 1881, as Garfield was in the Baltimore and Potomac railroad station in Washington, D.C., on his way to deliver the commencement address at his alma mater, Williams College, he was shot by Charles J. Guiteau. Guiteau shot the president once in the back and fired another bullet that grazed his arm. Garfield was taken to the White House, where he remained for two months while doctors unsuccessfully probed for the bullet that was lodged near his spine. On September 6 the president asked to be moved to Elberon, New Jersey, in the hope that the sea air would help him recover. He died in Elberon on September 19. Ironically, Garfield probably would have survived if his doctors had left the bullet undisturbed rather than searching for it with unsterile instruments, which spread infection.

Guiteau had been captured at the time of the assault and was put on trial in Washington, D.C., two months after the president's death. At the time of the attack the assassin had shouted, "I am a Stalwart; now Arthur is president!" Guiteau, however, was not associated with Roscoe Conkling and the Stalwarts. The assassin believed his distribution of pro-Republican Party literature during the 1880 presidential campaign entitled him to a diplomatic appointment. Repeated rejections by the White House angered him, and he claimed to have received a divine vision instructing him to kill the president. The assassin's lawyers argued that their client was insane and should be acquitted, but the jury found him guilty and sentenced him to death. Guiteau was hanged in Washington, D.C., on June 30, 1882.

Garfield married Lucretia Rudolph of Hiram, Ohio, on November 11, 1858. They had five sons and two daughters; two of the children died in infancy. One of their sons, James Rudolph Garfield, served as secretary of the interior under President Theodore Roosevelt.

Chester A. Arthur

BORN: October 5, 1830; Fairfield, Vermont
PARTY: Republican
TERM: September 20, 1881–March 4, 1885
VICE PRESIDENT: None
DIED: November 18, 1886; New York City
BURIED: Albany, New York

Chester Alan Arthur was one of the nine children of Malvina and William Arthur, a Baptist minister who had emigrated from Northern Ireland. Arthur claimed to have been born in Fairfield, Vermont, but some political enemies claimed that he actually had been born in Canada, where his father had lived at one time. This charge, if true, would have disqualified him for the presidency, but it was never substantiated.

In 1845 at the age of fifteen Arthur enrolled as a sophomore at Union College in Schenectady, New York, where he studied Greek and Latin. He graduated three years later and was one of six in his class to be elected to Phi Beta Kappa, a national honor society. He settled in North Pownal, Vermont, where he taught school at the North Pownal Academy, becoming principal in 1849. While teaching, Arthur studied law, and in 1853 he joined the New York City law firm of Parker and Culver as a clerk. The following year he passed the bar and became a member of the firm. As a lawyer, he often defended fugitive slaves and free blacks who suffered discrimination.

Arthur attended the first New York Republican National Convention in 1856 and became an active supporter of Republican candidates. In 1860 New York Republican governor Edward D. Morgan rewarded Arthur's political work by appointing him state engineer in chief with the military rank of brigadier general. During the Civil War Arthur served as assistant quartermaster general, inspector general, and finally quartermaster general of the troops of New York. He excelled in these administrative posts, spending state funds efficiently and keeping scrupulous books. He resigned his commission at the beginning of 1863 and returned to his law practice when Democrat Horatio Seymour became governor. He continued his rise in the New York Republican Party, however, and by the time Ulysses S. Grant was elected president in 1868, he was Sen. Roscoe Conkling's principal lieutenant in the state's Republican machine.

In 1871, with Conkling's support, President Grant appointed Arthur to one of the most lucrative and coveted offices in government—collector of the port of New York. In this post Arthur oversaw the activities of almost one thousand officials, was in charge of collecting about two-thirds of the country's tariff revenue, and earned an average income of $40,000 per year. But despite Arthur's administrative abilities and basic honesty, President Hayes fired him from the customhouse in 1878 as part of his fight against the spoils system.

The Republican National Convention of 1880 pitted New York boss senator Roscoe Conkling and his radical party faction known as the Stalwarts against James G. Blaine and the slightly more moderate Half-breed faction. Conkling supported former president Ulysses S. Grant for the nomination, but after thirty-six ballots the convention turned to a dark horse candidate, James A. Garfield of Ohio. In an effort to appease the Stalwarts and unify the party, Republican leaders offered the vice presidency to Levi P. Morton, one of Conkling's associates. Conkling, however, was not in a mood to be appeased, and he convinced Morton to reject the offer. When the same offer was made to Arthur, who had never held elective office, he gratefully accepted the nomination despite the objections of Conkling. Garfield and Arthur defeated the Democratic ticket of Winfield Scott Hancock and William H. English by less than ten thousand votes but won in the electoral college, 214–155.

Garfield served only 199 days of his presidential term, however. On July 2, 1881, he was shot by an assassin in Washington, D.C. The gunman, Charles J. Guiteau, declared after the attack, "I am a Stalwart; now Arthur is President!" Garfield initially survived his wounds but died on September 19, after months of failed attempts by his doctors to remove the bullet.

Although Arthur had no connection to Guiteau, he was sensitive to charges that he and the Stalwarts may have been involved in Garfield's death. Therefore, once Arthur had assumed the presidency, he severed his ties to Conkling and the New York political machine. The new president demonstrated his independence by backing the investigations of post office scandals in which several Stalwarts were implicated.

Arthur was not, however, ready to embrace civil service reform, which had been the cause of James Garfield. He advocated instead a continuation of the partisan system of dispensing patronage. Nevertheless, on January 16, 1883, Arthur signed the Pendleton Civil Service Reform Act. The act set up a commission to develop and administer examinations for many federal positions previously filled through patronage.

In economic policy Arthur sought to reduce the government's continuing budget surplus that took money out of the economy. He proposed reducing tariffs, building up the navy, and reducing the federal debt with the surplus. Arthur succeeded in making moderate improvements to the navy and reducing the national debt, but Congress rejected his proposals to cut tariffs.

Upon leaving office Arthur returned to New York City to practice law. He soon accepted the presidency of the New York Arcade Railway Company, which was trying to construct a subway in New York City. In February 1886 Arthur retired after a medical examination revealed that he had Bright's disease, a life-threatening kidney ailment. He died later that year in New York City.

Arthur married Ellen Lewis Herndon on October 25, 1859. They had two sons and one daughter, but their first son died in infancy. Ellen Arthur died on January 12, 1880, five months before her husband was nominated for the vice presidency. Arthur's sister, Mary Arthur McElroy, acted as White House hostess.

Grover Cleveland

BORN: March 18, 1837; Caldwell, New Jersey
PARTY: Democratic
TERMS: March 4, 1885–March 4, 1889; March 4, 1893–March 4, 1897
VICE PRESIDENTS: Thomas A. Hendricks; Adlai E. Stevenson
DIED: June 24, 1908; Princeton, New Jersey
BURIED: Princeton

Grover Cleveland was the fifth of the nine children born to Ann and Richard F. Cleveland, a Presbyterian minister. Grover was originally named Stephen Grover, but he dropped his first

name early in his life. In 1853, the year his father died, Grover moved to New York City, where he got a job at a school for the blind. After a year, however, he returned to his family in Holland Patent, New York.

In the spring of 1855 Cleveland traveled west to seek work in Cleveland, Ohio. On the way he stopped to visit relatives in Buffalo, New York, where he decided to stay when his uncle, Lewis F. Allen, offered him a job as a farmhand. A few months later Cleveland went to work as an apprentice clerk in a local law firm. In 1859 he was admitted to the bar and promoted to chief clerk in his firm.

Cleveland had been drafted to fight in the Civil War, but in accordance with the draft laws he had hired a substitute for $300 so he could continue to help support his mother and younger siblings. In 1863 Cleveland accepted an appointment as assistant district attorney of Erie County, New York. Two years later he was defeated in an election for district attorney. With the exception of a two-year term as sheriff of Buffalo from 1871 to 1873, he practiced law for the next sixteen years.

In 1881 he was elected mayor of Buffalo and immediately took action to reform the city administration. His well-deserved reputation as an uncompromising reformer earned him the Democratic nomination for governor of New York in 1882. He easily won the election and assumed office on January 3, 1883. As governor, Cleveland combated corruption and the spoils system with his veto power. He formed an alliance with Theodore Roosevelt, a Republican member of the New York State Assembly, to enact legislation reforming New York City's government.

The governor's successes and reform principles made him an attractive presidential candidate in 1884. The Republicans nominated James G. Blaine, a Republican senator from Maine, who had been linked to several scandals. Cleveland's supporters argued that if the Democratic Party nominated the reform governor, the reform-minded Republicans, known as Mugwumps might desert their party in sufficient numbers to elect a Democrat to the presidency for the first time since the Civil War. The Democratic delegates at the national convention in Chicago agreed with this strategy, and Cleveland was nominated on the second ballot.

Cleveland's election hopes were damaged, however, when a newspaper report disclosed that he had fathered an illegitimate child, which he continued to support. Cleveland admitted his paternity and instructed his campaign workers to "tell the truth." Cleveland also was attacked for not serving in the Civil War, although Blaine had avoided service as well. Blaine lost many Catholic votes when he failed to repudiate a supporter's accusation less than a week before the election that the Democrats represented "rum, Romanism, and rebellion." In the end Cleveland received just sixty thousand more votes than Blaine and defeated him 219–182 in the electoral college.

During his first term Cleveland attempted to bring to the presidency the same reformist principles that he had followed as governor of New York. For example, he implemented the Pendleton Civil Service Act, signed into law by Chester A. Arthur, which shifted thousands of government jobs from patronage to a merit system of hiring. He also vetoed numerous private pension bills for individual Civil War veterans. Cleveland was unsuccessful, however, in lowering the tariff, which he considered to be unfair to farmers and workers and unnecessary given the large federal budget surplus.

In 1888 Cleveland ran for reelection against Indiana Republican Benjamin Harrison. Despite defeating Harrison by 100,000 votes, Cleveland lost to Harrison in the electoral college 233–168. Had Cleveland won his home state's thirty-six electoral votes as he did in 1884, he would have won the election.

After leaving office Cleveland moved to New York City, where he practiced law. Four years later he was again nominated for president by his party. The 1892 election featured a rematch between Cleveland and President Benjamin Harrison. Cleveland easily defeated Harrison in the electoral college by 277–145 votes but received only 46.3 percent of the popular vote because the third party candidacy of James Baird Weaver of the People's Party drew more than one million votes.

Soon after Cleveland took office for the second time the Panic of 1893 sparked a deep economic depression. More than five hundred banks failed, and unemployment rose sharply as businesses went bankrupt. Cleveland believed the depression was caused by inflation and an erosion of business confidence. Thus, with the support of many congressional Republicans, he convinced Congress in 1893 to repeal the mildly inflationary Sherman Silver Purchase Act. He also authorized the purchase of several million ounces of gold from private holders to replenish the government's shrinking gold reserves. Cleveland's policies, however, did not ease the depression.

In 1894 the economic situation worsened when a local strike at the Pullman Palace Car Company near Chicago led to a debilitating railroad strike throughout the Midwest. When violence erupted in Chicago, Cleveland sent federal troops there to break the strike despite the protests of Illinois governor John P. Altgeld. Cleveland's action earned him support from the business community but the enmity of labor organizations. Although the depression had greeted Cleveland as he entered office, he received much of the blame for the nation's economic troubles. After Republicans gained congressional seats in the 1894 midterm elections, Cleveland had difficulty exerting much control over Congress or even his party. The 1896 Democratic convention nominated William Jennings Bryan for president, and many Democratic candidates distanced themselves from Cleveland.

In foreign affairs Cleveland withdrew in March 1893 a treaty negotiated in the closing months of the Harrison administration that would have annexed Hawaii. He considered the treaty unfair and blocked any further attempt to annex the islands. He also resisted the temptation to yield to public pressure and go to war with Spain over their suppression of a rebellion in Cuba that began in 1895.

Upon leaving office for the second time Cleveland settled in Princeton, New Jersey. He devoted his time to fishing, delivering lectures, and writing books and articles. In 1901 he was appointed to the board of trustees of Princeton University, and in 1904 he became the president of that board while future president Woodrow Wilson served as president of the university. In 1907 Cleveland was elected president of the Association of Presidents of Life Insurance Companies. During his last years Cleveland's heart and kidneys weakened. He died of a heart attack in Princeton, New Jersey, in 1908.

Cleveland married Frances Folsom, the twenty-one-year-old daughter of his former law partner, on June 2, 1886, in a White House ceremony. The couple had three daughters and two sons. Two of the children were born during Cleveland's second term.

Benjamin Harrison

BORN: August 20, 1833; North Bend, Ohio
PARTY: Republican
TERM: March 4, 1889–March 4, 1893
VICE PRESIDENT: Levi P. Morton
DIED: March 13, 1901; Indianapolis, Indiana
BURIED: Indianapolis

Benjamin Harrison was born at his grandfather's home at North Bend, Ohio, the second of the ten children of John and Elizabeth Harrison. Four of the ten children died in infancy. The Harrison family also included John's two surviving daughters from a previous marriage. When Benjamin was seven, his grandfather, William Henry Harrison, became the ninth president of the United States but died after one month in office. Benjamin's great-grandfather, Benjamin Harrison, had been governor of Virginia and a signer of the Declaration of Independence.

After receiving a primary education at a country school and from tutors, Benjamin attended Farmer's College in Cincinnati from 1847 to 1850. He then transferred to Miami University in Oxford, Ohio. He graduated with honors in 1852 and began studying law at a firm in Cincinnati. In 1854 he moved to Indianapolis and established his own practice. A year later he formed a law partnership with William Wallace, a more established Indianapolis lawyer. Within a few years their firm had become one of the most respected in the city.

Soon after moving to Indianapolis Harrison became active in the Republican Party. In 1857 he was elected Indianapolis city attorney. The following year he served as secretary of the Indiana Republican central committee, and in 1860 he was elected reporter of the Indiana Supreme Court.

In 1862, during the Civil War, Harrison was commissioned as a colonel and given command of the Seventieth Indiana Volunteers, which he had helped recruit. His regiment guarded railroads in Kentucky and participated in the Atlanta campaign. He gained a reputation as a cold disciplinarian and was unpopular with many of his troops. His unit fought well, however, and he was promoted to brigadier general in 1865.

When the war ended Harrison returned to Indianapolis, where his legal skill, war record, and speeches on behalf of Republican causes made him one of the most famous men in Indiana. In 1876 Harrison received the Republican nomination for governor but lost by five thousand votes to Democrat James D. Williams. Harrison had not sought the nomination and was happy to return to his law practice. He presided over the Indiana Republican convention in 1878 and was chairman of his state's delegation to the Republican National Convention in 1880.

In 1881 Harrison was elected to the U.S. Senate, where he chaired the committee on territories. In this capacity he defended the interests of homesteaders and Native Americans against the railroads. Harrison also was a strong advocate of Civil War veterans and worked to protect and expand their pensions. Harrison ran for reelection in 1886, but the Democrats had gained control of the Indiana legislature two years before and voted him out of office.

At the 1888 Republican National Convention in Chicago Harrison was nominated on the eighth ballot to run for president against incumbent Grover Cleveland. The primary issue of the campaign was the tariff, which Harrison promised to raise if elected. Harrison lost the popular vote but won in the electoral college 233–168 with the help of a narrow victory in New York that gave him that state's thirty-six electoral votes.

Harrison enjoyed the luxury of having both houses of Congress controlled by his party. As a result, he was able to implement much of his economic program. In July 1890 he signed the

Sherman Antitrust Act and the Sherman Silver Purchase Act. The former outlawed trusts and business combines that restrained trade, while the latter required the Treasury to purchase large quantities of silver with notes that could be redeemed in gold. The silver purchase was inflationary and strained the nation's gold reserves, but Harrison and the Republicans resisted the more damaging proposal of free coinage of silver desired by many indebted farmers from the South and West. Later, in 1890, Harrison signed the McKinley Tariff Act, which was sponsored by House member and future president William McKinley. The act sharply raised tariffs as Harrison had promised, providing protection to some U.S. industries but raising prices for many consumer goods. Harrison constructed several compromises that led to passage of the act.

In foreign policy the Harrison administration enjoyed several successes. Harrison's secretary of state, James G. Blaine, presided over the Inter-American Conference in Washington, D.C., in 1889 and 1890, out of which came the Pan American Union. Blaine also secured an agreement in 1889 with Britain and Germany to preserve the independence of the Samoa Islands under a tripartite protectorate. In 1892 Harrison demanded and received an apology and reparations from Chile for an attack by its citizens on U.S. sailors who were on shore leave in Valparaiso, Chile. He failed, however, in his attempt to annex

Hawaii late in his term. An 1893 coup, in which Americans participated, had led to the overthrow of the Hawaiian queen. Thus, the U.S. minister in Hawaii hastily concluded a treaty of ratification with the new provisional government, but Senate Democrats in the Senate blocked the treaty until Harrison's term expired. Incoming president Grover Cleveland withdrew the treaty.

At the end of his term Harrison attended the inauguration of Grover Cleveland, who four years before had accompanied Harrison to the Capitol as the outgoing president. Harrison then returned to Indianapolis, where he resumed his lucrative law practice. In the spring of 1894 he delivered a series of law lectures at Stanford University in Palo Alto, California. Supporters encouraged him to seek the Republican presidential nomination in 1896, but he refused to allow his name to be placed in nomination. From 1897 to 1899 he represented Venezuela in a boundary dispute with Great Britain that was to be decided by an international arbitration tribunal. After he traveled to Paris in 1899 to present his case, the tribunal upheld most of Venezuela's claims. Harrison then toured Europe with his second wife. He died in Indianapolis in 1901 from pneumonia.

On October 20, 1853, Harrison married Caroline Lavinia Scott, whom he had met while attending Miami University. The couple had two children, Russell and Mary. Mrs. Harrison died in the White House on October 25, 1892. Three years after he left office on April 6, 1896, Harrison married thirty-seven-year-old Mary Scott Lord Dimmick, a niece of his first wife. They had one daughter, Elizabeth, who was born when Harrison was sixty-three.

William McKinley

BORN: January 29, 1843; Niles, Ohio
PARTY: Republican
TERM: March 4, 1897–September 14, 1901
VICE PRESIDENTS: Garret A. Hobart; Theodore Roosevelt
DIED: September 14, 1901; Buffalo, New York
BURIED: Canton, Ohio

William McKinley was the seventh of the nine children born to Nancy and William McKinley, an iron founder. The McKinleys moved from Niles, Ohio, to Poland, Ohio, when William was nine. There he attended Union Seminary, a local private school. He enrolled in Allegheny College in Meadville, Pennsylvania, in 1859 but dropped out the following year because of illness and financial problems. William returned to Poland, where he taught in a country school and worked in the post office.

When the Civil War began in 1861, McKinley enlisted as a private in the Twenty-third Ohio Volunteers—the same unit in which Rutherford B. Hayes began his service as a major. McKinley steadily worked his way up through the ranks, becoming an officer in September 1862 after the battle of Antietam in Maryland. When the war ended he was a twenty-two-year-old major who had been decorated for bravery.

McKinley chose to leave the army, however, to study law. He

worked for two years in the law office of a Youngstown, Ohio, attorney and then polished his legal skills at Albany Law School in New York for a term. He was admitted to the bar in 1867 and opened a law practice in Canton, Ohio. He ran for prosecuting attorney of Stark County as a Republican in 1869 and won despite the county's traditional Democratic voting record. Two years later, however, he was narrowly defeated for reelection.

From 1871 to 1876, McKinley practiced law in Canton and campaigned for Republican candidates. In 1876, when his old commanding officer, Rutherford B. Hayes, was elected president, McKinley won a seat in the U.S. House of Representatives. He served seven consecutive terms in the House until 1891. As a member of Congress, McKinley supported civil service reform, voting rights for African Americans, and government coinage of silver. He was best known, however, for his staunch support of high tariffs as a means of protecting U.S. industries. While serving as the chairman of the House Ways and Means Committee he sponsored the McKinley Tariff of 1890, which raised tariff rates to new highs. The tariff brought higher prices for consumers and contributed to voter disaffection for the Republican Party. McKinley was voted out of office along with many other Republican members of Congress in 1890.

McKinley returned to Ohio, where he ran for governor successfully. He served two two-year terms, during which he was increasingly promoted as a presidential candidate. In 1892 he served as the chairman of the Republican National Convention in Chicago. President Benjamin Harrison was nominated on the first ballot, but McKinley came in second in the balloting.

McKinley's presidential nomination in 1896 did not result from a spontaneous movement on the floor of the Republican convention. With McKinley's approval, Ohio party boss Mark Hanna and other leading Republicans actively promoted McKinley's candidacy in the months leading up to the convention. His nomination was almost ensured when the St. Louis convention convened in June 1896, and the delegates nominated him on the first ballot.

Although McKinley had favored the coinage of silver, he renounced his former position and supported the gold standard in order to win conservative Democrats away from the Democratic nominee, William Jennings Bryan, who was an ardent silver advocate. McKinley waged his campaign from his front porch, speaking to crowds that came to Canton by railroad. In contrast, Bryan traveled more than eighteen thousand miles and delivered hundreds of speeches during his campaign. The Republican nominee received the strong support of business and financial leaders who feared that a Bryan presidency would bring inflation. They helped raise a formidable war chest for McKinley, who won in the electoral college 271–176.

McKinley was severely criticized by Democrats and some Republicans for appointing aging Ohio senator John Sherman as his secretary of state. The appointment was seen as a political payoff to Mark Hanna, who promptly was elected to the vacant Senate seat by the Ohio state legislature.

McKinley's top priority upon entering office was the economy, which had been mired in a depression during much of Cleveland's second term. Congress quickly passed the Dingley Tariff Act of 1897 in response to McKinley's requests. Thereafter, the economy began to grow. Although the tariff bill may not have been the cause of the recovery, McKinley took credit for the improvement of economic conditions.

McKinley's first term, however, was dominated by the Spanish-American War and its results. Americans were disturbed by numerous press accounts of atrocities perpetrated by Spanish colonialists upon Cuban natives. McKinley responded to public pressure for war by sending a war message to Congress on April 11, 1898. Congress declared war two weeks later on April 25. Although the United States was not prepared for the war, victory came easily. Spanish control of Cuba was broken, and the U.S. Asiatic squadron under Commodore George Dewey destroyed the Spanish Pacific fleet in the Battle of Manila Bay. The fighting was over by August. On December 10, 1898, Spain signed a treaty freeing Cuba and ceding the Philippines, Puerto Rico, and

Guam to the United States. McKinley agonized over how to deal with the Philippines but decided to take possession of them rather than grant them their independence. He resolved to "uplift and civilize and Christianize" the Filipinos. Insurgents in the Philippines, however, were determined to gain their independence. In 1899 they launched a guerrilla war against the U.S. occupying force, which ended in 1902 with the defeat of the insurgents. The bloody conflict cost more American lives and money than the Spanish-American War.

McKinley took several important steps in other parts of Asia and the Pacific. He oversaw the annexation of Hawaii in 1898 and the partition of the Samoan Islands with Germany in 1899. Secretary of State John Hay negotiated an agreement with European nations in 1900 that established an "Open Door" policy toward China, under which all nations doing business with China would enjoy equal trading rights.

McKinley was renominated without opposition in 1900. His close friend and first-term vice president, Garret Hobart, had died in 1899, however, and the Republican National Convention chose Theodore Roosevelt as his running mate. The Democrats again ran William Jennings Bryan, but the nation's economic recovery since McKinley took office gave the Republicans a strong election issue. McKinley improved upon the popular and electoral vote margins of victory he had enjoyed in 1896, defeating Bryan in the electoral college 292–155.

After Roosevelt's nomination, Mark Hanna, who regarded the vice-presidential candidate as an unpredictable reformer, wrote McKinley saying, "Your duty to the country is to live for four years from next March." McKinley would be unable to carry out this duty. Six months after his inauguration, he traveled to Buffalo, New York, to deliver an address at the Pan-American Exposition, a fair celebrating friendship in the Western Hemisphere. The following day the president greeted thousands of people who waited in line to shake his hand at a public reception. Leon Czolgosz, an anarchist disturbed by social injustice, waited in line until it was his turn to shake McKinley's hand. Czolgosz then fired two shots with a concealed .32-caliber revolver that struck McKinley in the chest and stomach.

McKinley was taken first to the emergency medical center at the exposition and then to Milburn House, his Buffalo lodgings. Doctors initially thought the president would recover. Vice President Roosevelt, who had cut his vacation short and rushed to Buffalo upon hearing that the president had been shot, even resumed his holiday when he was informed of the doctors' prognosis. After a week, however, gangrene set in, and McKinley's conditioned deteriorated. He died early in the morning on September 14.

McKinley married Ida Saxton, the daughter of a banker, on January 25, 1871, in Canton, Ohio. The couple had two daughters, but one died as an infant and the other at the age of four. Ida was afflicted with epilepsy and phlebitis for most of her adult life. Despite occasional seizures and her inability to walk without a cane, she presided over most White House social functions.

Theodore Roosevelt.

Theodore Roosevelt

BORN: October 27, 1858; New York City
PARTY: Republican
TERM: September 14, 1901–March 4, 1909
VICE PRESIDENT: Charles W. Fairbanks
DIED: January 6, 1919; Oyster Bay, New York
BURIED: Oyster Bay

Theodore Roosevelt was the second of the four children and the oldest son of Theodore and Martha Roosevelt. His father was a wealthy New York City banker and merchant. Young Theodore was educated by tutors and enjoyed several trips abroad with the family. Throughout his boyhood, he suffered from asthma and other illnesses. When he was thirteen he began a program of vigorous physical exercise that turned him into a healthy, robust young man. Throughout the rest of his life, he would preach the virtues of a strenuous life.

Roosevelt entered Harvard in 1876. An excellent student, he graduated twenty-first in his class in 1880 and was elected to the Phi Beta Kappa honor society. He then enrolled in Columbia Law School but dropped out after a year of study without taking a degree or seeking admission to the bar.

Roosevelt entered politics in 1881 when he was elected to the New York state legislature at the age of twenty-three. He led a group of reform Republicans who fought corruption in the state government. Roosevelt was reelected in 1882 and 1883 but declined to seek reelection after his wife, Alice, and his mother died within hours of each other on February 14, 1884.

From 1884 to 1886, Roosevelt sought refuge from his grief in the Dakota Territory, where he managed a cattle ranch and served for a period as deputy sheriff. He returned to New York City in 1886 and ran unsuccessfully for mayor. After marrying Edith Kermit Carow, he settled into his home, Sagamore Hill, in Oyster Bay, Long Island. There he wrote books on American history and life in the West. His works include *Hunting Trip of a Ranchman, Life of Thomas Hart Benton, Gouverneur Morris, The Winning of the West,* and *Ranch Life and the Hunting Trail.* During his lifetime, Roosevelt wrote more than forty books.

In 1889 Roosevelt returned to public service when President Benjamin Harrison appointed him U.S. civil service commissioner. He was reappointed in 1893 by Democrat Grover Cleveland and served until 1895. As commissioner, Roosevelt fought against the spoils system, which he considered a source of corruption. He revised civil service exams, doubled the number of government positions subject to examination, and increased government employment opportunities for women.

From 1895 to 1897 Roosevelt served as president of the Police Commission of New York City. He moved to Washington, D.C., in 1897 when President William McKinley appointed him assistant secretary of the navy. In this post he fought to increase the size of the U.S. Navy and advocated war with Spain over that country's suppression of an independence movement in Cuba. On February 25, 1898, with Navy Secretary John Long absent from the capital, Roosevelt ordered the Pacific fleet to go to Hong Kong and prepare to destroy the Spanish fleet in the event of a declaration of war. In issuing the order, Roosevelt overstepped the bounds of his authority, but when Commodore George Dewey defeated the Spanish fleet in the Battle of Manila Bay on May 1, 1898, Roosevelt's action was vindicated.

Soon after the United States declared war against Spain, Roosevelt resigned from the Navy Department so he could fight in Cuba. He secured the rank of lieutenant colonel and organized a regiment of cavalry that came to be known as the Rough Riders. Although the importance of the Rough Riders to the American victory over the Spanish in Cuba became exaggerated, Roosevelt demonstrated his courage in leading his regiment in the famous charge up one of the San Juan Hills overlooking Santiago. Despite suffering heavy casualties, the Rough Riders captured the hill.

Roosevelt's exploits in Cuba made him a celebrity in the United States. In November 1898 he received the Republican nomination for governor of New York and was narrowly elected. As governor his political independence and refusal to promote the interests of big business disturbed the power brokers of his party, particularly New York Republican boss Thomas Platt.

In 1900 Platt hoped to get rid of Roosevelt by promoting him as a candidate for vice president. Although Roosevelt declared he did not want the job, he was the popular choice at the Philadelphia Republican National Convention, and he accepted the nomination when it was offered to him. Party leaders had mixed feelings about Roosevelt. They recognized that his popularity could win votes for the ticket, but they feared what might happen if McKinley died. Mark Hanna, the Republican national chairman who had overseen McKinley's career, warned his colleagues, "Don't any of you realize that there's only one life between this madman and the White House?"

After the inauguration, Roosevelt presided over a five-day session of the Senate held to confirm presidential appointees. When the session was completed, Congress adjourned until December. Roosevelt, with no other vice-presidential duties to execute, returned to his home on Long Island. On September 6, 1901, Roosevelt was hunting and fishing in Vermont when he learned that President McKinley had been shot. He rushed to Buffalo, where doctors said McKinley would recover from his wounds. Roosevelt wanted to demonstrate to the public that the president was in no danger of death, so he resumed his vacation on September 10. Three days later, however, Roosevelt was informed that McKinley's condition had deteriorated. The vice president arrived in Buffalo on September 14, the day McKinley died. Later in the day he took the oath of office in Buffalo from U.S. District Court Judge John Hazel. At the age of forty-two, Roosevelt became the youngest person ever to serve as president.

PRESIDENCY

After McKinley's death, Roosevelt declared, "It shall be my aim to continue absolutely unbroken the policy of President McKinley for the peace, the prosperity, and the honor of our beloved country." Despite retaining McKinley's cabinet, Roosevelt promoted his own policies, which included measures to curb abuses by big business. Soon after taking office he had directed Attorney General Philander Knox to prepare an antitrust suit against Northern Securities Company, a giant railroad trust. The suit was successful in 1904 when the Supreme Court ruled that the company should be dissolved. Although the Roosevelt administration would initiate fewer antitrust suits than the Taft administration, Roosevelt became known as the trust-busting president. In 1902 when a coal strike in Pennsylvania caused shortages and rising coal prices, Roosevelt threatened to take over the mines unless the mine owners submitted to arbitration. The mine owners backed down, and Roosevelt appointed a commission that gave the miners a 10 percent raise.

Roosevelt's most famous act during his first term was his acquisition of land for the Panama Canal. Colombia owned Panama, but in August 1903 the Colombian senate refused to approve a treaty giving the United States the rights to a canal zone six miles wide. Determined to build the canal, Roosevelt later that year supported a revolution in Panama, which, with the help of the U.S. Navy, overthrew Colombian rule. The new Panamanian government agreed to lease the zone to the United States, and construction of the canal began.

In the 1904 presidential election, Roosevelt ran against New York judge Alton B. Parker. Roosevelt lost the South but received over 56 percent of the popular vote, swept the North and West, and easily won in the electoral college, 336–140. He became the first successor president to win the White House in his own right after serving the unfinished term of his predecessor.

During his second term Roosevelt championed many pieces of reform legislation including the Pure Food and Drug Act, the Meat Inspection Act, and the Hepburn Act, which empowered the government to set railroad rates. Roosevelt also continued his conservationist activities begun during his first term. Under Roosevelt the government initiated thirty major federal irrigation projects, added 125 million acres to the national forest reserves, and doubled the number of national parks.

In foreign affairs Roosevelt continued aggressively to promote U.S. interests abroad, often in a manner his critics described as imperialistic. In late 1904 he issued the Roosevelt Corollary to the Monroe Doctrine, which declared that the United States would intervene in Latin American affairs to prevent European nations from intervening there. The following year he put the corollary into practice by taking control of the Santo Domingo customhouses to guarantee that country's European debts. In 1905 he mediated an agreement ending the Russo-Japanese War and was awarded the Nobel Peace Prize for his efforts. In the face of congressional opposition Roosevelt also sent the U.S. fleet on a world cruise that lasted from late 1907 to early 1909. The show of strength was intended to impress other nations, especially Japan, with U.S. resolve to defend its interests and play an active role in world affairs.

FORMER PRESIDENT

Roosevelt's friend and secretary of war, William Howard Taft, was elected president in 1908 with Roosevelt's backing. Upon leaving office Roosevelt went to Africa to hunt big game with his son Kermit, then toured Europe with his wife before returning to the United States in June 1910. During the next two years Roosevelt became increasingly alienated from Taft, who he felt had abandoned his policies.

In 1912 Roosevelt declared his interest in the Republican nomination for president. He won most of the primaries, but the Republican National Convention in Chicago was controlled by supporters of President Taft, who received the nomination. Progressive Republicans organized the Progressive Party and persuaded Roosevelt to run. The party was dubbed the "Bull Moose" Party, because candidate Roosevelt declared that he felt "as fit as a bull moose."

On October 14, 1912, while campaigning in Milwaukee, Roosevelt was shot in the chest by an assailant. The candidate insisted on delivering a scheduled speech, which lasted almost an hour. He was then rushed from the amazed crowd to a hospital. Taft and the Democratic nominee, Woodrow Wilson, stopped their campaigns while Roosevelt recovered, but the former president was delivering speeches again within two weeks. Roosevelt's heroic campaigning, however, could not overcome the split he had caused among Republicans. Second-place Roosevelt and third-place Taft together received over a million more popular votes than Wilson, but with his opposition divided, Wilson won the election.

The Progressives asked Roosevelt to run for president again in 1916, but Roosevelt declined and supported Republican Charles Evans Hughes, who lost to President Wilson. In 1916 Roosevelt had begun to make plans for raising a volunteer division to command if the United States entered World War I. When the United States did enter the war in 1917, he went to the White House to request authority to implement his plans, but Wilson turned him down. During the war, Roosevelt was a leading Republican spokesperson and likely would have been his party's candidate for president in 1920 had he lived. He was hospitalized in November 1918 with a severe attack of rheumatism, an ailment from which he suffered during the last years of his life. He returned to Sagamore Hill for Christmas but remained ill. He died in his sleep on January 6, 1919, from an arterial blood clot.

Roosevelt married Alice Hathaway Lee on October 27, 1880, his twenty-second birthday. Alice died on February 14, 1884, of Bright's disease two days after giving birth to the couple's only child, Alice. Roosevelt's mother, Martha Roosevelt, died the same day of typhoid fever. On February 17, 1906, at the White House, Alice married Rep. Nicholas Longworth, who would serve as Speaker of the House from 1925 to 1931.

Roosevelt married Edith Kermit Carow, whom he had known since childhood, on December 2, 1886. They had four sons and one daughter. Their youngest child, Quentin, was killed during World War I while flying a mission over France. Their oldest child, Theodore Jr., served as assistant secretary of the navy, governor of Puerto Rico, and governor-general of the Philippines during the Harding, Coolidge, and Hoover administrations.

William Howard Taft

BORN: September 15, 1857; Cincinnati, Ohio
PARTY: Republican
TERM: March 4, 1909–March 4, 1913
VICE PRESIDENT: James S. Sherman
DIED: March 8, 1931; Washington, D.C.
BURIED: Arlington National Cemetery, Virginia

William Howard Taft was the second of the five children of Alphonso and Louisa Taft. William's older brother died in infancy. Alphonso Taft was a prominent Cincinnati lawyer, who served as secretary of war and attorney general under Ulysses S. Grant and later was ambassador to Austria-Hungary and Russia.

After excelling as a scholar and an athlete in high school, William enrolled in Yale in 1874. He graduated four years later, second in his class. He returned to Cincinnati, where he studied

law in his father's office and at the Cincinnati Law School. He gained admission to the bar in 1880 and was appointed assistant prosecutor of Hamilton County, Ohio, the following year. In 1882 he served briefly as collector of internal revenue for his Ohio district but resigned rather than fire several employees for political reasons. In 1883 he established a law partnership in Cincinnati with a former partner of his father.

In 1887 Taft was appointed to a vacancy on the state superior court, winning election to his own two-year term on the court the following year. In 1890 President Benjamin Harrison appointed him U.S. solicitor general. Two years later, Harrison appointed him judge of the U.S. Circuit Court, where Taft remained for eight years. During this period the judge also taught at the Cincinnati Law School.

In 1900 President William McKinley appointed Taft president of the U.S. Philippine Commission, which was charged with establishing a civil government on the islands. Taft was reluctant to leave his judgeship, but McKinley persuaded him to go to the Philippines by offering him an eventual appointment to the Supreme Court.

Taft expected to be in the Philippines only a short time, but in 1901 McKinley appointed him governor-general of the islands. In this capacity, Taft reorganized the Filipino court system, acquired land for the Filipinos from the Catholic Church, improved roads, harbors, and schools, and encouraged limited self-government. While in the Philippines, Taft twice refused appointment to the Supreme Court, the position he coveted most, because he believed he could not abandon the people of the islands. In 1904, however, he accepted Theodore Roosevelt's appointment as secretary of war under the condition that he would be able to continue supervising U.S. policy toward the Philippines.

As secretary of war, Taft's activities ranged beyond oversight of the army. He visited the Panama Canal site in 1904, negotiated a secret agreement with the Japanese in 1905 pledging noninterference with Japan's affairs in Korea in return for Japan's promise to recognize U.S. influence in the Philippines, served as temporary provisional governor of Cuba in 1906, and oversaw relief efforts after the 1906 San Francisco earthquake. By 1908, Taft's wide government experience, his close friendship with Theodore Roosevelt, and his well-known administrative abilities made him the front-runner for the Republican presidential nomination.

Taft was not anxious to run, but Theodore Roosevelt, Republican Party leaders, and his wife persuaded him to seek the presidency. As Roosevelt's chosen successor Taft won the nomination at the 1908 Republican National Convention in Chicago on the first ballot. He then defeated Democrat William Jennings Bryan 321–162 in the electoral college.

Upon entering office Taft urged Congress to reduce tariffs. The president, however, angered progressive Republicans, who favored lower tariffs, when he signed the Payne-Aldrich Tariff Act of 1909. The act reduced tariff rates by amounts that most progressives considered insignificant.

Taft showed stronger leadership in his pursuit of antitrust cases. Although Theodore Roosevelt is often remembered as the president who first made wide use of the Sherman Antitrust Act to break up monopolies, Taft's administration brought ninety antitrust suits in four years compared with forty-four during Roosevelt's seven-year presidency. The Standard Oil and American Tobacco companies were among those broken up by the Taft administration. Taft also successfully backed the passage of the Sixteenth Amendment, which authorized a federal income tax.

In foreign affairs Taft instituted a policy that came to be known as "dollar diplomacy." This policy sought to use investments and trade to expand U.S. influence abroad, especially in Latin America. Taft also was willing to use force to maintain order and to protect U.S. business interests in Latin America. He dispatched ships and troops to Honduras in 1911 and Nicaragua in 1910 and again in 1912 to protect American lives and property threatened by revolution. These interventions contributed to Latin American resentment toward the United States.

In 1911 Taft negotiated a trade reciprocity agreement with Canada, which significantly lowered tariffs between the two countries, but the Canadian parliament rejected the agreement later in the year. Taft suffered another foreign policy defeat in 1911 when the Senate attached crippling amendments to his treaty with Britain and France that would have established a process of arbitration to settle international disputes between the signatories. Taft withdrew the treaty rather than sign it.

Theodore Roosevelt had been one of the harshest critics of the arbitration treaty during the ratification fight. Roosevelt also criticized Taft for what the former president considered conservative departures from his progressive policies toward big business and the environment.

In 1912 Taft was nominated by the Republican Party for reelection. Roosevelt, who had won most of the Republican primaries that year, protested that he had not received a fair chance to win the nomination at the Republican National Convention, which was controlled by Taft supporters. Roosevelt launched a third party candidacy that doomed Taft's reelection bid. Roosevelt and Taft split the Republican vote, allowing Democrat Woodrow Wilson to capture the presidency. Taft finished in third place with just eight electoral votes.

When Taft's term expired, he accepted a professorship of law at Yale University. While teaching, Taft wrote for law journals and other publications and delivered many lectures around the country. In 1913 he was elected president of the American Bar Association. During World War I President Wilson named him joint chairman of the War Labor Board, which resolved wartime labor disputes.

Although Taft enjoyed his time at Yale, he continued to covet an appointment to the Supreme Court. The election of Taft's friend and fellow Republican Warren G. Harding to the presidency in 1920 opened the door to a Supreme Court appointment. When Chief Justice Edward White died on May 19, 1921, Harding chose Taft to take his place. Taft was a highly capable chief justice who usually rendered moderately conservative opinions. He improved the efficiency of the judicial system and fought successfully for passage of the Judiciary Act of 1925, which increased the Supreme Court's discretion in choosing which cases to accept. As chief justice, Taft administered the presidential oath of office to Calvin Coolidge in 1925 and Herbert Hoover in 1929. Taft resigned as chief justice on February 3, 1930, because of his weak heart. He died a few weeks later from heart failure on March 8.

Taft married Helen Herron June 19, 1886. They had one daughter and two sons. Their oldest son, Robert Alphonso Taft, became one of the most powerful Republicans in the Senate during the late 1940s and early 1950s and was considered as a possible presidential candidate in 1940, 1948, and 1952. Their youngest son, Charles Phelps Taft, served as mayor of Cincinnati from 1955 to 1957.

Woodrow Wilson

BORN: December 28, 1856; Staunton, Virginia
PARTY: Democrat
TERM: March 4, 1913–March 4, 1921
VICE PRESIDENT: Thomas R. Marshall
DIED: February 3, 1924; Washington, D.C.
BURIED: Washington, D.C.

Woodrow Wilson was the third of the four children born to Janet and Joseph Wilson, a Presbyterian minister. When Wilson was two, his family moved from Staunton, Virginia, to Augusta, Georgia, where his father became pastor of the First Presbyterian Church. As a boy Wilson witnessed the destruction of the Civil War. He claimed later in life that his earliest recollection was hearing a passerby tell his father that "Mr. Lincoln was elected and there was to be war." Although Joseph Wilson was originally from Ohio, he had strong Southern sympathies and served as a chaplain to Confederate troops in the area. The war prevented Woodrow from attending school until he was nine. In 1870, the Wilsons moved to Columbia, South Carolina, where his father taught at a seminary.

Wilson, who was originally named Thomas Woodrow,

dropped his first name as a young adult. He enrolled in Davidson College near Charlotte, North Carolina, in 1873. Before the end of the school year, illness forced him to withdraw. After his family moved to Wilmington, North Carolina, he entered Princeton University in 1875. There he earned recognition as a debater, developed a keen interest in government, and decided not to become a minister like his father. After graduation in 1879, he entered law school at the University of Virginia, but in 1880 poor health again forced him to abandon school. He finished his law degree through independent study while living in Wilmington and was admitted to the bar in 1882. He established a law partnership in Atlanta with a law school friend but quit the profession in 1883 to enroll in Johns Hopkins University as a graduate student of history and government.

EDUCATOR AND GOVERNOR

At Johns Hopkins, Wilson distinguished himself as a brilliant student. In 1885 he published his first book, *Congressional Government*, which argued that Congress had become the dominant branch of government and that it should adopt a system of governing patterned after the British Parliament. The book received critical acclaim and served as Wilson's dissertation. In 1885 Bryn Mawr College near Philadelphia hired Wilson as an associate professor of history. He was awarded his doctorate degree in 1886.

Wilson moved to Wesleyan University in Middletown, Connecticut, in 1888. There he taught history and political science and coached the football team. In 1890 he accepted a professorship at Princeton University. In 1902 Princeton's trustees unanimously elected him president of the university.

Wilson regarded his new job as an opportunity to implement his ideas about education. He introduced a system providing for small scholarly discussion groups and close faculty supervision of students. His most cherished reform, however, was his plan to reorganize the residential structure of the college around quadrangle units that he believed would refocus the life of the college away from social and sporting activities toward academics. His "quad plan" was opposed by Princeton's private clubs, which Wilson regarded as bastions of the privileged. Although Wilson's quad plan was eventually rejected, he became known as a crusader for democratic principles in education.

New Jersey's Democratic Party leaders proposed to Wilson that he run for governor in 1910. They hoped the notoriety he had gained while president of Princeton and his eloquence could carry him to the New Jersey statehouse. Once elected, party leaders expected to be able to dominate the scholarly Wilson, who had no political experience. Wilson accepted on condition that he would not have to fulfill any promises of patronage. He resigned from Princeton and was elected governor.

Once in office Wilson quickly demonstrated that he was swayed by no one and was in complete control. He pushed a series of reforms through the legislature that attracted national attention including laws establishing direct primaries, worker's compensation, and antitrust measures. His efforts also led to improved regulation of utilities and the reorganization of the public school system. By 1912 Democrats were considering him as a potential presidential candidate.

Wilson entered the 1912 Democratic National Convention in Baltimore as an underdog to Speaker of the House Champ Clark. Although Clark led Wilson in the early ballots, he could not muster a majority. On the fourteenth ballot Democratic patriarch William Jennings Bryan abandoned Clark to support Wilson. On the forty-sixth ballot Wilson was finally nominated.

Wilson's election to the presidency was virtually sealed when Teddy Roosevelt split the Republican Party by running for president as the candidate of the Progressive Party. Of the fifteen million votes cast, Wilson received only 6.3 million, but Republicans divided their votes between Roosevelt and President William Howard Taft. Wilson received 435 electoral votes, while Roosevelt and Taft received 88 and 8 votes, respectively.

PRESIDENCY

Once in office, Wilson demonstrated the same independence and innovation he had shown as governor and university president. He delivered his first annual message to Congress in person on April 8, 1913, which no president had done since John Adams. He also established weekly press conferences.

Wilson fulfilled a campaign promise to lower tariffs by signing the Underwood Tariff Act of 1913. The act cut tariff rates to their lowest levels since before the Civil War and provided for the levying of the first income tax since the Sixteenth Amendment had made such taxes legal. At Wilson's urging Congress passed the Federal Reserve Act of 1913, which created a system of regional federal banks to regulate currency and the banking industry. He supported the establishment of the Federal Trade Commission in 1914 to ensure fair business practices. That year he also signed the Clayton Anti-Trust Act, which strengthened the government's powers to break up monopolies. In 1916 Congress passed the Adamson Act at Wilson's request, which established the eight-hour day for railroad workers.

When World War I began in 1914, Wilson announced that the United States would stay out of the conflict. German submarines in the Atlantic Ocean, however, were not observing U.S. neutrality. In May 1915, a German submarine sank the British passenger ship *Lusitania* with more than one hundred Americans aboard. The incident led Wilson to issue several diplomatic protests, until the Germans agreed not to prey on passenger ships and to place other restrictions on their submarine warfare.

In 1916 Wilson did not have the luxury of facing a divided Republican Party as he had in 1912. The Republicans nominated Supreme Court justice Charles Evans Hughes, and Theodore Roosevelt declined a second third party candidacy to campaign for the Republican nominee. Wilson campaigned on his domestic accomplishments and his success in keeping the United States out of war. In one of the closest presidential elections in history, Wilson defeated Hughes 277–254 in the electoral college. Had Wilson lost any of the ten states he won with twelve or more electoral votes he would have lost the election.

Wilson, who tried to mediate an end to the war in Europe, called on January 22, 1917, for a "peace without victory" that would end the fighting and the establishment of a league of nations, an international body that would prevent and settle disputes between members. A week after Wilson's speech, however, the Germans, who expected the United States to enter the war soon, announced they would attack without warning any ship passing through a wide zone in the Atlantic. Wilson responded to the submarine offensive by severing diplomatic relations with Germany on February 3. When the Germans continued their submarine warfare in defiance of Wilson's protests, he asked Congress on April 2, 1917, for a declaration of war. Within four days both houses had overwhelmingly passed the declaration.

Congress delegated broad powers to Wilson to marshal the nations resources, build an army, and prosecute the war. He pushed the Selective Service Act through Congress, took control of the railroads, established the War Industries Board to oversee the economy, and instituted many other emergency measures.

With the addition of U.S. troops on the Allied side, the war went badly for Germany. An armistice was signed on November 11, 1918. After U.S. entry into the war, Wilson had outlined a plan for territorial adjustment and maintenance of world peace once the war was over. The basis of this plan was his "Fourteen Points," which included freedom of the seas, removal of trade barriers, an end to secret treaties, and a reduction of armaments. *(See "Wilson's 'Fourteen Points' Speech," p. 1594, in Reference Materials.)*

In December 1918, Wilson sailed to France to attend the Versailles peace conference. Europeans hailed the American president as a hero, and he dominated the deliberations of the Allies. Nevertheless, he was forced to make many concessions to European leaders to gain their endorsement of his Fourteen Points and the League of Nations. The treaty produced by the conference imposed a harsh peace on Germany that included heavy war reparations and the loss of its colonies.

Wilson submitted the Treaty of Versailles to the Senate for approval on July 10, 1919, but he could not persuade two-thirds of the Senate to support it. A group of senators led by Republican Henry Cabot Lodge of Massachusetts objected to the provision within the treaty establishing the League of Nations and would not vote for the treaty without attaching reservations that Wilson believed nullified the agreement. On September 4, 1919, Wilson launched a speaking tour of the western states designed to mobilize public support for the treaty. On September 26, after delivering speeches in twenty-nine cities, Wilson became ill in Pueblo, Colorado, and was forced to cancel the rest of his speaking tour. He returned to Washington, D.C., where he suffered a severe stroke on October 2.

The stroke left the president almost entirely incapacitated for several months, and he never completely recovered his strength. While Wilson recuperated, the Senate debated the Treaty of Versailles. Senators split into three major groups: those who supported the treaty, those who sided with Lodge in supporting it only if major reservations were attached, and those who were opposed to the treaty in any form. Wilson refused to compromise with Lodge to gain passage of the treaty and advised his supporters against accepting it with Lodge's reservations. The Senate rejected the treaty on November 19, 1919. Exactly four months later Senate Republican leaders again brought the treaty to a vote in the hope that Democrats would support the Lodge reservations. Democrats in the Senate, however, remained loyal to Wilson and rejected the amended treaty again, while the Republicans blocked the passage of the treaty in its original form. Wilson declared that the American people should decide the issue in the 1920 presidential contest. The public, however, overwhelmingly elected Republican Warren G. Harding over Democrat James M. Cox. Harding refused to back the treaty, and Wilson's fight for U.S. entry into the League of Nations was finished.

When Wilson left office he retired to a home on S Street in Washington, D.C. He formed a law partnership but did not practice. He lived in near seclusion until he died on February 3, 1924, from another stroke.

Wilson married Ellen Louise Axson, the daughter of a Presbyterian minister, on June 24, 1885. They had three daughters. Ellen died on August 6, 1914, in the White House. On December 18, 1915, Wilson married Edith Bolling Galt, a forty-three-year-old widow. After Wilson suffered his stroke in 1919, Edith restricted access to her husband. During Wilson's convalescence he conducted much of his presidential business through Edith. Historians have speculated that she may have made many presidential decisions for her husband.

Warren G. Harding

BORN: November 2, 1865; Corsica, Ohio (now Blooming Grove)

PARTY: Republican

TERM: March 4, 1921–August 2, 1923

VICE PRESIDENT: Calvin Coolidge

DIED: August 2, 1923; San Francisco, California

BURIED: Marion, Ohio

Warren Gamaliel Harding was the oldest of the eight children of Phoebe and George Harding, who owned a farm in north central Ohio. Warren did farm chores and attended local schools as a boy. He attended tiny Ohio Central College in Iberia, where he edited the school newspaper.

After Harding's graduation in 1882, he taught in a country school for one term, before giving up the profession and moving to Marion, Ohio. There he tried selling insurance and worked briefly for the *Marion Mirror* as a reporter. In 1884 he and two friends bought the *Marion Star,* a bankrupt, four-page newspaper. Harding bought out his friends in 1886 when they lost interest in the enterprise. Gradually, he made the paper a financial success and a political force in Ohio.

In 1892 Harding ran for county auditor but was defeated badly by his Democratic opponent. He remained active in state politics, however, frequently making campaign speeches for Republican candidates. In 1899 he ran for the state senate and was victorious. He won a second term in 1901 and was elected lieutenant governor in 1903. Two years later, however, he refused to be renominated for lieutenant governor in favor of returning to manage his paper in Marion.

In 1909, Harding ran for governor of Ohio but was defeated. He gained national prominence in June 1912 when he delivered the speech nominating William Howard Taft for president at the Republican National Convention in Chicago. Two years later, he ran for the U.S. Senate. After winning the Republican Party's first direct primary for senator in Ohio, Harding was elected.

As a senator, Harding followed the party line, made many friends, and avoided controversy. He frequently missed role calls and did not introduce any important legislation. He voted for Prohibition and women's suffrage but against the Versailles treaty. Much of his time in the capital was spent drinking, playing poker, and developing political allies.

Harding took his undistinguished record to the 1920 Republican National Convention in Chicago. His was one of many names entered into nomination for president, but he was not among the favorites in the early balloting. After four ballots, none of the front-runners could muster a majority of support. Fearing a deadlock that would threaten party unity, Republican leaders retired to a "smoke-filled room" at the Blackstone Hotel. At the urging of Harding's close friend and political mentor,

Harry Daugherty, they decided to give the nomination to Harding, who possessed good looks, an amiable personality, and a willingness to be led by the party.

During a "front porch" campaign reminiscent of William McKinley's 1896 campaign, Harding promised a "return to normalcy" after the Wilson years. This promise appealed to American voters, who had lived through a difficult period during World War I and were skeptical of outgoing president Woodrow Wilson's internationalist idealism. In the first presidential election in which women could vote, Harding defeated James M. Cox in a landslide, receiving over sixteen million votes to his opponent's nine million. Harding received 404 electoral votes, while Cox managed to win just eleven states, all in the South, for a total of 127 electoral votes.

In 1919 and 1920 the Senate had rejected Woodrow Wilson's Versailles treaty ending World War I because that body objected to U.S. membership in the League of Nations. Consequently, a separate agreement was needed to make formal the end of the war. In 1921 the Harding administration concluded treaties with Germany, Austria, and Hungary, officially making peace with those nations. In 1921, Harding also called the Washington Disarmament Conference. This meeting, masterminded by Secretary of State Charles Evans Hughes, succeeded in producing a treaty that reduced the navies of the United States, Great Britain, France, Germany, Japan, and Italy.

In domestic policy, Harding cut taxes on high incomes and signed the Fordney-McCumber Act, which raised tariff rates that had been lowered during the Wilson administration. A lasting contribution to U.S. government left by Harding was the Bureau of the Budget (now the Office of Management and Budget), which was created by the Budget Act of 1921.

Harding's administration is best known, however, for the scandals that were revealed after his death. Harding appointed to high government posts many friends and cronies who used their position for personal enrichment. Harding is not known to have participated in the crimes committed by his associates and advisers, but he did little to prevent the corruption within his administration. One of the most famous scandals involved Secretary of the Interior Albert Fall's leasing of government oil reserves at Teapot Dome, Wyoming, and Elk Hills, California, to private interests for a bribe. Fall was later fined and imprisoned for his actions. Secretary of the Navy Edwin Denby, Attorney General Harry Daugherty, and Charles Forbes, head of the Veterans Bureau, also were found to have participated in the scandals.

When the Republicans lost seats in both houses of Congress in the 1922 midterm election, Harding decided to go on a speaking tour in early 1923 to boost his party's and his own popularity. It is also probable that Harding wished to leave Washington to escape the developing rumors about the scandals within his administration.

In Seattle after visiting Alaska, Harding was stricken with pains that were diagnosed as indigestion but which may have been a heart attack. Harding improved but then died suddenly in San Francisco. His doctors suspected a blood clot in the brain may have killed him, but his wife refused to permit an autopsy. The absence of conclusive evidence about his death and the subsequent revelations of scandals led to public speculation that he may have committed suicide or been poisoned, but no evidence of an unnatural death exists. The news of Harding's death brought an outpouring of public grief, and he lay in state at the White House. As details of the scandals of his administration became known in 1923 and 1924, however, Harding's public reputation declined.

Harding married Florence Kling De Wolfe, a divorcee five years his senior, on July 8, 1891, in Marion, Ohio. The couple had no children but raised Florence's child by her first marriage. Harding carried on an affair with Nan Britton, a woman thirty years younger than he, whom he had known since he edited the *Marion Star*. When Harding was a senator, he helped Britton get a job in New York and often visited her. They had one daughter, who was born on October 22, 1919. Britton disclosed the affair three years after Harding's death in her book *The President's Daughter*.

Calvin Coolidge

BORN: July 4, 1872; Plymouth Notch, Vermont
PARTY: Republican
TERM: August 3, 1923–March 4, 1929
VICE PRESIDENT: Charles G. Dawes
DIED: January 5, 1933; Northampton, Massachusetts
BURIED: Plymouth, Vermont

Calvin Coolidge was the oldest of the two children of Victoria and John Coolidge, who farmed and owned a general store. Calvin was originally named John Calvin after his father, but he dropped his first name when he became an adult. As a boy, Calvin worked on the family farm and attended local public schools. His mother died in 1885 when he was twelve. His younger sister, Abigail, died five years later at the age of fifteen.

As a teenager, Coolidge attended Black River Academy, a local private preparatory school, graduating in 1890. He wanted to attend Amherst College but failed the school's entrance exam that year. He gained admission to Amherst after taking additional courses at St. Johnsbury Academy, another prep school. Coolidge graduated cum laude from Amherst in 1895.

After graduation Coolidge moved to nearby Northampton, Massachusetts, where he got a job as a law clerk. He was admitted to the bar in 1897, started his own law practice, and became involved in Northampton politics as a Republican. He served as a member of the city council, city solicitor, and chairman of the county Republican committee. He suffered his only political defeat in 1905 when he was beaten for a seat on the Northampton school board. In 1906, however, he was elected to the Massachusetts House of Representatives. After two terms, he returned to Northampton in 1909 and was elected mayor the following year.

In 1911 Coolidge won a seat in the state senate. After four one-year terms he was elected lieutenant governor in 1915. He

served three one-year terms in this office before being elected governor by a slim margin in 1918.

In September 1919, the Boston police staged a strike that opened the way for a criminal rampage. After two days, Governor Coolidge called out the state militia to keep order in Boston. When Samuel Gompers, head of the American Federation of Labor, accused Coolidge of acting unfairly, Coolidge sent him a wire declaring, "There is no right to strike against the public safety by anybody, anywhere, any time." The statement made Coolidge famous across the country.

Although Coolidge was one of many Republicans whose name was placed in nomination for the presidency at the 1920 Republican National Convention in Chicago, he was not a leading candidate for the nomination. The convention was deadlocked between several candidates during the early balloting but eventually turned to Sen. Warren G. Harding of Ohio as a compromise candidate. Harding had been chosen by party leaders who expected their choice for vice president, Wisconsin senator Irvine Lenroot, to be similarly ratified by the convention. When Coolidge's name was put into nomination for vice president after Lenroot's, however, the convention unexpectedly threw its support behind the popular governor. Coolidge received 674 votes to Lenroot's 146 and was chosen on the first ballot.

During the 1920 campaign, Harding and Coolidge promised to raise tariffs to protect U.S. industry and to keep the country out of war and entangling alliances. They won more than 60 percent of the popular vote on their way to a 404–127 victory in the electoral college over Democrats James M. Cox and Franklin D. Roosevelt.

In 1923 Vice President Coolidge was spending the summer in Vermont when a telegraph messenger arrived at his home after midnight on August 3 with the news that President Harding had unexpectedly died in San Francisco. Coolidge's father, who was a notary public, administered the oath of office. The next day Coolidge left for Washington.

Coolidge retained Harding's cabinet, but when the scandals that pervaded the Harding administration were revealed, he asked for the resignations of those involved, including Secretary of the Navy Edwin Denby and Attorney General Harry Daugherty. Coolidge dutifully prosecuted the former Harding administration officials who had committed crimes.

As president, Coolidge quickly became a symbol of simple, practical leadership. Coolidge was fondly called "Silent Cal" by the public because of his quiet, almost sphinxlike demeanor. He was an honest and successful administrator who made the national government more efficient and economical.

Coolidge ran for reelection in 1924 against John W. Davis. Despite the scandals of the Harding administration, Coolidge's personal honesty, his small-town image, and national prosperity carried him to victory. He defeated Davis in the electoral college, 382–136.

During his second term, Coolidge was successful in decreasing the national debt and cutting income taxes. These policies put more money into the hands of consumers and helped stimulate investment. Coolidge's hands-off policies toward business activities, however, deferred needed reforms of the financial industry and encouraged overspeculation that contributed to the stock market crash of 1929 and the subsequent depression.

In foreign relations, Coolidge reestablished diplomatic relations with Mexico severed under Woodrow Wilson and improved relations with other Latin American nations that had been strained since the turn of the century. Although Coolidge opposed U.S. entry into the League of Nations, he backed the multilateral Kellogg-Briand Pact of 1928, which naively outlawed war between nations.

After leaving office, Coolidge retired to Northampton, Massachusetts, where he bought Beeches, a nine-acre estate. During his short retirement Coolidge wrote newspaper columns and served on the board of directors of the New York Life Insurance Company. In January 1933, less than four years after leaving the White House, Coolidge died of a heart attack.

Coolidge married Grace Goodhue on October 4, 1905. Grace had been a teacher at Clarke Institute for the Deaf in Northampton. She died in Northampton in 1957 at the age of 78. The couple had two sons. Their younger son, Calvin Jr., died in 1924 after developing blood poisoning from a blister formed while playing tennis on the White House court.

Herbert Hoover

BORN: August 10, 1874; West Branch, Iowa
PARTY: Republican
TERM: March 4, 1929–March 4, 1933
VICE PRESIDENT: Charles Curtis
DIED: October 20, 1964; New York City
BURIED: West Branch

Herbert Clark Hoover was the second of the three children of Jesse and Huldah Hoover. His father, a blacksmith and farm implement merchant, died of typhoid when Herbert was six. When his mother died of pneumonia two years later, he was sent to Oregon to live with an aunt and uncle, who were Quakers like his parents. Herbert attended public schools and worked in his uncle's land settlement office in Salem. He also attended a local business school, where he sharpened his math skills and learned to type.

Hoover took entrance examinations to gain admission to Stanford University, an engineering school being established in California. Despite uneven education, his impressive math skills earned him a spot in Stanford's first freshman class in 1891. Hoover worked his way through college, earning his degree in 1895. After laboring for a few months at a menial mining job in

Nevada, Hoover went to San Francisco. There he worked as a typist before an international mining company hired him in 1897 as an engineering assistant. During the next seventeen years, Hoover managed mines in Africa, Asia, Europe, Australia, and the United States. Before the age of forty, he was one of the world's most successful mining engineers and worth several million dollars.

In 1914 when World War I began Hoover was living in London. He served as chairman of a committee of Americans who helped U.S. tourists stranded in Europe to secure passage home. He then became chairman of the Commission for Relief in Belgium, a private charity group. In this capacity he raised funds to aid the people of that war-torn country and made arrangements with the warring nations to distribute the aid.

When the U.S. Congress declared war on Germany in 1917, Hoover returned to the United States, where President Woodrow Wilson appointed him U.S. food administrator. In this post Hoover was responsible for stimulating food production and distributing and conserving food supplies. In 1918 Hoover was appointed chairman of the Allied Food Council, which distributed food to millions of Europeans left impoverished by the war. After the war Hoover attended the Versailles Peace Conference as an economic adviser to President Wilson.

Hoover's relief activities made him one of the most famous and admired Americans of his day and a prospective candidate for public office. But his political affiliation was unclear because he had supported Republican Theodore Roosevelt's third party candidacy in 1912 and had worked closely with President Wilson, a Democrat. In 1920, however, Hoover declared that he was a Republican and received some support for the party's presidential nomination, which eventually went to Warren G. Harding.

When Harding was elected president, he appointed Hoover secretary of commerce over the objections of Republican conservatives who regarded Hoover as a liberal. Hoover remained in this post for eight years. He reorganized the department and helped solidify the progress toward an eight-hour workday and a prohibition against child labor. He also became a close economic adviser to both President Harding and Vice President Calvin Coolidge, but he remained free of the scandals that plagued their administration.

Hoover was the popular choice of Republicans for the party's presidential nomination in 1928. Despite the opposition of some conservative party leaders, Hoover was nominated at the Kansas City Republican National Convention on the first ballot. He then won the general election over Democrat Al Smith of New York. Hoover received more than twenty-one million popular votes to Smith's fifteen million. Hoover even captured several traditionally Democratic southern states on his way to a 444–87 electoral vote victory.

Hoover had run on a Republican platform that took credit for the prosperity achieved during the 1920s. Ironically, seven months after Hoover's inauguration the October 1929 stock market crash began the economic depression that left about a quarter of the work force unemployed. After the crash Hoover tried to assure the nation that the economy was sound and that business activity would soon recover, but the depression grew worse during his term. Although he had not created the conditions that caused the depression, many Americans blamed him for it.

Hoover tried to fight the growing depression through limited public works projects, increased government loans to banks and businesses, reductions in the already low income tax, and personal appeals to industry to maintain wages and production levels. But these measures did little to ease the country's economic problems. Hoover's preoccupation with balancing the budget and his belief that federal relief violated the American principle of self-reliance prevented him from taking more sweeping actions. Thus, he opposed federal benefit programs to help the poor and unemployed and deficit spending that would have created jobs. He reluctantly signed the Smoot-Hawley Act of 1930, which dramatically raised tariff rates to protect U.S. industries, thereby initiating a trade war that hurt the American and world economies.

Hoover was nominated by the Republicans for a second term but the nation, desperate for relief from the depression, turned against him. His Democratic opponent, Franklin D. Roosevelt, won in a landslide.

Hoover returned to his home in Palo Alto, California, in March 1933. During Franklin Roosevelt's presidency Hoover actively criticized Roosevelt's New Deal programs and the U.S. alliance with the Soviet Union during World War II.

In 1946 President Harry S. Truman tapped Hoover's famine relief experience by appointing him chairman of the Famine Emergency Commission, which was charged with preventing starvation in post–World War II Europe. In 1947 Truman appointed Hoover chairman of the Commission on Organization of the Executive Branch of the Government. The "Hoover Commission" recommended hundreds of organizational changes, many of which were adopted, to make the executive branch more efficient. The commission submitted its final report in 1949, but in 1953 President Dwight D. Eisenhower appointed Hoover to chair a second commission on government organization. The second Hoover Commission functioned until 1955.

Hoover retired from government service after 1955 but continued to write on politics and speak at Republican conventions. In 1964 he died in New York City at the age of ninety. He had the second-longest life of any president, with John Adams living 136 days longer.

Hoover married Lou Henry, a fellow student at Stanford and the daughter of a Monterey, California, banker, on February 10, 1899. Their two sons, Herbert Jr. and Allan, were born while the Hoovers lived in London. Herbert served as under secretary of state from 1954 to 1957.

Franklin D. Roosevelt

BORN: January 30, 1882; Hyde Park, New York
PARTY: Democratic
TERM: March 4, 1933–April 12, 1945
VICE PRESIDENTS: John N. Garner; Henry A. Wallace; Harry S. Truman
DIED: April 12, 1945; Warm Springs, Georgia
BURIED: Hyde Park

Franklin Delano Roosevelt was the son of James and Sara Roosevelt. He was his mother's only child, but his father, a widower, had a son by his first wife. James Roosevelt was a wealthy lawyer and railroad executive who had inherited a fortune. Sara was also from a wealthy family and had married the fifty-two-year-old James when she was just twenty-six. She and James's first son were both born in 1854.

Franklin lived a sheltered early life. He received his elementary education from private tutors and traveled frequently with his family to Europe. At age fourteen Franklin enrolled in Groton, a private preparatory school in Groton, Massachusetts. After four years there he entered Harvard University in 1900. Although Franklin did not have a distinguished academic record, he graduated in three years and became editor of the campus newspaper.

Roosevelt stayed a fourth year at Harvard as a graduate student of history and economics. He then studied law at Columbia from 1904 until 1907 but left without graduating when he passed the bar. A New York City firm hired him as a law clerk.

POLITICAL CAREER

In 1910 Roosevelt ran for the New York State Senate as a Democrat from a traditionally Republican district and surprised Democratic Party leaders when he won. He was reelected in 1912 but gave up his seat in 1913, when President Woodrow Wilson appointed him assistant secretary of the navy, a post once held by his distant relative Theodore Roosevelt.

After war broke out in Europe in 1914, Roosevelt argued for greater military preparedness. When the United States entered the war, he twice asked Wilson to transfer him to active service, but the president turned him down saying he was needed where he was. Roosevelt made several trips to Europe to inspect U.S. naval forces. Near the end of the war he developed a plan to hinder German submarine attacks. His "North Sea Mine Barrage," a 240-mile cordon of antisubmarine mines in the Atlantic, reduced allied shipping losses and helped hasten the armistice.

In 1920 Roosevelt resigned from the Navy Department when the Democratic Party nominated him for the vice presidency on the ticket with presidential nominee James M. Cox. Democrats hoped that the promising young politician with the famous name could give the ticket a boost, but Cox and Roosevelt were beaten badly by Republicans Warren Harding and Calvin Coolidge.

After the defeat, Roosevelt became a partner in a New York City law firm and accepted a vice presidency in the Fidelity and Deposit Company of Maryland, a surety bond firm.

In 1921 Roosevelt suffered a personal tragedy. While vacationing in New Brunswick he was stricken with poliomyelitis. The attack left him severely crippled and his mother urged him to give up politics and retire to the family estate at Hyde Park. Roosevelt, however, struggled to rehabilitate himself. Over a period of years he built up his arms and chest and eventually was able to walk short distances with the aid of crutches and braces.

On June 26, 1924, Roosevelt returned to national politics when he delivered the presidential nomination speech for New York governor Alfred E. Smith at the Democratic National Convention in New York City. Smith did not receive the nomination, but Roosevelt's courageous appearance on crutches at Madison Square Garden increased his popularity and made him a leading figure in the Democratic Party. Later that year Roosevelt vacationed in Warm Springs, Georgia, where he hoped to regain the use of his legs by swimming in a natural pool of warm spring water. He made numerous trips to Warm Springs during the rest of his life. In 1927 he founded the Georgia Warm Springs Foundation, an inexpensive treatment center for polio victims.

Al Smith, nominated for president in 1928, urged Roosevelt to run for governor in New York to give the Democratic ticket a boost. Roosevelt at first declined, saying he wanted to concen-

trate on rehabilitating his legs, but he finally agreed to run when he was nominated by acclamation. Questions of Roosevelt's physical ability to function as governor were dispelled by his vigorous campaigning, often conducted from an automobile. Roosevelt won the election despite Republican presidential candidate Herbert Hoover's victory in New York.

As governor, Roosevelt gave tax relief to New York's farmers and lowered the cost of public utilities to consumers. He was reelected in a landslide in 1930. During his second term he concentrated on easing the suffering caused by the depression.

Roosevelt's success as governor made him a leading candidate for the Democratic presidential nomination in 1932. He entered the convention with a majority of delegates, but he had fewer than the two-thirds necessary to win the nomination. After three ballots he offered to endorse rival John Nance Garner, the Texan Speaker of the House, for vice president, if Garner released his presidential delegates. Garner, recognizing his chances of being nominated for president were slim, accepted the deal and released his ninety delegates to Roosevelt, who was nominated on the fourth ballot. The convention then nominated Garner for vice president.

During the campaign of 1932, Roosevelt exuded confidence and outlined his recovery program, which he called the "New Deal." Although he faced incumbent Republican president Herbert Hoover in the election, Roosevelt was favored to win because many voters blamed Hoover for the severity of the Great Depression. Roosevelt outpolled Hoover by more than seven million votes and won 472–59 in the electoral college.

Before Roosevelt was inaugurated, he became the only president-elect to be the target of an assassination attempt. After Roosevelt had delivered a speech in Florida on February 14, 1933, Giuseppe Zangara, an unemployed bricklayer, fired six shots from a handgun at Roosevelt from twelve yards away. The president-elect, who was sitting in an open car, was uninjured but five other people were shot, including Chicago mayor Anton Cernak, who was killed. Zangara, who had a pathological hatred for rich and powerful figures, was found guilty of murder and electrocuted.

PRESIDENCY

Roosevelt took office at the low point of the depression. Most of the nation's banks were closed, industrial production was about half of what it had been in 1928, and as many as 15 million people were unemployed. Roosevelt worked with the new Democratic Congress to enact many New Deal bills during the productive opening period of his presidency, known as the "First Hundred Days." He declared a four-day bank holiday to stop panic withdrawals, abandoned the gold standard, increased government loans to farmers and homeowners, and created federal bank deposit insurance. At Roosevelt's urging, Congress created the Civilian Conservation Corps, which employed tens of thousands of people on conservation projects and passed the Federal Emergency Relief Act, which provided grants to state and local governments for aid to the unemployed. Numerous other measures were passed during the First Hundred Days, which increased public confidence and stimulated the economy.

Business interests feared that the deficit spending required to finance the New Deal would lead to inflation, but injection of federal money into the economy eased the depression. Roosevelt promoted his policies through "fireside chats," radio addresses to the nation from the White House. A second wave of New Deal programs, including Social Security, unemployment insurance, and federal aid to dependent children, was passed in 1934 and 1935.

Roosevelt's New Deal successes made him a popular president. He defeated Kansas governor Alfred M. Landon in the 1936 presidential election in one of the largest landslides in presidential election history. Landon won only Maine and Vermont.

In 1937 Roosevelt suffered one of the biggest defeats of his presidency and squandered political capital won in the 1936 election when he proposed to expand the Supreme Court from nine to as many as fifteen justices. Roosevelt had been frustrated by the conservative court, which had struck down several of his New Deal measures. If the Court were expanded he could appoint justices who would accept his policies. Neither the public nor Congress, however, would go along with Roosevelt's court-packing scheme. Moreover, the episode hardened resistance to the New Deal from Republicans and conservative Democrats.

In 1940 Roosevelt ran for an unprecedented third term against the progressive Republican nominee, Wendell Willkie of Indiana. Roosevelt defeated Willkie 449 to 82 in the electoral college. His popular margin of victory narrowed from four years before, however, in part because some voters objected to Roosevelt's disregard of the unwritten rule that presidents should serve no more than two terms.

In September 1939 Adolph Hitler's Germany had invaded Poland, starting World War II in Europe. Despite strong neutralist sentiments among members of Congress and the general public, Roosevelt recognized that U.S. national security depended on Great Britain's survival. He promised to keep the United States out of the fighting but pressed for the authority to aid Britain and other allied nations in every way short of going to war. In September 1940 Roosevelt violated two neutrality statutes in trading Great Britain fifty outdated destroyers for the right to lease certain British territory in the western Atlantic for U.S. naval and air bases. In March 1941 Roosevelt persuaded Congress to pass the Lend-Lease Act, which gave the president the power to supply weapons and equipment to "any country whose defense the president deems vital to the defense of the United States." In September of that year, Roosevelt ordered U.S. warships providing protection for supply convoys bound for Britain to attack German vessels on sight. Thus, Roosevelt had engaged the United States in an undeclared naval war months before the nation would enter the war.

On December 7, 1941, the Japanese launched a surprise attack against the U.S. fleet at Pearl Harbor, Hawaii. The next day Roosevelt asked for and received a declaration of war from Congress. Roosevelt shifted his focus and national resources from New Deal reforms to winning the war.

Roosevelt oversaw the development of military strategy and conferred often with British prime minister Winston Churchill. Roosevelt and Churchill met with Soviet leader Joseph Stalin at Tehran in 1943 and Yalta in 1945. At these meetings, the leaders of the three principal Allied nations not only discussed wartime strategy, they planned for the postwar order. At Yalta Roosevelt secured a Soviet promise to enter the war against Japan when Germany was defeated in return for territorial concessions in Asia. The allies also set new Polish borders, scheduled a conference in 1945 to establish the United Nations, and agreed to allow occupied countries to construct new governments based on free elections after the war. Many historians have criticized Roosevelt for being too trusting of Stalin, who established communist puppet states in Eastern Europe after the war.

Although the strain of the wartime presidency had weakened Roosevelt, he ran for a fourth term in 1944. In a fateful move he agreed to the suggestion of his political advisers to drop his third-term vice president Henry A. Wallace, who was considered too liberal. The Democrats nominated Sen. Harry S. Truman from Missouri for vice president in Wallace's place. Roosevelt defeated his fourth Republican opponent, New York governor Thomas E. Dewey, 432–99 in the electoral college.

In April 1945, after returning from Yalta, Roosevelt went to Warm Springs, Georgia, for a rest before the conference on the establishment of the United Nations scheduled for later in the month in San Francisco. On April 12, while sitting for a portrait at his cottage, Roosevelt suddenly collapsed from a cerebral hemorrhage and died a few hours later. The same day in Washington, Truman was sworn in as president. The world mourned the dead president as a train carried his body back to the capital, where it lay in state at the White House. The train then resumed its journey north to Roosevelt's Hyde Park home, where he was buried.

Roosevelt married Anna Eleanor Roosevelt, a fifth cousin, on March 17, 1905. Eleanor's mother and father died when she was a child, so she was given away at her wedding by her father's brother, President Theodore Roosevelt. The Roosevelts had one daughter and five sons, one of whom died in infancy. Eleanor is regarded as the most active first lady in history up to her time. Besides promoting numerous social causes, she served as her crippled husband's representative at many political and ceremonial functions. After the president's death Eleanor continued to fight for social causes. She died on November 7, 1962.

Harry S. Truman

BORN: May 8, 1884; Lamar, Missouri
PARTY: Democratic
TERM: April 12, 1945–January 20, 1953
VICE PRESIDENT: Alben W. Barkley
DIED: December 26, 1972; Kansas City, Missouri
BURIED: Independence, Missouri

Harry S. Truman was the oldest of three children born to Martha and John Truman, a mule trader. Harry's parents wanted to give him a middle name in honor of a grandfather but could not decide between his two grandfathers, Anderson Shippe Truman and Solomon Young. Consequently they gave him the middle initial "S," which stood for nothing.

After living in several towns in Missouri, the Trumans settled in Independence, near Kansas City. Harry's poor eyesight prevented him from joining in some outdoor activities as a boy. Instead he learned to play the piano and became a voracious reader. At the age of sixteen he had his first political experience when he worked as a page at the 1900 Democratic National Convention in Kansas City, which nominated William Jennings Bryan for president.

After graduating from high school Truman held a succession of jobs, including mail room clerk, bank teller, and bookkeeper. He wanted to go to college, but he and his family could not afford it. In 1906, when Truman was twenty-two, he took over the management of his grandmother's 600-acre farm in Grandview, Missouri. He succeeded at farming and became active in local politics and community organizations.

When the United States entered World War I, Truman received a commission as a first lieutenant. He served with distinction in the Vosges and Meuse-Argonne campaigns as commander of an artillery battery and attained the rank of major before leaving the service in 1919.

POLITICAL CAREER

Upon returning to Missouri, Truman opened a haberdashery in Kansas City with a war buddy. When the store failed in 1922 he ran for judge of the eastern district of Jackson County. He won the election with the support of the powerful Kansas City political boss Tom Pendergast. He failed in his bid for reelection two years later but was elected presiding judge of the court in 1926 and was reelected in 1930. These judgeships were administrative rather than judicial positions. Truman controlled hundreds of patronage jobs and millions of dollars' worth of public works projects.

Truman became well known in the Kansas City area. He retained his close connections to Pendergast and the Kansas City machine but also developed a reputation for honesty. Using his Kansas City political base, Truman launched a campaign for the U.S. Senate and was elected in 1934.

In the Senate Truman supported Franklin D. Roosevelt's New Deal legislation. Despite the conviction of Tom Pendergast for income tax evasion, Truman was reelected by a narrow margin in 1940. During his second term, Truman chaired the Special Committee to Investigate the National Defense Program, which sought to eliminate waste and inefficiency among defense contractors. He also supported Roosevelt's efforts to aid the allies before the entry of the United States into World War II.

In 1944 the Democratic Party was set to nominate President Franklin Roosevelt for his fourth term, but the vice-presidential nomination remained in doubt. Vice President Henry Wallace had alienated many Democratic Party leaders, who considered his political views too liberal. Robert Hannegan, national chairman of the Democratic Party, recommended to Roosevelt that Truman be nominated in place of Wallace, and the president agreed. Truman was nominated for vice president on the second ballot at the Democratic National Convention in Chicago. Roosevelt and Truman then defeated Republicans Thomas E. Dewey and John W. Bricker in the general election.

PRESIDENCY

Truman served just eighty-two days as vice president. On April 12, 1945, he was summoned to the White House and informed by First Lady Eleanor Roosevelt that the president was dead. Later in the day he took the oath of office at the White House from Chief Justice Harlan F. Stone.

World events forced Truman to become an expert in foreign affairs, an area of policy in which he had little experience before becoming president. Truman's first priority was winning World War II. On May 7 Germany surrendered unconditionally to the allies. In July 1945 Truman traveled to Potsdam, Germany, to discuss the composition of the postwar world with British prime minister Winston Churchill and Soviet premier Joseph Stalin. There the three leaders agreed to divide Germany and its capital, Berlin, into occupation zones.

While at Potsdam, Truman was informed that the United States had successfully tested an atomic bomb. He authorized atomic attacks on Japanese cities to hasten the end of the war. On August 6, 1945, an atomic bomb dropped from a U.S. warplane on Hiroshima killed eighty thousand people. Three days later, another bomb destroyed the city of Nagasaki. Truman's decision to use atomic weapons has been debated by many scholars and military analysts since World War II. Before the bombs were dropped, Japan had sent signals that it might surrender, but Truman believed a quick end of the war was necessary to avoid any need for an invasion of Japan that would cost many U.S. lives. On September 2 the Japanese officially surrendered, ending the war.

Despite U.S.-Soviet cooperation during the war, differences between the two nations developed into a cold war by 1946. The United States objected in particular to the Soviet Union's creation of communist governments in the Eastern European states they had occupied while pushing the Nazi armies back into Germany. Truman vigorously protested Moscow's actions and resolved to contain further Soviet expansionism.

In March 1947 when Britain withdrew its assistance to Greek anticommunists for economic reasons, Truman proclaimed the Truman Doctrine and asked Congress for $400 million in economic and military aid to prevent Greece and Turkey from falling to communist insurgents. The Truman Doctrine declared that the United States would aid governments threatened by communist subversion. Later that year Truman and Secretary of State George Marshall asked Congress to expand foreign aid dramatically by approving the Marshall Plan, a multibillion-dollar program to rebuild the economies of Western Europe. Congress gave its approval in 1948, and the Marshall Plan became one of the foremost successes of the Truman administration. Later in 1948 when the Soviets closed passage between western Germany and Berlin, which was located within the Soviet occupation zone, Truman used a massive airlift to supply the parts of the city administered by Britain, France, and the United States. The Soviets had hoped to force the United States and its western allies to give up control of their part of Berlin, but Truman's airlift broke the blockade and the Soviets backed down without a military confrontation.

In domestic policy, Truman developed a plan to extend Franklin Roosevelt's New Deal, which the new president called the "Fair Deal." Republicans and conservative Democrats in Congress, however, blocked many of his proposals. He also unsuccessfully backed progressive civil rights legislation. In 1947

Congress overrode Truman's veto of the Taft-Hartley Act, which he claimed unfairly weakened the bargaining power of unions. Five years later he seized and operated steel mills shut down by a strike during the Korean War, a move that the Supreme Court declared unconstitutional. Truman battled postwar inflation with the modest tools at his disposal, but Congress rejected his proposals for more sweeping price-control legislation, and inflation continued to be the most troublesome domestic problem during Truman's years in office.

In 1948 Truman ran for reelection against Thomas E. Dewey. Truman's reelection chances appeared slim when ultraliberal Democrats nominated Henry Wallace for president, and southern Democrats who disliked Truman's strong civil rights platform formed the "Dixiecrat" Party and nominated Sen. Strom Thurmond of South Carolina. During the campaign public opinion polls indicated that Dewey would win. Truman, however, used a cross-country, whistle-stop campaign to take his message to the people and won a surprise victory, defeating Dewey 303–189 in the electoral college.

Truman's second term was dominated by the Korean War. On June 24, 1950, troops from communist North Korea invaded South Korea. Truman sent U.S. troops to Korea under the auspices of the United Nations. UN forces pushed the North Koreans out of South Korea and drove into North Korea in an attempt to unify the country. Communist China entered the war on the side of the North Koreans in late 1950, however, and pushed UN forces back into South Korea. Eventually the war became deadlocked near the thirty-eighth parallel that had divided the two Koreas before the start of the war. Truman was unable to attain a negotiated peace during his presidency.

In 1951 Truman fired Gen. Douglas MacArthur, commander of UN forces in Korea, for insubordination. MacArthur had criticized the Truman administration's conduct of the war, publicly advocated a provocative invasion of China, interfered with Truman's diplomatic gestures, and disobeyed orders. Nevertheless, MacArthur enjoyed a large following in Congress and among the American public, and Truman's popularity sank after he fired the general.

During Truman's years in office the country became consumed with paranoia over communist subversion. Sen. Joseph R. McCarthy, R-Wis., led a group in Congress who claimed that communist agents had infiltrated the U.S. government, especially the State Department. McCarthy pointed to the failure of the United States to stop the communist revolution in China in 1949 as evidence of the communist sympathies of key U.S. officials. Truman denounced McCarthy but was unable to rally public support against the senator, despite the lack of evidence backing up McCarthy's accusations. After Truman left office, McCarthy became chairman of a Senate investigative subcommittee and accused many citizens of procommunist activities before being censured by the Senate in 1954.

From November 1948 until March 1952 the Trumans lived in Blair House, across Pennsylvania Avenue from the White House, while the executive mansion was being renovated. On November 1, 1950, Harry Truman became the first incumbent president to be the target of an assassination attempt since William McKinley was killed in 1901. Two Puerto Rican nationalists, Griselio Torresola and Oscar Collazo, attacked Blair House with automatic weapons, hoping to fight their way inside to kill the president. Although Truman was not harmed, one Secret Service agent and one of the assassins were killed.

On March 29, 1952, Truman announced that he would not run for reelection in the fall. After leaving office he returned to his home in Independence, Missouri. Truman remained active during his retirement, delivering lectures, commenting on political developments, and overseeing construction of the Truman Library near his home. He published his two-volume memoirs in 1955 and 1956.

Truman married Elizabeth (Bess) Wallace, whom he had known since his boyhood, on June 28, 1919. The couple had one child, Margaret, who was born in 1924. Margaret attended George Washington University and launched a singing career during her father's presidency.

Dwight D. Eisenhower

BORN: October 14, 1890; Denison, Texas
PARTY: Republican
TERM: January 20, 1953–January 20, 1961
VICE PRESIDENT: Richard M. Nixon
DIED: March 28, 1969; Washington, D.C.
BURIED: Abilene, Kansas

Dwight David Eisenhower was the third of the seven sons of David and Ida Eisenhower. One of Dwight's younger brothers died in infancy. Dwight was born in Texas, but his family lived there for only a short period. When Dwight was a baby, they returned to Kansas, where they had lived before he was born. Settling in Abilene, David Eisenhower got a job as a mechanic in a creamery. Dwight attended public schools and worked in the creamery after classes. At the age of fourteen, he developed blood poisoning from a severely skinned knee. Dwight's doctor wanted to amputate the leg, warning the Eisenhowers that failure to do so could cost Dwight his life. Despite the risk, the boy refused to let the doctor amputate his leg, and he recovered from the blood poisoning.

Eisenhower lacked the money to attend college, so he worked in the creamery full time upon graduation from high school. After a year, he applied for admission to both the Naval Academy and the Military Academy. He was rejected by Annapolis because he was too old, but he was nominated to West Point. He played football and was an above-average student, graduating sixty-fifth in his class of 164 in 1915.

MILITARY CAREER

When the United States entered World War I in 1917, Eisenhower served as a troop instructor at several bases in the United States. After the war his assignments included a two-year posting in Panama. In 1925 Eisenhower received an appointment to

the Army General Staff School in Leavenworth, Kansas. He graduated in 1926 first in his class of 275, an accomplishment that greatly contributed to his advancement through the ranks. He attended the Army War College in Washington, D.C., in 1928 and then served on the staff of the assistant secretary of war until 1932, when he was appointed as an aide to army chief of staff Gen. Douglas MacArthur. When MacArthur went to the Philippines in 1934 to organize a Filipino army, Eisenhower, by this time a major, accompanied him as a staff officer. While in the Philippines he received his pilot's license.

Eisenhower returned to the United States in early 1940 as a lieutenant colonel. During the next three years he would be promoted above hundreds of senior officers on his way to becoming a full general. When the United States entered World War II in 1941, he was a brigadier general serving as chief of staff of the Third Army in San Antonio, Texas. In February 1942 he was called to Washington, D.C., where he took command of the War Plans Division of the War Department's general staff. In this post he helped draft global strategy and a preliminary plan for the invasion of France from Britain. Eisenhower's skill as a tactician and his reputation as a soldier who could unify military leaders holding diverse points of view led to his appointment in June 1942 as the commanding general of the European Theater of Operations.

In November 1942 Eisenhower directed the successful Allied invasion of North Africa. In 1943 he attained the rank of full general and commanded the Allied invasions of Sicily and Italy. In December 1943 President Roosevelt named Eisenhower supreme commander of all Allied forces in Europe and instructed him to develop a plan for an invasion of France. On June 6, 1944, the forces under Eisenhower's command landed in Normandy in the largest amphibious invasion ever undertaken. The troops gained a beachhead and began driving toward Germany. Eisenhower accepted the surrender of the German army on May 7, 1945.

When the war was over, Eisenhower was one of America's most prominent war heroes. Although he lacked the dramatic presence of Douglas MacArthur, who had commanded U.S. forces in the Pacific during the war, Eisenhower was praised for his ability to rally his troops and his diplomacy with the Allied leaders. After serving as commander of the U.S. occupation zone in Germany, Eisenhower was appointed army chief of staff in November 1945. In 1948 he retired from the military to become president of Columbia University. That year he was approached by both the Democrats and the Republicans as a possible presidential candidate. In 1945 President Harry S. Truman had told Eisenhower that he would support Eisenhower if the general wanted to run for president as a Democrat in 1948. Eisenhower, however, declined all offers to run for office and maintained his political neutrality.

In 1950 President Truman asked Eisenhower to return to active service to become supreme commander of the North Atlantic Treaty Organization (NATO) forces in Europe. During his time in Europe, Eisenhower was again courted by both major political parties. Finally in January 1952 he announced that he would accept the Republican nomination for president if it were offered. He resigned his NATO command in May and was nominated by the Republicans on the first ballot at their national convention in Chicago in July.

Eisenhower's opponent was Gov. Adlai E. Stevenson II of Illinois. Eisenhower avoided detailed discussions of his political positions and relied primarily on his outgoing personality and his popularity as a war hero to win votes. He won a landslide popular-vote victory and defeated Stevenson 442–89 in the electoral college.

PRESIDENCY

When Eisenhower became president in 1953 a Korean War settlement was within reach. In December 1952, after the election, he had fulfilled a campaign promise to go to Korea to survey the situation. On July 27, 1953, an armistice was signed ending the war.

Although superpower tensions eased somewhat with the death of Soviet leader Joseph Stalin in March 1953 and the Korean War settlement, the cold war continued. Eisenhower endorsed Harry Truman's policy of containing communist expansion but sought to avoid conflict when possible. In 1954 he refused to aid the French garrison surrounded at Dien Bien Phu, Vietnam, by Vietnamese nationalists, who eventually drove the French out of Indochina, and he protested the attack on Egypt by Great Britain, France, and Israel in 1956 over Egypt's nationalization of the Suez Canal. Following the Suez crisis, Eisenhower announced the Eisenhower Doctrine, a commitment by the United States to use force to stop international communist aggression in the Middle East. In accordance with this doctrine, he sent U.S. troops to Lebanon in 1958 when the Lebanese government requested assistance fighting insurgents.

On September 24, 1955, Eisenhower suffered a heart attack that limited his activity for several months. The following June he underwent an operation for an attack of ileitis, an inflammation of the small intestine. Eisenhower's illnesses raised questions about his fitness for a second term. In November 1956, however, the voters reelected him over Democrat Adlai Stevenson by an even larger margin than he had enjoyed in 1952. President Eisenhower was confined to bed a third time in 1957 after suffering a stroke. His periods of disability fueled efforts to develop a procedure for transferring power to the vice president when the president was incapacitated by illness. Such a procedure was established by the Twenty-fifth Amendment, ratified in 1967.

In domestic policy Eisenhower favored anti-inflation policies over measures to stimulate economic growth. He produced budget surpluses in three of the eight years of his presidency, an accomplishment that became all the more noteworthy in the three decades after his retirement, when the federal budget was balanced only once. He also warned of the dangers of the development of a "military-industrial complex" and sought to limit defense spending. He signed bills that compensated farmers for taking land out of production and that initiated the national interstate highway system. Although he was not a leading opponent of racial segregation, he enforced existing civil rights laws. In 1957 he sent federal troops to Little Rock, Arkansas, when local citizens and state officials tried to block integration of public schools.

Eisenhower held several summits with Soviet leaders in attempting to improve U.S.-Soviet relations. He met with Soviet premier Nikolai Bulganin and Allied leaders in 1955 at Geneva and with Soviet first secretary Nikita Khrushchev in 1959 at Camp David, Maryland. Eisenhower's plans for a 1960 summit, however, were soured when the Soviets shot down an American U-2 reconnaissance plane over the Soviet Union on May 1 of that year. Khrushchev protested the U-2 overflights and refused to attend a summit in Paris with Allied leaders later that month. Eisenhower took full responsibility for the missions and defended them as vital to the security of the United States.

Eisenhower left office at the age of seventy, the oldest person to serve as president up to that time. He retired to his 230-acre farm near Gettysburg, Pennsylvania, where he enjoyed a quiet retirement. He indulged his love for golf, scoring a hole in one in February 1968, and wrote his memoirs, which were published in two volumes in 1965 and 1966. In November 1965 he suffered two heart attacks but recovered. During the spring and summer of 1968 he had a series of heart attacks that confined him to a hospital. He died in March 1969 from a heart attack, two months after his former vice president, Richard Nixon, was elected president.

Eisenhower married Marie "Mamie" Doud on July 1, 1916. Eisenhower met Mamie, the daughter of a wealthy Denver businessman, shortly after his graduation from West Point. They had two sons, but their first, Doud, died when he was three. Their second son, John Sheldon Eisenhower, was the father of David Eisenhower, who married President Richard Nixon's daughter Julie in 1968. Dwight Eisenhower's youngest brother, Milton, was president of three universities, chaired several government committees, and advised every president from Calvin Coolidge to Richard Nixon.

John F. Kennedy

BORN: May 29, 1917; Brookline, Massachusetts
PARTY: Democratic
TERM: January 20, 1961–November 22, 1963
VICE PRESIDENT: Lyndon B. Johnson
DIED: November 22, 1963; Dallas, Texas
BURIED: Arlington, Virginia

John Fitzgerald Kennedy was the second of the nine children of Joseph and Rose Kennedy. John's mother was the daughter of a former mayor of Boston. His father was a millionaire who had made his fortune in banking, real estate, and other financial ventures. In 1937 Franklin D. Roosevelt appointed Joseph Kennedy ambassador to Great Britain, a position he resigned in December 1940 when he became pessimistic about Britain's chances for survival during World War II. He returned to the United States, where his advocacy of isolationism caused a falling out with Roosevelt, who did not appoint him to another post.

John graduated in the middle of his class from Choate, a preparatory school in Wallingford, Connecticut. After attending the London School of Economics during the summer of 1935, he enrolled at Princeton University, but an illness forced him to withdraw after two months. In 1936 he entered Harvard University, where he studied economics and political science. Kennedy was an average student, but his grades improved dramatically at the end of his college career, and he graduated with honors in 1940. *Why England Slept*, his senior thesis published in book form, was an examination of British appeasement of fascism before World War II.

In 1941 Kennedy tried to enter the army, but he was rejected because of a bad back caused by a football injury. He strengthened his back through exercise and passed the navy's physical later that year. He received a commission as an ensign in October 1941. After attending PT (patrol torpedo) boat training, he was given command of a PT boat in the South Pacific in April 1943. On August 2, 1943, his boat, PT-109, was rammed and sunk by a Japanese destroyer. Eleven of his thirteen crew members survived, and he led them on a four-hour swim to a nearby island. During the swim he towed an injured crew member by a life preserver strap. Kennedy and his crew were rescued after friendly natives took a message carved on a coconut to nearby Allied personnel. After the ordeal Kennedy was sent back to the United States, where he was hospitalized for malaria. In 1944 he underwent a disc operation and was discharged the following year.

Kennedy worked briefly as a reporter for the International News Service, then decided to run for Congress from his Massachusetts district. He was elected in 1946 and served three terms before being elected to the Senate in 1952. In 1954 and 1955, he underwent two more operations for his chronic back condition.

While convalescing, Kennedy wrote *Profiles in Courage*, a book about senators who had demonstrated courage during their careers. The book became a bestseller and earned Kennedy the 1957 Pulitzer Prize for biography.

In 1956 Kennedy tried to secure the Democratic vice-presidential nomination on the ticket with Adlai Stevenson. After leading on the second ballot at the Democratic National Convention in Chicago, Kennedy lost the nomination to Sen. Estes Kefauver of Tennessee. Despite this defeat Kennedy's political reputation continued to grow. In 1957 he was assigned to the Senate Foreign Relations Committee, where he gained foreign policy experience. In 1958 he won reelection to the Senate by a record margin in Massachusetts.

By 1960 Kennedy was the leading candidate for the Democratic presidential nomination. His rivals for the nomination were Senate Majority Leader Lyndon Johnson of Texas, Sen. Stuart Symington of Missouri, Sen. Hubert H. Humphrey of Minnesota, and former Democratic presidential candidate Adlai Stevenson. Kennedy prevailed on the first ballot at the Democratic National Convention in Los Angeles in July 1960 and convinced Lyndon Johnson, who had finished second, to be his running mate.

Kennedy's opponent was Vice President Richard Nixon. Kennedy and Nixon engaged in a series of four televised debates, the first in presidential election history. Out of almost 69 million votes cast, Kennedy received only 120,000 more than Nixon. Kennedy won in the electoral college 303–219.

Kennedy was the youngest person ever to be elected president, although Theodore Roosevelt was younger than Kennedy when he succeeded to the presidency after the death of William McKinley. Kennedy's youth, idealism, and attractive family would make him one of the most popular presidents of the twentieth century. His administration came to be known as "Camelot" because of its romantic image.

Soon after entering office Kennedy endorsed a CIA plan developed during the Eisenhower presidency to arm, train, and land fourteen hundred Cuban exiles in Cuba in an attempt to overthrow the communist regime of Fidel Castro. The April 17, 1961, operation, which came to be known as the Bay of Pigs invasion, was a complete failure as twelve hundred of the Cuban exiles were captured. The president accepted full responsibility for the blunder.

Cuba had been the site of Kennedy's greatest foreign policy failure, but it was also the place of his most memorable foreign policy success. In October 1962 Kennedy was informed that aerial reconnaissance photography proved conclusively that the Soviets were building offensive missile bases in Cuba. Kennedy believed Soviet missiles in there would seriously diminish U.S. national security and increase the chances that the Soviets would try to blackmail the United States into concessions in other parts of the world. The president demanded that the bases be dismantled, but he rejected the option of an air strike against the sites in favor of a naval blockade of the island. The confrontation brought the United States and Soviet Union to the brink of nuclear war, but the Soviets ultimately backed down and agreed to remove the missiles.

Tensions decreased following the Cuban Missile Crisis, but the incident spurred the Soviets to undertake a military buildup that enabled them to achieve nuclear parity with the United States by the late 1960s. In 1963 Kennedy concluded an important arms control treaty with Britain, France, and the Soviet Union that banned nuclear tests in the atmosphere, in outer space, and under water.

Outside of superpower relations, Kennedy increased U.S. involvement in the developing world. In 1961 he established the Peace Corps, an agency that sent skilled volunteers overseas to assist people of underdeveloped countries. He also initiated the Alliance for Progress, an aid program aimed at developing the resources of Latin America.

In domestic policy, Kennedy made substantial progress in furthering the cause of civil rights. He advocated school desegregation, established a program to encourage registration of African American voters, issued rules against discrimination in public housing built with federal funds, and appointed an unprecedented number of blacks to public office. Kennedy used federal troops several times to maintain order and enforce the law in the South during the civil rights movement. He sent federal troops and officials to oversee the integration of the University of Mississippi in 1962 and the University of Alabama in 1963. That year he proposed sweeping civil rights legislation, but it did not come to a vote during his lifetime.

Kennedy also tried unsuccessfully to convince Congress to cut taxes. The president's advisers convinced him that a tax cut would stimulate the economy and bring growth without large budget deficits or inflation. After Kennedy's death, President Lyndon Johnson was able to secure passage of the Kennedy tax cut and civil rights legislation.

During the fall of 1963 Kennedy made several trips around the country to build political support for his reelection bid the following year. In late November he scheduled a trip to Texas. While riding through Dallas in an open car on November 22, Kennedy was shot once in the head and once in the neck. He died at a nearby hospital without regaining consciousness. Vice President Lyndon Johnson was sworn in as president that afternoon.

Police quickly apprehended the alleged assassin, Lee Harvey Oswald, a former marine who had once renounced his U.S. citizenship and lived in the Soviet Union. Initial investigations concluded that Oswald had shot Kennedy with a rifle from a sixth-story window of the Texas School Book Depository building. Three days after the shooting, Oswald was murdered in front of millions of television viewers by Jack Ruby, owner of a Dallas nightclub. The Warren Commission, a seven-member panel appointed by President Johnson to investigate the assassination, determined that Oswald acted alone. But Oswald's violent death, his unknown motivation, the difficulty of a single marksman firing several accurate shots so quickly, and other peculiarities surrounding the assassination have fostered speculation that Oswald may have been part of a conspiracy.

Kennedy married Jacqueline Lee Bouvier on September 12, 1953. They had three children, but their youngest son, who had been born several weeks prematurely, died of a respiratory ailment two days after birth on August 9, 1963. Kennedy's children, Caroline and John Jr., the first young children of a president living in the White House since the Theodore Roosevelt administration, were favorite subjects of the news media. Kennedy's widow, Jacqueline, married Greek shipping millionaire Aristotle Onassis on October 29, 1968. She died May 19, 1994, at age sixty-four and was buried beside President Kennedy at Arlington National Cemetery.

Lyndon B. Johnson

BORN: August 27, 1908; Stonewall, Texas
PARTY: Democratic
TERM: November 22, 1963–January 20, 1969
VICE PRESIDENT: Hubert H. Humphrey
DIED: January 22, 1973; San Antonio, Texas
BURIED: Johnson City, Texas

Lyndon Baines Johnson was the oldest of the five children of Sam and Rebekah Johnson. Lyndon's father and mother were school teachers. His father and both his grandfathers had served in the Texas state legislature. At age five Lyndon moved with his family from Stonewall, Texas, to nearby Johnson City, a small town named for his grandfather. After graduating from high school in 1924, Lyndon traveled to California with a group of friends. He supported himself by working odd jobs, but after a year he hitchhiked his way back to Texas.

Johnson worked on a road gang for a year, then enrolled in Southwest Texas State Teachers College in San Marcos in 1927. He graduated in 1930 and taught high school in Houston for a

year before Richard Kleberg, a newly elected member of the U.S. House of Representatives, asked Johnson to come to Washington, D.C., as an aide. Johnson worked for Kleberg from 1931 until 1935. During this period he learned firsthand about the legislative process and became an ardent supporter of President Franklin D. Roosevelt's New Deal policies. Johnson also studied law at Georgetown University during the 1934–1935 school year. He gave up his law studies and his job with Kleberg, however, when Roosevelt appointed him Texas director of the National Youth Administration in 1935. This program sought to help the nation's unemployed youth find employment and go to school.

In 1937 Johnson suddenly was given the opportunity to run for Congress when James P. Buchanan, the House member from Johnson's Texas district, died. Johnson entered the special election held to fill his seat and beat several candidates by campaigning on a pro-Roosevelt platform.

Johnson won reelection to the House in 1938 and 1940 but was narrowly defeated when he ran for a Senate seat in 1941. After the Japanese attacked Pearl Harbor, Johnson was the first House member to volunteer for active duty in the armed forces. He was commissioned as a lieutenant commander in the navy and sent to the South Pacific, where he undertook a fact-finding mission of the Australian combat zone. Johnson's service was short, however, because in July 1942 President Roosevelt ordered all members of Congress to leave the military and return to Washington.

Johnson served in the House until January 1949, when he took the Senate seat he had won the previous November. After just four years his Democratic colleagues elected him minority leader. In January 1955 he was elected majority leader when the Democrats took control of the Senate. Johnson suffered a severe heart attack in July 1955 but recovered fully. During his six years as majority leader, Johnson became known as one of the most skilled legislative leaders in congressional history. His ability to use flattery, coercion, and compromise to get legislation passed was a valuable asset when he became president.

Johnson wanted to run for president in 1960, but he was defeated for the Democratic nomination by Sen. John F. Kennedy of Massachusetts. Kennedy offered the vice presidency to Johnson, however, and the majority leader accepted. Kennedy and Johnson defeated Republicans Richard Nixon and Henry Cabot Lodge in a close election. Many political observers believed Kennedy might not have won without Johnson on the ticket. Johnson's presence was valuable in helping Kennedy win five southern states, including Texas.

Although Johnson was not an insider in the Kennedy administration, he undertook many diplomatic missions, and the president frequently sought his advice, especially on legislative matters. When Kennedy was shot while he rode in a motorcade through Dallas, Johnson was riding in a car behind the president. He followed the president's car to a hospital, where Kennedy was pronounced dead. Johnson then proceeded to the Dallas airport and boarded *Air Force One*. He decided to take the oath of office immediately, rather than wait until he returned to Washington. While the plane sat on the runway, federal Judge Sarah T. Hughes administered the oath of office to Johnson, who became the thirty-sixth president.

In the days following the assassination, Johnson declared his intention to carry out Kennedy's programs and asked Kennedy's cabinet to remain. Johnson, recognizing that public sentiment for the slain president improved his chances of enacting Kennedy's legislative program, vigorously lobbied Congress to pass a civil rights bill and a tax cut. Congress passed both bills in 1964. The tax cut succeeded in stimulating the economy, and the Civil Rights Act of 1964 protected black voting rights, established the Equal Employment Opportunity Commission, and forbade discrimination on account of race or sex by employers, places of public accommodation, and labor unions.

In 1964 Johnson ran for a presidential term of his own against Republican Sen. Barry Goldwater of Arizona. Many Americans were apprehensive that Goldwater's conservative positions were too extreme. Johnson outpolled Goldwater by more than 15 million votes and defeated him 486–52 in the electoral college.

Johnson regarded his landslide victory as a mandate to enact the "Great Society" social programs that he had outlined in his campaign. Johnson's Great Society was a comprehensive plan designed to fight poverty, ignorance, disease, and other social problems. During his second term he guided numerous bills through Congress establishing federal programs that provided expanded aid for medical care, housing, welfare, education, and urban renewal.

Although Johnson had hoped that his administration would be able to concentrate on his Great Society programs, the involvement of the United States in Southeast Asia soon came to dominate his presidency. The government in North Vietnam and guerrillas in South Vietnam were attempting to unify the country under communist rule by defeating the South Vietnamese regime militarily. Since Vietnam had been split into North and South Vietnam in 1954, the United States had supported the South with weapons, U.S. military advisers, and economic aid. In 1965 Johnson increased the U.S. commitment by sending American combat troops to South Vietnam.

Johnson continued to escalate U.S. involvement in the war in response to communist provocations and the inability of the South Vietnamese government to defend its country. The growing war diverted attention and dollars away from Johnson's domestic programs. Although many citizens supported the war, by 1966 college campuses had erupted in protest against it. Johnson hoped that each increase in U.S. troop strength and expansion of bombing targets would produce a breakthrough on the battlefield that would lead to a negotiated settlement preserving the independence and security of South Vietnam, but the communists refused to give up their goal of reunification.

By early 1968 public opinion had swung decisively against the war and Johnson. He recognized that there was a good chance that he might not be renominated for president by his party. Sen. Eugene J. McCarthy of Minnesota and Sen. Robert F. Kennedy of New York, the late president's brother, were running for the Democratic presidential nomination on antiwar platforms and were receiving substantial support. On March 31, 1968, Johnson delivered a television address in which he announced a partial halt to U.S. air attacks on North Vietnam to emphasize the U.S. desire for peace. He then stunned the nation by saying that he would not seek or accept the Democratic nomination for president.

After leaving Washington in 1969, Johnson retired to his ranch near Johnson City, Texas. He wrote a book about his presidential years, *The Vantage Point*, which was published in 1971. On January 22, 1973, Johnson was stricken by a heart attack at his ranch and was pronounced dead on arrival at Brooke Army Medical Center in San Antonio.

Johnson married Claudia Alta Taylor, the daughter of a storekeeper and rancher, on November 17, 1934. During her tenure as first lady, Mrs. Johnson championed efforts to beautify America. Johnson and his wife, who was known as "Lady Bird," had two daughters, Lynda and Luci. Lynda married Charles Robb, who would later serve as governor of and then senator from Virginia.

Richard Nixon

BORN: January 9, 1913; Yorba Linda, California
PARTY: Republican
TERM: January 20, 1969–August 9, 1974
VICE PRESIDENTS: Spiro T. Agnew; Gerald R. Ford
DIED: April 22, 1994; New York City
BURIED: Yorba Linda, California

Richard Milhous Nixon was the second of the five sons of Hannah and Francis Nixon, a lemon farmer. When Richard was nine he moved with his family from Yorba Linda to Whittier, California. There his father managed a combination gas station and general store, and Richard and his brothers attended public schools.

Nixon entered Whittier College in 1930. While at Whittier he played football, participated on the debate team, and was elected president of the student body. He graduated second in his class in 1934 with a degree in history. His academic excellence earned him a tuition scholarship to Duke University law school in Durham, North Carolina. In 1937 he graduated third in his class. He returned to California and joined the law firm of Wingert and Bewley in Whittier, eventually becoming a partner.

When the United States entered World War II in 1941 Nixon quit the law firm and went to Washington, D.C., to help the war effort. He worked briefly as a lawyer in the Office of Price Administration before applying for a navy commission. He was given the rank of lieutenant (junior grade) and assigned to a navy air transport unit. He served for over a year in the Pacific before being reassigned to the states in 1944. Before leaving ac-

tive duty in 1946, he had attained the rank of lieutenant commander.

POLITICAL CAREER

In 1945 Nixon was persuaded by a California Republican committee to run for Congress. He faced Democratic House member Jerry Voorhis, who had represented his California district for ten years. In a series of debates Nixon put Voorhis on the defensive by accusing him of being a socialist. Nixon won the election and was reelected in 1948.

In the House Nixon gained a national reputation as an anticommunist crusader. In 1948 he was appointed chairman of a subcommittee of the House Committee on Un-American Activities. His subcommittee investigated charges that several government employees were communists, including Alger Hiss, a former State Department official. In testimony, Hiss denied that he was a communist. President Truman and other top officials, including some Republicans, denounced the hearings. But Nixon pressed the investigation and found discrepancies that led to Hiss's conviction for perjury.

Nixon won a Senate seat in 1950. Democrats accused him of employing dirty campaign tactics, but his aggressive campaigning and his huge margin of victory impressed many Republican leaders. He became an early supporter of Gen. Dwight D. Eisen-

hower for the 1952 Republican presidential nomination and was chosen as the party's vice-presidential candidate when Eisenhower was nominated. In September 1952, however, Nixon's candidacy was jeopardized by a *New York Post* story that accused him of using secret funds provided by California business interests for personal expenses. Eisenhower refused to dismiss his running mate but said that Nixon would have to prove that he was "as clean as a hound's tooth." In an emotional televised speech on September 23 viewed by sixty million people, Nixon denied any wrongdoing and said he and his family lived simple lives without the benefit of many luxuries. The address became known as the "Checkers Speech" because, after admitting that he had accepted the gift of a dog his daughter had named "Checkers," he asserted that he would not give it back. The address brought an outpouring of support from the American people and saved Nixon's candidacy.

Dwight Eisenhower's status as a war hero and his pledge to find a settlement to the Korean War brought victory to the Republican ticket. Four years later Nixon was renominated for vice president, despite a "dump Nixon" movement started by several Republican leaders, and was reelected with President Eisenhower. As vice president, Nixon was more visible than many of his predecessors. He chaired several domestic policy committees and made numerous trips overseas, including a 1958 goodwill tour of Latin America and a 1959 diplomatic visit to Moscow, where he engaged in a famous spontaneous debate with Soviet premier Nikita Khrushchev on the merits of capitalism and communism.

Nixon ran for president in 1960 and received the Republican nomination. He and his Democratic opponent, Sen. John F. Kennedy of Massachusetts, engaged in the first televised presidential debates in history. Nixon is considered to have lost the important first debate to Kennedy because he appeared tired on camera. Kennedy defeated Nixon by a slim 120,000-vote margin but won 303–219 in the electoral college.

After the defeat, Nixon returned to California to practice law. In 1962 he ran for governor but lost to Edmund G. Brown. Following the election he told reporters that they would not "have Richard Nixon to kick around anymore."

In 1963 he moved to New York City, where he joined a law firm. Nixon's political ambitions remained alive, however, and he continued to give speeches on foreign policy. He campaigned for Republican candidates in 1966 and maneuvered for the 1968 Republican presidential nomination. At the Republican National Convention in Miami in 1968 he was nominated for president on the first ballot. Nixon promised to end the war in Vietnam and combat rising inflation. In an election that was almost as close as his 1960 loss, Nixon defeated his Democratic opponent, Vice President Hubert H. Humphrey, 301–191 in the electoral college.

PRESIDENCY

Nixon's first priority as president was achieving "peace with honor" in Vietnam. He proposed a plan to "Vietnamize" the war by providing the South Vietnamese military with upgraded training and weaponry, while slowly withdrawing U.S. troops from Indochina. Nixon believed that the South Vietnamese armed forces could be built into a force capable of defending their country from North Vietnamese aggression. While this slow withdrawal was taking place, Nixon ordered several controversial military operations, including an invasion of Cambodia in 1970, that increased domestic protests against the war. Nevertheless, the majority of Americans supported Nixon's slow withdrawal. During this period, Nixon's national security adviser, Henry Kissinger, conducted negotiations with the North Vietnamese on ending the war. In January 1973 the Nixon administration finally concluded an agreement that ended direct U.S. participation in the Vietnam War and provided for an exchange of prisoners. Nixon secretly promised South Vietnamese president Nguyen Van Thieu that the United States would not allow his regime to be overthrown by the communists. These commitments would not be met. The communists conquered the South in 1975 after Nixon had left office and Congress had placed strict limitations on U.S. military activities in Southeast Asia.

The most notable successes of the Nixon administration came in relations with China and the Soviet Union. In 1972 he became the first American president to travel to communist China. His summit meeting with Chinese leaders signaled a new beginning for U.S.-Chinese relations, which had been hostile since the communists came to power in 1949. In 1972 Nixon also became the first incumbent president to travel to Moscow. His summit with Soviet leader Leonid Brezhnev was the result of a relaxation of tensions between the superpowers known as détente. Brezhnev and Nixon signed agreements limiting nuclear weapons and antiballistic-missile systems at the Moscow summit. The Soviet leader returned Nixon's visit in June 1973, when he came to Washington, D.C., for a summit meeting.

Nixon's most significant domestic policy action was his imposition of wage and price controls on August 15, 1971. Nixon took this drastic measure to combat rising inflation that he thought might threaten his reelection chances in 1972. The controls initially slowed inflation, but their removal late in Nixon's presidency, combined with a jump in the price of oil caused by an Arab oil embargo, led to sharp increases in inflation. Prices rose 6.2 percent in 1973 and 11.0 percent in 1974.

The 1971 wage and price controls allowed Nixon to stimulate the economy in 1972 without fear that inflation would skyrocket. With unemployment falling, peace at hand in Vietnam, and the memory of Nixon's dramatic 1972 trips to China and the Soviet Union fresh in the minds of voters, the president was reelected in a landslide. Democratic challenger Sen. George McGovern of South Dakota won only Massachusetts and the District of Columbia.

Despite Nixon's overwhelming election victory, his second term soon became consumed by the Watergate scandal. On June 17, 1972, during the presidential campaign, five men with ties to the Committee for the Reelection of the President were arrested while breaking into the Democratic National Committee headquarters in the Watergate Hotel in Washington, D.C. Investigations of the burglary and the White House's attempt to cover up its connections to the burglars led to disclosure of numerous crimes and improprieties committed by members of the Nixon administration. Several top Nixon officials, including former attorney general John N. Mitchell, chief of staff H. R. Haldeman, and chief domestic adviser John D. Ehrlichman, were indicted. Nixon claimed he was innocent of any wrongdoing, but evidence showed that he had participated in the coverup of illegal administration activities. In July 1974 the House Judiciary Committee recommended to the full House that Nixon be impeached for obstruction of justice, abuse of presidential powers, and contempt of Congress.

On August 9, 1974, Richard Nixon became the first president ever to resign from office. Vice President Gerald R. Ford became president. Nixon had chosen Ford to replace his first vice president, Spiro T. Agnew, who had resigned in 1973 because of a scandal unrelated to Watergate. Nixon did not have to face criminal proceedings, however, because on September 8 President Ford granted him a "full, free, and absolute pardon."

After leaving the presidency Nixon wrote extensively about his time in office and world affairs. Although he remained tainted by the Watergate scandal, he came to be regarded as an elder statesman by many Americans because of his successes in foreign policy. Presidents of both parties and other officials often asked his advice on dealing with the Soviets and other matters. Nixon died April 22, 1994, at age eighty-one.

Nixon married Thelma Catherine "Pat" Ryan, a high school typing teacher, on June 21, 1940. Nixon met her while acting in an amateur theater group in Whittier. The couple had two daughters, Patricia and Julie. Patricia married Edward Cox in a White House Rose Garden wedding in 1971. Julie married David Eisenhower, the grandson of President Dwight D. Eisenhower. Pat Nixon died June 22, 1993, at age eighty-one.

Gerald R. Ford

BORN: July 14, 1913; Omaha, Nebraska
PARTY: Republican
TERM: August 9, 1974–January 20, 1977
VICE PRESIDENT: Nelson A. Rockefeller

Gerald Rudolph Ford was the only child of Dorothy and Leslie King, a wool trader. Ford was originally named Leslie Lynch King Jr., but his parents divorced when he was two. His mother gained custody of the child and moved to her family home in Grand Rapids, Michigan, where she married Gerald R. Ford in 1916. Ford, a paint salesman, adopted young Leslie, who was renamed Gerald Rudolph Ford Jr. Dorothy and Gerald, Sr., had three sons in addition to Gerald Jr.

Young Gerald attended public schools in Grand Rapids and became a star football player in high school. He worked in his stepfather's small paint factory and in a restaurant while growing up.

In 1931 Ford enrolled in the University of Michigan. There he studied economics and political science and played center on the football team. Ford played on two national championship teams while at Michigan and was named his team's most valuable player in 1934. He graduated in 1935 with a B average.

Several professional football teams wanted Ford to play for them, but he turned down the offers to become Yale University's boxing coach and an assistant on the football coaching staff. In 1938 he was admitted to Yale's law school. He continued to coach to support himself and finished his law degree in 1941.

Ford practiced law in Grand Rapids for less than a year before joining the navy early in 1942. He was commissioned as an ensign and assigned as a physical education instructor in North Carolina. Ford requested sea duty in 1943 and was transferred to the Pacific, where he became a gunnery officer on the light aircraft carrier *Monterey*. He fought in several major naval battles and achieved the rank of lieutenant commander by the end of the war.

Ford returned to his Grand Rapids law practice in late 1945. He became involved in local politics and decided to run for the U.S. House of Representatives in 1948. With the support of Michigan's powerful Republican senator, Arthur H. Vanden-

berg, Ford defeated an isolationist Republican incumbent, Bartel Jonkman, in the primary. Ford's district was solidly Republican, so he had little trouble defeating the Democratic candidate in the general election.

Ford won thirteen consecutive terms in the House, always with at least 60 percent of the vote. He turned down an opportunity to run for the Senate in 1952 because he wished to continue in the House where he was building seniority. Ford rose gradually to leadership positions among House Republicans. In 1963 he became chairman of the House Republican Conference, and in 1964 President Lyndon B. Johnson appointed him to the Warren Commission, which investigated the assassination of president John F. Kennedy. The following year, Ford challenged Charles A. Halleck of Indiana for the post of House minority leader. Ford was the choice of most younger Republicans in the House, and he was elected by a vote of 73–67 on January 4, 1965. He remained minority leader for nine years.

In 1973 Vice President Spiro T. Agnew resigned after being accused of income tax evasion and accepting bribes. When the vice presidency is vacant, under terms of the Twenty-fifth Amendment, ratified in 1967, the president nominates a new vice president who then must be confirmed by both houses of Congress. Because the credibility of the administration had been seriously damaged by Agnew and the unfolding Watergate scandal, President Richard Nixon wanted a vice president of unquestioned integrity. He chose Ford, who had developed a reputation for honesty during his years in the House. Nixon announced the appointment of Ford on October 12, 1973, in the East Room of the White House. After two months of scrutiny by Congress, Ford's nomination was approved 92–3 by the Senate and 387–35 by the House. He was sworn in as vice president on December 6.

The Watergate scandal forced President Nixon to resign on August 9, 1974. Later that day Ford became the first president to gain that office without being elected either president or vice president. He nominated former New York governor Nelson A. Rockefeller to be vice president. After a congressional inquiry into Rockefeller's finances, he was confirmed and sworn into office on December 19, 1974.

After taking the oath of office, Ford declared that "our long national nightmare is over." Ford's honest reputation, his friendly relations with Congress, and the public's desire for a return to normalcy led to an initial honeymoon with the American public. Seventy-one percent of respondents to a Gallup poll expressed their approval of the new president, while just 3 percent disapproved.

Ford's honeymoon, however, did not last long. On Sunday morning September 8 he announced to a small group of reporters that he was granting Richard Nixon an unconditional pardon. Ford was sensitive to speculation that he had promised to pardon Nixon in return for his nomination as vice president, so he took the unprecedented action of voluntarily going before a House Judiciary subcommittee to explain the pardon. Ford justified the highly unpopular pardon by saying it was needed to heal the political and social divisions caused by the Watergate scandal. Although no evidence of a secret bargain with Nixon surfaced, the pardon severely damaged Ford's popularity and his chances for election to a term of his own in 1976.

The most pressing domestic problem facing Ford during his term was persistent inflation and a sluggish economy. The president initially attempted to fight inflation by vetoing spending bills and encouraging the Federal Reserve to limit the growth of the money supply. In 1975, however, unemployment had become the more serious problem, and Ford compromised with Congress on a tax cut and a spending plan designed to stimulate the economy. Although inflation and unemployment remained at historically high levels, the nation experienced an economic recovery during late 1975 and 1976.

In foreign affairs Ford attempted to build on President Nixon's expansion of relations with the Soviet Union and China. Congressional restrictions on U.S. military involvement in Southeast Asia prevented Ford from providing military assistance to South Vietnam, which North Vietnam conquered in 1975. When the U.S. merchant ship *Mayaguez* was seized by Cambodia that year, however, he ordered marines to rescue the crew. The operation freed the crew, but forty-one of the rescuers were killed.

In September 1975 Ford was the target of two assassination attempts. On September 5 Lynette Fromme pointed a loaded pistol at the president as he moved through a crowd in Sacramento. A Secret Service agent disarmed her before she could fire. Fromme, a follower of mass murderer Charles Manson, was convicted of attempted assassination and sentenced to life imprisonment. Two weeks later, on September 22, political activist Sara Jane Moore fired a handgun at Ford as he was leaving a hotel in San Francisco. The bullet struck a taxi driver, who received a minor wound. Moore was apprehended by a bystander and two police officers before she could fire a second shot. She, too, was convicted of attempted assassination and sentenced to life in prison.

In early 1976 Ford appeared unlikely to retain the presidency. Even his party's nomination was in doubt, as conservative former California governor Ronald Reagan made a strong bid for the nomination. Ford collected enough delegates in the primaries, however, to narrowly defeat Reagan at the party's convention. In late 1975 Ford had asked Vice President Rockefeller to remove himself from consideration for the vice-presidential nomination in 1976. The president chose Sen. Robert J. Dole of Kansas as his running mate.

Jimmy Carter, the Democratic presidential candidate, was heavily favored to defeat Ford in the general election, but Ford made up ground during the fall campaign. The president, however, was defeated by Carter 297–240 in the electoral college.

After leaving the presidency, Ford retired to Palm Springs, California. In 1979 he published his autobiography, *A Time to Heal*. Ronald Reagan approached Ford about becoming his vice-presidential running mate in 1980, but the former president turned down Reagan's offer.

Ford was not actively engaged in public affairs during his retirement, but he did occasionally campaign for Republican candidates. He also joined with other former presidents to endorse selected policies, including enactment of the revisions to the General Agreement on Tariffs and Trade, the North American Free Trade Agreement, and the deployment of U.S. troops to the former Yugoslavia.

Ford married Elizabeth "Betty" Bloomer Warren, a thirty-year-old divorcee and former professional dancer, on October 15, 1948. The Fords had three sons and one daughter. After undergoing medical treatment for her own alcoholism in 1978, Mrs. Ford established the Betty Ford Center for Drug and Alcohol Rehabilitation.

Jimmy Carter

BORN: October 1, 1924; Plains, Georgia
PARTY: Democratic
TERM: January 20, 1977–January 20, 1981
VICE PRESIDENT: Walter F. Mondale

James Earl Carter Jr. was the oldest of the four children of James and Lillian Carter. From childhood on, James preferred to be called "Jimmy." His father was a storekeeper, farmer, and insurance broker who believed in segregation. His mother, a registered nurse who provided health care to her poor neighbors, held more progressive views on social and racial issues. Jimmy attended public schools and became a member of the First Baptist Church of Plains, Georgia. This evangelical church profoundly influenced Carter's development, although he did not adopt its conservative political philosophy in his political career.

After high school, Carter briefly attended Georgia Southwestern College in Americus, before being appointed to the U.S. Naval Academy. Carter graduated fifty-ninth in his class of 820 in 1946. His first assignment was as an instructor aboard battleships anchored at Norfolk, Virginia. In 1948 he applied and was accepted for submarine duty. After two and a half years as a crew member on a submarine in the Pacific, he was selected to work in the navy's nuclear submarine program. He became an engineering officer on the *Sea Wolf*, a new atomic submarine under construction. He also took classes in nuclear physics at Union College in Schenectady, New York. After his father died in 1953, however, he decided to retire from the navy.

Carter returned to his home in Plains, where he took over the family peanut farm. He gradually increased his land holdings and started several agriculture-related businesses, including a peanut-shelling plant and a farm-supply business. As Carter's wealth grew he became involved in local politics. He was appointed to the Sumter County School Board in 1955 and served there for seven years. He also served as chairman of the county hospital authority.

In 1962 Carter ran for the Georgia State Senate. He lost a primary election but challenged the results because he had personally witnessed a ballot box being stuffed by a supporter of his

opponent. His protest was upheld, and he became the Democratic nominee. He was elected and served two terms before declaring his candidacy for governor in 1966. Carter campaigned vigorously but lost in the primary election. In 1970 he surprised political observers by defeating former governor Carl E. Sanders in the Democratic primary, then went on to win the general election.

As governor, Carter openly denounced racial segregation and became a symbol of the "New South." He also reorganized the state government, supported measures to protect the environment, and opened government meetings to the public.

Georgia law prohibited a governor from running for two consecutive terms, so Carter set his sights on the presidency. New federal election laws that provided presidential candidates with campaign funds made it possible for Carter to run for president without the support of wealthy campaign contributors or Democratic Party leaders. One month after leaving the Georgia governorship he announced that he was running for the 1976 Democratic presidential nomination.

Carter's candidacy was a long shot. He was an inexperienced, one-term governor from a southern state, who had to defeat several better-known Democrats for the nomination. Carter campaigned tirelessly during 1975 and 1976 and gained national attention by winning the Democratic caucuses in Iowa on January 19, 1976. When he won again in the New Hampshire primary on February 24, he suddenly became the front-runner. Before the June 1976 Democratic National Convention in New York he had earned enough delegates in primaries and caucuses to lock up the nomination.

Carter emerged from the convention with a solid lead in public opinion polls over Republican incumbent Gerald R. Ford, whose candidacy suffered from several years of economic troubles and his pardon of former president Richard Nixon. This gap narrowed as the election approached, but Carter won 297–240 in the electoral college.

One of Carter's early presidential goals was to "depomp" the presidency and make it more responsive to the people. He underscored his intention by walking back to the White House from the Capitol after his inauguration. Carter conducted frequent press conferences, held meetings in selected towns across the country, carried his own suitbag, and stopped the tradition of having a band play "Hail to the Chief" when he arrived at an occasion. The public liked Carter's open, informal style, but the president could not sustain his initial popularity.

In the late summer of 1977 journalists and government investigators disclosed that Carter's budget director, Bert Lance, had engaged in questionable financial practices during his career as a banker before he joined the Carter administration. For several months Carter defended Lance, a close personal friend, but on September 21, 1977, Lance resigned under the weight of the allegations. Lance was ultimately exonerated when a jury acquitted him of bank fraud charges in 1981, but the Lance affair appeared to contradict Carter's claim that he was holding the officials of his administration to a higher ethical standard than previous presidents had.

The state of the economy did even more damage to Carter's presidency. During the 1976 campaign Carter had criticized President Ford for the high inflation and unemployment the country was suffering. Under Carter, however, the economic situation worsened. Prices had risen 6.5 percent the year Carter took office, but they rose 11.3 percent in 1979 and 13.5 percent in 1980. Unemployment, which stood at about 7.7 percent in 1980 during Carter's reelection campaign, was also higher than most Americans would accept.

In foreign policy, Carter achieved several notable successes. He mediated negotiations between Prime Minister Menachem Begin of Israel and President Anwar Sadat of Egypt. The talks produced the 1979 Camp David Accords, which established peace between those two countries. He also formalized relations with the People's Republic of China on January 1, 1979, and secured Senate approval in 1978 of treaties transferring control of the Panama Canal to Panama on December 31, 1999.

The last two years of Carter's term, however, brought several foreign policy failures. On June 18, 1979, Carter and Soviet leader Leonid Brezhnev signed a treaty in Vienna to limit strategic nuclear weapons, but the Senate was hesitant to approve this agreement known as SALT II. In 1980 Carter withdrew the SALT II treaty after the Soviets invaded Afghanistan in December 1979 to prop up a procommunist government there. In response to the Soviet invasion, Carter also imposed a grain embargo and refused to allow the U.S. team to participate in the 1980 Olympic games in Moscow.

On November 4, 1979, Iranian militants stormed the U.S. embassy in Tehran, taking American diplomats and embassy personnel hostage. Carter's efforts to free the hostages, including an abortive helicopter raid in April 1980 in which eight soldiers died, proved ineffective. The hostage crisis dominated the last year of Carter's presidency, and the Iranians did not release the hostages until January 20, 1981, minutes after Carter had left office.

Despite these problems, Carter fought off a challenge for the 1980 Democratic presidential nomination from Sen. Edward M. Kennedy of Massachusetts. Carter's opponent in the general election was conservative former governor Ronald Reagan of California. Reagan defeated Carter 489–49 in the electoral college, with Carter winning only six states and the District of Columbia.

After leaving the presidency, Carter returned to his home in Plains. He lectured and wrote about world affairs and became involved in several voluntary service projects. In 1994 Carter carried out a series of high-profile diplomatic missions to North Korea, Bosnia, and Haiti. The Haiti trip produced a last-minute agreement that allowed U.S. military forces, which were set to invade Haiti, to enter the country peacefully. Critics of Carter's missions, however, argued that he was too willing to accommodate despotic leaders and his activities undermined standard diplomacy.

Carter married eighteen-year-old Rosalynn Smith, a close friend of his sister Ruth, on July 7, 1946. The Carters had three sons and one daughter. Several of Carter's relatives became national celebrities. His brother, Billy, capitalized on his brother's fame by making numerous public appearances and marketing "Billy Beer." Carter's mother, who had served in the Peace Corps while in her late sixties and early seventies, made several overseas journeys to represent her son at state funerals and other occasions.

Ronald Reagan

BORN: February 6, 1911; Tampico, Illinois
PARTY: Republican
TERM: January 20, 1981–January 20, 1989
VICE PRESIDENT: George Bush

Ronald Wilson Reagan was the youngest of the two sons of Nelle and John Reagan, a shoe salesman. When Ronald was nine the family moved from Tampico, Illinois, to nearby Dixon. He attended public schools and worked as a lifeguard at a swimming area in the Rock River. He enrolled in Eureka College near Peoria, Illinois, in 1928. There he played football and was elected president of the student body. He graduated in 1932 with a degree in economics and sociology.

After college Reagan worked as a sportscaster for radio stations in Davenport and Des Moines, Iowa. During a trip to California in 1937 to cover the spring training sessions of the Chicago Cubs baseball team, Reagan was persuaded by an agent for Warner Brothers movie studio to take a screen test. Reagan won the role of a small-town radio announcer in the movie *Love Is on the Air*. The movie began his twenty-eight-year acting career, during which he would make fifty-five movies, including *King's Row, The Hasty Heart,* and *Knute Rockne, All American*.

In 1942 Reagan entered the U.S. Army Air Corps as a second lieutenant and was assigned to make training films. He was discharged in 1945 with the rank of captain. After the war he continued to act in movies but devoted an increasing share of his time to move industry politics. In 1947 he was elected president of the Screen Actors Guild, a labor union representing Hollywood actors. He held that office until 1952 and was reelected to a one-year term in 1959. In October 1947 he appeared as a friendly witness before the House Un-American Activities Committee. He supported the blacklist created by Hollywood producers to deny work to actors and writers suspected of having communist ties.

Until the late 1940s Reagan had been a staunch Democrat, supporting presidents Franklin Roosevelt and Harry Truman. In the late 1940s his political sympathies began to shift to the right as he became more concerned about communist subversion. He voted for Dwight Eisenhower in 1952 and 1956 and Richard Nixon in 1960. From 1954 to 1962 he served as a spokesperson for General Electric. In addition to hosting the television show *GE Theater*, he made speeches to factory workers about the virtues of free enterprise and the dangers of too much government regulation. In 1962 Reagan finally abandoned the Democratic Party and registered as a Republican.

POLITICAL CAREER

In 1964 Reagan made a televised campaign speech on behalf of Republican presidential candidate Barry Goldwater. The speech established Reagan as an articulate spokesman for the conservative wing of the Republican Party and led California Republican leaders to ask him to run for governor. Reagan received the 1966 Republican nomination for governor after winning almost 65 percent of the vote in a five-candidate primary election. He then defeated incumbent Democrat Edmund G. Brown, who had beaten Richard Nixon four years before. Reagan was easily elected to a second term in 1970.

As governor, Reagan succeeded in passing a welfare reform bill that cut the number of Californians on welfare and increased the payments to the remaining welfare recipients. He campaigned for budget cuts and lower taxes, but early in his governorship he signed bills increasing taxes, because he claimed Brown had left the state in financial trouble. Reagan also harshly criticized student protesters on college campuses and cut state funds for higher education during his first term. During his second term, however, the cuts were restored, and by the time he left office state support for higher education was double what it had been when he was first elected.

Reagan received some support for the presidential nomination in 1968, but the party nominated Richard Nixon. Reagan backed President Nixon in 1972, but after declining to run for a third term as governor in 1974 he began campaigning for the presidency. Despite running against incumbent president Gerald R. Ford, Reagan came close to winning the 1976 Republican presidential nomination. Ford received 1,187 delegate votes to Reagan's 1,070 delegate votes at the Republican National Convention in Kansas City. When Ford lost the election to Democrat Jimmy Carter, Reagan became the favorite to receive the Republican nomination in 1980.

During the next four years Reagan campaigned for Republican candidates and raised money for his 1980 campaign. He was upset in the Iowa caucuses by George Bush but recovered with a win in the New Hampshire primary. Reagan went on to win all but four of the remaining Republican primaries. He then defeated incumbent Jimmy Carter in the general election, 489 electoral votes to 49.

PRESIDENCY

On March 30, 1981, less than three months after he became president, Reagan was shot as he was leaving the Washington Hilton Hotel, where he had spoken to a group of union officials. The assailant, John Hinckley Jr., fired six shots at Reagan with a .22-caliber pistol. One bullet struck Reagan in the chest and lodged in his left lung. A police officer, a Secret Service agent,

and presidential press secretary James Brady were also wounded in the shooting. Reagan was rushed to a nearby hospital, where surgeons removed the bullet. Reagan became the first incumbent president to be wounded by an assailant and survive. Hinckley, who declared he shot the president to impress Jodie Foster, a Hollywood actress, was found not guilty by reason of insanity and confined at St. Elizabeth's Hospital in Washington, D.C.

During 1981 the Reagan administration focused on economic policy. The president pushed a large tax cut through Congress, along with increases in the defense budget and decreases in funding for many domestic programs. Reagan claimed that the tax cut would produce an economic boom that would lower unemployment while ultimately increasing tax revenues that would balance the federal budget. A severe recession that began in late 1981, however, increased unemployment to postdepression highs.

In early 1983 the economy began to recover. Unlike economic recoveries during the 1970s, however, the expansion was not accompanied by high inflation. In the 1984 presidential election, with the economy prospering, Reagan overwhelmed his Democratic challenger, former vice president Walter F. Mondale, 525–13 in the electoral college. The economic expansion continued through the end of Reagan's term.

Although most Americans were satisfied with the economic recovery, critics charged that it was flawed because low-income groups had fared poorly during the Reagan years, the U.S. trade position had deteriorated, and the federal government had built up huge budget deficits. The last of these problems was particularly troublesome to Reagan, because he had promised in his 1980 campaign to balance the federal budget. Instead, Reagan's military buildup and tax cut had exacerbated the nation's budget deficit problem. In 1981 when Reagan entered office, the budget deficit was $78.9 billion. Two years later it had more than doubled to $207.8 billion, and in 1986 it stood at $221.2 billion. The national debt had risen from a little over one trillion dollars in 1981 to more than two trillion dollars in 1986. Reagan and the Democratic Congress addressed the debt problem by enacting the Gramm-Rudman-Hollings amendment in 1985. The measure mandated across-the-board spending cuts if the president and Congress could not agree on budget reductions that would reduce the deficit to specified yearly targets.

In foreign affairs, the first five years of Reagan's presidency were characterized by hard-line anticommunist rhetoric and efforts to block communist expansion and even overturn procommunist governments in the developing world. Reagan supported military funding to the anticommunist Nicaraguan rebels known as the "contras," who were fighting to overthrow the Marxist regime in their country. He also supported aid to anticommunist guerrillas fighting in Angola and Cambodia, and Afghan rebels fighting Soviet forces that had invaded Afghanistan in 1979. In 1983 Reagan dispatched U.S. troops to Grenada to overthrow the Marxist government and bring stability to the tiny Caribbean island.

With the rise of Mikhail Gorbachev as the leader of the Soviet Union in 1985, however, the president softened his anticommunist rhetoric and began developing a working relationship with the Soviet leader. During his last three years in office, Reagan held five summits with Gorbachev and signed a treaty banning intermediate nuclear missiles in Europe.

The Reagan administration also took actions to strike back at terrorists in the Middle East, including a 1986 bombing raid on Libya in retaliation for alleged Libyan support for a terrorist bombing of a Berlin nightclub. Reagan's tough antiterrorist posture was undercut late in 1986 when the administration disclosed that the president had approved arms sales to Iran that appeared to be aimed at securing the release of American hostages in Lebanon held by pro-Iranian extremists. Reagan denied that the sale was an arms-for-hostages swap, which would have contradicted his policy of not negotiating with terrorists, but the evidence suggested otherwise.

Investigations revealed that members of the president's National Security Council staff had used the arms sales profits to aid the contras, despite a congressional prohibition then in force against U.S. aid to the contras. Although investigators found no evidence that Reagan had been aware of the diversion of funds to the contras, the scandal led to the resignation of several administration officials. The Tower Commission, appointed by the president to investigate the Iran-contra affair, issued a report in 1987 that was highly critical of the president's detached style of management, which allowed his subordinates to operate without his knowledge.

Despite the Iran-contra affair, Reagan remained one of the most popular presidents of the twentieth century. After Vice President George Bush won the Republican presidential nomination in 1988, Reagan campaigned hard for him. Bush easily defeated Gov. Michael Dukakis of Massachusetts in the November election.

When Reagan's term ended, he returned to his home in Bel Air, California, and maintained a low public profile. In November 1994, Reagan announced in a handwritten note that he had been diagnosed with Alzheimer's disease, which causes progressive mental and physical deterioration. He said that he wanted his announcement to help raise awareness about the disease.

Reagan married Jane Wyman, an actress, on January 24, 1940. The couple had one daughter and adopted a son before divorcing in 1948. Reagan then married another actress, Nancy Davis, on March 4, 1952. They had one daughter and one son.

George Bush

BORN: June 12, 1924; Milton, Massachusetts
PARTY: Republican
TERM: January 20, 1989–January 20, 1993
VICE PRESIDENT: Dan Quayle

George Herbert Walker Bush was the second of the five children of Prescott and Dorothy Bush. George's father was a weal-

thy Wall Street banker who represented Connecticut in the U.S. Senate from 1952 to 1963.

George grew up in Greenwich, Connecticut, where he attended a private elementary school before enrolling in the Phillips Academy in Andover, Massachusetts. At this exclusive prep school he excelled in athletics and academics and was elected president of his senior class. He graduated in 1942 and joined the navy, becoming the youngest bomber pilot in that branch of the service.

On September 22, 1944, while flying a mission from the light aircraft carrier *San Jacinto*, Bush was shot down near the Japanese-held island of Chichi Jima. He parachuted safely into the Pacific Ocean and after four hours was rescued by a submarine. Bush received the Distinguished Flying Cross. In December 1944 he was reassigned as a naval flight instructor in Virginia, where he remained until his discharge in September 1945.

After the war Bush enrolled in Yale University and majored in economics. He was also captain of Yale's baseball team. He graduated Phi Beta Kappa in 1948.

Bush then moved to Texas, where he gradually made a small fortune in the oil business. He ran for the Senate in 1964 against incumbent Ralph Yarborough, a Democrat. Although he received 200,000 more votes in Texas than Republican presidential nominee Barry Goldwater, Bush lost the election.

In 1966 when reapportionment gave Houston another House seat, Bush ran for it and won. He served on the Ways and Means Committee and became an outspoken supporter of Richard Nixon. Bush was reelected to the House in 1968 when Nixon captured the presidency. Two years later Bush followed Nixon's advice and abandoned his safe House seat to run for the Senate. He was defeated by conservative Democrat Lloyd Bentsen, who would be the Democratic vice-presidential nominee in 1988 on the ticket opposing Bush.

After the 1970 election Nixon appointed Bush ambassador to the United Nations. When Nixon was reelected in 1972, he asked Bush to leave the UN to take over as chair of the Republican National Committee. Bush served in that post during the difficult days of the Watergate scandal. At first he vigorously defended President Nixon. In 1974, however, as the evidence against Nixon mounted, he privately expressed doubts about the president's innocence. Nevertheless, Bush avoided public criticism of the president and concentrated on maintaining Republican Party strength despite the president's troubles. On August 7, 1974, Bush wrote a letter asking Nixon to resign, which the president did two days later.

When Vice President Gerald R. Ford succeeded to the presidency upon Nixon's resignation, Bush was a leading candidate to fill the vice-presidential vacancy. Bush wanted the job, but he was bypassed in favor of Gov. Nelson A. Rockefeller of New York. Ford offered Bush the ambassadorship to Britain or France. Bush chose, however, to take the post of chief of the U.S. Liaison Office in the People's Republic of China.

In 1975 Ford called Bush back to the United States to become director of the Central Intelligence Agency. As CIA chief, Bush's primary goal was restoring the reputation of the agency, which had been damaged by revelations of its illegal and unauthorized activities during the 1970s, including assassination plots against foreign officials and spying on members of the domestic anti-war movement. Bush won bipartisan praise for his efforts to repair the agency's morale and integrity.

After being replaced as CIA director when Democrat Jimmy Carter became president in 1977, Bush returned to Houston to become chairman of First International Bank. He stayed active in politics by campaigning for Republican candidates before the 1978 midterm election. On January 5, 1979, he declared his intention to seek the presidency. Bush campaigned full-time during 1979 and established himself as the leading challenger to Republican front-runner Ronald Reagan when he won the Iowa caucuses on January 21, 1980. During the primary campaign Bush attacked Reagan as an ultraconservative and called his economic proposals "voodoo economics." Reagan, however, prevailed in the primaries and secured enough delegates for the nomination before the Republican National Convention in Detroit in July 1980.

At the convention Reagan's team approached former president Ford about running for vice president. When Ford declined, they asked Bush to be the vice-presidential nominee in an attempt to unify the party. Bush accepted, and the Republican ticket defeated President Jimmy Carter and Vice President Walter F. Mondale in a landslide.

Despite Bush's differences with Reagan during the campaign, as vice president he was extremely loyal to the president. When Reagan was wounded by an assailant in 1981, Bush emphasized that Reagan was still president and exerted leadership over the administration in the president's absence. Bush was frequently called upon to make diplomatic trips overseas. While vice president he visited more than seventy countries. His frequent attendance at state funerals led him to joke that his motto was "I'm George Bush. You die, I fly." Reagan and Bush won a second term in 1984 by easily defeating the Democratic ticket of Walter F. Mondale and Geraldine Ferraro.

Late in Reagan's second term Bush launched his campaign for the presidency. Despite his status as a two-term vice president, he was challenged for the nomination by Senate Minority Leader Robert Dole of Kansas and several other candidates. Dole defeated Bush in the Iowa caucuses, as Bush had defeated Reagan eight years before. In the first primary, in New Hampshire, however, Bush scored a decisive victory and secured the nomination before the end of the primary season.

Bush faced Gov. Michael S. Dukakis of Massachusetts in the general election. Bush attacked his opponent for liberal policies and promised to continue Ronald Reagan's diplomacy with the Soviet Union. Despite the presence of massive budget deficits, Bush also pledged not to raise taxes. Bush overcame speculation about his role in the Reagan administration's Iran-contra affair and criticism of Dan Quayle, his vice-presidential choice, to defeat Dukakis. Bush won the election decisively in the electoral college, 426–112.

Bush had pledged to carry on the conservative legacy of Ronald Reagan. However, he had also promised to preside over a "kinder, gentler America," implying that partisanship had gone too far during the Reagan period. Nevertheless, partisan battles with the Democratic Congress would characterize much of Bush's presidency. In November 1990, after months of partisan negotiation and posturing, Bush signed a budget bill that aimed to trim about $500 billion off the deficit over five years. Congressional Democrats forced Bush to accept a tax increase as part of the deal. Many Americans saw Bush's acquiescence to the tax increase as a betrayal of his campaign pledge.

The previous August, events in the Persian Gulf region had intruded on Bush's other priorities and provided a troubling backdrop to the budget negotiations. On August 2 Iraqi forces invaded and quickly occupied the small, oil-rich nation of Kuwait. Bush responded by rallying international opposition against Iraq and sending hundreds of thousands of American troops to join the coalition assembling in the region. The administration argued that this aggression by Iraqi leader Saddam Hussein had to be reversed because it threatened the stability of world oil markets and set a dangerous precedent that could encourage other acts of aggression. Bush also was concerned about mounting evidence that Iraq was engaged in an ambitious nuclear weapons program.

On January 17, 1991, Bush ordered a devastating bombing campaign against Iraqi military forces. On February 24, after thirty-eight days of sustained bombing, coalition ground forces attacked the Iraqi troops, routing them from Kuwait. The ground war lasted just one hundred hours before Bush gave the cease-fire order. The stunning success of the operation and the low casualty figures boosted the president's popularity to a high of 89 percent immediately following the war. Commentators speculated that Bush's victory in the Gulf might make him unbeatable for reelection in 1992, and several prominent Democrats declined to enter the race because of Bush's standing. But his popularity did not last. After the war, the American people turned their attention back to domestic matters. The nation had entered a recession in the summer of 1990. As wages stagnated and unemployment continued to rise after the war, Bush was perceived as having no answers to domestic problems. He also was seen as spending too much time on foreign affairs, the area of policy in which he had the most expertise and success.

Bush's reelection chances were further damaged when he was challenged for the Republican nomination by conservative political commentator Pat Buchanan. Although Bush's nomination was not seriously threatened by Buchanan, the challenger's attacks from the right weakened enthusiasm for Bush among conservatives and forced the president to defend himself instead of preparing for the fall election.

Governor Bill Clinton of Arkansas was nominated by the Democrats to face Bush. Billionaire Ross Perot mounted a self-financed independent candidacy that also drew significant attention. Clinton won the election with 43 percent of the popular vote and 370 electoral votes. Bush finished second with 37 percent of the popular vote and 168 electoral votes. Perot did not win any states, but finished with 19 percent of the popular vote. Clinton capitalized on Bush's inattention to domestic matters by promising to focus "like a laser beam" on the economy.

Bush left office declaring that he would spend time in retirement with his grandchildren. In 1993 he made a trip to Kuwait, where he was greeted as a liberator. Intelligence findings that Iraqi agents had plotted to assassinate Bush during the trip led President Clinton to launch a missile attack against Iraq on June 26, 1993. In 1994, two of Bush's sons, George Jr. and Jeb, ran for the governorships of Texas and Florida, respectively. George Jr. won in Texas, but Jeb lost a close election.

Bush married nineteen-year-old Barbara Pierce, the daughter of a prominent magazine publisher, on January 6, 1945. They had four sons and two daughters. Their daughter Robin died of leukemia in 1953.

Bill Clinton

BORN: August 19, 1946; Hope, Arkansas
PARTY: Democrat
TERM: January 20, 1993–
VICE PRESIDENT: Al Gore

Bill Clinton was the only child of William Jefferson Blythe III and Virginia Dwire. Bill originally was named William Jefferson Blythe, after his father. But the senior Blythe died in an automobile accident before his son was born. When Bill was four, his mother married Roger Clinton, a car salesman who legally adopted Bill. Bill's stepfather was an alcoholic who frequently quarreled with his mother.

Clinton grew up in Hot Springs, Arkansas, where he excelled in public schools and played saxophone in the band. In 1968 he graduated from Georgetown University in Washington, D.C., with a degree in international affairs. He earned a prestigious Rhodes Scholarship and attended Oxford University for two years, though he did not earn a degree. He returned to the United States in 1970 and entered Yale University Law School. He earned his law degree in 1973.

POLITICAL CAREER

Politics had been a childhood ambition for Clinton. In 1972 he managed the Texas campaign of Democratic presidential nominee George McGovern. After a brief stint as a staff member of the House Judiciary Committee, he began teaching law at the University of Arkansas in 1973. The next year, he ran unsuccessfully for a House seat from the Third Congressional District of Arkansas. Although he was defeated, his strong showing against a popular Republican incumbent established his position in Arkansas politics.

In 1976 Clinton was elected attorney general of Arkansas. Then in 1978, at age thirty-two, he decisively defeated a crowded field of Democratic contenders for the gubernatorial nomination. Clinton coasted to victory in the general election. Two years later, however, Clinton was defeated for reelection by Republican banker Frank White. Clinton's popularity had been weakened by rioting among 18,000 Cuban refugees housed at Fort Charles, Arkansas, by the Carter administration. He also was attacked by his opponent for raising gasoline taxes and automobile licensing fees to pay for road construction projects. In addition, many Arkansas voters resented Clinton's broader political ambitions, which he did little to hide.

After his defeat Clinton went to work for the Little Rock law firm Wright, Lindsay, and Jennings, but he spent much of his time preparing for a rematch with White. During the 1982 campaign he declared that his tax increases had been a mistake. He defeated White and was reelected in 1984 to a two-year term and in 1986 and 1990 to four-year terms.

At the 1988 Democratic National Convention in Atlanta, Clinton delivered a nominating speech for Michael Dukakis that was criticized as being long and tedious. Despite this setback, during the late 1980s and early 1990s Clinton achieved national prominence as a reform governor and was frequently mentioned as a future presidential candidate. He served two terms as chair of the National Governors Association. In 1990 and 1991 he also headed the Democrat Leadership Council, a national organization of Democrats who favored a realignment of the Democratic Party to more moderate positions.

On October 3, 1991, despite an earlier promise to serve out his full term as governor, Clinton officially announced his intention to seek the Democratic presidential nomination. He quickly emerged as one of the front-runners. The campaign was placed in jeopardy, however, by allegations of Clinton's marital infidelity and avoidance of military service during the Vietnam War. Without denying either charge, Clinton and his wife, Hillary, appealed for understanding. Clinton outlasted rivals Paul Tsongas and Jerry Brown to win the nomination.

In the general election Clinton faced incumbent George Bush and billionaire populist Ross Perot, who was running as an independent. Support for Bush had been weakened by a stagnant economy and perceptions that he had little interest in domestic policy. To capitalize on public perceptions, Clinton promised to make economic policy and the middle class his top priorities. He promoted himself as a fiscally conscientious agent of change who would reform the country's health care, welfare, and education systems. He chose Senator Al Gore of Tennessee as his vice-presidential running mate. The two Democrats (each of whom was in his mid-forties) projected a youthful energy that appealed to many younger voters. Clinton won the election with 43 percent of the popular vote and 370 electoral votes. Bush finished second with 37 percent and 168 electoral votes.

PRESIDENCY

Clinton's first hundred days in office were a mixed bag of successes and setbacks. His first two choices for attorney general were forced to withdraw after revelations that they had employed illegal immigrants as nannies; he was forced to compromise on his campaign pledge to lift outright the ban on gays serving in the military; and his economic stimulus bill was defeated by a Republican filibuster in the Senate. But Clinton succeeded in passing family leave legislation and a long-stalled motor-voter bill.

During the second half of 1993 Clinton scored three major victories. His aggressive lobbying led to the close passage of a budget plan that was projected to reduce the anticipated deficit by about $500 billion over five years. The House on August 5 passed the budget 218–216. The next day the Senate passed it 51–50, with Vice President Gore breaking the tie. Later in the year, Clinton scored major legislative successes by passing the North American Free Trade Agreement, primarily on the strength of Republican votes, and the Brady bill, which mandated a five-day waiting period for the purchase of a handgun. The Brady bill had been seven-years in the making and was the first major gun control legislation to pass Congress since 1968.

In 1994, however, the Clinton agenda was less successful. With Hillary Clinton serving as the head of the White House task force on health care, the administration attempted to advance a comprehensive health care reform plan. Republicans attacked the plan as overly complex, expensive, and bureaucratic. By early fall, it was apparent that the Clinton plan did not have sufficient congressional or public support. The bill was withdrawn without coming to a final vote in either house. Clinton's disappointment was tempered somewhat by passage of a major crime bill and revisions to the General Agreement on Tariffs and Trade.

The congressional elections of 1994 brought a stunning realignment in Washington. With many Republican candidates campaigning against the policies of Bill Clinton, Republicans gained control of both houses of Congress for the first time in four decades. Clinton suddenly was faced with an aggressive Republican-controlled Congress intent on rolling back years of Democratic legislation. The Republican-dominated Congress also reinvigorated a lingering ethics investigation arising from investments Clinton and his wife had made in an Arkansas land development deal known as "Whitewater" during his time as governor.

During 1995 Clinton blocked many Republican priorities

with his veto. Most notably, Clinton vetoed Republican legislation to balance the budget in seven years, saying that the proposed cuts in health care, education, environment, and welfare were draconian. The vetoes led to two shutdowns of government services and bitter partisan accusations as the two parties sought political advantage. With the polls showing the majority of Americans supporting his position on balancing the budget, Clinton was able to keep a firm hand in the budget negotiations. His stubborn style proved successful by April 1996, as the final 1996 fiscal spending bill reflected Clinton's priorities rather than the deeper cuts sought by the congressional Republicans.

As he had promised during his campaign, Clinton deemphasized foreign policy to focus on domestic problems, but he took an interest in several regions of the world. After Israel and the Palestine Liberation Organization reached a framework agreement in 1993 on achieving peace, Clinton actively promoted a broadening of the accord. Clinton also sought to advance negotiations between warring factions in Ireland. And he expanded the humanitarian mission in Somalia that had been launched during the Bush administration. But when U.S. military units began experiencing casualties, Clinton decided to evacuate American troops. In 1994 Clinton also sent American forces to Haiti to reestablish the deposed government of Jean-Bertrand Aristide.

But Clinton's largest foreign policy endeavor was his commitment in 1995 of 20,000 U.S. troops to a NATO peacekeeping mission in war-torn Bosnia. The deployment followed the signing of a complex U.S.-brokered peace agreement in Dayton, Ohio, on November 21. Critics charged that the United States had no vital interests in Bosnia, that the troops would be targets for rogue paramilitary units, and that the factions would resume their fighting when the NATO force was eventually withdrawn. But Clinton cited the need to follow through with his previous commitment to deploy American peacekeepers if a peace agreement was signed.

Clinton married Hillary Rodham on October 11, 1975. The couple met while students at Yale University Law School. They had one daughter, Chelsea, who was born in 1980.

CHAPTER 37

Biographies of the Vice Presidents

BY DANIEL C. DILLER

THE VICE PRESIDENCY often has been ridiculed, sometimes by vice presidents themselves, as an insignificant office. Nevertheless, the importance of the vice presidency is obvious given that fourteen vice presidents have become president. Nine succeeded to the presidency after the death or resignation of the incumbent; the five others were elected in their own right.

The biographies of the thirty-one vice presidents who never became president follow. Although their names are obscure today, they were among the most powerful politicians—and fascinating characters—of their times.

Aaron Burr

BORN: February 6, 1756; Newark, New Jersey
PARTY: Democratic-Republican
TERM: March 4, 1801–March 4, 1805
PRESIDENT: Thomas Jefferson
DIED: September 14, 1836; Staten Island, New York
BURIED: Princeton, New Jersey

Aaron Burr was born into a family of prominent ministers, headed by his grandfather, the famous theologian and preacher Jonathan Edwards. Burr's father, Rev. Aaron Burr, was the cofounder and second president of Princeton University. His uncle, Timothy Edwards, was a clergyman as well. Shortly after Aaron's birth his parents died, and he and his sister were left in the custody of his uncle.

Burr was only thirteen when he entered Princeton University as a sophomore. He graduated with honors three years later in 1772 and briefly studied theology before abandoning it for a law career. But he had barely begun his legal studies when he received a commission in the army in 1775. Burr joined Gen. George Washington's army at Cambridge, Massachusetts, and served as a captain in Gen. Benedict Arnold's force, which failed to capture Quebec. He then became a member of General Washington's staff until the mutual dislike of the two men resulted in Burr's transfer to the staff of Gen. Israel Putnam. After Burr's promotion to lieutenant colonel he commanded a regiment that fought in the battle of Monmouth (New Jersey) in 1778. The following year he resigned his commission because of illness.

Burr studied law in Albany, New York, until 1782, when he was admitted to the bar. After practicing law in New York City, he was elected to the New York State legislature in 1784. New York governor George Clinton appointed Burr the state's attorney general in 1789, and two years later Burr was elected to the U.S. Senate.

Burr served in the Senate until 1797, then returned to New York. He won a seat in the New York legislature a year later and helped the Democratic-Republican Party take control of that body through his organizational work. Burr's reputation for political intrigue and romantic affairs had made him a controversial figure, but his intelligence, charm, and service to the Democratic-Republicans led to his nomination for vice president by that party in 1800.

The electoral procedure in effect through the 1800 election dictated that the candidate who received the second highest number of electoral votes for president became vice president. Each elector voted for two candidates, with no distinction made between a vote for president and a vote for vice president. Although the parties distinguished between their presidential and vice-presidential candidates, nothing prevented a vice-presidential candidate from being elected president if that candidate received more electoral votes than his presidential running mate.

In the election of 1800 this voting procedure resulted in a tie between the Democratic-Republican presidential candidate, Thomas Jefferson, and Burr, his vice-presidential running mate. Both men received seventy-three electoral votes, and Burr refused to concede the election. The responsibility for selecting a president then fell to the House of Representatives, where the Federalists had a majority. After a week and thirty-six ballots, the weary representatives elected Jefferson president. (The confusion of the 1800 election led to the Twelfth Amendment to the Constitution, which was ratified in 1804; it separated the voting for president and vice president.) Predictably, Jefferson did not include Burr in the deliberations of his administration.

Because of Alexander Hamilton's historic reputation as one of the most important Founders of the United States, the romantic mystique that surrounds the antiquated practice of dueling, and the incomprehensibility of a vice president committing murder while in office, Burr will always be remembered as the man who shot and killed Hamilton in a duel on July 11, 1804, at Weehawken, New Jersey. The duel occurred when Burr challenged Hamilton for making derogatory remarks about him during the 1804 New York gubernatorial campaign, which Burr lost to Hamilton's candidate. After Burr mortally wounded Hamilton he fled south to avoid the warrants that had been issued for his arrest in New York and New Jersey. Because federal law did not yet provide for the extradition of criminals from the District of Columbia, Burr returned to the capital. Incredibly, he resumed his duties as presiding officer of the Senate as if nothing had happened.

Even before he left office in 1805 Burr had begun to formulate a treasonous conspiracy. Although the details of Burr's plot are unclear, it is known that he hoped to incite a rebellion in the western regions of the United States, conquer Mexico, and then establish a vast western empire with New Orleans as its capital. While vice president he had proposed to the British ambassador in Washington that he lead a revolt in the western United States in return for $110,000. The offer was rejected, but Burr raised money through other means. He assembled a small force in the summer of 1806 and was preparing to move against Mexico when one of his co-conspirators, James Wilkinson, exposed the plot. Burr eventually was arrested and tried for treason in 1807 with Chief Justice John Marshall personally presiding over the case. President Jefferson pushed for a conviction, but, despite evidence that he had planned the conspiracy, Burr was acquitted because he had not yet committed an overt act of treason.

Even after his trial Burr continued to plot ways to gain an empire. In Europe he tried unsuccessfully to convince Napoleon to help him conquer Florida. After living in Europe for four years he returned to the United States in 1812 to be with his only daughter, Theodosia, who was married to Joseph Alston, the governor of South Carolina. She sailed from South Carolina to meet him in New York, but her ship was lost at sea. Burr then settled in New York City and spent the rest of his years practicing law.

Burr had married Theodosia's mother, Theodosia Prevost, in 1782; she died in 1794. In 1833 Burr married Eliza Jumel, a wealthy widow twenty years his junior. She was granted a divorce the day Burr died.

George Clinton

BORN: July 26, 1739; Little Britain, New York
PARTY: Democratic-Republican
TERM: March 4, 1805–April 20, 1812
PRESIDENTS: Thomas Jefferson; James Madison
DIED: April 20, 1812; Washington, D.C.
BURIED: Kingston, New York

Unlike the majority of his contemporaries who reached high office, George Clinton did not have the advantage of being born into a wealthy family. His father was a poor Irish immigrant who could not afford to send George to college. Thus, George went to sea when he was eighteen but returned home after a year. He then fought in the French and Indian War as a lieutenant and gained combat experience during the campaign of 1760 in which the British and their colonial allies captured Montreal.

After the war Clinton studied law in New York City and eventually was admitted to the bar. He then practiced law in his native Ulster County, New York, and in 1765 became district attorney. In 1768 Clinton began his rise in politics when he was elected to the New York Assembly. He served in that body until 1775, when he was elected to the Second Continental Congress.

As a prominent public figure with military experience, Clinton was appointed a brigadier general in the New York militia. Gen. George Washington then ordered him to lead his troops in defense of New York in the summer of 1776. Consequently, he was absent from the Continental Congress when the Declaration of Independence was signed, but he had advocated independence before his departure.

Although Clinton's forces were unable to defend Fort Montgomery in the highlands of the Hudson River from advancing British forces under Sir Henry Clinton, the stiff resistance shown by the New York militia enhanced George Clinton's reputation despite his mediocre military skills. In March 1777 Congress granted him the rank of brigadier general in the Continental army to go along with his generalship in the New York militia. He gave up his commissions, however, when he was chosen governor of New York. He assumed the office on July 30, 1777, and served six successive terms until 1795. During the Revolutionary War Governor Clinton became known for his harsh treatment of New York's loyalists.

Clinton's power within his home state made him a natural opponent of the new federal Constitution, which, if approved, would limit state sovereignty and slice into his personal power. As the presiding officer at New York's ratifying convention, he did his best to prevent ratification, but the Constitution won approval, 30–27.

Clinton's preeminence in New York gubernatorial elections was not challenged until 1792, when he narrowly defeated John Jay only after he had the votes of three counties invalidated on a technicality. Clinton recognized that his popularity in New York had slipped, and he declined to run for reelection in 1795. Six years later, however, he won another three-year term as governor with the support of his powerful nephew DeWitt Clinton, who manipulated his aging uncle during his last term in office.

Clinton's nomination as the Democratic-Republican candidate for vice president in 1804 stemmed from the new Twelfth Amendment, which linked the fates of a party's presidential and vice-presidential candidates. Vice-presidential nominees were chosen according to their ability to attract votes for their running mates. Although at age sixty-five Clinton's physical and mental capacities were declining, he could still deliver many votes for the Democratic-Republicans in his native New York. As a northerner he also would provide geographic balance to the ticket with Virginian Thomas Jefferson. After Aaron Burr the Democratic-Republicans desired a noncontroversial figure like Clinton for the number two spot. Clinton, who had designs on the presidency, accepted the vice-presidential nomination in the hope that it would be a steppingstone to the higher office. The Jefferson-Clinton ticket won easily over Federalists Charles Cotesworth Pinckney and Rufus King.

Clinton was regarded unanimously as a poor presiding officer of the Senate. His forgetfulness and inattention to detail caused much parliamentary confusion. He complained that his duties were tiresome, and he spent an increasing proportion of his time at his home in New York rather than at the capital.

Clinton still desired the presidency in 1808, but he was widely regarded as senile. Thus, he had little chance of beating out Jefferson's chosen successor, James Madison, for the Democratic-Republican nomination. Even though Clinton declared his availability for the presidency, the party caucus, as expected, selected Madison as its nominee, and Clinton bitterly accepted the consolation of yet another vice-presidential nomination. Madison and Clinton were easily elected, but the victory did not soften the vice president's hard feelings. He refused to attend Madison's inauguration and openly opposed the president's policies.

In 1811 Clinton got his chance to strike a blow against Madison and other Democratic-Republican leaders whom he believed had denied him the presidential nomination that he deserved. When the vote on the bill to recharter the Bank of the United States, which Madison favored, was tied in the Senate, Clinton, as vice president, cast the deciding vote against rechartering the bank. On April 20, 1812, at the age of seventy-two, Clinton became the first vice president to die in office.

Clinton married Cornelia Tappan, who was a member of a politically powerful family in New York's Ulster County, on February 7, 1770. They had six children. Cornelia died in 1800, before her husband became vice president.

Elbridge Gerry

BORN: July 17, 1744; Marblehead, Massachusetts
PARTY: Democratic-Republican
TERM: March 4, 1813–November 23, 1814
PRESIDENT: James Madison
DIED: November 23, 1814; Washington, D.C.
BURIED: Washington, D.C.

Elbridge Gerry was the son of a prosperous Massachusetts merchant. Upon graduating from Harvard in 1752, he entered his father's lucrative importing and shipping business. His resentment of British efforts to tax American commerce drew him into revolutionary circles. Gerry was elected to the General Court of Massachusetts in 1772 and subsequently the Massachusetts Provincial Congress. From his position in this body he managed supply procurement operations for his state's patriot forces in the early days of the American Revolution.

From 1776 to 1781 Gerry served in the Continental Congress. An influential member of its treasury committee, he put his supply procurement experience to use in the service of the Continental army. He also represented Massachusetts in Congress under the Articles of Confederation from 1783 to 1785. Gerry signed both the Declaration of Independence and the Articles of Confederation. At the Constitutional Convention he advocated strengthening the federal government. He refused, however, to endorse the document that the convention eventually produced because he thought it gave the federal government too much power over the states. After the Constitution was adopted by Massachusetts, Gerry put his reservations aside and supported the document. He was elected to two terms in the House of Representatives (1789–1793).

In 1797 President Adams sent Gerry, along with John Marshall and Charles C. Pinckney, to France to negotiate a treaty that would head off war between France and the United States. The talks were abandoned by the American side when the French representatives demanded as preconditions to negotiations a bribe for Foreign Minister Talleyrand, a loan for the French government, and an apology for Adams's recent criticisms. Marshall and Pinckney, who were known to be unsympathetic toward France, left for home. But Gerry stayed in Paris until the following year in the vain hope that his pro-French reputation might create an opening with the French that could lead to a treaty. A bribery incident, which came to be known as the "XYZ affair," after the French representatives who were referred to as "X, Y, and Z" in documents released by Adams, outraged the American public and ushered in several years of undeclared naval warfare with France. Gerry's Federalist opponents accused him of conducting an accommodating diplomacy with an enemy nation, but his reports of France's desire to avoid war contributed to Adams's decision to send another negotiating team to France in 1799.

When Gerry returned to the United States, he ran for the governorship of Massachusetts four consecutive years (1800–1803) without winning. His prospects for election were hampered by his position as a Democratic-Republican in a traditionally Federalist state. Finally, in 1810 and 1811, Gerry was elected to consecutive terms as governor.

Before the Massachusetts elections of 1812, Gerry left his most indelible mark on U.S. political culture. He signed a bill that restructured the senatorial districts of his state so that his party, the Democratic-Republicans, would be likely to win more seats than their actual numbers warranted. Because the map of the new districts was perceived to resemble the outline of a salamander, the redistricting tactic was dubbed a "gerrymander." Gerry had not sponsored the bill, but Federalists were quick to blame him for it. That year he failed to win reelection to his third term as governor.

Despite Gerry's advanced age and his defeat in his home state, his political career was not over. In 1812 the Democratic-Republicans were searching for a northerner to balance their ticket with President James Madison. After DeWitt Clinton of New York and John Langdon of New Hampshire refused the second spot, the party turned to Gerry. He and Madison defeated DeWitt Clinton and Jared Ingersoll, who had formed a coalition of Federalists and maverick Democratic-Republicans.

Gerry fulfilled his constitutional duty of presiding over the Senate despite his weakening health. During his vice presidency he was an outspoken proponent of the War of 1812. He narrowly missed becoming president in 1813 when Madison was stricken by a severe fever. Madison recovered and lived twenty-three years longer, but Gerry died in 1814 while still in office.

Gerry married Ann Thompson, the twenty-year-old daughter of a New York merchant, on January 12, 1786. The couple had ten children. Because of Ann's poor health, she did not move to Washington, D.C., with her husband when he became vice president, but, ironically, she lived thirty-five years after his death.

Daniel D. Tompkins

BORN: June 21, 1774; Fox Meadows (now Scarsdale), New York
PARTY: Democratic-Republican
TERM: March 4, 1817–March 4, 1825
PRESIDENT: James Monroe
DIED: June 11, 1825; Tompkinsville, Staten Island, New York
BURIED: New York City

Daniel D. Tompkins was born into a family of wealthy farmers in Westchester County, New York. His parents did not give him a middle name, but he added a middle initial to distinguish himself from another boy with the same name. He graduated from Columbia College in 1795 and was admitted to the bar two years later.

Tompkins enjoyed a brilliant early career in New York State politics that was sponsored by New York political boss DeWitt Clinton; Clinton eventually became his political enemy, however. In 1803 Tompkins won a seat in the New York State Assembly. The following year he was elected to the U.S. House of Representatives, but he resigned after he was appointed to the New York Supreme Court. He occupied that post until he was elected governor in 1807. He remained New York's chief executive until his rise to the vice presidency in 1817.

As governor, Tompkins was one of the few political leaders in the Northeast who supported the War of 1812. He borrowed millions of dollars and oversaw the disbursement of funds to pay troops and buy supplies. During his ten years as New York's chief executive, Tompkins also worked for prison reform, better

Daniel D. Tompkins

treatment of Native Americans, and the abolition of slavery in his state. Following his lead, the state legislature passed a bill in 1817 that outlawed slavery as of 1827. In 1814 President James Madison offered Tompkins the post of secretary of state, but he declined the appointment to remain governor of New York.

Tompkins sought the presidential nomination in 1816, but he was forced to settle for the vice presidency because Madison supported James Monroe and Tompkins was not well known outside New York. Like his predecessors, George Clinton and Elbridge Gerry, Tompkins provided the Democratic-Republican ticket with geographic balance. Unlike Clinton and Gerry, however, Tompkins had the advantage of being a youthful forty-two years old.

Tompkins's term as vice president was dominated by his fight against charges that he had mismanaged New York finances while he was governor during the war. Tompkins had indeed failed to keep accurate, detailed records of wartime expenditures and had mixed his personal finances with those of the state. Accounts showed that he owed New York $120,000. In April 1819 the state legislature voted to cancel the vice president's debt by granting him a commission on money he had raised during the war, but Tompkins insisted on a higher commission that would have required the state to pay him a sum in addition to forgiving the debt. His influence in the New York legislature, however, had been damaged by his decision to run for governor against DeWitt Clinton in 1820. Tompkins lost the election and incurred the enmity of Clinton, who snuffed out a movement in the Assembly to give Tompkins the money he claimed. Under

Clinton's direction the state filed a suit against the vice president to recover the debt.

Despite the financial scandal, Tompkins was again chosen by the Democratic-Republican Party as its candidate for vice president in 1820. Monroe and Tompkins won easily, with only one electoral college vote cast against them. Throughout his second term Tompkins remained preoccupied with his debt problem and devoted little time to the duties of his office. He declined to travel to the capital for the inauguration and was instead given the oath of office in a private ceremony in New York. In 1823, at Tompkins's request, the Senate chose a president pro tempore to preside over its deliberations; Tompkins never again led that body. When his term ended in 1825, he made no attempt to run for another national or state office. Instead, he continued to work to exonerate himself. Weakened by the stress of the scandal and his heavy drinking, he died a year later.

After Tompkins's death, audits finally revealed that New York actually owed him money. His descendants were paid $92,000. In 1827 the law abolishing slavery that had been signed by Tompkins ten years before went into effect. To honor the governor for his efforts to end slavery in the state, a square in New York City was renamed after him.

Tompkins married Hannah Minthorne, a member of a prominent New York family, around 1797. They had eight children.

John C. Calhoun

BORN: March 18, 1782; Abbeville District, South Carolina
PARTY: Democratic-Republican
TERM: March 4, 1825–December 28, 1832
PRESIDENTS: John Quincy Adams; Andrew Jackson
DIED: March 31, 1850; Washington, D.C.
BURIED: Charleston, South Carolina

John Caldwell Calhoun hailed from a family of wealthy and prestigious South Carolina planters. He received his early education at a school in Georgia and entered Yale University in 1802. After graduating in 1804 he studied law in Litchfield, Connecticut, and Abbeville, South Carolina. He was admitted to the South Carolina bar in 1807 and opened a law office in Abbeville. The following year he won a seat in the state legislature, and in 1811 he was elected to the U.S. House of Representatives as a Jeffersonian Democrat.

During the War of 1812 Calhoun gained national fame as a leader of the War Hawks, a group of expansionist members of Congress who helped push the United States toward war with the British. He served three terms in the House and chaired the Foreign Relations Committee. In 1817 President James Monroe appointed Calhoun secretary of war, a post that he held throughout Monroe's presidency.

Calhoun sought the presidency in 1824, but he received less support for the office than either John Quincy Adams or Andrew Jackson. Thus, he gave up his immediate presidential aspirations and maneuvered for the vice presidency. He courted

John C. Calhoun

Jackson and Adams and received the support of both men for his vice-presidential candidacy. Adams was elected president by the House of Representatives after neither he nor Jackson received a majority of electoral votes; Calhoun's fence-straddling strategy thus paid off.

Calhoun's quest for the vice presidency was not motivated primarily by his ambition to serve in that office. He saw the post as a steppingstone to the presidency. Nevertheless, the talented former House member devoted himself to his duties as the presiding officer of the Senate. In this capacity he worked to foil the programs of President Adams, with whom he shared few political goals. The two men vented their antagonism toward one another through letters published in newspapers under pseudonyms.

Calhoun endured a political scandal during his first term as vice president. It was discovered that, while Calhoun had served as secretary of war under James Monroe, an assistant had awarded a $450,000 military construction contract to the assistant's brother-in-law. Calhoun was accused of receiving a cut of the profits from the deal. After declaring his innocence, the vice president asked the House of Representatives to investigate the matter, and he took a temporary leave of absence while a seven-member committee examined the charges. Six weeks later the committee exonerated Calhoun of any misconduct. The vice president confidently resumed his duties, but the scandal had damaged his reputation.

By 1828 Calhoun's break with John Quincy Adams was complete. The vice president threw his support behind Democratic

presidential candidate Andrew Jackson, who in turn backed Calhoun's nomination for a second vice-presidential term. The Jackson-Calhoun ticket easily defeated Adams and Richard Rush of Pennsylvania.

Like John Quincy Adams, Jackson soon became disaffected with his vice president. The split between the two men was first opened in early 1829 not by a political dispute, but by the refusal of Calhoun's wife to accept the wife of Secretary of War John H. Eaton into Washington society. Eaton had met his wife, Peggy O'Neale Timberlake, while he was living in a tavern owned by Peggy and her first husband. Eaton had carried on an affair with Mrs. Timberlake, and, after Mr. Timberlake's death at sea, Eaton followed the advice of his close friend Andrew Jackson and married her. When the wives of prominent politicians in Washington, led by Calhoun's wife, Floride, refused to accept Mrs. Eaton as an equal, Jackson blamed his vice president.

The Eaton affair was a small matter compared to Calhoun's increasingly radical opinions on states' rights. During his early career Calhoun had been known as a nationalist. He had not only called for war with the British in 1812, but also supported the National Bank, internal improvements, and a high tariff that many of his fellow southerners opposed. By 1827, however, Calhoun had begun to believe that the southern states needed protection from the high tariffs being imposed by the federal government and the growing antislavery movement in the North. He even wrote anonymously in support of nullification, a concept that allowed a state to nullify within its borders a federal law that it believed was against its interests. Andrew Jackson rejected nullification as an illegal usurpation of national sovereignty by the states. On April 13, 1830, at a Jefferson Day dinner, Jackson resolved to find out whether his vice president's first loyalties were to his country or to his state. The president stared directly at Calhoun as he delivered the toast: "Our Union—it must be preserved." When the vice president replied, "The Union, next to our liberties, most dear," he finally committed himself to South Carolina and the South. As a result, Calhoun no longer had much influence with Jackson, and he lost any chance of eventually attaining the presidency.

In 1832 the Nullification Crisis occurred when South Carolina declared that federal tariffs had no force in the state. But South Carolina leaders agreed to a compromise tariff after Andrew Jackson threatened to send 200,000 troops to that state to enforce the law. Two months before his term was to expire Calhoun resigned the vice presidency in response to Jackson's actions and accepted an appointment to a vacant Senate seat from South Carolina. He remained in that office until 1844, when he resigned to become secretary of state during John Tyler's last year in office. He returned to the Senate in 1845 and served there until his death in 1850. After he left the vice presidency Calhoun did not try to conceal his southern partisanship. He was celebrated in the South for his eloquent advocacy of slavery and states' rights.

Calhoun married Floride Bonneau Calhoun, a wealthy cousin, in January 1811. They had nine children.

Richard M. Johnson

BORN: October 17, 1780; Floyd's Station, Kentucky
PARTY: Democratic
TERM: March 4, 1837–March 4, 1841
PRESIDENT: Martin Van Buren
DIED: November 19, 1850; Frankfort, Kentucky
BURIED: Frankfort, Kentucky

The son of a wealthy Kentucky landowner, Richard Mentor Johnson studied law at Transylvania University in Lexington, Kentucky, and was admitted to the bar in 1802. After briefly practicing law, Johnson began his political career at the age of twenty-four when he was elected to the Kentucky legislature. Two years later, in 1806, he was elected to the U.S. House of Representatives, where he served until 1819.

Before the War of 1812 Johnson joined with other War Hawks from the South and West in calling for war with Great Britain. When the fighting began, he left the capital without resigning his seat in Congress to become a colonel in command of a regiment of his fellow Kentuckians. In 1813 he led his troops skillfully at the battle of Thames River, where U.S. forces defeated the British and their Indian allies. Johnson, who was seriously wounded in the battle, gained national fame for allegedly killing the Indian chief Tecumseh.

When his wounds healed, Johnson returned to Congress, where he worked to secure military pensions for veterans. In 1816 he authored a bill that granted members of Congress a $1,500 salary instead of a daily allowance for expenses. Although Johnson had justified the salary as a way to encourage Congress to expedite legislative business, the public saw only greed in the

law. Johnson responded by supporting the repeal of his own bill. In 1819 he retired from the House and returned to Kentucky, where the state legislature promptly elected him to an unexpired Senate seat. He served in that body until 1829, when he was again elected to the House after losing reelection to the Senate.

In 1824 Johnson backed Henry Clay's presidential bid but switched to Andrew Jackson when Clay threw his support behind John Quincy Adams. Because no candidate had received a majority of electoral votes, the election was decided by the House, which elected Adams. Thereafter, Johnson developed a close political association with Andrew Jackson, who became president in 1829. As a member of Congress, Johnson voted for the president's tariff policies and supported Jackson's stands against the Second Bank of the United States and the use of public funds for internal improvements.

Before the 1836 presidential election Andrew Jackson designated Martin Van Buren as the Democratic Party's presidential nominee and pushed for Johnson to be Van Buren's running mate. Jackson probably wanted to reward the Kentuckian for his political loyalty, but the outgoing president also may have believed that Johnson would strengthen Van Buren's candidacy. The Kentuckian gave the ticket geographical balance and a more heroic image. The lore surrounding Johnson's Indian fighting exploits helped to offset the popularity of William Henry Harrison, one of the Whig candidates, who also had a reputation as an Indian fighter and had been Johnson's commanding general at the battle of Thames River.

Despite these contributions to the ticket, the scandals surrounding Johnson's personal life would have prevented his nomination had he not had the support of Jackson, who was still the most powerful and popular political figure in the United States. Johnson was reviled by his fellow politicians for keeping a succession of black mistresses. He had two daughters by his first mistress, Julia Chinn, a mulatto slave he had inherited from his father. Johnson's attempts to introduce his daughters into society as equals offended many powerful southern slaveowners. His vulgar manners and shabby appearance also lost him support.

When it came time to select Van Buren's running mate in 1840, the Democratic Party initially ignored Johnson. Even Andrew Jackson had become convinced that Johnson was no longer fit to be vice president. Jackson denounced the colonel's candidacy, saying it would cost "thousands of votes." Thus, rather than renominate Johnson, the Democratic convention chose to allow individual states to nominate vice-presidential candidates. Enough states nominated Johnson, however, to get his name on the ballot. Van Buren and Johnson tried to repeat their success of 1836, but they faced a better-organized Whig Party, which had coalesced behind William Henry Harrison. The economic depression that had plagued Van Buren's presidency and a shrewd Whig campaign that relied on catchy slogans and generous quantities of hard cider brought Harrison victory.

After leaving the vice presidency in 1841 Johnson returned to

Kentucky, where he again served in the state legislature until 1842. Two years later he sought the Democratic presidential nomination at the Baltimore national convention, but his favorite-son candidacy received little support. In 1850 the ailing sixty-nine-year-old was elected to the Kentucky legislature for the final time; however, he died of a stroke without ever taking up his legislative duties.

George M. Dallas

BORN: July 10, 1792; Philadelphia, Pennsylvania
PARTY: Democratic
TERM: March 4, 1845–March 4, 1849
PRESIDENT: James K. Polk
DIED: December 31, 1864; Philadelphia
BURIED: Philadelphia

George Mifflin Dallas was born into a wealthy Philadelphia family. His father, Alexander Dallas, had served as secretary of the Treasury under James Madison. George was groomed for college by Philadelphia's best tutors. After graduating from Princeton University in 1810, he went to work in his father's law office. He was admitted to the bar in 1813. That year he traveled to Russia to serve as a private secretary to Albert Gallatin, the U.S. minister in St. Petersburg. When he returned in 1814, he worked for his father in the Treasury Department and later on the legal staff of the Second Bank of the United States. During the 1820s Dallas became increasingly active in politics. He supported the presidential candidacy of John C. Calhoun in 1824. After Andrew Jackson's strong showing in that election, however, Dallas became a Jacksonian Democrat.

Dallas began his own political career in 1828 when he was elected mayor of Philadelphia. In 1829 he accepted an appointment as U.S. district attorney for eastern Pennsylvania. Two years later his state legislature sent him to the U.S. Senate, where he served out an unexpired term. Although Dallas remained personally loyal to President Jackson, he favored the rechartering of the National Bank, which Jackson successfully opposed. When his senatorial term expired in 1833, Dallas returned to Pennsylvania, where he served as state attorney general until 1835. Martin Van Buren appointed him minister to Russia in 1837, but he resigned the post in 1839, claiming there was little work for a U.S. minister to do there. Upon his return to Pennsylvania, he reestablished his law practice while remaining active in state politics.

In 1844 the Democratic National Convention, meeting in Baltimore, Maryland, chose Sen. Silas Wright of New York as James K. Polk's running mate. Wright, who was in Washington, D.C., refused to accept the nomination because his close political associate, Martin Van Buren, had been denied the top spot on the ticket. Wright had received the news of his nomination by telegraph and had wired his answer back to the convention. Democratic leaders, however, wanted to make sure the new invention had not made a mistake and sent a messenger to Washington. By the time the confirmation of Wright's refusal reached Baltimore, many of the delegates had gone home.

Those delegates still in Baltimore gathered early the next morning to select another candidate. On the second ballot they nominated Dallas to balance the ticket with Polk, who was from Tennessee. Polk and Dallas defeated Whigs Henry Clay and Theodore Frelinghuysen by 170–105 in the electoral college, with Pennsylvania's twenty-six votes contributing to the margin of victory.

Dallas believed that a vice president should support the administration's policies even when in disagreement with them. In 1846 he demonstrated his devotion to this principle by breaking a tie vote in the Senate on a low-tariff bill supported by Polk, in spite of his state's strong protectionist sentiment. The vice president's action was attacked so bitterly in Pennsylvania that he arranged to move his family to Washington, D.C., because he feared for their safety.

By voting for the low-tariff bill, Dallas had hoped to win support in the South and West for his own presidential candidacy in 1848. At the Democratic National Convention that year he received only a handful of votes on the first ballot; Democrats were skeptical of a candidate who probably could not even win his home state. The convention chose instead Sen. Lewis Cass of Michigan, and Dallas retired from politics. In 1856 President Franklin Pierce appointed Dallas minister to Great Britain, a post he retained under James Buchanan. In 1861 he returned to Philadelphia, where he lived until he died suddenly on the last day of 1864.

Dallas married Sophia Nicklin in Philadelphia on May 23, 1816. The couple, who took their family with them on diplomatic missions to Europe, had eight children. Dallas, Texas, is named after George Dallas, who was vice president when Texas was admitted to the Union on December 29, 1845.

William R. King

BORN: April 7, 1786; Sampson County, North Carolina
PARTY: Democratic
TERM: March 24, 1853–April 18, 1853
PRESIDENT: Franklin Pierce
DIED: April 18, 1853; Dallas County, Alabama
BURIED: Selma, Alabama

William Rufus Devane King was the son of well-to-do North Carolina planters William and Margaret King. Young William graduated from the University of North Carolina in 1803. After studying law in Fayetteville, North Carolina, he was admitted to the bar in 1806.

King entered politics in 1807 at the age of twenty-one when he won a two-year term in the North Carolina House of Commons. In 1810 he was elected to the U.S. House of Representatives, where he sided with the War Hawks, who supported the War of 1812 with Great Britain. He resigned from the House in 1816, however, to undertake a diplomatic mission to Italy and Russia.

When he returned to the United States in 1818, King moved to Alabama and bought a plantation. He was a delegate to the convention that established Alabama's state government, and he was elected to the U.S. Senate in 1820 as one of Alabama's first senators. During his long career in the Senate King was a strong supporter of Andrew Jackson's policies. He served as president pro tempore of the Senate from 1836 to 1841.

In 1844 King left the Senate after twenty-four years when President John Tyler appointed him minister to France. While in Paris he helped secure French acquiescence to the U.S. annexation of Texas. He returned to Alabama in 1846 and was defeated for reelection to the Senate. Two years later, however, King was appointed by the governor of Alabama to fill an unexpired Senate seat. He served as chairman of the Senate Foreign Relations Committee, and, when Millard Fillmore became president following the death of Zachary Taylor in 1850, the Senate selected King to take over Fillmore's duties as presiding officer of the Senate.

During King's time in Washington, D.C., he was surrounded by an air of personal scandal. His lack of a wife and his intimate friendship with James Buchanan, with whom he shared an apartment while the two men served in the Senate, led to speculation that he was a homosexual. King also was ridiculed for his fastidious dressing habits and his insistence on wearing a wig long after they had gone out of style. Andrew Jackson referred to King as "Miss Nancy." Like Richard M. Johnson, however, King overcame the gossip about his private life to obtain the vice presidency.

In 1852 the Democrats chose King to balance the ticket with their dark horse presidential candidate, Franklin Pierce of New Hampshire. The choice of King was also intended to satisfy supporters of James Buchanan, who had sought the presidential nomination. King, however, was already ill with tuberculosis when he received the nomination. His condition deteriorated rapidly before the election, and he was not able to campaign. King's condition did not raise much concern among voters, however, as the Pierce-King team defeated Whigs Winfield Scott and William Alexander Graham by an electoral college vote of 254–42.

After the election King traveled to Cuba in the hope that the Caribbean climate would heal him. There on March 24, 1853, with the special permission of Congress, he became the only executive officer of the United States to take the oath of office on foreign soil. King realized that he was weakening and asked the U.S. government for a ship to take him back to the United States to die. The U.S. Navy steamship *Fulton* transported him to Mobile, Alabama. He reached his plantation, King's Bend, on April 17 and died the next day. King served just twenty-five days of his term, fewer than any other vice president.

John C. Breckinridge

BORN: January 21, 1821; Lexington, Kentucky
PARTY: Democratic
TERM: March 4, 1857–March 4, 1861
PRESIDENT: James Buchanan
DIED: May 17, 1875; Lexington
BURIED: Lexington

John Cabell Breckinridge was born into a prominent Kentucky family. His grandfather, John Breckinridge, had represented Kentucky in the Senate and had served as attorney general

John C. Breckinridge

under Thomas Jefferson. His father, Joseph Cabell Breckinridge, was an influential lawyer and politician.

Breckinridge attended Centre College in Danville, Kentucky, graduating in 1839. After studying law at the College of New Jersey (later Princeton University) and Transylvania College in Lexington, Kentucky, he was admitted to the bar in 1841. He opened a law practice in Burlington, Iowa, but returned to Kentucky after two years. By 1845 he had established a successful law partnership in Lexington.

In 1846 he declined to fight in the Mexican War. The following year, however, after delivering a moving speech honoring the state's war dead in front of thousands of people, he was given a commission as a major and sent to Mexico. Although he arrived after most of the fighting was over, he was able to add military experience to his political credentials.

In 1849 Breckinridge was elected to the Kentucky legislature as a Democrat. Two years later he upset the Whig candidate for a seat in the U.S. House of Representatives from Henry Clay's former district. In 1855, after two terms, Breckinridge left Congress to resume his law practice in Kentucky and improve his finances. That year he also turned down President Franklin Pierce's offer of the ambassadorship to Spain.

The 1856 Democratic National Convention nominated Pennsylvanian James Buchanan for president and Breckinridge for vice president. Buchanan easily defeated John C. Fremont of the new Republican Party, whose election many Americans feared would bring civil war. Breckinridge was a capable presiding

officer of the Senate. The handsome and eloquent vice president was so popular in his home state that, sixteen months before his vice-presidential term was to expire, he was elected to a term in the U.S. Senate, which was to begin when he left the vice presidency.

In 1860 southern Democrats nominated Breckinridge for the presidency, while Illinois senator Stephen A. Douglas was nominated by Democrats in the North. Breckinridge had not encouraged this split in his party, but he accepted the nomination. He declared that he favored preserving the Union and that it could be saved if slavery were not prohibited in the territories. Breckinridge finished second with seventy-two electoral votes from eleven southern states. Abraham Lincoln received less than 40 percent of the popular vote, but with three other candidates splitting the vote—Breckinridge, Douglas, and John Bell of the Constitutional Union Party—Lincoln won 180 electoral votes and the presidency.

As a lame-duck vice president, Breckinridge worked with Democratic leaders who searched vainly for a compromise that would prevent civil war. After Lincoln's inauguration Breckinridge returned to Kentucky, whose leaders were debating the future of their state. Breckinridge was in favor of secession, but he accepted the state's declaration of neutrality. When Congress reconvened on July 4, 1861, he took his seat in the Senate. Throughout the summer he defended the right of southern states to secede and opposed Lincoln's efforts to raise an army to put down the insurrection.

In September Union and Confederate armies invaded Kentucky. When the Union army won control of the state, Breckinridge offered his services to the South and was indicted for treason by the federal government. He joined the Confederate army and was commissioned as a brigadier general. After serving at the battle of Shiloh in April 1862, he was promoted to major general. He led troops at the battles of Vicksburg, Murfreesboro, Chickamauga, Chattanooga, and Cold Harbor. In February 1865 Confederate president Jefferson Davis appointed Breckinridge secretary of war.

When the South surrendered in April 1865, Breckinridge feared that he would be captured and prosecuted as a traitor. He and his small party eluded federal troops for two months as they made their way through the South and across the water to Cuba. For three and a half years Breckinridge lived in Europe and Canada while he waited for the treason charge against him to be dropped. On Christmas Day 1868 President Andrew Johnson declared an amnesty for all who had participated in the insurrection. The following March Breckinridge returned to Kentucky, where crowds greeted him as a hero. He settled in Lexington and resumed his law practice. He died at the age of fifty-four after undergoing his second unsuccessful liver operation.

Breckinridge married Mary Burch of Lexington, Kentucky, on December 12, 1843. They had five children. Although Mary suffered through several periods of poor health during her lifetime, she lived for thirty-two years after her husband's death.

Hannibal Hamlin

BORN: August 27, 1809; Paris Hill, Maine
PARTY: Republican
TERM: March 4, 1861–March 4, 1865
PRESIDENT: Abraham Lincoln
DIED: July 4, 1891; Bangor, Maine
BURIED: Bangor

Hannibal Hamlin's ancestors were among the first settlers in Maine. His father, Cyrus, was a Harvard-educated doctor who also dabbled in farming and small-town politics. Hannibal's parents intended to send him to college and even gave him a prep school education, but family financial troubles forced him to abandon his college plans. He worked as a surveyor, printer, schoolteacher, and farmer before deciding to study law.

In Portland, Maine, Hamlin studied law in the office of Samuel C. Fessenden, the leading antislavery activist in the state. Hamlin was admitted to the bar in 1833 and established a lucrative law practice in Hampden, Maine. In 1836 he was elected as a Democrat to the Maine House of Representatives. During his five years in that body he served three one-year terms as speaker.

In 1843 Hamlin was elected to the U.S. House of Representatives, where he served two terms. Then in 1847, after a brief stint back in the Maine legislature, that body elected him to the U.S. Senate. While in the Senate, Hamlin became an outspoken opponent of slavery. He supported Democrat Franklin Pierce in the 1852 presidential election, but in 1856 his abolitionist sentiments caused him to defect to the new Republican Party. He was elected governor of Maine in 1857 but resigned after serving

only a few weeks when he once again was elected to the Senate.

The 1860 Republican National Convention nominated Abraham Lincoln of Illinois for president. Republican leaders correctly saw that Lincoln had little chance to win electoral votes in the South, even if a southerner were nominated for the vice presidency. Consequently, giving the ticket geographic balance meant choosing a northeasterner for vice president. Republican leaders were also looking for a candidate who would satisfy William H. Seward, the powerful New York senator who had hoped to be the presidential nominee. The convention settled on Hamlin, who met both requirements and had the proper antislavery credentials. Lincoln and Hamlin faced a divided Democratic Party and won the election with less than 40 percent of the popular vote.

Hamlin, who criticized the president's circumspect approach to emancipation, had little influence within the Lincoln administration. Hamlin disliked the vice presidency, not only because of his lack of power, but also because the office did not allow him to dispense any patronage, which for Hamlin had been the foremost reward of political success. Although well qualified to preside over the Senate, Hamlin spent little time in this capacity. Routinely, he presided over a new session of the Senate only until it chose a president pro tempore, after which he returned to Maine.

Despite Hamlin's misgivings about the vice presidency, he wanted a second term. Lincoln, however, believed that Hamlin's view toward the South had become too radical and did not support his candidacy. The 1864 National Union Convention, a coalition of Republicans and pro-Union Democrats, nominated Tennessee Democrat Andrew Johnson to run with Lincoln. Republican leaders hoped Johnson would be better able than Hamlin to attract votes in border states and among northern Democrats.

After retiring from the vice presidency Hamlin served for a year as collector of the port of Boston and two years as president of a railroad company. In 1868 Maine again elected him to the Senate. He served two terms during which he was associated with the radical Republicans who advocated harsh Reconstruction policies. Hamlin retired from politics in 1881 but secured an appointment as minister to Spain. During his year and a half in Europe he and his wife traveled widely on the Continent, occasionally showing up in Madrid to perform the minimum duties of his post.

In late 1882 Hamlin returned to Maine, where he enjoyed a quiet retirement. He died of heart failure on July 4, 1891, at the age of eighty-one.

Hamlin married Sarah Emery on December 10, 1833, in Paris Hill, Maine. The couple had four children before she died in 1855. On September 25, 1856, Hamlin married Ellen Vesta Emery, a younger half-sister of his first wife. They had two sons; the younger was born while Hamlin was vice president.

Schuyler Colfax

BORN: March 23, 1823; New York City
PARTY: Republican
TERM: March 4, 1869–March 4, 1873
PRESIDENT: Ulysses S. Grant
DIED: January 13, 1885; Mankato, Minnesota
BURIED: South Bend, Indiana

Schuyler Colfax was the son of Schuyler and Hannah Colfax. His father died in 1822, and his mother married George Matthews in 1832. Schuyler attended public schools in New York City until he was ten. In 1836 he moved with his family to New Carlisle, Indiana, where he studied law but never passed the bar. His interest in politics stemmed from his writing for newspapers, which he began at age sixteen. In 1841 Schuyler's stepfather, who was county auditor, appointed his stepson deputy auditor, a post Schuyler then occupied for eight years.

Colfax became active in state politics in 1842 when he began a two-year term as enrolling clerk of the Indiana Senate. In 1845 Colfax became part owner of the *South Bend Free Press*. He changed its name to the *St. Joseph Valley Register* and used it to support Whig candidates and issues. Colfax attended several state and national Whig conventions and ran unsuccessfully for the U.S. House of Representatives in 1851. When the Republican Party was formed, Colfax became a member and helped build a Republican organization in Indiana. In 1855 he was elected to the U.S. House of Representatives, where he served for the next fourteen years until he became vice president in 1869. During his last five and a half years in the House, he held the office of Speaker.

At the 1868 Republican National Convention Colfax actively sought the vice presidency. He hoped the Republican presidential nominee, Ulysses S. Grant, would serve only one four-year term, thereby setting the stage for his own nomination for president in 1872. Colfax emerged from a crowd of favorite-son candidates to receive the vice-presidential nomination on the fifth ballot despite being from Indiana, a state contiguous to Grant's home state of Illinois. Grant, however, was the most celebrated hero of the Civil War, and a geographically balanced ticket was not necessary for victory. He and Colfax easily defeated Democrats Horatio Seymour and Francis P. Blair Jr. 214–80 in the electoral college. Like most nineteenth-century vice presidents, Colfax did not play a significant role in his running mate's administration.

During Colfax's rise in government he had gained a reputation for political intrigue. He was known as the "Smiler" and "Great Joiner" for his propensity to join any club or organization that would accept him. Abraham Lincoln had called Colfax a "friendly rascal." Events would show, however, that Colfax was not just an opportunistic and manipulative politician; he was also corrupt.

A September 1872 newspaper exposé implicated Colfax in the Crédit Mobilier scandal. In 1867 Congress had appropriated funds for the construction of the Union Pacific Railroad. The director of the railroad, Oakes Ames (R-Mass.), who was also a House member, set up a holding company, Crédit Mobilier of America, in which he deposited millions of dollars of money appropriated for the railroad. He proceeded to bribe other members of Congress not to expose his corruption and to support legislation favorable to the railroad by selling them shares of stock in the holding company at bargain prices. While Speaker of the House, Colfax had received twenty shares of Crédit Mobilier stock and substantial dividends from those shares. His defense of his actions was unconvincing, and he fell back on the argument that his mistakes while in Congress should not affect his tenure as vice president. Some members of Congress considered impeaching him, but, because his term was about to expire, they dropped the matter. Colfax then claimed he had been exonerated, but his political reputation was ruined.

When Colfax left office, he made a good living by touring the country delivering lectures. He died of a stroke in 1885 after changing trains in subzero weather during a lecture tour of Minnesota.

Colfax married Evelyn Clark on October 10, 1844. His wife, who had no children, died in 1863 while he was Speaker of the House. On November 18, 1868, he married Ellen Wade, a niece of Sen. Benjamin F. Wade (R-Ohio), who had been Colfax's primary rival for the 1868 vice-presidential nomination. The couple had one child, Schuyler Colfax III. Colfax's grandfather, William Colfax, had been the commander of George Washington's bodyguard during the Revolutionary War.

Henry Wilson

BORN: February 16, 1812; Farmington, New Hampshire
PARTY: Republican
TERM: March 4, 1873–November 22, 1875
PRESIDENT: Ulysses S. Grant
DIED: November 22, 1875; Washington, D.C.
BURIED: Natick, Massachusetts

Henry Wilson was born Jeremiah Jones Colbath, the son of Abigail and Winthrop Colbath, a poor New Hampshire sawmill worker. When Jeremiah was ten, he was indentured to a farmer, for whom he labored for over ten years for room and board. During his free hours he educated himself by reading hundreds of borrowed books. On his twenty-first birthday Jeremiah was given his freedom as well as six sheep and a pair of oxen. He broke with the hard life he had led by selling the livestock for eighty-five dollars and legally changing his name to Henry Wilson.

Wilson then walked over one hundred miles to Natick, Massachusetts, where he apprenticed himself to a shoemaker. He learned the trade within a month, bought his freedom from his master, and went into business for himself. By the time he was twenty-seven Wilson owned a shoe factory that employed as many as one hundred people. Although Wilson was accumulating a modest fortune, his political ambitions were stronger than his desire for wealth. He continued to read voraciously and developed his speaking skills at the Natick Debating Society. In 1840 Wilson was elected as a Whig to the Massachu-

setts legislature, where he served for most of the next twelve years.

Wilson left the Whig Party in 1848 because of its indecisiveness on the slavery issue. He helped form the Free Soil Party and edited the *Boston Republican*, a party organ, from 1848 to 1851. He joined the ultraconservative American (Know Nothing) Party in 1854 but walked out of its 1855 convention when it too failed to take a strong stand against slavery.

Earlier in 1855 Wilson had been elected to the U.S. Senate by the Massachusetts legislature to fill an unexpired term. He served in the Senate until 1873, when he became vice president. Wilson joined the Republican Party after his rejection of the Know Nothings. He made many enemies among southern members of Congress for his harsh attacks in the Senate against slavery. His fear of assassination led him to carry a pistol and make plans for his family to be provided for in the event of his death. In addition to his activism against slavery, Wilson also established himself as an advocate of the rights of factory workers.

During the Civil War Wilson served as chairman of the Senate Committee on Military Affairs. In this capacity he earned praise from military and political leaders for his effective legislative leadership in raising and supporting the huge Union army. After the war he supported the harsh Reconstruction program of the radical Republicans and voted for Andrew Johnson's impeachment in 1868. Wilson's Reconstruction views softened late in his Senate career after he toured the South and West extensively.

Wilson was nominated to be President Ulysses S. Grant's vice-presidential running mate at the 1872 Republican National Convention in Philadelphia. Like his vice-presidential predecessor, Schuyler Colfax, Wilson had been involved in the Crédit Mobilier scandal. A few weeks before the 1872 presidential election the *New York Sun* broke the story that several members of Congress, including Wilson, were involved in the bribery scheme. Wilson, however, claimed that he had returned the twenty Crédit Mobilier shares he had purchased before he reaped any profit from them. Although Wilson was not exonerated by the congressional committees investigating the scandal until several months after the election, his troubles did not affect the election's outcome. The highly popular president Grant easily defeated Democrat Horace Greeley 286–66 in the electoral college.

Shortly after the election Wilson suffered a stroke. When he recovered, he claimed to be in good health, but he was a poor presiding officer of the Senate. In 1875, he died from a second stroke with a year and a half left in his term.

Wilson married sixteen-year-old Harriet Malvina Howe on October 28, 1840. She died of cancer on May 28, 1870. They had one son, Henry Hamilton Wilson, who distinguished himself as a Union officer during the Civil War. He died in 1866 while still in the army.

William A. Wheeler

BORN: June 30, 1819; Malone, New York
PARTY: Republican
TERM: March 4, 1877–March 4, 1881
PRESIDENT: Rutherford B. Hayes
DIED: June 4, 1887; Malone
BURIED: Malone

William Almon Wheeler was the second of the two children of Eliza and Almon Wheeler. Although William's father was a lawyer, he left virtually no estate when he died in 1827. William worked his way through a preparatory academy, and in 1838 he enrolled in the University of Vermont, where he led a spartan existence. He had so little money that at one point he lived on bread and water for several weeks. After two years these financial problems forced Wheeler to drop out of college before graduating.

He returned to his home in Malone, New York, where he studied law with a local lawyer. He was admitted to the New York bar in 1845 and served as district attorney of Franklin County from 1846 to 1849. In 1850 he was elected to the New York State legislature as a Whig. Upon leaving the assembly in 1851 he took over the management of a Malone bank, and two years later he became a trustee for the mortgage holders of the Northern Railway. Like many northern Whigs, Wheeler switched his loyalty to the Republican Party in the mid-1850s. From 1858 to 1860 he served in the New York State Senate, where as president pro tempore he gained experience presiding over a legislature.

In 1861 Wheeler was elected to the U.S. House of Representatives, his first national office. He served only one term but remained active in New York politics. In 1867 he was chosen to preside over the New York constitutional convention because he was on good terms with the New York Republican machine while retaining his independence. He was reelected to the U.S. House in 1869 and served there until he became vice president in 1877.

Wheeler was best known not for his legislative skill or political acumen but for his scrupulous honesty. He demonstrated this quality during the "Salary Grab" of 1873, in which Congress voted itself a 50 percent pay raise and back pay of $5,000. Wheeler voted against the measure, and, when it was passed, he returned the back pay. His most notable accomplishment during his time in the House was his service on a congressional committee that investigated an election dispute in Louisiana in 1874. He developed a compromise known as the "Wheeler adjustment" that resolved the dispute and ended the threat of civil unrest.

When Wheeler's name was put into contention for the vice presidency at the 1876 Republican National Convention, he was virtually unknown. Earlier in the year when someone had suggested a Hayes-Wheeler ticket, Hayes commented in a letter to his wife, "Who is Wheeler?" Despite his lack of prominence, Wheeler received the vice-presidential nomination because he was from New York, he had a spotless reputation, and the convention delegates were anxious to go home.

The election of 1876 involved the uncontroversial Wheeler in one of the most intense political controversies in American history. Although the Hayes-Wheeler ticket received a minority of the popular vote and their Democratic opponents appeared to win the electoral college, Republican leaders challenged the election results in several southern states. After months of political maneuvers and backroom deals, a congressionally appointed electoral commission ruled in favor of Hayes and Wheeler.

Wheeler was a conscientious presiding officer of the Senate, but he had little enthusiasm for his office. He frequently referred to Benjamin Franklin's comment that the vice presidency was so insignificant that its occupant should be called "His Superfluous Highness."

Wheeler welcomed the end of his term as vice president. He quietly retired to Malone, where he lived the last six years of his life. He had married Mary King on September 17, 1845. She died in March 1876, three months before he was nominated for the vice presidency. The couple had no children, and, when Wheeler's sister died shortly after his wife, he was left without any immediate family. Although Hayes had never met Wheeler before 1876, they became close friends during their time in office. The widowed vice president spent many evenings at the White House with Hayes and his wife, Lucy.

Thomas A. Hendricks

BORN: September 7, 1819; near Zanesville, Ohio
PARTY: Democratic
TERM: March 4, 1885–November 25, 1885
PRESIDENT: Grover Cleveland
DIED: November 25, 1885; Indianapolis, Indiana
BURIED: Indianapolis

Thomas Andrews Hendricks was born in Ohio, the son of John and Jane Hendricks. In 1820, when Thomas was a baby, the family moved to Indiana, where Thomas grew up working on the family farm in Shelby County. He attended local schools before enrolling in Hanover College near Madison, Indiana. After his graduation in 1841, Thomas began to study law in Shelbyville, Indiana. In 1843 he traveled to Chambersburg, Pennsylvania, to study law under an uncle who was a judge. He returned to Shelbyville the following year, passed the bar, and established a successful law practice.

Hendricks entered politics in 1848 when he was elected to the Indiana legislature. In 1850 he served as a delegate to the convention called to revise the Indiana constitution. At the convention he supported a proposal to prohibit blacks from entering the state. He was elected to the U.S. House of Representatives in 1851 and again in 1852 when the state constitution mandated that House elections be held in even-numbered years. While in the House, Hendricks aligned himself with the policies of Democratic senator Stephen A. Douglas of Illinois. Hendricks was a strong supporter of Douglas's Kansas-Nebraska Act, which per-

mitted Kansas to decide for itself whether it would be a slave state or free state and precipitated a bloody war in that territory. Hendricks lost reelection to the House in 1854, but President Franklin Pierce appointed him commissioner of the general land office, a post he occupied until 1859.

In 1860 Hendricks ran for governor of Indiana but was defeated by Republican Henry S. Lane. When the Democratic Party gained control of the Indiana legislature in 1863, Hendricks was elected to the U.S. Senate. During his single term he was a leading critic of Lincoln's leadership during the war. Hendricks supported appropriations to pay for troops, weapons, and supplies, but he opposed the Emancipation Proclamation, the draft, and many other wartime measures. After the war he backed President Andrew Johnson's magnanimous Reconstruction plan and worked against the Thirteenth Amendment, which abolished slavery, and the Fourteenth Amendment, which gave African Americans the rights of U.S. citizens. Hendricks claimed that the black slave was "inferior and no good would come from his freedom."

In 1868 Hendricks again was nominated as his party's candidate for governor of Indiana, but he lost the election. The following year, when his Senate term expired, he retired to Indianapolis, where he resumed his law practice. In 1872, however, he ran for governor for the third time and was finally elected by a narrow 1,148-vote margin.

In 1872 the national prominence attained by Hendricks was demonstrated when he received forty-two of the sixty-two electoral votes for president won by fellow Democrat Horace Greeley, who had died between the election and the electoral college vote. Four years later the Democrats nominated Hendricks as Samuel J. Tilden's vice-presidential running mate. The presence of Hendricks on the ticket helped Tilden carry Indiana and seemingly the election. The Republicans, however, disputed the election results in several southern states, and an election commission that favored the Republicans ruled in favor of the Republican presidential candidate, Rutherford B. Hayes.

Hendricks was nominated again for vice president in 1884 to balance the ticket with New Yorker Grover Cleveland. Like eight years before, his popularity helped the Democrats carry Indiana, but this time they won the election. Cleveland and Hendricks defeated Republicans James G. Blaine and John A. Logan 219–182 in the electoral college and by just sixty thousand votes in the popular balloting.

As vice president, Hendricks presided over only a one-month session of the Senate called to consider President Cleveland's cabinet nominations. Hendricks died in his home in Indianapolis two weeks before the Senate was scheduled to resume its business in December. The vice president had served less than nine months of his term.

Hendricks married Eliza C. Morgan of North Bend, Ohio, on September 26, 1845. They had one child, Morgan, who died when he was three years old. Eliza died at the age of eighty in 1903.

Levi P. Morton

BORN: May 16, 1824; Shoreham, Vermont
PARTY: Republican
TERM: March 4, 1889–March 4, 1893
PRESIDENT: Benjamin Harrison
DIED: May 16, 1920; Rhinebeck, New York
BURIED: Rhinebeck

Levi Parsons Morton was the son of Lucretia and Daniel Morton, an Episcopalian minister. His ancestors arrived in New England before 1650. He received a modest education as a boy and never attended college.

Morton began his climb in the business world as a clerk in a Hanover, New Hampshire, store. He later worked in Boston for an import company and by 1855 owned a wholesale business in New York City. He suffered a financial setback in 1861 because the Civil War debts owed to him by southerners went unpaid. He was able to pay his creditors, however, and in 1863 established a Wall Street banking firm. Over the next thirteen years he accumulated a large personal fortune and developed his firm, Morton, Bliss & Company, into one of the most powerful financial institutions in the United States.

In 1876 Morton decided to try his hand at politics. He ran unsuccessfully for a seat in the U.S. House of Representatives from Manhattan's wealthy Eleventh District but won the seat two years later. Morton was reelected to Congress in 1880, but he resigned his House seat when President James A. Garfield appointed him minister to France.

The 1880 Republican National Convention nominated dark horse James A. Garfield of Ohio as president instead of former

president Ulysses S. Grant, who was allied with Morton's political mentor, Republican senator Roscoe Conkling of New York. As a gesture to the Conkling faction, Garfield offered the vice-presidential nomination to Morton, who refused on the instructions of Conkling. Instead, the nomination went to another Conkling ally, Chester A. Arthur, who accepted the nomination against Conkling's wishes.

Had Grant been nominated and elected, Morton would have likely been nominated Treasury secretary, a post that the New York banker coveted. After Garfield won the election, however, he sought to limit the influence of the Conkling faction and chose William Windom of Minnesota to be Treasury secretary. Morton's fund-raising efforts on behalf of Garfield were rewarded by an appointment as minister to France, where for four years Morton lived in splendor and threw lavish parties for European royalty. Morton, who had relinquished his House seat to go to France, returned to the United States in 1885 hopeful of winning a Senate seat, but his election campaigns for the Senate in 1885 and 1887 were unsuccessful.

In 1888 Morton was offered the vice-presidential slot on the Republican ticket with Indianan Benjamin Harrison. Having seen Chester Arthur succeed to the presidency when Garfield was killed by an assassin in 1881, Morton did not refuse the nomination a second time. During the 1888 campaign Morton concentrated on doing what he knew best—raising money. Although Harrison and Morton lost the popular election by ten thousand votes to President Grover Cleveland and Allen G. Thurman, they won in the electoral college 233–168.

Morton fulfilled his duties as presiding officer of the Senate conscientiously. During one Democratic filibuster in late 1890 and early 1891, Morton opposed the position of his party and refused to cooperate with Republican attempts to end the filibuster. The Democrats stopped the legislation, however, and Morton's standing in the Republican Party was damaged. He was willing to accept a second vice-presidential term, but Republican Party leaders dropped him for fellow New Yorker Whitelaw Reid.

In 1895 Morton ran successfully for governor of New York with the support of Sen. Thomas C. Platt (R-N.Y.), the most powerful figure in New York politics. Morton, however, displayed the same independence that he had shown as vice president and refused to be part of Platt's machine. In particular, he angered his machine supporters by advocating civil service reform. Morton hoped to be his party's presidential nominee in 1896 (his name was entered as a favorite-son candidate), but William McKinley was the clear choice of the party bosses and the convention. When Morton's term as governor ended in January 1897, he retired from politics to manage his business interests. He formed the Morton Trust Company in 1899 and merged it with the Guaranty Trust Company in 1909.

Morton spent much of his retirement traveling or at Ellerslie, his thousand-acre estate in Rhinebeck, New York. He died there in 1920 on his ninety-sixth birthday.

On October 15, 1856, Morton married Lucy Young Kimball,

who died in 1871 before her husband entered politics. They had one daughter, who died in infancy. Morton then married Anna Livingson Street on February 12, 1873, and the couple had five daughters. Anna died at Ellerslie in 1918, two years before her husband.

Adlai E. Stevenson

BORN: October 25, 1835; Christian County, Kentucky
PARTY: Democratic
TERM: March 4, 1893–March 4, 1897
PRESIDENT: Grover Cleveland
DIED: June 14, 1914; Chicago, Illinois
BURIED: Bloomington, Illinois

Adlai Ewing Stevenson was the second of the seven children of Eliza and John Stevenson, a slave-owning Kentucky planter. As a boy, Adlai worked on the farm and obtained an elementary education at local schools. When Adlai was sixteen his family moved to Bloomington, Illinois, where he taught school and attended briefly Illinois Wesleyan University. He then enrolled in Centre College in Danville, Kentucky. In 1857, after two years of study, he left Centre without a degree when the death of his father forced him to resume teaching to supplement his family's income. While teaching, Adlai studied law and was admitted to the bar in 1858.

That same year Stevenson opened a law office in Metamora, Illinois. He also became a Democrat and a follower of Illinois senator Stephen A. Douglas. In 1864 Stevenson won his first elective office, state's attorney for the Metamora judicial district.

After four years in the post Stevenson moved back to Bloomington and resumed his successful career as a lawyer.

In 1874 Stevenson was elected to the U.S. House of Representatives. He was defeated for reelection in 1876 but won his seat back in 1878. After his term expired in 1881 he returned to private life.

In 1885 President Grover Cleveland appointed Stevenson first assistant postmaster. In this office Stevenson was in charge of firing postmasters appointed by the previous Republican administrations. Cleveland believed that, despite the traditional practice, government employees should not be fired simply because they belonged to the party out of power. But Cleveland's fellow Democrats were not as magnanimous. They demanded that Cleveland replace Republicans with loyal Democrats. Stevenson agreed and wrote a letter to the *New York World,* a Democratic paper, supporting patronage. Under pressure from his party, Cleveland relented and gave Stevenson permission to proceed with the mass removal of Republican postmasters. Although Stevenson was known for his tact and amiability, he made many enemies in the process of firing tens of thousands of people and earned the nickname, the "Headsman." Cleveland appointed Stevenson to the Supreme Court in 1889, but the Republican majority in the Senate refused to confirm the nomination of a man who had just fired tens of thousands of their fellow party members.

Stevenson went to the 1892 Democratic National Convention as the chairman of the Illinois delegation. There he received the party's nomination for vice president. By choosing Stevenson, the Democrats improved their chances of winning Illinois, a large, traditionally Republican state. Stevenson's support of bimetallism, the coinage of money based on both gold and silver, also appealed to many citizens in the South and West who believed that having more money in circulation would increase their buying power and the country's economic health. With Stevenson on the ticket, Illinois voted for a Democratic presidential candidate for the first time since 1856. Cleveland and Stevenson defeated Republican incumbent Benjamin Harrison and vice-presidential candidate Whitelaw Reid 277–145 in the electoral college.

As vice president, Stevenson made many friends in the Senate, where he was regarded as a good presiding officer. And, although he was on friendly terms with President Cleveland, Stevenson was not a regular participant in policy making. In July 1893, when Cleveland secretly underwent surgery for mouth cancer, Stevenson was not even informed.

In 1900 Stevenson again received the Democratic nomination for vice president on a ticket with William Jennings Bryan, but they were defeated by incumbent William McKinley and vice-presidential nominee Theodore Roosevelt. In 1908 the Illinois Democratic Party honored the aging Stevenson with its nomination for governor. He lost, however, to Republican Charles Deneen in a close election. After this defeat Stevenson retired from politics. His book, *Something of Men I Have Known,* a collection of speeches and political anecdotes, was published in 1909. In 1914 Stevenson died of heart failure following prostate surgery.

On December 20, 1866, Stevenson married Letitia Green, whom he had met while attending Centre College, where her father served as president. They did not marry, however, until they met again nearly a decade later after she had moved to Illinois. Letitia died on Christmas Day in 1913, a few months before her husband. The Stevensons had three girls and a boy. Their son, Lewis, managed his father's vice-presidential campaign in 1892 and served as his father's private secretary while he was in office. Lewis was the father of Adlai Stevenson II, who was the Democratic nominee for president in 1952 and 1956.

Garret A. Hobart

BORN: June 3, 1844; Long Branch, New Jersey
PARTY: Republican
TERM: March 4, 1897–November 21, 1899
PRESIDENT: William McKinley
DIED: November 21, 1899; Paterson, New Jersey
BURIED: Paterson

Garret Augustus Hobart was the eldest son of Addison and Sophia Hobart, who owned a store and a small farm. When Garret was sixteen, he enrolled in Rutgers College in New Jersey. There he majored in math and English and graduated with honors in 1863. Garret then taught school briefly before moving to Paterson, New Jersey, to work in the law office of Socrates Tuttle, a close friend of his father. Garret was admitted to the bar in 1869.

After serving as Paterson city counsel in 1871, Hobart entered

state politics and in 1872 was elected to the state assembly. He became speaker in 1874 at the age of thirty. Two years later he won election to the state senate, where he served two three-year terms. Hobart left the state senate in 1882 but continued to be a leading figure in New Jersey politics. From 1880 to 1891 he was chairman of the state Republican committee. Although Hobart was not a well-known figure outside of New Jersey, he had become a member of the Republican National Committee in 1884 and was acquainted with the leading Republicans around the country, including Ohio boss Mark Hanna.

Although Hobart was enthusiastic about his political career, he considered it a hobby. Most of his energies went into his legal and business career. He served as president of the Passaic, New Jersey, water company and was director of several banks. By the time he entered national politics, he had amassed a fortune.

In 1896 the Republican Party was confident of recapturing the White House. Grover Cleveland and the Democrats had received much of the blame for the economic and labor troubles of the previous four years. The Democrats nominated William Jennings Bryan as president and Arthur Sewall as vice president. The Republicans countered with William McKinley of Ohio and a conservative platform that advocated the gold standard. Republican Party leaders wanted a gold supporter from the East as the vice-presidential candidate to balance the ticket and reinforce their commitment to hard money. They found their candidate in Hobart, who was an outspoken advocate of the gold standard. In his acceptance speech at the Republican National Convention in St. Louis, Hobart uttered one of the most famous quotes of his era: "An honest dollar, worth 100 cents everywhere, cannot be coined out of fifty-three cents of silver, plus a legislative fiat."

Despite Bryan's stirring campaign speeches, the Republicans won the 1896 election 271–176 in the electoral college. Hobart's presence on the ticket helped the Republicans win New Jersey for the first time since Ulysses S. Grant's success there in 1872.

The last vice president of the nineteenth century proved to be one of the most able and influential. Despite never having held national office, Hobart understood national political issues and became one of McKinley's closest friends and advisers. The press often referred to Hobart as the "Assistant President." He also was credited with presiding over the Senate with energy and fairness.

Hobart became ill in the spring of 1899. He left the capital to recuperate in New Jersey, but he died at his home in Paterson in November. Hobart received stirring eulogies in the nation's newspapers, and his funeral was attended by President McKinley and many other top government officials. Paterson erected a bronze statue of Hobart in front of its city hall next to a statue of Alexander Hamilton.

Hobart married Jennie Tuttle on July 21, 1869. While Hobart was vice president, they entertained lavishly at their rented mansion on Lafayette Square near the White House. The couple had two children, Garret Jr. and his older sister Fannie. Fannie died in 1895 from diphtheria while on a tour of Europe with her family. Mrs. Hobart died on January 8, 1941, at the age of ninety-one. She wrote two books about her experiences, *Memories*, published in 1930, and *Second Lady*, published in 1933.

Charles W. Fairbanks

BORN: May 11, 1852; near Unionville Center, Ohio
PARTY: Republican
TERM: March 4, 1905–March 4, 1909
PRESIDENT: Theodore Roosevelt
DIED: June 4, 1918; Indianapolis, Indiana
BURIED: Indianapolis

Charles Warren Fairbanks was born in a one-room log cabin on a farm in Ohio. His parents, Loriston and Mary Fairbanks, were Methodist abolitionists who helped runaway slaves before the Civil War. As a child, Charles worked on the family farm and attended a district school. Despite his humble background, he enrolled in Ohio Wesleyan University in Delaware, Ohio, at the age of fifteen. He worked his way through college and graduated in 1872.

He was admitted to the bar in 1874 and moved to Indianapolis. He quickly built a reputation as an attorney specializing in railroad litigation. While accumulating a fortune from his law practice, Fairbanks became involved in politics. He supported various Republican candidates, including fellow Indianan Benjamin Harrison. By 1896 he was one of the state's leading Republicans, although he had never held public office. That year his keynote address at the Republican National Convention brought him national acclaim. In 1897 he was elected to the U.S. Senate.

In the Senate Fairbanks was one of President William McKinley's most consistent supporters. Republican leaders considered Fairbanks for the vice-presidential nomination in 1900, but he decided to remain in the Senate. For Fairbanks, who had presidential ambitions, the decision was a bad one; Theodore Roosevelt was nominated instead.

Fairbanks had planned to run for the presidency after McKinley served out his second term, but McKinley's assassination in 1901 eliminated any chance of his nomination for the presidency in 1904. Theodore Roosevelt assumed the presidency and became so popular that he was the inevitable choice of his party for a second term.

In 1904 Fairbanks settled for the vice-presidential nomination. Roosevelt would have preferred someone else, but he accepted Fairbanks, who was the choice of the party's conservative wing. While Roosevelt remained aloof in Washington, Fairbanks campaigned vigorously across the country. Roosevelt and Fairbanks easily defeated Democrats Alton B. Parker and Henry G. Davis.

While serving as McKinley's vice president, Theodore Roosevelt had advocated a greater role for the occupant of nation's second highest office. As president, however, Roosevelt made no effort to involve Fairbanks in his administration. He had a low opinion of Fairbanks and was disdainful of Fairbanks's persistent maneuverings to set himself up as the Republican nominee in 1908. Roosevelt's endorsement of Secretary of War William Howard Taft ensured that Fairbanks would not get the nomination.

After finishing his vice-presidential term, Fairbanks never again held public office, but he remained a powerful figure in national and state politics. His fellow Indiana Republicans supported his bid for the presidential nomination in 1916, but his favorite-son candidacy was unsuccessful. He asked that his name not be placed in nomination for the vice presidency that year, but, when it was, he accepted. The election was extremely close and remained in doubt until the day after the voting. Fairbanks, responding to news reports that the Republican ticket had won, even sent a congratulatory telegram to his presidential running mate, Charles Evans Hughes. Woodrow Wilson and Thomas Marshall, however, won in the electoral college 277–254.

After the defeat Fairbanks retired from politics. When World War I began, he was appointed to the Indiana State Council of Defense. He died in 1918 at the age of sixty-six after a speaking tour supporting the war effort.

In 1874 Fairbanks married Cornelia Cole, whom he had met at Ohio Wesleyan University, where they coedited the college newspaper. The couple had five children. Cornelia died on October 24, 1913. The second largest city in Alaska is named after Fairbanks, who sat on a senatorial commission on Alaskan affairs.

James S. Sherman

BORN: October 24, 1855; Utica, New York
PARTY: Republican
TERM: March 4, 1909–October 30, 1912
PRESIDENT: William Howard Taft
DIED: October 30, 1912; Utica
BURIED: Utica

James Schoolcraft Sherman was the son of Richard and Mary Sherman. James's father was a newspaper editor and a Democratic politician who held minor offices at the state and national levels. After attending both public and private schools, James enrolled at Hamilton College in Clinton, New York, where he earned a bachelor's degree in 1878 and a law degree in 1879. He then moved back to Utica, where he joined his brother-in-law's law firm.

Despite his family's Democratic affiliation, Sherman chose to enter politics as a Republican. In 1884 he was elected mayor of Utica, an office once held by his brother, who was a Democrat. Two years later Sherman won a seat in the U.S. House of Representatives, where he served from 1887 to 1891 and 1893 to 1909. As a member of Congress, Sherman was known best for his amiability and his parliamentary skills. He became close friends with Republican leaders Thomas B. Reed (R-Maine) and Joseph G. Cannon (R-Ill.), both of whom served as Speaker during Sherman's tenure in the House. Reed and Cannon frequently called on Sherman to preside over House debates.

In 1908 Theodore Roosevelt had pushed Republican Party leaders to nominate William Howard Taft as his successor to the presidency, but Roosevelt did not express a strong preference for a vice-presidential candidate. When congressional Republicans led by Cannon backed Sherman's nomination for vice president, Taft and Roosevelt agreed. Sherman, like Taft, was nominated on the first ballot at the Republican National Convention in Chicago.

During the 1908 campaign Sherman was accused of misconduct. Edmund Burke, a California lawyer, claimed that he and Sherman had obtained tens of thousands of acres of Indian land in New Mexico at bargain prices through bribery and Sherman's influence as chairman of the House Committee on Indian Affairs. The Democrats, however, did not press the scandal issue, and the Republicans denounced the unproven charges as an attempt to slander their candidate. Taft and Sherman easily defeated William Jennings Bryan and John W. Kern 321–162 in the electoral college.

As vice president, Sherman got to do what he did best—preside over a legislative body. He won praise from both parties for his handling of the Senate. Sherman was not a close confidant of Taft, who did not like his vice president's ties to New York Republican machine politicians, but early in their term the two shared a regular golf game together and became more friendly.

Even before becoming vice president, Sherman suffered from Bright's disease, a kidney ailment. He became seriously ill in the spring of 1908 but recovered in time to accept the vice-presidential nomination. During his vice presidency he experienced occasional periods of illness that prevented him from presiding over the Senate. Nevertheless, he was renominated in 1912 along with Taft. In the fall he became very ill, and on October 30, 1912, he died of complications caused by his kidney condition. He was the only vice president who died before election day after having been nominated for a second term.

Because the election was just six days away, the Republican Party did not have time to choose a replacement for Sherman. His death, however, did not affect the outcome of the election. Democrat Woodrow Wilson swept to victory when Theodore Roosevelt's third party candidacy split the Republican vote.

Sherman married Carrie Babcock on January 26, 1881, while he practiced law in Utica; they had three sons. Sherman's wife died in 1931 in Utica at the age of seventy-four.

Thomas R. Marshall

BORN: March 14, 1854; North Manchester, Indiana
PARTY: Democratic
TERM: March 4, 1913–March 4, 1921
PRESIDENT: Woodrow Wilson
DIED: June 1, 1925; Washington, D.C.
BURIED: Indianapolis, Indiana

Thomas Riley Marshall was the son of Martha and Daniel Marshall, a country doctor. Thomas was born in Indiana, but as a boy he lived in Illinois, Kansas, and Missouri before his family resettled in Indiana. He was educated at public schools and at-

Thomas R. Marshall

tended Wabash College in Crawfordsville, Indiana. He graduated in 1873 and was selected for membership in Phi Beta Kappa, a national honor society.

After college Marshall studied law and was admitted to the bar in 1875. He then embarked on a successful legal career in Columbia City, Indiana. Although Marshall became friends with many prominent Democratic politicians, he never ran for office until he was nominated for governor of the state in 1908 at the age of fifty-four. Marshall's candidacy seemed a long shot, since Indiana had not had a Democratic governor since 1892. Nevertheless, he won the election by more than ten thousand votes, overcoming the coattails of Republican presidential nominee William Howard Taft, who carried Indiana by fifteen thousand votes.

As governor, Marshall opposed capital punishment (he issued many pardons), Prohibition, and voting rights for women. Because Indiana barred a governor from seeking two consecutive terms, Marshall planned to return to Columbia City when his four-year term expired. In 1912, however, Indiana Democratic Party leader Thomas Taggart backed Marshall for vice president. Marshall received the number two slot on the Democratic ticket with Woodrow Wilson. Wilson and Marshall faced a Republican Party divided by Theodore Roosevelt's third party candidacy. The Democrats received less than 42 percent of the popular vote but won 435 electoral votes to Roosevelt's 88 votes and President William Howard Taft's 8 votes.

While serving as vice president, Marshall gained a national reputation for his dry humor. After listening to Sen. Joseph L. Bristow (R-Kan.) deliver a long speech on the needs of the country, he remarked in a voice loud enough for many in the Senate chamber to overhear, "What this country needs is a really good five-cent cigar." This line was reported in newspapers and immediately became his most famous utterance. During his political career he declined to run for Congress on the grounds that he "might be elected."

The vice presidency was among the targets of Marshall's wit. He told a story about two brothers: "One ran away to sea; the other was elected vice president. And nothing was ever heard of either of them again." He also likened his position to "a man in a cataleptic fit; he cannot speak; he cannot move; he suffers no pain; he is perfectly conscious of all that goes on, but has no part in it."

Both President Wilson and Vice President Marshall were renominated for a second term. In the 1916 election, however, they were opposed by a Republican Party united behind Charles Evans Hughes and former vice president Charles W. Fairbanks. Wilson and Marshall narrowly defeated Hughes and Fairbanks 277–254 in the electoral college.

Marshall's most significant action as vice president may have been something he did not do. When President Wilson returned to the United States after negotiating the Versailles treaty, he encountered strong Senate opposition to U.S. entry into the League of Nations that was to be created by the treaty. In response, Wilson toured the country trying to build support for ratification. The stress of the tour caused Wilson to suffer a nervous breakdown and a stroke. With Wilson paralyzed, many people advised Marshall to assume the presidency. At that time, however, there was no provision in the Constitution for the removal of an incapacitated president by the vice president. Marshall refused to make any move to replace Wilson because he believed such a move would set a bad precedent and might divide the government and the nation. Marshall merely took over many of Wilson's ceremonial duties to lighten the weakened president's work load.

When Marshall's second term expired in 1921 he retired to Indianapolis. He was the first vice president since Daniel D. Tompkins to serve two full terms. Marshall occupied his time by writing syndicated articles, delivering lectures, and traveling. Just before his death at the age of seventy-one, he finished writing *Recollections,* a book containing many of his humorous stories and witticisms.

Marshall married twenty-three-year-old Lois Kimsey on October 2, 1895. The couple had no children but took care of a foster child for a period while they lived in Washington. It is said that the couple spent only two nights of their twenty-nine-year marriage apart.

Charles G. Dawes

BORN: August 27, 1865; Marietta, Ohio
PARTY: Republican
TERM: March 4, 1925–March 4, 1929
PRESIDENT: Calvin Coolidge
DIED: April 23, 1951; Evanston, Illinois
BURIED: Chicago, Illinois

Charles Gates Dawes was the son of Mary and Rufus Dawes, a Civil War general who served one term in the House of Representatives. Charles's great-great-grandfather was William Dawes, who rode with Paul Revere to alert the people near Boston that British troops were approaching on April 18, 1775.

Dawes attended Marietta College in Marietta, Ohio, graduating in 1884. He earned his law degree from Cincinnati Law School in 1886 and joined a Lincoln, Nebraska, law firm the following year. His practice grew as he became known for his expertise on banking issues and his opposition to discriminatory railway freight rates.

In 1894 Dawes bought gas and light companies in Evanston, Illinois, and LaCrosse, Wisconsin. He moved to Chicago to oversee his new business ventures. He soon expanded his profitable utility operations and was joined in business by his three brothers.

Since his days in Lincoln, Dawes had been active in the Republican Party. He directed William McKinley's early 1896 presidential campaign in Illinois and became the campaign finance director after McKinley won the nomination. After McKinley became president in 1897, he appointed Dawes comptroller of the currency. In 1902 Dawes resigned and ran unsuccessfully for the Senate in Illinois. He returned to Chicago, where he organized the Central Trust Company of Illinois and became its president. The bank's success made him one of the leading financiers in the nation.

When the United States entered World War I, Dawes asked for a commission and was made a major in the Seventeenth Engineers. Soon after, his close friend, Gen. John J. Pershing, commander of the American Expeditionary Force in Europe, appointed him chief purchasing agent for the American army. Dawes oversaw the purchase and transportation of millions of tons of supplies for the troops in Europe. He retired from the army in 1919 with the rank of brigadier general. He became a popular figure after the war when he answered a petty congressional inquiry into his wartime purchasing records by exclaiming, "Hell and Maria, we weren't trying to keep a set of books, we were trying to win the war!"

President Warren G. Harding offered to appoint Dawes secretary of the Treasury in 1921, but Dawes chose instead a one-year assignment as director of the new Bureau of the Budget. In 1923 Dawes was appointed chairman of the Allied Reparations Commission, formed to study Germany's budget and make recommendations on restructuring payments of its World War I reparations. He helped to develop the "Dawes Plan," adopted in August 1924, which reduced German reparation payments and provided for a foreign loan to stimulate the German economy. For his efforts Dawes was awarded the Nobel Peace Prize in 1925.

In 1924 the Republican Party nominated Gov. Frank Lowden of Illinois as the vice-presidential candidate on the ticket with President Calvin Coolidge. When Lowden turned down the nomination, the convention turned to Dawes, who accepted. Coolidge and Dawes defeated Democrats John W. Davis and Charles W. Bryan 382–136 in the electoral college.

On inauguration day Dawes stole some of the limelight from President Coolidge when he demanded in his inaugural speech that the Senate pass new rules limiting filibusters. As vice president, Dawes became active in Senate politics, where he worked behind the scenes for naval appropriations, banking reforms, and farm relief programs. When President Coolidge announced he would not run for another term, Dawes also declared he would not seek reelection.

After leaving the vice presidency, Dawes was appointed ambassador to Great Britain in 1929 by President Herbert Hoover. He served there until January 1932, when Hoover appointed him director of the Reconstruction Finance Corporation (RFC), a government agency charged with making loans to banks and businesses in financial trouble. He resigned after several months to return to Chicago to reorganize his old bank into the City National Bank and Trust Company. He was criticized for securing an RFC loan for the bank shortly after resigning as the agency's director, but the loan helped return his bank to financial stability and it was properly repaid.

Dawes married Caro Blymer on January 24, 1889. When Dawes died in 1951 at the age of eighty-five, they had been married sixty-two years. Mrs. Dawes died on October 3, 1957. The couple had two children and later adopted two more. Dawes was a talented amateur composer, whose "Melody in A Major" was published in 1911. The piece became a popular song in 1951, when it was set to lyrics and retitled, "It's All in the Game."

Charles Curtis

BORN: January 25, 1860; North Topeka, Kansas
PARTY: Republican
TERM: March 4, 1929–March 4, 1933
PRESIDENT: Herbert Hoover
DIED: February 8, 1936; Washington, D.C.
BURIED: Topeka, Kansas

Charles Curtis was the older of the two children of Oren and Ellen Curtis. Charles's father was a drifter who had two sons by a previous marriage, which had ended in divorce. When Ellen Curtis died in 1863, Oren left Charles and his sister in the care of their two grandmothers and joined the Union cavalry. He remained in the cavalry after the war and seldom saw his children. His daughter by a third marriage would develop a close relationship with Charles.

After living with his paternal grandmother, Permelia Curtis, from 1863 to 1866, Charles spent three years with his maternal grandmother, Julie Pappan. Mrs. Pappan, who was half Kaw Indian, lived on an Indian reservation in Kansas. During this period Charles became such a skilled horseman that he was able to supplement his income as a teenager by riding race horses at county fairs.

After 1869 Charles again lived with Permelia Curtis in North Topeka, Kansas. He had attended a mission school on the reservation, but he had fallen behind his classmates in North Topeka. Nevertheless, he graduated from a public high school in 1879. He then clerked for a Topeka lawyer and was admitted to the bar in 1881.

Curtis practiced law in Topeka for several years before being elected county attorney in 1885. His vigorous prosecution of Prohibition violators brought him statewide recognition. He returned to his law practice in 1889 but stayed active in local politics.

In 1892 Curtis was elected to the U.S. House of Representatives. His greatest strength as a politician was staying in contact with his constituents. He kept information about persons throughout his district so he would be able to answer their mail with a personal touch and call them by name on campaign trips. This attention to detail helped Curtis win seven consecutive terms.

In 1907 Curtis shifted from the House to the Senate when he was elected by the Kansas legislature to fill several months of an unexpired term. The legislature elected him to a term of his own that year, and he served until 1913, when he was defeated for reelection. In 1914, however, he was elected to the Senate in the first election in which senators were chosen by popular vote according to the new Seventeenth Amendment.

Curtis served in the Senate until 1929. He supported Prohibition, voting rights for women, and bills benefiting farmers and Indians. He rarely introduced bills or made speeches, preferring to influence legislation through personal consultations and backroom meetings with other senators. He became Republican whip in 1915 and Senate majority leader in 1924.

Curtis wanted the Republican presidential nomination in 1928, and his name was placed in nomination at the Republican National Convention in Kansas City, Missouri, along with several other candidates. Herbert Hoover, however, was nominated on the first ballot. Party leaders chose Curtis for vice president because he was a political conservative from a farm state who could balance the ticket with Hoover, a liberal Californian. With the nation enjoying prosperity after eight years of Republican presidential leadership, Hoover and Curtis had little trouble defeating Democrats Alfred E. Smith and Joseph T. Robinson.

As vice president, Curtis faithfully supported Republican policies. Although he had served thirty-four years in Congress, he considered the vice presidency to be an office with higher status and asked colleagues who had called him "Charley" for decades to address him as "Mr. Vice President."

Hoover and Curtis were renominated in 1932, but the Great Depression had turned voters against the Republicans. They were defeated by Franklin D. Roosevelt and John Nance Garner 472–59 in the electoral college. After leaving the vice presidency, Curtis practiced law in Washington, D.C. He died of a heart attack in 1936.

On November 27, 1884, Curtis married Anna E. Baird, whom he had met in high school. They had three children. Anna died in 1924, five years before Curtis became vice president. The vice president's half-sister, Dolly Gann, who worked as his secretary during his years in Congress, served as his official hostess.

John Nance Garner

BORN: November 22, 1868; near Detroit, Texas

PARTY: Democratic

TERM: March 4, 1933–January 20, 1941

PRESIDENT: Franklin D. Roosevelt

DIED: November 7, 1967; Uvalde, Texas

BURIED: Uvalde

John Nance Garner was the oldest of the six children of Sarah and John Garner, a former soldier in the Confederate cavalry. Young John attended a Texas country school until the fourth grade, when he stopped going because of poor health. Thereafter he was tutored by a maiden aunt.

Garner enrolled at Vanderbilt University in Nashville, Tennessee, when he was eighteen, but he returned to Texas in less than a month, considering himself scholastically unprepared for college. Rather than go back to school, he studied law under local attorneys. He was admitted to the bar in 1890 and opened a law practice in the northeast Texas city of Clarksville, about fifteen miles from where he was born.

While Garner was in Clarksville, doctors tentatively diagnosed him as having tuberculosis and advised him to move to a drier climate. He took their advice and in 1892 relocated to Uvalde, in west Texas, a town of about 2,500 people. He joined a local law firm and regained his health. Through shrewd investing, he gradually acquired thousands of acres of land, three banks, and numerous businesses that made him a millionaire.

Garner was elected a judge of Uvalde County in 1893. He served until 1896, when he returned to his law practice. Two years later he was elected to the Texas house of representatives. After two terms there, he won a seat in the U.S. House in 1902. When Woodrow Wilson was elected president in 1913, Garner

gained a seat on the powerful Ways and Means Committee and soon developed into one of Wilson's most important congressional allies. Garner served in the House continuously until 1933, becoming minority leader in 1928 and Speaker on December 7, 1931.

In 1932 Garner ran for the Democratic presidential nomination. In the early balloting at the party's national convention in Chicago, he was a distant third place behind front-runner Franklin D. Roosevelt and the 1928 Democratic presidential candidate, Alfred E. Smith. After the third ballot the convention appeared to be headed for a deadlock. More than half the delegates favored Roosevelt, but he could not secure the two-thirds needed for nomination. Rather than see the party divided, Garner agreed to release his ninety delegates from Texas and California. The addition of Garner's delegates gave Roosevelt enough votes for the nomination. Roosevelt then supported Garner for the vice-presidential nomination, which the Texas representative received on the first ballot. The Roosevelt and Garner camps claimed they had not traded Garner's delegates for his nomination, but they convinced few political observers. Roosevelt and Garner were swept into office by a landslide victory over President Herbert Hoover and Vice President Charles Curtis.

Garner had reservations about taking the vice presidency because he had long aspired to the speakership of the House and had attained his goal less than a year before being nominated for vice president. Indeed, during his vice presidency, Garner would remark that his office was "not worth a bucket of warm spit." Garner, however, had wanted the party to be united for the 1932 election and believed that holding the vice presidency increased his chances of eventually becoming president.

Unlike many previous vice presidents, Garner remained active. He attended cabinet meetings and used his congressional contacts and experience to help push Franklin Roosevelt's New Deal legislation through Congress in 1933. Roosevelt and Garner were reelected in 1936, but during their second term a split developed between them. Garner was alarmed by the enhancement of executive power under Roosevelt and opposed the president's plan to increase the number of Supreme Court justices in 1937. The vice president also thought that deficit spending on Roosevelt's New Deal social programs should be cut back. In response, the president excluded Garner from many important White House meetings.

In December 1939 Garner announced he was a candidate for president, but Roosevelt chose to break precedent and seek a third term. Garner denounced the president's action, but Roosevelt was nominated by acclamation in 1940, with Garner receiving only a handful of votes at the Democratic National Convention in Chicago. After this disappointment, Garner quit politics and retired to Uvalde. He died in 1967, two weeks before his ninety-ninth birthday. He lived longer than any other vice president or president.

Garner married Mariette Rheiner on November 25, 1895. They had met on a train shortly after he moved to Uvalde. Their one son, Tully, was born in 1896.

Henry A. Wallace

BORN: October 7, 1888; Adair County, Iowa
PARTY: Democratic
TERM: January 20, 1941–January 20, 1945
PRESIDENT: Franklin D. Roosevelt
DIED: November 18, 1965; Danbury, Connecticut
BURIED: Des Moines, Iowa

Henry Agard Wallace was the son of May and Henry C. Wallace, a magazine editor and secretary of agriculture under Warren G. Harding and Calvin Coolidge. Henry attended public school in central Iowa and graduated in 1910 from Iowa State University in Ames with a degree in animal husbandry.

After college Wallace worked as a writer and editor on his father's magazine, *Wallaces' Farmer,* one of the most influential agricultural journals in the United States. He also conducted plant breeding experiments and farmed a small plot of land. He became associate editor of the magazine in 1916 and editor in 1924.

Despite his father's Republicanism, Wallace left the party during the late 1920s because he believed the high tariffs advocated by the Republicans hurt farmers and he supported farm export bills that President Calvin Coolidge had vetoed. Wallace backed Democrat Alfred E. Smith for president in 1928 and Franklin D. Roosevelt in 1932.

In 1933 Wallace entered public service when President Roosevelt appointed him secretary of agriculture. Wallace traveled to all forty-eight states during his first year in office to survey the plight of the farmers, who had endured low commodity prices since the 1920s. Armed with the Agriculture Adjustment Act of 1933, a measure giving the secretary of agriculture broad powers to address the farm crisis, Wallace began subsidy payments to farmers who took fields out of production, authorized the slaughter of millions of hogs to raise prices, and introduced systematic controls to prevent overproduction. He also supported Secretary of State Cordell Hull's efforts to negotiate with foreign nations tariff reductions that increased world trade and opened up markets for U.S. agricultural products.

In 1940 a rift between Roosevelt and Vice President John Nance Garner caused Democratic leaders to look for a new vice-presidential candidate. During Wallace's two terms as agriculture secretary, he had supported virtually all of the president's programs, including his unpopular attempt to increase the number of Supreme Court justices in 1937. This loyalty and Wallace's popularity in farm states led Roosevelt to support him as Garner's replacement. Many Democrats, however, did not want Wallace. Not only did they consider him to be too liberal, they were suspicious of his unconventional personal philosophy, which was influenced by Eastern religions and mysticism. Nevertheless, when Roosevelt insisted that he would not run for a third term without Wallace as his running mate, the 1940 Democratic National Convention in Chicago gave Wallace the nomination on the first ballot. Roosevelt and Wallace easily defeated Republicans Wendell Willkie and Charles L. McNary 449–82 in the electoral college. The vice presidency was the only office to which Wallace was ever elected.

Wallace was an active vice president. He made goodwill tours of Latin America, China, and Soviet Asia. He also became an outspoken advocate of an internationalist post–World War II foreign policy in which the United States would cooperate closely with the Soviet Union and provide economic and technical assistance to underdeveloped nations.

By 1944 Wallace's liberal views had alienated many Democratic leaders, who urged Roosevelt to drop him from the ticket. Roosevelt said he wanted to keep Wallace, but that he would also accept either Supreme Court Justice William O. Douglas or Sen. Harry Truman of Missouri. This weak endorsement ended Wallace's chances for a second term, and Truman was nominated. Roosevelt and Truman then defeated Thomas E. Dewey and William W. Bricker in the general election.

Even after being dropped from the ticket, Wallace campaigned hard for Roosevelt and Truman. Roosevelt rewarded him by naming him secretary of commerce in 1945. After Roosevelt died in April of that month, Wallace became concerned that President Truman would abandon Roosevelt's policy of friendship toward the Soviet Union. In July 1946 he wrote to the president, urging him to recognize Soviet security interests that Wallace believed were legitimate. When Wallace spoke out against Truman's tough policy toward the Soviets in September 1946, Truman fired him.

While the people of the United States were becoming increasingly alarmed by the threat of communist expansion and subversion, Wallace continued to speak out in favor of cooperation between the superpowers. On December 29, 1947, he announced his intention to run for the presidency as the candidate of the Progressive Party. Wallace's candidacy hurt Truman's chances of being elected in 1948, especially since southern Democrats had also formed a separate party and nominated Sen. Strom Thurmond of South Carolina to run for president. The endorsement of Wallace by the American Communist Party, however, reinforced perceptions that he was at best a naive dreamer and at worst a communist. Wallace received barely more than 2 percent of the vote and won no states. Truman overcame the divisions within his party to win the election.

After his defeat, Wallace retired to his farm in South Salem, New York. By 1952 Wallace's attitudes toward the Soviet Union had undergone a transformation. He published *Why I Was Wrong*, a book that explained his newfound distrust of the Soviet Union.

Wallace married Ilo Browne on May 30, 1914. They had two sons and a daughter. Before his death in 1965, Wallace spent much of his retirement conducting agricultural experiments.

Alben W. Barkley

BORN: November 24, 1877; Lowes, Kentucky
PARTY: Democratic
TERM: January 20, 1949–January 20, 1953
PRESIDENT: Harry S. Truman
DIED: April 30, 1956; Lexington, Virginia
BURIED: Paducah, Kentucky

Alben William Barkley was the son of Electra and John Barkley, a poor tobacco farmer and railroad worker. Alben, who was born in a log cabin, worked on his father's farm and attended country schools.

At age fourteen he entered Marvin College in Clinton, Kentucky. He paid his tuition by working as a janitor at the college. After graduating in 1897, he studied law for a year at Emory University in Oxford, Georgia. He then moved to Paducah, Kentucky, and got a job in a law office. He was admitted to the bar in 1901 and attended the University of Virginia Law School during the summer of 1902 to sharpen his legal skills.

Entering Democratic politics, Barkley won his first election in 1905, becoming prosecuting attorney of McCracken County, Kentucky. In 1909 he was elected county judge, an administrative rather than a judicial position that was primarily responsible for building and maintaining public roads. Barkley ran for the U.S. House of Representatives in 1912 and won a seat he held continuously until he became a senator in 1927.

In Congress Barkley was a staunch supporter of President Woodrow Wilson. He backed Wilson's decision to enter World War I and voted for the Versailles treaty. Although he supported most liberal causes, he gained a reputation as a political compromiser who would make political deals when it was in the interests of his constituents. He also was renowned for his speak-

Alben W. Barkley

ing ability, which combined a bombastic style with homespun humor and wisdom. He delivered the keynote addresses at the 1932, 1936, and 1948 Democratic National Conventions.

After Barkley was reelected to the Senate in 1932, Democratic majority leader Joseph Robinson of Arkansas appointed him assistant majority leader. In 1937, with the support of the White House, Barkley was elected majority leader when Robinson died. Barkley supported both Roosevelt's New Deal social programs and his aid to Britain and its allies before World War II. He remained majority leader until 1946, when the Republicans gained control of the Senate and he became minority leader.

In 1948 Truman's first choice for vice president was Supreme Court Justice William O. Douglas, but Douglas turned him down. Barkley had long wanted to be president, but Franklin Roosevelt's four-term grip on the Democratic presidential nomination prevented him from running. Now, at the age of seventy, Barkley was unwilling to challenge an incumbent Democratic president for the nomination, but he decided that he wanted to be vice president. He telephoned Truman during the convention to tell him he would accept a nomination as his running mate. Truman agreed to support his candidacy, and the convention nominated him by acclamation. Although opinion polls indicated that the Democrats would lose, Truman and Barkley campaigned tirelessly around the country and defeated Republicans Thomas E. Dewey and Earl Warren.

Although Barkley, at seventy-one, was the oldest vice president ever to take office, he had an active term. He lobbied Congress to support administration programs and made many ceremonial appearances. His grandson called him the "Veep," a title that stuck with the office of vice president even after Barkley had left.

In 1952 Barkley announced his interest in the presidential nomination, but he received little support because of his age. He retired briefly but was elected to the Senate in 1954 by the voters of Kentucky. He died in 1956 from a heart attack suffered during a speaking engagement at Washington and Lee College in Lexington, Virginia.

Barkley married Dorothy Brower on June 23, 1903. They had four children. Dorothy died in 1947 after a long illness. Barkley became the only incumbent vice president ever to marry, when he wed Jane Rucker Hadley, a thirty-eight-year-old St. Louis widow, on November 18, 1949.

Hubert H. Humphrey

BORN: May 27, 1911; Wallace, South Dakota
PARTY: Democratic
TERM: January 20, 1965–January 20, 1969
PRESIDENT: Lyndon B. Johnson
DIED: January 13, 1978; Waverly, Minnesota
BURIED: Minneapolis, Minnesota

Hubert Horatio Humphrey Jr. was the second of the four children of Hubert and Christine Humphrey. His father was a druggist and his mother was a Norwegian immigrant who had come to the United States in her teens. Hubert Jr. was born above the family drugstore in Wallace, South Dakota. When he was four, the Humphreys moved to Doland, South Dakota, where his father ran another drugstore. Hubert attended public schools in Doland and was the valedictorian of his high school class.

Humphrey enrolled in the University of Minnesota in 1929, but he left the following year because of family financial troubles caused by the Great Depression. He helped his father run a drugstore in Huron, South Dakota, where his family had moved. In 1932 Humphrey entered the Denver School of Pharmacy and was licensed as a registered pharmacist in 1933. Humphrey managed the family drugstore when his father, who had been active in local politics as a Democrat, won a seat in the South Dakota state legislature.

In 1937 Humphrey returned to the University of Minnesota. He graduated magna cum laude in 1939 with a degree in political science and was elected to the Phi Beta Kappa honor society. He then enrolled in graduate school at Louisiana State University, where he had received a teaching assistantship. After earning his master's degree in 1940, he again returned to the University of Minnesota, hoping to earn a doctorate, but financial problems forced him to withdraw after less than a year.

Color blindness and a double hernia disqualified Humphrey from military service during World War II. Instead, he served as

Hubert H. Humphrey

state director for war production training and later became assistant director of the state War Manpower Administration. While serving in these administrative posts, he made many political contacts, especially among labor organizations.

In 1943 Humphrey ran for mayor of Minneapolis on the Democratic ticket. He had the support of labor unions and intellectuals at the University of Minnesota, but he lost by a close vote. Two years later, after helping to forge an alliance between the Minnesota Democratic and Farmer Labor Parties, he was elected mayor in his second try. He gained a reputation as a hardworking reformer and easily won a second term as mayor in 1947.

In 1948 Humphrey ran for the Senate. His advocacy of a civil rights platform at the 1948 Democratic convention in Philadelphia won him national recognition and helped him defeat his Republican opponent, Sen. Joseph Ball. In the Senate, Humphrey became a leading supporter of legislation promoting civil rights and welfare programs. He was easily reelected in 1954 and 1960.

Humphrey announced his candidacy for his party's presidential nomination in January 1960, but he withdrew after doing poorly against John F. Kennedy in the primaries. In 1961 Humphrey became Senate majority whip and helped guide several of President Kennedy's legislative proposals, including the nuclear test ban treaty and the Civil Rights Act of 1964, to approval.

In 1964 President Lyndon Johnson chose Humphrey as his running mate after securing a promise from the senator that he would remain loyal to the administration even if he disagreed with specific policies. Johnson and Humphrey defeated Republicans Barry M. Goldwater and William E. Miller by more than sixteen million popular votes.

As vice president, Humphrey was not a member of Johnson's inner circle of advisers. Nevertheless, he worked hard to help push Johnson's Great Society social programs through Congress and made several goodwill tours of foreign nations, including two trips to Vietnam.

After Johnson announced on March 31, 1968, that he would not seek another term, Humphrey entered the race. His nomination was secure when his main rival, Sen. Robert F. Kennedy of New York, was assassinated in Los Angeles on June 5. Humphrey's campaign was burdened by the unpopularity of the Vietnam War and the unfavorable media attention given violent protests at the Democratic National Convention in Chicago. He was defeated 301–191 in the electoral college but received only a half million fewer votes than Richard Nixon out of more than sixty-three million cast.

After leaving the vice presidency in 1969 Humphrey taught at Macalester College in St. Paul, Minnesota. In 1970 he returned to the Senate after winning the seat vacated by retiring Democrat Eugene J. McCarthy. Humphrey entered the race for the 1972 Democratic presidential nomination after the campaign of Sen. Edmund S. Muskie, his 1968 vice-presidential running mate, sputtered. The nomination, however, went to Sen. George McGovern of South Dakota. Humphrey considered running for the presidency again in 1976, but he announced in April of that year that he would not be a candidate.

In August 1976 doctors detected an advanced cancer in Humphrey's prostate and bladder. Surgery failed to arrest the cancer. Despite his illness, the voters of Minnesota reelected him to the Senate in 1976. His Senate colleagues honored him by electing him deputy president pro tempore, a post created especially for him. Humphrey's fortitude and high spirits during the year preceding his death won him admiration around the country. He died at his Waverly, Minnesota, home on January 13, 1978.

Humphrey married Muriel Buck on September 3, 1936. They had one daughter and three sons. Their oldest son, Hubert H. Humphrey III, became attorney general of Minnesota. Muriel Humphrey was appointed to her husband's Senate seat after his death and served until January 3, 1979.

Spiro T. Agnew

BORN: November 9, 1918; Baltimore, Maryland
PARTY: Republican
TERM: January 20, 1969–October 10, 1973
PRESIDENT: Richard M. Nixon

Spiro Theodore Agnew was the son of Theofrastos and Margaret Agnew. Spiro's father, whose original name was Anagnostopoulos, immigrated to the United States from Greece in 1897. He settled in Baltimore, Maryland, where he became the owner of a successful restaurant. Spiro's Greek ancestry was not a major factor in his childhood. He was raised in his mother's Episcopalian church, attended public schools, and preferred to be called "Ted."

Agnew enrolled in Johns Hopkins University in Baltimore in 1937 with the intention of studying chemistry, but he dropped out after two years. He then took classes at the Baltimore Law School at night, while holding a succession of jobs during the day, including supermarket manager and insurance claims adjuster.

In 1941 Agnew was drafted into the army and assigned to officer candidate school at Fort Knox, Kentucky. He was commissioned as a lieutenant in 1942. While serving with the Tenth Armored Division during World War II, he saw combat in France and Germany.

Agnew returned to the Baltimore Law School after the war and earned his law degree in 1947. He then opened a law office in Towson, Maryland, a Baltimore suburb. Agnew had been a Democrat, but he switched to the Republican Party in the late 1940s and actively supported local Republican candidates. In 1957 he was appointed to the Zoning Board of Appeals of Baltimore County. In 1962 he ran for executive of the county, a post with responsibilities similar to those of a mayor. He won the election, becoming the first Republican in the twentieth century to be elected executive of Baltimore County.

Agnew ran for governor of Maryland in 1966. During the campaign he acquired a reputation as a liberal, in part because his Democratic opponent, George Mahoney, was a segregationist, while Agnew took a strong stand on civil rights. Substantial support from blacks and liberal Democrats helped Agnew defeat Mahoney decisively, despite the Democratic Party's three-to-one advantage over the Republicans among Maryland's registered voters.

Agnew fulfilled many of his campaign promises in his first year as governor. With the cooperation of the Maryland legislature he reformed the state's tax code, increased aid to the poor, passed an open housing law, repealed the ban on racial intermarriage, liberalized the abortion law, and enacted strict regulations to reduce water pollution. In 1968, however, Agnew appeared to shift to the right. In particular, his uncompromising response to race riots in Baltimore after the assassination of civil rights leader Martin Luther King Jr. in April 1968 caused observers to question his liberal image. Agnew called out the National Guard and had thousands of blacks arrested. He then met with black leaders and scolded them for failing to control the rioting, even though many of the leaders had made an earnest effort to stop the riots.

On August 7, 1968, Agnew placed Richard Nixon's name in nomination for president at the Republican National Convention in Miami. The following morning, after Nixon had secured the nomination, he surprised many observers by announcing that he had chosen Agnew as his running mate. Agnew was virtually unknown outside of Maryland, but Nixon hoped that his new running mate would appeal to southern voters who might be drawn to the third party candidacy of former Alabama governor George C. Wallace.

During the 1968 campaign, Agnew made several political blunders that betrayed his lack of national political experience. His claim that Democratic presidential candidate Hubert H. Humphrey was "squishy soft on communism" rekindled memories of Nixon's extreme anticommunist rhetoric during the 1940s and 1950s. Agnew also used the derogatory term "Polack" in a statement referring to a person of Polish ancestry and remarked in an interview that "If you've seen one city slum, you've seen them all." Nixon and Agnew overcame these mistakes to defeat Democrats Hubert H. Humphrey and Edmund S. Muskie 301–191 in the electoral college.

As vice president, Agnew had little influence on policy decisions, but he became the administration's hard-line spokesperson against liberal members of the news media, Vietnam war protesters, and other Nixon opponents. In 1972 Nixon and Agnew were reelected in a landslide. Early in 1973 Agnew's noninvolvement in the Watergate scandal made him a potential contender for his party's presidential nomination in 1976.

In August 1973, however, the U.S. attorney in Baltimore disclosed that Agnew was under investigation for receiving bribes from contractors during his years as Baltimore County executive and governor of Maryland. Agnew claimed he was innocent, but his lawyers worked out a plea bargain in which the vice president agreed to resign, plead "no contest" to income tax evasion, and pay a $10,000 fine and $150,000 in back taxes. In return, the Justice Department agreed not to prosecute Agnew for taking bribes. Agnew resigned the vice presidency on October 10, 1973. Two days later Nixon nominated Gerald R. Ford to replace him.

Early in 1974 Agnew was disbarred. He decided to write a novel to pay his debts, and in 1976 he published *The Canfield Decision,* a story about a U.S. vice president who becomes involved with Iranian militants. Agnew also opened Pathlite, Inc., a profitable consulting service for firms doing business in the Middle East. In 1980 he published his autobiography, *Go Quietly . . . or Else,* in which he claims he was innocent of the crimes that forced his resignation.

In April 1994 Agnew made a rare public appearance when he attended the funeral of Richard Nixon. Agnew disclosed that he had not spoken with Nixon since he resigned from the vice presidency.

Agnew married Elinor "Judy" Judefind on May 27, 1942. The couple had met while Agnew worked in an insurance office. They had four children.

Nelson A. Rockefeller

BORN: July 8, 1908; Bar Harbor, Maine
PARTY: Republican
TERM: December 19, 1974–January 20, 1977
PRESIDENT: Gerald R. Ford
DIED: January 26, 1979; New York City
BURIED: North Tarrytown, New York

Nelson Aldrich Rockefeller was the second of the six children of Abby and John D. Rockefeller Jr. Nelson's paternal grandfather was John D. Rockefeller, the billionaire philanthropist who founded Standard Oil. Nelson's maternal grandfather was Nelson W. Aldrich, a senator from Rhode Island.

After attending private schools in New York City, Nelson enrolled in Dartmouth College in 1926. Although hindered by dyslexia, he graduated with a degree in economics in 1930 and was named to the Phi Beta Kappa honor fraternity. Rockefeller then helped manage the numerous holdings of the Rockefeller family, including real estate properties in New York City. From 1935 to 1940 he served as director of the Standard Oil subsidiary in Venezuela. During this period he developed an intense interest in Latin American affairs.

In 1940 Rockefeller entered public service when President Franklin D. Roosevelt appointed him coordinator of a new agency, the Office for Coordination of Commercial and Cultural Relations between the American Republics. During World War II the agency was renamed the Office of Inter-American Affairs. In 1944 Roosevelt transferred Rockefeller to the State Department, where he became assistant secretary for Latin American affairs. After clashing with other State Department officials in 1945, Rockefeller was asked by incoming secretary James F. Byrnes to resign. In 1950 Rockefeller returned to gov-

Nelson A. Rockefeller

ernment when President Harry Truman appointed him to chair the Advisory Board on International Development. When the president did not commit himself to acting on the board's recommendations, Rockefeller resigned in 1951.

Rockefeller supported Dwight Eisenhower's successful bid for the presidency in 1952, and in 1953 Eisenhower appointed him under secretary of the newly created Department of Health, Education, and Welfare. In 1954 Rockefeller became special assistant to the president for foreign affairs, but he resigned in 1955 after conflicts with Secretary of State John Foster Dulles. From 1953 to 1958 Rockefeller also chaired Eisenhower's Advisory Committee on Government Organization, which studied ways to reorganize the government.

Rockefeller was elected governor of New York as a Republican in 1958. In this office he supported civil rights legislation and urban renewal and oversaw the expansion of New York's state university system. He was reelected governor in 1962, 1966, and 1970. In September 1971, after inmates had taken hostages at the state prison in Attica, Rockefeller ordered more than a thousand policemen to storm the cellblock. This controversial action culminated in the deaths of thirty-four prisoners and nine hostages.

Rockefeller wanted to be president and unsuccessfully sought the Republican nomination before all three presidential elections during the 1960s. He was a leading candidate for the nomination in 1964, but he lost it to Sen. Barry M. Goldwater of Arizona. Rockefeller suffered from an image problem. Although he was conservative on many issues, including law enforcement,

military spending, and superpower relations, he was seen as an urbane liberal by the conservatives who dominated his party during the 1960s.

Rockefeller resigned from the governorship on December 18, 1973, to establish the National Commission on Critical Choices for Americans, an organization devoted to developing new national policy options.

On August 20, 1974, President Gerald R. Ford, who had succeeded to the presidency from the vice presidency after the resignation of President Richard Nixon, nominated Rockefeller for vice president. The sixty-six-year-old Rockefeller had considered another run for the presidency in 1976, but knowing his chances of being elected were small, he accepted the nomination. Under the Twenty-fifth Amendment, Rockefeller's appointment had to be approved by a majority of both houses of Congress. The confirmation hearings lasted throughout the fall as committees examined the nominee's vast financial holdings for potential conflicts of interest. Finally, on December 19, 1974, he was sworn in as the forty-first vice president.

Rockefeller chaired several boards and commissions as vice president, including a commission set up by the president to investigate the CIA. At Ford's request, Rockefeller announced on November 3, 1975, that he would not accept the Republican nomination for vice president. Ford believed he could attract more votes in the Republican primaries without Rockefeller. Nevertheless, the vice president remained loyal to Ford. He delivered the speech nominating Sen. Robert J. Dole of Kansas as the Republican vice-presidential nominee and campaigned for the Ford-Dole ticket.

After leaving the vice presidency in 1977, Rockefeller returned to New York to manage various family business and philanthropic enterprises. He died of a heart attack in his Manhattan townhouse while in the company of Megan Marshack, a twenty-six-year-old assistant.

Rockefeller married Mary Todhunter "Tod" Clark, a member of a prominent Philadelphia family, on June 23, 1930. They had three sons and two daughters. The couple became estranged during Rockefeller's first term as governor and divorced in 1962. In May 1963 he married Margaretta "Happy" Murphy, with whom he had two sons.

Walter F. Mondale

BORN: January 5, 1928; Ceylon, Minnesota
PARTY: Democratic
TERM: January 20, 1977–January 20, 1981
PRESIDENT: Jimmy Carter

Walter Frederick Mondale was the second of the three sons of Claribel and Theodore Mondale, a Methodist minister who served as pastor of a succession of churches in southern Minnesota. Theodore married Claribel in 1925 after the death of his first wife, with whom he also had three sons. In 1946 Walter, who was nicknamed "Fritz," graduated from Elmore (Minnesota) High School, where he excelled in athletics and music.

Walter F. Mondale

Mondale then entered Macalester College in St. Paul. He dropped out in 1949 when his father died, but he resumed his education at the University of Minnesota the following year. After graduating with honors in 1951, he enlisted in the army. He was discharged with the rank of corporal after serving two years at Fort Knox, Kentucky. Mondale then returned to the University of Minnesota, where he earned his law degree in 1956. That year he was admitted to the Minnesota bar and began practicing law.

Since Mondale's college years, he had been active in the Minnesota Democratic Party. He became a follower of Hubert H. Humphrey in 1946 when Humphrey was mayor of Minneapolis. In 1948, when Humphrey ran successfully for the Senate, Mondale managed Humphrey's campaign in Minnesota's Second Congressional District. Mondale also worked on the campaign of Orville Freeman, who was elected governor of Minnesota in 1954, and served as Freeman's campaign chairman in his successful bid for reelection in 1958.

That year Freeman appointed Mondale special assistant to Minnesota's attorney general. When the attorney general resigned in 1960, Freeman appointed Mondale to serve out the remaining eight months of the term. Mondale was elected to the post in 1960 and reelected in 1962. As attorney general, he won praise for his enforcement of civil rights, antitrust, and consumer protection laws.

When Humphrey resigned from the Senate in 1964 after be-

ing elected vice president, Minnesota governor Karl Rolvaag appointed Mondale to Humphrey's seat. Mondale was elected to a term of his own in 1966 and reelected in 1972. In the Senate Mondale compiled a consistently liberal voting record on domestic issues. He became a leading advocate of civil rights legislation, Lyndon Johnson's Great Society social programs, and bills benefiting farm workers, Native Americans, children, and the elderly. In foreign policy he was less consistent. He supported U.S. participation in the Vietnam War until 1968. He then sided with those members of Congress who sought to limit U.S. military involvement in Southeast Asia.

In 1974 Mondale took time off from his Senate duties to campaign across the country for the 1976 Democratic presidential nomination. He abandoned his candidacy after several months when he failed to attract significant support. Jimmy Carter, the eventual Democratic presidential nominee, however, selected Mondale to be his vice-presidential running mate. Carter said he chose Mondale because the Minnesota senator was qualified to assume the presidency, had substantial Washington experience that would complement Carter's "outsider" image, and gave the ticket geographic balance. On October 15, 1976, Mondale engaged Republican vice-presidential candidate Robert J. Dole in the first televised debate between vice-presidential candidates in U.S. election history. Most observers believed Mondale won the debate. Carter and Mondale defeated President Gerald R. Ford and Dole 297–240 in the electoral college.

Mondale was deeply involved in Carter administration policy making. He helped choose cabinet officers and draft policy proposals. He also met with Carter alone at least once a week and had an open invitation to attend any White House meeting. During Carter's first week in office he demonstrated Mondale's importance by sending him as a personal emissary to Western Europe and Japan. In 1980 Carter and Mondale were renominated, but a sagging economy and the Iran hostage crisis weakened their chances for reelection. They were easily defeated by Republicans Ronald Reagan and George Bush.

In 1984 Mondale was the front-runner of a pack of Democrats seeking the party's presidential nomination. Mondale overcame early primary successes by Sen. Gary Hart of Colorado to win the nomination. Mondale made history by choosing Rep. Geraldine Ferraro of New York as his running mate. She was the first woman to be nominated as vice president by a major political party. Mondale and Ferraro, however, faced President Ronald Reagan and Vice President George Bush, who were running for reelection during a period of economic prosperity. The Democrats won only Minnesota and the District of Columbia as they were buried in a forty-nine-state Republican landslide. After the election, Mondale retired from politics and returned to Minnesota.

On July 30, 1993, Mondale was confirmed by the Senate as U.S. ambassador to Japan, after being nominated by President Bill Clinton. The appointment of a former vice president to this post was intended to signal the importance of U.S.-Japanese relations.

Mondale married Joan Adams, the daughter of a Presbyterian minister, on December 27, 1955. They had two sons and a daughter.

Dan Quayle

BORN: February 4, 1947; Indianapolis
PARTY: Republican
TERM: January 20, 1989–January 20, 1993
PRESIDENT: George Bush

James Danforth Quayle III was the eldest of the four children of James and Corinne Quayle. Since childhood, James was called "Dan." His maternal grandfather, Eugene C. Pulliam, was a conservative Indiana newspaper publisher who amassed a fortune close to a billion dollars. In 1955 Dan moved with his family from Indiana to Phoenix, Arizona, where his father helped manage the family's newspaper interests in that state. When Dan was in high school, the Quayles moved back to Indiana, where his father took over as publisher of the *Huntington Herald-Press,* one of the family newspapers.

In 1965 Quayle enrolled in DePauw University, a small liberal arts college in Greencastle, Indiana, which was heavily endowed by his family. Quayle played on the golf team and compiled a mediocre academic record. Upon graduation in 1969 Quayle lost his student deferment and became eligible for the military draft. With the help of family friends, however, Quayle secured a place in the Indiana National Guard, an action that made military service in Vietnam unlikely.

While serving in the National Guard one weekend a month, Quayle held a series of jobs in Indiana state government and attended Indiana University Law School at night. With the help of his family he was hired as a clerk in the attorney general's office and later as an assistant to Indiana governor Edgar Whitcomb. After graduating from law school in 1974, Quayle opened a law practice in Huntington and worked as associate publisher of the *Huntington Herald-Press.*

In 1976 local Republican leaders asked Quayle to run for Congress against eight-term incumbent Democrat Edward Roush. Quayle waged an energetic campaign and won despite his inexperience. He served two terms in the House before challenging Democrat Birch Bayh for his Senate seat in 1980. With the help of conservative groups, Quayle unseated Bayh after a tough campaign.

Quayle showed greater diligence in the Senate than he had in the House. As a member of the Armed Services Committee he supported most defense spending programs, including President Ronald Reagan's Strategic Defense Initiative missile defense system, but he also advocated reforms in the Pentagon's procurement process. Although Quayle sided with Senate conservatives on most issues, he occasionally demonstrated independence. In 1982 he worked with liberal senator Edward M. Kennedy on a consensus job training bill that was enacted into law despite the initial opposition of the administration. In 1986 the Democrats were unable to attract a prominent challenger, and Quayle was reelected to his seat.

In August 1988 Republican presidential nominee George Bush surprised the nation by naming the forty-one-year-old Quayle to be his running mate. Quayle had been mentioned as a possible vice-presidential candidate, but he was considered a long shot behind several better-known Republicans. Within hours of the announcement, Quayle became the subject of controversy. Commentators focused on Quayle's use of family connections to enter the National Guard rather than risk being drafted. Negative reports also pointed to his unimpressive academic record and his apparent use of family influence to gain admittance to law school. The portrait of a wealthy underachiever who exploited his family's connections threatened to damage Bush's election chances. Some Republicans advised Bush to withdraw Quayle's nomination, but Bush stuck by his choice.

Bush campaign strategists sought to limit Quayle's visibility by seldom having him appear with Bush and assigning him to campaign in smaller cities. Most observers believed that Democratic vice-presidential nominee Lloyd Bentsen easily defeated Quayle in their one televised debate. Nevertheless, Bush and Quayle defeated Massachusetts governor Michael S. Dukakis and Bentsen 426–112 in the electoral college. Quayle took the oath of office on January 20, 1989, becoming the forty-fourth vice president of the United States.

As vice president, Quayle was prone to verbal gaffes that perpetuated perceptions of him as inexperienced and inept. Quayle sought to overcome these perceptions by taking on several high-profile assignments. He headed the Council on Competitiveness, a Bush administration working group charged with identifying and eliminating unnecessary or counterproductive regulations. Quayle also headed the president's National Space Council and provided advice to Bush on congressional matters. But like most vice presidents, Quayle spent much of his time on ceremonial and political duties and was not among the president's foremost advisers.

Before the 1992 election, many Republicans urged Bush to choose another vice-presidential running mate. Bush expressed his confidence in Quayle and declined to consider anyone else. During the campaign Quayle gained favor with many party conservatives by frequently promoting personal responsibility, the maintenance of two-parent families, the disciplined upbringing of children, and the preservation of religion in society. Quayle's activities may have helped to increase the ticket's popularity with conservatives, but support for Bush and Quayle among independents and moderates eroded. They were defeated by Bill Clinton and Al Gore 370–168 in the electoral college.

Upon leaving office, Quayle returned with his family to Indiana. He wrote a regular newspaper column and a book about his vice-presidential experience. His performance during the 1992 campaign had made him a favorite with the conservative wing of the Republican Party, which frequently enlisted him to appear at party events.

In 1994 Quayle began assembling a campaign team for a run at the 1996 Republican presidential nomination. In February 1995, however, he announced that he would not run. Quayle contended that he did not want to leave his family to campaign. But most observers believed that he had made a strategic decision not to enter the crowded Republican field after reviewing polling data and prospects for fund raising. He also declined to enter the 1996 gubernatorial race in Indiana, an office that he would have been favored to win if he ran.

Quayle married Marilyn Tucker on November 18, 1972. The couple met in law school and practiced law together for a brief period before Quayle entered politics. Marilyn Quayle functioned as a close political adviser to her husband and also was mentioned as a possible candidate for governor of Indiana. They had two sons and a daughter.

Al Gore

BORN: March 31, 1948; Washington, D.C.
PARTY: Democrat
TERM: January 20, 1993–
PRESIDENT: Bill Clinton

Albert Arnold Gore Jr. was the son of Al Gore Sr. and Pauline Gore. His father was a U.S. senator from Tennessee who served from 1953 to 1971. Before being elected to the Senate, Al Gore Sr. served seven terms in the House of Representatives. Pauline Gore was one of the first women to earn a law degree from Vanderbilt University.

Al Gore

Gore grew up in Washington, D.C., where he attended private schools. He spent summers and vacations on the family farm near Carthage, Tennessee. In 1969 he graduated from Harvard University with a degree in government. Gore opposed the Vietnam War, but he enlisted in the army and served as a military journalist in Vietnam. He was never involved in combat. Gore's decision to enter the military rather than seek a graduate school deferment was influenced by his concern that his father's reelection chances could be harmed if he avoided service. Despite Gore's action, his father was defeated for reelection in 1970 by William Brock.

From 1971 to 1976 Gore worked as a reporter for the *Tennessean,* a Nashville newspaper, writing investigative pieces and covering local politics. During that time he took classes at Vanderbilt Divinity School and Vanderbilt Law School, but he did not earn a degree.

In 1976 Gore won his father's former seat in the House of Representatives. He was easily reelected to the heavily Democratic district in 1978, 1980, and 1982. Gore successfully jumped to the Senate in 1984, winning with 61 percent of the vote despite Ronald Reagan's national landslide. During his years in Congress, Gore gained a reputation as a moderately liberal, detail-oriented lawmaker. He became an expert on the environment and many defense issues.

At age thirty-nine Gore entered the race for the 1988 Democratic presidential nomination. During the race he exhibited a stiff and uninspiring, yet substantive campaign style. He won five southern primaries but was unable to win a major primary in the North. Nevertheless, his third place showing behind Jesse Jackson and the eventual nominee, Michael Dukakis, established him as one of the top southern Democrat politicians and a contender for the nomination in 1992. He was easily reelected in 1990 to his Senate seat.

Gore was one of only ten Democrats in the Senate to vote for the authorization of the use of military force against Iraq in January 1991. His vote upset some Democratic Party loyalists, but he repaired the damage by vigorously defending Democrats who had voted against using force from charges that they were unpatriotic.

In 1992 Governor Bill Clinton of Arkansas emerged as the Democratic nominee. Clinton surprised many commentators by picking Gore as his vice-presidential running mate. Presidential candidates usually try to balance the ticket with a running mate who is from another region and who has a somewhat different political ideology. In contrast to this norm, Gore shared Clinton's moderate southern Democrat outlook and was from a state that borders Arkansas. Moreover, they were only a year and a half apart in age. But Clinton and Gore used this close identification to project an image of unity and youthful energy. Gore's service in Vietnam also aided Clinton, who had been accused of avoiding military service. Clinton and Gore defeated incumbents George Bush and Dan Quayle by an electoral vote of 370–168.

Gore became one of President Clinton's closest advisers. Their relationship departed from the usual pattern of vice presidents playing peripheral roles in the administration. Gore took on many critical assignments. He served as the head of the president's effort to "reinvent government." This was a long-term project to reduce the size of and reengineer the federal government to achieve efficiency and cost savings. Gore also functioned as the administration's point man on congressional relations, environmental protection, defense, and high technology.

One of Gore's most celebrated moments came on November 9, 1993, when he debated the merits of the North American Free Trade Agreement (NAFTA) with billionaire H. Ross Perot on the *Larry King Live* talk show. Through much of the fall, it appeared that Congress would reject the agreement, which was supported by Clinton. Clinton and Gore decided on the unorthodox strategy of challenging Perot, a vocal critic of the agreement, to a televised debate with Gore. Polls showed after the debate that Gore and the pro-NAFTA position had won decisively, giving proponents a big psychological boost. The outcome induced many wavering members of Congress to support the president and the agreement, which passed both houses.

Gore married Mary Elizabeth "Tipper" Aitcheson in 1970. They had three girls and one boy. Tipper Gore gained national attention in the mid-1980s when she waged a campaign to put warning labels on record albums to alert parents about lyrics that glorified violence and casual sex.

Reference Materials

APPENDIX A Documents and Texts

Documents and Texts

THE DOCUMENTARY HISTORY of the presidency is long and extensive. It begins before the actual creation of the office at the Constitutional Convention of 1787 with documents from the American Revolution that helped to prepare the way for the presidency. It includes official messages and orders by individual presidents, presidential speeches, Supreme Court decisions, congressional resolutions, and other official and unofficial documents.

In compiling this section, an effort has been made to include the most important presidential documents (a sort of "Top 40" from the history of the office), with an emphasis on the twentieth-century presidency. But no pretense is made to comprehensiveness; for reasons of space, many important documents had to be omitted. In addition, most of the documents in this Appendix have been edited to retain only the most important material. Omissions are indicated by ellipses (. . .).

A more complete and less heavily edited compilation of presidential documents may be found in Michael Nelson, ed., *Historic Documents on the Presidency: 1776–1989,* also published by Congressional Quarterly.

Declaration of Independence

On June 11, 1776, the responsibility to "prepare a declaration" of independence was assigned by the Continental Congress, meeting in Philadelphia, to five members: John Adams, Benjamin Franklin, Thomas Jefferson, Robert Livingston, and Roger Sherman. Impressed by his talents as a writer, the committee asked Jefferson to compose a draft. After modifying Jefferson's draft the committee turned it over to Congress on June 28. On July 2 Congress voted to declare independence; on the evening of July 4, it approved the Declaration of Independence.

The declaration is best remembered for its ringing preamble, which affirms the "self-evident" truths that "all men are created equal, that they are endowed by their Creator with certain unalienable Rights, that among these are Life, Liberty, and the pursuit of Happiness." But, at the time, the more important part of the Declaration was what followed the preamble: the list of "a long train of abuses and usurpations" against the American colonists by the British government. The charges detailed the abuses that made it "necessary for one people [the Americans] to dissolve the political bands which have connected them with another [the British]." Although many of the more than two dozen specific alleged abuses were acts of Parliament, all were attributed to King George III. The indictment—and the declaration as a whole—thus contributed to the idea that a strong executive was a threat to the fundamental liberties of the people.

In Congress, July 4, 1776,

THE UNANIMOUS DECLARATION OF THE THIRTEEN UNITED STATES OF AMERICA,

When in the Course of human events, it becomes necessary for one people to dissolve the political bands which have connected them with another, and to assume among the Powers of the earth, the separate and equal station to which the Laws of Nature and of Nature's God entitle them, a decent respect to the opinions of mankind requires that they should declare the causes which impel them to the separation.

We hold these truths to be self-evident, that all men are created equal, that they are endowed by their Creator with certain unalienable Rights, that among these are Life, Liberty and the pursuit of Happiness. That to secure these rights, Governments are instituted among Men, deriving their just powers from the consent of the governed. That whenever any form of Government becomes destructive of these ends, it is the Right of the People to alter or to abolish it, and to institute new Government, laying its foundation on such principles and organizing its powers in such form, as to them shall seem most likely to effect their Safety and Happiness. Prudence, indeed, will dictate that Government long established should not be changed for light and transient causes; and accordingly all experience hath shown, that mankind are more disposed to suffer, while evils are sufferable, than to right themselves by abolishing the forms to which they are accustomed. But when a long train of abuses and usurpations, pursuing invariably the same Object evinces a design to reduce them under absolute Despotism, it is their right, it is their duty, to throw off such Government, and to provide new Guards for their future security. — Such has been the patient sufferance of these Colonies; and such is now the necessity which constrains them to alter their former Systems of Government. The history of the present King of Great Britain is a history of repeated injuries and usurpations, all having in direct object the establishment of an absolute Tyranny over these States. To prove this, let Facts be submitted to a candid world.

He has refused his Assent to Laws, the most wholesome and necessary for the public good.

He has forbidden his Governors to pass Laws of immediate and pressing importance, unless suspended in their operation till his Assent should be obtained; and when so suspended, he has utterly neglected to attend to them.

He has refused to pass other Laws for the accommodation of large districts of people, unless those people would relinquish the right of Representation in the Legislature, a right inestimable to them and formidable to tyrants only.

He has called together legislative bodies at places unusual, uncomfortable, and distant from the depository of their Public Records, for the sole purpose of fatiguing them into compliance with his measures.

He has dissolved Representative Houses repeatedly, for opposing with manly firmness his invasions on the rights of the people.

He has refused for a long time, after such dissolutions, to cause others to be elected; whereby the Legislative Powers, incapable of Annihilation, have returned to the People at large for their exercise; the State remaining in the mean time exposed to all the dangers of invasion from without, and convulsions within.

He has endeavored to prevent the population of these States; for that purpose obstructing the Laws of Naturalization of Foreigners; refusing to pass others to encourage their migration hither, and raising the conditions of new Appropriations of Lands.

He has obstructed the Administration of Justice, by refusing his Assent to Laws for establishing Judiciary Powers.

He has made Judges dependent on his Will alone, for the tenure of their offices, and the amount and payment of their salaries.

He has erected a multitude of New Offices, and sent hither swarms of Officers to harass our People, and eat out their substance.

He has kept among us, in times of peace, Standing Armies without the Consent of our legislature.

He has affected to render the Military independent of and superior to the Civil Power.

He has combined with others to subject us to a jurisdiction foreign to our constitution, and unacknowledged by our laws; giving his Assent to their acts of pretended legislation:

For quartering large bodies of armed troops among us:

For protecting them, by a mock Trial, from Punishment for any Murders which they should commit on the Inhabitants of these States:

For cutting off our Trade with all parts of the world:

For imposing taxes on us without our Consent:

For depriving us in many cases, of the benefits of Trial by Jury:

For transporting us beyond Seas to be tried for pretended offences:

For abolishing the free System of English Laws in a neighbouring Province, establishing therein an Arbitrary government, and enlarging its Boundaries so as to render it at once an example and fit instrument for introducing the same absolute rule into these Colonies:

For taking away our Charters, abolishing our most valuable Laws, and altering fundamentally the Forms of our Governments:

For suspending our own Legislature, and declaring themselves invested with Power to legislate for us in all cases whatsoever.

He has abdicated Government here, by declaring us out of his Protection and waging War against us.

He has plundered our seas, ravaged our Coasts, burnt our towns, and destroyed the lives of our people.

He is at this time transporting large armies of foreign mercenaries to compleat the works of death, desolation and tyranny, already begun with circumstances of Cruelty & perfidy scarcely parallel in the most barbarous ages, and totally unworthy the Head of a civilized nation.

He has constrained our fellow Citizens taken Captive on the high Seas to bear Arms against their Country, to become the executioners of their friends and Brethren, or to fall themselves by their Hands.

He has excited domestic insurrections amongst us, and has endeavoured to bring on the inhabitants of our frontiers, the merciless Indian Savages, whose known rule of warfare, is an undistinguished destruction of all ages, sexes and conditions.

In every stage of these Oppressions We have Petitioned for Redress in the most humble terms: Our repeated Petitions have been answered only by repeated injury. A Prince, whose character is thus marked by every act which may define a Tyrant, is unfit to be the ruler of a free People.

Nor have We been wanting in attention to our British brethren. We have warned them from time to time of attempts by their legislature to extend an unwarrantable jurisdiction over us. We have reminded them of the circumstances of our emigration and settlement here. We have appealed to their native justice and magnanimity, and we have conjured them by the ties of our common kindred to disavow these usurpations, which would inevitably interrupt our connections and correspondence. They too have been deaf to the voice of justice and of consanguinity. We must, therefore, acquiesce in the necessity, which denounces our Separation, and hold them, as we hold the rest of mankind, Enemies in War, in Peace Friends.

We, therefore, the Representatives of the United States of America, in General Congress, Assembled, appealing to the Supreme Judge of the world for the rectitude of our intentions, do, in the Name, and by Authority of the good People of these Colonies, solemnly publish and declare, That these United Colonies are, and of Right ought to be Free and Independent States; that they are Absolved from all Allegiance to the British Crown, and that all political connection between them and the State of Great Britain, is and ought to be totally dissolved; and that as Free and Independent States, they have full Power to levy War, conclude Peace, contract Alliances, establish Commerce, and to do all other Acts and Things which Independent States may of right do. And for the support of this Declaration, with a firm reliance on the Protection of Divine Providence, we mutually pledge to each other our Lives, our Fortunes and our sacred Honor.

John Hancock.

New Hampshire:
Josiah Bartlett,
William Whipple,
Matthew Thornton.

Massachusetts-Bay:
Samuel Adams,
John Adams,
Robert Treat Paine,
Elbridge Gerry.

Rhode Island:
Stephen Hopkins,
William Ellery.

Connecticut:
Roger Sherman,
Samuel Huntington,
William Williams,
Oliver Wolcott.

New York:
William Floyd,
Philip Livingston,
Francis Lewis,
Lewis Morris.

Pennsylvania:
Robert Morris,
Benjamin Harris,

Benjamin Franklin,
John Morton,
George Clymer,
James Smith,
George Taylor,
James Wilson,
George Ross.

Delaware:
Caesar Rodney,
George Read,
Thomas McKean.

Georgia:
Button Gwinnett,
Lyman Hall,
George Walton.

Maryland:
Samuel Chase,
William Paca,
Thomas Stone,
Charles Carroll of
    Carrollton.

Virginia:
George Wythe,
Richard Henry Lee,
Thomas Jefferson,
Benjamin Harrison,

Thomas Nelson Jr.,
Francis Lightfoot
    Lee,
Carter Braxton.

North Carolina:
William Hooper,
Joseph Hewes,
John Penn.

South Carolina:
Edward Rutledge,
Thomas Heyward
    Jr.,
Thomas Lynch Jr.,
Arthur Middleton.

New Jersey:
Richard Stockton,
John Witherspoon,
Francis Hopkinson,
John Hart,
Abraham Clark.

Articles of Confederation

On June 11, 1776, the same day that it created a five-member com-mittee to prepare the Declaration of Independence, the Continental Congress appointed a thirteen-member committee (one from each state) to draft a "plan of confederation." The two decisions were closely con-nected: a new and independent nation needed a government of some sort. The committee recommended the Articles of Confederation to Con-gress on July 12; Congress adopted the plan on November 15, 1777; and unanimous ratification by the states finally came on March 1, 1781.

Written at a time when hostility against a strong central government (the British) and executive power (the king and his royal governors in each colony) was at its height, the Articles, not surprisingly, provided for a weak central government with no executive at all. Congress—a uni-cameral body in which each state was represented equally—was the sole organ of the new national government. It had no power to levy taxes or to enforce any laws that it passed. Even the powers that it did have— such as to raise an army and navy, regulate coinage and borrow money, and adjudicate disputes among the states—were hard to exercise, be-cause any proposed law required a two-thirds majority for passage. (To amend the Articles required unanimity.)

The Articles of Confederation provided a barely adequate framework for fighting and winning the Revolutionary War: the presence of a com-mon enemy fostered a certain amount of unity among the states. But when the British were defeated in 1783, the national government found it increasingly difficult to unite the country to confront the new chal-lenges of peace.

To all to whom these Presents shall come, we the undersigned Delegates of the States affixed to our Names send greeting. Whereas the Delegates of the United States of America in Congress assembled did on the fifteenth day of November in the Year of our Lord One Thousand Seven Hundred and Seventy seven, and in the Second Year of the Independence of America agree to certain articles of Confeder-ation and perpetual Union between the States of Newhampshire, Massachusetts-bay, Rhodeisland and Providence Plantations, Con-necticut, New York, New Jersey, Pennsylvania, Delaware, Maryland, Virginia, North-Carolina, South-Carolina and Georgia in the Words following, viz. "Articles of Confederation and perpetual Union be-tween the states of Newhampshire, Massachusetts-bay, Rhodeisland and Providence Plantations, Connecticut, New-York, New-Jersey, Pennsylvania, Delaware, Maryland, Virginia, North-Carolina, South-Carolina and Georgia.

Article I. The Stile of this confederacy shall be "The United States of America."

Article II. Each state retains its sovereignty, freedom and inde-pendence, and every Power, Jurisdiction and Right, which is not by this confederation expressly delegated to the United States, in Con-gress assembled.

Article III. The said states hereby severally enter into a firm league of friendship with each other, for their common defence, the security of their Liberties, and their mutual and general welfare, binding themselves to assist each other, against all force offered to, or attacks made upon them, or any of them, on account of religion, sov-ereignty, trade, or any other pretence whatever.

Article IV. The better to secure the perpetuate mutual friendship and intercourse among the people of the different states in this union, the free inhabitants of each of these states, paupers, vagabonds and fugitives from Justice excepted, shall be entitled to all privileges and immunities of free citizens in the several states; and the people of each state shall have free ingress and regress to and from any other state, and shall enjoy therein all the privileges of trade and commerce, subject to the same duties, impositions and restrictions as the inhabi-tants thereof respectively, provided that such restriction shall not ex-tend so far as to prevent the removal of property imported into any state, to any other state of which the Owner is an inhabitant; provid-ed also that no imposition, duties or restriction shall be laid by any state, on the property of the united states, or either of them.

If any Person guilty of, or charged with treason, felony, or other high misdemeanor in any state, shall flee from Justice, and be found in any of the united states, he shall upon demand of the Governor or executive power, of the state from which he fled be delivered up and removed to the state having jurisdiction of his offence.

Full faith and credit shall be given in each of these states to the records, acts and judicial proceedings of the courts and magistrates of every other state.

Article V. For the more convenient management of the general interests of the united states, delegates shall be annually appointed in such manner as the legislature of each state shall direct, to meet in Congress on the first Monday in November, in every year, with a power reserved to each state, to recall its delegates, or any of them, at any time within the year, and to send others in their stead, for the re-mainder of the Year.

No state shall be represented in Congress by less than two, nor by more than seven Members; and no person shall be capable of being a delegate for more than three years in any term of six years; nor shall any person, being a delegate, be capable of holding any office under the united states, for which he, or another for his benefit receives any salary, fees or emolument of any kind.

Each state shall maintain its own delegates in a meeting of the states, and while they act as members of the committee of the states.

In determining questions in the united states, in Congress assem-bled, each state shall have one vote.

Freedom of speech and debate in Congress shall not be im-peached or questioned in any Court, or place out of Congress, and the members of congress shall be protected in their persons from ar-rests and imprisonments, during the time of their going to and from, and attendance on congress, except for treason, felony, or breach of the peace.

Article VI. No state without the Consent of the united states in congress assembled, shall send any embassy to, or receive any em-bassy from, or enter into any conference, agreement, or alliance or treaty with any King, prince or state; nor shall any person holding any office of profit or trust under the united states, or any of them, accept of any present, emolument, office or title of any kind whatever from any king, prince or foreign state; nor shall the united states in con-gress assembled, or any of them, grant any title of nobility.

No two or more states shall enter into any treaty, confederation or alliance whatever between them, without the consent of the united states in congress assembled, specifying accurately the purposes for which the same is to be entered into, and how long it shall continue.

No state shall lay any imposts or duties, which may interfere with any stipulations in treaties, entered into by the united states in con-gress assembled, with any king, prince or state, in pursuance of any treaties already proposed by congress, to the courts of France and Spain.

No vessels of war shall be kept up in time of peace by any state, ex-cept such number only, as shall be deemed necessary by the united states in congress assembled, for the defence of such state, or its trade; nor shall any body of forces be kept up by any state, in time of peace, except such number only, as in the judgment of the united states, in congress assembled, shall be deemed requisite to garrison the forts necessary for the defence of such state; but every state shall always keep up a well regulated and disciplined militia, sufficiently armed and accoutred, and shall provide and constantly have ready for use, in public stores, a due number of field pieces and tents, and a proper quantity of arms, ammunition and camp equipage.

No state shall engage in any war without the consent of the united states in Congress assembled, unless such state be actually invaded by enemies, or shall have received certain advice of a resolution being formed by some nation of Indians to invade such state, and the danger is so imminent as not to admit of a delay, till the united states in congress assembled can be consulted: nor shall any state grant commissions to any ships or vessels of war, nor letters of marque or reprisal, except it be after a declaration of war by the united states in congress assembled, and then only against the kingdom or state and the subjects thereof, against which war has been so declared, and under such regulations as shall be established by the united states in congress assembled, unless such state be infested by pirates, in which case vessels of war may be fitted out for that occasion, and kept so long as the danger shall continue, or until the united states in congress assembled shall determine otherwise.

Article VII. When land-forces are raised by any state for the common defence, all officers of or under the rank of colonel, shall be appointed by the legislature of each state respectively by whom such forces shall be raised, or in such manner as such state shall direct, and all vacancies shall be filled up by the state which first made the appointment.

Article VIII. All charges of war, and all other expences that shall be incurred for the common defence or general welfare, and allowed by the united states in congress assembled, shall be defrayed out of a common treasury, which shall be supplied by the several states, in proportion to the value of all land within each state, granted to or surveyed for any Person, as such land and the buildings and improvements thereon shall be estimated according to such mode as the united states in congress assembled, shall from time to time direct and appoint. The taxes for paying that proportion shall be laid and levied by the authority and direction of the legislatures of the several states within the time agreed upon by the united states in congress assembled.

Article IX. The united states in congress assembled, shall have the sole and exclusive right and power of determining on peace and war, except in the cases mentioned in the sixth article—of sending and receiving ambassadors—entering into treaties and alliances, provided that no treaty of commerce shall be made whereby the legislative power of the respective states shall be restrained from imposing such imposts and duties on foreigners, as their own people are subjected to, or from prohibiting the exportation or importation of any species of goods or commodities whatsoever—of establishing rules for deciding in all cases, what capture on land or water shall be legal, and in what manner prizes taken by land or naval forces in the service of the united states shall be divided or appropriated—of granting letters of marque and reprisal in times of peace—appointing courts for the trial of piracies and felonies committed on the high seas and establishing courts for receiving and determining finally appeals in all cases of captures, provided that no member of congress shall be appointed a judge of any of the said courts.

The united states in congress assembled shall also be the last resort on appeal in all disputes and differences now subsisting or that hereafter may arise between two or more states concerning boundary, jurisdiction or any other cause whatever; which authority shall always be exercised in the manner following. Whenever the legislative or executive authority or lawful agent of any state in controversy with an-

other shall present a petition to congress, stating the matter in question and praying for a hearing, notice thereof shall be given by order of congress to the legislative or executive authority of the other state in controversy, and a day assigned for the appearance of the parties by their lawful agents, who shall then be directed to appoint by joint consent, commissioners or judges to constitute a court for hearing and determining the matter in question: but if they cannot agree, congress shall name three persons out of each of the united states, and from the list of such persons each party shall alternately strike out one, the petitioners beginning, until the number shall be reduced to thirteen; and from that number not less than seven, nor more than nine names as congress shall direct, shall in the presence of congress be drawn out by lot, and the persons whose names shall be so drawn or any five of them, shall be commissioners or judges, to hear and finally determine the controversy, so always as a major part of the judges who shall hear the cause shall agree in the determination: and if either party shall neglect to attend at the day appointed, without shewing reasons, which congress shall judge sufficient, or being present shall refuse to strike, the congress shall proceed to nominate three persons out of each state, and the secretary of congress shall strike in behalf of such party absent or refusing; and the judgment and sentence of the court to be appointed, in the manner before prescribed, shall be final and conclusive; and if any of the parties shall refuse to submit to the authority of such court, or to appear to defend their claim or cause, the court shall nevertheless proceed to pronounce sentence, or judgment, which shall in like manner be final and decisive, the judgment or sentence and other proceedings being in either case transmitted to congress, and lodged among the acts of congress for the security of the parties concerned: provided that every commissioner, before he sits in judgment, shall take an oath to be administered by one of the judges of the supreme or superior court of the state, where the cause shall be tried, "well and truly to hear and determine the matter in question, according to the best of his judgment, without favour, affection or hope of reward:" provided also that no state shall be deprived of territory for the benefit of the united states.

All controversies concerning the private right of soil claimed under different grants of two or more states, whose jurisdictions as they may respect such lands, and the states which passed such grants are adjusted, the said grants or either of them being at the same time claimed to have originated antecedent to such settlement of jurisdiction, shall on the petition of either party to the congress of the united states, be finally determined as near as may be in the same manner as is before prescribed for deciding disputes respecting territorial jurisdiction between different states.

The united states in congress assembled shall also have the sole and exclusive right and power of regulating the alloy and value of coin struck by their own authority, or by that of the respective states—fixing the standard of weights and measures throughout the united states—regulating the trade and managing all affairs with the Indians, not members of any of the states, provided that the legislative right of any state within its own limits be not infringed or violated—establishing and regulating post-offices from one state to another, throughout all the united states, and exacting such postage on the papers passing thro' the same as may be requisite to defray the expences of the said office—appointing all officers of the land forces, in the service of the united states, excepting regimental officers—appointing all the officers of the naval forces, and commissioning all officers whatever in the service of the united states—making rules for the government and regulation of the said land and naval forces, and directing their operations.

The united states in congress assembled shall have authority to appoint a committee, to sit in the recess of congress, to be denominated "A Committee of the States," and to consist of one delegate from each state; and to appoint such other committees and civil officers as may be necessary for managing the general affairs of the united states under their direction—to appoint one of their number to preside, provided that no person be allowed to serve in the office of president more than one year in any term of three years; to ascertain the necessary sums of Money to be raised for the service of the united states, and to appropriate and apply the same for defraying the public expences—to borrow money, or emit bills on the credit of the united states, transmitting every half year to the respective states an account of the sums of money so borrowed or emitted,—to build and equip a navy—to agree upon the number of land forces, and to make requisitions from each state for its quota, in proportion to the number of white inhabitants in such state; which requisition shall be binding, and thereupon the legislature of each state shall appoint the regimental officers, raise the men and cloath, arm and equip them in a soldier like manner, at the expence of the united states, and the officers and men so cloathed, armed and equipped shall march to the place appointed, and within the time agreed on by the united states in congress assembled: But if the united states in congress assembled shall, on consideration of circumstances judge proper that any state should not raise men, or should raise a smaller number than its quota, and that any other state should raise a greater number of men than the quota thereof, such extra number shall be raised, officered, cloathed, armed and equipped in the same manner as the quota of such state, unless the legislature of such state shall judge that such extra number cannot be safely spared out of the same, in which case they shall raise, officer, cloath, arm and equip as many of such extra number as they judge can be safely spared. And the officers and men so cloathed, armed and equipped, shall march to the place appointed, and within the time agreed on by the united states in congress assembled.

The united states in congress assembled shall never engage in a war, nor grant letters of marque and reprisal in time of peace, nor enter into any treaties or alliances, nor coin money, nor regulate the value thereof, nor ascertain the sums and expences necessary for the defence and welfare of the united states, or any of them, nor emit bills, nor borrow money on the credit of the united states, nor appropriate money, nor agree upon the number of vessels of war, to be built or purchased, or the number of land or sea forces to be raised, nor appoint a commander in chief of the army or navy, unless nine states assent to the same: nor shall a question on any other point, except for adjourning from day to day be determined, unless by the votes of a majority of the united states in congress assembled.

The congress of the united states shall have power to adjourn to any time within the year, and to any place within the united states, so that no period of adjournment be for a longer duration than the space of six Months, and shall publish the Journal of their proceedings monthly, except such parts thereof relating to treaties, alliances or military operations as in their judgment require secrecy; and the yeas and nays of the delegates of each state on any question shall be entered on the Journal, when it is desired by any delegate; and the delegates of a state, or any of them, at his or their request shall be furnished with a transcript of the said Journal, except such parts as are above excepted, to lay before the legislatures of the several states.

Article X. The committee of the states, or any nine of them, shall be authorised to execute, in the recess of congress, such of the powers of congress as the united states in congress assembled, by the consent of nine states, shall from time to time think expedient to vest them with; provided that no power be delegated to the said committee, for the exercise of which, by the articles of confederation, the voice of nine states in the congress of the united states assembled is requisite.

Article XI. Canada acceding to this confederation, and joining in the measures of the united states, shall be admitted into, and entitled

to all the advantages of this union: but no other colony shall be admitted into the same, unless such admission be agreed to by nine states.

Article XII. All bills of credit emitted, monies borrowed and debts contracted by, or under the authority of congress, before the assembling of the united states, in pursuance of the present confederation, shall be deemed and considered as a charge against the united states, for payment and satisfaction whereof the said united states, and the public faith are hereby solemnly pledged.

Article XIII. Every state shall abide by the determinations of the united states in congress assembled, on all questions which by this confederation are submitted to them. And the Articles of this confederation shall be inviolably observed by every state, and the union shall be perpetual; nor shall any alteration at any time hereafter be made in any of them; unless such alteration be agreed to in a congress of the united states, and be afterwards confirmed by the legislatures of every state.

And Whereas it has pleased the Great Governor of the World to incline the hearts of the legislatures we respectively represent in congress, to approve of, and to authorize us to ratify the said articles of confederation and perpetual union. Know Ye that we the undersigned delegates, by virtue of the power and authority to us given for that purpose, do by these presents, in the name and in behalf of our respective constituents, fully and entirely ratify and confirm each and every of the said articles of confederation and perpetual union, and all and singular the matters and things therein contained: And we do further solemnly plight and engage the faith of our respective constituents, that they shall abide by the determinations of the united states in congress assembled, on all questions, which by the said confederation are submitted to them. And that the articles thereof shall be inviolably observed by the states we respectively represent, and that the union shall be perpetual. In Witness whereof we have hereunto set our hands in Congress. Done at Philadelphia in the state of Pennsylvania the ninth Day of July in the Year of our Lord one Thousand seven Hundred and Seventy-eight, and in the third year of the independence of America.

New Hampshire:
Josiah Bartlett,
John Wentworth Jr.

Massachusetts:
John Hancock,
Samuel Adams,
Elbridge Gerry,
Francis Dana,
James Lovell,
Samuel Holten.

Rhode Island:
William Ellery,
Henry Marchant,
John Collins.

Connecticut:
Roger Sherman,
Samuel Huntington,
Oliver Wolcott,
Titus Hosmer,
Andrew Adams.

New York:
James Duane,
Francis Lewis,
William Duer,
Gouverneur Morris.

New Jersey:
John Witherspoon,
Nathaniel Scudder.

Pennsylvania:
Robert Morris,
Daniel Roberdeau,
Jonathan Bayard
    Smith,
William Clingan,
Joseph Reed.

Delaware:
Thomas McKean,
John Dickinson,
Nicholas Van Dyke.

Maryland:
John Hanson,
Daniel Carroll.

Virginia:
Richard Henry Lee,
John Banister,
Thomas Adams,
John Harvie,
Francis Lightfoot
    Lee.

North Carolina:
John Penn,
Cornelius Harnett,
John Williams.

South Carolina:
Henry Laurens,
William Henry
    Drayton,
John Mathews,
Richard Hutson,
Thomas Heyward Jr.

Georgia:
John Walton,
Edward Telfair,
Edward Langworthy.

The Virginia Plan of Union

James Madison of Virginia not only helped to orchestrate the calling of the Constitutional Convention of 1787, he arrived in Philadelphia several days before it began and drafted a proposed plan of government to lay before the delegates. Madison, who was only thirty-six years old and lacked a strong national reputation, persuaded the governor of his state, Edmund Randolph, to introduce the plan on May 29, the convention's first day of business.

The Virginia Plan proposed a radical departure from the Articles of Confederation—a strong, three-branch national government whose powers would make it superior to the states. The legislature would have two houses, not one, and would be apportioned according to population, not state equality. In addition, the new government would have an executive and a judicial branch. The executive would be chosen by the legislature, but was otherwise undefined in the plan.

The Virginia Plan was endorsed in principle by the delegates to the convention, and it provided a working agenda for their deliberations.

1. Resolved that the Articles of Confederation ought to be so corrected and enlarged as to accomplish the objects proposed by their institution; namely "common defence, security of liberty and general welfare."

2. Resolved therefore that the rights of suffrage in the National Legislature ought to be proportioned to the Quotas of contribution, or to the number of free inhabitants, as the one or the other rule may seem best in different cases.

3. Resolved that the National Legislature ought to consist of two branches.

4. Resolved that the members of the first branch of the National Legislature ought to be elected by the people of the several States every   for the terms of   ; to be of the age of   years at least, to receive liberal stipends by which they may be compensated for the devotion of their time to public service, to be ineligible to any office established by a particular State, or under the authority of the United States, except those peculiarly belonging to the functions of the first branch, during the term of service, and for the space of   after its expiration; to be incapable of reelection for the space of   after the expiration of their term of service, and to be subject to recall.

5. Resolved that the members of the second branch of the National Legislature ought to be elected by those of the first, out of a proper number of persons nominated by the individual Legislatures, to be of the age of   years at least; to hold their offices for a term sufficient to ensure their independency; to receive liberal stipends, by which they may be compensated for the devotion of their time to public service; and to be ineligible to any office established by a particular State, or under the authority of the United States, except those peculiarly belonging to the functions of the second branch, during the term of service, and for the space of   after the expiration thereof.

6. Resolved that each branch ought to possess the right of originating Acts; that the National Legislature ought to be impowered to enjoy the Legislative Rights vested in Congress by the Confederation and moreover to legislate in all cases to which the separate States are incompetent, or in which the harmony of the United States may be interrupted by the exercise of individual Legislation; to negative all laws passed by the several States, contravening in the opinion of the National Legislature the articles of Union; and to call forth the force of the Union against any member of the Union failing in its duty under the articles thereof.

7. Resolved that a National Executive be instituted; to be chosen by the National Legislature for the term of   years; to receive punctually, at stated times, a fixed compensation for the services rendered, in which no increase or diminution shall be made so as to affect the Magistracy, existing at the time of the increase or diminution, and to be ineligible a second time; and that besides a general authority to execute the National laws, it ought to enjoy the Executive rights vested in Congress by the Confederation.

8. Resolved that the Executive and a convenient number of the National Judiciary, ought to compose a Council or revision with authority to examine every act of the National Legislature before it shall operate, and every act of a particular Legislature before a Negative thereon shall be final; and that the dissent of the said Council shall amount to a rejection, unless the Act of the National Legislature be passed again, or that of a particular Legislature be again negatived by   of the members of each branch.

9. Resolved that a National Judiciary be established to consist of one or more supreme tribunals, and of inferior tribunals to be chosen by the National Legislature, to hold their offices during good behavior; and to receive punctually at stated times fixed compensation for their services, in which no increase or diminution shall be made so as to affect the persons actually in office at the time of such increase or diminution. That the jurisdiction of the inferior tribunals shall be to hear and determine in the first instance, and of the supreme tribunal to hear and determine in the dernier resort, all piracies and felonies on the high seas, captures from an enemy; cases in which foreigners or citizens of other States applying to such jurisdictions may be interested, or which respect the collection of the National revenue; impeachments of any National officers, and questions which may involve the national peace and harmony.

10. Resolved that provision ought to be made for the admission of States lawfully arising within the limits of the United States, whether from a voluntary junction of Government and Territory or otherwise, with the consent of a number of voices in the National legislature less than the whole.

11. Resolved that a Republican Government and the territory of each State, except in the instance of a voluntary junction of Government and territory, ought to be guaranteed by the United States to each State.

12. Resolved that provision ought to be made for the continuance of Congress and their authorities and privileges, until a given day after the reform of the articles of Union shall be adopted, and for the completion of all their engagements.

13. Resolved that provision ought to be made for the amendment of the Articles of Union whensoever it shall seem necessary, and that the assent of the National Legislature ought not to be required thereto.

14. Resolved that the Legislative, Executive and Judiciary powers within the several States ought to be bound by oath to support the articles of Union.

15. Resolved that the amendments which shall be offered to the Confederation, by the Convention ought at a proper time, or times, after the approbation of Congress to be submitted to an assembly or assemblies of Representatives, recommended by the several Legislatures to be expressly chosen by the people, to consider and decide thereon.

Constitution of the United States

The United States Constitution was written at a convention that Congress called on February 21, 1787, for the purpose of recommending amendments to the Articles of Confederation. Every state but Rhode Island sent delegates to Philadelphia, where the convention met that summer. The delegates decided to write an entirely new constitution, completing their labors on September 17. Nine states (the number the Constitution itself stipulated as sufficient) ratified by June 21, 1788.

The presidency is the most original feature of the Constitution. Described mainly in Article II, it was created as a strong, unitary office. The president was to be elected by an electoral college to a four-year term and was empowered, among other things, to recommend and veto congressional acts, appoint judges and executive officials, command the army and navy, negotiate treaties, and issue pardons. Congress could impeach and remove a president for committing acts of "Treason, Bribery, or other High Crimes and Misdemeanors." The Constitution also created the vice presidency and charged the vice president to be president of the Senate and standby successor to the president.

Numerous constitutional amendments have dealt with the presidency. For example, the Twenty-second Amendment (1951) imposes a two-term limit on the president, and the Twenty-fifth Amendment (1967) provides for both vacancies in the vice presidency and situations of presidential disability.

We the People of the United States, in Order to form a more perfect Union, establish Justice, insure domestic Tranquility, provide for the common defence, promote the general Welfare, and secure the Blessings of Liberty to ourselves and our Posterity, do ordain and establish this Constitution for the United States of America.

ARTICLE I

Section 1. All legislative Powers herein granted shall be vested in a Congress of the United States, which shall consist of a Senate and House of Representatives.

Section 2. The House of Representatives shall be composed of Members chosen every second Year by the People of the several States, and the Electors in each State shall have the Qualifications requisite for Electors of the most numerous Branch of the State Legislature.

No Person shall be a Representative who shall not have attained to the age of twenty five Years, and been seven Years a Citizen of the United States, and who shall not, when elected, be an Inhabitant of that State in which he shall be chosen.

[Representatives and direct Taxes shall be apportioned among the several States which may be included within this Union, according to their respective Numbers, which shall be determined by adding to the whole Number of free Persons, including those bound to Service for a Term of Years, and excluding Indians not taxed, three fifths of all other Persons.][1] The actual Enumeration shall be made within three Years after the first Meeting of the Congress of the United States, and within every subsequent Term of ten Years, in such Manner as they shall by Law direct. The Number of Representatives shall not exceed one for every thirty Thousand, but each State shall have at Least one Representative; and until such enumeration shall be made, the State of New Hampshire shall be entitled to chuse three, Massachusetts eight, Rhode-Island and Providence Plantations one, Connecticut five, New-York six, New Jersey four, Pennsylvania eight, Delaware one, Maryland six, Virginia ten, North Carolina five, South Carolina five, and Georgia three.

When vacancies happen in the Representation from any State, the Executive Authority thereof shall issue Writs of Election to fill such Vacancies.

The House of Representatives shall chuse their Speaker and other Officers; and shall have the sole Power of Impeachment.

Section 3. The Senate of the United States shall be composed of two Senators from each State, [chosen by the Legislature thereof,][2] for six Years; and each Senator shall have one Vote.

Immediately after they shall be assembled in Consequence of the first Election, they shall be divided as equally as may be into three Classes. The Seats of the Senators of the first Class shall be vacated at the Expiration of the second Year, of the second Class at the Expiration of the fourth Year, and of the third Class at the Expiration of the sixth Year, so that one third may be chosen every second Year; [and if Vacancies happen by Resignation, or otherwise, during the Recess of the Legislature of any State, the Executive thereof may make temporary Appointments until the next Meeting of the Legislature, which shall then fill such Vacancies.][3]

No Person shall be a Senator who shall not have attained to the Age of thirty Years, and been nine Years a Citizen of the United States, and who shall not, when elected, be an Inhabitant of that State for which he shall be chosen.

The Vice President of the United States shall be President of the Senate, but shall have no Vote, unless they be equally divided.

The Senate shall chuse their other Officers, and also a President pro tempore, in the Absence of the Vice President, or when he shall exercise the Office of President of the United States.

The Senate shall have the sole Power to try all Impeachments. When sitting for that Purpose, they shall be on Oath or Affirmation. When the President of the United States is tried, the Chief Justice shall preside: And no Person shall be convicted without the Concurrence of two thirds of the Members present.

Judgment in Cases of Impeachment shall not extend further than to removal from Office, and disqualification to hold and enjoy any Office of honor, Trust or Profit under the United States: but the Party convicted shall nevertheless be liable and subject to Indictment, Trial, Judgment and Punishment, according to Law.

Section 4. The Times, Places and Manner of holding Elections for Senators and Representatives, shall be prescribed in each State by the Legislature thereof; but the Congress may at any time by Law make or alter such Regulations, except as to the Places of chusing Senators.

The Congress shall assemble at least once in every Year, and such Meeting shall [be on the first Monday in December],[4] unless they shall by Law appoint a different Day.

Section 5. Each House shall be the Judge of the Elections, Returns and Qualifications of its own Members, and a Majority of each shall constitute a Quorum to do Business; but a smaller Number may adjourn from day to day, and may be authorized to compel the Attendance of absent Members, in such Manner, and under such Penalties as each House may provide.

Each House may determine the Rules of its Proceedings, punish its Members for disorderly Behaviour, and, with the Concurrence of two thirds, expel a Member.

Each House shall keep a Journal of its Proceedings, and from time to time publish the same, excepting such Parts as may in their Judgment require Secrecy; and the Yeas and Nays of the Members of either House on any question shall, at the Desire of one fifth of those Present, be entered on the Journal.

Neither House, during the Session of Congress, shall, without the Consent of the other, adjourn for more than three days, nor to any other Place than that in which the two Houses shall be sitting.

Section 6. The Senators and Representatives shall receive a Compensation for their Services, to be ascertained by Law, and paid out of the Treasury of the United States. They shall in all Cases, except Treason, Felony and Breach of the Peace, be privileged from Arrest during their Attendance at the Session of their respective Houses, and in going to and returning from the same; and for any Speech or Debate in either House, they shall not be questioned in any other Place.

No Senator or Representative shall, during the Time for which he was elected, be appointed to any civil Office under the Authority of the United States, which shall have been created, or the Emoluments whereof shall have been encreased during such time; and no Person holding any Office under the United States, shall be a Member of either House during his Continuance in Office.

Section 7. All Bills for raising Revenue shall originate in the House of Representatives; but the Senate may propose or concur with Amendments as on other Bills.

Every Bill which shall have passed the House of Representatives and the Senate, shall, before it become a Law, be presented to the President of the United States; If he approve he shall sign it, but if not he shall return it, with his Objections to that House in which it shall have originated, who shall enter the Objections at large on their Journal, and proceed to reconsider it. If after such Reconsideration two thirds of that House shall agree to pass the Bill, it shall be sent, together with the Objections, to the other House, by which it shall likewise be reconsidered, and if approved by two thirds of that House, it shall become a Law. But in all such Cases the Votes of both Houses shall be determined by yeas and Nays, and the Names of the Persons voting for and against the Bill shall be entered on the Journal of each House respectively. If any Bill shall not be returned by the President within ten Days (Sundays excepted) after it shall have been presented to him, the Same shall be a Law, in like Manner as if he had signed it, unless the Congress by their Adjournment prevent its Return, in which Case it shall not be a Law.

Every Order, Resolution, or Vote to which the Concurrence of the Senate and House of Representatives may be necessary (except on a question of Adjournment) shall be presented to the President of the United States; and before the Same shall take Effect, shall be approved by him, or being disapproved by him, shall be repassed by two thirds of the Senate and House of Representatives, according to the Rules and Limitations prescribed in the Case of a Bill.

Section 8. The Congress shall have Power To lay and collect Taxes, Duties, Imposts and Excises, to pay the Debts and provide for the common Defence and general Welfare of the United States; but all Duties, Imposts and Excises shall be uniform throughout the United States;

To borrow Money on the credit of the United States;

To regulate Commerce with foreign Nations, and among the several States, and with the Indian Tribes;

To establish an uniform Rule of Naturalization, and uniform Laws on the subject of Bankruptcies throughout the United States;

To coin Money, regulate the Value thereof, and of foreign Coin, and fix the Standard of Weights and Measures;

To provide for the Punishment of counterfeiting the Securities and current Coin of the United States;

To establish Post Offices and post Roads;

To promote the Progress of Science and useful Arts, by securing for limited Times to Authors and Inventors the exclusive Right to their respective Writings and Discoveries;

To constitute Tribunals inferior to the supreme Court;

To define and punish Piracies and Felonies committed on the high Seas, and Offences against the Law of Nations;

To declare War, grant Letters of Marque and Reprisal, and make Rules concerning Captures on Land and Water;

To raise and support Armies, but no Appropriation of Money to that Use shall be for a longer Term than two Years;

To provide and maintain a Navy;

To make Rules for the Government and Regulation of the land and naval Forces;

To provide for calling forth the Militia to execute the Laws of the Union, suppress Insurrections and repel Invasions;

To provide for organizing, arming, and disciplining, the Militia, and for governing such Part of them as may be employed in the Service of the United States, reserving to the States respectively, the Appointment of the Officers, and the Authority of training the Militia according to the discipline prescribed by Congress;

To exercise exclusive Legislation in all Cases whatso-ever, over such District (not exceeding ten Miles square) as may, by Cession of particular States, and the Acceptance of Congress, become the Seat of the Government of the United States, and to exercise like Authority over all Places purchased by the Consent of the Legislature of the State in which the Same shall be, for the Erection of Forts, Magazines, Arsenals, dock-Yards, and other needful Buildings;—And

To make all Laws which shall be necessary and proper for carrying into Execution the foregoing Powers, and all other Powers vested by this Constitution in the Government of the United States, or in any Department or Officer thereof.

Section 9. The Migration or Importation of such Persons as any of the States now existing shall think proper to admit, shall not be prohibited by the Congress prior to the Year one thousand eight hundred and eight, but a Tax or duty may be imposed on such Importation, not exceeding ten dollars for each Person.

The Privilege of the Writ of Habeas Corpus shall not be suspended, unless when in Cases of Rebellion or Invasion the public Safety may require it.

No Bill of Attainder or ex post facto Law shall be passed.

No Capitation, or other direct, Tax shall be laid, unless in Proportion to the Census or Enumeration herein before directed to be taken.[5]

No Tax or Duty shall be laid on Articles exported from any State.

No Preference shall be given by any Regulation of Commerce or Revenue to the Ports of one State over those of another; nor shall Vessels bound to, or from, one State, be obliged to enter, clear, or pay Duties in another.

No Money shall be drawn from the Treasury, but in Consequence of Appropriations made by Law; and a regular Statement and Account of the Receipts and Expenditures of all public Money shall be published from time to time.

No Title of Nobility shall be granted by the United States: And no Person holding any Office of Profit or Trust under them, shall, without the Consent of the Congress, accept of any present, Emolument, Office, or Title, of any kind whatever, from any King, Prince, or foreign State.

Section 10. No State shall enter into any Treaty, Alliance, or Confederation; grant Letters of Marque and Reprisal; coin Money; emit Bills of Credit; make any Thing but gold and silver Coin a Tender in Payment of Debts; pass any Bill of Attainder, ex post facto Law, or Law impairing the Obligation of Contracts, or grant any Title of Nobility.

No State shall, without the Consent of the Congress, lay any Imposts or Duties on Imports or Exports, except what may be absolutely necessary for executing it's inspection Laws: and the net Produce of all Duties and Imposts, laid by any State on Imports or Exports, shall be for the Use of the Treasury of the United States; and all such Laws shall be subject to the Revision and Controul of the Congress.

No State shall, without the Consent of Congress, lay any Duty of Tonnage, keep Troops, or Ships of War in time of Peace, enter into any Agreement or Compact with another State, or with a foreign Power, or engage in War, unless actually invaded, or in such imminent Danger as will not admit of delay.

ARTICLE II

Section 1. The executive Power shall be vested in a President of the United States of America. He shall hold his Office during the Term of four Years, and, together with the Vice President, chosen for the same Term, be elected, as follows

Each State shall appoint, in such Manner as the Legislature thereof may direct, a Number of Electors, equal to the whole Number of Senators and Representatives to which the State may be entitled in the Congress: but no Senator or Representative, or Person holding an Office of Trust or Profit under the United States, shall be appointed an Elector.

[The Electors shall meet in their respective States, and vote by Ballot for two Persons, of whom one at least shall not be an Inhabitant of the same State with themselves. And they shall make a List of all the Persons voted for, and of the Number of Votes for each; which List they shall sign and certify, and transmit sealed to the Seat of the Government of the United States, directed to the President of the Senate. The President of the Senate shall, in the Presence of the Senate and House of Representatives, open all the Certificates, and the Votes shall then be counted. The Person having the greatest Number of Votes shall be the President, if such Number be a Majority of the whole Number of Electors appointed; and if there be more than one who have such Majority, and have an equal Number of Votes, then the House of Representatives shall immediately chuse by Ballot one of them for President; and if no Person have a Majority, then from the five highest on the list the said House shall in like Manner chuse the President. But in chusing the President, the Votes shall be taken by States, the Representation from each State having one Vote; A quorum for this Purpose shall consist of a Member or Members from two thirds of the States, and a Majority of all the States shall be necessary to a Choice. In every Case, after the Choice of the President, the Person having the greatest Number of Votes of the Electors shall be the Vice President. But if there should remain two or more who have equal Votes, the Senate shall chuse from them by Ballot the Vice President.][6]

The Congress may determine the Time of chusing the Electors, and the Day on which they shall give their Votes; which Day shall be the same throughout the United States.

No Person except a natural born Citizen, or a Citizen of the United States, at the time of the Adoption of this Constitution, shall be eligible to the Office of President; neither shall any Person be eligible to that Office who shall not have attained to the Age of thirty five Years, and been fourteen Years a Resident within the United States.

In Case of the Removal of the President from Office, or of his Death, Resignation, or Inability to discharge the Powers and Duties of the said Office,[7] the Same shall devolve on the Vice President, and the Congress may by Law provide for the Case of Removal, Death, Resignation or Inability, both of the President and Vice President, declaring what Officer shall then act as President, and such Officer shall act accordingly, until the Disability be removed, or a President shall be elected.

The President shall, at stated Times, receive for his Services, a Compensation, which shall neither be encreased nor diminished during the Period for which he shall have been elected, and he shall not receive within that Period any other Emolument from the United States, or any of them.

Before he enter on the Execution of his Office, he shall take the following Oath or Affirmation:—"I do solemnly swear (or affirm) that I will faithfully execute the Office of President of the United States, and will to the best of my Ability, preserve, protect and defend the Constitution of the United States."

Section 2. The President shall be Commander in Chief of the Army and Navy of the United States, and of the Militia of the several States, when called into the actual Service of the United States; he may require the Opinion, in writing, of the principal Officer in each of the executive Departments, upon any Subject relating to the Duties of their respective Offices, and he shall have Power to grant Reprieves and Pardons for Offences against the United States, except in Cases of Impeachment.

He shall have Power, by and with the Advice and Consent of the Senate, to make Treaties, provided two thirds of the Senators present concur; and he shall nominate, and by and with the Advice and Consent of the Senate, shall appoint Ambassadors, other public Ministers and Consuls, Judges of the supreme Court, and all other Officers of the United States, whose Appointments are not herein otherwise provided for, and which shall be established by Law: but the Congress may by Law vest the Appointment of such inferior Officers, as they think proper, in the President alone, in the Courts of Law, or in the Heads of Departments.

The President shall have Power to fill up all Vacancies that may happen during the Recess of the Senate, by granting Commissions which shall expire at the End of their next Session.

Section 3. He shall from time to time give to the Congress Information of the State of the Union, and recommend to their Consideration such Measures as he shall judge necessary and expedient; he may, on extraordinary Occasions, convene both Houses, or either of them, and in Case of Disagreement between them, with Respect to the Time of Adjournment, he may adjourn them to such Time as he shall think proper; he shall receive Ambassadors and other public Ministers; he shall take Care that the Laws be faithfully executed, and shall Commission all the Officers of the United States.

Section 4. The President, Vice President and all civil Officers of the United States, shall be removed from Office on Impeachment for, and Conviction of, Treason, Bribery, or other high Crimes and Misdemeanors.

ARTICLE III

Section 1. The judicial Power of the United States, shall be vested in one supreme Court, and in such inferior Courts as the Congress may from time to time ordain and establish. The Judges, both of the supreme and inferior Courts, shall hold their Offices during good Behaviour, and shall, at stated Times, receive for their Services, a Compensation, which shall not be diminished during their Continuance in Office.

Section 2. The judicial Power shall extend to all Cases, in Law and Equity, arising under this Constitution, the Laws of the United States, and Treaties made, or which shall be made, under their Authority; — to all Cases affecting Ambassadors, other public Ministers and Consuls; —to all Cases of admiralty and maritime Jurisdiction; —to Controversies to which the United States shall be a Party; —to Controversies between two or more States; —between a State and Citizens of another State;[8] —between Citizens of different States; —between Citizens of the same State claiming Lands under Grants of different States, and between a State, or the Citizens thereof, and foreign States, Citizens or Subjects.[8]

In all Cases affecting Ambassadors, other public Ministers and Consuls, and those in which a State shall be Party, the supreme Court shall have original Jurisdiction. In all the other Cases before mentioned, the supreme Court shall have appellate Jurisdiction, both as to Law and Fact, with such Exceptions, and under such Regulations as the Congress shall make.

The Trial of all Crimes, except in Cases of Impeachment, shall be by Jury; and such Trial shall be held in the State where the said Crimes shall have been committed; but when not committed within any State, the Trial shall be at such Place or Places as the Congress may by Law have directed.

Section 3. Treason against the United States, shall consist only in levying War against them, or in adhering to their Enemies, giving them Aid and Comfort. No Person shall be convicted of Treason unless on the Testimony of two Witnesses to the same overt Act, or on Confession in open Court.

The Congress shall have Power to declare the Punishment of Treason, but no Attainder of Treason shall work Corruption of Blood, or Forfeiture except during the Life of the Person attainted.

ARTICLE IV

Section 1. Full Faith and Credit shall be given in each State to the public Acts, Records, and judicial Proceedings of every other State. And the Congress may by general Laws prescribe the Manner in which such Acts, Records and Proceedings shall be proved, and the Effect thereof.

Section 2. The Citizens of each State shall be entitled to all Privileges and Immunities of Citizens in the several States.

A Person charged in any State with Treason, Felony, or other Crime, who shall flee from Justice, and be found in another State, shall on Demand of the executive Authority of the State from which he fled, be delivered up, to be removed to the State having Jurisdiction of the Crime.

[No Person held to Service or Labour in one State, under the Laws thereof, escaping into another, shall, in Consequence of any Law or Regulation therein, be discharged from such Service or Labour, but shall be delivered up on Claim of the Party to whom such Service or Labour may be due.]

Section 3. New States may be admitted by the Congress into this Union; but no new State shall be formed or erected within the Jurisdiction of any other State; nor any State be formed by the Junction of two or more States, or Parts of States, without the Consent of the Legislatures of the States concerned as well as of the Congress.

The Congress shall have Power to dispose of and make all needful Rules and Regulations respecting the Territory or other Property belonging to the United States; and nothing in this Constitution shall be so construed as to Prejudice any Claims of the United States, or of any particular State.

Section 4. The United States shall guarantee to every State in this Union a Republican Form of Government, and shall protect each of them against Invasion; and on Application of the Legislature, or of the Executive (when the Legislature cannot be convened) against domestic Violence.

ARTICLE V

The Congress, whenever two thirds of both Houses shall deem it necessary, shall propose Amendments to this Constitution, or, on the Application of the Legislatures of two thirds of the several States, shall call a Convention for proposing Amendments, which, in either Case, shall be valid to all Intents and Purposes, as Part of this Constitution, when ratified by the Legislatures of three fourths of the several States, or by Conventions in three fourths thereof, as the one or the other Mode of Ratification may be proposed by the Congress; Provided [that no Amendment which may be made prior to the Year One thousand eight hundred and eight shall in any Manner affect the first and fourth Clauses in the Ninth Section of the first Article; and][10] that no State, without its Consent, shall be deprived of its equal Suffrage in the Senate.

ARTICLE VI

All Debts contracted and Engagements entered into, before the Adoption of this Constitution, shall be as valid against the United States under this Constitution, as under the Confederation.

This Constitution, and the Laws of the United States which shall be made in Pursuance thereof; and all Treaties made, or which shall be made, under the Authority of the United States, shall be the supreme Law of the Land; and the Judges in every State shall be bound thereby, any Thing in the Constitution or Laws of any State to the Contrary notwithstanding.

The Senators and Representatives before mentioned, and the Members of the several State Legislatures, and all executive and judicial Officers, both of the United States and of the several States, shall be bound by Oath or Affirmation, to support this Constitution; but no religious Test shall ever be required as a Qualification to any Office or public Trust under the United States.

ARTICLE VII

The Ratification of the Conventions of nine States, shall be sufficient for the Establishment of this Constitution between the States so ratifying the Same.

Done in Convention by the Unanimous Consent of the States present the Seventeenth Day of September in the Year of our Lord one thousand seven hundred and Eighty seven and of the Independence of the United States of America the Twelfth. IN WITNESS whereof We have hereunto subscribed our Names,

George Washington,
President and deputy from Virginia.

New Hampshire:
John Langdon,
Nicholas Gilman.

Massachusetts:
Nathaniel Gorham,
Rufus King.

Connecticut:
William Samuel Johnson,
Roger Sherman.

New York:
Alexander Hamilton.

New Jersey:
William Livingston,
David Brearley,
William Paterson,
Jonathan Dayton.

Pennsylvania:
Benjamin Franklin,
Thomas Mifflin,
Robert Morris,
George Clymer,

Thomas FitzSimons,
Jared Ingersoll,
James Wilson,
Gouverneur Morris.

Delaware:
George Read,
Gunning Bedford Jr.,
John Dickinson,
Richard Bassett,
Jacob Broom.

Maryland:
James McHenry,
Daniel of St. Thomas Jenifer,
Daniel Carroll.

Virginia:
John Blair,
James Madison Jr.

North Carolina:.
William Blount,
Richard Dobbs Spaight,
Hugh Williamson.

South Carolina:
John Rutledge,
Charles Cotesworth Pinckney,
Charles Pinckney,
Pierce Butler.

Georgia:
William Few,
Abraham Baldwin.

[The language of the original Constitution, not including the Amendments, was adopted by a convention of the states on September 17, 1787, and was subsequently ratified by the states on the following dates: Delaware, December 7, 1787; Pennsylvania, December 12, 1787; New Jersey, December 18, 1787; Georgia, January 2, 1788; Connecticut, January 9, 1788; Massachusetts, February 6, 1788; Maryland, April 28, 1788; South Carolina, May 23, 1788; New Hampshire, June 21, 1788.

Ratification was completed on June 21, 1788.

The Constitution subsequently was ratified by Virginia, June 25, 1788; New York, July 26, 1788; North Carolina, November 21, 1789; Rhode Island, May 29, 1790; and Vermont, January 10, 1791.]

AMENDMENTS

Amendment I

(First ten amendments ratified December 15, 1791.)

Congress shall make no law respecting an establishment of religion, or prohibiting the free exercise thereof; or abridging the freedom of speech, or of the press; or the right of the people peaceably to assemble, and to petition the Government for a redress of grievances.

Amendment II

A well regulated Militia, being necessary to the security of a free State, the right of the people to keep and bear Arms, shall not be infringed.

Amendment III

No Soldier shall, in time of peace be quartered in any house, without the consent of the Owner, nor in time of war, but in a manner to be prescribed by law.

Amendment IV

The right of the people to be secure in their persons, houses, papers, and effects, against unreasonable searches and seizures, shall not be violated, and no Warrants shall issue, but upon probable cause, supported by Oath or affirmation, and particularly describing the place to be searched, and the persons or things to be seized.

Amendment V

No person shall be held to answer for a capital, or otherwise infamous crime, unless on a presentment or indictment of a Grand Jury, except in cases arising in the land or naval forces, or in the Militia, when in actual service in time of War or public danger; nor shall any person be subject for the same offence to be twice put in jeopardy of life or limb; nor shall be compelled in any criminal case to be a witness against himself, nor be deprived of life, liberty, or property, without due process of law; nor shall private property be taken for public use, without just compensation.

Amendment VI

In all criminal prosecutions, the accused shall enjoy the right to a speedy and public trial, by an impartial jury of the State and district wherein the crime shall have been committed, which district shall have been previously ascertained by law, and to be informed of the nature and cause of the accusation; to be confronted with the witnesses against him; to have compulsory process for obtaining witnesses in his favor, and to have the Assistance of Counsel for his defence.

Amendment VII

In Suits at common law, where the value in controversy shall exceed twenty dollars, the right of trial by jury shall be preserved, and no fact tried by a jury, shall be otherwise re-examined in any Court of the United States, than according to the rules of the common law.

Amendment VIII

Excessive bail shall not be required, nor excessive fines imposed, nor cruel and unusual punishments inflicted.

Amendment IX

The enumeration in the Constitution, of certain rights, shall not be construed to deny or disparage others retained by the people.

Amendment X

The powers not delegated to the United States by the Constitution, nor prohibited by it to the States, are reserved to the States respectively, or to the people.

Amendment XI (Ratified February 7, 1795)

The Judicial power of the United States shall not be construed to extend to any suit in law or equity, commenced or prosecuted against one of the United States by Citizens of another State, or by Citizens or Subjects of any Foreign State.

Amendment XII (Ratified June 15, 1804)

The Electors shall meet in their respective states and vote by ballot for President and Vice-President, one of whom, at least, shall not be an inhabitant of the same state with themselves; they shall name in their ballots the person voted for as President, and in distinct ballots the person voted for as Vice-President, and they shall make distinct lists of all persons voted for as President, and of all persons voted for as Vice-President, and of the number of votes for each, which lists they shall sign and certify, and transmit sealed to the seat of the government of the United States, directed to the President of the Senate; — The President of the Senate shall, in the presence of the Senate and House of Representatives, open all the certificates and the votes shall then be counted; — The person having the greatest number of votes for President, shall be the President, if such number be a majority of the whole number of Electors appointed; and if no person have such majority, then from the persons having the highest numbers not exceeding three on the list of those voted for as President, the House of Representatives shall choose immediately, by ballot, the President. But in choosing the President, the votes shall be taken by states, the representation from each state having one vote; a quorum for this purpose shall consist of a member or members from two-thirds of the states, and a majority of all the states shall be necessary to a choice. [And if the House of Representatives shall not choose a President whenever the right of choice shall devolve upon them, before the fourth day of March next following, then the Vice-President shall act as President, as in the case of the death or other constitutional disability of the President. —][11] The person having the greatest number of votes as Vice-President, shall be the Vice-President, if such number be a majority of the whole number of Electors appointed, and if no person have a majority, then from the two highest numbers on the list, the Senate shall choose the Vice-President; a quorum for the purpose shall consist of two-thirds of the whole number of Senators, and a majority of the whole number shall be necessary to a choice. But no person constitutionally ineligible to the office of President shall be eligible to that of Vice-President of the United States.

Amendment XIII (Ratified December 6, 1865)

Section 1. Neither slavery nor involuntary servitude, except as a punishment for crime whereof the party shall have been duly convicted, shall exist within the United States, or any place subject to their jurisdiction.

Section 2. Congress shall have power to enforce this article by appropriate legislation.

Amendment XIV (Ratified July 9, 1868)

Section 1. All persons born or naturalized in the United States, and subject to the jurisdiction thereof, are citizens of the United States and of the State wherein they reside. No State shall make or enforce any law which shall abridge the privileges or immunities of citizens of the United States; nor shall any State deprive any person of life, liberty, or property, without due process of law; nor deny to any person within its jurisdiction the equal protection of the laws.

Section 2. Representatives shall be apportioned among the several States according to their respective numbers, counting the whole number of persons in each State, excluding Indians not taxed. But when the right to vote at any election for the choice of electors for President and Vice President of the United States, Representatives in Congress, the Executive and Judicial officers of a State, or the members of the Legislature thereof, is denied to any of the male inhabitants of such State, being twenty-one years of age,[12] and citizens of the United States, or in any way abridged, except for participation in rebellion, or other crime, the basis of representation therein shall be reduced in the proportion which the number of such male citizens shall bear to the whole number of male citizens twenty-one years of age in such State.

Section 3. No person shall be a Senator or Representative in Congress, or elector of President and Vice President, or hold any office, civil or military, under the United States, or under any State, who, having previously taken an oath, as a member of Congress, or as an officer of the United States, or as a member of any State legislature, or as an executive or judicial officer of any State, to support the Constitution of the United States, shall have engaged in insurrection or rebellion against the same, or given aid or comfort to the enemies thereof. But Congress may by a vote of two-thirds of each House, remove such disability.

Section 4. The validity of the public debt of the United States, authorized by law, including debts incurred for payment of pensions and bounties for services in suppressing insurrection or rebellion, shall not be questioned. But neither the United States nor any State shall assume or pay any debt or obligation incurred in aid of insurrection or rebellion against the United States, or any claim for the loss or emancipation of any slave; but all such debts, obligations and claims shall be held illegal and void.

Section 5. The Congress shall have power to enforce, by appropriate legislation, the provisions of this article.

Amendment XV (Ratified February 3, 1870)

Section 1. The right of citizens of the United States to vote shall not be denied or abridged by the United States or by any State on account of race, color, or previous condition of servitude.

Section 2. The Congress shall have power to enforce this article by appropriate legislation.

Amendment XVI (Ratified February 3, 1913)

The Congress shall have power to lay and collect taxes on incomes, from whatever source derived, without apportionment among the several States, and without regard to any census or enumeration.

Amendment XVII (Ratified April 8, 1913)

The Senate of the United States shall be composed of two Senators from each State, elected by the people thereof, for six years; and each Senator shall have one vote. The electors in each State shall have the qualifications requisite for electors of the most numerous branch of the State legislatures.

When vacancies happen in the representation of any State in the Senate, the executive authority of such State shall issue writs of election to fill such vacancies: *Provided,* That the legislature of any State may empower the executive thereof to make temporary appointments until the people fill the vacancies by election as the legislature may direct.

This amendment shall not be so construed as to affect the election or term of any Senator chosen before it becomes valid as part of the Constitution.

Amendment XVIII (Ratified January 16, 1919)

Section 1. After one year from the ratification of this article the manufacture, sale, or transportation of intoxicating liquors within, the importation thereof into, or the exportation thereof from the United States and all territory subject to the jurisdiction thereof for beverage purposes is hereby prohibited.

Section 2. The Congress and the several States shall have concurrent power to enforce this article by appropriate legislation.

Section 3. This article shall be inoperative unless it shall have been ratified as an amendment to the Constitution by the legislatures of the several States, as provided in the Constitution, within seven years from the date of the submission hereof to the States by the Congress.][13]

Amendment XIX (Ratified August 18, 1920)

The right of citizens of the United States to vote shall not be denied or abridged by the United States or by any State on account of sex.

Congress shall have power to enforce this article by appropriate legislation.

Amendment XX (Ratified January 23, 1933)

Section 1. The terms of the President and Vice President shall end at noon on the 20th day of January, and the terms of Senators and Representatives at noon on the 3d day of January, of the years in which such terms would have ended if this article had not been ratified; and the terms of their successors shall then begin.

Section 2. The Congress shall assemble at least once in every year, and such meeting shall begin at noon on the 3d day of January, unless they shall by law appoint a different day.

Section 3.[14] If, at the time fixed for the beginning of the term of the President, the President elect shall have died, the Vice President elect shall become President. If a President shall not have been chosen before the time fixed for the beginning of his term, or if the President elect shall have failed to qualify, then the Vice President elect shall act as President until a President shall have qualified; and the Congress may by law provide for the case wherein neither a President elect nor a Vice President elect shall have qualified, declaring who shall then act as President, or the manner in which one who is to act shall be selected, and such person shall act accordingly until a President or Vice President shall have qualified.

Section 4. The Congress may by law provide for the case of the death of any of the persons from whom the House of Representatives may choose a President whenever the right of choice shall have devolved upon them, and for the case of the death of any of the persons from whom the Senate may choose a Vice President whenever the right of choice shall have devolved upon them.

Section 5. Sections 1 and 2 shall take effect on the 15th day of October following the ratification of this article.

Section 6. This article shall be inoperative unless it shall have been ratified as an amendment to the Constitution by the legislatures of three-fourths of the several States within seven years from the date of its submission.

Amendment XXI *(Ratified December 5, 1933)*

Section 1. The eighteenth article of amendment to the Constitution of the United States is hereby repealed.

Section 2. The transportation or importation into any State, Territory, or possession of the United States for delivery or use therein of intoxicating liquors, in violation of the laws thereof, is hereby prohibited.

Section 3. This article shall be inoperative unless it shall have been ratified as an amendment to the Constitution by conventions in the several States, as provided in the Constitution, within seven years from the date of the submission hereof to the States by the Congress.

Amendment XXII *(Ratified February 27, 1951)*

Section 1. No person shall be elected to the office of the President more than twice, and no person who has held the office of President, or acted as President, for more than two years of a term to which some other person was elected President shall be elected to the office of the President more than once. But this Article shall not apply to any person holding the office of President when this Article was proposed by the Congress, and shall not prevent any person who may be holding the office of President, or acting as President, during the term within which this Article becomes operative from holding the office of President or acting as President during the remainder of such term.

Section 2. This article shall be inoperative unless it shall have been ratified as an amendment to the Constitution by the legislatures of three-fourths of the several States within seven years from the date of its submission to the States by the Congress.

Amendment XXIII *(Ratified March 29, 1961)*

Section 1. The District constituting the seat of Government of the United States shall appoint in such manner as the Congress may direct:

A number of electors of President and Vice President equal to the whole number of Senators and Representatives in Congress to which the District would be entitled if it were a State, but in no event more than the least populous State; they shall be in addition to those appointed by the States, but they shall be considered, for the purposes of the election of President and Vice President, to be electors appointed by a State; and they shall meet in the District and perform such duties as provided by the twelfth article of amendment.

Section 2. The Congress shall have power to enforce this article by appropriate legislation.

Amendment XXIV *(Ratified January 23, 1964)*

Section 1. The right of citizens of the United States to vote in any primary or other election for President or Vice President, for electors for President or Vice President, or for Senator or Representative in Congress, shall not be denied or abridged by the United States or any State by reason of failure to pay any poll tax or other tax.

Section 2. The Congress shall have power to enforce this article by appropriate legislation.

Amendment XXV *(Ratified February 10, 1967)*

Section 1. In case of the removal of the President from office or of his death or resignation, the Vice President shall become President.

Section 2. Whenever there is a vacancy in the office of the Vice President, the President shall nominate a Vice President who shall take office upon confirmation by a majority vote of both Houses of Congress.

Section 3. Whenever the President transmits to the President pro tempore of the Senate and the Speaker of the House of Representatives his written declaration that he is unable to discharge the powers and duties of his office, and until he transmits to them a written declaration to the contrary, such powers and duties shall be discharged by the Vice President as Acting President.

Section 4. Whenever the Vice President and a majority of either the principal officers of the executive departments or of such other body as Congress may by law provide, transmit to the President pro tempore of the Senate and the Speaker of the House of Representatives their written declaration that the President is unable to discharge the powers and duties of his office, the Vice President shall immediately assume the powers and duties of the office as Acting President.

Thereafter, when the President transmits to the President pro tempore of the Senate and the Speaker of the House of Representatives his written declaration that no inability exists, he shall resume the powers and duties of his office unless the Vice President and a majority of either the principal officers of the executive departments or of such other body as Congress may by law provide, transmit within four days to the President pro tempore of the Senate and the Speaker of the House of Representatives their written declaration that the President is unable to discharge the powers and duties of his office. Thereupon Congress shall decide the issue, assembling within forty-eight hours for that purpose if not in session. If the Congress, within twenty-one days after receipt of the latter written declaration, or, if Congress is not in session, within twenty-one days after Congress is required to assemble, determines by two-thirds vote of both Houses that the President is unable to discharge the powers and duties of his office, the Vice President shall continue to discharge the same as Acting President; otherwise, the President shall resume the powers and duties of his office.

Amendment XXVI *(Ratified July 1, 1971)*

Section 1. The right of citizens of the United States, who are eighteen years of age or older, to vote shall not be denied or abridged by the United States or by any State on account of age.

Section 2. The Congress shall have power to enforce this article by appropriate legislation.

Amendment XXVII *(Ratified May 7, 1992)*

No law varying the compensation for the services of the Senators and Representatives shall take effect, until an election of Representatives shall have intervened.

SOURCE: U.S. Congress, House, Committee on the Judiciary, *The Constitution of the United States of America, as Amended,* 100th Cong., 1st sess., 1987, H Doc 100–94.

NOTES: 1. The part in brackets was changed by section 2 of the Fourteenth Amendment. 2. The part in brackets was changed by the first paragraph of the Seventeenth Amendment. 3. The part in brackets was changed by the second paragraph of the Seventeenth Amendment. 4. The part in brackets was changed by section 2 of the Twentieth Amendment. 5. The Sixteenth Amendment gave Congress the power to tax incomes. 6. The material in brackets was superseded by the Twelfth Amendment. 7. This provision was affected by the Twenty-fifth Amendment. 8. These clauses were affected by the Eleventh Amendment. 9. This paragraph was superseded by the Thirteenth Amendment. 10. Obsolete. 11. The part in brackets was superseded by section 3 of the Twentieth Amendment. 12. See the Nineteenth and Twenty-sixth Amendments. 13. This amendment was repealed by section 1 of the Twenty-first Amendment. 14. See the Twenty-fifth Amendment.

The Federalist, No. 70

During the months that the proposed Constitution was being considered for ratification by the states, a number of newspaper articles were written by Alexander Hamilton, James Madison, and John Jay under the pseudonym "Publius" to explain and defend the Constitution. The papers later were gathered together in a book called The Federalist *(or* The Federalist Papers*).*

Federalist Nos. 69–77, written by Hamilton, deal with the presidency. His most memorable defense of the office may be found in No. 70. In it, he squarely addresses the argument that a one-person executive is a threat to liberty. Instead, Hamilton writes, only a properly designed unitary executive can provide those qualities of "energy" that a republican government needs.

There is an idea, which is not without its advocates, that a vigorous executive is inconsistent with the genius of republican government. The enlightened well-wishers to this species of government must at least hope that the supposition is destitute of foundation; since they can never admit its truth, without at the same time admitting the condemnation of their own principles. Energy in the executive is a leading character in the definition of good government. It is essential to the protection of the community against foreign attacks; it is not less essential to the steady administration of the laws; to the protection of property against those irregular and high-handed combinations which sometimes interrupt the ordinary course of justice; to the security of liberty against the enterprises and assaults of ambition, of faction, and of anarchy. Every man the least conversant in Roman history knows how often that republic was obliged to take refuge in the absolute power of a single man, under the formidable title of dictator, as well against the intrigues of ambitious individuals who aspired to the tyranny, and the seditions of whole classes of the community whose conduct threatened the existence of all government, as against the invasions of external enemies who menaced the conquest and destruction of Rome.

There can be no need, however, to multiply arguments or examples on this head. A feeble executive implies a feeble execution of the government. A feeble execution is but another phrase for a bad execution; and a government ill executed, whatever it may be in theory, must be, in practice, a bad government.

Taking it for granted, therefore, that all men of sense will agree in the necessity of an energetic executive, it will only remain to inquire, what are the ingredients which constitute this energy? How far can they be combined with those other ingredients which constitute safety in the republican sense? And how far does this combination characterize the plan which has been reported by the convention?

The ingredients which constitute energy in the executive are unity; duration; an adequate provision for its support; and competent powers.

The ingredients which constitute safety in the republican sense are a due dependence on the people, and a due responsibility.

Those politicians and statesmen who have been the most celebrated for the soundness of their principles and for the justness of their views have declared in favor of a single executive and a numerous legislature. They have, with great propriety, considered energy as the most necessary qualification of the former, and have regarded this as most applicable to power in a single hand; while they have, with equal propriety, considered the latter as best adapted to deliberation and wisdom, and best calculated to conciliate the confidence of the people and to secure their privileges and interests.

That unity is conducive to energy will not be disputed. Decision, activity, secrecy, and dispatch will generally characterize the proceedings of one man in a much more eminent degree than the proceedings of any greater number; and in proportion as the number is increased, these qualities will be diminished.

This unity may be destroyed in two ways: either by vesting the power in two or more magistrates of equal dignity and authority, or by vesting it ostensibly in one man, subject in whole or in part to the control and cooperation of others, in the capacity of counselors to him. Of the first, the two consuls of Rome may serve as an example; of the last, we shall find examples in the constitutions of several of the States. New York and New Jersey, if I recollect right, are the only States which have intrusted the executive authority wholly to single men. Both these methods of destroying the unity of the executive have their partisans; but the votaries of an executive council are the most numerous. They are both liable, if not equal, to similar objections, and may in most lights be examined in conjunction.

The experience of other nations will afford little instruction on this head. As far, however, as it teaches anything, it teaches us not to be enamored of plurality in the executive. . . .

Whenever two or more persons are engaged in any common enterprise or pursuit, there is always danger of difference of opinion. If it be a public trust or office in which they are clothed with equal dignity and authority, there is peculiar danger of personal emulation and even animosity. From either, and especially from all these causes, the most bitter dissensions are apt to spring. Whenever these happen, they lessen the respectability, waken the authority, and distract the plans and operations of those whom they divide. If they should unfortunately assail the supreme executive magistracy of a country, consisting of a plurality of persons, they might impede or frustrate the most important measures of the government in the most critical emergencies of the state. And what is still worse, they might split the community into the most violent and irreconcilable factions, adhering differently to the different individuals who composed the magistracy. . . .

Upon the principles of a free government, inconveniences from the source just mentioned must necessarily be submitted to in the formation of the legislature; but it is unnecessary, and therefore unwise, to introduce them into the constitution of the executive. It is here too that they may be most pernicious. In the legislature, promptitude of decision is oftener an evil than a benefit. The differences of opinion, and the jarring of parties in that department of the government, though they may sometimes obstruct salutary plans, yet often promote deliberation and circumspection, and serve to check excesses in the majority. When a resolution too is once taken, the opposition must be at an end. That resolution is a law, and resistance to it punishable. But no favorable circumstances palliate or atone for the disadvantages of dissension in the executive department. Here they are pure and unmixed. There is no point at which they cease to operate. They serve to embarrass and weaken the execution of the plan or measure to which they relate, from the first step to the final conclusion of it. They constantly counteract those qualities in the executive which are the most necessary ingredients in its composition—vigor and expedition, and this without any counterbalancing good. In the conduct of war, in which the energy of the executive is the bulwark of the national security, everything would be to be apprehended from its plurality.

It must be confessed that these observations apply with principal weight to the first case supposed—that is, to a plurality of magistrates of equal dignity and authority, a scheme, the advocates for which are not likely to form a numerous sect; but they apply, though not with equal yet with considerable weight to the project of a council, whose concurrence is made constitutionally necessary to the operations of the ostensible executive. An artful cabal in that council would be able to distract and to enervate the whole system of administration. If no such cabal should exist, the mere diversity of views and opinions would alone be sufficient to tincture the exercise of the executive authority with a spirit of habitual feebleness and dilatoriness.

But one of the weightiest objections to a plurality in the executive, and which lies as much against the last as the first plan is that it tends to conceal faults and destroy responsibility. . . . It often becomes impossible, admidst mutual accusations, to determine on whom the blame or the punishment of a pernicious measure, or series of pernicious measures, ought really to fall. . . .

A little consideration will satisfy us that the species of security sought for in the multiplication of the executive is unattainable. Numbers must be so great as to render combination difficult, or they are rather a source of danger than of security. The united credit and influence of several individuals must be more formidable to liberty than the credit and influence of either of them separately. When power, therefore, is placed in the hands of so small a number of men as to admit of their interests and views being easily combined in a common enterprise, by an artful leader, it becomes more liable to abuse, and more dangerous when abused, than if it be lodged in the hands of one man, who, from the very circumstance of his being alone, will be more narrowly watched and more readily suspected, and who cannot unite so great a mass of influence as when he is associated with others. . . .

I will only add that, prior to the appearance of the Constitution, I rarely met with an intelligent man from any of the States who did not admit, as the result of experience, that the UNITY of the executive of this State was one of the best of the distinguishing features of our Constitution.

Washington's Farewell Address

George Washington had hoped to retire from public life at the end of his first term as president—he even asked James Madison to draft a farewell address in 1792—but was prevailed upon to serve another term. In 1796 Washington resolved to retire after his second term expired in 1797. Weaving together Madison's draft, a new draft by Alexander Hamilton, and his own words and ideas, Washington wrote (the address was never spoken to an audience) a long address directly to his "friends and fellow citizens" (not Congress) and released it to the Daily American Advertiser, *a Philadelphia newspaper, where it was published on September 19. Newspapers around the country reprinted what soon became known as the "Farewell Address," setting off a national wave of tributes and expressions of thanks. By disseminating word of his decision to retire three months before the presidential election, Washington also forestalled any effort to reelect him.*

The Farewell Address reviews Washington's career of public service, then looks ahead to the long-term future of the new nation. Washington was especially concerned about threats to national unity. He dwelled at length on two such threats—the rise of political parties and the inclination among Americans to choose sides in disputes between England and France.

Friends, and Fellow-Citizens:

The period for a new election of a Citizen, to administer the Executive Government of the United States, being not far distant, and the time actually arrived, when your thoughts must be employed in designating the person, who is to be clothed with that important trust, it appears to me proper, especially as it may conduce to a more distinct expression of the public voice, that I should now apprise you of the resolution I have formed, to decline being considered among the number of those, out of whom a choice is to be made. . . .

The acceptance of, and continuance hitherto in, the office to which your suffrages have twice called me, have been a uniform sacrifice of inclination to the opinion of duty, and to a deference for what appeared to be your desire.—I constantly hoped, that it would have been much earlier in my power, consistently with motives, which I was not at liberty to disregard, to return to that retirement, from which I had been reluctantly drawn.—The strength of my inclination to do this, previous to the last election, had even led to the preparation of an address to declare it to you; but mature reflection on the then perplexed and critical nature of our affairs with foreign Nations, and the unanimous advice of persons entitled to my confidence, impelled me to abandon the idea.—

I rejoice that the state of your concerns, external as well as internal, no longer renders the pursuit of inclination incompatible with the sentiment of duty, or propriety; and am persuaded, whatever partiality may be retained for my services, that in the present circumstances of our country, you will not disapprove my determination to retire.

The impressions, with which I first undertook the arduous trust, were explained on the proper occasion.—In the discharge of this trust, I will only say, that I have, with good intentions, contributed towards the organization and administration of the government, the best exertions of which a very fallible judgment was capable.—Not unconscious, in the outset, of the inferiority of my qualifications, experience in my own eyes, perhaps still more in the eyes of others, has strengthened the motives to diffidence of myself; and every day the increasing weight of years admonishes me more and more, that the shade of retirement is as necessary to me as it will be welcome.—Satisfied, that, if any circumstances have given peculiar value to my services, they were temporary, I have the consolation to believe, that, while choice and prudence invite me to quit the political scene, patriotism does not forbid it. . . .

Here, perhaps, I ought to stop.—But a solicitude for your welfare, which cannot end but with my life, and the apprehension of danger, natural to that solicitude, urge me on an occasion like the present, to offer to your solemn contemplation, and to recommend to your frequent review, some sentiments; which are the results of much reflection, of no inconsiderable observation, and which appear to me all-important to the permanency of your felicity as a People.—These will be offered to you with the more freedom, as you can only see in them the disinterested warnings of a parting friend, who can possibly have no personal motive to bias his counsels.—Nor can I forget, as an encouragement to it your indulgent reception of my sentiments on a former and not dissimilar occasion.

Interwoven as is the love of liberty with every ligament of your hearts, no recommendation of mine is necessary to fortify or confirm the attachment.—

The Unity of Government which constitutes you one people, is also now dear to you.—It is justly so;—for it is a main Pillar in the Edifice of your real independence; the support of your tranquility at home; your peace abroad; of your safety; of your prosperity; of that very Liberty, which you so highly prize.—But as it is easy to foresee, that from different causes, and from different quarters, much pains will be taken, many artifices employed, to weaken in your minds the conviction of this truth;—as this is the point in your political fortress against which the batteries of internal and external enemies will be most constantly and actively (though often covertly and insidiously) directed, it is of infinite moment, that you should properly estimate the immense value of your national Union to your collective and individual happiness;—that you should cherish a cordial, habitual, and immoveable attachment to it; accustoming yourselves to think and speak of it as of the Palladium of your political safety and prosperity; watching for its preservation with jealous anxiety; discountenancing whatever may suggest even a suspicion that it can in any event be abandoned, and indignantly frowning upon the first dawning of every attempt to alienate any portion of our Country from the rest, or to enfeeble the sacred ties which now link together the various parts. . . .

. . . Let me now . . . warn you in the most solemn manner against the baneful effects of the Spirit of Party, generally.

This Spirit, unfortunately, is inseparable from our nature, having its root in the strongest passions of the human mind.—It exists under different shapes in all Governments, more or less stifled, controuled, or repressed; but, in those of the popular form, it is seen in its greatest rankness, and is truly their worst enemy. . . .

It serves always to distract the Public Councils, and enfeeble the Public administration.—It agitates the community with ill-founded jealousies and false alarms, kindles the animosity of one part against another, foments occasionally riot and insurrection.—It opens the doors to foreign influence and corruption, which find a facilitated access to the Government itself through the channels of party passions. Thus the policy and the will of one country, are subjected to the policy and will of another.

There is an opinion that parties in free countries are useful checks upon the Administration of the Government, and serve to keep alive the Spirit of Liberty.—This within certain limits is probably true—and in Governments of a Monarchical cast, Patriotism may look with indulgence, if not with favour, upon the spirit of party.—But in those of the popular character, in Governments purely elective, it is a spirit not to be encouraged.—From their natural tendency, it is certain there will always be enough of that spirit for every salutary purpose,—and there being constant danger of excess, the effort ought to be, by force of public opinion, to mitigate and assuage it.—A fire not to be quenched; it demands a uniform vigilance to prevent its bursting into a flame, lest, instead of warning, it should consume. . . .

Observe good faith and justice towards all Nations. Cultivate peace and harmony with all.—Religion and Morality enjoin this conduct; and can it be that good policy does not equally enjoin it?—It will be worthy of a free, enlightened, and, at no distant period, a great nation, to give to mankind the magnanimous and too novel example of a People always guided by an exalted justice and benevolence.—Who can doubt that in the course of time and things, the fruits of such a plan would richly repay any temporary advantages, which might be lost by a steady adherence to it? Can it be, that Providence has not connected the permanent felicity of a Nation with its virtue? The experiment, at least, is recommended by every sentiment which ennobles human nature.—Alas! is it rendered impossible by its vices?

In the execution of such a plan nothing is more essential than that permanent, inveterate antipathies against particular nations and passionate attachments for others should be excluded; and that in place

of them just and amicable feelings towards all should be cultivated.—The Nation, which indulges towards another an habitual hatred or an habitual fondness, is in some degree a slave. It is a slave to its animosity or to its affection, either of which is sufficient to lead it astray from its duty and its interest.—Antipathy in one nation against another disposes each more readily to offer insult and injury, to lay hold of slight causes of umbrage, and to be haughty and intractable, when accidental or trifling occasions of dispute occur.—Hence frequent collisions, obstinate, envenomed and bloody contests.—The Nation promoted by ill-will and resentment sometimes impels to War the Government, contrary to the best calculations of policy.—The Government sometimes participates in the national propensity, and adopts through passion what reason would reject;—at other times, it makes the animosity of the Nation subservient to projects of hostility instigated by pride, ambition, and other sinister and pernicious motives.—The peace often, sometimes perhaps the Liberty, of Nations has been the victim. . . .

The great rule of conduct for us, in regard to foreign Nations, is, in extending our commercial relations, to have with them as little Political connection as possible.—So far as we have already formed engagements, let them be fulfilled with perfect good faith.—Here let us stop. . . .

In offering to you, my Countrymen, these counsels of an old and affectionate friend, I dare not hope they will make the strong and lasting impression, I could wish,—that they will controul the usual current of the passions, or prevent our Nation from running the course which has hitherto marked the destiny of Nations.—But if I may even flatter myself, that they may be productive of some partial benefit; some occasional good; that they may now and then recur to moderate the fury of party spirit, to warn against the mischiefs of foreign intrigue, to guard against the impostures of pretended patriotism, this hope will be a full recompense for the solicitude for your welfare, by which they have been dictated.—

How far in the discharge of my official duties, I have been guided by the principles which have been delineated, the public Records and other evidences of my conduct must witness to You, and to the World.—To myself, the assurance of my own conscience is, that I have at least believed myself to be guided by them. . . .

. . . With me, a predominant motive has been to endeavour to gain time to our country to settle and mature its yet recent institutions, and to progress without interruption to that degree of strength and consistency, which is necessary to give it, humanly speaking, the command of its own fortunes.

Though, in reviewing the incidents of my Administration, I am unconscious of intentional error—I am nevertheless too sensible of my defects not to think it probable that I may have committed many errors.—Whatever they may be I fervently beseech the Almighty to avert or mitigate the evils to which they may tend.—I shall also carry with me the hope that my country will never cease to view them with indulgence; and that after forty-five years of my life dedicated to its service, with an upright zeal, the faults of incompetent abilities will be consigned to oblivion, as myself must soon be to the mansions of rest.

Relying on its kindness in this as in other things, and actuated by that fervent love towards it, which is so natural to a man, who views in it the native soil of himself and his progenitors for several generations;—I anticipate with pleasing expectation that retreat, in which I promise myself to realize, without alloy, the sweet enjoyment of partaking, in the midst of my fellow-citizens, the benign influence of good Laws under a free Government,—the ever favourite object of my heart, and the happy reward, as I trust, of our mutual cares, labours, and dangers.

Jefferson's First Inaugural Address

Despite George Washington's warnings about the dangers of party strife, his retirement from the presidency in 1797 loosed spirits of angry partisanship in the land. The Federalist Party, which won the election of 1796, passed laws (notably the Alien and Sedition Acts of 1798) to stifle public criticism and undermine the opposition Democratic-Republican Party; the Democratic-Republicans quickly passed resolutions in Kentucky and Virginia to deny the federal government's right to impose its laws on resisting states.

In an 1800 rematch of the 1796 presidential election, Thomas Jefferson, the Democratic-Republican candidate, ran against the Federalist president John Adams. This time Jefferson won. The very fact of his inaugural address on March 4, 1801, was significant—it was the first inauguration in the new capital city of Washington and it marked the first peaceful transfer of power from one political party to another in the new nation. But the address also was significant because of what Jefferson said. Resisting the temptation to proclaim a partisan triumph, the new president insisted that "every difference of opinion is not a difference of principle. We have called by different names brethren of the same principle. We are all Republicans, we are all Federalists."

Friends and Fellow-Citizens. . . .

During the contest of opinion through which we have passed the animation of discussions and of exertions has sometimes worn an aspect which might impose on strangers unused to think freely and to speak and to write what they think; but this being now decided by the voice of the nation, announced according to the rules of the Constitution, all will, of course, arrange themselves under the will of the law, and unite in common efforts for the common good. All, too, will bear in mind this sacred principle, that though the will of the majority is in all cases to prevail, that will to be rightful must be reasonable; that the minority possess their equal rights, which equal law must protect, and to violate would be oppression. Let us, then, fellow-citizens, unite with one heart and one mind. Let us restore to social intercourse that harmony and affection without which liberty and even life itself are but dreary things. And let us reflect that, having banished from our land that religious intolerance under which mankind so long bled and suffered, we have yet gained little if we countenance a political intolerance as despotic, as wicked, and capable of as bitter and bloody persecutions. During the throes and convulsions of the ancient world, during the agonizing spasms of infuriated man, seeking through blood and slaughter his long-lost liberty, it was not wonderful that the agitation of the billows should reach even this distant and peaceful shore; that this should be more felt and feared by some and less by others, and should divide opinions as to measures of safety. But every difference of opinion is not a difference of principle. We have called by different names brethren of the same principle. We are all Republicans, we are all Federalists. If there be any among us who would wish to dissolve this Union or to change its republican form, let them stand undisturbed as monuments of the safety with which error of opinion may be tolerated where reason is left free to combat it. I know, indeed, that some honest men fear that a republican government can not be strong, that this Government is not strong enough; but would the honest patriot, in the full time of successful experiment, abandon a government which has so far kept us free and firm on the theoretic and visionary fear that this Government, the world's best hope, may by possibility want energy to preserve itself? I trust not. I believe this, on the contrary, the strongest Government on earth. I believe it the only one where every man, at the call of the law, would fly to the standard of the law, and would meet invasions of the public order as his own personal concern. Sometimes it is said that man can not be trusted with the government of himself. Can he, then, be trusted with the government of others? Or have we found angels in the forms of kings to govern him? Let history answer this question.

Let us, then, with courage and confidence pursue our own Federal and Republican principles, our attachment to union and representative government. Kindly separated by nature and a wide ocean from the exterminating havoc of one quarter of the globe; too high-minded to endure the degradations of the others; possessing a chosen country, with room enough for our descendants to the thousandth and thousandth generation; entertaining a due sense of our equal right to the use of our faculties, to the acquisitions of our own industry, to honor and confidence from our fellow-citizens, resulting not from birth, but from our actions and their sense of them; enlightened by a benign religion, professed, indeed, and practiced in various forms, yet all of them inculcating honesty, truth, temperance, gratitude, and the love of man; acknowledging and adoring an overruling Providence, which by all its dispensations proves that it delights in the happiness of man here and his greater happiness hereafter—with all these blessings, what more is necessary to make us a happy and a prosperous people? Still one thing more, fellow-citizens—a wise and frugal Government, which shall restrain men from injuring one another, shall leave them otherwise free to regulate their own pursuits of industry and improvement, and shall not take from the mouth of labor the bread it has earned. This is the sum of good government, and this is necessary to close the circle of our felicities.

About to enter, fellow-citizens, on the exercise of duties which comprehend everything dear and valuable to you, it is proper you should understand what I deem the essential principles of our Government, and consequently those which ought to shape its Administration. I will compress them within the narrowest compass they will bear, stating the general principle, but not all its limitations. Equal and exact justice to all men, of whatever state or persuasion, religious or political; peace, commerce, and honest friendship with all nations, entangling alliances with none; the support of the State governments in all their rights, as the most competent administrations for our domestic concerns and the surest bulwarks against antirepublican tendencies; the preservation of the General Government in its whole constitutional vigor, as the sheet anchor of our peace at home and safety abroad; a jealous care of the right of election by the people—a mild and safe corrective of abuses which are lopped by the sword of revolution where peaceable remedies are unprovided; absolute acquiescence in the decisions of the majority, the vital principle of republics, from which is not appeal but to force, the vital principle and immediate parent of despotism; a well-disciplined militia, our best reliance in peace and for the first moments of war, till regulars may relieve them; the supremacy of the civil over the military authority; economy in the public expense, that labor may be lightly burthened; the honest payment of our debts and sacred preservation of the public faith; encouragement of agriculture, and of commerce as its handmaid; the diffusion of information and arraignment of all abuses at the bar of the public reason; freedom of religion; freedom of the press, and freedom of person under the protection of the habeas corpus, and trial by juries impartially selected. These principles form the bright constellation which has gone before us and guided our steps through an age of revolution and reformation. The wisdom of our sages and blood of our heroes have been devoted to their attainment. They should be the creed of our political faith, the text of civic instruction, the touchstone by which to try the services of those we trust; and should we wander from them in moments of error or of alarm, let us hasten to retrace our steps and to regain the road which alone leads to peace, liberty, and safety.

I repair, then, fellow-citizens, to the post you have assigned me. With experience enough in subordinate offices to have seen the difficulties of this the greatest of all, I have learnt to expect that it will rarely fall to the lot of imperfect man to retire from this station with the reputation and the favor which bring him into it. Without pretensions to that high confidence you reposed in our first and greatest revolutionary character, whose preeminent services had entitled him to the first place in his country's love and destined for him the fairest page in the volume of faithful history, I ask so much confidence only as may give firmness and effect to the legal administration of your affairs. I shall often go wrong through defect of judgment. When

right, I shall often be thought wrong by those whose positions will not command a view of the whole ground. I ask your indulgence for my own errors, which will never be intentional, and your support against the errors of others, who may condemn what they would not if seen in all its parts. The approbation implied by your suffrage is a great consolation to me for the past, and my future solicitude will be to retain the good opinion of those who have bestowed it in advance, to conciliate that of others by doing them all the good in my power, and to be instrumental to the happiness and freedom of all.

Relying, then, on the patronage of your good will, I advance with obedience to the work, ready to retire from it whenever you become sensible how much better choice it is in your power to make. And may that Infinite Power which rules the destinies of the universe lead our councils to what is best, and give them a favorable issue for your peace and prosperity.

The Monroe Doctrine

President James Monroe is best known for the doctrine that bears his name. It was proclaimed in response to two foreign policy disputes in which the United States was involved during the early 1820s. The first was a Russian claim of land along the Pacific coast, from the Bering Straits south to some unspecified location. The other arose from rumored European plans to recolonize the newly independent nations of previously Spanish South America.

After frequent consultations with the cabinet and with former presidents Thomas Jefferson and James Madison during the fall of 1823, Monroe and Secretary of State John Quincy Adams resolved to declare the "new world" of the Americas off-limits to new attempts at colonization by the "old world" of Europe.

The Monroe Doctrine had almost no immediate effect: as it turned out, Europe was not planning to recolonize South America anyway; as for the Russians, they continued their efforts in the Pacific northwest. In later years, however, presidents invoked the doctrine on several occasions to assert special U.S. influence in South America.

This document is without doubt the most famous public statement ever delivered by James Monroe. It is quite possibly the most renowned doctrine ever promulgated by an American statesman—anywhere, at any time. Contrary to popular opinion, however, it was not delivered as a separate, isolated statement of American policy; rather, it was contained in Monroe's Seventh Annual Message to Congress (1823). In essence, the Doctrine consists of two basic points: that the two American continents are no longer to be considered subjects for future European colonization, and that any attempt by European powers to extend their influence into the Western Hemisphere would be considered dangerous to the peace and safety of the United States.

Fellow-Citizens of the Senate and House of Representatives. . . .

At the proposal of the Russian Imperial Government, made through the minister of the Emperor residing here, a full power and instructions have been transmitted to the minister of the United States at St. Petersburg to arrange by amicable negotiation the respective rights and interests of the two nations on the northwest coast of this continent. A similar proposal had been made by His Imperial Majesty to the Government of Great Britain, which has likewise been acceded to. The Government of the United States has been desirous by this friendly proceeding of manifesting the great value which they have invariably attached to the friendship of the Emperor and their solicitude to cultivate the best understanding with his Government.

In the discussions to which this interest has given rise and in the arrangements by which they may terminate the occasion has been judged proper for asserting, as a principle in which the rights and interests of the United States are involved, that the American continents, by the free and independent condition which they have assumed and maintain, are henceforth not to be considered as subjects for future colonization by any European powers. . . .

It was stated at the commencement of the last session that a great effort was then making in Spain and Portugal to improve the condition of the people of those countries, and that it appeared to be conducted with extraordinary moderation. It need scarcely be remarked that the result has been so far very different from what was then anticipated. Of events in that quarter of the globe, with which we have so much intercourse and from which we derive our origin, we have always been anxious and interested spectators. The citizens of the United States cherish sentiments the most friendly in favor of the liberty and happiness of their fellow-men on that side of the Atlantic. In the wars of the European powers in matters relating to themselves we have never taken any part, nor does it comport with our policy to do so. It is only when our rights are invaded or seriously menaced that we resent injuries or make preparation for our defense. With the movements in this hemisphere we are of necessity more immediately connected, and by causes which must be obvious to all enlightened and impartial observers. The political system of the allied powers is essentially different in this respect from that of America. This difference proceeds from that which exists in their respective Governments; and to the defense of our own, which has been achieved by the loss of so much blood and treasure, and matured by the wisdom of their most enlightened citizens, and under which we have enjoyed unexampled felicity, this whole nation is devoted. We owe it, therefore, to candor and to the amicable relations existing between the United States and those powers to declare that we should consider any attempt on their part to extend their system to any portion of this hemisphere as dangerous to our peace and safety. With the existing colonies or dependencies of any European power we have not interfered and shall not interfere. But with the Governments who have declared their independence and maintained it, and whose independence we have, on great consideration and on just principles, acknowledged, we could not view any interposition for the purpose of oppressing them, or controlling in any other manner their destiny, by any European power in any other light than as the manifestation of an unfriendly disposition toward the United States. In the war between those new Governments and Spain we declared our neutrality at the time of their recognition, and to this we have adhered, and shall continue to adhere, provided no change shall occur which, in the judgment of the competent authorities of this Government, shall make a corresponding change on the part of the United States indispensable to their security.

The late events in Spain and Portugal shew that Europe is still unsettled. Of this important fact no stronger proof can be adduced than that the allied powers should have thought it proper, on any principle satisfactory to themselves, to have interposed by force in the internal concerns of Spain. To what extent such interposition may be carried, on the same principle, is a question in which all independent powers whose governments differ from theirs are interested, even those most remote, and surely none more so than the United States. Our policy in regard to Europe, which was adopted at an early stage of the wars which have so long agitated that quarter of the globe, nevertheless remains the same, which is, not to interfere in the internal concerns of any of its powers; to consider the government de facto as the legitimate government for us; to cultivate friendly relations with it, and to preserve those relations by a frank, firm, and manly policy, meeting in all instances the just claims of every power, submitting to injuries from none. But in regard to those continents circumstances are eminently and conspicuously different. It is impossible that the allied powers should extend their political system to any portion of either continent without endangering our peace and happiness; nor can anyone believe that our southern brethren, if left to themselves, would adopt it of their own accord. It is equally impossible, therefore, that we should behold such interposition in any form with indifference. If we look to the comparative strength and resources of Spain and those new Governments, and their distance from each other, it must be obvious that she can never subdue them. It is still the true policy of the United States to leave the parties to themselves, in the hope that other powers will pursue the same course. . . .

Jackson's Bank Bill Veto

Andrew Jackson's veto of a bill passed by Congress to renew the Bank of the United States's charter was politically important at the time and of enduring importance as a bold assertion of presidential power.

Politically, the bank was a bastion of everything Jackson opposed— the East, the commercial elite, and the National Republican Party (soon to be known as the Whigs). Indeed, bank president Nicholas Biddle, encouraged by Henry Clay, the National Republican candidate for president in 1832, asked Congress to renew the bank's charter four years before the old charter was scheduled to expire in 1836 because Clay thought (erroneously) that a veto by Jackson would be a good issue in the election.

Jackson's veto message reflected an expansive view of the powers of the presidency. Previously, presidents had felt constrained to veto bills only on constitutional grounds, and an earlier version of the bank bill had been judged constitutional by the Supreme Court. But Jackson, in the first part of his message, attacked the bank renewal as bad public policy, setting a precedent for future presidents casting future vetoes. He went on to assert that the president and Congress have as much right to interpret the Constitution as the Court.

To the Senate:

The bill "to modify and continue" the act entitled "An act to incorporate the subscribers to the Bank of the United States" was presented to me on the 4th July instant. Having considered it with that solemn regard to the principles of the Constitution which the day was calculated to inspire, and come to the conclusion that it ought not to become a law, I herewith return it to the Senate, in which it originated, with my objections. . . .

The present [bank]. . . enjoys an exclusive privilege of banking under the authority of the general government, a monopoly of its favor and support, and, as a necessary consequence, almost a monopoly of the foreign and domestic exchange. The powers, privileges, and favors bestowed upon it in the original charter, by increasing the value of the stock far above its par value, operated as a gratuity of many millions to the stockholders. . . .

The act before me proposes another gratuity to the holders of the same stock. . . .

Every monopoly and all exclusive privileges are granted at the expense of the public, which ought to receive a fair equivalent. The many millions which this act proposes to bestow on the stockholders of the existing bank must come directly or indirectly out of the earnings of the American people. . . .

It is maintained by the advocates of the bank that its constitutionality in all its features ought to be considered as settled by precedent and by the decision of the Supreme Court. To this conclusion I cannot assent. Mere precedent is a dangerous source of authority and should not be regarded as deciding questions of constitutional power except where the acquiescence of the people and the states can be considered as well settled. So far from this being the case on this subject, an argument against the bank might be based on precedent. One Congress in 1791 decided in favor of a bank; another in 1811 decided against it. One Congress in 1815 decided against a bank; another in 1816 decided in its favor. Prior to the present Congress, therefore, the precedents drawn from that source were equal. If we resort to the states, the expressions of legislative, judicial, and executive opinions against the bank have been probably to those in its favor as 4 to 1. . . .

If the opinion of the Supreme Court covered the whole ground of this act, it ought not to control the coordinate authorities of this government. The Congress, the executive, and the court must each for itself be guided by its own opinion of the Constitution. Each public officer who takes an oath to support the Constitution swears that he will support it as he understands it and not as it is understood by others. It is as much the duty of the House of Representatives, of the Senate, and of the President to decide upon the constitutionality of any bill or resolution which may be presented to them for passage or approval as it is of the supreme judges when it may be brought before them for judicial decision. The opinion of the judges has no more authority over Congress than the opinion of Congress has over the judges, and on that point the President is independent of both. The authority of the Supreme Court must not, therefore, be permitted to control the Congress or the executive when acting in their legislative capacities, but to have only such influence as the force of their reasoning may deserve. . . .

The government is the only "proper" judge where its agents should reside and keep their offices, because it best knows where their presence will be "necessary." It cannot, therefore, be "necessary" or "proper" to authorize the bank to locate branches where it pleases to perform the public service, without consulting the government and contrary to its will. The principle laid down by the Supreme Court concedes that Congress cannot establish a bank for purposes of private speculation and gain, but only as a means of executing the delegated powers of the general government. By the same principle a branch bank cannot constitutionally be established for other than public purposes. The power which this act gives to establish two branches in any state, without the injunction or request of the government and for other than public purposes, is not "necessary" to the due "execution" of the powers delegated to the Congress. . . .

The principle is conceded that the states cannot rightfully tax the operations of the general government. They cannot tax the money of the government deposited in the state banks nor the agency of those banks remitting it; but will any man maintain that their mere selection to perform this public service for the general government would exempt the state banks and their ordinary business from state taxation? Had the United States, instead of establishing a bank at Philadelphia, employed a private banker to keep and transmit their funds, would it have deprived Pennsylvania of the right to tax his bank and his usual banking operations? . . .

It can not be "necessary" to the character of the bank as a fiscal agent of the government that its private business should be exempted from that taxation to which all the state banks are liable, nor can I conceive it "proper" that the substantive and most essential powers reserved by the states shall be thus attacked and annihilated as a means of executing the powers delegated to the general government. It may be safely assumed that none of those sages who had an agency in forming or adopting our Constitution ever imagined that any portion of the taxing power of the states not prohibited to them nor delegated to Congress was to be swept away and annihilated as a means of executing certain powers delegated to Congress.

If our power over means is so absolute that the Supreme Court will not call in question the constitutionality of an act of Congress the subject of which "is not prohibited, and is really calculated to effect any of the objects entrusted to the government," although, as in the case before me, it takes away powers expressly granted to Congress and rights scrupulously reserved to the states, it becomes us to proceed in our legislation with the utmost caution. Though not directly, our own powers and the rights of the states may be indirectly legislated away in the use of means to execute substantive powers.

We may not enact that Congress shall not have the power of exclusive legislation over the District of Columbia, but we may pledge the faith of the United States that as a means of executing other powers it shall not be exercised for twenty years or forever. We may not pass an act prohibiting the states to tax the banking business carried on within their limits, but we may, as a means of executing our powers over other objects, place that business in the hands of our agents and then declare it exempt from state taxation in their hands. Thus may our own powers and the rights of the states, which we cannot directly curtail or invade, be frittered away and extinguished in the use of means employed by us to execute other powers. That a bank of the United States, competent to all the duties which may be required by the government, might be so organized as not to infringe on our own delegated powers or the reserved rights of the states I do not entertain a doubt. . . .

Under such circumstances the bank comes forward and asks a renewal of its charter for a term of fifteen years upon conditions which not only operate as a gratuity to the stockholders of many millions of dollars but will sanction any abuses and legalize any encroachments. . . .

The bank is professedly established as an agent of the executive branch of the government, and its constitutionality is maintained on that ground. Neither upon the propriety of present action nor upon the provisions of this act was the executive consulted. It has had no opportunity to say that it neither needs nor wants an agent clothed with such powers and favored by such exemptions. There is nothing in its legitimate functions which makes it necessary or proper. Whatever interest or influence, whether public or private, has given birth to this act, it cannot be found either in the wishes or necessities of the Executive Department, by which present action is deemed premature, and the powers conferred upon its agent not only unnecessary but dangerous to the government and country.

It is to be regretted that the rich and powerful too often bend the acts of government to their selfish purposes. Distinctions in society will always exist under every just government. Equality of talents, of education, or of wealth cannot be produced by human institutions. In the full enjoyment of the gifts of Heaven and the fruits of superior industry, economy, and virtue, every man is equally entitled to protection by law; but when the laws undertake to add to these natural and just advantages artificial distinctions, to grant titles, gratuities, and exclusive privileges, to make the rich richer and the potent more powerful, the humble members of society—the farmers, mechanics, and laborers—who have neither the time nor the means of securing like favors to themselves, have a right to complain of the injustice of their government. There are no necessary evils in government. Its evils exist only in its abuses. If it would confine itself to equal protection, and, as Heaven does it rains, shower its favors alike on the high and the low, the rich and the poor, it would be an unqualified blessing. In the act before me there seems to be a wide and unnecessary departure from these just principles.

Nor is our government to be maintained or our Union preserved by invasions of the rights and powers of the several states. In thus attempting to make our general government strong, we make it weak. Its true strength consists in leaving individuals and states as much as possible to themselves—in making itself felt, not in its power, but in its beneficence; not in its control, but in its protection; not in binding the states more closely to the center, but leaving each to move unobstructed in its proper orbit.

Experience should teach us wisdom. Most of the difficulties our government now encounters and most of the dangers which impend over our Union have sprung from an abandonment of the legitimate objects of government by our national legislation and the adoption of such principles as are embodied in this act. Many of our rich men have not been content with equal protection and equal benefits but have besought us to make them richer by act of Congress. By attempting to gratify their desires, we have in the results of our legislation arrayed section and section, interest against interest, and man against man, in a fearful commotion which threatens to shake the foundations of our Union.

It is time to pause in our career to review our principles and, if possible, revive that devoted patriotism and spirit of compromise which distinguished the sages of the Revolution and the fathers of our Union. If we cannot at once, in justice to interests vested under improvident legislation, make our government what it ought to be, we can at least take a stand against all new grants of monopolies and exclusive privileges, against any prostitution of our government to the advancement of a few at the expense of the many, and in favor of compromise and gradual reform in our code of laws and system of political economy.

The Emancipation Proclamation

To Abraham Lincoln, the Civil War was a crusade not to end slavery, but to preserve the Union. "If I could save the Union without freeing any slave, I would do it," he wrote in a letter to the New York Herald. *In the face of continuing Union frustration on the battlefield, however, Lincoln's hands-off policy on slavery jeopardized the support of abolitionists at home and European governments abroad. During the summer of 1862 Lincoln resolved to move against slavery, but he heeded the advice of his cabinet that he wait until after the Union army had won a battle. A partial military victory at Antietam in September was occasion enough, and on September 22, 1862, Lincoln issued a preliminary Emancipation Proclamation. The rebellious states were told that unless they laid down their arms by January 1, 1863, their slaves would be legally free.*

On New Year's Day, 1863, Lincoln signed the Emancipation Proclamation at a White House ceremony, saying, "I never, in my life, felt more certain that I was doing right than I do in signing this paper." Few slaves were freed right away, since the only slaves to whom the proclamation applied were in the states of the Confederacy. But abolitionists and European public opinion rallied to the North's cause and, in the long run, slavery was ended as the Union army regained more and more southern territory.

By the President of the United States of America:

A Proclamation.

Whereas on the 22d day of September, A.D. 1862, a proclamation was issued by the President of the United States, containing, among other things, the following, to wit:

"That on the 1st day of January, A.D. 1863, all persons held as slaves within any state or designated part of a State the people whereof shall then be in rebellion against the United States shall be then, thenceforward, and forever free; and the executive government of the United States, including the military and naval authority thereof, will recognize and maintain the freedom of such persons and will do no act or acts to repress such persons, or any of them, in any efforts they may make for their actual freedom.

"That the executive will on the 1st day of January aforesaid, by proclamation, designate the States and parts of States, if any, in which the people thereof, respectively, shall then be in rebellion against the United States; and the fact that any State or the people thereof shall on that day be in good faith represented in the Congress of the United States by members chosen thereto at elections wherein a majority of the qualified voters of such States shall have participated shall, in the absence of strong countervailing testimony, be deemed conclusive

evidence that such State and the people thereof are not then in rebellion against the United States."

Now, therefore, I, Abraham Lincoln, President of the United States, by virtue of the power in me vested as Commander-in-Chief of the Army and Navy of the United States in time of actual armed rebellion against the authority and government of the United States, and as a fit and necessary war measure for suppressing said rebellion, do, on this 1st day of January, A.D. 1863, and in accordance with my purpose so to do, publicly proclaim for the full period of one hundred days from the first day above mentioned, order and designate as the State and parts of States wherein the people thereof, respectively, are this day in rebellion against the United States the following, to wit:

Arkansas, Texas, Louisiana (except the parishes of St. Bernard, Plaquemines, Jefferson, St. John, St. Charles, St. James, Ascension, Assumption, Terrebonne, Lafourche, St. Mary, St. Martin, and Orleans, including the city of New Orleans), Mississippi, Alabama, Florida, Georgia, South Carolina, North Carolina, and Virginia (except the forty-eight counties designated as West Virginia, and also the counties of Berkeley, Accomac, Northhampton, Elizabeth City, York, Princess Anne, and Norfolk, including the cities of Norfolk and Portsmouth), and which excepted parts are for the present left precisely as if this proclamation were not issued.

And by virtue of the power and for the purpose aforesaid, I do order and declare that all persons held as slaves within said designated States and parts of States are, and henceforward shall be, free; and that the Executive Government of the United States, including the military and naval authorities thereof, will recognize and maintain the freedom of said persons.

And I hereby enjoin upon the people so declared to be free to abstain from all violence, unless in necessary self-defense; and I recommend to them that, in all cases when allowed, they labor faithfully for reasonable wages.

And I further declare and make known that such persons of suitable condition will be received into the armed service of the United States to garrison forts, positions, stations, and other places, and to man vessels of all sorts in said service.

And upon this act, sincerely believed to be an act of justice, warranted by the Constitution upon military necessity, I invoke the considerate judgment of mankind and the gracious favor of Almighty God.

The Gettysburg Address

Abraham Lincoln appeared at Gettysburg, Pennsylvania, on November 19, 1863, more than four months after the bloody battle that claimed more than 40,000 lives and provoked deep uncertainty on both sides about the strategy and objectives of the Civil War. The occasion was the dedication of the battlefield's cemetery. Realizing the symbolic potency of cemeteries and the uneasy state of the nation one year before his reelection campaign, Lincoln prepared intensely for his appearance.

Some scholars have argued that Lincoln's mere 272 words dramatically changed the basic creed of American politics. In the address, Lincoln raised the Declaration of Independence above the Constitution as

the nation's guiding light, stressed the notion of equality of citizens, and began the process of rebuilding a nation bitterly consumed by the war.

More specifically, Lincoln's brief remarks gave the war a transcendent meaning that was not obvious amid the conflict's confusion and misery. The president declared that the United States was a nation always in the process of becoming, not a nation already completed with the establishment of a constitutional system of government. He then called on his countrymen to "the great task remaining before us," which was to remake the nation out of the misery of the Civil War.

Four score and seven years ago our fathers brought forth on this continent, a new nation, conceived in Liberty, and dedicated to the proposition that all men are created equal.

Now we are engaged in a great civil war, testing whether that nation or any nation so conceived and so dedicated, can long endure. We are met on a great battle-field of that war. We have come to dedicate a portion of that field, as a final resting place for those who here gave their lives that that nation might live. It is altogether fitting and proper that we should do this.

But, in a larger sense, we can not dedicate—we can not consecrate—we can not hallow—this ground. The brave men, living and dead, who struggled here, have consecrated it, far above our poor power to add or detract. The world will little note, nor long remember what we say here, but it can never forget what they did here. It is for us the living, rather, to be dedicated here to the unfinished work which they who fought here have thus far so nobly advanced. It is rather for us to be here dedicated to the great task remaining before us—that from these honored dead we take increased devotion to that cause for which they gave the last full measure of devotion—that we here highly resolve that these dead shall not have died in vain—that this nation, under God, shall have a new birth of freedom—and that government of the people, by the people, for the people, shall not perish from the earth.

Lincoln's Second Inaugural Address

Abraham Lincoln delivered his second inaugural address, which could not have lasted more than five minutes, on March 4, 1865, almost four years after the beginning of the Civil War. Six hundred thousand people had died in the war, but it clearly was drawing to an end. (Indeed, Confederate general Robert E. Lee surrendered to Union general Ulysses S. Grant at Appomattox Courthouse in Virginia only a month later, on April 9.)

In style, Lincoln's second inaugural address is biblical—he quotes from the Old Testament, describes the hand of Providence in the war, and writes in cadences reminiscent of the King James Version. In substance, the address is tolerant and conciliatory toward the almost-defeated South, whose people he refers to as "adversaries," not enemies. His concluding plea for "malice toward none" in the effort to "bind up the nation's wounds" is almost as well remembered as the first and last sentences of the Gettysburg Address.

Fellow-Countrymen:

At this second appearing to take the oath of the presidential office there is less occasion for an extended address than there was at the first. Then a statement somewhat in detail of a course to be pursued seemed fitting and proper. Now, at the expiration of four years, during which public declarations have been constantly called forth on every point and phase of the great contest which still absorbs the attention and engrosses the energies of the nation, little that is new could be presented. The progress of our arms, upon which all else chiefly depends, is as well known to the public as to myself, and it is, I trust, reasonably satisfactory and encouraging to all. With high hope for the future, no prediction in regard to it is ventured.

On the occasion corresponding to this four years ago all thoughts were anxiously directed to an impending civil war. All dreaded it, all sought to avert it. While the inaugural address was being delivered from this place, devoted altogether to saving the Union without war, insurgent agents were in the city seeking to destroy it without war—seeking to dissolve the Union and divide effects by negotiation. Both parties deprecated war, but one of them would make war rather than let the nation survive, and the other would accept war rather than let it perish, and the war came.

One eighth of the whole population was colored slaves, not distributed generally over the Union, but localized in the southern part of it. These slaves constituted a peculiar and powerful interest. All knew that this interest was somehow the cause of the war. To strengthen, perpetuate, and extend this interest was the object for which the insurgents would rend the Union even by war, while the Government claimed no right to do more than to restrict the territorial enlargement of it. Neither party expected for the war the magnitude or the duration which it has already attained. Neither anticipated that the cause of the conflict might cease with or even before the conflict itself should cease. Each looked for an easier triumph, and a result less fundamental and astounding. Both read the same Bible and pray to the same God, and each invokes His aid against the other. It may seem strange that any men should dare to ask a just God's assistance in wringing their bread from the sweat of other men's faces, but let us judge not, that we be not judged. The prayers of both could not be answered. That of neither has been answered fully. The Almighty has His own purposes. "Woe unto the world because of offenses; for it must needs be that offenses come, but woe to that man by whom the offense cometh." If we shall suppose that American slavery is one of those offenses which, in the providence of God, must needs come, but which, having continued through His appointed time, He now wills to remove, and that he gives to both North and South this terrible war as the woe due to those by whom the offense came, shall we discern therein any departure from those divine attributes which the believers in a living God always ascribe to Him? Fondly do we hope, fervently do we pray, that this mighty scourge of war may speedily pass away. Yet, if God wills that it continue until all the wealth piled by the bondsman's two hundred and fifty years of unrequited toil shall be sunk, and until every drop of blood drawn with the lash shall be paid by another drawn with the sword, as was said three thousand years ago, so still it must be said, "The judgments of the Lord are true and righteous altogether."

With malice toward none, with charity for all, with firmness in the right as God gives us to see the right, let us strive on to finish the work we are in, to bind up the nation's wounds, to care for him who shall have borne the battle and for his widow and his orphan, to do all which may achieve and cherish a just and lasting peace among ourselves and with all nations.

Impeachment of Andrew Johnson

The Constitution stipulates that the president "shall be removed from Office on Impeachment for, and Conviction of, Treason, Bribery, or other High Crimes and Misdemeanors." The House of Representatives is charged to impeach the president by majority vote; the Senate, with the chief justice of the United States presiding, then tries the president and decides whether to convict and remove. A two-thirds majority of senators is required to do so. Andrew Johnson, who was elected vice president in 1864 and succeeded to the presidency when President Abraham Lincoln was assassinated in 1865, is the only president to undergo the entire impeachment process. Johnson was very unpopular in the Republican-controlled Congress because he wished to pursue a conciliatory policy of Reconstruction toward the southern states that had seceded from the Union and been defeated in the Civil War. The major formal charge against Johnson, however, was that he had violated the Tenure of Office Act of 1867 by firing Secretary of War Edwin M. Stanton without obtaining the Senate's approval. The House impeached him on that charge on March 2 and 3, 1868, and on May 16 and 26 the Senate voted for conviction and removal by a margin of 35 to 19—one vote shy of the required two-thirds majority. Johnson served out the remainder of the term.

ARTICLES OF IMPEACHMENT

ARTICLES EXHIBITED BY THE HOUSE OF REPRESENTATIVES OF THE UNITED STATES, IN THE NAME OF THEMSELVES AND ALL THE PEOPLE OF THE UNITED STATES, AGAINST ANDREW JOHNSON, PRESIDENT OF THE UNITED STATES, IN MAINTENANCE AND SUPPORT OF THEIR IMPEACHMENT AGAINST HIM FOR HIGH CRIMES AND MISDEMEANORS IN OFFICE.

Article I

That said Andrew Johnson, President of the United States, on the 21st day of February, A.D. 1868, at Washington, in the District of Columbia, unmindful of the high duties of his office, of his oath of office, and of the requirement of the Constitution that he should take care that the laws be faithfully executed, did unlawfully and in violation of the Constitution and laws of the United States issue an order in writing for the removal of Edwin M. Stanton from the office of Secretary for the Department of War, said Edwin M. Stanton having been theretofore duly appointed and commissioned, by and with the advice and consent of the Senate of the United States, as such Secretary; and said Andrew Johnson, President of the United States, on the 12th day of August, A.D. 1867, and during the recess of said Senate, having suspended by his order Edwin M. Stanton from said office, and within twenty days after the first day of the next meeting of said Senate—that is to say, on the 12th day of December, in the year last aforesaid—having reported to said Senate such suspension, with the evidence and reasons for his action in the case and the name of the person designated to perform the duties of such office temporarily until the next meeting of the Senate; and said Senate thereafterwards, on the 13th day of January, A.D. 1868, having duly considered the evidence and reasons reported by said Andrew Johnson for said suspension, and having refused to concur in said suspension, whereby and by force of the provisions of an act entitled "An act regulating the tenure of certain civil offices," passed March 2, 1867, said Edwin M. Stanton did forthwith resume the functions of his office, whereof the said Andrew Johnson had then and there due notice; and said Edwin M. Stanton, by reason of the premises, on said 21st day of February, being lawfully entitled to hold said office of Secretary for the Department of War; which said order for the removal of said Edwin M. Stanton is in substance as follows; that is to say:

EXECUTIVE MANSION,
Washington, D.C., February 21, 1868.

HON. EDWIN M. STANTON,
Washington, D.C.

SIR: By virtue of the power and authority vested in me as President by the Constitution and laws of the United States, you are hereby removed from office as Secretary for the Department of War, and your functions as such will terminate upon the receipt of this communication.

You will transfer to Brevet Major-General Lorenzo Thomas, Adjutant-General of the Army, who has this day been authorized and empowerd to act as secretary of War ad interim, all records, books, papers, and other public property now in your custody and charge.

Respectfully yours,
ANDREW JOHNSON.

Which order was unlawfully issued with intent then and there to violate the act entitled "An act regulating the tenure of certain civil offices," passed March 2, 1867, and with the further intent, contrary to the provisions of said act, in violation thereof, and contrary to the provisions of the Constitution of the United States, and without the advice and consent of the Senate of the United States, the said Senate then and there being in session, to remove said Edwin M. Stanton from the office of Secretary for the Department of War, the said Edwin M. Stanton being then and there Secretary for the Department of War, and being then and there in the due and lawful execution and discharge of the duties of said office; whereby said Andrew Johnson, President of the United States, did then and there commit and was guilty of a high misdemeanor in office. . . .

(ARTICLES II THROUGH IX OMITTED)

Article X

That said Andrew Johnson, President of the United States, unmindful of the high duties of his office and the dignity and proprieties thereof, and of the harmony and courtesies which ought to exist and be maintained between the executive and legislative branches of the Government of the United States, designing and intending to set aside the rightful authority and powers of Congress, did attempt to bring disgrace, ridicule, hatred, contempt, and reproach to the Congress of the United States and the several branches thereof, to impair and destroy the regard and respect of all the good people of the United States for the Congress and legislative power thereof (which all officers of the Government ought inviolably to preserve and maintain) and to excite the odium and resentment of all the good people of the United States against Congress and the laws by it duly and constitutionally enacted; and, in pursuance of his said design and intent, openly and publicly, and before divers assemblages of the citizens of the United States, convened in divers parts thereof to meet and receive said Andrew Johnson as the Chief Magistrate of the United States, did, on the 18th day of August, A.D. 1866, and on divers other days and times, as well before as afterwards, make and deliver with a loud voice certain intemperate, inflammatory, and scandalous harrangues, and did therein utter loud threats and bitter menaces, as well against Congress as the laws of the United States, duly enacted thereby, amid the cries, jeers, and laughter of the multitudes then assembled and in hearing, . . .

SCHUYLER COLFAX,
Speaker of the House of Representatives
EDWARD McPHERSON,
Clerk of the House of Representatives

Pendleton Act

The effort to reform the federal civil service by replacing the "spoils system" (under which government employees were hired and fired by elected officials) with a "merit system" (under which personnel decisions would be made nonpolitically, according to ability) was a prominent feature of American politics after the Civil War. In 1881 President James A. Garfield was assassinated by Charles Guiteau, who was enraged that he had not received a government job as reward for his labors on behalf of Garfield's candidacy in the 1880 election. In the atmosphere of revulsion against spoils that followed the assassination, Congress passed the Pendleton Act of 1883.

The Pendleton Act created the Civil Service Commission and stated several ideals that were to guide its labors. Partisan activity and family and personal connections as reasons for hiring, promoting, and firing government employees were to be replaced by competitive examinations and performance-based promotion and retention policies. In the short term, only 10 percent of the federal civil service was covered by the new rules, but the act empowered the president to extend the coverage to additional categories of employees. Over time, virtually the entire civil service became "merit"-based by virtue of presidential decisions.

An act to regulate and improve the civil service of the United States.

Be it enacted . . . , That the President is authorized to appoint, by and with the advice and consent of the Senate, three persons, not more than two of whom shall be adherents of the same party, as Civil Service Commissioners, and said three commissioners shall constitute the United States Civil Service Commission. Said commissioners shall hold no other official place under the United States.

SEC.2. That it shall be the duty of said commissioners:

FIRST. To aid the President, as he may request, in preparing suitable rules for carrying this act into effect, and when said rules shall have been promulgated it shall be the duty of all officers of the United States in the departments and offices to which any such rules may relate to aid, in all proper ways, in carrying said rules, and any modifications thereof, into effect.

SECOND. And, among other things, said rules shall provide and declare, as nearly as the first conditions of good administration will warrant, as follows:

First, for open, competitive examinations for testing the fitness of applicants for the public service now classified or to be classified hereunder. Such examinations shall be practical in their character, and so far as may be shall relate to those matters which will fairly test the relative capacity and fitness of the persons examined to discharge the duties of the service into which they seek to be appointed.

Second, that all the offices, places, and employments so arranged or to be arranged in classes shall be filled by selections according to grade from among those graded highest as the results of such competitive examinations.

Third, appointments to the public service aforesaid in the departments at Washington shall be apportioned among the several States and Territories and the District of Columbia upon the basis of population as ascertained at the last preceding census. . . .

Fourth, that there shall be a period of probation before any absolute appointment or employment aforesaid.

Fifth, that no person in the public service is for that reason under any obligations to contribute to any political fund, or to render any political service, and that he will not be removed or otherwise prejudiced for refusing to do so.

Sixth, that no person in said service has any right to use his official authority or influence to coerce the political action of any person or body. . . .

SEC.6. . . .That from time to time [the secretary of the Treasury,] the Postmaster-General, and each of the heads of departments mentioned in . . . [Section 158] . . . of the Revised Statutes, and each head of an office, shall, on the direction of the President, and for facilitating the execution of this act, respectively revise any then existing classification or arrangement of those in their respective departments and offices, and shall, for the purposes of the examination herein provided for, include in one or more of such classes, so far as practicable, subordinate places, clerks, and officers in the public service pertaining to their respective departments not before classified for examinations. . . .

SEC.8. That no person habitually using intoxicating beverages to excess shall be appointed to, or retained in, any office, appointment, or employment to which the provisions of this act are applicable.

SEC.9. That whenever there are already two or more members of a family in the public service in the grades covered by this act, no other member of such family shall be eligible to appointment to any of said grades.

SEC.10. That no recommendation of any person who shall apply for office or place under the provisions of this act which may be given by any Senator or member of the House of Representatives, except as to the character or residence of the applicant, shall be received or considered by any person concerned in making any examination or appointment under this act. . . .

Theodore Roosevelt's "New Nationalism" Speech

Theodore Roosevelt voluntarily stepped down as president at the end of his term in 1909, two years shy of his fiftieth birthday. His "New Nationalism" speech was delivered almost a year and a half later, at the August 31, 1910, dedication of the John Brown Battlefield at Osawatomie, Kansas. In between those two dates, Roosevelt had witnessed the inauguration of his chosen successor, William Howard Taft, as president, then had become increasingly disillusioned with Taft's conservative leadership.

When it was delivered, the New Nationalism speech (the phrase was writer Herbert Croly's) was widely regarded as the kickoff to another

presidential candidacy. In fact, Roosevelt did seek the Republican nomination in 1912 and, when Taft was nominated instead, ran as the Progressive, or "Bull Moose" candidate. (Both he and Taft lost to Woodrow Wilson.)

But Roosevelt's speech is of greatest enduring interest because it embodies the philosophy that he brought to political life in general and to the presidency in particular. He warned of the dangers of rising concentrations of corporate power and, by implication, union power. Bigness in the private sector was not intrinsically bad, Roosevelt argued, but big business and big labor were prone to commit abuses of power that could be checked only by a large and active federal government. Within that government, the president must be "the steward of the public welfare."

I stand for the square deal. But when I say that I am for the square deal, I mean not merely that I stand for fair play under the present rules of the game but that I stand for having those rules changed so as to work for a more substantial equality of opportunity and of reward for equally good service. . . .

Now, this means that our government, national and state, must be freed from the sinister influence or control of special interests. . . . We must drive the special interests out of politics. . . . For every special interest is entitled to justice, but not one is entitled to a vote in Congress, to a voice on the bench, or to representation in any public office. The Constitution guarantees protection to property, and we must make that promise good. But it does not give the right of suffrage to any corporation.

The true friend of property, the true conservative, is he who insists that property shall be the servant and not the master of the commonwealth; who insists that the creature of man's making shall be the servant and not the master of the man who made it. The citizens of the United States must effectively control the mighty commercial forces which they have themselves called into being. There can be no effective control of corporations while their political activity remains. To put an end to it will be neither a short nor an easy task, but it can be done.

We must have complete and effective publicity of corporate affairs so that the people may know beyond peradventure whether the corporations obey the law and whether their management entitles them to the confidence of the public. It is necessary that laws should be passed to prohibit the use of corporate funds directly or indirectly for political purposes; it is still more necessary that such laws should be thoroughly enforced. Corporate expenditures for political purposes, and especially such expenditures by public service corporations, have supplied one of the principal sources of corruption in our political affairs.

It has become entirely clear that we must have government supervision of the capitalization, not only of public service corporations, including, particularly, railways, but of all corporations doing an interstate business. I do not wish to see the nation forced into the ownership of the railways if it can possibly be avoided, and the only alternative is thoroughgoing and effective regulation, which shall be based on a full knowledge of all the facts, including a physical valuation of property. . . .

We have come to recognize that franchises should never be granted, except for a limited time, and never without proper provision for compensation to the public. It is my personal belief that the same kind and degree of control and supervision which should be exercised over public service corporations should be extended also to combinations which control necessaries of life, such as meat, oil, and coal, or which deal in them on an important scale. I have no doubt that the ordinary man who has control of them is much like ourselves. I have no doubt he would like to do well, but I want to have enough supervision to help him realize that desire to do well.

I believe that the officers, and, especially, the directors, of corporations should be held personally responsible when any corporation breaks the law.

Combinations in industry are the result of an imperative economic law which cannot be repealed by political legislation. The effort at prohibiting all combination has substantially failed. The way out lies, not in attempting to prevent such combinations but in completely controlling them in the interest of the public welfare. For that purpose the Federal Bureau of Corporations is an agency of first impor-

tance. Its powers, and, therefore, its efficiency, as well as that of the Interstate Commerce Commission, should be largely increased. We have a right to expect from the Bureau of Corporations and from the Interstate Commerce Commission a very high grade of public service. We should be as sure of the proper conduct of the interstate railways and the proper management of interstate business as we are now sure of the conduct and management of the national banks, and we should have as effective supervision in one case as in the other. . . .

There is a widespread belief among our people that, under the methods of making tariffs which have hitherto obtained, the special interests are too influential. Probably this is true of both the big special interests and the little special interests. These methods have put a premium on selfishness, and, naturally, the selfish big interests have gotten more than their smaller, though equally selfish, brothers. The duty of Congress is to provide a method by which the interest of the whole people shall be all that receives consideration. To this end there must be an expert tariff commission, wholly removed from the possibility of political pressure or of improper business influence. Such a commission can find the real difference between cost of production, which is mainly the difference of labor cost here and abroad. As fast as its recommendations are made, I believe in revising one schedule at a time. A general revision of the tariff almost inevitably leads to logrolling and the subordination of the general public interest to local and special interests.

The absence of effective state and, especially, national restraint upon unfair money getting has tended to create a small class of enormously wealthy and economically powerful men whose chief object is to hold and increase their power. The prime need is to change the conditions which enable these men to accumulate power which it is not for the general welfare that they should hold or exercise. . . . This, I know, implies a policy of a far more active governmental interference with social and economic conditions in this country than we have yet had, but I think we have got to face the fact that such an increase in governmental control is now necessary.

No man should receive a dollar unless that dollar has been fairly earned. Every dollar received should represent a dollar's worth of service rendered—not gambling in stocks but service rendered. The really big fortune, the swollen fortune, by the mere fact of its size, acquires qualities which differentiate it in kind as well as in degree from what is possessed by men of relatively small means. Therefore, I believe in a graduated income tax on big fortunes, and in another tax which is far more easily collected and far more effective—a graduated inheritance tax on big fortunes, properly safeguarded against evasion and increasing rapidly in amount with the size of the estate.

The people of the United States suffer from periodical financial panics to a degree substantially unknown among the other nations which approach us in financial strength. There is no reason why we should suffer what they escape. It is of profound importance that our financial system should be promptly investigated and so thoroughly and effectively revised as to make it certain that hereafter our currency will no longer fail at critical times to meet our needs. . . .

Nothing is more true than that excess of every kind is followed by reaction; a fact which should be pondered by reformer and reactionary alike. We are face to face with new conceptions of the relations of property to human welfare, chiefly because certain advocates of the rights of property as against the rights of men have been pushing their claims too far. The man who wrongly holds that every human right is secondary to his profit must now give way to the advocate of human welfare, who rightly maintains that every man holds his property subject to the general right of the community to regulate its use to whatever degree the public welfare may require it.

But I think we may go still further. The right to regulate the use of wealth in the public interest is universally admitted. Let us admit also the right to regulate the terms and conditions of labor, which is the chief element of wealth, directly in the interest of the common good. The fundamental thing to do for every man is to give him a chance to reach a place in which he will make the greatest possible contribution to the public welfare. Understand what I say there. Give him a chance, not push him up if he will not be pushed. Help any man who stumbles; if he lies down, it is a poor job to try to carry him; but if he is a worthy man, try your best to see that he gets a chance to show the worth that is in him.

No man can be a good citizen unless he has a wage more than sufficient to cover the bare cost of living and hours of labor short enough so that after his day's work is done he will have time and energy to bear his share in the management of the community, to help in carrying the general load. We keep countless men from being good citizens by the conditions of life with which we surround them. We need comprehensive workmen's compensation acts, both state and national laws to regulate child labor and work for women, and, especially, we need in our common schools not merely education in book learning but also practical training for daily life and work. We need to enforce better sanitary conditions for our workers and to extend the use of safety appliances for our workers in industry and commerce, both within and between the states. Also, friends, in the interest of the workingman himself we need to set our faces like flint against mob violence just as against corporate greed; against violence and injustice and lawlessness by wage workers just as much as against lawless cunning and greed and selfish arrogance of employers.

If I could ask but one thing of my fellow countrymen, my request would be that, whenever they go in for reform, they remember the two sides, and that they always exact justice from one side as much as from the other. I have small use for the public servant who can always see and denounce the corruption of the capitalist, but who cannot persuade himself to say a word about lawless mob violence. And I have equally small use for the man, be he a judge on the bench, or editor of a great paper, or wealthy and influential private citizen, who can see clearly enough and denounce the lawlessness of mob violence, but whose eyes are closed so that he is blind when the question is one of corruption in business on a gigantic scale. . . .

I do not ask for overcentralization; but I do ask that we work in a spirit of broad and far-reaching nationalism when we work for what concerns our people as a whole. We are all Americans. Our common interests are as broad as the continent. I speak to you here in Kansas exactly as I would speak in New York or Georgia, for the most vital problems are those which affect us all alike. The national government belongs to the whole American people, and where the whole American people are interested, that interest can be guarded effectively only by the national government. The betterment which we seek must be accomplished, I believe, mainly through the national government.

The American people are right in demanding that New Nationalism, without which we cannot hope to deal with new problems. The New Nationalism puts the national need before sectional or personal advantage. It is impatient of the utter confusion that results from local legislatures attempting to treat national issues as local issues. It is still more impatient of the impotence which springs from overdivision of governmental powers, the impotence which makes it possible for local selfishness or for legal cunning, hired by wealthy special interests, to bring national activities to a deadlock. This New Nationalism regards the executive power as the steward of the public welfare. It demands of the judiciary that it shall be interested primarily in human welfare rather than in property, just as it demands that the representative body shall represent all the people rather than any one class or section of people. . . .

One of the fundamental necessities in a representative government such as ours is to make certain that the men to whom the people delegate their power shall serve the people by whom they are elected and not the special interests. I believe that every national officer, elected or appointed, should be forbidden to perform any service or receive any compensation, directly or indirectly, from interstate corporations; and a similar provision could not fail to be useful within the states.

The object of government is the welfare of the people. The material progress and prosperity of a nation are desirable chiefly so far as they lead to the moral and material welfare of all good citizens. Just in proportion as the average man and woman are honest, capable of sound judgment and high ideals, active in public affairs—but, first of all, sound in their homelife, and the father and mother of healthy children whom they bring up well—just so far, and no farther, we may count our civilization a success. We must have—I believe we have already—a genuine and permanent moral awakening, without which no wisdom of legislation or administration really means anything; and, on the other hand, we must try to secure the social and economic legislation without which any improvement due to purely mortal agitation is necessarily evanescent.

Wilson's "Fourteen Points" Speech

Almost from the moment the United States entered World War I in 1917, President Woodrow Wilson wanted to issue a clear statement of U.S. objectives in the war against Germany. He was dissuaded from doing so by the argument that any such statement could foster disagreement among the other Allied governments. In December 1917, however, the new Bolshevik government in Russia released copies of the old tsarist government's secret treaties with the Allies, charging that the documents proved that both sides in the war were fighting only in pursuit of selfish national interests. In response to Russia's action, Wilson resolved to publish a statement of U.S. objectives that was more idealistic.

The "Fourteen Points" speech (each point described a U.S. war aim) was delivered to Congress on January 8, 1918. The speech was successful both as an answer to the Bolsheviks and as the initial framework for peace. The armistice agreement that ended the war on November 11,

1918, recognized the fourteen points as the basis for a negotiated settlement. Much of its idealism was lost in the writing of the Treaty of Versailles, but Wilson's proposal to create a League of Nations was accepted. Much to Wilson's disappointment, the U.S. Senate refused to allow the United States to join the league.

. . . We entered this war because violations of right had occurred which touched us to the quick and made the life of our own people impossible unless they were corrected and the world secured once for all against their recurrence. What we demand in this war, therefore, is nothing peculiar to ourselves. It is that the world be made fit and safe to live in; and particularly that it be made safe for every peace-loving nation which, like our own, wishes to live its own life, determine its own institutions, be assured of justice and fair dealing by the other peoples of the world as against force and selfish aggression. All the peoples of the world are in effect partners in this interest, and for our own part we see very clearly that unless justice be done to others it will not be done to us. The program of the world's peace, therefore, is our program; and that program, as we see it, is this:

I. Open covenants of peace, openly arrived at, after which there shall be no private international understandings of any kind but diplomacy shall proceed always frankly and in the public view.

II. Absolute freedom of navigation upon the seas, outside territorial waters, alike in peace and in war, except as the seas may be closed in whole or in part by international action for the enforcement of international covenants.

III. The removal, so far as possible, of all economic barriers and the establishment of an equality of trade conditions among all the nations consenting to the peace and associating themselves for its maintenance.

IV. Adequate guarantees given and taken that national armaments will be reduced to the lowest point consistent with domestic safety.

V. A free, open-minded, and absolutely impartial adjustment of all colonial claims, based upon a strict observance of the principle that in determining all such questions of sovereignty the interests of the populations concerned must have equal weight with the equitable claims of the government whose title is to be determined.

VI. The evacuation of all Russian territory and such a settlement of all questions affecting Russia as will secure the best and freest co-operation of the other nations of the world in obtaining for her an unhampered and unembarrassed opportunity for the independent determination of her own political development and national policy and assure her of a sincere welcome into the society of free nations under institutions of her own choosing; and, more than a welcome, assistance also of every kind that she may need and may herself desire. The treatment accorded Russia by her sister nations in the months to come will be the acid test of their good will, of their comprehension of her needs as distinguished from their own interests, and of their intelligent and unselfish sympathy.

VII. Belgium, the whole world will agree, must be evacuated and restored, without any attempt to limit the sovereignty which she enjoys in common with all other free nations. No other single act will serve as this will serve to restore confidence among the nations in the laws which they have themselves set and determined for the government of their relations with one another. Without this healing act the whole structure and validity of internal law is forever impaired.

VIII. All French territory should be freed and the invaded portions restored, and the wrong done to France by Prussia in 1871 in the matter of Alsace-Lorraine, which has unsettled the peace of the world for nearly fifty years, should be righted, in order that peace may once more be made secure in the interest of all.

IX. A readjustment of the frontiers of Italy should be effected along clearly recognizable lines of nationality.

X. The peoples of Austria-Hungary, whose place among the nations we wish to see safeguarded and assured, should be accorded the freest opportunity of autonomous development.

XI. Rumania, Serbia, and Montenegro should be evacuated; occupied territories restored; Serbia accorded free and secure access to the sea; and the relations of the several Balkan states to one another determined by friendly counsel along historically established lines of allegiance and nationality; and international guarantees of the political and economic independence and territorial integrity of the several Balkan states should be entered into.

XII. The Turkish portions of the present Ottoman Empire should be assured a secure sovereignty, but the other nationalities which are now under Turkish rule should be assured an undoubted security of life and an absolutely unmolested opportunity of autonomous development, and the Dardanelles should be permanently opened as a free passage to the ships and commerce of all nations under international guarantees.

XIII. An independent Polish state should be erected which should include the territories inhabited by indisputably Polish populations, which should be assured a free and secure access to the sea, and whose political and economic independence and territorial integrity should be guaranteed by international covenant.

XIV. A general association of nations must be formed under specific covenants for the purpose of affording mutual guarantees of political independence and territorial integrity to great and small states alike. . . .

We have spoken now, surely, in terms too concrete to admit of any further doubt or question. An evident principle runs through the whole program I have outlined. It is the principle of justice to all peoples and nationalities, and their right to live on equal terms of liberty and safety with one another, whether they be strong or weak. Unless this principle be made its foundation no part of the structure of international justice can stand. The people of the United States could act upon no other principle; and to the vindication of this principle they are ready to devote their lives, their honor, and everything that they possess. The moral climax of this the culminating and final war for human liberty has come, and they are ready to put their own strength, their own highest purpose, their own integrity and devotion to the test.

Teapot Dome Resolution

Warren G. Harding, who was president from 1921 until his death in 1923, presided over one of the most corrupt administrations in history. The most notorious scandal of his tenure involved the naval oil reserves at Teapot Dome, Wyoming, and Elk Hills, California. In 1921 Secretary of the Interior Albert B. Fall persuaded Secretary of the Navy Edwin Denby to transfer these oil fields to the Interior Department, with Harding's approval. Fall then leased them without competitive bidding—Teapot Dome to Harry Sinclair's Mammoth Oil Co. and Elk Hills to Edward L. Doheny's Pan-American Co. In October 1923, after an eighteen-month investigation and two months after Harding's death, a Senate committee exposed the scandal in public hearings.

The Teapot Dome scandal eventually led to the resignation of Denby, the cancellation of the oil leases, the firing of Attorney General Harry M. Daugherty, who had refused to cooperate with the Senate investigation and had ordered federal agents to spy on certain senators, and the imprisonment of Sinclair and Fall. Congress cancelled the leases by a joint resolution adopted February 8, 1924. President Calvin Coolidge, who succeeded Harding, heeded Congress's call to investigate and prosecute vigorously.

A joint resolution directing the President to institute and prosecute suits to cancel certain leases of oil lands and incidental contracts, and for other purposes.

Whereas it appears from evidence taken by the Committee on Public Lands and Surveys of the United States Senate that certain lease of naval reserve No. 3, in the State of Wyoming, bearing date April 7, 1922, made in form by the Government of the United States, through Albert B. Fall, Secretary of the Interior, and Edwin Denby, Secretary of the Navy, as lessor, to the Mammoth Oil Co., as lessee, and that certain contract between the Government of the United States and the Pan American Petroleum & Transport Co., dated April 25, 1922, signed by Edward C. Finney, Acting Secretary of the Interior, and Edwin Denby, Secretary of the Navy, relating among other things to the construction of oil tanks at Pearl Harbor, Territory of Hawaii, and that certain lease of naval reserve No. 1, in the State of California, bearing date December 11, 1922, made in form by the Government of the United States through Albert B. Fall, Secretary of the Interior, and Edwin Denby, Secretary of the Navy, as lessor, to the Pan American Petroleum Co., as lessee, were executed under circumstances indicating fraud and corruption; and

Whereas the said leases and contract were entered into without authority on the part of the officers purporting to act in the execution of the same for the United States and in violation of the laws of Congress; and

Whereas such leases and contract were made in defiance of the settled policy of the Government adhered to through three successive administrations, to maintain in the ground a great reserve supply of oil adequate to the needs of the Navy in any emergency threatening the national security: Therefore be it

Resolved, etc., That the said leases and contract are against the public interest and that the lands embraced therein should be recovered and held for the purpose to which they were dedicated; and

Resolved further, That the President of the United States be, and he hereby is, authorized and directed immediately to cause suit to be instituted and prosecuted for the annulment and cancellation of the said leases and contract and all contracts incidental or supplemental thereto, to enjoin further extraction of oil from the said reserves under said lease or from the territory covered by the same, to secure any further appropriate incidental relief, and to prosecute such other actions or proceedings, civil and criminal, as may be warranted by the facts in relation to the making of the said leases and contract.

And the President is further authorized and directed to appoint, by and with the advice and consent of the Senate, special counsel who shall have charge and control of the prosecution of such litigation, anything in the statutes touching the powers of the Attorney General of the Department of Justice to the contrary notwithstanding.

Franklin D. Roosevelt's First Inaugural Address

Franklin D. Roosevelt was the last president to be inaugurated on March 4; the Twentieth Amendment (1933) advanced the start of the president's term to January 20. During the long winter between Roosevelt's election victory over President Herbert C. Hoover in November 1932 (the most overwhelming defeat of an incumbent president in history) and his inauguration, the depression that had sunk the nation into economic inactivity had worsened. Factories to produce goods and land to grow food and other crops were abundant but had fallen into disuse.

Roosevelt saw his main challenge as restoring the people's confidence and raising their morale. In the best-remembered line from his address, he proclaimed that "the only thing we have to fear is fear itself—nameless, unreasoning, unjustified terror which paralyzes needed efforts to convert retreat into advance." Roosevelt pledged to pursue active and helpful government policies to combat the depression, using and perhaps extending the full powers of the presidency to do so.

Roosevelt's distant relative, former president Theodore Roosevelt, had been the first to describe the presidency as a "bully pulpit" for moral leadership. Franklin Roosevelt made full use of the pulpit in 1933 and afterward. In response to his first inaugural address, half a million people wrote him to express their thanks and support, an unprecedented outpouring of mail.

President Hoover, Mr. Chief Justice, my friends:

This is a day of national consecration, and I am certain that my fellow-Americans expect that on my induction into the Presidency I will address them with a candor and a decision which the present situation of our nation impels.

This is pre-eminently the time to speak the truth, the whole truth, frankly and boldly. Nor need we shrink from honestly facing conditions in our country today. This great nation will endure as it has endured, will revive and will prosper.

So first of all let me assert my firm belief that the only thing we have to fear is fear itself—nameless, unreasoning, unjustified terror which paralyzes needed efforts to convert retreat into advance.

In every dark hour of our national life a leadership of frankness and vigor has met with that understanding and support of the people themselves which is essential to victory. I am convinced that you will again give that support to leadership in these critical days.

In such a spirit on my part and on yours we face our common difficulties. They concern, thank God, only material things. Values have shrunken to fantastic levels; taxes have risen; our ability to pay has fallen, government of all kinds is faced by serious curtailment of income; the means of exchange are frozen in the currents of trade; the withered leaves of industrial enterprise lie on every side; farmers find no markets for their produce; the savings of many years in thousands of families are gone.

More important, a host of unemployed citizens face the grim problem of existence, and an equally great number toil with little return. Only a foolish optimist can deny the dark realities of the moment.

Yet our distress comes from no failure of substance. We are stricken by no plague of locusts. Compared with the perils which our forefathers conquered because they believed and were not afraid, we have still much to be thankful for. Nature still offers her bounty and human efforts have multiplied it. Plenty is at our doorstep, but a generous use of it languishes in the very sight of the supply.

Primarily, this is because the rulers of the exchange of mankind's goods have failed through their own stubbornness and their own incompetence, have admitted their failure and abdicated. Practices of the unscrupulous money changers stand indicted in the court of public opinion, rejected by the hearts and minds of men. True, they have tried, but their efforts have been cast in the pattern of an outworn tradition. Faced by failure of credit, they have proposed only the lending of more money.

Stripped of the lure of profit by which to induce our people to follow their false leadership, they have resorted to exhortations, pleading tearfully for restored confidence. They know only the rules of a generation of self-seekers.

They have no vision, and when there is no vision the people perish.

The money changers have fled from their high seats in the temple of our civilization. We may now restore that temple to the ancient truths.

The measure of the restoration lies in the extent to which we apply social values more noble than mere monetary profit.

Happiness lies not in the mere possession of money; it lies in the joy of achievement, in the thrill of creative effort.

The joy and moral stimulation of work no longer must be forgotten in the mad chase of evanescent profits. These dark days will be worth all they cost us if they teach us that our true destiny is not to be ministered unto but to minister to ourselves and to our fellowmen.

Recognition of the falsity of material wealth as the standard of success goes hand in hand with the abandonment of the false belief that public office and high political position are to be valued only by the standards of pride of place and personal profit; and there must be an end to a conduct in banking and in business which too often has given to a sacred trust the likeness of callous and selfish wrongdoing.

Small wonder that confidence languishes, for it thrives only on honesty, on honor, on the sacredness of obligations, on faithful protection, on unselfish performance. Without them it cannot live.

Restoration calls, however, not for changes in ethics alone. This nation asks for action, and action now.

Our greatest primary task is to put people to work. This is no unsolvable problem if we face it wisely and courageously.

It can be accomplished in part by direct recruiting by the government itself, treating the task as we would treat the emergency of a war, but at the same time, through this employment accomplishing greatly needed projects to stimulate and reorganize the use of our natural resources.

Hand in hand with this, we must frankly recognize the overbalance of population in our industrial centers and, by engaging on a national scale in the redistribution, endeavor to provide a better use of the land for those best fitted for the land.

The task can be helped by definite efforts to raise the values of agricultural products and with this the power to purchase the output of our cities.

It can be helped by preventing realistically the tragedy of the growing loss, through foreclosure, of our small homes and our farms.

It can be helped by insistence that the Federal, State and local governments act forthwith on the demand that their cost be drastically reduced.

It can be helped by the unifying of relief activities which today are often scattered, uneconomical and unequal. It can be helped by national planning for and supervision of all forms of transportation and of communications and other utilities which have a definitely public character.

There are many ways in which it can be helped, but it can never be helped merely by talking about it. We must act, and act quickly.

Finally, in our progress toward a resumption of work we require two safeguards against a return of the evils of the old order; there must be a strict supervision of all banking and credits and investments; there must be an end to speculation with other people's money, and there must be provision for an adequate but sound currency.

These are the lines of attack. I shall presently urge upon a new Congress in special session detailed measures for their fulfillment, and I shall seek the immediate assistance of the several States. . . .

I am prepared under my constitutional duty to recommend the measures that a stricken nation in the midst of a stricken world may require.

These measures, or such other measures as the Congress may build out of its experience and wisdom, I shall seek, within my constitutional authority, to bring to speedy adoption.

But in the event that the Congress shall fail to take one of these two courses, and in the event that the national emergency is still critical, I shall not evade the clear course of duty that will then confront me.

I shall ask the Congress for the one remaining instrument to meet the crisis—broad executive power to wage a war against the emergency as great as the power that would be given me if we were in fact invaded by a foreign foe.

For the trust reposed in me I will return the courage and the devotion that befit the time. I can do no less.

We face the arduous days that lie before us in the warm courage of national unity; with the clear consciousness of seeking old and precious moral values; with the clean satisfaction that comes from the stern performance of duty by old and young alike.

We aim at the assurance of a rounded and permanent national life.

We do not distrust the future of essential democracy. The people of the United States have not failed. In their need they have registered a mandate that they want direct, vigorous action.

They have asked for discipline and direction under leadership. They have made me the present instrument of their wishes. In the spirit of the gift I take it.

In this dedication of a nation we humbly ask the blessing of God. May He protect each and every one of us! May He guide me in the days to come!

United States v. Curtiss-Wright Export Corporation

This landmark Supreme Court case endorsed an expansive view of presidential power in foreign affairs, which was all the more remarkable because the Court had been unusually hostile to the New Deal domestic policies of President Franklin D. Roosevelt. Indeed, the author of the Court's December 21, 1936, opinion, Justice George Sutherland, was one of the New Deal's most ardent judicial foes. Yet in U.S. v. Curtiss-Wright (299 U.S. 304), Sutherland and all but one of his fellow justices (James C. McReynolds) promulgated a constitutional theory that regarded "the President as the sole organ of the federal government in the field of international relations."

The case was triggered by the government's effort to limit a war be-tween Bolivia and Paraguay. Congress had empowered the president to prohibit the sale of U.S.-made arms to the two nations. The Curtiss-Wright corporation was charged with conspiring to sell machine guns to Bolivia in violation of the president's order not to do so. It challenged the law under which the president acted by saying that it involved an unconstitutional delegation of power from Congress to the president.

. . . It will contribute to the elucidation of the question if we first consider the differences between the powers of the federal government in respect of foreign or external affairs and those in respect of domestic or internal affairs. That there are differences between them, and that these differences are fundamental, may not be doubted.

The two classes of powers are different, both in respect of their origin and their nature. The broad statement that the federal government can exercise no powers except those specifically enumerated in the Constitution and such implied powers as are necessary and proper to carry into effect the enumerated powers, is categorically true only in respect of our internal affairs. In that field, the primary purpose of the Constitution was to carve from the general mass of legislative powers then possessed by the states such portions as it was thought desirable to vest in the federal government, leaving those not included in the enumeration still in the States. That this doctrine applies only to powers which the states had, is self evident. And since the states severally never possessed international powers, such powers could not have been carved from the mass of state powers but obviously were transmitted to the United States from some other source. During the colonial period, those powers were possessed exclusively by and were entirely under control of the Crown....

As a result of the separation from Great Britain by the colonies acting as a unit, the powers of external sovereignty passed from the Crown not to the colonies severally, but to the colonies in their collective and corporate capacity as the United States of America....

The Union existed before the Constitution, which was ordained and established among other things to form "a more perfect Union."...

It results that the investment of the federal government with the powers of external sovereignty did not depend upon the affirmative grants of the Constitution. The powers to declare and wage war, to conclude peace, to make treaties, to maintain diplomatic relations with other sovereignties, if they had never been mentioned in the Constitution, would have vested in the federal government as necessary concomitants of nationality....

Not only, as we have shown, is the federal power over external affairs in origin and essential character different from that over internal affairs, but participation in the exercise of the power is signifi-

cantly limited. In this vast external realm, with its important, complicated, delicate and manifold problems, the President alone has the power to speak or listen as a representative of the nation. He makes treaties with the advice and consent of the Senate; but he alone negotiates. Into the field of negotiation the Senate cannot intrude; and Congress itself is powerless to invade it....

It is important to bear in mind that we are here dealing not only with an authority vested in the President by an exertion of legislative power, but with such an authority plus the very delicate, plenary and exclusive power of the President as the sole organ of the federal government in the field of international relations—a power which does not require as a basis for its exercise an act of Congress, but which, of course, like every other government power, must be exercised in subordination to the applicable provisions of the Constitution. It is quite apparent that if, in the maintenance of our international relations, embarrassment—perhaps serious embarrassment—is to be avoided and success for our aims achieved, congressional legislation which is to be made effective through negotiation and inquiry within the international field must often accord to the President a degree of discretion and freedom from statutory restriction which would not be admissible were domestic affairs alone involved. Moreover he, not Congress, has the better opportunity of knowing the conditions which prevail in foreign countries, and especially is this true in time of war. He has his confidential sources of information. He has his agents in the form of diplomatic, consular and other officials. Secrecy in respect of information gathered by them may be highly necessary and the premature disclosure of it productive of harmful results....

In the light of the foregoing observations, it is evident that this court should not be in haste to apply a general rule which will have the effect of condemning legislation like that under review as constituting an unlawful delegation of legislative power. The principles which justify such legislation find overwhelming support in the unbroken legislative practice which has prevailed almost from the inception of the national government to the present day....

Franklin D. Roosevelt's "Four Freedoms" Speech

After World War I the United States sank into a mood of isolationism in foreign policy that was embodied by the slogan, "America first!" Beginning in 1937 President Franklin D. Roosevelt tried to alert the nation to the "solidarity and interdependence about the modern world, ... which makes it impossible for any nation completely to isolate itself from political and economic upheavals in the rest of the world." But public response was tepid to his call to "quarantine" aggressor nations for the sake of national self-interest.

In 1941 Roosevelt took another tack in his effort to promote U.S. aid to nations that were at war with the Axis powers of Germany, Italy, and Japan. In his January 6, 1941, State of the Union Address, Roosevelt appealed to American idealism by citing "four essential human freedoms" to which all people were entitled. The first two—freedom of speech and expression and freedom of religion—derived from the Bill of Rights to the Constitution. The third—freedom from want—extended the New Deal view of economic sufficiency to the international arena. The fourth was freedom from fear, which ultimately meant widespread disarmament.

The "Four Freedoms" speech roused public support for Roosevelt's lend-lease program of military aid to Great Britain and the Soviet Union and was incorporated into the Atlantic Charter, which stated Allied war aims.

... Let us say to the democracies:

We Americans are vitally concerned in your defense of freedom. We are putting forth our energies, our resources and our organizing powers to give you the strength to regain and maintain a free world. We shall send you in ever-increasing numbers, ships, planes, tanks, guns. That is our purpose and our pledge....

Yes, and we must prepare, all of us prepare, to make the sacrifices that the emergency—almost as serious as war itself—demands. Whatever stands in the way of speed and efficiency in defense, in defense preparations at any time, must give way to the national need.

A free nation has the right to expect full cooperation from all groups. A free nation has the right to look to the leaders of business, of labor and of agriculture to take the lead in stimulating effort, not among other groups but within their own groups....

As men do not live by bread alone, they do not fight by armament alone. Those who man our defenses and those behind them who build our defenses must have the stamina and the courage which come from unshakable belief in the manner of life which they are defending. The mighty action that we are calling for cannot be based on a disregard for all the things worth fighting for.

The nation takes great satisfaction and much strength from the things which have been done to make its people conscious of their individual stakes in the preservation of democratic life in America. Those things have toughened the fiber of our people, have renewed their faith and strengthened their devotion to the institutions we make ready to protect.

Certainly this is no time for any of us to stop thinking about the social and economic problems which are the root cause of the social revolution which is today a supreme factor in the world. For there is nothing mysterious about the foundations of a healthy and strong democracy.

The basic things expected by our people of their political and economic systems are simple. They are:

Equality of opportunity for youth and for others.

Jobs for those who can work.

Security for those who need it.

The ending of special privilege for the few.

The preservation of civil liberties for all.

The employment of the fruits of scientific progress in a wider and constantly rising standard of living.

These are the simple, the basic things that must never be lost sight of in the turmoil and unbelievable complexity of our modern world. The inner and abiding strength of our economic and political systems is dependent upon the degree to which they fulfill these expectations....

I have called for personal sacrifice, and I am assured of the willingness of almost all Americans to respond to that call. A part of the sacrifice means the payment of more money in taxes. In my budget message I will recommend that a greater portion of this great defense program be paid for from taxation than we are paying for today. No person should try, or be allowed to get rich out of the program, and the principle of tax payments in accordance with ability to pay should be constantly before our eyes to guide our legislation.

If the Congress maintains these principles the voters, putting patriotism ahead of pocketbooks, will give you their applause.

In the future days which we seek to make secure, we look forward to a world founded upon four essential human freedoms.

The first is freedom of speech and expression—everywhere in the world.

The second is freedom of every person to worship God in his own way—everywhere in the world.

The third is freedom from want, which, translated into world terms, means economic understanding which will secure to every nation a healthy peacetime life for its inhabitants—everywhere in the world.

The fourth is freedom from fear, which, translated into world terms means a world-wide reduction of armaments to such a point and in such a thorough fashion that no nation will be in a position to commit an act of physical aggression against any neighbor—anywhere in the world.

That is no vision of a distant millennium. It is a definite basis for a kind of world attainable in our own time and generation. That kind of world is the very antithesis of the so-called "new order" of tyranny which the dictators seek to create with the crash of a bomb.

To that new order we oppose the greater conception—the moral order. A good society is able to face schemes of world domination and foreign revolutions alike without fear.

Since the beginning of our American history we have been engaged in change, in a perpetual, peaceful revolution, a revolution which goes on steadily, quietly, adjusting itself to changing conditions without the concentration camp or the quicklime in the ditch. The world order which we seek is the cooperation of free countries, working together in a friendly, civilized society.

This nation has placed its destiny in the hands, heads and hearts of its millions of free men and women, and its faith in freedom under the guidance of God. Freedom means the supremacy of human rights everywhere. Our support goes to those who struggle to gain those rights and keep them. Our strength is our unity of purpose.

To that high concept there can be no end save victory.

Truman's Point Four Message

On January 20, 1949, President Harry S. Truman delivered an inaugural address organized around four main points. He especially emphasized point four, in which he called for "a bold new program for making the benefits of our scientific advances and industrial progress available for the improvement and growth of underdeveloped areas." Part of Truman's motive was altruistic; the underdeveloped nations were suffering economically. Part of the motive was political. The United States had been laboring to halt the spread of communism in Europe and wanted to do the same in Africa, Asia, and South America.

The Point Four program was spelled out in detail in a special message that Truman sent to Congress on June 24, 1949. In 1950 Congress passed the Act for International Development and also appropriated money for the technical assistance program of the United Nations.

U.S. foreign aid falls into two main categories: military aid and economic aid. The latter originated with Truman's Point Four program.

To the Congress of the United States:

In order to enable the United States, in cooperation with other countries, to assist the peoples of economically under-developed areas to raise their standards of living, I recommend the enactment of legislation to authorize an expanded program of technical assistance for such areas, and an experimental program for encouraging the outflow of private investment beneficial to their economic development. These measures are the essential first steps in an undertaking which will call upon private enterprise and voluntary organizations in the United States, as well as the Government, to take part in a constantly growing effort to improve economic conditions in the less developed regions of the world.

The grinding poverty and the lack of economic opportunity for many millions of people in the economically under-developed parts of Africa, the Near and Far East, and certain regions of Central and South America, constitute one of the greatest challenges of the world today. In spite of their age-old economic and social handicaps, the peoples in these areas have in recent decades been stirred and awakened. The spread of industrial civilization, the growing understanding of modern concepts of government, and the impact of two world wars have changed their lives and their outlook. They are eager to play a greater part in the community of nations.

All these areas have a common problem. They must create a firm economic base for the democratic aspirations of their citizens. Without such an economic base, they will be unable to meet the expectations which the modern world has aroused in their peoples. If they are frustrated and disappointed, they may turn to false doctrines which hold that the way of progress lies through tyranny....

The major effort in such a program must be local in character; it must be made by the people of the under-developed areas themselves. It is essential, however, to the success of their effort that there be help from abroad. In some cases, the peoples of these areas will be unable to begin their part of this great enterprise without initial aid from other countries.

The aid that is needed falls roughly into two categories. The first is the technical, scientific and managerial knowledge necessary to economic development. This category includes not only medical and educational knowledge, and assistance and advice in such basic fields as sanitation, communications, road building and governmental services, but also, and perhaps most important, assistance in the survey of resources and in planning for long-range economic development.

The second category is production goods—machinery and equipment—and financial assistance in the creation of productive enterprises. The under-developed areas need capital for port and harbor development, roads and communications, irrigation and drainage projects, as well as for public utilities and the whole range of extractive, processing and manufacturing industries. Much of the capital required can be provided by these areas themselves, in spite of their low standards of living. But much must come from abroad.

The two categories of aid are closely related. Technical assistance is necessary to lay the groundwork for productive investment. Investment, in turn, brings with it technical assistance. In general, however, technical surveys of resources and of the possibilities of economic development must precede substantial capital investment. Furthermore, in many of the areas concerned, technical assistance in improving sanitation, communications or education is required to create conditions in which capital investment can be fruitful. . . .

In addition to our participation in this work of the United Nations, much of the technical assistance required can be provided directly by the United States to countries needing it. A careful examination of the existing information concerning the under-developed countries shows particular need for technicians and experts with United States training in plant and animal diseases, malaria and typhus control, water supply and sewer systems, metallurgy and mining, and nearly all phases of industry.

It has already been shown that experts in these fields can bring about tremendous improvements. For example, the health of the people of many foreign communities has been greatly improved by the work of United States sanitary engineers in setting up modern water supply systems. The food supply of many areas has been increased as the result of the advice of United States agricultural experts in the control of animal diseases and the improvement of crops. These are only examples of the wide range of benefits resulting from the careful application of modern techniques to local problems. The benefits which a comprehensive program of expert assistance will make possible can only be revealed by studies and surveys undertaken as a part of the program itself. . . .

Many of these conditions of instability in under-developed areas which deter foreign investment are themselves a consequence of the lack of economic development which only foreign investment can cure. Therefore, to wait until stable conditions are assured before encouraging the outflow of capital to under-developed areas would defer the attainment of our objectives indefinitely. It is necessary to take vigorous action now to break out of this vicious circle.

Since the development of under-developed economic areas is of major importance in our foreign policy, it is appropriate to use the resources of the government to accelerate private efforts toward that end. . . .

The enactment of these two legislative proposals, the first pertaining to technical assistance and the second to the encouragement of foreign investment, will constitute a national endorsement of a program of major importance in our efforts for world peace and economic stability. Nevertheless, these measures are only the first steps. We are here embarking on a venture that extends far into the future. We are at the beginning of a rising curve of activity, private, governmental and international, that will continue for many years to come. It is all the more important, therefore, that we start promptly. . . .

Before the peoples of these areas we hold out the promise of a better future through the democratic way of life. It is vital that we move quickly to bring the meaning of that promise home to them in their daily lives.

Youngstown Sheet and Tube Co. v. Sawyer

On April 8, 1952, President Harry S. Truman ordered Secretary of Commerce Charles Sawyer to seize the nation's privately owned steel mills and keep them in operation. Truman acted partly out of the fear that an impending strike of the steel unions would jeopardize U.S. ability to maintain its military effort in the Korean War. His order was challenged quickly and was ruled unconstitutional by the Supreme Court on June 2, 1952, in Youngstown Sheet and Tube Co. v. Sawyer *(343 U.S. 579).*

Although Truman lost the case, his constitutional claim that the president has an inherent, unstated constitutional power to act in national emergencies was accepted, to one degree or another, by a majority of the justices. Justice Hugo L. Black, delivering the opinion of the Court, rejected this claim (as did Justice William O. Douglas). But the three dissenting justices (Chief Justice Fred M. Vinson and Justices Sherman Minton and Stanley F. Reed) and at least two of the justices who voted with Black endorsed it to one degree or another. Justice Robert H. Jackson, for example, voted with Black, but only because Congress had expressly denied the president powers of seizure. But Jackson argued that an inherent executive power did exist.

[Justice Black delivered the opinion of the Court.]

We are asked to decide whether the President was acting within his constitutional power when he issued an order directing the Secretary of Commerce to take possession of and operate most of the Nation's steel mills. The mill owners argue that the President's order amounts to lawmaking, a legislative function which the Constitution has expressly confided to the Congress and not to the President. The Government's position is that the order was made on findings of the President that his action was necessary to avert a national catastrophe which would inevitably result from a stoppage of steel production, and that in meeting this grave emergency the President was acting within the aggregate of his constitutional powers as the Nation's Chief Executive and the Commander in Chief of the Armed Forces of the United States. . . .

Two crucial issues have developed: *First.* Should final determination of the constitutional validity of the President's order be made in this case which has proceeded no further than the preliminary injunction stage? *Second.* If so, is the seizure order within the constitutional power of the President? . . .

The President's power, if any, to issue the order must stem either from an act of Congress or from the Constitution itself. There is no statute that expressly authorizes the President to take possession of property as he did here. Nor is there any act of Congress to which our attention has been directed from which such a power can fairly be implied. Indeed, we do not understand the Government to rely on statutory authorization for this seizure. . . .

Moreover, the use of the seizure technique to solve labor disputes in order to prevent work stoppages was not only unauthorized by any congressional enactment; prior to this controversy, Congress had refused to adopt that method of settling labor disputes. When the Taft-Hartley Act was under consideration in 1947, Congress rejected an amendment which would have authorized such governmental seizures in cases of emergency. . . .

It is clear that if the President had authority to issue the order he did, it must be found in some provisions of the Constitution. And it is not claimed that express constitutional language grants this power to the President. The contention is that presidential power should be implied from the aggregate of his powers under the Constitution. Particular reliance is placed on provisions in Article II which say that "the executive Power shall be vested in a President . . ."; that "he shall take Care that the Laws be faithfully executed"; and that he "shall be Commander in Chief of the Army and Navy of the United States."

The order cannot properly be sustained as an exercise of the President's military power as Commander in Chief of the Armed Forces. The Government attempts to do so by citing a number of cases upholding broad powers in military commanders engaged in day-to-day fighting in a theater of war. Such cases need not concern us here. Even though "theater of war" be an expanding concept, we cannot with faithfulness to our constitutional system hold that the Commander in Chief of the Armed Forces has the ultimate power as such to take possession of private property in order to keep labor disputes from stopping production. This is a job for the Nation's lawmakers, not for its military authorities.

Nor can the seizure order be sustained because of the several constitutional provisions that grant executive power to the President. In the framework of our Constitution, the President's power to see that the laws are faithfully executed refutes the idea that he is to be a lawmaker. The Constitution limits his functions in the lawmaking process to the recommending of laws he thinks wise and the vetoing of laws he thinks bad. And the Constitution is neither silent nor equivocal about who shall make laws which the President is to execute. The first section of the first article says that "All legislative Powers herein granted shall be vested in a Congress of the United States. . . ." After granting many powers to the Congress, Article I goes on to provide that Congress may "make all Laws which shall be necessary and proper for carrying into Execution the foregoing Powers and all other Powers vested by this Constitution in the Government of the United States, or in any Department or Officer thereof." . . .

It is said that other Presidents without congressional authority have taken possession of private business enterprises in order to settle labor disputes. But even if this be true, Congress has not thereby lost its exclusive constitutional authority to make laws necessary and proper to carry out the powers vested by the Constitution "in the Government of the United States, or in any Department or Officer thereof."

The Founders of this Nation entrusted the law-making power to the Congress alone in both good and bad times. It would do no good to recall the historical events, the fears of power and the hopes for freedom that lay behind their choice. Such a review would but confirm our holding that this seizure order cannot stand.

The Judgment of the District Court is affirmed.

[Dissent by Chief Justice Vinson, in which Justice Reed and Justice Minton joined.]

. . . Those who suggest that this is a case involving extraordinary powers should be mindful that these are extraordinary times. A world not yet recovered from the devastation of World War II has been forced to face the threat of another and more terrifying global conflict. . . .

The steel mills were seized for a public use. The power of eminent domain, invoked in this case, is an essential attribute of sovereignty and has long been recognized as a power of the Federal Government. . . .

Admitting that the Government could seize the mills, plaintiffs claim that the implied power of eminent domain can be exercised only under an Act of Congress; under no circumstances, they say, can that power be exercised by the President unless he can point to an express provision in enabling legislation. This was the view adopted by the District Judge when he granted the preliminary injunction. . . .

Under this view, the President is left powerless at the very moment when the need for action may be most pressing and when no one, other than he, is immediately capable of action. Under this view, he is left powerless because a power not expressly given to Congress is nevertheless found to rest exclusively with Congress. . . .

Eisenhower's Farewell Address

President Dwight D. Eisenhower was the first president to deliver a televised farewell address, three days before the end of his second term on January 17, 1961. Eisenhower's departing speech is the best-remembered such address since George Washington's in 1796.

President Eisenhower was not renowned as an orator, yet his speech was both thoughtful and moving. Although he was best known as the general who had served as supreme commander of the Allied forces during World War II, his speech warned the nation to keep a close watch on the "military-industrial complex" (a term he coined). Eisenhower also cautioned against the excesses of technology and warned the nation not to overreact to crises foreign and domestic.

At the time, Eisenhower's farewell address was not so well suited to the mood of the country as President John F. Kennedy's bold and challenging inaugural address, which was delivered three days later. As time went by, however, the wisdom of the farewell address became better appreciated.

My fellow Americans:

Three days from now, after half a century in the service of our country, I shall lay down the responsibilities of office as, in traditional and solemn ceremony, the authority of the Presidency is vested in my successor.

This evening I come to you with a message of leave-taking and farewell, and to share a few final thoughts with you, my countrymen. . . .

Throughout America's adventure in free government, our basic purposes have been to keep the peace; to foster progress in human achievement, and to enhance liberty, dignity and integrity among people and among nations. To strive for less would be unworthy of a free and religious people. Any failure traceable to arrogance, or our lack of comprehension or readiness to sacrifice would inflict upon us grievous hurt both at home and abroad.

Progress toward these noble goals is persistently threatened by the conflict now engulfing the world. It commands our whole attention, absorbs our very beings. We face a hostile ideology—global in scope, atheistic in character, ruthless in purpose, and insidious in method. Unhappily the danger it poses promises to be of indefinite duration. To meet it successfully, there is called for, not so much the emotional and transitory sacrifices of crisis, but rather those which enable us to carry forward steadily, surely, and without complaint the burdens of a prolonged and complex struggle—with liberty the stake. Only thus shall we remain, despite every provocation, on our charted course toward permanent peace and human betterment.

Crises there will continue to be. In meeting them, whether foreign or domestic, great or small, there is a recurring temptation to feel that some spectacular and costly action could become the miraculous solution to all current difficulties. A huge increase in newer elements of our defense; development of unrealistic programs to cure every ill in agriculture; a dramatic expansion in basic and applied research—these and many other possibilities, each possibly promising in itself, may be suggested as the only way to the road we wish to travel.

But each proposal must be weighed in the light of a broader consideration: the need to maintain balance in and among national programs—balance between the private and the public economy, balance between cost and hoped for advantage—balance between the clearly necessary and the comfortably desirable; balance between our essential requirements as a nation and the duties imposed by the nation upon the individual; balance between actions of the moment and the national welfare of the future. Good judgment seeks balance and progress; lack of it eventually finds imbalance and frustration.

The record of many decades stands as proof that our people and their government have, in the main, understood these truths and have responded to them well, in the face of stress and threat. But threats, new in kind or degree, constantly arise. I mention two only. . . .

Until the latest of our world conflicts, the United States had no armaments industry. American makers of plowshares could, with time and as required, make swords as well. But now we can no longer risk emergency improvisation of national defense; we have been compelled to create a permanent armaments industry of vast proportions. Added to this, three and a half million men and women are directly engaged in the defense establishment. We annually spend on military security more than the net income of all United States corporations.

This conjunction of an immense military establishment and a large arms industry is new in the American experience. The total influence—economic, political, even spiritual—is felt in every city, every State house, every office of the Federal government. We recognize the imperative need for this development. Yet we must not fail to comprehend its grave implications. Our toil, resources and livelihood are all involved; so is the very structure of our society.

In the councils of government, we must guard against the acquisi-

tion of unwarranted influence, whether sought or unsought, by the military-industrial complex. The potential for the disastrous rise of misplaced power exists and will persist.

We must never let the weight of this combination endanger our liberties or democratic processes. We should take nothing for granted. Only an alert and knowledgeable citizenry can compel the proper meshing of the huge industrial and military machinery of defense with our peaceful methods and goals, so that security and liberty may prosper together.

Akin to, and largely responsible for the sweeping changes in our industrial-military posture, has been the technological revolution during recent decades.

In this revolution, research has become central; it also becomes more formalized, complex, and costly. A steadily increasing share is conducted for, by, or by the direction of, the Federal government.

Today, the solitary inventor, tinkering in his shop, has been overshadowed by task forces of scientists in laboratories and testing fields. In the same fashion, the free university, historically the fountainhead of free ideas and scientific discovery, has experienced a revolution in the conduct of research. Partly because of the huge costs involved, a government contract becomes virtually a substitute for intellectual curiosity. For every old blackboard there are now hundreds of new electronic computers.

The prospect of domination of the nation's scholars by Federal employment, project allocations, and the power of money is ever present—and is gravely to be regarded.

Yet, in holding scientific research and discovery in respect, as we should, we must also be alert to the equal and opposite danger that public policy could itself become the captive of a scientific-technological elite.

It is the task of statesmanship to mold, to balance, and to integrate these and other forces, new and old, within the principle of our democratic system—ever aiming toward the supreme goals of our free society.

Another factor in maintaining balance involves the element of time. As we peer into society's future, we—you and I, and our government—must avoid the impulse to live only for today, plundering, for our own ease and convenience, the precious resources of tomorrow. We cannot mortgage the material assets of our grandchildren without risking the loss also of their political and spiritual heritage. We want democracy to survive for all generations to come, not to become the insolvent phantom of tomorrow. . . .

To all the peoples of the world, I once more give expression to America's prayerful and continuing aspiration:

We pray that peoples of all faiths, all races, all nations, may have their great human needs satisfied; that those now denied opportunity shall come to enjoy it to the full; that all who yearn for freedom may experience its spiritual blessings; that those who have freedom will understand, also, its heavy responsibilities; that all who are insensitive to the needs of others will learn charity; that the scourges of poverty, disease and ignorance will be made to disappear from the earth, and that, in the goodness of time, all peoples will come to live together in a peace guaranteed by the binding force of mutual respect and love.

Kennedy's Inaugural Address

John F. Kennedy was elected president in 1960, at the end of Dwight D. Eisenhower's second term. The contrasts between the two presidents were dramatic and visible: the youngest man ever to be elected president was replacing the oldest man to leave the office up to that time; a Democrat was replacing a Republican; and an advocate of change and energy was replacing a defender of caution, prudence, and restraint.

Kennedy's inaugural, delivered January 20, 1961, on a bright but bitterly cold day, accentuated all of these contrasts. He emphasized his youth by noting that "the torch has been passed to a new generation of Americans—born of this century." He reached out to the Soviet Union: "Let us never negotiate out of fear. But let us never fear to negotiate." But he also pledged that "we shall pay any price, bear any burden, meet any hardship, support any friend, oppose any foe to assure the survival and the success of liberty." Finally, in the best-remembered phrase of his presidency, Kennedy summoned the idealism of the American people: "ask not what your country can do for you—ask what you can do for your country."

We observe today not a victory of party but a celebration of freedom—symbolizing an end as well as a beginning—signifying renewal as well as change. For I have sworn before you and Almighty God the same solemn oath our forebears prescribed nearly a century and three quarters ago.

The world is very different now. For man holds in his mortal hands the power to abolish all forms of human poverty and all forms of human life. And yet the same revolutionary beliefs for which our forebears fought are still at issue around the globe—the belief that the rights of man come not from the generosity of the state but from the hand of God.

We dare not forget today that we are the heirs of that first revolution. Let the word go forth from this time and place, to friend and foe alike, that the torch has been passed to a new generation of Americans—born in this century, tempered by war, disciplined by a hard and bitter peace, proud of our ancient heritage—and unwilling to witness or permit the slow undoing of those human rights to which this nation has always been committed, and to which we are committed today at home and around the world.

Let every nation know, whether it wishes us well or ill, that we shall pay any price, bear any burden, meet any hardship, support any friend, oppose any foe to assure the survival and the success of liberty.

This much we pledge—and more.

To those old allies whose cultural and spiritual origins we share, we pledge the loyalty of faithful friends. United, there is little we cannot do in a host of cooperative ventures. Divided, there is little we can do—for we dare not meet a powerful challenge at odds and split asunder.

To those new states whom we welcome to the ranks of the free, we pledge our word that one form of colonial control shall not have passed away merely to be replaced by a far more iron tyranny. We shall not always expect to find them supporting our view. But we shall always hope to find them strongly supporting their own freedom—and to remember that, in the past, those who foolishly sought power by riding the back of the tiger ended up inside.

To those peoples in the huts and villages of half the globe struggling to break the bonds of mass misery, we pledge our best efforts to help them help themselves, for whatever period is required—not because the communists may be doing it, not because we seek their votes, but because it is right. If a free society cannot help the many who are poor, it cannot save the few who are rich.

To our sister republics south of our border, we offer a special pledge—to convert our good words into good deeds—in a new alliance for progress—to assist free men and free governments in casting off the chains of poverty. But this peaceful revolution of hope cannot become the prey of hostile powers. Let all our neighbors know that we shall join with them to oppose aggression or subversion anywhere in the Americas. And let every other power know that this Hemisphere intends to remain the master of its own house.

To that world assembly of sovereign states, the United Nations, our last best hope in an age where the instruments of war have far outpaced the instruments of peace, we renew our pledge of support—to prevent it from becoming merely a forum for invective—to strengthen its shield of the new and the weak—and to enlarge the area in which its writ may run.

Finally, to those nations who would make themselves our adversary, we offer not a pledge but a request: that both sides begin anew the quest for peace, before the dark powers of destruction unleashed by science engulf all humanity in planned or accidental self-destruction.

We dare not tempt them with weakness. For only when our arms are sufficient beyond doubt can we be certain beyond doubt that they will never be employed.

But neither can two great and powerful groups of nations take comfort from our present course—both sides overburdened by the cost of modern weapons, both rightly alarmed by the steady spread of the deadly atom, yet both racing to alter that uncertain balance of terror that stays the hand of mankind's final war.

So let us begin anew—remembering on both sides that civility is not a sign of weakness, and sincerity is always subject to proof. Let us never negotiate out of fear. But let us never fear to negotiate.

Let both sides explore what problems unite us instead of belaboring those problems which divide us.

Let both sides, for the first time, formulate serious and precise proposals for the inspection and control of arms—and bring the absolute power to destroy other nations under the absolute control of all nations.

Let both sides seek to invoke the wonders of science instead of its terrors. Together let us explore the stars, conquer the deserts, eradicate disease, tap the ocean depths and encourage the arts and commerce.

Let both sides unite to heed in all corners of the earth the command of Isaiah—to "undo the heavy burdens . . . (and) let the oppressed go free."

And if a beach-head of cooperation may push back the jungle of suspicion, let both sides join in creating a new endeavor, not a new balance of power, but a new world of law, where the strong are just and the weak secure and the peace preserved.

All this will not be finished in the first one hundred days. Nor will it be finished in the first one thousand days, nor in the life of this Administration, nor even perhaps in our lifetime on this planet. But let us begin.

In your hands, my fellow citizens, more than mine, will rest the final success or failure of our course. Since this country was founded, each generation of Americans has been summoned to give testimony to its national loyalty. The graves of young Americans who answered the call to service surround the globe.

Now the trumpet summons us again—not as a call to bear arms, though arms we need—not a call to battle, though embattled we are—but a call to bear the burden of a long twilight struggle, year in and year out, "rejoicing in hope, patient in tribulation"—a struggle against the common enemies of man: tyranny, poverty, disease and war itself.

Can we forge against these enemies a grand and global alliance, North and South, East and West, that can assure a more fruitful life for all mankind? Will you join in that historic effort?

In the long history of the world, only a few generations have been granted the role of defending freedom in its hours of maximum danger. I do not shrink from this responsibility—I welcome it. I do not believe that any of us would exchange places with any other people or any other generation. The energy, the faith, the devotion which we bring to this endeavor will light our country and all who serve it—and the glow from that fire can truly light the world.

And so, my fellow Americans: ask not what your country can do for you—ask what you can do for your country.

My fellow citizens of the world: ask not what America will do for you, but what together we can do for the freedom of man.

Finally, whether you are citizens of America or citizens of the world, ask of us here the same high standards of strength and sacrifice which we ask of you. With a good conscience our only sure reward, with history the final judge of our deeds, let us go forth to lead the land we love, asking His blessing and His help, but knowing that here on earth God's work must truly be our own.

The Cuban Missile Crisis

On October 15, 1962, President John F. Kennedy received photographic evidence that the Soviet Union had installed offensive nuclear missiles, aimed at the United States, just ninety miles from U.S. soil in Cuba. Kennedy secretly formed an "executive committee" (ExCom) of high administration officials to prepare a U.S. response. With advice from the committee, Kennedy decided to confront the Soviet Union by imposing a naval blockade around Cuba to prevent Soviet ships from bringing in supplies. Publicly and privately, Kennedy then demanded that the Soviet missiles be withdrawn. Nuclear war between the United States and the Soviet Union seemed more likely than at any other time in history.

Soviet reaction to the U.S. blockade and demand was hard to ascertain. A conciliatory message from Soviet leader Nikita Khrushchev was received on October 26; a harsh one followed on October 27. Kennedy decided to ignore the latter and reply to the former. Kennedy's October 27 letter to Khrushchev laid out the basis of the agreement that ended the crisis: the Soviet missiles would be removed in return for a U.S. pledge not to invade Cuba.

PRESIDENT KENNEDY'S LETTER TO KHRUSHCHEV

Dear Mr. Chairman:

I have read your letter of October 26th with great care and welcomed the statement of your desire to seek a prompt solution to the problem. The first thing that needs to be done, however, is for work to cease on offensive missile bases in Cuba and for all weapons systems in Cuba capable of offensive use to be rendered inoperable, under effective United Nations arrangements.

Assuming this is done promptly, I have given my representatives in New York instructions that will permit them to work out this weekend—in cooperation with the Acting Secretary General and your representative—an arrangement for a permanent solution to the Cuban problem along the lines suggested in your letter of Octo-

ber 26th. As I read your letter, the key elements of your proposals—which seem generally acceptable as I understand them—are as follows:

1) You would agree to remove these weapons systems from Cuba under appropriate United Nations observation and supervision; and undertake, with suitable safeguards, to halt the further introduction of such weapons systems into Cuba.

2) We, on our part, would agree—upon the establishment of adequate arrangements through the United Nations to ensure the carrying out and continuation of these commitments—(a) to remove promptly the quarantine measures now in effect and (b) to give assurances against an invasion of Cuba. I am confident that other nations of the Western Hemisphere would be prepared to do likewise.

If you will give your representative similar instructions, there is no reason why we should not be able to complete these arrangements and announce them to the world within a couple of days. The effect of such a settlement on easing world tensions would enable us to work toward a more general arrangement regarding "other armaments," as proposed in your second letter which you made public. I would like to say again that the United States is very much interested in reducing tensions and halting the arms race; and if your letter signifies that you are prepared to discuss a detente affecting NATO and the Warsaw Pact, we are quite prepared to consider with our allies any useful proposals.

But the first ingredient, let me emphasize, is the cessation of work on missile sites in Cuba and measures to render such weapons inoperable, under effective international guarantees. The continuation of this threat, or a prolonging of this discussion concerning Cuba by linking these problems to the broader questions of European and world security, would surely lead to an intensification of the Cuban crisis and a grave risk to the peace of the world. For this reason I hope we can quickly agree along the lines outlined in this letter and in your letter of October 26th.

Lyndon B. Johnson's "Great Society" Speech

Vice President Lyndon B. Johnson succeeded to the presidency when President John F. Kennedy was assassinated on November 22, 1963. Although Johnson initially offered "Let us continue" as the watchwords of his presidency, he was more concerned to make his own mark on history. Within a few months, Johnson chose the phrase "Great Society" as the theme for his administration. In a May 22, 1964, commencement address at the University of Michigan, he developed the theme in detail.

According to Johnson, the United States already had become "the rich society and the powerful society" and now was challenged to reach "upward." The effort to build a Great Society would have two main goals. The first was "an end to poverty and racial injustice." The other was "to advance the quality of our American civilization."

As president, Johnson was able to create and enact a number of new programs to address the goals of the Great Society, including Medicare, Medicaid, highway beautification, the National Endowment for the Arts, civil rights legislation, and others.

. . . The purpose of protecting the life of our Nation and preserving the liberty of our citizens is to pursue the happiness of our people. Our success in that pursuit is the test of our success as a nation. For a century we labored to settle and to subdue a continent. For half a century, we called upon unbounded invention and untiring industry to create an order of plenty for all of our people. The challenge of the next half century is whether we have the wisdom to use that wealth to enrich and elevate our national life, and to advance the quality of our American civilization.

Your imagination, your initiative and your indignation will determine whether we build a society where progress is the servant of our needs, or a society where old values and new visions are buried under unbridled growth.

For in your time we have the opportunity to move not only toward the rich society and the powerful society, but upward to the Great Society. The Great Society rests on abundance and liberty for all. It demands an end to poverty and racial injustice, to which we are totally committed in our time. But that is just the beginning.

The Great Society is a place where every child can find knowledge to enrich his mind and to enlarge his talents. It is a place where leisure is a welcome chance to build and reflect, not a feared cause of boredom and restlessness. It is a place where the city of man serves not only the needs of the body and the demands of commerce, but the desire for beauty and the hunger for community.

It is a place where man can renew contact with nature. It is a place which honors creation for its own sake and for what it adds to the understanding of the race. It is a place where men are more concerned with the quality of their goals than the quantity of their goods. But most of all, the great society is not a safe harbor, a resting place, a final objective, a finished work. It is a challenge constantly renewed, beckoning us toward a destiny where the meaning of our lives matches the marvelous products of our labor.

So I want to talk to you today about three places where we begin to build the Great Society—in our cities, in our countryside, and in our classrooms. . . .

Aristotle said, "Men come together in cities in order to live, but they remain together in order to live the good life."

It is harder and harder to live the good life in American cities today. The catalogue of ills is long: There is the decay of the centers and the despoiling of the suburbs. There is not enough housing for our people or transportation for our traffic. Open land is vanishing and old landmarks are violated. Worst of all, expansion is eroding the precious and time-honored values of community with neighbors and communion with nature. The loss of these values breeds loneliness and boredom and indifference. Our society will never be great until our cities are great. Today the frontier of imagination and innovation is inside those cities, and not beyond their borders. . . .

A second place where we begin to build the Great Society is in our countryside. We have always prided ourselves on being not only America the strong and America the free, but America the beautiful. Today that beauty is in danger. The water we drink, the food we eat, the very air that we breathe, are threatened with pollution. Our parks are overcrowded. Our seashores overburdened. Green fields and dense forests are disappearing.

A few years ago we were greatly concerned about the Ugly American. Today we must act to prevent an Ugly America.

For once the battle is lost, once our natural splendor is destroyed, it can never be recaptured. And once man can no longer walk with beauty or wonder at nature, his spirit will wither and his sustenance be wasted.

A third place to build the Great Society is in the classrooms of America. There your children's lives will be shaped. Our society will not be great until every young mind is set free to scan the farthest reaches of thought and imagination. We are still far from that goal. . . . In many places, classrooms are overcrowded and curricula are outdated. Most of our qualified teachers are underpaid, and many of our paid teachers are unqualified.

So we must give every child a place to sit and a teacher to learn from. Poverty must not be a bar to learning, and learning must offer an escape from poverty.

But more classrooms and more teachers are not enough. We must seek an educational system which grows in excellence as it grows in size. This means better training for our teachers. It means preparing youth to enjoy their hours of leisure as well as their hours of labor. It means exploring new techniques of teaching, to find new ways to stimulate the love of learning and the capacity for creation.

These are three of the central issues of the Great Society. While our government has many programs directed at those issues, I do not pretend that we have the full answer to those problems. But I do promise this: We are going to assemble the best thought and the broadest knowledge from all over the world to find those answers for America. . . .

There are those timid souls who say this battle cannot be won, that we are condemned to a soulless wealth. I do not agree. We have the power to shape the civilization that we want. But we need your will, your labor, your hearts, if we are to build that kind of society.

Those who came to this land sought to build more than just a new country. They sought a free world.

So I have come here today to your campus to say that you can make their vision our reality. Let us from this moment begin our work so that in the future men will look back and say: It was then, after a long and weary way, that man turned the exploits of his genius to the full enrichment of his life.

Thank you. Goodbye.

Lyndon B. Johnson's Gulf of Tonkin Message

Two themes dominated the five-year presidency of Lyndon B. Johnson: the Great Society and the war in Vietnam. In early 1964 Johnson aides privately prepared a congressional resolution that would give the president a virtual blank check to conduct the Vietnam War as he saw fit. Johnson feared that such a proposal would generate too much controversy. But on August 4, 1964, reports reached Washington (they were proved false much later) that U.S. naval vessels had been attacked by North Vietnamese patrol boats in the Gulf of Tonkin near North Vietnam. The next day, Johnson sent a message to Congress urging passage of "a Resolution expressing the support of Congress for all necessary action to protect our armed forces and to assist nations covered by the SEATO [Southeast Asia Treaty Organization] treaty," including South Vietnam. On August 6 the Gulf of Tonkin Resolution passed unanimously in the House of Representatives and with only two dissenting votes in the Senate. In later years, as the U.S. war effort became much larger and more controversial, Johnson cited the resolution as providing ample justification for his administration's policies. Privately, he compared it to "grandma's nightshirt—it covered everything."

To the Congress of the United States:

Last night I announced to the American people that the North Vietnamese regime had conducted further deliberate attacks against U.S. naval vessels operating in international waters, and that I had therefore directed air action against gun boats and supporting facilities used in these hostile operations. This air action has now been carried out with substantial damage to the boats and facilities. Two U.S. aircraft were lost in the action.

After consultation with the leaders of both parties in the Congress, I further announced a decision to ask the Congress for a Resolution expressing the unity and determination of the United States in supporting freedom and in protecting peace in Southeast Asia.

These latest actions of the North Vietnamese regime have given a new and grave turn to the already serious situation in Southeast Asia. Our commitments in that area are well known to the Congress. They were first made in 1954 by President Eisenhower. They were further defined in the Southeast Asia Collective Defense Treaty approved by the Senate in February 1955.

This Treaty with its accompanying protocol obligates the United States and other members to act in accordance with their Constitutional processes to meet Communist aggression against any of the parties or protocol states.

Our policy in Southeast Asia has been consistent and unchanged since 1954. I summarized it on June 2 in four simple propositions:

1. America keeps her word. Here as elsewhere, we must and shall honor our commitments.

2. The issue is the future of Southeast Asia as a whole. A threat to any nation in that region is a threat to all, and a threat to us.

3. Our purpose is peace. We have no military, political or territorial ambitions in the area.

4. This is not just a jungle war, but a struggle for freedom on every front of human activity. Our military and economic assistance to South Vietnam and Laos in particular has the purpose of helping these countries to repel aggression and strengthen their independence.

The threat to the free nations of Southeast Asia has long been clear. The North Vietnamese regime has constantly sought to take over South Vietnam and Laos. This Communist regime has violated the Geneva Accords for Vietnam. It has systematically conducted a campaign of subversion, which includes the direction, training, and supply of personnel and arms for the conduct of guerrilla warfare in South Vietnamese territory. In Laos, the North Vietnamese regime has maintained military forces, used Laotian territory for infiltration into South Vietnam, and most recently carried out combat operations—all in direct violation of the Geneva Agreements of 1962.

In recent months, the actions of the North Vietnamese regime have become steadily more threatening. In May, following new acts of Communist aggression in Laos, the United States undertook reconnaissance flights over Laotian territory, at the request of the Government of Laos. These flights had the essential mission of determining the situation in territory where Communist forces were preventing inspection by the International Control Commission. When the Communists attacked these aircraft, I responded by furnishing escort fighters with instructions to fire when fired upon. Thus, these latest North Vietnamese attacks on our naval vessels are not the first direct attack on armed forces of the United States.

As President of the United States I have concluded that I should now ask the Congress, on its part, to join in affirming the national determination that all such attacks will be met, and that the U.S. will continue in its basic policy of assisting the free nations of the area to defend their freedom.

As I have repeatedly made clear, the United States intends no rashness, and seeks no wider war. We must make it clear to all that the United States is united in its determination to bring about the end of Communist subversion and aggression in the area. We seek the full and effective restoration of the international agreements signed in Geneva in 1954, with respect to South Vietnam, and again in Geneva in 1962, with respect to Laos.

I recommend a Resolution expressing the support of the Congress for all necessary action to protect our armed forces and to assist nations covered by the SEATO Treaty. At the same time, I assure the Congress that we shall continue readily to explore any avenues of political solution that will effectively guarantee the removal of Communist subversion and the preservation of the independence of the nations of the area.

The Resolution could well be based upon similar resolutions enacted by the Congress in the past—to meet the threat to Formosa in 1955, to meet the threat to the Middle East in 1957, and to meet the threat in Cuba in 1962. It could state in the simplest terms the resolve and support of the Congress for action to deal appropriately with attacks against our armed forces and to defend freedom and preserve peace in southeast Asia in accordance with the obligations of the United States under the southeast Asia Treaty. I urge the Congress to enact such a Resolution promptly and thus to give convincing evidence to the aggressive Communist nations, and to the world as a whole, that our policy in Southeast Asia will be carried forward—and that the peace and security of the area will be preserved.

The events of this week would in any event have made the passage of a Congressional Resolution essential. But there is an additional reason for doing so at a time when we are entering on three months of political campaigning. Hostile nations must understand that in such a period the United States will continue to protect its national interests, and that in these matters there is no division among us.

Nixon's China Trip Announcement

On July 15, 1971, President Richard Nixon appeared on national television to read a three-and-one-half minute announcement that he would be traveling to China sometime in early 1972 at the invitation of the Chinese government. The purpose would be "to seek the normalization of relations" between the United States and the People's Republic of China. Nixon made the trip, which was the product of two years of secret negotiations, in February 1972.

Nixon's visit ended more than twenty years of hostility between the two nations, tracing back to the 1949 revolution in China in which communist forces led by Mao Tse-tung had overthrown the government of Chiang Kai-shek, a close ally of the United States. Ironically, Nixon's entire political career had been based on anticommunism, including strong support for Chiang, who had fled to the island of Formosa, claiming to be leader of the true government of China. Yet, as president, Nixon saw an opportunity for the United States to take advantage of the hostility between China and the Soviet Union. Many analysts believed that only a staunch anticommunist like Nixon could have ended U.S. hostility to the most populous nation in the world without provoking widespread political opposition.

Good evening.

I have requested this television time tonight to announce a major development in our efforts to build a lasting peace in the world.

As I have pointed out on a number of occasions over the past three years, there can be no stable and enduring peace without the participation of the Peoples Republic of China and its 750 million people. That is why I have undertaken initiatives in several areas to open the door for more normal relations between our two countries.

In pursuance of that goal, I sent Dr. Kissinger, my Assistant for National Security Affairs, to Peking during his recent world tour for the purpose of having talks with Premier Chou En-lai. The announcement I shall now read is being issued simultaneously in Peking and in the United States.

Premier Chou En-lai and Dr. Henry Kissinger, President Nixon's Assistant for National Security Affairs, held talks in Peking from July 9 to 11, 1971. Knowing of President Nixon's expressed desire to visit the Peoples Republic of China, Premier Chou En-lai, on behalf of the Government of the Peoples Republic of China, has extended an invitation to President Nixon to visit China at an appropriate date before May 1972. President Nixon has accepted the invitation with pleasure.

The meeting between the leaders of China and the United States is to seek the normalization of relations between the two countries and also to exchange views on questions of concern to the two sides. In anticipation of the inevitable speculation which will follow this announcement, I want to put our policy in the clearest possible context.

Our action in seeking a new relationship with the Peoples Republic of China will not be at the expense of our old friends. It is not directed against any other nation. We seek friendly relations with all nations. Any nation can be our friend without being any other nation's enemy.

I have taken this action because of my profound conviction that all nations will gain from a reduction of tensions and a better relationship between the United States and the Peoples Republic of China.

It is in that spirit that I will undertake what I deeply hope will become a journey for peace, peace not just for our generation, but for future generations on this earth we share together.

Thank you and good night.

Resignation of Vice President Agnew

Vice President Spiro T. Agnew, who was elected with President Richard Nixon in 1968 and reelected in 1972, resigned on October 10, 1973, as part of a plea bargain with federal prosecutors. The Justice Department had uncovered extensive evidence that Agnew received bribes from contractors while serving as county executive of Baltimore County, Maryland, governor of Maryland, and vice president. It was prepared to indict Agnew on conspiracy, extortion, bribery, and tax charges. In return for his resignation, however, Agnew was allowed (also on October 10) to plead nolo contendere (no contest) to one count of income tax evasion. He was fined $10,000 and sentenced to three years of unsupervised probation.

On the day of Agnew's resignation, the Justice Department submitted a forty-page document to a federal grand jury in Baltimore that listed the payoffs Agnew had accepted.

II. THE RELATIONSHIP BETWEEN MR. AGNEW AND ALLEN GREEN.

Shortly after Mr. Agnew's election in November 1966 as governor of Maryland, he complained to Allen Green, principal of a large engineering firm, about the financial burdens to be imposed upon Mr. Agnew by his role as Governor. Green responded by saying that his company had benefited from state work and had been able to generate some cash funds from which he would be willing to provide Mr. Agnew with some financial assistance. Mr. Agnew indicated that he would be grateful for such assistance.

Beginning shortly thereafter, Green delivered to Mr. Agnew six to nine times a year an envelope containing between $2,000 and $3,000 in cash. Green's purpose was to elicit from the Agnew administration as much state work for his engineering firm as possible. The purpose was clearly understood by Governor Agnew. . . .

Green continued to make cash payments to Vice President Agnew three or four times a year up to and including December 1972. These payments were usually about $2,000 each. The payments were made both in Mr. Agnew's vice presidential office and at his residence in the Sheraton-Park Hotel, Washington, D.C. The payments were not discontinued until after the initiation of the Baltimore County investigation by the United States Attorney for the District of Maryland in January 1973.

III. THE RELATIONSHIP BETWEEN MR. AGNEW AND LESTER MATZ.

Lester Matz, a principal in another large engineering firm, began making corrupt payments while Mr. Agnew was County Executive of

Baltimore County in the early 1970s. In those days, Matz paid 5 percent of his fees from Baltimore County contracts in cash to Mr. Agnew through one of Mr. Agnew's close associates.

After Mr. Agnew became Governor of Maryland, Matz decided to make his payments directly to Governor Agnew. He made no payments until that summer of 1968 when he and his partner calculated that they owed Mr. Agnew approximately $20,000 in consideration for the work which their firm had already received from the Governor's administration. The $20,000 in cash was generated in an illegal manner and was given by Matz to Governor Agnew in a manila envelope in Governor Agnew's office on or about July 16, 1968. . . .

Matz made no further corrupt payments to Mr. Agnew until shortly after Mr. Agnew became Vice President, at which time Matz calculated that he owed Mr. Agnew approximately $10,000 more from jobs and fees which the Matz firm had received from Governor Agnew's administration since July 1968. After generating $10,000 in cash in an illegal manner, Matz met with Mr. Agnew in the Vice President's office and gave him approximately $10,000 cash in an envelope. . . .

In or around April 1971, Matz made a cash payment to Vice President Agnew of $2,500 in return for the awarding by the General Services Administration of a contract to a small engineering firm in which Matz had a financial ownership interest. An intermediary was instrumental in the arrangement for that particular corrupt payment.

Proposed Articles of Impeachment of Richard Nixon

On June 17, 1972, burglars secretly employed by the Committee to Re-elect the President were caught breaking into the offices of the Democratic National Committee in Washington's Watergate Hotel. The chain of command that had authorized the break-in, as well as a host of other illegal and unethical campaign activities, reached high into the Nixon administration. In an effort to avoid embarrassing revelations, President Richard Nixon and some of his closest aides responded to news of the burglary by trying to obstruct official investigations into what had happened.

Through a combination of activities—including diligent investigations by reporters Bob Woodward and Carl Bernstein of the Washington Post, *thorough hearings by a special bipartisan Senate committee chaired by Democratic senator Sam Ervin of North Carolina, testimony by John Dean and other participants in the Watergate affair, and the release of secret White House tape recordings—evidence of Nixon's involvement in the Watergate coverup was brought to light.*

In February 1974 the House of Representatives charged its Judiciary Committee to consider impeaching the president for "High Crimes and Misdemeanors." Between July 27 and 29 the committee voted to recommend three articles of impeachment to the full House. Article I describes Nixon's role in the Watergate coverup, Article II details other abuses of power by the president, and Article III charges Nixon with contempt of Congress for his failure to honor the Judiciary Committee's subpoenas, mostly for certain tape recordings. Two other proposed articles—one dealing with Nixon's secret bombings of Cambodia, the other with his income taxes—were rejected by the committee on July 30.

ARTICLE I

In his conduct of the office of President of the United States, Richard M. Nixon, in violation of his constitutional oath faithfully to execute the office of President of the United States and, to the best of his ability, preserve, protect, and defend the Constitution of the United States, and in violation of his constitutional duty to take care that the laws be faithfully executed, has prevented, obstructed, and impeded the administration of justice, in that: On June 17, 1972, and prior thereto, agents of the Committee for the Re-Election of the President committed unlawful entry of the headquarters of the Democratic National Committee in Washington, District of Columbia, for the purpose of securing political intelligence. Subsequent thereto, Richard M. Nixon, using the powers of his high office, engaged personally and through his close subordinates and agents, in a course of conduct or plan designed to delay, impede, and obstruct the investigation of such unlawful entry; to cover up, conceal and protect those responsible; and to conceal the existence and scope of other unlawful covert activities.

The means used to implement this course of conduct or plan included one or more of the following:

(1) making false or misleading statements to lawfully authorized investigative officers and employees of the United States;

(2) withholding relevant and material evidence or information from lawfully authorized investigative officers and employees of the United States;

(3) approving, condoning, acquiescing in, and counseling witnesses with respect to the giving of false or misleading statements to lawfully authorized investigative officers and employees of the United States and false or misleading testimony in duly instituted judicial and congressional proceedings;

(4) interfering or endeavoring to interfere with the conduct of investigations by the Department of Justice of the United States, the Federal Bureau of Investigation, the Office of Watergate Special Prosecution Force, and Congressional Committees;

(5) approving, condoning, and acquiescing in, the surreptitious payment of substantial sums of money for the purpose of obtaining the silence or influencing the testimony of witnesses, potential witnesses or individuals who participated in such unlawful entry and other illegal activities;

(6) endeavoring to misuse the Central Intelligence Agency, an agency of the United States;

(7) disseminating information received from officers of the Department of Justice of the United States to subjects of investigations conducted by lawfully authorized investigative officers and employees of the United States, for the purpose of aiding and assisting such subjects in their attempts to avoid criminal liability;

(8) making or causing to be made false or misleading public statements for the purpose of deceiving the people of the United States into believing that a thorough and complete investigation had been conducted with respect to allegations of misconduct on the part of personnel of the executive branch of the United States and personnel of the Committee for the Re-Election of the President, and that there was no involvement of such personnel in such misconduct; or

(9) endeavoring to cause prospective defendants, and individuals duly tried and convicted, to expect favored treatment and consideration in return for their silence or false testimony, or rewarding individuals for their silence or false testimony.

In all of this, Richard M. Nixon has acted in a manner contrary to his trust as President and subversive of constitutional government, to the great prejudice of the cause of law and justice and to the manifest injury of the people of the United States.

Wherefore Richard M. Nixon, by such conduct, warrants impeachment and trial, and removal from office.

[—Adopted July 27 by a 27–11 vote]

ARTICLE II

Using the powers of the office of President of the United States, Richard M. Nixon, in violation of his constitutional oath faithfully to execute the office of President of the United States and, to the best of his ability, preserve, protect, and defend the Constitution of the United States, and in disregard of his constitutional duty to take care that the laws be faithfully executed, has repeatedly engaged in conduct violating the constitutional rights of citizens, impairing the due and proper administration of justice and the conduct of lawful inquiries, or contravening the laws governing agencies of the executive branch and the purposes of these agencies.

This conduct has included one or more of the following:

(1) He has, acting personally and through his subordinates and agents, endeavored to obtain from the Internal Revenue Service, in violation of the constitutional rights of citizens, confidential information contained in income tax returns for purposes not authorized by law, and to cause, in violation of the constitutional rights of citizens, income tax audits or other income tax investigations to be initiated or conducted in a discriminatory manner.

(2) He misused the Federal Bureau of Investigation, the Secret Service, and other executive personnel, in violation or disregard of the constitutional rights of citizens, by directing or authorizing such agencies or personnel to conduct or continue electronic surveillance or other investigations for purposes unrelated to national security, the enforcement of laws, or any other lawful function of his office; he did direct, authorize, or permit the use of information obtained thereby for purposes unrelated to national security, the enforcement of laws, or any other lawful function of his office; and he did direct the concealment of certain records made by the Federal Bureau of Investigation of electronic surveillance.

(3) He has, acting personally and through his subordinates and agents, in violation or disregard of the constitutional rights of citizens, authorized and permitted to be maintained a secret investigative unit within the office of the President, financed in part with money derived from campaign contributions, which unlawfully utilized the resources of the Central Intelligence Agency, engaged in covert and unlawful activities, and attempted to prejudice the constitutional right of an accused to a fair trial.

(4) He has failed to take care that the laws were faithfully executed by failing to act when he knew or had reason to know that his close subordinates endeavored to impede and frustrate lawful inquiries by duly constituted executive, judicial, and legislative entities concerning the unlawful entry into the headquarters of the Democratic National Committee, and the cover up thereof, and concerning other unlawful activities including those relating to the confirmation of Richard Kleindienst as Attorney General of the United States, the electronic surveillance of private citizens, the break-in into the offices of Dr. Lewis Fielding and the campaign financing practices of the Committee to Re-elect the President.

(5) In disregard of the rule of law, he knowingly misused the executive branch, including the Federal Bureau of Investigation, the Criminal Division, and the Office of Watergate Special Prosecution Force, of the Department of Justice, and the Central Intelligence Agency, in violation of his duty to take care that the laws be faithfully executed.

In all of this, Richard M. Nixon has acted in a manner contrary to his trust as President and subversive of constitutional government, to the great prejudice of the cause of law and justice and to the manifest injury of the people of the United States.

Wherefore Richard M. Nixon, by such conduct, warrants impeachment and trial, and removal from office.

[—Adopted July 29 by a 28–10 vote]

ARTICLE III

In his conduct of the office of President of the United States, Richard M. Nixon, contrary to his oath faithfully to execute the office of President of the United States and, to the best of his ability, preserve, protect, and defend the Constitution of the United States, and in violation of his constitutional duty to take care that the laws be faithfully executed, has failed without lawful cause of excuse to produce papers and things as directed by duly authorized subpoenas issued by the Committee on the Judiciary of the House of Representatives on April 11, 1974, May 15, 1974, May 30, 1974, and June 24, 1974, and willfully disobeyed such subpoenas. The subpoenaed papers and things were deemed necessary by the Committee in order to resolve by direct evidence fundamental, factual questions relating to Presidential direction, knowledge, or approval of actions demonstrated by other evidence to be substantial grounds for impeachment of the President. In refusing to produce these papers and things Richard M. Nixon, substituting his judgment as to what materials were necessary for the inquiry, interposed the powers of the Presidency against the lawful subpoenas of the House of Representatives, thereby assuming to himself functions and judgments necessary to the exercise of the sole power of impeachment vested by the Constitution in the House of Representatives.

In all of this, Richard M. Nixon has acted in a manner contrary to his trust as President and subversive of constitutional government, to the great prejudice of the cause of law and justice, and to the manifest injury of the people of the United States.

Wherefore, Richard M. Nixon by such conduct, warrants impeachment and trial, and removal from office.

[—Adopted July 30 by a 21–17 vote]

Nixon's "Smoking-Gun" Tape

In 1973 the special Senate Watergate committee learned that President Richard Nixon had installed a secret, voice-activated taping system in the Oval Office and other presidential offices. Under severe political and legal pressure, Nixon released many of the tape recordings but withheld others. On July 24, 1974, just before the House Judiciary Committee voted to recommend articles of impeachment, a unanimous U.S.

Supreme Court ordered Nixon to release more tapes in the case of United States v. Nixon.

Included in the tapes, which Nixon made public August 5, was a ninety-five-minute Oval Office meeting between the president and his chief of staff, H. R. Haldeman. At that meeting, Nixon instructed Haldeman to have the Central Intelligence Agency (CIA) falsely tell the

Federal Bureau of Investigation (FBI) that the FBI should tread lightly in its investigation because the June 17, 1972, Watergate break-in was a CIA activity.

The June 23 tape was the "smoking gun" in the Watergate investigation—the first piece of evidence that indisputably demonstrated Nixon's active role in the coverup. Republicans in Congress, including members of the House Judiciary Committee who had voted against recommending impeachment, publicly denounced Nixon, all but guaranteeing that the House of Representatives would vote to impeach the president and that the Senate would vote to convict. On August 9, 1974, Nixon became the first U.S. president to resign the office.

Haldeman. Now, on the investigation, you know the Democratic break-in thing, we're back in the problem area because the FBI is not under control, because Gray [acting FBI director L. Patrick Gray III] doesn't exactly know how to control it and they have—their investigation is now leading into some productive areas—because they've been able to trace the money—not through the money itself—but through the bank sources—the banker. And, and it goes in some directions we don't want it to go. Ah, also there have been some things—like an informant came in off the street to the FBI in Miami who was a photographer or has a friend who is a photographer who developed some films through this guy Barker [Bernard L. Barker, one of the five men caught in the Watergate break-in] and the films had pictures of Democratic National Committee letterhead documents and things. So it's things like that that are filtering in. Mitchell [former attorney general John N. Mitchell] came up with yesterday, and [White House counsel] John Dean analyzed very carefully last night and concludes, concurs now with Mitchell's recommendation that the only way to solve this, and we're set up beautifully to do it, ah, in that and that—the only network that paid any attention to it last night was NBC—they did a massive story on the Cuban thing.

President. That's right.

H. That the way to handle this now is for us to have Walters [deputy CIA director Vernon A. Walters] call Pat Gray and just say, "Stay to hell out of this—this is ah, business here we don't want you to go any further on it." That's not an unusual development, and ah, that would take care of it.

P. What about Pat Gray—you mean Pat Gray doesn't want to?

H. Pat does want to. He doesn't know how to, and he doesn't have, he doesn't have any basis for doing it. Given this, he will then have the basis. He'll call Mark Felt in [W. Mark Felt, FBI deputy associate director in 1972], and the two of them—and Mark Felt wants to cooperate because he's ambitious—

P. Yeah.

H. He'll call him in and say, "We've got the signal from across the river to put the hold on this." And that will fit rather well because the FBI agents who are working the case, at this point, feel that's what it is.

P. This is CIA? They've traced the money? Who'd they trace it to?

H. Well they've traced it to a name, but they haven't gotten to the guy yet.

P. Would it be somebody here?

H. Ken Dahlberg.

P. Who the hell is Ken Dahlberg?

H. He gave $25,000 in Minnesota and, ah, the check went directly to this guy Barker.

P. It isn't from the Committee, though, from [Nixon reelection committee finance chairman Maurice H.] Stans?

H. Yeah. It is. It's directly traceable and there's some more through some Texas people that went to the Mexican bank which can also be traced to the Mexican bank—they'll get their names today.

H.—And (pause)

P. Well, I mean, there's no way—I'm just thinking if they don't cooperate, what do they say? That they were approached by the Cubans. That's what Dahlberg has to say, the Texans too, that they—

H. Well, if they will. But then we're relying on more and more people all the time. That's the problem and they'll stop if we could take this other route.

P. All right.

H. And you seem to think the thing to do is get them to stop?

P. Right, fine.

H. They say the only way to do that is from White House instructions. And it's got to be to Helms [CIA director Richard C. Helms] and to—ah, what's his name . . .? Walters.

P. Walters.

H. And the proposal would be that [domestic policy adviser John D.] Ehrlichman and I call them in, and say, ah—

P. All right, fine. How do you call him in—I mean you just—well, we protected Helms from one hell of a lot of things.

H. That's what Ehrlichman says.

P. Of course, this Hunt [E. Howard Hunt, Jr., a White House consultant], that will uncover a lot of things. You open that scab there's a hell of a lot of things and we just feel that it would be very detrimental to have this thing go any further. This involves these Cubans, Hunt, and a lot of hanky-panky that we have nothing to do with ourselves. Well what the hell, did Mitchell know about this?

H. I think so. I don't think he knew the details, but I think he knew.

P. He didn't know how it was going to be handled though—with Dahlberg and the Texans and so forth? Well who was the asshole that did? Is it Liddy? [G. Gordon Liddy, former FBI agent] Is that the fellow? He must be a little nuts!

H. He is.

P. I mean he just isn't well screwed on is he? Is that the problem?

H. No, but he was under pressure, apparently, to get more information, and as he got more pressure, he pushed the people harder to move harder—

P. Pressure from Mitchell?

H. Apparently.

P. Oh, Mitchell. Mitchell was at the point (unintelligible).

H. Yeah.

P. All right, fine, I understand it all. We won't second-guess Mitchell and the rest. Thank God it wasn't Colson [Charles W. Colson, White House special counsel]

H. The FBI interviewed Colson yesterday. They determined that would be a good thing to do. To have him take an interrogation, which he did, and that—the FBI guys working the case concluded that there were one or two possibilities—one, that this was a White House—they don't think that there is anything at the Election Committee—they think it was either a White House operation and they had some obscure reasons for it—non-political, or it was a—Cuban and the CIA. And after their interrogation of Colson yesterday, they concluded it was not the White House, but are now convinced it is a CIA thing, so the CIA turnoff would—

P. Well, not sure of their analysis, I'm not going to get that involved. I'm (unintelligible).

H. No, sir, we don't want you to.

P. You call them in.

H. Good deal.

P. Play it tough. That's the way they play it and that's the way we are going to play it.

H. O.K.

P. When I saw that news summary, I questioned whether it's a bunch of crap, but I thought, er, well it's good to have them off us awhile, because when they start bugging us, which they have, our little boys will not know how to handle it. I hope they will though.

H. You never know.

P. Good.

[Other matters are discussed. Then the conversation returns to the break-in coverup strategy.]

P. When you get in—when you get in (unintelligible) people, say, "Look the problem is that this will open the whole, the whole Bay of Pigs thing, and the President just feels that ah, without going into the details—don't, don't lie to them to the extent to say there is no involvement, but just say this is a comedy of errors, without getting into it, the President believes that it is going to open the whole Bay of Pigs thing up again. And, ah, because these people are plugging for (unintelligible) and that they should call the FBI in and (unintelligible) don't go any further into this case period! (Inaudible) our cause—

H. Get more done for our cause by the opposition than by us.

P. Well, can you get it done?

H. I think so.

Nixon's Resignation Speech

After protesting many times that he would defend his presidency until the end, President Richard Nixon announced in a televised address August 8, 1974, that he would resign effective noon the next day. Impeachment and conviction were certain—also for Nixon to fight on would cost him the extensive benefits that former presidents receive and increase the likelihood that he would be prosecuted for his role in the Watergate coverup.

In his speech, Nixon admitted only to having made mistaken judgments, claiming that even "they were made in what I believed at the time to be the best interest of the Nation." He also suggested that but for the political hopelessness of his position, and the paralysis that a long impeachment process would cause in the government, the right thing to do would be to continue his fight for vindication.

Good evening.

This is the 37th time I have spoken to you from this office, where so many decisions have been made that shaped the history of this Nation. Each time I have done so to discuss with you some matter that I believe affected the national interest.

In all the decisions I have made in my public life, I have always tried to do what was best for the Nation. Throughout the long and difficult period of Watergate, I have felt it was my duty to persevere, to make every possible effort to complete the term of office to which you elected me.

In the past few days, however, it has become evident to me that I no longer have a strong enough political base in the Congress to justify continuing that effort. As long as there was a base, I felt strongly that it was necessary to see the constitutional process through to its conclusion. . . .

But with the disappearance of that base, I now believe that the constitutional purpose has been served, and there is no longer a need for the process to be prolonged. . . .

I have never been a quitter. To leave office before my term is completed is abhorrent to every instinct in my body. But as President, I must put the interest of America first. America needs a full-time President and a full-time Congress, particularly at this time with problems we face at home and abroad.

To continue to fight through the months ahead for my personal vindication would almost totally absorb the time and attention of both the President and the Congress in a period when our entire focus should be on the great issues of peace abroad and prosperity without inflation at home.

Therefore, I shall resign the Presidency effective at noon tomorrow. Vice President Ford will be sworn in as President at that hour in this office.

As I recall the high hopes for America with which we began this second term, I feel a great sadness that I will not be here in this office working on your behalf to achieve those hopes in the next 2 and a half years. But in turning over direction of the Government to Vice President Ford, I know, as I told the Nation when I nominated him for that office 10 months ago, that the leadership of America will be in good hands. . . .

By taking this action, I hope that I will have hastened the start of that process of healing which is so desperately needed in America.

I regret deeply any injuries that may have been done in the course of the events that led to this decision. I would say only that if some of my judgments were wrong, and some were wrong, they were made in what I believed at the time to be the best interest of the Nation.

To those who have stood with me during these past difficult months, to my family, my friends, to many others who joined in supporting my cause because they believed it was right, I will be eternally grateful for your support.

And to those who have not felt able to give me your support, let me say I leave with no bitterness toward those who have opposed me, because all of us, in the final analysis, have been concerned with the good of the country, however our judgments might differ.

So, let us all now join together in affirming that common commitment and in helping our new President succeed for the benefit of all Americans.

I shall leave this office with regret at not completing my term, but with gratitude for the privilege of serving as your President for the past 5 and a half years. These years have been a momentous time in the history of our Nation and the world. They have been a time of achievement in which we can all be proud, achievements that represent the shared efforts of the Administration, the Congress, and the people.

But the challenges ahead are equally great, and they, too, will require the support and the efforts of the Congress and the people working in cooperation with the new Administration.

We have ended America's longest war, but in the work of securing a lasting peace in the world, the goals ahead are even more far-reaching and more difficult. We must complete a structure of peace so that it will be said of this generation, our generation of Americans, by the people of all nations, not only that we ended one war but that we prevented future wars.

We have unlocked the doors that for a quarter of a century stood between the United States and the People's Republic of China.

We must now ensure that the one quarter of the world's people who live in the People's Republic of China will be and remain not our enemies but our friends.

In the Middle East, 100 million people in the Arab countries, many of whom have considered us their enemy for nearly 20 years, now look on us as their friends. We must continue to build on that friendship so that peace can settle at last over the Middle East and so that the cradle of civilization will not become its grave.

Together with the Soviet Union we have made the crucial breakthroughs that have begun the process of limiting nuclear arms. But we must set as our goal not just limiting but reducing and finally destroying these terrible weapons so that they cannot destroy civilization and so that the threat of nuclear war will no longer hang over the world and the people.

We have opened the new relation with the Soviet Union. We must continue to develop and expand that new relationship so that the two strongest nations of the world will live together in cooperation rather than confrontation.

Around the world, in Asia, in Africa, in Latin America, in the Middle East, there are millions of people who live in terrible poverty, even starvation. We must keep as our goal turning away from production for war and expanding production for peace so that people everywhere on this earth can at last look forward in their children's time, if not in our own time, to having the necessities for a decent life.

Here in America, we are fortunate that most of our people have not only the blessings of liberty but also the means to live full and good and, by the world's standards, even abundant lives. We must press on, however, toward a goal of not only more and better jobs but of full opportunity for every American and of what we are striving so hard right now to achieve, prosperity without inflation.

For more than a quarter of a century in public life I have shared in the turbulent history of this era. I have fought for what I believed in. I have tried to the best of my ability to discharge those duties and meet those responsibilities that were entrusted to me.

Sometimes I have succeeded and sometimes I have failed, but always I have taken heart from what Theodore Roosevelt once said about the man in the arena, "whose face is marred by dust and sweat and blood, who strives valiantly, who errs and comes short again and again because there is not effort without error and shortcoming, but who does actually strive to do the deed, who knows the great enthusiasms, the great devotions, who spends himself in a worthy cause, who at the best knows in the end the triumphs of high achievements and who at the worst, if he fails, at least fails while daring greatly."

I pledge to you tonight that as long as I have a breath of life in my body, I shall continue in that spirit. I shall continue to work for the great causes to which I have been dedicated throughout my years as a Congressman, a Senator, a Vice President, and President, the cause of peace not just for America but among all nations, prosperity, justice, and opportunity for all of our people.

There is one cause above all to which I have been devoted and to which I shall always be devoted for as long as I live.

When I first took the oath of office as President 5 and a half years ago, I made this sacred commitment, to "consecrate my office, my energies, and all the wisdom I can summon to the cause of peace among nations."

I have done my very best in all the days since to be true to that pledge. As a result of these efforts, I am confident that the world is a safer place today, not only for the people of America but for the people of all nations, and that all of our children have a better chance than before of living in peace rather than dying in war.

This, more than anything, is what I hoped to achieve when I sought the Presidency. This, more than anything, is what I hope will be my legacy to you, to our country, as I leave the Presidency.

To have served in this office is to have felt a very personal sense of kinship with each and every American. In leaving it, I do so with this prayer: May God's grace be with you in all the days ahead.

Ford's Remarks on Becoming President

Section 2 of the Twenty-fifth Amendment (1967) charges the president to fill a vacancy in the vice presidency by nominating a new vice president, subject to the approval of both houses of Congress, voting separately. When Vice President Spiro T. Agnew resigned in 1973, President Richard Nixon nominated House minority leader Gerald R. Ford of Michigan to be vice president. Congress confirmed the nomination overwhelmingly.

From the moment of his appointment, Ford was aware that he might be called upon to serve as president if Nixon either resigned or was removed from office. When Nixon's resignation took effect at noon on August 9, 1974, Ford was sworn in by Chief Justice Warren E. Burger. In his brief remarks, Ford proclaimed that "our long national nightmare is over." Aware that he was the first unelected vice president to become president, Ford said: "I am acutely aware that you have not elected me your President by your ballots, and so I ask that you confirm me as your President with your prayers."

Mr. Chief Justice, my dear friends, my fellow Americans:

The oath that I have taken is the same oath that was taken by George Washington and by every President under the Constitution. But I assume the Presidency under extraordinary circumstances, never before experienced by Americans. This is an hour of history that troubles our minds and hurts our hearts.

Therefore, I feel it is my first duty to make an unprecedented compact with my countrymen. Not an inaugural address, not a fireside chat, not a campaign speech—just a little straight talk among friends. And I intend it to be the first of many.

I am acutely aware that you have not elected me as your President by your ballots, and so I ask you to confirm me as your President with your prayers. And I hope that such prayers will be the first of many.

If you have not chosen me by secret ballot, neither have I gained office by any secret promises. I have not campaigned either for the Presidency or the Vice Presidency. I have not subscribed to any partisan platform. I am indebted to no man, and only to one woman—my dear wife—as I begin this very difficult job.

I have not sought this enormous responsibility, but I will not shirk it. Those who nominated and confirmed me as Vice President were my friends and are my friends. They were of both parties, elected by all the people and acting under the Constitution in their name. It is only fitting then that I should pledge to them and to you that I will be the President of all the people.

Thomas Jefferson said the people are the only sure reliance for the preservation of our liberty. And down the years, Abraham Lincoln renewed this American article of faith saying, "Is there any better way or equal hope in the world?"

I intend, on Monday next, to request of the Speaker of the House of Representatives and the President pro tempore of the Senate the privilege of appearing before the Congress to share with my former colleagues and with you, the American people, my views on the priority business of the Nation and to solicit your views and their views. And may I say to the Speaker and the others, if I could meet with you right after these remarks, I would appreciate it.

Even though this is late in an election year, there is no way we can go forward except together and no way anybody can win except by serving the people's urgent needs. We cannot stand still or slip backwards. We must go forward now together.

To the peoples and the governments of all friendly nations, and I hope that could encompass the whole world, I pledge an uninterrupted and sincere search for peace. America will remain strong and united, but its strength will remain dedicated to the safety and sanity of the entire family of man, as well as to our own precious freedom.

I believe that truth is the glue that holds governments together, not only our Government, but civilization itself. That bond, though strained, is unbroken at home and abroad.

In all my public and private acts as your President, I expect to follow my instincts of openness and candor with full confidence that honesty is always the best policy in the end.

My fellow Americans, our long national nightmare is over. Our Constitution works; our great Republic is a Government of laws and not of men. Here the people rule. But there is a higher power, by whatever name we honor him, who ordains not only righteousness but love, not only justice but mercy.

As we bind up the internal wounds of Watergate, more painful and more poisonous than those of foreign wars, let us restore the golden rule to our political process, and let brotherly love purge our hearts of suspicion and of hate.

In the beginning, I asked you to pray for me. Before closing, I ask again your prayers, for Richard Nixon and his family. May our former President, who brought peace to millions, find it for himself. May God bless and comfort his wonderful wife and daughters, whose love and loyalty will forever be a shining legacy to all who bear the lonely burdens of the White House.

I can only guess at those burdens, although I have witnessed at close hand the tragedies that befell three Presidents and the lesser trials of others.

With all the strength and all the good sense I have gained from life, with all the confidence my family, my friends, and my dedicated staff impart to me, and with the good will of countless Americans I have encountered in recent visits to 40 states, I now solemnly reaffirm my promise I made to you last December 6: to uphold the Constitution, to do what is right as God gives me to see the right, and to do the very best I can for America.

God helping me, I will not let you down.

Thank you.

The Nixon Pardon

President Richard Nixon's resignation on August 9, 1974, left him subject to indictment, trial, and possible conviction for obstructing justice in the Watergate investigation. On September 8, President Gerald R. Ford used the pardon power of his office to grant Nixon a "full, free and absolute pardon . . . for all offenses against the United States which he . . . has committed or may have committed."

In announcing the pardon, Ford noted several reasons for his decision, including the former president's health and mental anguish and the difficulty of securing a fair trial. More than anything else, though, Ford argued that someone must write "The End" to the "American tragedy" of the Watergate affair, lest "ugly passions . . . again be aroused."

Ford paid a severe political price for the Nixon pardon. He was roundly criticized and his approval rating dropped 20 percentage points in the polls.

. . . The Constitution is the supreme law of our land and it governs our actions as citizens. Only the laws of God, which govern our consciences, are superior to it. As we are a nation under God, so I am sworn to uphold our laws with the help of God. And I have sought such guidance and searched my own conscience with special diligence to determine the right thing for me to do with respect to my predecessor in this place, Richard Nixon, and his loyal wife and family.

Theirs is an American tragedy in which we all have played a part. It could go on and on and on, or someone must write "The End" to it.

I have concluded that only I can do that. And if I can, I must.

There are no historic or legal precedents to which I can turn in this matter, none that precisely fit the circumstances of a private citizen who has resigned the presidency of the United States. But it is common knowledge that serious allegations and accusations hang like a sword over our former President's head, threatening his health, as he tries to reshape his life, a great part of which was spent in the service of this country and by the mandate of its people.

After years of bitter controversy and divisive national debate, I have been advised and I am compelled to conclude that many months and perhaps more years will have to pass before Richard Nixon could obtain a fair trial by jury in any jurisdiction of the United States under governing decisions of the Supreme Court.

I deeply believe in equal justice for all Americans, whatever their station or former station. The law, whether human or divine, is no respecter of persons but the law is a respecter of reality. The facts as I see them are that a former President of the United States, instead of enjoying equal treatment with any other citizen accused of violating the law, would be cruelly and excessively penalized either in preserving the presumption of his innocence or in obtaining a speedy determination of his guilt in order to repay a legal debt to society.

During this long period of delay and potential litigation, ugly passions would again be aroused, and our people would again be polarized in their opinions, and the credibility of our free institutions of government would again be challenged at home and abroad. In the end, the courts might well hold that Richard Nixon had been denied due process and the verdict of history would even more be inconclusive with respect to those charges arising out of the period of his presidency of which I am presently aware.

But it is not the ultimate fate of Richard Nixon that most concerns me—though surely it deeply troubles every decent and every compassionate person. My concern is the immediate future of this great country. In this I dare not depend upon my personal sympathy as a longtime friend of the former President nor my professional judgment as a lawyer. And I do not.

As President, my greatest concern must always be the greatest good of all the people of the United States, whose servant I am.

As a man, my first consideration is to be true to my own convictions and my own conscience. My conscience tells me clearly and certainly that I cannot prolong the bad dreams that continue to reopen a chapter that is closed.

My conscience tells me that only I, as President, have the constitutional power to firmly shut and seal this book. My conscience says it is my duty, not merely to proclaim domestic tranquility, but to use every means that I have to ensure it.

I do believe that the buck stops here, that I cannot rely upon public opinion polls to tell me what is right. I do believe that right makes might, and that if I am wrong 10 angels swearing I was right would make no difference. I do believe with all my heart and mind and spirit that I, not as President, but as a humble servant of God, will receive justice without mercy if I fail to show mercy.

Finally, I feel that Richard Nixon and his loved ones have suffered enough, and will continue to suffer no matter what I do, no matter what we as a great and good nation can do together to make his goal of peace come true.

Now, therefore, I, Gerald R. Ford, President of the United States, pursuant to the pardon power conferred upon me by Article II, Section 2, of the Constitution, have granted and by these presents do grant a full, free, and absolute pardon unto Richard Nixon for all offenses against the United States which he, Richard Nixon, has committed or may have committed or taken part in during the period from January 20, 1969, through August 9, 1974.

In witness whereof, I have hereunto set my hand this 8th day of September in the year of our Lord Nineteen Hundred Seventy Four, and of the independence of the United States of America the 199th.

Carter's Remarks on the Signing of the Camp David Accords

On September 17, 1978, American president Jimmy Carter, Israeli prime minister Menachem Begin, and Egyptian president Anwar Sadat concluded thirteen days of negotiations at Camp David by announcing that two agreements had been signed. Taken together, the two documents—called "A Framework for Peace in the Middle East Agreed to at Camp David" and "A Framework for the Conclusion of a Peace Treaty Between Egypt and Israel"—provided an outline for peace in the Middle East. The former attempted (unsuccessfully, it later turned out) to provide a structure to settle the issue of control of the West Bank, which Israel had seized from the Arab nation of Jordan in the June 1967 war. The latter, which proved to be more successful, provided in part for the return of Israeli-occupied territory in the Sinai desert to Egypt in return for a treaty of peace between the two nations. The agreements were announced jointly by Carter, Begin, and Sadat on the evening of September 17. Both foreign leaders praised Carter effusively for keeping the negotiations going and bringing them to a successful conclusion.

When we first arrived at Camp David, the first thing upon which we agreed was to ask the people of the world to pray that our negotiations would be successful. Those prayers have been answered far beyond any expectations. We are privileged to witness tonight a significant achievement in the cause of peace, an achievement none thought possible a year ago, or even a month ago, an achievement that reflects the courage and wisdom of these two leaders.

Through 13 long days at Camp David, we have seen them display determination and vision and flexibility which was needed to make this agreement come to pass. All of us owe them our gratitude and respect. They know that they will always have my personal admiration.

There are still great difficulties that remain and many hard issues to be settled. The questions that have brought warfare and bitterness to the Middle East for the last 30 years will not be settled overnight. But we should all recognize the substantial achievements that have been made.

One of the agreements that President Sadat and Prime Minister Begin are signing tonight is entitled, "A Framework For Peace in the Middle East."

This framework concerns the principles and some specifics in the most substantive way which will govern a comprehensive peace settlement. It deals specifically with the future of the West Bank and Gaza, and the need to resolve the Palestinian problem in all its aspects. The framework document proposes a five-year transitional period in the West Bank and Gaza during which the Israeli military government will be withdrawn and a self-governing authority will be elected with full autonomy.

It also provides for Israeli forces to remain in specified locations during this period to protect Israel's security.

The Palestinians will have the right to participate in the determination of their own future, in negotiations which will resolve the final status of the West Bank and Gaza, and then to produce an Israeli-Jordanian peace treaty.

These negotiations will be based on all the provisions and all the principles of the United Nations Security Council Resolution 242. And it provides that Israel may live in peace within secure and recognized borders.

This great aspiration of Israel has been certified without constraint with the greatest degree of enthusiasm by President Sadat, the leader of one of the greatest nations on earth.

The other document is entitled, "Framework For the Conclusion of a Peace Treaty," between Egypt and Israel.

It provides for the full exercise of Egyptian sovereignty over the Sinai. It calls for the full withdrawal of Israeli forces from the Sinai; and after an interim withdrawal which will be accomplished very quickly, the establishment of normal, peaceful relations between the two countries, including diplomatic relations.

Together with accompanying letters, which we will make public tomorrow, these two Camp David agreements provide the basis for progress and peace throughout the Middle East.

There is one issue on which agreement has not been reached. Egypt states that the agreement to remove Israeli settlements from Egyptian territory is a prerequisite to a peace treaty. Israel states that the issue of Israeli settlements should be resolved during the peace negotiations. That is a substantial difference.

Within the next two weeks, the Knesset [Israel's parliament] will decide on the issue of these settlements.

Tomorrow night, I will go before the Congress to explain these agreements more fully, and to talk about their implications for the United States, and for the world. For the moment, and in closing, I want to speak more personally about my admiration for all those who have taken part in this process, and my hope that the promise of this moment will be fulfilled.

During the last two weeks the members of all three delegations have spent endless hours, day and night, talking, negotiating, grappling with problems that have divided their people for 30 years. Whenever there was a danger that human energy would fail, or patience would be exhausted, or good will would run out—and there were such moments—these two leaders and the able advisers in all delegations found the resources within them to keep the chances for peace alive.

Well, the long days at Camp David are over. But many months of difficult negotiations still lie ahead.

I hope that the foresight and the wisdom that have made this session a success will guide these leaders and the leaders of all nations as they continue the process toward peace.

Thank you very much.

Carter's "Crisis of Confidence" Speech

Summer 1979 was a time of oil shortages, raging inflation, and widespread dissatisfaction with the leadership of President Jimmy Carter. In July, Carter cancelled a scheduled televised address on energy and retreated to the presidential compound at Camp David, Maryland, to reflect on the underlying causes of the energy crisis. During the course of the next week, he met there with more than a hundred invited visitors, including political, business, labor, and religious leaders. He also made some unannounced helicopter visits to speak with average families in their homes. On July 15 Carter gave a televised speech from the White House that, while dealing with energy, dwelt on the "crisis of confidence" that he believed was enfeebling the country.

Carter began with an extended mea culpa, quoting criticisms of his leadership from some of the people with whom he had spoken during his Camp David retreat. He then described "a fundamental threat to American democracy," namely, a "crisis of the American spirit" that was marked by loss of faith in the country and confidence in the future. "Restoring that faith and that confidence in America is now the most important task we face," Carter concluded.

Although Carter never spoke the word, his address soon became known as the "malaise" speech. In 1980 Republican Ronald Reagan defeated Carter in his bid for reelection after proclaiming repeatedly that the United States was not lacking in confidence, but in leadership.

Good evening.

This is a special night for me. Exactly three years ago on July 15, 1976, I accepted the nomination of my party to run for President of the United States. I promised you a President who is not isolated from the people, who feels your pain and who shares your dreams and who draws his strength and his wisdom from you.

During the past 3 years I have spoken to you on many occasions about national concerns, the energy crisis, reorganizing the Government, our Nation's economy and issues of war and especially peace. But over those years the subjects of the speeches, the talks and the press conferences have become increasingly narrow, focused more and more on what the isolated world of Washington thinks is important. Gradually you have heard more and more about what the Government thinks or what the Government should be doing and less and less about our Nation's hopes, our dreams and our vision of the future.

Ten days ago I had planned to speak to you again about a very important subject—energy. For the fifth time I would have described the urgency of the problem and laid out a series of legislative recommendations to the Congress. But as I was preparing to speak, I began to ask myself the same question that I now know has been troubling many of you. Why have we not been able to get together as a nation to resolve our serious energy problem?

It's clear that the true problems of our Nation are much deeper—deeper than gasoline lines or energy shortages, deeper even than inflation or recession. And I realize more than ever that as President I need your help. So, I decided to reach out and to listen to the voices of America.

I invited to Camp David people from almost every segment of our society—business and labor, teachers and preachers, Governors, mayors and private citizens. And then I left Camp David to listen to other Americans, men and women like you. It has been an extraordinary 10 days, and I want to share with you what I've heard.

First of all, I got a lot of personal advice. Let me quote a few of the typical comments that I wrote down.

This from a southern Governor: "Mr. President, you are not leading this Nation—you're just managing the Government."

"You don't see the people enough any more."

"Some of your Cabinet members don't seem loyal. There is not enough discipline among your disciples."

"Don't talk to us about politics or the mechanics of government, but about an understanding of our common good."

"Mr. President, we're in trouble. Talk to us about blood and sweat and tears."

"If you lead, Mr. President, we will follow."

Many people talked about themselves and about the condition of our Nation. This from a young woman in Pennsylvania: "I feel so far from government. I feel like ordinary people are excluded from political power."

And this from a young Chicano: "Some of us have suffered from recession all our lives."

"Some people have wasted energy, but others haven't had anything to waste."

And this from a religious leader: "No material shortage can touch the important things like God's love for us or our love for one another."

And I like this one particularly from a black woman who happens to be the mayor of a small Mississippi town: "The big shots are not the only ones who are important. Remember, you can't sell anything on Wall Street unless someone digs it up somewhere else first."

This kind of summarized a lot of other statements: "Mr. President, we are confronted with a moral and a spiritual crisis.". . .

These 10 days confirmed my belief in the decency and the strength and the wisdom of the American people, but it also bore out some of my longstanding concerns about our Nation's underlying problems.

I know, of course, being President, that government actions and legislation can be very important. That is why I've worked hard to put my campaign promises into law—and I have to admit, with just mixed success. But after listening to the American people I have been reminded again that all the legislation in the world can't fix what's wrong with America. So, I want to speak to you first tonight about a subject even more serious than energy or inflation. I want to talk to you right now about a fundamental threat to American democracy.

I do not mean our political and civil liberties. They will endure. And I do not refer to the outward strength of America, a nation that is at peace tonight everywhere in the world, with unmatched economic power and military might.

The threat is nearly invisible in ordinary ways. It is a crisis of confidence. It is a crisis that strikes at the very heart and soul and spirit of our national will. We can see this crisis in the growing doubt about the meaning of our own lives and in the loss of a unity of purpose for our Nation.

The erosion of our confidence in the future is threatening to destroy the social and the political fabric of America.

The confidence that we have always had as a people is not simply some romantic dream or a proverb in a dusty book that we read just on the Fourth of July. It is the idea we founded our Nation on and has guided our development as a people. Confidence in the future has supported everything else—public institutions and private enterprise, our own families, and the very Constitution of the United States. Confidence has defined our course and has served as a link between generations. We've always believed in something called progress. We've always had a faith that the days of our children would be better than our own.

Our people are losing that faith, not only in government itself, but in the ability as citizens to serve as the ultimate rulers and shapers of our democracy. As a people we know our past and we are proud of it.

Our progress has been part of the living history of America, even the world. We always believed that we were part of a great movement of humanity itself called democracy, involved in the search for freedom and that belief has always strengthened us in our purpose. But just as we are losing our confidence in the future, we are also beginning to close the door on our past.

In a Nation that was proud of hard work, strong families, close knit communities, and our faith in God, too many of us now tend to worship self-indulgence and consumption. Human identity is no longer defined by what one does, but by what one owns. But we've discovered that owning things and consuming things does not satisfy our longing for meaning. We've learned that piling up material goods cannot fill the emptiness of lives which have no confidence or purpose.

The symptoms of this crisis of the American spirit are all around us. For the first time in the history of our country the majority of our people believe that the next 5 years will be worse than the past 5 years. Two-thirds of our people do not even vote. The productivity of American workers is actually dropping and the willingness of Americans to save for the future has fallen below that of all other people in the Western world.

As you know, there is a growing disrespect for government and for churches and for schools, the news media, and other institutions. This is not a message of happiness or reassurance, but it is the truth and it is a warning.

These changes did not happen overnight. They've come upon us gradually over the last generation, years that were filled with shocks and tragedy.

We were sure that ours was a nation of the ballot, not the bullet, until the murders of John Kennedy and Robert Kennedy and Martin Luther King Jr. We were taught that our armies were always invincible and our causes were always just, only to suffer the agony of Vietnam. We respected the Presidency as a place of honor until the shock of Watergate.

We remember when the phrase "sound as a dollar," was an expression of absolute dependability, until 10 years of inflation began to shrink our dollars and our savings. We believed that our Nation's resources were limitless until 1973 when we had to face a growing dependence on foreign oil.

These wounds are still very deep. They have never been healed.

Looking for a way out of this crisis, our people have turned to the Federal Government and found it isolated from the mainstream of our Nation's life. Washington, D.C., has become an island. The gap between our citizens and our government has never been so wide. The people are looking for honest answers, not easy answers; clear leadership, not false claims and evasiveness and politics as usual.

What you see too often in Washington and elsewhere around the country is a system of government that seems incapable of action. You see a Congress twisted and pulled in every direction by hundreds of well-financed and powerful special interests.

You see every extreme position defended to the last vote, almost to the last breath by one unyielding group or another. You often see a balanced and a fair approach that demands sacrifice, a little sacrifice from everyone, abandoned like an orphan without support and without friends.

Often you see paralysis and stagnation and drift. You don't like it, and neither do I. What can we do?

First of all, we must face the truth and then we can change our course. We simply must have faith in each other, faith in our ability to govern ourselves and faith in the future of this Nation.

Restoring that faith and that confidence to America is now the most important task we face. It is a true challenge of this generation of Americans.

One of the visitors to Camp David last week put it this way: "We've got to stop crying and start sweating, stop talking and start walking, stop cursing and start praying. The strength we need will not come from the White House, but from every house in America."

We know the strength of America. We are strong. We can regain our unity. We can regain our confidence. We are the heirs of generations who survived threats much more powerful and awesome than those that challenge us now. Our fathers and mothers were strong men and women who shaped a new society during the Great Depression, who fought world wars and who carved out a new charter of peace for the world.

We ourselves are the same Americans who just 10 years ago put a man on the moon. We are the generation that dedicated our society to the pursuit of human rights and equality. And we are the generation that will win the war on the energy problem and in that process rebuild the unity and confidence of America. . . .

Reagan's First Inaugural Address

In the 1980 presidential election, Ronald Reagan defeated President Jimmy Carter by the largest electoral vote majority in history against an incumbent president. His inauguration also was unprecedented in some ways. Reagan was the oldest person ever to be inaugurated as president. He was inaugurated on the West Front of the Capitol, not the traditional East Front. And he coordinated part of his speech with television cameras, which showed pictures of the Washington Monument, the Jefferson and Lincoln Memorials, and Arlington National Cemetery as he spoke of them.

Reagan's inaugural on January 20, 1981, advanced the two main themes of his political career, his 1980 campaign, and, subsequently, of his presidency: the ills of big government and a fervent optimism that national problems could be overcome. "In this present crisis," he said, "government is not the solution to our problem; government is the problem."

To a few of us here today this is a solemn and most momentous occasion. And, yet, in the history of our Nation it is a commonplace occurrence. The orderly transfer of authority as called for in the Constitution routinely takes place, as it has for almost two centuries, and few of us stop to think how unique we really are. In the eyes of many in the world, this every-4-year ceremony we accept as normal is nothing less than a miracle.

Mr. President, I want our fellow citizens to know how much you did to carry on this tradition. By your gracious cooperation in the transition process you have shown a watching world that we are a united people pledged to maintaining a political system which guarantees individual liberty to a greater degree than any other, and I thank you and your people for all your help in maintaining the continuity which is the hallmark of our Republic.

The business of our Nation goes forward. These United States are confronted with an economic affliction of great proportions. We suffer from the longest and one of the worst sustained inflations in our national history. It distorts our economic decisions, penalizes thrift and crushes the struggling young and the fixed-income elderly alike. It threatens to shatter the lives of millions of our people.

Idle industries have cast workers into unemployment, human misery, and personal indignity. Those who do work are denied a fair return for their labor by a tax system which penalizes successful achievement and keeps us from maintaining full productivity.

But great as our tax burden is, it has not kept pace with public spending. For decades we have piled deficit upon deficit, mortgaging our future and our children's future for the temporary convenience of the present. To continue this long trend is to guarantee tremendous social, cultural, political, and economic upheavals.

You and I, as individuals, can, by borrowing, live beyond our means, but for only a limited period of time. Why, then, should we think that collectively, as a nation, we're not bound by that same limitation? We must act today in order to preserve tomorrow. And let there be no misunderstanding—we are going to begin to act, beginning today.

The economic ills we suffer have come upon us over several decades. They will not go away in days, weeks, or months, but they will go away. They will go away because we as Americans have the capacity now, as we've had in the past, to do whatever needs to be done to preserve this last and greatest bastion of freedom.

In this present crisis, government is not the solution to our problem; government is the problem. From time to time we've been tempted to believe that society has become too complex to be managed by self-rule, that government by an elite group is superior to government for, by, and of the people. Well, if no one among us is capable of governing himself, then who among us has the capacity to govern someone else? All of us together—in and out of government—must bear the burden. The solutions we seek must be equitable with no one group singled out to pay a higher price.

We hear much of special interest groups. Well, our concern must be for a special interest group that has been too long neglected. It knows no sectional boundaries or ethnic and racial divisions, and it crosses political party lines. It is made up of men and women who raise our food, patrol our streets, man our mines and factories, teach our children, keep our homes, and heal us when we're sick—professionals, industrialists, shopkeepers, clerks, cabbies, and truck drivers. They are, in short, "We the people," this breed called Americans.

Well, this administration's objective will be a healthy, vigorous, growing economy that provides equal opportunities for all Americans with no barriers born of bigotry or discrimination. Putting America back to work means putting all Americans back to work. Ending inflation means freeing all Americans from the terror of runaway living costs. All must share in the productive work of this "new beginning," and all must share in the bounty of a revived economy. With the idealism and fair play which are the core of our system and our strength, we can have a strong and prosperous America at peace with itself and the world.

So, as we begin, let us take inventory. We are a nation that has a government—not the other way around. And this makes us special among the nations of the Earth. Our government has no power except that granted it by the people. It is time to check and reverse the growth of government which shows signs of having grown beyond the consent of the governed.

It is my intention to curb the size and influence of the Federal establishment and to demand recognition of the distinction between the powers granted to the Federal Government and those reserved to the States or to the people. All of us need to be reminded that the Federal Government did not create the States; the States created the Federal Government.

Now so there will be no misunderstanding, it's not my intention to do away with government. It is rather to make it work—work with us, not over us; to stand by our side, not ride on our back. Government can and must provide opportunity, not smother it; foster productivity, not stifle it.

If we look to the answer as to why for so many years we achieved so much, prospered as no other people on Earth, it was because here in this land we unleashed the energy and individual genius of man to a greater extent than has ever been done before. Freedom and the dignity of the individual have been more available and assured here than in any other place on Earth. The price for this freedom at times has been high. But we have never been unwilling to pay that price.

It is no coincidence that our present troubles parallel and are proportionate to the intervention and intrusion in our lives that result from unnecessary and excessive growth of government. . . .

Well, I believe we, the Americans of today, are ready to act worthy of ourselves, ready to do what must be done to ensure happiness and liberty for ourselves, our children, and our children's children. And as we renew ourselves here in our own land, we will be seen as having greater strength throughout the world. We will again be the exemplar of freedom and a beacon of hope for those who do not now have freedom.

To those neighbors and allies who share our ideal of freedom, we will strengthen our historic ties and assure them of our support and firm commitment. We will match loyalty with loyalty. We will strive for mutually beneficial relations. We will not use our friendship to impose on their sovereignty, for our own sovereignty is not for sale.

As for the enemies of freedom, those who are potential adversaries, they will be reminded that peace is the highest aspiration of the American people. We will negotiate for it, sacrifice for it; we will not surrender for it now or ever.

Our forbearance should never be misunderstood. Our reluctance for conflict should not be misjudged as a failure of will. When action is required to preserve our national security, we will act. We will maintain sufficient strength to prevail if need be, knowing that if we do so we have the best chance of never having to use that strength.

Above all we must realize that no arsenal or no weapon in the arsenals of the world is so formidable as the will and moral courage of free men and women. It is a weapon our adversaries in today's world do not have. It is a weapon that we as Americans do have. Let that be understood by those who practice terrorism and prey upon their neighbors.

I'm told that tens of thousands of prayer meetings are being held on this day, and for that I'm deeply grateful. We are a nation under God, and I believe God intended for us to be free. It would be fitting and good, I think, if each Inaugural Day in future years it should be declared a day of prayer.

This is the first time in our history that this ceremony has been held, as you've been told, on this West Front of the Capitol. Standing here, one faces a magnificent vista, opening up on this city's special beauty and history. At the end of this open mall are those shrines to the giants on whose shoulders we stand.

Directly in front of me, the monument to a monumental man. George Washington, father of our country. A man of humility who came to greatness reluctantly. He led America out of revolutionary victory into infant nationhood. Off to one side, the stately memorial to Thomas Jefferson. The Declaration of Independence flames with his eloquence. And then, beyond the Reflecting Pool, the dignified columns of the Lincoln Memorial. Whoever would understand in his heart the meaning of America will find it in the life of Abraham Lincoln.

Beyond these monuments to heroism is the Potomac River, and on the far shore the sloping hills of Arlington National Cemetery, with its row upon row of simple white markers bearing crosses or Stars of David. They add up to only a tiny fraction of the price that has been paid for our freedom.

Each one of those markers is a monument to the kind of hero I spoke of earlier. Their lives ended in places called Belleau Wood, The Argonne, Omaha Beach, Salerno, and halfway around the world on Guadalcanal, Tarawa, Pork Chop Hill, the Chosin Reservoir, and in a hundred rice paddies and jungles of a place called Vietnam. Under one such marker lies a young man, Martin Treptow, who left his job in a small town barbershop in 1917 to go to France with the famed Rainbow Division. There, on the western front, he was killed trying to carry a message between battalions under heavy artillery fire.

We're told that on his body was found a diary. On the flyleaf under the heading, "My Pledge," he had written these words: "America must win this war. Therefore I will work, I will save, I will sacrifice, I will endure, I will fight cheerfully and do my utmost, as if the issue of the whole struggle depended on me alone."

The crisis we are facing today does not require of us the kind of sacrifice that Martin Treptow and so many thousands of others were called upon to make. It does require, however, our best effort, and our willingness to believe in ourselves and to believe in our capacity to perform great deeds, to believe that together and with God's help we can and will resolve the problems which confront us.

And after all, why shouldn't we believe that? We are Americans. God bless you, and thank you.

Reagan's Economic Plan Speech

President Ronald Reagan became known to the nation as the "Great Communicator" because of his skill, developed during a long career as a movie and television actor and public speaker, at appealing directly to the public in televised speeches from the Oval Office of the White House. Reagan's first such speech, delivered February 5, 1981, was one of his most successful. In it, he asked the American people to support his economic plan of dramatic reductions in a range of domestic federal programs and of sweeping reductions in federal income taxes. At one point, the president dramatized the nation's economic woes by holding a dollar in one hand and thirty-six cents (which he had borrowed from an aide) in the other: the coins represented the decline in the value of the dollar since 1960.

Reagan's speech had its intended effect: an unusually large outpouring of letters, telegrams, and telephone calls urging Congress to support the president's proposed policies. Within a few months, most of the Reagan economic plan was enacted.

Good evening. I am speaking to you tonight to give you a report on the state of our Nation's economy. I regret to say that we are in the worst economic mess since the Great Depression....

Let me try to put this in personal terms. Here is a dollar such as you earned, spent, or saved in 1960. Here is a quarter, a dime, and a penny—36¢ That's what this 1960 dollar is worth today. And if the present inflation rate should continue three more years, that dollar of 1960 will be worth a quarter. What initiative is there to save? And if we don't save we are short of the investment capital needed for business and industry expansion. Workers in Japan and West Germany save several times the percentage of their income than Americans do.

What's happened to that American dream of owning a home? Only ten years ago a family could buy a home and the monthly payment averaged little more than a quarter—27¢ out of each dollar earned. Today it takes 42¢ out of every dollar of income. So, fewer than 1 out of 11 families can afford to buy their first new home.

Regulations adopted by government with the best of intentions have added $666 to the cost of an automobile. It is estimated that altogether regulations of every kind, on shopkeepers, farmers, and major industries add $100 billion or more to the cost of the goods and services we buy. And then another $20 billion is spent by government handling the paperwork created by those regulations.

I'm sure you are getting the idea that the audit presented to me found government policies of the last few decades responsible for our economic troubles. We forgot or just overlooked the fact that government—any government—has a built-in tendency to grow. Now, we all had a hand in looking to government for benefits as if government had some sources of revenue other than our earnings. Many if not most of the things we thought of or that government offered to us seemed attractive....

By 1960 our national debt stood at $284 billion. Congress in 1971 decided to put a ceiling of $400 billion on our ability to borrow. Today the debt is $934 billion. So-called temporary increases or extensions in the debt ceiling have been allowed 21 times in these 10 years and now I have been forced to ask for another increase in the debt ceiling or the government will be unable to function past the middle of February and I've only been here 16 days. Before we reach the day when we can reduce the debt ceiling we may in spite of our best efforts see a national debt in excess of a trillion dollars. Now this is a figure literally beyond our comprehension.

We know now that inflation results from all that deficit spending. Government has only two ways of getting money other than raising taxes. It can go into the money market and borrow, competing with its own citizens and driving up interest rates, which it has done, or it can print money, and it's done that. Both methods are inflationary....

One way out would be to raise taxes so that government need not borrow or print money. But in all these years of government growth we've reached—indeed surpassed—the limit of our people's tolerance or ability to bear an increase in the tax burden.

Prior to World War II, taxes were such that on the average we only had to work just a little over one month each year to pay our total Federal, state and local tax bill. Today we have to work four months to pay that bill.

Some say shift the tax burden to business and industry but business doesn't pay taxes. Oh, don't get the wrong idea, business is being taxed—so much so that we are being priced out of the world market. But business must pass its costs of operation and that includes taxes, onto the customer in the price of the product. Only people pay taxes—all the taxes. Government just uses business in a kind of sneaky way to help collect the taxes. They are hidden in the price and we aren't aware of how much tax we actually pay. Today, this once great industrial giant of ours has the lowest rate of gain in productivity of virtually all the industrial nations with whom we must compete in the world market here in America against foreign automobiles, steel and a number of other products.

Japanese production of automobiles is almost twice as great per worker as it is in America. Japanese steel workers out-produce their American counterparts by about 25 percent.

Now this isn't because they are better workers. I'll match the American working man or woman against anyone in the world. But we have to give them the tools and equipment that workers in the other industrial nations have.

We invented the assembly line and mass production, but punitive tax policies and excessive and unnecessary regulations plus government borrowing have stifled our ability to update plant and equipment. When capital investment is made it's too often for some unproductive alterations demanded by government to meet various of its regulations.

Excessive taxation of individuals has robbed us of incentive and made overtime unprofitable. . . .

All of you who are working know that even with cost-of-living pay raises you can't keep up with inflation. In our progressive tax system as you increase the number of dollars you earn you find yourself moved up into higher tax brackets, paying a higher tax rate just for trying to hold your own. The result? Your standard of living is going down.

Over the past decades we've talked of curtailing government spending so that we can then lower the tax burden. Sometimes we've even taken a run at doing that. But there were always those who told us taxes couldn't be cut until spending was reduced. Well, you know, we can lecture our children about extravagance until we run out of voice and breath. Or we can cure their extravagance by simply reducing their allowance.

It is time to recognize that we have come to a turning point. We are threatened with an economic calamity of tremendous proportions and the old business as usual treatment can't save us.

Together, we must chart a different course. We must increase productivity. That means making it possible for industry to modernize and make use of the technology which we ourselves invented: that means putting Americans back to work. And that means above all bringing government spending back within government revenues which is the only way, together with increased productivity that we can reduce and, yes, eliminate inflation.

In the past we've tried to fight inflation one year and then when unemployment increased turn the next year to fighting unemployment with more deficit spending as a pump primer. So again, up goes inflation. It hasn't worked. We don't have to choose between inflation and unemployment—they go hand in hand. It's time to try something different and that's what we're going to do.

I've already placed a freeze on hiring replacements for those who retire or leave government service. I have ordered a cut in government travel, the number of consultants to the government, and the buying of office equipment and other items. I have put a freeze on pending regulations and set up a task force under Vice President Bush to review regulations with an eye toward getting rid of as many as possible. I have decontrolled oil. And I am eliminating that ineffective Council on Wage and Price Stability.

But it will take more, much more and we must realize there is no quick fix. At the same time, however, we cannot delay in implementing an economic program aimed at both reducing rates to stimulate productivity and reducing the growth in government spending to reduce unemployment and inflation.

On February 18th, I will present in detail an economic program to Congress embodying the features I have just stated. It will propose budget cuts in virtually every department of government. It is my belief that these actual budget cuts will only be a part of the savings. As our Cabinet Secretaries take charge of their departments, they will search out areas of waste, extravagance, and costly administrative overhead which could yield additional and substantial reductions.

Now at the same time we're doing this, we must go forward with a tax relief package. I shall ask for a 10 percent reduction across the board in personal income tax rates for each of the next three years. Proposals will also be submitted for accelerated depreciation allowances for business to provide necessary capital so as to create jobs.

Now, here again, in saying this, I know that language, as I said earlier, can get in the way of a clear understanding of what our program is intended to do. Budget cuts can sound as if we are going to reduce total government spending to a lower level than was spent the year before. This is not the case. The budgets will increase as our population increases and each year we'll see spending increases to match that growth. Government revenues will increase as the economy grows, but the burden will be lighter for each individual because the economic base will have been expanded by reason of the reduced rates. . . .

Now, in all of this we will of course work closely with the Federal Reserve System toward the objective of a stable monetary policy.

Our spending cuts will not be at the expense of the truly needy. We will, however, seek to eliminate benefits to those who are not really qualified by reason of need. . . .

We can create the incentives which take advantage of the genius of our economic system—a system, as Walter Lippmann observed more than 40 years ago, which for the first time in history gave men "a way of producing wealth in which the good fortune of others multiplied their own."

Our aim is to increase our national wealth so all will have more not just redistribute what we already have which is just a sharing of scarcity. We can begin to reward hard work and risk-taking, by forcing this government to live within its means.

Over the years we've let negative economic forces run out of control. We've stalled the judgment day. We no longer have that luxury. We're out of time.

And to you my fellow citizens, let us join in a new determination to rebuild the foundation of our society; to work together to act responsibly. Let us do so with the most profound respect for that which must be preserved as well as with sensitive understanding and compassion for those who must be protected.

We can leave our children with an unrepayable massive debt and a shattered economy or we can leave them liberty in a land where every individual has the opportunity to be whatever God intended us to be. All it takes is a little common sense and recognition of our ability. Together we can forge a new beginning for America.

Thank you and good night.

Temporary Transfer of Power from Reagan to Bush

Section 3 of the Twenty-fifth Amendment (1967) created a procedure for a disabled president to transfer temporarily the powers and duties of the office to the vice president. President Ronald Reagan was criticized for not invoking the amendment after he was shot in March 1981. On July 13, 1985, preparing for cancer surgery, Reagan transferred power to Vice President George Bush, the first such transfer in history. Following the constitutional procedure, Reagan sent separate letters to the Speaker of the House of Representatives and the president pro tempore of the Senate to announce both the beginning of the transfer and the end, later the same day. For eight hours, Bush was acting president.

Curiously, although Reagan's transfer of power to Bush clearly fell under the terms of the Twenty-fifth Amendment, his letter to the Speaker and president pro tempore stated that he thought the action was inappropriate to the situation.

Dear Mr. President: (Dear Mr. Speaker:)

I am about to undergo surgery during which time I will be briefly and temporarily incapable of discharging the Constitutional powers and duties of the Office of the President of the United States.

After consultation with my counsel and the Attorney General, I am mindful of the provisions of Section 3 of the 25th Amendment to the Constitution and of the uncertainties of its application to such brief and temporary periods of incapacity. I do not believe that the drafters of this Amendment intended its application to situations such as the instant one.

Nevertheless, consistent with my long-standing arrangement with Vice President George Bush, and not intending to set a precedent binding anyone privileged to hold this Office in the future, I have determined and it is my intention and direction that Vice President George Bush shall discharge those powers and duties in my stead commencing with the administration of anesthesia to me in this instance.

I shall advise you and the Vice President when I determine that I am able to resume the discharge of the Constitutional powers and duties of this Office.

May God bless this Nation and us all.

Dear Mr. President: (Dear Mr. Speaker:)

Following up on my letter to you of this date, please be advised I am able to resume the discharge of the Constitutional powers and duties of the Office of the President of the United States. I have informed the Vice President of my determination and my resumption of those powers.

Bush's War Address

No decision weighs more heavily on a president than the decision to commit American troops to war. Presidents must bear not only the moral burden of ordering Americans into harm's way but also the political burden. The Vietnam experience taught that presidents cannot sustain foreign military operations for long without the support of the American people and Congress.

When on August 2, 1990, Iraqi troops invaded neighboring Kuwait, President George Bush angrily denounced the move as "naked aggression" and vowed that it would not stand. In the months that followed, Bush conducted a two-track policy: trying through bilateral and multilateral diplomatic initiatives to convince Iraqi leader Saddam Hussein to withdraw his troops from Kuwait voluntarily, while simultaneously preparing the American military, the American people, and the international community for war. Through press releases, news conferences, and public addresses, Bush repeatedly stated his case for intervening. "In the life of a nation, we're called upon to define who we are and what we believe. Sometimes these choices are not easy. But today as President, I ask for your support in a decision I've made to stand up for what's right and condemn what's wrong, all in the cause of peace," Bush said in a television address to the nation on August 8.

By January 15, 1991, the deadline set by United Nations Resolution 678 for Iraqi withdrawal, President Bush had secured from the House and Senate authorization to use military force, and he had the support of a majority of the American people. The next day, the United States, in coalition with twenty-seven other nations, went to war with Iraq. Less than two hours after the first coalition aircraft began the attack, President Bush addressed the nation. Speaking from the Oval Office, Bush sought to assure the American people that the war's aims were just, necessary, and limited. And he sought to reassure them that "this will not be another Vietnam."

Just 2 hours ago, allied air forces began an attack on military targets in Iraq and Kuwait. These attacks continue as I speak. Ground forces are not engaged.

This conflict started August 2d when the dictator of Iraq invaded a small and helpless neighbor. Kuwait—a member of the Arab League and a member of the United Nations—was crushed; its people, brutalized. Five months ago, Saddam Hussein started this cruel war against Kuwait. Tonight, the battle has been joined.

This military action, taken in accord with United Nations resolutions and with the consent of the United States Congress, follows months of constant and virtually endless diplomatic activity on the part of the United Nations, the United States, and many, many other countries. Arab leaders sought what became known as an Arab solution, only to conclude that Saddam Hussein was unwilling to leave Kuwait. Others traveled to Baghdad in a variety of efforts to restore peace and justice. Our Secretary of State, James Baker, held an historic meeting in Geneva, only to be totally rebuffed. This past weekend, in a last-ditch effort, the Secretary-General of the United Nations went to the Middle East with peace in his heart—his second such mission. And he came back from Baghdad with no progress at all in getting Saddam Hussein to withdraw from Kuwait.

Now the 28 countries with forces in the Gulf area have exhausted all reasonable efforts to reach a peaceful resolution—have no choice but to drive Saddam from Kuwait by force. We will not fail.

As I report to you, air attacks are underway against military targets in Iraq. We are determined to knock out Saddam Hussein's nuclear bomb potential. We will also destroy his chemical weapons facilities. Much of Saddam's artillery and tanks will be destroyed. Our operations are designed to best protect the lives of all the coalition forces by targeting Saddam's vast military arsenal. Initial reports from General [Norman] Schwarzkopf are that our operations are proceeding according to plan.

Our objectives are clear: Saddam Hussein's forces will leave Kuwait. The legitimate government of Kuwait will be restored to its rightful place, and Kuwait will once again be free. Iraq will eventually comply with all relevant United Nations resolutions, and then, when peace is restored, it is our hope that Iraq will live as a peaceful and cooperative member of the family of nations, thus enhancing the security and stability of the Gulf.

Some may ask: Why act now? Why not wait? The answer is clear: The world could wait no longer. Sanctions, though having some effect, showed no signs of accomplishing their objective. Sanctions were tried for well over 5 months, and we and our allies concluded that sanctions alone would not force Saddam from Kuwait.

While the world waited, Saddam Hussein systematically raped, pillaged, and plundered a tiny nation, no threat to his own. He subjected the people of Kuwait to unspeakable atrocities—and among those maimed and murdered, innocent children.

While the world waited, Saddam sought to add to the chemical weapons arsenal he now possesses, an infinitely more dangerous weapon of mass destruction—a nuclear weapon. And while the world waited, while the world talked peace and withdrawal, Saddam Hussein dug in and moved massive forces into Kuwait.

While the world waited, while Saddam stalled, more damage was being done to the fragile economies of the Third World, emerging democracies of Eastern Europe, to the entire world, including to our own economy. The United States, together with the United Nations, exhausted every means at our disposal to bring this crisis to a peaceful end. However, Saddam clearly felt that by stalling and threatening and defying the United Nations, he could weaken the forces arrayed against him.

While the world waited, Saddam Hussein met every overture of peace with open contempt. While the world prayed for peace, Saddam prepared for war.

I had hoped that when the United States Congress, in historic debate, took its resolute action, Saddam would realize he could not prevail and would move out of Kuwait in accord with the United Nation[s] resolutions. He did not do that. Instead, he remained intransigent, certain that time was on his side.

Saddam was warned over and over again to comply with the will of the United Nations: Leave Kuwait, or be driven out. Saddam has arrogantly rejected all warnings. Instead, he tried to make this a dispute between Iraq and the United States of America.

Well, he failed. Tonight, 28 nations—countries from 5 continents, Europe and Asia, Africa, and the Arab League—have forces in the Gulf area standing shoulder to shoulder against Saddam Hussein. These countries had hoped the use of force could be avoided. Regrettably, we now believe that only force will make him leave.

Prior to ordering our forces into battle, I instructed our military commanders to take every necessary step to prevail as quickly as possible, and with the greatest degree of protection possible for American and allied servicemen and women. I've told the American people before that this will not be another Vietnam, and I repeat this here tonight. Our troops will have the best possible support in the entire world, and they will not be asked to fight with one hand tied behind their back. I'm hopeful that this fighting will not go on for long and that casualties will be held to an absolute minimum.

This is an historic moment. We have in this past year made great progress in ending the long era of conflict and cold war. We have before us the opportunity to forge for ourselves and for future generations a new world order—a world where the rule of law, not the law of the jungle, governs the conduct of nations. When we are successful—and we will be— we have a real chance at this new world order, an order in which a credible United Nations can use its peacekeeping role to fulfill the promise and vision of the U.N.'s founders.

We have no argument with the people of Iraq. Indeed, for the innocents caught in this conflict, I pray for their safety. Our goal is not the conquest of Iraq. It is the liberation of Kuwait. It is my hope that somehow the Iraqi people can, even now, convince their dictator that he must lay down his arms, leave Kuwait and let Iraq itself rejoin the family of peace-loving nations.

Thomas Paine wrote many years ago: "These are the times that try men's souls." Those well-known words are so very true today. But even as planes of the multinational forces attack Iraq, I prefer to think of peace, not war. I am convinced not only that we will prevail but that out of the horror of combat will come the recognition that no nation can stand against a world united. No nation will be permitted to brutally assault its neighbor.

No president can easily commit our sons and daughters to war. They are the Nation's finest. Ours is an all-volunteer force, magnificently trained, highly motivated. The troops know why they're there. And listen to what they say, for they've said it better than any President or Prime Minister ever could.

Listen to Hollywood Huddleston, Marine lance corporal. He says, "Let's free these people, so we can go home and be free again." And he's right. The terrible crimes and tortures committed by Saddam's henchmen against the innocent people of Kuwait are an affront to mankind and a challenge to the freedom of all.

Listen to one of our great officers out there, Marine Lieutenant General Walter Boomer. He said: "There are things worth fighting for. A world in which brutality and lawlessness are allowed to go unchecked isn't the kind of world we're going to want to live in."

Listen to Master Sergeant J. P. Kendall of the 82d Airborne: "We're here for more than just the price of a gallon of gas. What we're doing is going to chart the future of the world for the next 100 years. It's better to deal with this guy now than 5 years from now."

And finally, we should all sit up and listen to Jackie Jones, an Army lieutenant, when she says, "If we let him get away with this, who knows what's going to be next?"

I have called upon Hollywood and Walter and J. P. and Jackie and all their courageous comrades-in-arms to do what must be done. Tonight, America and the world are deeply grateful to them and to their families. And let me say to everyone listening or watching tonight: When the troops we've sent in finish their work, I am determined to bring them home as soon as possible.

Tonight, as our forces fight, they and their families are in our prayers. May God bless each and every one of them, and the coalition forces at our side in the Gulf, and may He continue to bless our nation, the United States of America.

Clinton's Inaugural Address

William Jefferson Clinton took the oath of office from Chief Justice William H. Rehnquist at 11:58 a.m., January 20, 1993. In his inaugural address he declared that "a new season of American renewal has begun." Pledging "an end to the era of deadlock and drift," the new president echoed the dominant theme of his election campaign, that the nation was in dire need of economic and political change. The fourteen-minute address urged sacrifice to "renew America" and elicited applause from the crowd of 250,000 onlookers assembled before the West Front of the Capitol in clear, crisp weather.

During the campaign, Clinton had persuaded a plurality of American voters that he, better than incumbent president George Bush or independent candidate Ross Perot, could revive a sluggish economy, scale back a soaring fiscal deficit, and address a host of social concerns. His triumph brought to office the first Democratic president in twelve years and placed control of the White House and Congress in the same party after twelve years of divided government—Republican presidents and Congresses controlled in whole or in part by Democrats.

But the victory was notable for its tenuousness. In the three-way race for president, Clinton had received 43 percent of the popular vote. Only three presidents—John Quincy Adams in 1824, Abraham Lincoln in 1860, and Woodrow Wilson in 1912—had won with smaller percentages.

My fellow citizens, today we celebrate the mystery of American renewal. This ceremony is held in the depth of winter, but by the words we speak and the faces we show the world, we force the spring, a spring reborn in the world's oldest democracy that brings forth the vision and courage to reinvent America. When our Founders boldly declared America's independence to the world and our purposes to the Almighty, they knew that America, to endure, would have to change; not change for change's sake but change to preserve America's ideals: life, liberty, the pursuit of happiness. Though we marched to the music of our time, our mission is timeless. Each generation of Americans must define what it means to be an American.

On behalf of our Nation, I salute my predecessor, President Bush, for his half-century of service to America. And I thank the millions of men and women whose steadfastness and sacrifice triumphed over depression, fascism, and communism.

Today, a generation raised in the shadows of the cold war assumes new responsibilities in a world warmed by the sunshine of freedom but threatened still by ancient hatreds and new plagues. Raised in unrivaled prosperity, we inherit an economy that is still the world's strongest but is weakened by business failures, stagnant wages, increasing inequality, and deep divisions among our own people.

When George Washington first took the oath I have just sworn to uphold, news traveled slowly across the land by horseback and across the ocean by boat. Now, the sights and sounds of this ceremony are broadcast instantaneously to billions around the world. Communications and commerce are global. Investment is mobile. Technology is almost magical. And ambition for a better life is now universal.

We earn our livelihood in America today in peaceful competition with people all across the Earth. Profound and powerful forces are shaking and remaking our world. And the urgent question of our time is whether we can make change our friend and not our enemy. This new world has already enriched the lives of millions of Americans who are able to compete and win in it. But when most people are working harder for less; when others cannot work at all; when the cost of health care devastates families and threatens to bankrupt our enterprises, great and small; when the fear of crime robs law-abiding citizens of their freedom; and when millions of poor children cannot even imagine the lives we are calling them to lead, we have not made change our friend.

We know we have to face hard truths and take strong steps, but we have not done so; instead, we have drifted. And that drifting has eroded our resources, fractured our economy, and shaken our confidence. Though our challenges are fearsome, so are our strengths. Americans have ever been a restless, questing, hopeful people. And we must bring to our task today the vision and will of those who came before us. From our Revolution to the Civil War, to the Great Depression, to the civil rights movement, our people have always mustered the determination to construct from these crises the pillars of our history. Thomas Jefferson believed that to preserve the very foundations of our Nation, we would need dramatic change from time to time. Well, my fellow Americans, this is our time. Let us embrace it.

Our democracy must be not only the envy of the world but the engine of our own renewal. There is nothing wrong with America that cannot be cured by what is right with America. And so today we pledge an end to the era of deadlock and drift, and a new season of American renewal has begun.

To renew America, we must be bold. We must do what no generation has had to do before. We must invest more in our own people, in their jobs, and in their future, and at the same time cut our massive debt. And we must do so in a world in which we must compete for every opportunity. It will not be easy. It will require sacrifice, but it can be done and done fairly, not choosing sacrifice for its own sake but for our own sake. We must provide for our Nation the way a family provides for its children.

Our Founders saw themselves in the light of posterity. We can do no less. Anyone who has ever watched a child's eyes wander into sleep knows what posterity is. Posterity is the world to come: the world for whom we hold our ideals, from whom we have borrowed our planet, and to whom we bear sacred responsibility. We must do what America does best: offer more opportunity to all and demand more responsibility from all. It is time to break the bad habit of expecting something for nothing from our Government or from each other. Let us all take more responsibility not only for ourselves and our families but for our communities and our country.

To renew America, we must revitalize our democracy. This beautiful Capital, like every capital since the dawn of civilization, is often a place of intrigue and calculation. Powerful people maneuver for position and worry endlessly about who is in and who is out, who is up and who is down, forgetting those people whose toil and sweat sends us here and pays our way. Americans deserve better. And in this city today there are people who want to do better. And so I say to all of you here: Let us resolve to reform our politics so that power and privilege no longer shout down the voice of the people. Let us put aside personal advantage so that we can feel the pain and see the promise of America. Let us resolve to make our Government a place for what Franklin Roosevelt called bold, persistent experimentation, a Government for our tomorrows, not our yesterdays. Let us give this Capital back to the people to whom it belongs.

To renew America, we must meet challenges abroad as well as at home. There is no longer a clear division between what is foreign and what is domestic. The world economy, the world environment, the world AIDS crisis, the world arms race: they affect us all. Today, as an older order passes, the new world is more free but less stable. Communism's collapse has called forth old animosities and new dangers. Clearly, America must continue to lead the world we did so much to make.

While America rebuilds at home, we will not shrink from the challenges nor fail to seize the opportunities of this new world. Together with our friends and allies, we will work to shape change, lest it engulf us. When our vital interests are challenged or the will and conscience of the international community is defied, we will act, with peaceful diplomacy whenever possible, with force when necessary. The brave Americans serving our Nation today in the Persian Gulf, in Somalia, and wherever else they stand are testament to our resolve. But our greatest strength is the power of our ideas, which are still new in many lands. Across the world we see them embraced, and we rejoice. Our hopes, our hearts, our hands are with those on every continent who are building democracy and freedom. Their cause is America's cause.

The American people have summoned the change we celebrate today. You have raised your voices in an unmistakable chorus. You have cast your votes in historic numbers. And you have changed the face of Congress, the Presidency, and the political process itself. Yes, you, my fellow Americans, have forced the spring. Now we must do the work the season demands. To that work I now turn with all the authority of my office. I ask the Congress to join with me. But no President, no Congress, no Government can undertake this mission alone.

My fellow Americans, you, too, must play your part in our renewal. I challenge a new generation of young Americans to a season of service: to act on your idealism by helping troubled children, keeping company with those in need, reconnecting our torn communities. There is so much to be done; enough, indeed, for millions of others who are still young in spirit to give of themselves in service, too. In serving, we recognize a simple but powerful truth: We need each other, and we must care for one another.

Today we do more than celebrate America. We rededicate ourselves to the very idea of America, an idea born in revolution and renewed through two centuries of challenge; an idea tempered by the knowledge that, but for fate, we, the fortunate and the unfortunate, might have been each other; an idea ennobled by the faith that our Nation can summon from its myriad diversity the deepest measure of unity; an idea infused with the conviction that America's long, heroic journey must go forever upward.

And so, my fellow Americans, as we stand at the edge of the 21st century, let us begin anew with energy and hope, with faith and discipline. And let us work until our work is done. The Scripture says, "And let us not be weary in well doing: for in due season we shall reap, if we faint not." From this joyful mountaintop of celebration we hear a call to service in the valley. We have heard the trumpets. We have changed the guard. And now, each in our own way and with God's help, we must answer the call.

Thank you, and God bless you all.

Clinton's 1996 State of the Union Address

Bill Clinton's first three years as president were as politically turbulent as any president's since Herbert Hoover. The year 1993 was marked by both triumphant political success—enactment of spending reductions and tax increases on the wealthy that promised to reduce the federal budget deficit by $500 billion over a five-year period—and stormy political controversy concerning issues such as gays in the military. The following year, 1994, was unrelentingly disappointing for the president. First, the administration's major legislative initiative—a proposed overhaul of the nation's health care system that was developed by First Lady Hillary Rodham Clinton at the president's behest—stalled in Congress. Then, in a crushing political blow, the Republicans took control of Congress in the midterm elections for the first time in forty years.

At the start of 1995, Clinton was already a lame duck president in the eyes of many political observers—at one news conference, he had to insist that "the president is relevant." Sen. Robert Dole of Kansas, an early contender for the 1996 Republican presidential nomination, was the new Senate majority leader. Rep. Newt Gingrich of Georgia, a strongly ideological conservative and a fiercely partisan Republican, was the new Speaker of the House. During the 1994 midterm election campaign, Gingrich had committed Republican congressional candidates to a ten-item "Contract with America" that included items such as welfare reform and a line-item veto. As speaker, Gingrich vowed that the contract would serve as Washington's political agenda for 1995, eclipsing the president's legislative program.

The Republican contract faltered during the first year of the 104th Congress. Even when the House of Representatives approved an item, either the Senate failed to pass it or Clinton cast a veto. By the end of 1995, Republicans were stymied in their effort pass a seven-year balanced budget plan. When the federal government shut down for several days for lack of appropriations, most voters blamed the Republicans.

Clinton's strategy during 1995 was to lie low, hoping that the Repub-licans would fail, then come out fighting at the start of the 1996 election year. In a sense, his State of the Union address, delivered to a joint session of Congress and televised to a live national audience on January 23, 1996, was the kickoff of his reelection campaign.

In the vigorously delivered speech, Clinton argued that "the state of the union is strong" because of the accomplishments of his administration. Stealing a popular theme from the Republicans, he also proclaimed, "The era of big government is over." Senator Dole, who gave the Republican response to Clinton's address, could do little more than complain that the president talked like a conservative Republican but governed as a liberal Democrat.

Mr. Speaker, Mr. Vice President, members of the 104th Congress, distinguished guests, my fellow Americans all across our land.

Let me begin tonight by saying to our men and women in uniform around the world, and especially those helping peace take root in Bosnia, and to their families, I thank you. America is very, very proud of you.

My duty tonight is to report on the state of the union, not the state of our government, but of our American community, and to set forth our responsibilities—in the words of our founders—to form a "more perfect union."

The state of the union is strong.

Our economy is the healthiest it has been in three decades. We have the lowest combined rates of unemployment and inflation in 27 years.

We have created nearly 8 million new jobs, over a million of them in basic industries like construction and automobiles. America is selling more cars than Japan for the first time since the 1970s, and for three years in a row we have had a record number of new businesses started in our country.

Our leadership in the world is also strong, bringing hope for a new peace. And perhaps most important, we are gaining ground in restoring our fundamental values. The crime rate, the welfare and food stamp rolls, the poverty rate, and the teen pregnancy rate are all down. And as they go down, prospects for America's future go up.

"AN AGE OF POSSIBILITY"

We live in an Age of Possibility. A hundred years ago we moved from farm to factory. Now we move to an age of technology, information and global competition. These changes have opened vast new opportunities for our people, but they have also presented them with stiff challenges. While more Americans are living better, too many of our fellow citizens are working harder just to keep up, in search of greater security for their families.

We must answer here three fundamental questions: First, how do we make the American dream of opportunity for all a reality for all Americans who are willing to work for it? Second, how do we preserve our old and enduring values as we move into the future? And third, how do we meet these challenges together, as one America?

We know big government does not have all the answers. We know there is not a program for every problem. We know and we have worked to give the American people a smaller, less bureaucratic government in Washington—and we have to give the American people one that lives within its means. The era of big government is over.

But we cannot go back to the time when our citizens were left to fend for themselves. We must go forward as one America—one nation working together, to meet the challenges we face together. Self-reliance and teamwork are not opposing virtues—we must have both.

I believe our new, smaller government must work in an old-fashioned American way—together with all our citizens, through state and local governments, in the workplace, in religious, charitable and civic associations. Our goal must be to enable all our people to make the most of their own lives with stronger families, more educational opportunity, economic security, safer streets, a cleaner environment, and a safer world.

To improve the state of our union, we must ask more of ourselves; we must expect more of each other; and we must face our challenges together.

Here, in this place, our responsibility begins with balancing the budget in a way that is fair to all Americans. There is now broad bipartisan agreement that permanent deficit spending must come to an end.

I compliment the Republican leadership and the membership for the energy and determination you have brought to this task of balancing the budget. And I thank the Democrats for passing the largest deficit reduction plan in history in 1993, which has already cut the deficit nearly in half in just three years.

Since 1993, we have all seen the benefits of deficit reduction: Lower interest rates have made it easier for businesses to borrow and to invest and to create new jobs. Lower interest rates have brought down the cost of home mortgages, car payments and credit card rates to ordinary citizens. Now it is time to finish the job and balance the budget.

Though differences remain among us that are significant, the combined total of the proposed savings common to both plans is more than enough, using the numbers from your Congressional Budget Office, to balance the budget in seven years and to provide a modest tax cut. These cuts are real, they will require sacrifice from everyone. But these cuts do not undermine our obligations to our parents, our children, and our future by endangering Medicare, Medicaid, education or the environment, or by raising taxes on working families.

I have said before and I'll say again that many good ideas have come out of our negotiations. I have learned a lot about the way both Republicans and Democrats view the debate before us. I have learned a lot about the good ideas that each side has that we could all embrace. We ought to resolve our remaining differences. I am willing to work to resolve them. I am ready to meet tomorrow. But I ask you to consider that we should at least enact these savings that both plans have in common and give the American people their balanced budget, a tax cut, lower interest rates and a brighter future. We should do that now and make permanent deficits yesterday's legacy.

CHILDREN AND FAMILIES

Now it is time for us to look also to the challenges of today and tomorrow, beyond the burdens of yesterday. The challenges are significant, but our nation was built on challenges. America was built on challenges, not promises. And when we work together, we never fail. That is the key to a more perfect union: Our individual dreams must be realized by our common efforts.

Tonight, I want to speak to you about the challenges we all face as a people.

Our first challenge is to cherish our children and strengthen America's families.

Families are the foundation of American life. If we have stronger families, we will have a stronger America. Before I go on, I'd like to take just a moment to thank my own family, and to thank the person who has taught me more than anyone else over 25 years about the importance of families and children. A wonderful wife, a magnificent mother, and a great first lady. Thank you, Hillary.

All strong families begin with taking more responsibility for our children. I've heard Mrs. Gore say that it's hard to be a parent today, but it's even harder to be a child. So all of us, not just as parents but all of us in our other roles—our businesses, our media, our schools, our teachers, our communities, our churches and synagogues, our government—all of us have a responsibility to help our children to make it, and to make the most of their lives and their God-given capacities.

To the media: I say you should create movies, CDs and television shows you would want your own children and grandchildren to enjoy. I call on Congress to pass the requirement for a "v-chip" in TV sets so that parents can screen out programs they believe are inappropriate for their children.

When parents control what their young children see, that is not censorship. That is enabling parents to assume more personal responsibility for their children's upbringing. And I urge them to do it. The v-chip requirement is part of the important telecommunications bill now pending in this Congress. It has bipartisan support, and I urge you to pass it now.

To make the v-chip work, I challenge the broadcast industry to do what movies have done to identify your programs in ways that help parents to protect their children. And I invite the leaders of major media corporations and the entertainment industry to come to the White House next month to work with us in a positive way on concrete ways to improve what our children see on television. I am ready to work with you.

I say to those who produce and market cigarettes: Every year, a million children take up smoking, even though it's against the law; 300,000 of them will have their lives shortened as a result.

Our administration has taken steps to stop the massive marketing campaigns that appeal to our children. We are simply saying: Market your products to adults, if you wish—but draw the line on children.

I say to those who are on welfare, and especially to those who have been trapped on welfare for a long time: For too long our welfare system has undermined the values of family and work instead of supporting them. The Congress and I are near agreement on sweeping welfare reform. We agree on time limits, tough work requirements, and the toughest possible child-support enforcement. But I believe we must also provide child care so that mothers who are required to go to work can do so without worrying about what is happening to their children. I challenge this Congress to send me a bipartisan welfare reform bill that will really move people from welfare to work and do the right thing by our children. I will sign it immediately.

But let us be candid about this difficult problem. Passing a law, even the best possible law, is only a first step. The next step is to make it work. I challenge people on welfare to make the most of this opportunity for independence. I challenge American businesses to give people on welfare the chance to move into the work force. I applaud the work of religious groups and others who care for the poor. More than anyone else in our society, they know the true difficulty of this task, and they are in a position to help. Every one of us should join them. That is the only way we can make real welfare reform a reality in the lives of the American people.

To strengthen the family, we must do everything we can to keep the teen pregnancy rate going down. I am gratified, as I'm sure all Americans are, that it has dropped for two years in a row. But we all know it is still far too high. Tonight I am pleased to announce that a group of prominent Americans is responding to that challenge by forming an organization that will support grassroots community efforts all across our country in a national campaign against teen pregnancy. And I challenge all of us and every American to join their efforts.

I call on American men and women in families to respect one another. We must end the deadly scourge of domestic violence in our country. And I challenge America's families to work harder to stay together. For families that stay together not only do better economically, their children do better as well.

In particular, I challenge the fathers of this country to love and care for their children. If your family has separated, you must pay your child support. We are doing more than ever to make sure you do, and we are going to do more. But let's admit something about that too: A check will never substitute for a father's love and guidance, and only you, only you can make the decision to help raise your children, no matter who you are, how low or high your station in life, it is the most basic human duty of every American to do that job to the best of his or her ability.

EDUCATIONAL OPPORTUNITIES

Our second challenge is to provide Americans with the educational opportunities we need for this new century.

In our schools, every classroom in America must be connected to the information superhighway, with computers, good software and well-trained teachers. We are working with the telecommunications industry, educators, and parents to connect 20 percent of California's classrooms by this spring, and every classroom and every library in the entire United States by the year 2000. I ask Congress to support our education technology initiative so that we can make sure this national partnership succeeds.

Every diploma ought to mean something. I challenge every community, every school, and every state to adopt national standards of excellence, to measure whether schools are meeting those standards, to cut bureaucratic red tape so that schools and teachers have more flexibility for grassroots reform, and to hold them accountable for results. That's what our Goals 2000 initiative is all about.

I challenge every state to give all parents the right to choose which public school their children will attend and to let teachers form new schools with a charter they can keep only if they do a good job.

I challenge all our schools to teach character education: to teach good values, and good citizenship. And if it means that teenagers will stop killing each other over designer jackets, then our public schools should be able to require the students to wear school uniforms.

I challenge our parents to become their children's first teachers. Turn off the TV. See that the homework is done. And visit your children's classroom. No program, no teacher, no one else can do that for you.

My fellow Americans, higher education is more important today than ever before. We have created a new student loan program that has made it easier to borrow and repay loans; and we have dramatically cut the student loan default rate. That's something we should all be proud of, because it was unconscionably high just a few years ago. Through AmeriCorps, our national service program, this year 25,000 young people will earn college money by serving in their local communities to improve the lives of their friends and neighbors. These initiatives are right for America, and we should keep them going.

And we should work hard to open the doors of college even wider. I challenge Congress to expand work study and help 1 million young Americans work their way through college by the year 2000; to provide a $1,000 merit scholarship for the top 5 percent of graduates in every high school in the U.S.; to expand Pell Grant scholarships for deserving and needy students; and to make up to $10,000 a year of college tuition tax deductible. It's a good idea for America.

ECONOMIC SECURITY

Our third challenge is to help every American who is willing to work for it achieve economic security in this new age.

People who work hard still need support to get ahead in the new economy. They need education and training for a lifetime, they need more support for families raising children, they need retirement security, they need access to health care.

More and more Americans are finding that the education of their childhood simply doesn't last a lifetime. So I challenge Congress to consolidate 70 overlapping, antiquated job training programs into a simple voucher worth $2,600 for unemployed or underemployed workers to use as they please for community college tuition or other training. This is a GI bill for America's Workers we should all be able to agree on.

More and more Americans are working hard without a raise. Congress sets the minimum wage. Within a year, the minimum wage will fall to a 40-year low in purchasing power. $4.25 an hour is no longer a minimum wage. But millions of Americans and their children are trying to live on it. I challenge you to raise their minimum wage.

In 1993, Congress cut the taxes of 15 million hard-pressed working families to make sure that no parents who worked full time would have to raise their children in poverty, and to encourage people to move from welfare to work. This expanded Earned Income Tax Credit is now worth about $1,800 a year to a family of four living on $20,000. The budget bill I vetoed would have reversed this achievement and raised taxes on nearly eight million of these people. We should not do that. We should not do that.

But I also agree that the people who are helped under this initiative are not all those in our country who are working hard to do a good job raising their children and at work. I agree that we need a tax credit for working families with children. That's one of the things most of us in this chamber, I hope, can agree on. I know it is strongly supported by the Republican majority and it should be part of any final budget agreement.

I want to challenge every business that can possibly afford it to provide pensions for your employees, and I challenge Congress to pass a proposal recommended by the White House Conference on Small Business that would make it easier for small businesses and farmers to establish their own pension plans. That is something we should all agree on.

We should also protect existing pension plans. Two years ago, with bipartisan support, it was almost unanimous on both sides of the aisle. We moved to protect the pensions of 8 million working people and to stabilize the pensions of 32 million more. Congress should not now let companies endanger those workers' pension funds. I know the proposal to liberalize the ability of employers to take money out of pension funds for other purposes would raise money for the treasury, but I believe it is false economy. I vetoed that proposal last year, and I would have to do so again.

Finally, if our working families are going to succeed in the new economy, they must be able to buy health insurance policies that they do not lose when they change jobs or when someone in their family gets sick. Over the past two years, over 1 million Americans in working families have lost their health insurance. We have to do more to make health care available to every American. And Congress should start by passing the bipartisan bill offered by Senator [Edward M.] Kennedy [D-Mass.] and Senator [Nancy Landon] Kassebaum [R-Kan.] that would require insurance companies to stop dropping people when they switch jobs, and stop denying coverage for pre-existing conditions. Let's all do that.

And even as we enact savings in these programs, we must have a common commitment to preserve the basic protections of Medicare and Medicaid, not just to the poor, but to people in working families, including children, people with disabilities, people with AIDS, and senior citizens in nursing homes. In the past three years, we have saved $15 billion just by fighting health care fraud and abuse. We have all agreed to save much more. We have all agreed to stabilize the Medicare trust fund. But we must not abandon our fundamental obligations to the people who need Medicare and Medicaid. America cannot become stronger if they become weaker.

The GI Bill for Workers, tax relief for education and child-rearing, pension availability and protection, access to health care, preservation of Medicare and Medicaid, these things—along with the Family and Medical Leave Act passed in 1993—these things will help responsible hard-working American families to make the most of their own lives.

But employers and employees must do their part as well, as they are in so many of our finest companies, working together, putting long-term prosperity ahead of short-term gains. As workers increase their hours and their productivity, employers should make sure they get the skills they need and share the benefits of the good years as well as the burdens of the bad ones. When companies and workers work as a team, they do better. And so does America.

TAKE BACK THE STREETS

Our fourth great challenge is to take back our streets from crime, gangs and drugs.

At last, we have begun to find the way to reduce crime—forming community partnerships with local police forces to catch criminals and to prevent crime. This strategy, called community policing, is clearly working. Violent crime is coming down all across America.

In New York City, murders are down 25 percent, in St. Louis 18 percent, in Seattle 32 percent. But we still have a long way to go before our streets are safe and our people are free of fear.

The Crime Bill of 1994 is critical to the success of community policing. It provides funds for 100,000 new police in communities of all sizes. We are already a third of the way there. And I challenge Congress to finish the job. Let us stick with the strategy that's working, and keep the crime rate coming down.

Community policing also requires bonds of trust between citizens and police. I ask all Americans to respect and support our law enforcement officers. And to our police I say: Our children need you as role models and heroes. Don't let them down.

The Brady Bill has already stopped 44,000 people with criminal records from buying guns. The assault weapons ban is keeping 19 kinds of assault weapons out of the hands of violent gangs. I challenge the Congress to keep those laws on the books.

Our next step in the fight against crime is to take on gangs the way we once took on the mob. I am directing the FBI and other investigative agencies to target gangs that involve juveniles in violent crime and to seek authority to prosecute as adults teen-agers who maim and kill like adults.

And I challenge local housing authorities and tenant associations: Criminal gang members and drug dealers are destroying the lives of decent tenants. From now on, the rule for residents who commit crime and peddle drugs should be: One strike and you're out.

I challenge every state to match federal policy: to assure that serious violent criminals serve at least 85 percent of their sentence.

More police and punishment are important, but they're not enough. We have got to keep more of our young people out of trouble, with prevention strategies not dictated by Washington, but developed in communities. I challenge all of our communities, all of our adults, to give our children futures to say yes to. And I challenge Congress not to abandon the crime bill's support of these grassroots prevention efforts.

Finally, to reduce crime and violence, we have to reduce the drug problem. The challenge begins in our homes, with parents talking to their children openly and firmly. It embraces our churches and synagogues, our youth groups and our schools. I challenge Congress not to cut our support for drug-free schools. People like these DARE [Drug Abuse Resistance Education] officers are making a real impression on grade school children that will give them the strength to say no when the time comes.

Meanwhile, we continue our efforts to cut the flow of drugs into America. For the last two years, one man in particular has been on the front lines of that effort. Tonight I am nominating a hero of the Persian Gulf and the commander in chief of the U.S. Military's Southern Command, Gen. Barry McCaffrey, as America's new drug czar.

Gen. McCaffrey has earned three Purple Hearts and two Silver Stars fighting for this country. Tonight I ask that he lead our nation's battle against drugs at home and abroad. To succeed, he needs a force far larger than he has ever commanded before. He needs all of us. Every one of us has a role to play on this team. Thank you, Gen. McCaffrey, for agreeing to serve your country one more time.

COMMITMENT TO THE ENVIRONMENT

Our fifth challenge: to leave our environment safe and clean for the next generation.

Because of a generation of bipartisan effort, we do have cleaner air and water. Lead levels in children's blood has been cut by 70 percent and toxic emissions from factories cut in half. Lake Erie was dead. Now it is a thriving resource.

But 10 million children under 12 still live within four miles of a toxic waste dump. A third of us breathe air that endangers our health. And in too many communities, water is not safe to drink. We still have much to do.

Yet Congress has voted to cut environmental enforcement by 25 percent. That means more toxic chemicals in our water, more smog in our air, more pesticides in our food. Lobbyists for the polluters have been allowed to write their own loopholes into bills to weaken laws that protect the health and safety of our children. Some say that the taxpayers should pick up the tab for toxic waste and let polluters who can afford to fix it off the hook.

I challenge Congress to re-examine those policies and to reverse them. I believe . . . This issue has not been a partisan issue. The most significant environmental gains in the last 30 years were made under a Democratic Congress and President Richard Nixon. We can work together. We have to believe some basic things. Do you believe we can expand the economy without hurting the environment? I do. Do you believe we can create more jobs over the long run by cleaning the environment up? I know we can. That should be our commitment.

We must challenge businesses and communities to take more initiative in protecting the environment and we have to make it easier for them to do it. To businesses, this administration is saying: If you can find a cheaper, more efficient way than government regulations require to meet tough pollution standards, do it—as long as you do it right.

To communities we say: We must strengthen community right-to-know laws requiring polluters to disclose their emissions, but you have to use the information to work with business to cut pollution. People do have a right to know that their air and water are safe.

AMERICAN WORLD LEADERSHIP

Our sixth challenge is to maintain America's leadership in the fight for freedom and peace throughout the world.

Because of American leadership, more people than ever before live free and at peace, and Americans have known 50 years of prosperity and security. We owe thanks especially to our veterans of World War II. I would like to say to Senator Bob Dole [R-Kan.] and to all others in this chamber who fought in World War II and to all others on both sides of the aisle who have fought bravely in all our conflicts since, I salute your service and so do the American people.

All over the world, even after the Cold War people still look to us, and trust us to help them seek the blessings of peace and freedom.

But as the Cold War fades into memory, voices of isolation say America should retreat from its responsibilities. I say they are wrong.

The threats we face today as Americans respect no nation's borders. Think of them—terrorism, the spread of weapons of mass destruction, organized crime, drug trafficking, ethnic and religious hatred, aggression by rogue states, environmental degradation. If we fail to address these threats today, we will suffer the consequences in all our tomorrows.

Of course, we can't be everywhere. Of course, we can't do everything. But where our interests and our values are at stake—and where we can make a difference—America must lead. We must not be isolationist; we must not be the world's policeman. But we can and should be the world's very best peacemaker.

By keeping our military strong, by using diplomacy where we can and force where we must, by working with others to share the risk and the cost of our efforts, America is making a difference for people here and around the world.

For the first time since the dawn of the nuclear age, there is not a single Russian missile pointed at America's children. North Korea has now frozen its dangerous nuclear weapons program. In Haiti, the dictators are gone, democracy has a new day, the flow of desperate refugees to our shores has subsided.

Through tougher trade deals for America, over 80 of them, we have opened markets abroad, and now exports are at an all-time high, growing faster than imports and creating good American jobs.

We stood with those taking risks for peace—in Northern Ireland, where Catholic and Protestant children now tell their parents that violence must never return, and in the Middle East, where Arabs and Jews, who once seemed destined to fight forever, now share knowledge and resources and even dreams.

And we stood up for peace in Bosnia. Remember the skeletal prisoners, the mass graves, the campaigns of rape and torture, the endless lines of refugees, the threat of a spreading war—all these threats all these horrors have now begun to give way to the promise of peace.

Now our troops and a strong NATO, together with our new partners from Central Europe and elsewhere, are helping that peace to take hold.

As all of you know, I was just there with a bipartisan Congressional group and I was so proud not only of what our troops were doing but at the pride they evidenced in what they were doing. They know what America's mission in this world is and they were proud to be carrying it out.

Through these efforts, we have enhanced the security of the American people. But make no mistake about it, important challenges remain. The Start II treaty with Russia will cut our nuclear stockpiles by another 25 percent; I urge the Senate to approve it—now. We must end the race to create new nuclear weapons by signing a truly comprehensive nuclear test ban treaty—this year. As we remember what happened in the Japanese subway, we can outlaw poison gas forever, if the Senate approves the Chemical Weapons Convention—this year. We can intensify the fight against terrorists and organized criminals at home and abroad, if Congress passes the anti-terrorism legislation I proposed after the Oklahoma City bombing—now. We can help more people move from hatred to hope all across the world in our own interest—if Congress gives us the means to remain the world's leader for peace.

RE-INVENTING GOVERNMENT

My fellow Americans, the six challenges I have discussed are for all of us. Our seventh challenge is really America's challenge to those of us in this hallowed hall here tonight—to reinvent our government and make our democracy work for them.

Last year, this Congress applied to itself the laws it applies to everyone else. This Congress banned gifts and meals from lobbyists. This Congress forced lobbyists to disclose who pays them and what legislation they are trying to pass or kill. This Congress did that and I applaud you for it.

Now I challenge Congress to go further, to curb special interest influence in politics by passing the first truly bipartisan campaign finance reform bill in a generation. You Republicans and Democrats alike can show the American people that we can limit spending and we can open the airwaves to all candidates.

And I also appeal to Congress to pass the line item veto you promised the American people. Our administration is working hard to give the American people a government that works better and costs less. Thanks to the work of Vice President [Al] Gore, we are eliminating 16,000 pages of unnecessary rules and regulations and shifting more decision-making out of Washington back to states and communities.

As we move into an era of balanced budgets and smaller government, we must work in new ways to enable people to make the most of their own lives. We are helping America's communities, not with more bureaucracy, but with more opportunities. Through our successful empowerment zones and community development banks we are helping people to find jobs, to start businesses.

And with tax incentives for the companies that clean up abandoned industrial property, we can bring jobs back to the places that desperately, desperately need them.

But there are some areas that the federal government should not leave and should address and address strongly. One of these areas is the problem of illegal immigration. After years and years of neglect, this administration has taken a strong stand to stiffen the protection of our borders. We are increasing border patrols by 50 percent. We are increasing inspections to prevent the hiring of illegal immigrants.

And tonight, I announce I will sign an executive order to deny federal contracts to businesses that hire illegal immigrants. Let me be very clear about this: We are still a nation of immigrants, we should be proud of it. We should honor every legal immigrant here working hard to be a good citizen, working hard to become a new citizen. But we are also a nation of laws.

I want to say a special word now to those who work for our federal government. Today, the federal work force is 200,000 employees smaller than it was the day I took office as president—our federal government today is the smallest it has been in 30 years, and it's getting smaller every day. Most of our fellow Americans probably don't know that and there's a good reason, a good reason. The remaining federal work force is composed of Americans who are now working harder and working smarter than ever before to make sure that the quality of our services does not decline.

I'd like to give you one example. His name is Richard Dean. He's a 49-year-old Vietnam veteran who's worked for the Social Security Administration for 22 years now. Last year, he was hard at work in the federal building in Oklahoma City when the blast killed 169 people and brought the rubble down all around him. He re-entered the building four times. He saved the lives of three women. He is here with us this evening, and I want to recognize Richard and applaud both his public service and his extraordinary personal heroism.

But Richard Dean's story doesn't end there. This last November, he was forced out of his office when the government shut down. And the second time the government shut down, he continued helping Social Security recipients, but he was working without pay. On behalf of Richard Dean and his family and all the other people who are out there working every day doing a good job for the American people, I challenge all of you in this chamber: Never—ever—shut the federal government down again. On behalf of all Americans, especially those who need their Social Security payments at the beginning of March, I also challenge the Congress to preserve the full faith and credit of the United States, to honor the obligations of this great nation as we have for 220 years, to rise above partisanship and pass a straightforward extension of the debt limit and show the people America keeps its word.

I know that this evening I have asked a lot of Congress and even more from America. But I am confident. When Americans work together in their homes, their schools, their churches, their synagogues, their civic groups, or their workplace, they can meet any challenge.

TORCH OF CITIZENSHIP

I say again: The era of big government is over. But we can't go back to the era of fending for yourself. We have to go forward, to the era of working together—as a community, as a team, as one America—with all of us reaching across these lines that divide us. The division, the discrimination, the rancor, we have to reach across it to find common ground. We have got to work together if we want America to work.

I want you to meet two more people tonight who do just that. Lucius Wright is a teacher in the Jackson, Mississippi, public school system. A Vietnam veteran, he has created groups to help inner city children turn away from gangs and build futures they can believe in. And Sergeant Jennifer Rodgers is a police officer in Oklahoma City. Like Richard Dean, she helped to pull her fellow citizens out of the rubble and deal with that awful tragedy. She reminds us that, in their response to that atrocity, the people of Oklahoma City lifted all of us with their basic sense of decency and community.

Lucius Wright and Jennifer Rodgers are special Americans, and I have the honor to announce tonight that they are the very first of several thousand Americans who will be chosen to carry the Olympic torch on its long journey from Los Angeles to the centennial of the modern Olympics in Atlanta this summer—not because they are star athletes, but because they are star citizens, community heroes meeting America's challenges. They are our real champions. Please stand up.

Now each of us must hold high the torch of citizenship in our own lives. None of us can finish the race alone. We can only achieve our destiny together—one hand, one generation, one American connecting to another. There have always been things we could do together, dreams we could make real, which we could never have done on our own. We Americans have forged our identity, our very union, from the very point of view that we can accommodate every point on the planet, every different opinion, but we must be bound together by a faith more powerful than any doctrine that divide us, by our belief in progress, our love of liberty, and our relentless search for common ground.

America has always sought and always risen to every challenge. Who would say that having come so far together, we will not go forward from here? Who would say that this age of possibility is not for all Americans? Our country is and always has been a great and good nation, but the best is yet to come if we all do our part.

Thank you, God bless you, and God bless the United States of America. Thank you.

APPENDIX B Tabular and Graphical Data

U.S. Presidents and Vice Presidents

President and political party	Born	Died	Age at inauguration	Native of	Elected from	Term of service	Vice president
George Washington (F)	1732	1799	57	Va.	Va.	April 30, 1789–March 4, 1793	John Adams
George Washington (F)			61			March 4, 1793–March 4, 1797	John Adams
John Adams (F)	1735	1826	61	Mass.	Mass.	March 4, 1797–March 4, 1801	Thomas Jefferson
Thomas Jefferson (DR)	1743	1826	57	Va.	Va.	March 4, 1801–March 4, 1805	Aaron Burr
Thomas Jefferson (DR)			61			March 4, 1805–March 4, 1809	George Clinton
James Madison (DR)	1751	1836	57	Va.	Va.	March 4, 1809–March 4, 1813	George Clinton
James Madison (DR)			61			March 4, 1813–March 4, 1817	Elbridge Gerry
James Monroe (DR)	1758	1831	58	Va.	Va.	March 4, 1817–March 4, 1821	Daniel D. Tompkins
James Monroe (DR)			62			March 4, 1821–March 4, 1825	Daniel D. Tompkins
John Q. Adams (DR)	1767	1848	57	Mass.	Mass.	March 4, 1825–March 4, 1829	John C. Calhoun
Andrew Jackson (D)	1767	1845	61	S.C.	Tenn.	March 4, 1829–March 4, 1833	John C. Calhoun
Andrew Jackson (D)			65			March 4, 1833–March 4, 1837	Martin Van Buren
Martin Van Buren (D)	1782	1862	54	N.Y.	N.Y.	March 4, 1837–March 4, 1841	Richard M. Johnson
W. H. Harrison (W)	1773	1841	68	Va.	Ohio	March 4, 1841–April 4, 1841	John Tyler
John Tyler (W)	1790	1862	51	Va.	Va.	April 6, 1841–March 4, 1845	
James K. Polk (D)	1795	1849	49	N.C.	Tenn.	March 4, 1845–March 4, 1849	George M. Dallas
Zachary Taylor (W)	1784	1850	64	Va.	La.	March 4, 1849–July 9, 1850	Millard Fillmore
Millard Fillmore (W)	1800	1874	50	N.Y.	N.Y.	July 10, 1850–March 4, 1853	
Franklin Pierce (D)	1804	1869	48	N.H.	N.H.	March 4, 1853–March 4, 1857	William R. King
James Buchanan (D)	1791	1868	65	Pa.	Pa.	March 4, 1857–March 4, 1861	John C. Breckinridge
Abraham Lincoln (R)	1809	1865	52	Ky.	Ill.	March 4, 1861–March 4, 1865	Hannibal Hamlin
Abraham Lincoln (R)			56			March 4, 1865–April 15, 1865	Andrew Johnson
Andrew Johnson (R)	1808	1875	56	N.C.	Tenn.	April 15, 1865–March 4, 1869	
Ulysses S. Grant (R)	1822	1885	46	Ohio	Ill.	March 4, 1869–March 4, 1873	Schuyler Colfax
Ulysses S. Grant (R)			50			March 4, 1873–March 4, 1877	Henry Wilson
Rutherford B. Hayes (R)	1822	1893	54	Ohio	Ohio	March 4, 1877–March 4, 1881	William A. Wheeler
James A. Garfield (R)	1831	1881	49	Ohio	Ohio	March 4, 1881–Sept. 19, 1881	Chester A. Arthur
Chester A. Arthur (R)	1830	1886	50	Vt.	N.Y.	Sept. 20, 1881–March 4, 1885	
Grover Cleveland (D)	1837	1908	47	N.J.	N.Y.	March 4, 1885–March 4, 1889	Thomas A. Hendricks
Benjamin Harrison (R)	1833	1901	55	Ohio	Ind.	March 4, 1889–March 4, 1893	Levi P. Morton
Grover Cleveland (D)	1837	1908	55	N.J.	N.Y.	March 4, 1893–March 4, 1897	Adlai E. Stevenson
William McKinley (R)	1843	1901	54	Ohio	Ohio	March 4, 1897–March 4, 1901	Garret A. Hobart
William McKinley (R)			58			March 4, 1901–Sept. 14, 1901	Theodore Roosevelt
Theodore Roosevelt (R)	1858	1919	42	N.Y.	N.Y.	Sept. 14, 1901–March 4, 1905	
Theodore Roosevelt (R)			46			March 4, 1905–March 4, 1909	Charles W. Fairbanks
William H. Taft (R)	1857	1930	51	Ohio	Ohio	March 4, 1909–March 4, 1913	James S. Sherman
Woodrow Wilson (D)	1856	1924	56	Va.	N.J.	March 4, 1913–March 4, 1917	Thomas R. Marshall
Woodrow Wilson (D)			60			March 4, 1917–March 4, 1921	Thomas R. Marshall
Warren G. Harding (R)	1865	1923	55	Ohio	Ohio	March 4, 1921–Aug. 2, 1923	Calvin Coolidge
Calvin Coolidge (R)	1872	1933	51	Vt.	Mass.	Aug. 3, 1923–March 4, 1925	
Calvin Coolidge (R)			52			March 4, 1925–March 4, 1929	Charles G. Dawes
Herbert Hoover (R)	1874	1964	54	Iowa	Calif.	March 4, 1929–March 4, 1933	Charles Curtis
Franklin D. Roosevelt (D)	1882	1945	51	N.Y.	N.Y.	March 4, 1933–Jan. 20, 1937	John N. Garner
Franklin D. Roosevelt (D)			55			Jan. 20, 1937–Jan. 20, 1941	John N. Garner
Franklin D. Roosevelt (D)			59			Jan. 20, 1941–Jan. 20, 1945	Henry A. Wallace
Franklin D. Roosevelt (D)			63			Jan. 20, 1945–April 12, 1945	Harry S. Truman
Harry S. Truman (D)	1884	1972	60	Mo.	Mo.	April 12, 1945–Jan. 20, 1949	
Harry S. Truman (D)			64			Jan. 20, 1949–Jan. 20, 1953	Alben W. Barkley
Dwight D. Eisenhower (R)	1890	1969	62	Texas	N.Y.	Jan. 20, 1953–Jan. 20, 1957	Richard Nixon
Dwight D. Eisenhower (R)			66		Pa.	Jan. 20, 1957–Jan. 20, 1961	Richard Nixon
John F. Kennedy (D)	1917	1963	43	Mass.	Mass.	Jan. 20, 1961–Nov. 22, 1963	Lyndon B. Johnson
Lyndon B. Johnson (D)	1908	1973	55	Texas	Texas	Nov. 22, 1963–Jan. 20, 1965	
Lyndon B. Johnson (D)			56			Jan. 20, 1965–Jan. 20, 1969	Hubert H. Humphrey
Richard Nixon (R)	1913	1994	56	Calif.	N.Y.	Jan. 20, 1969–Jan. 20, 1973	Spiro T. Agnew
Richard Nixon (R)			60		Calif.	Jan. 20, 1973–Aug. 9, 1974	Spiro T. Agnew / Gerald R. Ford
Gerald R. Ford (R)	1913		61	Neb.	Mich.	Aug. 9, 1974–Jan. 20, 1977	Nelson A. Rockefeller
Jimmy Carter (D)	1924		52	Ga.	Ga.	Jan. 20, 1977–Jan. 20, 1981	Walter F. Mondale
Ronald Reagan (R)	1911		69	Ill.	Calif.	Jan. 20, 1981–Jan. 20, 1985	George Bush
Ronald Reagan (R)			73			Jan. 20, 1985–Jan. 20, 1989	George Bush
George Bush (R)	1924		64	Mass.	Texas	Jan. 20, 1989–Jan. 20, 1993	Dan Quayle
Bill Clinton (D)	1946		46	Ark.	Ark.	Jan. 20, 1993–	Albert Gore Jr.

SOURCE: *Presidential Elections 1789–1992* (Washington, D.C.: Congressional Quarterly, 1995), 8.
NOTE: D—Democrat; DR—Democratic-Republican; F—Federalist; R—Republican; W—Whig.

President	Age at first political office	First political office	Last political office[a]	Age at becoming president	State of residence[b]	Father's occupation	Higher education[c]	Occupation
1. Washington (1789–1797)	17	County surveyor	Commander in chief	57	Va.	Farmer	None	Farmer, surveyor
2. Adams, J. (1797–1801)	39	Surveyor of highways	Vice president	61	Mass.	Farmer	Harvard	Farmer, lawyer
3. Jefferson (1801–1809)	26	State legislator	Vice president	57	Va.	Farmer	William and Mary	Farmer, lawyer
4. Madison (1809–1817)	25	State legislator	Secretary of state	57	Va.	Farmer	Princeton	Farmer
5. Monroe (1817–1825)	24	State legislator	Secretary of state	58	Va.	Farmer	William and Mary	Lawyer, farmer
6. Adams, J. Q. (1825–1829)	27	Minister to Netherlands	Secretary of state	57	Mass.	Farmer, lawyer	Harvard	Lawyer
7. Jackson (1829–1837)	21	Prosecuting attorney	U.S. Senate	61	Tenn.	Farmer	None	Lawyer
8. Van Buren (1837–1841)	30	Surrogate of county	Vice president	54	N.Y.	Tavern keeper	None	Lawyer
9. Harrison, W. H. (1841)	26	Territorial delegate to Congress	Minister to Colombia	68	Ind.	Farmer	Hampden-Sydney	Military
10. Tyler (1841–1845)	21	State legislator	Vice president	51	Va.	Planter, lawyer	William and Mary	Lawyer
11. Polk (1845–1849)	28	State legislator	Governor	49	Tenn.	Surveyor	U. of North Carolina	Lawyer
12. Taylor (1849–1850)	-	None	[a]	64	Ky.	Collector of internal revenue	None	Military
13. Fillmore (1850–1853)	28	State legislator	Vice president	50	N.Y.	Farmer	None	Lawyer
14. Pierce (1853–1857)	25	State legislator	U.S. district attorney	48	N.H.	General	Bowdoin	Lawyer
15. Buchanan (1857–1861)	22	Assistant county prosecutor	Minister to Great Britain	65	Pa.	Farmer	Dickinson	Lawyer
16. Lincoln (1861–1865)	25	State legislator	U.S. House of Representatives	52	Ill.	Farmer, carpenter	None	Lawyer
17. Johnson, A. (1865–1869)	20	City alderman	Vice president	56	Tenn.	Janitor-porter	None	Tailor
18. Grant (1869–1877)	-	None	[a]	46	Ohio	Tanner	West Point	Military
19. Hayes (1877–1881)	36	City solicitor	Governor	54	Ohio	Farmer	Kenyon	Lawyer
20. Garfield (1881)	28	State legislator	U.S. Senate	49	Ohio	Canal worker	Williams	Educator, lawyer
21. Arthur (1881–1885)	31	State engineer	Vice president	50	N.Y.	Minister	Union	Lawyer
22. Cleveland (1885–1889)	26	Assistant district attorney	Governor	47	N.Y.	Minister	None	Lawyer
23. Harrison, B. (1889–1893)	24	City attorney	U.S. Senate	55	Ind.	Military	Miami of Ohio	Lawyer

President	Age at first political office	First political office	Last political office[a]	Age at becoming president	State of residence[b]	Father's occupation	Higher education[c]	Occupation
24. Cleveland (1893–1897)			President	55				
25. McKinley (1897–1901)	26	Prosecuting attorney	Governor	54	Ohio	Ironmonger	Allegheny	Lawyer
26. Roosevelt, T. (1901–1909)	24	State legislator	Vice president	42	N.Y.	Businessman	Harvard	Lawyer, author
27. Taft (1909–1913)	24	Assistant prosecuting attorney	Secretary of war	51	Ohio	Lawyer	Yale	Lawyer
28. Wilson (1913–1921)	54	Governor	Governor	56	N.J.	Minister	Princeton	Educator
29. Harding (1921–1923)	35	State legislator	U.S. Senate	55	Ohio	Physician, editor	Ohio Central	Newspaper editor
30. Coolidge (1923–1929)	26	City councilman	Vice president	51	Mass.	Storekeeper	Amherst	Lawyer
31. Hoover (1929–1933)	43	Relief and food administrator	Secretary of commerce	54	Calif.	Blacksmith	Stanford	Mining engineer
32. Roosevelt, F. (1933–1945)	28	State legislator	Governor	51	N.Y.	Businessman, landowner	Harvard	Lawyer
33. Truman (1945–1953)	38	County judge (commissioner)	Vice president	60	Mo.	Farmer, livestock	None	Clerk, store owner
34. Eisenhower (1953–1961)	-	None	[a]	62	Kan.	Mechanic	West Point	Military
35. Kennedy (1961–1963)	29	U.S. House of Representatives	U.S. Senate	43	Mass.	Businessman	Harvard	Newspaper reporter
36. Johnson, L. (1963–1969)	28	U.S. House of Representatives	Vice president	55	Texas	Farmer, real estate	Southwest Texas State Teacher's College	Educator
37. Nixon (1969–1974)	34	U. S. House of Representatives	Vice president	56	Calif.	Streetcar conductor	Whittier	Lawyer
38. Ford (1974–1977)	36	U.S. House of Representatives	Vice president	61	Mich.	Businessman	U. of Michigan	Lawyer
39. Carter (1977–1981)	38	County board of education	Governor	52	Ga.	Farmer, businessman	U.S. Naval Academy	Farmer, businessman
40. Reagan (1981–1989)	55	Governor	Governor	69	Calif.	Shoe salesman	Eureka	Entertainer
41. Bush (1989–1993)	42	U.S. House of Representatives	Vice president	64	Texas	Businessman, U.S. senator	Yale	Businessman
42. Clinton (1993–)	30	State attorney general	Governor	46	Ark.	Car dealer	Georgetown	Lawyer

SOURCE: Norman C. Thomas, Joseph A. Pika, and Richard A. Watson, *The Politics of the Presidency*, 3d ed., revised (Washington, D.C.: CQ Press, 1994), 490–492.

NOTES: a. This category refers to the last civilian office held before the presidency. Taylor, Grant, and Eisenhower had served as generals before becoming president. b. The state is where the president spent his important adult years, not necessarily where he was born.   c. Refers to undergraduate education.

Electoral College Votes, 1789–1992

Article II, section 1 of the Constitution gives each state a number of electors equal to the number of senators and representatives to which it is entitled. Prior to ratification of the Twelfth Amendment in 1804, each presidential elector had two votes and was required to cast each vote for a different person. The person receiving the highest number of votes from a majority of electors was elected president; the person receiving the second highest total became vice president. Since there were sixty-nine electors in 1789, Washington's sixty-nine votes constituted a unanimous election. After ratification of the Twelfth Amendment, electors were required to designate which of their two votes was for president and which was for vice president. The first four tables show *all* electoral votes cast in the elections of 1789, 1792, 1796, and 1800; the tables for 1804 and thereafter show only the electoral votes cast for president. A breakdown of electoral votes for vice president is given elsewhere in Reference Materials. *(See "Electoral Votes for Vice President, 1804–1992," p. 1659.)*

SPLIT ELECTORAL VOTES

Throughout the history of presidential elections, the electoral votes of a state have occasionally been divided between two or more candidates. Such split votes, which became less common as the electoral process evolved, occurred for a variety of reasons.

The voting procedures prescribed by the Constitution were in part responsible for split votes in the first four presidential elections. The requirement that each of a state's several electors cast two votes, each vote for a different candidate, contributed to split votes; in the election of 1800, for example, Maryland's twenty electoral votes were equally divided among four candidates. Passage of the Twelfth Amendment prior to the election of 1804 reduced the occurrence of split votes, but other factors promoting split votes remained, among them:

• The district system of choosing electors. Under this system, different candidates each could carry several districts. This was the cause of split electoral votes in Maryland in 1804, 1808, 1812, 1824, 1828, and 1832; North Carolina in 1808; Illinois in 1824; Maine and New York in 1828; and Michigan in 1892.

• The selection of electors by the legislatures of some states. Party factionalism or political deals sometimes resulted in the choice of electors loyal to more than one candidate. This caused the division of electoral votes in New York in 1808 and 1824, Delaware in 1824, and Louisiana in 1824.

By 1836 all states except South Carolina had established a system of statewide popular election of electors. (In South Carolina the legislature continued to select electors until after the Civil War.) This practice limited the frequency of split votes, but a few states on occasion still divided their electoral votes among different presidential candidates because of the practice of listing on the ballot the names of all electors and allowing voters to cross off the names of any particular electors they did not like, or, alternatively, requiring voters to vote for each individual elector. Electors of different parties sometimes were chosen. This accounted for split votes in California in 1880, 1892, 1896, and 1912; New Jersey in 1860; North Dakota, Ohio, and Oregon in 1892; Kentucky in 1896; Maryland in 1904 and 1908; and West Virginia in 1916.

The increasing use of voting machines and straight-ticket voting—where the pull of a lever or the marking of an "X" results in automatically casting a vote for every elector—led to a further decline in the frequency of split electoral votes.

Since 1796 the so-called faithless elector has also been a source of split electoral votes. Electors are not legally bound to vote for any particular candidate; they may cast their ballots any way they wish. Although electors are almost always faithful to the candidate of the party with which they are affiliated, they have on occasion broken ranks and voted for a candiate not supported by their party.

This happened in 1796 when a Pennsylvania Federalist elector voted for Democratic-Republican Thomas Jefferson instead of Federalist John Adams; in 1820 when a New Hampshire Democratic-Republican elector voted for John Quincy Adams instead of the party nominee, James Monroe; in 1948 when Preston Parks, a Truman elector in Tennessee, voted for the States' Rights Democratic (Dixiecrat) nominee, Gov. Strom Thurmond of South Carolina; in 1956 when W. F. Turner, a Stevenson elector in Alabama, voted for a local judge, Walter B. Jones; in 1960 when Henry D. Irwin, a Nixon elector in Oklahoma, voted for Sen. Harry F. Byrd, D-Va.; in 1968 when Dr. Lloyd W. Bailey, a Nixon elector in North Carolina, voted for George C. Wallace, the American Independent Party candidate; in 1972 when Roger L. MacBride, a Nixon elector in Virginia, voted for John Hospers, the Libertarian Party candidate; in 1976 when Mike Padden, a Ford elector in Washington State, voted for former governor Ronald Reagan of California; and in 1988 when Margaret Leach, a Dukakis elector in West Virginia, voted for Dukakis's running mate, Sen. Lloyd Bentsen of Texas.

SOURCES: Electoral votes cast for presidential candidates are listed in the *Senate Manual* (Washington, D.C.: U.S. Government Printing Office, 1994), 961–1008. Total electoral votes for each state through the 1980 census were compiled from a chart of each apportionment of the House of Representatives, published in the *Biographical Directory of the United States Congress, 1774–1989* (Washington, D.C.: U.S. Government Printing Office, 1989), 47. The source for apportionment after the 1990 census was the Bureau of the Census.

1789

States	Electoral Votes[a]	Washington	Adams	Jay	Harrison	Rutledge	Hancock	Clinton	Huntington	Milton	Armstrong	Lincoln	Telfair
Connecticut[b]	(14)	7	5	-	-	-	-	-	2	-	-	-	-
Delaware	(6)	3	-	3	-	-	-	-	-	-	-	-	-
Georgia[b]	(10)	5	-	-	-	-	-	-	-	2	1	1	1
Maryland[c]	(16)	6	-	-	6	-	-	-	-	-	-	-	-
Massachusetts	(20)	10	10	-	-	-	-	-	-	-	-	-	-
New Hampshire	(10)	5	5	-	-	-	-	-	-	-	-	-	-
New Jersey[b]	(12)	6	1	5	-	-	-	-	-	-	-	-	-
New York[d]	(16)	-	-	-	-	-	-	-	-	-	-	-	-
North Carolina[e]	(14)	-	-	-	-	-	-	-	-	-	-	-	-
Pennsylvania[b]	(20)	10	8	-	-	-	2	-	-	-	-	-	-
Rhode Island[e]	(6)	-	-	-	-	-	-	-	-	-	-	-	-
South Carolina[b]	(14)	7	-	-	-	6	1	-	-	-	-	-	-
Virginia[f]	(24)	10	5	1	-	-	1	3	-	-	-	-	-
TOTALS	(182)	69	34	9	6	6	4	3	2	2	1	1	1

NOTES: a. Two votes for each elector; see explanation, p. 1634.   b. For explanation of split electoral votes, see p. 1634.   c. Two Maryland electors did not vote.   d. Not voting. Because of a dispute between its two chambers, the New York legislature failed to choose electors.   e. Not voting because had not yet ratified the Constitution. f. Two Virginia electors did not vote. For explanation of split electoral votes, see p. 1634.

1792

States	Electoral Votes[a]	Washington	Adams	Clinton	Jefferson	Burr
Connecticut	(18)	9	9	-	-	-
Delaware	(6)	3	3	-	-	-
Georgia	(8)	4	-	4	-	-
Kentucky	(8)	4	-	-	4	-
Maryland[b]	(20)	8	8	-	-	-
Massachusetts	(32)	16	16	-	-	-
New Hampshire	(12)	6	6	-	-	-
New Jersey	(14)	7	7	-	-	-
New York	(24)	12	-	12	-	-
North Carolina	(24)	12	-	12	-	-
Pennsylvania[c]	(30)	15	14	1	-	-
Rhode Island	(8)	4	4	-	-	-
South Carolina[c]	(16)	8	7	-	-	1
Vermont[b]	(8)	3	3	-	-	-
Virginia	(42)	21	-	21	-	-
TOTALS	(270)	132	77	50	4	1

NOTES: a. Two votes for each elector; see explanation, p. 1634.   b. Two Maryland electors and one Vermont elector did not vote.   c. For explanation of split electoral votes, see p. 1634.

1796

States	Electoral Votes[a]	J. Adams	Jefferson	T. Pinckney	Burr	S. Adams	Ellsworth	Clinton	Jay	Iredell	Henry	Johnston	Washington	C. Pinckney
Connecticut[b]	(18)	9	-	4	-	-	-	-	5	-	-	-	-	-
Delaware	(6)	3	-	3	-	-	-	-	-	-	-	-	-	-
Georgia	(8)	-	4	-	-	-	-	4	-	-	-	-	-	-
Kentucky	(8)	-	4	-	4	-	-	-	-	-	-	-	-	-
Maryland[b]	(20)	7	4	4	3	-	-	-	-	-	2	-	-	-
Massachusetts[b]	(32)	16	-	13	-	-	1	-	-	-	-	2	-	-
New Hampshire	(12)	6	-	-	-	-	6	-	-	-	-	-	-	-
New Jersey	(14)	7	-	7	-	-	-	-	-	-	-	-	-	-
New York	(24)	12	-	12	-	-	-	-	-	-	-	-	-	-
North Carolina[b]	(24)	1	11	1	6	-	-	-	-	3	-	-	1	1
Pennsylvania[b]	(30)	1	14	2	13	-	-	-	-	-	-	-	-	-
Rhode Island	(8)	4	-	-	-	-	4	-	-	-	-	-	-	-
South Carolina	(16)	-	8	8	-	-	-	-	-	-	-	-	-	-
Tennessee	(6)	-	3	-	3	-	-	-	-	-	-	-	-	-
Vermont	(8)	4	-	4	-	-	-	-	-	-	-	-	-	-
Virginia[b]	(42)	1	20	1	1	15	-	3	-	-	-	-	1	-
TOTALS	(276)	71	68	59	30	15	11	7	5	3	2	2	2	1

NOTES: a. Two votes for each elector; see explanation, p. 1634.   b. For explanation of split electoral votes, see p. 1634.

1800

States	Electoral Votes[a]	Jefferson[b]	Burr[b]	Adams	Pinckney	Jay	States	Electoral Votes[a]	Jefferson[b]	Burr[b]	Adams	Pinckney	Jay
Connecticut	(18)	-	-	9	9	-	North Carolina[c]	(24)	8	8	4	4	-
Delaware	(6)	-	-	3	3	-	Pennsylvania[c]	(30)	8	8	7	7	-
Georgia	(8)	4	4	-	-	-	Rhode Island[c]	(8)	-	-	4	3	1
Kentucky	(8)	4	4	-	-	-	South Carolina	(16)	8	8	-	-	-
Maryland[c]	(20)	5	5	5	5	-	Tennessee	(6)	3	3	-	-	-
Massachusetts	(32)	-	-	16	16	-	Vermont	(8)	-	-	4	4	-
New Hampshire	(12)	-	-	6	6	-	Virginia	(42)	21	21	-	-	-
New Jersey	(14)	-	-	7	7	-	TOTALS	(276)	73	73	65	64	1
New York	(24)	12	12	-	-	-							

NOTES: a. Two votes for each elector; see explanation, p. 1634.   b. Since Jefferson and Burr tied in the electoral college, the election was decided (in Jefferson's favor) by the House of Representatives. See "Jefferson's Revenge: 1800," p. 336, in Chapter 5, Vol. I.   c. For explanation of split electoral votes, see p. 1634.

1804

States	Electoral Votes	Jefferson	Pinckney	States	Votes	Jefferson	Pinckney
Connecticut	(9)	-	9	Ohio	(3)	3	-
Delaware	(3)	-	3	Pennsylvania	(20)	20	-
Georgia	(6)	6	-	Rhode Island	(4)	4	-
Kentucky	(8)	8	-	South Carolina	(10)	10	-
Maryland[a]	(11)	9	2	Tennessee	(5)	5	-
Massachusetts	(19)	19	-	Vermont	(6)	6	-
New Hampshire	(7)	7	-	Virginia	(24)	24	-
New Jersey	(8)	8	-	TOTALS	(176)	162	14
New York	(19)	19	-				
North Carolina	(14)	14	-				

NOTES: a. For explanation of split electoral votes, see p. 1634.

1808

States	Electoral Votes	Madison	Pinckney	Clinton	States	Electoral Votes	Madison	Pinckney	Clinton
Connecticut	(9)	-	9	-	Ohio	(3)	3	-	-
Delaware	(3)	-	3	-	Pennsylvania	(20)	20	-	-
Georgia	(6)	6	-	-	Rhode Island	(4)	-	4	-
Kentucky[a]	(8)	7	-	-	South Carolina	(10)	10	-	-
Maryland[b]	(11)	9	2	-	Tennessee	(5)	5	-	-
Massachusetts	(19)	-	19	-	Vermont	(6)	6	-	-
New Hampshire	(7)	-	7	-	Virginia	(24)	24	-	-
New Jersey	(8)	8	-	-					
New York[b]	(19)	13	-	6	TOTALS	(176)	122	47	6
North Carolina[b]	(14)	11	3	-					

NOTES: a. One Kentucky elector did not vote.   b. For explanation of split electoral votes, see p. 1634.

1812

States	Electoral Votes	Madison	Clinton	States	Electoral Votes	Madison	Clinton
Connecticut	(9)	-	9	North Carolina	(15)	15	-
Delaware	(4)	-	4	Ohio[b]	(8)	7	-
Georgia	(8)	8	-	Pennsylvania	(25)	25	-
Kentucky	(12)	12	-	Rhode Island	(4)	-	4
Louisiana	(3)	3	-	South Carolina	(11)	11	-
Maryland[a]	(11)	6	5	Tennessee	(8)	8	-
Massachusetts	(22)	-	22	Vermont	(8)	8	-
New Hampshire	(8)	-	8	Virginia	(25)	25	-
New Jersey	(8)	-	8				
New York	(29)	-	29	TOTALS	(218)	128	89

NOTES: a. For explanation of split electoral votes, see p. 1634.   b. One Ohio elector did not vote.

1816

States	Electoral Votes	Monroe	King	States	Electoral Votes	Monroe	King
Connecticut	(9)	-	9	North Carolina	(15)	15	-
Delaware[a]	(4)	-	3	Ohio	(8)	8	-
Georgia	(8)	8	-	Pennsylvania	(25)	25	-
Indiana	(3)	3	-	Rhode Island	(4)	4	-
Kentucky	(12)	12	-	South Carolina	(11)	11	-
Louisiana	(3)	3	-	Tennessee	(8)	8	-
Maryland[a]	(11)	8	-	Vermont	(8)	8	-
Massachusetts	(22)	-	22	Virginia	(25)	25	-
New Hampshire	(8)	8	-				
New Jersey	(8)	8	-	TOTALS	(221)	183	34
New York	(29)	29	-				

NOTE: a. One Delaware and three Maryland electors did not vote.

1820

States	Electoral Votes	Monroe	Adams	States	Electoral Votes	Monroe	Adams
Alabama	(3)	3	-	New Hampshire[b]	(8)	7	1
Connecticut	(9)	9	-	New Jersey	(8)	8	-
Delaware	(4)	4	-	New York	(29)	29	-
Georgia	(8)	8	-	North Carolina	(15)	15	-
Illinois	(3)	3	-	Ohio	(8)	8	-
Indiana	(3)	3	-	Pennsylvania[a]	(25)	24	-
Kentucky	(12)	12	-	Rhode Island	(4)	4	-
Louisiana	(3)	3	-	South Carolina	(11)	11	-
Maine	(9)	9	-	Tennessee[a]	(8)	7	-
Maryland	(11)	11	-	Vermont	(8)	8	-
Massachusetts	(15)	15	-	Virginia	(25)	25	-
Mississippi[a]	(3)	2	-				
Missouri	(3)	3	-	TOTALS	(235)	231	1

NOTES: a. One elector each from Mississippi, Pennsylvania, and Tennessee did not vote.   b. For explanation of split electoral votes, see p. 1634.

1824

States	Electoral Votes	Jackson	Adams	Crawford	Clay	States	Electoral Votes	Jackson	Adams	Crawford	Clay
Alabama	(5)	5	-	-	-	New Hampshire	(8)	-	8	-	-
Connecticut	(8)	-	8	-	-	New Jersey	(8)	8	-	-	-
Delaware[a]	(3)	-	1	2	-	New York[a]	(36)	1	26	5	4
Georgia	(9)	-	-	9	-	North Carolina	(15)	15	-	-	-
Illinois[a]	(3)	2	1	-	-	Ohio	(16)	-	-	-	16
Indiana	(5)	5	-	-	-	Pennsylvania	(28)	28	-	-	-
Kentucky	(14)	-	-	-	14	Rhode Island	(4)	-	4	-	-
Louisiana[a]	(5)	3	2	-	-	South Carolina	(11)	11	-	-	-
Maine	(9)	-	9	-	-	Tennessee	(11)	11	-	-	-
Maryland[a]	(11)	7	3	1	-	Vermont	(7)	-	7	-	-
Massachusetts	(15)	-	15	-	-	Virginia	(24)	-	-	24	-
Mississippi	(3)	3	-	-	-						
Missouri	(3)	-	-	-	3	TOTALS	(261)	99[b]	84	41	37

NOTES: a. For explanation of split electoral votes, see p. 1634.   b. As no candidate received a majority of the electoral votes, the election was decided (in Adams's favor) by the House of Representatives.

1828

States	Electoral Votes	Jackson	Adams	States	Electoral Votes	Jackson	Adams
Alabama	(5)	5	-	New Hampshire	(8)	-	8
Connecticut	(8)	-	8	New Jersey	(8)	-	8
Delaware	(3)	-	3	New York[a]	(36)	20	16
Georgia	(9)	9	-	North Carolina	(15)	15	-
Illinois	(3)	3	-	Ohio	(16)	16	-
Indiana	(5)	5	-	Pennsylvania	(28)	28	-
Kentucky	(14)	14	-	Rhode Island	(4)	-	4
Louisiana	(5)	5	-	South Carolina	(11)	11	-
Maine[a]	(9)	1	8	Tennessee	(11)	11	-
Maryland[a]	(11)	5	6	Vermont	(7)	-	7
Massachusetts	(15)	-	15	Virginia	(24)	24	-
Mississippi	(3)	3	-				
Missouri	(3)	3	-	TOTALS	(261)	178	83

NOTE: a. For explanation of split electoral votes, see p. 1634.

1832

States	Electoral Votes	Jackson	Clay	Floyd	Wirt	States	Votes	Jackson	Clay	Floyd	Wirt
Alabama	(7)	7	-	-	-	New Hampshire	(7)	7	-	-	-
Connecticut	(8)	-	8	-	-	New Jersey	(8)	8	-	-	-
Delaware	(3)	-	3	-	-	New York	(42)	42	-	-	-
Georgia	(11)	11	-	-	-	North Carolina	(15)	15	-	-	-
Illinois	(5)	5	-	-	-	Ohio	(21)	21	-	-	-
Indiana	(9)	9	-	-	-	Pennsylvania	(30)	30	-	-	-
Kentucky	(15)	-	15	-	-	Rhode Island	(4)	-	4	-	-
Louisiana	(5)	5	-	-	-	South Carolina	(11)	-	-	11	-
Maine	(10)	10	-	-	-	Tennessee	(15)	15	-	-	-
Maryland[a]	(10)	3	5	-	-	Vermont	(7)	-	-	-	7
Massachusetts	(14)	-	14	-	-	Virginia	(23)	23	-	-	-
Mississippi	(4)	4	-	-							
Missouri	(4)	4	-	-	-	TOTALS	(288)	219	49	11	7

NOTE: a. Two Maryland electors did not vote. For explanation of split electoral votes, see p. 1634.

1836

States	Electoral Votes	Van Buren	Harrison[a]	White[a]	Webster[a]	Mangum
Alabama	(7)	7	-	-	-	-
Arkansas	(3)	3	-	-	-	-
Connecticut	(8)	8	-	-	-	-
Delaware	(3)	-	3	-	-	-
Georgia	(11)	-	-	11	-	-
Illinois	(5)	5	-	-	-	-
Indiana	(9)	-	9	-	-	-
Kentucky	(15)	-	15	-	-	-
Louisiana	(5)	5	-	-	-	-
Maine	(10)	10	-	-	-	-
Maryland	(10)	-	10	-	-	-
Massachusetts	(14)	-	-	-	14	-
Michigan	(3)	3	-	-	-	-
Mississippi	(4)	4	-	-	-	-
Missouri	(4)	4	-	-	-	-
New Hampshire	(7)	7	-	-	-	-
New Jersey	(8)	-	8	-	-	-
New York	(42)	42	-	-	-	-
North Carolina	(15)	15	-	-	-	-
Ohio	(21)	-	21	-	-	-
Pennsylvania	(30)	30	-	-	-	-
Rhode Island	(4)	4	-	-	-	-
South Carolina	(11)	-	-	-	-	11
Tennessee	(15)	-	-	15	-	-
Vermont	(7)	-	7	-	-	-
Virginia	(23)	23	-	-	-	-
TOTALS	(294)	170	73	26	14	11

NOTE: a. For an explanation of the Whigs' strategy in running several candidates, see "Van Buren's 1836 Win," p. 344, in Chapter 7, Vol. I.

1840

States	Electoral Votes	Harrison	Van Buren	States	Electoral Votes	Harrison	Van Buren
Alabama	(7)	-	7	Missouri	(4)	-	4
Arkansas	(3)	-	3	New Hampshire	(7)	-	7
Connecticut	(8)	8	-	New Jersey	(8)	8	-
Delaware	(3)	3	-	New York	(42)	42	-
Georgia	(11)	11	-	North Carolina	(15)	15	-
Illinois	(5)	-	5	Ohio	(21)	21	-
Indiana	(9)	9	-	Pennsylvania	(30)	30	-
Kentucky	(15)	15	-	Rhode Island	(4)	4	-
Louisiana	(5)	5	-	South Carolina	(11)	-	11
Maine	(10)	10	-	Tennessee	(15)	15	-
Maryland	(10)	10	-	Vermont	(7)	7	-
Massachusetts	(14)	14	-	Virginia	(23)	-	23
Michigan	(3)	3	-				
Mississippi	(4)	4	-	TOTALS	(294)	234	60

1844

States	Electoral Votes	Polk	Clay	States	Electoral Votes	Polk	Clay
Alabama	(9)	9	-	Missouri	(7)	7	-
Arkansas	(3)	3	-	New Hampshire	(6)	6	-
Connecticut	(6)	-	6	New Jersey	(7)	-	7
Delaware	(3)	-	3	New York	(36)	36	-
Georgia	(10)	10	-	North Carolina	(11)	-	11
Illinois	(9)	9	-	Ohio	(23)	-	23
Indiana	(12)	12	-	Pennsylvania	(26)	26	-
Kentucky	(12)	-	12	Rhode Island	(4)	-	4
Louisiana	(6)	6	-	South Carolina	(9)	9	-
Maine	(9)	9	-	Tennessee	(13)	-	13
Maryland	(8)	-	8	Vermont	(6)	-	6
Massachusetts	(12)	-	12	Virginia	(17)	17	-
Michigan	(5)	5	-				
Mississippi	(6)	6	-	TOTALS	(275)	170	105

1848

States	Electoral Votes	Taylor	Cass	States	Electoral Votes	Taylor	Cass
Alabama	(9)	-	9	Missouri	(7)	-	7
Arkansas	(3)	-	3	New Hampshire	(6)	-	6
Connecticut	(6)	6	-	New Jersey	(7)	7	-
Delaware	(3)	3	-	New York	(36)	36	-
Florida	(3)	3	-	North Carolina	(11)	11	-
Georgia	(10)	10	-	Ohio	(23)	-	23
Illinois	(9)	-	9	Pennsylvania	(26)	26	-
Indiana	(12)	-	12	Rhode Island	(4)	4	-
Iowa	(4)	-	4	South Carolina	(9)	-	9
Kentucky	(12)	12	-	Tennessee	(13)	13	-
Louisiana	(6)	6	-	Texas	(4)	-	4
Maine	(9)	-	9	Vermont	(6)	6	-
Maryland	(8)	8	-	Virginia	(17)	-	17
Massachusetts	(12)	12	-	Wisconsin	(4)	-	4
Michigan	(5)	-	5				
Mississippi	(6)	-	6	TOTALS	(290)	163	127

1852

States	Electoral Votes	Pierce	Scott	States	Electoral Votes	Pierce	Scott
Alabama	(9)	9	-	Missouri	(9)	9	-
Arkansas	(4)	4	-	New Hampshire	(5)	5	-
California	(4)	4	-	New Jersey	(7)	7	-
Connecticut	(6)	6	-	New York	(35)	35	-
Delaware	(3)	3	-	North Carolina	(10)	10	-
Florida	(3)	3	-	Ohio	(23)	23	-
Georgia	(10)	10	-	Pennsylvania	(27)	27	-
Illinois	(11)	11	-	Rhode Island	(4)	4	-
Indiana	(13)	13	-	South Carolina	(8)	8	-
Iowa	(4)	4	-	Tennessee	(12)	-	12
Kentucky	(12)	-	12	Texas	(4)	4	-
Louisiana	(6)	6	-	Vermont	(5)	-	5
Maine	(8)	8	-	Virginia	(15)	15	-
Maryland	(8)	8	-	Wisconsin	(5)	5	-
Massachusetts	(13)	-	13				
Michigan	(6)	6	-	TOTALS	(296)	254	42
Mississippi	(7)	7	-				

1856

States	Electoral Votes	Buchanan	Fremont	Fillmore	States	Electoral Votes	Buchanan	Fremont	Fillmore
Alabama	(9)	9	-	-	Missouri	(9)	9	-	-
Arkansas	(4)	4	-	-	New Hampshire	(5)	-	5	-
California	(4)	4	-	-	New Jersey	(7)	7	-	-
Connecticut	(6)	-	6	-	New York	(35)	-	35	-
Delaware	(3)	3	-	-	North Carolina	(10)	10	-	-
Florida	(3)	3	-	-	Ohio	(23)	-	23	-
Georgia	(10)	10	-	-	Pennsylvania	(27)	27	-	-
Illinois	(11)	11	-	-	Rhode Island	(4)	-	4	-
Indiana	(13)	13	-	-	South Carolina	(8)	8	-	-
Iowa	(4)	-	4	-	Tennessee	(12)	12	-	-
Kentucky	(12)	12	-	-	Texas	(4)	4	-	-
Louisiana	(6)	6	-	-	Vermont	(5)	-	5	-
Maine	(8)	-	8	-	Virginia	(15)	15	-	-
Maryland	(8)	-	-	8	Wisconsin	(5)	-	5	-
Massachusetts	(13)	-	13	-					
Michigan	(6)	-	6	-	TOTALS	(296)	174	114	8
Mississippi	(7)	7	-	-					

1860

States	Electoral Votes	Lincoln	Breckinridge	Bell	Douglas
Alabama	(9)	-	9	-	-
Arkansas	(4)	-	4	-	-
California	(4)	4	-	-	-
Connecticut	(6)	6	-	-	-
Delaware	(3)	-	3	-	-
Florida	(3)	-	3	-	-
Georgia	(10)	-	10	-	-
Illinois	(11)	11	-	-	-
Indiana	(13)	13	-	-	-
Iowa	(4)	4	-	-	-
Kentucky	(12)	-	-	12	-
Louisiana	(6)	-	6	-	-
Maine	(8)	8	-	-	-
Maryland	(8)	-	8	-	-
Massachusetts	(13)	13	-	-	-
Michigan	(6)	6	-	-	-
Minnesota	(4)	4	-	-	-
Mississippi	(7)	-	7	-	-
Missouri	(9)	-	-	-	9
New Hampshire	(5)	5	-	-	-
New Jersey[a]	(7)	4	-	-	3
New York	(35)	35	-	-	-
North Carolina	(10)	-	10	-	-
Ohio	(23)	23	-	-	-
Oregon	(3)	3	-	-	-
Pennsylvania	(27)	27	-	-	-
Rhode Island	(4)	4	-	-	-
South Carolina	(8)	-	8	-	-
Tennessee	(12)	-	-	12	-
Texas	(4)	-	4	-	-
Vermont	(5)	5	-	-	-
Virginia	(15)	-	-	15	-
Wisconsin	(5)	5	-	-	-
TOTALS	(303)	180	72	39	12

NOTE: a. For explanation of split electoral votes, see p. 1634.

1864

States[a]	Electoral Votes	Lincoln	McClellan
California	(5)	5	-
Connecticut	(6)	6	-
Delaware	(3)	-	3
Illinois	(16)	16	-
Indiana	(13)	13	-
Iowa	(8)	8	-
Kansas	(3)	3	-
Kentucky	(11)	-	11
Maine	(7)	7	-
Maryland	(7)	7	-
Massachusetts	(12)	12	-
Michigan	(8)	8	-
Minnesota	(4)	4	-
Missouri	(11)	11	-
Nevada[b]	(3)	2	-
New Hampshire	(5)	5	-
New Jersey	(7)	-	7
New York	(33)	33	-
Ohio	(21)	21	-
Oregon	(3)	3	-
Pennsylvania	(26)	26	-
Rhode Island	(4)	4	-
Vermont	(5)	5	-
West Virginia	(5)	5	-
Wisconsin	(8)	8	-
TOTALS	(234)	212	21

NOTES: a. Eleven Southern states—Alabama, Arkansas, Florida, Georgia, Louisiana, Mississippi, North Carolina, South Carolina, Tennessee, Texas, and Virginia—had seceded from the Union and did not vote.   b. One Nevada elector did not vote.

1868

States[a]	Electoral Votes	Grant	Seymour	States[a]	Electoral Votes	Grant	Seymour
Alabama	(8)	8	-	Missouri	(11)	11	-
Arkansas	(5)	5	-	Nebraska	(3)	3	-
California	(5)	5	-	Nevada	(3)	3	-
Connecticut	(6)	6	-	New Hampshire	(5)	5	-
Delaware	(3)	-	3	New Jersey	(7)	-	7
Florida	(3)	3	-	New York	(33)	-	33
Georgia	(9)	-	9	North Carolina	(9)	9	-
Illinois	(16)	16	-	Ohio	(21)	21	-
Indiana	(13)	13	-	Oregon	(3)	-	3
Iowa	(8)	8	-	Pennsylvania	(26)	26	-
Kansas	(3)	3	-	Rhode Island	(4)	4	-
Kentucky	(11)	-	11	South Carolina	(6)	6	-
Louisiana	(7)	-	7	Tennessee	(10)	10	-
Maine	(7)	7	-	Vermont	(5)	5	-
Maryland	(7)	-	7	West Virginia	(5)	5	-
Massachusetts	(12)	12	-	Wisconsin	(8)	8	-
Michigan	(8)	8	-				
Minnesota	(4)	4	-	TOTALS	(294)	214	80

NOTE: a. Mississippi, Texas, and Virginia were not yet readmitted to the Union and did not participate in the election.

1872

States	Electoral Votes	Grant	Hendricks[a]	Brown[a]	Jenkins[a]	Davis[a]	States	Electoral Votes	Grant	Hendricks[a]	Brown[a]	Jenkins[a]	Davis[a]
Alabama	(10)	10	-	-	-	-	Nebraska	(3)	3	-	-	-	-
Arkansas[b]	(6)	-	-	-	-	-	Nevada	(3)	3	-	-	-	-
California	(6)	6	-	-	-	-	New Hampshire	(5)	5	-	-	-	-
Connecticut	(6)	6	-	-	-	-	New Jersey	(9)	9	-	-	-	-
Delaware	(3)	3	-	-	-	-	New York	(35)	35	-	-	-	-
Florida	(4)	4	-	-	-	-	North Carolina	(10)	10	-	-	-	-
Georgia[c]	(11)	-	-	6	2	-	Ohio	(22)	22	-	-	-	-
Illinois	(21)	21	-	-	-	-	Oregon	(3)	3	-	-	-	-
Indiana	(15)	15	-	-	-	-	Pennsylvania	(29)	29	-	-	-	-
Iowa	(11)	11	-	-	-	-	Rhode Island	(4)	4	-	-	-	-
Kansas	(5)	5	-	-	-	-	South Carolina	(7)	7	-	-	-	-
Kentucky	(12)	-	8	4	-	-	Tennessee	(12)	-	12	-	-	-
Louisiana[b]	(8)	-	-	-	-	-	Texas	(8)	-	8	-	-	-
Maine	(7)	7	-	-	-	-	Vermont	(5)	5	-	-	-	-
Maryland	(8)	-	8	-	-	-	Virginia	(11)	11	-	-	-	-
Massachusetts	(13)	13	-	-	-	-	West Virginia	(5)	5	-	-	-	-
Michigan	(11)	11	-	-	-	-	Wisconsin	(10)	10	-	-	-	-
Minnesota	(5)	5	-	-	-	-							
Mississippi	(8)	8	-	-	-	-	TOTALS	(366)	286	42	18	2	1
Missouri	(15)	-	6	8	-	1							

NOTES: a. Liberal Republican and Democratic presidential candidate Horace Greeley died November 29, 1872. In the electoral college, the electors who had been pledged to Greeley split their presidential electoral votes among four candidates, including 18 for Benjamin Gratz Brown, Greeley's running mate. b. Congress refused to accept the electoral votes of Arkansas and Louisiana because of disruptive conditions during Reconstruction. c. Three Georgia electoral votes cast for Greeley were not counted.

1876

States	Electoral Votes	Hayes	Tilden	States	Electoral Votes	Hayes	Tilden
Alabama	(10)	-	10	Missouri	(15)	-	15
Arkansas	(6)	-	6	Nebraska	(3)	3	-
California	(6)	6	-	Nevada	(3)	3	-
Colorado	(3)	3	-	New Hampshire	(5)	5	-
Connecticut	(6)	-	6	New Jersey	(9)	-	9
Delaware	(3)	-	3	New York	(35)	-	35
Florida[a]	(4)	4	-	North Carolina	(10)	-	10
Georgia	(11)	-	11	Ohio	(22)	22	-
Illinois	(21)	21	-	Oregon[a]	(3)	3	-
Indiana	(15)	-	15	Pennsylvania	(29)	29	-
Iowa	(11)	11	-	Rhode Island	(4)	4	-
Kansas	(5)	5	-	South Carolina[a]	(7)	7	-
Kentucky	(12)	-	12	Tennessee	(12)	-	12
Louisiana[a]	(8)	8	-	Texas	(8)	-	8
Maine	(7)	7	-	Vermont	(5)	5	-
Maryland	(8)	-	8	Virginia	(11)	-	11
Massachusetts	(13)	13	-	West Virginia	(5)	-	5
Michigan	(11)	11	-	Wisconsin	(10)	10	-
Minnesota	(5)	5	-				
Mississippi	(8)	-	8	TOTALS	(369)	185	184

NOTE: a. The electoral votes of Florida, Louisiana, Oregon, and South Carolina were disputed. See "The Compromise of 1876," p. 356, in Chapter 7, Vol. I.

1880

States	Electoral Votes	Garfield	Hancock	States	Electoral Votes	Garfield	Hancock
Alabama	(10)	-	10	Missouri	(15)	-	15
Arkansas	(6)	-	6	Nebraska	(3)	3	-
California[a]	(6)	1	5	Nevada	(3)	-	3
Colorado	(3)	3	-	New Hampshire	(5)	5	-
Connecticut	(6)	6	-	New Jersey	(9)	-	9
Delaware	(3)	-	3	New York	(35)	35	-
Florida	(4)	-	4	North Carolina	(10)	-	10
Georgia	(11)	-	11	Ohio	(22)	22	-
Illinois	(21)	21	-	Oregon	(3)	3	-
Indiana	(15)	15	-	Pennsylvania	(29)	29	-
Iowa	(11)	11	-	Rhode Island	(4)	4	-
Kansas	(5)	5	-	South Carolina	(7)	-	7
Kentucky	(12)	-	12	Tennessee	(12)	-	12
Louisiana	(8)	-	8	Texas	(8)	-	8
Maine	(7)	7	-	Vermont	(5)	5	-
Maryland	(8)	-	8	Virginia	(11)	-	11
Massachusetts	(13)	13	-	West Virginia	(5)	-	5
Michigan	(11)	11	-	Wisconsin	(10)	10	-
Minnesota	(5)	5	-				
Mississippi	(8)	-	8	TOTALS	(369)	214	155

NOTE: a. For explanation of split electoral votes, see p. 1634.

1884

States	Electoral Votes	Cleveland	Blaine	States	Electoral Votes	Cleveland	Blaine
Alabama	(10)	10	-	Missouri	(16)	16	-
Arkansas	(7)	7	-	Nebraska	(5)	-	5
California	(8)	-	8	Nevada	(3)	-	3
Colorado	(3)	-	3	New Hampshire	(4)	-	4
Connecticut	(6)	6	-	New Jersey	(9)	9	-
Delaware	(3)	3	-	New York	(36)	36	-
Florida	(4)	4	-	North Carolina	(11)	11	-
Georgia	(12)	12	-	Ohio	(23)	-	23
Illinois	(22)	-	22	Oregon	(3)	-	3
Indiana	(15)	15	-	Pennsylvania	(30)	-	30
Iowa	(13)	-	13	Rhode Island	(4)	-	4
Kansas	(9)	-	9	South Carolina	(9)	9	-
Kentucky	(13)	13	-	Tennessee	(12)	12	-
Louisiana	(8)	8	-	Texas	(13)	13	-
Maine	(6)	-	6	Vermont	(4)	-	4
Maryland	(8)	8	-	Virginia	(12)	12	-
Massachusetts	(14)	-	14	West Virginia	(6)	6	-
Michigan	(13)	-	13	Wisconsin	(11)	-	11
Minnesota	(7)	-	7				
Mississippi	(9)	9	-	TOTALS	(401)	219	182

1888

States	Electoral Votes	Harrison	Cleveland	States	Electoral Votes	Harrison	Cleveland
Alabama	(10)	-	10	Missouri	(16)	-	16
Arkansas	(7)	-	7	Nebraska	(5)	5	-
California	(8)	8	-	Nevada	(3)	3	-
Colorado	(3)	3	-	New Hampshire	(4)	4	-
Connecticut	(6)	-	6	New Jersey	(9)	-	9
Delaware	(3)	-	3	New York	(36)	36	-
Florida	(4)	-	4	North Carolina	(11)	-	11
Georgia	(12)	-	12	Ohio	(23)	23	-
Illinois	(22)	22	-	Oregon	(3)	3	-
Indiana	(15)	15	-	Pennsylvania	(30)	30	-
Iowa	(13)	13	-	Rhode Island	(4)	4	-
Kansas	(9)	9	-	South Carolina	(9)	-	9
Kentucky	(13)	-	13	Tennessee	(12)	-	12
Louisiana	(8)	-	8	Texas	(13)	-	13
Maine	(6)	6	-	Vermont	(4)	4	-
Maryland	(8)	-	8	Virginia	(12)	-	12
Massachusetts	(14)	14	-	West Virginia	(6)	-	6
Michigan	(13)	13	-	Wisconsin	(11)	11	-
Minnesota	(7)	7	-				
Mississippi	(9)	-	9	TOTALS	(401)	233	168

1892

States	Electoral Votes	Cleveland	Harrison	Weaver	States	Electoral Votes	Cleveland	Harrison	Weaver
Alabama	(11)	11	-	-	Nebraska	(8)	-	8	-
Arkansas	(8)	8	-	-	Nevada	(3)	-	-	3
California[a]	(9)	8	1	-	New Hampshire	(4)	-	4	-
Colorado	(4)	-	-	4	New Jersey	(10)	10	-	-
Connecticut	(6)	6	-	-	New York	(36)	36	-	-
Delaware	(3)	3	-	-	North Carolina	(11)	11	-	-
Florida	(4)	4	-	-	North Dakota[a]	(3)	1	1	1
Georgia	(13)	13	-	-	Ohio[a]	(23)	1	22	-
Idaho	(3)	-	-	3	Oregon[a]	(4)	-	3	1
Illinois	(24)	24	-	-	Pennsylvania	(32)	-	32	-
Indiana	(15)	15	-	-	Rhode Island	(4)	-	4	-
Iowa	(13)	-	13	-	South Carolina	(9)	9	-	-
Kansas	(10)	-	-	10	South Dakota	(4)	-	4	-
Kentucky	(13)	13	-	-	Tennessee	(12)	12	-	-
Louisiana	(8)	8	-	-	Texas	(15)	15	-	-
Maine	(6)	-	6	-	Vermont	(4)	-	4	-
Maryland	(8)	8	-	-	Virginia	(12)	12	-	-
Massachusetts	(15)	-	15	-	Washington	(4)	-	4	-
Michigan[a]	(14)	5	9	-	West Virginia	(6)	6	-	-
Minnesota	(9)	-	9	-	Wisconsin	(12)	12	-	-
Mississippi	(9)	9	-	-	Wyoming	(3)	-	3	-
Missouri	(17)	17	-	-					
Montana	(3)	-	3	-	TOTALS	(444)	277	145	22

NOTE: a. For explanation of split electoral votes, see p. 1634.

1896

States	Electoral Votes	McKinley	Bryan	States	Electoral Votes	McKinley	Bryan
Alabama	(11)	-	11	Nevada	(3)	-	3
Arkansas	(8)	-	8	New Hampshire	(4)	4	-
California[a]	(9)	8	1	New Jersey	(10)	10	-
Colorado	(4)	-	4	New York	(36)	36	-
Connecticut	(6)	6	-	North Carolina	(11)	-	11
Delaware	(3)	3	-	North Dakota	(3)	3	-
Florida	(4)	-	4	Ohio	(23)	23	-
Georgia	(13)	-	13	Oregon	(4)	4	-
Idaho	(3)	-	3	Pennsylvania	(32)	32	-
Illinois	(24)	24	-	Rhode Island	(4)	4	-
Indiana	(15)	15	-	South Carolina	(9)	-	9
Iowa	(13)	13	-	South Dakota	(4)	-	4
Kansas	(10)	-	10	Tennessee	(12)	-	12
Kentucky[a]	(13)	12	1	Texas	(15)	-	15
Louisiana	(8)	-	8	Utah	(3)	-	3
Maine	(6)	6	-	Vermont	(4)	4	-
Maryland	(8)	8	-	Virginia	(12)	-	12
Massachusetts	(15)	15	-	Washington	(4)	-	4
Michigan	(14)	14	-	West Virginia	(6)	6	-
Minnesota	(9)	9	-	Wisconsin	(12)	12	-
Mississippi	(9)	-	9	Wyoming	(3)	-	3
Missouri	(17)	-	17				
Montana	(3)	-	3	TOTALS	(447)	271	176
Nebraska	(8)	-	8				

NOTE: a. For explanation of split electoral votes, see p. 1634.

1900

States	Electoral Votes	McKinley	Bryan	States	Electoral Votes	McKinley	Bryan
Alabama	(11)	-	11	Nevada	(3)	-	3
Arkansas	(8)	-	8	New Hampshire	(4)	4	-
California	(9)	9	-	New Jersey	(10)	10	-
Colorado	(4)	-	4	New York	(36)	36	-
Connecticut	(6)	6	-	North Carolina	(11)	-	11
Delaware	(3)	3	-	North Dakota	(3)	3	-
Florida	(4)	-	4	Ohio	(23)	23	-
Georgia	(13)	-	13	Oregon	(4)	4	-
Idaho	(3)	-	3	Pennsylvania	(32)	32	-
Illinois	(24)	24	-	Rhode Island	(4)	4	-
Indiana	(15)	15	-	South Carolina	(9)	-	9
Iowa	(13)	13	-	South Dakota	(4)	4	-
Kansas	(10)	10	-	Tennessee	(12)	-	12
Kentucky	(13)	-	13	Texas	(15)	-	15
Louisiana	(8)	-	8	Utah	(3)	3	-
Maine	(6)	6	-	Vermont	(4)	4	-
Maryland	(8)	8	-	Virginia	(12)	-	12
Massachusetts	(15)	15	-	Washington	(4)	4	-
Michigan	(14)	14	-	West Virginia	(6)	6	-
Minnesota	(9)	9	-	Wisconsin	(12)	12	-
Mississippi	(9)	-	9	Wyoming	(3)	3	-
Missouri	(17)	-	17				
Montana	(3)	-	3	TOTALS	(447)	292	155
Nebraska	(8)	8	-				

1904

States	Electoral Votes	Roosevelt	Parker	States	Electoral Votes	Roosevelt	Parker
Alabama	(11)	-	11	Nevada	(3)	3	-
Arkansas	(9)	-	9	New Hampshire	(4)	4	-
California	(10)	10	-	New Jersey	(12)	12	-
Colorado	(5)	5	-	New York	(39)	39	-
Connecticut	(7)	7	-	North Carolina	(12)	-	12
Delaware	(3)	3	-	North Dakota	(4)	4	-
Florida	(5)	-	5	Ohio	(23)	23	-
Georgia	(13)	-	13	Oregon	(4)	4	-
Idaho	(3)	3	-	Pennsylvania	(34)	34	-
Illinois	(27)	27	-	Rhode Island	(4)	4	-
Indiana	(15)	15	-	South Carolina	(9)	-	9
Iowa	(13)	13	-	South Dakota	(4)	4	-
Kansas	(10)	10	-	Tennessee	(12)	-	12
Kentucky	(13)	-	13	Texas	(18)	-	18
Louisiana	(9)	-	9	Utah	(3)	3	-
Maine	(6)	6	-	Vermont	(4)	4	-
Maryland[a]	(8)	1	7	Virginia	(12)	-	12
Massachusetts	(16)	16	-	Washington	(5)	5	-
Michigan	(14)	14	-	West Virginia	(7)	7	-
Minnesota	(11)	11	-	Wisconsin	(13)	13	-
Mississippi	(10)	-	10	Wyoming	(3)	3	-
Missouri	(18)	18	-				
Montana	(3)	3	-	TOTALS	(476)	336	140
Nebraska	(8)	8	-				

NOTE: a. For explanation of split electoral votes, see p. 1634.

1908

States	Electoral Votes	Taft	Bryan	States	Electoral Votes	Taft	Bryan
Alabama	(11)	-	11	Nevada	(3)	-	3
Arkansas	(9)	-	9	New Hampshire	(4)	4	-
California	(10)	10	-	New Jersey	(12)	12	-
Colorado	(5)	-	5	New York	(39)	39	-
Connecticut	(7)	7	-	North Carolina	(12)	-	12
Delaware	(3)	3	-	North Dakota	(4)	4	-
Florida	(5)	-	5	Ohio	(23)	23	-
Georgia	(13)	-	13	Oklahoma	(7)	-	7
Idaho	(3)	3	-	Oregon	(4)	4	-
Illinois	(27)	27	-	Pennsylvania	(34)	34	-
Indiana	(15)	15	-	Rhode Island	(4)	4	-
Iowa	(13)	13	-	South Carolina	(9)	-	9
Kansas	(10)	10	-	South Dakota	(4)	4	-
Kentucky	(13)	-	13	Tennessee	(12)	-	12
Louisiana	(9)	-	9	Texas	(18)	-	18
Maine	(6)	6	-	Utah	(3)	3	-
Maryland[a]	(8)	2	6	Vermont	(4)	4	-
Massachusetts	(16)	16	-	Virginia	(12)	-	12
Michigan	(14)	14	-	Washington	(5)	5	-
Minnesota	(11)	11	-	West Virginia	(7)	7	-
Mississippi	(10)	-	10	Wisconsin	(13)	13	-
Missouri	(18)	18	-	Wyoming	(3)	3	-
Montana	(3)	3	-				
Nebraska	(8)	-	8	TOTALS	(483)	321	162

NOTE: a. For explanation of split electoral votes, see p. 1634.

1912

States	Electoral Votes	Wilson	Roosevelt	Taft	States	Electoral Votes	Wilson	Roosevelt	Taft
Alabama	(12)	12	-	-	Nevada	(3)	3	-	-
Arizona	(3)	3	-	-	New Hampshire	(4)	4	-	-
Arkansas	(9)	9	-	-	New Jersey	(14)	14	-	-
California[a]	(13)	2	11	-	New Mexico	(3)	3	-	-
Colorado	(6)	6	-	-	New York	(45)	45	-	-
Connecticut	(7)	7	-	-	North Carolina	(12)	12	-	-
Delaware	(3)	3	-	-	North Dakota	(5)	5	-	-
Florida	(6)	6	-	-	Ohio	(24)	24	-	-
Georgia	(14)	14	-	-	Oklahoma	(10)	10	-	-
Idaho	(4)	4	-	-	Oregon	(5)	5	-	-
Illinois	(29)	29	-	-	Pennsylvania	(38)	-	38	-
Indiana	(15)	15	-	-	Rhode Island	(5)	5	-	-
Iowa	(13)	13	-	-	South Carolina	(9)	9	-	-
Kansas	(10)	10	-	-	South Dakota	(5)	-	5	-
Kentucky	(13)	13	-	-	Tennessee	(12)	12	-	-
Louisiana	(10)	10	-	-	Texas	(20)	20	-	-
Maine	(6)	6	-	-	Utah	(4)	-	-	4
Maryland	(8)	8	-	-	Vermont	(4)	-	-	4
Massachusetts	(18)	18	-	-	Virginia	(12)	12	-	-
Michigan	(15)	-	15	-	Washington	(7)	-	7	-
Minnesota	(12)	-	12	-	West Virginia	(8)	8	-	-
Mississippi	(10)	10	-	-	Wisconsin	(13)	13	-	-
Missouri	(18)	18	-	-	Wyoming	(3)	3	-	-
Montana	(4)	4	-	-					
Nebraska	(8)	8	-	-	TOTALS	(531)	435	88	8

NOTE: a. For explanation of split electoral votes, see p. 1634.

1916

States	Electoral Votes	Wilson	Hughes	States	Electoral Votes	Wilson	Hughes
Alabama	(12)	12	-	Nevada	(3)	3	-
Arizona	(3)	3	-	New Hampshire	(4)	4	-
Arkansas	(9)	9	-	New Jersey	(14)	-	14
California	(13)	13	-	New Mexico	(3)	3	-
Colorado	(6)	6	-	New York	(45)	-	45
Connecticut	(7)	-	7	North Carolina	(12)	12	-
Delaware	(3)	-	3	North Dakota	(5)	5	-
Florida	(6)	6	-	Ohio	(24)	24	-
Georgia	(14)	14	-	Oklahoma	(10)	10	-
Idaho	(4)	4	-	Oregon	(5)	-	5
Illinois	(29)	-	29	Pennsylvania	(38)	-	38
Indiana	(15)	-	15	Rhode Island	(5)	-	5
Iowa	(13)	-	13	South Carolina	(9)	9	-
Kansas	(10)	10	-	South Dakota	(5)	-	5
Kentucky	(13)	13	-	Tennessee	(12)	12	-
Louisiana	(10)	10	-	Texas	(20)	20	-
Maine	(6)	-	6	Utah	(4)	4	-
Maryland	(8)	8	-	Vermont	(4)	-	4
Massachusetts	(18)	-	18	Virginia	(12)	12	-
Michigan	(15)	-	15	Washington	(7)	7	-
Minnesota	(12)	-	12	West Virginia[a]	(8)	1	7
Mississippi	(10)	10	-	Wisconsin	(13)	-	13
Missouri	(18)	18	-	Wyoming	(3)	3	-
Montana	(4)	4	-				
Nebraska	(8)	8	-	TOTALS	(531)	277	254

NOTE: a. For explanation of split electoral votes, see p. 1634.

1920

States	Electoral Votes	Harding	Cox	States	Electoral Votes	Harding	Cox
Alabama	(12)	-	12	Nevada	(3)	3	-
Arizona	(3)	3	-	New Hampshire	(4)	4	-
Arkansas	(9)	-	9	New Jersey	(14)	14	-
California	(13)	13	-	New Mexico	(3)	3	-
Colorado	(6)	6	-	New York	(45)	45	-
Connecticut	(7)	7	-	North Carolina	(12)	-	12
Delaware	(3)	3	-	North Dakota	(5)	5	-
Florida	(6)	-	6	Ohio	(24)	24	-
Georgia	(14)	-	14	Oklahoma	(10)	10	-
Idaho	(4)	4	-	Oregon	(5)	5	-
Illinois	(29)	29	-	Pennsylvania	(38)	38	-
Indiana	(15)	15	-	Rhode Island	(5)	5	-
Iowa	(13)	13	-	South Carolina	(9)	-	9
Kansas	(10)	10	-	South Dakota	(5)	5	-
Kentucky	(13)	-	13	Tennessee	(12)	12	-
Louisiana	(10)	-	10	Texas	(20)	-	20
Maine	(6)	6	-	Utah	(4)	4	-
Maryland	(8)	8	-	Vermont	(4)	4	-
Massachusetts	(18)	18	-	Virginia	(12)	-	12
Michigan	(15)	15	-	Washington	(7)	7	-
Minnesota	(12)	12	-	West Virginia	(8)	8	-
Mississippi	(10)	-	10	Wisconsin	(13)	13	-
Missouri	(18)	18	-	Wyoming	(3)	3	-
Montana	(4)	4	-				
Nebraska	(8)	8	-	TOTALS	(531)	404	127

1924

States	Electoral Votes	Coolidge	Davis	La Follette	States	Electoral Votes	Coolidge	Davis	La Follette
Alabama	(12)	-	12	-	Nevada	(3)	3	-	-
Arizona	(3)	3	-	-	New Hampshire	(4)	4	-	-
Arkansas	(9)	-	9	-	New Jersey	(14)	14	-	-
California	(13)	13	-	-	New Mexico	(3)	3	-	-
Colorado	(6)	6	-	-	New York	(45)	45	-	-
Connecticut	(7)	7	-	-	North Carolina	(12)	-	12	-
Delaware	(3)	3	-	-	North Dakota	(5)	5	-	-
Florida	(6)	-	6	-	Ohio	(24)	24	-	-
Georgia	(14)	-	14	-	Oklahoma	(10)	-	10	-
Idaho	(4)	4	-	-	Oregon	(5)	5	-	-
Illinois	(29)	29	-	-	Pennsylvania	(38)	38	-	-
Indiana	(15)	15	-	-	Rhode Island	(5)	5	-	-
Iowa	(13)	13	-	-	South Carolina	(9)	-	9	-
Kansas	(10)	10	-	-	South Dakota	(5)	5	-	-
Kentucky	(13)	13	-	-	Tennessee	(12)	-	12	-
Louisiana	(10)	-	10	-	Texas	(20)	-	20	-
Maine	(6)	6	-	-	Utah	(4)	4	-	-
Maryland	(8)	8	-	-	Vermont	(4)	4	-	-
Massachusetts	(18)	18	-	-	Virginia	(12)	-	12	-
Michigan	(15)	15	-	-	Washington	(7)	7	-	-
Minnesota	(12)	12	-	-	West Virginia	(8)	8	-	-
Mississippi	(10)	-	10	-	Wisconsin	(13)	-	-	13
Missouri	(18)	18	-	-	Wyoming	(3)	3	-	-
Montana	(4)	4	-	-					
Nebraska	(8)	8	-	-	TOTALS	(531)	382	136	13

1928

States	Electoral Votes	Hoover	Smith	States	Electoral Votes	Hoover	Smith
Alabama	(12)	-	12	Nevada	(3)	3	-
Arizona	(3)	3	-	New Hampshire	(4)	4	-
Arkansas	(9)	-	9	New Jersey	(14)	14	-
California	(13)	13	-	New Mexico	(3)	3	-
Colorado	(6)	6	-	New York	(45)	45	-
Connecticut	(7)	7	-	North Carolina	(12)	12	-
Delaware	(3)	3	-	North Dakota	(5)	5	-
Florida	(6)	6	-	Ohio	(24)	24	-
Georgia	(14)	-	14	Oklahoma	(10)	10	-
Idaho	(4)	4	-	Oregon	(5)	5	-
Illinois	(29)	29	-	Pennsylvania	(38)	38	-
Indiana	(15)	15	-	Rhode Island	(5)	-	5
Iowa	(13)	13	-	South Carolina	(9)	-	9
Kansas	(10)	10	-	South Dakota	(5)	5	-
Kentucky	(13)	13	-	Tennessee	(12)	12	-
Louisiana	(10)	-	10	Texas	(20)	20	-
Maine	(6)	6	-	Utah	(4)	4	-
Maryland	(8)	8	-	Vermont	(4)	4	-
Massachusetts	(18)	-	18	Virginia	(12)	12	-
Michigan	(15)	15	-	Washington	(7)	7	-
Minnesota	(12)	12	-	West Virginia	(8)	8	-
Mississippi	(10)	-	10	Wisconsin	(13)	13	-
Missouri	(18)	18	-	Wyoming	(3)	3	-
Montana	(4)	4	-				
Nebraska	(8)	8	-	TOTALS	(531)	444	87

1932

States	Electoral Votes	Roosevelt	Hoover	States	Electoral Votes	Roosevelt	Hoover
Alabama	(11)	11	-	Nevada	(3)	3	-
Arizona	(3)	3	-	New Hampshire	(4)	-	4
Arkansas	(9)	9	-	New Jersey	(16)	16	-
California	(22)	22	-	New Mexico	(3)	3	-
Colorado	(6)	6	-	New York	(47)	47	-
Connecticut	(8)	-	8	North Carolina	(13)	13	-
Delaware	(3)	-	3	North Dakota	(4)	4	-
Florida	(7)	7	-	Ohio	(26)	26	-
Georgia	(12)	12	-	Oklahoma	(11)	11	-
Idaho	(4)	4	-	Oregon	(5)	5	-
Illinois	(29)	29	-	Pennsylvania	(36)	-	36
Indiana	(14)	14	-	Rhode Island	(4)	4	-
Iowa	(11)	11	-	South Carolina	(8)	8	-
Kansas	(9)	9	-	South Dakota	(4)	4	-
Kentucky	(11)	11	-	Tennessee	(11)	11	-
Louisiana	(10)	10	-	Texas	(23)	23	-
Maine	(5)	-	5	Utah	(4)	4	-
Maryland	(8)	8	-	Vermont	(3)	-	3
Massachusetts	(17)	17	-	Virginia	(11)	11	-
Michigan	(19)	19	-	Washington	(8)	8	-
Minnesota	(11)	11	-	West Virginia	(8)	8	-
Mississippi	(9)	9	-	Wisconsin	(12)	12	-
Missouri	(15)	15	-	Wyoming	(3)	3	-
Montana	(4)	4	-				
Nebraska	(7)	7	-	TOTALS	(531)	472	59

1936

States	Electoral Votes	Roosevelt	Landon	States	Electoral Votes	Roosevelt	Landon
Alabama	(11)	11	-	Nevada	(3)	3	-
Arizona	(3)	3	-	New Hampshire	(4)	4	-
Arkansas	(9)	9	-	New Jersey	(16)	16	-
California	(22)	22	-	New Mexico	(3)	3	-
Colorado	(6)	6	-	New York	(47)	47	-
Connecticut	(8)	8	-	North Carolina	(13)	13	-
Delaware	(3)	3	-	North Dakota	(4)	4	-
Florida	(7)	7	-	Ohio	(26)	26	-
Georgia	(12)	12	-	Oklahoma	(11)	11	-
Idaho	(4)	4	-	Oregon	(5)	5	-
Illinois	(29)	29	-	Pennsylvania	(36)	36	-
Indiana	(14)	14	-	Rhode Island	(4)	4	-
Iowa	(11)	11	-	South Carolina	(8)	8	-
Kansas	(9)	9	-	South Dakota	(4)	4	-
Kentucky	(11)	11	-	Tennessee	(11)	11	-
Louisiana	(10)	10	-	Texas	(23)	23	-
Maine	(5)	-	5	Utah	(4)	4	-
Maryland	(8)	8	-	Vermont	(3)	-	3
Massachusetts	(17)	17	-	Virginia	(11)	11	-
Michigan	(19)	19	-	Washington	(8)	8	-
Minnesota	(11)	11	-	West Virginia	(8)	8	-
Mississippi	(9)	9	-	Wisconsin	(12)	12	-
Missouri	(15)	15	-	Wyoming	(3)	3	-
Montana	(4)	4	-				
Nebraska	(7)	7	-	TOTALS	(531)	523	8

1940

States	Electoral Votes	Roosevelt	Willkie	States	Electoral Votes	Roosevelt	Willkie
Alabama	(11)	11	-	Nevada	(3)	3	-
Arizona	(3)	3	-	New Hampshire	(4)	4	-
Arkansas	(9)	9	-	New Jersey	(16)	16	-
California	(22)	22	-	New Mexico	(3)	3	-
Colorado	(6)	-	6	New York	(47)	47	-
Connecticut	(8)	8	-	North Carolina	(13)	13	-
Delaware	(3)	3	-	North Dakota	(4)	-	4
Florida	(7)	7	-	Ohio	(26)	26	-
Georgia	(12)	12	-	Oklahoma	(11)	11	-
Idaho	(4)	4	-	Oregon	(5)	5	-
Illinois	(29)	29	-	Pennsylvania	(36)	36	-
Indiana	(14)	-	14	Rhode Island	(4)	4	-
Iowa	(11)	-	11	South Carolina	(8)	8	-
Kansas	(9)	-	9	South Dakota	(4)	-	4
Kentucky	(11)	11	-	Tennessee	(11)	11	-
Louisiana	(10)	10	-	Texas	(23)	23	-
Maine	(5)	-	5	Utah	(4)	4	-
Maryland	(8)	8	-	Vermont	(3)	-	3
Massachusetts	(17)	17	-	Virginia	(11)	11	-
Michigan	(19)	-	19	Washington	(8)	8	-
Minnesota	(11)	11	-	West Virginia	(8)	8	-
Mississippi	(9)	9	-	Wisconsin	(12)	12	-
Missouri	(15)	15	-	Wyoming	(3)	3	-
Montana	(4)	4	-				
Nebraska	(7)	-	7	TOTALS	(531)	449	82

1944

States	Electoral Votes	Roosevelt	Dewey	States	Electoral Votes	Roosevelt	Dewey
Alabama	(11)	11	-	Nevada	(3)	3	-
Arizona	(4)	4	-	New Hampshire	(4)	4	-
Arkansas	(9)	9	-	New Jersey	(16)	16	-
California	(25)	25	-	New Mexico	(4)	4	-
Colorado	(6)	-	6	New York	(47)	47	-
Connecticut	(8)	8	-	North Carolina	(14)	14	-
Delaware	(3)	3	-	North Dakota	(4)	-	4
Florida	(8)	8	-	Ohio	(25)	-	25
Georgia	(12)	12	-	Oklahoma	(10)	10	-
Idaho	(4)	4	-	Oregon	(6)	6	-
Illinois	(28)	28	-	Pennsylvania	(35)	35	-
Indiana	(13)	-	13	Rhode Island	(4)	4	-
Iowa	(10)	-	10	South Carolina	(8)	8	-
Kansas	(8)	-	8	South Dakota	(4)	-	4
Kentucky	(11)	11	-	Tennessee	(12)	12	-
Louisiana	(10)	10	-	Texas	(23)	23	-
Maine	(5)	-	5	Utah	(4)	4	-
Maryland	(8)	8	-	Vermont	(3)	-	3
Massachusetts	(16)	16	-	Virginia	(11)	11	-
Michigan	(19)	19	-	Washington	(8)	8	-
Minnesota	(11)	11	-	West Virginia	(8)	8	-
Mississippi	(9)	9	-	Wisconsin	(12)	-	12
Missouri	(15)	15	-	Wyoming	(3)	-	3
Montana	(4)	4	-				
Nebraska	(6)	-	6	TOTALS	(531)	432	99

1948

States	Electoral Votes	Truman	Dewey	Thurmond	States	Electoral Votes	Truman	Dewey	Thurmond
Alabama	(11)	-	-	11	Nevada	(3)	3	-	-
Arizona	(4)	4	-	-	New Hampshire	(4)	-	4	-
Arkansas	(9)	9	-	-	New Jersey	(16)	-	16	-
California	(25)	25	-	-	New Mexico	(4)	4	-	-
Colorado	(6)	6	-	-	New York	(47)	-	47	-
Connecticut	(8)	-	8	-	North Carolina	(14)	14	-	-
Delaware	(3)	-	3	-	North Dakota	(4)	-	4	-
Florida	(8)	8	-	-	Ohio	(25)	25	-	-
Georgia	(12)	12	-	-	Oklahoma	(10)	10	-	-
Idaho	(4)	4	-	-	Oregon	(6)	-	6	-
Illinois	(28)	28	-	-	Pennsylvania	(35)	-	35	-
Indiana	(13)	-	13	-	Rhode Island	(4)	4	-	-
Iowa	(10)	10	-	-	South Carolina	(8)	-	-	8
Kansas	(8)	-	8	-	South Dakota	(4)	-	4	-
Kentucky	(11)	11	-	-	Tennessee[a]	(12)	11	-	1
Louisiana	(10)	-	-	10	Texas	(23)	23	-	-
Maine	(5)	-	5	-	Utah	(4)	4	-	-
Maryland	(8)	-	8	-	Vermont	(3)	-	3	-
Massachusetts	(16)	16	-	-	Virginia	(11)	11	-	-
Michigan	(19)	-	19	-	Washington	(8)	8	-	-
Minnesota	(11)	11	-	-	West Virginia	(8)	8	-	-
Mississippi	(9)	-	-	9	Wisconsin	(12)	12	-	-
Missouri	(15)	15	-	-	Wyoming	(3)	3	-	-
Montana	(4)	4	-	-					
Nebraska	(6)	-	6	-	TOTALS	(531)	303	189	39

NOTE: a. For explanation of split electoral votes, see p. 1634.

1952

States	Electoral Votes	Eisenhower	Stevenson	States	Electoral Votes	Eisenhower	Stevenson
Alabama	(11)	-	11	Nevada	(3)	3	-
Arizona	(4)	4	-	New Hampshire	(4)	4	-
Arkansas	(8)	-	8	New Jersey	(16)	16	-
California	(32)	32	-	New Mexico	(4)	4	-
Colorado	(6)	6	-	New York	(45)	45	-
Connecticut	(8)	8	-	North Carolina	(14)	-	14
Delaware	(3)	3	-	North Dakota	(4)	4	-
Florida	(10)	10	-	Ohio	(25)	25	-
Georgia	(12)	-	12	Oklahoma	(8)	8	-
Idaho	(4)	4	-	Oregon	(6)	6	-
Illinois	(27)	27	-	Pennsylvania	(32)	32	-
Indiana	(13)	13	-	Rhode Island	(4)	4	-
Iowa	(10)	10	-	South Carolina	(8)	-	8
Kansas	(8)	8	-	South Dakota	(4)	4	-
Kentucky	(10)	-	10	Tennessee	(11)	11	-
Louisiana	(10)	-	10	Texas	(24)	24	-
Maine	(5)	5	-	Utah	(4)	4	-
Maryland	(9)	9	-	Vermont	(3)	3	-
Massachusetts	(16)	16	-	Virginia	(12)	12	-
Michigan	(20)	20		Washington	(9)	9	-
Minnesota	(11)	11	-	West Virginia	(8)	-	8
Mississippi	(8)	-	8	Wisconsin	(12)	12	-
Missouri	(13)	13	-	Wyoming	(3)	3	-
Montana	(4)	4	-				
Nebraska	(6)	6	-	TOTALS	(531)	442	89

1956

States	Electoral Votes	Eisenhower	Stevenson	Jones	States	Electoral Votes	Eisenhower	Stevenson	Jones
Alabama[a]	(11)	-	10	1	Nevada	(3)	3	-	-
Arizona	(4)	4	-	-	New Hampshire	(4)	4	-	-
Arkansas	(8)	-	8	-	New Jersey	(16)	16	-	-
California	(32)	32	-	-	New Mexico	(4)	4	-	-
Colorado	(6)	6	-	-	New York	(45)	45	-	-
Connecticut	(8)	8	-	-	North Carolina	(14)	-	14	-
Delaware	(3)	3	-	-	North Dakota	(4)	4	-	-
Florida	(10)	10	-	-	Ohio	(25)	25	-	-
Georgia	(12)	-	12	-	Oklahoma	(8)	8	-	-
Idaho	(4)	4	-	-	Oregon	(6)	6	-	-
Illinois	(27)	27	-	-	Pennsylvania	(32)	32	-	-
Indiana	(13)	13	-	-	Rhode Island	(4)	4	-	-
Iowa	(10)	10	-	-	South Carolina	(8)	-	8	-
Kansas	(8)	8	-	-	South Dakota	(4)	4	-	-
Kentucky	(10)	10	-	-	Tennessee	(11)	11	-	-
Louisiana	(10)	10	-	-	Texas	(24)	24	-	-
Maine	(5)	5	-	-	Utah	(4)	4	-	-
Maryland	(9)	9	-	-	Vermont	(3)	3	-	-
Massachusetts	(16)	16	-	-	Virginia	(12)	12	-	-
Michigan	(20)	20	-	-	Washington	(9)	9	-	-
Minnesota	(11)	11	-	-	West Virginia	(8)	8	-	-
Mississippi	(8)	-	8	-	Wisconsin	(12)	12	-	-
Missouri	(13)	-	13	-	Wyoming	(3)	3	-	-
Montana	(4)	4	-	-					
Nebraska	(6)	6	-	-	TOTALS	(531)	457	73	1

NOTE: a. For explanation of split electoral votes, see p. 1634.

1960

States	Electoral Votes	Kennedy	Nixon	Byrd	States	Electoral Votes	Kennedy	Nixon	Byrd
Alabama[a]	(11)	5	-	6	Nebraska	(6)	-	6	-
Alaska	(3)	-	3	-	Nevada	(3)	3	-	-
Arizona	(4)	-	4	-	New Hampshire	(4)	-	4	-
Arkansas	(8)	8	-	-	New Jersey	(16)	16	-	-
California	(32)	-	32	-	New Mexico	(4)	4	-	-
Colorado	(6)	-	6	-	New York	(45)	45	-	-
Connecticut	(8)	8	-	-	North Carolina	(14)	14	-	-
Delaware	(3)	3	-	-	North Dakota	(4)	-	4	-
Florida	(10)	-	10	-	Ohio	(25)	-	25	-
Georgia	(12)	12	-	-	Oklahoma[b]	(8)	-	7	1
Hawaii	(3)	3	-	-	Oregon	(6)	-	6	-
Idaho	(4)	-	4	-	Pennsylvania	(32)	32	-	-
Illinois	(27)	27	-	-	Rhode Island	(4)	4	-	-
Indiana	(13)	-	13	-	South Carolina	(8)	8	-	-
Iowa	(10)	-	10	-	South Dakota	(4)	-	4	-
Kansas	(8)	-	8	-	Tennessee	(11)	-	11	-
Kentucky	(10)	-	10	-	Texas	(24)	24	-	-
Louisiana	(10)	10	-	-	Utah	(4)	-	4	-
Maine	(5)	-	5	-	Vermont	(3)	-	3	-
Maryland	(9)	9	-	-	Virginia	(12)	-	12	-
Massachusetts	(16)	16	-	-	Washington	(9)	-	9	-
Michigan	(20)	20	-	-	West Virginia	(8)	8	-	-
Minnesota	(11)	11	-	-	Wisconsin	(12)	-	12	-
Mississippi[a]	(8)	-	-	8	Wyoming	(3)	-	3	-
Missouri	(13)	13	-	-					
Montana	(4)	-	4	-	TOTALS	(537)	303	219	15

NOTES: a. Six Alabama electors and all eight Mississippi electors, elected as "unpledged Democrats," cast their votes for Byrd.   b. For explanation of split electoral votes, see p. 1634.

1964

States	Electoral Votes	Johnson	Goldwater	States	Electoral Votes	Johnson	Goldwater
Alabama	(10)	-	10	Nebraska	(5)	5	-
Alaska	(3)	3	-	Nevada	(3)	3	-
Arizona	(5)	-	5	New Hampshire	(4)	4	-
Arkansas	(6)	6	-	New Jersey	(17)	17	-
California	(40)	40	-	New Mexico	(4)	4	-
Colorado	(6)	6	-	New York	(43)	43	-
Connecticut	(8)	8	-	North Carolina	(13)	13	-
Delaware	(3)	3	-	North Dakota	(4)	4	-
District of Columbia	(3)	3	-	Ohio	(26)	26	-
Florida	(14)	14	-	Oklahoma	(8)	8	-
Georgia	(12)	-	12	Oregon	(6)	6	-
Hawaii	(4)	4	-	Pennsylvania	(29)	29	-
Idaho	(4)	4	-	Rhode Island	(4)	4	-
Illinois	(26)	26	-	South Carolina	(8)	-	8
Indiana	(13)	13	-	South Dakota	(4)	4	-
Iowa	(9)	9	-	Tennessee	(11)	11	-
Kansas	(7)	7	-	Texas	(25)	25	-
Kentucky	(9)	9	-	Utah	(4)	4	-
Louisiana	(10)	-	10	Vermont	(3)	3	-
Maine	(4)	4	-	Virginia	(12)	12	-
Maryland	(10)	10	-	Washington	(9)	9	-
Massachusetts	(14)	14	-	West Virginia	(7)	7	-
Michigan	(21)	21	-	Wisconsin	(12)	12	-
Minnesota	(10)	10	-	Wyoming	(3)	3	-
Mississippi	(7)	-	7				
Missouri	(12)	12	-	TOTALS	(538)	486	52
Montana	(4)	4	-				

1968

States	Electoral Votes	Nixon	Humphrey	Wallace	States	Electoral Votes	Nixon	Humphrey	Wallace
Alabama	(10)	-	-	10	Nebraska	(5)	5	-	-
Alaska	(3)	3	-	-	Nevada	(3)	3	-	-
Arizona	(5)	5	-	-	New Hampshire	(4)	4	-	-
Arkansas	(6)	-	-	6	New Jersey	(17)	17	-	-
California	(40)	40	-	-	New Mexico	(4)	4	-	-
Colorado	(6)	6	-	-	New York	(43)	-	43	-
Connecticut	(8)	-	8	-	North Carolina[a]	(13)	12	-	1
Delaware	(3)	3	-	-	North Dakota	(4)	4	-	-
District of Columbia	(3)	-	3	-	Ohio	(26)	26	-	-
Florida	(14)	14	-	-	Oklahoma	(8)	8	-	-
Georgia	(12)	-	-	12	Oregon	(6)	6	-	-
Hawaii	(4)	-	4	-	Pennsylvania	(29)	-	29	-
Idaho	(4)	4	-	-	Rhode Island	(4)	-	4	-
Illinois	(26)	26	-	-	South Carolina	(8)	8	-	-
Indiana	(13)	13	-	-	South Dakota	(4)	4	-	-
Iowa	(9)	9	-	-	Tennessee	(11)	11	-	-
Kansas	(7)	7	-	-	Texas	(25)	-	25	-
Kentucky	(9)	9	-	-	Utah	(4)	4	-	-
Louisiana	(10)	-	-	10	Vermont	(3)	3	-	-
Maine	(4)	-	4	-	Virginia	(12)	12	-	-
Maryland	(10)	-	10	-	Washington	(9)	-	9	-
Massachusetts	(14)	-	14	-	West Virginia	(7)	-	7	-
Michigan	(21)	-	21	-	Wisconsin	(12)	12	-	-
Minnesota	(10)	-	10	-	Wyoming	(3)	3	-	-
Mississippi	(7)	-	-	7					
Missouri	(12)	12	-	-	TOTALS	(538)	301	191	46
Montana	(4)	4	-	-					

NOTE: a. For explanation of split electoral votes, see p. 1634.

1972

States	Electoral Votes	Nixon	McGovern	Hospers	States	Electoral Votes	Nixon	McGovern	Hospers
Alabama	(9)	9	-	-	Nebraska	(5)	5	-	-
Alaska	(3)	3	-	-	Nevada	(3)	3	-	-
Arizona	(6)	6	-	-	New Hampshire	(4)	4	-	-
Arkansas	(6)	6	-	-	New Jersey	(17)	17	-	-
California	(45)	45	-	-	New Mexico	(4)	4	-	-
Colorado	(7)	7	-	-	New York	(41)	41	-	-
Connecticut	(8)	8	-	-	North Carolina	(13)	13	-	-
Delaware	(3)	3	-	-	North Dakota	(3)	3	-	-
District of Columbia	(3)	-	3	-	Ohio	(25)	25	-	-
Florida	(17)	17	-	-	Oklahoma	(8)	8	-	-
Georgia	(12)	12	-	-	Oregon	(6)	6	-	-
Hawaii	(4)	4	-	-	Pennsylvania	(27)	27	-	-
Idaho	(4)	4	-	-	Rhode Island	(4)	4	-	-
Illinois	(26)	26	-	-	South Carolina	(8)	8	-	-
Indiana	(13)	13	-	-	South Dakota	(4)	4	-	-
Iowa	(8)	8	-	-	Tennessee	(10)	10	-	-
Kansas	(7)	7	-	-	Texas	(26)	26	-	-
Kentucky	(9)	9	-	-	Utah	(4)	4	-	-
Louisiana	(10)	10	-	-	Vermont	(3)	3	-	-
Maine	(4)	4	-	-	Virginia[a]	(12)	11	-	1
Maryland	(10)	10	-	-	Washington	(9)	9	-	-
Massachusetts	(14)	-	14	-	West Virginia	(6)	6	-	-
Michigan	(21)	21	-	-	Wisconsin	(11)	11	-	-
Minnesota	(10)	10	-	-	Wyoming	(3)	3	-	-
Mississippi	(7)	7	-	-					
Missouri	(12)	12	-	-	TOTALS	(538)	520	17	1
Montana	(4)	4	-	-					

NOTE: a. For explanation of split electoral votes, see p. 1634.

1976

States	Electoral Votes	Carter	Ford	Reagan	States	Electoral Votes	Carter	Ford	Reagan
Alabama	(9)	9	-	-	Nebraska	(5)	-	5	-
Alaska	(3)	-	3	-	Nevada	(3)	-	3	-
Arizona	(6)	-	6	-	New Hampshire	(4)	-	4	-
Arkansas	(6)	6	-	-	New Jersey	(17)	-	17	-
California	(45)	-	45	-	New Mexico	(4)	-	4	-
Colorado	(7)	-	7	-	New York	(41)	41	-	-
Connecticut	(8)	-	8	-	North Carolina	(13)	13	-	-
Delaware	(3)	3	-	-	North Dakota	(3)	-	3	-
District of Columbia	(3)	3	-	-	Ohio	(25)	25	-	-
Florida	(17)	17	-	-	Oklahoma	(8)	-	8	-
Georgia	(12)	12	-	-	Oregon	(6)	-	6	-
Hawaii	(4)	4	-	-	Pennsylvania	(27)	27	-	-
Idaho	(4)	-	4	-	Rhode Island	(4)	4	-	-
Illinois	(26)	-	26	-	South Carolina	(8)	8	-	-
Indiana	(13)	-	13	-	South Dakota	(4)	-	4	-
Iowa	(8)	-	8	-	Tennessee	(10)	10	-	-
Kansas	(7)	-	7	-	Texas	(26)	26	-	-
Kentucky	(9)	9	-	-	Utah	(4)	-	4	-
Louisiana	(10)	10	-	-	Vermont	(3)	-	3	-
Maine	(4)	-	4	-	Virginia	(12)	-	12	-
Maryland	(10)	10	-	-	Washington[a]	(9)	-	8	1
Massachusetts	(14)	14	-	-	West Virginia	(6)	6	-	-
Michigan	(21)	-	21	-	Wisconsin	(11)	11	-	-
Minnesota	(10)	10	-	-	Wyoming	(3)	-	3	-
Mississippi	(7)	7	-	-					
Missouri	(12)	12	-	-	TOTALS	(538)	297	240	1
Montana	(4)	-	4	-					

NOTE: a. For explanation of split electoral votes, see p. 1634.

1980

States	Electoral Votes	Reagan	Carter	States	Electoral Votes	Reagan	Carter
Alabama	(9)	9	-	Nebraska	(5)	5	-
Alaska	(3)	3	-	Nevada	(3)	3	-
Arizona	(6)	6	-	New Hampshire	(4)	4	-
Arkansas	(6)	6	-	New Jersey	(17)	17	-
California	(45)	45	-	New Mexico	(4)	4	-
Colorado	(7)	7	-	New York	(41)	41	-
Connecticut	(8)	8	-	North Carolina	(13)	13	-
Delaware	(3)	3	-	North Dakota	(3)	3	-
District of Columbia	(3)	-	3	Ohio	(25)	25	-
Florida	(17)	17	-	Oklahoma	(8)	8	-
Georgia	(12)	-	12	Oregon	(6)	6	-
Hawaii	(4)	-	4	Pennsylvania	(27)	27	-
Idaho	(4)	4	-	Rhode Island	(4)	-	4
Illinois	(26)	26	-	South Carolina	(8)	8	-
Indiana	(13)	13	-	South Dakota	(4)	4	-
Iowa	(8)	8	-	Tennessee	(10)	10	-
Kansas	(7)	7	-	Texas	(26)	26	-
Kentucky	(9)	9	-	Utah	(4)	4	-
Louisiana	(10)	10	-	Vermont	(3)	3	-
Maine	(4)	4	-	Virginia	(12)	12	-
Maryland	(10)	-	10	Washington	(9)	9	-
Massachusetts	(14)	14	-	West Virginia	(6)	-	6
Michigan	(21)	21	-	Wisconsin	(11)	11	-
Minnesota	(10)	-	10	Wyoming	(3)	3	-
Mississippi	(7)	7	-				
Missouri	(12)	12	-	TOTALS	(538)	489	49
Montana	(4)	4	-				

1984

States	Electoral Votes	Reagan	Mondale	States	Electoral Votes	Reagan	Mondale
Alabama	(9)	9	-	Nebraska	(5)	5	-
Alaska	(3)	3	-	Nevada	(4)	4	-
Arizona	(7)	7	-	New Hampshire	(4)	4	-
Arkansas	(6)	6	-	New Jersey	(16)	16	-
California	(47)	47	-	New Mexico	(5)	5	-
Colorado	(8)	8	-	New York	(36)	36	-
Connecticut	(8)	8	-	North Carolina	(13)	13	-
Delaware	(3)	3	-	North Dakota	(3)	3	-
District of Columbia	(3)	-	3	Ohio	(23)	23	-
Florida	(21)	21	-	Oklahoma	(8)	8	-
Georgia	(12)	12	-	Oregon	(7)	7	-
Hawaii	(4)	4	-	Pennsylvania	(25)	25	-
Idaho	(4)	4	-	Rhode Island	(4)	4	-
Illinois	(24)	24	-	South Carolina	(8)	8	-
Indiana	(12)	12	-	South Dakota	(3)	3	-
Iowa	(8)	8	-	Tennessee	(11)	11	-
Kansas	(7)	7	-	Texas	(29)	29	-
Kentucky	(9)	9	-	Utah	(5)	5	-
Louisiana	(10)	10	-	Vermont	(3)	3	-
Maine	(4)	4	-	Virginia	(12)	12	-
Maryland	(10)	10	-	Washington	(10)	10	-
Massachusetts	(13)	13	-	West Virginia	(6)	6	-
Michigan	(20)	20	-	Wisconsin	(11)	11	-
Minnesota	(10)	-	10	Wyoming	(3)	3	-
Mississippi	(7)	7	-				
Missouri	(11)	11	-	TOTALS	(538)	525	13
Montana	(4)	4	-				

1988

States	Electoral Votes	Bush	Dukakis	Bentsen	States	Electoral Votes	Bush	Dukakis	Bentsen
Alabama	(9)	9	-	-	Nebraska	(5)	5	-	-
Alaska	(3)	3	-	-	Nevada	(4)	4	-	-
Arizona	(7)	7	-	-	New Hampshire	(4)	4	-	-
Arkansas	(6)	6	-	-	New Jersey	(16)	16	-	-
California	(47)	47	-	-	New Mexico	(5)	5	-	-
Colorado	(8)	8	-	-	New York	(36)	-	36	-
Connecticut	(8)	8	-	-	North Carolina	(13)	13	-	-
Delaware	(3)	3	-	-	North Dakota	(3)	3	-	-
District of Columbia	(3)	-	3	-	Ohio	(23)	23	-	-
Florida	(21)	21	-	-	Oklahoma	(8)	8	-	-
Georgia	(12)	12	-	-	Oregon	(7)	-	7	-
Hawaii	(4)	-	4	-	Pennsylvania	(25)	25	-	-
Idaho	(4)	4	-	-	Rhode Island	(4)	-	4	-
Illinois	(24)	24	-	-	South Carolina	(8)	8	-	-
Indiana	(12)	12	-	-	South Dakota	(3)	3	-	-
Iowa	(8)	-	8	-	Tennessee	(11)	11	-	-
Kansas	(7)	7	-	-	Texas	(29)	29	-	-
Kentucky	(9)	9	-	-	Utah	(5)	5	-	-
Louisiana	(10)	10	-	-	Vermont	(3)	3	-	-
Maine	(4)	4	-	-	Virginia	(12)	12	-	-
Maryland	(10)	10	-	-	Washington	(10)	-	10	-
Massachusetts	(13)	-	13	-	West Virginia[a]	(6)	-	5	1
Michigan	(20)	20	-	-	Wisconsin	(11)	-	11	-
Minnesota	(10)	-	10	-	Wyoming	(3)	3	-	-
Mississippi	(7)	7	-	-					
Missouri	(11)	11	-	-	TOTALS	(538)	426	111	1
Montana	(4)	4	-	-					

NOTE: a. For explanation of split electoral vote, see p. 1634.

1992

States	Electoral Votes	Clinton	Bush	States	Electoral Votes	Clinton	Bush
Alabama	(9)	-	9	Nebraska	(5)	-	5
Alaska	(3)	-	3	Nevada	(4)	4	-
Arizona	(8)	-	8	New Hampshire	(4)	4	-
Arkansas	(6)	6	-	New Jersey	(15)	15	-
California	(54)	54	-	New Mexico	(5)	5	-
Colorado	(8)	8	-	New York	(33)	33	-
Connecticut	(8)	8	-	North Carolina	(14)	-	14
Delaware	(3)	3	-	North Dakota	(3)	-	3
District of Columbia	(3)	3	-	Ohio	(21)	21	-
Florida	(25)	-	25	Oklahoma	(8)	-	8
Georgia	(13)	13	-	Oregon	(7)	7	-
Hawaii	(4)	4	-	Pennsylvania	(23)	23	-
Idaho	(4)	-	4	Rhode Island	(4)	4	-
Illinois	(22)	22	-	South Carolina	(8)	-	8
Indiana	(12)	-	12	South Dakota	(3)	-	3
Iowa	(7)	7	-	Tennessee	(11)	11	-
Kansas	(6)	-	6	Texas	(32)	-	32
Kentucky	(8)	8	-	Utah	(5)	-	5
Louisiana	(9)	9	-	Vermont	(3)	3	-
Maine	(4)	4	-	Virginia	(13)	-	13
Maryland	(10)	10	-	Washington	(11)	11	-
Massachusetts	(12)	12	-	West Virginia	(5)	5	-
Michigan	(18)	18	-	Wisconsin	(11)	11	-
Minnesota	(10)	10	-	Wyoming	(3)	-	3
Mississippi	(7)	-	7				
Missouri	(11)	11	-	TOTALS	(538)	370	168
Montana	(3)	3	-				

Electoral Votes for Vice President, 1804–1992

The following list gives the electoral votes for vice president from 1804 to 1992. Unless indicated by a note, the state-by-state breakdown of electoral votes for each vice-presidential candidate was the same as for his or her party's presidential candidate.

Prior to 1804, under Article II, section 1, of the Constitution, each elector cast two votes—each vote for a different person. The electors did not distinguish between votes for president and vice president.

The candidate receiving the second highest total became vice president. The Twelfth Amendment, ratified in 1804, required electors to vote separately for president and vice president.

In some cases, persons received electoral votes although they had never been formally nominated. The word *candidate* is used in this section to designate persons receiving electoral votes.

Year	Candidate	Electoral votes
1804	George Clinton (Democratic-Republican)	162
	Rufus King (Federalist)	14
1808	George Clinton (Democratic-Republican)[a]	113
	John Langdon (Democratic-Republican)	9
	James Madison (Democratic-Republican)	3
	James Monroe (Democratic-Republican)	3
	Rufus King (Federalist)	47
1812	Elbridge Gerry (Democratic-Republican)[b]	131
	Jared Ingersoll (Federalist)	86
1816	Daniel D. Tompkins (Democratic-Republican)	183
	John E. Howard (Federalist)[c]	22
	James Ross (Federalist)	5
	John Marshall (Federalist)	4
	Robert G. Harper (Federalist)	3
1820	Daniel D. Tompkins (Democratic-Republican)[d]	218
	Richard Rush (Democratic-Republican)	1
	Richard Stockton (Federalist)	8
	Daniel Rodney (Federalist)	4
	Robert G. Harper (Federalist)	1
1824	John C. Calhoun (Democratic-Republican)[e]	182
	Nathan Sanford (Democratic-Republican)	30
	Nathaniel Macon (Democratic-Republican)	24
	Andrew Jackson (Democratic-Republican)	13
	Martin Van Buren (Democratic-Republican)	9
	Henry Clay (Democratic-Republican)	2
1828	John C. Calhoun (Democratic-Republican)[f]	171
	William Smith (Independent Democratic-Republican)	7
	Richard Rush (National Republican)	83
1832	Martin Van Buren (Democrat)[g]	189
	William Wilkins (Democrat)	30
	Henry Lee (Independent Democrat)	11
	John Sergeant (National Republican)	49
	Amos Ellmaker (Anti-Mason)	7
1836	Richard M. Johnson (Democrat)[h]	147
	William Smith (Independent Democrat)	23
	Francis Granger (Whig)	77
	John Tyler (Whig)	47
1840	John Tyler (Whig)	234
	Richard M. Johnson (Democrat)[i]	48
	L. W. Tazewell (Democrat)	11
	James K. Polk (Democrat)	1
1844	George M. Dallas (Democrat)	170
	Theodore Frelinghuysen (Whig)	105
1848	Millard Fillmore (Whig)	163
	William Orlando Butler (Democrat)	127

Year	Candidate	Electoral votes
1852	William R. King (Democrat)	254
	William Alexander Graham (Whig)	42
1856	John C. Breckinridge (Democrat)	174
	William L. Dayton (Republican)	114
	Andrew Jackson Donelson (Whig-American)	8
1860	Hannibal Hamlin (Republican)	180
	Joseph Lane (Southern Democrat)	72
	Edward Everett (Constitutional Union)	39
	Herschel V. Johnson (Democrat)	12
1864	Andrew Johnson (Republican)	212
	George H. Pendleton (Democrat)	21
1868	Schuyler Colfax (Republican)	214
	Francis P. Blair (Democrat)	80
1872	Henry Wilson (Republican)	286
	Benjamin Gratz Brown (Democrat)[j]	47
	Alfred H. Colquitt (Democrat)	5
	John M. Palmer (Democrat)	3
	Thomas E. Bramlette (Democrat)	3
	William S. Groesbeck (Democrat)	1
	Willis B. Machen (Democrat)	1
	George W. Julian (Liberal Republican)	5
	Nathaniel P. Banks (Liberal Republican)	1
1876	William A. Wheeler (Republican)	185
	Thomas A. Hendricks (Democrat)	184
1880	Chester A. Arthur (Republican)	214
	William H. English (Democrat)	155
1884	Thomas A. Hendricks (Democrat)	219
	John A. Logan (Republican)	182
1888	Levi P. Morton (Republican)	233
	Allen G. Thurman (Democrat)	168
1892	Adlai E. Stevenson (Democrat)	277
	Whitelaw Reid (Republican)	145
	James G. Field (Populist)	22
1896	Garret A. Hobart (Republican)	271
	Arthur Sewall (Democrat)[k]	149
	Thomas E. Watson (Populist)	27
1900	Theodore Roosevelt (Republican)	292
	Adlai E. Stevenson (Democrat)	155
1904	Charles W. Fairbanks (Republican)	336
	Henry G. Davis (Democrat)	140
1908	James S. Sherman (Republican)	321
	John W. Kern (Democrat)	162
1912	Thomas R. Marshall (Democrat)	435
	Hiram W. Johnson (Progressive)	88
	Nicholas Murray Butler (Republican)[l]	8

(table continues)

Year	Candidate	Electoral votes	Year	Candidate	Electoral votes
1916	Thomas R. Marshall (Democrat)	277	1960	Lyndon B. Johnson (Democrat)	303
	Charles W. Fairbanks (Republican)	254		Strom Thurmond (Democrat)[m]	14
1920	Calvin Coolidge (Republican)	404		Henry Cabot Lodge (Republican)	219
	Franklin D. Roosevelt (Democrat)	127		Barry Goldwater (Republican)	1
1924	Charles G. Dawes (Republican)	382	1964	Hubert H. Humphrey (Democrat)	486
	Charles W. Bryan (Democrat)	136		William E. Miller (Republican)	52
	Burton K. Wheeler (Progressive)	13	1968	Spiro T. Agnew (Republican)	301
1928	Charles Curtis (Republican)	444		Edmund S. Muskie (Democrat)	191
	Joseph T. Robinson (Democrat)	87		Curtis E. LeMay (American Independent)	46
1932	John N. Garner (Democrat)	472	1972	Spiro T. Agnew (Republican)	520
	Charles Curtis (Republican)	59		R. Sargent Shriver (Democrat)	17
1936	John N. Garner (Democrat)	523		Theodora Nathan (Libertarian)	1
	Frank Knox (Republican)	8	1976	Walter F. Mondale (Democrat)	297
1940	Henry A. Wallace (Democrat)	449		Robert Dole (Republican)[n]	241
	Charles L. McNary (Republican)	82	1980	George Bush (Republican)	489
1944	Harry S. Truman (Democrat)	432		Walter F. Mondale (Democrat)	49
	John W. Bricker (Republican)	99	1984	George Bush (Republican)	525
1948	Alben W. Barkley (Democrat)	303		Geraldine A. Ferraro (Democrat)	13
	Earl Warren (Republican)	189	1988	Dan Quayle (Republican)	426
	Fielding L. Wright (States' Rights Democrat)	39		Lloyd Bentsen (Democrat)[o]	111
1952	Richard Nixon (Republican)	442		Michael S. Dukakis (Democrat)	1
	John J. Sparkman (Democrat)	89	1992	Al Gore (Democrat)	370
1956	Richard Nixon (Republican)	457		Dan Quayle (Republican)	168
	Estes Kefauver (Democrat)	73			
	Herman Talmadge (Democrat)	1			

SOURCES: *Senate Manual* (Washington, D.C.: Government Printing Office, 1994) was the source used for vice-presidential electoral votes. For political party designation, the basic source was Svend Petersen, *A Statistical History of the American Presidential Elections* (Westport, Conn.: Greenwood Press, 1981). Petersen gives the party designation of presidential candidates only. Congressional Quarterly adopted Petersen's party designations for the running mates of presidential candidates. To supplement Petersen, Congressional Quarterly consulted the *Biographical Directory of the United States Congress, 1774–1989* (Washington, D.C.: Government Printing Office, 1989); the *Dictionary of American Biography* (New York: Charles Scribner's Sons, 1928–1936); the *Encyclopedia of American Biography*, ed. John A. Garraty (New York: Harper and Row, 1974); and *Who Was Who in America, 1607–1968* (Chicago: Marquis Co., 1943–1968).

NOTES: a. New York cast 13 presidential electoral votes for Democratic-Republican James Madison and 6 votes for Clinton; for vice president, New York cast 13 votes for Clinton, 3 votes for Madison, and 3 votes for Monroe. Langdon received Ohio's 3 votes and Vermont's 6 votes.   b. The state-by-state vote for Gerry was the same as for Democratic-Republican presidential candidate Madison, except for Massachusetts and New Hampshire. Massachusetts cast 2 votes for Gerry and 20 votes for Ingersoll; New Hampshire cast 1 vote for Gerry and 7 votes for Ingersoll.   c. Four Federalists received vice-presidential electoral votes: Howard—Massachusetts, 22 votes; Ross—Connecticut, 5 votes; Marshall—Connecticut, 4 votes; Harper—Delaware, 3 votes.   d. The state-by-state vote for Tompkins was the same as for Democratic-Republican presidential candidate Monroe, except for Delaware, Maryland, and Massachusetts. Delaware cast 4 votes for Rodney; Maryland cast 10 votes for Tompkins and 1 for Harper; Massachusetts cast 7 votes for Tompkins and 8 for Stockton. New Hampshire, which cast 7 presidential electoral votes for Monroe and 1 vote for John Quincy Adams, cast 7 vice-presidential electoral votes for Tompkins and 1 vote for Rush.   e. The state-by-state vice-presidential electoral vote was as follows: Calhoun—Alabama, 5 votes; Delaware, 1 vote; Illinois, 3 votes; Indiana, 5 votes; Kentucky, 7 votes; Louisiana, 5 votes; Maine, 9 votes; Maryland, 10 votes; Massachusetts, 15 votes; Mississippi, 3 votes; New Hampshire, 7 votes; New Jersey, 8 votes; New York, 29 votes; North Carolina, 15 votes; Pennsylvania, 28 votes; Rhode Island, 3 votes; South Carolina, 11 votes; Tennessee, 11 votes; Vermont, 7 votes. Sanford—Kentucky, 7 votes; New York, 7 votes; Ohio, 16 votes. Macon—Virginia, 24 votes. Jackson—Connecticut, 8 votes; Maryland, 1 vote; Missouri, 3 votes; New Hampshire, 1 vote. Van Buren—Georgia, 9 votes. Clay—Delaware, 2 votes.   f. The state-by-state vote for Calhoun was the same as for Democratic-Republican presidential candidate Jackson, except for Georgia, which cast 2 votes for Calhoun and 7 votes for Smith.   g. The state-by-state vote for Van Buren was the same as for Democratic-Republican presidential candidate Jackson, except for Pennsylvania, which cast 30 votes for Wilkins. South Carolina cast 11 presidential electoral votes for Independent Democratic presidential candidate Floyd and 11 votes for Independent Democratic vice-presidential candidate Lee. Vermont cast 7 presidential electoral votes for Anti-Masonic candidate Wirt and 7 vice-presidential electoral votes for Wirt's running mate, Ellmaker.   h. The state-by-state vote for Johnson was the same as for Democratic presidential candidate Van Buren, except for Virginia, which cast 23 votes for Smith. Granger's state-by-state vote was the same as for Whig presidential candidate Harrison, except for Maryland and Massachusetts. Maryland cast 10 presidential electoral votes for Harrison and 10 vice-presidential votes for Tyler; Massachusetts cast 14 presidential electoral votes for Whig candidate Webster and 14 vice-presidential votes for Granger. Tyler received 11 votes from Georgia, 10 from Maryland, 11 from South Carolina, and 15 from Tennessee. No vice-presidential candidate received a majority of the electoral vote. As a result, the Senate, for the only time in history, selected the vice president under the provisions of the Twelfth Amendment. Johnson was elected vice president by a vote of 33 to 16 over Granger.   i. The Democratic Party did not nominate a vice-presidential candidate in 1840. Johnson's state-by-state vote was the same as for presidential candidate Van Buren, except for South Carolina and Virginia. South Carolina cast 11 votes for Tazewell. Virginia cast 23 presidential electoral votes for Van Buren, 22 vice-presidential votes for Johnson, and 1 vice-presidential vote for Polk.   j. Liberal Republican and Democratic presidential candidate Horace Greeley died November 29, 1872. As a result, 18 electors pledged to Greeley cast their presidential electoral votes for Brown, Greeley's running mate. The vice-presidential vote was as follows: Brown—Georgia, 5 votes; Kentucky, 5 votes; Maryland, 8 votes; Missouri, 6 votes; Tennessee, 12 votes; Texas, 8 votes. Colquitt—Georgia, 5 votes. Palmer—Missouri, 3 votes. Bramlette—Kentucky, 3 votes. Groesbeck—Missouri, 1 vote. Machen—Kentucky, 1 vote. Julian—Missouri, 5 votes. Banks—Georgia, 1 vote.   k. The state-by-state vote for Sewall was the same as for Democratic-Populist candidate William Jennings Bryan, except for the following states, which cast electoral votes for Watson: Arkansas, 3 votes; Louisiana, 4; Missouri, 4; Montana, 1; Nebraska, 4; North Carolina, 5; South Dakota, 2; Utah, 1; Washington, 1.   l. Butler received the 8 electoral votes of Vice President James Sherman, who died Oct. 30, 1912, after being renominated on the Republican ticket. Butler was named as the substitute candidate.   m. Democratic electors carried Alabama's 11 electoral votes. Five of the electors were pledged to the national Democratic ticket of Kennedy and Johnson. Six electors ran unpledged and voted for Harry F. Byrd for president and Strom Thurmond for vice president. Mississippi's 8 electors voted for Byrd and Thurmond. In Oklahoma, the Republican ticket of Nixon and Lodge carried the state, but Henry D. Irwin, 1 of the state's 8 electors, voted for Byrd for president and Goldwater for vice president.   n. One Republican elector from the state of Washington cast his presidential electoral vote for Reagan instead of the Republican nominee, Ford. But he voted for Dole, Ford's running mate, for vice president. Dole thus received one more electoral vote than Ford.   o. Margaret Leach, a Democratic elector from West Virginia, cast her vice-presidential electoral vote for Dukakis, the Democratic nominee for president, and her presidential vote for his running mate, Bentsen.

Also-Rans: Electoral Vote Winners Who Did Not Become President or Vice President

This directory provides biographical summaries of candidates who received electoral votes for president or vice president but never served in those offices. Also included are a number of prominent third party and independent candidates who received popular votes but no electoral votes. The material is organized as follows: name, state of residence in the year or years when the individual received electoral votes, party or parties with which the individual identified when he or she received electoral votes, date of birth, date of death (where applicable), major offices held, and the year or years when the person received electoral votes. For third-party candidates who received no electoral votes, the dates indicate the year or years in which they were candidates. (*See Chapter 36, Biographies of the Presidents, and Chapter 37, Biographies of the Vice Presidents.*)

In the elections of 1789, 1792, 1796, and 1800, presidential electors did not vote separately for president and vice president. It was, therefore, difficult in many cases to determine whether an individual receiving electoral votes in these elections was a candidate for president or vice president. Where no determination could be made from the sources consulted by Congressional Quarterly, the year in which the individual received electoral votes is given with no specification as to whether the individual was a candidate for president or vice president.

The following sources were used: *American Leaders, 1789–1994: A Biographical Summary* (Washington, D.C.: Congressional Quarterly, 1994); *Biographical Directory of the United States Congress, 1774–1989* (Washington, D.C.: Government Printing Office, 1989); Jaques Cattell Press, ed. *Who's Who in American Politics, 1977–1978*, 6th ed. (New York: R. R. Bowker, 1977); *Dictionary of American Biography* (New York: Scribner's, 1928–1936); John A. Garraty, ed. *Encyclopedia of American Biography* (New York: Harper and Row, 1974); Svend Petersen, *A Statistical History of the American Presidential Elections* (Westport, Conn.: Greenwood Press, 1981); Richard M. Scammon, *America Votes 10* (1972) (Washington, D.C.: Congressional Quarterly, 1973); Richard M. Scammon and Alice V. McGillivray, *America Votes 12* (1976) (Washington, D.C.: Congressional Quarterly, 1977); Scammon and McGillivray, *America Votes 14* (1980) (Washington, D.C.: Congressional Quarterly, 1981); Scammon and McGillivray, *America Votes 18* (1988) (Washington, D.C.: Congressional Quarterly, 1989); Scammon and McGillivray, *America Votes 20* (1992) (Washington, D.C.: Congressional Quarterly, 1993); and *Who Was Who in America, 1607–1968* (Chicago: Marquis, 1943–1968).

Adams, Charles Francis - Mass. (Free Soil) August 18, 1807–November 21, 1886; House, 1859–1861; minister to Great Britain, 1861–1868. Candidacy: VP - 1848.

Adams, Samuel - Mass. (Federalist) September 27, 1722–October 2, 1803; Continental Congress, 1774–1781; signer of Declaration of Independence; governor, 1793–1797. Candidacy: 1796.

Anderson, John B. - Ill. (Republican, independent) February 15, 1922– ; state's attorney, 1956–1960; House, 1961–1981. Candidacy: P - 1980.

Armstrong, James - Pa. (Federalist) August 29, 1748–May 6, 1828; House, 1793–1795. Candidacy: 1789.

Banks, Nathaniel Prentice - Mass. (Liberal Republican) January 30, 1816–September 1, 1894; House, 1853–1857, 1865–1873, 1875–1879, 1889–1891; governor, 1858–1861. Candidacy: VP - 1872.

Bell, John - Tenn. (Constitutional Union) February 15, 1797–September 10, 1869; House, 1827–1841; Speaker of the House, 1834–1835; secretary of war, 1841; Senate, 1847–1859. Candidacy: P - 1860.

Benson, Allan Louis - N.Y. (Socialist) November 6, 1871–August 19, 1940; writer, editor; founder of *Reconstruction Magazine*, 1918. Candidacy: P - 1916.

Bentsen, Lloyd Millard Jr. - Texas (Democratic) February 11, 1921– ; House, 1948–1955; Senate, 1971–1993; secretary of the Treasury, 1993–1994. Candidacy: VP - 1988.

Bidwell, John - Calif. (Prohibition) August 5, 1819–April 4, 1900; California pioneer; major in Mexican War; House, 1865–1867. Candidacy: P - 1892.

Birney, James Gillespie - N.Y. (Liberty) February 4, 1792–November 25, 1857; Kentucky Legislature, 1816–1817; Alabama Legislature, 1819–1820. Candidacies: P - 1840, 1844.

Blaine, James Gillespie - Maine (Republican) January 31, 1830–January 27, 1893; House, 1863–1876; Speaker of the House, 1869–1875; Senate, 1876–1881; secretary of state, 1881, 1889–1892; president, first Pan American Congress, 1889. Candidacy: P - 1884.

Blair, Francis Preston Jr. - Mo. (Democratic) February 19, 1821–July 8, 1875; House, 1857–1859, 1860, 1861–1862, 1863–1864; Senate, 1871–1873. Candidacy: VP - 1868.

Bramlette, Thomas E. - Ky. (Democratic) January 3, 1817–January 12, 1875; governor, 1863–1867. Candidacy: VP - 1872.

Bricker, John William - Ohio (Republican) September 6, 1893–March 22, 1986; attorney general of Ohio, 1933–1937; governor, 1939–1945; Senate, 1947–1959. Candidacy: VP - 1944.

Brown, Benjamin Gratz - Mo. (Democratic) May 28, 1826–December 13, 1885; Senate, 1863–1867; governor, 1871–1873. Candidacy: VP - 1872.

Bryan, Charles Wayland - Neb. (Democratic) February 10, 1867–March 4, 1945; governor, 1923–1925, 1931–1935; Candidacy: VP - 1924.

Bryan, William Jennings - Neb. (Democratic, Populist) March 19, 1860–July 26, 1925; House, 1891–1895; secretary of state, 1913–1915. Candidacies: P - 1896, 1900, 1908.

Butler, Benjamin Franklin - Mass. (Greenback, Anti-Monopoly) November 5, 1818–January 11, 1893; House, 1867–1875, 1877–1879; governor, 1883–1884. Candidacy: P - 1884.

Butler, Nicholas Murray - N.Y. (Republican) April 2, 1862–December 7, 1947; president, Columbia University, 1901–1945; president, Carnegie Endowment for International Peace, 1925–1945. Candidacy: VP - 1912. (Substituted as candidate after October 30 death of nominee James S. Sherman.)

Butler, William Orlando - Ky. (Democratic) April 19, 1791–August 6, 1880; House, 1839–1843. Candidacy: VP - 1848.

Byrd, Harry Flood - Va. (States' Rights Democratic, Independent Democratic) June 10, 1887–October 20, 1966; governor, 1926–1930; Senate, 1933–1965. Candidacies: P - 1956, 1960.

Cass, Lewis - Mich. (Democratic) October 9, 1782– June 17, 1866; military and civil governor of Michigan Territory, 1813–1831; secretary of war, 1831–1836; minister to France, 1836–1842; Senate, 1845–1848, 1849–1857; secretary of state, 1857–1860. Candidacy: P - 1848.

Clay, Henry - Ky. (Democratic-Republican, National Republican, Whig) April 12, 1777–June 29, 1852; Senate, 1806–1807, 1810–1811, 1831–1842, 1849–1852; House, 1811–1814, 1815–1821, 1823–1825; Speaker of the House, 1811–1814, 1815–1820, 1823–1825; secretary of state, 1825–1829. Candidacies: P - 1824, 1832, 1844.

Clinton, De Witt - N.Y. (Independent Democratic-Republican, Federalist) March 2, 1769–February 11, 1828; Senate, 1802–1803; mayor of New York, 1803–1807, 1810, 1811, 1813, 1814; governor, 1817–1823, 1825–1828. Candidacy: P - 1812.

Colquitt, Alfred Holt - Ga. (Democratic) April 20, 1824–March 26, 1894; House, 1853–1855; governor, 1877–1882; Senate, 1883–1894. Candidacy: VP - 1872.

Cox, James Middleton - Ohio (Democratic) March 31, 1870–July 15, 1957; House, 1909–1913; governor, 1913–1915, 1917–1921. Candidacy: P - 1920.

Crawford, William Harris - Ga. (Democratic-Republican) February 24, 1772–September 15, 1834; Senate, 1807–1813; president pro tempore of the Senate, 1812–1813; secretary of war, 1815–1816; secretary of the Treasury, 1816–1825. Candidacy: P - 1824.

Davis, David - Ill. (Democratic) March 9, 1815–June 26, 1886; associate justice of U.S. Supreme Court, 1862–1877; Senate, 1877–1883; president pro tempore of the Senate, 1881. Candidacy: P - 1872.

Davis, Henry Gassaway - W.Va. (Democratic) November 16, 1823–March 11, 1916; Senate, 1871–1883; chairman of Pan American Railway Committee, 1901–1916. Candidacy: VP - 1904.

Davis, John William - W.Va. (Democratic) April 13, 1873–March 24, 1955; House, 1911–1913; solicitor general, 1913–1918; ambassador to Great Britain, 1918–1921. Candidacy: P - 1924.

Dayton, William Lewis - N.J. (Republican) February 17, 1807–December 1, 1864; Senate, 1842–1851; minister to France, 1861–1864. Candidacy: VP - 1856.

Debs, Eugene Victor - Ind. (Socialist) November 5, 1855–October 20, 1926; Indiana Legislature, 1885; president, American Railway Union, 1893–1897. Candidacies: P - 1900, 1904, 1908, 1912, 1920.

Dewey, Thomas Edmund - N.Y. (Republican) March 24, 1902–March 16, 1971; district attorney, New York County, 1937–1941; governor, 1943–1955. Candidacies: P - 1944, 1948.

Dole, Robert Joseph - Kan. (Republican) July 22, 1923– ; House, 1961–1969; Senate, 1969– ; Senate majority leader, 1985–1987, 1995– ; Senate minority leader, 1987–1995. Candidacy: VP - 1976.

Donelson, Andrew Jackson - Tenn. (Whig-American) August 25, 1799–June 26, 1871; minister to Prussia, 1846–1848; minister to Germany, 1848–1849. Candidacy: VP - 1856.

Douglas, Stephen Arnold - Ill. (Democratic) April 23, 1813–June 3, 1861; House, 1843–1847; Senate, 1847–1861. Candidacy: P - 1860.

Dukakis, Michael Stanley - Mass. (Democratic) November 3, 1933– ; governor, 1975–1979, 1983–1991. Candidacy: P - 1988.

Eagleton, Thomas Francis - Mo. (Democratic) September 4, 1929– ; attorney general of Missouri, 1961–1965; lieutenant governor, 1965–1968; Senate, 1968–1987. Candidacy: VP - 1972. (Resigned from Democratic ticket July 31; replaced by R. Sargent Shriver Jr.)

Ellmaker, Amos - Pa. (Anti-Masonic) February 2, 1787–November 28, 1851; elected to the House for the term beginning in 1815 but did not qualify; attorney general of Pennsylvania, 1816–1819, 1828–1829. Candidacy: VP - 1832.

Ellsworth, Oliver - Conn. (Federalist) April 29, 1745–November 26, 1807; Continental Congress, 1778–1783; Senate, 1789–1796; chief justice of United States, 1796–1800; minister to France, 1799. Candidacy: 1796.

English, William Hayden - Ind. (Democratic) August 27, 1822–February 7, 1896; House, 1853–1861. Candidacy: VP - 1880.

Everett, Edward - Mass. (Constitutional Union) April 11, 1794–January 15, 1865; House, 1825–1835; governor, 1836–1840; minister to Great Britain, 1841–1845; president of Harvard University, 1846–1849; secretary of state, 1852–1853; Senate, 1853–1854. Candidacy: VP - 1860.

Ferraro, Geraldine Anne - N.Y. (Democratic) August 26, 1935– ; assistant district attorney, Queens County, 1974–1978; House, 1979–1985. Candidacy: VP - 1984.

Field, James Gaven - Va. (Populist) February 24, 1826–October 12, 1901; major in the Confederate Army, 1861–1865; attorney general of Virginia, 1877–1882. Candidacy: VP - 1892.

Fisk, Clinton Bowen - N.J. (Prohibition) December 8, 1828–July 9, 1890; Civil War brevet major general; founder of Fisk University, 1866; member, Board of Indian Commissioners, 1874, president, 1881–1890. Candidacy: P - 1888.

Floyd, John - Va. (Independent Democratic) April 24, 1783–August 17, 1837; House, 1817–1829; governor, 1830–1834. Candidacy: P - 1832.

Frelinghuysen, Theodore - N.J. (Whig) March 28, 1787–April 12, 1862; attorney general of New Jersey, 1817–1829; Senate, 1829–1835; president of Rutgers College, 1850–1862. Candidacy: VP - 1844.

Fremont, John Charles - Calif. (Republican) January 21, 1813–July 13, 1890; explorer and Army officer in West before 1847; Senate, 1850–1851; governor of Arizona Territory, 1878–1881. Candidacy: P - 1856.

Goldwater, Barry Morris - Ariz. (Republican) January 1, 1909– ; Senate, 1953–1965, 1969–1987. Candidacies: VP - 1960; P - 1964.

Graham, William Alexander - N.C. (Whig) September 5, 1804–August 11, 1875; Senate, 1840–1843; governor, 1845–1849; secretary of the Navy, 1850–1852; Confederate Senate, 1864. Candidacy: VP - 1852.

Granger, Francis - N.Y. (Whig) December 1, 1792–August 31, 1868; House, 1835–1837, 1839–1841, 1841–1843; postmaster general, 1841. Candidacy: VP - 1836.

Greeley, Horace - N.Y. (Liberal Republican, Democratic) February 3, 1811–November 29, 1872; founder and editor, *New York Tribune*, 1841–1872; House, 1848–1849. Candidacy: P - 1872.

Griffin, S. Marvin - Ga. (American Independent) September 4, 1907–June 13, 1982; governor, 1955–1959. Candidacy: VP - 1968. (Substituted as candidate until permanent candidate Curtis LeMay was chosen.)

Groesbeck, William Slocum - Ohio (Democratic) July 24, 1815–July 7, 1897; House, 1857–1859; delegate to International Monetary Conference in Paris, 1878. Candidacy: VP - 1872.

Hale, John Parker - N.H. (Free Soil) March 31, 1806–November 19, 1873; House, 1843–1845; Senate, 1847–1853, 1855–1865; minister to Spain, 1865–1869. Candidacy: P - 1852.

Hancock, John - Mass. (Federalist) January 23, 1737–October 8, 1793; Continental Congress, 1775–1778, 1785–1786; president of Continental Congress, 1775–1777; governor, 1780–1785, 1787–1793. Candidacy: 1789.

Hancock, Winfield Scott - Pa. (Democratic) February 14, 1824–February 9, 1886; brigadier general, commander of II Army Corps, Civil War. Candidacy: P - 1880.

Harper, Robert Goodloe - Md. (Federalist) January 1765–January 14, 1825; House, 1795–1801; Senate, 1816. Candidacies: VP - 1816, 1820.

Harrison, Robert H. - Md. 1745–1790; chief justice, General Court of Maryland, 1781. Candidacy: 1789.

Henry, John - Md. (Democratic-Republican) November 1750–December 16, 1798; Continental Congress, 1778–1780, 1785–1786; Senate, 1789–1797; governor, 1797–1798. Candidacy - 1796.

Hospers, John - Calif. (Libertarian) June 9, 1918– ; director of school of philosophy at University of Southern California. Candidacy: P - 1972.

Howard, John Eager - Md. (Federalist) June 4, 1752–October 12, 1827; Continental Congress, 1788; governor, 1788–1791; Senate, 1796–1803. Candidacy: VP - 1816.

Hughes, Charles Evans - N.Y. (Republican) April 11, 1862–August 27, 1948; governor, 1907–1910; associate justice of U.S. Supreme Court, 1910–1916; secretary of state, 1921–1925; chief justice of United States, 1930–1941. Candidacy: P - 1916.

Huntington, Samuel - Conn., July 3, 1731–January 5, 1796; Continental Congress, 1776, 1778–1781, 1783; president of Continental Congress, 1779–1781, 1783; governor, 1786–1796. Candidacy: 1789.

Ingersoll, Jared - Pa. (Federalist) October 24, 1749–October 31, 1822; Continental Congress, 1780–1781; Constitutional Convention, 1787. Candidacy: VP - 1812.

Iredell, James - N.C. (Federalist) October 5, 1751–October 20, 1799; associate justice of U.S. Supreme Court, 1790–1799. Candidacy: 1796.

Jay, John - N.Y. (Federalist) December 12, 1745–May 17, 1829; Continental Congress, 1774–1776, 1778–1779; president of Continental Congress, 1778–1779; minister to Spain, 1779; chief justice of United States, 1789–1795; governor, 1795–1801. Candidacies: 1789, 1796, 1800.

Jenkins, Charles Jones - Ga. (Democratic) January 6, 1805–June 14, 1883; governor, 1865–1868. Candidacy: P - 1872.

Johnson, Herschel Vespasian - Ga. (Democratic) September 18, 1812–August 16, 1880; Senate, 1848–1849; governor, 1853–1857; senator, Confederate Congress, 1862–1865. Candidacy: VP - 1860.

Johnson, Hiram Warren - Calif. (Progressive) September 2, 1866–August 6, 1945; governor, 1911–1917; Senate, 1917–1945. Candidacy: VP - 1912.

Johnston, Samuel - N.C. (Federalist) December 15, 1733–August 18, 1816; Continental Congress, 1780–1781; Senate, 1789–1793. Candidacy: 1796.

Jones, Walter Burgwyn - Ala. (Independent Democratic) October 16, 1888–August 1, 1963; Alabama Legislature, 1919–1920; Alabama circuit court judge, 1920–1935; presiding judge, 1935–1963. Candidacy: P - 1956.

Julian, George Washington - Ind. (Free Soil, Liberal Republican) May 5, 1817–July 7, 1899; House, 1849–1851, 1861–1871. Candidacies: VP - 1852, 1872.

Kefauver, Estes - Tenn. (Democratic) July 26, 1903–August 10, 1963; House, 1939–1949; Senate, 1949–1963. Candidacy: VP - 1956.

Kern, John Worth - Ind. (Democratic) December 20, 1849–August 17, 1917; Senate, 1911–1917; Senate majority leader, 1913–1917. Candidacy: VP - 1908.

King, Rufus - N.Y. (Federalist) March 24, 1755–April 29, 1827; Continental Congress, 1784–1787; Constitutional Convention, 1787; Senate, 1789–1796, 1813–1825; minister to Great Britain, 1796–1803, 1825–1826. Candidacies: VP - 1804, 1808; P - 1816.

Knox, Franklin - Ill. (Republican) January 1, 1874–April 28, 1944; secretary of the Navy, 1940–1944. Candidacy: VP - 1936.

La Follette, Robert Marion - Wis. (Progressive) June 14, 1855–June 18, 1925; House, 1885–1891; governor, 1901–1906; Senate, 1906–1925. Candidacy: P - 1924.

Landon, Alfred Mossman - Kan. (Republican) September 9, 1887–October 12, 1987; governor, 1933–1937. Candidacy: P - 1936.

Lane, Joseph - Ore. (Southern Democratic) December 14, 1801–April 19, 1881; governor of Oregon Territory, 1849–1850, May 16–19, 1853; House (territorial delegate), 1851–1859; Senate, 1859–1861. Candidacy: VP - 1860.

Langdon, John - N.H. (Democratic-Republican) June 26, 1741–September 18, 1819; Continental Congress, 1775–1776, 1787; governor, 1805–1809, 1810–1812; Senate, 1789–1801; first president pro tempore of the Senate, 1789. Candidacy: VP - 1808.

Lee, Henry - Mass. (Independent Democratic) February 4, 1782–February 6, 1867; merchant and publicist. Candidacy: VP - 1832.

LeMay, Curtis Emerson - Ohio (American Independent) November 15, 1906– ; air force chief of staff, 1961–1965. Candidacy: VP - 1968.

Lemke, William - N.D. (Union) August 13, 1878–May 30, 1950; House, 1933–1941, 1943–1950. Candidacy: P - 1936.

Lincoln, Benjamin - Mass. (Federalist) January 24, 1733–May 9, 1810; major general in Continental Army, 1777–1781. Candidacy: 1789.

Lodge, Henry Cabot Jr. - Mass. (Republican) July 5, 1902–February 27, 1985; Senate, 1937–1944, 1947–1953; ambassador to United Nations, 1953–1960; ambassador to Republic of Vietnam, 1963–1964, 1965–1967. Candidacy: VP - 1960.

Logan, John Alexander - Ill. (Republican) February 9, 1826–December 26, 1886; House, 1859–1862, 1867–1871; Senate, 1871–1877, 1879–1886. Candidacy: VP - 1884.

Machen, Willis Benson - Ky. (Democratic) April 10, 1810–September 29, 1893; Confederate Congress, 1861–1865; Senate, 1872–1873. Candidacy: VP - 1872.

Macon, Nathaniel - N.C. (Democratic-Republican) December 17, 1757–June 29, 1837; House, 1791–1815; Speaker of the House, 1801–1807; Senate, 1815–1828; president pro tempore of the Senate, 1826, 1827. Candidacy: VP - 1824.

Mangum, Willie Person - N.C. (Independent Democrat) May 10, 1792–September 7, 1861; House, 1823–1826; Senate, 1831–1836, 1840–1853. Candidacy: P - 1836.

Marshall, John - Va. (Federalist) September 24, 1755–July 6, 1835; House, 1799–1800; secretary of state, 1800–1801; chief justice of United States, 1801–1835. Candidacy: VP - 1816.

McCarthy, Eugene Joseph - Minn. (Independent) March 29, 1916– ; House, 1949–1959; Senate, 1959–1971. Candidacy: P - 1976.

McClellan, George Brinton - N.J. (Democratic) December 3, 1826–October 29, 1885; general-in-chief of Army of the Potomac, 1861; governor, 1878–1881. Candidacy: P - 1864.

McGovern, George Stanley - S.D. (Democratic) July 19, 1922– ; House, 1957–1961; Senate, 1963–1981. Candidacy: P - 1972.

McNary, Charles Linza - Ore. (Republican) June 12, 1874–February 25, 1944; state supreme court judge, 1913–1915; Senate, May 29, 1917–November 5, 1918, December 18, 1918–February 25, 1944; Senate minority leader, 1933–1944. Candidacy: VP - 1940.

Miller, William Edward - N.Y. (Republican) March 22, 1914–June 24, 1983; House, 1951–1965; chairman of Republican National Committee, 1961–1964. Candidacy: VP - 1964.

Milton, John - Ga. circa 1740–circa 1804; secretary of state, Georgia, circa 1778, 1781, 1783. Candidacy: 1789.

Muskie, Edmund Sixtus - Maine (Democratic) March 28, 1914–March 26, 1996; governor, 1955–1959; Senate, 1959–1980; secretary of state, 1980–1981. Candidacy: VP - 1968.

Nathan, Theodora Nathalia - Ore. (Libertarian) February 9, 1923– ; broadcast journalist; National Judiciary Committee, Libertarian Party, 1972–1975; vice chairperson, Oregon Libertarian Party, 1974–1975. Candidacy: VP - 1972.

Palmer, John McAuley - Ill. (Democratic, National Democratic) September 13, 1817–September 25, 1900; governor, 1869–1873; Senate, 1891–1897. Candidacies: VP - 1872; P - 1896.

Parker, Alton Brooks - N.Y. (Democratic) May 14, 1852–May 10, 1926; chief justice of N.Y. Court of Appeals, 1898–1904. Candidacy: P - 1904.

Pendleton, George Hunt - Ohio (Democratic) July 19, 1825–November 24, 1889; House, 1857–1865; Senate, 1879–1885; minister to Germany, 1885–1889. Candidacy: VP - 1864.

Perot, Ross - Texas (Independent) June 27, 1930– ; business executive and owner. Candidacy: P - 1992.

Pinckney, Charles Cotesworth - S.C. (Federalist) February 25, 1746–August 16, 1825; president, state senate, 1779; minister to France, 1796. Candidacies: VP - 1800; P - 1804, 1808.

Pinckney, Thomas - S.C. (Federalist) October 23, 1750–November 2, 1828; governor, 1787–1789; minister to Great Britain, 1792–1796; envoy to Spain, 1794–1795; House, 1797–1801. Candidacy: 1796.

Reid, Whitelaw - N.Y. (Republican) October 27, 1837–December 15, 1912; minister to France, 1889–1892; editor-in-chief, *New York Tribune*, 1872–1905. Candidacy: VP - 1892.

Robinson, Joseph Taylor - Ark. (Democratic) August 26, 1872–July 14, 1937; House, 1903–1913; governor, January 16–March 8, 1913; Senate, 1913–1937; Senate minority leader, 1923–1933; Senate majority leader, 1933–1937. Candidacy: VP - 1928.

Rodney, Daniel - Del. (Federalist) September 10, 1764–September 2, 1846; governor, 1814–1817; House, 1822–1823; Senate, 1826–1827. Candidacy: VP - 1820.

Ross, James - Pa. (Federalist) July 12, 1762–November 27, 1847; Senate, 1794–1803. Candidacy: VP - 1816.

Rush, Richard - Pa. (Democratic-Republican, National-Republican) August 29, 1780–July 30, 1859; attorney general, 1814–1817; minister to Great Britain, 1817–1824; secretary of the Treasury, 1825–1829. Candidacies: VP - 1820, 1828.

Rutledge, John - S.C. (Federalist) September 1739–July 23, 1800; Continental Congress, 1774–1775, 1782–1783; governor, 1779–1782; Constitutional Convention, 1787; associate justice of U.S. Supreme Court, 1789–1791; chief justice of United States, 1795. Candidacy: 1789.

Sanford, Nathan - N.Y. (Democratic-Republican) November 5, 1777–October 17, 1838; Senate, 1815–1821, 1826–1831. Candidacy: VP - 1824.

Schmitz, John George - Calif. (American Independent) August 12, 1930– ; House, 1970–1973. Candidacy: P - 1972.

Scott, Winfield - N.J. (Whig) June 13, 1786–May 29, 1866; general-in-chief of U.S. Army, 1841–1861. Candidacy: P - 1852.

Sergeant, John - Pa. (National-Republican) December 5, 1779–November 23, 1852; House, 1815–1823, 1827–1829, 1837–1841. Candidacy: VP - 1832.

Sewall, Arthur - Maine (Democratic) November 25, 1835–September 5, 1900; Democratic National Committee member, 1888–1896. Candidacy: VP - 1896.

Seymour, Horatio - N.Y. (Democratic) May 31, 1810–February 12, 1886; governor, 1853–1855, 1863–1865. Candidacy: P - 1868.

Shriver, Robert Sargent Jr. - Md. (Democratic) November 9, 1915– ; director, Peace Corps, 1961–1966; director, Office of Economic Opportunity, 1964–1968; ambassador to France, 1968–1970. Candidacy: VP - 1972. (Replaced Thomas F. Eagleton on Democratic ticket August 8.)

Smith, Alfred Emanuel - N.Y. (Democratic) December 30, 1873–October 4, 1944; governor, 1919–1921, 1923–1929. Candidacy: P - 1928.

Smith, William - S.C., Ala. (Independent Democratic-Republican) September 6, 1762–June 26, 1840; Senate, 1816–1823, 1826–1831. Candidacies: VP - 1828, 1836.

Sparkman, John Jackson - Ala. (Democratic) December 20, 1899–November 16, 1985; House, 1937–1946; Senate, 1946–1979. Candidacy: VP - 1952.

Stevenson, Adlai Ewing II - Ill. (Democratic) February 5, 1900–July 14, 1965; assistant to the secretary of Navy, 1941–1944; assistant to the secretary of state, 1945; governor, 1949–1953; ambassador to United Nations, 1961–1965. Candidacies: P - 1952, 1956.

Stockton, Richard - N.J. (Federalist) April 17, 1764–March 7, 1828; Senate, 1796–1799; House, 1813–1815. Candidacy: VP - 1820.

Talmadge, Herman Eugene - Ga. (Democratic) August 9, 1913– ; governor, 1947, 1948–1955; Senate, 1957–1981. Candidacy: VP - 1956.

Taylor, Glen Hearst - Idaho (Progressive) April 12, 1904–April 28, 1984; Senate, 1945–1951. Candidacy: VP - 1948.

Tazewell, Littleton Waller - Va. (Democratic) December 17, 1774–May 6, 1860; House, 1800–1801; Senate, 1824–1832; president pro tempore of the Senate, 1832; governor, 1834–1836. Candidacy: VP - 1840.

Telfair, Edward - Ga. (Democratic-Republican) 1735–September 17, 1807; Continental Congress, 1778, 1780–1782; governor, 1789–1793. Candidacy: 1789.

Thomas, Norman Mattoon - N.Y. (Socialist) November 20, 1884–December 19, 1968; Presbyterian minister, 1911–1931; author and editor. Candidacies: P - 1928, 1932, 1936, 1940, 1944, 1948.

Thurman, Allen Granberry - Ohio (Democratic) November 13, 1813–December 12, 1895; House, 1845–1847; Ohio Supreme Court, 1851–1856; Senate, 1869–1881; president pro tempore of the Senate, 1879, 1880. Candidacy: VP - 1888.

Thurmond, James Strom - S.C. (States' Rights Democrat, Democratic, Republican) December 5, 1902– ; governor, 1947–1951; Senate, 1954–1956, 1956– ; president pro tempore of the Senate, 1981–1987. Candidacies: P - 1948; VP - 1960.

Tilden, Samuel Jones - N.Y. (Democratic) February 9, 1814–August 4, 1886; governor, 1875–1877. Candidacy: 1876.

Wallace, George Corley - Ala. (American Independent) August 25, 1919– ; governor, 1963–1967, 1971–1979, 1983–1987. Candidacy: P - 1968.

Warren, Earl - Calif. (Republican) March 19, 1891–July 9, 1974; governor, 1943–1953; chief justice of United States, 1953–1969. Candidacy: VP - 1948.

Watson, Thomas Edward - Ga. (Populist) September 5, 1856–September 26, 1922; House, 1891–1893; Senate, 1921–1922. Candidacies: VP - 1896; P - 1904, 1908.

Weaver, James Baird - Iowa (Greenback, Populist) June 12, 1833–February 6, 1912; House, 1879–1881, 1885–1889. Candidacies: P - 1880, 1892.

Webster, Daniel - Mass. (Whig) January 18, 1782–October 24, 1852; House, 1813–1817, 1823–1827; Senate, 1827–1841, 1845–1850; secretary of state, 1841–1843, 1850–1852. Candidacy: P - 1836.

Wheeler, Burton Kendall - Mont. (Progressive) February 27, 1882–January 6, 1975; Senate, 1923–1947. Candidacy: VP - 1924.

White, Hugh Lawson - Tenn. (Whig) October 30, 1773–April 10, 1840; Senate, October 25, 1825–March 3, 1835, October 6, 1835–January 13, 1840. Candidacy: P - 1836.

Wilkins, William - Pa. (Democratic) December 20, 1779–June 23, 1865; Senate, 1831–1834; minister to Russia, 1834–1835; House, 1843–1844; secretary of war, 1844–1845. Candidacy: VP - 1832.

Willkie, Wendell Lewis - N.Y. (Republican) February 18, 1892–October 8, 1944; utility executive, 1933–1940. Candidacy: P - 1940.

Wirt, William - Md. (Anti-Masonic) November 8, 1772–February 18, 1834; attorney general, 1817–1829. Candidacy: P - 1832.

Wright, Fielding Lewis - Miss. (States' Rights Democratic) May 16, 1895–May 4, 1956; governor, 1946–1952. Candidacy: VP - 1948.

Summary of Presidential Elections, 1789–1992

Year	No. of states	Candidates	Party	Electoral vote	Popular vote
1789[a]	10	**George Washington**	**Fed.**	**69**	—[b]
		John Adams	Fed.	34	
1792[a]	15	**George Washington**	**Fed.**	**132**	—[b]
		John Adams	Fed.	77	
1796[a]	16	**John Adams**	**Fed.**	**71**	—[b]
		Thomas Jefferson	Dem.-Rep.	68	
1800[a]	16	**Thomas Jefferson**	**Dem.-Rep.**	**73**	—[b]
		Aaron Burr	Dem.-Rep.	73	
		John Adams	Fed.	65	
		Charles Cotesworth Pinckney	Fed.	64	
1804	17	**Thomas Jefferson**	**Dem.-Rep.**	**162**	—[b]
		George Clinton			
		Charles Cotesworth Pinckney	Fed.	64	
		Rufus King			
1808	17	**James Madison**	**Dem.-Rep.**	**122**	—[b]
		George Clinton			
		Charles Cotesworth Pinckney	Fed.	64	
		Rufus King			
1812	18	**James Madison**	**Dem.-Rep.**	**128**	—[b]
		Elbridge Gerry			
		George Clinton	Fed.	89	
		Jared Ingersoll			
1816	19	**James Monroe**	**Dem.-Rep.**	**183**	—[b]
		Daniel D. Tompkins			
		Rufus King	Fed.	34	
		John Howard			
1820	24	**James Monroe**	**Dem.-Rep.**	**231**[c]	—[b]
		Daniel D. Tompkins			
1824[d]	24	**John Quincy Adams**	**Dem.-Rep.**	**99**	**113,122 (30.9%)**
		John C. Calhoun			
		Andrew Jackson	Dem.-Rep.	84	151,271 (41.3%)
		Nathan Sanford			
1828	24	**Andrew Jackson**	**Dem.-Rep.**	**178**	**642,553 (56.0%)**
		John C. Calhoun			
		John Quincy Adams	Nat.-Rep.	83	500,897 (43.6%)
		Richard Rush			
1832[e]	24	**Andrew Jackson**	**Dem.**	**219**	**701,780 (54.2%)**
		Martin Van Buren			
		Henry Clay	Nat.-Rep.	49	484,205 (37.4%)
		John Sergeant			
1836[f]	26	**Martin Van Buren**	**Dem.**	**170**	**764,176 (50.8%)**
		Richard M. Johnson			
		William Henry Harrison	Whig	73	550,816 (36.6%)
		Francis Granger			
1840	26	**William Henry Harrison**	**Whig**	**234**	**1,275,390 (52.9%)**
		John Tyler			
		Martin Van Buren	Dem.	60	1,128,854 (46.8%)
		Richard M. Johnson			
1844	26	**James K. Polk**	**Dem.**	**170**	**1,339,494 (49.5%)**
		George M. Dallas			
		Henry Clay	Whig	105	1,300,004 (48.1%)
		Theodore Frelinghuysen			
1848	30	**Zachary Taylor**	**Whig**	**163**	**1,361,393 (47.3%)**
		Millard Fillmore			
		Lewis Cass	Dem.	127	1,223,460 (42.5%)
		William O. Butler			
1852	31	**Franklin Pierce**	**Dem.**	**254**	**1,607,510 (50.8%)**
		William R. King			
		Winfield Scott	Whig	42	1,386,942 (43.9%)
		William A. Graham			
1856[g]	31	**James Buchanan**	**Dem.**	**174**	**1,836,072 (45.3%)**
		John C. Breckinridge			
		John C. Fremont	Rep.	114	1,342,345 (33.1%)
		William L. Dayton			
1860[h]	33	**Abraham Lincoln**	**Rep.**	**180**	**1,865,908 (39.8%)**
		Hannibal Hamlin			
		Stephen A. Douglas	Dem.	12	1,380,202 (29.5%)
		Herschel V. Johnson			
1864[i]	36	**Abraham Lincoln**	**Rep.**	**212**	**2,218,388 (55.0%)**
		Andrew Johnson			
		George B. McClellan	Dem.	21	1,812,807 (45.0%)
		George H. Pendleton			
1868[j]	37	**Ulysses S. Grant**	**Rep.**	**214**	**3,013,650 (52.7%)**
		Schuyler Colfax			
		Horatio Seymour	Dem.	80	2,708,744 (47.3%)
		Francis P. Blair Jr.			
1872	37	**Ulysses S. Grant**	**Rep.**	**286**	**3,598,235 (55.6%)**
		Henry Wilson			
		Horace Greeley	Dem.	—[k]	2,834,761 (43.8%)
		Benjamin Gratz Brown			
1876	38	**Rutherford B. Hayes**	**Rep.**	**185**	**4,034,311 (47.9%)**
		William A. Wheeler			
		Samuel J. Tilden	Dem.	184	4,288,546 (51.0%)
		Thomas A. Hendricks			

(table continues)

Year	No. of states	Candidates	Party	Electoral vote	Popular vote	Year	No. of states	Candidates	Party	Electoral vote	Popular vote
1880	38	**James A. Garfield** *Chester A. Arthur*	**Rep.**	**214**	**4,446,158 (48.3%)**	1932	48	**Franklin D. Roosevelt** *John N. Garner*	**Dem.**	**472**	**22,825,016 (57.4%)**
		Winfield S. Hancock *William H. English*	Dem.	155	4,444,260 (48.2%)			Herbert C. Hoover *Charles Curtis*	Rep.	59	15,758,397 (39.6%)
1884	38	**Grover Cleveland** *Thomas A. Hendricks*	**Dem.**	**219**	**4,874,621 (48.5%)**	1936	48	**Franklin D. Roosevelt** *John N. Garner*	**Dem.**	**523**	**27,747,636 (60.8%)**
		James G. Blaine *John A. Logan*	Rep.	182	4,848,936 (48.2%)			Alfred M. Landon *Frank Knox*	Rep.	8	16,679,543 (36.5%)
1888	38	**Benjamin Harrison** *Levi P. Morton*	**Rep.**	**233**	**5,443,892 (47.8%)**	1940	48	**Franklin D. Roosevelt** *Henry A. Wallace*	**Dem.**	**449**	**27,263,448 (54.7%)**
		Grover Cleveland *Allen G. Thurman*	Dem.	168	5,534,488 (48.6%)			Wendell L. Willkie *Charles L. McNary*	Rep.	82	22,336,260 (44.8%)
1892[l]	44	**Grover Cleveland** *Adlai E. Stevenson*	**Dem.**	**277**	**5,551,883 (46.1%)**	1944	48	**Franklin D. Roosevelt** *Harry S. Truman*	**Dem.**	**432**	**25,611,936 (53.4%)**
		Benjamin Harrison *Whitelaw Reid*	Rep.	145	5,179,244 (43.0%)			Thomas E. Dewey *John W. Bricker*	Rep.	99	22,013,372 (45.9%)
1896	45	**William McKinley** *Garret A. Hobart*	**Rep.**	**271**	**7,108,480 (51.0%)**	1948[o]	48	**Harry S. Truman** *Alben W. Barkley*	**Dem.**	**303**	**24,105,587 (49.5%)**
		William J. Bryan *Arthur Sewall*	Dem.	176	6,511,495 (46.7%)			Thomas E. Dewey *Earl Warren*	Rep.	198	21,970,017 (45.1%)
1900	45	**William McKinley** *Theodore Roosevelt*	**Rep.**	**292**	**7,218,039 (51.7%)**	1952	48	**Dwight D. Eisenhower** *Richard M. Nixon*	**Rep.**	**442**	**33,936,137 (55.1%)**
		William J. Bryan *Adlai E. Stevenson*	Dem.	155	6,358,345 (45.5%)			Adlai E. Stevenson II *John J. Sparkman*	Dem.	89	27,314,649 (44.4%)
1904	45	**Theodore Roosevelt** *Charles W. Fairbanks*	**Rep.**	**336**	**7,626,593 (56.4%)**	1956[p]	48	**Dwight D. Eisenhower** *Richard M. Nixon*	**Rep.**	**457**	**35,585,245 (57.4%)**
		Alton B. Parker *Henry G. Davis*	Dem.	140	5,028,898 (37.6%)			Adlai E. Stevenson II *Estes Kefauver*	Dem.	73	26,030,172 (42.0%)
1908	46	**William Howard Taft** *James S. Sherman*	**Rep.**	**321**	**7,676,258 (51.6%)**	1960[q]	50	**John F. Kennedy** *Lyndon B. Johnson*	**Dem.**	**303**	**34,221,344 (49.7%)**
		William J. Bryan *John W. Kern*	Dem.	162	6,406,801 (43.0%)			Richard Nixon *Henry Cabot Lodge*	Rep.	219	34,106,671 (49.5%)
1912[m]	48	**Woodrow Wilson** *Thomas R. Marshall*	**Dem.**	**435**	**6,293,152(41.8%)**	1964	50*	**Lyndon B. Johnson** *Hubert H. Humphrey*	**Dem.**	**486**	**43,126,584 (61.1%)**
		William Howard Taft *James S. Sherman*	Rep.	8	3,486,333 (23.2%)			Barry Goldwater *William E. Miller*	Rep.	52	27,177,838 (38.5%)
1916	48	**Woodrow Wilson** *Thomas R. Marshall*	**Dem.**	**277**	**9,126,300 (49.2%)**	1968[r]	50*	**Richard Nixon** *Spiro T. Agnew*	**Rep.**	**301**	**31,785,148 (43.4%)**
		Charles E. Hughes *Charles W. Fairbanks*	Rep.	254	8,546,789 (46.1%)			Hubert H. Humphrey *Edmund S. Muskie*	Dem.	191	31,274,503 (42.7%)
1920	48	**Warren G. Harding** *Calvin Coolidge*	**Rep.**	**404**	**16,133,314 (60.3%)**	1972[s]	50*	**Richard Nixon** *Spiro T. Agnew*	**Rep.**	**520**	**47,170,179 (60.7%)**
		James M. Cox *Franklin D. Roosevelt*	Dem.	127	9,140,884 (34.2%)			George McGovern *Sargent Shriver*	Dem.	17	29,171,791 (37.5%)
1924[n]	48	**Calvin Coolidge** *Charles G. Dawes*	**Rep.**	**382**	**15,717,553 (54.1%)**	1976[t]	50*	**Jimmy Carter** *Walter F. Mondale*	**Dem.**	**297**	**40,830,763 (50.1%)**
		John W. Davis *Charles W. Bryan*	Dem.	136	8,386,169 (28.8%)			Gerald R. Ford *Robert Dole*	Rep.	240	39,147,793 (48.0%)
1928	48	**Herbert C. Hoover** *Charles Curtis*	**Rep.**	**444**	**21,411,991 (58.2%)**	1980	50*	**Ronald Reagan** *George Bush*	**Rep.**	**489**	**43,904,153 (50.7%)**
		Alfred E. Smith *Joseph T. Robinson*	Dem.	87	15,000,185 (40.8%)			Jimmy Carter *Walter F. Mondale*	Dem.	49	35,483,883 (41.0%)

(table continues)

Year	No. of states	Candidates	Party	Electoral vote	Popular vote	Year	No. of states	Candidates	Party	Electoral vote	Popular vote
1984	50*	**Ronald Reagan** *George Bush*	**Rep.**	**525**	**54,455,074(58.8%)**	1992	50*	**Bill Clinton** *Al Gore*	**Dem.**	**370**	**44,908,233 (43.0%)**
		Walter F. Mondale *Geraldine Ferraro*	Dem.	13	37,577,137 (40.6%)			George Bush *Dan Quayle*	Rep.	168	39,102,282 (37.4%)
1988[u]	50*	**George Bush** *Dan Quayle*	**Rep.**	**426**	**48,881,278 (53.4%)**						
		Michael S. Dukakis *Lloyd Bentsen*	Dem.	111	41,805,374 (45.6%)						

SOURCE: Harold W. Stanley and Richard G. Niemi, *Vital Statistics on American Politics,* 5th ed. (Washington, D.C.: CQ Press, 1995), table 3-13.

NOTES: In the elections of 1789, 1792, 1796, and 1800, each candidate ran for the office of president. The candidate with the second highest number of electoral votes became vice president. For elections after 1800, italic indicates vice-presidential candidates. Dem.-Rep.—Democratic-Republican; Fed.—Federalist; Nat.-Rep.—National-Republican; Dem.—Democratic; Rep.—Republican.   a. Elections of 1789–1800 were held under rules that did not allow separate voting for president and vice president. b. Popular vote returns are not shown before 1824 because consistent, reliable data are not available.   c. Monroe ran unopposed. One electoral vote was cast for John Adams and Richard Stockton, who were not candidates.   d. 1824: All four candidates represented Democratic-Republican factions. William H. Crawford received 41 electoral votes, and Henry Clay received 37 votes. Since no candidate received a majority, the election was decided (in Adams's favor) by the House of Representatives. e. 1832: Two electoral votes were not cast.   f. 1836: Other Whig candidates receiving electoral votes were Hugh L. White, who received 26 votes, and Daniel Webster, who received 14 votes.   g. 1856: Millard Fillmore, Whig-American, received 8 electoral votes.   h. 1860: John C. Breckinridge, Southern Democrat, received 72 electoral votes. John Bell, Constitutional Union, received 39 electoral votes.   i. 1864: Eighty-one electoral votes were not cast.   j. 1868: Twenty-three electoral votes were not cast. k. 1872: Horace Greeley, Democrat, died after the election. In the electoral college, Democratic electoral votes went to Thomas Hendricks, 42 votes; Benjamin Gratz Brown, 18 votes; Charles J. Jenkins, 2 votes; and David Davis, 1 vote. Seventeen electoral votes were not cast.   l. 1892: James B. Weaver, People's Party, received 22 electoral votes. m. 1912: Theodore Roosevelt, Progressive Party, received 86 electoral votes.   n. 1924: Robert M. La Follette, Progressive Party, received 13 electoral votes.   o. 1948: J. Strom Thurmond, States' Rights Party, received 39 electoral votes.   p. 1956: Walter B. Jones, Democrat, received 1 electoral vote.   q. 1960: Harry Flood Byrd, Democrat, received 15 electoral votes.   r. 1968: George C. Wallace, American Independent Party, received 46 electoral votes.   s. 1972: John Hospers, Libertarian Party, received 1 electoral vote. t. 1976: Ronald Reagan, Republican, received 1 electoral vote.   u. 1988: Lloyd Bentsen, the Democratic vice-presidential nominee, received 1 electoral vote for president. *Fifty states plus the District of Columbia.

Political Party Nominees, 1831–1992

Following is a comprehensive list of major- and minor-party nominees for president and vice president since 1831, when the first nominating convention was held by the Anti-Masonic Party. In many cases, minor parties made only token efforts at a presidential campaign. Often, third party candidates declined to run after being nominated by the convention, or their names appeared on the ballots of only a few states. In some cases the names of minor candidates did not appear on any state ballots and they received only a scattering of write-in votes, if any.

The basic source used to compile the list was Joseph Nathan Kane, *Facts About the Presidents,* 6th ed. (New York: H. W. Wilson, 1993). To verify the names appearing in Kane, Congressional Quarterly consulted the following additional sources: Richard M. Scammon, *America at the Polls* (Pittsburgh: University of Pittsburgh Press, 1965); *America Votes 8* (Washington, D.C.: Congressional Quarterly, 1969); *America Votes 10* (Washington, D.C.: Congressional Quarterly,

1973); Richard B. Morris, ed., *Encyclopedia of American History* (New York: Harper and Row, 1965); *Dictionary of American Biography* (New York: Scribner's, 1928–1936); *Facts on File* (New York: Facts on File Inc., 1945–1975); Arthur M. Schlesinger Jr., ed., *History of U.S. Political Parties,* vols. I–IV (New York: McGraw-Hill, 1971); and *Who Was Who in America, 1607–1968,* vols. I–V (Chicago: Marquis, 1943–1968). The sources for the 1976 to 1992 elections were Richard M. Scammon and Alice V. McGillivray, *America Votes 12* (1977), *America Votes 14* (1981), *America Votes 16* (1985), *America Votes 18* (1989), and *America Votes 20* (1993), published in Washington, D.C., by Congressional Quarterly.

In cases where these sources contain information in conflict with Kane, the conflicting information is included in a footnote. Where a candidate appears in Kane *but could not be verified in another source,* an asterisk appears beside the candidate's name on the list.

1832 ELECTION

Democratic Party
President: Andrew Jackson, Tennessee
Vice president: Martin Van Buren, New York
National Republican Party
President: Henry Clay, Kentucky
Vice president: John Sergeant, Pennsylvania
Independent Party
President: John Floyd, Virginia
Vice president: Henry Lee, Massachusetts
Anti-Masonic Party
President: William Wirt, Maryland
Vice president: Amos Ellmaker, Pennsylvania

1836 ELECTION

Democratic Party
President: Martin Van Buren, New York
Vice president: Richard Mentor Johnson, Kentucky
Whig Party
President: William Henry Harrison, Ohio; Hugh Lawson White, Tenn.; Daniel Webster, Mass.
Vice president: Francis Granger, New York; John Tyler, Virginia

The Whigs nominated regional candidates in 1836 hoping that each candidate would carry his region and deny Democrat Van Buren an electoral vote majority. Webster was the Whig candidate in Massachusetts; Harrison in the rest of New England, the Middle Atlantic states, and the West; and White in the South.

Granger was the running mate of Harrison and Webster. Tyler was White's running mate.

1840 ELECTION

Whig Party
President: William Henry Harrison, Ohio
Vice president: John Tyler, Virginia

Democratic Party
President: Martin Van Buren, New York

The Democratic convention adopted a resolution that left the choice of vice-presidential candidates to the states. Democratic electors divided their vice-presidential votes among incumbent Richard M. Johnson (forty-eight votes), Littleton W. Tazewell (eleven votes), and James K. Polk (one vote).

Liberty Party
President: James Gillespie Birney, New York
Vice president: Thomas Earle, Pennsylvania

1844 ELECTION

Democratic Party
President: James Knox Polk, Tennessee
Vice president: George Mifflin Dallas, Pennsylvania
Whig Party
President: Henry Clay, Kentucky
Vice president: Theodore Frelinghuysen, New Jersey
Liberty Party
President: James Gillespie Birney, New York
Vice president: Thomas Morris, Ohio
National Democratic Party
President: John Tyler, Virginia
Vice president: None
Tyler withdrew in favor of the Democrat, Polk.

1848 ELECTION

Whig Party
President: Zachary Taylor, Louisiana
Vice president: Millard Fillmore, New York
Democratic Party
President: Lewis Cass, Michigan
Vice president: William Orlando Butler, Kentucky

Free Soil Party
President: Martin Van Buren, New York
Vice president: Charles Francis Adams, Massachusetts

Free Soil (Barnburners—Liberty Party)
President: John Parker Hale, New Hampshire
Vice president: Leicester King, Ohio
    Later John Parker Hale relinquished the nomination.

National Liberty Party
President: Gerrit Smith, New York
Vice president: Charles C. Foote, Michigan

1852 ELECTION

Democratic Party
President: Franklin Pierce, New Hampshire
Vice president: William Rufus De Vane King, Alabama

Whig Party
President: Winfield Scott, New Jersey
Vice president: William Alexander Graham, North Carolina

Free Soil
President: John Parker Hale, New Hampshire
Vice president: George Washington Julian, Indiana

1856 ELECTION

Democratic Party
President: James Buchanan, Pennsylvania
Vice president: John Cabell Breckinridge, Kentucky

Republican Party
President: John Charles Fremont, California
Vice president: William Lewis Dayton, New Jersey

American (Know-Nothing) Party
President: Millard Fillmore, New York
Vice president: Andrew Jackson Donelson, Tennessee

Whig Party (the "Silver Grays")
President: Millard Fillmore, New York
Vice president: Andrew Jackson Donelson, Tennessee

North American Party
President: Nathaniel Prentice Banks, Massachusetts
Vice president: William Freame Johnson, Pennsylvania
    Banks and Johnson declined the nominations and gave their support to the Republicans.

1860 ELECTION

Republican Party
President: Abraham Lincoln, Illinois
Vice president: Hannibal Hamlin, Maine

Democratic Party
President: Stephen Arnold Douglas, Illinois
Vice president: Herschel Vespasian Johnson, Georgia

Southern Democratic Party
President: John Cabell Breckinridge, Kentucky
Vice president: Joseph Lane, Oregon

Constitutional Union Party
President: John Bell, Tennessee
Vice president: Edward Everett, Massachusetts

1864 ELECTION

Republican Party
President: Abraham Lincoln, Illinois
Vice president: Andrew Johnson, Tennessee

Democratic Party
President: George Brinton McClellan, New York
Vice president: George Hunt Pendleton, Ohio

Independent Republican Party
President: John Charles Fremont, California
Vice president: John Cochrane, New York
    Fremont and Cochrane declined the nominations and gave their support to the Republicans.

1868 ELECTION

Republican Party
President: Ulysses Simpson Grant, Illinois
Vice president: Schuyler Colfax, Indiana

Democratic Party
President: Horatio Seymour, New York
Vice president: Francis Preston Blair Jr., Missouri

1872 ELECTION

Republican Party
President: Ulysses Simpson Grant, Illinois
Vice president: Henry Wilson, Massachusetts

Liberal Republican Party
President: Horace Greeley, New York
Vice president: Benjamin Gratz Brown, Missouri

Independent Liberal Republican Party (Opposition Party)
President: William Slocum Groesbeck, Ohio
Vice president: Frederick Law Olmsted, New York

Democratic Party
President: Horace Greeley, New York
Vice president: Benjamin Gratz Brown, Missouri

Straight-Out Democratic Party
President: Charles O'Conor, New York
Vice president: Charles Francis Adams, Massachusetts

Prohibition Party
President: James Black, Pennsylvania
Vice president: John Russell, Michigan

People's Party (Equal Rights Party)
President: Victoria Claflin Woodhull, New York
Vice president: Frederick Douglass

Labor Reform Party
President: David Davis, Illinois
Vice president: Joel Parker, New Jersey

Liberal Republican Party of Colored Men
President: Horace Greeley, New York
Vice president: Benjamin Gratz Brown, Missouri

National Working Men's Party
President: Ulysses Simpson Grant, Illinois
Vice president: Henry Wilson, Massachusetts

1876 ELECTION

Republican Party
President: Rutherford Birchard Hayes, Ohio
Vice president: William Almon Wheeler, New York

Democratic Party
President: Samuel Jones Tilden, New York
Vice president: Thomas Andrews Hendricks, Indiana

Greenback Party
President: Peter Cooper, New York
Vice president: Samuel Fenton Cary, Ohio

Prohibition Party
President: Green Clay Smith, Kentucky
Vice president: Gideon Tabor Stewart, Ohio

American National Party
President: James B. Walker, Illinois
Vice president: Donald Kirkpatrick, New York

1880 ELECTION

Republican Party
President: James Abram Garfield, Ohio
Vice president: Chester Alan Arthur, New York

Democratic Party
President: Winfield Scott Hancock, Pennsylvania
Vice president: William Hayden English, Indiana

Greenback Labor Party
President: James Baird Weaver, Iowa
Vice president: Benjamin J. Chambers, Texas

Prohibition Party
President: Neal Dow, Maine
Vice president: Henry Adams Thompson, Ohio

American Party
President: John Wolcott Phelps, Vermont
Vice president: Samuel Clarke Pomeroy, Kansas*

1884 ELECTION

Democratic Party
President: Grover Cleveland, New York
Vice president: Thomas Andrews Hendricks, Indiana

Republican Party
President: James Gillespie Blaine, Maine
Vice president: John Alexander Logan, Illinois

Anti-Monopoly Party
President: Benjamin Franklin Butler, Massachusetts
Vice president: Absolom Madden West, Mississippi

Greenback Party
President: Benjamin Franklin Butler, Massachusetts
Vice president: Absolom Madden West, Mississippi

Prohibition Party
President: John Pierce St. John, Kansas
Vice president: William Daniel, Maryland

American Prohibition Party
President: Samuel Clarke Pomeroy, Kansas
Vice president: John A. Conant, Connecticut

Equal Rights Party
President: Belva Ann Bennett Lockwood, District of Columbia
Vice president: Marietta Lizzie Bell Stow, California

1888 ELECTION

Republican Party
President: Benjamin Harrison, Indiana
Vice president: Levi Parsons Morton, New York

Democratic Party
President: Grover Cleveland, New York
Vice president: Allen Granberry Thurman, Ohio

Prohibition Party
President: Clinton Bowen Fisk, New Jersey
Vice president: John Anderson Brooks, Missouri*

Union Labor Party
President: Alson Jenness Streeter, Illinois
Vice president: Charles E. Cunningham, Arkansas*

United Labor Party
President: Robert Hall Cowdrey, Illinois
Vice president: William H. T. Wakefield, Kansas*

American Party
President: James Langdon Curtis, New York
Vice president: Peter Dinwiddie Wigginton, California*

Equal Rights Party
President: Belva Ann Bennett Lockwood, District of Columbia
Vice president: Alfred Henry Love, Pennsylvania*

Industrial Reform Party
President: Albert E. Redstone, California*
Vice president: John Colvin, Kansas*

1892 ELECTION

Democratic Party
President: Grover Cleveland, New York
Vice president: Adlai Ewing Stevenson, Illinois

Republican Party
President: Benjamin Harrison, Indiana
Vice president: Whitelaw Reid, New York

People's Party of America
President: James Baird Weaver, Iowa
Vice president: James Gaven Field, Virginia

Prohibition Party
President: John Bidwell, California
Vice president: James Britton Cranfill, Texas

Socialist Labor Party
President: Simon Wing, Massachusetts
Vice president: Charles Horatio Matchett, New York*

1896 ELECTION

Republican Party
President: William McKinley, Ohio
Vice president: Garret Augustus Hobart, New Jersey

Democratic Party
President: William Jennings Bryan, Nebraska
Vice president: Arthur Sewall, Maine

People's Party (Populist)
President: William Jennings Bryan, Nebraska
Vice president: Thomas Edward Watson, Georgia

National Democratic Party
President: John McAuley Palmer, Illinois
Vice president: Simon Bolivar Buckner, Kentucky

Prohibition Party
President: Joshua Levering, Maryland
Vice president: Hale Johnson, Illinois*

Socialist Labor Party
President: Charles Horatio Matchett, New York
Vice president: Matthew Maguire, New Jersey

National Party
President: Charles Eugene Bentley, Nebraska
Vice president: James Haywood Southgate, North Carolina*

National Silver Party (Bi-Metallic League)
President: William Jennings Bryan, Nebraska
Vice president: Arthur Sewall, Maine

1900 ELECTION

Republican Party
President: William McKinley, Ohio
Vice president: Theodore Roosevelt, New York

Democratic Party
President: William Jennings Bryan, Nebraska
Vice president: Adlai Ewing Stevenson, Illinois

Prohibition Party
President: John Granville Wooley, Illinois
Vice president: Henry Brewer Metcalf, Rhode Island

Social-Democratic Party
President: Eugene Victor Debs, Indiana
Vice president: Job Harriman, California

People's Party (Populist—Anti-Fusionist faction)
President: Wharton Barker, Pennsylvania
Vice president: Ignatius Donnelly, Minnesota

Socialist Labor Party
President: Joseph Francis Malloney, Massachusetts
Vice president: Valentine Remmel, Pennsylvania

Union Reform Party
President: Seth Hockett Ellis, Ohio
Vice president: Samuel T. Nicholson, Pennsylvania

United Christian Party
President: Jonah Fitz Randolph Leonard, Iowa
Vice president: David H. Martin, Pennsylvania

People's Party (Populist—Fusionist faction)
President: William Jennings Bryan, Nebraska
Vice president: Adlai Ewing Stevenson, Illinois

Silver Republican Party
President: William Jennings Bryan, Nebraska
Vice president: Adlai Ewing Stevenson, Illinois

National Party
President: Donelson Caffery, Louisiana
Vice president: Archibald Murray Howe, Massachusetts*

1904 ELECTION

Republican Party
President: Theodore Roosevelt, New York
Vice president: Charles Warren Fairbanks, Indiana

Democratic Party
President: Alton Brooks Parker, New York
Vice president: Henry Gassaway Davis, West Virginia

Socialist Party
President: Eugene Victor Debs, Indiana
Vice president: Benjamin Hanford, New York

Prohibition Party
President: Silas Comfort Swallow, Pennsylvania
Vice president: George W. Carroll, Texas

People's Party (Populist)
President: Thomas Edward Watson, Georgia
Vice president: Thomas Henry Tibbles, Nebraska

Socialist Labor Party
President: Charles Hunter Corregan, New York
Vice president: William Wesley Cox, Illinois

Continental Party
President: Austin Holcomb, Georgia
Vice president: A. King, Missouri

1908 ELECTION

Republican Party
President: William Howard Taft, Ohio
Vice president: James Schoolcraft Sherman, New York

Democratic Party
President: William Jennings Bryan, Nebraska
Vice president: John Worth Kern, Indiana

Socialist Party
President: Eugene Victor Debs, Indiana
Vice president: Benjamin Hanford, New York

Prohibition Party
President: Eugene Wilder Chafin, Illinois
Vice president: Aaron Sherman Watkins, Ohio

Independence Party
President: Thomas Louis Hisgen, Massachusetts
Vice president: John Temple Graves, Georgia

People's Party (Populist)
President: Thomas Edward Watson, Georgia
Vice president: Samuel Williams, Indiana

Socialist Labor Party
President: August Gillhaus, New York
Vice president: Donald L. Munro, Virginia

United Christian Party
President: Daniel Braxton Turney, Illinois
Vice president: Lorenzo S. Coffin, Iowa

1912 ELECTION

Democratic Party
President: Woodrow Wilson, New Jersey
Vice president: Thomas Riley Marshall, Indiana

Progressive Party ("Bull Moose" Party)
President: Theodore Roosevelt, New York
Vice president: Hiram Warren Johnson, California

Republican Party
President: William Howard Taft, Ohio
Vice president: James Schoolcraft Sherman, New York
    Sherman died October 30; he was replaced by Nicholas Murray Butler, New York.

Socialist Party
President: Eugene Victor Debs, Indiana
Vice president: Emil Seidel, Wisconsin

Prohibition Party
President: Eugene Wilder Chafin, Illinois
Vice president: Aaron Sherman Watkins, Ohio

Socialist Labor Party
President: Arthur Elmer Reimer, Massachusetts
Vice president: August Gillhaus, New York[a]

1916 ELECTION

Democratic Party
President: Woodrow Wilson, New Jersey
Vice president: Thomas Riley Marshall, Indiana

Republican Party
President: Charles Evans Hughes, New York
Vice president: Charles Warren Fairbanks, Indiana

Socialist Party
President: Allan Louis Benson, New York
Vice president: George Ross Kirkpatrick, New Jersey

Prohibition Party
President: James Franklin Hanly, Indiana
Vice president: Ira Landrith, Tennessee

Socialist Labor Party
President: Arthur Elmer Reimer, Massachusetts*
Vice president: Caleb Harrison, Illinois*

Progressive Party
President: Theodore Roosevelt, New York
Vice president: John Milliken Parker, Louisiana

1920 ELECTION

Republican Party
President: Warren Gamaliel Harding, Ohio
Vice president: Calvin Coolidge, Massachusetts

Democratic Party
President: James Middleton Cox, Ohio
Vice president: Franklin Delano Roosevelt, New York

Socialist Party
President: Eugene Victor Debs, Indiana
Vice president: Seymour Stedman, Illinois

Farmer Labor Party
President: Parley Parker Christensen, Utah
Vice president: Maximilian Sebastian Hayes, Ohio

Prohibition Party
President: Aaron Sherman Watkins, Ohio
Vice president: David Leigh Colvin, New York

Socialist Labor Party
President: William Wesley Cox, Missouri
Vice president: August Gillhaus, New York

Single Tax Party
President: Robert Colvin Macauley, Pennsylvania
Vice president: R. G. Barnum, Ohio

American Party
President: James Edward Ferguson, Texas
Vice president: William J. Hough

1924 ELECTION

Republican Party
President: Calvin Coolidge, Massachusetts
Vice president: Charles Gates Dawes, Illinois

Democratic Party
President: John William Davis, West Virginia
Vice president: Charles Wayland Bryan, Nebraska

Progressive Party
President: Robert La Follette, Wisconsin
Vice president: Burton Kendall Wheeler, Montana

Prohibition Party
President: Herman Preston Faris, Missouri
Vice president: Marie Caroline Brehm, California

Socialist Labor Party
President: Frank T. Johns, Oregon
Vice president: Verne L. Reynolds, New York

Socialist Party
President: Robert La Follette, New York
Vice president: Burton Kendall Wheeler, Montana

Workers Party (Communist Party)
President: William Zebulon Foster, Illinois
Vice president: Benjamin Gitlow, New York

American Party
President: Gilbert Owen Nations, District of Columbia
Vice president: Charles Hiram Randall, California[b]

Commonwealth Land Party
President: William J. Wallace, New Jersey
Vice president: John Cromwell Lincoln, Ohio

Farmer Labor Party
President: Duncan McDonald, Illinois*
Vice president: William Bouck, Washington*

Greenback Party
President: John Zahnd, Indiana*
Vice president: Roy M. Harrop, Nebraska*

1928 ELECTION

Republican Party
President: Herbert Clark Hoover, California
Vice president: Charles Curtis, Kansas

Democratic Party
President: Alfred Emanuel Smith, New York
Vice president: Joseph Taylor Robinson, Arkansas

Socialist Party
President: Norman Mattoon Thomas, New York
Vice president: James Hudson Maurer, Pennsylvania

Workers Party (Communist Party)
President: William Zebulon Foster, Illinois
Vice president: Benjamin Gitlow, New York

Socialist Labor Party
President: Verne L. Reynolds, Michigan
Vice president: Jeremiah D. Crowley, New York

Prohibition Party
President: William Frederick Varney, New York
Vice president: James Arthur Edgerton, Virginia

Farmer Labor Party
President: Frank Elbridge Webb, California
Vice president: Will Vereen, Georgia[c]

Greenback Party
President: John Zahnd, Indiana*
Vice president: Wesley Henry Bennington, Ohio*

1932 ELECTION

Democratic Party
President: Franklin Delano Roosevelt, New York
Vice president: John Nance Garner, Texas

Republican Party
President: Herbert Clark Hoover, California
Vice president: Charles Curtis, Kansas

Socialist Party
President: Norman Mattoon Thomas, New York
Vice president: James Hudson Maurer, Pennsylvania

Communist Party
President: William Zebulon Foster, Illinois
Vice president: James William Ford, New York

Prohibition Party
President: William David Upshaw, Georgia
Vice president: Frank Stewart Regan, Illinois

Liberty Party
President: William Hope Harvey, Arkansas
Vice president: Frank B. Hemenway, Washington

Socialist Labor Party
President: Verne L. Reynolds, New York
Vice president: John W. Aiken, Massachusetts

Farmer Labor Party
President: Jacob Sechler Coxey, Ohio
Vice president: Julius J. Reiter, Minnesota

Jobless Party
President: James Renshaw Cox, Pennsylvania
Vice president: V. C. Tisdal, Oklahoma

National Party
President: Seymour E. Allen, Massachusetts

1936 ELECTION

Democratic Party
President: Franklin Delano Roosevelt, New York
Vice president: John Nance Garner, Texas

Republican Party
President: Alfred Mossman Landon, Kansas
Vice president: Frank Knox, Illinois

Union Party
President: William Lemke, North Dakota
Vice president: Thomas Charles O'Brien, Massachusetts

Socialist Party
President: Norman Mattoon Thomas, New York
Vice president: George A. Nelson, Wisconsin

Communist Party
President: Earl Russell Browder, Kansas
Vice president: James William Ford, New York

Prohibition Party
President: David Leigh Colvin, New York
Vice president: Alvin York, Tennessee

Socialist Labor Party
President: John W. Aiken, Massachusetts
Vice president: Emil F. Teichert, New York

National Greenback Party
President: John Zahnd, Indiana*
Vice president: Florence Garvin, Rhode Island*

1940 ELECTION

Democratic Party
President: Franklin Delano Roosevelt, New York
Vice president: Henry Agard Wallace, Iowa

Republican Party
President: Wendell Lewis Willkie, New York
Vice president: Charles Linza McNary, Oregon

Socialist Party
President: Norman Mattoon Thomas, New York
Vice president: Maynard C. Krueger, Illinois

Prohibition Party
President: Roger Ward Babson, Massachusetts
Vice president: Edgar V. Moorman, Illinois

Communist Party (Workers Party)
President: Earl Russell Browder, Kansas
Vice president: James William Ford, New York

Socialist Labor Party
President: John W. Aiken, Massachusetts
Vice president: Aaron M. Orange, New York

Greenback Party
President: John Zahnd, Indiana*
Vice president: James Elmer Yates, Arizona*

1944 ELECTION

Democratic Party
President: Franklin Delano Roosevelt, New York
Vice president: Harry S. Truman, Missouri

Republican Party
President: Thomas Edmund Dewey, New York
Vice president: John William Bricker, Ohio

Socialist Party
President: Norman Mattoon Thomas, New York
Vice president: Darlington Hoopes, Pennsylvania

Prohibition Party
President: Claude A. Watson, California
Vice president: Andrew Johnson, Kentucky

Socialist Labor Party
President: Edward A. Teichert, Pennsylvania
Vice president: Arla A. Albaugh, Ohio

America First Party
President: Gerald Lyman Kenneth Smith, Michigan
Vice president: Henry A. Romer, Ohio

1948 ELECTION

Democratic Party
President: Harry S. Truman, Missouri
Vice president: Alben William Barkley, Kentucky

Republican Party
President: Thomas Edmund Dewey, New York
Vice president: Earl Warren, California

States' Rights Democratic Party
President: James Strom Thurmond, South Carolina
Vice president: Fielding Lewis Wright, Mississippi

Progressive Party
President: Henry Agard Wallace, Iowa
Vice president: Glen Hearst Taylor, Idaho

Socialist Party
President: Norman Mattoon Thomas, New York
Vice president: Tucker Powell Smith, Michigan

Prohibition Party
President: Claude A. Watson, California
Vice president: Dale Learn, Pennsylvania

Socialist Labor Party
President: Edward A. Teichert, Pennsylvania
Vice president: Stephen Emery, New York

Socialist Workers Party
President: Farrell Dobbs, New York
Vice president: Grace Carlson, Minnesota

Christian Nationalist Party
President: Gerald Lyman Kenneth Smith, Missouri
Vice president: Henry A. Romer, Ohio

Greenback Party
President: John G. Scott, New York
Vice president: Granville B. Leeke, Indiana*

Vegetarian Party
President: John Maxwell, Illinois
Vice president: Symon Gould, New York*

1952 ELECTION

Republican Party
President: Dwight David Eisenhower, New York
Vice president: Richard Milhous Nixon, California

Democratic Party
President: Adlai Ewing Stevenson II, Illinois
Vice president: John Jackson Sparkman, Alabama

Progressive Party
President: Vincent William Hallinan, California
Vice president: Charlotta A. Bass, New York

Prohibition Party
President: Stuart Hamblen, California
Vice president: Enoch Arden Holtwick, Illinois

Socialist Labor Party
President: Eric Hass, New York
Vice president: Stephen Emery, New York

Socialist Party
President: Darlington Hoopes, Pennsylvania
Vice president: Samuel Herman Friedman, New York

Socialist Workers Party
President: Farrell Dobbs, New York
Vice president: Myra Tanner Weiss, New York

America First Party
President: Douglas MacArthur, Wisconsin
Vice president: Harry Flood Byrd, Virginia

American Labor Party
President: Vincent William Hallinan, California
Vice president: Charlotta A. Bass, New York

American Vegetarian Party
President: Daniel J. Murphy, California
Vice president: Symon Gould, New York*

Church of God Party
President: Homer Aubrey Tomlinson, New York
Vice president: Willie Isaac Bass, North Carolina*

Constitution Party
President: Douglas MacArthur, Wisconsin
Vice president: Harry Flood Byrd, Virginia

Greenback Party
President: Frederick C. Proehl, Washington
Vice president: Edward J. Bedell, Indiana

Poor Man's Party
President: Henry B. Krajewski, New Jersey
Vice president: Frank Jenkins, New Jersey

1956 ELECTION

Republican Party
President: Dwight David Eisenhower, Pennsylvania
Vice president: Richard Milhous Nixon, California

Democratic Party
President: Adlai Ewing Stevenson II, Illinois
Vice president: Estes Kefauver, Tennessee

States' Rights Party
President: Thomas Coleman Andrews, Virginia
Vice president: Thomas Harold Werdel, California
    Ticket also favored by Constitution Party.

Prohibition Party
President: Enoch Arden Holtwick, Illinois
Vice president: Edward M. Cooper, California

Socialist Labor Party
President: Eric Hass, New York
Vice president: Georgia Cozzini, Wisconsin

Texas Constitution Party
President: William Ezra Jenner, Indiana*
Vice president: Joseph Bracken Lee, Utah*

Socialist Workers Party
President: Farrell Dobbs, New York
Vice president: Myra Tanner Weiss, New York

American Third Party
President: Henry Krajewski, New Jersey
Vice president: Ann Marie Yezo, New Jersey

Socialist Party
President: Darlington Hoopes, Pennsylvania
Vice president: Samuel Herman Friedman, New York

Pioneer Party
President: William Langer, North Dakota*
Vice president: Burr McCloskey, Illinois*

American Vegetarian Party
President: Herbert M. Shelton, California*
Vice president: Symon Gould, New York*

Greenback Party
President: Frederick C. Proehl, Washington
Vice president: Edward Kirby Meador, Massachusetts*

States' Rights Party of Kentucky
President: Harry Flood Byrd, Virginia
Vice president: William Ezra Jenner, Indiana

South Carolinians for Independent Electors
President: Harry Flood Byrd, Virginia

Christian National Party
President: Gerald Lyman Kenneth Smith
Vice president: Charles I. Robertson

1960 ELECTION

Democratic Party
President: John Fitzgerald Kennedy, Massachusetts
Vice president: Lyndon Baines Johnson, Texas

Republican Party
President: Richard Milhous Nixon, California
Vice president: Henry Cabot Lodge, Massachusetts

National States' Rights Party
President: Orval Eugene Faubus, Arkansas
Vice president: John Geraerdt Crommelin, Alabama

Socialist Labor Party
President: Eric Hass, New York
Vice president: Georgia Cozzini, Wisconsin

Prohibition Party
President: Rutherford Losey Decker, Missouri
Vice president: Earle Harold Munn, Michigan

Socialist Workers Party
President: Farrell Dobbs, New York
Vice president: Myra Tanner Weiss, New York

Conservative Party of New Jersey
President: Joseph Bracken Lee, Utah
Vice president: Kent H. Courtney, Louisiana

Conservative Party of Virginia
President: C. Benton Coiner, Virginia
Vice president: Edward M. Silverman, Virginia

Constitution Party (Texas)
President: Charles Loten Sullivan, Mississippi
Vice president: Merritt B. Curtis, District of Columbia

Constitution Party (Washington)
President: Merritt B. Curtis, District of Columbia
Vice president: B. N. Miller

Greenback Party
President: Whitney Hart Slocomb, California*
Vice president: Edward Kirby Meador, Massachusetts*

Independent Afro-American Party
President: Clennon King, Georgia
Vice president: Reginald Carter, Georgia

Tax Cut Party (America First Party; American Party)
President: Lar Daly, Illinois
Vice president: Merritt Barton Curtis, District of Columbia

Theocratic Party
President: Homer Aubrey Tomlinson, New York
Vice president: Raymond L. Teague, Alaska*

Vegetarian Party
President: Symon Gould, New York
Vice president: Christopher Gian-Cursio, Florida

1964 ELECTION

Democratic Party
President: Lyndon Baines Johnson, Texas
Vice president: Hubert Horatio Humphrey, Minnesota

Republican Party
President: Barry Morris Goldwater, Arizona
Vice president: William Edward Miller, New York

Socialist Labor Party
President: Eric Hass, New York
Vice president: Henning A. Blomen, Massachusetts

Prohibition Party
President: Earle Harold Munn, Michigan
Vice president: Mark Shaw, Massachusetts

Socialist Workers Party
President: Clifton DeBerry, New York
Vice president: Edward Shaw, New York

National States' Rights Party
President: John Kasper, Tennessee
Vice president: J. B. Stoner, Georgia

Constitution Party
President: Joseph B. Lightburn, West Virginia
Vice president: Theodore C. Billings, Colorado

Independent States' Rights Party
President: Thomas Coleman Andrews, Virginia
Vice president: Thomas H. Werdel, California*

Theocratic Party
President: Homer Aubrey Tomlinson, New York
Vice president: William R. Rogers, Missouri*

Universal Party
President: Kirby James Hensley, California
Vice president: John O. Hopkins, Iowa

1968 ELECTION

Republican Party
President: Richard Milhous Nixon, New York
Vice president: Spiro Theodore Agnew, Maryland

Democratic Party
President: Hubert Horatio Humphrey, Minnesota
Vice president: Edmund Sixtus Muskie, Maine

American Independent Party
President: George Corley Wallace, Alabama
Vice president: Curtis Emerson LeMay, Ohio
    LeMay replaced S. Marvin Griffin, who originally had been selected.

Peace and Freedom Party
President: Eldridge Cleaver
Vice president: Judith Mage, New York

Socialist Labor Party
President: Henning A. Blomen, Massachusetts
Vice president: George Sam Taylor, Pennsylvania

Socialist Workers Party
President: Fred Halstead, New York
Vice president: Paul Boutelle, New Jersey

Prohibition Party
President: Earle Harold Munn Sr., Michigan
Vice president: Rolland E. Fisher, Kansas

Communist Party
President: Charlene Mitchell, California
Vice president: Michael Zagarell, New York

Constitution Party
President: Richard K. Troxell, Texas
Vice president: Merle Thayer, Iowa

Freedom and Peace Party
President: Richard Claxton (Dick) Gregory, Illinois
Vice president: Mark Lane, New York

Patriotic Party
President: George Corley Wallace, Alabama
Vice president: William Penn Patrick, California

Theocratic Party
President: William R. Rogers, Missouri

Universal Party
President: Kirby James Hensley, California
Vice president: Roscoe B. MacKenna

1972 ELECTION

Republican Party
President: Richard Milhous Nixon, California
Vice president: Spiro Theodore Agnew, Maryland

Democratic Party
President: George Stanley McGovern, South Dakota
Vice president: Thomas Francis Eagleton, Missouri
    Eagleton resigned and was replaced on August 8, 1972, by Robert Sargent Shriver Jr., Maryland, selected by the Democratic National Committee.

American Independent Party
President: John George Schmitz, California
Vice president: Thomas Jefferson Anderson, Tennessee

Socialist Workers Party
President: Louis Fisher, Illinois
Vice president: Genevieve Gunderson, Minnesota

Socialist Labor Party
President: Linda Jenness, Georgia
Vice president: Andrew Pulley, Illinois

Communist Party
President: Gus Hall, New York
Vice president: Jarvis Tyner

Prohibition Party
President: Earle Harold Munn Sr., Michigan
Vice president: Marshall Uncapher

Libertarian Party
President: John Hospers, California
Vice president: Theodora Nathan, Oregon

People's Party
President: Benjamin McLane Spock
Vice president: Julius Hobson, District of Columbia

America First Party
President: John V. Mahalchik
Vice president: Irving Homer

Universal Party
President: Gabriel Green
Vice president: Daniel Fry

1976 ELECTION

Democratic Party
President: James Earl (Jimmy) Carter Jr., Georgia
Vice president: Walter Frederick Mondale, Minnesota

Republican Party
President: Gerald Rudolph Ford, Michigan
Vice president: Robert Joseph Dole, Kansas

Independent candidate
President: Eugene Joseph McCarthy, Minnesota
Vice president: none[d]

Libertarian Party
President: Roger MacBride, Virginia
Vice president: David P. Bergland, California

American Independent Party
President: Lester Maddox, Georgia
Vice president: William Dyke, Wisconsin

American Party
President: Thomas J. Anderson, Tennessee
Vice president: Rufus Shackleford, Florida

Socialist Workers Party
President: Peter Camejo, California
Vice president: Willie Mae Reid, California

Communist Party
President: Gus Hall, New York
Vice president: Jarvis Tyner, New York

People's Party
President: Margaret Wright, California
Vice president: Benjamin Spock, New York

U.S. Labor Party
President: Lyndon H. LaRouche Jr., New York
Vice president: R. W. Evans, Michigan

Prohibition Party
President: Benjamin C. Bubar, Maine
Vice president: Earl F. Dodge, Colorado

Socialist Labor Party
President: Jules Levin, New Jersey
Vice president: Constance Blomen, Massachusetts

Socialist Party
President: Frank P. Zeidler, Wisconsin
Vice president: J. Quinn Brisben, Illinois

Restoration Party
President: Ernest L. Miller
Vice president: Roy N. Eddy

United American Party
President: Frank Taylor
Vice president: Henry Swan

1980 ELECTION[e]

Republican Party
President: Ronald Wilson Reagan, California
Vice president: George Herbert Walker Bush, Texas

Democratic Party
President: James Earl (Jimmy) Carter Jr., Georgia
Vice president: Walter Frederick Mondale, Minnesota

National Unity Campaign
President: John B. Anderson, Illinois
Vice president: Patrick Joseph Lucey, Wisconsin

Libertarian Party
President: Edward E. Clark, California
Vice president: David Koch, New York

Citizens Party
President: Barry Commoner, New York
Vice president: LaDonna Harris, New Mexico

Communist Party
President: Gus Hall, New York
Vice president: Angela Davis, California

American Independent Party
President: John Richard Rarick, Louisiana
Vice president: Eileen M. Shearer, California

Socialist Workers Party
President: Andrew Pulley, Illinois
Vice president: Matilde Zimmermann, New York
President: Clifton DeBerry, California
Vice president: Matilde Zimmermann, New York
President: Richard Congress, Ohio
Vice president: Matilde Zimmermann, New York

Right to Life Party
President: Ellen McCormack, New York
Vice president: Carroll Driscoll, New Jersey

Peace and Freedom Party
President: Maureen Smith, California
Vice president: Elizabeth Barron, California

Workers World Party
President: Deirdre Griswold, New Jersey
Vice president: Larry Holmes, New York

Statesman Party
President: Benjamin C. Bubar, Maine
Vice president: Earl F. Dodge, Colorado

Socialist Party
President: David McReynolds, New York
Vice president: Diane Drufenbrock, Wisconsin

American Party
President: Percy L. Greaves, New York
Vice president: Frank L. Varnum, California
President: Frank W. Shelton, Utah
Vice president: George E. Jackson

Middle Class Party
President: Kurt Lynen, New Jersey
Vice president: Harry Kieve, New Jersey

Down with Lawyers Party
President: Bill Gahres, New Jersey
Vice president: J. F. Loghlin, New Jersey

Independent Party
President: Martin E. Wendelken

Natural Peoples Party
President: Harley McLain, North Dakota
Vice president: Jewelie Goeller, North Dakota

1984 ELECTION[f]

Republican Party
President: Ronald Wilson Reagan, California
Vice president: George Herbert Walker Bush, Texas

Democratic Party
President: Walter Frederick Mondale, Minnesota
Vice president: Geraldine Anne Ferraro, New York

Libertarian Party
President: David P. Bergland, California
Vice president: Jim Lewis, Connecticut

Independent Party
President: Lyndon H. LaRouche Jr., Virginia
Vice president: Billy Davis, Mississippi

Citizens Party
President: Sonia Johnson, Virginia
Vice president: Richard Walton, Rhode Island

Populist Party
President: Bob Richards, Texas
Vice president: Maureen Kennedy Salaman, California

Independent Alliance Party
President: Dennis L. Serrette, New Jersey
Vice president: Nancy Ross, New York

Communist Party
President: Gus Hall, New York
Vice president: Angela Davis, California

Socialist Workers Party
President: Mel Mason, California
Vice president: Andrea Gonzalez, New York

Workers World Party
President: Larry Holmes, New York
Vice president: Gloria La Riva, California
President: Gavrielle Holmes, New York
Vice president: Milton Vera

American Party
President: Delmar Dennis, Tennessee
Vice president: Traves Brownlee, Delaware

Workers League Party
President: Ed Winn, New York
Vice presidents: Jean T. Brust, Helen Halyard, Edward Bergonzi

Prohibition Party
President: Earl F. Dodge, Colorado
Vice president: Warren C. Martin, Kansas

1988 ELECTION[g]

Republican Party
President: George Herbert Walker Bush, Texas
Vice president: James Danforth Quayle, Indiana

Democratic Party
President: Michael Stanley Dukakis, Massachusetts
Vice president: Lloyd Millard Bentsen Jr., Texas

Libertarian Party
President: Ronald Ernest Paul, Texas
Vice president: Andre V. Marrou, Nevada

New Alliance Party
President: Lenora B. Fulani, New York
Vice president: Joyce Dattner

Populist Party
President: David E. Duke, Louisiana
Vice president: Floyd C. Parker

Consumer Party
President: Eugene Joseph McCarthy, Minnesota
Vice president: Florence Rice

American Independent Party
President: James C. Griffin, California
Vice president: Charles J. Morsa

National Economic Recovery Party
President: Lyndon H. LaRouche Jr., Virginia
Vice president: Debra H. Freeman

Right to Life Party
President: William A. Marra, New Jersey
Vice president: Joan Andrews

Workers League Party
President: Edward Winn, New York
Vice president: Barry Porster

Socialist Workers Party
President: James Warren, New Jersey
Vice president: Kathleen Mickells

Peace and Freedom Party
President: Herbert Lewin
Vice president: Vikki Murdock

Prohibition Party
President: Earl F. Dodge, Colorado
Vice president: George D. Ormsby

Workers World Party
President: Larry Holmes, New York
Vice president: Gloria La Riva, California

Socialist Party
President: Willa Kenoyer, Minnesota
Vice president: Ron Ehrenreich

American Party
President: Delmar Dennis, Tennessee
Vice president: Earl Jepson

Grassroots Party
President: Jack E. Herer
Vice president: Dana Beal

Independent Party
President: Louie Youngkeit, Utah

Third World Assembly
President: John G. Martin, District of Columbia
Vice president: Cleveland Sparrow

1992 ELECTION[h]

Democratic Party
President: William Jefferson "Bill" Clinton, Arkansas
Vice president: Albert Gore Jr., Tennessee

Republican Party
President: George Herbert Walker Bush, Texas
Vice president: James Danforth Quayle, Indiana

Independent
President: H. Ross Perot, Texas
Vice president: James Stockdale, California

Libertarian Party
President: Andre V. Marrou, Nevada
Vice president: Nancy Lord, Georgia

America First Party (Populist)
President: James "Bo" Gritz
Vice president: Cyril Minett

New Alliance Party
President: Lenora B. Fulani, New York
Vice president: Maria E. Munoz, California

Taxpayers Party
President: Howard Phillips, Virginia
Vice president: Albion W. Knight, Maryland

Natural Law Party
President: John Hagelin, Iowa
Vice president: Mike Tompkins, Iowa

Peace and Freedom Party
President: Ron Daniels
Vice president: Asiba Tupahache

Independent
President: Lyndon H. LaRouche Jr., Virginia
Vice president: James L. Bevel

Socialist Workers Party
President: James Warren, New Jersey
Vice president: Willie Mae Reid

Independent
President: Drew Bradford

Grassroots Party
President: Jack E. Herer
Vice president: Derrick P. Grimmer

Socialist Party
President: J. Quinn Brisben
Vice president: Barbara Garson

Workers League Party
President: Helen Halyard
Vice president: Fred Mazelis

Take Back America Party
President: John Yiamouyiannas
Vice president: Allen C. McCone

Independent
President: Delbert L. Ehlers
Vice president: Rick Wendt

Prohibition Party
President: Earl F. Dodge, Colorado
Vice president: George D. Ormsby

Apathy Party
President: Jim Boren
Vice president: Will Weidman

Third Party
President: Eugene A. Hem
Vice president: Joanne Roland

Looking Back Party
President: Isabell Masters
Vice president: Walter Masters

American Party
President: Robert J. Smith
Vice president: Doris Feimer

Workers World Party
President: Gloria La Riva, California
Vice president: Larry Holmes, New York

NOTES: * Candidates appeared in Joseph Nathan Kane, *Facts About the Presidents*, 6th ed. (New York: H. W. Wilson, 1993), but could not be verified in another source.
a. 1912: Arthur M. Schlesinger's *History of American Presidential Elections* (New York: McGraw-Hill, 1971) lists the Socialist Labor Party vice-presidential candidate as Francis. No first name is given.   b. 1924: Richard M. Scammon's *America at the Polls* (Pittsburgh: University of Pittsburgh Press, 1965) lists the American Party vice-presidential candidate as Leander L. Pickett.   c. 1928: *America at the Polls* lists the Farmer Labor Party vice-presidential candidate as L. R. Tillman.   d. 1976: McCarthy, who ran as an independent with no party designation, had no national running mate, favoring the elimination of the office. But as various state laws required a running mate, he had different ones in different states, amounting to nearly two dozen, all political unknowns.   e. 1980: In several cases vice-presidential nominees were different from those listed for most states, and the Socialist Workers and American Party nominees for president varied from state to state. For example, because Pulley, the major standard-bearer for the Socialist Workers Party was only twenty-nine years old, his name was not allowed on the ballot in some states (the Constitution requires presidential candidates to be at least thirty-five years old). Hence, the party ran other candidates in those states. In a number of states, candidates appeared on the ballot with variants of the party designations listed, without any party designation, or with entirely different party names.   f. 1984: Both Larry Holmes and Gavrielle Holmes were standard-bearers of the Workers World Party. Of the two, Larry Holmes was listed on more state ballots. Milton Vera was Gavrielle Holmes's vice-presidential running mate in Ohio and Rhode Island. The Workers League Party had three vice-presidential candidates: Jean T. Brust in Illinois; Helen Halyard in Michigan, New Jersey, and Pennsylvania; and Edward Bergonzi in Minnesota and Ohio.   g. 1988: The candidates listed include all those who appeared on the ballot in at least one state. In some cases, a party's vice-presidential candidate varied from state to state. Candidates' full names and states were not available from some parties.   h. 1992: The candidates listed include all those who appeared on the ballot in at least one state. In some cases a party's vice-presidential candidate varied from state to state. Candidates' states were not available from some parties.

Party Affiliations in Congress and the Presidency, 1789–1995

Year	Congress	House		Senate		President
		Majority party	*Principal minority party*	*Majority party*	*Principal minority party*	
1995–1997	104th	R-230	D-204	R-53	D-47	D (Clinton)
1993–1995	103rd	D-258	R-176	D-57	R-43	D (Clinton)
1991–1993	102nd	D-267	R-167	D-56	R-44	R (Bush)
1989–1991	101st	D-259	R-174	D-55	R-45	R (Bush)
1987–1989	100th	D-258	R-177	D-55	R-45	R (Reagan)
1985–1987	99th	D-252	R-182	R-53	D-47	R (Reagan)
1983–1985	98th	D-269	R-165	R-54	D-46	R (Reagan)
1981–1983	97th	D-243	R-192	R-53	D-46	R (Reagan)
1979–1981	96th	D-276	R-157	D-58	R-41	D (Carter)
1977–1979	95th	D-292	R-143	D-61	R-38	D (Carter)
1975–1977	94th	D-291	R-144	D-60	R-37	R (Ford)
1973–1975	93rd	D-239	R-192	D-56	R-42	R (Ford)
						R (Nixon)
1971–1973	92nd	D-254	R-180	D-54	R-44	R (Nixon)
1969–1971	91st	D-243	R-192	D-57	R-43	R (Nixon)
1967–1969	90th	D-247	R-187	D-64	R-36	D (L. Johnson)
1965–1967	89th	D-295	R-140	D-68	R-32	D (L. Johnson)
1963–1965	88th	D-258	R-177	D-67	R-33	D (L. Johnson)
						D (Kennedy)
1961–1963	87th	D-263	R-174	D-65	R-35	D (Kennedy)
1959–1961	86th	D-283	R-153	D-64	R-34	R (Eisenhower)
1957–1959	85th	D-233	R-200	D-49	R-47	R (Eisenhower)
1955–1957	84th	D-232	R-203	D-48	R-47	R (Eisenhower)
1953–1955	83rd	R-221	D-211	R-48	D-47	R (Eisenhower)
1951–1953	82nd	D-234	R-199	D-49	R-47	D (Truman)
1949–1951	81st	D-263	R-171	D-54	R-42	D (Truman)
1947–1949	80th	R-245	D-188	R-51	D-45	D (Truman)
1945–1947	79th	D-242	R-190	D-56	R-38	D (Truman)
1943–1945	78th	D-218	R-208	D-58	R-37	D (F. Roosevelt)
1941–1943	77th	D-268	R-162	D-66	R-28	D (F. Roosevelt)
1939–1941	76th	D-261	R-164	D-69	R-23	D (F. Roosevelt)
1937–1939	75th	D-331	R-89	D-76	R-16	D (F. Roosevelt)
1935–1937	74th	D-319	R-103	D-69	R-25	D (F. Roosevelt)
1933–1935	73rd	D-310	R-117	D-60	R-35	D (F. Roosevelt)
1931–1933	72nd	D-220	R-214	R-48	D-47	R (Hoover)
1929–1931	71st	R-267	D-167	R-56	D-39	R (Hoover)
1927–1929	70th	R-237	D-195	R-49	D-46	R (Coolidge)
1925–1927	69th	R-247	D-183	R-56	D-39	R (Coolidge)
1923–1925	68th	R-225	D-205	R-51	D-43	R (Coolidge)
1921–1923	67th	R-301	D-131	R-59	D-37	R (Harding)
1919–1921	66th	R-240	D-190	R-49	D-47	D (Wilson)
1917–1919	65th	D-216	R-210	D-53	R-42	D (Wilson)
1915–1917	64th	D-230	R-196	D-56	R-40	D (Wilson)
1913–1915	63rd	D-291	R-127	D-51	R-44	D (Wilson)
1911–1913	62nd	D-228	R-161	R-51	D-41	R (Taft)
1909–1911	61st	R-219	D-172	R-61	D-32	R (Taft)
1907–1909	60th	R-222	D-164	R-61	D-31	R (T. Roosevelt)
1905–1907	59th	R-250	D-136	R-57	D-33	R (T. Roosevelt)
1903–1905	58th	R-208	D-178	R-57	D-33	R (T. Roosevelt)
1901–1903	57th	R-197	D-151	R-55	D-31	R (T. Roosevelt)
						R (McKinley)
1899–1901	56th	R-185	D-163	R-53	D-26	R (McKinley)
1897–1899	55th	R-204	D-113	R-47	D-34	R (McKinley)
1895–1897	54th	R-244	D-105	R-43	D-39	D (Cleveland)

(table continues)

Year	Congress	House Majority party	House Principal minority party	Senate Majority party	Senate Principal minority party	President
1893–1895	53rd	D-218	R-127	D-44	R-38	D (Cleveland)
1891–1893	52nd	D-235	R-88	R-47	D-39	R (B. Harrison)
1889–1891	51st	R-166	D-159	R-39	D-37	R (B. Harrison)
1887–1889	50th	D-169	R-152	R-39	D-37	D (Cleveland)
1885–1887	49th	D-183	R-140	R-43	D-34	D (Cleveland)
1883–1885	48th	D-197	R-118	R-38	D-36	R (Arthur)
1881–1883	47th	R-147	D-135	R-37	D-37	R (Arthur)
						R (Garfield)
1879–1881	46th	D-149	R-130	D-42	R-33	R (Hayes)
1877–1879	45th	D-153	R-140	R-39	D-36	R (Hayes)
1875–1877	44th	D-169	R-109	R-45	D-29	R (Grant)
1873–1875	43rd	R-194	D-92	R-49	D-19	R (Grant)
1871–1873	42nd	R-134	D-104	R-52	D-17	R (Grant)
1869–1871	41st	R-149	D-63	R-56	D-11	R (Grant)
1867–1869	40th	R-143	D-49	R-42	D-11	R (A. Johnson)
1865–1867	39th	U-149	D-42	U-42	D-10	R (A. Johnson)
						R (Lincoln)
1863–1865	38th	R-102	D-75	R-36	D-9	R (Lincoln)
1861–1863	37th	R-105	D-43	R-31	D-10	R (Lincoln)
1859–1861	36th	R-114	D-92	D-36	R-26	D (Buchanan)
1857–1859	35th	D-118	R-92	D-36	R-20	D (Buchanan)
1855–1857	34th	R-108	D-83	D-40	R-15	D (Pierce)
1853–1855	33rd	D-159	W-71	D-38	W-22	D (Pierce)
1851–1853	32nd	D-140	W-88	D-35	W-24	W (Fillmore)
1849–1851	31st	D-112	W-109	D-35	W-25	W (Fillmore)
						W (Taylor)
1847–1849	30th	W-115	D-108	D-36	W-21	D (Polk)
1845–1847	29th	D-143	W-77	D-31	W-25	D (Polk)
1843–1845	28th	D-142	W-79	W-28	D-25	W (Tyler)
1841–1843	27th	W-133	D-102	W-28	D-22	W (Tyler)
						W (W. Harrison)
1839–1841	26th	D-124	W-118	D-28	W-22	D (Van Buren)
1837–1839	25th	D-108	W-107	D-30	W-18	D (Van Buren)
1835–1837	24th	D-145	W-98	D-27	W-25	D (Jackson)
1833–1835	23rd	D-147	AM-53	D-20	NR-20	D (Jackson)
1831–1833	22nd	D-141	NR-58	D-25	NR-21	D (Jackson)
1829–1831	21st	D-139	NR-74	D-26	NR-22	DR (Jackson)
1827–1829	20th	J-119	AD-94	J-28	AD-20	DR (John Q. Adams)
1825–1827	19th	AD-105	J-97	AD-26	J-20	DR (John Q. Adams)
1823–1825	18th	DR-187	F-26	DR-44	F-4	DR (Monroe)
1821–1823	17th	DR-158	F-25	DR-44	F-4	DR (Monroe)
1819–1821	16th	DR-156	F-27	DR-35	F-7	DR (Monroe)
1817–1819	15th	DR-141	F-42	DR-34	F-10	DR (Monroe)
1815–1817	14th	DR-117	F-65	DR-25	F-11	DR (Madison)
1813–1815	13th	DR-112	F-68	DR-27	F-9	DR (Madison)
1811–1813	12th	DR-108	F-36	DR-30	F-6	DR (Madison)
1809–1811	11th	DR-94	F-48	DR-28	F-6	DR (Madison)
1807–1809	10th	DR-118	F-24	DR-28	F-6	DR (Jefferson)
1805–1807	9th	DR-116	F-25	DR-27	F-7	DR (Jefferson)
1803–1805	8th	DR-102	F-39	DR-25	F-9	DR (Jefferson)
1801–1803	7th	DR-69	F-36	DR-18	F-13	DR (Jefferson)
1799–1801	6th	F-64	DR-42	F-19	DR-13	F (John Adams)
1797–1799	5th	F-58	DR-48	F-20	DR-12	F (John Adams)
1795–1797	4th	F-54	DR-52	F-19	DR-13	F (Washington)
1793–1795	3rd	DR-57	F-48	F-17	DR-13	F (Washington)
1791–1793	2nd	F-37	DR-33	F-16	DR-13	F (Washington)
1789–1791	1st	AD-38	Op-26	AD-17	Op-9	F (Washington)

SOURCES: *Congressional Quarterly Weekly Report*, various issues; U.S. Bureau of the Census, *Historical Statistics of the United States, Colonial Times to 1970* (Washington, D.C.: Government Printing Office, 1975); and U.S. Congress, Joint Committee on Printing, *Official Congressional Directory* (Washington, D.C.: Government Printing Office, 1967–).

NOTE: (Key to abbreviations: AD—Administration; AM—Anti-Masonic; D—Democratic; DR—Democratic-Republican; F—Federalist; J—Jacksonian; NR—National Republican; Op—Opposition; R—Republican; U—Unionist; W—Whig. Figures are for the beginning of the first session of each Congress.

Cabinet Members and Other Officials, 1789–1996

Following is a list of cabinet members by administration from George Washington to Bill Clinton. Included are dates of service. The list does not include those who served in ad interim appointments.

George Washington, 1789–1797

Chief Justice
John Jay
Oct. 19, 1789–June 29, 1795
Oliver Ellsworth
March 8, 1796–Dec. 15, 1800

Vice President
John Adams
April 21, 1789–March 4, 1797

Secretary of State
Thomas Jefferson
March 22, 1790–Dec. 31, 1793
Edmund Randolph
Jan. 2, 1794–Aug. 20, 1795
Timothy Pickering
Dec. 10, 1795–May 12, 1800

Secretary of the Treasury
Alexander Hamilton
Sept. 11, 1789–Jan. 31, 1795
Oliver Wolcott Jr.
Feb. 3, 1795–Dec. 31, 1800

Secretary of War
Henry Knox
Sept. 12, 1789–Dec. 31, 1794
Timothy Pickering
Jan. 2–Dec. 10, 1795
James McHenry
Jan. 27, 1796–May 13, 1800

Attorney General
Edmund Randolph
Sept. 26, 1789–Jan. 2, 1794
William Bradford
Jan. 27, 1794–Aug. 23, 1795
Charles Lee
Dec. 10, 1795–Feb. 18, 1801

Postmaster General
Samuel Osgood
Sept. 26, 1789–Aug. 18, 1791
Timothy Pickering
Aug. 19, 1791–Jan. 2, 1795
Joseph Habersham
July 1, 1795–Nov. 2, 1801

John Adams, 1797–1801

Chief Justice
Oliver Ellsworth
March 8, 1796–Dec. 15, 1800
John Marshall
Feb. 4, 1801–July 6, 1835

Vice President
Thomas Jefferson
March 4, 1797–March 4, 1801

Secretary of State
Timothy Pickering
Dec. 10, 1795–May 12, 1800
John Marshall
June 6, 1800–Feb. 4, 1801

Secretary of the Treasury
Oliver Wolcott Jr.
Feb. 3, 1795–Dec. 31, 1800
Samuel Dexter
Jan. 1–May 13, 1801

Secretary of War
James McHenry
Jan. 27, 1796–May 13, 1800
Samuel Dexter
May 13–Dec. 31, 1800

Attorney General
Charles Lee
Dec. 10, 1795–Feb. 18, 1801

Postmaster General
Joseph Habersham
July 1, 1795–Nov. 2, 1801

Secretary of the Navy
Benjamin Stoddert
June 18, 1798–March 31, 1801

Thomas Jefferson, 1801–1809

Chief Justice
John Marshall
Feb. 4, 1801–July 6, 1835

Vice President
Aaron Burr
March 4, 1801–March 4, 1805
George Clinton
March 4, 1805–April 20, 1812

Secretary of State
James Madison
May 2, 1801–March 3, 1809

Secretary of the Treasury
Samuel Dexter
Jan. 1–May 13, 1801
Albert Gallatin
May 14, 1801–Feb. 8, 1814

Secretary of War
Henry Dearborn
March 5, 1801–March 7, 1809

Attorney General
Levi Lincoln
March 5, 1801–March 3, 1805
John C. Breckinridge
Aug. 7, 1805–Dec. 14, 1806
Caesar Augustus Rodney
Jan. 20, 1807–Dec. 11, 1811

Postmaster General
Joseph Habersham
July 1, 1795–Nov. 2, 1801
Gideon Granger
Nov. 28, 1801–Feb. 25, 1814

Secretary of the Navy
Benjamin Stoddert
June 18, 1798–March 31, 1801
Robert Smith
July 27, 1801–March 7, 1809

James Madison, 1809–1817

Chief Justice
John Marshall
Feb. 4, 1801–July 6, 1835

Vice President
George Clinton
March 4, 1805–April 20, 1812
Elbridge Gerry
March 4, 1813–Nov. 23, 1814

Secretary of State
Robert Smith
March 6, 1809–April 1, 1811
James Monroe
April 6, 1811–Sept. 30, 1814, Feb. 28, 1815–March 3, 1817

Secretary of the Treasury
Albert Gallatin
May 14, 1801–Feb. 8, 1814
George Washington Campbell
Feb. 9–Oct. 5, 1814
Alexander James Dallas
Oct. 6, 1814–Oct. 21, 1816
William Harris Crawford
Oct. 22, 1816–March 6, 1825

Secretary of War
William Eustis
March 7, 1809–Jan. 13, 1813
John Armstrong
Jan. 13, 1813–Sept. 27, 1814
James Monroe
Oct. 1, 1814–Feb. 28, 1815
William Harris Crawford
Aug. 1, 1815–Oct. 22, 1816

Attorney General
Caesar Augustus Rodney
Jan. 20, 1807–Dec. 11, 1811
William Pinkney
Dec. 11, 1811–Feb. 10, 1814
Richard Rush
Feb. 10, 1814–Nov. 13, 1817

Postmaster General
Gideon Granger
Nov. 28, 1801–Feb. 25, 1814
Return Jonathan Meigs Jr.
April 11, 1814–June 30, 1823

Secretary of the Navy
Robert Smith
July 27, 1801–March 7, 1809
Paul Hamilton
May 15, 1809–Dec. 31, 1812
William Jones
Jan. 19, 1813–Dec. 1, 1814
Benjamin Williams Crowninshield
Jan. 16, 1815–Sept. 30, 1818

James Monroe, 1817–1825

Chief Justice
John Marshall
Feb. 4, 1801–July 6, 1835

Vice President
Daniel D. Tompkins
March 4, 1817–March 4, 1825

Secretary of State
John Quincy Adams
Sept. 22, 1817–March 3, 1825

Secretary of the Treasury
William Harris Crawford
Oct. 22, 1816–March 6, 1825

Secretary of War
John C. Calhoun
Oct. 8, 1817–March 7, 1825

Attorney General
Richard Rush
Feb. 10, 1814–Nov. 13, 1817
William Wirt
Nov. 13, 1817–March 3, 1829

Postmaster General
Return Jonathan Meigs Jr.
April 11, 1814–June 30, 1823
John McLean
July 1, 1823–March 9, 1829

Secretary of the Navy
Benjamin Williams Crowninshield
Jan. 16, 1815–Sept. 30, 1818
Smith Thompson
Jan. 1, 1819–Aug. 31, 1823
Samuel Lewis Southard
Sept. 16, 1823–March 3, 1829

John Quincy Adams, 1825–1829

Chief Justice
John Marshall
Feb. 4, 1801–July 6, 1835

Vice President
John C. Calhoun
March 4, 1825–Dec. 28, 1832

Secretary of State
Henry Clay
March 7, 1825–March 3, 1829

Secretary of the Treasury
Richard Rush
March 7, 1825–March 5, 1829

Secretary of War
James Barbour
March 7, 1825–May 23, 1828
Peter Buell Porter
May 26, 1828–March 9, 1829

Attorney General
William Wirt
Nov. 13, 1817–March 3, 1829

Postmaster General
John McLean
July 1, 1823–March 9, 1829

Secretary of the Navy
Samuel Lewis Southard
Sept. 16, 1823–March 3, 1829

Andrew Jackson, 1829–1837

Chief Justice
John Marshall
Feb. 4, 1801–July 6, 1835
Roger B. Taney
March 28, 1836–Oct. 12, 1864

Vice President
John C. Calhoun
March 4, 1825–Dec. 28, 1832
Martin Van Buren
March 4, 1833–March 4, 1837

Secretary of State
Martin Van Buren
March 28, 1829–March 23, 1831
Edward Livingston
May 24, 1831–May 29, 1833
Louis McLane
May 29, 1833–June 30, 1834
John Forsyth
July 1, 1834–March 3, 1841

Secretary of the Treasury
Samuel Delucenna Ingham
March 6, 1829–June 20, 1831
Louis McLane
Aug. 8, 1831–May 28, 1833
William John Duane
May 29–Sept. 22, 1833
Roger B. Taney
Sept. 23, 1833–June 25, 1834
Levi Woodbury
July 1, 1834–March 3, 1841

Secretary of War
John Henry Eaton
March 9, 1829–June 18, 1831
Lewis Cass
Aug. 1, 1831–Oct. 5, 1836

Attorney General
John Macpherson Berrien
March 9, 1829–July 20, 1831
Roger B. Taney
July 20, 1831–Sept. 23, 1833
Benjamin Franklin Butler
Nov. 15, 1833–Sept. 1, 1838

Postmaster General
John McLean
July 1, 1823–March 9, 1829
William Taylor Barry
April 6, 1829–April 30, 1835
Amos Kendall
May 1, 1835–May 25, 1840

Secretary of the Navy
John Branch
March 9, 1829–May 12, 1831
Levi Woodbury
May 23, 1831–June 30, 1834
Mahlon Dickerson
July 1, 1834–June 30, 1838

Martin Van Buren, 1837–1841

Chief Justice
Roger B. Taney
March 28, 1836–Oct. 12, 1864

Vice President
Richard M. Johnson
March 4, 1837–March 4, 1841

Secretary of State
John Forsyth
July 1, 1834–March 3, 1841

Secretary of the Treasury
Levi Woodbury
July 1, 1834–March 3, 1841

Secretary of War
Joel Roberts Poinsett
March 7, 1837–March 5, 1841

Attorney General
Benjamin Franklin Butler
Nov. 15, 1833–Sept. 1, 1838

Felix Grundy
Sept. 1, 1838–Dec. 1, 1839
Henry Dilworth Gilpin
Jan. 11, 1840–March 4, 1841

Postmaster General
Amos Kendall
May 1, 1835–May 25, 1840
John Milton Niles
May 26, 1840–March 3, 1841

Secretary of the Navy
Mahlon Dickerson
July 1, 1834–June 30, 1838
James Kirke Paulding
July 1, 1838–March 3, 1841

William Henry Harrison, 1841

Chief Justice
Roger B. Taney
March 28, 1836–Oct. 12, 1864

Vice President
John Tyler
March 4, 1841–April 6, 1841

Secretary of State
Daniel Webster
March 6, 1841–May 8, 1843,
July 23, 1850–Oct. 24, 1852

Secretary of the Treasury
Thomas Ewing
March 4–Sept. 11, 1841

Secretary of War
John Bell
March 5–Sept. 13, 1841

Attorney General
John Jordan Crittenden
March 5–Sept. 13, 1841, July 22, 1850–
March 3, 1853

Postmaster General
Francis Granger
March 8–Sept. 13, 1841

Secretary of the Navy
George Edmund Badger
March 6–Sept. 11, 1841

John Tyler, 1841–1845

Chief Justice
Roger B. Taney
March 28, 1836–Oct. 12, 1864

Vice President
None

Secretary of State
Daniel Webster
March 6, 1841–May 8, 1843, July 23, 1850–
Oct. 24, 1852

Abel Parker Upshur
July 24, 1843–Feb. 28, 1844
John C. Calhoun
April 1, 1844–March 10, 1845

Secretary of the Treasury
Thomas Ewing
March 4–Sept. 11, 1841
Walter Forward
Sept. 13, 1841–March 1, 1843
John Canfield Spencer
March 8, 1843–May 2, 1844
George Mortimer Bibb
July 4, 1844–March 7, 1845

Secretary of War
John Bell
March 5–Sept. 13, 1841
John Canfield Spencer
Oct. 12, 1841–March 3, 1843
James Madison Porter
March 8, 1843–Jan. 30, 1844
William Wilkins
Feb. 15, 1844–March 4, 1845

Attorney General
John Jordan Crittenden
March 5–Sept. 13, 1841, July 22, 1850–
March 3, 1853
Hugh Swinton Legare
Sept. 13, 1841–June 20, 1843
John Nelson
July 1, 1843–March 3, 1845

Postmaster General
Francis Granger
March 8–Sept. 13, 1841
Charles Anderson Wickliffe
Oct. 13, 1841–March 6, 1845

Secretary of the Navy
George Edmund Badger
March 6–Sept. 11, 1841
Abel Parker Upshur
Oct. 11, 1841–July 23, 1843
David Henshaw
July 24, 1843–Feb. 18, 1844
Thomas Walker Gilmer
Feb. 19–Feb. 28, 1844
John Young Mason
March 26, 1844–March 10, 1845, Sept. 10,
1846–March 7, 1849

James K. Polk, 1845–1849

Chief Justice
Roger B. Taney
March 28, 1836–Oct. 12, 1864

Vice President
George M. Dallas
March 4, 1845–March 4, 1849

Secretary of State
John C. Calhoun
April 1, 1844–March 10, 1845
James Buchanan
March 10, 1845–March 7, 1849

Secretary of the Treasury
George Mortimer Bibb
July 4, 1844–March 7, 1845
Robert John Walker
March 8, 1845–March 5, 1849

Secretary of War
William Wilkins
Feb. 15, 1844–March 4, 1845
William Learned Marcy
March 6, 1845–March 4, 1849

Attorney General
John Nelson
July 1, 1843–March 3, 1845
John Young Mason
March 11, 1845–Sept. 9, 1846
Nathan Clifford
Oct. 17, 1846–March 17, 1848
Isaac Toucey
June 21, 1848–March 3, 1849

Postmaster General
Charles Anderson Wickliffe
Oct. 13, 1841–March 6, 1845
Cave Johnson
March 7, 1845–March 5, 1849

Secretary of the Navy
John Young Mason
March 26, 1844–March 10, 1845, Sept. 10,
1846–March 7, 1849
George Bancroft
March 11, 1845–Sept. 9, 1846

Zachary Taylor, 1849–1850

Chief Justice
Roger B. Taney
March 28, 1836–Oct. 12, 1864

Vice President
Millard Fillmore
March 4, 1849–July 10, 1850

Secretary of State
James Buchanan
March 10, 1845–March 7, 1849
John Middleton Clayton
March 8, 1849–July 22, 1850

Secretary of the Treasury
Robert John Walker
March 8, 1845–March 5, 1849
William Morris Meredith
March 8, 1849–July 22, 1850

Secretary of War
William Learned Marcy
March 6, 1845–March 4, 1849

George Washington Crawford
March 8, 1849–July 23, 1850

Attorney General
Isaac Toucey
June 21, 1848–March 3, 1849
Reverdy Johnson
March 8, 1849–July 20, 1850

Postmaster General
Cave Johnson
March 7, 1845–March 5, 1849
Jacob Collamer
March 8, 1849–July 22, 1850

Secretary of the Navy
John Young Mason
March 26, 1844–March 10, 1845, Sept. 10, 1846–March 7, 1849
William Ballard Preston
March 8, 1849–July 22, 1850

Secretary of the Interior
Thomas Ewing
March 8, 1849–July 22, 1850

Millard Fillmore, 1850–1853

Chief Justice
Roger B. Taney
March 28, 1836–Oct. 12, 1864

Vice President
None

Secretary of State
John Middleton Clayton
March 8, 1849–July 22, 1850
Daniel Webster
March 6, 1841–May 8, 1843, July 23, 1850–Oct. 24, 1852
Edward Everett
Nov. 6, 1852–March 3, 1853

Secretary of the Treasury
William Morris Meredith
March 8, 1849–July 22, 1850
Thomas Corwin
July 23, 1850–March 6, 1853

Secretary of War
George W. Crawford
March 8, 1849–July 23, 1850
Charles Magill Conrad
Aug. 15, 1850–March 7, 1853

Attorney General
Reverdy Johnson
March 8, 1849–July 20, 1850
John Jordan Crittenden
March 5–Sept. 13, 1841, July 22, 1850–March 3, 1853

Postmaster General
Jacob Collamer
March 8, 1849–July 22, 1850

Nathan Kelsey Hall
July 23, 1850–Sept. 13, 1852
Samuel Dickinson Hubbard
Sept. 14, 1852–March 7, 1853

Secretary of the Navy
William Ballard Preston
March 8, 1849–July 22, 1850
William Alexander Graham
Aug. 2, 1850–July 25, 1852
John Pendleton Kennedy
July 26, 1852–March 7, 1853

Secretary of the Interior
Thomas Ewing
March 8, 1849–July 22, 1850
Thomas McKean Thompson McKennan
Aug. 15–Aug. 26, 1850
Alexander Hugh Holmes Stuart
Sept. 12, 1850–March 7, 1853

Franklin Pierce, 1853–1857

Chief Justice
Roger B. Taney
March 28, 1836–Oct. 12, 1864

Vice President
William R. King
March 4, 1853–April 18, 1853

Secretary of State
William Learned Marcy
March 8, 1853–March 6, 1857

Secretary of the Treasury
Thomas Corwin
July 23, 1850–March 6, 1853
James Guthrie
March 7, 1853–March 6, 1857

Secretary of War
Charles Magill Conrad
Aug. 15, 1850–March 7, 1853
Jefferson Davis
March 7, 1853–March 6, 1857

Attorney General
John Jordan Crittenden
March 5–Sept. 13, 1841, July 22, 1850–March 3, 1853
Caleb Cushing
March 7, 1853–March 3, 1857

Postmaster General
Samuel Dickinson Hubbard
Sept. 14, 1852–March 7, 1853
James Campbell
March 8, 1853–March 6, 1857

Secretary of the Navy
John Pendleton Kennedy
July 26, 1852–March 7, 1853
James Cochran Dobbin
March 8, 1853–March 6, 1857

Secretary of the Interior
Alexander Hugh Holmes Stuart
Sept. 12, 1850–March 7, 1853
Robert McClelland
March 8, 1853–March 9, 1857

James Buchanan, 1857–1861

Chief Justice
Roger B. Taney
March 28, 1836–Oct. 12, 1864

Vice President
John C. Breckinridge
March 4, 1857–March 4, 1861

Secretary of State
William Learned Marcy
March 8, 1853–March 6, 1857
Lewis Cass
March 6, 1857–Dec. 14, 1860
Jeremiah Sullivan Black
Dec. 17, 1860–March 5, 1861

Secretary of the Treasury
James Guthrie
March 7, 1853–March 6, 1857
Howell Cobb
March 7, 1857–Dec. 8, 1860
Philip Francis Thomas
Dec. 12, 1860–Jan. 14, 1861
John Adams Dix
Jan. 15–March 6, 1861

Secretary of War
John Buchanan Floyd
March 6, 1857–Dec. 29, 1860
Joseph Holt
Jan. 18–March 5, 1861

Attorney General
Caleb Cushing
March 7, 1853–March 3, 1857
Jeremiah Sullivan Black
March 6, 1857–Dec. 17, 1860
Edwin Stanton
Dec. 20, 1860–March 3, 1861

Postmaster General
James Campbell
March 8, 1853–March 6, 1857
Aaron Venable Brown
March 7, 1857–March 8, 1859
Joseph Holt
March 14, 1859–Dec. 31, 1860
Horatio King
Feb. 12–March 9, 1861

Secretary of the Navy
James Cochran Dobbin
March 8, 1853–March 6, 1857
Isaac Toucey
March 7, 1857–March 6, 1861

Secretary of the Interior
Robert McClelland
March 8, 1853–March 9, 1857
Jacob Thompson
March 10, 1857–Jan. 8, 1861

Abraham Lincoln, 1861–1865

Chief Justice
Roger B. Taney
March 28, 1836–Oct. 12, 1864
Salmon P. Chase
Dec. 15, 1864–May 7, 1873

Vice President
Hannibal Hamlin
March 4, 1861–March 4, 1865
Andrew Johnson
March 4, 1865–April 15, 1865

Secretary of State
Jeremiah Sullivan Black
Dec. 17, 1860–March 5, 1861
William Henry Seward
March 6, 1861–March 4, 1869

Secretary of the Treasury
John Adams Dix
Jan. 15–March 6, 1861
Salmon P. Chase
March 7, 1861–June 30, 1864
William Pitt Fessenden
July 5, 1864–March 3, 1865
Hugh McCulloch
March 9, 1865–March 3, 1869, Oct. 31, 1884–March 7, 1885

Secretary of War
Joseph Holt
Jan. 18–March 5, 1861
Simon Cameron
March 5, 1861–Jan. 14, 1862
Edwin Stanton
Jan. 20, 1862–May 28, 1868

Attorney General
Edwin Stanton
Dec. 20, 1860–March 3, 1861
Edward Bates
March 5, 1861–Sept. 1864
James Speed
Dec. 2, 1864–July 17, 1866

Postmaster General
Horatio King
Feb. 12–March 9, 1861
Montgomery Blair
March 9, 1861–Sept. 30, 1864
William Dennison Jr.
Oct. 1, 1864–July 16, 1866

Secretary of the Navy
Isaac Toucey
March 7, 1857–March 6, 1861

Gideon Welles
March 7, 1861–March 3, 1869

Secretary of the Interior
Caleb Blood Smith
March 5, 1861–Dec. 31, 1862
John Palmer Usher
Jan. 1, 1863–May 15, 1865

Andrew Johnson, 1865–1869

Chief Justice
Salmon P. Chase
Dec. 15, 1864–May 7, 1873

Vice President
None

Secretary of State
William Henry Seward
March 6, 1861–March 4, 1869

Secretary of the Treasury
Hugh McCulloch
March 9, 1865–March 3, 1869, Oct. 31, 1884–March 7, 1885

Secretary of War
Edwin Stanton
Jan. 20, 1862–May 28, 1868
John McAllister Schofield
June 1, 1868–March 13, 1869

Attorney General
James Speed
Dec. 2, 1864–July 17, 1866
Henry Stanberry
July 23, 1866–March 12, 1868
William Maxwell Evarts
July 15, 1868–March 3, 1869

Postmaster General
William Dennison Jr.
Oct. 1, 1864–July 16, 1866
Alexander Williams Randall
July 25, 1866–March 4, 1869

Secretary of the Navy
Gideon Welles
March 7, 1861–March 3, 1869

Secretary of the Interior
John Palmer Usher
Jan. 1, 1863–May 15, 1865
James Harlan
May 15, 1865–Aug. 31, 1866
Orville Hickman Browning
Sept. 1, 1866–March 4, 1869

Ulysses S. Grant, 1869–1877

Chief Justice
Salmon P. Chase
Dec. 15, 1864–May 7, 1873
Morrison R. Waite
March 4, 1874–March 23, 1888

Vice President
Schuyler Colfax
March 4, 1869–March 4, 1873
Henry Wilson
March 4, 1873–Nov. 22, 1875

Secretary of State
William Henry Seward
March 6, 1861–March 4, 1869
Elihu Benjamin Washburne
March 5–March 16, 1869
Hamilton Fish
March 17, 1869–March 12, 1877

Secretary of the Treasury
Hugh McCulloch
March 9, 1865–March 3, 1869, Oct. 31, 1884–March 7, 1885
George Sewel Boutwell
March 12, 1869–March 16, 1873
William Adams Richardson
March 17, 1873–June 3, 1874
Benjamin Helm Bristow
June 4, 1874–June 20, 1876
Lot Myrick Morrill
July 7, 1876–March 9, 1877

Secretary of War
John McAllister Schofield
June 1, 1868–March 13, 1869
John Aaron Rawlins
March 13–Sept. 6, 1869
William Tecumseh Sherman
Sept. 11–Oct. 25, 1869
William Worth Belknap
Oct. 25, 1869–March 2, 1876
Alphonso Taft
March 8–May 22, 1876
James Donald Cameron
May 22, 1876–March 3, 1877

Attorney General
Ebenezer Rockwood Hoar
March 5, 1869–June 23, 1870
Amos Tappan Akerman
June 23, 1870–Jan. 10, 1872
George Henry Williams
Jan. 10, 1872–May 15, 1875
Edwards Pierrepont
May 15, 1875–May 22, 1876
Alphonso Taft
May 22, 1876–March 11, 1877

Postmaster General
John Angel James Creswell
March 6, 1869–July 6, 1874
James William Marshall
July 7–Aug. 31, 1874
Marshall Jewell
Sept. 1, 1874–July 12, 1876
James Noble Tyner
July 13, 1876–March 12, 1877

Secretary of the Navy
Adolph Edward Borie
March 9–June 25, 1869
George Maxwell Robeson
June 26, 1869–March 12, 1877

Secretary of the Interior
Jacob Dolson Cox
March 5, 1869–Oct. 31, 1870
Columbus Delano
Nov. 1, 1870–Sept. 30, 1875
Zachariah Chandler
Oct. 19, 1875–March 11, 1877

Rutherford B. Hayes, 1877–1881

Chief Justice
Morrison R. Waite
March 4, 1874–March 23, 1888

Vice President
William A. Wheeler
March 4, 1877–March 4, 1881

Secretary of State
Hamilton Fish
March 17, 1869–March 12, 1877
William Maxwell Evarts
March 12, 1877–March 7, 1881

Secretary of the Treasury
Lot Myrick Morrill
July 7, 1876–March 9, 1877
John Sherman
March 10, 1877–March 3, 1881

Secretary of War
James Donald Cameron
May 22, 1876–March 3, 1877
George Washington McCrary
March 12, 1877–Dec. 10, 1879
Alexander Ramsey
Dec. 10, 1879–March 5, 1881

Attorney General
Alphonso Taft
May 22, 1876–March 11, 1877
Charles Devens
March 12, 1877–March 6, 1881

Postmaster General
James Noble Tyner
July 13, 1876–March 12, 1877
David McKendree Key
March 13, 1877–Aug. 24, 1880
Horace Maynard
Aug. 25, 1880–March 7, 1881

Secretary of the Navy
George Maxwell Robeson
June 26, 1869–March 12, 1877
Richard Wigginton Thompson
March 13, 1877–Dec. 20, 1880
Nathan Goff Jr.
Jan. 7–March 6, 1881

Secretary of the Interior
Zachariah Chandler
Oct. 19, 1875–March 11, 1877
Carl Schurz
March 12, 1877–March 7, 1881

James A. Garfield, 1881

Chief Justice
Morrison R. Waite
March 4, 1874–March 23, 1888

Vice President
Chester A. Arthur
March 4, 1881–Sept. 20, 1881

Secretary of State
William Maxwell Evarts
March 12, 1877–March 7, 1881
James G. Blaine
March 7–Dec. 19, 1881, March 7, 1889–
June 4, 1892

Secretary of the Treasury
William Windom
March 8–Nov. 13, 1881, March 7, 1889–Jan.
29, 1891

Secretary of War
Alexander Ramsey
Dec. 10, 1879–March 5, 1881
Robert Todd Lincoln
March 5, 1881–March 5, 1885

Attorney General
Charles Devens
March 12, 1877–March 6, 1881
Wayne MacVeagh
March 7–Oct. 24, 1881

Postmaster General
Horace Maynard
Aug. 25, 1880–March 7, 1881
Thomas Lemuel James
March 8, 1881–Jan. 4, 1882

Secretary of the Navy
Nathan Goff Jr.
Jan. 7–March 6, 1881
William Henry Hunt
March 7, 1881–April 16, 1882

Secretary of the Interior
Carl Schurz
March 12, 1877–March 7, 1881
Samuel Jordan Kirkwood
March 8, 1881–April 17, 1882

Chester A. Arthur, 1881–1885

Chief Justice
Morrison R. Waite
March 4, 1874–March 23, 1888

Vice President
None

Secretary of State
James G. Blaine
March 7–Dec. 19, 1881, March 7, 1889–
June 4, 1892
Frederick Theodore Frelinghuysen
Dec. 19, 1881–March 6, 1885

Secretary of the Treasury
William Windom
March 8–Nov. 13, 1881, March 7, 1889–Jan.
29, 1891
Charles James Folger
Nov. 14, 1881–Sept. 4, 1884
Walter Quintin Gresham
Sept. 5–Oct. 30, 1884
Hugh McCulloch
March 9, 1865–March 3, 1869,
Oct. 31, 1884–March 7, 1885

Secretary of War
Robert Todd Lincoln
March 5, 1881–March 5, 1885

Attorney General
Wayne MacVeagh
March 7–Oct. 24, 1881
Benjamin Harris Brewster
Jan. 2, 1882–March 5, 1885

Postmaster General
Thomas Lemuel James
March 8, 1881–Jan. 4, 1882
Timothy Otis Howe
Jan. 5, 1882–March 25, 1883
Walter Quintin Gresham
April 11, 1883–Sept. 24, 1884
Frank Hatton
Oct. 15, 1884–March 6, 1885

Secretary of the Navy
William Henry Hunt
March 7, 1881–April 16, 1882
William Eaton Chandler
April 16, 1882–March 6, 1885

Secretary of the Interior
Samuel Jordan Kirkwood
March 8, 1881–April 17, 1882
Henry Moore Teller
April 18, 1882–March 3, 1885

Grover Cleveland, 1885–1889

Chief Justice
Morrison R. Waite
March 4, 1874–March 23, 1888
Melville W. Fuller
Oct. 8, 1888–July 4, 1910

Vice President
Thomas A. Hendricks
March 4, 1885–Nov. 25, 1885

Secretary of State
Frederick Theodore Frelinghuysen
Dec. 19, 1881–March 6, 1885

Thomas Francis Bayard Sr.
March 7, 1885–March 6, 1889

Secretary of the Treasury
Hugh McCulloch
March 9, 1865–March 3, 1869, Oct. 31, 1884–March 7, 1885
Daniel Manning
March 8, 1885–March 31, 1887
Charles Stebbins Fairchild
April 1, 1887–March 6, 1889

Secretary of War
Robert Todd Lincoln
March 5, 1881–March 5, 1885
William Crowninshield Endicott
March 5, 1885–March 5, 1889

Attorney General
Benjamin Harris Brewster
Jan. 2, 1882–March 5, 1885
Augustus Hill Garland
March 6, 1885–March 5, 1889

Postmaster General
Frank Hatton
Oct. 15, 1884–March 6, 1885
William Freeman Vilas
March 7, 1885–Jan. 16, 1888
Donald McDonald Dickinson
Jan. 17, 1888–March 5, 1889

Secretary of the Navy
William Eaton Chandler
April 16, 1882–March 6, 1885
William Collins Whitney
March 7, 1885–March 5, 1889

Secretary of the Interior
Lucius Quintus Cincinnatus Lamar
March 6, 1885–Jan. 10, 1888
William Freeman Vilas
Jan. 16, 1888–March 6, 1889

Secretary of Agriculture
Norman Jay Colman
Feb. 15–March 6, 1889

Benjamin Harrison, 1889–1893

Chief Justice
Melville W. Fuller
Oct. 8, 1888–July 4, 1910

Vice President
Levi P. Morton
March 4, 1889–March 4, 1893

Secretary of State
Thomas Francis Bayard Sr.
March 7, 1885–March 6, 1889
James G. Blaine
March 7–Dec. 19, 1881, March 7, 1889–June 4, 1892
John Watson Foster
June 29, 1892–Feb. 23, 1893

Secretary of the Treasury
Charles Stebbins Fairchild
April 1, 1887–March 6, 1889
William Windom
March 8–Nov. 13, 1881, March 7, 1889–Jan. 29, 1891
Charles Foster
Feb. 25, 1891–March 6, 1893

Secretary of War
William Crowninshield Endicott
March 5, 1885–March 5, 1889
Redfield Proctor
March 5, 1889–Nov. 5, 1891
Stephen Benton Elkins
Dec. 17, 1891–March 5, 1893

Attorney General
Augustus Hill Garland
March 6, 1885–March 5, 1889
William Henry Harrison Miller
March 5, 1889–March 6, 1893

Postmaster General
Donald McDonald Dickinson
Jan. 17, 1888–March 5, 1889
John Wanamaker
March 6, 1889–March 7, 1893

Secretary of the Navy
William Collins Whitney
March 7, 1885–March 5, 1889
Benjamin Franklin Tracy
March 6, 1889–March 6, 1893

Secretary of the Interior
William Freeman Vilas
Jan. 16, 1888–March 6, 1889
John Willock Noble
March 7, 1889–March 6, 1893

Secretary of Agriculture
Norman Jay Colman
Feb. 15–March 6, 1889
Jeremiah McLain Rusk
March 6, 1889–March 6, 1893

Grover Cleveland, 1893–1897

Chief Justice
Melville W. Fuller
Oct. 8, 1888–July 4, 1910

Vice President
Adlai E. Stevenson
March 4, 1893–March 4, 1897

Secretary of State
Walter Quintin Gresham
March 7, 1893–May 28, 1895
Richard Olney
June 10, 1895–March 5, 1897

Secretary of the Treasury
Charles Foster
Feb. 25, 1891–March 6, 1893

John Griffin Carlisle
March 7, 1893–March 5, 1897

Secretary of War
Stephen Benton Elkins
Dec. 17, 1891–March 5, 1893
Daniel Scott Lamont
March 5, 1893–March 5, 1897

Attorney General
William Henry Harrison Miller
March 5, 1889–March 6, 1893
Richard Olney
March 6, 1893–June 7, 1895
Judson Harmon
June 8, 1895–March 5, 1897

Postmaster General
John Wanamaker
March 6, 1889–March 7, 1893
Wilson Shannon Bissel
March 8, 1893–April 3, 1895
William Lyne Wilson
April 4, 1895–March 5, 1897

Secretary of the Navy
Benjamin Franklin Tracy
March 6, 1889–March 6, 1893
Hilary Abner Herbert
March 7, 1893–March 5, 1897

Secretary of the Interior
John Willock Noble
March 7, 1889–March 6, 1893
Hoke Smith
March 6, 1893–Sept. 1, 1896
David Rowland Francis
Sept. 3, 1896–March 5, 1897

Secretary of Agriculture
Jeremiah McLain Rusk
March 6, 1889–March 6, 1893
Julius Sterling Morton
March 7, 1893–March 5, 1897

William McKinley, 1897–1901

Chief Justice
Melville W. Fuller
Oct. 8, 1888–July 4, 1910

Vice President
Garret A. Hobart
March 4, 1897–Nov. 21, 1899
Theodore Roosevelt
March 4, 1901–Sept. 14, 1901

Secretary of State
Richard Olney
June 10, 1895–March 5, 1897
John Sherman
March 6, 1897–April 27, 1898
William Rufus Day
April 28–Sept. 16, 1898
John Milton Hay
Sept. 30, 1898–July 1, 1905

Secretary of the Treasury
John Griffin Carlisle
March 7, 1893–March 5, 1897
Lyman Judson Gage
March 6, 1897–Jan. 31, 1902

Secretary of War
Daniel Scott Lamont
March 5, 1893–March 5, 1897
Russell Alexander Alger
March 5, 1897–Aug. 1, 1899
Elihu Root
Aug. 1, 1899–Jan. 31, 1904

Attorney General
Judson Harmon
June 8, 1895–March 5, 1897
Joseph McKenna
March 5, 1897–Jan. 25, 1898
John William Griggs
June 25, 1898–March 29, 1901
Philander Chase Knox
April 5, 1901–June 30, 1904

Postmaster General
William Lyne Wilson
April 4, 1895–March 5, 1897
James Albert Gary
March 6, 1897–April 22, 1898
Charles Emory Smith
April 23, 1898–Jan. 14, 1902

Secretary of the Navy
Hilary Abner Herbert
March 7, 1893–March 5, 1897
John Davis Long
March 6, 1897–April 30, 1902

Secretary of the Interior
David Rowland Francis
Sept. 3, 1896–March 5, 1897
Cornelius Newton Bliss
March 6, 1897–Feb. 19, 1899
Ethan Allen Hitchcock
Feb. 20, 1899–March 4, 1907

Secretary of Agriculture
Julius Sterling Morton
March 7, 1893–March 5, 1897
James Wilson
March 6, 1897–March 5, 1913

Theodore Roosevelt, 1901–1909

Chief Justice
Melville W. Fuller
Oct. 8, 1888–July 4, 1910

Vice President
Charles W. Fairbanks
March 4, 1905–March 4, 1909

Secretary of State
John Milton Hay
Sept. 30, 1898–July 1, 1905

Elihu Root
July 19, 1905–Jan. 27, 1909
Robert Bacon
Jan. 27–March 5, 1909

Secretary of the Treasury
Lyman Judson Gage
March 6, 1897–Jan. 31, 1902
Leslie Mortier Shaw
Feb. 1, 1902–March 3, 1907
George Bruce Cortelyou
March 4, 1907–March 7, 1909

Secretary of War
Elihu Root
Aug. 1, 1899–Jan. 31, 1904
William Howard Taft
Feb. 1, 1904–June 30, 1908
Luke Edward Wright
July 1, 1908–March 11, 1909

Attorney General
Philander Chase Knox
April 5, 1901–June 30, 1904
William Henry Moody
July 1, 1904–Dec. 17, 1906
Charles Joseph Bonaparte
Dec. 17, 1906–March 4, 1909

Postmaster General
Charles Emory Smith
April 23, 1898–Jan. 14, 1902
Henry Clay Payne
Jan. 15, 1902–Oct. 4, 1904
Robert John Wynne
Oct. 10, 1904–March 4, 1905
George Bruce Cortelyou
March 7, 1905–March 3, 1907
George von Lengerke Meyer
March 4, 1907–March 5, 1909

Secretary of the Navy
John Davis Long
March 6, 1897–April 30, 1902
William Henry Moody
May 1, 1902–June 30, 1904
Paul Morton
July 1, 1904–July 1, 1905
Charles Joseph Bonaparte
July 1, 1905–Dec. 16, 1906
Victor Howard Metcalf
Dec. 17, 1906–Nov. 30, 1908
Truman Handy Newberry
Dec. 1, 1908–March 5, 1909

Secretary of the Interior
Ethan Allen Hitchcock
Feb. 20, 1899–March 4, 1907
James Rudolph Garfield
March 5, 1907–March 5, 1909

Secretary of Agriculture
James Wilson
March 6, 1897–March 5, 1913

Secretary of Commerce and Labor
George Bruce Cortelyou
Feb. 18, 1903–June 30, 1904
Victor Howard Metcalf
July 1, 1904–Dec. 16, 1906
Oscar Solomon Straus
Dec. 17, 1906–March 5, 1909

William Howard Taft, 1909–1913

Chief Justice
Melville W. Fuller
Oct. 8, 1888–July 4, 1910
Edward D. White
Dec. 19, 1910–May 19, 1921

Vice President
James S. Sherman
March 4, 1909–Oct. 30, 1912

Secretary of State
Robert Bacon
Jan. 27–March 5, 1909
Philander Chase Knox
March 6, 1909–March 5, 1913

Secretary of the Treasury
George Bruce Cortelyou
March 4, 1907–March 7, 1909
Franklin MacVeagh
March 8, 1909–March 5, 1913

Secretary of War
Luke Edward Wright
July 1, 1908–March 11, 1909
Jacob McGavock Dickinson
March 12, 1909–May 21, 1911
Henry Lewis Stimson
May 22, 1911–March 4, 1913, July 10,
1940–Sept. 21, 1945

Attorney General
Charles Joseph Bonaparte
Dec. 17, 1906–March 4, 1909
George Woodward Wickersham
March 5, 1909–March 5, 1913

Postmaster General
George von Lengerke Meyer
March 4, 1907–March 5, 1909
Frank Harris Hitchcock
March 6, 1909–March 4, 1913

Secretary of the Navy
Truman Handy Newberry
Dec. 1, 1908–March 5, 1909
George von Lengerke Meyer
March 6, 1909–March 4, 1913

Secretary of the Interior
James Rudolph Garfield
March 5, 1907–March 5, 1909
Richard Achilles Ballinger
March 6, 1909–March 12, 1911

Walter Lowrie Fisher
March 13, 1911–March 5, 1913

Secretary of Agriculture
James Wilson
March 6, 1897–March 5, 1913

Secretary of Commerce and Labor
Oscar Solomon Straus
Dec. 17, 1906–March 5, 1909
Charles Nagel
March 6, 1909–March 4, 1913

Woodrow Wilson, 1913–1921

Chief Justice
Edward D. White
Dec. 19, 1910–May 19, 1921

Vice President
Thomas R. Marshall
March 4, 1913–March 4, 1921

Secretary of State
Philander Chase Knox
March 6, 1909–March 5, 1913
William Jennings Bryan
March 5, 1913–June 9, 1915
Robert Lansing
June 24, 1915–Feb. 13, 1920
Bainbridge Colby
March 23, 1920–March 4, 1921

Secretary of the Treasury
Franklin MacVeagh
March 8, 1909–March 5, 1913
William Gibbs McAdoo
March 6, 1913–Dec. 15, 1918
Carter Glass
Dec. 16, 1918–Feb. 1, 1920
David Franklin Houston
Feb. 2, 1920–March 3, 1921

Secretary of War
Henry Lewis Stimson
May 22, 1911–March 4, 1913, July 10, 1940–
Sept. 21, 1945
Lindley Miller Garrison
March 5, 1913–Feb. 10, 1916
Newton Diehl Baker
March 9, 1916–March 4, 1921

Attorney General
George W. Wickersham
March 5, 1909–March 5, 1913
James Clark McReynolds
March 5, 1913–Aug. 29, 1914
Thomas Watt Gregory
Sept. 3, 1914–March 4, 1919
Alexander Mitchell Palmer
March 5, 1919–March 5, 1921

Postmaster General
Frank Harris Hitchcock
March 6, 1909–March 4, 1913

Albert Sidney Burleson
March 5, 1913–March 4, 1921

Secretary of the Navy
George von Lengerke Meyer
March 6, 1909–March 4, 1913
Josephus Daniels
March 5, 1913–March 5, 1921

Secretary of the Interior
Walter Lowrie Fisher
March 13, 1911–March 5, 1913
Franklin Knight Lane
March 6, 1913–Feb. 29, 1920
John Barton Payne
March 15, 1920–March 4, 1921

Secretary of Agriculture
James Wilson
March 6, 1897–March 5, 1913
David Franklin Houston
March 6, 1913–Feb. 2, 1920
Edwin Thomas Meredith
Feb. 2, 1920–March 4, 1921

Secretary of Commerce
Charles Nagel
March 6, 1909–March 4, 1913
William Cox Redfield
March 5, 1913–Oct. 31, 1919
Joshua Willis Alexander
Dec. 16, 1919–March 4, 1921

Secretary of Labor
William Bauchop Wilson
March 4, 1913–March 4, 1921

Warren G. Harding, 1921–1923

Chief Justice
Edward D. White
Dec. 19, 1910–May 19, 1921
William Howard Taft
July 11, 1921–Feb. 3, 1930

Vice President
Calvin Coolidge
March 4, 1921–Aug. 3, 1923

Secretary of State
Bainbridge Colby
March 23, 1920–March 4, 1921
Charles Evans Hughes
March 5, 1921–March 4, 1925

Secretary of the Treasury
David Houston
Feb. 2, 1920–March 3, 1921
Andrew William Mellon
March 4, 1921–Feb. 12, 1932

Secretary of War
Newton Diehl Baker
March 9, 1916–March 4, 1921

John Wingate Weeks
March 5, 1921–Oct. 13, 1925

Attorney General
Alexander Mitchell Palmer
March 5, 1919–March 5, 1921
Harry Micajah Daugherty
March 5, 1921–March 28, 1924

Postmaster General
Albert Sidney Burleson
March 5, 1913–March 4, 1921
William Harrison Hays
March 5, 1921–March 3, 1922
Hubert Work
March 4, 1922–March 4, 1923
Harry Stewart New
March 4, 1923–March 5, 1929

Secretary of the Navy
Josephus Daniels
March 5, 1913–March 5, 1921
Edwin Denby
March 6, 1921–March 10, 1924

Secretary of the Interior
John Barton Payne
March 15, 1920–March 4, 1921
Albert Bacon Fall
March 5, 1921–March 4, 1923
Hubert Work
March 5, 1923–July 24, 1928

Secretary of Agriculture
Edwin Thomas Meredith
Feb. 2, 1920–March 4, 1921
Henry Wallace
March 5, 1921–Oct. 25, 1924

Secretary of Commerce
Joshua Willis Alexander
Dec. 16, 1919–March 4, 1921
Herbert Clark Hoover
March 5, 1921–Aug. 21, 1928

Secretary of Labor
William Bauchop Wilson
March 4, 1913–March 4, 1921
James John Davis
March 5, 1921–Nov. 30, 1930

Calvin Coolidge, 1923–1929

Chief Justice
William Howard Taft
July 11, 1921–Feb. 3, 1930

Vice President
Charles G. Dawes
March 4, 1925–March 4, 1929

Secretary of State
Charles Evans Hughes
March 5, 1921–March 4, 1925
Frank Billings Kellogg
March 5, 1925–March 28, 1929

Secretary of the Treasury
Andrew William Mellon
March 4, 1921–Feb. 12, 1932

Secretary of War
John Wingate Weeks
March 5, 1921–Oct. 13, 1925
Dwight Filley Davis
Oct. 14, 1925–March 5, 1929

Attorney General
Harry Micajah Daugherty
March 5, 1921–March 28, 1924
Harlan Fiske Stone
April 7, 1924–March 2, 1925
John Garibaldi Sargent
March 17, 1925–March 5, 1929

Postmaster General
Harry Stewart New
March 4, 1923–March 5, 1929

Secretary of the Navy
Edwin Denby
March 6, 1921–March 10, 1924
Curtis Dwight Wilbur
March 19, 1924–March 4, 1929

Secretary of the Interior
Hubert Work
March 5, 1923–July 24, 1928
Roy Owen West
July 25, 1928–March 4, 1929

Secretary of Agriculture
Henry Wallace
March 5, 1921–Oct. 25, 1924
Howard Mason Gore
Nov. 22, 1924–March 4, 1925
William Marion Jardine
March 5, 1925–March 4, 1929

Secretary of Commerce
Herbert C. Hoover
March 5, 1921–Aug. 21, 1928
William Fairfield Whiting
Aug. 22, 1928–March 4, 1929

Secretary of Labor
James John Davis
March 5, 1921–Nov. 30, 1930

Herbert C. Hoover, 1929–1933

Chief Justice
William Howard Taft
July 11, 1921–Feb. 3, 1930
Charles Evans Hughes
Feb. 24, 1930–July 1, 1941

Vice President
Charles Curtis
March 4, 1929–March 4, 1933

Secretary of State
Frank Billings Kellogg
March 5, 1925–March 28, 1929
Henry Lewis Stimson
March 28, 1929–March 4, 1933

Secretary of the Treasury
Andrew William Mellon
March 4, 1921–Feb. 12, 1932
Ogden Livingston Mills
Feb. 13, 1932–March 4, 1933

Secretary of War
Dwight Filley Davis
Oct. 14, 1925–March 5, 1929
James William Good
March 6–Nov. 18, 1929
Patrick Jay Hurley
Dec. 9, 1929–March 3, 1933

Attorney General
John Garibaldi Sargent
March 17, 1925–March 5, 1929
William DeWitt Mitchell
March 5, 1929–March 3, 1933

Postmaster General
Harry Stewart New
March 4, 1923–March 5, 1929
Walter Folger Brown
March 5, 1929–March 5, 1933

Secretary of the Navy
Curtis Dwight Wilbur
March 19, 1924–March 4, 1929
Charles Francis Adams
March 5, 1929–March 4, 1933

Secretary of the Interior
Roy Owen West
July 25, 1928–March 4, 1929
Ray Lyman Wilbur
March 5, 1929–March 4, 1933

Secretary of Agriculture
William Marion Jardine
March 5, 1925–March 4, 1929
Arthur Mastick Hyde
March 6, 1929–March 4, 1933

Secretary of Commerce
William Fairfield Whiting
Aug. 22, 1928–March 4, 1929
Robert Patterson Lamont
March 5, 1929–Aug. 7, 1932
Roy Dikeman Chapin
Aug. 8, 1932–March 3, 1933

Secretary of Labor
James John Davis
March 5, 1921–Nov. 30, 1930
William Nuckles Doak
Dec. 9, 1930–March 4, 1933

Franklin D. Roosevelt, 1933–1945

Chief Justice
Charles Evans Hughes
Feb. 24, 1930–July 1, 1941
Harlan Fiske Stone
July 3, 1941–April 22, 1946

Vice President
John Nance Garner
March 4, 1933–Jan. 20, 1941
Henry A. Wallace
Jan. 20, 1941–Jan. 20, 1945
Harry S. Truman
Jan. 20, 1945–April 12, 1945

Secretary of State
Cordell Hull
March 4, 1933–Nov. 30, 1944
Edward Reilly Stettinius Jr.
Dec. 1, 1944–June 27, 1945

Secretary of the Treasury
William Hartman Woodin
March 5–Dec. 31, 1933
Henry Morgenthau Jr.
Jan. 1, 1934–July 22, 1945

Secretary of War
George Henry Dern
March 4, 1933–Aug. 27, 1936
Harry Hines Woodring
Sept. 25, 1936–June 20, 1940
Henry Lewis Stimson
*May 22, 1911–March 4, 1913, July 10,
1940–Sept. 21, 1945*

Attorney General
Homer Stille Cummings
March 4, 1933–Jan. 2, 1939
Francis William Murphy
Jan. 17, 1939–Jan. 18, 1940
Robert Houghwout Jackson
Jan. 18, 1940–July 10, 1941
Francis Beverley Biddle
Sept. 15, 1941–June 30, 1945

Postmaster General
James Aloysius Farley
March 6, 1933–Aug. 31, 1940
Frank Comerford Walker
Sept. 11, 1940–June 30, 1945

Secretary of the Navy
Claude Augustus Swanson
March 4, 1933–July 7, 1939
Charles Edison
Jan. 2–June 24, 1940
William Franklin "Frank" Knox
July 11, 1940–April 28, 1944
James V. Forrestal
May 19, 1944–Sept. 17, 1947

Secretary of the Interior
Harold Ickes
March 4, 1933–Feb. 15, 1946

Secretary of Agriculture
Henry A. Wallace
March 4, 1933–Sept. 4, 1940
Claude Raymond Wickard
Sept. 5, 1940–June 29, 1945

Secretary of Commerce
Daniel Calhoun Roper
March 4, 1933–Dec. 23, 1938
Harry Hopkins
Dec. 24, 1938–Sept. 18, 1940
Jesse Holman Jones
Sept. 19, 1940–March 1, 1945
Henry A. Wallace
March 2, 1945–Sept. 20, 1946

Secretary of Labor
Frances Perkins
March 4, 1933–June 30, 1945

Harry S. Truman, 1945–1953

Chief Justice
Harlan Fiske Stone
July 3, 1941–April 22, 1946
Frederick M. Vinson
June 24, 1946–Sept. 8, 1953

Vice President
Alben W. Barkley
Jan. 20, 1949–Jan. 20, 1953

Secretary of State
Edward Reilly Stettinius Jr.
Dec. 1, 1944–June 27, 1945
James Francis Byrnes
July 3, 1945–Jan. 21, 1947
George C. Marshall
Jan. 21, 1947–Jan. 20, 1949
Dean Acheson
Jan. 21, 1949–Jan. 20, 1953

Secretary of the Treasury
Henry Morgenthau Jr.
Jan. 1, 1934–July 22, 1945
Frederick Moore Vinson
July 23, 1945–June 23, 1946
John Wesley Snyder
June 25, 1946–Jan. 20, 1953

Secretary of War
Henry Lewis Stimson
May 22, 1911–March 4, 1913, July 10, 1940–
Sept. 21, 1945
Robert Porter Patterson
Sept. 27, 1945–July 18, 1947
Kenneth Claiborne Royall
July 19–Sept. 17, 1947

Secretary of Defense
James Vincent Forrestal
Sept. 17, 1947–March 27, 1949
Louis Arthur Johnson
March 28, 1949–Sept. 19, 1950
George Catlett Marshall
Sept. 21, 1950–Sept. 12, 1951
Robert Abercrombie Lovett
Sept. 17, 1951–Jan. 20, 1953

Attorney General
Francis Beverley Biddle
Sept. 15, 1941–June 30, 1945
Thomas Campbell Clark
July 1, 1945–Aug. 24, 1949
James Howard McGrath
Aug. 24, 1949–April 7, 1952
James Patrick McGranery
May 27, 1952–Jan. 20, 1953

Postmaster General
Frank Comerford Walker
Sept. 11, 1940–June 30, 1945
Robert Emmet Hannegan
July 1, 1945–Dec. 15, 1947
Jesse Monroe Donaldson
Dec. 16, 1947–Jan. 20, 1953

Secretary of the Navy
James V. Forrestal
May 19, 1944–Sept. 17, 1947

Secretary of the Interior
Harold LeClair Ickes
March 4, 1933–Feb. 15, 1946
Julius Albert Krug
March 18, 1946–Dec. 1, 1949
Oscar Littleton Chapman
Dec. 1, 1949–Jan. 20, 1953

Secretary of Agriculture
Claude Raymond Wickard
Sept. 5, 1940–June 29, 1945
Clinton Presba Anderson
June 30, 1945–May 10, 1948
Charles Franklin Brannan
June 2, 1948–Jan. 20, 1953

Secretary of Commerce
Henry A. Wallace
March 2, 1945–Sept. 20, 1946
W. Averell Harriman
Oct. 7, 1946–April 22, 1948
Charles Sawyer
May 6, 1948–Jan. 20, 1953

Secretary of Labor
Frances Perkins
March 4, 1933–June 30, 1945
Lewis Baxter Schwellenbach
July 1, 1945–June 10, 1948
Maurice Joseph Tobin
Aug. 13, 1948–Jan. 20, 1953

Dwight D. Eisenhower, 1953–1961

Chief Justice
Frederick M. Vinson
June 24, 1946–Sept. 8, 1953
Earl Warren
Oct. 5, 1953–June 23, 1969

Vice President
Richard Nixon
Jan. 20, 1953–Jan. 20, 1961

Secretary of State
John Foster Dulles
Jan. 21, 1953–April 22, 1959
Christian Archibald Herter
April 22, 1959–Jan. 20, 1961

Secretary of the Treasury
George Magoffin Humphrey
Jan. 21, 1953–July 29, 1957
Robert Bernard Anderson
July 29, 1957–Jan. 20, 1961

Secretary of Defense
Charles Erwin Wilson
Jan. 28, 1953–Oct. 8, 1957
Neil Hosler McElroy
Oct. 9, 1957–Dec. 1, 1959
Thomas Sovereign Gates Jr.
Dec. 2, 1959–Jan. 20, 1961

Attorney General
Herbert Brownell Jr.
Jan. 21, 1953–Nov. 8, 1957
William Pierce Rogers
Nov. 8, 1957–Jan. 20, 1961

Postmaster General
Arthur Summerfield
Jan. 21, 1953–Jan. 20, 1961

Secretary of the Interior
Douglas McKay
Jan. 21, 1953–April 15, 1956
Fred Andrew Seaton
June 8, 1956–Jan. 20, 1961

Secretary of Agriculture
Ezra Taft Benson
Jan. 21, 1953–Jan. 20, 1961

Secretary of Commerce
Charles Sinclair Weeks
Jan. 21, 1953–Nov. 10, 1958
Frederick Henry Mueller
Aug. 10, 1959–Jan. 19, 1961

Secretary of Labor
Martin Patrick Durkin
Jan. 21–Sept. 10, 1953
James Paul Mitchell
Oct. 9, 1953–Jan. 20, 1961

Secretary of Health, Education and Welfare
Oveta Culp Hobby
April 11, 1953–July 31, 1955
Marion Bayard Folsom
Aug. 1, 1955–July 31, 1958
Arthur Sherwood Flemming
Aug. 1, 1958–Jan. 19, 1961

John F. Kennedy, 1961–1963

Chief Justice
Earl Warren
Oct. 5, 1953–June 23, 1969

Vice President
Lyndon B. Johnson
Jan. 20, 1961–Nov. 22, 1963

Secretary of State
David Dean Rusk
Jan. 21, 1961–Jan. 20, 1969

Secretary of the Treasury
C. Douglas Dillon
Jan. 21, 1961–April 1, 1965

Secretary of Defense
Robert S. McNamara
Jan. 21, 1961–Feb. 29, 1968

Attorney General
Robert F. Kennedy
Jan. 21, 1961–Sept. 3, 1964

Postmaster General
James Edward Day
Jan. 21, 1961–Aug. 9, 1963
John A. Gronouski Jr.
Sept. 30, 1963–Nov. 2, 1965

Secretary of the Interior
Stewart Lee Udall
Jan. 21, 1961–Jan. 20, 1969

Secretary of Agriculture
Orville Lothrop Freeman
Jan. 21, 1961–Jan. 20, 1969

Secretary of Commerce
Luther Hartwell Hodges
Jan. 21, 1961–Jan. 15, 1965

Secretary of Labor
Arthur Joseph Goldberg
Jan. 21, 1961–Sept. 20, 1962
William Willard Wirtz
Sept. 25, 1962–Jan. 20, 1969

Secretary of Health, Education and Welfare
Abraham Alexander Ribicoff
Jan. 21, 1961–July 13, 1962
Anthony Joseph Celebrezze
July 31, 1962–Aug. 17, 1965

Lyndon B. Johnson, 1963–1969

Chief Justice
Earl Warren
Oct. 5, 1953–June 23, 1969

Vice President
Hubert H. Humphrey
Jan. 20, 1965–Jan. 20, 1969

Secretary of State
David Dean Rusk
Jan. 21, 1961–Jan. 20, 1969

Secretary of the Treasury
C. Douglas Dillon
Jan. 21, 1961–April 1, 1965
Henry Hamill Fowler
April 1, 1965–Dec. 20, 1968
Joseph Walker Barr
Dec. 21, 1968–Jan. 20, 1969

Secretary of Defense
Robert S. McNamara
Jan. 21, 1961–Feb. 29, 1968
Clark McAdams Clifford
March 1, 1968–Jan. 20, 1969

Attorney General
Robert F. Kennedy
Jan. 21, 1961–Sept. 3, 1964
Nicholas de Belleville Katzenbach
Feb. 11, 1965–Oct. 2, 1966
William Ramsey Clark
March 2, 1967–Jan. 20, 1969

Postmaster General
John A. Gronouski Jr.
Sept. 30, 1963–Nov. 2, 1965
Lawrence Francis O'Brien
Nov. 3, 1965–April 26, 1968
William Marvin Watson
April 26, 1968–Jan. 20, 1969

Secretary of the Interior
Stewart Lee Udall
Jan. 21, 1961–Jan. 20, 1969

Secretary of Agriculture
Orville Lothrop Freeman
Jan. 21, 1961–Jan. 20, 1969

Secretary of Commerce
Luther Hartwell Hodges
Jan. 21, 1961–Jan. 15, 1965
John Thomas Connor
Jan. 18, 1965–Jan. 31, 1967
Alexander Buel Trowbridge
June 14, 1967–March 1, 1968
Cyrus Rowlett Smith
March 6, 1968–Jan. 19, 1969

Secretary of Labor
William Willard Wirtz
Sept. 25, 1962–Jan. 20, 1969

Secretary of Health, Education and Welfare
Anthony Joseph Celebrezze
July 31, 1962–Aug. 17, 1965
John William Gardner
Aug. 18, 1965–March 1, 1968
Wilbur Joseph Cohen
May 16, 1968–Jan. 20, 1969

Secretary of Housing and Urban Development
Robert Clifton Weaver
Jan. 18, 1966–Dec. 3, 1968

Secretary of Transportation
Alan Stephenson Boyd
Jan. 23, 1967–Jan. 20, 1969

Richard Nixon, 1969–1974

Chief Justice
Earl Warren
Oct. 5, 1953–June 23, 1969
Warren Earl Burger
June 23, 1969–Sept. 26, 1986

Vice President
Spiro T. Agnew
Jan. 20, 1969–Oct. 10, 1973
Gerald R. Ford
Dec. 6, 1973–Aug. 9, 1974

Secretary of State
William Pierce Rogers
Jan. 22, 1969–Sept. 3, 1973
Henry Alfred Kissinger
Sept. 22, 1973–Jan. 20, 1977

Secretary of the Treasury
David Matthew Kennedy
Jan. 22, 1969–Feb. 10, 1971
John Bowden Connally
Feb. 11, 1971–June 12, 1972
George Pratt Shultz
June 12, 1972–May 8, 1974
William Edward Simon
May 8, 1974–Jan. 20, 1977

Secretary of Defense
Melvin Robert Laird
Jan. 22, 1969–Jan. 29, 1973
Elliot Lee Richardson
Jan. 30–May 24, 1973
James Rodney Schlesinger
July 2, 1973–Nov. 19, 1975

Attorney General
John Newton Mitchell
Jan. 21, 1969–March 1, 1972
Richard Gordon Kleindienst
June 12, 1972–May 24, 1973
Elliot Lee Richardson
May 25–Oct. 20, 1973
William Bart Saxbe
Jan. 4, 1974–Feb. 3, 1975

Postmaster General
Winton Malcolm Blount
Jan. 22, 1969–Jan. 12, 1971

Secretary of the Interior
Walter Joseph Hickel
Jan. 24, 1969–Nov. 25, 1970
Rogers Clark Ballard Morton
Jan. 29, 1971–April 30, 1975

Secretary of Agriculture
Clifford Morris Hardin
Jan. 21, 1969–Nov. 17, 1971
Earl Lauer Butz
Dec. 2, 1971–Oct. 4, 1976

Secretary of Commerce
Maurice Hubert Stans
Jan. 21, 1969–Feb. 15, 1972
Peter George Peterson
Feb. 29, 1972–Feb. 1, 1973
Frederick Baily Dent
Feb. 2, 1973–March 26, 1975

Secretary of Labor
George Pratt Shultz
Jan. 22, 1969–July 1, 1970
James Day Hodgson
July 2, 1970–Feb. 1, 1973
Peter Joseph Brennan
Feb. 2, 1973–March 15, 1975

Secretary of Health, Education and Welfare
Robert Hutchinson Finch
Jan. 21, 1969–June 23, 1970
Elliot Lee Richardson
June 24, 1970–Jan. 29, 1973
Caspar Willard Weinberger
Feb. 12, 1973–Aug. 8, 1975

Secretary of Housing and Urban Development
George Wilcken Romney
Jan. 20, 1969–Feb. 2, 1973
James Thomas Lynn
Feb. 2, 1973–Feb. 10, 1975

Secretary of Transportation
John Anthony Volpe
Jan. 22, 1969–Feb. 1, 1973
Claude Stout Brinegar
Feb. 2, 1973–Feb. 1, 1975

Gerald R. Ford, 1974–1977

Chief Justice
Warren Earl Burger
June 23, 1969–Sept. 26, 1986

Vice President
Nelson A. Rockefeller
Dec. 19, 1974–Jan. 20, 1977

Secretary of State
Henry Alfred Kissinger
Sept. 22, 1973–Jan. 20, 1977

Secretary of the Treasury
William Edward Simon
May 8, 1974–Jan. 20, 1977

Secretary of Defense
James Rodney Schlesinger
July 2, 1973–Nov. 19, 1975
Donald Henry Rumsfeld
Nov. 20, 1975–Jan. 20, 1977

Attorney General
William Bart Saxbe
Jan. 4, 1974–Feb. 3, 1975
Edward Hirsh Levi
Feb. 6, 1975–Jan. 20, 1977

Secretary of the Interior
Rogers Clark Ballard Morton
Jan. 29, 1971–April 30, 1975
Stanley Knapp Hathaway
June 12–Oct. 9, 1975
Thomas Savig Kleppe
Oct. 17, 1975–Jan. 20, 1977

Secretary of Agriculture
Earl Lauer Butz
Dec. 2, 1971–Oct. 4, 1976
John Albert Knebel
Nov. 4, 1976–Jan. 20, 1977

Secretary of Commerce
Frederick Baily Dent
Feb. 2, 1973–March 26, 1975
Rogers Clark Ballard Morton
May 1, 1975–Feb. 2, 1976
Elliot Lee Richardson
Feb. 2, 1976–Jan. 20, 1977

Secretary of Labor
Peter Joseph Brennan
Feb. 2, 1973–March 15, 1975
John Thomas Dunlop
March 18, 1975–Jan. 31, 1976
William Julian Usery Jr.
Feb. 10, 1976–Jan. 20, 1977

Secretary of Health, Education and Welfare
Caspar Willard Weinberger
Feb. 12, 1973–Aug. 8, 1975
Forrest David Mathews
Aug. 8, 1975–Jan. 20, 1977

Secretary of Housing and Urban Development
James Thomas Lynn
Feb. 2, 1973–Feb. 10, 1975
Carla Anderson Hills
March 10, 1975–Jan. 20, 1977

Secretary of Transportation
Claude Stout Brinegar
Feb. 2, 1973–Feb. 1, 1975
William Thaddeus Coleman Jr.
March 7, 1975–Jan. 20, 1977

Jimmy Carter 1977–1981

Chief Justice
Warren Earl Burger
June 23, 1969–Sept. 26, 1986

Vice President
Walter F. Mondale
Jan. 20, 1977–Jan. 20, 1981

Secretary of State
Cyrus Roberts Vance
Jan. 23, 1977–April 28, 1980
Edmund Sixtus Muskie
May 8, 1980–Jan. 18, 1981

Secretary of the Treasury
Werner Michael Blumenthal
Jan. 23, 1977–Aug. 4, 1979
George William Miller
Aug. 7, 1979–Jan. 20, 1981

Secretary of Defense
Harold Brown
Jan. 21, 1977–Jan. 20, 1981

Attorney General
Griffin Boyette Bell
Jan. 26, 1977–Aug. 16, 1979
Benjamin Richard Civiletti
Aug. 16, 1979–Jan. 19, 1981

Secretary of the Interior
Cecil Dale Andrus
Jan. 23, 1977–Jan. 20, 1981

Secretary of Agriculture
Robert Selmer Bergland
Jan. 23, 1977–Jan. 20, 1981

Secretary of Commerce
Juanita Morris Kreps
Jan. 23, 1977–Oct. 31, 1979
Philip M. Klutznick
Jan. 9, 1980–Jan. 19, 1981

Secretary of Labor
Fred Ray Marshall
Jan. 27, 1977–Jan. 20, 1981

Secretary of Health, Education and Welfare
Joseph Anthony Califano Jr.
Jan. 25, 1977–Aug. 3, 1979
Patricia Roberts Harris
Aug. 3, 1979–May 4, 1980

Secretary of Health and Human Services
Patricia Roberts Harris
May 4, 1980–Jan. 20, 1981

Secretary of Housing and Urban Development
Patricia Roberts Harris
Jan. 23, 1977–Aug. 3, 1979
Maurice Edwin "Moon" Landrieu
Sept. 24, 1979–Jan. 20, 1981

Secretary of Transportation
Brockman "Brock" Adams
Jan. 23, 1977–July 22, 1979
Neil Goldschmidt
July 27, 1979–Jan. 20, 1981

Secretary of Energy
James Rodney Schlesinger
Aug. 6, 1977–Aug. 23, 1979
Charles William Duncan Jr.
Aug. 24, 1979–Jan. 20, 1981

Secretary of Education
Shirley Mount Hufstedler
Dec. 6, 1979–Jan. 19, 1981

Ronald Reagan, 1981–1989

Chief Justice
Warren Earl Burger
June 23, 1969–Sept. 26, 1986
William Rehnquist
Sept. 26, 1986–

Vice President
George Bush
Jan. 20, 1981–Jan. 20, 1989

Secretary of State
Alexander Meigs Haig Jr.
Jan. 22, 1981–July 5, 1982
George Pratt Shultz
July 16, 1982–Jan. 20, 1989

Secretary of the Treasury
Donald Thomas Regan
Jan. 22, 1981–Feb. 1, 1985
James Addison Baker III
Feb. 4, 1985–Aug. 17, 1988
Nicholas Frederick Brady
Sept. 16, 1988–Jan. 19, 1993

Secretary of Defense
Caspar Willard Weinberger
Jan. 21, 1981–Nov. 21, 1987
Frank Charles Carlucci
Nov. 23, 1987–Jan. 20, 1989

Attorney General
William French Smith
Jan. 23, 1981–Feb. 24, 1985
Edwin Meese III
Feb. 25, 1985–Aug. 12, 1988
Richard Lewis Thornburgh
Aug. 12, 1988–Aug. 9, 1991

Secretary of the Interior
James Gaius Watt
Jan. 23, 1981–Nov. 8, 1983
William Patrick Clark
Nov. 18, 1983–Feb. 7, 1985
Donald Paul Hodel
Feb. 8, 1985–Jan. 20, 1989

Secretary of Agriculture
John Rusling Block
Jan. 23, 1981–Feb. 14, 1986
Richard Edmund Lyng
March 7, 1986–Jan. 20, 1989

Secretary of Commerce
Malcolm Baldrige
Jan. 20, 1981–July 25, 1987
Calvin William Verity Jr.
Oct. 19, 1987–Jan. 20, 1989

Secretary of Labor
Raymond James Donovan
Feb. 4, 1981–March 15, 1985
William Emerson Brock III
April 29, 1985–Oct. 31, 1987
Ann Dore McLaughlin
Dec. 17, 1987–Jan. 20, 1989

Secretary of Health and Human Services
Richard Schultz Schweiker
Jan. 22, 1981–Feb. 3, 1983
Margaret Mary O'Shaughnessy Heckler
March 9, 1983–Dec. 13, 1985
Otis Ray Bowen
Dec. 13, 1985–Jan. 20, 1989

Secretary of Housing and Urban Development
Samuel Riley Pierce Jr.
Jan. 23, 1981–Jan. 20, 1989

Secretary of Transportation
Andrew Lindsay "Drew" Lewis Jr.
Jan. 23, 1981–Feb. 1, 1983
Elizabeth Hanford Dole
Feb. 7, 1983–Sept. 30, 1987
James Horace Burnley IV
Dec. 3, 1987–Jan. 30, 1989

Secretary of Energy
James Burrows Edwards
Jan. 23, 1981–Nov. 5, 1982
Donald Paul Hodel
Nov. 5, 1982–Feb. 7, 1985
John Stewart Herrington
Feb. 11, 1985–Jan. 20, 1989

Secretary of Education
Terrel Howard Bell
Jan. 23, 1981–Dec. 31, 1984
William John Bennett
Feb. 6, 1985–Sept. 20, 1988
Lauro Fred Cavazos
Sept. 20, 1988–Dec. 12, 1990

George Bush, 1989–1993

Chief Justice
William Rehnquist
Sept. 26, 1986–

Vice President
Dan Quayle
Jan. 20, 1989–Jan. 20, 1993

Secretary of State
James Addison Baker III
Jan. 27, 1989–Aug. 23, 1992
Lawrence Sidney Eagleburger
Dec. 8, 1992–Jan. 19, 1993

Secretary of the Treasury
Nicholas Frederick Brady
Sept. 16, 1988–Jan. 19, 1993

Secretary of Defense
Richard Bruce Cheney
March 21, 1989–Jan. 20, 1993

Attorney General
Richard Lewis Thornburgh
Aug. 12, 1988–Aug. 9, 1991
William Pelham Barr
Nov. 26, 1991–Jan. 15, 1993

Secretary of the Interior
Manuel Lujan Jr.
Feb. 8, 1989–Jan. 20, 1993

Secretary of Agriculture
Clayton Keith Yeutter
Feb. 16, 1989–March 1, 1991
Edward Rell Madigan
March 12, 1991–Jan. 20, 1993

Secretary of Commerce
Robert Adam Mosbacher
Feb. 3, 1989–Jan. 15, 1992
Barbara Hackman Franklin
Feb. 27, 1992–Jan. 20, 1993

Secretary of Labor
Elizabeth Hanford Dole
Jan. 30, 1989–Nov. 23, 1990
Lynn Morley Martin
Feb. 22, 1991–Jan. 20, 1993

Secretary of Health and Human Services
Louis Wade Sullivan
March 10, 1989–Jan. 20, 1993

Secretary of Housing and Urban Development
Jack French Kemp
Feb. 13, 1989–Jan. 20, 1993

Secretary of Transportation
Samuel Knox Skinner
Feb. 6, 1989–Dec. 16, 1991
Andrew Hill Card Jr.
Feb. 24, 1992–Jan. 20, 1993

Secretary of Energy
James David Watkins
March 9, 1989–Jan. 20, 1993

Secretary of Education
Lauro Fred Cavazos
Sept. 20, 1988–Dec. 12, 1990
Lamar Alexander
March 22, 1991–Jan. 20, 1993

Secretary of Veterans Affairs
Edward Joseph Derwinski
March 15, 1989–Sept. 26, 1992

Bill Clinton, 1993–

Chief Justice
William Rehnquist
Sept. 26, 1986–

Vice President
Albert Gore Jr.
Jan. 20, 1993–

Secretary of State
Warren Minor Christopher
Jan. 22, 1993–

Secretary of the Treasury
Lloyd Millard Bentsen Jr.
Jan. 22, 1993–Dec. 22, 1994
Robert E. Rubin
Jan. 10, 1995–

Secretary of Defense
Leslie Aspin
Jan. 22, 1993–Feb. 2, 1994

William James Perry
Feb. 3, 1994–

Attorney General
Janet Reno
March 12, 1993–

Secretary of the Interior
Bruce Edward Babbitt
Jan. 22, 1993–

Secretary of Agriculture
Albert Michael "Mike" Espy
Jan. 22, 1993–Dec. 31, 1994
Daniel Glickman
March 30, 1995–

Secretary of Commerce
Ronald Harmon Brown
Jan. 22, 1993–April 3, 1996

Secretary of Labor
Robert Bernard Reich
Jan. 22, 1993–

Secretary of Health and Human Services
Donna Edna Shalala
Jan. 22, 1993–

Secretary of Housing and Urban Development
Henry Gabriel Cisneros
Jan. 22, 1993–

Secretary of Transportation
Federico Fabia Pena
Jan. 22, 1993–

Secretary of Energy
Hazel Rollins O'Leary
Jan. 22, 1993–

Secretary of Education
Richard Wilson Riley
Jan. 22, 1993–

Secretary of Veterans Affairs
Jesse Brown
Jan. 22, 1993–

Presidential Approval Ratings, Gallup Poll, 1949–1995 (percent)

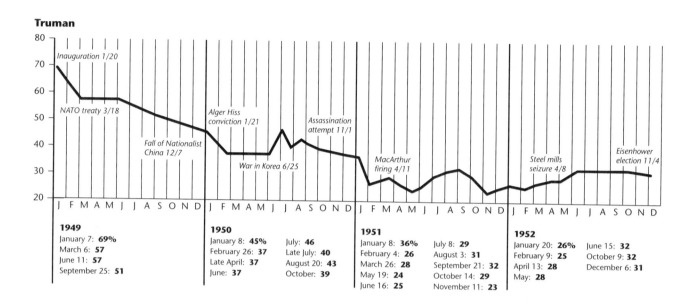

Truman

Inauguration 1/20

NATO treaty 3/18

Fall of Nationalist China 12/7

Alger Hiss conviction 1/21

War in Korea 6/25

Assassination attempt 11/1

MacArthur firing 4/11

Steel mills seizure 4/8

Eisenhower election 11/4

1949
January 7: **69%**
March 6: **57**
June 11: **57**
September 25: **51**

1950
January 8: **45%**
February 26: **37**
Late April: **37**
June: **37**

July: **46**
Late July: **40**
August 20: **43**
October: **39**

1951
January 8: **36%**
February 4: **26**
March 26: **28**
May 19: **24**
June 16: **25**

July 8: **29**
August 3: **31**
September 21: **32**
October 14: **29**
November 11: **23**

1952
January 20: **26%**
February 9: **25**
April 13: **28**
May: **28**

June 15: **32**
October 9: **32**
December 6: **31**

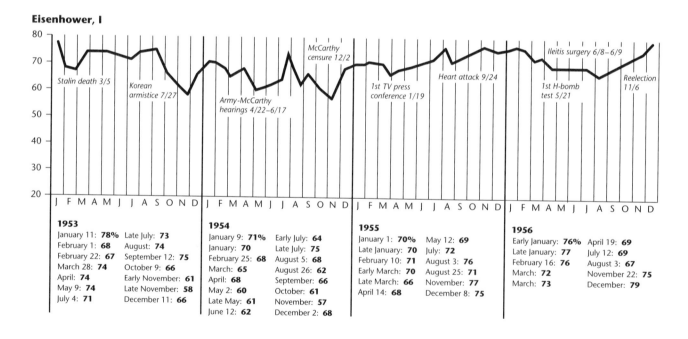

Eisenhower, I

Stalin death 3/5

Korean armistice 7/27

Army-McCarthy hearings 4/22–6/17

McCarthy censure 12/2

1st TV press conference 1/19

Heart attack 9/24

Ileitis surgery 6/8–6/9

1st H-bomb test 5/21

Reelection 11/6

1953
January 11: **78%**
February 1: **68**
February 22: **67**
March 28: **74**
April: **74**
May 9: **74**
July 4: **71**

Late July: **73**
August: **74**
September 12: **75**
October 9: **66**
Early November: **61**
Late November: **58**
December 11: **66**

1954
January 9: **71%**
January: **70**
February 25: **68**
March: **65**
April: **68**
May 2: **60**
Late May: **61**
June 12: **62**

Early July: **64**
Late July: **75**
August 5: **68**
August 26: **62**
September: **66**
October: **61**
November: **57**
December 2: **68**

1955
January 1: **70%**
Late January: **70**
February 10: **71**
Early March: **70**
Late March: **66**
April 14: **68**

May 12: **69**
July: **72**
August 3: **76**
August 25: **71**
November: **77**
December 8: **75**

1956
Early January: **76%**
Late January: **77**
February 16: **76**
March: **72**
March: **73**

April 19: **69**
July 12: **69**
August 3: **67**
November 22: **75**
December: **79**

Eisenhower, II

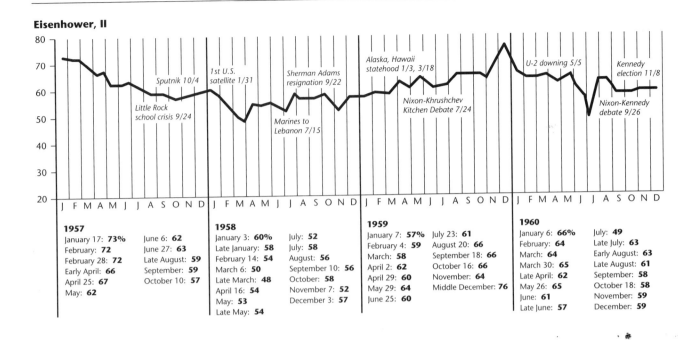

1957

January 17: **73%**	June 6: **62**
February: **72**	June 27: **63**
February 28: **72**	Late August: **59**
Early April: **66**	September: **59**
April 25: **67**	October 10: **57**
May: **62**	

1958

January 3: **60%**	July: **52**
Late January: **58**	July: **58**
February 14: **54**	August: **56**
March 6: **50**	September 10: **56**
Late March: **48**	October: **58**
April 16: **54**	November 7: **52**
May: **53**	December 3: **57**
Late May: **54**	

1959

January 7: **57%**	July 23: **61**
February 4: **59**	August 20: **66**
March: **58**	September 18: **66**
April 2: **62**	October 16: **66**
April 29: **60**	November: **64**
May 29: **64**	Middle December: **76**
June 25: **60**	

1960

January 6: **66%**	July: **49**
February: **64**	Late July: **63**
March: **64**	Early August: **63**
March 30: **65**	Late August: **61**
Late April: **62**	September: **58**
May 26: **65**	October 18: **58**
June: **61**	November: **59**
Late June: **57**	December: **59**

Kennedy   Kennedy/Johnson   Johnson

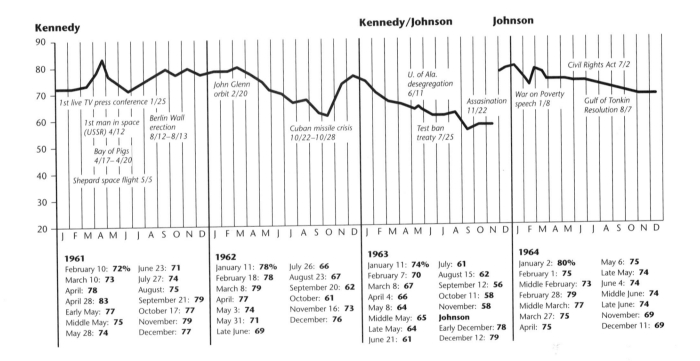

1961

February 10: **72%**	June 23: **71**
March 10: **73**	July 27: **74**
April: **78**	August: **75**
April 28: **83**	September 21: **79**
Early May: **77**	October 17: **77**
Middle May: **75**	November: **79**
May 28: **74**	December: **77**

1962

January 11: **78%**	July 26: **66**
February 18: **78**	August 23: **67**
March 8: **79**	September 20: **62**
April: **77**	October: **61**
May 3: **74**	November 16: **73**
May 31: **71**	December: **76**
Late June: **69**	

1963

January 11: **74%**	July: **61**
February 7: **70**	August 15: **62**
March 8: **67**	September 12: **56**
April 4: **66**	October 11: **58**
May 8: **64**	November: **58**
Middle May: **65**	**Johnson**
Late May: **64**	Early December: **78**
June 21: **61**	December 12: **79**

1964

January 2: **80%**	May 6: **75**
February 1: **75**	Late May: **74**
Middle February: **73**	June 4: **74**
February 28: **79**	Middle June: **74**
Middle March: **77**	Late June: **74**
March 27: **75**	November: **69**
April: **75**	December 11: **69**

Johnson

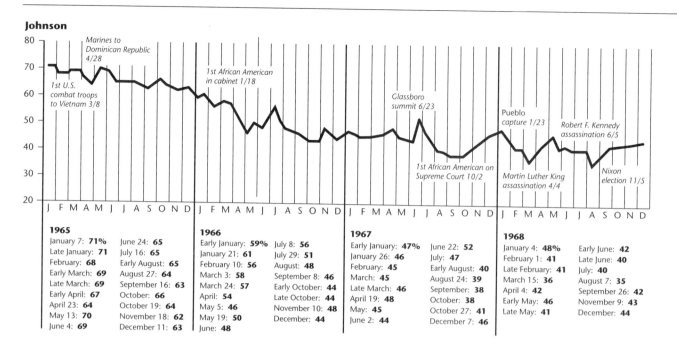

1965

January 7: **71%**	June 24: **65**
Late January: **71**	July 16: **65**
February: **68**	Early August: **65**
Early March: **69**	August 27: **64**
Late March: **69**	September 16: **63**
Early April: **67**	October: **66**
April 23: **64**	October 19: **64**
May 13: **70**	November 18: **62**
June 4: **69**	December 11: **63**

1966

Early January: **59%**	July 8: **56**
January 21: **61**	July 29: **51**
February 10: **56**	August: **48**
March 3: **58**	September 8: **46**
March 24: **57**	Early October: **44**
April: **54**	Late October: **44**
May 5: **46**	November 10: **48**
May 19: **50**	December: **44**
June: **48**	

1967

Early January: **47%**	June 22: **52**
January 26: **46**	July: **47**
February: **45**	Early August: **40**
March: **45**	August 24: **39**
Late March: **46**	September: **38**
April 19: **48**	October: **38**
May: **45**	October 27: **41**
June 2: **44**	December 7: **46**

1968

January 4: **48%**	Early June: **42**
February 1: **41**	Late June: **40**
Late February: **41**	July: **40**
March 15: **36**	August 7: **35**
April 4: **42**	September 26: **42**
Early May: **46**	November 9: **43**
Late May: **41**	December: **44**

Nixon, I

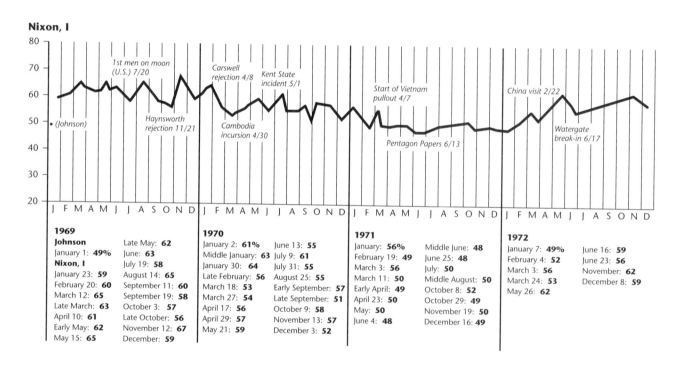

1969

Johnson

January 1: **49%**

Nixon, I

January 23: **59**	Late May: **62**
February 20: **60**	June: **63**
March 12: **65**	July 19: **58**
Late March: **63**	August 14: **65**
April 10: **61**	September 11: **60**
Early May: **62**	September 19: **58**
May 15: **65**	October 3: **57**
	Late October: **56**
	November 12: **67**
	December: **59**

1970

January 2: **61%**	June 13: **55**
Middle January: **63**	July 9: **61**
January 30: **64**	July 31: **55**
Late February: **56**	August 25: **55**
March 18: **53**	Early September: **57**
March 27: **54**	Late September: **51**
April 17: **56**	October 9: **58**
April 29: **57**	November 13: **57**
May 21: **59**	December 3: **52**

1971

January: **56%**	Middle June: **48**
February 19: **49**	June 25: **48**
March 3: **56**	July: **50**
March 11: **50**	Middle August: **50**
Early April: **49**	October 8: **52**
April 23: **50**	October 29: **49**
May: **50**	November 19: **50**
June 4: **48**	December 16: **49**

1972

January 7: **49%**	June 16: **59**
February 4: **52**	June 23: **56**
March 3: **56**	November: **62**
March 24: **53**	December 8: **59**
May 26: **62**	

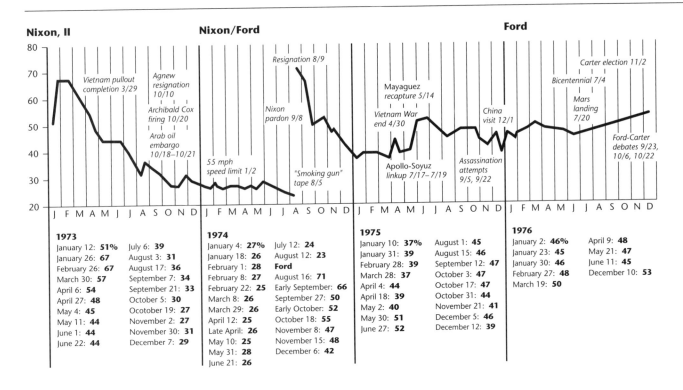

Nixon, II

Nixon/Ford

Ford

Vietnam pullout completion 3/29

Agnew resignation 10/10

Archibald Cox firing 10/20

Arab oil embargo 10/18–10/21

55 mph speed limit 1/2

Resignation 8/9

Nixon pardon 9/8

"Smoking gun" tape 8/5

Mayaguez recapture 5/14

Vietnam War end 4/30

Apollo-Soyuz linkup 7/17–7/19

China visit 12/1

Assassination attempts 9/5, 9/22

Carter election 11/2

Bicentennial 7/4

Mars landing 7/20

Ford-Carter debates 9/23, 10/6, 10/22

1973

January 12: **51%**	July 6: **39**
January 26: **67**	August 3: **31**
February 26: **67**	August 17: **36**
March 30: **57**	September 7: **34**
April 6: **54**	September 21: **33**
April 27: **48**	October 5: **30**
May 4: **45**	Ocotober 19: **27**
May 11: **44**	November 2: **27**
June 1: **44**	November 30: **31**
June 22: **44**	December 7: **29**

1974

January 4: **27%**	July 12: **24**
January 18: **26**	August 12: **23**
February 1: **28**	**Ford**
February 8: **27**	August 16: **71**
February 22: **25**	Early September: **66**
March 8: **26**	September 27: **50**
March 29: **26**	Early October: **52**
April 12: **25**	October 18: **55**
Late April: **26**	November 8: **47**
May 10: **25**	November 15: **48**
May 31: **28**	December 6: **42**
June 21: **26**	

1975

January 10: **37%**	August 1: **45**
January 31: **39**	August 15: **46**
February 28: **39**	September 12: **47**
March 28: **37**	October 3: **47**
April 4: **44**	October 17: **47**
April 18: **39**	October 31: **44**
May 2: **40**	November 21: **41**
May 30: **51**	December 5: **46**
June 27: **52**	December 12: **39**

1976

January 2: **46%**	April 9: **48**
January 23: **45**	May 21: **47**
January 30: **46**	June 11: **45**
February 27: **48**	December 10: **53**
March 19: **50**	

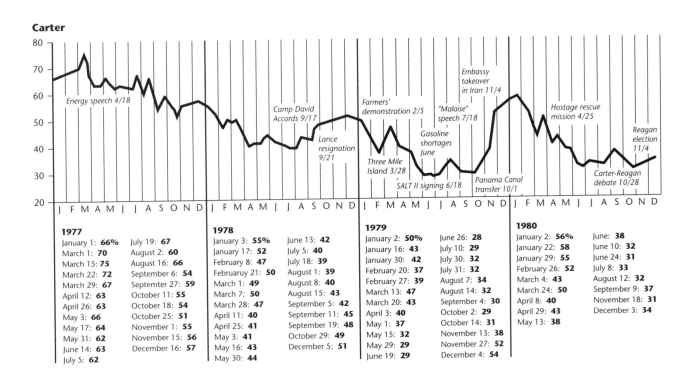

Carter

Energy speech 4/18

Camp David Accords 9/17

Lance resignation 9/21

Farmers' demonstration 2/5

Three Mile Island 3/28

SALT II signing 6/18

"Malaise" speech 7/18

Gasoline shortages June

Embassy takeover in Iran 11/4

Panama Canal transfer 10/1

Hostage rescue mission 4/25

Reagan election 11/4

Carter-Reagan debate 10/28

1977

January 1: **66%**	July 19: **67**
March 1: **70**	August 2: **60**
March 15: **75**	August 16: **66**
March 22: **72**	September 6: **54**
March 29: **67**	Septemter 27: **59**
April 12: **63**	October 11: **55**
April 26: **63**	October 18: **54**
May 3: **66**	October 25: **51**
May 17: **64**	November 1: **55**
May 31: **62**	November 15: **56**
June 14: **63**	December 16: **57**
July 5: **62**	

1978

January 3: **55%**	June 13: **42**
January 17: **52**	July 5: **40**
February 8: **47**	July 18: **39**
Februaruy 21: **50**	August 1: **39**
March 1: **49**	August 8: **40**
March 7: **50**	August 15: **43**
March 28: **47**	September 5: **42**
April 11: **40**	September 11: **45**
April 25: **41**	September 19: **48**
May 3: **41**	October 29: **49**
May 16: **43**	December 5: **51**
May 30: **44**	

1979

January 2: **50%**	June 26: **28**
January 16: **43**	July 10: **29**
January 30: **42**	July 30: **32**
February 20: **37**	July 31: **32**
February 27: **39**	August 7: **34**
March 13: **47**	August 14: **32**
March 20: **43**	September 4: **30**
April 3: **40**	October 2: **29**
May 1: **37**	October 14: **31**
May 15: **32**	November 13: **38**
May 29: **29**	November 27: **52**
June 19: **29**	December 4: **54**

1980

January 2: **56%**	June: **38**
January 22: **58**	June 10: **32**
January 29: **55**	June 24: **31**
February 26: **52**	July 8: **33**
March 4: **43**	August 12: **32**
March 24: **50**	September 9: **37**
April 8: **40**	November 18: **31**
April 29: **43**	December 3: **34**
May 13: **38**	

Reagan, I

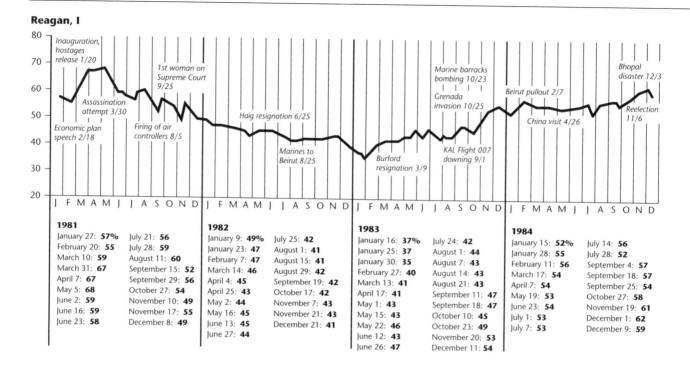

1981

January 27: **57%**
February 20: **55**
March 10: **59**
March 31: **67**
April 7: **67**
May 5: **68**
June 2: **59**
June 16: **59**
June 23: **58**

July 21: **56**
July 28: **59**
August 11: **60**
September 15: **52**
September 29: **56**
October 27: **54**
November 10: **49**
November 17: **55**
December 8: **49**

1982

January 9: **49%**
January 23: **47**
February 7: **47**
March 14: **46**
April 4: **45**
April 25: **43**
May 2: **44**
May 16: **45**
June 13: **45**
June 27: **44**

July 25: **42**
August 1: **41**
August 15: **41**
August 29: **42**
September 19: **42**
October 17: **42**
November 7: **43**
November 21: **43**
December 21: **41**

1983

January 16: **37%**
January 25: **37**
January 30: **35**
February 27: **40**
March 13: **41**
April 17: **41**
May 1: **43**
May 15: **43**
May 22: **46**
June 12: **43**
June 26: **47**

July 24: **42**
August 1: **44**
August 7: **43**
August 14: **43**
August 21: **43**
September 11: **47**
September 18: **47**
October 10: **45**
October 23: **49**
November 20: **53**
December 11: **54**

1984

January 15: **52%**
January 28: **55**
February 11: **56**
March 17: **54**
April 7: **54**
May 19: **53**
June 23: **54**
July 1: **53**
July 7: **53**

July 14: **56**
July 28: **52**
September 4: **57**
September 18: **57**
September 25: **54**
October 27: **58**
November 19: **61**
December 1: **62**
December 9: **59**

Reagan, II

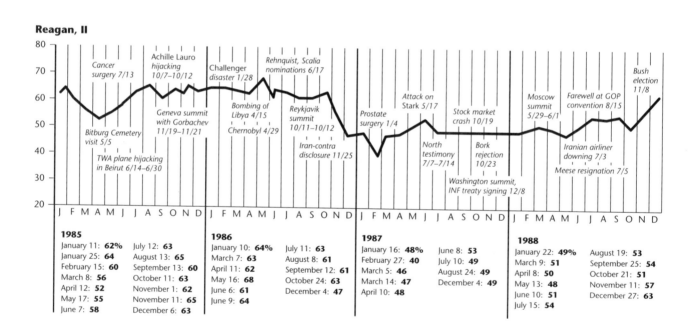

1985

January 11: **62%**
January 25: **64**
February 15: **60**
March 8: **56**
April 12: **52**
May 17: **55**
June 7: **58**

July 12: **63**
August 13: **65**
September 13: **60**
October 11: **63**
November 1: **62**
November 11: **65**
December 6: **63**

1986

January 10: **64%**
March 7: **63**
April 11: **62**
May 16: **68**
June 6: **61**
June 9: **64**

July 11: **63**
August 8: **61**
September 12: **61**
October 24: **63**
December 4: **47**

1987

January 16: **48%**
February 27: **40**
March 5: **46**
March 14: **47**
April 10: **48**

June 8: **53**
July 10: **49**
August 24: **49**
December 4: **49**

1988

January 22: **49%**
March 9: **51**
April 8: **50**
May 13: **48**
June 10: **51**
July 15: **54**

August 19: **53**
September 25: **54**
October 21: **51**
November 11: **57**
December 27: **63**

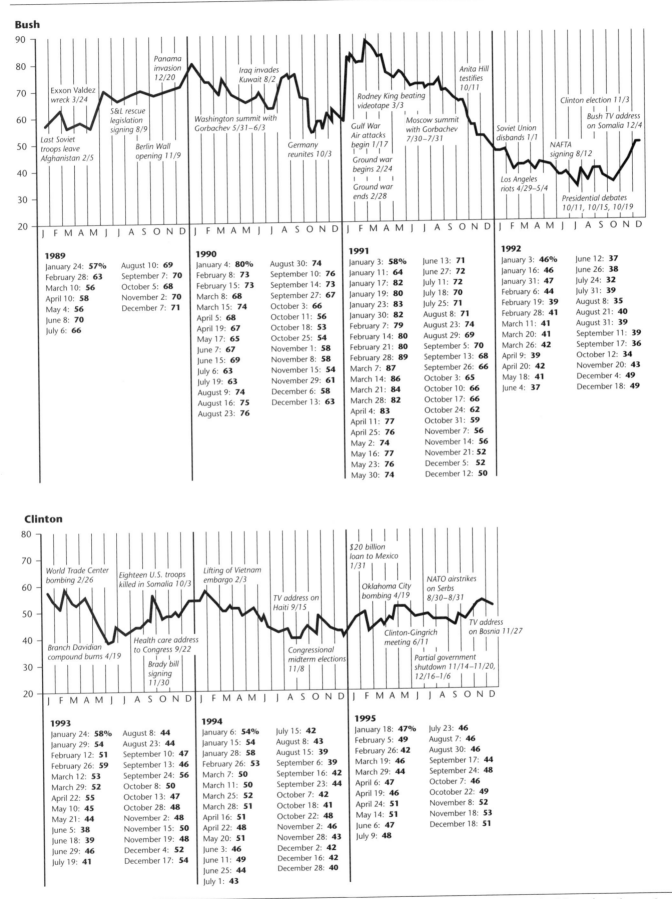

Bush

Panama invasion 12/20
Iraq invades Kuwait 8/2
Anita Hill testifies 10/11
Exxon Valdez wreck 3/24
S&L rescue legislation signing 8/9
Rodney King beating videotape 3/3
Clinton election 11/3
Bush TV address on Somalia 12/4
Washington summit with Gorbachev 5/31–6/3
Moscow summit with Gorbachev 7/30–7/31
Last Soviet troops leave Afghanistan 2/5
Berlin Wall opening 11/9
Gulf War Air attacks begin 1/17
Soviet Union disbands 1/1
NAFTA signing 8/12
Germany reunites 10/3
Ground war begins 2/24
Los Angeles riots 4/29–5/4
Ground war ends 2/28
Presidential debates 10/11, 10/15, 10/19

1989

January 24: **57%**	August 10: **69**
February 28: **63**	September 7: **70**
March 10: **56**	October 5: **68**
April 10: **58**	November 2: **70**
May 4: **56**	December 7: **71**
June 8: **70**	
July 6: **66**	

1990

January 4: **80%**	August 30: **74**
February 8: **73**	September 10: **76**
February 15: **73**	September 14: **73**
March 8: **68**	September 27: **67**
March 15: **74**	October 3: **66**
April 5: **68**	October 11: **56**
April 19: **67**	October 18: **53**
May 17: **65**	October 25: **54**
June 7: **67**	November 1: **58**
June 15: **69**	November 8: **58**
July 6: **63**	November 15: **54**
July 19: **63**	November 29: **61**
August 9: **74**	December 6: **58**
August 16: **75**	December 13: **63**
August 23: **76**	

1991

January 3: **58%**	June 13: **71**
January 11: **64**	June 27: **72**
January 17: **82**	July 11: **72**
January 19: **80**	July 18: **70**
January 23: **83**	July 25: **71**
January 30: **82**	August 8: **71**
February 7: **79**	August 23: **74**
February 14: **80**	August 29: **69**
February 21: **80**	September 5: **70**
February 28: **89**	September 13: **68**
March 7: **87**	September 26: **66**
March 14: **86**	October 3: **65**
March 21: **84**	October 10: **66**
March 28: **82**	October 17: **66**
April 4: **83**	October 24: **62**
April 11: **77**	October 31: **59**
April 25: **76**	November 7: **56**
May 2: **74**	November 14: **56**
May 16: **77**	November 21: **52**
May 23: **76**	December 5: **52**
May 30: **74**	December 12: **50**

1992

January 3: **46%**	June 12: **37**
January 16: **46**	June 26: **38**
January 31: **47**	July 24: **32**
February 6: **44**	July 31: **39**
February 19: **39**	August 8: **35**
February 28: **41**	August 21: **40**
March 11: **41**	August 31: **39**
March 20: **41**	September 11: **39**
March 26: **42**	September 17: **36**
April 9: **39**	October 12: **34**
April 20: **42**	November 20: **43**
May 18: **41**	December 4: **49**
June 4: **37**	December 18: **49**

Clinton

World Trade Center bombing 2/26
Eighteen U.S. troops killed in Somalia 10/3
Lifting of Vietnam embargo 2/3
$20 billion loan to Mexico 1/31
NATO airstrikes on Serbs 8/30–8/31
TV address on Haiti 9/15
Oklahoma City bombing 4/19
Branch Davidian compound burns 4/19
Health care address to Congress 9/22
Clinton-Gingrich meeting 6/11
TV address on Bosnia 11/27
Brady bill signing 11/30
Congressional midterm elections 11/8
Partial government shutdown 11/14–11/20, 12/16–1/6

1993

January 24: **58%**	August 8: **44**
January 29: **54**	August 23: **44**
February 12: **51**	September 10: **47**
February 26: **59**	September 13: **46**
March 12: **53**	September 24: **56**
March 29: **52**	October 8: **50**
April 22: **55**	October 13: **47**
May 10: **45**	October 28: **48**
May 21: **44**	November 2: **48**
June 5: **38**	November 15: **50**
June 18: **39**	November 19: **48**
June 29: **46**	December 4: **52**
July 19: **41**	December 17: **54**

1994

January 6: **54%**	July 15: **42**
January 15: **54**	August 8: **43**
January 28: **58**	August 15: **39**
February 26: **53**	September 6: **39**
March 7: **50**	September 16: **42**
March 11: **50**	September 23: **44**
March 25: **52**	October 7: **42**
March 28: **51**	October 18: **41**
April 16: **51**	October 22: **48**
April 22: **48**	November 2: **46**
May 20: **51**	November 28: **43**
June 3: **46**	December 2: **42**
June 11: **49**	December 16: **42**
June 25: **44**	December 28: **40**
July 1: **43**	

1995

January 18: **47%**	July 23: **46**
February 5: **49**	August 7: **46**
February 26: **42**	August 30: **46**
March 19: **46**	September 17: **44**
March 29: **44**	September 24: **48**
April 6: **47**	October 7: **46**
April 19: **46**	Ocotober 22: **49**
April 24: **51**	November 8: **52**
May 14: **51**	November 18: **53**
June 6: **47**	December 18: **51**
July 9: **48**	

SOURCES: 1995 ratings from Gallup. 1949–1994 ratings from Lyn Ragsdale, *Vital Statistics on the Presidency* (Washington, D.C.: Congressional Quarterly, 1996), 194–208. Ratings 1949–1976 adapted by Ragsdale from the *Gallup Opinion Index*, Report 182, October–November 1980, 13–59. Ratings 1977–1984 calculated by Ragsdale from original Gallup survey data. Ratings 1985–1994 calculated by Ragsdale from successive volumes of *Gallup Poll Monthly*.

Presidential Support in Congress, 1953–1995

Studies of congressional voting behavior have been a staple of Congressional Quarterly for more than forty years. For the presidential support study, CQ tries to determine what the president personally, as distinct from other administration officials, does and does not want in the way of legislative action by analyzing the president's messages to Congress, press conference remarks, and other public statements and documents. Members of Congress must be aware of the president's position when the vote is taken.

By the time proposed legislation reaches a vote, it may differ from the original form in which the president expressed opposition or support. In such cases, CQ analyzes the measure to determine whether, on balance, the features favored by the president outweigh those opposed or vice versa. Only then is the vote classified.

In general, analysts who use the CQ study should do so cautiously, taking into account its strengths and weaknesses. The study is a useful gauge of long-term trends in presidential-congressional relations, and it has served as a key yardstick for political scientists.

The study's usefulness diminishes, however, as the need for detail rises. It masks controversies that never reach a roll-call vote on the floor. In the Senate, particularly, legislation of considerable substance often passes by voice vote. When a committee kills a bill the president supports, this goes unrecorded in the vote study. Furthermore, the study gives equal weight to every vote, no matter its actual importance.

Presidential Success on Votes, 1953–1995

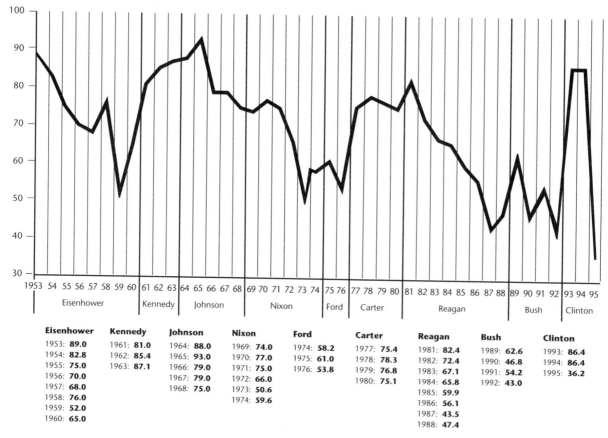

Eisenhower	Kennedy	Johnson	Nixon	Ford	Carter	Reagan	Bush	Clinton
1953: **89.0**	1961: **81.0**	1964: **88.0**	1969: **74.0**	1974: **58.2**	1977: **75.4**	1981: **82.4**	1989: **62.6**	1993: **86.4**
1954: **82.8**	1962: **85.4**	1965: **93.0**	1970: **77.0**	1975: **61.0**	1978: **78.3**	1982: **72.4**	1990: **46.8**	1994: **86.4**
1955: **75.0**	1963: **87.1**	1966: **79.0**	1971: **75.0**	1976: **53.8**	1979: **76.8**	1983: **67.1**	1991: **54.2**	1995: **36.2**
1956: **70.0**		1967: **79.0**	1972: **66.0**		1980: **75.1**	1984: **65.8**	1992: **43.0**	
1957: **68.0**		1968: **75.0**	1973: **50.6**			1985: **59.9**		
1958: **76.0**			1974: **59.6**			1986: **56.1**		
1959: **52.0**						1987: **43.5**		
1960: **65.0**						1988: **47.4**		

SOURCE: *Congressional Quarterly Weekly Report*, January 27, 1996, 193–198, 237–242.

Illustration Credits and Acknowledgments

1. Constitutional Beginnings

1 Library of Congress   7 Library of Congress   8 Library of Congress
9 Library of Congress   10 (all) Library of Congress   11 Library of Congress   12 Library of Congress   13 Library of Congress
14 Library of Congress   15 Library of Congress   19 Library of Congress   49 Library of Congress   50 Franklin D. Roosevelt Library   51 (top) Library of Congress, (bottom) White House   55 (left) Library of Congress, (right) White House   56 Library of Congress

2. History of the Presidency

62 (both) The Pierpont Morgan Library
63 Library of Congress   68 National Portrait Gallery, Smithsonian Institution   70 by permission of the Houghton Library, Harvard University   73 (both) Library of Congress
77 courtesy of the New-York Historical Society, New York City   79 Library of Congress
80 Library of Congress   81 Library of Congress   86 Library of Congress   89 Library of Congress   91 Library of Congress
96 Library of Congress   97 National Portrait Gallery   98 Library of Congress   103 Library of Congress   104 Library of Congress
111 Harvard College Library   117 Library of Congress   121 Library of Congress
123 AP/Wide World Photos   128 National Archives   130 Library of Congress   132 John F. Kennedy Library   134 National Park Service
135 *New York Review of Books*   137 National Archives   140 Frank Johnston, *Washington Post*   144 Ronald Reagan Library
147 R. Michael Jenkins   151 R. Michael Jenkins

3. History of the Vice Presidency

166 (both) Library of Congress
167 Smithsonian Institution   171 (left) Joe Houston, (right) R. Michael Jenkins
172 Library of Congress   173 Jimmy Carter Library   174 (left) White House, (right) Library of Congress

5. The Electoral Process

183 Congressional Quarterly   188 Library of Congress   189 Library of Congress
193 Library of Congress   194 (both) Library of Congress   196 Moorland-Spingarn Research Center   198 (left) National Portrait Gallery, Smithsonian Institution, (right) Library of Congress   200 Theodore Roosevelt Collection, Harvard College Library   205 (both) Library of Congress   207 Library of Congress
219 no credit   221 Library of Congress
223 UPI/Bettmann Newsphotos   242 (both) no credit   243 (both) Library of Congress   245 The Garrison Studio
251 UPI/Bettmann Newsphotos
252 R. Michael Jenkins   257 AP/Wide World Photos   259 Wide World Photos   263 Jimmy Carter Library   265 UPI/Bettmann Newsphotos   267 Library of Congress

270 no credit   271 R. Michael Jenkins
274 R. Michael Jenkins   275 Library of Congress   277 Library of Congress
279 Library of Congress   284 courtesy of Princeton University Library   285 Gerald R. Ford Library   288 AP/Wide World Photos
290 courtesy of League of Women Voters
292 UPI/Bettmann Newsphotos
295 Smithsonian Institution   296 Smithsonian Institution   301 (top) Judith Barry Smith, (bottom) UPI/Bettmann Newsphotos
303 UPI/Bettmann   304 no credit   308 (both) Library of Congress   310 (both) Library of Congress   312 (all) Library of Congress

6. Taking Office

325 R. Michael Jenkins   327 Library of Congress   329 R. Michael Jenkins   330 Ronald Reagan Library   331 Architect of the Capitol

7. Chronology of Presidential Elections

334 John Frost, *History of the United States, 1836*; The New York Public Library
335 Library of Congress   337 courtesy of the New-York Historical Society, New York City   342 Library of Congress   350 The Bettmann Archive   351 Library of Congress
353 Library of Congress   356 Library of Congress   359 Library of Congress
360 Library of Congress   361 Library of Congress   364 (left) Library of Congress, (right) Theodore Roosevelt Collection, Harvard College Library   366 Library of Congress   368 Franklin D. Roosevelt Library
369 Smithsonian Institute   371 The Bettmann Archive   372 Franklin D. Roosevelt Library
376 (left) Library of Congress, (center) Library of Congress, (right) courtesy of the New-York Historical Society, New York City   380 From the collection of the St. Louis Mercantile Library Association   381 courtesy of the Dwight D. Eisenhower Library   383 Charleston Gazette   386 Library of Congress
388 AP/Wide World Photos   392 Sygma
395 UPI/Bettmann Newsphotos   397 David Valdez, White House   401 Reuters/Bettmann   402 MTV

8. Selection by Succession

412 Abbie Rowe, National Park Service
416 Lyndon B. Johnson Library   418 Gerald R. Ford Library

9. Removal of the President

425 Library of Congress   432 Charles DeForest Fredericks, National Portrait Gallery
436 Ralph E. Becker Collection, Smithsonian Institution   437 Copyright 1963 by Bob Jackson, *Dallas Times Herald*   438 John F. Kennedy Library   439 Reuters/Bettmann
440 AP/Wide World Photos
451 UPI/Bettmann   455 Library of Congress

10. Removal of the Vice President

463 Library of Congress

11. Chief Executive

465 Susan Biddle, White House   469 Reuters/Bettmann   474 Marilynn K. Yee, *New York Times* Pictures   476 White House
478 White House   479 (top left) Ken Heinen, (top center) White House, (top right) Roger Sandler, (bottom) Karen Ruckman
481 R. Michael Jenkins   491 John F. Kennedy Library   492 Nixon Project, National Archives   493 *Washington Star*, courtesy of the Martin Luther King, Jr. Library   502 Steve Karafyllakis   528 Library of Congress
537 Associated Press   539 U.S. Coast Guard
541 Kathleen Beall   545 Library of Congress

12. Legislative Leader

562 R. Michael Jenkins   566 (both) Library of Congress   568 Library of Congress   577 John F. Kennedy Library   529 (left) courtesy of the Dwight D. Eisenhower Library, (right) John F. Kennedy Library   585 Gerald R. Ford Library

13. Chief Diplomat

595 Theodore Roosevelt Collection, Harvard College Library   600 John F. Kennedy Library   604 Jimmy Carter Library
607 Library of Congress   610 no credit
612 Reuters   615 (left) Bill Auth, (right) no credit   617 (top) National Archives, (bottom) White House   622 Reuters/Bettmann
624 White House

14. Commander in Chief

634 Library of Congress   635 Library of Congress   641 AP/Wide World Photos   648 George Bush Presidential Materials Project   650 United Nations Photo
653 Dwight D. Eisenhower Library
654 Library of Congress   655 Library of Congress   657 courtesy of the White House
660 Library of Congress   663 Library of Congress   664 U.S. Air Force

15. Chief of State

677 White House   679 UPI/Bettmann
682 Library of Congress   683 (top) Reuters/Bettmann, (bottom) Ronald Reagan Library
688 Library of Congress   695 George Tames, *New York Times*   698 Jimmy Carter Library
701 Reuters   703 Nixon Project, National Archives

16. Chief Economist

708 Library of Congress   711 Library of Congress   715 UPI/Bettmann   717 United Press International   723 Reuters/Luc Wovovitch Archive Photos   728 UPI/Bettmann   737 Bill Fitz-Patrick, White House   740 R. Michael Jenkins

17. Presidential Appearances

747 Lyndon B. Johnson Library   751 Pete Souza, White House   752 Library of Congress   753 Library of Congress

755 Library of Congress   757 Library of Congress   758 Franklin D. Roosevelt Library   759 John F. Kennedy Library   761 Scott J. Ferrell   764 Reuters   766 Lyndon B. Johnson Library   770 National Archives

18. The President and Political Parties

782 Library of Congress   783 Library of Congress   786 Library of Congress 793 (both) Library of Congress   797 Library of Congress   803 no credit   806 Franklin D. Roosevelt Library   811 National Republican Congressional Committee   815 Ray Lustig, *Washington Post*   823 (top) The Bettmann Archive, (bottom) Franklin D. Roosevelt Library   825 Library of Congress   829 no credit

19. The President and the News Media

836 Library of Congress   839 Library of Congress   841 Illinois State Historical Library   845 Library of Congress   851 Franklin D. Roosevelt Library   852 *Washington Post*   854 White House   855 Jimmy Carter Library   863 David Valdez, White House   864 AP/Wide World Photos   866 David Hume Kennerly, White House   867 no credit   876 R. Michael Jenkins

20. Public Support and Opinion

882 National Archives   884 Reuters   887 Library of Congress   889 R. Michael Jenkins   895 Library of Congress   897 George Bush Presidential Materials Project

21. The President and Interest Groups

906 Library of Congress   910 Pete Souza, White House   913 Franklin D. Roosevelt Library   915 Ronald Reagan Library   919 R. Michael Jenkins   923 Library of Congress

22. Housing of the Executive Branch

927 no credit   931 Library of Congress   932 Library of Congress   933 Library of Congress   934 White House Historical Association   937 Library of Congress   939 Library of Congress   942 National Park Service   944 Jon Preimesberger   945 Jon Preimesberger   946 White House   947 White House   949 Department of Defense photo by Eddie McCrossan

23. Executive Branch Pay and Perquisites

958 UPI/Bettmann   961 Bill Fitz-Patrick, White House   963 White House   964 John F. Kennedy Library   969 R. Michael Jenkins   976 Library of Congress   978 Library of Congress   985 no credit

24. Daily Life of the President

994 George Bush Presidential Materials Project   999 Library of Congress   1000 Dwight D. Eisenhower Library   1001 White House   1005 UPI/Bettmann

25. The First Lady, the First Family, and the President's Friends

1012 Franklin D. Roosevelt   1013 Lyndon B. Johnson Library   1014 R. Michael Jenkins   1017 Gerald R. Ford Library   1018 White House   1019 National Portrait Gallery

1020 Library of Congress   1021 Library of Congress   1022 Library of Congress   1023 Library of Congress   1024 Library of Congress   1025 Library of Congress   1027 Library of Congress   1028 Library of Congress   1029 Library of Congress   1030 Library of Congress   1031 Library of Congress   1032 Library of Congress   1033 Library of Congress   1034 Library of Congress   1035 Library of Congress   1036 Library of Congress   1037 Library of Congress   1038 Library of Congress   1039 Library of Congress   1040 Library of Congress   1041 Library of Congress   1042 Library of Congress   1043 Library of Congress   1044 Lyndon B. Johnson Library   1045 Library of Congress   1046 Library of Congress   1047 White House   1048 (left) Library of Congress, (right) White House   1049 White House   1051 Library of Congress   1054 R. Michael Jenkins   1059 Culver Pictures

26. Office of the Vice President

1064 no credit   1066 Newport News Shipbuilding   1069 AP/Wide World Photos   1068 (left) Library of Congress, (right) White House

27. Executive Office of the President: White House Office

1075 Franklin D. Roosevelt Library   1088 Bettmann   1089 no credit   1095 Library of Congress   1088 R. Michael Jenkins

28. Executive Office of the President: Supporting Organizations

1116 R. Michael Jenkins   1125 R. Michael Jenkins   1134 R. Michael Jenkins

29. The Cabinet and Executive Departments

1146 Library of Congress   1148 courtesy of Harry S. Truman Library   1151 Reuters   1155 Nixon Project, National Archives   1160 Library of Congress   1163 Library of Congress   1165 (top) Gail S. Rebhan, (bottom) AP/Wide World Photos   1166 no credit   1168 Reuters/Bettmann   1171 USDA   1174 Department of Defense   1186 Ken Heinen   1197 R. Michael Jenkins   1203 Department of Transportation   1207 National Archives

30. Government Agencies and Corporations

1217 U.S. Postal Service   1221 no credit   1225 R. Michael Jenkins   1235 Florida Department of Commerce

31. Presidential Commisssions

1253 Library of Congress   1256 Library of Congress   1259 Paul Hosefros, *New York Times*

32. Former Presidents

1271 The Bettmann Archive   1272 Library of Congress   1274 no credit   1276 Reuters/Bettmann

33. The President and Congress

1283 Air Photographics   1286 Library of Congress   1289 AP/Wide World Photos   1295 Black Star   1299 U.S. Navy

1313 Reuters   1326 no credit   1327 no credit   1337 (all) George Tames   1344 Pete Souza, White House

34. The President and the Supreme Court

1355 U.S. Supreme Court   1356 Library of Congress   1360 Ken Heinen for the Supreme Court   1365 Ken Heinen   1368 Library of Congress   1375 Library of Congress   1376 Franklin D. Roosevelt Library   1377 Library of Congress   1381 U.S. Supreme Court   1390 National Archives   1398 Library of Congress

35. The President and the Bureaucracy

1408 Franklin D. Roosevelt Library   1419 Barry Shapiro, *Marietta Daily Journal*   1426 no credit   1428 Air Photographics   1440 White House   1445 Library of Congress

36. Biographies of the Presidents

1455 National Park Service   1458 National Portrait Gallery, Smithsonian Institution   1461 Library of Congress   1463 Library of Congress   1465 Library of Congress   1467 Library of Congress   1469 Library of Congress   1471 Library of Congress   1473 Library of Congress   1474 Library of Congress   1476 Library of Congress   1477 Library of Congress   1479 Library of Congress   1480 Library of Congress   1481 Library of Congress   1483 Library of Congress   1484 Library of Congress   1486 Library of Congress   1488 Library of Congress   1490 Library of Congress   1491 Library of Congress   1493 Library of Congress   1494 Library of Congress   1496 Library of Congress   1497 Library of Congress   1499 Library of Congress   1501 Library of Congress   1503 Library of Congress   1505 Library of Congress   1507 Library of Congress   1508 Library of Congress   1509 Library of Congress   1512 U.S. Navy courtesy Harry S. Truman Library   1514 Library of Congress   1516 Library of Congress   1518 Lyndon B. Johnson Library   1520 White House   1522 Gerald R. Ford Library   1524 White House   1525 White House   1527 White House   1529 White House

37. Biographies of the Vice Presidents

1533 Library of Congress   1534 Library of Congress   1535 Library of Congress   1537 Library of Congress   1538 National Portrait Gallery, Smithsonian Institution   1539 Library of Congress   1540 Library of Congress   1541 Library of Congress   1542 Library of Congress   1543 Library of Congress   1544 Library of Congress   1545 Library of Congress   1546 Library of Congress   1547 Library of Congress   1548 Library of Congress   1549 Library of Congress   1550 Library of Congress   1551 Library of Congress   1552 Library of Congress   1553 Library of Congress   1554 Library of Congress   1555 Library of Congress   1556 Library of Congress   1557 Library of Congress   1558 Library of Congress   1559 Library of Congress   1560 Library of Congress   1562 White House   1563 White House   1564 Joe Houston   1565 White House

Index

treaty power, 603
war powers, 670–671, 1292
White House residence, 932
Buchanan, Patrick J., 403
campaign finance, 229
1992 candidacy, 246, 252, 401, 799, 829, 911
1996 candidacy, 252
Nixon speechwriter, 1080
presidential aspirations, 242, 258
Reagan communications adviser, 860, 861
Buckingham, Joseph, 838
Buckley, James L., 226, 817–818, 1338
Buckley, Jill, 289
Buckley v. Valeo, 226–227, 1316, 1382
Budget Act of 1974. *See* Congressional Budget and Impoundment Control Act of 1974
Budget and Accounting Act of 1921, 102, 119, 497, 507, 571, 573, 710, 723, 1112, 1290, 1319, 1320
Budget Circular 49, 1113
Budget committees, House and Senate, 138, 503, 725
Budget deficits
balanced budget amendment proposals, 43, 502, 727–729
deficit defined, 706
economic policy making constrained by, 720–723
economic stimulation, 712–713
historical perspective, 710, 725
negative effects, 725–726
selected years, 715, 719–722, 725, 726 (table)
statutory control, 502, 720, 727–728
Budget director, 735, 736
Budget Enforcement Act of 1990, 502
Budget politics, 496–506, 723–731
budget deficit effects, 725–729
budgeting theories, 500
budget timetable, 497–499
bureaucratic politics, 511–512, 1428, 1436, 1438, 1439
confidential and secret funding, 504
congressional role, 138, 501–504, 514, 1290
continuing resolutions, 723
controllable spending, 501
current services budget, 499
defense budget, 499, 505, 661, 663–665
election cycle effects, 724
"fiscal policy," definition, 706, 712
foreign policy affected by, 597–598
fund deferrals and rescissions, 483, 505, 506, 561, 729–730
funds reprogramming, 505
fund transfers, 504–505
historical perspective, 102, 496–497, 573, 710
impoundment powers, 138, 505–506, 560, 729–730, 1388, 1438
interest group politics, 727, 912–913, 919, 920
legislative veto, 483, 506, 730, 1316
line-item veto, 44, 502, 506, 560–561, 722, 730–731, 1315
OMB role, 469, 497–499, 508, 706, 728, 1112, 1114–1119, 1320
presidential discretionary spending, 504–505
presidential role, 83–84, 112, 119, 129, 497–501, 710, 723, 725, 1112–1114, 1290, 1320
redistributive programs, 1324, 1447
regulatory and law enforcement programs, 527, 540–541
uncontrollable spending, 499–501, 726–727
United Nations payments, 651
veto politics, 555–557
Buffalo, New York, 266
Bulletin boards. *See* Internet and bulletin boards

Bulletin of Labor, 1197
Bull Moose Party, 199, 218, 300, 303, 365, 1270
Bully pulpit, 364, 394, 566, 749, 772
Bumpers, Dale, 220
Bundy, McGeorge, 133, 473, 615, 624, 1078, 1088, 1120, 1155, 1156, 1162
Burch, Dean, 790
Bureaucracy
acronym list, 1414
appointments. *See* Appointment power and process
bureaucratic lingo, 1412
characteristics of bureaucrats, 1159, 1417, 1418
civil service. *See* Civil service system
components and functions, 468–470, 1413–1415
constitutional foundation, 468, 1405–1406
defense establishment, 659–661
functional and structural characteristics, 1411–1413
government organization chart, 1413
growth and reform, 470–471, 525, 568, 573, 974, 1406–1408
internet access to federal information, 1409
law enforcement agencies, 533–539
law enforcement personnel, 529–530
pay and perquisites, 970–973
policy advisory role, 576–578, 614, 619–626
policy making by, 1419–1420
public attitudes, 1410–1411
recruitment and hiring information, 1416
size and budget, 1408, 1410–1411
terms defined, 468, 802, 1405
Bureaucratic politics
appointment and removal powers, 487–496, 1432–1433
budgetary controls, 496–497
bureaucratic accountability, 1449–1450
bureaucratic power, sources and limits on, 1420–1430
congressional role, 481–484, 1424–1425, 1428
information management, 473–475, 1421, 1438–1439
iron triangles, 1443–1444
issue networks, 1444–1445
judicial involvement, 1428–1429
presidential administrative styles, 131, 475–481, 1092–1099
presidential control, 83–84, 126, 129, 137–138, 143–144, 150, 153, 323–327, 471–475, 511–512, 625–626, 989, 1430–1446
public politics, 1423, 1425–1426, 1429
reorganization efforts, 126, 484–487, 1161, 1436
supercabinet proposal, 137, 1096, 1156
Bureau of Administration, 1202
Bureau of Agricultural Economics, 1170
Bureau of Alcohol, Tobacco, and Firearms, 530, 533, 535, 538, 541, 1207, 1425
Bureau of the Budget (BOB), 1206
conversion to OMB, 137, 469, 486, 497, 512, 573, 710, 734, 1320
diminished influence, 135
origin and development, 119, 126, 129, 484, 491, 497, 499, 505, 573, 710, 734, 1110, 1112–1113, 1290, 1320
role expansion, 511–512, 573, 1113–1114, 1318
Bureau of Consular Affairs, 1202
Bureau of Democracy, Human Rights, and Labor, 1202
Bureau of Diplomatic Security, 1202
Bureau of Economic and Business Affairs, 1202
Bureau of Employment Security, 1183
Bureau of Engraving and Printing, 952, 981, 1207

Bureau of Export Administration, 1173
Bureau of Finance and Management Policy, 1202
Bureau of Indian Affairs, 1189, 1191
Bureau of Intelligence and Research, 620, 1202, 1221
Bureau of Internal Revenue, 1208
Bureau of International Communications and Information Policy, 1202
Bureau of International Narcotics and Law Enforcement Affairs, 1202
Bureau of International Organization Affairs, 1202
Bureau of Labor Statistics, 951, 1200
Bureau of Land Management, 473, 1191
Bureau of Legislative Affairs, 1202
Bureau of Mines, 951
Bureau of Oceans and International Environmental and Scientific Affairs, 1202
Bureau of Politico-Military Affairs, 1202
Bureau of Population, Refuges, and Migration, 1202
Bureau of Prisons, 539, 1195–1196
Bureau of Public Affairs, 1202
Bureau of the Public Debt, 1207, 1208
Bureau of Public Roads, 1173
Bureau of Reclamation, 1191
Bureau of War Risk Insurance, 952, 1208
Burford, Anne Gorsuch, 1422–1423
Burford, Robert F., 473
Burger, Warren E., 144, 419, 420, 1358, 1362, 1368, 1371
on executive privilege, 450, 1287, 1390
on legislative veto, 645, 1316, 1387
Burgess, Susan, 1373
Burke, Edmund, 187
Burke, John P., 1150
Burleson, Albert, 579
Burnett, John D., 101, 102
Burnham, Walter Dean, 149, 152
Burns, Arthur F., 325, 477, 714, 735, 736, 1080, 1128–1129
Burns, James MacGregor, 258, 307, 374, 777
Burnside, Ambrose E., 352
Burr, Aaron, 335, 461, 534, 696
biography, 1533–1534
1800 election events, 45, 68–69, 165, 191–192, 310–311, 336–337, 780
Hamilton duel, 165, 463
1796 election events, 66, 191, 335
treason trial, 1374
Burt, Richard, 614
Burton, Harold D., 818
Bush, Barbara, 297, 943, 946, 1014, 1017, 1048, 1279
Bush, George
administrative politics, 484, 510, 513, 514, 524, 1120–1121, 1125, 1131, 1139, 1140
administrative style, 477, 478, 480, 1098
appointment politics, 493, 614, 807–808, 822, 1109, 1111, 1308, 1418
assassination plot, 648, 897, 1008
biography, 1457, 1527–1529, 1633
budget politics, 146, 501, 502, 506, 729, 1116
bureaucratic politics, 1430, 1431, 1435, 1441
cabinet, 1696–1697
cabinet politics, 1149, 1150, 1153, 1156–1159, 1167, 1169, 1225
campaign finance, 220, 228, 229, 232, 236, 238, 288, 298, 316 n. 170
candidate debates, 265, 285, 294, 299
ceremonial duties, 679–681, 684, 685, 687–688
coattails effect, 307
daily life, 998, 1000–1002
deregulation efforts, 524, 1219

House of Commons, 3, 9, 241, 441
House of Lords, 3, 9, 17, 241, 441
House of Representatives
  apportionment formula, 13, 21, 786
  campaign finance disclosure, 222
  on direct election of president, 47
  Framers' ideas, 9, 18
  impeachment power, 20, 26, 27, 441, 442, 544
  lawmaking procedure, 574–575
  leadership reforms, 103, 111–112
  midterm elections, 563, 815, 1335–1336
  party affiliations in Congress and presidency,
    1789–1995 (table), 1681–1682
  qualifications for office, 18, 34, 35
  revenue bills, House initiation of, 1146
  selection of president, 20, 25, 43, 45, 46, 186,
    192
  Speaker. *See* Speaker of the House
  staff, 1086
  term of office, 563, 815
  treaty-making role, 32, 1297, 1298
Housing and Urban Development Department
    (HUD), 469
  bureaucratic politics, 486
  headquarters office, 950
  organization and functions, 1188–1189
  origin and development, 324, 1185–1188, 1408
Housing programs, 388
Houston, David F., 1170
Houston, Texas, 266–268
Howard, John Eager, 1663
Howard University, 1180
Howe, Louis McHenry, 913, 1059, 1074
Howell, Varina, 353
Hoxie, R. Gordon, 1146–1148, 1150, 1166
Huberman, Benjamin, 1136
Hubert H. Humphrey Building, 950
Huckshorn, Robert, 800
Huerta, Victoriano, 610
Hufstedler, Shirley M., 1178
Hughes, Charles Evans
  career profile, 1663
  judicial decisions, 1376, 1386
  1916 candidacy, 276, 367
  secretary of state, 118, 847
  supreme court justice, 376, 1375, 1381
Hughes, Emmet J., 710, 1090
Hughes, Harold, 212
Hughes, Howard, 1057
Hughes, Sarah T., 328, 437
Hughes Commission, 212
Hughes-Ryan Amendment, 621, 1306
Hull, Cordell, 376–377, 476, 738, 790, 947, 1160,
    1200
Human Events periodical, 226
Human Resources Department (proposed),
    486
Human rights issues, 237, 299, 597, 1303–1304
Hume, Brit, 835
Hume, David, 4, 187, 345
Humphrey, George M., 234, 1153, 1206
Humphrey, Hubert H., 47, 54, 270, 379, 383,
    438, 680
  biography, 1559–1560
  campaign finance, 220, 223, 224, 228, 233, 238,
    239
  ceremonial duties, 702
  Johnson successorship arrangement, 53, 456
  1960 candidacy, 383–384
  1968 candidacy, 164, 169, 175, 174, 201, 202,
    204, 210, 212, 252, 253, 258–259, 261, 270,
    286, 312, 388–389
  1972 candidacy, 202, 258, 390
  1976 candidacy, 202, 262, 392
  pay and perquisites, 970

political experience, 243
political ideology, 253
running mate selection, 792
vice presidency, 172, 386, 969, 1063, 1066,
    1068, 1069
Humphrey, William E., 495
Humphrey's Executor v. United States, 495, 1214,
    1375, 1382
Hungerford, Henry James, 1247
Hunkers movement, 347
Hunt, James B., Jr., 214
Hunt Commission, 211, 214–215, 281
Hunter, Floyd, 907
Hunter, James Davison, 883
Huntington, Samuel, 1214, 1663
Hurricane Andrew, 521
Hussein, Saddam, 147, 647, 762, 894, 1193, 1296,
    1297, 1339, 1344
Huston, Claudius H., 790
Hylton v. United States, 1355
Hyman, Harold, 93

I

Iceland, 666
Ickes, Harold L., 494, 805, 950, 1148, 1160, 1189
Idaho, 203, 207, 259, 668
Ideological parties, 301–302
Illinois, 88, 203, 260, 282, 307
Immigration, 349, 358, 524
Immigration and Naturalization Service (INS),
    533, 535, 537, 951, 1196
*Immigration and Naturalization Service v.
    Chadha*, 483–484, 506, 645, 730, 1161, 1316,
    1387–1388
Immunity, 528, 1389–1391
Impeachment, 441–452
  Belknap, 1060
  constitutional provision, 26, 441, 442, 544
  English origins, 441–442
  Framers' ideas, 8, 15, 16, 18, 20, 26–27, 441, 442
  grounds for, 442–443, 544
  historical precedents, 441
  Johnson, A., 95–96, 167, 354, 443–448, 494,
    544, 554, 594, 1288, 1389–1390, 1591 (text)
  judges, 1369
  nature of process, 443, 544
  Nixon, 137, 391, 448–452, 528, 544–545, 1288,
    1389, 1608 (text)
  pardon power excluded from, 31, 532
  procedures, 442, 544, 1288
  Tyler, 82
  vice president, 463
"Imperial presidency," 514, 518–519, 521
Impoundment powers, 138, 505, 560, 729–730,
    1388, 1438
Imus in the Morning radio show, 402
Inaugural addresses, 330–332, 764. *See also* specific presidents
Inauguration ceremony and celebration,
    327–332, 675–677, 687
Inauguration day, 43, 48, 327
Income tax, 59 n. 53, 142, 146, 365, 366, 710, 732,
    1208, 1370
Incumbency advantage, 246–247, 253, 284–286,
    293
Indentured servants, 205
Independence (aircraft), 962
Independence Hall, 12, 328
Independent agencies, 1414
  executive agencies, 468, 470, 1213, 1216
  regulatory commissions, 470, 1213
  size, for selected years (table), 1410
  See also specific agency names
Independent counsel (special prosecutor), 487,
    496, 1383

Independent Journal, 836
Independent Party, 300
Independent Safety Board Act of 1974, 1239
India, 650, 689
Indiana, 88, 193, 200, 282, 668
Indian Education Act, 1180
Indian Health Service, 1185
Indian Queen tavern, 11–12
Indian Removal Act of 1830, 343
Indians. *See* Native Americans
Indonesia, 650, 1293
Industrial Revolution, 105
Inflation, 707
  definition, 706
  emergency powers, 520
  funds impoundment to combat, 505
  1929–1995 (table), 711
Inflation Conference, 139
Information Agency, U.S. (USIA), 619, 772,
    1249
Information and Regulatory Affairs, Office of,
    1117–1118, 1130
Information management, 473–475
Ingersoll, Jared, 339, 1663
Ingersoll, Robert G., 358
Initiating ceremonies, 764
Injunctions, 112
Ink, Dwight A., Jr., 1123
Inman, Bobby Ray, 1177
Inouye, Daniel P., 272, 1306
*Inquiry into the Origin and Course of Political
    Parties in the United States, An* (Van
    Buren), 344
In re. See name of case
Insider strategy, 252, 253
Inspectors general, 538–539
Institute of Museum Services, 1237
Institute of Peace, U.S., 1249–1250
Institutional presidency, 491
Insurance industry, 235
Insurrection, 90
Intelligence activities, 472, 1003
  domestic surveillance, 513
  funding, 504, 505, 1221
  oversight, 621, 1221–1222, 1305–1307
  See also Iran-contra affair
Intelligence and Research, Bureau of, 620, 1202,
    1221
Intelligence and Security Command, 535
Intelligence Committee, House, 621, 1306
Intelligence Committee, Senate, 472, 603, 621,
    1306
Intelligence community
  agencies comprising, 620, 1221, 1297
  foreign policy–making role, 619, 625
Intelligence Oversight Act of 1980, 621
Intelligence Oversight Board, 614, 621, 1221
Intelligence Policy and Review, Office of, 1195
Interagency Committee on Internal Security,
    512–513
Interagency Council on the Homeless, 1188
Interagency Toxic Substances Data Committee,
    1138
Inter-American Foundation, 1233–1234
Intercontinental ballistic missiles (ICBMs), 655
Interest group politics
  budget politics, 727
  bureaucratic politics, 324, 1425, 1429,
    1443–1445
  cabinet advocacy, 1154–1156
  daily activities, 916
  effect on traditional politics, 209, 256, 258,
    262, 290
  goals and functions, 915–916
  government funding of, 220

war powers, 633–634
White House residence, 931, 940
Tyler, Julia, 1009, 1010, 1018, 1024, 1051
Tyler, Letitia, 1009, 1010, 1024, 1051
Tyler, Priscilla Cooper, 1053
Tyranny, 3, 4
Tyson, Laura D'Andrea, 1126, 1131
Tyson Chicken company, 229, 1172

U

U-2 incident, 685, 871–872, 1306
Udall, Morris K., 282, 392, 559
interior secretary, 1189
1976 candidacy, 230, 249, 253, 262, 264, 316 n.
123, 392
Uganda, 597, 1303
Un-American Activities Committee, House,
381, 1274, 1277, 1378
Unanimous consent agreement, 575
Under Fire (North), 1278
"Understandings," in lieu of executive agreements, 609
Underwood, Gilbert S., 951
Underwood, Oscar, 218, 366
Underwood-Simmons Tariff Act, 114, 738
Unemployment
election politics and, 724
1929–1995 (table), 711
Uniform Code of Military Justice, 1391
Union newspaper, 837
Union Pacific Railroad Co., 356, 463
Union Party, 352, 353
United Auto Workers, 318 n. 237, 916, 921
United Mine Workers, 395, 916
United Nations (UN), 430, 603, 771–772
Korean conflict, 129, 639–640
peacekeeping operations, effect on U.S. foreign policy, 591, 598, 599, 611–613,
649–651, 667
Security Council permanent members, 650
U.S. representative to, 1149
United Nations Conference on Trade and
Development, 1135
United Nations Participation Act of 1945, 129,
611, 639, 650, 651
United Press International (UPI), 871
United Public Workers v. Mitchell, 983
United States
v. Alvarez-Machain, 1397
v. Belmont, 127, 592, 606–607, 1397
v. Butler, 1375
v. Curtiss-Wright Export Corp., 127, 592–593,
606, 1290, 1291, 1395–1396, 1597 (text)
v. Eichman, 1370
v. Kelin, 1370
v. Laub, 1394
v. Nixon, 137, 450, 1287, 1359, 1390
v. Pink, 1397
v. Richardson, 1365
v. United States District Court, 1394
v. Wilson, 1384
United States agencies and corporations. *See*
other part of title
United States attorneys, 529, 530, 535, 539
United States Attorneys' Bulletin, 1195
United States Attorneys' Manual, 1195
*United States Civil Service Commission v.
National Association of Letter Carriers*, 983
United States Code, 327
*United States Government Organization
Manual*, 1070
*United States Government Policy and
Supporting Positions* (plum book), 487, 984
United States National Central Bureau, 1196
United States Telegraph, 837

United Way, 679
United We Stand America, 305, 922
*United We Stand: How We Can Take Back Our
Country* (Perot), 304
Unit rule, 189, 212, 215, 270–271, 274
University of Alabama, 303, 520
University of Arkansas, 682
University of Michigan Documents Center,
1409
University of Mississippi, 520, 525–527
Unmediated messages, 291–292
Unsafe at Any Speed (Nader), 1215
Untermeyer, Charles, 493, 1109, 1167, 1168
Uranium Mill Tailings Radiation Control Act,
1225
Urban Development Action Grants, 1187
Urban League, 920
Urban Mass Transportation Act of 1964, 1206
Urban Mass Transportation Administration,
1204, 1205
Urban Renewal Administration, 1186
U.S. agencies. *See* other part of title
U.S. News and World Report, 870, 963, 968
U.S. Reports, 1360
U.S.S. *C. Turner Joy*, 642, 872
U.S.S. *Greer*, 638
U.S.S. *Maddox*, 642, 872
U.S.S. *Nashville*, 109
U.S.S. *Princeton*, 426
U.S.S. *Stark*, 647, 1296
Utah, 207, 349

V

Valdez, David, 857
Valenti, Jack, 1091
Valis, Wayne, 912
Vallandigham, Clement L., 352, 1391
*Valley Forge Christian College v. Americans
United for Separation of Church and State*,
1364
Van Buren, Angelica Singleton, 1051, 1052
Van Buren, Hannah, 1055
Van Buren, Martin, 329, 347, 356, 462
administrative politics, 1254
biography, 1457, 1458, 1472–1474, 1632
budget policy, 710
cabinet, 1684–1685
on ceremonial function, 687
1832 vice-presidential nomination, 266, 343
1836 election, 46, 145, 165, 169, 174, 194, 217,
293, 312, 344
1840 election events, 93, 346, 681
1844 and 1848 election events, 83, 84, 300, 302,
347, 1270, 1272
news media relations, 79, 837
patronage, 342, 781, 976
political experience, 244, 342, 343, 1059
on political parties, 344–345
presidency, 80–81, 344
rating, 178, 180
retirement, 1273
speeches and rhetoric, 753, 754
vice presidency, 166, 217, 343
White House residence, 931
Vance, Cyrus R., 624, 962, 973, 1120, 1153, 1156,
1165, 1201
Vandenberg, Arthur H., 276, 374, 377, 379, 1298
Vandenberg Resolution, 603
Vanderbilt, Cornelius, 221
Vandergrift, Benjamin, 239
Van Devanter, Willis, 1363, 1375, 1376, 1378
Vanik, Charles A., 1303
Van Riper, Paul P., 118, 975, 977, 984
*Vantage Point, The: Perspectives on the
Presidency* (Johnson), 1277

Vermont, 188, 192, 193, 203, 260
Versailles treaty, 116, 117, 195, 367, 454, 583, 589,
596, 603, 605, 631, 689, 692, 765, 1318, 1396
Vesco, Robert, 224
Vesting clauses, 20, 30
Veterans, 371, 502
Veterans Administration, 952, 1187, 1209
Veterans Affairs Department
bureaucratic politics, 1424, 1449
headquarters office, 952–953
organization and functions, 534, 1199, 1210,
1408
origin and development, 324, 1208–1210
personnel system, 1416
Veterans' Bureau, 118, 1208, 1209
Veterans Day holiday, 682
Veterans Employment and Training Service,
1199
Veterans of Foreign Wars (VFW), 767, 915
Veterans' Preference Act of 1944, 984
Veto power
Framers' ideas, 15–17, 23
governors, 3, 5, 17
legislative veto, 483–484, 487, 506, 514, 645,
730, 1161, 1316, 1387–1388, 1428
line-item veto, 44, 502, 506, 560–561, 722,
730–731, 1312, 1315
See also Executive veto
Vice president/vice presidency
abolishment proposal, 44, 46, 165, 414
administration defender role, 1069
advisory role, 1067–1068
as appointive office, proposal, 44
attitudes toward, 163, 167, 293, 419, 701
cabinet membership, 1065–1066, 1145
candidate selection, 165, 168, 170–171
ceremonial duties, 684, 700, 701
commission chair, 1066–1067
death in office, 60 n. 85, 165–166, 409, 413,
415, 461–462
death or resignation of nominee, 280
diminished status, 46
disability, 417, 464
election campaign, 293–295
enhanced duties and status, 163–164, 167–169,
171–175, 1063, 1070–1071
EOP component, 1103
filling of office vacancy (Twenty-fifth
Amendment), 43, 44, 46, 48, 49, 52–55,
138, 139, 163, 171–173, 391, 406 n. 140, 409,
412, 413, 415–420, 442, 449, 456–457, 461,
462, 463–464
hybrid nature, 37, 164, 1287–1288
impeachment, 27, 463
legislative liaison, 1068
NSC membership, 164, 171, 469, 620, 1065
nomination, 277
oath of office, 327, 328, 425
office creation, 22, 25, 36, 164
office locations, 947, 970, 1067, 1070
pay and perquisites, 172, 968–970, 1070
personal and political characteristics, 165–
166
presidential relationships, 166, 168, 172–173
presidential successorship. *See* Succession
president of Senate, 20, 25, 36, 38, 41–42, 164,
165, 809, 1063–1064, 1287–1288, 1329
presumptive presidential candidacy, 51,
163–164
protection, 538, 542, 1003–1005
qualifications for office, 43, 45, 165, 240
removal, 461–464
residence, 172, 946–947, 970, 1070
resignation, 462–463
seal of office, 172, 1070

Guide to the Presidency was designed and typeset in Adobe Minion, Stone Print, and Stone Sans using QuarkXPress on a MacIntosh by Kachergis Book Design, Pittsboro, North Carolina. This book was printed on fifty-pound Finch Opaque and bound by RR Donnelley & Sons Company, Crawfordsville, Indiana.